DEVELOPMENTAL
PSYCHOPATHOLOGY

DEVELOPMENTAL PSYCHOPATHOLOGY

Volume 2:   Risk, Disorder, and Adaptation

Editors

DANTE CICCHETTI
AND
DONALD J. COHEN

A Wiley-Interscience Publication

John Wiley & Sons, Inc.

New York   •   Chichester   •   Brisbane   •   Toronto   •   Singapore

Library of Congress Cataloging-in-Publication Data:

Developmental psychopathology / Dante Cicchetti and Donald J. Cohen,
    editors.
        v. <1–   > cm. — (Wiley series on personality processes)
        Includes index.
        Contents: v. 1. Theory and methods — v.   2. Risk, disorder, and
    adaptation.
        ISBN 0-471-53257-6 (set). — ISBN 0-471-53243-6 (v. 1). — ISBN
    0-471-53244-4 (v. 2)
        1. Mental illness—Etiology.   2. Developmental psychology.
    3. Mental illness—Risk factors.   4. Adjustment (Psychology)
    I. Cicchetti, Dante.   II. Cohen, Donald J.   III. Series.
    RC454.4.D483   1995
    616.89´071–dc20   94-36391

Printed in the United States of America

10   9   8   7   6   5   4   3

To Alex Siegel and Phyllis Cohen

Contributors

Ilana Attie, Ph.D.
Supervising Psychologist
St. Luke's-Roosevelt Hospital Center
Department of Psychology
New York, New York

Paul B. Baltes, Ph.D.
Professor of Psychology and,
Director, Center for Psychology and Human Development
Max Planck Institute for Human Development and Education
Berlin, Germany

Daniel F. Becker, M.D.
Assistant Professor of Psychiatry
Yale University
New Haven, Connecticut

Jeanne Brooks-Gunn, Ph.D.
Virginia and Leonard Marx Professor of Child Development
  and Education
Teachers College
Columbia University
New York, New York

Alice S. Carter, Ph.D.
Assistant Professor
Department of Psychology and Yale Child Study Center
Yale University
New Haven, Connecticut

Avshalom Caspi, Ph.D.
Associate Professor
Department of Psychology
University of Wisconsin
Madison, Wisconsin

Dante Cicchetti, Ph.D.
Professor of Psychology, Psychiatry, and Pediatrics and
Director, Mt. Hope Family Center
University of Rochester
Rochester, New York

J. Douglas Coatsworth, Ph.D.
Research Assistant Professor
Center for Family Studies
University of Miami School of Medicine
Miami, Florida

Donald J. Cohen, M.D.
Director, Yale Child Study Center and,
Irving B. Harris Professor of Child Psychiatry, Pediatrics, and
  Psychology
Yale University
New Haven, Connecticut

Bertram J. Cohler, Ph.D.
William Rainey Harper Professor
College and Department of Psychology
University of Chicago
Chicago, Illinois

Roger D. Davis, M.A.
University Fellow
Department of Psychology
University of Miami
Miami, Florida

Melissa E. DeRosier, Ph.D.
Post Doctoral Fellow
Developmental Epidemiology
Duke University Medical Center
Durham, North Carolina

Thomas J. Dishion, Ph.D.
Research Scientist
Oregon Social Learning Center
Eugene, Oregon

Robert E. Emery, Ph.D.
Professor of Psychology
University of Virginia
Charlottesville, Virginia

Hiram E. Fitzgerald, Ph.D.
Professor
Department of Psychology
Michigan State University
East Lansing, Michigan

Doran C. French, Ph.D.
Professor
Department of Counseling Psychology
Lewis and Clark College
Portland, Oregon

Judy Garber, Ph.D.
Associate Professor
Department of Psychology and Human Development
Vanderbilt University
Nashville, Tennessee

Diane C. Gooding, B.A.
Ph.D. Candidate
Department of Psychology
University of Minnesota
Minneapolis, Minnesota

Robert M. Hodapp, Ph.D.
Associate Professor
Graduate School of Education
University of California at Los Angeles
Los Angeles, California

William G. Iacono, Ph.D.
Professor of Psychology and Neuroscience
University of Minnesota
Minneapolis, Minnesota

Robert A. King, M.D.
Associate Professor of Child Psychiatry
Yale University
New Haven, Connecticut

Katherine M. Kitzmann, M.A.
Graduate Student
Department of Psychology
University of Virginia
Charlottesville, Virginia

James F. Leckman, M.D.
Nelson Harris Professor of Child Psychiatry and Pediatrics
Yale Child Study Center and Pediatrics
Yale University
New Haven, Connecticut

Michael Lynch, Ph.D.
Assistant Professor
Department of Psychology
Mt. Hope Family Center
University of Rochester
Rochester, New York

Michael Marsiske, Ph.D.
Postdoctoral Research Fellow
Center for Psychology and Human Development
Max Planck Institute for Human Development
   and Education
Berlin, Germany

Ann S. Masten, Ph.D.
Associate Professor and
Associate Director, Institute of Child Development
University of Minnesota
Minneapolis, Minnesota

Thomas H. McGlashan, M.D.
Professor of Psychiatry
Yale University
New Haven, Connecticut

Steven L. Miller, Ph.D.
Research Fellow
Center for Molecular and Behavioral Neuroscience
Rutgers, The State University of New Jersey
Newark, New Jersey

Theodore Millon, Ph.D., D.Sc.
Professor
Department of Psychology
University of Miami
Miami, Florida and
Professor
Department of Psychiatry
Harvard Medical School
Boston, Massachusetts

Terrie E. Moffitt, Ph.D.
Professor
Department of Psychology
University of Wisconsin
Madison, Wisconsin

Helene D. Moses, M.A.
Ph.D. Candidate
Department of Psychology
Michigan State University
East Lansing, Michigan

Judith S. Musick, Ph.D.
Faculty
The Erikson Institute
Loyola University
Chicago, Illinois

Jeffrey G. Parker, Ph.D.
Assistant Professor
Department of Psychology
University of Michigan
Ann Arbor, Michigan

Gerald R. Patterson, Ph.D.
Research Scientist
Oregon Social Learning Center
Eugene, Oregon

David L. Pauls, Ph.D.
Associate Professor
Yale Child Study Center, Psychology and Genetics
Yale University
New Haven, Connecticut

Bradley S. Peterson, M.D.
Assistant Professor
Yale Child Study Center
Yale University
New Haven, Connecticut

Joseph M. Price, Ph.D.
Assistant Professor
Department of Psychology
San Diego State University
San Diego, California

Frank W. Putnam, M.D.
Chief, Unit on Dissociative Disorders
Laboratory of Developmental Psychology
National Institute of Mental Health
Bethesda, Maryland

Robert S. Pynoos, M.D., M.P.H.
Associate Professor
Department of Psychiatry and Behavioral Sciences and,
Director, Trauma Psychiatry Program
University of California at Los Angeles
Los Angeles, California

Nancy S. Robinson, Ph.D.
Research Associate
Department of Psychology and Human Development
Vanderbilt University
Nashville, Tennessee

Kenneth H. Rubin, Ph.D.
Professor
Department of Psychology
University of Waterloo
Waterloo, Ontario
Canada

Ursula M. Staudinger, Ph.D.
Research Scientist
Center for Psychology and Human Development
Max Planck Institute for Human Development and Education
Berlin, Germany

Alan M. Steinberg, Ph.D.
Research Health Scientist
Trauma Psychiatry Program
Department of Psychiatry and Behavioral Sciences
University of California at Los Angeles
Los Angeles, California

Frances M. Stott, Ph.D.
The Erikson Institute
Loyola University
Chicago, Illinois

Paula Tallal, Ph.D.
Professor of Neuroscience and,
Co-Director, Center for Molecular and Behavioral Neuroscience
Rutgers, The State University of New Jersey
Newark, New Jersey

Eric Taylor, FRCP, FRCPsych.
Professor of Developmental Neuropsychiatry
MRC Child Psychiatry Unit
Institute of Psychiatry
University of London
London, United Kingdom

Sheree L. Toth, Ph.D.
Associate Director
Mt. Hope Family Center and,
Associate Professor
Department of Psychology
University of Rochester
Rochester, New York

Fred R. Volkmar, M.D.
Harris Associate Professor of Child Psychiatry, Pediatrics, and
    Psychology
Yale University
New Haven, Connecticut

Ruth Wraith
Senior Child Psychotherapist
Royal Children's Hospital
Department of Child/Family Psychiatry
Parkville, Victoria
Australia

Edward Zigler, Ph.D.
Sterling Professor of Psychology
Department of Psychology and,
Director, Yale Bush Center in Child Development and Social
    Policy
Yale University
New Haven, Connecticut

Robert A. Zucker, Ph.D.
Professor of Psychology in Psychiatry and Psychology
Department of Psychiatry and,
Director, University of Michigan Alcohol Research Center
University of Michigan
Ann Arbor, Michigan

Series Preface

This series of books is addressed to behavioral scientists interested in the nature of human personality. Its scope should prove pertinent to personality theorists and researchers as well as to clinicians concerned with applying an understanding of personality processes to the amelioration of emotional difficulties in living. To this end, the series provides a scholarly integration of theoretical formulations, empirical data, and practical recommendations.

Six major aspects of studying and learning about human personality can be designated: personality theory, personality structure and dynamics, personality development, personality assessment, personality change, and personality adjustment. In exploring these aspects of personality, the books in the series discuss a number of distinct but related subject areas: the nature and implications of various theories of personality; personality characteristics that account for consistencies and variations in human behavior; the emergence of personality processes in children and adolescents; the use of interviewing and testing procedures to evaluate individual differences in personality; efforts to modify personality styles through psychotherapy, counseling, behavior therapy, and other methods of influence; and patterns of abnormal personality functioning that impair individual competence.

IRVING B. WEINER

Tampa, Florida

Preface

If the value of a scientific course of inquiry can be measured, then, at least in part, its contribution can be judged by the role it exerts on generating new questions and discovering new truths, and through its impact and visibility in the literature. By these criteria, the importance of the field of developmental psychopathology to the basic research and applied aspects of developmental and clinical psychology, psychiatry, the neurosciences, and related disciplines cannot be denied. In the past two decades, the presence of the developmental psychopathology perspective has been manifested in a number of arenas: through the growing number of theoretical, review, and empirical papers that reflect this orientation; through its enhanced influence on work in the fields of prevention and intervention; and through its increased application to the areas of advocacy and social policy. In addition, there has been a proliferation of journal special sections devoted to the topic, as well as the publication of a number of journal special issues, beginning with the landmark volume in *Child Development* (Cicchetti, 1984).

The scientific importance of developmental psychopathology also was formally acknowledged through its inclusion as a topic in the fourth edition of the *Handbook of Child Psychology* (Mussen, 1983; see the chapter by Rutter and Garmezy). In 1989, *Development and Psychopathology,* a journal devoted exclusively to the discipline of developmental psychopathology, was initiated. Moreover, there have been numerous scientific meetings focused on the theoretical and empirical advances that have been fostered by the developmental psychopathology framework.

Despite the relatively recent ascendance of developmental psychopathology, its roots can be traced to a variety of areas and disciplines (Cicchetti, 1990; Cohen, 1974). Although a more comprehensive historical perspective on the discipline of developmental psychopathology has been presented elsewhere (Cicchetti, 1990), some highlights of contributions to the formation of developmental psychopathology will be helpful in embedding this area of inquiry within a broader context. Specifically, the origins of developmental psychopathology can be seen in a number of developmental theories, including organismic-developmental theory (Werner, 1948), psychoanalytic theory (Freud, 1940/1955), and structural-developmental theory (Piaget, 1971), all of which stress the dynamic relationship between the individual and the environment.

For scientists working within each of these developmental traditions, the study of pathological populations resulted in the confirmation, expansion, or modification of the developmental principles on which their theories were based. As stated by Werner (1948), "[P]sychopathology will shed light on the genetic data of other developmental fields . . . the results of psychopathology . . . become valuable in many ways for the general picture of mental development, just as psychopathology is itself enriched and its methods facilitated by the adoption of the genetic approach" (pp. 33–34). In their recognition of the importance of understanding the abnormal in order to inform the normal, and vice versa, theoreticians and researchers such as Werner were promulgating a well-established tradition that can be traced to Goethe, who believed that psychopathology resulted from "regressive metamorphoses" and stressed the close connection between abnormal and normal functioning. In essence, for Goethe, the study of pathology allowed one to see, magnified, the normal processes of development and functioning. William James (1902), too, emphasized the role that abnormal mental functioning could play in enhancing the understanding of human nature. Much of psychoanalytic theory also has been grounded in the belief that a knowledge of normal development is a prerequisite to understanding abnormality (Marans & Cohen, 1991). Working within this tradition, Sigmund Freud (1940/1955) drew no sharp distinction between normal and abnormal functioning. Likewise, Anna Freud (1965) argued against adopting a symptomatological diagnostic system for psychopathology, advocating instead the evaluation of disturbances in children based on their ability to perform age-appropriate developmental tasks. Examples such as these serve to elucidate the historical origins of one of the central tenets of developmental psychopathology: that the studies of normal and abnormal development are mutually enriching.

In addition to the important contributions of the early developmental theorists to the emergence of developmental psychopathology, this young field owes much to the influences derived from a variety of disciplines, including cultural anthropology, epidemiology, embryology, genetics, the neurosciences, experimental psychology, and psychiatry (see Cicchetti, 1990). Many of the eminent theorists and great systematizers in these fields conceived of psychopathology as a magnification or distortion of the normal condition and believed that the examination of psychopathology could sharpen our understanding of normal biological and psychological processes.

The reason for the relatively recent crystallization of a number of subdisciplines into a line of inquiry subsumed under developmental psychopathology can be attributed to the maturation of related disciplines. Only after a sufficient corpus of research knowledge on normal biological and psychological development across the life span had been accumulated could researchers interpret the findings of their investigations of psychopathological processes and atypical development. The current work in developmental psychopathology, much of which is contained in these volumes, attests to the rich history that has contributed to this discipline, as well as to the promising future that remains to be discovered.

This two-volume set utilizes a developmental approach to elucidate processes and mechanisms associated with risk, disorder, and adaptation across the life course. As suggested by the title, *Developmental Psychopathology* applies a developmental perspective to the ever-fluctuating relationship between adaptive and maladaptive outcomes, between pathology and normality, and between intrinsic and extrinsic influences on ontogenesis. Because developmental psychopathologists are as invested in understanding those individuals who evidence adaptation despite risk as they are in examining manifestations of psychopathology, we have chosen not to organize these volumes exclusively around thematic psychiatric disorders. Rather, we have opted to explore developmentally relevant theories, methods of assessment, and domains of functioning. Although many chapters address specific disorders, processes that eventuate in psychopathology rather than the psychiatric disturbances per se are emphasized.

In Volume 1, *Theory and Methods*, various approaches to understanding developmental influences are presented. The volume begins with an explication of the discipline of developmental psychopathology. After issues of epidemiology, taxonomy, and assessment are examined, biological and genetic processes are addressed. The volume concludes with analyses of cognitive and social-cognitive processes, socioemotional processes, and systems theory approaches.

Volume 2, *Risk, Disorder, and Adaptation*, begins with a series of chapters that examine the impact of ecological and relational risk factors on development, ranging from societal to more micro-level processes. The volume then examines the emergence of disorder in a variety of populations. To conclude, in their discussions of adaptation and protective processes, a number of authors address the occurrence of resilient outcomes despite the presence of stressors often associated with maladaptation.

In a work of this breadth and scope, it is important that readers understand the goals of these volumes. *Developmental Psychopathology* was not intended to serve as a "how to" manual or as a compendium of research knowledge on the extensive array of psychiatric disorders across the life course. Rather, we invited premier scholars to conceptualize their work within a developmental psychopathology framework and to discuss the implications of their theory and research for enhancing knowledge of normal and atypical development. Toward this end, the utilization of dimensional approaches affecting development, as well as more categorical approaches, was considered to be necessary. We also chose to focus these volumes on theory and research. Although generalizations to implications for treatment of various disorders can be made by the knowledgeable reader, these volumes were not conceived to provide information on various psychotherapeutic approaches. Because we felt that a chapter or two on psychotherapy could not possibly provide the necessary depth to address the topic adequately, intervention techniques are not presented other than when an author chooses to incorporate therapeutic considerations into a chapter. These volumes are concerned with methods of approaching and understanding normal and atypical development, not with providing guidelines for intervention.

As the editors of *Developmental Psychopathology*, we are honored to contribute yet another link to the chain that has been forged from this exciting area of inquiry. The contributors to these volumes have many suggestions and recommendations for furthering the growth that has occurred, and we believe that developmental psychopathology will be enriched and will continue to exert a growing influence on theory and research in normal and abnormal development as a result of their insights.

Collectively, we wish to acknowledge the generations of developmentalists and the several decades of personal contributions of the individuals whose ideas flow throughout these volumes and whose foresight, vision, courage, and passion helped to create the field of developmental psychopathology.

Dante Cicchetti has had the privilege and good fortune of working closely with a number of scholars who have influenced his thinking and supported his work in this field, as well as provided inestimable sources of support, love, and friendship. Without the belief and guidance, as well as the ongoing love and "fatherly concern" of Alex Siegel, Dante would not have embarked on the "developmental psychopathology journey" that began in his undergraduate years and has continued through to the present. In following Alex's footsteps to the University of Minnesota, Dante studied with and was deeply influenced by three incredible intellects and persons: Norman Garmezy, Paul Meehl, and Alan Sroufe. Words cannot express Dante's indebtedness to these individuals for believing in him, providing a supportive environment, encouraging him to pursue his dreams to the fullest, and having the wisdom to look beneath the surface. When he left the University of Minnesota for Harvard University, a number of scholars and friends contributed to Dante's breadth and depth as a scientist, theorist, and clinician. In particular, his colleagues, Jules Bemporad, Phil Holzman, Jerome Kagan, Steve Kosslyn, Duncan Luce, Brendan Maher, and Shep White; his closest friends, David Buss, Heidi Mitke, Ross Rizley, and James Stellar; and his students, especially Larry Aber, Marjorie Beeghly, Vicki Carlson, Wendy Coster, Petra Hesse, and Karen Schneider-Rosen—all enhanced Dante's personal and professional growth. In his current environment at the Mt. Hope Family Center at the University of Rochester, Dante has been fortunate to be surrounded by a group of first-rate intellects and high-integrity individuals. First and foremost among these is Sheree

Toth, a phenomenal example of a scientist-clinician who has already made numerous contributions to this field. In addition, his colleagues and friends, Douglas Barnett, Kathleen Holt, Michael Lynch, Jody Todd Manly, and Fred Rogosch have greatly contributed to the exciting and productive environment that exists at Mt. Hope. Knowing that these talented individuals have chosen to become developmental psychopathologists bodes well for the continued growth of the field. Finally, Dante acknowledges the support, influence, and inspiration of Thomas Achenbach, William Charlesworth, Byron Egeland, Irving Gottesman, Larry Kohlberg, Ping Serafica, Michael Rutter, and Edward Zigler.

Donald Cohen acknowledges the influential role that his colleagues at the Yale Child Study Center have had in contributing to his thinking in the area of developmental psychopathology. Although the team is too large for everyone to be recognized by name, Donald extends special recognition to Albert Solnit and Edward Zigler.

REFERENCES

Cicchetti, D. (Ed.). (1984). Developmental psychopathology [Special issue]. *Child Development, 55,* 1–314.

Cicchetti, D. (1990). A historical perspective on the discipline of developmental psychopathology. In J. Rolf, A. Masten, D. Cicchetti, K. Nuechterlein, & S. Weintraub (Eds.), *Risk and protective factors in the development of psychopathology* (pp. 2–28). New York: Cambridge University Press.

Cohen, D. J. (1974). Competence and biology: Methodology in studies of infants, twins, psychosomatic disease and psychosis. In E. J. Anthony & C. Koupernik (Eds.), *The child in his family: Children at psychiatric risk* (pp. 361–394). New York: Wiley.

Freud, A. (1965). *Normality and pathology in childhood.* New York: International Universities Press.

Freud, S. (1955). An outline of psycho-analysis. In J. Strachey (Ed. and Trans.), *The standard edition of the complete works of Sigmund Freud* (Vol. 23, pp. 139–207). London: Hogarth Press. (Original work published 1940)

James, W. (1902). *The varieties of religious experience.* London: Longmans, Green.

Marans, S., & Cohen, D. J. (1991). Child psychoanalytic theories of development. In M. Lewis (Ed.), *Child and adolescent psychiatry: A comprehensive textbook* (pp. 613–621). Baltimore: Williams & Wilkins.

Mussen, P. (Ed.). (1983). *Handbook of child psychology* (4th ed.). New York: Wiley.

Piaget, J. (1971). *Biology and knowledge.* Chicago: University of Chicago Press.

Werner, H. (1948). *Comparative psychology of mental development.* New York: International Universities Press.

DANTE CICCHETTI
DONALD J. COHEN

Rochester, New York
New Haven, Connecticut
January 1995

Contents

Volume 2
Risk, Disorder, and Adaptation

Volume 1
Theory and Methods

PART ONE

Ecological and Relational Risk Factors

CHAPTER 1

The Child in the Family: Disruptions in Family Functions

ROBERT E. EMERY and KATHERINE M. KITZMANN

The rapidly evolving view of families in contemporary personal and political life has been reflected in changes in psychological theory and research. Psychological certainty about adaptive and maladaptive family forms has been replaced by a cornucopia of evidence about alternative family structures, functions, and processes. In fact, the injection of ambiguity has revitalized the study of the child in the family. Empirical evidence has undermined the assumption that single-parent families are invariably pathogenic, and in so doing, research on alternative families has revised thinking about child development in two-parent families. This research has demonstrated that family processes, not family structures, are critical influences on children's mental health. Thus, the overarching goal of this chapter is to review disruptions in functioning found across different family forms. These commonalities form the principles of developmental psychopathology in the family context.

The present review begins with a discussion of the psychological outcomes of children who have been reared in alternative family forms. This is an appropriate point of departure because it demonstrates the need for a developmental perspective. The term "outcome" implies stability, but research indicates that both children's psychological health and the functioning of families are best understood in the context of developmental change. The focus on outcomes also demonstrates that family structure is *not* of paramount importance to children's long-term emotional well-being. Rather than documenting their psychological risk, research indicates that children are resilient in coping with alternative family forms. This conclusion apparently holds across the variety of mental health outcomes that have been assessed, including externalizing problems, internalizing problems, self-esteem, relationships with the opposite sex, and psychological adjustment during adult life.

Despite children's resilience when measured in terms of emotional disturbance, alternative family structures are far from innocuous when children's broader psychological experience is considered. Thus, the first section of this chapter also discusses children's struggles in overcoming family adversity. The process of coping with sometimes dramatic changes in family life is distressing for almost all children (and parents). In fact, the construct of resilience implies that coping with stress takes a psychological toll. Thus, in addition to the traditional mental health concerns, it is essential to consider children's subclinical distress as a part of the experience of disruptions in family functioning. Uncertainty about oneself and one's relationships, painful memories of the past, and continued longing for things to be different often are among the feelings that form the residue of children's resilience.

Whereas the first section emphasizes normative coping processes, the second section of the chapter focuses on individual differences in children's experience of and reactions to disruptions in family functioning. It is clear that disruptions in family functioning are more common among alternative family forms than among families headed by the two biological parents. These disruptions include mother-child relationships that may be more inconsistent, negative, and less effective in terms of discipline, at least during periods when parenting support is missing. Father-child contact often is infrequent, contains less discipline, and grows increasingly distant across time. Finally, children's uncertain role in the broader system of family relationships is seen most clearly in the destructive impact of interparental conflict.

The third section of the chapter considers some functions that parents and families serve for children in addition to meeting their psychological needs by offering them love, socialization, and a network of close relationships. In particular, the family also is vital in promoting children's education and providing them with financial support. Emotional health is not the only outcome of importance to children's well-being, and recognition of these broader family functions demands that psychologists heed the wider body of multidisciplinary research on children and families. Broader domains of functioning are especially important to consider because evidence indicates that alternative family structures, particularly single-mother families, are more successful in meeting children's emotional needs than in guiding children's education and in ensuring their economic well-being. Thus, it is essential to temper conclusions about the developmental psychopathology of alternative family structures with an awareness of these broader consequences.

Although ethnic issues are considered throughout the review, the fourth and final section of the chapter explicitly acknowledges that research on children's development in families necessarily is embedded in and bounded by the limits of culture and time. Broad, cultural influences are evident both in the contemporary demographics of American families and in the history of American families of different ethnic backgrounds. It is especially important to recognize cultural and subcultural influences, because the vast majority of family research to date has focused on the experience of European Americans and on the alternative family structures found most commonly among whites: legal marriage, divorce, and remarriage. Comparatively little research has been conducted on African Americans or other ethnic minorities, or on childbirth outside of marriage, extended families, and informal marital unions and dissolutions. The present review can only cover the body of extant research, but it attempts to demonstrate the importance of broadening the focus of future investigation to include additional family issues and ethnicities. The need for a broader focus can be demonstrated initially with a brief overview of the demographics of contemporary American families.

AMERICAN FAMILIES IN DEMOGRAPHIC PERSPECTIVE

There is a strong tendency to define "family" in terms of the prototypical structure idealized in the 1950s: an employed husband and a homemaker wife in their first marriage and living with their two biological children. The U.S. Census Bureau defines family more broadly, as two or more persons residing together and related by birth, marriage, or adoption. In 1988, however, only 72% of all households were occupied by families, and only 36% contained children under the age of 18. Moreover, only 60% of children living in a family household resided with their two biological parents, and only 40% of these children had a mother who was not in the labor force (Select Committee on Children, Youth, and Families [SCCYF], 1989).

Ethnic Differences

These global statistics mask prominent differences in the composition of European American, African American, Hispanic American, and Asian American families that result from cultural, historical, and economic influences as discussed later in this chapter. In 1988, 79% of white children lived with two parents, as did 66% of Hispanic children. Only 39% of black children lived with two parents, however. Conversely, 51% of black children lived with a single mother, as did 27% of Hispanic children, and 16% of white children. About 3% of children from each ethnic group lived with their fathers, while 2% of whites, 4% of Hispanics, and 7% of blacks lived with neither parent (SCCYF, 1989). Other ethnic differences also are important to consider. For example, among Hispanic Americans, single-parenting is twice as high among Puerto Ricans as it is among Mexican Americans (Laosa, 1988). Finally, national data on the family living arrangements of Asian children are not currently available, but two-parent families are more common among Asians than among the other three most numerous American ethnic groups (Laosa, 1988). Family size also is smaller among this growing proportion of American families (Kitano & Daniels, 1988).

Divorce, Unmarried Parenting, and Remarriage

Divorce is a major cause of children's family living arrangements in a society where 56% of recent first marriages are expected to end in divorce within the first 40 years of marriage (Bumpass, 1990). In fact, 38% of white children and 75% of black children born to married parents are expected to experience a parental divorce before the age of 18 (Bumpass, 1984). Despite the prominence of divorce, the greatest ethnic differences in family composition result from childbirth outside of marriage. In 1986, 23% of all American births occurred outside of marriage, including 16% of the children born to whites, 32% of the children born to Hispanics, and 61% of the children born to blacks (SCCYF, 1989).

Remarriage is another, substantial influence on children's living circumstances. In 1988, 11% of children were living with one biological parent and one stepparent (8% with stepfathers and 3% with stepmothers) (SCCYF, 1989). The census bureau does not provide these data broken down by ethnic group, but other evidence indicates that three times as many white as black children (35% vs. 12%) experience a legal remarriage within five years following a divorce (Bumpass, 1984). Thus, out-of-wedlock birth, divorce, and remarriage all contribute to the substantial ethnic differences in family structure in the United States today.

Constantly Evolving Family Structures

Although changes in the composition of American families have been dramatic over the past 25 years, these changes have not been limited to the United States. The divorce rates in the United States are the highest in the world, but other European countries have experienced a similar surge in divorce and out-of-wedlock births since the 1960s (U.S. Department of Education, 1991). In fact, birth rates to unmarried women are considerably lower in the United States than in some European countries. In predominantly white Sweden, for example, the divorce rate in 1986 was about half of that of the United States. At the same time, 48% of childbirths occurred outside marriage in Sweden, compared with 23% in the United States (U.S. Department of Education, 1991).

All these statistics demonstrate that the 1950s image of the American family is grossly inaccurate (Cherlin, 1993), as are many psychological theories that were based on this narrow concept of the family (Emery, 1988). Contemporary family demographics do not represent an historical aberration, moreover, as the composition of family households in early American history did not conform with the idealized assumptions of the present day. For example, in New England in the 1700s, 35% of European-American couples were expecting children before they were legally married (Demos, 1986). In the 1800s, 25% of Mexican American and African American households were headed by a female with no male in the home (Altenbaugh, 1991; Franklin, 1988). Lower life expectancy also made broken homes and remarriage common among families of all ethnic backgrounds during earlier eras (Shorter, 1975). In short, family structures have evolved across history, and psychological research and theory must either label enormous numbers of families as being pathological or else take this diversity and change in family forms into account. A developmental psychopathology perspective promises to fulfill this latter goal.

FAMILY STRUCTURE AND CHILDREN'S PSYCHOLOGICAL OUTCOMES

Since the 1950s, much psychological research has been conducted on the adjustment of children living in various alternative family forms. Some of this research has been driven by psychological theory. For example, one interpretation of psychoanalytic theory suggested that because of the paramount importance of the resolution of the Oedipal conflict to children's identification with the parent of the same gender, boys are at risk of being feminized as a result of being reared in a fatherless home. The interpretation further suggested that these boys subsequently become overly aggressive as a defense against their hypothesized feminization (Miller, 1958).

Although investigators are well versed in challenging such theoretical constructions of psychology, other research on alternative family forms has been motivated by practical and political pressures. After all, terms like "divorce" and "single-parent families" are legal and social categories, not psychological ones. In short, psychological research has taken place within a sociopolitical context that surely has influenced the hypotheses, findings, and interpretation of psychological research. It may be impossible to document such contextual influences on empirical findings, but it is essential to recognize that the broad social context surely affects conclusions about psychological research on family structure (Halem, 1981).

Despite these caveats, the large body of research on children's adjustment in alternative family forms deserves careful examination. Notwithstanding potential biases and limits on research, there are many theoretical and practical reasons for examining the psychological adjustment of children living in different types of families. Another reason for examining this literature, however, is that it is at least as informative about children's resilience in the face of adversity, as it is about the risk to children's mental health that is posed by different family forms. Perhaps an even more important reason for considering the literature on children's outcomes is that it underscores the need for a developmental perspective on families and children's mental health (Cicchetti, 1993). There are predictable time- and age-graded changes in the psychological well-being of children living in different types of families. There also are predictable time- and age-graded changes in family composition and in difficulties in family functioning.

The Average Adjustment of Children in Married and Divorced Families

The debate about alternative family forms and the psychological adjustment of children has reached its pinnacle in the case of divorce. On one side of the debate are those who believe that the damaging psychological consequences for children have been ignored or overlooked. This position is common in the public media, and it has received particularly strong support from clinicians who rely primarily on case studies to reach

their conclusions. For example, in their influential book of case studies of families followed longitudinally up to 15 years after divorce, Wallerstein and Blakeslee (1989) concluded: "Many of the children emerged in young adulthood as compassionate, courageous, and competent people. . . . In this study [of divorce], however, almost half of the children entered adulthood as worried, underachieving, self-deprecating, and sometimes angry young men and women" (pp. 298–299).

In contrast, more benign conclusions have been reached by researchers who note the obvious problems with the case study method. These include unstandardized measurement, small and biased samples, the absence of comparison groups, and the failure to control for demographic background conditions (Emery, 1988). Allison and Furstenberg (1989), demographers who studied a nationally representative sample of divorced families, provide a good example of the other side of the debate: ". . . the proportion of variation in the outcome measures that could be attributed to marital dissolution was generally quite small, never amounting to more than 3%" (p. 546).

In fact, empirical researchers generally have demonstrated that the differences between children from married and divorced families are small in magnitude. These modest differences have been noted consistently in qualitative reviews of the literature on children and divorce (e.g., Amato, 1993; Atkeson, Forehand, & Rickard, 1982; Emery, 1982; 1988; Emery, Hetherington, & DiLalla, 1984; Furstenberg & Cherlin, 1991; Grych & Fincham, 1990, 1992; Hetherington, 1989), although some reviewers have come to a different conclusion (e.g., Wallerstein, 1991). The body of research on children and divorce has been summarized quantitatively, moreover, in a recent meta-analysis by Amato and Keith (1991a). These reviewers found an effect size of .14 standard deviation units when comparing children from divorced and married families across all measures of children's psychological difficulties. The authors noted that even this small difference may be an overestimate, because the effect sizes in their meta-analysis decreased as the methodological sophistication of research increased (Amato & Keith, 1991a). Specifically, smaller effect sizes were found in studies that included demographic control variables, matched subjects, used representative rather than convenience samples, or included more reliable measures of children's adjustment. When these conclusions are considered together with questions about third variables and reverse causality when interpreting the correlation between divorce and children's adjustment problems (Emery, 1988), it would seem that the most parsimonious conclusion is that there are only modest differences in the global psychological adjustment of children whose biological parents are married or divorced. Because more psychological difficulties typically are found among children whose parents are divorced than among those living with a parent who is single for other reasons (Emery, 1982), this conclusion can be applied to alternative family forms in general.

A number of qualifications apply to this conclusion, however. The magnitude of differences in the adjustment of children living with married and divorced parents may differ for various areas of psychological functioning, temporal and developmental factors may bear on children's outcomes, and mean data may mask variability in children's response to divorce (including variation related to children's age, gender, and ethnic background). Before delving into these specifics, however, it is worthwhile first to attempt to reconcile the debate between clinical observation and empirical research by considering the distinction between disturbance and distress.

A Focus on Resilience

Emery and Forehand (1994) have asserted that the construct of psychological resilience suggests a way of reconciling the findings of empirical research, which emphasize children's successful coping with divorce, and those of clinicians, which emphasize children's distress. Resilience has been defined as "the maintenance of competent functioning despite an interfering emotionality" (Garmezy, 1991, p. 466), an approach that emphasizes both children's success in overcoming the odds and the struggles involved in doing so. Research indicates that successful coping is the most common outcome of divorce for children, at least as judged by standard indexes of their mental health. The absence of psychological problems is not the same as the presence of positive mental health or life satisfaction, however, and other evidence attests to the difficulties involved in reaching the endpoint of adjustment.

Stressors in Divorce

Research on the family disruptions that result from divorce offers some of the most compelling evidence on the struggles that children face in coping with the family transition. As reviewed in more detail later in the chapter, family living standards fall dramatically after divorce. In fact, a number of single-mother families move into poverty as a result of divorce (Nichols-Casebolt, 1986). Contact with nonresidential parents (fathers in roughly 90% of divorces) also falls dramatically. According to one recent study, 32% of nonresidential divorced fathers had seen their children not at all or only a few times in the past year, 22% saw them several times a year, 21% saw them up to 3 times per month, and only 25% saw them weekly (Seltzer, 1991). Although less easily quantified, other evidence indicates that children's relationships with residential mothers also become more strained (Hetherington, 1991; Hetherington & Clingempeel, 1992), and depression and other mental health problems among parents increase (Gotlib & McCabe, 1990). In addition, conflict between parents, which theoretically is resolved by divorce, may actually escalate for some families following a marital separation, and it may become more focused on the children (Emery, Matthews, & Kitzmann, 1994; Maccoby & Mnookin, 1992). These are substantial stressors that challenge children's coping resources, even if researchers have not fully documented the difficulties involved.

Distress if Not Disturbance

Another indicator of children's distress can be found in clinical reports. Detailed observations have been made about divorce and children's resentment and longing about the past, torn loyalties in the present, and fears about their own and their parents' future (e.g., Emery, 1994; Wallerstein & Blakeslee, 1989; Wallerstein

& Kelly, 1980). Such observations are supported by empirical evidence indicating that substantial proportions of children from divorced families report fantasies of parental reconciliation, fears of being abandoned by both parents, and social embarrassment about divorce (Kurdek & Berg, 1987).

Research also consistently reveals that children from divorced families are overrepresented in the outpatient treatment population. In one national study, children from divorced families were two to three times as likely to have seen a mental health professional in comparison with children whose parents were married (Zill, 1978). Although seeking treatment for children sometimes may only reflect parental overconcern, this statistic surely must indicate increased distress among children as well. In fact, a follow-up study of this same national sample documented a variety of unhappy circumstances that were found significantly more often among children (who were now young adults) from divorced rather than married families: (a) 41% versus 22% had sought psychological help, (b) 30% versus 16% reported having a bad relationship with their mothers, and (c) 65% versus 29% said they had a bad relationship with their fathers (Zill, Morrison, & Coiro, 1993). Finally, in a different national survey, adults who had experienced a parental divorce during childhood were more likely than others to report that childhood was the "unhappiest time of their lives" (Kulka & Weingarten, 1979).

Thus, at the same time that it focuses attention on their psychological strengths, the resilience construct raises concerns about children's emotional distress. Children's life happiness is not equivalent to scores in the average range on behavior checklists or to the absence of unusual behavior during a brief, videotaped interaction. Few concerned parents would define their own children's mental health in such narrow terms. Although existing research is reassuring, psychologists cannot be complacent about null findings when so much goes unmeasured. Thus, one challenge for quantitative researchers is to develop new measures of children's well-being that tap the subtle sources of distress suggested by qualitative research. Another challenge is to extend the focus on resilience to other, alternative family forms in order to document both children's strengths and their struggles in living in families that are different from the ideal, even if they differ less from the ever-changing norm.

Different Mental Health Outcomes

In addition to the distinction between distress and disturbance, it is important to consider different areas of mental health functioning when evaluating the outcomes of children living in alternative family forms. Again, the literature on divorce offers the most evidence on this topic. Among the range of outcomes that have been considered are externalizing problems, internalizing problems, self-esteem, relationships with members of the opposite sex, and adjustment during adult life.

Much research on children from divorced and single-parent families has been motivated by concerns about excessive externalizing problems. Research initially emphasized increased rates of juvenile delinquency (e.g., Glueck & Glueck, 1950), and later investigation focused on difficulties in parenting aggressive and coercive children, particularly boys (e.g., Hetherington, Cox, &

Cox, 1982). This concern with and focus on externalizing problems among children has been justified by empirical evidence. In the meta-analysis discussed earlier, the largest effect size obtained for children's mental health problems was .23 for children's conduct problems, compared with an effect size of .12 for social functioning, .09 for self-concept, and .08 for general psychological adjustment (Amato & Keith, 1991a).

As children of divorce move through adolescence and into adult life, interpersonal relationships increasingly have been of concern to clinicians and researchers (e.g., Hetherington, 1972; Wallerstein & Blakeslee, 1989). A particular focal point has been the intergenerational transmission of divorce. Amato and Keith (1991b) have conducted a second meta-analysis of the literature on adjustment of children of divorce during adult life, and their review indicates that empirical findings also support the accuracy of this focus. They compared adults reared by parents who divorced with adults reared by parents who remained married, and found an effects size of .36 for the children's (now adults') likelihood of being single parents. The analysis also yielded an effect size of .22 for the likelihood that the children of divorce would divorce or separate themselves in comparison with children of married parents. Moderate effect sizes also were found for various measures of "psychological adjustment" (.32) and for use of mental health services (.21) when comparing adults from divorced versus married families. Other effect sizes were more modest (Amato & Keith, 1991b).

Many of the effect sizes that were obtained during adult life were larger than those obtained during childhood. Although this may indicate that many of the adverse consequences of divorce for children are delayed until adult life, some cautions suggest that it is premature to reach this conclusion. As with the child meta-analysis, the effect sizes obtained for adults grew smaller as the methodological sophistication of the study increased (Amato & Keith, 1991b). This may be a particularly important influence, since more research has been conducted on childhood than adult adjustment. In fact, while the former meta-analysis included 92 different studies, the latter was based on 37 investigations.

Cohort effects perhaps are the most important potential confound, however. Studies of adults necessarily involve cohorts born in an earlier historical period. In many cases, these adults experienced a parental divorce during a time before divorce rates increased to a level where divorce was "common." It therefore is likely that their families suffered from more distress in taking the extreme step of divorce during the earlier historical period. It also is likely that the social consequences of divorce involved more rejection and less support for both parents and children who experienced divorce in the 1950s and 1960s than in the 1970s and 1980s. In support of this speculation about cohort effects, larger effect sizes were found for both children and adults when studies had been conducted in earlier than in more recent historical periods (Amato & Keith, 1991a, 1991b). Thus, an unbiased comparison of child and adult outcome awaits longitudinal research that follows the same children from childhood into adult life during a time of relative stability in social views and practices regarding divorce.

Consideration of these more differentiated indexes of children's adjustment to divorce suggests the importance of a devel-

opmental perspective on the outcome of children living in alternative family forms. Age- and time-graded influences may alter children's experience of the family transition. In fact, theoretical, methodological, and empirical considerations all indicate the importance of taking a developmental psychopathology approach to understanding children's divorce adjustment, as numerous temporal influences must be taken into account.

Children's Divorce Outcomes in Developmental Perspective

The term "outcome" connotes stability, but developmental change would seem to be a more accurate means of conceptualizing the adjustment of children from married and divorced families. Some of children's emotional difficulties begin prior to the parents' marital separation, and others may continue not only after the legal divorce, but also after children form independent households as young adults. In fact, the developmental perspective suggests the need to look backward in time beyond the point of conception. Some of the "consequences of divorce" for children may be due to nonrandom selection into divorce (and into nonmarital or teenage childbearing), and these third variables may account both for children's family status and their psychological functioning. The most important, recent research on these developmental issues has compared children's adjustment before and after divorce.

Children's Adjustment Prior to Divorce

Children from divorced families traditionally have been studied only after the divorce takes place. This method leaves unanswered the question of whether or not any difficulties in their adjustment actually reflect preexisting problems. In fact, a handful of studies that were designed as longitudinal investigations of normal development have recently been used to compare the adjustment of children prior and subsequent to divorce. These investigations suggest that many of the problems found among children after divorce actually begin *before* divorce.

The first study to make this comparison focused on a small sample of children who had been assessed extensively in a longitudinal study of normal social development. Block, Block, and Gjerde (1986) examined children's predivorce adjustment by comparing children from to-be-divorced and to-remain-married families. Their analyses found more aggression among boys after a parental divorce, but this aggression also was present many years earlier when the boys were still living with their married parents.

Similar findings have been reported by investigators who have used much larger samples. Cherlin and colleagues (1991) found statistically significant differences in the behavior problems of children whose parents were divorced versus married in two nationally representative samples, one of American and another of British children. These differences were no longer significant, however, when various predivorce characteristics were statistically controlled. Children's predivorce adjustment was the most notable of the control variables, which also included demographic indexes and a family conflict measure. Although the marginal reliability and the narrow domains of measurement surely diminished the study's ability to detect differences, the large sample size gave the analyses substantial statistical power.

An independent analysis of the British sample also concluded that postdivorce differences are found predivorce. Compared with children whose parents were married, children from divorced families were found to be more "disruptive" and "unhappy and worried" when they were 16 years old. Differences of the same magnitude also were found between the two groups at age 7, however, when all the children's biological parents were still married to each other (Elliott & Richards, 1991). In fact, divorce did not alter the trajectory of children's preexisting differences on measures of psychological problems. In contrast, divorce exacerbated preexisting differences in children's math and reading achievement scores. Significant achievement discrepancies that were present at age 7 grew wider by age 16 (Elliott & Richards, 1991).

Nonrandom Selection into Divorce

If children's behavior problems are present before divorce, they may be explained by two major alternative hypotheses. One hypothesis is that differences are due to selection factors. Selection into alternative family forms is nonrandom, as indicated by demographic evidence (SCCYF, 1989) and by research on the increased likelihood of divorce when one partner has a severe psychological disorder (e.g., Emery, Weintraub, & Neale, 1982). Furthermore, recent evidence has indicated that genetic factors may play a role in explaining individual differences in selection into divorce (McGue & Lykken, 1992). Thus, a characteristic that is partially mediated by genetic factors, such as antisocial behavior patterns (Mednick, Gabrielli, & Hutchings, 1984), may be responsible for both an increased likelihood of parental divorce and an increased likelihood of externalizing problems among children.

An alternative hypothesis is that disruptions in family functioning begin before a marital separation, and these disruptions, not just divorce per se, are responsible for the psychological disturbance and distress found among children prior to divorce. Parental conflict is an obvious disruption that typically precedes a divorce and is related to increased adjustment difficulties among children (Emery, 1982; Grych & Fincham, 1990). Moreover, some further analysis of existing, longitudinal data sets indicates that difficulties in parenting after divorce actually begin before divorce, much in the same way that child behavior problems begin at an earlier period (Block et al., 1986, 1988; Shaw, Emery, & Tuer, 1993). Thus, like the selection hypothesis, the family disruption hypothesis also is a tenable explanation for the increase in children's behavior problems prior to divorce.

Parental Antisocial Behavior, Divorce, and Child Externalizing

Testing the selection and family process alternative hypotheses is an important challenge for researchers. In fact, the role of parental antisocial behavior and marital status (or marital conflict) in explaining behavior disturbances among children has been examined in a handful of studies. Rutter (1971), who tested the joint and independent contributions of parental personality disorder and an unhappy marriage in predicting conduct disorder among large community samples of children, found that parental personality did not account for the risk associated with

marital distress. The interaction between personality disorder and marital unhappiness fell just short of statistical significance, however (Rutter, 1971). Lahey and colleagues (1988) reported different results in an analysis of parental divorce, antisocial personality disorder, and conduct disorder in a small sample of clinic-referred children. In this study, parents' antisocial personality disorder did account for the relation between divorce and conduct disorder. In contrast, Capaldi and Patterson (1991) found that maternal antisocial behavior was related to multiple marital transitions in an analysis of a large, community sample of at-risk boys. However, neither maternal antisocial behavior nor marital transitions accounted for the children's behavior problems two years later. Instead, antisocial behavior was linked with parental involvement, which, in turn, accounted for the boys' problems (Capaldi & Patterson, 1991). Finally, Emery, Kitzmann, and Aaron (1993) found that maternal antisocial behavior predicted both subsequent marital status and children's externalizing behavior. Children's aggression was accounted for by parental divorce, not by a history of maternal antisocial behavior in the statistical analyses reported in this study. This last investigation was based on a large, national sample, and it was the only study to include measures that were prospectively ordered in the hypothesized sequence. Maternal antisocial behavior was assessed 1 to 9 years prior to marital status and 10 years before children's externalizing. Assessment of divorce also preceded measurement of child behavior by a minimum of a year (Emery et al., 1993).

Concerns about selection into divorce and about predivorce family processes both focus on important temporal issues occurring *before* divorce. Three additional time- and age-related issues that occur *after* divorce are of potential relevance to children's outcomes. These are the child's age at the time of divorce, the time that has elapsed since the divorce, and the child's current developmental stage.

Children's Age at Divorce

A number of theoretical perspectives suggest that children's age at the time of divorce may influence their subsequent adjustment to the family transition. Most of these viewpoints focus on separation during the preschool period as being most disturbing to children, a prediction consistent with Oedipal theory (Meissner, 1978), object relations theory (Goldstein, Freud, & Solnit, 1973), attachment theory (Bowlby, 1973), and social-cognitive theories, which emphasize the preschooler's limited understanding of divorce (e.g., Wallerstein & Kelly, 1980). Empirically, however, findings in relation to age at separation or divorce and children's later psychological outcomes have been mixed. Several investigators have found more problems among children whose parents divorced before a child reached the age of 6 years (Allison & Furstenberg, 1989; Hetherington, 1972; Peterson & Zill, 1986; Zill et al., 1993). Other researchers have found no effects due to age at separation (Power, Ash, Schoenberg, & Sorey, 1974), however, and in a handful of studies, more problems have been found in the late divorcing group (Gibson, 1969; McCord, McCord, & Thurber, 1962).

A factor in considering this mixed body of research findings is that parents themselves may believe that divorce is more harmful to preschoolers. Couples with young children are about half as likely to divorce as are childless couples who have been married for the same length of time (Waite, Haggstrom, & Kanouse, 1985), whereas divorce rates for families with school-age children are comparable to those of childless marriages of the same length (Cherlin, 1977). Nevertheless, because shorter marriages are much more likely to end in divorce than are longer ones, about twice as many preschoolers as school-age children experience a parental divorce (Furstenberg, Peterson, Nord, & Zill, 1983).

Thus, psychological theories and parental behavior suggest a stronger relation between age at divorce and children's adjustment than has been demonstrated in empirical research to date. One reason for this discrepancy likely is the modest global relation between divorce and child outcomes, which makes age-at-separation effects difficult to detect. Another reason for the inconsistent empirical evidence surely is that divorce is a process, not an event, and there is wide variation in the pre- and post-divorce family environments experienced by children of all ages. Finally, some of the lack of clarity about age at separation probably is caused by its being inextricably confounded with other temporal factors, as is discussed shortly.

Before turning to a discussion of these additional temporal influences on children's divorce adjustment, one age-at-separation effect should be noted in relation to children's coping and psychological distress. Children of different ages have differing interpretations of the personal and the abstract meanings of a parental divorce. Wallerstein and Kelly (1980) offer a sensitive descriptive account of how children interpret the family transition according to their own developmental level. Preschoolers commonly are full of bewilderment, fears of abandonment, and self-blame; early school-age children experience more grief, including sadness, yearning, and fantasies of reconciliation; older school-age children understand the concrete meaning of divorce, and they disapprove of and are embarrassed by it; finally, teenagers are able to understand a divorce more abstractly, and they struggle more with integrating the painful family disruption with their own, emerging sense of self (Wallerstein & Kelly, 1980).

Time since Divorce

Perhaps the most common developmental influence that alters children's divorce adjustment is the passage of time. As the crisis of divorce subsides, children's distress is thought to lessen (Hetherington, 1979). In fact, according to a meta-analysis of existing research, studies that have included information on the time since divorce find fewer conduct problems as more time has passed since the marital separation. Time since divorce was unrelated to the effect sizes of other outcome measures, however (Amato & Keith, 1991a).

While interesting, such cross-sectional research on a temporal variable can be called into question. Importantly, several longitudinal studies have reported improvement in children's functioning over time (Allison & Furstenberg, 1989; Ambert, 1984; Hetherington, Cox, & Cox, 1985; Wallerstein & Kelly, 1980). The multimethod research of Hetherington and colleagues (1985) is the most notable documentation of improvements in children's and the family's functioning as time passes beyond a divorce. A question that can be raised about the relief

children experience as the crisis of divorce is resolved, however, is whether children experience a decline in disturbance or merely in distress. It may be that more serious disruptions in family functioning related to truly dysfunctional child behavior are less likely to be alleviated merely as a function of the passage of time. Still, longitudinal research on divorce supports the common wisdom that time does heal.

Current Developmental Level

Children's current age or developmental level is a third and final temporal issue that may moderate their adjustment following divorce. This developmental issue perhaps can be conceptualized best in terms of the diathesis-stress model. The experience of a parental divorce may lead to problematic outcomes only when it is combined with the stressors that children confront as a part of normal, developmental transitions.

The idea that predisposing conditions may exacerbate or potentiate the struggles involved in normal developmental transitions is a familiar one. Researchers, however, have offered little theory or even much speculation about alternative family forms based on this model, a somewhat surprising circumstance. Probably the most commonly discussed hypothesis is that divorce has consequences that make it more difficult for children, especially girls, to form heterosexual relationships when they reach early (Hetherington, 1972) or late adolescence (Wallerstein & Blakeslee, 1989). Wallerstein and Blakeslee (1989) termed their proposed emergence of relationship difficulties a "sleeper effect," problems that, like a time bomb, are destined to explode eventually. Emergent problems with heterosexual relationships perhaps are better conceptualized from a developmental psychopathology perspective. Relationship difficulties (to the extent that they occur) likely reflect exaggerated difficulties in coping with predictably difficult developmental transitions. That is, the problem only is evident and will only emerge in a given social context.

Although predictions about developmental challenges or transitions are rare, even more sparse is research in which children of different ages are compared directly within a single study (Amato & Keith, 1991a). Many investigators have focused on the divorce adjustment of children of a circumscribed age range, however, and comparisons across studies of children of different ages are relevant to the present question. In the meta-analysis of children's outcomes, larger effect sizes tended to be found for children in primary or secondary school, as opposed to preschoolers or college students (Amato & Keith, 1991a). These findings are puzzling. They run counter both to the prediction that early divorce is more damaging to children, and to speculation that divorce predisposes children for troubles in forming intimate relationships with members of the opposite sex. If the limited theorizing, general absence of research, and confusing empirical findings do point to anything, it is the need for further investigation of how children from divorced families subsequently cope with normal developmental transitions.

The Age-at-Event, Time, Current-Age Problem

As investigators conduct further research on children's age at divorce, the time that has passed since divorce, or their current age, it is essential that they recognize that these three variables are perfectly confounded (Emery, 1988). Once any two of these variables is fixed, the third is determined perfectly. This observation can be made clear by briefly considering the very simple equation:

$$\text{Age at divorce} + \text{Time since divorce} = \text{Current age}$$

Whereas the formula is simple, it has infrequently been recognized that research on any one of these temporal variables is inevitably confounded by one or both of the other variables. For example, in an investigation of children who are all of the same age, a researcher could measure how much time has elapsed since the divorce, as this variable will differ among the children. Time since divorce would be perfectly confounded with age at divorce, however. (Current age − Time since divorce = Age at divorce.) Other research strategies would similarly lead to other confounds between the three variables (Emery, 1988). In fact, the age-at-event, time, current-age problem is analogous to the age-period-cohort problem in longitudinal research (Baltes, Cornelius, & Nesselroade, 1979), a methodological conundrum that has yet to be resolved even though it has been long recognized. To complicate the consideration of temporal issues even further, it can be noted that cohort effects also might affect research on children's divorce adjustment, as was briefly mentioned in the earlier discussion of adjustment during adult life.

Growth Curves

The many temporal issues related to children's divorce adjustment not only are difficult methodologically, they also can be confusing to grasp conceptually. Fortunately, the issues can be summarized simply and clearly if they are portrayed in terms of growth curves (Emery, 1988). Curves illustrating changes in children's physical stature provide excellent portrayals of time- and age-graded changes in children's physical and cognitive development (McArdle & Epstein, 1987), and similar chartings can summarize social development, including all five of the key developmental issues discussed to this point. As illustrated in Figure 1.1, age-graded growth curves of children's adjustment to divorce can capture many important points in a single diagram.

In examining Figure 1.1, first consider children's adjustment near the time of divorce. The growth curve indicates an increase in the adjustment difficulties of children around the time of divorce. These problems begin before divorce, and they diminish in the few years following divorce. Figure 1.1 also portrays nonrandom selection into divorce that may be genetically mediated (the divorce group begins life with more adjustment problems on average), and the curve further indicates that children from divorced families struggle more with normal, developmental transitions long after the divorce occurs. In this diagram, the transitions to adolescence and to adulthood are portrayed as more difficult struggles for children from divorced families than they are for children whose parents are married. Finally, Figure 1.1 illustrates the similar patterning but differing mean levels of adjustment difficulties that theoretically are experienced by children who are preschoolers rather than school-age when their parents divorce (compare the early-divorce and late-divorce curves). Cohort effects might be portrayed by adding further curves, but they are not included in Figure 1.1.

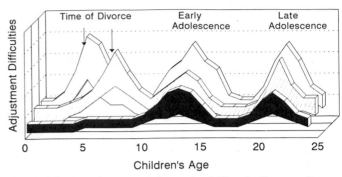

Figure 1.1   Developmental change in children's divorce adjustment—hypothetical growth curves.

Note: (a) nonrandom selection into divorce, (b) increased difficulties prior to divorce, (c) decline in problems after divorce, (d) exaggerated distress during developmental transitions, (e) greater effect of divorce at early age, (f) overlap of distributions, and (g) variability within all groups.

Figure 1.1 may or may not capture children's divorce experience accurately. It is based on theory, not evidence. Although the details may be called into question, this summary figure indicates the value of a developmental psychopathology perspective. Children's divorce outcomes are far from static.

Variability in Divorce Outcomes: Characteristics of the Child

In addition to the various temporal influences on children's divorce outcomes, Figure 1.1 also portrays considerable variability within the group of children from divorced families. At least some of this variation in divorce is attributable to characteristics of the child. Some of the most important child characteristics are gender, temperament, and race.

Gender as a Moderating Factor

A number of earlier studies of the adjustment of children from divorced families indicated that more difficulties were found among boys than girls (for a review, see Emery, 1982). More recent research on gender differences reveals a more clouded picture. Very few gender differences in children's (Amato & Keith, 1991a) or adults' (Amato & Keith, 1991b) postdivorce functioning were documented in two recent meta-analyses. Moreover, in a review specifically focused on gender differences, Zaslow (1988) found only weak and inconsistent support for the hypothesis that more severe or pervasive difficulties are found among boys. The conclusions of reviewers are echoed in very recent research, which has failed to find significant differences in the divorce adjustment of boys and girls (Hetherington, 1991; 1993; Zill et al., 1993).

It is not clear why earlier studies found gender differences, whereas they have not been uncovered in more recent investigations. Several possible alternative explanations are worth considering, however. One explanation is that investigators have confused main and interaction effects in some cases. Boys typically are found to have more behavior problems than girls, and when such gender differences are found in samples of children from divorced families, the main effect for gender can easily be misinterpreted as a reaction to divorce. What is missing in this analysis is a comparison group of children from married families, with the interaction between gender and marital status being critical to the sex difference. In fact, a complete test of gender differences in response to divorce would find not only a marital status by gender interaction, but also a three-way interaction with longitudinal data on pre- to postdivorce adjustment in the manner of research discussed earlier.

The custody arrangement studied is another possible influence on gender differences. Most children live in the custody of their mothers, and some research has found a gender-of-parent by gender-of-child interaction such that children fare best when living with their same-sex parent (Warshak, 1986). Recent evidence on much larger samples has challenged this finding, however (Downey & Powell, 1993). Additional factors that may explain why gender differences have been found less frequently in recent research include the increased use of larger, nonclinic samples, the extension of research from childhood into adolescence, and the development of more reliable measures of children's internalizing problems. In an earlier review, gender differences were found to be more pronounced when externalizing problems among clinic samples of school-age children were studied (Emery, 1982; Zaslow, 1988).

Thus, the magnitude of the distress of divorce does not appear to differ for boys and girls. Still, there are numerous reasons to continue to examine ways in which gender differences in response to divorce may manifest themselves in terms of the nature, timing, and course of boys', and girls', coping and adjustment. Perhaps the most accurate conclusion that can be reached based on present research is that gender does not moderate outcome in a straightforward manner, but it is one of several factors that may alter the trajectory of children's divorce adjustment.

Race as a Moderating Factor

As noted at the outset of this chapter, perhaps the most important thing to note about research on race, family status, and children's adjustment is the need to conduct more of it, a conclusion that also has been reached by other reviewers. (Amato and Keith, 1991a, found only five out of 92 studies contained all-black samples, and therefore had to drop race from their meta-analysis.) Some research on adults suggests more difficulties are found among whites than among blacks following divorce (Amato & Keith, 1991b), as does a recent investigation on children (Emery et al., 1993). Of course, any influence of race on outcome surely is mediated by social and subcultural differences between European Americans and African Americans, not by intraindividual factors. In fact, we consider the important topic of social and cultural influences on divorce adjustment at some length in the final section of this chapter.

Temperament as a Moderating Factor

Temperament is another factor that may be responsible for some of the variability in children's adjustment to divorce. One research group recently reported that a difficult temperament is associated with more problems in psychological adjustment following divorce (Tschann, Johnston, Kline, & Wallerstein, 1989). A difficult temperament also was linked with a better relationship with the father, however, a finding the authors attributed to fathers' attempts to protect temperamentally difficult children. Hetherington (1989) also found that temperament affected children's divorce adjustment, but the pattern of influence was a complex one. She found that temperamentally difficult children became less adaptable as stress increased, even when support was available. In contrast, temperamentally easy children benefited from support when they were exposed to moderate levels of stress, but support did not have a buffering effect when children were faced with high or low levels of stress.

Each of these sets of findings supports a diathesis-stress model, wherein a difficult temperament predisposes children toward having more problems following divorce. Hetherington's data (1989) suggest that this may result, in part, from temperamentally difficult children's inability to take advantage of resources in the environment, whereas Tschann et al. (1989) highlight the different reactions that a difficult temperament elicits from their divorced parents. Although both studies suggest interesting developmental models, caution is indicated by the small magnitude of obtained relations and the limited research conducted to date.

Summary

A number of key issues are highlighted when the literature on children and divorce is considered from a developmental psychopathology perspective. Children's divorce outcomes depend on a number of intraindividual characteristics and vary according to the outcome that is considered. Developmental influences are especially important to recognize, and they are quite numerous. As summarized in the theoretical growth curves in Figure 1.1, age- and time-graded influences include nonrandom selection into divorce, increased difficulties prior to divorce, diminishing problems in the few years after divorce, and particular struggles in coping with key developmental transitions. Furthermore, while divorce adjustment may follow the same trajectory, the average level of difficulties may differ when divorce occurs when children are younger or older, or for children born into different cohorts. Whatever the moderating influences, however, resilience, not risk, is the more accurate way to characterize the normative experience of children whose parents divorce. Still, the construct of resilience highlights both children's long-term emotional adjustment and the distress involved in coping with difficult changes in their lives.

FAMILY PROCESSES AND CHILD OUTCOMES

The wide variability in the psychological outcomes of divorce for children may be explained less by characteristics of the child and more by individual differences in family disruption associated with single parenting, divorce, or remarriage. For some children and their parents, a divorce is a relief from a conflict-ridden and perhaps abusive family life. For other children, the marital separation is a complete surprise. It is the end of a family life that they thought was happy, and it may be the beginning of a series of unwanted changes in their relationships with both of their parents, as well as in their parents' relationship with each other.

This section of the chapter reviews evidence on several key family relationships that have been demonstrated to be disrupted by divorce, single-parenting, and remarriage. Most of this discussion again focuses on divorce, reflecting the preponderance of the literature on the topic. The first subsection focuses on disruptions in parent-child relationships, including relationships between children and both of their biological parents, as well as between children and stepparents. The second subsection emphasizes relationships between the various parents themselves, with particular attention to interparental conflict and children's role in the broader system of family relationships.

Parent-Child Relationships

There is considerable evidence that parent-child relationships are strained in single-parent, divorced, and remarried families. Both mothers and fathers who parent alone confront a number of challenges, although their experiences can differ considerably. Mothers typically retain primary responsibility for rearing their children following divorce or nonmarital childbirth, and they thus face the sometimes overwhelming task of assuming sole responsibility for most day-to-day child rearing. Fathers, in contrast, typically see their children far less frequently, and they feel the effects of their "visitor" status. Fathers may be lonely and isolated, and they can feel as if their paternal role has been reduced to providing a bit of fun and a paycheck.

Issues are of relevance to postdivorce parenting, and differences between mothers' and fathers' experiences are particularly apparent from a developmental perspective. As time passes, the normative pattern is for mothers to overcome many of their difficulties with their children and establish or reestablish a more "normal" relationship. Often this occurs with the support of friends, relatives, or perhaps a new partner. Unfortunately, the normative pattern for fathers is to become less and less involved in their children's lives over time, particularly as they or their former spouse make major life changes such as residential moves or remarriage. As with child outcomes, a child's age at the time of separation and children's current age may be important developmental contributors to relationships between children and their parents, as is discussed in more detail shortly.

High rates of formal or informal remarriage following separation and divorce (and following informal marriages, in many cases, of nonmarital childbirth) introduce stepparents into children's lives. Stepparents can serve as key figures in children's lives, but unlike some earlier social science stereotypes, remarriage hardly is a simple reconstitution of the two-parent family. Stepparents may be viewed as rivals by the children (and by former spouses), and their authority as disciplinarians is established only over a period of time if at all. In addition to the amount of time in the stepparenting role, the age of the child when the new partner becomes a presence in the household can be a key developmental issue in stepparenting, as younger children typically are more accepting of stepparents than are older children, particularly adolescents.

Recognition of the development of all three sets of parent-child relationships is important for the accurate understanding of the family experience of a large proportion of American children. Parent-child relationships are of considerable relevance, moreover, because they appear to be partial mediators of children's psychological functioning in alternative family forms. The quality of parent-child relationships is of greatest importance to children's well-being. Before considering parent-child relationship quality in detail, however, it is first helpful to understand more about the amount of time children spend with their different parents by briefly turning to the demographic literature on parenting in alternative families.

Normative Childrearing Arrangements in Nontraditional Families

According to 1988 census data, across boys and girls, all ages, and races, 88% of children living with a single parent resided primarily with their mothers, and 12% lived primarily with their fathers (U.S. Bureau of the Census, 1989). However, children's gender, current age, race, and reason for single-parenting all influenced children's single-parent circumstances, at least somewhat. More boys (13%) than girls (10%) lived with single fathers, as did more children who are older than younger (e.g., 11% of children under 3 vs. 15% of children 15 to 17) (U.S. Bureau of the Census, 1988). The largest proportion of white children lived with single fathers (15%), followed by children of Hispanic origin (10%) and black children (5%). Finally, 8% of children of never-married parents lived with a single father, as opposed to 14% of children whose parents were separated or divorced (U.S. Bureau of the Census, 1988). In general, the interactions between gender, age, race, and reason for single status were not substantial in these data.

For children whose parents are separated or divorced, the cross-sectional finding that more older children live with their fathers could be due to age at separation, time since separation, current age, or some combination of the three. The cross-sectional statistics also are limited in that they likely mask a number of changes in residence that are canceled out by countervailing trends. To document such important developmental progressions in residential arrangements, longitudinal data are needed. Unfortunately, the U.S. Census Bureau does not track changes in custody status over time.

A recent longitudinal study conducted by Eleanor Maccoby and Robert Mnookin (1992) of a large sample of 1,416 California custody cases provides valuable information on these developmental changes. Although the California data depart from national norms, the age and time trends are likely to be similar in other states. When first studied shortly after their parents filed divorce, 66% of boys and 72% of girls in the sample lived primarily with their mothers, 14% of boys and 8% of girls were primarily with fathers, and 16% of boys and 13% of girls lived in a joint physical custody arrangement. An additional 4% of boys and 6% of girls lived in other arrangements, including split custody, where at least one child resided primarily with each parent.

The data from this study clearly indicated an age-at-separation effect. (Recall that all the families were recently separated.) Older children were more likely to live primarily with their fathers than were younger children. For example, 8% of children under 3 lived primarily with their fathers, compared with 17% of children 15 and older. Age at separation had little effect on the percentage of children living in the mother's custody (71% under 3 vs. 73% for children 15 and older). The increase in father custody therefore came primarily from a decrease in joint physical custody for older children (17% for children under 3 vs. 3% for children 15 and older) (Maccoby & Mnookin, 1992).

The percentage of families maintaining each custody arrangement remained relatively stable over the 3 years they were followed, although findings also indicated a time-since-separation effect. The largest change was found for father custody which increased from 14% to 17% of boys and from 8% to 11% of girls. Moreover, there was a significant interaction between age and time, such that children who were older at the time of divorce were more likely to move into father custody (Maccoby & Mnookin, 1992). For methodological reasons discussed earlier, however, some of these effects could be attributable to current age rather than time since separation.

The relative stability over time in the percentages of children living in different custody arrangements across families masked numerous additional developmental issues within families. Over 80% of mother residence families maintained this arrangement 3 years later, as did approximately 70% of father residence families. Only 54% of dual-residence families maintained this pattern, however, and less than one-third of families with split custody kept the arrangement three years later. As noted earlier, however, changes *into* the different patterns of residence were such that the percentages remained fairly constant over time (Maccoby & Mnookin, 1992).

Thus, single-parent living arrangements are best viewed within a developmental perspective. As time passes, children are more likely to move into primary residence with their fathers, especially when they become adolescents and especially if the children were older when the separation occurred. There also is considerable movement from father to mother custody, however, and in fact, longitudinal data indicated far more changes in residence than were apparent in cross-sectional studies. None of these developmental findings should obscure the fact that mother custody is the most likely living arrangement for children in single-parent families irrespective of their age at separation, current age, or the amount of time that has elapsed between these two periods.

Contact with Nonresidential Parents

Data on children's primary residence are important, but it is also important to recognize that children have two parents even when they live with only one of them. Children of never married or divorced mothers are not "fatherless," contrary to what was implied by the social stereotypes and social science research of a generation ago. The examination of data on children's contact with their nonresidential parents, both mothers and fathers, is a beginning step toward acknowledging the existence of this relationship. Such data are essential for testing the significance for children's emotional health of their relationships with both parents.

The straightforward question of how often children see their nonresidential parents quickly becomes quite complicated. Its answer is influenced by the sample studied, the length of time that has elapsed since divorce, the current age of the children, and the historical cohort that is studied. In short, the best answer to this question is a developmental one.

A starting point in understanding contact or access developmentally is to examine data on a nationally representative sample of a recent divorce cohort. Seltzer (1991) has conducted such an analysis of a nationally representative sample of adults living in the United States in 1987–1988. She found that, according to mothers' reports, 18% of these fathers had not seen their children in the past year, and another 14% saw them only once or several times in that year; 22% of fathers saw their children several times during the year, and 21% more saw them 1 to 3 times per month; 12% of divorced or separated fathers saw their children weekly, and another 12% saw them several times per week (Seltzer, 1991). This amount of contact was somewhat higher than that found in two other national surveys of earlier cohorts (Furstenberg et al., 1983; Seltzer & Bianchi, 1988), but all data point to a low level of involvement for a large number of fathers. In the more optimistic estimates, a third of fathers had seen their children several times or less in the past year, whereas only a quarter saw them weekly or more.

In the more recent survey, moreover, absent fathers were not found to make up for lack of contact with letters or phone calls. For example, only 10% of fathers who had not seen their children in the past year wrote or phoned them. In contrast, 77% of fathers who saw their children monthly or more also called or wrote them. In addition, decision making was left up to the mother in the majority of cases. Of the separated or divorced fathers, 18% spoke with the mothers about the child once a week or more, whereas 63% spoke with them several times a year or less. According to mothers, among those who discussed the children at all, only 17% of nonresidential fathers had "a great deal" of influence in decisions concerning their children's education, medical care, and religious training. Over 50% were reported to have no influence (Seltzer, 1991).

A developmental perspective begins to emerge from data indicating that the degree of father involvement was strongly related to time since separation. Among fathers separated for 2 years or less, for example, 13% had only seen their children once a year or less, whereas 43% saw them once a week or more. In contrast, among fathers separated for 11 years or more, 50% had only seen their children once a year or less, and only 12% saw them once a week or more. Time since separation also was related to the other measures of involvement. For example, 45% of fathers separated 2 years or less spoke with their children's mother about them at least weekly, whereas only 6% of parents separated 11 years or more spoke that often.

Other influences related to decreased paternal involvement in various studies include lower socioeconomic status, greater distance between residences, and the remarriage of either parent

(Furstenberg et al., 1983; Seltzer, 1991; Seltzer & Bianchi, 1988). In addition, all studies find substantially less contact between never-married fathers and their children than between children and divorced or separated fathers. Finally, at least two surveys have found considerably higher contact between children and their nonresidential mothers than between children and their nonresidential fathers (Furstenberg et al., 1983; Seltzer, 1991). Because no longitudinal study of children's contact with their nonresidential parents has been undertaken, it is uncertain whether age at separation or current age affects the frequency of contact. It should be noted that these influences, if present, may be responsible for some or all of the effect currently attributed to the passage of time.

In summary, a developmental perspective on children's living arrangements in alternative family forms provides valuable information both on normative patterns and developmental change. Most children living in single-parent families reside with and spend the vast majority of their time with their mothers. About a quarter of children in these families maintain substantial contact with their fathers; about a third see them little or not at all. A little over 10% of children reside primarily with their fathers, and contact with mothers is more frequent in this circumstance. Over time, residential arrangements change somewhat, as some older children move in with their fathers and other shifts take place. The most notable developmental pattern, however, is a decline in paternal involvement over time, a decrease that is more marked when parents are never married or when a marital separation occurs when children are younger.

The Quality of Parent-Child Relationships

In the era of "quality time," it is important to recognize that the extent of contact between children and their biological parents may be less important than the nature of the relationship. In this regard, it is evident that parent-child relationships are strained in nontraditional families, at least following separation and divorce. In the meta-analysis discussed earlier, the average effect sizes when comparing parenting in married and divorced families were .19 standard deviation units for mother-child relationships and .26 for father-child relationships (Amato & Keith, 1991a). In one important national survey, moreover, twice as many children from divorced as married families reported having bad relationships with both their mothers and their fathers (Zill et al., 1993).

Simple summary statistics mask many important differences in parenting, however. For example, mothers and fathers typically experience very different problems in their interactions with their children. Each is likely to confront more difficulties in attempting to perform the functions that are traditionally a part of the other gender's role in marriage. Women face more problems with disciplining their children, while fathers struggle more with offering warmth and affection. This section examines mother-child and father-child relationships in detail, with particular emphasis on a developmental perspective when data are available on age- and time-graded changes.

Mother-Child Relationships

Some of the most important research on mothering and children's mental health in alternative family forms comes from the studies of divorce and remarriage conducted by Hetherington and colleagues (Hetherington, 1989; 1991; 1993; Hetherington & Clingempeel, 1992). In this series of investigations, mother-child relationships were found to be troubled after divorce, and in some cases, they deteriorated following remarriage as well. Similar findings have been reported by other investigators. The parenting of recently divorced women is more authoritarian (Barber & Eccles, 1992), and at the same time, divorced mothers have been found to be more permissive (Dornbusch, Ritter, Leiderman, Roberts, & Fraleigh, 1987). Other researchers find single mothers to be more negative, inconsistent, and less affectionate than married mothers (e.g., Capaldi & Patterson, 1991; Fauber, Forehand, Thomas, & Wierson, 1990; Forehand, Thomas, Wierson, Brody, & Fauber, 1990; Hess & Camara, 1979; Wallerstein & Kelly, 1980). The composite picture is one of a mother who is struggling with parenting. As a result, she is less able to show her love, less effective in her discipline, and inconsistent in her attempts at both.

Hetherington's longitudinal studies paint a very different picture when the developmental trajectory is taken into account, however. Although the strains of parenting alone remain, particularly in relationships between single mothers and their sons, mother-child relationships have been found to improve considerably over time, especially in the second year following a divorce (Hetherington, 1991; 1993). Remarriage also has been found to relieve some of the strains on mother-son relationships, but it may challenge stepfather-stepdaughter dyads. Problems were found to be especially likely when stepfathers attempted to assume authority early in the relationship, before they had established stable, affective ties (Hetherington, 1991; 1993; Hetherington & Clingempeel, 1992). Overall, the changes over time suggest a process of adaptation in the parenting of residential mothers that in many respects seems to parallel the process of children's improving adjustment to divorce.

Further research that takes a developmental perspective suggests some caution in interpreting findings about the source of difficulties with postdivorce parenting. As with research on children's adjustment, at least two studies in which parenting was studied prospectively have found that less affectionate and more conflictual parent-child relationships were present *before* the divorce (Block et al., 1988; Shaw et al., 1993). It may be that marital problems produce problems in parenting prior to divorce, some of the parents' behavior may be a reaction to the children's difficulties, or preexisting personality factors may be responsible both for divorce and for less adequate parenting.

Developmental issues in the parenting of single mothers are not limited to normative changes over time. Research also reflects changes associated with discipline strategies that are appropriate for children of different ages. For example, research on younger children has emphasized disruptive child behavior and coercive parent-child interactions (Hetherington et al., 1982), while studies of adolescents focus on poor communication, problem solving, and monitoring (Capaldi & Patterson, 1991; Fauber et al., 1990; Forehand et al., 1990). Although mother-child warmth often is reported to be less strained than maternal discipline, the importance of giving children time, attention, and affection also is supported across studies. Finally, this review has focused exclusively on residential mother-child relationships. Virtually nothing is known about the quality of relationships between children and their nonresidential mothers.

Father-Child Relationships

Just as little is known about nonresidential mothers, very little systematic research has been conducted on residential fathers. The available research suggests that these men are of higher socioeconomic status to begin with (Chang & Deinard, 1982; Gersick, 1979) and are more likely to have a former spouse who is psychologically impaired (Orthner, Brown, & Ferguson, 1976). Others suggest that single parents of either gender have more troubles fulfilling tasks traditionally assumed by the opposite sex (Luepnitz, 1982). Still, most research indicates that residence, not gender, is the more powerful influence on parenting alone (Camara & Resnick, 1987; Warshak, 1986). The preponderance of existing research reflects the most common normative patterns of residential mothers and nonresidential fathers. It should be clear, however, that fathers can "mother" and that mothers sometimes are reduced to becoming "visitors" in their children's lives.

In fact, relatively little research has been conducted on single fathers at all, or on fathering in two-parent families for that matter. It is well established that contact between children and their nonresidential fathers is infrequent on average, but whether contact is frequent or rare, little is known about the quality of these relationships. Teenagers who have nonresidential, divorced fathers report feeling less close to them than do children whose parents are married (Peterson & Zill, 1986). (Surprisingly, the same is not true for mothers.) Children also indicate that nonresidential fathers have more lax rules and lower expectations for their conduct than do married fathers (Furstenberg & Nord, 1985). Some recent reports indicate that the relationship between nonresidential fathers and their children can be more positive and normal (Braver et al., 1993), but limited research precludes any firm conclusions. The meager data available to characterize father-child relationships thus point most clearly to the pressing need for more research.

Parent-Child Relationships and Children's Mental Health

Difficulties in mother-child and father-child relationships are important to note in alternative family forms, because a large body of research indicates that the effects of parenting on children's development are substantial across different family forms (Belsky, 1984; Luster & Okagaki, 1993; Maccoby & Martin, 1983). Although the dynamics of parenting differ according to family structure, the same dimensions (or categorizations) of mother-child relationships are associated with more positive child outcomes across family forms. Secure attachments, continued parental support, firm, consistent, and developmentally sensitive discipline, and continued monitoring of children's behavior all are related to more adequate child adjustment within different family structures. In short, both increased parental warmth and increased parental control are important to children, with the co-occurrence of warmth and control or authoritative parenting being the most adaptive parenting style (Maccoby & Martin, 1983). To be sure, differences in parenting styles are found

across ethnic groups, as is discussed later in the chapter. Still, the consistency of evidence across family forms suggests that authoritative parenting is a robust protective factor against the development of psychopathology.

In single-parent, divorced, and remarried families, the quality of mother-child relationships, in particular, has been linked to a wide variety of indexes of children's adjustment (Bray & Berger, 1993; Hetherington, 1989; 1991; 1993; Hetherington & Clingempeel, 1992; Maccoby, Buchanan, Mnookin, & Dornbusch, 1993). In fact, some researchers have concluded that lack of maternal warmth and supportiveness mediates the relation between child behavior problems, troubled family relationships, and single-parent families (Capaldi & Patterson, 1991; Fauber et al., 1990).

The quality of children's relationships with their nonresidential fathers or with their stepparents also has been linked with children's psychological well-being in several studies (Bray & Berger, 1993; Camara & Resnick, 1987; Hetherington, 1993; Hetherington & Clingempeel, 1992). Findings for nonresidential father-child relationships typically are not as strong as for residential mother-child relationships, however, and coparenting conflict can undermine the benefits of children's relationships with their nonresidential fathers or stepparents. As noted earlier, relatively little research has been conducted on father-child relationships. Whereas the importance of the quality of mother-child relationships in divorced and single-parent families is well documented, research on postdivorce fathering generally has focused on quantity not quality. The question that typically is asked is: Does more contact matter?

Father-Child Contact and Children's Mental Health

One attempt to answer this question came from a study of a nationally representative sample of 12- to 16-year-old children (Furstenberg, Morgan, & Allison, 1987). Nonresidential father-child contact was used as a predictor of various measures of children's behavioral and academic functioning, but no consistent relations were found in the entire sample or for boys versus girls, single versus remarried mothers, or data on the children's adjustment at ages 7 to 11. Children's ratings of closeness to their fathers were unrelated to adjustment measures, moreover, but closeness to the residential mother did predict child outcome (Furstenberg et al., 1987).

Although some investigators have found that nonresidential father-child relationships predict children's well-being (e.g., Camara & Resnick, 1987; Kurdek & Berg, 1987), an important, recent study again found that contact with nonresidential fathers was unrelated to the emotional functioning of adolescents (Maccoby et al., 1993). In this latter investigation, more contact with nonresidential *mothers* did predict better child adjustment, however (Maccoby et al., 1993).

A problem with studies of father-contact is its infrequency, even in the high contact groups formed by researchers. In the national study, for example, the *high* contact group of fathers saw their children only 25 days a year or more, or about one weekend per month (Furstenberg et al., 1987). Reflecting the research emphasis, another problem is that mothers often are used as informants about the frequency of father-child visitation (Braver et al., 1993). Perhaps more notable differences would appear when contact with both parents is very frequent, particularly when parents share joint physical custody.

Joint Custody

A fair amount of research has been done comparing children's adjustment in joint and sole custody families. A major problem with interpreting this research is that parents who choose joint physical custody differ from sole custody parents. Thus, the two groups are confounded by unmeasured third variables related to self-selection into custodial arrangements, and these variables may account for differences in child adjustment (Emery, 1988). With this caution in mind, the literature on joint custody still provides a window into the question of frequent father-child contact.

Several, careful empirical studies have now found that joint physical custody is related to improved mental health among children (Maccoby et al., 1993; see generally, Folberg, 1991). An important caveat in research findings is that joint physical custody has been found to be problematic for children when interparental conflict is intense and uncontained (Johnston, Kline, & Tschann, 1989). Perhaps what is most notable about the joint physical custody literature, however, is that demonstrated benefits for children are rather small in magnitude (Emery, 1988).

Together, the findings on visitation and joint physical custody suggest that a positive relationship with both parents is beneficial, but it is not a prerequisite for positive mental health among children. This interpretation of the literature is consistent with the earlier conclusion that there are only small differences in children's adjustment in married and divorced families. The same caveats raised in that earlier discussion apply to the present one, however. Although the relation between father-child contact and children's mental health is not strong, this does not imply that good relationships with both parents are unimportant. Empirically, there are few studies, and many areas of children's functioning have not been adequately assessed in relation to father contact. Indeed, children who see their divorced fathers infrequently still list them as members of their family (Furstenberg & Nord, 1985). Thus, relationships with fathers are of symbolic importance to children. Perhaps high father-child contact will prove to be most valuable in alleviating much emotional distress among children who are resilient in coping with unwanted changes in their lives, but who are happier when the unwanted changes are fewer.

The System of Parent-Child Relationships

Consideration of father-child relationships not only shows there is a great need for more research on fathering in alternative family forms, but also highlights the need for developmental psychopathologists to understand parenting systemically (Emery, 1988; 1992; Howes & Cicchetti, 1993). Parenting traditionally has been conceptualized in dyadic terms, with particular emphasis on the mother-child dyad. Researchers increasingly have documented, however, that family relationships must be considered triadically. For example, mothers' relationships with their adolescent boys have been found to improve in the physical presence of the father (e.g., Gjerde, 1986), and third family members have been shown to intervene frequently in disputes between other dyads in the home (Vuchinich, Emery, & Cassidy, 1988).

These considerations lead to a host of questions about child psychopathology generally, and about disruptions in family functioning in particular. For example, does a child with a loving but permissive mother and an aloof but firm father experience inconsistency or authoritative parenting? Such questions need to be addressed conceptually before they can be adequately tested empirically. A limited body of research has taken a more systemic view of parenting, however, and examined whether a good relationship with one parent can buffer children against a bad relationship with the other.

A handful of investigations of children living with married parents (Jenkins & Smith, 1990; Rutter, 1971) or from divorced families (Camara & Resnick, 1987; Hess & Camara, 1979; Hetherington et al., 1982) have found evidence for buffering effects, although the specific findings differ across reports. In one investigation, buffering was found only when there was an extremely good relationship with the mother (Hetherington et al., 1982). In other studies, a good relationship with either parent served as a buffer (Camara & Resnick, 1987; Hess & Camara, 1979; Rutter, 1971). An even broader context of buffering is indicated by evidence that a good relationship with parents, siblings, other relatives, and adult friends serves as a protective factor (Jenkins & Smith, 1990).

This last report is a reminder that, just as family relationships must be considered as a system, broader systems of influence on child development also must be recognized. An essential implication of this is that, because social supports differ across ethnic family groups in the United States today, the experience of different types of families is not the same for American children of all ethnic family backgrounds. This important issue is developed later in this chapter.

At present, consideration of the entire family system leads into the important topic of interparental conflict and children's adjustment across different family forms. Children are a part of a triad that includes both parents, even when the two parents are not living together, even when children rarely see their second parent, or even when one or both parents is remarried. A family systems approach to child psychopathology highlights the importance not only of children's relationships with all their parenting figures, but also of the quality of the relationships between these parental figures themselves.

Interparental Conflict

Interparental conflict increasingly has been recognized to be a critical contributor to children's psychological functioning across family forms. This recognition is based both on new, empirical research (Cummings, 1987; Emery, 1982; Grych & Fincham, 1990; Long & Forehand, 1987) and emergent conceptualizations (Emery, Fincham, & Cummings, 1992; Minuchin, 1985; Minuchin, 1974). Particularly in the past decade, parental conflict has been the focus of a considerable body of research on children's adjustment in married and divorced families. This evidence consistently indicates that high levels of conflict between parents are linked with more psychological difficulties among children (Emery, 1982, 1988; Grych & Fincham, 1990; 1992; Long & Forehand, 1987). In fact, interparental conflict may be more strongly related to children's adjustment than is marital status (e.g., Forehand et al., 1988). Such findings have led several reviewers to conclude that much of the relation between divorce and children's disturbance is mediated by parental conflict.

Interparental Conflict versus Divorce

Based on an extensive review of the literature through the early 1980s, one reviewer concluded that parental conflict was a more powerful risk factor for psychological difficulties among children than was marital status per se (Emery, 1982). The same conclusion was reaffirmed in subsequent reviews of the rapidly expanding literature on conflict (Emery et al., 1984; Emery, 1988), and it also has been reached in several other qualitative reviews (Cummings, 1987; Grych & Fincham, 1990; Long & Forehand, 1987) and two quantitative meta-analyses (Amato & Keith, 1991a; Reid & Crisafulli, 1990).

As the correlation between parental conflict and child behavior problems has been recognized, research increasingly has examined the processes by which conflict may adversely affect children. Several mechanisms have been proposed to account for the relation. Parental conflict has been suggested to lead to aggressive behavior among children by exposing them to inappropriate models (Long & Forehand, 1987). Conflict also has been conceptualized as a stressor that arouses negative affect in children and sensitizes them to further disputes (Cummings, 1987). Others have suggested that parental cooperation is more important than parental conflict, as parents can protect their children if they coordinate their child-rearing efforts despite their own disagreements (Camara & Resnick, 1987, 1988).

Interparental Conflict versus Parenting

Probably the most active area of research, however, has raised the question of whether the effects of conflict are mediated through disruptions in parenting. This is an important speculation, because parenting problems are correlated with parental conflict. In fact, less adequate parenting has been demonstrated to be caused by experimentally controlled parental conflict in a laboratory experiment (Jouriles & Farris, 1992).

Several investigations have found the statistical controls for parenting can account for the linkages between parental conflict and child outcome. In one analysis, for example, parenting problems statistically accounted for the link between conflict and adolescents' adjustment difficulties (Fauber et al., 1990). In another, both parenting skill and maternal depression were found to account for much of the association (Forehand et al., 1990). Problematic parenting also has been found to account for the statistical relation between single-parent family status and child outcome (Capaldi & Patterson, 1991). This has led some to conclude that parenting is the key mediating variable (Fauber & Long, 1991).

A systemic conceptualization indicates, however, that it is problematic to conclude that the effects of parental conflict are mediated primarily through parenting. Parenting problems may account for the effects of conflict statistically, but this is not the same as accounting for the effects conceptually (Emery et al., 1992). An important issue is recognition of the reductionist tendency to focus only on proximal influences in causal chains.

Even assuming a strictly linear model whereby interparental conflict causes dysfunctional parenting, which causes maladjustment among children, it is a mistake to conclude that parenting is the ultimate cause of children's problems. By way of analogy, in a chain collision of automobiles, damage to one car is caused by the vehicle immediately behind it, but this does not explain the ultimate cause of the accident (Emery et al., 1992). Notwithstanding the heuristic value of statistical models of causal pathways, it is a conceptual error to dismiss distal causes even when the variance they contribute is accounted for by other, more proximal causes.

Both laboratory and field research raise further empirical questions about the conclusion that the effects of conflict are entirely mediated through parenting. A 10-year series of laboratory studies by Cummings and colleagues demonstrated that conflict between adults directly affects children (e.g., Cummings, 1987; Cummings, Vogel, Cummings, & El-Sheikh, 1989). Moreover, recent research on a large sample of adolescents from divorced families is but one of several examples of studies in which parenting has *not* been found to fully account for the relation between conflict and indexes of children's adjustment (Buchanan, Maccoby, & Dornbusch, 1991). Similar findings were reported in another large-scale investigation (Jenkins & Smith, 1990).

A Model of Children's Involvement in Parental Conflict

Although some of the effects of conflict on children are likely to be mediated through parent-child relationships, Emery (1992) has proposed an account of conflict processes that highlights children's affect regulation and systemic processes in family interaction. In this model, children's immediate responses to episodes of parental conflict provide a microcosm for understanding the developmental psychopathology of interparental conflict over time. At the level of immediate, microsocial interaction, the three-stage model asserts that (a) conflict is an aversive event that (b) causes multiple reactions among children, including affective arousal and an increased likelihood of intervening in the dispute, and (c) when children's responses result in the resolution or the avoidance of parental conflict, the systemic pattern of interaction is maintained over time by negative reinforcement.

The model can be illustrated with a brief example. A parental argument may upset a child who responds to the situation (and attempts to regulate his or her own affect) by refocusing attention onto him- or herself through obvious antisocial (or prosocial) actions. If the child's actions succeed in distracting the parents from their dispute, then the pattern is likely to be maintained by negative reinforcement. That is, the reduction of the conflict, which is adversive both to parents involved in it and to the children exposed to it, reinforces an interaction pattern wherein conflicted parents focus on a child's behavior instead of their own disputes.

In broader terms, the child assumes the role of a scapegoat or a distractor for the parents (Minuchin, 1985). Because this role allows all family members to avoid the threatening, parental disputes, the pattern is maintained over time. The antisocial (or prosocial) behavior becomes a characteristic style for the child in relating to the parents and perhaps to others. The model further asserts that a child's immediate affective and cognitive reactions to conflict (fear, anger, self-blame, or a sense of responsibility) also become characteristic for the child who is caught in the middle of parental disputes (Emery, 1992).

Research in Support of the Model

Several findings support the importance of the first component of the model. In addition to demonstrating that conflict unequivocally affects children apart from any changes in parent-child relationships, a number of analogue experiments have shown that children are more distressed by certain forms of conflict. For example, physical aggression, which has been found to be more distressing to children than verbal conflict in field research (Christopolous et al., 1987; Jaffe, Wolfe, & Wilson, 1990), also has been demonstrated to cause greater affective distress in experimental analogues (Cummings et al., 1989; Cummings, Pellegrini, Notarius, & Cummings, 1989; O'Brien, Margolin, John, & Krueger, 1991). Similarly, children have been found to be more distressed by conflicts about topics that concern child rearing both in correlational field research (Block, Block, & Morrison, 1981) and in analogue experiments (Grych & Fincham, 1992).

The second component of the model highlights children's affective reactions to and appraisals of parental conflict. Laboratory simulations have documented that children report a variety of negative reactions in response to simulated anger (Cummings, 1987; Cummings, Pellegrini et al., 1989; Cummings, Vogel et al., 1989). Convincing evidence also has documented increased psychophysiological arousal among children who are exposed to anger and conflict between adults (Ballard, Cummings, & Larkin, 1993; El-Sheikh, Cummings, & Goetsch, 1989; Gottman & Katz, 1989). In addition, correlation research indicates that children's perceptions of interparental conflict are better predictors of parents' reports of child behavior problems than are the parents' own reports about their marital relationship (Emery & O'Leary, 1982; Grych & Fincham, 1992). Finally, clinical observation (Wallerstein & Kelly, 1980), correlational studies (Kurdek & Berg, 1987), and experimental analogue research (Grych & Fincham, 1992) all indicate that children often attribute responsibility for interparental conflict to themselves, particularly when the conflict is about children or child rearing.

The third component of the model is that children's actions that serve to reduce the conflict are maintained over time. School-age children have been documented to intervene in their parents' disputes according to diaries kept by their parents (Cummings, Zahn-Waxler, & Radke-Yarrow, 1981, 1984), as well as by behavioral observations in the laboratory (Cummings, Pellegrini et al., 1989). Children's intervention in their parents' conflicts (primarily distraction strategies) also are apparent in videotapes of routine family dinners (Vuchinich et al., 1988). In fact, children's ability to articulate their strategies for attempting to manage their parents' anger (e.g., Covell & Miles, 1992; Jenkins, Smith, & Graham, 1989), and their attempts to intervene even in violent disputes have been demonstrated in interviews with children of battered women (Christopolous et al., 1987). Finally, experimental analogue evidence indicates that children are more distressed by conflict that is unresolved rather than resolved (Cummings, Ballard, El-Sheikh, & Lake, 1991; Cummings, Simpson, & Wilson, 1993), suggesting that their successful interventions are negatively reinforcing.

Although considerable evidence thus supports the three-stage model at the level of microsocial interaction, evidence on the extent to which children adopt these roles over time is lacking in the empirical literature (Emery, Joyce, & Fincham, 1987). Clinical reports suggest that children take on distinct roles in relation to their parents' marriage, and more generally, that they adopt specialized roles in their family. There is a need for research on this issue, despite the difficulty in operationalizing abstractions such as family roles. A major goal of such research would be to link individual differences in family roles to individual differences in children's adjustment. It is worth noting that this suggestion is wholly consistent with the emphasis on within-family differences found in contemporary behavior genetic research (Plomin, 1986).

Summary

Like children's "outcomes," disruptions in family relationships that are associated with alternative family forms are best understood within a developmental perspective. Residential mother-child relationships may deteriorate near the time of marital transitions, but they generally improve over time. In contrast, nonresidential father-child relationships become more and more distant, on average, as time passes. Evidence links children's adjustment with the quality of their relationships with their residential mothers, but the amount of contact with nonresidential fathers is only weakly tied to child outcome. This latter conclusion holds even when the literature on joint custody is considered.

Children's relationships with both their parents must be understood systemically. Family systems theory leads to several conceptual challenges that await future research on developmental psychopathology. However, the empirical literature on the relation between interparental conflict and children's adjustment across family forms supports the systems approach. Empirically, conflict has been found to be a risk factor for psychological problems among children, and it may be a better predictor of some difficulties than is family status. Emerging empirical evidence also supports a more process-oriented approach to understanding children's role in relation to their biological parents and perhaps in relation to other parenting figures as well.

MULTIPLE FAMILY FUNCTIONS: ECONOMICS AND EDUCATION

For the most part, research on family processes and family structure leads to optimistic conclusions about children's mental health. Some difficult transitions and relationships are found among single-parent and divorced families, and these dysfunctional processes, not family structure, appear to be responsible for the significant, but small, increase in emotional and behavioral disturbances among children reared in these homes. This is an optimistic conclusion because distressed family relationships presumably can be changed, and, in fact, evidence suggests that strained relationships become more stable over time. Moreover, additional support for single parents and their children comes from nonmarital relationships, particularly among some ethnic minority groups. Together, these findings help to explain why the mental health of children living in alternative family forms has been found to be only slightly more disturbed than that of children living with their married parents.

It has been repeatedly noted, however, that the absence of emotional problems is not the same as the presence of emotional health. The very fact of children's resilience suggests that family disruptions are related to children's psychological distress if not to their psychological disorders. The children of the Great Depression were another resilient group, but the undesirability of an economic depression is obvious, children's resilience notwithstanding. The same can be said for disruptions in family forms and functions. In this section of the chapter, further concerns about children's coping are raised by considering some of the functions that families can serve for children in addition to protecting them against emotional disturbance.

Multiple Family Functions

Since the turn of the twentieth century, children's psychological needs have dominated social and legal discourse. This emphasis is embodied in the principle of the child's "best interests," a doctrine conceptualized in terms of maximizing children's psychological health or happiness while inventing new social institutions or resolving family disputes (Mnookin, 1985). As suggested by Maslow's (1968) straightforward hierarchy of human needs, the success of families, and of society, in meeting children's more basic needs is one reason for this emphasis. As industrialization, economic vitality, and improving health care have made survival of children (and adults) a less pressing concern, attention could be focused on children's psychological needs.

Maslow's (1968) hierarchy also serves as a reminder of children's more basic survival and safety needs, however. Meeting these needs also is part of what defines a family, as must be recognized in considering the needs of families globally and in noting the declining living conditions of a growing number of American children. Families are defined by the functions that the social unit fulfills, not just by household or relationship structures. No matter what its form, the family has as its functions the production and distribution of wealth, emotional and material support of its members, and the socialization and education of children (Sudarkasa, 1988). Of these multiple functions, education and economic support are among the most important in contemporary society.

Education

Public schooling has replaced the family and the church as the seat of children's education. Although some religious groups such as the Amish are allowed to educate their children outside the public school systems, most families are no longer responsible for children's formal education. However, one of the family's most important tasks is to socialize children for school and to prepare them to benefit from their education (Thompson, Alexander & Entwisle, 1988). Parent-child interaction and care influence early cognitive and social development, setting the stage for formal learning later. Families are responsible for providing nutrition and rest so that children can benefit from schooling. Thus, children's

experiences at home can have profound effects on their performance at school (Bronfenbrenner, 1986).

Economic Support

The earliest kin groups cooperated to allow the procurement and allocation of resources (Hughes, 1988), and modern spouses also form an economic unit (Becker, 1980). Marital partners share their wealth legally, but they also contribute to each other's and their children's financial well-being in other ways. Each spouse may generate shared income, or one spouse may support the other in a manner that increases their earning potential. Moreover, the sharing of a household and other resources reduces family expenses. Evidence on the financial status of one- and two-parent families, reviewed shortly, indicates the striking economic benefits of such shared economic goals.

Income, Education, and Single-Parent Families

Ironically, although alternative family forms in the United States today apparently succeed in meeting children's psychological needs, evidence indicates that some of children's more basic needs are better fulfilled by two-parent families. More substantial differences are found between children from single-parent families and children whose parents are married in terms of such basic measures as educational attainment, income loss, and poverty.

Family Structure and Children's Education

The family plays a critical role in children's cognitive development and academic success. Variables such as the number of parents, parent availability, family size, birth order, and gender vary in their importance for predicting children's intelligence and academic success (Milne, 1989). The specific family status variable reflecting whether or not the parents are married is unrelated to children's cognitive abilities as evidenced in IQ scores, but it seems to be related to children's school-related behavior and performance (Featherman, 1980). Children from single-parent families do less well in school than children from two-parent families. Although children with stepparents fare better than children whose parents have not remarried, they still do not do as well academically as children from always-married families (Astonc & McLanahan, 1991; Dornbusch et al., 1987; Zimiles & Lee, 1991). Children from always-married families have higher achievement scores and grades, have better classroom behavior, finish more years of schooling, and are more likely to graduate from high school. Moreover, prospective, longitudinal research documents that these differences are not due solely to selection factors, as academic performance declines after divorce (Elliott & Richards, 1991).

Differences among single-parent and two-parent children are more notable in terms of classroom grades than achievement scores. This may be because standardized achievement tests assess more general knowledge than material covered in class (Hetherington et al., 1983). However, grades are also subject to teacher stereotypes about single- and divorced-parent homes (Guttmann & Boudo, 1988) and are more likely to be influenced by the tendency to assign higher grades to children who are quiet and obedient (Hetherington et al., 1983). Disruptions in family life that affect children's study habits, attendance, and behavior are likely to affect grades, independent of any actual deficits in learning or performance.

Disruptions in family life are also associated with decreases in the number of years of education completed by children. In a study of the number of years of schooling completed by men in the United States between 1907 and 1951, Featherman and Hauser (1978) found that boys raised in single-parent families completed about three-fourths of a year less education than boys in two-parent families. More recent evidence also suggests that children from single-parent and divorced-parent families tend to complete fewer years of schooling and drop out of school at a younger age (McLanahan, 1985). In a large-scale study of young adults, Mueller and Cooper (1984) found that 10% of those raised in single-parent homes did not complete high school, compared with 4% from two-parent homes. On average, single-parent children completed 12.6 years of schooling, and two-parent children completed 13.7 years.

Parent remarriage may not help children in terms of keeping them in school. In fact, in a sample of white families, Zimiles and Lee (1991) found that children of single parents and of remarried parents were two to three times more likely to drop out of high school than were children in intact families. Children with step-parents were even more likely to drop out than children with a single parent of the same sex. In terms of their achievement scores and grades, dropouts from single-parent and stepparent homes are more similar to students who stay in school than they are to dropouts from intact families. This observation led Zimiles and Lee (1991) to concur with others (Dornbusch & Gray, 1988) that the effects of single-parent families on children's academic performance are evident not in cognitive deficits but in social and emotional maladjustment.

Despite the consistent evidence that family structure is related to the number of years of education completed by teenagers, the effects of family status appear to be more influential on the academic performance of young children than on that of teenagers or preschoolers (Milne, 1989). This may be due to the low variability in preschoolers' performance and to adolescents' involvement with extrafamilial influences, such as peer groups (Chase-Lansdale & Hetherington, 1990). For example, among teenagers attending school, those from single-parent families do not differ from those from two-parent families in terms of problem behaviors at school, academic difficulty, or school retention (Allison & Furstenberg, 1989). Similarly, Marsh (1990) found that students who remained in school and whose family status was stable for the last two years of high school did not differ in terms of achievement scores, grades, absences, or rates of university admission, after race, socioeconomic status (SES), and sophomore-year performance level were controlled.

Evidence also suggests that family status may be more influential on the academic performance of boys than on that of girls. Zimiles and Lee (1991) found that boys drop out of high school more often than do girls when living with a single mother. This may be because children living with the opposite-sex parent tend to do more poorly after a divorce (Hetherington et al., 1983). Boys living in mother-only homes seem especially affected by

lower scores on measures of quantitative reasoning; interestingly, girls living in mother-only homes actually show better verbal reasoning abilities than girls from two-parent homes (Hetherington et al., 1983), perhaps because they talk more with their mother than do girls in two-parent families (Astonc & McLanahan, 1991). In addition, after a divorce, boys are more likely to show disruptive behaviors that might affect their learning and their teachers' ratings of their performance.

Although differences in the academic functioning of children from married, remarried, and single-parent families are reliable, they are generally small when considered as a proportion of the total variance in academic measures. Amato and Keith's (1991a) meta-analysis of studies on the effects of divorce concluded that children from divorced families scored an average of .16 standard deviation below children from married families on a variety of academic measures. Overall, achievement scores show a delay of one year or less, and the number of years of schooling completed differs by ¾ of a year (Hetherington et al., 1983). Although in view of the wide range of academic outcomes, family status accounts for a small amount of the total variance, almost one year less of school completed is a figure that would seem to be of practical significance.

Academics and Family Processes under Stress

Differences in children's academic performance associated with having one or two parents in the home may reflect differences in family functioning, often associated with transitions after a divorce. For example, Kinard and Reinherz (1986) found that not all children whose parents were divorced showed deficits in academic measures. Only children from recently divorced families scored lower than children from intact families on measures of aptitude and achievement, after controlling for social class.

The academic difficulties encountered by children in divorced and single-parent homes are not necessarily due to the father's absence. There is some evidence that paternal contact is not influential for children's school achievement (Furstenberg et al., 1987). In general, the presence of any second adult in the home (not just the father) seems to have a beneficial effect on children's academics (Thompson et al., 1988). In more general terms, intelligence has been found to be related to time spent with adults, independent of whether these adults are male and female parents (Bisnaire, Firestone, & Rynard, 1990).

The resources of single parents, both in terms of money and time, are more limited than those of married or remarried parents. Especially if working outside the home, single parents have less time to spend on housework, meals, and helping with homework, and children may take on household responsibilities and chores at an earlier age (Hetherington et al., 1983). Children whose parents have recently divorced tend to watch more television and have less regular bedtimes (Guidubaldi, Perry, & Nastasi, 1987), perhaps as a function of less supervision (Barber & Eccles, 1992). Astonc and McLanahan (1991) found that children living with single parents or stepparents received less encouragement and less help with schoolwork than did children who lived in intact families. However, the single-parent children's poorer academic performance in this study was more directly due to truancy and negativity about school than to differences in parental behaviors per se. Wentzel (1991) found that teenagers from single-parent and remarried families miss more school; although absences and family structure were both significant predictors of grades, absences explained twice as much variance as family structure per se. This finding contrasts with that reported by Marsh (1990), described earlier, who found that family structure was unrelated to rates of absence among students whose family structure had been stable over the last two years of high school. This discrepancy suggests that children may show temporary disruptions in academics during periods of transition after changes in their parents' marital status, but that these disruptions may resolve over time.

Family Status, Race, and Income

The number of parents involved in raising a child and the type of parenting provided affect a child's educational performance. In fact, family status generally may be correlated *more* strongly with academic outcome than race, a factor that obviously has received substantial attention as a potential roadblock to education. In Featherman and Hauser's (1978) study of schooling completed by men between 1907 and 1951, race explained some of the educational differences in earlier-born cohorts but its influence declined for those born successively later in this century. As a result, family status and family economics became far better predictors than race or number of years of school completed.

Moreover, there is evidence that variables such as parental education and family status are less predictive of grades for black children than for white children, perhaps because of the greater community influences relative to family influences on African American families (Dornbusch, Ritter, & Steinberg, 1991). On the other hand, parental involvement in schoolwork seems more influential for black children than for white children, perhaps because of its effect on providing specific socialization for school (Thompson et al., 1988). Although the positive relationship between authoritative parenting and academic success has been shown to vary according to ethnic group and the amount of peer support (Dornbusch et al., 1987; Steinberg, Dornbusch, & Brown, 1992), across ethnic groups the relationship does not vary by family status; that is, authoritative parenting is associated with better achievement in single-parent and in two-parent homes (Lamborn, Mounts, & Steinberg, 1991).

When family economic status is controlled, differences in academics due to family status sometimes diminish or disappear, depending on the type of academic measure. Economic stressors associated with single-parenthood may be more influential on academic problems than on other behavior problems, which are apparent regardless of the effects of income (Guidubaldi et al., 1987). Children from single-parent homes are almost identical to children from *poor* two-parent homes in terms of their rates of dropping out of school and the number of years of schooling completed (Mueller & Cooper, 1984). However, as data on family economics indicate, in some ways it is misleading to examine educational data by family status with the effects of economics statistically controlled. Economic hardship is caused by family status, and although the concurrent

effects of poverty can be controlled statistically, they cannot be controlled in real life.

The direct effect of economic status on children's academic success also may vary by ethnic group, depending on other factors such as amount of parental contact with the school and extent of social support (Cooper, 1990). In addition, a decline in economic status may have a different influence on educational attainment than chronic poverty, which, in turn, would affect whites and blacks differently because of ethnic differences in divorce and childbirth outside marriage (Svanum, Bringle, & McLaughlin, 1982).

Family Structure and Children's Economic Well-Being

The percentage of children living in poverty in the United States has grown since the 1970s (Strawn, 1993), and children who live with single parents, particularly single mothers, suffer substantial financial hardships relative to children living with their two parents. In 1987, 16.2% of children in the United States were living below the poverty level. Of children living in different family types, 7.8% of children living in a household headed by a married couple were in poverty, as were 17.6% of children living in a household headed by a single male. For households headed by a single female, fully 46.1% of children were living in poverty (SCCYF, 1989).

Race and ethnicity account for some of these differences associated with family structure. In 1987, 12.5% of white children were living in poverty (median income of $32,217), while 37.3% of black children (median income of $15,005) and 32.1% of Hispanic children (median income of $17,962) were living in poverty. Still, marital status contributes enormously to children's economic well-being across ethnic groups. For those living with a married couple, 7.0% of white children and 13.6% of black children were living below the poverty level in 1987. (Data on Hispanic children are not available.) For those living with a single female, however, 38.7% of white children, 59.5% of black children, and 60.7% of Hispanic children were living in poverty. Economic hardship is particularly severe among young children. Among children under the age of 6, 54.8% of white children and 68.0% of black children who resided with a single mother were living in poverty in 1987 (SCCYF, 1989).

These dramatic differences in income and poverty rates are partially attributable to selection factors. Divorce and childbirth outside marriage are more common among the poor (Emery, 1988). Still, family status is the primary reason for the economic hardships experienced by single parents. Economies of scale dictate that single-parent families will suffer relative to two-parent families, because it is cheaper to live in one household than in two. The dramatically higher poverty rates of single-parent families also reflect that the majority of families, even those with young children, are dual-earner households. Many married women work out of economic necessity, not out of choice. If one income is insufficient in a married household, its insufficiency in a single-earner household is hardly surprising. Moreover, poverty is a particular problem for single women with children, because women continue to earn only about 60% of men's incomes.

Prospective, longitudinal research on the economic consequences of divorce demonstrates the causal role that family status plays in creating economic hardship for children living with single mothers. An analysis of a national sample of women found that their income dropped from approximately $26,000 to less than $15,000 (in 1981 dollars) in the year following divorce. This lower figure represented 91% of predivorce income relative to needs (with postdivorce needs levels adjusted for smaller family size) (Duncan & Hoffman, 1985). The critical role of family status in determining children's economic well-being was emphasized by the fact that the income of single women remained stable and below predivorce levels even five years after divorce, while the income of families who remained married rose substantially during this time. The subsequent income of women who remarried, however, was equivalent to that of always-married couples (Duncan & Hoffman, 1985).

Small child support awards and noncompliance with payment orders contribute to the poverty of single women and their children. There are substantial economic (and social) reasons for increasing both child payment levels and compliance among divorced and never-married fathers, and numerous state initiatives have been directed toward this end (Strawn, 1993). Still, according to 1987 census data, child support payments accounted for only 5.5% of the income of poor, single mothers (SCCYF, 1989). Public assistance programs, including AFDC, food stamps, and housing programs, were of greater benefit, as they accounted for 61.4% of poor, single mothers' income. (Poor women's earnings accounted for 25.3% of their income, SCCYF, 1989.) Despite these benefits, 71.5% of children living with a single mother either received no outside assistance or remained below the poverty level even *after* income transfers (SCCYF, 1989).

Thus, although child support payments and public assistance are of considerable benefit, increases in either source of income transfer are unlikely to alter the living conditions of impoverished women and children. Within the current cultural context and given current definitions of "family," it is painfully clear that one-parent families meet children's economic needs less well than two-parent families.

Understanding the causes of the poorer academic performance and economic deprivation in children of single parents is complicated by the fact that family status, race, and poverty are confounded. In addition, single-parent families are a diverse group. Ten percent of single-parent homes are male-headed, some "single-parent" homes are actually multigenerational (Thompson et al., 1988), and family status is likely to be unstable over short periods as families go through the multiple transitions surrounding marriage, divorce, and remarriage (Patterson, Kupersmidt, & Vaden, 1990).

ETHNIC DIFFERENCES IN FAMILY FORMS, DISRUPTION, AND COPING

This chapter has reviewed research on the consequences of family disruptions such as divorce on child development and the mediating processes thought to affect child adaptation to disruption.

As noted earlier, however, most of the research on child outcomes after divorce is conducted on European American families. The results of such research cannot always be generalized to families of other ethnic groups.

Like other social groups, families are systems that change in response to economic and cultural demands (Aries, 1962), and the American family is no exception (Macklin, 1987; Olson & Habenstein, 1992). The evolution of family forms occurs as a result of adaptation to cultural, social, and economic circumstances. Because the major ethnic groups in the United States have distinct histories with varying cultural traditions, circumstances, and access to societal resources, the families of various ethnic and racial groups that make up the U.S. population differ (Laosa, 1988). Across ethnic groups, differences can be seen in the prevalence of various family forms and the timing of family transitions. Ethnic groups also show differences in terms of family functioning in areas that affect the child's coping with family disruption, such as parenting styles, the nature of the marital relationship, and the involvement of extended family members.

Prevalence of Family Forms and Timing of Transitions

As noted early in the chapter, many statistics on families in the United States do not describe all ethnic groups equally well. Rates of divorce, the number of single-parent families, and family size show significant variability across European American, African American, Hispanic American, and Asian American groups. These differences have implications for understanding family disruption and child coping. Children's experiences in a single-parent home may differ substantially depending on the cause of the single parenting (never being married vs. divorce) and on the meaning and normative status of single parenthood in the child's cultural context.

On average, black and Hispanic women bear more children than do white women (Ponterotto & Casas, 1991). Asian groups in the United States, except the Japanese, are increasing in numbers due to immigration rather than due to births into families already in the United States (Gordon, 1990), and Asian families tend to have a smaller number of children than African, European, and Hispanic American families.

Among American ethnic groups, European American families (other than Hispanic American families) have the highest rate of divorce and remarriage. Hispanic Americans, with a strong Roman Catholic tradition, have low divorce rates. Although there is a shame associated with divorce, with acculturation, the number of female-headed households among some Asian American groups has come to be comparable to that found among European Americans (Kitano & Daniels, 1988).

Until the 1960s, 75% of African American families were two-parent households (Franklin, 1988). Since then, however, divorce and single-parenting have increased dramatically among this group, with many of the single parents being adolescents at the time of their child's birth. Disproportionate male-to-female ratios, due to high death and incarceration rates among young black males, contribute to this pattern (Peters & McAdoo, 1983). By contrast, Asian Americans have the lowest rate of single parenting (Laosa, 1988).

Contemporary Ethnic Differences in Family Processes

In addition to the differences in family structure and size across American ethnic groups, there also appear to be differences in terms of parenting styles and families' involvement with extended family. All these differences have implications for understanding children's development, especially child outcomes in divorced and single-parent homes.

Given the cultural and economic differences in the experiences of members of various ethnic groups in the United States, it is not surprising that family functioning and children's socialization would vary across ethnic groups. Ogbu (1981) notes that within a social group, there exist social roles and a system for survival depending on the group's economic ecology. Parents socialize their children to fit these roles and to be competent for survival within the context of the group's socioeconomic system. Rather than there being some universal ideal for parenting, effective parenting depends on the sociocultural context in which it takes place.

Parenting Styles

In Baumrind's (1972) original work on parenting styles, she found that authoritative, authoritarian, and permissive parenting styles were not equally distributed across ethnic groups. Black fathers tended to be more authoritarian, a pattern that has been more recently found among other minority parents in the United States, including Hispanic and Asian parents (Steinberg et al., 1992). In addition, black families have been shown to use more direct and physical discipline (Peters, 1986).

These differences in parenting styles may be related to differences in the ideals held by parents for their children's development, most notably in terms of the emphasis placed on autonomy versus obedience. Just as European American families focus on the nuclear family as autonomous from the extended family, European American parents often emphasize the importance of individualism, achievement, and their children's autonomy (Ponterotto & Casas, 1991). By contrast, Hispanic American parents often emphasize a child's respect for authority and good behavior more than a child's personal achievement (Garcia-Preto, 1982). African American parents' more explicit, directive parenting style also suggests a concern for obedience that is less apparent in European Americans' more suggestive, implicit parenting (Delpit, 1988). Among Asian Americans, subordination to the family is expected, and self-assertion is disapproved (Kitano, 1989). Personal acts reflect on the entire family, not just oneself. Traditionally, Asian children are expected to obey and care for their parents throughout life.

It is not clear how much of this difference in parenting styles is due to socioeconomic characteristics rather than ethnicity. Poor mothers and psychologically stressed middle-class mothers have similar styles of parenting, emphasizing obedience, power assertion, and low responsiveness to the child (McLoyd, 1990). Studies of poor families during the Great Depression showed that fathers who lost their jobs became more irritable, tense, explosive, and punitive (Elder & Caspi, 1988). In terms of the interplay of cultural and economic influences on parenting style, McLoyd (1990) asserts that power-assertive discipline may evolve in minority families from psychological stressors associated with poverty and then be rationalized as necessary to help children survive in hard circumstances.

Although some research has shown authoritative parenting to be associated with positive adjustment among adolescents across ethnic groups (Steinberg, Mounts, Lamborn & Dornbusch, 1991), researchers have also suggested that parenting styles may have different effects on children of different ethnic backgrounds. Baumrind (1972) found that daughters of black authoritarian families were actually more independent by the time of nursery school. In addition, whereas authoritative parenting has been found to have a direct positive effect on white children's academic performance, other factors such as socialization for school and peer group support have been found to be more influential for minority children's success (Cooper, 1990; Dornbusch et al., 1987; Steinberg et al., 1992). Thus, conclusions about the effects of family structure and family processes on children's emotional and academic performance must take into account preexisting differences across ethnic groups in parenting styles and the nature and extent of family influence on children's schooling. The effectiveness of various parenting styles must be evaluated in their proper sociocultural context.

Extended Family Involvement

Families of various ethnic groups also differ in the permeability of the boundary between the nuclear family and extended family, friends, and the community. These differences have implications for understanding child development in the context of family relationships.

Whereas European American families rely most heavily on the resources and support of nuclear family members, families of other ethnic groups show more involvement with extended family. The inclusion of extended family in the household is three times more likely among African American families than among European American families in the United States (Wilson & Tolson, 1988), especially in the case of single mothers (Tienda & Angel, 1982). More black elderly live with family members than do white elderly (53% vs. 40%), and 10% of black children live with a grandparent rather than a parent, a rate three times that of white children (Pearson & Hunter, 1990). The extended family structure persists in African American communities because of poverty, single parenting, and marital dissolution (Wilson, 1989a). The wide, informal network of kin often includes longtime friends as well as relatives. Kin social support is associated with increased authoritative parenting among single African American parents (Taylor, Casten, & Flickinger, 1993).

After marital dissolution, black mothers are more likely to move in with parents than are white mothers, even controlling for socioeconomic influences (Isaacs & Leon, 1987). Although black families report that grandmothers living in the home help significantly with child care (Wilson, 1986), observational data show that grandmothers actually have a more indirect influence. They model effective parenting, provide information (Stevens, 1984), and offer respites from child care (Wilson, 1989b).

Permeability in family boundaries is also seen in African American family members' willingness to informally adopt children whose own parents do not have the resources to parent (Wilson & Tolson, 1990). Black families also rely more than other families on what has been termed "fictive kin," friends who are incorporated as part of the family (Wilson, 1989a). This broadened concept of family is thought to have evolved in the face of poverty, marital dissolution, and extramarital birth (Wilson, 1989a), but broader family networks are evident even among established middle-class black families (McAdoo, 1986).

Hispanic American families also have an extended network of family relationships that may provide support after divorce, although Hispanic American families are less supportive than other ethnic groups of members who divorce, even after controlling for religious beliefs (Wagner, 1988). Still, Hispanic American women depend on their families more than do European American women in the first year of being a single parent. Although extended family members do not officially share a household, Hispanic American families view even third and fourth cousins as family, and family members often become "permanent visitors" in a household (Falicov, 1982). Godparents often have a prominent place in the family, and take an active role in socializing children.

Child Outcomes after Divorce

Much of the research on family processes, adaptation to divorce, and parenting is conducted on white families, with the standard of family functioning being that of the two-parent married household. Little is known about the normative, adaptive functioning of nonwhite children and families. Thus conclusions about the changes in family processes and child outcomes associated with disrupted family functioning in these groups are only speculative. It appears that current knowledge about developmental psychopathology still is culture-bound despite advances in developing principles that have more general application.

Perhaps the most important ethnic difference to address when studying child adaptation to family disruption is the cause of single parenthood and the meaning of that condition within the child's sociocultural group. Whereas European, Hispanic, and Asian American children are most likely to be living with a single parent because of divorce, African American children are more frequently born into single-parent homes. Most research on mothers who never marry is conducted on teenage mothers, with limited generalizability to older single parents (Mednick, 1987). In addition, the reality of single parenting differs across groups, depending on the group's norms for parenting and on the support available from extended family and the community. In European American families, single mothers may be more isolated in their efforts to raise their children than are their African American counterparts.

The different economic and social realities of single parents of various ethnic groups present a challenge to the concept of "family disruption." In many African American communities, for example, single parenting is a common family form that is accepted and effective in the context of extended community and multigenerational involvement in family life. Just as more recent cohorts of children in the general population show fewer negative consequences of divorce, perhaps associated with growing acceptance of one-parent families (Amato & Keith, 1991a), so too must the consequences of living with a never-married or divorced mother depend on the acceptability of these family forms within one's community.

Svanum and colleagues (1982) note that developmental stress may be more associated with changes in living circumstances than in static conditions. For example, in terms of the economic consequences of divorce, children who experience a drop in economic stability are coping with a different stressor than children already living in chronic poverty. Similarly, children who lose a father through separation or divorce are different from those who have been raised by a single parent. This is not to say that chronic poverty or being raised by a single parent has no developmental consequences for children. Rather, in understanding the consequences of divorce and single parenting for children, researchers must take into account what is normative, adaptive family functioning and what is family disruption.

The variables and processes mediating the effects of single parenting and divorce on children are also likely to differ by ethnic group. For example, ethnic groups differ in the extent to which they acknowledge and express family conflict. Future research could examine ethnic differences in the amount of resolved versus unresolved family conflict, and in how conflict in nonmarital relationships (such as those in multigenerational households) affects child outcomes.

Further research could also explore the mediating role of child gender on outcomes associated with single parenthood and divorce, given ethnic differences in parenting styles and socialization of children. For example, African American families have been noted for a less sex-stereotyped approach to assigning chores and child-care duties (Peters, 1986), and for a more egalitarian relationship between parents (Hines & Boyd-Franklin, 1982). These qualities differentiate African American families from most of the European American families that have been the subject of research on child adaptation to family disruption, and further suggest the need for research on normative family functioning within ethnic groups.

CONTRIBUTIONS OF THE STUDY OF RISK TO NORMAL DEVELOPMENT

Research on children's normal and abnormal behavior in alternative family forms highlights the benefits of a developmental psychopathology approach. The central conclusion is that psychological resilience, not risk, is the term that most accurately describes the experience of children who grow up in different types of families. Remember, however, that resilience refers both to children's ability to "bounce back" and to the struggles involved in doing so.

This conclusion about a group of children traditionally considered to be "at risk" holds implications for the study of normal development. Perhaps the most basic implication is that children's experiences in growing up in alternative family forms are a part of normal development in contemporary American life. At the present time, divorce and single-parenting are normative, not deviant, family living circumstances. The same basic rules of child development apply in traditional and nontraditional families, and it is intellectually inaccurate and a disservice to children and families to imply otherwise.

This does not mean that unique and extremely difficult stressors do not confront children whose parents divorce, remarry, or never marry. Evidence indicates that disruptions in family functions are substantial in alternative families compared with always-married two-parent families. Children's successful adjustment to these changes over the long run suggests a process of resilience more strongly than it suggests risk, however. Researchers have uncovered useful evidence about such risk processes as inconsistent parenting and parental conflict. In contrast, the processes that lead to resilience are not well understood despite the increasing frequency with which the term has been invoked. There is a pressing need to develop a basic understanding about how children achieve adaptive outcomes in the face of adversity. Such inquiry is not limited to the field of developmental psychopathology, but it is also basic to the study of normal development. Adversity and challenge are givens in life. The key to social and emotional development lies in successful coping, not in the avoidance of stress.

The focus on resilience also suggests the need to expand the content domain in assessing children's positive social and emotional development. It has been suggested here that resilience leaves a psychological residue, but we know little about the subclinical—the normal—distress that children experience. The absence of mental health problems is not the same as the presence of mental health. Until developmental researchers adequately define mental health, however, it will continue to be defined by exclusion.

Evidence on the adjustment of children who grow up in single-parent, divorced, or remarried families also indicates that their "outcomes" are far from fixed. A developmental perspective highlights numerous time- and age-graded influences on children's adjustment both before and after key family transitions. Some of the central developmental issues include nonrandom selection into particular family forms, the onset of difficulties prior to family transitions, the amelioration of problems over time, and the subsequent exacerbation of the challenges posed by the tasks of normal child development.

These age- and time-graded conclusions about children's experiences, particularly in divorced families, also hold implications for the study of normal development. One implication is methodological. The confound between the age at which an event is experienced, current age, and time since the event applies to research on all childhood experiences. Attempts are needed to disentangle these confounds across the study of normal development. Evidence that many of the adjustment difficulties found among children after divorce actually begin before divorce also strongly underscores the importance of prospective research in examining the "consequences" of normal and atypical life events. Finally, research on some specific domains of children's distress in alternative family forms suggests the need to chart the normal developmental course of these concerns. For example, many investigators have emphasized the concerns that children from divorced families have about forming intimate relationships. It is impossible to adequately evaluate such concerns, however, because there is little evidence on the normal progression of these worries.

Yet another central issue that emerges from the body of research on alternative family forms is the importance of family processes rather than family structures. Although researchers have found only modest differences in the mental health of children living in alternative family forms, children's psychological well-being consistently has been found to be associated with difficulties in key family relationships. In this circumstance, research on normal development has been extremely valuable in pinpointing key family processes. The presence of at least one authoritative parent-child relationship and the absence of conflict between children's parental figures both are substantial predictors of children's adjustment within and across family forms.

Research on children's experiences in nontraditional families directly suggests the need for a more systemic conceptualization of these processes in studies of normal development, however. Questions about the role of fathers, and particularly about the roles of mothers and fathers parenting together, are raised by concerns about interparental conflict and coparenting in two households. Parenting in two-parent families traditionally has been viewed in dyadic terms, but a broader awareness of the entire family system prompts basic questions. If one parent is indulgent and the other is authoritarian, is the net result inconsistency or authoritative parenting from the perspective of children's development? Such questions rarely have been asked, let alone answered, in developmental research.

Research on children's psychological adjustment in alternative family forms optimistically points to resilience, change, and the paramount importance of family processes. A thorough understanding of children's lives requires that other outcomes be considered, however, and here the conclusions reached are less sanguine. Research suggests that family structure may have a more detrimental effect on children's educational attainment, particularly the number of years of school completed, than it does on their emotional well-being. Evidence dramatically indicates that divorce and childbirth outside marriage directly cause substantial declines in children's standards of living. Far more children whose parents are divorced or never married live in poverty, an outcome that is of much relevance to children's lives.

These distressing conclusions about education and income indicate the need for broad, multidisciplinary approaches to the study of both normal development and developmental psychopathology. Developmental researchers cannot be complacent either with their individual measure or with their broad domains of inquiry. In research on children's normal and abnormal development, variables like income often are considered to be nuisance factors. At best, income is incorporated into developmental models as a worthy predictor of child adjustment. We would not want our own children to grow up in poverty, however, even if poverty were unrelated to any measure of psychological well-being. Poverty and other factors traditionally considered to be the domain of sociologists or economists are important developmental outcomes for children in their own right. Study of the family is not the exclusive domain of either developmental psychology or developmental psychopathology, and both disciplines need to demonstrate more recognition of broader family functions.

Finally, American children of various ethnic backgrounds come from families with very different structures on average. Key family relationships also differ somewhat across ethnic groups. The preponderance of research on children's adjustment in alternative family forms focuses on the experience of divorce among European Americans from middle-income groups. The same is true of studies of normal development. A consideration of the heritage and current experience of family life among the major American ethnic groups suggests directions for the major, future challenge for understanding child psychopathology in the family context: investigating children's normal and abnormal development in families that differ not only in structure, but also in ethnic background.

FUTURE DIRECTIONS FOR RESEARCH ON DISRUPTIONS IN FAMILY FUNCTIONS

Research on children's development and disruptions in family functions will be furthered by such efforts to expand the study of children's normal development within different family contexts. Several future directions also are suggested for researchers whose primary interests are focused on children's experiences in alternative family forms.

An area where research is likely to continue concerns further comparisons of the magnitude of the difference in the psychological functioning of children from two-parent and nontraditional families. Are these differences large, or are they small? The resilience perspective taken here and elsewhere (Emery & Forehand, 1994) suggests a resolution to this debate, which has strong political undertones. Rather than continue to attempt to resolve a matter of interpretation with data, this review suggests an integrative explanation. The chapter also suggests that a new and critical direction for future study is to broaden the domain of inquiry. Researchers have collected much data on the psychological outcomes that form the basic concerns about children's mental health in alternative family forms. Data are lacking on children's more hidden and subtle worries. These have been noted by clinicians, but have yet to be adequately measured by empirical investigators.

Another crucial direction for future research involves the further investigation of the timing of disruptions in children's functioning in relation to major family transitions. More prospective research is needed, and its added expense is justified by the valuable contributions of the existing prospective studies. In conducting prospective, longitudinal research, it is essential to investigate both nonrandom selection and the onset of dysfunctional family processes as explanations of the origins of difficulties in children's development prior to family transitions.

Another area ripe for further investigation is the exploration of individual differences in family stressors and in children's strategies for coping with them. For example, it is known that parental conflict is related to maladaptive child outcomes across all family forms. What is not clear is why conflict is pathogenic for some children and not for others. The answer may rest in the way parents manage conflict, or it may lie in the manner that children interpret conflict. More generally, researchers need to move from the study of risk factors to the identification of mediating processes to explain variability in individual outcomes when children are faced with the same or a similar stressor.

Finally, as noted previously, there is a pressing need to investigate children's development in alternative family forms within the context of different ethnic and socioeconomic backgrounds. At present, researchers and social policy makers are drawing conclusions about family disruptions based on research conducted on one segment of American society, the white middle class, and applying the findings to an entirely different part of the population, the black underclass. Advancement of scientific knowledge, and of political credibility, awaits the broadening of research so that findings are applied to the same ethnic groups that are studied.

REFERENCES

Allison, P., & Furstenberg, F. (1989). How marital dissolution affects children: Variations by age and sex. *Developmental Psychology, 25,* 540–549.

Altenbaugh, R. (1991). Urban immigrant families: A comparative study of Italians and Mexicans. In J. Hunter & P. Mason (Eds.), *The American family: Historical perspectives* (pp. 125–141). Pittsburg: Duquesne University Press.

Amato, P. R. (1993). Children's adjustment to divorce: Theories, hypotheses, and empirical support. *Journal of Marriage and the Family, 55,* 23-38.

Amato, P. R., & Keith, B. (1991a). Parental divorce and the well-being of children: A meta-analysis. *Psychological Bulletin, 110,* 26–46.

Amato, P. R., & Keith, B. (1991b). Parental divorce and adult well-being. *Journal of Marriage and the Family, 53,* 43–58.

Ambert, A. (1984). Longitudinal changes in children's behavior toward custodial parents. *Journal of Marriage and the Family, 46,* 463–467.

Aries, P. (1962). *Centuries of childhood.* New York: Vintage Books.

Astonc, N., & McLanahan, S. (1991). Family structure, parental practices, and high school completion. *American Sociological Review, 56,* 309–320.

Atkeson, B. M., Forehand, R. L., & Rickard, K. M. (1982). The effects of divorce on children. In B. B. Lahey & A. E. Kazdin (Eds.), *Advances in clinical child psychology* (Vol. 5, pp. 255–281). New York: Plenum.

Ballard, M. E., Cummings, E. M., & Larkin, K. (1993). Emotional and cardiovascular responses to adults' angry behavior and challenging tasks in children of hypertensive and normotensive parents. *Child Development, 64,* 500–515.

Baltes, P. B., Cornelius, S. W., & Nesselroade, J. R. (1979). Cohort effects in developmental psychology. In J.R. Nesselroade & P. B. Baltes (Eds.), *Longitudinal research in the study of behavior and development* (pp. 61–88). New York: Academic Press.

Barber, B., & Eccles, J. (1992). Long-term influences of divorce and single parenting on adolescent family- and work-related values, behaviors, and aspirations. *Psychological Bulletin, 111,* 108–126.

Baumrind, D. (1972). An exploratory study of socialization effects on black children: Some black-white comparisons. *Child Development, 43,* 261–267.

Becker, G. (1980). *A treatise on the family.* Chicago: University of Chicago Press.

Belsky, J. (1984). The determinants of parenting: A process model. *Child Development, 55,* 83–96.

Bisnaire, L., Firestone, P., & Rynard, D. (1990). Factors associated with academic achievement in children following parent separation. *American Journal of Orthopsychiatry, 60,* 67–76.

Block, J., Block, J. H., & Gjerde, P. F. (1988). Parental functioning and the home environment in families of divorce: Prospective and concurrent analyses. *Journal of the American Academy of Child and Adolescent Psychiatry, 27,* 207–213.

Block, J. H., Block, J., & Gjerde, P. F. (1986). The personality of children prior to divorce: A prospective study. *Child Development, 57,* 827–840.

Block, J. H., Block, J., & Morrison, A. (1981). Parental agreement-disagreement on child-rearing orientations and gender-related personality correlates in children. *Child Development, 52,* 965–974.

Bowlby, J. (1973). *Attachment and loss: Vol. 2. Separation.* New York: Basic Books.

Braver, S. L., Wolchik, S. A., Sandler, I. N., Sheets, V. L., Fogas, B., & Bay, R. C. (1993). A longitudinal study of noncustodial parents: Parents without children. *Journal of Family Psychology, 7,* 9–23.

Bray, J. H., & Berger, S. H. (1993). Developmental issues in Stepfamilies Research Project: Family relationships and parent-child interactions. *Journal of Family Psychology, 7,* 76–90.

Bronfenbrenner, U. (1986). Ecology of the family as a context for human development: Research perspectives. *Developmental Psychology, 22,* 723–742.

Buchanan, C. M., Maccoby, E. E., & Dornbusch, S. M. (1991). Caught between parents: Adolescents' experience in divorced homes. *Child Development, 62,* 1008–1029.

Bumpass, L. (1984). Children and marital disruption: A replication and update. *Demography, 21,* 71–82.

Bumpass, L. (1990). What's happening to the American family? Interactions between demographic and institutional change. *Demography, 27,* 483–498.

Camara, K. A., & Resnick, G. (1987). Marital and parental subsystems in mother-custody, father-custody and two-parent households: Effects on children's social development. In J. Vincent (Ed.), *Advances in family assessment, intervention and research* (Vol. 4, pp. 165–196). Greenwich, CT: JAI Press.

Camara, K. A., & Resnick, G. (1988). Interparental conflict and cooperation: Factors moderating children's post-divorce adjustment. In E. M. Hetherington & J. Arasteh (Eds.), *Divorced single-parent and stepparent families* (pp. 169–195). Hillsdale NJ: Erlbaum.

Capaldi, D. M., & Patterson, G. R. (1991). Relation of parental transitions to boys' adjustment problems: I. A. linear hypothesis. II. Mothers at risk for transitions and unskilled parenting. *Developmental Psychology, 3,* 489–504.

Caspi, A., & Elder, G. (1988). Emergent family patterns: The intergenerational construction of problem behavior and relationships. In R. Hinde & J. Stevenson-Hinde (Eds.), *Relationships within the family* (pp. 218–240). Oxford, England: Clarendon Press.

Chang, P., & Deinard, A. S. (1982). Single-father caretakers: Demographic characteristics and adjustment processes. *American Journal of Orthopsychiatry, 52,* 236–243.

Chase-Lansdale, P., & Hetherington, E. M. (1990). The impact of divorce on life-span development: Short- and long-term effects. In P. B. Baltes, D. L. Featherman, & R. M. Lerner (Eds.), *Life-span development and behavior* (Vol. 10, pp. 107–151). Hillsdale, NJ: Erlbaum.

Cherlin, A. J. (1977). The effect of children on marital dissolution. *Demography, 14,* 265–272.

Cherlin, A. J. (1993). *Marriage, divorce, remarriage* (2nd ed.). Cambridge, MA: Harvard University Press.

Cherlin, A. J., Furstenberg, F. F., Chase-Lansdale, P. L., Kiernan, K. E., Robins, P. K., Morrison, D. R., & Teitler, J. O. (1991). Longitudinal studies of effects of divorce on children in Great Britain and the United States. *Science, 252,* 1386–1389.

Christopoulos, C., Cohn, D. A., Shaw, D. S., Joyce, S., Sullivan-Hanson, J., Kraft, S., & Emery, R. E. (1987). Children of abused women: I. Adjustment at time of shelter residence. *Journal of Marriage and the Family, 49,* 611–619.

Cicchetti, D. (1993). Developmental psychopathology: Reactions, reflections, projections. *Developmental Review, 13,* 471–502.

Cooper, A. (1990). Fallacy of a single model for school achievement: Considerations for ethnicity. *Sociological Perspectives, 33,* 159–184.

Covell, K., & Miles, B. (1992). Children's beliefs about strategies to reduce parental anger. *Child Development, 63,* 381–390.

Cummings, E. M. (1987). Coping with background anger in early childhood. *Child Development, 58,* 976–984.

Cummings, E. M., Ballard, M., El-Sheikh, M., & Lake, M. (1991). Resolution and children's responses to interadult anger. *Development Psychology, 27,* 462–470.

Cummings, E. M., Simpson, K. S., & Wilson, A. (1993). Children's responses to interadult anger as a function of information about resolution. *Developmental Psychology, 29,* 978–985.

Cummings, E. M., Vogel, D., Cummings, J. S., & El-Sheikh, M. (1989). Children's responses to different forms of expression of anger between adults. *Child Development, 60,* 1392–1404.

Cummings, E. M., Zahn-Waxler, C., & Radke-Yarrow, M. (1981). Young children's responses to expressions of anger and affection by others in the family. *Child Development, 52,* 1274–1282.

Cummings, E. M., Zahn-Waxler, C., & Radke-Yarrow, M. (1984). Developmental changes in children's reactions to anger in the home. *Journal of Child Psychology and Psychiatry, 25,* 63–74.

Cummings, J. S., Pellegrini, D., Notarius, C., & Cummings, E. M. (1989). Children's responses to angry adult behavior as a function of marital distress and history of interparent hostility. *Child Development, 60,* 1035–1043.

Delpit, L. D. (1988). The silenced dialogue: Power and pedagogy in educating other people's children. *Harvard Educational Review, 58,* 280–297.

Demos, J. (1986). *Past, present, and future: The family and the life course in American history.* New York: Oxford University Press.

Dornbusch, S. M., & Gray, K. D. (1988). Single-parent families. In S. M. Dornbusch & M. H. Strober (Eds.), *Feminism, children, and the new families* (pp. 274–296). New York: Guilford.

Dornbusch, S., Ritter, P., Leiderman, P., Roberts, D., & Fraleigh, M. (1987). The relation of parenting style to adolescent school performance. *Child Development, 58,* 1244–1257.

Dornbusch, S., Ritter, P., & Steinberg, L. (1991). Community influences on the relation of family statuses to adolescent school performance: Differences between African Americans and non-Hispanic whites. *American Journal of Education, 99,* 543–567.

Downey, D. B., & Powell, B. (1993). Do children in single-parent households fare better living with same-sex parents? *Journal of Marriage and the Family, 55,* 55–71.

Duncan, G. J., & Hoffman, S. D. (1985). Economic consequences of marital instability. In M. David & T. Smeeding (Eds.), *Horizontal equity, uncertainty and well-being* (pp. 427–469). Chicago: University of Chicago Press.

Elder, G., & Caspi, A. (1988). Economic stress in lives: Developmental perspectives. *Journal of Social Issues, 44,* 25–45.

Elliott, B. J., & Richards, M. P. M. (1991). Children and divorce: Educational performance and behaviour before and after parental separation. *International Journal of Law and the Family, 5,* 258–276.

El-Sheikh, M., Cummings, E. M., & Goetsch, V. (1989). Coping with adults' angry behavior: Behavioral, physiological, and verbal responses in preschoolers. *Developmental Psychology, 25,* 490–498.

Emery, R. E. (1982). Interparental conflict and the children of discord and divorce. *Psychological Bulletin, 92,* 310–330.

Emery, R. E. (1988). *Marriage, divorce, and children's adjustment.* Beverly Hills, CA: Sage.

Emery, R. E. (1992). Family conflict and its developmental implications: A conceptual analysis of deep meanings and systemic processes. In C. U. Shantz & W. W. Hartup (Eds.), *Conflict in child and adolescent development* (pp. 270–297). London: Cambridge University Press.

Emery, R. E. (1994). *Child custody mediation: Negotiating agreements and renegotiating relationships.* New York: Guilford.

Emery, R. E., Fincham, F. F., & Cummings, M. (1992). Parenting in context: Systemic thinking about parental conflict and its influence on children. *Journal of Consulting and Clinical Psychology, 60,* 909–912.

Emery, R. E., & Forehand, R. (1994). Parental divorce and children's well-being: A focus on resilience. In R. J. Haggerty, N. Garmezy, M. Rutter, & L. Sherrod (Eds.), *Risk and resilience in children* (pp. 64–99). London: Cambridge University Press.

Emery, R. E., Hetherington, E. M., & DiLalla, L. F. (1984). Divorce, children, and social policy. In H. W. Stevenson & A. E. Siegel (Eds.), *Child development research and social policy* (pp. 189–266). Chicago: University of Chicago Press.

Emery, R. E., Joyce, S. A., & Fincham, F. D. (1987). The assessment of marital and child problems. In K. D. O'Leary (Ed.), *Assessment of marital discord* (pp. 223–262). Hillsdale, NJ: Erlbaum.

Emery, R. E., Kitzmann, K., & Aaron, J. (1993, March). *Mothers' aggression before marriage and children's aggression after divorce.* Paper presented at the biennial meeting of the Society for Research in Child Development, New Orleans.

Emery, R. E., Matthews, S., & Kitzmann, K. (1994). Child custody mediation and litigation: Parents' satisfaction and functioning a year after settlement. *Journal of Consulting and Clinical Psychology, 62,* 124–129.

Emery, R., & O'Leary, K. (1982). Children's perception of marital discord and behavior problems of boys and girls. *Journal of Abnormal Child Psychology, 10,* 11–24.

Emery, R. E., Weintraub, S., & Neale, J. M. (1982). Effects of marital discord on the school behavior of children of schizophrenic, affectively disordered, and normal parents. *Journal of Abnormal Child Psychology, 10,* 215–228.

Falicov, C. J. (1982). Mexican families. In M. McGoldrick, J. Pearce, & J. Giordano (Eds.), *Ethnicity and family therapy* (pp. 134–163). New York: Guilford.

Fauber, R., Forehand, R., Thomas, A. M., & Wierson, M. (1990). A mediational model of the impact of marital conflict on adolescent adjustment in intact and divorced families: The role of disruptive parenting. *Child Development, 61,* 1112–1123.

Fauber, R. L., & Long, N. (1991). Children in context: The role of the family in child psychotherapy. *Journal of Consulting and Clinical Psychology, 59,* 813–820.

Featherman, D. L. (1980). Schooling and occupational careers: Constancy and change in worldly success. In O. Brim & J. Kagan (Eds.), *Constancy and change in human development* (pp. 675–738). Cambridge, MA: Harvard University Press.

Featherman, D. L., & Hauser, R. M. (1978). *Opportunity and change.* New York: Academic Press.

Folberg, J. (1991). *Joint custody and shared parenting.* New York: Guilford.

Forehand, R., McCombs, A., Long, N., Brody, G., & Fauber, R. (1988). Early adolescent adjustment to recent parental divorce: The role of interparental conflict and adolescent sex as mediating variables. *Journal of Consulting and Clinical Psychology, 56,* 624–627.

Forehand, R., Thomas, A. M., Wierson, M., Brody, G., & Fauber, R. (1990). Role of maternal functioning and parenting skills in adolescent functioning following parental divorce. *Journal of Abnormal Psychology, 99,* 278–283.

Franklin, J. H. (1988). A historical note on black families. In H. P. McAdoo (Ed.), *Black families* (pp. 23–26). Beverly Hills, CA: Sage.

Furstenberg, F., & Cherlin, A. (1991). *Divided families: What happens to children when parents part.* Cambridge, MA: Harvard University Press.

Furstenberg, F., Morgan, S., & Allison, P. (1987). Paternal participation and children's well-being after marital dissolution. *American Sociological Review, 52,* 695–701.

Furstenberg, F. F., & Nord, C. W. (1985). Parenting apart: Patterns of childrearing after marital disruption. *Journal of Marriage and the Family, 47,* 893–904.

Furstenberg, F. F., Peterson, J. L., Nord, C. W., & Zill, N. (1983). The life course of children of divorce: Marital disruption and parental contact. *American Sociological Review, 48,* 656–668.

Garcia-Preto, N. (1982). Puerto Rican families. In M. McGoldrick, J. Pearce, & J. Giordano (Eds.), *Ethnicity and family therapy* (pp. 164–186). New York: Guilford.

Garmezy, N. (1991). Resilience in children's adaptation to negative life events and stressed environments. *Pediatric Annals, 20,* 459–466.

Gersick, K. E. (1979). Fathers by choice: Divorced men who receive custody of their children. In G. Levinger & O. C. Moles (Eds.), *Divorce and separation* (pp. 307–323). New York: Basic Books.

Gibson, H. B. (1969). Early delinquency in relation to broken homes. *Journal of Child Psychology and Psychiatry, 10,* 195–204.

Gjerde, P. F. (1986). The interpersonal structure of family interaction settings: Parent-adolescent relations in dyads and triads. *Developmental Psychology, 22,* 297–304.

Glueck, S., & Glueck, E. (1950). *Unraveling juvenile delinquency.* Cambridge, MA: Harvard University Press.

Goldstein, J., Freud, A., & Solnit, A. J. (1973). *Beyond the best interests of the child.* New York: Free Press.

Gordon, L. (1990). Asian immigration since World War II. In R. Tucker, C. Keely, & L. Wrigley (Eds.), *Immigration and U.S. foreign policy* (pp. 169–191). Boulder, CO: Westview Press.

Gotlib, I. H., & McCabe, S. B. (1990). Marriage and psychopathology. In F. Fincham & T. Bradbury (Eds.), *The psychology of marriage* (pp. 226–257). New York: Guilford.

Gottman, J. M., & Katz, L. F. (1989). Effects of marital discord on young children's peer interaction and health. *Developmental Psychology, 25,* 373–381.

Grych, J. H., & Fincham, F. D. (1990). Marital conflict and children's adjustment: A cognitive-contextual framework. *Psychological Bulletin, 108,* 267–290.

Grych, J. H., & Fincham, F. D. (1992). Interventions for children of divorce: Towards greater integration of research and action. *Psychological Bulletin, 111,* 434–454.

Guidubaldi, J., Perry, J., & Nastasi, B. (1987). Growing up in a divorced family: Initial and long-term perspectives on children's adjustment. *Applied Social Psychology Annual, 7,* 202–237.

Guttmann, J., & Boudo, M. (1988). Teachers' evaluations of pupils' performance as a function of pupils' sex, family type, and past school performance. *Educational Review, 40,* 105–113.

Halem, L. C. (1981). *Divorce reform.* New York: Free Press.

Hess, R. D., & Camara, K. A. (1979). Post-divorce relationships as mediating factors in the consequences of divorce for children. *Journal of Social Issues, 35,* 79–96.

Hetherington, E. M. (1972). Effects of parental absence on personality development in adolescent daughters. *Developmental Psychology, 7,* 313–326.

Hetherington, E. M. (1979). Divorce: A child's perspective. *American Psychologist, 34,* 851–858.

Hetherington, E. M. (1983). Coping with family transitions: Winners, losers, and survivors. *Child Development, 60,* 1–14.

Hetherington, E. M. (1991). Presidential address: Families, lies, and videotapes. *Journal of Research on Adolescence, 1,* 323–348.

Hetherington, E. M. (1993). An overview of the Virginia Longitudinal Study of Divorce and Remarriage with a focus on early adolescence. *Journal of Family Psychology, 7,* 39–56.

Hetherington, E. M., & Clingempeel, W. G. (1992). Coping with marital transitions. *Monographs of the Society for Research in Child Development* (Serial No. 227), *57,* 1–229.

Hetherington, E. M., Cox, M., & Cox, R. (1982). Effects of divorce on parents and children. In M. Lamb (Ed.), *Nontraditional families* (pp. 233–288). Hillsdale, NJ: Erlbaum.

Hetherington, E. M., Cox, M., & Cox, R. (1985). Long-term effects of divorce and remarriage on the adjustment of children. *Journal of the American Academy of Child Psychiatry, 24,* 518–530.

Hines, P. M., & Boyd-Franklin, N. (1982). Black families. In M. McGoldrick, J. Pearce, & J. Giordano (Eds.), *Ethnicity and family therapy* (pp. 84–107). New York: Guilford.

Howes, P. W., & Cicchetti, D. (1993). A family/relational perspective on maltreating families: Parallel processes across systems and social policy implications. In D. Cicchetti & S. L. Toth (1993), *Child abuse, child development, and social policy.* Norwood, NJ: Ablex.

Hughes, H. M. (1988). Psychological and behavioral correlates of family violence in child witnesses and victims. *American Journal of Orthopsychiatry, 18,* 77–90.

Isaacs, M., & Leon, G. (1987). Race, marital dissolution and visitation: An examination of adaptive family strategies. *Journal of Divorce, 11*(2), 17–31.

Jaffe, P. G., Wolfe, D. A., & Wilson, S. K. (1990). *Children of battered women.* Beverly Hills, CA: Sage.

Jenkins, J. M., & Smith, M. A. (1990). Factors protecting children living in disharmonious homes. *Journal of the American Academy of Child and Adolescent Psychiatry, 29,* 60–69.

Jenkins, J. M., Smith, M. A., & Graham, P. J. (1989). Coping with parental quarrels. *Journal of the American Academy of Child and Adolescent Psychiatry, 28,* 182–191.

Johnston, J. R., Kline, M., & Tschann, J. M. (1989). Ongoing post-divorce conflict: Effects on children of joint custody and frequent access. *American Journal of Orthopsychiatry, 59,* 576–592.

Jouriles, E. N., & Farris, A. M. (1992). Effects of marital conflict on subsequent parent-son interactions. *Behavior Therapy, 23,* 355–374.

Kinard, E. M., & Reinherz, H. (1986). Effects of marital disruption on children's school aptitude and achievement. *Journal of Marriage and the Family, 48,* 285–293.

Kitano, H. (1989). A model for counseling Asian-Americans. In P. Pedersen, J. Draguns, W. Lonner, & J. Trimble (Eds.), *Counseling across cultures* (pp. 139–152). Honolulu, Hawaii: University Press of Hawaii.

Kitano, H., & Daniels, R. (1988). *Asian-Americans: Emerging minorities.* Englewood Cliffs, NJ: Prentice-Hall.

Kulka, R. A., & Weingarten, H. (1979). The long-term effects of parental divorce in childhood on adult adjustment. *Journal of Social Issues, 35,* 50–78.

Kurdek, L. (1986). Custodial mothers' perceptions of visitation and payment support by noncustodial fathers in families with low and high levels of preseparation conflict. *Journal of Applied Developmental Psychology, 7,* 307–323.

Kurdek, L. A., & Berg, B. (1987). Children's beliefs about parental divorce scale: Psychometric characteristics and concurrent validity. *Journal of Consulting and Clinical Psychology, 55,* 712–718.

Lahey, B. B., Hartdagen, S. E., Frick, P. J., McBurnett, K., Connor, R., & Hynd, G. W. (1988). Conduct disorder: Parsing the confounded relations to parental divorce and antisocial personality. *Journal of Abnormal Psychology, 97,* 334–337.

Lamborn, S., Mounts, N., & Steinberg, L. (1991). Patterns of competence and adjustment among adolescents from authoritative, authoritarian, indulgent, and neglectful families. *Child Development, 62,* 1049–1065.

Laosa, L. (1988). Ethnicity and single parenting in the United States. In E. M. Hetherington & J. Arasteh (Eds.), *Impact of divorce, single parenting, and stepparenting on children* (pp. 23–52). Hillsdale, NJ: Erlbaum.

Long, N., & Forehand, R. (1987). The effects of parental divorce and parental conflict on children: An overview. *Developmental and Behavioral Pediatrics, 8,* 292–296.

Luepnitz, D. A. (1982). *Child custody: A study of families after divorce.* Lexington, MA: Lexington Books.

Luster, T., & Okagaki, L. (1993). *Parenting: An ecological perspective.* Hillsdale, NJ: Erlbaum.

Maccoby, E. E., Buchanan, C. M., Mnookin, R. H., & Dornbusch, S. M. (1993). Postdivorce roles of mothers and fathers in the lives of their children. *Journal of Family Psychology, 7,* 24–38.

Maccoby, E. E., & Martin, J. A. (1983). Socialization in the context of the family. In E. M. Hetherington (Ed.), *Handbook of child psychology* (pp. 1–101). New York: Wiley.

Maccoby, E. E., & Mnookin, R. H. (1992). *Dividing the child.* Cambridge, MA: Harvard University Press.

Macklin, D. (1987). Nontraditional family forms. In M. Sussman & S. Steinmetz (Eds.), *Handbook of marriage and the family* (pp. 317–353). New York: Plenum.

Marsh, H. (1990). Two-parent, stepparent, and single-parent families: Changes in achievement, attitudes, and behaviors during the last two years of high school. *Journal of Educational Psychology, 82,* 327–340.

Maslow, A. H. (1968). *Toward a psychology of being* (2nd ed.). New York: Van Nostrand.

McAdoo, H. (1986). Transgenerational patterns of upward mobility in African-American families. In H. P. McAdoo (Ed.), *Black families* (pp. 148–168). Beverly Hills, CA: Sage.

McArdle, J. J., & Epstein, D. (1987). Latent growth curves within developmental structural equation models. *Child Development, 58,* 110–133.

McCord, J., McCord, W., & Thurber, E. (1962). Some effects of paternal absence on male children. *Journal of Abnormal and Social Psychology, 64,* 361–369.

McGue, M., & Lykken, D. T. (1992). Genetic influence on risk of divorce. *Psychological Science, 3,* 368–373.

McLanahan, S. (1985). Family structure and the reproduction of poverty. *American Journal of Sociology, 90,* 873–901.

McLoyd, V. (1990). The impact of economic hardship on black families and children: Psychological distress, parenting, and socioemotional development. *Child Development, 61,* 311–346.

Mednick, M. (1987). Single mothers: A review and critique of current research. *Applied Social Psychology Annual, 7,* 184–202.

Mednick, S. A., Gabrielli, W. F., & Hutchings, B. (1984). Genetic influences in criminal convictions: Evidence from an adoption cohort. *Science, 224,* 891–894.

Meissner, W. W. (1978). The conceptualization of marriage and family dynamics from a psychoanalytic perspective. In T. J. Paolino & B. S. McCrady (Eds.), *Marriage and marital therapy* (pp. 25–88). New York: Brunner/Mazel.

Miller, W. B. (1958). Lower class culture as a generating milieu of gang delinquency. *Journal of Social Issues, 14,* 5–19.

Milne, A. (1989). Family structure and the achievement of children. In W. Weston (Ed.), *Education and the American family* (pp. 32–65). New York: New York University Press.

Minuchin, P. (1985). Families and individual development: Provocations from the field of family therapy. *Child Development, 56,* 289–302.

Minuchin, S. (1974). *Families and family therapy.* Cambridge, MA: Harvard University Press.

Mnookin, R. H. (1985). *In the interest of children.* New York: Freeman.

Mueller, D., & Cooper, P. (1984). Children of single-parent families: How they fare as young adults. *Family Relations Journal of Applied Family and Child Studies, 35,* 169–176.

Nichols-Casebolt, A. (1986). The economic impact of child support reform on the poverty status of custodial and noncustodial families. *Journal of Marriage and the Family, 48,* 875–880.

O'Brien, M., Margolin, G., John, R. S., & Krueger, L. (1991). Mothers' and sons' cognitive and emotional reactions to simulated marital and family conflict. *Journal of Consulting and Clinical Psychology, 59,* 692–703.

Ogbu, J. (1981). Origins of human competence: A cultural ecological perspective. *Child Development, 52,* 413–429.

Olson, R., & Habenstein, R. (1992). Families and children in history. In C. Walker & M. Roberts (Eds.), *Handbook of clinical child psychology* (2nd ed., pp. 3–18). New York: Wiley.

Orthner, D., Brown, R., & Ferguson, D. (1976). Single-parent fatherhood: An emerging family life style. *Family Coordinator, 25,* 429–437.

Patterson, C., Kupersmidt, J., & Vaden, N. (1990). Income level, gender, ethnicity, and household composition as predictors of children's school-based competence. *Child Development, 61,* 485–494.

Pearson, J., & Hunter, A. (1990). Black grandmothers in multigenerational households: Diversity in family structure and parenting involvement in the Woodlawn community. *Child Development, 61,* 434–442.

Peters, M. (1986). Parenting in black families with young children. In H. P. McAdoo (Ed.), *Black families* (pp. 228–241). Beverly Hills, CA: Sage.

Peters, M., & McAdoo, H. P. (1983). The present and future of alternative lifestyles in ethnic American cultures. In E. Macklin & R. Rubin (Eds.), *Contemporary families and alternative lifestyles* (pp. 288–307). Beverly Hills, CA: Sage.

Peterson, J. L., & Zill, N. (1986). Marital disruption, parent-child relationships, and behavior problems in children. *Journal of Marriage and the Family, 48,* 295–307.

Plomin, R. (1986). *Development, genetics, and psychology.* Hillsdale, NJ: Erlbaum.

Ponterotto, J., & Casas, J. M. (1991). *Handbook of racial/ethnic minority counseling research.* Springfield, IL: Thomas.

Power, M. J., Ash, P. M., Schoenberg, E., & Sorey, E. C. (1974). Delinquency and the family. *British Journal of Social Work, 4,* 17–18.

Reid, W. J., & Crisafulli, A. (1990). Marital discord and child behavior problems: A meta-analysis. *Journal of Abnormal Child Psychology, 18,* 105–117.

Rogers, K. (1992). *Poverty and children's externalizing behaviors.* Unpublished manuscript.

Rutter, M. (1971). Parent-child separation: Psychological effects on the children. *Journal of Child Psychology and Psychiatry, 12,* 233–260.

Rutter, M. (1981). The city and the child. *American Journal of Orthopsychiatry, 51,* 610–625.

Rutter, M. (1985). Resilience in the face of adversity: Protective factors and resistance to psychiatric disorder. *British Journal of Psychiatry, 147,* 598–611.

Rutter, M. (1986). Child psychiatry: Looking thirty years ahead. *Journal of Child Psychology, Psychiatry, and Allied Disciplines, 27,* 803–840.

Select Committee on Children, Youth, and Families (SCCYF). (1989). *U.S. children and their families: Current conditions and recent trends, 1989.* Washington, DC: U.S. Government Printing Office.

Seltzer, J. A. (1991). Relationships between fathers and children who live apart: The father's role after separation. *Journal of Marriage and the Family, 53,* 79–101.

Seltzer, J. A., & Bianchi, S. M. (1988). Children's contact with absent parents. *Journal of Marriage and the Family, 50,* 663–677.

Shaw, D. S., Emery, R. E., & Tuer, M. (1993). Parental functioning and children's adjustment in families of divorce: A prospective look. *Journal of Abnormal Child Psychology, 29,* 119–134.

Shorter, E. (1975). *The making of the modern family.* New York: Basic Books.

Steinberg, L., Dornbusch, S., & Brown, B. (1992). Ethnic differences in adolescent achievement: An ecological perspective. *American Psychologist, 47,* 723–729.

Steinberg, L., Mounts, N. S., Lamborn, S. D., & Dornbusch, S. M. (1991). Authoritative parenting and adolescent adjustment across varied ecological niches. *Journal of Research on Adolescence, 1,* 19–36.

Stevens, J. (1984). Black grandmothers' and black adolescent mothers' knowledge about parenting. *Developmental Psychology, 20,* 1017–1025.

Strawn, J. (1993). The states and the poor: Child poverty rises as the safety net shrinks. *SRCD Social Policy Report, 6,* 1–19.

Sudarkasa, N. (1988). Interpreting the African heritage in Afro-American family organizations. In H. P. McAdoo (Ed.), *Black Families* (2nd ed., pp. 27–45). Beverly Hills, CA: Sage.

Svanum, S., Bringle, R., & McLaughlin, J. (1982). Father absence and cognitive performance in a large sample of 6- to 11-year-old children. *Child Development, 53,* 136–143.

Taylor, R. D., Casten, R., & Flickinger, S. M. (1993). Influence of kinship social support on the parenting experiences and psychosocial adjustment of African-American adolescents. *Developmental Psychology, 29,* 382–388.

Thompson, M., Alexander, K., & Entwisle, D. (1988). Household composition, parental expectations, and school achievement. *Social Forces, 67,* 424–451.

Tienda, M., & Angel, R. (1982). Headship and household composition among blacks, Hispanics, and other whites. *Social Forces, 61,* 508–531.

Tschann, J. M., Johnston, J. R., Kline, M., & Wallerstein, J. S. (1989). Family process and children's functioning during divorce. *Journal of Marriage and the Family, 51,* 431–444.

U.S. Bureau of the Census. (1988). Marital status and living arrangements: March, 1988. *Current Population Reports* (Series P-20, No. 433). Washington, DC: U.S. Department of Commerce.

U.S. Bureau of the Census. (1989). Marital status and living arrangements: March, 1989. *Current Population Reports* (Series P-20, No. 445). Washington, DC: U.S. Department of Commerce.

U.S. Department of Education. (1991). *Youth indicators 1991.* Washington, DC: U.S. Government Printing Office.

Vuchinich, S., Emery, R. E., & Cassidy, J. (1988). Family members as third parties in dyadic family conflict: Strategies, alliances, and outcomes. *Child Development, 59,* 1293–1302.

Wagner, R. (1988). Changes in extended family relationships for Mexican-American and Anglo-Saxon single mothers. *Journal of Divorce, 11*(2), 69–87.

Waite, L. J., Haggstrom, G. W., & Kanouse, D. E. (1985). The consequences of parenthood for the marital stability of young adults. *American Sociological Review, 50,* 850–857.

Wallerstein, J. (1991). The long-term effects of divorce on children: A review. *Journal of the American Academy of Child and Adolescent Psychiatry, 30,* 349–360.

Wallerstein, J. S., & Blakeslee, S. (1989). *Second chances: Men, women, and children a decade after divorce.* New York: Ticknor & Fields.

Wallerstein, J., & Kelly, J. B. (1980). *Surviving the breakup: How children actually cope with divorce.* New York: Basic Books.

Warshak, R. A. (1986). Father-custody and child development: A review and analysis of psychological research. *Behavioral Sciences and the Law, 4,* 2–17.

Wentzel, K. (1991). Relations between social competence and academic achievement in early adolescence. *Child Development, 62,* 1066–1078.

Wilson, M. (1986). Perceived parental activity of mothers, fathers, and grandmothers in three-generational black families. *Journal of Black Psychology, 12,* 43–59.

Wilson, M. (1989a). The black extended family: An analytical review. *Developmental Psychology, 22,* 246–258.

Wilson, M. (1989b). Child development in the context of the black extended family. *American Psychologist, 44,* 380–385.

Wilson, M., & Tolson, T. (1988). Single parenting in the context of three-generational black families. In E. M. Hetherington & J. Arasteh (Eds.), *Impact of divorce, single parenting, and stepparenting on children* (pp. 215–244). Hillsdale, NJ: Erlbaum.

Wilson, M., & Tolson, T. (1990). Familial support in the black community. *Journal of Clinical Child Psychology, 19,* 347–355.

Zaslow, M. J. (1988). Sex differences in children's response to parental divorce: 1. Research methodology and postdivorce family forms. *American Journal of Orthopsychiatry, 58,* 355–378.

Zill, N. (1978, February). *Divorce, marital happiness, and the mental health of children: Findings from the FCD national survey of children.* Paper presented at the NIMH Workshop on Divorce and Children, Bethesda, MD.

Zill, N., Morrison, D. R., & Coiro, M. J. (1993). Long-term effects of parental divorce on parent-child relationships, adjustment, and achievement in young adulthood. *Journal of Family Psychology, 7,* 91–103.

Zimiles, H., & Lee, V. (1991). Adolescent family structure and educational progress. *Developmental Psychology, 27,* 314–320.

CHAPTER 2

Failures in the Expectable Environment and Their Impact on Individual Development: The Case of Child Maltreatment

DANTE CICCHETTI and MICHAEL LYNCH

What happens to individual development when there are severe disturbances in the early caretaking environment? Quinton and Rutter's studies of the effects of institutional rearing indicate that a wide range of psychosocial dysfunctions and parenting difficulties are evident in adulthood for individuals who were raised in settings having nonoptimal caregiving (Quinton & Rutter, 1988; Quinton, Rutter, & Liddle, 1984; Rutter & Quinton, 1984). Along these lines, recent debates in the developmental literature suggest that a number of paradigms may be useful in helping scientists understand the effects of environmental disturbance.

For example, the notion of an "average expectable environment" for promoting normal development, proposed by Hartmann (1958), connotes that there are a species-specific range of environmental conditions that elicit normal development in humans (see also Winnicott's, 1958, 1965, concept of the "good enough" environment). Through the process of natural selection, the human gene pool has been shaped to provide a match between species-specific phenotypes and the range of environments in which they are found. When presented with such an average expectable environment, a genetically normal organism will develop within the normal range for the species.

Scarr (1992, 1993) has elaborated this concept to apply it to contemporary models of development. Specifically, she proposes that infants and children may be *preadapted* by their genetic endowment to respond to a specific range of environmental experiences that provide opportunities for stimulation and knowledge acquisition. In addition, within the genetically specified range of environments, a *variety* of environmental conditions can promote normal human development. Central to Scarr's formulation is the claim that variations within this range of environments provide functionally equivalent opportunities for individuals to *construct* their own experiences (Scarr & McCartney, 1983). However, environments that fall outside this range impede normal development. With particular relevance for the central question of this chapter, Scarr (1992) states that violent, abusive, and neglectful home conditions do not fall within the range of average expectable environments.

As a result, normal development can occur under a variety of conditions, but not those lacking the average expectable experiences under which the species evolved. For infants, part of the species-specific expectable environment includes protective, nurturant adults and the presence of a larger social group to which the child will be socialized. For older children, a normal environment includes such features as a supportive family, contact with peers, and ample opportunities to explore and master the environment. Although the exact details of normal environments need to be specified, Scarr claims that what is crucial to normal development is having a rearing environment that falls within the limits of normal "expectable" conditions.

According to Scarr's perspective, individual differences in development in normal expectable environments are largely the result of differences in genotypes. The role of the environment is seen as providing opportunities for development and for the phenotypic expression of genes. The environment has nonlinear effects on development because the same environments do not have the same effects on all individuals (cf. Plomin & Daniels, 1987). Rather, individuals construct different experiences from the same environments based on their own prior experiences and on their genotypes (Scarr & McCartney, 1983). According to an evolutionary view that specifies the necessity of an average expectable environment, if individuals are given equal access to cultural knowledge and to other environmental opportunities for experience, then individual genetic variation plays a prominent role in the many individual differences that are observed in development. Heritability studies of the offspring of schizophrenic and healthy twins offer evidence in support of this position (Gottesman & Bertelsen, 1989).

Some caveats should be kept in mind with respect to the proposed role of average expectable environments in normal development and their link to genetic influences. As Gottlieb (1991a) points out, genetic activity does not by itself produce finished physical traits, let alone the development of more complex individual personality characteristics. Developmental differentiation requires influences above the strictly cellular level. As Scarr

(1993) also has noted, the environment plays a critical role in the unfolding expression of genes.

Some developmentalists have suggested that the concept of an average expectable environment may be too poorly specified to be useful in developmental theory (Baumrind, 1993). The mere absence of maltreatment or extreme disadvantage is not equivalent to the presence of a varied environment rich with opportunities. Moreover, variability in the environment does not guarantee that the environment is benign, nor that all children have adequate access to supportive environments (Baumrind, 1993). In fact, the increasing presence of problematic behavior among youth across diverse sectors of society suggests that there may not be an "average expectable environment" that robustly promotes normal development. A number of indicators point toward this conclusion including the rising levels of violent deaths among youth, increased rates of adolescent suicide, higher rates of alcohol and substance abuse, lower literacy scores and increased school dropout rates, increased prevalence of eating disorders, and the rising incidence of sexually transmitted diseases, including autoimmune deficiency syndrome (AIDS). These trends however, may be indicating that modern society deviates in some important ways from the evolutionarily selected average expectable environment. As a result, the construct of an average expectable environment may be especially important in helping to conceptualize environmental failure at many different levels.

A "systems view" of development (Gottlieb, 1991a, 1992) offers a slightly different perspective on how the environment interacts with genes in producing development. More specifically, a "systems view" of individual development sees development as being hierarchically organized into multiple levels that mutually influence each other (Cicchetti & Schneider-Rosen, 1986; Gottlieb, 1991a, 1992; Horowitz, 1987). "Top-down" as well as "bottom-up" bidirectional effects are expected to occur among the various levels. Thus, genetic activity ↔ neural activity ↔ behavior ↔ environment is a schematic representation of this systems view. In addition, these bidirectional effects among levels of the system result in a probabilistic conceptualization of epigenetic development.

This systems perspective of development also sees variations in the expression of phenotypes as a function of both the genotype and the environment. It is specifically these reciprocal interactions, or "coactions" as they are called by Gottlieb (1991a), among levels of the developing system that cause development to occur. Epigenetic development is probabilistically determined by active interactions among levels of the system (Gottlieb, 1991a, 1992). No single level of the system or single component of a coaction can cause development. It is the mutual relationship between at least two components of the developmental system that brings about development and phenotypic expression.

Gottlieb's (1991a) notion of "experiential canalization" of development is consistent with a systems view, as well. It was Waddington (1942, 1957) who first suggested that development was highly canalized. By this, he meant that early development could withstand great perturbations and still return to a normal developmental pathway. For Waddington, genes acted as a buffer against the environment to ensure species-typical phenotypic outcomes (Fishbein, 1976). According to Gottlieb (1991a)

and Turkheimer and Gottesman (1991), however, there are both genetic and environmental influences on the stability of species-typical development. It is likely that there are canalizing influences across all levels of the developing system. In particular, the organism's usual or typical experience can play a canalizing role that brings about species-specific behavior. For example, Gottlieb (1991b) discusses the role that a mallard duckling's own prenatal embryonic "contact call" plays in the development of its selective response to maternal calls. When a mallard duckling is prevented from hearing this contact call, it becomes susceptible to developing a preference for extraspecific maternal calls over the mallard maternal call. Exposure to the typical contact call prevents ducklings from developing a preference for extraspecific maternal calls. An example from the human literature on the possible canalizing role of experience is the finding that profoundly deaf children do not maintain vocalizations in later infancy, presumably because they lack the species-typical auditory experiences that play a role in language development (see Scarr, 1993).

When considering the nature of the interaction between an organism and its environment, experience can play at least three different roles in development (Gottlieb, 1976). The *inductive* function of experience is operating when some (particular) experience is necessary to bring about a developmental change that would not appear unless the experience occurred. Greenough (Greenough, Black, & Wallace, 1987) and Wachs (1992) refer to these changes as "experience expectant development." The *maintenance* function of development is occurring when some (particular) experience is necessary to sustain an already-achieved state of development. Lastly, the *facilitative* function of experience is in effect when experience is able to temporally regulate when a feature appears during development. These latter two changes in development are referred to as "experience dependent developments" (Greenough et al., 1987; Wachs, 1992). These functions of experience describe, for the most part, typical and expected interactions between the organism and environment during the course of normal development.

If we return to our original question, we still are presented with a dilemma. What happens to individual development when there are severe disturbances in the child-rearing environment? How do these atypical, unexpected organism-environment interactions influence development? The example that we use to explore these questions is derived from the child maltreatment literature.

By studying child maltreatment, we can learn more about the function of typical and atypical environments as they influence development. Both the concept of an average expectable environment and a systems view of development will help to formulate our analysis of the consequences of child maltreatment. As a result, in this chapter we examine how models focusing on average expectable environments and probabilistic epigenesis help us to understand the processes and mechanisms associated with individual development in the face of severe environmental challenge.

THE CASE OF CHILD MALTREATMENT

Child maltreatment may represent the greatest failure of the environment to provide opportunities for normal development.

With respect to the notion of an average expectable environment, maltreating families fail to provide many of the expectable experiences that theoretically are required for normal development. By definition, maltreating parents are at best an aberration of the supportive, nurturant adults that are expected by the organism in the evolutionary contexts of species-typical development. In addition, as we explicate more fully later, numerous studies indicate that maltreating families characteristically provide fewer supports and opportunities for mastery outside the family than are expected from an environment that is "good enough" (Scarr, 1992; Winnicott, 1958, 1965) to foster normal development. Moreover, from the perspective of a systems view of development, maltreatment experiences may provide serious challenges to the species-typical organism-environment "coactions" that play important roles in the emergence and timing of normal developmental change.

Significance of the Problem

Such challenges to normal development are important to understand, especially in light of their rising incidence. Child maltreatment has become a devastating social problem. In 1990, case reports involving maltreatment were made to local social service agencies within the United States for over 2 million children (National Research Council, 1993). In the period from 1979 through 1988, approximately 2,000 deaths per year for children between the ages of 0 and 17 were the result of abuse and neglect (McClain, Sacks, Froehlke, & Ewigman, 1993). Moreover, an additional 160,000 cases resulted in serious injuries to children in 1990 alone (Daro & McCurdy, 1991). Finally, nearly one woman in three reports having had one or more unwanted sexual experiences before the age of 16 (Anderson, Martin, Mullen, Romans, & Herbison, 1993). Altogether, the services required for children who have been abused or neglected cost more than $500 million annually, according to estimates by the General Accounting Office (1991).

Although these numbers are alarming, it is important to get a more precise understanding of what they mean. A significant number of cases reported to Child Protective Services (CPS) agencies are not substantiated. The most recent estimates indicate that as many as 47 percent of the Child Protective Services (CPS) cases of alleged maltreatment are unfounded (National Center on Child Abuse and Neglect, 1988). However, the process of substantiating a case of alleged maltreatment can be influenced by a range of social and economic factors (such as the number of caseworkers in a given locale and the size of their caseloads), in addition to the details of the case itself (Barnett, Manly, & Cicchetti, 1993). It is important for increased effort to be made in trying to comprehend the true scope of this insidious societal problem (see Cicchetti & Toth, 1993; Edelman, 1987; Hamburg, 1992).

Recognizing the need to estimate the actual occurrence of child maltreatment rather than simply relying on reported cases, the National Center on Child Abuse and Neglect (NCCAN) has implemented two national studies of the incidence and severity of child abuse and neglect. The first National Incidence Study (NIS-1) was conducted in 1979–1980. Data regarding reported and unreported cases of maltreatment were gathered from child protective agencies, investigatory agencies (e.g., courts, police), and professionals in other community agencies (such as physicians and educators). To apply some uniformity to the variety of data included, this study employed a uniform operational definition of maltreatment across all sources of information, with the further criteria that the harm resulting from the maltreatment needed to be rated as moderate or severe for the case to be classified as maltreatment. Based on these guidelines, NIS-1 estimated the incidence of maltreatment to include 10.5 per 1,000 children (NCCAN, 1981).

The second National Incidence Study (NIS-2) was compiled in 1986. This study was based on the same design as the first study, with the addition of a second set of criteria that included "endangered" children at risk for harm. Based on the inclusion criteria used in NIS-1, the new estimate of the incidence of maltreatment was at 14.8 per 1,000 children (NCCAN, 1988). If the broader "endangered" criteria were used, the estimated incidence reached 22.6 per 1,000 children (NCCAN, 1988). The more conservative estimate represents a 66% increase over the incidence reported in NIS-1 (NCCAN, 1988). Most of this increase was due to physical abuse (up 58 percent from NIS-1) and sexual abuse (up 300 percent) (NCCAN, 1988).

Employing a different approach to estimating the incidence of violence against children, Straus and Gelles (1986) surveyed a national probability sample of over 3,000 families with at least one child under 18 years of age (Gelles & Straus, 1987; Straus & Gelles, 1986). Conducting phone interviews with these families, they administered the Conflict Tactics Scale (CTS), an 18-item instrument describing a variety of tactics that are utilized in conflict situations ranging from rational discussion to acts of violence (Straus, 1979). They used the Severe Violence Index from the CTS to provide an estimate of the incidence of physical abuse against children. This index includes such acts as hitting someone with an object, kicking or biting a person, burning a person, and using a gun or a knife on someone. Based on parents' own reports of the violence that they committed against their children, this study estimated that 110 per 1,000 children were victims of severe violence (Gelles & Straus, 1987; Straus & Gelles, 1986).

Issues of Definition

Although child maltreatment is a major societal problem that constitutes environmental failure and has direct implications for the welfare and normal development of children, there remains a lack of consensus on what constitutes maltreatment and how it should be defined (Aber & Zigler, 1981; Barnett et al., 1993; Besharov, 1981; Cicchetti & Rizley, 1981; Emery, 1989; Juvenile Justice Standards Project, 1977). Despite vigorous debate over these issues, little progress has been made in producing clear, reliable, valid, and useful definitions of child abuse and neglect (Barnett, Manly, & Cicchetti, 1991; Cicchetti & Barnett, 1991b; Cicchetti & Rizley, 1981; McGee & Wolfe, 1991; National Research Council, 1993). The problems in constructing effective operational definitions include such factors as a lack of social consensus about what forms of parenting are unacceptable or dangerous; uncertainty about whether to define maltreatment based on adult behavior, child outcome, or some combination of the two; controversy over whether criteria of harm or endangerment should be included in definitions of maltreatment; and confusion about whether similar definitions should be used for scientific, legal, and clinical purposes.

The last issue in particular has presented a continuing source of disagreement because scientists, lawmakers, and clinicians all use separate definitions of maltreatment to best suit their particular needs. In legal settings, for example, definitions focusing on the demonstrable harm done to the child may be useful in prosecuting cases (Juvenile Justice Standards Project, 1977). However, Zuravin (1991) suggests that for researchers, definitions of maltreatment that focus on the specific acts that endanger children may be more appropriate (see also Barnett et al., 1991, 1993; Cicchetti & Barnett, 1991b). This allows researchers to concentrate on identifiable behaviors that make up part of the child's caretaking environment rather than the uncertain consequences of those parental actions, such as some form of harm that may or may not be demonstrable. The challenge for researchers, though, is to develop precise operational definitions that minimize relying on professional opinion. This lack of consensus about what constitutes maltreatment makes clear communication and collaboration among the respective fields difficult.

Although standardization of the definition of maltreatment is demanding and carries with it the risk of oversimplification, it is necessary to make progress in the identification, understanding, and treatment of child maltreatment. Moreover, for our purposes, it is necessary to capture the nature of experience that constitutes a nonaverage expectable environment. In general, four categories of child maltreatment are usually distinguished from each other: (a) *physical abuse,* which involves the infliction of bodily injury on a child by other than accidental means; (b) *sexual abuse,* which includes sexual contact or attempted sexual contact between a caregiver or other responsible adult and a child for purposes of the caregiver's sexual gratification or financial benefit; (c) *neglect,* which includes both the failure to provide minimum care and the lack of supervision; and (d) *emotional maltreatment,* which involves persistent and extreme thwarting of a child's basic emotional needs. McGee and Wolfe (1991) have expanded on the notion of emotional maltreatment to offer an operational definition of "psychological maltreatment" that subsumes both psychologically abusive and psychologically neglectful caretaking behaviors. Each of these subtypes of maltreatment represents a clear deviation from the average expectable environment. However, even an issue as seemingly straightforward as identifying maltreatment subtypes can become unclear. It would be a mistake to think that maltreatment always occurs in discrete subtypes. There is a high degree of comorbidity among maltreatment subtypes, indicating that many maltreated children experience more than one type of maltreatment (Cicchetti & Barnett, 1991b; Cicchetti & Rizley, 1981; Crittenden, Claussen, & Sugarman, 1994; Egeland & Sroufe, 1981). In many instances, it may be necessary to focus on the major subtype of maltreatment in a particular case, but the actual experience of many children is much more complicated, and this presents significant challenges for researchers and clinicians.

Cicchetti and Barnett (1991b) suggest that a number of additional issues need to be considered in trying to define child maltreatment. They propose a nosology that attempts to incorporate many important aspects of maltreatment, including its subtype. Features of maltreatment such as the severity of the incident, the frequency and chronicity of the maltreating acts, who the perpetrator is, and the developmental period of the child during which the maltreatment occurred all are considered to be influential and are relevant for specifying the nature of the environmental failure. The goal of such a detailed nosology is to provide as complete an account of each child's maltreatment experience as possible. By trying to quantify some of the major components of maltreatment, it may be possible to capture some of the qualitative meaning of the experience for the child. This ultimately would provide researchers with a set of powerful independent variables in studies of the consequences of maltreatment.

In a study of 5- to 11-year-old children from families of low socioeconomic status, Manly, Cicchetti, and Barnett (1994) have utilized this nosology and have found that various dimensions of maltreatment predict child functioning. Although maltreated children generally evidence poorer adaptation than nonmaltreated children, a more complete portrayal of functioning emerges when other aspects within the context of maltreatment are examined. Specifically, the severity of the maltreatment, the frequency of CPS reports, and the interaction between severity and frequency are significant predictors of children's functioning. The chronicity of the maltreatment in the family also significantly predicts peer ratings of aggression. Subtype differences emerge as well, with children in the sexual abuse group being more socially competent than other maltreated children, and children in the physical abuse group having more behavior problems than nonmaltreated children.

Wolfe and McGee (1994) have used an alternate classification system, but share the goal of examining the underlying structure of maltreatment and its relation to adjustment. In investigating the developmental period during which maltreatment occurs, the type of maltreatment experienced, and gender differences in maltreated adolescents, important differences have been revealed. In males, the relationship between early maltreatment and adjustment is strengthened when interactions between physical and psychological abuse and between partner abuse and neglect are entered into the analysis. Current adjustment for females is significantly related to the developmental period during which neglect or psychological abuse occurs, with elevated adjustment problems occurring when maltreatment increases during mid-childhood relative to early childhood.

Although adding complexity to an already difficult area, systematization efforts such as these emphasize the importance of comprehensively defining the variable of maltreatment if accurate depictions of the consequences of maltreatment are to be obtained. Researchers must continue to pursue increased specificity in the ways maltreatment is defined and measured so that we can better understand the experience of maltreated children and the environmental failure it represents. Likewise, proponents for maltreated children must be able to articulate the conceptualization of maltreatment that is being used in research and advocacy efforts (cf. Cicchetti & Toth, 1993; National Research Council, 1993).

Moving toward a uniform agreement on what constitutes maltreatment, and instituting a standardized means of recording the pertinent information regarding identified cases of maltreatment are necessary steps for the future. Despite some important groundbreaking work in this direction (Barnett et al.,

1993; Brassard, Hart, & Hardy, 1993; Cicchetti & Barnett, 1991b; McGee & Wolfe, 1991; Zuravin, 1991), the field still has a long way to go. The challenge is to adopt a consistent method of systematizing maltreatment that is feasible and that satisfies everyone's needs. Most of the research that we discuss in the sections to follow uses varying definitions of maltreatment, and we make clear the relevant distinctions where appropriate.

Etiology of Maltreatment

Discussion of the etiology of maltreatment is complicated by the recognition that most forms of maltreatment are part of a pattern of maladaptive behavior that emerges over time. Basic differences in viewing maltreatment either as part of a continuum of parenting behavior (from appropriate to inappropriate) or as a set of unique behavioral problems with distinct etiologies (Gelles, 1991) have contributed to a lack of clarity about the origins of such parental behaviors. Because no single risk factor or set of risk factors have been identified as providing a necessary or sufficient cause of maltreatment, a number of interactive etiological models have evolved that consider a combination of individual, familial, environmental, and cultural factors that may contribute to the occurrence of child maltreatment (Belsky, 1980, 1993; Cicchetti & Lynch, 1993; Cicchetti & Rizley, 1981; Garbarino, 1977; Lyons-Ruth, Zoll, Connell, & Grunebaum, 1989; Parke & Collmer, 1975; Wolfe, 1991).

Belsky has been especially articulate in helping to clarify the interrelationships among different factors in the etiology of maltreatment. His ecological model (Belsky, 1980) provides a framework for defining and understanding the broader environment in which child maltreatment occurs. Belsky views maltreatment as a social-psychological phenomenon that is influenced by forces within the individual, the family, the community, and the culture in which the family and the individual are embedded. His ecological model contains four levels of analysis: (a) ontogenic development, which includes factors within the individual that are associated with being a perpetrator of maltreatment; (b) the microsystem, which consists of factors within the family that contribute to the occurrence of maltreatment; (c) the exosystem, which contains aspects of communities that contribute to the incidence of maltreatment; and (d) the macrosystem, which encompasses the beliefs and values of the culture that contribute to perpetration of maltreatment. Conditions within all levels of the ecology interact with each other in influencing whether or not maltreatment takes place. Furthermore, this multilevel approach to understanding the ecology provides a more detailed analysis of the environment. As a result, it is possible to assess whether features at each level of the ecology fall within the range of evolutionarily selected conditions, or whether they represent a departure from the average expectable environment.

Along these lines, interactive etiological models suggest that child maltreatment occurs when multiple risk factors outweigh protective, compensatory, and buffering factors (Cicchetti & Carlson, 1989). As a result, these models take a probabilistic approach in assessing the risk for maltreatment. Cicchetti and Rizley (1981) have developed a transactional model to specify the processes through which probabilistic risk for maltreatment is determined and conceptualized.

In a transactional model, environmental forces, caregiver characteristics, and child characteristics all influence each other and make reciprocal contributions to the events and outcomes of child development (Sameroff & Chandler, 1975). This approach is similar to Gottlieb's (1991a, 1992) probabilistic epigenesis view of development. Cicchetti and Rizley's model focuses on the transactions among risk factors in determining the occurrence of maltreatment. These risk factors are divided into two broad categories: *potentiating* factors, which increase the probability of maltreatment, and *compensatory* factors, which decrease the risk for maltreatment. In addition, temporal distinctions are made for both categories of risk factor. For example, *transient* risk factors fluctuate and may indicate a temporary state of affairs. On the other hand, *enduring* risk factors represent more permanent conditions or characteristics.

By combining the categorical and temporal dimensions of risk factors in their model, Cicchetti and Rizley propose four classes of determinants for the occurrence of maltreatment. *Enduring vulnerability factors* include all relatively long-lasting factors, conditions, or attributes that function to potentiate maltreatment. These could include parental, child, or environmental characteristics. *Transient challengers* include short-term conditions and stresses that could contribute to the onset of maltreatment. Such circumstances as experiencing loss (of a job or a loved one), physical injury or illness, financial difficulties, legal difficulties, marital or family problems, discipline problems with children, and the emergence of a child into a new and more difficult developmental period are among the possible stressors included here.

Conversely, *enduring protective factors* include relatively permanent conditions that decrease the risk of maltreatment. Examples of likely protective factors are a parent's history of having received good parenting as a child and supportive intimate relationships between parent figures. *Transient buffers* consist of factors that may protect a family from stress such as sudden improvement in financial conditions, periods of marital harmony and a child's transition out of a difficult developmental period.

It is the combination of potentiating and protective factors that determines the likelihood of maltreatment (Cicchetti & Rizley, 1981). This cumulative risk perspective suggests that maltreatment results from complex constellations of variables whose influence may increase or decrease over different developmental and historical periods. The combined effects of these risk variables provide multiple pathways to the occurrence of maltreatment.

AN ECOLOGICAL-TRANSACTIONAL MODEL OF CHILD MALTREATMENT AND ITS CONSEQUENCES ON INDIVIDUAL DEVELOPMENT

Drawing from the work of Belsky (1980) and Cicchetti and Rizley (1981), Cicchetti and Lynch (1993) have proposed an ecological-transactional model that can be used to examine the way in which serious disturbances in caretaking environments, such as child maltreatment, impact individual development and adaptation. By combining powerful theoretical constructs such as the average expectable environment and probabilistic epigenesis, this model presents a broad integrative framework for examining the processes associated with child maltreatment and the resulting implications for development. More specifically, by taking an ecological-transactional perspective, this model explains how forces from each level of the environment as well as characteristics of the individual exert reciprocal influences on each other and shape the course of child development (cf. Cicchetti & Lynch, 1993; Sameroff & Chandler, 1975). Thus, the multilevel ecology of child maltreatment can be seen as demonstrating broad-based environmental failure and as indicating a deviation from the average expectable environment. In combination with characteristics of the individual, these environmental disturbances shape the probabilistic course of maltreated children's development.

According to Cicchetti and Lynch (1993) potentiating and compensatory risk factors associated with maltreatment are present at each level of the ecology. Risk factors within a given level of the model can influence outcomes and processes in surrounding levels of the environment. These constantly occurring transactions determine the amount of biological and psychological risk that the individual faces (Cicchetti, Toth, & Lynch, 1993). At higher, more distal levels of the ecology, such as the macrosystem and the exosystem, potentiating factors increase the potential of conditions that support maltreatment, whereas compensatory factors decrease the potential of such conditions. Risk factors within the microsystem also contribute to the presence or absence of maltreatment and to the adaptiveness of family functioning. Because it is the level of the ecology most proximal to the child, characteristics of the microsystem have the most direct effects on children's development.

The manner in which children handle the challenges presented to them by family, community, and societal dysfunction is seen in their own ontogenic development. It is the particular pathway that individual development takes that results in ultimate adaptation or maladaptation. An increased presence at all ecological levels of the enduring vulnerability factors and transient challengers associated with different forms of violence and maltreatment represents a deviation from the average expectable environment, and makes the successful resolution of stage-salient developmental issues problematic for children (Cicchetti, 1989). The result is a greater likelihood of negative developmental outcomes and psychopathology (Cicchetti, 1990). Conversely, such an ecological-transactional approach also should help to account for resilient outcomes in some children. The presence of enduring protective factors and transient buffers at any level of the ecology may approximate some conditions of an average expectable environment and, in accord with a systems perspective on development, may help to explain why some children display successful adaptation in the face of maltreatment and other disturbances in the caretaking environment.

In applying such a model to predictions about individual adaptation, it is critical to know the individual's level of adaptation before the maltreatment occurred. How individuals have adapted to their environment will play a significant role in how they respond to subsequent stress (Cicchetti, 1990; Cicchetti, Toth et al., 1993; Sroufe, 1979; Sroufe & Rutter, 1984). This statement, which reflects an organizational perspective on development, is in accord with Cicchetti and Lynch's (1993) ecological-transactional model of environmental influences on biological and psychological development. This model will be used as an heuristic for reviewing the literature on the consequences of child maltreatment for individual development and for addressing our initial question concerning the impact of aberrant experiences on the ontogenetic process.

The Macrosystem

The macrosystem includes the set of cultural values and beliefs that permeate individual and family lifestyles, and that are reflected in the community services offered by a society. Although researchers have had difficulty in specifying the effects of factors within the macrosystem, some cultural values of American society may contribute to child maltreatment. For example, there is evidence for a social acceptance of violence. Compared with other Western nations, the level of violent crime in the United States is inordinately high (Aber & Rappaport, 1994; Christoffel, 1990; Fingerhut & Kleinman, 1990; Lykken, 1993). Justice Department statistics suggest that approximately 1 out of every 10 American households is affected by violent crimes such as robbery, assault, rape, and burglary (U.S. Department of Justice, 1991). Among minority groups, these figures become even more alarming. The leading cause of death among African American adolescent males is gunshot wounds (National Center for Health Statistics, 1990, 1992). Overall, violent offenses among juveniles have been on the rise since 1985 (Butts & Connors-Beatty, 1993; Butts & Poe, 1993).

Of a more subtle nature with regard to maltreatment, racism can place undue stress on families. Racism can result in the unequal distribution of resources, and of job and educational opportunities. This undermines the ability of many ethnic minority families to support their children financially, placing increasing stress on the whole family and on the parents in particular. The term "societal neglect" has been suggested to characterize American tolerance of the situation in which one-fifth of all preschool-age children live below the poverty line (Children's Defense Fund, 1991; Edelman, 1987). These rates are substantially higher among minority children (Duncan, 1991; Edelman, 1987; Huston, 1991b; National Center for Children in Poverty, 1991). However, while there is a disproportionate representation of reports of child maltreatment in ethnic minorities (Holton, 1992), there is no support to claims that cultural practices among minority groups contribute to abuse and neglect (National Resource Council, 1993). Greater effort must be directed at differentiating culturally acceptable behaviors from individually deviant behavior in studies examining links among ethnicity, socioeconomic status, stress, and maltreatment.

Finally, sporadic attention has been paid to suggestions that a relationship exists between the availability of pornographic materials and child maltreatment, particularly sexual abuse. Only indirect influences of pornography on child sexual maltreatment have been reported (Knudsen, 1988). Basic to our ecological-transactional model is the assumption that societal willingness to tolerate violence, racism, children living in poverty, and pornography acts as an enduring vulnerability factor that sets the stage for the presence of additional stressors in the exosystem and the occurrence of maltreatment in the microsystem. With respect to implications for an average expectable environment, these aspects of the macrosystem may constitute diffuse environmental failure.

The Exosystem

The exosystem represents the formal and informal social structures that create the context in which individuals and families function. These social structures include neighborhoods, informal social networks, and formal support groups. The exosystem also encompasses characteristics of these extrafamilial social systems such as the availability of services, the availability of employment, and the pervasive socioeconomic climate. This conceptualization of the exosystem also draws from Bronfenbrenner's notion of a "mesosystem" that incorporates the interconnections among settings such as school, peer group, church, and workplace (Bronfenbrenner, 1977).

Several aspects of the exosystem have been associated with maltreatment. Poverty conditions, for example, place families under great stress (Edelman, 1987; Huston 1991a; McLoyd & Wilson, 1991) and may be an indirect precipitating factor in the occurrence of maltreatment. Although maltreatment occurs across the socioeconomic spectrum, it is disproportionately reported among impoverished families (Pelton, 1981). Self-reports on the Conflict Tactics Scale (CTS) indicate that low socioeconomic status (SES) is a risk factor for violent behavior against children (Gelles & Straus, 1988; Straus & Kaufman-Kantor, 1986; Wolfner & Gelles, 1993). This is especially true for mothers of young children who live below the poverty line (Connelly & Straus, 1992; Gelles, 1992).

There has been significant growth over the past two decades in the proportion of people living in areas of concentrated poverty that also are affected by a convergence of other social problems (Edelman, 1987; Garbarino, Kostelny, & Dubrow, 1991; Huston, 1991a; Jencks & Peterson, 1991; Lynn & McGeary, 1990; Ricketts & Mincy, 1990). Of particular note is the frequent co-occurrence of high rates of poverty and high rates of violence within communities. Poverty and violence, while not identical, are highly interrelated and reciprocally influential on individuals and families (Aber, 1994). It will be important in the future to disentangle the effects of community-level poverty and violence on family and individual functioning (Aber, 1994; Mayer & Jencks, 1989). Along these lines, a number of studies have begun to demonstrate the independent additive and interactive effects of low SES and maltreatment on children's development (see, e.g., Aber, Allen, Carlson, & Cicchetti, 1989; Kaufman & Cicchetti, 1989; Okun, Parker, & Levendosky, 1994; Trickett, Aber, Carlson, & Cicchetti, 1991; Vondra, Barnett, & Cicchetti, 1990). These studies illustrate how factors from the exosystem and the microsystem interact with each other in affecting children's development.

Unemployment is another aspect of the exosystem that has been associated with child maltreatment. Steinberg, Catalano, and Dooley (1981), using an aggregate longitudinal design replicated in two metropolitan communities, demonstrated that increases in child abuse are preceded by periods of high job loss. This is consistent with an ecological-transactional framework

suggesting that unemployment can lead to family stress which results in maltreatment. In fact, the link between unemployment and maltreatment has been documented in a number of studies (Gelles & Hargreaves, 1981; Gil, 1970; Krugman, Lenherr, Betz, & Fryer, 1986; Light, 1973; Whipple & Webster-Stratton, 1991; Wolfner & Gelles, 1993). The relationship between unemployment and violent behaviors toward children appears to be strongest among fathers (Straus & Kaufman-Kantor, 1986; Wolfner & Gelles, 1993). Although these studies have shown a connection between unemployment and maltreatment, the specific mechanisms (such as stress) by which unemployment may lead to maltreatment need to be identified.

The neighborhoods in which families live also may play a role in the incidence of maltreatment. A particular area of interest in this vein is the burgeoning literature on community violence (Cicchetti & Lynch, 1993; Freeman, Mokros, & Poznanski, 1993; Martinez & Richters, 1993; Richters & Martinez, 1993a). Neighborhoods with high rates of violence undoubtedly are stressful environments for family functioning. In addition, it is possible that there are links between the perpetrators of community violence and the perpetrators of child maltreatment (Patterson, 1982). These issues need to be explored more fully.

In looking at the prevalence of maltreatment in particular neighborhoods, Garbarino and his colleagues (Garbarino & Crouter, 1978; Garbarino & Sherman, 1980) have found that some neighborhoods have higher rates of maltreatment than would be expected and that some neighborhoods have lower rates of maltreatment than would be expected based on socioeconomic conditions alone. Child abuse rates have been found to be higher in poor neighborhoods with fewer social resources than in equally disadvantaged neighborhoods where social resources are perceived to be more plentiful. Parents in these high-abuse-rate neighborhoods do not use resources preventively, they do not use informal supports such as scouting or youth groups, and they usually rely on formal public agencies when intervention is necessary. During exchanges these neighborhoods, maltreating parents often try to exploit others. On the other hand, parents in neighborhoods with lower than expected abuse rates make more constructive use of resources and experience greater satisfaction with their neighborhoods as a context for child and family development. In fact, parents who are most successful in coping with these challenges from the exosystem appear to make active attempts to protect their children physically and psychologically from the dangers of their environment while employing more achievement-oriented socialization practices with their children (Dubrow & Garbarino, 1989; Jayaratne, 1993).

Social isolation from neighborhood networks, support groups, and extended family also is associated with maltreatment (Garbarino, 1977, 1982; Hunter & Kilstrom, 1979; Kempe, 1973; Parke & Collmer, 1975). As a result, maltreating families often lack a "lifeline" to emotional and material support during times of stress (Kempe, 1973). In particular, physically abusing mothers have been shown to have fewer peer relationships, more troubled relationships with relatives, and more limited contact with the wider community than nonabusing mothers (Corse, Schmid, & Trickett, 1990). This increased social isolation is associated with less positive parenting beliefs in physically abusing mothers, suggesting that they experience less enjoyment of and openness in parenting (Corse et al., 1990). Along these lines, child-rearing practices can be influenced by information from educational institutions, the media, and extended social networks (Belsky, 1984; Garbarino & Gilliam, 1980; Sigel, 1986). Maltreating parents who are isolated from the broader community may not be exposed to new information that could improve their child-rearing beliefs and practices (Trickett & Susman, 1988).

In general, the presence of social networks has been regarded as a protective factor against child maltreatment (Garbarino, 1977). Religious affiliation and participation, in particular, have been identified as countering social isolation and having important influences in protecting against child maltreatment, especially among African Americans (Garbarino, 1977; Giovannoni & Billingsley, 1970). However, social networks may not be de facto protective factors. Abusive parents may select networks of people who condone their parenting styles, thus increasing the likelihood of continued maltreatment. This tendency to affiliate with groups that share child-rearing beliefs can be seen in maltreating parents who belong to cultlike groups that advocate the use of strict corporal punishment. Further research needs to be directed at understanding the role of social networks in child maltreatment (National Research Council, 1993).

The possible cause of social isolation among maltreating families involves some interaction between characteristics of individual families and characteristics of the environment (Crittenden, 1985; Crittenden & Ainsworth, 1989; Garbarino, 1977). Even if resources are available, maltreating families often fail to make use of social supports (Garbarino, 1977). Whatever the cause of this isolation, the result is that maltreating families are likely to lack the support and resources that could ameliorate negative family functioning. Moreover, these additional supports are especially necessary in light of the many ecological risk factors that typically occur in families that maltreat their children (Cicchetti & Lynch, 1993).

An important point to consider in evaluating the influences of the exosystem on the maltreating family microsystem is that these potentiating factors most likely stimulate maltreatment and family dysfunction through the pressure and stress that they place on families, whether the exosystem factor is a transient challenger, such as social isolation and recent unemployment, or an enduring vulnerability factor, such as background community violence (Cicchetti & Lynch, 1993). To the extent that stress within the family is already high, the presence of any of these negative exosystem factors may increase the likelihood of child maltreatment. Also, if the parent's developmental history predisposes him or her to respond to stress with aggression (another enduring vulnerability factor), then the probability of child maltreatment increases even further. In any event, the features of the exosystem that are associated with maltreatment represent further departure from an average expectable environment.

The Microsystem

Following Belsky's (1980) usage, the microsystem represents the family environment. This is the immediate context in which child maltreatment takes place. In addition, the microsystem incorporates many other related components such as family dynamics and parenting styles, and the developmental histories and psychological resources of the maltreating parents. However, Bronfenbrenner (1977) does not limit the microsystem to the family alone. According to him, it includes any environmental setting (such as the home, school, or workplace) that contains the developing person.

With this expanded conceptualization of the microsystem, any form of violence directly experienced by children, whether it is physical abuse or some act of community violence, is considered to occur within the microsystem. This point has theoretical significance because it places all actual experiences of violence in an ecological level that is proximal to children's ontogenic development, suggesting that any experience of violence should have direct effects on children. Research on posttraumatic stress experienced by children is relevant in this regard. Several studies have documented that children exhibit posttraumatic symptoms over prolonged periods of time in response to being victimized by severe acts of personal violence (Pynoos et al., 1987; Terr, 1981, 1991; Udwin, 1993).

In the case of child maltreatment, the microsystem in which children develop is characterized by stressful, chaotic, and uncontrollable events (Cicchetti & Lynch, 1993; Howes & Cicchetti, 1993). The most obvious feature of this ecological level is the maltreatment experience itself. The type, severity, and chronicity of maltreatment are potent characteristics of the maltreating microsystem (Cicchetti & Barnett, 1991b). Furthermore, there is mounting evidence for the independent and interactive effects these factors exert on children's development (Manly et al., 1994).

Intergenerational Transmission of Child Maltreatment

Other related features of the maltreating microsystem are important as well. For example, parents' prior developmental histories may be the first contributors to evolving family microsystems. In general, research with nonmaltreating samples has suggested that there is evidence for the intergenerational transmission of parenting styles (Jacobvitz, Morgan, Kretchmar, & Morgan, 1991; Van IJzendoorn, 1992). Along these lines, the intergenerational transmission of child maltreatment in particular has received considerable attention by researchers and theorists. There is extensive evidence for the claim that maltreating parents are more likely than nonmaltreating parents to have had a history of abuse (Cicchetti & Aber, 1980; Conger, Burgess, Barrett, 1979; Egeland, Jacobvitz, & Papatola, 1987; Hunter & Kilstrom, 1979; Kaufman & Zigler, 1989; Widom, 1989). Not all parents who maltreat their children were themselves maltreated. As was stated earlier, maltreatment can occur in response to acute environmental challengers, especially in an unsupportive ecology, even if the parent has no personal history of abuse. However, reviews of the literature estimate that approximately one-third of all maltreating parents were maltreated themselves as children (Kaufman & Zigler, 1989; Oliver, 1993). Similarly, even though they are not currently maltreating their children, many nonmaltreating parents with childhood histories of maltreatment are especially vulnerable to the effects of social stress, and they may remain at risk for perpetrating maltreatment (Oliver, 1993).

It is believed that one way in which abusive parenting behaviors may be transmitted across generations is through socialization and social learning (Feshbach, 1978; Herzberger, 1983). In contrast, attachment theorists claim that representational models of attachment relationships are internalized and integrated into self structures (Bowlby, 1980; Sroufe, 1989; Sroufe & Fleeson, 1986). As a result, these representational models may act as the mechanism through which abusive parenting is transmitted from one generation to the next. In accord with an attachment theory conceptualization, Main and Goldwyn (1984) have found that women who remember their mothers as being rejecting are more likely to reject their own children. Such theoretical explanations deserve closer examination in linking different types of maltreatment during childhood and the multiple pathways to abusive parenting (Zeanah & Zeanah, 1989).

Despite the converging evidence for the intergenerational transmission of maltreatment, some controversy remains because this hypothesis is supported largely by retrospective analyses. Inherent limitations of a retrospective approach include the impossibility of knowing the proportion of maltreated children who do not become maltreating parents. Only longitudinal prospective studies can determine these rates. It is also difficult to assess whether maltreating parents provide distorted accounts of their own childhood. These factors can lead to an overestimate of the rate of intergenerational transmission of child maltreatment. For example, Hunter and Kilstrom's (1979) one-year prospective study of premature infants produced an intergenerational transmission rate of 18% when the data were examined prospectively. However, when the same data were looked at retrospectively, the rate of intergenerational transmission increased to 90%.

Not all adults who were maltreated as children become abusive parents. Several investigators have identified some possible protective factors in breaking the cycle of abuse (Egeland, Jacobvitz, & Sroufe, 1988; Hunter & Kilstrom, 1979). In prospective studies, parents with reported histories of maltreatment who do not maltreat their own children are more likely than parents who continue the cycle of abuse to have better current social support, including a supportive spouse. They also are more likely to have had a positive relationship with a significant adult during childhood. Finally, parents who have broken the cycle of abuse are more likely to have undergone therapy, either as an adolescent or an adult, and they can provide a clear account of their childhood experiences with appropriate anger, while directing responsibility for the abuse toward the perpetrator and not themselves.

Personal Resources of Maltreating Parents

The personal resources—psychological and biological—of maltreating parents also shape the microsystem. In a prospective study, Brunquell, Crichton, and Egeland (1981) have shown that parents who later become abusive are less psychologically complex and personally integrated than mothers who do not maltreat their children. Specifically, these mothers receive more negative scores than nonmaltreating mothers on summary scales of anxiety, locus of control, aggression, and defendence. In addition, parental drug use has been linked with increased violence toward children (Wolfner & Gelles, 1993). In general, higher rates of parental psychopathology, particularly depression, appear to be associated with maltreatment (Gilbreath & Cicchetti, 1991; Lahey, Conger, Atkeson, & Treiber, 1984; Sloan & Meier, 1983). Whereas most studies on personality characteristics and psychopathology in maltreating parents

have investigated legally identified child abusers, Dinwiddie and Bucholz (1993) employed three large databases of clinical, community, and family study participants to assess the lifetime prevalence of psychiatric diagnoses among self-reported maltreaters. These investigators have discovered that self-identified child maltreaters have increased lifetime rates of alcoholism, depression, and antisocial personality disorder. The interaction of parental psychopathology with the experience of maltreatment poses serious threats to normal child development (Walker, Downey, & Bergman, 1989).

More broadly, difficulty in coping with stress presents a challenge for many maltreating parents. A number of studies indicate that maltreating parents lack impulse control, especially when aroused and stressed (Altemeier, O'Connor, Vietze, Sandler, & Sherrod, 1982; Brunquell et al., 1981). In fact, these parents may be biologically predisposed to overreact to stressful stimuli (McCanne & Milner, 1991). For example, Frodi and Lamb (1980) have demonstrated that abusive mothers report more aversion to infant cries than nonabusers, and that they are more physiologically aroused. A separate study conducted by Wolfe and his colleagues suggests that, according to skin conductance and respiration data, abusive mothers display greater emotional arousal than nonabusive mothers in response to stressful stimuli, and that they *remain* more aroused during both stressful and nonstressful stimuli (Wolfe, Fairbank, Kelly, & Bradlyn, 1983).

These physiological findings, in combination with data on the psychological resources of maltreating parents, provide some insight into maltreating parents' failure to cope with stressful life events (Crittenden, 1985; Wolfe, 1985). Moreover, when maltreating parents' reports of feeling socially isolated and lacking in social supports (Egeland & Brunquell, 1979; Garbarino, 1976, 1982; Kotelchuck, 1982) are considered together with their inability to handle stress, it does not allow for an optimistic view that they will be able to handle the tasks of parenting successfully.

Family Dynamics

Disruptions in all aspects of family relationships are often present in the families of maltreated children. Maltreating parents interact less with their children and display more negative affect toward them than do comparison parents (Burgess & Conger, 1978). In addition, anger and conflict are pervasive features of maltreating families (Trickett & Susman, 1988), although interpersonal conflict may be more characteristic of abusive parents and social isolation may be more indicative of neglecting families (Crittenden, 1985). Overall, husbands and wives in maltreating families are less warm and supportive, less satisfied in their conjugal relationships, and more aggressive and violent than spousal partners in nonabusive families (Howes & Cicchetti, 1993; Rosenbaum & O'Leary, 1981a, 1981b; Rosenberg, 1987; Straus, Gelles, & Steinmetz, 1980; Straus & Kaufman-Kantor, 1986).

In general, family interactions in maltreating families tend to be unsupportive (Cicchetti & Howes, 1991). A distinctive feature of many maltreating families, especially neglecting families, is the chaotic and unstable nature of the family system. Neglecting families often are characterized by a shifting constellation of adult and child figures moving into and out of the home (Polansky, Gaudin, & Kilpatrick, 1992). To more fully understand how this lack of stability within neglecting families and how the other maladaptive characteristics of family interaction within maltreating families impact children's development, a systems approach to family functioning needs to be taken (Cicchetti & Howes, 1991; Crittenden, Partridge, & Claussen, 1991; Emery, 1989; Howes & Cicchetti, 1993; Kashani, Daniel, Dandoy, & Holcomb, 1992). Such a family systems approach, as described by Minuchin (1985), emphasizes the reciprocal relationships between various subsystems (i.e., family dyads, triads, tetrads, etc.) and the organized whole family system. In addition, it is important to understand the rules and patterns that help to maintain homeostasis within evolving family systems. As a result, behavior within maltreating families should be viewed as being multiply determined by a wide range of interactive factors (Cicchetti & Howes, 1991).

Parenting Styles

The actual parenting styles and attitudes that maltreating parents contribute to the family microsystem may have the most direct impact on children's ontogenic development (Cicchetti & Lynch, 1993). Trickett and her colleagues (Trickett et al., 1991; Trickett & Kuczynski, 1986; Trickett & Susman, 1988) have found that maltreating parents, when compared with nonmaltreating parents, are less satisfied with their children, perceive child rearing as more difficult and less enjoyable, use more controlling disciplinary techniques, do not encourage the development of autonomy in their children even though they maintain high standards of achievement, and promote an isolated lifestyle for themselves and their children. Observational studies indicate that, compared with nonabusive parents, physically abusing parents have less pleasant interactions with their children, even if they are not always more negative (Burgess & Conger, 1978; Mash, Johnston, & Kovitz, 1983). Abusing parents also are less supportive, affectionate, playful and responsive with their children (Burgess & Conger, 1978; Egeland, Breitenbucher, & Rosenberg, 1980; Kavanaugh, Youngblade, Reid, & Fagot, 1988; Reid, Kavanaugh, & Baldwin, 1987; Trickett & Susman, 1988; Twentyman & Plotkin, 1982). Even with infants, abusive parents are more controlling, interfering, and hostile (Crittenden, 1981, 1985). In addition, aversive behavior in abusive families is more likely to be reciprocated, with escalating negative exchanges of longer duration, than those found in nonabusive families (Lorber, Felton, & Reid, 1984).

Other distortions in parent-child relationships can be found among maltreating parents as well. It is common for maltreating parents to parentify their children, placing on them the inappropriate expectation that the child should act as a caretaker for the parent (Howes & Cicchetti, 1993). A frequent characteristic of maltreated children is that they seem to have traded roles with their caregiver (Dean, Malik, Richards, & Stringer, 1986). In such parent-child relationships, the child appears to be the more nurturing and sensitive member of the dyad.

Differences of disciplinary practices also have been observed in maltreating and nonmaltreating families. Inaccurate knowledge and expectations about child development, and negative attitudes and attributions about their children's behavior may contribute to these differences. For example, abusive parents, as opposed to nonabusive parents, are more likely to perceive their children to be aggressive, intentionally disobedient, and annoying, even when other observers fail to detect such attributes

in the children's behavior (Mash et al., 1983; Reid et al., 1987). These differences in maltreating parents' perceptions and expectations of their children could lead them to adopt different disciplinary practices (Milner & Chilamkurti, 1991).

Along these lines, abusive parents are more likely to use punishment, threats, coercion, and power assertion, and they are less likely to use reasoning and affection in disciplining and controlling their children (Chilamkurti & Milner, 1993; Lorber et al., 1984; Oldershaw, Walters, & Hall, 1986; Trickett & Susman, 1988). Moreover, the discipline used by maltreating parents is less likely to be contingent on the type of behavior exhibited by their children (Crittenden, 1981; Trickett & Kuczynski, 1986). Abusive parents also are more intrusive, more inconsistent, and less flexible in their attempts to gain compliance from their children (Oldershaw et al., 1986). Current research on normal populations suggests that the disciplinary practices of maltreating families will not effectively promote children's internalization of parental values (cf. Grusec & Goodnow, 1994). In fact, children of abusive mothers demonstrate far more noncompliant behavior than children of nonabusive mothers (Oldershaw et al., 1986; Wasserman, Green, & Allen, 1983).

In terms of the average expectable environment, the maltreating microsystem represents substantial environmental failure in providing the necessary conditions for normal ontogenesis. In general, at the level of the microsystem, maltreating parents do little to foster the successful adaptation of their children on the major tasks of individual development (cf. Cicchetti, 1989, 1990). Moreover, maltreating families as a whole do not successfully resolve the salient issues of family development (e.g., attachment, emotion regulation, autonomy, peer competence, school and work competence; cf. Cicchetti & Howes, 1991). All these negative potentiating inputs from the maltreating microsystem may be internalized and carried forward by maltreated children in the form of relatively enduring vulnerability factors as they proceed through the tasks of development. Sroufe and Fleeson (1988) contend that whole relationships (including complex family relationships) are internalized and perpetuated by the individual. As a result, the individual's internalized relationship history can influence his or her attitudes, affects, and cognitions, thus organizing the self and shaping individual development. For maltreated children, this does not bode well.

Ontogenic Development

It is in children's ontogenic development that the effects of maltreatment, and the environmental failure that maltreatment represents, can be seen. At the level of ontogenic development, the most critical determinant of eventual competence or incompetence is the negotiation of the central tasks of each developmental period (Cicchetti, 1989). An ecological-transactional perspective views child development as a series of negotiations of age- and stage-appropriate tasks. Although certain issues may be central at particular periods in time and subsequently decrease in importance, each issue must be coordinated and integrated with the environment, as well as with subsequently emerging issues across the life span (Cicchetti & Lynch, 1993; Cicchetti, Toth et al., 1993). Accordingly, each new development builds on and incorporates previous developments (i.e., these stage-salient tasks are hierarchically organized and integrated). How these issues are handled plays a pivotal role in determining subsequent adaptation. Although the previously described features of the macro-, exo-, and microsystems continue to transact with the individual to influence overall development, poor resolution of these issues ultimately may contribute to the development of psychopathology.

Because each stage-salient issue is also a lifelong task that is integrated and coordinated with each subsequent issue, no one is ever completely inoculated against or totally doomed to maladaptive and/or psychopathological outcomes. Consistent with Gottlieb's (1991a, 1992) notions of probabilistic epigenesis, we believe that individuals continue to be affected by new biological and psychological experiences, and thus, changing conditions in their lives and modifications in the course of adaptation, positive or negative, remain possible. Despite the possibility of change throughout the life span, however, prior adaptation does place constraints on subsequent adaptation. In particular, the longer an individual persists along a maladaptive pathway, the more difficult it is to reclaim a normal developmental trajectory.

We next examine how growing up in an environment that deviates from the average expectable conditions impacts children's individual development. Our review is organized around ascertaining how maltreated children resolve the central developmental tasks of infancy and childhood. Because each issue is operative throughout the life course, we begin with each task's period of ascendance as a salient issue and track what is known about each issue as it unfolds to become coordinated and integrated with later emerging developmental tasks.

Physiological Regulation

One of the first tasks of development is the maintenance of physiological or homeostatic regulation (Emde, Gaensbauer, & Harmon, 1976; Greenspan, 1981; Sroufe, 1979). The goal of a homeostatic system is to maintain a "set point" of functioning or homeostatic equilibrium. Departure from this point introduces tension into the system, which serves as the motivation for behavioral systems that subsequently act to dissipate tension and return the system once more to a state of homeostasis (Bischof, 1975).

During the first months of life, tension is defined in terms of changes in the infant's arousal level and the physiological discomfort caused by these experiences. An infant who is overly aroused or physically uncomfortable generates homeostatic tension. At later stages of development, however, with the onset of representational skills and the formation of a core sense of self, threats to psychological coherence and consistency create tension as well.

Throughout the first months of life, caregivers and infants gradually develop their own system of signals or language through which infants can effectively communicate their needs and caregivers can sensitively respond to them (Sroufe, 1979). In essence, we view the infant's homeostatic system as an open system, in which the caregiver plays an integral role in helping the infant modulate states and reduce internal tension.

To a large extent, maturation and development of physiological regulation may be guided by the infant's experiences with his or her caregiver during dyadic regulation (Sander, 1962). Caregivers play a critical role in the development of this homeostasis as they help the infant to establish basic cycles and rhythms of balance between inner need states and external stimuli (Hofer, 1987). By directly aiding infants in the maintenance of physiological homeostasis in the early weeks of life, caregivers may influence the development and organization of neurological systems (Black & Greenough, 1986). Such influences on the part of the caregiver during a period of rapid neurological growth and maturation may have long-term effects on the organization and development of the infant's brain. In fact, the existence of an open homeostatic system at this time in development suggests that interactions with the environment may be necessary for the brain to mature fully. Consequently, the development of some neurological systems may be "experience expectant"; that is, for complete differentiation and development to occur, certain types of external input by caregivers are essential and, usually, readily available (Greenough et al., 1987). By providing stable routines and responding appropriately to their infants' needs, caregivers help them modulate physiological tension and support their development of physiological regulation (Derryberry & Rothbart, 1984; Field, 1989).

Initial evidence for the negative impact of stressful rearing environments on neurobiological and psychophysiological development comes from primate studies. For example, primates raised in abnormal rearing conditions have manifested irregularities in their central noradrenergic functions. Specifically, mother-deprived infant primates show lower levels of cerebral spinal fluid norepinephrine than mother-reared infants (Kraemer, Ebert, Lake, & McKinney, 1984; Kraemer, Ebert, Schmidt, & McKinney, 1989). Likewise, Reite, Short, and Seiler (1978) have shown that in the absence of the mother, nonhuman primate infants experience physiologically disorganizing extremes of hypo- and hyperarousal (see also Krasnegor & Bridges, 1990; Reite & Field, 1985).

The level of maternal sensitivity and responsivity needed to support this kind of homeostatic regulation is a specific weakness of maltreating parents. As a result, signs of physiological dysregulation may be evident in maltreated children. For example, van der Kolk (1987) reports evidence suggesting that childhood maltreatment may enhance children's long-term hyperarousal and decrease their ability to modulate strong affect states. Additionally, van der Kolk (1987) hypothesizes that abused children may require much greater external stimulation to affect the endogenous opioid system for soothing than is the case for children whose good quality early caregiving enables them to more easily access the biological concomitants of comfort.

Specifically, a growing body of evidence suggests that parent-child attachment relationships are, in part, mediated by the endogenous opiate system (Krasnegor & Bridges, 1990; van der Kolk, 1987). Based on research with nonhuman primates, we now possess considerable knowledge of the links between the development of the attachment system and neurobiological functions. The areas of the brain thought to be most involved in the development of attachment behavior are those that are most richly endowed with opioid receptors (Kling & Stecklis, 1976; Panksepp, 1982). Early disruption of attachment in nonhuman primates brings about enduring psychobiological changes that both impair the ability to cope with subsequent social stresses and disrupt the capacity to parent in future generations (Krasnegor & Bridges, 1990; Panksepp, 1982).

A handful of studies with humans have been conducted that indicate atypical physiological processes in maltreated children. In particular, noradrenergic, dopaminergic, and glucocorticoid systems, which are activated by stress, may be affected. For example, abnormal noradrenergic activity, as indicated by lower urinary norepinephrine, has been found in children who have been abused and neglected (Rogeness, 1991). This finding is significant because noradrenergic functions are believed to be associated with attention, conditioning, internalization of values, anxiety, and inhibition (Rogeness, Javors, & Pliszka, 1992). In addition, sexually abused girls have been shown to excrete significantly greater amounts of the dopamine metabolite homovanillac acid (DeBellis, Lefter, Trickett, & Putnam, 1994). Furthermore, abnormal cortisol levels have been found in sexually abused girls, implicating altered glucocorticoid functions in the hypothalamic-pituitary-adrenal axis (Putnam et al., 1991). Relatedly, the attenuated plasma adrenocorticotropic hormone (ACTH) responses to the ovine corticotropin-releasing hormone (CRH) stimulation test in sexually abused girls further suggests a dysregulatory disorder of the hypothalamic-pituitary-adrenal axis (DeBellis et al., 1993).

Some studies have examined the timing of maltreatment and its impact on physiological development. Galvin and his colleagues have speculated that maltreatment at developmentally critical times may have particular effects on the noradrenergic system. In their studies, they have focused on serum dopamine beta hydroxylase (DBH), an enzyme involved in the conversion of dopamine to norepinephrine. In general, boys who were abused and/or neglected early in life (i.e., before 36 months of age) show lower DBH activity than those who were abused later in life or who were never maltreated (Galvin et al., 1991). The authors interpret their low DBH findings as indicative of a biological sequela of abuse and neglect brought about by an early impairment in the parent-child attachment relationship. This hypothesis is rendered plausible by the findings of animal studies and human investigations suggesting that serious disruptions in the formation of attachment relationships during developmentally sensitive or critical periods may result in regulatory failure of the noradrenergic system (Kandel, 1983; Sapolsky, Krey, & McEwen, 1984).

Other biological studies have examined the effects of different types of maltreatment. For example, Jensen and his colleagues have studied the growth hormone (GH) response patterns of sexually and physically abused boys (Jensen, Pease, ten Bensel, & Garfinkel, 1991). These investigators discovered that, compared with psychiatric controls and normal comparisons, boys who have experienced different types of abuse develop disparate patterns of neuroendocrine dysregulation. Specifically, sexually abused boys show an increased GH response to clonidine and a decreased response to L-dopa. This pattern may be linked to feelings of anxiety, isolation, mistrust, and depression, and a tendency toward revictimization and self-destructive behavior among sexually abused boys (Jensen et al., 1991; van der Kolk, 1987). On the other hand, physically abused boys show a decreased GH response to clonidine and an increased response to L-dopa. The pattern for physically abused boys may be associated with behavioral lessening of activity, increased learning or "over-learning," and increased fear and enhanced startle (Jensen et al., 1991). This pattern among physically abused boys may suggest a prelude to hypervigilance in some maltreated children.

Abused children also show a decreased heart rate over time when given repeated presentations of stressful scenes, indicating their increased attention to these nonnovel stimuli (Hill, Bleichfeld, Brunstetter, Hebert, & Steckler, 1989). The decreased heart rate shown by these children may indicate a general wariness of, and hypervigilance to, the environment not found in other children (Hill et al., 1989). Moreover, they may point out a link between the persistent psychological effects and the long-standing physiological changes that result from abuse (Lewis, 1992).

These findings are interesting in light of what is known about the physiology of maltreating parents. Maltreating parents exhibit a generalized heightened state of arousal, particularly under conditions of stress (see Frodi & Lamb, 1980; Wolfe et al., 1983). Subsequently, their children show distortions in their physiological stress-response systems, some of which may be associated with emerging hypervigilance. When these findings are examined together, we can gain some insight into the possible intergenerational transmission of biobehavioral organization. Early disturbances in the parent-child relationship may result from maltreating parents having aversive physiological reactions to the stresses of parenting, which in turn may contribute to their relative inability to respond sensitively to their infants. Problems in maintaining early homeostatic regulation, in combination with experiencing specific acts of maltreatment, may then lead to disturbances in maltreated children's own stress-response systems, thus shaping the organization of their subsequent behavioral response systems.

Affect Regulation and Differentiation

Affect regulation is defined as the intra- and extraorganismic factors by which emotional arousal is redirected, controlled, modulated, and modified so that an individual can function adaptively in emotionally challenging situations (Cicchetti, Ganiban, & Barnett, 1991). Appropriately developed affect regulation helps the individual to maintain arousal within a manageable range, thereby optimizing performance. Early parent-child interactions play an important role in the development of this emotional competency (Cicchetti & Schneider-Rosen, 1986; Kalin, Shelton, & Snowdon, 1993).

Unfortunately, maltreated children show numerous deficits in their emotional self-regulation (Cicchetti et al., 1991). Both the modulation and initiation of positive and negative effects is problematic for these children. Because serotonin is the neurotransmitter involved in the fine-tuning of arousal and aggression, it is conceivable that maltreatment experiences bring about a dysregulation of the neuromodulating serotonergic system. In addition, maltreated children exhibit distortions in the initial patterns of affect differentiation (Gaensbauer & Hiatt, 1984; Gaensbauer, Mrazek, & Harmon, 1981). Specifically, they manifest either excessive amounts of negative affect or, in contrast, blunted patterns of affect where they express neither positive nor negative emotions. Maltreated children also have difficulty in processing emotional stimuli. Because such children manifest difficulty in effectively modulating physiological arousal, they often have grave problems coping with emotionally stressful circumstances. Their hyperarousal and hypervigilant states seriously hinder their capacity to make rational assessments of stressful or ambiguous situations (Rieder & Cicchetti, 1989).

Furthermore, very early difficulties in the development of affective communication have been identified among maltreated children (Gaensbauer, 1982a; Gaensbauer et al., 1981; Gaensbauer & Sands, 1979). In general, abused and neglected infants show less adaptive affective regulation (Gaensbauer, 1982a). They demonstrate a variety of distorted affective communications that interfere with mutual engagement and elicit negative responses from caretakers (Gaensbauer & Sands, 1979). These distorted communications include affective withdrawal, lack of pleasure, inconsistency and unpredictability, shallowness, ambivalence and ambiguity, and negative affective communications. Overall, Gaensbauer and his colleagues (Gaensbauer et al, 1981) have identified four primary affective patterns that appear to represent the principal means of communication between maltreating mothers and their infants. *Affectively retarded* behavior patterns demonstrate a lack of social responsiveness, with emotional blunting and inattentiveness to the environment. *Depressed* affective patterns exhibit inhibition, withdrawal, aimless play, and sad and depressed facial expressions. *Ambivalent* or *affectively labile* patterns show sudden shifts from engagement and pleasure to withdrawal and anger. *Angry* behavior patterns manifest active disorganized play and a low frustration tolerance with frequent angry outbursts.

Other irregularities are observed in maltreated children's affective development. The facial expressions of 3- to 4-month-old physically abused infants reveal the early manifestation of a number of negative affects, including fear (Gaensbauer, 1980, 1982b). This early emergence of fear in abused infants is in contrast to the normal pattern seen in nonabused infants, where fear does not appear until approximately 8 to 9 months of age (Sroufe, 1979). It is possible that early maltreatment accelerates the development of fear in infancy and that this brings about corresponding neurobiological changes in these children (cf. Kalin, 1993). However, the lack of the cognitive capacity to process fear-inducing stimuli adequately at this early age may create problems for young infants as they attempt to modulate such a powerful negative affect (Cicchetti, Toth, & Lynch, 1993). The early emergence of fear, combined with distorted patterns of affective communication with caregivers, may result in severe impairments in the regulation and organization of affect for young maltreated children. In fact, they exhibit a profile of symptoms similar to that of individuals suffering from chronic stress including anxiety, low tolerance to stress, depression, and helplessness (Kaufman, 1991; Kazdin, Moser, Colbus, & Bell, 1985; Toth, Manly, & Cicchetti, 1992; Wolfe, 1985).

In addition to the affective anomalies found among maltreated infants, physically abused children also demonstrate later affect regulatory problems in the coping that they employ when confronted with interadult anger. For example, physically abused boys who observe simulated anger directed at their mother by an adult female confederate evidence more aggression (e.g., physical and verbal expressions of anger directed toward the female confederate) and more coping designed to minimize their mother's distress (e.g., helping mother; comforting mother) than do nonabused boys (Cummings, Hennessy, Rabideau, & Cicchetti, 1994). It appears that physically abused boys do not habituate to anger as a result of being exposed to familial hostility, but rather they are more aroused and angered by it, and more likely to try to stop it. In general, the hypervigilance and arousal in response to hostility seen among abused children might contribute to the development of their aggressive behavior, especially if conflict in the home is chronic.

In a related study, Hennessy, Rabideau, Cicchetti, and Cummings (1994) presented physically abused and nonabused boys with videotaped vignettes of adults in angry and friendly interactions. After viewing these vignettes, abused boys report experiencing more distress than nonabused boys in response to interadult hostility, especially when the hostility involves unresolved anger between adults. Moreover, physically abused boys describe more fear in response to different forms of angry adult behavior. These results support a sensitization model in which repeated exposure to anger and familial violence leads to greater, rather than less, emotional reactivity. Similarly, the distress responses to interadult anger that abused children display may provide an early indication of an increased potential for developing internalizing problems among children exposed to high levels of familial violence (cf. Kaufman, 1991; Kazdin et al., 1985; Toth et al., 1992).

Additional evidence about the affective coping strategies of maltreated children can be seen in studies of cognitive control functioning. Rieder and Cicchetti (1989) have found that maltreated children are more hypervigilant to aggressive stimuli and recall a greater number of distracting aggressive stimuli than do nonmaltreated children. Maltreated children also assimilate aggressive stimuli more readily even though this impairs their efficiency on tasks.

Although hypervigilance and quick assimilation of aggressive stimuli may emerge as an adaptive coping response in a maltreating environment, this strategy becomes less adaptive when children are faced with nonthreatening situations. Eventually, such a response pattern may adversely affect children's adaptation under normal conditions and impair their ability to negotiate subsequent tasks of development successfully. In support of this assertion, Shields, Cicchetti, and Ryan (1994) have shown in an observational study that maltreated children are deficient in affective and behavioral regulation, and that this attenuated self-regulation mediates the negative effects of maltreatment on children's social competence with peers.

Formation of Attachment Relationships

The capacity for preferential attachment originates during early affect regulation experiences and interactions with the caregiver. These early parent-child experiences provide a context for children's emerging biobehavioral organization. Specifically, the preattachment parent-child environment helps to shape children's physiological regulation and biobehavioral patterns of response (Gunnar & Nelson, 1994; Hofer, 1987; Pipp & Harmon, 1987; Spangler & Grossmann, 1993).

More overt manifestations of attachment become salient toward the end of the first year of life when infants derive feelings of security from their caregivers and use them as a base from which to explore the environment (Sroufe, 1979). Parent-child dyadic interactions characterized by relatedness and synchrony and by appropriate affective interchange are associated with successful adaptation during this stage of development. The knowledge that a caregiver is reliable and responsive also is critical because the absence of contingent responsiveness on the part of the caregiver can impede infants' ability to develop feelings of security in their primary attachment relationship (Sroufe & Waters, 1977). Ultimately, the task for the child is to be able to enter into a goal-corrected partnership where the caregiver and the child share internal states and goals (Bowlby, 1969/1982; Cicchetti, Cummings, Greenberg, & Marvin, 1990). Based on the relationship history with their primary caregivers, children form representational models of attachment figures, of themselves, and of themselves in relation to others (Bowlby, 1969/1982). Through these mental representational models, children's affects, cognitions, and expectations about future interactions are organized and carried forward into subsequent relationships (cf. Cicchetti & Lynch, 1993; Nash & Hay, 1993; Sroufe, 1989; Sroufe, Carlson, & Shulman, 1993).

A number of studies, using the Strange Situation (Ainsworth & Wittig, 1969), have shown that maltreated children are more likely to form insecure attachments with their caregivers than are nonmaltreated children (Crittenden, 1985; Egeland & Sroufe, 1981; Lamb, Gaensbauer, Malkin, & Schultz, 1985; Schneider-Rosen, Braunwald, Carlson, & Cicchetti, 1985). Using traditional classification schemes (Ainsworth, Blehar, Waters, & Wall, 1978), approximately two-thirds of maltreated children have insecure attachments to their mothers (either anxious avoidant "Type A" or anxious resistant "Type C"), whereas the remaining one-third of these children have secure attachments ("Type B"). The reverse pattern is observed in nonmaltreated children (Schneider-Rosen et al., 1985; Youngblade & Belsky, 1989). In addition, both cross-sectional and longitudinal studies reveal that with increasing age, maltreated infants' attachments are more likely to be classified as insecure-avoidant (Type A).

In a contribution to normal developmental theory and research made through observations of maltreated children, a number of investigators have observed patterns of attachment behavior that do not fit smoothly into the original attachment rating system (e.g., Egeland & Sroufe, 1981). For example, unlike infants with more typical patterns of attachment, infants from high-risk and maltreating populations often lack organized strategies for dealing with separations from and reunions with their caregiver. Main and Solomon (1990) describe this pattern of attachment as "disorganized/disoriented" ("Type D"). In addition, these infants display other bizarre symptoms in the presence of their caregiver such as interrupted movements and expressions, dazing, freezing, and stilling behaviors, and apprehension (see also Fraiberg, 1982).

Distortions in affect regulation may play a role in the disorganization found in maltreated children's attachment relationships (Barnett, Ganiban, & Cicchetti, 1992). The early emergence of fear that is elicited in these children may paralyze or severely impair their ability to regulate and organize affects when their attachment system is activated (Cicchetti & Lynch, 1993). Frightened and frightening behavior associated with the caregiver is believed to be a key factor in the emergence of disorganized attachments (Main & Hesse, 1990). When fear is connected to the caregiver, the child in effect loses the attachment figure as a secure base and a haven of safety, and the result can be a disorganized/disoriented orientation toward the attachment relationship with the caregiver. This type of loss is a devastating psychological insult and may lead to long-term psychobiological impairments such as those found in Posttraumatic Stress Disorder (Cicchetti et al., 1991; van der Kolk, 1987).

In a related vein, Crittenden (1988) has identified another atypical pattern of attachment in her observations of children who have experienced various forms of maltreatment. She has observed that a number of maltreated children in her sample display unusual patterns of moderate-to-high levels of avoidance of the mother in combination with moderate-to-high levels of resistance. She labels this pattern as avoidant-resistant ("Type A-C"). Although there are theoretical distinctions between Main and Solomon's (1990) and Crittenden's (1988, 1992) views of disorganization, most investigators have chosen to consider the A-C category as a subtype of the disorganized/disoriented Type D attachment pattern (Cicchetti, Toth, & Lynch, in press). All researchers consider the A-C and D classifications to represent atypical patterns of attachment.

Within a revised attachment classification scheme that includes these atypical patterns, maltreated infants and toddlers demonstrate a preponderance of insecure and atypical attachments (Carlson, Cicchetti, Barnett, & Braunwald, 1989; Crittenden, 1988; Lyons-Ruth, Connell, & Zoll, 1989; Lyons-Ruth, Connell, Zoll, & Stahl, 1987). Most of these studies show rates of attachment insecurity for maltreated children to be as high as 80% to 90%. Moreover, maltreated children show substantial stability of insecure attachment, whereas securely attached maltreated children generally become insecurely attached (Cicchetti & Barnett, 1991a; Schneider-Rosen et al., 1985). In contrast, for nonmaltreated children, secure attachments are highly stable, whereas insecure attachments are more likely to change (Lamb, Thompson, Gardner, & Charnov, 1985). Furthermore, in some samples, as many as 80% of maltreated infants exhibit disorganized attachments (Carlson et al., 1989). This is in comparison with only 20% of demographically matched nonmaltreated infants having disorganized attachments. Similar findings have been reported by Lyons-Ruth, Repacholi, McLeod, and Silva (1991). In addition, Crittenden (1988) finds that a high percentage of the abused and neglected children in her sample can be classified as having avoidant-resistant (A-C) patterns of attachment.

Of interest is the finding of substantial stability in these atypical attachments across the ages of 12, 18, and 24 months (Barnett et al., 1992). Approximately 60% of the infants who have disorganized attachments at 12 months of age maintain the same classification one year later, whereas over 90% of infants who are disorganized at 24 months have previously received the same classification.

Throughout the preschool years, maltreated children are more likely than nonmaltreated children to have insecure attachments (Cicchetti & Barnett, 1991a). As maltreated children grow older, though, it appears less certain that they will have an atypical pattern of attachment. In an investigation of the attachments of preschool-age maltreated children (Cicchetti & Barnett, 1991a), 30-month-old children who have been maltreated are significantly more likely to have atypical patterns of attachment (i.e., Types D or A-C) than are nonmaltreated children. However, even though approximately one-third of 36-month-old and 48-month-old maltreated children manifest these atypical patterns, this is not significantly greater than the proportion of same-age nonmaltreated children who have such patterns.

In a study of maltreated school-age children, a preponderance of nonoptimal patterns of relatedness was obtained, indicating continued disturbance in the representations of their relationships (Lynch & Cicchetti, 1991). Lynch and Cicchetti (1991) also have found that approximately 30% of maltreated children between the ages of 7 and 13 years report having a "confused" pattern of relatedness to their mothers. This pattern is characterized by children reporting that they feel warm and secure with their mothers despite not feeling close to them. The identification of a confused pattern of relatedness may be consistent with accounts that some maltreated children manifest a basic confusion, disorganization, or disorientation in how they mentally represent their relationships with their mothers (Cicchetti et al., in press; Lynch & Cicchetti, 1991). The finding of significantly more confused patterns of relatedness among maltreated school-age children than nonmaltreated children suggests that distortions in maltreated children's relationships with, and mental representations of, their caregivers may persist up through the preadolescent years at rates comparable to those found during the preschool years, but at lower rates than those observed during early infancy (Cicchetti & Lynch, 1993).

There are several possible explanations for the apparent decline in disorganized/atypical attachment patterns at older ages (Cicchetti & Lynch, 1993). It is conceivable that older children represent their maltreating attachment relationship in ways that are organized differently from the representations of younger children. Cognitive maturity may play a role in how children are able to represent maltreating relationships and themselves in such relationships, and how they are able to organize their attachment behavior strategies. For example, in middle childhood (age 6 years), youngsters who were classified as disorganized/disoriented in infancy tend to exhibit controlling strategies upon reunion with their caregiver (Main & Cassidy, 1988). Thus, disorganization may be a characteristic feature of less differentiated and integrated mental relationships and strategies (cf. Kaplan, 1966). Furthermore, severity, chronicity, and type of abuse most likely interact with cognitive maturity in determining the nature of mental representation. The decrease of disorganized and atypical attachments also may be a result of the expanded social networks that maltreated children are exposed to once they enter the school environment. As children are faced with increased numbers of nonthreatening potential relationship partners, their representational models may become more organized and consolidated. Many important questions remain to be answered regarding the manner in which relationship experiences and cognitive maturity interact as determinants of mental representation. The representational models of maltreated children will be discussed more specifically in the upcoming section on symbolic development.

Regardless of these issues, findings on the prevalence and stability of atypical and other insecure attachments in maltreated children point to the extreme risk these children face in achieving adaptive outcomes in other domains of self and interpersonal development (Cicchetti & Lynch, 1993). Quality of attachment is associated with the presence of externalizing and internalizing problems in high-risk populations (Lyons-Ruth & Easterbrooks, in press). Toth and Cicchetti (in press) have provided evidence that maltreated children's representational models (as indicated by their reported patterns of relatedness) may actually moderate the effects of maltreatment on children's perceived competence and depressive symptomatology.

Furthermore, attachment theory suggests that the organizing effects of earlier representational models are brought forward through later childhood and adulthood (Sroufe, 1989). For individuals who have had abusive or neglecting experiences in childhood, insecure patterns of adult attachment organization and difficulties in family relationships are likely to predominate (Bartholomew, 1990; Crittenden, 1988; Crittenden & Ainsworth, 1989; Feldman & Downey, 1994; Howes & Cicchetti, 1993; Main & Goldwyn, 1984). As an example, not only do the representational models of maltreating parents guide their behavior with their children, but they also may exert a powerful influence on the selection of and relational quality between spouses or partners (Crittenden et al., 1991). In examining the Adult Attachment Interviews of a sample of maltreating mothers and their spouses or partners, Crittenden and her colleagues have found rates of Dismissing or Preoccupied-Engaged adult attachment organizations in both women and men that exceed 90%. Comparison of their attachment organizations demonstrates two patterns. There is either a match between the adults' attachment organizations (i.e., both Dismissing or both Preoccupied-Engaged), or there is a complementary "mesh" between them with one partner Dismissing and the other Preoccupied-Engaged. In contrast, in low-income families that parent their children adequately, secure adult attachment organizations are more common, as are matches between spouses with both partners being secure. In the maltreating families, secure adult attachment organization, a match between partners with secure organizations, and a union between secure and insecure partners are all nearly nonexistent.

Representational models also may operate at other levels of the ecology. In this regard, Reiss (1981) describes family paradigms as the set of core assumptions, beliefs, and convictions that families hold about their environment. Reiss contends that these paradigms affect how families process information about the world. Like individual representational models, these family paradigms are relatively enduring, according to Reiss, and their core beliefs emerge over the course of family development (cf. Cicchetti & Howes, 1991). These family paradigms can be conceptualized as the family's representational model of itself and its relationship to the community in which it resides (Cicchetti & Lynch, 1993). These models may shape families' attitudes toward, and expectations about, their role and value in the community. Most likely there are interactions between the quality of children's representational models of relationships and the nature of shared family representational models. As a result, family models may provide a link between representational models that are formed over the course of individual ontogenesis and further disruption of the exosystem among individuals who have experienced maltreatment. The distorted individual and family representations of maltreated children may adversely affect their information processing in ways that result in these individuals functioning incompetently in their communities and contributing to the deterioration of the exosystem. Furthermore, links between shared family models and individual representations may facilitate the intergenerational transmission of family styles and dynamics. From the perspective of an ecological-transactional model, the negative expectations that accompany the representational models of children and families that experience and are exposed to violence may perpetuate violence both across generations and throughout all levels of the ecological system (Cicchetti & Lynch, 1993). Attachment is a developmental issue that remains salient across the life span.

The Development of an Autonomous Self

The infant's self-concept is believed to emerge from within the context of caregiving relationships (Bowlby, 1988; Bretherton & Waters, 1985; Emde, 1983; Mahler, Pine, & Bergman, 1975; Sroufe, 1989; Stern, 1989). In fact, attachment security to mother is associated with more complex self-knowledge in children aged 12 to 36 months (Pipp, Easterbrooks, & Harmon, 1992). Even among maltreated children, attachment security is associated with an increased likelihood of an early-onset of visual self-recognition (Schneider-Rosen & Cicchetti, 1984), an absence of internal state language deficits (Beeghly & Cicchetti, 1994), and higher levels of perceived competence (Toth & Cicchetti, in press) in comparison with insecurely attached maltreated children.

As development proceeds and the task of self *management* begins to move away from the context of the caregiver-infant relationship into the realm of autonomous functioning, the toddler becomes increasingly invested in self-management due to developmentally new capabilities, as well as to a more developed understanding of self and other. During this period, self-regulation and the regulation of affect gradually are transferred from the caregiver-child dyad to the child alone. The caregiver's sensitivity to, and tolerance of, the toddler's strivings for autonomy, in addition to the caregiver's ability to set age-appropriate limits, are necessary for the successful resolution of this issue. Caregivers who feel rejected as a result of their toddler's increasing independence, or who are stressed by their child's new demands, may inhibit the emergence of autonomy in their children.

As self-organization is brought forward to the new tasks of development, a number of aspects of maltreated children's self-development are likely to be affected, with possible implications for their subsequent interpersonal relationships. Studies on the self-recognition of maltreated children provide some insight into their emerging self-concept. Although there are no deficits in maltreated infants' ability to recognize their rouge-marked selves in a mirror, they are more likely than nonmaltreated infants to display neutral or negative affect on visual self-recognition (Schneider-Rosen & Cicchetti, 1984, 1991). In another study of self-differentiation in maltreated toddlers, Egeland and Sroufe (1981) employed a tool-use, problem-solving paradigm to investigate 24-month-old children's emerging autonomy, independent

exploration, and ability to cope with frustration. They found that maltreated children become more angry, frustrated with the mother, and noncompliant than comparison children do, suggesting that maltreated children at this age have difficulty making a smooth transition toward autonomy.

Other delays in maltreated children's self-systems have been noted as well. For example, maltreated children talk less about themselves and about their internal states than do nonmaltreated children (Beeghly & Cicchetti, 1994; Coster, Gersten, Beeghly, & Cicchetti, 1989). Maltreated children with insecure attachments display the most compromised internal state language (Beeghly & Cicchetti, 1994). The ability to talk about internal states and feelings is a development of late toddlerhood that is believed to reflect toddlers' emergent self-other understanding and to be fundamental to the regulation of social interaction (Beeghly & Cicchetti, 1994). Maltreated children's negative feelings about themselves and their inability to talk about their own activities and states may impede their ability to engage in successful social relationships.

In particular, maltreated children appear to be most reluctant to talk about their negative internal states (Beeghly & Cicchetti, 1994). This finding is corroborated by reports that maltreated children may actually inhibit negative affect, especially in the context of their relationship with their caregiver (Crittenden & DiLalla, 1988; Lynch & Cicchetti, 1991). It is possible that some maltreated children adopt a strategy designed to suppress the expression of their own negative feelings to avoid eliciting adverse responses from their caregivers (Cicchetti, 1991). Although this approach may be adaptive in the context of a maltreating relationship, it can become maladaptive and lead to incompetence in other interpersonal contexts. Additionally, the inability of maltreated children to identify and discuss their own distress may play a major role in these children's difficulties in displaying empathy toward their peers (Main & George, 1985; Troy & Sroufe, 1987).

The effects of exposure to the school setting on maltreated children's sense of self may have further implications for their subsequent relationships with others. Even by the preschool years, maltreated children already are described as lower in ego control and self-esteem (Egeland, Sroufe, & Erickson, 1983). Furthermore, maltreated children report lower self-concepts than demographically matched nonmaltreated children (Allen & Tarnowski, 1989; Oates, Forrest, & Peacock, 1985). In general, physically abused school-age children show deficits in self-esteem compared with nonabused children (Okun et al., 1994). However, there appear to be different patterns of findings for children of different ages. Young maltreated children actually express an exaggerated sense of self-competence compared with nonmaltreated children (Vondra, Barnett, & Cicchetti, 1989). By the age of 8 to 9 years, though, maltreated children perceive themselves as being less competent than do nonmaltreated children. Teachers' ratings of these children's competence indicate that the older maltreated children's perceptions are more accurate and in accord with their own ratings. Initially, young maltreated children's inflated sense of self may help them to gain feelings of competence in the midst of chaotic and uncontrollable family relationships. As maltreated children mature, though, and in the context of school are forced to make social comparisons between themselves and others, they begin to make more negative (and accurate) self-appraisals. These negative appraisals likely become internalized as part of their self-representations. Feeling less competent in comparison with others may have a further negative impact on maltreated children's ability to interact with others successfully.

Thus, maltreated children display major difficulties in autonomy and self-other differentiation (Cicchetti, 1990). Moreover, because maltreated children may assume the role of caretaker in the attachment relationship with their parents, they may be more effective in taking care of others than they are of themselves. The data on internal state language also suggest that maltreated children have difficulty recognizing their own needs (Beeghly & Cicchetti, 1994). Consequently, maltreated children may have trouble being alone, thereby exacerbating and contributing to their problems in self-other differentiation (Cicchetti, 1991).

In the most extreme cases, maltreatment experiences may lead to basic and severe disturbances in self-definition and self-regulation (Fischer & Ayoub, 1994; Westen, 1994). For example, adolescent girls who have experienced prolonged sexual abuse have been shown to have a negativity bias in the evaluations of their "core" self, while exhibiting a complex form of dissociation called "polarized affective splitting" in which they produce diametrically opposed descriptions of the "real me" (Calverley, Fischer, & Ayoub, 1994). There is evidence that traumatic abuse experiences such as these can play a role in the etiology of dissociative disorders (Cole & Putnam, 1992).

Symbolic Development

During the toddler years, various symbolic competencies evolve and become more differentiated. For example, the development of language and symbolic play allow children to represent their growing awareness of self and other (Cicchetti, 1990). There are strong cognitive maturational components to the development of these abilities, but socioemotional and environmental factors also play a role in their evolution. In addition, children demonstrate an increasing ability to form complex mental representations of people, relationships, and the world during this period. Their ability to manipulate these (so-called) representational models can be seen in the nature of their information-processing skills.

Language. A variety of environmental risk factors have been associated with children's language development, including family social status, maternal psychosocial functioning, and quality of mother-infant involvement (Morissey, Barnard, Greenberg, Booth, & Spieker, 1990). With regard to the specific effects of child maltreatment, a number of studies show that maltreatment, especially severe neglect, is related to a number of linguistic delays affecting both expressive and receptive language (Allen & Oliver, 1982; Culp et al., 1991; Fox, Long, & Langlois, 1988). These deficits are correlated with caretaking environments in which maltreating parents engage in less social language exchange with their children and provide less direct verbal teaching (Culp et al., 1991; Wasserman et al., 1983).

Attachment security is related to communication abilities for both maltreated and nonmaltreated children (Gersten, Coster, Schneider-Rosen, Carlson, & Cicchetti, 1986). In fact, a secure attachment may operate as a protective factor for language

competence among maltreated children (Gersten et al., 1986; Morisset et al., 1990). In general, though, communicative functioning in maltreated children shows signs of impairment. The mean length of utterance (MLU) for maltreated toddlers is significantly shorter than that observed in nonmaltreated children (Coster et al., 1989). In addition, they produce less internal state speech (Beeghly & Cicchetti, 1994; Coster et al., 1989) and proportionately less contingent speech (Coster et al., 1989) than do nonmaltreated toddlers. These findings suggest that maltreated toddlers have developed a communicative style in which language is not used as frequently as a medium for social or affective exchanges.

Play. The development of symbolic play reflects children's emerging conceptions of themselves and of others (Cicchetti, 1990). Over the course of the preschool years, children's symbolic play becomes more socially and cognitively complex. Maltreated children, however, show deficits in this symbolic capacity as well. The overall play patterns of maltreated children are less cognitively and socially mature than those of nonmaltreated children (Alessandri, 1991). Moreover, maltreated preschoolers in a free play setting engage in lower total amounts of play than do nonmaltreated preschoolers. In addition, the cognitive play of maltreated children is primarily functional, sensorimotor, and less symbolic in form. Maltreated children display routine, stereotyped use of play materials, engage in simple motoric activities, and demonstrate greater touching of toys without any direct manipulations. These play patterns occur in both solitary and parallel social situations (Alessandri, 1991).

Conversely, nonmaltreated children engage in greater constructive activity in which play is sequentially organized and purposeful. Although there appears to be no differences between maltreated and nonmaltreated children in the frequency of dramatic play, thematic differences have been found (Alessandri, 1991). The dramatic play of maltreated children is restricted in the type of themes that are used, in the affect that is expressed, and in the type of fantasy transformation that is involved. Maltreated children tend to engage in imitative play themes that focus on the reenactment of parental roles and concrete events. In comparison, nonmaltreated children engage in play involving more elaborate fantasy themes (Alessandri, 1991).

Differences in maltreated and nonmaltreated children's play are correlated with differences in mother-child interaction styles. Studies of maltreating mothers in play settings with their children reveal that, while they are more controlling, overall they are less involved with their children, use fewer physical and verbal strategies to direct their children's attention, and are more negative in comparison with nonmaltreating mothers (Alessandri, 1992; Mash et al., 1983). Both maltreated and nonmaltreated children who are exposed to a low level of maternal attention-directing behavior and to an aloof and critical mother are less likely to engage in higher forms of cognitive play (Alessandri, 1992). They are more likely to engage in simple manipulative sensorimotor play. On the other hand, when mothers frequently focus their children's attention on objects and events in the environment and interact with them in a positive reciprocal manner, children are more able to initiate, maintain, and engage in more complex forms of cognitive play (Alessandri, 1992). These findings provide evidence for how the maltreating caretaking environment can inhibit symbolic development.

Representational Models. The manner in which maltreatment affects the development of symbolic abilities related to the formation of mental representational models is of interest as well. These models are believed to play an important role in the continuity of development across different domains of functioning (Bowlby, 1969/1982; Cicchetti, Toth et al., in press; Lynch & Cicchetti, 1991; Sroufe, 1989). For example, in normal populations the quality of children's attachment relationships to their primary caregiver has been associated with the complexity of their knowledge of self and others (Pipp et al., 1992). Among maltreated children, links between their attachment histories and problems in their peer relationships have been demonstrated (Cicchetti, Lynch, Shonk, & Todd Manly, 1992; Youngblade & Belsky, 1989). More specifically, maltreated children's attachment histories appear to play a role in the victimization observed in these preschool children's relationships with their peers (Main & George, 1985; Troy & Sroufe, 1987). In addition, maltreated children's patterns of relatedness to their mothers have a significant effect on their feelings of relatedness to others (Lynch & Cicchetti, 1991).

Unfortunately, little direct research has been conducted that can provide clear information about the nature and development of representational models. There is not even a consensus about how and if such research can be done. Most of what is believed about the emergence and function of representational models derives from attachment theory and has been inferred from observations of behavior in the Strange Situation.

Initially, the young child develops expectations about the nature of future interpersonal contacts through repeated interactions with the caregiver. These expectations form the basis of representational models of the self, others, and the self in relation to others (Bowlby, 1969/1982). Children's models reflect expectations about the availability and probable actions of others with complementary models of how worthy and competent the self is.

Bretherton (1990) has suggested that representational models of the self and attachment figures may be hierarchically organized in terms of event schemas. Such a hierarchy would include low-level interactional schemas (e.g., "When I get hurt, my mother comes to help me") and more generalized schemas (e.g., "My mother is usually there for me when I need her"). At the top of the hierarchy are overarching schemas such as "My mother is a loving person" and "I am loved and worthy of love." Attachment theory proposes that these organized mental representations are internalized by the individual and used in subsequent interpersonal contexts.

In addition, it is believed that children are able to form independent models of different relationship figures with their complementary models of the self. Some supporting evidence for this claim has been found in maltreating and high-risk samples (Lynch & Cicchetti, 1991). Representational models of individual relationships contain information that is specific to those relationships. Expectations about the availability of the other person, how effective the self is likely to be in eliciting desired responses from that person, attitudes and commitment toward the relationship, and the affective tone of the relationship are the kinds of information that may be incorporated into models of specific relationships.

During the course of development, information from these specific models may become integrated as part of more generalized models of relationships (Crittenden, 1990). It is possible that internal representational models of early attachment relationships begin to provide the individual with general information and expectations about other potential social partners and the self in relation to them. These generalized models of self and other allow the individual to forecast how others will act and react, and how successful the self is likely to be in the broader social context.

This process is likely to be problematic for maltreated children. Once maltreated children have internalized their caregiving experiences, the resulting representational models of their insecure and atypical attachments may generalize to new relationships. Consequently, maltreated children may develop negative expectations of how others will behave, and of how successful the self will be in relation to others (Bowlby, 1973, 1980; Bretherton, 1991; Cicchetti, 1991; Lynch & Cicchetti, 1991).

In generating these expectations, children may evaluate information both from models that are specific to a given relationship, as well as from more generalized models of relationships (Crittenden, 1990; Lynch & Cicchetti, 1991). Factual knowledge about relationships and the affects connected to them may be activated within the relevant representational models. This is possible because similar relationship events are organized and encoded into episodic memory in the form of prototypical memories (Stern, 1989). These prototypes are representations of general emotions and cognitions, events, and behavioral patterns located in the semantic, episodic, and procedural memory systems respectively (Crittenden, 1990, 1992; Tulving, 1985, 1989).

Observed continuities in the quality and pattern of children's interactions with different relationship figures may be the result, in part, of children's increasing use of organized mental representations. A number of studies show that there are similarities in the quality of children's relationships with both of their parents, their siblings, their friends, and their teachers. More specifically, the quality of children's attachment with their mothers is related to the quality of their relationships with their fathers (Fox, Kimmerly, & Schafer, 1991), their siblings (Teti & Ablard, 1989), their preschool-age best friends (Park & Waters, 1989), and their teachers (Howes & Hamilton, 1992). This combination of findings suggests that representational models are at work creating coherence across children's relationships. Of particular interest with respect to maltreatment is the finding that maltreated children who have been removed from their homes exhibit attachment insecurity with their alternative caregivers at rates that are similar to what would be expected if the caregivers were their maltreating mothers (Howes & Segal, 1993). In addition, there is substantial concordance between maltreated children's patterns of relatedness with both their mothers and their teachers (Lynch & Cicchetti, 1992).

Initially, both specific and general models remain more or less open to new input and consequent readjustment (Crittenden & Ainsworth, 1989). Early on, as children experience additional interactions with their relationship partners, they are readily able to assimilate these experiences into their existing models, or to accommodate their models to new information if necessary.

Open models such as these are akin to Bowlby's notion of a "working" model (Bowlby, 1969/1982). With increasing verbal abilities and cognitive development, however, children's representational models may become more closed to experience (Crittenden & Ainsworth, 1989). Conceptual processes and symbolic function replace actual episodes of experience in the formulation and integration of representational models. It may not be until adolescence when children attain formal operations that a rethinking of previous experiences is likely to occur.

It is interesting to recall our earlier discussion of how "formalized" rethinking processes during adolescence and early adulthood can help individuals who were maltreated as children to avoid becoming maltreating parents (Egeland et al., 1988). For example, parents with "earned-secure" adult attachment classifications who have reworked their representations of early difficulties with their parents demonstrate competent parenting styles that are comparable to those of "continuous-secure" parents (Pearson, Cohn, Cowan, & Cowan, 1994). Despite their reconstruction of past difficulties, though, "earned-secure" adults may still possess emotional liabilities as evidenced by levels of depressed symptomatology similar to those seen in insecure adults (Pearson et al., 1994).

Having representational models that are closed to new interpersonal information may be especially detrimental to children who have experienced insecure attachments and maltreatment. Parents' explanations that their harsh (and perhaps maltreating) behavior is for their children's own good become organizing principles for children's models of themselves and others. Moreover, some children may begin to employ a form of cognitive screening for relationship-relevant information to avoid the emotional discomfort of an angry relationship (Bowlby, 1980). It has been shown, for example, that abused children tend to split off from consciousness the more negative aspects of their perceptions (Beeghly & Cicchetti, 1994; Stovall & Craig, 1990). As a result, these children's representations of themselves and others may not be open to alternative and potentially positive experiences with others. Instead, they approach their interactions with others based on more generalized negative expectations, leading to less competent dealings with others. Repeated experiences of incompetent interactions with others serve to confirm their negative representational models, making it even less likely that they will be open to positive interpersonal experiences in the future.

Recent research is beginning to document differences in maltreated and nonmaltreated children's representational models. For example, differences in maltreated and nonmaltreated children's patterns of relatedness are reflected in the complexity and organization of their person concepts (Lynch, 1992). More specifically, a child's pattern of relatedness with a particular person is significantly related to the descriptiveness, depth, evaluative consistency, and emotional tone of his or her open-ended description of that relationship figure. Children with optimal patterns of relatedness have relatively detailed conceptions of others that are associated with consistently positive affect, as opposed to the person concepts of children with nonoptimal patterns of relatedness (Lynch, 1992).

In addition, maltreated children differ from nonmaltreated children in their perceptions of self and other on a variety of projective assessments (Stovall & Craig, 1990), in the negativity of their view of the relational world demonstrated in projective stories (McCrone, Egeland, Kalkoske, & Carlson, 1994) and in their perceptions of their parents exhibited in a projective family measure (Sternberg et al., in press). Furthermore, maltreated children tell fewer stories than nonmaltreated children in which adults and peers reciprocate the kind acts of children, and they tell more stories in which they justify their parents' unkind acts on the basis of their own bad behavior (Dean et al., 1986). Thus, based on their early maltreatment experiences, these children may have developed negative, and perhaps closed, representational models of themselves and others. Consequently, in subsequent relationship situations maltreated children may be constricted in their ability to cognitively process events, may have difficulty regulating their own emotions, and may employ processes of defensive exclusion to manage their feelings of distress (McCrone et al., 1994).

Social Information Processing. Children may use their developing representational models to help them process social information. In addition, various aspects of experience have been shown to influence how children process social information. For example, normal children who are presented with negative affect conditions make more frequent information-processing errors (Bugental, Blue, Cortez, Fleck, & Rodriguez, 1992). This is especially true for young children (e.g., between 5 and 6 years old). Increases in heart rate are associated with these processing errors (Bugental et al., 1992). In a related vein, rape victims with Posttraumatic Stress Disorder (PTSD) show longer response latencies for processing rape-related words than those found in non-PTSD and nonvictim control subjects (Foa, Feske, Murdock, Kozak, & McCarthy, 1991). Finally, overwhelming empirical evidence supports the relationship between characteristic social-information-processing styles and children's social adjustment (Crick & Dodge, 1994). Some aspects of processing may be especially influential in leading to behaviors that affect social status (e.g., hostile attributional biases, intention cue detection accuracy, response access patterns, and evaluation of response outcomes).

Deficits in children's information processing are seen in association with harsh and maltreating parenting (Dodge, Pettit, & Bates, 1990). For example, maladaptive social-information-processing patterns that develop in response to harsh discipline appear to mediate the effects of harsh parenting on children's aggression (Weiss, Dodge, Bates, & Pettit, 1992). In addition, maltreated children, in comparison with nonmaltreated children, are less accurate in encoding social cues, and they generate a higher proportion of aggressive responses to problematic social situations (Price & Van Slyke, 1991).

As was described earlier, Rieder and Cicchetti (1989) have found that the cognitive control functioning of maltreated children is affected by the presence of aggressive stimuli. Moreover, maltreated children recall a greater number of these distracting aggressive stimuli than do nonmaltreated children. They readily assimilate these aggressive stimuli, even though it results in less cognitive efficiency and impaired task performance. Maltreated children's apparent hypervigilance for aggressive stimuli may have developed as an adaptive coping strategy with the maltreating environment, alerting children to signs of imminent danger and keeping emotions from rising so high that the children become incapacitated. However, this response pattern becomes less adaptive in nonthreatening situations. The poor-quality representational models that maltreated children develop of themselves and others may predispose them to the observed impairments in information processing. These impairments may interfere with subsequent interpersonal relationships (Crick & Dodge, 1994).

The Formation of Peer Relationships

Another important task on ontogenic development is the formation of effective peer relationships (Cicchetti, 1990). Because of their negative early relationship histories, peer relationships and friendships may provide an important opportunity for promoting positive adaptation in maltreated children (Cicchetti et al., 1992). Many important issues of children's social and emotional development are facilitated by being exposed to the world of peers (Hartup, 1983).

Unfortunately, maltreated children's relationships with their peers typically mirror the maladaptive representational models that they carry with them into this task of development. Originating in the context of atypical relationships with caregivers, the inner organization of maltreated children's models of self and others proves to be dysfunctional when they are faced with the task of interacting competently with peers. In general, maltreated children exhibit more disturbed patterns of interaction with peers than do nonmaltreated children. They interact less with their peers, and they display fewer prosocial behaviors than nonmaltreated children (Haskett & Kistner, 1991; Hoffman-Plotkin & Twentyman, 1984; Jacobson & Straker, 1982). A number of investigators have demonstrated that maltreated children display general maladjustment and incompetence with their peers (Kaufman & Cicchetti, 1989; Okun et al., 1994; Rogosch & Cicchetti, 1994). In addition, physically abused children are less popular with their peers, they show less positive reciprocity in their interactions, and they have social networks that are more insular and atypical with higher levels of negativity (Dodge, Pettit, & Bates, 1994; Haskett & Kistner, 1991; Salzinger, Feldman, Hammer, & Rosario, 1993). Moreover, the magnitude of some of these differences from nonmaltreated children may grow over time (Dodge et al., 1994). Maltreated children also express greater mistrust of peers (Bernath, Feshbach, & Gralinski, 1993). This lack of trust is related to diminished concern about affect and future interpersonal relationships, and somewhat heightened concern about the past (Bernath et al., 1993).

Overall, two main themes regarding maltreated children's relationships with their peers emerge from the literature (Cicchetti et al., 1992; Mueller & Silverman, 1989). One set of findings indicates that maltreated children, particularly physically abused children, show heightened levels of physical and verbal aggression in their interactions with peers (George & Main, 1979; Herrenkohl & Herrenkohl, 1981; Hoffman-Plotkin & Twentyman, 1984; Kaufman & Cicchetti, 1989; Salzinger et al., 1993). In addition, abused preschoolers are more likely to cause distress in their peers than are nonabused children (Klimes-Dougan & Kistner, 1990). More alarmingly, though, maltreated children have been observed to respond with anger and aggression both to friendly overtures from their peers (Howes & Eldredge, 1985) and to signs of distress in other children (Howes & Espinosa, 1985; Klimes-Dougan & Kistner, 1990; Main & George, 1985). In some instances physically abused children exhibit fear, along with alternating comforting and attacking behaviors, in response to peers in distress (Main & George, 1985).

Another set of findings indicates that there are high degrees of withdrawal from and avoidance of peer interactions among maltreated children, especially those who have been neglected (Dodge et al., 1994; George & Main, 1979; Hoffman-Plotkin & Twentyman, 1984; Howes & Espinosa, 1985; Jacobson & Straker, 1982). In many cases, it appears that this social withdrawal is an active strategy of avoidance on the part of maltreated children, and not merely a passive orientation toward peer interaction (George & Main, 1979; Howes & Espinosa, 1985).

Rogosch and Cicchetti (1994) recently have identified a subgroup of maltreated and nonmaltreated children who are perceived by their peers as demonstrating a combination of aggressive and withdrawn behavior. In particular, maltreated children who are viewed by their peers as relatively high on both aggression and withdrawal evidence substantially lower social effectiveness than is the case for nonmaltreated comparison youngsters. An attachment theory perspective may be useful to account for the effects of maltreatment among the children who exhibit the mixed aggressive and withdrawn presentation. Given the high prevalence of blending of avoidance and resistance in the attachment behavior of maltreated infants and toddlers and the patterns of disorganization and disorientation in those attachments (Carlson et al., 1989), it is interesting to speculate on the mixing of aggression and withdrawal found among maltreated children. Intense frightening experiences in the maltreating parent-child relationship may contribute to these intermingled patterns in that fearful and frightening behavior by caregivers has been associated with disorganized attachment behaviors (Main & Hesse, 1990). This co-occurrence of aggression and withdrawal may represent the continued operation of disorganized representational models of relationships carried forward from the attachment relationship into new social encounters, resulting in disturbance in social adaptation. The aggressive-withdrawn strategy may be used protectively to diminish the anticipated negative aspects of interpersonal relations; aggression may be employed to terminate perceived interpersonal threats, whereas isolation may be utilized to avoid threats.

By revealing indications of a predisposition to both "fight" and "flight" responses in maltreated children's interactions with their peers, these findings lend support to the claim that maltreated children internalize both sides of their relationship with their caregiver (Troy & Sroufe, 1987). As a result, maltreated children's representational models may include elements of being both a victim and a victimizer. Evidence in support of this notion comes from the absence of dominance hierarchies that is observed in classrooms of maltreated preschool children (Meisburger & Cicchetti, 1993). It is not possible to establish a dominance hierarchy when all members of the group are likely to be both a victim and a victimizer. Overall, heightened aggressiveness, avoidance of social interaction, and aberrant responses to friendly overtures and signs of distress leave maltreated children unprepared to develop effective relationships with their peers (Mueller

& Silverman, 1989). On the contrary, contact with peers seems to elicit stressful reactions from maltreated children that further decreases the likelihood of successful interaction.

The maladaptive pattern of maltreated children's relationship histories is among the factors that place them at risk for negative developmental outcomes. For example, poor peer relationships in childhood are associated with juvenile delinquency and other type of behavior disorders during adolescence (Cowen, Pederson, Babigian, Izzo, & Trost, 1973; Hartup, 1983; Janes & Hesselbrock, 1978; Kohlberg, LaCrosse, & Ricks, 1972; Parker & Asher, 1987; Robins, 1966; Roff, Sells, & Golden, 1972; Rutter & Giller, 1983). Recently, researchers have concluded that childhood aggression and peer rejection are relatively stable, and they are good predictors of negative outcomes including school dropout, criminality, delinquency, and psychological disturbance in adolescence and adulthood (Ollendick, Weist, Borden, & Greene, 1992; Parker & Asher, 1987; Rubin & Mills, 1988; Rubin & Ross, 1988). Conversely, there is some evidence that maltreated preschool-age children who have participated in a "peer treatment" intervention show short-term improvement in their social behavior (Fantuzzo et al., 1988).

For maltreated children, heightened aggressiveness and social withdrawal may represent serious obstacles to successful adaptation. Both forms of social dysfunction can lead to increasing isolation and peer rejection. Rubin and his colleagues (Rubin, LeMare, & Lollis, 1990; Rubin & Lollis, 1988) have proposed a model of peer rejection in which the active avoidance and increased aggression observed in maltreated children's interactions with peers may indicate two different developmental pathways, each with different sequelae (Cicchetti et al., 1992).

One pathway leads to the development of externalizing disorders. At the outset, a combination of factors such as temperamental difficulty, intrusive parenting, and negative social ecologies contribute to the formation of hostile relationships. These hostile and possibly aggressive relationships result in rejection by the peer group. Being rejected may cause children to turn against their peer group and eventually lead to the onset of externalizing problems.

A second pathway leads to the development of internalizing disorders. Showing a high degree of behavioral inhibition, some anxious, inhibited children react to the environment with increasing rates of withdrawal. Their deviance from age-appropriate social and emotional norms causes their peers to reject them. Such rejected children may respond with further withdrawal and the development of internalizing problems.

Although this model is somewhat speculative, several of the main linkages associated with each pathway have been supported empirically (Hymel, Rubin, Rowden, & LeMare, 1990). These alternative developmental pathways provide a framework for understanding the peer interactions of maltreated children and their implications for subsequent development. Particular maltreatment experiences may lead children along different pathways to peer rejection and isolation, with the individual child's response to integration of these issues resulting in different developmental outcomes (Aber et al., 1989).

Adaptation to School

A final example of a central task of ontogenic development is the successful adaptation to school (Cicchetti, 1990). As children grow older, they increasingly begin to function in contexts that extend beyond the home and family. School is the major extrafamilial environment in which children operate beginning in early childhood and extending through adolescence. In the school setting, children are exposed to a new community of unfamiliar peers and adults, and they are presented with a new set of context-specific challenges. In particular, integration into the peer group, acceptable performance in the classroom, and appropriate motivational orientations for achievement are all parts of this stage-salient developmental task.

Once again, however, maltreated children appear to be at risk for an unsuccessful resolution to this issue of development. A high percentage of high-risk children coming from backgrounds similar to those of representative samples of maltreated children have difficulty in school and are referred for educational services in relation to school-based problems (Egeland & Abery, 1991). Furthermore, Eckenrode and his colleagues have shown that maltreated children, in comparison with nonmaltreated children, perform worse on standardized tests, obtain lower grades, and are more likely to repeat a grade (Eckenrode & Laird, 1991; Eckenrode, Laird, & Doris, 1993). In addition, they receive significantly more discipline referrals and suspensions than nonmaltreated children (Eckenrode & Laird, 1991; Eckenrode et al., 1993). Other investigators have found that maltreated children are dependent on their teachers (Egeland, Sroufe, & Erickson, 1983), score lower on tests measuring cognitive maturity, perhaps due to motivational reasons (Barahal, Waterman, & Martin, 1981), and are rated by both parents and teachers as less ready to learn in school (Hoffman-Plotkin & Twentyman, 1984).

Neglected children display the most severe academic deficits (Eckenrode et al., 1993; Wodarski, Kurtz, Gaudin, & Howing, 1990). A history of sexual abuse also predicts poor academic performance. Specifically, sexually abused girls demonstrate poorer overall academic performance and receive more negative ratings of classroom social competence than do girls with no history of abuse (Trickett, McBride-Chang, & Putnam, 1994). In general, sexual abuse is negatively related to cognitive ability (Trickett et al., 1994).

Rogosch and Cicchetti (1994) have found that teachers consistently perceive maltreated children as evidencing greater disturbance in social functioning than nonmaltreated children. Specifically, teachers evaluate maltreated children as less socially competent, as less socially accepted by their peers, and as displaying higher levels of behavioral disturbance, particularly externalizing problems. Classroom peers also distinguish maltreated children as more rejected or isolated by peer groups. Physically abused children show the greatest differentiation from their nonmaltreated peers.

An important prospective study conducted by Erickson, Egeland, and Pianta (1989) on the antecedents and consequences of child maltreatment lends support to the findings of school incompetence in maltreated children. Erickson and her colleagues examined maltreated children's adaptation to school and the manner in which they respond to the task of school entry. They report that aggressive, noncompliant, acting-out behavior is common among physically abused children. These children also perform poorly on cognitive tasks in the classroom. The conduct of physically abused children is so problematic that approximately half of them have been either referred for services or retained by the end of their first year in school (Erickson et al., 1989).

Moreover, consistent with findings from other researchers' work on neglected children's performance in school (Eckenrode et al., 1993; Wodarski et al., 1990), Erickson et al. (1989) report that children with histories of neglect manifest the most severe and variable problems in school. They perform worse than other maltreated children on cognitive assessments. In addition, they are anxious and inattentive, lack initiative, rely on teachers for help, and are aggressive toward and withdrawn from their peers. They tend to be uncooperative with teachers and insensitive and unempathic with their peers. By the end of their first year in school, 65% of the neglected children in this sample were either referred for services or retained (Erickson et al., 1989).

Finally, the Erickson study indicates that sexually abused children also exhibit a variety of problems in school. In addition to being anxious, inattentive, and unpopular, sexually abused children are excessively dependent upon their teachers (Erickson et al., 1989). Overall, these children appear passive and lacking in autonomy in their school functioning.

Along these lines, an especially important factor in resolving the task of adaptation to school may be "secure readiness to learn." Aber and Allen (1987) have proposed that effectance motivation, which is the intrinsic desire to deal competently with one's environment, and successful relations with novel adults (i.e., relations characterized by neither dependency nor wariness) are important factors related to children's being able to adapt to their first major out-of-home environment. "Secure readiness to learn" is characterized by high effectance motivation and low dependency. Maltreated children consistently score lower than comparison children on secure readiness to learn (Aber & Allen, 1987; Aber et al., 1989). "Secure readiness to learn" appears to represent a dynamic balance between establishing secure relationships with adults and feeling free to explore the environment in ways that will promote cognitive competence. The findings from Aber and his colleagues are particularly compelling because they are congruent with prior research on how maltreatment affects development in infants and toddlers. At both of these developmental periods, maltreatment interferes with the balance between the motivation to establish secure relationships with adults and the motivation to explore the world in competency-promoting ways.

Maladaptation: The Emergence of Behavior Problems and Psychopathology

As opposed to what is expected in response to an average expectable environment, the ecological conditions associated with maltreatment set in motion a probabilistic path of ontogenesis for maltreated children characterized by an increased likelihood of failure in many stage-salient issues of development. These failures may be isolated to particular domains of functioning, or they may occur in combination with failures in other domains. Specifically, maltreated children are likely to exhibit atypical physiological responsiveness, difficulties in affect differentiation and regulation, dysfunctional attachment relationships, anomalies in self-system processes, deficits in representational

development, problematic peer relationships, and trouble adapting to school. These repeated developmental disruptions create a profile of relatively enduring vulnerability factors that places maltreated children at high risk for future maladaptation (Cicchetti & Lynch, 1993). Although not all maltreated children who have trouble resolving stage-salient issues will develop psychopathology, let alone the same form of pathology, later disturbances in functioning are likely to occur (Cicchetti, 1990).

In their review of the literature on the long-term consequences of childhood physical abuse, Malinosky-Rummell and Hansen (1993) have identified a number of maladaptive responses to maltreatment that may emerge later in adulthood. A major weakness of much of this research, however, is its reliance on retrospective research strategies. (However, see Brewin, Andrews, & Gotlib, 1993, who suggest that concerns about the reliability of retrospective reports may be exaggerated.) As a result, it is difficult to demonstrate the causal relationship between abuse and later outcomes. In addition, it is hard to determine whether the findings from these retrospective studies are generalizable to other abused populations because they usually focus on subjects with identified problems. Keeping these limitations in mind, a history of physical abuse may play a role in the etiology of various negative outcomes in adulthood.

A number of links between histories of abuse and aggressive and violent behavior in adolescents and adults have been demonstrated. For example, higher rates of physical abuse are reported in adolescents who have specified problems with violence and aggression (Lewis, Mallough, & Webb, 1989); adults who are convicted for violent offenses or who are institutionalized and have violent tendencies (Rosenbaum & Bennett, 1986; Sack & Mason, 1980); and adults who abuse their spouses (Kalmuss, 1984; Kroll, Stock, & James, 1985; Rosenbaum & O'Leary, 1981a, 1981b). Self-reported histories of physical abuse also predict nonviolent criminal behavior in adulthood (Pollock et al., 1990) and substance abuse during adolescence (Cavaiola & Schiff, 1988).

Histories of physical abuse also have been linked to other forms of psychological disturbance. For example, a higher incidence of suicide attempts and suicidal ideation among adolescents and adults is associated with childhood abuse (Cavaiola & Schiff, 1988; Deykin, Alpert, & McNamarra, 1985; Kroll et al., 1985). In addition, physically abused female inpatients demonstrate higher levels of psychiatric symptoms than do nonabused inpatients (Bryer, Nelson, Miller, & Kroll, 1987; Chu & Dill, 1990). Moreover, among inpatient and nonpatient women, self-reported physical abuse is related to more negative feelings about interpersonal interactions (Briere & Runtz, 1988; Bryer et al., 1987; Chu & Dill, 1990).

These studies on the long-term consequences of physical abuse are informative regarding the potential risk for negative outcomes that abused children face. However, to understand more clearly the individual developmental pathways that maltreated children take toward adaptation or maladaptation, prospective and longitudinal studies are needed. In a prospective cross-sectional study, Aber et al., (1989) have examined the relationship between parent-reported symptoms and two developmental constructs: secure readiness to learn and outer-directedness (defined as an orientation to problem solving in which children rely on external cues rather than their own cognitive resources). Among preschool-age children, these investigators report no differences between low-SES maltreated and demographically matched nonmaltreated children on parent-reported symptoms. However, the presence of symptoms in these children is associated with secure readiness to learn and outer-directedness in different ways for the two groups. Low secure readiness to learn predicts social withdrawal, aggression, and depression in *maltreated* preschoolers, whereas high outer-directedness predicts social withdrawal and aggression in *nonmaltreated* preschoolers.

The finding of different correlates of symptomatology in maltreated and nonmaltreated preschool children may reflect children's adaptation to the challenges of specific parenting styles. Even though both groups of preschool children appear equally depressed, withdrawn, and aggressive, there may be different underlying developmental pathways that account for similar patterns in the phenotypic expression of symptoms (cf. Cicchetti & Schneider-Rosen, 1986). At least during the preschool years, maltreated children may become symptomatic through a pathway of low secure readiness to learn, whereas nonmaltreated children may become symptomatic through a pathway of high outer-directedness. By the early school years, though, maltreated children are significantly more depressed and socially withdrawn than nonmaltreated children (Aber et al., 1989).

A number of recent studies provide evidence of heightened maladjustment for maltreated children as they progress through development. For example, Trupin, Tarico, Low, Jemelka, and McClellan (1993) have employed a criterion-referenced approach to assess the prevalence of serious emotional disturbances among children between the ages of 3 and 18 years receiving protective services in the state of Washington. These investigators report that over 70% of these children are statistically indistinguishable from children enrolled in the state's most intensive mental health treatment programs. The most common difficulties observed in these maltreated children are school problems, antisocial behaviors, and substance abuse (Trupin et al., 1993). Moreover, an array of investigations have revealed that school-age maltreated children and adolescents manifest higher levels of depressed symptomatology, behavior problems at home and at school, and juvenile delinquency than do nonmaltreated children (Crittenden et al., 1994; Okun et al., 1994; Zingraff, Leiter, Myers, & Johnsen, 1993). In general, problems seem to become more severe and differences between maltreated and nonmaltreated children become more significant as children get older (Crittenden et al., 1994; Dodge et al., 1994).

In addition to higher rates of adjustment problems, studies of maltreated children reveal a higher prevalence of psychiatric symptoms and diagnoses than is observed in nonmaltreated children. Maltreated children exhibit a significantly higher incidence of Attention Deficit/Hyperactivity Disorder, Oppositional Disorder, and Posttraumatic Stress Disorder than do nonmaltreated children according to both parent and child administrations of the Diagnostic Interview for Children and Adolescents (Famularo, Kinscherff, & Fenton, 1992). Child interviews reveal that maltreated children present a significant incidence of psychotic symptomatology, as well as personality and adjustment disorders. Parent interviews show a greater incidence of conduct and mood disorders among maltreated children (Famularo et al., 1992). In

general, maltreatment, especially physical and sexual abuse, is related to a number of psychiatric complaints in childhood and adulthood including panic disorders, anxiety disorders, depression, eating disorders, somatic complaints, dissociation and hysterical symptoms, sexual dysfunction, and borderline personality disorder (Browne & Finkelhor, 1986; Green, 1993; Merry & Andrews, in press; Salzman et al., 1993; Weaver & Clum, 1993; Wolfe & Jaffe, 1991).

Much research has been devoted to examining the effects of maltreatment on three clinical disorders in particular, namely: depression, Posttraumatic Stress Disorder, and Multiple Personality Disorder. Family histories of maltreatment have been linked to childhood depression in a number of studies (Downey, Feldman, Khuri, & Friedman, in press). Many studies show evidence of more depressive symptomatology in maltreated children than in nonmaltreated children (Sternberg et al., 1993; Toth et al., 1992). Moreover, a substantial number of maltreated children meet diagnostic criteria for major depression and/or dysthymia (Kaufman, 1991). A variety of factors appear to mediate the impact of maltreatment on depression including the subtype of maltreatment, children's patterns of relatedness to their mother, their social supports and stressful life events, their attributional styles, and their psychophysiology (Kaufman, 1991; Koverola, Pound, Heger, & Lytle, 1993; Toth & Cicchetti, in press; Toth et al., 1992).

The inherent severity of some forms of abuse may create especially high risk for psychopathology. Sexual abuse, in particular, presents a major source of chronic trauma for many children. Viewing the effects of sexual abuse from a model of chronic trauma, a number of interrelated areas of development are likely to be impaired including the development of self-esteem and self-concepts; beliefs about personal power, control, and self-efficacy; the development of cognitive and social competencies; and emotional and behavioral self-regulation (Putnam & Trickett, 1993). Such widespread impairment is highlighted in investigations of the links between sexual abuse and both Posttraumatic Stress Disorder and the dissociative states associated with Multiple Personality Disorder.

Posttraumatic Stress Disorder (PTSD) refers to a set of psychological symptoms that frequently occur in reaction to an acutely distressing event or series of events. According to the DSM (American Psychiatric Association, 1987, 1994), a diagnosis of PTSD requires the occurrence of a major stressor and the presence of the following symptoms: (a) frequent reexperiencing of the event through flashbacks, nightmares, or intrusive thoughts; (b) a numbing of general responsiveness to current events; and (c) persistent symptoms of increased arousal. Child sexual abuse has been shown to produce both immediate and long-term PTSD symptoms in some individuals (Briere & Runtz, 1993). For example, McLeer, Callaghan, Henry, and Wallen (1994) administered the Schedule for Affective Disorders and Schizophrenia for School-Age Children-Epidemiologic Version (Orvaschel, Puig-Antich, Chambers, Tabrizi, & Johnson, 1982) to a clinically referred sample of sexually abused children. These investigators found that sexually abused children are far more likely than a well-matched group of nonmaltreated disadvantaged children to develop Posttraumatic Stress Disorder. In general, sexually abused children display a variety of PTSD symptoms, and they exhibit them at higher rates than children experiencing other forms of abuse (Deblinger, McLeer, Atkins, Ralphe, & Foa, 1989; Kendall-Tackett, Williams, & Finkelhor, 1993; Kiser, Heston, Millsap, & Pruitt, 1991; Merry & Andrews, in press). Specific aspects of the abuse such as penetration, duration and frequency of the abuse, the use of force, and the perpetrator's relationship to the child all affect the degree of PTSD symptomatology (Alexander, 1993; Kendall-Tackett et al., 1993; Kiser et al., 1991).

Dissociation is a complex psychophysiological process manifested by a disruption in the normally integrative processes of memory, identity, and consciousness (American Psychiatric Association, 1987, 1994). Dissociation is conceptualized as occurring along a continuum ranging from the normal minor dissociations of everyday life, such as daydreaming, to the pathological manifestations seen in the profound disruptions to self and memory that occur in multiple personality disorder and fugue states (Fischer & Ayoub, 1994; Putnam & Trickett, 1993; Westen, 1994). In general, the experience of sexual abuse appears to render victims especially vulnerable to disturbances involving soma and self (Nash, Hulsey, Sexton, Harralson, & Lambert, 1993). Clinical work with victims of sexual abuse suggests that dissociation is used as a defense against the overwhelming trauma they have experienced. Higher rates of dissociation and affective splitting are seen in sexually abused children than in other comparison groups (Calverley et al., 1994; Kirby, Chu, & Dill, 1993; Nash, Hulsey, et al., 1993). These disturbances in self-functioning may be especially apparent in problems with self-definition and integration, and in problems with self-regulatory processes (Cole & Putnam, 1992). Once again, characteristics of the abuse such as age of onset, as well as the presence of family pathology, appear to be related to the development of dissociative symptoms (Kirby et al., 1993; Nash, Zivney, & Hulsey, 1993).

Resilient Outcomes

The notion that an average expectable environment is necessary for species-typical development suggests that competent outcomes in maltreated children are highly improbable due to wide-ranging disturbances in the maltreatment ecology. However, although there is documented risk for maladaptation associated with maltreatment, the absence of an average expectable environment does not condemn maltreated children to negative developmental outcomes later in life. Despite the relatively low probability of adaptive outcomes for maltreated children (in comparison with nonmaltreated children), individuals' self-righting tendencies (Waddington, 1942, 1957) in combination with the presence of any environmental protective factors may result in some maltreated children achieving developmental competence.

Very little work has been done investigating resilient outcomes in maltreated children. One reason for this is the lack of agreement on what constitutes resilient outcomes in children. Recently, a special issue of the journal *Development and Psychopathology* was devoted to examining such matters (Cicchetti & Garmezy, 1993). As an interesting example of this point, Kaufman and her colleagues have highlighted how variations in the source, type, and number of assessments that are obtained can affect the proportion of children who are classified as resilient (Kaufman, Cook, Arny, Jones, & Pittinsky, 1994). Changes in data collection and data reduction procedures can alter findings on resilient outcomes as well. However, in devising operational criteria to define resiliency, the use of multidimensional assessment strategies has some advantages. Primary among these is that they reduce the likelihood of falsely labeling a child as resilient who has competencies in one domain but significant problems in another (Kaufman et al., 1994).

With regard to resilience in maltreated children, some relevant work has been carried out with nonmaltreating populations that may shed light on this issue. For example, examining the presence of contextual risk and protective factors at distal and proximal levels of the child's ecology may provide insight into how some maltreated children demonstrate resilience (cf. Baldwin et al., 1993; Richters & Martinez, 1993b). Are there factors at other levels of the environment that can protect maltreated children from the negative influences of their family microsystems? Research that is guided by an ecological-transactional perspective may be informative. Unfortunately, initial studies of resilience that reflect such a perspective suggest even greater obstacles to resilient outcomes in maltreated children. For example, in children who are exposed to high levels of community violence (which is the case for many maltreated children), their chances of adaptational failure rise dramatically as a function of living in unstable and/or unsafe homes (Richters & Martinez, 1993b). A stable, safe home environment contributes to adaptational success in such children. By definition, this type of home environment is absent for most maltreated children.

The particular findings regarding resilient outcomes in maltreated children have been weak, largely because it is difficult to identify maltreated children who are doing well. Some studies have focused on specific positive outcomes, such as the avoidance of criminality in maltreated children. However, such avoidance does not necessarily demonstrate developmental competence (Widom, 1991). Even defining resilience by the relatively liberal criteria of "absence of significant problems" (as determined by normative cutoff scores on standardized assessments of adaptation) results in surprisingly few maltreated children being classified as resilient (Kaufman et al., 1994). Furthermore, Farber and Egeland's (1987) study of resilience in maltreated children indicates that *none* of the maltreated children in their sample were functioning competently across the entire period of infancy through preschool. A few of their maltreated children did show improved functioning in isolated domains. These improvements, however, were usually transient and were associated with factors such as placement in foster care, the availability of a caring adult, and intensive family intervention (Farber & Egeland, 1987). The most recent assessment of these children in the sixth grade shows that all these children are demonstrating clear dysfunction as the result of maltreatment (Egeland, Carlson, & Sroufe, 1993).

A peripheral issue that may be related to resilience is the occasional occurrence of secure attachments in maltreated children (Cicchetti, Toth et al., in press; Toth & Cicchetti, in press). Such an achievement could be considered an example of a stage-specific resilient outcome. The possibility of secure attachments in maltreated children is consistent with models that suggest that transactions among parent, child, and environmental factors determine quality of attachment (cf. Cicchetti & Schneider-Rosen, 1986; Cummings & Cicchetti, 1990). According to such conceptualizations, a maltreated child could manifest a secure attachment with the caregiver because of other factors that have protected the child, such as the provision of intervention services to the family. In these instances, the child may evidence resiliency over time (Cicchetti et al., in press). This outcome is most likely if the maltreatment has been transient. In cases of severe, chronic maltreatment perpetrated by the caregiver, secure attachment relationships are highly unlikely.

Finally, in a recent investigation of resilience, maltreated children as a group show lower overall competence across multiple areas of adaptation than nonmaltreated children (Cicchetti, Rogosch, Lynch, & Holt, 1993). However, whereas more maltreated children than nonmaltreated children exhibit low levels of competence, an equal proportion of maltreated and nonmaltreated children demonstrate moderate to high levels of competence. Ego resiliency, ego control, and self-esteem have been found to predict individual differences in competent functioning in these children (Cicchetti, Rogosch et al., 1993). More specifically, ego resiliency, ego overcontrol, and positive self-esteem account for significant amounts of variance in the adaptive functioning of maltreated children. In contrast, only ego resiliency and positive self-esteem contribute to adaptation in nonmaltreated children. This finding of a differential contribution of ego control for the two groups in predicting adaptive or resilient functioning suggests that ego overcontrol may serve a protective function for maltreated children. A reserved, controlled approach to the environment may help these children to be more attuned to adapting to the adverse conditions of their home environments and may protect them from being targets of continued maltreatment incidents (Cicchetti, Rogosch et al., 1993; cf. Crittenden & DiLalla, 1988).

LESSONS FOR NORMAL AND ABNORMAL DEVELOPMENT

The discipline of developmental psychopathology is built on the assumption that a developmental approach can be applied to any aspect of behavior and to all populations, both normal and atypical. Developmental psychopathologists believe that it is possible to learn more about an organism's normal functioning by studying its pathology and, likewise, more about its pathology by studying its normal condition (Cicchetti, 1984, 1990; Rutter, 1986; Sroufe & Rutter, 1984). To theorize about development without considering the deviations that might be expected from prominent and wide-ranging intra- and extra organismic disturbances, as well as the transactions that occur among them, would result in incomplete and ambiguous accounts of ontogenesis (Cicchetti, 1990). The study of child maltreatment provides researchers with an excellent opportunity to examine such developmental deviations and the ecological disturbances associated with them.

A powerful example of the effect of a nonoptimal caregiving environment on the process of ontogenesis and its potential for augmenting, challenging, and informing developmental theory can be gained from the case of "Genie," a child discovered in adolescence after having been subjected to a childhood of extreme maltreatment (Curtiss, 1977). Until her discovery at 13 ½ years of age, Genie existed in an environment largely devoid of visual, tactile, or auditory stimulation. It is reported that not only was Genie severely abused but also that she was virtually never spoken to. Observations of the unfolding of Genie's development after her discovery have provided insights into a number of issues of interest to developmentalists. For example, Genie's ability to acquire some aspects of language suggests that the original critical period proposed for language acquisition may have covered too narrow a span of time. Similarly, Genie's success in forming social relationships with the professionals who investigated her development suggests that individuals can still form attachment relationships later in life even if socially isolated during childhood.

Many additional lessons about development can be learned through the study of child maltreatment. For example, taking an ecological-transactional approach toward understanding normal development may help to organize current thinking about development in its multiple influences, as well as guide future research. As applied to the study of maltreatment, an ecological-transactional model of development points out that factors from many levels of the individual's ecology are operating simultaneously to influence ontogeny and adaptation. It emphasizes the linkages among the various psychological and biological domains of development and stresses that factors internal and external to the individual continually affect each other and influence the direction of the individual's developmental pathway.

By studying the effects of severe environmental disturbances (such as maltreatment) on individual development, it may be possible to examine processes that normally are so subtle and gradual that they are not observed (Cicchetti & Sroufe, 1976; Masten, 1989). For example, through investigating the development of children who have not received a benign rearing environment (e.g., youngsters who have been maltreated), researchers may be able to elucidate the impact that caregiving experiences can exert on brain function. Specifically, inquiries into the physiological development of maltreated children can help us to learn how caretaking experiences shape the ontogenesis of children's neurobiological and psychophysiological systems and consequent biobehavioral organization. Also, the ecological-transactional approach that has been applied to child maltreatment allows researchers to focus on periods of developmental transition and on how vulnerability and protective processes associated with each of these transitions operate for different children (Masten, 1989). In particular, studies of maltreated children make clear that failure on the major tasks of development results in cumulative risk for future maladaptation and psychopathology. Furthermore, there is evidence for various critical periods in development associated with different caregiving experiences. This idea is supported by the different experience-dependent effects that emerge when maltreatment occurs at different points in development. Overall, the study of child maltreatment provides a good initial test of the ecological-transactional model of development. However, additional theory and model testing needs to be carried out on other populations.

Research on child maltreatment also has shed light on several reputed mechanisms of development. As has been discussed, maltreated children's emerging patterns of physiological responsiveness play a role in their subsequent biobehavioral organization. These early patterns of responsiveness and organization are important factors in shaping the nature of children's interactions with the environment and, as a result, in influencing their developmental trajectories.

Representational models also are believed to be a mechanism in the continuity and coherence of individual development. Research with maltreated children has helped to inform us about the nature and function of these models. For example, as discussed earlier, there is evidence that people activate both specific and generalized representational models of themselves and others as they deal with their interpersonal environment (Lynch & Cicchetti, 1991). Moreover, maltreated children may be predisposed to employing generalized models that are closed to the processing of new information (Crittenden & DiLalla, 1988; Lynch, 1992; Lynch & Cicchetti, 1991). This preconscious cognitive strategy of utilizing generalized or closed representational models may be a defense that protects maltreated children from having to deal with the negative and angry affects that characterize their family interactions. Rather than openly evaluating and adjusting their representational models on the basis of new interpersonal information, the models of maltreated children may be more defensive in nature, thus closing them off to new experiences with caregivers and nonfamily members (Crittenden & DiLalla, 1988). Such a strategy may be maladaptive in other contexts, however, because it inhibits maltreated children from incorporating alternative information about themselves and others. If this is true, then it would suggest that having representational models that are open to new information, and that being able to appropriately employ both generalized and specific models, might be associated with more competent development in normal children. Children's representational models also influence the manner in which they process social information more generally. Evidence of this can be seen in the hypervigilance maltreated children display in attending to threatening stimuli (Rieder & Cicchetti, 1989).

Research on child maltreatment also informs, and can be informed by, the significant functions of normal parenting (Rogosch, Cicchetti, Shields, & Toth, in press). The specific acts and omissions that define child maltreatment are salient features of maltreated children's microsystems. It is in this immediate context of deviant parenting that maltreated children's atypical development takes shape. Closer analysis of the maltreating caregiving environment and its links with poor developmental outcomes can shed light on the protective processes associated with appropriate, normal parenting.

Finally, studies of resilience in maltreated children provide information about the multiple possible pathways of development. To begin, there is evidence for the principles of both equifinality and multifinality (Bertalanffy, 1968) in maltreated children's attempts at adaptation. Despite having different specific experiences, many maltreated children exhibit similar failures in the tasks of development (i.e., "equifinality"). On the other hand, not all maltreated children are equally affected by their experiences, with some children displaying resilient outcomes and the rest exhibiting developmental incompetence (i.e., "multifinality"). Examination of maltreated children's development and struggles with adaptation teaches us about the range and variability of individual response to challenge and adversity. Cases of maltreated children who succeed at particular tasks of development (such as forming a secure attachment) or who otherwise achieve competent levels of adaptation teach us about the self-righting properties inherent to development that result in a type of canalization of species-typical outcomes despite poor quality care (Sameroff & Chandler, 1975; Waddington, 1957). On the other hand, findings that indicate the extreme rarity with which maltreated children display resilient outcomes point out some of the real constraints on children's self-righting abilities.

FUTURE DIRECTIONS AND RECOMMENDATIONS

We began this chapter by posing the question: What happens to individual development when there are severe disturbances in the early caretaking environment? In addressing this question, we used child maltreatment as an example of profound environmental failure. The theoretical construct of an average expectable environment has been instrumental in formalizing our conceptualization of the ways in which maltreatment functions as a severe disruption of the child's caretaking environment. By failing to provide the species-typical expected conditions evolutionarily linked to normal ontogenesis, the ecology of child maltreatment places these children at risk for distortions and deviations in development. Furthermore, from a systems view of development, maltreatment experiences pose serious challenges to the organism-environment "coactions" that are the mechanism of ontogenetic change. Maltreated children progress along an array of probabilistic developmental pathways that often eventuate in the unsuccessful resolution of the salient ontogenetic tasks of the life course. The occurrence of resilient outcomes in some maltreated children, however, points out that the self-righting tendencies in human development may be strong, even in the face of deviance and failure in the environment.

Beyond these issues, given the scope of the problem of child maltreatment, there is a growing need for researchers to come to a more complete understanding of its etiology and sequelae. Furthermore, practitioners need to be able to use this information as they treat the causes and consequences of maltreatment. Most importantly, maltreated children need to be able to reap the benefits of this increased knowledge. Keeping in mind the limitations and the strengths of the existing work on child maltreatment, we make the following recommendations for the future.

1. Consistent and uniformly applied definitions of maltreatment need to be developed. The absence of such definitions seriously impedes efforts to attain a greater understanding of this grave problem. Initially, researchers need to agree among themselves about how they will define maltreatment and its different subtypes, and how they will identify maltreated subjects in their investigations. This will improve the generalizability of findings in these studies as well as bring about more precision in our understanding of the exact experiences that confront the children in these families. Eventually, there should be uniformity in the definitions of maltreatment that are utilized for different purposes (e.g., research, clinical work, legal issues) so that there can be clear communication among the various disciplines working in this area.

2. State and county data systems should be improved, and uniform information about maltreatment cases should be recorded. This will increase the clarity of the information that is known about particular cases of maltreatment. More precise information about maltreatment cases will assist researchers in the specification of the independent variable(s) used in their studies, and of the nature of the caregiving experienced by the children. Moreover, it will help clinicians to be better informed about the histories of the cases that they are involved with.

3. Continued research on the etiology of child maltreatment needs to be conducted. It is essential that large-scale prospective studies be initiated (cf. Cicchetti & Rizley, 1981; Erickson et al., 1989; Pianta, Egeland, & Erickson, 1989). Rather than focusing on specific precursors of maltreatment, interactions among variables at multiple ecological levels should be examined. In addition, competing models and theories of the etiology of maltreatment should be tested to improve our understanding of these processes. Similarities and differences among the etiologies of different forms of maltreatment should be specified to enhance the quality of future prevention and intervention efforts. In a related vein, studies of the etiology of maltreatment should be conducted across various social class, cultural, and ethnic populations (cf. Betancourt & Lopez, 1993).

4. Continued research on the consequences of maltreatment for children's development is needed as well. Increasingly, these studies should employ prospective longitudinal designs that will allow scientists to articulate the causal links between maltreatment and developmental outcomes. Moreover, additional research needs to be conducted on how varying aspects of maltreatment (including subtype, frequency, severity, chronicity, perpetrator, and age of onset) influence developmental outcome. For example, the timing of the maltreatment of the child's development could affect the differentiation, integration, and organization of experience-expectant and experience-dependent sensitive periods across biological and psychological domains. To capture a comprehensive understanding of the effects of maltreatment on children's development, a careful assessment must be obtained of when during the child's development the maltreatment occurred, how the experience impacted the emergence of competencies during that period, and what the long-term implications were for the child's later adaptation.

A multicontextual approach to maltreatment outcome research should be employed as well. These studies need to take place in the varied contexts in which maltreated children develop (including day care, out-of-home care, and foster care) to determine if there are context-specific effects of maltreatment. Additionally, empirical work must be conducted on culturally, racially, and ethnically diverse samples. As with research on the etiology of maltreatment, empirical work must be conducted on diverse samples.

In addition, interactions among variables at multiple ecological levels, and their impact on further development, should be examined. This will permit researchers to test competing models of the processes by which maltreatment influences development. It also will provide practitioners with more clear information about factors relevant to their treatment efforts.

5. The vast majority of the empirical investigations of the developmental sequelae of child maltreatment have focused on infancy and childhood. In keeping with the life-span perspective advocated by developmental systems theorists (cf. Erikson, 1950), cross-sectional and prospective longitudinal studies of the consequences of maltreatment must be conducted with adolescents and adults (see, e.g., Garbarino, 1989). Because the probabilistic epigenesis view of organizational and systems theorists holds that change is possible at any point in the life span (Cicchetti, 1993), the prospective longitudinal investigations are especially crucial for elucidating our understanding of the mechanisms that promote developmental continuity or discontinuity.

6. Sampling issues need to be addressed rigorously by maltreatment researchers. Different kinds of sampling biases in studies of maltreatment create problems for those who are trying to interpret their findings (Widom, 1988). *Criterion-dependent* biases are those that involve problems in the equivalence of definitions used by researchers and in the comparability of the populations they investigate. *Method-dependent* biases are those that are related to differences in the basic methods and sources of information that are used in determining the maltreatment status of subjects.

Other sampling issues need to be addressed as well. In longitudinal studies of the effects of maltreatment, it is critical to *confirm the maltreatment status of subjects over time*. The process of confirming maltreatment status is most important for subjects in the comparison groups of these studies. Most prospective studies of the effects of maltreatment include comparison groups of nonmaltreated children who, because they are demographically matched with the maltreated group, are at high risk for experiencing future maltreatment. If children's status is not periodically confirmed (e.g., by checking official records of reported maltreatment cases), then investigators run the risk at future assessment times of misclassifying some children who originally were recruited as nonmaltreated comparison subjects, but who have since experienced maltreatment. Failure to monitor maltreatment status carefully would result in a diluting of the accuracy of the comparison group that makes it difficult to identify true maltreatment-nonmaltreatment differences in outcome. This issue points out some of the considerable challenges faced in conducting longitudinal research on child maltreatment.

Two other sampling concerns typically receive little attention from maltreatment researchers. First, more studies including fathers need to be conducted. Most investigations focus on children and their maltreating mothers. Little is known about the role of mothers versus fathers on the consequences of maltreatment. Second, studies of maltreatment in samples from middle socioeconomic strata need to be conducted. Although overrepresented among low-SES families, maltreatment is found in families that range the span of socioeconomic status. Different patterns of effects may be observed in maltreated children who are not faced with the additional burden of economic disadvantage.

7. Basic research is needed to clarify the nature and function of proposed mechanisms of development. The study of child maltreatment has made important contributions to an improved understanding of several mechanisms that are believed to be important in the coherence of development. In particular, there has been substantial interest in the role that representational models of attachment figures, the self, and the self in relations to others play in maltreated children's development. However, much is still unknown about the nature of these models.

At the most fundamental level, researchers need to learn more about the formation of representational models, and their link to the episodic, semantic, and procedural memory systems (Crittenden, 1990; Tulving, 1985). What is known about the neural substrates of these memory systems? How does the ontogeny of these systems relate to the development of representational abilities? How do particular types of experience influence the transactions among biology, memory, and representation? Studies aimed at addressing these questions will help researchers and theorists to understand more about this proposed developmental mechanism.

Additionally, researchers need to delineate further the characteristics of representational models, and examine their function. For example, there is some evidence regarding the existence of both specific and generalized representational models. In addition, there is indirect evidence regarding the concordance found among children's representational models. However, there is no direct information about whether some children's representational models remain open versus closed to new information, despite speculation regarding such qualities in maltreated children's models. In addition, data are needed on whether and when children form single versus multiple models of the same person. A single model of a relationship figure is believed to reflect a coherent representation of that person. Conversely, some individuals may possess multiple models of the same person. These models may reflect different, affectively charged perceptions of the relationship figure that the individual is unable to integrate into a coherent, single representation.

Many of these questions have clinical significance. For example, do maltreated children tend to employ closed generalized models, and is this maladaptive in nonfamilial contexts? Could having discordant representational models be a predictor of greater adaptation in maltreated children? It is possible that possessing representational models that are discordant with the (negative) models of their caregiver may help maltreated children to experience greater interpersonal success outside the family (Lynch & Cicchetti, 1992). Finally, what adaptive function is served by forming multiple models of relationship figures, and could it impair the individual's ability to create coherent, integrated representations in other contexts?

An overarching challenge for researchers interested in this mechanism of development will be to devise appropriate assessments of representational models. For the most part, all that is known about the nature of children's representational models is inferred from the pattern of their behavior with their caregiver. Some self-report assessments asking children to discuss their relationships with others also are available. The recent

development of other narrative procedures may be fruitful in accessing children's representational models (cf. Bretherton, Ridgeway, & Cassidy, 1990; Buchsbaum, Toth, Clyman, Cicchetti, & Emde, 1992). Psychophysiological experiments such as investigations of cortical event-related potentials to emotional stimuli also may reveal something important about underlying representational models, including how caregiving can affect biological processes (and vice versa) and how representational models influence the processing of information. Most likely, researchers will need to converge on representational models through a variety of methodologies.

In general, the more that is understood about mechanisms of development such as representational models, the more we will know about the processes involved in developmental change and coherence. In the case of child maltreatment, this increased knowledge may help clinicians who are designing interventions to ameliorate maltreatment's negative effects.

8. Researchers need to identify the risk and protective mechanisms that influence maltreatment's impact on development. This line of inquiry should investigate the connections among different types of psychological, social, and biological risk and protective factors. Through such studies, it may be possible to identify factors that either mediate or moderate the effects of maltreatment on children's development.

In planning such studies on the pathways whereby maltreatment impacts the process of ontogenesis, it will be important to anticipate and address the diversity of possible developmental outcomes. For example, maltreated children may manifest deviations in the organization and integration of their development and in the resolution of salient tasks, with or without concomitant psychopathology. Conversely, some maltreated children may reveal a coherent developmental organization and successfully resolve salient issues, with or without psychopathology (Cicchetti, Rogosch et al., 1993). The diverse outcomes that eventuate from maltreatment shed light on the central question posed in this chapter. On the one hand, maltreated children who proceed along deviant ontogenetic pathways attest to the deleterious effects that nontypical environments can exert on individual development, and to the constraints they place on the self-righting mechanisms of ontogenesis. On the other hand, those resilient maltreated children who develop normally despite being exposed to extreme environmental adversity illustrate the multiple alternate pathways to competent adaptation and species-typical epigenesis.

9. Intergenerational studies of maltreatment should be conducted to identify the relevant cycles and key factors that contribute to the perpetuation of child maltreatment and its deleterious consequences across generations, as well as to uncover those factors that bring about its discontinuation.

10. Research on child maltreatment needs to be integrated with work from other relevant fields such as community violence, family violence, and spousal violence. Such an integration will contribute to a more ecologically complete perspective on maltreatment and related forms of trauma (see, e.g., Cicchetti & Lynch, 1993; Cicchetti, Toth, & Lynch, 1993).

11. Research on child maltreatment needs to be integrated into the social policy arena (Cicchetti & Toth, 1993). Many investigations on the causes and consequences of maltreatment have implications for prevention and intervention efforts (Institute of Medicine, 1994). For example, in a seminal preventive investigation influenced by developmental-ecological theory, Olds and Henderson (1989) have shown that the incidence of maltreatment can be greatly reduced in high-risk families. Moreover, the studies of the developmental consequences of child maltreatment suggest that intervention efforts should be targeted for the earliest possible time subsequent to the confirmation of maltreatment (Cicchetti & Toth, 1992). This will help to curtail the pattern of one developmental failure leading to another that is seen in many maltreated children (Toth & Cicchetti, 1993). Parents should be involved in the intervention and treatment process because an ecological-transactional model implicates the family system, and this is especially relevant in the case of maltreatment. Educators and clinicians working with maltreated children should understand the developmental consequences of maltreatment so that they can provide the appropriate therapeutic supports for fostering positive development. Teachers in particular must be sensitive to their role as potential alternative attachment figures who can ameliorate the negative development of maltreated children (Lynch & Cicchetti, 1992). Finally, sensitivity toward the ethnic, racial, and cultural milieu needs to be maintained in the provision of therapy to maltreated children (Toth & Cicchetti, 1993).

There needs to be an increased integration among the child welfare and mental health systems, the legal system, and the research community. Researchers must become increasingly invested in disseminating their findings in a form that is readily accessible by professionals from the legal and mental health systems. Furthermore, this same type of information should be provided to legislators and social policy advocates as they make decisions that affect children and families. Finally, educational efforts in preparing professionals to meet the needs of maltreated children must be improved.

Attention to all these recommendations should increase our understanding of what happens when there are severe disturbances in the caregiving environment and should improve our ability to respond effectively when they occur. Both research and applied endeavors will benefit from an attainment of these goals. Perhaps most importantly, the conceptualization of maltreatment as a dramatic departure from the average expectable environment enhances our understanding of functioning under both normal and atypical circumstances. Because developmental psychopathologists are interested in elucidating mechanisms contributing to adaptation in conditions of adversity, as well as to understanding the roots of maladaptive outcome, studies of conditions such as those associated with child maltreatment hold great promise for the advancement of developmental theory.

REFERENCES

Aber, J. L. (1994). Poverty, violence and child development: Untangling family and community level effects. In C. A. Nelson (Ed.), *Minnesota Symposia on Child Psychology: Vol. 27. Threats to optimal development: Integrating biological, psychological and social risk factors.* (pp. 229–272). Hillsdale, NJ: Erlbaum.

Aber, J. L., & Allen, J. P. (1987). The effects of maltreatment on young children's socio-emotional development: An attachment theory perspective. *Developmental Psychology, 23,* 406–414.

Aber, J. L., Allen, J., Carlson, V., & Cicchetti, D. (1989). The effects of maltreatment on development during early childhood: Recent studies and their theoretical, clinical, and policy implications. In D. Cicchetti & V. Carlson (Eds.), *Child maltreatment: Theory and research on the causes and consequences of child abuse and neglect* (pp. 579–619). New York: Cambridge University Press.

Aber, J. L., & Zigler, E. (1981). Developmental considerations in the definition of child maltreatment. *New Directions for Child Development, 11,* 1–29.

Aber, M., & Rappaport, J. (1994). The violence of prediction: The uneasy relationship between social science and social policy. *Applied and Preventive Psychology, 3,* 43–54.

Ainsworth, M. D. S., Blehar, M. C., Waters, E., & Wall, S. (1978). *Patterns of attachment: A psychological study of the Strange Situation.* Hillsdale, NJ: Erlbaum.

Ainsworth, M. D. S., & Wittig, B. A. (1969). Attachment and the exploratory behavior of one-year-olds in a strange situation. In B. M. Foss (Ed.), *Determinants of infant behavior* (Vol. 4, pp. 113–136). London: Methuen.

Alessandri, S. M. (1991). Play and social behavior in maltreated preschoolers. *Development and Psychopathology, 3,* 191–205.

Alessandri, S. M. (1992). Mother-child interactional correlates of maltreated and nonmaltreated children's play behavior. *Development and Psychopathology, 4,* 257–270.

Alexander, P. C. (1993). The differential effects of abuse characteristics and attachment in the prediction of long-term effects of sexual abuse. *Journal of Interpersonal Violence, 8,* 346–362.

Allen, D. M., & Tarnowski, K. J. (1989). Depressive characteristics of physically abused children. *Journal of Abnormal Child Psychology, 17,* 1–11.

Allen, R. E., & Oliver, J. M. (1982). The effects of child maltreatment on language development. *Child Abuse and Neglect, 6,* 299–305.

Altemeier, W., O'Connor, S., Vietze, P., Sandler, H., & Sherrod, L. (1982). Antecedents of child abuse. *Journal of Pediatrics, 100,* 823–829.

American Psychiatric Association. (1987). *Diagnostic and statistical manual of mental disorders (3rd ed., rev.).* Washington, DC: Author.

American Psychiatric Association. (1994). *Diagnostic and statistical manual of mental disorders* (4th ed.). Washington, DC: Author.

Anderson, J., Martin, J., Mullen, P., Romans, S., & Herbison, P. (1993). Prevalence of childhood sexual abuse experiences in a community sample of women. *Journal of the American Academy of Child and Adolescent Psychiatry, 32,* 911–919.

Baldwin, A. L., Baldwin, C. P., Kasser, T., Zax, M., Sameroff, A., & Seifer, R. (1993). Contextual risk and resiliency during late adolescence. *Development and Psychopathology, 5,* 741–762.

Barahal, R., Waterman, J., & Martin, H. (1981). The social-cognitive development of abused children. *Journal of Consulting and Clinical Psychology, 49,* 508–516.

Barnett, D., Ganiban, J., & Cicchetti, D. (1992, May). *Emotional reactivity, regulation, and attachment organization in children with Type D attachments: A longitudinal analysis across 12, 18, and 24 months of age.* Paper presented at the biennial meeting of the International Conference on Infant Studies, Miami, FL.

Barnett, D., Manly, J. T., & Cicchetti, D. (1991). Continuing toward an operational definition of psychological maltreatment. *Development and Psychopathology, 3,* 19–29.

Barnett, D., Manly, J. T., & Cicchetti, D. (1993). Defining child maltreatment: The interface between policy and research. In D. Cicchetti & S. L. Toth (Eds.), *Child abuse, child development, and social policy* (pp. 7–73). Norwood, NJ: Ablex.

Bartholomew, K. (1990). Avoidance of intimacy: An attachment perspective. *Journal of Social and Personal Relationships, 7,* 147–178.

Baumrind, D. (1993). The average expectable environment is not good enough: A response to Scarr. *Child Development, 64,* 1299–1317.

Beeghly, M., & Cicchetti, D. (1994). Child maltreatment, attachment, and the self system: Emergence of an internal state lexicon in toddlers at high social risk. *Development and Psychopathology, 6,* 5–30.

Belsky, J. (1980). Child maltreatment: An ecological integration. *American Psychologist, 35,* 320–335.

Belsky, J. (1984). The determinants of parenting: A process model. *Child Development, 55,* 83–96.

Belsky, J. (1993). Etiology of child maltreatment: A developmental-ecological analysis. *Psychological Bulletin, 114,* 413–433.

Bernath, M. S., Feshbach, N. D., & Gralinski, J. H. (1993, March). *Physical maltreatment and trust in peers: Feelings, reasons, and behavioral intentions.* Paper presented at the biennial meeting of the Society for Research in Child Development, New Orleans.

Bertalanffy, L. von. (1968). *General system theory.* New York: Braziller.

Besharov, D. (1981). Toward better research on child abuse and neglect: Making definitional issues an explicit methodological concern. *Child Abuse and Neglect, 5,* 383–389.

Betancourt, H., & Lopez, S. R. (1993). The study of culture, ethnicity, and race in American psychology. *American Psychologist, 48,* 629–637.

Bischof, N. (1975). A systems approach toward the functional connections of attachment and fear. *Child Development, 46,* 801–817.

Black, J., & Greenough, W. (1986). Induction of pattern in neural structure by experience: Implications for cognitive development. In M. Lamb, A. Brown, & B. Rogoff (Eds.), *Advances in developmental psychology* (Vol. 4, pp. 1–44). Hillsdale, NJ: Erlbaum.

Bowlby, J. (1982). *Attachment and loss: Vol. 1. Attachment.* New York: Basic Books. (Original work published in 1969.)

Bowlby, J. (1973). *Attachment and loss: Vol. 2. Separation.* New York: Basic Books.

Bowlby, J. (1980). *Attachment and loss: Vol. 3. Loss.* New York: Basic Books.

Bowlby, J. (1988). *A secure base.* New York: Basic Books.

Brassard, M., Hart, S., & Hardy, D. (1993). The psychological maltreatment rating scales. *Child Abuse and Neglect, 17,* 715–729.

Bretherton, I. (1990). Open communication and internal working models: Their role in the development of attachment relationships. In R. Thompson (Ed.), *Nebraska Symposium on Motivation: Vol. 36. Socioemotional development* (pp. 57–113). Lincoln: University of Nebraska Press.

Bretherton, I. (1991). Pouring new wine into old bottles: The social self as internal working model. In M. Gunnar & L. A. Sroufe (Eds.), *The Minnesota Symposia on Child Development: Vol. 23. Self processes and development* (pp. 1–41). Hillsdale, NJ: Erlbaum.

Bretherton, I., Ridgeway, D., & Cassidy, J. (1990). Assessing internal working models of the attachment relationship: An attachment story completion task for 3-year-olds. In M. Greenberg, D. Cicchetti, & E. M. Cummings (Eds.), *Attachment in the preschool years* (pp. 273–308). Chicago: University of Chicago Press.

Bretherton, I., & Waters, E. (Eds.). (1985). Growing points of attachment theory and research. *Monographs of the Society for Research in Child Development, 50,* No. 209.

Brewin, C., Andrews, B., & Gotlib, I. (1993). Psychopathology and early experience: A reappraisal of retrospective reports. *Psychological Bulletin, 113,* 82–98.

Briere, J., & Runtz, M. (1988). Multivariate correlates of childhood psychological and physical maltreatment among university women. *Child Abuse and Neglect, 12,* 331–341.

Briere, J., & Runtz, M. (1993). Childhood sexual abuse: Long-term sequelae and implications for psychological assessment. *Journal of Interpersonal Violence, 8,* 312–330.

Bronfenbrenner, U. (1977). Toward an experimental ecology of human development. *American Psychologist, 32,* 513–531.

Browne, A., & Finkelhor, D. (1986). Impact of child sexual abuse: A review of the literature. *Psychological Bulletin, 99,* 66–77.

Brunquell, D., Crichton, L., & Egeland, B. (1981). Maternal personality and attitude in disturbances of child rearing. *American Journal of Orthopsychiatry, 51,* 680–690.

Bryer, J. B., Nelson, B. A., Miller, J. B., & Krol, P. A. (1987). Childhood sexual and physical abuse as factors in adult psychiatric illness. *American Journal of Psychiatry, 144,* 1426–1430.

Buchsbaum, H. K., Toth, S. L., Clyman, R. B., Cicchetti, D., & Emde, R. N. (1992). The use of a narrative story stem technique with maltreated children: Implications for theory and practice. *Development and Psychopathology, 4,* 603–625.

Bugental, D. B., Blue, J., Cortez, V., Fleck, K., & Rodriguez, A. (1992). Influences of witnessed affect on information processing in children. *Child Development, 63,* 774–786.

Burgess, R. L., & Conger, R. D. (1978). Family interaction in abusive, neglectful, and normal families. *Child Development, 49,* 1163–1173.

Butts, J. A., & Connors-Beatty, D. J. (1993, April). The juvenile court's response to violent offenders: 1985–1989. *Juvenile Justice Bulletin: Office of Juvenile Justice and Delinquency Prevention Update on Statistics.* Washington, DC: U.S. Department of Justice.

Butts, J. A., & Poe, E. (1993, December). Offenders in juvenile court, 1990. *Juvenile Justice Bulletin: Office of Juvenile Justice and Delinquency Prevention Update on Statistics.* Washington, DC: U.S. Department of Justice.

Calverley, R. M., Fischer, K. W., & Ayoub, C. (1994). Complex splitting of self-representations in sexually abused adolescent girls. *Development and Psychopathology, 6,* 195–213.

Carlson, V., Cicchetti, D., Barnett, D., & Braunwald, K. (1989). Finding order in disorganization: Lessons from research on maltreated infants' attachments to their caregivers. In D. Cicchetti & V. Carlson (Eds.), *Child maltreatment: Theory and research on the causes and consequences of child abuse and neglect* (pp. 494–528). New York: Cambridge University Press.

Cavaiola, A. A., & Schiff, M. (1988). Behavioral sequelae of physical and/or sexual abuse in adolescents. *Child Abuse and Neglect, 12,* 181–188.

Chilamkurti, C., & Milner, J. S. (1993). Perceptions and evaluations of child transgressions and disciplinary techniques in high- and low-risk mothers and their children. *Child Development, 64,* 1801–1814.

Children's Defense Fund. (1991). *The state of America's children.* Washington, DC: Author.

Christoffel, K. K. (1990). Violent death and injury in U.S. children and adolescents. *American Journal of Disease Control, 144,* 697–706.

Chu, J. A., & Dill, D. L. (1990). Dissociative symptoms in relation to childhood physical and sexual abuse. *American Journal of Psychiatry, 147,* 887–892.

Cicchetti, D. (1984). The emergence of developmental psychopathology. *Child Development, 55,* 1–7.

Cicchetti, D. (1989). How research on child maltreatment has informed the development of child development: Perspectives from developmental psychopathology. In D. Cicchetti & V. Carlson (Eds.), *Child maltreatment: Theory and research on the causes and consequences of child abuse and neglect* (pp. 377–431). New York: Cambridge University Press.

Cicchetti, D. (1990). The organization and coherence of socioemotional, cognitive, and representational development: Illustrations through a developmental psychopathology perspective on Down syndrome and child maltreatment. In R. Thompson (Ed.), *Nebraska Symposium on Motivation: Vol. 36. Socioemotional development* (pp. 259–366). Lincoln: University of Nebraska Press.

Cicchetti, D. (1991). Fractures in the crystal: Developmental psychopathology and the emergence of self. *Developmental Review, 11,* 271–287.

Cicchetti, D. (1993). Developmental psychopathology: Reactions, reflections, projections. *Developmental Review, 13,* 471–502.

Cicchetti, D., & Aber, J. L. (1980). Abused children—abusive parents: An overstated case? *Harvard Educational Review, 50,* 244–255.

Cicchetti, D., & Barnett, D. (1991a). Attachment organization in maltreated preschoolers. *Development & Psychopathology, 3,* 397–411.

Cicchetti, D., & Barnett, D. (1991b). Toward the development of a scientific nosology of child maltreatment. In D. Cicchetti & W. Grove (Eds.), *Thinking clearly about psychology: Essays in honor of Paul E. Meehl* (pp. 346–377). Minneapolis: University of Minnesota Press.

Cicchetti, D., & Carlson, V. (Eds.). (1989). *Child maltreatment: Theory and research on the causes and consequences of child abuse and neglect.* New York: Cambridge University Press.

Cicchetti, D., Cummings, M., Greenberg, M., & Marvin, R. (1990). An organizational perspective on attachment theory beyond infancy: Implications for theory, measurement, and research. In M. Greenberg, D. Cicchetti, & M. Cummings (Eds.), *Attachment during the preschool years* (pp. 3–49). Chicago: University of Chicago Press.

Cicchetti, D., Ganiban, J., & Barnett, D. (1991). Contributions from the study of high risk populations to understanding the development of emotion regulation. In J. Garber & K. Dodge (Eds.), *The development of emotion regulation and dysregulation* (pp. 15–48). New York: Cambridge University Press.

Cicchetti, D., & Garmezy, N. (Eds.). (1993). Milestones in the development of resilience [Special issue]. *Development and Psychopathology, 5,* 497–794.

Cicchetti, D., & Howes, P. W. (1991). Developmental psychopathology in the context of the family: Illustrations from the study of child maltreatment. *Canadian Journal of Behavioural Science, 23,* 257–281.

Cicchetti, D., & Lynch, M. (1993). Toward an ecological/transactional model of community violence and child maltreatment. *Psychiatry, 56,* 96–118.

Cicchetti, D., Lynch, M., Shonk, S., & Todd Manly, J. (1992). An organizational perspective on peer relations in maltreated children. In R. D. Parke & G. W. Ladd (Eds.), *Family-peer relationships: Modes of linkage* (pp. 345–383). Hillsdale, NJ: Erlbaum.

Cicchetti, D., & Rizley, R. (1981). Developmental perspectives on the etiology, intergenerational transmission and sequelae of child maltreatment (pp. 31–56). In *New Directions for Child Development* (Vol. 11). San Francisco: Jossey-Bass.

Cicchetti, D., Rogosch, F. A., Lynch, M., & Holt, K. D. (1993). Resilience in maltreated children: Processes leading to adaptive outcomes. *Development and Psychopathology, 5,* 629–648.

Cicchetti, D., & Schneider-Rosen, K. (1986). An organizational approach to childhood depression. In M. Rutter, C. E. Izard, & P. B. Read (Eds.), Depression in young people: Developmental and clinical perspectives (pp. 71–134). New York: Guilford.

Cicchetti, D., & Sroufe, L. A. (1976). The relationship between affective and cognitive development in Down's syndrome infants. *Child Development, 47,* 920–929.

Cicchetti, D., & Toth, S. L. (1992). The role of developmental theory in prevention and intervention. *Development and Psychopathology, 4,* 489–493.

Cicchetti, D., & Toth, S. L. (Eds.). (1993). *Child abuse, child development, and social policy.* Norwood, NJ: Ablex.

Cicchetti, D., Toth, S. L., & Lynch, M. (1993). The developmental sequelae of child maltreatment: Implications for war-related trauma. In L. A. Leavitt & N. A. Fox (Eds.), *The psychological effects of war and violence on children* (pp. 41–71). Hillsdale, NJ: Erlbaum.

Cicchetti, D., Toth, S. L., & Lynch, M. (in press). Bowlby's dream comes full circle: The application of attachment theory to risk and psychopathology. In T. Ollendick & R. Prinz (Eds.), *Advances in clinical child psychology* (Vol. 17). New York: Plenum.

Cole, P. M., & Putnam, F. W. (1992). Effects of incest on self and social functioning: A developmental psychopathology perspective. *Journal of Consulting and Clinical Psychology, 60,* 174–184.

Conger, R., Burgess, R., & Barrett, C. (1979). Child abuse related to life change and perceptions of illness: Some preliminary findings. *Family Coordinator, 28,* 73–78.

Connelly, C. D., & Straus, M. A. (1992). Mother's age and risk for physical abuse. *Child Abuse and Neglect, 16,* 703–712.

Corse, S. J., Schmid, K., & Trickett, P. K. (1990). Social network characteristics of mothers in abusing and nonabusing families and their relationships to parenting beliefs. *Journal of Community Psychology, 18,* 44–59.

Coster, W., Gersten, M. S., Beeghly, M., & Cicchetti, D. (1989). Communicative functioning in maltreated toddlers. *Developmental Psychology, 25,* 1020–1029.

Cowen, E., Pederson, A., Babigian, H., Izzo, L., & Trost, M. (1973). Long-term follow-up of early detected children. *Journal of Consulting and Clinical Psychology, 41,* 438–446.

Crick, N. R., & Dodge, K. A. (1994). A review and reformulation of social information-processing mechanisms in children's social adjustment. *Psychological Bulletin, 115,* 74–101.

Crittenden, P. M. (1981). Abusing, neglecting, problematic, and adequate dyads: Differentiating by patterns of interaction. *Merrill-Palmer Quarterly, 27,* 1–18.

Crittenden, P. M. (1985). Social networks, quality of parenting, and child development. *Child Development, 56,* 1299–1313.

Crittenden, P. M. (1988). Relationships at risk. In J. Belsky & T. Nezworski (Eds.), *Clinical implications of attachment theory* (pp. 136–174). Hillsdale, NJ: Erlbaum.

Crittenden, P. M. (1990). Internal representational models of attachment relationships. *Infant Mental Health Journal, 11,* 259–277.

Crittenden, P. M. (1992). Quality of attachment in the preschool years. *Development and Psychopathology, 4,* 209–241.

Crittenden, P. M., & Ainsworth, M. (1989). Attachment and child abuse. In D. Cicchetti & V. Carlson (Eds.), *Child maltreatment: Theory and research on the causes and consequences of child abuse and neglect* (pp. 432–463). New York: Cambridge University Press.

Crittenden, P. M., Claussen, A. H., & Sugarman, D. B. (1994). Physical and psychological maltreatment in middle childhood and adolescence. *Development and Psychopathology, 6,* 145–164.

Crittenden, P., & DiLalla, D. L. (1988). Compulsive compliance: The development of an inhibitory coping strategy in infancy. *Journal of Abnormal Child Psychology, 16,* 585–599.

Crittenden, P. M., Partridge, M. F., & Claussen, A. H. (1991). Family patterns of relationships in normative and dysfunctional families. *Development and Psychopathology, 3,* 491–512.

Culp, R. E., Watkins, R. V., Lawrence, H., Letts, D., Kelly, D. J., & Rice, M. L. (1991). Maltreated children's language and speech development: Abused, neglected, and abused and neglected. *First Language, 11,* 377–389.

Cummings, E. M., & Cicchetti, D. (1990). Attachment, depression, and the transmission of depression. In M. T. Greenberg, D. Cicchetti, & E. M. Cummings (Eds.), *Attachment in the preschool years: Theory, research, and intervention* (pp. 339–372). Chicago: University of Chicago Press.

Cummings, E. M., Hennessy, K. D., Rabideau, G. J., & Cicchetti, D. (1994). Responses of physically abused boys to interadult anger involving their mothers. *Development and Psychopathology, 6,* 31–41.

Curtiss, S. (1977). *Genie: A psycholinguistic study of a modern-day "Wild Child."* New York: Academic Press.

Daro, D., & McCurdy, K. (1991). *Current trends in child abuse reporting and fatalities: The results of the 1990 annual fifty state survey.* Chicago: National Committee for Prevention of Child Abuse.

Dean, A. L., Malik, M. M., Richards, W., & Stringer, S. A. (1986). Effects of parental maltreatment on children's conceptions of interpersonal relationships. *Developmental Psychology, 22,* 617–626.

DeBellis, M., Chrousos, G., Dorn, L., Burke, L., Helmers, K., Kling, M., Trickett, P., & Putnam, F. (1993). Hypothalamic-pituitary-adrenal axis dysregulation in sexually abused girls. *Journal of Clinical Endocrinology and Metabolism, 77,* 1–7.

DeBellis, M. D., Lefter, L., Trickett, P. K., & Putnam, F. W. (1994). Urinary catecholamine excretion in sexually abused girls. *Journal of the American Academy of Child and Adolescent Psychiatry, 33,* 320–327.

Deblinger, E., McLeer, S. V., Atkins, M. S., Ralphe, D., & Foa, E. (1989). Post-traumatic stress in sexually abused, physically abused, and nonabused children. *Child Abuse and Neglect, 13,* 403–408.

Derryberry, D., & Rothbart, M. (1984). Emotion, attention, and temperament. In C. E. Izard, J. Kagan, & R. Zajonc (Eds.), *Emotions, cognition, and behavior* (pp. 132–166). New York: Cambridge University Press.

Deykin, E. Y., Alpert, J. J., & McNamarra, J. J. (1985). A pilot study of the effect of exposure to child abuse or neglect on adolescent suicidal behavior. *American Journal of Psychiatry, 142,* 1299–1303.

Dinwiddie, S., & Bucholz, K. (1993). Psychiatric diagnoses of self-reported child abusers. *Child Abuse and Neglect, 17,* 465–476.

Dodge, K. A., Pettit, G. S., & Bates, J. E. (1990). Mechanisms in the cycle of violence. *Science, 250,* 1678–1683.

Dodge, K. A., Pettit, G. S., & Bates, J. E. (1994). Effects of physical maltreatment on the development of peer relations. *Development and Psychopathology, 6,* 43–55.

Downey, G., Feldman, S., Khuri, J., & Friedman, S. (in press). Maltreatment and childhood depression. In W. M. Reynolds & H. F. Johnson (Eds.), *Handbook of depression in children.* New York: Plenum.

Dubrow, N. F., & Garbarino, J. (1989). Living in the war zone: Mothers and young children in a public housing project. *Child Welfare, 68,* 3–20.

Duncan, G. J. (1991). The economic environment of childhood. In A. C. Huston (Ed.), *Children in poverty: Child development and public policy* (pp. 23–50). New York: Cambridge University Press.

Eckenrode, J., & Laird, M. (1991, April). *Social adjustment of maltreated children in the school setting.* Paper presented at the biennial meeting of the Society for Research in Child Development, Seattle, WA.

Eckenrode, J., Laird, M., & Doris, J. (1993). School performance and disciplinary problems among abused and neglected children. *Developmental Psychology, 29,* 53–62.

Edelman, M. W. (1987). *Families in peril: An agenda for social change.* Cambridge, MA: Harvard University Press.

Egeland, B., & Abery, B. (1991). A longitudinal study of high-risk children: Educational outcomes. *International Journal of Disability, Development, and Education, 38,* 271–287.

Egeland, B., Breitenbucher, M., & Rosenberg, D. (1980). A prospective study of the significance of life stress in the etiology of child abuse. *Journal of Clinical and Consulting Psychology, 48,* 195–205.

Egeland, B., & Brunquell, D. (1979). An at-risk approach to the study of child abuse: Some preliminary findings. *Journal of the American Academy of Child Psychiatry, 18,* 219–235.

Egeland, B., Carlson, E., & Sroufe, L. A. (1993). Resilience as process. *Development and Psychopathology, 5,* 517–528.

Egeland, B., Jacobvitz, D., & Papatola, K. (1987). Intergenerational continuity of abuse. In R. J. Gelles & J. B. Lancaster (Eds.), *Child abuse and neglect: Biosocial dimensions* (pp. 255–276). New York: Aldine.

Egeland, B., Jacobvitz, D., & Sroufe, L. A. (1988). Breaking the cycle of abuse. *Child Development, 59,* 1080–1088.

Egeland, B., & Sroufe, L. A. (1981). Developmental sequelae of maltreatment in infancy. *New Directions for Child Development, 11,* 77–92.

Egeland, B., Sroufe, L. A., & Erickson, M. F. (1983). The developmental consequences of different patterns of maltreatment. *Child Abuse and Neglect, 7,* 459–469.

Emde, R. N. (1983). The pre-representational self and its affective core. *Psychoanalytical Study of the Child, 38,* 440–452.

Emde, R. N., Gaensbauer, T., & Harmon, R. (1976). *Emotional expression in infancy: A biobehavioral study.* New York: International Universities Press.

Emery, R. E. (1989). Family violence. *American Psychologist, 44,* 321–328.

Erickson, M., Egeland, B., & Pianta, R. (1989). The effects of maltreatment on the development of young children. In D. Cicchetti & V. Carlson (Eds.), *Child maltreatment: Theory and research on the causes and consequences of child abuse and neglect* (pp. 647–684). New York: Cambridge University Press.

Erikson, E. (1950). *Childhood and society.* New York: Norton.

Famularo, R., Kinscherff, R., & Fenton, T. (1992). Psychiatric diagnoses of maltreated children: Preliminary findings. *Journal of the American Academy of Child and Adolescent Psychiatry, 31,* 863–867.

Fantuzzo, J. W., Jurecic, L., Stovall, A., Hightower, A. D., Goins, C., & Schachtel, D. (1988). Effects of adult and peer social initiations on the social behavior of withdrawn, maltreated preschool children. *Journal of Consulting and Clinical Psychology, 56,* 34–39.

Farber, E., & Egeland, B. (1987). Abused children: Can they be invulnerable? In E. J. Anthony & B. Cohler (Eds.), *The invulnerable child* (pp. 253–288). New York: Guilford.

Feldman, S., & Downey, G. (1994). Rejection sensitivity as a mediator of the impact of childhood exposure to family violence on adult attachment behavior. *Development and Psychopathology, 6,* 231–247.

Feshbach, S. (1978). The development and regulation of aggression: Some research gaps and a proposed cognitive approach. In W. W. Hartup & J. de Wit (Eds.), *Origins of aggression* (pp. 163–187). New York: Mouton.

Field, T. (1989). Maternal depression effects on infant interaction and attachment behavior. In D. Cicchetti (Ed.), *Rochester Symposium on Developmental Psychopathology: Vol. 1. The emergence of a discipline* (pp. 139–163). Hillsdale, NJ: Erlbaum.

Fingerhut, L. A., & Kleinman, J. C. (1990). International and interstate comparisons of homicide among young males. *Journal of the American Medical Association, 263,* 3292–3295.

Fischer, F. W., & Ayoub, C. (1994). Affective splitting and dissociation in normal and maltreated children: Developmental pathways for self in relationships. In D. Cicchetti & S. L. Toth (Eds.), *Rochester Symposium on Developmental Psychopathology: Vol. 5. Disorders and dysfunctions of the self* (pp. 149–222). Rochester, NY: University of Rochester Press.

Fishbein, H. (1976). *Evolution, development, and children's learning.* Pacific Palisades, CA: Goodyear Publishing.

Foa, E. B., Feske, U., Murdock, T. B., Kozak, M. J., & McCarthy, P. R. (1991). Processing of threat-related information in rape victims. *Journal of Abnormal Psychology, 100,* 156–162.

Fox, L., Long, S. H., & Langlois, A. (1988). Patterns of language comprehension deficits in abused and neglected children. *Journal of Speech and Hearing Disorders, 53,* 239–244.

Fox, N. A., Kimmerly, N. L., & Schafer, W. D. (1991). Attachment to mother/attachment to father: A meta-analysis. *Child Development, 62,* 210–225.

Fraiberg, S. (1982). Pathological defenses in infancy. *Psychoanalytic Quarterly, 51,* 612–635.

Freeman, L. H., Mokros, H., & Poznanski, E. O. (1993). Violent events reported by normal urban school-aged children: Characteristics and depression correlates. *Journal of the American Academy of Child and Adolescent Psychiatry, 32,* 419–423.

Frodi, A. M., & Lamb, M. E. (1980). Child abusers' responses to infant smiles and cries. *Child Development, 51,* 238–241.

Gaensbauer, T. J. (1980). Anaclitic depression in a three-and-one-half-month-old child. *American Journal of Psychiatry, 137,* 841–842.

Gaensbauer, T. J. (1982a). Regulation of emotional expression in infants from two contrasting caretaking environments. *Journal of the American Academy of Child Psychiatry, 21,* 163–171.

Gaensbauer, T. J. (1982b). The differentiation of discrete affects. *Psychoanalytic Study of the Child, 37,* 29–66.

Gaensbauer, T. J., & Hiatt, S. (1984). Facial communication of emotion in early infancy. In N. A. Fox & R. J. Davidson (Eds.), *The psychobiology of affective development* (pp. 207–230). Hillsdale, NJ: Erlbaum.

Gaensbauer, T. J., Mrazek, D., & Harmon, R. (1981). Emotional expression in abused and/or neglected infants. In N. Frude (Ed.), *Psychological approaches to child abuse* (pp. 120–135). Totowa, NJ: Rowman & Littlefield.

Gaensbauer, T. J., & Sands, S. K. (1979). Distorted affective communications in abused/neglected infants and their potential impact on caretakers. *Journal of the American Academy of Child Psychiatry, 18,* 236–250.

Galvin, M. R., Shekar, A., Simon, J., Stilwell, B., Ten Eyck, R., Laite, G., Karwisch, G., & Blix, S. (1991). Low dopamine beta hydroxylase: A biological sequela of abuse and neglect? *Psychiatry Research, 39,* 1–11.

Garbarino, J. (1976). A preliminary study of some ecological correlates of child abuse: The impact of socioeconomic stress on mothers. *Child Development, 47,* 372–381.

Garbarino, J. (1977). The human ecology of child maltreatment: A conceptual model for research. *Journal of Marriage and the Family, 39,* 721–732.

Garbarino, J. (1982). *Children and families in the social environment.* Lexington, MA: Lexington Books.

Garbarino, J. (1989). Troubled youth, troubled families: The dynamics of adolescent maltreatment. In D. Cicchetti & V. Carlson (Eds.), *Child maltreatment: Theory and research on the causes and consequences of child abuse and neglect* (pp. 685–706). New York: Cambridge University Press.

Garbarino, J., & Crouter, A. (1978). Defining the community context for parent-child relations: The correlates of child maltreatment. *Child Development, 49,* 604–616.

Garbarino, J., & Gilliam, G. (1980). *Understanding abusive families.* Lexington, MA: Lexington Books.

Garbarino, J., Kostelny, K., & Dubrow, N. (1991). *No place to be a child: Growing up in a war zone.* Lexington, MA: Lexington Books.

Garbarino, J., & Sherman, D. (1980). High-risk neighborhoods and high-risk families: The human ecology of child maltreatment. *Child Development, 51,* 188–198.

Gelles, R. J. (1991). Physical violence, child abuse, and child homicide: A continuum of violence or distinct behaviors? *Human Nature, 2,* 59–72.

Gelles, R. J. (1992). Poverty and violence toward children. *American Behavioral Scientist, 35,* 258–274.

Gelles, R. J., & Hargreaves, E. F. (1981). Maternal employment and violence toward children. *Journal of Family Issues, 2,* 509–530.

Gelles, R. J., & Straus, M. A. (1987). Is violence toward children increasing? A comparison of 1975 and 1985 national survey rates. *Journal of Interpersonal Violence, 2,* 212–222.

Gelles, R. J., & Straus, M. A. (1988). *Intimate violence.* New York: Simon & Schuster.

General Accounting Office (1991). *Child abuse prevention: Status of the challenge grant program.* GAO:HRD91-95. Washington, DC: U.S. Government Printing Office.

George, C., & Main, M. (1979). Social interactions of young abused children: Approach, avoidance, and aggression. *Child Development, 50,* 306–318.

Gersten, M., Coster, W., Schneider-Rosen, K., Carlson, V., & Cicchetti, D. (1986). The socio-emotional bases of communicative functioning: Quality of attachment, language development, and early maltreatment. In M. E. Lamb, A. L. Brown, & B. Rogoff (Eds.), *Advances in developmental psychology* (Vol. 4, pp. 105–151). Hillsdale, NJ: Erlbaum.

Gil, D. (1970). *Violence against children: Physical child abuse in the United States.* Cambridge, MA: Harvard University Press.

Gilbreath, B., & Cicchetti, D. (1991). *Psychopathology in maltreating mothers.* Unpublished manuscript, Mt. Hope Family Center, University of Rochester, Rochester, NY.

Giovannoni, J. M., & Billingsley, A. (1970). Child neglect among the poor: A study of parental adequacy in families of three ethnic groups. *Child Welfare, 49,* 196–204.

Gottesman, I. I., & Bertelsen, A. (1989). Confirming unexpressed genotypes for schizophrenia. *Archives of General Psychiatry, 46,* 867–872.

Gottlieb, G. (1976). Conceptions of prenatal development: Behavioral embryology. *Psychological Review, 83,* 215–234.

Gottlieb, G. (1991a). Experiential canalization of behavioral development: Theory. *Developmental Psychology, 27,* 4–13.

Gottlieb, G. (1991b). Experiential canalization of behavioral development: Results. *Developmental Psychology, 27,* 35–39.

Gottlieb, G. (1992). *Individual development and evolution: The genesis of novel behavior.* New York: Oxford University Press.

Green, A. H. (1993). Child sexual abuse: Immediate and long-term effects and intervention. *Journal of the American Academy of Child and Adolescent Psychiatry, 32,* 890–902.

Greenough, W., Black, J., & Wallace, C. (1987). Experience and brain development. *Child Development, 58,* 539–559.

Greenspan, S. I. (1981). *Psychopathology and adaptation in infancy and early childhood.* New York: International Universities Press.

Grusec, J. E., & Goodnow, J. J. (1994). Impact of parental discipline methods on the child's internalization of values: A reconceptualization of current points of view. *Developmental Psychology, 30,* 4–19.

Gunnar, M. R., & Nelson, C. A. (1994). Event-related potentials in year-old infants: Relations with emotionality and cortisol. *Child Development, 65,* 80–94.

Hamburg, D. A. (1992). *Today's children: Creating a future for a generation in crisis.* New York: Times Books.

Hartmann, H. (1958). *Ego psychology and the problem of adaptation.* New York: International Universities Press.

Hartup, W. (1983). Peer relations. In P. Mussen (Ed.), *Handbook of child psychology* (Vol. 4, pp. 103–196). New York: Wiley.

Haskett, M. E., & Kistner, J. A. (1991). Social interactions and peer perceptions of young physically abused children. *Child Development, 62,* 979–990.

Hennessy, K. D., Rabideau, G. J., Cicchetti, D., & Cummings, E. M. (1994). Responses of physically abused and nonabused children to different forms of interadult anger. *Child Development, 65,* 815–828.

Herrenkohl, R. C., & Herrenkohl, E. C. (1981). Some antecedents and developmental consequences of child maltreatment. In R. Rizley & D. Cicchetti (Eds.), *Developmental perspectives on child maltreatment* (pp. 57–76). San Francisco: Jossey-Bass.

Herzberger, S. D. (1983). Social cognition and the transmission of abuse. In D. Finkelhor, R. Gelles, G. Hotaling, & M. Straus (Eds.), *The dark side of families: Current family violence research* (pp. 317–329). Beverly Hills, CA: Sage.

Hill, S. D., Bleichfeld, B., Brunstetter, R. D., Hebert, J. E., & Steckler, S. (1989). Cognitive and physiological responsiveness of abused children. *Journal of the American Academy of Child and Adolescent Psychiatry, 28,* 219–224.

Hofer, M. A. (1987). Early social relationships: A psychobiologist's view. *Child Development, 58,* 633–647.

Hoffman-Plotkin, D., & Twentyman, C. T. (1984). A multimodal assessment of behavioral and cognitive deficits in abused and neglected preschoolers. *Child Development, 55,* 794–802.

Holton, J. (1992). African American's needs and participation in child maltreatment prevention services: Toward a community response to child abuse and neglect. *Urban Research Review, 14,* 1–6.

Horowitz, F. D. (1987). *Exploring developmental theories: Toward a structural/behavioral model of development.* Hillsdale, NJ: Erlbaum.

Howes, C., & Eldredge, R. (1985). Responses of abused, neglected, and non-maltreated children to the behaviors of their peers. *Journal of Applied Developmental Psychology, 6,* 261–270.

Howes, C., & Espinosa, M. P. (1985). The consequences of child abuse for the formation of relationships with peers. *Child Abuse and Neglect, 9,* 397–404.

Howes, C., & Hamilton, C. E. (1992). Children's relationships with caregivers: Mothers and child care teachers. *Child Development, 63,* 859–866.

Howes, C., & Segal, J. (1993). Children's relationships with alternative caregivers: The special case of maltreated children removed from their homes. *Journal of Applied Developmental Psychology, 14,* 71–81.

Howes, P., & Cicchetti, D. (1993). A family/relational perspective on maltreating families: Parallel processes across systems and social policy implications. In D. Cicchetti & S. L. Toth (Eds.), *Child abuse, child development, and social policy,* (pp. 399–438). Norwood, NJ: Ablex.

Hunter, R. S., & Kilstrom, N. (1979). Breaking the cycle in abusive families. *American Journal of Psychiatry, 136,* 1320–1322.

Huston, A. C. (1991a). *Children in poverty: Child development and public policy.* New York: Cambridge University Press.

Huston, A. C. (1991b). Children in poverty: Developmental and policy issues. In A. C. Huston (Ed.), *Children in poverty: Child development and public policy* (pp. 1–22). New York: Cambridge University Press.

Hymel, S., Rubin, K. H., Rowden, L., & LeMare, L. (1990). Children's peer relationships: Longitudinal prediction of internalizing and externalizing problems from middle to late childhood. *Child Development, 61,* 2004–2021.

Institute of Medicine. (1994). *Reducing risks for mental disorders: Frontiers for preventive intervention research.* Washington, DC: National Academy Press.

Jacobson, R., & Straker, G. (1982). Peer group interaction of physically abused children. *Child Abuse and Neglect, 6,* 321–327.

Jacobvitz, D. B., Morgan, E., Kretchmar, M. D., & Morgan, Y. (1991). The transmission of mother-child boundary disturbances across three generations. *Development and Psychopathology, 3,* 513–527.

Janes, C. L., & Hesselbrock, V. (1978). Problem children's adult adjustment predicted from teacher's ratings. *American Journal of Orthopsychiatry, 48,* 300–309.

Jayaratne, T. E. (1993, March). *Neighborhood quality and parental socialization among single, African American mothers: Child gender differences.* Paper presented at the biennial meeting of the Society for Research in Child Development, New Orleans.

Jencks, C., & Peterson, P. (Eds.). (1991). *The urban underclass.* Washington, DC: Brookings Institution Press.

Jensen, J. B., Pease, J. J., ten Bensel, B. S., & Garfinkel, B. D. (1991). Growth hormone response patterns in sexually or physically abused boys. *Journal of the American Academy of Child and Adolescent Psychiatry, 30,* 784–790.

Juvenile Justice Standards Project. (1977). *Standards relating to child abuse and neglect.* Cambridge, MA: Ballinger.

Kalin, N. H. (1993). The neurobiology of fear. *Scientific American, 269,* 94–101.

Kalin, N. H., Shelton, S. E., & Snowdon, C. T. (1993). Social factors in regulating security and fear in infant rhesus monkeys. *Depression, 1,* 137–142.

Kalmuss, D. (1984). The intergenerational transmission of marital aggression. *Journal of Marriage and the Family, 46,* 11–19.

Kandel, E. (1983). From metapsychology to molecular biology: Explorations into the nature of anxiety. *American Journal of Psychiatry, 140,* 1277–1293.

Kaplan, B. (1966). The study of language in psychiatry: The comparative developmental approach and its application to symbolization and language in psychopathology. In S. Arieti (Ed.), *American handbook of psychiatry* (pp. 659–688). New York: Basic Books.

Kashani, J. H., Daniel, A. E., Dandoy, A. C., & Holcomb, W. R. (1992). Family violence: Impact on children. *Journal of the American Academy of Child and Adolescent Psychiatry, 31,* 181–189.

Kaufman, J. (1991). Depressive disorders in maltreated children. *American Journal of Child and Adolescent Psychiatry, 30,* 257–265.

Kaufman, J., & Cicchetti, D. (1989). The effects of maltreatment on school-aged children's socioemotional development: Assessments in a day camp setting. *Developmental Psychology, 25,* 316–324.

Kaufman, J., Cook, A., Arny, L., Jones, B., & Pittinsky, T. (1994). Problems defining resiliency: Illustrations from the study of maltreated children. *Development and Psychopathology, 6,* 215–229.

Kaufman, J., & Zigler, E. (1989). The intergenerational transmission of child abuse. In D. Cicchetti & V. Carlson (Eds.), *Child maltreatment: Theory and research on the causes and consequences of child abuse and neglect* (pp. 129–150). New York: Cambridge University Press.

Kavanaugh, K., Youngblade, L., Reid, J., & Fagot, B. (1988). Interactions between children and abusive control parents. *Journal of Clinical Child Psychology, 17,* 137–142.

Kazdin, A. E., Moser, J., Colbus, D., & Bell, R. (1985). Depressive symptoms among physically abused and psychiatrically disturbed children. *Journal of Abnormal Psychology, 94,* 298–307.

Kempe, C. (1973). A practical approach to the protection of the abused child and rehabilitation of the abusing parent. *Pediatrics, 51,* 804–812.

Kendall-Tackett, K. A., Williams, L. M., & Finkelhor, D. (1993). The impact of sexual abuse on children: A review and synthesis of recent empirical studies. *Psychological Bulletin, 113,* 164–180.

Kirby, J. S., Chu, J. A., & Dill, D. L. (1993). Correlates of dissociative symptomatology in patients with physical and sexual abuse histories. *Comprehensive Psychiatry, 34,* 258–263.

Kiser, L. J., Heston, J., Millsap, P. A., & Pruitt, D. B. (1991). Physical and sexual abuse in childhood: Relationship with Post-traumatic Stress Disorder. *Journal of the American Academy of Child and Adolescent Psychiatry, 30,* 776–783.

Klimes-Dougan, B., & Kistner, J. (1990). Physically abused preschoolers' response to peers' distress. *Developmental Psychology, 26,* 599–602.

Kling, A., & Stecklis, H. (1976). A neural substrate for affiliative behavior in non-human primates. *Brain, Behavior, and Evolution, 13,* 216–238.

Knudsen, D. D. (1988). Child sexual abuse and pornography: Is there a relationship? *Journal of Family Violence, 3,* 253–267.

Kohlberg, L., LaCrosse, J., & Ricks, D. (1972). The predictability of adult mental health from child behavior. In B. Wolman (Ed.), *Manual of child psychopathology* (pp. 1217–1284). New York: Wiley.

Kotelchuck, M. (1982). Child abuse and neglect: Prediction and misclassification. In R. H. Starr (Ed.), *Child abuse prediction* (pp. 67–104). Cambridge, MA: Ballinger.

Koverola, C., Pound, J., Heger, A., & Lytle, C. (1993). Relationship of child sexual abuse to depression. *Child Abuse and Neglect, 17,* 393–400.

Kraemer, G. W., Ebert, M. H., Lake, C. R., & McKinney, W. T. (1984). Hypersensitivity to *d*-amphetamine several years after early social deprivation in rhesus monkeys. *Psychopharmacology, 82,* 226–271.

Kraemer, G. W., Ebert, M. H., Schmidt, D. E., & McKinney, W. T. (1989). A longitudinal study of the effect of different social rearing conditions on cerebrospinal fluid norepinephrine and biogenic amine metabolites in rhesus monkeys. *Neuropsychopharmacology, 2,* 175–189.

Krasnegor, N. A., & Bridges, R. S. (Eds.). (1990). *Mammalian parenting: Biochemical, neurobiological, and behavioral determinants.* New York: Oxford University Press.

Kroll, P. D., Stock, D. F., & James, M. E. (1985). The behavior of adult alcoholic men abused as children. *Journal of Nervous and Mental Disease, 173,* 689–693.

Krugman, R. D., Lenherr, M., Betz, L., & Fryer, G. E. (1986). The relationship between unemployment and physical abuse of children. *Child Abuse and Neglect, 10,* 415–418.

Lahey, B., Conger, R., Atkeson, B., & Treiber, F. (1984). Parenting behavior and emotional status of physically abusive mothers. *Journal of Consulting and Clinical Psychology, 52,* 1062–1071.

Lamb, M., Gaensbauer, T. J., Malkin, C. M., & Schultz, L. A. (1985). The effects of child maltreatment on security of infant-adult attachment. *Infant Behavior and Development, 8,* 35–45.

Lamb, M., Thompson, R., Gardner, W., & Charnov, E. (1985). *Infant-mother attachment.* Hillsdale, NJ: Erlbaum.

Lewis, D. O. (1992). From abuse to violence: Psychophysiological consequences of maltreatment. *Journal of the American Academy of Child and Adolescent Psychiatry, 31,* 383–391.

Lewis, D. O., Mallough, C., & Webb, V. (1989). Child abuse, delinquency, and violent criminality. In D. Cicchetti & V. Carlson (Eds.), *Child maltreatment: Theory and research on the causes and consequences of child abuse and neglect* (pp. 707–721). New York: Cambridge University Press.

Light, R. (1973). Abused and neglected children in America: A study of alternative policies. *Harvard Educational Review, 43,* 556–598.

Lorber, R., Felton, D. K., & Reid, J. B. (1984). A social learning approach to the reduction of coercive processes in child abusive families: A molecular analysis. *Advances in Behavior Research and Therapy, 6,* 29–45.

Lykken, D. T. (1993). Predicting violence in the violent society. *Applied and Preventive Psychology, 2,* 13–20.

Lynch, M. (1992). *Modes of linkage between relationship disturbances and maladaptation: Issues in the area of child maltreatment.* Unpublished doctoral dissertation, University of Rochester, Rochester, NY.

Lynch, M., & Cicchetti, D. (1991). Patterns of relatedness in maltreated and nonmaltreated children: Connections among multiple representational models. *Development and Psychopathology, 3,* 207–226.

Lynch, M., & Cicchetti, D. (1992). Maltreated children's reports of relatedness to their teachers. In R. Pianta (Ed.), *Beyond the parent: The role of other adults in children's lives* (pp. 81–107). *New Directions for Child Development.* San Francisco: Jossey-Bass.

Lynn, L. E., & McGeary, M. G. H. (1990). *Inner-city poverty in the United States.* Washington, DC: National Academy Press.

Lyons-Ruth, K., Connell, D., & Zoll, D. (1989). Patterns of maternal behavior among infants at risk for abuse: Relations with infant attachment behavior and infant development at 12 months of age. In D. Cicchetti & V. Carlson (Eds.), *Child maltreatment: Theory and research on the causes and consequences of child abuse and neglect* (pp. 464–493). New York: Cambridge University Press.

Lyons-Ruth, K., Connell, D., Zoll, D., & Stahl, J. (1987). Infants at so-cial risk: Relations among infant maltreatment, maternal behavior, and infant attachment behavior. *Developmental Psychology, 23,* 223–232.

Lyons-Ruth, K., & Easterbrooks, M. A. (in press). Attachment relation-ships among children with aggressive behavior problems: The role of disorganized/controlling early attachment strategies. *Journal of Consulting and Clinical Psychology.*

Lyons-Ruth, K., Repacholi, B., McLeod, S., & Silva, E. (1991). Disor-ganized attachment behavior in infancy: Short-term stability, ma-ternal and infant correlated. *Development and Psychopathology, 3,* 377–396.

Lyons-Ruth, K., Zoll, D., Connell, D., & Grunebaum, H. U. (1989). Family deviance and family disruption in childhood: Associations with maternal behavior during the first two years of life. *Develop-ment and Psychopathology, 1,* 219–236.

Mahler, M., Pine, F., & Bergman, A. (1975). *The psychological birth of the infant.* New York: Basic Books.

Main, M., & Cassidy, J. (1988). Categories of response to reunion with parent at age six: Predictable from infant attachment classifications and stable over a one-month period. *Developmental Psychology, 24,* 415–426.

Main, M., & George, C. (1985). Responses of abused and disadvantaged toddlers to distress in agemates: A study in the daycare setting. *De-velopmental Psychology, 21,* 407–412.

Main, M., & Goldwyn, R. (1984). Predicting rejecting of her infant from mother's representation of her own experience: Implications for the abused-abusing intergenerational cycle. *Child Abuse and Ne-glect, 8,* 203–217.

Main, M., & Hesse, E. (1990). Parents' unresolved traumatic experi-ences are related to infant disorganized attachment status: Is fright-ened and/or frightening parental behavior the linking mechanism? In E. M. Greenberg, D. Cicchetti, & M. Cummings (Eds.), *Attach-ment during the preschool years* (pp. 161–182). Chicago: University of Chicago Press.

Main, M., & Solomon, J. (1990). Procedures for identifying infants as disorganized/disoriented during the Ainsworth Strange Situation. In M. Greenberg, D. Cicchetti, & E. M. Cummings (Eds.), *Attach-ment in the preschool years* (pp. 121–160). Chicago: University of Chicago Press.

Malinosky-Rummell, R., & Hansen, D. J. (1993). Long-term conse-quences of childhood physical abuse. *Psychological Bulletin, 114,* 68–79.

Manly, J. T., Cicchetti, D., & Barnett, D. (1994). The impact of subtype, frequency, chronicity, and severity of child maltreatment on social competence and behavior problems. *Development and Psychopathol-ogy, 6,* 121–143.

Martinez, P., & Richters, J. E. (1993). The NIMH community vio-lence project: II. Children's distress symptoms associated with vi-olence exposure. *Psychiatry, 56,* 22–35.

Mash, E. J., Johnston, C., & Kovitz, K. (1983). A comparison of the mother-child interactions of physically abused and nonabused chil-dren during play and task situations. *Journal of Clinical Child Psy-chology, 12,* 337–346.

Masten, A. S. (1989). Resilience in development: Implications of the study of successful adaptation for developmental psychopathology. In D. Cicchetti, (Ed.), *Rochester Symposium on Developmental Psycho-pathology: Vol. 1. The emergence of a discipline* (pp. 261–294). Hills-dale, NJ: Erlbaum.

Mayer, S. E., & Jencks, C. (1989). Growing up in poor neighborhoods: How much does it matter? *Science, 243,* 1441–1445.

McCanne, T. R., & Milner, J. S. (1991). Physiological reactivity of physically abusive and at-risk subjects to child-related stimuli. In J. S. Milner (Ed.), *Neuropsychology of aggression* (pp. 147–166). Boston, MA: Kluwer Academic Publishers.

McClain, P. W., Sacks, J. J., Froehlke, R. G., & Ewigman, B. G. (1993). Estimates of fatal abuse and neglect, United States, 1979 through 1988. *Pediatrics, 91,* 338–343.

McCrone, E. R., Egeland, B., Kalkoske, M., & Carlson, E. A. (1994). Relations between early maltreatment and mental representations of relationships assessed with projective storytelling in middle child-hood. *Development and Psychopathology, 6,* 99–120.

McGee, R. A., & Wolfe, D. A. (1991). Psychological maltreatment: To-ward an operational definition. *Development and Psychopathology, 3,* 3–18.

McLeer, S. V., Callaghan, M., Henry, D., & Wallen, J. (1994). Psychi-atric disorders in sexually abused children. *Journal of the American Academy of Child and Adolescent Psychiatry, 33,* 313–319.

McLoyd, V. C., & Wilson, L. (1991). The strain of living poor: Parenting, social support, and child mental health. In A. C. Huston (Ed.), *Children in poverty: Child development and public policy* (pp. 105–135). New York: Cambridge University Press.

Meisburger, D., & Cicchetti, D. (1993, March). *The lack of social orga-nization in peer groups of maltreated children.* Paper presented at the biennial meeting of the Society for Research in Child Develop-ment, New Orleans.

Merry, S. N., & Andrews, L. K. (in press). Psychiatric status of sexu-ally abused children 12 months after disclosure of abuse. *Journal of the American Academy of Child and Adolescent Psychiatry.*

Milner, J. S., & Chilamkurti, C. (1991). Physical child abuse perpetra-tor characteristics: A review of the literature. *Journal of Interper-sonal Violence, 6,* 345–366.

Minuchin, P. (1985). Families and individual development: Provocations from the field of family therapy. *Child Development, 56,* 289–302.

Morissey, C. E., Barnard, K. E., Greenberg, M. T., Booth, C. L., & Spieker, S. J. (1990). Environmental influences on early language development: The context of social risk. *Development and Psycho-pathology, 2,* 127–149.

Mueller, N., & Silverman, N. (1989). Peer relations in maltreated chil-dren. In D. Cicchetti & V. Carlson (Eds.), *Child maltreatment: The-ory and research on the causes and consequences of child abuse and neglect* (pp. 529–578). New York: Cambridge University Press.

Nash, A., & Hay, D. F. (1993). Relationships in infancy as precursors of later relationships and psychopathology. In D. F. Hay & A. Angold (Eds.), *Precursors and causes in development and psychopathology* (pp. 199–232). New York: Wiley.

Nash, M. R., Hulsey, T. L., Sexton, M. C., Harralson, T. L., & Lam-bert, W. (1993). Long-term sequelae of childhood sexual abuse: Per-ceived family environment, psychopathology, and dissociation. *Journal of Consulting and Clinical Psychology, 61,* 276–283.

Nash, M. R., Zivney, O. A., & Hulsey, T. (1993). Characteristics of sex-ual abuse associated with greater psychological impairment among children. *Child Abuse and Neglect, 17,* 401–408.

National Center for Child Abuse and Neglect. (1981). *National study of the incidence and severity of child abuse and neglect (NIS-1).* Washington, DC: U.S. Department of Health and Human Services.

National Center for Child Abuse and Neglect. (1988). *Study findings: Study of national incidence and prevalence of child abuse and neglect*

(NIS-2). Washington, DC: U.S. Department of Health and Human Services.

National Center for Children in Poverty. (1991). *Five million children: 1991 update.* New York: Columbia University School of Public Health.

National Center for Health Statistics. (1990). *Prevention profile: Health, United States, 1989* (DHHS Publication No. PHS 90-1232). Hyattsville, MD: U.S. Department of Health and Human Services.

National Center for Health Statistics. (1992). *Unpublished data tables from the NCHS mortality tapes, FBI-SHR.* Atlanta, GA: Centers for Disease Control.

National Research Council. (1993). *Understanding child abuse and neglect.* Washington, DC: National Academy Press.

Oates, R. D., Forrest, D., & Peacock, A. (1985). Self-esteem of abused children. *Child Abuse and Neglect, 9,* 159–163.

Okun, A., Parker, J. G., & Levendosky, A. A. (1994). Distinct and interactive contributions of physical abuse, socioeconomic disadvantage, and negative life events of children's social, cognitive, and affective adjustment. *Development and Psychopathology, 6,* 77–98.

Oldershaw, L., Walters, G. C., & Hall, D. K. (1986). Control strategies and noncompliance in abusive mother-child dyads: An observational study. *Child Development, 57,* 722–732.

Olds, D., & Henderson, C. (1989). The prevention of maltreatment. In D. Cicchetti & V. Carlson (Eds.), *Child maltreatment: Theory and research on the causes and consequences of child abuse and neglect* (pp. 722–763). New York: Cambridge University Press.

Oliver, J. E. (1993). Intergenerational transmission of child abuse: Rates, research, and clinical implications. *American Journal of Psychiatry, 150,* 1315–1324.

Ollendick, T. H., Weist, M. D., Borden, M. C., & Greene, R. W. (1992). Sociometric status and academic, behavioral, and psychological adjustment: A five-year longitudinal study. *Journal of Consulting and Clinical Psychology, 60,* 80–87.

Orvaschel, H., Puig-Antich, J., Chambers, W., Tabrizi, M., & Johnson, R. (1982). Retrospective assessment of child psychopathology with the Kiddie-SADS-E. *Journal of the American Academy of Child Psychiatry, 21,* 392–397.

Panksepp, J. (1982). Toward a general psychobiological theory of emotions. *Behavioral and Brain Sciences, 5,* 407–468.

Park, K. A., & Waters, E. (1989). Security of attachment and preschool friendships. *Child Development, 60,* 1076–1081.

Parke, R. D., & Collmer, C. W. (1975). Child abuse: An interdisciplinary analysis. In E. M. Hetherington (Ed.), *Review of child development research* (Vol. 5, pp. 509–590). Chicago: University of Chicago Press.

Parker, J. G., & Asher, S. R. (1987). Peer acceptance and later personal adjustment: Are low accepted children "at risk"? *Psychological Bulletin, 102,* 357–389.

Patterson, G. R. (1982). *Coercive family processes.* Eugene, OR: Castalia.

Pearson, J. L., Cohn, D. A., Cowan, P. A., & Cowan, C. P. (1994). Earned and continuous security in adult attachment: Relation to depressive symptomatology and parenting style. *Development and Psychopathology, 6,* 359–374.

Pelton, L. H. (1981). *The social context of child abuse and neglect.* New York: Human Sciences Press.

Pianta, R., Egeland, B., & Erickson, M. (1989). The antecedents of maltreatment: Results of the Mother-Child Interaction Research Project. In D. Cicchetti & V. Carlson (Eds.), *Child maltreatment:*

Theory and research on the causes and consequences of child abuse and neglect (pp. 203–253). New York: Cambridge University Press.

Pipp, S., Easterbrooks, M. A., & Harmon, R. J. (1992). The relation between attachment and knowledge of self and mother in one- to three-year-old infants. *Child Development, 63,* 738–750.

Pipp, S., & Harmon, R. J. (1987). Attachment as regulation: A commentary. *Child Development, 58,* 648–652.

Plomin, R., & Daniels, D. (1987). Why are children in the same family so different from each other? *Behavioral and Brain Sciences, 10,* 1–16.

Polansky, N. A., Gaudin, J. M., & Kilpatrick, A. C. (1992). Family radicals. *Children and Youth Services Review, 14,* 19–26.

Pollock, V. E., Briere, J., Schneider, L., Knop, J., Mednick, S. A., & Goodwin, D. W. (1990). Childhood antecedents of antisocial behavior: Parental alcoholism and physical abusiveness. *American Journal of Psychiatry, 147,* 1290–1293.

Price, J. M., & Van Slyke, D. (1991, April). *Social information processing patterns and social adjustment of maltreated children.* Paper presented at the biennial meeting of the Society for Research in Child Development, Seattle, WA.

Putnam, F. W., & Trickett, P. K. (1993). Child sexual abuse: A model of chronic trauma. *Psychiatry, 56,* 82–95.

Putnam, F. W., Trickett, P. K., Helmers, K., Susman, E. J., Dorn, L., & Everett, B. (1991, May). Cortisol abnormalities in sexually abused girls. In *New Research Programs and Abstracts,* paper presented at annual meeting of the American Psychiatric Association. New Orleans.

Pynoos, R. S., Frederick, C., Nader, K., Arroyo, W., Steinberg, A., Eth, S., Nunez, F., & Fairbanks, L. (1987). Life threat and posttraumatic stress in school-age children. *Archives of General Psychiatry, 44,* 1057–1063.

Quinton, D., & Rutter, M. (1988). *Parenting breakdown: The making and breaking of intergenerational links.* Aldershot, England: Avebury.

Quinton, D., Rutter, M., & Liddle, C. (1984). Institutional rearing, parenting difficulties and marital support. *Psychological Medicine, 14,* 107–124.

Reid, J. B., Kavanaugh, K., & Baldwin, D. V. (1987). Abusive parents' perceptions of child problem behaviors: An example of parental bias. *Journal of Abnormal Child Psychology, 15,* 457–466.

Reiss, D. (1981). *The family's construction of reality.* Cambridge, MA: Harvard University Press.

Reite, M., & Field, T. (Eds.) (1985). *The psychobiology of attachment and separation.* Orlando, FL: Academic Press.

Reite, M., Short, R., & Seiler, C. (1978). Physiological correlates of separation in surrogate-reared infants: A study in altered attachment bonds. *Developmental Psychobiology, 11,* 427–435.

Richters, J. E., & Martinez, P. (1993a). The NIMH community violence project: I. Children as victims and witnesses to violence. *Psychiatry, 56,* 7–21.

Richters, J. E., & Martinez, P. E. (1993b). Violent communities, family choices, and children's chances: An algorithm for improving the odds. *Development and Psychopathology, 5,* 609–628.

Ricketts, E., & Mincy, R. (1990). Growth of the underclass: 1970–1980. *Journal of Human Resources, 25,* 137–145.

Rieder, C., & Cicchetti, D. (1989). Organizational perspective on cognitive control functioning and cognitive-affective balance in maltreated children. *Developmental Psychology, 25,* 382–393.

Robins, L. N. (1966). *Deviant children grown up.* Baltimore: Williams & Wilkins.

Roff, M., Sells, B., & Golden, M. M. (1972). *Social adjustment and personality development in children.* Minneapolis: University of Minnesota Press.

Rogeness, G. A. (1991). Psychosocial factors and amine systems. *Psychiatry Research, 39,* 215–217.

Rogeness, G. A., Javors, M. A., & Pliszka, S. R. (1992). Neurochemistry and child and adolescent psychiatry. *Journal of the American Academy of Child and Adolescent Psychiatry, 31,* 765–781.

Rogosch, F. A., & Cicchetti, D. (1994). Illustrating the interface of family and peer relations through the study of child maltreatment. *Social Development, 3,* 291–308.

Rogosch, F. A., Cicchetti, D., Shields, A., & Toth, S. L. (in press). Facets of parenting dysfunction in child maltreatment. In M. H. Bornstein (Ed.), *Handbook of parenting: Vol. 4. Applied and practical considerations of parenting.* Hillsdale, NJ: Erlbaum.

Rosenbaum, A., & O'Leary, K. D. (1981a). Children: The unintended victims of marital violence. *American Journal of Orthopsychiatry, 51,* 692–699.

Rosenbaum, A., & O'Leary, K. D. (1981b). Marital violence: Characteristics of abusive couples. *Journal of Consulting and Clinical Psychology, 49,* 63–71.

Rosenbaum, M., & Bennett, B. (1986). Homicide and depression. *American Journal of Psychiatry, 143,* 367–370.

Rosenberg, M. S. (1987). New directions for research on the psychological maltreatment of children. *American Psychologist, 42,* 166–171.

Rubin, K. H., LeMare, L., & Lollis, S. (1990). Social withdrawal in childhood: Developmental pathways to peer rejection. In S. R. Asher & J. D. Coie (Eds.), *Peer rejection in childhood* (pp. 217–249). New York: Cambridge University Press.

Rubin, K. H., & Lollis, S. P. (1988). Beyond attachment: Possible origins and consequences of social withdrawal in childhood. In J. Belsky & T. Nezworski (Eds.), *Clinical implications of attachment* (pp. 219–252). Hillsdale, NJ: Erlbaum.

Rubin, K. H., & Mills, R. S. L. (1988). The many faces of isolation. *Journal of Consulting and Clinical Psychology, 6,* 916–924.

Rubin, K. H., & Ross, H. S. (1988). Toward the study of social competence, social status, and social relations. In C. Howes (Ed.), *Peer interaction in your children. Monographs of the Society for Research in Child Development, 53,* 79–87.

Rutter, M. (1986). The developmental psychopathology of depression: Issues and perspectives. In M. Rutter, C. Izard, & P. Read (Eds.), *Depression in young people: Developmental and clinical perspectives* (pp. 3–30). New York: Guilford.

Rutter, M., & Giller, H. (1983). *Juvenile delinquency: Trends and perspectives.* Hamondsworth, England: Penguin.

Rutter, M., & Quinton, D. (1984). Long-term follow-up of women institutionalized in childhood: Factors promoting good functioning in adult life. *British Journal of Developmental Psychology, 2,* 191–204.

Sack, W. H., & Mason, R. (1980). Child abuse and conviction of sexual crimes: A preliminary finding. *Law and Human Behavior, 4,* 211–215.

Salzinger, S., Feldman, R. S., Hammer, M., & Rosario, M. (1993). The effects of physical abuse on children's social relationships. *Child Development, 64,* 169–187.

Salzman, J. P., Salzman, C., Wolfson, A. N., Albanese, M., Looper, J., Ostacher, M., Schwartz, J., Chinman, G., Land, W., & Miyawaki, E.

(1993). Association between borderline personality structure and history of childhood abuse in adult volunteers. *Comprehensive Psychiatry, 34,* 254–257.

Sameroff, A., & Chandler, M. (1975). Reproductive risk and the continuum of caretaking casualty. In F. Horowitz (Ed.), *Review of child development research* (Vol. 4, pp. 187–244). Chicago: University of Chicago Press.

Sander, L. (1962). Issues in early mother-child interaction. *Journal of the American Academy of Child Psychiatry, 1,* 141–166.

Sapolsky, R., Krey, L., & McEwen, B. (1984). Glucocorticoid-sensitive hippocampal neurons are involved in terminating the adrenal stress response. *Proceedings of the National Academy of Sciences of the United States, 81,* 6174–6177.

Scarr, S. (1992). Developmental theories for the 1990s: Development and individual differences. *Child Development, 63,* 1–19.

Scarr, S. (1993). Biological and cultural diversity: The legacy of Darwin for development. *Child Development, 64,* 1333–1353.

Scarr, S., & McCartney, K. (1983). How people make their own environments: A theory of genotype → environment effects. *Child Development, 54,* 424–435.

Schneider-Rosen, K., Braunwald, K., Carlson, V., & Cicchetti, D. (1985). Current perspectives in attachment theory: Illustration from the study of maltreated infants. In I. Bretherton & E. Waters (Eds.), *Growing points in attachment theory and research. Monographs of the Society for Research in Child Development, 50* (Serial No: 209), 194–210.

Schneider-Rosen, K., & Cicchetti, D. (1984). The relationship between affect and cognition in maltreated infants: Quality of attachment and the development of visual self-recognition. *Child Development, 55,* 648–658.

Schneider-Rosen, K., & Cicchetti, D. (1991). Early self-knowledge and emotional development: Visual self-recognition and affective reactions to mirror self-image in maltreated and non-maltreated toddlers. *Developmental Psychology, 27,* 471–478.

Shields, A. M., Cicchetti, D., & Ryan, R. (1994). The development of emotional and behavioral self regulation and social competence among maltreated school-age children. *Development and Psychopathology, 6,* 57–75.

Sigel, I. E. (1986). Reflections on the belief-behavior connection: Lessons learned from a research program on parental belief systems and teaching strategies. In R. D. Ashmore & D. M. Brodzinsky (Eds.), *Thinking about the family: Views of parents and children* (pp. 35–65). Hillsdale, NJ: Erlbaum.

Sloan, M. P., & Meier, J. H. (1983). Typology for parents of abused children. *Child Abuse and Neglect, 7,* 443–450.

Spangler, G., & Grossmann, K. E. (1993). Biobehavioral organization in securely and insecurely attached infants. *Child Development, 64,* 1439–1450.

Sroufe, L. A. (1979). Socioemotional development. In J. Osofsky (Ed.), *Handbook of infant development,* (1st ed., pp. 462–516). New York: Wiley.

Sroufe, L. A. (1989). Relationships, self, and individual adaptation. In A. J. Sameroff & R. N. Emde (Eds.), *Relationship disturbances in early childhood: A developmental approach* (pp. 70–96). New York: Basic Books.

Sroufe, L. A., Carlson, E., & Shulman, S. (1993). Individuals in relationships: Development from infancy through adolescence. In D. C. Funder, R. D. Parke, C. Tomlinson-Keasey, & K. Widaman (Eds.), *Studying lives through time: Personality and development* (pp. 315–342). Washington, DC: American Psychological Association.

Sroufe, L. A., & Fleeson, J. (1986). Attachment and the construction of relationships. In W. Hartup & Z. Rubin (Eds.), *Relationships and development* (pp. 51–76). Hillsdale, NJ: Erlbaum.

Sroufe, L. A., & Fleeson, J. (1988). The coherence of family relationships. In R. A. Hinde & J. Stevenson-Hinde (Eds.), *Relationships within families* (pp. 27–47). Oxford, England: Clarendon Press.

Sroufe, L. A., & Rutter, M. (1984). The domain of developmental psychopathology. *Child Development, 55,* 17–29.

Sroufe, L. A., & Waters, E. (1977). Attachment as an organizational construct. *Child Development, 48,* 1184–1199.

Steinberg, L., Catalano, R., & Dooley, D. (1981). Economic antecedents of child abuse and neglect. *Child Development, 52,* 975–985.

Stern, D. N. (1989). The representations of relational patterns: Developmental considerations. In A. J. Sameroff & R. N. Emde (Eds.), *Relationship disturbances in early childhood: A developmental approach* (pp. 52–69). New York: Basic Books.

Sternberg, K. J., Lamb, M. E., Greenbaum, C., Cicchetti, D., Dawud, S., Cortes, R. M., Krispin, O., & Lorey, F. (1993). Effects of domestic violence on children's behavior problems and depression. *Developmental Psychology, 29,* 44–52.

Sternberg, K. J., Lamb, M. E., Greenbaum, C., Dawud, S., Cortes, R. M., & Lorey, F. (in press). The effects of domestic violence on children's perceptions of their perpetrating and nonperpetrating parents. *International Journal of Behavioral Development.*

Stovall, G., & Craig, R. J. (1990). Mental representations of physically abused and sexually abused latency-aged females. *Child Abuse and Neglect, 14,* 233–242.

Straus, M. A. (1979). Family patterns of child abuse in a nationally representative sample. *Child Abuse and Neglect, 3,* 23–25.

Straus, M. A., & Gelles, R. J. (1986). Societal change in family violence from 1975 to 1985 as revealed by two national surveys. *Journal of Marriage and the Family, 48,* 465–479.

Straus, M. A., Gelles, R. J., & Steinmetz, S. K. (1980). *Behind closed doors: Violence in the American family.* New York: Anchor Press.

Straus, M. A., & Kaufman-Kantor, G. (1986). Stress and physical child abuse. *Child Abuse and Neglect, 4,* 75–88.

Terr, L. C. (1981). Psychic trauma in children: Observations following the Chowchilla school-bus kidnapping. *American Journal of Psychiatry, 138,* 14–19.

Terr, L. C. (1991). Childhood traumas: An outline and overview. *American Journal of Psychiatry, 148,* 10–20.

Teti, D. M., & Ablard, K. E. (1989). Security of attachment and infant-sibling relationships: A laboratory study. *Child Development, 60,* 1519–1528.

Toth, S. L., & Cicchetti, D. (1993). Child maltreatment: Where do we go from here in our treatment of victims? In D. Cicchetti & S. L. Toth (Eds.), *Child abuse, child development, and social policy* (pp. 399–437). Norwood, NJ: Ablex.

Toth, S. L., & Cicchetti, D. (in press). Patterns of relatedness, depressive symptomatology, and perceived competence in maltreated children. *Journal of Consulting and Clinical Psychology.*

Toth, S. L., Manly, J., & Cicchetti, D. (1992). Child maltreatment and vulnerability to depression. *Development and Psychopathology, 4,* 97–112.

Trickett, P. K., Aber, J. L., Carlson, V., & Cicchetti, D. (1991). The relationship of socioeconomic status to the etiology and developmental sequelae of physical child abuse. *Developmental Psychology, 27,* 148–158.

Trickett, P., & Kuczynski, L. (1986). Children's behaviors and parental discipline in abusive and nonabusive families. *Developmental Psychology, 22,* 115–123.

Trickett, P. K., McBride-Chang, C., & Putnam, F. W. (1994). The classroom performance and behavior of sexually abused females. *Development and Psychopathology, 6,* 183–194.

Trickett, P., & Susman, E. J. (1988). Parental perceptions of child-rearing practices in physically abusive and nonabusive families. *Developmental Psychology, 24,* 270–276.

Troy, M., & Sroufe, L. A. (1987). Victimization among preschoolers: Role of attachment relationship history. *Journal of the American Academy of Child Psychiatry, 26,* 166–172.

Trupin, E., Tarico, V., Low, B., Jemelka, R., & McClellan, J. (1993). Children on child protective service caseloads: Prevalence and nature of serious emotional disturbance. *Child Abuse and Neglect, 17,* 345–355.

Tulving, E. (1985). How many memory systems are there? *American Psychologist, 40,* 385–398.

Tulving, E. (1989). Remembering and knowing the past. *American Scientist, 77,* 361–367.

Turkheimer, E., & Gottesman, I. I. (1991). Individual differences and the canalization of human behavior. *Developmental Psychology, 27,* 18–22.

Twentyman, C. T., & Plotkin, R. C. (1982). Unrealistic expectations of parents who maltreat their children: An educational deficit that pertains to child development. *Journal of Clinical Psychology, 38,* 497–503.

Udwin, O. (1993). Annotation: Children's reactions to traumatic events. *Journal of Child Psychology and Psychiatry, 34,* 115–127.

U.S. Department of Justice. (1991). *Criminal victimization, 1990* (Special Report No. NCJ-122743). Washington, DC: Author.

van der Kolk, B. (1987). The compulsion to repeat the trauma: Reenactment, revictimization, and masochism. *Psychiatric Clinics of North America, 12,* 389–411.

Van IJzendoorn, M. H. (1992). Intergenerational transmission of parenting: A review of studies in nonclinical populations. *Developmental Review, 12,* 76–99.

Vondra, J., Barnett, D., & Cicchetti, D. (1989). Perceived and actual competence among maltreated and comparison school children. *Development and Psychopathology, 1,* 237–255.

Vondra, J., Barnett, D., & Cicchetti, D. (1990). Self-concept, motivation, and competence among preschoolers from maltreating and comparison families. *Child Abuse and Neglect, 14,* 525–540.

Wachs, T. D. (1992). *The nature of nurture* (Individual Differences and Development Series, Vol. 3). Newbury Park, CA: Sage.

Waddington, C. H. (1942). Canalization of development and the inheritance of acquired characters. *Nature, 150,* 563–564.

Waddington, C. H. (1957). *The strategy of genes.* London: Allen & Unwin.

Walker, E., Downey, G., & Bergman, A. (1989). The effects of parental psychopathology and maltreatment on child behavior: A test of the diathesis-stress model. *Child Development, 60,* 15–24.

Wasserman, G. A., Green, A., & Allen, R. (1983). Going beyond abuse: Maladaptive patterns of interaction in abusing mother-infant pairs. *Journal of the American Academy of Child Psychiatry, 22,* 245–252.

Weaver, T., & Clum, G. (1993). Early family environments and traumatic experiences associated with borderline personality disorder. *Journal of Consulting and Clinical Psychology, 61,* 1068–1075.

Weiss, B., Dodge, K. A., Bates, J. E., & Pettit, G. S. (1992). Some consequences of early harsh discipline: Child aggression and a maladaptive social information processing style. *Child Development, 63,* 1321–1335.

Westen, D. (1994). The impact of sexual abuse on self structure. In D. Cicchetti & S. L. Toth (Eds.), *Rochester Symposium on Developmental Psychopathology: Vol. 5. Disorders and dysfunctions of the self* (pp. 223–250). Rochester, NY: University of Rochester Press.

Whipple, E. E., & Webster–Stratton, C. (1991). The role of parental stress in physically abusive families. *Child Abuse and Neglect, 15,* 279–291.

Widom, C. S. (1988). Sampling biases and implications for child abuse research. *American Journal of Orthopsychiatry, 58,* 260–270.

Widom, C. S. (1989). Does violence beget violence? A critical examination of the literature. *Psychological Bulletin, 106,* 3–28.

Widom, C. S. (1991). Avoidance of criminality in abused and neglected children. *Psychiatry, 54,* 162–174.

Winnicott, D. W. (1958). *Through pediatrics to psycho-analysis: Collected papers.* New York: Basic Books.

Winnicott, D. W. (1965). *The maturational processes and the facilitating environment: Studies in the theory of emotional development.* New York: International Universities Press.

Wodarski, J. S., Kurtz, J. S., Gaudin, J. M., & Howing, P. T. (1990). Maltreatment and the school-age child: Major academic, socioemotional, and adaptive outcomes. *Social Work, 35,* 506–513.

Wolfe, D. A. (1985). Child abusive parents: An empirical review and analysis. *Psychological Bulletin, 97,* 462–482.

Wolfe, D. A. (1991). *Preventing phsical and emotional abuse of children.* New York: Guilford.

Wolfe, D. A., Fairbank, J. A., Kelly, J. A., & Bradlyn, A. S. (1983). Child abusive parents' physiological responses to stressful and non-stressful behavior in children. *Behavioral Assessment, 5,* 363–371.

Wolfe, D. A., & Jaffe, P. (1991). Child abuse and family violence as determinants of child psychopathology. *Canadian Journal of Behavioural Science, 23,* 282–299.

Wolfe, D. A., & McGee, R. (1994). Dimensions of child maltreatment and their relationship to adolescent adjustment. *Development and Psychopathology, 6,* 165–181.

Wolfner, G. D., & Gelles, R. J. (1993). A profile of violence toward children: A national study. *Child Abuse and Neglect, 17,* 197–212.

Youngblade, L. M., & Belsky, J. (1989). Child maltreatment, infant-parent attachment security, and dysfunctional peer relationships in toddlerhood. *Topics in Early Childhood Special Education, 9,* 1–15.

Zeanah, C. H., & Zeanah, P. D. (1989). Intergenerational transmission of maltreatment. *Psychiatry, 52,* 177–196.

Zingraff, M. T., Leiter, J., Myers, K. A., & Johnsen, M. C. (1993). Child maltreatment and youthful problem behavior. *Criminology, 31,* 173–202.

Zuravin, S. J. (1991). Research definitions of child abuse and neglect: Current problems. In R. Starr & D. Wolfe (Eds.), *The effects of child abuse and neglect: Issues and research* (pp. 100–128). New York: Guilford.

CHAPTER 3

A Developmental Model of Childhood Traumatic Stress

ROBERT S. PYNOOS, ALAN M. STEINBERG, and RUTH WRAITH

Common wisdom has always held that certain childhood experiences are formative, indeed that both creativity and character are often born out of early tragedy. The past two decades have provided progressively more systematic knowledge about the reactions of children and adolescents to traumatic stress. As we make advances in our understanding of these reactions, however, we must ensure that our continued efforts increasingly incorporate and emphasize a sound developmental perspective.

This chapter attempts to synthesize current knowledge about child and adolescent exposure to traumatic stress into a developmental framework that recognizes the intricate matrix of a changing child and environment, evolving familial and societal expectations, and an essential linkage between disrupted and normal development. This developmental model of traumatic stress in childhood assigns a prominent role to the trauma-related formation of expectations as these are expressed in the thought, emotions, behavior, and biology of the developing child. By their very nature and degree of personal impact, traumatic experiences can skew expectations about the world, the safety and security of interpersonal life and the child's sense of personal integrity. These expectancies, as Bowlby discussed (1973), contribute to our inner plans of the world, and shape concepts of self and others and forecasts about the future that have a powerful influence on current and future behavior. After traumatic exposure(s), these altered expectations place the child at risk for proximal and distal developmental disturbances.

Modern developmental theory proposes that expectations arise from the progressive conceptualization of situational experiences and perceptions into prototypes or abstractions that synthesize average features of variable instances (Smith & Medin, 1981). For example, important research in child development has indicated that an infant develops an internal representation of the mother's face from a range of normal expressive variations (Stern, 1985). The extreme experience of witnessing the horrifying look on a mother's face as she screams for her life may seriously compromise the emerging composite image of the mother and, thereby, the relationship with her or subsequent primary attachment figures. The formation of traumatic expectations may represent a breach in the schematic "averaging," distorting emotional, cognitive, and moral concepts as well as inner representations of self, object relations, and the social environment. Of particular importance is the risk of a premature trauma-induced foreclosure of vital developmental and experiential revisions (Pynoos, 1993).

Figure 3.1 presents a detailed temporal model that has been expanded from a previous review of the complex interactions of trauma and development (Pynoos, 1993). This schema incorporates a tripartite model of the etiology of posttraumatic *distress,* deriving from the nature of the *traumatic experience(s)* and from the subsequent *traumatic reminders* and *secondary stresses. Resistance and vulnerability,* which directly mediate distress, are differentiated from *resilience,* which refers to early effective efforts at adjustment and recovery. Conceptualization of *adjustment processes* gives equal attention to the influence on, and the influence of both *proximal development* and *proximal stress-related psychopathology.* Ongoing adjustment interacts with *distal traumatic reminders* and *distal secondary stresses,* and, over time, interacts with *distal developmental disturbances* and *distal stress-related psychopathology.* The overall schema includes a permeable, pervasive interface with both the *ecology of the child's environment* and aspects of *the child's emerging personality.* This model incorporates a conceptualization of stress proposed by Steinberg and Ritzmann (1990), based on living systems theory (Miller, 1978).

A developmental model suggests important areas of clinical assessment and intervention and new avenues for future research. For example, this model indicates the need for more rigorous and refined typologies of traumatic exposures, traumatic reminders, and secondary stresses. A proper assessment of these categories is essential to the evaluation of a child, particularly in clarifying the relative contribution of each etiologic factor to subsequent posttraumatic distress, comorbid conditions, and developmental disturbances (see Cicchetti & Lynch, 1993).

With increased understanding of the complexity of traumatic stress, researchers are beginning to study such areas as the interaction of traumatic exposure to single or recurring extrafamilial violence within an environment of chronic danger; the impact of acute or repeated intrafamilial traumatic experiences within the context

The authors gratefully acknowledge support for the writing of this chapter from the John D. and Catherine T. MacArthur Foundation, the Robert Ellis Simon Foundation, and the Bing Fund.

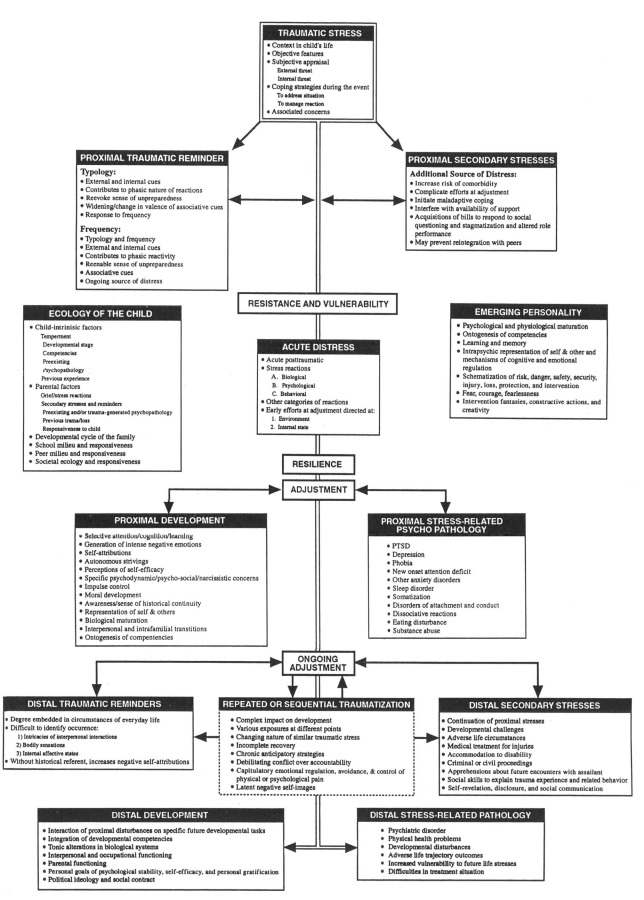

Figure 3.1 Model of the etiology of and reaction to childhood traumatic stress.

of a more general pathogenic family environment; and the potential interaction over time of these extra and intrafamilial traumatic experiences and their associated ecologies (Bell & Jenkins, 1991; Cicchetti & Carlson, 1989; Garbarino, Kostelny, & Dubrow, 1991; Macksoud, Dyregrov, & Raundalen, 1993; Martinez & Richters, 1993). For example, high crime rates and violence in a community may precipitate home acquisition of firearms for self-protection, which may, in turn, be associated with increased risk of intrafamilial firearm threats (Richters & Martinez, 1993), parental suicide by firearm (Groves, Zuckerman, Marans, & Cohen, 1993), and accidental shootings (Cotton, 1992).

In addition, traumatic exposure has been more clearly conceptualized as involving specific sequences of traumatic experiences. There may be a characteristic sequence associated with a type of traumatic situation, for example, violent political persecution (Keilson, 1979/1992) or major disaster (Sugar, 1988). On the other hand, in circumstances of family or community violence, children may experience a highly variable series of exposures occurring at different developmental stages. The typology of trauma also takes into consideration the developmental cycle of the family, which includes the current developmental phase of each family member as well as the developmental phase of the family as a whole (Brown, 1980; Cicchetti, 1993). Children suffering from life-threatening illnesses who undergo life-endangering medical procedures fall into a category where traumatic exposures require parental consent (Stuber, Nader, Yasuda, Pynoos, & Cohen, 1991).

In contrast to models that emphasize basic categories of acute, chronic, or cumulative/strain trauma (Khan, 1963; Terr, 1991), the proposed developmental schema indicates that new or repeated traumatic exposures are to be understood within this interactive framework. Subsequent traumatic experiences entail new sources of distress and are associated with their own reminders and secondary stresses, efforts at adjustment, and implications for developmental tasks, emerging personality, and stress-related psychopathology. Additional considerations include changes in the child from prior experiences, those initiated by the new experience, and those inherent in the evolution of the child's ecology and developmental progression.

In addition, this developmental model incorporates a multidimensional matrix that contributes to a changing liability of exposure to traumatic experiences throughout childhood and adolescence. Age, sex, and child-intrinsic factors interact with family, peer, community, and societal environments. In young children, affiliative dependence and reliance on the protection of caretakers is associated with increased risk of violent harm at the hands of a caretaker or injury due to adult negligence or inadequate supervision. Relative risk of accidental injury, dog bites, sexual molestation and exploitation, intentional severe physical injury, or life-threat from adult aggression vary with age, sex, and adult response to child-intrinsic factors.

As children mature, school milieu and neighborhood environment increasingly contribute to liability of exposure. In addition, progressive engagement in unsupervised activities such as walking to and from school or recreational activities may increase exposure to extrafamilial violence or accidental injury (e.g., hit-and-run accidents). In school-age children, the lack of adult presence at the time of violence or disaster may increase the nature and severity of exposure. During adolescence, peer group affiliation may increase the risk of violence and accidental life-threat, injury, and death. Moreover, adolescent experimentation with drugs and alcohol, inexperienced operation of a motor vehicle, later curfew hours, and geographic mobility changes the potential profile of traumatic exposures. Late adolescence and early adulthood are associated with additional risks of military combat exposure or voluntary involvement with disaster rescue work.

Over the past decade, research findings have substantiated the contribution of family, social, and political circumstances. There is significant evidence for the special risk of children's witnessing violence to a family member or peer, such as rape, murder, or suicide behavior, and interspousal violence or abuse of a sibling (Black & Kaplan, 1988; Carlson, 1984; Malmquist, 1984; Pynoos & Eth, 1985; Pynoos & Nader, 1988; Rosenberg, 1987). Family factors associated with increased risk of intrafamilial violence include parental psychopathology, lack of supervision, marital discord, maladaptive assortative mating, recent unemployment, and alcohol or other substance abuse by adult caretakers (Cicchetti & Lynch, 1993; Daly & Wilson, 1981). Changing family patterns also influence the rate of intrafamilial sexual abuse, such as the increased risk of sexual molestation by stepfathers (Russell, 1986).

Recently, the significant risk of exposure of even young children to community violence within the United States has been documented. Sociological findings have indicated that increased access to firearms is associated with children increasingly being victims, witnesses, and perpetrators of violent acts, and accidental shootings involving guns (Cotton, 1992). Even within the same community, intrafamilial factors mediate rates of exposure. For example, Osofsky (1992) reported that half of the children in one neighborhood in New Orleans exposed to acts of community violence were parented by adolescent mothers. In contrast, Richters and Martinez (1993) have reported on the protective role of grandparents' involvement in the upbringing of grandchildren. Emerging personality may contribute to risk of exposure, for example, by children or adolescents becoming engaged in activities where their own actions contribute to the risk of violence or injury. Genetic vulnerability may contribute to risk through a series of developmental interactions. For example, unaddressed Attention Deficit/Hyperactivity Disorder may lead to both school behavioral problems and peer rejection, and subsequent increased risk of substance abuse and juvenile offenses (Mannuzza, Klein, Bessler, Malloy, & LaPadula, 1993) that could involve an adolescent in a violent drug-related confrontation.

There is enhanced appreciation of the extent to which children are exposed to terrorism, war, atrocities against civilians, ethnic or religious violence, and political oppression and torture. Within intrafamilial and extrafamilial violent circumstances, the rates, nature, and severity of traumatic exposures vary with age, gender, and personality. For example, young children may not be able to remove themselves from repeated exposure to domestic violence, whereas by intervening, a late adolescent may either be injured by or injure a family member. During civil war or occupation, young children may be partially protected by being kept indoors, whereas older children or adolescents may become involved in supporting military or resistance activities. In addition, older boys may be targeted for elimination or imprisonment as potential enemy soldiers, and adolescent girls made victim to rape or abduction.

TABLE 3.1 Typology of Reported Traumatic Exposures in Children and Adolescents

Small and Large-Scale Natural and Technological Disasters
  Earthquake, flood, fire, tornado, hurricane, lightning-strike, cyclone, nuclear reactor accident
Accidents
  Transportation calamities—train, airplane, ship, automobile, etc.
  Severe accidental injury—burns, hit-and-run accidents, accidental shooting, etc.
Intra- and Extrafamilial Violence
  Kidnapping and hostage situations
  Community violence—gang violence, sniper attacks, etc.
  Political, racial or religious related violence—terrorism, war, atrocities, torture, etc.
  Massive catastrophic trauma—concentration camp, etc.
  Witnessing rape, murder, interspousal violence, and suicidal behavior
  Sexual molestation, incest, exploitation; physical abuse
Life-Threatening Illnesses and Life-Endangering Medical Procedures

Adapted from "Traumatic Stress and Developmental Psychopathology in Children and Adolescents" by R. Pynoos. In J. M. Oldham, M. B. Riba, and A. Tasman (Eds.), *American Psychiatric Press Review of Psychiatry* (Vol. 12, pp. 208). Washington, DC: American Psychiatric Press. Copyright 1993 by American Psychiatric Press. Adapted by permission.

The rates and severity of children's exposures to specific traumatic experiences during natural or technological disasters are strongly influenced by socioeconomic factors. For example, housing conditions, school building standards, advanced warning and evacuation plans, and disaster relief capabilities affect the rate at which children are injured or trapped, or witness injury or death to others. Whereas the morbidity and mortality rates associated with natural disasters are decreasing in the more industrialized countries, widespread death, injury, and destruction often occurs in developing countries, with large numbers of affected child survivors (Pynoos, Goenjian, Tashjian et al., 1993; Weisaeth, 1993). Also, as modern medical technology has advanced, children and adolescents are increasingly exposed to extremely intrusive medical procedures, aspects of which can be highly traumatizing. Mental health investigators are becoming appreciative of their traumatic elements, and of the child's experience of failure of parental protection, parental coercion, and entrapment in painful procedures.

The types of traumatic exposure reported in the literature on Posttraumatic Stress Disorder (PTSD) in children and adolescents fall into four major categories, which are presented in Table 3.1.

TRAUMATIC STRESS

The dualistic conceptualization of traumatic stress proposed in this model includes objective and subjective components.

Objective Features of the Traumatic Situation

Paralleling progress in the study of traumatic stress in adulthood, child investigations have provided more precise delineation of the specific features of traumatic experiences associated with risk for posttraumatic stress and other reactions. For example, recent studies of disasters and transportation accidents have indicated that such factors as exposure to direct life-threat, injury to self, witnessing of mutilating injury or grotesque death (especially to family members or friends), and hearing unanswered screams for help and cries of distress are strongly associated with the onset and persistence of Posttraumatic Stress Disorder (PTSD) in children and adolescents (Gleser, Green, & Winget, 1981; Pynoos, Goenjian, Tashjian et al., 1993; Yule & Williams, 1990).

The literature related to violence has identified additional objective features associated with risk, which include proximity to violent threat, the unexpectedness and duration of the experience(s), the extent of violent force and the use of a weapon or injurious object, the number and nature of threats during an episode, the witnessing of atrocities, the relationship to the assailant and other victims, use of physical coercion, violation of the physical integrity of the child, and degree of brutality and malevolence (Pynoos, Sorenson, & Steinberg, 1993). The posttrauma viewing of graphic details, such as photographs of atrocities or the mutilated corpse of a family member or friend constitutes an important secondary source of risk (Nader & Pynoos, 1993a).

The dose of exposure experimental model, which includes the use of co-temporaneous comparison groups, provides a scientific method for examining the casual relationship between objective features of a traumatic stress and its psychological sequelae (Pynoos, 1991). In this design, subjects are sorted by their relative exposure based on these refined typologies on a continuum from high exposure to nonexposure. Examination of the relatively homogeneous exposure subgroups permits a more accurate assessment of relative risk due to exposure or to other variables at differing levels of exposure. Studies of both children and adults exposed to disaster, interpersonal violence, and war have documented a direct relationship between dose of exposure, frequency, and severity of posttraumatic stress reactions, symptom profile, pattern of symptom accrual, and symptom improvement (Nader, Pynoos, Fairbanks, & Frederick, 1990; Pynoos et al., 1987).

Discrepancies in prior reports of rates of traumatic reactions in children may be attributable, in part, to the use of general categories of traumatic events rather than refined qualitative and quantitative exposure measures to define subject populations (Yule & Williams, 1990). For example, the pioneering investigations of children exposed to World War II often failed to differentiate among being under general threat during an air raid (Burt, 1943), being strafed by an airplane (Mercier, 1943), or witnessing atrocities and being subjected to daily life-threat in a concentration camp (Kuch & Cox, 1992). After major disasters or catastrophic political violence, children and adolescents exposed to specific risk factors such as those noted earlier, have been found to exhibit uniformly high rates of chronic PTSD (Kinzie, Sack, Angell, Manson, & Rath, 1986; Nader et al., 1990; Pynoos, Goenjian, et al., 1993; Yule & Williams, 1990).

Subjective Appraisal of Both External and Internal Threats

Historically, Freud's (1926) mature model of traumatic helplessness defined a traumatic situation as one where "external and internal, real and instinctual dangers *converge* [author's emphasis]" (p. 168). In traumatic situations, the experience of external threat involves an estimation of the extreme magnitude of the threat, the unavailability or ineffectualness of contemplated or actual protective actions by self or others, and the experience of physical helplessness at irreversible traumatic moments. The experience of internal threat includes a sense of inability to tolerate the affective responses and physiological reactions, as well as a sense of catastrophic personal consequence. The latter includes both dire external and psychodynamic consequences.

The experience of external and internal threats is influenced by subjective appraisals and the adequacy of efforts to address the situation and manage the internal responses. These appraisals and efforts at coping vary with the developmental and experiential maturation of the child, especially in regard to the degree of reliance on parents, adult caretakers, siblings, and peers. The internal responses include not only the autonomic or affective reactions, but also the emerging attribution of symbolic meaning and psychosexual interpretation. As Rosenblatt and Thickstun (1977) have noted, the autonomic arousal, which often continues beyond the direct perception of threat, may itself be appraised as a sign of danger, maintaining traumatic expectations, and "emergency emotions" (Rado, 1969) and behavior.

Recent studies have begun to examine the contribution of children's subjective perception of threat to intraexposure group differences in severity of posttrauma distress (Joseph, Brewin, Yule, & Williams, 1991; Schwarz & Kowalski, 1991). Guilt over acts of omission or commission perceived to have endangered others has been found to be associated with increased severity and persistence of posttraumatic stress reactions (Pynoos et al., 1987; Pynoos, Goenjian, Tashjian et al., 1993; Yule & Williams, 1990). The generation of other negative emotions, for example, shame and rage, can have a similar impact (Lansky, 1990).

The Complexity of Traumatic Experience(s) in Children and Adolescents

Recent empirical studies of acutely traumatized school-age children and adolescents have enhanced our appreciation of the complexity of their traumatic experiences. The following provides an overview of the interrelated components and specific developmental considerations. The context in the child's life contributes to the acute affective state, cognitive preoccupations, and developmental concerns at the onset of the traumatic stress (Fenichel, 1945). For example, a young child's readying himself after his mother's invitation to spend a special day at home with her constitutes an important antecedent in understanding his profound disillusionment in finding her that morning after a suicide attempt (Pynoos & Eth, 1985).

Traumatic experiences include intense moment-to-moment perceptual, kinesthetic, and somatic experiences accompanied by appraisals of external and internal threats. These may include misperceptions and primary appraisals that either minimize or exaggerate the extent of threat or harm. The child is challenged by the intensity and duration of the physiological arousal, affective responses, and psychodynamic threats, at the same time, making continuous efforts to address the situation in behavior,

thought and fantasy, and to manage physiological and emotional reactions.

The child's vantage point of concern or attention may vary. Young children may have their attention drawn away from (or suppress fear for) their own safety when there is imminent danger or actual injury to a parent, sibling, or friend, and experience unalleviated empathic distress (Hoffman, 1979). Alternatively, when the child is about to be harmed or sustains injury, he or she may experience a moment of unconcern, even estrangement from other family members who may also be under threat. When injury to self or other occurs, children may become suddenly preoccupied with concerns about the severity of injury, rescue, and repair. In violent circumstances, children may also feel compelled to inhibit wishes to intervene or to suppress retaliatory impulses out of fear of provoking counterretaliation.

A more radical change in the child's attention and concerns occurs when his or her physical integrity or autonomy begins to be compromised. The child's attention may be directed away from the monitoring of an assailant or imagining outside intervention toward fears of internal psychological and physical harm. The child may then engage self-protective mechanisms to meet these internal threats, including dissociative responses that allow the child to feel a physical distancing from what is happening, to feel it is not happening to him or her, to control autonomic arousal, anxiety, and pain, to protect certain ego functions, and to decrease a sense of active participation (Putnam, this volume; Rose, 1991). During an incestuous violation, sexual molestation, or hostage situation, there may be attempts either to disclaim or to invoke affiliative needs and desires as a means of warding off a sense of active participation or diminish conscious awareness of the physical menace, psychological abasement, and the accompanying distress (Bernstein, 1990).

Traumatic exposure may include additional traumatic moments after cessation of violence or threat, including the need to remain by an injured or dead family member until help arrives, attempts to stop bleeding or give resuscitation, the arrival and activities of the police or paramedics, an abrupt separation of family members, and the subsequent agonizing wait in the emergency room care or surgery to learn about the condition of a family member or friend.

A traumatic experience is often multilayered. Worry about the safety of a family member or friend, whether in the next room or at a different location, is a common source of additional stress. The danger may also remind the child of a previous situation, renewing old fears and anxieties that influence the immediate appraisal of threat and exacerbate physiological and psychological responses. Witnessing the death of an attachment figure or peer evokes concurrent acute reactions to the loss, even while the life-threat continues.

A number of key development concepts elucidate the developmental complexity of traumatic experiences. In the appraisal of external threat, infants and young toddlers rely on social referencing to attachment figures to respond to situations of uncertainty regarding safety and risk (Klinnert, Campos, Source, Emde, & Svejda, 1983), and initiate motoric and mental efforts aimed at searching for the protective figure (Krystal, 1991). Preschool children begin to rely on natural clues that elicit fearful responses and seek the company of attachment figures to diminish fearful apprehensions (Bowlby, 1979a). With maturity, school-age children rely less on cues from their caretakers and more fully appreciate situations of potential threat; they envision increasing self-efficacy in the face of danger and experience a sense of ineffectualness or culpability when that fails. Adolescents more readily rely on their own appraisals of threat and motivation, more fully envision the threatened harm and its later consequences, and struggle with decisions over whether to intervene (Pynoos & Nader, 1993).

The human infant, helpless to take any direct action in the face of external danger, is equipped with alarm reactions to elicit parental response and protection (Krystal, 1991). In preschool children, disruption of the expectation of a protective shield, coercive violation of physical integrity and psychological autonomy, and betrayal of basic affiliative assumptions are associated with intense fear, rage, or shame, and agitated motoric behavior or extreme passivity. Emerging catastrophic emotions "presage catastrophe" and enable the child to act more self-protectively to threats of invasion and bodily injury; failure to prevent harm is accompanied by terror (Rangell, 1991). The school-age child may experience an abrupt dissolution of expectations about a socially modulated world that elicits frightening, even murderous impulses. The more mature sense of surrender to a moment of unavoidable danger may challenge a compensatory sense of invulnerability during the transition to young adulthood and evoke narcissistic rage in an adolescent (Krystal, 1991; van der Kolk, 1985). Salient developmental consequences of a traumatic experience may result from specific failures in these evolving developmentally related expectations.

Traumatic Reminders

Traumatic reminders derive from trauma-specific features of the external and internal threats and subjective reactions of the child. They are ubiquitous in the aftermath of trauma and constitute an additional source of ongoing distress. Psychological and physiological reactivity to reminders contributes to the periodic or phasic nature of renewed traumatic anxiety or avoidant behavior. The unexpected nature of these reminders may reevoke a sense of unpreparedness and lack of control. Because of the complexity of a traumatic experience and its occurrence in a natural setting, there may be a large number of cues whose previous more neutral or even positive associations are now superseded by associations with the traumatic experience(s).

The frequency of traumatic reminders ranges from relatively infrequent to daily, for example, around the anniversary of a specific trauma, once every six months when it thunders and rains heavily, or every night going to bed in the room where a brother discovered the body of his sibling after a suicide. Fictional portrayals in fairy tales, novels, television, or films may serve as reminders to the child. After physical injury, a scar or handicap may act as a daily reminder of how it was incurred, threatening to bring back remembrance of the circumstances and associated distress. Hearing about, seeing, or being in the presence of a perpetrator may intensely challenge the child with reactivation of prior traumatic distress and unresolved

issues of accountability. For example, being in the company of an abusive parent, even years after cessation of sexual abuse, may trigger renewed traumatic expectations, especially if there has continued to be a conspiracy of silence.

Based on clinical descriptive accounts of children, Pynoos, Nader, and March (1991) have previously described categories of common traumatic reminders. These include the event-specific circumstances; precipitating conditions; characteristics of an assailant; signs of danger; endangering objects; associated affective exchanges; indicators of distress; unwanted results and signs of injury or death; parent or teacher reactions during or at reunion; internal reactions including kinesthetic, sensory, and bodily sensations; a sense of helplessness, fear, ineffectualness; and feelings of aloneness, shame, guilt, anger, and sadness.

There are important developmental questions to be investigated in regard to traumatic reminders. Their nature, context, frequency, and impact may vary with development and experience, and, in particular, with the capacity for appropriate cognitive discrimination. Development influences the degree to which a traumatic reminder exacerbates reactions to nontraumatic stress, reactivates or intensifies earlier traumatic distress, or recruits issues of risk and protection from an earlier developmental schema. The child may be challenged by two or more sets of reminders, to both current and past experiences (Pynoos et al., 1991).

Secondary Stresses and Adversities

Traumatic events are commonly associated with secondary stresses and adversities that may vary considerably with both the type of trauma and environmental responsiveness to the child. They constitute additional sources of distress and increase the risk of initial comorbidity of posttraumatic stress reactions with other adverse reactions. They complicate efforts at adjustment and may interfere with normal opportunities for developmental maturation, or initiate maladaptive coping responses that, over time, may be associated with chronic non-PTSD psychopathology. They may substantially interfere with the availability and/or effectiveness of support to the child from parents, family, school, and community.

These adversities fall into four interrelated categories: social structure and values; community and school organization; family function; and individual challenges to the child. Social structure and societal values govern the recognition of the needs of traumatized children and the allocation of resources. They help determine the extent of adversities associated with war, disasters, and interpersonal violence. Social institutions contribute to characteristics of the recovery environment, including the adjudication of blame and provision of restitution, and the type of resources for rehabilitation and child welfare services.

Community disruption resulting from war and large-scale disasters may be associated with deprivation, malnutrition, medical illness, family disruption, diminished social cohesion, dislocation, loss of educational opportunities, emigration and resettlement (see Cicchetti, Toth, & Lynch, 1993). For example, community disorganization and involuntary unemployment after the Mount Saint Helen's volcanic eruption was associated with increases in intrafamilial violence, adult substance abuse, and juvenile delinquency (Adams & Adams, 1984). The disruption and lack of recovery of the school community, including ongoing distress in school personnel, is a significant source of secondary adversity for children (Nader & Pynoos, 1993b; Yule, 1991).

A direct impact of a trauma on family functioning may include parental loss and subsequent impaired caretaking and/or separation of children from family members. Disharmonious offers and need of support due to differences in exposure and reactions among family members often occur (Pynoos, 1992a). Posttrauma disturbances in parental responsiveness and impairment in parental role function are a major source of secondary stress for children. These are often due to parent's own traumatic reactions or grief-related preoccupations, exacerbation of their preexisting psychopathology, and demands on them from secondary adversities.

Situations of chronic extra- and intrafamilial violence can erode the sense of safety, security, and affiliative commitments on which family life is predicated. In chronically violent environments, child-rearing practices may become more authoritarian and restrictive, thus altering parent-child interactions, decreasing opportunities for play, and disturbing family communication (Jensen, Richters, Ussery, Bloedau, & Davis, 1991). Extended family relationships may also be restructured. It may compromise the parental roles of disciplinarian, affection giver, and role model, which may influence long-term moral development in children (Garbarino et al., 1991; Hoffman, 1979).

Children may face a series of individual stressful challenges. They must respond to altered role performance in family or school due to their trauma-related symptoms, disruption of peer relationships, and the need to make new friends due to loss of residence or relocation. They must also respond to reactive changes in their own families and school systems. The aftermath of violent trauma may include the stress of disclosure, forensic examination, participation in criminal proceedings, engagement with social agencies with possible temporary placement, foster care or removal of a parent from the home, custody hearings, stigmatization, and the need to learn new social skills to respond to social questioning, including by peers. Physical injury to the child may require ongoing medical procedures, rehabilitation, adjustment to disability or handicap, and reintegration among one's peer group. The child is additionally challenged by the need to initiate personal or private communications that can bridge the sense of aloneness accompanying the intense subjective distress generated by the traumatic experience.

RESISTANCE AND VULNERABILITY TO TRAUMATIC EXPERIENCE(S)

Resistance and vulnerability refer to factors that mediate the impact of traumatic stress on the type and severity of acute posttraumatic distress. In the addendum to *Inhibitions, Symptoms and Anxiety* (1926), Freud suggested two parameters that affect resistance or vulnerability to experiencing an event as traumatic. These are the subjective estimations of the magnitude of danger and the perceived potential efficacy of one's own or other's efforts to take protective action.

The strength and importance of affiliative attachments (Lazarus & Folkman, 1984) constitute a critical developmental vulnerability. Because of the nature and intensity of children's affiliative needs and desires, they are particularly vulnerable to witnessing threat or harm to a parent or family member, or being victim to a violent betrayal of affiliative assumptions. Studies of children after disasters have identified other ways in which separation-attachment issues can mediate distress. For example, separating children from their parents during rescue efforts or the immediate postdisaster cleanup can measurably increase their postdisaster morbidity (Friedman & Linn, 1957; McFarlane, Policansky, & Irwin, 1987). In addition, during the Three Mile Island nuclear accident, adolescents who were worried about a younger sibling at another school reported greater postdisaster distress and more somatic complaints than their peers (Dohrenwend et al., 1981). Prior threats to important attachment bonds (e.g., parental illness, separation or divorce) may contribute to post-trauma anxiety reactions (Martini, Ryan, Nakayama, & Ramenofsky, 1990).

A crucial mediator of a child's distress is the response during the event(s) of parents or adult caretakers. During air raids or evacuation for disaster, children have reported greater anxiety if their parents or adult caretakers overreacted, appeared unable to respond competently, or appeared in conflict with each other over the appropriate response (Bat-Zion & Levy-Shiff, 1993; Handford et al., 1986). When adult caretakers have remained calm and appear in control, children's anxiety during and after the event is reduced. When adult caretakers, however, have underreacted or minimized an imminent danger which then results in injury or death, children exhibit increased anxiety and distrust (Pynoos & Nader, 1989).

Distress is also mediated by a number of child-intrinsic factors including current developmental competencies, temperament, self-esteem and locus of control, history of previous trauma and preexisting psychopathology, and the child's ability to make cognitive discriminations and to tolerate psychological and physiological reactions. Both resistance and vulnerability may be associated with positive or negative mental health attributes. For example, lack of empathy in a conduct-disturbed child may lead to less overt acute distress. Conversely, intelligence and empathy can increase distress, for example, when a child more fully recognizes the behavior of a hostage taker as erratic and disturbed.

Distress may also be related to the type of causality attributed to the traumatic occurrence. In a bidirectional model, causal attributions may lead to greater emotional distress whereas emotional upset may lead to an attributional search (Dollinger, O'Donnell, & Staley, 1984). Evolving theories of causal attribution have included more refined dimensions for coding causal beliefs (e.g., global-specific, personal-universal, internal-external, controllable-uncontrollable) and examination of their developmental determinants (Graham, Doubleday, & Guarino, 1984; Stratton et al., 1986; Weiner, 1986). These theories also propose a relationship between a causal attribution and such negative emotions as guilt, shame, fear, rage, anger, and pity.

Temperament and preexisting psychopathology may contribute to causal attributions and distress. For example, an inhibited, shy, or anxious child may overly attribute a lack of controllability, overgeneralize trauma-related fears, and thereby experience more intense posttrauma anxiety and display more social reticence. A depressed child may attribute undue guilt to his or her role, and, therefore, manifest a more severe than expected posttraumatic stress reaction. By making extreme external and controllable attributions, an impulsive child may increase their problematic behaviors. In addition, intrapsychic factors including traditional issues of impulse, ego strength and superego development may underlie fundamental differences in casual attribution.

Preschool children are more prone to ascribe pride or blame to themselves or others on the basis of an adventitious outcome, whereas older school-age children are more likely to link these positive and negative emotions with a sense of personal responsibility for the success or failure of protective actions (Pynoos & Eth, 1984). Outside attributions can influence children's own attributions or increase their distress because negative attributions about them from others may threaten affiliative needs and desires. There may be a complex interaction among age, sex, and resistance or vulnerability, depending on the type of traumatic exposure. For example, Pynoos and Nader (1988) reported that, among school-age children and adolescents who witnessed their mother's sexual assault, age was associated with a divergence of posttraumatic distress between boys and girls. Younger boys and girls felt equally fearful that this type of assault could happen to them, whereas adolescent boys and girls, who recognized that risk was associated with gender, differed in fear over personal vulnerability.

Causal attributions for the internal threats involve developmental efforts to externalize or internalize the source of the psychodynamic danger, to attribute responsibility for failures of developmentally linked expectations, and to address inadequacies in self-object representation of protective action. The correspondence of specific traumatic features with phase-specific psychosexual and narcissistic concerns (Eth & Pynoos, 1985; Pynoos & Nader, 1993), may generate intense guilt or shame, especially when current fantasy elements are experienced as "actualized" (Greenacre, 1952). Betrayal of affiliative assumptions may be particularly associated with excessive causal attributions of self-blame that vary with superego development. Failure in protective action may be associated with intense ego-ideal disillusionment with self or other and an unconscious reproach for the traumatic helplessness.

DISTRESS

Distress is the term used to encompass the biological, psychological, and behavioral manifestations of posttraumatic stress reactions. There is compelling evidence to suggest that by school age, children can provide adequate self-reports of their posttraumatic distress, including the full range of posttraumatic stress symptoms. The assessment of the preschool child remains problematic; however, valid and reliable assessment in this age group is an important area of current investigation (Marans et al., 1991; Nader & Pynoos, 1991; Nader, Stuber, & Pynoos, 1991; Sherkow, 1990).

Comprehensive assessment procedures include self-report instruments that provide a continuous scaling of frequency and severity of symptoms; special in-depth interview formats to explore the subjective experience of the child; structured clinical interviews that can reliably establish the presence of a disorder and multiassessment methods, including instruments designed to obtain information from parents, teachers, and significant others (Earls, Smith, Reich, & Jung, 1988; McNally, 1991; Pynoos & Eth, 1986; Pynoos et al., 1987; Saigh, 1989; Yule & Williams, 1990). Disparities in reports of a child's distress by the child, parent, and teacher have been repeatedly found (Nader & Pynoos, 1992; Yule & Williams, 1990; Zivcic, 1993) with children reporting more subjective symptoms and parents typically reporting changes in their children's aggressive, fearful, or regressive behaviors. Parents are least likely to be aware of children's negative emotional reactions or self-imposed restrictions on emotional range and daily activities, and often interpret children's avoidance of any mention of the trauma as a sign of successful recovery.

Posttraumatic stress reactions are difficult to categorize along the traditional spectrum of normal to pathological responses. The acute reactions can be conceptualized as understandable and expected. Professional and societal care must be taken not to impose psychopathological labels that can result in the attribution of additional psychopathology and stigma. Alternatively, acute reactions may involve severe subjective distress, altered behaviors, and neurophysiological disturbances that do not resolve spontaneously. Early identification and intervention may be critical to prevent these symptoms from becoming chronic and disabling.

The clinical diagnostic criteria for PTSD include symptoms of reexperiencing, avoidance and withdrawal, and increased arousal (American Psychiatric Association, 1987). Reexperiencing phenomena include recurrent intrusive distressing recollections of the trauma, traumatic play, dreams or nightmares of the event, behavioral reenactments and psychological and physiological reactivity to reminders of the event. Symptoms of avoidance and numbing of general responsiveness include efforts to avoid feelings or thoughts of the traumatic experience(s) or activities or situations that provoke such recollections, attempts to regulate the intensity of traumatic emotions (Janet's "vehement emotions," as cited in van der Kolk & van der Hart, 1989) "affective blocking" (Krystal, 1978) or "ego contraction" (Kardiner, 1941), feelings of detachment or estrangement from others, and memory disturbances. Disturbances of memory can include omissions, distortions, and amnestic or dissociative reactions. Symptoms of increased arousal include hypervigilance, exaggerated startle reactions, sleep disturbance, dysregulation of aggression, and interference with concentration and attention.

The reexperiencing of phenomena is as central to the disorder in children as it is in adults, as exemplified by the strong association found among exposure, intrusive images, and severity of PTSD reaction (Pynoos et al., 1987; Pynoos, Goenjian, Tashjian et al., 1993; Stuber et al., 1991). These phenomena, including images, smells, sounds, and bodily sensations, are markers of moments of traumatic helplessness, ongoing mental preoccupations and traumatic expectations. The nature and content of these phenomena are, in part, related to the maturity of both iconic memory (integration of isolated pictures into a single percept) and echoic memory (the brief sensory story), as components of autobiographical episodic memory (Baddeley, 1984). Typically, the younger the child, the more the recollection is confined to a single image, sound, or smell, usually representing the action most associated by the child with immediate threat or injury. Intrusive phenomena also incorporate subtle mental modifications to minimize or protect the child from the full horror of the experience, for example, by altering proximity to the immediate danger or freezing the action before irreversible injury. Development and experience influence the nature of these modifications.

Children's portrayal of traumatic images and themes in drawing and play underscore their important role as developmental intermediates "between symbolic play and the mental image" (Piaget & Inhelder, 1969) and between the realms of external and internal reality (Winnicott, 1971). Evolution in the traumatic dream content from specific trauma-related elements to more general threat to self or family, may reflect the developmental reliance on the safety and security of a protective shield. Dreams of their own death may not only represent a sense of life-threat but also a perceived absence, failure, or inadequacy of this shield.

Reenactment behavior to subsequent situations or cues associated with trauma-related actions, taken or imagined, may represent a developmental tendency toward "action memories" (Furman, 1973; Terr, 1988). Reenactments in fantasy, play, or action represent both an "anticipatory bias" in response to perceived threat and efforts to offset in action the original moments of traumatic helplessness. Older children and adolescents may actively seek out opportunities to engage in reenactments, ranging from thrill seeking (Balint, 1959) and controlled risk taking to more aggressively dangerous or violent actions (Cicchetti, Barnett, Rabideau, & Toth, 1991). Suppression or repression of traumatic images may be related to reenactment behaviors, especially in response to traumatic cues, and may underlie the appearance of increased impulsivity.

Avoidance and emotional constriction are difficult to measure in children. However, children do report becoming avoidant of specific thoughts, locations, concrete items, themes in their play and human characteristics and behaviors that remind them of a traumatic experience. Reduced interest in usual activities, including pleasurable ones, may not only reflect a depressed mood, but also traumatic expectations of recurrence. Developmental progression may influence and be influenced by the degree to which traumatic avoidance generalizes to more phobic behavior or leads to more selective restrictions on daily activities and the scope of circumstances to which traumatic expectations of recurrence apply.

A child's recognition of emotional numbing depends on a developmentally acquired capacity for self-perception, perhaps beginning in early adolescence. Younger children may indicate emotional constriction by their wish not to know how they are feeling or by a lack of relevant emotion in their recounting. They may report feeling alone with their subjective experience or describe efforts to keep an emotion from emerging, for example, by going to sit alone. Parents are not always aware of this sense of aloneness or isolation because the child may continue to cling or seek comfort. Children may experience a sense of estrangement, feeling that others, including parents, cannot fully understand or recognize what they went through. Efforts at avoidance and emotional regulation may reflect traumatic expectations of a fearful acceleration of pleasurable as well as unpleasurable emotions (Freud, 1936).

Memory disturbances may reflect specific modifications that occur during recall as well as perceptual, encoding, or storage errors (Bjork & Richardson-Klavehn, 1989). Distortions, omissions, reframing of aspects of the experience, and spatial or temporal misrepresentations of threat may reflect early efforts to minimize the objective threat and to regulate emotional distress during recall (Pynoos & Nader, 1989). Children may recount in detail other fearful moments to screen a memory of a more horrifying moment or may introduce premonitions. Traumatic expectations can acutely disturb memory processing when, for example, immediate preoccupation with future fearful situations distracts attention away from the initial experience. These retrieval modifications may become incorporated into future expectations and appraisals of danger, protection, and intervention. Lack of integration of traumatic moments, which may appear to be fragmentation of the memory, in young children may be due to the immaturity of their cognitive processing and strategy of recall, as well as their reliance on contextual cues. Dissociative memory disturbances may also occur, especially in response to physical coercion, torture, molestation, or abuse.

Children appear to show both tonic and phasic physiological reactivity (Pitman, 1989). The child is "on alert," ready to respond to any environmental threat (Kardiner, 1941). Highly exposed children may experience a serious sleep disturbance associated with changes in sleep architecture and the occurrence of parasomnia symptoms (Ornitz & Pynoos, 1989). Sleep may be fitful and not restful. The sleep disturbance may be intermittent and associated with the occurrence of traumatic reminders or sounds at night, indicating a fear-enhanced proneness to increased awakenings. Children may become afraid of sleep because of the autonomic reactivity associated with stage four awakenings (Fischer et al., 1970). A chronic sleep disturbance may be associated with problems in daytime concentration and learning (Pynoos et al., 1987).

Exaggerated startle reactions have been noted to predict increased overall severity of response in children exposed to major disasters or catastrophic violence (Pynoos, Goenjian, Tashjian et al., 1993; Yule & Williams, 1990). Persistent hypervigilance and exaggerated startle may alter a child's usual behavior by leading to constant efforts to ensure personal security or the safety of others. These recurrent bouts of fear may seriously affect a child's emerging self-concept. In addition, temporary or chronic difficulty in modulating aggression can make children more irritable and easy to anger. This may result in reduced tolerance of the normal behaviors and slights of peers and family members, followed by unusual acts of aggression or social withdrawal (Pynoos et al., 1991).

Acquisition of incident-specific new fears commonly occurs in children. Yule, Bolton, and Udwin (1992), in a comprehensive study of English adolescent students involved in a ferry disaster, found that, opposed to an increase in generalized fearfulness, the survivors developed new fears specifically linked to trauma-related cues. Saigh (1985) proposed that the extent of trauma-related fear acquisition in children is determined by perceived efficacy and anticipated consequences, whereas Dollinger,

O'Donnell, and Staley (1984) suggest an explanation based on a generalization gradient consistent with classical conditioning theory. Developmental progression, as well as trauma-specific features, contributes to potential fears at moments of feeling vulnerable, for instance when alone in the bathroom or when going to bed. In addition to age, gender may be associated with differences in the experiencing of fears and fear-related anxiety. Increased fears have been reported among girls, perhaps due to differences in perception of personal vulnerability and self-efficacy (Green et al., 1991; Lonigan, Shannon, Finch, Daugherty, & Taylor, 1991; Pynoos, Goenjian, Tashjian et al., 1993; Pynoos & Nader, 1988). However, these differences may also reflect reporting bias due to cultural discouragement of male expression of fears (Pynoos, Goenjian, Tashjian et al., 1993). These fears are an expression of traumatic expectations, constituting early warning signals intended to anticipate escalation of external danger and traumatic recurrence. In addition to posttraumatic stress reactions, posttrauma distress may include guilt, grief, worry about a significant other, and reactivation of symptoms associated with previous adverse life experiences (Pynoos & Nader, 1988). These reactions need not be related to degree of exposure. They may increase the severity of posttraumatic stress reactions and contribute to other comorbid conditions. Guilt reactions may reflect the experience of unalleviated distress over inability to prevent injury or death to others and self-blame for acts of omission and/or commission believed to have caused harm. Guilt reactions include exaggerated feelings of personal responsibility, intense survival guilt, and self-defeating behaviors. They are strongly dependent, not only on the specific features of a traumatic exposure, but also on complex developmental processes, including intrapsychic conflicts. For example, whereas a young boy may focus on his "bad" behavior that day as a precipitant of a spousal homicide, an adolescent may blame himself for failing to have anticipated the violent escalation and to have unloaded a household weapon that he discovered weeks before its fatal use.

The interplay of posttraumatic stress and grief reactions constitutes another dimension of acute posttraumatic distress (Pynoos, 1992a). The loss of a family member or friend initiates ongoing grief reactions and adjustment processes with many developmental determinants (Clark, Pynoos, & Goebel, 1994). Acute grief reactions in childhood are associated with symptoms and biological alterations that more closely resemble those of depressive than posttraumatic stress reactions (Weller, Weller, Fristad, & Bowes, 1991). The traumatic circumstances of a death, especially if witnessed by a child, complicates age-appropriate grief and mourning by prolonging preoccupation with the circumstances of the death (Pynoos, 1992a). The traumatic features give rise to painful, unbidden visual imagery, and rumination over the degree of brutality and accountability, and the meaning of the manner of death (Rynearson, 1990). For example, intrusive images of a mutilated parent interfere with the ability to summon positive remembrances of the deceased and can derail appropriate reminiscing. Efforts at alleviating traumatic anxiety appear to take psychological priority over mourning (Eth & Pynoos, 1985). These traumatic sequelae may increase the risk of pathological bereavement, depression, and chronic posttraumatic stress symptoms.

Children may increase attachment behaviors stemming from worries about the safety of family members or friends. These include continued apprehension about a parent, sibling, or friend being out of sight, nightly checking on the safety of a family member, and morbid dreams of catastrophe befalling family members.

Details of the current experience may serve as a significant reminder of past experiences, even in very young children. For example, a child who had a history of serious respiratory distress, focused in his retelling of his father's life-threatening experience with a fire on the threat of his father becoming asphyxiated more than on the risk of being burned. Acute posttraumatic distress may therefore include reactivation or exacerbation of posttraumatic symptoms associated with prior exposures or dangers.

PROXIMAL STRESS-RELATED PSYCHOPATHOLOGY

Children vary in their ability to tolerate and respond to acute distress, to adversities consequent to the event, and to subsequent challenges to self-concept and future expectations. Outcome may range from a relatively successful adaptation that includes restored psychological, interpersonal, and academic functioning to severe trauma-related pathology and pervasive developmental disturbance. The set of trauma-related reactions may constitute recognizable patterns of psychiatric disorder. Children and adolescents' posttrauma psychopathology have been reported to include PTSD, phobic and overanxious disorders, trauma-related disorders of attachment and conduct, new onset attention deficit disorder, depression, substance abuse, and dissociative, sleep, and somatization disorders. The International Classification of Diseases-10 (ICD-10) includes an attachment disorder secondary to intrafamilial abuse and violence (World Health Organization, 1990). Current diagnostic research is evaluating the overlap between criteria of PTSD and other comorbid conditions.

After catastrophic community violence, Pynoos and Nader (1992) reported that the most frequent diagnoses correlated with degree of exposure were PTSD, depression, attention deficit, and phobic disorder. Depression was also found to be correlated with the frequency and intensity of grief reactions. Overanxious behavior and separation anxiety were associated with other factors including worry about a significant other and past history of threats to important attachments (e.g., parental illness, separation, divorce, loss). In response to a catastrophic earthquake, Goenjian and his collaborators are investigating the association of chronic PTSD with an increased risk of concurrent depression (Pynoos, Goenjian, Tashjian et al., 1993). Several mechanisms may account for the risk of concurrent PTSD and depression: (a) the persistence of specific PTSD symptoms such as intrusive imagery may be directly associated with secondary depression; (b) chronic PTSD may curtail personal or family resourcefulness, leading to acute depressive reactions in response to subsequent adversity or undesirable life stresses; and (c) behavioral concomitants of chronic PTSD may include specific maladjustments that result in greater adversity or that directly constitute secondary psychopathology such as substance abuse.

Perry (1994) has proposed that the onset of secondary disorders to PTSD may be linked to specific familial predispositions, accounting for some of the variability in posttrauma psychiatric morbidity. The rate of comorbidity may represent an interplay between specific trauma-related reactions and those associated with the accumulation of secondary adversities (Rutter & Quinton, 1984). Traumatic events can also exacerbate preexisting conduct or learning disorders, which in turn can hamper the ability of the child to process traumatic experiences. Such reciprocal exacerbation may be especially characteristic of substance-abusing adolescents who may come to rely on drugs as a maladaptive coping strategy. The rate of adolescent substance abuse after trauma has been found to be culturally influenced (Kinzie et al., 1986).

THE POTENTIAL EFFECTS OF TRAUMATIC STRESS ON PROXIMAL DEVELOPMENT

The assessment of posttraumatic distress in children and adolescents should include consideration of proximal developmental tasks, including the ontogenesis of developmental competencies (Cicchetti, 1989), interpersonal and intrafamilial developmental transitions (Rutter, 1988) and biological plasticity and consolidation (Ornitz, 1991). Recently acquired developmental achievements may be particularly vulnerable to disruption (Rutter, 1988). A sense of safety and security throughout childhood provides a foundation for the achievement and integration of developmental competencies (Sandler, 1960).

Reexperiencing phenomena skew selective attention either toward or away from concrete and symbolic reminders, and, as proposed by Horowitz (1976), threaten to intrude and disrupt normal information processing. The following suggests potential developmental consequences for information processing in terms of acquisition, content, and functional impairment.

Preschool children may experience cognitive confusions that interfere with the achievement of narrative coherence (Osofsky et al., 1992) and may exhibit a general decrease in verbalization and/or more precocious use of trauma-related expressions. A failure in the appropriate use of fantasy may also occur (Mueller & Tingley, 1990). School-age children may engage in trauma related "detective" work (Pynoos & Eth, 1984) or exhibit selective inhibition of thought and nonreflective daydreaming and make repeated use of traumatic details and meanings that compromise their expanded use of metaphor and the shift from evocative to communicative symbols (Sarnoff, 1971). Adolescents may search for or shun motivational explanations and be challenged in the acquisition of abstract concepts where these concepts subsume more trauma-specific reminders (Pynoos & Nader, 1992). Further, an impairment in attention or learning may have quite different proximal impact for a child who is just learning to read than for a high school student whose sudden scholastic decline affects application to college. The marginal student may be at greatest academic risk (Yule, 1991), with school failure leading to significant loss of self-esteem and increased risk of secondary psychiatric morbidity (Saigh & Mrouegh, 1991).

The generation of intense negative emotions challenges the maturing mechanisms of emotional regulation (Parens, 1991). Fear of affective intensity may interfere with the preschool task of increasing differentiation of affective states, with the capacity for school-age children to elaborate on their affective expression, and with adolescents' efforts to achieve a more sophisticated understanding of the origin and consequences of negative emotions. Somatic complaints and wariness of even intense pleasurable responses may stem from biological similarities resembling the traumatic state of arousal. Self-attributions of shame, ineffectualness, or blame can initiate negative self-images that immediately challenge adaptive functioning. The generation of these intense, self-conscious emotions (Lewis, 1991) may lead to significant alterations in the privatization of internal life, empathic understanding, tendencies toward reparative behavior and prosocial actions. Particularly during latency and preadolescence, painful trauma-related emotions may accelerate an emerging awareness of discrepancies between subjective emotion and social expression and intensify the privatization of internal life.

Autonomous strivings may be subverted by trauma-related avoidant behavior that adversely restricts exploration and normal pleasurable activities; they may also be accelerated by trauma-generated adventuresome pursuits that may lie beyond the child's developmental capabilities. Early assault on the physical integrity of a preschool child or intentional psychological harm may interfere with a developing sense of physical and psychological autonomy by subduing an emerging resistance to coercive violation. As a consequence, there may be limitations on the attribution of similar boundaries to others, including peers.

A child's interpretation (or those proffered by others) of their own behavior during and after a traumatic experience may transform perceptions of self-efficacy. These include a sense of physical prowess or weakness; of passivity or activity; of cowardice, courage, and heroism; and of self-enhancement or diminishment. These appraisals may be linked to changes in self-confidence, self-esteem, and pride that mediate the acquisition or consolidation of new competencies in the immediate posttrauma period (Emde, 1991).

The correspondence of specific traumatic features with phase-specific psychodynamic psychosexual and narcissistic concerns may initiate prolonged developmental disturbances. Acute separation of young children from parents during a disaster may lead to exceptionally intense posttrauma preoccupation with fears of abandonment or desertion that may forestall attempts at individuation. A 5-year-old boy witnessing the use of a dildo during a mother's rape may subsequently be preoccupied with accentuated fears of dismemberment. A preadolescent boy's experience of lying helpless on the floor during a violent rampage in a fast food restaurant, where women were mutilated and killed, may generate unremitting conflicts over masculine and feminine self-attributions.

Unaddressed revenge and counterretaliatory fantasies may challenge the child's maturing capacity for restraint of aggression (Emde, 1991) and appropriate assertiveness. The developmental impact, in part, depends on the relative mobilization and endurance of hostile versus intrumental aggression. Absorption in hostile emotions may interfere with the appropriate instrumental use of aggression in such activities as competitive sports (Atkins, Stoff, Osborne, & Brown, 1993) or precise learning (Gardner, 1971). Witnessing or being victim to adult violence compromises the school-age child's reliance on adult augmentation of emerging impulse control (Schafer, 1976). The immediate social consequences of a dysregulation of aggression differ with age. Whereas the aggressive acts of younger children may be less injurious and more easily restrained, the combination of vengeful fantasy, narcissistic rage (van der Kolk, Perry, & Herman, 1991) and a sense of invulnerability in adolescence, coupled with accessibility of cars, weapons, alcohol, and drugs, provide the precursors to injurious or fatal violence.

The proximal impact on moral development, especially if there is nonadjudication of a violent crime or war-related atrocity, can be profound. In the preschool child, catastrophic violence represents an instantiation of the concept of "bad" that is far beyond its use in the child's daily life. Consequently, there may be interference with the emergence of moral concepts, resulting in behavior that is overly regulated by considerations of good or bad, or alternatively manifestly amoral. Nonadjudication of a parent's murder may undermine a school-age child's evolving reliance on rules to govern behavior. The early adolescent may experience an intense exaggeration of moral confusion (Stilwell, Galvin, & Kopta, 1991), and the late adolescent and young adult may incorporate themes of the threat of violence and revenge into a political ideology (Pynoos, 1992b).

Trauma disturbs the emerging awareness of historical continuity of the self. In preschool children, traumatic experiences embedded in "action memories" may result in their inaccessibility to the emerging verbal self (Stern, 1985; Terr, 1988; Wilson & Malatesta, 1989). Trauma-generated negative emotions may disturb the "affective core of the self," which contributes to one's sense of continuity across developmental progression (Emde, 1991). A trauma-induced sense of discontinuity can have a disrupting influence on the adolescent task of integrating past, present, and future expectations into a lasting sense of identity (Gordon & Wraith, 1993; Pynoos & Nader, 1993). Changes in future orientation, if they represent a discontinuity in expectation and forecast, may adversely affect the adolescent's emerging ambition, initiative, and assertiveness (Krystal, 1991), and alter current behavior by limiting the range of constructive plans for the future (Bowlby, 1979a).

Changes in the representation of self and other can affect critical transitions in child-parent relationships, upsetting the developmental balance between independent and dependent behavior. Cicchetti, Cummings, Greenberg, and Marvin (1990) emphasize that evolving forms of attachment throughout childhood serve the biological function of protecting children from danger while they develop skills to protect themselves. The mutual sense of a disrupted protective shield may alter a young child's reliance on parental efficacy and assurances of safety or security, and parental confidence in their own ability to protect their child. Posttraumatic-stress-related estrangement may deter a mid-adolescent from seeking the counsel of parents at a critical juncture of decision making or risk taking. In late adolescence, there may be a rapid thrust toward self-sufficiency or, out of concern for other family members' safety and security, postponement of plans to leave home.

Critical transitions in establishing peer relationships may be affected. Withdrawal, emotional constriction, and disrupted impulse control may interfere with the preschool tasks of cooperation, sharing, and discovery of the self in relationship to other children. Traumatic play may limit the flexibility of play for other developmental purposes and distort age-specific forms of play, for example, preschool coordinated fantasy play (Parker & Gottman, 1989). The school-age child may suffer an acute disturbance in relatedness to a best friend, may experience a sense of isolation from peers, or be ostracized as "different" because of posttraumatic behavior or physical injury. Reenactment behavior, especially inappropriate sexual or aggressive behavior, may acutely disrupt normative patterns of peer relationships and result in being labeled as deviant. Disturbance in achieving social competence with peers or peer rejection carries an important risk for the future adjustment of the child, secondary developmental consequences, and additional psychopathology (Howes, 1987; Ruben, LeMare, & Lollis, 1990). The adolescent may experience abrupt shifts in interpersonal attachments or heightened attachment in already existing relationships, increased identification with a peer group as a protective shield, or extreme isolation or ostracism, and a tendency toward aberrant rather than mainstream relationships (Pynoos & Nader, 1993).

There are different effects of traumatic stress during development periods characterized by relative neurophysiological plasticity or consolidation. The startle reaction provides a good example of potential neurophysiological vulnerability. It involves a well-elucidated neuroanatomical and biochemical pathway with known developmental maturation (Ornitz, 1991). Ornitz and Pynoos (1989) have provided preliminary evidence that traumatic exposure may interfere with the consolidation of inhibitory control of the startle reflex, representing a "neurophysiological regression" to an earlier pattern of startle modulation. The central nucleus of the amygdala regulates fear-enhanced startle (Ornitz, 1991) and, perhaps, the reactivity to novel stimuli of inhibited children (Kagan, 1991). The loss of inhibitory control over the startle reflex may interfere with the acquisition of a number of latency skills, for example, increased control over activity level, capacity for reflection, focused attention, and academic learning.

The recording, processing, and analyzing of sensory information may vary according to the specific sensory input, and the relative importance of sensory, kinesthetic, and somatic registration may have developmental determinants. For example, the smell of gunfire during a violent event may be registered with very little processing, perhaps, related to the underlying neuroanatomy of olfaction (Buck & Axel, 1991). Even very young children can discriminate accurately among smells (e.g., the ability of infants to respond to food smells with anticipation or rejection). Visual information, however, which utilizes a "visual-spatial pad" (Baddeley, 1984) to represent and manipulate distance and location of a threat, requires more ability to discriminate. In addition, because temporal registration in young children appears to require accurate spatial serialization of the event (Baddeley, 1976), temporal distortions are also commonly encountered.

Memory processing may also depend on the maturing capacity for understanding the metacognition of emotions (Saarni & Harris, 1991). The complexity of a traumatic situation may elicit two or more concurrent or successive emotions, for example, fear, sadness, excitement, and anger (Harter & Whitesell, 1991). The lack of a metacognition of concurrent emotions may interfere with preschool children's reconstruction of their experience, either by requiring the assignment of concurrent emotions to different portions of the experience or the omission of a competing emotion in their recount. The increasing capacity to make affective discriminations of such negative emotions as rage, anger, hostility, hatred, with more refined descriptions of the object and source (Parens, 1991) permits the formation of a more thorough memory of the complexity of the traumatic experience.

Developmental maturation also governs a progressive capacity to integrate unimodal sensory information, affective valence and spatial representation of threat among the interactive neuroprocessing system of the amygdala, hippocampus, and cortical feedbacks. This system tends toward stimulus completion (Rolls, 1989), whereby one sensory, affective, or cognitive reminder tends to elicit the fuller range of associated stimuli, affects, and meanings. At the interface of psychoanalysis and neurobiology, Freud first proposed that suppression, repression, lack of integration and fragmentation of stimuli in young children may constitute efforts to interrupt stimulus completion when presented with a frightening reminder (Freud, 1900). In latency, the combined maturation in cortical inhibitory control (Shapiro & Perry, 1976), and capacities for increased contextual discrimination and affective tolerance may begin to reduce the engagement of these protective mechanisms whereas trauma-related distortions, for example, spatial misrepresentation, may interfere with progressive topographical organization. Rieder and Cicchetti (1989) have suggested, even further, that chronic hypervigilance, for example, in physically abused children, can have a deleterious effect on information processing.

RESILIENCE AND ADJUSTMENT

Resilience and adjustment refer to the child's early and ongoing efforts to tolerate, manage, or alleviate the psychological, physiological, behavioral, and social consequences of traumatic experience(s). Effective adjustment includes the achievement of adequate understanding of the experience and subsequent reactions and, as two outcome measures, the absence of major deviation in the developmental course and distal traumatic stress-related pathology. The child may require different means of coping and support to adjust to trauma-specific features of the experience(s), contextual or affective reminders, secondary stresses, renewed responses to past experiences, subsequent distress, and proximal developmental disturbances.

Of special importance, traumatic experiences appear to activate neuromodulatory systems that enable their "personal consequentiality" (Conway, 1993) as well as their novelty, to influence both remembrance and expectation (McGaugh, 1990). In terms of remembrance, they initiate neurohormonal responses that appear to enhance and extend the period of reappraisal. From an evolutionary perspective, this period of reappraisal can facilitate a more accurate discrimination of potential dangers. At the same time, this "reworking" memory may incorporate other forms of mental modification that mediate the adaptational response, not only acutely, but also over time. From a developmental perspective, the child may be vulnerable to immature appraisals of future dangers and disturbances in emerging appraisal processes due to continued reliance on earlier forms of mental modifications.

Young children, especially, may also be highly vulnerable to inadequacies and incompleteness in these processes.

The goal of cognitive reprocessing is an enhanced age-appropriate understanding of the circumstances and meaning of the traumatic experience(s). It includes efforts to formulate constructive prevention and intervention strategies in relation both to what has occurred and to future situations. Emotional reprocessing represents an effort to understand the origins, legitimacy, and content of negative emotional reactions generated by the experience in order to increase tolerance, diminish self-punitive attributions, and maintain or repair the subjective sense of relatedness.

Parental responsiveness and support to the child or adolescent are major components of the recovery environment of the family and critical determinants of successful adjustment. Responding to the distress of a traumatized child requires the acquisition of relevant parental skills, for example, to address symptoms of increased arousal, reactivity to reminders and behavioral regressions. Parental responsiveness depends, in part, on such traditionally recognized factors as parental personality, preexisting psychopathology, marital satisfaction or discord, and prior relationship with a traumatized child. Parental responsiveness may be compromised by parental trauma and grief reactions, parental agency in the trauma, reactivation of residual or remitted symptoms, and latent self-images from prior children and adult traumatic or grief experiences, and emotional distress and practical problems associated with secondary adversities. Community responsiveness, social support, and socioeconomic factors mediate the influence of these secondary adversities on parental function. For example, Solomon (1986) has commented on the postdisaster vulnerability of single parents. Raundalen (1993) has brought special attention to the potentially profound developmental consequences of maternal depression on infants and toddlers reared in situations of chronic civil war or armed occupation.

Parental assistance in cognitive and emotional reappraisals may facilitate adjustment in providing a coconstruction of the contextual situation and meaning, as well as an empathic legitimization of the child's emotional experience. Parents, however, may be reluctant to participate with the child because they may feel too challenged by the traumatic material and by certain revelations that raise issues of accountability or call for interventions they are not prepared to undertake. Children may be under pressure from adult caretakers to disregard their own registration and attribution of meaning, through misleading explanations, prohibition, threats, or a covert conspiracy of silence. These tend to curtail efforts at adjustment, leading to impaired cognitive and emotional processing and failure to address issues of accountability (Bowlby, 1979b; Cain & Fast, 1972; Kestenberg, 1972).

A key indicator of how children are addressing trauma-specific features is the content and evolution of intervention fantasies. Pynoos and Nader (1989) observed that specific trauma-related "inner plans of action" (Lifton, 1979) are commonly incorporated into the memory representation of the experience(s). These fantasies represent complex mental efforts influenced by age, gender, and life experience, and demonstrate a developmental hierarchy in children's efforts to address the external and internal dangers

TABLE 3.2   Five Intervention Fantasies

1. To alter the precipitating events
2. To interrupt the traumatic action
3. To reverse the lethal or injurious consequences
4. To gain safe retaliation (fantasies of revenge)
5. To prevent future trauma

(Pynoos & Nader, 1993). Five categories of intervention fantasies are presented in Table 3.2. The intervention fantasies may vary as children focus on different moments of the experience, including the preceding circumstances and its aftermath (Pynoos & Nader, 1989).

In their conscious fantasies, children demonstrate a developmental hierarchy in their appraisal and responses to external and internal danger (Pynoos & Eth, 1984; Pynoos & Nader, 1993). For example, preschool children may desperately envision the need for outside help while invoking fantasies of superhuman powers, primarily to protect themselves and against attack. School-age children who entertain conscious fantasies of intervening, for example, by taking the gun out of an assailant's hand, may evoke fantasies of special powers in order to intervene without fear of harm, or may employ phase-appropriate fantasies of rescue and exile to procure safety for themselves or others. With maturity and appreciation of the surrounding circumstances, adolescents envision more opportunities for intervention. They can imagine themselves or peers taking direct action, sometimes reckless or endangering, while maintaining a sense of narcissistic invulnerability. Revenge fantasies also show a developmental progression. For example, preschool children may envision the police tearing an assailant limb from limb while in prison. The latency-age child may envision joining other family members in delivering vigilante justice, and the adolescent actually may contemplate taking revenge into his or her own hands, either directly or by recruiting peer assistance.

Curiously, there is correspondence in the slow maturation of neuroanatomical pathways of the acoustic startle reflex, an avoidant reflex associated with fearful situations, and the developmental evolution of intervention fantasies. For example, immature modulation of the startle reaction in preschool children corresponds to a behavioral disposition toward avoidant or escape behavior when "facing the danger" may be most ineffectual and to children's conscious thoughts of seeking external protection and intervention. Increased inhibitory control of the startle reaction occurs developmentally at an age when children engage in fantasies of personally addressing, disarming, or directly harming the source of the danger and anticipating dangerous situations in order to change them. By adolescence, when startle inhibition is more permanently consolidated, the adolescent not only fantasizes about intervention but also struggles with decisions about taking direct action.

Psychodynamic considerations are particularly germane in understanding the progressive developmental modifications of intervention fantasies as children attempt both to maintain a reality-based veridical memory representation and modify that representation to be more internally tolerable (Pruett, 1984). Unchanging intervention fantasies or role identification may lead to an inflexible, intrapsychic maladjustment which underlies processes that have been variably referred to as "repetition compulsion" (Freud, 1920), "fixation to the trauma" (Freud, 1916), or "identification with the aggressor" (Freud, 1936). This may result in a behavioral disposition that may become manifest in circumstances serving as contextual or emotional reminders.

Issues of accountability are among the most difficult to resolve, presenting potentially serious challenges to the child, the family, and society. They entail developmental phase-specific psychodynamic meanings and affects, and trauma-specific retaliatory and counterretaliatory fantasies. These issues vary depending on the type and degree of perceived human agency, particularly, whether the agent is perceived to be inside or outside the family or group affiliation. Intrafamilial accountability causes profound disturbances in the family matrix by creating intense conflicts of loyalty, different attributions of blame by family members, profound challenges to basic affiliative assumptions, and difficulties in resolving feelings of shame and guilt, and rage, hatred, and revenge. Extrafamilial agency can provoke extreme conscious fantasies of retaliation and counterretaliation that can be terrifying, and at the same time, deeply disruptive to the child's emerging sense of moral and social conscience. Family, group, or society may attempt to mobilize these intense retaliatory wishes into group hatreds, political persecution, and armed violence. Judicial adjudication of blame, which may include punishment and/or restitution, requires bringing a distressing private experience into the public domain. This step raises many secondary concerns for the child and family and links societal attitudes and actions with the attempts at trauma resolution. Responsiveness of the judicial system can help relieve the child and family of a sense of responsibility for retribution, and diminish fears of recurrence and hypervigilance. A child's aggressive traumatic play and dangerous reenactment behavior have been reported to abate in the weeks after the conviction and incarceration of the parent's murderer (Pynoos & Eth, 1984).

Unrealistic expectations about recovery on the part of the child, his or her family, friends and teachers, may exacerbate the child's distress, generate additional negative self-images and prevent help-seeking behaviors (Silver & Wortman, 1980). Successful efforts at adjustment to traumatic distress increase the child's understanding that these reactions are expectable, enhance the child's tolerance of them, and, over time, decrease their frequency and intensity. Recognition of reactivation of prior distress can prevent misinterpretations of these responses as "overreactions," temperamental traits, or moments of parental failure, and provide an opportunity for the child and family to approach the earlier experience within a more mature developmental framework.

Fear of recurrence is a common reaction across varying exposure levels. Addressing myths, rumors, and/or misconceptions can assist children in diminishing anxieties that interfere with daily functioning. Proactive interventions on the part of adult caretakers may be essential to restore a sense of safety and security. Lack of responsiveness on the part of parents, family, school, or community to real dangers of recurrence may not only exacerbate the child's distress but initiate primitive modes of accommodation to anticipatory fears.

A well-maintained interrelatedness with parent, sibling, or teacher is a prerequisite for the empathic understanding and communication of acute and recurrent posttraumatic distress. A child may need overt permission, encouragement, and assistance in describing specific intrusive symptoms, avoidant wishes based on fear, or arousal disturbances. Shared affective exchanges with a child, often requiring parental courage, are necessary to assist in increasing tolerance for negative emotions associated with the experience. Being able to listen to a child's description of his or her subjective experience and distress can generate a sense of authentic mutuality (Stern, 1985) that bridges a private feeling of estrangement.

Proper understanding of the neurophysiological basis of arousal symptoms and reactivity to reminders will prevent inappropriate expectations about the course of recovery. Children often experience traumatic reminders without any adequate assistance from others, increasing their sense of isolation, lack of protection and intervention, and inability to tolerate and understand their own reactions. Parental or teacher support includes becoming familiar with potential and anticipated reminders, assisting a child in contextual discriminations and emotional tolerance to reduce phasic reactivity, providing timely comfort to reduce the intensity and duration of renewed distress, and tolerating time-limited occurrences of unusual or regressive behaviors. The child can be assisted to increase support seeking at times of reminders and to gain an understanding of the traumatic references (Pynoos & Nader, 1993). Similar considerations apply in diminishing both the acquisition and intensity of new fears.

A proactive stance is essential to prevent or minimize secondary stresses and to enhance specific individual and family coping. The impact of secondary stresses on children is also commonly mediated by parental mood, behavior, and responsiveness. Relief of parental distress or intervention for stress-related psychopathology can make a significant contribution to strengthening the recovery environment. Promoting reunion with at least one parent, sibling, or relative after catastrophic family losses can improve outcome and help preserve or restore a sense of historical continuity (Danieli, 1985; Kinzie et al., 1986).

Schools can also assist in this effort. Restoration of the school milieu may be critical to academic and behavioral adjustment among students after major disasters or catastrophic community violence. Temporary modification of classroom activities and requirements may help restore or maintain a child's self-esteem during a period of recovery (Nader & Pynoos, 1993b; Yule, 1991). Consideration of possible traumatic origins of acute changes in school and peer behavior can prevent misattribution to other etiologies and inappropriate interventions.

Factors mediating resilience and adjustment to childhood stress in general have been described. These include a positive relationship with a competent adult, skill at learning and problem solving, engaging personality, competence and perceived efficacy by self or society, high IQ score, positive school experience, mastery motivation, and previous successful experiences (Masten, Best, & Garmezy, 1990). These factors are particularly relevant in mediating children's adjustment to the secondary adversities (Rutter, 1985).

In violent environments, each successive exposure may cause acute traumatic reactions from which there is only incomplete recovery, potentially increasing the risk of significant deviation in developmental trajectory. In an environment of ever-present threats of coercive violation of physical integrity and autonomy, coping mechanisms leading to primitive monitoring strategies, such as autohypnotic vigilance, serve as a means of gaining some sense of anticipatory control (Shengold, 1989; Terr, 1991). When these circumstances are seen as uncontrollable, primitive mechanisms of emotional regulation and avoidance may also be utilized (Band & Weisz, 1988). Many of these mechanisms, including those subsumed under the terms dissociation and repression, are complex mental operations directed at diminishing not only immediate or delayed distress but related issues of accountability or perceived involvement (Shengold, 1989; Pynoos & Nader, 1993). These mechanisms may then be represented in prominent intervention fantasies.

EFFECTS ON EMERGING PERSONALITY AND DISTAL DEVELOPMENT

Traumatic exposures in childhood occur during critical periods of personality formation when there are ongoing revisions of the inner model of the world, self, and other. This internal model includes conscious and unconscious expectations about others and one's own behavior, and forecasts about the future. There may be a developmental tendency for viridical and non-viridical representations of traumatic exposures to initiate the formation of coexisting, frequently incompatible working models (Bowlby, 1979a). These internal models, once organized, tend to operate outside conscious awareness and resist dramatic change (Cicchetti et al., 1990). Elements of the traumatic experience(s) may contribute to unconscious fantasies or pathogenic beliefs central to character formation (Arlow, 1969a, 1969b; Sampson, 1992).

Traumatic stress interacts with emerging personality in the areas of achievement of psychological and physiological maturation; hierarchical integration of competencies; intrapsychic structure of internal and external dangers, inner representation of self and other, mechanisms of cognitive and emotional regulation; schematization of security, safety, risk, injury, loss, protection and intervention; behavioral attributes of fear, courage, and fearlessness; and evolving intervention fantasies and their relationship to internal scripts, constructive actions, and creativity.

The emerging personality of a child may be particularly susceptible to traumatic influences, resulting in marked deviations in character and life attitude. What appears to be a discontinuity after trauma may often reflect an exaggeration of preexisting temperament or personality attributes. The maturation of temperamental qualities may also be interrupted at a critical stage of maturation. For example, a traumatic exposure during the preschool or early school years may potentially interfere with the frequently observed progression of inhibited, reticent children becoming more spontaneous, uninhibited, and sociable, perhaps reinforcing a biological vulnerability (Kagan, 1991). Conversely, a spontaneous, outgoing child may become shy and emotionally restrained.

One central personality axis affected by traumatic exposure is that of fear, courage, and fearlessness (Rachman, 1980), with reported oscillations toward each of the extremes (Gislason & Call, 1982). The incorporation of shifts on this dimension into character formation can result in enduring personality traits, including chronic fearfulness, compulsive heroism, or underreactivity to high-risk situations. These traits may be correlated with specific biological profiles, and associated with interpersonal choices and occupational pursuits. Successful adjustment restores a normative level of fear and promotes the capacity for courage in the face of ongoing subjective apprehension, conflicts over traumatic helplessness, and discomforting affects (Rachman, 1980).

Changes in the form and content of intervention fantasies over time reflect increasing maturity, additional outside information, and future life experiences. They may incorporate new reappraisals as well as revised intrapsychic conflicts and narcissistic accommodations. The evolving intervention fantasies, with embedded traumatic elements, can be instrumental in the construction of specific internal scripts that guide expectations and goals as well as interpersonal interactions (Emde, 1991). They may direct a child's attention toward future constructive actions, both short and long term, and may serve as an ongoing source of creativity in career or artistic pursuits. On the other hand, unaddressed or maladaptive revenge fantasies may contribute to a chronic pattern of dangerous reenactment behaviors. Compensatory fantasies of omnipotence and underestimation of the degree of threat may interfere with the development of appropriate self-protective capabilities and caution. Mental modification in the form of spatial misrepresentation of threat may, if incorporated into an evolving mental schema, increase the risk of further victimization. Lack of adequate schematization of protective intervention may compromise self-preservative and self-caring functions in children (Hartman & Burgess, 1989), and interfere with adult protective behavior (Wyatt, Guthrie, & Notgrass, 1992).

Acutely traumatized children demonstrate a flexibility in identificatory roles, varying even within a single interview session, in their identification with assailant, victim, or rescuer. Over time, there may be a rigidity and prominence of one such role, which becomes dominant in the emerging personality. Williams (1987) has described one set of children who became totally involved with aggressive revenge fantasies and another set who turned the aggression inward. Character traits and career interests may also reflect a lifelong preoccupation with rescue or reparative roles, or motivation for altruistic behavior. There may also be a chronic struggle against identification with a parent or sibling who died under traumatic circumstances (Furman, 1973). Negative self-attributions that arise out of the original experience(s), may, if uncorrected, also become embedded in character. Adult studies suggest that these negative self-images are vulnerable to reactivation after future traumatic exposure (Foa & Riggs, 1994), and compromise efforts at adjustment.

As Stoller (1989) notes, childhood masturbation fantasies may incorporate traumatic themes that, by adulthood, may become repetitive, compulsive, and aesthetic elements of erotic life. In two cases, we have observed that the witnessing of a rape in adolescence led to chronic disturbing, rape-related masturbatory themes and unresolved conflicts over hostility and tenderness in psychosexual development. Stoller has also suggested that consensual forms of sadomasochistic behavior in adults may derive from schematizations of danger, risk, mystery, secrecy, and negotiated consent relating to early childhood experiences with life-threatening medical illness, painful medical procedures, and required trust in parental oversight and medical restraint. In this manner, a perversion may represent a reparative fantasy, "an engineered reenactment" (Khan, 1979), and incorporate trauma-related intervention fantasies, including protective as well as "fantasized vengeful triumph" (Stoller, 1976).

A developmental psychopathology model of PTSD underscores the complex impact on developmental progression and personality of serial or sequential traumatization. There are long-range influences on psychosexual and narcissistic maturation, with the risk of prolonged psychosexual disturbances, narcissistic deficits, and impaired development of conscience. In situations of child abuse, additional exposures to spousal abuse, parental suicidal and homicidal behavior (at different points in the child's life) helps shape the form and content of these disturbances. The nature and circumstances of physical or sexual abuse or witnessing of violence necessarily changes over time, as both the child and the circumstances develop. The parent's expressed reason or threat, the child's attribution of meaning, and the content of retaliatory rage, protection, and escape fantasies may vary with developmental maturation. Mones (1991) has provided vivid descriptions of the extreme of this evolution, culminating in conscious and detailed parricidal plans carried out by a late adolescent after failed attempts to evoke familial, school, and societal intervention.

Trauma-induced changes in the reactivity of central catecholamine systems may produce a biological analogue of altered expectations by modulating the level of response of the central nervous system (CNS) with regard to specific traumatic related information, including reminders. It may also change the regulation of attentional balance between interoceptive (internal) and exteroceptive (environmental) cues, increasing focused attention on external stimuli to detect danger and make appropriate defensive response (Krystal et al., 1989). These changes may initiate "anticipatory bias" in the perception of environmental information including context errors, a "state of preparedness" for extremely negative emotions, and "anxiety of premonitions," which involves expectations of potentially dangerous future events (Kagan, 1991). These changes are commonly accompanied by increased autonomic and sympathetic reactivity, for example, in heart rate, blood pressure, and skin conductance, that may have long-term implications for the physical health of the child (Perry, 1994). Trauma-induced release of stress hormones in early childhood is likely to influence the selection and formation of neuronal networks that extend throughout the school age years and into adolescence (Chugani, Phelps, & Mazziotta, 1987). For example, resistance to extinction of traumatic expectations may be associated with the marking of memories as important through a mechanism of neural convergence (Garcia, Lasiter, Bermudez-Rattoni, & Deems, 1986) suggested by models of one-trial aversion learning associated with novel situations.

Where there is chronic environmental threat, arousal disturbances may be interpreted by the child and family as situationally appropriate monitoring, confrontational, or avoidant responses. The impact on personality and development may not be apparent until long after the perceived threat is over. This makes the assessment of children in war zones problematic, where self-perception as a good soldier or resistance fighter may maintain a child's self-esteem (Baker, 1990). Children and adolescents may seek out situations in the future where heightened arousal and accompanying intervention fantasies will feel ego-syntonic.

The influence of distal traumatic reminders may depend on the extent to which they are embedded in the circumstances of future everyday life. The more they involve intricacies of interpersonal interactions, bodily sensations and internal affective states, the more difficult they are to identify as sources of renewed hypervigilance or other arousal behavior, anxiety, or avoidance. Disturbances or distortion in a sense of historical continuity and conscious viridical representation increase the difficulty of making this association. The inability to identify the historical referent to a response to a distal traumatic reminder may lead to increased negative self-attributions that further compromise self-esteem and self-concept. The expression of traumatic expectations may only become apparent with the occurrence of specific reminders in later adult situations. The troubling aspects of the exposure are variable over time.

Distal secondary stresses may be a continuation of stresses that occurred in the immediate aftermath of the trauma, or they may arise out of new developmental challenges or life circumstances. These may include the need for future medical treatment and accommodations to disabilities, involvement in criminal or civil proceedings, renewed apprehension at the release of an assailant from prison, contact of an abusive parent or relative with children of the next generation or the need to acquire social skills to explain trauma-related behavior to intimate persons in one's later life including spouse, children, selected colleagues, and friends. Such later revelations may induce secondary changes in the developmental cycle of the family of origin, nuclear family, or interpersonal relations. Self-revelation, disclosure, and social communication mediate the long-term repercussions of childhood trauma, including psychosomatic symptoms. Conversely, ongoing inhibition of disclosure may operate as a distal secondary stress that may adversely affect physical and psychological well-being (Pennebaker & Susman, 1988).

COMPLEX OF DISTAL STRESS-RELATED PATHOLOGY

Distal posttraumatic-stress-related pathology includes chronic PTSD, comorbid psychiatric disorders and physical conditions, developmental and personality disturbances, and age-appropriate indications of dissatisfaction and lack of well-being. A future avenue for investigation concerns the deleterious effect on physical health of chronic child or adolescent PTSD. Persistent phasic reactivity may progress into more permanent forms of tonic physiological arousal, perhaps affecting cardiovascular risk. Maladaptive efforts at adjustment, especially substance abuse, may directly lead to later physical health problems.

In addition to the central role of traumatic insults at different developmental phases, pathology also derives from the interaction with other pathogenic environmental factors, the ongoing influences of secondary stresses and traumatic reminders, and the damaging consequences of the use of maladaptive coping mechanisms. There have been recent efforts to establish a set of diagnostic criteria to characterize the complex psychopathology associated with repeated or prolonged interpersonal brutality and abuse (Davidson, 1993). The diagnostic features cannot be properly understood without a developmental perspective that recognizes the etiologic importance of the interdigitating or layering of many of the preceding factors.

There have not as yet been prospective long-term follow-up studies of PTSD in children and adolescents using appropriate multimethod assessments. Adult clinical research suggests that after 3 to 6 months there may be relative stability of untreated PTSD symptoms (Foa & Riggs, 1994). Short-term posttrauma studies in children have so far supported the persistence of untreated posttraumatic stress symptoms in those who experienced severe initial reactions (Dyregrov & Raundalen, 1992; Nader et al., 1990; Yule et al., 1992). A longitudinal controlled comparison of adolescent Cambodian refugees, now young adults, revealed that although chronic PTSD remained related to the initial traumatic exposures, current depression was most strongly associated with current secondary stresses (Clarke, Sack, & Goff, 1993). A study of adolescents in residential treatment showed the advantage of rigorous adherence to DSM III-R criteria (American Psychiatric Association, 1987) to discern the frequency of chronic PTSD among other comorbid conditions including mood and disruptive behavioral disorders. Rediagnosis permitted more accurate identification of the role of current traumatic reminders in precipitating otherwise unexplained aggressive and avoidant behaviors (Doyle & Bauer, 1989).

Among a similar group of children in a residential treatment setting, Perry (1994) reported chronic alterations in neurochemical regulation and physiological function. These included tachycardia, alterations in alpha 2 platelet receptors, and marked reduction of symptoms in response to clonidine, an alpha 2 adrenergic blocker. He hypothesized that prolonged "alarm reactions" in childhood may induce chronic abnormal patterns of catecholamine activity altering brain stem functioning, including cardiovascular dysregulation, affective lability, increased anxiety, increased startle response, sleep abnormalities, and "sensitization" to future stressful events. Most recently, De Bellis, Lefter, Trickett, and Putnam (1994) reported apparent changes in noradrenergic status, as measured by urinary metabolites, in severely sexually abused girls, even years after the abuse.

A recent study of adolescents in treatment for multiple personality disorder found that improvement in integration of ego functions resulted in increased reporting of posttraumatic stress reactions to specific past traumatic experiences (Dell & Eisenhower, 1990). The core "personalities" were found to have originated during preschool years. The central types included fearful, protective-intervening, and avenging or aggressive selves, each of which was associated with specific traumatic episodes. A developmental psychopathology model suggests the importance of investigating to what degree these "selves" reflect a rigidification and persistence of age-related intervention fantasies and solitary and coordinated role play (Parker & Gottman, 1989).

Self-injurious behavior in adults presents an example in which childhood trauma, neglect, and deprivation each contribute to the factorial analysis of risk (van der Kolk et al., 1991). Symptoms of self-mutilation and suicidal behaviors in adolescents and young adults with borderline, narcissistic, or antisocial personality features may include behavioral reenactments of elements of childhood traumatic experiences and accompanying intervention fantasies. A history of multiple victimization in childhood serves as one of several complex antecedents to borderline personality disorder (Herman, Perry, & van der Kolk, 1989). Cooper (1986) has suggested that an unusual, isolated adult symptom may be etiologically related to a specific childhood traumatic experience. Stoller (1989) has commented that the more fixed and compulsive a perverse adult behavior, the more likely that traumatic exposures and family forces contributed to its origin and maintenance.

CONCLUSION

The theoretical model discussed in this chapter can provide a comprehensive framework for integrating the complex interactions involved in the etiology, course, and outcome of posttraumatic distress in children and adolescents. There should be attention to: the complexity of traumatic experiences; the role of traumatic reminders and secondary stresses; the differences among resistance, resilience, and vulnerability; and the nature, severity, and course of posttraumatic distress and its interactions with emerging personality, development, psychopathology, and the social ecology of the child. This model requires expanding our evaluation methods, prevention and intervention strategies, and treatment outcome measures, and suggests new research agendas.

A central developmental consideration is the formation of traumatic expectations and their consequences. Traumatic expectations have expression in biology, memory, and learning, behavioral predispositions, intrapsychic changes, object-relations, and family, community, and social organization. The study of traumatic expectations must therefore incorporate knowledge from a variety of such fields as neurobiology, memory and learning, cognition and behavior, psychoanalysis, adult and child development, and education. Conversely, knowledge derived from traumatic stress studies will continue to require revisions in explanatory models within these other disciplines.

We have especially emphasized the need for integration of the rapidly expanding knowledge from child developmental studies in order to identify specific developmental risks related to posttraumatic distress and secondary adversities. The field of traumatic stress must begin to utilize advances in child development research methodology and instrumentation, for example, developmental evaluations of narrative coherence (Buchsbaum, Toth, Clyman, Cicchetti, & Emde, 1992) in preschool children, affective discrimination and tolerance in school-age children, and moral development in adolescents. At the same time, the field of traumatic stress is contributing to a more refined developmental

assessment of perceptions of efficacy of self and others, of external and internal dangers, and of such related topics as altruism, courage, and intervention fantasies.

Animal models of PTSD can provide a potentially fruitful method to investigate selected issues in the neurobiology of traumatic expectations and their behavioral consequences. Beyond the "time-dependent sensitization" criteria recommended by Yehuda and Antelman (1993), a valid animal model must also include reactivity to situational reminders. The range of dependent variables should include behavioral manifestations of fear, anxiety, and learning and memory, as well as neurobiological indicators of stress. We are currently experimenting with an animal model to study the interactions of neurobiological maturity, neurophysiology, and behavior. Our pilot data suggests that there may be a bifurcation of both neurophysiological and behavioral responses. Such a bimodal distribution would permit further evaluation of the relative contributions of genetic, developmental, and social determinants (True et al., 1993). Important developmental issues to be investigated include potential disturbances in the maturation of key brain stem and midbrain mechanisms that underlie startle, sleep, affective valence and intensity, integration of sensory modalities, selective attention, and short- and long-term memory. Animal models will also prove useful in evaluating the timing and effectiveness of pharmacological interventions and their mechanisms of action (Davis, 1986).

A comprehensive framework should also incorporate continued research into principles of learning and memory. Different models of learning will provide alternative vantage points on aspects of traumatic memory. For example, one-trial learning models may be critical to understanding the encoding and storage of information related to experiences of extreme danger and the evolutionary significance of memories that are resistant to extinction. Classical models of conditioning and instrumental learning (Mowrer, 1947) suggests ways that continued exposure to traumatic cues can lead to chronic avoidant behavior. State-dependent learning (Weingartner, 1978) may explain the greater likelihood of the occurrence of reexperiencing phenomena under conditions of renewed anxiety. Current psychodynamic models provide another perspective to explore the subtle conscious and unconscious schematization of traumatic memories, the lack of revision with subsequent life experience, and their recruitment at later times in life.

A developmental model of traumatic stress needs to include an interactive historical perspective that can examine the interplay of previous and current trauma on adaptive functioning. This life-trajectory perspective points to the potential long-term consequences of traumatic expectations as they affect adult personal, interpersonal, occupational, and community functioning. Research is now beginning to examine the long-term effects on health-related behavior, parental character and competence, patterns of assortive mating, career choices, and quality and level of social involvement.

The inclusion of PTSD in DSM-III in 1980 led to a decade of research, principally examining the disorder and mediating variables. There are signs that the current decade will see increased attention to the refinement and integration of treatment techniques and to the conduct of controlled and comparative studies of the efficacy of preventive and therapeutic interventions. There is currently a healthy trend toward rapprochement among those oriented toward psychodynamic, family, cognitive-behavioral, and psychopharmacological approaches (Marmar, Foy, Kagan, & Pynoos, 1993). The four modalities provide complimentary perspectives in addressing the attribution of meaning, acquisition of new ears, reactivity to internal and external reminders, and disturbances in the stability of self-concepts and biological, familial, and social systems.

The model presented in this chapter suggests that the complex interaction over time of many critical factors plays a role in the outcome of traumatic exposure. Each of these factors can be seen as a potential focus for prevention and treatment. The model therefore implies that prevention and intervention must be multidimensional and that outcome measures must extend beyond those of traditional psychopathology. As Jensen and Shaw (1993) have commented, there is an urgent need to clarify the optimal level of intervention for children and their families, both acutely and over time. Because early intervention may prove most efficacious, there will be important public health and ethical issues regarding the conduct of biomedical research involving traumatized children and adolescents and the allocation of mental health resources.

Beyond the individual child, family, or community, traumatic stress studies are beginning to consider how the repercussions of regional catastrophic disasters or violence may alter the social and political character of a nation. After massive trauma, a whole generation of children may experience posttraumatic stress reactions. As evidenced by the rates of chronic psychiatric morbidity among Armenian children after the 1988 earthquake (Pynoos, Goenjian, Tashjian et al., 1993), the existence of thousands of traumatized children in different stages of recovery places special burdens on society. These can include the consequence of widespread maladaptation in terms of schooling, disturbances in intrafamilial and peer interactions, and diminished resistance or resilience to future stress. Changes in future orientation not only may affect the individual child but, on a massive scale, may permeate and transform cultural expectations, altering the social ecology of the next generation. Disasters and war can lead to radical shifts in fundamental beliefs and philosophical outlook. For example, Luke and Reeves (1978) reflect on how the famous Spanish earthquake of 1755 "not only shattered Lisbon but severely shook the optimistic theodocy of the Enlightenment" (p. 16). War and political violence can also radically alter expectations about the social contract, leading to upsurges in democratic convictions or more Machiavellian political ideologies (Pynoos, 1992b). Recently, out of an awareness of the alarming extent to which children are exposed to massive violence and the grave psychological repercussions, the United Nations General Assembly adopted a Convention on the Rights of the Child that requires countries to file and publicize regular progress reports on compliance (UNICEF, 1991). Researchers and clinicians in the field of traumatic stress may also help to make prevention more of a national and international concern by giving continued scientific voice to the legacy of trauma.

REFERENCES

Adams, P. R., & Adams, G. R. (1984). Mount St. Helens' Ashfall: Evidence for a disaster stress reaction. *American Psychologist, 39*(3), 252–260.

American Psychiatric Association (APA). (1987). *Diagnostic and statistical manual of mental disorders* (3rd ed. rev., DSM-III-R). Washington, DC: Author.

Arlow, J. (1969a). Unconscious fantasy and disturbances of conscious experience. *Psychoanalytic Quarterly, 38,* 1–27.

Arlow, J. (1969b). Fantasy, memory, and reality testing. *Psychoanalytic Quarterly, 38,* 28–51.

Atkins, M., Stoff, D., Osborne, M. L., & Brown, K. (1993). Distinguishing instrumental and hostile aggression: Does it make a difference? *Journal of Abnormal Child Psychology, 21,* 355–365.

Baddeley, A. D. (1976). *Psychology of memory.* New York: Basic Books.

Baddeley, A. D. (1984). Memory theory and memory therapy. In B. Wilson & N. Moffat (Eds.), *Clinical management of memory problems* (pp. 5–27). London: Aspen.

Baker, A. M. (1990). The psychological impact of the intifada on Palestinian children in the occupied West Bank and Gaza: An exploratory study. *American Journal of Orthopsychiatry, 60,* 496–505.

Balint, M. (1959). *Thrills and regressions.* New York: International Universities Press.

Band, E. B., & Weisz, J. (1988). How to feel better when it feels bad. Children's perspectives on coping with everyday stress. *Developmental Psychology, 24,* 247–253.

Bat-Zion, N., & Levy-Shiff, R. (1993). Children in war: Stress and coping reactions under the threat of the scud missile attacks and the effect of proximity. In L. Lewis & N. Fox (Eds.), *Effects of war and violence in children* (pp. 143–161). Hillsdale, NJ: Erlbaum.

Bell, C. C., & Jenkins, E. J. (1991). Traumatic stress and children. *Journal of Health Care for the Poor and Underserved, 2*(1), 175–186.

Bernstein, A. E. (1990). The impact of incest trauma on ego development. In H. B. Levine (Ed.), *Adult analysis and childhood sexual abuse* (pp. 65–91). Hillsdale, NJ: Analytic Press.

Bjork, R. A., & Richardson-Klavehn, A. (1989). On the puzzling relationship between environmental context and human memory. In *Current Issues in Cognitive Processes: The Tulane Flowertree Symposium on Cognition* (pp. 313–344). Hillsdale, NJ: Erlbaum.

Black, D., & Kaplan, T. (1988). Father kills mother: Issues and problems encountered by a child psychiatric team. *British Journal of Psychiatry, 153,* 624–630.

Bowlby, J. (1973). *Attachment and loss: Vol. 2. Separation.* New York: Basic Books.

Bowlby, J. (1979a). *The making and breaking of affectional bonds.* London: Tavistock.

Bowlby, J. (1979b). On knowing what you aren't supposed to know and feeling what you are not supposed to feel. *Canadian Journal of Psychiatry, 24,* 403–408.

Brown, S. L. (1980). Developmental cycle of family: Clinical implications. *Psychiatric Clinics of North America, 3*(3), 369–381.

Buchsbaum, H. K., Toth, S., Clyman, R., Cicchetti, C., & Emde, R. N. (1992). The use of a narrative story stem technique with maltreated children: Implications for theory and practice. *Development and Psychopathology, 4,* 603–625.

Buck, L., & Axel, R. (1991). A novel multigene family may encode odorant receptors: A molecular basis for odor recognition. *Cell, 65,* 175–187.

Burt, C. (1943). War neuroses in British children. *Nervous Child, 2,* 324–337.

Cain, A., & Fast, I. (1972). Children's disturbed reactions to parent suicide: Distortion and guilt, communication and identification. In A. Cain (Ed.), *Survivors of suicide,* (pp. 93–111). Springfield, IL: Thomas.

Carlson, B. E. (1984). Children's observations of interparental violence. In A. R. Roberts (Ed.), *Battered women and their families: Intervention strategies and treatment programs* (pp. 147–167). New York: Springer.

Chugani, H., Phelps, M., & Mazziotta, J. C. (1987). Positron emission tomography study of human brain functional development. *Annals of Neurology, 22*(4), 487–497.

Cicchetti, D. (1989). How research on child maltreatment has informed the study of child development: Perspectives from developmental psychopathology. In D. Cicchetti & V. Carlson (Eds.), *Child maltreatment: Theory and research on the causes and consequences of child abuse and neglect* (pp. 377–431). New York: Cambridge University Press.

Cicchetti, D. (1993). Developmental psychopathology: Reactions, reflections, projections. *Developmental Review, 13,* 471–502.

Cicchetti, D., Barnett, D., Rabideau, J., & Toth, S. L. (1991). Risk-taking and self-regulation in maltreated children. In L. Lipsitt & L. Mitnick (Eds.), *Risk-taking behavior* (pp. 165–198). Norwood, NJ: Ablex.

Cicchetti, D., & Carlson, V. (1989). *Child maltreatment: Theory and research on the causes and consequences of child abuse and neglect.* New York: Cambridge University Press.

Cicchetti, D., Cummings, E. M., Greenberg, M. T., & Marvin, R. (1990). An organizational perspective on attachment beyond infancy: Implications for theory, measurement, and research. In M. T. Greenberg, D. Cicchetti, E. M. Cummings (Eds.), *Attachment in the preschool years: Theory, research and intervention* (pp. 3–49). Chicago: University of Chicago Press.

Cicchetti, D., & Lynch, M. (1993). Toward an ecological/transactional model of community violence and child maltreatment: Consequences for children's development. *Psychiatry, 56,* 96–118.

Cicchetti, D., Toth, S. L., & Lynch, M. (1993). The developmental sequelae of child maltreatment: Implications for war-related trauma. In L. Leavitt & N. Fox (Eds.), *Psychological effects of war and violence on children* (pp. 41–71). Hillsdale, NJ: Erlbaum.

Clark, D. C., Pynoos, R. S., & Goebel, A. E. (1994). Mechanisms and processes of adolescent bereavement. In R. J. Haggerty, N. Garmezy, M. Rutter, & L. Sherrod (Eds.), *Risk and Resilience in children* (pp. 100–146). New York: Cambridge University Press.

Clarke, G., Sack, W. H., Goff, B. (1993). Three forms of stress in Cambodian adolescent refugees. *Journal of Abnormal Child Psychology, 21,* 65–77.

Conway, M. A. (1993). Emotion and memory. *Science, 261,* 369–370.

Cooper, A. M. (1986). Toward a limited definition of psychic trauma in the reconstruction of trauma: Its significance. In A. Rothstein & C. T. Madison (Eds.), *Clinical work* [Workshop Series of the American Psychoanalytic Association Monograph 2] (pp. 41–56). New York: International Universities Press.

Cotton, P. (1992). Gun-associated violence increasingly viewed as public health challenge, *Journal of the American Medical Association, 267*(9), 1171–1174.

Daly, M., & Wilson, J. (1981). Child maltreatment from a sociobiological perspective. *New Directions for Child Development, 11,* 93–112.

Danieli, Y. (1985). The treatment and prevention of long-term effects and intergenerational transmission of victimization: A lesson from Holocaust survivors and their children. In C. Figley (Ed.), *Trauma and its wake* (pp. 295–313). New York: Brunner/Mazel.

Davis, M. (1986). Pharmacological and anatomical analysis of fear conditioning using the fear potentiated startle paradigm. *Behavioral Neuroscience, 100,* 814–824.

Davidson, J. (1993). Issues in the diagnosis of posttraumatic stress disorder. In J. Oldham, M. Riba, & A. Tasman (Eds.), *Annual Review of Psychiatry* (Vol. 12, pp. 141–155). Washington, DC: American Psychiatric Press.

De Bellis, M. D., Lefter, L., Trickett, P., & Putnam, F. W. (1994). Urinary catecholamine excretion in sexually abused girls. *Journal of the American Academy of Child and Adolescent Psychiatry, 33,* 320–327.

Dell, P., & Eisenhower, J. (1990). Adolescent multiple personality disorder: A preliminary study of eleven cases. *Journal of the American Academy of Child and Adolescent Psychiatry, 29*(3), 359–366.

Dohrenwend, B. P., Dohrenwend, B. S., Warheit, G. J., Bartlett, G., Goldsteen, R., Goldsteen, K., & Martin J. (1981). Stress in the community: A report to the President's Commission on the Accident at Three Mile Island. *Annals New Year Academy Sciences, 365,* 159–174.

Dollinger, S. J., O'Donnell, J. P., & Staley, A. A. (1984). Lightning-strike disaster: Effects on children's fears and worries. *Journal of Consulting and Clinical Psychology, 52*(6), 1028–1038.

Doyle, J. S., & Bauer, S. (1989). Posttraumatic stress disorder in children: Its identification and treatment in a residential setting for emotionally disturbed youth. *Journal of Traumatic Stress, 2,* 275–288.

Dyregrov, A., & Raundalen, M. (1992, June). *The impact of the Gulf War on the children of Iraq.* Paper presented at the International Society for Traumatic Stress Studies World Conference "Trauma and Tragedy," Amsterdam.

Earls, F., Smith, E., Reich, W., & Jung, K. G. (1988). Investigating psychopathological consequences of a disaster in children: A pilot study incorporating a structured diagnostic interview. *Journal of the American Academy of Child and Adolescent Psychiatry, 27,* 90–95.

Emde, R. (1991). Positive emotions for psychoanalytic theory: Surprises from infancy research and new directions. *Journal of the American Psychoanalytic Association, 39,* 5–44.

Eth, S., & Pynoos, R. S. (1985). Developmental perspective on psychic trauma in childhood. In C. Figley, (Ed.), *Trauma and its wake* (Vol. I, pp. 36–52). New York: Brunner/Mazel.

Fenichel, O. (1945). *The psychoanalytic theory of neuroses.* New York: Norton.

Fisher, C., Byrne, J., Edwards, A., & Kahn, E. (1970). A psychophysiological study of nightmares. *Journal of the American Psychoanalytic Association, 18*(4), 747–782.

Foa, E. B., & Riggs, D. S. (1994). Posttraumatic stress disorder in rape. In R. Pynoos (Ed.), *Posttraumatic stress disorder: A clinical review* (pp. 133–163). Lutherville, MD: Sidron Press.

Freud, A. (1936). *The ego and the mechanisms of defence* (6th impression). London: Hogarth Press and the Institute of Psychoanalysis.

Freud, S. (1953). The interpretation of dreams. In J. Strachey (Ed. and Trans.), *The standard edition of the complete psychological works of Sigmund Freud* (Vol. 4). London: Hogarth Press. (Original work published 1900)

Freud, S. (1959). Introductory lectures on psychoanalysis. In J. Strachey (Ed. and Trans.), *The standard edition of the complete psychological works of Sigmund Freud* (Vol. 20). London: Hogarth Press. (Original work published 1916)

Freud, S. (1959). Inhibitions, symptoms and anxiety. In J. Strachey (Ed. and Trans.), *The standard edition of the complete psychological works of Sigmund Freud* (Vol. 20, pp. 87–156). London: Hogarth Press. (Original work published 1926)

Freud, S. (1962). Beyond the pleasure principle. In J. Strachey (Ed. and Trans.), *The standard edition of the complete psychological works of Sigmund Freud* (Vol. 18). London: Hogarth Press. (Original work published 1920)

Friedman, P., & Linn, I. (1957). Some psychiatric notes on the *Andrea Doria* disaster. *American Journal of Psychiatry, 114,* 426–432.

Furman, R. (1973). A child's capacity for mourning. In *The child in his family: The impact of disease and death* (pp. 225–231). New York: Wiley.

Garbarino, J., Kostelny, K., & Dubrow, N. (1991). What children can tell us about living in danger. *American Psychologist, 46*(4), 376–383.

Garcia, J., Lasiter, P. S., Bermudez-Rattoni, F., & Deems, A. (1986). A general theory of aversion learning. *Annals of the New York Academy of Sciences, 43,* 8–21.

Gardner, G. (1971). Aggression and violence—the enemies of precision learning in children. *American Journal of Psychiatry, 128,* 445–450.

Gislason, I. L., & Call, J. (1982). Dog bite in infancy: Trauma and personality development. *Journal of the American Academy of Child Psychiatry, 22,* 203–207.

Gleser, G., Green, B., & Winget, C. (1981). *Prolonged psychosocial effects of disaster: A study of Buffalo Creek.* New York: Academic Press.

Gordon, R., & Wraith, R. (1993). Responses of children and adolescents to disaster. In J. P. Wilson & B. Raphael (Eds.), *International handbook of traumatic stress syndromes* (pp. 561–575). New York: Plenum.

Graham, S., Doubleday, C., & Guarino, P. A. (1984). The development of relations between perceived controllability and the emotions of pity, anger, and guilt. *Child Development, 55,* 561–565.

Green, B., Korol, M., Grace, M., Vary, M., Leonard, A., Gleser, G., & Smitson-Cohen, S. (1991). Children and disaster: Age, gender, and parental effects on PTSD symptoms. *Journal of the American Academy of Child and Adolescent Psychiatry, 30*(6), 945–951.

Greenacre, P. (1952). *Trauma, growth and personality.* New York: Norton.

Groves, B. M., Zuckerman, B., Marans, S., & Cohen, D. J. (1993). Silent victims: Children who witness violence. *Journal of the American Medical Association, 269*(2), 262–264.

Handford, H. A., Mayes, S., Mattison, R., Humphrey, E., Bagnato, S., Bixler, E., & Kales, J. D. (1986). Child and parent reaction to the Three Mile Island nuclear accident. *Journal of the American Academy of Psychiatry, 25*(3), 346–356.

Harter, S., & Whitesell, N. (1991). Developmental changes in children's understanding of single, multiple and blended emotion concepts. In C. Saarni & P. L. Harris (Eds.), *Children's understanding of emotion* (pp. 81–116). New York: Cambridge University Press.

Hartman, C. R., & Burgess, A. (1989). Sexual abuse of children: Causes and consequences. In D. Cicchetti & V. Carlson, *Child maltreatment: Theory and research on the causes and consequences of child abuse and neglect* (pp. 95–128). New York: Cambridge University Press.

Herman, J. L., Perry, J. C., & van der Kolk, B. A. (1989). Childhood trauma in borderline personality disorder. *American Journal of Psychiatry, 146,* 490–495.

Hoffman, M. (1979). Development of moral thought, feeling, and behavior. *American Psychologist, 34,* 358–388.

Horowitz, M. (1976). *Stress response syndromes.* New York: Aronson.

Howes, C. (1987). Social competence with peers in young children: Developmental sequences. *Developmental Review, 7,* 252–272.

Jensen, P. S., Richters, J., Ussery, T., Bloedau, L., & Davis, H. (1991). Child psychopathology and environmental influences: Discrete life events versus ongoing adversity. *Journal of the American Academy of Child and Adolescent Psychiatry, 30,* 303–309.

Jensen, P. S., & Shaw, J. (1993). Children as victims of war: Current knowledge and future needs. *Journal of the American Academy of Child and Adolescent Psychiatry, 32,* 697–708.

Joseph, S. A., Brewin, C. R., Yule, W., & Williams, R. (1991). Causal attributions and psychiatric symptoms in survivors of the *Herald of Free Enterprise* disaster. *British Journal of Psychiatry, 159,* 542–546.

Kagan, J. (1991). A conceptual analysis of the affects. *Journal of the American Psychoanalytic Association, 39,* 109–130.

Kardiner, A. (1941). *The traumatic neurosis of war.* New York: Basic Books.

Keilson, H. (1992). *Sequential traumatization in children* (English ed.). Y. Bearne, H. Coleman, & D. Winter (Trans.). Jerusalem: Magnes Press. (Original work published 1979)

Kestenberg, J. S. (1972). How children remember and parents forget. *International Journal of Psychoanalytic Psychotherapy, 1,* 103–123.

Khan, M. (1963). The concept of cumulative trauma. *Psychoanalytic Study of the Child, 18,* 286–306.

Khan, M. (1979). *Alienation in perversions.* New York: International Universities Press.

Kinzie, D., Sack, W., Angell, R., Manson, S., & Rath, B. (1986). The psychiatric effects of massive trauma on Cambodian children: I. The children. *Journal of the American Academy of Child Psychiatry, 25,* 370–376.

Klinnert, M. D., Campos, J., Source, J. F., Emde, R. N., & Svejda, M. J. (1983). Social referencing. In P. Plutchik & H. Kellerman (Eds.), *The emotions in early development* (pp. 123–134). New York: Academic Press.

Krystal, H. (1978). Trauma and affects. *Psychoanalytic Study of the Child, 33,* 81–116.

Krystal, H. (1991). Integration and self-healing in post-traumatic states: A ten-year retrospective. *American Imago, 48*(1), 93–117.

Krystal, J., Kosten, T., Perry, B., Southwick, S., Mason, J., & Giller, E. L. (1989). Neurobiological aspects of PTSD: Review of clinical and preclinical studies. *Behavioral Therapy, 20,* 177–198.

Kuch, K., & Cox, B. J. (1992). Symptoms of PTSD in 124 survivors of the Holocaust. *American Journal of Psychiatry, 149,* 337–340.

Lansky, M. (1990). The screening function of posttraumatic nightmares. *British Journal of Psychotherapy, 6,* 384–400.

Lazarus, R. S., & Folkman, S. (1984). *Stress, appraisal and coping.* New York: Springer.

Lewis, M. (1991). Self-conscious emotions and the development of self. *Journal of the American Psychoanalytic Association, 39,* 45–73.

Lifton, R. J. (1979). *The broken connection.* New York: Simon & Schuster.

Lonigan, C., Shannon, M., Finch, A., Daugherty, T., & Taylor, C. (1991). Children's reactions to a natural disaster: Symptom severity and degree of exposure. *Advances in Behavior Research and Therapy, 13,* 133–154.

Luke, D., & Reeves, N. (1978). Introduction. In H. Von Kleist, *The Marquise of O—and Other Stories* (D. Luke & N. Reeves, Trans.). New York: Penguin.

Macksoud, M. S., Dyregrov, A., & Raundalen, M. (1993). Traumatic war experiences and their effects on children. In J. P. Wilson & B. Raphael (Eds.), *International handbook of traumatic stress syndromes* (pp. 625–633). New York: Plenum.

Malmquist, C. P. (1984). Children who witness parental murder: Posttraumatic and legal issues. *Journal of the American Academy of Child and Adolescent Psychiatry, 25,* 320–325.

Mannuzza, S., Klein, R., Bessler, A., Malloy, P., LaPadula, M. (1993). Adult outcome of hyperactive boys: Educational achievement, occupational rank, and psychiatric status. *Archives of General Psychiatry, 50,* 565–576.

Marans, S., Mayes, L., Cicchetti, D., Dahl, K., Marans, W., & Cohen, D. J. (1991). The child-psychoanalytic play interview: A technique for studying thematic content. *Journal of the American Psychoanalytic Association, 39*(4), 1015–1036.

Marmar, C., Foy, D., Kagan, V., & Pynoos, R. (1993). An integrated approach for treating posttraumatic stress. In J. Oldham, M. Riba, & A. Tasman (Eds.), *American Psychiatric Press review of psychiatry* (Vol. 12, pp. 238–272). Washington, DC: American Psychiatric Press.

Martinez, P., & Richters, J. (1993). NIMH community violence: II. Children's distress symptoms associated with violence exposure. *Psychiatry, 56,* 22–35.

Martini, D. R., Ryan, C., Nakayama, D., & Ramenofsky, M. (1990). Psychiatric sequelae after traumatic injury: The Pittsburgh Regatta accident. *Journal of the American Academy of Child and Adolescent Psychiatry, 29,* 70–75.

Masten, A., Best, K., & Garmezy, N. (1990). Resilience and development: Contributions from the study of children who overcome adversity. *Development and Psychopathology, 2,* 425–444.

McFarlane, A. C., Policansky, S. K., & Irwin, C. (1987). A longitudinal study of the psychological morbidity in children due to natural disaster. *Psychological Medicine, 17,* 727–738.

McGaugh, J. L. (1990). Significance and remembrance: The role of neuromodulatory systems. *Psychological Science, 1,* 15–25.

McNally, R. J. (1991). Assessment of posttraumatic stress disorder in children. *Psychological Assessment, 3*(4), 001–007.

Mercier, M. H. (1943). Children in an occupied land: The suffering of French children. *Nervous Child, 2,* 308–312.

Miller, J. G. (1978). *Living systems.* New York: McGraw-Hill.

Mones, P. (1991). *When a child kills: Abused children who kill their parents.* New York: Pocket Books.

Mowrer, O. H. (1947). On the dual nature of learning: A reinterpretation "of conditioning" and "problem-solving." *Harvard Educational Review, 17,* 102–148.

Mueller, E., & Tingley, E. (1990). The bears' picnic: Children's representations of themselves and their families. In I. Bretherton & M. W. Watson (Eds.), *Children's perspectives on the family. New Directions for Child Development, 48,* 47–65.

Nader, K., & Pynoos, R. (1991). Drawing and play in the diagnosis and assessment of childhood post-traumatic stress syndromes. In C. Schaefer, K. Gitlan, & A. Sandrgun (Eds.), *Play, Diagnosis and Assessment* (pp. 375–389). New York: Wiley.

Nader, K., & Pynoos, R. (1992). *Parental report of children's responses to life threat.* Paper presented at the annual meeting of the American Psychiatric Association, Washington, DC.

Nader, K., & Pynoos, R. (1993a). The children of Kuwait following the Gulf Crisis. In L. Leavitt & N. Fox (Eds.), *Psychological effects of war and violence on children* (pp. 181–195). Hillsdale, NJ: Erlbaum.

Nader, K., & Pynoos, R. (1993b). School disaster: Planning and initial interventions. *Journal of Social Behavior and Personality, Handbook of Post-disaster Interventions, 8,* 1–22.

Nader, K., Pynoos, R., Fairbanks, L., & Frederick, C. (1990). Children's PTSD reactions one year after a sniper attack at their school. *American Journal of Psychiatry, 147,* 1526–1530.

Nader, K., Stuber, M., & Pynoos, R. (1991). Posttraumatic stress reactions in preschool children with catastrophic illness: Assessment needs. *Comprehensive Mental Health Care, 1*(3), 223–239.

Ornitz, E. M. (1991). Developmental aspects of neurophysiology. In M. Lewis (Ed.), *Child and adolescent psychiatry: A comprehensive textbook* (pp. 38–51). Baltimore: Williams & Wilkins.

Ornitz, E., & Pynoos, R. (1989). Startle modulation in children with post-traumatic stress disorder. *American Journal of Psychiatry, 147,* 866–870.

Osofsky, J. D., Eberhart-Wright, A., Ware, L., & Hann, D. M. (1992). Children of adolescent mothers: A group at risk for psychopathology. *Infant Mental Health Journal, 13,* 119–131.

Parens, H. (1991). A view of the development of hostility in early life. *Journal of the American Psychoanalytic Association, 39,* 75–108.

Parker, J., & Gottman, I. (1989). Social and emotional development in a relational context. In T. Berndt & G. W. Ladd (Eds.), *Peer relationships in child development* (pp. 95–131). New York: Wiley.

Pennebaker, J. W., & Susman, J. R. (1988). Disclosure of traumas and psychosomatic processes. *Social Science Medicine, 26*(3), 327–332.

Perry, B. D. (1994). Neurobiological sequelae of childhood trauma. Post-traumatic stress disorders in children. In M. Murberg (Ed.), *Catecholamine function in post-traumatic stress disorder: Emerging concepts* (pp. 233–255). Washington, DC: American Psychiatric Press.

Piaget, J., & Inhelder, B. (1969). *The psychology of the child.* New York: Basic Books.

Pitman, R. K. (1989). Post-traumatic stress disorder, hormones, and memory [editorial]. *Biology Psychiatry, 26,* 221–223.

Pruett, K. (1984). A chronology of defensive adaptations to severe psychological trauma. *Psychoanalytic Study of the Child, 39,* 591–612.

Pynoos, R. (1991, November). *The dose exposure model in the study of child PTSD.* International Research on PTSD. Annual Convention, Association for the Advancement of Behavior Therapy, New York.

Pynoos, R. (1992a). Grief and trauma in children and adolescents. *Bereavement Care, 11*(1), 2–10.

Pynoos, R. (1992b). Violence, personality and politics. In A. Kales, C. M. Pierce, M. Greenblatt (Eds.), *The mosaic of contemporary psychiatry in perspective* (pp. 53–65). New York: Springer-Verlag.

Pynoos, R. (1993). Traumatic stress and developmental psychopathology in children and adolescents. In J. Oldham, M. Riba, & A. Tasman (Eds.), American Psychiatric Press review of psychiatry (Vol. 12, pp. 205–238). Washington, DC: American Psychiatric Press.

Pynoos, R., & Eth, S. (1984). The child as witness to homicide. *Journal of Social Issues, 40,* 87–108.

Pynoos, R., & Eth, S. (1985). Children traumatized by witnessing acts of personal violence: Homicide, rape and suicide behavior. In S. Eth & R. Pynoos (Eds.), *Post-traumatic stress disorder in children* (pp. 17–43). Washington, DC: American Psychiatric Press.

Pynoos, R. & Eth, S. (1986). Witness to violence: The child interview. *Journal of the American Academy of Child Psychiatry, 25*(3), 306–319.

Pynoos, R., Frederick, C., Nader, K., Arroyo, W., Steinberg, A., Eth, S., Nunez, F., & Fairbanks, L. (1987). Life threat and posttraumatic stress in school-age children. *Archives of General Psychiatry, 44,* 1057–1063.

Pynoos, R., Goenjian, A., Tashjian, M., Karakashian, M., Manjikian, R., Manoukian, G., Steinberg, A., & Fairbanks, L. (1993). Posttraumatic stress reactions in children after the 1988 Armenian earthquake. *British Journal of Psychiatry, 163,* 239–247.

Pynoos, R., & Nader, K. (1988). Children who witness the sexual assaults of their mothers. *Journal of the American Academy of Child and Adolescent Psychiatry, 27*(5), 567–572.

Pynoos, R., & Nader, K. (1989). Children's memory and proximity to violence. *Journal of the American Academy of Child and Adolescent Psychiatry, 28,* 236–241.

Pynoos, R., & Nader, K. (1992). Post-traumatic stress disorder in adolescents. In E. McAnarney, R. Kreipe, D. Orr, & G. Comerci (Eds.), *The textbook of adolescent medicine* (pp. 1003–1009). Philadelphia: Saunders.

Pynoos, R., & Nader, K. (1993). Issues in the treatment of post-traumatic stress in children and adolescents. In J. P. Wilson & B. Raphael (Eds.), *International handbook of traumatic stress syndromes* (pp. 535–549). New York: Plenum.

Pynoos, R., Nader, K., & March, J. (1991). Childhood post-traumatic stress disorder. In J. Weiner (Ed.), *The textbook of child and adolescent psychiatry* (pp. 955–984). Washington, DC: American Psychiatric Press.

Pynoos, R., Sorenson, S., & Steinberg, A. (1993). Interpersonal violence and traumatic stress reactions. In L. Goldberger & S. Breznitz (Eds.), *Handbook of stress: Theoretical and clinical aspects* (2nd ed., pp. 573–590). New York: Free Press.

Rachman, S. (1980). Emotional processing. *Behavior Research and Therapy, 18,* 51–60.

Rado, S. (1969). Adaptational psychodynamics. In J. Jameson & H. Klein (Eds.), *Motivation and control.* New York: Science House.

Rangell, L. (1991). Castration. *Journal of the American Psychoanalytic Association, 39*(1), 3–23.

Raundalen, M. (1993, June). *Family and war: Some observations and suggestions for further research.* Paper presented at the Third European Conference on Traumatic Stress, Bergen, Norway.

Richters, J., & Martinez, P. (1993). NIMH Community Violence Project: I. Children as victims of and witnesses to violence. *Psychiatry, 56,* 7–21.

Rieder, C., & Cicchetti, D. (1989). Organizational perspective on cognitive control functioning and cognitive-affective balance in maltreated children. *Developmental Psychology, 25,* 382–393.

Rolls, E. T. (1989). Functions of neuronal networks in the hippocampus and neocortex in memory. In J. Byrne & W. Berry (Eds.), *Neural models of plasticity: Experimental and theoretical approaches* (pp. 240–265). San Diego: Academic Press.

Rose, D. S. (1991). A model for psychodynamic psychotherapy with the rape victim. *Psychotherapy, 28,* 85–95.

Rosenberg, M. S. (1987). New directions for research on the psychological maltreatment of children. *American Psychologist, 42,* 166–171.

Rosenblatt, A. D., & Thickstun, J. T. (1977). *Modern psychoanalytic concepts in a general psychology.* New York: International Universities Press.

Rubin, K., LeMare, L., & Lollis, S. (1990). Social withdrawal in childhood: Developmental pathways to peer rejection. In S. Asher &

J. Cole (Eds.), *Peer rejection in childhood* (pp. 217–240). Cambridge, England: Cambridge University Press.

Russell, D. (1986). *The secret trauma.* New York: Basic Books.

Rutter, M. (1985). Resilience in the face of adversity. *British Journal of Psychiatry, 147,* 598–611.

Rutter, M. (1988). Epidemiological approaches to developmental psychopathology. *Archives of General Psychiatry, 45,* 486–495.

Rutter, M., & Quinton, D. (1984). Parental psychiatric disorder: Effects on children. *Psychoanalytic Medicine, 14,* 853–880.

Rynearson, E. K. (1990). Psychological adjustment to unnatural dying. In S. Zisook (Ed.), *Biopsychosocial aspects of bereavement* (pp. 77–93). Washington, DC: American Psychiatric Press.

Saarni, C., & Harris, P. L. (1991). *Children's understanding of emotion.* Cambridge, England: Cambridge University Press.

Sack, W. H., Clarke, G., Goff, B., & Ickason, D. (1991, November). *Three forms of stress in Cambodian adolescent refugees.* Paper presented at the 25th annual convention of the Association for Advancement of Behavior Therapy, New York.

Saigh, P. (1985). Adolescent anxiety following varying degrees of war exposure. *Journal of Clinical Child Psychology, 14,* 311–314.

Saigh, P. (1989). The validity of the DSM-III posttraumatic stress disorder classification as applied to children. *Journal of Abnormal Psychology, 98,* 189–192.

Saigh, P., & Mrouegh, A. (1991, November). Academic variations among traumatized Lebanese adolescents. Paper presented at the 25th annual convention of the Association for Advancement of Behavior Therapy, New York.

Sampson, H. (1992). The role of "real" experience in psychopathology and treatment. *Psychoanalytic Dialogues, 2,* 509–529.

Sandler, J. (1960). The background of safety. *International Journal of Psychoanalysis, 41,* 352–365.

Sarnoff, C. A. (1971). Ego structure in latency. *Psychoanalytic Quarterly, XL*(3), 387–414.

Schafer, R. (1976). A new language for psychoanalysis. New Haven: Yale University Press.

Schwarz, E. D., & Kowalski, J. M. (1991). Malignant memories: PTSD in children and adults after a school shooting. *Journal of the American Academy of Child Adolescent Psychiatry, 30,* 936–944.

Shapiro, T., & Perry, R. (1976). Latency revisited. *Psychoanalytic Study of the Child, 31,* 79–105.

Shengold, L. (1989). Autohypnosis and soul murder: Hypnotic evasion, autohypnotic vigilance and hypnotic facilitation. In H. Blum, E. Weinshel, & F. Rodman (Eds.), *The psychoanalytic core* (pp. 187–206). Madison, CT: International Universities Press.

Sherkow, S. P. (1990). Evaluation and diagnosis of sexual abuse of little girls. *Journal of the American Psychoanalytic Association, 38,* 347.

Silver, R. L., & Wortman, C. B. (1980). Coping with undesirable life events. In J. Garber & M. Seligman (Eds.), *Human helplessness: Theory and applications* (pp. 279–340). New York: Academic Press.

Smith, E. E., & Medin, D. L. (1981). *Categories and concepts.* Cambridge, MA: Harvard University Press.

Solomon, S. D. (1986). Mobilizing social support networks in times of disaster. In C. Figley (Ed.), *Trauma and its wake* (Vol. 2, pp. 232–263). New York: Brunner/Mazel.

Stoller, R. (1976). Sexual excitement. *Archives of General Psychiatry, 33,* 899–909.

Stoller, R. (1989). Consensual sadomasochistic perversions. In H. Blum, E. Weinshel, & F. Rodman (Eds.), *The psychoanalytic core* (pp. 265–282). Madison, CT: International Universities Press.

Steinberg, A., & Ritzmann, R. (1990). A living systems approach to understanding the concept of stress. *Behavioral Science, 35,* 138–146.

Stern, D. (1985). *The interpersonal world of the infant.* New York: Basic Books.

Stilwell, B., Galvin, M., & Kopta, S. (1991). Conceptualization of conscience in normal children and adolescents, ages 5–17. *Journal of the American Academy of Child and Adolescent Psychiatry, 30*(1), 16–21.

Stratton, P., Heard, D., Hanks, H. P. I., Munton, A. G., Brewin, C. R., & Davidson, C. (1986). Coding causal beliefs in natural discourse. *British Journal of Social Psychology, 25,* 299–313.

Stuber, M., Nader, K., Yasuda, P., Pynoos, R., & Cohen, S. (1991). Stress responses after pediatric bone marrow transplantation: Preliminary results of a prospective longitudinal study. *Journal of the American Academy of Child and Adolescent Psychiatry, 30*(6), 952–957.

Sugar, M. (1988). Children and the multiple trauma in a disaster. In E. T. Anthony & C. Chilano (Eds.), *The child in his family: Perilous development. Child raising and identity formation under stress* (pp. 429–442). New York: Wiley.

Terr, L. (1988). What happens to early memories of trauma? A study of twenty children under age five at the time of documented traumatic events. *Journal of the American Academy of Child and Adolescent Psychiatry, 27*(1), 96–104.

Terr, L. (1991). Childhood traumas: An outline and overview. *American Journal of Psychiatry, 148*(1), 10–20.

True, W. R., Rice, J., Eisen, S. A., Heath, A., Goldberg, J., Lyons, M., & Nowak, J. (1993). A twin study of genetic and environmental contributions to liability for posttraumatic stress symptoms. *Archives of General Psychiatry, 50,* 257–264.

UNICEF. (1991). *The state of the world's children.* New York: Oxford University Press.

van der Kolk, B. A. (1985). Adolescent vulnerability to post-traumatic stress. *Psychiatry, 48,* 365–370.

van der Kolk, B., Perry, J., & Herman, J. (1991). Childhood origins of self-destructive behavior. *American Journal of Psychiatry, 148,* 1665–1671.

van der Kolk, B., & van der Hart, O. (1989). Pierre Janet and the breakdown of adaption in psychological trauma. *American Journal of Psychiatry, 146,* 1530–1540.

Weiner, B. (1986). An attributional theory of motivation and emotion. New York: Springer.

Weingartner, H. (1978). Human state-dependent learning. In B. T. Ho, D. W. Richards, & D. C. Chute (Eds.), *Drug discrimination and state dependent learning.* New York: Academic Press.

Weisaeth, L. (1993). Disasters: Psychological and psychiatric aspects. In L. Goldberger & S. Breznitz (Eds.), *Handbook of stress: Theoretical and clinical aspects* (2nd ed., pp. 591–616). New York: Free Press.

Weller, E., Weller, R., Fristad, M., & Bowes, J. M. (1991). Depression in recently bereaved prepubertal children. *American Journal of Psychiatry, 148,* 11536–11540.

Williams, W. (1987). Reconstruction of an early seduction and its after effects. *Journal of the American Psychoanalytic Association, 35,* 145–163.

Wilson, A., & Malatesta, C. (1989). Affect and the compulsion to repeat: Freud's repetition compulsion revisited. *Psychoanalysis and Contemporary Thought, 12,* 265–312.

Winnicott, D. W. (1971). *Therapeutic consultations in child psychiatry.* New York: Basic Books.

World Health Organization (WHO). (1990). *Manual of the International Classification of Diseases (ICD-10), Mental and Behavioral Disorders* (Chapter V, p. 22). Geneva: DCR World Health Organization, Division of Mental Health.

Wyatt, G., Guthrie, D., & Notgrass, C. (1992). The differential effects of women's child sexual abuse and subsequent sexual assault. *Journal of Consulting and Clinical Psychology, 60,* 167–173.

Yehuda, R., & Àntelman, S. M. (1993). Criteria for rationally evaluating animal models of posttraumatic stress disorder. *Biological Psychiatry, 33,* 479–486.

Yule, W. (1991). Resilience and vulnerability in child survivors of disasters. In B. Tizare & V. Varma (Eds.), *Vulnerability and resilience in human development* (pp. 182–197). London: Jessie Kingsley.

Yule, W., Bolton, D., & Udwin, O. (1992, June). Objective and subjective predictors of PTSD in adolescence. Paper presented at the World Conference of the International Society for Traumatic Stress Studies, Amsterdam.

Yule, W., Udwin, O., & Murdoch, K. (1990). The *Jupiter* sinking: Effects on children's fears, depression and anxiety. *Journal of Child Psychology and Psychiatry, 31,* 1051–1061.

Yule, W., & Williams, R. (1990). Post-traumatic stress reactions in children. *Journal of Traumatic Stress, 3*(2), 279–295.

Zivcic, I. (1993). Emotional reactions of children to war stress in Croatia. *Journal of the American Academy of Child and Adolescent Psychiatry, 32,* 709–713.

CHAPTER 4

Peer Relationships, Child Development, and Adjustment: A Developmental Psychopathology Perspective

JEFFREY G. PARKER, KENNETH H. RUBIN, JOSEPH M. PRICE, and MELISSA E. DeROSIER

Scholarly discussion of children's peer experiences dates at least as far back as William James, Louis Terman, Charles H. Cooley, G. Stanley Hall, and the emergence of developmental psychology itself. Indeed, it is noteworthy that as early as the publication of the first *Handbook of Child Psychology* (Murchison, 1931), the literature on children's play and behavior with peers was sufficiently extensive that no fewer than *two* chapters—one by Charlotte Buhler and the other by Helen Marshall—of this landmark volume were broadly devoted to this topic.

The impressive historical continuity of scientific interest in children's peer relationships belies many important discontinuities, however. For one, empirical interest in the topic has waxed and waned several times during this century. For another, great gulfs in methodological rigor and sophistication separate early from recent work in this area such that very few, if any, of the studies showcased in Buhler's and Marshall's chapters are even familiar to most contemporary researchers.

Perhaps most importantly, a remarkable shift has occurred with regard to assumptions about the developmental significance of children's experiences with peers. A few early authors were convinced that children's experiences with peers shape their growth and subsequent adjustment. Cooley (1902, pp. 24–25), for example, observed, "Children, especially boys after about their twelfth year, live in fellowships in which their sympathy, ambition and honor are engaged even more often than they are in the family." Likewise, Puffer (1912, p. 8) concluded, "Three boys in every four are members of a gang; and the character of this gang determines in no small degree what sort of men these boys shall

Portions of this chapter were prepared while the first author was a fellow at the Summer Institute on Human Development and Psychopathology at the Center for Advanced Study in the Behavioral Sciences, Stanford, CA. We gratefully acknowledge the contributions to this chapter of our many wonderful collaborators and coauthors over the years, especially Steven Asher, Cathryn Booth, Kenneth Dodge, John Gottman, Shelley Hymel, Rosemary Mills, and Linda Rose-Krasnor. We are also grateful to Dante Cicchetti, John Coie, and Willard Hartup for their helpful feedback on earlier drafts of this manuscript, and to Jenny Bandyk for her tireless tracking and typing of references.

become." By and large, however, most early authors regarded variations in children's experiences with peers as derivative of broader achievements or failings of personality development and without developmental consequences of their own. As a result, the early literature on children's peer interaction and relationships was largely normative and descriptive, emphasizing developmental milestones in the form, salience, or complexity of peer interaction and relationships.

By contrast, most contemporary research on children's peer relationships is oriented toward individual differences at given ages, and nearly all contemporary scholars accept to some degree the hypothesis that experiences with peers directly promote, extend, discourage, or distort children's interpersonal and intrapersonal growth and adjustment. The ability to initiate and maintain positive peer relationships in childhood is regarded as an important developmental achievement, and most contemporary scholars are interested in the varying degrees to which individual children succeed at this task. It is assumed that children who are successful with peers are on track for adaptive and psychologically healthy outcomes, whereas those who fail to adapt to the peer milieu are at risk for maladaptive outcomes.

In this chapter, we examine the roots of and evidence for the thesis that adjustment with peers has broad developmental and clinical significance for children. Toward this end, we review empirical evidence suggesting links between problems of adjustment to peers and other concurrent and later psychological disturbances, including but not limited to some forms of traditional psychiatric disorders. As we will argue, although there is a sound basis for seeing problems in peer adjustment as part of a continuing pattern of maladaptation among some children, recent evidence also suggests that, once in place, problems in peer adjustment carry their own negative implications for the trajectories of children's lives and should not be dismissed as incidental to more deep-seated or long-standing disturbances.

However, the significance that contemporary scholars attach to children's peer experiences stems as much from an emerging understanding of the positive, promotive functions of peers in the normally developing child, as from concern surrounding the outcomes that may befall children with peer difficulties. Thus, a second general aim of this chapter is to review some of the arguments that have been advanced concerning the contributions of peer relationships in children's socialization in the ordinary course of development. We argue that many diverse lines of evidence and argument converge on the conclusion that interaction with friends and other agemates plays an important role in fostering cognitive and emotional development, and the growth of interpersonal skills, poise, and social competence. We also review evidence for the importance of social support from friends during childhood and adolescence.

Our third general ambition for this chapter is to contribute to an emerging interface between the large research literature on children's peer experiences and the theoretical framework of developmental psychopathology. Although children's peer experiences have relevance for understanding development and psychopathology, research on children's peer relationships has not been strongly influenced by nor identified with the emerging discipline of developmental psychopathology until recently. Thus, despite a common interest in adaptation, resilience, vulnerability, socialization, and other processes, peer relations researchers have been slow in explicitly recognizing the relevance to their work of many concepts from developmental psychopathology. In fact, a search of the indexes of the most often cited reference volumes in this area (e.g., Asher & Coie, 1990; Asher & Gottman, 1981; Berndt & Ladd, 1989; Schneider, Attili, Nadel, & Weissberg, 1989; Schneider, Rubin, & Ledingham, 1985) reveals only one, brief reference (Coie, 1990) to "developmental psychopathology." As a result, principles long taken for granted within the framework of developmental psychopathology are sometimes regarded as recent "discoveries" within the literature on peers. For example, considerable attention has focused on the previously unrecognized behavioral, emotional, and cognitive heterogeneity of children who are rejected by their peers. This finding has led to a considerable flurry of research on "subgroups" of rejected children (e.g., Boivin & Begin, 1989; Cillessen, van IJzendoorn, van Lieshout, & Hartup, 1992; French, 1988, 1990; Hymel, Bowker, & Woody, 1993; Parkhurst & Asher, 1992; Volling, MacKinnon-Lewis, Rabiner, & Baradaran, 1993; Williams & Asher, 1987). From the standpoint of developmental psychopathology, however, such heterogeneity is expectable, and an instance of the well-accepted principle of "equifinality" (Cicchetti, 1990)—that the same adjustment outcome can be reached through disparate pathways.

Measurement models and research designs simultaneously mirror the concerns of behavioral scientists and constrain what they contemplate and understand. The study of children's peer adjustment is characterized by a multiplicity of assessment approaches, each with its own technical jargon, repertoire of specific measures, and enthusiastic following. Methodological fashions and innovations, the personal penchants of key individual researchers, changes in funding priorities, or the opportunities afforded by specific research settings have all contributed to this diversity. And each approach has enjoyed periods of favored status and suffered periods of relative neglect. Heated polemics about the superiority or inferiority of different approaches have so far been rare, but the differences among measures should concern us. Statistical associations among different measures or

variables is seldom very high, and there is evidence that different procedures address somewhat different facets of adjustment. For this reason, a portion of this chapter is also devoted to issues surrounding the assessment of individual differences in children's peer experiences and adjustment. Our goal here is to document the diverse foci that have come under scrutiny in this area in the past and to advertise the spectrum of available techniques for those unfamiliar with them.

After a parenthetical review of the history of research on children's peer relations and adjustment, our chapter is divided roughly evenly into (a) a set of topics related to peer relationships in the normally developing child and (b) a set of topics addressing adjustment to peers, that is, the nature and significance of difficulties in peer relationships in childhood.

We begin our analyses of the role of peer experiences in the normally developing child with a sketch of the developmental course of children's peer experiences. Against this backdrop of normative trends, we turn to some of the major theoretical viewpoints on the role of peer experiences in children's socialization and development, and consider the supportive features of children's friendships. No unifying analytic framework exists yet for conceptualizing how peer experiences influence development and adjustment. Because several comprehensive treatments of these topics exist (e.g., Asher & Parker, 1989; Azmitia & Perlmutter, 1989; Berndt, in press; Berndt & Ladd, 1989; Bukowski & Hoza, 1989; Hartup, 1983, 1985, 1992b; Hartup & Laursen, 1991; Rubin & Coplan, 1992; Savin-Williams & Berndt, 1990), our effort in this area is not extended. Interested readers are referred to these earlier sources for more extensive treatment. Our aim is simply to provide a relatively comprehensive "annotated catalogue" of the divergent but sometimes intersecting schools of thought on this topic.

In the subsequent section, we address how to identify children with difficulties in peer relationships. This seemingly straightforward requirement belies an exceedingly complex conceptual and methodological task. We review specific assessment techniques for assessing children's peer group acceptance and involvement in friendships.

There are substantial individual differences in children's peer acceptance and success with friends. Such differences are obvious even from casual observation. A critical issue for parents, clinicians, and researchers is what do these differences imply for children's mental health and well-being? Three central questions concerning this issue may be posed:

The first question is essentially the epidemiological one: Are difficulties with peers associated with other behavioral and affective disturbances; that is, what are the contemporaneous mental health and adjustment correlates of difficulties with peers?

The second question concerns long-term sequelae: Do difficulties with peers forecast mental health and other disturbances in adulthood; that is, are children with poor peer relationships at risk for later maladaptive outcome? Note that the answer to this question is not contingent in any necessary way on the answer to the first question—peer difficulties need not be associated with contemporary disturbances to be predictive of later disturbances (so-called "sleeper effects") and contemporary correlations need not hold up over time. Nevertheless, faith in the continuity of individual development would lead one to expect some coherence of adaptation over time (Sroufe, 1979), and thus some consistency across the answers to these first two questions.

The third question is essentially the etiologic one: To what extent and under what circumstances can maladjustment to peers in childhood be said to *compromise* children's development and well-being? This question, which relates to the direction of causal effects between poor peer relationships and later adjustment, has been answered in different ways by different authors at different times.

These three central questions are taken up in successive sections. Specifically, first we explore several topics related to the links between peer relationships difficulties and other forms of maladjustment. This review focuses on the role of difficulties with peers in the children's referral to psychiatric clinics and in traditional differential psychiatric diagnosis and assessment. We also discuss (a) the role of peer relationships of children with specific types of psychiatric disturbances and (b) some concomitant affective and academic disturbances that accompany peer relationship difficulties. Next, we discuss research on the long-term links between difficulties in peer relationships and adjustment, focusing particularly on later criminal and mental health outcomes. Third, we discuss two prominent, albeit extreme, views of how to understand the long-term link between peer adjustment and personal adjustment. We suggest, as other authors have, that neither explanation is sufficient, and propose a more complex conceptualization borrowing concepts from recent transactive developmental models.

The final major section of the chapter considers the origins of difficulties with peers. The question of the origins of children's peer difficulties can be considered from two vantage points—one stressing the influence of earlier family (i.e., attachment and parenting history) factors that predispose children to later peer difficulties, and one stressing more proximal influences embedded in the spiraling processes of behavior, social cognition, and attributions that undergird children's reactions to their peers and their peers' reaction to them. The section reviews these proximal and distal influences.

The chapter ends with a comment on how research on children with difficulties in peer relationships extends our understanding of peer relationships and development, and with some suggestions for future research.

HISTORICAL SHIFTS IN RESEARCH ON CHILDREN'S PEER RELATIONSHIPS

The study of peer relationships and children's development has had a long and rich history. In her early review, Buhler (1931) credited Monroe (1899) with the first systematic investigation of this topic in North America. Using questionnaires, Monroe explored the "social consciousness" of 2,336 elementary school pupils in Massachusetts, asking, among other things, what qualities they valued in a "chum," their preferred social activities and games, and the organization of their gangs and clubs. Other examples of early research include that of Terman (1904), who

examined qualities of leadership and stability of status within experimentally constituted groups of elementary-school-age children, and that of Puffer (1912), who collected case histories of gangs and gang members.

In the 1920s, as Child Welfare Research Stations blossomed throughout North America, the empirical study of children's peer relationships attracted a large and influential following (see Renshaw, 1981, for a review of the peer relationships research conducted prior to 1940). In these new research laboratories, investigators developed novel methodologies to examine developmental and individual differences in children's peer acceptance and group composition (Moreno, 1934), their sociability and social participation (Parten, 1932; Thomas, Loomis, & Arrington, 1933), assertiveness (Dawe, 1934), sympathetic and altruistic behaviors (Murphy, 1937), aggression (Goodenough, 1931), choice of friends (Furfey, 1927), group dynamics (Hurlock, 1927; Lewin, Lippit, & White, 1938), and the correlates of individual differences in social skills and competence (Hanfmann, 1935; Jack, 1934; Koch, 1935).

The exigencies of World War II and related world events slowed progress in this area during the decade of the 1940s but did not halt it. During this decade, ambitious studies of sympathy and empathy (e.g., Dymond, 1948, 1949), social skills training (Chittenden, 1942), and individual differences in aggressiveness (Muste & Sharpe, 1947) were reported. A particularly important development during this time was the popularization of sociometric assessment techniques for studying children's social acceptance with peers and friendships. Thus, Lippitt (1941), Northway (1943), and Bonney (e.g., 1944, 1946, 1947), among many others, used sociometric techniques to discover the characteristics of popular and unpopular children. Other researchers reported on friendship fluctuations and children's reasons for selecting their friends (e.g., Austin & Thompson, 1948; Thompson & Horrocks, 1947).

In the 1950s, however, the scientific study of children's peer relationships slowed so considerably that by 1960, Thompson (1960, p. 821) declared this once-fashionable topic "a neglected area of inquiry." Thompson (1960) attributed much of the cause of this decline to the influence of the political climate of the Cold War. He noted that funding priorities at the time favored psychological research on behalf of national defense, and as a result, many topics that were once the focus of study within children's groups (leadership, popularity, aggression) were extended upward and became studied almost exclusively with young adults.

These influences and others continued to dampen interest and research in children's peer relationships during most of the 1960s. In the United States, for example, a national focus on poverty led to educational initiatives on behalf of high-risk children and minorities. Although these initiatives might have appropriately included concern for these children's social relationships and social skills, in fact, they were confined relatively narrowly to cognitive and language skills (Zigler & Trickett, 1978). Within developmental psychology, attention also shifted to the many provocative hypotheses offered by Piaget's developmental theory. Although Piaget had made important claims about the role of peer relationships in the development of cognitive skills and moral reasoning, this element of Piaget's theory received limited attention and cognitive and moral development was treated almost entirely as an individual rather than as a social achievement.

Nevertheless, there were a number of important milestones and developments in the study of peer relationships, even during this period of relative neglect. At the opening of the decade, for example, Coleman (1961) published a widely read treatise on the adolescent's values and lifestyles. Coleman's (1961) findings seemed to suggest that the values of adolescent peer society were very much at odds with those of the larger (adult) society, and in the face of such conflicting demands, teenagers were prone to acquiesce to peer pressure. Although Coleman's (1961) claims were subsequently qualified in important respects by a number of later investigations (see Brown, 1990), they influenced a great number of authors (e.g., Bronfenbrenner, 1970). Consequently, the view that parents and peers were engaged in a tug-of-war over socialization during adolescence dominated the literature for many years (Cooper & Cooper, 1992). Other examples of notable work during this period include a massive ($N = 37,913$) study of the correlates of sociometric status by Roff and Sells (1967); work by G. R. Patterson, Littman, and Bricker (1967) on aggression; work by Hartup and associates (Charlesworth & Hartup, 1967; Hartup, Glazer, & Charlesworth, 1967) on peer reinforcement; and, rich, naturalistic work by Sherif and colleagues (Sherif, Harvey, White, Hood, & Sherif, 1961; Sherif & Sherif, 1969) on the processes of group formation and group cohesion.

As the decade of the 1960s ended, research on children's peer relationships was at a low ebb. Yet, just a decade later, in the introduction to a special issue of the journal *Child Development* on peer relationships, Rubin (1983) described the field as "booming." That same year, Hartup (1983), reflecting on the staggering number of studies and papers available on children's peer relationships, remarked, "No one could have anticipated the surge of interest in peer relations that marked the 1970s" (p. 103).

A number of factors, both inside and outside the discipline, seem to have conspired to prompt the resurgence of interest in research on children's peer relationships that continues today (see Hartup, 1983; Parke & Asher, 1983; Rubin & Ross, 1982). Rubin and Ross (1982) have observed that a turning point for research concerning peer relationships and social skills was the publication of the third edition of *Carmichael's Manual of Child Psychology* (Mussen, 1970). Volume 2 of this *Manual* included a thorough and scholarly review by Hartup (1970) of research on children's groups, social acceptance, and friendships. Hartup urged developmental researchers to examine further the contributions of peers to children's socialization and development. Hartup's cogent appeal, and the datedness of much of the material in the chapter, was a call for further research that was heeded by many psychologists. Hartup's (1983) follow-up chapter in the subsequent fourth edition of this volume just over a decade later (retitled the *Handbook of Child Psychology,* Mussen, 1983) had much the same effect.

Additional factors were at work, however. To begin with, sociodemographic changes boosted the prominence of peers in children's lives by encouraging the increasingly early entry of the young children into organized peer group settings such as day-care centers and nursery schools. These changes included an upswing in the number of working mothers, more affordable day care, and the rise in the number of single-parent families. Many researchers and policymakers were drawn to the study of peer relationships and social adjustment because of an interest in the nature of children's experiences in these settings and the factors that fostered successful integration into these groups.

In addition, the shifts in theoretical orientation within developmental psychology that we alluded to earlier, especially the decline in influence of psychoanalytic theory and the rediscovery of various constructivist theories (e.g., Mead, 1934; Vygotsky, 1978) probably had an important impact. These shifts toppled the preoccupation of developmentalists with the unilateral influence of mothers, and opened the door for consideration of a whole host of instrumental figures, including peers (Maccoby, 1992). This prompted a rise in scholarly concern for children who have *difficulty* adjusting to peers. Such children were now viewed as missing out on socializing experiences that could not be duplicated elsewhere.

The upturn of interest in children's peer relationships in the 1970s and 1980s provided an impetus for methodological, statistical, and technical advances to capture the essence and nuances of peer interaction, peer acceptance and rejection, and group structure (e.g., Bakeman & Gottman, 1986; Coie, Dodge, & Coppotelli, 1982; Omark, Strayer, & Freedman, 1980; Strayer, 1980; Vaughn & Waters, 1981). These advances, including (a) the development of reliable methods for assessing preference, dominance, and affiliation patterns in peer groups; (b) the evolution of statistical procedures to examine causal and/or predictive relations between children's interactive behaviors (e.g., sequential analyses); and (c) the advent of high-quality, lightweight videotaping equipment for recording social behavior, all contributed significantly to the groundswell of interest in children's peer relationships. The upshot of these advances was that children's peer relationships and social skills could be studied in greater detail and in a wider array of age groups and settings than previously possible.

Finally, empirical evidence of a link between early problems in peer relationships and problematic adjustment later in life (Kupersmidt, Coie, & Dodge, 1990; Parker & Asher, 1987) has attracted clinicians, epidemiologists, and others to the study of peer adjustment in the hope of improving the early identification and prevention of adolescent and adult mental health disturbances.

Whatever the influences, vigorous research on children's peer relationships began in the early 1970s and continues unabated.

DEVELOPMENTAL TRENDS IN CHILDREN'S PEER INTERACTION AND RELATIONSHIPS

As with any class of complex behavior, understanding children's behavior with peers requires an appreciation of the child's developmental status and the dynamic organization of the behavior over time (Cairns, 1979; Cicchetti, 1990). Although the argument that the researcher must consider development when considering the meaning of behavior for actors and recipients seems obvious, in fact, the study of social development has been decidedly nondevelopmental for most of its history (Cairns, 1979; Sroufe & Jacobvitz, 1989). Moreover, an understanding of the major mileposts and transformations in peer experiences that occur with age is necessary to recognize and understand individual patterns of adaptation and maladaptation with peers (Cicchetti, 1993; Selman & Schultz, 1990; Sroufe & Rutter, 1984). Deviations, delays, or distortions in the development of peer relationships derive their meaning only through consideration of the timing, nature, and course of peer experiences in the average or expectable instance.

In this section, we examine children's peer experiences and relationships normatively from infancy through adolescence. Our concern is with the general developmental changes in the quantity, quality, and context of children's peer contacts and relationships. These normative patterns then provide a framework for considering the role of peer experiences in development and the considerable variation existing among individual children in the success of their adjustment with peers.

Infancy and Early Childhood

Early childhood is a period of rapid achievement of mileposts in social responsiveness and social skill. Infants have obvious motoric, cognitive, and verbal limitations that restrict their capabilities for, and interest in, peer interaction. Thus, peer interaction is absent in any meaningful sense during the first three to four months of life. Toward the end of the first half year of life, however, infants begin to demonstrate social interest toward peers, as inferred from the presence of behaviors such as smiling, vocalizing, and reaching toward peers. From this point forward, social skills are acquired rapidly (Field, 1979; Fogel, 1979).

Infants begin to coordinate their interactions with other children shortly after the first half year of life (Vandell, Wilson, & Buchanan, 1980). These initial exchanges are short, two-turn reciprocal chains, typically involving an infant exhibiting a social behavior, such as pointing or vocalizing toward another baby, and the other baby's responding in kind. Agonistic acts and object-centered activities are rare at this age. Interestingly, even at these early ages, considerable variability in interactive behavior is evident; some infants repeatedly direct social acts toward other children, whereas other infants do so very rarely (Vandell et al., 1980).

In contrast to the somewhat unpredictable social response sequences observed between young infants, the social exchanges of older infants and toddlers can be characterized as more predictable, more complex, more coordinated, and lengthier (Baudonniere, Garcia-Werebe, Michel, & Liegeois, 1989; Eckerman, Davis, & Didow, 1989; Eckerman & Stein, 1982, 1990; Goldman & Ross, 1978; Ross, 1982; Ross & Kay, 1980; Ross, Lollis, & Elliott, 1982). Around the time of the first birthday, children become capable of shared activity with peers. Initially, these activities center primarily around objects (Mueller & Brenner, 1977). Object struggles are common, but so, too, are exchanges involving imitation of other infants' behaviors toward objects. According to Mueller and Silverman (1989), imitation of other infants' actions toward objects may be common at this age because an agemate, capable of similar

actions with a toy, provides an ideal model of what to do with it. Further, Mueller and Silverman (1989) argue that these imitative exchanges mark the emergence of the earliest forms of parallel play, and these authors note that it is reasonable to assume that reciprocal exchanges of this type, although not intended as such, are experienced as shared activities by the participants.

The object-centeredness of children's peer interchanges declines from the beginning to the end of the second year of life (Mueller & Brenner, 1977). Mueller and Silverman (1989) suggest that this signals a subtle but significant transformation in peer relationships in that it marks a transition from an outward focus on activities to a more inward focus on the social relationship itself.

The period from 16 or 18 months to about 3 years is marked by social interaction that is increasing socially oriented, and more truly complementary and coordinated (e.g., Eckerman et al., 1989; Ross et al., 1982). The consolidation of locomotion and, especially, the emergence of the ability to communicate meaning through language, play a significant role in this transformation (e.g., Dunn, 1988; Howes, 1992). It is during this period that lighthearted and playful "games" can first be identified in toddlers' interactive exchanges (Ross, 1982).

Howes (1992) describes the gradually unfolding sequence that takes place over the span from 16 months to 3 years in the growth of children's skills at communicating meaning in the context of social pretense. At the beginning of this period, children's play and games have a complementary and reciprocal structure (e.g., run-chase); thus, their play is built on familiar and well-learned scripts or routines, permitting the children to play cooperatively with little need to communicate meaning. Social pretense at this point consists of little more than one child's imitation of the isolated pretense acts of another.

As language and symbolic capacity matures, however, social pretense undergoes regular, sequential changes. From 16 to 20 months, children's pretense becomes more abstract and distant from their sensorimotor actions. Children will not only match or imitate the pretense acts of other children, but also they will attempt to recruit the partner to join their pretend play. These efforts are not routinely successful, but children are beginning to understand that nonliteral meanings can be shared by partners.

From 21 to 24 months, children engage in similar pretend actions in the context of broader joint activity. Attempts to recruit others into pretense play are more frequent and more successful. Children organize materials for sociodramatic play, but there is little or no joint organization of the pretend play itself. Scripted joint play emerges from 25 to 30 months, and the assignment of social roles in play (e.g., doctor, mother, father, police officer) emerges shortly thereafter, from 31 to 36 months. At this point, children understand that nonliteral meaning can be shared and they can communicate these meanings effectively during pretense with partners.

The formation of specific friendships begins to be observed during the period from 18 to 36 months. These friendships are indexed by mutual interaction preference, shared affect, and differentially sophisticated play between peers (Bronson, 1981; Howes, 1983, 1988; Vandell, 1980; Zaslow, 1980). The percentage of children at these ages without friends is very small, at least among children in child-care settings (Howes, 1983, 1988).

Because toddlers' concepts of a "friend" and "friendship" are limited (Selman, 1980), it is sometimes assumed that these early friendships are of marginal importance. However, children with friends acquire social skills as a result of their participation in these relationships, especially if these relationships are maintained over time (Howes, 1983, 1988). Moreover, toddlers regularly and spontaneously discuss their friendship interactions with their parents at home, suggesting the salience of these relationships to even very young children (Krawczyk, 1985). Nevertheless, friendships at this age are less stable than friendships formed after 3 years of age (Howes, 1988).

Mileposts of the Preschool Years

Peer interaction after the third year and over the course of the remaining years preceding formal schooling continues to change in frequency and quality. Children direct increasing amounts of attention to peers, and spend increasing amounts of time with peers, especially if they are enrolled in child-care settings (Hartup, 1983; Schindler, Moely, & Frank, 1987). As might be expected from the increased contact and interest, conflictual exchanges between agemates increase in frequency and intensity over this period (Parke & Slaby, 1983). In comparison with older children, preschoolers' conflicts are more likely to involve struggles over objects (Killen, 1991; Shantz & Hobart, 1989). It may be misleading to dismiss these struggles as asocial, however, as object struggles almost always involve moral issues and elements of social control as well (see Hay & Ross, 1982; Killen, 1991).

Overall, however, the proportion of conflictual or aggressive interactions to friendly interaction declines across the preschool period (Parke & Slaby, 1983; see also Pepler & Rubin, 1991, for relevant reviews). Moreover, prosocial behavior (e.g., helping, sharing, empathy) is observed to increase from the toddler years to the early preschool years (e.g., Charlesworth & Hartup, 1967; Radke-Yarrow, Zahn-Waxler, & Chapman, 1983).

In a classic study, Parten (1932) described changes in peer play over the preschool period as following a rough progression from a tendency toward simple "parallel" activities to "associative" activities (simple shared activities) to more complex "cooperative play" (play involving a clear division of labor). More recent research has shown this characterization to be overly simplistic (see Rubin, Fein, & Vandenberg, 1983). Nonetheless, children's play increases in social complexity across the preschool period; the most notable changes occur with respect to sociodramatic play, which increases notably over this period (Gottman & Parkhurst, 1980; Howes, 1988; Rubin et al., 1983; Rubin, Watson, & Jambor, 1978).

The complexity of preschoolers' interactions may be related to the appearance at this age of behavior designed to protect their "interactive space" (Corsaro, 1985). According to Corsaro (1985), preschoolers' social interaction is especially "fragile," in that intrusions by other peers can lead interactive episodes to terminate quickly without formal marking or opportunity for negotiation. Realization of this fact leads children to develop a repertoire of interactional skills designed to insulate ongoing interaction from disruption, or, conversely, to counter resistance from peers to their attempts to join in play. This repertoire of skills and routines very often involves claims and counterclaims of friendship.

The skills of communicating meaning in social pretense are largely mastered by 3 years of age; thus, preschoolers' spontaneous social pretense is more likely to serve broader developmental functions (Corsaro, 1985; Fine, 1981; Gottman, 1983; Howes, 1992; Parker & Gottman, 1989). Spontaneous fantasy play is especially critical to the establishment and maintenance of friendships in preschool (see Corsaro, 1985; Gottman & Parkhurst, 1980; Howes, 1992; Parker & Gottman, 1989). In addition, it provides preschool children with a vehicle for working through major concerns and fears (see Breger, 1974; Corsaro, 1985; Howes, 1992; Kramer & Gottman, 1992; Parker & Gottman, 1989). Not surprisingly, then, spontaneous pretend play during the preschool ages, especially between best friends, is more frequent and elaborate than at any other point in development (e.g., Breger, 1974; Corsaro, 1985; Doyle, 1982; Forbes, Katz, & Paul, 1986; Gottman, 1983; Howes, 1992; Werebe & Baudonniere, 1988).

Developments in Later Childhood

The period of middle to late childhood has fewer of the obvious developmental mileposts that segment the periods of early childhood and preschool. Thus, the developmental timetable of this period is less explicitly punctuated. Nevertheless, this age span, covering roughly the period from 6 years to 13 or 14 years, is characterized by a great deal of change and growth in interpersonal skills and in the context and quality of children's peer relationships (see Hartup, 1984).

An increase in the size of the sphere of children's peer contacts is one of the most salient features separating peer experiences at this age from earlier ages. This change is wrought primarily by children's entry into formal schooling (Higgins & Parsons, 1983). A large proportion of children, however, also begin to participate in after-school or summertime extracurricular teams and lessons (e.g., organized sports, Girl or Boy Scouts) during this period. In addition to an increase in the *number* of available peers, children are likely to encounter unprecedented variability in the ascribed (e.g., race, ethnicity) characteristics and personalities of their peers in these contexts. The peer group also becomes increasingly segregated by sex, and to a lesser extent, race, and organized into more discernible hierarchies of power and popularity (Hartup, 1984; Higgins & Parsons, 1983).

Whereas preschoolers' cooperative play involves a great deal of spontaneous and unstructured fantasy and pretense, this type of play declines steadily across middle childhood, to the point of being almost entirely absent by the end of this period (Baumeister & Senders, 1989; Rubin et al., 1983). Simple roughhousing, or "rough-and-tumble" play, also declines with age, although it does not disappear entirely, at least among boys (Humphreys & Smith, 1987; Smith & Boulton, 1990). Instead, the cooperative play of elementary-school-age children increasingly involves adult-organized activities (e.g., playing sports) or games with formal (e.g., dodgeball, kickball, boardgames) or informal (e.g., tag, King-of-the-mountain, Hide-and-seek) rules. A common aspect of these activities, which sets them apart from earlier peer activities, is that they involve increasingly greater divisions of labor, differentiation of roles, and status, teamwork, and leadership.

Aggressive behavior also decreases from early to middle childhood, and changes in mode and content (see Parke & Slaby, 1983). Among other changes, verbal aggression (insults, derogation, threats) gradually replaces direct physical aggression over this period. Further, relative to early childhood, in middle childhood aggressive behavior is less instrumental (directed toward possessing objects or occupying specific space) and more specifically hostile toward others.

Reliable age trends have not been observed across middle childhood in children's general disposition to behave in a cooperative, helpful, or generous way toward peers (see Eisenberg, 1990; Hartup, 1984, for reviews). Instead, the pattern of growth and maturation in this connection is one of increasing complexity, flexibility, and responsivity to situational, intrapersonal, and interpersonal exigencies. This pattern is well illustrated by Berndt and colleagues who studied children ranging in age from 5 to 13 years (see Berndt, 1986b). In these studies, children were interviewed about their own and others' prosocial intentions, and observed while working under various incentive conditions on tasks with friends, former friends, or nonfriend classmates.

Berndt's findings indicated few overall developmental changes in either children's expectations regarding their own and their partner's inclination for prosocial behavior or their actual prosocial behavior with agemates. Instead, complex interactions among age, subjects' sex, and the friendship and incentive context of the interaction were evident or suggested. For example, among friends, a developmental increase was observed from 6 or 7 years of age to 9 or 10 years of age in the tendency of partners to work for equal rewards, but only when the possibility of equal rewards was salient. When the possibility of equal rewards was ambiguous or when equal rewards were not possible, findings were highly influenced by the children's sex, friendships status, and, to a lesser extent, age. After 9 to 10 years of age, both boys and girls showed a growing tendency to share more with friends than nonfriends. Nine- to ten-year-old girls suggested that they would share and assist friends more than nonfriends but, in fact, treated friends and nonfriends equally. Nine- to ten-year-old boys espoused equal treatment of friends and nonfriends but, in fact, behaved more competitively with friends than with nonfriends. According to Berndt (1983), the development of prosocial intentions and behavior over this age span reflects, not a single unfolding skill, but a complex confluence of developmental changes, including changes in the basis of social comparison among children, growing sex differences in children's preferences for small versus large social networks, and conceptual advances in children's understanding of reciprocity.

Middle childhood spans a period of considerable transformation in children's understanding of friendship. These changes have been charted by Selman (e.g., 1980; Selman & Schultz, 1990), among others (e.g., Berndt, 1986a; Damon, 1977; Youniss, 1980). Prior to middle childhood, children's understanding of friendship is little more than the concept of momentary playmate.

Chief among the constraints in preschoolers' thinking about friendship are difficulties they have in distinguishing their own perspectives from those of others, and in appreciating the distinction between the psychological versus manifest basis for people's behavior.

As they move into middle childhood, children's discussion of friendship and friendship issues begins to indicate a maturing appreciation that feelings and intentions, not just manifest actions, keep friends together or drive them apart. Children also begin to appreciate that others' thoughts and feelings concerning social events may differ from their own. Even in the face of this advance in perspective taking, however, children of this age for a time remain unilaterally concerned with their own, not their partner's, subjective experiences in the relationship. This unilateral perspective subsides eventually, however, and children begin to express an understanding that both parties in a relationship must coordinate and adjust their needs and actions to one another in mutually satisfying ways. But their understanding of friendship does not include an expectation that friendships can weather specific arguments or negative events. By the close of middle childhood, however, most children understand that friendship is an affective bond with continuity over time, space, and events.

Changes in children's understanding of friendship are accompanied by changes in the patterns and nature of children's involvement in friendships across middle childhood. Children's friendship choices are more stable and more likely to be reciprocated in middle childhood than at earlier ages, although it is not clear that either the reciprocity or stability of friendships increases across the period of middle childhood itself (Berndt & Hoyle, 1985; Epstein, 1986). In addition, the number of selections of close friends that children make has been reported to increase with age up to about 11 years of age, after which it begins to decline (see Epstein, 1986). Moreover, as is commonly observed, children's liking for and friendship involvement with opposite-sex peers drops off precipitously after 7 years of age (Epstein, 1986; Hartup, 1983; Hayden-Thompson, Rubin, & Hymel, 1987).

Studies in which elementary-school-age children have been asked to describe their friendships also indicate that children draw sharper distinctions between the supportiveness of friends and nonfriends with age (Berndt & Perry, 1986, 1990). Moreover, children's descriptions of their friendships indicate that loyalty, self-disclosure, and trust increase with age, although these trends are more likely to be observed in girls than in boys (Berndt, 1986a; Berndt & Perry, 1986; Furman & Buhrmester, 1985; Richey & Richey, 1980; Sharabany, Gershoni, & Hofman, 1981). Older children of both sexes also possess more intimate knowledge of their friends (Diaz & Berndt, 1982), describe their friends in a more differentiated and integrated manner (Peevers & Secord, 1973), and see their friendships as more exclusive and individualized (Sharabany et al., 1981; Smollar & Youniss, 1982).

During middle childhood, children express more implicit and explicit insecurity about their social position and acceptance among peers than younger children (Gavin & Furman, 1989; Parker & Gottman, 1989). In part this may be due to changes in social comparison processes that accompany the entry into middle childhood (Markus & Nurius, 1984; Ruble, 1983). Whereas the younger child is likely to evaluate his or her behavioral performance against a set of absolute standards, in middle childhood evaluations are more likely to be based on comparisons with others. On the other hand, children's insecurity is almost certainly also fueled by the sometimes capricious manner by which in-group and out-group status can shift. In a survey of 232 eleven-year-olds, for example, Kanner, Feldman, Weinberg, and Ford (1987) found that close to one-third of children report losing a friend or being picked last by peers for an activity in the previous month, and almost two-thirds of children report being teased by peers within the previous month.

During middle childhood, concerns about acceptance motivate children to devote a good deal of their energy, thought, and conversation with friends toward buttressing their social status and guarding against rejection (Eder, 1985; Fine, 1987; Parker & Gottman, 1989). Gossip, especially humorous gossip, which increases in salience and frequency among friends at this time, plays a significant role in this process (Fine, 1977, 1986; Parker & Gottman, 1989). Gossip serves at once to reaffirm membership in important same-sex social groups and to reveal the core attitudes, beliefs, and behaviors that constitute the basis for inclusion in or exclusion from these groups.

Finally, stable, polydyadic social groups, or cliques, emerge in middle childhood (Crockett, Losoff, & Peterson, 1984; Eder, 1985; Hallinan, 1981; Hartup, 1983). Cliques are construed as voluntary and friendship-based groups, and stand in contrast to the activity or work groups to which children can be assigned by circumstance or by adults. Cliques generally range in size from three to nine members, and are almost always same-sex (Epstein, 1986). The prevalence of cliques has generally not been investigated among children younger than 10 or 11 years of age. By 11 years of age, however, children report that most of their peer interaction takes place in the context of the clique, and nearly all children report being a member of a clique (Crockett et al., 1984). Ethnographic studies of cliques in middle childhood or early adolescence provide some of the richest data currently available on the nature and nuances of peer social life at this age. Eder (1985), for example, has described the plight of members of popular or elite female cliques, who, by virtue of their membership in an especially tight-knit and stable group, can earn negative reputations with others for being "snobbish." Involvement in cliques generally increases with age, at least through early adolescence (Epstein, 1986).

Developments in Adolescence

As with middle childhood, the period of adolescence is not punctuated by obvious and discrete developmental mileposts in children's relationships and activities with peers. Nonetheless, there are a number of developments in children's peer relationships over this period. Many of these developments continue trends begun in middle childhood, others reverse earlier trends, or otherwise represent developmental discontinuities.

The trend in middle childhood toward spending increasingly substantial amounts of time with peers continues in adolescence. This fact is readily apparent to anyone familiar with adolescents, but the results of formal assessments can be quite startling. For example, Csikszentmihalyi and Larson (1984) had adolescents indicate their activities, moods, and companions at random intervals across a one-week period. They calculated that during a typical week, even discounting time spent in classroom instruction, high school students spend almost a third (29%) of their waking hours with peers. This is an amount more than double the amount spent with parents and other adults (13%). Moreover, adolescent peer interaction takes place with less adult guidance and control than peer interaction in middle childhood, and is more likely to involve individuals of the opposite-sex (Brown, 1990).

In the area of friendship, adolescents have been reported to have fewer friends on average than children in middle childhood (Epstein, 1986). Nonetheless, same-sex friends account for an increasingly larger proportion of adolescents' perceived primary social network, and friends equal or surpass parents as sources of support and advice to adolescents in many significance domains (e.g., Adler & Furman, 1988). In a review of developmental trends in friendship selection, Epstein (1986) concluded that the stability of adolescent friendships is generally low, but increases with age. Subsequent research by Berndt and his colleagues (Berndt, Hawkins, & Hoyle, 1986; Berndt & Hoyle, 1985), however, indicates that most adolescent friendships are stable over the school year, and any developmental trend toward increasing stability is slight. School transitions, such as at entry to middle school, junior high school, and high school can disrupt the maintenance of friendships, however (Hirsch & Dubois, 1989). Although complete developmental data are lacking, it also appears that, in comparison with younger children, it is more important in adolescence for friendships with school friends to extend to nonschool settings such as the neighborhood.

A hallmark of friendship in adolescence is an increased emphasis on intimacy and self-disclosure (Savin-Williams & Berndt, 1990). Interviews and self-report assessments with adolescents consistently indicate that adolescents report greater levels of intimacy in their friendships than do younger children (Furman & Buhrmester, 1985; Sharabany et al., 1981; Youniss & Smollar, 1985). Further, observations of adolescent friends indicate that intimate self-disclosure becomes a salient feature of friendship interaction at this age (Gottman & Metettal, 1986; Parker & Gottman, 1989). Parker and Gottman (1989; Gottman & Parker, 1986) speculate that the salience of self-disclosure in friendship at this age is proportionate to the role it plays in assisting adolescents' efforts to understand themselves and their own and others' significant relationships. These authors note that self-disclosure *is* sometimes apparent in the interactions of younger friends. Unlike at earlier ages, however, self-disclosure in adolescent friendships prompts lengthy, and sometimes emotionally laden, psychological discussions about personal problems and possible avenues to their resolution.

Adolescence also heralds a final and key advance in the individual's abstract understanding of friendship (Selman, 1980; Selman & Schultz, 1990). Preadolescents understand a great deal about the reciprocal operations and obligations of friendship, about the potential of friendships to withstand conflict, and about the psychological motives that motivate friends' behavior. But preadolescents' understanding of issues such as trust and jealousy in friendship is very narrowly tied to their perceptions of loyalty and friendship exclusivity. In particular, preadolescents tend to view friendships in overly exclusive terms. They regard relationships with third parties as inimical to the basic nature of friendship commitment. The significant change at adolescence, however, is that individuals begin to accept the other's need to establish relationships with others and to grow through such experiences. In particular, adolescents recognize an obligation to grant friends a certain degree of autonomy and independence. Thus, their discussions of friendship and friendship issues show fewer elements of possessiveness and jealousy, and more concern with how the relationship helps the partners enhance their respective self-identities.

As in middle childhood, cliques are readily observed in adolescence, and membership in cliques is related to adolescents' psychological well-being and ability to cope with stress (Hansell, 1981, 1982). Across the late elementary school years and early adolescent years, there is a trend toward greater involvement in cliques (e.g, Crockett et al., 1984; Epstein, 1986; Hallinan, 1981). Whether this trend continues into late adolescence is not clear, however. Epstein (1986) concludes that the available evidence is supportive of such a trend. On the other hand, in a sociometric analysis of the clique structure of a large school, Shrum and Cheek (1987) found a sharp decline from 11 to 18 years of age in the proportion of students who were definitely clique members, and a corresponding increase with age in the proportion of children who had ties to many cliques or children whose primary ties were to other children who existed at the margins of one or more cliques.

Shrum and Cheek (1987) concluded that there is a general loosening of clique ties across adolescence, a social process they label "degrouping." This interpretation would appear to fit with recent data suggesting that both the importance of belonging to a group and the extent of intergroup antagonism decline steadily across the high school years (Brown, Eicher, & Petrie, 1986; Gavin & Furman, 1989). It is also consistent with the observations of several ethnographers, who report a dissipation of clique boundaries and a new sense of cohesiveness among senior high school class members (see Brown, 1990).

Whether cliques undergo progressive structural change, especially heterosexual integration, across adolescence is also not clear. A classic and familiar description of this process was provided by Dunphy (1963). According to Dunphy's five-stage developmental model, initially isolated, single-sex cliques in early adolescence eventually build closer ties to opposite-sex cliques. These ties eventually draw these cliques into a loose association of several cliques, which permits new social activities. Toward the end of adolescence, these larger associations dissolve into isolated but now fully heterosexual cliques and dating relationships. However, Brown (1989) points out that Dunphy's ethnographic description has never been formally replicated and that the ecology of Dunphy's study (Australia in the 1950s) probably restricts its utility as a description of structural changes in cliques among contemporary youth.

Brown (1990) argues that structural features of the transition to high school may account for some portion of the attraction of early adolescents to cliques, and the tendency for cliques to become increasingly heterosexual with age. He notes that the size of high schools and the fact that students are no longer assigned to self-contained classrooms mean that children of this age must confront a large and constantly shifting array of peers, many of whom are strangers. "Securing one's place in a clique prevents a student from having to confront this sea of unfamiliar faces alone. Including members of the opposite sex in one's circle of friends ensures participation in the heterosexually oriented series of school-sponsored social activities (mixers, proms)" (p. 181).

Whereas cliques represent small groups of individuals linked by friendship selections, the concept of peer subcultures, or "crowds" (Brown, 1990), is a more encompassing organizational framework for segmenting adolescent peer social life. A crowd is a reputation-based collective of similarly stereotyped individuals who may or may not spend much time together (Brown, 1990). Crowds are defined by the primary attitudes or activities their members share. Thus, crowd affiliation is assigned through the consensus of peer group, not selected by the adolescents themselves. Brown (1990) lists the following as common crowd labels among high school students: jocks, brains, loners, rogues, druggies, populars, and nerds (see also Castlebury & Arnold, 1988). Crowds place important restrictions on children's social contacts and relationships with peers (Brown, 1989; Eder, 1985). For example, cliques are generally formed within (versus across) crowds. Crowd labels may also constrain children's ability to change their lifestyle or explore new identities (Brown, 1990).

Crowd membership is an especially salient feature of adolescent social life, and children's perceptions of crowds change in important ways with age. For example, O'Brien and Bierman (1987) reported a general shift from 13 to 16 years in the basis by which students identify and describe the crowds and other significant groups in their school. Whereas preadolescents and young adolescents focus on group members' specific behavioral proclivities, older adolescents focus on members' dispositional characteristics and values. This shift mirrors broader changes that have been identified in children's and adolescents' perceptions of others (Barenboim, 1981). Moreover, this shift is accompanied by a concomitant developmental increase in the perception that peer groups have global and far-reaching influences on individuals, affecting their appearance, illicit acts, attitudes, and values (O'Brien & Bierman, 1987).

As another example, the prototypicality and exhaustivity of crowd labels also wax and wane with development. Brown and Clasen (1986) found that, when students were asked to name the major crowds in their school, the proportion of responses that fell into typical crowd categories rose from 80% in 6th grade to 95% in 9th grade, then fell steadily through 12th grade. The average number of crowds named increased across development, from just under eight at 11 years to over ten by 18 years. Adolescence also marks the appearance of crowd types ("druggies," "brains," "punkers") that are rarely mentioned by younger children. Finally, the percentage of students who are able to correctly identify their peer-rated crowd membership increases with age (Brown, Clasen, & Neiss, 1987).

Comment

In this section, we have tried to sketch how the nature and context of children's peer interactions change from infancy to adolescence. Our treatment was brief and limited largely to listing major, well-recognized, developmental markers and mileposts in this area. Doubtless, further developmental changes might be specified. For example, developmental sequences have been described in the growth of communicative competence (e.g., Shantz, 1983), interpersonal problem-solving skills (e.g., Rubin & Krasnor, 1986), and cross-race (e.g., Carter, Detine-Carter, & Benson, 1980) and cross-sex (e.g., Hayden-Thompson et al., 1987) peer relationships. Further, to do justice to this exponentially expanding field, we restricted our review to developments over the first approximately 18 years of life. It should be noted that we are not arguing that developments beyond these years are uninteresting or inconsequential. On the contrary, friendships serve most of the same functions in early-, middle-, and late-adulthood as they do in childhood and adolescence (for reviews, see Antonucci, 1990; Blieszner & Adams, 1992; Rawlins, 1992). Moreover, as individuals move in and through adulthood, their friendships and peer relationships are increasingly shaped by entirely new constraints, including the demands of work, love relationships, and family. These new constraints present new challenges, but also the potential for new rewards. In any case, despite these limitations, our review is sufficient to serve as a backdrop to our discussion in the following sections of the significance of individual differences in peer adjustment.

Two comments seem warranted, however. First, progress in peer relationships is not a simple unfolding developmental sequence, but rather a complex braiding of developmental changes across many levels of description, including the intrapersonal (changes in social understanding and concerns), the interpersonal (changes in the frequency or forms of specific behaviors), the dyadic (changes in qualities of friendships or patterns of involvement in friendships), and the group (changes in configurations of and involvement in cliques and crowds). What is more, development must be described as interlocking across levels. For example, we discussed developmental changes in how children view their behavior, their friendships, and the salient peer groups in their schools. And friendship experiences change children's expectations of friends; but changing friendship expectations lead children to change friends or to take existing friendships in new directions.

Second, the recent history of the study of social development has been one of allegiance to "dispositional" rather than "situational" explanations of developmental change (Higgins & Parsons, 1983). In other words, it has been common to assume that the impetus for major developmental change rests in facets of individual development (cognitive growth, physical maturation, etc.) rather than regularities in the organizational features of the social-cultural matrix within which the individual is embedded. Our review makes the limitations of this assumption apparent. Organizational features of the environment help to define the timetable for many developments in peer relationships. Were status hierarchies not such salient structural features of social life in middle childhood, it is doubtful that children of this age would express as much concern over this issue, and that gossip would play as central a role in their conversations as it does (Parker & Gottman, 1989). Likewise, as Brown (1990) notes somewhat facetiously, for too long, the tendency has been to regard adolescents'

interest in and allegiance to cliques and crowds as a collective expression of a biologically timed "herding instinct," rather than to recognize that the depersonalized and complex routine of high school can motivate young teenagers toward this form of involvement with peers (Brown, 1990). Without attention to the social-cultural matrix underlying development, our understanding of many of the major mileposts in the development of peer relationships would be hopelessly handicapped.

PEER INTERACTION IN DEVELOPMENT AND SOCIALIZATION: CONTRASTING THEORETICAL VISIONS

The role of peer interaction in development and socialization has been discussed in many contexts and from a diverse range of theoretical perspectives. No single framework has emerged for organizing this eclectic array of theoretical and other lines of argument, any more than a single framework exists for describing the influence on development of mothers, fathers, siblings, grandparents, teachers, schools, communities, and so on. Indeed, different authors and traditions have tended to emphasize different aspects of the process and outcome of peer interaction and relationships. However, several broad perspectives seem especially important to recognize, both for their influence on scholarship in this area and for their contrasting views of the significance of children's peer experiences.

Perspectives from Personality Theory

Psychoanalytic and Neopsychoanalytic Views

Childhood peer experiences do not figure prominently in most psychoanalytically inspired grand theories of personality development. Sigmund Freud, Erikson, Fromm, Mahler, Horney, Adler, and Jung, for example, devoted only tangential attention to children's friendships and peer experiences. Instead, these theorists focused primarily on the contributions of parents to children's healthy self-perceptions and behavioral functioning and tended to dismiss the importance of peer relationships or downplay their significance. Whereas the individual who begins life with a good start vis-à-vis parent-child relationships is assumed to succeed in peer relationships, the peer experiences themselves are not seen as central to adaptive or maladaptive personality development (Adelson & Doehrman, 1980; Cooper & Cooper, 1992; Grunebaum & Solomon, 1987; Youniss & Smollar, 1985).

An exception to this general trend is the attention devoted within the psychoanalytic framework to peer experiences at adolescence. Psychoanalytic authors have supposed that adolescents are drawn to peer friendships and peer groups in reaction to intrapsychic turmoil (see Blos, 1979; Douvan & Adelson, 1966; Freud, 1952). As articulated principally in the work of Anna Freud (1952) and Blos (1962), hormonal changes at puberty repotentiate sexual and aggressive drives to such an extent that children's earlier, hastily constructed defenses against oedipal feelings are seriously compromised and threatened. As refuge from these reawakened drives, children seek the companionship of peers at this time:

Erotic and aggressive drives toward family members become so intense that the youngster must have a neutral arena in which to work them out. . . . All and all, it would seem that the adolescent does not choose friendship, but is driven into it. . . . Erotic and aggressive drives, and to some degree sublimation, are the cement of adolescent peer relations. (Douvan & Adelson, 1966, p. 197)

Blos (1979), in particular, has suggested that changes at adolescence precipitate a "second individuation" process (the first, described by Mahler (1952) occurring in very early childhood) or severing of parental identifications and internalizations. According to Blos, adolescents must shed their family dependencies and loosen their infantile object ties to parents to become a member of the adult world. Within Blos's widely accepted framework, attachment to peers and identification with peer groups can play an important role in this process for several reasons:

1. Because peers can serve as important sounding boards without arousing anxiety or guilt, adolescents can use discussions with peers to resolve internal conflicts.
2. The peer group respects competencies, allowing the adolescent to develop an identity based on personal skills, especially athletic and social ones.
3. The peer group provides practical and personal guidance in social situations, especially in heterosexual relationships and behavior.
4. The peer group provides honest and critical evaluative feedback about the individual's behavior and personality attributes.

In Blos's view, because adolescents cannot find sexual gratification within the family and need to sever family dependencies, they turn to the peer group for support and security. Other psychoanalytic authors are less sanguine about the shift in dependency to peers at adolescence, though no less convinced of its necessity. Douvan and Adelson (1966) worried that in an attempt to free themselves from the control and restrictions of parents, adolescents may fall prey to the tyranny of a peer group that requires conformity in return for security. Douvan and Adelson (1966, p. 179) also expressed some skepticism over adolescents' ability to completely sublimate powerful erotic and aggressive feelings in the context of friendship:

If the sublimations fail (as they often do during this time), the drives spill over into the friendship and spoil it. Adolescent friendships . . . are based to a considerable extent on narcissism, identifications, and projections . . . All these circumstances join to make the adolescent friendship a tempestuous, changeable affair . . . If we look back to adolescence, we may be stupefied to recall friendships with the most unlikeliest, the most alien of partners, to whom we were bonded by a momentary, yet critical mutuality of needs. Even our solid and enduring adolescent friendships may turn out, if we remember them closely enough, not to have been quite so unbroken and harmonious as they first appear in retrospect.

Whatever their specific merits, the claims of theorists such as Douvan, Adelson, Anna Freud, and Blos rest in an important

way on assumptions about adolescents' intrapsychic turmoil and emotional lability. These assumptions have been difficult to substantiate, and have been challenged in many instances or in specific ways (e.g., Csikszentmihalyi & Larson, 1984; Eccles et al., 1993; Montemayor, 1982; Offer, Ostrov, & Howard, 1981; Rutter, Graham, Chadwich, & Yule, 1976; Steinberg, 1987). That adolescence heralds dramatic increase in children's interest in and attachment to peers seems undeniable, however, as we have discussed.

Sullivan's Psychiatry of Interpersonal Relationships

The psychiatrist Sullivan's (1953) views on children's and adolescents' peer relationships and friendships are similar in some ways, and sharply contrasting in others, from those of classic psychoanalysts, and have received a great deal of attention (see Berndt, in press; Buhrmester & Furman, 1986; Youniss, 1980). Sullivan's formal theory of personality development is fraught with fanciful and arcane constructs, but his observations on the growth of human social motives and relationships have proved surprisingly trenchant. Like Sigmund Freud, Sullivan accepted that much of human behavior is motivated by underlying biological drives. In contrast to Sigmund Freud, however, Sullivan assumed that anxiety is unavoidable, always has a interpersonal context, interferes with need fulfillment, and leads individuals to construct elaborate "security operations" to minimize the experience. An important construct within Sullivan's theory is that of "personifications," or mental representations of self and others based on the individual's accumulated experiences interacting in personal relationships. Sullivan's construct of personifications is quite close to Bowlby's (1982) better known, hypothesized "internal working models" and may have influenced Bowlby's views (Bretherton, 1990).

Sullivan also described the emergence of five basic *social needs* across the period from infancy to adolescence: tenderness, coparticipation in playful activity, acceptance by others, interpersonal intimacy, and sexual contact. According to Sullivan, these needs were fulfilled by specific individuals— parents, peers, same-sex best friends, and opposite-sex partners—in both a sequential and cumulative fashion. Of interest, the period of late childhood (the "Juvenile era," ages 6 to 9 years) is marked by the increase in the need for acceptance by peers and the development of "compeer" relationships founded along lines of egalitarian exchange. Somewhat later, during the period of "Preadolescence" (9 to 12 years), children's needs shift from a more general need for group approval to a need for a close, intimate tie to a specific other same-sex peer, or "chum." "Chumships" are true intimate relationships, prototypical of later love and other "collaborative" relationships; "chumships" revolve around the expression of "consensual validation" of one another's viewpoints and self.

In addition to offering a general age/stage descriptive framework, Sullivan (1953) speculated on the many positive and negative interpersonal and intrapersonal consequences of peer experiences for children. For example, he considered the development of skills for cooperation, compromise, and competition and perspective-taking, empathy, and altruism to emerge from peer experiences in the Juvenile and Preadolescent eras, respectively. He also emphasized the role of peer experiences in constructing and correcting children's perceptions of self through "consensual validation." And, along lines similar to the concept of a developmental deviation in developmental psychopathology, Sullivan offered speculations about "malevolent transformations" that might accompany developmental arrests of one form or another at specific periods of childhood. Children showing forms of developmental arrest included the "malevolent child," the "isolated child," the "disparaging child," and the "ostracized child."

Sullivan had a particularly deep interest in, and concern with, the affective consequences of peer experiences for children. For example, he offered many speculations as to the motivational origins of loneliness, its relation to estrangement in peer relationships, and its role in development and psychopathology. Sullivan defined loneliness as "the exceedingly unpleasant and driving experience connected with the inadequate discharge of the need for human intimacy, for interpersonal intimacy" (p. 290). He felt that intimacy and loneliness defined reciprocal sides of the same developmental-motivational coin, the need for interpersonal integration. According to Sullivan, loneliness "so terrible that it practically baffles recall" (p. 261) ordinarily was not experienced until after preadolescence, although precursors of loneliness could be found throughout development. In preadolescence, the potential of the loneliness experience becomes "really intimidating" (p. 261). At this age, loneliness arises out of "the need for intimate exchange with a fellow being, whom we may identify as a chum, a friend, or a loved one—that is, the need for most intimate type of exchange with respects to satisfaction and security" (p. 261). In Sullivan's view, loneliness rather than anxiety was the motivational force behind most significant distortions of development.

Finally, Sullivan also stressed the therapeutic potential of peer experiences. He believed that the supportive atmosphere of childhood friendships could wholly or partially ameliorate certain developmental arrests resulting from earlier disturbances in relationships with parents and peers. Buhrmester and Furman (1986, p. 50) note in this connection: "It is difficult to overestimate the importance Sullivan gave to the therapeutic potential of chumships. In fact, his innovative treatment for schizophrenia involved a form of milieu therapy in which the aim was to recreate preadolescent chumships."

Research based on interviews and questionnaires generally supports Sullivan's claim that intimacy becomes salient during preadolescence, primarily within the context of same-sex friendships (see Asher & Parker, 1989; Berndt, in press; Berndt & Perry, 1986, 1990; Buhrmester, 1992). Children's perceptions of their competence with peers also becomes more central to their self-definition and self-esteem in preadolescence (Bukowski & Newcomb, 1987), as Sullivan predicted. Research also supports Sullivan's claims about the circumstances of loneliness and its significance as a motivational force in development and adjustment (see Asher, Parkhurst, Hymel, & Williams, 1990; Rotenberg & Whitney, 1992), and his predictions regarding the role of close friendships in the development of social perspective taking skills and prosocial orientations (see Berndt, 1987b; Parker & Asher, 1993b).

Sullivan's provocative thesis about the therapeutic potential of friendships seems to have received less attention than other aspects of his theory. Nevertheless, the work of Selman and his colleagues (e.g., Selman & Schultz, 1990), though only partly motivated by Sullivan's views, is worth citing in this connection. In Selman's "pair therapy," two young adolescents with socioemotional and interpersonal difficulties are paired, along with a therapist, for long-term therapy. The dyad is encouraged to play together and the partners are asked to reflect on their interaction together and their relationship. The aim is to achieve a restructuring of the children's immature interpersonal functioning and understanding, improving their individual and joint capacities for engaging in productive interaction with each other and other children. Thus, a legacy of Sullivan's theory can be identified in recent, productive clinical interventions.

Havighurst's "Developmental Task" Approach

Havighurst (1953) drew early attention to the significance of adjustment with peers for children's well-being and personality development. He argued that adaptation to peers can be viewed as one of many important "tasks" in development. According to Havighurst (1953, p. 2), developmental tasks are "those things a person is to learn if he is to be judged and to judge himself to be a reasonably happy and successful person." They are *tasks* in the sense that "successful achievement . . . leads to [an individual's] happiness and success with later tasks, while failure leads to unhappiness in the individual, disapproval by the society, and difficulty with later tasks" (p. 2). They are *developmental* in the sense that each has a period of ascendance and is subject to arrest. Each "arises at or about a certain period in the life of the individual" (p. 2) and "if the task is not achieved at the proper time it will not be achieved well, and failure in this task will cause partial or complete failure in the achievement of other tasks yet to come" (p. 3).

According to Havighurst, developmental tasks have multiple origins. Some tasks, such as learning to walk, arise mainly from physical maturation. Tasks arising from physical maturation are more universal than other tasks. Other tasks, such as learning to read, arise primarily from cultural pressure. Such tasks are culturally or subculturally relative. The expectations, values, and aspirations of the individual represent the third source of developmental tasks. Like cultural tasks, these vary with the historical-cultural context of the individual.

Havighurst (1953) placed considerable emphasis on peer relationships as a task of childhood. He wrote:

> The process of learning to get along with agemates is really the process of learning a "social personality" or acquiring social stimulus value. The child learns ways of approaching strangers, shy or bold, stand-offish or friendly. He [sic] learns how to treat friends. He learns what it means to "play fair" in games. Once he has learned these social habits, he tends to continue them throughout life. (pp. 30–31)

Getting along with peers, Havighurst felt, was important in its own right, as well as for its role in helping children attain other tasks in middle childhood, including the development of social skills, a rational conscience, and "a scale of values"; the learning of appropriate social attitudes; and the achievement of personal independence. He suggested that getting along with peers was a primary task in middle childhood; but he recognized that this challenge was, in a very real sense, a lifelong one. Indeed, he anticipated considerable continuity in adaptation over development, speculating (p. 31): "The nine- or ten-year-old already shows what he will be like, socially, at fifty." In this way, Havighurst anticipated the contemporary interest in the long-term adjustment of children with peer relationships difficulties (see Kupersmidt et al., 1990; Parker & Asher, 1987, for reviews).

Ultimately, Havighurst's concept of "developmental tasks" had limited influence on human development research. However, this concept is represented in most of its essential elements, including its focus on the significance of peer relationships, in contemporary "organizational" or "adaptational" accounts of development (e.g., Cicchetti & Schneider-Rosen, 1984, Sroufe, 1979, 1989a, 1989b). Organizational theorists, however, disagree with Havighurst's characterization of development as a series of unfolding tasks that need to be accomplished and then decrease in importance. Instead, organizational theorists stress the life-span nature of most developmental tasks: "[Development consists] of a number of important age and stage-appropriate tasks that, upon emergence, remain critical to the child's continual adaptation although decrease in salience relative to other newly-emerging developmental tasks" (Cicchetti & Schneider-Rosen, 1984).

Developmental Constructivist Approaches

Besides contributing to a view of children as actively engaged in efforts to interpret, organize, and use information from the environment, developmental constructivists such as Piaget (1932) and Vygotsky (1978) have stressed how structural features of interpersonal relationships influence the development of knowledge, language, social problem-solving skills, and moral behavior. An important distinction within this framework involves the differential affordances of adult-child and child-child interpersonal exchanges, a distinction that Hartup (1989b, p. 120) characterized recently as the distinction between horizontal versus vertical relationships:

> [Children's *vertical* attachments are] attachments to individuals who have greater knowledge and social power than they do. These relationships, most commonly involving children and adults, encompass a wide variety of interactions among which complementary exchanges are especially salient. For example, adult actions toward children consist mainly of nurturance and controlling behaviors, whereas children's actions toward adults consist mainly of submission and appeals for succorance (Youniss, 1980). [Children's *horizontal* attachments are] relationships with individuals who have the same amount of social power as themselves. Ordinarily, these relationships involve other children and are marked by reciprocity and egalitarian expectations.

The concept of the differential socialization opportunities in horizontal (peer) versus vertical (adult) interpersonal contexts has been especially influential in the domains of cognitive and moral development.

Cognitive Development

Constructivist approaches to cognitive development have been reviewed in a number of connections recently (e.g., Azmitia & Perlmutter, 1989; Doise & Mugny, 1984; Dorval & Eckerman, 1984; Garvey, 1986; Hartup, 1985; Killen, 1989; Overton, 1983; Rogoff, 1990; Smith, 1988; Tudge & Rogoff, 1989). These reviews generally conclude that under specific circumstances, including many that occur frequently and spontaneously in the course of peer interaction, conversation with other children can promote children's perspective-taking skills, problem-solving, language skills, academic achievement, scientific and logical reasoning, and a host of other important cognitive and social cognitive accomplishments.

Piaget's (1952) influential proposal was that peers promote the advancement of one another's cognitive development through attempts to resolve discrepancies deriving from the differences in their perspectives on a problem. As children interact with other children, they become aware of the contradictions between their own view of a problem and that of the partner. This conflict provokes disequilibrium that can propel children to newer and higher levels of reasoning. Importantly, in Piaget's view, it was not so much the simple exposure to the new or better problem-solving strategies of the partner, as the opportunity to confront one's own thinking that was critical; unless children appreciated the inefficiency of their old cognitive strategies they were unlikely to abandon them. According to Piaget, this type of real conceptual advance was not likely to happen in discussion with adults or others with greater status, because children were likely to unilaterally accept the conclusions of higher status individuals.

Whereas Piaget emphasized the contribution of symmetrical relationships (i.e., friends, children of similar social and cognitive status), Vygotsky (1978) emphasized the contribution of asymmetrical (i.e., parent-child, sibling-child, expert child-novice child) relationships to cognitive development. Thus, Vygotsky also saw peers as important to cognitive development, though by comparison to Piaget, less uniquely so.

The ideas of Piaget and Vygotsky have been explored in a great many experimental and other studies. Most of this work has been carried out by Willem Doise and his collaborators (e.g., Doise & Mugny, 1984; Doise, Mugny, & Perret-Clermont, 1975; Perret-Clermont & Brossard, 1985) in Europe, and Bearison (1982; Bearison & Cassel, 1975) and others (e.g., Ames & Murray, 1982; Azmitia, 1988; Azmitia & Montgomery, 1993; Messer, Joiner, Loveridge, Light, & Littleton, 1993; Tudge, 1992; Tudge & Winterhoff, 1993; Turiel, 1983) in the United States. A review of this work suggests:

1. In line with both Piaget's and Vygotsky's assertions, children working together can solve problems that neither child is capable of solving alone. Further, children working with other children show real cognitive advances from pre- to posttesting and these advances are stable and in most circumstances generalize to other problems.

2. It is important that the partners bring conflicting perspectives to the problem; when two children share an understanding of the problem, little cognitive advance is noted.

3. In line especially with Vygotsky's thinking, children also make cognitive gains when they work with partners who have a superior understanding of a problem such as the conservation of length or number (though this is not a prerequisite for advancement).

4. Children with less advanced partners sometimes show a *regression* in their thinking about a task. Thus, peer collaboration is not always uniformly facilitative or even neutral. An important interactional constraint seems to be children's certainty of the correctness of their own thinking. When children are more certain of the correctness of their thinking or the task permits children to be more certain, they are more likely to influence their partners.

5. Certain types of conflicts are more promotive of growth than others. Especially critical are "transactive" discussions, which involve noticing and resolving contradictions in one's partner's rather than one's own logic.

6. Collaborations with friends may foster greater developmental change than collaborations with nonfriends, at least when the task is a complex one requiring metacommunication skills. Friends seem more inclined to take the important steps of anticipating their partner's conclusions and spontaneously justifying and elaborating their own thinking and rationales.

Overall, it appears that the research literature generally supports many of the theoretical assertions of Piaget and Vygotsky regarding the importance of peers in children's cognitive development, even as it suggests some qualifications.

Moral Development

Disputes over objects, distributions of resources, personal norms, customs and rules, respecting others, loyalty, and personal rights are all common features of peer interaction. So, too, are acts of cooperation, forgiveness, kindness, concern, respect, and altruism. In view of the ubiquity of such events, it should not be terribly surprising that peer relationships are important contexts for moral development and socialization.

Psychoanalytic and social learning socialization theories have traditionally viewed moral development as children's internalization of adults' skills, knowledge, and conventions. Peer experiences generally have not figured prominently in these formulations, although social learning theorists have recognized the importance of peers as social models and reinforcers of prosocial and antisocial behavior.

Developmental constructivists such as Piaget (1932) and Kohlberg (1969) present a contrasting view. In this view, peer interaction is uniquely suited to the promotion of higher moral reasoning (and presumably behavior). Piaget was dismissive of the ability of parents to affect any real, meaningful change in children's development in this area. In *The Moral Judgment of the Child,* Piaget (1932) suggested that parent-child relationships were a poor context for moral development because they are marked by unilateral authority or constraint. Although children obey their parents, they do so unreflectively. As a result, the moral issues behind rules parents establish are shrouded from and necessarily mysterious to children. With peers, on the other hand, the child is aware that both participants have

equal knowledge and authority. When a conflict of interest arises, therefore, the child is led to recognize that others have perspectives that differ from his or her own. Since neither of these perspectives have special authority, both children's views have an equal claim to validity, and children are motivated to use discussion, debate, negotiation, and compromise to integrate their conflicting views. The morality of peer interaction is a morality of reciprocity and mutual respect.

As might be imagined, Piaget's hypotheses about the special significance of peer interaction in moral socialization are difficult to evaluate; disentangling the contribution of peer experiences from other influences on moral judgment is an exceedingly challenging task. However, a number of studies, reviewed by Schlaefli, Rest, and Thoma (1985) and Walker (1986), indicate that peer debate can in fact encourage higher levels of moral reasoning in children. In one of the best known of these studies, Damon and Killen (1982) videotaped 5- to 9-year-old children in triads during discussion of a distributive justice problem. Pre- and posttests established that the children who participated in these discussions were more likely to advance in their moral reasoning than were children who discussed a similar justice problem with an adult or children who were merely exposed to the pre- and posttests. Similarly, Arbuthnot (1975) found that dyads who debated moral dilemmas toward consensus showed more change in moral reasoning than dyads who passively heard arguments about the dilemmas or who performed extraneous tasks.

These studies, and others (e.g., Berkowitz & Gibbs, 1985; Berkowitz, Gibbs, & Broughton, 1980; Kruger & Tomasello, 1986) further suggest, in line with Piaget's thinking, that the process of "transactive discussion" is a crucial impetus to developmental change in the context of peer discussion. Transactive exchanges are exchanges in which each discussant performs mental operations on the reasoning of his or her partner (e.g., critiques, refinements, extensions, paraphrases of the partner's ideas). Children have been found to employ more transactive statements in the discussions of moral issues with peers than their discussions with mothers (Kruger & Tomasello, 1986), and the use of transactive statements has been found to be an important condition for moral developmental change through peer interaction (e.g., Damon & Killen, 1982).

Cognitive-Social Learning Perspectives

Writers influenced by cognitive social learning theory have emphasized the ways in which peers extend, elaborate, and alter children's social skills, behavioral tendencies, and self-attributions (see Grusec & Lytton, 1988; Ollendick & Schmidt, 1987). According to social learning theory, children generate internal rules linking social behaviors to consequences (praise, criticism, rebuke, rejection) and guide their behavior according to these rules. In part, these rules are learned through direct experience of peer punishment and reinforcement; very simply, children tend to repeat behaviors their peers approve of, and they learn to inhibit actions that peers discourage. In addition, much learning is presumably also vicarious; that is, children learn through observation of other children's behavior and the consequences that other children receive for performing various behaviors. Observation of peers introduces children to new modes of behavior and to the situational and other exigencies governing their performance.

Increasingly, social learning theorists (Bandura, 1989; Rotter, 1954) have also stressed that much behavior is controlled by self-generated consequences, concerns, and expectations as well as external forces. Children set standards of achievement for themselves, and self-administering reinforcement when those standards are met and punishment when they are not. The intensity of children's self-reinforcement or self-punishment is governed by many features, but one important factor is social comparison to peers, or the child's assessment of how well his or her behavior compares with that of other children. Bandura (1989) proposes that when children wish to estimate their competence at an activity they tend to compare their performance at the activity with that of their peers, especially children who are similar or slightly higher in ability than themselves.

Social learning theory has also emphasized the role of social comparison, and hence peers, in the development of attitudes of personal agency or self-efficacy (Bandura, 1989). Children's beliefs about their abilities, characteristics, and vulnerabilities guide their behavior by determining what actions they attempt and how much effort and persistence they invest in these.

Within the social learning framework, peers influence the developing child according to the same laws of social learning that apply to other socialization agents, including parents, teachers, and television. However, owing to the special features and challenges of membership in peer groups, the content of what children learn from their peers is assumed to be very different in many instances from what they learn from adults. For instance, many authors note that peer experiences have powerful emotional concomitants, suggesting that children develop important emotion regulation competencies in this context (Saarni, 1988). Observations of preschoolers, for example, suggest that friendship interaction has the implicit goal of maximizing the level of children's enjoyment during play (Parker & Gottman, 1989). For this to occur, friends must be successful in coordinating their behavior; this, in turn, necessitates that children learn skills for inhibiting action and maintaining organized behavior and attention in the face of arousal, excitement, and frustration. Other authors (Fine, 1981; Hartup, 1983; Thornburg, 1991) have noted the especially strong influence of peers on the amount of specific information about sex learned during early adolescence.

Particular progress has been made in the application of cognitive-social learning concepts to the study of the development of aggressive (Patterson et al., 1967; Perry & Bussey, 1977; Perry, Perry, & Rasmussen, 1986) and prosocial (Masters, 1971; Masters & Furman, 1981; Ollendick & Schmidt, 1987; Saltzstein & Goldhammer, 1990) tendencies, and to the development of sex-typed behavior (see Beal, 1994; Huston, 1983; Huston & Alvarez, 1990). In the latter instance, for example, a great deal of research suggests preschool children reward "sex-appropriate" and punish "sex-inappropriate" behavior and toy choices (e.g., Bussey & Perry, 1982; Eisenberg, Tyron, & Cameron, 1984; Serbin, Connor, Burchardt, & Citron, 1979). In addition to such direct influences, many authors have noted that the de facto gender segregation of children's play groups during most of childhood and adolescence suggests that boys and girls inhabit almost entirely "separate worlds" in childhood, with important implications for their social learning (Ignico, 1989; Lever, 1976; Zarbatany, Hartmann, & Rankin, 1990). It has been suggested that one consequence of growing up in separate worlds is that as children learn a style of interaction that works well with same-sex peers, they become progressively less effective with the opposite sex (Beal, 1994; Leaper, 1991; Maccoby, 1990).

Cooley, Mead, and the Symbolic Interaction View

The idea that children's experiences with peers contribute to the development of their self-concepts seems an especially attractive one. This proposal is at the heart of symbolic interaction theories, and, as Bukowski and Hoza (1989) note, can in fact, be traced back to the earliest days of American psychology. One of the first authors to emphasize this point was Cooley (1902), whose ideas were later extended by Mead (1934; see Corsaro, 1985). Mead, like Cooley before him, suggested that children experience themselves indirectly through the responses of other members of their significant peer groups. Mead suggested that the ability to reflect on the self developed gradually over the early years of life, first through imitation of peers (and adults) and later primarily as a function of peer play and games. Mead argued that participation in rule-governed games and activities with peers led children to understand and coordinate the perspectives of others in relation to the self. Thus, perspective-taking experiences resulted in an understanding of the "generalized other" or the organized perspective of the social group. This development, in turn, led to the emergence of an organized sense of self. Therefore, to Mead, peer interaction was essential for the development, not only of perspective-taking skills, but also for the development of the self-system.

Authors influenced by this perspective have emphasized the contributions of peer relationships to specific social skills and, particularly, to children's self-presentational or "impression management" skills—skills for positioning oneself effectively and adaptively in social situations (e.g., Denzin, 1977; Fine, 1981, 1987). Fine (1981), for example, has argued that childhood peer relationships, especially friendships, are important arenas for testing the bounds of acceptable behavior and developing poise under stress. He noted that within the bounds of friendship, inadequate displays will typically be ignored or corrected without loss of face. In this connection, Grunebaum and Solomon (1987) observe:

> Much childhood play takes the form of deliberately perpetuating a "loss of poise." Children everywhere play pranks, induce dizziness, trip one another, disarrange clothing, "kid" or tease one another. In peer relations, these tests of social poise help prepare the child for the maintenance of identity and self-control later in life. (p. 480)

Interpretive Approaches to Peer Culture and Child Socialization

"Interpretive" writers have been highly critical of psychoanalytic, social learning, and other conceptualizations of socialization that describe socialization as the private and unilateral internalization of adult skills and knowledge (see Corsaro & Miller, 1992; Corsaro & Rizzo, 1988; Rizzo, 1989). In common with symbolic interaction and developmental constructivist authors, they stress children's proclivity to interpret, organize, and exploit information from the environment and thereby shape their own socialization experiences and outcomes. However, the interpretive approach extends the constructivist one by stressing that the "environment" itself is a social construction—a world of habitual interactive routines and shared understandings that permit children to participate further in social activity. In development,

> Children enter into a social system and, by interacting and negotiating with others, establish understandings that become fundamental social knowledge on which they continually build. (Corsaro & Rizzo, 1988, p. 880)

Interaction with peers plays an indispensable role in this process:

> By interacting with playmates in organized play groups and schools, children produce the first in a series of peer cultures in which childhood knowledge and practices are gradually transformed into the knowledge and skills necessary to participate in the adult world. (Corsaro & Rizzo, 1988, p. 880)

An especially valuable aspect of the interpretive approach to children's peer interaction is the stress placed on documenting the socially shared and culturally relevant meaning behind many of the recurrent and predictable interactional routines that make up much of the day-to-day social life of children with their peers. Corsaro (1985), for example, has described the shared concerns underlying the common spontaneous themes in preschoolers' social fantasy play. More generally, interpretive authors have emphasized that children are frequently exposed to social knowledge in adult-child interactions they do not fully grasp. Such ambiguities will often go unresolved in that context because the orderly nature of adult-child interaction does not demand their resolution. However, these uncertainties may be readdressed later in the interactional routines that make up peer culture. Contrariwise, children also seem to appropriate certain elements of the adult culture to deal with practical problems in the peer culture. In such reciprocal fashion, children produce and reproduce their culture through their socialization experiences in the peer group.

Insights from Comparative Social Ethology

Extended contact with peers is ubiquitous among juvenile nonhuman primates and some species of nonprimate mammals. For this reason, and because experiments involving social deprivation are possible with nonhuman primates, comparative social ethology has served as a wellspring of hypotheses concerning the significance of adjustment or maladjustment to peers in development (see Cheney & Seyfarth, 1990; de Waal, 1989; Hartup, 1970; Lewis & Rosenblum, 1975; Savin-Williams, 1987; Smuts, 1985). Particularly noteworthy in the present context are a series of classic studies by Harlow, Suomi, and associates (see Suomi, 1979; Suomi & Harlow, 1975).

Harlow and his colleagues examined the development of rhesus monkeys reared (a) in total social isolation, (b) with mothers, but no contact with peers, and (c) with peer contact but without mothers. Total social isolation predictably had quite profound negative impacts on species-appropriate social, sexual, aggressive, and maternal behavior. These monkeys exhibited varying degrees of psychopathology. More interesting were the patterns of adjustment of mother-only reared infants:

> We have found that monkeys reared with biological mothers but denied the opportunity to interact with peers early in life also fail to develop appropriate patterns of interactive behavior when finally exposed to peers. . . . [T]heir social behaviors are often far from satisfactory. These monkeys are generally contact-shy. They tend to avoid most play interactions, and they engage in activity associated with grooming far less often than normal monkeys of comparable age. Furthermore, infants reared by mother only (MOs) are likely to be hyperaggressive when they do contact peers. In short, they do not make good playmates. We have found that the longer such monkeys are chronologically denied the opportunity to interact with peers, the more gross are their social inadequacies. (Suomi & Harlow, 1975, pp. 165–166)

Moreover, peer contact played a compensatory role in adjustment when contact with mothers was lacking or atypical. Animals reared only with peers developed strong attachments to one another and manifested intense proximity seeking. However, as long as these animals were exposed to several different peers in early childhood, later disturbances in affective and instrumental behavior with other animals were not apparent.

For obvious reasons, there are no parallel studies with humans, but studies of children on isolated farms in Norway (e.g., Hollos & Cowan, 1973) are of interest. Children on these farms have extensive contact with their parents but grow up virtually without agemates. Sibling activities tend to be parallel rather than playful and interactive and are predominantly nonverbal. Studies of these children have suggested that, compared with controls, social role-taking skills are impaired, but tasks involving nonsocial logical cognitive operations are not. In other words, the problems that the peer-isolated children displayed were specifically social.

Comment

In this section, we have reviewed theory and research pointing to the importance of peer relationships in many domains of development and socialization. As apparent, in some formulations, peer experiences are suggested to contribute to development in ways that are unique from children's experiences with adults; in others, peer experiences offer an important countervailing influence to the influence of adults; in still others, peer experiences and adult influences are seen to share many similarities. In addition, some perspectives do not distinguish between children's experiences in especially close peer relationships (i.e., friendships) and children's experiences with agemates generally. Other perspectives, however, focus more specifically on the functions of children's friendships. Further, in some cases, the implications of unsuccessful adjustment with peers are drawn out explicitly, whereas in others they are only implied.

FEATURES AND PROCESSES OF SOCIAL SUPPORT IN CHILDHOOD AND ADOLESCENT FRIENDSHIPS

The supportive features and functions of children's and adolescents' friendships have received a great deal of attention recently. Particular progress has occurred concerning the assessment of the supportive qualities of children's friendships, and there have been several demonstrations of links between the supportive features of children's friendships and indexes of subjective distress or adjustment in children (see Adler & Furman, 1988; Cauce, 1986; Hartup, 1992b; Parker & Asher, 1993b). Somewhat less progress has been made in understanding friendship support and children's adjustment in relation to stressful life experiences (see Compas, 1987), although headway has been made recently in this area as well (e.g., Dubow & Tisak, 1989).

The Supportive Features of Friendships

There appears to be a broad consensus concerning the dimensions that make up friendship support and the overall significance of these dimensions to children's adjustment and development (e.g., Adler & Furman, 1988; Asher, Parker, & Walker, in press; Berndt, 1989, in press; Berndt & Perry, 1990; Buhrmester, 1992; Cauce, 1986; Parker & Asher, 1993a). Progress in this area has benefited greatly from investigations of friendship support in adults (e.g., Cohen & Wills, 1985), from research on children's conceptions of friendship (e.g., Berndt, 1986a), and from theoretical accounts of children's and adults' interpersonal needs (e.g., Buhrmester, 1992). In all, at least five major features of friendships and categories of social support have been discussed with some regularity.

A first important supportive feature of children's friendships is *self-esteem enhancement and self-evaluation:* Friendships help children develop and maintain an image of themselves as competent, attractive, and worthwhile. Because friends compliment one another, express care and concern over one another's problems, and boast to others about one another's accomplishments, friendships are thought to play an especially important role in children's self-esteem and self-image (see, e.g., Asher & Parker, 1989; Berndt, in press; Bukowski & Hoza, 1989; Cauce, 1986). Further, as Rawlins (1992) notes:

> Interaction with a friend is widely and duly celebrated for its potential to validate one's self-concept and enhance one's self-esteem (Sullivan, 1953). People are at ease with their friends because they feel liked and accepted by someone familiar with both their strengths and their weakness, their charming and their irritating qualities. (p. 22)

The self-esteem enhancing and self-validating properties of friendships have been hypothesized to be especially important when children are going through normative changes such as school transitions or puberty or undergoing stress (Sandler, Miller, Short, & Wolchik, 1989), but they are undoubtedly important at other times as well.

Quite apart from such directly reinforcing properties, friendships may represent especially significant contexts for social comparison. Festinger's (1954) original social comparison theory postulates that humans have a drive to evaluate their opinions and abilities, and, in the absence of objective standards, prefer to compare themselves with other similar people. Because friends are selected on the basis of similarity and become more similar over time (Hartup, 1992b), friendships may be especially potent contexts for social comparison goals.

Although Festinger stressed the *self-evaluative* function of social comparisons, other authors (see Wood, 1989) have also noted that social comparisons can be motivated by *self-enhancement* goals as well. Research on adults, for example, suggests that downward comparisons with significant, but less fortunate others can reduce distress and enhance self-esteem and coping; likewise, upward comparisons with the accomplishments of close others can inspire people to redouble their own efforts and improve their chances of eventual success. There is every reason to believe that these same processes can take place in the context of children's friendships.

A second important function of friendship is the provision of *emotional security* in novel or threatening situations. Even the simple presence of a friend may boost children's reassurance and confidence. This can have important implications for whether children are willing to explore new environments, try new behaviors, or take the kind of small and large risks often associated with growth.

The emotional security function of friendship has not been well studied. With very young children, however, there has been some interest in comparing the level of security that children derive from friends and other peers with that of parents (Ipsa, 1981; Schwarz, 1972). The basic design of these studies is to place a toddler or preschool-age child in a moderately threatening situation, such as in a novel room with an unfamiliar adult and to observe the child either alone or in the company of his or her mother, a friend, or another unfamiliar peer. The basic finding is that the presence of a friend is often as powerful as that of a parent in promoting exploration and security in these circumstances. Similar experiments have not been done with older children; however, Asher and Parker (1989) point out certain parallels between the security that very young friends provide one another in a strange experimental situation and the ways in which older children and their friends deal with novel and potentially threatening circumstances.

Third, friendships are important nonfamilial contexts for *intimacy and affection.* The expression of caring, concern, and affection for one's partner have been rightly identified as important, perhaps even defining, characteristics of children's friendships. As they get older, children increasingly emphasize intimacy, self-disclosure, openness, and affection as components of friendship, both in their general beliefs about friendships and in their descriptions of their actual friendships (see Berndt, 1989; Berndt & Perry, 1990; Hartup, 1993). Not surprisingly, children of all ages report more intimacy in same-sex as opposed to cross-sex friendships, although this difference may disappear in late adolescence among girls (Sharabany et al., 1981).

Fourth, friends provide *informational or instrumental assistance* to one another. Like adults, children count on their friends' physical assistance with difficult or time-consuming tasks and look to their friends to provide constructive criticism, counsel, and information.

Finally, friends provide one another with *companionship and stimulation*. As Asher et al. (in press) note, the companionship aspects of childhood friendship provide some of the most enduring and romantic images of childhood friendship. Friends of all ages emphasize the enjoyment they derive from one another and from the activities they undertake jointly, although the nature of friendship companionship changes developmentally, of course. Successful and stimulating shared experiences contribute to a sense of shared history, joint fate, and a perception of investment in the relationship.

Friendship Support, Stress, and Children's Adjustment

Stressful life experiences—such as those wrought by illnesses, deaths of family members or relatives, and family transitions and relocations—are a major contributor to children's mental and physical health problems (see Compas, 1987; Garmezy & Rutter, 1983; Johnson & Bradlyn, 1988; Sandler & Block, 1979). However, some children seem to be relatively resilient to the effects of life stressors, and it has long been suggested that the social support offered these children by their friendships is at least one factor that buffers them from the negative effects of stress.

The number of studies of children focusing on friendship support, stress, and adjustment is limited, and disentangling the causal pathways among these variables can be a formidable challenge. The available evidence, however, supports the conclusion that friendship support contributes to children's ability to cope with life stressors of many types (see Belle, 1989; Berndt, 1987a; Compas, 1987; Dubow & Tisak, 1989; Dubow, Tisak, Causey, Hryshko, & Ried, 1991; Kramer & Gottman, 1992). How and under what circumstances supportive friendships are beneficial in helping children and adolescents weather stress is less clear. In an insightful analysis of this problem, Berndt (1989) offers the following hypotheses and conclusions, however:

1. Friendships do not buffer children from stress if the friendships themselves do not survive the stressor. In other words, evidence for an inoculating effect of positive friendships is weak. Children with better friendships do not endure stressful events better than children with less adequate friendships if the stressful event separates children from their friends. School transitions and family relocations are good examples of stressful events that increase the mortality of friendships. Further, the loss of important friendships under these circumstances is, in all likelihood, itself a stressful event for children.

2. Supportive friendships have the greatest influence on children's adjustment when they offer the specific type of support needed to deal with a particular stressor. For example, "When a child needs help with homework, a friend who answers questions about the assignment . . . may render more effective support than a friend who simply tries to make the child feel better about his or her abilities" (Berndt, 1989, p. 318). Indeed, support that does not match the stressor may under some circumstances be less productive than no support at all.

3. Finally, the child must access or take advantage of the support that is available to him or her under the stressful circumstances. In many instances, this must be an active, purposeful process. As Asher et al. (in press) note, to do so effectively, children must recognize that a problem exists, and understand the seriousness of the problem, the problem details, and the specific emotions associated with the problem. And supportive friends must ensure that their affection and advice are perceived and received as selflessly motivated and genuine.

In a similar manner, Sandler et al. (1989) discuss the compensating, coacting, and coopting effects of friendship support and stress on children's coping and perceived control and security. First, these authors note that friendship support can sometimes *prevent* the occurrence of stressful events. In the face of stress, however, friendship support can also play a *moderating* role, reducing the negative impact of stressful events on the coping processes that support adjustment. A *counteracting* role of support would be indicated in circumstances where, independent of stress, support enhances the skills children possess for coping with stress. Finally, these authors, in line with Berndt, note some of the effects of stress on support itself. Stress may lead to increased support if the network becomes mobilized to provide the resources necessary to meet the coping demands of the situation. Alternatively, stress may lead to a deterioration of the social network, and this deterioration may be responsible for the negative effects of stress on adjustment.

IDENTIFYING CHILDREN WITH PEER RELATIONSHIPS DIFFICULTIES: FRIENDSHIP, PEER ACCEPTANCE, AND SOCIOMETRIC STATUS

The literature on peer adjustment has yet to offer a definitive framework for identifying children experiencing consequential difficulties in their peer relationships. It is important at the outset to acknowledge the distinction between not getting along with peers and displaying troublesome behavior such as aggressiveness toward peers and social withdrawal (see Furman, 1984; Parker & Asher, 1987; Putallaz & Gottman, 1983). Behavioral assessment is one of the oldest traditions of differential child psychology (see, e.g., pioneering studies of "character" by Buhler, 1931, and Hartshorne & May, 1929), but behavioral assessments are only indirect assessments of difficulties with peers. As Parker and Asher (1987) propose, this issue should be understood as the issue of whether measures of *what* the child is like with peers can substitute for measures of *whether* the child is liked by peers. In general, they cannot. Whether a child is liked by peers is manifestly a question about that child's adjustment with peers. Although issues arise about how best to address this question, its status as a question about adjustment with peers is unassailable. On the other hand, whether what a child is like—that is, how the child behaves—measures adjustment with peers depends partly on the focus of the assessment. Some dimensions of behavioral differences, of course, are irrelevant or presumably only very indirectly indicative of success or failure with peers. Nonsocial behavior, behavior directed toward adults, or behavior that is very academically oriented may fall in this category (but see Krehbiel & Milich, 1986). By contrast, it is difficult to argue that behaviors such as aggressiveness and social withdrawal are not signs of social failure with peers. Even so, the relation between what a child is like and whether a child is liked is an imperfect one, and the task of deciding which behaviors, if any, should be taken as signs of adjustment or maladjustment with peers is a thorny one (Furman, 1984).

A second important distinction that must be borne in mind in considering the assessment of children's adjustment with peers is the distinction between the objective circumstances of children's experiences with peers and children's subjective appraisals, such as their social outlook, motivational orientation to social participation, and attitudes and affect surrounding peers and peer relationships. Attention to children's views of their peer relationships has been scant until very recently (Bierman & McCauley, 1987; Hymel & Franke, 1985), when attention has begun to focus on children's peer-related self-perceptions (e.g., Boivin & Begin, 1989; Hymel et al., 1993; Patterson, Kupersmidt, & Griesler, 1990), social concerns (Parkhurst & Asher, 1992), social anxiety (LaGreca, Dandes, Wick, Shaw, & Stone, 1988), sense of self-efficacy with peers (Ollendick, Oswald, & Francis, 1989), and levels of loneliness (e.g., Asher & Wheeler, 1985; Parker & Asher, 1993b) and depression (Altmann & Gottlib, 1988; Jacobsen, Lahey, & Strauss, 1983; Vosk, Forehand, Parker, & Rickard, 1982). These studies support the important conclusion that children with objective peer difficulties experience subjective distress over their circumstances. However, a great deal of heterogeneity of opinion among even extremely rejected children is routinely observed in these studies (see Asher et al., 1990; Boivin & Begin, 1989). Further, other data suggest that children's views of their social success can be widely disparate from their objective circumstances (see Bierman & McCauley, 1987; Hymel & Franke, 1985). Together, such findings support the broader point that targeting children on the basis of their interpersonal outlook is an important and potentially profitable pursuit in its own right, but it should not be confused with the task of identifying children with objective peer difficulties.

These distinctions bring us immediately to another distinction more centrally involved in the task of identifying children experiencing problems in peer relationships. Research into children's adjustment with peers has made especially vigorous progress in two domains: the study of children's involvement in friendships and the study of children's acceptance by peers and sociometric status. The distinction between friendship, on the one hand, and acceptance or social status, on the other, emphasizes the dyadic versus aggregate sense of peer adjustment. As Furman (1984; Furman & Robbins, 1985), Hartup (1983), Berndt (1984), Cairns (1983), and a number of other authors (e.g., Asher & Hymel, 1981; Bukowski & Hoza, 1989; Gottman, 1983; Parker & Asher, 1993a) have discussed, friendship and acceptance-rejection represent different frameworks for describing peer adjustment. Peer acceptance or rejection is a group-referent construct. It describes the central tendency but not the variability of a set of peers' liking for a specific child. Like all measures of central tendency, the construct assumes both conceptually and operationally that the preferences and attitudes of individual members of the child's peer group are independent, additive, and interchangeable. That is, what matters in the assessment of peer acceptance is the nature (positive/negative, liking/dislike,) and not the source (Child A versus Child B) of the judgment.

By contrast, friendship refers to a specific type of relationship a child might have with a specific individual. Thus, friendship is an inherently dyadic- rather than group-referent construct, although the number of friends a child has, their connections to one another, and the role of a child's friendships in the larger peer group can and should be of interest (e.g., Parker & Asher, 1993a). Implicit in the definition of friendship is what Wright (1978) refers to as the "person-qua-person" component of interpersonal relationships: Friends perceive and respond to one another as unique and irreplaceable. Whereas a child's acceptance status is scarcely affected by the dissent of a single member, the secession of either party to a friendship destroys the whole. In the operationalization of friendship, then, the *source* as well as the nature of the judgment matters greatly and must be preserved. As such, a comprehensive assessment strategy probably requires attention to both friendships and group acceptance.

In the following sections, we consider the assessment of friendship and peer acceptance, emphasizing their distinct measurement objectives, issues, and alternatives. Although we discuss specific measurement strategies and measures in each area, detailed review of the now substantial catalog of specific assessment options available in even one of these areas is beyond the scope of this chapter. The intent here is to highlight some general trends and emerging issues in the research. For more in-depth consideration of specific assessment options, the reader is directed to Asher and Hymel (1981), Berndt (1984), Furman (1984), Hartup (1983), Hymel and Rubin (1985), Krehbiel and Milich (1986), Landau and Milich (1990), Michelson, Foster, and Richey (1981), Parker and Asher (1987), and Price and Ladd (1986). These sources, as well as Parker and Asher (1993a; Asher et al., in press), Bukowski and Hoza (1989), Furman and Robbins (1985), Newcomb, Bukowski, & Pattee (1993), Rubin and Cohen (1986), among others, also discuss some of the concerns that have surfaced regarding distinctions between specific measurement strategies.

Friendship

What Is a Friendship?

Valid assessment of friendship adjustment depends on the ability to specify a set of sufficient conditions for the identification of friendships. As Hays (1988) observes, the term "friend" is often used very loosely and idiosyncratically, by both children and researchers. Such slippage poses an obvious challenge to the assessment of friendship adjustment. The issue of what constitutes friendship is a venerable philosophical debate beyond the scope of this chapter. However, some points from this debate warrant noting because of their operational significance.

First, one point of unanimous opinion is that friendship is a *reciprocal* relationship and must be affirmed or recognized by both parties. It is this reciprocity that separates friendship, on the one hand, from simple interpersonal attraction or liking on the other. From an assessment standpoint, if procedures do not verify in some way that the perception of friendship is shared, they run into difficulty because children are sometimes motivated by self-presentational goals to designate as friends other children who do not view them as friends in return (Berndt, 1984). Without verification of reciprocity, assessment procedures run the risk of confusing desired relationships with actual relationships.

Second, there is consensus that friendships are voluntary rather than obligatory or prescribed. In some cultures and in some circumstances, children and adults may be assigned their "friends," sometimes even at birth (Brain, 1977). Although these relationships may take on some of the features and serve some of the same interpersonal ends as voluntary relationships, most scholars would agree that their involuntary nature argues against confusing them with friendship. Likewise, some prescribed relationships, such as parent-child relationships, teacher-student relationships, and sibling relationships, may have many features in common with friendships but should not be confused with them.

A third point of consensus is that reciprocity of affection or liking should serve as the essential, though not necessarily exclusive, tie that binds the participants to one another (Hays, 1988). In other words, the interdependence of the two children should derive primarily from socioemotional rather than instrumental motives. Children may seek out and affiliate with one another for reasons other than primarily liking. Similar or compensating special talents and interests may draw children together in committed ways, for example, as members of work teams, sports teams, musical or singing groups, or even delinquent gangs. It is a mistake, however, to consider all children drawn together in these ways as friends. Similarities or complementarities of talents and interests will often lead to friendships and can help sustain them, but they do not constitute the basis of the friendship itself. That basis is reserved for reciprocal affection.

Identification of Friendships

To identify friends or gauge the extent of a child's participation in friendship, researchers have relied primarily on reciprocal sociometric nomination assessments (Bukowski & Hoza, 1989; Hartup, 1992b; Price & Ladd, 1986). In the typical procedure, children are presented with a roster of their same-sex classmates (or some other functionally similar group) and asked to circle or otherwise indicate which members are their best or close friends. The pattern of choices is then examined to identify children who nominate one another. Often only a limited number of choices is permitted, usually three.

Sociometric nomination procedures have compelling face validity. They are also inexpensive, can be group administered and, depending on the child's age and the circumstances, testing can take only a few minutes. The simplicity of the procedure is slightly deceiving, however. The issue of limiting choices, for example, entails certain trade-offs. Limiting the number of choices has the advantage of suggesting to the respondent the degree of closeness to employ when deciding whether to include a particular other child among the list. If the research questions dictate further stringency, children can be asked to rank order their choices or to designate one friend from among the list as their "very best" friend. On the other hand, limiting choices may arbitrarily restrict the number of friendships a child may

have. Limited nomination procedures, then, trade definitional stringency and homogeneity for inclusivity, and the decision to employ a limited procedure should always be evaluated in the context of the broader research question under study. When the number of choices is specified, it should also be made clear to children that it is acceptable to specify *fewer* than the maximum number. Otherwise, children may feel compelled to name as best friends other children who are not actually their best friends (Hallinan, 1981), opening the possibility for overestimating the actual number of friendships children have.

A problem of a different, and perhaps more serious, nature occurs when the reciprocity of children's friendship choices is not verified. Unless verified, nominations by a single child are suspicious because, as previously noted, children are sometimes motivated to nominate others who do not view them as friends in return. Thus, a definitional prerequisite of friendship is violated, or, at least left unassessed.

Although reciprocity is occasionally ignored out of methodological oversight or ignorance, a more common and understandable case occurs in studies involving index children selected for reasons other than their social adjustment (e.g., children with specific organic problems, attachment or parenting histories, etc.). In such studies, it is typically necessary to evaluate a cohort of cases located singly in classrooms scattered across a large geographic area. This makes it unfeasible or impossible to obtain the sociometric nominations of the classmates of each and every index child. Nonetheless, with some resourcefulness it might still be possible and advisable to individually approach the designated friends of each particular index child and verify that the targeted child feels similarly about the relationship. Where this is not possible, it might be advisable for researchers to, at least, verify children's choices against the reports of children's parents or teachers (e.g., Gottman, 1983).

Once children's friends have been identified, both quantitative and qualitative questions may be pursued (see Berndt, 1984; Bukowski & Hoza, 1989; Parker & Asher, 1993a).

Quantitative Variables

Quantitative variables index the extent of children's involvement in friendship relations. At the simplest level, a dichotomy between children with friends and friendless children is immediately evident. Despite its seeming simplicity, whether or not a child has a friend appears to mark an important threshold in children's friendship adjustment. Regardless of their level of overall group acceptance, children with friends are less lonely than other children (Parker & Asher, 1993b). Other evidence suggests that friended and friendless children also differ behaviorally in important ways and reason differently about social events (see Parker & Asher, 1993a).

Beyond the distinction of having versus not having a friend, the researcher can examine both the number of friends a child has as well as their interconnectedness. Individual differences in the number of friends children have has been examined in several studies, though not often in studies in which the reciprocity of the friendship nominations given has been independently verified. The size of children's social networks does not appear to be as predictive of other aspects of adjustment as whether or not the child has a friend or the quality of the child's friendships (e.g., Berndt & Hawkins, 1987; Parker & Asher, 1993a). Some authors (e.g., Benenson, 1993) have argued that the dynamics of issues surrounding the separation-individuation of children from their mothers implies that girls should prefer to have fewer friends than boys. In fact, simple differences in the size of boys' and girls' friendship networks are not often observed, especially in studies where the reciprocity of choices is verified (e.g., Eder & Hallinan, 1978; Ladd, 1983; Parker & Asher, 1993a; see also Crockett et al., 1984; Feltham, Doyle, Schwartzman, Serbin, & Ledingham, 1985; Reisman & Schorr, 1978).

Another quantitative variable, *network density,* describes the degree to which children's friends are friends with each other (Wellman, 1981). Like network size, network density does not appear to be strongly related to children's adjustment, at least among preadolescent children. Ladd (1983), for example, examined the friendships among children's frequent play companions and found no gender differences or relation to children's popularity-rejection by peers.

Qualitative Assessments

Children's friendships vary widely in their qualitative features, even among children of the same age. The assessment of the qualities of children's friendships has made great strides recently with the appearance of several self-report questionnaire/interview measures for elementary school children and adolescents (Berndt & Perry, 1986; Buhrmester, 1990; Bukowski & Newcomb, 1987; Furman & Buhrmester, 1985; Parker & Asher, 1993b; Reid, Landesman, Treder, & Jaccard, 1989; Sharabany et al., 1981). These measures are very similar insofar as they attempt to describe friendship with respect to specific features that are presumed to be important to the functions of friendships (e.g., provision of companionship, level of intimate disclosure, degree of helpful advice) rather than attempt to arrive at a single, overall conclusion as to the relationship's adequacy or inadequacy. In most cases, these measures also assess children's perceptions of the degree of conflict as well as support present in their friendship, under the assumption (now substantiated) that conflict and disagreement occur in even the closest of friendships (see Adler & Furman, 1988; Hartup, 1992a; Laursen, 1993; Parker & Asher, 1993a; Rizzo, 1992). Some of these measures (i.e., Furman & Buhrmester, 1985; Reid et al., 1989) also ask children to describe the qualities of their relationships to parents and other social network members (e.g., grandparents, teachers), thereby making it possible to compare qualitative features across relationships. Another important feature of most of these measures is that they require children to describe *particular* (i.e., specified) friendships they have, in some cases based on actual prior sociometric testing (Berndt & Perry, 1986; Buhrmester, 1990; Parker & Asher, 1993b). This step is important because children who are simply asked to describe their friendships (i.e., are not explicitly given a particular relationship to describe) are likely to provide an idealized abstraction that does not fit any single friendship. The requirement to describe a particular friendship also probably helps to reduce the influence of social desirability on children's responses.

A recent example of these measures is the *Friendship Quality Questionnaire* (FQQ) developed by Parker & Asher (1993b). This questionnaire contains 40 primary items plus an initial "warm-up" item. For each item, children are required to indicate on a 5-point scale how true a particular quality is of their relationship with a specific friend (e.g., "Jamie and I loan each other things all the time"). The scale ranges from "Not at all true" (0) to "Really true" (4). The questionnaire is group administered in the child's classroom and each item is read aloud to make as few demands as possible on children's reading ability. Children complete the questionnaire with reference to a specific friend, whose name is embedded in each individual item. Children receive scores on four dimensions of support (companionship and recreation, validation and caring, help and guidance, intimate exchange) and two subscales related to conflict (conflict and betrayal, conflict resolution). Parker and Asher report good internal consistency for the subscales and links in two studies between the features of children's friendships and their levels of general peer group acceptance, satisfaction with the friendship, and loneliness in general.

Although the observation of friends' behavior with one another is an important tradition within the study of children's peer relationships (see Berndt, 1987b; Gottman & Parker, 1986; Hartup, 1989a; 1992a), observation has not often been used to assess individual differences between children in the context of their close friendships (Hartup, 1992a; Price & Ladd, 1986). Part of the reluctance of researchers may stem from the very formidable task of isolating the contributions of individual members to the observed patterns of dyadic interaction (Furman, 1984; Hinde, 1979; Hinde & Stevenson-Hinde, 1986). It is unfortunate that this very real concern has led researchers to place so much emphasis on children's self-reports. In the first place, self-reports have this ambiguity as well; when children report that their friendship lacks intimacy, for example, it is not always clear whether the child, his or her friend, or (most likely) both children are responsible. More importantly, description of a child's friendship experiences is an important objective even when the child's own contribution to the observed patterns cannot be isolated.

Recently, some promising methods for describing variation from dyad to dyad in friendships based on observations have appeared (e.g., Gottman & Katz, 1989; Howes, 1988; Kramer & Gottman, 1992; Park & Waters, 1989; Youngblade, Park, & Belsky, 1993). So far, these assessments have focused exclusively on young children (i.e., younger than 7 or 8 years of age), but their applicability to older children is clear and in some cases extensions along these lines have begun (K. Park, personal communication, November 1992). Representative of this approach is the *Dyadic Relationships Q-set* (DRQ) developed by Park and Waters (1989). This system utilizes the powerful Q-sort technique (Block, 1978) to obtain observers' global ratings of several a priori areas of dyadic involvement: positive social orientation, cohesiveness, harmony, control, responsiveness, self-disclosure, and coordinated play. Good internal consistency and other forms of reliability have been found for this measure, and the subscale scores have been found to define two broad dimensions of dyadic functioning—positive versus negative tone and coordinated versus asynchronous interaction (Youngblade et al., 1993). The DRQ was developed to explore links between children's attachment histories and their social functioning in close relationships. Consistent with theoretical expectations, dyads of insecurely attached children have been found to look problematic on most dimensions of the DRQ relative to dyads of securely attached children (Park & Waters, 1989).

Acceptance in the Peer Group

Two distinct approaches to measuring children's group acceptance can be identified. The first approach relies on sociometric nomination procedures. Although we introduced sociometric nomination procedures in connection with identifying friendships, this technique has historically found its primary use as an assessment of group acceptance. Indeed, the vast majority of the available literature on children's peer acceptance is based on this technique. The sociometric nomination technique was originally designed to describe the structural features of the networks of positive interpersonal relationships in a group (Moreno, 1934). The potential of this technique for describing individual differences in peer adjustment was quickly recognized, however (e.g., Northway, 1943). Unfortunately, so too were some of the limitations of this approach. Recognition of some of the limitations of the positive nomination technique has led researchers to include negative as well as positive nominations in their studies and to the recent development of several multidimensional taxonomies for classifying children on the basis of nomination data (see Newcomb et al., 1993).

The second approach involves the use of "roster-and-rating" sociometric techniques. Notwithstanding the appropriate reference to "sociometric" in its name, this technique is more allied with conventional psychometric approaches to measurement than with Moreno's original approach.

Sociometric Nomination Methods and Classification Schemes

The sociometric nomination procedure begins by asking children for the names of their friends or children they particularly like. Either a limited (usually three) or unlimited number of nominations may be permitted. To facilitate more accurate data, rosters of the names of classmates, or for younger children, pictures of available classmates, are provided. In the assessment of friendship, reciprocities in patterns of these positive choices are sought. In the assessment of group acceptance, the number of choices a child receives is simply tallied (and often standardized within classrooms). Thus, a rank ordering of group members is produced, from the most to least popular. In the past, these standardized positive nominations were often the only data collected.

Currently, it is usual for researchers to collect negative nominations (i.e., to ask children for the names of the children they dislike the most) in a separate assessment. These negative nominations are handled in manner analogous to positive nominations; that is, the number of negative nominations children receive are tallied and standardized to form an index of peer rejection.

Negative nominations became increasingly standard as recognition grew that using only positive nominations may obscure two conceptually different types of low-accepted children: children who are actively disliked by their peers (i.e., rejected) and

children who are neither highly liked or disliked (i.e., neglected). In support, researchers reported that positive nomination scores and negative nomination scores did not correlate highly (e.g., Goldman, Corsini, & de Urioste, 1980; Gottman, 1977; Hartup et al., 1967).

Consideration of these issues led to the development of several multidimensional classification schemes based on the conjunction of positive and negative sociometric nomination data (e.g., Coie et al., 1982; Newcomb & Bukowski, 1983; Peery, 1979). The two most widely used classification schemes are those proposed by Coie et al. (1982) and Newcomb and Bukowski (1983). Although these schemes differ from one another in certain important operational respects (see Newcomb et al., 1993; Terry & Coie, 1991), their underlying approach and assumptions are the same. Both schemes consider the balance of positive to negative nominations in assigning children to categories. In addition, both schemes also consider the number of nominations of either type (positive and negative) that children receive. The latter, an index of social impact, is important as the child's visibility could be expected to qualify the meaning of the valence (positive-negative balance) of peer opinion. Each scheme also identifies four types of extreme status groups: *popular* children, who receive many nominations and who have a very favorable ratio of positive to negative nominations; *rejected* children, who also receive many nominations but have a very unfavorable ratio of positive to negative nominations; *neglected* children, who receive exceptionally low numbers of nominations of any type, especially positive ones; and *controversial* children, who, as the name implies, receive many positive and many negative nominations simultaneously. Some or all of the remaining children are classified as *Average* in status. The proportion of children classified into the extreme groups varies from about 3% for controversial children to about 7% to 15% for other groups (Terry & Coie, 1991). Average children can represent from 60% to 65% of children.

Experience with these classification schemes has led to the conclusion that the more extreme sociometric classifications are relatively stable over time. Thus, regardless of the particular sociometric classification system employed, popular children tend to remain popular, whereas rejected children remain rejected (Coie & Dodge, 1983; Newcomb & Bukowski, 1983). It has been demonstrated consistently that the "neglected" and "controversial" categories are the least stable (e.g., Terry & Coie, 1991). When a change occurs, it is usually from popular to average and vice versa or from neglected to average. Rarely do popular children become rejected, and even more rarely do rejected children become popular.

In addition, a great deal of research now supports the validity of the distinctions contained in these classification schemes insofar as behavioral differences between the categories are regularly and consistently observed (see Newcomb et al., 1993). Of particular interest here are the categories of peer rejection and peer neglect. Based on a recent meta-analysis of the available research literature, Newcomb et al. (1993) concluded that rejected children are more aggressive and withdrawn than children of average status, and less sociable and cognitively skilled. Neglected children can also be distinguished behaviorally from average status children, although the neglected group is the least behaviorally distinct of the available extreme groups. Neglected children are less aggressive and disruptive than average children, and show less social interaction and display fewer prosocial skills than average children. We address the question of the differential risk of these two groups in the following subsection.

Sociometric Rating Scales

An alternative sociometric procedure, the "roster-and-rating" rating scale technique (Roistacher, 1974; Singleton & Asher, 1977), requires children to rate each of his or her classmates on a Likert-type scale, according to how much they like or would like to play with the child. Scale points usually range from *Not at all* (1) at the low end to "*Very much*" or "*A lot*" (5) at the high end. By averaging the ratings that a specific child receives from his or her classmates, the researcher obtains a direct summary measure of the child's acceptance in the group. Researchers also often standardize these ratings within sex and classroom to correct for biases that may exist when children are asked to rate opposite sex classmates and to facilitate the aggregation of data across classrooms.

Although rating-scale and nomination sociometric scores have been found to be highly correlated (e.g., Asher & Hymel, 1981; Asher, Singleton, Tinsley, & Hymel, 1979; Bukowski & Hoza, 1989), misperceptions sometimes surround the relation between these two alternative approaches. For example, it has sometimes been asserted that rating scales are preferable to nomination techniques because rating scale scores are based on the perceptions *of all* peers *by all* peers within the group. Strictly speaking, nomination procedures have this feature as well. What differs between the two procedures is the nature of the judgment required. Whereas rating scale procedures require children to give a graded appraisal of their liking for each child, nomination procedures require only binary judgments (e.g., friend/not a friend; liked/not liked) by respondents concerning each classmate. Thus, rating scale scores have more attractive scaling properties than simple tallies of choices. As a consequence, rating scales result in a greater range, variability, and more normal distribution in scores than nominations (see Michelson & Wood, 1980). The rating scale has also been shown to have better test-retest reliability than nomination scores for young children (see Asher & Hymel, 1981; Gresham, 1981; Wanless & Prinz, 1982).

Alternatively, rating scales are sometimes criticized for not permitting distinctions between subclasses of unpopular children (i.e., rejected versus neglected). This criticism is apt, but in certain specific ways. Sociometric rating data do not consider variability from member to member in peer opinion. Thus, distinguishing controversial children (who would presumably receive many very high ratings and many very low ratings) from children who receive ratings in the middle ranges from most children is problematic. Similarly, to the extent that neglected children would be expected to receive unremarkable ratings from peers, they should be difficult to distinguish from other children with unremarkable ratings, which appears to be the case (Rubin, Hymel, Le Mare, & Rowden, 1989). Neglected status is defined primarily in terms of social impact, rather than the positive-negative valence of peer opinion. On the other hand, rating scales do not confound children who are disliked by peers with children who are not disliked, as children who receive many negative

nominations and few positive nominations (i.e., rejected children) are also the same children who are likely to be rated as highly disliked (versus liked) by many peers on rating scale measures (i.e., children with low rating scale scores; see Rubin, Chen, & Hymel, 1993; Rubin et al., 1989).

DIFFICULTIES WITH PEERS: CONTEMPORANEOUS CORRELATES AND CLINICAL SIGNIFICANCE

Children show substantial variation in the quantity and quality of their peer experiences. This variation can be reliably assessed along dimensions of friendship and group acceptance. A critical issue for researchers, clinicians, and parents is whether and how children's development and well-being is compromised by persistent difficulties with peers in these areas. Note that this issue is distinct from the broader question of how peer interaction contributes to development; the emphasis, in this case, is on the consequences of rejection by peers or other forms of negative peer experiences. However, the two issues are obviously closely related—the more we understand of the contributions of peer interaction and friendships to development, the more the implications of peer ostracism become apparent.

In this section and the next, we consider evidence bearing on the significance of poor peer relationships and children's adjustment. In keeping with the distinction we highlighted earlier, we limit our review just to the implications of peer rejection or friendship difficulties; we do not attempt to examine systematically the implications of allied social behaviors, such as social withdrawal or aggression, except where these bear on other findings.

As a rule, clinical child psychologists and psychiatrists are vastly more familiar with the literature on parent-child relationships than the literature on peer-peer relationships. In part, this is because the psychoanalytic framework has traditionally dominated the training of clinical professionals. As previously noted, psychoanalytic theories have generally focused their attention on the contributions of parents to children's healthy functioning, and otherwise not attended to peer relationships. Nonetheless, skilled clinicians are probably familiar with and at least intuitively attentive to disturbances of childhood peer relationships owing to the close connections between difficulties with peers and clinical disorders and subclinical disturbances that bring children to the attention of clinicians.

Rates of Clinical Referral for Disturbances in Peer Relationships

Estimates of the rates of psychiatric or other referrals specifically for disturbances in peer relationships are difficult to come by. The available evidence suggests that poor peer relationships are common reasons for children's referrals to child specialists. Achenbach and Edelbrock (1981) reported that 30% to 75% (depending on age) of children referred to child guidance clinics are reported by their mothers to experience peer difficulties. Peer difficulties are roughly twice as common among clinic children as among nonreferred children. Similarly, Hutton (1985) examined the records of 215 students referred to school psychologists by teachers in five different school districts. The most common reason for referral for both boys and girls was "poor peer relationships." Poor peer relationships were cited as the basis of referral in 26.5% of the children. Moreover, problems of peer adjustment were implied (but not explicit) in other reasons for referral. For example, "fighting" and "shy, withdrawn" made up an additional 13.8% and 14.4% of the reasons for referral, respectively.

In an interesting analysis of this issue, Janes, Hesselbrock, and Schechtman (1980), divided a sample of 298 boys and 98 girls seen at a child guidance clinic over a period of years into those with and without poor peer relationships according to assessments obtained from teachers. Because of the way the assessments were conducted, Janes et al. could examine the role that poor peer relationships played in prompting the original clinic referral. Although children having difficulty getting along with peers were sometimes referred to the clinic for this reason, they were more likely to be referred because of poor school achievement and behavioral problems at home and school. In other words, difficulties with peers were not likely to prompt a clinic referral unless they were accompanied by other behavior that was (presumably) more worrisome to teachers and parents. Indeed, only one in eight children identified by teachers as having difficulties with peers was seen at the clinic primarily for that reason. Janes et al.'s (1980) findings suggest that clinic referrals may grossly underestimate the prevalence of difficulties with peers unless those difficulties are combined with other difficulties that pose more problems for teachers and parents.

Comorbidity and Co-Occurrence with Childhood Psychiatric Disorders

Disturbances in peer relationships have traditionally played little formal role in differential diagnosis and psychiatric classification (Bierman, 1987). For example, there is no formal diagnostic category for disturbed peer relationships in childhood in either the multiaxial diagnostic taxonomy of the *Diagnostic and Statistical Manual of Mental Disorders,* Third edition-Revised (DSM-III-R), (American Psychiatric Association, 1987) or the taxonomy offered by the International Statistical Classification of Diseases (ICD-9; Commission on Professional and Hospital Activities, 1980), as there are, for example, for developmental disturbances of gender identity (Gender Identity Disorder, DSM-III-R), reading (Developmental Reading Disorder, DSM-III-R), speech production (Developmental Expressive Language Disorder, DSM-III-R), and attachment difficulties (Reactive Attachment Disorder of Infancy or Early Childhood, DSM-III-R).

Nonetheless, field evaluations of nosological taxonomies have suggested a high comorbidity of poor peer relationships with some specific childhood psychiatric disturbances. Gould, Shaffer, and Rutter (1984), for example, reported that the proportions of children with disturbed peer relationships among children classified under ICD-9 as Conduct Disordered, Emotional Disordered, Hyperkinetic, or Neurotic were 55.9, 50.8, 63.6, and 47.5, respectively. Thus, a substantial number of children evidencing

significant psychopathology appear also to have serious disturbances of peer relationships.

Moreover, the quality of children's peer adjustment enters into the diagnostic process at several points. Within the rubric of DSM-III-R, evidence of recent or chronic interpersonal difficulties with peers is implied by some subtypes of Disruptive Behavior Disorders and Anxiety Disorders of Childhood and Adolescence. Moreover, children's habitual level of interpersonal functioning with peers influences the clinician's global assessment of functioning (Axis V), appraisal of the child's exposure to psychosocial stress (Axis IV), and targeting of treatment objectives (V-codes).

Though still widely used, DSM-III-R has been replaced by a revised version, DSM-IV (1994). It is noteworthy that peer relationships play a somewhat more prominent role in DSM-IV compared with DSM-III-R. For example, Axis IV has been restructured so that the clinician records the presence of stress in separate specific classes of stressors rather than giving a global estimate of stress across all possible stressors. Thus, in DSM-IV, stressors for social relationships outside the family (e.g., loss of a friend or inadequate social support) are explicitly considered in the diagnostic taxonomy. Peer relationships continue to play a role in specific disorders in a similar manner to that of DSM-III-R. However, the Pervasive Developmental Disorders have been expanded to include three new classifications of disorders where a primary symptom is the child's inability to engage in appropriate social interaction (i.e., Rett's Disorder, Asperger's Disorder, and Childhood Disintegrative Disorder; American Psychiatric Association, 1994). Of particular interest is Asperger's Disorder for which chronic, severe impairment in social interaction, communication, and behavior (without the language, cognitive, and self-help skill delays seen in autism) are the essential diagnostic features.

Problems of peer adjustment also appear prominently in the makeup of most dimensions of maladjustment arising from the behavioral assessment approach. For example, the Child Behavior Checklist (CBCL; Achenbach & Edelbrock, 1986) is probably the most widely recognized example of the behavioral assessment/dimensional approach to child psychopathology. The CBCL identifies two broad dimensions of child functioning—internalizing problems (inhibition, shy-anxious behavior) and externalizing problems (acting out, aggressive behavior)—as well as several more specific (i.e., narrow) dimensions of functioning (e.g., anxiousness, schizoid behavior, sleep disturbances, aggressiveness). Peer relationship problems are reflected in several of the items (e.g., "poor peer relations," "bad friends") that make up both the broad-band and narrow-band subscales of this measure.

The Peer Relationships of Children with Psychiatric Disorders

Though peer problems play a role in the diagnosis of psychiatric disorders, the peer relationships of children with specific psychiatric disorders have received substantially less interest compared with normal and distressed, but subclinical, populations of children. Therefore, relatively little is known about the type and quality of peer interactions and the impact of those interactions on the emergence and maintenance of psychiatric disorders. Prospective studies of psychiatric disorders with low prevalence rates are difficult to achieve and costly, particularly because sociometric assessments are the most common and most defensible methodologies for assessing adjustment with peers, and these techniques require large numbers of informants (e.g., every peer within the same grade at school). The use of clinical samples is more feasible, but because the disorder has emerged, this research is limited in its ability to assess premorbid developmental trends. With this in mind, we will discuss several specific psychiatric disorders of childhood and adolescence in relation to their association with peer relationship problems.

Attention Deficit/Hyperactivity Disorder (ADHD)

The diagnosis for ADHD does not include problematic peer relationships as an essential symptom; however, the symptomatology included under the diagnosis has major implications for peer relationships (e.g., difficulty sustaining attention in tasks or play activities, difficulty waiting his or her turn, and talks and fidgets excessively). Children with ADHD display large social skills deficits; they are seen as intrusive, loud, annoying, and generally aversive by their peers (see Landau & Moore, 1991, for review). In addition, there is evidence that the social reasoning of ADHD children may be more negative. For example, Whalen, Henker, and Granger (1990) compared 25 ADHD and 14 normal boys aged 6 to 12 years and found that the ADHD boys saw their peers in a more negative way, identifying more undesirable behaviors in peers than did the non-ADHD boys. Overall, ADHD children have been found to be more likely to experience disturbed peer relationships and rejection by peers (Landau & Moore, 1991). In fact, Barkley (1981) found that 81% of a sample of hyperactive children had problematic peer interactions according to parents compared with 7% of control, nonhyperactive children.

A further complicating factor in this picture, is the high degree of comorbidity of ADHD with other psychiatric diagnoses, particularly the other Disruptive Behavior Disorders (i.e., Conduct Disorder and Oppositional and Defiant Disorder) (August, Ostrander, & Bloomquist, 1992; Barkley, Anastopoulos, Guevremont, & Fletcher, 1991) and Learning Disorders (LD) (Flicek, 1992). This comorbidity may additionally contribute to peer disturbances. For example, in a study of 249 second through sixth graders, Flicek (1992) found that children with both ADHD and LD (n = 18) were most likely to be rejected and displayed the most disturbed social behavior compared with all other children.

Children with ADHD are frequently treated with stimulant medication, particularly methylphenidate (Ritalin). Results indicate that treatment with Ritalin improves the social interactions, through decreasing aversive behavior, and enhances the social status of children with ADHD (Whalen, Henker, Buhrmester, & Hinshaw, 1989).

Conduct Disorder (CD)

As with ADHD, children with Conduct Disorder tend to have problematic peer relationships and to be highly disliked or rejected by their peers (Cole & Carpentieri, 1990). However, unlike ADHD, the primary peer difficulty in CD tends to be aggressiveness. Rather than being simply intrusive, irritating, and disruptive

to peers, CD children tend to bully and otherwise aggress toward peers, to intimidate and victimize peers, and to violate the rights of peers (e.g., steal, lie, or destroy property).

It is hypothesized that CD children experience early maladaptive patterns of reinforcement for aggressive behavior as well as exposure to hostile role-models, resulting in a hostile, self-defensive view of the world, so that, in the end, aggression becomes the response of choice to deal with interpersonal situations (Dodge, 1993). Aggression can be a very effective tool for achieving goals and for controlling the behavior of others, but it also increases the likelihood that others will reciprocate the aggression. This pattern develops into a self-perpetuating negative cycle between the child and the social context where both the child's aggressive behavior and his or her self-defensive view of the world are continually reinforced and maintained (Dodge, 1993).

There is some evidence that peer rejection may play a causal role in the development of CD (Cairns & Cairns, 1991; Patterson, Capaldi, & Bank, 1991; Vuchinich, Bank, & Patterson, 1992). When aggressive children are rejected from the broader peer group, they tend to associate with other aggressive and rejected peers like themselves (Cairns, Cairns, Neckerman, Gest, & Gariépy, 1988). Involvement in a deviant peer group exposes them further to deviant models and restricts their opportunities to interact with nondeviant peers. Involvement in deviant peer groups has been found to predict adolescent substance use and delinquency as well as early school dropout (Cairns, Cairns, & Neckerman, 1989). Thus, peer rejection may set in motion an escalating cycle toward Conduct Disorder.

In DSM-IV, there are two subtypes of CD: Childhood-Onset (i.e., before age 10) and Adolescent-Onset (i.e., between ages 10 and 18) (American Psychiatric Association, 1994). Children with Childhood-Onset CD experience more disturbed peer relationships and are more likely to have persistent CD throughout adolescence and develop Antisocial Personality Disorder in adulthood (Hinshaw, Lahey, & Hart, 1993). In contrast, children with Adolescent-Onset CD tend to display less aggressive behavior and to have more normative peer relationships (Hinshaw et al., 1993).

Pervasive Developmental Disorders (PDD) (Autism, Rett's, Childhood Disintegrative, and Asperger's)

Unlike the previous two disorders, the primary symptom related to peer relationships for the PDDs is extreme social withdrawal (Erwin, 1993). Autism and Asperger's are, in large part, defined by the child's inability to engage in age-appropriate social interactions (American Psychiatric Association, 1994). (Rett's and Child Disintegrative Disorder include a loss of social engagement and social skills from a previously normal developmental level and are associated with severe or profound mental retardation.) Children with autism and Asperger's prefer solitary activities and appear to have no interest in forming friendships. They may be completely unresponsive to and detached from social relationships, interacting with others in a nonemotional, instrumental way. In addition, their social sensitivity or awareness of the thoughts and feelings of others may be severely limited.

Autistic (but not Asperger's) children also have language (delay or absent), communication (e.g., difficulty initiating a conversation), and cognitive impairments (e.g., about 75% of autistic children also have mental retardation) (American Psychiatric Association, 1994). However, autistic children's social deficits are not simply a function of their cognitive limitations. For example, Volkmar, Carter, Sparrow, and Cicchetti (1993) examined the social skills of 71 autistic children using the Vineland Adaptive Behavior Scale. They found that the autistic children's social skills were extremely impaired with social functioning at a level well below (i.e., greater than 2 standard deviations below the mean) what would be expected for their cognitive capabilities (i.e., mental age). Thus, it appears that social interaction difficulties is a central, rather than secondary, feature of autism.

There is no research to date on the sociometric status of PDD children. However, given the preceding description, we would expect PDD children to have grave difficulties with peer acceptance and to experience peer rejection more than non-PDD children. Peer rejection may be particularly probable given the higher incidence of unpopularity for children with mental retardation and learning disorders (e.g., Brewer & Smith, 1989; LaGreca & Stone, 1990).

Depression

Although deficiencies in social relationships are not required for the diagnosis of depression, current conceptualizations of the etiology and maintenance of depression symptoms emphasize the role of social skills and dysfunctional interpersonal behavior (e.g., Coyne, 1976; Youngren & Lewinsohn, 1980). Furthermore, on the evidence that childhood friendships serve as sources of social support, one can predict that the absence of involvement in friendship, by undermining self-esteem and depriving children of important pleasurable experiences, can contribute to the development of depressive symptomology. Because friends also may be important in buffering children against stress, the presence of close satisfying relationships with friends could be expected to protect children from depressive affect in connection with stress.

The available literature generally supports a link between depression and difficulties with peers (Cole & Carpentieri, 1990; Jacobsen et al., 1983; Panak & Garber, 1992; Peterson et al., 1993; Puig-Antich et al., 1985; Vernberg, 1990). In an interesting study of this issue, Vernberg (1990), for example, found that among young adolescents, less closeness with a best friend, infrequent contact with friends, and more experiences of victimization by peers contributed to increases over time in depressive affect. Likewise, in a 5-year longitudinal study of young boys, Cillessen, van Lieshout, and Haselager (1992) found the experience of peer rejection led to higher levels of loneliness, which in turn increased the risk for developing depression.

On the other hand, there is also support for the view that depressive affect contributes to problems with peer relationships (Faust, Baum, & Forehand, 1985), possibly because peers make unflattering generalizations about other children's behavioral characteristics in the face of evidence of depressive affect (Peterson, Mullins, & Ridley-Johnson, 1985).

Less evidence is available concerning the protective role of friendships vis-à-vis depression. Based on their review of the literature, Peterson et al. (1993) concluded that good peer relationships in early adolescence do not appear to provide a protective influence; later in adolescence, close peer relationships do appear to be protective, particularly when parent relationships are impaired in some way (Peterson, Sarigiani, & Kennedy, 1991; Peterson et al., 1993).

Loneliness and Subjective Distress

As noted, Sullivan (1953) attached considerable significance to loneliness as a motivational force in development and adjustment. At the same time, Sullivan (pp. 260–261) was pessimistic about the promise of measuring loneliness with any precision:

> Now loneliness is possibly most distinguished, among the experiences of human beings, by the toneless quality of the things said about it . . . I, in common apparently with all denizens of the English-speaking world, feel inadequate to communicate a really clear impression of the experience of loneliness in its quintessential force.

Sullivan's pessimism notwithstanding, there is a growing body of research on loneliness in childhood (Asher, Hymel, & Renshaw, 1984; Heinlein & Spinner, 1985; Marcoen & Brumagne, 1985). This research suggests that children have a basic understanding of the concept of loneliness (Cassidy & Asher, 1992; Williams & Asher, 1992), that a substantial number of children feel lonely (Asher et al., 1984), that feelings of loneliness can be reliably measured (Asher et al., 1984; Marcoen & Brumagne, 1985), and that feelings of loneliness are rather stable even over a one-year period (Hymel et al., 1993; Renshaw & Brown, 1993).

Research supports an association between difficulties with peers and children's feelings of loneliness although instances of negative findings can also be found (e.g., Rubin, Hymel, et al., 1991). In most instances, researchers have studied this relation by comparing children with membership in different sociometric status groups. This evidence shows that rejected sociometric status is associated with greater feelings of loneliness and social dissatisfaction in early adolescence (Parkhurst & Asher, 1992), during middle childhood (e.g., Asher & Wheeler, 1985; Crick & Ladd, 1993), and during early childhood (Cassidy & Asher, 1992). Neglected sociometric status has not been found to be associated with risk for loneliness. Recently, Cillessen et al. (1992) reported that the links between the experience of peer rejection and levels of loneliness hold up longitudinally and may be implicated in the development of depression.

Focusing on friendship indexes rather than sociometric status group membership, Parker and Asher (1993b) reported that elementary school children without friends are more lonely than other children. Interestingly, this relation between loneliness and having a friend held for children at all levels of group acceptance, suggesting that popularity and involvement in friendships contribute additively rather than interactively to feelings of loneliness. Parker and Asher (1993b) also examined the relation between loneliness and six qualitative features of children's closest friendships—levels of companionship, conflict, conflict resolution, intimate disclosure, help and guidance, and personal validation. Loneliness was found to be strongly, albeit redundantly, associated with each of these six aspects of friendships. Once again, these effects were independent of the contributions of peer acceptance.

Before leaving the topic of children's loneliness, recent findings concerning children's requests for help with their peer relationships might be briefly noted. Direct requests for help with peer relationships can be seen as further evidence of the subjective distress experienced by children with problematic peer relationships. This issue has been studied by Asher and his colleagues (Asher, Zelis, Parker, & Bruene, 1991). They found that poorly accepted children were significantly more interested in receiving help than other children. For example, in one study, 46.7% of poorly accepted children replied "yes," 37.8% replied "maybe," and only 15.6% indicated "no" to the question of whether they would be interested in specialized help in developing their social skills and forming friendships. By contrast, 8.5% of highly accepted children said "yes," 48.9% said "maybe," and 42.6% said "no."

Academic Functioning

Problems in peer relationships have been repeatedly linked to problems in academic functioning (Coie, Lochman, Terry, & Hyman, 1992; Dishion, 1990; Green, Forehand, Beck, & Vosk, 1980; Ollendick, Weist, Borden, & Greene, 1992; Olson & Lifgren, 1988). This association has been found in both cross-sectional and short-term longitudinal studies, and across multiple measures of academic functioning, including standardized achievement test scores, academic grades, absenteeism, and grade retention. As an illustration, Ollendick et al. (1992) reported that children who were actively disliked by many of their peers were anywhere from 2 to 7 times more likely to fail a subsequent grade than better accepted children. Similarly, Coie et al. (1992) report findings from a 3-year longitudinal study indicating that higher levels of social rejection are predictive of later grade retention and poorer adjustment to the transition to middle school (Coie et al., 1992). Likewise, based on a 4-year longitudinal study, DeRosier, Kupersmidt, and Patterson (1993) reported that the experience of peer rejection in any one of the first 3 years of the study placed children at significantly greater risk for absenteeism in the 4th year, even after statistically controlling for initial levels of absenteeism.

An interesting issue in this connection concerns the positive, stress-buffering role of friendships at critical school transitions. Ladd (1990) obtained repeated measures of friendship, sociometric status, and school adjustment during the transition to kindergarten. Although children's personal attributes (mental age and prior school experience) predicted early school performance, measures of social adjustment with peers were much better by comparison. Children with many friends at school entrance developed more favorable school perceptions in the early months than children with fewer friends. Those who maintained these friendships also liked school better as the year went by. Making new friends in the classroom also predicted gains in school performance. By comparison, measures of school performance at the start of the transition to kindergarten did not generally forecast gains in social adjustment. Positive, harmonious close friendships also have been found to facilitate the school adjustment of Head Start preschoolers (Taylor & Machida, 1993) and adolescents' transitions to

middle school (Berndt & Keefe, 1993; Terry, Coie, Lochman, & Jacobs, 1992).

Over a longer time frame, the literature also generally supports a link between poor peer relationships and risk for dropping out of school (DeRosier et al., 1993; Kupersmidt & Coie, 1990; Ollendick et al., 1992; see Kupersmidt et al., 1990, and Parker & Asher, 1987, for reviews). Based on their review of this literature up to 1986, Parker and Asher (1987) reported that multiple studies have found that unaccepted children, particularly girls, drop out of school at a rate 2 to 8 times greater than that of accepted children; approximately one-quarter of low-accepted elementary school children drop out compared with about 8% of other children. More recently, Ollendick and colleagues (1992) found in a 5-year longitudinal study that 17.5% of rejected children had dropped out of school before the end of 9th grade compared with 3.1% of neglected children and 5.4% of popular or average children.

Although the literature is generally supportive of a link between poor peer relationships and later dropping out, at least one methodologically rigorous study (Cairns et al., 1989) suggests otherwise. In a longitudinal study with a representative sample of 475 twelve-year-olds, Cairns et al. (1989) found little reason to conclude that peer rejection by itself carries risk of later dropping out. Instead, the most powerful precursors of later dropping out were aggression and academic difficulties, especially when they were simultaneously present. Many dropouts appeared to have very satisfactory social lives. Cairns et al. caution against viewing dropping out as a purely individual phenomenon. Potential school dropouts in their study appeared to gravitate to peers who share their negative dispositions toward school.

POOR CHILDHOOD PEER RELATIONSHIPS AND LATER ADULT ADJUSTMENT

From the earliest days of research on children's peer relationships, there has been interest in the implications of problematic relationships with peers for children's long-term behavioral and psychological adjustment. Indeed, as Parker and Asher (1987) point out, the premise that children with relationship problems are at risk for later life difficulties is one of the most widely shared professional and popular beliefs about development and psychopathology and has played an important role in motivating research on children's adjustment with peers. But, whereas the existence of such long-term linkages has enjoyed almost universal acceptance, opinions diverge surrounding the causal basis of this presumed association.

Researchers generally address this issue in one of two ways. One way is to ask whether deviant (e.g., schizophrenic) adults and nondeviant adults differed as children in terms of their adjustment with peers. This type of design is known as a "case-control" or "follow-back" design. The second approach is to ask whether accepted and nonaccepted children differ in terms of their incidence of later behavioral abnormalities. This type of approach is known as a "cohort," "prospective," or "follow-up" approach. The two approaches tell us somewhat different things about the relation between acceptance and later adjustment.

Do Disturbed Adults Have a History of Poor Peer Relationships?

Interviews with psychiatric patients or relatives and friends of psychiatric patients very often suggest that a high proportion of such individuals had difficulties with peers as children (see Parker & Asher, 1987). For example, Kohn and Clausen (1955) interviewed 45 adult schizophrenics and a matched group of nondisordered control subjects and found that 18% of the disordered subjects reported that they, as children, had played alone nearly all the time, and an additional 27% reported that they had played primarily alone. By comparison, these rates among nondisordered adults were about 2%. Similarly, Bower, Shellhammer, and Dailey (1960) interviewed the former teachers of adult male schizophrenics and found that, relative to controls, the schizophrenics were recalled as having been less well liked, having been less interested in their environment, having shown fewer leadership skills, having been less interested in the opposite sex, and having participated less frequently in athletics.

Retrospective interviews may invite conscious or unconscious distortion by soliciting information from respondents who are often disturbed, defensive, denying, or guilt ridden (see Garmezy, 1974; Yarrow, Campbell, & Burton, 1970). Even if such distortions can be minimized—for example, by efforts to ensure that respondents do not know the true purpose of the inquiry—the unreliability inherent in asking someone to recall events that may have happened as much as a decade earlier is still present. To avoid this limitation, authors have often turned to available child guidance clinic records to gain an understanding of the disordered individual's peer adjustment history (e.g., Friedlander, 1945; Nameche, Waring, & Ricks, 1964; Ricks & Berry, 1970; Roff, 1963; Rolf, Knight, & Wertheim, 1976). The advantage of this approach is that the peer relations data were collected more or less systematically by teachers and social workers *while the patient was still a child,* thereby avoiding potential inaccuracies from memory limitations and selective recall. Illustrative of this approach is a series of pioneering studies by Roff published in the late 1950s and early 1960s (Roff, 1957, 1960, 1961, 1963).

Roff searched military service records to locate servicemen who, in middle childhood, had been referred to either of two guidance clinics in Minnesota and who later showed problematic military adjustment in the form of either a diagnosis by military psychiatrists as neurotic (Roff, 1957, 1960) or psychotic (Roff, 1961) or a dishonorable discharge for antisocial conduct (Roff, 1963). The child clinic records of these servicemen were then reviewed for evidence of earlier difficulties with peers (e.g., dislike by the general peer group, inability to keep friends, and being regarded as "odd," "peculiar," or "queer" by other children) and compared with those of former clinic patients who had exemplary later military service records.

Roff's analyses indicated a strong association between disorder and poor childhood peer relationships. For example, the initial studies of neurotic servicemen (Roff, 1957, 1960) indicated that about half of these servicemen had shown poor peer adjustment when seen at the clinic in childhood compared with only one in eight normal servicemen. Similarly, the study of psychotic servicemen (Roff, 1961) indicated that about two-thirds of the psychotics, but only one-fourth of the normals, had shown poor peer adjustment. Finally, the study of dishonorably discharged servicemen (Roff, 1963) indicated that twice as many of these servicemen had shown poor peer adjustment as control servicemen (54% and 24%, respectively). In short, depending on the psychiatric or behavioral disorder, disordered servicemen were anywhere from 2 to 4 times as likely as nondisordered servicemen to have had a history of poor peer relationships.

Roff's findings are consistent with those of other follow-back researchers working with child guidance clinic files (see Parker & Asher, 1987). For example, Frazee (1953) examined the child clinic files of 23 adult schizophrenics and 23 adults with no history of psychiatric hospitalization and found that 12 (52%) of the later schizophrenics had no friends and had been isolated from agemates in childhood, compared with only 5 (22%) of the controls. Indeed, none of the psychotics had shown normal associations with other children. Similarly, Ricks and colleagues (Fleming & Ricks, 1970; Nameche et al., 1964; Ricks & Berry, 1970) examined the clinic files of schizophrenic adults and noted that, compared with controls, preschizophrenics "showed longstanding histories of difficulty in establishing or maintaining peer relationships" (Fleming & Ricks, 1970, p. 249). Adults with impulsive character disorders were like schizophrenics, in that they had also evidenced very poor peer relationships according to their clinic files. Interestingly, alcoholic adults, by contrast, had a history of relatively good peer relationships and integration into the peer group. In fact, there was evidence that prealcoholics were excessively dependent on their peers, often at the expense of relationships with parents and siblings.

Collectively, then, case-control studies with child clinic samples add credence to the notion that disordered individuals have a history of peer disturbance. Case-control studies represent an improvement over retrospective interview studies, but they are not without limitations (see Garmezy, 1974; Neale & Oltmanns, 1980; Offer & Cross, 1969; Parker & Asher, 1987; Robins, 1972). Among the most serious is the question of whether the findings can be generalized to the majority of disordered adults. Most schizophrenics, for example, have no history of child clinic contact (Neale & Oltmanns, 1980). Children seen at guidance clinics are children with adjustment difficulties severe enough to warrant their referral for evaluation or treatment, and thus represent a select subset of children.

Fortunately, other case-control or follow-back studies have avoided some of the problems of generalization endemic to child guidance clinic studies and thereby provide the most pertinent data yet on the general issue of whether disturbed adults have histories of problematic peer acceptance. In these studies, researchers used samples that did not have a history of being seen in a childhood guidance clinic (see Kupersmidt et al., 1990; Parker & Asher, 1987). One of the best known of these studies is that by Cowen and colleagues (1973). As part of a statewide program for early detection and prevention of school maladaptation, a battery of school adjustment measures had been administered to a large cohort of third-grade children and their teachers. This battery included indexes of poor physical health (school nurse referrals, absenteeism), intellectual capacity (IQ scores), achievement (standardized test scores, grade-point average, over- or underachievement), and socioemotional adjustment (behavioral ratings, anxiety, self-esteem). In particular, the children had been asked to select from among their classmates those children who they thought would be most appropriate for certain roles in a hypothetical class play (Bower & Lambert, 1961). Children who received many nominations for undesirable roles in the hypothetical class play (e.g., "a bully") were presumed to be generally disliked by their classmates. The fortuitous establishment of a countywide psychiatric registry shortly thereafter made it possible to establish which of the third-grade children, 11 to 13 years later, had received public or private psychiatric care. Registry adults were matched with former classmates whose names did not later appear in the psychiatric registry, and the two groups were compared in terms of their class play nominations.

The results indicated that, compared with nonregistry adults, adults under psychiatric care had received significantly more class play nominations for undesirable roles, a greater proportion of undesirable to total role nominations, and more overall nominations (desirable and undesirable). In short, registry adults had been viewed quite negatively by their peers. Moreover, the authors were surprised to find that class play scores were the *only* childhood index to discriminate reliably between registry and nonregistry adults—proving more effective than indexes of past physical health, intelligence, academic achievement, and socioemotional well-being.

Another example of work of this type is the work of Watt and colleagues (Lewine, Watt, Prentky, & Fryer, 1978, 1980; Watt, 1972, 1978; Watt & Lubensky, 1976; Watt, Stolorow, Lubensky, & McClelland, 1970). These authors examined the ad lib comments of teachers in the cumulative records of pupils who later did and did not develop schizophrenia. Watt et al. found that schizophrenics were less socially competent as children than controls. Likewise, Warnken and Siess (1965) reported that preschizophrenics are reported by teachers to be less well liked by peers than controls, and Barthell and Holmes (1968) noted that preschizophrenics were less likely than controls to have participated in social extracurricular activities in their senior year.

Moreover, psychiatric patients are not the only group of later disordered individuals to show evidence of problematic peer acceptance in childhood. For example, Conger and Miller (1966) studied the comments of teachers in the cumulative records of later juvenile delinquents and nondelinquents. They presented evidence that, as early as age 8, future delinquents are distinguishable from future nondelinquents in the quality of their adjustment with peers. Similarly, Lambert (1972) examined the behavioral nominations given at age 10 to students who were either successful or unsuccessful academically their last year of high school. She reported that seniors with low (versus average or high) academic success (high grade-point averages and achievement test scores) or high academic failure (reports of discipline problems, remedial instruction, probationary academic standing, or dropping out) tended to be those children who, at age 10, had received a disproportionate number of

undesirable role nominations using the class play technique, suggesting that they were disliked by peers.

In summary, there seems to be consistent empirical support for the commonsense view that disturbed adults have a longstanding history of problematic peer relationships. This pattern is not limited to adults with serious psychiatric disorders, but also may be characteristic of juvenile delinquents, dropouts, and high school students who do poorly academically and socially. Moreover, this finding seems relatively unaffected by changes in methods of collecting childhood peer data since it occurs in studies that use retrospective interviews, studies that abstract guidance clinic records, and studies that use school records. Childhood peer adjustment variables under some circumstances may even distinguish disordered from nondisordered adults when many other intellectual and demographic variables do not (e.g., Cowen et al., 1973).

Are Children with Poor Peer Relationships Likely to Be Maladjusted Later?

Several authors (e.g., Garmezy, 1974; Kohlberg, LaCross, & Ricks, 1972; Kupersmidt et al., 1990; Parker & Asher, 1987) have pointed out that case-control or follow-back studies are useful for suggesting connections between adult symptoms and childhood behavior but cannot provide data interpretable in terms of predictive risk. That is, case-control approaches do not address whether children with a certain level or type of acceptance, when compared with others with higher or more adaptive types of acceptance, have an increased likelihood of experiencing later maladjustment. Such probabilistic prediction is possible only from cohort prospective studies that first identify samples of accepted and nonaccepted children and then follow these children over time to determine the proportion of children in each of these two groups that subsequently develop disorder. This reduces the possibility of overestimating the importance of a particular childhood characteristic (such as peer rejection) in the etiology of a subsequent disorder.

Follow-up studies are expensive, inflexible, and may require decades to complete. Moreover, to ensure that a sufficient number of individuals later develop some specific disorder, acceptance data ideally must be gathered on a large number of individuals in childhood. For these reasons, there are fewer prospective than case-control studies of acceptance and later adjustment (see Kupersmidt et al., 1990; Parker & Asher, 1987). One of the earliest follow-up studies that included measures of peer acceptance was that conducted by Janes and her colleagues (Janes & Hesselbrock, 1978; Janes, Hesselbrock, Myers, & Penniman, 1979). Janes et al. interviewed 187 adult men and women who had been referred to a child guidance clinic more than a decade earlier. At the time of their clinic referral, the subjects' elementary school teachers had completed a lengthy behavioral checklist that assessed classroom academic performance and attitudes, relationships with other children, shyness and withdrawal, neurotic behaviors, and leadership. The follow-up interview covered a wide range of adult adjustment outcomes, including educational and employment progress, contacts with police, and psychiatric hospitalization. In addition, clinical ratings of the quality of each subject's present social adjustment were obtained.

The results indicated that teachers' simple notation that the child "fails to get along with other children" related to six separate adulthood variables. Compared with boys whose teachers did not check this item, boys whose teachers indicated that they failed to get along with other children were twice as likely to report later not finishing high school, having been fired because of something they had done, having been in trouble with the law, or having been arrested. They were also somewhat more likely to enter the military or to report that they had been hospitalized for psychiatric disorder. (Girls were not examined in this analysis.) No other teacher item, including indications of aggressiveness or shyness predicted later problematic adult outcomes. In addition, boys and girls who failed to get along with other children, as adults had significantly lower clinician adjustment ratings than other children, even after intelligence and socioeconomic status had been statistically controlled.

Although the Janes et al. (1979) study supported a connection between childhood peer difficulties and later adult disorder, the fact that it was based on a clinic sample was a limitation. Several subsequent authors have corrected this problem, however.

Based on the results of Roff's earlier retrospective studies, Roff, Sells, and Golden (1972) conducted a large-scale study of the relation between childhood difficulties and later delinquency. Peer status information was collected for approximately 38,000 eight- to eleven-year-old children in schools in Minnesota and Texas. Children were given limited positive nomination and limited negative nomination sociometric assessments and standardized liked-most and liked-least sociometric scores were calculated on children in the sample. Liked-most and liked-least scores were then summed into social preference scores (i.e., liked-most nominations received minus liked-least nominations received) and used to classify children as high, middle, or low in peer acceptance. Three to four years later, delinquency information was obtained for a selected number of male children in the sample. Delinquency was defined as contact with juvenile authorities resulting in the preparation of a case file.

Results indicated that the chances for children with very low social preference scores to become delinquent prior to age 14 were 1.5 to 2 times greater than those of other children, depending on the sex of the child (differences were more dramatic for girls) and the geographic location of the school (differences were less dramatic in schools located in severely economically depressed areas). In fact, these data showed that in most schools the risk of delinquency increased more or less monotonically with decreasing peer status. In a subsequent reanalysis of a portion of the original sample ($n = 2,453$), J. D. Roff and Wirt (1984) reported an inverse relationship between the level of preference and the risk of delinquency at any age, regardless of the sex of the child or the location of the school.

At the time of J. D. Roff and Wirt's (1984) reanalysis, data were also available for the children's adult psychiatric status through statewide public psychiatric hospitalization records. A significant but low negative correlation between childhood sociometric status and later psychiatric hospitalization was obtained for both boys and girls.

Because the studies of M. Roff et al. (1972) and J. D. Roff and Wirt (1984) predated current concern for sociometric status classification, in these studies the risk attached to active rejection was not clearly separated from the risk attached to neglected peer status. Two subsequent studies have addressed this issue.

In the first of these, Kupersmidt and Coie (1990) followed a small sample of 19 sociometrically rejected 10-year-old children for 7 years, and compared their later school adjustment and involvement in delinquency activities to that of 63 average, 14 popular, and 11 neglected children. School difficulties were indexed by subsequent truancy, high absenteeism, grade retention, and dropping out. Delinquency was defined as police or juvenile court contacts. Perhaps because of the small sample size, Kupersmidt and Coie found little support for the specific hypothesis that rejected status places children at risk for subsequent adjustment difficulties. Rejected status alone was not a statistically significant predictor of the specific outcomes of delinquent activity, school dropout status, truancy, and school suspensions, although rejected children were more at risk for these outcomes than children in other sociometric status classifications. There was no evidence that neglected peer status was associated with any of these subsequent outcomes.

Utilizing a much larger sample ($n = 600$) and hence employing a more powerful design, Ollendick et al. (1992) followed sociometrically rejected, neglected, popular, controversial, and average status 9-year-old children for 5 years, documenting the incidence of subsequent academic, delinquent, behavioral, and psychological disturbance. Ollendick et al.'s findings strongly supported the risk status of rejected children. At 5-year follow-up, rejected children were perceived by their peers as less likable and more aggressive than popular children. Rejected children were also perceived by their teachers as having more conduct problems, aggression, motor excess, and attentional problems than their popular counterparts. Moreover, rejected children reported a more external locus of control and higher levels of conduct disturbance and substance abuse, performed less well academically, failed more grades, and were more likely to drop out of school and to commit delinquent offenses than the popular children. Rejected children were undoubtedly at risk when compared with popular children. Furthermore, rejected children differed from average children on most of these same measures, including failed grades, dropping out of school, and commission of delinquent offenses. Thus, it cannot be said that they differed only from a well-accepted group; rather, they also differed from the average child in the class.

Ollendick et al.'s findings suggested a similar pattern for controversial children. Controversial children differed from popular and average children on most of the academic, behavioral, and social measures. In fact, they were similar to rejected children on most measures. For example, a similar number of controversial children (27.3%) as rejected children (33.3%) failed at least one grade and the children in the two groups committed similar numbers of delinquent offenses. Neglected children, on the other hand, did not differ from average children on any measure and differed from popular children only on the locus of control and peer evaluation measures.

Overall, the pattern of findings from studies that use prospective designs are consistent with the conclusion that early difficulties with peers place children at risk for subsequent, sometimes serious, disorders. This finding emerges not only from studies employing clinic samples but also from follow-up studies of school samples. Certain questions, however, have not been completely resolved. One issue concerns the specificity of the outcomes associated with early difficulties with peers. Although Kupersmidt and Coie's (1990) results were not strongly supportive of links between rejection and specific later outcomes, somewhat stronger support was found when peer rejection was considered as a predictor *of some sort of* negative outcome later in life. Kupersmidt and Coie interpreted this finding as supportive of earlier arguments that, because problems in peer relationships reflect stress on children, they will be better at predicting the outbreak of later disorder rather than its specific form (Sroufe & Rutter, 1984).

A related unresolved issue relates to the heterogeneity among children with peer difficulties; specifically, it is possible that certain subgroups of rejected children may be more at risk for later disorder, or at risk for different later disorders, than other subgroups of rejected children. Children with poor peer relationships can vary widely in their behavioral and social-cognitive profiles, and consideration of the particular profile displayed by rejected children has been shown to enhance predictability of specific outcomes. For example, although aggressiveness is correlated with peer rejection, many rejected children are not aggressive and some aggressive children are not rejected. Coie and colleagues (Coie et al., 1992; Kupersmidt & Coie, 1990), as well as other investigators (e.g., Bierman, 1993; Bierman et al., 1993; Hymel et al., 1993), have found evidence of a conditional relationship between aggressive behavior, rejection, and adjustment, wherein a rejected child's risk is enhanced for some outcomes when that child is characteristically aggressive. Examining differences in rejected children's social cognitions may also be useful for enhancing predictability. For example, only about half of rejected children accurately perceive themselves to have problematic peer relationships while the other half overestimate their acceptance to a greater or lesser degree (Boivin & Begin, 1989; Hymel et al., 1993). Current work suggests that accuracy may mediate the impact of rejection such that accurate rejected children are at greatest risk for depression, loneliness, and negative self-esteem (Boivin & Begin, 1989; Panak & Garber, 1992). Overall, these findings underscore the need to broaden our conceptualization of risk beyond the mere presence or absence of difficulties with peers.

A third unresolved issue concerns whether risk for later maladjustment varies according to the chronicity of peer ostracism. Recent research suggests that there is great variability among rejected children in the likelihood that peer rejection will continue from one year to the next (e.g., Coie & Dodge, 1983). Researchers have not examined whether the level and pattern of risk of later negative outcomes is equivalent for children with chronic versus episodic and transient rejection by peers. An exception is research by DeRosier and colleague (DeRosier et al., 1993). DeRosier et al.

followed 640 seven- to nine-year-old children for 4 years. They found that children who were more chronically rejected over the first 3 years of the study were at greater risk for behavior problems in the 4th year, even after controlling for initial level of adjustment. It is reasonable to expect that prolonged peer rejection induces more significant negative changes than transient rejection in children's views of themselves and the world. More attention to the chronicity of children's poor peer adjustment should lead to more accurate identification of children at risk for developing later behavioral and psychological disorders.

Understanding the Link between Poor Peer Relationships and Later Adjustment Problems

Our review indicates considerable support for a link between early difficulty with peers and maladjustment later in life. How can this link be understood?

Simple Incidental and Causal Explanations

Several years ago, Parker and Asher (1987) offered a characterization and critique of two alternative interpretations of the link between poor peer relationships and later personal adjustment. Both positions represent attempts to understand the links over time between deviant behavior, problems relating to peers, and subsequent academic, behavioral, and psychiatric disturbances. The interpretations differ, however, in the extent to which they view problems in adjustment to peers as tangentially or centrally (i.e., causally) involved in the etiology of the later difficulties.

The first, or *incidental,* interpretation makes no assumption that problems with peers cause the interpersonal and intrapersonal difficulties they later predict. Instead, on this view, an association between these variables exists because behavioral precursors and subclinical symptoms of later disorders and deviancies perturb relationship with peers early on. As we have seen, there is considerable comorbidity between mental health disturbances and maladjustment with peers in childhood, and children respond negatively to the flat affect and social withdrawal that characterizes depressed children, for example (Faust, Baum, & Forehand 1985). Disturbances in peer relationships may make particularly good bellweathers to later disorder, but there is no assumption that poor peer relationships make any independent contribution to later maladjustment and no reason to suspect that children who are rejected by peers for reasons other than underlying disorder will have later maladjustment.

A schematic representation of the extreme incidental view of peer disturbances and later maladjusted outcomes, based on Parker and Asher's (1987) conceptualization, is shown in Figure 4.1. The model presupposes an underlying disposition to later psychopathology. This disposition may be a constitutional (e.g., a biological diathesis) or derive from early environmental influences (e.g., poor early parenting or maltreatment resulting in insecure attachment) or some process of coacting constitutional and environmental factors—its origins need not concern us here. The important feature is that this pathognomic process unfolds over time, resulting eventually in disordered outcome. The child's peer relationships are disrupted along the way (upward arrows) by the

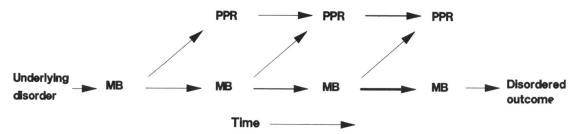

Figure 4.1 Simple "incidental" model of the link between peer relationships problems and later disorder. *Note:* PPR = Problems in peer relationships; MB = Maladaptive behavior toward peers. Adapted from "Peer Relations and Later Personal Development: Are Low-Accepted Children at Risk?" by J. G. Parker and S. R. Asher, 1987, *Psychological Bulletin, 102.* Copyright 1987 by American Psychological Association. Adapted by permission.

negative behavioral manifestations of the underlying pathognomic process. One might suppose that, because of reputational or other factors, these disruptions make it less likely for children to establish satisfactory peer relationships over time (horizontal arrows increasing in thickness). The important influence, however, is the underlying pathognomic process that disrupts behavior, and the peer disruptions themselves are epiphenomenal to the later maladjustment. As reviewed by Garmezy (1974), this type of model characterizes a number of early conceptualizations of the ontogeny of schizophrenia, and Parker and Asher (1987) note that it is more likely to be invoked to account for psychiatric outcomes than for outcomes such as school dropout or involvement in criminal activity. Note, too, that the model characterizes the role of *peer* disturbances in genesis of later maladjustment; the model is not necessarily incompatible with the view that parents contribute in an ongoing way to eventual disorder.

The alternative extreme position attributes later disturbance directly to the experience of earlier disruptions in peer relationships. Owing much to the developmental task framework, this *causal* position holds that many later disturbances can be traced to children's failure to establish effective and positive relationships with peers in childhood and adolescence. Because they are deprived of the important socialization experiences that positive peer interaction affords, and because they lack important sources of social support, children with peer difficulties experience more stress, have less mature and flexible social and cognitive skills, have less well-developed moral reasoning and less

commitment to conventional behavior, are less socialized generally, and have more idiosyncratic patterns of thought and behavior. These factors leave them less capable of meeting social responsibilities and expectations; less able to form subsequent, satisfactory interpersonal relationships; and more vulnerable to stress and breakdown. As we have reviewed, some of Sullivan's (1953) views of children's peer relationships and later disorder exemplify this type of causal argument. And, some elements of this argument are certainly consistent with the growing evidence (reviewed earlier) that peer interaction ordinarily plays multiple indispensable roles in the socialization of social, cognitive, and moral development.

A schematic representation of the extreme causal position appears in Figure 4.2. Again, some hypothetical representative time points appear along the X-axis, and the relations among problems with peers, behavioral problems, and later maladjusted outcome are shown. In this instance, maladjustment is shown as the result of the cumulative experience of peer ostracism and failure rather than as the unfolding of an underlying pathognomic process. The process of disruption begins with signs of maladaptive behavior with peers. The model is silent on the issue of the origins of this maladaptive behavior, although it is not incompatible with the argument that unspecified constitutional and early experiential factors contribute to original behavioral problems that, in turn, contribute to the development of problems with peers. Otherwise, like the incidental model, the causal model assumes that problematic behavior influences and maintains problems with

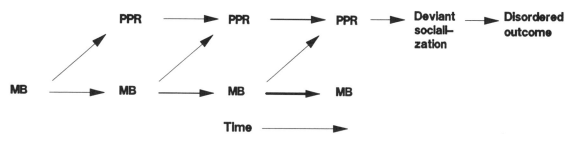

Figure 4.2 Simple "causal" model of the link between peer relationships problems and later disorder. *Note:* PPR = Problems in peer relationships; MB = Maladaptive behavior toward peers. Adapted from "Peer Relations and Later Personal Development: Are Low-Accepted Children at Risk?" by J. G. Parker and S. R. Asher, 1987, *Psychological Bulletin, 102.* Copyright 1987 by American Psychological Association. Adapted by permission.

peers at all ages (upward arrows) and has its own momentum (horizontal arrows).

Few studies have directly pitted causal and incidental explanations in the prediction of later maladjustment, and, indeed, because of the complexity of each explanation, it seems unlikely that any single study could do so effectively. An important prerequisite for accepting a causal model is evidence that poor peer relationships has a significant, negative impact on later maladjustment beyond the influence of child characteristics, such as behavioral style. In recent years, covariance multivariate models and cross-lagged stability models have been exploited to examine this issue. Findings from these studies indicate that peer rejection contributes uniquely to multiple forms of later adjustment problems, including internalizing and externalizing symptomatology and declines in academic performance (e.g., Bierman, 1993; Coie et al., 1992; DeRosier et al., 1993). Insofar as these findings suggest that peer problems are not simply a marker of a pathognomic process, a strictly incidental explanation for these linkages seems inadequate then.

Interactional and Transactional Interpretations

As Parker and Asher (1987) suggest, the incidental and causal views are caricatures and not likely to be steadfastly held by many actual authors. Even so, these models have exerted an influence on how researchers conduct and interpret longitudinal research on the long-term sequelae of early problems (see Parker & Asher, 1987). Importantly, neither view is likely to provide a satisfactory explanation for the link between problems with peers and later adjustment. As Parker and Asher (1987) observe:

> The extreme incidental model seemingly denies the very real possibility that the experience of peer rejection, especially prolonged peer rejection, leads a child to view the world and him- or herself negatively. . . . Ongoing rejection by peers must negatively affect many aspects of the child's social, academic, affective, and moral development. . . . Alternatively, an extreme causal view ignores the fact that factors that antedate poor interpersonal relationships continue to play a role in subsequent outcomes. It seems likely that factors that contribute to poor peer adjustment also continue to shape the course and nature of subsequent adjustment. (p. 379)

More generally, students of developmental models will recognize the preceding incidental and causal views as specific instances of "main effects" models emphasizing the contributions of the child or environment, respectively (Sameroff, 1987; Wachs, 1992). According to the incidental model, information concerning the child's constitutional nature is sufficient to predict later outcomes accurately. Likewise, the causal model implies that, whereas characteristics of the child, such as aggressive or withdrawn behavioral styles, may contribute initially to peer rejection, subsequent peer interactions and socialization process are responsible for later maladjustment. Missing from both models is any appreciable attention to (a) how characteristics of the child might condition the impact of ostracism by peers, and (b) how rejection by peers contributes to what is characteristic of the child.

In other areas of psychology, "interactional" models have proven useful for understanding the conditional impact of

environmental events on development (Sameroff, 1987; Wachs, 1992). The diathesis-stress model is an example of an interactional model that is frequently drawn on in the study of developmental psychopathology (see, for example, Garmezy, 1974). In this view, every child has a particular genotypic profile that defines his or her constitutional vulnerability to disorder. However, this genotypic vulnerabilty must be activated by an environmental stressor for the disorder to be manifested. The impact of a particular stressor is not invariant across individuals. Rather, whether a stressor produces maladjustment depends on the child's particular constitutional make up. A low level of stress may produce disorder for children whose genotypic vulnerability is high, but not for other children. Similarly, an extremely stressful event may produce disorder in almost all children, except those with a very low level of vulnerability. Thus, an interactional model, such as the diathesis-stress model, states that developmental outcomes can be predicted only when the interaction between child and environmental influences is taken into account.

As we noted earlier, in the study of peer relationships, very little longitudinal work has examined whether the combination of child characteristics, such as behavioral or social-cognitive style, and peer rejection places children at differential risk for later maladjustment. Several lines of research suggest, however, that there are considerable differences in the behavioral and social-cognitive profiles of low-accepted children and that considering both child features and social influences may greatly enhance the predictability of disorder, both in general and for specific types (e.g., Bierman, Smoot, & Aumiller, 1993; Dodge, 1993; Kupersmidt & Coie, 1990). For example, in a study of 95 six- to twelve-year-old boys, Bierman and colleagues (1993) found that peer-rejected children who also displayed excessive aggressive behavior were most likely to exhibit severe conduct problems, whereas children who were rejected but not aggressive were most likely to exhibit passivity.

Although an interactional interpretation addresses the need for a more conditional understanding of the impact of poor peer relationships on later adjustment, it falls short of being a comprehensive model of this process that allows for feedback among the causes of problems with peers, the consequences of poor peer relationships, and the course of later maladjustment. In other words, we are lacking a "transactional model" (Sameroff, 1987) of the link between difficulties with peers and later adjustment. Transactional models have been extremely helpful for conceptualizing and understanding a variety of phenomena in other areas, including schizophrenia (Barocas & Sameroff, 1982), day care (Sroufe, 1988), community violence and child maltreatment (Cicchetti & Lynch, 1993), and parent-child relationships (LaFreniere & Dumas, 1992; Lytton, 1990; Sameroff, 1975; Sameroff & Chandler, 1975). The basic tenets of transactional models have been cogently described by Sameroff (1987). Within transactional systems, development is viewed as a dynamic process wherein characteristics of the child and characteristics of the environment undergo continual change through processes of mutual influence over time. The influence of any element of the system is complex and is always bidirectional. The organism (child) in a transactional model is actively involved in attempts to organize and alter his or her environment. Changes in the environment as a result of a child's actions, on the other hand, subsequently function to produce changes in the child:

> The child is in a perpetual state of active reorganization and cannot properly be regarded as maintaining inborn characteristics as static qualities. In this view, the constants in development are not some set of traits, but rather the processes by which these traits are maintained in the transactions between organism and environment (Sameroff, 1975, p. 281)

From a transactional perspective, the development of psychopathology is neither a product of the child nor of the environment, but rather the result of child-environmental transactions that reinforce and sustain maladaptive patterns over time.

Figure 4.3 presents one possible way of representing the link between poor peer relationships in childhood and later disordered outcomes as a transactional developmental process. As in the earlier models, Figure 4.3 begins with the assumption that biogenetic and early experiential factors combine to contribute to a behavioral style that is maladaptive to forming friendships and interacting successfully in a peer group. The specific nature of this predisposing process is left unspecific for the moment, but is the focus of subsequent sections of this chapter. It is also explicit in Figure 4.3 that these early experiences influence not only the child's initial maladaptive behavior toward peers (MB_1 in the model), but also the child's self-perceptions and social outlook, social motivation, and social attributions ($NSOC_1$ in the model). These negative self-other cognitive processes, in turn, also contribute to initial behavior toward peers. Importantly, as with the other two models, children's behavior toward peers is suggested to contribute (upward arrows) to initial difficulties forming friendships and peer rejection (PPR_1 in the model).

At this point, the model departs notably from the other two models. Whereas the incidental and causal models attribute the development of disorder from this point to either processes in place in the child or stable processes set off by the environmental rejection, the transactional model in Figure 4.3 posits the operation of a dynamic pattern of continuous and reciprocal

influence of children's behavior toward peers, problems in peer relationships, and children's negative self- and other cognitions. Thus, peer rejection negatively influences children's perceptions of self and others. This, in turn, influences them to behave in further maladaptive ways toward peers, which, in turn, negatively influences peers' attitudes toward and behavior toward them, and so on, in a spiraling fashion. One iteration of this spiraling cycle of cognition-behavior-rejection-cognition is represented by the pathway $NSOC_1 \rightarrow MB_2 \rightarrow PPR_3 \rightarrow NSOC_4$ and this feature of the hypothesized model is discussed at greater length in the next section. The end point of this model indicates two (rather than one) sets of disordered outcomes. This duplication is deliberate, and intended to emphasize that most disorders have cognitive/affective as well as behavioral/symptom referents.

Several specific elements of the model require further mention. First, a path from each point of difficulty with peers to each successive point of difficulty with peers is articulated, and these paths are indicated with increasing thickness. This convention is adopted to recognize that, once in place, reputational and other factors contribute momentum to peer rejection, adding coherence to the process over time (see following section).

A similar convention is adopted from each point of behavior toward peers to each subsequent point of behavior toward peers (see Figure 4.3). This pattern is included as a means to represent the increasing canalization of behavior that results from the transactional operation of this cycle over time (Gottlieb, 1991; Sameroff, 1987). Likewise, the increasingly thick pathways from each point of self- and other-cognition to each subsequent point of self- and other-cognition are intended to recognize that these internal processes are somewhat self-perpetuating and have their own coherence over time, as we will discuss.

The elements in the model in Figure 4.3 have discrete subscripts at each hypothetical time point. This convention is adopted to highlight an important point about the transactional model: Even as they retain a certain lawful coherence over time, the elements of this model can be expected to change over time as a function of their participation in the recursive cycles of influence (Sameroff, 1987). For example, initially active and

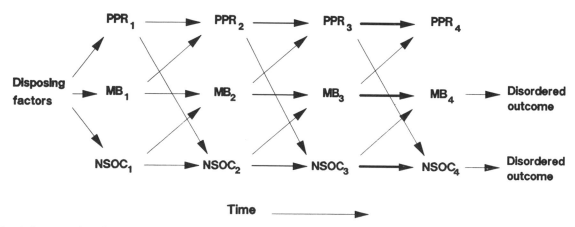

Figure 4.3 A "transactional" model of the link between peer relationships problems and later disorder. *Note:* PPR = Problems in peer relationships; MB = Maladaptive behavior toward peers; NSOC = Negative self- and other-cognitions.

aggressive children may, after experiencing peer rejection, appear sullen, withdrawn, and avoidant of peers later (Rubin et al., 1991; Rubin, LeMare & Lollis, 1990). As another example, children who behave unskillfully with peers may experience peer group rejection initially, but not initially have problems forming one or two same-sex friendships (Parker & Asher, 1993a). Friendship problems may follow later and, still later, problems relating to cross-sex others and romantic partners (Coie, 1990; Sullivan, 1953). Presumably, system-exogenous factors, such as how opportunities for cross-sex interaction are structured in the broader culture, partly dictate the specific nature of each element at a given timepoint. The broader point intended by the subscripts in Figure 4.3 is that the elements in the model should not be expected to stay constant—or even show homotypic similarity—over time (see Sroufe & Jacobvitz, 1989).

Transactional-like explanatory models have been increasingly invoked within the literature on children's peer relationships (Coie, 1990; Crick & Dodge, 1994; Rubin et al., 1990, 1991; Terry et al., 1992). An illustration is the discussion by Rubin et al. (1990, 1991; Rubin, Booth, Rose-Krasnor, & Mills, 1993). Noting that a broad distinction is often drawn between internalizing and externalizing disordered outcomes, Rubin and his colleagues describe the transactional pathways leading to these disparate eventual outcomes, and the complicity of peer rejection in these processes. Rubin et al. note that the distinction between externalizing and internalizing disordered outcomes parallels in certain respects the distinction between two types of at-risk infants, infants with difficult temperaments (difficult to soothe, fussy, overactive) and inhibited infants with low thresholds for stimulation and arousal. Rubin et al. argue that this correspondence is not coincidental, and describe two hypothetical transactive pathways that might respectively link difficult temperament to later externalizing disorders and early inhibition to later internalizing disorder. Both pathways start with the assumption that when children with problematic temperaments are born into early risky caretaking environments (e.g., poverty, poor parenting skills), the result is often a disruption in early parent-child attachment. In the instance of an infant with a difficult/fussy temperament, the result is often the creation of an avoidant-insecure attachment and a pattern of subsequent parenting that is authoritarian and hostile, and shows little concern for socializing social competence. As a result, as preschoolers, these children behave more aggressively than other children, and hold less positive and trusting attitudes toward their peers. Because peers reject these children, their attitudes toward peers become even more hostile, and their behavior toward peers becomes even more aggressive. Teachers label these children as "problematic," and the parents of these children respond by becoming even more controlling and autocratic. Powerful reputational biases in the peer group are also set in motion, which make it even less likely for these children to be accepted by peers. Over time, this reciprocal cycle of peer rejection-negative attitudes-aggression-hostile parenting-peer rejection leads to the full exclusion and isolation of these children from the peer group. By the end of elementary school, these initially aggressive children may even begin displaying higher-than-normal rates of social withdrawal as a reaction to the group exclusion. Rubin et al. suggests that the eventual prognosis for children who follow this pathway is the development of externalizing disorders (e.g., delinquency).

The pathway for children with initially inhibited temperaments is very different, however (Rubin & Lollis, 1988). When early caretaking circumstances exacerbate these children's difficulties, they will be prone to show difficulties characteristic of certain subtypes of avoidant and resistant categories of insecure attachment. They will be reluctant to explore their environment, will have less well-developed social and cognitive skills, and will show anxious, inhibited behavior with peers and high rates of nonsocial play as preschoolers. Rubin and his colleagues suggest that, for a variety of reasons, the parents of these children may react to their children's social difficulties by distancing themselves, exacerbating their children's sense of insecurity. Rubin and his colleagues suggest that, initially, peers do not necessarily reject these children, although they may come to be seen as "easy marks" for teasing. As they move into elementary school, however, the children themselves come to recognize their social failure and develop even more negative self-perceptions. Eventually, too, peers begin to regard these children's withdrawn behavior as atypical, and reject them. Rubin and his colleagues predict that, as rejection by peers increases, these children react by becoming depressed and lonely, and eventually by showing internalizing disorders and difficulties relating to others as young adults.

Transactional models such as the one offered by Rubin et al. (1990) present formidable research challenges. Children's peer relationships, behavior, social-cognition, and adjustment are not expected to remain constant over time, and patterns of change over time must be used to predict subsequent changes and organism states. Progress in this area has been helped by the development of statistical techniques (e.g., structural equation modeling, growth curve analyses, survival analyses) for examining bidirectional and reciprocal influences in multivariate longitudinal data sets, but the number of investigations incorporating these techniques is still very limited. A recent example is the work of Terry and colleagues (1992). Terry et al. (1992) investigated the adjustment of over 600 eleven-year-old, middle school students. Using information available from assessments of peer acceptance, antisocial behavior, and prosocial behavior at ages 8 and 10, Terry et al. (1992) found support for a transactional model, insofar as peer relationships and behavior were found to mutually influence one another over time. That is, it appeared that the peer group reinforced behavioral style, and at the same time, behavioral style reinforced the child's social status. In addition, the influence of low peer acceptance on children's adjustment to the transition to middle school occurred, in large part, indirectly by reinforcing antisocial behavioral patterns.

In summary, authors have offered simple main effects, interactional, and transactional explanations for why research has shown a link between early difficulties with peers and later maladjustment. Main effects explanations differ in the extent to which they view early difficulties with peers as involved in the etiology of the later disorders, with the incidental and causal being two extreme models. Such simple linear models seem insufficient explanations on the whole, however. Interactional models recognize that any attempt to specify how difficulties with peers affect later adjustment must consider aspects of the child, such as his or her preferred behavioral style and internal attributions and understandings. Interactional models, however, are still static characterizations. Dynamic, transactional models have begun to influence how authors conceptualize and analyze the link between early peer difficulties and later adjustment. These transactional models offer many advantages over other explanations because they recognize that the child and the peer group form a dynamic, interacting system that changes over time. Two especially significant elements of this system are (a) the mechanisms of reciprocal influence among the child's cognitions of the self and others, the child's behavior toward peers, and the peer group's collective appraisal of and behavior toward the child; and (b) the initial parameters of the system in terms of the interpersonal orientations, social competencies, and behavioral tendencies that children bring to peer interaction from their early caretaking environment. These two elements are the focus of the next two sections.

THE ORIGINS OF PEER DIFFICULTIES: PROCESSES OF RECIPROCAL BEHAVIOR AND SOCIAL COGNITION IN PEER GROUPS

In the preceding discussion of transactional models, we described a hypothetical spiraling cycle of influence, wherein children and their peers form impressions and perceptions of one another that guide their behavioral responses toward each other and determine the direction of their relationships. The components of this process included the child's cognitions about him- or herself, the child's characteristic behavior toward peers, the influence of the child's behavior on the peer group's collective appraisal and acceptance of the child, and the resulting influence of these attitudes on the peer group's collective behavior toward the child. Although this reciprocal process was presented abstractly earlier, in fact a great deal is already known about many of these variables and pathways of influence. Theory and research on the mechanisms that govern adult social interaction has a long history (e.g., Kelly, 1955) and continues to flourish (e.g., Fincham & Bradbury, 1987; Scott, Fuhrman, & Wyer, 1991), and recently several models of the mechanisms that govern the social interaction of children have also been presented (e.g., Dodge, 1986; Furman, 1984; Howes, 1988; Parker & Gottman, 1989; Price & Dodge, 1989; Rubin & Krasnor, 1986; Rubin & Rose-Krasnor, 1992). Also, as we have reviewed, the study of the behavioral correlates of difficulties with peers is one of the oldest traditions within the literature on children's peer relationships. Interestingly, it was the empirical evidence indicating that children who experience peer difficulties are at risk for both concurrent and later maladjustment that served as the major impetus for what is now a substantial body of research focusing on the social-cognitive and behavioral processes underlying peer difficulties.

Our purpose in this section is to flesh out this emerging general model of how children's cognitions and behavior affect the establishment of negative reputations among peers and peer group rejection by reviewing the existing research bearing on its key components and pathways. In several respects, the research in this area has followed a developmental psychopathological perspective. First, there is an implicit understanding that the study of social maladjustment is linked with the study of normal social development. One of the major tenets of developmental psychopathology is that our understanding of risk and pathology can be enhanced by knowledge about normal development. Likewise, our understanding of normal development is expanded by knowledge about deviations in development (Cicchetti, 1993). Much of the research on the social-cognitive and behavioral correlates of peer difficulties has involved identifying children who are experiencing social difficulties (e.g., children who are rejected, withdrawn, or friendless), assessing their social cognition or behavioral orientations, and then comparing their orientations to those of children who are functioning successfully within their peer groups. As a consequence, a great deal has been learned about the social-cognitive and behavioral processes underlying both successful and unsuccessful peer relationships. For example, in an attempt to better understand the behavioral antecedents of social rejection, researchers have discovered that inadequate group entry skills can lead to social rejection. In the process, the sequence of group entry behaviors that lead to social acceptance has also been identified (Putallaz & Wasserman, 1990).

Second, there is the recognition by researchers in this area that there are likely to be different pathways by which children come to experience peer difficulties. The view that the same developmental outcome may be achieved through different avenues is advocated by developmental psychopathologists. For example, whereas some children can become rejected because they behave aggressively and disruptively, others may become rejected because they withdraw from peers and engage in developmentally inappropriate play (Rubin et al., 1990).

Finally, there is the realization, as there is in developmental psychopathology, that there are multiple mechanisms and processes involved in determining a particular maladaptive outcome. Consequently, a variety of cognitive and behavioral mechanisms and processes have been examined, including the social cognitive and behavioral characteristics of children who are experiencing social difficulties, as well as the social cognitive and behavioral responses of the peers with whom the child interacts.

Although the general outline of the process we wish to describe was embedded in Figure 4.3, this process is shown in a different and clearer form in Figure 4.4. The cycle shown in Figure 4.4 is one in which the processing of social cues and the social behavior of both the target child and the members of the peer group contribute to difficulties in peer relationships or peer rejection. Figure 4.4 is a representation of the conclusions of recent research and theorizing in this area, including models offered by Coie (1990), Crick and Dodge (1994), Dodge (1986), Furman (1984), Howes (1988), Price and Dodge (1989), and Rubin (e.g., Rubin & Krasnor, 1986; Rubin & Rose-Krasnor, 1992), among others. The model in Figure 4.4 is guided by several assumptions. First, it is assumed that each individual brings into the interactive context broad representations of him- or herself and his or her relationships. These representations guide children's expectations for interaction and direct them to pursue some social goals but not others. They also influence how children interpret the behavioral cues of their interactive partners and how children evaluate alternative response options.

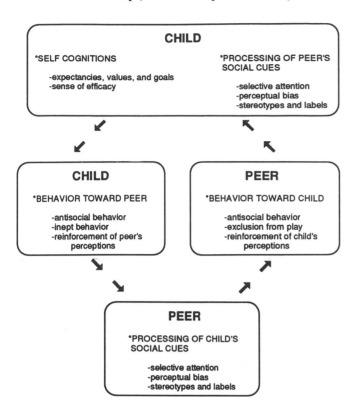

Figure 4.4 Processes of reciprocal influence in peer transactions involving children with poor adjustment with peers. Adapted from "Peers' Contribution to Social Maladjustment: Description and Intervention" by J. M. Price and K. A. Dodge, 1989. In *Peer Relations in Child Development*, T. J. Berndt and G. W. Ladd (Eds.). Copyright 1989 by John Wiley & Sons. Adapted by permission.

Second, the model assumes that from the earliest periods of interaction, participants form specific expectations and representations of their particular partner. These representations may include the behavioral characteristics of the other, as well as emotional reactions that were experienced at the time the representation was formed. These person representations are integrated into previously existing knowledge structures, and in concert with these structures, guide each participant's behavioral responses. The valence of these person representations is extremely important. If primarily positive, then future interaction with the partner is welcomed and pursued. If, however, the valence of the behavioral and affective features of the representation of the other are primarily negative, then further interaction with that particular individual might be avoided. This process of forming person perceptions is considered to be dynamic rather than static. As such, as long as two individuals are continuing to have contact with one another, there is the potential for the modification of existing representations and perceptions.

Finally, and consequently, the model assumes that the social outcomes of interactions (e.g., the degree to which the individuals like one another or whether they become friends) follow from the person perceptions that are formed during the course of interaction.

We turn next to some of the specific components of the model in Figure 4.4.

The Child's Self and Social Cognitions

The first component of interaction consists of the child's self and social cognitions. When a child interacts with a peer, he or she applies a set of knowledge structures about the self, about relationships in general, and if there has been prior experience with a particular peer, specific knowledge and memories about that peer. He or she also applies a set of specific social goals and expectations for the interaction. These goals and expectations also reflect the child's beliefs about his or her personal efficacy in relationships in general and in the specific relationship at hand. It is hypothesized that during social interaction, these knowledge structures and expectancies influence how the individual processes the social information available (Dodge, 1993; Rieder & Cicchetti, 1989; Rubin & Rose-Krasnor, 1992). In turn, the manner in which this information is processed serves to guide the child's behavior during interaction with the peer. Thus, positive views and expectations of self and relationships, along with effective processing of information, should be conducive to the formation of positive and supportive relationships with peers. Conversely, negative views and expectations of self and others, along with processing biases and deficits, should lead to social difficulties with peers.

Self-Cognitions

Children's self-regard and self-appraisals of their social competencies should have some bearing on the ways they initiate and maintain social exchanges with peers. Positive self-appraisals are likely to prove advantageous for the initiation of social interaction; negative self-evaluations may prove disadvantageous in promoting social exchange. The dialectic between self-regard and social interaction tendencies is an area that requires serious inquiry. At present, what is known is that popular children tend to view themselves as more socially competent than their less popular agemates, with the association between acceptance and self-appraisal increasing with age (Harter, 1982; Kurdek & Krile, 1982; Ladd & Price, 1986). Peer rejection, on the other hand, is associated with negative thoughts and feelings about the self. Unpopular or rejected children are more likely than their popular counterparts to express a less positive self-concept in the social area (Hymel, 1983); they are also more likely to perceive social situations as difficult (Wheeler & Ladd, 1982). Furthermore, unpopular children are more likely to report greater anxiety in social situations (Hymel & Franke, 1985; La Greca et al., 1988).

Although these findings suggest the general conclusion that children already experiencing difficulties with peers approach social situations feeling poorly about their social relationships and social skills, an important issue not yet resolved is whether *all* children with poor peer relationships approach social situations in this negatively disposed way. Recent evidence suggests that this is not the case. Studies of sociometrically rejected children indicate that one subset of these children, those who behave aggressively, do not report thinking poorly about their social relationships with peers (Patterson, Kupersmidt, & Griesler, 1990). Rejected children who are anxious and socially reticent do, however (Boivin &

Begin, 1989; Hymel et al., 1993). These findings are in keeping with the results of recent studies concerning extremely withdrawn and extremely aggressive children; it is only the former group that reports having difficulty with their social skills and peer relationships (Hymel et al., 1993; Rubin, 1985; Rubin, Chen, & Hymel, 1993).

Social Cognitions

In addition to perspectives on the self, cognitions about others and relationships are expected to be associated with, and predictive of, social difficulties with peers. Although little is known about the role of latent knowledge structures in children's social adjustment, considerable information exists on the relation between social information processing patterns of children and social outcomes (e.g., Dodge, Pettit, McClaskey, & Brown, 1986; Dodge & Price, in press; Rubin & Daniels-Beirness, 1983; Slaby & Guerra, 1988). Several theoretical models of the link between social information processing and behavior have been formulated. For example, in the social information processing model described by Rubin and Krasnor (1986), when children face an interpersonal dilemma (e.g., making new friends or acquiring an object from someone else), their thinking follows a particular sequence. First, children may select a *social goal*. This entails the establishment of a representation of the desired *end state* of the problem-solving process. Second, they *examine the task environment;* this involves reading and interpreting all the relevant social cues. For example, boys and girls are likely to produce different solutions when faced with a social dilemma involving same-sex as opposed to opposite-sex peers (Rubin & Krasnor, 1983). As well, the social status, familiarity, and age of the participants in the task environment are likely to influence the child's goal and strategy selection (Krasnor & Rubin, 1983). Third, they *access and select strategies;* this process involves generating possible plans of action for achieving the perceived social goal, and choosing the most appropriate one for the specific situation. Fourth, they *implement the chosen strategy*. Finally, it is proposed that children *evaluate the outcome of the strategy;* this involves assessing the situation to determine the relative success of the chosen course of action in achieving the social goal. If the initial strategy is unsuccessful, the child may repeat it or he or she may select and enact a new strategy, or abandon the situation entirely.

In an attempt to understand the production of aggression in children, Dodge (1986) has proposed a similar model of social information processing. This model also consists of five stages, namely, (a) the encoding of social cues; (b) the interpretation of encoded cues; (c) the accessing and generation of potential responses; (d) the evaluation and selection of responses; and (e) the enactment of the chosen response.

Children who have difficulties in their peer relationships demonstrate characteristic deficits or qualitative differences in thinking at various steps of these models. Several types of deficits or differences have been identified:

1. Children with problems in peer relationships have difficulty discriminating a peer's social intentions. Dodge, Murphy, and Buchsbaum (1984), for example, found that popular children are better than other children at discriminating a peer's intentions, whereas rejected children are significantly worse. The importance of attending to relevant social cues is that these cues are then used to interpret another's intentions.

2. Rejected children, particularly rejected children who are aggressive, are more likely than their more popular counterparts to assume malevolent intent when they are faced with negative circumstances, especially when the social cues are ambiguous (Dodge, 1980, 1986; Rubin, Bream, & Rose-Krasnor, 1991).

3. Socially accepted (popular) children tend to attribute social successes to internal causes and expect success to continue in the future (Sobol & Earn, 1985). They also view social outcomes as more controllable than do socially unaccepted children. Alternately, children experiencing social difficulties tend to perceive their social successes as unstable and externally caused and to perceive their social failures as stable and internally caused (Goetz & Dweck, 1980; Hymel & Franke, 1985; Rubin & Krasnor, 1986; Sobol & Earn, 1985).

Interestingly, this attributional pattern is similar to that found in lonely adults (Anderson, Horowitz & French, 1983; Peplau, Russell, & Heim, 1979). Peplau et al. (1979) have taken these latter findings as supportive of a cognitive model of loneliness in adults, which suggests that the individual's own cognitions and self-evaluations serve as mediating factors in the relation between loneliness and social behavior. According to this model, the negative attributional pattern exhibited by lonely adults affects subsequent expectations, motivation for social interaction and, ultimately, actual social behavior. Individuals who view their social problems as internally or personally caused are less likely to attempt to change their social situations and may even feel that they cannot change them. With children, results of research by Goetz and Dweck (1980) suggest a similar mediating link between attributional interpretations and subsequent social behavior. They demonstrated that children who attributed their failure to be accepted into a pen-pal club to personal causes were debilitated in later attempts to gain entry into the club.

4. Accepted and unaccepted children differ in their social problem-solving skills. Children who are well liked tend to generate competent and effective solutions to interpersonal dilemmas, whereas disliked children tend to generate incompetent or aggressive solutions (e.g., Asarnow & Callan, 1985; Ladd & Oden, 1979; Rubin & Daniels-Beirness, 1983), especially if they view the other's intentions as hostile (Dodge, 1980).

5. Socially accepted children differ from disliked children in the manner they evaluate the probable outcomes for their behavior. In general, well-liked children are more accurate in their evaluations of the outcomes of their behavior. Disliked children, however, expect that positive outcomes will accrue if they act aggressively and that less positive outcomes will result from nonaggressive solutions (Perry et al., 1986).

Complementing this research on the link between social cognition and peer difficulties is research on the relation between social information processing and behavior. Results from research with both extreme and normal samples indicate that the manner in which children process information is related to their actual behavior, particularly when aggregated assessments of processing are conducted (e.g., Dodge et al., 1986; Dodge & Price, in press). Thus, there is empirical evidence that children's social cognitions serve to guide their behavioral orientations and responses with peers.

Finally, there are even experimental data supporting the link between children's social cognitions and their social behavior and adjustment. In a novel experiment by Rabiner and Coie (1989), rejected subjects were given the assignment of entering a room to initiate play with a group of peers with whom they were unacquainted. Half the boys were told that the peers liked them and wanted them to play with them. The other half were not given any kind of expectation. Consistent with evidence presented in this section, relative to the boys not given an expectation, rejected boys who expected to be liked came to be liked more by the peers. Presumably, a child's expectations of being liked led him to behave in ways that led the peers to like him.

Children's Behavior toward Peers

The second component of the reciprocal influence model is the behavior the individual displays toward other children. Children's behavior toward other children is presumed to be driven by their self-cognitions and social cognitions. In turn, children's behavior is expected to influence the perceptions that other children develop of the child (see Figure 4.4).

A considerable body of research suggests that, although children are sometimes rejected by peers for nonbehavioral reasons such as physical stigmata, behavior plays a substantial, if not overriding, role. Many studies have documented behavioral differences between socially successful children and children experiencing difficulties in their relationships with peers (see Coie, Dodge, & Kupersmidt, 1990; Newcomb et al., 1993; Rubin & Coplan, 1992). Much of this work is based on cross-sectional research designs utilizing existing peer groups. Such studies are open to the alternative interpretation that the behavioral differences are the result of rather than responsible for the children's difficulties with peers. Children's behavior is undoubtedly affected by being rejected by peers; however, enough research now exists to safely conclude that how children behave shapes their reception by the peer group in the first place. Longitudinal studies and studies utilizing artificial play groups, for example, show that behavioral assessments made before or during the earliest stages of acquaintanceship *predict* children's subsequent social acceptance (e.g., Coie & Kupersmidt, 1983; Dodge, 1983; Hymel, Rubin, Rowden, & LeMare, 1990; Putallaz, 1983; Rubin, 1993; Rubin, Hymel, & Mills, 1989). More importantly, intervention studies designed to reduce children's negative behaviors or increase their repertoire of social skills have shown increases in acceptance by peers as a result of behavioral changes (see Asher, et al., in press, for a review).

Which behaviors matter? Most research has focused on the behavioral basis of peer acceptance or rejection. Research on the behavioral correlates of sociometric standing is a several-decades-old tradition, and many lawful associations between specific behaviors and rejection by the peer group have been documented (see Coie et al., 1990; Newcomb et al., 1993; Rubin & Coplan, 1992). One broad class of behavior that has proven to be especially significant is aggression. Aggressive behavior has been found to correlate with rejection by peers

regardless of whether peer evaluations (Cantrell & Prinz, 1985; Carlson, Lahey, & Neeper, 1984; Coie et al., 1982; Rubin et al., 1993), teacher ratings (Coie & Kupersmidt, 1983; Dodge, 1983; Dodge, Coie, & Brakke, 1982; Rubin & Clark, 1983), or direct observations (Coie & Kupersmidt, 1983; Dodge, 1983) are used to assess children's social behavior. In addition, extremely withdrawn children have been found to be more actively disliked by peers than are their more sociable agemates (French, 1988, 1990; Rubin et al., 1993; Rubin et al., 1989), especially during the mid-to-late years of childhood.

On the other hand, observational studies also suggest that children who engage in high rates of positive social behavior (e.g., conversation, smiling, prosocial sharing and helping), who make efforts to initiate contact with others, who join ongoing play in a fluid and natural way, who cooperate, and who respect peer norms, are likely to receive more positive behavioral responses from peers and to have higher peer sociometric rating and nomination scores than other children (see Coie et al., 1990; Newcomb et al., 1993). Similarly, children who are described by their peers as helpful, supportive, cooperative, friendly, nice, calm, understanding, good at games, and good leaders are more likely to receive high sociometric ratings and many positive and few negative sociometric nominations (see Coie et al., 1990; Newcomb et al., 1993; Rubin & Coplan, 1992). Thus, the presence of positive social skills as well as the absence of aggressive or extremely withdrawn behavior seems critical to acceptance by peers (Bierman, 1986).

Although the correlates of acceptance and rejection appear to be similar across age groups, Coie et al. (1990) point out that a few developmental differences that have been identified. For example, as children enter elementary school, both athletic and academic competence become increasingly important determinants of social adjustment in the peer group. Children who display competence in either one or both of these domains are better liked by their peers who are less competent. In addition, with age, verbal aggression, disruptiveness in the classroom, and social withdrawal become increasingly important contributors to social rejection. And, although much less is known about this issue, it appears that the behavioral correlates of peer acceptance and rejection also differ somewhat for children of different genders and from different socioeconomic circumstances (see Bierman, 1986; Coie et al., 1990).

Specific behaviors have also been shown to be related to the development and maintenance of friendships, although much less is known about this process (Hartup, 1989a, 1992a). It has been demonstrated that among children who are "hitting it off," communication becomes increasingly connected, conflicts that arise are successfully resolved, and play activities are coordinated (Gottman, 1983). As the relationship progresses, communication clarity and self-disclosure become increasingly important. Once friendships are established, cooperation and reciprocity become key elements of successful relationships (see Hartup, 1989a, 1992a). Thus, the child's ability to engage in joint communication and cooperative activities with a peer as well as successfully resolve conflicts with that peer, appear to be important behavioral skills for friendships.

On the negative side, children's behavioral orientations also have been found to contribute to the development of less desirable relationships, such as antagonistic/conflictual relationships and bully/victim relationships (Dodge, Price, Coie, & Christopoulos, 1990; Olweus, 1993). For example, Dodge et al. (1990) identified high-conflict, low-conflict, asymmetric (bully/victim relationships), and low-interaction dyads that developed in small play groups. Their results indicated that the rate of aggressing toward a peer was positively correlated with the rate of being the object of the peer's aggression. Furthermore, these aggressive exchanges contributed to the development of stable high-conflict relationships. Once developed, participants of high-conflict dyads were more aggressive toward one another and engaged in less prosocial behavior than other dyads. Not surprisingly, participants of these relationships came to dislike each other.

A vast array of positive and negative behaviors have been linked to the development of successful and unsuccessful relationships with peers, and any attempt to catalog the hundreds of specific behaviors that have been studied in relation to various social outcomes quickly becomes unwieldy. In an effort to impose some conceptual organization on the existing litany of behavioral correlates and to identify areas of relative neglect, Asher and Williams (1987) suggested a useful framework for considering the kinds of behaviors that should relate to adjustment with peers.

According to Asher and Williams (1987), when considering the kinds of behavior that are likely to contribute to adjustment with peers, it is helpful to consider how children decide whether they like or dislike another child. These authors suggest that children ask themselves six metaphoric questions stemming from what Asher and Williams (1987) presume to be children's minimal requirements for fulfilling interpersonal interaction. Asher and Williams (1987) suggest that the more children find that these requirements are met, the more they are attracted to another individual. The core issues for children are (a) whether they find the partner entertaining, (b) whether they feel that they can trust the partner, (c) whether they find that the partner influences them in ways that they find acceptable, (d) whether they find that the partner facilitates rather than undermines their personal goals, (e) whether the partner makes them feel good about themselves, and (f) whether the partner shares their fundamental values and priorities.

Asher and Williams (1987) suggest that by considering these core issues for children, one can better understand which behaviors should and should not be expected to be related to success with peers, and why some behaviors are more robust correlates of social success than others. Behaviors that simultaneously address several core issues for children are expected to be stronger correlates of social success than behaviors that address only one concern. This argument, for example, would explain why aggression is such a strong correlate of adjustment with peers: Children who are aggressive are not fun to be around (issue (a)), humiliate others (issue (e)), are unpredictable (issue (b)), disrupt activities (issue (d)), and generate resentment (issue (c)). A further important element of Asher and Williams' (1987) framework is that it assumes the configuration of children's behavioral assets and liabilities is most important, not the presence or absence of any single specific behavioral tendency. Thus, aggressive children who nonetheless possess skills for behaving in ways that leave others feeling good about themselves or to find them entertaining, trustworthy, persuasive, and so on, are not expected to run the same risk of peer rejection as aggressive children without these additional social skills (see Bierman, 1986). The significance of particular negative behaviors such as aggressiveness or social withdrawal, therefore, depends partly on whether the child also possesses offsetting social skills. In the following section, peers' perception of the child will be explored in greater detail.

Peers' Social Cognitions

One of the basic propositions of the social interaction model is that from their initial encounter, social partners are forming representations and perceptions of one another. These cognitive processes are depicted in the third component of Figure 4.4. As is supported by the research reviewed in the previous section, children's representations and perceptions of one another are, at least in part, based on the behaviors they direct to one another. There is also evidence that children's memories and perceptions of one another are influenced by their own behavioral reputation, level of peer status, age, and liking for the peer target; situational factors (e.g., the levels of aggression within the peer group); and the peer target's gender, age, and sociometric status (Hymel, 1986; Rogosch & Newcomb, 1989; Younger & Boyko, 1987; Younger & Piccinin, 1989; Younger, Schwartzman, & Ledingham, 1986).

Once children's perceptions of one another are formed, they appear to remain moderately stable over time (Coie et al., 1990). Thus, the impressions that are formed of a child within a particular peer group are likely to be maintained over time. One explanation for the stability of person perceptions is that the structure of social cognitive processes appears to be favorable to the maintenance of the perceptions and impressions.

To begin with there is evidence that individuals selectively attend to certain types of behavior displayed by their interactive partner, depending on their attitudes and perceptions of that particular partner. Research with adults suggests that knowledge structures (person representations) guide attentional processes (Scott, Fuhrman, & Wyer 1991). Relevant information (i.e., information that is either consistent or inconsistent with the knowledge structure) is attended to rather than irrelevant or neutral information. Thus, when interacting with a child, the types of behavioral displays that are likely to be attended to will be based, at least in part, on the peer's perceptions of the child. If the child is perceived to be friendly or is liked by peers, then prosocial or cooperative behavior may be a part of the peers' scheme for the child. These behaviors would be likely to be attended to. If, however, the child was perceived as aggressive or was disliked, then antisocial behaviors would be a part of the peers' schema, and as a consequence, future aggression would be likely to be attended to. In both scenarios, peers' original perceptions and representations of the child would be reinforced.

Attributional processes also appear to be oriented toward the maintenance of previously developed person perceptions. According to social information processing theorists, attributional processes primarily occur at an unconscious, automatic level, unless the individual behaves in an unexpected manner, is highly negative, or there is some kind of affective arousal (the peer threatens the child). These particular conditions are hypothesized to trigger explicit, conscious processing (Dodge, 1986; Rubin & Rose-Krasnor, 1992; Weiner, 1985), which may lead to a modification of the original representations of the child. Thus, when interacting with a child, a peer will consciously engage in attributional activity only when the child is particularly negative or acts in a manner inconsistent with the peer's perceptions or schema for the child.

The automation of attributional processes also appears to be guided by a number of biases. Research with adults indicates that when interpreting another's behavior, individuals tend to show a bias toward confirming rather than disconfirming their existing perceptions (Sherman, 1987). Thus, unless the behaviors displayed by the partner are so highly inconsistent with developed person perceptions as to lead to conscious processing, behavioral displays are interpreted as being consistent with person perceptions (Hymel, 1986). For example, if a child accidently bumps into a peer, and the peer has a person perception of the child as aggressive, then the child's behavior is likely to be interpreted in a manner that confirms the peer's perceptions. Thus, Dodge (1980) found that children were five times more likely to attribute hostile intentions to a child they knew was aggressive than to a child known to be nonaggressive.

Additional biases have been observed among children. For example, Hymel (1986) found that children's explanations of a child's behavior varied as a function of both affect toward the child and the valence of the child's behavior. For liked children, positive behaviors were attributed to stable causes (e.g., traits), whereas for disliked children, negative behaviors were attributed to stable causes.

Peers' Behavior toward Child

The final component in the model of children's social interactions as depicted in Figure 4.4, is the behavioral responses directed toward the child by the peer group. Once formed, children's reputations guide other children's behavior toward them. In a persuasive study, Dodge (1980) presented children with hypothetical stores about classmates with differing reputations for aggressiveness with peers. Dodge (1980) found that children were more likely to retaliate aggressively when an act was performed by a classmate with a reputation for aggressiveness than when the same act was performed by a nonaggressive classmate. Consistent with these findings, Feldman and Ruble (1986) found that children's generosity to another child was dependent on whether the child was viewed as "generous" or "stingy," especially if they expected future interaction with that particular child.

The reputational frames that guide children's behavior toward a specific child are important, as they may entice the child who is the object of a negative reputation to behave, in turn, in ways that affirm this reputation. Indeed, research with adults indicates that when an individual expects another individual to behave in a certain way (e.g., to be friendly or unfriendly; hostile or nonhostile), the partner's behavior may indeed fall in line with these expectations. Thus, when an individual is led to expect unfriendly behavior from a partner, their behavior may indeed inspire unfriendly behavior from their partners. In addition, research with adults (e.g., Bem, 1972) indicates that individuals sometimes make inferences about other people's characteristics by referencing their own behavior. In a similar

fashion, to the extent that children reference their own behavior to make inferences about another child, and their own behavior is motivated by reputational frames, those reputational frames may be strengthened. In this way, the spiral cycle of the child's cognition → child's behavior → peers' cognitions → peers' behavior is reinforced.

The reciprocal model of children's social interactions in Figure 4.4 indicates that a child's level of peer adjustment is an outcome of the dynamic relations among the construal and behavioral processes of the child and his or her social partners. Thus, to fully understand the origins of children's peer difficulties, it is necessary to understand the reciprocal nature of children's social exchanges, as well as each of the cognitive and behavioral components composing these exchanges. As noted earlier, the cognitive and behavioral components of children's social interactions represent the proximal origins of children's peer difficulties. In the following section, an important set of distal influences on children peer difficulties is discussed.

THE ORIGINS OF PEER DIFFICULTIES: INFLUENCES OF EARLY FAMILY EXPERIENCES AND TEMPERAMENT

Successful adjustment with peers may depend on highly heritable behavioral traits (i.e., temperament and personality dispositions) as well as on the kind of interaction style children have learned through previous interactions with their parents. The behavior of parents toward their children, in turn, is influenced by the parents' personalities, mental health status, belief systems, and own childhood experiences (Belsky, 1984). Thus, such variables may also have implications for children's adjustment with peers. Finally, expanded theoretical conceptualizations of families as systems suggest the importance of contextual factors, such as poverty or marital conflict, in promoting or jeopardizing children's social competence and later adjustment with peers. These family context factors may influence the development of peer difficulties *directly,* by influencing how children interpret, process, and respond to social stimuli and affective arousal. For example, exposure to interadult anger is associated with distressed, angry, self-blaming, and physically aggressive reactions in children (Cummings, 1987; Cummings, Iannotti, & Zahn-Waxler, 1985; Grych, Seid, & Fincham, 1991). On the other hand, these contextual factors may *indirectly* influence adjustment with peers via their deleterious impact on parenting practices (e.g., Campbell, Pierce, March, & Ewing, 1991; Dodge, Pettit, & Bates, 1994; Snyder, 1991).

Research has not yet been able to definitively specify the distinct, relative, and interactive contributions of children's traits, parental behavior, and contextual factors to children's social competence and later success with peers. For example, efforts in this area have been complicated by the need for multivariate, prospective studies, and by the formidable statistical problems inherent to analyses of direct and indirect effects in nonexperimental data sets. In addition, controversies exist over the interpretation of the "direction of effects" in many important areas of socialization (see Dodge, 1990; Kochanska, 1993; Lytton, 1990; Maccoby, 1992; Stafford & Bayer, 1993). Nevertheless, steady progress has been made in understanding the origins of children's peer difficulties over the past decade, to the point that the research literature in some areas is relatively well-developed.

In this section, we review some of the arguments and empirical evidence related to the origins of children's peer difficulties. We begin with a short discussion of the role of temperament and biological factors. As we have discussed, temperament has been a factor in some models of how peer experiences influence later adjustment (i.e., Rubin et al., 1990, 1991). Following this, we briefly examine the link between the parent-child and child-child relational systems. Research on the parenting antecedents of children's peer difficulties has accelerated especially rapidly in recent years, accompanying the general rise in scholarly appreciation of the importance of peer relationships in child development (e.g., Duck, 1993; Dunn, 1993; Ladd, 1991; Parke & Ladd, 1992; Rubin, Booth, Rose-Krasnor, & Mills, 1994). We first review research conducted within the framework of attachment theory. Attachment theory has had a pervasive influence on scholarship in this area, and has already generated a good deal of empirical work. However, alternative or broader conceptualizations of this link are also possible (e.g., Dunn, 1993; Hartup & Laursen, 1991; see also Duck, 1993; Parke & Ladd, 1992), and some authors (i.e., Dunn, 1993; Lamb & Nash, 1989) have pointed to important limits to existing research within the attachment framework with respect to children' peer relationships. Accordingly, following our discussion of attachment theory work we focus on research representative of two other traditions in this area—research on parents' general disciplinary practices and research on parents' specific efforts to manage their child's peer relationships or to coach their child around social skills. Although neither of these research traditions is dominated by a single theoretical framework, much of the work in both areas can be readily interpreted from within the framework of social learning theory. Finally, we very briefly present some examples of family contextual factors that might be influential to children's peer relationships and social skills.

Temperament and Later Peer Relationships

Several years ago, Rowe (1989) appealed for the more systematic application of behavioral genetic approaches to understanding the development of peer relationships, including increased research on the relations between highly heritable child traits, especially temperament, and sociometric outcomes. Despite periodic calls of this type, behavioral genetic and other approaches that emphasize biologically-based explanations of behavior have not received much attention within the literature on children's adjustment with peers. The relative neglect of temperament seems particularly unfortunate, as the implications for children's later peer relationships of differing constellations of temperamental qualities are not difficult to draw.

Temperament researchers generally distinguish three dispositional characteristics in infancy and toddlerhood—difficult temperament, activity level, and inhibition versus sociability. *Difficult temperament* refers to the frequent and intense expression of negative affect (Thomas & Chess, 1977). Fussiness and irritability would be characteristic of a "difficult" infant or toddler.

The highly *active* baby or toddler is one who is easily excited and motorically facile. Infants or toddlers who are timid, vigilant, and fearful when faced with novel social stimuli are labeled *inhibited;* those who are outgoing and open in response to social novelty are described as *sociable* (Kagan, 1989).

Each of these temperamental characteristics is relatively stable, and each is related to particular constellations of social behaviors known to be characteristic of children with difficulties in peer relationships. For example, difficult and active temperament in infancy and toddlerhood are associated predictively with developmental problems of undercontrol in early childhood (e.g., aggression; Bates, Bayles, Bennett, Ridge, & Brown, 1991; Bates, Maslin, & Frankel, 1985). In turn, undercontrolled, impulsive, and aggressive behavior is characteristic and predictive of peer rejection (Bates et al., 1991). Similarly, indexes of inhibition in infancy and toddlerhood predict social withdrawal in early and middle childhood (Kagan, 1989). Like aggression, social withdrawal in middle childhood is a strong correlate of peer rejection.

The current evidence is not completely consistent, however, in that instances of low or no predictability have also been reported (e.g., Katz & Gottman, 1993). Moreover, although informative, these studies provide an incomplete perspective on the role of temperament in the origins of difficulties with peers because behavioral problems cannot be taken as unambiguous evidence of difficulty with peers, as we have already discussed.

In one of the few studies to explore this issue directly, Stocker and Dunn (1990) obtained parent and teacher ratings of 124 5- to 10-year-old children's sociability and emotionality, and related these scores to various parent, teacher, and child self-report indexes of adjustment with peers. Importantly, Stocker and Dunn (1990) distinguished between children's success in establishing close, harmonious friendships with others and children's overall acceptance or popularity with peers. Consistent with the arguments above, both aspects of temperament were found to be related to the quality of children's friendships and general acceptance by peers. As is a common finding in the temperament literature, relations among measures differed somewhat according to who supplied the information on the child's temperament (mothers versus teachers). In general, however, children reported to be more sociable were rated as having more positive relationships with friends and judged to be more popular with peers than children who were less sociable. Contrariwise, children who were reportedly high in emotionality were found to have less successful relationships with friends and peers than children who were low in emotionality. The cross-sectional nature of the Stocker and Dunn (1990) study leaves open the question of the longitudinal link between temperament and adjustment, however.

Parent-Child to Child-Child Relationships:
Attachment Perspectives

Children usually grow up living with their parents and one or more siblings. The relationships and interactions that children have with their siblings and especially their parents must assuredly influence their developing social repertoires and their subsequent child-child relationships. In an attempt to understand

and predict differences in children's later adjustment with peers from their earliest relationships with parents, authors have increasing drawn on the guiding tenets and hypotheses of attachment theory (Ainsworth, Blehar, Waters, & Wall, 1978; Bowlby, 1969; Bretherton, 1985; Sroufe, 1983). As expressed by Sroufe and Fleeson (1986, p. 52), one of the basic premises of attachment theory is that "The young child seeks and explores new relationships within the framework of expectations for self and others that emerges from the primary relationship." In most instances, an infant's most significant earliest relationship is with his or her mother. Thus, according to the theory, the early mother-child relationship lays the groundwork for the children's understanding of and participation in subsequent familial and extrafamilial relationships. Since the quality of infants' attachments with their mothers vary, children's later social outlook and success with peers is expected to vary as well.

In the case of children with secure attachment histories, an internalized or "working" model of relationships is built up comprising the beliefs that the parent is available and will be responsive to the child's needs for protection, nurturance, and physical care; in a reciprocal fashion, the child with a secure attachment history is also expected to come to regard him- or herself as competent and worthy of parental love and nurturance. In particular, according to Elicker, Englund, and Sroufe (1992), attachment theory predicts at least three specific, salutary influences on children's internal working models and ultimate success with peers. First, a secure attachment relationship with the primary caregiver promotes *positive social expectations*. Children are disposed to engage other children and expect peer interaction to be rewarding. Second, their experience with a responsive and empathic caregiver builds the rudiments of a social understanding of *reciprocity:*

> . . . by participating in a relationship with an empathic, responsive caregiver, the child not only learns how to receive care (and count on aid from others) but learns the very nature of empathic relating. . . . Later, in more symmetrical relationships (such as peer relationships), this child will know how to respond empathically when the other is in need (Elicker et al., 1992, p. 80).

Finally, through a history of responsive care and support for autonomy within the relationship, the child *develops a sense of self-worth and efficacy*. This internal outlook is thought to be important to promoting curiosity, enthusiasm, and positive affect, characteristics that other children find attractive.

On the other hand, when parental insensitivity and unresponsivity contribute to the development of an insecure primary attachment, children are thought to develop an internal working model of relationships that stresses their unpredictable nature, and images of themselves as unworthy and ineffectual (Bretherton, 1985; Egeland & Farber, 1984; Spieker & Booth, 1988). According to Bowlby (1973), an attachment relationship that provides neither comfort nor support is likely to arouse anxiety and anger. This may lead to the insecure child's behaving in the peer group "by shrinking from it or doing battle with it" (Bowlby, 1973, p. 208). Children who "shrink" anxiously away from peers preclude themselves from the positive outcomes associated with exploration and peer play. Children who "do battle" with their peers will likely engage in aggression, thereby leading to rejection and isolation by the peer group (Rubin et al., 1990; Rubin et al., 1994).

Attachment theory, then, suggests a number of hypotheses concerning aspects of the quality of children's attachment with caregivers and children's later relationships, including those with peers. Attachment theorists stress that, although the working models of relationships that children form from their earliest attachments can change with divergent experiences, they would not ordinarily be expected to do so. Once working models form, they shape and explain experience. They are thereby usually conserved and self-perpetuating.

Recent research appears generally to support many of the predictions of attachment theory concerning the influence of early attachment on the quality of subsequent peer relationships. A number of researchers, for example, have examined the general social orientation and specific social skills of young children with secure and insecure attachment histories. This work suggest that infants who have experienced a secure attachment relationship are more likely than their insecure counterparts to demonstrate socially competent behaviors among peers during the toddler (e.g., Pastor, 1981), preschool (e.g., Booth, Rose-Krasnor, & Rubin, 1991; Erickson, Sroufe, & Egeland, 1985; Lieberman, 1977; Waters, Wippman, & Sroufe, 1979), and elementary school periods (e.g., Booth, Rose-Krasnor, McKinnon, & Rubin, 1994; Elicker et al., 1992; Grossman & Grossman, in press; Renkin, Egeland, Marvinney, Mangelsdorf, & Sroufe, 1989).

Of more direct interest, evidence suggests that infants with secure attachment histories are later more popular in the peer group during the preschool (LaFreniere & Sroufe, 1985) and elementary school years (Elicker et al., 1992; Grossman & Grossman, in press) than their insecurely attached counterparts. Furthermore, there appears to be a contemporaneous association between the security of parent-child attachment and peer popularity (Cohn, 1990).

Finally, research suggests an association between children's attachment histories and the qualities of their later best friendships. As several authors note (e.g., Hartup, 1986; Youngblade et al., 1993), studies of children's friendships represent a better test of specific hypotheses raised by attachment theory than studies of children's broader peer acceptance, as the theory predicts that the quality of parent-child attachment is related to the quality of a child's subsequent close *relationships*. In a recent study using this specific strategy, Youngblade and Belsky (1992) reported that infants who had a secure attachment relationship with the mother were less likely to have negative and asynchronous friendships at 5 years of age. Their data replicated and extended the findings of Park and Waters (1989). Park and Waters (1989) observed dyads of 4-year-old best friends. In dyads where both members were securely attached, the interaction was more harmonious, less controlling, more responsive, and more positive than in dyads in which one member was insecurely attached.

Beyond Attachment: Parenting and Peer Relationships

In attempting to understand the ways in which parenting practices influence children's social relationships with peers, authors have found it useful to draw broad distinctions between different putative pathways of influence. Pettit and Mize (1993), among others, have proposed a particularly useful distinction between (a) parents' specific efforts to manage their children's opportunities for contact with peers or to coach their children around specific peer tasks and social skills, and (b) broader elements of parent-child interaction, especially in disciplinary encounters, that influence children's social orientation and social competence with peers. Research on parental coaching is quite new but is already showing great promise. Research on parental discipline and other practices is, of course, quite venerable; however, efforts to link parental practices specifically to children's adjustment with peers is much more recent.

Parenting Style and Children's Adjustment with Peers

Research on parenting styles related to children's social orientations, social competence, and success with peers has been reviewed recently by Cohn, Patterson, and Christopoulos (1991); Parke, Cassidy, Burks, Carson, and Boyum (1992); Pettit and Mize (1993); Putallaz & Heflin, 1990; and Rubin and colleagues (Rubin, Chen, & Stewart, in press; Rubin, Bootin, Rose-Krasnor, & Mills, 1994). In general, this literature suggests many differences in the disciplinary practices of the parents of socially successful and socially unsuccessful children, as well as in the general tone and positiveness of successful and unsuccessful children's overall relationships with their parents.

To illustrate, Hart, DeWolf, Wozniak, and Burt (1992) coded mothers' and fathers' responses to hypothetical discipline situations along a continuum from induction to power-assertion. Although the findings were qualified to some extent by the child's gender and age, parents of preschoolers who were popular with peers and prosocial were found to be more likely to use inductive disciplinary styles, whereas parents of unpopular and antisocial preschoolers were more likely to use power-assertive strategies. Similar findings are reported by Pettit, Dodge, and Brown (1988). These researchers interviewed mothers and asked them to respond to hypothetical stories involving discipline. Peer competence, assessed through peer and teacher ratings, was associated with less use of restrictive discipline by mothers.

As another example, Dishion (1990) examined the relations among grade-school boys' sociometric status, academic skills, antisocial behavior, and several elements of parental discipline practices and family circumstances. Parental discipline was assessed through observations in the home, and a broad index of parent discipline skill was derived from observers' ratings of parents' use of coercive, ineffectual, and negative discipline strategies. Results indicated that, compared with other boys, sociometrically rejected boys had parents who were significantly more likely to engage in inept and negative disciplinary practices. Disadvantaged family circumstances (e.g., poverty, low SES) and stressful events were also linked to poor adjustment with peers, but further analysis of this relation suggested that the link was indirect, that is, mediated primarily by parenting practices. Causal modeling further suggested that the relation between inept parenting and peer rejection was itself mediated by boys' antisocial behavior and academic difficulties. That is, lower levels of parental skill were associated with higher levels of antisocial behavior and lower levels of academic performance. Antisocial behavior and poor academic performance, in turn, were associated with higher levels of peer rejection.

Research by MacDonald (MacDonald & Parke, 1984) provides another example with a slightly different focus. MacDonald and his colleagues studied the affective quality of parent-child play as a predictor of children's peer acceptance and social competence. In an initial study, MacDonald and Parke (1984) videotaped mothers and fathers in their homes as they interacted with their preschool-age children. Parental verbal stimulation and affectively positive style of play were found to be associated with children's competence with peers. In a subsequent study, MacDonald observed popular, rejected, and neglected preschool children with their parents during two brief laboratory play sessions. Results indicated that parents of popular boys engaged them in high levels of physical play, and the boys displayed positive affect during these play bouts. By comparison, peer-rejected boys were found to be more often overstimulated, and their interactions with their parents were less smooth and coordinated. Preschool neglected boys were generally passive in responding to their parents during play, and the parents of these neglected boys were less likely to engage them in play in the first place.

Many methodological and other issues remain in this area. However, the existing research supports the general conclusion that socially successful children have mothers (and, where examined, fathers) who are more feelings-oriented, more positive, more skillful, more likely to use inductive reasoning, and less negative and coercive in their interactions with their children than their socially unsuccessful counterparts. The magnitude of these relations are often modest, but the links themselves are robust and generally consistent with our broader understanding of the effects of parental discipline styles (Baldwin, 1955; Baumrind, 1967). The limits that the correlational nature of this work place on our interpretation should be recognized, however. Although it is likely that parents' behaviors influence their children's behavior and success with peers, it must be acknowledged that parental behavior may be elicited by their children's characteristics (Lytton, 1990). With few exceptions, research in this area focuses on the *concurrent* relations between parental practices and children's social adjustment with peers, and not these relations over time. Thus, although we take this work as generally supportive of a link between early parental behaviors and children's later social success, this link has not been explicitly demonstrated. In this regard, a recent study by Weiss, Dodge, Bates, and Pettit (1992) bears mention. These authors interviewed mothers of 4-year-old children about their discipline practices. Mothers' reports of harsh, punitive discipline toward their children at age 4 were found to predict their children's later aggression toward peers (a composite measure based on peer, teacher, and observer reports) at kindergarten. Although aggressiveness is not an unambiguous index of poor peer relationships, the two constructs are highly related, as we have reviewed.

Parental Structuring and Coaching

Recent research suggests that parents vary widely in the extent of their efforts to provide opportunities for peer interaction for their children and to coach their children in specific social skills. Moreover, the available evidence suggests that parents' efforts in these areas have implications for their children's success with peers (see Ladd, Profilet, & Hart, 1992; Lollis, Ross, & Tate, 1992; Pettit & Mize, 1993).

In an early study in this area, Ladd and Golter (1988) gathered data on parents' (a) tendencies to create opportunities for their preschool children to contact other children, and (b) tendencies to directly or indirectly supervise their children's play with other children. Fifty-eight middle-class parents were trained to keep detailed daily logs of their children's nonschool peer contacts, noting whether the contact was suggested by the parent or requested by the child. They were also asked to note how the contact had been monitored by the parent. These investigators found that about half the parents in the sample regularly arranged opportunities for their child to play with other children, and almost all of preschoolers' play with other children was monitored in some form by parents. Direct monitoring by parents was found to be less likely than indirect monitoring, however. Parents who actively arranged peer contacts and who indirectly supervised these contacts had children who were better liked by their peers. In addition, children whose parents relied on indirect rather than direct monitoring of their children's peer contacts were less hostile toward peers.

In a subsequent follow-up study using a short-term longitudinal design, Ladd and Hart (1992) found that mothers' over- as well as underinvolvement in arranging and monitoring peer contacts could be detrimental to children's social success, at least among boys. Boys whose mothers were moderately involved in initiating their child's peer contacts displayed significant gains in peer status over time compared with boys with over- and underinvolved mothers. Girls made significant gains in peer status only when their own efforts to initiate contact with other children were large in comparison with those of their mothers (i.e., when their mothers were underinvolved).

As another example, Bhavnagri and Parke (1991) interviewed mothers of 2- through 6-year-old children about their management activities. Consistent with the research by Ladd and colleagues, Bhavnagri and Parke found that it was common for mothers to arrange for and supervise play sessions with peers for their children. These authors also found that mothers were far more likely than fathers to arrange and supervise children's contacts with other children, a disparity that was also noted by Ladd and Golter (1988) in their earlier study.

In addition to studying parental efforts to initiate peer contact and to support it indirectly through distal monitoring, researchers have also observed the supervisory and other behaviors of parents as their children interact with other children (e.g., Bhavnagri & Parke, 1991; Finnie & Russell, 1988; Parke & Bhavnagri, 1989; Russell & Finnie, 1990). Finnie and Russell (1988), for example, examined the communication of mothers with their preschool children during their children's initial play encounters with unfamiliar peers. Mothers of low-social-status children (based on teacher reports) were found to be more likely to avoid supervising their children and to supervise their children less skillfully than mothers of high-status children. Mothers of high-status children tended to use more active and more effective supervising strategies than mothers of low-status children (e.g., by making relevant group-oriented statements). Further, in subsequent interviews,

mothers of high-status children were found to be more likely to suggest positive and assertive strategies for handling hypothetical problems involving children's peer relationships than mothers of low-status children. Mothers of low-status children were more likely than mothers of high-status children to suggest avoidant strategies in response to hypothetical problems involving peers.

In a follow-up study using a similar methodology, Russell and Finnie (1990) extended their work to examine mothers' instructions to their child immediately prior to the child's opportunity to play with another unfamiliar child. In this study, teachers were also asked to distinguish between rejected and neglected low-status children. Mothers of high-status children were found to be more likely than mothers of low-status children to make group-oriented statements during both the anticipatory instruction period as well as during the play session itself. Mothers of low-status children were found to be more likely to disrupt play by taking charge than were mothers of high-status children. Few differences were found between mothers of rejected and neglected low-status children. The authors acknowledge, however, that the absence of differences between neglected and rejected children may have been influenced by the nonstandard procedure used to make this distinction (i.e., use of teacher rankings versus sociometric data).

Taken together, the preceding research suggests that when parents are involved in effective ways in coaching their children through difficulties with peers, facilitating their child's play with peers, and providing their children with opportunities to play with peers their children are more successful with peers. Once again, however, the correlational nature of all research in this area must be stressed. As all of these authors have acknowledged, it is possible that the observed differences between the mothers of socially successful and unsuccessful children are a consequence rather than the cause of their children's social competence and success with peers. It is also worth noting that parental management of children's peer relationships is not a task that is shared equally by both parents. Where both parents have been studied, mothers have been found to be more actively involved than fathers in both arranging and supervising their young children's contacts with peers (e.g., Bhavnagri & Parke, 1991; Ladd & Golter, 1988).

Determinants of Parenting and Family Contextual Factors

Space allows only a sketching of some important determinants of parenting and family contextual factors that influence adjustment with peers. Instead, the reader is referred to Belsky (1984), Dix (1991), and Rubin, Chen, and Stewart (in press). Nevertheless, it is appropriate to briefly note several factors that are particularly relevant to the study of children's peer relationships.

First, *parental psychopathology* is associated with parenting styles known to be related to children's maladaptive social behaviors and peer relationships. For example, maternal depression is associated with a lack of parental involvement, responsivity, spontaneity, and emotional support (Downey & Coyne, 1990; Gelfand & Teti, 1990; Hammen, 1988; Kochanska, Kuczynski, & Maguire, 1989; Miller, Cowan, Cowan, Hetherington, & Clingempeel, 1993; Zahn-Waxler et al., 1988). Given that depression is associated with maternal feelings of hopelessness and helplessness (Gurland, Yorkston, Frank, & Stone, 1967), the pattern of parenting behaviors noted here is not surprising. Furthermore, families in which one or both parents are depressed have been found to be less cohesive and emotionally expressive than families in which the parents are psychologically well (Billings & Moos, 1985).

Second, *marital distress and conflict* has been shown to be linked to poor social outcomes in children, including friendship difficulties and child behaviors related to peer rejection (e.g., Fainsilber-Katz & Gottman, 1993; Gottman & Katz, 1989; see Grych & Fincham, 1990, for a review). Marital distress and conflict may exert its negative impact on children's social adjustment indirectly, through its debilitating effect on parenting behavior. For example, mothers who experience affectionate and relatively conflict-free marital relationships have been shown to feel competent in their parenting roles and have been observed to be sensitive, affectionate caregivers (Engfer, 1986). On the other hand, marital conflict and dissatisfaction predict negative attitudes about child rearing as well as insensitive, unresponsive parenting behaviors (e.g., Jouriles, Barling, & O'Leary, 1987; Jouriles et al., 1991). As previously noted, these parenting styles are associated with the development of social behaviors in children that are known to predict peer rejection. Furthermore, spousal conflict and hostility can affect children directly by providing them with models of coercive interpersonal behavior (Emery, 1992).

Third, it is likely that *parents' recollections and reconstructions of their own childhood peer experiences* shape their concern over their child's peer experiences and their strategies for assisting their children through problems they encounter in peer relationships (see Putallaz, Costanzo, & Klein, 1993). At the moment, evidence on this point is extremely limited. However, important initial efforts in this regard have been made by Putallaz, Costanzo, and Smith (1991). These authors reported that mothers who recall their own childhood peer relationships positively report being more nurturing as parents and judge their children to be more socially competent than mothers who regard their childhood peer interaction negatively. Negative recollections of childhood peer relationships were not necessarily connected to poor child outcomes, however. Specifically, one group of mothers who regarded their early peer relationships negatively were distinctive in their tendency to recall anxious/lonely peer experiences. These mothers described themselves as nurturent of their children and made more efforts than other mothers to positively influence their own children's peer experiences (by enrolling them in social activities, for example). Although these mothers did not view their children as particularly socially competent, their children were rated as the most socially competent by other peers, by teachers, and by objective observers. Other researchers (Cohen & Woody, 1991) similarly report that mothers who recall being socially withdrawn in childhood exert special effort to orchestrate successful peer experiences for their own children.

Finally, *poverty and parental unemployment* produce sufficient stress in the family so as to interfere with the ability of a parent to be sensitive and responsive to the needs of a child (e.g., Belsky, Robins, & Gamble, 1984; Booth et al., 1991;

Dodge, Pettit, & Bates, 1994; McLoyd, 1989). Poverty is also associated with anger, inconsistency, and punitiveness in child rearing (Conger, McCarty, Yang, Lahey, & Kropp, 1984; Dodge et al., 1994; Patterson, 1983; Radke-Yarrow, Richters, & Wilson, 1988). Given these findings, it should not be surprising that behavioral maladaptation, as well as peer rejection are associated with the chronic stress and economic disadvantage (Conger, Conger, Elder, Lorenz, Simons, & Whitbeck, 1992, 1993; Conger, Ge, Elder, Lorenz, & Simons, 1994; Dishion, 1990; Dodge et al., 1994; Patterson, Kupersmidt, & Vaden, 1990; Patterson, Vaden, & Kupersmidt, 1991). However, as Dishion's (1990) findings indicate, links between these factors and children's adjustment with peers are likely to be complex and not necessarily direct.

Summary

There is good evidence that the quality of children's relationships with their peers is affected by the parenting behaviors they experience, by the quality of their relationships with their parents, and by ecological factors that impinge on the family unit. Thus, children who experience harsh or neglectful parenting, who develop insecure relationships with their parents, and who live in ecologically stressful environments may be considered at risk for (a) developing maladaptive social and emotional behavioral styles and (b) experiencing peer rejection. There is also reason to expect that infant temperament may set the stage for the development of particular types of parent-child relationships and for the development of social behavioral profiles that ultimately predict the quality of children's peer relationships.

THE STUDY OF PEER RELATIONSHIPS PROBLEMS: ANOTHER AVENUE TO UNDERSTANDING NORMAL PEER RELATIONSHIPS

One of the distinctive features of the emerging discipline of developmental psychopathology is the emphasis placed on the close connection between typical and deviant forms of adjustment (Achenbach, 1990; Cicchetti, 1993; Masten & Braswell, 1989; Sroufe & Rutter, 1984). As Cicchetti (1993, p. 472) notes, "knowledge of normal development is necessary to understand deviations or distortions from normality. Similarly, information obtained from studying pathology can be utilized to enhance the understanding of normal development." In the initial sections of this chapter, we reviewed the now substantial evidence bearing on the developmental course and functions of peer experiences in the typically developing child. We noted that knowledge of the typical forms and functions of peer relationships can assist in understanding the origins and significance of maladaptive relationships with peers. We subsequently highlighted the assessment, origins, and short- and long-term implications of difficulties in adjustment with peers in childhood, in many cases drawing from literature on normal development to aid our interpretations. Thus far, however, we have devoted little explicit attention to the reciprocal relation; namely, how research on children with significant peer relationships disturbances can and has furthered our understanding of normal development, including the normal development of peer relationships. A few comments in this regard therefore seem warranted.

Research on children with difficulties in peer relationships has furthered our understanding of the development of peer relationships in several significant ways. First, research on the behavioral and social cognitive correlates of peer rejection has advanced our understanding of the social skills necessary for effective and satisfying interpersonal relationships. As was noted in the section on the origins of children's peer difficulties, the literature on the social-cognitive and behavioral characteristics of children experiencing problems with peers (e.g., sociometric rejection) is well developed. In this research, children with poor peer relationships (e.g., sociometrically rejected children; friendless children) are compared with children who have typical (e.g., average status children; children with friends) or even exemplary (e.g., popular children) peer relationships. Where differences result, these differences can be understood to point to the social skills deficits and behavioral incompetencies that underlie peer rejection. These findings have important implications for the selection of program content for interventions on behalf of poorly accepted, at-risk children (Ladd & Mize, 1983). However, they also bring us closer to a full understanding of the behavioral and cognitive processes that operate normally in peer interaction. That is, differences between rejected and nonrejected children indicate what other children do *right* as well as what rejected children do *wrong*. Thus, as a result of the substantial effort to isolate the important and unimportant factors that contribute to children's difficulties with peers, our understanding of the requirements of successful peer interaction has become more comprehensive.

In addition, as advocated by Cicchetti (1989), the study of high-risk children can help to explain the nature of the relation between domains of development. Already, substantial literature exists on the relation between children's behavior with peers and children's social cognitive development. This research shows that children who behave in problematic ways with peers also possess particular deficits or biases in the manner in which they process social information (e.g., Dodge et al., 1986; Rubin & Krasnor, 1986). In contrast, children who are successful with their peers lack these biases and deficits and process social information efficiently and effectively. Contrariwise, as Rabiner & Coie (1989) demonstrated in their study of the influence of expectancy inductions of rejected children's acceptance by peers, the manipulation of children's social cognitions has an impact on children's behavior and peer relationships. Studies of rejected children have also yielded insights into how affect is linked to behavior with peers (e.g., Denham, McKinley, Couchoud, & Holt, 1990).

Finally, research on children with peer difficulties has enhanced our understanding of the role of peer experiences in children's development. As we have seen, peer interaction has been suggested to play many roles in children's subsequent adjustment and development. Our ability to evaluate some of these suggested functions is severely hampered by the ethical impossibility of conducting experiments that deprive children of important peer experiences or expose children to peer experiences that may compromise their psychological well-being. Long-term research on rejected children can circumvent some of these ethical issues, however. As we have seen, there is evidence suggesting

that peer rejection is predictive of later maladjustment, even after controlling initial maladjustment and for the contributions of other important predictors, such as poverty. Although the link between peer relationships and adjustment is still not yet fully understood, these data do suggest that peer relationships may play an important role in children's development and that children who have difficulties establishing positive and supportive relationships with peers are at risk for later psychopathology.

CONCLUDING COMMENTS AND SUGGESTIONS FOR FUTURE RESEARCH

After varying initial experiences with parents and siblings, children enter into increasingly complex and varying relationships with peers. In this chapter, we have reviewed evidence that children's experiences with other children are significant to their growth and adjustment. We have reviewed some of the ways in which peer experiences complement children's experiences with family members, particularly parents, and some of the ways in which peer experiences may be unique experiences in development. We also examined the supportive features and functions of childhood and adolescent friendships.

Much of the chapter was devoted to considering the wide individual variability in children's peer experiences, which we suggested could be organized powerfully along two basic dimensions—success with friends and acceptance by the peer group. Consideration of friendship adjustment suggested both qualitative and quantitative aspects that may be linked to developmental processes and outcomes. At the acceptance level, we considered especially the child's membership in sociometrically identifiable status groups (i.e., popular, rejected, neglected, controversial, and average). Evidence was found for the validity of parsing children's social worlds into such categories; members of different groups show distinct behavioral profiles, for example. Finally, we devoted considerable attention to the origins, concomitant correlates, and long-term consequences of individual differences in adjustment with peers.

We noted at the outset that investigators seeking to understand children's relationships with peers have seldom done so explicitly within a developmental psychopathology framework. This omission hardly seems to have handicapped scholarship in this area. Quite the contrary, as our review makes clear, the area continues to be an area of active, vigorous research. But, insofar as so much of the interest within this literature focuses on the origins, maintenance, and consequences of deviant adjustment with peers, we find it disappointing that it has remained somewhat disconnected from the interpretive framework and tenets of developmental psychopathology. In our view, the framework of developmental psychopathology can sharpen our understanding of some of the new and well-established findings in this area, as well as reveal directions for future work. Thus, throughout this chapter, we have attempted to highlight significant areas of intersection.

For their part, developmental psychopathologists have recognized the importance of adjustment with peers in childhood and have emphasized some of the negative consequences for children of cumulative peer rejection or friendship difficulties. Even so, it can be argued that developmental psychopathologists have not taken full advantage of many of the insights of researchers who have studied children's peer relationships from outside that framework. Indeed, research on children's peer relationships can in some ways be seen as paradigmatic of the developmental psychopathology approach. For example, one of the guiding propositions underlying a developmental psychopathology perspective is that individuals develop both toward increasing flexibility and increasing organization (Cicchetti, 1990; Sroufe & Rutter, 1984). This proposition aptly characterizes the pattern of development in several areas of children's peer relationships, such as the growth of children's conceptions of friendship and the developmental patterns in very young children's play. Another example is the concept of *directedness,* encompassing the idea that individuals selectively receive, respond to, and create experience based on past experiences and cognitive frameworks and biases. As we reviewed, much attention within the literature on children's peer relationships has been directed toward the biases and inappropriately selective social information processing of children with peer relationship difficulties; we are beginning to learn how such biases operate in peer interaction and exacerbate the problems of certain children with budding peer relationship difficulties. As a final example, the evidence that we reviewed presented a convincing case for viewing disturbed adjustment to peers as a condition of risk. However, peer rejection has been very seldom included among the litany of illustrative risk conditions (e.g., Down syndrome, maltreatment, failure-to-thrive, insecure attachment, depression) that are commonly cited by developmental psychopathologists (cf. Cicchetti, Toth, & Bush, 1988).

Almost at every turn in our review, gaps in current knowledge were identified. As these gaps were discussed in their respective contexts, there is little need to recapitulate those discussions here. However, some emergent concerns merit note in closing.

First, there has been little attention to the cultural context of children's peer experiences and the implications of culture for our conclusion about the significance of peer relationships in development. The vast literature on the correlates and consequences of children's acceptance and rejection by peers, for example, focuses almost exclusively on children who live in North American and Western European communities. Thus, little, if anything, is known about the development of peer relationships in other cultures. This is a disturbing omission; we simply do not know whether the predictors, correlates, and consequences of acceptance or rejection by peers vary from culture to culture. Indeed, we do not know whether the meaning of maladaptation and psychopathology, and the developmental course of particular social behaviors are cross-culturally universal.

This neglect of cross-cultural differences is highlighted by the recent research program of Chen and colleagues in Shanghai, P.R. China (e.g., Chen & Rubin, 1992, 1994; Chen, Rubin, & Sun, 1992). Chen et al. found that acceptance by peers was predicted by social competence and that rejection by peers was predicted by hostile, aggressive behavior. These findings are in keeping with those reported in the Western literature. However, contrary to Western studies, socially wary, withdrawn behavior

was associated with popularity, not rejection in the middle years of childhood. Chen and colleagues explain their findings by contrasting the cultural values of Chinese and Western communities vis-à-vis the meanings and importance of sociability, social interaction, deference, and compliance to adult norms and standards. It would be in the best interests of psychological scholars not to generalize culture-specific theories of the development of psychopathology to other cultures.

Second, further work is also needed on the links between children's family experiences and children's peer experiences. Much progress has been made on this front, but as Ladd (1991, p. 307) notes, the literature on family and the literature on peers "have remained relatively independent because each has been built on differing research agendas and questions." Interest in children's attachment has played a critical, catalytic role in bringing researchers who study the family together with researchers who study children in peer groups. Drawing on Bowlby's construct of internal working models, researchers using an attachment framework have begun to examine children's peer relationships in an attempt to define more precisely how early relationships affect later development (Booth, Rose-Krasnor, MacKinnon, & Rubin, 1994; Cicchetti, Lynch, Shonk, & Manly, 1992; Elicker et al., 1992).

The alliance of attachment research with research on children's peer relationships has unquestionably already yielded rich dividends in understanding important developmental processes. But it has probably also meant that some issues receive more attention than others. For example, research on the parenting antecedents of children's peer relationships skills is almost singularly focused on the putative contributions of mothers. Future research must address the dearth of information on how fathers influence children's peer relationships (see Parke et al., 1992). Generally speaking, fathers have not received much attention within the attachment literature, and controversy surrounds the validity of father-child attachment classifications (see Dunn, 1993). It would be unfortunate if the very salutary influence of attachment research on the study of children's peer relationships has the unintended consequence of further directing attention away from fathers. The same general point can be made about the need for further research on sibling influences, another area that has received scant attention in the literature on children's peer relationships (Buhrmester, 1992; Dunn, 1993).

One way to affirm, extend, or challenge our understanding of how family experiences influence peer adjustment is through the study of maltreated children and their families (Cicchetti et al., 1992; Rogosch & Cicchetti, in press). Children who experience some form of maltreatment have been found to manifest a variety of behavioral problems and experience difficulties establishing positive and supportive relationships with peers (e.g., Conway & Hansen, 1989; Dodge, Pettit, & Bates, 1990; Kaufman & Cicchetti, 1989; Okun, Parker, & Levendosky, 1994; Rogosch & Cicchetti, 1994; Salzinger, Feldman, Hammer & Rosario, 1993; Shields, Cicchetti, & Ryan, 1994). Insofar as maltreatment appears to jeopardize the development of peer relationships, research directed toward understanding the mechanisms of this influence would appear to represent an important avenue for isolating family factors that contribute to development of social skills and adequate peer relationships. Although work in this direction has begun (see Cicchetti et al., 1992), on the whole this strategy seems underutilized.

The study of maltreated children can contribute to our understanding of peer relationships, development, and adjustment in another way; namely, through the identification of protective factors and resilience among children at risk for poor adjustment with peers. One of the tenets of developmental psychopathology is the need to understand the functioning of individuals who do not succumb to the risks that eventuate in maladaptive outcomes in others (see Cicchetti, Rogosch, Lynch, & Holt, 1993; Masten & Braswell, 1989; Sroufe & Rutter, 1984). As we have just suggested, parental maltreatment is generally associated with difficulties with peers. However, very little attention has been directed toward understanding the variability in maltreated children's experiences with peers. By examining factors that pull maltreated children toward or away from problems in adjustment with peers, insight can be gained into the requirements for successful adjustment with peers.

The variability in maltreated children's success with peers also affords an opportunity to examine some of the hypotheses offered by Sullivan (1953) and others concerning the therapeutic possibilities of friendships for children. As we indicated earlier, Sullivan (1953) believed that close friendships could ameliorate certain developmental arrests stemming from problematic relationships with parents by providing children with offsetting positive social experiences and opportunities for the development of social skills (see Buhrmester & Furman, 1986; Cooper & Cooper, 1992; Price, in press).

There is another sense in which thinking about resilience might move us a little closer to a fuller understanding of peer relationships, child development, and adjustment. Experiencing difficulties with peers is a consistent risk factor for later mental health and personal adjustment. Although this link is robust, it remains the case that only a subset of children with poor peer relationships—perhaps about one-third (Parker & Asher, 1987)—actually experience later maladjustment beyond adolescence. Apparently, most children with poor peer relationships ultimately escape the most deleterious consequences of this experience. Comparisons among rejected children who do and do not ultimately develop later disorders may offer clues to family, genetic, demographic, behavioral, and other factors that either increase the risk or protect children from later disorder in this group, and should be an important agenda for future research. Data of this type should also be useful in constructing preventive interventions for children with poor peer relationships.

The identification of children experiencing difficulties with peers relies heavily on sociometric assessments of children's liking, disliking, and judgments of friendship toward others. On the basis of children's ratings or nominations of liking and disliking, children's rejection by the peer group can be gauged. Children who lack friends can be identified from the reciprocal patterns of choices in matrices of children's friendship designations. The available literature strongly supports researchers' faith in the power of sociometric assessments of adjustment with peers as well as the distinction between friendship adjustment and overall acceptance by the peer group. As we have reviewed, children

with good and poor overall group acceptance may or may not always be involved in friendships, and friendship and group acceptance seem to make distinct (as well as overlapping) contributions to children's sense of well-being and adjustment.

Although the large quantity of research employing sociometric assessment procedures may suggest to some that further efforts to refine these techniques are unnecessary, the existing research is quite lopsided. Important strides have been made in understanding how to assess children's group acceptance and assign children to sociometric status classification (popular, rejected, neglected, etc.). By comparison, our understanding of how to assess children's involvement in friendship and children's friendship experiences is still in its infancy. The identification of friendships relies on sociometric techniques developed and refined principally in the context of efforts to gauge children's peer acceptance or group standing. As a result, a great deal is known about how the assessment of acceptance by peers and the assignment of children to sociometric status groups is affected by variations in the instructions given to children, the testing context, and the mathematical algorithms employed (see Newcomb et al., 1993). Notably lacking, however, is much understanding of how these and other parameters of sociometric assessment affect the identification of friendships. Some authors (e.g., Asher et al., in press; Parker & Asher, 1993a, 1993b) have argued that operational decisions such as how sociometric nomination items are worded, the number of nominations children are permitted, whether children nominate other children rather than rate them on a continuum, and how sociometric data are aggregated affect the interpretation of friendship variables. In particular, these authors have worried that some decisions conflate the association between friendship involvement and acceptance by the peer group. Other authors (e.g., Bukowski, Hoza, & Newcomb, in press) have countered that most of these operational factors are nuances that do not have large practical significance. The current literature provides little guidance on assessment issues and controversies of this type.

A further point is that the distinction between friendship and group acceptance may be important for understanding differences in the eventual outcomes of children with peer difficulties. Because most of the risk literature predates concern for this distinction, the existing literature is not particularly helpful. It may be, as Gottman (1983, p. 2) warned a decade ago, that "the correlation between peer sociometric data and later functioning can be accounted for, to some extent, by the problems encountered by . . . [the subset of] . . . children who go through childhood without any friends." At the very least, it seems that the long-term implications of difficulties in each domain will be different.

Finally, although sociometric assessments of friendships and peer acceptance are appropriate and valid, it must be remembered that, by themselves, they do not provide insights into the day-to-day experiences of children with significant difficulties in peer relationships. Few data exist, for example, on the frequency with which peer-rejected children are excluded from playground games, experience teasing and taunts, or are otherwise victimized by other children (Asher & Gabriel, 1993). The high levels of loneliness and social dissatisfaction reported by rejected children suggest that their day-to-day commerce with peers is generally negative (Asher et al., 1990). As we have reviewed, there is substantial variability among rejected children in their reports of loneliness and other signs of subjective distress however. This variability may partly account for the heterogeneity that rejected children show in their long-term adjustment and positive responses to remedial interventions (Asher et al., 1990). An important direction for future research, then, should be greater systematic effort to obtain observational data on rejected children's experiences with peers, especially outside the classroom (Asher & Gabriel, 1993). In other words, we recommend that researchers step up their efforts to understand the experiences that contribute to making rejection by peers and friendlessness stressful for children.

Another area in which development has been somewhat lopsided is in friendship support. As we reviewed, researchers have made considerable progress in developing techniques for assessing children's perceptions of the features of their friendships, especially with respect to the level of emotional support provided. We are also beginning to understand something about the significance of friendship support to children's sense of well-being and adjustment. Yet, the amount of observationally based research on children's friendships is embarrassingly thin. As a result, we know a great deal more about support as a *property* of children's friendships than we do about the *process* of support in these relationships. Very little is understood, for example, about how children respond when their friends raise emotional issues, how self-disclosure unfolds in the course of the conversations among friends of different ages or genders, or how advice is offered or received in friendships. Further efforts are needed to stimulate work in this area.

Although peer relationships are an important consideration in the diagnosis of many of the psychiatric disorders of childhood and adolescence, relatively little is known about the quality and type of the peer interactions of children with psychiatric diagnoses. Moreover, the link between poor peer relationships and traditional psychiatric disorders has seldom been studied developmentally. Thus, the role that adjustment with peers plays in the emergence and maintenance of psychiatric disorders remains unclear. Further research on the peer relationships of children with various psychiatric diagnoses would be helpful to understanding the etiology, prognosis, and treatment of these children.

A final point concerns the thorny issue of causality that has dogged much theorizing in this area. As noted earlier, many authors have assumed that where poor peer adjustment is found to predict later problematic outcomes, the poor peer adjustment is in some way *responsible*, at least in part, for the later negative outcome. We noted that this assumption probably has merit, owing to the evidence that poor peer adjustment constitutes a stressor for children and deprives children of important socialization opportunities. Indeed, we explored what a transactional model—containing embedded, reciprocal paths of causal influence—might look like. There now exists an extensive literature addressing how to improve children's social skills (see Asher, 1985; Asher et al., in press; Bond & Compas, 1989; Pepler & Rubin, 1991). Elsewhere, we (Parker & Asher, 1987; Rubin, Hymel, Mills, & Rose-Krasnor, 1991) suggested that the advances of this literature provide an opportunity to test some of the causal pathways implicated in the link between poor peer relationships and later adjustment. Specifically, by intervening with children who have poor peer relationships, researchers can learn whether improvements in adjustment with peers also reduce children's relative risk for subsequent adjustment disturbances. The importance of conducting methodologically rigorous interventions as tests of causal pathways and developmental theories is an important cornerstone of the developmental psychopathology framework (see Cicchetti & Toth, 1992). This strategy has not been sufficiently exploited to date.

REFERENCES

Achenbach, T. M., & Edelbrock, C. S. (1981). Behavioral problems and competencies reported by parents of normal and disturbed children aged four through sixteen. *Monographs of the Society for Research in Child Development, 46* (1, Serial No. 188).

Achenbach, T. M., & Edelbrock, C. S. (1986). *Child Behavior Checklist and Youth Self-Report.* Burlington, VT: Author.

Adelson, J., & Doehrman, M. J. (1980). The psychodynamic approach of adolescence. In J. Adelson (Ed.), *Handbook of adolescent psychiatry* (pp. 99–116). New York: Wiley.

Adler, T., & Furman, W. (1988). A model for children's relationships and relationship dysfunctions. In S. W. Duck (Ed.), *Handbook of personal relationships: Theory, research, and interventions* (pp. 211–228). London: Wiley.

Ainsworth, M. D. S., Blehar, M. C., Waters, E., & Wall, S. (1978). *Patterns of attachment.* Hillsdale, NJ: Erlbaum.

Altmann, E. O., & Gottlib, I. H. (1988). The social behavior of depressed children: An observational study. *Journal of Abnormal Child Psychology, 16,* 29–44.

American Psychiatric Association (1987, 1994). *Diagnostic and Statistical Manual of Mental Disorders* (3rd ed. rev., 4th ed.). Washington, DC: Author.

Ames, G. J., & Murray, F. B. (1982). When two wrongs make a right: Promoting cognitive change by social conflict. *Developmental Psychology, 18,* 894–897.

Anderson, C. A., Horowitz, L. M., & French, R. (1983). Attributional style of lonely and depressed people. *Journal of Personality and Social Psychology, 45,* 127–136.

Antonucci, T. C. (1990). Social supports and social relationships. In R. H. Binstock & L. K. George (Eds.), *Handbook of aging and the social sciences* (3rd ed., pp. 205–226). San Diego, CA: Academic Press.

Arbuthnot, J. (1975). Modification of moral development through role playing. *Developmental Psychology, 11,* 319–324.

Asarnow, J. R., & Callan, J. W. (1985). Boys with peer adjustment problems: Social cognitive processes. *Journal of Consulting and Clinical Psychology, 53,* 80–87.

Asher, S. R. (1985). An evolving paradigm in social skills training research with children. In B. H. Schneider, K. Rubin, & J. E. Ledingham (Eds.), *Children's peer relations: Issues in assessment and intervention* (pp. 157–174). New York: Springer-Verlag.

Asher, S. R., & Coie, J. D. (Eds.). (1990). *Peer rejection in childhood.* New York: Cambridge University Press.

Asher, S. R., & Gabriel, S. (1993). Using a wireless transmission system to observe conversations and social interaction on the playground. In C. H. Hart (Ed.), *Children on playgrounds: Research perspectives and applications (pp. 184–209).* Albany, NY: SUNY Press.

Asher, S. R., & Gottman, J. M. (Eds.). (1981). *The development of children's friendships*. New York: Cambridge University Press.

Asher, S. R., & Hymel, S. (1981). Children's social competence in peer relations: Sociometric and behavioral assessment. In J. D. Wine & M. D. Smye (Eds.), *Social competence* (pp. 125–157). New York: Guilford.

Asher, S. R., Hymel, S., & Renshaw, P. D. (1984). Loneliness in children. *Child Development, 55,* 1456–1464.

Asher, S. R., & Parker, J. G. (1989). Significance of peer relationship problems in childhood. In B. H. Schneider, G. Attili, J. Nadel, & R. P. Weissberg (Eds.), *Social competence in developmental perspective* (pp. 5–23). Dordrecht: Kluwer.

Asher, S. R., Parker, J. G., & Walker, D. L. (in press). Distinguishing friendship from acceptance: Implications for intervention and assessment. In W. M. Bukowski, A. F. Newcomb, & W. W. Hartup (Eds.), *The company they keep: Friendship during childhood and adolescence*. New York: Cambridge University Press.

Asher, S. R., Parkhurst, J. T., Hymel, S., & Williams, G. A. (1990). Peer rejection and loneliness in childhood. In S. R. Asher & J. D. Coie (Eds.), *Peer rejection in childhood* (pp. 253–273). New York: Cambridge University Press.

Asher, S. R., Singleton, L., Tinsley, B., & Hymel, S. (1979). A reliable sociometric measure of preschool children. *Developmental Psychology, 15,* 433–444.

Asher, S. R., & Wheeler, V. A. (1985). Children's loneliness: A comparison of rejected and neglected peer status. *Journal of Consulting and Clinical Psychology, 53,* 500–505.

Asher, S. R., & Williams, G. A. (1987). Helping children without friends in home and school contexts. In *Children's social development: Information for teachers and parents* (pp. 1–26). Urbana, IL: ERIC Clearinghouse on Elementary and Early Childhood Education.

Asher, S. R., Zelis, K. M., Parker, J. G., & Bruene, C. M. (1991, April). *Self-referral for peer relationship problems among aggressive and withdrawn low-accepted children*. Paper presented at the biennial meeting of the Society for Research in Child Development, Seattle.

August, G. J., Ostrander, R., & Bloomquist, M. J. (1992). Attention deficit hyperactivity disorder: An epidemiological screening method. *American Journal of Orthopsychiatry, 62,* 387–396.

Austin, M. C., & Thompson, G. G. (1948). Children's friendships: A study of the bases on which children select and reject their best friends. *Journal of Educational Psychology, 39,* 101–116.

Azmitia, M. (1988). Peer interaction and problem solving: When are two heads better than one? *Child Development, 59,* 87–96.

Azmitia, M., & Montgomery, R. (1993). Friendship, transactive dialogues, and the development of scientific reasoning. *Social Development, 2,* 202–221.

Azmitia, M., & Perlmutter, M. (1989). Social influences on children's cognition: State of the art and future directions. In H. W. Reese (Ed.), *Advances in child development and behavior* (Vol. 22, pp. 89–144). New York: Academic Press.

Bakeman, R., & Gottman, J. M. (1986). *Observing interaction: An introduction to sequential analysis*. New York: Cambridge University Press.

Baldwin, J. (1955). *Behavior and development in childhood*. New York: Dreyden.

Bandura, A. (1989). Social cognitive theory. In R. Vasta (Ed.), *Annals of child development: Six theories of child development: Revised formulations and current issues* (Vol. 6, pp. 1–60). Greenwich, CT: JAI Press.

Barenboim, C. (1981). The development of person perception in childhood and adolescence: From behavioral comparisons to psychological constructs to psychological comparisons. *Child Development, 52,* 129–144.

Barkley, R. A. (1981). Hyperactivity. In E. Mash & L. Terdal (Eds.), *Behavioral assessment of childhood disorders* (pp. 127–184). New York: Guilford.

Barkley, R. A., Anastopoulos, A. D., Guevremont, D. C., & Fletcher, K. E. (1991). Adolescents with ADHD: Patterns of behavioral adjustment, academic functioning, and treatment utilization. *Journal of the American Academy of Child and Adolescent Psychiatry, 30,* 752–761.

Barocas, R., & Sameroff, A. J. (1982). Social class, maternal psychopathology, and mediational processes in young children. *Advances in Child Behavioral Analysis and Therapy, 2,* 43–77.

Barthell, C. N., & Holmes, D. S. (1968). High school yearbooks: A nonreactive measure of social isolation in graduates who later became schizophrenic. *Journal of Abnormal Psychology, 4,* 40–45.

Bates, J. E., Bayles, K., Bennett, D. S., Ridge, B., & Brown, M. M. (1991). Origins of externalizing behavior problems at eight years of age. In D. J. Pepler & K. H. Rubin (Eds.), *The development and treatment of childhood aggression* (pp. 93–120). Hillsdale, NJ: Erlbaum.

Bates, J. E., Maslin, C. A., & Frankel, K. A. (1985). Attachment security, mother-child interaction, and temperament as predictors of behavior-problem ratings at age three years. *Monographs of the Society for Research in Child Development, 50,* 167–193.

Baudonniere, P., Garcia-Werebe, M., Michel, J., & Liegeois, J. (1989). Development of communicative competencies in early childhood: A model of results. In B. H. Schneider, G. Attili, J. Nadel, & R. P. Weissberg (Eds.), *Social competence in developmental perspective*. Boston, MA: Kluwer.

Baumeister, R. F., & Senders, P. S. (1989). Identity development and the role of structure of children's games. *Journal of Genetic Psychology, 150,* 19–37.

Baumrind, D. (1967). Child care patterns anteceding three patterns of preschool behavior. *Genetic Psychology Monographs, 75,* 43–88.

Beal, C. R. (1994). *Boys and girls: The development of gender roles*. New York: McGraw-Hill.

Bearison, D. J. (1982). New directions in studies of social interaction and cognitive growth. In F. Serafica (Ed.), *Social-cognitive development in context* (pp. 199–221). New York: Guilford.

Bearison, D. J., & Cassel, T. (1975). Cognitive decentration and social codes: Communicative effectiveness in young children from differing family contexts. *Developmental Psychology, 11,* 29–36.

Belle, D. (1989). *Children's social networks and social supports*. New York: Wiley.

Belsky, J. (1984). The determinants of parenting: A process model. *Child Development, 55,* 83–96.

Belsky, J., Robins, E., & Gamble, W. (1984). The determinants of parental competence: Toward a contextual theory. In M. Lewis (Ed.), *Beyond the dyad* (pp. 251–279). New York: Plenum.

Bem, S. L. (1972). Self-perception theory. In L. Berkowitz (Ed.), *Advances in experimental social psychology* (Vol. 6, pp. 2–62). New York: Academic Press.

Benenson, J. F. (1993). Greater preference among females than males for dyadic interaction in early childhood. *Child Development, 64,* 544–555.

Berkowitz, M., & Gibbs, J. (1985). The process of moral conflict resolution and moral development. In M. Berkowitz (Ed.), *Peer conflict and psychological growth*. San Francisco: Jossey-Bass.

Berkowitz, M., Gibbs, J., & Broughton, J. (1980). The relation of moral judgment stage disparity to developmental effects of peer dialogues. *Merrill-Palmer Quarterly, 26*, 341–357.

Berndt, T. J. (1983). Social cognition, social behavior, and children's friendships. In E. T. Higgins, D. N. Ruble, & W. W. Hartup (Eds.), *Social cognition and social development: A sociocultural perspective*. Cambridge, England: Cambridge University Press.

Berndt, T. J. (1984). Sociometric, social-cognitive, and behavioral measures for the study of friendship and popularity. In T. Field, J. L. Roopnarine, & M. Segal (Eds.), *Friendship in normal and handicapped children* (pp. 31–52). Norwood, NJ: Ablex.

Berndt, T. J. (1986a). Children's comments about their friendships. In M. Perlmutter (Ed.), *Minnesota Symposia on Child Psychology: Vol. 18. Cognitive perspectives on children's social and behavioral development* (pp. 189–212). Hillsdale, NJ: Erlbaum.

Berndt, T. J. (1986b). Sharing between friends: Contexts and consequences. In E. C. Mueller & C. R. Cooper (Eds.), *Process and outcome in peer relationships* (pp. 105–127). New York: Academic Press.

Berndt, T. J. (1987a, April). *Changes in friendship and school adjustment after the transition to junior high school*. Paper presented at the biennial meeting of the Society for Research in Child Development, Baltimore.

Berndt, T. J. (1987b). The distinctive features of conversations between friends: Theories, research, and implications for socio-moral development. In W. M. Kurtines & J. L. Gewitz (Eds.), *Moral development through social interaction* (pp. 281–300). New York: Wiley.

Berndt, T. J. (1989). Obtaining support from friends in childhood and adolescence. In D. Belle (Ed.), *Children's social networks and social supports*. New York: Wiley.

Berndt, T. J. (in press). Friendship quality affects adolescents' self-esteem and social behavior. In W. M. Bukowski, A. F. Newcomb, & W. W. Hartup (Eds.), *The company they keep: Friendship during childhood and adolescence*. New York: Cambridge University Press.

Berndt, T. J., & Hawkins, J. A. (1987). *The contribution of supportive friendships to adjustment after the transition to junior high school*. Unpublished manuscript, Purdue University.

Berndt, T. J., Hawkins, J. A., & Hoyle, S. G. (1986). Changes in friendship during a school year: Effects on children's and adolescents' impressions of friendship and sharing with friends. *Child Development, 57*, 1284–1297.

Berndt, T. J., & Hoyle, S. G. (1985). Stability and change in childhood and adolescent friendships. *Developmental Psychology, 21*, 1007–1015.

Berndt, T. J., & Keefe, K. (1993, March). *How friends influence adolescents' adjustment to school*. Paper presented at the biennial meeting of the Society for Research in Child Development, New Orleans.

Berndt, T. J., & Ladd, G. W. (1989). *Peer relationships in child development*. New York: Wiley.

Berndt, T. J., & Perry, T. B. (1986). Children's perceptions of friendships as supportive relationships. *Developmental Psychology, 22*, 640–648.

Berndt, T. J., & Perry, T. B. (1990). Distinctive features and effects of early adolescent friendships. In R. Montemayor, G. R. Adams, & T. P. Gullotta (Eds.), *From childhood to adolescence: A translation period?* (pp. 269–287). Newbury Park, CA: Sage.

Bhavnagri, N., & Parke, R. D. (1991). Parents as direct facilitators of children's peer relationships: Effects of age of child and sex of parent. *Journal of Social and Personal Relationships, 8*, 423–440.

Bierman, K. L. (1986). The relation between social aggression and peer rejection in middle childhood. In R. J. Prinz (Ed.), *Advances in behavioral assessment of children and families* (Vol. 2, pp. 151–178). Greenwich, CT: JAI Press.

Bierman, K. L. (1987). The clinical significance and assessment of poor peer relations: Peer neglect versus peer rejection. *Journal of Developmental and Behavioral Pediatrics, 8*, 233–240.

Bierman, K. L. (1993, March). *Social adjustment problems of aggressive-rejected, aggressive, and rejected boys: A longitudinal analysis*. Paper presented at the biennial meeting of the Society for Research in Child Development, New Orleans.

Bierman, K. L., & McCauley, E. (1987). Children's descriptions of their peer interactions: Useful information for clinical child assessment. *Journal of Clinical Child Psychology, 16*, 9–18.

Bierman, K. L., Smoot, D. L., & Aumiller, K. (1993). Characteristics of aggressive-rejected, aggressive (nonrejected), and rejected (nonaggressive) boys. *Child Development, 64*, 139–151.

Billings, A. G., & Moos, R. H. (1985). Children of parents with unipolar depression: A controlled 1 year follow-up. *Journal of Abnormal Child Psychology, 14*, 149–166.

Blieszner, R., & Adams, R. G. (1992). *Adult friendship*. Newbury Park, CA: Sage.

Block, J. (1978). *The Q-sort method*. Palo Alto, CA: Consulting Psychologists Press.

Blos, P. (1962). *On adolescence: A psychoanalytic interpretation*. New York: Free Press.

Blos, P. (1979). The second individuation process of adolescence. In P. Blos, *The adolescent passage: Developmental issues*. New York: International University Press.

Boivin, M., & Begin, G. (1989). Peer status and self-perception among early elementary school children: The case of rejected children. *Child Development, 60*, 591–596.

Bond, L. A., & Compas, B. E. (Eds.). (1989). *Primary prevention and promotion in the schools*. Newbury Park, CA: Sage.

Bonney, M. E. (1944). Relationship between social success, family size, socioeconomic background, and intelligence among school children grades three to five. *Sociometry, 7*, 26–39.

Bonney, M. E. (1946). A sociometric study of the relationship of some factors to mutual friendships in the elementary, secondary, and college levels. *Sociometry, 7*, 26–39.

Bonney, M. E. (1947). Popular and unpopular children. *Sociometric Monographs, 9*.

Booth, C. L., Rose-Krasnor, L., MacKinnon, J., & Rubin, K. H. (1994). Predicting social adjustment in middle childhood: The role of preschool attachment security and maternal style. *Social Development, 3*, 189–204.

Booth, C. L., Rose-Krasnor, L., & Rubin, K. H. (1991). Relating preschoolers' social competence and their mothers' parenting behaviors to early attachment security and high-risk status. *Journal of Social and Personal Relationships, 8*, 363–382.

Bower, E. M., & Lambert, N. (1961). *A process for in-school screening of emotionally handicapped children*. Princeton, NJ: Educational Testing Service.

Bower, E. M., Shellhammer, T. A., & Dailey, J. M. (1960). School characteristics of male adolescents who later become schizophrenic. *American Journal of Orthopsychiatry, 30*, 712–729.

Bowlby, J. (1969). *Attachment and loss: Vol. 1. Attachment*. New York: Basic Books.

Bowlby, J. (1973). *Attachment and loss: Vol. 2. Separation, anxiety and anger*. New York: Basic Books.

Bowlby, J. (1982). *Attachment and loss: Vol. 1. Attachment* (2nd ed.). London: Hogarth Press.

Brain, R. (1977). *Friends and lovers*. New York: Pocket Books.

Breger, L. (1974). *From instinct to identity: The development of personality*. Englewood Cliffs, NJ: Prentice-Hall.

Bretherton, I. (1985). Attachment theory: Retrospect and prospect. In I. Bretherton & E. Waters (Eds.), Growing points in attachment theory and research. *Monographs of the Society for Research in Child Development, 50*, (1-2, Serial No. 209).

Bretherton, I. (1990). Open communication and internal working models. In R. A. Thompson (Ed.), *Socioemotional development: Nebraska symposium on motivation* (Vol. 36, pp. 57–114). Lincoln, NE: University of Nebraska Press.

Brewer, N., & Smith, J. M. (1989). Social acceptance of mentally retarded children in regular schools in relation to years mainstreamed. *Psychological Reports, 64*, 375–380.

Brofenbrenner, U. (1970). *Two worlds of childhood: U.S. and U.S.S.R.* New York: Sage.

Bronson, W. C. (1981). Toddlers' behaviors with agemates: Issues of interaction, cognition, and affect. *Monographs of Infancy, 1,* 127.

Brown, B. B. (1989). The role of peer groups in adolescents' adjustment to secondary school. In T. J. Berndt & G. W. Ladd (Eds.), *Peer relationships in child development* (pp. 188–216). New York: Wiley.

Brown, B. B. (1990). Peer groups and peer cultures. In S. S. Feldman & G. R. Elliott (Eds.), *At the threshold* (pp. 171–196). Cambridge, MA: Harvard University Press.

Brown, B. B., & Clasen, D. R. (1986, March). *Developmental changes in adolescents' conceptions of peer groups.* Paper presented at the biennial meeting of the Society for Research in Adolescence, Madison, WI.

Brown, B. B., Clasen, D. R., & Niess, J. D. (1987, April). *Smoke through the looking glass: Adolescents' perceptions of the peer group status.* Paper presented at the biennial meeting of the Society for Research in Child Development, Baltimore, MD.

Brown, B. B., Eicher, S. A., & Petrie, S. (1986). The importance of peer group ("crowd") affiliation in adolescence. *Journal of Adolescence, 9*, 73–96.

Buhler, C. (1931). The social behavior of the child. In C. Murchinson (Ed.), *Handbook of child psychology* (pp. 392–431). Worchester, MA: Clark University Press.

Buhrmester, D. (1990). Intimacy of friendship, interpersonal competence, and adjustment during preadolescence and adolescence. *Child Development, 61,* 1101–1111.

Buhrmester, D. (1992). The development courses of sibling and peer relationships. In F. Boer & J. Dunn (Eds.), *Children's sibling relationships: Developmental and clinical issues* (pp. 19–40). Hillsdale, NJ: Erlbaum.

Buhrmester, D., & Furman, W. (1986). The changing functions of friends in childhood. A neo-Sullivan perspective. In V. J. Derlega & B. A. Winstead (Eds.), *Friendship and social interaction* (pp. 41–62). New York: Springer-Verlag.

Bukowski, W. M., & Hoza, B. (1989). Popularity and friendship: Issues in theory, measurement, and outcome. In T. J. Berndt & G. W. Ladd (Eds.), *Peer relations in child development* (pp. 15–45). New York: Wiley.

Bukowski, W. M., Hoza, B., & Newcomb, A. F. (in press). Using rating scale and nomination techniques to measure friendships and popularity. *Journal of Social and Personal Relationships.*

Bukowski, W. M., & Newcomb, A. F. (1987, April). *Friendship quality, popularity, and the self during early adolescence.* Paper presented at the biennial meeting of the Society for Research in Child Development, Baltimore.

Bussey, K., & Perry, D. G. (1982). Same-sex initiation? *Sex Roles, 8,* 773–784.

Cairns, R. B. (1979). *Social development: The origins and plasticity of interchanges.* San Francisco: Freeman.

Cairns, R. B. (1983). Sociometry, psychometry, and social structure: A commentary on six recent studies of popular, rejected, and neglected children. *Merrill-Palmer Quarterly, 29,* 429–438.

Cairns, R. B., & Cairns, B. D. (1991). Social cognition and social networks: A developmental perspective. In D. J. Pepler & K. H. Rubin (Eds.), *The development and treatment of childhood aggression* (pp. 249–276). Hillsdale, NJ: Erlbaum.

Cairns, R. B., Cairns, B. D., & Neckerman, H. J. (1989). Early school dropout: Configurations and determinants. *Child Development, 60,* 1437–1452.

Cairns, R. B., Cairns, B. D., Neckerman, H., Gest, S., & Gariépy, J. L. (1988). Social networks and aggressive behavior: Peer support or peer rejection? *Developmental Psychology, 24,* 815–823.

Campbell, S. B., Pierce, E. W., March, C. L., & Ewing, L. J. (1991). Noncompliant behavior, overactivity, and family stress as predictors of negative maternal control with preschool children. *Development and Psychopathology, 3,* 175–190.

Cantrell, S., & Prinz, R. J. (1985). Multiple perspectives of rejected, neglected, and accepted children: Relationship between sociometric status and behavioral characteristics. *Journal of Consulting and Clinical Psychology, 53,* 884–889.

Carlson, C. L., Lahey, B. B., & Neeper, R. (1984.) Peer assessment of social behavior of accepted, rejected, and neglected children. *Journal of Abnormal Child Psychology, 12,* 189–198.

Carter, D. E., Detine-Carter, L., & Benson, F. W. (1980). Interracial acceptance in the classroom. In H. C. Foot, A. J. Chapman, & J. R. Smith (Eds.), *Friendship and social relations in children* (pp. 117–143). New York: Wiley.

Cassidy, J., & Asher, S. R. (1992). Loneliness and peer relations in young children. *Child Development, 63,* 350–365.

Castlebury, S., & Arnold, J. (1988). Early adolescent perceptions of informal groups in a middle school. *Journal of Early Adolescence, 8,* 97–107.

Cauce, A. M. (1986). Social networks, and social competence: Exploring the effects of early adolescent friendships. *American Journal of Community Psychology, 14,* 607–628.

Charlesworth, R., & Hartup, W. W. (1967). Positive social reinforcement in the nursery school peer group. *Child Development, 38,* 993–1002.

Chen, X., & Rubin, K. H. (1992). Correlates of peer acceptance in a Chinese sample of six-year-olds. *International Journal of Behavioral Development, 15,* 259–273.

Chen, X., & Rubin, K. H. (1994). Family conditions, parental acceptance, and social competence and aggression in Chinese children. *Social Development, 3,* 269–290.

Chen, X., Rubin, K. H., & Sun, Y. (1992). Social reputation and peer relationships in Chinese and Canadian children: A cross-cultural study. *Child Development, 63,* 1336–1343.

Cheney, D. L., & Seyfarth, R. M. (1990). The representation of social relations by monkeys. *Cognition, 37,* 167–196.

Chittenden, G. E. (1942). An experimental study in measuring and modifying assertive behavior in young children. *Monographs of the Society for Research in Child Development, 7*(1, Serial No. 31).

Cicchetti, D. (1989). How research on child maltreatment has informed the study of child development: Perspectives from developmental psychopathology. In D. Cicchetti & V. Carlson (Eds.), *Child maltreatment: Research and theory on the causes and consequences of child abuse and neglect* (pp. 377–431). New York: Cambridge University Press.

Cicchetti, D. (1990). A historical perspective on the discipline of developmental psychopathology. In J. Rolf, A. Masten, D. Cicchetti, K. Nuechterlein, & S. Weintraub (Eds.), *Risk and protective factors in the development of psychopathology* (pp. 2–28). New York: Cambridge University Press.

Cicchetti, D. (1993). Developmental psychopathology: Reactions, reflections, projections. *Developmental Review, 13,* 471–502.

Cicchetti, D., & Lynch, M. (1993). Toward an ecological/transactional model of community violence and child maltreatment: Consequences for children's development. *Psychiatry: Interpersonal and Biological Processes, 56,* 96–118.

Cicchetti, D., Lynch, M., Shonk, S., & Manly, J. T. (1992). An organizational perspective on peer relations in maltreated children. In R. D. Parke & G. W. Ladd (Eds.), *Family-peer relationships: Modes of linkage* (pp. 345–384). Hillsdale, NJ: Erlbaum.

Cicchetti, D., Rogosch, F. A., Lynch, M., & Holt, K. D. (1993). Resilience in maltreated children: Processes leading to adaptive outcomes. *Development and Psychopathology, 5,* 6–43.

Cicchetti, D., & Schneider-Rosen, K. (1984). Toward a transactional model of child depression. *New Directions for Child Development.* No. 26, pp. 5–27.

Cicchetti, D., & Toth, S. L. (1992). The role of developmental theory in prevention and intervention. *Development and Psychopathology, 4,* 489–493.

Cicchetti, D., Toth, S. L., & Bush, M. (1988). Developmental psychopathology and incompetence in childhood: Suggestions for intervention. In B. Lahey & A. Kazdin (Eds.), *Advances in clinical child psychology* (pp. 1–71). New York: Plenum.

Cillessen, A. H., van IJzendoorn, H. W., van Leishout, C. F., & Hartup, W. W. (1992). Heterogeneity among peer-rejected boys: Subtypes and stabilities. *Child Development, 63,* 893–905.

Cillessen, A. H., van Leishout, C. F., & Haselager, G. J. (1992, August). *Children's problems caused by consistent rejection in early elementary school.* Paper presented at the Centennial Convention of the American Psychological Association, Washington, DC.

Cohen, S., & Wills, T. A. (1985). Stress, social support, and the buffering hypothesis. *Psychological Bulletin, 98,* 310–357.

Cohen, J. S., & Woody, E. (1991, April). *Maternal involvement in children's peer relationships in middle childhood.* Paper presented at the biennial meeting of the Society for Research in Child Development, Seattle.

Cohn, D. A. (1990). Child-mother attachment of six-year-olds and social competence at school. *Child Development, 61,* 152–162.

Cohn, D. A., Patterson, C., & Christopoulos, C. (1991). The family and children's peer relations. *Journal of Social and Personal Relationships, 8,* 315–346.

Coie, J. D. (1990). Towards a theory of peer rejection. In S. R. Asher & J. D. Coie (Eds.), *Peer rejection in childhood* (pp. 365–401). Cambridge, MA: Cambridge University Press.

Coie, J. D., & Dodge, K. A. (1983). Continuities and changes in children's social status: A five-year longitudinal study. *Merrill-Palmer Quarterly, 29,* 261–281.

Coie, J. D., Dodge, K. A., & Coppotelli, H. (1982). Dimensions and types of social status: A cross-age perspective. *Developmental Psychology, 18,* 557–570.

Coie, J. D., Dodge, K., & Kupersmidt, J. B. (1990). Peer group behavior and social status. In S. R. Asher & J. D. Coie (Eds.), *Peer rejection in childhood.* New York: Cambridge University Press.

Coie, J. D., & Kupersmidt, J. (1983). A behavioral analysis of emerging social status in boys' groups. *Child Development, 54,* 1400–1416.

Coie, J. D., Lochman, J. E., Terry, R., & Hyman, C. (1992). Predicting early adolescent disorder from childhood aggression and peer rejection. *Journal of Consulting and Clinical Psychology, 60,* 783–792.

Cole, D. A., & Carpentieri, S. (1990). Social status and the comorbidity of child depression and conduct disorder. *Journal of Consulting and Clinical Psychology, 58,* 748–757.

Coleman, J. S. (1961). *The adolescent society.* New York: Free Press.

Compas, B. E. (1987). Coping with stress during childhood and adolescence. *Psychological Bulletin, 101,* 393–403.

Conger, J. J., & Miller, W. C. (1966). *Personality, social class, and delinquency.* New York: Wiley.

Conger, R. D., Conger, K. L., Elder, G. H., Jr., Lorenz, F., Simons, R., & Whitbeck, L. (1992). A family process model of economic hardship and adjustment of early adolescent boys. *Child Development, 63,* 526–541.

Conger, R. D., Conger, K. L., Elder, G. H., Jr., Lorenz, F., Simons, R., & Whitbeck, L. (1993). Family economic stress and adjustment of early adolescent girls. *Developmental Psychology, 29,* 206–219.

Conger, R. D., Ge, X., Elder, G. H., Lorenz, F. O., & Simons, R. L. (1994). Economic stress, coercive family process, and developmental problems of adolescents. *Child Development, 65,* 541–561.

Conger, R. D., McCarty, J. A., Yang, R. K., Lahey, B. B., & Kropp, J. P. (1984). Perception of child, child-rearing values, and emotional distress as mediating links between environmental stressors and observed maternal behavior. *Child Development, 55,* 2234–2247.

Conway, L. P., & Hansen, D. J. (1989). Social behavior of physically abused and neglected children: A critical review. *Clinical Psychology Review, 9,* 627–652.

Cooley, C. H. (1902). *Human nature and the social order.* New York Scribner's.

Cooper, C. R., & Cooper, R. G. (1992). Links between adolescents' relationships with their parents and peers: Models, evidence, and mechanisms. In R. D. Parke & G. W. Ladd (Eds.), *Family-peer relationships: Modes of linkage* (pp. 135–158). Hillsdale, NJ: Erlbaum.

Corsaro, W. A. (1985). *Friendship and peer culture in the early years.* Norwood, NJ: Ablex.

Corsaro, W. A., & Miller, P. J. (Eds.). (1992). *Interpretative approaches to children's socialization.* San Francisco: Jossey-Bass.

Corsaro, W. A., & Rizzo, T. A. (1988). *Discussione* and friendship: So cialization processes in the peer culture of Italian nursery school children. *American Sociological Review, 53,* 879–894.

Cowen, E. L., Pedersen, A., Babigian, H., Izzo, L. D., & Trost, M. A. (1973). Long-term follow-up of early detected vulnerable children. *Journal of Consulting and Clinical Psychology, 41,* 438–446.

Coyne, J. C. (1976). Toward an interactional description of depression. *Psychiatry, 39,* 28–40.

Crick, N. R., & Dodge, K. A. (1994). A review and reformulation of so cial information-processing mechanisms in children's social adjust ment. *Psychological Bulletin, 115,* 74–101.

Crick, N. R., & Ladd, G. W. (1993). Children's perceptions of their peer experiences: Attributions, loneliness, social anxiety, and so cial avoidance. *Developmental Psychology, 29,* 244–254.

Crockett, L., Losoff, M., & Peterson, A. C. (1984). Perceptions of the peer group and friendship in early adolescence. *Journal of Early Adolescence, 4,* 155–181.

Csikszentmihalyi, M., & Larson, R. (1984). *Being adolescent.* New York: Basic Books.

Cummings, E. M. (1987). Coping with background anger in early child hood. *Child Development, 58,* 976–984.

Cummings, E. M., Iannotti, R. J., & Zahn-Waxler, C. (1985). The influ ence of conflicts among adults on the emotions and aggression of young children. *Developmental Psychology, 21,* 495–507.

Damon, W. (1977). *The social world of the child.* San Francisco: Jossey-Bass.

Damon, W., & Killen, M. (1982). Peer interaction and the process of change in children's moral reasoning. *Merrill-Palmer Quarterly, 28,* 347–378.

Dawe, H. C. (1934). Analysis of two hundred quarrels of preschool chil dren. *Child Development, 5,* 135–157.

Denham, S. A., McKinley, M., Couchoud, E. A., & Holt, R. (1990). Emotional and behavioral predictors of preschool peer ratings. *Child Development, 61,* 1145–1152.

Denzin, N. K. (1977). *Childhood socialization.* San Francisco: Jossey-Bass.

DeRosier, M. E., Kupersmidt, J. B., & Patterson, C. (1993). *Children's academic and behavioral adjustment as a function of the chronicity and proximity of peer rejection.* Manuscript submitted for publication.

de Waal, F. B. M. (1989). *Peacemaking among primates.* Cambridge, MA: Harvard University Press.

Diaz, R. M., & Berndt, T. J. (1982). Children's knowledge of a best friend: Fact or fancy? *Developmental Psychology, 18,* 787–794.

Dishion, T. J. (1990). The family ecology of boys' peer relations in middle childhood. *Child Development, 61,* 874–892.

Dix, T. (1991). The affective organization of parenting: Adaptive and maladaptive processes. *Psychological Bulletin, 110,* 3–25.

Dodge, K. A. (1980). Social cognition and children's aggressive behav ior. *Child Development, 51,* 162–170.

Dodge, K. A. (1983). Behavioral antecedents of peer social status. *Child Development, 54,* 1386–1399.

Dodge, K. A. (1986). A social information processing model of social competence in children. In M. Perlmutter (Ed.), *Minnesota Sym posium on Child Psychology* (Vol. 18. pp. 77–125). Hillsdale, NJ: Erlbaum.

Dodge, K. A. (1990). Nature versus nurture in childhood conduct disor der: It is time to ask a different question. *Developmental Psychol ogy, 26,* 698–701.

Dodge, K. A. (1993). Social-cognitive mechanism in the development of conduct disorder and depression. *Annual Review of Psychology, 44,* 559–584.

Dodge, K. A., Coie, J. D., & Brakke, N. P. (1982). Behavior patterns of socially rejected and neglected preadolescents: The role of social approach and aggression. *Journal of Abnormal Child Psychology, 10,* 389–410.

Dodge, K. A., Murphy, R. R., & Buchsbaum, K. (1984). The assessment of intention-cue detection skills in children: Implications for devel opmental psychopathology. *Child Development, 55,* 163–173.

Dodge, K. A., Pettit, G. S., & Bates, J. E. (1990). Mechanisms in the cycle of violence. *Science, 250,* 1678–1683.

Dodge, K. A., Pettit, G. S., & Bates, J. E. (1994). Socialization media tors of the relation between socioeconomic status and child conduct problems. *Child Development, 65,* 649–665.

Dodge, K. A., Pettit, G. S., McClaskey, C. L., & Brown, M. M. (1986). Social competence in children. *Monographs of the Society for Re search in Child Development, 51(2),* 1–80.

Dodge, K. A., & Price, J. M. (in press). On the relation between social information processing and socially-competent behavior in early school-aged children. *Child Development.*

Dodge, K. A., Price, J. M., Coie, J. D., & Christopoulos, C. (1990). On the development of aggressive dyadic relationships in boys' peer groups. *Human Development, 33,* 20–270.

Doise, W., & Mugny, G. (1984). *The social development of the intellect.* Oxford: Pergamon.

Doise, W., Mugny, G., & Perret-Clermont, A.-N. (1975). Social interac tion and the development of cognitive operations. *European Journal of Social Psychology, 5,* 367–383.

Dorval, B., & Ekerman, C. O. (1984). Developmental trends in the qual ity of conversation achieved by small groups of acquainted peers. *Monographs of the Society for Research in Child Development, 49,* 1–72. (Serial No. 206).

Douvan, E., & Adelson, J. (1966). *The adolescent experience.* New York: Wiley.

Downey, G., & Coyne, J. C. (1990). Children of depressed parents: An integrative review. *Psychological Bulletin, 108,* 50–76.

Doyle, A. (1982). Friends, acquaintances, and strangers: The influence of familiarity and ethnolinguistic background on social interaction. In K. H. Rubin & H. S. Ross (Eds.), *Peer relations and social skills in childhood.* New York: Springer-Verlag.

Dubow, E. F., & Tisak, J. (1989). The relation between stressful life events and adjustment in elementary school children: The role of so cial support and social problem-solving skills. *Child Development, 60,* 1412–1423.

Dubow, E. F., Tisak, J., Causey, D., Hryshko, A., & Ried, G. (1991). A two-year longitudinal study of stressful life events, social support, and social problem-solving skills: Contributions to children's be havioral and academic adjustment. *Child Development, 62,* 583–599.

Duck, S. (Ed.). (1993). *Learning about relationships.* Beverly Hills: Sage.

Dunn, J. (1988). *The beginnings of social understanding.* Cambridge, MA: Harvard University Press.

Dunn, J. (1993). *Young children's close relationships: Beyond attach ment.* Newbury Park, CA: Sage.

Dunphy, D. C. (1963). The social structure of urban adolescent peer groups. *Sociometry, 26,* 230–246.

Dymond, R. F. (1948). A preliminary investigation of the relation of in sight and empathy. *Journal of Consulting Psychology, 12,* 228–233.

Dymond, R. F. (1949). A scale for the measurement of empathic ability. *Journal of Consulting Psychology, 13,* 127–133.

Eccles, J. S., Midgley, C., Wigfield, A., Buchanan, C. M., Rueman, D., Flanagan, C., & MacIver, D. (1993). Development during adolescence: The impact of stage-environmental fit on young adolescents' experiences in schools and in families. *American Psychologist, 48,* 90–101.

Eckerman, C. O., Davis, C. C., & Didow, S. M. (1989). Toddlers' emerging ways of achieving social coordinations with a peer. *Child Development, 60,* 440–453.

Eckerman, C. O., & Stein, M. R. (1982). The toddler's emerging interactive skills. In K. H. Rubin & H. S. Ross (Eds.), *Peer relationships and social skills in childhood* (pp. 47–71). New York: Springer-Verlag.

Eckerman, C. O., & Stein, M. R. (1990). How imitation begets imitation and toddler's generation of games. *Developmental Psychology, 26,* 370–378.

Eder, D. (1985). The cycle of popularity: Interpersonal relations among female adolescents. *Sociology of Education, 58,* 154–165.

Eder, D., & Hallinan, M. T. (1978). Sex differences in children's friendships. *American Sociological Review, 13,* 237–250.

Egeland, B., & Farber, E. A. (1984). Infant-toddler attachment: Factors related to its development and changes over time. *Child Development, 55,* 753–771.

Eisenberg, N. (1990). Prosocial development in early and mid-adolescence. In R. Montemayor, G. R. Adams, T. P. Gullotta (Eds.), *From childhood to adolescence: A transitional period?* (pp. 240–268). Beverly Hills, CA: Sage.

Eisenberg, N., Tyron, K., & Cameron, E. (1984). The relation of preschoolers' peer interaction to their sex-typed toy choices. *Child Development, 55,* 1044–1050.

Elicker, J., Englund, M., & Sroufe, L. A. (1992). Predicting peer competence and peer relationships in childhood from early parent-child relationships. In R. Parke & G. Ladd (Eds.), *Family-peer relationships: Modes of linkage.* Hillsdale, NJ: Erlbaum.

Emery, R. E. (1992). Family conflicts and their developmental implications: A conceptual analysis of meanings for the structure of relationships. In C. U. Shantz & W. W. Hartup (Eds.), *Conflict in child and adolescent development* (pp. 270–298). New York: Cambridge University Press.

Engfer, A. (1986). Antecedent of problem behaviors in infancy. In G. A. Kohnstamm (Ed.), *Temperament discussed: Temperament and development in infancy and childhood* (pp. 155–180). Amsterdam: Stwets & Zeitlinger.

Epstein, J. L. (1986). Friendship selection: Developmental and environmental influences. In E. Mueller & C. Cooper (Eds.), *Process and outcome in peer relationships.* New York: Academic Press.

Erickson, M. F., Sroufe, L. A., & Egeland, B. (1985). The relationship between quality of attachment and behaviour problems in preschool in a high-risk sample. In I. Bretherton & E. Waters (Eds.), *Growing points of attachment theory and research: Monographs of the Society for Research in Child Development, 50* (1-2, Serial No. 209), 147–166.

Erwin, P. (1993). *Friendship and peer relations in children.* New York: Wiley.

Fainsilber-Katz, L., & Gottman, J. M. (1993). Patterns of marital conflict predict children's internalizing and externalizing behaviors. *Developmental Psychology, 29,* 940–950.

Faust, J., Baum, C. G., & Forehand, R. (1985). An examination of the association between social relationships and depression in early adolescence. *Journal of Applied Developmental Psychology, 6,* 291–297.

Feldman, N. S., & Ruble, D. N. (1986). *The effect of personal relevance on dispositional inference: A developmental analysis.* Unpublished manuscript.

Feltham, R. F., Doyle, A. B., Schwartzman, A. E., Serbin, L. A., & Ledingham, J. E. (1985). Friendship in normal and socially deviant children. *Journal of Early Adolescence, 5,* 371–382.

Festinger, L. (1954). A theory of social comparison processes. *Human Relations, 7,* 117–140.

Fincham, F. D., & Bradbury, T. N. (1987). Cognitive processes and conflict in close relationships: An attribution-efficacy model. *Journal of Personality and Social Psychology, 53,* 1106–1118.

Field, T. (1979). Infant behaviors directed towards peers and adults in the presence and absence of mother. *Infant Behavior and Development, 2,* 47–54.

Fine, G. A. (1977). The social components of children's gossip. *Journal of Communications, 27,* 281–286.

Fine, G. A. (1981). Friends, impression management, and preadolescent behavior. In S. R. Asher & J. M. Gottman (Eds.), *The development of children's friendships* (pp. 29–52). New York: Cambridge University Press.

Fine, G. A. (1986). The social organization of adolescent gossip: The rhetoric of moral evaluation. In J. Cook-Gumperz, W. A. Corsaro, & J. Streek (Eds.), *Children's social worlds and children's language* (pp. 404–423). New York: Mouton de Gruyter.

Fine, G. A. (1987). *With the boys: Little league baseball and preadolescent culture.* Chicago: University of Chicago Press.

Finnie, V., & Russell, A. (1988). Preschool children's social status and their mothers' behavior and knowledge in the supervisory role. *Developmental Psychology, 24,* 789–801.

Fleming, D., & Ricks, D. F. (1970). Emotions of children before schizophrenia and before character disorder. In M. Roff & D. F. Ricks (Eds.), *Life history research in psychopathology* (Vol. 1, pp. 240–264). Minneapolis: University of Minnesota Press.

Flicek, M. (1992). Social status of boys with both academic problems and attention-deficit hyperactivity disorder. *Journal of Abnormal Child Psychology, 20,* 353–366.

Fogel, A. (1979). Peer- vs. mother-directed behavior in 1- to 3-month-old infants. *Infant Behavior and Development, 2,* 215–226.

Forbes, D., Katz, M., & Paul, B. (1986). "Frame talk": A dramatistic analysis of children's fantasy play. In E. C. Mueller & C. R. Cooper (Eds.), *Process and outcome in peer relationships* (pp. 249–266). New York: Academic.

Frazee, H. E. (1953). Children who later become schizophrenic. *Smith College Studies in Social Work, 23,* 125–149.

French, D. C. (1988). Heterogeneity of peer rejected boys: Aggressive and nonaggressive subtypes. *Child Development, 59,* 976–985.

French, D. C. (1990). Heterogeneity of peer rejected girls. *Child Development, 61,* 2028–2031.

Freud, A. (1952). The role of bodily illness in the mental life of children. *Psychoanalytic Study of the Child, 7,* 69–81.

Friedlander, D. (1945). Personality development of twenty-seven children who later become psychotic. *Journal of Abnormal Social Psychology, 40,* 330–335.

Furfey, P. H. (1927). Some factors influencing the selection of boys' chums. *Journal of Applied Psychology, 11,* 47–51.

Furman, W. (1984). Issues in the assessment of social skills of normal and handicapped children. In T. Field, M. Siegal, & J. Roopnarine

(Eds.), *Friendships of normal and handicapped children*. New York: Ablex.

Furman, W., & Buhrmester, D. (1985). Children's perceptions of the personal relationships in their social networks. *Developmental Psychology, 21,* 1016–1024.

Furman, W., & Robbins, P. (1985). What's the point: Selection of treatment objectives. In B. Schneider, K. H. Rubin, & J. E. Ledingham (Eds.), *Children's peer relations: Issues in assessment and intervention* (pp. 41–54). New York: Springer-Verlag.

Garmezy, N. (1974). Children at risk: The search for antecedents of schizophrenia: Part 1. Conceptual models and research methods. *Schizophrenia Bulletin, 1,* 14–89.

Garmezy, N., & Rutter, M. (Eds.). (1983). *Stress, coping, and development in children*. New York: McGraw-Hill.

Garvey, C. (1986). Peer relations and the growth of communication. In E. Mueller & C. Cooper (Eds.), *Process and outcome in peer relationships*. New York: Academic Press.

Gavin, L. A., & Furman, W. (1989). Age differences in adolescents' perceptions of their peer groups. *Developmental Psychology, 25,* 827–834.

Gelfand, D. M., & Teti, D. M. (1990). The effects of maternal depression on children. *Clinical Psychological Review, 10,* 329–353.

Goetz, T. E., & Dweck, C. S. (1980). Learned helplessness in social situations. *Child Development, 39,* 246–255.

Goldman, J. A., Corsini, D. A., & de Urioste, R. (1980). Implications of positive and negative sociometric status for assessing the social competence of young children. *Journal of Applied Developmental Psychology, 1,* 209–220.

Goldman, B. D., & Ross, H. S. (1978). Social skills in action: An analysis of early peer games. In J. Glick & K. A. Clarke-Stewart (Eds.), *Studies in social and cognitive development: Vol. 1. The development of social understanding*. New York: Gardner Press.

Goodenough, F. L. (1931). *Anger in young children*. Minneapolis: University of Minnesota Press.

Gottlieb, G. (1991). Experiential canalization of behavioral development: Theory. *Developmental Psychology, 27,* 4–13.

Gottman, J. M. (1977). Toward a definition of social isolation in children. *Child Development, 48,* 513–517.

Gottman, J. M. (1983). How children become friends. *Monographs of the Society for Research in Child Development, 48* (3, Serial No. 201).

Gottman, J. M., & Katz, L. F. (1989). Effects of marital discord on young children's peer interactions and health. *Developmental Psychology, 25,* 373–381.

Gottman, J. M., & Metettal, G. (1986). Speculations about social and affective development: Friendship and acquaintanceship through adolescence. In J. M. Gottman & J. G. Parker (Eds.), *Conversation of friends: Speculations on affective development* (pp. 192–237). New York: Cambridge University Press.

Gottman, J. M., & Parker, J. G. (Eds.). (1986). *Conversation of friends: Speculations on affective development*. New York: Cambridge University Press.

Gottman, J. M., & Parkhurst, J. T. (1980). A developmental theory of friendship and acquaintanceship processes. In W. A. Collins (Ed.), *Minnesota symposia on child development: Vol. 13. Development of cognition, affect, and social relations* (pp. 197–253). Hillsdale, NJ: Erlbaum.

Gould, M. S., Shaffer, D., & Rutter, M. (1984, Sept.). *UK/WHO Study of ICD-9*. Working paper for NIMH conference on the definition and measurement of psychopathology in children and adolescents. Washington, DC.

Green, K. D., Forehand, R., Beck, S. J., & Vosk, B. (1980). An assessment of the relationship among measures of children's social competence and children's academic adjustment. *Child Development, 51,* 1149–1156.

Gresham, F. (1981). Validity of social skills measures for assessing social competence in low-status children: A multivariate investigation. *Developmental Psychology, 17,* 390–398.

Grossman, K. E., & Grossman, K. (in press). Attachment quality as an organizer of emotional and behavioral responses. In P. Marris, J. Stevenson-Hinde, & C. Parkes (Eds.), *Attachment across the life cycle*. New York: Rutledge.

Grunebaum, H., & Solomon, L. (1987). Peer relationships, self-esteem, and the self. *International Journal of Group Psychotherapy, 37,* 475–513.

Grusec, J. E., & Lytton, H. (1988). *Social development*. New York: Springer-Verlag.

Grych, J. H., & Fincham, F. D. (1990). Marital conflict and children's adjustment: A cognitive-contextual framework. *Psychological Bulletin, 108,* 267–290.

Grych, J. H., Seid, M., Fincham, F. D. (1991, April). *Children's cognitive and affective responses to different forms of interparental conflict*. Paper presented at the biennial meeting of the Society for Research in Child Development, Seattle, WA.

Gurland, B., Yorkston, N., Frank, L., & Stone, A. (1967). *The structured and scaled interview to assess maladjustment*. Mimeographed booklet, Biometric Research, Department of Mental Hygiene, New York.

Hammen, C. (1988). Self-cognitions, stressful events and the prediction of depression in children of depressed mothers. *Journal of Abnormal Child Psychology, 16,* 347–360.

Hallinan, M. T. (1981). Recent advances in sociometry. In S. R. Asher & J. M. Gottman (Eds.), *The development of children's friendships* (pp. 91–115). New York: Cambridge University Press.

Hanfmann, E. P. (1935). Social structure of a group of kindergarten children. *American Journal of Orthopsychiatry, 5,* 407–410.

Hansell, S. (1981). Ego development and peer friendship networks. *Sociology of Education, 54,* 51–63.

Hansell, S. (1982). *The adolescent friendship network as a source of stress and support in school*. Paper presented at the National Conference on Social Stress, University of New Hampshire.

Hart, C. H., DeWolf, D., Wozniak, P., & Burt, D. C. (1992). Maternal and paternal disciplinary styles: Relations with preschoolers' playground behavioral orientations and peer status. *Child Development, 63,* 879–892.

Harter, S. (1982). The perceived competence scale for children. *Child Development, 53,* 89–97.

Hartup, W. W. (1970). Peer interaction and social organization. In P. H. Mussen (Ed.), *Carmichael's manual of child psychology* (Vol. 2, pp. 361–456). New York: Wiley.

Hartup, W. W. (1983). Peer relations. In P. H. Mussen (Ed.), *Handbook of child psychology: Vol. 4. Socialization, personality, and social development* (pp. 103–196). New York: Wiley.

Hartup, W. W. (1984). The peer context in middle childhood. In W. A. Collins (Ed.), *Development during middle childhood: The years from six to twelve* (pp. 240–282). Washington, DC: National Academy Press.

Hartup, W. W. (1985). Relationships and their significance in cognitive development. In R. A. Hinde, A. Perret-Clermont, & J. Stevenson-

Hinde (Eds.), *Social relationships and cognitive development* (pp. 66–82). Oxford, England: Clarendon Press.

Hartup, W. W. (1986). On relationships and development. In W. W. Hartup & Z. Rubin (Eds.), *Relationships and development* (pp. 1–26). Hillsdale, NJ: Erlbaum.

Hartup, W. W. (1989a). Behavioral manifestations of children's friendships. In T. J. Berndt & G. W. Ladd (Eds.), *Peer relationships in child development* (pp. 46–70). New York: Wiley.

Hartup, W. W. (1989b). Social relationships and their developmental significance. *American Psychologist, 44,* 120–126.

Hartup, W. W. (1992a). Conflict and friendship relations. In C. U. Shantz & W. W. Hartup (Eds.), *Conflict in child and adolescent development* (pp. 185–215). Cambridge, England: Cambridge University Press.

Hartup, W. W. (1992b). Friendships and their developmental significance. In H. McGurk (Ed.), *Childhood social development: Contemporary perspectives* (pp. 175–205). Hillsdale, NJ: Erlbaum.

Hartup, W. W. (1993). Adolescents and their friends. In B. Laursen, *Close friendships in adolescence* (pp. 3–22). San Francisco: Jossey-Bass.

Hartup, W. W., Glazer, J. A., & Charlesworth, R. (1967). Peer reinforcement and sociometric status. *Child Development, 38,* 1017–1024.

Hartup, W. W., & Laursen, B. (1991). Relationships as developmental contexts. In R. Cohen & A. W. Siegel (Eds.), *Context and development* (pp. 253–279). Hillsdale, NJ: Erlbaum.

Hartshorne, H., & May, M. S. (1929). *Studies in the nature of character: Vol. 1. Studies in self-control.* New York: Macmillan.

Havighurst, R. J. (1953). *Human development and education.* New York: Longmans, Green.

Hay, D., & Ross, H. (1982). The social nature of early conflict. *Child Development, 53,* 105–113.

Hayden-Thompson, L., Rubin, K. H., & Hymel, S. (1987). Sex preferences in sociometric choices. *Developmental Psychology, 23,* 559–562.

Hays, R. B. (1988). Friendship. In S. W. Duck (Ed.), *Handbook of personal relationships: Theory, research, and interventions* (pp. 391–408). London: Wiley.

Heinlein, L., & Spinner, B. (1985, April). *Measuring emotional loneliness in children.* Paper presented at the biennial meeting of the Society for Research in Child Development, Toronto.

Hetherington, E. M., Cox, M., & Cox, R. (1979). Play and social interaction in children following divorce. *Journal of Social Issues, 35,* 26–49.

Higgins, E. T., & Parsons, J. E. (1983). Social cognition and the social life of the child: Stages as subcultures. In E. T. Higgins, D. N. Ruble, & W. W. Hartup (Eds.), *Social cognition and social development* (pp. 15–62). Cambridge, England: Cambridge University Press.

Hinde, R. A. (1979). *Towards understanding relationships.* London: Academic Press.

Hinde, R. A., & Stevenson-Hinde, J. (1986). Relating childhood relationships to individual characteristics. In W. W. Hartup & Z. Rubin (Eds.), *Relationships and development.* Hillsdale, NJ: Erlbaum.

Hinshaw, S. P., Lahey, B. B., & Hart, E. L. (1993). Issues of taxonomy and comorbidity in the development of conduct disorder. *Development and Psychopathology, 5,* 31–49.

Hirsch, B. J., & DuBois, D. L. (1989). The school-nonschool ecology of early adolescent friendships. In D. Belle (Ed.), *Children's social networks and social supports* (pp. 260–274). New York: Wiley.

Hollos, M., & Cowan, P. A. (1973). Social isolation and cognitive development: Logical operations and role-taking abilities in three Norwegian social settings. *Child Development, 44,* 630–641.

Howes, C. (1983). Patterns of friendship. *Child Development, 54,* 1041–1053.

Howes, C. (1988). Peer interaction of young children. *Monographs of the Society for Research in Child Development, 53* (Serial No. 217).

Howes, C. (1992). *The collaborative construction of pretend.* New York: SUNY Press.

Humphreys, A. P., & Smith, P. K. (1987). Rough and tumble, friendship, and dominance in schoolchildren: Evidence of continuity and change with age. *Child Development, 58,* 201–212.

Hurlock, E. B. (1927). The use of group rivalry as an incentive. *Journal of Abnormal Social Psychology, 22,* 278–290.

Huston, A. C. (1983). Sex-typing. In P. H. Mussen (Ed.), *Handbook of child psychology* (Vol. 4, pp. 103–196). New York: Wiley.

Huston, A. C., & Alvarez, M. (1990). The socialization context of gender role development in early adolescence. In R. Montemayor, G. R. Adams, & T. P. Gullotta (Eds.), *From childhood to adolescence: A transitional period?* (pp. 156–179). Newbury Park, CA: Sage.

Hutton, J. B. (1985). What reasons are given by teachers who refer problem behavior students? *Psychology in the Schools, 22,* 79–84.

Hymel, S. (1983, April). *Social isolation and rejection in children: The child's perspective.* Paper presented at the biennial meeting of the Society for Research in Child Development, Detroit.

Hymel, S. (1986). Interpretations of peer behavior: Affective bias in childhood and adolescence. *Child Development, 57,* 431–445.

Hymel, S., Bowker, A., & Woody, E. (1993). Aggressive versus withdrawn unpopular children: Variations in peer and self-perceptions in multiple domains. *Child Development, 64,* 879–896.

Hymel, S., & Franke, S. (1985). Children's peer relations: Assessing self-perceptions. In B. H. Schneider, K. H. Rubin, & J. E. Ledingham (Eds.), *Children's peer relationships: Issues in assessment and intervention* (pp. 75–92). New York: Springer-Verlag.

Hymel, S., & Rubin, K. H. (1985). Children with peer relationship and social skills problems: Conceptual, methodological, and developmental issues. In G. J. Whitehurst (Ed.), *Annals of Child Development* (Vol. 2). Greenwich, CT: JAI Press.

Hymel, S., Rubin, K. H., Rowden, L., & Le Mare, L. (1990). Children's peer relationships: Longitudinal predictions of internalizing and externalizing problems from middle to late childhood. *Child Development, 61,* 2004–2021.

Ignico, A. A. (1989). Development and verification of a gender-role stereotyping index for physical activities. *Perceptual and Motor Skills, 68,* 1067–1075.

International Classification of Diseases, 9th revision: Clinical modification (2nd ed.). (1980), Ann Arbor, MI: Commission on Professional and Hospital Activities.

Ipsa, J. (1981). Peer support among Soviet day care toddlers. *International Journal of Behavioral Development, 4,* 255–269.

Jack, L. M. (1934). An experimental study of ascendant behavior in preschool children. *University of Iowa Studies in Child Welfare, 9.*

Jacobsen, R. H., Lahey, B. B., & Strauss, C. C. (1983). Correlates of depressed mood in normal children. *Journal of Abnormal Child Psychology, 11,* 29–39.

Janes, C. L., & Hesselbrock, V. M. (1978). Problem children's adult adjustment predicted from teacher's ratings. *American Journal of Orthopsychiatry, 48,* 300–309.

Janes, C. L., Hesselbrock, V. M., Myers, D. G., & Penniman, J. H. (1979). Problem boys in young adulthood: Teachers' ratings and twelve-year follow-up. *Journal of Youth and Adolescence, 8,* 453–472.

Janes, C. L., Hesselbrock, V. M., & Schechtman, J. (1980). Clinic children with poor peer relations: Who refers them and why? *Child Psychiatry and Human Development, 11,* 113–125.

Johnson, J. H., & Bradlyn, A. S. (1988). Life events and adjustment in childhood and adolescence: Methodological and conceptual issues. In L. H. Cohen (Ed.), *Life events and psychological functioning: Theoretical and methodological issues* (pp. 64–96). Beverly Hills, CA: Sage.

Jouriles, E. N., Barling, J., O'Leary, K. D. (1987). Predicting child behavior problems in maritally violent families. *Journal of Abnormal Child Psychology, 15,* 165–173.

Jouriles, E. N., Murphy, C. M., Farris, A. M., Smith, D. A., Richters, J., & Waters, E. (1991). Marital adjustment, parental disagreements about child rearing and behavior problems in boys: Increasing the specificity of the marital assessment. *Child Development, 62,* 1424–2433.

Kagan, J. (1989). *Unstable ideas: Temperament, cognition, and self.* Cambridge, MA: Harvard University Press.

Kanner, A. D., Feldman, S. S., Weinburg, D. A., & Ford, M. E. (1987). Uplifts, hassles, and adaptational outcomes in early adolescents. *Journal of Early Adolescence, 7,* 371–394.

Katz, L. F., & Gottman, J. G. (1993). Patterns of marital conflict predict children's internalizing and externalizing behaviors. *Developmental Psychology, 29,* 940–950.

Kaufman, J., & Cicchetti, D. (1989). The effects of maltreatment on school-aged children's socioemotional development: Assessments in a day camp setting. *Developmental Psychology, 25,* 516–524.

Kelly, G. A. (1955). *The psychology of personal constructs.* New York: McGraw-Hill.

Killen, M. (1989). Context, conflict, and coordination in social development. In L. T. Winegar (Ed.), *Social interaction and the development of children's understanding* (pp. 119–146). Norwood, NJ: Ablex.

Killen, M. (1991). Social and moral development in early childhood. In W. Kurtines & J. Gewirtz (Eds.), *Handbook of moral behavior and development* (pp. 115–138). Hillsdale, NJ: Erlbaum.

Koch, H. (1935). Popularity among preschool children: Some related factors and technique for its measurement. *Child Development, 4,* 164–175.

Kochanska, G. (1993). Toward a synthesis of parental socialization and child temperament in early development of conscience. *Child Development, 64,* 325–347.

Kochanska, G., & Kuczynski, L., & Maguire, M. (1989). Impact of diagnosed depression and self-reported mood on mothers' control strategies: A longitudinal study. *Journal of Child Psychology, 17,* 493–511.

Kohlberg, L. (1969). Stage and sequence: The cognitive-developmental approach to socialization. In D. A. Goslin (Ed.), *Handbook of socialization theory and research.* Chicago: Rand McNally.

Kohlberg, L., LaCross, J., & Ricks, D. (1972). The predictability of adult mental health from childhood. In B. Wolman (Ed.), *Manual of child psychopathology.* New York: McGraw-Hill.

Kohn, M., & Clausen, J. (1955). Social isolation and schizophrenia. *American Sociological Review, 20,* 265–273.

Kramer, L., & Gottman, J. M. (1992). Becoming a sibling: "With a little help from my friends" *Developmental Psychology, 28,* 685–699.

Krasnor, L., & Rubin, K. H. (1983). Preschool social problem solving: Attempts and outcomes in naturalistic interaction. *Child Development, 54,* 1545–1558.

Krawczyk, R. (1985, April). *What toddlers talk about when they talk about friends.* Paper presented at the biennial meetings of the Society for Research in Child Development, Toronto.

Krehbiel, G., & Milich, R. (1986). Issues in the assessment and treatment of socially rejected children. In R. J. Prinz (Ed.), *Advances in behavioral assessment of children and families* (Vol. 2, pp. 249–270). Greenwich, CT: JAI Press.

Kruger, A. C., & Tomasello, M. (1986). Transactive discussions with peers and adults. *Developmental Psychology, 22,* 681–685.

Kupersmidt, J. B., & Coie, J. D. (1990). Preadolescent peer status, aggression, and school adjustment as predictors of externalizing problems in adolescence. *Child Development, 61,* 1350–1362.

Kupersmidt, J. B., Coie, J. D., & Dodge, K. A. (1990). The role of poor peer relationships in the development of disorder. In S. R. Asher & J. D. Coie (Eds.), *Peer rejection in childhood.* Cambridge: Cambridge University Press.

Kurdek, L. A., & Krile, D. (1982). A developmental analysis of the relation between peer acceptance and both interpersonal understanding and perceived social self-competence. *Child Development, 53,* 1485–1491.

Ladd, G. W. (1983). Social networks of popular, average, and rejected children in a school setting. *Merrill Palmer Quarterly, 29,* 283–307.

Ladd, G. W. (1990). Having friends, keeping friends, making friends, and being liked by peers in the classroom: Predictors of children's early school adjustment? *Child Development, 61,* 312–331.

Ladd, G. W. (1991). Family-peer relations during childhood: Pathways to competence and pathology? *Journal of Social and Personal Relationships, 8,* 307–314.

Ladd, G. W., & Golter, B. S. (1988). Parents' initiation and monitoring of children's peer contacts: Predictive of children's peer relations in nonschool and school settings? *Developmental Psychology, 24,* 109–117.

Ladd, G. W., & Hart, C. H. (1992). Creating informal play opportunities: Are parents' and preschoolers' initiations related to children's competence with peers? *Developmental Psychology, 28,* 1179–1187.

Ladd, G. W., & Mize, J. (1983). Social skills training and assessment with children: A cognitive-social learning approach. *Child and Youth Services, 5,* 61–74.

Ladd, G. W., & Oden, S. (1979). The relationship between peer acceptance and children's ideas about helpfulness. *Child Development, 50,* 402–408.

Ladd, G. W., & Price, J. M. (1986). Promoting children's cognitive and social competence: The relation between parents' perceptions of task difficulty and children's perceived and actual competence. *Child Development, 57,* 446–460.

Ladd, G. W., Profilet, S., & Hart, C. H. (1992). Parent's management of children's peer relations: Facilitating and supervising children's activities in the peer culture. In R. D. Parke & G. W. Ladd (Eds.), *Family-peer relationships: Modes of linkage* (pp. 215–254). Hillsdale, NJ: Erlbaum.

LaFreniere, P. J., & Dumas, J. E. (1992). A transactional analysis of early childhood anxiety and social withdrawal. *Development and Psychopathology, 4,* 385–402.

LaFreniere, P. J., & Sroufe, L. A. (1985). Profiles of peer competence in the preschool: Interrelations between measures, influence of social ecology, and relations to attachment history. *Developmental Psychology, 21,* 56–69.

LaGreca, A. M., Dandes, S. K., Wick, P., Shaw, K., & Stone, W. L. (1988). Development of the Social Anxiety Scale for Children:

Reliability and concurrent validity. *Journal of Clinical Child Psychology, 17,* 84–91.

LaGreca, A. M., & Stone, W. L. (1990). LD status and achievement: Confounding variables in the study of children's social status, self-esteem, and behavioral functioning. *Journal of Learning Disabilities, 23,* 483–490.

Lamb, M. E., & Nash, A. (1989). Infant-mother attachment, sociability, and peer competence. In T. J. Berndt & G. W. Ladd (Eds.), *Peer relations in child development* (pp. 219–245). New York: Wiley.

Lambert, N. (1972). Intellectual and nonintellectual predictors of high school status. *Journal of Scholastic Psychology, 6,* 247–259.

Landau, S., & Milich, R. (1990). Assessment of children's social status and peer relations. In A. M. La Greca (Ed.), *Through the eyes of the child: Obtaining self-reports from children and adolescents* (pp. 259–291). Needham Heights, MA: Allyn & Bacon.

Landau, S., & Moore, L. A. (1991). Social skills deficits in children with attention-deficit hyperactive disorder. *School Psychology Review, 20,* 235–251.

Laursen, B. (1993). Conflict management among close peers. In B. Laursen (Ed.), *Close friendships in adolescence* (pp. 39–54). San Francisco: Jossey-Bass.

Leaper, C. (1991). Influence and involvement in children's discourse: Age, gender, and partner effects. *Child Development, 62,* 797–811.

Lever, J. (1976). Sex differences in games children play. *Social Problems, 23,* 478–487.

Lewin, K., Lippit, R., & White, R. K. (1938). Patterns of aggressive behavior in experimentally created "social climates." *Journal of Social Psychology, 10,* 271–299.

Lewine, R. J., Watt, N. E., Prentky, R. A., & Fryer, J. H. (1978). Childhood behavior in schizophrenia, personality disorder, depression, and neurosis. *British Journal of Psychiatry, 132,* 347–357.

Lewine, R. J., Watt, N. E., Prentky, R. A., & Fryer, J. H. (1980). Childhood social competence in functionally disordered psychiatric patients and normals. *Journal of Abnormal Psychology, 89,* 132–138.

Lewis, M., & Rosenblum, L. A. (1975). *Friendship and peer relations.* New York: Wiley.

Lieberman, A. F. (1977). Preschoolers' competence with a peer: Relations with attachment and peer experience. *Child Development, 48,* 1277–1287.

Lippitt, R. (1941). Popularity among preschool children. *Child Development, 12,* 305–332.

Lollis, S. P., Ross, H. S., & Tate, E. (1992). Parents' regulation of children's peer interactions: Direct influences. In R. D. Parke & G. W. Ladd (Eds.), *Family-peer relationships: Modes of linkage* (pp. 255–281). Hillsdale, NJ: Erlbaum.

Lytton, H. (1990). Child and parent effects in boys' conduct disorder: A reinterpretation. *Developmental Psychology, 26,* 683–697.

Maccoby, E. E. (1990). Gender and relationships. *American Psychologist, 45,* 513–520.

Maccoby, E. E. (1992). The role of parents in the socialization of children: An historical overview. *Developmental Psychology, 28,* 1006–1017.

MacDonald, K., & Parke, R. D. (1984). Bridging the gap: Parent-child play interactions and peer interactive competence. *Child Development, 55,* 1265–1277.

Marcoen, A., & Brumagne, M. (1985). Loneliness among children and young adolescents. *Developmental Psychology, 21,* 1025–1031.

Markus, H. J., & Nurius, P. S. (1984). Self-understanding and self-regulation in middle childhood. In W. A. Collins (Ed.), *Development during middle childhood: The years from six to twelve* (pp. 147–183). Washington, DC: National Academy Press.

Masten, A. S., & Braswell, L. (1989). Developmental psychopathology: An integrative framework for understanding behavioral problems in children and adolescents. In P. R. Martin (Ed.), *Handbook of behavior therapy and psychological science: An integrative approach.* New York: Pergamon.

Masters, J. C. (1971). Effects of social comparison on children's self-reinforcement and altruism toward competitors and friends. *Developmental Psychology, 5,* 64–72.

Masters, J. C., & Furman, W. (1981). Popularity, individual friendship selection, and specific peer interaction among children. *Developmental Psychology, 17,* 344–350.

McLoyd, V. C. (1989). Socialization and development in a changing economy: The effects of paternal job and income loss on children. [Special issue] Children and their development: Knowledge base, research agenda, and social policy application. *American Psychologist, 44,* 293–302.

Mead, G. H. (1934). *Mind, self, and society.* Chicago: University of Chicago Press.

Messer, D. J., Joiner, R., Loveridge, N., Light, P., & Litteton, K. (1993). Influences on the effectiveness of peer interaction: Children's level of cognitive development and the relative ability of partners. *Social Development, 2,* 279–294.

Michelson, L., Foster, S. L., & Richey, W. L. (1981). Social-skills assessment of children. In B. B. Lahey & A. E. Kazdin (Eds.), *Advances in clinical child psychology* (Vol. 4, pp. 119–165). New York: Plenum.

Michelson, L., & Wood, R. (1980). A group assertive training program for elementary schoolchildren. *Child Behavior Therapy, 2,* 1–9.

Miller, N. B., Cowan, P. A., Cowan, C. P., Hetherington, E. M., & Clingempeel, W. G. (1993). Externalizing in preschoolers and early adolescents: A cross-study replication of a family model. *Developmental Psychology, 29,* 3–18.

Montemayor, R. (1982). The relationship between parent-adolescent conflict and the amount of time adolescents spend alone and with parents and peers. *Child Development, 53,* 1512–1519.

Moreno, J. L. (1934). *Who Shall Survive? A new approach to the problem of human interrelations.* Washington, DC: Nervous and Mental Disease.

Mueller, E., & Brenner, J. (1977). The origins of social skills and interaction among playgroup toddlers. *Child Development, 48,* 854–861.

Mueller, E., & Silverman, N. (1989). Peer relations in maltreated children. In D. Cicchetti & V. Carlson (Eds.), *Child maltreatment: Theory and research on the causes and consequences of child abuse and neglect* (pp. 529–578). New York: Cambridge University Press.

Murchison, C. A. (1931). *A handbook of child psychology.* Worchester, MA: Clark University Press.

Murphy, L. B. (1937). *Social behavior and child psychology: An exploratory study of some roots of sympathy.* New York: Columbia University Press.

Mussen, P. H. (Ed.). (1970). *Carmichael's manual of child psychology.* New York: Wiley.

Mussen, P. H. (Ed.). (1983). *Handbook of child psychology.* New York: Wiley.

Muste, M. J., & Sharpe, D. F. (1947). Some influential factors in the determination of aggressive behavior in preschool children. *Child Development, 18,* 11–28.

Nameche, G., Waring, M., & Ricks, D. (1964). Early indicators of outcome in schizophrenia. *Journal of Nervous and Mental Disease, 139,* 232–240.

Neale, J. M., & Oltmanns, T. F. (1980). *Schizophrenia.* New York: Wiley.

Newcomb, A. F., & Bukowski, W. M. (1983). Social impact and social preference as determinants of children's peer group status. *Developmental Psychology, 19,* 856–867.

Newcomb, A. F., Bukowski, W. M., & Pattee, L. (1993). Children's peer relations: A meta-analytic review of popular, rejected, neglected, controversial, and average sociometric status. *Psychological Bulletin, 113,* 99–128.

Northway, M. L. (1943). Social relationships among preschool children: Abstracts and interpretations of three studies. *Sociometry, 6,* 429–433.

O'Brien, S. F., & Bierman, K. L. (1987). Conceptions and perceived influence of peer groups: Interviews with preadolescents and adolescents. *Child Development, 59,* 1360–1365.

Offer, D. R., & Cross, L. A. (1969). Behavioral antecedents of adult schizophrenia. *Archives of General Psychiatry, 21,* 267–283.

Offer, D. R., Ostrov, E., & Howard, K. I. (1981). The mental health professional's concept of the normal adolescent. *Archives of General Psychiatry, 38,* 149–152.

Okun, A., Parker, J. G., & Levendosky, A. A. (1994). Distinct and interactive contributions of physical abuse, socioeconomic disadvantage, and negative life events to children's social, cognitive, and affective development. *Development and Psychopathology, 6,* 77–98.

Ollendick, T. H., Oswald, D. P., & Francis, G. (1989). Validity of teacher nominations in identifying aggressive, withdrawn, and popular children. *Journal of Clinical Child Psychology, 18,* 221–229.

Ollendick, T. H., & Schmidt, C. R. (1987). Social learning constructs in the prediction of peer interaction. *Journal of Clinical Child Psychology, 16,* 80–87.

Ollendick, T. H., Weist, M. D., Borden, M. G., & Greene, R. W. (1992). Sociometric status and academic, behavioral, and psychological adjustment: A five-year longitudinal study. *Journal of Consulting and Clinical Psychology, 60,* 80–87.

Olson, S. L., & Lifgren, K. (1988). Concurrent and longitudinal correlates of preschool sociometrics: Comparing rating scale and nomination measures. *Journal of Applied Developmental Psychology, 9,* 409–420.

Olweus, D. (1993). Victimization by peers: Antecedents and long-term outcomes. In K. H. Rubin & J. B. Asendorpf (Eds.), *Social withdrawal, inhibition and shyness in childhood* (pp. 315–341). Hillsdale, NJ: Erlbaum.

Omark, D. R., Strayer, F., & Freedman, D. G. (1980). *Dominance relations: An ethological view of human conflict and social interaction.* New York: Garland.

Overton, W. F. (1983). *The relationships between social and cognitive development.* Hillsdale, NJ: Erlbaum.

Panak, W. F., & Garber, J. (1992). Role of aggression, rejection, and attribution in the prediction of depression in children. *Development and Psychopathology, 4,* 145–165.

Park, K. A., & Waters, E. (1989). Security of attachment and preschool friendships. *Child Development, 60,* 1076–1081.

Parke, R. D., & Asher, S. R. (1983). Social and personality development. *Annual Review of Psychology, 34,* 465–509.

Parke, R. D., & Bhavnagri, N. (1989). Parents as managers of children peer relationships. In D. Belle (Ed.), *Children's social networks and social supports* (pp. 241–259). New York: Wiley.

Parke, R. D., Cassidy, J., Burks, V. M., Carson, J. L., & Boyum, L. (1992). Familial contributions to peer competence among young children: The role of interactive and affective processes. In R. D. Parke & G. W. Ladd (Eds.), *Family-peer relationships: Modes of linkage* (pp. 107–134). Hillsdale, NJ: Erlbaum.

Parke, R. D., & Ladd, G. W. (1992). *Family-peer relationships: Modes of linkage.* Hillsdale, NJ: Erlbaum.

Parke, R. D., & Slaby, R. G. (1983). The development of aggression. In P. H. Mussen (Ed.), *Handbook of child psychology: Vol. 4. Socialization, personality, and social development* (pp. 547–611). New York: Wiley.

Parker, J. G., & Asher, S. R. (1987). Peer relations and later personal adjustment: Are low-accepted children at risk? *Psychological Bulletin, 102,* 357–389.

Parker, J. G., & Asher, S. R. (1993a). Beyond group acceptance: Friendship and friendship quality as distinct dimensions of children's peer adjustment. In D. Perlman & W. Jones (Eds.), *Advances in personal relationships* (Vol. 4, pp. 261–294). London: Kingsley.

Parker, J. G., & Asher, S. R. (1993b). Friendship and friendship quality in middle childhood: Links with peer group acceptance and feelings of loneliness and social dissatisfaction. *Developmental Psychology, 29,* 611–621.

Parker, J. G., & Gottman, J. M. (1989). Social and emotional development in a relational context: Friendship interaction from early childhood to adolescence. In T. J. Berndt & G. W. Ladd (Eds.), *Peer relations in child development* (pp. 95–131). New York: Wiley.

Parkhurst, J. T., & Asher, S. R. (1992). Peer rejection in middle school: Subgroup differences in behavior, loneliness, and interpersonal concerns. *Developmental Psychology, 28,* 231–241.

Parten, M. B. (1932). Social participation among preschool children. *Journal of Abnormal and Social Psychology, 27,* 342–269.

Pastor, D. L. (1981). The quality of mother-infant attachment and its relationships to toddlers' initial sociability with peers. *Developmental Psychology, 17,* 326–335.

Patterson, C. J., Kupersmidt, J. B., & Griesler, P. C. (1990). Children's perceptions of self and of relations with others as a function of sociometric status. *Child Development, 61,* 1335–1349.

Patterson, C. J., Kupersmidt, J. B., & Vaden, N. A. (1990). Income level, gender, ethnicity, and household composition as predictors of children's school-based competence. *Child Development, 61,* 485–494.

Patterson, C. J., Vaden, N. A., & Kupersmidt, J. B. (1991). Family background, recent life events, and peer rejection during childhood. *Journal of Social and Personal Relationships, 8,* 347–361.

Patterson, G. R. (1983). Stress: A change agent for family process. In N. Garmezy & M. Rutter (Eds.), *Stress, coping, and development in children* (pp. 235–264). New York: McGraw-Hill.

Patterson, G. R., Capaldi, D., & Bank, L. (1991). An early starter model for predicting delinquency. In D. J. Pepler & K. H. Rubin (Eds.), *The development and treatment of childhood aggression* (pp. 139–168). Hillsdale, NJ: Erlbaum.

Patterson, G. R., Littman, R., & Bricker, W. (1967). Assertive behavior in children: A step toward a theory of aggression. *Monographs of the Society for Research in Child Development, 32* (Serial No. 113).

Peery, J. C. (1979). Popular, amiable, isolated, rejected: A reconceptualization of sociometric status in preschool children. *Child Development, 50,* 1231–1234.

Peevers, B. H., & Secord, P. F. (1973). Developmental changes in attribution of descriptive concepts to persons. *Journal of Personality and Social Psychology, 27,* 120–128.

Peplau, L. A., Russell, D., & Heim, M. (1979). An attributional analysis of loneliness. In I. Frieze, D. Bar-Tal, & J. S. Carroll (Eds.), *New approaches to social problems* (pp. 53–78). San Francisco: Jossey-Bass.

Pepler, D. J., & Rubin, K. H. (Eds.). (1991). *The development and treatment of childhood aggression.* Hillsdale, NJ: Erlbaum.

Perret-Clermont, A. N., & Brossard, A. (1985). *Social interaction and cognitive development in children.* London: Academic Press.

Perry, D. G., & Bussey, K. (1977). Self-reinforcement in high- and low-aggressive boys following acts of aggression. *Child Development, 48,* 653–658.

Perry, D. G., Perry, L. C., & Rasmussen, P. (1986). Cognitive social learning mediators of aggression. *Child Development, 57,* 700–711.

Peterson, A. C., Compas, B. E., Brooks-Gunn, J., Stemmler, M., Ey, S., & Grant, K. E. (1993). Depression in adolescence. *American Psychologist, 48,* 155–168.

Peterson, A. C., Sarigiani, P. A., & Kennedy, R. E. (1991). Adolescent depression: Why more girls? *Journal of Youth and Adolescence, 20,* 247–271.

Peterson, L., Mullins, L. L., & Ridley-Johnson, R. (1985). Childhood depression: Peer reactions to depression and life stress. *Journal of Abnormal Child Psychology, 13,* 597–609.

Pettit, G. S., Dodge, K. A., & Brown, M. (1988). Early family experience, social problem-solving patterns, and children's social competence. *Child Development, 59,* 107–120.

Pettit, G. S., & Mize J. (1993). Substance and style: Understanding the ways in which parents teach children about social relationships. In S. Duck (Ed.), *Learning about relationships* (pp. 118–151). Newbury Park, NJ: Sage.

Piaget, J. (1932). *The moral judgment of the child.* Glencoe, IL: Free Press.

Piaget, J. (1952). *The origins of intelligence in children.* New York: Norton. (Originally published in 1936)

Price, J. M. (in press). Friendships of maltreated children and adolescents: Contexts for expressing and modifying relationship history. In B. Bukowski, A. Newcomb, & W. W. Hartup (Eds.), *The company they keep: Friendship during childhood and adolescence.* New York: Cambridge University Press.

Price, J. M., & Dodge, K. A. (1989). Peers' contribution to children's social maladjustment: Description and intervention. In T. J. Berndt & G. W. Ladd (Eds.), *Peer relations in child development* (pp. 341–370). New York: Wiley.

Price, J. M., & Ladd, G. W. (1986). Assessment of children's friendships: Implications for social competence and social adjustment. In R. J. Prinz (Ed.), *Advances in behavioral assessment of children and families* (Vol. 2, pp. 121–150). Greenwich, CT: JAI Press.

Puffer, J. A. (1912). *The boy and his gang.* Boston: Houghton Mifflin.

Puig-Antich, J., Lukens, E., Davies, M., Goetz, D., Brennan-Quattrock, J., & Todak, G. (1985). Psychosocial functioning in prepubertal major depressive disorders. *Archives of General Psychiatry, 42,* 500–517.

Putallaz, M. (1983). Predicting children's sociometric status from their behavior. *Child Development, 54,* 1417–1426.

Putallaz, M., Constanzo, P. R., & Klein, T. P. (1993). Parental ideas as influences on children's social competence. In S. Duck (Ed.), *Learning about relationships* (pp. 63–97). Newbury Park, NJ: Sage.

Putallaz, M., Constanzo, P. R., & Smith, R. B. (1991). Maternal recollections of childhood peer relationships: Implications for their children's social competence. *Journal of Social and Personal Relationships, 8,* 403–422.

Putallaz, M., & Gottman, J. M. (1983). Social relationship problems in children: An approach to intervention. In B. B. Lahey & A. E. Kazdin (Eds.), *Advances in clinical child psychology* (Vol. 6, pp. 1–39). New York: Cambridge University Press.

Putallaz, M., & Heflin, A. H. (1990). Parent child interaction. In S. R. Asher & J. D. Coie (Eds.), *Peer rejection in childhood* (pp. 189–216). Cambridge, England: Cambridge University Press.

Putallaz, M., & Wasserman, A. (1990). Children's entry behaviors. In S. R. Asher & J. D. Coie (Eds.), *Peer rejection in childhood.* New York: Cambridge University Press.

Rabiner, D., & Coie, J. D. (1989). Effect of expectancy inductions on rejected children's acceptance by unfamiliar peers. *Developmental Psychology, 25,* 450–457.

Radke-Yarrow, M., Richters, J., & Wilson, W. E. (1988). Child development in a network of relationships. In R. A. Hinde & J. Stevenson-Hinde (Eds.), *Relationships within families* (pp. 48–67). Oxford, England: Clarendon.

Radke-Yarrow, M., Zahn-Waxler, C., & Chapman, M. (1983). Children's prosocial dispositions and behavior. In P. H. Mussen (Ed.), *Handbook of child psychology: Vol. 4. Socialization, personality, and social development* (pp. 469–545). New York: Wiley.

Rawlins, W. K. (1992). *Friendship matters: Communication, dialetics, and the life course.* New York: Aldine de Gruyter.

Reid, M., Landesman, S., Treder, R., & Jaccard, J. (1989). "My family and friends": Six- to twelve-year-old children's perceptions of social support. *Child Development, 60,* 896–910.

Reisman, J. M., & Schorr, S. E. (1978). Friendship claims and expectations among children and adults. *Child Development, 49,* 913–916.

Renkin, B., Egeland, B., Marvinney, D., Mangelsdorf, S., & Sroufe, L. A. (1989). Early childhood antecedent of aggression and passive-withdrawal in early elementary school. *Journal of Personality, 57,* 257–281.

Renshaw, P. E. (1981). The roots of peer interaction research: A historical analysis of the 1930s. In S. R. Asher & J. M. Gottman (Eds.), *The development of children's friendships.* New York: Cambridge University Press.

Renshaw, P. D., & Brown, P. J. (1993). Loneliness in middle childhood: Concurrent and longitudinal predictors. *Child Development, 64,* 1271–1284.

Richey, M. H., & Richey, H. W. (1980). The significance of best-friend relationships in adolescence. *Psychology in the Schools, 17,* 535–540.

Ricks, D., & Berry, J. C. (1970). Family and symptom patterns that precede schizophrenia. In M. Roff & D. Ricks (Eds.), *Life history research in psycho-pathology* (Vol. 1, pp. 31–39). Minneapolis: University of Minnesota Press.

Rieder, C., & Cicchetti, D. (1989). Organizational perspective on the cognitive control functioning and cognitive-affective balances in maltreated children. *Developmental Psychology, 25,* 382–393.

Rizzo, T. A. (1989). *Friendship development among children in school.* Norwood, NJ: Ablex.

Rizzo, T. A. (1992). The role of conflict in children's friendship development. In W. A. Corsaro & P. J. Miller (Eds.), *Interpretive approaches to children's socialization* (pp. 93–112). San Francisco: Jossey-Bass.

Robins, L. N. (1972). Follow-up studies of behavior disorders in children. In H. C. Quay & J. S. Weery (Eds.), *Psychopathological disorders of childhood* (pp. 415–450). New York: Wiley.

Roff, J. D., & Wirt, D. (1984). Childhood aggression and social adjustment as antecedents of delinquency. *Journal of Abnormal Child Psychology, 12,* 111–126.

Roff, M. (1957). Preservice personality problems and subsequent adjustments to military service: The prediction of psychoneurotic reactions. *U.S. Air Force School of Aviation Medical Report,* No. 57-136.

Roff, M. (1960). Relations between certain preservice factors and psychoneurosis during military duty. *Armed Forces Medical Journal, 11,* 152–160.

Roff, M. (1961). Childhood social interactions and young adult bad conduct. *Journal of Abnormal Social Psychology, 63,* 333–337.

Roff, M. (1963). Childhood social interactions and young adult psychosis. *Journal of Clinical Psychology, 19,* 152–157.

Roff, M., & Sells, S. B. (1967). The relations between the status of chooser and chosen in a sociometric situation at the grade school level. *Psychology in the Schools, 4,* 101–111.

Roff, M., Sells, B. B., & Golden, M. M. (1972). *Social adjustment and personality development.* Minneapolis: University of Minnesota Press.

Rogoff, B. (1990). *Apprenticeship in thinking: Cognitive development in social context.* Oxford, England: Oxford University Press.

Rogosch, F. A., & Cicchetti, D. (in press). Illustrating the interface of family and peer relations through the study of child maltreatment. *Social Development.*

Rogosch, F. A., & Newcomb, A. F. (1989). Children's perceptions of peer reputations and their social reputations among peers. *Child Development, 60,* 597–610.

Roistacher, R. C. (1974). A microeconomic model of sociometric choice. *Sociometry, 37,* 219–238.

Rolf, J. E., Knight, R., & Wertheim, E. (1976). Disturbed preschizophrenics: Childhood symptoms in relation to adult outcomes. *Journal of Nervous and Mental Disease, 162,* 274–279.

Ross, H. S. (1982). The establishment of social games amongst toddlers. *Developmental Psychology, 18,* 509–518.

Ross, H. S., & Kay, D. A. (1980). The origins of social games. In K. H. Rubin (Ed.), *Children's play: New directions for child development (Vol. 9).* San Francisco: Jossey-Bass.

Ross, H. S., Lollis, S. P., & Elliott, C. (1982). Toddler-peer communication. In K. H. Rubin & H. S. Ross (Eds.), *Peer relationships and social skills in childhood.* New York: Springer-Verlag.

Rotenberg, K. J., & Whitney, P. (1992). Loneliness and disclosure in preadolescence. *Merrill-Palmer Quarterly, 38,* 401–416.

Rotter, J. B. (1954). *Social learning and clinical psychology.* New York: Prentice-Hall.

Rowe, D. C. (1989). Families and peers: Another look at the nature-nurture question. In T. J. Berndt & G. W. Ladd (Eds.), *Peer relationships in child development* (pp. 274–300). New York: Wiley.

Rubin, K. H. (1983). Recent perspectives on sociometric status in childhood: Some introductory remarks. *Child Development, 54,* 1383–1385.

Rubin, K. H. (1985). Socially withdrawn children: An "at risk" population? In B. Schneider, K. H. Rubin, & J. Ledingham (Eds.), *Children's peer relations: Issues in assessment and intervention.* (pp. 125–139). New York: Springer-Verlag.

Rubin, K. H. (1993). The Waterloo Longitudinal Project: Continuities of social withdrawal from early childhood to early adolescence. In K. H. Rubin & J. Asendorpf (Eds.), *Social withdrawal, shyness, and inhibition in childhood.* Hillsdale, NJ: Erlbaum.

Rubin, K. H., Booth, C., Rose-Krasnor, L., & Mills, R. S. L. (1994). Family relationships, peer relationships and social development: Conceptual and empirical analyses. In S. Shulman (Ed.), *Close relationships and socio-emotional development* (pp. 63–94). New York: Ablex.

Rubin, K. H., Bream, L., & Rose-Krasnor, L. (1991). Social problem solving and aggression in childhood. In D. J. Pepler & K. H. Rubin (Eds.), *The development and treatment of childhood aggression* (pp. 219–248). Hillsdale, NJ: Erlbaum.

Rubin, K. H., Chen, X., & Hymel, S. (1993). Socioemotional characteristics of withdrawn and aggressive children. *Merrill-Palmer Quarterly, 39,* 518–534.

Rubin, K. H., Chen, X., & Stewart, S. (in press). Parenting factors associated with aggression and social withdrawal in children. In M. Bornstein (Ed.), *Handbook of parenting* (Vol. 1). Hillsdale, NJ: Erlbaum.

Rubin, K. H., & Cohen, J. S. (1986). Predicting peer ratings of aggression and withdrawal in the middle childhood years. In R. J. Prinz (Ed.), *Advances in behavioral assessment of children and families* (Vol. 2, pp. 179–206). Greenwich, CT: JAI Press.

Rubin, K. H., & Coplan, R. (1992). Peer relationships in childhood. In M. Bornstein & M. Lamb (Eds.), *Developmental psychology: An advanced textbook* (pp. 519–578). Hillsdale, NJ: Erlbaum.

Rubin, K. H., & Daniels-Beirness, T. (1983). Concurrent and predictive correlates of sociometric status in kindergarten and grade one children. *Merrill-Palmer Quarterly, 29,* 337–351.

Rubin, K. H., Fein, G., & Vandenberg, B. (1983). Play. In P. H. Mussen (Series Ed.); E. M. Hetherington (Vol. Ed.), *Handbook of child psychology: Vol. 4. Socialization, personality and social development* (pp. 693–774). New York: Wiley.

Rubin, K. H., Hymel, S., Le Mare, L. J., & Rowden, L. (1989). Children experiencing social difficulties: Sociometric neglect reconsidered. *Canadian Journal of Behavioral Science, 21,* 94–111.

Rubin, K. H., Hymel, S., Mills, R. S. L., & Rose-Krasnor, L. (1991). Conceptualizing different developmental pathways to and from social isolation in childhood. In D. Cicchetti & S. L. Toth (Eds.), *Rochester Symposium on Developmental Psychopathology: Vol. 2. Internalizing and externalizing expressions of dysfunction* (pp. 91–122). Hillsdale, NJ: Erlbaum.

Rubin, K. H., & Krasnor, L. R. (1983). Age and gender differences in the development of a representative social problem solving skill. *Journal of Applied Developmental Psychology, 4,* 463–475.

Rubin, K. H., & Krasnor, L. R. (1986). Social-cognitive and social behavioral perspectives on problem solving. In M. Perlmutter (Ed.), *Minnesota Symposia on Child Psychology: Vol. 18. Cognitive perspectives on children's social and behavioral development* (pp. 1–88). Hillsdale, NJ: Erlbaum.

Rubin, K. H., LeMare, L. J., & Lollis, S. (1990). Social withdrawal in childhood: Developmental pathways to peer rejection. In S. R. Asher & J. D. Coie (Eds.), *Peer rejection in childhood* (pp. 217–249). New York: Cambridge University Press.

Rubin, K. H., & Lollis, S. (1988). Origins and consequences of social withdrawal. In J. Belsky & T. Nezworski (Eds.), *Clinical implications of attachment* (pp. 219–252). Hillsdale, NJ: Erlbaum.

Rubin, K. H., & Rose-Krasnor, L. (1992). Interpersonal problem solving. In V. B. Van Hassett & M. Hersen (Eds.), *Handbook of social development* (pp. 283–323). New York: Plenum.

Rubin, K. H., & Ross, H. S. (Eds.). (1982). *Peer relationships and social skills in childhood.* New York: Springer-Verlag.

Rubin, K. H., Watson, K., & Jambor, T. (1978). Free play behaviors in pre-school and kindergarten children. *Child Development, 49,* 534–536.

Ruble, D. (1983). The development of social comparison processes and their role in achievement-related self-socialization. In E. T. Higgins, D. Ruble, & W. W. Hartup (Eds.), *Social cognition and social behavior: Developmental perspectives* (pp. 134–157). New York: Cambridge University Press.

Russell, A., & Finne, V. (1990). Preschooler's social status and maternal instructions to assist group entry. *Developmental Psychology, 26,* 602–611.

Rutter, M., Graham, P., Chadwick, O. F. D., & Yule, W. (1976). Adolescent turmoil: Fact or fiction? *Journal of Child Psychology and Psychiatry, 17,* 35–56.

Saarni, C. (1988). Children's understanding of the interpersonal consequences of dissemblance of nonverbal emotional-expressive behavior. Deception [Special Issue]. *Journal of Nonverbal Behavior, 12,* 275–294.

Saltzstein, H. D., & Goldhammer, E. (1990). Developmental changes in children's criteria for rewarding a peer in an experimental game. *Merrill-Palmer Quarterly, 36,* 557–571.

Salzinger, S., Feldman, R. S., Hammer, M., & Rosario, M. (1993). The effects of physical abuse on children's social relationships. *Child Development, 64,* 169–187.

Sameroff, A. J. (1975). Early influences on development: Fact or fantasy. *Merrill-Palmer Quarterly, 21,* 267–294.

Sameroff, A. J. (1987). The social context of development. In N. Eisenberg (Ed.), *Contemporary topics in developmental psychology* (pp. 273–291). New York: Wiley.

Sameroff, A. J., & Chandler, M. J. (1975). Reproductive risk and the continuum of caretaking casualty. In F. D. Horowitz, M. Hetherington, S. Scarr-Salapatek, & G. Siegel (Eds.), *Review of child development research* (Vol. 4, pp. 187–244). Chicago: University of Chicago Press.

Sandler, E. N., Miller, P., Short, J., & Wolchik, S. A. (1989). Social support as a protective factor for children in stress. In D. Belle (Ed.), *Children's social networks and social supports* (pp. 277–307). New York: Wiley.

Sandler, I. N., & Block, M. (1979). Life stress and maladaptation of children. *American Journal of Community Psychology, 7,* 425–440.

Savin-Williams, R. (1987). *Adolescence: An ethological perspective.* New York: Springer-Verlag.

Savin-Williams, R. C., & Berndt, T. J. (1990). Friendship and peer relations. In S. S. Feldman & G. R. Elliott (Eds.), *At the threshold* (pp. 277–307). Cambridge, MA: Harvard University Press.

Schindler, P. J., Moely, B. E., & Frank, A. L. (1987). Time in day care and social participation of young children. *Developmental Psychology, 23,* 255–261.

Schlaefli, A., Rest, J. R., & Thoma, S. J. (1985). Does moral education improve moral judgement? A meta-analysis of intervention studies using the Defining Issues Test. *Review of Educational Research, 55,* 319–352.

Schneider, B. H., Attili, G., Nadel, J., & Weissberg, R. P. (1989). *Social competence in developmental perspective.* Boston: Kluwer.

Schneider, B. H., Rubin, K. H., & Ledingham, J. E. (Eds.). (1985). *Children's peer relations: Issues in assessment and intervention.* New York: Springer-Verlag.

Schofield, W., & Balian, L. (1959). A comparative study of the personal histories of schizophrenic and nonpsychiatric patients. *Journal of Abnormal and Social Psychology, 59,* 216–225.

Schwartz, J. C. (1972). Effects of peer familiarity on the behavior of preschoolers in a novel situation. *Journal of Personality and Social Psychology, 24,* 276–284.

Scott, C. K., Fuhrman, R. W., & Wyer, R. S. (1991). Information processing in close relationships. In G. J. Fletcher & F. D. Fincham (Eds.), *Cognition in close relationships* (pp. 37–67). Hillsdale, NJ: Erlbaum.

Selman, R. L. (1980). *The growth of interpersonal understanding: Developmental and clinical analyses.* New York: Academic Press.

Selman, R. L., & Schultz, L. H. (1990). *Making a friend in youth: Developmental theory and pair therapy.* Chicago: University of Chicago Press.

Serbin, L. A., Connor, J. M., Burchardt, C. J., & Citron, C. C. (1979). Effects of peer presence of sex-typing of children's play behavior. *Journal of Experimental Child Psychology, 27,* 303–309.

Shantz, C. U. (1983). Social cognition. In J. H. Flavell & E. M. Markman (Eds.), *Handbook of child psychology:* Vol. 3. *Cognitive development* (pp. 495–555). New York: Wiley.

Shantz, C. U., & Hobart, C. J. (1989). Social conflict and development: Peers and siblings. In T. J. Berndt & G. W. Ladd (Eds.), *Peer relationships in child development.* New York: Wiley.

Sharabany, R., Gershoni, R., & Hofman, J. (1981). Girlfriend, boyfriend: Age and sex differences in intimate friendship. *Developmental Psychology, 17,* 800–808.

Sherif, M., Harvey, O. J., White, B. J., Hood, W. R., & Sherif, C. (1961). *Inter-group conflict and cooperation: The Robbers Cave experiment.* Norman, OK: University of Oklahoma Press.

Sherif, M., & Sherif, C. W. (1969). Adolescent attitudes and behavior in their reference groups within differing sociocultural settings. In J. P. Hill (Ed.), *Minnesota Symposia on Child Psychology* (Vol. 3, pp. 97–130). Minneapolis: University of Minnesota Press.

Sherman, S. J. (1987). *Hypothesis-confirmation biases.* Paper presented at the Nags Head International Conference on Social Cognition, Nags Head, NC.

Shields, A., Cicchetti, D., & Ryan, R. (1994). The development of emotional and behavioral self-regulation and social competence among maltreated school-age children. *Development and Psychopathology, 6,* 121–143.

Shrum, W., & Cheek, N. H. (1987). Social structure during the school years: Onset of the degrouping process. *American Sociological Review, 52,* 218–223.

Singleton, L. C., & Asher, S. R. (1977). Peer preferences and social interaction among third-grade children in an integrated school district. *Journal of Educational Psychology, 69,* 330–336.

Slaby, R. G., & Guerra, N. B. (1988). Cognitive mediators of aggression in adolescent offenders: 1. Assessment. *Developmental Psychology, 24,* 580–588.

Smith, P. K. (1988). Children's play and its role in early development: A re-evaluation of the "play ethos." In A. D. Pellegrini (Ed.), *Psychological bases for early education* (pp. 207–226). Chichester, England: Wiley.

Smith, P. K., & Boulton, M. (1990). Rough-and-tumble play, aggression and dominance: Perception and behavior in children's encounters. *Human Development.*

Smollar, J., & Youniss, J. (1982). Social development through friendship. In K. H. Rubin & H. S. Ross (Eds.), *Peer relationships and social skills in childhood* (pp. 277–298). New York: Springer-Verlag.

Smuts, B. (1985). *Sex and friendship in baboons.* New York: Aldine.

Snyder, J. (1991). Discipline as a mediator of the impact of maternal stress and mood on child conduct problems. *Development and Psychopathology, 3,* 263–276.

Sobol, M. P., & Earn, B. M. (1985). Assessment of children's attributions for social experiences: Implications for social skills training. In B. H. Schneider, K. H. Rubin, & J. E. Ledingham (Eds.), *Children's peer relations: Issues in assessment and intervention* (pp. 93–110). New York: Springer-Verlag.

Sroufe, L. A. (1979). The coherence of individual development: Early care, attachment, and subsequent developmental issues. *American Psychologist, 34,* 834–841.

Sroufe, L. A. (1983). Infant-caregiver attachment and patterns of adaptation in preschool: The roots of competence and maladaptation. In R. N. Emde & R. J. Harmon (Eds.), *The development of attachment and affiliative systems* (pp. 281–292). New York: Plenum.

Sroufe, L. A. (1988). The role of infant-caregiver attachment in development. In J. Belsky & T. Nezworski (Eds.), *Clinical implication of attachment* (pp. 18–38). Hillsdale, NJ: Erlbaum.

Sroufe, L. A. (1989a). Relationships and relationship disturbances. In A. J. Sameroff & R. N. Emde (Eds.), *Relationship disturbances in early childhood: A developmental approach* (pp. 97–124). New York: Basic Books.

Sroufe, L. A. (1989b). Relationships, self, and individual adaptation. In A. J. Sameroff & R. N. Emde (Eds.), *Relationship disturbances in early childhood: A developmental approach* (pp. 70–96). New York: Basic Books.

Sroufe, L. A., & Fleeson, J. (1986). Attachment and the construction of relationships. In W. W. Hartup & Z. Rubin (Eds.), *Relationships and development* (pp. 36–54). Hillsdale, NJ: Erlbaum.

Sroufe, L. A., & Jacobvitz, D. (1989). Diverging pathways, developmental transformations, multiple etiologies, and the problem of continuity in development. *Human Development, 32,* 196–203.

Sroufe, L. A., & Rutter, M. (1984). The domain of developmental psychopathology. *Child Development, 55,* 17–29.

Stafford, L., & Bayer, C. L. (1993). *Interaction between parents and children.* Newbury Park, CA: Sage.

Strayer, F. F. (1980). Child ethology and the study of preschool social relations. In H. C. Foot, A. J. Chapman, & J. R. Smith (Eds.), *Friendship and social relations in children* (pp. 235–265). New York: Wiley.

Steinberg, L. (1987). Impact of puberty on family relations: Effects of pubertal status and pubertal timing. *Developmental Psychology, 23,* 451–460.

Stocker, C., & Dunn, J. (1990). Sibling relationships in childhood: Links with friendships and peer relationships. *British Journal of Developmental Psychology, 8,* 227–244.

Sullivan, H. S. (1953). *The interpersonal theory of psychiatry.* New York: Norton.

Suomi, S. J. (1979). Peers, play, and primary prevention in primates. In M. K. Whalen & J. E. Rolf (Eds.), *Primary prevention of psychopathology: Vol. 3. Social competence in children.* Hanover, VT: University of Vermont.

Suomi, S. J., & Harlow, H. F. (1975). The role and reason of peer relationships in rhesus monkeys. In M. Lewis & L. A. Rosenblum (Eds.), *Friendship and peer relations* (pp. 153–186). New York: Wiley.

Taylor, A. R., & Machida, S. (1993). *The contribution of peer relations to social competence in low-income children.* Paper presented at the biennial meeting of the Society for Research in Child Development, New Orleans.

Terman, L. M. A. (1904). A preliminary study of the psychology and pedagogy of leadership. *Pedagogical Seminary, 11,* 413–451.

Terry, R., & Coie, J. D. (1991). A comparison of methods for defining sociometric status among children. *Developmental Psychology, 27,* 867–880.

Terry, R. A., Coie, J. D., Lochman, J. E., & Jacobs, M. (1992, August). Dynamic social development and its relation to middle school adjustment. In J. B. Kupersmidt (Chair), *Longitudinal research in child psychopathology: Peer rejection and children's behavioral adjustment.* Symposium conducted at the Centennial Convention of the American Psychological Association, Washington, DC.

Thomas, A., & Chess, S. (1977). *Temperament and development.* New York: Brunner/Mazel.

Thomas, D. S., Loomis, A. M., & Arrington, R. E. (1933). *Observational studies of social behavior.* New Haven, CT: Yale University.

Thompson, G. G. (1960). Children's groups. In P. H. Mussen (Ed.), *Handbook of research methods in child development* (pp. 821–853). New York: Wiley.

Thompson, G. G., & Horrocks, J. E. (1947). A study of the friendship fluctuations of urban boys and girls. *Journal of Genetic Psychology, 70,* 53–63.

Thornburg, H. D. (1991). The amount of sex information learning obtained during early adolescence. *Journal of Early Adolescence, 1,* 171–183.

Tudge, J. R. H. (1992). Processes and consequences of peer collaborations. A Vygotskian analysis. *Child Development, 63,* 1364–1379.

Tudge, J. R. H., & Winterhoff, P. (1993). Can young children benefit from collaborative problem solving? Tracing the effects of partner competence and feedback. *Social Development, 2,* 242–259.

Tudge, J. R. H., & Rogoff, B. (1989). Peer influences on cognitive development: Piagetian and Vygotskian perspectives. In M. Bornstein & J. Bruner (Eds.), *Interaction and human development.* Hillsdale, NJ: Erlbaum.

Turiel, E. (1983). Domains and categories in social-cognitive development. In W. F. Overton (Ed.), *The relationship between social and cognitive development* (pp. 53–89). Hillsdale, NJ: Erlbaum.

Vandell, D. L. (1980). Sociability with peer and mother during the first year. *Developmental Psychology, 16,* 355–361.

Vandell, D. L., Wilson, K. S., & Buchanan, N. R. (1980). Peer interaction in the first year of life: An examination of its structure, content, and sensitivity to toys. *Child Development, 51,* 481–488.

Vaughn, B., & Waters, E. (1981). Attention structure, sociometric status, and dominance: Interrelations, behavioral correlates and relationships to social competence. *Developmental Psychology, 17,* 275–288.

Vernberg, E. M. (1990). Psychological adjustment and experiences with peers during early adolescence: Reciprocal, incidental, or unidirectional relationships? *Journal of Abnormal Child Psychology, 18,* 187–198.

Volkmar, F. R., Carter, A., Sparrow, S. S., & Cicchetti, D. (1993). Quantifying social development in autism. *Journal of the American Academy of Child and Adolescent Psychiatry, 32,* 627–632.

Volling, B. L., MacKinnon-Lewis, C., Rabiner, D., Baradaran, L. P. (1993). Children's social competence and sociometric status: Further exploration of aggression, social withdrawal, and peer rejection. *Developmental and Psychopathology, 5,* 459–483.

Vosk, B., Forehand, R., Parker, J., & Rickard, K. (1982). A multimethod comparison of popular and unpopular children. *Developmental Psychology, 18,* 571–575.

Vuchinich, S., Bank, L., & Patterson, G. R. (1992). Parenting, peers, and the stability of antisocial behavior in preadolescent boys. *Developmental Psychology, 28,* 510–521.

Vygotsky, L. S. (1978). *Mind in society: The development of higher psychological processes.* Cambridge, MA: Harvard University Press.

Wachs, T. D. (1992). *The nature of nurture.* London: Sage.

Walker, L. J. (1986). Experiential and cognitive sources of moral development in adulthood. *Human Development, 29,* 113–124.

Wanless, R. L., & Prinz, R. J. (1982). Methodological issues in conceptualizing and treating childhood social isolation. *Psychological Bulletin, 92,* 39–55.

Warnken, R. G., & Siess, T. F. (1965). The use of the cumulative record in the prediction of behavior. *Personnel and Guidance Journal, 31,* 231–237.

Waters, E., Wippman, J., & Sroufe, L. A. (1979). Attachment, positive affect, and competence in the peer group: Two studies in construct validation. *Child Development, 50,* 821–829.

Watt, N. E. (1972). Longitudinal changes in the social behavior of children hospitalized for schizophrenia as adults. *Journal of Nervous and Mental Disease, 155,* 42–54.

Watt, N. E. (1978). Patterns of childhood social development in adult schizophrenics. *Archives of General Psychiatry, 35,* 160–165.

Watt, N. E., & Lubensky, A. (1976). Childhood roots of schizophrenia. *Journal of Consulting and Clinical Psychology, 44,* 363–375.

Watt, N. E., Stolorow, R. D., Lubensky, A. W., & McClelland, D. C. (1970). School adjustment and behavior of children hospitalized for schizophrenia as adults. *American Journal of Orthopsychiatry, 40,* 637–657.

Weiner, B. (1985). Spontaneous causal thinking. *Psychological Bulletin, 97,* 74–84.

Weiss, B., Dodge, K. A., Bates, J. E., & Pettit, G. S. (1992). Some consequences of early harsh discipline: Child aggression and maladaptive social information processing study. *Child Development, 63,* 1312–1335.

Wellman, B. (1981). Applying network analyses to the study of social support. In B. H. Gottlieb (Ed.), *Social networks and social support* (pp. 171–200). Beverly Hills: Sage.

Werebe, M. J., & Baudonniere, P. M. (1988). Communication competence and privileged relations among children: Comparison between two age groups. *International Journal of Psychology, 23,* 619–635.

Whalen, C. K., Henker, B., Buhrmester, D., & Hinshaw, S. P. (1989). Does stimulant medication improve the peer status of hyperactive children? *Journal of Consulting and Clinical Psychology, 57,* 545–549.

Whalen, C. K., Henker, B., & Granger, D. A. (1990). Social judgment processes in hyperactive boys: Effects of methylphenidate and comparisons with normal peers. *Journal of Abnormal Child Psychology, 18,* 297–316.

Wheeler, V. A., & Ladd, G. W. (1982). Assessment of children's self-efficacy for social interactions with peers. *Developmental Psychology, 18,* 795–805.

Williams, G. A., & Asher, S. R. (1987, April). *Peer- and self-perceptions of peer rejected children: Issues in classification and subgrouping.* Paper presented at the biennial meeting of the Society for Research in Child Development, Baltimore.

Williams, G. A., & Asher, S. R. (1992). Assessment of loneliness at school among children with mild mental retardation. Social skills [Special Issue]. *American Journal on Mental Retardation, 96,* 373–385.

Wood, J. V. (1989). Theory and research concerning social comparisons of personal attributes. *Psychological Bulletin, 106,* 231–248.

Wright (1978). Toward a theory of friendship based on a conception of self. *Human Communication Research, 4,* 196–207.

Yarrow, M. R., Campbell, J. D., & Burton, R. V. (1970). Recollections of childhood: A study of the retrospective method. *Monographs of the Study for Research in Child Development, 35* (Series No. 138).

Youngblade, L. M., & Belsky, J. (1992). Parent-child antecedents of five-year-olds' close friendships: A longitudinal analysis. *Developmental Psychology, 1,* 107–121.

Youngblade, L. M., Park, K. A., & Belsky, J. (1993). Measurement of young children's close friendship: A comparison of two independent assessment systems and their associations with attachment security. *International Journal of Behavioral Development, 16,* 563–587.

Younger, A. J., & Boyko, K. A. (1987). Aggression and withdrawal as social schemas underlying children's peer perceptions. *Child Development, 58,* 1094–1100.

Younger, A. J., & Piccinin, A. M. (1989). Children's recall of aggressive and withdrawn behaviors: Recognition memory and likability judgments. *Child Development, 60,* 580–590.

Younger, A. J., Schwartzman, A. E., & Ledingham J. E. (1986). Age-related changes in children's perceptions of social deviance: Changes in behavior or in perspective? *Developmental Psychology, 22,* 531–542.

Youngren, M. A., & Lewinsohn, P. M. (1980). The functional relation between depression and problematic interpersonal behavior. *Journal of Abnormal Psychology, 89,* 333–341.

Youniss, J. (1980). *Parents and peers in social development: A Sullivan-Piaget perspective.* Chicago: University of Chicago Press.

Youniss, J., & Smollar, J. (1985). *Adolescent relations with mothers, fathers, and friends.* Chicago: University of Chicago Press.

Zahn-Waxler, C., Mayfield, A., Radke-Yarrow, M., McKnew, D. H., Cytryn, L., & Davenport, D. (1988). A follow-up investigation of offspring of parents with bipolar disorder. *American Journal of Psychiatry, 145,* 506–509.

Zarbatany, L., Hartmann, D. P., & Rankin, D. B. (1990). The psychological functions of preadolescent peer activities. *Child Development, 61,* 1067–1980.

Zaslow, M. (1980). Relationships among peers in kibbutz toddler groups. *Child Psychiatry and Human Development, 10,* 178–189.

Zigler, E., & Trickett, P. (1978). IQ, social competence, and evaluation of early childhood interventions programs. *American Psychologist, 33,* 789–798.

CHAPTER 5

Social Support and Psychopathology across the Life Span

NANCY S. ROBINSON and JUDY GARBER

The study of the relation between social support and adaptation has a long history represented in multiple disciplines including anthropology, sociology, psychology, epidemiology, medicine, and child development. The construct of a "social network" was used by anthropologists and sociologists as a metaphor for studying the number and kinds of social contacts among individuals (Barnes, 1954; Bott, 1971; Mitchell, 1969). Bott (1971) used open-ended interviews to examine the relation between social organization and social class, and between personal social networks and individual role functioning in the family. Anthropologists conducted social network analyses for the purpose of providing qualitative descriptions of concrete living systems in complex societies. Barnes (1954) was particularly influential in moving social anthropology away from the concepts of administrative structures and social categories toward a focus on social relationships and linkages among individuals. Thus, early work in this area was primarily descriptive of the relations among individuals and the larger systems in which they operated. Research then began to show that enhanced social networks were valuable to individuals (Brim, 1974; McKinlay, 1973; Pilisuk & Froland, 1979; Walker, Macbride, & Vachon, 1977), whereas the absence of social support could be harmful (Caplan, 1974). As early as 1897, Durkheim suggested that a lack of social relationships could increase the probability of suicide. Epidemiologists formulated the social disorganization hypothesis, which was concerned with the structure and function of individuals' social networks, in order to explain differences in rates of disease and psychopathology among different populations and in different geographic regions (Leighton et al., 1963; Murphy, 1977; Struening, 1975). Cassel (1976) noted that the social environment, particularly the presence or absence of other members of the same species, influenced organisms' susceptibility to environmental disease agents. Cassel

suggested that the best way to prevent disease was strengthening individuals' social support systems rather than trying to decrease their exposure to stress.

Cobb (1976) similarly emphasized the importance of social support during times of stress. He suggested that social support protected individuals from disease, accelerated recovery, and increased the likelihood of compliance with medical regimens. Thus, according to Cobb, social support was an important buffer during times of illness or other crises.

Family therapists and psychiatrists have emphasized the role of the social environment including the nuclear and extended family, the workplace, and community in the etiology and course of psychiatric disorders (Speck & Rueveni, 1969). Community psychologists (Auerbach & Kilmann, 1977; Whitcher & Fisher, 1979) have observed the important contribution of health care professionals to the well-being of the socially isolated and economically disadvantaged. Finally, developmental psychologists have emphasized the connection between attachment theory and social support (Bowlby, 1969, 1980) and the importance of secure interpersonal relationships for successful adaptation over the life span.

Thus, the construct of social support is truly multidisciplinary. An advantage of this is that it has been studied from diverse perspectives. A disadvantage, however, is that there is no coherent theory of social support nor is there a consistent operational definition. The present review first outlines the definition and dimensions of social support for which there is some consensus in the literature. Next, the development of the major components of social support are discussed and the cognitive and social skills relevant to social support are reviewed. The remainder of the chapter highlights the relations among social support, stress, and psychopathology. The major models hypothesized to explain these relations are outlined, and the role of social support in the development and course of three different psychopathological disorders (depression, schizophrenia, and conduct disorder) are reviewed. Although the current chapter is not an exhaustive review of these literatures, it does highlight the major findings in each area and suggests important directions for future research.

This chapter was completed while Nancy S. Robinson was supported in part by a training grant from the National Institute of Mental Health (T32MH18921) and Judy Garber was supported in part by a Faculty Scholar Award from the W. T. Grant Foundation (88-1214-88) and a FIRST Award from the National Institute of Mental Health (R29-MH4545801A1).

DEFINING SOCIAL SUPPORT

Despite numerous attempts in the literature to define and measure social support, no single operational definition of the construct exists. Much of the work designed to better understand the multidimensional nature of support has focused on predicting overall well-being or functioning rather than specific psychopathological syndromes. Adjustment and well-being in this work also have been assessed using a wide range of criteria. Hence, the outcomes referred to in this section are concerned with a broad-based concept of functioning, typically measured with some combination of psychiatric symptom inventories, job or school performance indexes, global functioning within the social environment, or subjective ratings of emotional or physical distress, rather than the presence or absence of a particular psychopathological syndrome.

Reviews of this literature suggest that how the support construct is operationally defined greatly affects how the various findings can be interpreted (e.g., Barrera, 1986; Cohen & Wills, 1985; Coyne & Downey, 1991; Heitzmann & Kaplan, 1988; Leavy, 1983; Wolchik, Beals, & Sandler, 1989; Wolchik, Sandler, & Braver, 1987; Wortman & Dunkel-Schetter, 1987). According to this literature, there are at least three important levels of analysis to consider when defining social support: The dimension or nature of support measured, the sources of support, and the types or functions of support.

Dimensions of Support

Dimensions of support are concerned with how support is measured. In a review of the literature concerning social support and its relation to life stress in adults, Barrera (1986) proposed three dimensions: *Social embeddedness* means the connections or linkages individuals have to significant others in the environment with a focus on the size of network or the number of organizations a person belongs to; *perceived support* consists of subjective appraisal of support, satisfaction with relationships and perceived closeness to network members; and *enacted support* is captured by the frequency of supportive transactions or how much help an individual actually receives from his or her network. Wolchik et al. (1987; Wolchik, Beals, & Sandler, 1989) advocated for these same three dimensions in conceptualizing children's social support and its effect on well-being and adaptive coping in children experiencing stressors such as divorce, school transitions, poverty, and teen pregnancy.

Interestingly, past research has found these social support dimensions to be only mildly related to each other and differentially associated with stress (e.g., Barrera, 1986; Cohen & Wills, 1985; Tucker, 1982). B. R. Sarason, Shearin, Pierce, and I. G. Sarason (1987) examined the relation among the different dimensions of support and various personality measures in a sample of college students. Overall, measures of received support and the size of support networks were not strongly related to measures of perceived available support. The lack of a strong relation between perceived and received support measures suggests that perceiving a supportive social network and

positive relationships with significant others does not ensure that the individual will utilize them more when in need of help.

B. R. Sarason et al. (1987) also found that perceived support was more highly correlated with well-being than received support or size of social network (see also Vega, Kolody, Valle, & Weir, 1991), reinforcing the notion that these two dimensions may have different roles to play in the support process. Barrera (1986) suggested that there is a positive relation between distress and enacted support, but a negative relation between distress and perceived social support. That is, when a person encounters a relatively high number stressful events and the level of distress due to those encounters rises, he or she actually seeks more support or is provided with such support by members of his or her network. However, perceiving the availability of a supportive network, whether or not the individual actually uses it, appears to be related to lower levels of distress. Only a limited amount of research focusing on the relation between the social embeddedness dimension of support and adjustment exists, but preliminary findings suggest that measures of social embeddedness may be useful in predicting psychological distress independent of life stress (Barrera, 1986).

Although these differences should be interpreted cautiously because they are based largely on correlations among data collected at a single point in time, they suggest several important issues for future investigation. It may be that persons who are more distressed seek out more aid than do those who are less distressed. This could result in a negative correlation between received support and well-being due to the greater level of distress such persons are exhibiting even before utilizing their support system. On the other hand, the support that is received may or may not be effective in relieving distress, resulting in a nonsignificant relation or in some cases where the "botched" or mismatched support actually exacerbates distress, a negative relation with distress. That is, it is the quality rather than the quantity of support that results in a positive association between support and distress.

For example, consider the common scenario of someone providing information to a person in distress. The informational support provided could actually cause more distress if that information turns out to be inaccurate, is delivered in an unfeeling manner, or the person dealing with the problem is not ready to receive the information being provided. On the other hand, the positive relation between perceived support and well-being may be due to the positive effects of high-quality relationships, regardless of whether support is actually provided in response to a *particular* stressful event. In fact, in the preceding situation, just knowing where helpful information can be obtained should it be needed may decrease the amount of anxiety experienced, thereby allowing the person to deal directly and more competently with stressful situations.

An alternative explanation for the stronger relation between well-being and perceived rather than received support could be that perceived support is confounded with subjective appraisals of distress since it is a less objective measure. Although all three support dimensions are often measured using self-report, both social embeddedness and received support are based on more concrete behaviors than the more subjective perceived support or quality-of-relationships measures. Thus, the relation between perceived support and well-being may be more inflated by simple method variance.

In sum, three dimensions of support have been identified in both the adult and child literatures. These dimensions, labeled social embeddedness, perceived support, and received support, have been found to be differentially associated with general measures of adaptation and distress. The relations of these three distinct dimensions to specific forms of psychopathology are described in later sections of the chapter.

Sources of Support

Wolchik et al. (1987; Wolchik, Beals, & Sandler, 1989) noted that different sources of support also can differentially impact well-being. Various categories have been used to classify sources of support ranging from global ratings of kin and nonkin, to more specific labels such as parents, peers (coworkers), teachers and supervisors, friends, siblings, and extended family (e.g., grandparents, aunts, uncles, cousins). Research suggesting that support from various sources has a different impact on adjustment highlights the importance of the source distinction (e.g., Cauce, Felner, & Primavera, 1982; Harter, 1990; Reid, Landesman, Treder, & Jaccard, 1989; Wolchik, Ruehlman, Braver, & Sandler, 1989; Wortman & Dunkel-Schetter, 1987). Cauce, Felner, and Primavera, (1982) found that although perceived helpfulness of family members, teachers, and counselors or clergy was associated with academic adjustment as measured by grades and school attendance in an inner-city high school, high levels of support from friends and other adults were actually associated with poorer grades and higher rates of absenteeism. Presumably, the friends and other adults did things that detracted from students' schoolwork and school attendance. Alternatively, the students with poor grades and school attendance may have utilized more support from these network members because of their high level of distress, and this support may not have helped to ameliorate the problems in these two areas.

Wortman and Dunkel-Schetter (1987) have found that whether cancer patients perceive certain behaviors as supportive depends on who provides the assistance. Advice concerning their cancer from physicians is viewed as helpful, whereas the same sort of advice from friends is not perceived as helpful. Thus, the distinction in sources of support becomes particularly salient when trying to understand the relation between support and adjustment. The importance of these different sources and their impact on adjustment may vary at different points in the life span.

Functions of Support

Another level of analysis to consider when defining social support is the function of the support. That is, what is the type or purpose of the support? Various categories of function of support have been proposed (e.g., Berndt & Perry, 1986; Caplan, 1979; Cobb, 1976; Cohen & Wills, 1985; Furman & Buhrmester, 1985; Hirsch & Reischl, 1985; House, 1981; House & Kahn, 1985; Kahn & Antonucci, 1980; Reid et al., 1989; Robinson, 1991, in press; Sarason et al., 1987; Thoits, 1985; Wortman & Dunkel-Schetter,

1987). These researchers differ somewhat with regard to the particular categories and terminology used, although they all refer to similar supportive behaviors. The following categories of support function are noted frequently: *Approval* or positive regard, which also is known as self-esteem enhancing or affirmation; *emotional support* including affection (e.g., hugs, expressions of caring and concern) and intimacy/disclosure (e.g., degree of trust and closeness); *instrumental or informational aid,* which includes both advice and material aid as well as tangible assistance and cognitive guidance with tasks; and *social companionship,* which consists of doing activities together (e.g., watching a movie, playing games) not necessarily directed at meeting the other three purposes. Some other taxonomies have divided the instrumental aid category into informational support and instrumental support (Hirsh & Reischl, 1985; House, 1981; Reid et al., 1989; Wolchik et al., 1987; Wortman & Dunkel-Schetter, 1987), and some combine emotional support and positive regard (e.g., Reid et al., 1989).

Generalists versus Specialists Models: Integration of Source and Function of Support

Bogat, Caldwell, Rogosch, and Kriegler (1985) introduced the framework of support generalists and specialists. A support generalist is a core member of an individual's network, who provides many types of support, whereas a support specialist provides more limited support. For example, a good friend may give emotional support, approval, companionship, and occasionally some important instrumental aid, thereby fitting the description of a generalist. A lawyer, on the other hand, may provide excellent instrumental aid, but not meaningful emotional support, approval, or social companionship, and thus would be more of a support specialist.

Cauce, Reid, Landesman, and Gonzales (1990) found this distinction to be quite useful in describing the support profiles of children 5 to 12 years old. They reported that parents serve as support generalists, whereas friends, teachers, and even siblings tend to be more support specialists for young children. The particular sources who are the support generalists versus specialists change somewhat over the course of development.

Although most researchers agree that both the source or provider of support and the type or function of support are legitimate distinctions to make when defining support, it is difficult to assess both these levels of analysis in a comprehensive yet cost-effective way. Therefore, some researchers have tried to determine which distinction, source, or function is more useful in explaining individual and developmental differences in the relation between support and adjustment (e.g., Cauce et al., 1990; Wolchik, Beals, & Sandler, 1989). These researchers have compared the amount of variance in well-being accounted for by models utilizing support scores based on source, function, and a combination of the two.

Cauce et al. (1990) compared how well the following three models described the relation between first-grade children's perceived support and their behavioral adjustment: The provider model in which scores were created for each source of support (i.e., parents, peers, teachers), summing across all functional indexes; the functional model in which scores were created for each type of support (i.e., emotional, informational, companionship, and instrumental), summing across all sources; and the interactional model whereby separate scores were created for each type of support provided by each source (e.g., parent emotional support, peer companionship, etc.). Cauce et al. (1990) found the provider model to be the "more sensitive barometer of adjustment" (p. 83), with support from parents being positively related to maternal report of social adjustment and self-esteem, and support from peers being positively related to adjustment on the first day of school but negatively associated with cognitive competence and curiosity. None of the correlations for the functional model were significant; the interactional model provided some additional information, however. In particular, emotional and instrumental support from parents was most strongly associated with social adjustment, whereas the relation between parental support and self-esteem did not vary as much across the different support functions. Informational support from peers was the function most highly negatively correlated with cognitive competence and curiosity, although it was also positively correlated with adjustment to school on the first day.

Wolchik, Beals, and Sandler (1989) evaluated the provider and function distinction for 8- to 16-year-old children's reports of the quality of support from their social networks following stressors such as the death of a parent, parental divorce, or exacerbation of asthma symptoms. Their measure of support assessed function (play, advice, provisions of goods and services, emotional support, and positive feedback) across five provider categories (household adults, household children, extended family, nonfamily adults, and nonfamily children or peers). Confirmatory factor analyses indicated that both the provider and function models fit the data better than did the single factor model, although neither was acceptable as indicated by the ratio of chi-square to degrees of freedom and the normed fit indexes. The model that best described the support process in this sample incorporated both provider and function distinctions, with the provider distinction being the most prominent. Thus, the notion of generalist and specialist models of support providers appears to be a meaningful distinction for both children and adults.

Attitudes toward Help-Seeking and Support Utilization

Several researchers have suggested that attitudes toward help-seeking can influence the social support process (Gottlieb, 1983; Mitchell & Trickett, 1980; Tolsdorf, 1976; Vaux, Burda, & Stewart, 1986). Such attitudes do not represent a different dimension of support, but they are important for the prediction of the effects of support utilization. If obtaining help from another person is seen as a sign of weakness or failure, then the effect of help-seeking on indexes of adjustment such as self-esteem might be quite different from the effect of help-seeking that is viewed more positively. Such individual differences in attitudes toward support utilization are probably the result of multiple socialization forces such as cultural or family values.

The relation between social support and adjustment might vary across the life span as a result of developmental differences in attitudes toward help-seeking. Even within a particular culture or family setting, obtaining support in the form of instrumental assistance or emotional reassurance among young children might

be viewed as quite acceptable and even encouraged, whereas for adolescents and young adults the same degree of assistance might be viewed as inappropriate or at least something to be enacted only as a last resort. Thus, the "cost-benefit" ratio of support utilization depends, in part, on attitudes held by the person receiving assistance; although support from others may be of help in obtaining an immediate goal, it could invoke a cost to the person's sense of self-efficacy depending on his or her attitudes about receiving such help. More needs to be learned about developmental differences in help-seeking attitudes so that such factors can be incorporated into theoretical models of the relation between social support and well-being.

Current theories and research on social support indicate that it is a multifaceted construct. The three dimensions of support (social embeddedness, perceived support, and enacted support) appear to be only mildly related to each other and differentially related to well-being, with perceived support having the strongest positive association with adjustment. The distinctions between who provides support and the function of that support also appear to be meaningful in mapping the support experience. Finally, attitudes about help-seeking and the meaning of obtaining assistance for the individual's sense of self also should be incorporated into our models of the relation between social support and psychopathology across the life span.

DEVELOPMENT AND SOCIAL SUPPORT

How does development influence the experience of social support and the relation between support and psychopathology? The following section describes some of the empirical evidence for age differences in the nature of social support along the three dimensions of social embeddedness, perceived support, and enacted support. Developmental changes in goals, cognitive and social ability, and social environment that are associated with developmental shifts in the social support experience also are discussed. It is first necessary to understand these developmental shifts in the normative social support experience to appreciate how the relation between social support and psychopathology might differ across the life span. We present a selective review of the literature that highlights those developmental changes in support that are most relevant to psychopathology in both children and adults. This framework can serve as a guide to the study of both social support and psychopathology from a developmental perspective, and the examination of how the relation between the two constructs changes over the course of the life span.

Developmental Differences in Social Networks

An infant's world is filled with a variety of family members, professionals, and friends, although most of the infant's supportive interactions are centered around caregivers. Despite continued debate concerning when infants intentionally interact with others, there seems to be agreement that almost from birth, infants initiate and respond to social interactions with caregivers (Damon, 1983; Hartup, 1986). Who those caregivers are depends on the culture, economic status, and family constellation. Typically during the early years, it is limited to family members and professional caretakers in day-care settings. The precise age at which infants naturally begin to interact with peers is unclear. There appears to be a gradual interest in peers starting during the first 6 months and increasing in complexity to the point that by age 2 years, children have been observed to take turns with one another, imitate behaviors of peers, and engage in primitive vocal exchanges (Eckerman, Whatley, & Kutz, 1975; Damon, 1983).

Parents or other caregivers orchestrate most of children's early social activities. Parke and Bhavnagri (1989) note that parents (or other caregivers) manage their children's activities in two important ways: (a) They arrange opportunities for interaction with others by living in safe neighborhoods, organizing play groups, and enrolling their children in activities with peers and other adults; and (b) they encourage relationships, especially with peers by directly monitoring and supervising interactions to facilitate the development of social skills.

The degree and form of parental management varies with the age of the children. For example, Bhavnagri (1987, as cited in Parke & Bhavnagri, 1989) found that mothers reported that their young preschoolers (2 to 3½ years old) participated in less unsupervised play with other peers and had fewer friends in the neighborhood than did older preschool children (3½- to 6-year-olds). In addition, young preschoolers' play with peers was reported to be more often initiated by mothers than by children. Not only did the amount of supervised play differ across the two age groups studied, but Bhavnagri and Parke (1991) found that the impact of parental supervision also varied with age. Supervision facilitated interaction with peers for younger children but did not have much of an impact on the peer interactions of older children.

Thus, preschoolers' social networks and experiences in those networks are significantly affected by caretakers' management tactics. Management by caretakers continues to have an impact during early childhood, although it takes a different form. For example, families' participation in sponsored organizations with structured activities for children (i.e., clubs, Brownies or Cub Scouts, sports teams, other community-based activities) increases as children get older and is most prevalent among preadolescents (Bryant, 1985; O'Donnell & Stueve, 1983).

Bryant (1985) used a "neighborhood walk" measure to study the social support network and sources of support among 7- and 10-year-old children. Subjects were asked about their access to and interactions with friends, relatives, and recreational facilities in their community as they walked with an experimenter around their neighborhood. Bryant found that 10-year-olds had more elaborate sources of support (a greater number of diverse persons in their reported social network) and reported more effective use of their social support network than did 7-year-olds.

Other researchers have found developmental differences in the amount of time children and adolescents spend with social network members (i.e., companionship). In general, two shifts seem salient: First, there is an increase with age in the amount of time spent with peers beginning at about age 6 and continuing into adolescence (e.g., Buhrmester & Furman, 1984; Larson & Richards, 1991; Wright, 1967). Second, prior to early adolescence, relatively little time is spent with opposite-sex peers (Asher, Oden, & Gottman, 1977). During late adolescence and adulthood, transitions such as going to college

(Shaver, Furman, & Buhrmester, 1985), pregnancy, and parenthood (Belsky & Rovine, 1984; Gottlieb & Pancer, 1988; McCannell, 1988) typically lead to changes in the size and time spent with various network members.

Finally, the social networks of the elderly also show some shifts with increasing age. Interactions with more distant kin decline over the life cycle due to death and limited mobility; interactions with adult children remain fairly constant across later life with a small decline during the time adult children are raising a family, a trend probably due to lack of geographic proximity (Hanson & Sauer, 1985). During times of crisis, however, parents and adult children often become central support providers for one another. Parents have been found to provide valuable support to their adult children experiencing stressful events such as divorce or the birth of a preterm infant (Hetherington & Camara, 1984; Parke & Anderson, 1987), and adult children are often cited as providing support to their parents in times of crisis (Hagestad, 1985; Tinsley & Parke, 1984). Nevertheless, on a daily basis, Larson and colleagues (Larson, Csikszentmihalyi, & Graef, 1982; Larson, Zuzanek, & Mannell, 1985) have found that, in general, adults over 65 years of age spend more of their waking time alone (48%) than do younger adults and adolescents (25–30%). Thus, there is evidence for significant shifts in the social embeddedness experienced by adults as they grow older.

Developmental Differences in Perceived Support

The dimension of perceived quality or satisfaction with support is more easily assessed in children who are old enough to communicate verbally their feelings about others. Researchers studying social support and relationships in older children and adults, however, recently have started to draw parallels between their work and research on attachment (e.g., Antonucci, 1991; Kahn & Antonucci, 1980; Sarason, Pierce, & Sarason, 1990). At the same time, there has been a surge of interest in viewing attachment as a life-span concept (e.g., Ainsworth, 1989; Belsky & Nezworski, 1988; Bretherton, 1985; Cicchetti, Cummings, Greenberg, & Marvin, 1990; Skolnick, 1986). It is difficult to know how this work, which is dyadic in nature and derived from behavioral observation rather than self-report, fits with the dimensions of social support. During infancy and early childhood, attachment is largely assessed using behavior observations. The work initially begun by Ainsworth (Ainsworth, Blehar, Waters, & Wall, 1978) and Bowlby (1969) has enabled researchers to derive qualitative ratings of mother-infant interactions (e.g., secure and insecure) that predict to later ratings of the same relationship, more general social behavior, and other aspects of development (Belsky & Nezworski, 1988; Erickson, Egeland, & Sroufe, 1985; Lewis, Feiring, McGuffog, & Jaskir, 1984; Parkes & Stevenson-Hinde, 1982). These qualitative ratings of behavior include some examples of enacted support, such as when a distressed child seeks physical comfort and reassuring words or glances from his or her caretaker on seeing a stranger or following separation from the primary caretaker. Later work using the attachment framework with adults relies on their self-reported global ratings of their early relationships with their parents (e.g., Hazan & Shaver, 1987; Ricks, 1985). This attachment work seems more aligned with what is referred to here as perceived support.

In addition, a central theme of the attachment construct is the security felt in relationships with significant others whether they are physically present or the person is simply aware of their availability. The notion of perceiving that people are there to help if that help is needed (perceived support) is often hard to disentangle from received or enacted support. This distinction, however, might be quite important in understanding the relation of support to adjustment. Regardless of whether research on attachment is classified as being most relevant to perceived or enacted support dimensions, it is relevant to the early social support experience.

Furman and associates (Furman, 1989; Furman & Buhrmester, 1985) have focused on understanding how children's perceptions of relationships with significant others change with development. Students in 4th grade, 7th grade, 10th grade, and college completed Furman and Buhrmester's (1985) Network of Relationship Inventories describing their relationships with parents, siblings, grandparents, teachers, friends, and boy/girlfriends. Furman found that the size of the correlations between different relationship scores (e.g., parents and friends) was lower in older (adolescents) than younger (elementary school) children. He concluded that relationships appear to become more differentiated and more specialized with age.

Furman (1989) also has found developmental differences in the perceived level of support and other relationship qualities. Adolescent subjects reported that they perceived their parents to be less supportive than did younger subjects; the largest decrease in reported support from parents was between 4th and 7th grades. Students in 7th grade reported greater parental conflict and punishment than did 4th graders, and 7th and 10th graders reported having less power in their interactions with their parents than did 4th graders. Perceptions of support from siblings and grandparents were lower in the 7th grade than for the 4th grade, although the level of perceived conflict and punishment did not increase in these relationships as much as they did in relationships with parents.

A very different set of developmental shifts were found in the reported quality of peer relationships. Ratings of support from peers were greater in the 7th grade than the 4th grade but lower in the 10th grade and college. This difference between 4th graders and 10th graders and college students can be attributed to changes in specific supportive provisions rather than an overall decrease in all types of support. That is, older adolescents' ratings of peers' level of companionship and nurturance were lower than younger subjects' ratings, whereas their ratings of the other supportive provisions from peers (reliable alliance, enhancement of worth, instrumental help, affection, intimacy and satisfaction) were about the same or slightly higher than ratings made by younger adolescents. Thus, the nature of the support from peers changes with age.

The shift toward perceiving greater intimacy and support from peers during late childhood and early adolescence found by Furman (1989) is consistent with other studies in the literature (Berndt, 1982; Berndt & Hoyle, 1985; Blyth & Traeger, 1988; Buhrmester, 1990; Hunter & Youniss, 1982). During later adolescence and early adulthood, this shift encompasses cross-sex relationships as well, with intimacy in opposite-sex relationships (romantic and friendship based) becoming increasingly important (e.g., Shaver et al., 1985; Wheeler, Reis, & Nezlek, 1983). Buhrmester and Furman (1986) pointed out, however, that there is still no consensus on precisely when this shift occurs. Moreover, gender differences complicate things even further. Across late childhood and early adolescence, girls tend to report higher levels of intimacy and support from friends than do boys (Foot, Chapman, & Smith, 1980; Rivernbark, 1971; Rubin, 1985; Sharabany, Gershoni, & Hoffman, 1981). It is also noteworthy that, although intimacy from parents has been reported to become more secondary during early adolescence (Buhrmester & Furman, 1984) and there is a shift away from dependency on parents (Steinberg & Silverberg, 1986), the level of closeness to and support from parents remains fairly high even during adolescence (Hill & Holmbeck, 1986; Robinson, in press; Ryan & Lynch, 1989).

The importance of continued connectedness with parents has recently been emphasized by researchers of adolescent development (e.g., Bogat et al., 1985; Cooper, Grotevant, & Condon, 1983; Ryan & Lynch, 1989), and some research has suggested that, at least for young adults attending college, relationships with parents may actually be perceived as more positive on leaving home than during adolescence. This trend could be due to either subjective reappraisal or objective changes in their interactions with their parents (Furman, 1989; Shaver et al., 1985). Thus, although perceived supportiveness and level of intimacy experienced with peers becomes increasingly important, perceiving parents and other family members as being supportive remains important.

Developmental shifts in perceptions of the quality of support and the level of intimacy experienced in relationships with others during midadulthood certainly exist, although it is difficult to disentangle such shifts from individual differences because the developmental milestones during this part of the life span are not necessarily age-related. During older adulthood, a combination of physical and societal changes common to more same-age cohorts allows for greater confidence in mapping developmental change in perceived support. An interesting finding is that older adults report less loneliness than do other age groups (Peplau, Bikson, Rook, & Goodchilds, 1982). Older adults are also less likely to report that they wish they had more friends (Antonucci, 1985). Given that research suggests older adults spend less time with others than younger adults and adolescents (Larson et al., 1982; Larson et al., 1985), these two findings seem to reflect either older adults' success in surrounding themselves with relationships that are satisfying, or a tendency to deny social needs in an effort to protect emotional well-being (Rook, 1990).

Finally, older adults also report that they experience greater arousal and positive effect when they are with their friends than with their family members. Presumably this is due to either the type of activities they are engaged in or the quality of the relationships they have with friends and family members (Larson, Mannell, & Zuzanek, 1986; Lowenthal & Robinson, 1976; Wood & Robertson, 1978).

Developmental Differences in Enacted/Received Support

From birth, human beings must receive some form of support in order to survive. In fact, even very young infants have the communication skills to elicit a soothing response from their caretaker. Some of these early signals, such as crying when hungry, may be largely reflexive and even biologically determined. By the end of the first year, infants' repertoire of support-eliciting signals is relatively elaborate and does not appear to rely solely on reflexes (e.g., Kopp, 1989). For example, infants about 1 year of age will look toward a caretaker when presented with a novel or fear-inducing event, a phenomenon known as social referencing (i.e., Feinman, 1982; Klinnert, Campos, Sorce, Emde, & Svejda, 1983; Walden & Ogan, 1988). Presumably, infants are seeking information from their caretaker, in the form of facial expressions or more dramatic physical intervention. Although subtle, this social referencing represents an early form of seeking informational support.

In an elaborate effort to emphasize that even infants are capable of utilizing their social environment to obtain a desired goal, Rogoff and colleagues (1990; Rogoff, Mistry, Radziszewska, & Germond, 1992) have described infants' and toddlers' instrumental social interaction with unfamiliar adults. Rogoff (1990) emphasized the importance of the social environment for learning a variety of skills (i.e., language, object exploration and construction, and remembering and planning), a process she refers to as "guided participation." Rogoff (1990) described the following example of guided participation as seen in everyday interactions between a parent and child:

> David, age 7.5 months, was at a restaurant with his parents and seemed to be getting bored. His mother handed him a dinner roll, although until then he had eaten only strained foods, zwieback toast, and Cheerios. David happily took the roll, examined it, looked up at his mother, and said, "Da?" as he held the roll up near his mouth. His mother replied automatically, "Yes, you can eat it." (p. 151)

Although subtle, David's quizzical look at his mother was an attempt to get information from her that would help him know what to do with this new object. This act could be classified as enacted support in which the support provided is geared to further the young child's understanding of the objects with which he or she comes into contact.

Another example of the importance of guided participation can be seen in the work on language development by Tomasello and Farrar (1986). These researchers have found that the extent to which mothers refer to objects already in the focus of their toddlers' attention is correlated with the size of the children's vocabulary 6 months later. Interestingly, this relation between mothers' informational support and the size of children's subsequent vocabulary was not as strong when mothers redirected their children's attention away from an object of interest to the child in order to convey such informational support. Thus, the way in which support is provided as well as the amount of informational support appear to be important to developing language skills.

The question of developmental differences in help-seeking behavior, or enacted support, once children are in school has received a fair amount of attention by counseling and school psychologists. Much of this research has been driven by the pragmatic interest in learning how to best meet the needs of children of different ages through formal help-providing systems, such as school counselors and administrators. There is some evidence that children seek more help or support from peers as they get older,

although the level of help sought from parents and other adults remains consistently high from early childhood to adolescence (e.g., Hetherington & Camara, 1984; Kneisel, 1987; Nelson-LeGall & Gumerman, 1984; Northman, 1978). The types of support sought appear to vary slightly with age. Whereas younger children focus more on instrumental or "make it all better" type of help (i.e., basic emotional support), older children tend to seek out others for more complex forms of emotional support and approval as well as instrumental aid (e.g., Band & Weisz, 1988; Kliewer, Lepore, Broquet, & Zuba, 1990).

Finally, several other interesting developmental trends in help-seeking are worth noting. Nelson-Le Gall (1987) examined the help-seeking behavior of children in the third and fifth grade while they were participating in an experimental problem-solving task. She found that, compared with third graders, children in the fifth grade sought more necessary than unnecessary help. Help was judged as "necessary" when the child gave an incorrect and tentative answer and asked for help prior to giving the final answer, whereas help was rated as "unnecessary" when the child gave a correct tentative answer but still requested help before providing the final answer. Older children in this study also showed a preference for indirect (hints) versus direct (answers) help more than did the younger children.

Newman (1990; Newman & Goldin, 1990) has found developmental differences in children's reported reasons for seeking help in math class. Whereas third and fifth grade students reported that they sought help because of an intrinsic preference for challenge, external dependence on the teacher, and attitudes concerning the benefits of help-seeking, seventh graders explained their help-seeking in terms of both the benefits as well as the costs of help-seeking. Interestingly, no age difference was found in students' reported tendency to seek help or in their awareness of the costs of help-seeking. Rather, the difference was isolated to the degree to which such awareness affected their reported likelihood of help-seeking. Newman suggested that heightened fear of embarrassment and sensitivity regarding peer acceptance and conformity during early adolescence (Berndt, 1979; Hartup, 1983) may be responsible for the older students showing more inhibition to help-seeking when greater costs are perceived.

In a sample of 5- to 12-year-old children, Cauce et al. (1990) found several developmental changes in the sources of support from whom children reported seeking emotional, informational, companionship, and instrumental help. Whereas ratings of all types of support from mothers were consistently high across these ages, ratings regarding fathers as sources of support increased with age. There were fluctuations in how often siblings were rated as being providers of the various types of support, with elementary school students citing siblings less than 5-year-olds; middle school children cited siblings more often than did elementary school students. The frequency with which teachers were named as providers of informational support increased with age, whereas the frequency with which they were named as companions decreased with age. Friends were named as providers of informational and instrumental support at a consistent rate over the age span assessed, but older children named friends as providers of companionship and emotional support more often than did younger children.

Cauce et al. (1990) concluded that the distinctions among support providers become less relevant as children get older. That is, even friends, who are initially cited as providing only specific forms of support, come to provide all types of support; family members were cited as doing so all along. This is not to say "support specialists" do not exist in adulthood. Rather highly specialized help may come from more tangential members of the social network, such as lawyers, therapists, physicians, and so on.

A limitation of the empirical work just reviewed is that the majority of the studies suggesting developmental differences in the nature of social support have been cross-sectional in design. To understand the changes that occur in social support across the life span, researchers need to conduct longitudinal studies. This seems particularly important given the individual differences evident within age groups. Without rigorous longitudinal designs, it is difficult to tease apart individual and developmental differences in the support experience. Although truly life-span longitudinal work may be impractical, research that follows the same group of children at least over a substantial number of years (e.g., from preschool through early adolescence) would be invaluable in trying to understand social support developmentally.

Changes in Social Goals and the Need for Support

Sullivan (1953; also see Buhrmester & Furman, 1986 and Furman, 1989 for discussions of Sullivan's perspective) suggested a developmental progression in social needs. Social needs, as used in this framework, refer to the preferred or central social activity; underlying these needs are emotional tensions (or negative emotions, such as fear, sadness, loneliness, boredom, or anxiety) that encourage social interaction. During infancy, the need for tenderness is the most salient social need. Tenderness refers to the care provided when infants require protection or help in obtaining some immediate physical or emotional comfort. This need for tenderness from members of one's social network continues throughout the life span, particularly during times of helplessness and distress, but it is especially pervasive during infancy. During early childhood (from about 2 to 5 years), the need for adult participation and interest (often involving a parent or other primary caregiver) in play becomes central. Through joint "play" activities, the child learns that compliance with powerful others can bring tangible rewards and fulfillment of certain social needs.

Throughout the elementary school years, children's social need for companionship with other children becomes increasingly salient. These exchanges are more egalitarian than the earlier exchanges with adult playmates. Along with this gradual shift toward the importance of companionship with peers comes the individual's need for acceptance by peers, and during preadolescence, the need for intimate exchanges or "chumships" becomes central. Sullivan (1953) proposed that these chumships foster social competence and lead to feelings of reassurance that others think and feel as preadolescents do themselves. He also claimed these early intimate exchanges formed the basis for later adult friendships, romantic, marital, and parenting relationships. During early adolescence, opposite-sex peers become increasingly important as the difficult task of blending the need for sexuality and intimacy is undertaken.

Research describing developmental changes in the understanding of friendships suggests a similar developmental trend, although the focus usually has been limited to the peer context (e.g., Berndt, 1981; Gottman & Parkhurst, 1980; Youniss & Volpe, 1978). Bigelow (1977) described changes in the concept of friendship using a three-stage approach. Initially, friendship is determined by common activities and proximity: "My best friend plays next to me with the same toys." Then, the notion of mutual understanding and liking become central, leading to some constancy over time: "My best friend is someone who likes me and whom I like whether or not he [she] is right beside me." Finally, friendship becomes characterized by loyalty, commitment, trust, and mutual obligation or give-and-take.

For the most part, the social needs just described emphasize the importance of developing a sense of self as a part of a particular social network. As children grow into adolescents and adults, however, the goal of developing a self that can be differentiated from others also becomes increasingly important (Damon, 1983; Harter, 1983; Veroff & Veroff, 1980). The need for support from and connectedness to others must be balanced with the need for autonomy (Bryant, 1989) and this balancing act has repercussions for the social support process across the life span. Bryant (1989) pointed out that theories of psychosocial development, such as those by Erikson (1964), Wertheim (1978), and Kegan (1982), all emphasize that at different points in development the need for independence from others is balanced with the need to remain connected to others:

> . . . Erikson does *not* propose a list of achievements beginning with trust, followed by autonomy, then initiative, industry, and so forth. Rather, Erikson proposes that it is necessary to acquire a sense of trust along with a sense of mistrust, a sense of autonomy along with a sense of shame and doubt, a sense of initiative along with a sense of guilt, and so on. While trust requires social connectedness, mistrust requires some detachment from others; while autonomy requires some independence from others, shame and doubt brought about in part by parental sanctions or limits of the child's autonomous functioning and parental responses to a child's experiences of failure firmly plant these issues in a social context. At each stage of development the need for some sort of mastery to keep us independent from others is to be balanced by a kind of mastery to keep us connected with others. (p. 334)

The manner in which support is delivered affects this balance. For example, Bryant (1989) emphasized the importance of both supervised and unsupervised peer activities for healthy social-emotional functioning in elementary school children. Thus, parental support in the form of close supervision is important to children this age but at a moderate level; too much "support" or involvement, even if it is positive, can create conflict with the need for independence as children learn to interact with their peers.

The developmental changes in the needs and goals of social behavior impact the nature of social support across the life span. The developmental shifts in core needs may be one of the main reasons for developmental changes in the size of social networks, the sources of support perceived as being central, and the ways in which network members display their support.

Changes in Cognitive and Social Abilities in Relation to Support

As children develop new cognitive and social abilities, their experience of the world around them, including their relationships with others, changes significantly. In this section, we discuss some of these changes in ability that are associated with and possibly drive some of the shifts in the social support experience. First, we focus on two broadly defined social-cognitive abilities, perspective-taking and empathy, and then move to some of the relevant social skills. It should be noted that although we have chosen to emphasize this particular causal direction, others have studied how specific aspects of children's social networks influence the development of important cognitive and social abilities (e.g., Cochran & Brassard, 1979). The processes certainly work both ways in that the social support experience can influence the development of cognitive and social skills as well as the reverse.

Perspective-Taking Skills

Rosenberg (1979) noted that Mead's (1934) and Cooley's (1902) social models of the self are dependent on quite elaborate perspective-taking skills. A person must have the ability to appreciate another's perspective toward the self in order to use it in forming his/her looking-glass self or generalized-other.

Selman (1980) proposed a developmental progression of perspective-taking containing five levels. First, children (between 3 and 6 years old) hold an egocentric viewpoint. Although they are able to recognize the subjective states of self and other, the states are often not distinguishable from one another. This results in difficulty realizing that others may view a situation differently than they do themselves.

As children approach 5 to 9 years of age, they are able to display a higher level of reasoning called social-informational role taking, in which they understand that even in similar social circumstances, the self and others' perspectives may be either the same or different, and that people have unique physical and psychological characteristics. Self-reflective role taking is possible once children are able to reflect their own thoughts and feelings from another person's perspective, a skill that usually is evident in children aged 7 to 12. Between ages 10 and 15, children display mutual role taking that relies on their understanding of the recursiveness of reciprocal perspectives. They have the ability to observe the self as both actor and subject simultaneously through adopting the position of the "generalized other."

The most advanced level of perspective-taking Selman (1980) proposed is that of social and conventional system role taking that can be displayed by children around 12 years of age or older. This final level is marked by an understanding that thoughts or feelings are psychologically determined, but not necessarily understood by the self, thus allowing for an understanding of societal or moral perspectives held by some individuals but not all.

The developmental progression in perspective-taking ability has important implications for perceived support. Perceiving support presumably requires the ability to form cognitive abstractions from experiences with others across time. As children gain the necessary cognitive skills and the motivation to use these skills, they can form more elaborate perceptions of how much the people in their lives care about them, are available when they might need help, and approve of them.

Rosenberg's (1979) work with children and adolescents suggests that not only are there developmental trends in the ability to utilize others' perspectives of the self, but there are shifts in just whose perspective has the greatest impact on self-esteem. In late childhood and early adolescence, the general peer group appears to be a critical source of information concerning one's self-esteem, but by late adolescence, best friends are more likely to be the primary source for feedback affecting self-esteem.

Empathy

Somewhat related to the notion of perspective-taking is the construct of empathy. Hoffman (1975) suggested that even newborns have the ability to experience purely affective empathic reactions, although increasing cognitive skills allow children to develop an even more refined ability to empathize. He proposed several general stages through which this cognitive component of empathy develops. Initially, infants merely experience empathic distress in which the emotion of another is truly shared, such as when infants cry or become upset when another infant cries. Between 1 and 2 years of age, this global shared feeling of discomfort becomes a feeling of concern for the other person who is distressed (Zahn-Waxler, Radke-Yarrow, Wagner & Chapman, 1992). Children experiencing this level of empathy might bring their mothers over to a crying friend in an effort to comfort the friend in the same way that they themselves might be comforted.

By age 6 years, children come to realize that others can sometimes feel the same emotions they do and sometimes feel different emotions. This allows children to not only put themselves in another's place, but also to more effectively assess what might be useful in treating another's specific distress. Finally, by age 9, children have developed an increasing awareness of themselves and others as persons with continuing identities that transcend the immediate situation. This allows them to become concerned with general conditions of persons rather than only situational distress (e.g., becoming concerned about the "general blight" of the poor or handicapped).

This growing ability to empathize helps children to build more supportive relationships with both family and peers, and thus, impacts both social embeddedness and perceived support. For example, the ability to empathize could result in children being more helpful to others (Eisenberg, Miller, Shell, McNalley, & Shea, 1991) and result in a greater level of intimacy. Although some relationships are not necessarily marked by reciprocity, many are, especially those with peers. Mannarino (1976, 1979) and McGuire and Weisz (1982) found that children with close friends had higher scores of altruism (derived from self-report and/or laboratory assessment) than did those without close friends. However, the direction of this relationship is not clear. It could be that having close friends provides the types of experiences that assist in the development of empathy (McGuire & Weisz, 1982). Nevertheless, developmental changes in the ability to empathize with others may be associated with important changes in network membership and perceived quality of the relationships within those networks.

Social Skills

Much of the literature concerning social skills has focused on individual differences rather than normative developmental changes in such skills. Moreover, the developmental changes in social skills may be driven by the social-cognitive abilities just discussed. That is, the ability to perspective-take and empathize can result in being more skilled in making and keeping friends and having positive exchanges with others in the social network. It seems useful, however, to review in brief some skills that are believed to be associated with being socially competent since they may affect the size and scope of children's and adults' social networks. Certain social skills also may impact the ways in which others are utilized in times of distress or need (enacted support).

Dodge, Pettit, McClaskey, and Brown (1986; see also Dodge, 1985) emphasized the importance of social information processing skills in predicting social competence in children. These skills include encoding social cues, interpreting social cues in an accurate and meaningful way, generating potential behavioral responses, evaluating the consequences of the various possible responses, and enacting the chosen response (which requires a repertoire of verbal and motor skills). These social information processing skills have been found to be associated with peer status, such as popular, rejected, or socially isolated (see Ladd, 1985 for review of this literature). Although Dodge and associates originally generated their model to explain two specific examples of social behavior, peer group entry and response to peer provocation, the same information-processing skills may be important in eliciting social support or help from one's social network. For example, perceiving social cues and interpreting them accurately could be important in determining whether or not another person might be willing and able to provide support and assistance. Generating a number of different potential sources of support and a variety of methods to elicit such support also could be important in effectively obtaining useful support. Finally, having the language and other communication skills to ask for or elicit support from others, and being able to evaluate what about the support provided is useful and what might not be useful should also have repercussions for effective use of others in times of need.

The normative developmental differences in these skills have not received the same degree of attention as that received by individual variation in such skills. Nevertheless, we speculate that as children gain more experience within the social context, they can encode and retrieve more diverse relevant information, and become more facile with language and other communicative skills, their social information processing abilities may change both quantitatively and qualitatively. Such improving skills might then be associated with developmental shifts in the social support process.

As children gain more elaborate social information processing skills, they might find forming and maintaining supportive relationships with a variety of other people easier, thereby increasing the size of the social network in which they are embedded. Some of the same skills also may allow children to become more facile at obtaining useful support in times of need (enacted support) and might impact perceived support indirectly through their influence on both social embeddedness and enacted support. Having a greater number of support sources with whom they have had positive support experiences would probably lead to children perceiving a higher level of support availability and intimacy from the members of their social network.

The abilities to cooperate, compromise, and express competitiveness in a socially appropriate manner are additional skills that may be important in building a supportive social network of friends once in the school environment. The finding that popular children are rated as being more competent at these skills than unpopular children supports this premise (Buhrmester & Furman, 1986; Ladd, 1985). The abilities to cooperate, compromise, and express competitiveness in socially acceptable ways, however, are not skills children display from birth. Rather these skills develop during late childhood and early adolescence (Berndt, 1982). What impact do such normative changes in social skills have on the social support experience? As with the development of more elaborate social information processing skills, the development of these other social skills assists children in creating and maintaining a supportive social network and in getting their various needs met through their interactions with the members of their expanded network.

Although developmentalists have studied social support across the life span, little work has been done to trace the types of social-cognitive abilities that may influence the social support experience at different ages. A relatively strong association has been found between social skills in adulthood and the size and quality of support networks (Cohen, Sherrod, & Clark, 1986; Mitchell & Trickett, 1980; Sarason, Sarason, Hacker, & Basham, 1985). How do developmental changes in various social and cognitive abilities impact children's and adolescents' social support experiences? A few studies have examined the link between social competence and help-seeking in children with regard to a specific problem-solving experimental task (Tyler & Varma, 1988) or in math class (Newman, 1990). These studies have found that children who are more socially competent are also more likely to be competent help-seekers (i.e., seeking task-relevant help when needed and rejecting it when not needed). More research is needed that specifically links the social and cognitive abilities at various points in the life span to the perception and enactment of social support.

Changes in the Social Environment in Relation to Support

Social networks change dramatically from infancy to adulthood. During infancy, family members, particularly the primary caretakers, provide most of the support. As children grow, their social network expands to include peers and other adult caretakers, and eventually evolves to include a spectrum of colleagues and friends, all of whom have varying amounts of significance in the person's daily life.

Not only do the members of the social environment change with development, but the nature of the groups changes, largely as a reflection of the shift in goals and needs discussed earlier. The social milieu of children around age 6 or 7 has been described as "play groups" in which there are few rules, limited structure, few defined roles if any, and a constant shift in membership depending on who is nearby at the moment. By age 9 or so, children's social groups involve "formal clubs" characterized by shared interests, planned activities, and rules concerning initiations and exclusions. Finally, as adolescence nears, "informal cliques" become the norm, usually consisting of two or three core members who provide each other with support and guidance in dealing with the pressures of growing up, particularly regarding relations with the opposite sex. These changes in the social environment across the life span have implications for the type of support obtained from peers (Bronfenbrenner, 1979; Hirsch, Engel-Levy, DuBois, & Hardesty, 1990; see Tietjen, 1989 for a discussion of cultural differences in the social environment of children that affect the form, function, and impact of social support).

As developmental researchers, often the best we can do is get glimpses through narrow windows at a process as it changes across development. Because of this snapshot nature of the information collected, we need to be aware of other shifts in the environment that could account for the changes we see in children of particular ages. For example, as Berndt (1982) points out, the transition from elementary to junior high school may result in shifts in friendship patterns that have more to do with the shift in social environment than any social or cognitive ability developing within children and young adolescents making this shift. Entry into day care, first grade, and entry into and exit from college are other environmental shifts that could have a dramatic influence on a person's social support experience regardless of age and developmental status. Although it may not be critical to separate these within-person and environmental forces because they often interact in a bidirectional fashion, the possibility of multiple explanations for developmental differences should be acknowledged.

The current review indicates that there is clear evidence of developmental differences in social embeddedness, perceptions of support, and enacted support. Social networks during infancy are often limited to family and other caretakers but expand during early childhood to include peers and other adults. There also is a shift toward greater intimacy and perceived support from peers during late childhood, which is at first limited to friendships and then expands to include romantic relationships. Older adults report smaller networks and spend less time with others than younger adults and children, but they also report less loneliness.

Even infants are reasonably skilled at eliciting support, but as children get older, the function of the support they seek becomes more complex. Initially, young children seek instrumental or informational aid and simple emotional support in the form of immediate comfort. During middle childhood and adolescence, more complex forms of support such as emotional understanding and approval from significant others become an important aspect of the support experience. Who provides this support also shifts, with peers becoming progressively more central for a greater variety of support.

The developmental shifts in goals and social needs or desires may provide the driving force behind some of these developmental differences. In addition, increases in cognitive abilities such as perspective taking and information processing, as well as increases in the social skills necessary for cooperation, compromise, and expressing competitiveness presumably impact the nature of social support. Moreover, normative shifts in the social environment most likely affect who is available for support and how that support may or may not be utilized across the life span. Future studies should assess changes in the needs, social and cognitive abilities, and environment of children as they develop, while simultaneously collecting information about their social support experience using a multidimensional approach assessing social networks, perceptions of the quality and availability of support, and actual use of support.

SOCIAL SUPPORT AND PSYCHOPATHOLOGY

> Social support, like nutrition, is not a concept that can be readily applied from health to illness. Each mental illness has its own special sensitivity to factors of environmental support. (Beels, Gutwirth, Berkeley, & Struening, 1984, p. 399).

The Relation among Social Support, Stress, and Well-Being

Much of the research on social support has focused on the processes by which social support affects well-being. A great deal of this literature has evaluated whether or not social support moderates the impact of stressful life events on well-being or more severe forms of psychopathology. The models described in this section are by no means exhaustive; many variations have been proposed. Consistent with comprehensive reviews by Barrera (1988) and Cohen and Wills (1985), we have chosen to summarize those models that have received the most empirical attention. Most of this work has not systematically defined social support as the multidimensional construct described in this chapter. Nevertheless, in the following summary of this literature, we will suggest how the three dimensions of support (social network, perceived support, and enacted support) may play different roles in the leading process models.

Social Support Deterioration Model

In this model, the deterioration of existing social support is linked to distress. Several mechanisms have been proposed to describe this model (Barrera, 1988; Fondacaro & Moos, 1987). Certain life events, such as divorce or death of a loved one, can change the structure of social relationships and lead to increased distress (e.g., Leslie & Grady, 1985). On the other hand, because of their own discomfort, people sometimes intentionally or unintentionally avoid others who have experienced traumatic events, such as being diagnosed with cancer or losing a child (e.g., Wortman & Lehman, 1985). By having less contact with network members while experiencing a stressful life event, the individual receives less support during this time of possible increased need. This shift in contact with network members may ultimately impact whether or not certain persons remain significant members in that person's social network. Thus, both the dimensions of enacted support and social embeddedness are implicated in this model.

Certain coping efforts by the individual encountering stress also may reduce social support utilization (i.e., enacted support). Some individuals choose to solve problems alone without the added strain of social comparison with others who are not affected by the stress. The use of such autonomous coping strategies may in turn actually decrease the frequency of contact with others, decrease the size of their social network (i.e., social embeddedness), and/or affect perceptions of available support (Barrera, 1988).

Direct Effect or Additive Model

According to the direct effect model, social support contributes to well-being by meeting a basic human need for affiliation and attachment. That is, regardless of the amount of stress encountered, social support has a negative relation with distress and a positive relation with adjustment. Having supportive relationships with family and friends lessens distress and thus helps individuals to live happy and productive lives. Consequently, those persons who lack supportive affiliations are more likely to feel distress and less likely to lead productive lives regardless of life circumstances and the level of stress encountered.

A variation of the main effect model is the stress prevention model. In this model, social support is hypothesized to prevent the initial occurrence of stressful life events that would add to distress and maladaptive outcomes. Barrera (1988) suggested, for example, that living in a neighborhood where persons are part of a cohesive and vigilant Neighborhood Watch program may prevent certain negative life events such as burglaries, vandalism, and other crimes.

Social support also could simply affect whether or not a particular event is considered to be potentially threatening. For example, a person going on vacation who knows he or she can leave a pet in the care of a trustworthy friend may lead to the appraisal that this absence from the pet is neither threatening nor distressing. This second mechanism is similar to the buffering model. The difference is that here social support actually leads to the appraisal of the event as "nonstressful" rather than simply "less stressful," with the latter being more of a buffering effect. In other words, having a supportive network of friends and/or family decreases the chances of encountering certain stressful life events or increases a person's tendency to "roll with the punches" and view certain life events as being nonstressful.

Much of the empirical support for these main effect models has come from research in which social embeddedness or other structural approaches have been used to operationally define social support (e.g., Bell, LeRoy, & Stephenson, 1982; Cohen, Teresi, & Holmes, 1986; Costello, 1982). Some research using measures of perceived support and the quality of relationships with others also has been cited as evidence for this direct effect model (e.g., Barrera, 1988; Cohen & Wills, 1985; Dubow, Tisak, Causey, Hryshko, & Reid, 1991; Henderson, Byrne, Duncan-Jones, Scott, and Adcock, 1980; Husaini, Neff, Newbrough, & Moore, 1982; Paykel, Emms, Fletcher, & Rassaby, 1980; Pearlin, Menaghan, Lieberman, & Mullan, 1981; Windle, 1992a). The third dimension, enacted support, is not directly relevant to this model because it involves actually receiving support in response to some need or stressor; in the main effect models, such stressors are avoided at least in part because of the positive effects of having a social network of sufficient size and perceiving the relationships with members of the network to be satisfying. However, the quality of enacted support experienced would indirectly feed back into social embeddedness and perceived support. Those members of the social network providing useful support when a

person is dealing with various crises certainly have a greater chance of remaining central to his or her social network, and enacted support experiences certainly provide information that presumably is integrated into the individual's perceptions of the supportiveness of network members.

Stress-Buffering Models

Stress-buffering models propose that social support lessens the distress or maladjustment associated with negative life events (e.g., Heller & Swindle, 1983; Kessler & McLeod, 1985; Kessler, Price, & Wortman, 1985; Leavy, 1983; Mitchell, Billings, & Moos, 1982; Thoits, 1982). The traditional stress buffering model asserts that social support interacts with stress but that it is not independently related to either stress or adaptation. One way that having a supportive social network can reduce the likelihood of maladaptive responses to life events is by assisting the individual to make realistic cognitive appraisals of these events and to cope effectively with them (Cohen & Wills, 1985). For example, although moving to a new city is typically viewed as a stressful event, awareness of having a supportive friend or relative in that city might help the individual view such a move as less threatening. Not surprisingly, perceived support seems to be the dimension that best fits this model. Under conditions of high stress, having or perceiving the support of others helps to buffer a person against high levels of distress, whereas under conditions of low stress there is a less noticeable effect of social support on adjustment.

In the suppression model, social support acts to suppress the effects of stress by mitigating adverse reactions to stressful events. A friend or a relative living in a city to which a person is moving can provide help in finding a place to live and introductions to a new circle of friends, thereby reducing the amount of distress encountered as a result of the move. Thus, the distress resulting from exposure to a stressor can be minimized by the presence of and the behavioral assistance from supportive others.

The buffering qualities of social support can affect the person's interpretation of the stressor, knowledge of coping strategies, and sense of self-esteem or self-efficacy; all these factors can, in turn, affect the level of distress experienced. Cohen and McKay (1984) proposed a specificity hypothesis to explain the complex nature of the buffering effect of social support. They suggested that stressors vary in the types of adaptation demands, and various categories of social support differ in the type of demands they can moderate. For example, the stress of job loss due to a layoff results in several adaptation demands, one of which is to find another job, a task for which instrumental or tangible aid from a variety of sources can be helpful. On the other hand, if the stressor results in the self-attribution of failure or inadequacy, such as losing a job because of the person's own incompetence, an important category of support might be positive regard or approval from similar others who can relate to his or her predicament. Therefore, social support may be particularly effective in minimizing the negative effects of the stressor when there is congruence between the demands of the stressor and the support resources.

Three Important Intervening Processes

Sandler, Miller, Short, and Wolchik (1989) proposed that social support may have its positive effects on well-being through three important intervening processes: Increasing self-esteem, increasing appropriate control perceptions, and enhancing the perceived security of the individual's social network. These positive effects then result in higher levels of adaptive functioning.

Sandler et al. (1989) outlined the ways in which support operates in each of these intervening processes for children experiencing stress. First, support may act to prevent the occurrence of esteem-threatening events, reduce the negative effects of stressors on self-esteem, and counteract the effects of negative events by providing self-esteem enhancing experiences. Second, social support may prevent control-threatening events by helping to maintain a predictable social environment in the face of stressors and may moderate maladaptive control beliefs by helping the person realistically assess his or her ability to control events. Through direct contributions to perceptions of control and efficacy, social support thereby counteracts negative events, or creates environmental conditions that enhance the development of internal control beliefs apart from the stress effects. Finally, social support may act to increase the security of social relations by providing continuity in the face of threatening circumstances, preventing the disruptions of social relationships during times of stress, and moderating the effects of stress on well-being.

Disentangling Stress, Support, and Adjustment

Although the various models of the relations among stress, support, and adjustment differ in their emphasis, all of them assert that social support plays a central, and possibly a causal, role in promoting psychological and physical well-being. Research examining the causal link between support and well-being has received serious criticism, however, because frequently the measures used to operationalize the constructs of support, adjustment, and stress overlap in content and therefore, are confounded with one another (Blazer & Hughes, 1991; Dohrenwend & Shrout, 1985; Dohrenwend, Dohrenwend, Dodson, & Shrout, 1984; DuBois, Felner, Brand, Adan, & Evans, 1992; Monroe & Steiner, 1986). For example, life events checklists used for assessing level of stress typically include events such as divorce, death of loved ones, and even increases in arguments with spouse or other primary network members; measures of social support often include marital status and quality of relationships with primary network members. Thus, both measures assess the extent and quality of the individual's social environment.

Recent reviews have found that although this is certainly an important issue to address in interpreting any association among support, stress, and adjustment, the correlations among these variables remain significant even when procedures for dealing with this possible confounding are used. These procedures include using multiple or different informants about stress and adjustment, or not counting those stressful events that are likely to be confounded with adjustment, particularly those events that could be a function of the individual's psychopathology such as interpersonal conflict or being sent to prison (Compas, 1987; Johnson, 1986; Rowlison & Felner, 1988).

Monroe and Steiner (1986) argue quite convincingly that in studying the relation between social support and psychopathology, researchers need to focus more attention on the influence of preexisting disorder because particular disorders may lead to decreases in social support. Thus, unless preexisting symptoms are controlled for, it is hard to establish how much of the relation between support and psychopathology is due to prior symptomology (Monroe, 1982, 1983) and how much of the relation is due to the direct or indirect effects of social support itself.

These methods of disentangling stress, support, and adjustment empirically or statistically do not solve the theoretical quandary. In fact, such methodological solutions may lead us to falsely believe that a clear distinction is possible. In real life, support, stressors, and distress *are* confounded under many circumstances, or they at least mutually and simultaneously influence each other, making it difficult to operationalize each construct independently.

Is Social Support an Artifact of Personality or a Product of Environment?

Just as modern-day developmentalists are required to integrate both nature and nurture in their theories, social psychologists are faced with a similar task of integrating forces within both the person and the environment. This task has generated considerable debate with regard to the study of individuals' reactions to stressful life events. Coping theories propose that individuals' efforts to alter stressful situations or regulate their emotions contribute to the distress they experience when encountering stressful events (Lazarus & Folkman, 1984), whereas other theories propose that personality dispositions, such as neuroticism, explain why some people become distressed and others remain resilient when faced with stressful events (Eysenck & Eysenck, 1985; McCrae & Costa, 1986).

This debate between a trait and a process orientation to personality is reflected in the literature concerning social support as well. Several theorists have raised the concern that the positive stress-buffering effects of social support may be artifacts of trait-like characteristics of personality such as neuroticism (Bolger & Eckenrode, 1991; Monroe & Steiner, 1986) or social competence (Heller & Swindle, 1983; B. R. Sarason et al., 1985). Is it that people who are very socially skilled tend to cope better with life stressors as well as attract social support, or do people in environments characterized by strong social ties with supportive others cope better with life stressors because of these environmental features? Overall, the findings are mixed with regard to this issue (e.g., Cohen, 1991; Cohen, Sherrod, & Clark, 1986; Sarason et al., 1985). Most likely, some of both mechanisms are responsible for the stress-buffering effects of social support. In other words, social support is probably best understood from an interactional perspective (Bolger & Eckenrode, 1991; Mitchell & Trickett, 1980; Sarason, Sarason, & Pierce, 1990; Vinokur, Schul, & Caplan, 1987; also see Bolger, 1990 who used a similar tactic concerning more general coping). Therefore, establishing the primacy of person or environment becomes less important, and understanding how the two forces interact as well as have their independent effects on well-being becomes more central.

An example of this approach is the research on locus of control and social support. Persons with internal control beliefs for negative events and low levels of support are more likely to become depressed, or otherwise distressed than are people with internal control beliefs and access to support under conditions of stress (Lefcourt, Martin, & Saleh, 1984; Sandler & Lakey, 1982). This suggests that control beliefs and support interact to moderate the effect of stress on well-being. Lefcourt et al. (1984) also found that adults with internal control beliefs derived greater benefit from support than did adults with external control beliefs, presumably because they are more discriminating and strategic in their use of support.

This more integrative perspective of the relation between the individual personality and the environment allows researchers to begin asking questions about process. For example, how do people's skills in obtaining and maintaining social networks, encouraging positive relationships, and expressing needs so that support is utilized in an optimal way contribute to their level of social support (Carpenter, Hansson, Rountree, & Jones, 1984; Sarason, Sarason, & Shearin, 1986)? This leads to an even more intriguing question from a developmental point of view: Does the nature of this relation differ across the life span? Early in development, social support may be more of an environmentally based phenomenon, although certainly temperament and other genetic factors (Bergeman, Plomin, Pedersen, & McClearn, 1991; Kessler, Kendler, Health, Neale, & Eaves, 1992), often categorized as within-child variables, can affect the quality of interactions an infant has with primary caretakers and other network members. Early experiences with social support may lead to particular personality characteristics, which in turn may lead to certain support experiences in later life (Sarason, Pierce, & Sarason, 1990). Sarason, Pierce, Shearin, Sarason, Waltz, and Poppe (1991) in their recent work with college students have found that perceptions of support from others are positively related to perceptions of others, as well as self-perceptions, beliefs about others' views, and parents' and friends' actual opinions about the target person. They assert that such findings substantiate the view that perceived support is not simply a global assessment of the person's relationships. Rather:

> In a sense, perceived social support is a cognitive adaptation that individuals make given the constraints and opportunities, both real and imagined, that are placed upon them by a history of experiences that result in working models of self and others. (Sarason et al., 1991, p. 285)

What is particularly appealing about this view is that it emphasizes that social support, in particular perceived support in this example, evolves over time. To locate its center solely within a person or in the environment ignores its dynamic nature.

There are several important and distinct models of the relations among social support, stress, and well-being. The support deterioration model suggests that deterioration and changes in the social network (social embeddedness) or how much support is received from the social network (enacted support) can result in increased distress and possible psychopathology. The main or direct effect model proposes that the presence of supportive relationships lessens distress either by keeping potentially stressful events from happening or by causing individuals to interpret events as nonstressful. Although much of the evidence for the

direct effect model has utilized a social embeddedness or structural definition of support, some evidence for this model has been found utilizing perceived support measures as well. Enacted or received support most likely plays a more tangential role in the direct effect model. Finally, stress-buffering models propose that social support lessens distress brought on by events that are appraised as stressful at least initially. According to these models, high levels of social support may result in individuals interpreting events as less stressful when they first occur, may increase coping options, or may boost individuals' self-esteem and sense of self-efficacy. Much of the research supporting this model has utilized measures of perceived support. All three models are helpful in understanding the relation between social support and psychopathology, although which model is the most useful may depend on the particular psychopathology being examined.

The following sections review the dimensions of social support (social networks, perceived, and enacted) with regard to three important and different forms of psychopathology: depression, schizophrenia, and conduct disorder. Although other diagnoses also have been found to be affected by social support including eating disorders (e.g., Garner, Garfinkel, & Olmsted, 1983; Grissett & Norvell, 1992) and anxiety (e.g., Pyke & Roberts, 1987), it is beyond the scope of this chapter to review these other literatures as well. The present discussion focuses on the role of social support in the onset and maintenance of depression, schizophrenia, and conduct disorder in relation to the various models just outlined.

Social Support and Depression

Most of the symptoms that define depressive disorder (e.g., sadness, sleep and appetite problems, fatigue, concentration difficulties, psychomotor changes, and suicidal ideation) are not particularly social in nature. A few depressive symptoms, however, do involve some interpersonal processes. For example, anhedonia is characterized by a loss of interest in usual activities, some of which typically include interactions with others. Such anhedonia can lead to the person's withdrawal from members of his or her social network. Feelings of guilt also often involve others in terms of the depressed person's belief of having failed to meet others' standards and of having let others down. Thus, it is possible for a diagnosis of an affective disorder to be made in a social vacuum, although depressive symptoms can have a serious impact on many aspects of social functioning, and the social environment can contribute to the onset and exacerbation of depressive symptoms.

Of all forms of psychopathology, perhaps most has been written about the relation of social support to depression and its milder forms of distress. There have been several scholarly and thorough reviews of the topic (e.g., Alloway & Bebbington, 1987; Barrera, 1988; Billings & Moos, 1982; Cohen & Wills, 1985; Coyne & Downey, 1991; Kessler et al., 1985; Leavy, 1983; Lin, Dean, & Ensel, 1986; Thoits, 1983), some of which have been concerned with identifying the direct and moderating effects of social support on psychological symptoms, particularly depression. Therefore, the present discussion does not provide a comprehensive review of this extensive literature, but rather it highlights the important findings concerning the relation of the three dimensions of social support (networks, perceptions, and enacted support) to depression across the life span).

Social Theories of Depression

Many of the leading theories of depression either implicitly or explicitly recognize the importance of interpersonal relationships in the development and maintenance of depression. Moreover, one of the more effective interventions for depression—interpersonal psychotherapy (IPT)—is based on the premise that depression usually occurs in an interpersonal context, often as the result of an interpersonal loss or dispute (Klerman, Weissman, Rounsaville, & Chevron, 1984).

Several models of depression are considered interpersonal theories and specifically emphasize the importance of social interactions. Early social theorists (Meyer, 1957; Sullivan, 1953) suggested that depression occurs when individuals have difficulty adapting to their current psychosocial and interpersonal environment. Lewinsohn and colleagues (1974; Lewinsohn, Mischel, Chaplin, & Barton, 1980; Libet & Lewinsohn, 1973; Youngren & Lewinsohn, 1980) argued that depression results, in part, from a deficiency in social skills that leads to a reduction in positive reinforcement and support from others. In a review of the literature concerning psychosocial factors and depression, Barnett and Gotlib (1988; also see Hammen, 1992) concluded that disturbances in interpersonal functioning may be an important antecedent or sequela of depression. Other theorists have speculated that depression is the result of insecure early attachments and the loss of intimate connectedness (Bowlby, 1969, 1980; Cummings & Cicchetti, 1990; Hammen, 1991; Weiss, 1974). That is, the absence or loss of positive and supportive social attachments is hypothesized to lead to depression particularly among individuals who have a history of less than adequate interpersonal relationships.

G. W. Brown (1987; Brown & Harris, 1978) has emphasized the buffering role of social support in relation to stress and depression. He posited that stressful life events are provoking agents that can trigger depression in individuals who are particularly vulnerable to the disorder. Contextual factors such as social support or individual factors such a self-esteem can either buffer or exacerbate the impact of negative life events. According to Brown and colleagues (Brown, Bifulco, & Harris, 1987; Brown & Harris, 1978) highly personal stressful events, especially those that occur in the context of chronic ongoing difficulties and low social support are especially predictive of depression. Brown (1987) further argued that it is the presence of support *at the time* of the negative event that is critical rather than necessarily the existence of an ongoing confidant relationship.

In perhaps the most extensive interactional perspective on depression, Coyne and colleagues (1976a; Coyne, Burchill, & Stiles, 1991) have suggested that the characteristic responses that depressed individuals receive from others can serve to maintain and exacerbate depressive symptoms by perpetuating an unsatisfactory situation. This perspective focuses on how depressed people get along with key people in their lives as well as how they affect and are affected by the people with whom they interact.

Coyne's (1976a; Coyne et al., 1991) model is particularly relevant for explaining the role of social support in the maintenance rather than the onset of depressive symptoms. He suggested, "Regardless of the precipitants for depression, it can be anticipated that depressed people will make demands and depend on their relationships in ways that leave others feeling depressed or annoyed themselves" (Coyne et al., 1991, p. 328). Thus, depressed individuals may cause their social network to shrink because people begin staying away from them. In addition, members of their social network might not provide support or help (enacted support) as much or as well as they did before the person became depressed because they themselves are annoyed by the depressed individual and might not want to spend as much time around him or her. The depressed individual then perceives this rejection from others and becomes less satisfied with his or her social relationships (perceived support). Thus, according to Coyne's perspective, depression is associated with all three social support dimensions.

Coyne (1976a; Coyne et al., 1991) has detailed some of the behaviors of depressed individuals that are particularly likely to annoy or distress the members of their social network. For example, although other people initially try to be helpful and supportive, depressed individuals are likely to express dissatisfaction with these attempts and push for further assistance and approval. Their excessive neediness and dependence on others for helping them to feel better often lead to frustration and hostility among members of the support system. As a result, these members begin providing less support and actually might become more rejecting, thereby perpetuating the dissatisfaction and the depressive symptoms.

Finally, even cognitive theories of depression (Abramson, Metalsky, & Alloy, 1989; Beck, 1976, 1983) recognize the importance of the social context and have suggested the notion of specific vulnerability. According to this view, individuals who are particularly affiliative or sociotropic (Beck, 1983; Hammen, Ellicott, Gitlin, & Jamison, 1989), that is, those who highly value interpersonal relationships, are especially vulnerable to depression when negative life events occur within the interpersonal domain, such as rejection or loss of a loved one. Moreover, these cognitive-stress models of depression acknowledge that social support can be a further moderator of the interaction between cognitions and stress. That is, stressful life events can precipitate depression in cognitively vulnerable individuals, and the presence of positive and supportive social relationships can buffer the negative impact of such negative events in these vulnerable individuals. Although this is often difficult to demonstrate empirically because it requires a three-way interaction, it is a more complex and conceptually rich model.

Thus, social relationships in general and social support in particular are hypothesized to play an important role in the onset and maintenance of depressive symptoms and disorders. The relation among stress, social support, and depression involves a complex, nonlinear system of feedback loops among these constructs and thus is an interactive process. Moreover, these relations appear to be bidirectional (Monroe & Steiner, 1986). Whereas low levels of social support alone or in the context of stress have been found to be associated with and to predict depressive symptoms (Cohen & Wills, 1985), it also is true that depression can seriously affect the nature of the person's social relationships and thereby alter the extent and nature of the social support available and received.

Social Networks

The size and characteristics of the social network have been found to covary with, directly predict, and buffer against depression. Studies that have used global structural support measures to assess a composite of the amount of contact with members of the person's social network, neighborhood interaction, and community participation have been found to be directly related to depressive symptoms (Bell, LeRoy, & Stephenson, 1982) and to buffer the effect of stressors on symptoms (Frydman, 1981; Miller & Ingham, 1979). Several studies have found that having a smaller social network, fewer close relationships, less contact with friends, and less supportive relationships all are associated with depression (Billings & Moos, 1984; Leaf, Weissman, Myers, Tischler, & Holzer, 1984; Schaefer, Coyne, & Lazarus, 1981). Weissman and Paykel (1974) reported that depressed people had relatively few social contacts and limited support systems. Billings, Cronkite, and Moos (1983) found that, compared with controls, depressed subjects reported having fewer contacts with members of their social network, which was comprised of significantly fewer friends and fewer close relationships.

Evidence of a buffering effect for support also has been found. In a study of pregnant teens between 15 and 19 years old, Barrera (1981) reported a significant interaction between network size and stress in the prediction of depressive symptoms. That is, the relation between stressful life events and depression was smaller for adolescents with larger total networks and larger unconflicted networks than for adolescents with small total networks.

Stiffman, Chueh, and Earls (1992) conducted a large longitudinal study of over 5,000 youth who used public primary health-care facilities in 10 cities across the country. They found that the level of social activities that subjects participated in (e.g., clubs, hobbies, sports, church) was associated with lower depression scores among those youths who had experienced many stressful circumstances over the year, whereas there was not this relation among youths with low levels of stress. The authors suggested that such social activities may play a protective role for children from disrupted environments. Thus, there is some evidence of a buffering effect of social networks on the relation between stress and depression.

Why do depressed individuals have less dense social networks or lower levels of social resources? Some of the symptoms of depression might directly or indirectly impact social relationships. For example, depressed individuals might not engage in the behaviors necessary for obtaining and maintaining friendships because they are too tired, don't care (anhedonic), or want to be by themselves (social withdrawal). Their lack of confidence and low self-esteem might keep them from pursuing relationships. Depressed people also might turn off their networks as a result of such symptoms as irritability, anger, hostility, complaining, lack of interest, social withdrawal, interpersonal passivity and underresponsiveness, preoccupation with their own concerns, and frequent expressions of pessimism, self-devaluation, helplessness, and vulnerability to others (Altman & Wittenborn, 1980; Blumberg & Hokanson, 1983; Coyne, Aldwin, & Lazarus, 1981;

Howes, Hokanson, & Lowenstein, 1985; Lewinsohn et al., 1980). Howes et al. (1985), for example, found in a study of college roommates that depressed students were more dependent, distrustful, and self-devaluing than nondepressed students. Such social behaviors seem to elicit a variety of reactions in others, including dysphoria, anger, negative evaluations, and rejection (Coyne, 1976b; Strack & Coyne, 1983; see discussion of enacted support below). These conflictual reactions set into motion negative interactional patterns that maintain or exacerbate the depression over time (Coates & Wortman, 1980; Coyne, 1976b).

Thus, there is a direct association between network size and depression. This relation appears to be bidirectional: Few supportive persons in a person's network and lack of connection with the people in the community can contribute directly to feelings of isolation, distress, and depression. On the other hand, depressive symptoms also can irritate and annoy members of the network so that they are less likely to keep coming around. This reduction in contact with network members then can result in emotional distress and other depressive symptoms.

Regardless of the absolute size of the social network, having one or two confiding relationships has been found to have beneficial effects, especially in the context of stress. The distinction among the three dimensions of support becomes blurred with regard to confidant relationships. Simply the presence of a confidant (or other members of the social network) is considered here in the discussion of social networks; the extent to which individuals utilize these confidants to receive support is discussed with regard to enacted support.

Important work concerning social networks, confidants, and depression has been done by Brown and colleagues (Brown, 1974; Brown, Bhrolchain, & Harris, 1975; Brown & Harris, 1978). They found in their Camberwell study that the single most powerful factor moderating the effect of negative life events on clinical depression was the *presence* of an "intimate, confiding relationship with a boyfriend or husband" (Brown et al., 1975, p. 225). Women who did not have an intimate confidant and who experienced stressful life events were about 10 times more likely to develop clinical depression than those with similar levels of stress who had a confidant.

Several other studies (Habif & Lahey, 1980; Paykel et al., 1980; Roy, 1978; Slater & Depue, 1981; Surtees, 1980) have similarly reported that having an open and confiding relationship is associated with lower levels of depression. Slater and Depue (1981), for example, found that among depressed patients, those who had made a suicide attempt were significantly less likely to have a confidant. Warheit (1979) found that simply the presence of a spouse or a close friend significantly predicted lower depression scores, particularly among individuals experiencing high levels of negative events.

The presence of a significant interpersonal relationship such as a spouse, sibling, parent, or close friendship, has a buffering effect, particularly in relation to specific stressors related to health, marriage, school, or employment (Linn & McGranahan, 1980; Monroe, Imhoff, Wise, & Harris, 1983). Monroe et al. (1983) found that among college students, living at home with parents was significantly associated with lower levels of depressive symptoms during the time of their final examinations.

In addition, Monroe et al. reported that having fewer friends also predicted higher levels of depressive symptoms in the context of undesirable life events.

Among elderly individuals, Murphy (1982) similarly found that having no confiding relationship at all significantly increased the risk of their developing depression in the context of a serious life difficulty. Thus, results from these various studies are consistent with those of Brown and Harris (1978) who found that an intimate confiding relationship afforded protection from symptoms of distress in the presence of stressful life events; therefore, confidants may play a particularly important buffering role in the relation between stress and depression.

In a review of the literature on marriage and depression, Coyne and Downey (1991) concluded that being married provided a modest reduction in the risk for clinical depression over that associated with being single, separated, or divorced presumably through emotional support and intimacy. However, individuals who are married and unable to communicate with their spouse are at much greater risk for depression (Weissman, 1987). Thus, simply being married may not be sufficient to buffer against stress; rather the quality of the person's interactions with his or her spouse may be even more important in reducing the risk for depression (see discussion of enacted support).

Surtees (1980) found that depressed patients who reported having a confidant with whom they had a reciprocal confiding relationship had significantly fewer severe symptoms at follow-up about 7 months later than did either those with a nonreciprocal relationship or those with a very poor (relationship) or no confidant. Those patients with at least some potentially supportive others in their network (e.g., relatives, neighbors, coworkers) had significantly fewer symptoms at follow-up than did those with a very limited supportive network. The key characteristic of the confidant relationship identified in this study was reciprocity in disclosure between the patient and confidant. Thus, once again, it may be that particular qualitative features of relationships with significant others, rather than merely their presence, results in fewer depressive symptoms. This notion is discussed further in the following sections addressing the relation between depression and both perceived and enacted support.

The benefits of confiding relationships also have been found for children and adolescents. Sandler (1980) reported that both the presence of two parents or an older sibling were associated with lower levels of maladjustment in children. Belle and Longfellow (1983, 1984) measured support using Saunders' (1977) Nurturance Scale that operationalizes support in terms of the number of confidants children have across a variety of situations. Those who reported having more confidants (typically mothers and friends) exhibited higher self-esteem, more internal locus of control, and less loneliness, whereas having no confidant was significantly associated with lower self-esteem and more external locus of control. Although Belle and Longfellow did not measure depressive symptoms directly, low self-esteem, external locus of control, and loneliness all have been found to be associated with depression in children (Garber & Hilsman, 1992).

Several studies have implicated the absence of an intimate relationship as a risk factor for depression in both adults (Brown & Prudo, 1981; Costello, 1982) and children (Hirschfeld & Cross,

1982; Pelligrini et al., 1986; Roy, 1978). Pelligrini et al. found that the risk of having an affective disorder compared with no disorder was 4.9 times as great for children who did not have a best friend as for those who did have a best friend. Thus, the presence of even one confiding relationship seems to make a substantial difference among individuals experiencing life stress.

Finally, one other important question concerns whether the associations between social networks and depression are stable or change when the depressed individual is no longer in an episode. Billings and Moos (1985) found that remitted depressives (tested 12 months after admission to treatment) had fewer friends and fewer close relationships, although not fewer social network contacts, than did normal controls. Thus, remitted depressives appear able to maintain a normal level of superficial acquaintances, but they may have greater difficulty sustaining close or intimate relationships.

In sum, depressed individuals tend to have smaller social networks during their depressive episodes. Prospective studies are needed to examine the extent to which having a small or decreasing network precedes the onset of the depressive symptoms or whether decreasing networks are the result of the expression of depressive symptoms, and thereby serve to maintain these symptoms. In addition, the presence of a confidant seems to buffer the effects of stress on depression in both children and adults. Thus, the quantity of relationships in the social network is directly associated with depression, and the quality of these relationships may be particularly important for predicting depressive symptoms in the context of stress.

Perceived Support

Perceived support in the depression literature has been assessed using measures of subjects' ratings of their satisfaction with support from specific individuals as well as broader measures of the perceived quality of family, marital, or peer relationships. The main thing these measures have in common is that they assess individuals' subjective appraisals of the social support available to them.

In general, studies that assess the concurrent relation between perceived support and depression in adults have found that low support satisfaction is significantly correlated with higher levels of distress and depressive symptoms (Barrera, 1981, 1986). Depressed individuals in both community (e.g., Leaf et al., 1984; O'Hara, 1986) and clinical samples (e.g., Billings & Moos, 1984) report less satisfaction with friends and relatives, less confiding in their spouse, and less satisfactory marital relationships. Billings and Moos and colleagues (Billings et al., 1983; Billings & Moos, 1982, 1984; Holahan & Moos, 1981) consistently have found that perceived cohesiveness and supportiveness in the family is more highly negatively correlated with depression than is the number of people in one's network. Billings et al. (1983) reported that currently depressed patients perceived the quality of their significant relationships, family support, and work support to be significantly less than did controls. In a sample of pregnant women, O'Hara (1986; O'Hara, Rehm, & Campbell, 1983) found that depressed women reported significantly more dissatisfaction with the frequency of supportive behaviors from social network members than did nondepressed women. Women who became depressed postpartum also reported significantly less marital satisfaction than did nondepressed women.

A significant concurrent relation between perceived support and depression also has been observed in children and adolescents. Friedrich, Reams, and Jacobs (1982) found that higher self-reported depression on the Beck Depression Inventory (BDI) was associated with less perceived support, more family conflict, and less family cohesion in adolescents. Among 8- to 13-year-old children hospitalized for psychiatric problems, Asarnow, Carlson, & Guthrie (1987) found that suicide attempters reported lower perceived support than did nonsuicidal patients. In a community sample of children, Kaslow, Rehm, and Siegel (1984) revealed that self-reported depressed children perceived their parents as being less available and less nurturing than did nondepressed children. Harter, Marold, & Whitesell (1992) also have found perceptions of approval or positive regard from peers and parents (along with hopelessness about obtaining that approval) were associated with depressive symptoms in a nonclinical sample of young adolescents.

Compas, Slavin, Wagner, and Vannatta (1986) used a measure that assessed the average number of support persons across a variety of hypothetical situations, and their perceived level of satisfaction with the support they received in each situation in adolescents. They found that whereas the average number of support persons was not related to symptom level measured on the Hopkins symptom checklist (HSCL), lower satisfaction with social support was significantly correlated with symptoms (-.27 with depression). Compas et al. (1986) did not find a significant buffering effect for perceived support on the relation between negative events and symptoms, however.

Gad and Johnson (1980) also did not find that perceived social support moderated the relation between stress and adjustment. Using a global measure of respondents' subjective ratings of support from a number of different sources, Gad and Johnson found significant relations between negative life events and maladaptation in subjects who were both high and low in social support.

Some studies, however, have found a significant buffering effect for perceived support. In adults, Cohen and colleagues (Cohen & Hoberman, 1983; Cohen, Mermelstein, Kamarck, & Hoberman, 1985) used the Interpersonal Support Evaluation List (ISEL) to assess the perceived availability of advice, material aid, and "approval" (i.e., feedback involving favorable comparison with others), and social companionship, and found a significant buffering effect of such perceived support on depressive symptoms. In a study of men experiencing occupational stress, House and Wells (1978) reported that perceived support from wives was associated with less depression among those men experiencing high levels of occupational stress. Perceived support from supervisors or coworkers, however, was not associated with depressive symptoms among these men. Using a community sample of older adults, Phifer and Murrell (1986) found that perceived social support both directly and in interaction with health or loss events significantly predicted to increases in self-reported depression. Finally, in a sample of 6- to 9-year-old children, Wertlieb, Weigel, and Feldstein (1987) reported evidence for a buffering effect of perceived

support on the relation between stress and behavior symptoms. Low levels of support and greater numbers of life events were associated with higher levels of symptoms.

Thus, cross-sectional studies consistently have found a significant relation between measures of perceived support and depressive symptoms. The results have been mixed, however, with regard to whether perceived support buffers the effect of stress on symptoms. These studies differ in many ways including the measures of perceived support, measures of depressive symptoms, age of the subjects, sources of support, and types of stressors. A particularly important factor that could partially explain the different results concerns the extent to which the measures of perceived support, stress, and depression were confounded in the different studies. That is, the relations among stress, support, and depression will be affected by how much the measures of each construct overlap (Monroe, 1983).

A related limitation of these cross-sectional studies is the potential problem of rater bias. Critics of the literature linking social support to adjustment have argued that this relation is the result of shared self-report bias that affects responses to both support and symptom measures (Cutrona, 1989; Henderson, Byrne, & Duncan-Jones, 1981; Monroe, 1983). When people are depressed, they tend to evaluate themselves and others more negatively than when they are not depressed (Alloy & Abramson, 1988; Beck, 1967, 1976), and this negativity may account for the association between perceived support and depression rather than a true absence of support.

To examine whether the association between perceived support and depression was simply a function of a negative reporting bias, Billings et al. (1983) assessed the relation between subjects' and their spouses' reports about family supportiveness. They found substantial agreement among informants and therefore concluded that the reported lack of family support by depressed patients might accurately reflect the nature and level of the resources available in these families.

Other evidence of the veridicality of individuals' descriptions of their social networks has been found (Antonucci & Israel, 1986; Cutrona, 1989; Repetti, 1987). Cutrona (1989) reported moderate concordance between adolescents' and another informant's (typically parents) ratings of the supportiveness received from their parents, and somewhat lower agreement regarding support from friends. Cutrona also found that informants' social support ratings significantly predicted depression scores both concurrently and prospectively even after controlling for the adolescents' self-reported support ratings. Cutrona concluded that "neither self-report nor informant assessments of social support can be viewed as mirrors of objective social reality" (p. 729). Moreover, the extent to which an individual's perceptions of his or her support relate to other variables of interest (e.g., symptoms) may be more important for our understanding of the relation between social support and psychopathology than the accuracy of these perceptions per se.

Another method of exploring the relation between social support and depression that is presumed to be less affected by reporting bias and the potential influences of dysphoric mood or depressogenic thinking on subjective ratings of support has been to examine the perceptions of formerly depressed individuals when they are no longer symptomatic. Billings and Moos (1985) reported that remitted depressives perceived the quality of their family interactions to be significantly less supportive than did normal controls although they did not differ from controls with regard to their ratings of the quality of their close relationships or support received at work.

Armsden, McCauley, Greenberg, Burke, & Mitchell (1990) compared the perceived security of parent and peer attachment of adolescents with clinical depression, nondepressed psychiatric disorders, no psychiatric disorder, and remitted depressives. Currently depressed adolescents reported significantly less secure parent attachment than the never depressed groups, and less secure peer attachments than the nonpsychiatric controls. The remitted depressed group were not significantly different from the other groups although they reported attachments at about the level of the nonpsychiatric controls who were significantly higher than currently depressed patients.

Thus, there is evidence that remitted depressed individuals continue to perceive some people in their network as less supportive than nondepressed individuals although they do not appear to be as dissatisfied as are currently depressed individuals. Future studies need to compare the same individuals during and after a depressive episode with regard to their perceptions of support. It could be that as they become less depressed they become more satisfied, and thus, their perceived support would be linked to their depressive state. It also could be that as they become less depressed their relationships with others improves and therefore other people actually provide them with more support. Prospective studies of the same individuals over time that measure both the perceptions and behaviors of depressed patients as well as the responses of members of their social networks are needed to test these various hypotheses.

In addition, prospective studies that assess support *prior* to the onset of depressive symptoms can begin to examine the potential causal role of perceived support on depression. It is possible that perceptions of support are the consequence rather than the cause of the depressive symptoms. Instead of such dissatisfaction preceding the onset of depressive symptoms and possibly contributing to their development, depressed individuals might perceive their networks to be unsatisfactory only while they are depressed.

Monroe and colleagues (Monroe, 1983; Monroe, Bromet, Connell, & Steiner, 1986) have tried to disentangle these relations by studying the role of social support in the onset of depressive symptoms. They assessed perceived support and marital discord in women who were not showing any symptoms of depression at the time of the first assessment. They reassessed these women one year later and found that the higher the support satisfaction measured a year earlier, the lower the subsequent depression symptom score. Marital support did not buffer the effect of stressful life events on symptoms, however. This is consistent with other studies that have found a direct effect of perceived social support on depression (Aneshensel & Stone, 1982; S. Cohen & McKay, 1984; Lin & Ensel, 1984). Lin and Ensel (1984) asked a community sample of subjects to rate their satisfaction with their close friends. They found that, controlling for initial levels of symptoms, deterioration in perceived social support predicted increases in depressive symptoms one year later.

Using a community sample of older adults, Krause, Liang, and Yatomi (1989) similarly found that changes in satisfaction with support preceded changes in depressive symptoms, whereas initial levels of depression were unrelated to subsequent changes in satisfaction with social support.

Cutrona (1984) reported that a global measure of total perceived social support predicted to depressive symptoms 8 weeks postpartum. Cutrona suggested that simply knowing that others are available during the stressful time right after a baby is born may decrease the likelihood of feeling overwhelmed and depressed about all the new responsibilities that accompany this period.

Several prospective studies of children and adolescents have found that perceived support predicted depressive symptoms several months later, controlling for initial levels of symptoms (DuBois et al., 1992; Stiffman et al., 1992; Windle, 1992b). DuBois et al. (1992) conducted a longitudinal study over a 2-year period that examined the relations among life stressors, social support, and psychological and academic adjustment in young adolescents. They included measures of major life events and daily hassles, and perceived support from family, peers, and school personnel. Analyses of the cross-sectional relations indicated that higher levels of perceived support from family and friends were associated with lower levels of distress; friend support related to higher grades; teacher support was not associated with either outcome. In the prospective analyses, higher perceived support from school personnel, although not from friends or family, was related to reduced levels of distress at follow-up after controlling for initial level of distress, life events, and hassles.

DuBois et al. (1992) also found two significant interactions with regard to support. First, major life events were more strongly related to distress among subjects who reported low levels of support from school personnel than among those who reported high levels of such support. Second, ratings of support from school personnel were more strongly related to reduced psychological distress among adolescents who reported low levels of support from family members than among those who reported higher levels of family support. DuBois et al. (1992) also examined the potential reciprocal influence of distress on social support. Psychological distress was significantly related to increased daily hassles and reduced family support at Time 2, whereas lower grades were predictive of higher levels of perceived friend support.

This study was important because it found evidence of a prospective relation between social support and psychological distress, controlling for initial levels of distress. It also found interactive and reciprocal patterns of associations among these constructs. DuBois et al. (1992) noted that supportive ties to school personnel may buffer or compensate for potential problems in the home environment. They also found support for the notion that distressed individuals may interact with their environment in ways that reduce their access to supportive resources and increase the stressfulness of their daily experiences.

These results also highlight the importance of examining different sources of support separately in relation to adjustment. Several other studies in the child literature have shown different findings with regard to perceived parental versus peer support. In a review of the social support literature in children, Wolchik et al. (1989) concluded that whereas social support from peers has been found to be positively related to distress, support from adults was negatively related to symptoms. Similarly Cauce, Felner, Primavera, and Ginter (1982) found a positive association between perceived family support and good scholastic self-concept, and a negative relation between perceived support from friends and scholastic achievement.

Barrera and Garrison-Jones (1992) compared family versus peer support in relation to depression in adolescent psychiatric patients. They found that greater perceived family support, particularly satisfaction with support from fathers was associated with fewer depressive symptoms. In contrast, the multiplexity of the peer network was positively related to depression. This is consistent with other studies that have found a deleterious effect of peer support with other child outcomes such as academic achievement and smoking (e.g., Cauce et al., 1982; Chassin, Presson, Sherman, Montello, & McGrew, 1986; Wolchik, Ruehlman, Braver, & Sandler, 1989).

It is not clear what accounts for this negative relation between perceived peer support and adjustment. Is it that highly distressed youth seek out greater contact with their peers or actually receive more support from peers; or is there something about these peer interactions that leads to depression? A third possibility is that some third variable such as increased stress leads to greater contact with peers and also to greater feelings of distress. Future studies need to test among these alternative explanations.

Barrera and Garrison-Jones (1992) also found several interesting interactions between peer and family support. For adolescents with low family support, low levels of perceived peer support were associated with greater depressive symptoms. Similarly, at low levels of perceived support from fathers, low levels of satisfaction with peer support were associated with greater depressive symptoms. This was not the case with regard to perceived maternal support, however. Thus, adolescents who perceived low levels of family support were more depressed than were those who perceived high levels of family support. When family support was perceived to be low, peer support was negatively related to depression. That is, perceived peer support may be particularly important in the context of low perceived family support, but less so when family support is high.

Parent versus peer support also may be differentially related to various forms of psychopathology. In a cross-sectional study of the relations among temperament, perceived support, and internalizing and externalizing symptoms in 975 adolescents, Windle (1992b) found that low perceived family emotional support was significantly correlated with higher levels of depressive symptoms and delinquency, indicating the generality of family support for both internalizing and externalizing problems. Low perceived friend emotional support, however, was significantly related to depressive symptoms but not to delinquency, suggesting more specificity of friend support relative to family support for adolescents.

Windle (1992b) also reported the interesting finding that perceived family and peer support partially mediated the relation between temperament and depressive symptoms. Windle speculated that higher levels of temperamental difficulty may lead to more interpersonal conflict and less interpersonal reciprocity. These interpersonal difficulties then lead to perceptions of lower levels of social support, which result in greater levels of depressive symptoms.

In sum, subjective dissatisfaction with the perceived availability of support is linked to depressive symptoms in both children and adults. Such dissatisfaction can occur when there is not a fit between a person's expectations and experiences of support. Barrera (1986) suggested that the negative relation between perceived support and psychological distress is consistent with attachment theory (Bowlby, 1969; Henderson, 1977). That is, social connections and the perceived adequacy of these relationships in meeting the individual's needs are hypothesized to be a primary requisite for psychological well-being, and the absence of such attachments is a sufficient cause of distress (Barrera, 1986).

The role of perceived support as a buffer against stress is less clear. Future studies of the relation between perceived support and depression need to address the problem of rater bias and the potential influence of depression on subjective ratings. Prospective studies of the same individuals both during and after a depressive episode, as well as studies that assess perceived support prior to the onset of symptoms are needed. Finally, perceptions of support from different sources (e.g., parents, peers, coworkers, spouse) might be differentially associated with adjustment and therefore should be assessed separately.

Enacted Support

Enacted support in the depression literature has been concerned with the amount of help provided by members of the social network and the quality of this support. Patterns of interactions among family members are particularly relevant to the construct of enacted support. There is a growing literature showing that both the absence of supportive interactions and the presence of negative, conflictual interpersonal exchanges are associated with depression (Burbach & Borduin, 1986; Coyne & Downey, 1991; Downey & Coyne, 1990; McCauley & Meyers, 1992). The quality of interactions with close relationships, most notably that with the spouse, has a particularly strong association with depression (Leaf et al., 1984).

In general, a positive relation has been found between enacted support, defined in terms of frequency of help provided, and depressive symptoms (Barrera, 1981; Coyne et al., 1981; Fiore, Becker, & Coppel, 1983). Barrera (1986) suggested several explanations for this relation including (a) individuals who show the greatest amount of distress receive and/or seek the most enacted support; (b) the relation is the result of a shared association with stress which leads to both receiving more support from others and to depression; or (c) receiving assistance from others could be experienced negatively if it was not delivered satisfactorily. Thus, bad support can actually increase the level of distress.

A significant buffering effect for received support also has been found. Paykel et al. (1980) reported that among postpartum women who experienced negative life events, those who received no help from their husbands were 10 times more likely to be depressed than were those who received instrumental and emotional support from their spouses. Furthermore, Campbell, Cohn, Flanagan, Popper, and Meyers (1992) found that among women experiencing postpartum depression, the level of instrumental and emotional support from spouses at 2 months postpartum predicted chronicity of depression, with less support from spouses being associated with more chronic versus short-lived depressions. Gore (1978) found that among married men who had recently lost their jobs, those who received emotional support from their wives were significantly less likely to become depressed than those who did not have such supportive wives.

Several studies that have used the Inventory of Socially Supportive Behaviors (ISSB; Barrera, Sandler, & Ramsey, 1981) to assess respondents' reports of the amount of different types of support received during the past month have found both a direct and a buffering effect for enacted support, although the direction of the relation between support and depression has not been consistent. Barrera (1981) found that amount of received support positively correlated with symptomatology. Sandler and Lakey (1982) reported that received support was associated with higher levels of symptoms for low-stress persons, and lower levels of symptoms for high-stress persons. In contrast, Cohen and Hoberman (1983) found a negative relation between received support and depressive symptoms under low stress, but not under high stress. After reviewing these findings, Cohen and Wills (1985) argued that measures such as the ISSB that assess recent past use of support reflect psychological distress that then leads to more support being provided and used, although in some cases the received support can help to reduce the symptom level.

Wolchik, Ruehlman, Braver, and Sandler (1985) used a children's version of the ISSB known as the Children's Inventory of Social Support (CISS) to examine its relation to parent and child report measures of adjustment. The CISS assesses the number of support functions provided by different members of their network during a specific period of time (e.g., the previous 3 months). Wolchik et al. found that the relations between social support and adjustment differed depending on the source of support and the informant about adjustment. Higher levels of family support were significantly positively related to parental report of children's adjustment, whereas support from peers and nonfamily adults were not related to adjustment. None of the support scores across all potential providers (i.e., family, nonfamily adult, peers) were significantly correlated with children's report of symptoms.

Wolchik et al. (1985) also found significant stress by support interactions for family support and nonfamily adult support, but not for peers. Under conditions of high stress, children who reported receiving high levels of support were better adjusted than were children with low support. Under conditions of low stress, children with high support reported more adjustment problems than did children with low support. Wolchik et al. (1987) speculated that perhaps children who have very helpful networks but few stressors interpret this helpfulness as indicating that they are less able to do things themselves and therefore perceive themselves as having more problems. It also could be that those children who get a lot of support during nonstressful times may receive it because they are already having symptoms.

In addition, the type of support provided by members of an individual's social network and who provides that support also might change when the person is manifesting depressive symptoms. For example, whereas friends and relatives still might be willing to provide information or instrumental aid, they might be less likely to show approval and positive regard, which is probably what the depressed person most needs at that time. O'Hara (1986) found that depressed women both during and after their pregnancy reported receiving more emotional support from a friend, but less instrumental support from their spouses than did nondepressed women. O'Hara concluded that distressed individuals might be more likely to receive support from a nonmarital confidant, particularly if support from their spouses has decreased.

As mentioned in the discussion concerning social networks, the presence of even one confiding relationship seems to make a substantial difference among individuals experiencing life stress (e.g., Brown & Prudo, 1981; Pelligrini et al., 1986). What are the processes by which confiding relationships assist vulnerable individuals? Brown (1987) suggested that at the time of a crisis, support characterized by a confiding and emotionally supportive relationship without negative reactions was the most helpful and least likely to be associated with depression. In addition to the instrumental and informational assistance and guidance with cognitive reappraisal that these close relationships make available, they are particularly important because of the unconditional approval and positive regard they provide (see Harter et al., 1992, for a discussion of importance of conditionality of support in explaining depressive symptoms in young adolescents). Brown (1987) asserted that those women who did not receive the support they expected became more depressed, in part, as a result of a fall in their self-esteem over and above the negative effects of the event itself. Indeed, some researchers (Husaini et al., 1982; Pearlin et al., 1981) have found that the relation between support from a confidant and depressive symptoms is mediated by self-esteem or self-efficacy.

There are aspects of marital quality that are particularly relevant to the issue of enacted social support. Much has been written about the relation between marriage and depression (e.g., Bothwell & Weissman, 1977; Monroe et al., 1986; O'Hara, 1986) that is beyond the scope of this chapter. We highlight here only some of the major findings from this literature that are relevant to social support.

There is increasing evidence of a relation between disturbances in intimate interpersonal functioning and depression both as an antecedent and a sequela of the disorder (Barnett & Gotlib, 1988). The marriages of depressed people tend to have problems, and this is true as rated by both the depressed person and the spouse (Coleman & Miller, 1975; Coyne et al., 1991; Kahn, Coyne, & Margolin, 1985). The marital interactions of depressed people tend to be tense, hostile, critical, and conflictual (Coyne et al., 1991; Hinchcliffe, Hopper, & Roberts, 1978; Leff & Vaughn, 1985). Such critical interactions have been linked to increased risk for relapse among formerly depressed patients. In particular, the level of expressed emotion, specifically the number of hostile, critical comments about a depressed patient that the spouse makes in an interview during the patient's hospitalization, is predictive of posthospital relapse independent of the patient's level of symptomatology (Hooley, Orley, & Teasdale, 1986; Leff & Vaughn, 1985; Vaughn & Leff, 1976a).

There also is evidence that the marital problems persist beyond the time of the acute depressive episode. Paykel and Weissman (1973) found that asymptomatic formerly depressed women had disturbed intimate interpersonal functioning 8 months after remission of their symptoms. Four years after the remission of their symptoms, recovered female depressives continued to experience more interpersonal friction and to be more impaired in their marital roles than control subjects (Bothwell & Weissman, 1977).

Thus, the social difficulties of depressed individuals seem to endure. This could be the result of their depressive symptoms causing subsequent interpersonal problems, a more stable personality characteristic, or social skills deficits. Whatever the cause, these individuals are less likely to receive adequate social support from their networks even beyond the time of their depressive episode.

Coyne and Downey (1991) commented about the relation between marriage and depression, and concluded that "the apparent benefits of having support may in large part represent freedom from the deleterious effects of relationships that are conflictual, insecure, or otherwise not sustaining" (p. 23). "The notion of a stress buffering functioning of social support becomes transformed into a question of how involvement in dysfunctional relationships impairs coping with stress" (p. 24).

One difficulty of conceptualizing the effects of social support in terms of the deleterious effects of being in a problematic relationship, however, is that it is then difficult to know where low support ends and stress begins. Lennon (1989) stated that "the distinction between stressors and support blur when we conceptualize the unit of study as actors embedded in social relations . . . support and stressors often reside in the same set of interactions and cannot be understood part from this relational context" (p. 262). Thus, it is important to differentiate between the constructs of marital conflict and marital support in trying to understand the role of intimate relationships in the process of becoming depressed (Monroe et al., 1986; O'Hara, 1986).

Another important issue with regard to the relation between enacted support and depression is why the amount and nature of support changes for individuals when they become depressed. Coyne (1976a, 1976b) suggested that because interacting with depressed individuals is aversive, others tend to respond negatively or to avoid them. Indeed, several studies have found that individuals tend to be more rejecting of depressed persons than nondepressed persons (Coyne, 1976b; Hammen & Peters, 1978; Howes & Hokanson, 1979; Strack & Coyne, 1983; although see also Gotlib & Robinson, 1982; King & Heller, 1984). Robbins, Strack, and Coyne (1979) found that subjects reacted less positively to depressed individuals, and Hokanson, Sacco, Blumberg, and Landrum (1980) reported that subjects reported expressing more irritation toward depressed individuals than controls. Moreover, it is not simply that others report feeling more negatively toward depressed individuals, but depressed subjects report experiencing fewer positively reinforcing responses from others as well (Youngren & Lewinsohn, 1980). Thus, depressed individuals appear to actually receive less support from others.

Hops et al. (1987) also suggested that the behavior of depressed individuals tends to be aversive and controlling. They found that although depressive behavior in the short run inhibited angry displays by others, it also tended to suppress caring behavior and was often associated with subsequent hostility by members of their network. Thus, although depressed individuals

might initially receive increased levels of support from others, they begin to anger members of their network because they express dissatisfaction with this support, and gradually receive reduced levels of support from others.

Depressed individuals also tend to be overly sensitive and avoidant of conflict or any other situation that would involve criticism or rejection. This makes them less willing to directly confront and deal with interpersonal difficulties, thereby letting them continue or escalate (Kahn et al., 1985). Moreover, depressed individuals have been found to be relatively deficient in general social competence (Lewinsohn, Steinmetz, Larson, & Franklin, 1981), so they are less able to obtain or sustain friendships (Heller, 1979).

Only a few studies have examined the interactions of depressed children and their families. Cole and Rehm (1986) found that, compared with parents of nondepressed children, parents of depressed children attended more to failure rather than success on a structured laboratory task, and rewarded their children less. Dadds, Sanders, Morrison, and Rebgetz (1992) observed parents and children during a typical dinner. They found that depressed children were exposed to higher levels of parental aversive behaviors (e.g., negative social attention) than a nonpsychiatric comparison group. The depressed children however, did not manifest higher levels of aversive behavior themselves. Thus, parents of depressed children were more negative in their interactions with their children than were parents of normal children, although the children themselves were not engaging in observably negative behaviors.

Hirsch and Reischl (1985) compared the adolescent children of depressed, arthritic, and normal parents with regard to the social support received from members of their social networks. They found that among children of depressed parents, increased interactions with friends and parents were associated with poorer adjustment. Such contact, if characterized by increased demands, conflict, and role reversals, is likely to contribute to greater distress in these children. They might then have sought out greater contact with friends because of the difficulties at home. Hirsch and Reischl suggested that the developmental demands of adolescence that involve separation and individuation (Josselson, 1980) might be especially difficult when there is a sick and needy parent for whom the adolescent feels some caretaking responsibility. This can then create distress among these adolescents.

In sum, studies have found both a direct and buffering effect for enacted support in relation to depression. The direction of the correlation between enacted support and depression has been both positive and negative. The positive association could be due to depressed individuals receiving increased support from others when they become symptomatic. On the other hand, it could be that they receive high levels of unsatisfactory support, which then results in distress. The negative association between enacted support and depression could result when high levels of support serve to reduce the symptomatology. Prospective observational studies are needed that assess the quality of received support and the extent to which this support precedes or follows the onset of symptoms. Observational studies also can be used to examine the extent to which positive supportive interactions buffer the impact of stress, or negative interactions themselves are a stressor that then leads to distress.

Development, Social Support, and Depression

There are several intriguing developmental questions with regard to the relation between social support and depression. Although there is some literature that has addressed these issues, much more needs to be learned about the relation between these constructs. For example, how might developmental changes in social support impact the development of depression? How does the relation between social support and depression change over the course of development? How does social support influence the onset and maintenance of depression at different points in development? How might changes in the nature of social support contribute to the increased rate of depression during early adolescence, especially in girls?

The intriguing developmental observation that the rates of depression increase during early adolescence (Rutter, 1986) is an ideal place to begin the study of the relation between social support and depression. How is social support changing during this important developmental period, and how might these changes influence the development of depression? Young adolescents are faced with an increasing number of developmental challenges including physiological changes associated with puberty, increasing academic demands during the transition to junior high school, changing relationships with parents centering around issues of separation and individuation, and increasing focus on peer and heterosexual relationships. If the amount of the social support available or the type of support perceived or received is not consistent with the demands of these new challenges, then this could lead to feeling overwhelmed and distressed; if the challenges are too great and the distress persists, then this could eventually result in depressive symptoms. This is consistent with the buffering model that suggests the absence of necessary support in times of stress leads to depression.

Second, the providers of support change during early adolescence. Although the amount of support received from parents does not necessarily decrease during adolescence, the desire for and the actual amount of contact and support from peers generally tends to increase during this time. If this normative developmental increase in peer contact does not occur, this could lead to feelings of distress. A low rate of supportive interactions with peers during early adolescence can lead to lower satisfaction with perceived support and subsequent unhappiness. Thus, depressive symptoms among adolescents could result from either the absence of positive peer relationships or the presence of negative and rejecting interactions with others. This would be consistent with the direct model of the impact of social support on depression.

A third and related process that might lead to increases in depression during early adolescence concerns the parent-child relationship. How the young teen negotiates the salient developmental task of individuation and separation from parents can impact the quality of the support perceived and received from parents. If there is a great deal of conflict, the young adolescent might perceive or actually experience a decrease in the amount and quality of support received from parents. This reduction in parental support could lead directly to depressive symptoms. It also could be that a decrease in available parental support is especially a problem when there are also high levels of stress, which are common during this age period. Thus, this change in the parent-child relationship during early adolescence can directly impact adjustment as well as create greater risk for depression if parents are no longer available to help buffer against the increasing challenges during this age period.

A different kind of developmental question that is relevant across the life span is, "What is the role of social support in the onset and maintenance of depression?" The current review highlighted the evidence that low rates of perceived and received support are associated with depression both directly and in combination with stress. Although there is good evidence of concurrent associations among social support, stress, and depression, more prospective studies are needed to more directly examine the role of social support in the development of depression. Such studies need to control for initial levels of depressive symptoms and should predict to the onset of depressive disorder as well as to increases in depressive symptoms.

The onset model of social support and depression suggests that individuals become depressed because they do not have an adequate social support system. This could be due to either characteristics of the individual or characteristics of others in the network. For example, individuals who do not have good social skills may not develop meaningful social relationships. It also could be that their behavior is so aversive that it causes others to move away from them. In either case, poor social skills could result in a smaller support network. The absence of a supportive network can then lead to feelings of loneliness, lower rates of positive reinforcement from others, and the lack of available social resources during times of stress, all of which can result in depression.

Thus, children who do not develop adequate social skills and the social cognitive abilities that are associated with such skills such as empathy and perspective-taking may be at particular risk for peer difficulties and subsequent depression. There is growing evidence of a relation between peer rejection and depression in children (Cole, 1990; Panak & Garber, 1992), and of a link between poor social skills and depression (Lewinsohn et al., 1981). Further prospective studies are needed that identify individuals lacking in social skills prior to the onset of depressive symptoms and observe both others' reactions to them and their specific behaviors toward others.

Another possibility is that an inadequate social support system could lead to the onset of depression if it is itself a significant source of stress for the individual. For example, members of the social network who are very negative, critical, rejecting, or abusive could represent a significant stressor that provokes feelings of distress. If the rejection or abuse becomes chronic and the individual cannot cope with or escape from it, then this could bring on feelings of helplessness and depression.

Social support also can have a more distal effect on depression through its role in the development of the self-schema. Cognitive models of depression (Beck, 1967, 1976) have suggested that individuals who have negative schema about themselves and who experience negative life events within a life domain relevant to that negative self-schema are particularly vulnerable to becoming depressed. The nature of the social support that a person receives from others early in life can play a role in the development of the self-schema (Rosenberg, 1979). For example, individuals who chronically do not receive positive regard or admiration from significant others, or who receive high rates of negative and critical interactions with others within their social networks, are likely to develop negative views of themselves. If these individuals are then confronted with stressors relevant to their negative self-schema, then they are at risk for becoming depressed. Furthermore, just whose positive regard or approval is important to self-schema may differ across the life span. For example, during early childhood, approval from parents may be crucial to children's sense of who they are and their self-esteem. Later on, during middle childhood, approval from peers may play a more active role in the development of self-schema. Thus, social support across the life span can play an important role in the development of the negative cognitions that are then vulnerability factors for the onset of depression in the face of stressful life events.

In contrast to onset models of social support and depression, the maintenance model suggests that regardless of how individuals become depressed, the absence of adequate social support or the presence of negative social relationships can serve to maintain and exacerbate the depressive condition (Hooley, 1985). That is, individuals might have had adequate social relationships prior to the onset of depression, but once they are depressed they might tend to perceive their social interactions more negatively. Moreover, changes in their behavior, such as increased irritability or social withdrawal, might actually create strain and rejection in their formerly adequate relationships (Coyne, 1976a).

Thus, an inadequate social network and poor social relationships can lead to distress; distressed individuals are likely to be less satisfied with their relationships; and this dissatisfaction as well as the depressive symptoms themselves can create even greater disruptions in their relationships with members of their social networks. Longitudinal studies of individuals who have never had a depressive episode should be conducted to explore the role of social support in the onset of the disorder. Such a study with early adolescents would be particularly informative about how social support might contribute to the increased rate of depression during this age period. In addition, prospective studies of currently depressed individuals are needed to understand how and why the nature of their received support changes during the course of a depressive episode and how such changes contribute to the maintenance of depressive symptoms over time.

Social Support and Schizophrenia

Schizophrenia is almost invariably characterized by difficulties in interpersonal relationships. These difficulties are often in the form of social withdrawal and emotional detachment, although some schizophrenics also show excessive clinginess and difficulties maintaining personal boundaries. Thus, it is not surprising that individuals with schizophrenia have problems establishing and maintaining social relationships. Such social difficulties impact the extent and nature of the social support schizophrenic patients receive.

The need for stronger social networks for patients with mental illness has been increasing since the move toward deinstitutionalization of the chronically mentally ill. Greater levels of social support have been found to be associated with a lower dependency on hospital inpatient care (Faccincani, Mignolli, & Platt, 1990), whereas impoverished and deficient social networks are associated with more frequent hospitalizations (Cohen & Sokolovsky, 1978). Interventions that are aimed at building and strengthening schizophrenics' social skills and social networks are more likely to prolong and enhance their community living (Collins & Pancoast, 1976). Thus, the adequacy of the social networks of patients with mental illness has very real implications for their aibility to function within the community.

Social Theories of Schizophrenia

Current theories of schizophrenia suggest a diathesis-stress perspective in which individuals who have a genetic or biological diathesis are vulnerable to developing schizophrenia if they are confronted with significant stressors (Gottesman & Shields, 1972; Meehl, 1962; Zubin & Spring, 1977). Modifications of this theory have been proposed that incorporate the construct of social support as well (Nuechterlein et al., 1992). Nuechterlein et al. suggested that social support can be an environmental protective factor, whereas the absence of supportive relationships or the presence of negative interpersonal interactions can serve as environmental potentiators or stressors. Thus, there are both buffering and main effect models of social support and schizophrenia. According to the buffering model, social support can help to reduce the level of stress encountered thereby decreasing the likelihood of the onset or relapse of symptoms of schizophrenia. In contrast, the main effect perspective suggests that the presence of nonsupportive, negative interpersonal interactions can serve as a stressor that exacerbates symptoms of schizophrenia and leads to relapse.

One of the most widely studied forms of negative social interactions with regard to schizophrenia involves criticism and overinvolvement, which are the defining components of the construct of expressed emotion. Expressed emotion is concerned with the quality and nature of relationships, and it is probably most relevant to the dimension of enacted support. Expressed emotion (EE) is defined in terms of the negative and intrusive attitudes that relatives express about their schizophrenic family member. It is measured by assessing the number of critical comments made by relatives about the patient, the global level of hostility and rejection, and the degree of emotional overinvolvement, overprotection, and overidentification with the patient. Typically, expressed emotion is assessed by coding interviews of significant family members talking about the patient, or coding interactions between the patient and his or her relatives (Goldstein, 1987; Vaughn & Leff, 1976b).

Schizophrenic patients exposed to relatives who are characterized by high levels of EE are two to four times more likely to have a relapse in the year following hospitalization than are patients whose relatives do not express such attitudes (Bebbington & Kuipers, 1988; Kavanagh, 1992). Another perspective on this is that schizophrenics who live with relatives who are characterized by low EE have a significantly lower rate of relapse than those from high-EE families. It is not clear to what extent low EE is an active protective factor or high EE is a vulnerability factor that increases the amount of stress the patient encounters. According to the definition of expressed emotion, high EE is characterized by criticism, hostility, and overinvolvement. An important issue to study in the future is whether low-EE families simply are absent of such negativity or also provide positive forms of support such as instrumental aid, affection, and companionship (see discussion of enacted support later in this chapter).

Does expressed emotion impact the onset of schizophrenia? Some supportive evidence was found by Goldstein and colleagues (Doane, West, Goldstein, Rodnick, & Jones, 1981; Goldstein, 1987) who examined the prevalence of schizophrenic spectrum disorders (schizophrenia, schizoid, schizotypal, paranoid, and borderline personality) among individuals who had been behaviorally disordered 15 years earlier when they were adolescents. Individuals whose relatives had previously shown high EE or a negative affective style in their family interactions were at higher risk of schizophrenic spectrum disorders than were subjects from low-EE families. There is no published evidence yet, however, that high EE influences the onset of schizophrenia among individuals who do not already have some behavior problems. Kavanagh (1992) suggested that whereas EE might not primarily cause schizophrenia, it may impact the timing of the onset of the first episode. Although the evidence does not appear to be consistent with this hypothesis (Mintz, Nuechterlein, Goldstein, Mintz, & Snyder, 1989; Vaughn, Snyder, Jones, Freeman, & Falloon, 1984), the appropriate longitudinal studies of well subjects that would be needed to really address the issue of the relation between EE and the timing and onset of schizophrenia have not yet been conducted.

Most of the research on EE has focused on schizophrenics, as noted earlier, but there also is evidence that EE affects outcomes in depression (Hooley et al., 1986; Hooley & Teasdale, 1989), bipolar disorder (Miklowitz, Goldstein, Nuechterlein, Snyder, & Mintz, 1988), and eating disorders (Szmukler, Eisler, Russell, & Dare, 1985). Nevertheless, it is still possible that social support in general and EE in particular can contribute to the onset and maintenance of each of these disorders if it is part of a more complex causal model (Garber & Hollon, 1991).

Social Networks

Much of the research concerning social support and schizophrenia has focused on describing the size and nature of social networks. In general, schizophrenics tend to have smaller networks with fewer social linkages, and the networks comprise mostly kin and some nonkin, particularly professionals (Beels et al., 1984; Henderson, 1980; Pattison & Pattison, 1981; Sokolovsky, Cohen, Berger, & Geiger, 1978; Tolsdorf, 1976). Sokolovsky et al. (1978) reported that whereas normal individuals have over 20 people in their networks, schizophrenics have an average of 10.2 persons, and these relationships lack reciprocity and multiplexity. That is, they tend to be unidimensional and dependent.

Schizophrenic patients may have more of a need for tangible material and instrumental support than for admiration and affection. Beels et al. (1984) argued that frequent contact with network members who can provide assistance may be more important for schizophrenics than the availability of an intimate confidant. In contrast, Faccincani et al. (1990) found that having a confidant was significantly correlated with higher functioning. The direction of this relation, however, is unclear.

Faccincani et al. also found that being a confidant was associated with higher functioning. Thus, it may be that higher functioning schizophrenics are more able to establish a reciprocal relationship that serves to maintain interactions with a confidant. In general, however, most schizophrenic patients do not have a relationship with a close confidant that is characterized by such reciprocity (Cohen & Sokolovsky, 1978).

Schizophrenics' need for social support may change depending on where they are in their psychotic episode. For example, Breier and Strauss (1984) noted that whereas material support and nonkin professionals were important during the early months of treatment, social approval particularly from family members became increasingly significant during their recovery. Thus, the sources and nature of their networks change with the course of their illness.

What accounts for the differences in schizophrenics' networks compared with nonclinical populations? Whereas some clinicians have suggested that the bizarre hallucinations and delusions of schizophrenics scare others away, others have suggested that it is the interpersonal inappropriateness and blandness that accounts for their social isolation and possible rejection. Hamilton, Ponzoha, Cutler, and Weigel (1989) examined the relation of these positive and negative symptoms to the size and quality of the social networks of 39 chronic schizophrenic patients. They found that patients with more severe negative symptoms (e.g., blunted affect, apathy) had significantly smaller and more dysfunctional networks, whereas positive symptoms (e.g., hallucinations, delusions) were not significantly associated with network characteristics. Those patients who lacked emotional responsiveness and expressive relatedness had the most impoverished social networks. Thus, it would seem that the ability to engage in social exchanges with others is important for obtaining and maintaining a network of social relationships.

This is an example of how the study of a psychopathological population can inform us about the nature of processes necessary for normal development. By identifying the skills that are apparently lacking in very disturbed psychiatric patients such as the ability to relate to others emotionally, we can learn about the relation of such skills to adaptation within an important domain such as social relationships.

Perceived Support

Two aspects of perceived support are important to consider. First, how do schizophrenic patients appraise the quality of the support they receive? In particular, how satisfied are they with this support? Second, how do schizophrenics perceive the actual amount and type of support, and how do these perceptions compare with the ratings of others who are in their networks? Because schizophrenics' symptoms can affect their perceptions of their world and the people around them, it is important to obtain information about their social networks from other sources as well as from the patients themselves. For example, whereas schizophrenic patients with depressive or paranoid symptoms might underestimate their level of social support, patients with grandiose delusions or euphoric affect might tend to overestimate it. Thus, information from significant members of schizophrenics' social networks can enhance our understanding of their social environment.

Although schizophrenics tend to recognize that their social networks are small and are not always supportive (Crotty & Kulys, 1985), they are not necessarily dissatisfied with this. Hirschberg (1985) reported that compared with a sample of elderly individuals, schizophrenics reported lower levels of alienation and loneliness. Hirschberg speculated that schizophrenics may be less adversely affected by their social isolation because some social withdrawal allows them to maintain their "psychological balance between excessive and deficient social stimulation" (p. 176). Henderson (1980) similarly suggested that some social withdrawal can be self-protective for schizophrenics who find it difficult enduring highly emotionally charged social transactions.

Schizophrenics' satisfaction with their social networks also seems to change with increasing age. Cohen and Kochanowicz (1989) reported that older schizophrenics reported greater satisfaction with their network members than did younger patients. They reported being happier with their current relationships and they felt less criticized and controlled by their network members. Cutler, Tatum, and Shore (1987) similarly found that compared with younger schizophrenics, older patients were more satisfied with their social environment and their level of functioning. These findings are consistent with the notion that patients with serious mental disorders go through a series of changes and adjustments until they finally accept some of the less stressful identities, roles, and niches in society that are available to them (Cutler et al., 1987; Strauss, Hafez, Lieberman, & Harding, 1985).

To address the second aspect of perceived support concerning the extent to which schizophrenic patients perceive their social networks accurately, Crotty and Kulys (1985) examined the congruence of schizophrenic patients' perceptions of their network with that of their significant others, most of whom were family members. They found that although schizophrenics and their significant others agreed that their social networks were relatively small and generally not very supportive, schizophrenics still reported their social networks to be significantly larger than did their significant others, and this was particularly with regard to the number of nonfamily relationships. Schizophrenics also reported that nonfamily members (e.g., friends, therapists, physicians) were the most supportive, whereas family members rated themselves or other family members to be more supportive than nonkin. In addition, schizophrenics had a more positive assessment of their own social competency in that they perceived themselves as having more interactions with members of their social networks and as both providing and receiving more support than was perceived by their significant others.

Without additional ratings by objective observers, it is impossible to know which perceptions are more accurate. Moreover, the fact that schizophrenics and their relatives agree at times does not necessarily make the perceptions valid. Nevertheless, their own and others' perceptions of their social network can either enhance or hinder the schizophrenic's functioning and impact the extent and nature of the third dimension of support, enacted or received support. For example, significant others who perceive that their schizophrenic relative is not receiving adequate social support may make more of an effort to provide such support themselves or see to it that relevant others in their network do so.

On the other hand, Crotty and Kulys (1985) suggested that significant others' negative perceptions of the social competency of schizophrenics may lead to lower expectations for their social performance, which could, in turn, adversely affect that performance. Indeed, high family expectations have been found to correlate with higher performance among schizophrenic patients (Freeman & Simmons, 1963; Greenley, 1979). It is not clear, however, whether family members have higher expectations for higher functioning schizophrenics or if high expectations contribute to better adaptation. Nonetheless, the perception of significant others (perceived support) can influence the type and amount of support actually given to their schizophrenic relatives (enacted support).

Enacted Support

Enacted support is concerned with the actual amount of contact with members within the network and the extent and type of support received. Compared with normal individuals, schizophrenic patients tend to have lower rates of enacted support; among schizophrenics, low-density and low-frequency contacts are associated with a higher risk for rehospitalization (Sokolovsky et al., 1978). Moreover, Hamilton et al. (1989) reported that the frequency of instrumental support by nonkin was inversely related to schizophrenics' negative symptoms. Higher levels of emotional and practical support provided by nonkin were significantly associated with greater motivation, emotional responsivity, and expressive relations in schizophrenic patients. This could reflect that others are less responsive to the needs of schizophrenics who are emotionally nonresponsive and anhedonic. It also could be that the negative symptoms are maintained by the absence of emotional and instrumental support from their social network.

Crotty and Kulys (1985) similarly found that schizophrenic patients rated the support received from their social network to be limited. Less than half the patients interviewed reported receiving strong practical or emotional support. Ratings by their significant others were consistent with this, although the significant others tended to rate the amount of support received by the schizophrenics as even lower than did the patients themselves.

Significant others also indicated that although schizophrenic patients tended to have relatively high frequency of contact with members of their social network, particularly family members, the actual amount of emotional and practical support received was quite low. Thus, although the frequency of contact with others can be high, the amount of actual social support received can be low. Therefore, simply counting the frequency of interactions with network members is not the best index of enacted support nor is it the best predictor of subsequent adjustment. Rather, a better index might be the ratio of the actual support received to the total amount of contact with members of their social network.

As previously mentioned, one of the prominent social theories of schizophrenia focuses on specific characteristics, referred to as expressed emotion (EE), of the interactions between schizophrenics and family members. Schizophrenia patients whose interactions with relatives are characterized by high EE appear to be at greater risk for relapse than those whose interactions are characterized by low levels of EE. Expressed emotion was originally concerned with both the level of warmth and positive comments about the patient as well as the extent of hostile and critical statements and emotional overinvolvement by significant others (Vaughn & Leff, 1976b). Earlier studies found that warmth was not a predictor of relapse (Brown, Birley, & Wing, 1972), and therefore it was dropped from studies of expressed emotion. Brown et al. (1972), however, noted that warmth was confounded with emotional overinvolvement, and when this confound was removed, warmth was associated with positive outcomes. Kavanagh (1992) suggested that more research needs to be conducted examining "noninvasive support" that is characterized by practical assistance and nonintrusive emotional support. Future studies of the relation between social support and schizophrenia need to examine the impact of both the presence of positive kinds of support as well as the absence of negative interactions that define expressed emotion.

Another important issue with regard to expressed emotion and schizophrenia is whether the amount of actual contact with the *relevant* family members impacts the course of the disorder. Expressed emotion has been found to have little effect on relapse when contact with the relatives is low (i.e., less than 35 hours a week) (Brown et al., 1972; Vaughn & Leff, 1976a; Vaughn et al., 1984). Moreover, those studies that have not found a particularly strong predictive effect of EE on relapse did not include many subjects who had high contact with their relatives (e.g., Dulz & Hand, 1986; McCreadie & Robinson, 1987).

Thus, the individual's frequent contact with members of his or her social network is not necessarily a good thing. The quality of the interactions that occur during these contacts can significantly impact schizophrenic patients' adjustment. Therefore, interventions designed to reduce the negative effect of expressed emotion on schizophrenics have been directed at either changing the nature of the interactions among family members, reducing the amount of contact the schizophrenic patient has with certain individuals, or both (Leff, Kuipers, Berkowitz, Eberlein-Fries, & Sturgeon, 1982; Tarrier et al., 1988). In general, such family intervention studies have found a significant reduction in the rate of relapse among schizophrenics from treated families compared with no treatment controls (Barrowclough & Tarrier, 1984; Strachan, 1986).

Finally, although most of the research concerning EE has focused on family members, there is some evidence EE also may be relevant to other relationships within schizophrenic patients' social networks (e.g., mental health professionals and friends). For example, overly intensive supervision by hospital staff has been found to be associated with increased risk for relapse (Drake & Sederer, 1986). Interpersonal interactions between schizophrenic patients and their coresidents that are characterized by high levels of criticism and hostility also tend to be associated with worsening of symptoms (Herzog, 1992, Higson & Kavanagh, 1988). Thus, the quality of the relationships with both kin and nonkin members of schizophrenics' social networks may be important predictors of the course and outcome of the disorder.

In sum, schizophrenics tend to have smaller and less reciprocal social networks; they are generally not very satisfied by these smaller networks, particularly when they receive high levels of criticism from network members. Such negative interactions are associated with higher rates of relapse among schizophrenic

patients. Decreasing the amount of contact with highly critical network members and increasing the amount of instrumental and emotional support provided by other network members are two potential strategies for improving the functioning and outcome of schizophrenic patients that are in need of further study.

Development, Social Support, and Schizophrenia

As noted previously, older schizophrenics report being more satisfied with their social environment than do younger patients (Cohen & Kochanowicz, 1989; Cutler et al., 1987). The networks of older schizophrenics also tend to be significantly smaller, with decreases in both kin and nonkin members. Their relationships with the members of their social network, however, continue to be highly dependent and nonreciprocal. Cohen and Kochanowicz (1989) also found that older schizophrenics were less bothered by being criticized and controlled, and they expressed a significantly greater preference to be by themselves.

What accounts for these changes in the social support of schizophrenics with increasing age? It could be that schizophrenics have learned that they do better when they have less contact with others and therefore they actively try to avoid contact with others. On the other hand, it also could be that they have fewer exacerbations of their illness with increasing age, and therefore they place fewer demands on their network members leading to fewer negative exchanges. It also is possible that older members of their networks such as parents may have died off, thereby decreasing the amount of contact with potentially stressful others. Finally, older schizophrenics may have gained some skills in managing their social environment in a way that makes it less stressful for them. Longitudinal studies of the same schizophrenic patients over their adult years are needed to better understand these developmental differences in the nature and perception of schizophrenics' social support systems.

Social Support and Conduct Disorder

Conduct disorder is defined by a wide range of behaviors in which the "basic rights of others and major age-appropriate societal norms or rules are violated" (American Psychiatric Association, p. 53; 1994). It is characterized by such behaviors as aggression toward other people or animals, destruction of property, stealing, school truancy, and running away from home (American Psychiatric Association, 1994). Historically, social context has been important in defining conduct disorder. DSM-III-R (American Psychiatric Association, 1987) divided conduct disorder into three subtypes depending on whether the antisocial behavior occurred in groups, was solitary and aggressive, or was a mixture of these types. Another classification that has been used to describe conduct disorder in the past has been socialized versus unsocialized (American Psychiatric Association, 1980; Rutter & Garmezy, 1983). Children and adolescents with unsocialized conduct disorder display disturbed interpersonal relationships whereas those with socialized delinquency have adequate social relationships.

In discussing the relation between conduct disorder and social support, we use a broad definition of social support. Much of the research in this area has not assessed social support in as direct a way as the research presented earlier concerning depression and schizophrenia. However, a fair amount is known about the relation between conduct disorder and some constructs that are closely related to social support as defined in this chapter. In fact, although not labeled as such by the investigators, the constructs studied often are synonymous with what has been called social support. In this section, we refer to literature that focuses on the characteristics of neighborhoods and communities because of its relevance to the support dimension of social embeddedness. The empirical work focusing on the perception and presence of conflict and/or other negative characteristics of interactions among network members also is discussed because of its relevance to both perceived and enacted support. Although reviewing this research broadens the definition of social support somewhat, it is important to our understanding of social support and its relation to psychopathology across the life span.

Social Theories of Conduct Disorder and Delinquency

Several theories of delinquency focus on social relationships on some level. Communities and neighborhoods represent an important part of youths' expanded social network. One explanation for delinquency revolves around certain characteristics of society and specific communities that put youth at risk for delinquency. In particular, neighborhood standards convey what forms of behavior are acceptable, and certain neighborhoods may inadvertently communicate that delinquent behavior is an acceptable way of life through actual example or images of violence in the media (Coie & Jacobs, 1993; McCord, 1990, 1993). The lack of employment opportunities within a community also has been linked to increases in the amount of serious crime committed by youth (McCord, 1990). In these communities, very needy families compete for limited resources. Violence and criminal acts may be perceived as the only effective method for overcoming barriers to achievement (Coie & Jacobs, 1993; Owens & Straus, 1975).

Another explanation for delinquent behaviors that has received theoretical and empirical attention focuses on parent inadequacies and family dysfunction. Conflict between parents and inadequate discipline have been found to be associated with increased delinquency, early sexual activity, and drug use (McCord, 1990, 1993). Several studies have found family adversity factors such as poor housing, large family size, low employment status, marital discord, maternal social isolation, parental criminology and psychological illness (e.g., maternal depression, parental alcoholism, or drug abuse) are also associated with increases in juvenile delinquency, adult criminality, and nondelinquent disturbances in conduct (Barron & Earls, 1984; Dumas & Wahler, 1983; Richman, Stevenson, & Graham, 1982; Rutter, Tizard, & Whitmore, 1970; Rutter et al., 1975; see Gardner, 1992; Rutter & Garmezy, 1983; and Yoshikawa, 1994 for reviews). Broken homes are cited as one of the strongest predictors of delinquency, conduct disorder (McCord, 1990; Rutter & Garmezy, 1983), and gang membership (Bowker & Klein, 1983; Lowney, 1984).

Several theorists (see Rutter & Garmezy, 1983) have proposed that this link is due to the family discord that characterizes broken homes rather than the broken homes per se. Rutter and Garmezy (1983) described several possible mechanisms connecting family discord with conduct disorder and delinquency. For example, family discord is often associated with erratic, deviant, and inefficient methods of discipline and

parental supervision (Wilson, 1974, 1980). Such parenting behavior, in turn, may encourage problem behaviors in children. Family discord or conflict may provide children with a model of aggression, inconsistency, hostility, and antisocial behavior that they emulate in their own social interactions (Bandura, 1969). Family discord also may set up coercive family interaction patterns in which hostile or coercive behaviors perpetuate aggressiveness (Patterson, 1982). These negative patterns make parents less available and less likely to provide positive support as well as more likely to participate in negative, unsupportive interactions. Thus, family discord makes it difficult for parents to maintain loving relationships that may be crucial for appropriate social behavior later in life (Bowlby, 1969).

Unfortunately, many of the family adversity factors just described are highly correlated with one another, making it difficult to tease apart the unique effects each has on delinquency and conduct disorder (Gardner, 1992; McCord, 1990). Another problem with most of the parent inadequacy and family dysfunction theories and empirical work generated in this area is the possibility of bidirectional relations. Often, the children studied have been displaying conduct problems for some time prior to the assessment and thus may already be trapped in a cycle of eliciting negative responses from others, particularly parents (Cantor & Gelfand, 1977; Patterson, 1976; Rauh, Achenbach, Nurcombe, Howell, & Teti, 1988; Tremblay, Larivee & Gregoire, 1985).

Despite this difficulty in teasing apart the effects of various family adversity factors, the link between such factors and chronic delinquency is important to consider when designing prevention programs. In a recent review of the effects of early family support and education on chronic delinquency, Yoshikawa (1994) suggested that family support intervention (including elements such as providing parenting and child development information, making home visits that involve discussion of the child, providing food or emergency assistance, and providing child care) may be a necessary component in any program attempting to reduce later delinquency. Family support intervention, which presumably addresses some of these family adversity factors, has been found to be associated with reductions in later delinquency (Yoshikawa, 1994).

Another social relationship theory of delinquency described by McCord (1990) proposes that vulnerability to peer influence is the main risk factor for problem behaviors. Children who develop conduct disorder may be more easily swayed by peers who are already delinquent. Snyder, Dishion, and Patterson (1986) found that having delinquent friends predicted first arrest within three years. Several factors may produce such a vulnerability. Friendships among delinquents often involve closer ties and greater mutual influence than do friendships among nondelinquents (Bowker & Klein, 1983; Giordano, Cernkovich, & Pugh, 1986); thus such relationships may be quite rewarding if friendship needs are not being met in other ways. In fact, susceptibility to peer influences has been found to be inversely related to interactions with parents (Kandel, 1980; Kandel & Andrews, 1987; Steinberg, 1987). Children in these "rewarding" friendships may be unwilling to compromise or threaten these ties by not "following the pack." McCord (1990) also noted that co-offending and committing crimes with others is common in adolescence. Such activities may form the basis for friendships among juvenile delinquents.

Children at risk for conduct disorder may be especially vulnerable to the influence of deviant peers due to deficits in the social skills necessary for normal peer relationships. Joffe, Dobson, Fine, Marriage, and Haley (1990) have shown that conduct-disordered adolescents, compared with normal and depressed adolescents, were less able to generate relevant means to a social end, to anticipate obstacles to be dealt with in pursuit of a social end, and to generate directly assertive social responses when solving difficult social problem tasks. Gard, Turone, and Devlin (1985) also found behaviorally disturbed youths to have fewer social skills than normal children as assessed in terms of proximity to peers and frequency of social interactions. McGee et al. (1990) found that adolescents with externalizing disorders or multiple disorders tended to have poor social competence, as defined using indexes of parent attachment, peer attachment, school involvement, leisure activities, support and coping behaviors, and part-time employment. Thus, conduct-disordered and delinquent youth may be less competent in enacting support and maintaining a support network due to deficits in basic social skills necessary for these processes. This may result in higher levels of peer and parent rejection, which in turn may act to maintain problem behaviors.

During the early school years, aggressive behaviors may be reinforced by peers who allow them to achieve more immediate social and material goals through threats and physical force (Coie, Dodge, Terry, & Wright, 1991; Patterson, Littman, & Bricker, 1967). Immediate gratification may trap these children into behavior patterns with short-term gains but long-term losses (Coie & Jacobs, 1993). Thus, lack of social support from parents in families with marked discord and selective support from deviant peers are likely to be associated with conduct problems.

Social Networks

Krohn (1986) described two dominant social psychological perspectives on delinquent behavior, both of which focus on the characteristics of the social network: Sutherland's (1939) differential association theory and Hirschi's (1969) social control theory. Sutherland's theory concentrates on the impact of juveniles' interaction with significant others, whereas Hirschi's theory places greater emphasis on the bonding of individuals to groups, institutions, goals, and beliefs. Hirschi proposed that the more links a person has to these groups, the stronger the bond to conventional society. Juveniles without such bonds are freer from constraints and therefore are more likely to become delinquent.

Combining these two perspectives, Krohn proposed a network approach that involves examining two characteristics of social networks: Network multiplexity, defined as the number of roles, activities, or exchanges in which the same people interact jointly; and network density, defined as the extent to which all actors in the social network are connected by direct relationships. The greater the network multiplexity in social relationships, the more consistency there will be in behavior. The greater the network density, the greater constraint on behavior within the social network. Hence, the lower the levels of social network multiplexity and density in a particular community, the higher the rate of delinquency. Krohn cited multifamily housing and greater mobility in certain urban areas as factors that result in low levels of social network multiplexity and density, which presumably lead to higher rates of delinquency in these communities.

Krohn used his social network theory to interpret past findings concerning the association between a variety of family and community factors and delinquent behavior. For example, Hirschi (1969) found that the less adolescents are attached to their parents, the greater the likelihood of delinquent behavior. Short and Strodtbeck (1965) found that, compared with nongang members, gang members were less likely to report joint activities with adults. Krohn suggested that these findings indicated that delinquents and gang members may lack multiplexity in their relationships with parents and adults, and this lower level of multiplexity may be what leads such youth to seek out support through other gang members and thus continue to engage in antisocial behaviors.

Lower social status (in terms of educational and economic levels) areas have higher rates of delinquency (Braithwaite, 1981; Clark & Wenninger, 1962; Johnstone, 1978; McDonald, 1969; Reiss & Rhodes, 1961). Krohn suggested that this is the result of there being more residential mobility, lower overall network density, and lower multiplexity. Maccoby, Johnson, and Church (1958) compared two lower working class neighborhoods, one with a very high rate of delinquency and one with a low rate of delinquency. The members of the neighborhood with the high rate of delinquency were slightly more transient, knew fewer of their neighbors, and were less ethnically and religiously homogeneous, resulting in lower levels of network multiplexity and density. Lower status youth also are less likely to participate in extracurricular activities than are middle and upper status youth (Campbell & Alexander, 1965; Otto, 1976), and lower status adults are less likely to participate in voluntary associations, such as parent-teacher organizations or Cub Scouts, than are middle or upper status adults (Otto, 1976). Thus, lower status adults have fewer activities that link them with their children. This results in lower levels of social network multiplexity, which in turn contributes to higher levels of juvenile delinquency (Krohn, 1986).

As suggested by the vulnerability to peer influence theories described earlier (Bowker & Klein, 1983; Giordano et al., 1986; Kandel, 1980; McCord, 1990; Steinberg, 1987), certain characteristics of network members may also be important in predicting conduct disorder. Members of some groups may reinforce delinquent or aggressive behaviors. For example, Wright, Giammarino, and Parad (1986) have found that whether or not aggressiveness or socially withdrawn behavior predicted social acceptance depended on how aggressive the members of the peer group were to begin with. Rejected children in the highly aggressive groups tended to be withdrawn, whereas rejected children in the nonaggressive groups tended to be relatively more aggressive. Wright et al. did find, however, that prosocial interaction was a necessary factor for peer popularity regardless of the aggressive nature of the group members. In sum, there appears to be considerable evidence for a link between delinquent or conduct problem behavior and certain features of the social network, such as multiplexity and density, as well as characteristics of the members of that social network.

Perceived Support

Several researchers have argued that early parent-child attachment relationships are related to conduct disorder or delinquency (see Greenberg, Speltz, & DeKlyen, 1993 for a recent review).

Although the literature on attachment is relevant for both perceived and received support dimensions, this literature is discussed here with regard to perceived support because much of the focus of the longitudinal work is on the cognitive abstractions of the security the individual feels with others (i.e., "internal working models"). Insecure attachment assessed prior to age 2 years has been found to be related to lower sociability, anger, poorer peer relations, and poorer behavioral self-control during the preschool years (Greenberg & Speltz, 1988). The question of whether or not insecure attachment during the first 2 years of life is related to higher rates of disruptive behavior problems among 4- to 6-year-olds is still being debated. Some research has failed to find a significant main effect for insecure attachment (Bates, Bayles, Bennett, Ridge, & Brown, 1991; Fagot & Kavanaugh, 1990; Lewis et al., 1984), whereas other research with high-risk samples has found a significant relation between early attachment and later externalizing behaviors (see Greenberg et al., 1993). Studies in the latter category suggest that children in high social risk environments showing early insecure attachments are significantly more likely to have poor peer relationships and to display moodiness, depression, and aggression during the preschool years (Erickson et al., 1985; Sroufe 1983; Troy & Sroufe, 1987), the elementary school years (Renken, Egeland, Marvinney, Mangelsdorf, & Sroufe, 1989; Sroufe, 1988; Sroufe, Egeland, & Kreutzer, 1990), and even during preadolescence (Urban, Carlson, Egeland, & Sroufe, 1991) than those children showing early secure attachments.

Greenberg et al. (1993) argued that important transactual processes should be given more attention when studying the association between early attachment relations and later conduct disorder. For example, an examination of some insecurely attached infants who did not display problem behaviors revealed that they had more appropriate play materials and higher levels of maternal involvement than those insecurely attached infants displaying problem behaviors. Thus, the association between early attachment and behavior problems may be moderated in some cases by subsequent variations in the parent-child relationship and family circumstances (Greenberg et al., 1993). Greenberg et al. (1993) concluded:

> . . . it is unlikely that insecure attachment is either a necessary or sufficient cause of later disruptive disorders. Thus, main effect models are of little use and there is a need to examine these processes in populations that share one or more other important risk factors as well as to examine more closely the operation of these processes in children already showing disruptive behaviors. (p. 203)

Holcomb and Kashani (1991) found that conduct-disordered adolescents reported lower levels of satisfaction with family life relative to a sample of non-conduct-disordered adolescents. According to these adolescents, family life was typified by a lack of nurturance along with a high level of conflict and turmoil. Conduct-disordered adolescents also reported an indifference to the feelings and concerns of others suggesting they did not put much effort into maintaining positive reciprocal supportive relationships.

Wells and Rankin (1983) found lower scores on male adolescents' reports of positive family relationships were associated with higher rates of school rebellion and more general delinquency both concurrently and predictively. Positive family relationships were operationally defined using a combination of adolescents' ratings of how close they felt to their parents and the degree of parental reasoning and communication and parental punitiveness. This measure of family relationships seems most closely tied to the perceived support dimension, although it probably encompasses enacted support as well. In addition, adolescent males who reported more school rebellion also reported higher levels of peer rejection or exclusion based on their perceptions of being unwanted, lonely, and unloved. However, social rejection, as measured in this study, was not a significant predictor of later delinquency.

Other research has failed to find a relation between perceived social support and conduct disorder. Barrera and Garrison-Jones (1992) found that although perceptions of the quality of the family environment and the availability of and satisfaction with social support of various types from parents and peers (i.e., intimacy, material aid, advice, positive feedback, physical assistance, and social participation) were related to depressive symptoms, these indexes of perceived support were not related to conduct disorder symptoms in their sample of adolescent inpatients.

The *source* of perceived support was found to be quite important in a recent study of perceived support and adjustment of isolated and aggressive sixth graders. East and Rook (1992) reported that isolated, but not aggressive, children compensated for unsatisfactory school friendships by deriving support from siblings and nonschool friends. Compared with average and aggressive sixth graders, isolated children perceived their school friendships as less supportive and their relationships with their favorite sibling as most supportive. High support from favorite siblings was associated with better adjustment among isolated children on selected outcomes, such as immaturity and anxiety, although overall these children were still less well adjusted. High support from a favorite sibling, however, was associated with greater anxiety among aggressive children, possibly due to sibling relationships triggering more conflict and aggression in these children. Reports of support from nonschool friends did not show a compensatory effect. In fact, perceived support from nonschool friends was associated with more self-rated aggressive and disruptive behavior among aggressive children. Thus, perceptions of non-school peer and sibling support were actually associated with more adjustment difficulties for children who were currently categorized as being aggressive.

Windle (1992b) also found source of perceived support to be important in explaining the association between social support and depressive symptoms as well as delinquent behaviors in a large sample of middle-class, white adolescents. Lower levels of emotional support from family members were associated with higher rates of both depressive symptoms and delinquent behaviors, whereas lower levels of emotional support from friends were significantly associated with higher rates of depressive symptoms but not delinquent behaviors.

Descriptive work concerning street gangs also can add to our understanding of what characteristics of perceived support may be involved in the onset and maintenance of conduct disorder and delinquency. Riley (1991) stated that the personal motivations for joining a street gang are pride, prestige, peer pressure, adventure, self-presentation, the lure of money, and limited life options. Hochhaus and Sousa (1987) interviewed nine gang members and found that although the most frequent motives for joining a gang were the desire for more and closer friends (companionship), protection, and excitement, these needs were not getting met through gang membership at the time of the interview. Thus, even though gang membership may satisfy some social needs, many gang members may be dissatisfied with the "social support" (i.e., companionship, instrumental aid, and emotional support) the gangs provide.

In sum, the research addressing perceived support and conduct disorder or delinquency is limited and the findings are still inconclusive. Although some studies suggest low levels of satisfaction, higher levels of conflict, and negative interactions with family and peers are associated with and may even be predictive of problem behaviors, other recent work has found either a positive or a nonsignificant relation, especially in the case of peer support and aggressive behavior (Barrera & Garrison-Jones, 1992; East & Rook, 1992; Windle, 1992a, 1992b). Moreover, it is difficult to establish the importance of perceived support for the onset of conduct disorder. More longitudinal work assessing children's and adolescents' perceptions of the quality of the support and their satisfaction with that support prior to their displaying delinquent or problem behaviors is needed to understand the contributions of perceived support to the onset of conduct disorder.

Enacted Support

Research on enacted support and conduct disorder and delinquency has focused primarily on relationships with family members, in particular, mothers. Aside from the link between peer rejection and aggressive behavior (Gottman, Gonso, & Rasmussen, 1975; Hartup, 1983; Snyder & Brown, 1983), very little is known about the association between received or enacted support from peers and externalizing behaviors. Thus, the work reviewed in this section is limited to characteristics of family interaction. Presumably, family interactions represent one route through which support is obtained (or not obtained). However, it is important to emphasize that interactions involve two active participants. The child or adolescent is not a passive recipient of the negative or supportive gestures displayed by family members. The process is truly bidirectional.

In a review of the literature examining family risk factors for conduct disorder and delinquency, Rutter and Garmezy (1983) concluded that there is an association between conduct disorder and weak parental relationships. Although the relation between aspects of parent-child relationships and conduct disorder is not always a strong one, a number of studies have found conduct disorder to be associated with a lack of joint family leisure activities (West & Farrington, 1973), a lack of intimate parent-child communication (Hirschi, 1969), and a lack of parental warmth (W. McCord & J. McCord, 1959; Rutter, 1971; West & Farrington, 1973). In addition, parents of children with conduct disorder often report that they cannot get through to their children and that they don't feel attached to them (Patterson, 1982).

In a more recent review, Loeber and Stouthamer-Loeber (1986) found that poor parental supervision and lack of parenting

involvement in their children's activities (two processes central to potential supportive interactions with parents) were two of the strongest correlates of severe conduct problems. Recent studies have continued to replicate these findings (Cernkovich & Giordano, 1987; Voorhis, Cullen, Mathers, & Garner, 1988; Wells & Rankin, 1988), and have also linked harsh or abusive forms of discipline (Brown, 1984; Farrington, 1978; Patterson, 1982; Voorhis et al., 1988; Wells & Rankin, 1988) and inconsistent discipline (Patterson & Stouthamer-Loeber, 1984; Wells & Rankin, 1988) to conduct disorder in children.

Several studies have also found an association between particular parent-reported family characteristics and conduct disorder (see Yoshikawa, 1994 for a recent review). For example, Haddad, Barocas, and Hollenbeck (1991) found that after controlling for SES, family status, stress level, and parental satisfaction, parents of children with conduct disorder reported lower levels of family cohesion and active-recreational orientation and higher levels of conflict than parents of children who were diagnosed with an anxiety disorder or who were without a disorder. Parents' reports of family organization and control and their emphasis on personal growth or moral control did not differ as a function of their children's diagnostic status, however.

Schachar and Wachsmuth (1991) also found that parents of children with conduct disorder reported relatively higher levels of parent-child dysfunction compared with normal and clinic controls. Parent-child dysfunction was defined as problems in task accomplishment, communication, role performance, affective expression, affective involvement, control, and explicitness, flexibility, and consistency of family values and norms. Frick, Lahey, Loeber, Stouthamer-Loeber, Christ, and Hanson (1992) found that mothers of children with conduct disorder reported more deviant parenting practices (supervision and persistence in discipline) than mothers of children in a clinical comparison group (none of whom had conduct disorder but many of whom were diagnosed with attention deficit/hyperactivity disorder or anxiety disorders). However, when both paternal diagnosis of antisocial personality disorder and maternal parenting were entered into a logit-model analysis, only the presence of paternal antisocial personality disorder was significantly associated with conduct disorder in the children, suggesting that correlates of maternal parenting, such as paternal diagnoses, may be as important as the parenting process itself in predicting conduct disorder.

Other literature that has addressed the relation between enacted support and conduct disorder includes studies examining parent-child interaction in families with and without children having conduct problems. Gardner's (1992) recent review groups this research into three categories based on the nature of the observations made. The first group of studies focused on parents and children in conflict. Children with conduct disorder have been found to engage in a higher rate of aversive behavior when interacting with their parents or their entire families than normal children (e.g., Anderson, Lytton, & Romney, 1986; Patterson, Dishion, & Bank, 1984). Gardner (1989) found that mothers of children with conduct disorder were eight times more likely to end conflicts by failing to follow through with their stated demands to their children than mothers of children in a control group. Thus, the problem behavior of conduct-disordered children displayed in the family context may be reinforced both by escape from parental demands and parental compliance to their children's demands during conflictual interactions. In addition, these negative behavior patterns make it less likely that these children will experience the supportive interactions that have been found to be related to adjustment and well-being. This is an area in need of more empirical work. In particular, although it seems likely that conflictual interactions result in a parent-child environment less conducive to supportive interactions, more research needs to document this possibility and assess its role in the onset and maintenance of conduct disorder.

Patterson (1982, 1986b) proposed that disrupted family management skills, resulting in patterned exchanges of aversive behaviors and coercive exchanges, lead to the development of antisocial child behavior. The noncompliant and coercive features of this antisocial behavior place children at risk for both rejection by parents and normal peers, and academic failure. This in turn causes children to develop low self-esteem. The combination of academic failure, rejection by peers, and possibly low self-esteem result in a higher likelihood that these children will continue to behave in aggressive and antisocial ways. Patterson (1986a) cited evidence that many of the links in this chain of events lead to antisocial behavior. For example, aggressiveness within normal peer groups has been found to be correlated with peer rejection (Gottman et al., 1975; Hartup, 1983; Snyder & Brown, 1983), and coercive behavior has been shown to contribute to this peer rejection (Coie & Kupersmidt, 1983; Dodge, 1983). In a study described by Patterson (1986b), maternal rejection was related to discipline confrontation, conflict with siblings, and antisocial behaviors. Furthermore, deviant behavior (hyperactivity and aggression) displayed by children in this study reduced parental involvement and support.

The second category of studies examining parent-child interactions of children with conduct disorder involves indiscriminate caretaking (Gardner, 1992). Wahler (Sansbury & Wahler, 1992; Wahler & Dumas, 1986) proposed that the maladaptive parenting style that has been linked to conduct disorder comprises two processes: Parent compliance with child refusals to obey commands and inconsistent parental reactions to prosocial or positive behavior, along with consistent parental aversive reactions in response to children's antisocial behavior. Both of these processes seem marked by an absence or a lesser degree of enacted support. Several studies have shown that children with conduct disorder may evoke a maladaptive pattern of behavior in their parents (Anderson et al., 1986; Barkely, Karleson, Pollard, & Murphey, 1985; Olweus, 1980). A number of stressors, such as socioeconomic disadvantage (Emery, 1982; Loeber & Stouthamer-Loeber, 1986; Robins, 1966), marital distress (Emery, Weintraub, & Neale, 1982), and social isolation (Wahler, 1980) in mothers' ecosystem are also associated with the use of a maladaptive parenting style with conduct-disordered children.

Wahler and Dumas (1986) found that parents of conduct-disordered children reacted in an unpredictable manner to their children's behavior, sometimes even reacting negatively to their children's appropriate behavior to a greater extent than parents of normal children (also see Patterson, 1976; Snyder, 1977).

This unpredictability is hypothesized to be aversive to the children, and so they engage in problem behavior because it elicits a more predictable response from their parents than when they behave in positive or neutral ways.

Interestingly, Sansbury and Wahler (1992) found that the compliance and inconsistency processes they observed in mother-child dyads were not correlated, and the two processes had different associations with mothers' perceptions. In particular, mothers showing a maladaptive parenting style characterized by inconsistency displayed a bias to perceive their children's behavior in a highly personalized and diffused way that did not match closely with their children's objective behaviors. Those mothers whose maladaptive parenting style could be described as overly compliant with children's refusals tended to miss or undercode what professional observers considered aversive child behaviors. Thus, not only do mothers of conduct-disordered children appear to use different maladaptive parenting techniques, the processes that lead them to a pattern of inconsistent or compliant parenting differ as well.

The final category of studies examining parent-child interactions in families with and without children displaying conduct problems focuses on parents and children engaging in positive activities and joint play (Gardner, 1992; also see Yoshikawa, 1994). Parent-child dyads in which the child has a history of behavior problems engage in less joint play and conversation than parent-child dyads in which the child does not have such a history (Dunn & Kendrick, 1982; Gardner, 1987). Pettit and Bates (1989) found affectively positive and educative exchanges between mother and child dyads were concurrently related to the absence of problem behavior (i.e., social withdrawal and aggression). Mothers of children with relatively severe behavior problems rarely initiated joint play activity with their children and were more likely to ignore bids for attention from their children. In addition, ratings of family coercion obtained when the children were younger were predictive of problem behavior when the children were 4 years old. Early family coercion, however, was not as strong a predictor of behavior problems as was the absence of early positive behaviors. Because the problem behaviors reported in this study were a combination of social withdrawal and aggression, however, it is not clear if these findings reflect the relation between these parent-child interactions and conduct disorder specifically.

Recent work by Dadds and Sanders (Dadds et al., 1992; Sanders, Dadds, Johnston, & Cash, 1992) suggests that certain negative interaction patterns, assessed both in the laboratory setting and in the home, characterize the exchanges between conduct-disordered children and their families. Sanders et al. (1992) found that conduct-disordered children displayed lower levels of effective problem-solving behavior and higher levels of aversive verbal content during problem-solving discussions with their mothers than did depressed or nonproblem children. This tendency for more aversive interactions was also evident in children's behavior at home with their families during an evening meal. Children with conduct disorder exhibited relatively high levels of demanding, noncompliant, and oppositional behaviors compared with children who suffered from depression or had no diagnosed problems (Dadds et al., 1992). Moreover, the aversive behavior and anger expressed by these conduct-disordered children appeared to be reciprocated by both parents and siblings and, thus, may be a part of a family system characterized by conflict and aggression (Dadds et al., 1992).

In sum, supportive interactions between parents and children appear to be associated with fewer problem behaviors, whereas aversive, punitive, or aggressive interactions between parents and their children seem to be associated with more conduct problems. Little is known about the relation of supportive interactions with peers to conduct disorder. In addition, although differences in the enacted support experience of children and adolescents with conduct disorder have been established, more longitudinal studies with at-risk or normative populations are needed to better understand how particular characteristics of enacted support may or may not contribute to the onset of conduct disorder.

Development, Social Support, and Conduct Disorder

There are a number of developmental shifts in the context children and adolescents display conduct problems. These shifts parallel the developmental differences in the nature of the normative social support experience discussed earlier. During early childhood, conduct disorder develops within the context of parent-child and sibling relationships, whereas later the antisocial behavior, such as bullying, vandalism, and stealing, generalizes to interactions with peers and other adults outside the family (Gardner, 1992). Normatively, during the preschool years, over half the angry outbursts displayed by children arise from some conflict with parental authority. Initially, this conflict is centered around toileting and prohibited activities, but around 5 years of age, these angry outbursts occur around refusal to put toys away and clashes over clothes (Goodenough, 1931). Before age 4, disagreement with playmates is relatively infrequent, but between ages 4 and 5, disagreements among playmates make up 20% of the angry outbursts displayed by children (Goodenough, 1931). Appel (1942) described a shift in the topic of quarrels. Possessions are often the topic of quarrels of very young children around 2 years of age, whereas later disputes are more likely to arise during play with other children.

The conduct problem behaviors displayed also change with age (see Loeber et al., (1993) for discussion of individual differences in the developmental sequence of disruptive behaviors). The destructiveness, bullying, and lying diminish slightly between 5 and 9 years of age (Macfarlane, Allen, & Honzik, 1954; Rutter & Garmezy, 1983; Shepherd, Oppenheim, & Mitchell, 1971), whereas school truancy increases during high school (Rutter & Garmezy, 1983). Theft and property offenses decrease in frequency during the transition to adulthood, whereas the frequency of violent crime increases during adolescence and peaks in the early 20s (Cline, 1980; West, 1982).

What is constant across different ages is that all antisocial acts involve some kind of violation of age-appropriate *social* rules and are distressing or painful to others. Furthermore, they tend to provoke hostile, irritable, punitive, or avoidant reactions from others (Gardner, 1992). Thus, both currently and historically, the nature of social relationships has been important in defining subcategories of conduct disorder, has been involved in the symptomatology, and has been tied to both the etiology and maintenance of the disorder.

Several of the theories concerning the origin of conduct disorder and antisocial behaviors rely on the differential impact of particular social relationships across the life span. Thus, the focus of the models used to explain the origin and maintenance of conduct disorder and delinquency parallel the developmental differences in the normative social experience. Patterson, DeBaryshe, and Ramsey (1989) presented a developmental model of antisocial behavior. According to Patterson et al., during early childhood, poor parental discipline and monitoring leads to conduct problems. These conduct problems and coercive behavior patterns that developed out of negative interactions with parents, in turn lead to rejection by the normal peer group and/or academic failure during middle childhood. These experiences encourage commitment to the deviant peer group during late childhood and adolescence. These deviant peers positively reinforce delinquent behavior and punish socially conforming acts, resulting in higher rates of delinquent and antisocial behavior central to the definition of conduct disorder. Although research is still underway to test the complete model, there is empirical evidence for many of the links.

Coie and Jacobs (1993) also emphasized the importance of social context in explaining conduct disorder and possible routes to prevention across the life span. During the early school years, peers may inadvertently reinforce the use of threats and physical force to achieve personal goals by backing down when such behaviors are used and allowing the children using such tactics to get what they want (Coie et al., 1991; Patterson et al., 1967). This positive reinforcement in combination with a tendency for a hostile attributional bias (Dodge & Coie, 1987) and a lack of awareness of any negative consequences for much of their early deviant behavior may serve to increase antisocial behavior both in early childhood and later. During the middle school years, the social context of a neighborhood with a high crime rate along with a deviant peer group may reinforce delinquent behavior by creating a setting where such behavior is actually normative and may be even somewhat adaptive (Coie & Jacobs, 1993). Thus, although the peer social context may influence conduct problems both in early and middle school years, the exact nature of reinforcement (or lack of reinforcement) may differ depending on the developmental period.

In sum, some of the developmental shifts in the normative social support experience across the life span are evident in the context and kinds of conduct problems displayed and the focus of the models used to explain the origin and maintenance of conduct disorder and delinquency. Initially, the context in which externalizing behaviors are seen and are reinforced may be the family, but gradually, during early and middle childhood, the peer context becomes increasingly important in reinforcing such problem behaviors. During the early school years, aggressive or problem behavior may be largely driven by short-term goals of material possessions, attention, or intimidation, whereas during the middle school years in addition to these short-term gains, aggressive or delinquent behavior may be used to gain approval and acceptance in the deviant peer group. Recognizing developmental differences in the nature of social support and the relation it bears to conduct disorder and delinquent behaviors has important implications not only for understanding the etiology of conduct disorder but also for intervention. Future research would benefit from a developmental approach in which various risk factors, both biological and social, were studied simultaneously over development in an effort to understand how risk and protective factors work together in a multidimensional model and how these processes might vary during different developmental periods (Cicchetti & Richters, 1993; McCord, 1993).

THE CONTRIBUTION OF PSYCHOPATHOLOGY TO THE UNDERSTANDING OF NORMAL PROCESSES RELEVANT TO SOCIAL SUPPORT

A central feature of a developmental psychopathological perspective is that knowledge gained through the study of normal development can contribute greatly to our understanding of psychopathology and knowledge gained through the study of psychopathology can, in turn, enhance our understanding of normal development (Cicchetti, 1990, 1993). Much of this chapter has emphasized the importance of incorporating what is known about normal development in the study of the relation between social support and psychopathology across the life span. At the same time, the literature examining the link between social support and psychopathology has revealed some features of the social support experience that give us greater insight about the nature of social support normatively.

First, several studies reviewed here showed that individuals with psychopathology differ from their significant others with regard to their perceptions of the extent and nature of their social support (Crotty & Kulys, 1985). It remains to be studied whether or not this is simply a normative trend for people to know more about their own social network than do the people who compose it. It seems reasonable to assume that individuals know best all the people with whom they have contact, and that others in the network might not be aware of all these individuals. However, other research suggests that people may not seek out the support they receive and may not label that support as support (Coyne & Bolger, 1990). Many times, the process of obtaining support from significant others may occur so subtly that recipients may be unable to assess accurately the level of support they have received (Bolger & Eckenrode, 1991; Lieberman, 1986). Thus, although the recipient of support and a significant other may not always be concordant, the report of significant others still can be quite informative in predicting well-being as well as reflect the complexity of the normative social support experience.

A related normative question is, "To what extent does the discrepancy between self and others' report about social support vary as a function of development?" For example, although parents of young children are likely to know the entire social network of their children, this might change during adolescence. When discrepancies are found between target subjects' and their significant others' report about their social support, are these differences greater or less for psychopathological versus normal populations? What accounts for differences in self and other's perceptions of social support, and are there different processes for normal versus deviant populations? Thus, the discrepancy between self and others' report of the extent and

nature of the individual's social network could reflect deviation particularly noteworthy among psychopathological populations, or it could reflect a normal process in need of further study across a variety of samples.

Second, the study of the perception of and satisfaction with social networks highlights the need also to assess individuals' expectations and aspirations about these networks. For example, although schizophrenic patients tend to have smaller social networks, there is some evidence that they are not necessarily dissatisfied with this situation because it may be consistent with what they desire or are able to handle. Depressed individuals, on the other hand, might report being very dissatisfied with the support they receive even if it is objectively higher than that available to most individuals. Adolescents who engage in delinquent behavior may be motivated to do so in part by a desire to belong to a particular gang and reap the expected benefits of companionship, protection, and excitement. The power of such desires for affiliation to encourage antisocial behavior highlights the importance of these needs during adolescence, not just for delinquent youth but for the normative population of adolescents as well. Thus, it is not enough to ask individuals how satisfied they are with their social network and the support they receive. Rather, it also is important to evaluate what they expect and want from the individuals in their network.

Third, it is probably generally assumed that a person's greater frequency of contact with his or her social support network will be positively associated with well-being. However, if the valence of this contact tends to be negative, as in the case of high expressed emotion families, then possibly the less contact the better for the patient. The study of psychopathological populations such as individuals with schizophrenia or depression underscores the need to consider not only the amount of contact but also the quality of this contact. The work on expressed emotion and psychopathology particularly highlights the importance of evaluating the quality of the interactions that are occurring in addition to the simple count of the frequency of contact with members of the network. Although normatively more contact with friends and family should have a positive outcome, if the valence of these interactions is negative, then the effect may be even more detrimental than no contact at all.

A negative association between enacted support and well-being could be the result of at least two different processes. First, as previously noted, high-frequency contact with members of a social network who provide negative and critical interactions may produce higher levels of distress and symptomatology. Second, individuals who are already experiencing high levels of distress may be more likely to seek out members of their social network and thereby receive a greater amount of support from them. Both of these explanations are possible and are not mutually exclusive. Studies testing these alternative views with both psychopathological and normal populations are an important direction for future research.

Another way in which understanding the relation between social support and psychopathology can enhance our knowledge of normal development is by helping to identify certain social skills that may be especially important in creating and maintaining a supportive network. Are there particular social skills that depressed, schizophrenic, or delinquent individuals lack relative to nonpsychopathological individuals? By examining social skill deficits that are related to the social support experience of these populations, we can begin to identify which skills may be primary in the normative social support experience. Further study of these skills could then prove quite helpful in understanding the social support process as it changes across the life span.

Finally, the study of psychopathology can enhance our understanding of normal processes relevant to social support through a closer analysis of what *types* of support may be linked to particular pathological symptoms. For example, many depressed individuals have low self-esteem. Particular types of support, such as approval or emotional support, may be particularly important in predicting low self-esteem. Identifying links between specific types of support and particular symptoms or associated features of psychopathology may be helpful in deciding which aspects of support should be studied longitudinally in a normative sample. Because of the time and expense required for longitudinal designs, research that helps us formulate clear hypotheses about the links between specific aspects of support and normal developmental processes is critical.

In sum, the study of psychopathological populations highlights the need for more intensive study of what goes on in the context of social interactions with members of the individual's social network. What kinds of social exchanges serve as buffers against the onset or maintenance of disorder, and conversely what social processes actually exacerbate symptomatology? Studies of psychopathological populations have helped to identify some of the processes that have gone awry. Further research is needed regarding what these processes look like in normal individuals, how they develop over time, and how they result in abnormal rather than normal outcomes.

CONCLUSIONS AND FUTURE DIRECTIONS

Social support is a complex and multifaceted construct comprised of several dimensions, sources, and functions. Dividing the dimensions of social support into social networks, perceived support, and enacted support has provided a useful framework for describing the literature concerning development, social support, and psychopathology. Each of the three dimensions of social support is associated somewhat differently with psychopathology, and the relation between social support and psychopathology varies depending on the type of disorder. There also are important normative developmental changes in each of these dimensions of support, and these developmental changes can affect the relation between social support and psychopathology differently across the life span.

Although there is a growing body of literature about social support, development, and psychopathology, several important and interesting questions still lack answers. These include issues concerning developmental changes in social support, the role of social support in the onset and maintenance of psychopathology, and the implications of this basic knowledge for interventions aimed at preventing or ameliorating maladaptation. First, developmental questions require longitudinal studies that follow the same cohort of children to identify the processes underlying the developmental changes in children's social networks, perceptions, and received support. How do children enlarge and alter their social networks as they develop, and what is responsible for these changes? What is the role of parents, peers, and teachers in the development and maintenance of children's social networks? What social and cognitive abilities influence the social support experience differentially across the life span? We need to move beyond simple correlations between social competence and social support and begin untangling the direction of this relation and the processes that underlie it. As mentioned in the previous section, in addition to longitudinal research with normative populations, longitudinal research with at-risk or psychopathological populations may shed some light on the direction of the normative processes driving particular social support experiences.

Second, how does the relation between social support and psychopathology change as a function of development? How do developmental changes in children's social networks, perceived and received support impact adaptation? For example, the child who perceives that members of his or her social network are intentionally hostile may become aggressive and subsequently may be rejected by peers in that social network. How does the need for social support change with the varying salient developmental tasks of each age period? How might disruption in a child's social support system impact the successful negotiation of these normal developmental tasks? For example, during middle childhood, an important task is the development of appropriate peer relations. If a child has a limited social network for some reason (e.g., lives in a remote area), then this child may not learn the necessary social skills to maintain a meaningful social network. This could lead to other interpersonal problems later if the child does not have an opportunity to develop these skills.

The relation between social support and psychopathology needs to be studied more extensively from a developmental perspective. This means having a clear understanding of the normative processes linked with the development and maintenance of a social support system, as well as knowing how and when these normal processes can go awry. It then is necessary to identify the processes by which problems in the social support system can produce, exacerbate, or maintain symptoms of psychopathology.

The converse relation also needs to be studied. How do the various types of psychopathology differentially affect a social support system, and how does this change over time? Whereas early in a depressive episode, an individual might receive a great deal of positive social support, over time this often changes as the result of the increasing frustration among members of the depressive's social network. Schizophrenic patients who have particularly conflictual relationships with family members are more likely to have families characterized by hostility and criticism (i.e., expressed emotion), and this then affects the subsequent course of the disorder. Young children who display aggressive and antisocial behavior are more likely to be rejected by peers (and adults) who are behaving in more socially sanctioned ways, and thus these young aggressive children may end up in a social group that encourages later delinquent behavior. Social support can play a role in the onset and maintenance of psychopathology, and psychopathology can significantly alter the nature of an individual's social support system.

Finally, the implications of basic research concerning development, psychopathology, and social support for treatment and prevention provide an important direction for future study. Should the focus of intervention be on increasing social networks, changing the individual's perceptions of the quality of a network, or learning how to actually obtain support from members of that network? At what points in development are these different interventions likely to be the most effective? Can strategies designed to obtain and maintain an adequate social support system be developed to prevent the onset of psychopathology in high-risk samples? These are crucial questions for researchers in developmental psychopathology to address as part of their quest not only to understand the etiology and maintenance of psychopathology but also to apply the knowledge gained to the treatment and prevention of psychopathology across the life span.

REFERENCES

Abramson, L. Y., Metalsky, G. I., & Alloy, L. B. (1989). Hopelessness depression: A theory-based subtype of depression. *Psychological Review, 96,* 358–372.

Ainsworth, M. D. S. (1989). Attachments beyond infancy. *American Psychologist, 44,* 709–716.

Ainsworth, M. D. S., Blehar, M. C., Waters, E., & Wall, S. (1978). *Patterns of attachment.* Hillsdale, NJ: Erlbaum.

Alloway, R., & Bebbington, P. (1987). The buffer theory of social support—A review of the literature. *Psychological Medicine, 17,* 91–108.

Alloy, L. B., & Abramson, L. Y. (1988). Depressive realism: Four theoretical perspectives. In L. B. Alloy (Ed.), *Cognitive processes in depression* (pp. 223–265). New York: Guilford.

Altman, J. H., & Wittenborn, J. R. (1980). Depression-prone personality in women. *Journal of Abnormal Psychology, 89,* 49–74.

American Psychiatric Association. (1980, 1987, 1994). *Diagnostic and statistical manual of mental disorders* (3rd ed., 3rd ed. rev., 4th ed.). Washington, DC: Author.

Anderson, K. E., Lytton, H., & Romney, D. M. (1986). Mothers' interactions with normal and conduct-disordered boys: Who affects whom? *Developmental Psychology, 22,* 604–609.

Aneshensel, C. S., & Stone, J. D. (1982). Stress and depression: A test of the buffering model of social support. *Archives of General Psychiatry, 39,* 1392–1396.

Antonucci, T. (1985). Personal characteristics, social support, and social behavior. In R. H. Binstock & E. Shanas (Eds.), *Handbook of aging and the social sciences* (2nd ed., pp. 94–128). New York: Van Nostrand-Reinhold.

Antonucci, T. (1991). Attachment, social support, and coping with negative life events in mature adulthood. In E. M. Cummings, A. L. Greene, & K. H. Karraker (Eds.), *Life-span developmental psychology: Perspectives on stress and coping* (pp. 261–276). Hillsdale, NJ: Erlbaum.

Antonucci, T. C., & Israel, B. A. (1986). Veridicality of social support: A comparison of principal and network members' responses. *Journal of Consulting and Clinical Psychology, 54,* 432–437.

Appel, M. H. (1942). Aggressive behavior of nursery school children and adult procedures in dealing with such behaviour. *Journal of Experimental Education, 11,* 185–199.

Armsden, G. C., McCauley, E., Greenberg, M. T., Burke, P. M., & Mitchell, J. R. (1990). Parent and peer attachment in early adolescent depression. *Journal of Abnormal Child Psychology, 18,* 683–697.

Asarnow, J. R., Carlson, G. A., & Guthrie, D. (1987). Coping strategies, self-perceptions, hopelessness, and perceived family environment in depressed and suicidal children. *Journal of Consulting and Clinical Psychology, 55,* 361–366.

Asher, S. R., Oden, S. L., & Gottman, J. M. (1977). Children's friendships in school settings. In L. G. Katz (Ed.), *Current topics in early childhood education* (pp. 33–61). Norwood, NJ: Ablex.

Auebach, S. M., & Kilmann, P. R. (1977). Crisis intervention: A review of outcome research. *Psychological Bulletin, 84,* 1189–1217.

Band, E. B., & Weisz, J. R. (1988). How to feel better when it feels bad: Children's perspectives on coping with everyday stress. *Developmental Psychology, 24,* 247–253.

Bandura, A. (1969). Social-learning theory of identificatory processes. In D. A. Goslin (Ed.), *Handbook of socialization theory and research* (pp. 213–262). New York: Rand McNally.

Barkley, R. A., Karleson, J., Pollard, S., & Murphey, F. V. (1985). Developmental changes in the mother-child interactions of hyperactive boys: Effects of two dose levels of Ritalin. *Journal of Child Psychology and Psychiatry, 26,* 705–715.

Barnes, J. A. (1954). Class and committees in a Norwegian island parish. *Human Relations, 1,* 39–58.

Barnett, P. A., & Gotlib, I. H. (1988). Psychosocial functioning and depression: Distinguishing among antecedents, concomitants, and consequences. *Psychological Bulletin, 104,* 97–126.

Barrera, M. (1981). Social support in the adjustment of pregnant adolescents: Assessment of issues. In B. Gottlieb (Ed.), *Social networks and social support* (pp. 69–96). Beverly Hills, CA: Sage.

Barrera, M. (1986). Distinctions between social support concepts, measures, and models. *American Journal of Community Psychology, 14,* 413–445.

Barrera, M. (1988). Models of social support and life stress: Beyond the buffering hypothesis. In L. H. Cohen (Ed.), *Life events and psychological functioning: Theoretical and methodological issues* (pp. 211–235). Newbury Park: Sage.

Barrera, M., & Garrison-Jones, C. (1992). Family and peer social support as specific correlates of adolescent depressive symptoms. *Journal of Abnormal Child Psychology, 20,* 1–16.

Barrera, M., Sandler, I. N., & Ramsey, T. B. (1981). Preliminary development of a scale of social support: Studies on college students. *American Journal of Community Psychology, 9,* 435–447.

Barron, A. P., & Earls, F. (1984). The relation of temperament and social factors to behavior problems in three-year-old children. *Journal of Child Psychology and Psychiatry, 25,* 23–33.

Barrowclough, C., & Tarrier, N. (1984). Psychosocial interventions with families and their effects on the course of schizophrenia: A review. *Psychological Medicine, 14,* 629–642.

Bates, J. E., Bayles, K., Bennett, D. S., Ridge, B., & Brown, M. M. (1991). Origins of externalizing behavior problems at eight years of age. In D. J. Pepler & K. H. Rubin (Eds.), *The development and treatment of childhood aggression* (pp. 93–120). Hillsdale, NJ: Erlbaum.

Bebbington, P., & Kuipers, L. (1988). Social influences on schizophrenia. In P. Bebbington & P. McGuffin (Eds.), *Schizophrenia: The major issues* (pp. 201–225). Oxford: Heinemann.

Beck, A. T. (1967). *Depression: Clinical, experimental, and theoretical aspects.* New York: Harper & Row.

Beck, A. T. (1976). *Cognitive therapy and the emotional disorders*. New York: International Universities Press.

Beck, A. T. (1983). Cognitive therapy of depression: New perspectives. In P. J. Clayton & J. E. Barrett (Eds.), *Treatment of depression: Old controversies and new approaches* (pp. 265–290). New York: Raven Press.

Beels, C. C., Gutwirth, L., Berkeley, J., & Struening, E. (1984). Measurements of social support in schizophrenia. *Schizophrenia Bulletin, 10*, 399–411.

Bell, R. A., LeRoy, J. B., & Stephenson, J. J. (1982). Evaluating the mediating effects of social supports upon life events and depressive symptoms. *Journal of Community Psychology, 10*, 325–340.

Belle, D., & Longfellow, C. (1983, April). *Emotional support and children's well-being: An exploratory study of children's confidants.* Paper presented at the biennial meeting of the Society for Research in Child Development, Detroit.

Belle, D., & Longfellow, C. (1984, August). *Turning to others: Children's use of confidants.* Paper presented at the annual meeting of the American Psychological Association, Toronto.

Belsky, J., & Nezworski, T. (Eds.). (1988). *Clinical implications of attachment.* Hillsdale, NJ: Erlbaum.

Belsky, J., & Rovine, M. (1984). Social network contact, family support, and the transition to parenthood. *Journal of Marriage and the Family, 45*, 567–579.

Bergeman, C. S., Plomin, R., Pedersen, N. L., & McClearn, G. E. (1991). Genetic mediation of the relationship between social support and psychological well-being. *Psychology and Aging, 6*(4), 640–646.

Berndt, T. J. (1979). Developmental changes in conformity to peers and parents. *Developmental Psychology, 15*, 608–616.

Berndt, T. J. (1981). Relations between social cognition, nonsocial cognition, and social behavior: The case of friendship. In J. H. Flavell & L. D. Ross (Eds.), *Social cognitive development* (pp. 176–199). New York: Cambridge University Press.

Berndt, T. J. (1982). The features and effects of friendship in early adolescence. *Child Development, 53*, 1447–1460.

Berndt, T. J., & Hoyle, S. G. (1985). Stability and change in childhood and adolescent friendships. *Developmental Psychology, 21*, 1007–1015.

Berndt, T. J., & Perry, T. B. (1986). Children's perceptions of friendships as supportive relationships. *Developmental Psychology, 22*, 640–648.

Bhavnagri, N. P., & Parke, R. D. (1991). Parents as direct facilitators of children's peer relationships: Effects of age of child and sex of parent. *Journal of Social and Personal Relationships, 8*, 423–440.

Bigelow, B. J. (1977). Children's friendship expectations: A cognitive-developmental study. *Child Development, 48*, 246–53.

Billings, A. G., Cronkite, R. C., & Moos, R. H. (1983). Social-environmental factors in unipolar depression: Comparisons of depressed patients and nondepressed controls. *Journal of Abnormal Psychology, 92*, 119–133.

Billings, A. G., & Moos, R. H. (1982). Stressful life events and symptoms: A longitudinal model. *Health Psychology, 1*, 99–117.

Billings, A. G., & Moos, R. H. (1984). Coping, stress, and social resources among adults with unipolar depression. *Journal of Personality and Social Psychology, 46*, 877–891.

Billings, A. G., & Moos, R. H. (1985). Psychosocial processes of remission in unipolar depression: comparing depressed patients with matched community controls. *Journal of Consulting and Clinical Psychology, 53*, 314–325.

Blazer, D. G., & Hughes, D. C. (1991). Subjective social support and depressive symptoms in major depression: Separate phenomena or epiphenomena. *Journal of Psychiatric Research, 25*, 191–203.

Blumberg, S. R., & Hokanson, J. E. (1983). The effects of another person's response style on interpersonal behavior in depression. *Journal of Abnormal Psychology, 92*, 196–209.

Blyth, D. A., & Traeger, C. (1988). Adolescent self-esteem and perceived relationships with parents and peers. In S. Salzinger, J. Antrobus, & M. Hammer (Eds.), *Social networks of children, adolescents, and college students* (pp. 171–194). Hillsdale, NJ: Erlbaum.

Bogat, G. A., Caldwell, R. A., Rogosch, F. A., & Kriegler, J. A. (1985). Differentiating specialists and generalists within college students' social support networks. *Journal of Youth and Adolescence, 14*, 23–35.

Bolger, N. (1990). Coping as a personality process: A prospective study. *Journal of Personality and Social Psychology, 59*, 525–537.

Bolger, N., & Eckenrode, J. (1991). Social relationships, personality, and anxiety during a major stressful event. *Journal of Personality and Social Psychology, 61*, 440–449.

Bothwell, S., & Weissman, M. M. (1977). Social impairments four years after an acute depressive episode. *American Journal of Orthopsychiatry, 47*, 231–237.

Bott, E. (1971). *Family and social network* (2nd ed.). London: Tavistock Publications.

Bowker, L. H., & Klein, M. W. (1983). The etiology of female juvenile delinquency and gang membership: A test of psychological and social structural explanations. *Adolescence, 18*, 739–751.

Bowlby, J. (1969). *Attachment and loss: Vol. 1. Attachment.* London: Hogarth Press.

Bowlby, J. (1980). *Attachment and loss: Vol. 3. Loss: Sadness and depression.* New York: Basic Books.

Braithwaite, J. (1981). The myth of social class and criminality reconsidered. *American Sociological Review, 35*, 63–77.

Breier, A., & Strauss, J. S. (1984). The role of social relationships in the recovery from psychotic disorders. *American Journal of Psychiatry, 141*, 949–955.

Bretherton, I. (1985). Attachment theory: Retrospect and prospect. In I. Bretherton & E. Waters (Eds.), *Growing points of attachment theory and research* (pp. 3–35). *Monographs of the Society for Research in Child Development, 50* (1-2, Serial No. 209).

Brim, J. A. (1974). Social network correlates of avowed happiness. *Journal of Nervous and Mental Disease, 158*, 432–439.

Bronfenbrenner, U. (1979). *The ecology of human development.* Cambridge, MA: Harvard University Press.

Brown, G. W. (1974). Meaning, measurement and stress of life events. In B. S. Dohrenwend & B. P. Dohrenwend (Eds.), *Stressful life events: Their nature and effects* (pp. 217–243). New York: Wiley.

Brown, G. W. (1987). Social factors and development and course of depressive disorders in women. *British Journal of Social Work, 17*, 615–634.

Brown, G. W., Bhrolchain, M. N., & Harris, T. (1975). Social class and psychiatric disturbance among women in an urban population. *Sociology, 9*, 225–254.

Brown, G. W., Bifulco, A., & Harris, T. O. (1987). Life events, vulnerability and onset of depression: Some refinements. *British Journal of Psychiatry, 150*, 30–42.

Brown, G. W., Birley, J. L. T., & Wing, J. K. (1972). The influences of family life on the course of schizophrenic disorders: A replication. *British Journal of Psychiatry, 121*, 241–258.

Brown, G. W., & Harris, T. (1978). *The social origins of depression: A study of psychiatric disorder in women.* New York: Free Press.

Brown, G. W., & Prudo, R. (1981). Psychiatric disorder in a rural and urban population: 1. Etiology of depression. *Psychological Medicine, 11,* 581–599.

Brown, S. F. (1984). Social class, child maltreatment, and delinquent behavior. *Criminology, 22,* 259–278.

Bryant, B. K. (1985). The neighborhood walk: Sources of support in middle childhood (with commentary by Ross D. Parke). *Monographs of the Society for Research in Child Development, 50* (3, Serial No. 210).

Bryant, B. K. (1989). The need for support in relation to the need for autonomy. In D. Belle (Ed.), *Children's social networks and social supports* (pp. 332–351). New York: Wiley.

Buhrmester, D. (1990). Intimacy of friendship, interpersonal competence, and adjustment during preadolescence and adolescence. *Child Development, 61,* 1101–1111.

Buhrmester, D., & Furman, W. (1984, July). *The need fulfilling role of friendship in children's social networks.* Paper presented at the Second International Conference on Personal Relations, Madison, WI.

Buhrmester, D., & Furman, W. (1986). The changing functions of friends in childhood: A Neo-Sullivanian perspective. In V. J. Derlega & B. A. Winstead (Eds.), *Friendship and social interaction* (pp. 41–62). New York: Springer-Verlag.

Burbach, D. J., & Borduin, C. M. (1986). Parent-child relations and the etiology of depression: A review of methods and findings. *Clinical Psychology Review, 6,* 133–153.

Campbell, E. R., & Alexander, C. N. (1965). Structural effects and interpersonal relationships. *American Journal of Sociology, 71,* 284–289.

Campbell, S. B., Cohn, J. F., Flanagan, C., Popper, S., & Meyers, T. (1992). Course and correlates of postpartum depression during the transition to parenthood. *Development and Psychopathology, 4,* 29–47.

Cantor, N. L., & Gelfand, D. M. (1977). Effects of responsiveness and sex of children on adults' behavior. *Child Development, 48,* 232–238.

Caplan, G. (1974). *Support systems and community mental health.* New York: Behavioral Publications.

Caplan, R. D. (1979). Social support, person-environment fit and coping. In L. F. Furman & J. Gordis (Eds.), *Mental health and the economy* (pp. 89–131). Kalamazoo, MI: UpJohn Institute for Employment Research.

Carpenter, B. N., Hansson, R. O., Rountree, R., & Jones, W. H. (1984). Relational competence and adjustment in diabetic patients. *Journal of Social and Clinical Psychology, 1,* 359–369.

Cassel, J. (1976). The contribution of the social environment to host resistance. *American Journal of Epidemiology, 104,* 107–123.

Cauce, A. M., Felner, R. D., & Primavera, J. (1982). Social support in high-risk adolescents: Structural components and adaptive impact. *American Journal of Community Psychology, 10,* 417–428.

Cauce, A. M., Reid, M., Landesman, S., & Gonzales, N. (1990). Social support in young children: Measurement, structure, and behavioral impact. In B. R. Sarason, I. G. Sarason, & G. R. Pierce (Eds.), *Social support: An interactional view* (pp. 64–94). New York: Wiley.

Cernkovich, S. A., & Giordano, P. C. (1987). Family relationships and delinquency. *Criminology, 25,* 295–319.

Chassin, L., Presson, C. C., Sherman, S. J., Montello, D., & McGrew, J. (1986). Changes in peer and parent influence during adolescence: Longitudinal versus cross-sectional perspectives on smoking initiation. *Developmental Psychology, 22,* 327–334.

Cicchetti, D. (1990). Perspectives on the interface between normal and atypical development. *Development and Psychopathology, 2,* 329–333.

Cicchetti, D. (1993). Developmental psychopathology: Reactions, reflections, projections. *Developmental Review, 13,* 471–502.

Cicchetti, D., Cummings, E. M., Greenberg, M. T., & Marvin, R. S. (1990). An organizational perspective on attachment beyond infancy: Implications for theory, measurement, and research. In M. Greenberg, D. Cicchetti, & E. M. Cummings (Eds.), *Attachment in the preschool years: Theory, research, and intervention* (pp. 3–50). Chicago: University of Chicago Press.

Cicchetti, D., & Richters, J. E. (1993). Developmental considerations in the investigation of conduct disorder. *Development and Psychopathology, 5,* 331–344.

Clark, J. P., & Wenninger, E. P. (1962). Socioeconomic class and area as correlates of illegal behavior among juveniles. *American Sociological Review, 27,* 826–834.

Cline, H. F. (1980). Criminal behavior over the life span. In O. G. Brim, Jr. & J. Kagan (Eds.), *Constancy and change in human development* (pp. 641–674). Cambridge: Harvard University Press.

Coates, D., & Wortman, C. B. (1980). Depression maintenance and interpersonal control. In A. Baum & J. E. Singer (Eds.), *Advances in environmental psychology* (Vol. 2, pp. 149–181). Hillsdale, NJ: Erlbaum.

Cobb, S. (1976). Social support as a moderator of life stress. *Psychosomatic Medicine, 38,* 300–314.

Cochran, M. M., & Brassard, J. A. (1979). Child development and personal social networks. *Child Development, 50,* 601–616.

Cohen, C. I., & Kochanowicz, N. (1989). Schizophrenia and social network patterns: A survey of black inner-city outpatients. *Community Mental Health Journal, 25,* 197–207.

Cohen, C. I., & Sokolovsky, J. (1978). Schizophrenia and social networks: Ex-patients in the inner city. *Schizophrenia Bulletin, 4,* 546–560.

Cohen, C. I., Teresi, J., & Holmes, D. (1986). Assessment of stress-buffering effects of social networks on psychological symptoms in an inner-city elderly population. *American Journal of Community Psychology, 14,* 75–91.

Cohen, S. (1991). Social supports and physical health: Symptoms, health behaviors, and infectious disease. In E. M. Cummings, A. L. Greene, & K. H. Karraker (Eds.), *Life-span developmental psychology: Perspectives on stress and coping* (pp. 261–276). Hillsdale, NJ: Erlbaum.

Cohen, S., & Hoberman, H. M. (1983). Positive events and social supports as buffers of life change stress. *Journal of Applied Social Psychology, 13,* 19–125.

Cohen, S., & McKay, G. (1984). Social support stress and the buffering hypothesis: A theoretical analysis. In A. Baum, S. E. Taylor, & J. E. Singer (Eds.), *Handbook of psychology and health: Social psychological aspects of health,* (Vol. IV, pp. 253–267). Hillsdale, NJ: Erlbaum.

Cohen, S., Mermelstein, R., Kamarck, T., & Hoberman, H. (1985). Measuring the functional components of social support. In I. G. Sarason & B. Sarason (Eds.), *Social support: Theory, research and applications* (pp. 73–94). The Hague, The Netherlands: Martinus Nijhoff.

Cohen, S., Sherrod, D. R., & Clark, M. S. (1986). Social skills and the stress-protective role of social support. *Journal of Personality and Social Psychology, 50,* 963–973.

Cohen, S., & Wills, T. A. (1985). Stress, social support, and the buffering hypothesis. *Psychological Bulletin, 98,* 310–357.

Coie, J. D., Dodge, K. A., Terry, R., & Wright, V. (1991). The role of aggression in peer relations: An analysis of aggression episodes in boys' play groups. *Child Development, 62,* 812–826.

Coie, J. D., & Jacobs, M. R. (1993). The role of social context in the prevention of conduct disorder. *Development and Psychopathology, 5,* 263–275.

Coie, J. D., & Kupersmidt, J. B. (1983). A behavioral analysis of emerging social status in boys' groups. *Child Development, 54,* 1400–1416.

Cole, D. A. (1990). Relation of social and academic competence to depressive symptoms in childhood. *Journal of Abnormal Psychology, 99,* 422–429.

Cole, D. A., & Rehm, L. P. (1986). Family interaction patterns and childhood depression. *Journal of Abnormal Child Psychology, 14,* 297–314.

Coleman, R. E., & Miller, R. E. (1975). The relationship between depression and marital maladjustment in a clinic population: A multitrait-multimethod study. *Journal of Consulting and Clinical Psychology, 43,* 647–651.

Collins, A. H., & Pancoast, D. L. (1976). *Natural helping networks: A strategy for prevention.* Washington, DC: National Association of Social Workers.

Compas, B. E. (1987). Stress and life events during childhood and adolescence. *Clinical Psychology Review, 7,* 275–302.

Compas, B. E., Slavin, L. A., Wagner, B. M., & Vannatta, K. (1986). Relationship of life events and social support with psychological dysfunction among adolescents. *Journal of Youth and Adolescence, 15,* 205–221.

Cooley, C. H. (1902). *Human nature and the social order.* New York: Scribner's.

Cooper, C. R., Grotevant, H. D., & Condon, S. M. (1983). Individuality and connectedness both foster adolescent identity formation and role taking skills. In H. D. Grotevant & C. R. Cooper (Eds.), *Adolescent development in the family. New directions for child development* (pp. 43–59). San Francisco: Jossey-Bass.

Costello, C. G. (1982). Social factors associated with depression: A retrospective community study. *Psychological Medicine, 12,* 329–339.

Coyne, J. C. (1976a). Toward an interactional description of depression. *Psychiatry, 39,* 28–40.

Coyne, J. C. (1976b). Depression and the response of others. *Journal of Abnormal Psychology, 85,* 186–193.

Coyne, J. C., Aldwin, C., & Lazarus, R. S. (1981). Depression and coping in stressful episodes. *Journal of Abnormal Psychology, 90,* 439–447.

Coyne, J. C., & Bolger, N. (1990). Doing without social support as an explanatory concept. *Journal of Social and Clinical Psychology, 9,* 148–158.

Coyne, J. C., Burchill, S. A. L., & Stiles, W. B. (1991). An interactional perspective on depression. In C. R. Snyder & D. O. Forsyth (Eds.), *Handbook of social and clinical psychology: The health perspective* (pp. 327–349).

Coyne, J. C., & Downey, G. (1991). Social factors and psychopathology: Stress, social support, and coping processes. *Annual Review of Psychology, 42,* 401–425.

Crotty, P., & Kulys, R. (1985). Social support networks: The views of schizophrenic clients and their significant others. *Social Work, 4,* 301–309.

Cummings, E. M., & Cicchetti, D. (1990). Toward a transactional model of relations between attachment and depression. In M. T. Greenberg, D. Cicchetti, & E. M. Cummings (Eds.), *Attachment in preschool years* (pp. 339–372). Chicago: University of Chicago Press.

Cutler, D., Tatum, E., & Shore, J. H. (1987). A comparison of schizophrenic patients in different community support treatment approaches. *Community Mental Health Journal, 23,* 103–113.

Cutrona, C. E. (1984). Social support and stress in the transition to parenthood. *Journal of Abnormal Psychology, 92,* 161–172.

Cutrona, C. E. (1989). Rating of social support by adolescents and adult informants: Degree of correspondence and prediction of depressive symptoms. *Journal of Personality and Social Psychology, 57,* 723–730.

Dadds, M. R., Sanders, M. R., Morrison, M., & Rebgetz, M. (1992). *Journal of Abnormal Psychology, 101,* 505–513.

Damon, W. (1983). *Social and personality development: Infancy through adolescence.* New York: Norton.

Doane, J. A., West, K. L., Goldstein, M. J., Rodnick, E., Jones, J. E. (1981). Parental communication deviance and affective style: Predictors of subsequent schizophrenia spectrum disorders in vulnerable adolescents. *Archives of General Psychiatry, 38,* 679–685.

Dodge, K. A. (1983). Behavioral antecedents: A peer social status. *Child Development, 54,* 1386–1399.

Dodge, K. A. (1985). Facets of social interaction and the assessment of social competence in children. In B. H. Schneider, K. H. Rubin, & J. E. Ledingham (Eds.), *Children's peer relations: Issues in assessment and intervention* (pp. 243–269). New York: Springer-Verlag.

Dodge, K. A., & Coie, J. D. (1987). Social-information processing factors in reactive and proactive aggression in children's peer groups. *Journal of Personality and Social Psychology, 53,* 1146–1158.

Dodge, K. A., Pettit, G. S., McClaskey, C. L., & Brown, M. M. (1986). Social competence in children (with commentary by J. M. Gottman). *Monographs of the Society for Research in Child Development, 51* (2, Serial No. 213).

Dohrenwend, B. S., Dohrenwend, B. P., Dodson, M., & Shrout, P. E. (1984). Symptoms, hassles, social supports and life events: Problems of confounded measures. *Journal of Abnormal Psycholgoy, 93,* 222–230.

Dohrenwend, B. P., & Shrout, P. E. (1985). "Hassles" in the conceptualization and measurement of life stress variables. *American Psychologist, 40,* 780–785.

Downey, G., & Coyne, J. C. (1990). Children of depressed parents: An integrative review. *Psychological Bulletin, 108,* 50–76.

Drake, R. E., & Sederer, L. I. (1986). The adverse effects of intensive treatment of chronic schizophrenia. *Comprehensive Psychiatry, 27,* 313–326.

DuBois, D. L., Felner, R. D., Brand, S., Adan, A. M., & Evans, E. G. (1992). A prospective study of life stress, social support and adaptation in early adolescence. *Child Development, 63,* 542–557.

Dubow, E. F., Tisak, J., Causey, D., Hryshko, A., & Reid, G. (1991). A two-year longitudinal study of stressful life events, social support, and social problem-solving skills: Contributions to children's behavioral and academic adjustment. *Child Development, 62,* 583–599.

Dulz, B., & Hand, I. (1986). Short-term relapse in young schizophrenics: Can it be predicted and affected by family (CFI), patient and treatment variables? An experimental study. In M. J. Goldstein, I. Hand, & K. Hahlweg (Eds.), *Treatment of schizophrenia: Family assessment and intervention* (pp. 59–75). Berlin: Springer-Verlag.

Dumas, J. E., & Wahler, R. G. (1983). Predictors of treatment outcome in parent training: Mother insularity and socioeconomic disadvantage. *Behavioral Assessment, 5,* 301–313.

Dunn, J., & Kendrick, C. (1982). *Siblings: Love, envy and understanding.* London: Grant McIntyre.

East, P. L., & Rook, K. S. (1992). Compensatory patterns of support among children's peer relationships: A test using school friends, nonschool friends, and siblings. *Developmental Psychology, 28,* 163–172.

Eckerman, C. O., Whatley, J., & Kutz, S. (1975). Growth of social play with peers during the second year of life. *Developmental Psychology, 11,* 42–49.

Eisenberg, N., Miller, P. A., Shell, R., McNalley, S., & Shea, C. (1991). Prosocial development in adolescence: A longitudinal study. *Developmental Psychology, 27,* 849–857.

Emery, R. E. (1982). Interparental conflict and the children of discord and divorce. *Psychological Bulletin, 92,* 310–330.

Emery, R. E., Weintraub, S., & Neale, J. M. (1982). Effects of marital discord on the school behavior of children of schizophrenic, affectively disordered, and normal parents. *Journal of Abnormal Child Psychology, 10,* 215–228.

Erikson, E. H. (1964). *Insight and responsibility: Lectures on the ethical implications of psychoanalytic insight.* New York: Norton.

Erickson, M., Egeland, B., & Sroufe, L. A. (1985). The relationship between quality of attachment and behavior problems in preschool in a high risk sample. In I. Bretherton & E. Waters (Eds.), *Growing points in attachment theory and research* (pp. 147–186). *Monographs of the Society for Research in Child Development, 50*(1-2, Serial No. 209).

Eysenck, H. J., & Eysenck, M. W. (1985). *Personality and individual differences.* New York: Plenum.

Faccincani, C., Mignolli, G., & Platt, S. (1990). Service utilization, social support and psychiatric status in a cohort of patients with schizophrenic psychoses: A 7-year follow-up study. *Schizophrenia Research, 3,* 139–146.

Fagot, B. I., & Kavanaugh, K. (1990). The prediction of antisocial behavior from avoidant attachment classifications. *Child Development, 61,* 864–873.

Farrington, D. P. (1978). The family backgrounds of aggressive youths. In L. A. Hersov & M. Berger (Eds.), *Aggression and antisocial behavior in childhood and adolescence* (pp. 73–93). London: Pergamon.

Feinman, S. (1982). Social referencing in infancy. *Merrill-Palmer Quarterly, 28,* 445–470.

Fiore, J., Becker, J., & Coppel, D. B. (1983). Social network interactions: A buffer or a stress. *American Journal of Community Psychology, 11,* 423–439.

Fondacaro, M. R., & Moos, R. H. (1987). Social support and coping: A longitudinal analysis. *American Journal of Community Psychology, 15,* 653–673.

Foot, H., Chapman, A., & Smith, J. (1980). Patterns of interaction in children's friendships. In H. C. Foot, A. J. Chapman, & J. R. Smith (Eds.), *Friendship and social relations in children* (pp. 267–292). New York: Wiley.

Freeman, H. E., & Simmons, O. G. (1963). *The mental patient comes home.* New York: Wiley.

Frick, P. J., Lahey, B. B., Loeber, R., Stouthamer-Loeber, M., Christ, M. A. G., & Hanson, K. (1992). Familial risk factors to oppositional defiant disorder and conduct disorder: Parental psychopathology and maternal parenting. *Journal of Consulting and Clinical Psychology, 60*(1), 49–55.

Friedrich, W., Reams, R., & Jacobs, J. (1982). Depression and suicidal ideation in early adolescents. *Journal of Youth and Adolescence, 11,* 403–407.

Frydman, J. I. (1981). Social support, life events and psychiatric symptoms: A study of direct, conditional and interaction effects. *Social Psychiatry, 16,* 69–78.

Furman, W. (1989). The development of children's social networks. In D. Belle (Ed.), *Children's social networks and social supports* (pp. 151–172). New York: Wiley.

Furman, W., & Buhrmester, D. (1985). Children's perceptions of personal relationships in their social networks. *Developmental Psychology, 21,* 1016–1024.

Gad, M. T., & Johnson, J. H. (1980). Correlates of adolescent life stress as realted to race, SES, and levels of perceived social support. *Journal of Clinical Child Psychology, 3,* 13–16.

Garber, J., & Hilsman, R. (1992). cognitions, stress, and depression in children and adolescents. *Child and Adolescent Psychiatric Clinics of North America, 1,* 129–167.

Garber, J., & Hollon, S. D. (1991). What can specificity designs say about causality in psychopathology research? *Psychological Bulletin, 110,* 129–136.

Gard, G. C., Turone, R., & Devlin, B. (1985). Social interaction and interpersonal distance in normal and behaviorally disturbed boys. *Journal of Genetic Psychology, 146,* 189–196.

Gardner, F. (1987). Positive interaction between mothers and children with conduct problems: Is there training for harmony as well as fighting? *Journal of Abnormal Child Psychology, 15,* 283–293.

Gardner, F. (1989). Inconsistent parenting: Is there evidence for a link with children's conduct problems? *Journal of Abnormal Child Psychology, 17,* 223–233.

Gardner, F. (1992). Parent-child interaction and conduct disorder. *Educational Psychology Review, 4,* 135–163.

Garner, D. M., Garfinkel, P. E., & Olmsted, M. (1983). An overview of sociocultural factors in the development of anorexia nervosa. In P. L. Darby, P. E. Garfinkel, D. M. Garner, & D. V. Coscina (Eds.), *Anorexia nervosa: Recent development in research* (pp. 65–82). New York: Liss.

Giordano, P. C., Cernkovich, S. A., & Pugh, M. D. (1986) Friendships and delinquency. *American Journal of Sociology, 91,* 1170–1202.

Goldstein, M. J. (1987). The UCLA high risk project. *Schizophrenia Bulletin, 13,* 505–514.

Goodenough, F. L. (1931). *Anger in young children.* Minneapolis: University of Minnesota Press.

Gore, S. (1978). Effects of social support in moderating health consequences of unemployment. *Journal of Health and Social Behavior, 19,* 157–165.

Gotlib, I. H., & Robinson, A. (1982). Responses to depressed individuals: Discrepancies between self-report and observer-rated behavior. *Journal of Abnormal Psychology, 91,* 231–240.

Gottesman, I. I., & Shields, J. (1972). *Schizophrenia and genetics: A twin study vantage point.* New York: Academic Press.

Gottlieb, B. H. (1983, March). Social support as a focus for integrative research in psychology. *American Psychologist,* pp. 278–287.

Gottlieb, B. H., & Pancer, S. M. (1988). Social networks and the transition to parenthood. In G. Y. Michaels & W. A. Goldberg (Eds.), *The transition to parenthood: Current theory and research* (pp. 235–269). Cambridge: Cambridge University Press.

Gottman, J. M., Gonso, J., & Rasmussen, B. (1975). Social interactions, social competence, and friendship in children. *Child Development, 46,* 709–718.

Gottman, J., & Parkhurst, J. (1980). A developmental theory of friendship and acquaintance processes. In W. A. Collins (Ed.), *Development of cognition, affect, and social relations* (Minnesota Symposium on Child Psychology, Vol. 13, pp. 197–253). Hillsdale, NJ: Erlbaum.

Greenberg, M. T., & Speltz, M. L. (1988). Contributions of attachment theory to the understanding of conduct problems during the preschool years. In J. Belsky & T. Nezworski (Eds.), *Clinical implications of attachment* (pp. 177–218). Hillsdale, NJ: Erlbaum.

Greenberg, M. T., Speltz, M. L., & DeKlyen, M. (1993). The role of attachment in the early development of disruptive behavior problems. *Development and Psychopathology, 5,* 191–213.

Greenley, R. (1979). Family expectations, post-hospital adjustment, and the societal reaction perspective on mental illness. *Journal of Health and Social Behavior, 20,* 217–227.

Grissett, N. I., & Norvell, N. K. (1992). Perceived social support, social skills, and quality of relationships in bulimic women. *Journal of Consulting and Clinical Psychology, 60,* 293–299.

Habif, V. L., & Lahey, B. B. (1980). Assessment of the life stress-depression relationship: The use of social support as a moderator variable. *Journal of Behavioral Assessment, 2,* 167–173.

Haddad, J. D., Barocas, R., & Hollenbeck, A. R. (1991). Family organization and parent attitudes of children with conduct disorder. *Journal of Clinical Child Psychology, 20,* 152–161.

Hagestad, G. O. (1985). Continuity and connectedness. In V. L. Bengston & J. F. Robertson (Eds.), *Grandparenthood* (pp. 31–34). Beverly Hills, CA: Sage.

Hamilton, N. G., Ponzoha, C. A., Cutler, D. L., & Weigel, R. M. (1989). Social networks and negative versus positive symptoms of schizophrenia. *Schizophrenia Bulletin, 15,* 625–633.

Hammen, C. (1991). *Depression runs in families: The social context or risk and resilience in children of depressed mothers.* New York: Springer-Verlag.

Hammen, C. (1992). Cognitive, life stress, and interpersonal approaches to a developmental psychopathology model of depression. *Development and Psychopathology, 4,* 189–206.

Hammen, C., Ellicott, A., Gitlin, M., & Jamison, K. R. (1989). Sociotropy/autonomy and vulnerability to specific life events in unipolar and bipolar patients. *Journal of Abnormal Psychology, 98,* 154–160.

Hammen, C., & Peters, S. D. (1978). Interpersonal consequences of depression: Response to men and women enacting a depressed role. *Journal of Abnormal Psychology, 87,* 322–332.

Hanson, S. M., & Sauer, W. J. (1985). Children and their elderly parents. In W. J. Sauer & R. T. Coward (Eds.), *Social support networks and the care of the elderly* (pp. 41–66). New York: Springer.

Harter, S. (1983). Developmental perspectives on the self-system. In P. Mussen (Ed.), *Handbook of child psychology: Vol. 4 Socialization, personality and social development* (pp. 275–385). New York: Wiley.

Harter, S. (1990). Causes, correlates and the functional role of global self-worth: A life-span perspective. In J. Kolligan & R. Sternberg (Eds.), *Perceptions of competence and incompetence across the lifespan* (pp. 67–97). New Haven, CT: Yale University Press.

Harter, S., Marold, D. B., & Whitesell, N. R. (1992). Model of psychosocial risk factors leading to suicidal ideation in young adolescents. *Development and Psychopathology, 4,* 167–188.

Hartup, W. W. (1983). Peer relations. In P. Mussen (Ed.), *Handbook of child psychology: Vol. 4 Socialization, personality and social development* (pp. 103–196). New York: Wiley.

Hartup, W. W. (1986). On relationships and development. In W. W. Hartup & Z. Rubin (Eds.), *Relationships and development* (pp. 1–26). Hillsdale, NJ: Erlbaum.

Hazan, C., & Shaver, P. (1987). Romantic love conceptualized as an attachment process. *Journal of Personality and Social Psychology, 52*(3), 511–524.

Heitzmann, C. A., & Kaplan, R. M. (1988). Assessment of methods for measuring social support. *Health Psychology, 7*(1), 75–109.

Heller, K. (1979). The effects of social support: Prevention and treatment implications. In A. P. Goldstein & F. H. Kanfer (Eds.), *Maximizing treatment gains: Transfer enhancement in psychotherapy.* New York: Academic Press.

Heller, K., & Swindle, R. W. (1983). Social networks, perceived social support, and coping with stress. In R. D. Felner, L. A. Jason, J. N. Moritsugu, & S. S. Farber (Eds.)., *Preventive psychology: Theory, research and practice* (pp. 87–103). New York: Pergamon.

Henderson, S. (1977). The social network, support, and neurosis. *British Journal of Psychiatry, 131,* 185–191.

Henderson, S. (1980). Personal networks and the schizophrenics. *Australian and New Zealand Journal of Psychiatry, 14,* 255–257.

Henderson, S., Byrne, D. G., & Duncan-Jones, P. (1981). *Neurosis and the social environment.* Sydney: Academic Press.

Henderson, S., Byrne, D. G., Duncan Jones, P., Scott, R., & Adcock, S. (1980). Social relationships, adversity and neurosis: A study of associations in a general population sample. *British Journal of Psychiatry, 136,* 354–383.

Herzog, T. (1992). Nurses, patients and relatives: A study of family patterns on psychiatric wards. In C. L. Cazzullo & G. Invernizzi (Eds.), *Family intervention in schizophrenia: Experiences and orientations in Europe.* Milan: ARS.

Hetherington, E. M., & Camara, K. (1984). Families in transition: The processes of dissolution and reconstitution. In R. D. Parke (Ed.), *Review of child development research: Vol. 7. The family* (pp. 398–439). Chicago: University of Chicago Press.

Higson, M., & Kavanaugh, D. J. (1988). A hostel-based psychoeducational intervention for schizophrenia: Programme development and preliminary findings. *Behavior Change, 5,* 85–89.

Hill, J. P., & Holmbeck, G. N. (1986). Attachment and autonomy during adolescence. In G. J. Whitehurst (Ed.), *Annals of child development* (Vol. 3, pp. 145–189). Greenwich, CT: JAI Press.

Hinchcliffe, M., Hopper, D., & Roberts, F. J. (1978). *The melancholy marriage.* New York: Wiley.

Hirsch, B. J., Engel-Levy, A., DuBois, D. L., & Hardesty, P. H. (1990). The role of social environments in social support. In B. R. Sarason, I. G. Sarason and G. R. Pierce (Eds.), *Social support: An interactional view* (pp. 367–393). New York: Wiley.

Hirsch, B. J., & Reischl, T. M. (1985). Social networks and developmental psychopathology: A comparison of adolescent children of depressed, arthritic, or normal parents. *Journal of Abnormal Psychology, 94,* 272–281.

Hirschberg, W. (1985). Social isolation among schizophrenic outpatients. *Social Psychiatry, 20,* 171–178.

Hirschfield, R. M., & Cross, C. K. (1982). Epidemiology of affective disorders. *Archives of General Psychiatry, 39,* 35–46.

Hirschi, T. (1969). *Causes of delinquency.* Berkeley & Los Angeles: University of California Press.

Hochhaus, C., & Sousa, F. (1987). Why children belong to gangs: A comparison of expectations and reality. *High School Journal, 71,* 74–77.

Hoffman, M. L. (1975). Developmental synthesis of affect and cognition and its implications for altruistic motivation. *Developmental Psychology, 11,* 607–622.

Hokanson, J. E., Sacco, W. P., Blumberg, S. R., & Landrum, G. C. (1980). Interpersonal behavior of depressive individuals in a mixed-motive game. *Journal of Abnormal Psychology, 89,* 320–332.

Holahan, C. J., & Moos, R. H. (1981). Social support and psychological distress: A longitudinal analysis. *Journal of Abnormal Psychology, 90,* 365–370.

Holcomb, W. R., & Kashani, J. H. (1991). Personality characteristics of a community sample of adolescents with conduct disorders. *Adolescence, 26*(103), 579–586.

Hooley, J. M. (1985). Expressed emotion: A review of the critical literature. *Clinical Psychology Review, 5,* 119–139.

Hooley, J. M., Orley, J., & Teasdale, J. D. (1986). Levels of expressed emotion and relapse in depressed patients. *British Journal of Psychiatry, 148,* 642–647.

Hooley, J. M., & Teasdale, J. D. (1989). Predictors of relapse in unipolar depressives: Expressed emotion, marital distress, and perceived criticism. *Journal of Abnormal Psychology, 98,* 229–235.

Hops, H., Biglan, A., Sherman, L., Arthur, J., Friedman, L. S., & Osteen, V. (1987). Home observations of family interactions of depressed women. *Journal of Consulting and Clinical Psychology, 55,* 341–346.

House, J. S. (1981). *Work stress and social support.* Reading, MA: Addison-Wesley.

House, J. S., & Kahn, R. L. (1985). Measures and concepts of social support. In S. Cohen & S. L. Syme (Eds.), *Social support and health* (pp. 83–108). New York: Academic Press.

House, J. S., & Wells, J. A. (1978). Occupational stress, social support and health. In A. McLean, G. Black, & M. Colligan (Eds.), *Reducing occupational stress: Proceedings of a conference* (HEW Publication No. 78-140, pp. 8–29). Washington, DC: U.S. Government Printing Office.

Howes, M. J., & Hokanson, J. E. (1979). Conversational and social responses to depressive interpersonal behavior. *Journal of Abnormal Psychology, 6,* 625–634.

Howes, M. J., Hokanson, J. E., & Lowenstein, D. A. (1985). The induction of depressive affect after prolonged exposure to a mildly depressed individual. *Journal of Abnormal Psychology, 49,* 1110–1113.

Hunter, F. T., & Youniss, J. (1982). Changes in function of three relations during adolescence. *Developmental Psychology, 18,* 806–811.

Husani, B. A., Neff, J. A., Newbrough, J. R., & Moore, M. C. (1982). The stress-buffering role of social support and personal confidence among the rural married. *Journal of Community Psychology, 10,* 409–426.

Joffe, R. D., Dobson, K. S., Fine, S., Marriage, K., & Haley, G. (1990). Social problem-solving in depressed, conduct-disorder, and normal adolescents. *Journal of Abnormal Child Psychology, 18,* 565–575.

Johnson, J. H. (1986). *Life events as stressors in childhood and adolescence.* Beverly Hills, CA: Sage.

Johnstone, J. W. C. (1978). Social class, social areas and delinquency. *Sociology and Social Research, 63,* 49–72.

Josselson, R. (1980). Ego development in adolescent. In J. Adelson (Ed.), *Handbook of adolescent psychology* (pp. 188–210). New York: Wiley.

Kahn, J., Coyne, J. C., & Margolin, G. (1985). Depression and marital disagreement: The social construction of despair. *Journal of Social and Personal Relationships, 2,* 447-461.

Kahn, R. L., & Antonucci, T. C. (1980). Convoys over the life course: Attachment, roles, and social support. In P. B. Baltes & O. G. Brim, Jr. (Eds.), *Life-span development and behavior* (Vol. 3, pp. 253–286). New York: Academic Press.

Kandel, D. B. (1980). Drug and drinking behavior among youth. *Annual Review of Sociology, 6,* 235–285.

Kandel, D. B., & Andrews, K. (1987). Process of adolescent socialization by parents and peers. *International Journal of the Addictions, 22,* 319–342.

Kaslow, N. J., Rehm, L. P., & Siegel, A. W. (1984). Social cognitive and cognitive correlates of depression in children. *Journal of Abnormal Child Psychology, 12,* 605–620.

Kavanagh, D. J. (1992). Recent developments in expressed emotion and schizophrenia. *British Journal of Psychiatry, 160,* 601–620.

Kegan, R. (1982). *The evolving self: Problem and process in human development.* Cambridge, MA: Harvard University Press.

Kessler, R. C., Kendler, K. S., Health, A., Neale, M. C., & Eaves, L. J. (1992). Social support, depressed mood, and adjustment to stress: A genetic epidemiologic investigation. *Journal of Personality and Social Psychology, 62*(2), 257–272.

Kessler, R. C., & McLeod, J. D. (1985). Social support and mental health in community samples. In S. Cohen & S. L. Syme (Eds.), *Social support and health* (pp. 219–240). New York: Academic Press.

Kessler, R. C., Price, R. H., & Wortman, C. B. (1985). Social factors in psychopathology: Stress, social support, and coping processes. *Annual Review of Psychology, 36,* 531–572.

King, D. A., & Heller, K. (1984). Depression and the response to others: A reevaluation. *Journal of Abnormal Psychology, 93,* 477–480.

Klerman, G. L., Weissman, M. M., Rounsaville, B. J., & Chevron, E. S. (1984). *Interpersonal psychotherapy of depression.* New York: Basic Books.

Kliewer, W., Lepore, S. J., Broquet, A., & Zuba, L. (1990). Developmental and gender differences in anonymous support-seeking: Analysis of data from a community help line for children. *American Journal of Community Psychology, 18,* 333–339.

Klinnert, M. D., Campos, J. J., Sorce, J. F., Emde, R. N., & Svejda, M. (1983). Emotions as behavior regulators: Social referencing in infancy. In R. Plutchik & H. Kellerman (Eds.), *Emotion: Theory, research and experience: Vol. 2. Emotions in early development* (pp. 57–86). Orlando, FL: Academic Press.

Kneisel, P. J. (1987, April). Social support preferences of female adolescents in the context of interpersonal stress. Poster presented at the biennial meeting of the Society for Research in Child Development, Baltimore.

Kopp, C. B. (1989). Regulation of distress and negative emotions: A developmental view. *Developmental Psychology, 25,* 343–354.

Krause, N., Liang, J., & Yatomi, N. (1989). Satisfaction with social support and depressive symptoms: A panel analysis. *Psychology and Aging, 4,* 88–97.

Krohn, M. D. (1986). The web of conformity: A network approach to the explanation of delinquent behavior. *Social Problems, 33,* S81–S93.

Ladd, G. W. (1985). Documenting the effects of social skill training with children: Process and outcome assessment. In B. H. Schneider, K. H. Rubin, & J. E. Ledingham (Eds.), *Children's peer relations: Issues in assessment and intervention* (pp. 243–269). New York: Springer-Verlag.

Larson, R., Csikszentmihalyi, M., & Graef, R. (1982). Time alone in daily experience: Loneliness or renewal? In L. A. Peplau & D. Perlman (Eds.), *Loneliness: A source book of current theory, research and therapy* (pp. 41–53). New York: Wiley.

Larson, R., Mannell, R., & Zuzanek, J. (1986). Daily well-being of older adults with friends and family. *Psychology and Aging, 1,* 117–126.

Larson, R., & Richards, M. H. (1991). Daily companionship in late childhood and early adolescence: Changing developmental contexts. *Child Development, 62,* 284–300.

Larson, R., Zuzanek, J., & Mannell, R. (1985). Being alone versus being with people: Disengagement in the daily experience of older adults. *Journal of Gerontology, 40,* 375–381.

Lazarus, R. S., & Folkman, S. (1984). *Stress, appraisal and coping.* New York: Springer.

Leaf, P. J., Weissman, M. M., Myers, J. K., Tischler, G. L., & Holzer, C. E. (1984). Social factors related to psychiatric disorder: Yale Epidemiologic Catchment Area Study. *Social Psychiatry, 19,* 53–61.

Leavy, R. L. (1983). Social support and psychological disorder: A review. *Journal of Community Psychology, 11,* 3–21.

Lefcourt, H. M., Martin, R. A., & Saleh, W. E. (1984). Locus of control and social support: Interactive moderators of stress. *Journal of Personality and Social Psychology, 47,* 378–389.

Leff, J. P., Kuipers, L., Berkowitz, R., Eberlein-Fries, R., & Sturgeon, D. (1982). A controlled trial of intervention in the families of schizophrenic patients. *British Journal of Psychiatry, 141,* 121–134.

Leff, J. P., & Vaughn, C. E. (1985). *Expressed emotion in families.* New York: Guilford.

Leighton, A., Lambo, T., Hughs, D., Leighton, D., Murphy, J., & Macklin, D. (1963). *Psychiatric disorder among the Yoruba.* Ithaca, NY: Cornell University Press.

Lennon, M. C. (1989). The structural contexts of stress. *Journal of Health and Social Behavior, 30,* 241–256.

Leslie, L. A., & Grady, K. (1985). Changes in mothers' social networks and social support following divorce. *Journal of Marriage and the Family, 47,* 663–673.

Lewis, M., Feiring, C., McGuffog, C., & Jaskir, J. (1984). Predicting psychopathology in six-year-olds from early social relations. *Child Development, 55,* 123–137.

Lewinsohn, P. M. (1974). A behavioral approach to depression. In R. J. Friedman & M. M. Katz (Eds.), *The psychology of depression: Contemporary theory and research* (pp. 331–359). New York: Academic Press.

Lewinsohn, P. M., Mischel, W., Chaplin, W., & Barton, R. (1980). Social competence and depression: The role of illusory self-perceptions. *Journal of Abnormal Psychology, 89,* 203–212.

Lewinsohn, P. M., Steinmetz, J. L., Larson, D. W., & Franklin, J. (1981). Depression related cognitions: Antecedent or consequences? *Journal of Abnormal Psychology, 91,* 213–219.

Libet, J., & Lewinsohn, P. M. (1973). The concept of social skill with special reference to the behavior of depressed persons. *Journal of Consulting and Clinical Psychology, 40,* 304–312.

Lieberman, M. A. (1986). Social supports—The consequences of psychologizing: A commentary. *Journal of Consulting and Clinical Psychology, 54,* 461–465.

Lin, N., Dean, A., & Ensel, W. (1986). *Social support, life events, and depression.* Orlando, FL: Academic Press.

Lin, N., & Ensel, W. M. (1984). Depression mobility and its social etiology: The role of life events and social support. *Journal of Health and Social Behavior, 25,* 176–188.

Linn, J. G., & McGranahan, D. A. (1980). Personal disruptions, social integration, subjective well-being, and predisposition toward the use of counseling services. *American Journal of Community Psychology, 8,* 87–100.

Loeber, R., & Stouthamer-Loeber, M. (1986). Family factors as correlates and predictors of juvenile conduct problems and delinquency. In M. Tonry & N. Morris (Eds.), *Crime and justice* (Vol. 7, pp. 29–149). Chicago: University of Chicago Press.

Loeber, R., Wung, P., Keenan, K., Giroux, B., Stouthamer-Loeber, M., VanKammen, W. B., & Maughan, B. (1993). Developmental pathways in disruptive child behavior. *Development and Psychopathology, 5,* 103–133.

Lowney, J. (1984). The wall gang: A study of interpersonal process and deviance among twenty-three middle-class youths. *Adolescence, 19,* 527–538.

Lowenthal, M. F., & Robinson, B. (1976). Social networks and isolation. In R. H. Binstock & W. Shanas (Eds.), *Handbook of aging and the social sciences* (pp. 432–456). New York: Van Nostrand-Reinhold.

Maccoby, E. E., Johnson, J. P., & Church, R. M. (1958). Community integration and the social control of juvenile delinquency. *Journal of Social Issues, 14,* 38–51.

Macfarlane, J. W., Allen, L., & Honzik, M. P. (1954). *Developmental study of the behavior problems of normal children between twenty-one months and fourteen years.* Berkeley: University of California Press.

Mannarino, A. P. (1976). Friendship patterns and altruistic behavior in preadolescent males. *Developmental Psychology, 12,* 555–556.

Mannarino, A. P. (1979). The relationship between friendship and altruism in preadolescent girls. *Psychiatry, 42,* 280–284.

McCannell, K. (1988). Social networks and the transition to motherhood. In R. Milardo (Ed.), *Families and social networks* (pp. 83–106). Beverly Hills, CA: Sage.

McCauley, E., & Myers, K. (1992). Family interactions in mood-disordered youth. *Child and Adolescent Psychiatric Clinics of North America, 1,* 111–127.

McCord, J. (1990). Problem behaviors. In S. S. Feldman & G. R. Elliott (Eds.), *At the threshold: The developing adolescent.* Cambridge, MA: Harvard University Press.

McCord, J. (1993). Conduct disorder and antisocial behavior: Some thoughts about processes. *Development and Psychopathology, 5,* 321–329.

McCord, W., & McCord, J. (1959). *Origins of crime: A new evaluation of the Cambridge-Somerville study.* New York: Columbia University Press.

McCrae, R. R., & Costa, P. T. (1986). Personality, coping, and coping effectiveness in an adult sample. *Journal of Personality, 54,* 384–405.

McCreadie, R. G., & Robinson, A. D. T. (1987). The Nithsdale schizophrenia survey. VI. Relatives' expressed emotion: Prevalence, patterns, and clinical assessment. *British Journal of Psychiatry, 150,* 640–644.

McDonald, L. (1969). *Social class and delinquency.* Garden City, NY: Doubleday.

McGee, R., Feehan, M., Willimas, S., Partridge, F., Silva, P. A., & Kelly, J. (1990). DSM-III disorders in a large sample of adolescents. *Journal of the American Academy of Child and Adolescent Psychiatry, 29,* 611–619.

McGuire, K. D., & Weisz, J. R. (1982). Social cognition and behavior correlates of preadolescent chumship. *Child Development, 53,* 1478–1484.

McKinlay, J. E. (1973). Social networks, lay construction and help-seeking behavior. *Social Forces, 51,* 275–291.

Mead, G. H. (1934). *Mind, self and society.* Chicago: University of Chicago Press.

Meehl, P. E. (1962). Schizotaxia, schizotypy, schizophrenia. *American Psychologist, 17,* 827–838.

Meyer, A. (1957). *Psychobiology: A science of man.* Springfield, IL: Thomas.

Miklowitz, D. J., Goldstein, M. J., Nuechterlein, K. H., Snyder, K. S., & Mintz, J. (1988). Family factors and the course of bi-polar affective disorder. *Archives in General Psychiatry, 45,* 225–231.

Miller, P. M., & Ingham, J. G. (1979). Reflections on the life events to illness link with some preliminary findings. In I. G. Sarason & C. D. Spielberger (Eds.), *Stress and anxiety* (pp. 313–336). New York: Hemisphere.

Mintz, L. I., Nuechterlein, K. H., Goldstein, M. J., Mintz, J., & Snyder, K. S. (1989). The initial onset of schizophrenia and family expressed emotion: Some methodological considerations. *British Journal of Psychiatry, 154,* 212–217.

Mitchell, J. C. (1969). (Ed.), *Social networks in urban situations,* Manchester, England: University Press.

Mitchell, R. E., Billings, A. G., & Moos, R. H. (1982). Social support and well-being: Implications for prevention programs. *Journal of Primary Prevention, 3,* 77–98.

Mitchell, R. E., & Trickett, E. J. (1980). Task Force Report: Social networks as mediators of social support: An analysis of the effects and determinants of social networks. *Community Mental Health Journal, 16,* 27–44.

Monroe, S. M. (1982). Life events and disorder: Event-symptom associations and the course of disorder. *Journal of Abnormal Psychology, 91,* 14–24.

Monroe, S. M. (1983). Social support and disorder: Toward an untangling of cause and effect. *American Journal of Community Psychology, 11,* 81–97.

Monroe, S. M., Bromet, E. J., Connell, M. M., & Steiner, S. C. (1986). Life events, social support, and depressive symptoms: A one-year prospective study of initially nondepressed women in nonconflicted marriages. *Journal of Consulting and Clinical Psychology, 54,* 424–431.

Monroe, S. M., Imhoff, D. F., Wise, B. D., & Harris, J. E. (1983). Prediction of psychological symptoms under high-risk psychosocial circumstances: Life events, social support, and symptom specificity. *Journal of Abnormal Psychology, 92,* 338–350.

Monroe, S. M., & Steiner, S. C. (1986). Social support and psychopathology: Interrelations with preexisting disorder, stress, and personality. *Journal of Abnormal Psychology, 95*(1), 29–39.

Murphy, E. (1982). Social origins of depression in old age. *British Journal of Psychiatry, 141,* 135–142.

Murphy, H. B. M. (1977). Migration, culture and mental health. *Psychological Medicine, 7,* 677–684.

Nelson-LeGall, S. A. (1987). Necessary and unnecessary help-seeking in children. *Journal of Genetic Psychology, 148,* 53–62.

Nelson-LeGall, S. A., & Gumerman, R. A. (1984). Children's perceptions of helpers and helper motivation. *Journal of Applied Developmental Psychology, 5,* 1–12.

Newman, R. S. (1990). Children's help-seeking in the classroom: The role of motivational factors and attitudes. *Journal of Educational Psychology, 82,* 71–80.

Newman, R. S., & Goldin, L. (1990). Children's reluctance to seek help with schoolwork. *Journal of Educational Psychology, 82,* 92–100.

Northman, J. E. (1978). Developmental changes in preferences for help. *Journal of Clinical Child Psychology,* Summer, 129–132.

Nuechterlein, K. H., Dawson, M. E., Gitlin, M., Ventura, J., Goldstein, M. J., Snyder, K. S., Yee, C. M., & Mintz, J. (1992). Developmental processes in schizophrenic disorders: Longitudinal studies of vulnerability and stress. *Schizophrenia Bulletin, 18,* 387–424.

O'Donnell, L., & Steuve, A. (1983). Mothers as social agents: Structuring the community activities of school aged children. In H. Lopata & J. H. Pleck (Eds.), *Research in the interweave of social roles: Jobs and Families: Vol. 3. Families and Jobs.* Greenwich, CT: JAI Press.

O'Hara, M. W. (1986). Social support, life events, and depression during pregnancy and the puerperium. *Archives of General Psychiatry, 43,* 569–573.

O'Hara, M. W., Rehm, L. P., & Campbell, S. B. (1983). Postpartum depression: A role for social network and life stress variables. *Journal of Nervous and Mental Diseases, 171,* 333–341.

Olweus, D. (1980). Familial and temperamental determinants of aggressive behavior in adolescent boys: A causal analysis. *Developmental Psychology, 16,* 644–660.

Otto, L. B. (1976). Status integration and the status attainment process. *American Journal of Sociology, 81,* 1360–1383.

Owens, D. J., & Strauss, M. A. (1975). The social structure of violence in children and approval of violence as an adult. *Aggressive Behavior, 1,* 193–211.

Panak, W. F., & Garber, J. (1992). Role of aggression, rejection, and attributions in the prediction of depression in children. *Development and Psychopathology, 4,* 145–165.

Parke, R. D., & Anderson, E. (1987). Fathers and their at-risk infants: Conceptual and empirical analyses. In P. Berman & F. Pedersen (Eds.), *Men's transitions to parenthood: Longitudinal studies of early family experience* (pp. 197–215). Hillsdale, NJ: Erlbaum.

Parke, R. D., & Bhavnagri, N. P. (1989). Parents as managers of children's peer relationships. In D. Belle (Ed.), *Children's social networks and social support* (pp. 241–259). New York: Wiley.

Parkes, C. M., & Stevenson-Hinde, J. (1982). *The place of attachment in human behavior.* New York: Basic Books.

Patterson, G. R. (1976). The aggressive child: Victim and architect of a coercive system. In E. J. Mash, L. A. Hamerlynck, & L. C. Handy (Eds.), *Behavior modification and families: Vol. I. Theory and Research* (pp. 287–316). New York: Brunner/Mazel.

Patterson, G. R. (1982). *Coercive family process.* Eugene, OR: Castalia.

Patterson, G. R. (1986a). Performance models for antisocial boys. *American Psychologist, 41,* 432–444.

Patterson, G. R. (1986b). Maternal rejection: Determinants or product for deviant child behavior? In W. Hartup & Z. Rubin (Eds.), *Relationships and development* (pp. 73–94). Hillsdale, NJ: Erlbaum.

Patterson, G. R., DeBaryshe, B. D., & Ramsey, E. (1989). A developmental perspective on antisocial behavior. *American Psychologist, 44*(2), 329–335.

Patterson, G. R., Dishion, T. J., & Bank, L. (1984). Family interaction: A process model of deviancy training. In L. Eron (Ed.), *Aggressive Behavior [Special issue], 10,* 253–267.

Patterson, G. R., Littman, R. A., & Bricker, W. (1967). *Monographs of the Society for Research in Child Development, 32*(5, Serial No. 113).

Patterson, G. R., & Stouthamer-Loeber, M. (1984). The correlation of family management practices and delinquency. *Child Development, 55,* 1299–1307.

Pattison, E. M., & Pattison, M. L. (1981). Analysis of a schizophrenic psychosocial network. *Schizophrenia Bulletin, 7,* 135–143.

Paykel, E. S., Emms, E. M., Fletcher, J., & Rassaby, E. S. (1980). Life events and social support in puerperal depression. *British Journal of Psychiatry, 136,* 339–346.

Paykel, E. S., & Weissman, M. M. (1973). Social adjustment and depression: A longitudinal study. *Archives of General Psychiatry, 28,* 659–663.

Pelligrini, D., Kosisky, S., Nackman, D., Cytryn, L., McKnew, D. H., Gershon, E., Hamovit, J., & Cammuso, K. (1986). Personal and social resources in children of patients with bipolar affective disorder and children of normal control subjects. *American Journal of Psychiatry, 143,* 856–861.

Pearlin, L. I., Menaghan, E. G., Lieberman, M. A., & Mullan, J. T. (1981). The stress process. *Journal of Health and Social Behavior, 22,* 337–356.

Peplau, L. A., Bikson, T. K., Rook, K. S., & Goodchilds, J. D. (1982). Being old and living alone. In L. A. Peplau & D. Perlman (Eds.), *Loneliness: A sourcebook of current theory, research and therapy* (pp. 135–151). New York: Wiley.

Pettit, G. S., & Bates, J. E. (1989). Family interaction patterns and children's behavior problems from infancy to 4 years. *Developmental Psychology, 25,* 413–420.

Phifer, J. R., & Murrell, S. A. (1986). Etiologic factors in the onset of depressive symptoms in older adults. *Journal of Abnormal Psychology, 95,* 282–291.

Pilisuk, M., & Froland, C. (1979). Kinship, social networks, social support and health. *Social Science Medicine, 12,* 273–280.

Pyke, J., & Roberts, J. (1987). Social support and married agoraphobic women. *Canadian Journal of Psychiatry, 32,* 100–104.

Rauh, V. A., Achenbach, T. M., Nurcombe, B., Howell, C. T., & Teti, D. M. (1988). Minimizing the adverse effects of low birthweight: Four-year results of an early intervention program. *Child Development, 59,* 544–553.

Reid, M., Landesman, S., Treder, R., & Jaccard, J. (1989). My family and friends: Six- to twelve-year-old children's perceptions of social support. *Child Development, 60,* 896–910.

Reiss, A., & Rhodes, A. L. (1961). The distribution of juvenile delinquency in social class structure. *American Sociological Review, 26,* 720–732.

Renken, B., Egeland, B., Marvinney, D., Mangelsdorf, S., & Sroufe, L. A. (1989). Early childhood antecedents of aggression and passive-withdrawal in early elementary school. *Journal of Personality, 57,* 257–281.

Repetti, R. (1987). Individual and common components of the social environment at work and psychological well-being. *Journal of Personality and Social Psychology, 52,* 710–720.

Richman, N., Stevenson, J. E., & Graham, P. (1982). *Preschool to school: A behavioral study.* London: Academic Press.

Ricks, M. H. (1985). The social transmission of parental behavior: Attachment across generations. In I. Bretherton & E. Waters (Eds.), *Growing points of attachment theory and research* (pp. 211–227). *Monographs of the Society for Research in Child Development, 50* (1-2, Serial No. 209).

Riley, K. W. (1991). *Street gangs in the schools: A blueprint for intervention.* Bloomington, IN: Phi Delta Kappa Educational Foundation.

Rivenbark, W. H. (1971). Self-disclosure patterns among adolescents. *Psychological Reports, 28,* 35–42.

Robbins, B., Strack, S., & Coyne, J. C. (1979). Willingness to provide feedback to depressed persons. *Social Behavior and Personality, 7,* 199–203.

Robins, L. N. (1966). *Deviant children grown up.* Baltimore: Williams & Wilkens.

Robinson, N. S. (1991, April). *Evaluating the importance of type and source distinctions in assessing adolescents' perceptions of social support.* Poster presented at the meeting of the Society for Research in Child Development, Seattle.

Robinson, N. S. (in press). Evaluating the nature of perceived support and its relation to perceived self-worth in adolescents. *Journal of Research on Adolescence.*

Rogoff, B. (1990). *Apprenticeship in thinking: Cognitive development in social context.* New York: Oxford University Press.

Rogoff, B., Mistry, J., Radziszewska, B., & Germond, J. (1992). Infants' instrumental social interaction with adults. In S. Feinman (Ed.), *Social referencing and the social construction of reality in infancy* (pp. 323–348). New York: Plenum.

Rook, K. S. (1990). Social relationships as a source of companionship: Implications for older adults' psychological well-being. In B. R. Sarason, I. G. Sarason, & G. R. Pierce (Eds.), *Social support: An interactional view* (pp. 219–250). New York: Wiley.

Rosenberg, M. (1979). *Conceiving the self.* New York: Basic Books.

Rowlison, R. T., & Felner, R. D. (1988). Major life events, hassles, and adaptation in adolescence: Confounding in the conceptualization and measurement of life stress and adjustment revisited. *Journal of Personality and Social Psychology, 55,* 432–444.

Roy, A. (1978). Risk factors and depression in Canadian women. *Journal of Affective Disorders, 3,* 69–70.

Rubin, L. (1985). *Just friends: The role of friendship in our lives.* New York: Harper & Row.

Rutter, M. (1971). Parent-child separation: Psychological effects on the children. *Journal of Child Psychology and Psychiatry, 12,* 233–260.

Rutter, M. (1986). The developmental psychopathology of depression: Issues and perspectives. In. M. Rutter, C. E. Izard & P. B. Read (Eds.), *Depression in young people: Developing and clinical perspectives* (pp. 3–30). New York: Guilford.

Rutter, M., & Garmezy, N. (1983). Developmental psychopathology. In E. M. Hetherington (Ed.), *Handbook of child psychology: Vol IV. Socialization, personality and social development* (pp. 775–911). New York: Wiley.

Rutter, M., Tizard, J., & Whitmore, K. (Eds.), (1970). *Education, health and behavior.* London: Longmans.

Rutter, M., Yule, B., Quinton, D., Rowlands, O., Yule, W., & Berger, M. (1975). Attainment and adjustment in two geographical areas: III. Some factors accounting for area differences. *British Journal of Psychiatry, 126,* 520–523.

Ryan, R. M., & Lynch, J. H. (1989). Emotional autonomy versus detachment: Revisiting the vicissitudes of adolescence and young adulthood. *Child Development, 60,* 340–356.

Sanders, M. R., Dadds, M. R., Johnston, B. M., & Cash, R. (1992). Childhood depression and conduct disorder: I. Behavioral, affective, and cognitive aspects of family problem-solving interactions. *Journal of Abnormal Psychology, 101,* 495–504.

Sandler, I. N. (1980). Social support resources, stress, and maladjustment of poor children. *American Journal of Community Psychology, 7,* 425–440.

Sandler, I. N., & Lakey, B. (1982). Locus of control as a stress moderator: The role of control perceptions and social support. *American Journal of Community Psychology, 10,* 65–80.

Sandler, I. N., Miller, P., Short, J., & Wolchik, S. A. (1989). Social support as a protective factor for children in stress. In D. Belle (Ed.), *Children's social support networks and social supports* (pp. 191–220). New York: Wiley.

Sansbury, L. L., & Wahler, R. G. (1992). Pathways to maladaptive parenting with mothers and their conduct disordered children. *Behavior Modification, 16,* 574–592.

Sarason, B. R., Pierce, G. R., & Sarason, I. G. (1990). Social support: The sense of acceptance and the role of relationships. In B. R. Sarason, I. G. Sarason, & G. R. Pierce (Eds.), *Social support: An interactional view* (pp. 97–128). New York: Wiley.

Sarason, B. R., Pierce, G. R., Shearin, E. N., Sarason, I. G., Waltz, J. A., & Poppe, L. (1991). Perceived social support and working models of self and actual others. *Journal of Personality and Social Psychology, 60,* 273–287.

Sarason, B. R., Sarason, I. G., Hacker, T. A., & Basham, R. B. (1985). Concomitant of social support: Social skills, physical attractiveness, and gender. *Journal of Personality and Social Psychology, 49,* 469–480.

Sarason, B. R., Sarason, I. G., & Pierce, G. R. (1990). *Social support: An interactional view.* New York: Wiley.

Sarason, B. R., Shearin, E. N., Pierce, G. R., & Sarason, I. G. (1987). Interrelations of social support measures: Theoretical and practical implications. *Journal of Personality and Social Psychology, 52,* 813–832.

Sarason, I. G., Sarason, B. R., & Shearin, E. N. (1986). Social support as an individual difference variable: Its stability, origins, and relational aspects. *Journal of Personality and Social Psychology, 50,* 845–855.

Saunders, E. B. (1977). *The nurturance scale.* Unpublished report, Stress and Families Project, Harvard University.

Schachar, R. J., & Wachsmuth, R. (1991). Family dysfunction and psychosocial adversity: Comparison of attention deficit disorder, conduct disorder, normal and clinical controls. *Canadian Journal of Behavioral Science, 23,* 332–348.

Schaefer, C., Coyne, J. C., & Lazaraus, R. S. (1981). The health-related functions of social support. *Journal of Behavioral Medicine, 4,* 381–406.

Selman, R. L. (1980). *The growth of interpersonal understanding.* New York: Academic Press.

Sharabany, R., Gershoni, R., & Hoffman, J. E. (1981). Girlfriend, boyfriend: Age and sex differences in intimate friendships. *Developmental Psychology, 1,* 800–808.

Shaver, P., Furman, W., & Buhrmester, D. (1985). Transition to college: Network changes, social skills, and loneliness. In S. Duck & D. Perlman (Eds.), *Understanding personal relationships: An interdisciplinary approach* (pp. 193–219). London: Sage.

Shepherd, M., Oppenheim, B., & Mitchell, S. (Eds.). (1971). *Childhood behavior and mental health.* London: University of London Press.

Short, J. F., & Strodtbeck, F. L. (1965). *Group process and gang delinquency.* Chicago: University of Chicago Press.

Skolnick, A. (1986). Early attachment and personal relationships across the life course. In P. B. Baltes, D. L. Featherman, & R. M. Lerner (Eds.), *Life-span development and behavior* (Vol. 7, pp. 173–206). Hillsdale, NJ: Erlbaum.

Slater, J., & Depue, R. A. (1981). The contributions of environmental events and social support to serious suicide attempts in primary depressive disorder. *Journal of Abnormal Psychology, 90,* 275–285.

Snyder, J. J. (1977). A reinforcement analysis of interaction in problem and non-problem families. *Journal of Abnormal Psychology, 86,* 528–535.

Snyder, J. J., & Brown, K. (1983). Oppositional behavior and noncompetence in preschool children: Environmental correlates and skill deficits. *Behavioral Assessment, 5,* 333–348.

Snyder, J. J., Dishion, T. J., & Patterson, G. R. (1986) Determinants and consequences of associating with deviant peers during preadolescence and adolescence. *Journal of Early Adolescence, 6,* 29–43.

Sokolosky, J., Cohen, C., Berger, D., & Geiger, J. (1978). Personal networks of ex-mental patients in a Manhattan SRO hotel. *Human Organization, 37,* 5–15.

Speck, R. V., & Rueveni, V. (1969). Network therapy—A developing concept. *Family Process, 8,* 182–191.

Sroufe, L. A. (1983). Infant caregiver attachment and patterns of adaptation in preschool: The roots of maladaptation and competence. In M. Perlmutter (Ed.), *Minnesota Symposium on Child Psychology* (Vol. 16, pp. 41–81). Hillsdale, NJ: Erlbaum.

Sroufe, L. A. (1988). The role of infant-caregiver attachment in development. In J. Belsky & T. Nezworski (Eds.)., *Clinical implications of attachment* (pp. 18–38). Hillsdale, NJ: Erlbaum.

Sroufe, L. A., Egeland, B., & Kreutzer, T. (1990). The fate of early experience following developmental change: Longitudinal approaches to individual adaptation in childhood. *Child Development, 61,* 1363–1373.

Steinberg, L. (1987). Single parents, stepparents, and the susceptibility of adolescents to antisocial peer pressure. *Child Development, 58,* 269–275.

Steinberg, L., & Silverberg, S. B. (1986). The vicissitudes of autonomy in early adolescence. *Child Development, 57,* 841–851.

Stiffman, A. R., Chueh, H., & Earls, F. (1992). Predictive modeling of change in depressive disorder and counts of depressive symptoms in urban youths. *Journal of Research on Adolescence, 2,* 295–316.

Strachan, A. M. (1986). Family intervention for the rehabilitation of schizophrenia. *Schizophrenia Bulletin, 12,* 678–698.

Strack, S., & Coyne, J. C. (1983). Social confirmation of dysphoria: Shared and private reactions to depression. *Journal of Personality and Social Psychology, 44,* 806–814.

Strauss, J. S., Hafez, H., Lieberman, P., & Harding, C. M. (1985). The course of psychiatric disorder. III: Longitudinal principles. *American Journal of Psychiatry, 142,* 289–296.

Struening, E. L. (1975). Social area analysis as a method of evaluation. In E. L. Struening & M. L. Guttentag (Eds.), *Handbook of evaluation research* (Vol. 1, pp. 519–536). Beverly Hills, CA: Sage.

Sullivan, H. S. (1953). *The interpersonal theory of psychiatry.* New York: Norton.

Surtees, P., (1980). Social support, residual adversity and depressive outcome. *Social Psychiatry, 15,* 71–80.

Sutherland, E. H. (1939). *Principles of criminology* (3rd ed.). Philadelphia: Lippincott.

Szmukler, G. I., Eisler, I., Russell, G. F. M., & Dare, C. (1985). Anorexia nervosa, parental expressed emotion and dropping out of treatment. *British Journal of Psychiatry, 147,* 265–271.

Tarrier, N., Barrowclough, C., Vaughn, C., Bamrak, J. S., Porceddu, K., Watts, S., & Freeman, H. (1988). The community management of schizophrenia: A controlled trial of a behavioural intervention with families to reduce relapse. *British Journal of Psychiatry, 153,* 532–542.

Thoits, P. A. (1982). Conceptual, methodological, and theoretical problems in studying social support as a buffer against life stress. *Journal of Health and Social Behavior, 23,* 145–159.

Thoits, P. A. (1983). Multiple identities and psychological well-being: A reformulation and test of the social isolation hypothesis. *American Sociological Review, 48,* 174–187.

Thoits, P. A. (1985). Social support and psychological well-being: Theoretical possibilities. In I. G. Sarason & B. R. Sarason (Eds.), *Social support: Theory, research and applications* (pp. 51–72). Dordrecht, The Netherlands: Martinus Nijhoff.

Tietjen, A. M. (1989). The ecology of children's social support networks. In D. Belle (Ed.) *Children's social networks and social supports* (pp. 37–69). New York: Wiley.

Tinsely, B. J., & Parke, R. D. (1984). The contemporary impact of the extended family on the nuclear family: Grandparents as support and socialization agents. In M. Lewis (Ed.), *Beyond the dyad* (pp. 161–194). New York: Plenum.

Tolsdorf, C. C. (1976). Social networks, support, and coping: An exploratory study. *Family Process, 15,* 407–417.

Tomasello, M., & Farrar, M. J. (1986). Joint attention and early language. *Child Development, 57,* 1454–1463.

Tremblay, R. E., Larivee, S., & Gregoire, J. C. (1985). The association between early adolescent boys' cognitive development, father attitudes, and nonverbal behavior. *Journal of Early Adolescence, 5,* 45–58.

Troy, M., & Sroufe, L. A. (1987). Victimization among preschoolers: Role of attachment relationship history. *Journal of American Academy of Child and Adolescent Psychiatry, 26,* 166–172.

Tucker, M. B. (1982). Social support and coping: Applications for the study of female drug abuse. *Journal of Social Issues, 38,* 117–137.

Tyler, F. B., & Varma, M. (1988). Help-seeking and helping behavior in children as a function of psychosocial competence. *Journal of Applied Developmental Psychology, 9,* 219–231.

Urban, J., Carlson, E., Egeland, B., & Sroufe, L. A. (1991). Patterns of individual adaptation across childhood. *Development and Psychopathology, 3,* 445–460.

Vaux, A., Burda, P., & Stewart, D. (1986, April). Orientation toward utilization of support resources. *Journal of Community Psychology, 14,*(2), 159–170.

Vaughn, C. E., & Leff, J. (1976a). The influence of family and social factors on the course of psychiatric illness: A comparison of schizophrenic and depressed neurotic patients. *British Journal of Psychiatry, 129,* 125–137.

Vaughn, C. E., & Leff, J. (1976b). The measurement of expressed emotion in the families of psychiatric patients. *British Journal of Social and Clinical Psychology, 15,* 157–165.

Vaughn, C. E., Snyder, K. S., Jones, S., Freeman, W. B., & Falloon, I. R. H. (1984). Family factors in schizophrenic relapse: Replication in California of British research on expressed emotion. *Archives of General Psychiatry, 41,* 1169–1177.

Vega, W. A., Kolody, B., Valle, R., & Weir, J. (1991). Social networks, social support, and their relationship to depression among immigrant Mexican women. *Human Organization, 50,* 154–162.

Veroff, J., & Veroff, J. B. (1980). *Social incentives: A life-span developmental approach.* New York: Academic Press.

Vinokur, A., Schul, Y., & Caplan, R. D. (1987). Determinants of perceived social support: Interpersonal transactions, personal outlook, and transient affect states. *Journal of Personality and Social Psychology, 53,* 1137–1145.

Voorhis, P. V., Cullen, F. T., Mathers, R. A., & Garner, C. C. (1988). The impact of family structure and quality on delinquency: A comparative assessment of structural and functional factors. *Criminology, 26,* 235–248.

Wahler, R. G. (1980). The insular mother: Her problems in parent-child treatment. *Journal of Applied Behavior Analysis, 13,* 207–219.

Wahler, R. G., & Dumas, J. E. (1986). Maintenance factors in coercive mother-child interaction: The compliance and predictability hypotheses. *Journal of Applied Behavioral Analysis, 19,* 13–22.

Walden, T. A., & Ogan, T. A. (1988). The development of social referencing. *Child Development, 59,* 1230–1240.

Walker, K. N., Macbride, A., & Vachon, M. L. S. (1977). Social support networks and the crisis of bereavement. *Social Science Medicine, 11,* 35–41.

Warheit, G. (1979). Life events, coping, stress, and depressive symptomatology. *American Journal of Psychiatry, 136,* 502–507.

Weiss, R. S. (1974). The provisions of social relationships. In Z. Rubin (Ed.), *Doing unto others* (pp. 17–26). Englewood Cliffs, NJ: Prentice-Hall.

Weissman, M. M. (1987). Advances in psychiatric epidemiology: Rates and risks for depression. *American Journal of Public Health, 77,* 445–451.

Weissman, M. M., & Paykel, E. S. (1974). *The depressed woman.* Chicago: University of Chicago Press.

Wells, L. E., & Rankin, J. H. (1983). Self-concept as a mediating factor in delinquency. *Social Psychology Quarterly, 46,* 11–22.

Wells, L. E., & Rankin, J. H. (1988). Direct parental controls and delinquency. *Criminology, 26,* 263–284.

Wertheim, E. S. (1978). Developmental genesis of human vulnerability: Conceptual re-evaluation. In E. J. Anthony, C. Koupernik, & C. Chiland (Eds.), *The child in his family: Vol. 4. Vulnerable children* (pp. 17–36). New York: Wiley.

Wertlieb, D., Weigel, C., & Feldstein, M. (1987). Stress, social support, and behavior symptoms in middle childhood. *Journal of Clinical Child Psychology, 16,* 204–211.

West, D. J. (1982). *Delinquency: Its roots, careers and prospects.* London: Heinemann.

West, D. J., & Farrington, D. P. (1973). *Who becomes delinquent?* London: Heinemann.

Wheeler, L., Reis, H., & Nezlek, J. (1983). Loneliness, social interaction, and sex roles. *Journal of Personality and Social Psychology, 45,* 943–953.

Whitcher, S. J., & Fisher, J. D. (1979). Multi-dimensional reacton to therapeutic touch in a hospital setting. *Journal of Personality and Social Psychology, 36,* 87–96.

Wilson, H. (1974). Parenting in poverty. *British Journal of Social Work, 4,* 241–254.

Wilson, H. (1980). Parental supervision: A neglected aspect of delinquency. *British Journal of Criminology, 20,* 203–235.

Windle, M. (1992a). A longitudinal study of stress buffering for adolescent problem behaviors. *Developmental Psychology, 28,* 522–530.

Windle, M. (1992b). Temperament and social support in adolescence: Interrelations with depressive symptoms and delinquent behaviors. *Journal of Youth and Adolescence, 21*(1), 1–21.

Wolchik, S. A., Beals, J., & Sandler, I. N. (1989). Mapping children's support networks: Conceptual and methodological issues. In D. Belle (Ed.), *Children's social support networks and social supports* (pp. 191–220). New York: Wiley.

Wolchik, S. A., Ruehlman, L. S., Braver, S. L., & Sandler, I. N. (1985, August). *Social support of children of divorce: Direct and stress buffering effects.* Poster presented at the annual meeting of the American Psychological Association, Los Angeles.

Wolchik, S. A., Ruehlman, L. S., Braver, S. L., & Sandler, I. N. (1989). Social support of children of divorce: Direct and stress buffering effects. *American Journal of Community Psychology, 17,* 485–501.

Wolchik, S. A., Sandler, I. N., & Braver, S. L. (1987). Social support: Its assessment and relation to children's adjustment. In N. Eisenberg (Ed.), *Contemporary topics in developmental psychology* (pp. 319–349). New York: Wiley.

Wood, V., & Robertson, J. F. (1978). Friendship and kinship interaction: Differential effect on the morale of the elderly. *Journal of Marriage and the Family, 40,* 367–375.

Wortman, C. B., & Dunkel-Schetter, C. (1987). Conceptual and methodological issues in the study of social support. In A. Baum & J. E. Singer (Eds.), *Handbook of psychology and health: Vol. 5. Stress* (pp. 63–108). Hillsdale, NJ: Erlbaum.

Wortman, C. B., & Lehman, D. R. (1985). Reactions to victims of life crises: Support attempts that fail. In I. G. Sarason & B. R. Sarason (Eds.), *Social support: Theory, research, and applications* (pp. 463–489). Dordrecht, The Netherlands: Martinus Nijhoff.

Wright, H. F. (1967). *Recording and analyzing child behavior.* New York: Harper & Row.

Wright, J. C., Giammarino, M., & Parad, H. W. (1986). Social status in small groups: Individual-group similarity and the social "misfit." *Journal of Personality and Social Psychology, 50,* 523–536.

Yoshikawa, H. (1994). Prevention as cumulative protection: Effects of early family support and education on chronic delinquency and its risks. *Psychological Bulletin, 115,* 28–54.

Youngren, M. A., & Lewinsohn, P. M. (1980). The functional relationship between depression and interpersonal behavior. *Journal of Abnormal Psychology, 89,* 333–341.

Youniss, J., & Volpe, J. (1978). A relationship analysis of children's friendship. In W. Damon (Ed.), *Social cognition* (New Directions for Child Development, No. 1) (pp. 1–22). San Francisco: Jossey-Bass.

Zahn-Waxler, C., Radke-Yarrow, M., Wagner, E., & Chapman, M. (1992). Development of concern for others. *Developmental Psychology, 28,* 126–136.

Zubin, J., & Spring, B. (1977). Vulnerability: A new view of schizophrenia. *Journal of Abnormal Psychology, 86,* 103–126.

PART TWO

Disorders

CHAPTER 6

Tourette's Syndrome: A Genetically Predisposed and an Environmentally Specified Developmental Psychopathology

BRADLEY S. PETERSON, JAMES F. LECKMAN, and DONALD J. COHEN

Tourette's syndrome (TS) is a familial disorder characterized by chronic motor and phonic tics that wax and wane in severity. TS is often accompanied by an array of behavioral, emotional, and cognitive problems, including some forms of obsessive-compulsive and attention deficit disorders. (Cohen, Friedhoff, Leckman, & Chase, 1992; Cohen & Leckman, 1994). From the time of its recognition in the 1880s by the young Charcot-trained neurologist, Georges Gilles de la Tourette, this syndrome has been important to neurologists, psychiatrists, and psychologists interested in exploring the vague boundaries between voluntary and involuntary behaviors, and to investigators studying the neural substrate of complex, perplexing mentations and behaviors.

The syndrome initially was studied toward the end of the nineteenth century, in the context of the hysterias and choreas. In the 1940s, it was approached from the perspective of psychoanalytic theories of character, obsessive compulsive neurosis, and narcissism (Mahler, Luke, & Daltroff, 1945). When the efficacy of haloperidol in reducing tics was discovered in the 1960s, TS became an exemplary disorder of neurochemical regulation (Shapiro, Shapiro, Young, & Feinberg, 1988a). Recently, attention has turned to defining the disorder's underlying genetic vulnerability and its range of phenotypic expression (Pauls & Leckman, 1986; Pauls, Leckman, & Cohen, 1993; Pauls, Towbin, Leckman, Zahner, & Cohen, 1986). Current conceptualization of the pleiomorphic expression of TS phenotype increasingly emphasizes

This work was supported in part by grants MH49351, MH44843, and MH30929 from the National Institute of Mental Health, grants NS16648, HD03008, RR06022, and RR00125 from the National Institutes of Health, the Tourette Syndrome Association, and the Gatepost Foundation.

The authors would like to acknowledge the vital contributions to this work from Drs. David L. Pauls, Robert A. King, Mark A. Riddle, Phillip B. Chappell, Paul J. Lombroso, and Ms. Sharon I. Ort and Mr. Lawrence Scahill.

Portions of this work appear in the following articles: Cohen, 1991; Cohen & Leckman, 1994; Leckman et al., 1992; Leckman & Peterson, 1993; Peterson, Riddle, Cohen, Katz, Smith, Hardin & Leckman, 1993; Peterson et al., 1994.

the pathophysiologic importance of a wide variety of complex environmental determinants. These environmental determinants act during critical periods of development on the particular genetic burden of an individual who has a unique set of adaptive capacities, all of which together specify changes in symptom profile and functional ability throughout maturation and development (Cohen, 1991; Leckman, Pauls, Peterson, Riddle, Anderson, & Cohen, 1992; Leckman & Peterson, 1993). This current conceptualization of TS will likely serve as a basic model of pathophysiology for many other childhood and adult neuropsychiatric illnesses, including schizophrenia, affective illness, infantile autism, and attention deficit disorder, because the central features of their pathophysiologies are all now thought to emphasize genetic vulnerabilities interacting with mostly undefined environmental determinants.

The emerging model of TS pathogenesis originated in clinical phenomenology, genetics, and developmental neuroscience (Cohen & Leckman, 1994; Leckman et al., 1992; Leckman & Peterson, 1993). Appreciation of these aspects of the disorder aids in the understanding not only of developmental psychopathology but also of normal human development; because the determinants of that development are uniform and ubiquitous, they can be more readily discerned when viewed in contrast to the perturbed developing central nervous system. The TS vulnerability gene, moreover, has a real possibility of being a gene that is expressed in the normal course of development of some individuals. Understanding the multiple determinants that can lead to its expression as disease will also aid in understanding the response of the central nervous system to constitutional and environmental stress, and ultimately the mechanisms that attempt to compensate for the presence of those stressors through the course of development.

PHENOMENOLOGY AND NATURAL HISTORY

Significance

As with other clinical syndromes, the understanding and treatment of TS begins with a thorough exploration of the phenomenology and natural history of the disorder. This knowledge is fundamental to informing effective treatment, and it provides a basis for patient education and counseling. This knowledge is also helpful in the development of diagnostic instruments and research protocols for clinical, genetic, and epidemiological studies, and for molecular and neuroimaging studies of the TS neurobiological substrate. Lastly, an appreciation of the full range of phenotypic expression of the disorder facilitates an appreciation of its continuities with normal childhood development, and of the ways in which development can go awry to produce functional disability.

Tic Symptoms

Phenomenology

Tics are sudden repetitive movements, gestures, or utterances that in isolation typically mimic some aspect of normal behavioral repertoire. Usually of brief duration, individual tics rarely last more than a second. Motor tics vary from simple abrupt movements such as eye blinking, head jerks, or shoulder shrugs, to more complex purposive-appearing behaviors such as facial expressions, or gestures of the face or hands. In extreme cases, motor tics can be obscene in character or self-injurious. Phonic or vocal tics range from simple throat clearing and guttural sounds, to fragments of speech that include isolated syllables, words, and even whole phrases. Tics tend to occur in bouts, with brief intertic intervals. Individual tics can either occur singly, or together in a seemingly orchestrated pattern.

Subjectively, the tics are initially experienced as "meaningless" events, as isolated movements or sounds that simply and rapidly pop out of the body or throat. A child may be unaware of the occurrence of his or her tics, although over months or years, most children do become conscious of them. Many adolescents and adults then experience the impending tic as an irresistible urge, need, or temptation that is impossible to suppress or deny. Being asked or told not to tic, blurt, or curse often only heightens the need to do so, which often induces a sense of shame and guilt, especially after innumerable capitulations to the urges, transgressions of social norms, and failures to conform to a self-ideal.

Just as they are exquisitely sensitive to their need to move prior to the tic act, TS patients also are remarkably sensitive to and easily captured by changes in their sensory world—both by the events of the external world and by the sensations within their own bodies (Cohen & Leckman, 1992). As first noted by Gilles de la Tourette, patients with the syndrome may unintentionally and unknowingly mirror the behavior (echopraxia) and speech (echolalia) of others and themselves (palilalia): they do and say what they have just seen or heard.

Continuity of Tic Phenomenology with Normal Behaviors

The brief, rapid, spontaneous, and nonpurposive motor and vocal tics are, in some ways, very similar to movements produced by the vast majority of normal people to varying degrees. These normal movements can occur in any body region but most frequently seem to occur in the face, shoulders, and distal extremities. They too are very rapid, brief, and nonpurposive movements that may or may not be preceded by a conscious "need" or "urge" to move, and that are thought by many to originate from muscular tension in the periphery (Keller & Heckhausen, 1990). These movements

and the urges preceding them are often only noted through active introspection and during conscious attempts to willfully inhibit them—the difficulty in totally inhibiting movement for prolonged periods can be appreciated readily if one simply attempts it.

A normal spontaneous motor act that is particularly difficult to inhibit is blinking. The urge to blink that ensues from blink inhibition may be very similar in quality to the urge to tic in TS patients; both tics and blinking can be inhibited voluntarily, though not for indefinite periods of time. Many normal individuals blink frequently, and benign tics often involve the orbital musculature (Nomoto & Machiyama, 1990). It may not be coincidence that the tics of TS also frequently involve this same musculature, and in fact often first appear there (Shapiro, Shapiro, Young, & Feinberg, 1988b). The frequency of eye blinking has been reported to correlate with the overall number and severity of tics in TS (Karson, Kaufmann, Shapiro, & Shapiro, 1985), suggesting that the modulator of central nervous system tonus in the normal motor act of eye blinking may also modulate the tonus of tic severity. The study of TS may benefit from study of these normal spontaneous movements, the understanding of which is remarkably limited.

Other behaviors in childhood that closely resemble those of TS are transient and chronic motor tics. These tics phenomenologically are very similar to, if not indistinguishable from, the tics of TS, and involve blinking, head jerking, shoulder shrugging, mouth twitching, throat clearing, sniffing, and vocalizations (Nomoto & Machiyama, 1990). The prevalence in the general population of these more benign tic syndromes is between 5% and 20% (Achenbach & Edelbrock, 1978; Lapouse & Monk, 1964; Nomoto & Machiyama, 1990; Rutter & Hemming, 1970; Rutter, Yule, Berger, Yule, Morton, & Bagley, 1974; Verhulst, Akkerhuis, & Althaus, 1985), and may represent one aspect of normal behavioral repertoire. Although the neural systems subserving these tics conceivably could confer some kind of behavioral advantage to the individuals in whom they are found, such an advantage has not yet been discerned. These tics, like those of TS, most commonly appear in early childhood, probably as a consequence of normal central nervous system maturational changes, and like the tics of TS, are also stress sensitive. Unlike the TS tics, however, transient tics by definition disappear within months of their occurrence, suggesting that additional central nervous system (CNS) maturational changes attenuate tics in normal children and may be absent or arrested in TS.

Assessing Tic Severity

Clinical rating instruments presently in widespread use focus on the number, frequency, intensity, and complexity of the tics, as well as on the degree to which they interfere with routine activities or speech (Leckman et al., 1989). Other instruments focus on how noticeable the tics are to others, whether they elicit comments or curiosity, and the extent to which they render the patient's appearance odd or bizarre (Shapiro et al., 1988b). Videotaped tic counts can also provide a valuable adjunct to clinical ratings in medication trials (Chappell, McSwiggan-Hardin et al., 1994; Leckman, Hardin et al., 1991; Shapiro et al., 1989) and challenge studies (Chappell et al., 1992; Lombroso, Mack, Scahill, King, & Leckman, 1991).

Comorbid Conditions

Tics in TS frequently are not the child's first (or only) trouble. In 40% to 50% of cases seen in clinic settings, the child who develops tics already has a history of being impulsive, overly active, and inattentive; often, frustration intolerance and troubles in the regulation of activity appear or else worsen with the onset of tics (Cohen et al., 1992; Comings, 1987). Mildly self-injurious behaviors such as lip and finger biting are not infrequently seen. Severe self-injury is uncommon but, when present, can be extremely disturbing to others in the environment and, very rarely, even potentially lethal to the patient. Many of these symptoms are often confluent with the tic symptoms, and together they can produce disastrous effects on peer and family relationships, and on the child's capacity for academic success (Dykens et al., 1990).

Approximately 60% of TS children who present to clinic have attentional problems of sufficient severity to satisfy criteria for attention deficit/hyperactivity disorder (ADHD). These attentional problems, in fact, can be a source of greater impairment than are the tics themselves. These children tend to be more severely affected and impaired by TS, which may simply represent the phenomenon of Berkson, in which children with one or more comorbid illnesses of any kind are more likely to present to clinic and have more severe disease than children with only one illness (Berkson, 1946). Family studies suggest that some Tourette's syndrome children have both TS and ADHD as independent disorders, whereas others manifest attentional problems that are phenomenologically similar to run-of-the-mill ADHD but which result from disturbances to attentional neural substrates that are intrinsic to the TS disease process (Comings & Comings, 1984; Pauls, Hurst et al., 1986; Pauls, Leckman, & Cohen, 1993). Some data indicate that the sharing of neurobiological substrates by both tic-generating and attentional networks may be responsible for the clinical observation that the presence of ADHD correlates with the presence of more severe tic disorder (Randolph, Hyde, Gold, Goldberg, & Weinberger, 1993).

About 50% of adult TS patients also have sudden, intrusive, repetitive thoughts or urges to action that formally meet criteria for obsessive-compulsive disorder (OCD). The urges to action associated with TS frequently have an aggressive or sexual quality (George, Trimble, Ring, Sallee, & Robertson, 1993), although a sizable proportion of patients have more classically defined OCD symptoms that include contamination and contagion obsessions, and checking and cleaning compulsions (Leckman, Walker, Goodman, Pauls, & Cohen, 1994). These and other TS patients often have obsessive-compulsive personality characteristics that demand extreme order and regularity in their lives, and they may need to collect, arrange, and rearrange their belongings. They often have an obsessional preoccupation with "evening up" the feelings of clothes, muscular tension, or actions on one side of their bodies, for instance, by invoking similar feelings on the other side of the body until the symmetry is "just right" (Leckman, Walker, & Cohen, 1993).

Often these obsessional concerns blur with and can become nearly indistinguishable from the conscious awareness of the "need" to tic, which has been termed a "premonitory urge." For many of the subjects, these premonitory urges are described as the "cause" of their tics (if they did not have the urge, they would not have the tic). For some, these urges are incessant and are experienced as being more troublesome than the tics themselves (Cohen & Leckman, 1992). The almost obsessive urge to act can manifest in more complex movements and compulsions. Patients may, for instance, have an urge to blurt out an obscenity, hit a loved one, or touch their own or someone else's genitals. Obsessions and compulsions thus blur not only with simple and complex tics, but also with voluntary and involuntary actions. It can be extraordinarily difficult for parents, friends, and teachers to know how best to respond to what appear to be provocative, "voluntary" behaviors such as these.

Continuity of Comorbid Symptoms with Normal Childhood Development

Both the motorically disinhibited, inattentive characteristics of ADHD and the obsessive-compulsive, anxious qualities of OCD that are commonly present in TS, are commonly seen in varying degrees at different stages of normal child development. Preschool children could be considered to be behaviorally disinhibited compared with older age norms. Normal age-related behavioral "disinhibition" in preschool children, for instance, includes relatively poor control of basic physiological activities such as nocturnal urinary continence and sleep arousal, relatively poor affective self-regulation seen in tantrum behaviors, and cognitive immaturity seen in their relatively short attention spans. Similarly, obsessive-compulsive and anxiety symptoms are common in normal children, especially in the early school years. The appearance of simple phobias, for example, is considered part of normal early childhood development that subsides spontaneously without treatment. Varying degrees of somatic preoccupation and anxiety about the maintenance of bodily integrity are ubiquitous in oedipal-aged children. These preoccupations and anxieties tend to be transformed in the ensuing years into more rigid, rule-governed behaviors, more constricted and more highly regulated affective states, and more obsessional cognitive styles, all of which are thought to represent psychological defenses against sexual and aggressive concerns of the preceding years.

The normal unfolding of these motoric, affective, and cognitive characteristics according to a universal developmental timetable must be determined in part by the maturation of many neuronal systems, including myelination of white matter tracts and commissures, axonal growth and synaptogenesis, the normal ontogeny of neurochemical and neurotransmitter receptor systems, and the environmentally determined differences in structural and functional expression of cytoarchitectural potentialities established in utero. The prominent behavioral disinhibition seen in TS, as well as the inattention, somatic concerns and anxieties, and obsessive-compulsive features that often erupt into frank disorder, all suggest that the phenomenology of TS and its common comorbid illnesses share broad features of the affective, cognitive, and behavioral manifestations of early childhood development that normally either subside, mature, or transfigure into forms and styles that are interpersonally, emotionally, and educationally more adaptive. The shared features of TS and normal early childhood development also suggest that certain key aspects of development may either be arrested or delayed in TS, and that although the complex interplay between normal psychological, social-emotional, and biological development are still poorly understood, evidence for delayed maturation should be sought in each of those domains. In fact, much of the literature on TS pathobiology to be reviewed here supports an interpretation of the presence in these children of a delay or arrest in the development of neuroregulatory centers important in sensorimotor functioning, cognition, and affective regulation that is commensurate with the apparent immaturities in the social-emotional functioning of these children, and with the residua of those immaturities in adulthood.

Epidemiology

Once thought to be a rare condition, the prevalence of TS is currently estimated to be between one and eight cases per thousand boys, and between 0.1 and 4 cases per thousand girls (Apter et al., 1993; Burd, Kerbeshian, Wikenheiser, & Fisher, 1986; Comings, Himes, & Comings, 1990). The reported population based sex-specific prevalence differences of TS (not including other potential variants such as OCD) have ranged from a 2:1 to 10:1 preponderance of males.

The differences in prevalence data reflect in part differing ascertainment of the sampled populations (e.g. treated cases vs. community samples), varying ages at diagnosis (children vs. adults), and differing diagnostic instruments. Differences in ascertainment of the study populations, for example, have included identification of referrals to mental health clinics (Comings et al., 1990; Debray-Ritzen & Dubois, 1980), self-reports or physician reports in community surveys (Burd et al., 1986; Caine et al., 1988), and examination of military service recruits (Apter et al., 1993). Ascertainment from mental health clinics has produced the highest prevalence estimates of 2.3–5 in 1,000, which is an order of magnitude larger than the estimates of 3–5 in 10,000 found in community survey ascertainment estimates. Studies of children tend to produce higher prevalence estimates (.29–5 in 1,000) than do studies of adolescents and adults (0.5–4.3 in 10,000), probably due to the average postpubertal diminution of tic severity. Studies that rely solely on surveys for the diagnosis of cases probably underestimate TS prevalence due to an underreporting of symptoms of the disorder, whereas studies that rely only on direct examination probably overestimate rates of comorbid illnesses, since the human resources required to perform the diagnoses tend to make necessary the examination of clinically ascertained subjects, with individuals having more severe illness and more frequent comorbidities being more likely to present to the clinic for treatment.

It is important to recognize that TS prevalence estimates will depend critically both on the age distribution of the population being sampled, and on how sensitive and specific the diagnostic instruments are in detecting mild variants of the disorder. Mild forms of familial TS are likely to occur in a sizable percentage of the pediatric population as a subset of chronic motor tic (CMT) disorder, for instance (Zahner, Clubb, Leckman, & Pauls, 1988), although probably not all forms of CMT or the commonly seen transient tics of childhood represent TS variants.

Given the high prevalence of childhood tic disorders (nearly 20% of the population), even small differences in the sensitivities and specificities of the epidemiological diagnostic instruments used in screening and diagnosing TS will have a potentially large impact on its reported prevalence when those differing instruments are applied to this large portion of the pediatric population. Because of the high prevalence of tic disorders in the population, diagnostic specificity (the percentage of true negatives detected by the instrument, reflecting also the false positives that it yields) is particularly important in prevalence estimates. Conservatively estimating, for instance, a prevalence of CMT in the general pediatric population of 10% (100 in 1,000) and a "true" TS prevalence of 1 in 1,000, a small difference in diagnostic specificity of 5% (decreasing from 99% to 94%, for example) in just the 100 children with other tic disorders (assuming perfect specificity in the other 900) will yield 5 more false positive cases and increase fivefold the population prevalence estimates for TS.

As a more specific example, in the methodologically most sophisticated epidemiological study of TS to date, a three-stage ascertainment procedure was used to diagnose affected 16- to 17-year-old Israeli army recruits, who constitute the vast majority of the male Israeli population in that age group (Apter et al., 1993). Stage 1 of ascertainment consisted of a screening self-report questionnaire assessing the lifetime occurrence of tics. Each subject was briefly questioned by trained interviewers and the self-report tic questionnaire was reviewed. Any subject responding positively to any of the queries about tics was then examined by a child psychiatrist in Stage 2 of ascertainment. If the psychiatrist believed the individual might meet diagnostic criteria, the subject was then entered into Stage 3, a structured diagnostic interview schedule for TS, which served as the "gold standard" by which to judge the sensitivity and specificity of the first two ascertainment stages. Although the sensitivity of the initial self-report screening questionnaire for detecting true cases of tics was high (91%), an estimate of the specificity for detecting tics was low, as a false positive rate of the screening questionnaire was 16%.

Because determining the true specificity of the entire ascertainment procedure (all three stages) in this kind of an epidemiological study is financially and logistically prohibitive, the overall specificity of this study is unknown. Even if the specificity were known, however, the gold standard structured interview may be less than golden, since the similarities in the presentation of TS and of the more benign tic disorders in this screen-positive population make their clinical distinction particularly difficult; thus the specificity of even the gold standard structured interview is suboptimal for detecting true TS cases, especially when applied to this population with a high prevalence of CMT and transient tics, the presence of which make the specificity of the diagnostic instrument—its ability to avoid false positive diagnoses—difficult but all the more important. Furthermore, sampling a population with a high percentage of children will increase proportionally the percentage of benign tic disorders that must be distinguished from TS and likely will increase the estimated population prevalence of TS, not because the disorder is in fact more common in that population, but simply because of inherent limitations in diagnostic specificity. This would explain the higher prevalence estimates found in epidemiological studies of children. Thus the apparent continuity of TS phenomenology with that of normal childhood development takes on added significance when researchers estimate population prevalence. These same considerations—the importance of the diagnostic specificity, the population composition, and the population prevalence of not only TS but of phenomenologically similar syndromes as well (their "prior probabilities" in Bayesian terms) (Feinstein, 1985)—are equally applicable to the "population" of extended family pedigrees in TS family-genetic studies, in which false positive diagnoses are highly detrimental to segregation and linkage analyses of familial transmission.

Natural History

Onset

As described by Gilles de la Tourette, and as seen in every published series, the modal age of onset of motor tics in TS is around age 7 years, although there are children who may have their first tics as early as one year of age or as late as the early 20s (Burd & Kerbeshian, 1987). Late-onset, nonfamilial illness warrants a more aggressive workup for other primary causes. Most commonly, TS has a gradual onset, with one or several transient episodes of "innocent" childhood tics being followed by more persistent motor and phonic tics of sufficient severity to move the child's symptoms into the range of clinical disorder.

The first tics seen are most often subtle motor tics of the face, most commonly eye tics, but nose twitching, facial grimacing, licking or biting of the lips, or vocalizations are also possible (Bruun, 1988). Subsequently, new tics usually follow a generally cephalocaudal progression, affecting other head and neck structures most commonly, then the upper extremities, and lastly and least frequently, the lower extremities. Rarely, TS may erupt with volcanic force, literally within a few days transforming a normal tic-free child into one tormented by dozens of tics every minute.

During the first years of a chronic tic disorder, there is an unfolding of symptoms: the original single tics may be joined by tics of the limbs and body; noises become sounds and then words and phrases; simple, rapid tics crescendo into complex, orchestrated movements that make use of one or many muscle groups; the full potential of the vocal apparatus and musculoskeletal system becomes recruited into often explosive bouts of discharge. Tic repertoires appear to be unique to any given individual. Fragments of actions and phonetic patterns surface in bursts of behavior that are assembled in chaotic bouts. The overall severity of tics usually waxes and wanes in poorly defined cycles lasting weeks or months, although at times a stimulus for exacerbation may be detected in major losses, upsets, or nonspecific stress.

Attentional disturbances typically manifest in this general period, whether or not those problems are associated with the TS vulnerability gene. If children are to have attentional disturbances, they usually appear by age 4, and in that instance they may precede the onset of tic symptoms. Obsessive-compulsive symptomatology, in contrast, typically follows tics in age of onset. Children with TS also are often motorically active and behaviorally impulsive, which in some children can be particularly volatile in combination with what appear to be inherently strong sexual and aggressive drives. The severity of the ensuing behavioral disturbances cannot be predicted by TS tic symptom severity, and often children with mild tic symptoms have very debilitating behavioral problems.

Early Intramorbid Course

By age 10 or 11, many children recognize and report the premonitory experiences that precede the tics and that are relieved by performing the tics (Bliss, 1980; Cohen & Leckman, 1992; Kurlan, Lichter, & Hewitt, 1989; Lang, 1991; Leckman, Walker, & Cohen, 1993). These sensory experiences, which may be intrinsic to the phenomenology of the tic, typically consist of a feeling of tightness, tension, or increased sensitivity located in a specific part of the body and accompanied by a mounting discomfort and anxiety. The sensory prodrome, which is likened to the expectation preceding a sneeze or an itch, is felt to require some type of vigorous, quick, ticlike action for its relief. Although the performance of a tic may lead to short-term relief, the child soon feels the mounting of renewed tension to which he or she will inevitably and perhaps shamefully capitulate. This cycle of tension—motor or phonic tic activity, amelioration of anxiety, and then a mounting crescendo of tension in varying loci of the body—may be repeated many times an hour and lead to paroxysms of physically exhausting tics. Sometimes the patient feels that an effective action must include a dangerous or aggressive quality as an essential constituent (and not merely a secondary effect) of the tic experience.

For perhaps 30% to 60% of patients with TS, obsessive thoughts and compulsive rituals emerge several years after the onset of motor tics, during late latency, or in the preadolescent or early adolescent years (Leckman, Walker, Goodman, Pauls, & Cohen, 1994). Compulsive behaviors often appear first and can be very difficult, if not impossible, to distinguish from complex motor tics. Initially, even classic dressing or washing rituals may be free of obsessional thoughts or other complex mental elaborations (Swedo, Rapoport, Leonard, Lenane, & Cheslow, 1989). If asked, many of these children will report that they do not know why they engage in these rituals; others will describe a need for things to look or feel "just right" (Leckman, Walker, & Cohen, 1993).

Obsessive-compulsive disorder, unassociated with tics, makes its appearance around this age (Swedo, Rapoport, Leonard, Lenane, & Cheslow, 1989). This is also when many normal children engage in collecting and ordering, or in using other obsessive-compulsive defenses, to help allay anxieties around newly aroused sexual and aggressive drives. For youngsters with tic syndromes, however, obsessive-compulsive processes may not be primarily defensive, or defensive at all, and they may become their most persistent and disabling impairment (Leonard, Goldberger, Rapoport, Cheslow, & Swedo, 1990).

Tics and behavioral disturbances are often the source of much ridicule for TS school children. They see themselves as physically less attractive than their peers (Carter, Pauls, Leckman, & Cohen, 1994), and indeed they usually are in reality less popular than their classmates, who along with their teachers see TS children as withdrawn and aggressive (Stokes, Bawden, Camfield, Backman, & Dooley, 1991). Aggressive impulsivity, often associated with ADHD, seems to be particularly detrimental to peer relations

(Stokes et al., 1991), and is also more likely to bring the child to clinical attention (Caine et al., 1988).

Postpubertal Intramorbid Course

For most children, adolescence may be marked by greater awareness and self-control, and by an abatement of tic symptom severities. Nearly 75% of older adolescents experience some degree of attenuation of tic symptom severity, although many of these patients still take medication for their tics. For some, adolescence may be disastrous, with an upsurge of aggression (self- and other-directed), impulsions, compulsions, obsessions, anxieties, and depression, and a concomitant, profound worsening of highly disturbing, complex tics. For most adolescents, however, some degree of continuing morbidity, either in tic symptoms, level of academic and social functioning, or quality of self-esteem and emotional well-being, seems to be the rule (Bruun, 1988).

The normal adolescent psychological processes of separation and individuation, the developmental need for privacy of experience and physical movement away from the family, may be distorted as the adolescent with TS at once both requires and resents the continued engagement of parents around the child's symptoms and their treatment. Any physical stigmata have powerful psychological repercussions in adolescence, when there is a heightened cathexis of the body and a preoccupation with its role in revealing and satisfying desire. Thus it is easy to imagine the ways in which the very visible, audible, and tangible somatic manifestations of TS—the coprolalia, copropraxia, sexual touching, aggression, and weird tics—can distort the reformation and crystallization of adolescent identity. Socialization frequently continues to suffer (Dykens et al., 1990), irrespective of the severity of tic symptoms (Stokes et al., 1991). Many continue to be seen as immature, withdrawn, and aggressive. Unfortunately, as their peers struggle with aggressive and libidinal urges of their own, TS children can become the real target of others' aggressive fantasies.

Adult Outcomes

Most TS follow-up studies agree that the overall outcome of tic severity has stabilized and can be gleaned by the early 20s (Bruun, 1988; Erenberg, Cruse, & Rothner, 1987). Patients only rarely experience symptom exacerbation in the third or fourth decades (Nee, Polinsky, & Ebert, 1982). The severity of illness during childhood and adolescence may have some predictive power for severity in adulthood. Adults who as children had mild illness generally will have mild illness as adults; roughly two-thirds of the children who have moderately severe illness will be rated mild as adults; and fewer than one in five who are severe in childhood will be rated as mild in adulthood (Bruun, 1988). Associated behavioral disorders such as ADHD, OCD, and disruptive behaviors appear to be controlled or substantially improved with treatment, in approximately half of TS clinic patients who present with them (Park, Como, Cui, & Kurlan, 1993).

Despite the relative improvement in tic symptoms during adulthood, preliminary data from a follow-up study (Erenberg et al., 1987) indicates that nearly 90% of patients report experiencing some degree of interference in daily functioning due to tic symptoms alone, and about one-third of patients feel that this interference is severe. More than half continue to require pharmacotherapy for tics in adulthood. Learning and behavioral problems continue to plague nearly the same proportion of adult patients, and frequently are more distressing than the actual tic symptoms. Nearly 40% report difficulties coping with the illness as adults, although only 5% report serious coping difficulties. On the other hand, more than half of former child patients report bright spirits and good functioning. These follow-up data must be interpreted with caution, however, in that the relatively poor response to the inquiries (60%) is likely to skew the outcome findings.

A follow-up telephone or in-person interview of adult TS patients provided similar findings (Goetz, Tanner, Stebbins, Leipzig, & Carr, 1992), in which nearly 25% of subjects had moderate to severe tic symptoms, compared with 60% at their time of worst prior illness, which occurred for most at the time of puberty. Only 4% had coprolalia at follow-up, compared with 22% previously. All subjects continued to have at least mild tics, in contrast to prior reports of complete remission from follow-up questionnaires. The severity of tics during childhood generally did not predict adult tic severity, although severe tics in late youth had some value for predicting severe tics in adulthood. Despite a high rate of school and behavioral problems in the past, 98% nevertheless graduated from high school, and 90% were either full-time students or fully employed at follow-up. These data also need to be interpreted with caution, as only 58 (62%) of the 93 identified eligible subjects participated in the interviews.

Few data are available on the social and emotional functioning of TS adults, irrespective of the outcome severity of tic and comorbid symptoms. It seems unlikely that having a stigmatizing and socially debilitating developmental disorder like TS in childhood could leave the adult without residual social or emotional difficulties. This, however, awaits further study.

Difficulties Predicting Outcome

Unfortunately, predicting with certainty the longitudinal course of TS for any given patient is still not possible. Some children with relatively milder tics may become chronic patients, whereas others with quite severe tics as children may later become outgoing, happily married, successful young adults. Despite the difficulty in predicting the long-term outcome for any individual child, generalities can still be made regarding the natural history of the disorder. Fortunately, for most patients, TS improves during late adolescence and early adulthood, and a relative decrement in the number of symptoms, reduced social impairment, and new ways of coping are the norm in this stage of development.

HEREDITY AND GENETIC VULNERABILITY

Gilles de la Tourette's original papers hypothesized an etiological role for hereditary factors. For the next century, genetics of the disorder tended to be ignored. A decade ago, clinical observations of multigenerational transmission of tics and associated problems led researchers to begin systematic studies on genetic and familial factors (Kidd, Prusoff, & Cohen, 1980), an enterprise which has now brought together collaborators from throughout the world. During the past several years, twin and family-genetic studies have clearly revealed TS to be familial and genetic.

Twin Studies

Twin studies indicate that genetic factors play an important role in the transmission and expression of TS and related phenotypes. Specifically, monozygotic (MZ) twin pairs have been found to be highly concordant (50%–90%) for TS and (77%–100%) for tic disorders (Hyde, Aaronson, Randolph, Rickler, & Weinberger, 1992; Price, Kidd, Cohen, Pauls, & Leckman, 1985; Walkup et al., 1988). Although fewer dizygotic (DZ) twin pairs have been studied, the concordance rates for TS (8%) and tic disorders (23%) are much lower. This MZ-DZ difference in concordance rates provides compelling evidence for the etiological importance of genetic factors in TS.

Family-Genetic Studies

Family-genetic studies of first-degree relatives have also provided valuable information concerning the pattern of vertical transmission within families. In the largest series to date, 86 TS probands and 338 biological relatives were studied, along with control subjects who included the unrelated relatives of adopted individuals with TS (Pauls, Raymond, Stevenson, & Leckman, 1990).

Mode of Genetic Transmission

These family-genetic data have shown that about 8% of the relatives of TS probands are likely to have the syndrome themselves (Pauls et al., 1990). Visual inspection of typical family pedigrees constructed with data obtained from structured psychiatric interviews of all family members suggests an autosomal, dominant mode of genetic transmission of the underlying vulnerability; this is supported by the exclusion of alternative mathematical models (recessive, polygenic, single locus with polygenic background) (Pauls & Leckman, 1986). Findings with large, multigenerational pedigrees are consistent with the studies of nuclear families in supporting an autosomal, single dominant locus model for the transmission of TS (Kurlan et al., 1986).

This putative dominant gene appears to have a high penetrance, up to 0.99, for males and a somewhat lower penetrance, perhaps about 0.7, for females. Within families, and thus, presumably, as an expression of the "same" genetic diathesis, there is a broad range of impairment or severity of tic disorder. In the majority of cases, TS is a mild condition of chronic motor tics or recurrent episodes of transient tics; most individuals who can formally be diagnosed, using standardized criteria and assessment methods, do not come to medical attention (Caine et al., 1988). Today, they are recognized through family studies and because of increased public and physician awareness. When diagnosed, such individuals are found to have little impairment associated with their tic disorder. For a minority of individuals, however, TS is as serious and impairing as any neuropsychiatric disorder known.

Genetic Linkage Studies

Molecular biological approaches to locating the TS vulnerability gene are well underway, with DNA available from carefully evaluated, multigenerational pedigrees. The genome is being probed using restriction fragment length polymorphisms (RFLPs) and newer methods to detect polymorphisms based on polymerase chain reaction techniques (Weber & May, 1989). Using the methods of genetic linkage, more than 90% of the genome has been excluded, and it likely will be only a matter of time before a vulnerability locus is detected (Pakstis et al., 1991). If and when this occurs, methods are available to move toward the precise localization, cloning, and characterization of the gene and its products.

Alternate Linkage Analytic Strategies

If, however, the entire genome is in fact excluded using the current model of autosomal dominant transmission, it will then be time to reexamine some of the underlying assumptions that have thus far guided the search. One assumption has been that TS is genetically homogeneous, and that the exclusion of a particular genetic locus within any of the large linkage families is sufficient to eliminate that site from consideration in any of the other families.

Another assumption has been that TS and chronic multiple tics are alternate expressions of the same underlying genetic vulnerability. Individuals diagnosed with either condition are therefore counted as "affected" in the linkage analyses. Although this assumption may well be correct in the majority of cases, it may not always be correct. "Phenocopies" (individuals with tics stemming from some other etiological mechanism) will then be introduced into the linkage analyses as true cases. These false positives can play havoc with the linkage results, so that more conservative and stringent diagnostic standards will need to be adopted (Cohen et al., 1992).

Finally, there is the assumption of a single autosomal locus. Although the family data are consistent with this model of transmission, there is no guarantee that this is the correct model, and other oligogenic models may need to be considered.

The Range of Phenotypic Variability in Genetic Expression

Among the most intriguing findings from the twin and family-genetic studies concern the etiological relationship between TS and the associated psychopathological conditions of CMT, OCD, and ADHD. When TS, CMT, and OCD are combined, the autosomal dominant pattern of transmission becomes clearer than when TS is considered as the only manifestation of the genetic diathesis. In addition, when variability in severity of expression of these disorders is assessed in the family and twin studies, it is apparent that symptom severities span a large range along what appears to be a continuous spectrum of severity. The inclusion of varying degrees and quality of phenotypic expression actually strengthens a Mendelian pattern of inheritance which suggests that the putative TS vulnerability gene may not be a disease gene per se; instead, TS as a disorder may represent an extreme form of expression of an otherwise normally expressed developmental gene.

Chronic Motor Tics

Family studies support the concept that one form of CMT may be an alternate manifestation of the TS gene. Stated another way, the phenotype for the genetic diathesis is broad. The diathesis may be expressed as anything on the continuum from chronic single or multiple motor tics, through the full-blown, persistent, multiple motor and phonic tics of Tourette's disorder (Price et al., 1985). The recurrence risk for chronic multiple tics in family studies is about 17%, in contrast to only 2% to 3% in relatives of normal controls (Pauls et al., 1990).

Obsessive-Compulsive Disorder

Recent genetic research (Leonard et al., 1992; Pauls & Leckman, 1986; Pauls, Towbin, Leckman, Zahner, & Cohen, 1986) has sustained the clinical impression that TS and OCD are intimately related disorders. They have been associated, in fact, in both directions: TS has been described as a variant form of OCD, and OCD has been conceptualized as a variant of TS. Currently, at least one form of OCD, with or without tics, seems to be a variant expression of the putative TS vulnerability gene (Pauls, Towbin, Leckman, Zahner, & Cohen, 1986). In family studies of TS probands, a marked elevation of OCD is found in first-degree relatives (23%), who may or may not also have tics. Female relatives of TS probands appear more likely to have OCD without tics than do male relatives. Approximately 30% of OCD patients seen in mental health clinics have a personal history of TS or tics, and another 10% to 15% of these patients have a family history of tic disorder. Recent family studies of OCD support this hypothesis that some, but not all, cases of OCD are genetically related to TS (Pauls et al., in press; van de Wetering & Heutink, 1993).

Clinical Import of Tourette's Syndrome and Obsessive-Compulsive Disorder Relatedness

As a direct consequence of the family studies demonstrating that some forms of OCD are a manifestation of the putative TS genetic diathesis, numerous phenomenological studies that explore and treatment studies that exploit the pathophysiological differences between tic- and non-tic-related OCD have arisen. One follow-up study of childhood-onset OCD, for instance, reported that nearly 60% of those patients who initially present without TS later display tics at follow-up, and that nearly 25% of those patients actually meet diagnostic criteria for TS; the OCD children who later manifest TS appear to have an earlier onset of obsessive-compulsive symptoms than those who do not develop TS (Leonard et al., 1992). A lifetime history of tics in these children predicted more severe OCD symptoms at follow-up (Leonard et al., 1993).

Adult patients who have both TS and OCD, when compared with OCD patients without TS, may have more aggressive, sexual, and symmetry-related obsessions, as well as more touching, blinking, counting, and self-damaging compulsions (George, Trimble, Ring, Sallee, & Robertson, 1993). The perceptually mediated "just right" urges experienced by these two groups of OCD patients appear to be identical (Leckman, Walker, Goodman, Pauls, & Cohen, 1994).

In addition to these phenomenological differences between tic- and non-tic-related OCD, preliminary biochemical data support the pathophysiological distinction between these two forms of OCD. Markedly elevated levels of the neurohormone and neurotransmitter oxytocin have been detected in the non-tic-related OCD group compared with tic-related OCD, TS, and normal control subjects (Leckman, Goodman et al., 1994a, 1994b). Oxytocin levels were found to correlate with OC symptom severity.

Lastly, the motor tics of TS are unresponsive to the specific serotonin reuptake inhibitor (SSRI) therapy that is typically helpful for OC symptoms (Riddle, Scahill et al., 1992). In contrast, however, adult OCD subjects who have a past history of tics and who are unresponsive to SSRIs experience significant improvement in their OC symptoms on the addition to their SSRI treatment of high-potency neuroleptics, the agents most commonly helpful in treating tic disorders (McDougle et al., 1994). These phenomenological and clinical treatment data provide further support for the hypothesis that some forms of OCD represent variant expressions of the TS vulnerability gene.

Attention Deficit/Hyperactivity Disorder

In contrast to the genetic connection that has been established between TS and OCD, the basis of the relation between TS and attentional and activity problems (ADHD) remains less certain. In studies of TS clinic patients, the majority have attentional and activity problems consistent with the diagnosis of ADHD (Cohen, Leckman, & Shaywitz, 1984; Cohen et al., 1979; Jagger et al., 1982). That many children have these difficulties before the onset of their tics has suggested that ADHD-like problems are prodromal to the eventual tic disorder (Comings & Comings, 1984, 1987). If so, the genetic diathesis, manifested as disturbances in regulatory and inhibitory processes, would have its emergence on average far earlier than the age of onset of the tics.

The first family-genetic studies, however, failed to support a tight association between TS and ADHD (Pauls, Hurst et al., 1986). The recurrence risk of ADHD was elevated only in the families of those probands who had ADHD (in contrast to the pattern with OCD, which had an elevated recurrence risk in families regardless of whether the proband had OCD). In addition, the risk of having both TS and ADHD in any of the families was no greater than that expected by chance. As ADHD is fairly common in childhood, affecting up to 6% or more of schoolchildren, it seemed possible that the co-occurrence of ADHD and TS in clinic populations was a reflection of a referral bias, with the sickest children (those with comorbid TS and disruptive disorders) being brought for care more often than children with TS alone.

More recent analyses of a larger cohort of TS patients, however, has further complicated the understanding of TS and ADHD comorbidity (Pauls, Leckman, & Cohen, 1993). In this series, the families of probands with both TS and ADHD again had a higher rate of ADHD than did the families in which the proband had only TS, replicating the group's earlier findings. In contrast to the earlier study, however, TS and ADHD were associated at a greater than chance expectancy within the families. Individuals with CMT did not show such an association, suggesting that the severity of tic symptoms may impact the cognitive processes needed for sustained attention, and that if CMT is also on the spectrum of tic continuity with TS, then ADHD becomes a manifestation of TS genetic vulnerability as the severity of tic symptoms increases. This interpretation is consistent with the findings that more severe tic symptoms are associated with more severe impairment in measures of inattention and impulsivity in monozygotic TS twin pairs (Randolph et al., 1993).

ADHD is most likely a heterogeneous assortment of conditions encompassing multiple genotypes and a broad spectrum of phenotypes. Thus, to explicate the precise relations between any forms of ADHD and TS may require more precise diagnostic methods and other advances in defining the clinical syndromes.

Other Comorbidities

In addition to CMT, OCD, and ADHD, some investigators have proposed that other behavioral disorders are part of an hypothesized spectrum expressing the putative TS vulnerability gene. Comings and Comings in particular have advanced the hypothesis that this putative gene produces in its carriers an enormous array of behavioral manifestations that includes anxiety disorders, alcoholism, eating disorders, bipolar disorder, and agoraphobia (Comings & Comings, 1984, 1987). The primary evidence marshaled in support of this hypothesis is the observation that the designation of an "any behavioral disorder" disease category in family studies produces highly significant differences between TS and control families in this "disease" frequency. Pedigree analyses of the inheritance in these families of the "any behavioral disorder" disease entity suggests its presence on both the maternal and paternal sides of the family. The inheritance is interpreted by these investigators as a semidominant, semirecessive mode of transmission, by which they mean that the more severe cases are homozygous for the "any behavioral disorder" gene (i.e., it is inherited from both sides of the family), whereas the less severe cases are heterozygous (inherited from only one side) (Comings & Comings, 1993).

Difficulties Inherent in Comorbidity Analyses

It has long been recognized that the high rate of comorbidity seen in TS clinic patients could result from an ascertainment bias of the type first described by Berkson (1946). Berkson proved through astoundingly concise and lucid mathematical arguments that in clinic populations, the rates of comorbid illness are much greater than the rates found in the general population. The increase in comorbidity rates of clinic populations can be attributed to selection pressures in the community that act through compounding probabilities that a given person with that illness will present to clinic for treatment. These probabilities individually are assumed to be independent, such that having any two diseases does not increase the likelihood of clinic presentation above what would be expected by chance. With this assumption of independent probabilities, the ratio of multiple diagnoses to single diagnoses in the clinic will always be greater than in the general population, such that two diagnoses will be nearly double, three diagnoses triple, and four quadruple the ratio seen in the community. These ratios will be even higher if the probabilities of clinic presentation are not independent, which is likely with neuropsychiatric disorders like TS that share a neurobiological substrate with other disorders like OCD and ADHD, and that are therefore likely to be more severe in the presence of these comorbidities. Thus, TS probands in family studies are more likely than community controls to have comorbid illnesses such as OCD and ADHD, or any other disorder that would independently have some likelihood of bringing the proband to clinical attention. Even when TS probands do not themselves have these comorbid illnesses, however, increased rates of these disorders, with or without tics, are still observed in their families compared with controls, which at first consideration seems to point to the variability of TS gene expression (Pauls, Leckman, & Cohen, 1993).

Nevertheless, an additional interpretation of Berkson's ascertainment bias that has not been addressed in family studies of neuropsychiatric disorder is the possibility that *families*, not just individual *probands*, are what present to clinics, so that the consideration of selection pressures for clinic presentation should be applied not only to the probands, but to the entire family as an individual entity as well. This would mean, for instance, that proband families with other neuropsychiatric illnesses, such as OCD, ADHD, and even the other behavioral disorders proposed by Comings and Comings (1984, 1987), are more likely to present for treatment than are proband families with less psychopathology. Just as ascertainment bias will increase when disorders share the same neurobiological substrate, increased ascertainment bias may also obtain if the comorbid conditions share the same "family substrate," so to speak, as could occur when the psychological functioning of family members are particularly conflictual and mutually provocative. This mutually noxious provocation will increase the likelihood of clinic presentation above what would be expected if each of the family members' illnesses contributed independently to the probability of bringing the family to clinical attention. A hypersexual and aggressive TS child, for example, may have a parent who has prominent obsessive-compulsive features, including moral and cognitive rigidity, behavioral inhibition, and other defensive reactions to his or her fears of sex and aggression; these psychological characteristics make the parent-child dyadic fit inherently strained and tenuous. Such families would be much more prone to clinic presentation than would families having only the child or the parent as one of its members.

This interpretation of Berkson's bias has considerable intuitive appeal, as it is a clinical truism in mental health centers that the families of clinic patients are often more severely disturbed than are community norms. This interpretation also could explain the finding of Comings and Comings (1993) that by considering their "any behavioral disorder" gene in pedigree analyses, TS and control group differences in the rate of multiple familial comorbidities increases beyond that when only TS is considered to be a manifestation of the gene. It also explains their finding that both sides of the family appear to be affected when this larger designation is considered.

The only way to overcome fully the formidable obstacles posed by this larger interpretation of ascertainment bias is to assess the rate of comorbidities in the families of TS subjects identified through large, population-based epidemiological surveys. No family studies of this kind have yet been performed. The large, elegant epidemiological study of TS in late adolescent Israeli defense recruits did not assess family psychopathology; nevertheless, the high rate of OCD in TS subjects (42%) compared with controls (3%), and the similar rates of ADHD in the two groups (8% and 4%, respectively), lend support to the contention that OCD is one manifestation of the TS vulnerability gene and speaks against the inclusion of ADHD in the TS disease spectrum (Apter et al., 1993). The strengthening of the autosomal dominant modeling of TS genetic inheritance when OCD is included in the analysis provides other indirect evidence for the genetic relatedness of TS and OCD that is not obviously vulnerable to the familywide interpretation of ascertainment bias (Pauls & Leckman, 1986). The only way in which family ascertainment bias could produce this finding is if genetically independent TS and OCD, when present together on one side of the family, could increase selection pressure for clinical presentation of the proband. Although not out of the realm of possibility, this seems unlikely. Thus, even though the variable expression of the putative TS gene is not conclusively demonstrated, the balance of evidence favors the inclusion of OCD as part of the TS spectrum of disorders. The inclusion of ADHD in that spectrum awaits more definitive further study. Insufficient evidence currently exists to include other behavioral disorders as a part of the phenotypic expression of the putative vulnerability gene.

ENVIRONMENTAL RISK FACTORS

In addition to providing evidence for the importance of genetic factors in TS, studies of monozygotic (MZ) twins also provide strong evidence that epigenetic and environmental determinants play an important role in the disorder. Environmental factors appear to be important in determining whether the putative gene is expressed as CMT, TS, OCD, or some combination of them, and whether the severity of symptoms of each clinical syndrome will be mild or severe. Although concordance rates for MZ twins are nearly 90% for the expression of the full Tourette syndrome (Walkup et al., 1988), the majority of these twin pairs have worst-ever and current tic symptom severity that differ substantially (Hyde et al., 1992). These differences in symptom severity cannot be due to genetic influences, since the monozygotic twin pairs are by definition genetically identical. Hence, the inciting events that determine symptom severity differences between these cotwins must be nongenetic in nature. These nongenetic determinants appear to include both pre- and postnatal experience.

Adverse Perinatal Events

Children with tics have been reported to have sustained significantly more complications in pregnancy than did a matched control group (Pasamanick & Kawi, 1956). Preliminary evidence suggests that prenatal events may be important nongenetic determinants of the full Tourette syndrome as well. Among monozygotic twin pairs who are concordant for the presence of TS, but who nevertheless are discordant for symptom severity, it has been reported that the more severely affected cotwin has the lower birth weight (Leckman, Price et al., 1987), a finding that has been

confirmed in a larger series (Hyde et al., 1992). Other studies in TS singletons have suggested that additional predictors of more severe illness in TS children could include the degree of maternal stress during pregnancy, and the severity of nausea and vomiting in the first trimester (Leckman et al., 1990). Pregnancy complication rates were also elevated in this TS cohort compared with population norms.

The neurobiological mechanisms mediating the effects of these prenatal events on symptom severity are unknown. Animal studies of fetal stress have shown that exposing pregnant mothers to a variety of stressors can induce an enduring heightened neurobiological responsivity to stress (Takahashi, Turner, & Kalin, 1992), and an altered neurochemical and neuroendocrine central nervous system milieu (Fride & Weinstock, 1988, 1989; Insel, Kinsley, Mann, & Bridges, 1990; Peters, 1982, 1990). Additionally, numerous obstetrical complications render the watershed territories of the brain, particularly the subcortical basal ganglia nuclei and periventricular parenchyma, vulnerable to hypoxic-ischemic injury (Vannucci, 1989).

Evidence for the importance of similar prenatal risk factors in the pathophysiology of other neuropsychiatric disorders includes reports of an increased rate of pregnancy and delivery complications in nonfamilial, highly comorbid ADHD (Sprich-Buckminster, Biederman, Milberger, Faraone, & Lehman, 1993), more frequent family discord, maternal stress, and obstetrical complications in the pregnancies giving birth to autistic children (Ward, 1990; Nelson, 1991), and prenatal exposure to influenza virus, maternal malnutrition, and obstetrical complications in genetically vulnerable children associated with the development of schizophrenia (Cannon et al., 1993; Marcus, Hans, Auerbach, & Auerbach, 1993; Mednick, Machohn, Huttunen, & Bonett, 1988; Sham et al., 1992; Susser & Lin, 1992; Takei et al., 1994). The similarities of these risk factors to those implicated thus far in TS pathophysiology raise the question of their specificity in producing any given neurodevelopmental disorder. At least in the case of ADHD, it appears that pregnancy and obstetrical complications predispose equally to ADHD and to general neuropsychiatric illness, and that the ADHD that they produce, being nonfamilial, may represent phenocopies of a putative ADHD gene (Sprich-Buckminster et al., 1993). Thus pre- and perinatal insults may either produce sporadic phenocopies of genetic disorders, or nonspecifically induce more severe symptomatology within genetically predisposed individuals.

Postnatal Factors

Other environmental risk factors may influence the intramorbid course of TS. The list of suspected factors includes psychosocial stress (being punished or severely criticized for having the tic symptoms, for example), exposure to CNS stimulants (Erenberg et al., 1987; Mesulam, 1986), and thermal stress in a few well-documented cases (Lombroso et al., 1991).

A potential postnatal environmental risk factor that may be important in illuminating elements of TS and OCD pathophysiologies is the presence in tic-related OCD of antineuronal antibodies (presumably directed against putamen and caudate tissue) that are nearly twice as frequent as in non-tic-related OCD, and which are likely to be found in either of these disorders more frequently than in psychiatric control children (Kiessling, Marcotte, & Culpepper, 1993a, 1993b). Children with movement disorders also were more likely than children without movement disorders to have at least one elevated antistreptococcal titer. Similar antibodies have been documented in the serum of patients with Sydenham's chorea, a late manifestation of rheumatic fever, which itself is thought to be a consequence of infection with the bacteria Group A beta-hemolytic streptococcus (Husby, Van de Rijn, Zabriskie, Abdin, & Williams, 1956; Taranta & Stollerman, 1956). Group A beta-hemolytic streptococcal infection, a common pharyngitis in children, may thus initiate an autoimmune disorder in which antibodies to the streptococci initiate a cross-reactive antibody response to antigens in the CNS, including those in the basal ganglia, producing movement disorders that include tics and chorea. Obsessive-compulsive symptoms may be a concomitant of this putative poststreptococcal syndrome, since these symptoms have been reported to occur more commonly in children who have Sydenham's chorea than they do in children who have rheumatic fever without Sydenham's (Swedo, Rapoport, Cheslow et al., 1989).

Interpretation of these data is complicated by the high rate of strongly positive antineuronal antibody titers in children without movement disorders (21%–37%) (Kiessling et al., 1993a, 1993b), and by the likelihood that the antineuronal antibodies are not specifically directed against basal ganglia tissue, but are instead more probably reactive with tissue from many brain regions nonspecifically. If the antibodies have a causal role in the development of tics or OCD, that role may be pathogenic only in the context of other prior constitutional vulnerabilities in children who develop the antibody titers.

NEUROBIOLOGICAL SUBSTRATE

The Mediator of Clinical Phenotype

Between the putative TS gene and its clinical expression there is, presumably, a cascade of pathophysiological processes in numerous brain regions that involves multiple, intertwined neuroanatomic, neurochemical, and neurodevelopmental processes (Young, Halperin, Leven, Shaywitz, & Cohen, 1988). In recent decades, a converging set of empirical data from the full range of clinical neuroscience disciplines has led to significant advances in the delineation of the neurobiological substrate of TS-related illnesses, and the formulation of hypotheses about the ways in which normal and pathological neurodevelopment may produce some of the most salient features of the syndrome. Those features include the varying ages of onset of tic, attention-deficit, and obsessive-compulsive symptoms, as well as other characteristics of the disorder's developmental progression, and its range and location of symptoms—the simple and complex movements (tics and compulsions), sensory premonitions, impaired cognitions (obsessions and inattention), and disinhibited behavioral

disturbances—all of which are modulated by a heightened responsivity to anxiety and arousal.

Neurobiological investigations in TS support the hypothesis that some kind of a combined inherent TS genetic vulnerability and perinatal insult produces a symptom diathesis that is unmasked and in part phenotypically specified by normal central nervous system maturational and developmental events. These events, in the absence of the symptom diathesis, would otherwise produce behavioral, affective, and cognitive manifestations falling within the range of normal biological variability. Neuropathological, neuroradiological, and neurosurgical data are consistent in implicating developmental disturbances of the basal ganglia, and of related thalamic and cortical structures, as determinants of TS pathobiology and natural history (Leckman, Knorr, Rasmusson, & Cohen, 1991).

Histopathology

Despite the description of the syndrome more than a century ago, structural neuropathological studies are exceedingly rare. Only three TS histopathological case reports exist, and in only two of the studies were detailed cell counts and morphological analyses performed. The validity of the negative findings of one of those two studies has been questioned because the patient's presentation was atypical. Findings in the other case revealed small striatal volumes, as well as a reduced neuropil and an increased number of small neurons per unit volume (i.e., an increased neuronal packing density) throughout the putamen. The author likened the basal ganglia appearance to that seen in control basal ganglia specimens taken from young infants, prompting his speculation that the growth of the basal ganglia in TS is either delayed or arrested (Balthazar, 1957; Richardson, 1982).

This histopathological report of a single patient must be considered preliminary, and it will need to be replicated using more modern neurohistochemical staining methodologies and cell counting techniques. The difficulties in obtaining postmortem tissue samples, however, and the problems inherent in their interpretability, make it likely that postmortem morphological, functional, and receptor binding studies will be supplanted at least in part by in vivo neuroimaging methodologies.

Neuroanatomy

Basal Ganglia

Stimulants applied directly to basal ganglia nuclei often produce ticlike stereotypies in animals (Kelley, Lang, & Gauthier, 1988), and either chemical or electrical stimulation of afferent inputs to the putamen in both primates and humans can produce motor and phonic stereotypies similar to tics seen in TS subjects (Baldwin, Frost, & Wood, 1954; McLean & Delgado, 1953). Lesions in regions anatomically and functionally related to the basal ganglia, such as the thalamus, cingulum, and prefrontal cortex, attenuate some tic and TS-related OC symptoms in humans (Leckman, de Lotbinière et al., 1993). Chemical interference with nigrostriatal afferents is the mechanism whereby neuroleptic medications are believed to produce Parkinsonian side effects, and through which they are thought to attenuate TS symptoms.

Corticostriatothalamocortical (CSTC) Circuitry

The basal ganglia are part of an intricate, somatotopically organized circuit running from the cortex to the basal ganglia, and then to the thalamus before returning to the cortex (Alexander, Crutcher, DeLong, 1990; Goldman-Rakic & Selemon, 1990). Evidence for the involvement of the basal ganglia and the related corticostriatothalamocortical (CSTC) circuit in TS pathophysiology comes from neurosurgical case reports which document the effects of stimulating or lesioning the various brain nuclei or fiber tracts compromising the CSTC circuit (Leckman, de Lotbinière et al., 1993). Most of this work emphasizes the importance of thalamic nuclei (intralaminar, ventrolateral, and dorsal medial), as well as thalamic efferent projections to the cortex and afferents from the cerebellum.

Central Nervous System Sexual Dimorphisms

Central nervous system sexual dimorphisms are by definition brain regions that differ between the sexes in either anatomic structure or neurophysiological function. These regions are believed to be responsible for much of the broad range of behavioral, affective, and cognitive differences between the sexes. Numerous brain regions in humans have been reported to be sexually dimorphic: they include the preoptic and medial preoptic areas, as well as the suprachiasmatic and arcuate nuclei in the brain stem; and the forebrain anterior commissure, corpus callosum, thalamic massa intermedia, medial amygdala, and bed nucleus of the stria terminalis in the forebrain. Several of these regions contain newly characterized neurotransmitters such as arginine vasopressin that are important in learning, attachment, and sexual and aggressive behaviors (see Peterson, Leckman, Scahill et al., 1993 for a review).

The sexual dimorphism of these brain structures seems to be established in utero by steroid hormone surges that occur during critical periods of CNS development. Changes in the magnitude and timing of these hormone surges in animals appear to alter the morphologies and neurochemical specifications of the dimorphic regions (DeVries, Best, & Sluiter, 1983; DeVries, Buijs, Van Leeuwen, Caffe, & Swaab, 1985; Simerly, Swanson, & Gorski, 1985), which are thought to induce in turn the dramatic changes in some of the behaviors evidenced by these animals (Ward, 1984; Ward & Weisz, 1984).

Although no direct evidence yet exists for the involvement of sexually dimorphic brain regions in TS pathophysiology, it seems likely that one or more of these brain regions compose at least part of the neurobiological substrate that mediates the sex-specific prevalence differences in phenotypic expression of TS genetic vulnerability, and that perhaps modulates the severity of TS symptom expression as well. Most of the known sexually dimorphic brain regions are thought to be regulators and neuromodulators of the basal ganglia, CSTC circuits, and frontal cortex, regions believed to be more centrally involved in the pathogenesis of either TS and its related disorders. Clinical evidence for the involvement of sex-specific neuronal or hormonal systems in affecting TS symptoms includes case reports of the use of anabolic steroids, androgens, antiandrogens, and antiestrogens in TS patients, as well as reports of tic exacerbation in women prior to and during their menses (Leckman & Scahill, 1990; Peterson, Leckman, Scahill et al., 1993; Peterson, Leckman, Scahill et al., 1994; Sandyk, 1988; Schwabe & Konkol, 1992). It is currently not possible to say conclusively what specific effect, if any, the many sex hormones have on TS symptoms.

Neurochemistry

Extensive immunohistochemical studies of the basal ganglia have demonstrated the presence of a wide spectrum of differently distributed classic neurotransmitters, neuromodulators, and neuropeptides (Graybiel, 1984, 1990). Mesencephalic monoaminergic (dopaminergic, noradrenergic, and serotonergic) projections that modulate the activity of the CSTC circuits have been implicated repeatedly in both TS and OCD. Group differences reported in measures of TS monoaminergic neurotransmitter and metabolite levels, however, cannot be assumed to be causal in the disorder. Group differences could just as easily represent cerebral compensatory mechanisms in response to more central deficits elsewhere, or even nonspecific epiphenomena of the disorder.

Dopaminergic Systems

Probably because of the long history of neuroleptic use in the treatment of TS, dopaminergic systems have been the neurotransmitter most frequently implicated in its pathophysiology. Dopaminergic neurons arise from the substantia nigra pars compacta and ascend to the basal ganglia. They also arise from the ventral tegmental area (VTA) and project to the ventral striatum, prefrontal cortex, and cingulum—all regions implicated in the genesis of the symptoms of TS or related disorders. The activities of dopaminergic systems are modulated by the sex steroids, which may explain some of the sex differences seen in the prevalence of numerous neurodevelopmental disorders, including TS (Hruska & Nowak, 1988; Morissette, Levesque, Belanger, & DePaolo, 1990).

In addition, the ontogeny of certain dopamine neurotransmitter and receptor systems is known to parallel average tic symptom severity reasonably closely through development (Riddle et al., 1986; Seeman et al., 1987; Shaywitz, Cohen, Leckman, Young, & Bowers, 1980). D_1 densities in the human striatum increase dramatically (more than threefold) in the school-age years when tic symptoms are at their worst, and then fall rapidly in early adolescence, when symptoms tend to subside. D_2 receptor densities, on the other hand, rise rapidly in the toddler years, falling abruptly to reach adult levels by the age of 5 years. Both receptor system densities gradually decline with age thereafter. D_1/D_2 receptor density ratios are thought to be important in normal behavioral control, and this ratio is greatest in the school-age years when tics are most prominent.

Dopamine receptor blocking agents like neuroleptics act on the projective fields of these dopaminergic systems, which is probably the basis for their therapeutic effect. Agents that deplete these neurons of dopamine, such as alpha-methyl-para-tyrosine and tetrabenazine, also can suppress tic symptoms (Jankovic, Glaze, & Frost, 1984; Sweet, Bruun, Shapiro, & Shapiro, 1976). Conversely, dopamine agonists, such as L dopa and stimulants, can with varying reliability exacerbate tic symptoms (Golden,

1974; Lowe, Cohen, Detlor, Kremenitzer, & Shaywitz, 1982). Finally, levels of the major dopamine metabolite in the brain, homovanillic acid (HVA), appear to be altered in TS (Butler, Koslow, Seifert, Caprioli, & Singer, 1979; Cohen et al., 1979; Leckman et al., 1988).

A postmortem analysis of the synaptic neurochemical specification of presynaptic dopamine uptake sites in three TS adults revealed a large increase in caudate and putamen carrier sites compared with controls (Singer, Hahn, & Moran, 1991), whereas levels of dopamine and its metabolites were not significantly different from control levels, consistent with other postmortem analyses (Anderson et al., 1992). If these findings of increased presynaptic dopamine uptake sites are replicated, it is unclear whether they would represent an increased number of dopaminergic neurons or an increase in the concentration of carrier sites in an otherwise normal number of neurons. They also may simply represent compensatory responses to chronic neuroleptic exposure in this set of patients.

Functional neuroimaging studies using novel radiolabeled ligands with specific affinity for this dopamine reuptake site are underway. Although in very preliminary reports positron emission tomography (PET) studies using such ligands have not indicated abnormal dopa metabolism or D_2 receptor numbers (Brooks, Turjanski, Sawle, Playford, & Lees, 1992; Singer et al., 1992), future studies will prove useful in the improved in vivo quantitation of these important neurotransmitter and receptor systems, including the newly characterized D_3, D_4, and D_5 receptor systems. They will also confirm or refute the preliminary dopamine uptake site postmortem findings. They will also be helpful in exploring the association of receptor levels with clinical ratings of symptom severity in living subjects.

Noradrenergic Systems

The primary impetus for implicating noradrenergic neurotransmitter systems in the pathogenesis of TS is the now widespread use of the alpha-2 adrenergic receptor agonist clonidine in the treatment of TS (Leckman, Hardin et al., 1991). In addition, TS is an exquisitely stress-sensitive disorder, and adrenergic mechanisms are the most obvious candidates for mediating symptom exacerbation in response to acute environmental stress. Although the adrenergic pathways that may be involved in the generation or modulation of tic symptoms are still unspecified, adrenergic projections from the locus ceruleus are widespread to virtually all cortical areas and to the basal ganglia, and adrenergic systems could thereby easily modulate any number of TS-related symptoms. CSF levels of 2-methoxy-4-hydroxyphenylethylene glycol (MHPG), the primary norepinephrine metabolite in brain, previously have not been found to differ between TS subjects and controls (Cohen et al., 1979; Leckman, Walkup, & Cohen, 1987), which tends to speak to more of a neuromodulatory than a primary etiologic role for noradrenergic systems in TS.

Compared with normal controls, TS adults may have a heightened reactivity of the hypothalamic-pituitary-adrenal axis and related noradrenergic sympathetic systems (Chappell, Riddle et al., 1994). In response to the stress of a lumbar puncture procedure, TS patients secreted significantly more ACTH into the systemic circulation than did controls. Consistent with the exaggerated stress response, TS patients had increased CSF (cerebrospinal fluid) corticotropin releasing factor hormone and elevated norepinephrine levels (Chappell et al., personal communication, April 1994). These subjects also excreted more urinary norepinephrine on the day preceding the procedure, the levels of which correlated with clinical ratings of tic severity. The latter finding tends to support the hypothesized neuromodulatory role for noradrenergic systems in the TS CNS, and is consistent with the use of clonidine in attenuating symptoms.

Serotonergic Systems

In contrast to the dopaminergic and noradrenergic systems, little clinical evidence exists to support the contention that serotonergic systems are important in TS pathophysiology. Instead, evidence for the importance of serotonin systems derives primarily from neurochemical studies. Preliminary postmortem analyses of four TS brains have demonstrated global reductions throughout the basal ganglia of serotonin, its primary metabolite, 5-hydroxy-indoleacetic acid (5-HIAA), and especially its precursor tryptophan, with normal indexes of presynaptic serotonin reuptake receptor densities and, presumably, serotonergic innervation (Anderson et al., 1992). The same group reported reduced serotonin and 5-HIAA levels, and increased 5-HT_{1A} receptor levels, measured in five cortical regions (Akbari, Anderson, Pollak, & Cohen, 1993). Similarly, lower levels of CSF 5-HIAA, plasma tryptophan, and whole blood serotonin have been reported in TS (Cohen et al., 1979; Comings, 1990; Leckman, Anderson, et al., 1984) and are consistent with the histopathological findings. The diffuse nature of the findings within the CNS is suggestive of either a more global CNS insult, or else a central defect or compensatory response in a diffusely projecting neuroregulatory system, which the serotonergic system from the dorsal raphe is known to be. The neuroanatomic pathways by which serotonin may impact tic and tic-related symptoms include afferents from the dorsal raphe nucleus to the striatum, the internal segment of the globus pallidus, and the substantia nigra pars reticulata (Parent, 1990).

Other Neurochemical Systems

Other studies have focused attention on the endogenous opioid projections from the striatum to the pallidum and substantia nigra (Chappell et al., 1992). Much of the recent work on endogenous opioid systems in TS was spurred by a postmortem report of markedly reduced levels of dynorphin A(1–17) polypeptide immunoreactivity in the striatum of a single patient (Haber, Kowall, Vonsattel, Bird, & Richardson, 1986). Dynorphin(1–8) may be increased in the CSF of TS patients, and its concentration in the CSF has correlated with obsessive-compulsive, but not tic, symptom severity (Leckman et al., 1988). Dynorphin and related opioid peptides produce a large array of motor and other behavioral effects, and seem to be involved in the regulation of motor function. Numerous exogenous opioid agonists and antagonists have been reported to produce variable changes in TS symptoms (Chappell, Leckman, Pauls, & Cohen, 1990).

The presence of cholinergic interneurons in the striatum, and the projection of cholinergic fibers from the nucleus basalis to much of the cortex, would suggest that these systems could be important in the modulation of tic symptoms, although the experimental data are conflicting. An increase in red blood cell choline levels in TS has been reported (Hanin, Merikangas, Merikangas, & Kopp, 1979). Cholinergic precursors such as lecithin and choline do not seem to affect tic symptom severity (Moldofsky & Sandor, 1983; Polinsky, Ebert, Caine, Ludlow, & Bassich, 1980). The cholinergic agonist physostigmine has been reported either to decrease (Stahl & Berger, 1981) or increase (Tanner, Goetz, & Klawans, 1982) symptoms, while the cholinergic antagonist scopolamine has been reported to attenuate motor tics while exacerbating phonic tics (Tanner et al., 1982).

In one neurochemical report of four TS patients (Singer, Hahn, Krowiak, Nelson, & Moran, 1990), reduced mean concentrations of adenosine 3',5'-monophosphate (cyclic AMP) were found in four cortical regions, whereas all other neurochemical analyses were within normal range. It is unclear whether the findings, if replicated, would represent a central etiologic deficit in the syndrome, or whether reduced cAMP levels reflect alterations in neuroanatomic or neurochemical systems that could in turn alter cortical metabolic activity and lower cAMP. In four patients, an impressive reduction in the neurotransmitter glutamate was noted within the globus pallidus and the substantia nigra pars reticulata (Anderson et al., 1992).

More recently, novel neurotransmitters like arginine vasopressin (AVP) and oxytocin, which are found in sexually dimorphic brain regions, have gained some prominence in postulated disease mechanisms of TS-related disorders. The intuitive appeal of these transmitters resides in their potential for mediating both the sex-specific differences in TS prevalence and the variability in its clinical phenotype that presumably expresses the putative vulnerability gene (Peterson, Leckman, Scahill et al., 1993). These neurotransmitters are potent modulators of dopaminergic activity in the ventral striatum, frontal cortex, and limbic forebrain (DeVries et al., 1985; Doris, 1984).

Although no direct evidence yet implicates them in TS pathophysiology, abnormalities in the vasopressin and oxytocin neurotransmitter systems have been implicated in the pathobiology of OCD. Elevated AVP levels have been reported in the CSF of adult OCD patients (Altemus et al., 1992), and CSF AVP levels have been reported to correlate negatively with childhood OCD symptom severity (Swedo, Leonard et al., 1992). In a large CSF study, markedly elevated CSF oxytocin levels have been reported in non-tic-related OCD, providing further evidence for the pathophysiological distinctness of tic-related and non-tic-related forms of OCD (Leckman et al., 1994b).

Preclinical data on the neuropharmacology of oxytocin suggest that this neurohormone and neurotransmitter could mediate at least some of the most prominent symptoms of OCD (Leckman et al., 1994a). In adult animals, for instance, oxytocin receptors are prominent in the ventral pallidum, dorsal subiculum, hypothalamus, the bed nucleus of the stria terminalis, and the central nucleus of the amygdala (Elands, Beetsma, Barberis, & de Kloet, 1988). Postmortem studies of adult human brains report similar receptor distributions (Loup, Tribollet, DuBois-Dauphin, Pizzolato, & Dreifuss, 1991), and numerous of these regions have been implicated in the pathophysiology of both OCD and TS. The behavioral effects of centrally administered oxytocin include variable effects on memory, as well as on grooming and sexual behaviors, which in humans could manifest pathologically as obsessional concerns about contagion and sexuality, symptoms commonly seen in OCD (see Leckman et al., 1994a, for a review).

Neuroimaging Studies

Basal Ganglia Volume Reductions

Lenticular nucleus volume reductions were first reported in a magnetic resonance imaging study of 14 medication-free, neuroleptic-naive, adult TS patients and 14 individually matched normal controls (Peterson, Riddle, Cohen, Katz, Smith, Hardin, & Leckman, 1993). The volume reductions, 10.7% on the left and 3.8% on the right, attained statistical significance only on the left side, and volume reductions in both the globus pallidus and putamen nuclei (which together compose the lenticular nucleus) seemed to contribute equally to the group differences.

From this report alone, it is impossible to exclude the possibility that the basal ganglia volume differences are the consequence of plastic changes in the adult TS CNS in response to having had a chronic neuropsychiatric disorder since early childhood. The predominantly left-sided reduction, however, has been confirmed in children with TS, which speaks against the likelihood that the differences are plastic changes caused by chronic illness (Singer et al., 1993). The confirmation also places the determination of morphological changes in an earlier period of development, at least into early childhood, and perhaps even before, into fetal or perinatal life.

Loss of Basal Ganglia Volume Asymmetries

Normal right-handed subjects are known to have volumetrically asymmetrical basal ganglia, in which left-sided structures predominate (Kooistra & Heilman, 1988; Peterson, Riddle, Cohen, Katz, Smith, & Leckman, 1993; Singer et al., 1993). In contrast to their matched controls, the TS group's mean basal ganglia volumes on the left were not significantly different from those on the right. This apparent loss of (or failure to develop) normal left-right asymmetry in TS subjects was borne out in a group comparison of basal ganglia asymmetries with normal controls: TS subjects had reduced or reversed asymmetries in their globus pallidi, lenticular nuclei, and total basal ganglia volumes.

Another group reported MRI basal ganglia volumetric findings in 37 TS children, half of whom also had ADHD (Singer et al., 1993). In the entire TS group, an absence of the normal asymmetry was seen in the putamen and in the lenticular nuclei. Subgroup analyses demonstrated, in the males-only TS cohort, trends to smaller left lenticular, putamen, and globus pallidus nuclei compared with normals. The TS subjects with comorbid ADHD had smaller left globus pallidi than either the TS subjects without ADHD or controls.

The basal ganglia structural alterations in TS may simply represent activity-mediated plastic changes due to differing degrees of lateralized motor dominance, although this seems improbable, as controlling for motor dominance did not alter the asymmetry findings. The basal ganglia changes then would seem more likely to reflect either a pathological process centrally involving those structures, a pathological process more directly involving structures anatomically and functionally related to the basal ganglia, or else an epiphenomenon from pathology in remote brain regions that could affect basal ganglia structure without causing basal ganglia dysfunction. Numerous cortical regions displaying structural and functional asymmetry, for instance, are known to project somatotopically to specific subregions of the basal ganglia nuclei (Alexander, DeLong, & Strick, 1986), and trophic effects from these regions conceivably could be responsible for normal basal ganglia asymmetries. Dysfunction and aberrant lateralization in TS cortical regions could conceivably then lead to aberrant basal ganglia lateralization.

The apparent contribution of both globus pallidus and putamen to the differences in lenticular nucleus volume reduction and asymmetry would tentatively suggest that the inciting pathophysiological event, however proximal or distal to the basal ganglia it may be, affects the normal lateralization of both structures. Despite their physical and functional relatedness postnatally, during fetal life the putamen and globus pallidus derive at different times from different regions of the developing cerebrum. The *anlage* of the globus pallidus is first evident at week 7 of human gestation in the diencephalon, while that of the putamen and caudate are visible at week 8 in the lateral ventricular eminence, which itself appears at week 7 (Müller & O'Rahilly, 1990a, 1990b). It is reasonable to hypothesize that the inciting event occurs sometime after both globus pallidus and putamen have made their appearance. Many CNS asymmetries appear to be established at about this same time under the effects of testosterone surges, which in the developing human fetus begins around gestational week 8 and peaks by week 20, corresponding with periods of rapid cell birth, migration, differentiation, and synaptogenesis throughout the cerebrum (Abramovich & Rowe, 1973; Forest, 1989). It is also possible, however, that an inciting event has occurred even before they appear, and has affected the determinants of later lateralization in precursor and progenitor cells in the embryonic cerebrum. Thus, placing a lower limit on the time window in which the inciting pathophysiological event in TS CNS lateralization occurs is not yet possible.

Corpus Callosum Morphologic Abnormalities

Peterson and colleagues (Peterson, Leckman, Wetzles et al., 1994) hypothesized that the alteration of structural lateralization found in TS basal ganglia might also be seen in other structures of the cerebral hemispheres that are lateralized. Given the massive funneling of interhemispheric axons through the corpus callosum (CC) and the subsequent potential sensitivity of CC size as an index of change in cortical anatomy, it was also hypothesized that those changes in cerebral asymmetries, if present, might be reflected as changes in TS CC morphology. Overall, CC area was significantly decreased by nearly 20% in the TS group compared with controls. Subregional areas appeared all to be reduced to a similar degree, and decreases in both curvilinear length and width of the CC appeared to be responsible for overall size reductions. Preliminary shape analyses also suggested that TS CCs are generally less curved than those of normals. The CC size reductions suggest that structural interhemispheric connectivity may be aberrant in the TS CNS and provide further indirect supportive evidence that TS cerebral lateralization may be aberrant.

The size and shape of the CC change throughout development, with fibers first appearing in the 11th week of gestation. The CC is initially a thin structure, but it widens gradually, first in the body and then in the rostrum and splenium. Axons increase in number until shortly after birth, when the first rapid, massive elimination of axons occurs, followed by a more protracted phase of axonal elimination prior to puberty (LaMantia & Rakic, 1990; Ramaekers, 1991). The perinatal period of axonal elimination coincides with the rapid phase of cortical synaptogenesis. Although CC myelination begins in the third trimester of pregnancy, myelination is not evident on MR images until infancy. Myelination and increasing axonal size are thought to produce CC elongation. By age 10 years, CC myelination is usually complete (Ramaekers, 1991), and after age 20, CC cross-sectional area on MR images progressively decreases (Allen, Richey, Chai, & Gorski, 1991; Hayakawa et al., 1989; Witelson, 1989). The shape of the CC appears to be under primarily genetic control, although twin studies indicate that environment also has an important influence (Oppenheim, Skerry, Tramo, & Gazzaniga, 1989). Thus, the CC morphological changes in TS could arise as early as 11 weeks' gestation, or even earlier if disturbances in cortical progenitor cells that give rise to CC axonal projections are the source of the abnormalities. Given the limitation of current developmental data on CC morphology in TS to the study of adults, it is possible that the changes also could appear as late as adult life. Thus CC developmental considerations do not yet aid in defining the timing of pathophysiological events in the genesis of structural abnormalities in the TS cerebrum.

Nevertheless, if the CC really is involved in some way in TS pathophysiology, knowledge of normal CC maturation may be helpful in understanding aspects of TS natural history. The progressive myelination of the CC in the school-age years, for instance, could in some way be responsible for the unmasking of a tic diathesis in a genetically vulnerable child. The CC myelination presumably facilitates normal interhemispheric lateralization and integration of function (Ramaekers, 1991), and CC structural and functional integrity is necessary for the manifestation of unilateral basal ganglia and nigral lesions (Sullivan, Parker, & Szechtman, 1993). Perhaps left-sided basal ganglia disturbances and aberrant asymmetries, through the normal maturation of CC structure and function, are rendered functionally visible as dyscontrol of motor and phonic acts, whether or not CC size reductions are central to TS pathophysiology.

Evidence of Other Changes in Structural Asymmetries

It is possible that the apparent abnormalities in TS cerebral lateralization might also be seen in actual tissue characterizations of the TS CNS. T_1 and T_2 relaxation times are tissue characteristics that describe the recovery of the bulk nuclear magnetization from hydrogen nuclei when those nuclei have been disturbed by appropriate radiofrequency energy during the process of MR imaging. The relaxation times determine how much NMR signal is recorded for each tissue, and differences in relaxation times between different tissues are the physical basis for radiographic tissue contrast seen in MR images.

T_2 relaxation times appear to be asymmetric throughout the cerebrum of normal individuals, with the differences seen between T_2 times of corresponding regions of both cerebral hemispheres being small in magnitude (2%–5%), but of a high degree of statistical significance throughout the cortex, subcortex, and brain stem (Peterson, Riddle, Gore, Cohen, & Leckman, in press). Altered T_2 relaxation time asymmetries have been noted in the TS insular cortex and frontal white matter, and in the putamen and caudate nuclei. T_2 times appear to be shorter in the TS right amygdala and right red nucleus, with similar trends in the corresponding left-sided structures. Because the determinants of relaxation times are many and complex, it is at this time impossible to say precisely what is responsible for the observed normal and abnormal asymmetries. Nonetheless, the differences in TS T_2 relaxation time asymmetries are consistent with the hypothesis of altered CNS lateralization in the disorder.

Functional Correlates of Structural Findings

A test battery was designed specifically to assess aspects of basal ganglia contribution to functional lateralization and interhemispheric transfer. It included tasks assessing the accuracy of line bisection and the biases in turning behavior exhibited by TS adults (Yazgan, Peterson, Wexler, & Leckman, in press). Normal right-handed subjects are known to have a mild "pseudo-neglect" of the right external hemispace (Bowers & Heilman, 1980; Manning, Halligan, & Marshall, 1990) that is thought to derive from left cerebral dominance of the CSTC circuits, and which is characterized by a leftward shift in line bisection and by a leftward bias in turning (Alexander et al., 1990; Mesulam, 1990). The adult TS subjects actually performed better on the line bisection task, dividing it more accurately than did controls. Similarly, these same TS subjects demonstrated virtually no bias in turning, unlike the control subjects, who displayed a leftward turning bias while reversing the direction of their gait. These simple tasks demonstrate that the loss of normal structural brain asymmetries seen in TS subjects may have functional correlates.

Functional Neuroimaging Studies

TS functional imaging studies generally mutually corroborate findings of reduced basal ganglia metabolism or perfusion, and frequently report associated decreases in metabolism/perfusion in associated CSTC circuitry, such as the frontal cortex and thalamus. Less commonly reported are changes in the anatomically related regions of the cingulum, and in the temporal and insular cortices.

A PET study using ^{18}F-labeled deoxyglucose (FDG) as the tracer in 12 TS adults reported a 15% decrement in nonnormalized glucose utilization in the frontal, cingulate, and insular cortices, as well as in the "inferior corpus striatum." A significant inverse correlation was also seen between the tic severity and glucose utilization in these same regions (Chase, Geoffrey, Gillespie, & Burrows, 1986).

A more recent [^{18}F]-FDG PET study using a higher resolution scanner in 16 medication-free TS adults reported decreased glucose utilization in the orbitofrontal, parahippocampal (entorhinal), and inferior insular cortices, as well as in the ventral striatum (nucleus accumbens, ventromedial caudate, and left anterior putamen) and midbrain (Braun et al., 1993; Stoetter et al., 1992). These changes were most pronounced in the left cerebral hemisphere. Increased, nonlateralized metabolic activity was seen in the sensorimotor cortices (supplementary motor, lateral premotor, and Rolandic regions).

Single photon emission computed tomography (SPECT) studies have the clinical advantage over PET studies of employing lower doses of radiation, but suffer the research disadvantage of providing lower resolution of regional brain metabolic activity. One SPECT study found differences in frontal lobe/basal ganglia ratios in "pure TS" compared with TS + OCD subjects, although the differences were not statistically significant (George et al., 1992). Another SPECT study found a 5% reduction in regional blood flow to the left lenticular nucleus and a 2% reduction in flow to the right frontal cortex in TS adults (Riddle, Rasmusson, Woods, & Hoffer, 1992).

Obsessive-Compulsive Disorder and Attention-Deficit/Hyperactivity Disorder Neuroimaging Studies

OCD structural studies have conflicted over reports of caudate nucleus volume changes (Kellner et al., 1991; Luxenberg et al., 1988; Scarone et al., 1992; Stein et al., 1993), and one study reported increased ventricular brain ratios (Behar et al., 1984). OCD functional studies are in generally good agreement in finding increased frontal cortex metabolism and perfusion (Baxter et al., 1987; Baxter et al., 1988; Machlin et al., 1991; Nordahl et al., 1989; Rubin, Villanueva-Meyer, Ananth, Trajmar, & Mena, 1992; Swedo, Schapiro et al., 1989; Swedo, Pietrini et al., 1992), with varying reports of hypermetabolism in the caudate nucleus, cingulum, and other cortical regions (Baxter et al., 1987, 1988; Rauch et al., 1994).

ADHD structural studies are rare. One study of primary ADHD reported widened cerebral sulci (Nasrallah et al., 1986), which if real could represent the underlying neural substrate for the global hypometabolism reported in PET studies (Zametkin et al., 1990). Very preliminary studies in a small number of subjects reported reversal of asymmetries in cross-sectional area of the head of the caudate nucleus (Hynd et al., 1993), and reduced cross-sectional area of the corpus callosum in its anterior and posterior regions (Giedd et al., 1994; Hynd et al., 1991; Semrud-Clikeman et al., 1994). The ADHD that occurs comorbidly with TS has been associated with reduced volumes and with a loss of normal asymmetry in the left lenticular nucleus, perhaps in the globus pallidus in particular (Singer et al., 1993). When regional metabolic rates are normalized by overall cerebral metabolism, the PET work in ADHD is suggestive of left anterior frontal and possibly striatal hypometabolism (Zametkin et al., 1990; Zametkin et al., 1993).

Additional Pathophysiological Implications of Neuroimaging Studies

The basal ganglia volume reductions and hypometabolism seen in TS are suggestive of some kind of CNS developmental abnormality. The apparent morphological abnormalities in more than one set of brain regions (in the basal ganglia and CC at least) would suggest that the underlying pathoetiologic processes impact on the developing TS CNS diffusely. The CC findings suggest that widespread cortical connectivity may be aberrant in TS, and that other cortical and subcortical abnormalities in both structure and function should be sought. The differences in performance of lateralized behavioral tasks, the apparently common occurrence of lateralized neurological soft signs in TS subjects (Sweet, Solomon, Wayne, Shapiro, & Shapiro, 1973), and the preliminary findings of altered asymmetries of tissue magnetic resonance characteristics in numerous regions of the cerebrum support the contention that the pathoetiologic determinants of TS affect the cerebrum diffusely.

Animal data implicate as a cause of altered cerebral anatomic asymmetries in utero exposure of the fetus to prenatal maternal stress (Fleming, Anderson, Rhees, Kinghorn, & Bakaitis, 1986). Stressed fetuses also demonstrate in adulthood a loss in amphetamine-induced rotations, enduring changes in striatal dopaminergic asymmetries, and heightened stress responsivities (Fride & Weinstock, 1989; Takahashi et al., 1992). Maternal emotional stress during pregnancy and nonspecific indexes of prenatal fetal physiological stress, such as low birth weight, have been reported to correlate with adult tic severity (Hyde et al., 1992; Leckman, Price et al., 1987). It may be that what has been imaged are the CNS vestiges of some diverse prenatal stressors.

Electrophysiology

Electroencephalograms (EEGs)

Although early EEG studies in medicated TS subjects suggested the frequent presence of nonspecific sharp waves and diffuse slowing (Bergen, Tanner, & Wilson, 1982; Krumholz, Singer, Niedermeyer, Burnite, & Harris, 1983; Volkmar et al., 1984), more recent studies have conclusively demonstrated that routine EEGs in unmedicated TS subjects do not differ significantly from those in normals (Neufeld, Berger, Chapman, & Korczyn, 1990; Van Woerkom, Fortgens, Rompel-Martens, & van de Wetering, 1988). Preliminary quantitative EEG analyses, in which the relative power contributions of each of the EEG frequency bands in specified electrode positions are compared between TS and normal subjects, also have been unable to demonstrate differences in scalp recordings of TS brain electrical activity (Drake et al., 1992; Neufeld et al., 1990). Brain stem auditory and visual evoked responses have proved similarly unrevealing (Syrigou-Papavasiliou, Verma, & LeWitt, 1988).

Event-Related Potential Studies (ERPs)

Task-related electrophysiological studies have been moderately more successful in differentiating TS from normal subjects, although they also have highlighted some of the important continuities with normal behaviors. One study has demonstrated the apparent absence in TS of the normal slow premotor movement potential (Bereinshaftspotential) preceding simple motor tics, which the authors interpret as evidence for an involuntary, subcortical initiation of tics (Obeso, Rothwell, & Marsden, 1981). Keller and Heckhausen (1990) studied in normal subjects the premovement potentials of the unplanned spontaneous motor acts that closely resemble tics and which are thought to originate from muscular tension in the periphery, and compared them with the premovement potentials of preplanned motor acts initiated in response to an urge to move. Sometimes the spontaneous movements were preceded by a conscious urge to move, and sometimes they were not preceded by conscious sensations. Premovement potentials associated with movements (whether preplanned or spontaneous) that were preceded by consciously perceived sensations were centered, as expected, over the medial premotor system of the supplementary motor area. Movements not preceded by conscious urges to move, in contrast, were centered over the contralateral lateral premotor system and primary motor cortex. In addition, the amplitude of the premovement potentials associated with unconscious motor acts were significantly smaller in amplitude than those associated with conscious motor acts preceded by an urge to move. These authors agree that unconsciously performed spontaneous motor acts may be generated by subcortical nuclei, such as the basal ganglia, that might bypass the usual initiation of movement by the supplementary motor area. These findings in normal subjects may illuminate those of Obeso et al. (1981), in which only one of six TS subjects demonstrated a tic-related premovement potential, which was much reduced in amplitude compared with voluntary imitations of the tic. Perhaps the tics in these patients were not detected because they were not preceded by conscious urges, so that their premovement potentials were reduced to undetectable amplitudes. This hypothesis can be tested by comparing the premovement potentials of tics preceded by conscious premonitory urges with those not preceded by such urges. The important point, however, is that not only are the phenomenologies of tics and normal spontaneous motor acts similar, but so are their apparent electrophysiologies, further underscoring the potential continuity between TS and normal behavior.

Auditory event-related potential (ERP) studies have been hindered by small numbers of subjects, and by the confusion presented by comorbid illnesses (Drake et al., 1992; Van Woerkom et al., 1988). Nevertheless, the preliminary findings suggest that cerebral attentional and arousal mechanisms are differentially involved in TS depending on the presence or absence of comorbid OCD or ADHD.

Another study assessed changes in autonomic arousal during sound and light habituation, as measured by skin conductance changes (Bock & Goldberger, 1985). TS subjects showed less change in tonic autonomic arousal during habituation than did controls and they tended also to have generally less tonic autonomic arousal overall. The authors interpreted these findings as evidence for the presence of excessively active arousal and reticular activating systems in the disorder.

Sleep Studies

Disordered arousal system theories of TS have been supported by numerous reports of sleep disturbances in TS that could again point to potential abnormalities in the TS reticular activating system. Sleepwalking, enuresis, night terrors, and nightmares are frequent, although it is not clear whether these problems are significantly more prevalent than in the normal population (Barabas, Matthews, & Ferrari, 1984). Parent reports of these and other behaviors associated with arousal disturbances support the findings of increased sleep disturbances in TS, and provide preliminary evidence that the presence of comorbid ADHD may more frequently be associated with arousal disorders in TS children than in normal, ADHD alone, or TS alone children (Allen, Singer, Brown, & Salam, 1992). TS patients may have less delta sleep (Stages 3 and 4 combined) than normals (Mendelson, Caine, Goyer, Ebert, & Gillin, 1980). Polysomnographic recordings also indicate that body movements are more frequent in all sleep stages, and that arousal patterns are abnormal in TS subjects, who experience more frequent awakenings than do normals, particularly in Stage IV sleep (Glaze, Frost, & Jankovic, 1983). The awakenings are characterized by intense arousal, disorientation, confusion, and increased tic activity, which coincides with changes in the EEG from a typical Stage IV pattern to a generalized, high-voltage, rhythmic delta activity that is reminiscent of immature arousal patterns seen in infants and young children (Glaze et al., 1983). These immature EEG patterns in sleep again suggest the possibility of some kind of developmental delay or arrest in the TS CNS.

Startle Paradigms

The startle reflex is a sudden, involuntary contraction of the facial or skeletal musculature in response to an abrupt, intense sensory stimulus. Abnormalities have been described in the TS blink reflex startle response to electrical stimulation of the supraorbital nerve (Castellanos et al., 1993; Smith & Lees, 1989). The amplitude of the startle reflex is normally inhibited by a weak prestimulus (a "prepulse") occurring 30 to 500 milliseconds prior to the actual startling stimulus. In 26 adult patients, the mean duration of the blink reflex was increased compared with that in 10 control subjects, and the degree of inhibition in amplitude induced by the conditioning (prepulse) stimulus was significantly reduced (Smith & Lees, 1989). This reduction in prepulse inhibition was confirmed in seven TS boys with comorbid ADHD (Castellanos et al., 1993). Whether the impairment in prepulse inhibition can be attributed to TS or ADHD in the latter report is open to question, however, since similar impairment has been seen in studies of acoustic startle in ADHD children (Ornitz, Hanna, & DeTraversay, 1992).

A loss of prepulse inhibition is generally thought to reflect a loss of detectability of the prestimulus, which then suggests that the gating of sensory information within the sensory processing neural circuitry is fundamentally impaired. The psychological utility of sensory gating mechanisms is hypothesized to consist of a lessening of the behavioral and cognitive impact of stronger subsequent stimuli. Sensory gating thus prevents the flooding and potential overload of cognitive information and minimizes the loss of discrete elements of the ensuing salient sensory information rising above excessive background noise (Swerdlow, Caine, Braff, & Geyer, 1992). Impaired sensory gating in TS may result in the intrusion of irrelevant sensory, motor, and cognitive stimuli from both the internal and external environments. Perhaps the urges to move or vocalize prior to a motor or phonic tic represent impaired gating of normal internal sensations that would otherwise never reach the level of conscious awareness. The aggressive and sexual behaviors associated with TS may be similarly ungated internal stimuli that normally would be screened from awareness and from admission into the normal behavioral repertoire.

The brain systems that subserve startle reflexes are primarily located in the brain stem. The systems that subserve prepulse inhibition of startle reflexes, in contrast, are located in the forebrain. Animal studies suggest that elements of the limbic cortex and basal ganglia modulate prepulse inhibition. In particular, glutamate efferents from the hippocampus to the ventral striatum (including nucleus accumbens), and in turn GABA efferents from the striatum to the ventral pallidum that are modulated by dopaminergic striatal receptors, appear to be important in modulating prepulse inhibition; the pallidal efferents to the mesencephalic pontine reticular formation then appear to modulate neural activity of the cellular elements composing the primary startle reflex (Swerdlow et al., 1992). All components of this neural circuitry have been implicated in TS pathophysiology. Reduced prepulse inhibition of electrically induced startle in TS could represent an epiphenomenon of dysfunctional neural systems that generate tics, and that could also impair prepulse inhibition simply by virtue of physical and functional proximity to the putative TS "lesion." Alternatively, the disordered neural systems implicated in TS could produce much of TS symptomatology by disrupting sensory, behavioral, and cognitive gating mechanisms of internal and external stimuli. Lastly, normal prepulse inhibition follows a sex-specific developmental trajectory, with prepulse inhibition of startle amplitude increasing with increasing age in both sexes, but with young girls showing less inhibition than same-age boys (Ornitz, Guthrie, Kaplan, Lane, & Norman, 1986; Ornitz, Guthrie, Sadeghpour, & Sugiyama, 1991; Ornitz et al., 1992); reduced prepulse inhibition in TS could conceivably *again* reflect delayed or arrested development of important neuromodulatory and neuroregulatory centers, including those involved in prepulse inhibition.

Neuropsychology

Early neuropsychological studies of TS were hindered by either small subject numbers or by suboptimal design. More recent studies generally have been consistent in reporting decreased performance on tasks of fine motor dexterity, visual-constructional ability, and executive functioning (Bornstein, 1990; Denckla et al., 1991). Relative weaknesses in attention, sensory perception, and mathematics have also been observed (Incagnoli & Kane, 1981; Joschko & Rourke, 1982). Commonly used medications in the treatment of TS do not appear to impair significantly neuropsychological test performance in children (Bornstein, 1990, 1991).

The variable neuropsychological test findings may be due to the variable clinical presentations and the presence of important comorbid illnesses, such as OCD, ADHD, and learning disabilities. Recent studies have tried to control for these potentially important confounds. TS children with clinically diagnosed ADHD, compared with children who have TS only, may perform more poorly on measures of full-scale IQ, visual motor integration, perceptual organization, and social functioning (Dykens et al., 1990). These children, as expected, also have more problems with the attentional processing elements of encoding, sustaining, and focusing/executing during tasks designed to tap those abilities. These children do not seem to have difficulty shifting cognitive set (Yeates & Bornstein, 1994). In addition, the severity of OCD in TS children may predict performance on tests sensitive to frontal lobe dysfunction (Bornstein, 1991).

One particularly elegant study deserves special note. Neuropsychological test performance was studied in 12 monozygotic twin child-pairs in which at least one of the pairs had TS

(Randolph et al., 1993). Five of the cotwins had diagnosable TS, five had a CMT disorder, one had a transient tic disorder, and the last had no tic disorder. Eight of the TS twins and five cotwins also had ADHD. The use of MZ twin-pairs controlled for all of the genetic, and much of the environmental, variance between the related twins, and allowed for a powerful assessment of the relationship between symptom severity and neuropsychological test performance. In each and every twin-pair, the twin with the more severe tic symptoms had a lower global neuropsychological test score than did the cotwin. The neuropsychological tests that most contributed to this global differentiation of the cotwins on the basis of symptom severity were tests that assess attention and impulsivity (continuous performance tests), visuospatial perception (the Benton Facial Recognition Test), and motor function (the Purdue Pegboard Test). These results suggest that the neurobiological substrates of tic generation are shared with those substrates subserving attention, visuospatial ability, and motor function. These functions almost certainly involve disparate (though anatomically related) brain regions, which further speaks to the likelihood of a diffuse, though pathophysiologically linked, environmentally determined central nervous system insult in TS.

Lastly, compared with normals, TS children were significantly impaired in their ability to perform the Luria Hand-Alternation Task, in which one hand closes as the other is simultaneously opened (Baron-Cohen, Cross, Crowson, & Robertson, 1994). These children also demonstrated impairment in their ability to provide appropriate, *non*stereotyped verbal responses to questions that normally elicit a stereotyped response (i.e., the questions used typically elicit "yes" and "no" answers). These TS children, who averaged 12 years of age, performed at the level of the 4-year-old control subjects and significantly below the level of the 5- and 6-year-old controls. The authors hypothesize the existence in normal individuals of an "intention editor," by which they mean a psychological entity that allows an individual to choose correctly from among several similar competing intentions to act. They interpret the experimental data as evidence for impairment in TS subjects of this intention editor. They also hypothesize that the neurobiological substrate of the intention editor resides in the frontal cortex. They do not mention that the Luria task which they employ almost certainly requires interhemispherically coordinated basal ganglia, as well as an intact corpus callosum, which is myelinating rapidly by the ages of 4, 5, and 6, the ages of their normal control subjects. Both of these structures have been implicated in TS pathophysiology. Their results further emphasize the potential importance in TS of a maturational delay or arrest in cerebral structure and function.

SOCIAL COMPETENCE AND ADAPTIVE FUNCTIONING

Not all TS children manifest disruptive behaviors apart from their tics and ADHD symptoms, although on average they display more behavioral disturbances than children without psychiatric illness (Wilson, Garron, Tanner, & Klawans, 1982). Compared with normal children they also report more somatic complaints on the Child Behavior Checklist (CBCL) (Frank, Sieg, & Gaffney, 1991). The severities of behavioral disturbances generally do *not* seem to correlate with the severity of tic symptoms or anxiety. Like normal children, the perception by TS children that their parents accept them is positively correlated with their own self-concept and self-esteem, whereas the child's perception of the parents as using guilt or hostility to control the child's behavior is negatively correlated with the child's self-concept, and positively correlated with trait anxiety (Edell & Motta, 1989).

Peer relationships and socialization are significantly impaired for many TS children. The Vineland Adaptive Behavior Scales Interview administered to the mothers of 30 TS children revealed significant weaknesses in the socialization domain (interpersonal relationships, use of play and leisure time, and coping skills) (Dykens et al., 1990). In an independent assessment of peer acceptance and socialization, the Pupil Evaluation Inventory (PEI) was administered to the classmates of 29 TS children (Stokes et al., 1991). The PEI assesses peer relationships in schoolchildren by asking them to rate each of their classmates' social behaviors. The classmates rated the TS children as much more withdrawn and less popular than other children in the classroom. Although teachers rated these children as more aggressive and withdrawn than their peers, mothers judged their children's social competence to be average, as assessed by the CBCL, despite the mothers' acknowledgment of numerous behavioral problems in their children. Measures of verbal ability from intelligence tests correlated negatively with ratings of aggression, and positively with ratings of likability of the TS children; it may be that language skills are important in these children in modulating aggressive drives and improving social relations. The TS children with comorbid ADHD were rated as more aggressive than TS children without ADHD, although the latter children were still less popular than their classmates. None of the socialization or behavioral ratings correlated with TS symptom severity.

In a preliminary report from a prospective longitudinal study of 21 children who are siblings of TS probands, and who therefore are also at risk for developing the disorder, the comorbidities, social-emotional functioning, and family functioning of 5 siblings who have developed TS, and 4 siblings with either motor or phonic tics, were compared with those siblings who have not manifested TS (Carter et al., 1994). Comorbidities included OCD in 4 (19%), ADHD in 5 (24%), and developmental disorders in 6 (29%). Tic-affected children rated their perceived physical attractiveness as significantly lower, and maternal acceptance as higher, compared with unaffected children. No family variables were identified that discriminated tic from nontic groups. In contrast, children with attentional problems were more likely to be found in families that were low in control and low in achievement orientation. For both affected and unaffected children, family environment measures (marital adjustment, family cohesion, independence promotion, and recreational activities) were strongly correlated with measures of parent and teacher ratings of the child's adaptive and maladaptive behaviors, as well as with indexes of the child's self-esteem. Thus, family environment as measured to date does not seem to influence the development of tic disorders, although they may play a role in the emergence of attentional problems and maladaptive behaviors.

A STATEMENT OF THE DEVELOPMENTAL MODEL

The emerging conceptualization of TS is thus one of a syndrome that develops in persons who carry a specific genetic burden and who, in certain prenatal and childhood environmental circumstances, develop motor and phonic tic symptoms that may or may not be of sufficient severity to cause interference in school, family, and social functioning to a degree requiring clinical care. It has become increasingly clear that the severity of tic symptoms often have little to do with the functional impairment experienced by children in terms of social competence, academic performance, and self-esteem. Rather, common comorbid illnesses such as OCD, ADHD, aggressive behavioral disturbances, and learning disabilities seem to be more predictive of functional impairment. Although these comorbidities may be intimately associated with the pathophysiology of the disorder, it is possible that their common association with TS could represent the product of a clinic ascertainment bias operating within individual TS probands as well as in their families. The magnitude of this ascertainment bias is likely to increase as comorbid conditions share with TS more of the same neurobiological substrate, as for example TS and OCD, or TS and ADHD, are thought to do. Ascertainment bias will also increase as certain family psychopathologies increase the intolerance of TS related behaviors. Families with high loading for the rigid, anxious, and inhibited styles of obsessive-compulsive individuals may be less likely, for example, to tolerate the disinhibited, aggressive, and sexual behaviors of their TS child. The clinical presentation of these children thus is individualized and contextualized by the many nuances of their physiological, psychological, and familial adaptive functioning.

Genetic Vulnerability

It is clear from twin and family studies that genetic determinants are important in producing the TS phenotype. Despite the problems inherent in comorbidity analyses in case control and family studies, the variable expressivity of these same genetic determinants appears important in producing at least one subset of chronic motor tic disorder, obsessive-compulsive disorder, and perhaps attention deficit disorder. It also appears, however, that carrying the same TS genetic predisposition within any twin-pair or within any given family is neither necessary nor sufficient to produce any of the known phenotypic expressions of the gene.

Carrying the putative TS gene is *not necessary* for producing TS because 10% to 15% of TS cases detected in family studies are sporadic (no family members have TS or a related disorder), and thus represent either new genetic mutations or TS phenocopies. Although a nuisance to genetic linkage studies in which the inclusion of false positive cases is highly detrimental, and perhaps fatal, recognizing the existence of phenocopies is important for a full understanding of the disease and of the ways that its underlying neural substrate can generate symptoms. Because the same symptoms can be produced by apparently nongenetic mechanisms, indicates that the range of biologic variability in the neural substrate or the "normal" CNS is, given exposure to the appropriate environmental determinants for that particular individual capable of producing the symptom profile of TS to a degree sufficient enough to be clinically identified for inclusion in TS family studies. Whether those environmental determinants are the same as those producing "real" TS remains to be seen, and warrants more attention and study.

Carrying the TS gene is also not always *sufficient* for producing bona fide familial TS or a related disorder, because obligate carriers do not always express the gene. Monozygotic TS twin studies show that, although the concordance rate for expressing a tic disorder in the cotwin is high, it is not perfect, and that, furthermore, the severity of the tic symptoms in each of the twins is often substantially different. Because these twins are genetically identical, environmental determinants are necessarily operative. The TS family studies have also demonstrated an incomplete penetrance of the gene, regardless of which constellation of TS-related disorders are included in the "affected" status of the family members, indicating that nongenetic factors are affecting expression of the vulnerability gene in known carriers. Thus, if the TS vulnerability gene ultimately proves to be homogeneous, then it can be stated without qualification that factors other than just the TS gene (epigenetic contributors) are necessary in determining the quality and severity of the disease phenotype. If the gene proves to be heterogeneous, on the other hand, then the most that can be said is that, for at least some allelic variants of the gene, epigenetic factors are necessary for its expression.

Because the TS gene is neither necessary nor sufficient to produce the Tourette syndrome, the concept of genetic *vulnerability* for developing the disorder seems most appropriate. This vulnerability endows individuals carrying the gene with a nonspecific diathesis to tic symptoms, obsessive-compulsive traits, and perhaps attention deficit syndromes. In the vast majority of people carrying the gene, such symptoms, if present at all, will be mild and not warrant clinical attention. In a minority of people, however, determinants other than the vulnerability gene—they may be purely environmental, or they may be physiological and therefore in part genetic—will play an important role in determining the degree to which such symptoms are expressed, who will suffer impairment, and who will require treatment for them.

What may, in fact, prove to be crucial in the successful localization of the putative gene is an appreciation for its enormous range of phenotypic expression in both quality and degree, be it expression as tics, obsessive-compulsive phenomena, attentional disturbances, or impulse dyscontrol, or as mild symptoms continuous with many normal, ubiquitous behaviors. The appreciation of this range of genetic expression is important for recognizing the very real difficulties in obtaining a gold standard diagnostic instrument specific enough to exclude false positive diagnoses (TS phenocopies) that can be lethal to the success of genetic linkage studies. The diagnostic difficulty is only exacerbated when that instrument is applied to the population of a TS proband family that may, by virtue of familywide ascertainment bias, have a higher frequency of tics and other nonspecific comorbidities. The appreciation of the continuity of TS tics with normal behaviors exhibited through development is also important in recognizing the real possibility that the putative TS vulnerability gene may be a gene that is not usually expressed pathologically and that might have a higher frequency in the population than is generally assumed. The confluence of this otherwise normal vulnerability gene with other unique constitutional and environmental factors may contribute to overt dysfunctional symptom expression that brings the proband of family-genetic studies to clinical attention.

Environmentally Determined Specificity

Whereas genetic determinants are important in establishing a nonspecific susceptibility to an array of TS-related disease phenotypes, environmental and epigenetic factors nevertheless will need to be specified before we can understand the full panoply of phenotypic expression of the TS gene. Evidence is mounting that epigenetic determinants play a pivotal role not only in defining who manifests the tic disorder conferred by carrying the TS vulnerability gene, but also in determining who manifests which TS-related illness, who suffers from more and who from less severe illness, and finally even who in neuroimaging studies manifests the various brain-based manifestations of these epigenetic effects on neuronal substrate.

Differences in degree of clinical phenotypic expression between genetically identical MZ twins indicates that epigenetic determinants must somehow be responsible for the differences between the twins in their severity of clinical presentation. This is a question of *degree* of expression of the vulnerability gene. Family studies also indicate the existence of a difference in degree of gene expression, in that most family members simply have a chronic motor tic disorder, while some have the full TS syndrome. Despite the inherent difficulties in assessing comorbidities in family studies, however, the balance of evidence argues for an epigenetic specification of the *quality* of gene expression as well, in that some family members express the tic symptoms, whereas others express only obsessive-compulsive symptoms, and still others may show just attentional deficits.

The precise epigenetic contributions to the specification of TS phenotype can at present only be surmised. The male preponderance of the tic disorder, for instance, and the apparent female preponderance of OCD without tics in the expression of the TS vulnerability gene, both strongly indicate the importance of sex-specific epigenetic contributions to phenotype specification, particularly in view of the apparent autosomal (i.e., non-sex-linked) mode of genetic transmission. Markers for adverse pre- and perinatal adverse events—low birth weight, maternal stress, and obstetrical complications—have been implicated in the degree of expression of the TS vulnerability gene, as assessed by measures of clinical severity. Finally, psychosocial stressors are undoubtedly environmental determinants of symptom severity in the short term, although consequences in the long term are as yet unknown.

The vestiges of these environmental determinants seem to be evident not only through clinical experience with patients, but also through various research probes that peer into the neurobiological substrate mediating between gene and external environment. Anatomic disruptions are evident in the basal ganglia and related CSTC circuitry, brain systems that we know are of paramount importance not only in the control of movement, but in the regulation of thought and affect as well. The TS CNS may have lost, in some neural systems, normal structural and functional lateralization. In animal models, similar losses of (or failures in developing) cerebral asymmetry appear to be prenatally and environmentally determined. Documented abnormalities in measures of neurotransmitter precursors, products, and metabolites within these same neural systems and other diffusely separate brain regions could be indexing some central pathological defect of the disorder, but arguably more likely reflect either a more generalized, disordered neuronal activity, or else some kind of neural compensatory response to the presence of the central defect elsewhere.

Subtle neuropsychological deficits may be either another phenotypic manifestation of the TS vulnerability gene, or else a product of whatever environmental insults may be operative. The preliminary correlations between the degree of neuropsychological deficits and symptom severity, however, suggest that the deficits and symptoms may share some of the same neurobiological substrate. Symptom severity also appears to correlate with the degree of perinatal risk factor exposure, and it may be that certain of these risk factors are responsible for injury to genetically vulnerable neural substrate, which then produces symptom exacerbation and cognitive deficits.

Other epigenetic influences on diffuse cortical and subcortical centers that are components of the CSTC circuitry could include the biological mediators of acute psychological stress, such as the brain stem reticular activating system, the hypothalamic-pituitary-adrenal axis, the locus ceruleus, and the dorsal raphe nucleus. In addition to mediating the effects of acute stress on the CSTC system, disturbances inherent to these regulatory centers may also contribute to the severity of symptom expression. Such disturbances in these systems could represent either extremes in the range of normal biological variability of functioning, or else real disorders that are biologically or environmentally determined in their own right. Either way, their dysregulation could worsen symptom expression and bring the patient to clinical attention, then resulting in an ascertainment bias in electrophysiological and sleep studies, for instance, that are suggestive of reticular activating system dysfunction. It is thus most reasonable to conjecture that even in these patients, the neurobiological substrate of the genetic predisposition to TS probably resides in the CSTC circuitry, and that brain stem neuroregulatory centers exert important modulatory effects on those other disordered systems.

Maturational Processes and the Specifying Environment

It is impossible to say when during CNS development the epigenetic insults occur that tip the genetic diathesis to TS-related illness over into determined disease phenotype. The normal basal ganglia and corpus callosum maturational morphologic changes seen in adults can occur anywhere between the first trimester of pregnancy and adult life. The observation by Singer and colleagues (1993) of similar left-sided lenticular nucleus volume reductions and loss of normal basal ganglia asymmetry in children, however, places the upper age limit of the genesis of those morphological abnormalities in early childhood. The histopathological case report of an infantile appearance of the basal ganglia, and the reports of immature-appearing electroencephalographic activity in Stage IV sleep, are consistent with these constraints on the timing of environmental insults that could produce basal ganglia abnormalities, and also hint that some type of CNS maturational arrest may be the consequence of the epigenetic insult.

The animal models of an environmentally determined loss of normal cerebral asymmetries suggests by analogy that the defining environmental insult in TS might occur prenatally although this evidence is circumstantial. The case for perinatal insults is considerably strengthened, however, by the preliminary data correlating symptom severity with the markers for the severity of adverse perinatal events such as low birth weight, maternal nausea and vomiting, and nonspecific maternal emotional stress. These kinds of prenatal insults are likely to have a diffuse, rather than a highly localized, effect on the developing CNS.

It is also possible that certain perinatal insults, when superimposed on a preexisting TS genetic vulnerability early in the course of CNS development, establish in the brain structural changes whose functional consequences are revealed later when other normal CNS postnatal maturational changes occur. For example, the functional manifestations of a congenitally pathological corpus callosum could remain in a state of relative symptomatic silence until the age of 6 or 7, when the most rapid period of corpus callosum myelination occurs, and when TS symptoms most commonly begin. Alternatively, normal but critically important events in the developing cortex, such as fetal growth cone formation or postnatal axonal elimination, could alter callosal morphology and function in ways that could later unmask TS symptoms. An intact corpus callosum appears to be necessary for the appearance of at least some of the behavioral manifestations of unilateral nigrostriatal lesions (Sullivan et al., 1993), and presumably of unilateral basal ganglia lesions like those that may be present in TS. Finally, extensive synaptic pruning early in the course of puberty is triggered in part by pubertal sex hormone surges and may underlie the exacerbation of peripubertal symptoms occurring prior to the late adolescent attenuation of tic symptom severities.

In addition to structural maturational changes that occur during development, functional maturational changes may appear during childhood and adolescence that are nevertheless environmentally determined prenatally. The cytoarchitectures of CNS sexual dimorphisms and their ranges of responsiveness to future hormonal challenges, for example, are established during critical windows of biological vulnerability in the developing fetal CNS. These brain systems are likely responsible for the sex-specific phenotype and prevalence differences in expression of the vulnerability gene in early childhood, and may have an important influence on symptom expression due to differing biological responsivities of these neuroregulatory systems to new hormonal changes in puberty.

Superimposed on the biologically determined maturational changes is psychological development, which in some general ways is as orderly and sequential as biological maturation. Schoolchildren will have many somatic and cosmetic preoccupations about their bodies in addition to the stigmatizing tic symptoms, which are the source of disdain and ridicule from classmates. Ironically, social relatedness and academic functioning generally do not seem to be dependent on the severity of tic symptoms. Inability to suppress aggressive and sometimes sexual impulses seems to most alienate peers, leaving the child with TS isolated and withdrawn, vulnerable to excessive use of obsessional defenses commonly seen in normal children of that age, but which are potentially problematic for these children, who have an apparent genetic vulnerability for becoming disabled by them. The verbal skills of these children may be particularly important for maintaining better social relatedness through the inevitable challenges posed by their symptoms. Nonjudgmental, nonpunitive, and appropriately structured family environments seem to be important in maintaining the child's self-esteem through these difficult times, particularly in the early pubertal years when aggressive and sexual urges are most prominent, when tic symptoms are at their worst, and when the recathexis of the adolescent's body is only heightening the individual's crisis in self-image formation and interpersonal relatedness. Parental support during this period is particularly important as the processes of separation and individuation, and physical movement away from family, take center stage, and as the attenuation in tic symptom severities affords the opportunity for a rejuvenation of self-image and self-esteem.

THE MODEL'S HEURISTIC VALUE

Much of the power of the proposed model derives from the potential application of multidisciplinary approaches to studying the interaction of biological and psychological variables through the course of development. These approaches have the potential of illuminating normal central nervous system developmental processes, and of advancing our understanding of TS and other neuropsychiatric disorders.

Determining the Range of Phenotypic Expression

In its various manifestations as TS, CMT, OCD, and possibly ADHD, the variability in expression of the putative autosomal dominant TS vulnerability gene is impressive. The full range of phenotypic expression may yet only be partially defined. It is crucial for the success of the genetic linkage studies that this range of expression be rigorously and accurately determined because the linkage mathematical models depend critically on accurate and valid diagnosis. The use of twin and family-genetic studies in helping to define valid nosological categories is well known (Leckman, Weissman, Pauls, & Kidd, 1987; Robins & Guze, 1970). In providing an independent source of data, these genetic studies allow investigators to assess directly the importance of various phenotypic features that are regularly part of the clinical presentation such as OCD and ADHD symptoms. Conversely, when the putative TS vulnerability gene is finally discovered, it will be possible to define exactly and unequivocally the range of phenotypic expression associated with each of the genetic abnormalities identified.

Molecular Studies of Gene-Environment Interactions

If the linkage studies succeed in identifying the chromosome carrying the TS vulnerability gene, the gene will then be physically mapped and isolated. Once the gene is located, the enormous task will begin of determining the gene's products and of following those products through the cascade of multiple levels of biological organization, from the proximal molecular aberrations to the distal clinical phenotype. The TS gene sequence and genomic organization will first be determined, and factors mediating the gene's cellular transcription will be characterized. Investigators will then be able to develop transgenic animal models, which will allow the precise determination of the spatial and temporal expression of the gene throughout the CNS.

Improving the Understanding of Normal Development

With eventual localization of the putative gene, characterization of its product, and elucidation of its impact on brain structure and function at each of the molecular, cellular, multineuronal information processing, and overt behavioral levels, the understanding of normal growth and development will improve enormously. Perhaps the greatest opportunities for improved understanding will include the ability to study what is likely to be the range of expression of a normal gene product that probably affects sensorimotor, affective, cognitive, and impulse control centers in the brain, and to study the combination of other constitutional and environmental determinants that tip normal gene expression over into functional debility. The study and understanding of normal compensatory processes, occurring in response to the presence of constitutional vulnerability and environmental stress, will also improve at all levels of structural and functional organization, from subcellular to social, as will understanding of the ways in which those compensatory capacities change through all stages of human development.

Exploiting Gene-Environment Interactions

With the anticipated success of the genetic linkage studies, it will be possible to identify precisely, in prospective longitudinal studies of high-risk families, those individuals carrying the TS vulnerability gene. Investigators will be able to explore the impact of specific epigenetic and environmental influences on vulnerable children. Determination of the chromosomal locus of the TS vulnerability gene, for instance, will provide researchers with an important tool to evaluate putative prenatal risk factors, such as first trimester nausea and vomiting and the burden of severe maternal stress, which then will allow identification of potentially at-risk pregnancies, if indeed these prenatal risk factors are confirmed. The identification of high-risk pregnancies in turn may lead to intervention strategies during critical developmental periods that can limit the future severity of expression of the syndrome within the vulnerable fetus. The development of animal models in molecular biological studies will permit the design of novel prevention and treatment strategies to help reduce the burden and suffering associated with the disease.

INTEGRATING GENE AND ENVIRONMENT

Ongoing Tourette's syndrome research will increasingly identify the causes and developmental course of a psychopathology,

the understanding of which will likely generalize to other disorders. The model of psychopathology that this research has thus far yielded is one of an illness in which individuals with a genetic burden, in specified adverse environmental situations, develop a particular kind of symptom that changes over the course of development. The study of this genetic burden, the endocrine modulation, the environmental interaction, and the developmental changes tells us about potential ways of understanding developmental psychopathology, the ways in which genes and environment interact in the production of a given disorder within a particular child. The interaction of these genetic and environmental determinants is further contextualized by the child's biologically and environmentally determined adaptive functioning, so that the final individual is the composite of his or her environmental and genetic vulnerability, and of the kinds of experience that have helped to shape the child's adaptive competence and functioning.

The study of childhood neuropsychiatric disorders has sometimes generated heated controversies over the primacy of psychosocial and biological determinants in the etiology and outcome of disease. More integrated biological and psychological approaches to research, however, will allow for a better explication of the multiple, interactive, and diverse determinants of normal maturation and human development. This kind of research will also provide an evolving theoretical framework for the ongoing study and improved understanding of the continuities and discontinuities between health and illness, both within and between developmental stages.

REFERENCES

Abramovich, D. R., & Rowe, P. (1973). Foetal plasma testosterone levels at mid-pregnancy and at term: Relationship to foetal sex. *Endocrinology, 56,* 621–622.

Achenbach, T. M., & Edelbrock, C. S. (1978). The classification of child psychopathology: A review and analysis of empirical efforts. *Psychology Bulletin, 85,* 1275–1301.

Akbari, H. M., Anderson, G. M., Pollak, E. S., & Cohen, D. J. (1993). Serotonin receptor binding and tissue indoles in postmortem cortex of Tourette's syndrome individuals. *Society for Neuroscience Abstracts, 83,* 838.

Alexander, G., & Crutcher, M. (1990). Functional architecture of basal ganglia circuits: Neural substrates of parallel processing. *Trends in Neuroscience, 13,* 266–271.

Alexander, G. E., Crutcher, M. D., & DeLong, M. R. (1990). Basal ganglia-thalamocortical circuits: Parallel substrates for motor, oculomotor, "prefrontal," and "limbic" functions. *Progress in Brain Research, 85,* 119–146.

Alexander, G. E., DeLong, M. R., & Strick, P. L. (1986). Parallel organization of functionally segregated circuits linking basal ganglia and cortex. *Annual Review of Neuroscience, 9,* 357–381.

Allen, L. S., Richey, M. F., Chai, Y. M., & Gorski, R. A. (1991). Sex differences in the corpus callosum of the living human being. *Journal of Neuroscience, 11,* 933–942.

Allen, R. P., Singer, H. S., Brown, J. E., & Salam, M. M. (1992). Sleep disorders in Tourette syndrome: A primary or unrelated problem? *Pediatric Neurology, 8,* 275–280.

Altemus, M., Pigott, T., Kalogeras, K. T., Demitrack, M., Dubbert, B., Murphy, D. L., & Gold, P. W. (1992). Abnormalities in the regulation of vasopressin and corticotropin releasing factor secretion in obsessive-compulsive disorder. *Archives of General Psychiatry, 49*, 9–20.

Anderson, G. M., Pollak, E. S., Chatterjee, D., Leckman, J. F., Riddle, M. A., & Cohen, D. J. (1992). Postmortem analyses of brain monoamines and amino acids in Tourette's syndrome: A preliminary study of subcortical regions. *Archives of General Psychiatry, 49*, 584–586.

Apter, A., Pauls, D. L., Bleich, A., Zohar, A. H., Kron, S., Ratzoni, G., Dycian, A., Kotler, M., Weizman, A., Gadot, N., & Cohen, D. J. (1993). An epidemiological study of Gilles de la Tourette's syndrome in Israel. *Archives of General Psychiatry, 50*, 734–738.

Baldwin, M., Frost, L. L., & Wood, C. D. (1954). Investigation of the primate amygdala. Movements of the face and jaws. *Neurology, 4*, 586–598.

Balthazar, K. (1957). Über das anatomische substrat der generalisierten tic-krankeit (maladie des tics, Gilles de la Tourette): Entwicklungshemmung des corpus striatum. *Archiv für Psychiatrie und Zeitschrift f.d.ges. Neurologie, 195*, 531–549.

Barabas, G., Matthews, W. S., & Ferrari, M. (1984). Disorders of arousal in Gilles de la Tourette's syndrome. *Neurology, 34*, 815–817.

Baron-Cohen, S., Cross, P., Crowson, M., & Robertson, M. (1994). Can children with Gilles de la Tourette syndrome edit their intentions? *Psychological Medicine, 24*, 29–40.

Baxter, L. R., Jr., Phelps, M. E., Mazziotta, J. C., Guze, B. H., Schwartz, J. M., & Selin, C. E. (1987). Local cerebral glucose metabolic rates in obsessive-compulsive disorder: A comparison with rates in unipolar depression and in normal controls. *Archives of General Psychiatry, 44*, 211–218.

Baxter, L. R., Jr., Schwartz, J. M., Mazziotta, J. C., Phelps, M. E., Pahl, J. J., Guze, B. H., & Fairbanks, L. (1988). Cerebral glucose metabolic rates in nondepressed patients with obsessive-compulsive disorder. *American Journal of Psychiatry, 145*, 1560–1563.

Behar, D., Rapoport, J. L., Berg, C. J., Denkla, M. D., Mann, L., Cox, C., Fedio, P., Zahn, T., & Wolfman, M. G. (1984). Computerized tomography and neuropsychological test measures in adolescents with obsessive-compulsive disorder. *American Journal of Psychiatry, 141*, 363–369.

Bergen, D., Tanner, C. M., & Wilson, R. (1982). The electroencephalogram in Tourette syndrome. *Annals of Neurology, 11*, 382–385.

Berkson, J. B. (1946). Limitations of the application of fourfold table analysis to hospital data. *Biometrics, 2*, 47–51.

Bliss, J. (1980). Sensory experiences of Gilles de la Tourette syndrome. *Archives of General Psychiatry, 37*, 1343–1347.

Bock, R. D., & Goldberger, L. (1985). Tonic, phasic, and cortical arousal in Gilles de la Tourette's syndrome. *Journal of Neurology, Neurosurgery, and Psychiatry, 48*, 535–544.

Bornstein, R. A. (1990). Neuropsychological performance in children with Tourette's syndrome. *Psychiatry Research, 33*, 73–81.

Bornstein, R. A. (1991). Neuropsychological correlates of obsessive characteristics in Tourette's syndrome. *Journal of Neuropsychiatry and Clinical Neurosciences, 3*, 157–162.

Bornstein, R. A., & Yang, V. (1991). Neuropsychological performance in medicated and unmedicated patients with Tourette's disorder. *American Journal of Psychiatry, 148*, 468–471.

Bowers, D., & Heilman, K. M. (1980). Pseudoneglect: Effects of hemispace on a tactile line bisection task. *Neuropsychologia, 18*, 491–498.

Braun, A. R., Stoetter, B., Randolph, C., Hsiao, H. K., Vladar, K., Gernert, J., Carson, R. E., Herscovitch, P., & Chase, T. N. (1993). The functional neuroanatomy of Tourette's syndrome: An FDG-PET study. I. Regional changes in cerebral glucose metabolism differentiating patients and controls. *Neuropsychopharmacology, 9*, 277–291.

Brooks, D. J., Turjanski, N., Sawle, G. V., Playford, E. D., & Lees, A. J. (1992). PET studies on the integrity of the pre and postsynaptic dopaminergic system in Tourette syndrome. In T. N. Chase, A. J. Friedhoff, & D. J. Cohen (Eds.), *Advances in neurology—Tourette syndrome: Genetics, neurobiology, and treatment* (Vol. 58, pp. 227–231). New York: Raven Press.

Bruun, R. D. (1988). The natural history of Tourette's syndrome. In D. J. Cohen, R. D. Bruun, & J. F. Leckman (Eds.), *Tourette's syndrome and tic disorders: Clinical understanding and treatment* (pp. 21–39). New York: Wiley.

Burd, L., & Kerbeshian, J. (1987). Onset of Gilles de la Tourette's syndrome before 1 year of age. *American Journal of Psychiatry, 144*, 1066–1067.

Burd, L., Kerbeshian, L., Wikenheiser, M., & Fisher, W. (1986). Prevalence of Gilles de la Tourette's syndrome in North Dakota adults. *American Journal of Psychiatry, 143*, 787.

Butler, I. J., Koslow, S. H., Seifert, W. E., Caprioli, R. M., & Singer, H. S. (1979). Biogenic amine metabolism in Tourette syndrome. *Annals of Neurology, 6*, 37–39.

Caine, E. D., McBride, M. C., Chiverton, P., Bamford, K. A., Rediess, S., & Shiao, S. (1988). Tourette syndrome in Monroe county schoolchildren. *Neurology, 38*, 472–475.

Cannon, T. D., Mednick, S. A., Parnas, J., Schulsinger, F., Praestholm, J., & Vestergaard, A. (1993). Developmental brain abnormalities in the offspring of schizophrenic mothers. I. Contributions of genetic and perinatal factors. *Archives of General Psychiatry, 50*, 551–564.

Carter, A. S., Pauls, D. L., Leckman, J. F., & Cohen, D. J. (1994). A prospective longitudinal study of Gilles de la Tourette's syndrome. *Journal of the American Academy of Child and Adolescent Psychiatry.*

Castellanos, F. X., Fine, E. J., Kaysen, D. L., Kozuch, P. L., Hamburger, S. D., & Rapoport, J. L. (1993). Sensorimotor gating in boys with Tourette's syndrome (TS) and attention deficit hyperactivity disorder (ADHD) [abstract]. *Society for Neuroscience Abstracts, 19*(2), 991.

Chappell, P. B., Leckman, J. F., Pauls, D., & Cohen, D. J. (1990). Biochemical and genetic studies of Tourette's syndrome: Implications for treatment and future research. In S. Deutsch, A. Weizman, & R. Weizman (Eds.), *Application of basic neuroscience to child psychiatry* (pp. 241–260). New York: Plenum.

Chappell, P. B., Leckman, J. F., Riddle, M. A., Anderson, G. M., Listwak, S. J., Ort, S. I., Hardin, M. T., Scahill, L. D., & Cohen, D. J. (1992). Neuroendocrine and behavioral responses to naloxone in Tourette's syndrome. In T. N. Chase, A. J. Friedhoff, & D. J. Cohen (Eds.), *Advances in neurology—Tourette syndrome: Genetics, neurobiology, and treatment* (Vol. 58, pp. 253–262). New York: Raven Press.

Chappell, P. B., McSwiggan-Hardin, M. T., Scahill, L., Rubenstein, M., Walker, D. E., Cohen, D. J., & Leckman, J. F. (1994). Videotape tic counts in the assessment of Tourette's syndrome: Stability, reliability, and validity. *Journal of the American Academy of Child and Adolescent Psychiatry, 33*, 386–393.

Chappell, P. B., Riddle, M. A., Anderson, G. M., Scahill, L. D., Hardin, M. T., Walker, D. E., Cohen, D. J., & Leckman, J. F. (1994). Enhanced stress responsivity of Tourette syndrome patients undergoing lumbar puncture. *Biological Psychiatry, 36*, 35–43.

Chase, T. N., Geoffrey, V., Gillespie, M., & Burrows, G. H. (1986). Structural and functional studies of Gilles de la Tourette's syndrome. *Revue Neurologique (Paris), 142,* 851–855.

Cohen, A., & Leckman, J. F. (1992). Sensory phenomena associated with Gilles de la Tourette syndrome. *Journal of Clinical Psychiatry, 53,* 319–323.

Cohen, D. J. (1991). Tourette's syndrome: A model disorder for integrating psychoanalytic and biological perspectives. *International Review of Psychoanalysis, 18,* 195–209.

Cohen, D. J., Friedhoff, A. J., Leckman, J. F., & Chase, T. N. (1992). Tourette syndrome: Extending basic research to clinical care, the clinical phenotype, and natural history. In T. N. Chase, A. J. Friedhoff, & D. J. Cohen (Eds.), *Advances in neurology—Tourette syndrome: Genetics, neurobiology, and treatment* (Vol. 58, pp. 341–362). New York: Raven Press.

Cohen, D. J., & Leckman, J. F. (1994). Developmental psychopathology and neurobiology of Tourette's syndrome. *Journal of the American Academy of Child and Adolescent Psychiatry, 33,* 2–15.

Cohen, D. J., Leckman, J. F., & Shaywitz, B. A. (1984). The Tourette's syndrome and other tics. In D. Shaffer, A. A. Ehrhardt, & L. Greenhill (Eds.), *Diagnosis and treatment in pediatric psychiatry* (pp. 3–28). New York: Macmillan.

Cohen, D. J., Shaywitz, B. A., Young, J. G., Carbonari, C. M., Nathanson, J. A., Lieberman, D., Bowers, M. B., & Maas, J. W. (1979). Central biogenic amine metabolism in children with the syndrome of chronic multiple tics of Gilles de la Tourette: Norepinephrine, serotonin and dopamine. *Journal of the American Academy of Child Psychiatry, 18,* 320–341.

Comings, D. E. (1987). A controlled study of Tourette syndrome. I–VI. *American Journal of Human Genetics, 41,* 701–838.

Comings, D. E. (1990). Blood serotonin and tryptophan in Tourette syndrome. *American Journal of Medical Genetics, 36,* 418–430.

Comings, D. E., & Comings, B. G. (1984). Tourette syndrome and attention deficit disorder with hyperactivity—are they genetically related? *Journal of the American Academy of Child Psychiatry, 23,* 138–144.

Comings, D. E., & Comings, B. G. (1987). Hereditary agoraphobia and obsessive-compulsive behavior in relatives of patients with Gilles de la Tourette's syndrome. *British Journal of Psychiatry, 151,* 195–199.

Comings, D. E., & Comings, B. G. (1993). Comorbid behavioral disorders. In R. Kurlan (Ed.), *Handbook of Tourette's syndrome and related tic and behavioral disorders* (pp. 111–147). New York: Marcel Dekker.

Comings, D. E., Himes, J. A., & Comings, B. G. (1990). An epidemiological study of Tourette's syndrome in a single school district. *Journal of Clinical Psychiatry, 51,* 463–469.

Debray-Ritzen, P., & Dubois, H. (1980). Maladies des tics de l'enfant [children's tic disorders]. *Revue Neurologique, 136,* 15–18.

Denckla, M. B., Harris, E. L., Aylward, E. H., Singer, H. S., Reiss, A. L., Reader, M. J., Bryan, R. N., & Chase, G. A. (1991). Executive functions and volume of the basal ganglia in children with Tourette's syndrome and attention deficit hyperactivity disorder. *Annals of Neurology, 30,* 476.

DeVries, G. J., Best, W., & Sluiter, A. A. (1983). The influence of androgens on the development of a sex difference in the vasopressinergic innervation of the rat lateral septum. *Developmental Brain Research, 8,* 377–380.

DeVries, G. J., Buijs, R. M., Van Leeuwen, F. W., Caffe, A. R., & Swaab, D. F. (1985). The vasopressinergic innervation of the brain in normal and castrated rats. *Journal of Comparative Neurology, 233,* 236–254.

Doris, P. A. (1984). Vasopressin and central integrative processes. *Progress in Neuroendocrinology, 38,* 75–85.

Drake, M. E., Hietter, S. A., Padamadan, H., Bogner, J. E., Andrews, J. M., & Weate, S. (1992). Auditory evoked potentials in Gilles de la Tourette syndrome. *Clinical Electroencephalography, 23,* 19–23.

Dykens, E. M., Leckman, J. F., Riddle, M. A., Hardin, M. T., Schwartz, S., & Cohen, D. J. (1990). Intellectual, academic, and adaptive functioning of Tourette syndrome children with and without attention deficit disorder. *Journal of Abnormal Child Psychology, 18,* 607–614.

Edell, B. H., & Motta, R. W. (1989). The emotional adjustment of children with Tourette's syndrome. *Journal of Psychology, 123,* 51–57.

Elands, J., Beetsma, A., Barberis, C., & de Kloet, E. R. (1988). Topography of the oxytocin receptor system in rat brain: An autoradiographical study with a selective radioiodinated oxytocin antagonist. *Journal of Clinical Neuroanatomy, 1,* 293–302.

Erenberg, G., Cruse, R. P., & Rothner, A. D. (1987). The natural history of Tourette syndrome: A follow-up study. *Annals of Neurology, 22,* 383–385.

Feinstein, A. R. (1985). *Clinical epidemiology. The architecture of clinical research* (pp. 434–437). Philadelphia: Saunders.

Fleming, B. E., Anderson, R. H., Rhees, R. W., Kinghorn, E., & Bakaitis, J. (1986). Effects of prenatal stress on sexually dimorphic asymmetries in the cerebral cortex of the rat. *Brain Research Bulletin, 16,* 395–398.

Forest, M. G. (1989). Physiological changes in circulating androgens. *Pediatric and Adolescent Endocrinology, 19,* 104–129.

Frank, M. S., Sieg, K. G., & Gaffney, G. R. (1991). Somatic complaints in childhood tic disorders. *Psychosomatics, 32,* 396–399.

Fride, E., & Weinstock, M. (1988). Prenatal stress increases anxiety related behavior and alters cerebral lateralization of dopamine activity. *Life Sciences, 42,* 1059–1065.

Fride, E., & Weinstock, M. (1989). Alterations in behavioral and striatal dopamine asymmetries induced by prenatal stress. *Pharmacology, Biochemistry, & Behavior, 32,* 425–430.

George, M. S., Trimble, M. R., Costa, D. C., Robertson, M. M., Ring, H. A., & Ell, P. J. (1992). Elevated frontal cerebral blood flow in Gilles de la Tourette syndrome: A ^{99}Tc^m-HMPAO SPECT study. *Psychiatry Research: Neuroimaging, 45,* 143–151.

George, M. S., Trimble, M. R., Ring, H. A., Sallee, F. R., & Robertson, M. M. (1993). Obsessions in obsessive-compulsive disorder with and without Gilles de la Tourette's syndrome. *American Journal of Psychiatry, 150,* 93–97.

Giedd, J., Castellanos, F., Casey, B., Kozuch, P., King, A., Hamburger, S., & Rapoport, J. (1994). Quantitative morphology of the corpus callosum in attention deficit hyperactivity disorder. *American Journal of Psychiatry, 151,* 665–669.

Glaze, D. G., Frost, J. D., & Jankovic, J. (1983). Sleep in Gilles de la Tourette's syndrome: Disorder of arousal. *Neurology, 33,* 586–592.

Goetz, C. G., Tanner, C. M., Stebbins, G. T., Leipzig, G., & Carr, W. C. (1992). Adult tics in Gilles de la Tourette's syndrome: Description and risk factors. *Neurology, 42,* 784–788.

Golden, G. S. (1974). Gilles de la Tourette syndrome following methylphenidate administration. *Developmental Medicine and Child Neurology, 16,* 76–78.

Goldman-Rakic, P. S., & Selemon, L. D. (1990). New frontiers in basal ganglia research. *Trends in Neuroscience, 13,* 241–244.

Graybiel, A. M. (1984). Neurochemically specific subsystems in the basal ganglia. In E. V. Evarts (Ed.), *Functions of the basal ganglia* (pp. 114–149). London: Pittman (CIBA Foundation Symposium 107).

Graybiel, A. M. (1990). Neurotransmitters and neuromodulators in the basal ganglia. *Trends in Neuroscience, 13,* 244–254.

Haber, S. N., Kowall, N. W., Vonsattel, J. P., Bird, E. D., Richardson, E. P., Jr. (1986). A postmortem neuropathological and immunohistochemical study. *Journal of Neurological Sciences, 75,* 225–241.

Hanin, I., Merikangas, J. R., Merikangas, K. R., & Kopp, U. (1979). Red-cell choline and Gilles de la Tourette syndrome. *New England Journal of Medicine, 301,* 661–662.

Hayakawa, K., Konishi, Y., Matsuda, T., Kuriyama, M., Konishi, K., Yamashita, K., Okumura, R., & Hamanaka, D. (1989). Development and aging of brain midline structures: Assessment with MR imaging. *Radiology, 172,* 171–177.

Hruska, R. E., & Nowak, M. W. (1988). Estrogen treatment increases the density of D_1 dopamine receptors in the rat striatum. *Brain Research, 442,* 349–350.

Husby, G., Van de Rijn, I., Zabriskie, J. B., Abdin, Z. H., & Williams, R. C. (1956). Antibodies reacting with cytoplasm of subthalamic and caudate nuclei neurons in chorea and acute rheumatic fever. *Journal of Experimental Medicine, 144,* 1094–1110.

Hyde, T. M., Aaronson, B. A., Randolph, C., Rickler, K. C., & Weinberger, D. R. (1992). Relationship of birth weight to the phenotypic expression of Gilles de la Tourette's syndrome in monozygotic twins. *Neurology, 42,* 652–658.

Hynd, G. W., Hern, K. L., Novey, E. S., Eliopulos, D., Marshall, R., Gonzalez, J. J., & Voeller, K. K. (1993). Attention deficit-hyperactivity disorder and asymmetry of the caudate nucleus. *Journal of Child Neurology, 8,* 339–347.

Hynd, G. W., Semrud-Clikeman, M., Lorys, A. R., Novey, E. S., Eliopulos, D., & Lyytinen, H. (1991). Corpus callosum morphology in attention deficit-hyperactivity disorder: Morphometric analysis of MRI. *Journal of Learning Disabilities, 24,* 141–146.

Incagnoli, T., & Kane, R. (1981). Neuropsychological functioning in Gilles de la Tourette's syndrome. *Journal of Clinical Neuropsychology, 3,* 165–169.

Insel, T. R., Kinsley, C. H., Mann, P. E., & Bridges, R. S. (1990). Prenatal stress has long-term effects on brain opiate receptors. *Brain Research, 511,* 93–97.

Jagger, J., Prusoff, B. A., Cohen, D. J., Kidd, K. K., Carbonari, C. M., & John, K. (1982). The epidemiology of Tourette syndrome: A pilot study. *Schizophrenia Bulletin, 8,* 267–278.

Jankovic, J., Glaze, D. G., & Frost, J. D. (1984). Effect of tetrabenazine on tics and sleep of Gilles de la Tourette's syndrome. *Neurology, 34,* 688–692.

Joschko, M., & Rourke, B. P. (1982). Neuropsychological dimensions of Tourette syndrome: Test-retest stability and implications for intervention. In A. J. Friedhoff & T. N. Chase (Eds.), *Gilles de la Tourette syndrome* (pp. 297–304). New York: Raven Press.

Karson, C. N., Kaufmann, C. A., Shapiro, A. K., & Shapiro, E. (1985). Eye-blink rate in Tourette's syndrome. *Journal of Nervous and Mental Disease, 173,* 566–569.

Keller, I., & Heckhausen, H. (1990). Readiness potentials preceding spontaneous motor acts: Voluntary versus involuntary control. *Electroencephalography and Clinical Neurophysiology, 76,* 351–361.

Kelley, A. E., Lang, C. G., & Gauthier, A. M. (1988). Induction of oral stereotype following amphetamine microinjection into a discrete subregion of the striatum. *Psychopharmacology (Berl), 95,* 556–559.

Kellner, C. H., Jolley, R. R., Holgate, R. C., Austin, L., Lydiard, R. B., Laraia, M., & Ballenger, J. C. (1991). Brain MRI in obsessive-compulsive disorder. *Psychiatry Research, 36,* 45–49.

Kidd, K. K., Prusoff, B. A., & Cohen, D. J. (1980). The familial pattern of Gilles de la Tourette syndrome. *Archives of General Psychiatry, 37,* 1336–1339.

Kiessling, L. S., Marcotte, A. C., & Culpepper, L. (1993a). Antineuronal antibodies: Tics and obsessive compulsive symptoms. *Journal of Developmental and Behavioral Pediatrics, 14,* 281–282.

Kiessling, L. S., Marcotte, A. C., & Culpepper, L. (1993b). Antineuronal antibodies in movement disorders. *Pediatrics, 92,* 39–43.

Kooistra, C. A., & Heilman, K. M. (1988). Motor dominance and lateral asymmetry of the globus pallidus. *Neurology, 38,* 388–390.

Krumholz, A., Singer, H. S., Niedermeyer, E., Burnite, R., & Harris, K. (1983). Electrophysiological studies in Tourette's syndrome. *Annals of Neurology, 14,* 638–641.

Kurlan, R., Behr, J., Medved, L., Shoulson, I., Pauls, D., Kidd, J. R., & Kidd, K. K. (1986). Familial Tourette's syndrome: Report of a large pedigree and potential for linkage analysis. *Neurology, 36,* 772–776.

Kurlan, R., Lichter, D., & Hewitt, D. (1989). Sensory tics in Tourette's syndrome. *Neurology, 41,* 223–228.

LaMantia, A.-S., & Rakic, P. (1990). Axon overproduction and elimination in the corpus callosum of the developing rhesus monkey. *Journal of Neuroscience, 10,* 2156–2175.

Lang, A. (1991). Patient perception of tics and other movement disorders. *Neurology, 41,* 223–228.

Lapouse, R., & Monk, M. A. (1964). Behavior deviations in a representative sample of children: Variation between sex, age, race, social class, and family size. *American Journal of Orthopsychiatry, 34,* 436–446.

Leckman, J. F., Anderson, G. M., Cohen, D. J., Ort, S., Harcherik, D. F., Hoder, E. L., & Shaywitz, B. A. (1984). Whole blood serotonin and tryptophan levels in Tourette's disorder: Effects of acute and chronic clonidine. *Life Science, 35,* 2497–2503.

Leckman, J. F., de Lotbinière, A. J., Marek, K., Gracco, C., Scahill, L. D., & Cohen, D. J. (1993). Severe disturbances in speech, swallowing, and gait following stereotactic infrathalamic lesions in Gilles de la Tourette's syndrome. *Neurology, 43,* 890–894.

Leckman, J. F., Dolnansky, E. S., Hardin, M. T., Clubb, M., Walkup, J. T., Stevenson, J., & Pauls, D. L. (1990). Perinatal factors in the expression of Tourette's syndrome: An exploratory study. *Journal of the American Academy of Child and Adolescent Psychiatry, 2,* 220–226.

Leckman, J. F., Goodman, W. K., North, W. G., Chappell, P. B., Price, L. H., Pauls, D. L., Anderson, G. M., Riddle, M. A., McDougle, C. J., Barr, L. C., & Cohen, D. J. (1994a). The role of central oxytocin in obsessive compulsive disorder and related normal behavior. *Psychoneuroendocrinology, 19,* 742–758.

Leckman, J. F., Goodman, W. K., North, W. G., Chappell, P. B., Price, L. H., Pauls, D. L., Anderson, G. M., Riddle, M. A., McSwiggan-Hardin, M., McDougle, C. J., Barr, L. C., & Cohen, D. J. (1994b). Elevated levels of CSF oxytocin in obsessive compulsive disorder: Comparison with Tourette's syndrome and healthy controls. *Archives of General Psychiatry, 51,* 782–792.

Leckman, J. F., Hardin, M. T., Riddle, M. A., Stevenson, J., Ort, S. I., & Cohen, D. J. (1991). Clonidine treatment of Gilles de la Tourette's syndrome. *Archives of General Psychiatry, 48,* 324–328.

Leckman, J. F., Knorr, A., Rasmusson, A. M., & Cohen, D. J. (1991). Another frontier for basal ganglia research: Tourette's syndrome and related disorders. *Trends in Neuroscience, 3,* 207–211.

Leckman, J. F., Pauls, D. L., Peterson, B. S., Riddle, M. A., Anderson, G. M., & Cohen, D. J. (1992). Pathogenesis of Tourette's syndrome: Clues from the clinical phenotype and natural history. In T. N. Chase, A. J. Friedhoff, & D. J. Cohen (Eds.), *Advances in neurology—Tourette syndrome: Genetics, neurobiology, and treatment* (Vol. 58, pp. 15–23). New York: Raven Press.

Leckman, J. F., & Peterson, B. S. (1993). The pathogenesis of Tourette's syndrome: Role of epigenetic factors active in early CNS development. *Biological Psychiatry, 34,* 425–427.

Leckman, J. F., Price, R. A., Walkup, J. T., Ort, S. I., Pauls, D. L., & Cohen, D. J. (1987). Birth weights of monozygotic twins discordant for Tourette's syndrome. *Archives of General Psychiatry, 44,* 100.

Leckman, J. F., Riddle, M. A., Berrettini, W. H., Anderson, G. M., Hardin, M. T., Chappell, P. B., Bissette, G., Nemeroff, C. B., Goodman, W. K., & Cohen, D. J. (1988). Elevated CSF dynorphin A[1–8] in Tourette's syndrome. *Life Sciences, 43,* 2015–2023.

Leckman, J. F., Riddle, M. A., Hardin, M. T., Ort, S. I., Swartz, K. L., Stevenson, J., & Cohen, D. J. (1989). The Yale Global Tic Severity Scale (YGTSS): Initial testing of a clinician-rated scale of tic severity. *Journal of the American Academy of Child and Adolescent Psychiatry, 28,* 566–573.

Leckman, J. F., & Scahill, L. (1990). Possible exacerbation of tics by androgenic steroids. *New England Journal of Medicine, 322,* 1674.

Leckman, J. F., Walker, D. E., & Cohen, D. J. (1993). Premonitory urges in Tourette's syndrome. *American Journal of Psychiatry, 150,* 98–102.

Leckman, J. F., Walker, D. E., Goodman, W. K., Pauls, D. L., & Cohen, D. J. (1994). "Just right" perceptions associated with compulsive behaviors in Tourette's syndrome. *American Journal of Psychiatry, 151,* 675–680.

Leckman, J. F., Walkup, J. T., & Cohen, D. J. (1987). Tic disorders. In H. Meltzer (Ed.), *Psychopharmacology: The third generation of progress* (pp. 1239–1246). New York: Raven Press.

Leckman, J. F., Weissman, M. M., Pauls, D. L., & Kidd, K. K. (1987). Family-genetic studies and the identification of valid diagnostic categories in adult and child psychiatry. *British Journal of Psychiatry, 151,* 39–44.

Leonard, H. L., Goldberger, E. L., Rapoport, J. L., Cheslow, D. L., & Swedo, S. E. (1990). Childhood rituals: Normal development or obsessive-compulsive symptoms? *Journal of the American Academy of Child and Adolescent Psychiatry, 29,* 17–23.

Leonard, H. L., Lenane, M. C., Swedo, S. E., Rettew, D. C., Gershon, E. S., & Rapoport, J. L. (1992). Tics and Tourette's syndrome: A 2- to 7-year follow-up of 54 obsessive-compulsive children. *American Journal of Psychiatry, 149,* 1244–1251.

Leonard, H. L., Swedo, S. E., Lenane, M. C., Rettew, D. C., Hamburger, S. D., Bartko, J. J., & Rapoport, J. L. (1993). A 2- to 7-year follow-up study of 54 obsessive-compulsive children and adolescents. *Archives of General Psychiatry, 50,* 429–439.

Lombroso, P. J., Mack, G., Scahill, L., King, R., & Leckman, J. F. (1991). Exacerbation of Tourette's syndrome associated with thermal stress: A family study. *Neurology, 41,* 1984–1987.

Loup, R., Tribollet, E., DuBois-Dauphin, M., Pizzolato, G., & Dreifuss, J. J. (1991). Localization of high-affinity binding sites for oxytocin and vasopressin in the human brain: An autoradiographic study. *Brain Research, 555,* 320–322.

Lowe, T. L., Cohen, D. J., Detlor, J., Kremenitzer, M. W., & Shaywitz, B. A. (1982). Stimulant medications precipitate Tourette's syndrome. *Journal of the American Medical Association, 247,* 1729–1731.

Luxenberg, J. S., Swedo, S. E., Flament, M. F., Friedland, R. P., Rapoport, J., & Rapoport, S. I. (1988). Neuroanatomical abnormalities in obsessive-compulsive disorder detected with quantitative X-ray computed tomography. *American Journal of Psychiatry, 145,* 1089–1093.

Machlin, S. R., Harris, G. J., Pearlson, G. D., Hoehn-Saric, R., Jeffery, P., & Camargo, E. E. (1991). Elevated medial-frontal cerebral blood flow in obsessive-compulsive patients: A SPECT study. *American Journal of Psychiatry, 148,* 1240–1242.

Mahler, S. M., Luke, J. A., & Daltroff, W. (1945). Clinical and follow-up study of the tic syndrome in children. *American Journal of Orthopsychiatry, 15,* 631–647.

Manning, L., Halligan, P. W., & Marshall, J. C. (1990). Individual variation in line bisection: A study of normal subjects with application to the interpretation of visual neglect. *Neuropsychologia, 28,* 647–655.

Marcus, J., Hans, S. L., Auerbach, J. G., & Auerbach, A. G. (1993). Children at risk for schizophrenia: The Jerusalem infant development study. *Archives of General Psychiatry, 50,* 797–809.

McDougle, C. J., Goodman, W. K., Leckman, J. F., Lee, N. C., Heninger, G. R., & Price, L. H. (1994). Haloperidol addition in fluvoxamine-refractory obsessive compulsive disorder: A double-blind, placebo-controlled study in patients with and without tics. *Archives of General Psychiatry, 51,* 302–308.

McLean, P., & Delgado, J. (1953). Electrical and chemical stimulation of frontotemporal portion of limbic system in the waking animal. *Electroencephalography and Clinical Neurophysiology, 5,* 91–100.

Mednick, S. A., Machon, R. A., Huttunen, M. O., & Bonett, D. (1988). Adult schizophrenia following prenatal exposure to an influenza epidemic. *Archives of General Psychiatry, 45,* 189–192.

Mendelson, W. B., Caine, E. D., Goyer, P., Ebert, M., & Gillin, J. C. (1980). Sleep in Gilles de la Tourette syndrome. *Biological Psychiatry, 15,* 339–343.

Mesulam, M. M. (1986). Cocaine and Tourette's syndrome. *New England Journal of Medicine, 315,* 398.

Mesulam, M. M. (1990). Large-scale neurocognitive networks and distributed processing for attention, language, and memory. *Annals of Neurology, 28,* 597–613.

Moldofsky, H., & Sandor, P. (1983). Lecithin in the treatment of Gilles de la Tourette's syndrome. *American Journal of Psychiatry, 140,* 1627–1629.

Morissette, M., Levesque, D., Belanger, A., & DePaolo, T. (1990). A physiological dose of estradiol with progesterone affects striatum biogenic amines. *Canadian Journal of Physiology and Pharmacology, 68,* 1520–1526.

Müller, F., & O'Rahilly, R. (1990a). The human brain at stages 18–20, including the choroid plexuses and the amygdaloid and septal nuclei. *Anatomy and Embryology, 182,* 285–306.

Müller, F., & O'Rahilly, R. (1990b). The human brain at stages 21–23, with particular reference to the cerebral cortical plate and to the development of the cerebellum. *Anatomy and Embryology, 182,* 375–400.

Nasrallah, H. A., Loney, J., Olson, S. C., McCalley-Whitters, M., Kramer, J., & Jacoby, C. G. (1986). Cortical atrophy in young adults with a history of hyperactivity in childhood. *Psychiatry Research, 17,* 241–246.

Nee, L. E., Polinsky, R. J., & Ebert, M. H. (1982). Tourette syndrome: Clinical and family studies. In A. J. Friedhoff & T. N. Chase (Eds.), *Gilles de la Tourette syndrome* (pp. 291–295). New York: Raven Press.

Nelson, K. B. (1991). Prenatal and perinatal factors in the etiology of autism. *Pediatrics, 87,* 761–766.

Neufeld, M. Y., Berger, Y., Chapman, J., & Korczyn, A. D. (1990). Routine and quantitative EEG analysis in Gilles de la Tourette's syndrome. *Neurology, 40,* 1837–1839.

Nomoto, F., & Machiyama, Y. (1990). An epidemiological study of tics. *Japanese Journal of Psychiatry and Neurology, 44,* 649–655.

Nordahl, T. E., Benkelfat, C., Semple, W. E., Gross, M., King, A. C., & Cohen, R. M. (1989). Cerebral glucose metabolic rates in obsessive-compulsive disorder. *Neuropsychopharmacology, 2,* 23–28.

Obeso, J. A., Rothwell, J. C., & Marsden, C. D. (1981). Simple tics in Gilles de la Tourette's syndrome are not prefaced by a normal premovement EEG potential. *Journal of Neurology, Neurosurgery, and Psychiatry, 44,* 735–738.

Oppenheim, J. S., Skerry, J. E., Tramo, M. J., & Gazzaniga, M. S. (1989). Magnetic resonance imaging morphology of the corpus callosum in monozygotic twins. *Annals of Neurology, 26,* 100–104.

Ornitz, E. M., Guthrie, D., Kaplan, A. R., Lane, S. J., & Norman, R. J. (1986). Maturation of startle modulation. *Psychophysiology, 23,* 624–634.

Ornitz, E. M., Guthrie, D., Sadeghpour, M., & Sugiyama, T. (1991). Maturation of prestimulation-induced startle modulation in girls. *Psychophysiology, 28,* 11–20.

Ornitz, E. M., Hanna, G. L., & DeTraversay, J. (1992). Prestimulation-induced startle modulation in attention-deficit hyperactivity disorder and nocturnal enuresis. *Psychophysiology, 29,* 437–451.

Pakstis, A., Heutink, P., Pauls, D. L., Kurlan, R., van de Wetering, B. J. M., Leckman, J. F., Sandkuyl, L. A., Kidd, J. R., Breedveld, G. J., Castiglione, C. M., Weber, J., Sparkes, R. S., Cohen, D. J., Kidd, K. K., & Oostra, B. A. (1991). Progress in the search for genetic linkage with Tourette syndrome: An exclusion map covering more than 50% of the autosomal genome. *American Journal of Human Genetics, 48,* 281–294.

Parent, A. (1990). Extrinsic connections of the basal ganglia. *Trends in Neuroscience, 13,* 254–258.

Park, S., Como, P. G., Cui, L., & Kurlan, R. (1993). The early course of the Tourette's syndrome clinical spectrum. *Neurology, 43,* 1712–1715.

Pasamanick, B., & Kawi, A. (1956). A study of the association of prenatal and perinatal factors in the development of tics in children. *Journal of Pediatrics, 48,* 596.

Pauls, D. L., Alsobrook, J. P., Goodman, W. K., Rasmussen, S., & Leckman, J. F. (in press). A family study of obsessive compulsive disorder. *American Journal of Psychiatry.*

Pauls, D. L., Hurst, C. R., Kruger, S. D., Leckman, J. F., Kidd, K. K., & Cohen, D. J. (1986). Gilles de la Tourette's syndrome and attention deficit disorder: Evidence against a genetic relationship. *Archives of General Psychiatry, 43,* 1177–1179.

Pauls, D. L., & Leckman, J. F. (1986). The inheritance of Gilles de la Tourette syndrome and associated behaviors: Evidence for autosomal dominant transmission. *New England Journal of Medicine, 315,* 993–997.

Pauls, D. L., Leckman, J. F., & Cohen, D. J. (1993). Familial relationship between Gilles de la Tourette's syndrome, attention deficit disorder, learning disabilities, speech disorders, and stuttering. *Journal of the American Academy of Child and Adolescent Psychiatry, 32,* 1044–1050.

Pauls, D. L., Raymond, C., Stevenson, J., & Leckman, J. F. (1990). A family study of Gilles de la Tourette syndrome. *American Journal of Human Genetics, 48,* 154–163.

Pauls, D. L., Towbin, K. E., Leckman, J. F., Zahner, G., & Cohen, D. J. (1986). Gilles de la Tourette's syndrome and obsessive-compulsive disorder: Evidence supporting a genetic relationship. *Archives of General Psychiatry, 43,* 1180–1182.

Peters, D. A. V. (1982). Prenatal stress: Effects on brain biogenic amine and plasma corticosterone levels. *Pharmacology, Biochemistry, and Behavior, 17,* 721–725.

Peters, D. A. V. (1990). Maternal stress increases fetal brain and neonatal cerebral cortex 5-hydroxytryptamine synthesis in rats: A possible mechanism by which stress influences brain development. *Pharmacology, Biochemistry, and Behavior, 35,* 943–947.

Peterson, B. S., Leckman, J. F., Scahill, L., Naftolin, F., Keefe, D., Charest, N. J., & Cohen, D. J. (1993). Hypothesis: Steroid hormones and CNS sexual dimorphisms modulate symptom expression in Tourette's syndrome. *Psychoneuroendocrinology, 17,* 553–563.

Peterson, B. S., Leckman, J. F., Scahill, L., Naftolin, F., Keefe, D., Charest, N. J., King, R. A., Hardin, M. T., & Cohen, D. J. (1994). Steroid hormones and Tourette's syndrome: Early experience with antiandrogen therapy. *Journal of Clinical Psychopharmacology, 14,* 131–135.

Peterson, B. S., Leckman, J. F., Wetzles, R., Duncan, J., Riddle, M. A., Hardin, M. T., & Cohen, D. J. (1994). Corpus callosum morphology from MR images in Tourette's syndrome. *Psychiatry Research: Neuroimaging, 55,* 85–99.

Peterson, B. S., Riddle, M. A., Cohen, D. J., Katz, L. D., Smith, J. C., Hardin, M. T., & Leckman, J. F. (1993). Reduced basal ganglia volumes in Tourette's syndrome using 3-dimensional reconstruction techniques from magnetic resonance images. *Neurology, 43,* 941–949.

Peterson, B. S., Riddle, M. A., Cohen, D. J., Katz, L., Smith, J., & Leckman, J. F. (1993). Human basal ganglia volume asymmetries on magnetic resonance images. *Magnetic Resonance Imaging, 11,* 493–498.

Peterson, B. S., Riddle, M. A., Gore, J. C., Cohen, D. J., & Leckman, J. F. (in press). CNA T_2 relaxation time asymmetries in Tourette's syndrome. *Psychiatric Research: Neuroimaging.*

Polinsky, R. J., Ebert, M. H., Caine, E. D., Ludlow, C., & Bassich, C. J. (1980). Cholinergic treatment in the Tourette syndrome [let]. *New England Journal of Medicine, 302,* 1310.

Price, R. A., Kidd, K. K., Cohen, D. J., Pauls, D. J., & Leckman, J. F. (1985). A twin study of Tourette's syndrome. *Archives of General Psychiatry, 42,* 815–820.

Ramaekers, G. (1991). Embryology and anatomy or the corpus callosum. In G. Ramaekers & C. Njiokiktjien (Eds.), *The child's corpus callosum* (pp. 34–39). Amsterdam, The Netherlands: Suyi Publications.

Randolph, C., Hyde, T. M., Gold, J. M., Goldberg, T. E., & Weinberger, D. R. (1993). Tourette's syndrome in monozygotic twins: Relationship of tic severity to neuropsychological function. *Archives of Neurology, 50,* 725–728.

Rauch, S. L., Jenike, M. A., Alpert, N. M., Baer, L., Breiter, H. C. R., Savage, C. R., & Fischman, A. J. (1994). Regional cerebral blood flow measured during symptom provocation in obsessive-compulsive disorder using oxygen 15-labeled carbon dioxide and positron emission tomography. *Archives of General Psychiatry, 51,* 62–70.

Richardson, E. P. (1982). Neuropathological studies of Tourette syndrome. In A. J. Friedhoff & T. N. Chase (Eds.), *Gilles de la Tourette syndrome* (pp. 83–87). New York: Raven Press.

Riddle, M. A., Anderson, G. M., McIntosh, S., Harcherik, D. F., Shaywitz, B. A., & Cohen, D. J. (1986). Cerebrospinal fluid monoamine precursor and metabolite levels in children treated for leukemia: Age and sex effects and individual variability. *Biological Psychiatry, 21,* 69–83.

Riddle, M. A., Rasmusson, A. M., Woods, S. W., & Hoffer, P. B. (1992). SPECT imaging of cerebral blood flow in Tourette syndrome. In T. N. Chase, A. J. Friedhoff, & D. J. Cohen (Eds.), *Advances in neurology—Tourette syndrome: Genetics, neurobiology, and treatment* (Vol. 58, pp. 207–211). New York: Raven Press.

Riddle, M. A., Scahill, L., King, R. A., Hardin, M. T., Anderson, G. M., Ort, S. I., Smith, J. C., Leckman, J. F., & Cohen, D. J. (1992). Double-blind, crossover trial of fluoxetine and placebo in children and adolescents with obsessive-compulsive disorder. *Journal of the American Academy of Child and Adolescent Psychiatry, 31,* 1062–1069.

Robins, E., & Guze, S. B. (1970). Establishment of diagnostic validity in psychiatric illness: Its application to schizophrenia. *American Journal of Psychiatry, 126,* 107–111.

Rubin, R. T., Villanueva-Meyer, J., Ananth, J., Trajmar, P. G., & Mena, I. (1992). Regional Xenon 133 cerebral blood flow and cerebral Technetium 99m HMPAO uptake in unmedicated patients with obsessive-compulsive disorder and matched normal control subjects. Determination by high-resolution single-photon emission computed tomography. *Archives of General Psychiatry, 49,* 695–702.

Rutter, M., & Hemming, M. (1970). Individual items of deviant behavior: Their prevalence and clinical significance. In M. Rutter, J. Tizard, & K. Whitmore (Eds.), *Education, health, and behavior* (pp. 202–232). London: Longman.

Rutter, M., Yule, W., Berger, M., Yule, B., Morton, J., & Bagley, C. (1974). Children of West Indian immigrants: I. Rates of behavioral deviance and psychiatric disorder. *Journal of Child Psychology and Psychiatry, 15,* 241–262.

Sandyk, R. (1988). Clomiphene citrate in Tourette's syndrome. *International Journal of Neuroscience, 43,* 103–106.

Scarone, S., Colombo, C., Livian, S., Abbruzzese, M., Ronchi, P., Locatelli, M., Scotti, G., & Smeraldi, E. (1992). Increased right caudate nucleus size in obsessive-compulsive disorder: Detection with magnetic resonance imaging. *Psychiatry Research: Neuroimaging, 45,* 115–121.

Schwabe, M. J., & Konkol, R. J. (1992). Menstrual cycle-related fluctuations of tics in Tourette syndrome. *Pediatric Neurology, 8,* 43–46.

Seeman, P., Bzowej, N. H., Guan, H.-C., Bergeron, C., Becker, L. E., Reynolds, G. P., Bird, E. D., Riederer, P., Jellinger, K., Watanabe, S., & Tourtellotte, W. W. (1987). Human brain dopamine receptors in children and aging adults. *Synapse, 1,* 339–404.

Semrud-Clikeman, M., Filipek, P. A., Biederman, J., Steingard, R., Kennedy, D., Renshaw, P., & Bekken, K. (1994). Attention-deficit hyperactivity disorder: Magnetic resonance imaging morphometric analysis of the corpus callosum. *Journal of the American Academy of Child and Adolescent Psychiatry, 33,* 875–881.

Sham, P. C., O'Callaghan, E., Takei, N., Murray, G. K., Hare, E. H., & Murray, R. M. (1992). Schizophrenia following pre-natal exposure to influenza epidemics between 1939 and 1960. *British Journal of Psychiatry, 160,* 461–466.

Shapiro, A. K., Shapiro, E. S., Young, J. G., & Feinberg, T. E. (1988a). History of Tourette and tic disorders. In A. K. Shapiro, E. S. Shapiro, J. G. Young, & T. E. Feinberg (Eds.), *Gilles de la Tourette syndrome* (pp. 1–27). New York: Raven Press.

Shapiro, A. K., Shapiro, E. S., Young, J. G., & Feinberg, T. E. (1988b). Signs, symptoms, and clinical course. In A. K. Shapiro, E. S. Shapiro,

J. G. Young, & T. E. Feinberg (Eds.), *Gilles de la Tourette syndrome* (pp. 127–193). New York: Raven Press.

Shapiro, E. S., Shapiro, A. K., Fulop, G., Hubbard, M., Mandeli, J., Nordlie, J., & Phillips, R. A. (1989). Controlled study of haloperidol, pimozide, and placebo for the treatment of Gilles de la Tourette's syndrome. *Archives of General Psychiatry, 46,* 722–730.

Shaywitz, B. A., Cohen, D. J., Leckman, J. F., Young, J. G., & Bowers, M. B. (1980). Ontogeny of dopamine and serotonin metabolites in the cerebrospinal fluid of children with neurological disorders. *Developmental Medicine and Child Neurology, 22,* 748–754.

Simerly, R. B., Swanson, L. W., & Gorski, R. A. (1985). Reversal of the sexually dimorphic distribution of serotonin-immunoreactive fibers in the medial preoptic nucleus by treatment with perinatal androgen. *Brain Research, 340,* 91–98.

Singer, H. S., Hahn, I.-H., Krowiak, E., Nelson, E., & Moran, T. (1990). Tourette's syndrome: A neurochemical analysis of postmortem cortical brain tissue. *Annals of Neurology, 27,* 443–446.

Singer, H. S., Hahn, I.-H., & Moran, T. H. (1991). Abnormal dopamine uptake sites in postmortem striatum from patients with Tourette's syndrome. *Annals of Neurology, 30,* 558–562.

Singer, H. S., Reiss, A. L., Brown, J., Aylward, E. H., Shih, B., Chee, E., Harris, E. L., Reader, M. J., Chase, G. A., Bryan, N., & Denckla, M. B. (1993). Volumetric MRI changes in basal ganglia of children with Tourette's syndrome. *Neurology, 43,* 950–956.

Singer, H. S., Wong, D. F., Brown, J. E., Brandt, J., Krafft, L., Shaya, E., Dannals, R. F., & Wagner, H. N. (1992). Positron emission tomography evaluation of dopamine D-2 receptors in adults with Tourette syndrome. In T. N. Chase, A. J. Friedhoff, & D. J. Cohen (Eds.), *Advances in neurology—Tourette syndrome: Genetics, neurobiology, and treatment* (Vol. 58, pp. 233–239). New York: Raven Press.

Smith, S. J. M., & Lees, A. J. (1989). Abnormalities of the blink reflex in Gilles de la Tourette syndrome. *Journal of Neurology, Neurosurgery, and Psychiatry, 52,* 895–898.

Sprich-Buckminster, S., Biederman, J., Milberger, S., Faraone, S. V., & Lehman, B. K. (1993). Are perinatal complications relevant to the manifestation of ADD? Issues of comorbidity and familiality. *Journal of the American Academy of Child and Adolescent Psychiatry, 32,* 1032–1037.

Stahl, S. M., & Berger, P. A. (1981). Physostigmine in Tourette syndrome: Evidence for cholinergic underactivity. *American Journal of Psychiatry, 138,* 240–242.

Stein, D. J., Hollander, E., Chan, S., DeCaria, C. M., Hilal, S., Liebowitz, M. R., & Klein, D. F. (1993). Computed tomography and neurological soft signs in obsessive-compulsive disorder. *Psychiatry Research: Neuroimaging, 50,* 143–150.

Stoetter, B., Braun, A. R., Randolph, C., Gernert, J., Carson, R. E., Herscovitch, P., & Chase, T. N. (1992). Functional neuroanatomy of Tourette syndrome: Limbic-motor interactions studied with FDG PET. In T. N. Chase, A. J. Friedhoff, & D. J. Cohen (Eds.), *Advances in neurology—Tourette syndrome: Genetics, neurobiology, and treatment* (Vol. 58, pp. 213–226). New York: Raven Press.

Stokes, A., Bawden, H. N., Camfield, P. R., Backman, J. E., & Dooley, J. M. (1991). Peer problems in Tourette's disorder. *Pediatrics, 87,* 936–942.

Sullivan, R. M., Parker, B. A., & Szechtman, H. (1993). Role of the corpus callosum in expression of behavioral asymmetries induced by a unilateral dopamine lesion of the substantia nigra in the rat. *Brain Research, 609,* 347–350.

Susser, E. S., & Lin, S. P. (1992). Schizophrenia after prenatal exposure to the Dutch hunger winter of 1944–1945. *Archives of General Psychiatry, 49,* 983–988.

Swedo, S. E., Leonard, H. L., Kruesi, M. J. P., Rettew, D. C., Listwak, S. J., Berrettini, W., Stipetic, M., Hamburger, S., Gold, P. W., Potter, W. Z., & Rapoport, J. L. (1992). Cerebrospinal fluid neurochemistry in children and adolescents with obsessive-compulsive disorder. *Archives of General Psychiatry, 49,* 29–36.

Swedo, S. E., Pietrini, P., Leonard, H. L., Schapiro, M. B., Rettew, D. C., Goldberger, E. L., Rapoport, S. I., Rapoport, J. L., & Grady, C. L. (1992). Cerebral glucose metabolism in childhood-onset obsessive-compulsive disorder. Revisualization during pharmacotherapy. *Archives of General Psychiatry, 49,* 690–694.

Swedo, S. E., Rapoport, J. L., Cheslow, D. L., Leonard, H. L., Ayoub, E. M., Hosier, D. M., & Wald, E. R. (1989). High prevalence of obsessive-compulsive symptoms in patients with Sydenham's chorea. *American Journal of Psychiatry, 146,* 246–249.

Swedo, S. E., Rapoport, J. L., Leonard, H., Lenane, M., & Cheslow, D. (1989). Obsessive-compulsive disorder in children and adolescents. Clinical phenomenology of 70 consecutive cases. *Archives of General Psychiatry, 46,* 335–341.

Swedo, S. E., Schapiro, M. B., Grady, C. L., Cheslow, D. L., Leonard, H. L., Kumar, A., Friedland, R., Rapoport, S. I., & Rapoport, J. L. (1989). Cerebral glucose metabolism in childhood-onset obsessive-compulsive disorder. *Archives of General Psychiatry, 46,* 518–523.

Sweet, R. D., Bruun, R., Shapiro, E., & Shapiro, A. K. (1976). Presynaptic catecholamine antagonists as treatment for Tourette syndrome: Effects of alpha-methyl-para-tyrosine and tetrabenazine. *Archives of General Psychiatry, 31,* 857–861.

Sweet, R. D., Solomon, G. E., Wayne, H., Shapiro, E., & Shapiro, A. K. (1973). Neurological features of Gilles de la Tourette's syndrome. *Journal of Neurology, Neurosurgery, and Psychiatry, 36,* 1–9.

Swerdlow, N. R., Caine, S. B., Braff, D. L., & Geyer, M. A. (1992). The neural substrates of sensorimotor gating of the startle reflex: A review of recent findings and their implications. *Journal of Psychopharmacology, 6,* 176–190.

Syrigou-Papavasiliou, A., Verma, N. P., & LeWitt, P. A. (1988). Sensory evoked responses in Tourette syndrome. *Clinical Electroencephalography, 19,* 108–110.

Takahashi, L. K., Turner, J. G., & Kalin, N. H. (1992). Prenatal stress alters brain catecholaminergic activity and potentiates stress-induced behavior in adult rats. *Brain Research, 574,* 131–137.

Takei, N., Sham, P., O'Callaghan, E., Murray, G. K., Glover, G., & Murray, R. M. (1994). Prenatal exposure to influenza and the development of schizophrenia: Is the effect confined to females? *American Journal of Psychiatry, 151,* 117–119.

Tanner, C. M., Goetz, C. G., & Klawans, H. L. (1982). Cholinergic and anticholinergic effects in Tourette syndrome. *Neurology, 32,* 1315–1317.

Taranta, A., & Stollerman, G. H. (1956). The relationship of Sydenham's chorea to infection with Group A Streptococci. *American Journal of Medicine, 20,* 170–175.

van de Wetering, B. J. M., & Heutink, P. (1993). The genetics of the Gilles de la Tourette syndrome: A review. *Journal of Laboratory and Clinical Medicine, 121,* 638–645.

Vannucci, R. C. (1989). Acute perinatal brain injury: Hypoxia-ischemia. In W. R. Cohen, D. B. Acker, & E. A. Riedman (Eds.), *Management of labor* (2nd ed., pp. 183–243). Rockville, MD: Aspen Press.

Van Woerkom, T. C. A. M., Fortgens, C., Rompel-Martens, C. M. C., & van de Wetering, B. J. M. (1988). Auditory event-related potentials in adult patients with Gilles de la Tourette's syndrome in the oddball paradigm. *Electroencephalography and Clinical Neurophysiology, 71,* 443–449.

Verhulst, F. C., Akkerhuis, G. W., & Althaus, M. (1985). Mental health in Dutch children: (1) A cross-cultural comparison. *Acta Psychiatrica Scandinavica, 72*(Suppl), 323.

Volkmar, F., Leckman, J. F., Cohen, D. J., Detlor, J., Harcherik, D., Pritchard, J., & Shaywitz, B. A. (1984). EEG abnormalities in Tourette's syndrome. *Journal of the American Academy of Child Psychiatry, 23,* 352–353.

Walkup, J. T., Leckman, J. F., Price, A. R., Hardin, M. T., Ort, S. I., & Cohen, D. J. (1988). The relationship between obsessive compulsive disorder and Tourette's syndrome: A twin study. *Psychopharmacology Bulletin, 24,* 375–379.

Ward, A. J. (1990). A comparison and analysis of the presence of family problems during pregnancy of mothers of "autistic" children and mothers of normal children. *Child Psychiatry and Human Development, 20,* 279–288.

Ward, I. L. (1984). The prenatal stress syndrome: Current status. *Psychoneuroendocrinology, 9,* 3–11.

Ward, I. L., & Weisz, J. (1984). Differential effects of maternal stress on circulating levels of corticosterone, progesterone, and testosterone in male and female rat fetuses and their mothers. *Endocrinology, 114,* 1635–1644.

Weber, J. L., & May, P. E. (1989). Abundant class of human DNA polymorphisms which can be typed using polymerase chain reaction. *American Journal of Human Genetics, 44,* 388–396.

Wilson, R. S., Garron, D. C., Tanner, C. M., & Klawans, H. L. (1982). Behavior disturbance in children with Tourette syndrome. In T. N. Chase & A. J. Friedhoff (Eds.), *Advances in neurology— Gilles de la Tourette syndrome* (Vol. 35, pp. 329–333). New York: Raven Press.

Witelson, S. F. (1989). Hand and sex differences in the isthmus and genu of the human corpus callosum. *Brain, 112,* 799–835.

Yazgan, Y., Peterson, B. S., Wexler, B. E., & Leckman, J. F. (in press). Functional correlates of basal ganglia alterations in Tourette's syndrome, *Biological Psychiatry.*

Yeates, K. O., & Bornstein, R. A. (1994). Attention deficit disorder and neuropsychological functioning in children with Tourette's syndrome. *Neuropsychology, 8,* 65–74.

Young, J. G., Halperin, J., Leven, L., Shaywitz, B., & Cohen, D. J. (1988). Developmental neuropharmacology: Clinical and neurochemical perspectives on the regulation of attention, learning and movement. In L. Iversen, S. Iversen, & S. Snyder (Eds.), *Handbook of psychopharmacology* (Vol. 19, pp. 59–121). New York: Plenum.

Zahner, G. E. P., Clubb, M. M., Leckman, J. F., & Pauls, D. L. (1988). The epidemiology of Tourette's syndrome. In D. J. Cohen, R. D. Bruun, & J. F. Leckman (Eds.), *Tourette's syndrome and tic disorders* (p. 79). New York: Wiley.

Zametkin, A. J., Liebenauer, L. L., Fitzgerald, G. A., King, A. C., Minkunas, D. V., Herscovitch, P., Yamada, E. M., & Cohen, R. M. (1993). Brain metabolism in teenagers with attention-deficit hyperactivity disorder. *Archives of General Psychiatry, 50,* 333–340.

Zametkin, A. J., Nordahl, T. E., Gross, M., King, A. C., Semple, W. E., Rumsey, J., Hamburger, S., & Cohen, R. M. (1990). Cerebral glucose metabolism in adults with hyperactivity of childhood onset. *New England Journal of Medicine, 323,* 1361–1366.

CHAPTER 7

Dysfunctions of Attention

ERIC TAYLOR

The world of phenomena is complex and detailed beyond our understanding. The information that reaches our sense organs is vast; we perceive, analyze, and act on only a fraction of it. All psychological theories therefore need to give an account of how it is that the organism can effectively regulate its receptiveness to stimuli and its readiness to respond to them. This discourse is the area of attention. God does not attend; omniscience would have no need of concentrating selectively on a part of its world. It is the limitation of knowledge and understanding that imposes the need for an effective way of selecting. Dysfunctions of the abilities involved can be expected to have profound influences on the ability of people to think and to react.

TYPES OF ATTENTION

Both in lay and scientific usage, "attention" has many meanings. Many processes are involved in being selective. In everyday use, the word often refers to an active process of effortful mental activity. Children are exhorted to "pay" or "give" attention; adults try to concentrate hard; soldiers, at the command to "come to attention," are expected to be alert and ready for action. These are the *intensive* aspects of attention, and scientific study has correspondingly focused on the effects of volition on a mental performance and the deployment of effort in keeping with the demands of a task. Not only does attention need to be paid intensely on occasion, but it must be prolonged over periods of time. *Sustained* attention is required when a child must work for increasing periods at a set task, when an adult has a job requiring perseverance, and indeed when a child who plays at a self-chosen task spends enough time with it to extract its lesson. Furthermore, sustained and intense attention must of necessity be selective. To focus on one thing means to ignore others, and the ability to do this is often studied scientifically in the various paradigms of *selective* attention. Selectiveness is required not only at the perceptual level but also at the level of response; inappropriate responses must be inhibited in some way and the inhibitory function can also be considered as a part of the mechanism of attention. Selective, intense attention must be directed in an efficient manner, and correspondingly, it is necessary to consider the *control* of attention. The scope of attentional focus can, for instance, be narrowed or broadened; its focus can be captured by extraneous stimuli, divided over several sources of

stimuli or concentrated on a single one, and switched from one to another. The orientation of an organism to novel stimuli, and the way that it explores or searches in a new environment without a specific task are also aspects of the way in which the direction of attention is controlled.

These divisions of attention—intensive, sustained, selective, and controlled—are not in themselves psychological processes. Rather they represent spheres of activity for which a scientific understanding is important. The importance of keeping them separate is that the researcher must not assume too readily that all these types of attention have very much in common. In principle at least, one aspect may be impaired while the others are intact. The clinician, trying to understand how a patient with schizophrenia seems to be overwhelmed by a mass of irrelevant stimuli, may be more confused than helped by a scientific literature addressing different questions, such as the abnormalities of response selection that may be found in attention deficit disorders. Neurophysiologists, experimental psychologists, developmentalists, and clinicians have in the past often investigated rather different processes under the same name, and it should not be surprising if confusion has sometimes resulted. This chapter will therefore emphasize distinctions between different concepts and theories that have surrounded attention and its dysfunctions. This does not imply that the processes are independent. To the contrary, they must work together. But their interaction can only be understood after they have been analyzed.

TYPES OF IMPAIRMENT

Impairments in these various aspects of attention are likely to be associated with different forms of psychopathology. An inability to engage attention intensely is likely to be described by other people as a weak concentration. Persons who are not successfully selecting between different sources of information are likely to be described as distractible, in that their attention is being captured by many irrelevant aspects of the world. Difficulties in sustaining attention will presumably be manifest in a short attention span so that behavior will be impersistent and activities brief. Abnormalities in the control of attention are likely to give rise to a variety of descriptions of altered behavior. A failure to inhibit inappropriate responses might be thought of as an impulsive style of responding. Increased breadth of the focus of attention might also give rise to descriptions of distractibility, since presumably a person afflicted in this way would orient to a large number of potentially irrelevant aspects of the world. Difficulties in shifting attention might give rise to complaints of perseveration and inflexible rigidity in activities. Clinicians describe psychopathology in these kinds of terms, and distinguish between different types of behavior impairment, in the belief that this precision will reflect the underlying psychological process. The belief might, however, be misplaced. These different aspects of attention are not unitary psychological processes and may have many antecedents and many consequences. Thus, impersistence and impaired selectivity sound like very different sorts of problems. Nevertheless, a person described as "distractible" might be showing either or both of them. The behaviors that would give rise to the description would be brief engaging in any given activity and frequent changes between activities. Observation alone could not distinguish between the endogenous explanation of a short attention span and the notion of capture of the organism's attention by external stimuli. Short attention span and distractibility would therefore represent statements about underlying theories concerning behavior, not observations of behavior itself.

It will be necessary to distinguish between different types of dysfunction of attention, and to make sharp boundaries between the behaviors of attentiveness, the test performance from which attentiveness is inferred, and the psychological processes that are associated with attentiveness. This review will take a historical approach to describing some of the theories and concepts of attention. It will then describe some of the tests that scientists and clinicians use to make operational the idea of attentional dysfunction. The normal course of development on these tests will be described with reference to the kinds of impairments that are seen in mental disorders and handicaps, together with the main influences on individual differences. The impairment of attention in different forms of psychiatric disorder will then be described, with particular reference to studies that have analyzed the possible developmental mechanisms and the reasons for test impairment in terms of underlying function. The implications of psychopathology for normal development will then be considered, together with the appropriate future directions for research.

HISTORICAL REVIEW OF CONCEPTS

Introspectionism

Introspectionist psychology at the turn of the century found that attention was a crucial concept. For writers such as James (1842–1910) and Titchener (1867–1927), thought resided in consciousness. It was therefore essential for a scientific account that they should consider what determined the contents of consciousness. William James used attention both to explain the way in which the mind focused on one sensation or one train of thought at a time; and to consider how the mind formed the kind of representation of an action that constituted the will. A major difficulty at once presented itself. Since so much of mental life depended on what became conscious, then decision making had

to be involved in the process; yet by definition it could not be a part of consciousness itself. Attention therefore became of high theoretical importance because it was the key mechanism by which mental objects were presented to consciousness.

Titchener's program of research focused on questions such as these. For example, when two stimuli were presented simultaneously, it was possible to prepare people by designating beforehand which of them was to be attended to. When this was done, then the relevant signal proved to be present in awareness before the other. This finding of "prior entry" suggested the idea of attention as a kind of gate through which stimuli queued for the bright circle of conscious awareness.

The corresponding notion in psychopathology was of a consciousness overwhelmed by a multitude of irrelevant stimuli—too many to be coped with and therefore confusing and strange. The infant, in whom the faculty had not fully developed, was memorably seen as living in a "buzzing, booming confusion." By the same token, mental illness (which was often conceptualized as a regression to earlier stages of development) could lead to the same kind of confusion and incapacity. Kraepelin's (1896) description of "hyperprosexia" in schizophrenia embodied just this idea of an overwhelming diversity of distractions, that could neither be ignored nor satisfactorily understood.

The same kind of notion was present in studies of pediatric pathology. Still (1902) devoted his Coulstonian lectures to the Royal College of Physicians in London to a series of accounts of "moral defects in children." These descriptions were the forerunner of modern concepts of hyperactivity. They stressed the normality of the family and the abnormality of brain function in such children, and considered an impairment of attention to be the key mechanism by which learning failed in school and behavior was inchoate and endlessly distractible.

Behaviorism

The rise of behaviorist psychology initially left little room for concepts such as attention that were tainted by mentalist connotations. The explanations for why one stimulus rather than another guided behavior was now to be sought in the reinforcement history of the previous associations of the stimuli. The active and self-regulating processes of attention were not admitted. However, it became harder to explain how one aspect of a stimulus rather than another came to be chosen for the strengthening of a stimulus-response (S-R) link and increasing complexity of theory was necessary.

Eventually, the study of animal behavior found it necessary to include active selecting mechanisms. Transfer of generalization experiments were a case in point. An animal that had learned to distinguish between two objects was tested with pairs of different objects that could vary in the same way. Qualities such as the shape and size of the objects could be the basis for this kind of transfer of learning. However, it was often found that different qualities of the objects did not generalize in quite the same way. Animals that had learned to choose one object that differed in both shape and size would, when tested for transfer to other objects, generalize on the basis of size only or shape only. Prior experience with the objects could manipulate which dimension was the more salient. Differential attention to one or another aspect therefore had to be inferred.

These ideas of differential attention could readily be applied to dysfunctional learning. Zeaman and House (1963) produced a widely influential theory and program of experiments in individuals suffering from learning disabilities. Their analysis of visual discriminative learning—often using procedures such as transfer of generalization derived from animal behavioral work—led to the argument that two stages were involved in learning. The first was to attend to the stimulus dimension that carried the key information; the second was to memorize the correct cues of that dimension. People with learning disability had difficulties in the first process, not the second.

Once an intellectually retarded child attended to the relevant aspects of a discriminative problem, then he or she would learn as quickly as other children. Correspondingly, a task for the educator was to increase the salience of the relevant cues. Rather similarly, O'Connor and Hermelin (1963) found that the learning of experimental material by intellectually retarded people was enhanced if the relevant stimuli were presented at a higher degree of intensity. Their argument was that acquisition was impaired because of an inability to focus attention on the relevant stimulus features. This was a very different model of attentional dysfunction from that provided by the notion of stimulus overload.

Neurological Approaches

Another way of thinking about attention dysfunction came, not from the psychological laboratory but from clinical observations of people with brain damage. Neurologists recognized parietal syndromes associated with the sensory neglect of a part of the body or a part of the physical field. In such conditions, sensation and perception were quite normal on, for instance, one side of the body when tested in isolation; but the same stimulus, if it was combined with another stimulus, for instance on the opposite side of the body, disappeared from consciousness. This could be interpreted as a problem in the distribution of attention between two stimuli, and experimental investigations of the processes involved in this division of attention were forthcoming. For instance, Birch, Belmont, and Karp (1967) studied the extinction of awareness to double simultaneous homologous stimulation in patients with unilateral cerebral damage and attributed it to an alteration in the processing rate of stimuli within a damaged hemisphere.

Developmental applications were soon forthcoming in the work of Luria (1961). He studied children with a "cerebro asthenic syndrome" (i.e., distractible, impulsive, and uninhibited children who were failing in school and behaviorally disturbed in spite of a normal intelligence). He used another experimental way of examining the distribution of attention between two stimuli. He trained children in choice response tests with one signal requiring a positive motor response and another the inhibition of a response. At rapid rates of presentation, the discriminative ability of affected children broke down. They would either respond to none of the signals or respond indiscriminately to both kinds. They could perform the task quite well if only verbal equivalent responses were required: The difficulty arose with conflicting motor activities. Remedial education therefore took the form of

associating verbal responses with the other types of discrimination that the children were required to learn. The concept of lack of inhibition of motor responses arose from this neurologically inspired work and as described later in this chapter, remains an active field of inquiry that calls for more basic psychological and developmental understanding.

Information Processing

Although both behaviorist and neurological approaches evolved means of accounting for selection of stimuli and distribution of attention between stimuli, attention did not become a central topic in either field. In the late 1950s, however, attention once again became a subject at the forefront of mainstream psychological debate. The need for it followed on social changes. World War II and subsequent technological advances made increasing demands on human beings as operators of complex machinery with multiple sources of information. An aircraft controller or radio operator was expected to receive several competing messages, all requiring a response, at the same time. Successful design of operating systems required a better understanding of how people would cope successfully.

Broadbent (1958) presented an illuminating and fruitful theory. Like many theorists before and since, he applied a modern technological analogy to understanding an obscure brain function. The core idea was that of a single central information processing channel in the brain, which could process the information only at a limited rate, and which was confined to one sensory input channel at a time. Such an analogy worked very well for many experimental situations. For instance, the channel was limited in the rate with which it could switch between sources of information; information coming in when the channel was engaged elsewhere could be held for a few seconds in a short-term memory mechanism but was then lost. When different sets of digits were presented to each ear at exactly the same time, then the brain did not recall them in the order in which they had arrived but rather recalled all those that had been presented to one ear, followed by all those that had been presented to the other. The finding was striking, and implied a mechanism by which the limited capacity channel was engaged first to one ear and then switched to the other.

This "filter theory" made attention a crucial topic for a reason similar to that which commended it to the introspectionists. Both emphasized the limitations of what could be analyzed at any one time, and therefore the means by which stimuli were selected for processing became a crucial part of the efficiency of the organism's reaction. The ability to study selective attention was greatly enhanced by the availability of methods such as the multiple channel tape recorder, which allowed the controlled presentation of several stimuli at the same time. Many properties of stimuli were found that made them more likely to command the attention of the observer. Separation in space of two auditory signals, difference in pitch, and difference in rate of change of the stimulation all enhanced the ability of the brain to focus on one rather than the other. Stimuli, if they were easily discriminable on the basis of their physical properties, could be ignored by passing through the filter only those stimuli that belonged to a physical class that had previously been chosen as relevant. Such a model allowed psychopathology to arise, not only by the overwhelming of the limited capacity channel, but also by inefficiencies in selecting stimuli.

Subsequent research amended the simple theory in several respects (Deutsch & Deutsch, 1963; Broadbent, 1971; Treisman, 1969). Several complexities arose. For one thing, the filter could choose stimuli not only on the basis of simple physical properties but also on the basis of quite complex structural and linguistic qualities. Experiments in which a subject was asked to repeat aloud a passage that had been read in the competing presence of other messages clarified the dimensions of stimuli on the basis of which the filter could select. They included a difference in the timbre of the voice between speakers, the degree of statistical redundancy in the content of the messages, and the contextual probability of words. This seemed to import a difficulty analogous to that never really solved by introspectionist psychology. The filter, which was supposed to be operating before processing the stimulus, did in fact require a good deal of stimulus processing before it operated.

Another complication to the simple theory came from experiments indicating that the ignoring of nonselected channels of information was not total. Emotionally important words, for instance, could be perceived and recalled even when they had been embedded in the signal source that was being rejected on the basis of its physical properties. The theory was therefore amended (Broadbent, 1971) to allow both for "filtering"—the process by which stimuli were attenuated (rather than wholly rejected) on the basis of their physical properties—and "pigeonholing," in which the surviving stimuli were assigned to different categories on the basis of decisions about the probabilities and relative importance of the categories. Selection could be not only by complex sensory and even linguistic stimuli but also by classes of response.

Attention, in short, did not operate once and for all at a peripheral level but took place at successive stages of information processing through the nervous system. The increasing complexity of the operations involved was reflected in some changes in terminology. "Analyzers" rather than "filters" became the units that could be selectively biased by the voluntary attention of the subject. A hierarchical and complex system was now required by the experimenters and the selection of stimuli was no longer the result only of rather simple, machinelike processes. Selection depended on high-level executive decisions of what was relevant within the central nervous system, and these decisions were influenced by the nature of the sensory stimuli reaching the higher decision-making centers.

Another profound modification of the original Broadbent theory was also in store. Information processing was not always as limited in rate as had been envisaged by the original model. Indeed, under some circumstances information could be processed at such a rate that the protective and guiding mechanisms of attention became much less crucial. If, for example, a test was highly practiced, or if the material on which it was based was familiar, then it could proceed without interfering greatly with other activities. The kind of distinction was that between a man driving a car along a familiar road, who could readily perform the task and have plenty of spare capacity left over for chatting and noticing the scenery; and the same man who in an unfamiliar car and surroundings, or when a sudden emergency had arisen, focused all activity on that task and had no capacity left over for any other activity at all. Shiffrin and Schneider (1977) formalized the distinction into that of *automatic* and *controlled* processing. Controlled processing is slow and narrow in focus and can deal with unfamiliar information. Attention is much more critical for controlled, effortful processing, because the latter is so rate limited. It is, however, by no means the same thing. Effortful processing requires many abilities other than attention; and by the same token, automatic processing will still involve attentional processes. To return to the analogy of the driver along a familiar road, there must still be an attentional mechanism in operation that will identify warning signals of an emergency and lead to the adoption of the controlled processing mode when it is appropriate. There have been many recent attempts to analyze people with attention deficit in terms of information-processing mechanisms. Many have been fruitful as considered later in this chapter. However, their success has come from identifying experimental variables that alter information processing—not from relying simply on an overall score of performance on the test.

These increasing complexities in the picture of how the brain selects and regulates its own input have been paralleled by increasing complexity in the picture of the neurological basis for the process. Corticofugal pathways to sense receptors were demonstrated both anatomically and physiologically. Some of the central effect on perception could be explained by effects on the most peripheral possible level, for instance whether the eyes are open or closed and whether the ears are oriented toward the sound source. Not all of it, however, could be explained in this way and the effect of the cortex on perceptual pathways seemed a good basis for the process whereby attentional mechanisms primed and tuned the limited information-processing channel. A more complex picture of a hierarchically organized system of processing emerged from the developing technology of single neuron recording. The classical experiments by Hubel and Weisel (1962) showed how single neurons in the central nervous system might be sensitive only to specific classes of sensory stimuli and later research by these and other investigators showed how the output of such neurons might themselves stimulate other neurons attuned only to high-level properties of stimuli. Cells were discovered that responded specifically to lines of particular orientation, to movement at particular speeds, to repeated trains of stimuli at particular frequencies, and even to specific objects (Tanaka, 1993).

There were several major consequences for the kind of neuropsychological theory of attention that could be considered. It became apparent that properties of the nervous system itself might lead to very rapid reductive coding of very large quantities of information. This was in keeping with experimental psychological findings of the circumstances in which a very high rate of information transmission could be achieved. A protective function of attention no longer seemed so crucial. Furthermore, the neurophysiological findings emphasized that selectiveness and organization were a property of every level of central nervous system functioning. To seek a single mechanism or center for attention was not a tempting goal.

Energetics of Attention

Psychological theorists correspondingly shifted formulations about what kind of explanation was desirable for the processes of attention. Theoretical formulations shifted from attention in the early processing of information to more "energetic" considerations of how processing effort was expended in different ways on different kinds of stimulus. At a neurological level, the theory of Pribram and McGuinness (1975) was influential. They distinguished three sorts of neurological mechanism controlling the responsiveness of the organism. The first, which they called *activation*, was the tonic readiness of an animal to respond. This system maintained readiness over longer periods under the control of activity in the dorsal thalamus and the basal ganglia. It was also necessary to consider the way that short-term changes in responsiveness occurred in response to the nature of the stimulus itself. This *phasic responsiveness* was, in the theory, under the control of circuits centering on the amygdala. A third system had the function of coordinating the tonic and phasic levels. Circuits focusing on the hippocampus were responsible for this high-level coordination of effort.

At a psychological level, these ideas of energy pools as determinants of cognitive performance were elaborated by Kahnemann (1973). It was possible to distinguish different energy pools according to experimental manipulations such as the level of ambient noise or the presence of incentives for good performance. Theories such as these generated a substantial amount of experimental work. Experimentalists also took up theoretical approaches to selectiveness that emphasized what happened in the choice of response rather than in the filtering of stimuli. It is possible to consider the human brain as capable of absorbing an enormous amount of stimuli and processing a great deal of it; competition between signals is then not accounted for by an initial level of filtering, but at a much later level of response choice based on the signal value of the stimuli (Norman, 1968). Experimental work has not suggested either that this approach or the filtering approach is wrong, but that both apply in different kinds of experimental situations.

Dysfunctions of Controlled Processing

It will be seen that the second half of the twentieth century has seen a ferment of theoretical and experimental approaches to the basic understanding of the neuropsychological processes involved in the selective and intensive aspects of attention. The result, for those trying to understand dysfunction, has been an increasing range of theoretical explanations and experimental paradigms that can be deployed to analyze clinical and educational impairments. The most widespread approaches have probably been the application of Broadbent's theories to the explanation of attention impairment in schizophrenia; and of information-processing theory to the explanation of attention deficit disorders in childhood. Both invited experimental work because of the key roles that inattentiveness played in clinicians' formulations of the

psychopathology and pathogenesis of the disorders. Both have yielded many positive results, in the sense that impairments of performance on tests related to attention have been found in both conditions. In both, the relationship between attention dysfunction and clinical syndrome remains obscure.

A developmental approach to psychopathology seems a promising way of understanding some of the complexities involved. First, however, the nature of the dysfunctions in these and other clinical disorders needs to be described. No condition has been unequivocally identified with the breakdown of any single hypothetical construct of attention process. This may result in part from the lack of simple and unequivocal tests of component processes. It may also be because the theories available have been elaborated for quite different purposes than the explanations of psychopathology. Indeed, the attempt to understand psychopathology has given rise to a need for theory in other aspects of attentional control, such as the way that attention is directed, the way that exploration and search are guided, and the way that inappropriate responding is inhibited.

Modular and Executive Processes

The study of psychopathology has drawn out the need for new kinds of theory. An example has been the need to understand how different types of brain damage have different consequences for cognitive performance of affected individuals. Shallice (1988) reviewed a range of different types of dysfunction. In the study of attention, just as in other types of perception, it has become necessary to distinguish between modular and executive processes. A modular process takes place at a relatively simple level of processing and represents a simple and defined cognitive operation, which can sometimes be localized to specific brain areas. An executive function combines the elements of operations into a strategically appropriate program that completes the necessary tasks. Such high-level aspects of control are often distributed over wide areas of cortex and are often affected by frontal lobe pathology. It has been possible to distinguish simple operations in attention as well as in perception. The disengagement, movement, and engagement of attention between stimuli (the distributional aspect of attention) have been localized to different types of lesion (e.g., Posner, Walker, Friedrich, & Rafal, 1984). It therefore becomes possible to think of any type of attention (such as selection) as the result of both low-level, machinelike functions (e.g., the filtering out of a stimulus identified as irrelevant) and higher executive aspects (e.g., the identification of which aspects of a situation are likely to be relevant and the engagement of filtering mechanisms). It would be wrong to pretend that the different components and the way that they are assembled are clear yet. However, studies of normal development have been particularly helpful in disentangling some of the processes involved. Although these developmental analyses have not been brought into full registration with the psychopathological, or indeed the basic theoretical literature; there seems a real chance that they will do so effectively in the future.

As high-level control processes have been integrated into theoretical accounts of attention, it has also been possible to think about ways in which they might interact with the development of affect. This has brought new interest to older formulations about the ways in which cognition and emotion might affect one another. Santostefano (1978) described "cognitive controls" as mental mechanisms determining how the individual organizes information; they were considered to maintain a balance between the demands for action from information in the outside world, and the inner world of emotions, needs, and fantasies. For example, a stimulus arousing aggressive thoughts will be handled in different ways from a neutral stimulus, and the extent to which it dictates behavior will depend on the individual's unique experience. Tests derived from this theory were applied by Rieder and Cicchetti (1989) to children who had been abused or neglected. For example, tests of field articulation (Fruit Distraction Test) assessed children's ability to direct their attention selectively to information designated as relevant. When the "irrelevant" information had aggressive connotations, then maltreated children were less able to withhold their attention from it. Emotional experience is likely to enter into the way that all children make decisions about where they will deploy their attention.

TESTS OF DYSFUNCTIONAL ATTENTION

Desired Qualities of Tests

An ideal psychological test would be rooted in a theoretical formulation of attentional dysfunction. It would represent a pure test of one process, uncontaminated by other psychological abilities and skills. It would be reliable between testers and stable over time. These are exacting requirements, and it should be said right away that no test fares very well against these standards. Even if there were good tests at a research level, the demands for the testing of clinically referred patients and people with special educational needs would be more demanding still. They would require that the test should be simple enough and robust enough to be reliably administered in the range of different situations that the real world makes necessary. Furthermore, it is not enough that tests are valid in the sense of discriminating significantly between criterion groups: they must also have acceptably high sensitivity and specificity so that individuals are classified correctly enough that their categorization is of predictive value.

One particular difficulty with most available tests for clinical and educational purposes is that an impaired performance is not necessarily a sign of impaired attention, for many other processes can limit performance. A few tests in frequent current use will be described, to give a critical appraisal of their value and prepare an understanding of their application to the analysis of clinical syndromes. There are many other tests and paradigms that have been used in research on attention. The aim is not to be exhaustive, nor to imply that there is an existing technology of satisfactory tests. Rather, the purpose is to show how ideas of attention dysfunction have been operationalized and to emphasize the caution that needs to be brought to interpretation by practitioners. Examples will be chosen from tests that have set out to tap the functions of sustained and selective attention, the orientation to a new signal, the maintenance of readiness to respond, and the inhibition of inappropriate responses. The complexity of determinants of performance on each test will be emphasized, so it needs to be stressed at the outset that for clinical purposes a test may still be useful even if it taps several aspects of attention. It is possible that the predictive value of a test may be even greater if it is sensitive to several different types of impairment of attention.

Routine Clinical Assessment

The standard mental state assessment carried out by a psychiatrist will usually include a request to perform some repetitive mental operations. The serial sevens test, for instance, requires prolonged mental arithmetic in which the subject successively subtracts sevens, first from 100 and then from each resulting figure. Although this is traditionally called a test of concentration, the term is in this case only a label of convenience. One person with a poor performance may be having difficulty with the calculations or with a generalized slowness of processing information. Another may have problems with short-term memory so that he or she forgets the intervening numbers, or the entire task. A third may be lacking in motivation and application to the task. A fourth may be distracted by ambient stimulation to the point of an inability to carry it out. Yet another may begin satisfactorily but be unable to prolong the effort required, so the performance tails off toward the end. The value of the test is as one component of a battery whose cumulative score will successfully detect signs of organic affliction of the brain. It is not suitable for making inferences about the nature of an individual's problems.

Something of the same criticism applies to the inferences sometimes made from subtests in an overall intellectual assessment. The Wechsler Intelligence Scale for Children has yielded, on factor analysis, a dimension that has been labeled "freedom from distractibility" (Wechsler, 1974). Tests loading on it include the digit span, the coding subtest, and the test of mental arithmetic. At an intuitive level, it is reasonable to think that what these tests have in common is a requirement for the sustained use of successive mental operations involving memory. However, there is no good reason to think that whatever they have in common is more closely related to attention than the other subtests of an intellectual assessment.

Specialized Clinical Psychometric Tests

The purpose of using more specialized tests is to try to get beyond the clinical assessment of a general cognitive impairment to a level of analysis that says something more specific about a dysfunction of attention.

Information-Processing Tests

Many tests aim to examine the efficiency of controlled information processing. An unfamiliar task is set and the reaction time—the time from the initial presentation of the stimulus to the first response by the subject—is taken to index the speed with which the information is processed. The technology for achieving this was greatly enhanced by the introduction of microcomputer-controlled tests in which visual stimuli are presented on the screens of portable computers or on imaging devices that are controlled by microcomputers. This has enabled general access, outside specialized laboratories, to tests meeting the basic requirements that stimuli are presented more or less instantaneously, that there is an accurate measurement of the time between the presentation of the stimulus and the subject's reaction, and that the details of the way the tests are presented can conveniently be altered.

Stages of Processing

The purpose of altering details of stimulus and response is often to test the notions of stages of information processing, such as those involved by Sternberg's (1966) theory. This conceives the reaction to a complex stimulus as taking place in several stages that must follow one another. First the stimulus must be encoded, then processed, then a response selected and enacted. The different stages of processing can then be affected differentially by experimental manipulations. For example, the task would be made more difficult if the initial stimulus presented is more complex or harder to perceive (e.g., if the stimulus is degraded). Correspondingly, to increase the number of response alternatives is in theory to affect the response stage of information processing but not the earlier steps in the chain.

Such tests are only tests of attention in the sense that they measure controlled information processing. As we have already seen, this cannot be identified with attention—though it is certainly a topic worthy of analysis in its own right. Reaction time tests do not in themselves address strategic aspects of stimulus selection, though they can help by showing whether slow information processing in a psychiatric syndrome is disproportionately affected by the stage of stimulus selection. The value of such tests has appeared to particular advantage in disorders that are associated with slow rates of processing information. They are for instance a good way of monitoring effects of anticonvulsant drugs on cognitive processes. Because the major effect to be expected is a general psychomotor slowing, then accurate timing of reaction in cognitive processes is a valuable way of detecting toxicity or of comparing the effects of different forms of medication (Cull & Trimble, 1989). Commercial batteries of information-processing tests are quite widely used for the assessment of individual cases of attention deficit. It is important, however, that practitioners appreciate some difficulties here. First of all, the sensitivity and specificity of such tests against an agreed criterion have never been established so it is not clear whether they have passed beyond the level of useful indicators of group differences to indexes of individual status. Second, the tests are quite crucially dependent on details of their administration. Because of differences in the screens on which the tests are projected, the same software run on two different computers may produce quite profound differences, for instance, in the timing of stimulus presentation or in the visual details. Satisfactory normative data are generally lacking. An abnormal individual score on such test batteries must therefore be treated circumspectly. It is not necessarily a valid measure of poor performance in the real world. Even if it is associated with real-life difficulties, it should not be taken to imply that the problem is an attentional one. It may be as much the result of overall limitation of resources as the way that resources are distributed.

Developmental Trends

Considering that tests using reaction time as an index of processing speed have been the backbone of experimental research into controlled information processing, it is perhaps surprising that we know rather little at present about developmental trends during childhood. From the age of about 6 until adolescence, there is a steady decrease in reaction time in simple and choice reaction time tests (Rourke & Czudner, 1972). Children with learning difficulties lag behind in the acceleration of reaction time, so that at any given age their response latencies are slower than those of their normally intelligent peers. This older literature does not provide the kind of analysis according to stages of information processing that might clarify the reasons for the acceleration with time. It is possible that it is a rather global change involving the speed of all mental operations; it is also possible that it reflects an increasing ability to select effectively from large numbers of stimuli or to establish or maintain a prepared motor response.

By contrast, the course of development in later life has been more thoroughly charted. An increase in reaction times is one of the best established of all the changes in mental processes that occur in senescence. Systematic research quite soon made it clear that such a slowing down could not be explained only in terms of delays in the transmission of information from sense organs to the brain, nor in muscular response. The marked slowing down in old age is in contrast to the minimal slowing in the conductive rate of peripheral nerves (Birren & Bottwinck, 1955). The notion that this reflected a rather general biological process, which affected many aspects of mental processing was supported by correlations between reductions in brain weight and increases in reaction time (Talland, 1965); and between reaction time and diminished electroencephalogram (EEG) reactivity (Surwillo, 1961). The changes are robust across many different types of test (Welford, 1980) and are substantial in size, so that in the seventh decade of life compared with the third the reaction time on simple tests is about 20% longer (Birren, Woods, & Williams, 1980).

What psychological processes might account for this slowing down? Poor attention has often been suggested as the reason for other types of cognitive impairment during later life, such as forgetfulness (Craik & Byrd, 1982). This does not, however, reflect any rigorous analysis of attention processes, but rather the finding that high-level processes such as grasping the nature of the task in hand are likely to be involved. It may well be, nevertheless, that the ability to recognize, and profit from, regularities in stimuli may suffer disproportionately during old age. For example, a program of studies by Rabbitt and colleagues has made a variety of experimental manipulations to the stimulus qualities of tests showing deficits. Rabbitt (1963) used a card-sorting test to show that there was a disproportionate increase in the time taken to categorize cards according to the letters printed on them, if there was an increase in the amount of irrelevant information that each card contained. This suggested a less efficient approach to discarding irrelevant information. In another experiment, when the stimulus requiring a response was a particular sequence of light signals, then older people were more impaired than younger ones for repetitive and predictable sequences;

whereas the differences were much less marked for irregular sequences of stimuli. The suggestion is therefore that there is a particular problem for elderly people in the ability to identify or make use of redundancies in stimulus information (Rabbitt & Birren, 1967).

The increases with age in reaction time for tests involving choice between signals tend to disappear when intensive practice is provided beforehand on the tests (Rabbitt, 1980). Attention processes involved in the selection of stimuli for controlled processing are therefore likely to become less efficient with increasing age. It would be of interest to know whether the same kind of analysis can account for the way that children normally accelerate their speed of reacting during development, and whether the same processes account for the increases of reaction time that have frequently been seen in groups of people with learning disabilities and attention deficit disorders.

Sustaining Attention

Research studies of the ability to sustain attention over long periods of time quite rapidly developed techniques for testing that took account of developing information on psychological processes involved in vigilance. For example, the Broadbent (1958) filter theory conceived the limited information-processing channel as something that could switch between different signal sources. These switches could be quite brief and their frequency could vary from time to time. Accordingly, self-paced tasks and highly predictable trains of signals could fail to pick up a decrement in performance over time that was shown in real-life situations. The sort of test that was required was one in which stimuli requiring responses were presented over lengthy periods of time, but with the occurrence of each stimulus being unpredictable. In this way, each stimulus had a chance of arriving at one of the periods in which the information channel was switched to a different source of stimuli and therefore of being neglected. In self-paced tasks, brief lapses of attention need not necessarily have very much overall effect on the amount of work that is done. In experimenter-paced tests that last at least 30 minutes, vigilance decrements can be readily detected and shown to be influenced by qualities in the individual, the test, and the surrounding environment (Stroh, 1971).

In studying dysfunctions of attention, these methodological requirements are often ignored and the interpretation of test findings is correspondingly difficult. By far, the most common test to be used is the *Continuous Performance Test* (CPT). It was introduced by Rosvold and colleagues in 1956, and researchers in psychopathology have used it very widely. In many parts of the world, it is used for the clinical diagnosis of attention deficit and to monitor the effects of treatment. Developmental norms have been provided by Levy (1980) showing that average scores improve with age through the early school years (Klee & Garfinkel, 1983). In spite of its popularity, the CPT has serious limitations as a test of attention, and is often applied without recognition of its limitations. It therefore needs further description.

There are many forms of the CPT. In the most common, letters are presented visually on a screen. Each presentation lasts for about half a second; a new stimulus appears about every 2 seconds. The stimuli appear very regularly, and most do not require a response. One particular letter is the target, and every time it appears the subject must press a button. Target stimuli usually make up about 10% of the stimuli presented.

The stimuli were originally presented as slides, from mechanically driven carousels on a standard slide projector. This is still the mechanism in some versions, but nowadays microcomputer programs are usually used to generate the images on a video screen. Traces of the older technology remain in the newer versions: For example, the interstimulus interval is kept fixed, even though a more sensitive test of vigilance might be obtained if stimuli were presented unpredictably. As it is, accuracy of time perception may help to determine performance—subjects can ready themselves at the moment of presentation. The slide projector version provided very obvious auditory warning stimuli as the slides clicked into place.

Apparently minor differences in stimulus presentation can make fundamental differences to the theoretical processes being measured. In some versions of the CPT, a letter (e.g., "X") is the target and requires a response whenever it appears (the "X" presentation). In others, it is only a target if it is preceded by another letter, say "A" (the "A-X" type of test). In others again, it is only a target if it occurs twice in succession (the "X-X" type of test). The "A-X" and "X-X" types are ways of making the test harder so that it discriminates better. But they also convert it into a warning-signal paradigm of sustained attention, and rather different abilities are therefore being tested. Often, it is not at all clear just what psychological abilities are determining performance in different experiments. Many processes are involved. Because the stimuli are usually letters presented visually, the ability to recognize them quickly will obviously affect the score obtained. Scores therefore correlate with reading ability and this may confound both developmental changes and differences between psychopathological groups and controls.

There are similar problems even when the test does not use letters. Auditory stimuli and nonverbal visual stimuli are widely used by some workers, but they all involve some kind of discrimination between stimuli that require a response and stimuli that require the response to be withheld. The difficulty of the discrimination is likely to be determined partly by the information-processing capacities of the subject. Available capacity will therefore contribute to the score as well as the way attention is deployed. In an attempt to avoid this, some versions of the test continuously adjust the level of test difficulty according to the performance of the child. The intention is laudable—to standardize the difficulty and therefore the load on information-processing capacity. Unfortunately, this is nearly always done by altering the speed of presentation of stimuli and this is a much more complex manipulation than simply adjusting difficulty. A bright child, for example, will do well and therefore receive a faster stream of stimuli. A faster rate will entail a shorter warning period; it may actually make the test easier to attend to. In practice, the best solution is probably to use a test without warning stimuli (e.g., by requiring a response to any stimulus that is identical to the previous one), to have different levels of difficulty determined by the complexity of differentiation, and to find beforehand the appropriate task for the subject. But even then interpretation is problematic.

It is possible that level of performance on the test results from overt rather than covert attention. Visual versions are highly susceptible to gaze aversion. The stimuli subtend a small angle to the eye; look away from the screen for a moment and you miss a stimulus. Experiments have not in general been able to control well for this. It is therefore possible that the test's sensitivity to off-task behavior explains the high associations between test scores and psychopathological conditions. If so, its popularity is perhaps ill founded and it should not be seen as giving insight into the psychological basis of inattentive behavior.

Another complexity in the test stems from the response required. Discrimination is needed between target stimuli and others, so it is a form of speeded classification test. The correct action to a nontarget stimulus is to withhold a motor response. As discussed later in this chapter, a lack of inhibitory motor control can give a poor score due to many false responses (errors of commission) and the test can therefore be seen as an index of impulsiveness rather than of sustained attention. However, it is hard to sort this out. Errors of commission are often used as an index of impulsive responding; yet not even this is valid, since they can also result from a confusion between target and nontarget, or a sensible economic choice to press all the time if there is no response cost for an error. Signal detection theory is widely used to differentiate patterns of error; but the assumptions of that theory are not in practice met and so the validity of inferring different processes from patterns of false positive and false negative scores is not established.

In summary, the CPT is a complex performance measure influenced by processing capacity, response readiness, and overt behavior as well as by the ability to sustain attention. Considerable research is therefore still needed before the reasons for developmental change become clear. One way forward seems to be by manipulating the experimental parameters of the CPT to illuminate the processes involved, as described earlier for warning stimuli, and including incentives, length of test, and presence of distractors (Taylor, 1986a). Other promising lines are the developmental study of simpler tests, such as the variable-foreperiod reaction time described by Sonuga-Barke and Taylor (1992); and the analysis of how and why children take more or less time over a test (see discussion of inhibitory control in the section "What Is the Nature of the Attention Deficit?").

Tests of Selectiveness

The great majority of experimental tests of attention are based on a relatively simple perceptuomotor task, which is complicated by the presence of irrelevant information. If attention mechanisms did not operate at all, and all stimuli were analyzed with equal weight, then the amount of time required for processing a stimulus array would rise as a function of the number of elements in the array. In practice, performance on a centrally relevant task is very much better than that on stimuli initially designated as irrelevant. Furthermore, reaction times with increasing complexity rise much more slowly than would be the case if every single stimulus required separate and successive analysis.

The main findings in the research literature have come from differences attributable to experimental manipulations of simple tests. Accordingly, a test designed to measure dysfunction does not yield a simple performance score on a test item. Rather, the key factor must be the difference between different ways in which the same test is presented. There is the corresponding problem that standardization of the test and consideration of the reliability of individual differences needs to be based on difference scores rather than on simple performance. The problems involved have not been fully overcome and no satisfactory normative data can be said to exist for tests of selective attention.

Developmental Trends

Even early in childhood, it is quite easy for subjects to ignore an obviously irrelevant stimulus. Many experimental studies, even of prepubertal children, have failed to demonstrate any effect of irrelevant stimuli at all. Doleys (1976) commented after reviewing the field that it was hard to find anything more than a myriad of contradictory results. Even when experiments did find that irrelevant stimuli worsened performance, the effect was dependent on contextual details. Belmont and Ellis (1968) reported that irrelevant stimuli could improve performance at one time and worsen it at another; White (1966) found that the presence of irrelevant visual stimuli worsened performance, as predicted, before the age of 5, but improved performance after that age. Findings such as these emphasize how wrong it would be to regard the human's capacity to process selectively as being merely a function of the stimuli presented. Attention is not captured by every accidental feature of the world—or not, at least, in normal development at any age. Rather, active processes are at work.

Tests that fail to show a worsening with irrelevant stimuli do not prove the absence of distractibility. They simply show that a particular test has failed to elicit it, and that it is not suitable for investigating the mechanisms of selective attention. Several qualities of tests make it more likely that irrelevant information will impair performance. Most of these have the effect of making it less obvious what is relevant and what is irrelevant. For instance, an outline drawing embedded in confusing lines is much harder to recognize than such a figure presented without confusing material; and individual differences in this ability can be related to other qualities such as emotional dependence and impulse control (Witkin, Dyk, Paterson, Goodenough, & Karp, 1962). The difficulty with this kind of test is that it is not clear that normal development would bring the ability to solve it successfully by suppressing information about the nonrelevant lines. Rather, it is a test that demands that all the information is synthesized before the outlined figure can be perceived. Unless some kind of information is available before analysis that can guide the selection of stimuli, such tests need to be regarded as indexes of complex spatial analysis rather than selective attention.

Another way of setting up tests to show the effects of distractors is by requiring some kind of response for the distractor itself. In this way, for instance, Hagen and Hale (1973) found that an auditory task could interfere with a learning test in the visual modality. However, this is not a matter of ignoring irrelevant information. The "irrelevant" task is only designated as such for the purposes of the analysis: a good performance on the whole task as presented to the child requires that the "irrelevant" auditory task is not ignored.

Tasks with competing inputs can be useful in demonstrating the bias toward one or other type of stimulus dimension. The "Stroop test" is perhaps the most famous way of eliciting this kind of conflict. The subject is presented with names of colors written in different colored inks. If, for instance, the word "yellow" is written in red ink then it is possible to read the word rapidly without the color of the ink causing interference, but it is very difficult to name the color of the ink. Modifications of this test have been useful in indicating how the brain biases itself toward one or other type of information in the light of past experience and the needs of the moment. They do not, however, by themselves indicate the nature of the process at work.

Processes Involved in Selecting Information

All tests that show an effect of distractibility also show that there is an improvement during the school years in the ability to resist the distraction. Visual search and speeded classification tests have been the main ways of showing this. They both require scanning of the full visual field, and the distinction between relevant and irrelevant stimuli is maintained through task instructions and response requirement. On all these tests 12-year-olds perform considerably better than 6- to 7-year-olds (Day, 1978; Gibson & Yonas, 1966; Strutt, Anderson, & Well, 1975; von Wright & Nurmi, 1979).

The physical properties of stimulus presentation makes a difference to the power of a distractor. When complex visual stimuli need a rapid response, then the presence of irrelevant information is more detrimental to performance if it is physically close to the relevant stimuli than if it is more widely separated (Enns & Girgus, 1985). The same experiment showed that the distracting effect of more closely spaced information was disproportionately greater in 8-year-olds than in 10-year-olds and in 10-year-olds compared with university students. Another experiment from the same laboratory eliminated the possibility that eye movements might account for the way that visual information was explored and therefore for the way that relevant information was selected (Enns & Brodeur, 1989). They used a speeded classification test in which a warning signal was presented before the main visual test. The time between the warning and the target was, at 200 msecs, too short for eye movements to have been made toward the warning signal. Nevertheless, the warning signal made a difference. If it was presented in a place that was physically remote from the later stimulus requiring a response, then the reaction times were longer than they would have been had the warning signal appeared in the same place as the target. Internal, covert shifting of attention could therefore take place and lead to a reduction in responsiveness to stimuli outside the field of shifted attention. This effect was stronger for children age 6 than it was for older children or for adults. The younger children could therefore be seen as equally able to shift their attention covertly but less able to extract information from a signal presented after a misleading warning. If the predictive value of a warning signal was manipulated (e.g., if it only sometimes predicted a target) this made rather little difference to the performance of 6- and 8-year-olds but it improved the performance of adults. Adults, in short, can work out when a warning signal is relevant and use its information to guide their attention. Children are more prone to be distracted by misleading information, but this is not because they admit all stimuli with equal weight.

The lesson was rather similar to one that could be taken from earlier work by Pick, Christy, and Frankel (1972). These workers investigated schoolchildren's ability to select relevant material in a visual display as a function of whether they were given distractions before or after the visual display. Older children were better at using the previous instructions and their performance on the selective attention test correspondingly increased. All these experiments suggest that the increasing ability to ignore distractors comes from an increasing knowledge and understanding about what is likely to be relevant in a given situation.

This is not the full story. It is likely that a simple filtering mechanism may be working better as children get older. When Enns and Akhtar (1989) manipulated the details of distracting stimuli in a speeded classification test, they found that the mere presence of irrelevant information had a disproportionate effect on younger children; attention set also had an influence, but it could not account for the whole of the age difference. Two types of experimental investigation will therefore be of particular relevance to understanding further the resistance to distractors. One is the way that children filter out stimuli on the basis of their physical properties. The second is the way that they make decisions about what is relevant.

Filtering and Breadth of Attention

Several metaphors have been applied from technology to explain how filtering might take place. A spotlight can expand its range at the expense of the intensity at any one part; a zoom lens can include a wider field at the expense of the amount of detail that is included. A variable width filter can tune to one wave length and exclude others without any particular loss in definition. All the models imply that the more selective attention of the older child and adult is obtained at a cost. Some of the increasing ability to respond accurately to relevant stimuli will entail a decreasing accuracy of response to stimuli that are not relevant to a task in progress. Hagen and Hale (1973) therefore predicted different developmental trends in central learning (where children knew beforehand what to concentrate on) and incidental learning (where they were tested on material that had not been relevant according to the test instructions). For example, children were asked to look at picture cards of animals and to recall the positions in which they had seen them. They were instructed beforehand in the task and were presumed to be concentrating on it, and indeed were at the end of the task asked to remember where each card had been. In addition, however, they were asked to recall other features about the pictures themselves. Because this information had not been discussed in the instructions, it could not have been preferentially included into analytic mechanisms by the operation of selective attention. On the central task, accuracy of recall increased with age. For the ages of 8 up to 12 years, the incidental learning task showed only a slight improvement; after the age of about 12 years, performance on the incidental task declined. (Siegal & Stevenson, 1966, had also found a curvilinear relationship between age and incidental learning with a peak of incidental learning at about 10 to 12 years).

The suggestion is therefore that some of the increasing selectiveness during development is brought about by the active ignoring of stimuli that are not relevant to the task in hand. Several conclusions follow. Some of the development of the filtering mechanism happens during adolescence. It may therefore be that older children become more confident in their judgments about what is relevant and what is not. In younger children, up to about the age of primary schooling, this selectiveness is not achieved by progressive exclusion of stimuli from being considered but through a more accurate concentration of resources on what is centrally relevant.

Decision Making about the Relevance of Stimuli

Although the experiments reviewed here have indicated that decision making is likely to be an important aspect of a final developmental account, research in it has barely begun. The majority of experimental approaches have deliberately excluded this area from their scope. When an investigator tells a child, with the maximum clarity that can be obtained, about what aspect of a task is relevant, then the whole purpose is to remove the potentially complicating factor of how the children themselves decide what will be relevant. Nevertheless, the technology does now exist for further study of this—both through the inferred operation of selective mechanisms, as in tests described earlier, and in direct observation about where attention is directed and how it is controlled, as will be discussed. It is likely that in infancy selective attention will be guided largely by properties of the stimuli themselves, or their immediate motivational significance; whereas during later childhood, there will be the development of a progressively more complex *theory of relevance*. Experience, and the instruction of others, will have guided children toward strategies of examination that focus differentially on those aspects of a stimulus array that are most likely to contain useful information about it. Dysfunctions of attention in mental disorders might therefore be a consequence of bias or inefficiency in this form of decision making, just as much as it might be due to impairment of the mechanisms of selection.

During adult life, the ability to select is well engrained. In fact, it may even be too rigidly set. It is a commonplace of scientific research that it may be very hard to leave a cherished hypothesis or line of approach to follow the significance of accidental observations. Often, people are unobservant to the responses of others, or to changes in the physical world, because they are too highly focused on a task in hand. We have already seen how some of the decrement in speed of response during senescence may be attributable to different ways in which older people take instructions about the nature of the task in hand. It is not necessarily to be thought of simply as a deterioration— their responses may be more conservative rather than less good. Advances in the study of selective attention are likely to come as experimenters increasingly shift their attention to the contextual and interpersonal aspects of the testing situations that have in the past been controlled out in the interests of experimental simplicity and rigor.

Control of the Direction of Attention

All the tests considered so far have been measures of performance. However, one of the most interesting aspects of the study of attention is that it embraces behavioral as well as cognitive functions. It is not always necessary to ask about what aspects of the world are governing performance; the researcher can watch people behave and see how they are orienting themselves. This is possible with the greatest sensitivity in the observation of eye movements and the direction of gaze. When such measures were introduced into infant psychology, they wrought a revolution in the range and depth of cognitive analysis that could be employed.

The observation of visual orientation has often served purposes other than the study of attention itself. For example, *habituation* can be elicited from an early age. A novel stimulus is fixated for longer than a familiar one, and repetitive presentation of a stimulus will lead to decreasing lengths of eye gaze on it. This rapidly opened up the possibility of studying the process of memory. The development of habituation must involve the formation of an internal trace of the object that is being looked at. Experimental ingenuity allowed habituation to be used for the studies of other types of infant cognition, reviewed elsewhere in this volume.

Only relatively recently have the methods of observing visual orientation been turned to studying how children attend, rather than using attention to investigate other processes. The same techniques of recording visual movements apply throughout the age span, and have been used in experimental work on adults operating complex machines. Such studies have and will yield much useful information about the best ways of designing control panels and complex information systems such as those that must be operated by pilots. Dysfunctions of eye movement also play a strong part in adult psychopathological research, especially in the study of schizophrenia: though not necessarily with the prime intention of clarifying attention mechanisms.

Developmental Trends in Directing Attention

Scanning

Even in the first days of life, babies use plans to sample information systematically. There is order in the way that neonates scan with their eyes depending on whether they are in the light or the dark and whether or not a sound is also present (Mendelson & Haith, 1976). It is not entirely necessary for the infant to learn what must be examined: some strategies of examination are innate. Neonates look at moving stimuli with high contrast in preference to those that are still and homogeneous (Fantz, 1966; Salapatek & Kesson, 1966). Their eyes fixate on the edges of contours; if there are no edges in the visual field then their eyes continue to search around (Mendelson & Haith, 1976). Figures with a moderate amount of edge seem to evoke more steadfast gaze than figures with none or a great deal (Karmel, 1969). There is a corresponding set of preferences in auditory attention. An intermittent tone produces more behavioral quietening than does a continuous tone (Brackbill, Adams, Crowell, & Gray, 1966), and an intense tone produces more cardiac deceleration than does a quiet tone (Moffitt, 1973).

Haith (1980) was able to unify many of the findings on the visual preferences of very young children into a set of rules that govern visual gaze. The simplest rule, which applies in a patternless visual field, is to scan systematically with broad and rather jerky sweeps of the eyes. However, when an edge of high contrast is encountered, then a new rule appears: that it should be selectively fixated. Shorter, finer eye movements then cross, systematically, backward and forward across the edge.

This kind of process is sometimes summarized by saying that the neonate's attention is passively captured by qualities of the stimuli. This, however, does not take into account the extent to which the neonate is actively following strategies and modifying dispositions of visual gaze according to the circumstances that are encountered. The distribution of attention is from the start an active process.

Visual Preferences

The active contribution of the baby is also emphasized by the finding that novel stimuli attract gaze preferentially over familiar stimuli; for the difference between a novel and a familiar stimulus depends on the infant's memory of a previous experience. The same phenomenon, of a novel stimulus creating a greater internal effect than a familiar one, can be detected with other means of assessing the response of the child. The extent to which the stimulus will interrupt an ongoing activity such as sucking has been used in some laboratories; the autonomic orienting response of changes in heart rate, skin resistance, and other peripheral measures is also useful. Physiological measures such as these have shown that the enhanced effect of a novel stimulus cannot be dependent on experience after birth, for it is detectable even during embryonic life (Hepper & Shahidullah, 1992).

There has in the past been some controversy over the age at which the visual preference for novelty appears. Earlier work suggested that neonates prefer familiar stimuli and that it is not until the age of about 3 months that a preference for novelty appears (Greenberg, Uzgiris, & Hunt, 1970; Wetherford & Cohen, 1973). The conclusion has been reversed by more recent work, finding a preference for novelty from the very first weeks of life (Freidman, 1972, 1975; Slater, Morison, & Rose, 1982). The reasons for the disagreement are not completely resolved. However, the most salient change in methodology over this time was the advance toward an "infant control" procedure in which the stimuli are presented only when the children are ready and the lengths of presentation are determined by the children's fixation on them. This means that stimuli for assessing the direction of attention are only given during the relatively short periods when a child is alert and attentive in manner. It might be objected that this is to take a very atypical set of states. In a sense, this is true, but it is preferable for measures to concentrate on those periods during which the responsiveness of the neonate can best be assessed.

One of the great difficulties of experimentation in this age group is the variability of state over quite short time periods. After the age of about 3 months, there are much longer and stabler periods of alert attentiveness. Novel stimuli continue to attract longer periods of gaze than do familiar ones, but many other aspects of stimuli come preferentially to be the targets of the gaze. These stimulus aspects include curved rather than straight edges, symmetrical rather than asymmetrical stimulus presentations, and moderately complex rather than simple stimuli. Karmel and Maisel (1975) synthesize these findings into the suggestion that the infant prefers an optimal level of contour density and that the optimal level becomes progressively denser over the first year of life.

A large amount of developmental research has focused on the visual preference for novel stimuli. This is not only because it offers a major route into the attention and other cognitive abilities of the infant but also because it is predictive of later cognitive qualities (see following section). A standardized test has therefore been developed by Fagan and Shepherd (1987) and widely used as a test of infant intelligence. Limited norms are available. The significance of individual differences on this test are not yet entirely clear, and the rapid variability of the infant introduces an uncontrolled factor. Benasich and Bejar (1992) argue for caution in the application of Fagan and Shepherd's test. About 40% of infants were misclassified into low- or high-risk status on the basis of the test.

The stability of infant tests of attention is also quite low. Bornstein and Benasich (1986) reported significant but modest correlations between the scores of children tested a couple of weeks apart. Pecheux and Lecuyer (1989) found that measures performed on the same children at 3 months and at 8 months had a correlation of about zero. There is an interesting paradox that measures of such low stability are also quite highly predictive. As discussed in the following section, the preference for a novel over a familiar stimulus predicts the later IQ quite strongly; indeed, it is a better predictor of IQ in later childhood than are infant tests of general development. The association is at its strongest when the predicting assessments are made between 2 and 8 months of age (McCall & Carriger, 1993)—the period in which stability in individual differences is very low. The implication appears to be not that measures of visual attention are unreliable but that they are determined by different factors at different stages of development.

Experimental Analyses of Changes in Visual Attention

The question of what is measured by visual attention has been taken further by experimental analyses. Although novel stimuli are fixated for longer periods than familiar ones, it is the infants who look for shorter periods at 3 months who are the best performers when they are tested on other cognitive measures in later childhood (Bornstein & Sigman, 1986). Colombo, Mitchell, Coldren, and Freeseman (1991) presented discrimination tasks to 4-month-old children. The tasks emphasized either global processing of the whole stimulus array, or the processing of details of the stimuli. The children who looked for the shortest periods did better than longer looking infants on the global task rather than on the detailed task; and their superiority was more evident when there was less time available for the discrimination to be carried out. There seem to be two main possibilities in present knowledge: either, as Colombo et al. concluded, children who look for short periods do so because they are rapid and efficient at cognitive processing and extract information rapidly from visual stimuli; or the short lookers are using a style of global rather than detailed processing and this manner of processing information is predictive of later performance. The implication is therefore that the chief determinants of individual differences in these measures of visual attention are not primarily visual attention itself. The "attention" explanation would imply that the infants who fixated on a new stimulus for the longest period would also be the ones who extracted the most information from it. Such a prediction is falsified by the longitudinal data. Individual differences in attending behavior are therefore determined by a more general aspect of cognitive performance.

During later childhood, there is an increasing preference for more complex patterns. This goes hand in hand with a decrease in the average time for which any given stimulus holds the attention. Because any one stimulus is inspected for a shorter period, it is possible to look at more things in a given period and correspondingly to extract more information about the world. Visual attention becomes more active and varied; it is correspondingly important that the distribution of attention is governed by efficient rules. The possibilities for exploration are dramatically increased with the ability to link auditory and visual information together and especially with the ability to explore manually and therefore to learn the properties of the outside world by experiment.

Kagan (1970) proposed a general rule to guide the distribution of attention over the first 2 years of life: children seek an optimum level of discrepancy between what is expected and what is actually present. Testing the theory has involved the complexities of determining what is expected by a child, in effect, of specifying the nature of the child's concepts. The most persuasive evidence quoted by Kagan found a curvilinear relationship between the attention that was paid to a test stimulus and its discrepancy from a stimulus that had frequently been presented to the child in the past. This in effect provided an experimental control of the child's concepts. The implication is that increasing knowledge about the world is increasingly the major force that determines how attention is distributed.

The importance of knowledge and theory in guiding the distribution of attention increases during later childhood. Grabbe and Campione (1969) found that stimuli previously associated with reward come to evoke longer gazes than do novel stimuli. Ruff and Lawson (1990) made longitudinal descriptions of children's orienting behavior. Children's focused attention (involving intent facial expression and manipulation) increases from 1 to 5 years. Casual attention—the mere tendency to look at toys—did not increase over this period. The focused attention, however, nearly always followed on a period of casual attention. They suggested that a first, casual exploration of the world set in motion a set of ideas and the full deployment of active and focused orientation followed.

Wright and Vlietstra (1975) reviewed a wide range of observational studies about the direction of attention during childhood. They concluded that there was a developmental line in which an early form of perceptual *exploration* of the most salient and novel aspects of the world gradually gave rise to an active, logically organized *search*. Such a process has several components, some of which have been tested. Scanning the world probably does become more logical. It has been known for many years that young children begin by fixing their eyes on a focal point in a pattern and working away from it, while the eye movements of older children

represent a more systematic and predictable way of scanning from the top to the bottom (Braine, 1965). Older children are more capable than younger ones of adapting their strategy to the changing demands of a task (Lehman, 1972). Older children will explore more dimensions of an object (e.g., shape, texture, size) if they are not given any information about which is relevant; on the other hand, if the important and relevant dimension of the stimulus is made clear in advance then older children will explore that dimension only and will therefore orient themselves to fewer stimulus dimensions than a younger child. Their strategy of exploration has been more successfully adapted to the changing demands of the task.

The study of psychopathology suggests that it would be worthwhile to develop and standardize this kind of observational test. The behavior of children with attention deficit disorder is characterized by rapid changes of activity, and it would be helpful to know to what extent this represents a disorganized distribution of attention, and how far it is logical even though rapid. The concept of logical organization is not an easy one to operationalize, but the developmental tasks applied to describing normal development indicate how this might be done.

In practice, other kinds of test have been used to study the distribution of attention in later childhood and adult life. One approach is to consider how the individual can switch attention between multiple sources of information that are present simultaneously. Experimenters here have typically followed Broadbent's (1958, 1971) emphasis on testing the recall of material, with the complexity of information as a parameter of experimental presentation. Maccoby (1967) played to children tape recordings of words that were spoken simultaneously by two different voices. Younger children found it harder than older children to recall words from one voice when another voice was also present. Older children were more successfully able to divide their attention. Posner and his colleagues have made extensive and fruitful use of tests in which multiple and visual stimuli are presented and attention needs to be shifted from one to the other (Posner et al., 1984). For example, the direction of attention can be "cued" by a signal to show subjects where a target will be presented, and the time needed to respond is less if the cue is accurate than if it is misleading. Some of the processes involved in this were described in the preceding discussion of selective attention. Different types of brain lesions can produce relatively specific impairments in disengaging and moving the focus of attention (see the section "Contributions of Psychopathology to Normal Development"). Tests such as these have their predominant value in distinguishing between psychopathological and control groups, but their potential importance in individual diagnosis calls for the development of standardized tests that will reliably measure individual differences in performance.

Maintenance and Inhibition of Responsiveness

The main test for assessing readiness to respond is a reaction time paradigm, in which a signal (requiring a response as soon as possible) is preceded by a warning stimulus. The reaction time to the signal is then determined in part by the length of time by which the warning precedes the signal. If the time interval is too short—less than about 500 milliseconds—then full readiness is not reached (Posner & Boies, 1971). A more prolonged interval sees reaction times lengthening again, as the readiness to respond fades. This is a relatively simple test experimentally, and it is capable of showing differences between groups defined by their behavior as hyperactive or normally active (Sonuga-Barke & Taylor, 1992); and of distinguishing between people with and without schizophrenia (Shakow, 1963). The developmental course, however, is not satisfactorily described.

Stop Tests

The inhibition of responsiveness can also be tested in a simple setting. A reaction time test is set up in which a signal such as a light requires a motor response (e.g., pressing a button). The experimental variable is the presence of a "stop" stimulus, indicating that the presentation of the signal should be followed by no response. Schachar and Logan (1990b) compared children at second grade and undergraduate students on their abilities to inhibit a response in this way, with the length of time between the stop stimulus and the reaction time signal the experimentally manipulated variable. No developmental trend was found over this age period.

Matching Familiar Figures Test

Tests can also be contrived that require much longer periods of orientation than do the brief reaction time tests considered so far. Kagan, Rasman, Day, Albert, and Phillips (1964) elaborated the Matching Familiar Figures Test, which has attracted a good deal of research by developmentalists. A target picture is presented at the same time as six very similar pictures, only one of which is identical to the target. The task is to identify the one that is identical. This task requires quite detailed scanning and has latencies typically in excess of 10 seconds—very long by comparison with the fractions of a second required in reaction tests. On this kind of test, the developmental trend is not only for children to become more accurate in their responses but also for their latencies to increase. The developmental change is not one simply of increased ability to do the task and more rapid information processing. Rather, children develop the long latency cognitive processes that are required and inhibit their immediate response so that they can fully analyze the stimulus. Children who are "impulsive" (i.e., rapid and inaccurate) on this task also tend to obtain poorer scores on prolonged tests of vigilance (Zelniker, Jeffrey, Ault, & Parsons, 1972). They tend to be unsystematic in their scanning of a picture (Ault, Crawford, & Jeffrey, 1972).

Components of Attention

Hierarchy of Functions

The developmental studies considered so far have made it possible to identify different aspects of the abilities involved in a good performance on the various tests that have been applied to the study of attention. It is necessary to consider both elementary components and higher level executive functions. The more modular functions include the following: to orientate to a new signal; to filter out stimuli that differ in their physical properties from those that have been selected as relevant; to sustain and to inhibit

the readiness to respond to a particular signal; to shift attention from one area to another by disengaging, moving, and engaging; to search for relevant stimuli and to halt when they are found. A slightly higher level of decision making in the deployment of these elementary abilities is seen in the decisions that are made to allot longer attention to novel and relevant material. High levels of executive control are required for decisions about deploying adequate and prolonged processing resources to difficult and complex stimuli, and in deciding what aspects of a stimulus array are relevant. This suggestion of a hierarchy of functions in attention will require more research.

Independence of Functions

It is not clear how far the components of attending can be considered as independent. In later childhood and adult life, the different tests of attention typically intercorrelate to a very low degree (Moray, 1969; Spring, 1980). In infancy, there is rather more evidence that the different components of attention share processing resources. For instance, those infants whose gaze at an object is considered to be more intensive because it is accompanied by sustained heart deceleration are also rather less distractible than other children: the intensive and selective aspects appear to be correlated (Richards, 1987). In later childhood, covert orientation toward a stimulus (indexed by the worsening on test performance brought about by a misleading cue) interacts with resistance to distractibility (indexed by the worsening in performance brought about by incompatible distracting stimuli). The simultaneous presence of a misleading cue and distracting stimuli produces a much greater interference with performance than does either taken alone. Such findings require replication, but they suggest that covert orienting and filtering may share resources, at least in early childhood. It is also possible that the simple processes are entirely separate and that the interaction between the two happens at a higher level of executive control.

All these components are possible ways in which attention might be impaired in psychopathology. All of them require, not just evidence of impairment on a single type of test, but an interaction between subject group and experimental parameters imposed by the tester. Analysis of the nature of a deficit is therefore always required before the researcher can say more than that a psychopathological syndrome is associated with reduced information processing.

ATTENTION IN PSYCHIATRIC SYNDROMES

Attention Deficit Disorders

Development of the Concept

The various behaviors described as "hyperactivity" can be enduring problems that place personality development at risk. A syndrome of antisocial and inattentive behavior, in association with neurodevelopmental abnormalities, was described by Still at the beginning of the century and has continued to generate a great deal of clinical research and practice. The concept of minimal brain damage (or dysfunction) as a unifying biological cause, with a coherent symptomatology including attention deficit, became more and more important through the first half of the 20th century. The driven quality of the overactivity shown by some children after encephalitic disease gave rise to an increasing recognition of hyperkinetic syndrome (Kahn & Cohen, 1934). Indeed, the idea became overgeneralized. It was supported by ideological as much as by scientific, clinical findings and became a way of attributing behavior disturbances, rightly or wrongly, to an organic cause (Schachar, 1986). The discovery of the rapid action of central nervous system sympathomimetic stimulant drugs (Bradley, 1937) lent a pressing clinical urgency to the diagnosis, and neurophysiological explanations of the basic pathology of amphetamine sensitive individuals soon became available (Laufer, Denhoff, & Solomons, 1957). Correspondingly, practice in the United States saw a rapid increase in the second half of the 20th century in the rate with which hyperactivity was diagnosed. It quite rapidly became the most common child psychiatric, and perhaps the most common pediatric diagnosis.

Dissatisfaction with the notion of minimal brain dysfunction grew, as it became clear that no unitary picture of psychological disturbance was to be seen in children with brain dysfunction (Rutter, Graham, & Yule, 1970) and that no unitary biological dysfunction was to be seen or expected in children with disturbances of behavior (Bax & Mac Keith, 1962). The diagnosis became founded on more explicit criteria that were grounded in behavioral change rather than in an organic etiology. The *Diagnostic and Statistical Manual of Mental Disorders* (DSM-III, DSM-III-R, DSM-IV; American Psychiatric Association, 1980, 1987, 1994) schemes all considered that the basic and underlying pathology was a disturbance of attention; and the disorders were therefore referred to as "attention deficit disorder." DSM-III recognized separate conditions of attention deficit with and without hyperactivity; DSM-III-R followed a clinical consensus that there was a unitary condition to which both attention deficit and hyperactivity could be witness and renamed it Attention Deficit/Hyperactivity Disorder; DSM-IV has retained the general idea of a widespread unitary condition, but has recognized predominantly inattentive and predominantly overactive/impulsive subtypes so that attention deficit with no other problem is diagnosed in a separate subcategory.

This consensus within the North American schemes has not been matched on an international basis. Heavy criticism was expressed of the whole idea of an attention deficit disorder (e.g., Prior & Sanson, 1986). The current 10th edition of the World Health Organization's *International Classification of Diseases* named the condition hyperkinetic disorder, preferring not to consider it as an attention deficit disorder because of the lack of evidence that attention mechanisms are in fact involved (World Health Organization, 1992). Together with this disagreement about the nature of the basic underlying pathology goes a massive difference in the prevalence with which disorders are diagnosed. Hyperkinetic syndrome cannot be regarded as a mere synonym for attention deficit disorder, for it is much more rarely diagnosed. In clinical practice, hyperkinetic syndrome was diagnosed, according to a case register study in the United Kingdom, some 20 times less frequently than attention deficit disorder was diagnosed in the United States (Taylor, 1994a).

A case vignette study of the differences in diagnosis was reported by Prendergast et al. (1988) and showed that British psychiatrists diagnosing a common bank of case histories and videotapes made the diagnosis of hyperkinetic syndrome much less frequently than American psychiatrists made the diagnosis of attention deficit disorder. The reason came from different weight being given to different components of the syndrome. The presence of hyperactivity, and indeed the DSM-III diagnosis of attention deficit disorder, was made just as frequently by the English as by the North American diagnosticians. The difference came when a single category diagnosis scheme, such as the ICD-9, was applied: Then, the Americans tended to give greater weight to the hyperactivity symptoms and diagnosed attention deficit, whereas the British gave greater weight to the conduct disorder symptoms and diagnosed conduct disorder. Most children with hyperactivity problems showed conduct disorder too, and the disagreement about how to consider the nature of this comorbidity was responsible for major differences in clinical practice. This is not merely a matter of terminology, but also of treatment decisions; for the rarity of amphetamine treatment in most countries following the ICD tradition of diagnosis is in great contrast to the very high prevalence in those following the criteria recommended by the American Psychiatric Association.

The perspective of developmental psychopathology, and the distinctions between different lines of attention emphasized earlier, raise several issues that will need to be addressed before there is a clear understanding of the morbidity of the condition: Is attention deficit associated with conditions involving hyperactivity? If so, what types of attention mechanisms are involved? What are the developmental relationships between different components of the syndrome—attention deficit, overactivity, disruptive behavior, cognitive impairment? How do etiological influences interact to produce the various components of attention deficit syndromes, and how do they in turn relate with the outside world to lead to social malfunction? What is the developmental impact of therapies, and what should be the targets of intervention at different developmental stages?

Are "Attention Deficit" Syndromes Characterized by Abnormalities of Attention?

At the level of rating scale information, there is no doubt that children with hyperactivity are frequently described by their parents and teachers as inattentive. Because of the way the diagnosis is made, this is virtually a tautology. Doubts about the specificity come for several reasons. First, inattentiveness is a common complaint about children who do not have any psychiatric diagnosis—some 30% of the general population in the Isle of Wight survey (Rutter, Tizard, & Whitmore, 1970). Rates of inattentiveness are elevated in virtually all psychiatric disorders, including conduct and emotional disorders (Shaffer & Greenhill, 1979). Second, the validity of the rating of inattentiveness is in doubt. We do not know just what it is that parents and teachers mean when they say that a child is "inattentive." It might, for example, be that they are rating a social quality of unresponsiveness to themselves rather than anything unusual about the way the children alter their responsiveness to the outside world.

Answering the question of the role of attention therefore requires more observational methodologies. Such studies have been surprisingly scanty. A few investigators, however, have used ethological techniques of observing children in naturalistic or conversational settings. Dienske, de Jonge, and Sanders-Woudstra (1985) reported differences between children, not only in activity level, but also in orientation to objects and in the sustaining of activity. Luk, Thorley, and Taylor (1987) used systematic time and events sampling of behaviors during playroom activity and concluded that children with a diagnosis of hyperkinetic disorder were more impersistent in their activity as well as more unsystematically exploratory, disinhibited, and overactive. Taylor (1986a) described observations during psychological testing, together with investigator-based interview approaches, to conclude that brief duration of activity and rapid changes of activity were characteristic of children with diagnosed hyperactivity syndromes in a way that did not apply to other psychiatric conditions such as conduct disorder. At the behavioral level, therefore, the diagnosis of hyperkinetic syndrome and attention deficit disorder are indeed accompanied by inattentiveness.

By itself, this conclusion does not tell us that attention deficits are primary to hyperactivity. The relationship between the various components of the "syndrome" will be a key point for a developmental understanding. The simplest relationship—that overactive and impulsive behaviors are symptoms of an attention deficit—is probably not correct. The main argument against it stems from the existence of children whose attending behavior is impaired yet in whom there is no suggestion of overactive, impulsive, or disruptive behavior. This "pure attention deficit" is to be found in primary school age populations with a frequency of about 1 in 100 children (Szatmari, Offord, & Boyle, 1989; Taylor, Sandberg, Thorley, & Giles, 1991). Taylor et al. (1991) identified such boys at the age of 8 years in a total population neighborhood survey. They were inattentive and dreamy in their school behavior, but their activity levels according to teachers' ratings were within 1 SD of the population norm. When such children were studied more intensively, then they were indeed inattentive in the sense that they obtained poor scores on conventional psychometric tests of attention. However, they did not seem to be at risk for developing the other aspects of hyperactivity, for when followed up at a mean of 9 months later they were no more active, impulsive, or disruptive than controls drawn randomly from the nondeviant population. Furthermore, they seemed to have a rather different pattern of associations to hyperactive children: They lacked the signs of adverse family relationships and they showed, by contrast, a tendency to come from more disadvantaged socioeconomic groupings.

Perhaps it would be more accurate to think of more than one type of attention deficit. The relationship with hyperactivity needs more study. Genetic evidence might be very helpful here, if for example there was an excess of inattentiveness without overactivity/impulsiveness in the other members of the families of people with hyperactivity disorders. Developmental studies might show that inattentiveness was the antecedent of overactivity and impulsiveness, rather than the other way around. Therapeutic procedures might be developed that would affect inattentiveness without a direct effect on the other components of hyperactivity; so that an experimental approach might be taken to determining whether inattentiveness was primary to the other components. In the absence of clear conclusions from this type of evidence, researchers can only register it as an important aspect for future study. The vast majority of studies of the neuropsychological concomitants and developmental course of children with "attention deficit disorders" have in fact focused on children with a mixed group of disorders, including not only inattentiveness but also overactivity, impulsiveness, and disruptive behaviors.

What Is the Nature of the Attention Deficit?

The next issue is the type of psychological disturbance that is in fact indexed by the tests. Earlier parts of this chapter indicated that these "attention" tests could be influenced by many factors other than attention.

The ability to perform well on tests can be seen as a rather general ability, indexed by the IQ. IQ may account for some of the difference between hyperactive and control groups. The reduction in scores is found in a wide variety of tests, and the IQ is reduced in hyperactive children in most of these studies. However, some abnormalities are still to be found even after IQ has been controlled for by analysis of covariance.

Impairment can also be seen in a number of tests that are not particularly intended to assess attention—such as short-term memory (the Digit Span Test, Taylor et al., 1991), speed of response (serial and choice reaction time tests, Sykes, Douglas, & Morgenstern, 1973), new learning (Paired Associate Learning Tests, Swanson & Kinsbourne, 1976)—and even tachistocopically presented tests that were originally designed to avoid effects of attention (McIntyre, Blackwell, & Denton, 1978).

Controlled information processing is therefore likely to be impaired in hyperactivity. However, the subtractive analysis of different stages of information processing has not indicated anything that looks much like a modular attention deficit. Attempts to implicate encoding, search and decision stages of processing information (Sergeant & Scholten, 1985) and overall attentional capacity (Schachar & Logan, 1990a) have been unsuccessful. There is some evidence of abnormalities at the later stages of response selection and enaction—as witnessed, for example, by a disproportionate effect on hyperactive children of making the response incompatible with the stimulus (van der Meere & Sergeant, 1988a). An impairment of response stages of information processing could still be compatible with a specific disability in one of the elementary processes of attention whose development was previously considered.

Sustained attention failure is suggested by the poor scores on the CPT, but not supported when the experimental variable is the time for which the test must be done. For example, the deficit is manifest in tests lasting a few seconds just as it is in those lasting for 10 minutes or more (Taylor et al., 1991) and is much the same in tests lasting for several hours (van der Meere & Sergeant, 1988b). The primary problem is therefore unlikely to be one of sustaining attention over time.

Selective attention failure is often suggested, if only because it seems self-evident that distractibility is a part of hyperactivity. However, this too gets little support from the experimental literature based on psychopathological groups. Although hyperactivity may well be associated with distractibility in the behavioral sense that the child changes activities often, this is not the same as the disruptive effect of irrelevant information that is sought by the experimentalist. The addition of irrelevant information to test stimuli does not worsen performance disproportionately in children with hyperactivity (Douglas & Peters, 1979; Sergeant & Scholten, 1985). Some have suggested that the deficit lies in an excessive breadth of attention, so that performance on incidental tests should be improved to the same extent as performance on a central test is reduced. The evidence is contradictory here. One investigation did find a shift of attention from what is centrally relevant to what is peripheral (Ceci & Tishman, 1984); but the majority of studies investigating this possibility have not found it (Douglas & Peters, 1979; Taylor et al., 1991).

Intensity of attention has been studied with psychophysiological measures in children diagnosed as showing hyperactivity or ADDH. A number of studies have found that such children—while showing no changes in their basal activation—have a reduced phasic response of the autonomic nervous system to stimuli with novelty or signal value (reviewed by Taylor, 1986a). The P300 component of the auditory evoked response to stimuli requiring a response is also reduced (Loiselle, Stamm, Maitinsky, & Whipple, 1980).

However, we cannot proceed from these findings to infer an impairment in the intensity of attention in hyperactivity. Unlike the scores on attention tests, these measures have not yet been shown to be specific to hyperactivity. Some evidence suggests that they are not; Conners (1975) reported that whereas reduced amplitude of the skin conductance response characterized a hyperactive group, it correlated, not with levels of hyperactivity within that group, but rather with neuromuscular incoordination. The orienting response is smaller in children with intellectual retardation (Luria, 1963) and specific learning disorders (Cousins, 1976; Sroufe, Sonies, West, & Wright, 1973); these conditions are often comorbid with hyperactivity.

Inhibitory control has a much stronger claim to being a process that is impaired in hyperactivity. The best-known way of testing the idea of impulsiveness is through Kagan's Matching Familiar Figures Test discussed earlier (Kagan et al., 1964). In conditions of uncertainty, impulsive children make rapid and inaccurate responses; in the theory, they are inaccurate because they are too rapid. The analysis applies well in some epidemiological research. Not only are hyperactive children unduly quick in their response, but accuracy falls as they take less time to do it (Fuhrman & Kendall, 1986; Taylor et al., 1991). In clinical research, the analysis has not always worked very well. In some studies, especially of pervasive hyperactivity, children with hyperactivity have proved to be less accurate but no faster in their responses than clinically referred controls (Firestone & Martin, 1979; Sandberg, Rutter, & Taylor, 1978). The likely reason for this comes from the high rate of other developmental disabilities in these series. Such children are likely to have slower reactions because their processing time takes longer. Many studies have shown that they have slow reactions in conventional information-processing experiments (Sergeant, 1989). Their responses may

therefore be premature, even when they take the same amount of time as ordinary children. Their usual tendency is still to take less time in inspecting new material than most children do; when this is prevented by the experimenter's controlling the amount of time that they spend looking at a visual test, then their performance is no worse than anybody else's (Sonuga-Barke, Taylor, & Heptinstall, 1992).

Schachar and Logan (1990b) have directly tested the idea that children with hyperactivity are less able to inhibit a response than others, and found that the prediction holds for children with the serious problem of hyperkinetic disorder (not for those with ADHD). Rapport, Tucker, DuPaul, Merlo, and Stoner (1986) tied this more closely to the obtaining of reward with the finding that children with hyperactivity were more likely to respond for a small immediate reward than for a large delayed one. More recently still, investigators have made a systematic examination of the effects of delay and size of incentive on children's choices (Sonuga-Barke, Taylor, Sembi, & Smith, 1992). In one sense, this confirmed the impulsiveness of children with pervasive hyperactivity: Under some circumstances they were indeed maladaptive in responding too quickly and not waiting for a reward. But the research also showed that, when the total amount of time they had to wait was controlled, they were no more impulsive than ordinary children. The difficulty should not be seen as a fixed impairment of inhibitory control but as a change in the decision making about when to inhibit.

The result of this impulsiveness is that children choose to take less time over tasks they are given. If the task needs more time to be completed accurately, then their accuracy will suffer. If this is so, then their performance should increase to normal levels when the time taken is controlled experimentally; in one experiment involving new learning, this has proved to be the case (Sonuga-Barke, Taylor, & Heptinstall, 1992).

Such a formulation is rather different from the traditional explanations of hyperactivity, and more study will be needed to test its predictions. It is not yet clear whether all the impairments in attention tests that have been noted can be accounted for by cognitive impulsiveness.

Direction of Causality

The preceding analysis of the nature of attention deficit opens up the possibility of complex relationships between constitution and environment. A "traditional" theory conceives the effect of developmental abnormality of the brain as impairing the powers of concentration and thereby leading to disorders of behavior and learning. This is one possibility, but it has not been demonstrated. It is also possible, for instance, that qualities of the caretaking relationship in the early years of life determine a style of the child's approaching the world in which brief inspection and avoidance of delay are the norm; it could also be that this style of impulsive exploration leads to the child living in a less socially responsive world as well as a less stimulating one.

There may also be complex relationships between impairment of attention and learning disabilities. Pennington, Groisser, and Welsh (1993) have recently described a comparison between reading disability and attention deficit suggesting that the two disorders have different associated patterns of neuropsychological deficits and that the coexistence of both problems can be seen as the secondary elaboration of attention deficit symptoms in children at risk for reading impairment. The pathways involved are not yet clear, but the general issue is that the relationship between attention deficit and other psychological problems is likely to be more complex than that between a disease and its complications. Developmental understanding will be needed.

Developmental Course of Attention Deficit Disorders

Longitudinal studies offer a powerful way of clarifying developmental mechanisms. The first need, of course, is simply to describe the course. To what extent, and for what outcomes, is hyperactivity a risk? Infants vary greatly in their activity levels, but individual differences are not very strongly predictive: In one study, there was actually a negative correlation between activity at the age of 3 days and at 2.5 years (Bell, Weller, & Waldrop, 1971).

In the preschool period, overactivity is a common complaint made by parents. It is often hard to evaluate because activity is high in normal children and there are few demands on sustained concentration; thus it is difficult to determine whether the complaint is a valid comment on a deviation of development or whether it reflects a parent's reduced tolerance of a developmentally unremarkable level of demandingness. Sometimes "hyperactivity" is used by caretakers to refer to quite different problems from those in this chapter, such as sleeplessness and oppositionality.

Nevertheless, the complaint of overactivity at 3 years is a predictor of the presence of conduct disorder in later childhood (Campbell, 1987; Stevenson, Richman, & Graham, 1985). After the age of 3, the normal course of development involves a reduction of the general level of activity in some settings but not others (Routh, 1980).

Starting school makes prolonged attention more necessary. Some children—especially the most intelligent—cope with this transition well and meet all the requirements even if they are still distressingly uncontrolled at home. The persistence of unmodulated and inattentive behavior beyond this age becomes more and more of a problem as schooling proceeds. It carries risks for failing to learn, and other children are antagonized and begin to withdraw from them.

Hyperactivity is a risk factor for outcome in later childhood and adolescence. The major outcome is the development of aggressive and antisocial behavior and delinquency (August, Stewart, & Holmes, 1983; Barkley, Fischer, Edelbrock, & Smallish, 1990; Gittelman, Mannuzza, Shenker, & Bonagura, 1985; Hoy, Weiss, Minde, & Cohen, 1978; Riddle & Rapoport, 1976; Satterfield, Hoppe, & Schell, 1982). Affected children also tend to remain inattentive and impulsive, become isolated and unpopular among their peers, and do not achieve academically as they should (Hechtman, Weiss, & Perlman, 1984). These studies and conclusions are all based on clinically referred children compared with nonreferred controls. The risk factors might, therefore, be the other problems that lead to referral, not hyperactivity itself. However, a few epidemiological studies have been done; they suggest that, even when conduct disorder has developed, hyperactivity is still a predictor of a more antisocial outcome (Farrington, Loeber, & van Kammen, 1990; Schachar, Rutter, &

Smith, 1981). Its developmental importance is therefore not confined to acting as an entry route into conduct disorder; it also modulates the course of the antisocial behavior. This may be partly because it increases the impact of conduct disorder on other people and therefore the vicious cycle of angry untrusting and coercive relationships. It is not yet known whether attention deficit and hyperactivity compromise development in adolescence in themselves, rather than as epiphenomena of true risk factors. Longitudinal study of epidemiologically defined populations is urgently required.

The stormy course in adolescence can sometimes be followed by a relatively happy adult adjustment. For example, Thorley (1984) followed a group of children who had been identified from clinical records as hyperactive, over a 15-year period to their early adult life. The worst of the outcome had been during their adolescence. Then, they were even more at risk than a group of children referred at the same time for psychiatric help—usually because of conduct disorder. They were more likely to be expelled from school, to be the subjects of psychiatric treatment, to suffer multiple accidents, and to have seizures. But, by the time they were in their adult life, their outcome was little worse than that of the psychiatric controls and was more determined by their intelligence, social class, and aggression than by just how hyperactive they had been as children.

A comparable picture comes from the Montreal cohort, on which most of our knowledge is based (Weiss & Hechtman, 1986). Many children grow out of their hyperactivity and escape disablement. Those who do not avoid the risk are likely to show an explosive or an immature kind of personality, and this risk is mediated as much or more by aggression and family relationships as by the original degree of hyperactivity.

Both these follow-up studies may be optimistic. Attrition of the cohorts may well remove those who have the worst outcome, and their initial selection ensured that they had all been treated. The Montreal studies have excluded some of the worst-outcome cases, such as those with brain damage and intellectual retardation. Nevertheless, they make it reasonable for clinicians to advise patients and their families that there is a fair chance of a good eventual outcome provided that the worst traps in development can be avoided.

Developmental Issues in Hyperactivity

It may be concluded from the preceding section that there is a considerable (though not a complete) continuity between childhood hyperactivity and a range of hyperactive and antisocial behaviors in adolescence and early adult life. What accounts for this continuity? The syndromically oriented research has commonly been based on the premise that the stability of symptoms reflects the direct continuity of an underlying medical condition. This may be the case, but current research has not yet established it. It is also possible that more indirect chains of causality account for the predictive value of hyperactivity in childhood. Several issues need to be addressed. They include the issues of whether hyperactivity works developmentally as a risk factor or as a discrete disorder, whether there is heterogeneity with the risk factor, and which components of hyperactivity account for later outcome, and what factors operate to mediate the risk of hyperactivity.

Disorder or Risk Factor

A dominant theme in research on hyperactivity proposes a distinct category of mental disturbance. Debate centers on the best diagnostic criteria to use and the exact prevalence. One implication is that only the diagnostic level of severity constitutes a risk for later social adjustment. Sub threshold levels by contrast can be seen as the normal range of variation and would be unlikely in this view to constitute a developmental impairment. It is, however, equally possible that the behaviors of hyperactivity might constitute a continuum of severity with development being affected, to a greater or lesser degree, at all points in the range.

The empirical evidence does not settle the matter. Indeed, it is somewhat contradictory. On the one hand, the longitudinal study into late adolescence by Gittelman et al. (1985) has suggested that attention deficit disorder symptoms in themselves are the key to outcome. Only the clinical diagnosis was a risk factor; subthreshold levels of disturbance were not associated with the same kinds of adverse outcome; furthermore, only those in whom attention deficit symptoms persisted were at risk for an adult DSM diagnosis. The contrasting position comes from epidemiological studies in which risk appears to be associated with quite minor degrees of elevation of rated hyperactivity (e.g., Fergusson, Horwood, & Lloyd, 1991). There are real methodological problems. In the clinically based series, there are doubts whether any of the children can truly be "subclinical" because of the very high rates of comorbidity with other disorders; in the population-based studies, it is still not clear how far the poor outcome of those with minor degrees of risk is due to the presence within them of some children at great risk. Magnusson and Bergman (1990) analyzed the short-term outcome of children with conduct disorder, and found that the poor outcome was not a function of severity of disturbance across the whole range of behaviors, but only of a subgroup of antisocial children who were also characterized by hyperactivity, early onset, and poor peer relationships. This work raises the possibility that studies of hyperactivity will find the same: that only a subgroup is at developmental risk and that it is a pattern of symptoms rather than the level of hyperactivity that constitutes the risk. The point is of some practical importance, as well as carrying strong theoretical implications, and new generations of longitudinal study seem to be needed to answer this and the other developmental questions.

Heterogeneity

It is possible that children with hyperactive behavior are a heterogeneous grouping of several types of disorder; it is also possible that they represent a single large and common group. The latter is the view implicitly held by most biological researchers. Neurochemical, neuroimaging, and genetic strategies are based on widely defined groupings. The possibility of heterogeneity, however, has several times been suggested (e.g., Taylor et al., 1987).

The first possible way of subdividing is according to the predominance of one or another subtype of hyperactive behavior—especially attention deficit or overactivity/impulsivity. Limited evidence on this matter suggests that the risk resides in the over-activity/impulsivity component. For example, in the epidemiological study by Taylor et al. (1991), those children defined as having pure attention deficit without overactivity were not at risk for psychiatric symptoms at 1-year follow-up; those screened as being pervasively hyperactive were. If this proves to be the case, then it will raise issues of how far the overactivity/impulsivity component can be distinguished from that of oppositional/antisocial behaviors.

Another form of heterogeneity lies in the extent to which hyperactive symptoms are comorbid with other types of childhood psychopathology. The best known and largest overlap is that with conduct disorder symptoms. The separation of these forms of disturbance has been affirmed by several reviewers, notably Hinshaw (1987), Schachar (1991), and Taylor (1988). All these have emphasized the rather different predictive associations of hyperactivity and conduct disorder, and especially the neurodevelopmental associations of attention deficit. The developmental significance of the distinction may be that of different developmental tracks (Hinshaw, Lahey, & Hart, 1993). It is not yet clear whether hyperactivity is still a risk factor when the researcher allows for comorbidity with oppositional-defiant symptomatology. An epidemiological study of 7-year-old boys by Taylor et al. (1991) suggested that it was: Children rated as hyperactive but not defiant were at risk for both hyperactivity and defiance-aggression 9 months later; whereas children who were defiant but not hyperactive were at risk for defiant-aggressive symptoms later but not for hyperactivity.

This is in some contrast to the findings by Fergusson et al. (1993). These workers used latent dimension analysis of an epidemiologically defined cohort to predict the course of later development. Children with aggression and defiance were indeed at risk for antisocial behaviors and criminality in their later outcome. However, children with attention deficit symptomatology were not. They were, unlike the defiant-aggressive, at risk for poor educational outcomes. A possible resolution of these disparate findings is to suppose that the risk factors interact in different ways at different points in development. In earlier childhood, hyperactivity is a risk for later conduct disorder; but the risk is all expressed by the age of about 8 or 9 years. Thereafter—during the period studied by Fergusson et al.—the two types of disorder pursue rather different developmental tracks.

A third form of heterogeneity may also exist within the group of children who show consistently hyperactive behaviors. For example, Taylor et al. (1987) contrasted, on the basis of cluster analysis, several different types of hyperactive behavior. Two important ones were (a) a group of children with pervasive and severe hyperactive behaviors, of very early onset in development, accompanied by neurodevelopmental delays; (b) a group of children with a later onset of hyperactivity confined largely to classroom settings, found in association with various forms of learning disability. The separability of an early onset and pervasive group has also been suggested by a lower gender ratio and a different pattern of affected family members in hyperkinesis than is normally reported in studies of attention deficit with hyperactivity (James & Taylor, 1990). This form of heterogeneity may also be of developmental importance: It raises the possibility that the poor outcome in groups of children with attention deficit disorder may result from the existence within them of a subtype of particularly high risk, as already suggested by Magnusson and Bergman (1990).

Predictive and Mediating Factors

We do not yet know the mediating pathways involved in the longitudinal course. The mechanism may be the continuation of a hyperactivity disorder, in which case the key to treatment should be the meticulous and prolonged control of the symptoms. However, against this notion is the clear finding of a very poor outcome in series of children who have been thoroughly treated at famous clinics specializing in the management of hyperactivity (Barkley et al., 1990; Satterfield et al., 1982). Accordingly, it is also possible that the risk is mediated through other factors such as self-esteem or the critical reactions of other people. A poor outcome in hyperactive children is predicted not only by severity of symptomatology and the presence of conduct disorder but also by discordant family relationships, depression in mothers, and antisocial fathers (Barkley et al., 1990; Lambert, 1988; Taylor et al., 1991; Wallander, 1988; Weiss & Hechtman, 1986). Recent work by Crouch (1992) has made multivariate predictions of outcome in a group of children initially studied as part of an epidemiological study, with the conclusion that family adversity and adverse peer relationships predict the later outcome independently of the extent to which they are associated with hyperactivity to begin with. It therefore seems very likely that treatment will fail to be maximally effective if, as is usually the case, it is confined to measures such as stimulant medication whose impact is on the behavior of the child. Stimulants are powerful agents in reducing hyperactivity in the short term; but in the long term, they may have little developmental impact on the majority of children for whom they are prescribed (Jacobvitz, Sroufe, Stewart, & Leffert, 1990).

Influences on Development of Attention Deficits

Our knowledge of the factors affecting dysfunction of attention remains confounded by the extent to which nearly all studies have defined groups not only on the basis of attentional problems but also on the basis of overactivity and impulsiveness. It is hard to know just what the specific influences may be. Reviews of the etiology of attention deficit disorder are based on an extensive literature that is reviewed elsewhere (see, e.g., Taylor, 1994a). From a developmental perspective, the important aspects to emphasize are the likely interaction of genetic inheritance and the psychological environment in shaping problems.

Genetic Inheritance

Several twin studies have indicated a genetically inherited component in hyperactivity. Monozygotic twins have been known for some time to be more concordant than dizygotic twins for several temperamental dimensions, including activity (Buss & Plomin, 1975; Goodman & Stevenson, 1989; Torgersen & Kringlen, 1978). This could not be accounted for by the greater physical similarity of the monozygotic, for the finding still held when considering cases where parents were mistaken about their children's zygosity (Goodman & Stevenson, 1989). Large nongenetic effects were also to be found.

Even these large series of twins include few who could be expected to show a clinically diagnosable disorder. We do not yet know the genetic contribution to the disorder, nor do we know very much about just what is inherited. The study by Goodman and Stevenson suggested that pervasive hyperactivity in the probands was accompanied by pervasive or school-based hyperactivity in the cotwins, suggesting that home-specific problems might have a rather different basis. The inheritance of attention deficit is not known, nor whether it segregates with hyperactive behavior in the way that must be expected if inattentiveness is indeed to be seen as a fundamental pathology. (Alberts-Corush, Firestone, & Goodman, 1986, argued for increased inattentiveness in the relatives of hyperactive children, but could not allow for sampling problems.)

An older literature comparing relatives of different degrees of relatedness has been reviewed elsewhere (Taylor, 1986b). Full siblings of hyperactive children are more likely than half-siblings to be hyperactive themselves (Safer, 1973). Biological parents, who are living with their own hyperactive children, are more likely to have had behavioral problems than the adoptive parents of hyperactive children—but this could reflect some other factor such as the selection of problem-free people as adopters (Cantwell, 1975). The adopted-away offspring of psychiatric patients are particularly likely to be hyperkinetic (Cunningham, Cadoret, Loftus, & Edwards, 1975). A complex set of findings from a Scandinavian register-based study suggested that the link between hyperactivity in children and antisocial behavior in their parents was partly genetic (Bohman, Cloninger, Sigvardsson, & von Knorring, 1982). This is circumstantial evidence, but it all points in the same direction toward a genetically inherited basis without saying exactly what that basis is.

The inherited basis might be rather nonspecific. Studies of psychopathology in the parents of children with hyperactivity have shown an increase in antisocial behaviors, which is very similar to the increased rate in the parents of antisocial children (Biederman et al., 1986; Lahey, Schaughency, Hynd, Carlson, & Nieves, 1987; Schachar & Wachsmuth, 1990; Stewart, deBlois, & Cummings, 1980). Schachar (1991) suggests that this is all due to the presence of comorbid antisocial disorder in the hyperactive children, and that hyperactivity in itself has no association with parental psychopathology; but epidemiological findings suggest that even children with a pure pattern of hyperactivity and nothing else may have high rates of parents who show psychopathology (Szatmari et al., 1989). The argument is complex and not yet resolved: There may well be several mechanisms through which behavior disorders in parents may be transmitted to their children, and some parental depression is probably the result of caring for a difficult child. The genetic contribution may need to be disentangled from a mixture of other influences, so more research here is badly needed.

Associations with Psychosocial Factors

Researchers have given less attention to the psychological environment than they have to the working of the brain. Nevertheless, a number of associations are known that could have etiological importance.

Social Adversity

The external disadvantages that affect family life should be distinguished from the alterations of personal relationships that they may cause. Poverty, bad housing, and low socioeconomic status have been investigated several times but their role is still uncertain. In some surveys, there has been no association at all (Campbell & Redfering, 1979; Goyette, Conners, & Ulrich, 1978; Szatmari et al., 1989; Taylor et al., 1991). Pervasive hyperactivity has been linked with lower social class (Schachar et al., 1981), but this could be due to the effect of co-existing conduct disorder.

Institutional upbringing is associated with inattentive and impulsive behavior (Roy, 1983; Tizard & Hodges, 1978). This is not likely to reflect material disadvantage, for the children's homes studied were on the whole reasonably well provided. Rather, the experience of changing caretakers and the lack of opportunity for stable attachments seem to be at the heart of the problem. Children who have grown up in this way are particularly likely to be inattentive in their classrooms, even after they have been adopted into a family home and their other psychological problems have improved.

Family Relationships

Adversity in close personal relationships is a robust association with hyperactive behavior. Hyperactive children are more common in families characterized by marital discord (Brandon, 1971), hostile parent-child relationships (Battle & Lacey, 1972; Tallmadge & Barkley, 1983) and discordant family life (Gillberg, Carlstrom, & Rasmussen, 1983).

All these associations have emerged from studies in which the cases are ascertained on the basis of their behavioral disturbance. This evidently allows the possibility that all the changes in family life were secondary to the abnormal behavior of the children. Some of the changes probably are secondary: Schachar, Taylor, Wieselberg, Thorley, and Rutter (1987) used the response to stimulant medication as a tool to investigate the family relationships and reported that critical expressed emotion from the parents was markedly reduced when the child's behavior was made more normal. Some of the changes in family life are probably not secondary, for they antedate the development of hyperactivity. This is particularly clear from evidence that hyperactivity is common in children who were at risk even before they were born because they had parents who had sought a termination of the pregnancy (Matejccek, Dytrych, & Schuller, 1985). Rieder and Cicchetti (1989) found that children who had been maltreated showed abnormal cognitive control function: This is not to be equated with hyperactivity but is of particular value in suggesting that the effects of family adversity are to be found in attention dysfunction and not only in disruptive or disobedient behavior.

Other investigators have used longitudinal strategies to test the possibility that family adversity can cause attention deficit disorders. Jacobvitz and Sroufe (1987) assessed some parenting problems in a prospective longitudinal study of children followed from 6 months to 42 months. An intrusive pattern of maternal care was predictive of teachers' ratings of hyperactivity when the children were in kindergarten. This seems to be all the more noteworthy because qualities of the child did not predict later hyperactivity. However, the negative conclusion was not so secure: better measures of the children's development and temperament might well have yielded significant predictions. It remains possible that the predictive effect of family variables was seen because the very early behavior of the child had shaped parenting practices. The research has not yielded definite conclusions, but it has pointed to the kind of longitudinal and observational investigation that needs to be done to correct the overemphasis on organic factors that has marred etiological research.

Virtually all the studies of family antecedents of hyperactivity fail to allow for the likely presence of conduct disorder as well. This is a serious lack. When, for example, Jacobvitz and Sroufe (1987) identified their cases of hyperactivity on the basis of teacher ratings, they were almost certainly selecting a group with high levels of conduct disorder. The family associations of conduct disorder are well known and strong; it is essential to determine whether they have any effect on attention deficit and whether different factors cause hyperactivity from those implicated in conduct disorder. Epidemiological evidence is needed because of the likelihood that adverse family relationships will be one of the factors leading to referral to clinical services. In one such study, poor coping and critical emotion from parents were characteristic of hyperactivity even allowing for conduct disorder (Taylor et al., 1991). In this last study, adverse family relationships were associated with the persistence of disorder over time: their developmental role may be the maintenance rather than the initiation of disorder. Alternatively, there may be qualities of the parent-child relationship that impair the development of self-regulation and therefore lead directly to the appearance of attention deficit disorder. Alternatively again, the role of adversity in family life might be to make more likely the development of conduct disorder in children who are predisposed because they have the risk factor of hyperactivity.

SCHIZOPHRENIA

Changes in Attention Tests

Attention changes have been thought to be important in schizophrenia for many years. Bleuler (1911/1950) thought there were several types: At one extreme were patients who were highly distractible and entirely governed by the stimuli from the environment, with almost all the information that reached them being registered. At the other extreme were patients who seemed to care nothing about the environment; though even in them there was the possibility that they were overwhelmed by unfiltered sense impressions. The introspective descriptions of sufferers have sometimes included similar experiences, such as "it's diversion of attention that troubles me," "everything seems to grip my attention although I am not particularly interested in anything," "I had very little ability to sort the relevant from the irrelevant" (McGhie, 1969). These clinical descriptions encouraged theoretical formulations in which thought disorder was conceived as a failure to filter out irrelevant associations and half-formed thoughts from consciousness. In fact, it is not at all clear in any rigorous sense that normal people do in fact generate such associations and thoughts that need to be screened out, nor that they would experience anything approaching thought disorder if such filtering failed. Nevertheless, the ideas have generated many cross-sectional case control comparisons on experimental tasks. There are now many findings of altered information processing from decades of study (reviewed by Holzman, 1987). For example, a continuous performance test is performed poorly by nearly half of parents with schizophrenia, even after the acute episode is over (Wohlberg & Kornetsky, 1973). Reaction time has long been known to be prolonged in schizophrenia and used as an index of impaired set (Rodnick & Shakow, 1940). Irrelevant, distracting information impairs performance on simple tests of memory in schizophrenia (Lawson, McGhie, & Chapman, 1964). The amplitude of the P300 component of the evoked potential is reduced (Baribeau-Brown, Picton, & Gosselin, 1983).

The research must, however, take things further if a developmental understanding is to be achieved (Taylor, 1994b). We would need to know, for example, whether the information-processing deficits result from changes in any of the previously noted developmental lines of attention; the time course of the deficits and whether they parallel clinical changes; whether they are a deviant form of information processing or an incomplete development and whether they are similar to alterations of attention encountered in other developmental contexts; how the deficits are affected by the interaction of genes and experience; and how they relate to the different components of the clinical syndrome of schizophrenia.

Developmental Perspectives: Type of Attention Impairment

The most promising experimental analyses suggest that there are changes of *selective attention*. The poor scores on the continuous performance test are not a function of vigilance, for they are not a function of the length of time for which the test is given. Rather they depend on the load that is placed on the early stages of information processing. Perceptual sensitivity, as assessed from signal-to-noise discrimination, is the measure that is most impaired; the offspring of schizophrenics also show a deficit when the perceptual difficulty is increased by presenting a very blurred image to be detected (degraded-stimulus CPT) (Nuechterlein, 1983). A "span of apprehension" task also showed a difference between people with schizophrenia and normal controls (Asarnow & MacCrimmon, 1981). Superficially, this is a memory task, requiring recognition of very briefly presented letters. However, the deficit only appears when irrelevant letters are presented at the same time and is worse when there is more irrelevant information. It can therefore be taken as further evidence for a breakdown in selection between stimuli. A failure of selective attention has also been implicated in analyses of the problems that people with schizophrenia (and depression) have in memory for dichotic listening (Hemsley & Zawada, 1976). Their difficulty came especially in distinguishing between relevant and irrelevant digits that were read out loud by different voices.

The studies of the normal development of selective attention reviewed here indicated that resistance to distraction could be seen in part as a relatively mechanical "filtering" process, but also that higher-level decisions about what is relevant had to be included in the account. Research on what is treated as irrelevant in different circumstances therefore deserves a good deal more emphasis. A simple related experimental paradigm is that of *latent inhibition*. A stimulus X is consistently paired with a signal for some other task (T); and then itself becomes a signal for a new task. Under these circumstances, stimulus X is less well processed: The new task based on it is learned less efficiently and reaction time is longer. It is arguable that the person originally learned that X was irrelevant during the course of task T and so does not pay much attention to it. People with schizophrenia, by comparison with normal controls, show less of this inhibition of responsiveness to X. Their reactions to X in the new task are actually faster than those of controls (Baruch, Hemsley, & Gray, 1988). This is not to be explained by filter breakdown and increased incidental learning, for then people with schizophrenia should be predicted to have learned more about X during the initial task, including that it is irrelevant. Rather it implies that schizophrenia is associated with a diminished ability to form or use knowledge about the previous importance of stimuli.

This clinical finding raises a new question for developmental research. How do people develop the ability to identify the relevance of signals and to apply their previous knowledge about them? Preliminary studies of latent inhibition in normal and hyperactive children have suggested a complex developmental course (Lubow & Josman, 1993); but more work is needed to give a systematic account and allow for effects of IQ and behavior. Developmental analyses of similar problems in selective attention have made much use of experimental manipulations of instructions and the relevance of precues. These approaches from developmental psychology could be usefully applied to schizophrenia.

Developmental Perspectives: Longitudinal Course

We know that poor test performance is relatively stable over periods of a few months after a first schizophrenic illness (Asarnow & MacCrimmon, 1981; Harvey, Docherty, Serper, & Rasmussen, 1990). This does not by itself mean that attention dysfunction is a trait problem nor that it enters into the etiology. Concentration may take months to recover after an acute schizophrenic episode even when recovery is eventually complete. However, Erlenmeyer-Kimling and Cornblatt (1987) have provided some long-term evidence. They found, like others, that children at risk because their parents had a schizophrenic illness showed deficits on a range of "attention tests" (CPT, span of apprehension, and digit span). The study was able to follow the children to their early adult life, by which time a few had undergone psychiatric hospitalization. Their breakdown could be predicted from childhood status by their score on these attention tests.

It is tempting to conclude that the impairment of attention is in itself the risk factor for schizophrenia. This, however, would go too far. For one thing, many children in the general population (around 5%) will show comparable impairment of attention and it is not at all clear that they are also at risk. If it is only a risk in those with a schizophrenic inheritance, then perhaps it is an indirect marker rather than a specific vulnerability. Another query arises from a report by the same study that those who later broke down had also had a lower IQ in childhood (Erlenmeyer-Kimling, Kestenbaum, Bird, & Hilldoff, 1984). Perhaps the risk factor was not specifically a failure of selective attention, but a more general cognitive problem.

A better understanding of developmental course will also need information about the relationship between disturbances of attention and different types of symptomatology. Schizophrenia is not a homogeneous syndrome, and several of the previously described disturbances of attention are also encountered in mania and depression. Evidence has appeared that poor performance on the CPT and span of apprehension tasks is correlated with the severity of the "negative" symptoms of mental impoverishment, not with the "positive" symptoms of bizarre thinking (Nuechterlein, Edell, Norris, & Dawson, 1986). There is also some evidence that direct tests of distractibility may be linked to positive rather than negative symptoms (Harvey et al., 1990), so further analyses of the selective attention deficit will be required.

The time course of changes in attention may be related to the development of psychotic episodes. Nuechterlein and Dawson (1984) presented an influential model of stress and vulnerability. Environmental stress interacted with the previous limitations of the person to produce vicious circles of breakdown: overload of processing capacity, autonomic hyperarousal, and a reduced sensitivity to social stimuli. These were seen as the immediate antecedents of psychotic episodes.

In summary, present understanding suggests that some of the information-processing deficit in schizophrenia is due to an alteration of the development of selective attention that antedates the symptoms of illness. Impaired attention could be a marker of the schizophrenia genotype that impairs social information processing, so that stress and social avoidance are both indirect consequences. Developmental research should have a good deal to contribute to clarifying the ways in which the genotype is expressed. Fruitful next steps include the further analysis of the nature of the problem in adults; the comparison of attention in people at high risk for schizophrenia with those who show other patterns of attention deficit; and the identification and follow-up of children in the general population with impairments of selective attention.

INTELLECTUAL RETARDATION

Inattentive behavior is associated with low intelligence. This truism has sometimes been obscured by researchers selecting groups with "attention deficit" in such a way that all those with learning difficulties are excluded. Nevertheless, unbiased estimates yield a consistent association. For example, children selected from an epidemiological survey on the basis of teachers' ratings of poor concentration had a mean IQ one standard deviation below that of children who were not behaviorally deviant (Taylor et al., 1991).

Scores on tests intended to measure attention also correlate with IQ (Taylor, 1986a). The correlations are usually significant but small. Attention is one of the functions assessed by intellectual testing; modern test batteries often include items that were originally introduced as measures of attention. On the other hand, individually administered IQ tests are usually designed so as to be insensitive to changes of attention. The psychologist structures the situation, gives clear instructions, controls the setting and often shows the subject what is relevant. All these can be expected to reduce the load on attention and make it less probable that poor attention will limit performance. The relationship between measured attention and IQ is therefore complex, and neither of them is a single entity. Both are convenient terms for large domains of mental function, and it is not surprising that they overlap.

Intellectual and attending functions will influence one another in several ways. Both may, in principle, be affected by similar causes—genetic, neurodevelopmental, and psychosocial. Intelligence can be expected to affect attending through a better metacognitive understanding about where the child should orient in different circumstances—one of the determinants of selective attention considered earlier. Attention might also affect intelligence. Visual attention to novelty has already been described as an infancy predictor of later cognitive development. The pathways involved are not known; one possibility is that a preference for novelty spurs on intellectual development. According to this idea, infants' attention shapes the complexity of the world they experience. If they prefer novel stimuli, then they are experiencing more interesting stimulation and more information that contradicts their expectations; consequently, they develop more complex cognitive structures. Intelligence in later life could even be seen as one kind of response to novelty: intellectual grasp of familiar material reflects primarily what the person has learned, so the powers of understanding are only really tested when they are needed for something outside previous experience. According to this view, the infant inspecting a novel stimulus and the child solving a novel problem are at different points along the same line of development.

Clinicians are often seeking evidence that will clarify whether a developmental delay is specific or general. They therefore need concepts that differentiate sharply between intellectual retardation and attention deficits, even while they acknowledge the interrelatedness of the two. The ICD-10 criteria for hyperkinetic syndrome, and other specific developmental delays, do this by excluding the diagnosis if the IQ is less than 70 (World Health Organization, 1992). This solution cannot be recommended. For one thing, it is essential in clinical and educational practice to recognize specific deficits in people who also show generalized delay. For another, individual differences in IQ above 70 may still account for apparent attention deficit.

A better solution to the conceptual problems of studying inattentiveness in people with generalized learning disability would be to use an idea of *specific attention retardation*. This would exist if scores on tests of attention were substantially less than those that would be predicted from the age and IQ of the child. Standardization of attention tests would be required for this, an enterprise widely neglected. It would then be possible to inquire empirically into whether specific retardation were different from inattentiveness that is merely in keeping with general developmental level.

AGING AND DEMENTIA

As people age, a decline in performance on tests of effortful information processing is very common (Welford, 1980). As considered earlier (see "Information-Processing Tests: Developmental Trends"), reaction time increases markedly and choice reaction time increases even more rapidly with aging. The processes involved in this normal aging process are not yet worked out. Poor attention could be the explanation, but it has already been stressed that there are many other possible reasons for a slowness in processing information. In other kinds of cognitive tests, such as short-term memory, attention has also been invoked as an explanation of the changes seen during aging (Craik & Byrd, 1982); but again the concept is being used in a rather vague and global sense, and not tested experimentally. Some high-level impairments are probably involved; for instance, a failure to grasp instructions (Rabbitt, 1979).

The cognitive changes in *dementia* are more extensive and varied. They include abnormalities on tests that are conventionally regarded as measuring attention; but have not yet shown that poor attention is the reason for poor scores. *Reaction times* are slowed in patients with dementia, even more than in age-matched controls (Hart & Semple, 1990). The difference is found both in simple tests and choice tests where a discrimination is expected. Continuous performance tests are also sensitive to dementia, and are more likely to be impaired than in normal aging or in functional psychiatric disorders such as depression (Alexander, 1973). There have been a few attempts to analyze why information processing is slowed in this way. For example, the speed and spacing of stimuli in reaction time tests have been varied experimentally (Hart & Semple, 1990). The prolongation of reaction times is more pronounced when stimuli come more rapidly and unpredictably. The implications of this for theories of attention are rather mixed. It can be taken as evidence that the abilities required to cope with unexpected stimuli are particularly lacking, and this is in keeping with the work cited earlier. It is also in keeping with the extensive evidence that effortful, controlled information processing shows a marked impairment even at the early stages of Alzheimer's disease (Jorm, 1986). It does not, however, tell us whether information processing is disturbed because of changes in attention, and it could well follow from a diminution of information-processing capacity rather than from any strategy change.

Selective attention has been studied with the Stroop Test (see above) (Hart & Semple, 1990). Patients with dementia were impaired in their speed and accuracy on this test, and disproportionately impaired when the stimuli were at their most confusing. A poor performance on an embedded figures test in dementia was found by Capitani, Della Sala, Lucchelli, Soave, and Spinnler (1988) and construed as a selective attention deficit. This sort of test certainly requires a figure to be picked out from a confusing background, but since the picture has to be analyzed before they can tell what is relevant and what is not, the finding is perhaps evidence of a problem in spatial perception rather than selective attention.

The *intensive* aspects of attention in dementia have been investigated using the P300 component of the auditory averaged evoked potential (Blackwood & Christie, 1986; Blackwood, St. Clair, Blackburn, & Tyrer, 1987). The amplitude is decreased and the latency increased; and as dementia progresses, the changes become more marked (St. Clair, Blackburn, Blackwood, & Tyrer, 1988).

The *control* of attending has been stressed by Baddeley's (1988) analysis of the changes in memory that are seen in senile dementia of Alzheimer type. In some experiments, for example, patients with dementia can remember experimental material well when the interval between items allows them to rehearse; but forget particularly quickly when a second task is presented in the interval so that rehearsal is suppressed. The interpretation is that new learning may be impaired chiefly by the resource demands of carrying out two tasks simultaneously. More research would be needed to determine whether this is truly a matter of attention, for it might result from a restriction of the capacity for effortful processing rather than from altered strategies about how to deploy those resources. Baddeley's analysis emphasizes the interdependence of different types of impairment of mental performance. The problem is to understand the significance of changes in tests of attention when all cognitive tests are to some extent impaired. Experimental analyses of the reasons for deteriorating performance, along the lines of those used to describe increasing abilities during development, should be illuminating.

CONTRIBUTIONS OF PSYCHOPATHOLOGY TO NORMAL DEVELOPMENT

Findings about people with psychiatric disorders have contributed to our knowledge of normal function from the beginnings of the scientific study of attention (see "Historical Review of Concepts"). Historically, the major role of psychopathology has been to indicate topics that needed study rather than to provide the methods and concepts for detailed inquiry. Thus, clinicians' descriptions of the neglect syndromes encountered in neurological disease were instrumental in giving rise to the original idea that the intensity of applying attention could be distinguished from the ability to perform a task. This is an example of a major role of pathology: to indicate what processes can be distinguished from one another. In a rather similar way, the clinical study of children with attention deficit disorder has emphasized the importance of allocating sufficient time to a task and tolerating delay to achieve reward. This should direct the focus of future developmental inquiry toward considering how this form of decision making about the use of mental resources appears in normal children, and whether the abnormality in attention deficit is an immaturity of development or a deviant pathway. The analysis of the disorder has, in effect, created a new area of study. However, psychopathology does not necessarily provide the intellectual tools that will be needed. They may come from any source of theory, including adult psychology and animal research.

Investigators often hope that their conclusions about the etiology of disorder will have direct implications for understanding the determinants of normal development. This may be the case, but researchers cannot assume it. Some forms of pathology can be seen as representing the extreme effect of the same causes that generate individual differences within the general population;

but others have no counterpart in normal development. There is no shortcut here; both have to be studied independently. Nevertheless, ideas about cause taken from one domain can be fertile suggestions about the other.

The neurological localization of some attention processes was suggested by the findings from parietal lobe pathology and from people with frontal lobe dysfunction (Shallice, 1988). This cannot be more than a suggestion, for the localization of dysfunction is not to be equated directly with the areas serving normal function. The advent of neuroimaging techniques will probably be the future means of clarifying the way in which different parts of the brain take part in the processes of selecting information; but clinico-pathological correlations have played and will play a useful role. Thus, parietal lobe lesions have long been known to produce sensory phenomena such as visual ignoring—in which visual information in the sensory field contralateral to a lesion is not detected even though peripheral pathways are intact, and extinction—in which stimuli contralateral to a lesion are seen when presented on their own but not when ipsilateral stimuli are present at the same time.

Neuropsychological analyses have suggested specific psychological deficits in association with specific lesions (Posner et al., 1984). For example, the shifting of visuospatial attention can be decomposed into components of disengaging, moving, and engaging. If a warning signal is given to indicate where a target will be presented, then the reaction time will be shorter because attention has been focused on that place. In lateralized parietal lesions, a misleading warning that summons attention to the side of the lesion produces a great increase in reaction time to targets presented contralaterally. The interpretation is that there is a difficulty in disengaging from a stimulus on the same side as a lesion. The neurological analysis suggests how shifts of attention may be carried out in the normal functioning of the brain, and this can be tested with methods such as positron emission tomography.

Neuropathological findings can also be helpful in suggesting alternative routes through which the brain may normally achieve its ends. One might, for example, find a dissociation of function at different developmental stages. An "attention" task such as maintaining a readiness to respond in spite of delay could be served by lower centers such as the caudate nucleus in earlier development and taken over by more rostral structures such as the frontal cortex in later childhood. Lesions would therefore have different effects according to the stage of development at which the individual is tested. These effects would both suggest the staging of brain function and direct attention to the possibility that differences in performance (both within the normal range and between normal and pathological groups) could result from the strategy difference of using the "wrong" part of the brain to carry out the task.

Etiological brain lesions can also suggest a deep similarity between apparently disparate tasks. For example, progressive supranuclear palsy is a brain disease that handicaps the control of eye movements. It also impairs the control of covert visual attention, in which the focus is shifted even though the eyes remain stationary. Posner, Cohen, and Rafal (1982) presented warning and target stimuli so quickly that the eyes themselves did not have time to move between them; yet patients still showed longer reaction times when they had to shift the focus of their attention. It is therefore possible that the same brain structures used in shifting overt attention via the eyes are involved in covert attention processes.

The role of factors outside the brain is very largely based on the study of psychopathological groups. This review of the development of attention deficit disorders in childhood drew attention to the range and likely importance of associations with psychosocial adversity. In considering the potential developmental pathways involved, it has been very helpful to examine cohorts of children defined by their exposure to the putative risk factors rather than concentrate on diagnostic groupings. Maltreated children, rejected children, and institutionalized children have all been shown to have attention problems of one kind or another—though it is far from clear that they all have the same type of problem or that the routes into it are similar in all groups. It might prove, for instance, that understimulated children failed to develop the usual skills of organizing their responsiveness to stimuli, whereas abused children used intact organizing skills to withhold attention from some whole classes of distressing stimuli. The result in both cases would be children appearing not to concentrate, but the remedial action needed would vary profoundly.

The argument can therefore be made that minor degrees of understimulation or harsh treatment are responsible for the variation in attention found in normal populations, and that close personal relationships are important in moving children to successively higher stages of attending. The argument cannot be resolved in present knowledge. The stressed groups may or may not be good witnesses to the factors responsible in the rest of the population. The continuities and discontinuities, between the reasons for individual differences found in the majority of children and those found in extreme subgroups, are a key subject for developmental psychopathology. They will be clarified by empirical study, not argument about what should be expected a priori. The importance of the psychopathological studies for normal development so far has not been to answer the questions about the origins of individual differences but to raise them.

CONCLUSIONS

The research that is called for to answer specific questions has been indicated throughout the chapter. It can be summarized into a few broad themes.

The first theme is the need for basic research into the development of functions whose importance has been indicated by the emerging understanding of psychopathology. It has not usually been very fruitful to apply ideas developed to account for the performance of radar and switchboard operators, directly to explaining mental disorders. Rather, as in the case of the so-called attention deficit disorder, it has proved a better strategy to analyze the nature of the cognitive impairment. This has produced a need for a deeper understanding of what is meant by "impulsiveness," and whether it reflects a deficit in the ability to inhibit or in how decisions are made about the regulation of responsiveness; and for a fuller understanding of how exploration becomes an organized process; so as to understand the uninhibited and disorganized behaviors seen in psychopathology.

Nevertheless, the distinctions made by developmental psychology, about the processes involved in the acquisition of increased attending skills with age, are likely to be useful in providing subtler analyses of the impairments in psychopathology. The notion of a hierarchy of abilities is far removed from the rather mechanical notions of the breakdown of a peripheral filter. The development of techniques for the measurement of decision-making processes in the control of the direction of attention should be a priority.

Psychosocial determinants of attention should be another theme for the research of the next decade. Theorizing in this area was inhibited while it seemed that attention could only be thought of as a basic and elementary process linked closely to neurophysiological processes. The work should be liberated by the realization of how the developing child evolves strategies of exploration and self-regulation, and accordingly of how adults and other children might collaborate in the process. Observational studies of how social interactions guide and direct children's attention are feasible in normal and deviant populations.

The neurological determinants of attention have attracted less studies in recent years than they once did. However, the sophistication of functional neuroimaging techniques raises the possibility of a renaissance of such studies. At the simplest level, neuroimaging can seek a physiological deficit corresponding to impaired psychological ability. This approach leads, for example, to the finding that adults, identified because they are both the parents of children with ADHD and the bearers of ADHD symptoms, show hypofrontality in positron emission tomography (Zametkin et al., 1990). This does not necessarily add much conceptually to our understanding of the problem; rather, it describes the same events with a different technology. More complex levels of analysis will also be possible. The different components of attention seem to have identifiably distinct bases in brain function, and in itself this will help the analysis of psychopathology; furthermore, it is quite possible that the brain basis of self-regulation changes as children mature. Developmental changes in the brain areas subserving selective attention and the inhibition of inappropriate responses are possible: they would allow for an understanding of whether impaired performance on attention tests reflects a delay or a deviation in development, or an altered strategy.

The relationship between attention dysfunction and psychopathology seems likely to be complex. The need for longitudinal studies has already been stressed. The study of several disorders has raised the issues of what is cause and what is consequence. Case-control studies have given such clear evidence of associations that it will be justifiable to proceed to cohort studies in which individuals are identified on the basis of attention dysfunctions and the spectrum of developmental consequences is examined. Cross-sectional studies could also help if the controls are matched on the basis of their performance on attention tests (e.g., because they are younger than the cases or globally less intelligent). The psychological processes leading to a specific impairment of attention might then be disentangled from those that result from inattention. The power of genetic studies to determine whether attention dysfunction is a cause, result, or epiphenomenon of mental disorder has so far been underexploited.

Treatment and education will need to be improved before they have a major impact on attending. The strength of controlled trials may not be apparent until an improved developmental understanding of attention dysfunction has clarified what the targets of intervention should be and what treatments should be applied.

REFERENCES

Alberts-Corush, J., Firestone, P., & Goodman, J. T. (1986). Attention and impulsivity characteristics of the biological and adoptive parents of hyperactive and normal control children. *American Journal of Orthopsychiatry, 56,* 413–423.

Alexander, D. A. (1973). Attention dysfunction in senile dementia. *Psychological Reports, 32,* 229–230.

American Psychiatric Association. (1980, 1987, 1994). *Diagnostic and statistical manual of mental disorders* (3rd ed., 3rd ed. rev., 4th ed.). Washington, DC: Author.

Asarnow, R. F., & MacCrimmon, D. J. (1981). Span of apprehension deficits during postpsychotic stages of schizophrenia: A replication and extension. *Archives of General Psychiatry, 38,* 1006–1011.

August, G. J., Stewart, M. A., & Holmes, C. S. (1983). A four-year follow-up of hyperactive boys with and without conduct disorder. *British Journal of Psychiatry, 143,* 192–198.

Ault, R. L., Crawford, D. E., & Jeffrey, W. E. (1972). Visual scanning strategies of reflective, impulsive, fast-accurate and slow-inaccurate children in the Matching Familiar Figures Test. *Child Development, 43,* 1412–1417.

Baddeley, A. (1988). *Working memory.* Oxford Psychology Series No. 11. Oxford, England: Clarendon Press.

Baribeau-Brown, J., Picton, T. W., & Gosselin, J. Y. (1983). Schizophrenia: A neurophysiological evaluation of abnormal information processing. *Science, 219,* 874–876.

Barkley, R. A., Fischer, M., Edelbrock, C. S., & Smallish, L. (1990). The adolescent outcome of hyperactive children diagnosed by research criteria: I. An 8-year prospective follow-up study. *Journal of the American Academy of Child and Adolescent Psychiatry, 29,* 546–557.

Baruch, I., Hemsley, D. R., & Gray, J. A. (1988). Differential performance of acute and chronic schizophrenics in a latent inhibition task. *Journal of Nervous and Mental Disease, 176,* 598–606.

Battle, E. S., & Lacey, B. (1972). A context for hyperactivity in children over time. *Child Development, 43,* 757–773.

Bax, M., & Mac Keith, R. (Eds.). (1962). *Minimal cerebral dysfunction.* Little Club Clinics in Developmental Medicine No. 10. London: Spastics Society/Heinemann.

Bell, R. Q., Weller, G. M., & Waldrop, M. F. (1971). Newborn and preschooler: Organisation of behavior and relations between periods. *Monographs of the Society for Research in Child Development, 36* (Serial No. 142), 1–145.

Belmont, J. M., & Ellis, N. R. (1968). Effects of extraneous stimulation upon discrimination learning in normals and retardates. *American Journal of Mental Deficiency, 72,* 525–532.

Benasich, A. A., & Bejar, I. I. (1992). The Fagan Test of Infant Intelligence: A Critical Review. *Journal of Applied Developmental Psychology, 13,* 153–171.

Biederman, J., Munir, K., Knee, D., Habelow, W., Armentano, M., Autor, S., Hodge, S. K., & Waternaux, C. (1986). A family study of patients with attention deficit disorder and normal controls. *Journal of Psychiatric Research, 20*, 263–274.

Birch, H. G., Belmont, L., & Karp, E. (1967). Delayed processing and extinction. *Brain, 90*, 113–124.

Birren, J., & Bottwinck, J. (1955). Speed of response as a function of perceptual difficulty and age. *Journal of Gerontology, 10*, 433–436.

Birren, J. E., Woods, A. M., & Williams, M. V. (1980). Behavioral slowing with age: Causes, organization and consequences. In L. W. Poon (Ed.), *Ageing in the 1980s—Psychological Issues* (pp. 293–308). Washington, DC: American Psychological Association.

Blackwood, D. H. R., & Christie, J. E. (1986). The effects of physostigmine on memory and auditory P300 in Alzheimer-type dementia. *Biological Psychiatry, 21*, 557–560.

Blackwood, D. H. R., St. Clair, D. M., Blackburn, I. M., & Tyrer, G. (1987). Cognitive brain potentials in Alzheimer's dementia and Korsakoff amnesic syndrome. *Psychological Medicine, 17*, 349–358.

Bleuler, E. (1950). *Dementia praecox of the group of schizophrenias.* New York: International Universities Press. (Original work published 1911)

Bohman, M., Cloninger, C. R., Sigvardsson, S., & von Knorring, A. -L. (1982). Predisposition of petty criminality in Swedish adoptees: I. Genetic and environmental heterogeneity. *Archives of General Psychiatry, 29*, 1233–1241.

Bornstein, M. H., & Benasich, A. A. (1986). Infant habituation: Assessments of short-term reliability and individual differences at 5 months. *Child Development, 57*, 87–99.

Bornstein, M. H., & Sigman, M. D. (1986). Continuity in mental development from infancy. *Child Development, 57*, 251–274.

Brackbill, Y., Adams, G., Crowell, D. H., & Gray, M. C. (1966). Arousal levels in newborns and preschool children under continuous auditory stimulation. *Experimental Child Psychology, 3*, 176–188.

Bradley, C. (1937). The behavior of children receiving benzedrine. *American Journal of Psychiatry, 94*, 557–585.

Braine, L. G. (1965). Age changes in the mode of perceiving geometric forms. *Psychonomic Science, 2*, 155–156.

Brandon, S. (1971). Overactivity in childhood. *Journal of Psychosomatic Research, 15*, 411–415.

Broadbent, D. E. (1958). *Perception and communication.* London: Pergamon Press.

Broadbent, D. E. (1971). *Decision and stress.* London: Academic Press.

Buss, A. H., & Plomin, R. (1975). *A temperament theory of personality development.* New York: Wiley.

Campbell, E. S., & Redfering, D. L. (1979). Relationships among environmental and demographic variables and teacher-rated hyperactivity. *Journal of Abnormal Child Psychology, 1*, 77–81.

Campbell, S. B. (1987). Parent-referred problem three-year-olds: Developmental changes in symptoms. *Journal of Child Psychology and Psychiatry, 28*, 835–845.

Cantwell, D. (1975). Genetic studies of hyperactive children: Psychiatric illness in biologic and adopting parents. In R. Fieve, D. Rosenthal, & H. Brill (Eds.), *Genetic research in psychiatry* (pp. 273–280). Baltimore: Johns Hopkins University Press.

Capitani, E., Della Sala, S., Lucchelli, F., Soave, P., & Spinnler, H. (1988). Gottschaldt's hidden figure test: Sensitivity of perceptual attention to ageing and dementia. *Journal of Gerontology, 43*, 157–163.

Ceci, S. J., & Tishman, J. (1984). Hyperactivity and incidental memory: Evidence for attentional diffusion. *Child Development, 55*, 2192–2203.

Colombo, J., Mitchell, D. W., Coldren, J. T., & Freeseman, L. J. (1991). Individual differences in infant visual attention: Are short lookers faster processors or feature processors? *Child Development, 62*, 1247–1257.

Conners, C. K. (1975). Minimal brain dysfunction and psychopathology in children. In A. Davids (Ed.), *Child personality and psychopathology: Current topics.* (Vol. 2). New York: Wiley.

Cousins, L. (1976). Individual differences in the orienting reflex and children's discrimination learning. *Psychophysiology, 13*, 479–487.

Craik, F. I. M., & Byrd, M. (1982). Aging and cognitive deficits: The role of attentional resources. In F. I. M. Craik & S. Trehub (Eds.), *Aging and cognitive processes* (pp. 191–211). New York: Plenum.

Crouch, E. (1992). *Continuity and discontinuity of hyperactivity in a general population sample.* Unpublished doctoral dissertation, University of Reading, Reading, England.

Cull, A., & Trimble, M. R. (1989). Effects of anticonvulsant medications on cognitive functioning in children with epilepsy. In B. P. Hermann & M. Seidenberg (Eds.), *Childhood Epilepsies: Neuropsychological, Psychosocial and Intervention aspects* (pp. 83–103). Chichester, England: Wiley.

Cunningham, L., Cadoret, R., Loftus, R., & Edwards, J. E. (1975). Studies of adoptees from psychiatrically disturbed biological parents. *British Journal of Psychiatry, 126*, 534–539.

Day, M. C. (1978). Visual search by children: The effect of background variation and the use of visual cues. *Journal of Experimental Child Psychology, 25*, 1–16.

Deutsch, J. A., & Deutsch, D. (1963). Attention: Some theoretical considerations. *Psychological Review, 70*, 80–90.

Dienske, H., de Jonge, G., & Sanders-Woudstra, J. A. R. (1985). Quantitative criteria for attention and activity in child psychiatric patients. *Journal of Child Psychology and Psychiatry, 26*, 895–916.

Doleys, D. M. (1976). Distractibility and distracting stimuli: Inconsistent and contradictory results. *Psychological Record, 26*, 279–287.

Douglas, V. I., & Peters, K. G. (1979). Toward a clearer definition of the attentional deficit of hyperactive children. In G. A. Hale & M. Lewis (Eds.), *Attention and the development of cognitive skills.* New York: Plenum.

Enns, J. J., & Akhtar, N. (1989). A developmental study of filtering in visual attention. *Child Development, 60*, 118–119.

Enns, J. T., & Brodeur, D. A. (1989). A developmental study of covert orienting to peripheral visual cues. *Journal of Experimental Child Psychology, 48*, 171–189.

Enns, J. T., & Girgus, J. S. (1985). Developmental changes in selective and integrative visual attention. *Journal of Experimental Child Psychology, 40*, 319–337.

Erlenmeyer-Kimling, L., & Cornblatt, B. (1987). The New York High Risk Project: A follow up report. *Schizophrenia Bulletin, 13*, 451–461.

Erlenmeyer-Kimling, L., Kestenbaum, C. J., Bird, H., & Hilldoff, U. (1984). Assessment of the New York High Risk Project subjects in sample A who are now clinically deviant. In N. F. Watt, E. J. Anthony, L. C. Wynne, & J. E. Rolf (Eds.), *Children at risk for schizophrenia: A longitudinal perspective* (pp. 227–239). New York: Cambridge University Press.

Fagan, J. F., & Shepherd, P. A. (1987). *Fagan Test of Infant Intelligence: Training manual.* Cleveland, OH: Infantest Corp.

Fantz, R. L. (1966). Pattern discrimination and selective attention as determinants of perceptual development from birth. In A. H. Kidd & J. J. Rivoire (Eds.), *Perceptual development in children.* New York: International Universities Press.

Farrington, D. P., Loeber, R., & van Kammen, W. B. (1990). Long-term criminal outcomes of hyperactivity-impulsivity-attention deficit and conduct problems in childhood. In L. N. Robins & M. Rutter (Eds.), *Straight and devious pathways from childhood to adulthood* (pp. 62–81). Cambridge, England: Cambridge University Press.

Fergusson, D. M., Horwood, L. J., & Lloyd, M. (1991). Confirmatory factor models of attention deficit and conduct disorder. *Journal of Child Psychology and Psychiatry, 32,* 257–274.

Firestone, P., & Martin, J. E. (1979). An analysis of the hyperactive syndrome: A comparison of hyperactive, behavior problem, asthmatic and normal children. *Journal of Abnormal Child Psychology, 7,* 261–273.

Friedman, S. (1972). Habituation and recovery of visual response in the alert human newborn. *Journal of Experimental Child Psychology, 13,* 339–349.

Friedman, S. (1975). Infant habituation: Process, problems and possibilities. In N. Ellis (Ed.), *Aberrant development in infancy.* Hillsdale, NJ: Erlbaum.

Fuhrman, M. J., & Kendall, P. C. (1986). Cognitive tempo and behavioural adjustment in children. *Cognitive Therapy and Research, 10,* 45–50.

Gibson, E. J., & Yonas, A. (1966). A developmental study of visual search behaviour. *Perception and Psychophysics, 1,* 169–171.

Gillberg, C., Carlstrom, G., & Rasmussen, P. (1983). Hyperkinetic disorders in children with perceptual, motor and attentional deficits. *Journal of Child Psychology and Psychiatry, 24,* 233–246.

Gittelman, R., Mannuzza, S., Shenker, R., & Bonagura, N. (1985). Hyperactive boys almost grown up: 1. Psychiatric status. *Archives of General Psychiatry, 42,* 937–947.

Goodman, R., & Stevenson, J. (1989). A twin study of hyperactivity: I. An examination of hyperactivity scores and categories derived from Rutter Teacher and Parent Questionnaires: II. The aetiological role of genes, family relationships, and perinatal adversity. *Journal of Child Psychology and Psychiatry, 30,* 671–710.

Goyette, C. H., Conners, C. K., & Ulrich, R. F. (1978). Normative data on revised Conners' parent and teacher rating scales. *Journal of Abnormal Child Psychology, 6,* 221–236.

Grabbe, W., & Campione, J. C. (1969). A novelty interpretation of the Moss-Harlow effect in pre-school children. *Child Development, 40,* 1077–1084.

Greenberg, D. J., Uzgiris, I. C., & Hunt, J. M. (1970). Attentional preference and experience: III. Visual familiarity and looking time. *Journal of Genetic Psychology, 117,* 123–135.

Hagen, J. W., & Hale, G. A. (1973). The development of attention in children. In A. D. Pick (Ed.), *Minnesota Symposia on Child Psychology* (Vol. 7, pp. 117–140). Minneapolis: University of Minnesota Press.

Haith, M. M. (1980). *Rules that babies look by: The organization of newborn visual activity.* Hillsdale, NJ: Erlbaum.

Hart, S., & Semple, J. M. (1990). *Neuropsychology and the dementias* (pp. 187–199). London: Taylor & Francis.

Harvey, P. D., Docherty, N. M., Serper, M. R., & Rasmussen, M. (1990). Cognitive deficits and thought disorder: II. An 8-month follow-up study. *Schizophrenia Bulletin, 16,* 147–156.

Hechtman, L., Weiss, G., & Perlman, T. (1984). Young adult outcome of hyperactive children who received long-term stimulant treatment. *Journal of the American Academy of Child Psychiatry, 23,* 261–269.

Hemsley, D. R., & Zawada, S. L. (1976). Filtering and the cognitive deficits in schizophrenia. *British Journal of Psychiatry, 128,* 456–461.

Hepper, P. G., & Shahidullah, S. (1992). Habituation in normal and Down's syndrome fetuses. *Quarterly Journal of Experimental Psychology, 44,* 305–317.

Hinshaw, S. P. (1987). On the distinction between attentional deficits/hyperactivity and conduct problems/aggression in child psychopathology. *Psychological Bulletin, 101,* 443–463.

Hinshaw, S. P., Lahey, B. B., & Hart, E. L. (1993). Issues of taxonomy and comorbidity in the development of conduct disorder. *Development and Psychopathology, 5,* 31–49.

Holzman, P. S. (1987). Recent studies of psychophysiology in schizophrenia. *Schizophrenia Bulletin, 13,* 49–75.

Hoy, E., Weiss, G., Minde, K., & Cohen, N. (1978). The hyperactive child at adolescence: Cognitive, emotional, and social functioning. *Journal of Abnormal Child Psychology, 6,* 311–324.

Hubel, D., & Weisel, T. (1962). Receptive fields, binocular interaction, and functional architecture in the cat's visual cortex. *Journal of Physiology, 160,* 106–154.

Jacobvitz, D., & Sroufe, L. A. (1987). The early caregiver-child relationship and attention-deficit disorder with hyperactivity in kindergarten: A prospective study. *Child Development, 58,* 1488–1495.

Jacobvitz, D., Sroufe, L. A., Stewart, M., & Leffert, N. (1990). Treatment of attentional and hyperactivity problems in children with sympathomimetic drugs: A comprehensive review. *Journal of the American Academy of Child and Adolescent Psychiatry, 29,* 677–688.

James, A., & Taylor, E. (1990). Sex differences in the hyperkinetic syndrome of childhood. *Journal of Child Psychology and Psychiatry, 31,* 437–446.

Jorm, A. F. (1986). Controlled and automatic information processing in senile dementia: A review. *Psychological Medicine, 16,* 77–88.

Kagan, J. (1970). The determinants of attention in the infant. *American Scientist, 38,* 298–306.

Kagan, J., Rasman, B. L., Day, D., Albert, J., & Phillips, W. (1964). Information processing in the child: Significance of analytic and reflective attitudes. *Psychological Monographs, 78*(1 whole No. 578).

Kahn, E., & Cohen, L. H. (1934). Organic driveness: A brain-stem syndrome and an experience with case reports. *New England Journal of Medicine, 210,* 748–756.

Kahnemann, D. (1973). *Attention and effort.* Englewood Cliffs, NJ: Prentice-Hall.

Karmel, B. Z. (1969). The effect of age, complexity and amount of contour on pattern preferences in human infants. *Journal of Experimental Child Psychology, 7,* 338–354.

Karmel, B. Z., & Maisel, E. B. (1975). A neuronal activity model for infant visual attention. In L. B. Cohen & B. Salapatek (Eds.). *Infant perception: Vol. 1. From sensation to cognition.* New York: Academic Press.

Klee, S. H., & Garfinkel, B. D. (1983). The computerized continuous performance task: A new measure of inattention. *Journal of Abnormal Child Psychology, 11,* 487–496.

Kraepelin, E. (1896). *Psychiatrie. Ein Lehrbuch fur Studirende und Aerzte* (5th ed.). Leipzig: Barth.

Lahey, B. B., Schaughency, E. A., Hynd, G. W., Carlson, C. L., & Nieves, W. (1987). Attention deficit disorder with and without hyperactivity: Comparison of behavioural characteristics of clinic-referred children. *Journal of the American Academy of Child and Adolescent Psychiatry, 26,* 718–723.

Lambert, N. M. (1988). Adolescent outcomes for hyperactive children: Perspectives on general and specific patterns of childhood risk for adolescent, educational, social and mental health problems. *American Psychologist, 43,* 786–799.

Laufer, M., Denhoff, E., & Solomons, G. (1957). Hyperkinetic impulse disorder in children's behavior problems. *Psychosomatic Medicine, 19,* 38–49.

Lawson, J. S., McGhie, A., & Chapman, J. (1964). Perception of speech in schizophrenia. *British Journal of Psychiatry, 110,* 375–380.

Lehman, E. B. (1972). Selective strategies in children's attention to task-relevant information. *Child Development, 43,* 197–210.

Levy, F. (1980). The development of sustained attention (vigilance) and inhibition in children: Some normative data. *Journal of Child Psychology and Psychiatry, 21,* 77–84.

Loiselle, D. L., Stamm, J. S., Maitinsky, S., & Whipple, S. C. (1980). Evoked potential and behavioural signs of attentive dysfunctions in hyperactive boys. *Psychophysiology, 17,* 193–201.

Lubow, R. E., & Josman, Z. E. (1993). Latent inhibition deficits in hyperactive children. *Journal of Child Psychology and Psychiatry, 34,* 959–973.

Luk, S. L., Thorley, G., & Taylor, E. (1987). Gross overactivity: A study by direct observation. *Journal of Psychopathology and Behavioral Assessment, 9,* 173–182.

Luria, A. R. (1961). *The role of speech in the regulation of normal and abnormal behavior.* New York: Liverlight.

Luria, A. R. (1963). *The mentally retarded child.* London: Pergamon Press.

McCall, R. B., & Carriger, M. S. (1993). A meta-analysis of infant habituation and recognition memory performance as predictors of later IQ. *Child Development, 64,* 57–79.

Maccoby, E. E. (1967). Selective auditory attention in children. In L. Lipsitt & C. Spiker (Eds.), *Advances in child development and behavior* (Vol. 3, pp. 99–125). New York: Academic Press.

McGhie, A. (1969). *Pathology of attention* (pp. 44–49). Harmondsworth, UK: Penguin.

McIntyre, C. W., Blackwell, S. L., & Denton, C. L. (1978). Effect of noise distractibility on the span of apprehension of hyperactive boys. *Journal of Abnormal Child Psychology, 6,* 483–492.

Magnusson, D., & Bergman, L. R. (1990). A pattern approach to the study of pathways from childhood to adulthood. In L. Robins & M. Rutter (Eds.), *Straight and devious pathways from childhood to adulthood* (pp. 101–115). Cambridge, England: Cambridge University Press.

Matejccek, Z., Dytrych, Z., & Schuller, V. (1985). Follow-up study of children born to women denied abortion. In R. Porter & M. O'Connor (Eds.), *Abortion: Medical progress and social implications.* CIBA Foundation Symposium 115. London: Pitman.

Mendelson, M. J., & Haith, M. M. (1976). The relation between audition and vision in the human newborn. *Monographs of the Society for Research in Child Development, 41*(4, Serial No. 167).

Moffitt, A. R. (1973). Intensity discrimination and cardiac reaction in young infants. *Developmental Psychology, 8,* 357–359.

Moray, N. (1969). *Attention: Selective processes in vision and hearing.* London: Hutchinson Educational.

Norman, D. A. (1968). Toward a theory of memory and attention. *Psychological Review, 75,* 522–536.

Nuechterlein, K. H. (1983). Signal detection in vigilance tasks and behavioral attributes among offspring of schizophrenic mothers and among hyperactive children. *Journal of Abnormal Psychology, 92,* 4–28.

Nuechterlein, K. H., & Dawson, M. E. (1984). A heuristic vulnerability/stress model of schizophrenic episodes. *Schizophrenia Bulletin, 10,* 300–312.

Nuechterlein, K. H., Edell, W. S., Norris, M., & Dawson, M. E. (1986). Attention vulnerability indicators, thought disorder, and negative symptoms. *Schizophrenia Bulletin, 12,* 408–426.

O'Connor, N., & Hermelin, B. (1963). *Speech and thought in severe subnormality.* Oxford, England: Pergamon Press.

Pecheux, M. G., & Lecuyer, R. (1989). A longitudinal study of visual habituation between 3, 5, and 8 months of age. *British Journal of Developmental Psychology, 7,* 159–169.

Pennington, B. F., Groisser, D., & Welsh, M. C. (1993). Contrasting cognitive deficits in attention deficit hyperactivity disorder versus reading disability. *Developmental Psychology, 29,* 511–523.

Pick, A. D., Christy, M. D., & Frankel, G. W. (1972). A developmental study of visual selective attention. *Journal of Experimental Child Psychology, 14,* 165–175.

Posner, M., & Boies, J. (1971). Components of attention. *Psychological Review, 78,* 391–408.

Posner, M. I., Cohen, Y., & Rafal, R. D. (1982). Neural systems control of spatial orienting. *Philosophical Transaction of the Royal Society of London (Biology), 298,* 187–198.

Posner, M. I., Walker, J. A., Friedrich, F. J., & Rafal, R. D. (1984). Effects of parietal injury on covert orienting of attention. *Journal of Neuroscience, 4,* 1863–1874.

Prendergast, M., Taylor, E., Rapoport, J. L., Bartko, J., Donnelly, M., Zametkin, A., Ahearn, M. B., Dunn, G., & Wieselberg, H. M. (1988). The diagnosis of childhood hyperactivity: A U.S.-U.K. cross-national study of DSM-III and ICD-9. *Journal of Child Psychology and Psychiatry, 29,* 289–300.

Pribram, K. H., & McGuinness, D. (1975). Arousal, activation and effort in the control of attention. *Psychological Review, 82,* 116–149.

Prior, M., & Sanson, A. (1986). Attention deficit disorder with hyperactivity: A critique. *Journal of Child Psychology and Psychiatry, 27,* 307–319.

Rabbitt, P. (1963). Age and discrimination between complex stimuli. In A. T. Welford & J. E. Birren (Eds.), *Behaviour, ageing and the nervous system.* Springfield, IL: Thomas.

Rabbitt, P. M. A. (1979). Some experiments and a model for changes in attentional selectivity with old age. In F. Hoffmeister & C. Muller (Eds.), *Brain function in old age: Evaluation of changes and disorders* (pp. 82–94). Berlin: Springer-Verlag.

Rabbitt, P. M. A. (1980). A fresh look at changes in reaction times in old age. In D. G. Stein (Ed.), *The psychobiology of aging: Problems and perspectives* (pp. 425–442). Amsterdam, The Netherlands: Elsevier.

Rabbitt, P., & Birren, J. E. (1967). Age and responses to sequences of repetitive and interruptive signals. *Journal of Gerontology, 22,* 143–150.

Rapport, M. D., Tucker, S. B., DuPaul, G. J., Merlo, M., & Stoner, G. (1986). Hyperactivity and frustration: The influence of control over and size of rewards in delaying gratification. *Journal of Abnormal Child Psychology, 14,* 191–204.

Richards, J. E. (1987). Heart rate responses and heart rate rhythms, and infant visual sustained attention. In P. K. Ackles, J. R. Jennings, & M. G. H. Coles (Eds.), *Advances in psychophysiology* (Vol. 3, pp. 189–221). Greenwich, CT: JAI Press.

Riddle, K. D., & Rapoport, J. L. (1976). A 2-year follow-up of 72 hyperactive boys. *Journal of Nervous and Mental Diseases, 162,* 126–134.

Rieder, C., & Cicchetti, D. (1989). Organizational perspective on cognitive control functioning and cognitive-affective balance in maltreated children. *Developmental Psychology, 25,* 382–393.

Rodnick, E. H., & Shakow, D. (1940). Set in the schizophrenic as measured by a composite reaction time index. *American Journal of Psychiatry, 97,* 214–215.

Rosvold, H. E., Mirsky, A. F., Sarason, I., Bransome, E. D., & Beck, L. H. (1956). A continuous performance test of brain damage. *Journal of Consulting Psychology, 20,* 343–352.

Rourke, B. P., & Czudner, G. (1972). Age differences in auditory reaction time of "brain-damaged" and normal children under regular and irregular preparatory internal conditions. *Journal of Experimental Child Psychology, 14,* 372–378.

Routh, D. K. (1980). Developmental and social aspects of hyperactivity. In C. K. Whalen & B. Henker (Eds.), *Hyperactive children: The social ecology of identification and treatment* (pp. 55–74). New York: Academic Press.

Roy, P. (1983, March). *Is continuity enough? Substitute care and socialisation.* Paper presented at the Spring Scientific Meeting, Child and Adolescent Specialist Section, Royal College of Psychiatrists, London.

Ruff, H. A., & Lawson, K. R. (1990). Development of sustained, focused attention in young children during free play. *Developmental Psychology, 26,* 85–93.

Rutter, M., Graham, P., & Yule, W. (1970). *A neuropsychiatric study in childhood.* London: Heinemann.

Rutter, M., Tizard, J., & Whitmore, K. (1970). *Education, health and behaviour.* London: Longman.

Safer, D. J. (1973). A familial factor in minimal brain dysfunction. *Behavior Genetics, 3,* 175–186.

Salapatek, P., & Kesson, W. (1966). Visual scanning of triangles by the human newborn. *Journal of Experimental Child Psychology, 3,* 155–157.

Sandberg, S., Rutter, M., & Taylor, E. (1978). Hyperkinetic disorder in psychiatric clinic attenders. *Developmental Medicine and Child Neurology, 20,* 279–299.

Santostefano, S. (1978). *A bio-developmental approach to clinical child psychology.* New York: Wiley

Satterfield, J., Hoppe, C. M., & Schell, A. M. (1982). A prospective study of delinquency in 100 adolescent boys with attention deficit disorder and 88 normal adolescent boys. *American Journal of Psychiatry, 139,* 795–798.

Schachar, R. J. (1986). Hyperkinetic syndrome: Historical development of the concept. In E. A. Taylor (Ed.), *The overactive child: Clinics in developmental medicine* (No. 97, pp. 19–40). London/Oxford: MacKeith Press/Blackwell.

Schachar, R. (1991). Childhood hyperactivity. *Journal of Child Psychology and Psychiatry, 32,* 155–192.

Schachar, R., & Logan, G. D. (1990a). Are hyperactive children deficient in attentional capacity? *Journal of Abnormal Child Psychology, 18,* 493–513.

Schachar, R., & Logan, G. D. (1990b). Impulsivity and inhibitory control in development and psychopathology. *Developmental Psychology, 26,* 1–11.

Schachar, R. J., Rutter, M., & Smith, A. (1981). The characteristics of situationally and pervasively hyperactive children: Implications for syndrome definition. *Journal of Child Psychology and Psychiatry, 22,* 375–392.

Schachar, R., Taylor, E., Wieselberg, M., Thorley, G., & Rutter, M. (1987). Changes in family function and relationships in children who respond to methylphenidate. *Journal of the American Academy of Child Psychiatry, 26,* 728–732.

Schachar, R., & Wachsmuth, R. (1990). Hyperactivity and parental psychopathology. *Journal of Child Psychology and Psychiatry, 31,* 381–392.

Sergeant, J. (1989). Attention deficit from an information processing perspective. In L. M. Bloomingdale & J. Sergeant (Eds.), *Attention deficit disorder—Criteria, cognition, intervention* (pp. 65–81). New York/Oxford: Pergamon Press.

Sergeant, J. A., & Scholten, C. A. (1985). On data limitations in hyperactivity. *Journal of Child Psychology and Psychiatry, 26,* 111–124.

Shaffer, D., & Greenhill, L. (1979). A critical note on the predictive validity of "the hyperkinetic syndrome." *Journal of Child Psychology and Psychiatry, 20,* 61–72.

Shakow, D. (1963). Psychological deficit in schizophrenia. *Behavioral Science, 8,* 275–305.

Shallice, T. (1988). *From Neuropsychology to Mental Structure.* Cambridge, England: Cambridge University Press.

Shiffrin, R. M., & Schneider, W. (1977). Controlled and automatic human information processing: II. Perceptual learning, automatic attending, and a general theory. *Psychological Review, 84,* 127–190.

Siegel, A. W., & Stevenson, H. W. (1966). Incidental learning: A developmental study. *Child Development, 37,* 811–818.

Slater, A., Morison, V., & Rose, D. (1982). Visual memory at birth. *British Journal of Psychology, 73,* 519–525.

Sonuga-Barke, E. J. S., & Taylor, E. (1992). The effect of delay on hyperactive and non-hyperactive children's response times: Research note. *Journal of Child Psychology and Psychiatry, 33,* 1091–1096.

Sonuga-Barke, E. J. S., Taylor, E., & Heptinstall, E. (1992). Hyperactivity and delay aversion: II. The effects of self versus externally imposed stimulus presentation periods on memory. *Journal of Child Psychology and Psychiatry, 33,* 399–410.

Sonuga-Barke, E. J. S., Taylor, E., Sembi, S., & Smith, J. (1992). Hyperactivity and delay aversion: I. The effect of delay on choice. *Journal of Child Psychology and Psychiatry, 33,* 387–398.

Spring, B. J. (1980). Shift of attention in schizophrenia, siblings of schizophrenics, and depressed patients. *Journal of Nervous and Mental Disease, 168,* 133–140.

Sroufe, L. A., Sonies, B., West, W., & Wright, F. (1973). Anticipatory heart rate deceleration and reaction time in children with and without referral for learning disability. *Child Development, 44,* 267–273.

St. Clair, D. M., Blackburn, I. M., Blackwood, D. H. R., & Tyrer, G. (1988). Measuring the course of Alzheimer's disease: A longitudinal study of neuropsychological function and changes in P3 event-related potential. *British Journal of Psychiatry, 152,* 48–54.

Sternberg, S. (1966). High speed scanning in human memory. *Science, 153,* 652–662.

Stevenson, J., Richman, N., & Graham, P. (1985). Behaviour problems and language abilities at three years and behavioural deviance at eight years. *Journal of Child Psychology and Psychiatry, 26,* 215–230.

Stewart, M. A., deBlois, C. S., & Cummings, C. (1980). Psychiatric disorder in the parents of hyperactive boys and those with conduct disorder. *Journal of Child Psychology and Psychiatry, 21,* 283–292.

Still, G. F. (1902). The Coulstonian lectures on some abnormal psychical conditions in children. *Lancet, i,* 1008–1012.

Stroh, C. M. (1971). *Vigilance: The problem of sustained attention.* Oxford, England: Pergamon Press.

Strutt, G., Anderson, D. R., & Well, A. D. (1975). A developmental study of the effects of irrelevant information on speeded classification. *Journal of Experimental Child Psychology, 20,* 127–135.

Surwillo, W. W. (1961). Frequency of the alpha rhythm, reaction time and age. *Nature, 191,* 823–824.

Swanson, J., & Kinsbourne, M. (1976). Stimulant related state-dependent learning in hyperactive children. *Science, 192,* 1354–1356.

Sykes, D. H., Douglas, V. I., & Morgenstern, G. (1973). Sustained attention in hyperactive children. *Journal of Child Psychology and Psychiatry, 14,* 213–220.

Szatmari, P., Offord, D. R., & Boyle, M. H. (1989). Ontario Child Health Study: Prevalence of attention deficit disorder with hyperactivity. *Journal of Child Psychology and Psychiatry, 30,* 219–230.

Talland, G. A. (1965). Initiation of response and reaction time in ageing and with brain damage. In A. T. Welford & J. E. Birren (Eds.), *Behaviour, ageing and the nervous system* (pp. 526–561). Springfield, IL: Thomas.

Tallmadge, J., & Barkley, R. A. (1983). The interactions of hyperactive and normal boys with their fathers and mothers. *Journal of Abnormal Child Psychology, 11,* 565–579.

Tanaka, K. (1993). Neuronal mechanisms of object recognition. *Science, 262,* 685–688.

Taylor, E. (1986a). Attention deficit. In E. Taylor (Ed.), *The overactive child* (pp. 73–106). London/Oxford: MacKeith Press/Blackwell.

Taylor, E. (1986b). The causes and development of hyperactive behaviour. In E. Taylor (Ed.), *The overactive child* (pp. 118–160). London/Oxford: MacKeith Press/Blackwell.

Taylor, E. (1988). Attention deficit and conduct disorder syndromes. In M. Rutter, A. H. Tuma, & I. S. Lann (Eds.), *Assessment and diagnosis in child psychopathology* (pp. 377–407). New York: Guilford.

Taylor, E. (1994a). Syndromes of attention deficit and overactivity. In M. Rutter, E. Taylor, & L. Hersov (Eds.), *Child and adolescent psychiatry: Modern approaches,* (3rd ed.) (pp. 285–307). Oxford, England: Blackwell.

Taylor, E. (1994b). The development and psychopathology of attention. In M. Rutter & D. F. Hay (Eds.), *Development through life: A handbook for clinicians.* Oxford, England: Blackwell.

Taylor, E., Sandberg, S., Thorley, G., & Giles, S. (1991). *The epidemiology of childhood hyperactivity* (Maudsley Monographs No. 33). Oxford, England: Oxford University Press.

Taylor, E., Schachar, R., Thorley, G., Wieselberg, M., Everitt, B., & Rutter, M. (1987). Which boys respond to stimulant medication? A controlled trial of methylphenidate in boys with disruptive behaviour. *Psychological Medicine, 17,* 121–143.

Thorley, G. (1984). *Clinical characteristics and outcome of hyperactive children.* Unpublished doctoral dissertation, University of London, London, England.

Tizard, B., & Hodges, J. (1978). The effect of early institutional rearing on the development of eight year old children. *Journal of Child Psychology and Psychiatry, 19,* 99–118.

Torgersen, A. M., & Kringlen, E. (1978). Genetic aspects of temperamental differences in infants: Their cause as shown through twin studies. *Journal of the American Academy of Child Psychiatry, 17,* 433–444.

Treisman, A. M. (1969). Strategies and models of selective attention. *Psychological Review, 76,* 282–299.

van der Meere, J., & Sergeant, J. (1988a). Focused attention in pervasively hyperactive children. *Journal of Abnormal Child Psychology, 16,* 627–639.

van der Meere, J., & Sergeant, J. (1988b). Acquisition of attention skills in pervasively hyperactive children. *Journal of Child Psychology and Psychiatry, 29,* 301–310.

von Wright, J., & Nurmi, L. (1979). Effects of white noise and irrelevant information on speeded classification: A developmental study. *Acta Psychologia, 43,* 157–166.

Wallander, J. L. (1988). The relationship between attention problems in childhood and antisocial behaviour eight years later. *Journal of Child Psychology and Psychiatry, 29,* 53–61.

Wechsler, D. (1974). *Manual for the Wechsler Intelligence Scale for Children—Revised.* New York: Psychological Corp.

Weiss, G., & Hechtman, L. T. (1986). *Hyperactive children grown up.* New York: Guilford.

Welford, A. T. (1980). Relationship between reaction time and fatigue, stress, age and sex. In A. T. Welford (Ed.), *Reaction times* (pp. 321–354). New York: Academic Press.

Wetherford, M. J., & Cohen, L. B. (1973). Developmental changes in infant visual preferences for novelty and familiarity. *Child Development, 44,* 416–424.

White, S. H. (1966). Age differences in reaction to stimulus variation. In O. J. Harvey (Ed.), *Experience, structure and adaptability.* New York: Springer.

Witkin, H. A., Dyk, R. B., Paterson, H. F., Goodenough, D. R., & Karp, S. A. (1962). *Psychological differentiation: Studies of development.* New York: Wiley.

Wohlberg, G. W., & Kornetsky, C. (1973). Sustained attention in remitted schizophrenia. *Archives of General Psychiatry, 28,* 533–537.

World Health Organization. (1992). *The ICD-10 Classification of mental health and behavioural disorders: Clinical descriptions and diagnostic guidelines.* Geneva: Author.

Wright, J. C., & Vlietstra, A. G. (1975). The development of selective attention: From perceptual exploration to logical search. In H. W. Reese (Ed.), *Advances in child development and behaviour* (Vol. 10). New York: Academic Press.

Zametkin, A. J., Nordahl, T. E., Gross, M., King, A.C., Semple, W. E., Rumsey, J., Hamburger, S., & Cohen, R. M. (1990). Cerebral glucose metabolism in adults with hyperactivity of childhood onset. *New England Journal of Medicine, 323,* 1361–1366.

Zeaman, D., & House, B. J. (1963). The role of attention in retardate discrimination learning. In N. R. Ellis (Ed.), *Handbook of mental deficiency.* New York: McGraw-Hill.

Zelniker, T., Jeffrey, W. E., Ault, R., & Parsons, J. (1972). Analysis and modification of search strategies of impulsive and reflective children on the Matching Familiar Figures Test. *Child Development, 431,* 321–335.

CHAPTER 8

A Behavioral Neuroscience Approach to Developmental Language Disorders: Evidence for a Rapid Temporal Processing Deficit

STEVEN L. MILLER and PAULA TALLAL

Language represents a set of skills used by people to represent or communicate through speaking, writing, or gesture their thoughts, feeling, and emotions. Most individuals' language is acquired with relative ease. For approximately 3% to 19% of children in the general population, however, the acquisition of language skills occurs significantly later, as compared to other children in their age group, and with greater difficulty (Beitchman, Nair, & Patel, 1986; Fundulis, Kolvin, & Garside, 1979; Jenkins, Bax, & Hart, 1980; Silva, McGee, & Williams, 1983; Stevenson & Richman, 1986). The term specific language impairment (SLI) is used to refer to a heterogeneous group of behaviorally diagnosed syndromes where, in the presence of normal intellectual ability and educational opportunity, an individual fails to achieve acceptable language performance. In addition, the diagnosis of a specific language impairment calls for ruling out environmental causes and frank neurological impairments (e.g., seizures, stroke). Implicit in the definition of a specific language disorder or any other learning disability is the assumption of domain specificity underlying the disorder. This assumption requires that the causal deficits underlying the disorder are confined to a specific cognitive area or domain, such as language in the present context. Therefore, a thorough understanding into the etiology and/or consequences of SLI can help lead to the treatment of the disorder while providing rare insights into the development of normal language as well as the role it plays in cognition.

Since the initial suggestion by Benton (1964) that children who fail to develop normal language represent a distinct clinical syndrome, many studies have compared language-impaired and non-language-impaired individuals. In apparent contrast to the specificity assumption, numerous behavioral tasks that differentiate normal and language-disabled children have been identified ranging from various measures of sensation and perception to measures of higher cognitive, linguistic, and emotional functioning. Not surprisingly, researchers can easily be overwhelmed at the plethora of findings and be at a complete loss for developing a conceptual framework that synthesizes these data.

The causal deficits underlying a specific language impairment are particularly difficult to identify because of the critical role language plays in the acquisition and maintenance of various social, emotional, and behavioral skills. In fact, children with a specific language impairment are at an increased risk for developing various behavioral, psychiatric (Beitchman, 1985; Beitchman, Hood, Rochon, & Peterson, 1989; Beitchman, Hood, Rochon, Peterson, Mantini, & Majumdar, 1989), and academic difficulties (Rissman, Curtiss, & Tallal, 1990). Recent research suggests that the psychiatric and behavioral disturbances identified in language-impaired children may be related, at least in part, to neurodevelopmental delays in these children. For example, group differences in behavioral and emotional status among 81 language-impaired and 60 control subjects, matched in age, race, socioeconomic status, and intellectual performance, were significantly reduced when group differences in attention, perception, and motor functioning were statistically controlled (Tallal, Dukette, & Curtiss, 1989).

Performance on these same perceptual/motor tasks has previously been shown to be significantly lower in language-impaired subjects than in control subjects (Tallal, Stark, & Mellits, 1985a) and to correlate highly with receptive language performance (Tallal, Stark, & Mellits, 1985b). In addition, these SLI subjects showed a significant decrease in Leiter International Performance Scale (Leiter, 1952) from 4 to 8 years of age, a measure of intellectual ability that minimizes the oral language instructions and responses (Benasich, Curtiss, & Tallal, 1993). These findings suggest that, at least in part, the factors related to the increased incidence for later behavioral and psychiatric problems are related to nonverbal aspects of specific language impairments.

Research with a developmental, longitudinal perspective indicates that, for a large number of children, delayed language development represents a serious problem which may have cascading effects throughout development. Furthermore, the relevant issues and criteria for characterizing the deficits involved in specific language impairments may be different across the life span due to the critical role language plays at different stages of development. These deficits put an SLI child at increased risk for developing numerous behavioral, psychiatric, and academic difficulties at great cost to both the individual and society. Therefore, understanding the underlying etiology of this disorder is crucial, if we are to make progress toward adequate remediation.

Although the vast proportion of research and clinical focus on SLI has taken a linguistic approach, recent methodological advances in the area of neuroscience have provided a new source of information about the mechanisms underlying language development that might aid in the organization of data pertaining to SLI. The present chapter will focus on several of the reported behavioral and neural manifestations of developmental language impairments. These findings will be presented within a framework that borrows from the principles of information processing models of higher cognitive functions for relating these two areas of research. The hypothesis that these findings suggest a homogeneous deficit in rapid temporal processing in individuals with a developmental language impairment also is presented. In addition, the developmental disorders that frequently co-occur with a specific language impairment (i.e., reading disability and childhood autism) are compared to assess the specificity of these findings with developmental language impairments. Evidence regarding the heritability of developmental language disorders is then presented along with their implications concerning the developmental mechanisms of the temporal processing disorder. Finally, suggestions for the further characterization of the neurobehavioral deficits to enhance our understanding of normal and disordered language also are discussed.

A BEHAVIORAL NEUROSCIENCE APPROACH TO SPECIFIC LANGUAGE DISORDERS

Our approach for examining specific developmental language disorders is based on an information-processing approach to understanding higher cognitive processes. This approach views behavior as the product of interrelated component processes such as sensation, perception, attention, and memory. These are considered to be constantly active processes. Further, this approach posits that these subprocesses can be isolated and empirically studied. In the present context, the normal development of sensory and perceptual functions is considered prerequisite to the development of higher cognitive speech and language processes. Specifically, the ability to process rapidly occurring auditory temporal[1] and spectral[2] changes is considered fundamental for perceiving much of the information present in the ongoing speech signal. Further, deficits in the processing of rapidly presented information are used to account for many of the speech perception, production, and language rule learning deficits that characterize developmentally language-impaired individuals. In addition, changes in rapid processing performance with age are invoked to provide insights into the developmental symptomatology and outcomes of this clinical disorder. Evidence for the cross-generational transmission (i.e., heritability) of these processing deficits is presented to examine the etiology of this developmental disorder.

[1] The temporal characteristics of a stimulus refer to the distribution in time of the spectral parameters of a stimulus (duration, onset time, and offset time).

[2] The spectral aspects of a stimulus refer to the distribution in frequency of the magnitude and/or phase of a stimulus.

The contribution from neuroscience to this approach is that insights into these component processes can be gained through an understanding of the system's underlying anatomy and physiology. It is assumed that the behavioral and physiological levels of analysis can be directly related to each other. Thus, the identification of independent processing systems at one level of analysis (behavioral) suggests a similar representation at the other level (physiological). The use of stimulus parameters in behavioral tasks shown to be important at the physiological level should provide an advantage for examining the fundamental properties of information-processing systems. Frequently, these tasks are based on animal models of behavior and, thus, have the additional advantage of examining these processing systems at a much more basic level. The incorporation of this dual approach of using both physiological and behavioral methods in the investigation of higher cognitive functions can provide more than just complementary evidence regarding plausible models of higher cognitive functions. It can actually drive future experiments at both levels of analysis.

The present approach also proposes that specific dissociations in models of impaired perception reflect dissociations in nonimpaired processing systems. For example, deuteranopia is a type of color blindness in which the green part of the color spectrum is perceived inadequately. This suggests that the visual system has separate processing channels for the perception of the color spectrum, and this finding maps directly on to the type of photosensitive receptors present in the retina (Regan, 1989). Similarly, the identification of specific rapid processing deficits in language-impaired individuals are used to suggest that specific channels exist for the processing of rapidly presented information in the nonimpaired language system. Data from experiments with normal as well as dissociations in performance among individuals with acquired focal brain lesions are presented to suggest that the processing of rapidly presented information is functionally specialized in the left hemisphere and might underlie the hemispheric specialization for speech perception.

BEHAVIORAL STUDIES

Attempts to characterize the behavioral deficits manifest in developmental language impairment are numerous. In large part, two main approaches—linguistic and sensory-perceptual—have been used to characterize these deficits. Intuitively, the sensory-perceptual deficit hypothesis for developmental language impairments appears in opposition to the linguistic domain specificity of the deficits implied in the classification of this developmental disorder. However, if language is determined through the development of prerequisite sensory, perceptual, motor, and cognitive processes, then the failure of one or more of these functions would result in a developmentally delayed or disordered language system. Further, if the behavioral impact of these perceptual deficits can be demonstrated to be specific in their disruption for language development, then the specificity assumption remains intact. The following section summarizes the sensory-perceptual deficits found in a majority of language-impaired individuals and suggests a fundamental deficit in their rapid perceptual processing. In addition, specific predictions about the impact of these perceptual deficits on the development of higher cognitive functions, particularly linguistic processes, are outlined.

Behavioral Evidence for a Rate-Processing Deficit

In an attempt to determine the fundamental processing deficits in individuals with a developmental language impairment, it is important to determine the functional integrity of various sub-skills or precursor skills to the linguistic processing system. These include various aspects of sensory, perceptual, motor, and memory functioning. Borrowing from previous models and experimental results pertaining to simple auditory perception (Hirsch, 1959), Tallal and Piercy (1973a) developed a hierarchical series of new experimental tests called the Repetition Test of Information Processing (see Table 8.1) to examine systematically, in the same subjects, levels of information processing in specifically language-impaired children. These tasks assess the ability to detect, discriminate, and sequence various verbal and nonverbal stimuli, while varying the rate processing and serial memory requirements of the tasks. It is within this model that the sensory-perceptual deficits in specific language-impaired individuals was first revealed.

Before a person can process complex acoustic information such as speech or language, it is necessary to be able to adequately

detect or discriminate acoustic differences between sounds. Initial comparisons of language-impaired and control children on auditory perceptual tasks did not permit any firm conclusions regarding the ability of language-impaired children to detect or discriminate changes in the acoustic signal (Haggerty & Stamm, 1978; Lowe & Campbell, 1965). Lowe and Campbell (1965) reported that language-impaired individuals significantly differed from control children on tasks requiring the identification of the sequence (temporal order) of two rapidly presented auditory tones. However, the interval between the two tones (interstimulus interval) required to identify the presence of two tones, as compared with one, failed to differentiate language-impaired children from control children. In contrast, Haggerty and Stamm (1978) reported that language-impaired subjects required a longer interstimulus interval (ISI) for 1 msec clicks presented to both ears (binaural presentation) to accurately identify whether a single or a pair of tones was presented.

Following the lead of these early studies, Tallal and colleagues have investigated the temporal processing abilities of SLI children. Over the past 20 years, they have demonstrated that language-impaired subjects are significantly impaired only on those tasks requiring the processing of stimulus information that is brief and followed in rapid succession by another stimulus (Tallal, Miller, & Fitch, 1993). For example, the data in Figure 8.1 show that normally developing children ages 6 to 9 years can discriminate the temporal sequence of two 75 msec duration nonverbal tones at better than a 75% level of accuracy with an ISI of 8 msec (see Figure 8.1).

In contrast, a matched group of language-impaired children required an ISI of over 300 msec to respond at the same level of accuracy. Further, the data in Figure 8.1 show that if the task

TABLE 8.1   The Hierarchical Series of Subtests Included in the Repetition Test of Information Processing

DETECTION
Stimulus 1 (until 10 correct responses)
Stimulus 2 (until 10 correct responses)

↓

ASSOCIATION/DISCRIMINATION
(Stimulus 1 or Stimulus 2) Stimuli are presented one at a time until 10 out of 12 consecutive correct responses are obtained. If the criterion has not been reached after 24 trials, discontinue testing.

↓

TEMPORAL ORDERING
Sequencing Subtest: Two stimuli (Stimulus 1 and Stimulus 2) are presented in random sequence with a 500 mss interstimulus interval. The number correct for 12 trials is recorded.

Rate Subtest: Stimulus pairs are presented with 10 or 70 ms interstimulus intervals. The number correct for 12 trials is recorded.

↓

SERIAL MEMORY
The same two stimuli (Stimulus 1 and Stimulus 2) are presented in sequential patterns of three to seven elements. Ten stimulus patterns at each level are presented with either a *slow* or *rapid* interstimulus interval.

Slow Subtest: Stimulus elements are presented with a 500 ms interstimulus interval.

Rapid Subtest: Stimulus elements are presented with either a 10 or 70 ms interstimulus interval. Testing on either subtest continues until the subject fails to correctly reproduce the stimulus pattern on 6 out of 10 trials on two consecutive levels (e.g., 4- and 5-element Rapid Subtests).

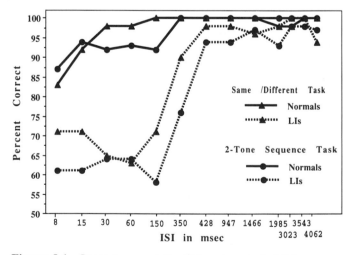

Figure 8.1   Percent correct for SLI and control children on a variable ISI task requiring either a same-different or temporal order judgment of two 75 msec nonverbal tones (tone 1 = 100 Hz, tone 2 = 305 Hz). From "Developmental Aphasia: Impaired Rate of Non-Verbal Processing as a Function of Sensory Modality" by P. Tallal and M. Piercy, 1973, *Neuropsychologia, 11.* Copyright 1973 by Elsevier Science Ltd. Reprinted by permission.

requires a response as to whether the two 75 msec stimuli are the same or different, as compared with a response that reproduces the temporal sequence, performance on this task is still significantly worse for the SLI group at the faster rates of presentation. At longer tone durations of 250 msec, these group differences in temporal processing performance were no longer significant, indicating that total signal duration rather than interstimulus interval alone contributed to these deficits (Tallal & Piercy, 1973a, 1973b, 1974).

A similar rapid processing deficit was also found in serial memory performance. In this study, language-impaired children were unable to correctly remember the temporal order of a series of three 75 msec duration tones; however, the same children were able to correctly report the sequence of five successive tones when the duration of each tone was increased to 250 msec (Tallal & Piercy, 1973b). The specificity of these deficits observed in language-impaired children provides evidence for separate information channels for the processing of rapid as compared with slower presentation rates of auditory information.

The extent to which a functional dissociation in language-impaired individuals between the processing of rapid versus more sustained auditory events is a useful distinction would be supported by evidence of a similar dissociation at the physiological level. In an attempt to provide such evidence, Tallal and Newcombe (1978) examined performance on the Repetition tasks in subjects with focal brain lesions. In this study, 20 male subjects with either a left- or right-hemisphere focal brain lesion, acquired as the result of a missile wound, were compared with six control subjects. In performance on the Repetition tasks, subjects with a left- but not right-hemisphere lesion were selectively impaired in the processing of rapidly presented (interstimulus intervals less than 300 msec) 75 msec nonverbal stimuli (see Figure 8.2).

Performance on this task failed to reliably differentiate between the control and/or the lesion groups on these sounds when the nonverbal tones were presented with a longer ISI (greater than 300 msec). These data provide additional support for the presence of separate information-processing systems for the processing of rapid compared with slower presentation rates of auditory information. Further, these data suggest that these information-processing systems are, at least in part, functionally lateralized in the cerebral hemispheres with normal functioning of the left hemisphere being critical for the successful discrimination of rapidly changing acoustic information, within 10s of milliseconds. Because SLI children show a similar behavioral deficit in rapid temporal processing performance, they might be expected to show a similar physiological deficit in the left hemisphere, a topic that will be explored in greater detail in a later section.

Rapid Auditory Processing and Speech Processing Deficits

The characterization that individuals with a developmental language impairment suffer from an inability to process rapidly presented nonverbal information in addition to verbal information may appear difficult to reconcile with the specific language deficits that characterize this disorder. However, it is well established that important acoustic cues in speech perception occur over relatively brief time periods. For example, in a complex speech signal, consonants are frequently characterized by rapidly changing acoustic parameters that are very brief (40–50 msec), whereas vowels are characterized by a more steady-state spectrum of longer duration (see Figure 8.3). These brief time periods, not unlike those that characterize the rapid timing deficits in language-impaired children, occur in the 10s of milliseconds

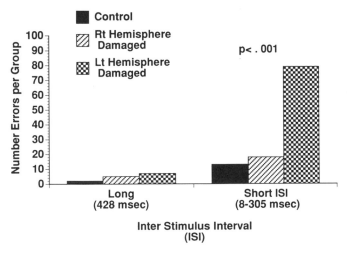

Figure 8.2 Rate processing performance for left- and right-hemisphere-damaged adults for 75 msec nonverbal tones with varying interstimulus intervals. From "Impairment of Auditory Perception and Language Comprehension in Dysphasia" by P. Tallal and F. Newcombe, 1978, *Brain and Language, 5.* Copyright 1978 by Academic Press. Reprinted by permission.

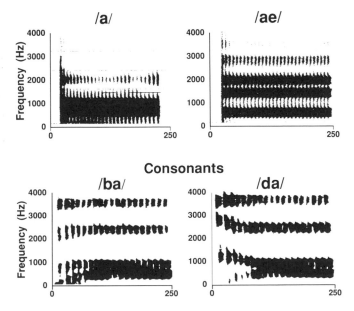

Figure 8.3 Computer-generated steady-state vowels and consonant stimuli.

range. Thus, it would be predicted based on psychophysical results with tones that language-impaired individuals would have more difficulty processing consonant-vowel (CV) syllables compared with vowels.

Figure 8.3 shows the spectrogram for two pairs of computer-generated speech stimuli with equal stimulus durations. The first pair shows the spectra of two steady-state vowels, /a/ and /ae/. The acoustic spectra of these speech stimuli are constant (and differ from each other) throughout the 250 msec duration. The second pair represent the acoustic spectra of the syllables /ba/ and /da/. These syllables differ only over the initial 40 msec, during which the frequencies change very rapidly in time, followed immediately by the vowel /a/, which is steady-state throughout the remainder of both 250 msec syllables. That is, for most of the 250 msec, both syllables comprise identical steady-state formant frequencies for the vowel /a/. Consequently, discrimination of these two syllables critically depends on an accurate analysis of the initial 40 msec formant transitions. Based on the previously described data, this is a temporal period that SLI children have difficulty resolving.

The direct comparison of language-impaired and control subjects on the processing of consonant-vowel, compared with equally long, but steady-state vowel stimuli, has supported a rapid temporal processing deficit in language-impaired subjects. Using the same behavioral paradigm described for the nonverbal acoustic studies previously described (Repetition Test of Information Processing), Tallal and Piercy (1974) reported that language-impaired children were able to successfully discriminate two 250 msec duration steady-state vowels /e/ and /ae/ but were significantly impaired in their ability to discriminate two computer generated 250 msec duration constant-vowel syllables (/ba/ and /da/). The critical difference acoustically is that the consonant-vowel syllables /ba/ versus /da/ differ in acoustic frequency changes that occur within the initial 40 msec of the 250 msec signal (see the bottom of Figure 8.3).

In a subsequent experiment, these authors showed further that the ability to differentiate control and language-impaired individuals failed to reach statistical significance for these same speech sounds when the formant transitions were computer extended to occur over 80 msec. Thus, increasing the temporal duration over which the formant transitions occur within speech syllables significantly improved subject performance for the SLI group, comparable to performance of the control subjects. To date, numerous experiments have been reported using a number of synthetic stimuli, including fricative-vowel syllables, consonant-vowel-consonant syllables, consonant cluster syllables, and phonemes in varying vowel contexts (Stark, Tallal, & Mellits, 1985; Tallal & Stark, 1981). Overwhelmingly, the findings from these studies show that the perceptual deficits of language-impaired children are not best characterized by the verbal aspects of the information to be processed. Rather, their deficit is characterized by difficulty in processing information (verbal or nonverbal) that is of brief duration and followed in rapid succession by other stimuli. The temporal boundary in the perceptual processing for these group effects appears to be on the order of 10s of milliseconds.

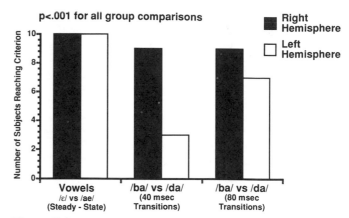

Figure 8.4 Perception of computer-generated speech by left- and right-hemisphere-damaged adults. From "Impairment of Auditory Perception and Language Comprehension in Dysphasia" by P. Tallal and F. Newcombe, 1978, *Brain and Language, 5.* Copyright 1978 by Academic Press. Reprinted by permission.

Additional support that deficits in rapid nonverbal auditory processing and speech processing are directly related comes from patients with acquired lesions. Remember, adults with acquired left- but not right-hemisphere lesions showed a specific deficit in processing rapidly presented nonverbal tones. Therefore, if rapid nonverbal auditory processing is related to the rapid acoustic nature of certain speech stimuli, then patients with left-hemisphere lesions also should have difficulties processing speech stimuli that incorporated rapidly changing acoustic parameters. In addition, these same subjects should show no performance differences from control subjects on stimuli which incorporated longer transition durations or are steady-state. The data in Figure 8.4 show the results from a study comparing subjects with acquired left and right hemisphere lesions to discriminate between the steady-state vowels / ε / and /æ/ as well as the consonant-vowels /ba/ and /da/ with formant transitions of 40 or 80 msec. As shown in Figure 8.4, the data indicate that the left-hemisphere lesion and right-hemisphere lesion groups could discriminate the two 250 msec steady-state vowels at a high level of task accuracy that failed to differentiate the groups. In contrast, task accuracy for discriminating the speech sounds /ba/ and /da/ when the critical acoustic transitions differing in these stimuli occurred in the initial 40 msec of the 250 msec stimuli showed significantly worse performance for the left-hemisphere, compared with the right-hemisphere, lesion group. Further, Tallal and Newcombe (1978) found that there was no difference between the lesion groups on these speech sounds when the critical acoustic formant transitions were extended to 80 msec.

The extent to which the same mechanism(s) underlie the perception of rapid nonverbal and verbal auditory processing is further supported by the data in Figure 8.5. These data show a significant relationship ($r = .83$) between rapid auditory processing and language comprehension performance within the group of subjects with acquired lesions in the left hemisphere. The subjects within this group that performed the most errors on the rapid

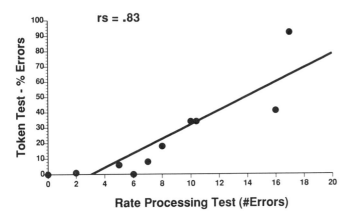

Figure 8.5 Adult aphasics: Correlation between language comprehension and auditory rate processing. From "Impairment of Auditory Perception and Language Comprehension in Dysphasia" by P. Tallal and F. Newcombe, 1978, *Brain and Language, 5.* Copyright 1978 by Academic Press. Reprinted by permission.

	b	p	d	t	g	k
b	100					
p		99				
d			97.9		3.6	
t				100		0.75
g					94	0.75
k					2.4	97.75
?						0.75
Other		1	2.1			

CONTROLS

	b	p	d	t	g	k
b	64.3	9.5		1.7		
p	27.4	80.9	4.2	3.3		0.8
d	1.2	1.2	66.7	3.3	14.3	3
t	3.6	1.2	15.6	80.8	10.7	9.1
g	1.2	1.2	2.1		50	2.3
k		1.2	2.1	8.3	17.8	79.5
?	1.2	4.8	2.1		3.6	2.3
Other	1.2		7.3	3.3	3.6	3

LANGUAGE IMPAIRED

Figure 8.6 Production of stop-consonants elicited by imitation and in response to pictures. The percentages of correct productions for each stop-consonant for both groups are shown. From "Analysis of Stop Consonant Production Errors in Developmentally Dysphasic Children" by R. E. Stark and P. Tallal, 1979, *Journal of the Acoustical Society of America, 66,*(6). Copyright 1979 by American Institute of Physics. Reprinted by permission.

auditory processing task also had the most errors in language comprehension, as demonstrated by performance on the Token Test (DeRenzi & Vignolo, 1962). These results, considered with the previous findings comparing left and right lesion groups, suggest that the functional integrity of the left hemisphere is important in the processing of rapid acoustic information for both nonverbal and verbal information. These data also suggest that normal functioning of the left hemisphere is required for successfully discriminating acoustic information that changes within 10s of milliseconds. Further, performance deficits in this time domain are highly related to performance deficits in processing speech stimuli, which rely on discriminating acoustic changes within this same time frame. In contrast, right-hemisphere lesions do not lead to similar performance deficits.

If a nonverbal auditory temporal processing deficit interferes with the ability of SLI children to perceive certain speech stimuli, do these same subjects have similar problems in speech production? Specifically, SLI children with deficits in perceiving the rapid acoustic segments that differentiate certain speech sounds should show a similar deficit in the production of these same speech sounds. The data in Figure 8.6 quantify the speech output characteristics of SLI and control children for producing stop-consonants /b/, /f/, /d/, /t/, /g/, /k/ elicited through imitation or picture naming. These data show that control subjects seldom misproduce stop-consonants. In contrast, SLI subjects frequently misproduce the correct stop-consonant. In addition, when SLI subjects fail to produce the correct stop-consonant, the errors usually consist of the production of a different stop-consonant and not the introduction of a different class of speech sounds. This suggests that these errors may result, at least in part, from an inability to control the rapid motor movements that differentiate the stop-consonants. For example, when a stop-consonant is the final sound in a word (e.g., /b/ as in tub), the duration of the preceding vowel is the salient cue as to whether the final stop is perceived as voiced /b/ or voiceless /p/. Studies of

the speech production of SLI children demonstrate that they prolong the duration of the vowel preceding a final-stop consonant, resulting in perceptual confusion in speech output. In an attempt to better quantify the temporal nature of the speech production deficits, Stark and Tallal (1979) examined the temporal nature of the speech production deficits of SLI subjects for the production of the stop-consonants. As indicated in Figure 8.7, control subjects show a rather distinct temporal boundary at approximately 35 msec, in producing the voiced (e.g., /ba/) versus voiceless stop-consonants (e.g., /ta/). The SLI group shows a more variable response overall with a substantial amount of overlap between the latencies observed in the creation of these speech sounds. These speech production data suggest that whereas SLI subjects appear to have some conceptualization

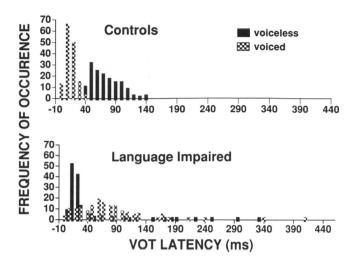

Figure 8.7 Voice onset time for voiced and voiceless final stop-consonants in SLI and control children. From "Analysis of Stop Consonant Production Errors in Developmentally Dysphasic Children" by R. E. Stark and P. Tallal, 1979, *Journal of the Acoustical Society of America, 66,*(6). Copyright 1979 by American Institute of Physics. Reprinted by permission.

about which speech sounds should be produced, their ability to make the rapid and precise motor movements required for producing the sounds is less well developed.

In another study, SLI subjects were asked to rapidly produce the stop-consonants (/pa/, /da/, and /ta/). Because the rapid sequential production of these sounds relies heavily on fine motor coordination, varying in 10s of milliseconds, individuals with SLI might be expected to show difficulties on this measure. Stark and Tallal (1988) recorded the number of sequentially repeated syllables that SLI and matched controls could produce in a 5-second period. They found that as a group, SLI children could produce significantly fewer repetitions of these sounds. In addition, a similar group difference was found for the rapid repetition of multisyllabic words (e.g., refrigerator, buttercup), suggesting that these deficits in production occurred for both individual speech sounds and for whole words. Importantly, it was found that the more speech problems an SLI child had in rapid production, the more severe his or her temporal problems in perception.

Up to this point, the data strongly suggest that in developmentally SLI individuals or adults with acquired brain lesions leading to aphasia, auditory information is processed independently as a function of the presentation rate. These data further suggest that a similar dissociation might occur in normal auditory processing systems. That is, it is hypothesized that the rate of these frequency changes in speech may reflect processes that are hemispherically specialized in normal individuals. To investigate this hypothesis, Schwartz and Tallal (1980) used a discrimination task that presented auditory information simultaneously to both ears (dichotic presentation) in normal adult listeners. A right ear advantage (which is considered to reflect left hemispheric functional specialization) was observed for speech syllables incorporating 40 msec duration transitions. However,

with longer acoustic transitions (80 msec), the right ear advantage was significantly smaller. These data strongly suggest that the left hemisphere's specialization for speech may be due, at least in part, to the presence of rapid acoustic changes that provide important cues in the perception of these speech stimuli.

These results combined with the previously discussed data from subjects with acquired focal lesions suggest a mechanism in the left hemisphere that is specialized for the processing of rapidly changing acoustic stimuli, on which speech processing relies. Abnormal hemispheric lateralization for speech processing has been suggested to underlie the language and reading deficits present in many language- and reading-disabled individuals (Geschwind & Galaburda, 1985a, 1985b, 1985c). Tallal (1981) has hypothesized that the disordered left hemisphere's specialized processing of very rapid acoustic change (in the order of 10s of milliseconds) may lead to deficits in speech perception and subsequently impair language and reading development.

Evidence has now been presented from normal adults, adults with acquired focal brain lesions, and from children with developmental language impairments suggesting that the rapid perception of auditory events is processed relatively independently from the perception of longer or slower events. Further, this perceptual dissociation appears to be represented differentially by the two hemispheres, with normal functioning of the left hemisphere being specifically important for the accurate processing of rapidly changing acoustic information. However, the extent to which this processing dissociation (rapid vs. extended processing) is specific to the auditory system is unclear. In fact, evidence supporting multiple sensory deficits or a single pansensory deficit in these individuals has also been reported.

Multimodal/Amodal Rate-Processing Deficits

In the previously discussed studies by Tallal and Piercy (1973a, 1973b, 1974), rapid auditory processing deficits for nonverbal tones in language-impaired children were reported. These studies also examined the rapid processing abilities for visual stimuli, two shades of the color green, and did not find group differences among the language-impaired and control subjects. However, the modality specificity of these findings conflicted with earlier reports suggesting that the perceptual processing deficits in language-impaired individuals were not confined to the auditory modality, but also involved the visual system (Furth & Pufall, 1966; Poppen, Stark, Eisenson, Forrest, & Wertheim, 1969; Stark, 1967). In an attempt to reconcile these findings, Tallal and colleagues conducted a subsequent set of experiments comparing information-processing performance for auditory, visual, and cross-modal (visual and auditory) perception in language-impaired and control subjects (see Figure 8.8; Tallal, Stark, Kallman, & Mellits, 1981). As indicated in Figure 8.8, SLI subjects had more errors in processing rapidly presented for auditory, visual, and cross-modal information. In addition, the subjects that participated in these experiments spanned a broader age range from 5 to 8 years and thus enabled the comparison of the groups as a function of age.

This study replicated the earlier findings (Tallal & Piercy, 1973b), which demonstrated that older language-impaired children have selective auditory processing deficits for information

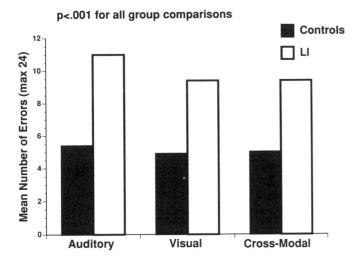

Figure 8.8 Mean number of errors for the rapid presentation of auditory, visual, and crossmodal information in SLI and Control subjects. From "A Re-examination of Some Nonverbal Perceptual Abilities of Language Impaired and Normal Children as a Function of Age and Sensory Modality" by P. Tallal, R. E. Stark, C. Kallman, and D. Mellitis, 1981, *Journal of Speech and Hearing Research, 24*, pp. 351–357. Copyright 1981 by the American Speech-Language-Hearing Association. Reprinted by permission.

that is rapidly presented. However, the extent to which the deficits were also present in the visual modality was dependent on the age of the subjects. For subjects ranging in age from 5 to 6 years, the language-impaired group showed impaired performance on both the auditory and visual tasks. In subjects between 7 and 8 years of age, only performance on the auditory task reliably differentiated the groups. Performance on the cross-modal task for both groups was significantly better than on either the visual or auditory tasks alone and this performance also failed to differentiate the groups.

These findings suggest that a rapid processing deficit appears to be present across both the visual and auditory modalities early in development but is selective to the auditory modality in older subjects. However, the auditory and visual stimuli used in this study were not equated in complexity, perceptual saliency, or difficulty, and thus interpretations based on the direct comparison of performance on these tasks should be considered tentative. The developmental change in the modality specificity of rate-processing deficits for language-impaired children could be the result of differing sensitivities of the tasks for evaluating rapid processing system(s) in each of these modalities at various ages.

Experimental evidence from these same language-impaired and control subjects on tasks designed to examine perceptual processing in somatosensory perception also have reported that language-impaired subjects show significant deficits in the abilities to discriminate simultaneously presented tactile information, and to produce rapid alternating and sequential movements (Johnston, Stark, Mellits, & Tallal, 1981; Tallal et al., 1985a). These data appear to support a specific, but multisensory processing deficit. Although later in development these processing deficits appear to become specific only to the auditory modality,

more sensitive measures in several modalities need to be used to confirm these findings. Furthermore, direct investigations into the extent to which these sensory/perceptual timing deficits are related to specific linguistic deficits of these individuals should provide insight into why it is that language is so particularly disrupted in SLI individuals.

Tallal et al., (1985b) directly examined whether these temporal processing deficits were related to the degree of receptive language impairments of language-impaired individuals. As indicated in Figure 8.9, the results of this study showed that the degree of perceptual impairment for rapidly presented information (nonverbal acoustic tones or speech stimuli) was highly correlated to the degree of receptive language impairment, as assessed by standardized receptive language measures ($r = .81$, $p < .001$). Furthermore, statistical analyses (multiple regression procedures) showed that 72% of the variability in the level of receptive language performance for the language-impaired group was accounted for by the ability to discriminate and sequence nonverbal acoustic tones separated by a short ISI or speech stimuli containing brief duration temporal cues (/ba/ vs. /da/).

In a later evaluation, Tallal and colleagues administered an extensive neuropsychological test battery including measures of auditory, visual, motor, and memory tests to a large group of language-impaired and age-matched control subjects. A stepwise discriminant function analysis was then used to determine which set of independent variables would correctly assign individuals to the defined language-impaired and control groups. The results demonstrated that six variables, when combined, correctly classified 100% ($n = 33$) of the control subjects and 96% ($n = 26$) of the language-impaired subjects. The six variables were rapid syllable production; two separate measures of two-point tactile discrimination; discrimination of two rapidly presented speech stimuli that were characterized by rapid acoustic transitions; crossmodal integration of rapidly presented information; and sequencing the rapid visual presentation of the letters "E" and

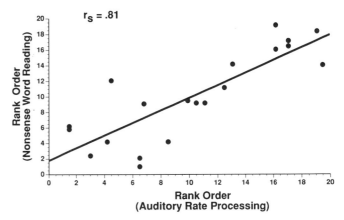

Figure 8.9 Dyslexics-correlation between nonword reading and auditory rate processing. From "Auditory Temporal Perception, Phonics and Reading Disabilities in Children" by P. Tallal, 1980, *Brain and Language, 9.* Copyright by Academic Press. Adapted by permission.

"K." These same tasks given at slower presentation rates failed to differentiate these populations.

In conclusion, these studies demonstrate that individuals with a developmental language impairment show specific deficits in the rapid processing of information. The nature and developmental course of these temporal processing deficits are directly related to an individual's deficit(s) in the perception and production of speech stimuli. The perception of rapid acoustic changes, within 10s of milliseconds, is crucial for determining the phonological and morphological linguistic forms being used in language.

In contrast, deficits in the use of syntax by language-impaired individuals may appear less well understood in terms of their rapid temporal processing deficits. Recent data, however, suggest that nonlinguistic temporal processing performance may also be directly related to specific aspects of processing syntax in speech. For example, individuals with a specific language impairment show an inverse relationship between the degree of their temporal processing deficit and their processing of grammatical and thematic information (Curtiss & Tallal, 1991). This relationship was observed specifically when linguistic information was provided by word order, as is frequently the case in spoken language. A similar relation in control subjects failed to reach statistical significance. These results suggest that a nonlinguistic temporal processing impairment may impact directly on the processing of linguistic structures in which the sequential order of linguistic elements uniquely signals grammatical and semantic information. Research is pending, however, to determine the relationship, if any, between perceptual processing and other forms of linguistic information.

Although the present discussion suggests a homogeneous deficit in rapid temporal processing, language-impaired children represent a heterogeneous group. Thus different subpopulations may, in part, reflect different levels of expression of these and other processing deficits or alternatively have different etiologies. To the extent to which they have been demonstrated as deficient, however, rapid timing deficits may represent an excellent measure for identifying different subtypes of language-impaired individuals, particularly where receptive phonology is compromised (Frumkin & Rapin, 1980). Nevertheless, in our experience, a temporal processing deficit reflects a large majority of developmentally language-impaired individuals. This area requires further investigation and supports the use and analysis of language development in single cases as well as in large groups of developmentally language-impaired individuals.

Syndrome Specificity for Rate-Processing Deficits

Growing evidence exists with regard to the frequent comorbidity among several of the developmental disabilities. The extent to which these clinical populations overlap in their behavioral manifestations, such as the similar linguistic deficits found in children with autism, specific language impairments, or reading impairment, has not yet been fully characterized much less understood. The extent to which a proposed causal deficit underlying any one disorder is equally manifest in the other clinical populations questions the specificity of the neurobiology underlying the disorder. Thus, the determination of the specificity of rapid timing deficits for developmental language impairment is particularly crucial to determine the specificity of the processing disorder. In the following section, evidence regarding the overlap between developmental disorders is discussed.

Autism. Autism is a pervasive developmental disorder characterized by impaired social, cognitive, and language development, typically not in keeping with the intellectual level of the person (Rutter, 1978). In addition, autistic patients frequently exhibit disturbances of motor and sensory systems (Rutter, 1978). Of all the symptoms associated with autism, the language impairment is frequently considered the central feature (Rutter, 1978). All children diagnosed with autism exhibit some form of language impairment, and the prognosis for future functioning can often be correlated with the degree of language impairment (Benton, 1964). It has been suggested that many of the other behaviors associated with autism are directly due to a failure to develop language (Rutter, 1978). However, the extent to which the language difficulties observed in autism reflect a similar etiology to that shown in other language-impaired individuals is not well understood.

Rutter and colleagues have compared the language disturbances of autistic and developmentally language-impaired boys. In general, the main findings suggest that the language disorder was more severe in the autistic than specifically language-impaired children, and the impairments for the autistic children included deviance as well as delay in the usage of spoken and gestural language (Rutter, 1978). Indeed, it has been suggested that the degree of language impairment may best differentiate these groups (Beitchman & Inglis, 1991).

In contrast to the similarity in linguistic performance, comparison of individuals suffering from childhood autism and SLI show significant differences in temporal processing abilities (Lincoln, Dickstein, Courchesne, Elmasian, & Tallal, 1993). In this study, teenagers and young adults with a documented childhood diagnosis of (a) autism or (b) language impairment were compared with age- and IQ-matched controls and with each other in auditory temporal processing. Results demonstrated that teenagers and young adults, with a documented childhood history of a language impairment, continued to be significantly impaired on the temporal processing subtests of the Tallal Repetition Test compared with matched controls ($P < .01$), as well as with autistic individuals ($P < .05$). These results demonstrate the specificity of the temporal processing disorder to SLI, as autistic individuals (despite their more impaired linguistic development) were not significantly different from controls on these temporal processing tests. These findings are particularly important for several reasons. First, these findings do not demonstrate poorer performance for autistic individuals compared with specifically language-impaired individuals as has so frequently been the case for linguistic and other cognitive measures, suggesting that there may be fundamentally different neurobiological underpinnings to these disorders, although both involved delayed language development. This is in concert with MRI results on these two groups of children, which also show vastly different anatomic signatures (see Courchesne, Lincoln, Yeung-Courchesne, Elmasian, & Grillon, 1989; Courchesne, Townsend, & Saitoh, 1994; Jernigan, Hesselink, & Tallal, 1991 for reviews of MRI data on these populations).

Specific Reading Disorders. The rapid temporal processing deficits described for specific language impaired subjects also appear to characterize individuals suffering from a developmental reading impairment. At present, studies conducted by several independent laboratories have shown that individuals with a specific reading disability also demonstrate a disruption in rapid auditory temporal processing (Reed, 1989; Steffens, Eilers, Gross-Glenn, & Jallad, 1992; Tallal, 1980). The extent of these deficits in reading impaired subjects has also been shown to be significantly related to their reading comprehension and nonword reading (decoding) abilities (Tallal, 1980). However, these findings only apply to some reading-impaired children. Importantly, measures of rapid temporal processing failed to differentiate reading-impaired children without concomitant oral language deficits (including phonics skills) from control children (Tallal & Stark, 1982). Thus, the extent to which reading-impaired individuals show oral language and phonological difficulties may be an important clue to the etiology of different subtypes of dyslexia. Future studies need to make direct comparisons between various subgroups of reading-impaired children on measures of perceptual processing.

Measures of visual temporal processing also appear to differentiate developmentally reading and language-impaired individuals from controls. However, unlike the relatively new concept of separate processing systems in audition, a well-established and dominant concept in visual perception is that visual processing is accomplished through the synergy of at least two separate, but highly interactive, systems. These systems are best characterized according to their spatiotemporal response preferences for visual information (Livingstone & Hubel, 1987): a "transient" visual processing system that is more sensitive to visual stimuli of lower spatial frequencies (number of light wave oscillations per unit distance) and higher temporal frequencies, and a "sustained" visual processing system that is more sensitive to visual stimuli of higher spatial frequencies and lower temporal frequencies (for a review, see Breitmeyer, 1989). Providing additional support for the existence of separate visual processing systems along the transient and sustained stimulus dimensions are data showing that individuals with a developmental reading impairment appear best differentiated from nonimpaired control subjects on tasks that emphasize processing in the "transient," as compared with the "sustained," visual processing system (Livingstone, Rosen, Drislane, & Galaburda, 1991; Lovegrove, Garzia, & Nicholson, 1990; Williams & LeCluyse, 1990).

For example, a group of reading-impaired, as compared with non-reading-impaired individuals, required longer interstimulus intervals of low spatial frequency gratings (1–4 c/deg) for detection of a gap (Lovegrove, Heddle, & Slaghuis, 1980). At higher spatial frequencies (i.e., gratings of 8 c/deg or greater), when visual processing in the transient system is minimal, task performance failed to differentiate the groups. Further, these visual processing differences were more pronounced when stimuli were presented at higher temporal frequencies (e.g., 25 Hz), when visual processing in the transient system is maximal (Martin & Lovegrove, 1987).

Thus, the visual processing deficits present in reading-impaired subjects, compared with controls, may represent a selective deficit in the transient visual processing system. However, the previously described studies examining temporal processing performance in reading-impaired subjects failed to screen subjects for a positive history or concurrent developmental language impairments, a factor that may contribute to the current overlap in temporal processing performance among these clinical populations. At present, the transient visual system deficits found in a large majority of reading-impaired individuals have been discussed almost exclusively within the context of integrating visual fixations and eye movements during the reading process (Breitmeyer, 1989; Williams & LeCluyse, 1990) and as being independent of the phonological processing deficits considered primary in reading-disabled individuals (Stanovich, 1988; Vellutino, Steger, Moyer, Harding, & Niles, 1977).

In apparent contrast to the theories postulating a phonologically based model of developmental language/reading impairments, language-impaired as well as reading-impaired children have also been found to be impaired in comparison with controls on the rapid temporal processing of visual as well as auditory information (Tallal, 1981). Consequently, Tallal has proposed a theory unifying these two lines of research. She suggests that a generalized "pansensory" deficit in processing sensory information, which converges in the nervous system in rapid succession (in the grain of 10s of msecs), may underlie both the phonological as well as auditory and visual psychophysical deficits that characterize these children.

In conclusion, both language-impaired and reading-impaired groups, in comparison with control subjects, have been found to demonstrate visual and auditory rate-processing deficits. However, due to differences in temporal processing tasks and subject selection procedures used across many of these studies, the extent to which these clinical populations differ in the precise pattern and/or degree of perceptual processing performance is unclear. Further complicating a synthesis of these findings is that few studies have included separate language-impaired and reading-impaired groups or screened subjects for the co-occurrence of these disorders. The extent to which these temporal processing deficits represent modality specific or pansensory rate-processing mechanisms is also difficult to determine because few studies have carefully examined and compared both auditory and visual rate processing performance on tasks specifically designed to equate task difficulty. Thus, direct and detailed comparisons of well-defined language-impaired and reading-impaired populations on theoretically relevant and equated temporal processing tasks across modalities are a high priority for future research. These important comparisons would provide necessary insight into the syndrome specificity of the mechanism(s) underlying the rate-processing deficits found in these clinical populations.

Outcomes of Language-Impaired Children

In reviewing the linguistic literature as it relates to language impairments, several fundamental findings have emerged. Language-impaired children frequently show deficits in comparison with normally developing individuals in the acquisition of numerous components of the linguistic system (Curtiss & Tallal, 1991). These include both receptive and expressive deficits in phonology, morphology, syntax, and semantics of language. The developmental pattern of these deficits is frequently similar to the acquisition patterns present in younger, non-language-impaired children. Thus, the pattern of linguistic deficits appears best characterized as a developmental delay in the acquisition of language, in contrast to a description of frank deviance of language development. More specifically, it is rarely reported that children with language impairments produce utterances that are not characteristic of normal language development (Curtiss & Tallal, 1990; Tomblin, 1991). The proposal that the underlying deficits in language-impaired individuals represent a developmental delay or lag, and not frank deviance, suggests that these individuals would eventually catch up to their same-age peers in language development (Schonhaut & Satz, 1983). However, recent evidence examining the outcomes of individuals diagnosed in childhood with a specific language impairment fail to support a simple developmental-lag hypothesis.

Evidence is mounting regarding the adult outcomes of specific language impairments. Taking into consideration the various developmental differences in educational, interventional, and compensatory influences available to adults with a history of a specific language impairment as well as the present lack of normative data on adult language performance, the diagnosis of a specific language impairment in adulthood presents a formidable task. Self-report questionnaire data represent some of the first evidence regarding the outcomes of specific developmental language disorders in adulthood. Hall and Tomblin (1978) found that adults with a childhood history of a specific language impairment were frequently viewed as continuing to present language difficulties. Direct evaluations further support the persistence of behavioral, cognitive, intellectual, and achievement deficits in language-impaired individuals into late childhood and early adolescence (Aram, Ekelman, & Nation, 1984; Benasich et al., 1993; Lincoln et al., 1993; Rissman et al., 1990; Weiner, 1974).

Recently, Tomblin and colleagues (Tomblin, Freese, & Records, 1992) reported the results from a series of diagnostic measures obtained from a group of 35 teenagers and adults, ages 15 to 25 years, with well-documented histories of specific language impairments. Measures of comprehension and production for words and sentences, as well as verbal memory and auditory temporal perceptual abilities were lower in adults with a childhood history of specific language impairments, compared with well-matched controls. These data fail to support the developmental-lag hypothesis regarding the nature and persistence of the underlying deficits involved in specific language impairments. In addition, these data support previous findings from other learning-disabled adults showing persistent deficits into adulthood of various language, cognitive, and intellectual abilities (Buchanan & Wolf, 1986; McCue, Shelly, & Goldstein, 1986; Naylor, Felton, & Wood, 1989; O'Donnall, Kurtz, & Ramanaiah, 1983; Steffens et al., 1992).

Social and Emotional Development

There is little debate that language plays a crucial role in the acquisition and maintenance of various social, emotional, and behavioral skills. Therefore, SLI children could provide a unique opportunity for evaluating the relationship between emerging language skills (or lack thereof) and social and emotional development. Furthermore, it could be hypothesized that SLI children might possess a greater risk for developing various social and emotional problems.

Support for a relationship between abnormal language development and social and/or emotional problems can be found in a number of previous studies. Griffiths (1969) reported a high incidence of psychiatric problems in the case histories of language-delayed children. Disturbances noted included for some children a wide range of behavioral problems in the home, enuresis, truancy from school, hyperactivity, aggression, and destructive behavior, and for other children excessive shyness and inhibition. Comparative studies of language-impaired and normal children found that a similar set of behavioral abnormalities differentiated these groups (Affolter, Brubaker, & Bischofberger, 1974). In a large study, nearly 50% of a national sample of children classified as having marked speech difficulties were assessed by their teachers as being maladjusted (Butler, Peckman, & Sheridan, 1973), suggesting that behavioral problems are not uncommon in the language-impaired population.

Similarly, the studies of Baker and Cantwell (1987a, 1987b), Cantwell and Baker (1977), Cantwell, Baker, and Mattison (1979, 1980), and Baker, Cantwell, & Mattison (1980) found that psychiatric evaluation of 100 consecutive cases of children seen in a community speech and hearing clinic revealed the presence of a diagnosable psychiatric disorder, according to DSM-III criteria (American Psychiatric Association, 1980), in approximately half (50%) of the cases. Developmental learning disorders, such as reading and math deficits, were found in approximately 25% of these same children. In an epidemiological longitudinal study of children from 8 to 13 years of age, Esser and colleagues (Esser, Schmidt, & Woerner, 1990) reported that the development of psychiatric disorders in subjects determined to be free of psychiatric disturbance at 8 years of age was related to prior learning disabilities and stressful life events. Promisingly, the remission of these disturbances was related to improvement within the psychosocial family environment.

A higher incidence of speech, language, and reading problems in a psychiatric population, compared with the general population, also provides additional evidence regarding a possible link between language and psychiatric problems (Chess & Rosenberg, 1974; Grinnell, Scott-Hartnet, & Glasier, 1983; Gualtieri, Koriath, Van Bourgondein, & Saleeby, 1983; Livingston, 1990). Chess and Rosenberg (1974) found that over a 3-year period, 24% of the children referred for psychiatric treatment had some type of a language disorder. The psychiatric diagnoses for the children examined by Chess and Rosenberg (1974) included a wide range of disorders including cerebral dysfunction, developmental lag, thought disorder, and neurotic behavior disorder. In at least some cases, the development and/or expression of a psychiatric disturbance appears to occur after the identification of a learning disability. However, the extent to which the speech and language disorders in these children were specific to a particular category of psychiatric disturbance was not addressed in these studies.

Recent evidence, however, suggests a relationship between the degree and type of behavioral problems that language-impaired children develop and neurodevelopmental delay. Baker et al. (1980) reported the nature of the linguistic deficit was related to the degree of psychiatric disturbance in SLI children. Children with speech articulation problems, without concomitant language disorders, were found to show the least prevalence for psychiatric disorders. The children with speech and language disorders, or language disorders alone, were at higher risk for psychiatric problems. In addition, attention deficit/hyperactivity disorder was found to be the predominant psychiatric disturbance in this language-impaired sample (Baker & Cantwell, 1987b). The language-impaired sample studied by Beitchman et al., (1986) was also found to show a relationship between hyperactivity and language impairments. The increased comorbidity of language impairments and attention deficit/hyperactivity disorder suggests a common factor that occurs prior to or early in the development of these two disorders.

Neurodevelopmental Delay and Rapid Processing Deficits

Beitchman (1985) has suggested that neurodevelopmental immaturity may be the common antecedent that relates specific language impairments and attention deficit/hyperactivity disorder. In support of this hypothesis, a recent study reported by Tallal et al. (1989) showed that the psychiatric and behavioral disturbances identified in language-impaired children appear to be related, at least in part, to neurodevelopmental delays in these children. For example, group differences in behavioral and emotional status among 81 language-impaired and 60 control subjects, matched in age, race, socioeconomic status, and intellectual performance, were significantly reduced when group differences in attention, perception, and motor functioning were statistically controlled (Tallal et al., 1989).

Performance on these same perceptual/motor tasks has previously been shown to be significantly lower in language-impaired subjects compared with controls (Tallal et al., 1985a) and to correlate highly with receptive language performance (Tallal et al., 1985b). In addition, these SLI subjects showed a significant decrease in Leiter intellectual performance (Leiter, 1952) in 4- to 8-year-old children, a measure designed to minimize the oral language instructions and responses. These findings suggest that, at least in part, the factors related to the increased incidence for later behavioral and psychiatric problems are related to the nonverbal perceptual/motor aspects of specific language impairments. Thus, the extent to which the neural developmental delays in SLI appear to be related to the social and emotional problems suggest that a further opportunity for understanding the complex developmental etiology of this disorder can be gained through better understanding the neurodevelopmental aspects of SLI.

HERITABILITY OF SPECIFIC LANGUAGE IMPAIRMENTS

Evidence is growing that specific language and learning disabilities appear to "run in families." The extent to which these patterns of heritability can be demonstrated can provide valuable insight into the developmental etiology underlying these disorders. Several methods for investigating heritable patterns of complex behaviors, such as language, currently exist. The most frequently used method has been to determine whether the inci-

dence of a specified condition—in the present context, a developmental language disorder—is greater in the relatives of an individual with that condition (hereafter designated probands[3]) than in the relatives of controls without that condition. At present, three types of methodological designs have been employed to examine the issue of the heritability of a developmental language impairment. These include the prevalence of developmental language disorders (a) within a single family with a large pedigree, (b) in a group of unrelated families regardless of pedigree size, or (c) the comparison among monozygotic and dizygotic twin pairs. The comparison across these measures may yield unique and complementary information regarding the heritability of developmental language disorders.

Evidence of Heritable Transmission

Family Studies

Case history reports provide some of the earliest reports of familial patterns of specific language impairments. A limited number of case histories of families with language-impaired members have been reported (Arnold, 1961; Borges-Osorio & Salzano, 1985; Hurst, Baraitser, Auger, Graham, & Norell, 1990; McReady, 1926; Samples & Lane, 1985). The regularity in the mode of transmission across generations reported in these studies was the first suggestion of a heritable etiology for developmental language impairments. Most recently, Hurst et al. (1990) described the pedigree of a three-generation extended family containing 30 members. Fifty percent of the family members were affected with speech and language disabilities. The rate and pattern of the affected family members within this study were consistent with an autosomal (nonsex chromosome) dominant mode of inheritance, with full penetrance. In autosomal dominant disorders, an affected parent has a 50% chance of transmitting the disorder to each offspring, regardless of their gender. However, the extent to which the pattern of inheritance from this single pedigree can be generalized to other families with a history of specific language impairments requires further examination.

Large group studies of language-impaired children and their immediate families can also provide information into the heritability of specific language impairments. The earliest data pertaining to family histories of language-impaired children appeared within the context of larger group studies. Ingram (1959) obtained family histories on 75 language-impaired children. Eighteen (24%) of these children had at least one parent with a history of a language impairment. In addition, 30 of the 131 siblings of these probands carried a diagnosis of a language impairment, which was confirmed by direct observation in 23. Luchsinger (1970) reviewed the cases of 127 language-impaired children. He reported that 35% of the parents of these children presented speech defects. Similarly, Byrne, Willerman, and Ashmore (1974) studied the family characteristics of 38 language-impaired children and reported that 37% had relatives (degree of relationship not specified) with language-related

---

[3] A proband is a family member on which the selection of the family is made.

disabilities. In a study focused on the neurological status of language-impaired children, Hier and Rosenberger (1980) reported that 63% of the language-impaired children participating in the study had a family history of a language impairment. Unfortunately, none of these previously described studies provide enough information to determine the extent or nature of the communication problems in either the probands or in the affected family members.

Two recent studies (Bishop & Edmundson, 1986; Robinson, 1987) provide evidence of family aggregation in the first quantitatively assessed populations of language-impaired children. Bishop and Edmundson's study demonstrated a significant increased frequency of affected primary and secondary relatives in language-impaired children compared with controls, but only brief mention was made of these data in the context of a larger study. Robinson (1987) reported family history results from three separate data sets. He found that 28% of language-impaired probands had a first-degree relative (parents, siblings) with a reported history of speech delay, whereas 20% reported a history of learning problems. Unfortunately, no control group was included to allow the significance of these results to be determined.

More recently, case-control family study designs have been used to assess family aggregation in language impairment. Neils and Aram (1986) reported the occurrence of a spectrum of language disorders in the immediate family members of 74 language-impaired children compared with 35 age-matched controls. They found that 20% of the family members of the language-impaired group, compared with only 3% of the control group, reported speech and language impairments.

Tomblin (1989) studied the family histories of 51 language-impaired and 146 controls. Family members were only considered affected when the parent reported that the problem had been treated by a speech-language clinician. Results showed 23% of the language-impaired, but only 3% of the control family members, reported a positive history, a highly significant group difference. The highest rate of impairment was found for the brothers of the language-impaired probands (40%). Approximately 20% of fathers as well as mothers and 17% of sisters of language-impaired probands also reported a history of language impairment. In contrast, rates fell below 5% for the control probands.

Two studies have focused on specific subtypes of language-impaired children. Whitehurst et al. (1991) reported the result of a familial aggregation study of young children with expressive language delay, without concomitant receptive language impairment. Unlike the previous studies reviewed, these authors failed to find evidence of significantly increased familial aggregation in this selected subtype of children compared with a control group. However, the probands with expressive language impairment in this study were only 2 years old, and Whitehurst et al. (1991) reported that at longitudinal follow-up, they found most of these children to be within normal limits by age 3 or 4 years. Thus, these children may better be classified as "late talkers" than language impaired. This study demonstrates the importance of specifying the diagnostic criteria used for including proband cases in familial aggregation studies.

Emphasizing the potential importance of subtype classification in specifying the phenotype of language-impaired probands

in family studies, Lewis, Ekelman, and Aram (1989) studied the siblings of children with specific phonological disorders. They also report the only quantitative data (as opposed to parent-report data) on family members of impaired probands. Despite initial subtype classification for specific phonological disorders, subsequent testing study results demonstrated significant deficits in receptive and expressive language abilities in these probands. Furthermore, they found that siblings of phonologically impaired probands were significantly impaired on a broad spectrum of tests including phonological production and reading, but not language, in comparison with siblings of matched controls. Thus, although this study showed increased aggregation based on evaluation of family members, the phenotypic pattern was not restricted to subtype classification of the probands.

Tallal, Ross, and Curtiss (1989a) report the results of the only family aggregation study to date using a case-control genetic design. Both the language-impaired and control probands were selected based on standardized speech, language, and intelligence tests, with groups matched on age, race, socioeconomic status (SES), and IQ. Both the biological mother and father of each proband were requested to fill-out questionnaires related to family history of speech, language, and academic achievement. Because of the lack of a good diagnostic criteria when the parents were children, and because of the relationship between language disorders and subsequent academic achievement, parents were classified as affected if any of the following were reported: (a) a history of speech or language problems; (b) a history of below-average achievement, up to the eighth grade, in reading, writing, or both; (c) a history of ever being kept back a grade in school through the eighth grade. Siblings were diagnosed as affected if parents reported for them a positive history for difficulty in reading, writing, language, or other learning disabilities. Data were analyzed according to a case-control genetic family design.

Results demonstrated highly significant between-group differences across family member types within the language-impaired children. Thirty-seven percent of mothers of language impaired children and 19% of mothers of controls met the criteria as affected ($P < .05$). Fathers of language impaired children were also significantly different from fathers of controls ($P < .02$) with 43% of the fathers of language impaired versus 20% of the fathers of controls meeting the criteria as affected. Similarly, control subjects had a significantly lower affected-sibling frequency than the siblings of the impaired children. Further analyses demonstrated that there was a significant effect of the number of affected parents on the number of affected offspring (not including proband). Whereas 25% of the siblings of probands without an affected parent were affected, 32% were affected in families with one affected parent and 53% were affected in families with both parents affected.

The preceding data set also was used to determine if any known mode(s) of genetic transmission patterns were suggested. Tallal, Ross, and Curtiss (1989b) examined the relationship between the proband's sex and parental impairment. For language-impaired boys, 23% had both parents affected, 18% had only an affected mother, and 25% had only an affected father. For the language-impaired girls, 11% had both parents affected, 11% had only a mother affected, and 33% had only a father affected.

There was no statistically significant difference between the number of language-impaired boys and girls with or without an affected parent. Combining language-impaired girls and boys, 63% had at least one affected parent.

To determine whether the sex of the proband is associated with the sex of the affected parent, only families with one affected parent were used. No significant association was demonstrated between the sex of the probands and the sex of the affected parent. Within the group of language-impaired children without an affected parent, although there were more boys than girls, this difference was not statistically different from the expected 1:1 sex ratio in the general population (15 boys, 8 girls; 1.9:1 ratio). However, for the language-impaired children who did have an affected parent, there were almost three times as many boys as girls, a highly significant ratio difference ($p < 0.01$). Thus, a higher sex ratio of language-impaired boys to girls was only found in those families with an affected parent. Further analyses showed no significant difference between the number of language-impaired boys and girls with affected siblings. That is, the sex of the proband is not significantly associated with either the impairment rate or sex of their affected siblings. The data from our preliminary studies of family aggregation in language impairment therefore fail to support a sex-linked mode of genetic transmission, but are consistent with an autosomal dominant mode of genetic transmission.

Twin Studies

The twin study design has been well established as a highly effective means of establishing heritability estimates for behavioral and cognitive abilities, and has been utilized with great success in the study of psychiatric disorders as well as cognitive disorders such as developmental dyslexia (see Rutter et al., 1990, for review). Monozygotic twins are genetically identical, and therefore differences between monozygotic twins can be considered due to differences in environmental factors during development. However, monozygotic twins that are reared together frequently share similar environmental experiences. Thus, similarities (concordance) in the development of monozygotic twins may represent shared environmental influences. In contrast, dizygotic twins have approximately 50% of the same genotype and thus provide an excellent comparison group for monozygotic concordance rates.

A few twin studies have investigated heritability of language abilities in normal twins (Koch, 1966; Mittler, 1969; Munsinger & Douglass, 1976; Osborne, Gregor, & Miele, 1968). All these studies report higher concordance rates for monozygotic than dizygotic twins supporting a genetic component to normal language development. Although twin studies provide one of the most direct ways of differentiating genetic from environmental effect on disorders that first manifest in childhood, until a recent study in Britain, no study of heritability in language-impaired twins had been reported.

At present, only preliminary findings from this important study of language-impaired twins have been presented (Bishop, North, & Donlan, 1994). However, a number of interesting points have emerged from the early data. On the one hand, they offer support for a genetic basis of language impairments, but they also suggest that other nongenetic influences are important. The preliminary data reported include 61 twin pairs where zygosity was unambiguous and at least one twin has a concurrent or previous language impairment status. When assessing concordance between twins, it was noted that in many cases where twins were discordant for past or present language impairment, the cotwin nevertheless was not developing normally. These cases included (a) mentally retarded children with nonverbal IQs below 70; (b) "spectrum" disorders—those with nonverbal IQs in the range 70 to 85, with language scores below the 5th percentile; (c) "borderline" cases—those with IQs in the range 70–85 with normal language scores; and (d) reading disabled—those with nonverbal IQs of 85 or above, who had severe problems with reading and/or spelling (scaled scores of 75 or below), but normal scores on language tests.

Although the number of twins tested thus far does not allow for firm conclusions, there appear to be closer similarities in the type of disorder seen in cotwins of affected monozygotic twins than in cotwins of affected dizygotic twins. Low nonverbal ability, in most cases above the level of mental retardation but within the borderline range, was common in all cotwins, but monozygotic cotwins seemed more likely to have specific language impairment, either at the time of assessment or in the past. The results of this preliminary study of higher monozygotic than dizygotic concordance rates provide substantial evidence supporting a heritability factor in the disorder.

However, Rutter (1978) has pointed out that although twin studies provide a powerful opportunity for potentially differentiating environmental and genetic effects, they also have several important limitations. It has been argued that family environment may not be comparable for monozygotic and dizygotic twins, with monozygotic twins being more likely than dizygotic twins to be treated alike by their parents (Jackson, 1960). The concern has also been raised that congenital abnormalities may be more frequent in twins than in singletons and more frequent still in monozygotic than in dizygotic pairs (Propping & Vogel, 1976). There is also concern that the unusually close relationship between some twins, resulting in "secret" languages (cryptoglossia), may predispose behavioral concordance (Bakker, 1987). A related concern pertains to a documented increase in language and reading disabilities in twins compared with singletons (Hay, O'Brien, Johnston, & Prior, 1984). To date, the evidence suggests that the raised incidence of these disabilities in twins is a consequence of environmental factors. Thus, twin studies are likely to seriously overestimate the influence of genetic factors as they apply to nontwin populations. Despite these limitations, twin studies have the important advantage of allowing calculations of the strength of genetic influences on developmental disorders.

Identifying the Phenotype of Familially Transmitted Language Disorders. As previously presented, Tallal, Townsend, and colleagues (1991) suggested that the significant increase in familial aggregation in the families of language-impaired children may result from interacting genetic and environmental factors. Although the specific etiologic influences are yet to be determined, it is clear that a subset of language-impaired children have a family history of developmental language/learning impairment, whereas others do not. Differences in family history may define unique subtypes of language impairment, displaying different behavioral (phenotypic) profiles. To investigate this possibility, these authors examined whether language-impaired children, with or without an affected parent, showed different phenotypic profiles. A comprehensive battery of speech, language, neuropsychological and academic achievement tests, as well as a child behavioral checklist, was used.

Twenty-three language-impaired subjects, for whom direct data from both biological parents were available to determine affected status, participated as subjects in this study. Results demonstrated that approximately 70% of these probands met criteria for a positive family history, with fathers reportedly being affected about twice as often as mothers. Statistical analyses showed that family history positive and family history negative language-impaired probands were not significantly different in age, WISC-R performance IQ, or distribution of gender. In addition, there was no significant differences in either receptive or expressive language abilities, based on standardized speech and language tests, found for the family history positive group compared with the family history negative group. However, a significant difference between the family history positive and negative groups was found on the Child Behavior Checklist (Achenbach & Edelbrock, 1983), based on both parent and teacher reports. More problems were reported for the family history positive language-impaired children. Narrowband scales developed from factor analysis of the checklist show that family history positive language-impaired children were rated by parents as being more "hyperactive" and by teachers as being more "inattentive" than language-impaired children with a negative family history. There is considerable overlap in items composing these scales. Items with the highest loadings that are common to both scales relate to attention as well as academic performance. No other behaviors on the checklist proved significantly different for the two SLI groups.

A broad battery of neuropsychological as well as academic achievement abilities were also assessed. Significant between-group differences were only found for a series of measures assessing auditory processing, attention, and memory performance (see Figure 8.10). Language-impaired children with a positive family history performed significantly more poorly on these measures than language-impaired children with a negative family history ($P < .01$). There were no significant differences between groups of family history positive and negative language-impaired children for performance on clusters of measures representing academic performance, language abilities, visual-spatial skills, audiological competence, speech, or oral/motor abilities. The results of this study underscore the sensitivity of auditory attention, temporal processing, and memory abilities in differentiating phenotypic patterns that may be most associated with familial transmission of language impairments.

Biological Trait Markers

One approach used in an attempt to better classify family members across generations has been to identify a biological trait marker that has been shown to be highly associated with the condition that is the focus of genetic study (Gershon & Goldin, 1986). The assumption is that specific biological trait markers may be

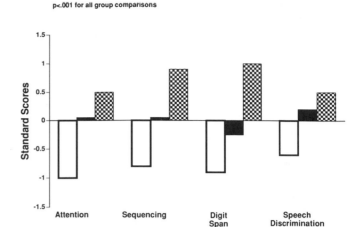

Figure 8.10 Phenotypic profiles for SLI children as a function of family history for a language-based learning disability and control children on measures requiring temporal processing. From "Phenotypic Profiles of Language Impaired Children Based on Genetic/Family History" by P. Tallal, J. Townsend, S. Curtiss and B. Wulfeck, 1991, *Brain and Language, 41*. Copyright 1991 by Academic Press. Reprinted by permission.

easier to quantify in a reliable fashion, and at the same time show less change across generations. As such, they may be particularly useful in identifying in adults disorders that manifest initially in childhood (e.g., specific language disorders), when the disorder itself is more difficult to quantify using standardized testing. Four criteria have been established for biological trait markers: (a) that the marker has been demonstrated to be consistently associated with the specific condition of interest; (b) that the marker is heritable; (c) that the marker is associated with an increased risk of the condition in relatives; and (d) that it is state independent, that is, it is present when the condition itself is no longer active. The strategy is a potentially powerful one, but to date no markers have been established for developmental learning disabilities.

Considerable evidence suggests that rapid temporal processing deficits are consistently associated with specific language impairments, fulfilling the first criterion for a biological risk marker. In addition, preliminary evidence is also now available to provide support for criteria 2 through 4. Studies are currently underway to determine whether rapid processing deficits may represent or be associated with a biological trait marker for developmental language impairments. Isolating a specific processing deficit as a biological trait marker would substantially improve precision in identifying family members as affected in future gene linkage studies.

The results of the phenotypic analysis of language-impaired children with or without an affected parent are particularly exciting in this context. These data suggest that the profile of temporal perceptual deficits, which has been reported consistently by Tallal and colleagues to characterize language-impaired children, occur significantly more often in language-impaired children with a positive family history than without and thus may have a familial or genetic basis.

NEUROPHYSIOLOGICAL STUDIES

The dominant role of the left hemisphere, particularly the cortical area surrounding the sylvian fissure (perisylvian region), in language performance is well established (Ojemann, 1991). Injury to the cortical tissue surrounding this area typically results in an acquired language disorder "aphasia," the inability to understand and/or produce speech. The extent to which damage in the perisylvian region interrupts the language system depends on several factors, one of which is the age of the individual patient (see Damasio & Damasio, 1989, for a review of this literature). Further support for this neural-behavioral relationship is the finding that in neurologically normal control subjects this area appears to be anatomically lateralized. For example, in a classic study, Geschwind and Levitski (1968) examined the brains of 100 neurologically normal controls. They found that in the region of the planum temporale, an anatomic landmark in the region of the sylvian fissure, 65% of the brains were significantly longer on the left, compared with the right side; 11% of the brains were longer on the right side than the left in this region; and 24% had relatively symmetrical measurements. Thus, this landmark has been considered to represent an anatomic marker reflecting the functional dominance of the cerebral hemispheres for language processing.

The hemispheric asymmetries in the area of the planum temporale, proposed to constitute the morphological correlate of the functional left cerebral dominance for language processes, has been used to base a theory on the development of learning disabilities. This model posited by Geschwind and Galaburda (1985a, 1985b, 1985c) proposes that deviations in the left greater than right (L > R) hemispheric asymmetry of the planum temporale are related to deviations in the development of handedness, the immune system, and certain types of language-based learning disabilities (developmental dyslexia and language impairments). More specifically, they propose that the development of the normal hemispheric lateralization of the planum temporale, occurs prenatally or very early postnatally, since approximately 56% of fetuses show a greater left than right hemisphere planum temporal at 31 weeks gestation (Chi, Doolings, & Gilles, 1977; Wada, Clarke, & Hamms, 1975). In addition, they hypothesize that normal hemispheric lateralization is partly dependent on the functional levels of gonadal hormones, particularly testosterone, during this time period. Support for this theory is based, in part, on the well-documented influence of prenatal hormones on morphological and functional lateralizations in animals (for a review, see Tallal & McEwen, 1991).

In the initial presentation of the Geschwind and Galaburda hypothesis, developmental learning disabilities (particularly language and reading impairments) were proposed to be due to an abnormal underdevelopment of the left hemisphere's planum temporale (Geschwind & Galaburda, 1985a, 1985b, 1985c). A more recent reformulation of this hypothesis proposes that a lack of neuronal cell death in the right hemisphere results in an abnormal hemispheric lateralization of the language areas (Galaburda, 1988). Based on the preceding data, the early anatomic and pathological studies of developmental disorders with some form of language impairment focused almost exclusively on detecting anomalies in this region. The hypothesis was that asymmetries in the left language areas provide a neurological substrate for the development of language and deviations in this pattern may underlie or provide a neurological marker for developmental learning disorders (Geschwind & Galaburda, 1985a, 1985b, 1985c).

In partial support of the Geschwind and Galaburda hypothesis, numerous lines of physiological and morphological evidence suggest that the brains of language-impaired individuals are not characterized by gross neural-anatomic abnormalities (i.e., frank lesions), but instead by subtle differences in volume and/or hemispheric lateralization gradients (Hynd & Semrud-Clikeman, 1989). However, these anatomic differences have been found in both cortical (Cohen, Campbell, & Yaghami, 1989; Jernigan et al., 1991; Plante, Swisher, & Vance, 1989) and subcortical thalamic and basal ganglia brain regions (Jernigan et al., 1991; Landau, Goldstein, & Kleffner, 1960).

One of the most significant modifications in recent theories regarding the neural representation of language has been the inclusion of subcortical nuclei in neural models of language. Data from electrical brain stimulation (Ojemann, 1991) and acquired language syndromes (Damasio, Damasio, Rizzo, Varney & Gersh, 1982; Robin & Schienberg, 1990) have suggested more than a secondary role for subcortical brain structures, particularly the basal ganglia and thalamic nuclei, in language processes (see Crosson, 1992, for a review of this literature). The extent to which these subcortical brain areas are abnormal may directly reflect both the outcome and nature of language impairments in children (Aram, Gillespie, & Yamashita, 1990; Ludlow et al., 1986).

Neuroanatomic Evidence

Landau et al. (1960) reported the first clinicopathological findings from a 10-year-old individual with a developmental language impairment. The subject had exhibited both expressive and receptive speech impairments. The neuropathology examination found a bilateral loss of tissue posterior to the insular region, through the sylvian fissure, and extending to the occipital lobe. A degeneration in the medial geniculate, probably resulting from the lesion of the insular and surrounding regions, was also noted. Because this subject had experienced many medical problems during the first year of life, the examiners could not determine the extent to which the brain pathology was developmental in origin or came about as a result of perinatal trauma.

A similar pattern of neuropathological findings, to those reported by Landau et al. (1960), was reported in a case study of a 7-year-old girl with a clinical diagnosis of developmental language impairment as well as an attention deficit disorder with hyperactivity (Cohen et al., 1989). The subject had both dysfunctional expressive and receptive language deficits but normal hearing ability. A clinical neurological examination performed prior to her death indicated no neurological abnormalities. Gross examination of the brain found it to be smaller in weight than normal brains for girls of this age group but with no apparent atrophy. The size of the planum temporale was reported to be symmetrical with a single dysplastic gyrus located on the inferior surface of the anterior portion of the sylvian fissure. Further, gross morphological examination and histological staining of tissue samples from adjacent subcortical structures and from the cerebellar region found no other abnormalities. The authors concluded that this pattern of findings was indicative of an abnormal migration of cells during midgestation in these brain regions and strikingly consistent with findings previously reported in dyslexic patients (Cohen et al., 1989).

Providing complementary evidence to the postmortem neuropathological studies, several studies using *in vivo* neuroimaging techniques have been conducted on language-impaired individuals. Both computed tomography (CT) and magnetic resonance imagery (MRI) are imaging techniques that provide structural information about the in vivo brain, with the MRI procedure providing better anatomic resolution. The findings from the CT/MRI research, while providing less structural resolution about the brain than the postmortem studies, can give information based on a substantially larger number of subjects with well-documented evaluations based on their current achievement status. Typically, these studies have reported findings almost exclusively in reference to the perisylvian areas of the brain. For example, Plante and colleagues (Plante, 1991; Plante et al., 1989) examined the left and right perisylvian area in eight language-impaired and control subjects using MRI. While clinical examination of the scans revealed no abnormalities, six of the language-impaired subjects had abnormal patterns of asymmetry in the perisylvian region. In each case, where an atypical perisylvian lateralization (L < R or L = R), was observed, this finding was due to a significantly larger right hemisphere in the language-impaired subjects compared with controls. Similar comparisons over the left perisylvian region failed to differentiate the groups.

In a more comprehensive evaluation to determine the neural correlates of developmental language impairments, Jernigan and colleagues (Jernigan, Hesselink, Sowell, & Tallal, 1991) compared MRI scans obtained from 20 language-impaired and 12 non-language-impaired children matched for age, race, IQ, and SES. Semiautomated measures of hemispheric volume and asymmetry in cortical, as well as adjoining caudate and diencephalic brain regions, were used to compare the groups. In the brain regions that correspond to the perisylvian area, a bilateral reduction in volume but no abnormal asymmetry was found for the language-impaired subjects compared with the controls. Further, a trend toward reduced volume in the adjoining diencephalic and caudate structures was also reported. Importantly, this study found that these differences in neuroanatomical lateralization do not appear to be restricted to perisylvian structures or a specific hemisphere. Measures of hemispheric asymmetry in the inferior frontal and superior posterior brain regions also differentiated language-impaired and control groups. Language-impaired subjects compared with controls, had a larger asymmetry (R > L) in the inferior frontal brain regions and less asymmetry in the superior posterior parietal region.

The findings reported by Jernigan et al. (1991) are not consistent with the previously reported findings of abnormal asymmetry in the posterior (perisylvian) regions of dyslexics (Hynd & Semrud-Clikeman, 1989) and language-impaired subjects (Plante, 1991). Direct comparisons between a large number of dyslexics and language-impaired patients will need to be made before any conclusions can be made regarding the specificity of these

morphological patterns to language-impaired or dyslexic patients. These findings are not consistent with the previous studies, which found reduced volumes bilaterally in this region. The increase in asymmetry in the frontal brain regions may also represent a unique neural marker for language-impaired individuals. Although differences over posterior brain regions have dominated the search for neural anomalies related to developmental language disorders, this may reflect that these were the primary regions (and in many cases the only regions) evaluated.

Developmental dyslexics have been found to show more anomalies in the cellular architectonics of the frontal brain regions, although asymmetry measures have not been systematically included. However, children with attention deficit disorder (ADD), a disorder found at higher than chance occurrence in learning-disabled populations, also differ from control subjects in the anterior frontal brain regions (Hynd, Semrud-Clikeman, Lorys, Novey, & Eliopulos, 1990). These findings suggest that subsequent studies examining the neuroanatomic indicants of developmental learning disabilities should include measurements within and across the hemispheres while including nonimpaired and clinical control populations (e.g., children with attention deficit/hyperactivity disorder (ADHD)) for comparison.

Two other studies also provide some evidence for reversed asymmetries in language impaired children. Hier, LeMay, Rosenberger, and Perlo (1978) included five language-delayed subjects in a population of dyslexics and measured parietal-occipital symmetry with CT. They found the usual increase in incidence of reversed asymmetry and symmetry in this population. However, four out of the five language-delayed subjects showed reversed asymmetry and this was significantly correlated with lower mean verbal IQ. If the language-delayed group is separated from the dyslexics, the dyslexics alone fail to show a significantly increased incidence of reverse asymmetry (Hynd et al., 1990). Rosenberger and Hier (1980) performed CT scans on 53 children with learning disorders, 22 of whom had delayed speech (onset after 36 months). Twelve of the 22 language-delay subjects showed a reverse asymmetry of the parieto-occipital region, a significantly larger proportion than was observed in the normal population (Galaburda, LeMay, Kemper, & Geschwind, 1978; Geschwind & Levitski, 1968; Wada et al., 1975). Further, the asymmetry in this region was correlated with the degree of discrepancy between verbal and performance IQ in these learning-impaired individuals. The authors concluded that the discordance between anatomical asymmetry and hemispheric specialization may provide a neural substrate for developmental language disorders (Rosenberger & Hier, 1980).

Preliminary evidence examining the perisylvian area in the family members of language-impaired individuals suggests that the lack of normal asymmetry (L > R) in these individuals may be heritable. Plante and colleagues examined the MRI scans from a set of dizygotic twins and from family members of four of the language-impaired boys discussed earlier. Both twins, seven of the eight parents and four of the five siblings examined in the families of the language-impaired children were found to show atypical perisylvian asymmetries, a larger than expected occurrence than has been found in the general population (approximately 35%) (Geschwind & Levitsky, 1968). The extent to which rapid temporal processing deficits and atypical perisylvian asymmetries, both which are more prevalent in individuals with specific language impairments and their family members, represent the same underlying deficit has yet to be systematically examined. The few postmortem analyses of the brains from language-impaired and reading-impaired individuals have demonstrated structurally abnormal lateral (Livingstone et al., 1991) and medial geniculate nuclei (Galaburda, 1992; Galaburda & Eidelberg, 1985; Landau et al., 1960). The autopsy cases with the thalamic cellular anomalies reported by Livingstone et al. (1991) included some, if not all, of the same cases that showed cortical anomalies in the perisylvian region as reported by Galaburda, Sherman, Rosen, & Geschwind (1985).

Neurophysiological Evidence of Rate-Processing Deficits

The functional brain activity of individuals with a developmental language impairment has been measured using scalp-recording electrodes to record the electrophysiological activity of the brain. Physiological investigations using event-related potentials (ERPs), while sacrificing spatial resolution to the regional cerebral blood flood (RCBF) and positron emission tomography (PET) methodologies, offer distinct advantages over these techniques and other electrophysiological methodologies. Electrophysiological measures record the functional aspects of the brain over milliseconds with spatial resolution on the order of centimeters. These functional measures of brain activity are noninvasive and have the potential to provide unique insight into assessing the relationship between the behavioral and neural deficits associated with developmental learning disorders. The physiological specificity of the neural anomalies that differentiate language-impaired and control groups appears, at least in part, to be related to their functional specificity for the processing of rapidly presented or transient visual (Livingstone et al., 1991) and auditory information (Tallal et al., 1991; Wood, Flowers, Buchsbaum, & Tallal, 1991).

For example, Neville and colleagues (Neville, Coffey, Holcomb, & Tallal, 1993) examined the electrophysiological recordings from 22 language impaired subjects and 12 controls during visual and auditory sensory processing tasks and also during a visually presented sentence processing task. Findings from this study suggest that multiple levels of neural processing differentiated the groups and that these differences were heterogeneous within the language-impaired group. Complementary to the MRI findings reported earlier, abnormal hemispheric specialization was observed in the language-impaired group with poor performance on tests of grammatical processing. Further, auditory ERP components considered to represent activity in the perisylvian area (particularly the superior temporal sulcus) were abnormal in a subset of children who had difficulties in rapid auditory processing (Neville et al., 1993). On a visual perceptual task, short latency ERP measures, considered to reflect activity in the visual system specialized in rapid visual processing, were reduced in the language-impaired subjects further supporting a pansensory or multisensory transient processing deficit (Neville et al., 1993).

Further support for the task specificity of these group differences has been reported by Stefanatos and colleagues (Stefanatos, Green, & Ratcliff, 1989). This study found that children with primary receptive language problems, as compared with primary expressive difficulties or normal control children, showed reduced auditory evoked responses specific to frequency modulated tones. Responses to pure tone stimuli failed to differentiate the groups. In the visual modality, Livingstone et al. (1991) obtained visually recorded evoked responses to pattern reversal checkerboard patterns at both high (40%) and low contrasts (4%). Group differences between adult language-based, learning-disabled individuals and control subjects were specific to the low contrast condition. A recent PET activation study suggests that these functional brain measures are compatible with the anatomic findings previously discussed, suggesting dysfunctional subcortical and perisylvian cortical brain regions in language-based, learning-impaired individuals (Hagman et al., 1992). In this study, a lack of statistical relationship between glucose uptake in the left hemisphere's cortical and diencephalic areas was found in a group of dyslexic adults during an auditory task that required the discrimination of syllables differing only in brief duration formant transitions (see Figure 8.11). In contrast, a strong positive relationship between these left hemisphere brain regions was present in a group of carefully matched control subjects, and for both groups in the right hemisphere.

Evidence from two laboratories suggests that electrophysiological recordings also may provide valuable insights into the early identification of children at risk for developing later language and learning problems. Molfese and colleagues have reported that auditory evoked potentials recorded in newborn infants in response to computer-synthesized speech sounds significantly discriminate between children who perform at different levels on standardized tests of language performance (Molfese & Molfese, 1985). Electrophysiological recordings from infants at risk for later developmental language and learning abilities showed evidence of a physiological impairment during the presentation of speech sounds, as indexed by ERP recordings. Further, these measures proved to be a substantially robust predictor of later language delay (Kurtzberg, Stapells, & Wallace, 1988). Thus, these measures serve as a practical means for assessing the discriminative abilities of the newborn and provide substantial input into the neural basis for these deficits.

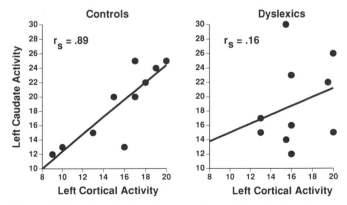

Figure 8.11   Correlation between the left hemisphere's caudate and cortical metabolism in control subjects and dyslexics.

IMPLICATIONS FOR NORMAL LANGUAGE DEVELOPMENT

Earlier in the chapter, the hypothesis was put forth that aspects of normal language development could be better understood by examining the etiology and/or consequences of an impaired language system. Further, we concur with Cicchetti's (1993) assertions that ". . . pathology calls for a life-span approach to understanding the developmental processes and that it is only by examining a variety of conditions and populations from infancy through adulthood that developmental continuities and discontinuities will be elucidated fully" (p. 473). It is our opinion that the following hypotheses about normal language and its development are supported from the literature on SLI.

The ability to process short duration, rapidly presented auditory information appears closely associated with or represents a perceptual prerequisite for the normal acquisition of language. Numerous lines of evidence now suggest that SLI can be characterized as a specific deficit in the rapid processing of information in the auditory, visual, and somatosensory systems (see Tallal et al., 1993, for review). The extent to which the processing of rapidly presented information is impaired can be used to predict a SLI classification and more specifically, to predict deficits in speech perception, speech production, language comprehension, and nonword reading ability. In addition, the strong quantitative link between nonverbal temporal processing performance and the perception/production deficits for classes of speech stimuli with rapid acoustic changes within 10s of milliseconds (e.g., stop-consonants) suggest that temporal processing deficits could represent a sufficient inclusionary criterion for classifying specific language impairment. Thus, the research data now overwhelmingly support the hypothesis that rapid temporal processing abilities (temporal integration, sequential memory) represent a perceptual precursor for the normal development of various aspects of speech and language development.

The development of phonological perception in infants shows that infants within the first months of life can discriminate the phonetic aspects of speech sounds (Eimas, Miller, & Jusczyk, 1987). Many of these discriminations rely on precisely those temporal perceptual contrasts that specific language-impaired children find so difficult. Thus, we can assume that the normal time frame for sufficient rapid temporal processing abilities for phonological development occurs in prenatal or early postnatal development. Further, because language-impaired children show delays in the onset and subsequent acquisition of language, which occurs within the first years of life, we can propose that the factors that result in an impaired temporal processing system occur within a similar time frame.

It is currently unclear whether temporal processing deficits cause, at least in part, some specific language impairments or whether these perceptual timing deficits are a manifestation of some other factor that underlies the disorder. We believe that such evidence will ultimately be obtained from looking longitudinally at the early perceptual development of infants at risk for developing specific language impairments.

Separate neural systems may exist for the processing of short duration information presented in rapid succession, within 10s of milliseconds, as compared with information presented within 100s of milliseconds. The specificity of the temporal processing deficits in SLI supports the contention that rapid temporal processing reflects a separate information-processing system(s) for the processing of short-duration rapidly changing information, as compared with information that changes more slowly. Further, this deficiency is not modality specific or even limited to sensory systems (as motor production has been shown to be similarly affected). This separate rapid processing system appears to be fundamental throughout the life span as evidenced by a performance dissociation in adults with acquired focal brain lesions of the left hemisphere, compared with the right hemisphere (Tallal & Newcombe, 1978), and normal adult subjects during a dichotic listening task (Schwartz & Tallal, 1980).

However, an important caveat must be presented. Separate information-processing systems does not exclude a high level of interactions between these systems. Quite the contrary, physiology frequently provides us with insights into complex interactions within and between systems. For example, while still quite controversial, behavioral and physiological evidence from both animal and human studies suggests a rather complex level of interaction between the proposed different rapid and sustained temporal processing systems in vision. Recent neuropathological studies of the brains of dyslexics provide evidence for separate physiological representation(s) for rapid and sustained processing systems in the auditory modality (medial geniculate nucleus [MGN] of the thalamus) as well. Further, these studies provide the first clear evidence of a neurophysiological basis for a rapid temporal processing deficit in SLI individuals by demonstrating selective anatomical differences in the large (magno) cells that support rapid, neural transmission. That these changes were seen in the left MGN, but not the right, is of particular relevance to issues of aberrant laterality in SLI individuals (Galaburda, Menard, & Rosen, 1994).

An interaction exists between the development of language and social-emotional behavior. Language appears to play a fundamental role in the acquisition and/or maintenance of social and emotional skills. Support for this hypothesis, at least in part, can be found in the higher than expected incidence of psychiatric problems in children with speech and language impairments. Similarly, social and emotional development appears to play a reciprocal role in the normal development of speech and language abilities, evidenced by the finding that difficulties in speech and language are found at higher levels than expected in psychiatric populations. Specifically, the increased comorbidity of language impairments and attention deficit/hyperactivity disorder suggests a common factor occurring prior to or early in the development of these two disorders.

Several studies have suggested that perceptual/motor neurodevelopmental immaturity may be the common antecedent that relates these two disorders (Beitchman, 1985; Tallal, Dukette & Curtiss, 1989). Infants who vary in their sustained attention, as measured by duration of fixation to two-dimensional stimuli, are responded to differently in the amount of time and level of interaction their caregivers provide (Sigman & Beckwith, 1980). Early mother-child attachment also has been shown to be related to subsequent language development (Gerston,

Coster, Schneider-Rosen, Carlson, & Cicchetti, 1986). Thus, neurodevelopmental immaturity, which can be measured in part by temporal processing ability, might be expected to have an impact on the ability of the child to form normal relationships with peers and with caregivers within the first year of life.

Language processes, at least in part, appear to be heritable. Growing evidence exists that language-based learning difficulties appear to run in families. Evidence from large single families, group studies of unrelated families regardless of family size, and twin concordance rates all provide converging evidence that SLI is heritable. In at least some families, the transmission rate appears to follow an autosomal dominant mode of transmission, affecting approximately 50% of the offspring from an affected parent. Evidence suggesting that SLI is equally transmitted in males and females has been particularly important for ruling out a sex-linked mode of genetic transmission in SLI. However, the exact nature of the language processes that appear to be transmitted or the genetic and environmental mechanism(s) of transmission are not well understood.

The results of the phenotypic analysis of language-impaired children with or without an affected parent are particularly exciting. These data suggest that the profile of temporal perceptual deficits, which has been consistently found to characterize language-impaired children, occur significantly more often in SLI children with a positive family history for a language-based learning disability than without, and thus may have a familial or genetic basis. These results underscore the sensitivity of auditory attention, temporal processing, and memory abilities in differentiating phenotypic patterns that may be most associated with familial transmission of language impairments. Further, these data support the hypothesis that what may be heritable in SLI is inadequate auditory temporal resolution. These findings not only suggest that inadequate temporal resolution may restrict or canalize language abilities across an individual's life span, but also potentially across generations. Future research examining individuals at risk for a language impairment, based on their family history for language disorders, but differing in their affected status (impaired/nonimpaired) should provide additional insight into the gene-environment interactions that occur in specific language impairments.

New evidence suggests that auditory temporal processing abilities may represent a biological risk marker for SLI. The four criteria that have been established for biological risk markers are (a) that the marker has been demonstrated to be consistently associated with the specific condition of interest; (b) that the marker is heritable; (c) that the marker is associated with an increased risk of the condition in relatives; and (d) that it is state independent (i.e., present when the condition itself may no longer be active) (Gershon & Goldin, 1986). Data are now available which demonstrate that temporal processing performance fulfill at least three of the preceding criteria. We are currently investigating the fourth. The strategy used for selecting biological risk markers is a potentially powerful one, but to date no markers have been established for developmental learning disabilities, at least partly because the difficulty of identifying the phenotype in adulthood.

Subcortical nuclei from the thalamus and basal ganglia, as well as the left frontal and perisylvian cortical structures, are important for the functional integrity of language processes. Numerous lines of physiological and morphological evidence suggest that RI and/or SLI individuals cannot be characterized by gross neural anatomic abnormalities (i.e., frank lesions), but instead by subtle differences in volume, cytoarchitecture, and/or hemispheric lateralization gradients in the frontal and perisylvian cortical (Galaburda, 1988; Hynd & Semrud-Clikeman, 1989; Jernigan et al., 1991) and subcortical (particularly thalamic and basal ganglia) brain regions (Galaburda & Eidelberg, 1982; Hagman et al., 1992; Jernigan et al., 1991; Livingstone et al., 1991; Landau et al., 1960).

The physiological specificity of these neural anomalies appears to be, at least in part, related to their functional specificity for the processing of rapidly presented or transient visual (Livingstone et al., 1991) and auditory (Tallal et al., 1990; Wood et al., 1991) information. In addition, rapid temporal processing performance appears to depend on the functional integrity of the left hemisphere with related subcortical structures. In addition, evidence from Hagman et al. (1992) suggests that the relational (correlational) activation of subcortical and cortical areas may be crucial for understanding the underlying neuropathology involved in SLI.

CONCLUSIONS

In looking toward future research studies, several major issues remain underdeveloped. Progress in both research and clinical practice for specifically language-impaired individuals has been hampered due to differences in the classification of this disorder. Agreement exists regarding the heterogeneity of the disorder, but not its characterization. With little conceptual agreement for the characterization of developmental learning disabilities, classification remains one of exclusion. The circularity of how best to characterize a developmental disorder without a complete understanding of either the etiologic or changing pattern of the disorder across the life span represents a difficult dilemma. In the present discussion, we suggest an initial inclusionary criterion of rapid auditory temporal processing deficits for identifying specifically language-impaired individuals. Auditory temporal processing deficits present a potentially new powerful diagnostic instrument for classifying some SLI subjects. Subsequent research should focus on identifying other inclusionary criteria, while delineating the extent to which rapid temporal processing deficits provide a useful characterization for all language-impaired children.

Language-impaired as well as reading-impaired children have also been found to be impaired, comparison with controls, on the rapid temporal processing of visual and tactile as well as auditory information (Tallal, 1981). Consequently, Tallal has hypothesized that a generalized pansensory deficit in processing sensory information, which converges in the nervous system in rapid succession, may underlie both the phonological as well as psychophysical deficits that characterize these children (Tallal et al., 1993). At the physiological level, a lack of normal anatomic hemispheric lateralization in the frontal and perisylvian brain region appears to be highly indicative of both developmental language and reading disorders. However, the sufficiency of perisylvian symmetry to underlie these disorders is questionable because approximately one-third of randomly selected normal individuals also show a lack of left > right asymmetry in the area of the planum temporale (Galaburda et al., 1978). A pansensory deficit may provide a better characterization of the extended network of neuroanatomic differences in cortical and subcortical areas, both in volume and/or hemispheric gradients observed in SLI. Studies in our laboratory are currently underway to better characterize the neurobiological substrates of rapid temporal processing deficits in developmental language and reading disorders.

There exists a growing need for a broader scientific approach to studying issues of developmental language processes. Although cross-sectional and static investigations have provided useful data, more multidisciplinary information (e.g., neuropsychological, linguistic, neurophysiological, psychiatric) from longitudinal studies of normal and abnormally developing individuals is required to more adequately address questions of language development. A broader, neurobiologically driven theoretical approach also is warranted for investigating the neural basis of SLI. Until recently, animal research has been excluded as a research tool for providing insights into understanding language development (see Dooling & Hulse, 1989, for a review). Although animals do not talk or read, they do process sensory information in rapid succession. Thus, specification of a basic, nonverbal temporal processing deficit as a potential precursor to developmental language impairments may now allow us to explore these same processes in animals. An animal model of SLI would provide a crucial research avenue for investigating aspects of etiology and remediation that are nonaccessible for direct experimentation in humans. Recent findings by Fitch, Brown, and Tallal (1993) support the development of an animal model of temporal processing performance in the rat and suggest that auditory temporal processing may be a phylogenetic precursor for language.

In summary, developmental language impairments present a serious problem for many children and adults. Our present understanding of the mechanisms underlying this disorder appears to have developed from two bodies of research involving neural and behavioral levels of analysis, both of which have evolved relatively independently. Integration of these two levels of analysis have led to a better understanding of the factors underlying normal and abnormal language development.

REFERENCES

Achenbach, T. M., & Edelbrock, C. S. (1983). *Manual for the Child Behavior Checklist and Revised Child Behavior Profile.* Burlington, VT: University of Vermont Press.

Affolter, F., Brubaker, R., & Bischofberger, W. (1974). Comparative studies between normal and language disturbed children based on performance profiles. *Acta Oto-laryngology, Supplement, 323,* 1–32.

American Psychiatric Association. (1980). *Diagnostic and Statistical Manual of Mental Disorders* (3rd ed.). Washington, DC: American Psychiatric Association.

Aram, D. M., Ekelman, B. L., & Nation, J. E. (1984, June). Preschoolers with language disorders: 10 years later. *Journal of Speech and Hearing Research, 27,* 232–244.

Aram, D. M., Gillespie, L. L., & Yamashita, T. S. (1990). Reading among children with left and right brain lesions. *Developmental Neuropsychology, 6*(4), 301–317.

Arnold, G. E. (1961). The genetic background of developmental language disorders. *Folia phoniat, 13,* 246–254.

Baker, L., & Cantwell, D. P. (1987a). Comparison of well, emotionally disordered, and behavioral disordered children with linguistic problems. *Journal of American Academy of Child and Adolescent Psychiatry, 26,* 193–196.

Baker, L., & Cantwell, D. P. (1987b). A prospective follow-up of children with speech/language disorders. *Journal of American Academy of Child and Adolescent Psychiatry, 26,* 546–553.

Baker, L., Cantwell, D. P., & Mattison, R. E. (1980). Behavior problems in children with pure speech disorders and children with combined speech and language disorder. *Journal of Abnormal Child Psychology, 8,* 245–256.

Bakker, P. (1987). Autonomous language of twins. *Acta Geneticae Medicae et Gemellologiae, 36,* 233–238.

Beitchman, J. H. (1985). Speech and language impairment and psychiatric risk: Toward a model of neurodevelopmental immaturity. *Psychiatric Clinics of North America, 8,* 721–735.

Beitchman, J. H., Hood, J., Rochon, J., & Peterson, M. (1989). Empirical classification of speech/language impairments in children: II. Behavioral characteristics. *Journal of the American Academy of Child and Adolescent Psychiatry, 28*(1), 118–123.

Beitchman, J. H., Hood, J., Rochon, J., Peterson, M., Mantini, T., & Majumdar, S. (1989). Empirical classification of speech/language impairments in children: I. Identification of speech/language categories. *Journal of the American Academy of Child and Adolescent Psychiatry, 28*(1), 112–117.

Beitchman, J. H., & Inglis, A. (1991). The continuum of linguistic dysfunction from pervasive developmental disorders to dyslexia. *Pervasive Developmental Disorders, 14*(1), 95–111.

Beitchman, J. H., Nair, R., & Patel, P. G. (1986). Prevalence of speech and language disorders in 5-year-old kindergarten children in the Ottawa-Carlton region. *Journal of Speech and Hearing Disorders, 51,* (98–110).

Benasich, A. A., Curtiss, S., & Tallal, P. (1993). Language, learning, and behavioral disturbances in childhood: A longitudinal perspective. *Journal of the American Academy of Child and Adolescent Psychology,* 1–19.

Benton, A. (1964). Developmental aphasia and brain damage. *Cortex, 1,* 40–52.

Bishop, D. V., & Edmundson, A. (1986). Is otitis media a major cause of specific developmental language disorder? *Disorder of Communication, 21,* 321–338.

Bishop, D. V. M., North, T., & Donlan, C. (1994). Genetic basis of specific language impairment: Evidence from a twin study. *Developmental Medicine and Child Neurology, 36,* 921–923.

Borges-Osorio, M. R., & Salzano, F. M. (1985). Language disabilities in three twin pairs and their relatives. *Acta Geneticae Medicae et Gemellologiae, 34,* 95–100.

Breitmeyer, B. G. (1989). A visually based deficit in specific reading disability. *Irish Journal of Psychology, 10*(4), 534–541.

Buchanan, M., & Wolf, J. (1986). A comprehensive study of learning disabled adults. *Journal of Learning Disabilities, 19,* 34–38.

Butler, N. R., Peckman, C., & Sheridan, M. (1973). Speech defects in children aged seven years: A national study. *British Medical Journal, 1,* 253–257.

Byrne, B., Willerman, L., & Ashmore, L. (1974). Severe and moderate language impairment: Evidence for distinctive etiologies. *Behavior Genetics, 4,* 331–345.

Cantwell, D. P., & Baker, L. (1977). Psychiatric disorder in children with speech and language retardation. *Archives of General Psychiatry, 34,* 589–591.

Cantwell, D. P., Baker, L., & Mattison, R. E. (1979). The prevalence of psychiatric disorder in children with speech and language disorder: An epidemiological study. *Journal of American Academy of Child Psychiatry, 18*(3), 450–461.

Cantwell, D. P., Baker, L., & Mattison, R. E. (1980). Factors associated with the development of psychiatric disorder in children with speech and language retardation. *Archives of General Psychiatry, 37,* 423–426.

Chess, S., & Rosenberg, M. (1974). Clinical differentiation among children with initial language complaints. *Journal of Autism and Childhood Schizophrenia, 4,* 99–109.

Chi, J. G., Dooling, E. C., & Gilles, F. H. (1977). Left-right asymmetries of the temporal speech area of the human fetus. *Archives of Neurology, 34,* 346–348.

Cicchetti, D. (1993). Review. Developmental Psychopathology: Reactions, reflections, projections. *Developmental Review, 13,* 471–502.

Cohen, M., Campbell, R., & Yaghami, F. (1989). Neuropathological abnormalities in developmental dysphasia. *Annals of Neurology, 25,* 567–570.

Courchesne, E., Lincoln, A. J., Yeung-Courchesne, R., Elmasian, R., & Grillon, C. (1989). Pathophysiologic findings in nonretarded autism and receptive developmental language disorders. *Journal of Autism and Developmental Disorders, 19,* 1–17.

Courchesne, E., Townsend, J., & Saitoh, O. (1994). *The brain in infantile autism: Posterior fossa structures are abnormal. Neurology, 44,* 214–223.

Crosson, B. (1992). *Subcortical functions in language and memory.* New York: Guilford.

Curtiss, S., & Tallal, P. (1991). On the nature of the impairment in language-impaired children. In J. Miller (Ed.), *Research on child language disorders: A decade of progress* (pp. 189–210). Austin, TX: Pro-Ed.

Damasio, A. R., & Damasio, H. (1989). *Lesion analysis in neuropsychology.* New York: Oxford University Press.

Damasio, A. R., Damasio, H., Rizzo, M., Varney, N., & Gersh, F. (1982). Aphasia with nonhemorrhagic lesions in the basal ganglia and internal capsule. *Archives of Neurology, 39,* 15–20.

DeRenzi, E., & Vignolo, L. A. (1962). The token test: A sensitive test to detect receptive disturbances in aphasia. *Brain, 85,* 665–678.

Dooling, R. J., & Hulse, S. H. (Ed.). (1989). *The Comparative Psychology of Audition: Perceiving Complex Sounds.* Hillsdale, NJ: Lawrence Erlbaum Associates.

Eimas, P. D., Miller, J. L., & Jurszyk, P. W. (1987). On infant speech perception and the acquisition of language. In S. Harnard (Ed.), *Categorical perception: The groundwork of cognition* (pp. 161–195). New York: Cambridge University Press

Esser, G., Schmidt, M. H., & Woerner, W. (1990). Epidemiology and course of psychiatric disorders in school-age children: Results of a longitudinal study. *Journal of Child Psychology and Psychiatry and Allied Disciplines, 31*(2), 243–263.

Fitch, R. H., Brown, C. P., O'Connor, K., & Tallal, P. (1993). Functional lateralization for auditory temporal processing in male and female rats. *Behavioral Neuroscience, 107*(5), 844–850.

Frumkin, B., & Rapin, I. (1980). Perception of vowels and consonant-vowels of varying duration in language impaired children. *Neuropsychologia, 18,* 443–454.

Fundulis, T., Kolvin, I., & Garside, R. F. (1979). *Speech retarded and deaf children. Their psychological development.* London: Academic Press.

Furth, H. G., & Pufall, P. B. (1966). Visual and auditory sequence learning in hearing impaired children. *Journal of Speech and Hearing Research, 9,* 441–449.

Galaburda, A. M. (1988). The pathogenesis of childhood dyslexia. In F. Plum (Ed.), *Language, communication and the brain* (pp. 127–137). New York: Raven Press.

Galaburda, A. M. (1992). Neurology of developmental dyslexia. *Current Opinion in Neurology and Neurosurgery, 5,* 71–76.

Galaburda, A. M., & Eidelberg, D. (1982). Symmetry and asymmetry in the human posterior thalamus. II. Thalamic lesions in a case of developmental dyslexia. *Archive of Neurology, 39,* 333–336.

Galaburda, A. M., LeMay, M., Kemper, T. L., & Geschwind, N. (1978). Right-left asymmetries of the brain. *Science, 199*(24), 852–856.

Galaburda, A. M., Menard, M. T., & Rosen, G. D., (1994). Evidence for aberrant auditory anatomy in developmental dyslexia. *Proceedings of the National Academy of Sciences USA, 91,* 8010–8013.

Galaburda, A. M., Sherman, G. F., Rosen, G. D., & Geschwind, A. F. (1985). Developmental dyslexia: Four consecutive patients with cortical anomalies. *Annals of Neurology, 18*(2), 222–233.

Gershon, E. S., & Goldin, L. R. (1986). Clinical methods in psychiatric genetics: I. Robustness of genetic marker investigative strategies. *Acta Psychiatra Scandinavica, 74,* 113–118.

Gerston, M., Coster, W., Schneider-Rosen, K., Carlson, V., & Cicchetti, D. (1986). The socio-emotional basis of communicative functioning: Quality of attachment, language development and early maltreatment. In M. E. Lamb, A. L. Brown, & B. Rogoff (Eds.), *Advances in developmental psychology* (Vol. 4, pp. 105–151).

Geschwind, N., & Galaburda, A. M. (1985a). Biological mechanisms, associations, and pathology: I. A hypothesis and a program for research. *Archives of Neurology, 42,* 428–459.

Geschwind, N., & Galaburda, A. M. (1985b). Biological mechanisms, associations, and pathology: II. A hypothesis and a program for research. *Archives of Neurology, 42,* 536–556.

Geschwind, N., & Galaburda, A. M. (1985c). Biological mechanisms, associations, and pathology: III. A hypothesis and a program for research. *Archives of Neurology, 42,* 634–654.

Geschwind, N., & Levitski, W. (1968). Human brain left-right asymmetries in temporal speech regions. *Science, 161,* 186–187.

Griffiths, C. P. S. (1969). A follow up study of children with disorders of speech. *British Journal of Disorders of Communication, 4,* 45–56.

Grinnell, S. W., Scott-Hartnet, D., & Glasier, J. L. (1983). Language disorders [Letter to the Editor]. *Journal of the American Academy of Child Psychiatry, 22,* 580–581.

Gualtieri, C. T., Koriath, U., Van Bourgondein, M., & Saleeby, N. (1983). Language disorders in children referred for psychiatric services. *Journal of American Child Psychiatry, 22,* 165–171.

Haggerty, R., & Stamm, J. S. (1978). Dichotic auditory fusion levels in children with learning disabilities, *Neuropsychologia, 16,* 349–360.

Hagman, J. O., Wood, F. B., Buchsbaum, M. S., Tallal, P., Flowers, L., & Katz, W. (1992). Cerebral brain metabolism in adult dyslexics assessed with positron emission tomography during performance of an auditory task. *Archives of Neurology, 49,* 734–739.

Hall, P. K., & Tomblin, J. B. (1978). A follow-up study of children with articulation and language disorders. *Journal of Speech and Hearing Disorders, 43,* 227–241.

Hay, D. A., O'Brien, P. J., Johnston, C. J., & Prior, M. (1984). The high incidence of reading disability in twin boys and its implications for genetic analyses. *Acta Geneticae Medicae et Gemellologia, 33,* 223–236.

Hier, D. B., LeMay, M., Rosenberger, P. B., & Perlo, V. P. (1978). Developmental dyslexia: Evidence for a subgroup with a reversal of cerebral asymmetry. *Archives of Neurology, 35,* 90–92.

Hier, E., & Rosenberger, P. (1980). Focal left temporal lobe lesions and delayed speech acquisition. *Developmental and Behavioral Pediatrics, 1,* 54–57.

Hirsch, I. J. (1959). Auditory perception of temporal order. *Journal of the Acoustical Society of America, 31*(6), 759–767.

Hurst, J. A., Baraitser, M., Auger, E., Graham, F., & Norell, S. (1990). An extended family with a dominantly inherited speech disorder. *Developmental Medicine and Child Neurology, 32,* 352–355.

Hynd, G., & Semrud-Clikeman, M. (1989). Dyslexia and brain morphology, *Psychological Bulletin, 106,* 447–482.

Hynd, G. W., Semrud-Clikeman, M., Lorys, A. R., Novey, E. S., & Eliopulos, D. (1990). Brain morphology in developmental dyslexia and attention deficit disorder/hyperactivity. *Archives of Neurology, 47,* 919–926.

Ingram, T. T. S. (1959). Specified developmental disorders of speech in childhood. *Brain, 82,* 450–454.

Jackson, D. D. (1960). A critique of the literature of the genetics of schizophrenia. In (pp. 37–87). New York: Basic Books.

Jenkins, S., Bax, M., & Hart, H. (1980). Behavior problems in preschool children. *Journal of Child Psychology and Psychiatry, 21,* 5–17.

Jernigan, T., Hesselink, J., Sowell, T., & Tallal, P. (1991). Cerebral structure on magnetic resonance imaging in language-learning impaired children. *Archives of Neurology, 48,* 539–545.

Johnston, R. B., Stark, R. E., Mellits, E. D., & Tallal, P. (1981). Neurological status of language-impaired and normal children. *Annals of Neurology, 10,* 159–163.

Koch, H. (1966). *Twins and twin relations.* Chicago: University of Chicago Press.

Kurtzberg, D., Stapells, D. R., & Wallace, I. F. (1988). Event-related potential assessment of auditory system integrity: Implications for language development. In P. Vietze & H. G. Vaughan (Eds.), *Early identification of infants with developmental disabilities* (pp. 160–180). Philadelphia: Grune & Stratton.

Landau, W. M., Goldstein, R., & Kleffner, F. R. (1960). Congenital aphasia. A clinicopathologic study. *Neurology, 10,* 915–921.

Leiter, G. (1952). *Arthur adaptation of the Leiter International Performance Scale.* Washington, DC: Psychological Services Center Press.

Lewis, B. A., Ekelman, B. L., & Aram, D. M. (1989). A familial study of severe phonological disorders. *Journal of Speech and Hearing Disorders, 32,* 713–724.

Lincoln, A., Dickstein, P., Courchesne, E., Elmasian, R., & Tallal, P. (1993). Auditory processing abilities in non-retarded adolescents and young adults with developmental language disorder and autism. *Brain and Language, 43,* 613–622.

Livingston, R. (1990). Psychiatric comorbidity with reading disability: A clinical study. In *Advances in learning and behavioral disabilities* (Vol. 6, pp. 143–155). Greenwich, CT: JAI Press.

Livingstone, M. S., Rosen, G. D., Drislane, F. W., & Galaburda, A. M. (1991). Physiological and anatomical evidence for a magnocellular deficit in developmental dyslexia. *Proceedings of the National Academy of Sciences USA, 88,* 7943–7947.

Livingstone, M. S., & Hubel, D. H. (1987). Psychophysical evidence for separate channels for the perception of form, color, movement, and depth. *Neuroscience, 11*(7), 3416–3468.

Livingstone, M. S., Rosen, G. D., Drislane, F. W., & Galaburda, A. M. (1991). Physiological and anatomical evidence for a magnocellular deficit in developmental dyslexia. *Proceedings of the National Academy of Sciences USA, 88,* 7943–7947.

Lovegrove, W. J., Garzia, R. P., & Nicholson, S. B. (1990). Experimental evidence for a transient system deficit in specific reading disability. *Journal of the American Optometric Association, 61*(2), 137–146.

Lovegrove, W. J., Heddle, M., & Slaghuis, W. (1980). Reading disability: Spatial frequency specific deficits in visual information store. *Neuropsychologia, 18,* 111–115.

Lowe, A., & Campbell, R. (1965). Temporal discrimination in aphasoid and normal children. *Journal of Speech and Hearing Research, 8,* 313–314.

Luchsinger, R. (1970). Inheritance of speech deficits. *Folia Phoniatrica, 22,* 216–230.

Ludlow, C. L., Rosenberg, J., Fair, C., Buck, D., Schesselman, S., & Salazar, A. (1986). Brain lesions associated with nonfluent aphasia fifteen years following penetrating head injury. *Brain, 109,* 55–80.

Martin, F., & Lovegrove, W. (1987). Flicker contrast sensitivity in normal and specifically disabled readers. *Perception, 16,* 215–221.

McCue, P. M., Shelly, C., & Goldstein, G. (1986). Intellectual, academic and neuropsychological performance levels in learning disabled adults. *Journal of Learning Disabilities, 19,* 34–38.

McReady, E. B. (1926). Defects in the zone of language (word-deafness and word-blindness) and their influence on education and behavior. *American Journal of Psychiatry, 6,* 267.

Mittler, P. (1969). *Psycholinguistic skills in four-year-old twins and singletons.* Unpublished doctoral dissertation, University of London.

Molfese, D. L., & Molfese, V. J. (1985). Electrophysiological indices of auditory discrimination in newborn infants: The bases for predicting later language development? *Infant Behavior and Development, 8,* 197–211.

Munsinger, H., & Douglass, A. (1976). The syntactic abilities of identical twins, fraternal twins and their siblings. *Child Development, 47,* 40–50.

Naylor, C. E., Felton, R. H., & Wood, F. B. (1989). Adult Outcome in developmental dyslexia. *Perspectives on dyslexia, 2,* 213–227.

Neils, J., & Aram, D. (1986). Family history of children with developmental language disorders. *Perceptual and Motor Skills, 63,* 655–658.

Neville, H. J., Coffey, S. A., Holcomb, P. J., & Tallal, P. (1993). The neurobiology of sensory and language processing in language-impaired children. *Journal of Cognitive Neuroscience, 5*(2), 235–253.

O'Donnall, J., Kurtz, J., & Ramanaiah, N. (1983). Neuropsychological test findings for normal, learning-disabled and brain-damaged young adults. *Journal of Consulting and Clinical Psychology, 51,* 726–729.

Ojemann, G. A. (1991). Cortical organization of language. *Neuroscience, 11*(8), 2281–2287.

Osborne, R. T., Gregor, A. J., & Miele, F. (1968). Heritability of factor V: Verbal comprehension. *Perceptual and Motor Skills, 26,* 191–202.

Plante, E. (1991). MRI findings in the parents and siblings of specifically language-impaired boys. *Brain and Language, 41,* 67–80.

Plante, E., Swisher, L., & Vance, R. (1989). Anatomical correlates of normals and impaired language in a set of dizygotic twins. *Brain and Language, 37,* 643–655.

Poppen, R., Stark, J., Eisenson, J., Forrest, T., & Wertheim, G. (1969). Visual sequencing performance of aphasic children. *Journal of Speech and Hearing Research, 12,* 288–300.

Propping, P., & Vogel, F. (1976). Twin studies in medical genetics. *Acta Geneticae Medicae et Gemellologiae, 25,* 249–258.

Reed, M. A. (1989). Speech perception and the discrimination of brief auditory cues in reading disabled children. *Journal of Experimental Child Psychology, 48,* 270–292.

Regan, D. (1989). *Human brain electrophysiology: Evoked potentials and evoked magnetic fields in science and medicine.* New York: Elsevier.

Rissman, M., Curtiss, S., & Tallal, P. (1990). School placement outcomes of young language impaired children. *Journal of Speech-Language Pathology and Audiology, 14*(2), 49–58.

Robin, D. A., & Schienberg, S. (1990). Subcortical lesions and aphasia. *Journal of Speech and Hearing Disorders, 55,* 90–100.

Robinson, R. J. (1987). Introduction and overview. In *Proceedings of the First International Symposium on Specific Speech and Language Disorders in Children* (pp. 123–145). London: AFASIC.

Rosenberger, P. B., & Hier, D. B. (1980). Cerebral asymmetry and verbal intellectual deficits. *Annals of Neurology, 8*(3), 300–304.

Rutter, M. (1978). Diagnosis and definition. In M. Rutter & E. Schopler (Eds.), *Autism: A reappraisal of concepts and treatments.* New York: Plenum.

Rutter, M., Bolton, P., Harrington, R., LeCouteur, A., MacDonald, H., & Simonoff, E. (1990). Genetic factors in child psychiatric disorders: I. A review of research strategies. *Journal of Child Psychology and Psychiatry, 31,* 3–37.

Samples, J. M., & Lane, V. W. (1985). Genetic possibilities in six siblings with specific language learning disorders. *ASHA, 27*(12), 27–32.

Schonhaut, S., & Satz, P. (1983). Prognosis for children with learning disabilities: A review of follow up studies. In M. Rutter (Eds.), *Developmental Neuropsychiatry* (pp. 542–563). New York: Guilford.

Schwartz, J., & Tallal, P. (1980). Rate of acoustic change may underlie hemispheric specialization for speech perception. *Science, 207,* 1380–1381.

Sigman, M., & Beckwith, L. (1980). Infant visual attentiveness in relation to caregiver-infant interaction and developmental outcome, *Infant Behavior and Development, 3,* 141–154.

Silva, P. A., McGee, R. O., & Williams, S. M. (1983). Developmental language delay from three to seven years of age and its significance for low intelligence and reading difficulties at age seven. *Developmental Medicine and Child Neurology, 25,* 783–793.

Stanovich, K. E. (1988). The right and wrong places to look for the cognitive locus of reading disability. *Annals of Dyslexia, 38,* 155–177.

Stark, J. (1967). A comparison of the performance of aphasic children on three sequencing tasks. *Journal of Communication Disorders, 1,* 31–34.

Stark, R., & Tallal, P. (1979). Analysis of stop consonant production errors in developmentally dysphasic children. *Journal of the Acoustical Society of America, 66,* 1703–1712.

Stark, R., & Tallal, P. (1988). *Language, Speech and Reading Disorders in Children: Neuropsychological Studies.* Boston: College-Hill Press.

Stark, R., Tallal, P., & Mellits, D. (1985). Expressive language and the perceptual and motor abilities in language-impaired children. *Human Communication Canada, 9(4),* 23–28.

Stefanatos, G. A., Green, G. G. R., & Ratcliff, G. G. (1989). Neurophysiological evidence of auditory channel anomalies in developmental dysphasia. *Archives of Neurology, 46,* 871–875.

Steffens, M. L., Eilers, R. E., Gross-Glenn, K., & Jallad, B. (1992). Speech perception in adult subjects with familial dyslexia. *Journal of Speech and Hearing Research, 35,* 192–200.

Stevenson, J., & Richman, N. (1976). The prevalence of language delay in a population of three-year-old children and its association with general retardation. *Developmental Medicine and Child Neurology, 18,* 431–441.

Tallal, P. (1980). Language and reading: Some perceptual prerequisites. *Bulletin of the Orton Society, 30,* 170–178.

Tallal, P. (1981). Temporal processing as related to hemispheric-specialization for speech perception in normal and language-impaired populations. *Behavioral and Brain Sciences, 4,* 77–78.

Tallal, P., Durkette, D., & Curtiss, S. (1989). Behavioral/emotional profiles of preschool language-impaired children. *Development and Psychopathology, 1,* 51–67.

Tallal, P., & McEwen, B. (Eds.). (1991). The effects of hormones on cognitive behavior [Special issue]. *Psychoneuroendocrinology, 16* (1–3).

Tallal, P., Miller, S. L., & Fitch, R. H. (1993). Neurobiological basis of speech: A case for the preeminence of temporal processing. In P. Tallal, A. M. Galaburda, R. R. Llinas, & C. V. Euler (Eds.), *Temporal information processing in the nervous system: Special reference to dyslexia and dysphasia.* Volume 682, Annals of the New York Academy of Sciences, June 14, 1993.

Tallal, P., & Newcombe, F. (1978). Impairment of auditory perception and language comprehension in dysphasia. *Brain and Language, 5,* 13–24.

Tallal, P., & Piercy, M. (1973a). Defects of non-verbal auditory perception in children with developmental aphasia. *Nature, 241,* 468–469.

Tallal, P., & Piercy, M. (1973b). Developmental aphasia: Impaired rate of non-verbal processing as a function of sensory modality. *Neuropsychologia, 11,* 389–398.

Tallal, P., & Piercy, M. (1974). Developmental aphasia: Rate of auditory processing and selective impairment of consonant perception. *Neuropsychologia, 12,* 83–93.

Tallal, P., Ross, R., & Curtiss, S. (1989a). Familial aggregation in specific language impairment. *Journal of Speech and Hearing Disorders, 54,* 167–173.

Tallal, P., Ross, R., & Curtiss, S. (1989b). Unexpected sex-ratios in families of language/learning-impaired children. *Neuropsychologia, 27*(7), 987–998.

Tallal, P., & Stark, R. E. (1981). Speech acoustic-cue discrimination abilities of normally developing and language-impaired children. *Journal of the Acoustical Society of America, 69,* 568–574.

Tallal, P., & Stark, R. E. (1982). Perceptual/motor profiles of reading impaired children with or without concomitant oral language deficits. *Annals of Dyslexia, 32,* 163–176.

Tallal, P., Stark, R., Kallman, C., & Mellits, D. (1981). A reexamination of some nonverbal perceptual abilities of language-impaired and normal children as a function of age and sensory modality. *Journal of Speech and Hearing Research, 24,* 351–357.

Tallal, P., Stark, R. E., & Mellits, D. (1985a). Identification of language-impaired children on the basis of rapid perception and production skills. *Brain and Language, 25,* 314–322.

Tallal, P., Stark, R. E., & Mellits, D. (1985b). The relationship between auditory temporal analysis and receptive language development: Evidence from studies of developmental language disorder. *Neuropsychologia, 23,* 527–534.

Tallal, P., Townsend, J., Curtiss, S., & Wulfeck, B. (1991). Phenotypic profiles of language impaired children based on genetic/family history. *Brain and Language, 41,* 81–95.

Tallal, P., Wood, F., Buchsbaum, M., Flowers, L., Brown, I., & Katz, W. (1990). Decoupling of PET measured left caudate and cortical metabolism in adult dyslexics. *Society for Neuroscience Abstracts, 16*(2), 1241.

Tomblin, J. B. (1989). Familial concentration of developmental language impairment. *Journal of Speech and Hearing Disorders, 54,* 287–295.

Tomblin, J. B. (1991). Examining the cause of specific language impairment. *Language, Speech, and Hearing Services in Schools, 22,* 69–74.

Tomblin, J. B., Freese, P. R., & Records, N. L. (1992). Diagnosing specific language impairment in adults for the purpose of pedigree analysis. *Journal of Speech and Hearing Research, 35,* 832–843.

Vellutino, F. R., Steger, B. M., Moyer, S. C., Harding, C. J., & Niles, J. A. (1977). Has the perceptual deficit led us astray? *Journal of Learning Disabilities, 10,* 375–385.

Wada, J. A., Clarke, R., & Hamms, A. (1975). Cerebral hemispheric asymmetry in humans. *Archives of Neurology, 32,* 239–246.

Weiner, P. (1974). A language delayed child at adolescence. *Journal of Speech and Hearing Disorders, 39,* 202–212.

Whitehurst, G. J., Arnold, D. S., Smith, M., Fischel, J. E., Lonigan, C. J., & Valdez-Menchana, M. C. (1991). Family history in developmental expressive language delay. *Journal of Speech and Hearing Research, 34,* 1150–1157.

Williams, M. C., & LeCluyse, K. (1990). Perceptual consequences of a temporal processing deficit in reading disabled children. *Journal of the American Optometric Association, 61*(2), 111–121.

Wood, F. B., Flowers, L., Buchsbaum, M., & Tallal, P. (1991). Investigation of abnormal left temporal functioning in dyslexia through rCBF, auditory evoked potentials, and positron emission tomography. *Reading and Writing: An Interdisciplinary Journal, 4,* 81–95.

CHAPTER 9

Past, Present, and Future Issues in the Developmental Approach to Mental Retardation and Developmental Disabilities

ROBERT M. HODAPP and EDWARD ZIGLER

Like many topics in developmental psychopathology, the developmental approach to mentally retarded and other disabled populations is both old and new. It is old, or at least established, in that for over 50 years workers have attempted to apply the theories, findings, and approaches of nonretarded development to conceptualize and intervene with children with disabilities. Yet at the same time, a formal field of "the developmental approach to mental retardation" is relatively new, dating only to the late 1960s and early 1970s. Even today, many aspects of development in children with retardaton and other disabilities remain almost totally unknown. Thus, although researchers have examined children with disabilities through the lens of normal development for over 50 years, we are only now approaching what might be considered an elaborated developmental approach to mental retardation and developmental disabilities.

Given the old and new status of the developmental approach, this chapter will address past, present, and future concerns. It begins with a brief overview tracing attempts to apply developmental theories and findings to children with retardation from the 1930s until the present day. The bulk of the chapter is then devoted to present-day issues: sequences; cross-domain relations; rates of development; transitions in development; mother-child interactions; family systems; and personality-motivational development. The chapter then ends with discussions of three remaining issues, how best to perform developmentally based research in mental retardation, what role etiology should play in mental retardation research, and how data from mentally retarded and other disabled populations can best be employed to inform us about nonimpaired populations. This last issue, in particular, brings us full circle, supplementing the examination of disabled populations through the lens of normal development with a perspective that uses developmental findings from retarded and otherwise disabled populations to provide us with a fuller, more complete view of normal development (Cicchetti & Cohen, Chapter 1, Volume 1).

HISTORY OF EXAMINING RETARDED POPULATIONS THROUGH THE LENS OF NORMAL DEVELOPMENT

As the longest- and best-studied of all disabled groups, children with mental retardation have historically served as a group to which the latest developmental and educational ideas have been applied. Itard's experiment with Victor, the "wild boy of Aveyron" (Lane, 1976), was an attempt to apply the late 18th century's new educational approaches to a child totally uninfluenced by modern society. In a similar way, Eduourd Seguin, the founder of modern services in mental retardation, was simply applying to children with retardation the latest and most scientific educational theories. Although we today might question some aspects of Seguin's program (e.g., its emphasis on sensory training; see Scheerenberger, 1983, pp. 78–80), these techniques were thought very beneficial during the mid to late 1800s.

But it was not until the emergence of developmental psychology in the 20th century that more developmentally based approaches to mental retardation were explored. Three strands can be identified in these early developmental approaches: those of Heinz Werner, of Jean Piaget and Barbel Inhelder, and of the Soviet psychologists Lev Vygotsky and Alexander Luria. Although each of these schools developed independently, they all attempted to apply developmental theories and findings to retarded populations. The influence of each school can be seen in current work on the developmental approach to mental retardation.

Early Applications of Developmental Perspectives to Retarded Populations

Heinz Werner and Work at the Wayne County Training School

As one of the great figures in developmental psychology, Heinz Werner is most closely associated with work at Clark University on comparative developmental approaches (e.g., Werner, 1948, 1957) and symbol formation (Werner & Kaplan, 1963). In addition to this more famous work, however, Werner served as senior research psychologist at the Wayne County (Michigan) Training School from 1937 to 1943. During this time, he published approximately 30 papers on functioning in children with mental retardation, a particularly sizable body of work given the period (Witkin, 1964).

Several themes characteristic of Werner's work in other areas can also be seen in his mental retardation studies. The first, most fully discussed in his article "Process and Achievement" (Werner, 1937), was the need to go beyond the behavior of the child (what he called "achievement") to examine underlying functional processes. In contrast to those relying exclusively on IQ tests, Werner (1941) noted: "In works on testing and remedial teaching the term 'diagnosis' is frequently applied to the analysis at the superficial level of achievement alone. . . . This fallacy consists in mistaking the effect of impaired functions appearing at the achievement level for the deficiency itself" (p. 234).

Related to getting beyond the child's achievement was the need to examine the child developmentally. In all his work, including research on children with retardation, Werner advocated the orthogenetic principle, the idea that development "proceeds from a state of relative globality and lack of differentiation to a state of increasing differentiation, articulation, and hierarchic integration" (Werner, 1957, p. 126). As individuals less developed in cognition, children with retardation were therefore examined to determine if indeed they displayed developmentally earlier patterns of thought. For example, in examining functioning on picture completion tasks, Werner and Strauss (1939) noted that nonretarded children are sometimes hindered by their sense of the completed picture, whereas children with retardation "merely put the parts together quite mechanically, taking care only that the edges of the different pieces agreed perfectly with each other. By this 'chain-like' procedure, characteristic of a genetically lower level, they performed better than most children of the same age but of far superior intellectual ability" (p. 39).

A third focus of Werner and his coworkers was attention to the reasons for the child's developmental delays. Like other workers of the time (e.g., Lewis, 1933; Strauss & Lehtinen, 1947), Werner and Alfred Strauss (his main collaborator in mental retardation) differentiated between those children who showed endogenous delay, or delay unconnected to identifiable brain pathology, and those of exogenous etiology, or deficits caused by one or another type of specific brain injury. Based on earlier findings from Goldstein (1939) and others working with soldiers who had received head injuries in World War I, Werner and Strauss (1939) predicted that performance in the two types of child might differ. In a series of studies, Werner and Strauss found that endogenous children performed more like nonretarded children of younger ages, whereas exogenous children were more likely to show the uncoordinated and perseverative behavioral patterns of brain-damaged adults.

Werner and his colleagues thus offered at least the beginnings of a developmental approach to mental retardation. They can be criticized in that their more global sense of development has been difficult to operationalize and their research, although acceptable

for its time, today seems inadequate in its statistical procedures and descriptions of subjects (e.g., exact diagnosis, living status). Nevertheless, Werner foreshadowed much developmental thought, including the emphasis on the processes underlying behavior (e.g., Overton & Reese, 1973) and the developmental analysis of functioning in children with at least one type of retardation—those demonstrating no clear organic pathology. Even Werner and Strauss's distinction between endogenous and exogenous mental retardation, and their examination of only the endogenous, or familial, child within the developmental perspective, is very similar to later work. Although unspecified in many ways, Werner and his colleagues performed much important work applying developmental principles to retarded populations.

Piaget, Inhelder, and the Genevan Approach

In contrast to Werner, Jean Piaget presented a clear sequence of behaviors through which children proceed. This sequence encompassed both the four larger stages of cognitive development and the numerous smaller substages within each stage. In addition, over a long and productive career, Piaget enumerated developments in many areas of children's thought, including six domains of sensorimotor functioning; conservation of number, weight, and volume; class inclusion; transitivity; probability; concepts of time and space; and relative and hypothetical thinking. Sequences in other areas, such as morality, were also enumerated by Piaget.

Like Werner, Piaget's focus was not on behaviors per se, but on the processes that underlie such behavior. As an assistant to Dr. Theophile Simon (who, with Binet, had earlier constructed the first IQ tests), Piaget became disenchanted with the rigid ways in which IQ test questions were asked and the focus in IQ tests on behavior as opposed to the child's underlying processes of reasoning (Ginsburg & Opper, 1979). To go beyond behavior, Piaget developed what has come to be called his "méthod clinique," the practice of asking a question then following up with clinical probes to elicit more elaborate understandings of the child's reasoning. This method was felt to be an improvement on the simple correct or incorrect answers obtainable from IQ tests (see Cronbach, 1957, 1975, for discussions of the relationship between experimental psychology—including Piagetian research—and individual differences work).

Piaget's methods had important implications for the study of functioning in persons with mental retardation. First, Piaget's techniques could be used with children who were untestable by standard psychometric instruments. Woodward (1961) found, for example, that although many children with retardation perform below basal levels on standardized IQ tests, some nonetheless possess conservation of number and other concrete operational abilities that allow for the introduction of simple mathematical concepts. This sense of "readiness," common in intervention programs today, is an outgrowth of examining the child's conceptual development within a particular area of functioning.

A second contribution involves the sequential nature of Piagetian developmental theory. In contrast to Werner and other developmentalists of the day, Piaget offered straightforward developmental sequences that could be applied in research and intervention. In addition, the claim that such sequences were logically sequential, that they built one on another in successively more complex, hierarchically organized structures, made the traversing of Piagetian cognitive stages likely for retarded as well as for nonretarded children (Piaget & Inhelder, 1947).

Given these advantages, Piaget's sequences of development were gradually examined in children with retardation as these sequences became known to developmental psychologists throughout the 1940s, 1950s, and 1960s. Abel (1941) studied moral judgment in subjects with retardation; Lovell, Healey, and Rowland (1962) studied Piagetian classification, class inclusion, and geometric problems; and Woodward (1962) examined children with severe and profound levels of mental retardation on several sensorimotor tasks (see Woodward, 1963, 1979, for reviews). Although Weisz, Yeates, and Zigler (1982) note the lack of careful statistical analyses in much of this research, these studies nevertheless strongly suggested that children with retardation proceed in the same order of development as do nonretarded children.

A third contribution of Piaget and his colleagues was an appreciation for the nature of thinking processes in children with retardation. In studies of the conservation of mass, weight, and volume, Piaget's colleague Barbel Inhelder (1943/1968) found that, while children and adults with retardation generally progressed through stages and substages in the hypothesized order, these individuals often showed patterns of reasoning that were different from younger nonretarded children. In particular, Inhelder identified oscillations between two stages at a single point in time, regressions in thought over a single session, leakages of lower-level thought into higher-level reasoning (which Inhelder termed "viscosity"), and fixations of reasoning at lower-level stages without an appreciation for the inherent contradictions that might lead the child to develop higher-level thought. These phenomena, some of which have recently been examined in specific etiological groups, show the Piagetian interest in the thinking processes undertaken by children with retardation.

Although Piaget and Inhelder laid the groundwork for a more elaborated developmental approach, certain aspects were lacking in work of the Genevan school. Specifically, scant attention was paid to organicity, and most of the early Piagetian studies examine together subjects with different types of mental retardation (Inhelder's use of retarded groups including both organically and familial retarded children may account for the greater amounts of oscillation and regression observed; Weisz et al., 1982). This inattention to etiology is understandable, given the Piagetian view of logically ordered developmental sequences and the general finding that children with organic retardation proceed as do nonretarded (and familial retarded) children through Piagetian stages in the hypothesized invariant order (e.g., Woodward, 1959, 1962, for early similar sequence findings in children with organic retardation). Similarly, although Piaget (1972) and Inhelder (1943/1968) mentioned horizontal décalage, discussions of cross-domain relationships are generally absent from early Piagetian-based studies in mental retardation.

Still, Piaget and Inhelder offered significant early contributions toward a developmental approach to mental retardation. They presented specific developmental sequences in many areas, and these sequences have a logical base that leads to their possible use with children with retardation. Early (and more recent) work showed that these sequences do characterize development

in children with mental retardation. Like Werner and his colleagues, Piaget and Inhelder also focused on the underlying processes of behavior, not behavior in and of itself. Inhelder's work, in particular, identified differences in underlying processes between children with and without retardation. Many of these ideas are evident in current developmental approaches in the mental retardation field.

Luria, Vygotsky, and the Soviet Study of "Defectology"

In line with the long-standing interest in "defectology" in the Soviet Union, Alexander Luria addressed the issue of retarded children's functioning over a career lasting more than 50 years. His main contribution in mental retardation was to characterize the language of children with mental retardation as less efficient at controlling behavior than the verbalizations of nonretarded individuals. Partly because of these views, Luria has generally been considered to be among the "defect theorists" in mental retardation, or those theorists holding that a particular psychological and/or physiological deficit is the cause of all retardation.

As shown by Cascione (1982), however, Luria's views arise from the Soviet interest in the development of verbal mediation. Children develop in their abilities to use language to control behavior, and the inability of children with mental retardation to use language in this way may be one of their cognitive problems. It remains unknown, however, whether the linguistic deficits of children with retardation are more pronounced than their general levels of retardation; this issue was first debated mainly in relation to those persons who show no clear organic etiology for their mental retardation (see Zigler & Balla, 1971; and Milgram, 1973 for two sides of this debate).

Although Luria held strong views about verbal mediation, he and other Soviet psychologists must be evaluated within the broader developmental framework provided by their teacher, Lev Vygotsky (1962, 1978). As the main proponent of a Marxist, dialectical vision of developmental psychology during the early years of the Soviet Union (Wertsch & Youniss, 1985), Vygotsky inspired a long line of Soviet psychologists over the past 60 years. Although he died in 1934, his works have only been organized and translated in the past two decades, with the result that there has been a revival—or late arrival—of Vygotskian thought into Western developmental psychology (e.g., Griffin & Cole, 1984; Wertsch, 1985; Wertsch & Rogoff, 1984). This recent period has also seen the first preliminary attempts to apply some of Vygotsky's ideas to retarded populations (e.g., Brown & Ferrara, 1985; Budoff, 1974; Campione, Brown, & Ferrara, 1982).

The main feature of Vygotsky's theory is that development consists of a progression from external to internal, that behaviors first shown in interactions with responsive adults gradually become internalized into the child's own cognitive schemes. Development to Vygotsky can only occur as a result of the interaction between the child and his or her surrounding culture, with mothers, fathers, and other family members serving as the representatives of that culture. Behaviors first developed within interactions with adults can then gradually become a part of the child's own internal schemes.

Because of its role in the enculturation of the child and in the development of higher-level thought, language has received much attention from Soviet psychologists. From Pavlov on, language has been considered as the "second signal system" that mediates higher-level thought (the first signal system involves perceptual-motor systems underlying "primitive" thought). To Vygotsky (1962), language first appears within social interactions, then gradually influences the child's behavior (as when children direct themselves by talking out loud while performing a difficult task). At a later point, just as adults mediate the child's behavior within adult-child interactions, internalized language (or, to Vygotsky, language that has "gone underground") serves to mediate thought for the developing child. Luria (1961) later proposed a four-stage process for this movement from social to mediational language.

This progression from external to internal regulation has specific consequences for the child. Vygotsky (1978) talked of how the adult helps the child accomplish tasks slightly ahead of current functioning (see Bruner, 1985; Wertsch, 1979, for examples). As a result, a discrepancy exists between behaviors that children can currently perform on their own (the *actual* level of development) and those that the child can perform only with adult help (the level of *potential* development). Vygotsky called this discrepancy between actual and potential levels the "zone of proximal development." The zone of proximal development is a prospective view of development, in that it emphasizes "functions which could be termed the 'buds' or 'flowers' of development rather than the 'fruits' of development" (p. 86).

Besides identifying a zone of proximal development that results from interactions with sensitive adults, Vygotsky also distinguished between two aspects of development, the natural line and the cultural line (Wertsch, 1985). The natural line consists of those developments occurring independently of social interaction. Wertsch (1985) suggests that Piagetian sensorimotor development might be one example of natural development. The cultural line involves all those functions that involve interaction with more advanced members of the culture. Although Vygotsky has been criticized for considering these two lines as completely separate during the early years (and for not realizing the degree to which even the youngest of infants live in a "social world"; van der Meer & van Ijzendoorn, 1985), the distinction remains useful for developmental analyses.

Although developmentally oriented workers continue to debate Vygotsky's theories, several aspects can be applied to retarded populations. The first is the zone of proximal development. Like both Werner and Piaget, Vygotsky was disenchanted with IQ tests. Vygotsky's concern, however, was with the testing of transitional as opposed to "achieved" development. He noted that two children at similar levels of development (e.g., mental age, or MA) might be able to perform at vastly different levels when attempting higher-level problems with adult help. The child with the greater "zone"—the one able to perform at very high levels when given adult help—would seem to have a better developmental prognosis. This child would appear to be struggling more with higher-level concepts than the child who is unable to solve difficult problems even with adult help. The zone of proximal development therefore complements ideas that concerned both Werner and Piaget: readiness and diagnosing the child's level of functioning.

A second outgrowth of Vygotsky's perspective is the focus on surrounding adults. For the most part, the concerns of both Werner and Piaget were with the child's development in interaction with a world of objects. It may be that Piaget simply chose to study nonsocial problems (Youniss, 1978), or that children interacting on their own with the environment may perform behaviors analogous to those performed by adults in adult-child interactions (Hodapp & Goldfield, 1985). Furthermore, because of the dialectical character of both theories, Piaget's theoretical differences with Vygotsky may actually be more apparent than real (Bidell, 1988). Nevertheless, neither Piaget nor Werner gave much weight to the child's interactions with others. In contrast, interaction with surrounding adults holds a central place in Vygotskian theory. Indeed, Vygotsky considered development within an interpersonal world the hallmark of human development (especially of the higher functions), and to Vygotsky, the job of the developmental psychologist was to examine the nature of the child's development in collaboration with others.

Through his own work and the work of Luria and other of his students, Lev Vygotsky opened up several unexplored avenues for a developmental approach to mental retardation. Unlike Piaget, he did not advance a particular developmental sequence in any area, and Luria's (1961) subsequent four-stage sequence of verbal mediation has rarely served as a developmental sequence as have Piagetian stages and substages. Similarly, Vygotsky did not concern himself with many issues addressed by modern developmentalists (e.g., sequences in the many subdomains of cognition or social development; cross-domain relations).

Still, Vygotsky's theories have begun to influence workers both within developmental psychology and, increasingly, within the developmental approach to mental retardation. His zone of proximal development has begun to be used for both testing and intervention, and his emphasis on surrounding adults has served as one of several influences on the "other regulation" movement in developmental psychology (e.g., Wertsch & Lee, 1984; Youniss, 1984) and the developmental approach to mental retardation. Although not a complete developmental approach, Vygotsky provides many important, and as yet relatively unexplored, ideas for developmentalists working with individuals with retardation.

Zigler's Developmental Approach to Mental Retardation

Although the ideas of Werner, Piaget, and Vygotsky formed the background for developmental analyses with retarded populations, none established a "developmental approach to mental retardation" per se. The formal establishment of this discipline can best be traced to work by Edward Zigler (1967, 1969) and his colleagues during the late 1960s and 1970s.

In many ways, Zigler's developmental approach to mental retardation combines and reinterprets the previously discussed developmental strands. Joined to these strands are personality and motivational factors affecting functioning in individuals with retardation (e.g., Zigler, 1971) and etiological considerations following from Strauss, Penrose, and others (for a review, see Burack, 1990).

As originally proposed by Zigler, the developmental approach to mental retardation involved three ideas: that children with mental retardation traverse the same invariant stages of development (e.g., Piagetian stages) as do nonretarded children; that children with retardation show the same structure to their intellectual abilities as do nonretarded children; and that any differences shown between children with retardation and MA-matched nonretarded children are caused by personality-motivational factors that appear as a consequence of children with retardation's peculiar life histories (Zigler & Balla, 1982; Zigler & Hodapp, 1986). Let us briefly address each in turn:

1. *Similar Sequence Hypothesis.* The similar sequence hypothesis asserts that children with retardation, like nonretarded children, traverse hypothesized sequences of development in correct order. Thus, children with retardation will develop from sensorimotor to preoperational to concrete operational thought (they generally will not reach formal operations), just as they will traverse in order the many substages within the larger stages. These stages may be Piagetian stages or other, presumably universal, stages of development; the important point is that, just as nonretarded children traverse hypothesized stages in a single, invariant order, so too will children with retardation develop through the same stages of development, in the same order.

2. *Similar Structure Hypothesis.* The similar structure hypothesis holds that children with retardation will demonstrate the same behaviors and underlying processes as will nonretarded children at the same level of functioning. Specifically, if children with retardation are matched to nonretarded children on overall levels of mental functioning (usually considered to be MA), then children with retardation should show equivalent performance to nonretarded children on other cognitive tasks. As such, there is no particular area of deficit in the functioning of children with mental retardation, and no single psychological or physiological deficit causing the child's retardation.

3. *Similar Reactions Hypothesis.* The similar reactions hypothesis holds that children with retardation will react as do nonretarded children to life experiences. When compared with nonretarded children, however, the life histories of children with retardation are different: because of their lower cognitive abilities, children with retardation suffer from more failure experiences and are more likely to experience institutionalization or other experiences that nonretarded children rarely undergo. Consequently, children with retardation differ from nonretarded children along a series of personality-motivational variables, and these differences can sometimes influence their performance on cognitive tasks.

These three tenets comprised the essence of Zigler's original developmental approach. In line with Strauss and others, Zigler (1969) originally proposed that only those children showing no clear organic cause for their mental retardation, the child with so-called familial retardation, definitely can be considered within this developmental perspective. His rationale was that children with familial retardation constitute the lower end of the Gaussian distribution of intelligence and are not different in kind from children of higher levels of intelligence. Children with familial retardation therefore should develop in ways similar to nonretarded children with higher IQs. Any differences between familial retarded and nonretarded children should be quantitative, not qualitative: children with familial retardation may develop more slowly and reach a lower asymptote in their development, but the processes of development (sequences, structures, reactions to external environment) should be identical to developmental processes shown by nonretarded children.

Zigler (1969) did not at first apply his developmental approach to the group of children who do show identifiable organic pathology. He noted: "If the etiology of the phenotypic intelligence (as measured by an IQ) of two groups differs, it is far from logical to assert that the course of development is the same, or that even similar contents in their behaviors are mediated by exactly the same cognitive process" (Zigler, 1969, p. 533). In this application to only children with familial retardation, Zigler followed the lead of Werner and Strauss, who considered children with familial retardation as delayed in development, but children with organic (exogenous) retardation as suffering from brain damage.

As the first formal developmental approach to mental retardation, Zigler's developmental approach has given rise to many studies of the development of persons with retardation. In particular, much work has now been performed to determine if the sequences of development—as proposed by Kohlberg (1969), Piaget (1953, 1955) and others—are indeed followed by these children (e.g., Weisz & Zigler, 1979). Similarly, whether children with retardation, particularly those with familial retardation, show similar structures of intelligence has been widely examined along domains ranging from linguistic (Achenbach, 1970, 1971), to Piagetian (Weisz & Yeates, 1981), to information processing (Weiss, Weisz, & Bromfield, 1986) tasks.

In a similar way, the exploration of personality-motivational functioning continues to be among "the richest legacies" (Weisz, 1982) of the developmental approach. In many ways, Zigler's developmental formulations arose as a response to Lewin's (1936) idea that persons with retardation were more "rigid" in their intelligence than are similar level nonretarded children (Zigler, 1984). Instead, however, as shown in a number of studies (see Zigler, 1971, for a review), children with retardation possess a set of personality and motivational characteristics that make them appear more rigid on some experimental tasks. These personality-motivational characteristics arise due to the greater number of failures that children with retardation have experienced compared with nonretarded children.

In focusing on characteristics such as positive and negative reaction tendencies, outerdirectedness, expectancy of success, and self-concept in persons with retardation (to be discussed more fully later), Zigler (1971) thus attempted to go beyond cognition in examining functioning in children with mental retardation. In contrast to other developmentally oriented workers of the time, he noted that the child with mental retardation should be considered (and studied as) a "whole child" (Zigler, 1971), not simply as a thinking or language-using organism. This perspective, like the formal introduction of sequences, stages, and attention to etiology, continues to play an important role in developmental work with retarded populations.

Recent Expansions of the Developmental Approach to Mental Retardation

When originally proposed in the late 1960s, Zigler's developmental approach was an accurate reflection of the state of developmental psychology and of those developmental principles that could be applied to retarded populations. Since that time, however, several expansions have occurred both within mental retardation and within the field of developmental psychology itself. Because of these additions, the developmental approach to mental retardation has itself expanded.

The first expansion of the developmental approach is to children with organic retardation. This expansion reflects changes in our understandings about mental retardation and about how development occurs in children with different types of retardation. Its genesis dates from early (cf. Woodward, 1963) and later (cf. Weisz & Zigler, 1979) studies showing that children with all types of retardation, regardless of etiology, proceed in order through Piagetian and other developmental sequences. Partly as a result of such findings, workers from the early 1960s on (e.g., Woodward, 1963) attempted to apply developmental approaches to children with different types of organic retardation. In the early 1980s, Cicchetti and Pogge-Hesse (1982) formally called for a more "liberal" developmental approach to mental retardation that would go beyond Zigler's "conservative" developmental approach by including within the developmental perspective children with both familial and organic mental retardation. Cicchetti and Pogge-Hesse (1982) felt that all children with retardation should be conceptualized within the framework of nonretarded development.

Related to the more liberal application of the developmental approach has been the move to distinguish among different etiological groups. In his original developmental approach, Zigler (1967, 1969) called for a "two-group approach" in mental retardation, or a separation of those persons showing no clear organic etiology (the familial retarded group) from those demonstrating one of several hundred (Grossman, 1983) types of organic retardation. In more recent years, Burack, Hodapp, and Zigler (1988) have advocated a further differentiation of organic retardation into its many different etiological groups. Burack et al. noted, for example, that children with Down syndrome, cerebral palsy, and fragile X syndrome differ in their trajectories of intellectual development over time, and intellectual strengths and weaknesses may also vary from one etiological group to another (Dykens, Hodapp, & Leckman, 1987; Hodapp, Leckman et al., 1992; Pueschel, Gallagher, Zartler, & Pezzullo, 1987). This increasing differentiation of organic mental retardation has led to a renewed interest in development of children with several different types of organic etiology (e.g., Cicchetti & Beeghly, 1990; Cohen & Donellan, 1987; Dykens, Leckman, & Hodapp, 1994; Hodapp, Burack, & Zigler, 1990).

In the course of work on the liberal developmental approach, developmentalists have been forced to work harder at the developmental approach, as they attempt to apply the theories of nonretarded development to those children who do show clear areas of deficit over and above their general levels of retardation. In a

sense, those attempting to apply nonretarded development to organically retarded populations are attempting to understand development "in the face of defect," to make clear how developmental processes operate in spite of particular, organically based deficits. This understanding of how developmental approaches can be applied to children with organic retardation promises to tell us much about both typical and atypical developmental processes.

In addition to the extension of the developmental approach to all persons with retardation, regardless of etiology, the approach itself has widened to reflect expansions in the field of developmental psychology. Compared with only 25 years ago, developmental psychologists are now concerned with issues of mother-child interactions and transactions over time (Sameroff & Chandler, 1975; Sameroff, this work, Volume 1, Chapter 21), of development of the child in collaboration with adults (e.g., Wertsch & Rogoff, 1984), and of the child's development and changing role within the family and larger social units (Bronfenbrenner, 1979; Emery & Kitzman, this volume, Chapter 1). Each of these expansions and elaborations has begun to be integrated into the developmental approach to mental retardation.

The resultant developmental approach incorporates the best of forerunners such as Werner, Piaget and Inhelder, and Vygotsky, of Zigler's original developmental formulation, and of the expansions caused by increased knowledge about mental retardation and human development. It is this combination of perspectives that we will attempt to outline in the following pages.

DEVELOPMENT IN PERSONS WITH MENTAL RETARDATION

Although we could overview current developmental work in mental retardation in many ways, the following review attempts to identify several important issues and to tie these issues to the earlier work already reviewed. Several of these areas were present in Zigler's original developmental approach to mental retardation. For these areas, including such issues as sequences, structures, and personality-motivational functioning, the following sections offer reviews of recent work and a brief sense of how the issues themselves have evolved over the past two decades. Other areas, while not formally within Zigler's developmental approach, have often been implicit in developmental work. Issues of this type include concerns about changing rates of development and transitions between stages in the development of children with mental retardation. Finally, there are issues such as mother-child interactions and family perspectives that owe much of their current emphases to changes in the field of developmental psychology over the past 20 to 30 years. In each case, the goal is to provide as complete a "developmental approach to mental retardation" as possible, as we discuss the seven areas of (a) sequences; (b) structures; (c) rates; (d) developmental transitions; (e) mother-child interactions; (f) families; and (g) motivation-personality development in children with mental retardation.

The Similar Sequence Hypothesis and Beyond

Among the main tenets of the developmental approach is that children with retardation develop in the same order as do nonretarded children. This view, typically referred to as the similar sequence hypothesis (Zigler, 1969), is probably the most researched of all developmental issues in mental retardation, with studies numbering into the hundreds. Sequences of development of children with retardation have been examined in numerous Piagetian domains (Weisz & Zigler, 1979; Woodward, 1979), in symbolic play (e.g., Beeghly & Cicchetti, 1987; Beeghly, Weiss-Perry, & Cicchetti, 1990), and in morality (Kohlberg, 1969), as well as in such linguistic domains as categorization-word meaning (Mervis, 1990), grammar (Fowler, 1988, 1990), and pragmatics, or the uses of language (Cicchetti & Ganiban, 1990; Leifer & Lewis, 1984).

In recent years, however, the idea of universal sequences of development within a single domain has been criticized in developmental psychology. Even the Piagetian ideal of progressively more adequate logical structures has been questioned, with Buck-Morss (1975) noting that Piaget's focus on "pure" thought, as separated from the content to which that thought is applied, reflects a distinction between structures and content that is valued only in industrialized societies. Empirically as well, the search for "universals" in development has often been unsuccessful, particularly as concerns formal operational thought (e.g., Dasen, 1972) and moral reasoning (Miller, 1984). Although most developmentalists agree that it is necessary to consider contextual factors within development (e.g., Bronfenbrenner, Kessel, Kessen, & White, 1987), some have gone so far as to question whether any sequences of development are universal (Kessen, 1984).

Before discussing findings on this issue relevant to children with retardation, it is important first to list reasons that have historically supported the hypothesis of sequentiality in developmental work (Hodapp, 1990). The first, from Piaget (1966) and others, is that certain skills serve as natural, logical prerequisites to other skills. Whether a high-level behavior embeds within it an earlier behavior (inclusion), or adds to an existing behavior, or coordinates two existing, but heretofore separate, behaviors (Flavell, 1972), some developments logically precede others. Second, biological propensities "channel" development, such that it is oftentimes very difficult for development to proceed in an "other-than-usual" pathway (e.g., Scarr-Salapatek, 1975; McCall, 1982). Third, the structure of human information processing and the nature of the world predispose some developments to occur before others. For example, humans notice and talk about objects and events that are new and unique as opposed to old or "given" (Bruner, 1985). Finally, some aspects of the environment may be universal, forming a "staged curriculum" for children; Kaye (1982) suggests that the burst-pause rhythm of early breastfeeding constitutes the beginnings of a universal pattern of communicative interactions between mothers and their infants.

Given the reasons for and against developmental sequences in work with nonretarded children, it is in some sense surprising that mental retardation findings are so clear: with only a few exceptions (to be discussed shortly), children with mental retardation

traverse Piagetian and other developmental stages in invariant order, just like nonretarded children. Assessing 28 cross-sectional and 3 longitudinal studies using Piagetian tasks, Weisz and Zigler (1979) note that virtually all studies show children with retardation to be as sequential as nonretarded children. On occasion, as in the development of moral concepts, children with retardation were only partially sequential (Mahaney & Stephens, 1974), but so too were the nonretarded children. In addition, the findings of sequential development held for children with both familial and organic retardation, lending further support to a "liberal" developmental approach to mental retardation.

There are, however, some exceptions. Children with severe electroencephalogram (EEG) abnormalities, that is, uncontrolled seizures, may not demonstrate sequential development (Weisz & Zigler, 1979). This lack of sequentiality may be due to atypical sequences in seizure-disordered children, or, possibly, to the extreme difficulties in testing severely seizure-prone children. More work is needed in this area.

A second exception is the recent finding that autistic children have their own, etiology-specific sequences for at least some aspects of development. In several studies, Wetherby (1986) and Prizant and Wetherby (1987) note that children with autism always use language first for imperative functions such as getting others to retrieve objects or to take care of their needs. Only at much later ages (if at all) do children with autism use language to comment on the world, greet people, show off, or otherwise engage in language's many social functions. In contrast, nonretarded children talk about social and object functions in their earliest communications, even before using formal words per se. To quote Wetherby (1986), "The function of directing another's attention to an object or event for a social end appears to be a 'later emerging' function for autistic children" (p. 305).

The findings of etiology-specific sequences in linguistic pragmatics, as well as earlier findings on moral development in children with retardation, lead to some speculations about sequences in both retarded and nonretarded children. In line with Scarr-Salapatek (1975), McCall (1982), and others (e.g., Brauth, Hall, & Dooling, 1991), two factors may influence the sequentiality of development: age at which the development usually occurs and the degree to which the domain of interest is "biological" as opposed to "social" (Hodapp, 1990). Thus, it would appear, as in the Mahaney and Stephens (1974) study of moral development, that developments that are both later occurring and more social in nature might be the least sequential, both for retarded and nonretarded children. In the same way, pragmatics, or the uses of language, would be less sequential than early semantic or grammatical developments in language or Piagetian sensorimotor developments in cognition. Those behaviors that are most biologically based *and* that occur earliest would appear most resistent to disruption for different types of children with disabilities. As Kopp (1983) notes with regard to early visual perceptual abilities and reduplicated babbling in infants with Down syndrome, "Both of these may be so basic to human existence and so tied to biological underpinnings and maturational factors that Down syndrome conditions are not severe enough to disrupt the timing of their emergence" (p. 1119). In short, the earlier developments occur, especially in domains that might be considered more "hardwired" or biologically based, the more sequential they are likely to be for all children, retarded or nonretarded.

This suggestion, while admittedly speculative, is similar to both early and recent theoretical formulations. Thus, Vygotsky (1978) suggests that there might be a distinction between natural and cultural lines of development, with the natural line requiring minimal environmental support. In a similar way, Horowitz's (1987) distinction between Universals I and II reflects this movement from early, more biologically based developments into later, more culturally based developments. According to Horowitz (1987), Universal I behaviors are those behaviors about which, given a normal, species-typical, human environment, "What will be expressed is largely the same in every normal human organism" (p. 145). She proposes perceptual capacities and eye-hand coordination as examples of Universal I behaviors (Gamble and Zigler's, 1986, idea that some domains are more "buffered" from environmental disturbances than others is similar in this regard). Universal II behaviors are slightly less hardwired, or behaviors that will usually, but not always, be expressed within widely different environments (speed and quality of these developments might also be more open to environmental effects). Horowitz nominates as examples of this category such developments as motor locomotion, the capacity to learn language, and sensorimotor skills. To these Universal I and II behaviors can be added an entire set of nonuniversal behaviors, or those developments that are very much socially derived, based somewhat on learning, and culturally dependent. Yet even for these nonuniversal behaviors, "The species-typical aspects of stages and system organization influence some of when and how these mechanisms operate and partially determine some of the content of the non-universal behaviors acquired" (p. 140; see also Kopp & Recchia, 1990).

A good example of the interplay between universal and cultural factors might be seen in the development of moral reasoning skills in children from widely differing cultures. For example, Miller (1984, 1986) has found that children in the United States and in India (Hindus) eventually develop very different systems of social reasoning: Americans attend more to dispositions of the person (e.g., the person's personality), whereas Hindus attribute action to contextual factors. At early ages, however, 8-year-old American and Hindu children give identical types of concrete, instance-oriented explanations to explain another's social and antisocial behavior (Miller, 1986). For instance, in explaining why a Hindu girl bandaged a boy's cut face, a Hindu 8-year-old noted that "his face was cut"; in explaining a girl's getting help when a boy got his pants caught in his bicycle chain, an American child noted that "there was no one else around/and she had her bike also" (p. 518). Thus, even in the expressly social and culturally-determined domain of reasoning about the actions of others, the earliest behaviors are influenced by the (presumably universal) concrete operational thinking of 8-year-olds.

Our suggestion is that different types of mental retardation be used to examine the effects of biological variability in sequential development (Hodapp & Burack, 1990). Those times during development or domains of development showing identical, invariant sequences in both retarded and nonretarded children would seem more "truly sequential" in nature, in much the way that Piaget talks about universal invariant sequences. Those behaviors showing variations in sequence due to the child's particular etiology of retardation, like social versus object uses of language in children with autism, would seem more open to effects from differences in the child's neurobiological structures.

This proposal, to use different types of mental retardation to test the effects of biological variability, operates in much the same way that cross-cultural studies help determine the effects of environmental variability (Cicchetti & Mans-Wagener, 1987). In both cases, the goal is to determine which developments *must* occur in invariant sequences versus which developments are more idiosyncratic due to the child's interests, the child's neurobiological structures, or the child's culture and environment. Although the idea of using biological variability to examine sequences remains relatively unexplored, studies of sequences in different retarded populations should tell us much about both retarded and nonretarded development in the years to come.

From Similar Structures to More Intricate Cross-Domain Relationships

The second major tenet of the developmental approach involves what has been called the "similar structure hypothesis" (Zigler, 1969). The view here is that, when matched on overall level of cognitive functioning, mentally retarded and nonretarded children will demonstrate identical levels of functioning on cognitive or linguistic tasks. The similar structure hypothesis was first applied by Zigler (1969) only to children with familial retardation, although subsequent work has examined the similar structure hypothesis both for children with familial and organic retardation (Weisz & Yeates, 1981; Weisz et al., 1982).

The original impetus for the idea of similar structures was Zigler's debate with the so-called "defect theorists" in mental retardation. Defect theorists make up a loosely connected group of mental retardation workers who hold that all of mental retardation is caused by one or another particular defect. In contrast, Zigler (1969) hypothesized that children with familial retardation, as simply the lower end of the Gaussian distribution of normal intelligence (roughly, from IQ 50 to IQ 150), should have no particular defects that are causing their subnormal intellectual abilities. In essence, the child with familial retardation who has an IQ of 60 should differ from the nonretarded child of IQ 90 in the same (albeit unspecified) way that the normal child of IQ 100 differs from the normal child of IQ 130. Just like groups of nonretarded children at any IQ level, children with familial retardation should show no particular domains or types of intellectual functioning that are impaired over and above general overall delays.

Given this reasoning—and the corollary that children with organic retardation *are* qualitatively different from nonretarded children—there may be a distinction between similar structure findings for children with organic versus familial retardation. This, indeed, has been the case. As reviewed by Weisz and Yeates (1981), children with organic retardation have shown less adequate performance compared to nonretarded children when the two groups have been matched on overall levels of intelligence (MA).

The findings for children with familial retardation have been more complicated. Weisz et al. (1982; also Weisz & Yeates, 1981) note that, on a series of Piagetian-based tasks, the performance of children with familial retardation is comparable to performance of MA-matched nonretarded children. But when children with familial retardation were given information-processing tasks involving learning, memory, learning-set formation, and distractibility and selective attention, they performed worse than MA-matches in approximately half of the studies (Weiss et al., 1986). In essence, there may be a "defect" in the functioning of children with familial retardation, but this defect only shows itself on information-processing tasks, not on Piagetian-based measures.

How to account for such puzzling findings? At present, there really is no definitive answer, but at least two explanations have been proposed. Weisz (1990) points to the possibility of task differences, with Piagetian tasks being more "ecologically valid" and therefore more interesting to children with familial retardation than are the more laboratory-based, often repetitive, information-processing measures. Conversely, Mundy and Kasari (1990) propose that distinctions can be made between tasks that they consider more "rate-related" (i.e., information-processing) versus those that are more "level-rated" (i.e., Piagetian). Although Mundy and Kasari (1990) acknowledge that performance on these two types of tasks must be correlated, the relationship may not be perfect. Conceivably, children with familial retardation could be defective in the more molecular information-processing tasks and not on the more molar Piagetian measures. Although both the Weisz (1990) and Mundy and Kasari (1990) views are interesting, neither has yet been tested empirically.

To date, issues of similar structure have revolved around children with familial retardation. But with the interest of liberal developmentalists in applying developmental principles to organically retarded populations (e.g., Cicchetti & Pogge-Hesse, 1982), issues of cross-domain organization have also arisen for children with organic retardation. Furthermore, current work focuses not solely on children with different organic syndromes grouped together, but on the interdomain organization of children with many different types of organic mental retardation divided into separate etiological groups.

The first point here is that specific etiologies of mental retardation differ in their particular intellectual strengths and weaknesses. For example, in a review of development in children with Down syndrome, Cicchetti and Ganiban (1990) note that, compared with other aspects of their (respective) language abilities, children with Down syndrome are particularly strong in linguistic pragmatics, whereas children with autism demonstrate particularly poor pragmatic abilities. Similarly, whereas children with Down syndrome show relative strengths in imitating a series of hand movements (Pueschel et al., 1987), this is an area of particular deficit for boys with fragile X syndrome (Dykens et al., 1987). As a result, the recently implemented strategy of teaching sign language to children with retardation (e.g., Abrahamson, Cavallo, & McCluer, 1985; see also Acredolo & Goodwyn, 1990) appears to help children with Down syndrome in their entry into language, whereas instruction using sign language might be expected to prove disappointing for children with fragile X syndrome (Hodapp & Dykens, 1991).

In addition to this expansion within the mental retardation field, the field of developmental psychology per se has also seen a change of focus from similar structures to cross-domain relations. As shown by Flavell (1982) and others, individual nonretarded children often show pronounced patterns of intellectual strengths and weaknesses. Gardner (1983) has even gone so far as to speak of independent "multiple intelligences," such that verbal, math, spatial, music, or other types of intelligence may be virtually unrelated for at least some children (see also Curtiss, 1989). Conversely, others note that, across groups of children, those scoring high on one intellectual task tend to score higher on other intellectual tasks, thereby supporting a general factor in intelligence (or g) that leads to more cross-domain consistency (Humphreys, 1979). Developmental psychology has thus gone from the view that all functioning was at the identical level (Piaget's idea of unified stages; cf. Kessen, 1962) to the possibility that developments in diverse areas are almost totally unrelated (Gardner, 1983), to various viewpoints in the middle. At the very least, cross-domain interrelations are currently under debate among researchers interested in nonretarded development.

One solution is that, even in the absence of unified Piagetian stages or other *structures d'ensemble* in development, there might remain smaller areas of organization. Bates, Benigni, Bretherton, Camaioni, and Volterra (1979) call these units of organization "local homologies of shared origin" and note that they involve two or more behavioral manifestations of a single underlying scheme or concept. Behaviors reflective of a homology should appear at approximately the same time in development, that is, when the child is beginning to master that homology's underlying concept. For example, the infant's use of one object as a means to retrieve another (e.g., using a rake to obtain a desired object) seems to develop at about the same time (10–12 months) as pointing to a desired object while looking to the mother (for her to retrieve it) (Bates, Camaioni, & Volterra, 1975). In both cases, the child is showing a knowledge that either an object (rake) or person (mother) can be used as a means to obtain a particular end (the desired object).

Retarded children of diverse etiologies might also demonstrate such local homologies (Mundy, Siebert, & Hogan, 1984; Hodapp & Zigler, 1990). In nonretarded children, for instance, levels of early language and symbolic behavior are related in that prelinguistic infants mouth objects, whereas children uttering one-word sentences engage in single-schemed play (e.g., combing the doll's hair), and children producing multiword utterances engage in multischemed play (combing, then feeding the doll). This relationship has been shown for nonretarded children (McCune-Nicholich & Bruskin, 1982), for children with Down syndrome (Beeghly & Cicchetti, 1987; Beeghly et al., 1990; Hill & McCune-Nicholich, 1981), and even for children with autism (Mundy, Sigman, Ungerer, & Sherman, 1987). In the same way, means-ends behaviors with objects and early intentional communication with people have been related in nonretarded children (Bates, Camaioni, & Volterra, 1975), in children with autism (Curcio, 1978), and in a heterogeneous group of retarded subjects (Mundy et al., 1984). Other relationships have also been found between levels of development in different domains for both retarded and nonretarded children (see Hodapp & Burack, 1990), leading to the belief that there are several smaller, "local" cross-domain connections.

There may also be other, "bigger" types of cross-domain organization. These larger cross-domain relations may be of several types, but the most obvious involves limits in the extent to which one domain can be ahead of another. For example, children with Down syndrome are more advanced in social adaptive skills than in their levels of general intelligence. As Cornwell and Birch (1969) discovered, however, the degree to which social behaviors can be advanced over mental age in children with Down syndrome is limited because relatively high levels of communication and cognitive reasoning are needed to perform many high-level social tasks.

In addition, cross-domain relations may not remain stable as children with different types of retardation get older. For example, although boys with fragile X syndrome show deficits in sequential, or step-by-step, processing throughout childhood (Dykens et al., 1987; Kemper, Hagerman, & Altshul-Stark, 1988), at later ages sequential processing skills stop developing, whereas other types of intellectual processing (e.g., simultaneous processing) continue to develop. As a result, boys with fragile X syndrome come to have an increasingly pronounced deficit in sequential processing as they get older (Hodapp, Dykens, Ort, Zelinsky, & Leckman, 1991). In a similar way, as children with Down syndrome get older, they become increasingly deficient in levels of grammar relative to overall levels of mental age (Miller, 1987). In short, the issue of cross-domain relations, already made more complicated by the movement from larger to smaller units of organization, may become even more complicated because strengths and weaknesses become more pronounced in certain etiological groups as children get older.

A final issue in the area of cross-domain relations involves new work on children with Williams syndrome, a rare, newly discovered, genetic disorder. In a series of studies, Ursula Bellugi and her colleagues have found that these children appear to show linguistic abilities vastly in advance of their levels of intelligence. Furthermore, such sparing of language appears in both linguistic grammar (Bellugi, Marks, Bihrle, & Sabo, 1988) and in narrative abilities (Reilly, Bellugi, & Klima, 1991). These children therefore appear to display "language in the (relative) absence of thought," an unusual, even unique, pattern of abilities. Although future studies of Williams and other mental retardation syndromes will determine the degree to which developments in different domains go together, the entire issue of cross-domain relations and organization of development remains problematic (see also Courchesne, Townsend, Chase, this work, Volume 1, Chapter 7, and Pennington & Welsh, this work, Volume 1, Chapter 9).

Changing Rates of Development: Why Do Children with Mental Retardation Show Varying Rates of Development during Childhood?

With a few notable exceptions, developmental psychologists have shown relatively little interest in issues of rate of cognitive development. Although clinical psychologists have long employed IQ tests, achievement tests, and other measures comparing individual children to same-age peers, this approach has been ignored by most developmental workers, particularly those interested in more "basic" issues of children's development. Of the three ways to examine cognition in children—Piagetian, information-processing, and psychometric approaches—the psychometric approach is probably the least prevalent method of study in developmental psychology.

This lack of interest in psychometric instruments is historically based on the developmentalist's quest for underlying processes. Thus we see Werner's interest in process as opposed to achievement, Piaget's creation of the méthod clinique to examine the child's underlying cognitive reasoning, and Vygotsky's concern with transitional rather than achieved development: Each reflects the desire to get beyond performance to understand the underlying processes of thinking engaged in by the developing child.

This interest in underlying process has generally translated into studies designed to assess how the prototypical child develops, instead of how development differs from one child to another. Piaget probably held this view most strongly. He derided psychologists who were interested in the rate of development, even those who were concerned about the precise ages at which children achieved Piagetian stages. To Piaget, such concerns reflected what he called the "American problem," the preoccupation in American society with quicker, faster, and better development. As Kessen (1962) notes, "Piaget has little interest in individual variation among children in the rate at which they achieve a stage . . . ; he is a student of the development of thinking more than he is a student of children" (1962, p. 77).

There have, however, been occasions during which developmentalists have used psychometric instruments to very good effect. For example, Nancy Bayley (1955) examined IQ test performance over time to determine whether children demonstrating above-average performance early in life showed similar above-average performance in later years. Her interest in the stability of intellectual development remains an important developmental issue.

In a similar way, some developmental workers have examined IQ test performance to help identify underlying developmental changes common to all children. McCall, Eichorn, and Hogarty (1977) examined Bayley test performance over the infancy period in groups of nonretarded infants. Through correlational analyses of DQ (developmental quotient, or infant IQ) scores over time, McCall et al. (1977) identified 2, 8, 13, and 21 months as those points during development when the nature of intelligence changed qualitatively. These periods closely relate to sensorimotor cognitive changes as described by Piaget and others (Uzgiris, 1987; see DeVries, 1974, and Kuhn, 1976, for studies of the relationship between Piagetian and psychometric measures in later childhood).

This use of IQ tests in "developmental ways" has recently been extended to address issues in children with retardation's rate of development (as Zigler, 1969, notes, IQ is a measure of rate of intellectual development). The issue is not that children with retardation develop at slower rates than nonretarded children, but that even these slowed rates of development change over time. For example, infants with Down syndrome appear to progress at slower and slower rates over the childhood years (e.g., Gibson, 1978). Bayley DQ scores decrease over the first several years of life (Carr, 1990; Dameron, 1963; Dicks-Mireaux, 1972; although see also Reed, Pueschel, Schnell, & Cronk, 1980) and may also decline in later childhood (Cornwell & Birch, 1969; Melyn & White, 1973; Morgan, 1979). This is not to say that children with Down syndrome stop developing, only that their cognitive development progresses at slower rates as they get older.

Similar findings can be observed in other etiologies as well. Boys with fragile X syndrome also decline in their IQ scores with increasing chronological age (Hagerman et al., 1989; Lachiewicz, Gullion, Spiridigliozzi, & Aylsworth, 1987). With fragile X boys, however, the decline does not appear to be uniform over the childhood years. Instead, fragile X boys appear to develop in a relatively steady fashion until the period from approximately 10 to 15 years, after which their rates of intellectual and adaptive development noticeably slow (Dykens et al., 1989; Dykens, Hodapp, Ort, & Leckman, 1992; Hodapp, Dykens et al., 1990).

These findings, occurring in the face of near steady IQ scores in other retarded groups (e.g., cerebral palsy; see Burack et al., 1988, for a review), suggest that there might be different mechanisms affecting rate of development in different etiological groups. These possibilities include *mental age* factors and *chronological age* factors, and we will briefly detail each factor.

In mental age factors, the child is slowed in development by difficulties in mastering one or more intellectual tasks. Thus, in Figure 9.1, two children are progressing at differing rates of speed. At the point in development when each child reaches the troublesome task, development slows compared with prior rates. Although Child 1 reaches the "developmental wall" at an earlier age than Child 2, both slow down in their rates of development once the difficult developmental task has been reached. Changes of this type will occur at later ages for lower IQ children (i.e., Child 2), but should affect all children once they attempt the more difficult developmental tasks (roughly related to mental age).

In Down syndrome, this type of "developmental wall" may occur even during the infancy period. Recall that Carr (1990) and others found that the Bayley DQ scores of children with Down syndrome decrease over the infancy years. In a study using an

adaptation of the Uzgiris and Hunt (1975) Ordinal Scales of Infant Development (Dunst, 1980), Carl Dunst (1988) found that infants with Down syndrome decreased in their rates of development across several sensorimotor stages. These decreases in rate of development were noted on Uzgiris-Hunt and on Bayley measures (Dunst, 1990), and were apparent even when the already slowed rate of development in Down syndrome infants was taken into account. Although not all Piagetian-stage transitions were equally difficult, chldren with Down syndrome experienced difficulties in making many of the "qualitative leaps" in cognitive reasoning that occur in nonretarded children over the 0- to 2-year period.

The second type of factor slowing development involves chronological age factors. As shown in Figure 9.2, two children slow in rate of development (IQ) when they reach a particular chronological age. This slowing appears related to the age of the child, not the level of development (MA) achieved at that particular chronological age. The best example of a "wall" due to chronological age factors appears to be fragile X syndrome, where boys with this disorder appear to slow in development during ages 10 to 15 years. Although the exact reason for this slowing continues to be debated (Hagerman et al., 1989), "the regulatory factors responsible for the initiation of puberty may play an important role in the plateauing of MA seen in these subjects" (Dykens et al., 1989, p. 425).

Other examples may also exist for CA-related slowing in developmental rates. Fowler (1988) notes, for example, that the development of grammar in children with Down syndrome seems partially age related. Although certain language stages are more difficult than others, children with Down syndrome appear to plateau in grammatical development during the period from 7.5 to 10.5 years. At earlier and later ages, high-IQ children (i.e., those with IQs above 50) make more progress than low-IQ children (IQs below 50), but progress stops for all children with Down syndrome during the middle childhood years. Similar slowing of children with Down syndrome during the middle childhood years may also occur relative to overall mental age as measured in IQ tests (Gibson, 1966, 1978) and, possibly, to adaptive age-equivalent

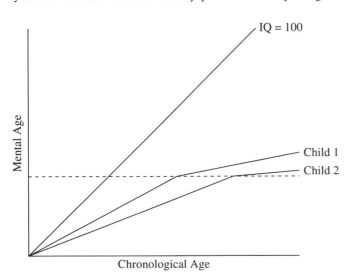

Figure 9.1 Task-related slowing of development.

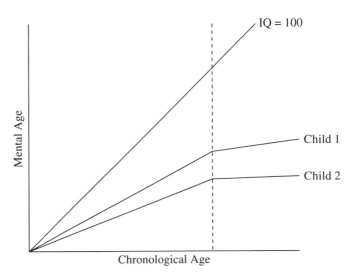

Figure 9.2 Age-related slowing of development.

scores as measured on the Vineland Scales of Adaptive Behavior (Dykens, Hodapp, & Evans, 1994).

The remaining problem is how MA- and CA-related factors—presumably related to underlying task and neurobiological factors—relate to one another. Given that children with Down syndrome show task-related difficulties during infancy and upon entering into language, what etiology-specific mechanisms in Down syndrome cause this slowing of development? Conversely, although puberty may be responsible for the slowing of development seen in fragile-X males, what exactly causes these changes?

An additional issue concerns ways that either task or neurobiological factors relate to similar findings in nonretarded children. For example, current work (based on Lenneberg, 1967) hints that at least some areas of language development show a "critical" or "sensitive" period such that second language learning is impaired at the onset of puberty (Johnson & Newport, 1989; Mayberry & Eichen, 1991). Such neurobiological changes have yet to be tied to development in mentally retarded populations.

Although much more work remains to be done in this area, a valid distinction exists between MA- and CA-related factors. Such factors are becoming more evident and more related to specific developments in particular etiological groups. At least in mental retardation work, the use of IQ and other "rate of development" measures seems capable of providing clues as to underlying mechanisms and processes of development.

Transitions in Development: Making the Qualitative "Leaps" Necessary for Higher-Level Thought

In conceptualizing issues of rate, developmentalists have attempted to think in terms of qualitative, as opposed to quantitative, change. Thus, whereas the behaviorist envisions development as the child's ability to engage in more and more behaviors (i.e., as quantitative change), the developmentalist sees development as different from one stage to the next (e.g., Reese & Overton, 1970). The best example of such qualitative change might be the child's entrance into language. Although there may well be cognitive, social, gestural, or other prerequisites for language, the actual entrance into language entails the achievement of a qualitatively different skill that is irreducible to what has come before. Like "paradigm shifts" in the history of science (Kuhn, 1962), the world is never again the same to the developing child once he or she has developed language.

Because of the difficulties that at least children with Down syndrome demonstrate in accomplishing many of the qualitative "leaps" in development (Dunst, 1988), there has recently been an attempt to characterize the nature of the transitions across stages in several retarded groups. These efforts are reminiscent of Inhelder's work on the processes of thinking in children with retardation. Recall that Inhelder (1943/1968), examining a heterogeneous group of children with retardation, discovered incomplete or less-than-stable development from one level of reasoning to the next. She noted the difficulties that children with retardation experienced in truly mastering high-level modes of thought, as they vacillated between higher and lower levels of reasoning,

showed intrusions of lower-level thought into higher-level reasoning, and in other ways showed difficult and tenuous transitions from lower to higher modes of reasoning.

This idea of difficult transitions in mentally retarded populations, although originally proposed almost 50 years ago, has only recently been re-examined in developmental work with children with mental retardation. This work has mainly focused on *regressions in development,* or the inability at later ages to perform high-level tasks previously performed, and *oscillations,* or the inability at one time to consistently perform at high levels. Let us address each in turn.

Regressions occur in most children as they develop. It is relatively common for a child to perform a higher-level task on one test session, then to be unable to perform at the same high level on the next session. Children develop in this "two steps forward, one step backward" manner even as they are (in general) sequentially progressing through Piagetian or other developmental stages.

This pattern of development is probably best detailed during infancy. In examining Piagetian sensorimotor stages from one month to the next, Uzgiris (1987) and Kopp, Sigman, and Parmelee (1974) found low overall rates of regression, with 7% (Uzgiris) and 9% (Kopp et al.) of tests showing regressions across all infants and all ages. Uzgiris (1987) notes, however, that regressions occurred on 22% of sessions following change in the child's highest level functioning during the prior session. Different sensorimotor domains also showed different degrees of regression, with regressions from one session to the next most likely to occur in the domains of vocal imitation, causality, and gestural imitation.

In addition, the amount of regression from session to session does not appear to be constant over time. Uzgiris (1987) notes that nonretarded infants were more likely to demonstrate regressions at roughly 8, 13, and 20–22 months, the ages at which McCall et al. (1977) suggest that the nature of intelligence changes. Although the Kopp et al. (1974) findings are less clear-cut, it remains possible that nonretarded infants show more variability during times of most qualitative change, when they are struggling with those intellectual tasks that are most different from tasks performed during previous sessions.

Although these regressions are relatively common in all children, regressions in development occur much more often in infants with Down syndrome (they have rarely been examined in other mentally retarded groups). Dunst (1990) has found that regressions occur roughly twice as often in Down syndrome versus nonretarded infants, with all sensorimotor scales showing more regression in the Down syndrome group. Morss (1987) further observed that the patterns of regressions do not always indicate strategies reflective of immediately preceding behavioral stages. In contrast to nonretarded infants, who during regressions perform behaviors "just below" their levels on the prior session, "For Down syndrome infants, achievement does not emerge from such a coherent background of performance. Previous acquisitions are not so well consolidated, and error patterns are not so conducive to developmental progress" (Morss, 1987, pp. 45–46; see also Wishart & Duffy, 1990).

Similarly, in a study of object permanence abilities at monthly intervals over a one-year span, Wohlheuter and Sindberg (1975) also found large amounts of regression in a heterogeneous group of children with severe and profound retardation. Wohlheuter and Sindberg (1975) noted that they could divide their subjects into those children demonstrating slow upward change across Piagetian stages; those who were essentially even across the one-year period; and those who were extremely variable from month to month. This last group, consisting mainly of children with severe EEG disturbances, were characterized by performance that varied widely, "showing approximately as great and as frequent downward as upward movement" (p. 515). But regressions occurred even among those children whose general pattern was one of advance over the one-year span. Thus, children with Down syndrome, with severe seizure disorders, and possibly with other types of retardation appear to show regressions much more often than do nonretarded children.

In addition to regressions from one month to the next, children with Down syndrome may also oscillate between higher and lower levels within a single session. In examining development of symbolic play, Beeghly and Cicchetti (1987; see also Beeghly et al., 1990) noted that children with Down syndrome performed about equal to their MA-matched nonretarded controls, but this equivalence was only seen if the child's highest level behavior was examined. If comparisons were made between children with Down syndrome and MA-matched nonretarded children on the *average level* of symbolic play, the nonretarded children showed superior performance. This discrepancy between MA-matches on average but not highest level behavior was true only for the older group of children with Down syndrome, who were 6-years-old and 4 years in mental age. Beeghly et al. (1990) suggest that children with Down syndrome might have been more perseverative in their play, repeating (lower-level) play schemes more often than the control children. Of importance here, however, is the finding that where as children with Down syndrome could sometimes perform high-level symbolic play, they were prone to mix a few high-level behaviors with many low-level symbolic behaviors. In much the same way as described by Inhelder (1943/1968), then, this particular group of children was not quite as secure as MA-matched nonretarded children in their acquisition of high-level concepts.

The preceding studies examined the child's variable transitions from one month to the next or over a single session. Another way to think about transitions is the child's ongoing struggle with a particular concept at a single moment. Similar to the clinician's concept of "testing the child's limits," here the goal is to understand the nature and extent of those concepts with which the child is struggling, obtaining a more dynamic, in-the-moment sense of transitional development.

Explicitly based on the work of Vygotsky, the idea of a more dynamic transitional state has been used in both assessment and intervention. In assessment, Brown and Ferrara (1985; see also Campione et al., 1982) have examined Vygotsky's "zone of proximal development" in children with different IQ levels. In line with Vygotsky, they maintain that two children might have identical MAs but nevertheless differ in their "zones," or the types of behaviors each could perform on their own as opposed to with adult help. Brown and her colleagues define differing zones by the number of standardized prompts the child needs in learning to perform any of several IQ test items (letter series completion,

block design, etc.). Although higher-IQ children learn faster—that is, they require fewer adult prompts to learn a new behavior—the relationship between learning speed and IQ is not perfect. Thus, there are some fast learners who are of lower IQs, just as there are some slow learners who have average IQ scores.

In accordance with the developmental idea that a person truly understands a concept only when he or she can use it appropriately across a range of situations, Brown and Ferrara (1985) then test transfer of the learned behavior to tasks both "near" and "far" from the original situation. Near transfer involves problems that are nearly identical to those on which the child was trained. For example, in the letter series task, a training task might involve learning a letter set using the rules "same first letter, then next letter of the alphabet." An example of a series of this type would be the series "R A R B R C." The child asked to give the next two letters in the series would be trained to respond "R D." On the near transfer task, the child would be given a new set of letters, but one that involved the same principle (C L C M C N), and asked to give the next two letters (C O). Far transfer tasks involve principles that were not taught in the original learning situation (e.g., same, then backward in alphabet: M D M C M B). In this way, the degree to which the child can generalize rules learned during the original training task can be examined.

Transfer of training is defined as narrow or wide depending on whether children can perform on these analogous and untrained tasks. Brown and Ferrara (1985) thus developed profiles of "consistent learning" type children (slow to learn, narrow transfer; fast to learn, wide transfer), as well as "context bound" children (fast learning, narrow transfer). Although for the most part, Brown and her colleagues have extended Vygotsky's zone of proximal development only to average IQ and borderline retarded children, these ideas, especially as they are gradually applied to more "real world" tasks, should help in the diagnosis and training of children with mental retardation.

In conceptualizing the work on transitions, it appears that children with at least some types of retardation exhibit less solid, more "fragile" developments of their highest stages. This idea, from Inhelder, seems definitely true of children with Down syndrome and with seizure disorders, although it remains unexamined in individuals with other types of retardation. Moreover, transitions occur not only from session to session and over a single session, but in a Vygotskian sense can even be seen at a single moment in interaction with tutoring adults. How well Vygotsky's zone of proximal development can be employed for either assessment or intervention work remains an open question at this time (although see Feurstein, Rand, Hoffman, Hoffman, & Miller, 1979, for preliminary efforts along this line).

Mother-Child Interactions: Going beyond Individual Development

In describing the zone of proximal development, we have focused on one aspect of Vygotsky's work, his interest in the processes by which children come to develop a particular concept. A second, related concept is that adults help children to learn, that they tutor or scaffold development. Vygotsky (1978) argued that the development of all higher-level concepts occurs first in collaboration with surrounding adults, only later within the child's own internal cognitive schemes. This second, more social, aspect of Vygotsky fits well with work on mother-child interaction that has recently become prominent in child development research.

The area of mother-child relations has undergone several important changes over the past 20 to 30 years. In developmental work prior to the late 1960s, there was a strong emphasis on the processes of socialization, or the ways that parents shape, reinforce, punish, and in other ways affect their children's development. Diana Baumrind's (1967) work, showing the effects of different parenting styles on children's personalities, is probably the best example of studies in the socialization tradition. In all of these studies, the emphasis is on the ways that parents affect their developing offspring (for a review, see Zigler, Lamb, & Child, 1982).

Beginning with Bell's (1968) "discovery" of interaction in the late 1960s, the focus of work on parents and their children changed dramatically. According to Bell, children affect their parents just as parents affect children. Bell endeavored to reinterpret studies of socialization through this bidirectional perspective, which he called interactionism. Partly as a result of Bell's article, the 1970s and 1980s were filled with studies examining how children and parents mutually affect one another.

Probably the best example of interaction occurs in language development. Whereas Chomsky (1975) thought of language development as innately determined (through what he called the "language acquisition device," or LAD), later work showed that mothers do, in fact, tailor their language to the child's level of abilities. Thus, Phillips (1973) and Snow (1972) found that mothers shorten their speech, speak in a higher pitch, and emphasize and repeat the important words when speaking to young nonretarded children. Murray, Johnson, and Peters (1990) have further noted that such modifications in maternal speech occur only when the child turns about 1 year of age, or when children are beginning to understand the language that is spoken to them. All these changes in the input that children hear constitute what Bruner (1985) calls the "language acquisition support system" (or LASS) that accompanies the child's innate propensities for language (or LAD).

From the input language and interaction studies of the 1970s and 1980s, researchers interested in the development of children with retardation have examined whether interactions are "the same or different" in dyads composed of children with retardation and their mothers. Across many studies, these interactions appear to be both the same *and* different. That is, mothers of children with retardation, just like those of nonretarded children, shorten their sentences, emphasize and repeat key words, and in other ways engage in the "motherese" demonstrated by mothers of nonretarded children. Rondal (1977) has noted that mothers of children with Down syndrome, when matched with mothers of nonretarded children whose children are at the same mean length of utterance, or MLU, are equivalent on most of these more "structural" aspects of input language.

In contrast to the structural similarity of maternal input language, other aspects of communication between mothers and children with retardation are very different from those seen in mother-nonretarded child interactions. Compared with mothers of nonretarded children at the same level of language, mothers of children with retardation have been found to be more didactic, to initiate interactive bids more often, and to more often speak at the same time as their children with retardation (cf. Marfo, 1984, 1988). As a result, these mothers may not allow their children with retardation to themselves initiate interactions, thereby (possibly) exacerbating already-existing communicative difficulties (Cardoso-Martins & Mervis, 1985; Jones, 1977).

One possible explanation for this "same but different" pattern of interaction in mothers of children with retardation involves the idea of "meaning." In contrast to interaction work during the 1970s, which showed how children and mothers influence one another in a back-and-forth, "ping-pong game" style of analysis, more recent work has focused on the meaning of the interaction to both participants (Hodapp, 1988). Thus, the late 1970s and 1980s was a time of much work on the concept of "intersubjectivity" between mothers and their infants (e.g., Bruner, 1982; Trevarthen, 1979) and on "mutual efficacy" (Goldberg, 1977) as the goal of mother-child interactions. There have also been many studies on meaning in interactions with disabled children, from Tronick and Field's (1986) work examining mothers who are depressed to the idea of the "readability" of the infant to the mother when the infant is born prematurely (Goldberg, 1977) or has Down syndrome (Cicchetti & Sroufe, 1976, 1978).

Given this background, mothers may possess a different set of "meanings" when the child has a disability. Jones (1977) notes, for example, that mothers of children with Down syndrome conceptualize interactions with their children as teaching sessions, as opposed to the more playful, looser, less goal-oriented interactions of similar MA nonretarded children and their mothers. Similarly with regard to the children themselves, Cardoso-Martins and Mervis (1985) and Jones (1980) both found that mothers were afraid that their children with Down syndrome would never learn language. As a result, the tendency of these mothers was to be more directive and more didactic in their interactive styles.

This is not to imply that all mothers of children with disabilities are poor interactors with their children or that these mothers do not differ one from another. Crawley and Spiker (1983) found large individual differences in interactive styles among mothers of children with Down syndrome. Further, they noted that, just as in work with mothers of nonretarded children, directiveness and sensitivity are at least partially separable. The interactive pattern most conducive to child progress seemed to be one that combines both highly sensitive *and* highly directive maternal behaviors.

Mothers of children with disabilities may also benefit from interventions that make them more comfortable and that teach them how to interact with their children. In work with mothers of children with several types of disability, Bromwich (1980, 1990) has had great success using a six-step program teaching mothers of children with disabilities to be comfortable in interacting with their babies. On a more molecular level, Mahoney (1988) has successfully taught mothers of infants with retardation to watch and imitate their children's behaviors, thus allowing the child to take a more active role in mother-child interaction.

Future interventions will promote better mother-child interactions by focusing on specific aspects of interactions with specific outcomes. For example, Curtiss's (1989) finding that different subdomains of language appear separable in children with different disabilities suggests the usefulness of different interactive strategies to tutor different aspects of language. An example in linguistic pragmatics is Curcio and Paccia's (1987) finding that children with autism communicate much better when responding to "Yes-No" questions and utterances that are conceptually simple and contingent on the child's topic of conversation. This type of "pragmatically based" interaction might be particularly useful for children with this disorder.

As implied by Curcio and Paccia (1987), interactions may also need to be tailored to the child's etiology of retardation. If children with autism do indeed show such strong pragmatic deficits, whereas children with Down syndrome show relatively high pragmatic abilities (e.g., Beeghly et al., 1990; Leifer & Lewis, 1984), certain etiology-specific strategies of intervention might be called for. These intervention strategies, in turn, will require different types of interactive behaviors between adults and children with disabilities. Again, specificity will be called for. As Bruner and Bornstein (1989) note for nonretarded children, "Again and again research and theory point to specific interaction experiences at specific times in development affecting specific facets of growth in specific ways" (Bruner & Bornstein, 1989, p. 12). It remains to be seen how such specificity works in interactions between children with mental retardation and the surrounding adult world.

Families of Children with Mental Retardation

Although families have long been of interest in the mental retardation field (Farber, 1959, 1960), this area has recently experienced what can only be described as an explosion of new work. Studies focus on individual family members and on the family as a whole, and are being performed by researchers in developmental psychology, sociology, clinical psychology, developmental pediatrics, nursing, social work, and human ecology (Ramey, Krauss, & Simeonsson, 1989). This multifocused, multidisciplinary effort has probably taught us more about functioning in families with a child with retardation in the past 10 to 15 years than we knew in the previous 30.

Within the field of developmental psychology, this renewed family focus is closely aligned with Bronfenbrenner's (1979) views on the ecology of human development, the idea that children develop within families and larger ecological systems. Some of these systems directly affect children (e.g., the family), whereas some are indirect in their effects (national or local economy, the media). In addition, the interrelations among different systems (e.g., schools and parents) serve to strengthen or lessen each system's effects on the developing child (see Emery & Kitzman, this volume, Chapter 1).

Although Bronfenbrenner's ecological ideas are relatively new to developmental psychology, an interest in families is at least 40 years old in the field of family therapy. Writers such as Minuchin, Haley, and Satir have long conceptualized the family as a living system in much the same way that children themselves are a system to Piaget and Werner. Ideas such as the whole (i.e., the family system) being irreducible to the sum of the parts, change as an inherent feature of the system, organization among different parts

of the system, hierarchies of subsystems, boundaries, and behavior as reflective of underlying organization, are all family systems concepts that are similar to ideas prominent in work with the child alone (Minuchin, 1985). Yet partly due to difficulties in operationalizing many family system concepts, family research is somewhat sparse in developmental psychology, at least until recent years.

It is not surprising, then, that the bulk of family work in mental retardation is relatively new. As a result, we have now learned a great deal about particular aspects of family functioning, but are only beginning to draw together the many separate strands. Consequently, the following review will examine mothers, fathers, siblings, overall family functioning, and extrafamilial factors in a style that is admittedly more "elemental" than "systemic." Several themes in current and future family work will then be explored.

Mothers

When thinking of surrounding environments, researchers in mental retardation began by examining the emotional reactions of mothers to the birth and development of the child with disabilities. Two main strands have characterized this work. The first, from Solnit and Stark (1961), is that the mother of any baby with disabilities "mourns" the loss of the idealized perfect infant. This mourning process, akin to the grieving that takes place upon the death of a loved one, can last for variable amounts of time during the early years, but is generally considered to be comprised of a three-stage process of shock, then emotional disorganization (i.e., depression or anger), and finally, emotional reorganization (see Blacher, 1984 for a review). In contrast, a second model conceptualizes mourning as recurrent, as occurring again and again as the child gets older (Olshansky, 1962). Recurrent mourning might be triggered by any number of events, recollections, or times of parental or familial stress, but the idea is that mourning is not finished in the first few years after the child's birth and diagnosis.

Although the three-stage mourning and recurrent mourning models may both be partially correct, there is at least some suggestion that mothers of children with disabilities continue to experience depression over the childhood years. In several studies (cf. Hagamen, 1980), mothers of children with disabilities of several ages have been shown to be more depressed than are mothers of same-age nondisabled children. Further, bouts of depression may occur at various times over the childhood years. In a study of mothers of children with Down syndrome over the first year of life, Emde and Brown (1978) found that several mothers showed renewed bouts of depression at approximately 4 months. It is at about this age that children with Down syndrome demonstrate the inconsistent smiles and dampened affect that begin to set these infants apart from same-age nonretarded children. As a result, mothers who had gradually accepted their Down syndrome infant after the baby's birth were now reacting to the first behavioral manifestations of the disorder. Renewed periods of maternal depression sometimes occurred.

Similarly, there may be renewed periods of maternal depression at later ages. In examining children with cerebral palsy and their mothers over an 8-year period, Minde (1978) found that mothers distanced themselves both emotionally and physically (e.g., not "babying" the child) from the middle childhood to the early adolescent years. These mothers seemed both to be giving up trying to control their children and to be preparing their children to become as independent as possible; only by learning to do things on their own could these children hope to live independently in their upcoming adult years. Similar concerns with adult transitions have been noted by Wikler, Wasow, and Hatfield (1981), who asked parents of children with disabilities and social service providers to rank order the concern each felt about various developmental milestones. Mothers of children with retardation were much more concerned about milestones occurring later during childhood (e.g., 21st birthday) than were service providers, who focused more on parental and family needs during the early years. This difference between parents and service providers may reflect the parents' increasing difficulties in dealing with children with retardation as they get older, as parents use support services less, become more isolated, and suffer a pileup of stress, as compared with the years directly after the child's birth (Minnes, 1989).

These findings lead to several hypotheses concerning maternal emotional reactions during the childhood years. First, as in the environmental effects involved in other areas of psychopathology (e.g., depression; Cicchetti & Schneider-Rosen, 1986), a "transactional model" may more accurately depict maternal reactions. These reactions might thus occur in response to different developmental issues throughout the childhood years. Some of these issues might relate to concerns over the child's inability to perform developmentally appropriate tasks, others to reminders about the child's retardation at certain chronological ages (e.g., entrance into puberty and into early adulthood, Wikler, 1986; cultural milestones such as first communion or entering high school). Still other periods of concern might relate to instances when younger nonimpaired children in a family perform behaviors that the older child with retardation cannot yet do. These three senses of time—developmental, chronological, and familial—might each bring about feelings of depression and loss to parents of children with mental retardation.

A second hypothesis is that maternal reactions may be partly specific to the child's particular handicapping condition. Although most work to date has examined together many different types of "disabled children," there are some preliminary suggestions that mothers of children with different types of disabilities respond differently. In a study comparing mothers of children with autism versus those with Down syndrome, Holroyd and MacArthur (1976) found that mothers of children with autism were more upset and disappointed about the child and were more concerned about the child's dependency and the child's effects on the rest of the family. Similarly, Hodapp, Dykens, Evans, and Merighi (1992) have found that, whereas mothers of 1- to 6-year-old children with cerebral palsy and other motor impairments were concerned about their child's motor abilities, mothers of children with Down syndrome were concerned both about motor and cognitive-language milestones, particularly those related to later academic behaviors (e.g., says ABCs; reads). In addition, mothers of children with motor impairments were more closely attuned to the child's degree of communicative impairments than were mothers of children with Down syndrome, who became more worried when levels of communication were markedly below the child's abilities in other areas. Other studies have found that added stresses may arise when parents do not have a clear, identifiable organic cause to which to attribute the child's problems (Goldberg, Marcovitch, MacGregor, & Lojkasek, 1986), and other child characteristics may also influence levels of maternal stress and concern (Beckman, 1983; Bristol & Shopler, 1984).

Fathers

In contrast to mothers, fathers have been much less studied in developmental work. The sense has been that fathers tend to withdraw from the family unit, becoming more involved in work or even leaving the family altogether (the divorce rate among families with children with Down syndrome has sometimes been shown to be higher than among families without disabled children; Gath, 1978). In addition, the worries of fathers are often primarily around practical issues such as the financial strains involved in raising a child with disabilities (Price-Bonham & Addison, 1978).

Fathers may also differ from mothers in the degree and pattern of their emotional reactions. Goldberg et al. (1986) found that fathers as opposed to mothers of children with disabilities feel more "in control" of the situation, have a higher self-esteem, and are less depressed (see also Bristol, Gallagher, & Shopler, 1988). Whereas mothers describe their emotional reactions over time in the up-and-down pattern characteristic of recurrent mourning, fathers are most distressed after the child's birth, and feel increasingly less distress as the child gets older (Domrosch & Perry, 1989). Although much more work is needed in this area, fathers and mothers appear to differ in several aspects of emotional and practical adaptation to children with retardation.

For both mothers and fathers, recent work has shown a movement from a "psychopathology-based" view to a more positive, coping perspective. Thus, in an issue of the *American Journal on Mental Retardation* specifically devoted to families (Krauss, Simeonsson, & Ramey, 1989), several articles described those aspects of family structure or social support networks that allow more successful coping by these parents. For example, Frey, Greenberg, and Fewell (1989) found that the presence of supportive social networks promotes better coping on the part of mothers of children with disabilities, whereas fathers cope better when there is a minimal amount of criticism from extended families. Both mothers and fathers cope better if the other spouse is coping well and if each feels a strong measure of personal control in raising the child with disabilities. Bristol et al. (1988) even note that, when matched to parents of same-age nondisabled children, mothers and fathers of children with autism and severe language disorders experienced more disruptions in family life and demonstrated less effective parenting skills but did not differ in their overall degree of depression or marital difficulties. Such findings emphasize "the importance of differentiating stress related to having a disabled child from the general stress of parenting young children" (Bristol et al., 1988, p. 449).

Siblings

The movement from negative to more positive views of family members also extends to the nonimpaired siblings. Whereas early work emphasized the role tensions (e.g., Farber, 1959) that siblings feel in being brother or sister to a child with disabilities, more recent work has noted that siblings as a group may not be more at risk for psychiatric disorder than are other, same-age children (Lobato, 1983). Risks of disorder may increase, however, if the nonimpaired sibling is the oldest girl, if the parents themselves have difficulty dealing with the child's disabilities, or if the child's condition is not clearly diagnosed and/or requires a great deal of parental care and attention (McHale, Simeonsson, & Sloan, 1984).

Growing up with a child with disabilities can also sometimes help to make siblings more concerned, more empathic, and more tolerant of individual differences of many types (Wilson, Blacher, & Baker, 1989). Grossman (1972) found that the effects of growing up with a sibling with retardation can be either positive or negative: As young adults, some nonimpaired siblings were angry and resentful of the lack of time and attention given to them while growing up, whereas others were altruistic, empathic, and felt that growing up with a child with retardation gave them a more mature, fuller view of life. Just as mothers, fathers, the marital couple, and families as a whole may be either beneficially or adversely affected by raising a child with disabilities, so too with the nonimpaired siblings.

Extrafamilial Variables

In employing the ecological perspective, researchers must also go beyond the family alone to examine those "out-of-family" variables that appear to affect family functioning (Crnic, 1990). Several of these variables appear particularly important. For example, higher SES families appear to cope better than poorer families, and the support of the mother's close friends and extended families may be particularly important (Crnic, 1990). It also appears that, in contrast to mothers of nondisabled children, mothers of children with disabilities possess smaller, more intimate social networks (Kazak & Marvin, 1984). Such contacts with only a few close friends and extended family members may be both beneficial and detrimental in that these contacts provide support for parents but at the same time parents have less chance to discuss network-related stress or to seek out alternative views about their problems (Kazak & Marvin, 1984; Waisbren, 1980). At the very least, issues of extrafamilial factors appear complex and only superficially understood at the present time (Byrne & Cunningham, 1985; Robinson & Garber, this volume, Chapter 5).

In summarizing the work on families with mentally retarded members, four themes would seem to characterize present and future work. The first is that the field has increasingly moved from a view centering on psychopathology to one focused on adaptation and coping. As opposed to the early emphases on mourning in mothers of children with disabilities, on psychopathology in siblings, and on the difficulties faced by families with children with retardation, there now seems a more even-handed view of individual family members and families as a whole. This more optimistic view does not deny that families of children with retardation have problems, or that the nature and degree of such problems may change over time, but instead provides a sense that these families are managing to cope with raising a child with retardation and providing for other family members.

Much of this more positive view has come about as researchers have reconceptualized the nature and effects of having a retarded child within the family. Crnic, Friedrich, and Greenberg (1983) note that the child with retardation is a stressor in the family system, with coping dependent on characteristics of the child, of the family as a whole, and of each member. In other work, McCubbin and Patterson (1983) have modified Hill's (1949) ABCX model of family stress in order to understand stress and coping in families with a retarded member. In this model, the initial crisis (X in their model) is due to specific characteristics of the child (the "stressor event," A) mediated by the family's internal and external resources (B) and by the family's perceptions of the child (C). But as the child develops, new stressors (A'), resources (B'), and perceptions (C') arise and change over time. Thus, stressors may pile up as children with retardation get older, even as parents less often use such resources as support networks (Suelzle & Keenan, 1981) and professionals underestimate parental needs (Wikler et al., 1981). Perceptions of the child may also change as parents attempt to deal with the child's upcoming issues (Minde, 1978). This Double ABCX model, while complicated, would appear to include many important variables in the family's adaptation to the child with disabilities over the childhood years (Minnes, 1989).

In addition to the more positive, more stress-coping models of family adaptation, a second theme of family work is that all families of children with retardation are not the same. Just as mothers of children with Down syndrome differ in their interactions with their children (Crawley & Spiker, 1983), so too do families of children with retardation differ one from another. Mink, Nihira, and Meyers (1983) identified five different clusters of families of children with severe retardation: (a) cohesive, harmonious families; (b) control-oriented, somewhat unharmonious families; (c) low-disclosure, unharmonious families; (d) child-oriented, expressive families; and (e) disadvantaged, low-morale families. Similar (although not identical) family groupings were found for families of children with mild and borderline retardation (Mink, Meyers, & Nihira, 1984). Future work should further refine such categories and examine each type's adaptive strengths and weaknesses, those intra- or extrafamilial factors leading to each, and how each can best be helped to cope with raising a child with retardation.

A third focus of family work is the etiology of the child. Although rarely examined until recently, different etiologies appear to differentially influence family functioning. Thus, the concerns of mothers of children with Down syndrome versus motor impairments may differ (Hodapp, Dykens, Evans, & Merighi, 1992) and mothers of children with different types of retardation appear to experience different levels of stress (Goldberg et al., 1986; Holroyd & MacArthur, 1976). Further, Mink et al., (1983) found that almost two-thirds of their "cohesive harmonious" families had children with Down syndrome, whereas much lower percentages of families with Down syndrome children were found in the other four clusters. As Mink et al. (1983) noted, "Taking into consideration the effects of children on their caretakers, we may speculate that Down syndrome children will have a positive effect on the climate of the home" (p. 495). For whatever reason, etiology may be related to particular types of family functioning.

A final theme of family work in mental retardation is the need for an approach that examines changes in families with retarded members over time. To date, virtually all studies have been cross-sectional, and more importantly, results are generally given in terms of "families of children with retardation," as opposed to "families of children with retardation of a particular age." As in the field of mother-child interactions, then, family work will need to become much more specific in the years to come.

Personality-Motivational Development in Children with Mental Retardation

Our final discussion of current developmental issues overviews motivational and personality functioning in persons with mental retardation. Although each of the issues discussed earlier falls within the developmental approach, an attention to motivational factors has often been called the hallmark of the developmental approach to mental retardation. Indeed, Zigler and his collaborators have published numerous studies in this area, and other workers (e.g., Haywood, 1987; MacMillan & Keough, 1971; Weisz, 1982) have also noted the importance of motivational and personality factors in the functioning of individuals with retardation.

Work on motivational factors has been so successful and so well known that several researchers have called Zigler's developmental approach a "motivational" theory of mental retardation (Milgram, 1969; Zeaman, 1968). Focusing on Zigler's contention that motivational factors lead children with retardation to perform worse than they otherwise might, these workers concluded that the original developmental formulation ascribed mental retardation to motivational factors. As Zigler (1984) notes, however, "While I have conducted much research on the role of motivational variables in the performance of children with retardation, I have been specific in asserting that the essential problem in mental retardation is an intellectual or cognitive one" (p. 190). Still, these criticisms, although incorrect, demonstrate the importance that motivational-personality work has assumed among developmentally oriented workers.

A brief history helps in an understanding of motivational-personality functioning in persons with mental retardation. In a series of papers in the 1930s and 1940s, Kounin (1941a, 1941b, 1948) and Lewin (1936) proposed that children with retardation were more "rigid" in their thinking. Although this concept was never adequately defined and many failed to distinguish between the construct and its measurement (Zigler & Balla, 1982), Lewin's (1936) idea was that, with development, children come to have a greater differentiation between "regions" of cognition. Persons with retardation, who also possess a greater number of regions with increasing mental age, were also predicted to have a "greater stiffness, a smaller capacity for dynamic rearrangement" (p. 210) among these cognitive regions than do MA-matched nonretarded children.

Early work by Lewin and Kounin, as well as criticisms of this work by Goldstein (1942–1943) and by Werner (1946), emphasized cognitive-neurological interpretations for differences between retarded and nonretarded children on concept switching, satiation, and other rigidity tasks (see Zigler, 1972). Yet in a series of experiments examining Lewin-Kounin's formulations, Zigler found that the institutional subjects used in most experiments were highly influenced by the amount of social support received from the experimenter (e.g., Zigler, Hodgden, & Stevenson, 1958). Furthermore, those institutionalized children

with retardation who had experienced the most depriving environments prior to institutionalization were most likely to play experimental games longer and to appear more "rigid" compared with nonretarded MA-matches (e.g., Zigler, Balla, & Butterfield, 1968). For at least children with familial retardation, motivational and experiential factors were influencing what had heretofore been considered a strictly "organismic" feature of persons with retardation.

As a result of these and other personality-motivational studies, Zigler (1984) concluded that "many retarded persons develop traits such as high needs for social reinforcement, strong social approach and avoidance tendencies, and vexing 'I can't do it' attitudes" (Zigler, 1984, p. 181). These traits are not related to the lower levels of cognitive functioning of individuals with retardation per se, but to the history of failure that these children have experienced. By adding these personality-motivational factors to functioning in children with mental retardation, Zigler (1971) emphasized how persons with retardation are not only thinking or language-using beings, but individuals who undergo particular life experiences and show particular personality and motivational characteristics. His approach was aimed at understanding the "whole child" with mental retardation, in all of that child's psychological complexity.

These thoughts led to the formulation of a series of personality-motivational factors affecting functioning in persons with mental retardation. Six of these factors have received much attention over the past several decades: (a) positive reaction tendency, (b) negative reaction tendency, (c) expectancy of success, (d) outerdirectedness, (e) effectance motivation, and (f) self-concept. Although other motivational factors may also influence functioning, we overview work with these six to provide a flavor of motivational factors (for more detailed reviews of personality-motivational functioning in persons with retardation, see Zigler & Burack, 1989; Zigler & Hodapp, 1986).

Positive Reaction Tendency

In early work among institutionalized children with retardation, Zigler noticed that these individuals were much more attentive to, and dependent on, the adult examiner. In a series of studies, Zigler (1958, 1961) tested this hypothesis by giving these children a boring, repetitive game with the examiner present. He found that children with retardation played this game for longer periods of time than did MA-matched nonretarded children. Furthermore, institutionalized retarded children played longer than did noninstitutionalized retarded children of the same MA and CA (Green & Zigler, 1962), and those children with retardation who played the game for the longest periods of time were most likely to have suffered from the greatest amounts of preinstitutional social deprivation (Zigler et al., 1968). Furthermore, positive reaction tendencies were motivated by the institutionalized child's desire to obtain social reinforcement from surrounding adults, not from same-age peers (Harter & Zigler, 1968).

Negative Reaction Tendency

At the same time as children with retardation were likely to play the boring, repetitive game for longer periods of time, their initial approach to a strange examiner was one of wariness. When the examiner divided the game into two, nearly identical parts, children with retardation played much longer on the second part than on the first part (Zigler, 1958). The idea was that, as opposed to the usual interactions with strange adults (e.g., doctors), children with retardation gradually realized that they had nothing to fear from the examiner, who really was there only to play with the child. Having gotten over their initial feelings of distrust and wariness, these children with retardation could then proceed to play the game with the adult examiner (see also Harter & Zigler, 1968, and Shallenberger & Zigler, 1961).

Expectancy of Success

Due to their less efficient cognitive processes, children with retardation fail more often than do nonretarded children. As a result, these children come to feel that they will not succeed when given difficult problems. This tendency was most easily seen when children with retardation were given a three-choice discrimination problem in which one stimulus is partially reinforced and the other two stimuli are never reinforced. In contrast to MA-matched nonretarded children, children with retardation were more likely to settle for the reinforcing stimulus, even though this stimulus never allowed them 100% success (Gruen & Zigler, 1968). This pattern of settling for lower levels of reward is similar to the learned helplessness behaviors examined by Weisz and his colleagues (see Weisz, 1982, 1990, for reviews). In these studies, children with retardation were found to be increasingly passive and "helpless" both over time (older children with retardation were more helpless than younger children) and in response to immediate feedback (e.g., the examiner's provision of negative feedback on performance). For both effectance motivation and learned helplessness, then, a history of failure served to make these children settle for lesser degrees of success and to develop a more passive, helpless style of problem solving.

Outerdirectedness

Besides settling for lower levels of success, persons with retardation also look outside themselves for cues to solve intellectual problems. In contrast, nonretarded children are more likely to rely on their own, internally generated solutions to problems, a tendency that increases in nonretarded children as they get older (MacMillan & Wright, 1974; Yando & Zigler, 1971; Zigler & Yando, 1972). This tendency to look outside for the solution to problems can be seen both in regard to looking to persons and to external cues (lights, other indicators); furthermore, such solutions are used by children with retardation even when cues are presented that are either extraneous or misleading to solving the task at hand (Bybee & Zigler, 1992).

Effectance Motivation

In addition to settling for lesser degrees of success and looking outside themselves for solutions, children with retardation appear to show less interest and pleasure in solving difficult problems. Based on the work of White (1959), nonretarded children and adults appear to have a strong, intrinsic desire to solve problems in their environment. This sense of "mastery motivation" accounts for why people tackle both big (e.g., mountains) and little (crossword puzzles) problems that appear to provide them with

little or no tangible "reward." Compared with nonretarded children, however, children with retardation are more influenced by tangible as opposed to intangible reward (Zigler & deLabry, 1962; Zigler & Unell, 1962). Harter and Zigler (1974) have further divided the effectance motivation concept into the areas of variation seeking, curiosity, mastery for the sake of competence, and preference for challenging tasks. On all these measures, retarded as opposed to nonretarded children were much less likely to choose new or difficult tasks. In contrast to nonretarded children, then, children with mental retardation received less intrinsic reward simply from attempting and solving difficult tasks.

Self-Concept

Self-concept is a construct that plays a central role in personality theory but that has only recently come under examination in work with individuals with retardation. Recently, the concept itself has come to be divided in several ways. As opposed to a single, general "sense of self," children with and without retardation are now thought to have several senses of self, as they conceptualize themselves in terms of their functioning in any number of domains (Harter, 1983). In line with Werner's orthogenetic principle, children come to have a greater number of domains of the self as they develop: Whereas 7- to 10-year-old children see themselves only in terms of scholastic, social, athletic, and physical appearance, and global senses of self (Harter, 1982), adolescents' self-concepts include these domains and the three additional domains of job performance, romantic relationships, and close friendships (Harter, 1988).

A second distinction involves how one sees oneself (the *real* self-image) and how one would ideally like to be, or the *ideal* self-image. The difference between how one is and how one would ideally like to be is called the *self-image disparity*. In accordance with developmental theory, children come to have a greater self-image disparity as they get older (Katz & Zigler, 1967), reflecting their greater capacity for guilt and their greater appreciation for ideals and ideal performance.

Although self-image work with mentally retarded children remains controversial (Zetlin, Heriot, & Turner, 1985), it appears that persons with retardation are affected both by their lower levels of development and by their history of failure experiences. Thus, Silon and Harter (1985) have noted that, in line with their lower developmental levels, persons with retardation have a less differentiated self-image—compared with nonretarded children of the same chronological age (CA-matches), they have fewer discrete domains of the self. In terms of the self-image disparity, Zigler, Balla, and Watson (1972; also Leahy, Balla, & Zigler, 1982) found that children with retardation possess lower ideal self-images than nonretarded CA- and MA-matches. Children with retardation appear to lower their goals and aspirations over time, at least partially due to the greater number of failures that they experience.

These six areas do not exhaust all the possible personality-motivational variables, but are merely those that have received the longest and most sustained research attention. From these variables, however, come several important themes.

The first theme is that motivational and personality variables may differ between individuals with different types of retardation. In a study of outerdirectedness (including measures of imitation), Yando, Seitz, and Zigler (1989) found that children with organic retardation differed widely from children with familial retardation. Compared with children with familial retardation, children with organic retardation imitated a greater percentage of the experimenter's acts that they remembered (i.e., they showed a more imitative style of problem solving). Children with organic mental retardation imitated both the experimenter's relevant and irrelevant acts and did not show the lessening of imitation with greater chronological age shown by nonretarded and familial retarded children.

Functioning on certain personality-motivational variables may also differ due to the specific nature of the child's disability. In an ongoing study, Adler and Zigler (in preparation) examined levels of effectance motivation in two groups of children with cerebral palsy, those with severe degrees of motor impairment and those with milder motor impairments (age and levels of intelligence were equated in the two groups). Children with milder motor impairments showed higher levels of interest and enjoyment in solving some types of motor problems than did children with more severe levels of motor impairment, even as the two groups were identical on verbal problems. These preliminary findings point to the possibility that particular types of impairments (e.g., motor, mental) might differentially influence the child's degree of interest and pleasure in solving problems of different types.

A second extension of personality-motivational work is to more real-world settings. Bybee and Zigler (1992) have recently discovered that the behavior of children with mental retardation can be changed as a result of relatively simple manipulations. Specifically, those children with retardation who received relatively easy tasks of outerdirectedness on initial trials were much less likely to imitate on subsequent, harder tasks; conversely, those children who were initially given difficult tasks continued to imitate and to look to others for help, even when the tasks later became easier (rigidity may also increase on harder tasks, Kreitler, Zigler, & Kreitler, 1990). These findings indicate that personality-motivational variables may be relatively easy to influence. Although the relative modifiability of personality-motivational factors has long been known (Zigler & Seitz, 1982), the findings of Bybee and Zigler provide yet another example of the real-world consequences of such modifiability.

Although so far confined primarily to experimental studies, the importance of personality-motivational factors is becoming more and more recognized in the field of mental retardation. In a study of 19-year-old Swedish young men, for example, K. Granat and S. Granat (1973, 1978) noted that only about half of the persons with below 70 IQs had been identified as being mentally retarded. Others, who were equally impaired intellectually, only became identified after taking an IQ test upon entrance into the army (see Windle, 1962, for similar findings). The features that distinguished the two groups were not intelligence, but instead personality and motivational factors such as getting along with others, not being depressed, being prompt, and staying on task at school or work.

More recent work in the United States has also pointed to the importance of factors apart from intelligence as the major determinants of life success. In a study of individuals with IQs between 70 and 84 (borderline mental retardation) during the year directly following high school, Zetlin and Murtaugh (1990) found that many of these young adults were performing poorly in work and school. They noted that "these former students left school without direction, and during this first year floundered further" (p. 468). Although many of their difficulties could be traced to lack of specific job training and counseling, at least some problems were due to disagreements with bosses or other workers, inability to persist at a job or school over many months, and other, more motivational problems. Moreover, issues with personality-motivational functioning may become more critical over the next few years, as public schools continue to declassify students previously identified as mildly mentally retarded; as MacMillan (1989) notes, these declassified students appear to fall through the cracks in educational and posteducational service systems.

In summarizing work on personality and motivational factors, it appears that we have moved from a state of examining persons with mental retardation as solely cognitive beings to one in which persons with retardation are considered to be "whole persons," with corresponding personality, emotional, and motivational characteristics. Such characteristics can only become more important in future years, as persons with retardation increasingly enter the mainstream of society. In essence, we now need to examine the whole child within the whole environment, to understand how personality and motivational characteristics of persons with retardation help or hinder these individuals as they take their place within society.

LOOKING TO THE FUTURE: REMAINING ISSUES IN THE DEVELOPMENTAL APPROACH TO MENTAL RETARDATION

The previous section provides an overview of work in the seven areas of sequences, structures, rates, transitions, mother-child interactions, families, and personality-motivational functioning in individuals with retardation. In these discussions, several unresolved issues have arisen concerning the best ways to perform research in mental retardation, the importance of etiology, and the use of children with mental retardation to inform us about nonretarded development. Each of these issues seems critical for how future work will be performed.

How Best to Perform Developmentally Based Research in Mental Retardation?

From the mid-1960s on, there have been numerous controversies about how best to perform mental retardation research. One issue is between those who feel that it is best to compare children with retardation to nonretarded children of the same chronological age (i.e., CA-matches) versus those advocating comparisons of children with retardation to nonretarded children of the same mental age (MA-matches). For the most part, this debate has paralleled the controversy between defect theorists and developmentalists, with defect theorists generally using CA-matches in their research and developmentalists employing MA-matches.

The argument in favor of CA-matching is that such matching shows areas of deficit in retarded samples. In studies examining issues such as language, attention, and other intellectual processes, defect theorists have compared children with retardation to nonretarded children of the same chronological age. They have then interpreted the lower performances of their mentally retarded samples as evidence for a defect in the domain of interest.

As implied in our earlier discussions of similar structures, however, simply showing that children with retardation perform at levels lower than those predicted by their chronological ages tells us very little about their intellectual strengths and weaknesses. Only occasionally do children with retardation function at their chronological ages and, by the logic of defect theorists, all performance that is below CA-levels is evidence for defects. Indeed, if only one area of functioning is examined in a particular study (the usual practice), children with mental retardation will be shown to be "defective" in virtually every area. Moreover, some areas of "defect" will, in fact, be domains of relative strength compared with functioning in other areas. As Cicchetti and Pogge-Hesse (1982) summarize the limitations of CA-matching, "*We know that they are retarded; the important and challenging research questions concern the developmental process*" (p. 279; italics in original).

But the strategy of MA-matching also has its critics. In particular, Baumeister (1967; also, Detterman, 1987; Sternberg & Spear, 1985) notes that mental age is a global measure, combining functioning on a host of diverse intellectual tasks. Two children can therefore attain identical mental ages in very different ways, a problem noted (e.g., Zigler, 1969) but rarely addressed in research by developmental researchers. In essence, if two children are matched on MA but each one's particular MA level is attained in vastly different ways, what exactly are the two children being matched on?

Although such criticisms are partially valid, it has rarely been shown, at least for familial retarded children, that these children *are* achieving their mental ages in such different ways compared with MA-matched nonretarded children. When examining individual items on IQ tests, children with familial retardation pass similar items as do MA-matched nonretarded children (Achenbach, 1970, 1971). Similarly, when IQ tests are factor analyzed into factors such as verbal comprehension, perceptual organization, and freedom from distractibility, children with mental retardation again show no consistent relative strengths or weaknesses compared with MA-matched nonretarded children (Groff & Linden, 1982). At least for children with familial retardation, then, there do not appear to be differences from nonretarded children in the ways each group achieves their respective mental ages.

An interest in more specific matching has, however, led to a greater ability to match retarded and nonretarded samples on particular levels of functioning within specific domains. In studies of infant cognition, for example, Wagner, Ganiban, and Cicchetti (1990) advocate matching on habituation and other information-processing measures that do not involve motor behavior (and that may be more correlated with later intelligence; Bornstein & Sigman, 1986). Similarly, language researchers have long compared research groups that are equivalent not on MA but on the two groups' mean length of utterance, or MLU. The idea is that language itself is a multifaceted development, one for which levels of component subdomains might vary in specific etiological groups. Comparing, say, children with autism or Down syndrome with nonretarded children of the same MA obscures that a particular group might be strong or weak in grammar, semantics, pragmatics, or vocabulary. Instead, MLU provides the child's general level of language (particularly in grammar), against which other areas of language can be examined. Using this design, Beeghly et al. (1990) note that children with Down syndrome are relatively high in pragmatic abilities, whereas children with autism show pragmatic deficits relative to their abilities in grammar. Only by employing designs that match on measures that are more specific to the domain of interest can the researcher hope to reveal these more precise findings (Cicchetti & Wagner, 1990).

Such interest in more precise, process-oriented research can even be seen in those creating IQ tests. Compared with earlier psychometric instruments, which paid little attention to underlying cognitive processes, several recent tests are very much process oriented. Probably the best example of such an instrument is the Kaufman Assessment Battery for Children, or K-ABC (Kaufman & Kaufman, 1983). Although the ultimate merits of the K-ABC's approach remains uncertain (Sattler, 1988), this test seems able to distinguish between tasks that utilize sequential, or serial, bit-by-bit processing, as opposed to tasks involving simultaneous processing, or the analysis of items in a holistic, Gestalt-like way. Furthermore, such a distinction between sequential and simultaneous processing has so far been particularly useful in examining functioning in some etiologies of mental retardation (e.g., sequential deficits in fragile X syndrome; Dykens et al., 1987). Especially with process-oriented instruments, then, IQ tests are beginning to go beyond amorphous collections of intellectual tasks to get at issues of underlying process that have always been of interest to developmental psychologists (see Sparrow, Carter, Racusin, & Morris, this work Volume 1, Chapter 4).

It may also be useful to employ both MA- (or more precise measures of level of functioning) and CA-matches in the same study or, in the case of children with different types of retardation, to match on both at once. The suggestion to compare different retarded groups matched on both MA and CA, although repeatedly made over the years, becomes even more important with the finding that in certain etiological groups relative strengths and weaknesses become more pronounced over time. In a study of boys with fragile-X syndrome, Hodapp, Dykens, Ort, Zelinsky, and Leckman (1991) have found that, whereas all boys with fragile X syndrome show relative weaknesses in sequential processing compared with simultaneous processing, this weakness is much more accentuated for older than for younger children. Longitudinal analyses suggest that these children continue to make slow progress in simultaneous processing over time, but may not progress in sequential processing after the middle-childhood years. A weakness that was already apparent at earlier ages therefore becomes increasingly pronounced as the child gets older. Such changes over time in degree of relative strength or weakness can be seen in other etiological groups as well, as in the age-related increase in the relative strength of vocabulary skills compared with mental age in the

Down syndrome population (Miller, 1987). It is becoming apparent that *both* the child's level of functioning (MA or more specific measure) and chronological age need to be considered in developmentally oriented work in mental retardation.

If the child's level of functioning and chronological age are both important in terms of developments in the children themselves, CA may be the more important variable when examining issues involving parents, siblings, and family systems. Stoneman (1989) notes that the best work on families of children with retardation compares families with same-age retarded and nonretarded children. Thus, the family of a 6-year-old Down syndrome child with a mental age of 4 years seems most comparable to the family with a 6-year-old nonretarded child (CA-match), as opposed to the family with a 4-year-old nonretarded child (MA-match). In family work, CA-matching as opposed to MA-matching is preferable because families develop along life courses, and these family life courses may be more related to children's chronological as opposed to mental ages. Families of children with mental retardation are therefore best compared with those families who have nonretarded children of similar chronological ages.

Finally, there is a need for developmental researchers to become more cognizant of the different meanings of time. As mentioned in our discussions of maternal emotional reactions, the point at which a child achieves a particular development (e.g., first words, walking) is one type of time (developmental time), whereas more culturally based points (e.g., first birthday, entrance into school) might constitute another. There may even be senses of time that differ from one family to another, as when a younger, nondisabled child surpasses an older child with retardation (a sort of "family" time). Yet work has scarcely begun on the many senses of time and how each is experienced by children with retardation and their families (e.g., Hodapp, 1988; Hodapp, Dykens, Evans, & Merighi, 1992).

Importance of Etiology and Other Specific Characteristics of Children with Retardation and Their Families

A recurrent theme in all seven areas discussed earlier concerns etiology and other specific characteristics of children with retardation and their families. Whereas earlier work in the developmental approach examined sequences, structures, and other aspects of development to examine whether each occurred the same or differently for children with retardation, current work examines different etiological groups, different types of mother-child interactions, and different family types. In each of these areas, there is a search for specificity, for going beyond an examination of development in all children with retardation grouped together.

Although the search for specificity could be traced to a number of sources, the utilization of the two-group approach seems a good place to start in developmental work. Beginning with a distinction between those persons who show no clear organic cause for their mental retardation (the so-called familial retarded group) versus those who do show organic causes for their retardation (Zigler, 1967, 1969), researchers examining development in children with retardation are increasingly separating

research groups into each individual etiological group (Burack et al., 1988).

In a sense, then, the field has gone beyond Cicchetti and Pogge-Hesse's (1982) "liberal" developmental approach to an approach that is even more specific and that promises more detailed, precise information about any number of organic etiologies. In response to Zigler's (1967, 1969) limitation of the developmental approach to children with familial retardation, Cicchetti and Pogge-Hesse (1982) explicitly called for a developmental approach that included children with organic retardation. Furthermore, through their studies of children with Down syndrome, Cicchetti and Pogge-Hesse implied that examinations should focus on individual etiological groups. The current approach makes explicit this emphasis on different, individual etiological groups; to use Wagner et al.'s (1990) terms, it includes the Uniqueness Hypothesis (whether a particular etiological group differs from other retarded children) as an explicit and important part of the revised developmental formulation. Partly because of this focus on particular etiological groups, information has been accruing rapidly about development in children with Down syndrome (Cicchetti & Beeghly, 1990), fragile X syndrome (Dykens & Leckman, 1990; Dykens et al., 1994), motor impairments and multiple disabilities (Kopp & Recchia, 1990), autism (Cohen & Donellan, 1987; Volkmar, Burack, & Cohen, 1990), and Prader-Willi syndrome (Taylor & Caldwell, 1988), to name just a few. Such a linking of behavioral characteristics to the child's specific etiology of mental retardation also promises to close the gap between the two research "cultures"—the behavioral and the biomedical—in the mental retardation field (Hodapp & Dykens, 1994).

Furthermore, the child's etiology of mental retardation seems important in shedding light on the processes of the child's development *and* on the processes of familial reactions. Within children themselves, the relative strengths or weaknesses in the pragmatics of language by children with Down syndrome versus autism; the different trajectories of IQ shown by children with fragile X syndrome, cerebral palsy, and Down syndrome; and the late development of social uses of language by children with autism show that etiology matters for some developments. Although every individual etiological group will not differ from every other group on all aspects of development, there are many differences based on etiology, enough to justify a search for etiology-specific strategies of intervention for children with different types of mental retardation (Gibson, 1991; Hodapp & Dykens, 1991).

But etiology might also matter for parents and families of children with disabilities. Parents of children with autism appear to suffer from more stress than do parents of children with Down syndrome (Holroyd & MacArthur, 1976), and mothers of children with Down syndrome versus those with cerebral palsy appear to have different types of worries about their respective offspring (Hodapp, Dykens, Evans, & Merighi, 1992). In terms of families, Mink et al. (1983) note that proportionately more families of children with Down syndrome are "cohesive and harmonious," again highlighting the ways in which etiology affects systems outside the children with retardation themselves.

In many ways, though, a focus on the child's specific etiology of mental retardation is but the most obvious example of a general trend in the mental retardation field toward greater specificity. Other instances of this trend are the use of diversity *within* different etiological groups and the use of several tasks in a single study (Wagner et al., 1990). The use of multiple measures when comparing, say, children with Down syndrome versus nonretarded children allows for a better understanding of the true strengths and weaknesses of children with Down syndrome. Differences in fatigue, or motivation, or other factors can be ruled out as possible explanations for group differences, allowing for stronger statements about cognitive or other processing in children with Down syndrome. As Wagner et al. (1990) note, the usual practice—of both MA- and CA-matched studies—examines performance of retarded versus nonretarded children on only one task, allowing only for a "main effect" finding that children with retardation perform the same as, better than, or worse than nonretarded children. A more effective strategy would attempt to examine performance on several tasks at once, such that it is possible to generate findings that retarded groups do less well on Task A, but not on Tasks B, C, and D. Although such "interaction effects" studies remain rare, they will become increasingly necessary to understand the processes of development in many different etiologies of mental retardation.

Children with Mental Retardation as "Experiments of Nature" for Typical Developmental Processes

A basic tenet of developmental psychopathology is the interplay between typical and atypical development (Cicchetti & Cohen, Vol. 1, Chapter 1). Just as developmentalists attempt to examine retarded development through the lens of nonretarded development, so too should the process be reversed, with retarded development shedding light on nonretarded development. As Cicchetti (1984) notes, "We can understand more about the normal functioning of an organism by studying its pathology, more about its pathology by studying its normal condition" (p. 1; see also Cicchetti, 1990). Although this dictum has become almost a truism among developmental psychopathologists, it nevertheless has interesting and important ramifications within the developmental approach to mental retardation.

All uses of pathological populations to tell us about typical development make use of what has been called "the experiment of nature" (Bronfenbrenner, 1979; Hodapp & Burack, 1990). Experiments of nature involve the use of unusual, but naturally occurring, organismic or environmental situations to inform us about normal development. In the field of developmental disability, for example, Hans Furth (1966) examined deaf children who had not acquired sign or spoken language to determine if language was a necessary condition for the performance of Piagetian preoperational and concrete operational tasks. In a similar way, Kopp and Shaperman (1973) examined a child born without limbs who was newly introduced to prosthesis to determine if motor manipulation was a necessary prerequisite of sensorimotor understandings. In both cases, the lack of either language (Furth) or motor manipulation (Kopp and Shaperman) did not hinder children from acquiring concrete operational and sensorimotor abilities, respectively.

The logic of the experiment of nature has also been used in recent studies of mental retardation and other developmental

disabilities. Mental retardation too is a naturally occurring condition that allows us to examine typical developmental processes. Compared with nonretarded children, children with retardation show the extent to which sequences must be followed in a single, invariant order. In addition, these children often display increased discrepancies between levels of functioning in different domains, and they show the effects of different factors on rate of development. Furthermore, children with mental retardation may also ultimately help to elucidate how family systems operate. Let us briefly turn to each of these issues.

Sequences: Which Developments Must Occur in Set Order versus Which Can Show Idiosyncratic Orderings?

Children with mental retardation can tell us much about which developments are more sequential or "channeled" in development and which are more variable, open to changes due to biological disturbance, cultural differences, or simply the child's interests and propensities. Our suggestion, detailed in the section on similar sequences, is that researchers can distinguish between Vygotsky's "natural" and "cultural" lines of development (Wertsch, 1985), or between Horowitz's (1987) Level I and II universals versus nonuniversal developments. Tentatively at least, those developments that appear earlier and that are more "biologically based" seem to be more sequential and more channeled in development, whereas those developments that appear later and that are more social are less hardwired and more open to different sequences (Hodapp, 1990).

Although these suggestions remain speculative, we should note a few recent studies on children with different types of disabilities. The first involves Pettito and Marentette's (1991) finding that congenitally deaf children exposed to sign language perform "hand babbling" at approximately the same ages (around 6 months) as the linguistic babbling shown by hearing infants. Even with no oral language input, there seems a highly channelized propensity to develop language, and babbling—be it with one's hand or vocal systems—seems the naturally occurring precursor.

A second example concerns the autistic child's sequence of developments in "theory of mind" tasks. As described by Baron-Cohen (1991, this work, Volume 1, Chapter 12) and others, children with autism may not show the identical ordering of developments in various theory of mind tasks as do nonretarded children. If true, these and similar findings show the degree to which certain developments must occur in invariant developmental sequences, the degree to which certain other developments need not occur in set sequence, and the residual or side-effects of atypical developmental sequences for any area of functioning. Again, although both the findings and suggestions remain speculative, they do provide a sense of the types of information attainable from work on individuals with various types of retardation and developmental disabilities.

Cross-Domain Relations: Using Consistencies across Different Etiologies

Examining children of different etiologies of mental retardation allows us to determine which developments must go together versus those that often do, but need not, go together in nonretarded development. To date, there are a host of developments in seemingly disparate domains that go together in nonretarded development and in development in children with several different types of retardation. The relationship between levels of symbolic play and early language; the ability to perform means-ends tasks during infancy and to engage in intentional communication; the performance of certain sensorimotor cognitive tasks and laughter and crying: All are connections that were first observed in nonretarded children but that have subsequently been noted in retarded children of diverse etiologies.

In terms of mental retardation, the reasoning is that of the "signal-to-noise" ratio, the idea of an electrical or radio signal coming through against background static or noise (Hodapp & Burack, 1990). Here we see that, despite the great differences between children with Down syndrome and those with autism, or fragile X syndrome, or some other etiology, there remain developmental connections such as those previously mentioned that continue to be demonstrated across a variety of studies. If such developmental connections (the "signals") continue to be apparent in spite of such large amounts of etiology-specific idiosyncrasies (the "noise"), then such connections would appear to be true connections in development, for different types of retarded children *and* for nonretarded children (Hodapp & Burack, 1990).

But as recent work on particular etiologies of mental retardation has shown, there may also be disconnections in development, and the nature and effects of such cross-domain disconnectedness remains unclear. The most exciting work in this area involves Williams syndrome. Although this work is more fully described in the section From Similar Structures to More Intricate Cross-Domain Relationships, research on Williams syndrome serves to demonstrate that language and thought—or at least certain aspects of thought—need not be so closely linked in development (Reilly et al., 1991). The exact nature of the deficit in children with Williams syndrome will receive more attention in the years to come, as will the effects of the Williams syndrome deficits on functioning in other areas. At present it is impossible to know for certain whether development from one domain to another is "organized" or "modularized" (Fodor, 1983), but findings such as those emanating from the Williams syndrome research will surely be involved in this controversy.

Factors Affecting Rates of Development: MA-Walls, CA-Walls and Brain-Behavior Relationships

Although much less examined than either sequences or cross-domain relations, the MA-walls and CA-walls discussed earlier constitute important factors affecting rate of development. More importantly, the ways in which the tasks that constitute MA-walls impede the progress of children with Down syndrome need to be determined, just as the specific neurobiological changes that constitute CA-related slowing in certain etiologies (e.g., fragile X syndrome) need greater explanation. The job here is to join several different levels of analysis, to determine what specific domains of cognition are deficient in a particular etiological group, but then to relate these deficient psychological processes to deficient neurobiological functioning (the "softwiring") or structurization (the "hardwiring"). To date, we have barely traced out which MA- and CA-walls exist in only a few groups; explanations

are almost totally lacking about why such slowings of development might occur.

Still, there are at least some beginning understandings of brain-behavior relations in nonretarded development (Crnic & Pennington, 1987), and these understandings promise to inform and be informed by mental retardation work. For example, Goldman-Rakic (1987) has demonstrated the neural circuitry by which nonhuman primates solve delayed response tasks such as Piaget's "A, not B" problem. Furthermore, development of the ability to solve this problem is related to a growth in the number of synaptic connections throughout the monkey's brain at approximately 4 months. Fischer (1987) has taken Goldman-Rakic's data and hypothesized similar brain growth-behavior relationships during human infancy, particularly to the developmental reorganizations occurring at 2, 8, 13, and 21 months (see studies by Diamond, 1987; Diamond & Goldman-Rakic, 1983). The fact that children with Down syndrome have difficulty in making "qualitative leaps" during infancy may (or may not) relate to the nature of synaptogenesis during the infancy period. Similarly, there should be some connection between the impaired sequential processing of fragile X boys throughout childhood and the (possibly abnormal) structure of their prefrontal cortex, which supposedly controls such behavior (Kaufmann, Leckman, & Ort, 1989; Pennington, O'Connor, & Sudhalter, 1991; Pennington & Walsh, this work, Volume 1, Chapter 9). Again, however, work remains preliminary that connects the child's behavior with changed rates of neurological development or with abnormalities in neurological structure in retarded populations.

Families of Children with Retardation: Viewing "Systems" in a Wider Perspective

Although there have been many studies in recent years on families of children with mental retardation, this work has yet to be used to help inform us about family functioning in families with same-age nonretarded children. Yet it would seem, in theory, that families of children with mental retardation are reacting in ways that might help elucidate many issues within the larger field of family systems theory.

In part, the fact that developmentalists have yet to employ families of children with retardation as an experiment of nature is not surprising. As Minuchin (1985) notes, even the work of Bronfenbrenner (1979) and other family-oriented researchers in developmental psychology has not fully drawn on family systems theory and family therapy. Changes in family structure due to events such as the birth of a baby have only begun to be explicitly joined with changes in subsystems such as the sibling system (e.g., Dunn, 1985) or marital changes (Grossman, Pollack, Golding, & Fedele, 1987), and little work has yet been performed on the changes in mothers, fathers, siblings, or extended family networks at many different ages or stages of development in nonretarded children.

Furthermore, families are only one part of the child's total ecology (Crnic, 1990), families are not all alike one to another (Mink et al., 1983), and outside support or lack of support might differentially affect individual family members (e.g., mothers, families, siblings) and family subsystems (e.g., sibling subsystem, marital relationship; see Meisels & Shonkoff, 1990). These concerns are as true of families with family members who are retarded as they are for families with a nonretarded child.

The task for future years is to show how families of children with retardation react to the child in ways that might elucidate familial reactions in families with same-age nonretarded children. It may be, as Crnic (1990) suggests, that mental retardation is similar to other stressors on a family—if so, models of familial stress and coping such as the Double ABCX model (McCubbin & Patterson, 1983) might operate for families with retarded offspring. Conversely, other, yet-to-be-discovered patterns of reactions might be idiosyncratic to families with retarded family members. In short, the connections have yet to be made between family work in families with retarded and with nonretarded children. Ironically, although family work is arguably the most exciting and—in terms of number of recent studies—among the most productive areas of research in the developmental approach to mental retardation, the use of families of children with mental retardation as an "experiment of nature" has scarcely begun.

TOWARD MORE COMPREHENSIVE DEVELOPMENTAL APPROACHES

After overviewing past, present, and future work, we are not quite certain how to evaluate the developmental approach to mental retardation. On one hand, the developmental approach has been formally in place for over 20 years, and developmentally based work has been implicitly present in mental retardation for the past 50 to 60 years. As a result, issues such as sequences, structures, and personality-motivational development have received quite a bit of study, whereas other issues, such as transitions in development, have continued to interest developmentalists for over a half a century.

But on the other hand, we have not yet even begun to scratch the surface in terms of developmental analyses of mental retardation. We know little about most aspects of development in the large majority of the 300 etiologies of mental retardation, have identified only a small number of cross-domain connections, and possess few studies that examine development in children with retardation during later ages. The areas of mother-child interaction and families, while burgeoning, remain even less detailed, with almost no information at present about any number of issues. Almost totally absent are understandings of the connections of our behavioral findings to brain functioning, or of how family functioning in families with retarded members relates to family systems theory.

Is it any wonder, then, that the wider field of mental retardation research has such a conflicted view of the developmental approach? Thus, leading workers such as Al Baumeister have on different occasions noted the importance of the developmental approach (Baumeister, 1987) and, conversely, decried, "One may, in the final analysis, question whether the developmental theory of mental retardation is really a theory at all" (Baumeister, 1984, p. 25). As with any area of scientific work, developmental workers must themselves explain what they do and why they do it to their coworkers in mental retardation, developmental psychology, developmental psychopathology, clinical psychology, and psychiatry. Only by clearly and consistently explaining the developmental formulation will workers in mental retardation and in related fields be able to evaluate realistically the merits of this approach.

Still, it is heartening to note that there has been so much work examining mentally retarded populations from a developmental approach, particularly as that approach has only begun to be explained in its fuller and more up-to-date form. It is hoped that this chapter's "map of the territory" will further encourage future work, as we attempt to more explicitly examine mental retardation through the lens of normal development (and vice versa). Almost as a by-product, these extensions and elaborations help to flush out the mental retardation portion of the larger field of developmental psychopathology.

REFERENCES

Abel, T. M. (1941). Moral judgments among subnormals. *Journal of Abnormal and Social Psychology, 36,* 378–392.

Abrahamson, A., Cavallo, M., & McCluer, J. (1985). Is the sign language advantage a robust phenomenon? From gesture to language in two modalities. *Merrill-Palmer Quarterly, 31,* 177–209.

Achenbach, T. (1970). Comparison of Stanford-Binet performance of nonretarded and retarded persons matched for MA and sex. *American Journal of Mental Deficiency, 74,* 488–494.

Achenbach, T. (1971). Stanford-Binet short-form performance of retarded and nonretarded persons matched for MA. *American Journal of Mental Deficiency, 76,* 30–32.

Acredolo, L., & Goodwyn, S. (1990). Sign language in babies: The significance of symbolic gesturing for understanding language development. *Annals of Child Development, 7,* 1–42.

Adler, A., & Zigler, E. (in preparation). *The impact of a physical handicap on effectance motivation.*

Baron-Cohen, S. (1991). The development of a theory of mind in autism: Deviance and delay? *Psychiatric Clinics of North America, 14,* 33–51.

Bates, E., Benigni, L., Bretherton, I., Camaioni, I., & Volterra, V. (1979). *The emergence of symbols: Cognition and communication in infancy.* New York: Academic Press.

Bates, E., Camaioni, I., & Volterra, V. (1975). The acquisition of performatives prior to speech. *Merrill-Palmer Quarterly, 21,* 205–226.

Baumeister, A. (1967). Problems in comparative studies of mental retardates and normals. *American Journal of Mental Deficiency, 71,* 869–875.

Baumeister, A. (1984). Some methodological and conceptual issues in the study of cognitive processes with retarded children. In P. Brooks, R. Sperber, & C. McCauley (Eds.), *Learning and cognition in the mentally retarded* (pp. 1–38). Hillsdale, NJ: Erlbaum.

Baumeister, A. (1987). Mental retardation: Some concepts and dilemmas. *American Psychologist, 42,* 796–800.

Baumrind, D. (1967). Child care practices anteceding three patterns of preschool behavior. *Genetic Psychology Monographs, 75,* 43–88.

Bayley, N. (1955). On the growth of intelligence. *American Psychologist, 10,* 805–818.

Beckman, P. (1983). Influence of selected child characteristics on stress in families of handicapped infants. *American Journal of Mental Deficiency, 88,* 150–156.

Beeghly, M., & Cicchetti, D. (1987). An organizational approach to symbolic development in children with Down syndrome. In D. Cicchetti & M. Beeghly (Eds.), *Symbolic development in atypical children. New directions for child development.* No. 36 (pp. 5–29). San Francisco: Jossey-Bass.

Beeghly, M., Weiss-Perry, B., & Cicchetti, D. (1990). Beyond sensorimotor functioning: Early communicative and play development of children with Down syndrome. In D. Cicchetti & M. Beeghly (Eds.), *Children with Down syndrome: A developmental perspective* (pp. 329–368). New York: Cambridge University Press.

Bell, R. Q. (1968). A re-examination of the direction of effects in studies of socialization. *Psychological Review, 75,* 81–95.

Bellugi, U., Marks, S., Bihrle, A. M., & Sabo, H. (1988). Dissociation between language and cognitive functions in Williams syndrome. In D. Bishop & K. Mogford (Eds.), *Language development in exceptional circumstances* (pp. 177–189). London: Churchill Livingstone.

Bidell, T. (1988). Vygotsky, Piaget, and the dialectic of development. *Human Development, 31,* 329–348.

Blacher, J. (1984). Sequential stages of parental adjustment to the birth of a child with handicaps: Fact or artifact? *Mental Retardation, 22,* 55–68.

Bornstein, M., & Sigman, M. (1986). Continuity in mental development from infancy. *Child Development, 57,* 251–274.

Brauth, S. E., Hall, W. S., & Dooling, R. J. (Eds.). (1991). *Plasticity of development.* Cambridge, MA: MIT Press.

Bristol, M., Gallagher, J., & Shopler, E. (1988). Mothers and fathers of young developmentally disabled and nondisabled boys: Adaptation and spousal support. *Developmental Psychology, 24,* 441–451.

Bristol, M., & Shopler, E. (1984). A developmental model of stress and coping in families of autistic children. In J. Blacher (Ed.), *Families of severely handicapped children* (pp. 91–134). New York: Academic Press.

Bromwich, R. (1980). *Working with parents of infants.* Baltimore: University Park Press.

Bromwich, R. (1990). The interaction approach to early intervention. *Infant Mental Health Journal, 11,* 66–79.

Bronfenbrenner, U. (1979). *The ecology of human development.* Cambridge, MA: Harvard University Press.

Bronfenbrenner, U., Kessel, F., Kessen, W., & White, S. (1986). Toward a critical social history of developmental psychology: A propaedeutic discussion. *American Psychologist, 41,* 1218–1230.

Brown, A., & Ferrara, R. (1985). Diagnosing zones of proximal development. In J. V. Wertsch (Ed.), *Culture, communication, and cognition: Vygotskian perspectives* (pp. 273–305). New York: Cambridge University Press.

Bruner, J. (1982). The organization of action and the nature of adult-infant transaction. In E. Z. Tronick (Ed.), *Social interchange in infancy* (pp. 23–35). Baltimore: University Park Press.

Bruner, J. (1985). Vygotsky: A historical and conceptual perspective. In J. V. Wertsch (Ed.), *Culture, communication, and cognition: Vygotskian perspectives* (pp. 21–34). New York: Cambridge University Press.

Bruner, J., & Bornstein, M. (1989). On interaction. In M. Bornstein & J. Bruner (Eds.), *Interaction and human development* (pp. 1–14). Hillsdale, NJ: Erlbaum.

Buck-Morss, S. (1975). Socio-economic bias in Piaget's theory and its implications for cross-culture studies. *Human Development, 18,* 35–49.

Budoff, M. (1974). *Learning potential and educability among the educable mentally retarded.* Cambridge, MA: Research Institute for Educational Problems.

Burack, J. A. (1990). Differentiating mental retardation: The two-group approach and beyond. In R. M. Hodapp, J. A. Burack, & E. Zigler (Eds.), *Issues in the developmental approach to mental retardation* (pp. 27–48). New York: Cambridge University Press.

Burack, J. A., Hodapp, R. M., & Zigler, E. (1988). Issues in the classification of mental retardation: Differentiating among organic etiologies. *Journal of Child Psychology and Psychiatry, 29,* 765–779.

Bybee, J., & Zigler, E. (1992). Is outerdirectedness employed in a harmful or beneficial manner by students with and without mental retardation? *American Journal on Mental Retardation, 96,* 512–521.

Byrne, E., & Cunningham, C. (1985). The effects of mentally handicapped children on families: A conceptual review. *Journal of Child Psychology and Psychiatry, 26,* 847–864.

Campione, J. C., Brown, A. L., & Ferrara, R. A. (1982). Mental retardation and intelligence. In R. Sternberg (Ed.), *Handbook of human intelligence* (pp. 392–490). New York: Cambridge University Press.

Cardoso-Martins, C., & Mervis, C. (1985). Maternal speech to prelinguistic children with Down syndrome. *American Journal of Mental Deficiency, 89,* 451–458.

Carr, J. (1990). Down syndrome. In J. Hogg, J. Sebba, & L. Lambe (Eds.), *Profound retardation and multiple impairment: Vol. 3. Medical and physical care and management* (pp. 40–53). London: Chapman & Hall.

Cascione, R. (1982). The developmental-difference controversy in verbal mediation of behavior. In E. Zigler & D. Balla (Eds.), *Mental retardation: The developmental-difference controversy* (pp. 99–120). Hillsdale, NJ: Erlbaum.

Chomsky, N. (1975). *Reflections on language.* New York: Pantheon.

Cicchetti, D. (1984). The emergence of developmental psychopathology. *Child Development, 55,* 1–7.

Cicchetti, D. (1990). An historical perspective on the discipline of developmental psychopathology. In J. Rolf, A. Masten, D. Cicchetti, K. Neuchterlein, & S. Weintraub (Eds.), *Risk and protective factors in the development of psychopathology* (pp. 2–28). New York: Cambridge University Press.

Cicchetti, D., & Beeghly, M. (Eds.). (1990). *Children with Down syndrome: A developmental perspective.* New York: Cambridge University Press.

Cicchetti, D., & Ganiban, J. (1990). The organization and coherence of developmental processes in infants and children with Down syndrome. In R. M. Hodapp, J. A. Burack, & E. Zigler (Eds.), *Issues in the developmental approach to mental retardation* (pp. 169–225). New York: Cambridge University Press.

Cicchetti, D., & Mans-Wagener, L. (1987). Sequences, stages, and structures in the organization of cognitive development in infants with Down syndrome. In I. Uzgiris & J. McV. Hunt (Eds.), *Infant performance and experience: New findings with the Ordinal Scales* (pp. 281–310). Urbana: University of Illinois Press.

Cicchetti, D., & Pogge-Hesse, P. (1982). Possible contributions of the study of organically retarded persons to developmental theory. In E. Zigler & D. Balla (Eds.), *Mental retardation: The developmental-difference controversy* (pp. 277–318). Hillsdale, NJ: Erlbaum.

Cicchetti, D., & Schneider-Rosen, K. (1986). An organizational approach to childhood depression. In M. Rutter, C. Izard, & P. Read (Eds.), *Depression in young people: Clinical and developmental perspectives* (pp. 71–134). New York: Guilford.

Cicchetti, D., & Sroufe, L. A. (1976). The relationship between affective and cognitive development in Down syndrome infants. *Child Development, 47,* 920–929.

Cicchetti, D., & Sroufe, L. A. (1978). An organizational view of affect: Illustration from the study of Down's syndrome infants. In M. Lewis & L. Rosenblum (Eds.), *The development of affect* (pp. 309–350). New York: Plenum.

Cicchetti, D., & Wagner, S. (1990). Alternative assessment strategies for the evaluation of infants and toddlers: An organizational perspective. In S. Meisels & J. Shonkoff (Eds.), *Handbook of early childhood intervention* (pp. 246–277). New York: Cambridge University Press.

Cohen, D., & Donellan, A. (Eds.). (1987). *Handbook of autism and pervasive developmental disorders.* New York: Wiley.

Cornwell, A., & Birch, H. (1969). Psychological and social development in home-reared children with Down's syndrome (mongolism). *American Journal of Mental Deficiency, 74,* 341–350.

Crawley, S., & Spiker, D. (1983). Mother-child interactions involving two-year-olds with Down syndrome: A look at individual differences. *Child Development, 54,* 1312–1323.

Crnic, K. (1990). Families of children with Down syndrome: Ecological contexts and characteristics. In D. Cicchetti & M. Beeghly (Eds.), *Children with Down syndrome: A developmental perspective* (pp. 399–423). New York: Cambridge University Press.

Crnic, K., Friedrich, W., & Greenberg, M. (1983). Adaptation of families with mentally retarded children: A model of stress, coping, and family ecology. *American Journal of Mental Deficiency, 88,* 125–138.

Crnic, L., & Pennington, B. (1987). Developmental psychology and the neurosciences: An introduction. *Child Development, 58,* 533–538.

Cronbach, L. (1957). The two disciplines of scientific psychology. *American Psychologist, 12,* 671–684.

Cronbach, L. (1975). Beyond the two disciplines of scientific psychology. *American Psychologist, 30,* 116–127.

Curcio, F. (1978). Sensorimotor functioning and communication in mute autistic children. *Journal of Autism and Childhood Schizophrenia, 12,* 264–287.

Curcio, F., & Paccia, J. (1987). Conversations with autistic children: Contingent relationships between features of adult input and children's response adequacy. *Journal of Autism and Developmental Disorders, 17,* 81–93.

Curtiss, S. (1989). The independence and task-specificity of language. In M. Bornstein & J. Bruner (Ed.), *Interaction in human development* (pp. 105–137). Hillsdale, NJ: Erlbaum.

Dameron, L. (1963). The development of intelligence in infants with mongolism. *Child Development, 34,* 733–738.

Dasen, P. (1972). Cross-cultural Piagetian research: A summary. *Journal of Cross-Cultural Psychology, 3,* 23–29.

Detterman, D. (1987). Theoretical notions of intelligence and mental retardation. *American Journal of Mental Deficiency, 92,* 2–11.

DeVries, R. (1974). Relationships among Piagetian, IQ, and achievement assessments. *Child Development, 45,* 746–756.

Diamond, A. (1987). Development of the ability to use recall to guide action, as indicated by infants' performance on AB. *Child Development, 56,* 868–883.

Diamond, A., & Goldman-Rakic, P. (1983). Comparison of performance on a Piagetian object permanence task in human infants and rhesus monkeys: Evidence for involvement of prefrontal cortex. *Society of Neuroscience Abstracts, 9,* 274.

Dicks-Mireaux, M. (1972). Mental development of infants with Down's syndrome. *American Journal of Mental Deficiency, 77,* 26–32.

Domrosch, S., & Perry, L. (1989). Self-reported adjustment, chronic sorrow, and coping of parents of children with Down syndrome. *Nursing Research, 38,* 25–30.

Dunn, J. (1985). *Sisters and brothers.* Cambridge, MA: Harvard University Press.

Dunst, C. J. (1980). *A clinical and educational manual for use with the Uzgiris-Hunt Scales for infant development.* Baltimore: University Park Press.

Dunst, C. J. (1988). Stage transitioning in the sensorimotor development of Down's syndrome infants. *Journal of Mental Deficiency Research, 32,* 405–410.

Dunst, C. J. (1990). Sensorimotor development of infants with Down syndrome. In D. Cicchetti & M. Beeghly (Eds.), *Children with Down syndrome: A developmental perspective* (pp. 180–230). New York: Cambridge University Press.

Dykens, E. M., Hodapp, R. M., & Evans, D. W. (1994). Profiles and development of adaptive behavior in children with Down syndrome. *American Journal on Mental Retardation, 98,* 580–587.

Dykens, E. M., Hodapp, R. M., & Leckman, J. F. (1987). Strengths and weaknesses in the intellectual functioning of males with fragile X syndrome. *American Journal of Mental Deficiency, 92,* 234–236.

Dykens, E. M., Hodapp, R. M., & Leckman, J. F. (1994). *Development and psychopathology in fragile X syndrome. Sage Series on Developmental Clinical Psychology and Psychiatry* (Alan E. Kazdin, Ed.). Newbury Park, CA: Sage.

Dykens, E. M., Hodapp, R. M., Ort, S., Finucane, B., Shapiro, L., & Leckman, J. (1989). The trajectory of cognitive development in males with fragile X syndrome. *Journal of the American Academy of Child and Adolescent Psychiatry, 28,* 422–428.

Dykens, E. M., Hodapp, R. M., Ort, S. I., & Leckman, J. F. (1993). Trajectory of adaptive behavior in males with fragile X syndrome. *Journal of Autism and Developmental Disorders, 23,* 135–145.

Dykens, E. M., & Leckman, J. F. (1990). Developmental issues in fragile X syndrome. In R. M. Hodapp, J. A. Burack, & E. Zigler (Eds.), *Issues in the developmental approach to mental retardation* (pp. 226–245). New York: Cambridge University Press.

Emde, R., & Brown, C. (1978). Adaptation to the birth of a Down's syndrome infant: Grieving and maternal attachment. *Journal of the American Academy of Child Psychiatry, 17,* 299–323.

Farber, B. (1959). Effects of a severely mentally retarded child on family integration. *Monographs of the Society for Research in Child Development, 24* (Whole No. 71).

Farber, B. (1960). Family organization and crisis: Maintenance of integration in families with a severely retarded child. *Monographs of the Society for Research in Child Development, 25,* 1–95.

Feurstein, R., Rand, Y., Hoffman, M., Hoffman, M., & Miller, R. (1979). Cognitive modifiability in retarded adolescents: Effects of instrumental enrichment. *American Journal of Mental Deficiency, 83,* 539–550.

Fischer, K. (1987). Relations between brain and cognitive development. *Child Development, 58,* 623–632.

Flavell, J. (1972). An analysis of cognitive-developmental sequences. *Genetic Psychology Monographs, 86,* 279–350.

Flavell, J. (1982). Structures, stages, and sequences of cognitive development. In W. A. Collins (Ed.), *The concept of development: The Minnesota symposia on child psychology* (Vol. 15, pp. 1–27). Hillsdale, NJ: Erlbaum.

Fodor, J. A. (1983). *The modularity of mind.* Cambridge, MA: MIT Press.

Fowler, A. (1988). Determinants of rate of language growth in children with Down syndrome. In L. Nadel (Ed.), *The psychobiology of Down syndrome* (pp. 217–245). Cambridge, MA: MIT Press.

Fowler, A. (1990). The development of language structure in children with Down syndrome. In D. Cicchetti & M. Beeghly (Eds.), *Children with Down syndrome: A developmental perspective* (pp. 302–328). New York: Cambridge University Press.

Frey, K., Greenberg, M., & Fewell, R. (1989). Stress and coping among parents of handicapped children: A multi-dimensional approach. *American Journal on Mental Retardation, 94,* 240–249.

Furth, H. (1966). *Thinking without language.* New York: Free Press.

Gamble, T., & Zigler, E. (1986). Effects of infant day care: Another look at the evidence. *American Journal of Orthopsychiatry, 56,* 26–42.

Gardner, H. (1983). *Frames of mind: The theory of multiple intelligences.* New York: Basic Books.

Gath, A. (1978). *Down's syndrome and the family: The early years.* New York: Academic Press.

Gibson, D. (1966). Early developmental staging as a prophesy index in Down's syndrome. *American Journal of Mental Deficiency, 70,* 825–828.

Gibson, D. (1978). *Down's syndrome: The psychology of mongolism.* London: Cambridge University Press.

Gibson, D. (1991). Down syndrome and cognitive enhancement: Not like the others. In K. Marfo (Ed.), *Early intervention in transition: Current perspectives on programs for handicapped children* (pp. 61–90). New York: Praeger.

Ginsburg, H., & Opper, S. (1979). *Piaget's theory of intellectual development* (2nd ed.). Englewood Cliffs, NJ: Prentice-Hall.

Goldberg, S. (1977). Social competence in infancy: A model of parent-infant interaction. *Merrill-Palmer Quarterly, 23,* 263–277.

Goldberg, S., Marcovitch, S., MacGregor, D., & Lojkasek, M. (1986). Family responses to developmentally delayed preschoolers: Etiology and the father's role. *American Journal on Mental Retardation, 90,* 610–617.

Goldman-Rakic, P. (1987). Development of cortical circuitry and cognitive function. *Child Development, 58,* 601–622.

Goldstein, K. (1939). *The organism.* New York: American Book.

Goldstein, K. (1942–1943). Concerning rigidity. *Character and Personality, 11,* 209–226.

Granat, K., & Granat, S. (1973). Below-average intelligence and mental retardation. *American Journal of Mental Deficiency, 78,* 27–32.

Granat, K., & Granat, S. (1978). Adjustment of intellectually below-average men not identified as mentally retarded. *Scandinavian Journal of Psychology, 19,* 41–51.

Green, C., & Zigler, E. (1962). Social deprivation and the performance of retarded and normal children on a satiation type task. *Child Development, 33,* 499–508.

Griffin, P., & Cole, M. (1984). Current activity for the future: The Zo-ped. In B. Rogoff & J. Wertsch (Eds.), *Children's learning in the "Zone of Proximal Development": New directions for child development* No. 23, pp. 45–64. San Francisco: Jossey-Bass.

Groff, M., & Linden, K. (1982). The WISC-R factor score profiles of cultural-familial mentally retarded and nonretarded youth. *American Journal of Mental Deficiency, 87,* 147–152.

Grossman, F. (1972). *Brothers and sisters of retarded children.* Syracuse, NY: Syracuse University Press.

Grossman, F. K., Pollack, W., Golding, E., & Fedele, N. (1987). Autonomy and affiliation in the transition to parenthood. *Family Relations, 36,* 263–269.

Grossman, H. (1983). *Classification in mental retardation.* Washington, DC: American Association on Mental Deficiency.

Gruen, G., & Zigler, E. (1968). Expectancy of success and the probability learning of middle-class, lower-class, and retarded children. *Journal of Abnormal Psychology, 73,* 343–352.

Hagamen, M. (1980). Family adaptation to the diagnosis of mental retardation in a child and strategies of intervention. In L. Szymanski & P. Tanguay (Eds.), *Emotional disorders of mentally retarded persons* (pp. 149–171). Baltimore: University Park Press.

Hagerman, R., Schreiner, R., Kemper, M., Wittenberger, M., Zahn, B., & Habicht, K. (1989). Longitudinal IQ changes in fragile X syndrome males. *American Journal of Medical Genetics, 33,* 513–518.

Harter, S. (1982). The perceived competence scale for children. *Child Development, 53,* 87–97.

Harter, S. (1983). Developmental perspectives on the self system. In E. M. Hetherington (Ed.), *Handbook of child psychology: Vol. 4. Socialization, personality, and social development* (pp. 275–386). New York: Wiley.

Harter, S. (1988). *Self perception profile for adolescents.* Denver: University of Denver Press.

Harter, S., & Zigler, E. (1968). The effectiveness of adult and peer reinforcement on the performance of institutionalized and noninstitutionalized retardates. *Journal of Abnormal Psychology, 73,* 144–149.

Harter, S., & Zigler, E. (1974). The assessment of effectance motivation in normal and retarded children. *Developmental Psychology, 10,* 169–180.

Haywood, H. C. (1987). The mental age deficit: Explanation and treatment. *Upsala Journal of Medical Sciences,* Supp. 44, 191–203.

Hill, P., & McCune-Nicholich, L. (1981). Pretend play and patterns of cognition in Down's syndrome infants. *Child Development, 23,* 43–60.

Hill, R. (1949). *Families under stress.* New York: Harper & Row.

Hodapp, R. M. (1988). The role of maternal emotions and perceptions in interactions with young handicapped children. In K. Marfo (Ed.), *Parent-child interaction and developmental disabilities: Theory, research, and intervention* (pp. 32–46). New York: Praeger.

Hodapp, R. M. (1990). One road or many? Issues in the similar sequence hypothesis. In R. M. Hodapp, J. A. Burack, & E. Zigler (Eds.), *Issues in the developmental approach to mental retardation* (pp. 49–70). New York: Cambridge University Press.

Hodapp, R. M., & Burack, J. A. (1990). What mental retardation tells us about typical development: The examples of sequences, rates, and cross-domain relations. *Development and Psychopathology, 2,* 213–226.

Hodapp, R. M., Burack, J. A., & Zigler, E. (Eds.). (1990). *Issues in the developmental approach to mental retardation.* New York: Cambridge University Press.

Hodapp, R. M., & Dykens, E. M. (1991). Toward an etiology-specific strategy of early intervention with handicapped children. In K. Marfo (Ed.), *Early intervention in transition: Current perspectives on programs for handicapped children* (pp. 41–60). New York: Praeger.

Hodapp, R. M., & Dykens, E. M. (1994). Mental retardation's two cultures of behavioral research. *American Journal on Mental Retardation, 98,* 675–687.

Hodapp, R. M., Dykens, E. M., Evans, D. W., & Merighi, J. R. (1992). Maternal reactions to young children with different types of handicaps. *Journal of Developmental and Behavioral Pediatrics, 13,* 118–123.

Hodapp, R. M., Dykens, E., Hagerman, R., Schreiner, R., Lachiewicz, A., & Leckman, J. (1990). Developmental implications of changing trajectories of IQ in males with fragile X syndrome. *Journal of the American Academy of Child and Adolescent Psychiatry, 29,* 214–219.

Hodapp, R. M., Dykens, E., Ort, S., Zelinsky, D., & Leckman, J. (1991). Changing profiles of intellectual strengths and weaknesses in males with fragile X syndrome. *Journal of Autism and Developmental Disorders, 21,* 503–516.

Hodapp, R. M., & Goldfield, E. C. (1985). Self- and other regulation during the infancy period. *Developmental Review, 5,* 274–288.

Hodapp, R. M., Leckman, J. F., Dykens, E. M., Sparrow, S., Zelinsky, D., & Ort, S. (1992). K-ABC profiles in children with fragile X syndrome, Down syndrome, and nonspecific mental retardation. *American Journal on Mental Retardation, 97,* 39–46.

Hodapp, R. M., & Zigler, E. (1990). Applying the developmental perspective to individuals with Down syndrome. In D. Cicchetti & M. Beeghly (Eds.), *Children with Down syndrome: A developmental perspective* (pp. 1–28). New York: Cambridge University Press.

Holroyd, J., & MacArthur, D. (1976). Mental retardation and stress on parents: A contrast between Down's syndrome and childhood autism. *American Journal of Mental Deficiency, 80,* 431–436.

Horowitz, F. (1987). *Exploring developmental theories: Toward a structural/behavioral model of development.* Hillsdale, NJ: Erlbaum.

Humphreys, L. (1979). The construct of general intelligence. *Intelligence, 3,* 105–120.

Inhelder, B. (1968). *The diagnosis of reasoning in the mentally retarded.* New York: John Day. (Originally published in 1943)

Johnson, J. S., & Newport, E. (1989). Critical period effects in second language learning: The influence of maturational state on the acquisition of English as a second language. *Cognitive Psychology, 21,* 60–99.

Jones, O. (1977). Mother-child communication with prelinguistic Down's syndrome and normal infants. In H. R. Schaffer (Ed.), *Studies in mother-infant interaction* (pp. 379–401). New York: Academic Press.

Jones, O. (1980). Prelinguistic communication skills in Down's syndrome and normal infants. In T. Field, S. Goldberg, D. Stern, & A. Sostek (Eds.), *High-risk infants and children: Adult and peer interactions* (pp. 205–225). New York: Academic Press.

Katz, P., & Zigler, E. (1967). Self-image disparity: A developmental approach. *Journal of Personality and Social Psychology, 5,* 186–195.

Kaufman, A., & Kaufman, N. (1983). *Kaufman Assessment Battery for Children.* Circle Pines, MN: American Guidance Service.

Kaufmann, P., Leckman, J. F., & Ort, S. I. (1989). Delayed response performance in males with fragile X syndrome. *Journal of Clinical and Experimental Neuropsychology, 12,* 69.

Kaye, K. (1982). *The mental and social life of babies.* Chicago: University of Chicago Press.

Kazak, A., & Marvin, R. (1984). Differences, difficulties, and adaptation: Stress and social networks in families with a handicapped child. *Family Relations, 33,* 67–77.

Kemper, M., Hagerman, R., & Altshul-Stark, D. (1988). Cognitive profiles of males with fragile X syndrome. *American Journal of Medical Genetics, 30,* 191–200.

Kessen, W. (1962). Stage and structure in the study of young children. In W. Kessen & C. Kuhlman (Eds.), *Thought in the young child. Monographs of the Society for Research in Child Development, 27,* 53–70.

Kessen, W. (1984). The end of the age of development. In R. Sternberg (Ed.), *Mechanisms of cognitive development* (pp. 1–17). New York: Freeman.

Kohlberg, L. (1969). Stage and sequence: The cognitive-developmental approach to socialization. In D. Goslin (Ed.), *Handbook of socialization theory and research* (pp. 347–480). Chicago: Rand McNally.

Kopp, C. (1983). Risk factors in development. In P. Mussen (Ed.), *Handbook of child psychology: Vol. 2. Infancy and developmental psychobiology* (pp. 1081–1188). New York: Wiley.

Kopp, C., & Recchia, S. (1990). The issue of multiple pathways in the development of handicapped children. In R. M. Hodapp, J. A. Burack, & E. Zigler (Eds.), *Issues in the developmental approach to mental retardation* (pp. 272–293). New York: Cambridge University Press.

Kopp, C., & Shaperman, J. (1973). Cognitive development in the absence of object manipulation during infancy [brief report]. *Developmental Psychology, 9,* 3.

Kopp, C., Sigman, M., & Parmelee, A. (1974). Longitudinal study of sensorimotor development. *Developmental Psychology, 10,* 687–695.

Kounin, J. (1941a). Experimental studies of rigidity: I. The measurement of rigidity in normal and feebleminded persons. *Character and Personality, 9,* 251–272.

Kounin, J. (1941b). Experimental studies of rigidity: II. The explanatory power of the concept of rigidity as applied to retarded persons. *Character and Personality, 9,* 273–282.

Kounin, J. (1948). The meaning of rigidity: A reply to Heinz Werner. *Psychological Review, 55,* 157–166.

Krauss, M. W., Simeonsson, R., & Ramey, S. L. (Eds.). (1989). Special issue on research on families. *American Journal on Mental Retardation, 94* (whole No. 3).

Kreitler, S., Zigler, E., & Kreitler, H. (1990). Rigidity in mentally retarded and nonretarded children. *American Journal on Mental Retardation, 94,* 550–562.

Kuhn, D. (1976). Relation of two Piagetian stage transitions to IQ. *Developmental Psychology, 12,* 157–161.

Kuhn, T. (1962). *The structure of scientific revolutions.* Chicago: University of Chicago Press.

Lachiewicz, A., Gullion, C., Spiridigliozzi, G., & Aylsworth, A. (1987). Declining IQs of males with fragile X syndrome. *American Journal of Mental Retardation, 92,* 272–278.

Lane, H. (1976). *The wild boy of Aveyron.* Cambridge, MA: Harvard University Press.

Leahy, R., Balla, D., & Zigler, E. (1982). Role taking, self-image, and imitation in retarded and nonretarded individuals. *American Journal of Mental Deficiency, 86,* 372–379.

Leifer, J., & Lewis, M. (1984). Acquisition of conversational response skills by young Down syndrome and nonretarded children. *American Journal of Mental Deficiency, 88,* 610–618.

Lenneberg, E. (1967). *Biological foundations of language.* New York: Wiley.

Lewin, K. (1936). *A dynamic theory of personality.* New York: McGraw-Hill.

Lewis, E. O. (1933). Types of mental deficiency and their social significance. *Journal of Mental Science, 79,* 298–304.

Lobato, D. (1983). Siblings of handicapped children: A review. *Journal of Autism and Developmental Disorders, 13,* 347–364.

Lovell, K., Healey, D., & Rowland, A. (1962). Growth of some geometric concepts. *Child Development, 33,* 751–767.

Luria, A. (1961). *The role of speech in the regulation of normal and abnormal behavior.* New York: Pergamon.

MacMillan, D. (1989). Equality, excellence, and the EMR population: 1970–1989. *Psychology in Mental Retardation and Developmental Disabilities, 15,* 1–10.

MacMillan, D., & Keough, B. (1971). Normal and retarded children's expectancy for failure. *Developmental Psychology, 4,* 343–348.

MacMillan, D., & Wright, D. (1974). Outerdirectedness in children of three ages as a function of experimentally induced success and failure. *Journal of Educational Psychology, 68,* 919–925.

Mahaney, E., & Stephens, B. (1974). Two-year gains in moral judgement by retarded and nonretarded persons. *American Journal of Mental Deficiency, 79,* 134–141.

Mahoney, G. (1988). Enhancing the developmental competence of handicapped infants. In K. Marfo (Ed.), *Parent-child interactions and developmental disabilities: Theory, research, and intervention* (pp. 203–219). New York: Praeger.

Marfo, K. (1984). Interactions between mothers and their mentally retarded children: Integration of research findings. *Journal of Applied Developmental Psychology, 5,* 45–69.

Marfo, K. (Ed.) (1988). *Parent-child interactions and developmental disabilities: Theory, research, and intervention.* New York: Praeger.

Mayberry, R. I., & Eichen, E. B. (1991). The long-lasting advantage of learning sign language in childhood: Another look at the critical period for language acquisition. *Journal of Memory and Language, 30,* 486–512.

McCall, R. B. (1982). Nature-nurture and the two realms of development: A proposed integration with respect to mental development. *Child Development, 52,* 1–12.

McCall, R. B., Eichorn, D., & Hogarty, P. (1977). Transitions in early mental development. *Monographs of the Society for Research in Child Development, 42.*

McCubbin, H., & Patterson, J. (1983). Family transitions: Adaptation to stress. In H. McCubbin & C. Figley (Eds.), *Stress and the family: Vol. 1. Coping with normative transitions.* New York: Brunner/Mazel.

McCune-Nicholich, L., & Bruskin, C. (1982). Combinatorial competency in symbolic play and language. In D. Pepler & K. Rubin (Eds.), *The play of children* (pp. 30–45). New York: Karger.

McHale, S., Simeonsson, R., & Sloan, J. (1984). Children with handicapped brothers and sisters. In E. Shopler & G. Mesibov (Eds.), *The effects of autism on the family* (pp. 327–342). New York: Plenum.

Meisels, S., & Shonkoff, J. (Eds.). (1990). *Handbook of early intervention.* New York: Cambridge University Press.

Melyn, M., & White, D. (1973). Mental and developmental milestones of noninstitutionalized Down's syndrome children. *Pediatrics, 52,* 542–545.

Mervis, C. (1990). Early conceptual development of children with Down syndrome. In D. Cicchetti & M. Beeghly (Eds.), *Children with Down syndrome: A developmental perspective* (pp. 252–301). New York: Cambridge University Press.

Milgram, N. (1969). The rationale and irrational in Zigler's motivational approach to mental retardation. *American Journal of Mental Deficiency, 73,* 527–532.

Milgram, N. (1973). Cognition and language in mental retardation: Distinctions and implications. In D. K. Routh (Ed.), *The experimental study of mental retardation* (pp. 157–230). Chicago: Aldine.

Miller, J. F. (1987). Language and communication characteristics of children with Down syndrome. In S. M. Pueschel, C. Tingey,

J. Rynders, A. Crocker, & D. Crutcher (Eds.), *New perspectives on Down syndrome* (pp. 233–262). Baltimore: Brookes.

Miller, J. G. (1984). Culture and the development of everyday social cognition. *Journal of Personality and Social Psychology, 46,* 961–978.

Miller, J. G. (1986). Early cross-cultural commonalities in social explanation. *Developmental Psychology, 22,* 514–520.

Minde, K. (1978). Coping styles of 34 adolescents with cerebral palsy. *American Journal of Psychiatry, 135,* 1344–1349.

Minnes, P. M. (1989). Family stress associated with a developmentally handicapped child. *International Review of Research in Mental Retardation, 15,* 195–226.

Mink, I., Meyers, C., & Nihira, K. (1984). Taxonomy of family life styles: II. Homes with slow-learning children. *American Journal of Mental Deficiency, 89,* 111–123.

Mink, I., Nihira, K., & Meyers, C. (1983). Taxonomy of family life styles: I. Homes with TMR children. *American Journal of Mental Deficiency, 87,* 484–497.

Minuchin, P. (1985). Families and individual development: Provocations from the field of family therapy. *Child Development, 56,* 289–302.

Morgan, S. (1979). Development and distribution of intellectual and adaptive skills in Down syndrome children: Implications for early intervention. *Mental Retardation, 17,* 247–249.

Morss, R. J. (1987). Cognitive development in the Down's syndrome infant: Slow or different? *British Journal of Educational Psychology, 53,* 40–47.

Mundy, P., & Kasari, C. (1990). The similar structure hypothesis and differential rate of development in mental retardation. In R. M. Hodapp, J. A. Burack, & E. Zigler (Eds.), *Issues in the developmental approach to mental retardation* (pp. 71–92). New York: Cambridge University Press.

Mundy, P., Seibert, J., & Hogan, A. (1984). Relationship between sensorimotor and early communication abilities in developmentally delayed children. *Merrill-Palmer Quarterly, 30,* 33–48.

Mundy, P., Sigman, M., Ungerer, J., & Sherman, T. (1987). Nonverbal communication and play correlates of language development in autistic children. *Journal of Autism and Developmental Disorders, 17,* 349–364.

Murray, A. D., Johnson, J., & Peters, J. (1990). Fine-tuning of utterance length of preverbal infants: Effects on later language development. *Journal of Child Language, 17,* 511–525.

Olshansky, S. (1962, April). Chronic sorrow: A response to having a mentally defective child. *Social Casework,* pp. 190–193.

Overton, W., & Reese, H. (1973). Models of development: Methodological implications. In J. Nesselroade & H. Reese (Eds.), *Life span developmental psychology* (pp. 65–86). New York: Academic Press.

Pennington, B., O'Connor, R., & Sudhalter, V. (1991). Toward a neuropsychology of fragile X syndrome. In R. Hagerman & A. Silverman (Eds.), *Fragile X syndrome: Diagnosis, treatment, research* (pp. 173–201). Baltimore: Johns Hopkins Press.

Petitto, L. A., & Marentette, P. F. (1991). Babbling in the manual mode: Evidence for the ontogeny of language. *Science, 235,* 1493–1496.

Phillips, J. (1973). Syntax and vocabulary of mothers' speech to young children: Age and sex comparisons. *Child Development, 44,* 182–185.

Piaget, J. (1953). *The origins of intelligence in the child.* London: Routledge & Kegan Paul.

Piaget, J. (1955). *The construction of reality in the child.* London: Routledge & Kegan Paul.

Piaget, J. (1966). Need and significance of cross-cultural studies in genetic psychology. *International Journal of Psychology, 1*, 3–13.

Piaget, J. (1972). Intellectual evolution from adolescence to adulthood. *Human Development, 15*, 1–12.

Piaget, J., & Inhelder, B. (1947). Diagnosis of mental operations and theory of intelligence. *American Journal of Mental Deficiency, 51*, 401–406.

Price-Bonham, S., & Addison, S. (1978). Families and mentally retarded children: Emphasis on the father. *The Family Coordinator, 27*, 221–230.

Prizant, B., & Wetherby, A. (1987). Communicative intent: A framework for understanding social-communicative behavior in autism. *Journal of the American Academy of Child and Adolescent Psychiatry, 26*, 472–479.

Pueschel, S., Gallagher, P., Zartler, A., & Pezzullo, J. (1987). Cognitive and learning processes in children with Down syndrome. *Research in Developmental Disabilities, 8*, 21–37.

Ramey, S. L., Krauss, M. W., & Simeonsson, R. (1989). Research on families: Current assessment and future opportunities. *American Journal on Mental Retardation, 94*, ii–vi.

Reed, R., Pueschel, S., Schnell, R., & Cronk, C. (1980). Interrelationships of biological, environmental, and competency variables in young children with Down syndrome. *Applied Research in Mental Retardation, 1*, 161–174.

Reese, H., & Overton, W. (1970). Models of development and theories of development. In L. R. Goulet & P. Baltes (Eds.), *Life-span developmental psychology: Research and theory* (pp. 113–145). New York: Academic Press.

Reilly, M., Bellugi, U., & Klima, E. (1991). Once more with feeling: Affect and language in atypical populations. *Development and Psychopathology, 2*, 367–391.

Rondal, J. (1977). Maternal speech in normal and Down's syndrome children. In P. Mittler (Ed.), *Research to practice in mental retardation: Vol. 2. Education and training.* Baltimore: University Park Press.

Sameroff, A., & Chandler, M. (1975). Reproductive risk and the continuum of caretaking casualty. In F. D. Horowitz, M. Hetherington, S. Scarr-Salapatek, & G. Siegel (Eds.), *Review of child development research* (Vol. 4, 187–244). Chicago: University of Chicago.

Sattler, J. (1988). *Assessment of children* (3rd ed.). San Diego, CA: Sattler.

Scarr-Salapatek, S. (1975). An evolutionary perspective on infant intelligence: Species patterns and individual variations. In M. Lewis (Ed.), *Origins of intelligence* (pp. 165–197). New York: Plenum.

Scheerenberger, R. C. (1983). *A history of mental retardation.* Baltimore: Brookes.

Shallenberger, P., & Zigler, E. (1961). Negative reaction tendencies and cosatiation effects in normal and feebleminded children. *Journal of Abnormal and Social Psychology, 63*, 20–26.

Silon, E., & Harter, S. (1985). Assessment of perceived competence, motivational orientation, and anxiety in segregated and mainstreamed educable mentally retarded children. *Journal of Educational Psychology, 77*, 217–230.

Snow, K. (1972). Mothers' speech to children learning language. *Child Development, 43*, 549–565.

Solnit, A., & Stark, M. (1961). Mourning and the birth of a defective child. *Psychoanalytic Study of the Child, 16*, 523–537.

Sternberg, R., & Spear, J. (1985). A triarchic theory of mental retardation. *International Review of Research in Mental Retardation, 13*, 301–326.

Stoneman, Z. (1989). Comparison groups in research on families with mentally retarded members: A methodological and conceptual review. *American Journal on Mental Retardation, 94*, 195–215.

Strauss, A., & Lehtinen, L. (1947). *Psychopathology and education of the brain-injured child.* New York: Grune & Stratton.

Suelzle, M., & Keenan, V. (1981). Changes in family support networks over the life cycle of mentally retarded persons. *American Journal of Mental Deficiency, 86*, 267–274.

Taylor, R., & Caldwell, M. (Eds.). (1988). *Prader-Willi syndrome: Selected research and management issues.* New York: Springer-Verlag.

Trevarthen, C. (1979). Communication and cooperation in early infancy. In M. Bullowa (Ed.), *Before speech.* Cambridge: Cambridge University Press.

Tronick, E., & Field, T. (Eds.). (1986). *Maternal depression and infant disturbance: New directions for child development.* No. 34. San Francisco: Jossey-Bass.

Uzgiris, I. (1987). The study of sequential order in cognitive development. In I. Uzgiris & J. McV. Hunt (Eds.), *Infant performance and experience: New findings with the Ordinal Scales* (pp. 131–167). Urbana: University of Illinois Press.

Uzgiris, I., & Hunt, J. McV. (1975). *Assessment in infancy: Ordinal scales of psychological development.* Urbana: University of Illinois Press.

van der Meer, R., & van Ijzendoorn, M. (1985). Vygotsky's theory of higher psychological processes: Some criticisms. *Human Development, 28*, 1–9.

Volkmar, F., Burack, J. A., & Cohen, D. (1990). Deviance and developmental approaches in the study of autism. In R. M. Hodapp, J. A. Burack, & E. Zigler (Eds.), *Issues in the developmental approach to mental retardation* (pp. 246–271). New York: Cambridge University Press.

Vygotsky, L. S. (1962). *Thought and language.* Cambridge, MA: MIT Press.

Vygotsky, L. S. (1978). *Mind in society.* Cambridge, MA: MIT Press.

Wagner, S., Ganiban, J., & Cicchetti, D. (1990). Attention, memory, and perception in infants with Down syndrome: A review and commentary. In D. Cicchetti & M. Beeghly (Eds.), *Children with Down syndrome: A developmental perspective* (pp. 147–179). New York: Cambridge University Press.

Waisbren, S. (1980). Parents' reaction after the birth of a developmentally disabled child. *American Journal of Mental Deficiency, 84*, 345–351.

Weiss, B., Weisz, J., & Bromfield, R. (1986). Performance of retarded and nonretarded persons on information-processing tasks: Further tests of the similar-structure hypothesis. *Psychological Bulletin, 100*, 157–175.

Weisz, J. (1982). Learned helplessness and the retarded child. In E. Zigler & D. Balla (Eds.), *Mental retardation: The developmental-difference controversy* (pp. 27–40). Hillsdale, NJ: Erlbaum.

Weisz, J. (1990). Cultural-familial mental retardation: A developmental perspective on cognitive performance and "helpless" behavior. In R. M. Hodapp, J. A. Burack, & E. Zigler (Eds.), *Issues in the developmental approach to mental retardation* (pp. 137–168). New York: Cambridge University Press.

Weisz, J., & Yeates, K. (1981). Cognitive development in retarded and nonretarded persons: Piagetian tests of the similar structure hypothesis. *Psychological Bulletin, 90*, 153–178.

Weisz, J., Yeates, K., & Zigler, E. (1982). Piagetian evidence and the developmental-difference controversy. In E. Zigler & D. Balla

(Eds.), *Mental retardation: The developmental-difference controversy* (pp. 213–276). Hillsdale, NJ: Erlbaum.

Weisz, J., & Zigler, E. (1979). Cognitive development in retarded and nonretarded persons: Piagetian tests of the similar sequence hypothesis. *Psychological Bulletin, 86*, 831–851.

Werner, H. (1937). Process and achievement: A basic problem of education and developmental psychology. *Harvard Educational Review, 7*, 353–368.

Werner, H. (1941). Psychological approaches investigating deficiencies in learning. *American Journal of Mental Deficiency, 46*, 233–235.

Werner, H. (1946). The concept of rigidity—A critical evaluation. *Psychological Review, 53*, 43–52.

Werner, H. (1948). *Comparative psychology of mental development* (rev. ed.). New York: Follett.

Werner, H. (1957). The concept of development from a comparative and organismic point of view. In D. Harris (Ed.), *The concept of development* (pp. 125–148). Minneapolis: University of Minnesota Press.

Werner, H., & Kaplan, B. (1963). *Symbol formation.* New York: Wiley.

Werner, H., & Strauss, A. (1939). Problems and methods of functional analysis in mentally deficient children. *Journal of Abnormal & Social Psychology, 34*, 37–62.

Wertsch, J. (1979). From social interaction to higher psychological processes: A clarification and application to Vygotsky's theory. *Human Development, 22*, 1–22.

Wertsch, J. (1985). *Vygotsky and the social formation of mind.* Cambridge, MA: Harvard University Press.

Wertsch, J., & Lee, B. (1984). The multiple levels of analysis in a theory of action. *Human Development, 27*, 193–196.

Wertsch, J., & Rogoff, B. (Eds.). (1984). *Children's learning in the "Zone of Proximal Development": New directions for child development.* No. 23. San Francisco: Jossey-Bass.

Wertsch, J., & Youniss, J. (1987). Contextualizing the investigator: The case of developmental psychology. *Human Development, 30*, 18–31.

Wetherby, A. M. (1986). Ontogeny of communicative functions in autism. *Journal of Autism and Developmental Disorders, 16*, 295–316.

White, R. (1959). Motivation reconsidered: The concept of competence. *Psychological Review, 66*, 297–333.

Wikler, L. (1986). Periodic stresses of families of older mentally retarded children: An exploratory study. *American Journal of Mental Deficiency, 90*, 703–706.

Wikler, L., Wasow, M., & Hatfield, E. (1981). Chronic sorrow revisited: Parent versus professional depiction of the adjustment of parents of mentally retarded children. *American Journal of Orthopsychiatry, 51*, 63–70.

Wilson, J., Blacher, J., & Baker, B. (1989). Siblings of children with severe handicaps. *Mental Retardation, 27*, 167–173.

Windle, C. (1962). Prognosis for mental subnormals. *American Journal of Mental Deficiency, 66* (Monograph supplement to No. 5).

Wishart, J. G., & Duffy, L. (1990). Instability of performance on cognitive tests in infants and young children with Down's syndrome. *British Journal of Education Psychology, 60*, 10–22.

Witkin, H. (1964). Heinz Werner: 1890–1964. *Child Development, 30*, 307–328.

Wohlheuter, M. J., & Sindberg, R. (1975). Longitudinal development of object permanence in mentally retarded children: An exploratory study. *American Journal of Mental Deficiency, 79*, 513–518.

Woodward, M. (1959). The behavior of idiots interpreted by Piaget's theory of sensorimotor development. *British Journal of Educational Psychology, 29*, 60–71.

Woodward, M. (1961). Concepts of number of the mentally subnormal studied by Piaget's method. *Journal of Child Psychology and Psychiatry, 2*, 249–259.

Woodward, M. (1962). Concepts of space and time in the mentally subnormal studied by Piaget's method. *British Journal of Social and Clinical Psychology, 1*, 25–37.

Woodward, M. (1963). The application of Piaget's theory to research in mental deficiency. In N. Ellis (Ed.), *Handbook of mental deficiency* (pp. 297–324). New York: McGraw-Hill.

Woodward, M. (1979). Piaget's theory and the study of mental retardation. In N. Ellis (Ed.), *Handbook of mental deficiency: Psychological theory and research* (2nd ed.) (pp. 169–195). Hillsdale, NJ: Erlbaum.

Yando, R., Seitz, V., & Zigler, E. (1989). Imitation, recall, and imitativeness in children with low intelligence of organic and familial etiology. *Research in Developmental Disabilities, 10*, 383–397.

Yando, R., & Zigler, E. (1971). Outerdirectedness in the problem-solving of institutionalized and noninstitutionalized normal and retarded children. *Developmental Psychology, 5*, 290–299.

Youniss, J. (1978). Dialectical theory and Piaget on social knowledge. *Human Development, 21*, 234–247.

Youniss, J. (1984). Discussion: Single mind and social mind. *Human Development, 27*, 133–135.

Zeaman, D. (1968). Review of N. Ellis, *International review of research in mental retardation (Vol. 1). Contemporary Psychology, 13*, 142–143.

Zetlin, A., Heriot, M. J., & Turner, J. L. (1985). Self-concept measurement in mentally retarded adults: A micro-analysis of response styles. *Applied Research in Mental Retardation, 6*, 113–125.

Zetlin, A., & Murtaugh, M. (1990). Whatever happened to those with borderline IQs? *American Journal on Mental Retardation, 94*, 463–469.

Zigler, E. (1958). *The effect of preinstitutional social deprivation on the performance of feebleminded children.* Unpublished doctoral dissertation, University of Texas.

Zigler, E. (1961). Social deprivation and rigidity in the performance of feebleminded children. *Journal of Abnormal and Social Psychology, 62*, 413–421.

Zigler, E. (1967). Familial mental retardation: A continuing dilemma. *Science, 155*, 292–298.

Zigler, E. (1969). Developmental versus difference theories of mental retardation and the problem of motivation. *American Journal of Mental Deficiency, 73*, 536–556.

Zigler, E. (1971). The retarded child as a whole person. In H. E. Adams, & W. K. Boardman (Eds.), *Advances in experimental clinical psychology* (pp. 47–121). Oxford, England: Pergamon.

Zigler, E. (1972). Rigidity in the retarded: A reexamination. In E. Trapp & P. Himelstein (Eds.), *Readings on the exceptional child: Research and theory* (2nd ed.) (pp. 123–160). Englewood Cliffs, NJ: Prentice-Hall.

Zigler, E. (1984). A developmental theory on mental retardation. In B. Blatt & R. Morris (Eds.), *Perspectives in special education: Personal orientations* (Vol. 1, pp. 173–209). Santa Monica, CA: Scott, Foresman.

Zigler, E., & Balla, D. (1971). Luria's verbal deficiency theory of mental retardation and performance on sameness, symmetry, and opposition tasks: A critique. *American Journal of Mental Deficiency, 75,* 400–413.

Zigler, E., & Balla, D. (Eds.). (1982). *Mental retardation: The developmental-difference controversy.* Hillsdale, NJ: Erlbaum.

Zigler, E., & Balla, D. (1982). Rigidity—A resilient concept. In E. Zigler & D. Balla (Eds.), *Mental retardation: The developmental-difference controversy* (pp. 61–82). Hillsdale, NJ: Erlbaum.

Zigler, E., Balla, D., & Butterfield, E. (1968). A longitudinal investigation of the relationship between preinstitutional social deprivation and social motivation in institutionalized retardates. *Journal of Personality and Social Psychology, 10,* 437–445.

Zigler, E., Balla, D., & Watson, N. (1972). Developmental and experiential determinants of self-image disparity in institutionalized and noninstitutionalized retarded and normal children. *Journal of Personality and Social Psychology, 23,* 81–87.

Zigler, E., & Burack, J. (1989). Personality development and the dually diagnosed person. *Research in Developmental Disabilities, 10,* 225–240.

Zigler, E., & deLabry, J. (1962). Concept switching in middle-class, lower-class, and retarded children. *Journal of Abnormal and Social Psychology, 65,* 267–273.

Zigler, E., & Hodapp, R. M. (1986). *Understanding mental retardation.* New York: Cambridge University Press.

Zigler, E., Hodgden, L., & Stevenson, H. (1958). The effect of support on the performance of normal and feebleminded children. *Journal of Personality, 26,* 106–122.

Zigler, E., Lamb, M., & Child, I. (1982). *Socialization and personality development* (2nd ed.). New York: Oxford University Press.

Zigler, E., & Seitz, V. (1982). Social policy and intelligence. In R. Sternberg (Ed.), *Handbook of human intelligence* (pp. 586–641). New York: Cambridge University Press.

Zigler, E., & Unell, E. (1962). Concept switching in normal and feebleminded children as a function of reinforcement. *American Journal of Mental Deficiency, 66,* 651–657.

Zigler, E., & Yando, R. (1972). Outerdirectedness and imitative behavior of institutionalized and noninstitutionalized younger and older children. *Child Development, 43,* 413–425.

CHAPTER 10

The Development of Eating Regulation across the Life Span

ILANA ATTIE and JEANNE BROOKS-GUNN

Despite accumulated evidence supporting a multidimensional model of eating problems and disorders, current research lacks a developmental framework for integrating findings from sociocultural, biogenetic, personality, family, and behavioral studies. Developmental psychopathology offers a conceptual paradigm for examining how eating problems and eating disorders arise within these domains, and the complex associations among them (Attie, Brooks-Gunn, & Petersen, 1990). A developmental perspective on the study of psychopathology takes into account the continuities and discontinuities between normal growth and psychopathology, age-related changes in modes of adaptation and symptom expression, reorganizations that occur around salient developmental transitions, internal and external sources of competence and vulnerability, and the effects of development on pathology and of pathology on development (Carlson & Garber, 1986; Cicchetti, 1984; Cicchetti & Schneider-Rosen, 1986; Rutter, 1986). Integral to this approach is the use of cross-sectional and longitudinal research designs aimed at delineating patterns of continuity and change as these become manifest across the life span.

If psychopathology is defined as developmental deviation (A. Sroufe, 1989), what can be considered deviant in the realm of eating behavior? For the purposes of this chapter, we consider eating pathology as those abnormal patterns of eating that reflect a disruption of developmental processes and are associated with maladaptive biological, cognitive, psychosocial, and emotional outcomes. Although eating disorders have long been considered disorders of adolescence, relatively little research has assumed a developmental orientation. In part, this is because of the paucity of theoretical models that would facilitate an integrative understanding of individual and familywide sources of vulnerability, biological predispositions, and the roles of cultural ideals and social contexts as mediators of risk.

This chapter focuses on the two major eating disorders, anorexia nervosa and bulimia nervosa, from a developmental perspective. Feeding disorders associated with failure to thrive in infancy will be considered insofar as they shed light on possible dimensions underlying food refusal. Findings from studies of obesity are included to the extent that they inform us about the genetics of weight regulation, the cultural context for eating disorders, and the effects of dieting on individuals at different weight levels. Contrary to earlier views, current research suggests that obese individuals show no greater psychopathology than nonobese individuals (Brownell & Wadden, 1992). However, they may be at increased risk for psychological disturbance resulting from social and economic discrimination as well as cycles of unsuccessful dieting and associated binge eating (Garner & Wooley, 1991; Marcus, Smith, Santelli, & Kaye, 1992). Weight is highly heritable, rendering it difficult for many to avoid high weights or to maintain low weights (Stunkard et al., 1986). In fact, many characteristics that have been attributed to obesity are now understood as correlates of frequent dieting and associated overeating (Heatherton & Polivy, 1992).

The study of eating disorders has only recently incorporated research strategies that emphasize continuities and discontinuities over time, and that address distinctions between normality and pathology. We have organized this chapter around eight themes reflecting the interplay of risk, continuity, and change in the development and expression of eating problems and disorders. First, historical continuity is examined with respect to recent studies that document cases of female self-starvation from the Middle Ages to the present. The meaning of food restriction and its association with female adolescent development across historical periods offers a context within which to understand contemporary eating-related psychopathology. The second theme concerns similarities and differences among different eating disorders and eating disorder subtypes. Changes in syndrome definition over the past 15 years provide a window on what are considered the core features of anorexia nervosa and bulimia nervosa. The third theme focuses on the epidemiology of eating disorders, by reviewing available prevalence rates in terms of age, gender, social class, and ethnicity. The fourth section considers the co-occurrence of eating disorders with other psychiatric conditions and the ways in which comorbidity may shed light on risk factors and their interaction. The fifth section focuses on phase-specific issues of adolescence and their relevance to the intensification of eating disorders at this time. Taking an organizational approach, we examine the onset of eating disorders in relation to adolescent challenges and transitions. We also look at the roles of nonfamilial and familial contexts in augmenting or diminishing the risk for developing an eating disorder during adolescence. The sixth section highlights continuities and discontinuities across age periods through a discussion of early onset eating problems and their possible links with adolescent and adult onset disorders. The seventh section adopts a transactional perspective, illustrating the interaction between biogenetic risk and environmental response. We then consider continuity between eating problems (dieting, binge eating) and eating disorders, as well as the complexity of developmental links between early adaptation and later disorder. In our discussion of future directions, we speculate about the ways in which eating problems may shed light on normal development and pose questions for further research.

FASTING FROM THE MIDDLE AGES TO THE PRESENT: HISTORICAL CONTINUITY AND DISCONTINUITY

The rising prevalence of eating disorders in Westernized cultures, together with the intensification of weight concerns among women in certain classes, has highlighted the potential role of sociocultural factors in the emergence of eating disorders (Pate, Pumariega, Hester, & Garner, 1992). In her analysis, the historian Joan Brumberg (1988) attempts to understand why women and girls in certain social and historical contexts become susceptible to exaggerated behavior centering on food. She locates the origins of eating disorders in the complex interplay of cultural forces, gender and family influences, the psychological and biological orientation of the individual, and the response of medical and/or the religious establishments of the day.

Brumberg and Striegel-Moore (1993) propose a two-stage model for the emergence of eating disorders in different historical eras. The first stage, "recruitment," considers how the cultural milieu shapes prevailing symptom constellations, which become expressions of predominant cultural preoccupations. The second stage, "career," explains why some individuals and not others are vulnerable, by virtue of their own biology and psychology, to the development of an eating disorder.

Refusal of food in women can be traced back to the Middle Ages, when saintly women fasted to gain recognition in God's eye. The 13th-century "miraculous maids" were regarded with reverence because of their ability to fast for long periods, seeming to survive on little more than "the juice of a roasted raisin" (Brumberg, 1985). The presence of self-starvation among religious women in medieval culture and among anorectic women of modern times raises an essential question about the nature of continuity in female fasting behavior: Does historical continuity in symptomatic expression (fasting, covert eating, asceticism) imply continuity in the diagnostic entity that is known as anorexia nervosa? According to Brumberg (1988), "In the earlier era, control of appetite was linked to piety and belief; through fasting, the medieval ascetic strove for perfection in the eyes of her God. In the modern period, female control of appetite is embedded in patterns of class, gender, and family relations established in the 19th century; the modern anorectic strives for perfection in terms of society's ideal of physical, rather than spiritual, beauty" (p. 46).

Habermas (1989) distinguishes the fasting of historical figures from the starvation seen in 20th-century anorectics on

several counts: (a) restraint of food intake was only one of several ascetic experiences, including sleeping on stone, scalding, and self-flagellation, that women undertook to heighten spirituality; (b) fasting was interpreted by those who wrote about it as a religious experience; and (c) unlike the contemporary anorectic's denial of emaciation and overactivity, the food refusal of postmedieval women had more direct symbolic meaning (hysterical conversion) and was associated with inactivity. Habermas (1989) concludes that anorexia nervosa existed historically without its predominant aspect—"the morbid dread of fatness despite a state of emaciation" (p. 261). Although Brumberg (1988) would agree that the saintly woman's "anorexia mirabilis" (miraculously inspired loss of appetite) and contemporary anorexia nervosa are not equivalent, her interpretation of historical material suggests that the modern syndrome of anorexia nervosa existed before the emergence of the preoccupation with thinness and dieting in Western cultures.

Anorexia nervosa was first identified in the 1870s by William Gull and Charles Lasegue in England and France. These physicians described the refusal to eat, extreme weight loss, amenorrhea, constipation, and low pulse rate. The anorectic patient's emaciation was distinguished from several of the wasting diseases (e.g., tuberculosis) that dominated 19th-century medicine by its etiology and selectivity: It was a mental (nervous) condition that afflicted adolescent daughters, not sons, in middle- to upper-middle-class families (Brumberg & Striegel-Moore, 1993). Although anorexia nervosa was relatively rare, it was not unusual for late 19th-century adolescent girls to develop peculiarities of eating and appetite. Chlorosis, a form of anemia characterized by various somatic symptoms and scanty appetite, was so common that it was considered by some medical authorities to be a nearly normative aspect of female adolescent development (Brumberg, 1988).

Physicians of the day linked the refusal of food to the struggles of adolescent daughters growing up in middle-class families (Brumberg, 1988). As a result of social and economic changes related to industrialization, secularization, and class stratification, Western European families in the late 19th century became smaller, more child-centered, and increasingly organized around an ideology of love and nurturance. Food, femininity, and marriageability were intertwined for privileged adolescent girls. Adolescent and adult women were admired for their fragility and suffering, which came to symbolize femininity, spirituality, and high social breeding. Displays of appetite could be interpreted as an exhibition of unchecked sensuality, whereas dietary restraint connoted self-control and moral superiority. It was the task of middle-class mothers to help their daughters develop appropriate social and moral aspirations. Indeed, physicians linked the onset of anorexia nervosa to several "events" related to the transition to adulthood: inappropriate romantic choices, blocked educational or social opportunities, and conflicts with parents. By the turn of the 20th century, slimness came to symbolize asexuality and gentility, both of which implied social distance from the working classes.

According to Brumberg and Striegel-Moore (1993), certain features of anorexia have remained salient throughout history, including the meaning of food and eating for female identity, the role of family and social class factors in etiology, and the use of weight regulation as a metaphor for self-regulation and self-control as the adolescent faces multiple developmental challenges. Three aspects of eating disorders are more recent developments— the chronic refusal of food, the emphasis on overactivity, and the emergence of bulimic symptoms of bingeing and purging. These changes make anorexia nervosa a more dangerous disease; the anorectic is thinner today than ever before. Bulimia requires certain features of contemporary Western culture, including personal freedom, an emphasis on instant gratification, the availability of food at any time, a desocialized eating environment, lack of supervision, and the cultural ideal of diet and exercise for weight loss. Although binge eating has been documented since the second century, its connection with weight-related concerns did not emerge until after World War II, when food became plentiful (Casper, 1983). As a syndrome, bulimia nervosa appears to have developed in the context of anorexia nervosa and is new in the 20th century (Habermas, 1989).

SIMILARITIES AND DIFFERENCES AMONG DIFFERENT EATING DISORDERS

Diagnostic Criteria

Andersen (1990) reviewed the core diagnostic criteria for the two major eating disorders, drawing on Russell's research diagnostic criteria. The diagnosis of anorexia nervosa requires (a) the behavior of self-induced starvation; (b) the psychopathological fear of becoming fat, even though underweight; and (c) a biological abnormality in reproductive functioning, which in females is manifest in primary or secondary amenorrhea (Morgan & Russell, 1975). Bulimia nervosa requires (a) a history of recurrent binges (ingestion of large amounts of food, eaten rapidly against one's initial resistance); (b) a fear of becoming fat; and (c) attempts to compensate for the unwanted calories whether by self-induced vomiting, strenuous exercising, subsequent fasting, or abuse of laxatives, diuretics, or other medications.

The diagnostic criteria for anorexia nervosa and bulimia nervosa have been revised with each edition of the *Diagnostic and Statistical Manual of Mental Disorders* (Wilson & Walsh, 1991). In *DSM-III-R,* the weight loss requirement for anorexia nervosa was reduced from 25 percent (in *DSM-III*), to 15 percent (American Psychiatric Association, 1987). The *DSM-IV* (American Psychiatric Association, 1994) has incorporated further diagnostic refinements: (a) different expressions of body image disturbance, including a distortion of the experience and significance of body shape and weight, or a denial of the seriousness of current low weight; and (b) subtyping anorexia nervosa into those who restrict food intake (Restricting Type) and those who regularly engage in bulimic episodes (Binge-Eating/Purging Type).

Bulimia nervosa was officially recognized in the third edition of the *Diagnostic and Statistical Manual of Mental Disorders* (American Psychological Association, 1980). With *DSM-III-R,* the criteria became more restrictive, specifying that there be an attitudinal disturbance ("persistent overconcern with shape or weight") as well as a severity criterion, i.e., the frequency of binge episodes must be an average of two a week for three months. The *DSM-IV* includes additional changes: (a) the term "binge" is

operationally defined as "eating, in a discrete period of time (e.g., within any 2-hour period), an amount of food that is definitely larger than most people would eat during a similar period of time and under similar circumstances," accompanied by a sense of lack of control; and (b) bulimia nervosa is subtyped according to the presence or absence of purging methods as a means to compensate for binge eating (Purging and Nonpurging Types). In current practice, the diagnosis of bulimia nervosa should not be given if it occurs only during episodes of anorexia nervosa.

Subthreshold eating disorders (*DSM-IV* Eating Disorder Not Otherwise Specified, EDNOS) apply to individuals with eating disturbances who fulfill some but not all of the diagnostic criteria for anorexia nervosa or bulimia nervosa.

Finally, several research groups are investigating the validity of an additional eating disorder characterized by recurrent binge eating in the absence of compensatory behaviors used to avoid weight gain. The so-called binge eating disorder (BED) has been found to be strongly associated with a lifetime history of obesity and weight cycling, impairment in work and social functioning, overconcern with body shape and weight, a history of depression or substance abuse, and previous treatment for emotional problems (Spitzer et al., 1993).[1]

Restricter and Bulimic Subgroups

A great deal of research has been devoted to distinguishing between groups of anorexia nervosa patients on the basis of whether they consistently restrict food intake ("restricters"), or whether they also binge and purge ("bulimics"). Bulimic anorectics have been found to differ from restricting anorectics on a number of personality and family dimensions. Compared with restricters, anorectics who binge and purge tend to experience greater affective instability, more impulsivity, and a higher likelihood of substance abuse (Wilson & Walsh, 1991). Paralleling personality differences, a dichotomy of family interaction patterns has also been suggested: Families of restricters exhibit more rigidity and enmeshment, whereas bulimic families show more hostility, incohesion, and lack of nurturance. Some authors fail to find support for a bulimic-restricter dichotomy along personality (Steiger, Liquornik, Chapman, & Hussain, 1991) or family dimensions (Wonderlich & Swift, 1990b). One explanation for the inconsistent findings is the age of subjects studied; Steiger suggests that restricter-bulimic differences may be prominent at early stages of the disorder but may be eliminated by the secondary effects of a chronic eating disorder on personality and family functioning.

Clinton and Glant (1992) propose that there may be an underlying sequential course of illness in anorexia and bulimia reflecting a common core of psychopathology centered around a pathological fear of weight gain and a tendency to define self-worth in terms of body shape and weight. Among 86 consecutive referrals to an adult clinic in Sweden, they found six times as many cases of bulimia nervosa compared with anorexia nervosa, diagnosed according to DSM-III-R criteria. This figure contrasts

---

[1] Fairburn, Welch, and Hay (1993) question the usefulness of the binge eating disorder diagnosis, arguing that too little is known about the disorder, and premature subclassification of the EDNOS category could enhance diagnostic confusion.

with studies of younger adolescents, in which anorexia nervosa is diagnosed more frequently than other eating disorders (Rastam, Gillberg, & Garton, 1989). In more than half the bulimia nervosa cases, anorexia nervosa preceded bulimia, lending support to the notion of a sequential course of illness.

Subtyping of eating disorders has significant implications for outcome (Herzog, Sacks et al., 1993). Herzog and his colleagues have conducted a prospective, naturalistic study of 225 women with anorexia nervosa, bulimia nervosa, and mixed anorexia and bulimia nervosa. Results of follow-up at one year revealed that the anorectic group, primarily young adult women who had been ill for several years, had the lowest recovery rate of all three groups. The full recovery rate for anorexia nervosa was 10%; for mixed anorexia and bulimia, 18%; and for bulimia nervosa, 56%. Of the eating disorder characteristics studied (including intake diagnosis, age of onset, episode duration, and percentage of ideal body weight), percentage of ideal body weight was found to have the strongest predictive value across the three groups. Partial recovery was more characteristic of the anorectic subjects; nearly half of the anorectic and mixed subjects dropped below full DSM-III-R criteria for at least 8 consecutive weeks during the first year follow-up. Whether the bulimia nervosa subjects who recovered will remain symptom-free must await further follow-up, given the high probability of relapse among bulimia nervosa patients (Keller, Herzog, Lavori, Bradburn, & Mahoney, 1992).

Studies of bulimic symptomatology have investigated the relative significance of binge eating as compared with purging behaviors, in terms of associated dysfunction. Some studies of patients with bulimia nervosa suggest that binge eating is the prime determinant of associated psychopathology, whereas others suggest that purging is the critical factor, with laxative abuse being the most pathognomonic form of purging (Tobin, Johnson, Steinberg, Staats, & Dennis, 1991). Tobin, Johnson, and Dennis (1992) found that the majority of bulimia nervosa patients (80%) relied on two or more purging behaviors. The number of purging strategies was a better predictor of personality disturbance, depression, and body dissatisfaction than was any single purging behavior. Along parallel lines, D. M. Garner, M. V. Garner, and Rosen (1993) provide support for subtyping anorexia nervosa according to the presence or absence of purging behaviors rather than binge eating, especially in view of the difficulties associated with defining criteria for binge size and frequency among patients with anorexia nervosa.

Physiological Factors

Dysregulation of eating behavior involves the complex interaction of biological, sensory, affective, cognitive, and social processes that override the normal physiological regulatory pressures of hunger and satiety (Polivy & Herman, 1987). Consequently, the eating disorders are not, at their core, disruptions of appetite, although appetitive adaptations may occur as a result of changed eating patterns (Lowe, 1993).[2] There is little evidence, for example, that individuals who develop anorexia nervosa do not experience hunger. During the early stages, the anorectic may feel intensely hungry but will tolerate food deprivation in response to psychological imperatives (Polivy & Herman, 1987).[3] For some restrained eaters who have dieted repeatedly but cannot effectively suppress their weight, dieting failures render them vulnerable to disinhibition of self-control (i.e., binge eating) in response to a variety of triggering factors (Lowe, 1993). At the same time, individuals with bulimia nervosa typically report difficulty knowing when they are full at the end of a meal, suggesting an impairment of satiety (Walsh, Kissileff, & Hadigan, 1989).

Recent research suggests that specific psychobiological markers of anorexia nervosa and bulimia nervosa may promote an understanding of the underlying pathology or diathesis. Kaplan and Woodside (1987) have reviewed the neurophysiological aspects of anorexia nervosa and bulimia, which include disturbances in the hypothalamic-pituitary axes regulating gonadal, adrenal, and thyroid functions; the disruption of neurotransmitter synthesis and release; alterations in endogenous opioid activity; changes in carbohydrate metabolism; and hyper- or hyposecretion of gastrointestinal hormones. The weight of available evidence does not implicate primary pathophysiology; most biological changes are considered secondary to weight loss or binge/purge cycles. However, these neuroendocrine and metabolic changes play an important role in the perpetuation of eating disorders, because of their effects on appetite, mood, perception, and energy regulation. For example, abnormalities of gastrointestinal hormone secretion may contribute to delayed gastric emptying and impaired satiety, while alterations of central opioid function may affect feeding behavior and mood; such neuroregulatory disruptions contribute to disturbed eating patterns and body image distortion (Brewerton, Lydiard, Laraia, Shook, & Ballenger, 1992; Walsh et al., 1989).

Psychological changes associated with starvation include impaired concentration, loss of general interests, depressive symptomatology, social withdrawal, and a focus on food-related concerns. Starvation-induced physiological changes include sleep disturbance, diminished libido, amenorrhea, hypotension, bradycardia, reduced core temperature, insensitivity to pain, loss of scalp hair, and lunago (fine downy) hair (Warren, 1986). Starvation effects are not specific to eating disorders; they are seen in all starving individuals (Keys, Brozek, Henschel, Mickelsen, & Taylor, 1950). Complications related to bingeing and purging include dermatological changes, salivary gland enlargement, erosion of tooth enamel, pancreatitis, esophageal or gastric dilation, electrolyte imbalances (associated with vomiting, and with diuretic and laxative abuse), and possible seizure activity. Although most physiological changes are thought to be reversible with symptom remission, recent evidence suggests that bone demineralization (associated with amenorrhea, reduced calcium absorption, hypercortisolism, and inactivity) in anorexia nervosa may not be reversible with weight gain (Salisbury & Mitchell, 1991).

Methodological problems have precluded a fuller understanding of possible commonalities between the different eating

---

[2] Studies of weight-suppressed individuals suggest that sustained weight reduction is associated with appetitive changes (decreased appetite, sweetness aversion) that enhance weight control (Lowe, 1993).

[3] Approximately 50% of restricting anorectics report low appetite, low palatability of meals, and high satiety after meals (Halmi, Sunday, Puglisi, & Marchi, 1989).

disorders and within subgroups of patients with anorexia nervosa and bulimia (Shaw & Garfinkel, 1990). First, subject selection is biased toward an overrepresentation of the most seriously ill, with relatively few samples drawn from community settings. Thus, comparative studies rarely include the full spectrum of eating pathology. Second, the absence of prospective research makes it difficult to tease out possible antecedents of different eating disorders from the effects of starvation or semistarvation. Without reliable and valid criteria for "weight recovery" or "normal nutritional status," it is not possible to determine when starvation effects have been eliminated. Moreover, individuals who are biologically predisposed to obesity may suffer from the effects of semistarvation despite normal weight. Third, abnormal laboratory findings have been described in both anorexia nervosa and bulimia nervosa, but it is not clear which factors contribute to etiology, which are maintaining the illness, and which are sequelae of a changed organism. Fourth, the interaction of biological vulnerabilities with psychosocial factors is poorly understood. Preliminary neuropsychological studies suggest that inherited and acquired central nervous system dysfunction may predispose some women to become "addicted" to thinness in response to psychosocial stressors (Braun & Chouinard, 1992). Neurodevelopmental or constitutional vulnerabilities may become activated under certain circumstances, resulting in progressive adaptation to chronic starvation and a shutdown of reproductive functions (Bakan, Birmingham, & Goldner, 1991; Mogul, 1989).

RATES OF EATING DISORDERS BY AGE, GENDER, AND SOCIAL CLASS

Prevalence of Eating Disorders

Anorexia nervosa and bulimia nervosa are generally viewed as uncommon disorders and therefore have not been studied as completely as other disorders. Complicating identification studies is the shame and secretiveness surrounding eating disorders as well as the referral biases of physicians. Although most adolescents with anorexia nervosa report using mental health services (Whitaker et al., 1990), only a minority of those with bulimia nervosa are in treatment (Fairburn & Beglin, 1990). For the most part, eating disorders are underrecognized and undertreated. They tend to be overrepresented among those who choose not to participate in prevalence studies, suggesting that available prevalence estimates may be underestimates of the true rate (Beglin & Fairburn, 1992).[4]

Prevalence data derives from three types of studies: (a) those relying on self-report questionnaires to make diagnoses, (b) those

using a two-stage design to screen potential cases with a self-report measure followed by an interview, and (c) those studies that either evaluate the sensitivity and specificity of the screening instrument or use no screening phase and interview the entire sample (Fairburn & Beglin, 1990). Large samples are needed to identify relatively rare disorders such as anorexia nervosa and bulimia nervosa. For instance, several large-scale surveys of schoolgirls failed to identify any cases of anorexia nervosa and very few cases of bulimia nervosa (Johnson-Sabine, Wood, Patton, Mann, & Wakeling, 1988; Szmukler, 1985).

Whitaker et al. (1990) conducted a two-stage epidemiological study of DSM-III psychiatric disorders in a secondary school population in New Jersey. Of 5,596 adolescents surveyed, they identified 12 lifetime cases of anorexia nervosa and 18 cases of bulimia. The eating behaviors screening test identified all cases with past or current anorexia but was less sensitive for normal weight bulimia. The lifetime prevalence estimate was 0.2% for anorexia nervosa, 0.1% for bulimia with past or current anorexia, and 2.5% for bulimia at normal weight. The rates for anorexia nervosa are similar to the lifetime prevalence estimates for the general adult population at three sites in the Epidemiological Catchment Area Study (Robins et al., 1984). Prevalence rates for anorexia nervosa were estimated to be 1 case per 500 girls, which is lower than estimates from Great Britain, where Crisp, Palmer, and Kalucy (1976) found 1 case per 200 girls and Szmukler (1985) found 1 case per 120 girls in state schools.

Fairburn and Beglin (1990) reviewed over 50 studies conducted on the prevalence of bulimia nervosa. Over the past 10 years, such studies have become increasingly sophisticated and have incorporated refined diagnostic criteria. Based on the better designed studies, bulimia nervosa appears to have a prevalence rate of about 1% among adolescent and young adult women. Interview-based studies of bulimia produce lower estimates for the point prevalence in women than questionnaire studies: 1.5% using DSM-III and 0.9% using DSM-III-R criteria (Fairburn & Beglin, 1990). In a recent interview study of an entire epidemiological sample, Kendler et al. (1991) used DSM-III-R criteria to determine the lifetime prevalence of bulimia nervosa among female twins born in the Commonwealth of Virginia. Results of their study revealed a lifetime prevalence of 2.8% and a lifetime risk of 4.2%, with these estimates rising to 5.7% and 8% respectively if bulimia spectrum diagnoses were included.

Despite their prevalence, subclinical eating disorders have received relatively little attention. Several authors believe that the DSM-III-R criteria for anorexia nervosa may underestimate the number of children and adolescents suffering from distressing eating disorder symptoms. Bennell, Shenker, Nussbaum, Jacobson, and Cooper (1990) assessed 60 referrals to a Pediatric Eating Disorder clinic and found that the 21 patients with subclinical anorexia nervosa showed levels of psychological disturbance comparable to those with a definite diagnosis. Conversely, the 8 patients with subclinical bulimia nervosa did not manifest the same degree of affect and impulse dysregulation as those with a definite diagnosis of bulimia nervosa.

Using an instrument developed for children (*The Kids' Eating Disorder Survey, KEDS*), Childress, Brewerton, Hodges, and Jarrell (1993) surveyed fifth- through eighth-grade children enrolled

---

[4] Beglin and Fairburn (1992) examined the records of 39 women who chose not to participate in a survey on eating disorders and found that 10.3% had a history of anorexia nervosa, 5.1% had a current eating disorder, 12.8% had other significant problems with eating, and 15.4% were clinically overweight. These authors suspect that it may not be possible to obtain accurate prevalence figures in community samples because many may choose not to take part.

in public and private schools in two counties of South Carolina. Of the 3,129 respondents, approximately 45% "wanted to lose weight" and/or "felt looked fat to others," and one-third had "dieted." Of the 165 participants who completed the second stage interviews, one (0.6%) met criteria for anorexia nervosa, and an alarming 22 (13.3%) endorsed anorectic or bulimic symptoms consistent with Eating Disorder Not Otherwise Specified.

Clinton and Glant (1992) found that "atypical" eating disorders were the second most common eating-disordered group presenting to adult psychiatric services in the community, constituting 20% of their sample of 86 consecutive cases from a defined urban catchment area of Stockholm. Many of these patients appeared to be in a transitional state between other eating disorders or in the process of successful remission of key symptoms, presenting with low normal weight, relatively little binge eating, relatively greater laxative abuse, and longer duration of illness. Over half had previously been anorectic. Similarly, 52% of the adolescent and adult women screened for inclusion in a large-scale, naturalistic study of eating disorders did not meet full DSM-III-R criteria for either anorexia nervosa or bulimia; yet their symptoms were troubling enough that they sought treatment at an eating disorder clinic (Herzog, Sacks et al., 1993).

Changes in the Rate of Eating Disorders

Both anorexia nervosa and bulimia nervosa are believed to be on the rise over recent decades, although it is not clear whether this represents an increase in true morbidity or an increase in the proportion of cases referred and reported (Lask & Bryant-Waugh, 1992). Lucas, Beard, O'Fallon, and Kurland (1991) examined long-term trends in the incidence of anorexia nervosa in Rochester, Minnesota, during the period between 1935 and 1984. Although they found no significant trend for all females over the 50-year-span, age-specific differences emerged. During the 5-year period from 1980 to 1984, they found a marked rise in the incidence of anorexia among Rochester girls aged 10 to 19, and particularly among 15- to 19-year-olds. The incidence for older women remained relatively constant and the rates for males did not change over time (the disorder was 11.6 times more frequent in females than in males). Given this prevalence, anorexia nervosa is the third most common chronic illness among adolescent girls after obesity and asthma, occurring in 0.48% of 15- to 19-year-old girls in Rochester.

Social Class

Reports of family demographics have documented a social class bias for eating disorders, which may be of etiological importance through the mediated effects of child-rearing practices and cultural values. Anorexia nervosa has been found to be more prevalent among the upper classes in Britain and the United States (Dolan, Evans, & Lacey, 1989). An epidemiological survey of Monroe County, New York, revealed an association between anorexia nervosa and social class for females age 15 and older but not among younger adolescents and children (Jones, Fox, Babigan, & Hutton, 1980). Crisp et al. (1976) found higher rates of anorexia in British private schools (1 per 200) compared with public schools (1 per 330) among 16- to 18-year-old girls. However, in their twin study, Kendler et al. (1991) found no strong evidence for an association between bulimia and social class or college attendance. Similarly, in a sample of normal-weight bulimic patients in a defined British catchment area, Dolan et al. (1989) found no difference in social class distribution between the clinic sample and a matched comparison group.

More generally, weight and social class are inversely related among women but not among men in developed societies (Sobal & Stunkard, 1989). The reverse may be true in undeveloped nations, suggesting that weight regulation has different meanings in different classes and cultures. Women in higher social economic status (SES) groups in Western cultures are more likely to adhere to a thin ideal, to have greater resources to facilitate dieting, to have more leisure time and opportunity for recreational exercise, and if thin, to be more upwardly mobile (Sobal & Stunkard, 1989). Obese women are more likely to be downwardly mobile, and if they are low SES, to have a greater number of pregnancies, higher stress, and possibly ethnic differences in female adiposity. These differences combined with inherited predispositions may account for the genetic transmission of weight propensities along SES lines (Garner & Wooley, 1991). When SES is controlled, African American women are more likely to be obese than white women, suggesting less restrictive standards for acceptable weight in the former group (Rand & Kuldau, 1990).

Gender

Most epidemiological studies document a marked preponderance of females among cases of anorexia nervosa, with a female-to-male ratio of approximately 10 to 1 (Lucas et al., 1991). In Whitaker et al.'s (1990) two-stage study of 13- to 18-year-olds, only one boy met the criteria for an eating disorder (normal weight bulimia). In younger samples, the proportion of boys with anorexia and bulimia appears to be somewhat higher, ranging from 20% to 30% (Lask & Bryant-Waugh, 1992). The diagnosis of eating disorders in males may be neglected not only because of its relative scarcity, but because of biases in diagnosis, referral patterns, and sampling procedures (Carlat & Camargo, 1991).

Andersen (1990) notes that the basic criteria for diagnosing eating disorders in males and females are similar but that the words males use to describe their body shape and dieting concerns are different. Males are less concerned with the number of pounds gained or lost, and more concerned with achieving a muscular, classically "masculine" physique. They tend to rationalize their dieting behavior in ways that sound plausible, for instance, by expressing a fear of present or future medical illness. In addition, males report less guilt and dysphoria about binge eating (Carlat & Carmago, 1991). When compared with females, males with eating disorders are more likely to belong to subgroups where weight control is demanded for professional athletic reasons or where thinness is emphasized as an important aspect of male beauty, such as gay male communities (Striegel-Moore, 1992). Although studies suggest that gay men and heterosexual women are more affected by societal norms about weight than are lesbians and heterosexual men (Herzog, Newman, Yeh, & Warshaw, 1992), a recent comparative study revealed that gender was more salient than sexual orientation in influencing concern with weight and dieting (Brand, Rothblum, & Solomon, 1992).

The promotion of gender-specific norms idealizing thinness for women has been hypothesized to contribute to sex-related differences in eating dysregulation and weight-related concerns. D. M. Garner, Garfinkel, Schwartz, and Thompson (1980) documented a significant shift toward a thinner "ideal" image of female beauty, reflected in the steady decrease in weights of Miss America participants and *Playboy* centerfolds during the period between 1959 and 1979, despite actual increases in weight in the general population of same-age young women. Wiseman, Gray, Mosimann, and Ahrens (1992) reported a continuation of this trend for the years between 1979 and 1988. Remarkably, Miss America contestants' weights have stabilized at 13% to 19% below expected weight, a level that would enable these women to fulfill one of the major diagnostic criteria for anorexia nervosa. In addition, the study found a dramatic rise in the number of diet, exercise, and diet/exercise articles between 1959 to 1988, with exercise articles surpassing diet articles in the past 8 years. Andersen and DiDomenico (1992) found that magazines read most frequently by young women contained 10 times as many diet-promoting articles and advertisements compared with those read primarily by men in the same age range of 18 to 24 years old. Magazines read by men tended to emphasize shape more than diet. The parallel between the gender ratio of diet articles and the ratio of females to males with eating disorders (10 to 1) led the authors to consider a possible "dose-response" curve to explain the prevalence of eating disorders in relation to sociocultural reinforcements for dieting behavior.

Age

Eating disorders have generally been viewed as adolescent and young adult disturbances, although evidence suggests that anorexia nervosa and bulimia nervosa are spreading beyond their original 14- to 25-year age range. Crisp (1984) found the peak age of onset for anorexia nervosa to be 15 years (with a mean of 17 to 18 years), whereas others have reported a bimodal distribution, with peaks at 14.5 and 18 years (Halmi, Casper, Eckert, Goldberg, & Davis, 1979). In their population study of twins, Kendler et al. (1991) found the mean age of onset for bulimia nervosa to be 20 years, several years later than that reported from clinical samples. Woodside and Garfinkel (1992) retrospectively studied the age of onset in anorexia nervosa and bulimia, acknowledging that there is no consensus for what constitutes "onset" in these disorders. Symptoms of anorexia nervosa and bulimia nervosa seem to have independent patterns of onset (even if both occur in the same individual); in addition, age of risk for the onset of bulimia nervosa is shorter than the age of risk for onset of anorectic symptoms. Among 323 patients attending a treatment center for *adults* with eating disorders, they found that onset of anorexia nervosa and bulimia nervosa was similar up to age 25; after age 25, there were few new cases of bulimia but a significant occurrence of new anorexia nervosa symptoms. Mynors-Wallis, Treasure, and Chee (1992) found that late onset anorexia nervosa (after age 25) was more likely to be preceded by life events and chronic stress than either early onset cases (before age 25) or chronic cases (onset before age 25 who were being treated after age 25). Concurrent severe depression was more often associated with late onset cases than early onset cases.

Lask and Bryant-Waugh (1992) have reviewed the literature on childhood onset eating disorders. Drawing on the few epidemiological studies available, they conclude that the number of children under age 14 presenting for treatment of an eating disorder is low in comparison with other age groups, but their number appears to be increasing. It is unclear whether the increase represents a true rise in incidence or enhanced detection of cases. Prevalence figures are difficult to obtain because of diagnostic difficulties, limited assessment instruments, and poor recognition. Many prepubertal children do not meet the full diagnostic criteria for anorexia nervosa: they have a lower percentage of body fat, leading to emaciation more quickly; and they are more likely to generalize their food restriction to fluid intake as well (Irwin, 1981). Moreover, starvation can lead to delayed puberty, blurring the pubertal/prepubertal distinction. Weight loss may be less prominent than failure to gain weight with age, leading to primary amenorrhea. Furthermore, detection of younger patients is hampered by a lack of developmentally appropriate assessment methods.

Several population studies failed to find any children who fulfilled diagnostic criteria for anorexia nervosa; in three studies, the lifetime prevalence estimates were as low as 0.1% to 0.6% (Ben Tovim & Morton, 1990; Childress et al., 1993; Whitaker et al., 1990). Bulimia nervosa is thought to be very rare in children below age 14 years but has been identified in 1% to 2.5% of secondary school populations.

Ethnicity and Culture

The few epidemiological surveys available suggest that the incidence of eating disorders among ethnic minorities is lower than that of whites in Western cultures. Compared with white women, African American women are less likely to develop eating disorders (Dolan, 1991). It appears that minority adolescents at risk are those who are from upper middle class, achievement-oriented families, who are trying to be accepted into the dominant white culture or are caught between two different sets of cultural values (Silber, 1986; Yates, 1989).[5] Among female college students from middle to upper middle class backgrounds, Abrams, Allen, and Gray (1993) found that African American students reported significantly less eating disordered attitudes and behaviors than white students. Weight loss efforts and body dissatisfaction were positively associated with actual weight among black but not white students, and were more prevalent among blacks who reported attitudes idealizing white identity and rejecting black

---

[5] A preliminary comparative study of African American and white prepubertal girls (mean age = 10.12 years) revealed that black girls scored significantly higher than white girls on five subscales of the Eating Disorder Inventory; yet they also reported more positive body images. When girls scoring high and low on the Drive for Thinness scale were compared, black and white girls showed similar psychological profiles (Striegel-Moore, Pike, Rodin, Schreiber, & Wilfley, 1993).

identity on a measure of racial identity consciousness. In a comparative study of white and Hispanic adolescent girls between 16 and 18 years of age, Pumariega (1986) found a significant association between acculturation and EAT (Eating Attitude Test) scores among the Hispanic adolescents. Among Asian and Caucasian schoolgirls living in Britain, Mumford, Whitehouse, and Platts (1991) found a relatively higher prevalence of bulimia nervosa among the Asian girls (3.4% vs. 0.6%). Contrary to expectation, the Asian girls diagnosed as bulimic had significantly higher "traditional scores" compared with the rest of the Asian girls. The stresses related to immigration and acculturation, and the struggle to reconcile two sets of sociocultural values may predispose these adolescents to heightened internal conflict and identity confusion. Dolan (1991) suggests that attempts to adapt to a new culture can lead to an exaggerated overidentification with aspects of that culture, such as the pursuit of thinness. She considers that the study of eating disorders in nonindigenous ethnic groups within Western society will enhance our understanding of acculturative influences on the development of eating-related psychopathology.

The scarcity of eating disorders in developing countries, their predominance in Western societies and Japan, and their emergence among "Westernized" groups in Third World countries has led to their classification as "culture-bound syndromes" (Prince, 1985). In their review of cross-cultural patterns in eating disorders, Pate and colleagues suggest that the rise in eating disorders among different cultural groups may be the result of a widening adherence to the thin ideal in different regions and countries, an ideal that has come to symbolize self-control, success, upward mobility, as well as the hallmark of female attractiveness (Pate et al., 1992). However, Dolan (1991) stresses that the prevailing attitudes of the social and political system in which the clinician/researcher works are linked to how cases are presented, researched, and diagnosed, possibly leading to biased conclusions about the occurrence of eating disorders in ethnic minorities.

CO-OCCURRENCE OF EATING DISORDERS WITH OTHER PSYCHIATRIC CONDITIONS

The co-occurrence of eating disorders with other psychiatric conditions or disorders has been the subject of much research. However, comorbidity rates may be misleading because individuals with two disorders are more likely to present for treatment than those with one disorder. In their review of comorbidity in childhood psychopathology, Caron and Rutter (1991) stress that clinic data cannot be used to calculate comorbidity rates unless the general population rates, and referral rates and biases for each disorder are known.

Caron and Rutter (1991) consider the potential utility of studying co-occurring disorders. First, the findings of many psychopathology studies may be misleading because the presumed correlates of a disorder may represent correlates of some unspecified comorbid condition. Recent studies suggest that family environment differences reported between eating-disordered individuals and controls or among eating disorder subtypes may in fact be accounted for by coexisting depression (Blouin, Zuro, &

Blouin, 1990) or personality disorders (Wonderlich, 1992). Second, it cannot be assumed that the meaning of a disorder remains the same regardless of the presence or absence of other disorders. For instance, studies suggest that eating-disordered individuals with borderline characteristics have poorer clinical outcomes at short-term follow-up than those without such features (Johnson, Tobin, & Dennis, 1990; Sansone & Fine, 1992). According to Caron and Rutter (1991), the study of true comorbidity may shed light on the nature of the disorders involved: The two disorders may share the same risk factors; risk factors may be associated; the comorbid pattern may constitute a meaningful syndrome; and one disorder may create an increased risk for the other.

Determination of comorbidity in eating disorders is limited on two fronts. First, there is a lack of fully representative epidemiological data. Second, the validity of the comorbid condition may be questionable due to the patient's clinical state. For instance, results of one short-term psychotherapy study suggested that mood disturbances and personality disorders observed in bulimia nervosa patients may be secondary elaborations of chronic dietary chaos that are alleviated with successful treatment of eating-disordered symptoms (Garner et al., 1990).

Eating Disorders and Depressive Disorders

Several research groups have documented large proportions of patients with an eating disorder who meet criteria for major depression. Approximately 50% of eating-disordered patients present with concomitant affective disorder, a rate significantly higher than that found in the general population (Katz, 1987). Herzog, Keller, Sacks, Yeh, and Lavori (1992) recently published the largest study to date of psychiatric comorbidity in 229 treatment-seeking, eating-disordered women, aged 13 to 45. They found comorbidity for Axis I disorders greatly exceeded comorbidity for Axis II disorders, with major depression being the most commonly diagnosed comorbid disorder. Among both anorectic and bulimic patients (analyzed separately), the prevalence of lifetime major depression was 63%. The patients with mixed anorexia and bulimia had the highest rates of past and current affective disorders, particularly major depressive disorder.

In a total population study of Swedish 16-year-olds with anorexia nervosa and sex-, age-, and school-matched comparison cases, Rastam (1992) found that only 6% of the cases had not been severely depressed (major depression, depressive disorder, or dysthymia) at some time before or after the onset of anorexia nervosa. By comparison, 75% of control cases had never been depressed. Depression was more likely to occur *following* the onset of the eating disorder.

Support for the presence of affective disturbance in eating-disordered individuals derives from longitudinal course and outcome, family pathology, response to pharmacotherapy, and biological characteristics. Eating disorders and affective disorders may co-occur for a variety of reasons: A depressive diathesis may be a risk factor for developing an eating disorder, a depressive episode could precipitate the onset of an eating disorder, depression could be a consequence of neurogenic changes secondary to starvation or weight fluctuations, or depression may be part of the affective instability associated with borderline personality or grief reactions caused by losses and interpersonal problems associated with the illness (Katz, 1987; Levy, Dixon, & Stern, 1989; Swift, Andrews, & Barklage, 1986).

Because of the prevalence of depression among subgroups of eating-disordered patients, efforts have been made to elucidate the nature of this association. Recent work in genetic epidemiology reveals that anorexia nervosa and depression show independent familial transmission. The presence of depression among relatives of anorectic probands is accounted for by a subset of anorectics with coexisting depression (Strober, Lampert, Morrell, Burroughs, & Jacobs, 1990). However, some controlled family studies of bulimia nervosa patients, employing different methodologies (family history, family interview), reveal elevated rates of familial mood disorders that cannot be attributed solely to the contribution of bulimic probands who themselves have a mood disorder (Keck et al., 1990). Given the absence of large-scale, controlled studies of depression and bulimia in the general population, the nature of the association between these disorders remains unclear (Levy et al., 1989).

Eating Disorders and Personality Disorders

High rates of personality disorders have been documented among anorectic and bulimic patients referred for treatment, with prevalence estimates ranging from 27% to 93% (Skodol et al., 1993). Inconsistent findings are most likely the result of the different diagnostic methods for assessing personality disorders, as well as differences in patient populations. In their comorbidity study, Herzog, Keller, Sacks, Yeh, and Lavori (1992) found relatively low rates of Axis II disorders among female patients seeking treatment for an eating disorder. Twenty-seven percent of their sample over age 18 had a comorbid personality disorder, with the most common being compulsive (7%) and avoidant (7%) among anorectics, borderline (6%) and histrionic (6%) among bulimics, and borderline for mixed disorder subjects (12%).[6] Gartner, Marcus, Halmi, and Loranger (1989) found that 57% of patients hospitalized for treatment of an eating disorder met the criteria for at least one Axis II diagnosis, with borderline, self-defeating, and avoidant being the most frequent. Of these patients, 40% received two or more diagnoses. The distribution of personality disorder diagnoses did not differ among anorectic, bulimic, or anorectic plus bulimic subtypes. Interestingly, a large number of patients met 20 or more Axis II criteria in the absence of a specific diagnosis. Furthermore, there were indications that state depression and anxiety affected personality assessment, highlighting the need for longitudinal follow-up to clarify the persistence versus transience of affective and personality disorder symptoms among eating-disordered patients.[7]

Using conservative personality disorder diagnoses, Skodol et al. (1993) examined rates of personality disorders and eating disorders among 100 patients referred to an inpatient unit specializing in the treatment of personality disorders, and another 100 applicants to an outpatient clinic for low-cost psychoanalysis. In this heterogenous population of inpatients and outpatients, the odds of an eating disorder occurring in association with a personality disorder were nearly four times the odds of these disorders occurring alone. Consistent with the findings of Herzog, Keller et al. (1992), Skodol et al. (1993) found a differential association of borderline personality disorder with current and lifetime bulimia nervosa, and avoidant personality disorder with current and lifetime anorexia nervosa.

Wonderlich and Swift (1990a) studied borderline and nonborderline personality disorders among eating-disordered patients and found that all personality-disordered groups displayed equivalently disordered eating, but significantly higher rates of other psychiatric symptoms in comparison with non-personality-disordered groups. Eating-disordered patients with borderline personality disorders differed from those with other personality disorders in their histories of sexual abuse and self-destructiveness during adolescence, higher frequency of suicidal gestures, and perceptions of hostility in their parental (particularly maternal) relationship. Eating-disordered subjects without personality disorders were much less disturbed and differed minimally from controls on eating attitudes, emotional distress, and parental ratings.

Based on intensive, semistructured trauma interviews with 20 patients drawn randomly from their large-scale longitudinal study, Herzog, Staley, Carmody, Robbins, and van der Kolk (1993) have proposed that childhood trauma may be a risk factor for the development of eating disorders and comorbid conditions.[8]

---

[6] Herzog, Keller et al. (1992) also found low rates of alcohol and drug use disorders in his sample; none of the anorectics, 5% of bulimic, and 8% of mixed subjects received diagnoses of substance abuse. These findings contrast with other clinical studies that document elevated levels of concurrent addictive disorders and eating disorders, particularly bulimia nervosa, in young adults (Katz, 1992). In a catchment area study, Lacey (1993) found that a substantial minority of bulimic patients reported self-damaging and addictive behaviors, including alcohol use, overdosing, cutting, and stealing. He proposes that this subgroup of bulimic patients may be distinguished by their "multi-impulsive personality disorder." As a group, they tended to be older, less likely to be employed or in a stable union, but more likely to have an alcohol-abusing partner and a family history of alcohol abuse.

[7] Several studies document a strong association between self-reported dysthymia or major depressive disorder and borderline or dependent personality disorders (Pope, Frankenburg, Hudson, Jonas, & Yurgelun-Todd, 1987; Wonderlich, Swift, Slotnick, & Goodman, 1990). Pope and Hudson (1989) caution that primary affective disorders may inflate the prevalence of borderline personality diagnoses in eating-disordered patients because of the overlap in symptoms.

[8] Whether there is a meaningful relationship between child sexual abuse and eating disorders is a subject of considerable debate. Pope and Hudson (1992) reviewed the literature pertaining to sexual abuse and bulimia nervosa, and found that prevalence rates of childhood sexual abuse for bulimics were comparable to the rates found for the general population. Palmer and Oppenheimer (1992) found that non-eating-disordered women with other psychiatric diagnoses had significantly higher rates of reported childhood sexual experiences compared with eating-disordered women. From their review of this literature, Connors and Morse (1993) suggest that methodological problems may account for widely disparate findings across studies. They also suggest that "the correlation between sexual trauma and general personality disturbance may turn out to be

In this pilot sample, 65% of patients had experienced childhood sexual abuse; in nearly all cases, the abuse occurred prior to the onset of their eating disorder. Compared with nonabused eating-disordered subjects, the abused eating-disordered subjects reported significantly higher rates of comorbid affective and personality disorders, self-destructive acts (including overdosing, poisoning, and cutting), and dissociative experiences.

In her population-based study of Swedish 16-year-old adolescents with anorexia nervosa and a matched comparison group, Rastam (1992) found a high rate of premorbid personality disorders in the anorexia nervosa group, particularly of the obsessive-compulsive type.[9] Thirty-five percent of the anorectic group compared with 4% of normal controls were diagnosed with obsessive-compulsive disorder by an examiner blind to diagnosis, and nearly 60% of the anorexia nervosa group had pronounced obsessional traits such as perfectionism. Of relevance is a study by Noshirvani, Kasvikis, Marks, Tsakiris, and Monteiro (1991) which found an excess of past anorexia nervosa among women with obsessive-compulsive disorder; 12% of the women and none of the men had a history of anorexia nervosa. Wonderlich et al. (1990) found obsessive-compulsive personality disorder to be common in restricting but not bulimic anorectics whereas normal-weight bulimics showed a high prevalence of histrionic personality disorder.

Rothenberg (1990) conceptualizes anorexia nervosa as the "modern obsessive-compulsive syndrome" among adolescent girls. He speculates that girls with obsessive-compulsive tendencies may become overwhelmed by the competitive demands of the adolescent period (in social, physical, and academic contexts), and because of peer and cultural pressures, may focus their intense achievement orientation on the pursuit of thinness. He regards the frequent occurrence of depressive symptoms among anorectic patients as a breakdown of obsessive-compulsive defenses. Further research is needed to test out this proposed pathway, in which obsessive-compulsive features are viewed as the essential, underlying character structure predisposing to the development of anorexia, and secondarily to depressive symptoms.

THE ONSET OF EATING DISORDERS DURING THE ADOLESCENT PERIOD: A DEVELOPMENTAL PERSPECTIVE

Developmental psychopathology research assumes an organizational approach to the study of development and psychopathology

---

stronger than the relationship between trauma and eating pathology, which, like depression, anxiety, and substance abuse, is present across a range of personality functioning" (p. 10).

[9] The distinction between obsessive-compulsive disorder (OCD) and obsessive-compulsive personality disorder (OCPD) is not consistently maintained in these studies. Several authors have found significant comorbidity of eating disorders with anxiety disorders, including OCD, generalized anxiety disorder, and social phobia (Fornari et al., 1992). A recent review of obsessive-compulsive disorders and eating disorders highlights the frequent occurrence of OCD symptoms among eating-disordered patients, as well as possibly overlapping correlates and outcomes (Hsu, Kaye, & Weltzin, 1993).

(Cicchetti & Schneider-Rosen, 1986). Briefly stated, an organizational perspective attempts to delineate the complex interactions among cognitive, social, emotional, and biological processes that contribute to the child's adaptation at each developmental level. Development proceeds by means of qualitative reorganizations of behaviors, which become increasingly differentiated and hierarchically incorporated into subsequent patterns. Psychopathology is thought to arise from a lack of integration among various competencies at certain developmental phases or transitions. Developmental transitions may be conceptualized along several dimensions: reproductive transitions (puberty, menopause), family transitions (leaving home, marriage, parenting), and school transitions (entering junior high school, going away to college). A transitional period for the developing adolescent also creates challenges and opportunities for the entire system in which she is embedded: Parents, siblings, and friends also must reorganize their interactional patterns (Minuchin, 1985).

From a transactional perspective, the organization of developmental competencies within the child interacts with characteristics of the environment to shape adaptive and maladaptive developmental pathways (Sameroff, 1975). As these reciprocal transactions evolve over time, they transform affective, interpersonal, and representational structures within the child and her social environment. Developmental transitions may be sensitive periods for these transformations because they propel a reorganization of biological, psychological, and contextual influences.

Challenges and Transitions of Adolescence

Eating disorders, and to a lesser extent eating problems (dieting, bingeing), are believed to occur modally at two developmental transitions: during the passage into adolescence, and during the movement out of adolescence into young adulthood. An organizational approach requires that we study the emergence of eating problems in the context of the multitude of developmental opportunities and challenges that confront most adolescents during these transitions. Normative challenges of the early- to middle-adolescent transition include the integration of a changing body shape, body image, and reproductive capacity into one's self-representation; gradual disengagement from internalized parental representations with moves toward greater autonomy in the context of connectedness; the development of confiding relationships; the development of sexual relationships; the internalization of achievement goals; and the organization of a relatively stable and cohesive self-structure for the regulation of mood, impulse, and self-esteem.

Late adolescent challenges include the establishment of intimacy, the pursuit of an education and an occupation, the synthesis of one's own values and goals, and the development of an identity apart from the family (Attie et al., 1990). It is the adolescent's ability to organize experience, particularly at critical transitions, that most likely will predict subsequent adaptive or maladaptive functioning.

Transitions into Adolescence

Dieting concerns intensify during early adolescence and may be related to pubertal changes in body composition. As girls mature sexually, they accumulate large quantities of fat in subcutaneous tissue, as indicated by increased skinfold thickness (Young, Sipin, & Roe, 1968). For the adolescent girl, this "fat spurt" is one of the most dramatic physical changes associated with puberty, adding an average of 11 kilograms of weight in the form of body fat (Brooks-Gunn & Warren, 1985; Gross, 1984). Increases in body fat during the pubertal years are associated with desires to be thinner (Dornbusch et al., 1984). Other pubertal changes such as breast development may be associated with efforts to restrict food intake, particularly in girls from higher social class backgrounds (Crisp, 1984; Dornbusch et al., 1984; Garguilo, Attie, Brooks-Gunn, & Warren, 1987). The timing of maturation may also influence the emergence of dieting behavior. Early maturers are at greater risk for eating problems, in part because they are likely to be heavier than their late maturing peers (Brooks-Gunn, 1988; Faust, 1983; Tanner, 1962).

For the early adolescent, the process of integrating changes in physical appearance, bodily feelings, and reproductive status requires a fundamental reorganization of the adolescent's body image and other body and self-representations (Blos, 1962). Physical attractiveness is more important to girls' as compared with boys' bodily satisfaction and self-esteem; yet girls are more unhappy with their appearance than boys are. For girls, but not for boys, body image is intimately bound up with subjective perceptions of weight, and especially with girls' satisfaction with weight; pubescent girls who perceive themselves as underweight are most satisfied, followed by those who think they are simply average (Tobin-Richards, Boxer, & Petersen, 1983).

For most girls, significant pubertal changes are timed with entry into junior high school. The modal girl reaches the peak of pubertal development in the seventh grade, whereas the modal boy does so $1\frac{1}{2}$ to 2 years later, in the ninth grade. The work of Simmons and her colleagues reveals that the transition to junior high school—with the move to a new, impersonal school environment, social pressures to date, the disruption of prior peer networks, and the increased achievement demands—is potentially more disruptive and detrimental to girls' as compared with boys' self-image and self-esteem. The greater number of simultaneous changes a girl experiences, the more her self-esteem, social participation, and grade point average suffer (Simmons, Burgeson, Carlton-Ford, & Blyth, 1987). Yet, school transitions may provide opportunities as well as challenges. In a series of studies, Harter (1990) found that changes in self-esteem that accompany the junior high transition correspond, both positively and negatively, to shifts in the adolescent's perceived competence and social support.

Attie and Brooks-Gunn (1989) examined the proposition that the development of eating problems represents a mode of accommodation to the multiple changes of the pubertal transition. In a short-term prospective study of nonclinically referred adolescent girls, they explored the relative impact of pubertal change, personality development, and family relationships on the emergence of eating problems. In short, 193 white upper-middle-class adolescents and their mothers were seen initially when the girls were in Grades 7 through 10, with follow-up 2 years later. Regression models tested the relative contributions of grade in school, physical maturation indexes, body image, psychopathology,

and perceptions of the family environment to the prediction of eating problems, both longitudinally and concurrently. The findings suggested that eating problems emerge in response to physical changes of the pubertal period, specifically body fat accumulation and associated body image dissatisfaction. Controlling for these variables, psychopathology was associated with problem eating whereas family relationships were not.

Two years later, when adolescents had completed their pubertal development, the pattern of influence among predictors had changed. The more developmental factors (i.e., grade-in-school and physical maturation indexes) were no longer influential, whereas psychological dimensions, namely a negative body image and psychopathology, accounted for significant variance increments. Eating behavior was associated with affective overcontrol (i.e., depression) as opposed to undercontrol (aggression, delinquency, hyperactivity). Longitudinal analyses revealed that once initial eating scores were taken into account, only initial body image significantly and negatively predicted change in eating problems; girls who early in adolescence felt most negatively about their bodies were significantly more likely to develop eating problems beyond what would be expected based on their earlier scores, controlling for variability in physical maturation, psychopathology, and family relationships. Perhaps at puberty, a pattern of eating behavior is set in motion with the subsequent trajectory defined, in part, by pubertal transformations in body image.

Because body image predicts long-term change in eating behavior, it is important to examine the meaning of body image and the mechanisms by which it may mediate changes in eating behavior among young adolescent girls. Studies of body image disturbance have focused predominantly on two different operationalizations of body image (Slade, 1985; Wardle & Foley, 1989): perceptual dimensions (size overestimation, image distortion) and affective dimensions (shape dissatisfaction and disparagement).[10] Based on their review of body image research, Hsu and Sobkiewicz (1991) conclude that body attitudes and feelings, such as fear of fatness, weight phobia, and pursuit of thinness are more relevant and significant than size overestimation for understanding the psychopathology of eating disorders.[11] They consider that "Crisp's concept that anorectics fear normal weight, not fatness (i.e., fear of fatness is normal in our

---

[10] With regard to affective components of body image, Cooper and Fairburn (1993) make a distinction between overvalued ideas about body shape and weight, and dissatisfaction with body shape. Dissatisfaction with body shape is usually present in eating-disordered patients but is also common among noneating-disordered women; it tends to be unstable and is closely associated with level of depressed mood. Conversely, overvalued ideas about body shape and weight are relatively stable, are closely linked to self-esteem, and are defining features of anorexia nervosa and bulimia nervosa.

[11] Using a silhouette method of body image assessment, Williamson, Cubic, and Gleaves (1993) found that both bulimic and anorectic patients judge their actual body size to be larger and their ideal body size to be thinner relative to normal control subjects. These authors stress that the method of measuring body image may account for widely disparate findings across studies, and that it is critical to control for actual body size of the subject when evaluating body image.

culture whereas fear of normal weight is pathological) has never been studied thoroughly" (p. 29).[12]

Several studies suggest that the preference for thinness and dissatisfaction with weight among female adolescents is the continuation of a developmental process by which girls learn about cultural ideals of femininity and bodily acceptability (Collins, 1991; Moore, 1988, 1990). However, research has not considered developmental transformations in body image in relation to adolescents' increasing cognitive sophistication, which may bring not only an enhanced capacity for abstraction and self-reflection, but an increased awareness of ideal-self discrepancies, greater emotional introspection, and a tendency to think in terms of global, rather than specific self-concepts (Keating, 1990; Rutter & Rutter, 1993). Although these cognitive shifts facilitate the complexity and subtlety of adolescent thinking, they also may become a source of cognitive distortion, confusion, and affective distress.

Late Adolescent Transitions

Schools play a significant role in the transmission of cultural ideals. From a contextual viewpoint, it is not known whether there are differences in the incidence of eating disorders depending on the type of school attended (Rutter & Rutter, 1993). In a recent study, Striegel-Moore, Connor-Greene, and Shime (1991) examined the relationship of the high school milieu to disordered eating. Contrary to expectation, girls from competitive environments that encourage traditional sex role behavior (emphasis on physical appearance, dating, or conformist behaviors) were not more likely to develop eating-disordered symptoms. A modest association was found between perception of the school milieu as low in social involvement and feelings of ineffectiveness and loneliness.

Few researchers have examined late adolescent transitions in relation to eating disorders, despite the developmental significance of "leaving home" for the emergence of certain forms of psychopathology and the clinical reports of "social contagion" of disordered eating on college campuses (Crandall, 1988). Striegel-Moore, Silberstein, Frensch, and Rodin (1989) conducted a prospective study of disordered eating among college freshman, assessed at the beginning and end of the freshman year. They hypothesized that the academic and social pressures of college life, combined with the competitive school environment may promote an emphasis on the achievement of thinness. Results of their study showed that few incoming freshman met the probable criteria for bulimia nervosa based on questionnaire assessment—less than 0.2% of males and 3.8% of females. Few students developed bulimia nervosa over the first year, but a significant number experienced an increase in one or more symptoms of disordered eating. About one-fourth of students dieted for the first time and about 15% of women began to binge for the first time. Worsening of disordered eating during the freshman year was associated with high perceived stress, an increased sense of ineffectiveness, and negative feelings about weight. The links between these factors and weight control efforts are not clear—stress may lead to a sense of ineffectiveness and then to weight concerns, or women who felt worse about their weight and began dieting and bingeing may have developed a greater sense of ineffectiveness.

Gender Issues in Adolescence

The social reorganization of gender relations during the early adolescent transition generates different stressors and coping strategies among girls and boys (Bush & Simmons, 1987; Galambos, Almeida, & Petersen, 1990; Steiner-Adair, 1990). In their review of research on adolescent socialization and development, Hill and Lynch (1983) offer support for their gender intensification hypothesis; that is, the notion that gender-differentiated role expectations intensify during early adolescence. First, young adolescent girls are reported to be more self-conscious, anxious, and insecure than boys, and are more likely to cope with novelty by being compliant or by avoiding negative interactions. Second, during adolescence, boys and girls become more aware of traditionally defined, gender-specific standards for achievement. In girls, academic achievement, educational aspirations, and risk taking all begin to decline. Third, self-esteem becomes less stable for adolescent girls, in part because of the greater emphasis girls place on the importance of peer regard and looks. Fourth, adolescent girls are more likely than boys to seek friendships based on intimacy and mutuality. Finally, expressions of anger and aggression are increasingly inhibited among adolescent girls and are tolerated less by parents and peers.

Recent research has emphasized gender differences in the developmental processes mediating self-differentiation and identity formation in adolescent development. Despite the emphasis on separation and individuation that has dominated the language of adolescent developmental theory, boys and girls may differ in their conceptions of self and relationships in adolescence: Girls have been hypothesized to retain a much stronger relational focus, whereas boys may be concerned more directly with the development of autonomy (Gilligan, 1982; Gilligan, Rogers, & Brown, 1990). Although gender "difference" feminist theories, such as Gilligan's, have earned wide appeal, they have been criticized on theoretical and scientific grounds (Pollitt, 1992).

Nonetheless, the emergence of eating disorders has been linked to contradictory messages regarding what it means to approach womanhood in contemporary society. According to Gilligan and colleagues, the adolescent girl is faced with a developmental double bind when cultural imperatives demand that she shift away from the relational mode which has been integral to her development throughout childhood, to "androcentric" cultural norms that stress competition, self-sufficiency, and individualism. In an interview study of high school girls attending a single-sex private school, Steiner-Adair (1990) found that those who described themselves in "superwoman" terms were more likely to associate thinness with autonomy, success, and recognition for independent achievement; they also were more at risk for eating disorders, as indicated by their clinically elevated scores on the EAT questionnaire. Conversely, girls

---

[12] In a subsequent paper, Hsu and Lee (1993) document cases of anorexia nervosa in developing countries that present with all the diagnostic features except for a weight phobia. These findings raise the question, alluded to in our earlier historical overview, as to whether fear of fatness (or other body image disturbance) is central to the pathogenesis of anorexia nervosa, or whether it more accurately represents the influence of sociohistorical forces on symptom expression.

who were able to repudiate the contemporary superwoman ideal as detrimental to their developmental needs (i.e., "wise women"), uniformly scored in the noneating-disordered range.

Levine and Smolak (1992) propose that the co-occurrence of multiple stressors during adolescence creates a vulnerability to eating disorders among girls who subscribe to the "superwoman" complex—that is, the notion that a woman must be successful in both traditionally feminine and traditionally masculine roles. They hypothesize that the interactive influence of pubertal weight gain, changes in heterosocial relationships, and threats to achievement status combine to promote body dissatisfaction, distress, and perceived loss of control in young adolescents. In their study of middle school girls, they found support for a cumulative stress model, in which simultaneous change (onset of menarche and dating in the same year), combined with academic pressure, a slender body ideal, as well as peer and parental investment in slenderness, best discriminated adolescents with and without self-reported disordered eating. The notion of a "superwoman complex" has yet to be validated within either this model or the one proposed by Steiner-Adair (i.e., the cumulative stress model may be sufficient to explain Levine and Smolak's findings); however, such a construct needs to be assessed within a social cognitive framework that considers the meaning of the "superwoman" ideal to developing adolescents across different age, socioeconomic, and ethnic groups.

Recent research by Silverstein and colleagues suggests an association between disordered eating and the discrepancy between women's career aspirations and the likelihood of their fulfillment. Eating-disordered symptoms are prevalent among adolescent women with academic and professional strivings, among those who perceive their gender as an impediment to success, and in those with gender role conflicts (Silverstein, Carpman, Perlick, & Perdue, 1990; Silverstein & Perdue, 1988). The link between gender role conflicts and disordered eating is most pronounced among women with professional aspirations whose mothers did not achieve academically and professionally (Silverstein, Perdue, Wolf, & Pizzolo, 1988). Herzog found a 15% lifetime history of an eating disorder among female medical students, which is substantially higher than the incidence in other groups (Herzog, Perpose, Norman, & Rigotti, 1985). More recently, Silverstein and Perlick (1991) examined historical patterns for rates of depression and found that gender differences in depression in adults age 40 and older are highest among cohorts who reached adolescence during periods of increasing opportunities for female achievement. The authors suggest possible overlapping risk factors for disordered eating and depression, including the rise in prevalence of both disorders over recent decades, the dramatic rise among females but not males during adolescence, and the significant relationships among disordered eating, depression, and poor body image (Cash & Pruzinsky, 1990).

Contextual Factors

Peer Relationships

The relationship between social competence, social support, and eating/weight-related concerns has not been studied systematically, although adolescence is a period when the nature and significance of friendships change. Among 13- to 16-year-old adolescents, close and intimate friendships have been linked to higher levels of mental health, interpersonal competence, and self-esteem (Buhrmester, 1990). In the co-construction of friendships, adolescents seek mutual validation, feedback, caring, respect, and trust. From interviews with normal adolescents, Youniss and Smollar (1985) demonstrate that friendship "provides a contrasting experience that may help adolescents evaluate their position in their parental relationships . . . The interplay of friendship with parental relations allows adolescents to test the limits of both their individuality and connectedness" (p. 157). Furthermore, studies of adolescent coping behavior reveal that girls are more likely than boys to use coping skills that involve relationships with others, such as "developing social support" and "turning to family members" (Patterson & McCubbin, 1987).

Monck (1991) examined confiding relationships among 15- to 20-year-old adolescent girls who were assessed as being depressed or having an eating disorder according to a screening instrument. She found that these girls tended to use other females (mothers, sisters, and girlfriends) as problem solvers and intimate confidants through age 19. Only the oldest girls selected boyfriends (but not brothers or fathers) for advice in practical matters. At all ages, mothers were cited as the closest confidants for intimate concerns, whereas fathers hardly featured as primary confidants. The preference for mothers over fathers was particularly marked if the parents' marriages were poor.

Harter, Marold, and Whitesell (1992) studied changes in the self that accompany the movement into adolescence. Self-awareness, self-consciousness, introspectiveness, and preoccupation with self-image increase markedly. The impact of peer relationships increases dramatically. The adolescent makes moves toward autonomy but also struggles to stay connected. Harter hypothesized that the adolescent's feelings of self-worth are linked to competence in domains of importance to the adolescent and to her parents. In a study of middle school students, she found that self-concept domains fell into two distinct clusters: appearance, peer likability, and athletic competence formed one factor and scholastic competence and behavioral conduct formed a second factor. Each of these clusters was differentially associated with sources of social support—scholastic competence and behavioral conduct had the largest impact on perceived parental support, and physical appearance, peer likability, and athletic competence were more related to the perceived level of peer support. These self-concept clusters predicted depressive symptomatology (affect, global self-worth, and hopelessness), which in turn mediated suicidal ideation. Based on Harter's work, researchers could speculate that high levels of preoccupation with physical appearance may predispose the adolescent toward dieting as a way of managing vulnerabilities in self-esteem and social competence, increasing the risk for development of an eating disorder.[13]

The association between peer relationships and eating disorders is not directly addressed by current literature. Teasing is

---

[13] Of relevance is a study by Casper, Hedeker, and McClough (1992), which revealed that feelings of social ineffectiveness among eating-disordered patients were accounted for by the coexistence of eating-disordered psychopathology and depressed mood.

perhaps the most often mentioned social variable in studies of adolescent adjustment and eating or weight-related concerns (Brown, Cash, & Lewis, 1989). Fabian and Thompson (1989) found a significant relationship between being teased about appearance, and depression, eating disturbance, and body dissatisfaction among younger adolescents, irrespective of their menarcheal status. In a study of 15 consecutive inpatients with early onset anorexia nervosa (onset of symptoms by age 13), Walford and McCune (1991) found that 7 children related the onset of their illness to comments made by others about their weight. Teasing may be especially stressful to younger adolescents who are anticipating or experiencing bodily changes. Without more indepth study, however, it is not clear whether teasing reflects the adolescent's popularity, quality of friendships, increased sensitivity to teasing due to preexisting characteristics, or perhaps differential treatment by family members. In view of recent research linking adolescents' levels of attachment, parental support, and emotional security with friends, it will be important to expand current family research in eating disorders to consider how the family system enhances or diminishes the adolescent's social development (Hill, 1993).

Several clinical reports have documented sexual and social maladjustment among eating-disordered patients. Three studies of eating-disordered adolescent inpatients (predominantly anorectic) revealed remarkably similar profiles on the *Offer Self-Image Questionnaire* (Casper, Offer, & Ostrov, 1981; Steinhausen & Vollrath, 1993; Swift, Bushnell, Hanson, & Logemann, 1986). Among the most disturbed components of self-concept were social relationships and sexual identity. In a sample of adult outpatients, Haimes and Katz (1988) found significant immaturity in sexual and social experiences of restricting anorectics, compared with bulimics and matched noneating-disordered patients with borderline personality disorder. Although the restricting anorectics were the least mature, most withdrawn, and most inhibited, they surpassed the other two groups as well as normal comparison groups in terms of their exquisite sensitivity to social expectations. In addition, only the two eating disorder groups felt that their psychological difficulties stemmed originally from their sexual problems.

Among nonclinically referred girls, Attie (1987) found that a measure of social competence, dating, best discriminated binge eaters from exclusive dieters, defined according to high scores on the Diet and Bulimia scales of the *EAT-26* Inventory. Those who scored low on the discriminant function, binge eaters, could be distinguished from dieters on the basis of their lower self-reported dating experience, higher depressive symptoms, less positive body image, and somewhat decreased impulse control. Lacey, Coker, and Birtchnell (1986) found that a substantial proportion of normal-weight bulimic women associated the onset of their bulimia with chronic social difficulties, including doubts about their attractiveness to men and poor relationships with peers of both sexes. In a naturalistic study of young adult patients with bulimia nervosa, having several good friends predicted recovery at 3-year follow-up (Keller et al., 1992).

The Family Context: Parent-Child Relationships

Early theorizing about eating disorders attributed a causal role to disturbances within the family, based mainly on inferences about

the mother-daughter relationship gained through psychotherapy with anorectic patients. Bruch (1973) was one of the first to describe the seemingly untroubled childhood of her adolescent anorectic patients. From predominantly privileged families, these girls were described by their parents as unusually compliant, successful, and gratifying children. As they reached adolescence, they manifested a negativism and mistrust that centered around their adamant refusal to eat. Bruch (1985) writes:

> In therapy, they reveal that underneath this self-assertive facade they experience themselves as acting only in response to demands coming from others, and not doing anything because they want to. Perceptions of their bodily and emotional sensations are often inaccurate, and they do not trust themselves to identify their own needs and feelings accurately. They claim not to "see" the severe emaciation and do not consider it abnormal or ugly; on the contrary, they take pride in their skeleton-like appearance. They also fail to experience their bodies as being their own, but look upon them as something extraneous, separate from their psychological selves, or as being possessions of their parents. This split between body and self is a basic issue and yields only slowly to therapeutic efforts. (p. 10)

The preceding passage describes what Bruch (1973) regarded as the three core clinical features of the anorectic syndrome: (a) a disturbance of body image and of body concept of possibly delusional proportions; (b) a disturbance of perceptual and cognitive interpretations of internal feeling states related to bodily and affective needs; and (c) a paralyzing sense of ineffectiveness, related to the belief that parental recognition is predicated on dutiful compliance at the expense of the child's own sense of agency and self-expression. According to Bruch, these ego deficiencies result from chronically disturbed parent-child interactions that leave the child with limited capacities to negotiate adolescent developmental challenges.

From an object relational perspective, adolescence has been characterized as a second individuation process, comparable to the one that takes place in early childhood (Blos, 1967). Whereas in childhood, the task is to separate from the parents of infancy, in adolescence, the task is to disengage emotionally from the now inner representations, a process that allows the individual to develop relationships outside the family. Disruptions in the early separation individuation process lay the groundwork for disturbances in internal object relations, those affectively-toned representational structures that ordinarily mediate the capacity for self-regulation and interpersonal relationships. Self-regulation may be viewed as a progressive developmental achievement that culminates in the ability to accurately identify needs and organize responses, to modulate activity level, to symbolically represent wishes and impulses, to tolerate delay and frustration, and soothe dysphoric affects while maintaining constructive engagement with others (Kopp, 1982).

Johnson and Connors (1987) trace the emergence of anorexia nervosa and bulimia nervosa to hypothesized disturbances in early object relationships that manifest as disorders of self-regulation and interpersonal regulation as the child confronts adolescent demands for differentiation and identity formation. Two dimensions of early caretaking are thought to contribute to the child's capacity for self-regulation: maternal (parental) involvement (overinvolvement and underinvolvement), and maternal affective tone (malevolent and nonmalevolent caretaking).[14] These authors speculate that the expression of disordered eating, in terms of restricting anorectic versus bulimic symptoms corresponds to the level of maternal overinvolvement or underinvolvement, respectively. Concurrently, the affective tone of the parental response contributes to the level of personality organization of individuals who become anorectic or bulimic. Specifically, hostility, negligence, and rejection in the caretaking environment are thought to be developmental antecedents to later borderline personality organization, as reflected in the malevolent object representations of borderline adolescent and adult patients (Westen, Ludolph, Lerner, Ruffins, & Wiss, 1990). Alternatively, eating-disordered patients with a history of nonmalevolent caretaking may be predisposed to develop a "false self" personality organization (Winnicott, 1965), in the context of disturbances in parental involvement. The level of maternal involvement combines with the affective tone of the relationship to produce two interacting dimensions of eating-disordered psychopathology: restricting versus bulimic mode, and borderline versus false self personality organization.

The restricting anorectic may have experienced her mother as intrusive, overprotective, and discouraging of separation and individuation (Johnson & Conners, 1987). She reaches puberty with fundamental deficits in interoceptive awareness (i.e., the ability to differentiate internal states), a deficient sense of separateness and connectedness, and poor self-regulatory capacities. Self-starvation becomes "a desperate attempt to assert some autonomy, defend the fragile self against further maternal intrusiveness, and protect the fragile ego from the psychobiological demands of adulthood" (p. 100). The predominant defensive structure of the restricting anorectic is paranoid—a restriction of entry by rigid, avoidant defenses.

In contrast to restricting anorectics, bulimic patients may have experienced their mothers as disengaged and emotionally unavailable. Unable to turn to the mother for soothing and comfort, the child seeks self-regulatory substitutes, such as food. Thus, the bulimic's eating behavior "may reflect a desperate attempt to compensate for an 'empty experience' resulting from maternal underinvolvement" (Johnson & Connors, 1987, p. 101). Although she may attempt a restricting stance, the would-be bulimic is often unable to sustain self-starvation because it intensifies her sense of emptiness and deficient holding. She is more likely to rely on diffuse, frantic, hysterical defenses against painful affects and the absence of positive introjects.

When parental overinvolvement has been malevolently intrusive (i.e., the caretaker has attempted to enmesh the child in a hostile dependent relationship), the restricting patient is at risk for developing a borderline personality organization. The symbolic focus of her paranoid system becomes body fat, which is to be avoided at all costs. The restricter experiences a sense of purpose, autonomy, and control as she organizes herself against the perceived threat (fat). Conversely, when parental underinvolvement is experienced as malevolent neglect, the bulimic patient is at risk for developing a borderline character. In this instance, parental withholding or disengagement is experienced as deliberate and aggressive, leaving the child with the feeling that she is worthless and unlovable. The borderline bulimic may later develop relationships patterned on earlier oscillations between desperate clinginess and rageful withdrawal, reflecting profound anxieties around separation and relatedness, and associated feelings of abandonment and confusion.

Eating-disordered individuals who present with "false self" organizations have not experienced their caretaking as predominantly malevolent. In response to accumulated parental "impingements" or misattunements, the child may develop a compliant adaptation to the caretaker's needs, while inwardly feeling nonexistent, fraudulent, and ineffectual (Winnicott, 1965). The anorectic with a false self deals with maternal intrusiveness by becoming pleasing and accommodating, relying on others for her sense of security and self-esteem. Her predominant anxiety around separation centers around fears of loss and depletion, not retaliation or annihilation. Rather than rely on paranoid defenses, the restricting anorectic develops obsessive-compulsive and phobic defenses.

In contrast to the restricter's preoccupation with her mother's overinvolvement, the bulimic manages maternal disengagement by developing a pseudomature adaptation, taking care of others and disavowing her own needs for comfort and nurturance. Lacking adequate structure to handle her more nurturant needs, she splits them off and experiences that part of herself as out-of-control and dangerous. Denial, intellectualization, and avoidance are employed as defenses, while food is invested with the ability to regulate painful or needy affect states.

Although Johnson and Connor's theoretical model is coherent and clinically meaningful, it has not been empirically tested. Given the salience of such constructs as malevolent object relations, the caregiver's parenting capacities, and false self development, future research should incorporate developmentally oriented measures of object relations (Diamond & Blatt, 1994; Westen et al., 1990), adult attachment history (Main, Kaplan, & Cassidy, 1985), and true versus false self experiences (Harter, Marold, & Whitesell, 1993).[15] Disturbed parent-child relationships do not necessarily imply that the earliest developmental years are critical, nor that disturbed self and object representations are a risk factor for specific forms of psychopathology, rather than being a more general risk factor. Cognitive-developmental research lends support to the notion of different object-relational processes (possibly coexisting) within individuals with severe psychopathology—some that derive from developmental arrests in the preschool (or preoedipal) years, some that reflect pathogenic disturbances during the

---

[14] As in other areas of psychopathology, the role of fathers in the development of their daughters' eating disorders has not been studied extensively (Phalen, 1992). Our reference to mothers reflects the current emphasis in the literature and is not meant to diminish the importance of paternal influences.

[15] In a recent study of false self phenomena and disordered eating, Striegel-Moore, Silberstein, & Rodin (1993) found that bulimic patients showed higher levels of Public Self-Consciousness, Social Anxiety, and Perceived Fraudulence when compared with matched, noneating-disordered college students.

preschool period that do not resemble normal functioning, and others that are related to developmental experiences in later childhood (Westen, 1989).

Early parent-child relationships have also been considered under the organizational principle of attachment. Recent research on the development of attachment has extended the focus from normal and atypical infants to older children, adolescents, and adults at risk for, or suffering from, psychopathology. Representations or internal working models of self and other in attachment relationships are formed during early childhood and tend to shape the individual's experience and construction of later relationships. Continuity in attachment organization has been documented in terms of the organizational coherence of behavior manifested during situations that normatively elicit attachment (i.e., the stable propensity to seek comfort from a primary caretaker during times of stress), although relatively little is known about developmental transformations in corresponding internal working models (Diamond & Blatt, 1994; Main et al., 1985; Steinberg, 1990). Kobak and Sceery (1988) have shown that different working models of attachment relationships are associated with different styles of self-regulation, understood in terms of the rules that organize the individual's response to distressing or challenging situations. For instance, attachment security, assessed retrospectively by the *Adult Attachment Interview,* was associated with greater ego resilience, less hostility, and less anxiety among late adolescents during the transition to college.

The relationship between security of attachment and vulnerability to eating disorders has not been systematically studied, despite the theoretical emphasis on separation distress among patients with eating-related psychopathology. A growing body of research is devoted to the individual's recollection of patterns of parental caregiving. In a preliminary study of attachment using a projective measure to tap Bowlby's construct of attachment (the *Hansburg Separation Anxiety Test*), Armstrong and Roth (1989) found that the majority of their sample of hospitalized eating-disordered patients demonstrated anxious attachment and extreme separation depression.

Several authors have used the *Parental Bonding Instrument* (Parker, Tupling, & Brown, 1979) to assess separation concerns in eating-disordered patients. The *PBI* is a 25-item self-report instrument that elicits information about the respondent's recollections of both parents during the first 16 years. Normative data from the scales are used to define four parenting styles: optimal parenting (High care-Low overprotection), affectionate constraint (High care-High overprotection), affectionless control (Low care-High overprotection), and neglectful parenting (Low care-Low overprotection).

An examination of studies using the *PBI* with eating-disordered patients reveals inconsistent findings with regard to the association between different parenting styles and the development of eating-disordered psychopathology. Palmer and colleagues failed to find an association between parenting style and different eating disorders (Palmer, Oppenhimer, & Marshall, 1988). Some investigators report that mothers are more likely to be rated in the affectionless control quandrant (Rhodes & Kroger, 1991), whereas others have found that fathers are perceived as more overprotective (Calam, Waller, Slade, & Newton, 1990) or lower

in empathic care (Steiger, Van der Feen, Goldstein, & Leichner, 1989). In a European study, adolescent anorectics were more likely than other psychiatric groups to describe their parenting as optimal (Russell, Kopec-Schrader, Rey, & Beaumont, 1992). Such a wide disparity in findings suggests three possible explanations: (a) the attachment relationships of eating-disordered patients are quite variable, paralleling the range of underlying personality organization discussed previously (from neurotic or false self to borderline); (b) the *PBI* may not be sufficiently sensitive to assess the quality of attachment relationships among eating-disordered patients; or (c) the constructs tapped by the *PBI* may not be relevant (or subtle enough) to capture the family processes that are operating in eating-disordered families.

The Family Context: Family Processes and Systems

Gradually, conceptualizations of the family in terms of the parent-child relationship have broadened to include the larger family system. Family theories of anorexia nervosa and bulimia nervosa have been studied in self-report and direct observation studies. Wonderlich (1992) offers a cogent critical review of family research in bulimia that is pertinent to eating disorders in general. First, most studies examine the "main effect" of family influences, minimizing variability among families in spite of accumulated evidence supporting heterogeneity (Kog & Vandereycken, 1989a; Rastam & Gillberg, 1991). Second, it has not been determined whether observed family characteristics are specific to eating disorders since most studies lack appropriate clinical control groups and very few are longitudinal or prospective, precluding an understanding of causality. Third, because of the dearth of comparative studies, available research cannot account for why the individual chooses disordered eating, as opposed to depression or some other breakdown in functioning. Fourth, until fairly recently, studies of families with an eating-disordered member failed to consider how family perceptions might be influenced by starvation, bulimic symptoms, or associated mood disturbance. Fifth, research has yet to examine nonshared influences, that is, the experiences within the family that differ for two children growing up together—despite evidence that the nonshared environment plays a key role in the divergence of siblings' or individuals' developmental paths. Is the risk familywide, or does it emanate from a specific parent-child relationship?

From a life cycle perspective, few studies have systematically examined the emergence of eating disorders in the context of developmental change, such as the pubertal transition for the developing adolescent or "leaving home" for the late adolescent. Very few studies have examined the reciprocal, transactional influences of co-occurring generational events and their respective developmental implications. For example, research has shown that marital dissatisfaction increases when children are adolescents, that rearing adolescents is harder, and that parents reevaluate their occupational achievements, health status, and sexual concerns (cf. Silverberg & Steinberg, 1990). Although family research has become more systems-oriented, the role of sibling relationships, and the ways in which they may contribute to vulnerability or protection against eating disorders, has been neglected (Plomin & Daniels, 1987). A recent review of findings pertaining to siblings of patients with an eating disorder focuses on static variables, such as family size, birth order, eating disorders and psychopathology in siblings, and self-reported sibling rivalry or incest (Vandereycken & Van Vrekem, 1992).

Furthermore, an overemphasis on psychopathology has prevented researchers from placing family observational findings in a developmental context. For instance, family interaction studies with psychologically healthy adolescents and their parents suggest that it is not so much the level of family conflict or cohesion that matters but the balance between them; that is, the ability to negotiate conflict in the context of emotional cohesion (Steinberg, 1990). Finally, researchers have yet to consider ways in which the child or adolescent contributes to her own risk for the development and maintenance of an eating disorder (Cook, Kenny, & Goldstein, 1991). Each of these areas requires process-oriented studies of different contextual systems and their interactions, concurrently and over time.

In the previous section, we discussed the potential role of early parent-child relationships in the development of eating disorders. Here, we take a more systemic approach, considering familywide influences from three theoretical perspectives. The first is Minuchin's conceptualization of patients with anorexia nervosa in terms of the "psychosomatic family model." The second is Humphrey's view of nurturance deficits in bulimic families and the areas of divergence between restricter and bulimic families. Third, we consider recent evidence suggesting that observed differences between families could be a function of some other mediating variable, such as comorbid disorders or the individual's clinical state.

From a structural family perspective, Minuchin and his colleagues identified five predominant characteristics of interaction in families with an anorectic member: enmeshment, overprotectiveness, rigidity, lack of conflict resolution, and the triangulation of the child in marital conflict (Minuchin, Rosman, & Baker, 1978; Sargent, Liebman, & Silver, 1985). According to Schwartz, Barrett, and Saba (1985), bulimic families share these five interaction patterns but show three additional characteristics: isolation, consciousness of appearances, and a special meaning attached to food and eating. Similarly, Selvini-Palazzoli (1974) characterized eating-disordered families in terms of the importance of self-sacrifice, filial loyalty, preserving appearances, marital discord, a rejection of communicated messages, poor conflict resolution, and secret coalitions.

Kog and his colleagues conducted a controlled comparative study of eating-disordered families in Belgium in an attempt at concept-validation of the "psychosomatic family" model (Kog, Vandereycken, & Vertommen, 1989). They used observational and self-report data to operationalize Minuchin's model along four dimensions: the intensity of intrafamilial boundaries ("enmeshment"), the degree of family adaptability or stability ("rigidity"), the degree of avoidance or recognition of intrafamilial tension ("overprotectiveness"), and the family's way of handling disagreements ("conflict resolution"). Results of a cluster analysis of the behaviorally measured dimensions (boundaries, adaptability, and conflict) among 55 eating-disordered families revealed seven types of families: some families conformed to Minuchin's psychosomatic model; others were less

extreme on these dimensions; and still others showed patterns opposite to what would be expected. The type of eating disorder was not correlated with a particular type of family functioning.

Preliminary findings from their questionnaire study, based on results of the *Leuven Family Questionnaire,* suggested that the family's social status and life cycle phase may have an impact on family functioning (Kog et al., 1989).[16] Although all eating-disordered groups reported more conflict and disorganization than normal controls, these differences diminished as social status increased such that differences were no longer significant for upper social class families. Comparing families in the same phase of the family life cycle, eating-disordered families with a pubertal adolescent reported less cohesion than their normal counterparts, whereas families in the launching phase reported more cohesion than corresponding normal families. In the adolescent phase proper, the eating-disordered families reported less conflict and disorganization than normals. These findings need to be replicated, since a subsequent study failed to find a significant effect for the age of the eating-disordered family member on any subscale of the LFQ (Kog & Vandereycken, 1989b).

Wood et al., (1989) have questioned Kog's operationalization of key concepts of the psychosomatic model, such as enmeshment, triangulation, and overprotection. More critically, they propose that the term "psychosomatic" be reserved for the processes that directly influence psychophysiology. In eating disorders, behaviors mediate between family patterns of functioning and the "disease activity" of weight loss and other symptoms. Although eating-disordered families were not included in their study, they found support for the five dimensions of the "psychosomatic family" among families of children with Chrohn's disease, ulcerative colitis, and functional recurrent abdominal pain syndrome. Laboratory scores of disease activity were correlated with triangulation and marital dysfunction but not with enmeshment, overprotection, rigidity, and conflict avoidance.

Large-scale comparative studies of families with and without eating disorders are rare. Rastam and Gillberg (1991) conducted a total population study in Sweden and found that families with children with anorexia nervosa were similar to a comparison group of families with age-, sex-, and school-matched children without anorexia nervosa. The two groups were similar in terms of size, sibship position, and family interaction according to the *FACES.* The anorectic families did not evidence greater enmeshment, rigidity, and overprotectiveness. Contrary to expectation, the anorectic families were less "problem denying" and were more open about conflicts and major family problems.

Humphrey and her colleagues have attempted to integrate family systems theory with object relations theory to account for the origin and maintenance of eating disorders (Humphrey, 1991; Humphrey & Stern, 1988). Based on their integration of these theoretical perspectives with family observation studies,

---

[16] The Leuven Family Questionnaire consists of three scales: Conflict, Cohesion, and Disorganization. Eating-disordered families reported more conflict and disorganization than normal families, but levels of cohesion did not differ. Restricting anorectics were more similar to normal families and bulimic anorectics reported more conflict and disorganization and lower levels of cohesion.

they hypothesize that families of eating-disordered individuals are deficient in the provision of a parental "holding environment" and in the development of healthy object relations. The holding environment refers to the capacity of empathically available parents to soothe and contain the child's negative affects, normal grandiosity, and sexual impulses (Winnicott, 1965).

According to Humphrey, the holding environment in anorectic and bulimic families fails them in nurturance, tension regulation, and affirmation of separate identities. These developmental deficits are transmitted across generations by means of the ongoing interpersonal relationships within the family and the corresponding internalized object relations of its members. Defensively, the family maintains an idealized view of itself as "perfect" and splits off the unwanted or unacceptable aspects, which are projected onto the eating-disordered child who "accepts" this role. Through the mechanisms of splitting, idealization, devaluation, and projective identification, the anorectic or bulimic daughter emerges as the family heroine or victim, protecting the parents from confronting their own sense of inadequacy, conflict, or vulnerability.

Eating-disordered families diverge in their "solutions" to deficits in nurturance, soothing, and individuation (Humphrey, 1991). Anorectic families are nurturant so long as the child does not attempt to separate, at which point they may be likely to negate or abandon their daughters. In bulimic families, all members are "hungry" for love and affection, and the daughter's developmental strivings may elicit criticism and rejection. Binge-purge cycles are conceptualized as a metaphoric expression of unfulfilled nurturant cravings (binges), coupled with the expulsion of anger and frustration (purges) that abounds within such families. The anorectic family tends to be constricted, superficial, and denying, whereas the bulimic family is more likely to be chaotic, hostile, and understructured.[17]

Humphrey (1986, 1987, 1988) and others have used the Structural Analysis of Social Behavior (*SASB;* Benjamin, 1974, 1984) to test family theories of eating disorders. The *SASB* is a circumplex model of interpersonal relations and intrapsychic representations organized around two orthogonal dimensions, affiliation (love-hate) and interdependence (freedom-enmeshment). Combinations of varying degrees of affiliation and interdependence characterize three clusters: focus on other, focus on self, and intrapsychic. In conjunction with a self-report measure *(Intrex),* there is a behavioral coding system that parallels the model (Wonderlich, 1992).

Comparing bulimics, bulimic anorectic, anorectic, and normal controls on *SASB* ratings, Humphrey (1986) found that both bulimic groups experienced deficits in parental nurturance and empathy relative to normal young women, whereas restricting anorectics did not report nurturance deficits. These findings were more consistent for bulimics' relationships with their fathers than with their mothers. All eating-disordered groups experienced

their relationships with parents as more hostile and less supportive than did normal controls. These interpersonal experiences were paralleled by an inability to nourish and accept the self. In support of Humphrey's theory, only deficits in parental nurturance and comfort were specific to bulimia and not anorexia.

In a subsequent study, Humphrey (1988) used the *SASB* to study family relations in 74 mother-father-daughter triads. As in the preceding study, both bulimic groups reported greater mutual neglect, rejection, and blame, and also less understanding, nurturance, and support in their families relative to normal controls. The restricting anorectic families tended to deny such problems but demonstrated severe marital distress, at least by maternal report. The findings lend support to both Minuchin's and Humphrey's models: The positive view of parent-child relationships in anorectic families is thought to divert attention from the parents' troubled marriages, and the higher need for nurturance and greater hostility in bulimic families is given metaphoric expression in the symptoms of bingeing and purging.

Humphrey's conceptualization of familial dysfunction is noteworthy, but some of the constructs have not been researched and are too broad to account for eating pathology. Familywide deficits in nurturance, containment of affect, and support for individuation may be characteristic of many eating-disordered families, but they are not specific to such families. It would be important to examine the moderating role of personality functioning because (a) primitive defenses (e.g., splitting, projective identification) and relationships based on part-object representations are characteristic of severe personality and family disturbance (organized at a borderline level); and (b) a significant proportion of eating-disordered patients exhibit comorbid personality and/or affective disorders.

In a study comparing subgroups of eating-disordered patients on the *SASB,* Wonderlich and Swift (1990b) found that differences among subgroups and controls were no longer significant once level of dysthymic mood was statistically controlled. Among the eating-disordered groups, only those with high dysthymia scores differed from controls on their ratings of relationships with parents, perceiving more hostility in their parental relationships. The failure to find restricter-bulimic differences is consistent with the Belgian studies but differs from Humphrey's findings. The authors suggest several possible explanations, including their exclusive reliance on self-reports, their use of older, as opposed to younger restricting anorectics, and their different usage of the *SASB.* Further longitudinal study is needed to determine the relative contributions of affective, eating, and personality disturbance to family functioning, and the temporal relationships among them.

Less is known about the degree to which observed patterns of family interaction are affected by parental psychopathology. An eating disorder, depressive illness, or impulse disturbance in a parent will impinge differentially on children in the family, depending on the life-cycle stage, gender, and personality characteristics of parent and child. Recent research suggests that maternal attitudes and behaviors, particularly in the realm of diet and weight, have an impact on parenting behavior and may be associated with disordered eating in their children. Clinical reports suggest that mothers with bulimia nervosa may have difficulties parenting their preschool children, particularly during episodes of

---

[17] Consistent with Humphrey's findings, studies of expressed emotion among eating-disordered families reveal significantly higher levels of critical comments from family members toward a bulimic offspring, compared with an anorectic offspring. See Hodes and LeGrange (1993) for a review of expressed emotion research and eating disorders.

bingeing and purging. Bulimic mothers have been reported to be less tolerant of their children's demands, to respond more punitively, and to have problems with feeding, related to efforts to limit the amount of food in the house and/or undue concern about their children's weight (Fahy & Treasure, 1989; Stein & Fairburn, 1989).

In Attie and Brooks-Gunn's (1989) nonclinical adolescent sample, a trend ($p < .10$) emerged for mothers' disordered eating to predict daughters' disordered eating during follow-up testing. Pike and Rodin (1991) found that mothers of adolescent daughters with disordered eating had a longer history of dieting and were more eating disordered themselves, compared with mothers of girls without disordered eating. Furthermore, these mothers were more critical of their daughters' appearance and eating than of their own, and thought their daughters should lose more weight than comparison mothers. Also unlike comparison mothers, mothers of daughters with disordered eating rated their daughters as significantly less attractive than the daughters rated themselves.

EATING DISORDERS IN INFANCY AND CHILDHOOD: CONTINUITY WITH ADOLESCENT ONSET EATING DISORDERS

Prepubertal Onset of Eating Disorders

The occurrence of anorexia nervosa in prepubertal children presents a challenge to theories that emphasize the pivotal role of puberty in the development of the disorder. Crisp (1984) is a major proponent of the view of anorexia as a retreat from the maturational demands of adolescence, which include separating from the family, forging peer relationships, and integrating one's emerging sexuality. Alessi, Krahn, Brehm, and Wittekindt (1989) consider the possibility that pathological levels of body and weight preoccupation are now emerging at earlier ages. In one study, nearly 7% of third- through sixth-grade children scored above the cutoff for severe eating pathology on the children's version of the *Eating Attitude Test* (ChEAT; Maloney, McGuire, & Daniels, 1988).

In a retrospective controlled study, Jacobs and Isaacs (1986) compared a group of prepubertal anorectics with postpubertal anorectics and age-matched prepubertal neurotic controls. The prepubertal and postpubertal anorectic groups were similar to one another in showing a high rate of intrafamilial communication difficulties and disturbances in the father-child relationship. Both anorectic groups also showed high levels of sexual anxiety as well as self-injurious behaviors and suicide attempts. Conversely, reports of sexual anxiety or self-injury were low or nonexistent in the prepubertal neurotic group. Prepubertal anorectics differed from postpubertal anorectics in two important respects: They reported more childhood feeding problems and family preoccupation with feeding, and they reported more major life events as possible precipitants for the eating disorder. In addition, there was a slightly (nonsignificant) higher proportion of boys in the prepubertal group compared with the postpubertal group.

In their review, Lask and Bryant-Waugh (1992) identified four salient characteristics of children with anorexia nervosa: (a) preoccupation with body weight and shape, with a desire to be thinner; (b) the child's stated belief of being larger than in reality (body disparagement); (c) low self-esteem manifested in interpersonal problems and perfectionistic strivings; (d) and a high incidence of depression. Available outcome studies suggest that early onset anorexia nervosa is a serious disorder that often carries a poor prognosis.

In addition to anorexia nervosa, a number of atypical eating disorders have been described in prepubertal children, including food avoidance emotional disorder, pervasive refusal syndrome, selective eating, and food fads. In two case series, Jaffe and Singer (1989) and Singer, Ambuel, Wade, and Jaffe (1992) described developmentally normal children who presented with prepubertal eating disorders that did not meet DSM-III-R criteria for anorexia nervosa or bulimia nervosa. The patients were boys and girls (mean age 5.4 years) who refused to eat normal amounts or types of food, displayed ritualistic behaviors during meals, and as a result, showed compromised nutritional and growth status. None of the children reported a fear of fatness or body image disturbance; rather, they tended to display a phobic aversion to solid foods. In the first study, seven of the eight children reported elevated scores on the internalizing scales of the *Achenbach Child Behavior Checklist* (Achenbach, 1978), and their family histories were remarkable for alcoholism and affective disorders. For all three children in the second sample, onset of feeding difficulties followed a potentially anxiety-provoking physical event such as choking or acute medical illness. Family stressors also appeared to contribute to the child's avoidant response to food.

Pugliese, Lifshitz, Grad, Fort, and Marks-Katz (1983) identified a subgroup of children with short stature and delayed puberty due to self-imposed caloric restriction arising from a fear of becoming obese. The children differed from prepubertal anorectic cases in several respects: they reported no body image distortion, a male predominance, and no vomiting, laxative abuse, or compulsive exercise. These patients responded well to nutritional and psychiatric counseling within the pediatric endocrinology center.

These studies provide evidence for both continuity and discontinuity between prepubertal and postpubertal eating disorders. First, although the incidence is not known, school-age children do present with determined food refusal associated with fears of fatness or obesity, preoccupation with body weight, and/or a phobic avoidance of solid foods. These children are at risk for delayed puberty, short stature or slowed growth. Second, depression is a frequent concomitant of eating disorders in children, leading some authors to suggest that the two disorders may be more closely intertwined in young children (DiNicola, Roberts, & Oke, 1989). Alessi et al. (1989) observed that weight loss is a less frequent manifestation of major depression in children; however, starvation may trigger a depressive syndrome in children through its effect on cortisol levels. Third, gender differences in the prevalence of eating disorders are less pronounced among prepubertal children than adolescents and adults. Yet, the preponderance of females among childhood eating disorders is significant given the male preponderance of most child psychiatric disorders and the equal rates of depression in prepubertal males and females (Angold & Rutter, 1992). Finally, retrospective studies suggest that prepubertal anorexia nervosa and food-avoidant disorders are often associated with family stress, major life events, or traumatic feeding episodes.

Family events may represent alternative stressors to puberty for the younger child, who developmentally is probably less concerned with appearance and identity and more dependent on his or her family (DiNicola et al., 1989).

Infant Onset of Eating Problems: The Case of Failure to Thrive

Research on childhood eating disorders has been impeded by diagnostic and conceptual difficulties. Mixed etiologies, complex biological and environmental interactions, and varied syndrome expression contribute to conceptual confusion. Eating disorders of childhood tend to be grouped into those that have their onset during infancy and those that begin in early or later childhood. Disorders occurring in infancy (birth to 2 years) are typically referred to as feeding disorders, to emphasize the dyadic nature of the disturbance. Infant feeding disorders include a variety of conditions characterized by insufficient or atypical food intake such as swallowing difficulties, poor appetite, selective food refusal, pica, and ruminative vomiting after or during feeding (Budd et al., 1992). These disorders can create, coexist with, or appear as sequelae of failure to thrive (FTT), defined as the child's weight, height, or growth rate below the third or fifth percentile (Budd et al., 1992).

Although FTT was formerly divided into nonorganic (NOFT) and organic (OFT) syndromes based on the absence or presence of a known physical problem contributing to growth failure, it is now viewed as a final common pathway for multiple biological, psychological, and social influences. Growth disturbances that have their onset in the preschool or school-age years are typically referred to as psychosocial dwarfism. A substantial proportion of children with chronic feeding disorders may not meet criteria for growth failure, suggesting the need for a more comprehensive classification system for childhood feeding disorders (Budd et al., 1992).

Several models have been proposed to explain infantile FTT and feeding disorders. Most authors regard FTT primarily as a syndrome of malnutrition, brought about by biological and psychosocial risk factors (Drotar, 1991; Frank & Zeisel, 1988). Others stress the phenomenological similarity between the affective disturbance seen in FTT children and clinically depressed adults (Powell & Bettes, 1992). Earlier, Spitz and Wolf (1946) described a syndrome of anaclitic depression in infants suffering from emotional deprivation, characterized by apathy, irritability, sadness, weight loss, and growth failure. Finally, some investigators have focused on the heightened levels of anger and aggression in the feeding interaction of older infants and toddlers, drawing a parallel between infantile and adolescent eating disorders as struggles for autonomy (Chatoor & Egan, 1987).

In his review of the family context of failure-to-thrive infants, Drotar (1991) stresses the contributions of economic disadvantage, family routines, social support, and level of family cohesion to early childhood malnutrition in nonorganic failure-to-thrive children. Families with FTT children are typically from lower socioeconomic backgrounds which may contribute, directly and indirectly, to the family's ability to provide sufficient caloric and nutritional input. Direct effects of poverty include limits on the amount and quality of food available to the child due to diminished economic resources and sometimes, misallocation of food. Indirect effects include family conflict or disorganization, which can disrupt the parent-child interaction through inconsistent feeding schedules, faulty responses to the child's feeding initiatives, family discord during mealtimes, and poor monitoring of the child's food intake and growth patterns. Parents of nonorganic failure-to-thrive children have been shown to have inadequate social and emotional support, compared with parents of demographically similar, normally growing children. They also are at greater risk for mood or other psychological disturbance.

Comparative studies, however, have questioned the role of parental distress, family disorganization, and economic hardship on the development of FTT in children with and without physical handicaps (Budd et al., 1992; Singer, Song, Hill, & Jaffe 1990). From a transactional perspective, the child's physical and temperamental characteristics may contribute to poor parental responsiveness, which may create and maintain negative patterns of interaction. Risk factors such as prematurity, intrauterine growth retardation, and acute physical illnesses are overrepresented in populations of FTT children.

Other authors suggest that some children with FTT manifest a form of infantile depression in which positive affect, appetite, and caloric intake are all compromised as a manifestation of a depressive syndrome. In a comparison of FTT children with a group of normally growing children, FTT children showed less positive affect across feeding and nonfeeding activities and heightened negative affect during a meal (Polan et al., 1991). Failure-to-thrive children who were both acutely and chronically malnourished expressed the highest levels of negative affect during feeding, suggesting that affective distress may in part reflect the child's malnourished state. The authors pose a pertinent question, "Do children who develop FTT first become depressed and then stop eating or do they develop blunted affect and apathy as a psychophysiological complication of primary malnutrition?" Prospective research is needed to determine the temporal relationship between affective disturbance and eating/weight changes in infancy and the coherence or transformation of these developmental trajectories over time.

Drawing on the work of A. Freud, Greenspan and Lourie, and others, Chatoor and Egan (1987) have proposed a developmental classification of infantile feeding disorders, corresponding to three developmental tasks of infancy: disorders of homeostasis, disorders of attachment, and disorders of separation and individuation. A "posttraumatic feeding disorder" has been added to characterize infants and toddlers who refuse food intake after painful or traumatic experiences associated with feeding (Chatoor, Conley, & Dickson, 1988). Although their original tripartite classification scheme has not been empirically validated, it offers a developmentally oriented framework. Feeding disorders may arise in the first 2 months of life, when the infant is learning to regulate states of hunger and satiation, with self-motivated oral feedings. Feeding problems that develop at this stage are often associated with medical difficulties such as autonomic dysregulation (colicky baby), delayed oral musculature development, respiratory problems, and congenital abnormalities of the gastrointestinal tract.

Disorders of attachment emerge during the next phase (2 to 6 months), when infants are developing an attachment with their primary caretaker. Disturbed mother-infant interactions are frequent concomitants of these feeding disorders: Mothers and infants are often listless and disengaged, sometimes secondary to mother's affective illness, character pathology, social isolation, and economic hardship. Disorders of separation and individuation emerge between 6 months and 3 years, when the infant's motoric and cognitive maturation supports move toward emotional separation and self-definition. Anxiety about issues of control and autonomy dominate the feeding situation, which becomes a battle of wills between mother and child. Disturbed parent-child interactions during feeding are hypothesized to interfere with normal somatopsychological differentiation, the process by which infants, beginning in the second half of the first year of life, begin to distinguish physical sensations (hunger, satiety) from emotional states (affection, anger, distress).

Chatoor and colleagues have used the term "infantile anorexia nervosa" to characterize the subgroup of feeding-disordered infants and toddlers that manifest a developmental disorder of separation and individuation. In one study, they observed 42 infants and toddlers with infantile anorexia nervosa and 30 matched controls during a feeding period followed by a play period (Chatoor, Egan, Getson, Menvielle, & O'Donnell, 1987). The sample was of mixed SES and racial background; mean age of the children was 20 months. The "anorectic infants" met the following criteria: food refusal or extreme food selectivity resulting in inadequate food intake and growth failure; onset of feeding problem between 6 months and 3 years; and intense parental involvement, anxiety, and frustration about the infant's poor food intake.

Significant differences in mother-infant interaction emerged in both feeding and play situations: The feeding-disordered group demonstrated less dyadic reciprocity, less maternal contingency, more dyadic conflict, and more struggle for control. In addition, mothers in the feeding-disordered group appeared more sad, distressed, and angry, and their infants displayed more gaze aversion, stiffening on being touched, and angry, distressed affect. Conversely, the mothers of control group infants tended to wait for the infant to initiate interactions, allowed more give-and-take in feeding and play situations, and were more cheerful and encouraging.

Chatoor, Egan, and Getson (1990) have written, "We consider both the infantile and adolescent forms of anorexia nervosa developmental disorders of separation and individuation in which the drive for autonomy and control is expressed through food refusal" (p. 317). In both infants and adolescents, food refusal is thought to be rooted in the mother's early failure to reflect back to the child the child's own self (mirroring), and instead to impose her own fixed view and will on the child. These relational difficulties interfere with the child's ability to differentiate somatic from emotional experiences, so that food intake becomes dominated by anger and the need to assert oneself rather than by internal hunger cues. However, unlike the feeding-disordered infants, who are described as willful and active, adolescents with anorexia nervosa are described retrospectively as having been easy babies. Chatoor postulates that temperamental differences may enable the adolescent to observe and conform to parental needs throughout childhood, until the developmental challenges of adolescence force a break in this compliant adaptation.

Sturm and Stancin (1990) question the utility and validity of applying the adolescent and adult diagnosis of anorexia to infants,

highlighting significant areas of discontinuity between the infant and adolescent disorders. Epidemiological differences are salient: Estimates of feeding problems in infants and toddlers range from 12% to 34%, a rate significantly higher than the 1% to 2% of adolescents with anorexia nervosa. Gender and socioeconomic differences are also pronounced, with a significantly higher proportion of boys and lower SES families among the feeding-disordered group. Essential criteria for the diagnosis of anorexia nervosa, including disturbances of body image and of reproductive functioning, are not applicable to infants. Sturm and Stancin (1990) suggest that infantile anorexia nervosa might better be described as a "control relationship syndrome," the term Anders (1989) developed to characterize how "a feeding disturbance may become a control disturbance when hunger, satiety, and homeostatic regulation become struggles over food preferences and feeding styles" (p. 137).

Continuity in Eating Disorders across Age Periods

The study of these early and prepubertal disorders highlights continuities and discontinuities across eating disorders at different developmental periods. In feeding-disordered youngsters and eating-disordered adolescents, food intake becomes derailed from its primary function of nourishing the body, to a means of controlling or expressing distressing emotions. Across age periods, children with eating disturbances appear to be at increased risk for affective disturbance. Although the stage-salient tasks may differ, developmental issues related to emotion regulation, self-esteem, and struggles for recognition and autonomy seem to underlie the eating disturbances of young children and adolescents. The concept of a "phobia" also threads through the childhood onset cases and has been central to Crisp's (1984) view of anorexia nervosa as a phobic avoidance of a postpubertal body weight and its sexual and psychosocial connotations.

Whether feeding disorders of infancy are related to eating disorders of adolescence is not known, given the absence of prospective research.[18] Marchi and Cohen (1990) traced maladaptive eating patterns in an epidemiological sample of over 800 children. Six eating behaviors were assessed by maternal interview at three time periods, when children were 1 through 10, 9 through 18, and 2.5 years later when they were 12 through 20. In late childhood and adolescence, children and mothers were interviewed for DSM-III-R disorders. Results indicated that children who show early feeding problems are at risk for subsequent problems. Pica in early childhood was related to bulimic symptoms in adolescence, suggesting developmental continuity in uncontrolled eating. Fights at mealtimes were predictive of bulimic symptoms. Digestive problems and picky eating were predictive of anorectic symptoms, reflecting a general tendency to eat less. Weight concerns and weight reduction efforts were not a risk factor for subsequent symptoms of anorexia nervosa.

---

[18] Early feeding difficulties have been described in some retrospective reports of anorectic patients. In her population study of Swedish 16-year-old adolescents with anorexia nervosa, Rastam (1992) found an excess of severe gastrointestinal problems and feeding problems in the developmental histories of anorectics compared with matched controls. Jacobs and Isaacs (1986) found that a history of mealtime feeding difficulties after age 5 years distinguished prepubertal anorectics from both postpubertal anorectics and prepubertal psychiatric controls.

TRANSACTIONS BETWEEN BIOLOGICAL FACTORS AND ENVIRONMENTAL RESPONSE

Another source of vulnerability to eating disorders derives from the interaction between a biological predisposition toward an illness or personality trait, and environmental factors affecting the individual. The possibility of a genetic contribution to the development of an eating disorder has been researched in family aggregation studies, twin studies, and studies of personality traits.

Family Aggregation and Twin Studies

Family aggregation studies document the occurrence of eating disorders and other psychiatric illnesses among biological relatives, usually first-degree relatives (parents, offspring, and siblings) who share both heredity and family environment. Strober et al. (1990) found evidence for the intergenerational transmission of anorexia nervosa, which was eight times as common among female first-degree relatives of anorectic women compared with nonpsychiatric and psychiatric controls. Eating disorders were not more common among relatives of unipolar and bipolar affective disorder probands, suggesting that anorexia nervosa and affective disorders show independent familial transmission. Affective disorders were more common among relatives of anorectic probands, but this association was accounted for by the subset of anorectics with coexisting major depression. Bulimia nervosa did not aggregate in families to the same degree although the lifetime prevalence of bulimia was somewhat elevated among female relatives of anorectic probands compared with affective disorder groups. Other studies also have failed to find an elevated risk of bulimia in relatives of patients with bulimia (Hudson, Pope, Jonas, Yurgelun-Todd, & Frankenburg, 1987). One exception is a study by Kassett and colleagues, which revealed an increased risk for bulimia (9.6% vs. 3.5%) in relatives of hospitalized probands compared with relatives of normal controls (Kassett et al., 1989).

Twin studies examine the concordance rates among twin pairs. To date, researchers have investigated twins raised within the same family environment; conclusions about the relative roles of nature and nurture will have to await studies of twins adopted away, twins reared apart, and cross-fostering. However, small sample twin studies report a higher concordance rate for monozygotic compared with dizygotic twins with anorexia nervosa (Holland, Hall, Murray, Russell, & Crisp, 1984) and, more recently, twins with bulimia nervosa (Fichter & Noegel, 1990; Hsu, Chesler, & Santouse, 1990). Kendler et al. (1991) interviewed 2,163 female twins from a population-based registry and found a significant difference in the probandwise concordance rate for narrowly defined and broadly defined bulimia nervosa. Among monozygotic twins, the concordance rate for narrowly defined bulimia was 22.9%, compared with 8.7% in dizygotic twins.

Personality Characteristics

Another group of studies considers the presence of certain personality or temperamental characteristics as potential risk factors for the development of an eating disorder or for the expression of a particular eating disorder pattern. Drawing on Cloninger's neuroadaptive model of personality, Strober (1991) proposes that the interaction between heritable variations in personality traits and environmental response underlies the child's vulnerability to develop an eating disorder. Cloninger (1987) has described three independent, bipolar dimensions of personality, which he calls novelty seeking, harm avoidance, and reward dependence. Novelty seeking (behavioral activation) is viewed as a tendency toward exhilaration or excitement in response to novel or rewarding stimuli. Harm avoidance (behavioral inhibition) refers to a tendency to inhibit behavior in response to uncertainty or threat. Reward dependence (behavioral maintenance) is posited as an innate propensity to seek out emotional support and to respond with heightened sensitivity to approval or rejection.

Strober (1991) hypothesizes that individuals with anorexia nervosa tend toward avoidance of harm, low novelty seeking, and reward dependence. This triad of temperamental characteristics renders the individual vulnerable to disruptions in self-experience and dysregulation of feeling states. He writes:

> Genetically extreme temperaments and personality traits can predispose an individual to a lower-than-optimal threshold for experiencing inner tensions and to a correspondingly greater sensitivity to disruption of self-object ties; when such individuals are inclined by nature to avoid novelty and harm and are possessed of an unusual responsiveness to environmental cues, they will inevitably experience a more pressing intrapsychic need to maintain unwavering control over threatening affective states. (p. 363)

In Strober's model, these reciprocal influences determine how self-experiences are restructured at times of developmental change. For instance, pubertal change may be experienced as an impetus for differentiation and expansion or as a humiliating betrayal that threatens to expose a weakened self structure. The individual who is likely to avoid harm and novelty will protect the self by adopting highly patterned and compulsively ritualized adaptive (defensive) behaviors, predicated on a repudiation of any awareness of affectivity, desire, or neediness.

Casper et al. (1992) investigated adaptive personality dimensions among 50 hospitalized eating-disordered patients and 19 healthy controls of similar age (range 12 to 39 years). Results showed that anorectic patients differed significantly from bulimic patients and healthy controls on personality dimensions reflecting behavioral control (impulsivity), emotional control (danger seeking), and cognitive control (traditionalism). Contrary to expectation, bulimic patients did not show greater than normal impulsivity or risk taking. Restricting anorectics showed high levels of self-discipline, emotional caution, and conscientiousness. These findings are consistent with previous studies that characterize restricting anorectics as more socially withdrawn, controlling, perfectionistic, avoidant, and sensitive to culturally desirable norms.

According to Casper, the adolescent who is poorly equipped to manage developmental challenges focuses on the pursuit of the thin ideal to cope with deficits in self-definition and self-esteem. The proclivity for emotional overcontrol, inhibition, and conformity is likely to support the decision to diet and to increase the likelihood that dieting may become excessive and precipitate anorexia nervosa. Tendencies toward inhibition enable the anorectic to suppress appetite and maintain rigid restraint. Self-starvation is further reinforced by a sense of achievement, control, and adherence to a demanding conscience.

The preceding findings are consistent with parental reports that described anorectics as having been shy, inhibited, and perfectionistic children (Bruch, 1973; Casper et al., 1981). Reznick, Hegeman, Kaufman, Woods, and Jacobs (1992) have shown that extreme inhibition in childhood can be a prodromal sign of, or indicator of risk for poor adult mental health, particularly anxiety and depression. They define behavioral inhibition is as "a temperamentally based disposition of children to react consistently to unfamiliar events, both social and nonsocial, with initial restraint" (p. 301). For about one-half inhibited children, behavioral inhibition remains stable from infancy through early adolescence. Because of the potential significance of childhood inhibition for the development of anorexia nervosa, prospective studies of inhibited children should include a regular assessment of eating behavior and weight-related outcomes, as well as the relationship between inhibition and other internalizing styles, such as perfectionism and overcontrol.

Although temperamental dispositions may increase vulnerability toward a particular developmental trajectory, transactions within the family context may further modify an evolving developmental pathway. The child vulnerable to anorexia nervosa may be growing up in a family environment that supports her propensity to retreat from the unfamiliar; in this instance, there may be a positive "match" between the child's temperamental predispositions and the environmental response (Strober, 1991). Because of their own temperaments and attachment histories, parents may fail to provide a relational context that fosters autonomy, competence, and self-regulation in stage-appropriate ways. Conversely, certain temperamental profiles may predispose the child to develop insecure attachments as a function of the lack of "fit" between these biological predispositions and the parental response.

CONTINUITY BETWEEN EATING PROBLEMS AND DISORDERS

One of the most challenging questions raised by a developmental approach to the study of eating problems and eating disorders concerns the nature and degree of continuity, first between dieting behavior and clinical syndromes, and second, between early adaptational patterns and later eating disorders.

The issue of a continuum of eating pathology, from dieting to clinical syndromes, is complex because most dieting adolescent and adult women do not go on to develop an eating disorder. Yet these normal dieters share many characteristics with eating-disordered individuals particularly in the realms of weight preoccupation, concern with appearance, and eating behaviors (Garner, Olmsted, Polivy, & Garfinkel, 1984; Polivy & Herman, 1987). With regard to the continuity issue, Sameroff and Seifer (1990) point out, "Developmental psychopathologists make no prior assumptions about either continuity or discontinuity. They are concerned centrally with both the connections and lack of connections between normality and disorder" (p. 52).

Normative is not synonymous with normality; dieting is pervasive among certain groups of adolescent and adult women, despite its deleterious effects on health and well-being (Attie & Brooks-Gunn, 1987; Polivy & Herman, 1987). Health hazards associated with weight-control efforts for teenagers include retardation of physical growth, delayed pubertal development, menstrual abnormalities, weakness, persistent irritability, constipation, poor concentration, sleep difficulties, and impulses to binge.

Results of a comprehensive, school-based survey administered to 36,320 Minnesota public school students in Grades 7 through 12 during 1987 to 1988 revealed that almost two-thirds of adolescent girls reported having been on a diet during the previous year (Story et al., 1991). Of these, 12% were chronic dieters who had been on a diet more than 10 times or were always dieting during the past year. Conversely, 2% of the boys were chronic dieters. The percentage of chronic dieters was significantly lower in Grades 7 and 8 compared with Grades 9 through 12. Few SES or location (rural, urban, suburban) differences were found for the prevalence of chronic dieting. Black girls were less likely to diet than white girls, but other ethnic differences did not emerge. Excessive dieting was strongly related to bulimic symptoms (bingeing and purging); chronic dieters were 7 to 13 times more likely to use purging techniques compared with other teenagers.

Restrained eating (i.e., the cognitively mediated effort to combat the urge to eat) is common among adolescent and adult women attempting to control their weight. In a series of studies, Herman, Polivy and colleagues have shown that self-reported restrained eaters are vulnerable to disinhibition of dietary restraint in laboratory and nonlaboratory settings; that is, they tend to overeat after a disruption of self-control (Polivy & Herman, 1987). Disinhibition or "counterregulation" may be triggered in a variety of contexts: after the consumption of a high-calorie preload or one believed to be high in calories; after the consumption of alcohol; or in response to negative mood states (Ruderman, 1986).

Similar factors have been shown to elicit binges in normal-weight patients with bulimia nervosa (Wardle & Beinart, 1981), as well as obese binge eaters (Loro & Orleans, 1981; Wardle & Beales, 1988). Ogden and Wardle (1991) found that whereas depression disrupts the self-control of the dieter, eating a "forbidden food" is associated with increased guilt but lessens anxiety, suggesting a "comforting" effect. Of relevance is a study by Lehman and Rodin (1989) that showed individuals with bulimia nervosa were less likely than restrained and nonrestrained eaters to nurture themselves in ways unrelated to food. These findings are consonant with Humphrey's (1991) theory of nurturance deficits in bulimic families.

Heatherton and Polivy (1992) have proposed a "spiral model" to explicate the causes and consequences of dietary restraint. The "decision to diet" is a complex one, since dieting is prevalent among adolescent and adult women, even among those who are not overweight (Attie & Brooks-Gunn, 1987; Rosen, Gross, & Vara, 1987). Studies show that the discrepancy between ideal and current body shape is central to body dissatisfaction, which is a significant predictor of dieting (Heatherton & Polivy, 1992). Low self-esteem and distress may also predispose the individual to diet (Striegel-Moore et al., 1989), whereas dieting behavior, in turn, increases stress levels among teenage girls (Rosen, Tacy, & Howell, 1990). Dieting is rarely successful; in fact, it is likely to result in weight fluctuations and metabolic changes that lead to less efficient weight loss and increased weight gain. Rather than give up dieting, however, the dieter typically continues to diet and becomes a restrained eater, or chronic dieter. Dietary failure is associated with lowered self-esteem, which in turn may render the dieter more susceptible to dietary disinhibitors. The chronic dieter may then enter a spiral in which each failure intensifies affective instability, making the dieter more vulnerable to external food cues and cognitive (as opposed to physiological) controls of eating. At this point in the spiral, the dieter is at risk for binge eating.

Heatherton and Baumeister (1991) propose that dieters may shift to low levels of self-awareness to reduce the threatening implications of ideal-self discrepancies and to escape from negative affect. At low levels of awareness, narrow and concrete meanings prevail, resulting in a suspension of usual inhibitions and an increased chance of overeating. Lowered levels of awareness have been implicated in a range of disinhibited behaviors including binge eating, suicide, alcohol abuse, and masochism (Baumeister, 1990; Heatherton & Baumeister, 1991). Once the individual enters the spiral, the cycle of dieting, overeating, dietary failure, and affective distress deepens and is difficult to break.

Although the counterregulatory model has generated considerable research on dietary restraint and its relationship with overeating, restraint theory has been challenged on methodological and theoretical grounds. In his critique of restraint theory, Lowe (1993) presents evidence in support of the view of dieting as a complex, multidimensional construct. Although they are used interchangeably, the terms "restrained eating" (i.e., frequent cycles of dieting and overeating), "dieting" (current dieting), and "weight suppression" (successful long-term dieting) are not equivalent; each is associated with a different pattern of eating regulation. Lowe (1993) concludes that highly restrained eaters' "vulnerability to counterregulatory eating, negative-affect eating, and salivary hyperresponsiveness stems not from their current dieting behavior but from the cumulative effects of their past dieting behavior" (p. 113). In addition, recent research has raised questions about the ecological validity of counterregulation as an analogue for the clinical phenomenon of bulimic episodes. Dritschel, Cooper, and Charnock (1993) found that overeating in the laboratory was not necessarily associated with a tendency to eat excessively or to lose control over eating in naturalistic settings.

Because of the paucity of developmentally oriented research, researchers do not know whether there are developmental transformations in the meaning and expression of dieting behaviors. For example, it is not clear what young adolescents mean when they report having been on a diet. A recent study of 431 preadolescent and adolescent girls from a working-class area revealed substantial variability in the behaviors construed as "dieting" across age groups (Field, Wolf, Herzog, Cheung, & Colditz, 1993). Although the percentage of girls who reported usually or always dieting was similar from 5th through 12th grade, there was no association between self-reported dieting and objective measures of either nutritional intake or physical activity among the preadolescent and middle school girls. Only among high school girls was dieting associated with decreased energy intake. These findings suggest that there are developmental changes in the manifestations of "dietary restraint" during the adolescent period, although the mechanisms involved have not been specified.

Few researchers have followed young dieters to describe the various outcomes of adolescent dieting. One exception is a study by Graber and colleagues, who followed Attie and Brooks-Gunn's (1989) adolescent sample into young adulthood (Graber, Brooks-Gunn, Paikoff, & Warren, in press). A total of 116 girls were seen at three age periods, first in early adolescence, then in middle adolescence, and the third time, during late adolescence. Scores above a cutoff on a measure of disordered eating *(EAT-26)* at the first two assessments were used to categorize girls into one of four risk groups: no risk, decreasing risk, increasing risk, or chronic risk. Although approximately one-quarter of the girls reported clinically significant levels of disordered eating at each assessment, girls shifted in their relative rank order across age periods.

At long-term follow-up, girls in the chronic group (i.e., those scoring above a clinical cutoff on the *EAT-26* at all three age periods) could be distinguished by their earlier maturational timing, higher percentages of body fat, elevated levels of depressed affect, and poorer body image. Taken together, this constellation of physical and psychological factors may be considered a risk pattern for the development of persistent and possibly severe eating problems.

A developmental perspective presumes an underlying coherence of individual functioning across periods of growth and transition despite changes in manifest behavior or symptomatology. Yet, research has yet to discover early patterns of developmental achievement and failure that might forecast subsequent disordered eating. Because of the relative absence of prospective research, we have speculated about "the complexity of developmental links" by examining eating disorders that have their onset before the adolescent period.

IMPLICATIONS OF STUDYING EATING DISORDERS FOR UNDERSTANDING NORMAL DEVELOPMENT

In studying the interface between normal development and psychopathology, developmental psychopathologists have devoted increasing attention to the ways in which psychopathological conditions can shed light on normal development (Cicchetti, in press; Sroufe, 1990). As noted throughout this chapter, the boundaries and direction of effects between normality and pathology in eating behavior are not well defined. Yet, the study of eating disorders may contribute to developmental theory in several ways:

1. The research conducted on individuals with failure to thrive, anorexia nervosa, and bulimia nervosa highlight the complex developmental processes that underlie eating behavior in disordered and nondisordered populations: Relational dysfunction at dyadic and familial levels centered around parental responses to the child's efforts at differentiation and connection;

the communicative meaning of eating-related symptoms, including food refusal, bingeing, and purging; the interrelation between appetite regulation, affect regulation, and self-regulation; and the role of the body in consolidating gender identity, self-other differentiation, and sexual identity.

2. The study of eating disorders highlights the gendered aspects of development in terms of the differences between boys and girls in their psychosexual development; the differential vulnerability of women and men to developmental challenges concerning sexuality, identity, and achievement; and the structuring of psychopathology within the cultural hierarchies of gender, class, and race/ethnicity.

3. Biological studies of the concomitants and consequences of dieting and exercise have altered our understanding of the psychobiological mechanisms involved in female development.

Developmental Processes Underlying Eating Regulation

Object-relational and self-psychological perspectives emphasize the role of the primary caretaker (usually the mother) in mediating the child's organization of early experience. The development of a sense of self-cohesion, object constancy, and resilient self-esteem regulation evolves gradually through the mutual regulation of exchange between caretaker and infant (Stern, 1985). The repetitive cycles of hunger, nursing, and satisfaction provide the mother-infant dyad with countless opportunities for affective interchange. As the mother responds to solicitations by the infant, the baby develops a sense of herself. The baby's capacity to experience and hold a sense of herself as real depends on the mother's recognizing and mirroring back to the child what she is like.

Over time, the child's subjective experience of these affective exchanges is internalized and becomes a part of her body and self-representations. Disruptions of engagement and attunement in the caregiver-child relationship at different developmental stages may interfere with the emergence of self-regulatory competencies, including the development of physiological regulation, the sense of initiative and curiosity, the capacity for play and learning, and the ability to organize, modulate, and communicate feelings (Anders, 1989).

Much has been written about the failure of symbolization in eating-disordered patients, whose needs, affects, and desires are expressed at somatic or bodily level. In their discussion of the development of self and object representations, Diamond and Blatt (1994) describe how "representational structures follow an epigenetic sequence from enactive to imagistic to lexical modalities as they are transformed from preoperational habitual motor patterns into symbolic cohesive representations of self, other and their interaction" (pp. 90–91). Drawing on attachment research, they present evidence linking the quality of early dyadic attachment patterns to the child's capacity to move from concrete, enactive modes to sensory and visual images to more abstract, verbal modes of representing the affective and experiential components of parent-child transactions.

In the context of a secure attachment relationship, the primary caregiver facilitates the shift from sensorimotor to verbal-symbolic modes of expression and representation. As the child becomes increasingly able to organize, reflect on, and verbally narrate her experience, she internalizes the regulation of affect and desire as an integral part of her self-representation. Conversely, negative attachment experiences (possibly emanating from the parent's attachment history or psychological vulnerability) may interfere with the development of more mature, symbolic modes of representation. Especially under the pressure of intense conflict, the child may be predisposed to represent unverbalized and unverbalizable experiences in the form of bodily enactments or poorly delineated visual images (Diamond & Blatt, 1994).[19]

Perhaps, when this enactive modality becomes a repetitive way of organizing experience, a split (nonintegration) may develop between the body self and the psychological self (Sugarman, 1991). Parental nonrecognition of the child's psychological experience may intensify the estrangement between the psychic self and body self, so that the body is experienced as the only part of the self that is noticed and therefore, real. From a self-psychological perspective,[20] the child vulnerable to

[19] The development of one's body image, defined as the mental representation of the body self, is a developmental process that is intertwined with the construction of the psychological self and its derivative representation, the self-image. According to Krueger (1990), early developmental disruptions in the establishment of a stable, integrated body image may result from three types of relationship disturbances. The first is overintrusiveness and overstimulation (what Anders, 1989, might call an overregulated relationship), which predisposes to the development of a body image experienced as indistinct and blurred, or as small, prepubescent, or undifferentiated. Intrusiveness can result from sexual assault, forced feedings, repeated illnesses and operations, and from invasion of the child's emotional world by manipulation, devaluation, or negation of feelings and developmental strivings. The second form of interaction pattern involves parental unavailability and nonresponsiveness to the child's physical and affective experiences (or Anders' underregulated relationship). Insecure holding and diminished affective exchange contribute to poor body boundaries, decreased sensory awareness, and the sense of fragmentation. The third type of interaction is characterized by inconsistency or selectivity of the parental response (e.g., responding only to the child's pain), which reinforces somatization and prevents affects and needs from being experienced at a symbolic level.

[20] Several theorists understand eating disorders to be a form self pathology; that is, a chronic disturbance of parental empathic responsiveness that eventuates in a "fear of psychic emptiness, loss of creative living, and fragmentation, resulting in psychological depletion, loss of vitality, and threats to self cohesion" (Geist, 1989, p. 10). Eating-disordered patients rely on a range of compulsive behaviors to compensate for structural deficits in the self, including "frantic business, sexualization of isolated drives, overstimulating physical activities, petty thefts, [and] hyperinvestment in intellectual aspects of communication" (Geist, 1989, p. 16). These strategies are ineffective in protecting the adolescent from feelings of disintegration anxiety and emptiness that reemerge in response to normative and nonnormative stressors, such as loss of a best friend, teasing, acceptance to college, or depression of a parent. According to Geist (1989), eating-disordered symptoms, including feeling fat, controlled eating, bingeing, and vomiting represent efforts to express and overcome unbearable feelings of emptiness. Quoting Winnicott, he notes that the adolescent "who fears the awfulness of emptiness" will defensively "organize a controlled emptiness by not eating . . . or else will ruthlessly fill up by a greediness which is compulsive and feels mad" (Winnicott, 1974, p. 107).

anorexia nervosa "resorts to striving for perfection and outstanding performance to experience a sense of being alive and at least seen, through action or behavior, by a mother who is incapable of mirroring" (Rizzuto, Peterson, & Reed, 1981). Alternatively, the child who later develops bulimia may turn to food and eating rituals to express missing self-regulatory and self-soothing functions. According to Sands (1991), "food is . . . a particularly compelling self-object substitute, since it is developmentally a first bridge between self and self-object . . . it provides soothing and comfort [and] helps regulate painful affect states" (p. 35). Bulimic symptoms express both protest and desire, both danger to self and efforts at self-restoration: "The binges reveal the need for nurturance and connection with the self-object; the purges express the needs for self-definition and separation from the self-object . . . the bulimic behavior is thus an assertion of self and a punishment for it" (pp. 38–39).

The Gendered Nature of Eating Disorders

Paradoxically, the split between the body self and the psychological self is precisely what is embodied in the aesthetic of femininity in this culture; that is, the core elements of disturbed body image development are "requirements" of normative femininity. Sands (1991) observes that the recruitment of the female body to express basic needs is supported at the level of culture and family: "First, there is the general societal preoccupation with the female body and encouragement for females to display their exhibitionistic strivings through their physical appearance. Second, all evidence suggests that in families of eating-disordered patients there is particular emphasis on physical appearance, and more precisely, a pathological focus on body fragments," leading to a loss of cohesion of the body self (Sands, 1991, p. 41).

To fully understand the gender specificity of eating disorders (that 90% of those afflicted are women), it must be acknowledged that these disorders have emerged and proliferated during a particular historical and cultural era. In the present historical moment compared with earlier periods, women in Western cultures are less confined to the domestic sphere, have more sexual freedom, and have greater access to paid work outside the home. However, with women's growing independence has come an escalating objectification of women's bodies (Bartsky, 1990).

In contemporary cultural representations of gender, normative femininity is increasingly centered on a discipline of the body, whose objectification and inferiorization have become integral to women's sense of identity. Media images leave no doubt that exhaustive practices of bodily care are required; women are expected to regulate their body size and contours, to curb their appetites, to constrict their movements, and to ornament and disguise their body surfaces: "To subject oneself to the new disciplinary power is to be up-to-date, to be 'with it'; . . . Since it is women who practice this discipline on and against their own bodies, men get off scot-free" (Bartsky, 1990, p. 80). What Bartsky is saying here is that women's subjectivities are constituted within a patriarchical organization of power, family, and gender relations.

In her critique of family theories, Goldner (1988) reminds us that "gender and the gendering of power are not secondary mediating variables *affecting* family life; they *construct* family life in

the deepest sense" (p. 28). In her view, "Every family . . . is as much about the politics and meaning of gender as it is about the politics and meaning of growing up" (p. 27). This conceptualization of the family is particularly relevant for understanding the development of eating disorders. The most frequent precipitants of anorexia nervosa and bulimia nervosa have to do with becoming a grown woman, including feminine identity, sexuality, romantic relationships, and the achievement of a woman's creative/productive potential in work and in love (Mogul, 1989). Although young women are being challenged and expected to realize unprecedented political, economic, and sexual freedoms, they are simultaneously being deprived of recognition and support from our collective values and institutions.

A problem arises when we attempt to consider how the study of eating disorders sheds light on normal development. The difficulty lies in our theories of development and psychopathology, which perpetuate prevailing cultural constructions of femininity and masculinity. In psychoanalytic theory, the vulnerability of women to eating disorders is commonly understood in terms of "inevitable" developmental differences in children's early psychosexual development (Chodorow, 1989). Because girls are not required to "disidentify" from the primary maternal caretaker in the same way as boys, they are thought to have greater difficulty with the psychological task of differentiation. According to Benjamin (1988), the psychoanalytic position maintains a split between the mother of attachment and the father of separation. The developmental issues of recognition and independence are conceptualized within a gender dichotomy that equates desire, power, and subjectivity with masculinity (Benjamin, 1988). The father represents the "outside world"; he liberates the child from the perpetual threat of maternal engulfment. Gender inequality is perpetuated through the reification of women's exclusive role as the (idealized and devalued) protector of private life while men are viewed as the (rational and autonomous) authors of social organization and agency (Benjamin, 1988).

Biological Consequences of Eating Disorders

Another contribution of the study of eating disorders to our understanding of normal development centers on the biological concomitants and consequences of disordered-eating behavior. Eating dysregulation and exercise have been shown to disrupt normal reproductive functioning in ways that have forced a reconceptualization of the complex mechanisms involved in the initiation of pubertal change.

Studies of the reproductive biology of anorexia nervosa illustrate the delicate equilibrium of physiological mechanisms underlying normal reproductive functioning. In about a quarter of patients with anorexia nervosa, amenorrhea occurs before the emergence of significant food restriction and weight loss (Weiner, 1989). With weight recovery, the anorectic may not ovulate or menstruate for months or even years. Studies of hypothalamic-pituitary gonadal (HPG) functions indicate that anorectic patients exhibit a pattern of pulsatile fluctuations of gonadotropins (FSH and LH) consistent with a reversion to a prepubertal state (Boyar et al., 1974). The regulation of the HPG is finely tuned by catecholamines, GABA, sex steroids, and peptides (Weiner, 1989). Studies also suggest that adreno-corticotrophin hormone (ACTH) and cortisol response to cor-ticotrophin-releasing factor (CRF) are blunted in anorectic women and are only restored to normal after long-term weight restoration (Gold et al., 1986); how such changes in the adrenal (HPA) axis might influence reproductive functioning is not clear. Yet, studies of neuroendocrine functioning in anorectic women have elucidated the role of normal hypothalamic-pituitary responsiveness in the onset of pubertal change, and how easily these processes can go into a state of disequilibrium.

Studies of adolescents and adults with anorexia nervosa have demonstrated the multidirectional relationships among eating behavior, exercise, and reproductive functioning. Delays in pubertal development have been demonstrated among adolescents girls with anorexia nervosa, as well as those engaged in high levels of exercise or competitive athletics (Brooks-Gunn, Burrow, & Warren, 1988; Malina, 1983; Warren, 1980; Warren, Brooks-Gunn, Hamilton, Warren, & Hamilton, 1986). The overlap among these three groups is substantial; for example, girls with anorexia nervosa may exercise three to four hours a day, and women who engage in athletics that require a thin body shape are at greater risk for the development of an eating disorder (Brooks-Gunn, Attie, Burrow, Rosso, & Warren, 1989). Warren's (1980) longitudinal study of ballet dancers highlights the ways in which different types of energy drain, in the form of exercise and diet, may perturb the normal processes of puberty. She followed 13- to 15-year-old ballet dancers over 4 years and found that three reproductive events—the progression of puberty, the onset of menarche, and the reversal of secondary amenorrhea—were most likely to occur when dancers had discontinued exercise or had been injured, forcing them to rest for a period of at least 2 months. The pubertal effects occurred despite the fact that body weights and percentage of body fat were well above those determined to be necessary for menarche in normal girls. These findings suggest that physical activity and body fat have independent but also interactive effects on reproductive functioning.

Studies of abnormal appetite regulation have also elucidated the processes involved in female skeletal growth and its relationship to normal reproductive functioning. In developing adolescents with anorexia nervosa, inadequate calcium absorption secondary to self-starvation may interfere with the attainment of peak skeletal mass through a disruption of hormonal functioning. Because estrogen is involved with the maintenance of calcium balance, delayed menarche or prolonged amenorrhea may be a risk factor for slowed maturation of bone or bone demineralization (Salisbury & Mitchell, 1991).

Research with young adult dancers with disordered eating suggests that low levels of estrogen, inferred from late pubertal development and amenorrhea, are linked to stress fractures and higher rates of scoliosis (Warren et al., 1986). In further studies, adolescent girls who were amenorrheic or premenarcheal and who exercised a great deal had lower bone mineral densities and more stress fracture injuries (Dhuper, Warren, Brooks-Gunn, & Fox, 1990; Warren et al., 1991). Although some forms of exercise can prevent loss of bone tissue, extremely low body weight may attenuate the protective effects of exercise on bone mineralization in women with anorexia nervosa (Salisbury & Mitchell, 1991). If almost one-half of bone growth happens

during the adolescent years, as it is believed, than high levels of diet and exercise may alter bone accretion. Such problems could predispose to the development of osteoporosis in adulthood (Warren et al., 1991).

As a final example of the usefulness of developmental models based on clinical samples, we consider current work regarding the effects of psychological disturbance on hormonal functioning (Brooks-Gunn, Graber, & Paikoff, 1994). Research with girls who exercise and girls who have eating problems elegantly demonstrates how behavior influences the HPG and HPA axes. Extending this line of research, investigators have been exploring the possibility that other behavioral and interpersonal dysfunction might influence pubertal functioning. Three studies have demonstrated that familial conflict and father absence are associated with accelerated pubertal development (Graber, Brooks-Gunn, & Warren, in press; Moffitt, Caspi, Belsky, & Silva, 1992; Surbey, 1990). The hormonal mechanisms underlying these findings are not well understood.

STRATEGIES FOR STUDYING CONTINUITY AND CHANGE IN EATING DISORDERS

Developmental psychopathology does not constitute a theory but rather "a means of bringing together a set of research strategies that have been little used until now" (Rutter, 1988, p. 486). As Rutter asserts, the aim of developmental psychopathology is to go beyond identification of risk factors toward an understanding of the chain of events or processes that lead to or protect from disorder. However, the study of eating regulation and dysregulation has not yet incorporated research approaches that emphasize continuities and discontinuities over time, or between pathology and normality. Following Rutter (1988), we consider several research strategies that may enhance our understanding of the pathogenesis of eating disorders from a developmental perspective.

The prospective study of vulnerable children is considered paradigmatic developmental psychopathology. In the case of anorexia nervosa, the low base rate is a factor that may pose problems for prospective research. Anorexia nervosa, however, has a relatively short latency period (the incidence rising sharply and reaching a peak during adolescence), making it relatively accessible to prospective study. Bulimia nervosa has a less stable prevalence rate, with the modal period of risk extending well into adulthood. Its detection among normal-weight individuals may be difficult because those afflicted tend to be secretive and do not "wear" their diagnosis.

Longitudinal designs are the method of choice for demonstrating the temporal relationships among different causal processes, the covariation between domain-specific developmental pathways, and the continuities in adaptational patterns despite apparent discontinuities in behavioral manifestations. Accelerated longitudinal designs and the risk group approach may prove especially useful for the study of low base rate disorders, such as the eating disorders.

The identification of risk variables, vulnerability, and protective processes is more problematic. At this relatively early stage of our understanding of the etiology of eating disorders, we have identified, at a descriptive level, certain variables that may constitute risk factors for the development of these disorders. For the adolescent girl, gender-related sources of risk include a culturally mediated focus on body shape and weight (Attie & Brooks-Gunn, 1987), the intensification of gender-specific expectations during the middle-school transition (Simmons & Blyth, 1987), conflicts between public sphere demands and the relational focus of female identity formation (Gilligan et al., 1990), and an increased risk of depression (Strober & Katz, 1987).

Familial risk factors may exert their influence through a number of constitutional and experiential pathways, including disturbed family interaction patterns, internalizing and externalizing psychopathology in both parents, and the transmission of biogenetic predispositions in several domains, including physical characteristics (obesity, pubertal timing, physical attractiveness), personality traits (temperamental variations in behavioral inhibition or impulsivity), and vulnerability to psychopathology (eating disorders, affective illness, personality disorders, and substance abuse). Research paradigms that examine the family in relation to different developmental tasks would help elucidate how family functioning affects adaptation to pubertal change, friendship development, school experiences, parental adjustment, and the transition into adult roles in the areas of work, marriage, and parenthood (Bronfenbrenner, 1986).

Although the family context has been implicated in the development of eating disorders, research suggests that it is the specifically experienced environment, not the shared environment, that accounts for individual differences in behavior and development (Plomin & Daniels, 1987). Especially during periods of developmental transition, the "goodness of fit" between the adolescent and her caretaking, social, or academic environment may break down, stressing the relationship and engendering shifts in coping and defensive processes. Nonshared family experiences, such as birth complications, early attachment patterns, differences within the sibling relationship, and different experiences with social groups outside the family may influence personality development more than global constructs such as family cohesion or parenting style (Wonderlich, 1992). For children in some families, specific developmental vulnerabilities such as insulin-dependent diabetes mellitus (Striegel-Moore, Nicholson, & Tamborlane, 1992), childhood sexual maltreatment (Herzog, Staley et al., 1993), alcohol abuse (Striegel-Moore & Huydic, 1993), or aesthetically demanding vocational pursuits, such as ballet (Brooks-Gunn et al., 1988; Brooks-Gunn et al., 1989), may create a unique risk for the development of an eating disorder, despite the fact that these factors do not appear to be elevated among eating-disordered populations in general.

From a developmental perspective, epidemiological studies should be concerned with mapping out continuities and discontinuities in symptom patterns over time (Costello & Angold, 1993). Large-scale studies of representative samples are needed to document expected base rates of eating-disordered symptoms from childhood through adulthood, age and sex trends, modal points of developmental breakdown, and the likelihood that symptoms will persist or remit over time. How are children who are vulnerable to "infantile anorexia" (FTT variant) different from those who will develop anorexia nervosa in adolescence? Is there continuity between childhood and adolescent eating disorders, even though the early onset cases may not be associated with distorted body image or fear of fatness (Jaffe & Singer, 1989)? What are the underlying mechanisms for the finding that childhood appetite disorders, including digestive problems, pickiness, problem meals, and pica, predicted at least one problem 8 to 10 years later (Marchi & P. Cohen, 1990)?

Studying age differences in onset is important for delineating developmental pathways because the onset of these disorders is often linked to developmental challenges and transitions. Patterns of risk factors may differ when onset occurs at "nonnormative" times (especially early or unusually late) or following nonnormative transitions (illness in the family, divorce, family moves). Timing of onset also may have different long-term effects, depending on which developmental outcome is being considered. For example, the emergence of amenorrhea closer to menarche places the anorectic at greater risk for decreased bone mineral density (Salisbury & Mitchell, 1991). Furthermore, research suggests that prepubertal and adult onset cases are more likely to be associated with depression and life stress (Jacobs & Isaacs, 1986; Mynors-Willis et al., 1992), suggesting that some forms of eating disorders may be stress-related and possibly implicating neurobiological mechanisms. Post (1992) has proposed that stress-related alterations in endocrine, neurotransmitter, and peptide substances may create an enduring vulnerability to recurrent affective episodes through their sensitizing effects on neural brain systems. Whether similar mechanisms are involved in the onset of eating disorders or in the emergence of comorbid patterns is not known.

Prospective studies are needed to distinguish episodic eating problems that will resolve spontaneously from those that will become chronic, especially given the high rates of chronicity in anorexia nervosa and bulimia, and the 5% mortality rate in anorexia nervosa (Bakan et al., 1991; Hsu et al., 1993). In addition, an understanding of *the process of recovery* from anorexia nervosa and bulimia nervosa may shed light on the defining features of these disorders and provide a conceptual basis for designing and evaluating prevention and intervention programs. Beresin, Gordon, and Herzog (1989) reviewed available outcome studies along the dimensions of weight, menses, body attitudes, eating behavior, psychosexual function, interpersonal relationships, family relationships, work history, and psychiatric symptoms and found that only 40% of patients are totally recovered and nearly one-third show persistent social and psychological impairments.

Another research strategy involves an assessment of eating-disordered symptoms in different social contexts, including culturally diverse settings. The rise in disordered eating in Western cultures may be linked to cultural changes in eating habits, which include the consumption of fast foods, the decline of family meals, and an increasingly sedentary lifestyle (Brumberg, 1988). On the one hand, children may not have the privacy to binge and purge in their homes, militating against the development of bulimic symptoms at young ages (Thelen, Lawrence, & Powell, 1992). On the other hand, children are being recruited by marketing experts in diet, beauty, entertainment, and toy industries to promote weight loss and health risk behaviors (Striegel-Moore, 1992). The impact of these social changes has not been studied in any systematic fashion. Moreover, in some non-Western cultures, anorexia nervosa presents without fear of fatness and body image disturbance, raising questions about the core dimensions of eating disorders and the role of cultural factors in shaping the expression of eating-related psychopathology (Hsu & Lee, 1993).

Continuities and discontinuities between normality and pathology are still not well understood. Dieting does not really shade into anorexia nervosa or bulimia nervosa in terms of prognosis. Yet, the manifest features of eating disorders are mostly exaggerations of normative behaviors, at least for females. A partial continuum seems to exist among nonpathological dieting, subclinical eating disturbances, and eating disorders (Levine & Smolak, 1992; Polivy & Herman, 1987). How do we distinguish those weight-preoccupied individuals who will go on to develop a disorder from those who will not? The prospective study of different dimensions of disorder (such as dieting, overeating, purging, and excessive exercise) would clarify whether the presence of these behaviors below a diagnostic threshold presents a risk factor for the development of an eating-disorder syndrome.

Because of the high rates of comorbidity, comparative studies are needed to identify the antecedents and correlates of comorbid conditions versus "pure" eating disorders. Are clinical and prognostic features similar when anorexia nervosa or bulimia nervosa occur as part of a mixed eating disorder (AN-BN) compared with either one alone? Does comorbidity of eating disorders with depression or personality disorders coevolve over time, or do these trajectories develop independently? The longitudinal study of comorbid patterns has the potential to reveal common and specific risk factors, shared pathophysiological mechanisms, the temporal sequencing between different disorders, and differential response to treatment (Skodol et al., 1993).

We believe that the study of eating and its disorders is in need of an overarching organizational framework. The discipline of developmental psychopathology has evolved to the point that it can offer investigators a "language" for conceptualizing and integrating contributions from diverse fields of inquiry. To understand how eating disorders develop, research designs must be theory driven, grounded in epidemiologically sound sampling procedures, and broad enough to encompass the complexity of multiple and interactive influences. It is not sufficient to identify risk and protective factors; we need to determine how they operate over time, the influence of meaningful patterns of risk processes, and the cumulative effects of successive developmental outcomes (Rutter, 1988). A transactional perspective requires further that we consider the meaning of events, challenges, and developmental transitions to the individual within her social system of relationships and beliefs. With a more indepth understanding of the diverse pathways that lead from risk to disorder to recovery, we will be in a better position to treat those who suffer from eating disorders and other forms of developmental psychopathology.

REFERENCES

Abrams, K. K., Allen, L. R., & Gray, J. J. (1993). Disordered eating attitudes and behaviors, psychological adjustment, and ethnic identity: A comparison of black and white female college students. *International Journal of Eating Disorders, 14,* 59–63.

Achenbach, T. (1978). The child behavior profile. *Journal of Consulting Psychology, 46,* 473–488.

Alessi, N. E., Krahn, D., Brehm, D., & Wittekindt, J. (1989). Prepubertal anorexia nervosa and major depressive disorder. *Journal of the American Academy of Child and Adolescent Psychiatry, 28,* 380–384.

American Psychiatric Association (1980, 1987, 1994). *Diagnostic and statistical manual of mental disorders* (3rd ed., 3rd ed. rev., 4th ed.). Washington, DC: Author.

Anders, T. (1989). Clinical syndromes, relationship disturbances, and their assessment. In A. J. Sameroff & R. N. Emde (Eds.), *Relationship disturbances in early childhood: A developmental approach* (pp. 125–144). New York: Basic Books.

Andersen, A. E. (1990). *Males with eating disorders.* New York: Brunner/Mazel.

Andersen, A. E., & DiDomenico, L. (1992). Diet vs. shape content of popular male and female magazines: A dose response relationship to the incidence of eating disorders? *International Journal of Eating Disorders, 11,* 283–287.

Angold, A., & Rutter, M. (1992). Effects of age and pubertal status on depression in a large clinical sample. *Development and Psychopathology, 4,* 5–28.

Armstrong, J. G., & Roth, D. M. (1989). Attachment and separation difficulties in eating disorders: A preliminary investigation. *International Journal of Eating Disorders, 8,* 141–155.

Attie, I. (1987). *Development of eating problems in adolescence: A follow-up of girls at risk.* Unpublished doctoral dissertation, Catholic University of America.

Attie, I., & Brooks-Gunn, J. (1987). Weight concerns as chronic stressors in women. In R. C. Barnett, L. Biener, & G. K. Baruch (Eds.), *Gender and stress* (pp. 218–254). New York: Free Press.

Attie, I., & Brooks-Gunn, J. (1989). Development of eating problems in adolescent girls: A longitudinal study. *Developmental Psychology, 25,* 70–79.

Attie, I., Brooks-Gunn, J., & Petersen, A. C. (1990). The emergence of eating problems: A developmental perspective. In M. Lewis & S. Miller (Eds.), *Handbook of developmental psychopathology* (pp. 409–420). New York: Plenum.

Bakan, R., Birmingham, C. L., & Goldner, E. M. (1991). Chronicity in anorexia nervosa: Pregnancy and birth complications as risk factors. *International Journal of Eating Disorders, 10,* 631–645.

Bartsky, S. L. (1990). *Femininity and domination: Studies in the phenomenology of oppression.* New York: Routledge.

Baumeister, R. F. (1990). Suicide as escape from self. *Psychological Review, 97,* 90–113.

Beglin, S. J., & Fairburn, C. G. (1992). Women who choose not to participate in surveys on eating disorders. *International Journal of Eating Disorders, 12,* 113–116.

Ben Tovim, D. I., & Morton, J. (1990). The prevalence of anorexia nervosa. *New England Journal of Medicine, 320,* 736–737.

Benjamin, J. (1988). *The bonds of love: Psychoanalysis, feminism, and the problem of domination.* New York: Pantheon.

Benjamin, L. S. (1974). Structural analysis of social behavior. *Psychological Review, 81,* 392–425.

Benjamin, L. S. (1984). Principles of prediction using structural analysis of social behavior (SASB). In R. A. Zucker, J. Aronoff, & A. J. Rabin (Eds.), *Personality and prediction of behavior* (pp. 121–174). New York: Academic Press.

Beresin, E. V., Gordon, C., & Herzog, D. B. (1989). The process of recovering from anorexia nervosa. *American Academy of Psychoanalysis, 17,* 103–130.

Blos, P. (1962). *On adolescence: A psychoanalytic interpretation.* New York: Free Press.

Blos, P. (1967). The second individuation process of adolescence. *Psychoanalytic Study of the Child, 22,* 162–186.

Blouin, A. G., Zuro, C., & Blouin, J. H. (1990). Family environment in bulimia nervosa: The role of depression. *International Journal of Eating Disorders, 9,* 649–658.

Boyar, R. M., Katz, J., Finkelstein, J. W., Kapen, S., Weiner, H., Weitzman, E. D., & Hellman, L. (1974). Anorexia nervosa: Immaturity of the 24 hour luteinizing hormone secretory pattern. *New England Journal of Medicine, 291,* 861–865.

Brand, P. A., Rothblum, E. D., & Solomon, L. J. (1992). A comparison of lesbians, gay men, and heterosexuals on weight and restrained eating. *International Journal of Eating Disorders, 11,* 253–259.

Braun, C. M. J., & Chouinard, M. (1992). Is anorexia nervosa a neuropsychological disease? *Neuropsychology Review, 3,* 171–212.

Brewerton, T. D., Lydiard, R. B., Laraia, M. T., Shook, J. E., & Ballenger, J. C. (1992). CSF B-endorphin and dynorphin in bulimia nervosa. *American Journal of Psychiatry, 149,* 1086–1090.

Bronfenbrenner, U. (1986). Ecology of the family as a context for human development: Research perspectives. *Developmental Psychology, 27,* 723–742.

Brooks-Gunn, J. (1988). Antecedents and consequences of variations in girls' maturational timing. *Journal of Adolescent Health Care, 9*(5), 365–373.

Brooks-Gunn, J., Attie, I., Burrow, C., Rosso, J. T., & Warren, M. P. (1989). The impact of puberty on body and eating concerns in athletic and nonathletic contexts. *Journal of Early Adolescence, 9,* 269–290.

Brooks-Gunn, J., Burrow, C., & Warren, M. P. (1988). Attitudes toward eating and body weight in different groups of female adolescent athletes. *International Journal of Eating Disorders, 7,* 749–758.

Brooks-Gunn, J., Graber, J. A., & Paikoff, R. L. (1994). Studying links between hormones and negative affect: Models and measures. *Journal of Research on Adolescence, 4,* 469–486.

Brooks-Gunn, J., & Warren, M. P. (1985). Effects of delayed menarche in different contexts: Dance and nondance students. *Journal of Youth and Adolescence, 14,* 285–300.

Brown, T. A., Cash, T. F., & Lewis, R. J. (1989). Body-image disturbances in adolescent female binge-purgers: A brief report of the results of a national survey in the U.S.A. *Journal of Child Psychology and Psychiatry, 30,* 605–613.

Brownell, K. D., & Wadden, T. A. (1992). Etiology and treatment of obesity: Understanding a serious, prevalent, and refractory disorder. *Journal of Consulting and Clinical Psychology, 60,* 505–517.

Bruch, H. (1973). *Eating disorders.* New York: Basic Books.

Bruch, H. (1985). Four decades of eating disorders. In D. M. Garner & P. E. Garfinkel (Eds.), *Handbook of psychotherapy for anorexia nervosa and bulimia* (pp. 7–18). New York: Guilford.

Brumberg, J. J. (1985). "Fasting girls": Reflections on writing the history of anorexia nervosa. In A. Boardman Smuts & J. W. Hagen (Eds.), History and research in child development. *Monographs of the Society for Research in Child Development, 50* (4–5, Serial No. 211), 93–104.

Brumberg, J. J. (1988). *Fasting girls: The emergence of anorexia nervosa as a modern disease.* Cambridge, MA: Harvard University Press.

Brumberg, J. J., & Striegel-Moore, R. (1993). Continuity and change in the symptom choice: Anorexia nervosa in historical and psychological perspective. In G. H. Elder, J. F. Modell, & R. Parke (Eds.), *Children in time and place* (pp. 131–146). Cambridge, England: University of Cambridge Press.

Budd, K. S., McGraw, T. E., Farbisz, R., Murphy, T. M., Hawkins, D., Heilman, N., Werle, M., & Hochstadt, N. J. (1992). Psychosocial concomitants of children's feeding disorders. *Journal of Pediatric Psychology, 17,* 81–94.

Buhrmester, D. (1990). Intimacy of friendship, interpersonal competence, and adjustment during preadolescence and adolescence. *Child Development, 61,* 1101–1111.

Bunnell, D. W., Shenker, I. R., Nussbaum, M. P., Jacobson, M. S., & Cooper, P. (1990). Subclinical versus formal eating disorders: Differentiating psychological features. *International Journal of Eating Disorders, 9,* 357–362.

Bush, D. M., & Simmons, R. (1987). Gender and coping with the entry into early adolescence. In R. C. Barnett, L. Biener, & G. K. Baruch (Eds.), *Gender and stress* (pp. 185–217). New York: Free Press.

Calam, R., Waller, G., Slade, P., & Newton, T. (1990). Eating disorders and perceived relationships with parents. *International Journal of Eating Disorders, 9,* 479–485.

Carlat, D. J., & Camargo, C. A. (1991). Review of bulimia nervosa in males. *American Journal of Psychiatry, 148,* 831–843.

Carlson, G. A., & Garber, J. (1986). Developmental issues in the classification of depression in children. In M. Rutter, C. E. Izard, & P. B. Read (Eds.), *Depression in young people: Clinical and developmental perspectives* (pp. 399–434). New York: Guilford.

Caron, C., & Rutter, M. (1991). Comorbidity in child psychopathology: Concepts, issues and research strategies. *Journal of Child Psychology and Psychiatry, 32,* 1063–1080.

Cash, T. F., & Pruzinsky, T. (1990). *Body images: Development, deviance, and change.* New York: Guilford.

Casper, R. C. (1983). On the emergence of bulimia nervosa as a syndrome: A historical view. *International Journal of Eating Disorders, 2,* 3–16.

Casper, R., Hedeker, D., & McClough, J. F. (1992). Personality dimensions in eating disorders and their relevance for subtyping. *Journal of the American Academy of Child and Adolescent Psychiatry, 31,* 830–840.

Casper, R. C., Offer, D., & Ostrov, E. (1981). The self-image of adolescents with acute anorexia nervosa. *Journal of Pediatrics, 98,* 656–661.

Chatoor, I., Conley, C., & Dickson, L. (1988). Food refusal after an incident of choking: A posttraumatic eating disorder. *Journal of the American Academy of Child and Adolescent Psychiatry, 27,* 105–110.

Chatoor, I., & Egan, J. (1987). Etiology and diagnosis of failure to thrive and growth disorders in infants and children. In J. Noshpitz (Ed.), *Basic handbook in child psychiatry* (Vol. V, pp. 272–279). New York: Basic Books.

Chatoor, I., Egan, J., & Getson, P. (1990). Reply to Sturm and Stancin. *Journal of the American Academy of Child and Adolescent Psychiatry, 29,* 317–318.

Chatoor, I., Egan, J., Getson, P., Menvielle, E., & O'Donnell, R. (1987). Mother-infant interactions in infantile anorexia nervosa. *Journal of the American Academy of Child and Adolescent Psychiatry, 27,* 535–540.

Childress, A. C., Brewerton, T. D., Hodges, E. L., & Jarrell, M. P. (1993). The kids' eating disorders survey (KEDS): A study of middle school students. *Journal of the Academy of Child and Adolescent Psychiatry, 32,* 843–850.

Chodorow, N. (1989). *Feminism and psychoanalytic theory.* New Haven: Yale University Press.

Cicchetti, D. (1984). The emergence of developmental psychopathology. *Child Development, 55,* 1–7.

Cicchetti, D. (in press). Developmental theory: Lessons from the study of risk and psychopathology. In S. Matthysse, D. Levy, J. Kagan, & F. Benes (Eds.), *Psychopathology: The evolving science of mental disorder.* New York: Cambridge University Press.

Cicchetti, D., & Schneider-Rosen, K. (1986). An organizational approach to childhood depression. In M. Rutter, C. E. Izard, & P. B. Read (Eds.). *Depression in young people: Clinical and developmental perspectives* (pp. 71–134). New York: Guilford.

Clinton, D. N., & Glant, R. (1992). The eating disorders spectrum of DSM-III-R: Clinical features and psychosocial concomitants of 86 consecutive cases from a Swedish urban catchment area. *Journal of Nervous and Mental Disease, 180,* 244–250.

Cloninger, C. R. (1987). A systematic method for clinical description and classification of personality variants. *Archives of General Psychiatry, 44,* 573–587.

Collins, M. E. (1991). Body figure perceptions and preferences among preadolescent children. *International Journal of Eating Disorders, 10,* 199–208.

Connors, M. E., & Morse, W. (1993). Sexual abuse and eating disorders: A review. *International Journal of Eating Disorders, 13,* 1–11.

Cook, W. L., Kenny, D. A., & Goldstein, M. J. (1991). Parental affective style risk and the family system: A social relations model analysis. *Journal of Abnormal Psychology, 100,* 492–501.

Cooper, P. J., & Fairburn, C. G. (1993). Confusion over the core psychopathology of bulimia nervosa. *International Journal of Eating Disorders, 13,* 385–389.

Costello, E. J., & Angold, A. (1993). Toward a developmental epidemiology of disruptive behavior disorders. *Development and Psychopathology, 5,* 91–101.

Crandall, C. S. (1988). Social contagion of binge eating. *Journal of Personality and Social Psychology, 55,* 588–598.

Crisp, A. H. (1984). The psychopathology of anorexia nervosa: Getting the "heat" out of the system. In A. J. Stunkard & E. Stellar (Eds.), *Eating and its disorders* (pp. 209–234). New York: Raven Press.

Crisp, A. H., Palmer, R. S., & Kalucy, R. S. (1976). How common is anorexia nervosa? A prevalence study. *British Journal of Psychology, 128,* 549–554.

Dhuper, S., Warren, M. P., Brooks-Gunn, J., & Fox, R. (1990). Effects of hormonal status on bone density in adolescent girls. *Journal of Clinical Endocrinology Society, 71,* 1083–1088.

Diamond, D., & Blatt, S. J. (1994). Internal working models and the representational world in attachment and psychoanalytic theories. In M. B. Sperling & W. H. Berman (Eds.), *Attachment in adults: Clinical and developmental perspectives* (pp. 72–97). New York: Guilford.

DiNicola, V. F., Roberts, N., & Oke, L. (1989). Eating and mood disorders in young children. *Psychiatric Clinics of North America, 12,* 873–893.

Dolan, B. (1991). Cross-cultural aspects of anorexia nervosa and bulimia: A review. *International Journal of Eating Disorders, 1,* 67–68.

Dolan, B. M., Evans, C., & Lacey, H. (1989). Family composition and social class in bulimia: A catchment area study of a clinical and a comparison group. *Journal of Nervous and Mental Disease, 177,* 267–272.

Dornbusch, S. M., Carlsmith, J. M., Duncan, P. D., Gross, R. T., Martin, J. A., Ritter, P. L., & Siegel-Gorelick, B. (1984). Sexual maturation, social class, and the desire to be thin among adolescent females. *Developmental and Behavioral Pediatrics, 5,* 308–314.

Dritschel, B., Cooper, P. J., & Charnock, D. (1993). The problematic counter-regulation experiment: Implications for the link between dietary restraint and overeating. *International Journal of Eating Disorders, 13,* 297–304.

Drotar, D. (1991). The family context of nonorganic failure to thrive. *American Journal of Orthopsychiatry, 61,* 23–34.

Fabian, L. J., & Thompson, J. K. (1989). Body image and eating disturbances in young females. *International Journal of Eating Disorders, 8,* 63–74.

Fahy, T., & Treasure, J. (1989). Children of mothers with bulimia nervosa. *British Medical Journal, 299,* 1031.

Fairburn, C. G., & Beglin, S. J. (1990). Studies of the epidemiology of bulimia nervosa. *American Journal of Psychiatry, 147,* 401–408.

Fairburn, C. G., Welch, S. L., & Hay, P. J. (1993). The classification of recurrent overeating: The "Binge eating disorder" proposal. *International Journal of Eating Disorders, 13,* 155–159.

Faust, M. S. (1983). Alternative constructions of adolescent growth. In J. Brooks-Gunn & A. C. Petersen (Eds.), *Girls at puberty: Biological and psychosocial perspectives.* New York: Plenum.

Fichter, M. M., & Noegel, R. (1990). Concordance for bulimia nervosa in twins. *International Journal of Eating Disorders, 9,* 255–263.

Field, A. E., Wolf, A. M., Herzog, D. B., Cheung, L., & Colditz, G. A. (1993). The relationship of caloric intake to frequency of dieting among preadolescent and adolescent girls. *Journal of the American Academy of Child and Adolescent Psychiatry, 32,* 1246–1252.

Fornari, V., Kaplan, M., Sandberg, D. E., Matthews, M., Skolnick, N., & Katz, J. (1992). Depressive and anxiety disorders in anorexia nervosa and bulimia nervosa. *International Journal of Eating Disorders, 12,* 21–29.

Frank, D. A., & Zeisel, S. H. (1988). Failure to thrive. *Pediatric Clinics of North America, 35,* 1187–1206.

Galambos, N. L., Almeida, D. M., & Petersen, A. C. (1990). Masculinity, femininity, and sex role attitudes in early adolescence: Exploring gender intensification. *Child Development, 61,* 1905–1914.

Gargiulo, J., Attie, I., Brooks-Gunn, J., & Warren, M. P. (1987). Dating in middle-school girls: Effects of social context, maturation, and grade. *Developmental Psychology, 23,* 730–737.

Garner, D. M., Garfinkel, P. E., Schwartz, D., & Thompson, M. (1980). Cultural expectations of thinness in women. *Psychological Reports, 47,* 483–491.

Garner, D. M., Garner, M. V., & Rosen, L. W. (1993). Anorexia nervosa "restricters" who purge: Implications for subtyping anorexia nervosa. *International Journal of Eating Disorders, 13,* 171–185.

Garner, D. M., Olmsted, M., Davis, R., Rockert, W., Goldbloom, D., & Eagle, M. (1990). The association between bulimic symptoms and reported psychopathology. *International Journal of Eating Disorders, 9,* 1–15.

Garner, D. M., Olmsted, M. P., Polivy, J., & Garfinkel, P. E. (1984). Comparison between weight-preoccupied women and anorexia nervosa. *Psychosomatic Medicine, 46,* 255–266.

Garner, D. M., & Wooley, S. C. (1991). Confronting the failure of behavioral and dietary treatments for obesity. *Clinical Psychology Review, 11,* 729–780.

Gartner, A. F., Marcus, R. N., Halmi, K., & Loranger, A. W. (1989). DSM-III-R personality disorders in patients with eating disorders. *American Journal of Psychiatry, 146,* 1585–1591.

Geist, R. A. (1989). Self psychological reflections on the origins of eating disorders. *Journal of the American Academy of Psychoanalysis, 17,* 5–27.

Gilligan, C. (1982). *In a different voice.* Cambridge, MA: Harvard University Press.

Gilligan, C., Rogers, A., & Brown, L. M. (1990). Epilogue: Soundings into development. In C. Gilligan, N. P. Lyons, & T. J. Hammer (Eds.), *Making connections: The relational worlds of adolescent girls at Emma Willard School* (pp. 314–334). Cambridge, MA: Harvard University Press.

Gold, P. W., Gwirtswan, H., Avgerinos, P. C., Nieman, L. K., Gallucci, W. T., Kaye, W., Jimerson, D., Ebert, M., Rittmaster, R., Loriaux, D. L., & Chrousos, G. P. (1986). Abnormal hypothalamic-pituitary-adrenal function in anorexia nervosa. *New England Journal of Medicine, 314,* 1335–1342.

Goldner, V. (1988). Generation and gender: Normative and covert hierarchies. *Family Process, 27,* 17–31.

Graber, J. A., Brooks-Gunn, J., Paikoff, R. L., & Warren, M. P. (in press). Prediction of eating problems: An eight year study of adolescent girls. *Developmental Psychology.*

Graber, J. A., Brooks-Gunn, J., & Warren, M. P. (in press). The antecedents of menarcheal age. *Child Development.*

Gross, R. T. (1984). Patterns of maturation: Their effects on behavior and development. In M. D. Levine & P. Satz (Eds.), *Middle childhood: Development and dysfunction.* Baltimore: University Park Press.

Habermas, T. (1989). The psychiatric history of anorexia nervosa and bulimia nervosa: Weight concerns and bulimic symptoms in early case reports. *International Journal of Eating Disorders, 8,* 259–273.

Haimes, A. K., & Katz, J. L. (1988). Sexual and social maturity versus social conformity in restricting anorectic, bulimic and borderline women. *International Journal of Eating Disorders, 7,* 331–341.

Halmi, K. A., Casper, R. C., Eckert, E. D., Goldberg, S. C., & Davis, J. M. (1979). Unique features associated with age of onset of anorexia nervosa. *Psychiatry Research, 1,* 209–215.

Halmi, K. A., Sunday, S., Puglisi, A., & Marchi, P. (1989). Hunger and satiety in anorexia and bulimia nervosa. *Annals of the New York Academy of Sciences, 575,* 431–445.

Harter, S. (1990). Self and identity development. In S. Feldman & G. R. Elliott (Eds.), *At the threshold: The developing adolescent* (pp. 352–387). Cambridge, MA: Harvard University Press.

Harter, S., Marold, D. M., & Whitesell, N. R. (1992). Model of psychosocial risk factors leading to suicidal ideation in young adolescents. *Development and Psychopathology, 4,* 167–188.

Harter, S., Marold, D. M., & Whitesell, N. R. (1993, March). *A model of conditional parent support and adolescent false self behavior.* Paper presented at the meeting of the Society for Research in Child Development, New Orleans.

Heatherton, T. F., & Baumeister, R. F. (1991). Binge eating as escape from self-awareness. *Psychological Bulletin, 110,* 86–108.

Heatherton, T. F., & Polivy, J. (1992). Chronic dieting and eating disorders: A spiral model. In J. H. Crowther, D. L. Tennenbaum, S. E. Hobfuoll, & M. A. P. Stephens (Eds.), *The etiology of bulimia nervosa: The individual and familial context* (pp. 133–155). Washington: Hemisphere.

Herzog, D. B., Keller, M. B., Sacks, N. R., Yeh, C. J., & Lavori, P. W. (1992). Psychiatric comorbidity in treatment-seeking anorexics and bulimics. *Journal of Child and Adolescent Psychiatry, 31,* 810–818.

Herzog, D. B., Newman, K. L., Yeh, C. J., & Warshaw, M. (1992). Body image satisfaction in homosexual and heterosexual women. *International Journal of Eating Disorders, 11,* 391–396.

Herzog, D. M., Perpose, M., Norman, D. K., & Rigotti, M. A. (1985). Eating disorders and social maladjustment in female medical students. *Journal of Nervous and Mental Disease, 173,* 734–737.

Herzog, D. B., Sacks, N. R., Keller, M. B., Lavori, P. W., von Ranson, K. B., & Gray, H. M. (1993). Patterns and predictors of recovery in anorexia nervosa and bulimia nervosa. *Journal of the American Academy of Child and Adolescent Psychiatry, 32,* 835–842.

Herzog, D. B., Staley, J. E., Carmody, S., Robbins, W. M., & van der Kolk, B. A. (1993). Child sexual abuse in anorexia nervosa and bulimia nervosa: A pilot study. *Journal of Child and Adolescent Psychiatry, 32,* 962–966.

Hill, J. P., & Lynch, M. E. (1983). The intensification of gender-related role expectations during early adolescence. In J. Brooks-Gunn & A. C. Petersen (Eds.), *Girls at puberty: Biological and psychosocial perspectives.* New York: Plenum.

Hill, P. (1993). Recent advances in selected aspects of adolescent development. *Journal of Child Psychology and Psychiatry, 34,* 69–99.

Hodes, M., & LeGrange, D. (1993). Expressed emotion in the investigation of eating disorders: A review. *International Journal of Eating Disorders, 13,* 279–288.

Holland, A. J., Hall, A., Murray, R., Russell, G. F. M., & Crisp, A. H. (1984). Anorexia nervosa: A study of 34 twin pairs and one set of triplets. *British Journal of Psychiatry, 145,* 414–419.

Hsu, L. K. G., Chesler, B. E., & Santhouse, R. (1990). Bulimia nervosa in eleven sets of twins: A clinical report. *International Journal of Eating Disorders, 9,* 275–282.

Hsu, L. K. G., Kaye, W., & Weltzin, T. (1993). Are eating disorders related to obsessive compulsive disorder? *International Journal of Eating Disorders, 14,* 305–318.

Hsu, L. K. G., & Lee, S. (1993). Is weight phobia always necessary for a diagnosis of anorexia nervosa? *American Journal of Psychiatry, 150,* 1466–1471.

Hsu, L. K. G., & Sobkiewicz, T. A. (1991). Body image disturbance: Time to abandon the concept for eating disorders? *International Journal of Eating Disorders, 10,* 15–30.

Hudson, J. I., Pope, H. G., Jonas, J. M., Yurgelun-Todd, D., & Frankenburg, F. R. (1987). A controlled family history study of bulimia. *Psychological Medicine, 17,* 883–890.

Humphrey, L. L. (1986). Structural analysis of parent-child relationships in eating disorders. *Journal of Abnormal Psychology, 95,* 395–402.

Humphrey, L. L. (1987). Comparison of bulimic-anorexic and nondistressed families using structural analysis of social behavior. *Journal of the American Academy of Child and Adolescent Psychiatry, 26,* 248–255.

Humphrey, L. L. (1988). Relationships within subtypes of anorexics, bulimics, and normal families. *Journal of the American Academy of Child and Adolescent Psychiatry, 27,* 544–551.

Humphrey, L. L. (1991). Object relations and the family system: An integrative approach to understanding and treating eating disorders. In C. Johnson (Ed.), *Psychodynamic treatment of anorexia nervosa and bulimia* (pp. 321–353). New York: Guilford.

Humphrey, L. L., & Stern, S. (1988). Object relations and the family system in bulimia: A theoretical integration. *Journal of Marital and Family Therapy, 14,* 337–350.

Irwin, M. (1981). Diagnosis of anorexia nervosa in children and the validity of DSM-III. *American Journal of Psychiatry, 138,* 1382–1383.

Jacobs, B. W., & Isaacs, S. (1986). Pre-pubertal anorexia nervosa: A retrospective controlled study. *Journal of Child Psychology and Psychiatry, 27,* 237–250.

Jaffe, A. C., & Singer, L. T. (1989). Atypical eating disorders in young children. *International Journal of Eating Disorders, 8,* 575–582.

Johnson, C., & Connors, M. E. (1987). *The etiology and treatment of bulimia nervosa: A biopsychosocial perspective.* New York: Basic Books.

Johnson, C., Tobin, D. L., & Dennis, A. (1990). Differences in treatment outcome between borderline and nonborderline bulimics at one-year follow-up. *International Journal of Eating Disorders, 9,* 617–627.

Johnson-Sabine, E., Wood, K., Patton, G., Mann, A., & Wakeling, A. (1988). Abnormal eating attitudes in London schoolgirls—a prospective epidemiological study: Factors associated with abnormal response on screening questionnaires. *Psychological Medicine, 18,* 615–622.

Jones, D. J., Fox, M. M., Babigan, H. M., & Hutton, H. E. (1980). Epidemiology of anorexia nervosa in Monroe County, New York: 1960–1976. *Psychosomatic Medicine, 42,* 551–558.

Kaplan, A. S., & Woodside, D. B. (1987). Biological aspects of anorexia nervosa and bulimia nervosa. *Journal of Consulting and Clinical Psychology, 55,* 645–653.

Kassett, J. A., Gershon, E. S., Maxwell, M. E., Guroff, J. J., Kazuba, D. M., Smith, A. L., Brandt, H. A., & Jimerson, D. C. (1989). Psychiatric disorders in the first-degree relatives of probands with bulimia nervosa. *American Journal of Psychiatry, 146,* 1468–1471.

Katz, J. (1987). Eating disorder and affective disorder: Relatives or merely chance acquaintances? *Comprehensive Psychiatry, 28,* 220–228.

Katz, J. (1992). Eating disorders and substance abuse disorder. In A. Tasman & M. B. Riba (Eds.), *Review of psychiatry,* (Vol. II, pp. 436–452). Washington, DC: American Psychiatric Press.

Keating, D. P. (1990). Adolescent thinking. In S. S. Feldman & G. R. Elliott (Eds.), *At the threshold: The developing adolescent* (pp. 54–89). Cambridge, MA: Harvard University Press.

Keck, P. E., Pope, H. G., Hudson, J. I., McElroy, S. L., Yurgelun-Todd, D., & Hundert, E. (1990). A controlled study of phenomenology and family history in outpatients with bulimia nervosa. *Comprehensive Psychiatry, 31,* 275–283.

Keller, M. B., Herzog, D. B., Lavori, P. W., Bradburn, I. S., & Mahoney, E. M. (1992). The natural history of bulimia nervosa: Extraordinarily high rates of chronicity, relapse, recurrence and psychosocial morbidity. *International Journal of Eating Disorders, 12,* 1–9.

Kendler, K. S., MacLean, C., Neale, M., Kessler, R., Heath, A., & Eaves, L. (1991). The genetic epidemiology of bulimia nervosa. *American Journal of Psychiatry, 148,* 1627–1637.

Keys, A., Brozek, J., Henschel, A., Mickelsen, O., & Taylor, H. L. (1950). *The biology of human starvation.* Minneapolis: University of Minnesota Press.

Kobak, R. R., & Sceery, A. (1988). Attachment in late adolescence: Working models, affect regulation, and representations of self and others. *Child Development, 59,* 135–146.

Kog, E., & Vandereycken, W. (1989a). The speculations: An overview of theories about eating disorder families. In W. Vandereycken, E. Kog, & J. Vanderlinden (Eds.), *The family approach to eating disorders* (pp. 7–24). New York: PMA Publishing.

Kog, E., & Vandereycken, W. (1989b). Family interaction in eating disorder patients and normal controls. *International Journal of Eating Disorders, 8,* 11–23.

Kog, E., Vandereycken, W., & Vertommen, H. (1989). Multimethod investigation of eating disorder families. In W. Vandereycken, E. Kog, & J. Vanderlinden (Eds.), *The family approach to eating disorders: Assessment and treatment of anorexia nervosa and bulimia* (pp. 81–106). New York: PMA Publishing.

Kopp, C. B. (1982). Antecedents of self-regulation: A developmental perspective. *Developmental Psychology, 18,* 199–214.

Krueger, D. W. (1990). Developmental and psychodynamic perspectives on body-image change. In T. F. Cash & T. Pruzinsky (Eds.), *Body images: Development, deviance, and change* (pp. 255–271). New York: Guilford.

Lacey, J. H. (1993). Self-damaging and addictive behavior in bulimia nervosa: A catchment area study. *British Journal of Psychiatry, 163,* 190–194.

Lacey, J. H., Coker, S., & Birtchnell, S. A. (1986). Bulimia: Factors associated with its etiology and maintenance. *International Journal of Eating Disorders, 5,* 475–488.

Lask, B., & Bryant-Waugh, R. (1992). Early-onset anorexia nervosa and related eating disorders. *Journal of Child Psychology and Psychiatry, 33,* 281–300.

Lehman, A. K., & Rodin, J. (1989). Styles of self-nurturance and disordered eating. *Journal of Consulting and Clinical Psychology, 57,* 117–122.

Levine, M. L., & Smolak, L. (1992). Toward a model of the developmental psychopathology of eating disorders: The example of early adolescence. In J. H. Crowther, D. L. Tennenbaum, S. E. Hobfoll, & M. A. P. Stephens (Eds.), *The etiology of bulimia nervosa: The individual and familial context* (pp. 59–80). Washington, DC: Hemisphere.

Levy, A. B., Dixon, K. N., & Stern, S. L. (1989). How are depression and bulimia related? *American Journal of Psychiatry, 146,* 162–169.

Loro, A. D., & Orleans, C. S. (1981). Binge-eating in obesity: Preliminary findings and guidelines for behavioral analysis and treatment. *Addictive Behaviors, 6,* 155–166.

Lowe, M. R. (1993). The effects of dieting on eating behavior: A three-factor model. *Psychological Bulletin, 114,* 100–121.

Lucas, A. R., Beard, C. M., O'Fallon, W. M., & Kurland, L. T. (1991). Fifty-year trends in the incidence of anorexia nervosa in Rochester, Minnesota: A population-based study. *American Journal of Psychiatry, 148,* 917–922.

Main, M., Kaplan, N., & Cassidy, J. (1985). Security in infancy, childhood, and adulthood: A move to the level of representation. In I. Bretherton & E. Waters (Eds.), *Growing points of attachment theory and research.* Monographs of the Society for Research in Child Development, *50*(1-2, Serial No. 209), 66–104.

Malina, R. M. (1983). Menarche in athletes: A synthesis and hypothesis. *Annals of Human Biology, 10,* 1–24.

Maloney, M. J., McGuire, J. B., & Daniels, S. R. (1988). Reliability testing of a children's version of the Eating Attitude Test. *Journal of the American Academy of Child and Adolescent Psychiatry, 27,* 541–543.

Marchi, M., & Cohen, P. (1990). Early childhood eating behaviors and adolescent eating disorders. *Journal of the American Academy of Child and Adolescent Psychiatry, 29,* 112–117.

Marcus, M. D., Smith, D., Santelli, R., & Kaye, W. (1992). Characterization of eating disordered behavior in obese binge eaters. *International Journal of Eating Disorders, 12,* 249–255.

Minuchin, P. (1985). Families and individual development: Provocations from the field of family therapy. *Child Development, 56,* 289–302.

Minuchin, S., Rosman, D. L., & Baker, L. (1978). *Psychosomatic family: Anorexia nervosa in context.* Cambridge, MA: Harvard University Press.

Moffitt, T. E., Caspi, A., Belsky, J., & Silva, P. A. (1992). Childhood experience and the onset of menarche: A test of a sociobiological model. *Child Development, 63,* 47–58.

Mogul, S. L. (1989). Sexuality, pregnancy, and parenting in anorexia nervosa. *Journal of the American Academy of Psychoanalysis, 17,* 65–88.

Monck, E. (1991). Patterns of confiding relationships among adolescent girls. *Journal of Child Psychology and Psychiatry, 32,* 333–345.

Moore, D. C. (1988). Body image and eating behavior of adolescent girls. *American Journal of Diseases of Childhood, 142,* 1114–1118.

Moore, D. C. (1990). Body image and eating behavior of adolescent boys. *American Journal of Diseases of Childhood, 144,* 475–479.

Morgan, H. G., & Russell, G. F. M. (1975). Value of family background and clinical features as predictors of long-term outcome in anorexia nervosa: A four year follow-up study of 41 patients. *Psychological Medicine, 5,* 355–371.

Mumford, D. B., Whitehouse, A. M., & Platts, M. (1991). Sociocultural correlates of eating disorders among Asian schoolgirls in Bradford. *British Journal of Psychiatry, 158,* 222–228.

Mynors-Wallis, L., Treasure, J., & Chee, D. (1992). Life events and anorexia nervosa: Differences between early and late onset cases. *International Journal of Eating Disorders, 11,* 369–376.

Noshirvani, H. F., Kasvikis, Y., Marks, I. M., Tsarkiris, F., & Monteiro, W. O. (1991). Gender-divergent aetiological factors in obsessive-compulsive disorder. *British Journal of Psychiatry, 158,* 260–263.

Ogden, J., & Wardle, J. (1991). Cognitive and emotional responses of food. *International Journal of Eating Disorders, 10,* 297–311.

Palmer, R. L., & Oppenheimer, R. (1992). Childhood sexual experiences with adults: A comparison of women with eating disorders and those with other diagnoses. *International Journal of Eating Disorders, 12,* 359–364.

Palmer, R. L., Oppenheimer, R. L., & Marshall, P. D. (1988). Eating-disorder patients remember their parents: A study using the Parenting Bonding Instrument. *International Journal of Eating Disorders, 7,* 101–106.

Parker, G., Tupling, H., & Brown, L. B. (1979). A parental bonding instrument. *British Journal of Medical Psychology, 52,* 1–10.

Pate, J. E., Pumariega, A. J., Hester, C., & Garner, D. M. (1992). Cross-cultural patterns in eating disorders: A review. *Journal of the American Academy of Child and Adolescent Psychiatry, 31,* 802–809.

Patterson, J. M., & McCubbin, H. I. (1987). Adolescent coping style and behaviors: Conceptualization and measurement. *Journal of Adolescence, 10,* 163–186.

Phalen, V. (1992). Where's Poppa? The relative lack of attention to the role of fathers in child and adolescent psychopathology. *American Psychologist, 47,* 656–664.

Pike, K. M., & Rodin, J. (1991). Mothers, daughters, and disordered eating. *Journal of Abnormal Psychology, 100,* 198–204.

Plomin, R., & Daniels, D. (1987). Why are children in the same family so different from one another? *Behavioral and Brain Sciences, 10,* 1–60.

Polan, H. J., Leon, A., Kaplan, M. D., Kessler, D. B., Stern, D. N., & Ward, M. J. (1991). Disturbances of affect expression in failure-to-thrive. *Journal of the American Academy of Child and Adolescent Psychiatry, 30,* 897–903.

Polivy, J., & Herman, C. P. (1987). Diagnosis and treatment of normal eating. *Journal of Consulting and Clinical Psychology, 55,* 635–644.

Pollitt, K. (1992, December 28). Are women morally superior to men? *The Nation,* pp. 799–807.

Pope, H. G., Frankenburg, F. R., Hudson, J. I., Jonas, J. M., & Yurgelun-Todd, D. (1987). Is bulimia associated with borderline personality disorder? A controlled study. *Journal of Clinical Psychiatry, 48,* 181–184.

Pope, H. G., & Hudson, J. I. (1989). Are eating disorders associated with borderline personality disorder? A critical review. *International Journal of Eating Disorders, 8,* 1–9.

Pope, H. G., & Hudson, J. L. (1992). Is childhood sexual abuse a risk factor for bulimia nervosa? *American Journal of Psychiatry, 149,* 455–463.

Post, R. M. (1992). Transduction of psychosocial stress into the neurobiology of recurrent affective disorder. *American Journal of Psychiatry, 149,* 999–1007.

Powell, G. F., & Bettes, B. A. (1992). Infantile depression, nonorganic failure to thrive and DSM-III-R: A different perspective. *Child Psychiatry and Human Development, 22,* 185–198.

Prince, R. (1985). The concept of culture-bound syndromes: Anorexia nervosa and brain-fag. *Social Science Medicine, 21,* 197–203.

Pugliese, M. T., Lifshitz, F., Grad, G., Fort, P., & Marks-Katz, M. (1983). Fear of obesity: A cause of short stature and delayed puberty. *New England Journal of Medicine, 309,* 513–518.

Pumariega, A. J. (1986). Acculturation and eating attitudes in adolescent girls: A comparative and correlational study. *Journal of the American Academy of Child and Adolescent Psychiatry, 25,* 276–279.

Rand, C., & Kuldau, J. M. (1990). The epidemiology of obesity and self-defined weight problem in the general population: Gender, race, age, and social class. *International Journal of Eating Disorders, 9,* 329–343.

Rastam, M. (1992). Anorexia nervosa in 51 Swedish adolescents: Premorbid problems and comorbidity. *Journal of the American Academy of Child and Adolescent Psychiatry, 31,* 819–828.

Rastam, M., & Gillberg, C. (1991). The family background in anorexia nervosa: A population-based study. *Journal of the American Academy of Child and Adolescent Psychiatry, 30,* 283–289.

Rastam, M., Gillberg, C., & Garton, M. (1989). Anorexia nervosa in a Swedish urban region. *British Journal of Psychiatry, 155,* 642–646.

Reznick, J. S., Hegeman, I. M., Kaufman, E. R., Woods, S. W., & Jacobs, M. (1992). Retrospective and concurrent self-report of behavioral inhibition and their relation to adult mental health. *Development and Psychopathology, 4,* 301–321.

Rhodes, B., & Kroger, J. (1991, April). Parental bonding and separation-individuation difficulties among late adolescent eating disordered women. Paper presented at the biennial meeting of the Society for Research in Child Development, Seattle.

Rizzuto, A., Peterson, R. K., & Reed, M. (1981). The pathological sense of self in anorexia nervosa. *Psychiatric Clinics of North America, 4,* 471–487.

Robins, L. N., Helzer, J. E., Weissman, M. M., Orvaschel, H., Gruenberg, E., Burke, J. D., & Regier, D. A. (1984). Lifetime prevalence of specific psychiatric disorders in three sites. *Archives of General Psychiatry, 41,* 949–958.

Rosen, J. C., Gross, J., & Vara, L. (1987). Psychological adjustment of adolescents attempting to lose or gain weight. *Journal of Consulting and Clinical Psychology, 55,* 742–747.

Rosen, J. C., Tacy, B., & Howell, D. (1990). Life stress, psychological symptoms and weight reducing behavior in adolescent girls: A prospective analysis. *International Journal of Eating Disorders, 9,* 17–26.

Rothenberg, A. (1990). Adolescence and eating disorder: The obsessive-compulsive syndrome. *Psychiatric Clinics of North America, 13,* 469–488.

Ruderman, A. (1986). Dietary restraint: A theoretical and empirical review. *Psychological Bulletin, 99,* 247–262.

Russell, J. D., Kopec-Schrader, E., Rey, J. M., & Beaumont, P. J. V. (1992). The parental bonding instrument in adolescent patients with anorexia nervosa. *Acta Psychiatrica Scandanavica, 86,* 236–239.

Rutter, M. (1986). The developmental psychopathology of depression: Issues and perspectives. In M. Rutter, C. E. Izard, & P. B. Read (Eds.), *Depression in young people: Clinical and developmental perspectives* (pp. 3–32). New York: Guilford.

Rutter, M. (1988). Epidemiological approaches to developmental psychopathology. *Archives of General Psychiatry, 45,* 486–495.

Rutter, M., & Rutter, M. (1993). *Developing minds: Challenge and continuity across the life span.* New York: Basic Books.

Salisbury, J. J., & Mitchell, J. E. (1991). Bone mineral density and anorexia nervosa in women. *American Journal of Psychiatry, 148,* 768–774.

Sameroff, A. J. (1975). Transactional models in early social relations. *Human Development, 18,* 65–79.

Sameroff, A. J., & Seifer, R. (1990). Early contributors to developmental risk. In J. Rolf, A. S. Masten, D. Cicchetti, K. H. Neuchterlein, & S. Weintraub (Eds.), *Risk and protective factors in the development of psychopathology* (pp. 52–66). Cambridge, England: Cambridge University Press.

Sands, S. (1991). Bulimia, dissociation, and empathy: A self-psychological view. In C. L. Johnson (Ed.), *Psychodynamic treatment of anorexia nervosa and bulimia.* New York: Guilford.

Sansone, R. A., & Fine, M. A. (1992). Borderline personality as a predictor of outcome in women with eating disorders. *Journal of Personality Disorders, 6,* 176–186.

Sargent, J. Liebman, R., & Silver, M. (1985). Family therapy for anorexia nervosa. In D. M. Garner & P. E. Garfinkel (Eds.), *Handbook of psychotherapy for anorexia nervosa and bulimia* (pp. 257–279). New York: Guilford.

Schwartz, R. C., Barrett, M. J., & Saba, G. (1985). Family therapy for bulimia. In D. M. Garner & P. E. Garfinkel (Eds.), *Handbook of psychotherapy for anorexia nervosa and bulimia* (pp. 280–307). New York: Guilford.

Selvini-Palazzoli, M. (1974). *Self-Starvation: From individual to family therapy in the treatment of anorexia nervosa.* New York: Aronson.

Shaw, B. R., & Garfinkel, P. E. (1990). Research problems in the eating disorders. *International Journal of Eating Disorders, 9,* 545–555.

Silber, T. J. (1986). Anorexia nervosa in blacks and Hispanics. *International Journal of Eating Disorders, 5,* 121–128.

Silverberg, S., & Steinberg, L. (1990). Psychological well-being of parents with early adolescent children. *Developmental Psychology, 26,* 658–666.

Silverstein, B., Carpman, S., Perlick, D., & Perdue, L. (1990). Nontraditional sex roles aspirations, gender identity conflict, and disordered eating among college women. *Sex Roles, 3,* 687–695.

Silverstein, B., & Perdue, L. (1988). The relationship between role concerns, preferences for slimness, and symptoms of eating problems among college women. *Sex Roles, 1,* 101–106.

Silverstein, B., Perdue, L., Wolf, C., & Pizzolo, C. (1988). Bingeing, purging, and estimates of parental attitudes regarding female achievement. *Sex Roles, 1,* 723–733.

Silverstein, B., & Perlick, D. (1991). Gender differences in depression: Historical changes. *Acta Psychiatrica Scandinavica, 84,* 327–331.

Simmons, R. G., & Blyth, D. A. (1987). *Moving into adolescence: The impact of pubertal change and school context.* New York: Aldine De Gruyter.

Simmons, R. G., Burgeson, R., Carlton-Ford, S., & Blyth, D. A. (1987). The impact of cumulative change in early adolescence. *Child Development, 58,* 1220–1234.

Singer, L. T., Ambuel, B., Wade, S., & Jaffe, A. (1992). Cognitive-behavioral treatment of health-impairing food phobias in children. *Journal of the American Academy of Child and Adolescent Psychiatry, 31,* 847–852.

Singer, L. T., Song, L. Y., Hill, B. P., & Jaffe, A. (1990). Stress and depression in mothers of failure-to-thrive children. *Journal of Pediatric Psychology, 15,* 711–720.

Skodol, A. E., Oldham, J. M., Hyler, S. E., Kellman, H. D., Doidge, N., & Davies, M. (1993). Comorbidity of DSM-III-R eating disorders and personality disorders. *International Journal of Eating Disorders, 14,* 403–416.

Slade, P. (1985). A review of body-image studies in anorexia nervosa and bulimia nervosa. *Journal of Psychiatric Research, 19,* 255–265.

Sobal, J., & Stunkard, A. J. (1989). Socioeconomic status and obesity: A review of the literature. *Psychological Bulletin, 105,* 260–275.

Spitz, R., & Wolf, K. M. (1946). Anaclitic depression: An inquiry into the genesis of psychiatric conditions in early childhood. *Psychoanalytic Study of the Child, 2,* 313–342.

Spitzer, R. L., Stunkard, A., Yanovski, S., Marcus, M. D., Wadden, T., Wing, R., Mitchell, J., & Hasin, D. (1993). Binge eating disorder should be included in DSM-IV: A reply to Fairburn et al.'s "The classification of recurrent overeating: The binge eating disorder proposal." *International Journal of Eating Disorders, 13,* 161–169.

Sroufe, A. (1989). Pathways to adaptation and maladaptation: Psychopathology as developmental deviation. In D. Cicchetti (Ed.), *Rochester Symposium on Developmental Psychopathology* (Vol. 1). Hillsdale, NJ: Erlbaum.

Sroufe, L. A. (1990). Considering normal and abnormal together: The essence of developmental psychopathology. *Development and Psychopathology, 2,* 335–347.

Steiger, H., Liquournik, K., Chapman, J., & Hussain, N. (1991). Personality and family disturbances in eating-disorder patients: Comparison of "restricters" and "bingers" to normal controls. *International Journal of Eating Disorders, 10,* 501–512.

Steiger, H., Van der Feen, J., Goldstein, C., & Leichner, P. (1989). Defense styles and parental bonding in eating-disordered women. *International Journal of Eating Disorders, 8,* 131–140.

Stein, A., & Fairburn, C. G. (1989). Children of mothers with bulimia nervosa. *British Medical Journal, 299,* 777–778.

Steinberg, L. (1990). Autonomy, conflict, and harmony in the family relationship. In S. S. Feldman & G. R. Elliott (Eds.), *At the threshold:*

The developing adolescent (pp. 255–276). Cambridge, MA: Harvard University Press.

Steiner-Adair, C. (1990). The body politic: Normal female adolescent development and the development of eating disorders. In C. Gilligan, N. P. Lyons, & T. J. Hanmer (Eds.), *Making connections: The relational worlds of adolescent girls at Emma Willard School* (pp. 162–182). Cambridge, MA: Harvard University Press.

Steinhausen, H. C., & Vollrath, M. (1993). The self-image of adolescent patients with eating disorders. *International Journal of Eating Disorders, 13,* 221–227.

Stern, D. N. (1985). *The interpersonal world of the infant.* New York: Basic Books.

Striegel-Moore, R. H. (1992). Prevention of bulimia nervosa: Questions and challenges. In J. H. Crowther, D. L. Tennenbaum, S. E. Hobfoll, M. A. P. Stephens (Eds.), *Bulimia nervosa: The individual and familial context* (pp. 203–224). Washington, DC: Hemisphere.

Striegel-Moore, R. H., Connor-Greene, P. A., & Shime, S. (1991). School milieu characteristics and disordered eating in high school graduates. *International Journal of Eating Disorders, 10,* 187–192.

Striegel-Moore, R. H., & Huydic, E. S. (1993). Problem drinking and symptoms of disordered eating in female high school students. *International Journal of Eating Disorders, 14,* 417–425.

Striegel-Moore, R. H., Nicholson, T. J., & Tamborlane, W. V. (1992). Prevalence of eating disorder symptoms in preadolescent and adolescent girls with IDDM. *Diabetes Care, 15,* 1361–1368.

Striegel-Moore, R., Pike, K., Rodin, J., Schreiber, G., & Wilfley, D. (1993, March). Predictors and correlates of drive for thinness: A comparison of 600 black and white girls. Paper presented at *The Society for Research in Child Development,* New Orleans.

Striegel-Moore, R. H., Silberstein, L. R., Frensch, P., & Rodin, J. (1989). A prospective study of disordered eating among college students. *International Journal of Eating Disorders, 8,* 499–509.

Striegel-Moore, R. H., Silberstein, L. R., & Rodin, J. (1993). The social self in bulimia nervosa: Public self-consciousness, social anxiety, and perceived fraudulence. *Journal of Abnormal Psychology, 102,* 297–303.

Strober, M. (1991). Disorders of the self in anorexia nervosa: An organismic-developmental paradigm. In C. Johnson (Ed.), *Psychodynamic treatment of anorexia nervosa and bulimia* (pp. 354–373). New York: Guilford.

Strober, M., & Katz, J. L. (1987). Do eating disorders and affective disorders share a common etiology? *International Journal of Eating Disorders, 6,* 171–180.

Strober, M., Lampert, C., Morrell, W., Burroughs, J., & Jacobs, C. (1990). A controlled family study of anorexia nervosa: Evidence of familial aggregation and lack of shared transmission with affective disorders. *International Journal of Eating Disorders, 9,* 239–253.

Stunkard, A. J., Sorensen, T. I. A., Hanis, C., Teasdale, T. W., Chakraborty, R., Schull, W. J., & Schulsinger, F. (1986). An adoption study of obesity. *New England Journal of Medicine, 314,* 193–198.

Sturm, L., & Stancin, T. (1990). Do babies get anorexia? *Journal of Child and Adolescent Psychiatry, 29,* 316–317.

Sugarman, A. (1991). Bulimia: A displacement from psychological self to body self. In C. L. Johnson (Ed.), *Psychodynamic treatment of anorexia nervosa and bulimia* (pp. 3–33). New York: Guilford.

Surbey, M. K. (1990). Family composition, stress, and the timing of human menarche. In T. E. Ziegler & F. B. Bercovitch (Eds.), *Socioendocrinology of primate reproduction* (pp. 11–32). New York: Wiley.

Swift, W. J., Andrews, D., & Barklage, N. E. (1986). The relationship between affective disorder and eating disorders: A review of the literature. *American Journal of Psychiatry, 143,* 290–299.

Swift, W. J., Bushnell, N. J., Hanson, P., & Logemann, T. (1986). Self-concept of adolescent anorexics. *Journal of the American Academy of Child and Adolescent Psychiatry, 25,* 826–835.

Szumkler, G. I. (1985). The epidemiology of anorexia nervosa and bulimia. *Journal of Psychiatric Research, 19,* 143–145.

Tanner, J. M. (1962). *Growth in adolescence* (2nd ed.). Oxford, England: Blackwell.

Thelen, M. H., Lawrence, C. M., & Powell, A. L. (1992). Body image, weight control, and eating disorders among children. In J. H. Crowther, D. L. Tennebaum, S. E. Hobfoll, & M. A. P. Stephens (Eds.), *The etiology of bulimia nervosa: The individual and familial context* (pp. 81–109). Washington, DC: Hemisphere.

Tobin, D. L., Johnson, C. L., & Dennis, A. B. (1992). Divergent forms of purging behavior in bulimia nervosa patients. *International Journal of Eating Disorders, 11,* 17–24.

Tobin, D. L., Johnson, J. C., Steinberg, S., Staats, M., & Dennis, A. B. (1991). Multifactorial assessment of bulimia nervosa. *Journal of Abnormal Psychology, 100,* 14–21.

Tobin-Richards, M. H., Boxer, A. M., & Petersen, A. C. (1983). The psychological significance of pubertal change: Sex differences in perceptions of self during early adolescence. In J. Brooks-Gunn & A. C. Petersen (Eds.), *Girls at puberty: Biological and psychosocial perspectives* (pp. 127–154). New York: Plenum.

Vandereycken, W., & Van Vrekem, E. V. (1992). Siblings of patients with an eating disorder. *International Journal of Eating Disorders, 12,* 273–280.

Walford, G., & McCune, N. (1991). Long-term outcome in early-onset anorexia nervosa. *British Journal of Psychiatry, 159,* 383–389.

Walsh, B. T., Kissileff, H. R., & Hadigan, C. M. (1989). Eating behavior in bulimia. In L. H. Schneider, S. J. Cooper, & K. A. Halmi (Eds.), The psychology of human eating disorders: Preclinical and clinical perspectives. *Annals of the New York Academy of Sciences, 575,* 446–455.

Wardle, J., & Beales, S. (1988). Control and loss of control over eating: An experimental investigation. *Journal of Abnormal Psychology, 97,* 35–40.

Wardle, J., & Beinart, H. (1981). Binge eating: A theoretical review. *British Journal of Clinical Psychology, 20,* 97–109.

Wardle, J., & Foley, E. (1989). Body image: Stability and sensitivity of body satisfaction and body size estimation. *International Journal of Eating Disorders, 8,* 55–62.

Warren, M. P. (1980). The effects of exercise on pubertal progression and reproductive function in girls. *Journal of Clinical Endocrinology and Metabolism, 51,* 1150–1157.

Warren, M. P. (1986). Anorexia nervosa. In *Precis III. An update in obstetrics and gynecology* (pp. 283–288). Washington, DC: American College of Obstetricians and Gynecologists.

Warren, M. P., Brooks-Gunn, J., Fox, R. P., Lancelot, C., Newman, D., & Hamilton, W. G. (1991). Lack of bone accretion and amenorrhea: Evidence for a relative osteopenia in weight-bearing bones. *Journal of Clinical Endocrinology and Metabolism, 72,* 847–853.

Warren, M. P., Brooks-Gunn, J., Hamilton, L. H., Warren, L. F., & Hamilton, W. G. (1986). Scoliosis and fractures in young ballet dancers. *New England Journal of Medicine, 314,* 1348–1353.

Weiner, H. (1989). Psychoendocrinology of anorexia nervosa. *Psychiatric Clinics of North America, 12,* 187–206.

Westen, D. (1989). Are "primitive" object relations really preoedipal? *American Journal of Orthopsychiatry, 59,* 331–345.

Westen, D., Ludolph, P., Lerner, H., Ruffins, S., & Wiss, F. C. (1990). Object relations in borderline adolescents. *Journal of the Academy of Child and Adolescent Psychiatry, 29,* 338–348.

Whitaker, A., Johnson, J., Shaffer, D., Rapoport, J. L., Kalikow, K., Walsh, B. T., Davies, M., Braiman, S., & Dolinksy, A. (1990). Uncommon troubles in young people: Prevalence estimates of selected psychiatric disorders in a nonreferred adolescent population. *Archives of General Psychiatry, 47,* 487–496.

Williamson, D. A., Cubic, B. A., & Gleaves, D. H. (1993). Equivalence of body image disturbances in anorexia and bulimia nervosa. *Journal of Abnormal Psychology, 102,* 177–180.

Wilson, G. T., & Walsh, B. T. (1991). Eating disorders. *Journal of Abnormal Psychology, 100,* 362–365.

Winnicott, D. W. (1965). Ego distortion in terms of true and false self. In *The maturational processes and the facilitating environment.* New York: International Universities Press.

Winnicott, D. W. (1974). Fear of breakdown. *International Review of Psychoanalysis, 1,* 103–107.

Wiseman, C. V., Gray, J. J., Mosimann, J. E., & Ahrens, A. H. (1992). Cultural expectations of thinness in women: An update. *International Journal of Eating Disorders, 11,* 85–89.

Wonderlich, S. (1992). Relationship of family and personality factors in bulimia. In J. H. Crowther, D. L. Tennenbaum, S. E. Hobfuoll, & M. A. P. Stephens (Eds.), *The etiology of bulimia nervosa: The individual and familial context* (pp. 103–126). Washington, DC: Hemisphere.

Wonderlich, S. A., & Swift, W. J. (1990a). Borderline versus other personality disorders in the eating disorders: Clinical description. *International Journal of Eating Disorders, 9,* 629–638.

Wonderlich, S. A., & Swift, W. J. (1990b). Perceptions of parental relationships in the eating disorders: The relevance of depressed mood. *Journal of Abnormal Psychology, 99,* 353–360.

Wonderlich, S. A., Swift, W. J., Slotnick, H. B., & Goodman, S. (1990). DSM-III-R personality disorders in eating-disorder subtypes. *International Journal of Eating Disorders, 9,* 607–616.

Wood, B., Atkins, J. B., Boyle, J. T., Nogueira, J., Zimand, E., & Carroll, L. (1989). The "psychosomatic family" model: An empirical and theoretical analysis. *Family Process, 28,* 399–417.

Woodside, D. B., & Garfinkel, P. E. (1992). Age of onset in eating disorders. *International Journal of Eating Disorders, 12,* 31–36.

Yates, A. (1989). Current perspectives on the eating disorders: I. History, psychological, and biological aspects. *Journal of Child and Adolescent Psychiatry, 28,* 813–828.

Young, C. M., Sipin, S. S., & Roe, D. A. (1968). Density and skinfold measurements: Body composition of preadolescent girls. *Journal of American Dietetic Association, 53,* 25–31.

Youniss, J., & Smollar, J. (1985). *Adolescent relations with mother, father and friends.* Chicago: University of Chicago Press.

CHAPTER 11

Developmental Psychopathology and Disorders of Affect

DANTE CICCHETTI and SHEREE L. TOTH

The mood disorders have long captured the rapt attention of philosophers, physicians, therapists, theoreticians, and researchers alike (see, e.g., Burton, 1621/1948; Haslam, 1809; Kagan, 1994; Siegel, 1973). Jackson's (1986) chronicling of the history of depression from Hippocratic times to contemporary views provides compelling documentation of a number of aspects of this troubling disorder. After presenting the myriad ways in which depression has been described throughout the ages, surveying the etiologic hypotheses of depression that have been promulgated, and detailing the treatment approaches that have been used with depressed persons, Jackson (1986) concluded that, despite the changes that have characterized the conceptualization of this disorder, there has been a remarkable amount of continuity over the past 2,500 years.

Manic-depressive illness, too, has been assiduously portrayed in the literature over the centuries (Bleuler, 1924; Goodwin & Jamison, 1990; Jamison, 1993). As Jackson (1986) explicated, "Disorders similar to our mania and our melancholia constituted significant portions of the larger groupings of mental disorders that were subsumed under those rubrics in ancient times" (p. 249). Moreover, when depression and mania have been deliberated in the clinical literature throughout time—even though early on they were conceived as separate illness entities—links between them have almost invariably been made (Goodwin & Jamison, 1990).

Nonetheless, it has been only since the middle of the 19th century that manic-depressive illness has been depicted as a unique disease entity (Goodwin & Jamison, 1990). Two French psychiatrists, Falret and Baillarger, independently and virtually contemporaneously, proposed the thesis that mania and depression represented distinct manifestations of an underlying unitary illness (Sedler, 1983). It was the great German psychiatrist, Kraepelin, who presented an elegant synthesis of the disorder in the early part of the 20th century. Kraepelin's (1921) integration emphasized the features of the disorder that distinguished it from "the group of schizophrenias" (Bleuler, 1911/1950): its episodic nature, more benign prognosis, and positive family history of the disorder (Goodwin & Jamison, 1990).

In the Kraepelinian framework, virtually all melancholia other than several involutional forms were included under the category of manic-depressive illness (Depue & Monroe, 1978; Goodwin & Jamison, 1990). It took until 1957, when Leonhard (1957/1979) proposed that patients with depression and mania (bipolar disorder) should be differentiated from those who exhibited recurrent depressions only (unipolar disorder). Despite Leonhard's observations and recommendations, as well as the long-standing and growing recognition of the limitations inherent in Kraepelin's unitary disease notion of manic-depressive illness (e.g., Angst, 1966; Perris, 1966), in the main the Kraepelinian nosology was embraced by the nomenclature of the American Psychiatric Association (1968) as late as the second edition of the *Diagnostic and Statistical Manual of Mental Disorders* (DSM-II).

In the years since researchers have adopted the unipolar-bipolar distinction when investigating the mood disorders, recognition of the differences between unipolar and bipolar disorder (Akiskal & McKinney, 1975; Depue & Monroe, 1978), as well as of the heterogeneity characterizing both depressive and manic-depressive illness, has come to the fore (Akiskal, 1981, 1983; Dunner, Dwyer, & Fieve, 1976; Dunner, Gershon, & Goodwin, 1976; Himmelhoch, 1979; Kupfer, Pickar, Himmelhoch, & Detre, 1975; Winokur, 1975, 1979; Winokur, Clayton, & Reich, 1969). Unipolar and bipolar illness are characterized by between- and within-disorder heterogeneity in a number of areas with which we must be concerned: in symptom pattern, in etiology, in course and psychological and biological sequelae, and in response to treatment. As researchers have begun to attend to these sources of inter- and intradisorder heterogeneity, our understanding of the mood disorders has grown with commensurate complexity.

Although the mood disorders of children and adolescents have been investigated for a shorter period than their adult counterparts, nonetheless, during recent years research activity has proliferated in the area of childhood and adolescent depression and manic-depressive illness. Whereas earlier beliefs questioned whether or not depressive or manic-depressive illness could occur prior to puberty (e.g., Anthony & Scott, 1960; Lefkowitz & Burton, 1978; Rie, 1966), the focus of contemporary research has shifted from debating which criteria should

Our work on this chapter was supported by a grant from the Prevention Research Branch of the National Institute of Mental Health (MH45027).

be used to diagnose childhood mood disorders, to more sophisticated examinations of the epidemiology, causes, courses, sequelae, and treatment responses of mood-disordered children, as well as of children who have one or more relatives with a mood disorder (Angold, 1988a, 1988b; Downey & Coyne, 1990; Hammen, 1992b; Kashani, Husain et al., 1983; Kovacs, 1989; Puig-Antich, 1980a; Strober & Carlson, 1982; Trad, 1986, 1987).

GOALS OF THE CHAPTER

This chapter takes a developmental psychopathology perspective in examining theory and research on the affective disorders. After describing epidemiological aspects of depressive and manic-depressive illness, we present a developmental psychopathology approach. Research on how individuals at risk for or suffering from a depressive or manic-depressive disorder negotiate illustrative issues of development is then discussed. To emphasize the importance of integrating biological and psychological domains, we then address the respective roles of parenting, genetics, and biology in the emergence of disorders of affect. Because a developmental psychopathology approach stresses investigating adaptation across the life span, various temporal periods of development are examined whenever possible. The chapter concludes by calling for intensified efforts to investigate affective disorders from an integrative, interdisciplinary, developmental framework.

EPIDEMIOLOGY OF THE MOOD DISORDERS ACROSS THE LIFE SPAN

With the increased knowledge of the epidemiology of the mood disorders throughout the life span, it is not surprising that researchers have conducted so many studies on the affective disorders. According to the Institute of Medicine (1989), the prevalence of depression in prepubertal children is approximately 2% (Kashani, McGee et al., 1983). Moreover, Weissman and her colleagues (Weissman et al., 1987) have discovered that prepubescent and adolescent children of clinically depressed parents had a greater prevalence of major depressive disorder than did children of parents without a psychiatric disorder.

Investigations indicate that the prevalence of depression in adolescence increases substantially, with between 5% and 10% of adolescents manifesting a major depressive disorder at any point in time (Fleming & Offord, 1990; Lewinsohn, Hops, Roberts, Seeley, & Andrews, 1993; Petersen et al., 1993). An epidemiological investigation of over 1,500 adolescents in a randomly selected community sample revealed that the mean age of onset of first depressive episode was approximately 15 years (Lewinsohn, Clark, Seeley, & Rohde, 1994). Early onset of depressive disorder in this adolescent community sample was associated with being female and having thoughts about committing suicide (Lewinsohn et al., 1994).

Comorbidity (the contemporaneous existence of two or more mental disorders) appears to occur commonly in depressed children and adolescents (Institute of Medicine, 1989). Conduct disorders and anxiety disorders frequently co-occur in depressed children (Angold & Costello, 1993; Capaldi, 1992; Caron & Rutter, 1991; Cole & Zahn-Waxler, 1992; Fleming & Offord, 1990; Kovacs, Gatsonis, Paulauskas, & Richards, 1989; Puig-Antich, 1980b, 1982), while substance abuse and alcohol abuse accompany the aforementioned disorders in affectively ill adolescents, as well as in the offspring of parents with a mood disorder (Kovacs, 1989).

According to some estimates, major depressive disorder is the most common serious adult mental health problem (Weissman, Bruce, Leaf, Florio, & Holzer, 1991). The affective or mood disorders are among the most devastating in terms of prevalence, mortality, family functioning, and mental health costs (Institute of Medicine, 1985). Epidemiological studies estimate that 9 to 16 million people currently have a mood disorder and that 8% (Weissman et al., 1991) to nearly 20% (Institute of Medicine, 1985; Kessler, McGonagle, Zhao et al., 1994) of persons experience a minimum of one serious bout of clinical depression at some point in their lives (see also Blazer, Kessler, McGonagle, & Swartz, 1994; Burke, Burke, Rae, & Regier, 1991). Furthermore, between 3% and 6% of adults develop the chronic disorder, dysthymia, in their lifetimes (Kessler, McGonagle, Zhao et al., 1994; Weissman et al., 1991).

Moreover, two large-scale epidemiological investigations have found lower lifetime prevalence rates of depression and dysthymia in the elderly (Kessler, McGonagle, Zhao et al., 1994; Weissman et al., 1991). Most researchers concur that there is no evidence that these mood disorders increase with age (Stoudemire & Blazer, 1985).

Adults with unipolar depression can expect to experience a mean number of five or six episodes during their lifetime (Zis & Goodwin, 1979). Most of these episodes resolve in 6 to 9 months, with 20% persisting for nearly 2 years (Post & Ballenger, 1984).

Comorbid mental disorders, including anxiety disorders, substance abuse, and alcohol abuse commonly accompany adult depressive disorders and dysthymia (Maser & Cloninger, 1990). Furthermore, personality disorders frequently co-occur with depression, and this comorbidity is associated with an earlier onset of depression, poorer recovery from the illness, more life stress, and more frequent suicide attempts (Pfol, Stangl, & Zimmerman, 1984).

Additionally, depressed persons tend to select mates with a psychiatric illness or a family history of psychopathology (termed assortative mating) (Merikangas & Spiker, 1982). As such, chronic interpersonal problems are common occurrences in these close relationships (Coyne, 1976; Downey & Coyne, 1990). Not surprisingly, depressed persons have a high rate of marital discord, with such conflicts continuing up to 4 years after the onset of an episode (Downey & Coyne, 1990; Hooley, 1986).

Mania is rare prior to the onset of puberty (Kovacs, 1989) although it increases in frequency by midadolescence (Rutter, 1986). Nonetheless, when major depressive disorder is accompanied by psychotic symptoms in advance of puberty, bipolar disorder is often an outcome later on in life, especially if one of the parents has a history of manic-depressive illness (Kovas, 1989; Puig-Antich, 1980a). For example, Geller, Fox, and Clark (1994), in a prospective longitudinal study, blindly rated 79 children with major depressive disorder and 31 normal control children matched on age, gender, and socioeconomic status. Geller and her colleagues found that nearly one-third of the children with major depressive disorder developed bipolar illness and that 80% of those who were bipolar were prepubertal. In contrast, none of the children in the normal group developed bipolar disorder. Both Strober and Carlson (1982) and Akiskal et al. (1983) have demonstrated that psychotically depressed adolescents had a greater probability of changing from unipolar to bipolar illness over time.

Approximately 1% to 2% of the population will merit the diagnosis of bipolar disorder in their lifetime (Kessler, McGonagle, Zhao, et al., 1994; Weissman et al., 1991). In addition, several epidemiological studies have demonstrated that bipolar disorder is less prevalent in the elderly (Kessler, McGonagle, Zhao et al., 1994; Weissman et al., 1991). Bipolar disorder that occurs for the first time late in life is seen predominantly in persons where there are relatively low rates of affective disorder and an increased frequency of drug abuse (Young & Klerman, 1992).

Persons with bipolar disorder experience a similar number of recurrences in their lifetime as do persons with unipolar disorder (Goodwin & Jamison, 1984, 1990). However, a recent prospective longitudinal study of patients with unipolar and bipolar disorder discovered that bipolar patients were more likely to experience multiple episodes at the 2-year and 5-year follow-ups than were the unipolar patients (Winokur, Coryell, Keller, Endicott, & Akiskal, 1993).

Hammen, Burge, Burney, and Adrian (1990) administered a semistructured psychiatric interview to the school-age children of women who had unipolar depression, bipolar illness, a chronic medical condition, and to a control group of youngsters of medically and psychiatrically healthy women. Hammen and her colleagues (1990) found that the offspring of mothers with unipolar disorder had the highest rates of disorder, including major depression. However, the children of the bipolar and medically ill women likewise manifested significant rates of mental disorder. The majority of the children with a psychiatric diagnosis had their first episode in preadolescence and continued on a chronic or intermittent course of disorder throughout the approximate 3-year follow-up period. The presence of a maternal mood disorder not only increases the risk of subsequent disorder in the short term but also portends the unfolding of a deleterious course that often includes the development of recurrent disorders, either affective illness alone or comorbid with other psychiatric problems.

Additionally, Warner, Weissman, Fendrich, Wickramaratne, and Moreau (1992) examined the 2-year course, first onset, recurrence, and recovery from major depression in a sample of 174 children with a parent who had a major depressive disorder. At 2 years, the incidence rate of major depression in these children was 8.5%. Moreover, 16.1% of the children also had experienced a recurrent episode. Congruent with the conclusion of Kovacs (1989), one of the best predictors of recurrent depression in these children was a prior comorbid diagnosis of dysthymic disorder.

Within the 2-year period, the majority of these children had recovered (87%), with the mean time to recovery being 54 weeks. Children who experienced their first affective disorder at or before the age of 13, and those who had been exposed to multiple parental depressions, displayed protracted courses of recovery. In particular, children whose first episode occurred prior to age 13 took an average of 74 weeks to recover, and those who had experienced two or more bouts of parental depression needed nearly 79 weeks to recover on average.

As part of a seminal prospective longitudinal investigation of the development of major depressive disorder in childhood, Kovacs and her colleagues (Kovacs, Feinberg, Crouse-Novak, Paulauskas, & Finkelstein, 1984; Kovacs, Feinberg, Crouse-Novak, Paulauskas, Pollock, & Finkelstein, 1984) examined the duration of the first illness, the course of recovery from this initial episode onset, and the time to recurrence of a subsequent major depressive bout in a school-age, clinically referred sample. The investigators discovered that dysthymia had an earlier age of onset than did major depressive disorder. Moreover, dysthymia persisted for approximately 3 years, whereas depressive disorders took nearly 8 months to remit. When these depressed children recovered, they continued to be examined until they developed a recurrent episode of major depression. Forty-percent of the children developed a subsequent depression and none of these youngsters had a recovery period of more than 2 years before they experienced their first remission. Those children who had an underlying dysthymic disorder had an elevated risk for experiencing recurrent or periodic depressive disorder.

In a more protracted prospective longitudinal investigation of this sample, Kovacs, Akiskal, Gatsonis, and Parrone (1994) compared the course of functioning in a group of 60 children whose first mood disorder was dysthymic disorder, and a group whose first affective illness was major depressive disorder. Kovacs and her colleagues (1994) found that children with first-onset dysthymic disorder had an earlier age of onset, similar symptoms of affect dysregulation, lower rates of anhedonia and vasovegetative symptoms, and a greater overall risk for developing any subsequent mood disorder than was the case for the youngsters whose first affective disorder was major depressive illness. Kovacs et al. (1994) found that 76% of dysthymic children developed a first-episode major depressive disorder and that 69% combined dysthymia and depression (i.e., manifested "double depression"). Moreover, 40% of the dysthymic youngsters had comorbid anxiety disorders, and 31% of dysthymic children had comorbid conduct disorder. Furthermore, 13% of the dysthymics subsequently "switched" to bipolar disorder diagnoses. After the first episode, the course and the subsequent rates of recurrent mood disorders of the dysthymic children were similar to those exhibited by the children whose first affective disorder was major depression.

In a noteworthy study, Strober and his colleagues (Strober, Lampert, Schmidt, & Morrell, 1993) found that in a 24-month longitudinal follow-up of adolescents with major depressive disorder, a substantial number of the adolescents had recovered within this period of time (90%), although for the majority of children the recovery was protracted in length (i.e., greater than 5 months). Moreover, only those adolescents with psychotic depression subsequently "switched" into mania (Strober et al., 1993). The 28% risk of "switching" found among the psychotically depressed adolescents is far greater than the 4%–8% rates of switching found in follow-up investigations of adults with unipolar disorder (e.g., Dunner, Dwyer, & Fieve,

1976) and suggests that the presence of psychotic features in adolescents has a greater affinity to manic-depressive illness than is the case for adults.

A recent investigation of the episode duration and time to recurrence of major depressive disorder in an adolescent community sample revealed that the average episode length was 26 weeks and the median length of 8 weeks (Lewinsohn et al., 1994). Those adolescents who took longer to recover were characterized by an earlier age of onset for the first episode, the presence of suicidal ideation, and the seeking of treatment for the mood disorder. Five percent of the recovered adolescents relapsed within 6 months, 12% developed a recurrent/depressive episode within a year, and nearly one-third became subsequently depressed within 4 years (Lewinsohn et al., 1994).

Harrington, Fudge, Rutter, Pickles, and Hill (1990, 1991) examined the adult outcomes of childhood and adolescent depression. Utilizing the clinical data summaries of children who attended the Maudsley Hospital in London, Harrington and his colleagues identified a cohort of 80 children and adolescents who were operationally defined as depressed and a demographically matched control group of nondepressed psychiatric patients. Over 80% of these children and adolescents were studied at approximately 18 years from their original contact at the Maudsley. The depressed and nondepressed psychiatric controls, assessed blindly to their status, did not differ with respect to the number of nondepressive adult psychiatric disorders. The depressed group, however, demonstrated an enhanced risk for affective disorder in adulthood, suggesting that substantial specificity exists in the continuity of mood disorders between childhood and adulthood (Harrington et al., 1990).

In a subsequent reanalysis of this sample, Harrington and his collaborators (1991) discovered that depressed children who were comorbid for conduct disorder had a poorer short-term outcome and engaged in significantly more criminal activity in adulthood than did the depressed children who were without conduct problems. Furthermore, depressed children with conduct disorder displayed patterns of maladaptation in adulthood that were similar to those of conduct-disordered children without depression. Finally, although findings did not quite reach statistical significance, Harrington et al., (1991) uncovered suggestive evidence that depressed children with conduct problems were less likely to develop depression in adulthood than were depressed children without conduct problems.

A recent investigation of the time course of nonchronic major depressive disorder in adults found that for 40% of the episodes, recovery occurred within a 3-month period. Within a year, 80% of the episodes remitted, and only 20% exhibited more protracted courses (Coryell et al., 1994). Maj, Veltro, Pirozzi, Lobrace, and Magliano (1992) likewise conducted a prospective longitudinal study aimed at investigating the pattern of recurrence of affective illness in a group of adult patients who had recovered from an episode of primary nonbipolar, nonpsychotic major depressive disorder. Maj and his colleagues found that the probability of persisting in a nondisordered condition was 76% at 6 months, 63% at 1 year, and 25% at 5-year follow-up. Moreover, these investigators discovered that a history of three or more major depressive episodes was the best predictor of an early recurrence after recovery from the index episode. Furthermore, Maj et al. (1992) observed a pattern of increasing severity from the index episode to the subsequent three prospective episodes of major depressive disorder.

Wells, Burnam, Rogers, Hays, and Camp (1992) examined the course of depression over a 2-year period in four groups of adult outpatients: (a) individuals with major depression; (b) individuals with dysthymia; (c) individuals with both major depression and dysthymia (i.e., "double depression"); and (d) individuals with depressive symptoms but no current depressive disorder. Wells and his colleagues (1992) found that patients who were diagnosed as dysthymic, with or without a contemporaneous major depression, had the poorest outcomes. In addition, patients who were diagnosed with major depression had intermediate outcomes, whereas those who had depressed symptoms but no depressive disorder had the best prognosis. Even the group of individuals with subthreshold depressed symptoms only had a high incidence of major depression (25%) within two years of follow-up (see Wells et al., 1992).

In a 5-year prospective follow-up investigation of over 400 subjects who were participants in the National Institute of Mental Health Collaborative Depression Study of Adult Depression, Keller et al. (1992) discovered that the rate of recovery from major depressive disorder decreased with the passage of time. Although 50% of the participants remitted within 6 months, the recovery rate diminished markedly thereafter, especially between years 1 and 5.

Additionally, a one-year prospective longitudinal investigation of 127 elderly patients with major depressive disorder revealed that interpersonal factors in the patients' family predicted whether or not the elderly person would recover from his or her episode. Of these patients, 72% recovered within the year, and 19% of them subsequently relapsed (Hinrichsen, 1992; Hinrichsen & Hernandez, 1993).

Finally, a number of researchers have investigated gender differences in depression across the life course. The majority of these investigations have found that, prior to age 12 or 13, boys are more likely to be depressed than girls (Angold & Rutter, 1992). Beginning in adolescence, there is a shift that appears to persist throughout all stages of the life course: Girls and women are far more likely to develop a mood disorder than boys and men (Angold & Rutter, 1992; Kessler, McGonagle, Zhao et al., 1994; Nolen-Hoeksema, 1987; Peterson et al., 1993; Radloff, 1975; Stoudemire & Blazer, 1985; Weissman et al., 1991; Weissman & Paykel, 1974; Winokour et al., 1993). A number of investigators who have studied community samples have found that retrospectively reported prevalence rates rise sharply from 9 to 19 years of age, especially for females (see, e.g., Kessler, McGonagle, Nelson et al., 1994; Lewinsohn et al., 1994). Although there do not appear to be any gender differences in the development of bipolar disorder (Goodwin & Jamison, 1990; Kessler, McGonagle, Zhao et al., 1994; Weissman et al., 1991), nonetheless, rapid cycling bipolar disorder appears to occur more frequently in females (Goodwin & Jamison, 1990).

A number of hypotheses have been put forth to explain the developmental transformation in gender differences in depression at adolescence, including the emergence of biological changes associated with puberty, varying socialization experiences and societal expectations, and different styles of coping with stressful life events in men and women (Angold & Rutter, 1992; Nolen-Hoeksema, 1987, 1991; Radloff, 1975). In particular, women appear to ruminate about their problems more than men, who are more prone to take action to distract themselves (Nolen-Hoeksema, 1987). Moreover, ruminative response styles, characterized by a focus on depressed symptoms, and the possible causes as outcomes of these symptoms, are associated with longer durations of depressive episodes (Nolen-Hoeksema, 1993).

A DEVELOPMENTAL PSYCHOPATHOLOGY PERSPECTIVE

Developmental psychopathology is an emerging discipline that seeks to unify, within a developmental, life-span framework, the many contributions to the study of the mood disorders emanating for multiple fields of inquiry, including psychology, psychoanalytic theory, psychiatry, the neurosciences, sociology, cultural anthropology, and epidemiology (Abraham, 1911; Angold, 1988a; Brown & Harris, 1978; Freud, 1917; Kleinman & Good, 1985; Meyersburg & Post, 1979; Post & Ballenger, 1984). Achenbach (1990) has described developmental psychopathology as a macroparadign rather than a unitary theory. Accordingly, developmental psychopathology represents a movement toward comprehending the causes and determinants, course, sequelae, and treatment of the affective disorders through its synthesis of knowledge from multiple disciplines within a developmental framework. The undergirding developmental orientation impels theoreticians and investigators to pose new questions about the phenomena they study. For example, it becomes necessary to move beyond identifying features that differentiate depressed and nondepressed children and adults (e.g., attributional distortions, affect dysregulation) to articulating how such differences have evolved developmentally (see, e.g., Cicchetti, Ganiban, & Barnett, 1991; Cole & Zahn-Waxler, 1992; Dodge, 1993; Fincham & Cain, 1986; Post, Rubinow, & Ballenger, 1986; Quiggle, Garber, Panak, & Dodge, 1992; Rose & Abramson, 1992). Likewise, rather than being concerned with merely describing the symptoms of unipolar and bipolar illness in children and adults, the focus shifts to ascertaining how similar and/or different organizations of biological, cognitive, socioemotional, and representational systems and processes contribute to the expression of specific depressive or manic symptoms (e.g., dysphoric mood, excessive guilt, thoughts about suicide, hallucinations, sleep disturbances, anhedonia, hypomania, flight of ideas) at each specific developmental level (see, e.g., Borst, Noam & Bartok, 1991; Chandler, 1994; Garber, 1984; Kegan, 1982; Post, 1992; Rierdan & Koff, 1993; Zahn-Waxler & Kochanska, 1990).

What Is Developmental?

Though seemingly straightforward, the effort to understand what "developmental" signifies often results in confusion and conflicting views. It is frequently presumed that any study involving children represents a "developmental" investigation. However, it is certainly possible to study children from a nondevelopmental perspective. Age, in and of itself, does not necessarily signify that a developmental process has been specified (Rutter, 1989; Wohlwill, 1973). Developmental psychopathology is concerned not only with children but also with individuals across the life span. A developmental analysis is as applicable to the study of the gene or cell as it is to the investigation of the individual, family, or society.

The developmental approach is charged with two interrelated goals. First, the developmental perspective seeks to examine the specific evolving capacities that are characteristic of individuals at varying developmental stages across the life span. This requires formulating questions about a phenomenon in terms of what capacities are inherent in an individual during a particular developmental stage and how a given process or mechanism becomes manifested in view of those developmental capacities and attainments of the individual. For example, the cognitive capacities of a toddler versus a third grader versus an adolescent are progressively more advanced. As a result, meanings attributed to events and cognitive capacities for dealing with experiences are vastly different. Thus, to understand a phenomenon, researchers must consider developmental variations in cognitive and social-cognitive capacities, in addition to other psychological and biological domains of functioning, to ascertain how particular outcomes are manifested during different developmental periods. Second, a developmental analysis seeks to examine the prior sequence of adaptations in development contributing to an outcome in a particular developmental period. This requires that the current status of an individual's functioning be examined in the context of how that status was attained across the course of development. In this way, the life-span view strives to move beyond the proximal causes of current outcomes to an examination of the developmental progression of distal sources of influences that eventuated in current outcomes (see, e.g., Post, 1992).

In keeping with these goals, Hammen (1992a) has offered an exemplary developmental analysis of major contributors to depression in adults. Historically, factors such as biased cognitive appraisals, life stress, and interpersonal difficulties each have been examined extensively for their effects on depressive outcomes. Hammen, however, has begun to ask the developmental questions of how individual differences in these proximal influences evolved. Her analysis places the sources of the current depression in the stream of the developmental process. The conceptualization of these constructs within a developmental perspective provides a richer, more in-depth understanding of the origins of depression and of the processes contributing to its continuation.

Tenets of Developmental Psychopathology

A focus on the boundary between normal and abnormal development is central to a developmental psychopathology analysis (Cicchetti, 1993; Cicchetti & Toth, 1991). Such a perspective emphasizes not only how knowledge from the study of normal development can inform the study of high-risk conditions and psychopathology but also how the investigation of risk and pathology can enhance our comprehension of normal development. Thus, the application of knowledge of normal biological, cognitive/social-cognitive, representational, and socioemotional, development to the understanding of unipolar and bipolar illness results in an articulation of how components of individual functioning in depressed persons contribute to their symptomatic presentation (cf. Kegan, 1982).

For example, many of the internal processes implicated in existing theories of unipolar and bipolar illness do not exist in isolation (cf. Walker, Downey, & Nightingale, 1989). Deficits in social information processing; social-cognition; neurobiological, neurochemical, and neuropsychological development and functioning; emotion regulation; parent-child attachment; impulse control; and other systems tend to covary significantly in samples of mood-disordered children and adults (see, e.g., Barnett & Gotlib, 1988; Cole & Zahn-Waxler, 1992; Collins & Depue, 1992; Cummings & Cicchetti, 1990; Davidson, 1991; Depue & Iacono, 1989; Dodge, 1993; Downey & Coyne, 1990; Gold, Goodwin, & Chrousos, 1988a, 1988b; Kinsbourne, 1988; Kupfer & Thase, 1983; Panak & Garber, 1992; Post, Weiss, & Leverich, 1994; Siever & Davis, 1985). This covariance, in turn, often renders difficult the important task of disentangling causal processes (Downey & Coyne, 1990). In some instances, suspected causal processes actually may be the products of other covarying systems and only spuriously related to depressive or manic-depressive illness. In other cases, a process may indeed influence depressive or hypomanic behavior, but the nature and extent of its causal influence may be masked or clouded by the influence of other interacting systems.

A strategy for disentangling causal influences among multiple, interactive systems is to identify and examine the functioning of individuals who possess particular functioning deficits and not others. Multiple processes studied individually in this manner may provide significant insights into the individual role(s) they play in normal adaptation, and into how those roles might change and require reconceptualization within a broader matrix of functioning deficits among persons with unipolar or bipolar illness.

In turn, the examination of aberrations in the biological, cognitive/social-cognitive, representational, and socioemotional domains in mood-disordered individuals assists in a more complete understanding of how these systems function in normal development (Hesse & Cicchetti, 1982). The study of abnormal and normal are intimately intertwined. For example, an understanding of the ramifications of a secure attachment relationship are best comprehended by contrasting children with secure and insecure attachments. Knowledge of the unfolding complications and difficulties that children with insecure attachments experience contributes to the understanding of how secure attachment relationships function to promote an adaptive course of development (Sroufe, 1979, 1989). It is through this dialectic that knowledge advances in the study of both normal and abnormal development.

In essence, developmental psychopathology is not primarily the study of disorders. That is not to say that the field does not seek to enhance understanding of psychopathology, including the affective disorders. However, the central focus of developmental psychopathology is the elucidation of developmental processes and how they function as indicated and elaborated by the examination of extremes in developmental outcome. Radke-Yarrow and Zahn-Waxler (1990) have highlighted how this contrasts with developmental psychology, which seeks to examine the central tendency of groups and uniformities and constancies in developmental progression. Extreme deviations from the mean in distributions are often viewed by developmental psychologists as problematic outliers that are best disregarded or that require adjustments through statistical transformation to bring their scores closer to the mean. In contrast, the developmental psychopathologist is keenly interested in these extremes in their own right. Such extremes contribute substantial diversity to the possible outcomes in development, thereby enhancing our understanding of developmental processes. In addition to an interest in extremes in the distribution (i.e., children and adults with disorders), the developmental psychopathologist also is interested in variations in the continuum between the mean and the extremes. These variations may represent individuals who are currently not divergent enough to be considered disordered but who may progress to further extremes as development continues. Such individuals may be vulnerable to developing future disordered outcomes. Or, viewed within Wakefield's (1992) concept of harmful dysfunction, developmental deviations may for some individuals reflect either the earliest signs of an emerging dysfunction or an already-existing dysfunction that is partially compensated for by other processes within (i.e., competencies) or outside (i.e., protective factors) the individual (cf. Cicchetti & Aber, 1986; Cicchetti & Garmezy, 1993). Therefore, tracking the ontogenetic course of these individuals is likely to broaden the complexity of understanding of developmental processes.

Diversity in process and outcome are hallmarks of the perspective of developmental psychopathology. It is expected that there are multiple contributors to mood-disordered outcomes in any individual, that the contributors vary between individuals with a mood-disordered outcome, that there is heterogeneity among persons with an affective disorder in the features of their behavioral and biological disturbances and (in some instances) underlying dysfunctions, and that there are numerous pathways to any mood-disordered outcome. The principles of equifinality and multifinality derived from general systems theory are relevant in this regard (von Bertalanffy, 1968). Equifinality refers to the observation that a diversity of paths may lead to the same outcome. This alerts us to the possibility that a variety of developmental progressions may eventuate in a mood disorder, rather than positing a singular primary pathway to disorder.

In contrast, multifinality suggests that any one component may function differently depending on the organization of the system in which it operates. Thus, loss of a major attachment figure in childhood will result in numerous outcomes for children depending on the context of their environment and the individual competencies and coping capacities of the child. Depression may be one such outcome in, for example, a child who already had insecure representational working models of attachment figures and of the self, and who faces extremes of additional stress in conjunction with minimal support or nurturance from caregivers (Cummings & Cicchetti, 1990).

Because of the diversity in process and outcome apparent in development, the approach to the affective disorders of developmental psychopathology does not proffer a simple unitary etiologic explanation. The occurrence of unipolar or bipolar illness during the life course likely results from a multiplicity of pathways in different individuals. Although commonalities in pathways in different clusters of depressed or manic persons may be delineated, it also is possible that a mood disorder is not the only outcome associated with each pathway. As further work exploring the developmental trajectories leading to mood-disordered outcomes is conducted, pathways may be delineated that are depression or manic-depression specific in some individuals. There are, however, also likely to be generic pathways that contribute to a range of dysfunctions and disorders (e.g., anxiety disorders, substance abuse, personality disorders), of which an affective disorder may be one (Maser & Cloninger, 1990). Thus, the study of affective disorders needs to be conceptualized within a larger body of inquiry into the developmental patterns promoting adjustment difficulties and psychopathology.

Consequently, developmental psychopathologists must be aware of normal developmental pathways, determine when deviations from these pathways occur, delineate the developmental transformations that emerge as individuals progress through these deviant ontogenetic courses, and identify the factors and mechanisms that may affect development (Cicchetti, 1993; Sroufe, 1989). A central tenet of developmental psychopathology is the assertion that individuals may move between pathological and nonpathological forms of functioning. Even in the presence of pathology, adaptive coping mechanisms may be present (Cicchetti & Garmezy, 1993; Zigler & Glick, 1986). Therefore, it is only through the consideration of both adaptive and maladaptive processes that it becomes possible to delimit the presence, nature, and boundaries of the underlying psychopathology.

Developmental psychopathology is especially applicable to the investigation of transitional turning points in development across the life span (Erikson, 1950; Staudinger, Marsiske, & Baltes, 1993). This is due to its acknowledgment that disorders may appear for the first time in later life (for examples in adolescence and adulthood, see Benes, Turtle, Khan, & Farol, 1994; Breslin & Weinberger, 1990; Moffitt, 1993; Rogers & Kegan, 1990), and because of its advocacy for the examination of the course of disorders once manifest, including their phases and sequelae (cf. Post et al., in press; Zigler & Glick, 1986). The nature of the developmental process elucidates a clear perspective on how to conceptualize empirical research on the origins and course of late-emerging psychopathology. Researchers have found it necessary to expand their studies of the antecedents of psychopathology beyond the search for isomorphic patterns of behavior in the early years and toward a focus on the adaptational failure on the stage-salient issues of particular developmental periods (Cicchetti & Aber, 1986; Noam & Valiant, 1994).

Rigorous empirical studies attempting to identify early precursors of later depressive or manic-depressive disorder face numerous conceptual and methodological challenges. Because of developmental changes in neurobiological and physiological systems, as well as parallel developments in cognitive, socioemotional, and representational systems, investigators cannot presume phenotypic similarity between early precursors and later impairments. Therefore, studies of the early precursors of later psychopathology should conceptualize and measure features of early development that are theoretically related but not necessarily behaviorally identical to later depression- or manic-depression-related impairments.

The developmental psychopathology perspective also emphasizes the need to understand the functioning of individuals who, after having diverged onto deviant developmental pathways, resume more positive functioning and achieve adequate adaptation, as well as the functioning of those who do not succumb to the stresses that eventuate in developmental deviation in others. Future research on the mood disorders would do well to increase its focus on the protective mechanisms underlying such resilient adaptations (see, e.g., Beardslee & Podorefsky, 1988; Conrad & Hammen, 1993; Jamison, 1993; Jamison, Gerner, Hammen, & Padesky, 1980; Radke-Yarrow & Brown, 1993; Radke-Yarrow & Sherman, 1990).

Likewise, the course of adaptation once an effective disorder has remitted (see, e.g., Belsher & Costello, 1988; Kovacs, 1989; Maj et al., 1992) could benefit from a developmental perspective. It would be informative, for example, to examine the functioning characteristics of individuals formerly diagnosed with an affective disorder who have returned to a nondisordered condition. Congruent with the concept of multifinality described earlier, it may be possible to identify core characteristics of functioning that remain stable but that no longer give rise to an affective disorder because of compensatory factors in the environment or within the individual (Cicchetti & Schneider-Rosen, 1986). Conceivably, research such as this might reveal that certain functioning characteristics that were causally relevant to unipolar or bipolar disorder in an earlier environment have become positively adaptive in a new environment. They not only may not detract from, but also actually facilitate, adaptive and successful functioning. It also may be erroneous to assume that normalized behavior necessarily reflects improvements in processes that were once causal to the development of a mood disorder. Thus, a developmental psychopathology perspective encourages us to remain open to the possibility that many of the characteristics we typically view as functioning deficits in fact may be neutral. That is, they may translate into deficits or assets depending on other characteristics of the individual and/or environment.

Finally, a multigenerational perspective also is extremely important to a developmental psychopathology approach to the affective disorders. Because mood disorders tend to occur more frequently in the relatives of depressed individuals, a multigenerational perspective can help to discover the processes whereby the transactions of genetic and environmental factors eventuate in normal and abnormal developmental outcomes (Cohen & Leckman, 1993).

AN ORGANIZATIONAL PERSPECTIVE ON DEVELOPMENT

Drawing from Werner's (1948; Werner & Kaplan, 1963) organismic-developmental theory, the organizational approach to development (Cicchetti & Schneider-Rosen, 1986; Sroufe & Rutter, 1984) offers developmental psychopathology a powerful theoretical framework for conceptualizing the intricacies of the life span perspective on psychopathology more generally, and on the mood disorders more specifically. According to the organizational perspective, development may best be understood as a series of structural reorganizations within and between the biological and behavioral systems of the individual that proceed by means of differentiation and hierarchical integration (i.e., Werner's "orthogenetic principle"). The relationship between the relatively immature person and the relatively mature one is the relationship between a state of globality and lack of articulation and a state of greater differentiation, articulation, complexity, and consolidation, effectively organized into hierarchical systems and subsystems (von Bertalanffy, 1968; Werner, 1948).

A distinction can thus be drawn between chronological age and developmental age, where the latter is determined by the individual's state of articulation and hierarchical integration (Wohlwill, 1973). An important consequence of the orthogenetic principle for the investigation of psychopathology in general and the mood disorders in particular is that, because development must be viewed in terms of integration and qualitative reorganization rather than mere accretion or expansion, the researcher should not necessarily expect behavioral isomorphism in depressive or manic symptomatology across developmental levels.

At each juncture of reorganization in development, the concept of hierarchical motility specifies that prior developmental structures are incorporated into later ones by means of hierarchical integration. In this way, early experience and its effects on the organization of the individual are carried forward within the individual's organization of systems rather than having reorganizations override previous organizations. As a result, hierarchical motility suggests that previous areas of vulnerability or strength within the organizational structure may remain present although not prominent in the current organizational structure. Nevertheless, the presence of prior structures in times of stress or crisis may exert an influence on the outcome. Thus, a behavioral or symptomatic presentation of a depressed or hypomanic individual may appear discrepant with recently evidenced adaptation, but in effect indicates the activation of prior maladaptive structures that were retained in the organizational structure through hierarchical integration.

Each stage of development poses new challenges to which the individual must adapt. At each stage, successful adaptation or competence is signified by an adaptive integration within and among the biological, cognitive, socioemotional, and representational domains, as the person masters current developmental challenges. Because earlier structures of the individual's organization are incorporated into later structures in the successive process of hierarchical integration, early competence tends to promote later competence. An individual who has adaptively met the developmental challenges of the particular stage will be better equipped to meet successive new challenges in development. This is not to say that early adaptation ensures successful later adaptation, because major changes or stresses in the internal and external environment may tax subsequent adaptational capacities. However, early competence provides a more optimal organization of behavioral and biological systems, thus offering, in a probabilistic manner, the greatest likelihood that adaptive resources are available to encounter and cope with new developmental demands.

In contrast, incompetence in development is fostered by difficulties or maladaptive efforts to resolve the challenges of a developmental period. Inadequate resolution of developmental challenges may result in a developmental lag or delay in, for example, one of the behavioral systems such as the emotional system. As a result, less than adequate integration within that domain will occur, and that poor within-domain integration will compromise adaptive integration among domains as hierarchical integration proceeds. Thus, incompetence in development may be viewed as a problematic integration within and among the biological, cognitive, socioemotional, and representational domains as the individual adapts to the challenges of his or her period of ontogenesis (see Figure 11.1).

Of particular importance are advances and lags in one biological or behavioral system with respect to the others, because the presence of capacities of one of these systems may be a necessary condition for the development or exercise of capacities of another system. For example, in infancy certain social capacities (i.e., those associated with a secure attachment) may be necessary for the age-appropriate development of cognitive abilities. Likewise, certain cognitive skills may be necessary for the development of particular affectual expressions and experiences (Hesse & Cicchetti, 1982). Lags in these systems may then result in compensatory development, which may in some instances leave the child vulnerable to psychopathology. Over time, difficulty in the organization of one biological or behavioral system may tend to promote difficulty in the way in which other systems are organized as hierarchical integration between the separate systems occurs. The organization of the individual may then appear to consist of poorly integrated component systems. As the converse of the effects of early competence, early incompetence will tend to promote later incompetence because the individual arrives at successive developmental stages with less than optimal resources available for responding to the challenges of that period. Again, however, this progression is not inevitable but probabilistic. Changes in the internal and external environment may lead to improvements in the ability to grapple with developmental challenges, resulting in a redirection in the developmental course.

When psychopathology is conceptualized in this manner, it becomes crucial to identify the specific developmental arrests or the unsuccessfully resolved developmental tasks implicated in a depressive episode, the environmental stressors involved, and the biological familial circumstances that may have interfered with the resolution of the developmental issues. Furthermore, it is essential to characterize depression in terms of specific forms of nonintegration, in such a way as to distinguish it from other forms of psychopathology, each of which leaves its own fingerprint of incompetence by leading to peculiar patterns of maladaption.

This conceptualization of psychopathology acknowledges human development and functioning in its complexity and subtleness. In contrast to the often dichotomous world of disorder/nondisorder in clinical psychology and psychiatry, it recognizes that normality frequently fades into abnormality, adaptive and maladaptive may take on differing definitions depending on whether the time referent is immediate circumstance or long-term

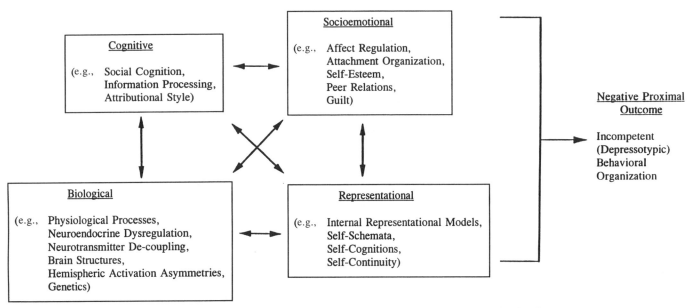

Figure 11.1 Emerging competence as the organization of biological and behavioral systems.

development, and that processes within the individual can be characterized as having shades or degrees of psychopathology.

Given the importance of a life-span view of developmental processes and an interest in delineating how prior development influences later development, a major issue in developmental psychopathology involves how to determine continuity in the quality of adaptation across developmental time. Sroufe (1979; Sroufe & Rutter, 1984) has articulated the concept of coherence in the organization of behaviors in successive developmental periods as a means of identifying continuity in adaptation despite changing behavioral presentations of the developing individual. Crucial to this concept is a recognition that the same behaviors in different developmental periods may represent quite different levels of adaptation. Behaviors indicating competence within a developmental period may indicate incompetence when evidenced within subsequent developmental periods. Normative behaviors early in development may indicate maladaptation when exhibited later in development. Thus, the manifestation of competence in different developmental periods is rarely indicated by isomorphism in behavioral presentation. Homotypic continuity is likely to be an unusual occurrence, particularly early in development.

Additionally, because the same function in an organized behavioral system can be fulfilled by two dissimilar behaviors, whereas the same kind of behavior may serve two different functions (Werner & Kaplan, 1963), and because the same behavior also may play different roles in different behavioral domains, it is especially important in this regard to distinguish between similarities and differences in *molar* and *molecular* symptomatology during different developmental periods. The reorganization of biological and behavioral systems that takes place at each new level of development means researchers could not expect to see, for any symptom, behavioral isomorphism at the molecular level, even if there is isomorphism at the molar

level. For example, the child whose depressive episode spans the transition form preoperational to concrete-operational thought may display excessive and inappropriate guilt, a loss of self-esteem, and a decrease in activity throughout the episode. Consequently, at a molar level, the depressive symptoms at the later period will be isomorphic to those of the earlier. Nonetheless, the particular manifestation of the guilt feelings, loss of self-esteem, and psychomotor retardation may change and develop during the transition, when the child's cognitive, representational, socioemotional, and behavioral competencies undergo a rather radical development. In this way, there may be noteworthy differences at the molecular level.

An illustration of different behaviors representing continuity of adaptation (i.e., heterotypic continuity) is provided by Sroufe, Fox, and Pancake (1983) in their discussion of attachment and dependency over the early years of life. The surface interpretation of behaviors of infants in the Strange Situation, an experimental paradigm devised to assess parent-child attachment relations (Ainsworth & Wittig, 1969), might suggest that those who typically exhibit little distress on separation from their mothers and little affective response when reunited (Type A or anxious/avoidant classification) are exhibiting early signs of independence and autonomy. In contrast, infants who may exhibit distress and crying when separated and who eagerly approach and seek comfort from their mothers when reunited (subgroups of the Type B or secure attachment classification) might be considered to exhibit high dependence on their mothers. However, the organization of behaviors in the securely attached children is regarded as indicating a secure attachment to the caregiver, a more developmentally competent attainment, whereas the anxious/avoidant children's behavior is regarded as signifying anxiety and insecurity in the attachment relationship. Later in development, the anxious/avoidant group of children exhibit helplessness and dependency, whereas the securely attached children are more likely to be autonomous and independent.

This example illustrates that if isomorphism in behaviors were to be the standard for judging continuity in development, the prior descriptions would suggest developmental discontinuity. However, when examined in the context of the coherence of the organization of behaviors across time, the presence of phenotypically different behaviors at different time points suggests continuity in the quality of adaptation (i.e., heterotypic continuity, rather than discontinuity). The underlying meaning of behaviors rather than the behaviors themselves is perpetuated across development. At the level of meaning in the preceding example, the securely attached children's behaviors on separation and reunion indicate trust in the supportive presence of the mother and expectations of being comforted when distressed. This confidence in the ability to rely on the mother is internalized, resulting in more self-confident and autonomous behavior later in development. In contrast, the anxious/avoidant infant's behavior indicates doubts in the mother's availability to provide comfort and a restriction in affect to avoid unpredictable behavior from the mother. Later in development, the child has internalized this sense of doubt and uncertainty, exhibiting dependent and helpless behaviors.

In a related vein, Zahn-Waxler and Kochanska (1990) provide another example of behavior that might appear developmentally appropriate if the underlying organization and meaning of the behavior is not considered. Zahn-Waxler and Kochanska examined the development of guilt feelings in the children of depressed and nondepressed mothers. Although there were increases with age for all children in the guilt feelings they experienced, the underlying motives and functions of the guilt feelings varied for the children of depressed and nondepressed mothers. For the children of depressed mothers, guilt feelings were more frequently associated with primitive reasoning and irrationality, whereas the guilt feelings of children with nondepressed mothers were shown to function more adaptively. Thus, behaviors that might phenotypically appear appropriate and developmentally expected may be considered to be problematic when the context in which those behaviors occur is considered. The molar organization and meanings of behavior and the coherence of themes underlying the molecular behavioral presentation is likely to be more informative with respect to continuities in development. Transformations in the behavioral presentation may occur despite continuity in the coherence of the underlying organization of behavior.

Because development typically involves the organization through integration of previously differentiated behaviors, we can predict that the expression of unipolar and bipolar illness may indeed be characterized by molar continuities but additionally by molecular discontinuities and changes. At the molar level, continuity will be preserved by an orderly development in the organization of behaviors; however, at the molecular level, the behaviors that are present at different periods may vary. We believe that the study of the development of the mood disorders over the life course is likely to be fruitful, and to reveal the relationship between pathological processes and normal development, only if the behavior of individuals with an affective disorder is examined simultaneously at the molar and molecular levels.

During development, there may be prototypic organizations of behavioral systems with the potential for transformation into a spectrum of depressive or manic-depressive presentations. There may be numerous forms of such prototypic organizations that, depending on subsequent experiences in development, may eventuate in depression, manic-depression, or other forms of psychopathology, or in the event of corrective experiences, adaptive outcomes. It is important that early forms of incompetent organization of biological and behavioral systems may not phenotypically resemble later unipolar or bipolar disorder, although a coherence in molar organization between a prior prototype and later depression or manic-depression may be discerned. For example, difficulty in managing anger may be an early prototypical feature with linkages to later depression. Difficulty in anger regulation through development may become integrated with changes in cognition and interpersonal relations that can eventually result in a depressive presentation. Alternatively, problems in regulating anger, given disparate developmental experiences, might eventuate in a different form of disorder (i.e., antisocial personality) or comorbidity of disorders (i.e., depression and antisocial personality). Nevertheless, for some individuals there may be continuity between early difficulties in affect regulation and later depression, although the phenotypic behavioral presentation, poor early anger control versus later dysphoria and chronic sadness, might appear discontinuous.

In view of the multiplicity of pathways that can eventuate in depressive and manic-depressive disorders, various forms of prototypical organizations should be anticipated. An example of a fairly typical outcome can be drawn from the attributional theory literature. Within the cognitive domain, the child has developed a negative attributional style, blaming the self for negative occurrences and brushing off successes as a result of luck (Abramson, Seligman, Teasdale, 1978; Fincham & Cain, 1986; Peterson & Seligman, 1984). There is a feeling of hopelessness about the future and a belief that the individual is unable to alter the situation (Abramson, Metalsky, & Alloy, 1989). Emotionally, the child has low self-esteem and feelings of worthlessness and guilt. Sadness and dejection are frequently experienced in response to minor difficulties. There is little capacity to enjoy daily experiences. Socially, the child has poor relationships with family members and peers and does not expect that others desire contact with him or her. Withdrawal from relationships has contributed to poor interpersonal skills. Biologically, a genetic propensity toward irritability exacerbates social encounters. In summary, this prototypical depressive organization suggests an integration of maladaptive features across the different behavioral and biological systems. Difficulties may arise in one component system and, subsequently, through hierarchical integration, affect other behavioral systems. Such a prototypical organization will have high potential for transforming into a depressive disorder with further experiences in development. This likelihood increases even more with the realization that the child's cognitive schemata and inner mental representations will perpetuate involvement in situations that confirm prior experiences and a negative self-view (Peterson & Seligman, 1984).

A TRANSACTIONAL APPROACH TO THE AFFECTIVE DISORDERS

Much of our discussion up to this point has focused on the organization of biological and psychological processes occurring within the developing individual. Our emphasis shifts now to examining the means by which individual differences in developmental outcomes are conceptualized. A transactional model, which recognizes the importance of transacting genetic, constitutional, neurobiological, biochemical, psychological, and sociological factors in the determination of behavior, and which states that those factors change through their dynamic transaction, provides the framework for a developmental perspective on how internal and external sources of influence are coordinated to shape the organizational structure of individuals along alternate pathways over the course of ontogenesis. A transactional model thus decries reductionism; in particular, it denies that the pathological process of depression or manic-depressive illness can be viewed as an emerging characteristic of, for example, some biological, psychological, or environmental process *alone,* except perhaps in the most extreme cases. Rather, various factors operate together through a hierarchy of dispositions. For example, a genetic diathesis may constitute a disposition to biochemical anomalies only under the action of some psychological mechanism; these biochemical anomalies in turn may constitute a disposition to the development of psychological anomalies only under a particular pattern of socialization (cf. Cicchetti & Aber, 1986). Thus, some factors act as *permissive* causes by constituting dispositions; others act as *efficient* causes by realizing these dispositions. Furthermore, it need not be the case that, as in the traditional diathesis-stress model, only genetic or biological factors act as permissive causes, whereas psychological or environmental factors function only as efficient causes. For example, long-standing patterns of social interaction in a child's immediate social environment may constitute a permissive cause for depression, or what may be called a "vulnerability" factor, whereas transient biological or biochemical changes during development may be efficient causes of depression, or "challengers" (Cicchetti & Schneider-Rosen, 1986). Moreover, in the words of Schildkraut and Kety (1967):

> . . . the demonstration of . . . a biochemical abnormality would not necessarily imply a genetic or constitutional, rather than an environmental or psychological, etiology of depression . . . Whereas specific genetic factors may be of importance in the etiology of some, and possibly all, depressions, it is equally conceivable that early experiences of the infant or child may cause enduring biochemical changes and that these may predispose some individuals to depressions in adulthood. (p. 28)

Furthermore, the particular vulnerability factors and challengers may vary in significance over time, as well as in relative importance with regard to the operation of alternative permissive or efficient causes (Post et al., 1986; Post et al., in press). Similarly, with development, the organization of the various biological and psychological systems, and the integration between the systems, may introduce protective factors or buffers against the overt manifestation of a mood disorder.

The transactional model specifies that the interrelationships between the organization of developmental domains (biological, socioemotional, cognitive, representational) and the environment (society, community, family) are in a progressive exchange of mutual influence. Not only is the individual influenced by environmental inputs resulting in transformation and reorganization, but also the environment is influenced by and responds to characteristics of the individual. At successive points in development, the organizational structure of both the individual and the environment are in a state of bidirectional influence. For example, early temperamental differences in children are transformed into a range of attachment organizations in response to variations in responses from caregivers. Subsequently, there also are likely to be alterations within caregivers as they respond to new variations in behavioral presentations of the child. Both qualities of the child and of the environment are being mutually influenced as each evolves. These transactions of bidirectional influence will generate variations in the quality of the organization of their different biological and behavioral systems. At subsequent points in development, variations in the organization of the child (i.e., competent vs. incompetent) will alter the manner in which the child is able to respond to new experiences, positive or negative, and the pathways toward adaptation or maladaptation that unfold.

The study of risk, vulnerability, and protective factors as they relate to the development of psychopathology has been an area of active inquiry consistent with transactional concepts of development (Rolf, Masten, Cicchetti, Nuechterlein, & Weintraub, 1990). In keeping with our developmental formulation, it is likely that a multitude of rather general factors across the broad domains of biology, psychology, and sociology will be at least indirectly related to depressive and manic-depressive outcomes because they represent the gamut of potential determinants of individual adaptation. A comprehensive articulation of the processes and mechanisms that have promoted or inhibited the development of competence during development and, in particular, have resulted in a prototypic depressive or manic-depressive organization of the individual may be more important than specific predictors of the immediate or proximal onset of unipolar or bipolar disorder. This approach is important because numerous characteristics related to depression and/or manic-depression, such as problems with emotion regulation, psychomotor and vegetative anomalies, liability of affect, impulsivity, distorted attributional style, interpersonal relationship difficulties, feelings of helplessness and hopelessness, and low self-esteem, are inevitably arrived at developmentally, and they will function as vulnerability factors for these disorders in and of themselves.

Vulnerability factors are typically regarded as enduring or long-standing life circumstances or conditions that function as potentiating processes for maladaptation. Major areas of influence on the child, including external (family, social-environmental) and internal (biological, psychological), may serve as sources of vulnerability as they detract from the achievement of successful adaptation and competence. For example, parental psychopathology, parental drug abuse and alcoholism, marital conflict, divorce, child maltreatment, parental hostility, and lack of parental nurturance all have been shown to have detrimental effects on the developing child and his or her striving for adaptation (Hetherington, 1989; Toth, Manly, & Cicchetti, 1992; Walker, Downey, & Bergman, 1989). Similarly, factors such as low socioeconomic status, unsupportive social and familial networks, inadequate schools, high crime, and frequent hassles in daily living create stressful conditions that aggravate coping and detract from competent development. Biologically, a genetic predisposition to depression, biogenic amine anomalies, temperamental difficulties, and hyperreactive physiological responses to stress are among those issues that represent long-standing conditions that are likely to complicate the ease of attaining competent developmental achievements. Through development, these vulnerability factors transact with the evolving organization of behavioral systems of the individual to detract from the attainment of competence and may promote a prototypic depressive or manic-depressive organization across the cognitive, socioemotional, representational, and biological systems.

In contrast, enduring protective factors also serve as compensatory processes to promote competent adaptation in the child. Many of these are the polar opposite of the vulnerability factors and are likely to enhance rather than hinder development. They would include parental mental health, harmonious marital relations, effective parenting, warmth and nurturance, adequate income levels, supportive social and familial networks, good schools, low crime, and no genetic predisposition for unipolar or bipolar illness.

In addition to these enduring competence-detracting and competence-promoting factors, transient influences, though temporary in duration, may have a critical positive (i.e., act as a buffer) or negative (i.e., function as a challenger) impact, depending on the timing of such events or transitions in circumstances and the pertinent developmental issues for the child at the time. Further, the potency of specific risk and protective factors in influencing development will vary as a result of the developmental period in which they occur; a specific factor may be more influential in one developmental period compared with another. As shown in Figure 11.2, for any individual, the specific enduring (both vulnerability and protective) and transient (both challenger and buffer) features will vary and exist within a dynamic balance. A greater likelihood for the development of incompetence and a prototypic depressive or manic-depressive organization will occur for those for whom vulnerability and challenger factors outweigh the protective and buffering influences (Cicchetti & Schneider-Rosen, 1984, 1986; Cummings & Cicchetti, 1990). To provide an example, depressive disorders have the potential to emerge in those individuals for whom a depressotypic organization has evolved transactionally through development and whose coping capacities and protective resources are no longer effective in counteracting long-standing vulnerabilities and current stressors or acute risk factors.

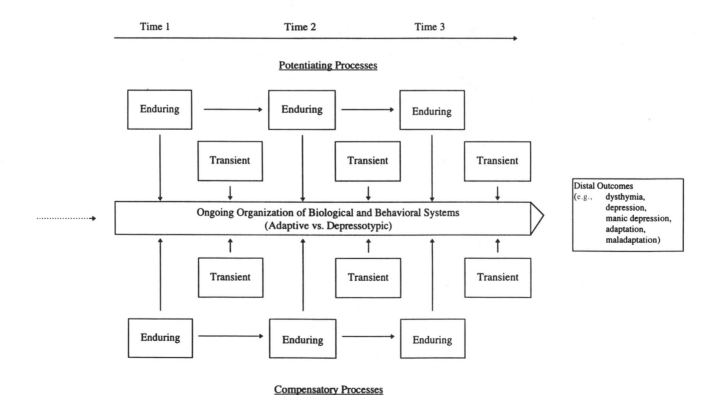

Figure 11.2 Balance of potentiating versus compensatory processes affecting biological and behavioral organization and mood-disordered outcomes.

Rutter (1990) has cautioned that risk, vulnerability, and protective factors are not variables causing pathological outcomes per se, but rather that they are indicators of more complex processes and mechanisms impacting individual adaptation. Specifying the process or mechanism involved is essential. In our conceptualization, these factors are expected to operate chiefly by the significance they have in promoting or detracting from the development of competence at progressive stages of development and the consequent likelihood of an emerging prototypical depressive or manic-depressive organization. For example, parental death per se does not cause depressive disorder, but in some children it may contribute to a sequence of negative transformations in the psychological and biological subsystems over the course of development. These changes, in turn, may result in the emergence of a prototypical depressive organization and a strong potential for depressive outcomes.

The manner in which vulnerability, risk, and protective mechanisms exert their effects is likely to vary depending on the developmental period in which they occur. Some factors may have a much stronger influence at one developmental period compared with another. High blood lead levels, for example, are likely to be far more detrimental early in development. Additionally, the same factor may function differently depending on the context in which it occurs. A parent losing a job may have varying degrees of impact on children depending on the socioeconomic conditions of the family. Thus, it is important to evaluate the effect of risk and protective processes based both on the developmental and social environmental context in which they occur.

ILLUSTRATIVE DEVELOPMENTAL ISSUES

Because adaptation at any point is viewed as the product of extant circumstances and conditions as well as prior experiences and adaptations (Sroufe, Egeland, & Kreutzer, 1990), unipolar and bipolar illness may best be understood in terms of current risk and protective factors within the context of prior developmental experiences that have been hierarchically integrated into the individual's organization of biological and behavioral systems. Understanding the developmental pathways between successive prior adaptations and current functioning is central to the developmental psychopathology approach (Cicchetti, 1993). We think that the developmental perspective holds considerable promise for expanding and unifying various theoretical models of unipolar and bipolar illness within a developmental psychopathology framework (see, e.g., Hammen, 1992b; Post et al., in press; Rose & Abramson, 1992). The perspective of developmental psychopathology allows for new questions to be addressed and enables us to move beyond a description of the symptomatological, biological, and psychological differences inherent among mood-disordered individuals to an examination of how such differences evolved. To achieve this goal, we examine a number of issues of development that we consider to be especially pertinent to the evolution of a mood disorder.

At each period of development, specific issues confront individuals for the first time and require them to garner and expand available resources in attempts to master new challenges.

Adaptation at a particular developmental level implies the successful resolution of the developmental task or tasks most salient for that period. Rather than construing development as a series of unfolding tasks that need to be accomplished and then decrease in importance, we perceive development as consisting of a number of important age and stage-appropriate tasks that, on emergence, remain critical to other newly emerging developmental tasks (Cicchetti & Schneider-Rosen, 1986; Cicchetti, Toth, & Bush, 1988).

For example, we do not conceive attachment as a developmental issue of the later part of the first year of life alone; rather, once an attachment relationship develops, it continues to undergo transformations and reintegrations with subsequent accomplishments such as emerging autonomy and entrance into the peer world. As a result, throughout the life span, from infancy to old age, individuals are continually renegotiating the balance between being connected to others and being independent and autonomous as they encounter each new developmental issue (cf. Erikson, 1950; Sroufe, 1979). Consequently, each of the issues represent life-span developmental tasks that require continual coordination and integration in the individual's adaptation to the environment. Each stage-salient issue, thematically, becomes a lifelong feature of importance for adaptation.

In extending this depiction of stage-salient developmental issues to the assessment of competence at various stages of the life span, several points require emphasis:

1. Each stage-salient developmental issue is marked by a new, more differentiated and integrated level of organization in the cognitive, socioemotional, representational, and biological systems.

2. Competent resolution of the salient developmental tasks at one period will exert a positive influence toward achieving competence at the next period.

3. Early competent adaptation also exerts a subtle influence toward adaptation throughout the life span because each developmental issue, although most salient at one developmental period, is of continuing importance throughout the life cycle.

4. The failure to achieve competent adaptation at one period makes adaptation that much more difficult at the next, and, in a lesser way, more difficult throughout the life span since each issue continues to assume importance throughout the individual's development.

5. However, successful resolution of stage-salient tasks does not inoculate the individual from future difficulties. Likewise, unsuccessful resolution does not doom the individual to future dysfunction. Individuals continue to be affected by new experiences and changing conditions in their lives, and changes in the course of adaptation remain possible. Many factors may mediate between early and later adaptation or maladaptation to permit alternative outcomes. Early problems or deviations in the successful resolution of a developmental task may be countered by major changes in the individual's experiences and/or by newly acquired strengths and competencies that could result in the successful negotiation of subsequent developmental tasks. Conversely, an individual's early successful

resolution of a developmental task may be undermined or challenged by major changes in life experiences and/or by newly emerging vulnerabilities that could result in the problematic or unsuccessful resolution of subsequent salient issues.

6. Nonetheless, the quality of resolution of stage-salient issues tends to constrain and canalize developmental pathways, making change probabilistically less likely. (Sroufe, 1989)

In the next section, we describe the principal features of a number of stage-salient issues across the life course in normal development and trace what is known about the unfolding of these issues in individuals who either have, or are at increased risk for, the development of an affective disorder. Rather than discussing all stage-salient issues, we focus on those that have generated the most research that is relevant to the etiology of mood disorders and also that are clinically relevant to our understanding of the development and course of these disorders. Specifically, we examine homeostatic and physiological regulation, affect differentiation and modulation of attention and arousal, attachment, and the development of the self system. Because of the interrelations and hierarchical reorganizations that occur among these issues, however, clear compartmentalization is impossible. Therefore, data that are relevant, for example, to homeostatic regulation may be referred to in subsequent discussions of the modulation of arousal. Rather than serving as categorical entities, all stage-salient issues flow into one another.

We provide illustrative data on how offspring of unipolar or bipolar parents resolve each of these stage-salient issues, as well as on how mood-disordered children and adults fare on these tasks. Where empirical evidence exists, we document how these individuals negotiate each of these issues as they go beyond their period of ascendancy to become coordinated and integrated with subsequent tasks. As will become apparent, much work remains to be conducted before a complete and definitive picture can be presented.

Our chief concern here is to ascertain how either a child of a parent with unipolar or bipolar illness or a child or an adult with a mood disorder expresses the self in terms of competence, how it may lead to deviations in adaptation at various developmental periods, and how such deviation may be assessed. Although failure to resolve the stage-salient tasks of a developmental period successfully is not indicative of psychopathology per se, such incompetent organization, in concert with the genotype and/or environmental stressors that predispose for a mood disorder or biological anomalies that constitute a diathesis for unipolar or bipolar illness, might signal a prototypical depressive or manic-depressive organization that forebodes the subsequent development of a mood disorder.

The following questions are of central importance as we examine research on stage-salient issues of development:

1. Do unipolar and bipolar illness manifest themselves at every developmental level in terms of incompetence?

2. If so, in what manner do mood disorders, as opposed to some other type of psychopathology, manifest themselves as a lack of competence?

3. Does having a mood disorder at one developmental period affect an individual's ability to attain competence at later developmental periods?

4. Does the presence of unipolar or bipolar illness in a caregiver affect the child's ability to resolve the stage-salient developmental issues in a competent fashion? Incompetence will have a variety of effects, some of which will be likely to perpetuate incompetent adaptation, others of which may constitute a vulnerability to depressive or manic-depressive illness, and still others which may potentiate later adaptation. If a depressive or manic episode arose, it would lead to maladaptations, and these again would eventuate in a variety of effects, some perhaps maintaining the mood disorder, others predisposing for future maladaptation and still others leading to adaptation that may buffer against the experience of subsequent depressive or manic-depressive episodes. Both maladaptation and the presence of any mood disorder will have sequelae that are depending in part on the ontogenesis of the neurobiological, genetic, and biochemical systems that serve as the biological/physiological underpinnings of unipolar and bipolar illness.

Homeostatic and Physiological Regulation

In the early months of life, infant affect expression is propelled by the infant's internal, physiological states. As infants gain control over their own internal states, they also gain control over the affects they express.

At a basic level, homeostasis describes a dynamic process through which individuals achieve internal consistency and stability. In this regard, the goal of a homeostatic system is to maintain a "set point" of functioning or homeostatic equilibrium. Departure from this point introduces tension into the system, which serves as the motivation for behavioral systems that subsequently act to dissipate tension and return the system once more to a state of homeostatic equilibrium.

During the first months of life, tension is defined in terms of changes in the infant's arousal level and physiological discomfort caused by these experiences; when the infant is overly aroused or physically uncomfortable, homeostatic tension is generated. At later stages of development, however, with the onset of representational skills and the formation of a core sense of self, threats to psychological coherence and consistency generate tension as well.

At birth, infants possess a number of motoric reflexes that enable them to counteract physiological disequilibrium independently. Despite the presence of such reflexes, however, not all of an infant's internal, physiological needs can be met by their activation. Consequently, the infant requires additional help from the environment to modulate physiological states and reduce internal tension. The primary affects of pleasure, distress, and discomfort accomplish this task, enabling infants to appraise their current physiological state and to communicate their needs to caregivers (Bowlby, 1969/1982).

The effectiveness of such expressions depends on the caregiver's ability to understand their meaning as well as the infant's ability to generate readable cues about internal states. Therefore, during the first months of life, caregivers and infants gradually develop their own system of signals or language through which infants can effectively communicate their needs and caregivers can sensitively respond to them (see Izard & Malatesta, 1987; Sroufe, 1979). In this view, the infant's homeostatic system is an open one, in which the caregiver plays an integral role in helping the infant modulate arousal states and reduce internal tension.

Within the first 2 to 3 months of life, infants gradually become more self-sufficient in modulating arousal generated by physiological tension. As the infant's neuroregulatory systems develop, their homeostatic control is internalized and, as a result, is less externally regulated by caregivers (Sroufe, 1979). This transition is made possible by the maturation of forebrain inhibitory tracts and neurotransmitter systems that permit increasing control of lower brain structures. These developments provide the neurological foundation for self-regulation and, thus, homeostasis.

To a large extent, maturation and development may be guided by the infant's experiences with his or her caregiver during dyadic regulation. By directly aiding infants in the maintenance of physiological homeostasis in the early weeks of life, caregivers may influence the development and organization of neurological systems (Black & Greenough, 1986). This influence, during a period of rapid neurological growth and maturation, may have long-term effects on the organization and development of the infant's brain. In fact, the existence of an open homeostatic system at this time in development suggests that interactions with the environment may be necessary for the brain to mature fully. Consequently, the development of some neurological systems may be "experience expectant"; that is, for complete differentiation and development, certain types of external input by caregivers are essential and, usually, readily available (Greenough, Black, & Wallace, 1987).

In fact, three processes underlie infants' growing ability to regulate their emotions in the first year of life: the maturation of neurological inhibitory systems, cognitive development, and parental socialization. The development of neurological inhibitory systems and cognitive abilities further enables infants to regulate their behavior and to adapt and coordinate it to meet the demands of the environment. Conversely, the caretaking environment and socialization provide the context within which this development occurs and to which the children must adapt.

The growth and further development and differentiation of the central nervous system serves as the foundation for the voluntary control of behavior. Such developments provide the neurological "hardware" necessary for the intentional control of affect expressions. During the first months of life, the development of forebrain inhibition and neurotransmitter systems supports self-regulation, through the formation of neuronal tracts that link lower hindbrain or midbrain limbic structures with cortical regions. In addition, the development of interhemispheric connections enhances the infants' ability to self-regulate and inhibit their behavior during the first years of life. The interaction of the two hemispheres, with their functional asymmetries, allows for the development and production of increasingly more complex behaviors that can be controlled by the individual (see, e.g., Fox & Davidson, 1984).

Various research groups have related the right and left hemispheres to different types of behavioral responsivity. Whereas the right hemisphere alerts the brain to new experiences or changes in the environment, the left hemisphere is biased toward redundancy and is sensitive to stability in the environment (Tucker & Williamson, 1984). Right-brain activation has also been associated with distress. In contrast, left-brain activation and the simultaneous inhibition of right-brain activity occur together with the expression of positive affect.

Either extremely novel experiences or an unstable environment may prompt right-brain activation, leading to the expression of negative affect. If children are exposed to situations such as these, they may become overly stimulated and thus respond with distress. But the development of interhemispheric tracts may enable infants to regulate such overarousal. That is, activation of the left hemisphere may modulate or inhibit right-brain activity, thereby enabling the infant to regulate arousal levels and distress. This interaction makes it possible for the infant to reach a steady state or equilibrium. Modulation of the right hemisphere by the left hemisphere may be reflected behaviorally in the child's growing ability to self-soothe and increased positive affect.

To some extent, the caregiving environment may influence the development and integrity of these transhemispheric tracts (Malatesta & Izard, 1984). In our view, parents may offer external support for the development of these tracts by providing environmental stability and consistency in the caretaking environment, particularly for the development of the left-hemisphere inhibitory tracts. Recall that the left hemisphere is biased toward responding to redundancy or constancy in the environment and that the activation of this hemisphere may support the child's ability to self-soothe. Caretaking stability may support left-brain activation during times of stress and, in so doing, perhaps strengthens the development of its inhibitory effects on arousal.

Thus, interhemispheric connections support arousal modulation and also emotion regulation at a very basic level. These developments, coupled with improved motor skills, enable infants to regulate and blend the expressions of different affects, leading to their increasing articulation and complexity.

Advances in the cognitive domain relevant to emotion regulation develop concurrently with neurological maturation and interhemispheric communication. Sroufe (1979) argued that a person feels psychological tension when his or her current experiences are discrepant with previous experiences and expectations. The internally felt tension that results from such psychological disequilibrium is similar to the tension generated by physiological disequilibrium. In both cases, tension permeates the infant's "inner ring" of experience (Bowlby, 1969/1982) and motivates the expression of affect. Similar to physiological disequilibrium, the intensity of such psychological tension varies among infants and determines the affective value (positive or negative) of the experience. Unlike physiological tension in the earliest stages of development, however, the tension that results from novelty or discrepancy is not immediately translated into the overt expression of affect. Rather, additional cognitive processes that intercede between the infant's internal world and the environment, such as the understanding of causality and the development of representational skills, come into play (e.g., cortical-limbic loops are formed; see Cicchetti & Sroufe, 1978).

The presence of an open homeostatic system in the first weeks of life also allows caregivers to regulate their infants' physiological systems directly. Consequently, it seems feasible that the full maturation of neuroregulatory systems also is experience expectant. By providing stable routines and responding appropriately to their infants' needs, caregivers help them modulate physiological tension and support their development of physiological regulation (Field, 1989). In this view, caregivers are expected to provide a stable, external scaffold or "buttress" for the infant's development of internal control, by structuring the infant's world.

Homeostatic physiological and affect regulatory systems are essential if the individual is to maintain a flexible range of adaptive functioning across the life span. Feedback components of homeostatic systems also serve a critical role in the development of self-evaluation and self-regulation.

Information pertaining to the homeostatic regulation of infants of parents with an affective disorder stems from a number of sources. As early as the neonatal period, infant offspring of depressed parents have been shown to have more difficult temperaments as indexed by greater difficulty in self-quieting, irritability, less social responsiveness, lower activity levels, and more negative affect (Cummings & Davies, 1994; Field, 1992; Sameroff, Seifer, & Zax, 1982).

In an important experiment, Cohn and Tronick (1983) investigated the face-to-face interaction of nondepressed mothers with their 3-month-old infants. In one of the counterbalanced experimental conditions, mothers were requested to simulate depressive affect during interaction with the baby. During periods of simulated depression, infants evidenced wariness, protest, and gaze aversion. Cohn and Tronick (1983) concluded that even simulated depression could result in negative infant affectivity, subsequently impairing the infant's capacity to engage in effective self-regulation. These findings revealed that the flexibility in rhythms evidenced during sequences of normal interaction were significantly impaired during phases of simulated depression. Additionally, Field (1984) compared dyadic interactions between a sample of mothers suffering from postpartum depression and a sample of normal mothers simulating depression. A difference in coping strategy emerged, with infants in the postpartum group evidencing resigned, passive, and mimicking behavior, whereas infants in the simulated depression group were active in their protests (Field, 1984).

Relatedly, Cohn, Campbell, Matias, and Hopkins (1990) examined the unstructured and structured mother-infant interactions at the infant's age of 2 months in a sample of postpartum-depressed and nondepressed mother-infant dyads. With the exception of depressed mothers who were employed outside home for more than 20 hours per week, depressed mothers and their babies exhibited more negative contingent responsiveness and less positive behaviors than nondepressed comparison mothers. Interestingly, Cohn, Campbell, and Ross (1991) demonstrated that infants, half of whose mothers had experienced postpartum depression, who had been observed longitudinally in the still-face paradigm (Cohn & Tronick, 1983) and exhibited positive affect expression were more likely to be securely attached, whereas those who failed to show positive expressions were more likely to evidence insecure avoidant attachment organization.

Field and her colleagues (Field, Healy, Goldstein, & Guthertz, 1990; Field, Healy, & LeBlanc, 1989) have conducted several studies of behavior-state matching and synchrony in depressed and nondepressed mother-infant dyads. Field et al. (1990) studied 48 depressed and nondepressed mother-infant dyads when the babies were 3 months old. These investigators discovered that the depressed mothers and their babies matched negative behavior states more frequently and positive behavior states less frequently than did the nondepressed dyads.

In another study, Field et al. (1989) found that African American depressed mothers and their 3-month-old infants not only shared negative behavior states more often and positive behavior states less frequently than nondepressed dyads but also revealed less coherence of mother-infant behavior states than nondepressed dyads (i.e., depressed mothers were less behaviorally *attuned* to their babies). Moreover, Field et al. (1989) discovered that nondepressed mothers and their babies likewise revealed a greater coherence of maternal heart rate and infant behavior (i.e., nondepressed mothers also were more physiologically attuned to their babies than were the depressed mothers).

Empirical evidence of affect regulatory difficulties beyond the early months of life can be seen throughout the toddler and childhood periods and in the behavior of depressed and bipolar children, adolescents, and adults. Zahn-Waxler, Iannotti, Cummings, and Denham (1990) found that toddlers of mothers with unipolar depression were more likely to manifest dysregulated out-of-control aggressive behavior than toddlers of nondepressed mothers. Moreover, the maladaptive aggression displayed by the toddlers of depressed mothers predicted externalizing behaviors in these youngsters at age five (mother report) and age six (child self-report). However, toddlers of depressed mothers who exerted modulated control, provided structure and organization during mother-toddler play, and could take the child's viewpoint, exhibited fewer externalizing behavior problems than toddlers of depressed mothers who did not employ these proactive child-rearing methods.

Gaensbauer, Harmon, Cytryn, and McKnew (1984) also found dysregulation of emotion in infants and toddlers of parents with an affective disorder. When compared with control children, youngsters of parents with a unipolar and/or bipolar disorder exhibited more fear in situations where one would normally experience less fear (e.g., during free play and during reunion with mother after a brief separation at 12 months) and displayed less fear in situations where more would be expected (e.g., during a brief maternal separation at 15 months). These investigators interpreted these findings as indicating that the children of mood-disordered parents appear to prolong the experience and expression of affect (e.g., a slow recovery time from a disruptive emotion). In their research, this general tendency was inferred from the children apparently carrying affect into a subsequent episode when its expression was most relevant to coping with the prior episode.

Another example of the dysregulation of emotion is the finding reported by Zahn-Waxler, McKnew, Cummings, Davenport, and Radke-Yarrow (1984) that, when compared with children of nondisordered mothers, youngsters with a mother who had bipolar illness expressed more aggression not toward mother but toward peers after a brief separation. The pattern of increased anger and aggression toward the mother on reunion after a brief separation is an empirically well-understood characteristic of infants and toddlers who are insecurely attached to their mothers. However, the expression of anger and aggression toward peers fulfills several nonidentical functions that only become apparent when the findings of the dysregulation of affect are placed in the context of the organization and functioning of the child's attachment behavioral system.

If children of manic-depressive parents cross upper-limit boundaries of peer aggression, then they may be avoided by peers and thereby be deprived of a common pathway for the proper socialization of angry feelings and aggressive behaviors (e.g., rough-and-tumble play). Likewise, if these children cross an upper-limit boundary for peer aggression, then they may serve to reinforce mood-disordered parents' already existent tendency toward over protectiveness. Finally, to the extent that children of parents with bipolar disorder inappropriately or atypically prolong their affective responses to past situations, or to the extent that they displace feelings typically directed toward their primary caretaker onto other social partners, then such children's behavior and affect are harder to read and interpret than those of other children.

In a review of the peer relations literature of toddler and preschool youngsters of parents with depressive or manic-depressive illness, Zahn-Waxler, Denham, Cummings, and Iannotti (1992) concluded that these youngsters characteristically engage in uncontrolled and poorly regulated social exchanges with their agemates. Relatedly, Hay, Zahn-Waxler, Cummings, and Iannotti (1992) investigated the beliefs that 5-year-old children of depressed and nondepressed women had about social conflict, justice, and attitudes toward persons who assumed different roles in a dispute. Utilizing a staged disagreement between two hand-held puppets, the female and male children of well and depressed mothers were queried about hypothetical conflicts between peers. Girls who had a depressed mother were least likely to propose aggressive solutions to peer conflict, whereas boys with a depressed mother were most likely among all groups of children to recommend aggressive tactics.

The regulatory difficulties evidenced by the offspring of depressed caregivers during infancy and childhood possess important implications for continued development. Unless these youngsters become able to modulate their behaviors more effectively, they will be at high risk for the development of mood disorders, as well as for personality disorders that are characterized by impulsivity and affective lability (e.g., borderline personality disorder).

Affect Differentiation and Modulation of Attention and Arousal

Following the establishment of physiological homeostasis, the infant's abilities rapidly develop in all domains of functioning. During this time, these new characteristics are organized hierarchically, with broad constructs defining the infant's basic qualities and capacities and specific behaviors reflecting the infant's adaptation to his or her specific environment. Consequently, the behavioral patterns that emerge at this time are "experience dependent" (Greenough et al., 1987).

The process of differentiation is apparent in the development of affect expression. With the establishment of physiological homeostasis, infants start to turn their attention to their social surroundings. As a result, they become more interactive in exchanges with caregivers and more sensitive to the behaviors that elicit responses from caregivers. When this occurs, the expression of affect becomes more refined as infants start to regulate and adapt their behaviors to those of their caregivers.

In this sense, the expression of affect is not only mediated by the infant's own physiological needs but also is now regulated by the infant's understanding and continual appraisal of his or her environment. This leads to the differentiation of affect as infants gradually modify their behaviors to simultaneously meet their own needs and the qualities and expectations of their environments.

Additionally, neurological maturation and cognitive growth promote affect differentiation. These developments occur within the context of the infant-caregiver interactions and so are expected to be influenced by the nature and quality of these interactions, at the levels of both the infant's internal experience of affect and the expression of affect to the environment.

One way in which a caregiver influences an infant's inner world of affect experiences is through shaping the infant's expectations of the environment. The infant's perceptions of the world as responsive, stable, and secure are largely dependent on the caregiver's sensitivity to the baby's needs. Thus, the history of interactions between caregivers and their infants is expected to color children's interpretation of and reaction to events in the world (Bowlby, 1973).

As in the homeostatic stage of development, during this phase caregivers also help infants modulate and manage arousal and tension. At this point in their development, however, tension may be generated by the infants' evaluations of the environment as threatening, overly stimulating, or too different from previous experiences to be assimilated and understood (Sroufe & Waters, 1976). Caregivers who are sensitive to their infants' arousal states or who are affectively attuned to them can help them tolerate and cope with increasing amounts of tension (Sroufe, 1979). Thus, at this stage, caregivers support the infants' development of psychological self-regulation and their continual adaptation to the world.

Finally, through socialization, infants adapt their overt displays of affect to meet the expectations and qualities of their environments. For example, by rewarding only certain affective expressions with positive responses or through imitation, caregivers may actively encourage the expression of some affects and, at the same time, extinguish or discourage the expression of other affects (Hesse & Cicchetti, 1982). Caregivers may also introduce to their infants new ways of expressing affect through modified imitation.

The central role of affect in the mood disorders suggests that the differentiation of affect in infancy could be a task subject to disruption in children with a depressive or manic-depressive parent. Although little empirical information exists on this important issue, relevant studies have focused on parental responses to infant affect and the effect that this could have on future development. By the time infants are 3 months of age, caregivers are able to identify correctly a range of infant emotional responses (Johnson, Emde, Pannabecker, Stenberg, & David, 1982). Thus, it may be hypothesized that depressed caregivers, because of their emotional difficulties, may be intolerant of or may respond differentially to certain affects in their children (Zahn-Waxler & Wagner, 1993).

Maternal imitation of infant affect may serve a number of functions for infants, including increasing eye contact with their mothers, promoting imitation, facilitating a sense of control over the environment, and enhancing the quality of the mother-child attachment relationship. Research with nondisordered populations reveals patterns of maternal imitation that correspond to periods in infant development. For example, mothers of 3-month-old babies tend to imitate mainly positive infant affect, but tend to make more imitations of the negative facial expressions of their 6-month-old infants (Malatesta & Izard, 1984). It is possible that depressed mothers engage in less imitation, or that they tend to imitate negative affect more readily than positive affect. Some support for this possibility has been obtained.

Pickens and Field (1993) examined the facial expressions of 84 3-month-old infants of mothers classified as depressed, nondepressed, or low scoring on the Beck Depression Inventory (BDI; Beck, 1967). Facial expressions were coded from videotaped mother-infant interactions by research assistants who were unaware of group membership. Pickens and Field (1993) discovered that infants of depressed mothers displayed sadness and anger expressions significantly more often, and interest expressions less often, than babies with well mothers. Infants whose mothers scored low on the BDI also exhibited higher incidence of sadness and anger, paralleling the emotion expression of the infants of depressed mothers. Although the higher frequency of sadness expressions is not surprising, the greater rate of anger expressions suggests that infants of depressed mothers may be more upset during interactions with their mothers (Pickens & Field, 1993).

Analogously, Field et al. (1988) found that infants are physiologically stressed (e.g., elevated heart rate, lower vagal tone) during interactions with their depressed mothers. Finally, the lower incidence of interest expressions on the faces of infants in the depressed and low-BDI groups may be because these mothers display a diminished facial repertoire when compared with well mothers.

In addition, Field and her collaborators (1988) examined 74 3- to 6-month-old infants of depressed and nondepressed mothers in videotaped face-to-face interactions with their mothers and with a nondepressed female stranger. Not surprisingly, depressed mothers and their babies displayed less positive behavior during their interaction than did well dyads. However, the infants of depressed mothers exhibited the same depressed style of interacting with a stranger as they did with their mother. The only exception to this finding was that infants of depressed mothers showed more head and gaze aversion with the mother than the stranger. This result suggests that the infants of depressed mothers utilized self-regulatory behaviors (e.g., gaze aversion) to reduce the negative affect elicited by the unresponsive maternal behavior (Tronick & Gianino, 1986). Field et al. (1988) hypothesized that the interactions with the stranger were less stressful to the infant.

Even though the strangers were not aware of the diagnostic status of the infants' mothers, the infants of depressed mothers impacted negatively on the behavior of the nondepressed strangers.

Thus, the depressed style of interacting of the infants of depressed mothers not only generalized to their actions with nondepressed female strangers, but also appeared to engender depressionlike behavior in the nondepressed adult.

Zahn-Waxler, Kochanska, Krupnick, and McKnew (1990; see also Zahn-Waxler & Kochanska, 1990) investigated patterns of guilt in 5- to 9-year-old children of depressed and nondepressed mothers. The younger children of depressed mothers in this sample displayed patterns of overarousal to projective stimuli depicting hypothetical situations of distress and interpersonal conflict. Specifically, these youngsters exhibited high levels of involvement and responsibility in their responses to the hypothetical problems of others. In contrast, the older children (i.e., the 9-year-olds) of depressed mothers did not reveal explicit guilt themes to these projective stimuli. Rather than assuming that these older children of depressed mothers were not experiencing guilt, Zahn-Waxler, Kochanska, Krupnick, and McKnew (1990) hypothesized that these children were engaged in an inner struggle against experiencing it.

Overall, patterns of guilt in children of depressed mothers of all ages did not cohere with assessments of their other areas of adaptation such as empathy. The differing patterns of organization for children of depressed and well mothers may reflect different developmental pathways or trajectories for these groups of children. In keeping with the organizational perspective on development, Zahn-Waxler, Kochanska et al. (1990) speculated that the intense involvement and arousal in the problems of others from an early point in development may alter how children of depressed mothers resolve the salient tasks of attachment and self-other differentiation. In addition, having a needy, dysregulated caregiver may make it difficult for children to become integrated into the peer group. Being deprived of these peer group experiences, thought to be crucial for developing morality and social competence, may diminish the ability of depressed mothers' children to experience guilt and responsibility in relationships in an adaptive fashion (Zahn-Waxler & Kochanska, 1990).

The narrative themes of the children of depressed mothers to the hypothetical situations contained distortions that reflect defensiveness against experiencing guilt feelings. Zahn-Waxler, Kochanska et al. (1990) discovered several types of distortions in the guilt reactions of these children. For some, the narrative response conveyed a striking sensitivity to others' problems, a quality that could eventuate in either problematic or constructive later outcomes (see also Hay, 1994). For example, Beardslee and Podorefsky (1988) hypothesized that one pathway to resilience in adolescent children of parents with an affective disorder is developing high levels of role taking, interpersonal maturity, and empathy. As noted by Zahn-Waxler, Kochanska et al. (1990), children who develop empathic overinvolvement with their parents' problems may also need to develop the ability to protect themselves by distancing from the burden of parental depression. A potential risk of adopting such a stance is that, as their feelings of guilt and responsibility persist without resolution, these children may develop an affective disorder later in life.

In observing depressed mothers with toddlers in a clinical context, support for the findings of affect anomalies during infancy and subsequent overinvolvement in parental problems can be further documented. Depressed mothers frequently present as asynchronous with their young children. Either an overly intrusive interactional style results in toddler avoidance of the mother, or maternal preoccupation with self-concerns inhibits responsivity to the toddler. Depressed mothers often experience difficulty reading the affective signals of their youngsters. Conversely, we have found that the toddlers of depressed mothers are extremely attuned to maternal negative affective expressions. In fact, when mothers are distressed, toddlers have been observed to engage in efforts to alleviate the negative affect by offering the mother hugs, tissues, and teddy bears. Moreover, while recognizing that this "caregiving" stance may be developmentally inappropriate for a toddler, depressed mothers often foster this behavior, either covertly or overtly.

Thus, research findings taken in conjunction with clinical observations underscore the risk that parental depression exerts on the socialization of affect in young children. Because the sensitivity to negative affect may be interpreted as prosocial behavior by depressed caregivers, these affective patterns may be difficult to modify.

As was true of the regulatory difficulties discussed earlier, the affective anomalies in children with depressed caregivers also possess implications for the emergence of psychopathology in the adult years. Although investigations of the role that perturbations in affect in childhood exert on affective disorders of adulthood remain to be conducted, it is quite feasible that these difficulties play a role in the etiology of affective disorders, as well as in the emergence of personality disorders.

The Development of A Secure Attachment Relationship

Patterns of interactions and expectations formed during previous stages are integrated to define a child's affective relationship with his or her caregiver. The formation of a secure attachment relationship with the primary caregiver is considered the paramount developmental issue of the latter half of the first year of life (Sroufe, 1979). At this phase, affect, cognition, and behavioral expression become organized around the physical and emotional availability of the attachment figure. Ainsworth, Blehar, Waters, and Wall (1978) identified individual differences in the patterning of infant-caregiver attachment relationships based on infants' responses to maternal separations and reunions in a laboratory paradigm known as the Strange Situation. Traditionally, children have been classified as securely attached (Type B), insecurely attached avoidant (Type A), or insecurely attached resistant (Type C). The differences in the quality and patterning of this relationship are thought to reflect different styles of emotion regulation that have developed out of the children's history of distress remediation and emotional synchrony with their caregivers. These regulatory strategies are believed to persist and remain influential into adulthood. The various patterns of insecure attachment organization are important to our understanding of depression because they represent early forms of aberrant organization of the biological, socioemotional, cognitive, and representational behavioral systems with potential implications for an evolving prototypic depressive or manic-depressive organization.

Apparently, those infants who are less prone to outward expressions of distress either turn away from the caregiver in their attempt to modulate their arousal or are able to share their affect directly with the caregiver, establishing a positive emotional connection. Those babies who are prone to higher levels of distress either are able to seek and be comforted by the parent or experience relatively longer periods of negative arousal. In addition, this special relationship with the primary caregiver seems to have hierarchical salience over other attachment relationships in determining children's subsequent affect regulatory styles.

It is important to keep in mind that children typically develop attachments to more than their primary caregiver. Although the representations associated with the primary caregiver may assume primacy, usually the other representations of, for example, the father, likely also develop. These representations may be largely consistent in quality and character with the internal representations of the mother and self in relation to the mother if the child experiences similar relationships with both parents. Some children however, may experience quite discrepant relationships with their parents. For example, a child may have a positive relationship with the mother and a negative relationship with the father. How this inconsistency is processed by the child and how it affects internal representational models is uncertain (Bretherton, 1985). Children may derive separate models of other and self consistent with their different caregiver relationships. Aspects of experience with the other attachment figure may be hierarchically integrated within this more general model and accessed later in development if experiences are consistent with qualitative features that were previously incorporated, though dormant.

Representational models of attachment figures are thought to develop through interactions with the primary caregiver. They are regarded as a system of expectations about the caregiver's relative responsiveness and effectiveness in modulating and alleviating the child's physical and psychological needs, including the regulation of tension (Bretherton, 1987; Cicchetti, Cummings, Greenberg, & Marvin, 1990). The internal working models are formed in the early stages of homeostatic regulation and affect differentiation.

A securely attached child has an internalized representation of a caregiver who is available and sensitive to their emotional needs and signals. Such children feel free to express their negative affects directly, and they expect to be soothed and reassured by their caregivers during times of stress. They thus are likely to spend less time distressed and more time engaged in positive interchanges. Through positive relationships with their caregivers, securely attached children experience emotion modulation. Consequently, regulation—as opposed to dysregulation—becomes familiar and anticipated. The internalization of this caregiving pattern, therefore, also includes the internalization of emotion regulation. But this is not the case in children with insecure attachment relationships.

Type A infants are believed to develop functional models that anticipate rejection, especially when they seek comfort. Their avoidance is an organized defensive strategy against becoming overwhelmed by negative affect. In support of this viewpoint, children and adults with avoidant representational models have been characterized as being angry and hostile, having less resilient egos, and having trouble with directly expressing negative affect. Children with insecure-resistant attachments (Type C) are thought to be more impulsive and helpless and less controlled. Their representational model is of a caregiver who is not available and is not effective in meeting their needs. Thus their relationship with that parent is one of dependence and helplessness (Cummings & Cicchetti, 1990). Although individuals with Type C attachments are able to express their affect directly, they are likely to become overwhelmed by negative emotion and to be preoccupied with fear, anger, and/or sadness.

Different evolving memory systems contribute to the structure of the representational models. Crittenden (1990) has discussed a type of memory system, procedural memory, thought to develop in the sensorimotor period, in which information about relationships is encoded, retrieved, and expressed in the form of patterns of behavior. Bowlby (1980), applying the work of Tulving (1985, 1989) to attachment, has discussed two other memory systems, semantic and episodic. In the semantic memory system, information in the form of generalizations about relationships is stored and retrieved. In contrast, the episodic memory system involves autobiographical information about events or episodes and actions of the self and others as well as associated affects at the time of specific events. The character of the different memory systems composing the internal representational model is not necessarily consistent across the memory systems, and the ease of access between systems may be variable.

Throughout his writings on separation and loss, Bowlby (1969/1982, 1973, 1980) argues that, when faced with separation from their primary caregiver, children experience anxiety. In cases of prolonged or sustained loss, an intense mourning process, with its socioemotional, cognitive, representational, and biological components, ensues, and if continued beyond the normally expected period of grieving, is viewed as a reflection of an unresolved loss. Without the presence of a secure internal representational model of the primary caregiver. Bowlby believed that any loss would be experienced as paramount. Conversely, the development of a good quality representational model of the major attachment figure was thought to serve as a buffer for minimizing the extent and duration of devastation experienced in the face of loss.

In terms of the development of internal representational models, the psychological unavailability of parents for long periods can be viewed as a powerful influence in shaping expectations that attachment figures are unavailable and the self is unlovable. The implicit communication to the child is that he or she is unworthy of love—worthless and rejected—and that the parent is "lost" to the child. The recurrent "loss" of the parent as a function of the decreased emotional availability that accompanies major depressive episodes may be equivalent in impact on the child's self-concept to the effects of recurrent major separations. This loss also can be seen as parallel to the perceptions of loss that precipitate depressive patterns (Beck, 1967). Early experiences of loss may be particularly powerful because they mold fundamental biological, cognitive, socioemotional, and representational response patterns (Akiskal & McKinney, 1973). The psychological unavailability of parents, the development of insecure attachments and representational models of attachment figures and of the self in relation to others in children,

and children's developing precursors of depression or clinical depression thus may be conceptualized as interrelated processes (cf. Blatt & Homann, 1992).

Children of depressed parents are particularly likely to be faced with the psychological unavailability of parents for long periods, especially during, but not necessarily restricted to, episodes of depression (Field, 1989). Such children are exposed to sad and dysphoric affect, helplessness and hopelessness, irritability, confusion, and, in bipolar illness to these episodes sometimes alternating with periods of euphoria and grandiosity. Thus, there are compelling reasons for considering psychological unavailability of the parent to be a risk factor for the development of insecure attachment in children of depressed parents.

On the other hand, not all children of depressed parents will develop insecure attachments. A secure relationship with a nondepressed parent may act as a protective factor against attachment insecurity. This psychological protection might be especially salient if the nondepressed parent is able to be emotionally available to the child at times when the spouse is experiencing more acute episodes of depression (Cummings & Cicchetti, 1990; Downey & Coyne, 1990). Additionally, it is the nature of the caregiving provided, not depression per se, that will contribute to child insecurity (Hammen, 1992a).

A number of studies have been conducted that have examined the quality of attachment relationships in the offspring of parents with a mood disorder. Gaensbauer and his colleagues (1984) found no differences in the percentage of infants securely attached to affectively ill and healthy parents at 12 months (77% for each group); however, by 18 months there was a dynamic shift in the percentage of securely attached infants of parents with an affective disorder (to 14%) but not for the infants of the healthy parents (58%). These results parallel short-term longitudinal findings reported by Egeland and Sroufe (1981). As part of a larger prospective study of children at developmental risk due to poverty, they assessed infant security of attachment at 12 months and again at 18 months for a subsample of infants whose maltreating mothers were "psychologically unavailable" (but not physically abusive) to their infants and for a subsample of comparison infants whose mothers were at risk for maltreating their infants because of psychosocial disadvantage but who had not maltreated their children to date. For the subsample of infants of psychologically unavailable mothers who were not physically abused, the number of securely attached infants fell from 57% at 12 months to 0% at 18 months. This compares with a slight rise, from 67% to 71%, in secure attachments among the control infants from 12 to 18 months.

Although the psychologically unavailable mothers in the Egeland and Sroufe (1981) study were not formally diagnosed as clinically depressed, the descriptions of their interactions with their infants and toddlers resemble both clinical and research descriptions of the effects of depression on adult social interaction in general, and parental caretaking behavior in particular (Downey & Coyne, 1990). Perhaps psychological unavailability is a shared feature of some maltreating parents and most depressed parents that affects the security of the attachment relationship between parent and infant.

Radke-Yarrow, Cummings, Kuczynski, and Chapman (1985) compared patterns of attachment in children of mothers with major unipolar and bipolar depression, minor depression, and no affective disorder. The children ranged in age from 15 to 52 months when they were observed in the Strange Situation and all sessions were coded using Ainsworth's original classification system, with adaptations made to the coding system to accommodate the developmental changes in the older children of their sample.

When these investigators examined the patterns of attachment in their four groups, they found a higher proportion of insecure attachments in children of parents with major unipolar and bipolar depressive illness than in children from the other two groups. Among children with a caregiver with major unipolar depression, 47% had insecure attachments with their primary caregiver and 53% were classified as securely attached. In contrast, 25% of the offspring of parents with a minor depression and 29% of the no depression group were classified as insecurely attached. Additionally, children of bipolar-depressed parents were most likely to develop insecure attachments; only 21% were securely attached.

In families in which the mothers were depressed, the presence of depression in the father did not exacerbate the likelihood that an insecure attachment would develop between the mother and child. However, if depressed mothers did not have a husband within the household, then the risk of an insecure mother-child attachment relationship developing increased.

DeMulder and Radke-Yarrow (1991) recoded the Strange Situations of the children described in the aforementioned Radke-Yarrow et al. (1985) study. DeMulder and Radke-Yarrow (1991) utilized the Ainsworth et al. (1978) infant coding system for children under 30 months of age and employed the Cassidy and Marvin (1992) preschool classification system when categorizing the attachments of children 30 months of age and older. Because of using more age-sensitive coding schemes DeMulder and Radke-Yarrow's (1991) results differed somewhat from the initial report. Across ages studied, 42% of the offspring of the unipolar and no affective disorder groups were insecurely attached to their caregiver. In contrast, 67% of bipolar offspring had developed insecure attachments. Because the investigators combined the major unipolar depression and minor depression groups from the earlier study into one unipolar group and added some additional new subjects to this recoding of the data, it is difficult to comment about the lack of differences found between the unipolar and well groups. The rate of insecurity in the bipolar groups, however, was comparable to that reported in the prior paper. Approximately 50% of the offspring of bipolar mothers were found to have very insecure or disorganized-disoriented attachments, a rate of atypical attachment consistent with those found in other high-risk samples (Carlson, Cicchetti, Barnett, & Braunwald, 1989; Lyons-Ruth, Connell, Zoll, & Stahl, 1987). Disorganized attachments (Type D—see Main & Solomon, 1990) are a recently discovered pattern characterized by a number of anomalous behaviors on the part of the child in the presence of the mother (e.g., dazing, stilling, apprehension, approaching mother with head down).

In a recent prospective longitudinal follow-up investigation of this sample, Radke-Yarrow et al. (in press) assessed the links between quality of attachment rated during the toddler or preschool years and psychosocial development during the early school-age years. Radke-Yarrow and her colleagues examined the influence of attachment and stressor conditions (e.g., maternal mood disorder, abusive relationships, marital discord) in combination as they relate to later problematic and adaptive child outcomes. These investigators found that, under some circumstances, secure attachment may not be protective for all children, and insecure attachment may confer some advantages, because some children who had developed a secure attachment relationship with a severely ill mother with unipolar illness exhibited problems that were of clinical concern by the early school years. Moreover, the development of an insecure attachment relationship with a mother with bipolar illness was associated with the absence of problematic anxiety during the early school years. The children of bipolar mothers who did not develop anxiety problems at age 6 were typically uninhibited temperamentally and often took refuge in autonomous activities. Continued longitudinal data are necessary on these children to distinguish between adaptive and maladaptive insecure attachments. Additionally, it will be important to ascertain how these children of bipolar parents fare on the other developmental issues at different points in the life span.

Lyons-Ruth, Connell, Grunebaum, and Botein (1990; see also Lyons-Ruth et al., 1987) found that infants of depressed mothers who had been receiving a 1-hour weekly home-visiting service for 9 or more months were twice as likely to develop a secure attachment (40% vs. 20%, respectively) and only one-sixth as likely to develop an insecure attachment (9% vs. 54%, respectively) than infants whose mothers were depressed and untreated. Unserved infants of depressed mothers displayed particularly high rates of disorganized-disoriented attachments compared with infants of depressed mothers who received the family support treatment (54% vs. 22%, respectively).

As is apparent, the rates of insecurity are far higher in the Lyons-Ruth et al. sample than in the DeMulder and Radke-Yarrow sample. However, there are important differences in social-class background and other demographic factors between the two groups of depressed women. The sample of Lyons-Ruth and her colleagues is a multirisk, low-SES one, and includes some infants who had also been maltreated, whereas the DeMulder and Radke-Yarrow sample primarily comprises middle and upper-middle SES families (see also Cohn & Campbell, 1992, for similar results to DeMulder & Radke-Yarrow, 1991, from a large community-based screening of middle-SES women for depression during the postpartum period).

When these children were between 4 and 6 years of age (mean age = 59 months), approximately 80% (N = 62) of the original sample participated in a subsequent investigation (Lyons-Ruth, Alpern, & Repacholi, 1993). During the follow-up assessment period, teachers completed the Preschool Behavior Questionnaire (PBQ) (Behar & Stringfield, 1974b) for the children in the study, as well as for three same-sex classmates nearest in age. Factor analyses of the PBQ have yielded three factors: anxious, hostile, and hyperactive (Behar & Stringfield, 1974a).

The most powerful single predictor of deviant levels of hostile behavior being exhibited toward peers was disorganized-disoriented attachment status. Looking backward from the teacher assessment to earlier assessments, it was found that 71% of hostile preschoolers were classified as having a disorganized attachment at their 18-month Strange Situation assessment. In contrast, only 12% of children manifesting deviant hostile behavior were securely attached during infancy. It is likely that for some infants, disorganized attachment may prove to be a precursor of later maladaptation, long before actual childhood disorders develop and become manifest.

In the most recent longitudinal follow-up assessment of the Lyons-Ruth et al. (1987, 1990) sample, Easterbrooks, Davidson, and Chazan (1993) located 45 of the 62 children seen at 5 years of age. When the children were 7, security of attachment to their mothers was assessed in an hour-long separation-reunion procedure in the laboratory. In addition, the mothers and teachers of these children provided reports of the children's behavior problems using the Child Behavior Checklist (CBCL; Achenbach & Edelbrock, 1981, 1986).

The Main and Cassidy (1988) separation-reunion codings revealed that 45% of the sample were insecurely attached to their caregivers (19% A, 12% C, 14% D,). Quality of attachment also was related to children's reported behavior problems. Specifically, both mothers and teachers rated children who were securely attached to manifest fewer internalizing and externalizing symptoms and to evidence fewer total behavior problems than children who were classified as insecurely attached.

In a further exploration of the behavior problems data, classifications were made as to whether the children's behavior problem scores fell into the "clinical range" using the standard Achenbach and Edelbrock (1981, 1986) cutoff scores. The results of these analyses revealed that maternal reports placed 42% of the children in the clinical range, whereas teachers' ratings resulted in a 24% placement above the clinical cutoff. Examinations of the relationship between attachment status and the presence of behavior problems in the clinical range revealed that securely attached children were significantly less likely to be placed in the clinical range by either mother or teacher CBCL ratings. Finally, 45% of the children with a secure attachment relationship to their mother received scores above the clinical cutoff from either their mothers or teachers, compared with 83% of those with insecure attachment relationships (88% of A's; 60% of C's; and 100% of the D groups).

Relatedly, Toth and Cicchetti (in press) applied an attachment theory framework toward understanding the emergence of depressive symptomatology and lower perceived competence in maltreated and nonmaltreated school-age children. Children's reports of relatedness with mother were examined in conjunction with maltreatment status. Maltreated children with nonoptimal patterns of relatedness (insecure) evidenced elevated depressive symptomatology and lower perceived competence, whereas nonmaltreated children with optimal/adequate patterns of relatedness (secure) exhibited the least depressive symptomatology and higher perceived competence. In addition, differentiations between maltreated children with and without secure patterns of relatedness emerged, suggesting that optimal/adequate relatedness may mitigate against the adverse effects of maltreatment. Of particular interest, results were especially striking in this regard with respect to sexual abuse.

Specifically, sexually abused children who reported confused (disorganized) patterns of relatedness to their mothers had clinically significant levels of depression.

Rubin, Both, Zahn-Waxler, Cummings, & Wilkinson (1991) studied the links between quality of attachment and peer relationships. Children of depressed and nondepressed mothers were seen in the Strange Situation (Ainsworth et al., 1978) at 2 years of age and observed interacting with a familiar same-sex peer in a free-play context at age 5. Results supported a link between attachment insecurity, maternal depression, and subsequent withdrawn, passive, and inhibited behavior in early childhood. Although the small sample size precluded examinations of subtype of attachment insecurity and child outcome, Rubin and his colleagues (Rubin, LeMare, & Lollis, 1990; Rubin & Mills, 1988) have hypothesized that insecure-resistant (Type C) attachments are associated with inhibited/withdrawn outcomes, whereas insecure-avoidant (Type A) attachments are associated with hostile/aggressive outcomes (cf. Lyons-Ruth et al., 1993).

Armsden, McCauley, Greenberg, Burke, and Mitchell (1990) examined the security of parent attachment in several groups of young adolescents, including clinically depressed, nondepressed psychiatric controls, and nonpsychiatric controls. Depressed adolescents reported significantly less secure attachments to their parents than either control group. Moreover, consistent with the predictions of cognitive models of depression (e.g., Abramson et al., 1978; Beck, 1967), associations were found among attachment security to parents, attributional style, and presence of a depressive disorder (cf. Rose & Abramson, 1992). These findings provide support for the belief that insecure attachment, and the concomitant negative representational models of self and other that it engenders, promote the development of negative cognitive schemata that contribute to the development of a depressive disorder and problems in interpersonal relations.

In a related vein, Kandel and Davies (1986) investigated the adult sequelae of adolescent depression nine years later. Kandel and Davis found that the long-term consequences of adolescent depression primarily were manifest in a decreased ability to form an intimate relationship with a person of the opposite gender. Moreover, these depressed symptoms were associated with deficits in establishing close emotional relationships, both with parents during adolescence and with spouses and parents during young adulthood.

Kobak, Sudler, and Gamble (1991) examined the relations between adolescents' quality of attachment on the Adult Attachment Interview (Main & Goldwyn, in press) and their self-reported depressive symptoms. The Adult Attachment Interviews were scored using the Q-Set developed by Kobak. Adolescents who were characterized by insecure attachment strategies had elevated levels of depressive symptomatology, both concurrently and 10 to 11 months prior to receiving the Adult Attachment Interview. In contrast, teenagers who had secure strategies had significantly lower levels of depressed symptomatology. Thus, an adolescent's ability to generate coherent discourse about him- or herself in relation to attachment figures appeared to act as a protective factor against depressive symptoms. The findings reported by Kobak and his colleagues (1991) dovetail nicely with an earlier study by Kobak and Sceery (1988) that found an association between adolescent secure attachment strategies and positive outcomes during the transition to college. Furthermore, the reported association between insecure attachment strategies and depressive symptoms provides important evidence that attachment remains as an important developmental task in adolescence.

Research also has been conducted to examine links among attachment history, depression, and current relationship functioning in adults. Carnelley, Pietromonaco, and Jaffe (1994) assessed the working models of others and the relative contribution of these models and depression to relationship functioning in mildly depressed college women and in women recovering from a major depressive disorder. Mildly depressed college women evidenced more preoccupation and fearful avoidance in romantic relationships than nondepressed college women. Women who were recovering from a major depressive disorder also evidenced greater fearful avoidance in relationships. Relationship functioning was predicted more strongly by adult attachment style than by depression status for both mildly depressed and recovering women. Additionally, both groups of depressed women were less likely to report positive childhood relationships with their parents. These investigators conclude that an insecure working model is linked with vulnerability to depression (Carnelley et al., 1994) and that these findings are consistent with the work of Blatt and others (Blatt, Quinlan, Chevron, MacDonald, & Zuroff, 1982; see also Cummings & Cicchetti, 1990). This study posits that interpersonal cognitions based on childhood experiences lead to depression. These investigators also conclude that adult romantic attachment style is more closely linked to current relationship functioning than is depression status, a finding consistent with results in the offspring literature that stress the importance of interacting risk factors and not of parental depression per se in predicting child outcome.

Pearson, Cohn, Cowan, and Cowan (1994) also have investigated the association between the quality of attachment and depressed symptomatology in an adult population. These investigators administered the Adult Attachment Interview in conjunction with an assessment of depressive symptoms to adults predominantly in their mid-30s. Using the Main and Goldwyn (in press) classification system for rating the nature of early relationships and coherency of discourse, Pearson and her colleagues identified three types of adult attachment: earned-security, continuous security, and insecurity. Earned-secure classifications were assigned to individuals who were classified as securely attached despite their discussion of difficult or adverse early and current secure models of attachment. Those classified as insecure had adverse early attachment relationship experiences as well as a current insecure state of mind with respect to attachment issues.

When Pearson et al. (1994) examined the relation between attachment security and depressive symptomatology, interesting findings emerged. Adults who received earned-secure classifications had depressive symptoms comparable to those of adults who were rated as insecurely attached. Thirty percent of the insecures and 40% of the earned-secures had depression scores that exceeded the clinical cutoff on the self-report measure employed in this investigation (i.e., the Center for Epidemiological Studies

Depression (CES-D) Scale; Radloff, 1977). In contrast, only 10% of the adults classified as having continuous-secure attachments exceeded the clinical cutoff on the CES-D. The increased amount of depressive symptomatology in the earned-secure than in the continuous-secure group provides suggestive evidence that adult reconstructions of past relationship difficulties may remain as emotional vulnerabilities despite the presence of a currently secure working model of attachment relationships.

Additionally, ratings of the parenting style of these adults were made based on observations of a series of structured and unstructured parent-child interactional tasks conducted in the laboratory. Consistent with the predictions of attachment theory, the parenting styles of the earned-secure adults were remarkably similar to those of the continuously secure adults.

Because developmental psychopathologists are interested in alternate pathways to competence and in how adverse experiences and adaptational failures in early development place children at risk for subsequent difficulties, we believe that attachment research will profit greatly from future examinations of the similarities and differences between individuals with earned-secure and those with continuous-secure attachments. As is apparent, secure attachment does not ensure absence of psychopathology, nor is insecure attachment a sufficient cause for clinical difficulties. It is conceivable that certain insecure strategies (in particular, the deactivation of attachment or dismissing strategy observed in the Pearson et al., 1994 study) may prevent the adult from becoming too in touch with his or her emotional difficulties, whereas a secure strategy against the backdrop of early adversity may be associated with a greater openness to dealing directly with emotional pain (i.e., becoming depressed) (cf. Zigler & Glick, 1986). Although individuals with insecure and secure working models are trying to cope with their histories in an adaptive fashion, longitudinal investigations of individuals with earned-secure working models develop more competently than insecures, even if at some points they experience periods of emotional difficulty.

In another investigation of adult attachment organization, Patrick, Hobson, Castle, Howard, and Maughan (1994) administered the Adult Attachment Interview to 12 adults on the psychotherapy waiting list at a major hospital who were diagnosed as dysthymic. Patrick and his colleagues (1994) found that 10 of the 12 dysthymic persons they interviewed (83%) were classified as insecurely attached. Utilizing the Main and Goldwyn (in press) system of considering the entire transcript of the interview, Patrick et al. discovered that 6 of the dysthymic adults (50%) had insecure Dismissing attachment organizations, 4 received insecure Preoccupied-Entangled classifications (33%), and 2 (17%) were considered to be Free or Autonomous (i.e., secure). In addition, 2 of the 12 dysthymic individuals also received the Unresolved/disoriented classification.

A wealth of data has accumulated from research conducted with groups of infants, toddlers, preschoolers, and school-age children who have depressed caregivers. Additionally, studies examining links between attachment organization and the development of depression in nonrisk and high-risk samples, as well as in individuals with dysthymia and major depression have begun to emerge. To date, however, direct evidence of a relationship between early insecure attachment and later clinical depression has not been obtained. Insecure attachment can only be regarded as a risk factor for deviant outcomes, including depression, within the context of a complex developmental model (see Cummings & Cicchetti, 1990). It is important to remember that there are diverse parental mechanisms through which depression might be linked with insecure attachment and risk for depression. These include maternal attributions toward the child, child-rearing practices associated with the socialization of affect, and facial expressions and body posture as aspects of the caregiver's emotion language (Cicchetti & Schneider-Rosen, 1986; Cohn, Matias, Tronick, Connell, & Lyons-Ruth, 1986). Identification of the links between parental depression and insecure attachment is only an initial step toward delimiting the bases for such relations. If depression in parents is linked with insecure attachment, it may be attributable to the effect that it has in influencing aspects of parent-child interaction, as well as to its role in determining broader aspects of the child-rearing environment. An important aspect of this caregiving environment is likely to be the psychological unavailability of the parent during periods of depression.

Early insecure attachment relationships may lead children to be more vulnerable to depression by causing them to have very low internalized feelings of felt security. When faced with stress, such children are likely to have few resources for coping and may easily be prone to developing lower self-esteem, intensified feelings of insecurity, and sad affect. In addition, the cognitions that the insecurely attached individual develops in the context of attachment relationships may contribute to the emergence of thought processes and affect that are associated with depression. As noted by Cummings and Cicchetti (1990), these cognitions that center around loss and the unacceptability of the self are likely to resemble patterns of cognitive processes that have been linked with depression in adults (Beck, 1967).

Another mechanism whereby maternal depression may bring about insecure attachment may be neurobiological in nature. It is conceivable that each developmental reorganization throughout ontogenesis is a "sensitive period" during which biological and psychological developments either render an individual vulnerable to psychopathology or allow for the development of new strengths that buffer or protect against pathological outcomes. Thus, parental depression, with its concomitant interpersonal, biological, affective, and cognitive difficulties that render sensitive parenting problematic, may either delay or impair the development of brain mechanisms that are the biological substrates of interpersonal attachments, and/or facilitate the development of genetically vulnerable neuronal circuits to the loss of reinforcement (cf. Akiskal & McKinney, 1973). Because depression is associated with the withdrawal of contact from significant persons and the dissolution of attachment relationships (Akiskal & McKinney, 1975; Gentile, Cicchetti, Rogosch, & O'Brien, 1992; Lewinsohn, 1974), children of depressed caregivers may develop a biological reward system that is especially susceptible to abandonment, unavailability, disappointment, and loss. Akin to Akiskal and McKinney's (1973) conceptualization, it is conceivable that, although reversible, the punishment system of the brain (e.g., the periventricular system) could assume an imbalanced dominance over the reward system (e.g.,

the medial forebrain bundle). Moreover, these genetically and/or psychologically induced neurobiological anomalies may form the basis of a neurobiology of representational models that sets the tone for: depressed individuals' views of themselves as hopeless and helpless with respect to their fate (Abramson et al., 1989); the dysregulation of the organization of the serotonergic, dopaminergic, nonadrenergic and cholinergic neurotransmitter systems; neuronal excitability and hyperarousal; and ineffective coping (Akiskal & McKinney, 1975; Antelman & Caggiula, 1977; Schildkraut & Kety, 1967).

Regardless of the processes and mechanisms that contribute to the evolution of an insecure attachment relationship, the presence of such an attachment organization has been linked with the seriousness of psychopathology in adulthood, as well as with responsivity to psychotherapeutic intervention. Dozier (1990) administered the Adult Attachment Interview to 40 adults with serious psychopathological disorders. Adults who were rated as more secure were more likely to have affective disorders than thought disorders. Additionally, greater security was associated with more treatment compliance, whereas stronger avoidant tendencies were accompanied by increased rejection of therapists, less self-disclosure, and poorer treatment utilization (Dozier, 1990). These findings suggest that attachment history exerts a role not only in the emergence of psychopathology, but also in the potential effectiveness of intervention.

The Development of the Self-System: Self-Awareness and Self-Other Differentiation

During the second half of the second year of life, children begin to develop a sense of themselves as autonomous agents (Emde, Gaensbauer & Harmon, 1976; Lewis & Brooks-Gunn, 1979). Before this age, development is primarily sensorimotor in nature. However, with the acquisition of a sense of self, the child's development is characterized by a transition from sensorimotor to representational capacities.

The infant must build on the attachment relationship to explore the environment during this period. The infant begins to understand the self as a separate and independent entity that has an effect on the environment and others. Self-regulation becomes increasingly important and is channeled through developing delay of gratification and frustration tolerance.

In normally developing children, play and language are age-appropriate ways to represent conceptions of the self and relationships that typically emerge and become more elaborated and differentiated during the second and third year of life. In addition, children become increasingly able to label the emotional states, intentions, and cognitions of both themselves and others (Bretherton & Beeghly, 1982; Kagan, 1981).

Consequently, children are able to use symbolic means of communicating their complex needs and feelings, thereby permitting more effective means of modulating arousal. Similarly, they are able to rely on the representations of caregivers, or negotiation, to calm their distress when separated from their parents (Cicchetti et al., 1990).

These growing symbolic capacities are accompanied by underlying, internal representational models. In addition to representational models of attachment figures, representational models of the self are formed (Bowlby, 1973; Bretherton, 1987), with emotional and cognitive components. Emotions, in particular, give meaning to the self and, as such, must be regulated for an individual to function adaptively (Malatesta & Wilson, 1988; Sroufe, 1990; Stern, 1985).

Although children share greater responsibility for their own functioning at this stage, caregivers continue to remain necessary for facilitating the children's achievement of this task. As we discussed, the experience of having a caretaker who is reliably available and emotionally responsive enables children to construct an accessible, responsive internal working model of their attachment figure, as well as a reciprocal representational model of the self as acceptable in the eyes of the attachment figure. In contrast, the psychological unavailability of parents for long periods can exert powerful expectations that attachment figures are unavailable and that the self is unlovable (Cummings & Cicchetti, 1990).

Evidence on the effects of parental depression on the self-system of young children emerges from a number of investigations. Radke-Yarrow, Belmont, Nottelmann, and Bottomly (1990) studied mothers with unipolar ($N = 13$) and bipolar ($N = 4$) disorder, as well as a group of control mothers with no psychiatric disorder, interacting with their $2\frac{1}{2}$-year-old toddlers. Although this investigation revealed that mood-disordered mothers were similar to non-mood-disordered mothers in the quantity and content of their attributions, mood-disordered mothers conveyed significantly more negatively toned affect in their attributions. This occurred most often with respect to negative attributions about child emotions. These findings are significant, because as we will demonstrate later, depressed children have been shown to selectively process negative self-referent words as opposed to positive self-referent words.

Additionally, mood-disordered mother-child dyads evidenced higher correspondence of affect tone of attributions and of self-reference than non-mood-disordered dyads (e.g., mother says "I hate myself," child says "I'm bad"). The researchers interpreted these results as suggesting a heightened vulnerability to maternal attributions in the offspring of mood-disordered mothers. The potential for increases in negative self-attributions for these children and the impact of this vulnerability for the development of a later mood-disorder are strikingly evident in these findings. Moreover, these results emphasize the importance of mother-child discourse for the development of children's emerging sense of self.

Cole, Barrett, and Zahn-Waxler (1992) observed a group of toddlers during two mishaps: a doll breaking and juice spilling. In general, toddlers exhibited two reactions to these mishaps— (a) concerned reparation and (b) tension and frustration. Moreover, consistent with Kagan's (1981) notions that self-awareness, the appreciation of standards, and a moral sense emerge during this period, most toddlers tried to repair the mishap. The presence of depressed/and anxious symptomatology in mothers was associated with a suppression of frustration and tension in their toddlers. It may be that the toddlers' exposure to mothers with depressed and anxious symptomatology served to inhibit the development of more normal affective expression, thereby contributing to a sense of a lack of efficacy in interfacing with the environment.

Kochanska (1991) studied patterns of inhibition to the unfamiliar in toddlers of nondepressed, unipolar, and bipolar mothers. Toddlers of recently symptomatic mothers with unipolar depression were the most inhibited (cf. Kagan, 1994). Toddlers of well mothers and of mothers with bipolar illness did not manifest inhibition to a new environment or to a stranger. Kochanska proffered two possible interpretations of these findings. First, she stated that the inhibition observed in toddlers of depressed mothers may be part of a more general response to living in a highly stressed environment brought on by the mother's depression. Alternatively, Kochanska theorized that the depressed mothers may have reacted anxiously to the experimental context and communicated their tension to the child.

Kochanska and Kuczynski (1991) examined preschool children's noncompliance strategies for asserting autonomy. Groups of depressed and well mothers and their toddlers were observed during spontaneous interactions in a naturalistic, apartmentlike setting. No differences were found in the extent to which depressed and nondepressed mothers granted or denied their children's requests; however, the determinants of autonomy granting differed for the two groups. In particular, the depressed mother's self-reported mood prior to interacting with her child, in combination with the child's concurrent behavior, was a predictor of the manner in which a depressed mother would respond to her child's autonomy requests. Specifically, depressed mothers whose self-reported mood was negative and whose children were commonly uncooperative often did not acquiese to their children's requests.

In a study of communication patterns among mothers and older children, Tarullo, DeMulder, Martinez, and Radke-Yarrow (1994) examined the interactions of unipolar, bipolar, and well mothers with their preadolescent and adolescent children. Preadolescent children of well mothers were rated as more happy/comfortable than were children of mood-disordered mothers. Mothers and their children were rated as more irritable/critical with each other when the child had a psychiatric illness. Whenever mothers met diagnostic criteria for a major depressive episode within the preceding month, their interactions with their adolescent daughters were rated as more critical.

Adolescents with a mother who had bipolar illness were less happy/comfortable than adolescents with a mother who had unipolar disease, especially if the children were free of psychiatric problems within the past year. In contrast, the dyadic interactions of younger children of unipolar mothers were rated as less comfortable/happy than those of younger children of bipolar mothers.

For the child who develops an insecure representational model of the self and others based on experiences in the attachment relationship, we observe what may be regarded as the germinal signs of a depression—or manic-depression-like organization— with interpersonal, emotional, cognitive, representational, and biological components. By extending this analysis to later points in development, we can examine how affective components of the self that are relevant to the mood disorders (e.g., self-esteem), are intertwined with growing cognitive and representational components of the self (e.g., self-understanding, self-cognitions, self-schemata). Such a developmental perspective may then provide insights into comprehending how cognitive distortions, learned helplessness, hopelessness, and other responses to one's own mood disorder, may have evolved throughout ontogenesis. To understand how perturbations in the emerging self-system may contribute to depression, it is important to understand how the self develops in nondisordered populations.

Self-understanding is a cognitive construction regarding oneself; it is the person's self-representation, which has roots in the early evolving self-representations of the internal models of the attachment relationship. Self-esteem (and the loss of self-esteem), a central component of many theories of depression (Abramson et al., 1978; Beck, 1967; Bibring, 1953), is the affective component of the self; it is positively or negatively valenced in accord with how the self is represented. A self-cognition represents a particular usage of the cognitive structure in regard to the self. Self-schemata are structuralized representations of the self that result from repeated self-cognitions and accompanying affect over time. Self-schemata are hierarchically organized sets of self-cognitions with similar content. Self-schemata take on an enduring character over time, becoming the core structure of how the self is understood.

Self-cognitions are characterized by both content and style. Content refers to those aspects of the self that are being represented, whereas style refers to the particular manner or process in which a person derives a specific thought about the self. In contrast, self-esteem is an affect that is dimensional in nature, varying from positive to negative. Negative or low self-esteem found in the intense dysphoria of depression may contrast with normal sadness not only in its quantitative intensity but also qualitatively by way of different cognitive processes or styles that compose the self-cognitions. Self-cognitions and self-esteem are likely to influence each other reciprocally. Negative self-cognitions engender consistent associated affect or low self-esteem. In turn, low self-esteem as an affective state is likely to be accompanied by further negative self-cognitions. A negative cycle between affect and cognition (i.e., self-esteem and self-cognitions) is likely to perpetuate depressive experience.

Following Damon and Hart (1988), four characteristics of the self can be represented. These include material characteristics (e.g., possessions, physical characteristics); active characteristics (e.g., activities and skills); social characteristics (e.g., roles, relationships); and psychological characteristics (e.g., thoughts, emotions, personality processes). These domains may receive different emphasis in the self-representations of different individuals. More importantly, there is a distinctive developmental aspect to the complexity of these domains. A number of self and person perception researchers have noted a significant transition in the 7- to 8-year-old range in how self-cognitions are constructed. This age shift corresponds to the cognitive transition from preoperational to operational thinking in the nonsocial arena and is associated with other social cognitive transitions as well in relation to self-cognitions (Selman, 1980). Prior to the shift, children tend to view themselves in concrete, physical terms, such as physical appearance, possessions, games they like to play, and where they go to school (i.e., materialistic and active characteristics). Following the cognitive shift, children increasingly begin to abstract qualitative features from their experience and to view themselves in psychological terms,

such as personal characteristics and traits, that are enduring over time.

Other important cognitive shifts also occur during this transitional period. Children move from viewing themselves in relation to absolute standards to engaging in more social comparison, contrasting themselves with others. Children also shift from thinking of themselves in terms of their usual actions or habits to evaluating their competencies and skills in various areas. These shifts from physical to psychological, from absolute standards to comparative evaluations, and from habit-based to competency-based self-cognitions have implications for the affective disorders. Before the shift, there is likely to be some degree of variability in the affective valence of self-cognitions (e.g., whether children like their hair style or the friends they sit with at lunch). However, these self-cognitions relate to features that are subject to change and are specific and concrete, and associated affects are likely to be context-specific and transient. However, after the shift, as children become more abstract and form generalizations across situations and time, they begin to evaluate themselves in psychological, comparative, and competency-based terms. As a result, their cognitive capacities allow for self-cognitions to become more personal, global, and stable. These generalized self-evaluations will be accompanied by congruent affect regarding the self. For children making negative self-evaluations, there will be a trend for greater stability in associated negative affect regarding the self, or low self-esteem. Consequently, after the shift, there may be a greater tendency for negative self-cognitions to generate and perpetuate low self-esteem and dysphoria, contributing to depressive outcomes. Thus, advancing capacities for self-understanding may have negative consequences for children who are at risk for an affective disorder.

The features of self-cognition made possible after the cognitive transition are relevant for understanding developmental aspects of the reformulated learned helplessness theory of depression (Abramson et al., 1978). In this framework, learned helplessness is conceptualized as a result of an individual's perception of noncontingency between responses and resulting rewards and punishments. This noncontingency is attributed based on perceptions of failures that are a result of personal traits or characteristics, but not characteristics that apply universally. Further, the personal failings are viewed as global rather than situation-specific; they are considered to be stable rather than transient and thus are expected to endure over time. These attributions of personal, global, and stable features, used to explain noncontingency, are attributions that become possible after the previously discussed cognitive transition. Thus, attainments in normal cognitive development may serve as preconditions for generating self-cognitions that may contribute to depression through attributions of noncontingency.

More broadly, the character of self-cognitions attainable after the cognitive transition is likely to contribute to more ingrained self-schemata, and these internal structural representations, when negative, may be seen as contributing to the likelihood of depressive outcomes. Beck's cognitive theory of depression (Beck, 1967) centers around a cognitive triad of attributions, including negative cognitions about the self, about the world, and about the future. Again, these types of attributions become possible when children are able to form cognitions about the self and others that are psychological rather than physical, stable and enduring rather than unstable and changing, and global rather than specific.

Although advances in cognitive development appear to provide the conditions under which certain forms of negative self-cognitions may be linked to depressive outcomes, these advances do not explain why some children and not others going through these universal transitions become depressed. For example, Beardslee and Podorefsky (1988) discovered that the adolescents who were functioning adaptively, despite being offspring of depressed parents, were characterized by higher levels of self-understanding, the ability to think and function separately from their parents, and a deep commitment to relationships. We believe that the individual's balance of risk and protective factors will influence the affective valence of the types of self-cognitions made (see Cummings & Cicchetti, 1990). More importantly, the representational models of self and others, derived from early experiences in the attachment relationship and elaborated through ongoing experience, are believed to contribute to the pathways taken in conjunction with advances in cognitive capacities. That is, insecure representational models that are part of a prototypic depressive or manic-depressive organization of biological and behavioral systems, will contribute to cognitive advances being used to confirm and elaborate negative self-schemata, thereby increasing the risk for mood-disordered outcomes.

Recently, Dodge (1993) formulated a theoretical model of the etiology of depression by integrating the constructs of social information processing and various knowledge structures into a developmental framework. Dodge (1993) hypothesized that experience in early life and biologically based limits on memory and neural functioning interact to yield constantly evolving knowledge structures that comprise schemata for experiences in the past, expectations about future occurrences, and affectively-charged vulnerabilities. Dodge speculated that when an individual encounters particular stimuli, these knowledge structures organize the manner in which information is processed. With regard to depression, Dodge conjectured that either early life experiences of interpersonal loss and instability or excessive pressure to achieve at an unrealistic level (both of which are increasingly likely if a child has grown up with a mood-disordered parent) may lead children to develop in memory both negative self-schemata and low self-esteem. As such children encounter loss, abandonment, or failure, the negative self-schemata held in memory cause these children to give heightened attention to the negative aspects of these stressful events and to attribute their occurrence to internal, stable, and global characteristics of the self. The children, in turn, then readily retrieve depressive memories and present in a depressed fashion. Because of the depressogenic processing patterns that are utilized and the negative self-schemata that are formed, it becomes increasingly likely that such children will develop chronic dysthymia or depression.

Quiggle and her colleagues (1992) examined the social information-processing patterns of depressed, aggressive, depressed and aggressive, and normal children. The children, between 9 and 12 years of age, reported on their depressive symptomatology and were administered intention cue detection vignettes to detect potential attributional biases in their information processing. In addition, their classmates rated their peer relationship skills and teacher ratings were utilized to index levels of child aggression.

The aggressive children displayed hostile attributional biases and stated that they could readily commit aggressive acts. Whereas depressed children likewise revealed hostile attributional biases, they attributed these negative situations to internal, stable, and global causes. Moreover, the depressed children stated that they would not be likely to employ assertive responses and believed that engaging in such aggressive acts would be more likely to eventuate in negative outcomes. The comorbid aggressive and depressive children manifested the cognitive patterns of both the aggressive and the depressed children. In particular, for those variables associated with aggression, comorbid children performed like aggressive children, and for those variables related to depression, they mirrored the responses of depressed children. Although the results of this study cannot address the origins of these biased patterns of social-information processing, they are consistent with a number of developmental cognitive formulations (e.g., Cummings & Cicchetti, 1990; Dodge, 1993; Rose & Abramson, 1992).

In a related study, Lauer et al. (1994) investigated the effects of clinical depression on memory and metamemory performances in 9- to 12-year-old children. Memory impairment was found only in the most severely depressed children; in addition, all depressed children, regardless of their level of severity, exhibited performance deficits on the metamemory battery. Specifically, depressed children were more likely to overestimate their memory abilities. The authors suggest two interesting hypotheses to account for their findings. They speculate that the overestimation of memory ability attributions exhibited by depressed children may be their attempt to compensate for feelings of inferiority or inadequacy brought about by their overly critical thought processes. Alternatively, depressed children could set themselves up to fail by setting unrealistic standards for themselves, thereby confirming their negative self-cognitions. Of especial relevance, these distortions or overestimations may cause depressed children's information processing to be impaired, resulting in poor judgment in selecting how to respond appropriately to ambiguous or negative situations.

Based on the findings of a number of laboratory investigations and field studies, Nolen-Hoeksema (1991) demonstrated that the manner in which individuals respond to their depressed symptoms is related to the duration of these symptoms. She found that persons who engage in ruminative responses to their depressions, focusing on their symptoms and their possible causes and consequences, will have depressions of a more prolonged duration than individuals who strive to actively distract themselves from their symptoms. Nolen-Hoeksema (1991) discovered that a ruminative style perpetuates the depression by enabling the depressed mood to exert a negative bias on behavior, thereby disrupting problem solving and instrumental action. In particular, women were more likely to utilize ruminative response styles to their depressed symptoms, whereas men more frequently engaged in distraction.

In an important study, Nolen-Hoeksema, Girgus, and Seligman (1992) conducted a 5-year prospective longitudinal investigation examining the interrelationships among children's depressed symptoms, negative life events, explanatory style, and helplessness behaviors in school and achievement contexts. The children were enrolled in the study when they were in the third grade and were assessed on the constructs noted above at 6-month intervals. Nolen-Hoeksema and her colleagues (1992) found that in early childhood it was negative events, and not explanatory style, that predicted later depressive symptoms. However, in later childhood, a pessimistic explanatory style (cf. Peterson & Seligman, 1984) surfaced as a predictor of depressive symptoms, either alone or in combination with negative events. During episodes of depression, children's explanatory styles not only worsened but also remained pessimistic even when the depression remitted. Thus, a pessimistic explanatory style increased the risk for future depressive episodes. Moreover, depressed children exhibited consistent helplessness in both interpersonal and achievement contexts.

A number of the major psychological theories of adult depression have focused on the cognitive processing and functioning of depressed persons. Beck's (1967) theory placed emphasis on the "cognitive triad" of faulty information processing, distorted cognitions, and negative self-schemata of depressed individuals. Beck (1967) hypothesized that individuals who are depressed possess negative self-schemata, processes believed to be a stable characteristic of the way depressed individuals process information even during nondepressed periods.

Likewise, Rehm (1977) hypothesized that deficits in various aspects of self-system processing (i.e., self-monitoring, self-evaluation, and self-reinforcement) could account for the development of depression. Specifically, Rehm (1977) contended that depressed persons attended more prominently to the negative events that followed their behavior, to the relative exclusion of positive events; engaged in a far greater frequency of self-punishment than self-reinforcement; set unrealistically high self-standards; and made inaccurate causal attributions of events in their lives. Depressed patients also have been shown to ascribe fewer positive aspects not only to the self, but also to their parents and significant others (Gara et al., 1993). Moreover, depressed patients described more negative aspects of these people. Furthermore, for both depressed patients and nonpsychiatric controls, views of the self were highly correlated with corresponding views of parents and significant others.

Longitudinal work on the development of self-schemata would help illuminate the role that they play in the development or sequelae of depression. Our position, although speculative, is that early loss, inadequate maternal care, an insecure attachment relationship, poor quality representational models of the self and the self in relation to others, an impoverished environment, maternal mood disorder, or a temperamental predisposition to heightened awareness or social unease may lead to the formation of depressogenic schemata, which make an individual vulnerable. Through time, these cognitive structures may then be elaborated and organized by experiences congruent with them (Rose & Abramson, 1992). Though the basic cognitive distortions may remain relatively stable, new information can be systematically integrated and organized into them. These structures can then be activated either by general or specific stress, or by prolonged negative affect.

A number of studies have demonstrated that children exhibit enhanced recall of personal adjectives considered to be self-descriptive. Depressed and nondepressed children also show differential facilitated memory for negative and positive adjectives, respectively (Hammen, 1992a). For example, Zupan, Hammen, and Jaenicke (1987) found that children between the ages of 8 and 16 years of age who had current or prior histories of depression demonstrated greater recall of negative self-descriptive adjectives. The number of previous depressions, however, was not predictive of the degree of negativity of the children's self-schemata over and above that predicted by their current mood. Zupan and his colleagues (1987) viewed their findings as congruent with a developmental model of self-schemata in which prior negative experiences may enhance the accessibility of negative thoughts once the self-schemata were activated (see also Hammen & Zupan, 1984).

In an especially impressive culling of normal developmental theory to address the cause of adolescent suicide, Chandler (1994) argues that the identity formation demands associated with the transition to adolescence can strip away the sense of identity necessary for maintaining an investment in the future. In the absence of a sense of self-continuity, Chandler believes that suicide may result. In efforts to test this hypothesis, Chandler (1994) classified hospitalized adolescents into those at "low" or "high" risk for suicide. Remarkably, more than 80% of the high-risk adolescents failed to find any means of justifying their own or other's self-continuity in the face of change. Only 8% of the low-risk adolescents, and none of the nonpatient controls evidenced this inability.

Research investigations of self-reference and of the encoding of personal information with adults also have revealed that self-schemata operate in the encoding and interpretation of incoming information, and that these internal cognitive structures appear to be most influential in the selection and organization of information concerning the self (Hammen, 1992a). For example, Hammen, Marks, Mayol, and DeMayo (1985) found that dependent depressed subjects showed significantly stronger associations between depression and schema-relevant interpersonal life events than between depression and schema-irrelevant negative achievement events. Hammen and her colleagues (1985) obtained the predicted opposite results for the self-critical depressed subjects, although the findings were not consistently as strong. These results are congruent with the identification of interpersonal and self-critical factors in depression (Abramson et al., 1978, 1989; Beck, 1967; Bibring, 1953), whereby dependency or helplessness/hopelessness and negative beliefs about the self are conceived as central issues in depression (see also Blatt & Zuroff, 1992).

Research has consistently demonstrated clear links between perturbations in the self-system and depression. Though causal relationships cannot be clearly documented, the hierarchical model of development suggests that self-system difficulties may emanate from the parent-child relationship and, in turn, contribute to a vulnerability to depression across the life course. Increased credibility for this conceptualization can be garnered from clinical work with depressed individuals. The origins of the pervasive negative self-views, passivity, and hopelessness that permeate the presentation of many depressed persons can be traced back to insults to the self experienced during childhood. Although therapists may opt to modify current self-views through techniques involving cognitive restructuring and may obtain success, it is rare for the underpinnings of a depressive style to originate from current experiences. Rather, self-conceptualizations and the resulting processing of information about the self and the world develop out of the caregiving history that has been experienced. Although departures from a negative history certainly are possible, individuals who present with depression are often struggling with a historically based negative self-view.

As will be addressed later, Post's (1992) discussion of the parallels between behavioral sensitization and electrophysiological kindling and the neurobiology of recurrent affective disorders suggests that different types of intervention may be differentially effective based on the temporal stage of the depressive illness. For example, psychodynamic interventions may be more effective for initial episodes of depression, whereas recurrent episodes may be treated more effectively with cognitively based or behavioral therapies that can address the more automatic neurobiological onset depressions.

Parenting and the Childrearing Context

As our discussion of the functioning of children with a depressed caregiver on a number of stage-salient issues has revealed, these youngsters are at risk for a range of difficulties. There is little doubt that the caregiving provided by the depressed parent as well as genetically transmitted vulnerability place these children at risk. In this section, we discuss findings on the parenting provided by depressed caregivers, as well as aspects of the child-rearing context that, in combination with a parental depressive illness, contribute to the difficulties that have been documented in children with a depressed caregiver.

To understand the potential impact of having a depressed caregiver, it is helpful to consider parenting in nondisordered populations. Moreover, although knowledge of normative parental functioning can assist us in forming a context in which to understand deviations from normality, the study of the parenting of depressed persons also sheds light on normative parenting by illuminating the effects on parent, child, and family when adaptive parenting is not present.

Belsky has delineated a general model of the determinants of parenting (Belsky, 1984; Belsky & Vondra, 1989). In Belsky's model, three primary forces are conceptualized as determining parenting quality: (a) parental developmental history and personal psychological resources, (b) social contextual sources of stress and support (marriage, work, social networks), and (c) the influences of individual child characteristics. In focusing on these three broad areas, the determinants-of-parenting model incorporates components of the psychiatric, sociological, and effect-of-child-on-caregiver models that have been separately linked to parenting. In Belsky's model, however, these separate components are seen as mutually influencing each other as well as affecting parenting quality. As such, a multiplicity of pathways, both direct and indirect, contribute to parenting quality.

A parent's developmental history is seen as directly contributing to parental personality functioning, which in turn directly influences parenting. Thus, the parent's developmental history is conceptualized as indirectly influencing parenting by the effects it has had on shaping personality. For example, a history of depression could contribute to personal difficulties and personality aberrations such as low self-esteem, excessive anger, excessive dependency, and criticality, to name a few, and these personal features could act directly to diminish parenting adequacy. Conversely, a benign and self-enhancing developmental history would result in adaptive personality characteristics (e.g., well-being, patience, personal self-efficacy, competence, interpersonal sensitivity) that would enhance parenting quality. These linkages are but one component of the model. Parental personality also is seen as influencing the social contextual features of marital relations, the social network, and employment, and each of these directly influences parenting positively or negatively, creating further indirect linkages between parental personality and parenting. Each of the social contextual features, in turn, influences personality functioning. In so doing, they may ameliorate or exacerbate personality strengths, thus further indirectly influencing parenting quality. Finally, child characteristics are conceptualized as directly influencing parenting quality and child developmental outcomes. Child characteristics may either stress parenting, as in the case of children with difficult temperaments, chronic physical illness, or mental retardation, or simplify parenting, as is true of children who are cooperative, independent, or socially competent.

Thus, Belsky's model of the determinants of parenting depicts multiple pathways of influence among developmental history and personality, social context, and child characteristics as they relate to individual differences in parenting quality as well as interrelationships among the separate components in the model. No one component is independently responsible for determining parenting, and there is a substantial degree of mutual influence operating between the various components. Despite this complexity, some hierarchy of influence is hypothesized, with personality assuming a prominent position, followed by social contextual features, and then child characteristics. Parenting is seen as a buffered system—and is likely to be optimal when all three major components evidence adaptive levels. A parent with a positive developmental history who has adaptive personality attributes, harmonious marital relations, a supportive social network, and fulfilling employment—in conjunction with a child with an easy temperament and good health—would likely be in the best position to parent effectively and adaptively. Parenting may continue to remain adaptive and functional even when some components of the model are not optimal. For example, a parent is likely to manage parenting a child with a difficult temperament when there are beneficial supports from social network members and the spouse, and when the parent has a calm, patient, and sensitive personality. Parenting quality and effectiveness begin to be jeopardized as fewer of the components of the model are optimal. In Belsky's model, dysfunctions in parenting are most likely to occur when all the components of the model are nonadaptive.

Another conceptualization of parenting with relevance for understanding the parenting provided by a depressed caregiver is described by Dix (1991), who synthesizes theory and research on how the coordination of emotional processes with parental cognitions and behavior contribute to parental functioning. The model specifies components of emotion activation, emotion engagement, and emotion regulation.

In emotion activation, goals or concerns of parents contribute to how parent-child interaction is appraised, with differences in appraisal contributing to variations in the emotions activated in parents. Differences in child behavior and stresses from other areas of the parent's life also contribute to the appraisals made and the emotions that are activated. When parent concerns are incompatible with child concerns and mutually satisfying behaviors and outcomes are not achieved, parents experience more negative and less positive emotion. Negative emotion is more likely when parents select forceful and coercive strategies to reduce incompatibility between parent and child concerns because this approach does not promote child concerns, restricts cooperation between parent and child, and heightens child resistance and noncompliance.

Through their effects on parental motivation, cognition, communication patterns, and behavior, activated emotions engage and organize processes affecting parenting (Dix, 1991). Chronically high levels of activated negative emotion are likely to contribute to disturbances in parenting through poor impulse control, cognitive distortions, and reduced sensitivity. High negative emotion in parents increases tendencies to focus on immediate reduction in the negative affect, resulting in an emphasis on short-term, parent goals over long-term, child developmental goals and the exertion of power tactics in parenting to gain immediate control (Maccoby & Martin, 1983). High negative emotion can disrupt parental reasoning and can contribute to more reflexive emotional responding from parents in efforts to gain control (Vasta, 1982). Negative expectations, perceptions, and evaluations of children also are more likely when negative affect is aroused in parents. Dix (1991) proposes that high negative emotion contributes to parental cognitive distortions, disrupts parental problem solving, and interferes with appropriate monitoring and attention. Each of these processes may reduce parental effectiveness. High negative emotion in parents is also expressed to children directly, increasing the likelihood of eliciting reciprocal negative emotion in children and contributing to negative, coercive interchanges.

Attempts of parents to regulate their emotions also are important for understanding parenting effectiveness (Dix, 1991). Whereas adequate parents may use a variety of cognitive and affective strategies to control or inhibit their expression of negative emotion (Dix, 1991), lack of control over negative emotion is likely to be present in parents who are struggling with a depressive illness.

Both the models of Belsky (1984) and Dix (1991) are useful in helping to conceptualize research findings on parenting and the caregiving context in instances of parental depression. Specifically, departures from these models may serve to elucidate the pathways through which depression in caregivers eventuates in poor-quality parenting and child maladaptation.

Parenting

A number of difficulties in children with depressed caregivers have been linked to dysfunctional parenting. Compared with nondepressed caregivers, parents with depression have been described as more inconsistent, lax, and ineffective in their child management and discipline (Cunningham, Benness, & Siegel, 1988; Forehand, Lautenschlager, Faust, & Graziano, 1986; Zahn-Waxler, Iannotti, Cummings, & Denham, 1990). In contrast, depressed caregivers also have been found to utilize more forceful control strategies (Fendrich, Warner, & Weissman, 1990). Overall, it appears that depressed caregivers try to avoid conflict with their children by accommodating to their child's demands and tolerating noncompliance. However, when efforts are made to set limits on child demands, depressed caregivers also are less likely to reach a compromise with their children (Kochanska, Kuczynski, Radke-Yarrow, & Welsh, 1987). Because relations have been reported between inconsistent, controlling, and lax parenting and externalizing child behavior problems (Loeber & Dishion, 1984), this style of parenting may contribute to the externalizing symptomatology reported in offspring of depressed caregivers. Increased inhibition to unfamiliar situations also has been noted in toddlers with depressed mothers, especially those with the most severe illnesses (Kochanska, 1991). This inhibition has been attributed to less involvement and less sensitivity in response to child wariness by depressed caregivers, in combination with infrequent encouragement of child exploration and frequent angry criticism of the child (Kochanska, 1991).

The self-critical styles of depressed caregivers also appear to be transmitted to offspring. One such mode of transmission relates to the speech used by depressed parents. Murray, Kempton, Woolgar, and Hooper (1993) found that the speech used by depressed women to their infants expressed more negative affect, was less focused on infant experience, and evidenced less acknowledgment of infant agency. Even in adolescence, increased irritability has been observed in the verbal interchanges between affectively ill mothers and their adolescents (Tarullo et al., 1994). The emotion socialization that is conveyed by depressed caregivers also may be especially important to consider for child development. In describing the emotions depicted by photographs of infants, Zahn-Waxler and Wagner (1993) reported that depressed mothers tended to view infants as more tearful and less joyous than did well mothers. Depressed mothers also were either more or less likely to identify sorrow in infants, a finding that suggests that depressed mothers may either deny the existence of sadness in their own infants or overattribute its presence (Zahn-Waxler & Wagner, 1993). Depressed mothers also have been shown to make more negative attributions about their children during mother-child interactions than well mothers (Radke-Yarrow et al., 1990). Depressed caregivers also have been shown to use more anxiety-and-guilt-inducing methods of discipline in combination with voiced disappointment in their children (Susman, Trickett, Iannotti, Hollenbeck, & Zahn-Waxler, 1985). The criticality of depressed caregivers also has been found to manifest itself through shouting and slapping (Panaccione & Wahler, 1986) and, in its more extreme forms, may result in hostile, coercive parenting.

Childrearing Context

In addition to the previously discussed dysfunctional parenting that characterizes the depressed caregiver, research concerning the marital relationship and the role of the nondisordered parent needs to be considered. Depressed persons tend to reside in adverse circumstances that may precede, co-occur with, and persist beyond their depression (Downey & Coyne, 1990). Chronic interpersonal difficulties commonly occur, particularly in close relationships (Coyne, 1976), and depressed women have a high rate of marital conflict (Weissman & Paykel, 1974). Moreover, research findings suggest that the interpersonal difficulties of depressed persons are more serious during an episode (Weissman & Paykel, 1974) and that persons' experiencing an active depression exert a markedly greater impact on their spouse's adjustment than recovered depressed persons (Coyne et al., 1987). Moreover, because of the tendency for assortative mating in depressed persons (Merikangas & Spiker, 1982) and for depression in one spouse to arouse stress in the marital partner (Coyne, 1976), children with a depressed parent are at high risk for poor parenting from both caregivers. Thus, it is unlikely that the nondepressed spouse can compensate adequately for the poor quality caregiving of depressed persons.

In an especially relevant study, Keller et al. (1986) investigated the effect of severity and chronicity of parental depression and marital discord on child psychopathology and adaptive functioning in a large group of children of unipolar depressed parents. Both severity of parental illness and marital distress were associated with poor adaptive functioning on current and lifetime DSM-III diagnoses (Keller et al., 1986). Likewise, Emery, Weintraub, and Neale (1982) found that marital discord was a stronger predictor of child competence in the offspring of depressives than in the offspring of schizophrenics or in controls. The role of the marital relationship and of the nondisordered spouse are important for understanding the sources of influences on the caregiving environment.

Rutter and Quinton (1984) have identified three possible mechanisms through which marital discord may contribute to child outcomes in children with a depressed caregiver. Specifically, they discuss: (a) marital discord as predating the emergence of a psychiatric disorder; (b) psychiatric disorder as causing impaired marital relationships; and (c) a process by which marital discord and psychiatric disorder are caused by prior conditions. Because research has shown that children are affected not only by their interactions with others, but also by what they observe (Cummings & Zahn-Waxler, 1992), exposure to negative parental interactions may constitute a major risk. In fact, after reviewing the literature on parental depression and child outcome, Downey and Coyne (1990) concluded that marital discord provides an alternative explanation for adjustment problems evidenced by the offspring of depressives.

The difficulties evidenced by children with a depressed caregiver also may be exacerbated by factors external to the nuclear family. Because depression frequently accompanies other adverse circumstances (e.g., poverty, limited knowledge of child development, stressful life events), disruptions in parenting are especially likely to occur. Similarly, these stressors may exacerbate parental depression, resulting in a negative cycle of depression, adverse circumstances, and maladaptive parenting. Over time, child behavior problems may emerge and enter into the negative cycle.

The isolated lifestyles of depressed persons also may result in increased adversity for children, as children with a depressed caregiver may be prevented from developing an extrafamilial support network (Cummings & Davies, 1994). Additionally, Zahn-Waxler and her colleagues have found that the few individuals the child may access outside the family are themselves frequently mentally ill or emotionally disturbed (Zahn-Waxler, Iannotti et al., 1990).

Thus, findings on the parenting provided by depressed caregivers, as well as the caregiving context within which they raise their children, may conspire to place these children at substantial risk for developmental failure and emotional difficulties. However, whereas a depressive illness may be immodifiable during its emergence and course, this is not the case for parenting and associated aspects of the caregiving context. Therefore, although parenting difficulties and a negative caregiving context may be present in conjunction with parental depression, it is also possible that even in the midst of parental depression positive parenting and/or related family circumstances may serve to buffer the adverse consequences of parental depression.

Genetics and the Development of Affective Disorders

The development of a mood disorder, as well as the age of its onset, is influenced not only by the emergence of salient issues or tasks that must be confronted throughout the life course, but also by timed biological events that create challenges and provide new opportunities as they figure prominently in every developmental phase. These genetic factors, though not all expressed at the earliest moments of life, contribute sources of vulnerability as well as resilience to the probabilistic unfolding of unipolar and bipolar illness.

For approximately three quarters of a century, we have possessed evidence that mood disorders are more commonly present among the relatives of depressed persons than in the general population. For example, the family members of patients with unipolar or bipolar disorder manifest an elevated risk for developing depressive or manic-depressive illness, respectively (McGuffin & Katz, 1989, 1993). Moreover, the empirical literature reveals that, in general, the greater the percentage of genes shared with the proband (i.e., the affected individual), the greater the probability that the relative will be similarly affected (Faraone, Kremen, & Tsuang, 1990; Tsuang & Faraone, 1990).

Additionally, the results of the small number of adoption studies conducted to date have largely documented that there is an increased rate of affective disorder in the biological relatives and not in the adopted relatives of the adoptees (see McGuffin & Katz, 1989; and Tsuang & Faraone, 1990 for reviews). Of note, the most methodologically sophisticated adoption studies have supported the importance of biological relatedness (over adoptive relationships) in the etiology of the affective disorders (see, e.g., Mendlewicz & Rainer, 1977; Wender et al., 1986).

Twin studies of affective illness have consistently revealed the concordance rates for monozygotic (MZ) twins to be substantially higher than in dizygotic (DZ) twins. For example, in their review of the early twin studies of the affective disorders, conducted prior to the era when depressive and manic-depressive illness were routinely differentiated from each other, Gershon, Bunney, Leckman, Van Eerdewegh, and Debauche (1976) concluded that the overall MZ concordance for affective illness was 69% compared with the DZ concordance of 13%. Additionally, in a more recent twin study that utilized cases ascertained from the Danish National Twin Register, Bertelsen, Harvald, and Hauge (1977) concluded that the genetic influences on bipolar illness were exceptionally strong. These investigators reported a heritability of bipolar disorder in excess of 80%, thereby underscoring the prominent role that genetic influences play in the evolution of bipolar illness.

Furthermore, several contemporary twin investigations have been carried out with probands who had unipolar disorder and with their cotwins. One of these studies focused on depressed patients derived from the Maudsley Hospital twin register in London (McGuffin, Katz, & Rutherford, 1991), whereas the other enrolled a sample of over 1,000 female-female twin pairs from a general population-based registry (Kendler, Neale, Kessler, Heath, & Eaves, 1992). In both of these studies, varying diagnostic definitions of depression were employed. Regardless of the divergence in how the depressed phenotype was delimited, the constant finding was of a higher concordance rate for unipolar depressive disorder in MZ twins than in DZ twins.

For example, Kendler and his colleagues (1992) utilized nine commonly employed definitions of depression, resulting in a range or continuum from narrowly to broadly conceptualized unipolar disorder. For the two most restrictive definitions of depression (i.e., including only cases of primary depression), the heritability coefficients were slightly over 20%. In contrast, the seven more broadly defined phenotypes yielded an estimated heritability of liability to unipolar depression that ranged between 33% and 45%. Thus, the results of the Kendler et al. (1992) study portray only a moderate amount of familial aggregation for depression, a finding that also is congruent with that obtained in family investigations (see, e.g., Weissman, Kidd, & Prusoff, 1982).

An intriguing conclusion from the findings of the Kendler et al. (1992) twin study is that environmental experiences are more critical than genes in increasing these female twins' liability to depression. The data of Kendler et al. (1992) show that environmental factors causally related to depression are those of the individual-specific environment (i.e., nonshared environment) and not of the shared family environment. In other words, in this investigation, the environmental factors that affected the development of depression were those that make twins growing up in the same family no more similar than pairs of children picked at random from the population (see Plomin & Daniels, 1987).

Although caution must be exerted before unequivocally accepting the conclusions of the Kendler et al. (1992) study as generalizable to the universe of individuals with unipolar depression, the findings support the hypothesis that stressful personal life events may exert a more powerful influence on the development of depression in members of an adult twin pair than do shared family experiences. Additional twin, family, adoption, and sibling studies, utilizing different designs, sampling techniques, and age periods need to be conducted to buttress and elaborate on these interesting results.

In addition to the similar findings that were previously noted between the twin studies conducted by Kendler et al. (1992) and McGuffin et al. (1991), a number of differences were obtained between the general population female twin sample of Kendler and colleagues (1992) and the patient twin sample of McGuffin

and colleagues (1991). Specifically, in contrast to Kendler et al. (1992), when McGuffin and his colleagues employed a broad definition of depression in the cotwins, additive genetic factors accounted for only 39% of the variance, with shared environment explaining 46%, and the remainder due to nonshared aspects of the environment. It appeared that it was the incorporation of hospital treatment into the broad definition of depression that eventuated in the substantial contribution of the shared family environment to the variance in liability. McGuffin and colleagues (1991) speculated that one of the major contributions of the family environment to depressive illness may be its role in facilitating the seeking of treatment.

In contrast, when McGuffin et al. (1991) utilized a narrow definition of the depression phenotype (i.e., DSM-III-R criteria), unlike in the Kendler et al. (1992) study, they found that 79% of the variance could be explained by additive genetic effects, with the remainder accounted for by nonshared environment.

In moving away from discussions about heritability coefficients and amount of variance accounted for by genetic, shared and nonshared environmental factors, two complex questions must be addressed: (a) what is the mode of genetic transmission in unipolar and bipolar illness?; and (b) what is it that persons with depressive and manic-depressive illness inherit?

In a review and synthesis of the existing literature, Faraone and his colleagues (1990) critically surveyed two major types of studies that focus on uncovering the mode of inheritance of the mood disorders: quantitative models of genetic transmission and linkage analyses. The major types of genetic models of the affective disorders that have been investigated are single major locus models, multifactorial polygenic models, and mixed models that include components of both single major locus and multifactorial polygenic models.

Based on their review, Faraone et al. (1990) concluded that specific support for a particular mode of genetic inheritance has yet to be found. Of note, some of the mixed models of genetic transmission that have been investigated yield data that support single major locus patterns of inheritance; however, the mathematical transmission probabilities are not in accord with the predictions emanating from a Mendelian model.

In efforts to provide more rigorous tests of the single gene hypothesis, linkage analyses have been carried out. Just as is the case with the results of the quantitative models studies, the findings from linkage investigations also have yielded inconsistent and equivocal support for a single gene model. To date, the linkage investigations have examined a small number of genetic loci. Perhaps as our knowledge of the human genome expands, researchers may discover loci that are consistently linked to certain subtypes of unipolar and bipolar disorders.

Despite these future possibilities, it is important to keep in mind the developmental psychopathology principles of equifinality and multifinality discussed earlier. Specifically, although we possess an ever-expanding knowledge of the genetics of adult (see e.g., Gottesman, 1991; Mullan & Murray, 1989; Pardes, Kaufmann, Pincus, & West, 1989) and childhood/adolescent (Plomin, Rende, & Rutter, 1991; Rutter et al., 1990) mental disorders, it has become widely recognized that psychiatric disorders pose difficulties for genetic research because of their etiologic heterogeneity (i.e., a given behavioral pattern can have different genetic pathways in different individuals) and pleiotropy (i.e., a single genotype can have different behavioral manifestations in different individuals). The genetic concepts of etiologic heterogeneity and pleiotropy bear striking resemblance to the systems-theory notions of equifinality and multifinality, respectively. The investigator who combines these principles with the oft-reported findings of incomplete penetrance and variable genetic expressivity encounters several possibilities: that there can be phenocopies of a given behavioral pattern without any genetic roots, that there are distal as well as proximal causes of psychiatric disorders, and that there certainly may exist individuals with no genetic risk factors who develop psychopathology (Richters & Cicchetti, 1993). Thus, it becomes quickly apparent why genetic investigations of the mood disorders must face many daunting challenges. Because the mode of inheritance of most forms of child and adult psychopathology appears to be multifactorially determined (i.e., due to the operation of several genes that act in combination), significant research lies ahead.

Over the past several decades, developmental theorizing has become increasingly infused into quantitative behavioral genetics (Cohen & Leckman, 1993; Plomin, 1986; Rutter, 1991; Scarr & McCartney, 1983). Moreover, there appears to be great promise for collaboration between the fields of developmental behavioral genetics and molecular genetics (Plomin et al., 1991). Much of this exciting progress can be traced to Gottesman's (1974) call for collaboration between developmentalists in psychology and genetics.

Developmental geneticists must strive to uncover the ontogenetic processes whereby genetic and environmental factors conspire to orchestrate normal and abnormal patterns of adaptation. For example, in the affective disorders it is important to ascertain how genetic as well as shared and nonshared environmental factors transact throughout ontogenesis. Especially helpful in this regard would be the identification of the factors that turn particular genes on and off during specific phases of development.

We now possess strong evidence from the field of molecular genetics that genes exert a dynamic and not a static influence on ontogenesis (see Gottesman & Goldsmith, 1994; Watson, Hopkins, Roberts, Steitz, & Weiner, 1987). Although all genes are present at birth, their effects may not be exerted until much later. Molecular geneticists have discovered that genetic activation may occur either for transient periods or be more enduring in nature (Watson et al., 1987). Noteworthy here, the presence of heterochromatin, a form of chromosomal structure that is not transcribed, denotes genetic inactivation for genes that contain this marker. In contrast, euchromatin, a form a chromosomal structure that undergoes transcription, signifies the activation of genes with this marker. During ontogenesis, certain genes apparently are genetically programmed to become activated at particular developmental periods, while becoming functionally inactive in other periods. For example, some regions of the genome are euchromatic during the early stages of life but become inactivated or heterochromatic during old age (Gottesman & Goldsmith, 1994; Watson et al., 1987). It is estimated that approximately 1% of our genes are undergoing transcription at any moment in time (Gottesman & Goldsmith, 1994). Additionally, a different 1% of genes are transcribed in the various types of cells that exist in humans. To complicate matters further, but

consistent with the characteristics of all developmental phenomena, geneticists believe that the percentage of genes that are expressed during a given temporal period are likely to differ according to the type of tissue involved. Furthermore, the nervous system is thought to be the most physiologically active site (Gottesman & Goldsmith, 1994).

As such, gene action, like psychological growth, persists throughout the life span and is not only a phenomenon of the early period of existence. Consequently, both genetic factors and psychological experiences can bring about developmental change across the life course. Furthermore, just as is true for psychologically mediated effects, consequences that are genetically mediated may be modified from infancy through senescence, both by subsequent experience and/or through later mechanisms of gene action (Gottesman & Goldsmith, 1994). So, genes may create particular physical structures early in ontogenesis (e.g., receptors for particular neurotransmitters in a specific tissue type), and the functioning of these structures subsequently may play a role in the unfolding of a particular normal or pathological behavioral disposition (e.g., withdrawal, negative affectivity, passivity). Nevertheless, gene action may occur at any point in the life course that could either modify these structures or cause a physiological process to unfold that affects particular individual behavioral dispositions (Gottesman & Goldsmith, 1994).

Furthermore, with regard to heritability coefficients, proportions of genetic and environmental variance that exist for a particular phenomenon (e.g., depression) at one period of development do not necessarily generalize to earlier or later phases of ontogenesis. Thus, with respect to twin, adoption, and family studies, it is essential not only to examine a variety of samples and age periods, but also to follow up the samples over time. In essence, each period of development conceivably may be characterized by different gene-environment relations for each individual and for each disorder.

A reasonable strategy for achieving an increased scientific understanding of the contribution of genetics to the causes and sequelae of psychopathology has been proposed by Gottesman, Carey, and Hanson (1983). These investigators recommended an epigenetic approach to the scientific investigation of a developmental psychopathology informed by human genetics. Gottesman and his colleagues (1983) advocate the viewpoint articulated by Waddington (1957) with respect to the fields of developmental genetics and embryology. In his classic book, *The Strategy of the Genes,* Waddington (1957) noted that to provide an analysis that is commensurately complex enough to account for human development, the investigator must consider the impact that three types of temporal change exert on this process. Moreover, each of these temporal elements operates contemporaneously and continuously throughout life.

In this epigenetic framework, Waddington stated that the macroscale of evolution provides the first temporal scale whereby humans are viewed as a species emanating from a long line of genetically related ancestors modified since the beginning of time by the process of natural selection. Concomitantly, in his discussions of the middle time scale, Waddington professed that it is essential to conceptualize human development from a life-span perspective, considering on the one extreme the importance of gathering knowledge from the scientific study of embryological processes, and on the other extreme, emphasizing the essential knowledge gleaned from the investigation of the aging process. Finally, on the microlevel, Waddington urged that researchers must devote their energies to molecular biological processes, including how genes are regulated, as well as to physiological processes (see Gottesman et al., 1983).

At this point in time, research on the genetics of mood disorders has yet to incorporate all three of the temporal dimensions proposed by Waddington concurrently. We see parallels between the ideas of Waddington (1957) and Gottesman et al. (1983) and the theoretical framework of the organizational perspective on development that we share with many individuals in the field of developmental psychopathology. In particular, it is essential to incorporate a longitudinal perspective over developmental time on the ever-changing interplay between molecular and molar biological and psychological systems across the life span and across generations—a central tenet of organizational developmental psychopathology. This approach captures the spirit of Waddington's and Gottesman et al.'s proposal for enhancing our understanding of biological-psychological interactions in psychopathological disorders throughout ontogenesis.

We believe that future research must focus on integrating the important lessons learned from molecular and behavioral genetics, with a concomitantly sophisticated developmental examination of biological, psychological, and environmental processes. Such work will greatly enhance our understanding of the role of genetics in the development of the neurobiological and behavioral characteristics displayed by individuals with unipolar and bipolar illness. Likewise, the communication of these developmental genetic principles to biologically and nonbiologically oriented researchers and clinicians will help to facilitate the elimination of any unidirectional biases in investigations of normal and abnormal development. It also will promote integrative research on the affective disorders that measures salient psychological and biological issues with the same individuals over developmental time.

Developmental Biology of the Affective Disorders

In addition to genetics, a developmental perspective on neurobiology, neurochemistry, neuropsychology, psychobiology, and psychophysiology can greatly enhance our understanding of normal and pathological affective processes. There has been a growing appreciation of the advantages and, indeed, the necessity of incorporating developmental principles into research on the biology and chemistry of the mood disorders. The investigation of these abnormal affective states can enhance our knowledge of the biological mechanisms involved in the regulation of normal socioemotional processes (see, e.g., Puig-Antich, 1986).

In a series of groundbreaking preliminary studies (Puig-Antich, Davies et al., 1984; Puig-Antich, Goetz, Davies, Fein, et al., 1984; Puig-Antich, Goetz, Davies, Tabrizi, et al., 1984; Puig-Antich, Novacenko et al., 1984), Puig-Antich and his colleagues demonstrated that prepubertal depressed children, like depressed adults, hyposecreted growth hormone in response to insulin-induced hypoglycemia, a finding that persisted during a medication-free recovery period. Moreover, children with major depressive disorder secreted increased sleep-stimulated

growth hormone, a result that likewise continued during recovery from a depressed episode.

Although Puig-Antich, Goetz, Hanlon, Davies, Thompson, Chambers, Tabrizi, and Weitzman (1982) did not discover any differences in sleep cytoarchitecture during the episode of depression, on recovery from the illness, the depressed children displayed reduced rapid eye movement (REM) latency (Puig-Antich et al., 1983). Finally, there were no differences between depressed and control children on either serum cortisol measures (Puig-Antich et al., 1989), or on response to the dexamethasone suppression test (DST) (Birmaher et al., 1992).

In more recent examinations of the psychobiology of prepubertal major depressive disorders, Ryan, Birmaher et al. (1992) and Ryan et al. (1994) have investigated depressed children's growth hormone (GH) responses, first to the serotonin precursor L-5-hydroxytryptophan (Ryan et al., 1992) and subsequently to several pharmacological probes, two operating at the level of the hypothalamus (i.e., insulin-induced hypoglycemia and clonidine) and one operating at the level of the pituitary gland (i.e., growth hormone-releasing hormone; GHRH) (Ryan et al., 1994).

In the first study, Ryan and his colleagues (1992) administered intravenous L-5-hydroxytryptophan over a 1-hour period to a group of depressed and nondepressed prepubertal children, after preloading with oral carbidopa. When given after carbidopa, L-5-hydroxytryptophan increases central nervous system turnover of serotonin. After this stimulation of the serotonergic system, prolactin, cortisol, and GH secretion were measured. Depressed children were found to secrete significantly less cortisol, and significantly more prolactin than was the case for the nondepressed controls. No significant differences were obtained between the two groups of children on GH secretion. Moreover, the hypersecretion of prolactin was observed only in depressed girls. Ryan et al. (1992) interpreted this array of findings as consistent with a dysregulation of central serotonergic systems in depressed children.

In a subsequent investigation, Ryan and his colleagues (1994) found, congruent with the results of their earlier study, that depressed children manifested blunted GH following insulin-induced hypoglycemia. Although the clonidine probe did not bring about the predicted hyposecretion of GH, nonetheless, Ryan et al. (1994) did find a blunted GH response to clonidine in those depressed children who had longer episode durations. Finally, contrary to the investigators' hypotheses, GHRH stimulation also yielded blunted GH responses in the depressed children. Taken in tandem, the results of the experiments of Puig-Antich, Ryan, Dahl, and their collaborators strongly suggest that GH dysregulation is characteristically observed in children with major depressive disorders. Based predominantly on the unexpected blunted GH response to GHRH, reflective of a hyporesponsive pituitary gland, Ryan and his colleagues (1994) have suggested that, consistent with their interpretation of the results of the investigation of Ryan et al. (1992), a dysregulation of the serotonergic systems could account for the blunted GH.

Extending their research to older ages, the investigative team of Puig-Antich, Ryan, and Dahl assessed the GH responses and sleep regulation of depressed adolescents. In one study, Ryan et al. (1988) examined the GH responses of depressed and suicidal adolescents to the pharmacological intramuscular injection of desmethylimipramine (DMI). The depressed adolescents were found to secrete significantly less GH than was the case for the normal control adolescents. Additionally, the largest subgroup differences were accounted for by the adolescents with suicidal major depressive disorder.

In another investigation, no significant differences of EEG sleep were found between depressed and nondepressed adolescents; however, subgroup analyses revealed that REM differences had occurred in the suicidal inpatient adolescents (Dahl et al., 1990). Likewise, 24-hour baseline cortisol measures did not differentiate the depressed and nondepressed adolescent outpatients (Dahl et al., 1989), but an investigation of inpatient depressives revealed that elevated cortisol occurred near sleep onset, a time when cortisol suppression is typically manifested (Dahl et al., 1991). Just as was the case with the sleep findings, Dahl and his colleagues (1991) discovered that the vast majority of the between-group differences were accounted for by the suicidal subgroup.

Dahl and his collaborators (1992) interpreted these results to reflect dysregulation around sleep onset in the suicidal adolescents with major depressive disorder. Specifically, Dahl et al. (1992) hypothesized that because sleep onset typically suppresses cortisol and enhances GH release, the findings of hyposecretion of GH and increased cortisol are interpreted as congruent with the presence of an impaired or weakened sleep-onset mechanism. Furthermore, the increased latency to falling asleep and the diminished REM latency likewise were consistent with the sleep onset dysregulation hypothesis proffered by Dahl et al. (1992).

Investigations of EEG sleep in adult depressed patients also reveal a number of disturbances thought to reflect a pathological state of arousal (Thase, Frank, & Kupfer, 1985). For example, dysregulations of sleep continuity occur, characterized by difficulty in falling asleep, frequent nighttime awakenings, and early morning wakening. In addition, a decreased arousal threshold and a decreased intensity and duration of slow-wave sleep and diminished REM latency time are observed. Furthermore, there is an increased amount of REM sleep activity and a shift of REM sleep activity into the initial hours of sleep (Kupfer & Thase, 1983; Thase et al., 1985).

Similarly, in the aggregate, investigations of hypothalamic-pituitary-adrenal (HPA) axis dysregulation in adults with major depressive disorder reveal a number of regulatory difficulties (Gold et al., 1988b). The results of these studies suggest the presence of diminished negative feedback sensitivity in a number of locations of the HPA axis (Yehuda, Giller, Southwick, Lowy, & Mason, 1991). Hypersecretion of urinary cortisol (and occasionally nonsuppression in the cortisol response to the DST—see Ribeiro, Tandon, Grunhaus, & Greden, 1993), a decrement in the typical number of glucocorticoid receptors, and an attenuated adrenocorticotropin hormone (ACTH) response to exogenous corticotropin-releasing factor (CRF), consistent with hypercortisolemia stemming from CRF hypersecretion (Yehuda, et al., 1991), characterize the HPA functioning of depressed adults. Moreover, Gold and his colleagues (1988b) conclude from their analysis of neuroendocrine abnormalities in adult patients with depression that a functional connection between the

corticotropin-releasing hormone (CRH) and the noradrenergic systems is of relevance to a series of central nervous system disturbances in depression. Finally, compared with nondepressed controls, adult depressed patients have elevated mean temperatures, as well as a flattened temperature curve, during sleep, again suggesting that depressed patients are in a chronic state of arousal (Gold et al., 1988b).

Finally, it is instructive to examine the developmental changes that normally occur in sleep across the life span. Dahl et al. (1992) describe children as very deep and highly efficient sleepers, who are hard to arouse from sleep and who sleep for long periods of time. During normal adolescence, sleep witnesses a large (40%) decrease in the duration and intensity of slow-wave sleep, a 30% to 40% decrement in REM latency, and an elevated sleepiness during the day (Dahl et al., 1992). Adults display a continued and steady decrease in slow-wave sleep, a diminished sleep efficiency, a decreased threshold of arousal from sleep, and a reduced REM latency.

Consequently, the EEG sleep changes found in the sleep of children and adolescents with major depressive disorder are somewhat similar to the age and developmental changes that occur in sleep during the normal process of aging (Kupfer & Thase, 1983; Thase et al., 1985). The most current interpretation of these findings of which we are aware holds that patients with major depressive disorder appear to manifest the normal age-related change of EEG sleep, but at an accelerated pace (Knowles & MacLean, 1990). Thus, as Puig-Antich (1986) aptly urged, to aid in the interpretation of patient data, investigators should break down EEG sleep profiles by the appropriate developmental period of the life span.

Within the past several decades, there has been a burgeoning recognition that neurotransmitter systems have dynamic characteristics (Siever & Davis, 1985). The time-dependent and stimulus-regulation properties of neurotransmitters, both mediated by multiple homeostatic mechanisms, are but a few examples of a broader reformulation that is occurring in research on the neurochemistry and neurobiology of mood disorders. Original neurochemical hypotheses that the levels of various neurotransmitter systems are either too high or too low (e.g., Prange, Wilson, Lynn, Alltop, & Stikeleather, 1974; Schildkraut, 1965; Van Praag, 1977), despite the great impact they have had in generating research on the pathophysiology of the mood disorders, are being reconsidered (Antelman & Caggiula, 1977; Siever & Davis, 1985).

In this regard, one exciting hypothesis that has great relevance to a developmental psychopathology perspective has been proposed by Siever and Davis (1985). Recognizing that there are a number of abnormalities in the pattern and degree of responsiveness of the activity of the neurotransmitter systems implicated in the mood disorders, and that various pharmacological agents function through the reequilibration of these neurotransmitters' activity, Siever and Davis (1985) proposed a dysregulation model of depression positing that a persistent impairment in one or more neurotransmitter regulatory or homeostatic mechanisms in depressed persons confers an enduring vulnerability to high variable, unstable, or erratic neurotransmitter output. Furthermore, Siever and Davis (1985) delimit additional criteria that are suggestive of a dysregulated neurotransmitter system in depression: inappropriate (i.e., less selective) environmental responsiveness, defective habituation (i.e., a slower return to baseline functioning following a perturbation), and restoring of normal functioning through the administration of the appropriate pharmacological agents of the dysregulated neurotransmitter system. Siever and Davis (1985) use data on noradrenergic system functioning in depressed persons to illustrate how their dysregulation model can address the criteria by which a dysregulated neurotransmitter system can be established.

In a related vein, in her integrative review of the literature on serotonin role in human information processing, Spoont (1992) concludes that serotonin functions in a nonspecific modulatory capacity in all mammals. More generally, Spoont (1992) proposed that the modulation of neurobiological systems may be conceived as a component of a homeostatic system, whereby the activity of the modulator helps to confer stability (i.e., regulation) on the system's output.

The role of serotonin in information processing is to regulate the flow of information through a neural system. Spoont conceptualized serotonin's constraining information flow in a regulatory system as having a dual purpose: preventing an overshoot of other dynamic elements within the neural system and controlling how the neural system responds to the perturbation of new elements entering into it.

Based on her synthetic review of the literature, Spoont (1992) contended that deviations in serotonin activity disrupt or dysregulate phase coherence and result in altered neural information processing and destabilization of affect, cognition, and behavior. In essence, Spoont postulates that there is a dissociation between affect and behavior, two systems that in the normal course of development are coupled under the modulatory function of serotonin.

Key to Spoont's (1992) thesis is that alterations in neurotransmitter functioning do not elicit specific pathological conditions such as violent suicide and aggression. Instead, these neurotransmitter alterations are associated with a biased processing of information that affects how the neural system responds to novel elements that enter it, thereby modifying the typical stability that exists between serotonin activity, affect, and behavior. In essence, alterations in the neurotransmitter serotonin may be portrayed as a vulnerability factor to developing behavioral and affective instability.

Based on an intriguing set of clinical, experimental, and pharmacological observations, Post and his colleagues (Post, 1992; Post et al., 1986; Post et al., in press) have proposed that a subgroup of depressed patients become increasingly vulnerable, or sensitized, to recurrent episodes of affective disorder. Essentially, Post and his colleagues suggest that patients with recurrences of affective disorders exhibit the characteristics of a process similar to electrophysiological kindling, in which the biological processes involved in the patient's mood disorder become triggered more readily by the same circumstances or precipitants with each successive bout of the illness (see Post et al., 1986).

Several clinical and epidemiological aspects of the mood disorders served as the foundation for the hypotheses and experiments carried out in Post's laboratory. As noted earlier in this chapter, in the majority of patients with unipolar and bipolar disorder, multiple recurrences are common (Goodwin & Jamison, 1990; Kraepelin, 1921; Perris, 1966; Zis & Goodwin, 1979). In addition, the frequency of recurrence and rapid cycling increase as a function not only of age, but also of the number of previous episodes (Kraepelin, 1921; Zis & Goodwin, 1979). Moreover, episodes that occur later in the course of a mood disorder may be characterized by increasing severity and a more precipitous onset than earlier episodes. Finally, persons who experience recurrent affective disorders display progressively shorter interepisode periods of remission, and the illness appears to take on a life of its own, evolving with its own spontaneity and rhythmicity. In contrast to the first episode of a depressive or manic-depressive illness, which often is associated with major psychosocial precipitants, episodes that occur later in the course of an affective disorder often take place without any apparent relation to the depressed person's current life events (see Post, 1992; Post et al., 1986).

These data led Post and his colleagues (Post et al., 1986) to observe that two models of the development of progressive behavioral dysfunction—electrophysiological kindling and behavioral sensitization—could offer important insight into the biological and clinical variables operating in unipolar and bipolar illness. Both of these paradigms bring about long-lasting, perhaps permanent, changes in neuronal excitability that have parallels to the natural evolution of unipolar and bipolar illness.

In the electrophysiological model of amygdala-kindled seizures, there is a progression from a number of repeated occurrences of full-blown seizures that take place in response to intermittent, previously subconvulsant stimulation current, to seizures that take place autonomously, in the absence of any exogenous stimulation. This kindlinglike process can be observed in some patients with unipolar and bipolar illness who, with each subsequent episode, become more readily triggered by the same precipitant and who may develop the episodes in the absence of these circumstances (e.g., the rapid or continuous cycling of mood observed in some patients with manic-depression).

Behavioral sensitization serves as another model of long-term changes in the responsivity of the central nervous system that can serve as a paradigm for spontaneous episodes that appear in recurrent affective illness. When sensitization takes place, stimulants or moderate doses of local anesthetics produce behavioral changes that develop with a more rapid onset, an increased magnitude, and a longer duration. Analogous to the sensitization paradigm, depressed persons who become manic during their first treatment with a monoamine ozidase inhibitor (MAOI) enter into mania sooner in the course of subsequent MAOI treatment (Goodwin & Jamison, 1990). Post and his colleagues (1986) believe that similar sensitizations may take place in manic episodes that are not drug induced.

Post (1992) postulates that there is both sensitization to stressors and episode sensitization and that these become encoded at the level of gene expression. Moreover, the neurochemical and microstructural synaptic mechanisms of the affective disorders may differ as a function of the particular stage in their temporal course. If Post's theoretical notions prove to be correct, then a sequentially unfolding developmental reconceptualization of the neurobiology of affective disorder would need to replace prior static depictions. In essence, Post's viewpoint conceives the neurobiology of the mood disorders as a dynamic, moving process that changes depending on the temporal stage in the longitudinal progression of the illness.

Of critical clinical import, based on the electrophysiological kindling and behavioral sensitization models, early treatment of affective disorders appears necessary to minimize the development of later phases of the illness, such as multiple recurrences and rapid cycling. Moreover, the parallels between these models and the course of affective illness implicate a crucial role for psychopharmacological prophylaxis.

Because "episodes beget episodes" in a number of patients with depressive and manic-depressive illness, the repeated occurrence of episodes triggered by circumstances and precipitating stressors can result in episodes without apparent external provocation, suggesting that long-term pharmacological prevention is extremely important. The biological mechanisms underlying episode and stressor sensitization may confer a lifelong vulnerability to recurrent mood disorder in some patients with unipolar and bipolar illness (Post, 1992; Post et al., in press).

Clinical evidence congruent with the sensitization model documents that even several decades of successful lithium treatment do not ensure the absence of episode recurrence on cessation of drug treatment (Post, 1990). Post (1990) also has reported that a subgroup of patients who have been episode-free for significant periods of time while on lithium develop breakthrough episodes that are consistent with the development of drug tolerance. Moreover, Post, Leverich, Altshuler, and Mikalauskas (1992) have described a small series of patients who were initially responsive to lithium, developed recurrent episodes upon discontinuation of the drug, and were nonresponsive to subsequent reinstatement of lithium prophylaxis. Post (1992) speculates that it is conceivable that not only may episodes of affective illness leave behind neurobiological residues that produce a vulnerability to future relapses, but also that the occurrence of these episodes may generate new mechanisms that can cause a previously successful intervention to no longer be effective. A logical corollary is that different medications may be effective at different points in the illness.

Finally, Post and his colleagues (Post, 1992; Post et al., 1986) have put forth the intriguing hypothesis that sensitization to the recurrent stressors related to intense dysphoria (e.g., separation, loss, assaults on self-esteem) might play a role in the natural evolution of recurrent mood disorder. Not unlike our earlier discussion of the neurobiology of representational models of attachment figures and of the self in relation to others, it is feasible that anticipation of separation from a loved one, loss, abandonment, blows to self-esteem, and the like could produce depression. Conceivably, the thoughts and feelings consistently evoked by memory of the events associated with a depressive episode could acquire the properties of a conditioned stimulus, thereby generating an episode of depression even without any actual external perturbation.

Evidence from converging lines of research has contributed to an enhanced comprehension of the role of the cerebral hemispheres in emotional functioning in normal infants, children, and adults (see, e.g., Fox & Davidson, 1984; Tucker & Williamson, 1984). Although controversy has surrounded their interpretation, the findings generated by these investigations have provided a firm foundation of knowledge regarding the hemispheric substrates of emotion. Moreover, in that the emotional dysfunctions of infants, children, and adults can be conceptualized and understood as distortions of normal emotional processes, a developmental neuropsychological perspective of the mood disorders across the life course can inform us about the normal ontogenesis of these hemispheric substrates of emotion.

One important source of information about the neural bases of emotion in adults derives from neuropsychological assessments of patients in whom there is evidence of emotional dysfunction as a result of brain damage, epilepsy, or psychopathology. Other information has come from studies that have utilized the electroencephalogram (EEG) to assess the patterns of brain activation associated with normal emotional functioning. The findings from these investigations suggest that various key aspects of emotional perception and production are lateralized. For example, patients with left frontal brain damage consistently have been found to show a "catastrophic depressive reaction," whereas patients with right frontal brain damage demonstrate euphoria and indifference to their condition (see Davidson, 1991, for a historical review).

Within the central nervous system, hemispheric asymmetries and the lateralization of neurotransmitter systems also may influence arousability to stimulation and individual differences in emotion processing. Tucker and Williamson (1984) have proposed that the right hemisphere is associated with the general arousal or activation of the brain. Through the interaction of noradrenergic and serotonergic systems, this hemisphere is particularly sensitive to change and helps to alert the brain to novelty in the environment. In contrast, Tucker and Williamson (1984) argue, the left hemisphere is dominated by dopaminergic and cholinergic motor systems that appear to be relatively nonresponsive to novelty. Rather, through the interaction of both neurotransmitter systems, the left hemisphere appears to be biased toward redundancy; novel environmental occurrences do not disrupt their activation, thereby enabling the person to carry out motor acts within a changing environment.

Several EEG studies of subjects engaged in normal emotional functioning have identified different patterns of frontal hemispheric activation asymmetries associated with positive versus negative emotions. In the main, there appears to be relatively less left frontal activation and/or greater right frontal activation during negative emotional states, such as sadness, disgust, and fear. This asymmetry is reversed for positive emotions, such as happiness and interest.

Because information regarding the underlying brain mechanisms is still not definitive, the results of these experiments have led researchers to different conclusions about how affect is lateralized. Although some researchers have attributed a greater role to the left hemisphere in the production of negative affect, others have stated that it has a positive bias that results in negative affect. It also has been argued that, depending on the level of activation associated with the frontal region of the right hemisphere, affect will shift from negative to positive.

Because interhemispheric connections are underdeveloped at birth has led some to hypothesize that behavior may be characterized by a simple continuum of approach (i.e., redundancy) or withdrawal (i.e., activation) behaviors (Davidson, 1991; Fox & Davidson, 1984). The infant's position on this continuum is dependent on which hemisphere is activated and the intensity of its response. Thus, a person's emotionality may reflect individual differences in the relative dominance and reactivity of the left and right hemispheres to stimulation. For example, infants with greater right-brain activation may be more prone to overstimulation and distress than other infants. Consequently, they may be extremely sensitive and distracted by changes in their environment. Conversely, infants with greater left-brain activation may be perceived as less distressed by change in their environment and more persistent. This latter group of babies also may demonstrate difficulties in shifting and/or refocusing attention (Rothbart, Posner, & Hershey, in this work, Volume 1, Chapter 11).

Although a consistent pattern of hemispheric specialization for emotion appears to be emerging from the adult literature, it was not until the past several decades that systematic investigations of such patterns were conducted in other periods of ontogenesis. In the first study that examined the existence of EEG activation frontal asymmetry in infants, Davidson and Fox (1982) recorded the EEG of 10-month-old infants in response to positive and negative videotapes. The babies exhibited greater relative left-sided frontal activation in response to the happy video segment and greater relative right-sided activation in response to the sad segment.

Studies of adults have indicated that resting EEG differences among subjects are related to differences in emotional style. A similar finding has been reported for infants (Davidson & Fox, 1989). Ten-month-old babies with resting right frontal activation were more likely to cry in response to brief maternal separation than were those with left frontal activation during rest. Such a finding suggests that important individual differences in hemispheric asymmetries may effect a predisposition toward a particular affective style—either positive or negative (see, e.g., Watson & Clark, 1984; Watson, Clark, & Carey, 1988; Watson & Tellegen, 1985).

Fox and Davidson (1984) have hypothesized that sadness is a complex emotion whose expression is mediated bilaterally and that, therefore, requires maturation of the cerebral commissures. In support of this hypothesis, Fox and Davidson cite evidence for a close link between the onset of locomotion and the concomitant development of the expression of fear and sadness. In their view, both developments have their neural substrates in the maturation of certain cerebral commissural pathways. Consequently, they believe that a clear experience of sadness is not possible until the first half of the second year of life. From this perspective, it would appear that if a depressive episode can occur during infancy (see, e.g., Trad, 1986), it might not be accompanied by feelings of sad affect until the second year of life.

The suggestion by Fox and Davidson (1984) that the ability to inhibit negative affect during the second year of life may have a neural basis in the increased inhibition by the left hemisphere of the right hemisphere, made possible by the development of transcallosal pathways, also is of interest to understanding the affective disorders in childhood. Fox and Davidson argue that, in addition to the more advanced differentiation that occurs in the functional development of the commissural pathways, the increased functional activity of the left hemisphere associated with language development may be the underlying change in brain function responsible for the greater affective regulation that is observable in the middle of the second year (Kagan, 1981). Thus, infants who are old enough to express fully developed sadness, but who have not yet developed the neural substrates for the inhibition of negative affect, may be at particular risk for the development of depression. This is especially likely if the infant is the offspring of one or both parents with an affective disorder. Moreover, based on work conducted by Goldman (1971) on the development of the prefrontal cortex in early life in nonhuman primates, and by Diamond and Goldman-Rakic (1989) on comparative studies of human infants and rhesus monkeys on Piaget's AB task of object permanence, we think it highly likely that the dorsolateral prefrontal cortex may be the neural mechanism that inhibits negative affect.

In an impressive series of programmatic investigations, Davidson and his colleagues have studied asymmetric brain function in subclinically depressed college students chosen on the basis of extreme scores on the DBI and in actual clinically depressed persons (see, e.g., Davidson, 1991, 1993; Henriques & Davidson, 1991; Tomarken & Davidson, 1994). Davidson (1991) hypothesizes that depression is a disorder of approach, a viewpoint that receives support from the clinical presentation of depressed persons, who often display decreased interest in objects and people, anhedonia, and motor retardation. Decreased left-hemisphere activation often results in depressive symptomatology (see, e.g., Allen, Iacono, Depue, & Arbisi, 1993) and is characterized by decreased approach behaviors and an increased vulnerability to negative affect. According to Davidson (1991), activation asymmetries are necessary but not sufficient to cause depression. Consistent with a diathesis-stress experience-dependent model, the environmental elicitors also must be present.

Davidson's studies have revealed that, concordant with his thesis that there is a deficit in approach mechanisms in depression, persons with a mood-disorder display less left-sided activation than is the case with nondepressed control subjects (Henriques & Davidson, 1991). Moreover, Davidson (1991) found that depressed persons showed greater relative right-hemisphere frontal activation and concomitant decreased left-hemisphere activation. Additionally, in a replication of this experiment, Davidson (1991) found that depressed persons exhibited decreased relative right-sided parietal activation. Based on these results, Davidson speculated that there may be two underlying vulnerabilities to depression, decreased left anterior activation and decreased right posterior activation.

Because the latter deficit may be associated with visuospatial processing impairments, Davidson assessed the performance of subclinically depressed and nondepressed individuals on verbal and spatial tasks. The subclinically depressed persons manifested a selective deficit on the spatial task, documenting that they have an impairment on right-hemisphere cognitive tasks. Davidson conjectured that these right-hemisphere cognitive impairments may contribute to the deficits in social skills and in the perception of nonverbal emotional expression often seen in depressed persons. We believe that it might be the case that the depression associated with a subgroup of children may be mediated through a neuropsychological deficit involving the right posterior regions of the brain. Because of their inability to rely on social cues to negotiate increasingly complex social situations throughout their development, these children may become increasingly isolated and alienated, leading to depression (cf. Dodge, 1993). Such an example highlights our earlier point that there is a heterogeneity of etiological pathways to depressive illness.

Davidson (1991) also reports the results of a study comparing the hemispheric activation asymmetries of individuals who had never experienced a bout of depression with a group of depressed persons who had been devoid of a depressive episode for one year and who were currently not taking any antidepressant medication. Although the two groups did not differ in their current level of depression, differences in hemispheric activation asymmetries were obtained. Specifically, the group of previously depressed individuals displayed decreased activation in the left frontal area when compared with the never-depressed group of individuals.

These findings suggest that hypoactivation of the left hemisphere may be a trait marker or vulnerability factor that predisposes a person to depression. The identification of these persons before their first depressive episode and the provision of appropriate intervention might prevent these individuals from developing a depressive disorder. Alternatively, this biological marker may have appeared during the person's first depressive episode and never attained normalcy during periods of remission. Thus, such a scenario suggests that the biological anomaly is like a scar or sequela of the first depressive episode, and not a veridical trait marker.

Davidson, Finman, Rickman, Straus, and Kagan (1993) have demonstrated that behaviorally inhibited children (see Kagan, 1994), who may be at an elevated risk for affective or anxiety disorders (see, e.g., Kochanska, 1991), display relative left anterior hypoactivation during resting EEG when compared with uninhibited children. Samples of high-risk children such as these must be followed up prospectively to ascertain whether left frontal hypoactivation is a trait marker specific to depression, or a more general marker of risk for psychopathology. Because the temperamental quality of behavioral inhibition can undergo change with socialization throughout development (Kagan, 1994), it also is conceivable that the relative left anterior hypoactivation may normalize during ontogenesis.

Whereas nondepressed persons often demonstrate unrealistic optimism and overestimate their abilities and the amount of control that they have over environmental contingencies (see, e.g., Shedler, Mayman, & Manis, 1993), depressed individuals do not engage in this self-enhancing cognitive style and instead are characterized by what Alloy and Abramson (1988) have called "depressive realism." The breakdown of the "self-deceptive" mechanisms in depressed persons is thought to enhance their risk for developing psychopathology (Alloy & Abramson, 1988). Tomarken and Davidson (1994) have provided evidence suggesting that relative left frontal activation may be associated with a self-enhancing regulatory style that might conceivably promote a lowered risk for depression and, perhaps, other forms of psychopathology. The ultimate fate of this intriguing hypothesis awaits confirmation (or refutation) by prospective longitudinal research.

The results of these psychophysiological investigations suggest that there may be individuals who are vulnerable to depression, as evidenced by long-term hemispheric activation asymmetries. A plausible explanation is that the hypoactivation of the left hemisphere and the overactivation of the right hemisphere may have a genetic basis. On the other hand, particular experiences, conceivably, can affect the developing brain structures and prime them for chronic activation asymmetry (see, e.g., Tucker, 1981). In that hemispheric asymmetries may be mediated by both genetic factors and socialization, the offspring of depressives may be especially at risk for developing a negative affect bias. Work by Dawson and her colleagues is beginning to shed important light on this topic (Dawson, Grofer Klinger, Panagiotides, Hill, & Spieker, 1992; Dawson, Grofer Klinger, Panagiotides, Spieker, & Frey, 1992; Dawson, Hessl, & Frey, in press).

In Dawson, Grofer Klinger, Panagiotides, Hill, and Spieker's (1992) first investigation addressing frontal lobe activation and affective behavior, EEG frontal and parietal activity were recorded from a group of infants whose mothers had elevated depressed symptomatology. A second group of babies whose mothers did not display increased depressive symptomatology served as the comparison group.

The EEGs of these babies, 14 months old on average, were recorded during resting and several emotion-eliciting conditions. In comparison with infants of nonsymptomatic mothers, the babies whose mothers exhibited elevated depressed symptomatology displayed reduced left frontal brain activation during baseline and playful interactions with their mothers. Moreover, infants of mothers with elevated depressed symptoms did not display the typical pattern of greater right frontal activation that was shown by the infants of nonsymptomatic mothers during a condition that elicits distress (i.e., maternal separation). In view of earlier discussion about the neural bases of inhibition of negative emotion occurring during the second year of life, as well as the finding that left hemisphere inhibitory mechanisms appear to regulate particular negative affects (e.g., sadness, fear), the findings that the infants of mothers with elevated depressive symptomatology had both reduced stress and enhanced left frontal activation during the maternal separation condition is especially intriguing.

Additionally, the infants of symptomatic mothers manifested less distress during the maternal separation condition than did the infants of nonsymptomatic mothers. The two groups of infants also did not differ in their behavior during the playful condition with mother. Finally, the infants of symptomatic mothers did not differ in their patterns of parietal lobe brain activity, suggesting that the differences obtained in brain activation were specific to the frontal lobe region.

In a further examination of this same sample, Dawson, Grofer Klinger, Panagiotides, Spieker, and Frey (1992) investigated the relation between quality of infant-mother attachment and frontal and parietal brain activation patterns in response to the positive- and negative-emotion-eliciting conditions described in their initial paper. Both during baseline and the free-play interaction with their mothers, securely attached infants of symptomatic mothers displayed left frontal hypoactivation asymmetries compared with securely attached babies of nonsymptomatic mothers. Additionally, during the maternal separation condition, infants of symptomatic mothers, independent of their attachment classification, exhibited reduced right frontal activation patterns and lower levels of behavioral upset. Dawson, Grofer Klinger, Panagiotides, Spieker, and Frey (1992) interpret these findings as evidence that both the emotional wellness of the mother and the quality of her attachment relationship with her infant can influence infant frontal lobe brain activation and emotional behavior.

The results of the aforementioned Dawson, Grofer Klinger, Panagiotides, Hill, and Spieker (1992) and Dawson, Grofer Klinger, Panagiotides, Spieker, and Frey (1992) studies parallel those of Davidson and his colleagues (e.g., Davidson, 1991), who also discovered that depressed adults exhibited left frontal activation asymmetries during resting EEGs. Thus, the EEGs of infants with symptomatic mothers may be interpreted either as reflecting a lower threshold for the experience of negative affect or a higher threshold for the experience of positive emotions (Davidson & Fox 1989; Dawson, Grofer Klinger, Panagiotides, Hill, & Spieker 1992). Consequently, the infants with symptomatic mothers appear to have an enhanced tendency toward developing negative emotionality (cf. Watson & Clark, 1984; Watson & Tellegen, 1985).

The securely attached offspring of the depressed mothers displayed the reduced left frontal activation, whereas the insecurely attached infants of depressed mothers did not differ from the infants of the nondepressed mothers. Although preliminary, these results suggest that the negative effects of maternal depression on infant brain activation are not mediated exclusively through an insecure attachment relationship. In fact, the development of an insecure relationship with a symptomatic mother may protect the infant from developing some of the negative sequelae associated with her condition. Finally, when the effects of maternal depressive symptoms and attachment security on parietal EEG were investigated, no statistically significant findings occurred, suggesting that the obtained group differences in attachment security and elevated maternal depressed symptomatology were specific to the frontal lobe area. These data also are consistent with those reported in the adult depression literature (see, e.g., Davidson, 1988, 1991).

Although additional work needs to be conducted utilizing larger samples (e.g., to have large enough cell sizes of securely and insecurely attached babies) and mothers who either have had and/or are experiencing a clinical depression, the findings of Dawson and her colleagues are exciting. In his important book, *Neural Darwinism,* Edelman (1987) describes the great variability that is found in patterns of synaptic connection and states that some of this heterogeneity takes place as a result of differential experiences during sensitive periods for synaptogenesis. Consistent with Edelman's (1987) thesis, the findings of Dawson and her colleagues suggest that a mother's emotional condition (and implicitly her interactions with her baby) can impact on developing patterns of synaptogenesis in the early years of life (see, e.g., Dawson et al., in press; also see Cicchetti & Tucker, 1994).

CONCLUSIONS

Despite its exciting beginnings, there is a great deal to be accomplished in advancing an integrative developmental understanding of the affective disorders. The burgeoning literature emanating from attachment theory should prove to be fruitful in enhancing our comprehension of how organizations of cognitive, socioemotional, and representational experiences are internalized and carried forward throughout development, affecting the course of adaptation and the evolution of the mood disorders. Future research on attachment organization must pay increased attention to the interface between the psychological and biological domains. How, for example, might insecure internal representational models affect brain function or modify brain organization, neurophysiological functioning, and information processing, and how might genetic heritage alter tendencies for certain forms of representational processes to occur (cf. Dawson, Grofer Klinger, Panagiotides, Spieker, & Frey 1992)? It also will be important to ascertain whether, for example, the changes in brain organization that precede and/or are consequences of a mood disorder can be normalized through appropriate intervention.

Future research also should provide more detail regarding the differential strength of various risk and protective factors and how these vary during different developmental periods. For example, might there be certain "sensitive periods" in development during which a confluence of factors is likely to result in the emergence of a manic or a depressive episode (cf. Post et al., in press)? Interdisciplinary collaborative research among neuroscientists, epidemiologists, sociologists, and developmental psychopathologists bodes well for advancing our knowledge about the weighing of these risk and protective factors throughout ontogenesis. Increased consideration of the various types of precursor prototypic dysthymic, depressive and manic-depressive organizations that may exist and of how risk and protective factors and processes may influence these organizations throughout the life course also hold great promise.

In addition, increased attention must be paid to the heterogeneity that characterizes the mood disorders. As Hammen (1992b) has pointed out, theoreticians, researchers, and clinicians often utilize the singular term depression to refer to a heterogeneous group of disorders. It is conceivable that each of these various subgroups of depressive and manic-depressive disorders possess differential risk and protective factors at different points in the life cycle. Moreover, there are treatments that are more effective for various depressive and manic-depressive subtypes (Belsher & Costello, 1988; Post et al., in press; Schildkraut, 1976), as well as times during the course of an affective disorder when it may be preferable to use a particular psychological and/or biological intervention (Post, 1992).

Along these lines, increased clarity and specification of the nature of the sampling techniques and the samples employed in each investigation must be provided by the investigators. For example, individuals drawn from randomly selected community samples are likely to differ in many respects from clinic samples of child, adolescent, and adult inpatients and outpatients. In addition, psychological investigations of the mood disorders often center on less severely depressed individuals, whereas biologically oriented studies generally include more severely ill samples of depressed persons. Moreover, if investigators lump together various mood disorder subtypes, the resultant data-analytic strategies utilized will obscure the equifinality, genetic heterogeneity, multifinality, and pleiotropy that are inherent to a developmental analysis of the affective disorders.

For example, there is growing consensus that there are multiple pathways to depression. Moreover, not all depressed or manic-depressive individuals experience each potential biological or psychological dysfunction that is examined. Likewise, various modalities of psychological intervention and medication show differential rates of effectiveness with different people. Additionally, because not all biological and psychological systems are investigated concurrently in each person, much valuable information about the mood disorders is being lost by focusing on groups of individuals and by forming overly inclusive subgroups. Furthermore, most investigations of the biological and psychological causes and consequences of depressive and manic-depressive illness do not note the possibility that females and males may traverse through differential developmental pathways (for notable exceptions to the lack of attention to gender in depression, see Gjerde & Block, in press; Kendler, Kessler, Neale, Heath, & Eaves, 1993; Petersen et al., 1993; Rierdan & Koff, 1993; Zahn-Waxler & Kochanska, 1990). It would be interesting to ascertain, for example, whether females exhibit a greater frequency of left frontal hypoactivation asymmetries as a result of their ruminative depressed styles and other risk factors than is the case for males. Likewise, it will be important to determine the similarities and differences that may exist in the depressotypic organization of psychological and biological systems in females and males. We share Hammen's (1992b) belief that integrative theories of mood disorder subtypes are woefully lacking and that more attention should be paid to their formulation and testing (see, e.g., Abramson et al., 1989).

The multiplicity of pathways contributing to the development of an affective disorder directs us toward studying the interface between normal and abnormal development. Developmental psychopathology draws attention to both the similarities and differences among normal and psychopathological conditions. Consequently, researchers can discern both the specific pathways leading to the mood disorders, as well as discover the commonalities underlying normal development, affective illness, and related disorders. In particular, increased attention to the pathways and trajectories taken by individuals who avoid developing a mood disorder despite the presence of enduring vulnerabilities and transient challengers may help inform prevention and intervention efforts.

In contrast to earlier writings that claimed mood disorders arising in childhood will diminish over time if left to run their course, we now possess longitudinal data demonstrating that once a mood disorder remits, it often reemerges and impairs children's ability to negotiate developmental tasks competently. Likewise, a number of investigations have followed up adults with depressive and manic-depressive disorders over time and found that serious psychological impairments often occur both during the illness proper and in the period of remission. Now that developmental psychopathologists have discovered how depressed individuals negotiate a number of the stage-salient issues throughout the life course, we are in a position to assess not only how an incompetent organization of biological and behavioral

systems can contribute to the development of a mood disorder, but also to discern how the presence of a mood disorder affects competence both during an episode and in remission. We urge that further longitudinal research on the differentiation of each of these tasks throughout the life course be investigated more fully.

To achieve this important goal, researchers in normal and abnormal development must work together. Thus, because each stage-salient issue cuts across multiple developmental domains (e.g., biological, cognitive, socioemotional, and representational), there is a need for continued application of knowledge of basic research in these domains from normal development to the field of developmental psychopathology. Conversely, developmental psychologists must realize that the study of these domains in children and adults with mood disorders can enhance our knowledge of developmental theory (e.g., the nature of the relation between cognition and emotion—see Beck, 1967; Hesse & Cicchetti, 1982). As such, investigations of how depressed adults and elderly depressed persons negotiate the critical issues of their respective periods (cf. Erikson, 1950) must be conducted. Moreover, because research on bipolar disorder is increasingly adopting a unidirectional biological focus, it is essential that research on the psychological developments that take place in concert with biological processes throughout the life span be undertaken in individuals with manic-depressive illness and their offspring.

Relatedly, the developmental considerations raised in this chapter make clear that progress toward a process-level understanding of the mood disorders will require research designs and strategies that allow for the simultaneous consideration of multiple domains of variables within and outside the individual. For some questions, reference to variables measured in other domains is essential to clarify the role(s) of variables of interest. In other cases, variables from other domains are necessary to consider as competing explanations for hypothesized etiologic pathways. We believe that the most pressing and important research questions are those that can be answered only in the broader context of theoretically informed variables within and outside the mood-disordered individual, particularly as these variables change and influence one another over developmental time. Moreover, the organizational perspective, with its emphasis on understanding the organization of biological and psychological development and its focus on studying the "whole person" in context, will play an important role in framing the questions as we seek to explore the nature of the relation between psychological and biological factors in the symptoms, causes, course, sequelae, and treatment responsivity of affective disorders.

In a seminal article on the biology of emotion, Schildkraut and Kety (1967) pointed out that few studies had examined the concurrent links between the psychological and biological aspects of normal and abnormal emotion. As they noted:

The interactions between environmental determinants of affect, various physiological factors, and the complexity of psychological determinants, *including cognitive factors derived from the individual's remote and immediate past experiences,* have received only limited study under adequately controlled conditions. (Schildkraut & Kety, 1967, p. 28, emphasis ours)

Likewise, they presciently argued:

It is not likely that changes in the metabolism of the biogenic amines alone will account for the complex phenomena of normal or pathological affect . . . any comprehensive formulation of the physiology of affective state will have to include many other concomitant biochemical, physiological, and psychological factors. (Schildkraut & Kety, 1967, p. 28)

We, too, believe that cross-fertilization of the neurosciences with psychology will result in major advances in our comprehension of the mood disorders, especially if a developmental perspective to these collaborative ventures is adopted by the investigators. In this regard, we wish to underscore a fundamental maxim that must characterize any interdisciplinary research: Adequate and state-of-the-art assessments must be made of each domain, biological, psychological, or environmental, that is examined. Moreover, the problem is compounded when we add the future requirement that the measurement strategy, design of the study, and the actual measures all must reflect a sensitivity to a variety of cultural and developmental issues (see, e.g., Kleinman & Good, 1985).

Although the challenges are great in the quest to arrive at a sufficiently integrative approach to understanding the depressive and manic-depressive disorders, we believe that a developmental psychopathology approach holds great promise for elucidating necessary questions and suggesting strategies to apply to such an undertaking. As this chapter illustrates, those who have been the pioneers in this endeavor have already contributed much to our knowledge of the affective disorders.

REFERENCES

Abraham, K. (1966). Notes on the psychoanalytical investigation and treatment of manic-depressive insanity and allied conditions. In J. Coyne (Ed.), *Essential papers on depression* (pp. 31–47). New York: New York University Press. (Original work published 1911)

Abramson, L., Metalsky, G., & Alloy, L. (1989). The hopelessness theory of depression: A theory-based subtype of depression. *Psychological Review, 96,* 358–372.

Abramson, L., Seligman, M., & Teasdale, J. (1978). Learned helplessness in humans: Critique and reformulation. *Journal of Abnormal Psychology, 87,* 49–74.

Achenbach, T. (1990). What is "developmental" about developmental psychopathology? In J. Rolf, A. Masten, D. Cicchetti, K. Nuechterlein, & S. Weintraub (Eds.), *Risk and protective factors in the development of psychopathology* (pp. 29–48). New York: Cambridge University Press.

Achenbach, T. M., & Edelbrock, C. S. (1981). Behavioral problems and competencies reported by parents of normal and disturbed children aged four through sixteen. *Monographs of the Society for Research in Child Development, 46*(188).

Achenbach, T. M., & Edelbrock, C. S. (1986). *Child Behavior Checklist and Profile for Ages 2–3.* Burlington: University of Vermont Department of Psychiatry.

Ainsworth, M. D. S., Blehar, M. C., Waters, E., & Wall, S. (1978). *Patterns of attachment: A psychological study of the Strange Situation.* Hillsdale, NJ: Erlbaum.

Ainsworth, M. D. S., & Wittig, B. A. (1969). Attachment and the exploratory behavior of one-year-olds in a strange situation. In B. M. Foss (Ed.), *Determinants of infant behavior* (Vol. 4, pp. 113–136). London: Methuen.

Akiskal, H. (1981). Subaffective disorders: Dysthymic, cyclothymic, and bipolar II disorders in the "borderline" realm. *Psychiatric Clinics of North America, 4,* 25–46.

Akiskal, H. (1983). The bipolar spectrum: New concepts in classification and diagnosis. In L. Grinspoon (Ed.), *Psychiatry update,* (Vol. II, pp. 271–292). Washington, DC: American Psychiatric Press.

Akiskal, H., & McKinney, W. (1973). Depressive disorders: Toward a unified hypothesis. *Science, 162,* 20–29.

Akiskal, H., & McKinney, W. (1975). Overview of recent research in depression. *Archives of General Psychiatry, 32,* 285–305.

Akiskal, H., Walker, P., Puzantian, V., King, D., Rosenthal, T., & Drannon, M. (1983). Bipolar outcome in the course of depressive illness: Phenomenologic, familial, and pharmacologic predictors. *Journal of Affective Disorders, 5,* 115–128.

Allen, J., Iacono, W., Depue, R., & Arbisi, X. (1993). Regional EEG asymmetries in bipolar seasonal affective disorder before and after phototherapy. *Biological Psychiatry, 33,* 642–646.

Alloy, L., & Abramson, L. (1988). Depressive realism: Four theoretical perspectives. In L. Alloy (Ed.), *Cognitive processes in depression* (pp. 223–265). New York: Guilford.

American Psychiatric Association (1968, 1980, 1987). *Diagnostic and Statistical Manual of Mental Disorders* (2nd ed., 3rd ed., 3rd ed. rev.) Washington, DC: Author.

Angold, A. (1988a). Childhood and adolescent depression: I. Epidemiological and aetiological aspects. *British Journal of Psychiatry, 152,* 601–617.

Angold, A. (1988b). Childhood and adolescent depression: II. Research in clinical populations. *British Journal of Psychiatry, 153,* 476–492.

Angold, A., & Costello, E. J. (1993). Depressive comorbidity in children and adolescents: Empirical, theoretical and methodological issues. *American Journal of Psychiatry, 150,* 1779–1791.

Angold, A., & Rutter, M. (1992). Effects of age and pubertal status on depression in a large clinical sample. *Development and Psychopathology, 4,* 5–28.

Angst, J. (1966). *Zur Atiologie und Nosologie endogener depressiver Psychosen.* Berlin: Springer.

Antelman, S., & Caggiula, A. (1977). Norepinephrine-dopamine interactions and behavior. *Science, 195,* 646–651.

Anthony, E. J., & Scott, P. (1960). Manic-depressive psychosis in childhood. *Child Psychology and Psychiatry, 1,* 53–72.

Armsden, G., McCauley, E., Greenberg, M., Burke, P., & Mitchell, J. (1990). Parent and peer attachment in early adolescent depression. *Journal of Abnormal Child Psychology, 18,* 683–697.

Barnett, P., & Gotlib, I. (1988). Psychosocial functioning and depression: Distinguishing among antecedents, concomitants, and consequences. *Psychological Bulletin, 104,* 97–126.

Beardslee, W., & Podorefsky, D. (1988). Resilient adolescents whose parents have serious affective and other psychiatric disorders: Importance of self-understanding and relationships. *American Journal of Psychiatry, 145,* 63–69.

Beck, A. (1967). *Depression: Clinical, experimental, and theoretical aspects.* New York: Harper & Row.

Behar, L. B., & Stringfield, S. (1974a). A behavior rating scale for the preschool child. *Developmental Psychology, 10,* 601–610.

Behar, L. B., & Stringfield, S. (1974b). *Manual for the Preschool Behavior Questionnaire* (Available from Dr. Lenore Behar, 1821 Woodburn Road, Durham, NC 27705).

Belsher, G., & Costello, C. (1988). Relapse after recovery from unipolar depression: A critical review. *Psychological Bulletin, 104,* 84–96.

Belsky, J. (1984). The determinants of parenting: A process model. *Child Development, 55,* 83–96.

Belsky, J., & Vondra, J. (1989). Lessons from child abuse: The determinants of parenting. In D. Cicchetti & V. Carlson (Eds.), *Child maltreatment: Research and theory on consequences of child abuse and neglect* (pp. 153–202). New York: Cambridge University Press.

Benes, F., Turtle, M., Khan, Y., & Farol, P. (1994). Myelination of a key relay zone in the hippocampal formation occurs in the human brain during childhood, adolescence, and adulthood. *Archives of General Psychiatry, 51,* 477–484.

Bertelsen, A., Harvald, B., & Hauge, M. (1977). A Danish twin study of manic-depressive disorders. *British Journal of Psychiatry, 130,* 330–351.

Bibring, E. (1953). The mechanism of depression. In P. Greenacre (Ed.), *Affective disorders.* New York: International Universities Press.

Birmaher, B., Ryan, N., Dahl, R., Rabinovich, H., Ambrosini, P., Williamson, D., Novacenko, H., Nelson, B., Lo, E., & Puig-Antich, K. (1992). Dexamethasone suppression test in children with major depressive disorder. *Journal of the American Academy of Child and Adolescent Psychiatry, 31,* 291–297.

Black, J., & Greenough, W. (1986). Induction of pattern in neural structure by experience: Implications for cognitive development. In M. Lamb, A. Brown, & B. Rogoff (Eds.), *Advances in developmental psychology* (Vol. 4, pp. 1–44). Hillsdale, NJ: Erlbaum.

Blatt, S., & Homann, E. (1992). Parent-child interaction in the etiology of dependent and self-critical depression. *Clinical Psychology Review, 12,* 47–91.

Blatt, S. J., Quinlan, D., Chevron, E., MacDonald, C., & Zuroff, D. (1982). Dependency and self-criticism: Psychological dimensions of depression. *Journal of Consulting and Clinical Psychology, 50,* 113–124.

Blatt, S., & Zuroff, D. (1992). Interpersonal relatedness and self-definition: Two prototypes for depression. *Clinical Psychology Review, 12,* 527–562.

Blazer, D., Kessler, R., McGonagle, K., & Swartz, M. (1994). The prevalence and distribution of major depression in a national community sample: The national comorbidity survey. *American Journal of Psychiatry, 151,* 979–986.

Bleuler, E. (1950). *Dementia praecox or the group of schizophrenias.* New York: International Universities Press. (Original work published 1911)

Bleuler, E. (1924). *Textbook of psychiatry.* New York: Macmillan.

Borst, S., Noam, G., & Bartok, J. (1991). Adolescent suicidality: A clinical-developmental approach. *Journal of the American Academy of Child and Adolescent Psychiatry, 30,* 796–803.

Bowlby, J. (1982). *Attachment and loss: Vol. 1. Attachment.* New York: Basic Books. (Original work published 1969)

Bowlby, J. (1973). *Attachment and loss: Vol. 2. Separation.* New York: Basic Books.

Bowlby, J. (1980). *Loss: Sadness and depression.* New York: Basic Books.

Breslin, N. A., & Weinberger, D. R. (1990). Schizophrenia and the normal functional development of the prefrontal cortex. *Development and Psychopathology, 2,* 409–424.

Bretherton, I. (1985). Attachment theory: Retrospect and prospect. In I. Bretherton & E. Waters (Eds.), *Growing points of attachment theory and research. Monographs of the Society for Research in Child Development, 50* (Serial No. 209, Nos. 1–2, 5–38).

Bretherton, I. (1987). New perspectives on attachment relations: Security, communication, and internal working models. In J. Osofsky (Ed.), *Handbook of infant development* (2nd ed.) (pp. 1061–1100). New York: Wiley.

Bretherton, I., & Beeghly, M. (1982). Talking about internal states: The acquisition of an explicit theory of mind. *Developmental Psychology, 18,* 906–921.

Brown, G., & Harris, T. (1978). *Social origins of depression: A study of psychiatric disorder in women.* London: Tavistock.

Burke, K., Burke, J., Rae, D., & Regier, D. (1991). Comparing age at onset of major depression and other psychiatric disorders by birth cohorts in five U.S. community populations. *Archives of General Psychiatry, 48,* 789–795.

Burton, R. (1948). *The anatomy of melancholy.* New York: Tudor. (Original work published 1621)

Capaldi, D. (1992). Co-occurrence of conduct problems and depressive symptoms in early adolescent boys: II. A 2-year follow-up at grade 8. *Development and Psychopathology, 4,* 125–144.

Carlson, V., Cicchetti, D., Barnett, D., & Braunwald, K. (1989). Disorganized/disoriented attachment relationships in maltreated infants. *Developmental Psychology, 25,* 525–531.

Carnelley, K., Pietromonaco, P., & Jaffee, K. (1994). Depression, working models of others, and relationship functioning. *Journal of Personality and Social Psychology, 66,* 127–140.

Caron, C., & Rutter, M. (1991). Comorbidity in child psychopathology: Concepts, issues, and research strategies. *Journal of Child Psychology and Psychiatry, 32,* 1063–1080.

Cassidy, J., & Marvin, R. (1992). *Attachment organization in preschool children: Procedures and coding manual.* Unpublished manuscript, Pennsylvania State University and University of Virginia.

Chandler, M. (1994). Adolescent suicide and the loss of personal continuity. In D. Cicchetti & S. L. Toth (Eds.), *Rochester Symposium on Developmental Psychopathology: Vol. 5. Disorders and dysfunctions of the self* (pp. 371–390). Rochester, NY: University of Rochester Press.

Cicchetti, D. (1993). Developmental psychopathology: Reactions, reflections, projections. *Developmental Review, 13,* 471–502.

Cicchetti, D., & Aber, J. L. (1986). Early precursors to later depression: An organizational perspective. In L. Lipsitt & C. Rovee-Collier (Eds.), *Advances in infancy* (Vol. 4, pp. 87–137). Norwood, NJ: Ablex.

Cicchetti, D., Cummings, M., Greenberg, M., & Marvin, R. (1990). Attachment beyond infancy. In M. Greenberg, D. Cicchetti, & E. M. Cummings (Eds.), *Attachment during the preschool years* (pp. 3–49). Chicago: University of Chicago Press.

Cicchetti, D., Ganiban, J., & Barnett, D. (1991). Contributions from the study of high risk populations to understanding the development of emotion regulation. In J. Garber & K. Dodge (Eds.), *The development of emotion regulation and dysregulation* (pp. 15–48). New York: Cambridge University Press.

Cicchetti, D., & Garmezy, N. (Eds.). (1993). Milestones in the development of resilience [Special issue]. *Development and Psychopathology, 5*(4), 497–783.

Cicchetti, D., & Schneider-Rosen, K. (1984). Toward a developmental model of the depressive disorders. *New Directions for Child Development, 26,* 5–27.

Cicchetti, D., & Schneider-Rosen, K. (1986). An organizational approach to childhood depression. In M. Rutter, C. Izard, & P. Read (Eds.), *Depression in young people: Clinical and developmental perspectives* (pp. 71–134). New York: Guilford.

Cicchetti, D., & Sroufe, L. A. (1978). An organizational view of affect: Illustration from the Study of Down's Syndrome Infants. In M. Lewis & L. Rosenblum (Eds.), *The development of affect* (pp. 309–350). New York: Plenum.

Cicchetti, D., & Toth, S. L. (1991). The making of a developmental psychopathologist. In J. Cantor, C. Spiker, & L. Lipsitt (Eds.), *Child behavior and development: Training for diversity* (pp. 34–72). Norwood, NJ: Ablex.

Cicchetti, D., Toth, S. L., & Bush, M. (1988). Developmental Psychopathology and incompetence in childhood: Suggestions for intervention. In B. Lahey & A. Kazdin (Eds.), *Advances in clinical child psychology* (pp. 1–71). New York: Plenum.

Cicchetti, D., & Tucker, D. (Eds.). (1994). Neural plasticity, sensitive periods, and psychopathology [Special issue]. *Development and Psychopathology, 6*(4).

Cohen, D. J., & Leckman, J. (1993). Developmental psychopathology and neurobiology of Tourette's syndrome. *Journal of the American Academy of Child and Adolescent Psychiatry, 33,* 2–15.

Cohn, J., & Campbell, S. (1992). Influence of maternal depression on infant affect regulation. In D. Cicchetti & S. L. Toth (Eds.). *Rochester Symposium on Developmental Psychopathology: Vol. 4. Developmental perspectives on depression* (pp. 103–130). Rochester, NY: University of Rochester Press.

Cohn, J., Campbell, S., Matias, R., & Hopkins, J. (1990). Face-to-face interactions of postpartum depressed and nondepressed mother-infant pairs. *Developmental Psychology, 26,* 15–23.

Cohn, J., Campbell, S., & Ross, S. (1991). Infant response in the still-face paradigm at 6 months predicts avoidant and secure attachment at 12 months. *Development and Psychopathology, 3,* 367–376.

Cohn, J., Matias, R., Tronick, E., Connell, D., & Lyons-Ruth, K. (1986). Face-to-face interactions of depressed mothers and their infants. *New Directions for Child Development, 34,* 31–45.

Cohn, J., & Tronick, E. (1983). Three-month-old infants' reaction to simulated maternal depression. *Child Development, 54,* 185–193.

Cole, P., Barrett, K., & Zahn-Waxler, C. (1992). Emotion displays in two-year-olds during mishaps. *Child Development, 63,* 314–324.

Cole, P., & Zahn-Waxler, C. (1992). Emotional dysregulation in disruptive behavior disorders. *Rochester Symposium on Developmental Psychopathology: Vol. 4. Developmental perspectives on depression* (pp. 173–209). Rochester, NY: University of Rochester Press.

Collins, P., & Depue, R. (1992). A neurobehavioral systems approach to developmental psychopathology: Implications for disorders of affect. In D. Cicchetti & S. L. Toth (Eds.). *Rochester Symposium on Developmental Psychopathology: Vol. 4. Developmental perspectives on depression* (pp. 29–101). Rochester, NY: University of Rochester Press.

Connelley, K. B., Pietromonaco, P. R., & Jaffe, K. (1994). Depression, working models of others, and relationship functioning. *Journal of Personality and Social Psychology, 66,* 127–140.

Conrad, M., & Hammen, C. (1993). Protective and resource factors in high- and low-risk children: A comparison of children with unipolar, bipolar, medically ill, and normal mothers. *Development and Psychopathology, 5,* 593–607.

Coryell, W., Akiskal, H., Leon, A., Winokur, G., Maser, J., Mueller, T., & Keller, M. (1994). The time course of nonchronic major depressive disorder. *Archives of General Psychiatry, 51,* 405–410.

Coyne, J. (1976). Toward an interactional description of depression. *Psychiatry, 39,* 28–40.

Coyne, J. C., Kessler, R., Tal, M., Turnball, J., Worthman, C., & Greden, J. (1987). Living with a depressed person: Burden and psychological distress. *Journal of Consulting and Clinical Psychology, 55,* 347–352.

Crittenden, P. (1990). Internal representational models of attachment relationships. *Infant Mental Health Journal, 11,* 259–277.

Cummings, E. M., & Cicchetti, D. (1990). Attachment, depression, and the transmission of depression. In M. T. Greenberg, D. Cicchetti, & E. M. Cummings (Eds.), *Attachment in the preschool years* (pp. 339–372). Chicago: University of Chicago Press.

Cummings, E. M., & Davies, P. (1994). Maternal depression and child development. *Journal of Child Psychology and Psychiatry, 35,* 73–112.

Cummings, E. M., & Zahn-Waxler, C. (1992). Emotions and the socialization of aggression: Adults' angry behavior and children's arousal and aggression. In A. Fraczek & H. Zumkley (Eds.), *Socialization and aggression* (pp. 61–84). New York and Heidelberg: Springer.

Cunningham, C. E., Benness, B. B., & Siegel, L. (1988). Family functioning, time allocation, and parental depression in families of normal and ADDH children. *Journal of Clinical Child Psychology, 17,* 169–177.

Dahl, R., Puig-Antich, J., Ryan, N., Nelson, B., Novacenko, H., Twomey, J., Williamson, D., Goetz, R., & Ambrosini, P. J. (1989). Cortisol secretion in adolescents with major depressive disorder. *Acta Psychiatrica Scandinavia, 80,* 18–26.

Dahl, R., & Puig-Antich, J., Ryan, N., Cunningham, S., Nelson, B., & Klepper, T. (1990). EEG sleep in adolescents with major depression: The role of suicidality and inpatient status. *Journal of Affective Disorders, 19,* 63–75.

Dahl, R., Ryan, N., Puig-Antich, J., Nyugen, N., Al-Shabbout, M., Meyer, V., & Perel, J. (1991). 24-hour cortisol measures in adolescents with major depression: A controlled study. *Biological Psychiatry, 30,* 25–36.

Dahl, R., Ryan, N., Williamson, D., Ambrosini, P., Rabinovich, H., Novacenko, H., Nelson, B., & Puig-Antich, J. (1992). Regulation of sleep and growth hormone in adolescent depression. *Journal of the American Academy of Child and Adolescent Psychiatry, 31,* 615–621.

Damon, W., & Hart, D. (1988). *Self-understanding in childhood and adolescence.* New York: Cambridge University Press.

Davidson, R. (1988). Cerebral asymmetry, affective style, and psychopathology. In M. Kinsbourne (Ed.), *Cerebral hemisphere function in depression* (pp. 1–22). Washington, DC: American Psychiatric Press.

Davidson, R. (1991). Cerebral asymmetry and affective disorders: A developmental perspective. In D. Cicchetti & S. L. Toth (Eds.), *Rochester Symposium on Developmental Psychopathology: Vol. 2. Internalizing and externalizing expressions of dysfunction* (pp. 123–154). Hillsdale, NJ: Erlbaum.

Davidson, R. (1993). Parsing affective space: Perspectives from neuropsychology and psychophysiology. *Neuropsychology, 7,* 464–475.

Davidson, R., Finman, R., Rickman, M., Straus, A., & Kagan, J. (1993). *Childhood temperament and frontal lobe activity: Patterns of asymmetry differentiate between wary and outgoing children.* Unpublished manuscript, University of Wisconsin, Madison.

Davidson, R., & Fox, N. (1982). Asymmetrical brain activity discriminates between positive versus negative affective stimuli in human infants. *Science, 218,* 1235–1237.

Davidson, R., & Fox, N. (1989). Frontal brain asymmetry predicts infants' response to maternal separation. *Journal of Abnormal Psychology, 98,* 127–131.

Dawson, G., Grofer Klinger, L., Panagiotides, H., Hill, D., & Spieker, S. (1992). Frontal lobe activity and affective behavior of infants of mothers with depressive symptoms. *Child Development, 63,* 725–737.

Dawson, G., Grofer Klinger, L., Panagiotides, H., Spieker, S., & Frey, K. (1992). Infants of mothers with depressive symptoms: Electroencephalographic and behavioral findings related to attachment status. *Development and Psychopathology, 4,* 67–80.

Dawson, G., Hessl, D., & Frey, K. (in press). The role of the social environment in shaping early-developing biological and behavioral systems involved in the expression and regulation of emotion and risk for affective disorder. *Development and Psychopathology.*

DeMulder, E., & Radke-Yarrow, M. (1991). Attachment with affectively ill and well mothers: Concurrent behavioral correlates. *Development and Psychopathology, 3,* 227–242.

Depue, R., & Iacono, W. (1989). Neurobehavioral aspects of affective disorders. *Annual Review of Psychology, 40,* 457–492.

Depue, R., & Monroe, S. (1978). The unipolar-bipolar distinction in the depressive disorders. *Psychological Bulletin, 85,* 1001–1029.

Diamond, A., & Goldman-Rakic, P. (1989). Comparison of human infants and rhesus monkeys on Piaget's AB task. Evidence for dependence on dorsolateral prefrontal cortex. *Experimental Brain Research, 74,* 24–40.

Dix, T. (1991). The affective organization of parenting: adaptive and maladaptive processes. *Psychological Bulletin, 110,* 3–25.

Dodge, K. (1993). Social-cognitive mechanisms in the development of conduct disorder and depression. *Annual Review of Psychology, 44,* 559–584.

Downey, G., & Coyne, J. (1990). Children of depressed parents: An integrative review. *Psychological Bulletin, 106,* 50–76.

Dozier, M. (1990). Attachment organization and treatment use for adults with serious psychopathological disorders. *Development and Psychopathology, 2,* 47–60.

Dunner, D., Dwyer, T., & Fieve, R. (1976). Depressive symptoms in patients with unipolar and bipolar affective disorder. *Comprehensive Psychiatry, 17,* 447–451.

Dunner, D., Gershon, E., & Goodwin, F. (1976). Heritable factors in the severity of affective illness. *Biological Psychiatry, 129,* 40–44.

Easterbrooks, M. A., Davidson, C., & Chazan, R. (1993). Psychosocial risk, attachment, and behavior problems among school-aged children. *Development and Psychopathology, 5,* 389–402.

Edelman, G. (1987). *Neural Darwinism.* New York: Basic Books.

Egeland, B., & Sroufe, L. A. (1981). Developmental sequelae of maltreatment in infancy, *New Directions for Child Development, 11,* 77–92.

Emde, R. N., Gaensbauer, T., & Harmon, R. (1976). *Emotional expression in infancy: A biobehavioral study.* New York: International Universities Press.

Emery, R., Weintraub, S., & Neale, J. (1982). Effects of marital discord on the school behavior of children of schizophrenic, affective disordered, and normal parents. *Journal of Abnormal Child Psychology, 16,* 215–225.

Erikson, E. H. (1950). *Childhood and society.* New York: Norton.

Faraone, S., Kremen, W., & Tsuang, M. (1990). Genetic transmission of major affective disorders: Quantitative models and linkage analyses. *Psychological Bulletin, 108,* 109–127.

Fendrich, M., Warner, V., & Weissman, M. M. (1990). Family risk factors, parental depression, and psychopathology in offspring. *Developmental Psychology, 26,* 40–50.

Field, T. M. (1984). Early interactions between infants and their postpartum depressed mothers. *Infant Behavior and Development, 7,* 517–522.

Field, T. (1989). Maternal depression effects on infant interaction and attachment behavior. In D. Cicchetti (Ed.), *Rochester Symposium on Developmental Psychopathology: Vol. 1. The emergence of a discipline* (pp. 139–163). Hillsdale, NJ: Erlbaum.

Field, T. (1992). Infants of depressed mothers. *Development and Psychopathology, 4,* 49–66.

Field, T., Healy, B., Goldstein, S., & Guthertz, M. (1990). Behavior-state matching and synchrony in mother-infant interactions of nondepressed versus depressed dyads. *Developmental Psychology, 26,* 7–14.

Field, T., Healy, B., Goldstein, S., Perry, S., Bendell, D., Schanberg, S., Zimmerman, E., & Kuhn, C. (1988). Infants of depressed mothers show "depressed" behavior even with nondepressed adults. *Child Development, 59,* 1569–1579.

Field, T., Healy, B., & LeBlanc, W. (1989). Sharing and synchrony of behavior states and heart rate in nondepressed versus depressed mother-infant interactions. *Infant Behavior and Development, 12,* 357–376.

Fincham, F., & Cain, K. (1986). Learned helplessness in humans: A developmental analysis. *Developmental Review, 6,* 301–333.

Fleming, J., & Offord, D. (1990). Epidemiology of childhood depressive disorders: A critical review. *Journal of the American Academy of Child and Adolescent Psychiatry, 29,* 571–580.

Forehand, R., Lautenschlager, G. J., Faust, J., & Graziano, W. G. (1986). Parent perceptions and parent-child interactions in clinic-referred children: A preliminary investigation of the effects of maternal depressive moods. *Behavior Research and Therapy, 24,* 73–75.

Fox, N., & Davidson, R. (1984). Hemispheric substrates of affect. In N. A. Fox & R. J. Davidson (Eds.), *The psychobiology of affective development* (pp. 353–381). Hillsdale, NJ: Erlbaum.

Freud, S. (1966). Mourning and melancholia. In J. Coyne (Ed.), *Essential papers on depression* (pp. 48–63). New York: New York University Press. (Original work published 1917)

Gaensbauer, T. J., Harmon, R. J., Cytryn, L., & McKnew, D. H. (1984). Social and affective development in infants with a manic-depressive parent. *American Journal of Psychiatry, 141,* 223–229.

Gara, M., Woolfolk, R., Cohen, B., Goldstron, R., Allen, L., & Novalany, J. (1993). Perception of self and other in major depression. *Journal of Abnormal Psychology, 102,* 93–100.

Garber, J. (1984). Classification of childhood psychopathology: A developmental perspective. *Child Development, 55,* 30–48.

Gershon, E., Bunney, W., Leckman, J., Van Eerdewegh, M., & Debauche, B. (1976). The inheritance of affective disorders: A review of data and of hypotheses. *Behavior Genetics, 6,* 227–261.

Geller, B., Fox, L., & Clark, K. (1994). Rate and predictors of prepubertal bipolarity during follow-up of 6- to 12-year-old depressed children. *Journal of the American Academy of Child and Adolescent Psychiatry, 33,* 461–468.

Gentile, J., Cicchetti, D., Rogosch, F., & O'Brien, R. (1992). Functional deficits in the self and depression in widows. *Development and Psychopathology, 4,* 323–339.

Gjerde, P., & Block, J. (in press). Depressive symptoms in adolescence: A developmental perspective on gender differences in concurrent manifestations, childhood antecedents, and young adult sequelae. In D. Cicchetti & S. L. Toth (Eds.) *Rochester Symposium on Developmental Psychopathology: Vol. 7. Adolescence: Opportunities and challenges.* Rochester, NY: University of Rochester Press.

Gold, P., Goodwin, F., & Chrousos, G. (1988a). Clinical and biochemical manifestations of depression: Relation to the neurobiology of stress (Part I). *New England Journal of Medicine, 319,* 348–353.

Gold, P., Goodwin, F., & Chrousos, G. (1988b). Clinical and biochemical manifestations of depression: Relation to the neurobiology of stress (Part II). *New England Journal of Medicine, 319,* 413–420.

Goldman, P. (1971). Functional development of the prefrontal cortex in early life and the problem of neuronal plasticity. *Experimental Neurology, 32,* 366–387.

Goodwin, F., & Jamison, K. (1984). The natural course of manic-depressive illness. In R. Post & J. Ballenger (Eds.), *Neurobiology of mood disorders* (pp. 20–37). Baltimore: Williams & Wilkins.

Goodwin, F., & Jamison, K. (1990). *Manic-depressive illness.* New York: Oxford University Press.

Gottesman, I. I. (1974). Developmental genetics and ontogenetic psychology: Overdue detente and propositions from a matchmaker. In A. Pick (Ed.), *Minnesota Symposium on Child Psychology* (pp. 55–80). Minneapolis: University of Minnesota Press.

Gottesman, I. (1991). *Schizophrenia genesis.* San Francisco: Freeman.

Gottesman, I. I., Carey, G., & Hanson, D. (1983). Pearls and perils in epigenetic psychopathology. In S. Guze, F. Earls, & J. Barrett (Eds.), *Childhood psychopathology and development* (pp. 287–299). New York: Plenum.

Gottesman, I. I., & Goldsmith, H. (1994). Developmental psychopathology of antisocial behavior: Inserting genes into its genesis and epigenesis. In C. A. Nelson (Ed.), *Minnesota Symposia on Child Psychology: Vol. 27. Threats to optimal development: Integrating biological, psychological, and social risk factors.* Hillsdale, NJ: Erlbaum.

Greenough, W., Black, J., & Wallace, C. (1987). Experience and brain development. *Child Development, 58,* 539–559.

Hammen, C. (1992a). Cognitive, life stress, and interpersonal approaches to a developmental psychopathology model of depression. *Development and Psychopathology, 4,* 189–206.

Hammen, C. (1992b). The family-environmental context of depression: A perspective on children's risk. In D. Cicchetti & S. L. Toth (Eds.), *Rochester Symposium on Developmental Psychopathology: Vol. 4. Developmental perspectives on depression* (pp. 251–281). Rochester, NY: University of Rochester Press.

Hammen, C., Burge, D., Burney, E., & Adrian, C. (1990). Longitudinal study of diagnoses in children of women with unipolar and bipolar affective disorder. *Archives of General Psychiatry, 47,* 1112–1117.

Hammen, C., Marks, T., Mayol, A., & DeMayo, R. (1985). Depressive self-schemas, life stress, and vulnerability to depression. *Journal of Abnormal Psychology, 94,* 308–319.

Hammen, C., & Zupan, B. (1984). Self-schemas, depression, and the processing of personal information in children. *Journal of Experimental Child Psychology, 37,* 598–608.

Harrington, R., Fudge, H., Rutter, M., Pickles, A., & Hill, J. (1990). Adult outcomes of childhood and adolescent depression: I. Psychiatric status. *Archives of General Psychiatry, 47,* 465–473.

Harrington, R., Fudge, H., Rutter, M., Pickles, A., & Hill, J. (1991). Adult outcomes of childhood and adolescent depression: II. Risk for antisocial disorders. *Journal of American Academy of Child and Adolescent Psychiatry, 30,* 434–439.

Haslam, J. (1809). *Observations on madness and melancholy.* London: J. Callow.

Hay, D. (1994). Prosocial development. *Journal of Child Psychology and Psychiatry, 35,* 29–71.

Hay, D., Zahn-Waxler, C., Cummings, E. M., & Iannotti, R. (1992). Young children's views about conflict with peers: A comparison of the daughters and sons of depressed and well women. *Journal of Child Psychology and Psychiatry, 33,* 669–693.

Hetherington, E. M. (1989). Coping with family transitions: Winners, losers, and survivors. *Child Development, 60,* 1–14.

Henriques, J., & Davidson, R. (1991). Left frontal hypoactivation in depression. *Journal of Abnormal Psychology, 100,* 535–545.

Hesse, P., & Cicchetti, D. (1982). Perspectives on an integrated theory of emotional development. In D. Cicchetti & P. Hesse (Eds.), *New Directions for Child Development, 16,* 3–48.

Himmelhoch, J. (1979). Mixed states, manic-depressive illness, and the nature of mood. *Psychiatric Clinics of North America, 2,* 449–459.

Hinrichsen, G. (1992). Recovery and relapse from major depressive disorder in the elderly. *American Journal of Psychiatry, 149,* 1575–1579.

Hinrichsen, G., & Hernandez, N. (1993). Factors associated with recovery from and relapse into major depressive disorders in the elderly. *American Journal of Psychiatry, 150,* 1820–1825.

Hooley, J. M. (1986). Expressed emotion and depression: Interactions between patients and high-versus-low expressed-emotion spouses. *Journal of Abnormal Psychology, 95,* 237–246.

Institute of Medicine. (1985). Research on mental illness and addictive disorders: Progress and prospects [Supplement]. *American Journal of Psychiatry, 1142,* 1–41.

Institute of Medicine. (1989). *Research on children and adolescents with mental, behavioral, and developmental disorders.* Washington, DC: National Academy Press.

Izard, C. E., & Malatesta, C. Z. (1987). Perspectives on emotional development: I. Differential emotions theory of early emotional development. In D. J. Osofsky (Ed.), *Handbook of infant development* (2nd ed.) (pp. 494–554). New York: Wiley.

Jamison, K. (1993). *Touched with fire: Manic-depressive illness and the artistic temperament.* New York: Free Press.

Jamison, K., Gerner, R., Hammen, C., & Padesky, C. (1980). Clouds and silver linings: Positive experiences associated with primary affective disorders. *American Journal of Psychiatry, 137,* 198–202.

Jackson, S. (1986). *Melancholia and depression: From Hippocratic times to modern times.* New Haven: Yale University Press.

Johnson, W. F., Emde, R. W., Pannabecker, B. J., Stenberg, C., & David, H. (1982). Maternal perception of infant emotion from birth through 18 months. *Infant Behavior and Development, 5,* 313–322.

Kagan, J. (1981). *The second year: The emergence of self-awareness.* Cambridge, MA: Harvard University Press.

Kagan, J. (1994). *Galen's prophecy: Temperament in human nature.* New York: Basic Books.

Kandel, D., & Davies, M. (1986). Adult sequelae of adolescent depressive symptoms. *Archives of General Psychiatry, 43,* 255–262.

Kashani, J., Husain, A., Shekim, W., Hodges, K., Cytryn, L., & McKnew, D. (1983). Current perspectives on childhood depression: An overview. *American Journal of Psychiatry, 138,* 143–153.

Kashani, J., McGee, R. O., Clarkson, S. E., Anderson, J. C., Walton, L., Williams, S., Silva, P., Robins, A., Cytryn, L., & McKnew, D. (1983). The nature and prevalence of major and minor depression in a sample of nine-year-old children. *Archives of General Psychiatry, 40,* 1217–1227.

Kegan, R. (1982). *The evolving self.* Cambridge, MA: Harvard University Press.

Keller, M., Beardslee, W., Dorer, D., Lavori, P., Samuelson, H., & Klerman, G. (1986). Impact of severity and chronicity of parental affective illness on adaptive functioning and psychopathology in children. *Archives of General Psychiatry, 43,* 930–937.

Keller, M., Lavori, P., Mueller, T., Endicott, J., Coryell, W., Hirschfield, R., & Sheat, T. (1992). Time to recovery, chronicity, and levels of psychopathology in major depression: A 5-year prospective follow-up of 431 subjects. *Archives of General Psychiatry, 49,* 809–816.

Kendler, K., Kessler, R., Neale, M., Heath, A., & Eaves, L. (1993). The prediction of major depression in women: Toward an integrated etiologic model. *American Journal of Psychiatry, 150,* 1139–1148.

Kendler, K., Neale, M., Kessler, R., Heath, A., & Eaves, L. (1992). A population-based twin study of major depression in women: The impact of varying definitions of illness. *Archives of General Psychiatry, 49,* 257–266.

Kessler, R., McGonagle, K., Nelson, C., Hughes, M., Swartz, M., & Blazer, D. (1994). Sex and depression in the National Comorbidity Survey: II. Cohort effects. *Journal of Affective Disorders, 30,* 15–26.

Kessler, R., McGonagle, K., Zhao, S., Nelson, C., Hughes, M., Eshleman, S., Wittchen, H., & Kendler, K. (1994). Lifetime and 12-month prevalence of DSM-III-R psychiatric disorders in the United States: Results from the national comorbidity survey. *Archives of General Psychiatry, 51,* 8–19.

Kinsbourne, M. (1988). Hemispheric interactions in depression. In M. Kinsbourne (Ed.), *Cerebral hemisphere function in depression* (pp. 99–131). Washington, DC: American Psychiatric Press.

Kleinman, A., & Good, B. (Eds.). (1985). *Culture and depression.* Berkeley: University of California Press.

Knowles, J., & MacLean, A. (1990). Age-related changes in sleep in depressed and healthy subjects. *Neuropsychopharmacology, 3,* 251–259.

Kobak, R., & Sceery, A. (1988). Attachment in late adolescence: Working models, affect regulation and perceptions of self and others. *Child Development, 59,* 135–146.

Kobak, R., Sudler, N., & Gamble, W. (1991). Attachment and depressive symptoms during adolescence: A developmental pathways analysis. *Development and Psychopathology, 3,* 461–474.

Kochanska, G. (1991). Patterns of inhibition to the unfamiliar in children of normal and affectively ill mothers. *Child Development, 62,* 250–263.

Kochanska, G., & Kuczynski, L. (1991). Maternal autonomy granting: Predictors of normal and depressed mothers' compliance with the requests of five-year-olds. *Child Development, 62,* 1449–1459.

Kochanska, G., Kuczynski, L., Radke-Yarrow, M., & Welsh, J. D. (1987). Resolution of control episodes between well and affectively ill mothers and their young child. *Journal of Abnormal Child Psychology, 15,* 441–456.

Kovacs, M. (1989). Affective disorders in children and adolescence. *American Psychologist, 44,* 209–215.

Kovacs, M., Akiskal, H., Gatsonis, C., & Parrone, P. (1994). Childhood-onset dysthymic disorder: Clinical features and prospective naturalistic outcome. *Archives of General Psychiatry, 51,* 365–374.

Kovacs, M., Feinberg, T., Crouse-Novak, M., Paulauskas, S., & Finkelstein, R. (1984). Depressive disorders in childhood: I. A longitudinal prospective study of characteristics and recovery. *Archives of General Psychiatry, 41,* 229–237.

Kovacs, M., Feinberg, T., Crouse-Novak, M., Paulauskas, S., Pollock, M., & Finkelstein, R. (1984). Depressive disorders in childhood: II. A longitudinal study of the risk for a subsequent major depression. *Archives of General Psychiatry, 41,* 643–649.

Kovacs, M., Gatsonis, C., Paulauskas, S., & Richards, C. (1989). Depressive disorders in childhood: IV. A longitudinal study of comorbidity with and risk for anxiety disorders. *Archives of General Psychiatry, 46,* 776–782.

Kraepelin, E. (1921). *Manic depressive insanity and paranoia.* Edinburgh: Livingstone.

Kupfer, D., Pickar, D., Himmelhoch, J., & Detre, T. (1975). Are there two types of unipolar depression? *Archives of General Psychiatry, 16,* 125–131.

Kupfer, D., & Thase, M. (1983). The use of the sleep laboratory in the diagnosis of affective disorders. *Psychiatric Clinics of North America, 5,* 3–25.

Lauer, R., Giordani, B., Boivin, M., Halle, N., Glasgow, B., Alessi, N., & Berent, S. (1994). Effects of depression on memory performance and metamemory in children. *Journal of the American Academy of Child and Adolescent Psychiatry, 33,* 679–685.

Lefkowitz, M. M., & Burton, N. (1978). Childhood depression: A critique of the concept. *Psychological Bulletin, 135,* 716–726.

Leonhard, K. (1979). *The classification of endogenous psychoses* (English translation). New York: Wiley. (Original work published 1957)

Lewinsohn, P. M. (1974). A behavioral approach to depression. In R. J. Freidman & M. M. Katz (Eds.), *The psychology of depression: Contemporary theory and research.* Washington, DC: Winston.

Lewinsohn, P., Clarke, G., Seeley, J., & Rohde, P. (1994). Major depression in community adolescents: Age at onset, episode duration, and time to recurrence. *Journal of the American Academy of Child and Adolescent Psychiatry, 33,* 809–818.

Lewinsohn, P., Hops, H., Roberts, R., Seeley, J., & Andrews, J. (1993). Adolescent psychopathology: I. Prevalence and incidence of depression and other DSM-III-R disorders in high school students. *Journal of Abnormal Psychology, 102,* 133–144.

Lewis, M., & Brooks-Gunn, J. (1979). *Social cognition and the acquisition of self.* New York: Plenum.

Loeber, R., & Dishion, T. J. (1984). Boys who fight at home and school: Family conditions influencing cross-setting consistency. *Journal of Consulting and Clinical Psychology, 52,* 759–768.

Lyons-Ruth, R., Alpern, L., & Repacholi, B. (1993). Disorganized infant attachment classification and maternal psychosocial problems as predictors of hostile-aggressive behavior in the preschool classroom. *Child Development, 64,* 572–585.

Lyons-Ruth, K., Connell, D., Grunebaum, H., & Botein, S. (1990). Infants at social risk: Maternal depression and family support services as mediators of infant development and security of attachment. *Child Development, 59,* 1569–1579.

Lyons-Ruth, K., Connell, D., Zoll, D., & Stahl, J. (1987). Infants at social risk: Relations among infant maltreatment, maternal behavior, and infant attachment behavior. *Developmental Psychology, 3,* 223–232.

Maccoby, E. E., & Martin, J. A. (1983). Socialization in the context of the family: Parent-child interaction. In P. H. Mussen (Ed.), *Handbook of child psychology: Vol. 4. Socialization, personality, and social development* (pp. 1–102). New York: Wiley.

Main, M., & Cassidy, J. (1988). Categories of response to reunion with a parent at age 6: Predictable from infant attachment classifications and stable over a 1-month period. *Developmental Psychology, 24,* 415–426.

Main, M., & Goldwyn, R., (in press). Interview-based adult attachment classifications: Related to infant-mother and infant-father attachment. *Developmental Psychology.*

Main, M., & Solomon, J. (1990). Procedures for identifying infants as disorganized/disoriented during the Ainsworth Strange Situation. In M. Greenberg, D. Cicchetti, and E. M. Cummings (Eds.), *Attachment during the preschool years* (pp. 121–160). Chicago: University of Chicago Press.

Maj, M., Veltro, F., Pirozzi, R., Lobrace, S., & Magliano, L. (1992). Pattern of recurrence of illness after recovery from an episode of major depression: A prospective study. *American Journal of Psychiatry, 149,* 795–800.

Malatesta, C. Z., & Izard, C. (1984). The ontogenesis of human social signals: From biological imperatives to symbol utilization. In N. A. Fox & R. J. Davidson (Eds.), *The psychobiology of affective development* (pp. 161–206). Hillsdale, NJ: Erlbaum.

Malatesta, C. Z., & Wilson, A. (1988). Emotion-cognition, interaction in personality development: A discrete emotions, functionalist analysis. *British Journal of Social Psychology, 27,* 91–112.

Maser, J., & Cloninger, C. R. (Eds.). (1990). *Comorbidity of mood and anxiety disorders.* Washington, DC: American Psychiatric Press.

McGuffin, P., & Katz, R. (1989). The genetics of depression and manic-depressive illness. *British Journal of Psychiatry, 155,* 294–304.

McGuffin, P., & Katz, R. (1993). Genes, adversity, and depression. In R. Plomin & G. McLearn (Eds.), *Nature, nurture, and psychology* (pp. 217–230). Washington, DC: American Psychological Association.

McGuffin, P., Katz, R., & Rutherford, J. (1991). Nature, nurture, and depression: A twin study. *Psychological Medicine, 21,* 329–335.

Mendlewicz, J., & Rainer, J. (1977). Adoption study supporting genetic transmission in manic-depressive illness. *Nature, 268,* 327–329.

Merikangas, K., & Spiker, D. (1982). Assortative mating among inpatients with primary affective disorder. *Psychological Medicine, 12,* 753–764.

Meyersburg, H., & Post, R. (1979). An holistic developmental view of neural and psychological processes: A neurobiologic-psychoanalytic integration. *British Journal of Psychiatry, 135,* 139–155.

Moffitt, T. E. (1993). "Life-course-persistent" and "adolescent-limited" antisocial behavior: A developmental taxonomy. *Psychological Review, 100.*

Mullan, M., & Murray, R. (1989). The impact of molecular genetics on our understanding of the psychoses. *British Journal of Psychiatry, 154,* 591–595.

Murray, L., Kempton, C., Woolgar, M., & Hooper, R. (1993). Depressed mothers' speech to their infants and its relation to infant gender and cognitive development. *Journal of Child Psychology and Psychiatry, 34,* 1083–1101.

Noam, G., & Valiant, G. (1994). Clinical-developmental psychology in developmental psychopathology: Theory and research of an emerging perspective. In D. Cicchetti & S. L. Toth (Eds.), *Rochester Symposium on Developmental Psychopathology: Vol. 5. Disorders and dysfunctions of the self* (pp. 299–331). Rochester, NY: University of Rochester Press.

Nolen-Hoeksema, S. (1987). Sex differences in unipolar depression: Evidence and theory. *Psychological Bulletin, 101,* 259–282.

Nolen-Hoeksema, S. (1991). Responses to depression and their effects on the duration of depressive episodes. *Journal of Abnormal Psychology, 100,* 569–582.

Nolen-Hoeksema, S. (1993). Response styles and the duration of episodes of depressed mood. *Journal of Abnormal Psychology, 102,* 20–28.

Nolen-Hoeksema, S., Girgus, J., & Seligman, M. (1992). Predictors and consequences of childhood depressive symptoms; A 5-year longitudinal study. *Journal of Abnormal Psychology, 101,* 405–422.

Panaccione, V. F., & Wahler, R. G. (1986). Child behavior, maternal depression, and social coercion as factors in the quality of child care. *Journal of Abnormal Child Psychology, 14*(2), 263–278.

Panak, W., & Garber, J. (1992). Role of aggression, rejection, and attributions in the prediction of depression in children. *Development and Psychopathology, 4,* 145–165.

Pardes, H., Kaufmann, C., Pincus, H., & West, A. (1989). Genetics and psychiatry: Past discoveries, current dilemmas, and future directions. *American Journal of Psychiatry, 146,* 435–443.

Patrick, M., Hobson, R. P., Castle, D., Howard, R., & Maughan, B. (1994). Personality disorder and the mental representation of early social experience. *Development and Psychopathology, 6,* 375–388.

Pearson, J. L., Cohn, D. A., Cowan, P., & Cowan, C. P. (1994). Earned and continuous-security in adult attachment: Relation to depression and parenting style. *Development and Psychopathology, 6,* 359–373.

Perris, C. (1966). A study of bipolar (manic-depressive) and unipolar depressive psychosis. *Acta Psychiatrica Scandinavica, 194,* 1–88.

Petersen, A., Compas, B., Brooks-Gunn, J., Stemmler, M., Ey, S., & Grant, K. (1993). Depression in adolescence. *American Psychologist, 48,* 155–168.

Peterson, C., & Seligman, M. (1984). Causal explanations as a risk factor for depression: Theory and evidence. *Psychological Review, 91,* 347–374.

Pfol, B., Stangl, D., & Zimmerman, M. (1984). The implications of DSM-III-R personality disorders for patients with major depression. *Journal of Affective Disorders, 7,* 309–318.

Pickens, J., & Field, T. (1993). Facial expressivity in infants of depressed mothers. *Developmental Psychology, 29,* 986–988.

Plomin, R. (1986). *Development, genetics, and psychology.* Hillsdale, NJ: Erlbaum.

Plomin, R., & Daniels, D. (1987). Why are children in the same family so different from each other? *Behavioral and Brain Sciences, 10,* 1–16.

Plomin, R., Rende, R., & Rutter, M. (1991). Quantitative genetics and developmental psychopathology. In D. Cicchetti and S. L. Toth (Eds.), *Rochester Symposium on Developmental Psychopathology: Vol. 2. Internalizing and externalizing expressions of dysfunction* (pp. 155–202). Hillsdale, NJ: Erlbaum.

Post, R. (1990). Prophylaxis of bipolar affective disorders. *International Review of Psychiatry, 2,* 165–208.

Post, R. (1992). Transduction of psychosocial stress into the neurobiology of recurrent affective disorder. *American Journal of Psychiatry, 149*, 999–1010.

Post, R., & Ballenger, J. (Eds.). (1984). *Neurobiology of mood disorders.* Baltimore: Williams & Wilkins.

Post, R., Leverich, G., Altshuler, L., & Mikalauskas, K. (1992). Lithium-induced refractoriness. *American Journal of Psychiatry, 149*, 1727–1729.

Post, R., Rubinow, D., & Ballenger, J. (1986). Conditioning and sensitisation in the longitudinal course of affective illness. *British Journal of Psychiatry, 149*, 191–201.

Post, R., Weiss, S., & Leverich, G. (in press). Recurrent affective disorder: Roots in developmental neurobiology and illness progression based on changes in gene expression. *Development and Psychopathology.*

Prange, A., Wilson, I., Lynn, C., Alltop, L., & Stikeleather, R. (1974). L-trytophan in mania: Contribution to a permissive hypothesis of affective disorders. *Archives of General Psychiatry, 30*, 56–62.

Puig-Antich, J. (1980a). Affective disorders in childhood: A review and perspective. *Psychiatric Clinics of North America, 3*, 403–424.

Puig-Antich, J. (1980b). Major depression and conduct disorder in prepuberty. *Journal of the American Academy of Child Psychiatry, 19*, 291–293.

Puig-Antich, J. (1982). Major depression and conduct disorder in prepuberty. *Journal of the American Academy of Child Psychiatry, 21*, 118–128.

Puig-Antich, J. (1986). Psychobiological markers: Effects of age and puberty. In M. Rutter, C. C. Izard, & P. B. Read (Eds.), *Depression in young people: Developmental and clinical perspectives* (pp. 341–381). New York: Guilford.

Puig-Antich, J., Dahl, R., Ryan, N., Novacenko, H., Goetz, D., Twomey, J., & Klepper, T. (1989). Cortisol secretion in prepubertal children with major depressive disorder. *Archives of General Psychiatry, 46*, 801–809.

Puig-Antich, J., Davies, M., Novacenko, H., Tabrizi, M., Ambrosini, P., Goetz, R., Bianca, J., & Sachar, E. (1984). Growth hormone secretion in prepubertal major depressive children: III. Response to insulin induced hypoglycemia in a drug-free, fully recovered clinical state. *Archives of General Psychiatry, 41*, 471–475.

Puig-Antich, J., Goetz, R., Davies, M., Fein, M., Hanlon, C., Chambers, W. J., Tabrizi, M. A., Sachar, E. J., & Weitzman, E. D. (1984). Growth hormone secretion in prepubertal children with major depression: II. Sleep-related plasma concentrations during a depressive episode. *Archives of General Psychiatry, 41*(5), 463–466.

Puig-Antich, J., Goetz, R., Davies, M., Tabrizi, M. A., Novacenko, H., Hanlon, C., Sachar, E. J., & Weitzman, E. D. (1984). Growth hormone secretion in prepubertal children with major depression: IV. Sleep-related plasma concentration in a drug-free, fully recovered clinical state. *Archives of General Psychiatry, 41*(5), 479–483.

Puig-Antich, J., Goetz, R., Hanlon, C., Davies, M., Thompson, J., Chambers, W., Tabrizi, M., & Weitzman, E. (1982). Sleep architecture and REM sleep measures in prepubertal children with major depression. *Archives of General Psychiatry, 39*, 932–939.

Puig-Antich, J., Goetz, R., Hanlon, C., Tabrizi, M., Davies, M., & Weitzman, E. (1983). Sleep architecture and REM sleep measures in prepubertal major depressives: Studies during recovery from a major depressive episode in a drug free state. *Archives of General Psychiatry, 40*, 187–192.

Puig-Antich, J., Novacenko, H., Davies, M., Chambers, W. J., Tabrizi, M. A., Krawiec, V., Ambrosini, P. J., & Sachar, E. J. (1984). Growth hormone secretion in prepubertal children with major depression: I. Sleep related plasma concentrations during a depressive episode. *Archives of General Psychiatry, 41*(5), 455–460.

Quiggle, N., Garber, J., Panak, W., & Dodge, K. (1992). Social information processing in aggressive and depressed children. *Child Development, 63*, 1305–1320.

Radke-Yarrow, M., Belmont, B., Nottelmann, E., & Bottomly, L. (1990). Young children's self-conceptions: Origins in the natural discourse of depressed and normal mothers and their children. In D. Cicchetti & M. Beeghly (Eds.), *The self in Transition* (pp. 345–361). Chicago: University of Chicago Press.

Radke-Yarrow, M., & Brown, E. (1993). Resilience and vulnerability in children of multiple-risk families. *Development and Psychopathology, 5*, 581–592.

Radke-Yarrow, M., Cummings, E. M., Kuczynski, L., & Chapman, M. (1985). Patterns of attachment in two-and-three-year-olds in normal families and families with parental depression. *Child Development, 56*, 884–893.

Radke-Yarrow, M., McCann, K., DeMulder, E., Belmont, B., Martinez, P., & Richardson, D. (in press). The role of attachment in the context of other relationships. *Development and Psychopathology.*

Radke-Yarrow, M., & Sherman, T. (1990). Hard growing: Children who survive. In J. Rolf, A. Masten, D. Cicchetti, K. Nuechterlein, & S. Weintraub (Eds.), *Risk and protective factors in the development of psychopathology* (pp. 97–119). New York: Cambridge University Press.

Radke-Yarrow, M., & Zahn-Waxler, C. (1990). Research on children of affectively ill parents: Some considerations for theory and research on normal development. *Development and Psychopathology, 2*, 349–366.

Radloff, L. (1975). Sex differences in depression: The effects of occupation and marital status. *Sex Roles, 1*, 249–265.

Radloff, L. (1977). The CES-D Scale: A self-report depression scale for research in the general population. *Applied Psychological Measurement, 1*, 385–401.

Rehm, L. (1977). A self control model of depression. *Behavior Therapy, 8*, 787–804.

Ribeiro, S., Tandon, R., Grunhaus, L., & Greden, J. (1993). The DST as a predictor of outcome in depression: A meta-analysis. *American Journal of Psychiatry, 150*, 1618–1629.

Richters, J. E., & Cicchetti, D. (1993). Mark Twain meets DSM-III-R: Conduct disorder, development, and the concept of harmful dysfunction. *Development and Psychopathology, 5*, 5–29.

Rie, H. (1966). Depression in childhood: A survey of some pertinent contributions. *Journal of the American Academy of Child Psychiatry, 5*, 653–685.

Rierdan, J., & Koff, E. (1993). Developmental variables in relation to depressive symptoms in adolescent girls. *Development and Psychopathology, 5*, 653–685.

Rogers, L., & Kegan, R. (1990). Mental growth and mental health as distinct concepts in the study of developmental psychopathology: Theory, research, and clinical applications. In D. Keating & H. Rosen (Eds.), *Constructivist perspectives on developmental psychopathology and atypical development* (pp. 103–147). Hillsdale, NJ: Erlbaum.

Rolf, J., Masten, A., Cicchetti, D., Nuechterlein, K., & Weintraub, S. (Eds.). (1990). *Risk and protective factors in the development of psychopathology.* New York: Cambridge University Press.

Rose, D., & Abramson, L. (1992). Developmental predictions of depressive cognitive style: Research and theory. In D. Cicchetti & S. L. Toth (Eds.), *Rochester Symposium on Developmental Psychopathology: Vol. 4. Developmental perspective on depression* (pp. 323–349). Rochester, NY: University of Rochester Press.

Rubin, K., Both, L., Zahn-Waxler, C., Cummings, E. M., & Wilkinson, M. (1991). Dyadic play behaviors of children of well and depressed mothers. *Development and Psychopathology, 3,* 243–251.

Rubin, K., LeMare, L., & Lollis, S. (1990). Social withdrawal in childhood: Developmental pathways to peer rejection. In S. Asher & J. Coie (Eds.), *Peer rejection in childhood* (pp. 217–249). New York: Cambridge University Press.

Rubin, K. H., & Mills, R. S. L. (1988). The many faces of social isolation in childhood. *Journal of Consulting and Clinical Psychology, 56,* 916–924.

Rutter, M. (1986). The developmental psychopathology of depression: Issues and perspectives. In M. Rutter, C. Izard, & P. Read (Eds.), *Depression in young people* (pp. 3–30). New York: Guilford.

Rutter, M. (1989). Age as an ambiguous variable in developmental research: Some epidemiological considerations from developmental psychopathology. *International Journal of Behavioral Development, 12,* 1–34.

Rutter, M. (1990). Psychosocial resilience and protective mechanisms. In J. Rolf, A. S. Masten, D. Cicchetti, K. H. Nuechterlein, & S. Weintraub (Eds.), *Risk and protective factors in the development of psychopathology* (pp. 181–214). New York: Cambridge University Press.

Rutter, M. (1991). Nature, nurture, and psychopathology. *Development and Psychopathology, 3,* 125–136.

Rutter, M., Macdonald, H., LeCouteur, A., Harrington, R., Bolton, P., & Bailey, A. (1990). Genetic findings in child psychiatric disorders—II. Empirical findings. *Journal of Child Psychology and Psychiatry, 31,* 39–83.

Rutter, M., & Quinton, D. (1984). Parental psychiatric disorder: Effects on children. *Psychological Medicine, 14,* 853–880.

Ryan, N., Birmaher, B., Perel, J., Dahl, R., Meyer, V., Al-Shabbout, M., Iyengar, S., & Puig-Antich, J. (1992). Neuroendocrine response to L-5-hydroxytryptophan challenge in prepubertal major depression. *Archives of General Psychiatry, 49,* 843–851.

Ryan, N., Dahl, R., Birmaher, B., Williamson, D., Iyengar, S., Nelson, B., Puig-Antich, J., & Perel, J. (1994). Stimulatory tests of growth hormone secretion in prepubertal major depression: Depressed versus normal children. *Journal of the American Academy of Child and Adolescent Psychiatry, 33,* 824–833.

Ryan, N., Puig-Antich, J., Rabinovich, H., Ambrosini, P., Robinson, D., Nelson, B., & Novacenko, H. (1988). Growth hormone response to desmethylimipramine in depressed and suicidal adolescents. *Journal of Affective Disorders, 15,* 323–332.

Sameroff, A. J., Seifer, R., & Zax, M. (1982). Early development of children at risk for emotional disorder. *Monographs of the Society for Research in Child Development, 47* (Serial No. 199).

Scarr, S., & McCartney, K. (1983). How people make their own environments: A theory of genotype-environment effects. *Child Development, 54,* 424–435.

Schildkraut, J. (1965). The catecholamine hypothesis of affective disorders: A review of supporting evidence. *American Journal of Psychiatry, 122,* 509–522.

Schildkraut, J. (1976). The current status of biological criteria for classifying the depressive disorders and predicting responses to treatment. *Psychopharmacological Bulletin, 10,* 5–25.

Schildkraut, J., & Kety, S. (1967). Biogenic amines and emotion. *Science, 156,* 21–30.

Sedler, M. (1983). Falret's Discovery: The origin of the concept of bipolar affective illness. *American Journal of Psychiatry, 140,* 1127–1133.

Selman, R. (1980). *The growth of interpersonal understanding: Developmental and clinical analyses.* New York: Academic Press.

Shedler, J., Mayman, M., & Manis, M. (1993). The *illusion* of mental health. *American Psychologist, 48,* 1117–1131.

Siegel, R. (1973). *Galen on psychology, psychopathology, and function and disease of the nervous system.* Basel: Karger.

Siever, L., & Davis, K. (1985). Overview: Toward a dysregulation hypothesis of depression. *American Journal of Psychiatry, 142,* 1017–1031.

Spoont, M. (1992). Modulatory role of serotonin in neural information processing: Implications for human psychopathology. *Psychological Bulletin, 112,* 330–350.

Sroufe, L. A. (1979). The coherence of individual development: Early care attachment, and subsequent developmental issues. *American Psychologist, 34,* 834–841.

Sroufe, L. A. (1989). Pathways to adaptation and maladaptation: Psychopathology as developmental deviation. In D. Cicchetti (Ed.), *Rochester Symposium on Developmental Psychopathology: Vol. 1. The emergence of a discipline* (pp. 13–40). Hillsdale, NJ: Erlbaum.

Sroufe, L. A. (1990). An organizational perspective on the self. In D. Cicchetti & M. Beeghly (Eds.), *The self in transition: Infancy to childhood* (pp. 281–307). Chicago: University of Chicago Press.

Sroufe, L. A., Egeland, B., & Kreutzer, T. (1990). The fate of early experience following developmental change: Longitudinal approaches to individual adaptation in childhood. *Child Development, 61,* 1363–1373.

Sroufe, L. A., Fox, N., & Pancake, V. (1983). Attachment and dependency in developmental perspective. *Child Development, 54,* 1615–1627.

Sroufe, L. A., & Rutter, M. (1984). The domain of developmental psychopathology. *Child Development, 55,* 17–29.

Sroufe, L. A., & Waters, E. (1976). The ontogenesis of smiling and laughter: A perspective on the organization of development in infancy. *Psychological Review, 83,* 173–189.

Staudinger, U., Marsiske, M., & Baltes, P. (1993). Resilience and levels of reserve capacity in later adulthood: Perspectives from life-span theory. *Development and Psychopathology, 5,* 541–566.

Stern, D. (1985). *The interpersonal world of the infant.* New York: Basic Books.

Stoudemire, A., & Blazer, D. (1985). Depression in the elderly. In E. Beckham & W. Leber (Eds.), *Handbook of depression: Treatment, assessment, and research* (pp. 556–586). Homewood IL: Dorsey Press.

Strober, M., & Carlson, G. (1982). Bipolar illness in adolescents with major depression. *Archives of General Psychiatry, 39,* 549–555.

Strober, M., Lampert, C., Schmidt, S., & Morrell, W. (1993). The course of major depressive disorder in adolescents: I. Recovery and risk of manic switching in a follow-up of psychotic and nonpsychotic subtypes. *Journal of the American Academy of Child and Adolescent Psychiatry, 32,* 34–42.

Susman, E. J., Trickett, P. K., Iannotti, R. J., Hollenbeck, B. E., & Zahn-Waxler, C. (1985). Childrearing patterns in depressed abusive, and normal mothers. *American Journal of Orthopsychiatry, 55*(2), 237–251.

Tarullo, L., DeMulder, E., Martinez, P., & Radke-Yarrow, M. (1994). Dialogues with preadolescents and adolescents: Mother-child interaction patterns in affectively ill and well dyads. *Journal of Abnormal Psychology, 22,* 33–51.

Thase, M., Frank, E., & Kuper, D. (1985). Biological processes in depression. In E. Beckham & W. Leber (Eds.), *Handbook of depression: Treatment, assessment, and research* (pp. 816–913). Homewood, IL: Dorsey Press.

Tomarken, A., & Davidson, R. (1994). Frontal brain activation in repressors and nonrepressors. *Journal of Abnormal Psychology, 103,* 339–349.

Toth, S. L., & Cicchetti, D. (in press). Patterns of relatedness, depressive symptomatology, and perceived competence in maltreated children. *Journal of Consulting and Clinical Psychology.*

Toth, S. L., Manly, J. T., & Cicchetti, D. (1992). Child maltreatment and vulnerability to depression. *Development and Psychopathology, 4,* 323–339.

Trad, P. (1986). *Infant depression.* New York: Springer-Verlag.

Trad, P. (1987). *Infant and childhood depression: Developmental factors.* New York: Wiley.

Tronick, E. Z., & Gianino, A. F. (1986). The transmission of maternal disturbances to the infant. In E. Z. Tronick & T. Field (Eds.), *Maternal depression and infant disturbances* (pp. 5–11). San Francisco: Jossey-Bass.

Tsuang, M., & Faraone, S. (1990). *The genetics of mood disorders.* Baltimore: Johns Hopkins University Press.

Tucker, D. (1981). Lateral brain function, emotion and conceptualization. *Psychological Bulletin, 89,* 19–46.

Tucker, D., & Williamson, P. (1984). Asymmetric neural control systems in human self-regulation. *Psychological Review, 91,* 185–215.

Tulving, E. (1985). How many memory systems are there? *American Psychologist, 40,* 385–398.

Tulving, E. (1989). Remembering and knowing the past. *American Scientist, 77,* 361–398.

Van Praag, H. (1977). New evidence of serotonin-deficient depression. *Neuropsychobiology, 3,* 56–63.

Vasta, R. (1982). Physical child abuse: A dual-component analysis. *Developmental Review, 2,* 125–149.

von Bertalanffy, L. (1968). *General system theory.* New York: Braziller.

Waddington, C. H. (1957). *The strategy of genes.* London: Allen & Unwin.

Wakefield, J. C. (1992). Disorder as harmful dysfunction: A conceptual critique of DSM-III-R's definition of mental disorder. *Psychological Review, 99,* 232–247.

Walker, E., Downey, G., & Bergman, A. (1989). The effects of parental psychopathology and maltreatment on child behavior: A test of the diathesis-stress model. *Child Development, 60,* 15–24.

Walker, E., Downey, G., & Nightingale, N. (1989). The non-orthogonal nature of risk factors: Considerations for investigations of children at risk for psychopathology. *Journal of Primary Prevention, 9,* 143–163.

Warner, V., Weissman, M., Fendrich, M., Wickramaratne, P., & Moreau, D. (1992). The course of major depression in the offspring of depressed parents: Incidence, recurrence, and recovery. *Archives of General Psychiatry, 49,* 795–801.

Watson, D., & Clark, L. (1984). Negative affectivity: The disposition to experience aversive emotional states. *Psychological Bulletin, 96,* 465–490.

Watson, D., & Clark, L. A., & Carey, G. (1988). Positive and negative affectivity and their relation to anxiety and depressive disorders. *Journal of Abnormal Psychology, 97,* 346–353.

Watson, D., & Tellegen, A. (1985). Toward a consensual structure of mood. *Psychological Bulletin, 98,* 219–235.

Watson, J., Hopkins, N., Roberts, J., Steitz, J., & Weiner, A. (1987). *Molecular biology of the gene: Vol. 1. General principles; Vol. 2. Specialized aspects.* Menlo Park, CA: Benjamin/Cummings.

Weissman, M., Bruce, M., Leaf, P., Florio, L., & Holzer, C. (1991). Affective disorders. In L. Robins & D. Reigier (Eds.), *Psychiatric disorders in America* (pp. 53–80). New York: Free Press.

Weissman, M., Gammon, G., John, K., Merikangas, K., Warner, V., Prusoff, B., & Sholmskas, D. (1987). Children of depressed parents. *Archives of General Psychiatry, 44,* 847–853.

Weissman, M., Kidd, K., & Prusoff, B. (1982). Variability in rates of affective disorders in relatives of depressed and normal probands. *Archives of General Psychiatry, 39,* 1397–1403.

Weissman, M., & Paykel, E. (1974). *The depressed woman: A study of social relationships.* Chicago, IL: University of Chicago Press.

Werner, H. (1948). *Comparative psychology of mental development.* New York: International Universities Press.

Werner, H., & Kaplan, B. (1963). *Symbol formation: An organismic-developmental approach to language and the expression of thought.* New York: Wiley.

Wells, K., Burnam, A., Rogers, W., Hays, R., & Camp, P. (1992). The course of depression in adult outpatients: Results from the medical outcomes study. *Archives of General Psychiatry, 49,* 788–794.

Wender, P., Kety, S., Rosenthal, D., Schulsinger, F., Ortmann, J., & Lunde, I. (1986). Psychiatric disorders in the biological and adoptive families of adopted individuals with affective disorders. *Archives of General Psychiatry, 43,* 923–929.

Winokur, G., (1975). The Iowa 500: Heterogeneity and course of manic-depressive illness (bipolar). *Comprehensive Psychiatry, 16,* 125–131.

Winokur, G. (1979). Unipolar depression: Is it divisible into autonomous subtypes? *Archives of General Psychiatry, 36,* 47–52.

Winokur, G., Clayton, P., & Reich, T. (1969). *Manic-depressive illness.* St. Louis, MO: Mosby.

Winokur, G., Coryell, W., Keller, M., Endicott, J., & Akiskal, H. (1993). A prospective follow-up of patients with bipolar and primary unipolar affective disorder. *Archives of General Psychiatry, 50,* 457–465.

Wohlwill, J. (1973). *The study of behavioral development.* New York: Academic Press.

Yehuda, R., Giller, E., Southwick, S., Lowy, M., & Mason, J. (1991). Hypothalamic-pituitary adrenal dysfunction in posttraumatic stress disorder. *Biological Psychiatry, 30,* 1031–1048.

Young, R., & Klerman, G. (1992). Mania in late life: Focus on age at onset. *American Journal of Psychiatry, 147,* 867–876.

Zahn-Waxler, C., Denham, S., Cummings, E. M., & Iannotti, R. (1992). Peer relations in children with a depressed caregiver. In R. Parke & G. Ladd (Eds.), *Family-peer relationships: Modes of linkage* (pp. 317–344). Hillsdale, NJ: Erlbaum.

Zahn-Waxler, C., Iannotti, R., Cummings, E. M., & Denham, S. (1990). Antecedents of problem behaviors in children of depressed mothers. *Development and Psychopathology, 2,* 271–291.

Zahn-Waxler, C., & Kochanska, G. (1990). The origins of guilt. In R. Thompson (Ed.), *Nebraska Symposium on Motivation: Vol. 36. Socio-emotional development* (pp. 183–258). Lincoln: University of Nebraska Press.

Zahn-Waxler, C., Kochanska, G., Krupnick, J., & McKnew, D. (1990). Patterns of guilt in children of depressed and well mothers. *Developmental Psychology, 26,* 51–59.

Zahn-Waxler, C., McKnew, D. H., Cummings, E. M., Davenport, Y. B., & Radke-Yarrow, M. (1984). Problem behaviors and peer interactions of young children with a manic depressive parent. *American Journal of Psychiatry, 141,* 236–240.

Zahn-Waxler, C., & Wagner, E. (1993). Caregivers' interpretations of infant emotions: A comparison of depressed and well mothers. In R. Emde, J. Osofsky, & P. Butterfield (Eds.), *Clinical infant reports: The I Feel pictures* (pp. 175–184). Madison, CT: International Universities Press.

Zigler, E., & Glick, M. (1986). *A developmental approach to adult psychopathology.* New York: Wiley.

Zis, A. P., & Goodwin, F. K. (1979). Major affective disorder as a recurrent illness: A critical review. *Archives of General Psychiatry, 36,* 835–839.

Zupan, B. A., Hammen, C., & Jaenicke, C. (1987). The effects of current mood and prior depressive history on self-schematic processing in children. *Journal of Experimental Child Psychology, 43,* 149–158.

CHAPTER 12

The Development and Ecology of Antisocial Behavior

THOMAS J. DISHION, DORAN C. FRENCH, and GERALD R. PATTERSON

THE ANTISOCIAL PATTERN

Antisocial behavior is disruptive to the individual, to relationships, and to the community at large. Antisocial children fail at school and are often disliked by peers and rejected by parents (Patterson, Reid, & Dishion, 1992). Not surprisingly, such behavior is often accompanied by feelings of depression (Patterson & Stoolmiller, 1991). Childhood antisocial behavior is of major concern to adults in the community; nearly half of all childhood referrals to outpatient clinics are for antisocial behavior (Kazdin, 1987). Having a history of antisocial behavior is associated with an array of adult mental health problems (Robins, 1966). Antisocial adults are at greater risk for work failure, troubled marriages, and expensive sanctions from police and penal institutions (Robins, 1966). As parents, antisocial adults tend to elicit antisocial behavior in their children (Patterson & Dishion, 1988), thus perpetuating those patterns across generations.

Pessimism regarding the efficacy of interventions is a constant burden for clinicians working with antisocial people. It is tempting to resort to "bad seed" models when tools and resources are lacking to change antisocial behavior. Bad seed models emphasize traits of the person over environmental effects in explaining the stability and continuity of antisocial behavior. Indeed, the stability and continuity of antisocial behavior is such that the use of the term *trait* is empirically justified (Loeber & Dishion, 1983; Olweus, 1979). A trait model, on the other hand, helps very little in the design of remedial interventions.

In this chapter, we will apply the developmental psychopathology perspective to the development and ecology of antisocial behavior. In doing so, we will review the state of the art of etiologic research, addressing the onset, chronicity, and desistance of antisocial behavior as well as correlated features such as frequency and seriousness. We will attempt to integrate interdisciplinary findings, especially those of developmental psychology, sociology, and biology, with findings from clinical psychology. We consider antisocial behavior as a continuum, but one in which the form of expression changes over time (Patterson, 1993). Because researchers vary considerably in their approach to measurement and definition, this issue requires some attention. So we now turn to the question, how can we define and measure antisocial behavior.

Definition and Measurement

A key factor in aggression research has been the need to incorporate intentions of the actor in the definition of aggressive behavior (Parke & Slaby, 1983). An act is considered aggressive if the actor *intended* to inflict harm on another. For example, swinging a baseball bat at a family member is considered extremely aggressive, regardless whether the bat met its mark, as long as the act was intended. In contrast, running over a pedestrian with a car would not be considered aggressive or antisocial if the event were accidental.

The obvious difficulty with intention as a definitional component for antisocial behavior is the black box problem. How do we know if an act was intentional? What about "accidents" that are subconsciously intended? Although intentions are important in our everyday experience of antisocial behavior, they are not terribly useful when doing research on antisocial behavior because the research depends on loose inferences regarding the actor's labeling of his or her own behavior.

Another approach is to consider the function of antisocial behavior within social interaction or behavioral contexts (Patterson, 1982). In this approach, the cornerstone of the coercion model, the investigator determines behaviors that contingently follow certain classes of events (Patterson & Cobb, 1971). Coercive antisocial behavior is defined as contingent aversive behavior. Such acts tend to contingently follow aversive stimuli (e.g., demands by adults) or negative emotional states (e.g., arguing, whining, temper, biting, hunger, boredom, etc.). The contingent connection between two aversive events can be established without referring

Preparation of this chapter was supported in part by grants to Dr. T. J. Dishion from the National Institute on Drug Abuse (R01 DA 05304, R01 DA 07031), to Dr. G. R. Patterson from the National Institute of Mental Health (R01 MH 37940), and to Dr. John B. Reid from the National Institute of Mental Health (P50 MH 46690). Margaret McKean, Mary Perry, and Carol Kimball are gratefully acknowledged for their support in preparing this manuscript, which entailed more than a few hours of editing, reference retrieval, and patience. Many of the figures in this chapter were prepared by Will Mayer.

to intention (e.g., what the dentist does is aversive, but it is not contingent).

Patterson and Cobb (1971) defined classes of traits and revealed the enormous amount of work entailed in empirically establishing which acts are part of a general antisocial response class. High correlations between aversive behaviors are generally taken as sufficient evidence of there being a common response class. As it turns out, different measures of antisocial behavior tend to intercorrelate quite highly, resembling what Allport (1937) originally defined as a trait: "dynamic and flexible dispositions, resulting, at least in part, from the integration of specific habits, expressing characteristic modes of adaptation to one's surroundings" (pp. 39–140). Antisocial behavior tends to be consistent across settings and informants (Achenbach, McConaughy, & Howell, 1987; Bernal, Delfini, North, & Kreutzer, 1976; Charlesbois, Tremblay, Gagnon, Larivee, & Laurent, 1989; Loeber & Dishion, 1984; Patterson, 1986; Patterson, Dishion, & Bank, 1984). Antisocial behavior in childhood is also quite stable over time (Loeber, 1982; Loeber & Dishion, 1983; Olweus, 1979; Patterson, Capaldi, & Bank, 1991). In all respects, child antisocial behavior seems to be a form of adaptation that is relatively consistent across diverse settings.

One problem with a functional approach to studying antisocial behavior is how to get from the reductionistic microsocial exchanges (e.g., noncompliance, threats, criticism) to behaviors considered more seriously antisocial (e.g., robbery, shoplifting, vandalism). From a social interactional point of view, the antisocial trait can be seen as an aggregation of many discrete events (Epstein, 1979). This includes thousands of social exchanges with parents, peers, teachers, siblings, and other agents of socialization (Patterson, Reid, & Dishion, 1992). As we discussed later in this chapter, the frequency and variety of antisocial acts are the best predictors of more serious forms of antisocial behavior, including violence. We hypothesize that frequency predicts violence or severity. The common thread between microsocial coercive acts and more serious antisocial behavior is that both are powerful means of changing the individual's environment. The coercive acts themselves are experienced as aversive by the victims.

Formal diagnostic systems also define antisocial behavior. There have been dramatic shifts, however, in the way that antisocial behavior has been categorized. In the third edition of the *Diagnostic and Statistical Manual of Mental Disorders* (DSM-III, American Psychiatric Association, 1980), several discrete diagnoses were associated with child antisocial behavior. Oppositional Disorder was defined as a lesser form of antisocial behavior, in contrast to the Conduct Disorder classifications. Four different categories of Conduct Disorder were defined: Undersocialized-Aggressive; Undersocialized-Nonaggressive; Socialized-Aggressive, and Socialized-Nonaggressive. These classifications were based on two dimensions. The first was the aggressive-nonaggressive aspect of the antisocial behavior; and the second was the child's capability to form close relationships. The latter classification relied heavily on Quay's (1964) influential distinction.

In the DSM-III-R (American Psychiatric Association, 1987), the four subtypes of Conduct Disorder were dropped, leaving the categories of Conduct Disorder and Oppositional Defiant Disorder. In the DSM-IV (American Psychiatric Association, 1994), Oppositional Disorder developmentally precedes Conduct Disorder, and both are representative of a more general class of disruptive behavior disorders (Loeber, Green, Lahey, Christ, & Frick, 1992).

The diagnosis of Antisocial Personality for adults in the DSM system has undergone less change. Although a history of antisocial behavior is certainly an important part of this diagnosis, other intrapersonal factors are also considered such as the lack of empathy, manipulativeness, and superficial interpersonal relationships. This diagnosis was heavily influenced by dynamic theorizing concerning what researchers once referred to as the *sociopath* or the *psychopath*. Research and modeling of adult antisocial behavior falls far behind the research in childhood and adolescence.

Dimensionality

Underlying the major shifts in diagnostic strategies are questions regarding the extent to which antisocial behavior represents a single dimension or is, in fact, multidimensional. A unidimensional perspective assumes that the psychiatric categories of Oppositional Defiant Disorder (ODD), Conduct Disorder (CD), and Antisocial Personality Disorder (APD) are three interrelated points on a continuum. The unidimensional perspective proposes that the three diagnostic categories represent a developmental progression where the basic case of ODD begins with noncompliance, abrasive temper, and argumentativeness followed by the emergence of behaviors such as stealing and fighting for CD and disorganized work and marital problems for APD. The progression is cumulative. If this is true, then there are not three distinct categories, but a dynamic representation of the same disorder manifested at three points in time.

Loeber and Schmaling (1985) suggested that antisocial behavior should be seen as a bipolar dimension, with one end of the dimension being Covert and the other being Overt. Covert antisocial behavior describes acts such as lying, stealing, and vandalism. These acts are, by and large, performed outside the view of supervisors. Overt antisocial behaviors, on the other hand, are interpersonal and confrontational and include arguing, yelling, and hitting. Loeber and Schmaling (1985) examined 22 studies that included over 11,000 children with recorded referral symptoms. Using a nonmetric, multidimensional scaling approach, they found that the Overt-Covert bipolar dimension accounted for 69% of the variance. Behaviors that loaded high on the Covert end of the bipolar dimension were alcohol use, truancy from school, and association with deviant peers. Those that loaded high on the Overt dimension were hyperactivity, screaming, stubbornness, moodiness, attention seeking, arguing, teasing, impulsiveness, attacking people, jealousy, sulking, and displaying temper tantrums.

Several questions emerge when evaluating this position. One is the generalizability of these analyses to the main population. Patterson, Reid, and Dishion (1992) used structural equation modeling (SEM) to construct a multitrait, multimethod test of the hypothesis that overt and covert behaviors form a unitary construct. They analyzed data from 140 fourth- and seventh-grade boys who participated in a planning study for the Oregon Youth Study (OYS)

(Loeber & Dishion, 1984; Patterson & Stouthamer-Loeber, 1984) and who were rated by parents, teachers, and peers on both their overt and covert behaviors. A confirmatory model was run to assess the relative fit of a two-factor (i.e., Clandestine and Overt) versus a one-factor (i.e., General Antisocial) model. The two-factor model satisfactorily fit the data, but there was an extremely high correlation between the two constructs, which approached 1.0. The chi-square difference between the one- and two-factor models was not statistically different, indicating that the one-factor model sufficed to explain the pattern of correlations between teacher, peer, and parent report of Overt and Clandestine behavior in boys ranging in age from 9 to 15. These findings were replicated in the Oregon Youth Study (Patterson, Reid, & Dishion, 1992). The failure to find family interaction differences between covert and overt antisocial boys leads to further questions regarding the utility of this distinction (Patterson, 1982).

Another literature relevant to the issue of dimensionality is the area of specialization in criminology. Much of this discussion has focused on whether the offenders specialized in committing violent or nonviolent crimes. Farrington's (1991) analysis of the Cambridge study data showed no tendency for London males in the sample to specialize in property or person crimes. There was, however, a tendency for those individuals who committed a variety of antisocial acts throughout childhood and adolescence to escalate to more serious violent acts, and frequent offenders tended to be arrested for violent offenses, $p = .49$. Thus the frequency and variety of antisocial acts seemed to be the best predictor of escalation to more serious antisocial behavior.

A systematic test of the variety and frequency hypothesis was conducted by Loeber and Schmaling (1985), who compared the family and peer adjustment profiles of youths who were classified as Pure Fighters, Pure Stealers, Versatile (i.e., fighters and stealers), and Not Antisocial. The Versatile boys, in comparison with boys in the other three groups, engaged in both overt and clandestine behaviors and exhibited more deficits in parental monitoring, showed increased association with deviant peers, and displayed a variety of problem behaviors including hyperactivity. Similarly, Loeber and Dishion (1984) found differences among boys who fought only at school, those who fought at home, those who fought both at home and school, and those who were nonfighters. The fighters in all situations experienced less monitoring by parents, associated with more deviant peers, and experienced more inept parent discipline practices than boys who fought only at home or school or who were nonfighters.

One of the simplest and yet most powerful differentiations is age of onset of delinquent behavior. Robins (1966) noted that boys arrested early had more serious outcomes than those arrested later. Patterson and Yoerger (1993) demonstrated that boys showing high levels of antisocial behavior in middle childhood were at risk for arrest in early adolescence (13.9 years). An event-history analysis showed that half the boys scoring at the 70th percentile on a multiagent-defined antisocial trait score had early arrest status. Of these, 77% were chronic offenders (three or more arrests) by age 18. Half the early arrest boys were violent offenders. Furthermore, 94% of all these violent offenders were also chronic offenders (Patterson & Yoerger, 1993). The Capaldi and Patterson (1994) study showed that early-arrest boys lived in contexts that

were significantly different from late-arrest boys. They came from homes with lower SES and the parents were antisocial and unemployed. The early-arrest boys also experienced more disruptive parenting practices. This early-arrest model seems promising in that these boys were characterized both by different histories and different outcomes.

As clinicians, we appreciate that antisocial behavior may often be presented by parents as specific (e.g., lying, stealing, difficulties with anger). Research, on the other hand, suggests that age of onset and frequency and variety of offense are most prognostic of significant development outcomes (Moffitt, 1993a). Therefore, in this chapter, we focus on the general trait *antisocial*, which represents both the covert and overt dimensions of antisocial behavior. The one-factor model is useful because the component behaviors are highly intercorrelated and are relatively stable across settings, as seen in multiagent and multimethod data. An example of this extensive measurement approach is provided in *Antisocial Boys* by Patterson, Reid, and Dishion (1992). The extensive convergence of the diverse measures of antisocial behavior in middle childhood is shown in Figure 12.1. The variety of antisocial acts, frequency, variety, and severity across settings is probably the best

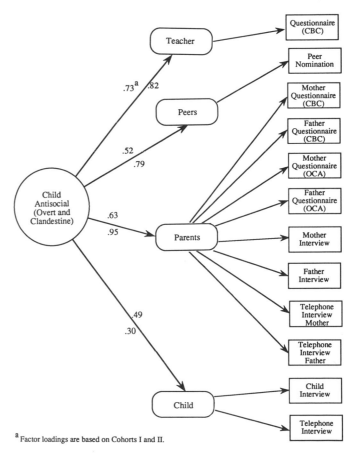

[a] Factor loadings are based on Cohorts I and II.

Figure 12.1 A multiagent and multimethod approach to the measurement of antisocial behavior. From *Antisocial Boys* by G. R. Patterson, J. B. Reid, and T. J. Dishion, 1992, (p. 28). Copyright 1992 by Castalia Publishing Co. Used by permission.

index of severity. This approach is consistent with findings that measurements taken from an aggregate of situations are more likely to predict behavior in new settings (Buss & Craik, 1983; Epstein, 1979; Moskowitz, 1982).

This general antisocial score is also highly predictive of subsequent delinquent offending. Patterson and Yoerger (1993) found that an Antisocial construct score that represented frequency, variety, and number of settings predicted delinquent offending at age 15 to 16 with a relative improvement over chance of 63%.

Continuity

Antisocial behavior is among the most stable of the behavioral characteristics, with stabilities close to those seen for intellectual ability scores. Olweus (1979) reviewed 16 studies and found a strong stability for aggression in boys from ages 2 through 18. There was, however, less apparent stability from preschool to middle childhood than there was from middle childhood to adolescence.

The longitudinal study by R. B. Cairns, B. D. Cairns, and Neckerman (1989) is among the few studies that carefully examined the stability of aggression in boys and girls from childhood to adolescence. Both short-term and long-term stability were observed in teacher- and self-ratings of aggressiveness in boys and girls. For boys, the stability of teacher ratings of aggressive behavior from Grade 4 to 9 was .45; for girls, the comparable stability coefficient was .33. Self-ratings of aggressiveness, however, revealed higher 5-year stability for boys (.36) compared with girls (.13). Although short-term stabilities within middle childhood were quite similar for boys and girls, there appeared to be less stability for girls in adolescence.

There is also continuity from childhood aggression to delinquency. In reviewing the literature, Loeber (1982) summarized data suggesting a tendency for children who were originally high on the antisocial behavior trait to exhibit high adolescent delinquency. Loeber and Dishion (1983) used a meta-analytic approach and found that antisocial behavior in middle childhood was among the best predictors of adolescent delinquency.

More recently, Patterson and Yoerger (1993) assessed the stability of antisocial behavior over a 6-year time span for 200 boys in the Oregon Youth Study. Multiagent and multimethod definitions of antisocial behavior were employed. The Antisocial construct measured at age 9 to 10 years included parent, teacher, and peer ratings, and direct observations. The Delinquency construct, measured at age 15 to 16, was defined by official records of police contact and self-reported delinquency. Antisocial behavior was extremely stable from middle childhood, as shown by a SEM stability coefficient above .80. This stability was particularly dramatic because the constructs were defined by different assessment methods, avoiding the monomethod bias that results in inflated estimates of stability due to correlating two measures sharing the same assessment method (Cook & Campbell, 1979).

Equally dramatic is the continuity of antisocial behavior over long time periods, including across generations. Huesmann, Eron, Lefkowitz, and Walder (1984) found significant correlations between peer nominations of male aggression at age 8 compared with measures of male antisocial behavior at age 30. These varied from .19 for traffic violations to .30 for driving while intoxicated.

The evidence for stability in antisocial behavior for females was more limited. Peer nominated aggression at age 8 correlated only with MMPI 4/9 profile (i.e., Psychopathic Deviate) ($r = .15$) and punishment practices of children ($r = .19$) at age 30. The concept of continuity in function by variety of form is referred to as heterotypic continuity within a developmental psychopathology framework (Cicchetti, 1990). Simply put, the topography of antisocial behavior shifts over the life span. The divergence in form of antisocial behavior suggests that there are age-related progressions in antisocial behavior, a question to which we now turn.

Progressions

Patterson (1982) described how preschool children "coerce" their parents to get their own way and consequently learn to maximize short-term gain. In this sense, the antisocial individual is considered the ultimate "here-and-now" person. The net result of this overlearned tendency is a failure to develop strategies for forestalling immediate relief for the sake of long-term objectives. Patterson (1982) places noncompliance and avoidance at the core of the antisocial child's adaptive style, overlearned in thousands of transactions with his or her environment. The overlearned quality of the interaction suggests that children with considerable practice in coercive behavior will automatically (i.e., unconsciously) adapt to novel circumstances with functionally equivalent behavior.

Patterson (1982) demonstrated a progression from noncompliance to temper tantrums to physical attack for toddlers at 18 months of age. According to mother ratings, almost all boys who used physical attack also had temper tantrums. It was particularly interesting that most boys who were in this progression remained there through age 5. Patterson and Duncan (1993) showed that this same sample, with intact, middle-class families had mother and father ratings that predicted ODD status by Grade 2. The multiple correlation of .623 showed that highly coercive preschool boys were perceived by teachers and parents to be ODD several years later. This provides strong support for coercive behavior as the pathway from preschool to childhood ODD.

Patterson and Dawes (1975) used cross-sectional data to test the hypothesis that noncompliant behavior progresses to aggression, stealing, and eventually to fire setting. The conditional probabilities relating less serious forms of antisocial behavior to the most serious forms (e.g., fire setting) fit the Guttman statistical model of invariant progressions. This model, however, was based on behavior patterns existing at the time of intake into treatment for children referred for behavior problems. Patterson, Reid, and Dishion (1992) used longitudinal data on a nonclinical sample to test the same hypothesis. The data base consisted of 200 boys in the Oregon Youth Study (OYS) as they matured from age 9 to age 12. An ordered relation over time was found between parent-reported disobedience, parent-reported temper tantrums, teacher-reported physical fighting, and finally teacher-reported stealing. Teacher reports of fighting and stealing were predicted at better-than-chance levels from parent reports of less serious behaviors occurring in the home. This noncompliance progression did not, however, account for all the boys' antisocial behavior exhibited in schools. This suggests the possibility of alternative pathways for about a third of all antisocial individuals (Patterson, Reid, & Dishion, 1992).

Less studied are progressions in antisocial behavior that occur in adolescence and adulthood. For youngsters who start later, do noncompliance and temper tantrums signal the beginning of the same progressions, or are other prodromal behaviors more relevant at different points in the life span? In a national probability sample, Elliott, Huizinga, and Menard (1989) explored progressions of delinquent behavior and substance use in middle adolescence. They found that minor delinquency (in conjunction with alcohol use) tended to precede other more serious forms of problem behaviors including index crimes, marijuana, and polydrug use.

Loeber (1988) hypothesized that three pathways account for the development of problem behavior. Within the Aggressive-Versatile path are those children who start early by showing interpersonal aggression, poor peer relations, hyperactivity, and educational failure. Those in the Nonaggressive-Antisocial path have an onset during middle childhood or early adolescence that is perpetuated by deviant peer involvement. A third pathway describes individuals without early or concurrent antisocial behavior who exhibit substance use problems. The extent to which a common progression applies to early and late initiators of antisocial behavior is an unresolved issue. We know very little about the antecedents of late-starting adolescent antisocial behavior. Moreover, there are virtually no data on individuals who suddenly initiate a pattern of antisocial behavior as adults and eventually commit serious crimes.

Summary

Perhaps because of the disruptive impact of antisocial behavior on society, there is a vast literature on its measurement and developmental course. Age of onset appears to be the most prognostic of developmental course, with frequency and variety of antisocial acts serving as a robust dependent variable. A functional perspective seems promising in understanding the continuity of antisocial behavior, with the fundamental process being noncompliance and avoidance of the demands of social living.

The developmental progression of antisocial behavior appears to follow a pattern of hierarchical integration, with new forms of antisocial acts from middle childhood through adulthood embellishing the central theme of noncompliance and avoidance. Thus, heterotypic continuity is to be expected. This is observed when examining the behavior of antisocial individuals over the life course, changing with transforming contexts of each developmental stage. Early forms of antisocial behavior may be direct noncompliance with a parent's requests (e.g., temper tantrums). In middle childhood, stealing and lying might be added to the pattern; in adulthood, noncompliance with traffic or other laws might be evident. Difficulties with close intimate relationships seem to become a central feature in adulthood. Because of the differential course of early and late onset, it is quite likely that each has somewhat different adaptive functions and/or etiologies.

Associated and Comorbid Features

A variety of characteristics tend to be associated with antisocial behavior that are not, in themselves, antisocial. These include skill deficits, substance use, and precocious sexual activity. Antisocial behavior also co-occurs or is prominent in the disruptive behavior disorders in DSM-III-R classification, among which is Attention Deficit with Hyperactivity Disorder (ADHD). The comorbidity between classifications that are purely antisocial behaviors (ODD, CD) and ADHD is quite high.

Although such associated features may not be causal, they could be organized into three groups. Some features may simply be mutual developmental outcomes from the same process. For example, skill deficits may be a *concomitant* of antisocial behavior in the sense that they arise out of the same child-rearing circumstances that lead to child antisocial behavior. Other factors may be *potentiating,* that is, comorbid characteristics that potentiate the development of antisocial behavior within the same environmental conditions (Cicchetti, 1993). Other associated features might best be considered *sequelae,* as the available evidence suggests that these features are actually outcomes of the antisocial behavior.

Skill Deficits

Most antisocial children exhibit skill deficits across multiple domains, including academic, interpersonal, and intellectual (Dishion, Loeber, Stouthamer-Loeber, & Patterson, 1984; Patterson, 1982). Farrington (1991) noted that more than 80% of boys who became adult frequent offenders dropped out of school prior to matriculation. These low skills are so salient that some investigators suggest that they cause antisocial behavior. This hypothesis is captured by the criminological theory referred to as *strain* (Cloward & Ohlin, 1960). Strain theory proposes that the individual's inability to access material culture due to his or her socioeconomic status and lack of social and academic skills is a necessary but not sufficient condition for engaging in antisocial behavior. Interventionists have also set out to reduce antisocial behavior by improving the social (Spence & Marzillier, 1981) or academic skills (Cohen, 1977) of antisocial youngsters. In general, they have found that improvements in skills are not associated with reductions in antisocial behavior.

Substance Use

The association between antisocial behavior, other problem behavior, and substance use has been interpreted as indicative of a general problem-behavior syndrome (Gottfred & Hirschi, 1990; Jessor & Jessor, 1977). Early antisocial behavior is a risk factor for adolescent substance use. This was established by studies in the United States (e.g., Dishion, Capaldi, & Ray, in press; Kellam, Brown, Rubin, & Ensminger, 1983; Smith & Fogg, 1979), Britain (West & Farrington, 1977), and Finland (Pulkinnen, 1983). It also appears that early antisocial behavior is a vulnerability factor for excessive use or abuse of substances (Hirschi & Gottfredson, 1983; Kellam et al., 1983; McCord, 1988; Miller & Brown, 1991). Miller and Brown (1991) hypothesized that antisocial or aggressive behavior in childhood underlies delayed skills in self-regulation that translate to the development of alcohol and drug problems by young adulthood.

Drug use is not restricted to antisocial adolescents. As noted earlier, Loeber (1988) described a group of nonantisocial adolescents involved in substance use. These adolescents were less pathogenic on both peer and family socialization indexes (Dishion & Loeber, 1985). Individuals who are not antisocial but begin using substances during young adulthood appear to be at a particular risk for the development of substance abuse disorders (Robins & Przybeck, 1985). Although strongly associated with antisocial behavior, substance use appears to be different from antisocial behavior with respect to its etiology and life course and should be considered separately.

To some degree, adolescent substance use may exacerbate adjustment difficulties, especially for the antisocial adolescent; this may contribute to the continuation of antisocial behavior into adulthood. Farrington (1991) examined the adolescent characteristics of frequent adult offenders, both violent and nonviolent, and found a distinguishing feature of these offenders as adolescents was their use of tobacco, alcohol, and marijuana prior to age 15.

Substance use may also lead the marginally adjusted adolescent into deviant social contexts that support a wide range of problem behavior. Drug use and drug sales may be particularly important in coalescing deviant peer groups. Many gangs organize their social commerce around drug use, drug sales, and other antisocial behaviors (Fagin, 1989). There is also a consistent relation between drug and alcohol use and delinquent behavior. Elliott et al. (1989) found that increases in prevalence as well as offending rate were a function of substance use severity (alcohol, marijuana, and polydrug use). During the year in which the National Youth Study sample was between the ages of 15 and 21, 12.5% of the sample who were classified as polydrug users committed 47% of the felony assaults, 70% of the felony thefts, and 54% of index offenses.

Sexual Behavior

Antisocial adolescents are at risk for exhibiting early and risky sexual behavior. For example, Biglan et al. (1990) found that self-reports of aggressive and delinquent behavior were associated with reports of high-risk sexual behavior (e.g., involvement with multiple partners and failure to use contraceptives). Elliott and Morse (1989), using data from the National Youth Study, found that sexual activity in adolescence was associated with both delinquency and substance use.

Child antisocial behavior is also predictive of early sexual activity. Ensminger (1990) found that aggressive behavior in Grade 1 was associated with sexual activity in later adolescence. Capaldi (1991, April) demonstrated that antisocial behavior and deviant peer involvement at Grade 4 predicted the initiation of sexual intercourse by the time the OYS boys were 13 to 14 years old.

Implicated in the development of early sexual behavior are factors also important in the development of antisocial behavior. These include low family cohesion, communication, and stability (Zabin & Hayward, 1993) as well as limited parental supervision and monitoring (Biglan et al., 1990; Miller, McCoy, Olson, & Wallace, 1986). There is also evidence that involvement with peers who exhibit problem behavior is associated with high-risk sexual behavior (Biglan et al., 1990).

Findings of the common occurrence of sexual activity, delinquency, and substance use have been used to support a general problem behavior model (Donovan & Jessor, 1985). Thus, it is assumed that initiation of sexual behavior can be explained by a general tendency to engage in problem behavior. As noted by Zabin and Hayward (1993), however, this clustering can be explained as well by common risk factors across problem behavior (Ensminger, 1990). Further, some adolescents exhibit sexual behavior in the absence of other problem behaviors. More research is needed if we are to disentangle the interrelations between antisocial behavior and sexual behavior.

In accomplishing this, we need to differentiate between models predicting early sexual initiation from those predicting later initiation. As Capaldi (1991, April) has shown, antisocial behavior is more strongly associated with early than late onset. Early onset is likely to be seen as a violation of norms and is in part dependent on lax parental supervision. Later onset is normative and is likely a product of socially sanctioned adolescent dating activities.

Additionally, these models may also need to be developed separately for males and females. Ensminger (1990) found that a general problem model was less satisfactory for predicting sexual behavior of males than females. It may also be necessary to account for ethnicity in these models because there is evidence that the timing and meaning of sexual activity varies (Zabin & Hayward, 1993).

More research is needed to explore the relation between antisocial behavior and sexual activity. This is an area of some priority in view of the AIDS epidemic, the importance of sexual behavior to delinquency in females, and the role that youth pregnancy plays in perpetuating the transmission of antisocial behavior across generations (Zabin & Hayward, 1993). Unfortunately, there are limited high-quality longitudinal data currently available to answer these questions. Investigators comparing multiple problem behaviors frequently rely exclusively on self-reports, with the consequence that any associations found may be attributable to measurement error.

Depression

Antisocial behavior also co-occurs with depressed mood as well as the affective disorders of Major Depression and Dysthymia. The degree of this overlap varies and depends on the age and gender of the study population, the diagnostic criteria employed, and whether epidemiological or clinical samples were assessed. Correlations between depressed mood and conduct problems were between 37% and 51% in a large community sample of adolescents (Hops, Lewinsohn, Andrews, & Roberts, 1990). Generally, somewhat larger associations were found for boys than for girls (Gjerde, Block, & Block, 1988; Jacobson, Lahey, & Strauss, 1983). Jackson (1992) investigated a sample of young adolescent children who were referred on the basis of risk for substance use. She found that antisocial behavior, substance use, and depressed mood were highly correlated for boys, but depressed mood was virtually uncorrelated with these problem behaviors in girls.

In clinical populations, approximately 33% of depressed children and adolescents also received a diagnosis of CD (Asarnow, 1988; Carlson & Cantwell, 1980; Marriage, Fine, Moretti, & Haley, 1986; Puig-Antich, 1982). Again, boys were disproportionately represented in this comorbid population. In a New Zealand epidemiological sample, Anderson, Williams, McGee, and Silva (1987) found that 16% of a depressed child sample exhibited conduct disorders. In contrast, greater comorbidity is seen when ODD is also considered. Kashani et al. (1987) found that 50% of the children experiencing depression also exhibited ODD. In a Puerto Rican sample, Bird, Canino, Rubio-Stipec, and Ribera (1988) also found a high degree of overlap (45%) between depression and a combined classification of CD/ODD.

The causal interrelations between depression and conduct disorders have been a subject of some controversy. Beginning with the concept of *masked depression,* it has been commonly assumed that conduct problems are a symptom of depressive disorders (Carlson & Cantwell, 1980). This view was based on clinical observations that depression often preceded the display of acting-out behavior in some children. These conclusions must be tempered because of the lack of studies implementing formal child assessments prior to onset of a depressive episode, as well as failure to assess subclinical levels of antisocial behavior. Puig-Antich (1982) found that both depression and conduct disorder were reduced by treatment with imipramine, suggesting that the disorders stemmed from a common etiology. Alternatively, however, Kovacs, Paulauskas, Gatsonis, and Richards (1988) found that antisocial behavior continued following the remission of the depressive characteristics, suggesting that the two disorders are independent.

An alternative etiological perspective is that some forms of depression arise as a consequence of the antisocial behavior trajectory. The theoretical basis for this position comes from Lewinsohn's (Lewinsohn, Hobermand, Teri, & Hautzinger, 1985) observation that deficits in social skills and failure to obtain positive reinforcement underlie depressed moods. Patterson and Stoolmiller (1991) tested a model that related depressed mood to boys' peer rejection and academic skill deficits. The model replicated well in three groups of boys, supporting the idea that depression in boys may result from experiences of failure in the social and academic arenas.

Capaldi (1992) provided the best test of the interrelation between depressed mood and antisocial behavior in a study of two cohorts of boys who were 11 to 12 years old and 13 to 14 years old at the beginning of the study. She compared four groups: (a) conduct problems and depressed, (b) depressed only, (c) conduct problems only, and (d) neither. The psychosocial correlates for the two antisocial groups were similar, including experiencing poor parenting practices, associating with deviant peers, and having academic skill deficits. There was a marginal trend for the depressed-antisocial group to show more severe pathologies, such as suicide ideation and arrests. Log linear analyses were conducted to detect reciprocal effects over time between depression and antisocial behavior. It was found that antisocial behavior at age 11 to 12 was prognostic of increases in depression by age 13 to 14, but the reverse was not true. This analysis seems to support the contention that some portion of the comorbidity of depression and antisocial behavior, at least in boys, is secondary to failure experiences, low social reinforcement, and conflict with peers and parents. Obviously missing from this picture is the co-occurrence of depression and antisocial behavior in girls. The incidence of depression increases for girls in adolescence compared with boys, and co-occurrence of antisocial behavior and depression is lower, so the etiology of the two disorders is likely somewhat independent in girls. It is also true that boys who are depressed but show no indication of antisocial behavior have quite different developmental courses from boys with depression and antisocial behavior.

Summary

We have suggested three classes of comorbid features of antisocial behavior: those that are *concomitants* of antisocial behavior, those that *potentiate* antisocial behavior, and those that are simply *sequelae.* The literature suggests that skill deficits are concomitants of antisocial behavior in the sense that such skill deficits may share a common etiology. Substance use and early sexual promiscuity may potentiate future antisocial conduct, as antisocial behavior may become a means for attaining substances or engaging in sex. Although many individuals who are depressed do not display the antisocial pattern, evidence suggests that antisocial behavior often leads to depression, after failure in the social realm. There is an emerging sense that these comorbid features of antisocial behavior represent developmentally specific adaptations that are highly predictable based on the onset and course of the antisocial pattern.

A Conceptual Framework

Model Building

Behavioral models serve two functions: They provide accurate predictions concerning future behavior and guidance as to appropriate targets of intervention. These two functions are probably best approached sequentially, with the development of models that predict as the first step and testing the models within the context of intervention trials as the second step (Dishion, Reid, & Patterson, 1988; Patterson, Reid, & Dishion, 1992).

In applying the prediction criteria, we might search for models that optimally account for antisocial behavior in terms of the amount of variance that is accounted for or percentage of accurate predictions made (Loeber & Dishion, 1983). When developing models explaining variance in antisocial behavior, investigators must allow for the high percentage caused by previous antisocial behavior. Because stability is so high, it is difficult for most competing variables to significantly exceed the prediction accounted for by prior antisocial behavior. Second, some variables might produce substantial variance, but have little to do with the development of this behavior and are not appropriate targets of intervention. For example, a measure of antisocial attitude might be an excellent predictor but is arguably less useful as an explanation or intervention target.

The sophistication of behavioral research has grown along with an increasing reliance of multivariate statistics, in particular, the use of structural equation modeling (SEM) (Bentler, 1989; Joreskog & Sorbom, 1989). The practice of model testing has led behavioral researchers to an increasing awareness of the issues of measurement and the testing of competing models. Testing competing models is probably the most productive way of gaining knowledge of developmental processes and encouraging interdisciplinary collaboration. Thus model A can be compared with model B by measuring each of the key constructs and testing how well these competing constructs account for antisocial behavior. The models can be compared using a chi square goodness-of-fit test (Bentler & Bonnett, 1980) to determine which model best accounts for performance of antisocial behavior.

There are pitfalls in the use of SEM, or any other statistical tool, to test competing models. The most common is the "straw man" problem. This occurs when the researcher weakly measures variables from a competing model or oversimplifies an alternative explanation. Consequently, the competing model will perform poorly in explaining variance. As discussed so poignantly by Meehl (1978), testing any model requires a network of measurement hypothesis *and* the causal hypotheses. Without the explicit measurement hypothesis, an investigator can squirm in the face of null findings by playing the "rotating measures game" (e.g., if parent-report of Construct A is uncorrelated with antisocial behavior, yet the child-report of Construct A is correlated, then pick the child-report). Playing the rotating measures game eliminates the need to grapple with the rather complex issue of why there are different patterns of findings for the two alternative measures of the same construct.

The other weakness in model testing is the monomethod bias problem (Cook & Campbell, 1979). Assessing all constructs with the same measure introduces method variance into estimates as accounted variance. Bank, Dishion, Skinner, and Patterson (1990) fondly refer to this as the *glop* problem. The "fast food" approach to behavioral research is assessing independent and dependent measures using questions from the same agent. The correlation between the independent and dependent variables may be entirely accounted by for method variance. For example, a tendency to admit to less than desirable behavior might account for the correlation between the child's report of deviant peers and delinquent behavior.

Methodological issues are often raised when considering the empirical literature in a review such as the present one. We offer the following guidelines for model development, to facilitate reference and discussion of these methodological issues:

1. If dependent and independent variables are derived from the observations of a single reporting agent (or are derived from a single measurement method), then the problem of monomethod bias (Cook & Campbell, 1979) operates as a confound in estimating the magnitude of covariation.

2. Are the correlations between implied "causes" and antisocial outcomes based on cross-sectional or longitudinal data sets? How much of the variance is accounted for in the outcome variable? Given sample sizes in the several hundreds, then very small effect sizes could be significant but could be of little theoretical or clinical significance. We arbitrarily use 10% of the variance as a minimal level to establish the credentials of a model. In the effort to understand the etiology of antisocial behavior, we prefer liberal inclusion of viable hypotheses. As discussed earlier, the effect of some variables may be mediated by another variable. These variables are important in understanding the developmental processes leading to antisocial behavior.

3. Have the effects been replicated by other investigators? Is the effect limited to some special subsample, or is it generalizable across samples?

4. Have the causal implications been appropriately tested using experimental designs? A strong test requires random assignment of subjects to interventions that place the candidate for causal status at serious risk of being falsified (Popper, 1972). A strong theory should tell us something about how to change an emerging or extant maladaptive pattern. As previously stated, the model would not only target intervention variables but would also provide a guide to the measurement of change.

A major issue in statistically testing causal models is the problem of specification. If key variables are excluded from a prediction equation (linear or nonlinear), then estimates of the effects of the hypothesized causal influence are biased, usually in the direction of having too liberal an effect. Gollob and Reichardt (1987) concluded that excluding measures of prior behavior in longitudinal causal models results in misspecifying the causal influence under consideration. For example, if peer relationships in middle childhood are used to predict adolescent antisocial behavior without controlling for measures of the child's antisocial behavior in middle childhood, then the researcher is likely to overestimate the contribution of peer relations. Not including other key causal influences (e.g., parenting practices, academic skills, etc.) also may result in bias.

There is an infinite regress flavor to the specification problem. How can we know which variables to include in a causal model, when at any time there are likely to be unconsidered variables that, if entered into the model as competing constructs, would change the findings? One way to think about what variables could be missing from a model is to think broadly about the context in which development unfolds and to consider what conditions and processes may have been excluded. An ecological framework provides us with a basis for considering influences on the development of antisocial behavior and for judging the completeness of the empirical literature on the development of antisocial behavior.

The Ecology of Causation

Several research programs are in progress that promote an ecological focus on normative and maladaptive development (Bolger, Caspi, Downey, & Moorehouse, 1987; Hinde, 1989; Kellam, 1990; Magnusson, 1988; Rutter, 1989; Sameroff, 1981; Scarr, 1985). Bronfenbrenner's (1979, 1986, 1989) model provides a convenient and organized conceptual framework for considering the network of findings related to the etiology of antisocial behavior. Taking a systems view, the ecology of child development is conceptualized as a hierarchy of nested systems, beginning with face-to-face interactions among people (microsystems within relationships), continuing on to behavior settings in which relationships take place, and on to more macrocontextual influences that are usually referred to as cultural and community practices. The focus on the impact of larger social units on development has been referred to as a macrosystem model.

The subsequent review of research on antisocial behavior adapts the Bronfenbrenner model into four spheres of causative influence: (a) intrapersonal factors, (b) relationship processes, (c) behavior settings, and (d) community contexts.

Intrapersonal factors are those characteristics of individuals that alone or by interacting with environmental circumstances increase the propensity to use antisocial behavior. Because behavior does not occur in a vacuum, it is assumed that intrapersonal factors require some environmental stimulus to produce antisocial behavior. Constructs that are important to the development of antisocial behavior include temperament, social-cognitive style, and intelligence.

The second ecological level describes *relationship processes.* Socialization takes place within the context of relationships that evolve in constituency, structure, and quality over the life course. Synchronized mother-child interactions are particularly salient during infancy. In later development, other family members become involved. During their preschool years, children begin to spend as much time with peers as they do with parents (Ellis, Rogoff, & Cromer, 1981). Teachers become significant social agents when children enter school. Relationships with supervisors become increasingly important with entry into the workforce.

Also changing over the course of development are the *behavior settings* in which relationships occur, a term borrowed from Barker's ecological model (1960). These are primarily the physical settings (e.g., neighborhood, school, etc.) in which relation-

ships transpire that are assumed to have an impact, directly and indirectly, on social development.

The fourth level of ecological analysis is *community contexts.* This includes cultural processes that potentiate or reduce antisocial behavior, including television violence, economic practices (i.e., employment, income resources, etc.), cultural patterns that eventually influence the structure of family and peer interactions, governmental policies, population density, and available family resources. Probably the factors most relevant to antisocial behavior are the cultural policies that affect minority citizens (see Figure 12.2).

Summary

We propose that findings concerning the development of antisocial behavior be considered with respect to the construction of one or more models. Models serve two interrelated functions: first, as guides to predict and explain the occurrence of antisocial behavior, and second, as tools to prevent it. Several methodological issues are discussed that ultimately bear on interpretation of findings to date. Most findings are vulnerable to the specification problem, where estimates of causal effects are biased due to what is *left out* of the model. An ecological framework is offered as an organizing structure to consider strengths and weaknesses of the empirical literature.

ETIOLOGY

Intraindividual Factors

Overview

In this section, we discuss a variety of person characteristics implicated in the development of antisocial behavior. Biosocial factors refer to genotype characteristics that may, in consort with the environment, contribute to the development of antisocial behavior. The section on social cognition focuses on Dodge's social information-processing model in the development of antisocial behavior in middle childhood and adolescence.

Biosocial Factors

In this section, we critically review suggestive evidence that biological characteristics of individuals predispose them toward antisocial behavior. The term *biosocial* was selected to imply a fundamental link between biological characteristics and environmental experiences in establishing antisocial trajectories. As articulated by Plomin and Hershberger (1991), there are virtually no inherited behavioral characteristics that do not depend on environmental conditions to materialize. In this sense, behavior geneticists and developmental psychologists are united in their interest to better understand the extent to which genotype characteristics of the individual qualify the impact of social interaction on developmental outcomes. As discussed by Hoffman (1991), however, this is about the extent of common ground between the two areas of research. As of this writing, no studies have combined process-oriented developmental research with family studies of genetic transmission

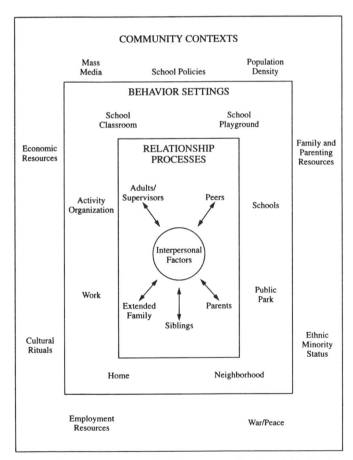

Figure 12.2 Framework for the ecology of antisocial behavior.

or research on physiological mechanisms related to possible genotype-environment interactions.

What follows is a review of the most promising areas of research relating possible biological characteristics of the person to the etiology, form, and course of antisocial behavior. These include the areas of gender differences, hyperactivity, behavior genetics, and temperament.

Gender Differences

The literature does not show pervasive differences in antisocial behavior between males and females. In general, the differences are not ubiquitous or clear (Zoccolillo, 1993). On the one hand, being male is a risk factor for severe forms of antisocial behavior across the life span, including childhood conduct problems (Kazdin, 1987), adult APD (Cloninger & Gottesman, 1987; Robins et al., 1984), delinquent behavior (Elliott, Huizinga, & Ageton, 1985), and adult criminality (Federal Bureau of Investigation, 1989). On the other hand, beyond differences in incidence of serious antisocial behavior, the findings of gender differences seem to vary from study to study, apparently depending on the level of antisocial behavior and the reporting agent.

In reviewing the evidence from developmental studies of aggressive behavior, Maccoby and Jacklin (1974) reported pervasive gender differences at the normative level of aggressive behavior. In the absence of clear differences in parenting practices for boys and girls, these authors concluded that there must be some biological component. This bold statement certainly fueled debate regarding the issue of gender differences in aggressive, antisocial behavior as well as its origin. Tieger (1980) reanalyzed the Maccoby and Jacklin (1974) studies using a more rigorous meta-analytic technique and found statistically marginal ($p < .12$) differences between girls and boys on observation measures of aggression. Tieger (1980) also took issue with the use of equivalent measures of aggressive and antisocial behavior for boys and girls, emphasizing the need to consider differences in the form of antisocial behavior for the two genders at various developmental stages.

R. B. Cairns, B. D. Cairns, Neckerman, Gest, and Gariepy (1988) conducted one of the few longitudinal studies (Grade 4 through Grade 8) on antisocial behavior that included both boys and girls and used multiple measures to assess aggressive and antisocial behavior. Teachers in general rated boys as more antisocial than girls. Surprisingly, self-ratings of aggressiveness for boys and girls were equal from Grade 4 to Grade 9. More intensive interviews with the children regarding aggressive episodes suggested that the function of aggression shifted for girls as they moved into early adolescence. Girls' conflicts centered around group acceptance and affiliation, whereas boys' conflicts tended to be more directly confrontational. In adolescence, girls increased their use of more subtle, indirect aggression (e.g., social manipulation, ostracism, and gossiping). These findings support Tieger's (1980) point that careful consideration of the form and function of antisocial behavior as it occurs for boys and girls is necessary before making statements regarding gender differences.

Boys are much more likely to be referred for intervention for their conduct problems than are girls. There are, however, fewer differences between male and female referred children. Reid (1978) found only marginal differences between clinically referred girls and boys in observed aversive behavior in the home. Similarly, Dishion and Andrews (in press) found no differences in the observed rate of negative behavior in videotaped observations of 11- to 14-year-old referred teens interacting with their parents, nor were there differences in parents' global reports of antisocial behavior. In contrast, teacher reports of antisocial behavior in school rated boys as more antisocial than girls. R. B. Cairns, B. D. Cairns, et al. (1988) also found that teachers rated boys much higher than girls on their antisocial behavior in school.

Thus it seems that gender differences in antisocial behavior become increasingly dramatic in middle childhood in settings such as school. During adolescence, there may be major developmental shifts in the form of the antisocial pattern that vary for males and females. This depends, in part, on the new socioemotional demands of this period, including heterosexual relationships, larger social groupings, and diverse strategies for acquiring the benefits of adult status (Moffitt, 1993b).

The most comprehensive model of the development of antisocial behavior in girls comes from Caspi, Lynam, Moffitt, and Silva (1993). They found evidence of two trajectories into female delinquent behavior. Females in one pathway exhibited antisocial behavior during childhood. At adolescence, they associated with deviant peer groups and exhibited delinquent behavior and drug use. These females followed a path similar to that outlined by Patterson, Reid, and Dishion (1992) for boys. Girls without a history of childhood antisocial behavior followed a different path to delinquency. Early menarche had an indirect effect on delinquency through increased involvement with deviant peers. This model is intriguing, but requires replication and further empirical analysis with more complete specification of family and peer relationship components of the models.

It is particularly important to understand the development of antisocial behavior in females because of the contribution this makes to perpetuation of antisocial behavior across generations. It has been consistently found that antisocial females are likely to develop relationships with antisocial males (Caspi, Elder, & Bem, 1987; Robins et al., 1984), become pregnant at an early age, and display dysfunctional parenting (Serbin, Moskowitz, Schwarzman, & Ledingham, 1991). Patterson and Dishion (1988) found that the mother's antisocial behavior had both a direct and an indirect effect on the antisocial behavior of her male offspring. These mothers provided an optimal environment for rearing conduct-disordered children. Tremblay (1991) argues convincingly that it is necessary for us to understand the antisocial behavior of females if we are to prevent this intergenerational transmission. Greater emphasis needs to be placed on developing a life-course model of antisocial behavior in females. In developing a model, we need to consider biological as well as relationship and societal influences.

Behavior Genetics

Genetic and environmental influences work in tandem to produce antisocial behavior (Gottesman & Goldsmith, in press; Rende & Plomin, 1992; Rutter, et al., 1990). Much of the emphasis of behavior geneticists, however, has been on assessing the strength of the genetic contribution. No studies have disentangled the ambiguous nature and nurture effects on antisocial behavior (Hoffman, 1991). Lack of research employing intensive measurement of environmental conditions associated with the display of a trait in families with adopted or biological offspring has been the major barrier to such understanding. The complexities of such investigations are revealed by R. B. Cairns and Gariepy (1990) who note that nature and nurture seldom compete, but rather work together to produce adaptive outcomes.

Compelling evidence exists of a genetic contribution to what Moffitt (1993b) has labeled the life-course-persistent pattern of antisocial behavior, as reflected in either adult criminal behavior or diagnoses of Antisocial Personality. Cloninger and Gottesman (1987) concluded on the basis of their review of the Scandinavian adoption studies that extreme levels of antisocial lifestyle behavior and problem drinking appear to have a common heritable component in males. The socialization component, however, was also seen in the unique contribution to adult antisocial behavior of the adoptive family. Thus, children whose adoptive fathers were of low socioeconomic status or were criminals had elevated rates of adult criminality.

Reviewers of the literature (Plomin, Nitz, & Rowe, 1990; Rutter et al., 1990) have concluded that the genetic component of antisocial behavior is more clearly demonstrated in adult rather than child or adolescent populations. This is particularly the case when considering juvenile delinquency or aggression in middle childhood (for review, see Rutter et al., 1990). Most convincing was the failure to find differences between the correlation for monozygotic and dizygotic twins on observed antisocial behavior in the laboratory (Plomin, Foch, & Rowe, 1981). Thus, there was no demonstrated effect of shared genetic endowment observed in childhood antisocial behavior. We are again confronted in this review with the confounding issue of method effects. It turns out that the degree of similarity between two siblings varied as a function of the measure used. Parent-report tended to provide findings that were supportive of a genetic component; direct observations, on the other hand, supported a strong environmental component.

The issue of similarity, or lack thereof, has engendered one of the more interesting debates on the relative contribution of nature versus nurture on psychological traits. Plomin and Daniels (1987) assert that environmental effects often exert influence in making siblings more different than similar. Hoffman (1991) has pointed out that this may be true for some traits and not for others. As indicated in the Plomin et al. (1990) review, siblings appear to be quite similar on observed measures of aggression in the laboratory. More recently, Lewin, Hops, Davis, and Dishion (1993) found siblings in middle childhood to be quite similar with respect to their behavior in school-based multiagent and multimethod constructs that measured their antisocial behavior ($r = .62$, $p < .05$), peer relations ($r = .52$, $p < .05$), and academic competence ($r = .49$, $p < .05$), but significantly dissimilar with respect to a construct score of the children's social withdrawal ($r = -.58$, $p < .05$). All constructs consisted of teacher ratings, peer nominations, objective tests, and direct observations. Thus, adjustment of siblings in school is quite similar on a number of dimensions, with a suggestion of trait complementarity on social withdrawal.

Research on the heritability of temperament for 14-month-old children indicates that there is some heritability for children's behavioral inhibition (reaction to novel stimuli) at an early age but not for the expression of anger or negative emotion (Emde et al., 1992). Animal studies also suggest that environmental influences on antisocial behavior are stronger early rather than later in development. The findings are most supportive of a genetic link to antisocial behavior that is displayed in adolescence and adulthood. R. B. Cairns, Gariepy, and Hood (1988) reported the same tendency in studies of breeding for aggressiveness in mice. Differences in pedigree, in terms of aggressive behavior, did not emerge until puberty.

DiLalla and Gottesman (1989) failed to find a heritable component to antisocial behavior in adolescents when self-reported behavior was used as the dependent variable. These investigators considered the distinction between Continuous Antisocial (early starters) and Transitory Delinquents (normative and trivial delinquency) and Late Bloomers (adult criminals who were not antisocial in middle childhood). They speculated that the Continuous group was genetically at risk, whereas the Transitory group had little if any inheritable tendency toward antisocial behavior. Thus, researchers who combine these two groups are unlikely to find a heritable component to adolescent antisocial behavior. Indexes of more serious antisocial behavior in adolescence such as recidivism, serious violent physical offenses, or property offenses do seem to be related to genetic pedigree (DiLalla & Gottesman, 1989). These findings are also consistent with those reported earlier regarding the genetic contributions to adult criminal careers and antisocial personalities. An early history of antisocial behavior is definitional to a DSM diagnosis of Antisocial Personality and is an important precursor to adult criminality (Nagin & Farrington, 1991).

The evidence suggests that genetic components may contribute to early-starting antisocial behavior that persists into adulthood, but this explains nothing about the possible mechanism contributing to this persistence. Theorists agree that the influence is polygenic and certainly interacts with adverse environmental conditions. In a recent discussion of seratype in the etiology of antisocial behavior, Gottesman and Goldsmith (in press) suggest that there is a dynamic interplay between genotype and environment. They also suggest that the most promising strategy is to understand how genotype might influence broader characteristics of the child and how these in turn may interact with environmental circumstances to yield persistent patterns of antisocial behavior. To this end, we now turn our discussion to hyperactivity.

Hyperactivity

The constellation of overactivity and distractibility comprising ADHD is implicated in the development of antisocial behavior. ADHD and Oppositional and Conduct Disorders are grouped together under the category of disruptive disorders in DSM-III-R and are clustered under the category of Externalizing Disorders in Achenbach's (1992) influential taxonomy. The overlap between these disorders is so extensive that there has been controversy as to whether they constitute different disorders. Part of this difficulty has emerged from the diversity in the diagnosis of ADHD over time and across settings. Hyperactivity and difficulties with following rules are symptoms common to both Conduct Disorder and ADHD, while excessive motor activity and difficulty sustaining attention are more easily pulled apart in the two disorders (Werry, 1988). This recognition has resulted in clarification of the distinctive features of the two disorders, as well as recognition that the two disorders frequently co-occur (Barkley, 1989).

Precise estimates of the overlap between antisocial behavior and ADHD disorders are difficult to make because of differences in diagnostic criteria and differences in characteristics of samples across studies. In general, the overlap is greater in clinical samples than in normative samples. Steward, DeBlos, and Cummings (1979) found that about 60% of the conduct-disordered children seen in a clinic setting had a dual diagnosis of hyperactivity. In a New Zealand epidemiological sample, Anderson et al. (1987) found that 35% of the diagnosed population who were conduct disordered and oppositional defiant also had a dual diagnosis of ADHD. Antisocial behavior may even be more difficult to disentangle in preschoolers than in older school-age populations (Campbell, Breaux, Ewing, & Szumowski, 1986).

Evidence of the distinctiveness as well as the co-occurrence of these disorders comes from a variety of sources. Separate aggression and hyperactivity factors consistently emerge from factor analyses of parent and teacher ratings of hyperactivity, attention deficits, and conduct problems (Hinshaw, 1987). Nevertheless, these scale scores are highly correlated. On the Child Behavior Checklist, for example, correlations between Aggression and Hyperactivity scales ranged between .51 and .71 (Achenbach & Edelbrock, 1981).

New studies have taken a multiagent and multimethod approach to address the question of whether hyperactivity (or ADHD) is distinguishable from antisocial behavior. Figure 12.3 provides an overview on how this might be approached. Attention deficit and hyperactivity are considered as possibly separate constructs, as suggested in the work by Lahey, Schaughency, Strauss, and Frame (1984). The idea is relatively simple. By using confirmatory factor analysis (Dwyer, 1983; Long, 1983) through structural equation modeling, the investigator can systematically test the viability of a one-, two- or three-factor solution to these data. Fergusson, Horwood, and Lloyd (1991) used the approach shown in Figure 12.3 to test the validity of a two-factor model (ADHD versus CD) on a large, nonreferred sample of 9- to 10-year-old boys and girls. The alternative model was that parent and teacher ratings of the two sets of behaviors best fit a general Disruptive Behavior factor. The two-factor model provided a superior fit to the data, whereas the one-factor model did not. Consistent with other findings regarding high overlap between these two constructs, these investigations found correlations between the two in the .85 and .90 range.

Other evidence of distinctiveness comes from comparisons of children who are either aggressive or ADHD and those who are both aggressive and ADHD. Comparisons of these subgroups reveal that the two hyperactive groups can be differentiated from purely aggressive groups on the basis of their greater cognitive impairment (McGee, Williams, & Silva, 1984; Moffitt, 1990), early motor deficits (Moffitt, 1990), and inattentive behavior in structured academic settings (Roberts, 1990).

The parental characteristics of children in these groups also differ. Lahey et al. (1988) found that pure ADHD was not

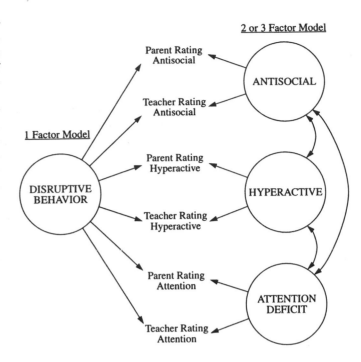

Figure 12.3   One-, two-, and three-factor models.

associated with parental psychiatric disorder. In contrast, both mothers and fathers of CD children and CD-ADHD children were disproportionately diagnosed APD and had a history of fighting. Mothers were more likely to have experienced recent depression, whereas fathers abused alcohol and other drugs. Two analyses of Silva's New Zealand sample indicated that the combined hyperactive-aggressive group showed more family adversity in middle childhood (McGee et al., 1984). Moffitt (1990) also documented that the adverse family environments of the hyperactive-aggressive group persisted through early adolescence.

There are some indications that CD-ADHD children exhibit the most problematic features of each disorder and appear to be at greater risk for concurrent and later disorders than individuals without this comorbidity (Werry, Reeves, & Elkind, 1987). J. L. Walker, Lahey, Hynd, and Frame (1987) found that children who received dual diagnoses of ADHD and CD were more likely to exhibit a versatile pattern of disruptive behavior (i.e., both overt and covert antisocial behavior) (Loeber & Schmaling, 1985) than were CD children who were not ADHD. The CD-ADHD children were also more likely to exhibit more serious symptoms (e.g., fire-setting, cruelty to animals). Moffitt's (1990) group of hyperactive-antisocial youngsters also reported more violent offenses at age 15.

Magnusson (1988) found that 13-year-old boys who exhibited a combination of aggressiveness and restlessness were more likely to exhibit criminal behavior between the ages of 18 and 26 than were boys who displayed either aggression or restlessness in isolation. Schachar, Rutter, and Smith (1981) also found that children with CD and ADHD exhibited a poorer prognosis than CD children who were not diagnosed with hyperactivity. Thus it appears that the combination of antisocial behavior and ADHD is associated with a poorer late adolescent and adult outcome than either disorder in isolation.

The role of ADHD in the etiology of antisocial behavior is somewhat unclear. Loeber, Stouthamer-Loeber, and Green (1991) used retrospective data to argue that ADHD symptoms are an initial risk factor for a progression toward more serious conduct problems. For example, as early as age 1 to 2, referred CD boys showed hyperactive symptoms such as "moves much in sleep" and at age 3 "climbs," "runs around outside," and "has difficulty playing quietly." Behaviors included as indicators of ADHD (e.g., climbs, has difficulty playing quietly) may be indications of how well the child is socialized. Further, some of the ADHD and antisocial behaviors may be confounded because they are caused by the same environmental factors. Moreover, not paying attention in class and restlessness may be a by-product of an uncooperative approach to task demands in school. In this sense, the combination of antisocial behavior and hyperactive behavior may indicate the extreme nature of the child's adjustment problems. Others would say that hyperactivity reflects a very real biological predisposition for social development problems; chief among them is antisocial behavior. Various structural deficits in the brain (e.g., frontal lobe, left hemisphere, or hippocampal dysfunctions) have been proposed to account for the behavior of the hyperactive child. Evidence considered supportive of this structural perspective is the tendency for the antisocial, hyperactive child to score lower on verbal intelligence, executive functioning, and attention modulation (e.g., Hirschi & Hindelang, 1977; Moffitt, 1990, 1993a). Moffitt (1993a) proposed the hypothesis that these deficits, along with other minor neurological and physical anomalies, are key factors for the diathesis process that accounts for the maladaptive behavior exhibited during the life course of antisocial youth. Evidence in favor of structural abnormalities preceding the onset of conduct disorders is derived from literature relating soft neurological problems to difficulties in temperament (Rothbart & Derryberry, 1981). At this point, the link between early difficult temperament and later antisocial behavior is weak. In addition, the ability to use intelligence to predict future delinquency is quite low (Loeber & Dishion, 1983). Two key methodological issues cloud interpretation in this area of research. The first is the failure to consider prediction errors when estimating longitudinal effects (i.e., false positives). The second is to control for competing environmental factors, as they may account for the majority of variance in antisocial behavior. Although the hypothesis that structural deficits are key factors in the etiology of the life-course-persistent patterns of antisocial behavior is interesting, we await more data to determine the level of variance accounted for by key variables in the developmental process.

Another challenge of testing a structural hypothesis is resolving the "chicken or the egg" question. Recent research reveals that, although brain development affects behavior, behavior can also affect brain development (Kolb, 1989; Rosenzweig, 1984). Presumably, the life-course-persistent children with antisocial behavior would have been exposed to the most dysfunctional environments during critical periods of brain development, thereby resulting in suboptimal neurological development of higher cortical functions. For example, special classrooms for language-impaired 5-year-olds typically comprise at least 50%

of children from abusive and deprived home environments who have both serious language deficits (syntax, pragmatics) and behavioral problems. We know that myelinization of the neural pathways in the brain is not complete until late adolescence at best. Myelinization is critical for attentional and higher cortical processing (language, verbal reasoning, etc.). It seems reasonable to hypothesize that environmental deprivation would compromise the neurological integrity of the developing child. Thus it would seem important to test the structural deficit hypothesis to control for these prenatal and postnatal environmental experiences.

Temperament

In some respects, research on temperament is troubled by the same issue. However, recent developments in conceptualization of psychophysiological processes suggests promising mechanisms in which a diathesis between genotype and environmental experiences might contribute to the development of life-course-persistent patterns of antisocial behavior, as articulated by Moffitt (1993a). An advantage the temperament perspective enjoys over the structuralist hypothesis is that the researcher can make conceptual and empirical connections with the behavioral-genetic literature on heritability of socio-emotional traits.

Research on temperament is beginning to point the way to viable and testable hypotheses regarding the mechanism by which environmental experience and genotype combine to produce antisocial behavior. Research on temperament is vast and complex; therefore, only those studies attempting to establish a relation between temperament and the etiology of antisocial behavior are discussed here. Temperament characteristics associated with antisocial behavior vary as a function of the age of the individual. In early childhood, it seems to be the difficult-child syndrome (e.g., Chess & Thomas, 1984), in adolescence it is the sensation-seeking teenager (Zuckerman, 1979), and in adulthood it is the hypoaroused, amotivated, self-centered psychopath (e.g., Hare, 1968; Newman, Widom, & Nathan, 1985). These constitutional constructs have been conceptualized within two psychophysiological processes, namely, the Behavioral Activation System (BAS) and the Behavior Inhibition System (BIS) (Gray, 1982). We will first review the research on temperament types and then proceed to discuss the viability of Gray's model as this is applied to antisocial behavior across the life span.

Any parent will tell you that some children are more difficult to socialize than others. A parent-client of the first author, who had two sons, described one as a *voice-activated* learner and the other as a *hands-on* learner. The point of the parent was that one of his sons simply required more attention, structure, and consistency than the other son, for whatever reason. When that issue was accepted and dealt with through improved behavior management practices, the "difficult" son's behavior was no longer a "problem."

Chess and Thomas's (1984) longitudinal study provided enticing morsels of data suggesting that difficult children may be at an increased risk for antisocial behavior. These authors found that ratings of difficult temperament at age 3 were predictive of more serious subsequent behavior problems. Bates, Bayles,

Bennett, Ridge, and Brown (1991) also found difficult temperament ratings at 6 months old to be prognostic of externalizing problems in boys and girls in middle childhood. For boys, the effect of difficult temperament was additive to the mother's negative control tactics in the preschool years.

The data supporting the concept of an optimal fit between the characteristics of the child and the family provide an important contribution to thinking about person and environment interactions (Chess & Thomas, 1984). The main point of the optimal-fit perspective is that some children's temperaments fit quite nicely with the temperaments of their parents and other children's do not.

Researchers have tried to identify individual characteristics that are correlated with adolescents' problem behavior. Zuckerman (1979) has offered the Sensation Seeking construct as a possibility. The hypothesis states that some youngsters physiologically require higher levels of arousal than others and thus seek arousal experiences. In adolescence, problem behavior is one mode of increasing arousal. Indeed, there is a correlation between teenagers' report of sensation seeking and their reports of problem behavior in adolescence. Although sensation seeking seemingly would predict other outcomes as well, such as sports injuries among athletes (i.e., high sensation seekers would take more risks and be more likely to sustain an injury), this has not been found. In fact, in a study by Smith, Ptacek, and Smoll (1992), there was no correlation between a youngster's sensation seeking and any index of sports functioning, including likelihood of sports injury. On the contrary, in this study, sensation seeking seem to function as a stress-resiliency factor, although a weak one, $r = .14$, $n = 425$.

An alternative statement of the sensation-seeking idea is that antisocial people are hyporesponsive. Classic research on adult psychopaths suggests that these individuals are less sensitive to aversive stimuli as indicated by measures of skin conductance (Hare, 1968). The most recent literature on adults has updated the hypoarousal construct to include deficits in passive avoidance (Newman, Widom, & Nathan, 1985). Indeed, experimental laboratory studies show that individuals characterized as psychopathic, either incarcerated or not, do not inhibit behavior as readily under conditions of punishment. This seems to be the case, as well, for adults with high scores on the extroversion personality dimension. The studies fit the concept of the psychopath being hypoaroused in the sense that he or she requires high amplitudes of punishment to inhibit behavior. Considered together with the literature on sensation seeking, there is also a good chance that such individuals may be quite sensitive to positive reinforcement, and at the same time less responsive to aversive stimuli.

Although these findings suggest a temperament effect on antisocial behavior, serious conceptual and methodological problems exist, especially with research on child and adolescent temperament. First, the sample sizes of studies assessing the role of temperament tend to be quite limited, especially considering that boys and girls require separate analyses. Second, the concept of the difficult child is vague, consisting of several dimensions (Rothbart & Derryberry, 1981) that may show differential, predictive validity (e.g., activity level, emotional lability, etc.). Third, studies to date tend to be restricted in terms of assessment methods. Studies of temperament in infancy and toddlerhood tend

to rely exclusively on parent ratings of temperament. Researchers are gradually becoming aware that such ratings contain systematic biases (Patterson & Duncan, 1993; Rutter et al., 1990). Factors such as parent mood or rejection of the child can influence ratings of temperament as well as those of behavior problems (Patterson, Reid, & Dishion, 1992).

In adolescence, measurement of both temperament and problem behavior relies on self-report. To make matters worse, some of the items of some sensation-seeking questionnaires contain direct or indirect statements of preferences for adolescent problem behavior ("I like wild parties"). Observational studies of adolescent affect do not identify the level of arousal as a key factor in adolescent temperament. As discussed earlier, sensation seeking does not appear to be predictive of other outcomes related to risk taking in prosocial activities. To this extent, much of the research relating temperament in childhood and adolescence to antisocial behavior is plagued by the monomethod bias (Cook & Campbell, 1979).

Few studies have collected physiological data and measures of antisocial behavior outside the laboratory. Magnusson (1988) compared the adrenaline levels in the urine of aggressive boys with those of nonaggressive boys. If aversive stimuli have less impact on aggressive children, then there should be lower basal levels of adrenaline in their urine (because adrenaline and cortisol levels are associated with the experience of stress) compared with nonaggressive children. This hypothesis was supported. He found that motor restlessness contributed to the prediction of subsequent criminality. Motor restlessness might be considered an additional indicator of the hypoaroused status of extremely aggressive children and children who have poor impulse control.

Using a sample of adolescent boys, Olweus (1987) correlated testosterone levels taken from blood samples and adrenaline from urine samples with aggressive behavior in adolescence. Adrenaline and testosterone seemed to correlate with different types of adolescent aggressive behavior. Testosterone levels predicted *provoked* aggressive behavior. Adrenaline level, on the other hand, correlated negatively with *unprovoked* aggressive behavior. These data support the hypothesis that youngsters who are responsive to aversive stimuli are less likely to be antisocial. In addition, self-reported low frustration tolerance was also correlated with aggressive behavior. This finding ties in with the work of Caprara et al. (1985), who related irritability and emotional susceptibility, as assessed by measures of systolic blood pressure and heart rate, to provoked aggressive behavior in laboratory settings.

Studies on temperament across the life span have lacked theoretical coherence. However, exciting recent developments have resulted from a better understanding of the neurophysiology of anxiety and impassivity in theoretical and empirical research by Gray (1982, 1987). Gray's model of impassivity and behavioral inhibition has recently been applied to antisocial behavior, conduct problems, and hyperactivity (Fowles, 1984, 1987; Quay, 1983, 1993). The overarching conceptual model is elegantly simple (see Figure 12.4). Behavior is presumed to be a product of environmental contingencies and physiological/affective reactivity. Two opponent processes define the nature of an individual's reaction. The Behavioral Inhibition System (BIS) underlies the emotion of anxiety and the tendency to inhibit action and respond to punishment. The Behavioral Activation System (BAS) underlies

Behavioral Inhibition System   Behavioral Activation System (i.e., reward seeking)

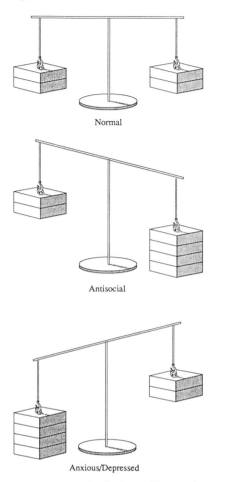

Normal

Antisocial

Anxious/Depressed

Figure 12.4 Three physiological profiles and potential for psychopathology.

the reinforcement-seeking component of behavior and the tendency to respond through action in the presence of reinforcement. The physiological processes and neurotransmitters that are hypothesized to underlie these systems are quite complex and beyond the scope of this chapter (see Gray, 1987; Quay, 1993).

The basic patterns and predictions for psychopathology, in which potential for psychopathology results from an imbalance between the BIS and BAS, are shown in Figure 12.4. It was originally hypothesized that antisocial behavior (and hyperactivity) was a result of a dominant BAS compared with the BIS. By nature, these individuals tend to be impulsive in the presence of reinforcement. In the presence of both aversive and hedonically positive stimuli, they would be more influenced by the latter. Anxious children and adults, however, are plagued by an overly active BIS. They readily inhibit behavior in the presence of aversive stimuli, even in the presence of potential reinforcement. An imbalance in the BAS/BIS systems, in combination with pathogenic environments, produces diagnosable disorders. Neither pattern, however, leads to disorder within the normal range of environmental experiences. At this stage, the conceptual model is not clear as to one crucial point: Would the same pathogenic environments produce

different (e.g., anxious versus antisocial) psychopathologies among individuals with the two different inherited dispositions?

Quay (1993) has been highly influential in promoting the Gray model to explain the undersocialized conduct disorder, a disorder, he argues, that is partially determined by genetic disposition. Quay and colleagues (Daugherty & Quay, 1991; Shapiro, Quay, Hogan, & Schwartz, 1988) have pursued systematic laboratory tests of Gray's model. In their most recent research, CD children were more likely to perseverate in responding to conditions of no reinforcement than were Normal and Anxious-Withdrawn children. CD children were also more responsive to positive reinforcing conditions in these tasks. These findings provide preliminary support for the hypothesis that a predisposition for antisocial behavior in early childhood is associated with a heightened sensitivity to reward. In a review of this issue, Quay (1993) concluded that the undersocialized CD group was most differentiated by underactive BIS systems. They simply failed to respond to aversive stimuli.

Gray's conceptual model is interesting and has received some empirical support. The model addresses the conceptual vagueness of temperament explanations of antisocial behavior, as well as providing a sense of coherence to the findings of Chess and Thomas (1984), Hare (1968), Newman (1987), and Zuckerman (1979). The model also maps well onto findings from behavioral genetic studies, demonstrating the heritability of traits such as extroversion and introversion (Goldsmith, 1988). Particularly dramatic is evidence that children may inherit a tendency to inhibit behavior that lasts through adulthood (Emde et al., 1992; Kagan, Reznick, & Snidman, 1988).

As of this writing, more data are needed on three crucial issues. First, it remains necessary to map a physiological substrate of the inhibition and reward system and relate it back to the performance of antisocial behavior. The juxtaposition of social and physiological measurement, characteristic of the work by Gottman and Levenson (1986), would provide the potential bridge between physiological processes and the performance of behavior.

Second, children are often comorbid for anxiety and conduct disorders. Consistent with Gray's model, it has been found that CD children who also exhibit disorders (indicating an active BIS) are less antisocial than children in these groups who differ as well in physical processes. This was shown by McBurnett et al. (1991), who demonstrated that boys who were comorbid for conduct and anxiety disorders had higher levels of salivary cortisol (which is linked to BIS) than boys with only conduct disorders. To date, however, attempts to distinguish comorbid groups on the basis of responsiveness to aversive stimuli have not been successful (Pliszka, Rogeness, Hatch, Borcherding, & Maas, 1992).

Third, we need to know to what extent pathogenic environments shape the relative strength and dominance of the BIS and BAS. Do children who are raised in punitive, erratic, and stressful social environments develop patterns of responding that are reflected on these physiological dimensions? It is quite likely that the influence from experience to neural development is every bit as strong as the reverse (Kolb, 1989). The findings by Bates et al. (1991) suggest that the "difficult child" syndrome is identifiable as early as 6 months of age. The environmental contributors to temperamental differences throughout development require exploration.

Social Cognition

Characteristics of the individual do not necessarily need to be innate to be attributed as causes of antisocial behavior (Bandura, 1989). Social cognition research attempts to define how the individual "reads" social stimuli as an individual difference variable. Within the developmental psychopathology arena, there is a concern for social cognitive *biases* or *deficits*. Deficits in social perception and social problem solving have been hypothesized to contribute to antisocial behavior (Rubin, Bream, & Rose-Krasnor, 1991). A variety of social cognitive models share the common idea that cognitions mediate the relation between environmental stimuli and aggressive behavior (Meyers & Craighead, 1984).

We present a schematic of a mediational model in Figure 12.5. The individual's experience with the environment is labeled a *social exchange*. The individual's interpretation of this act underlies a tendency to react, perhaps aggressively. In this sense, a tendency to perceive aggressive intentions in social exchanges mediates the relation between environmental events and reaction tendencies.

There is probably no idea more intuitively appealing in psychology than the notion that thoughts determine actions. Such mediational models appeal to our perception of individuals as agents of free will, choosing behavior patterns and trajectories rather than being forced into paths within the developmental life stream. Mediational models also provide a sense of optimism that it is possible to alter antisocial behavior simply by altering how people perceive events. Indeed, psychotherapists spend considerable time

(a) Mediational models

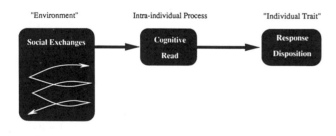

(b) Social interactional models

Figure 12.5 Contrasting mechanisms underlying social development, stability, and change.

and energy diplomatically persuading clients to reconsider their interpretation of the world. In this sense, the social cognitive model reflects how we live our lives and conduct ourselves professionally. However, as we shall see, careful consideration of the data unveils subtleties, ambiguities, and nuances that confront those who empirically test the relation between social cognition and antisocial behavior.

Often, social cognition is studied by using a problem-solving metaphor: Social exchanges are considered as problems requiring resolution. Using this approach, Kendall and Fischler (1984) did not find a relation between aspects of problem solving (i.e., means-to-an-end thinking, alternative solution generation, and consequential thinking) and parent or teacher ratings of social adjustment. After controlling for IQ, they found that these structural aspects were unrelated to either externalizing or internalizing problem behaviors. In later research, Fischler and Kendall (1988), however, did find that solution effectiveness was related to adjustment as assessed by teachers and parents. These findings are consistent with those of other investigators in showing that aggressive children frequently selected ineffective and aggressive solutions, but they did not differ from normal children in the number of solutions that they generated (Waas & French, 1989).

Presently, the most influential social cognitive research is guided by the *Social Information Processing* (SIP) model, outlined by Dodge and colleagues (Dodge, 1990, 1993; Dodge & Coie, 1987; Dodge, Murphy, & Buchsbaum, 1984; Dodge & Tomlin, 1987). Within this framework, social cognition is organized information processing, using a computer metaphor, in which the steps intervening between the environmental stimulus and the outcome response are schematically rendered. This model is an attempt to provide a comprehensive explanation for the origins and maintenance of antisocial behavior in young children, as well as attempting to explain the behavior of violent, aggressive, incarcerated adolescents (Dodge, Price, Bachorowski, & Newman, 1990). Maladaptive behavior is presumed to arise from the breakdown of sequential cognitive processing steps that mediate the individual's reaction to a stimulus. These steps are referred to as *encoding, response-accessing, response-decision,* and *enactment*.

The first step is to *encode* (or record in short-term memory) relevant features of the environmental stimulus. The individual learns to selectively attend to certain features of the environment to make sense out of a complex and overwhelming stimulus picture. In a series of studies (Dodge & Newman, 1981; Slaby & Guerra, 1988), aggressive children were found to search for less information than nonaggressive children before making a decision about another child's intentions, and selectively focused on hostile cues. *Response-accessing* refers to the process whereby the mental representation elicits one or more behaviors or emotional responses. Deficits are seen in the antisocial child's limited behavior response generation with a preponderance of aggressive and ineffective solutions. *Response-decision* refers to the process by which the individual evaluates responses according to their likely payoff and acceptability. Deficits in this component are seen in the antisocial child's propensity to value aggressive solutions and to devalue the negative consequences of aggressive behavior. Finally, *enactment* refers to the process by which the selected response is performed. Deficits are seen in the child's failure to display socially competent behavior despite his or her successful problem solving.

These information-processing competencies are hypothesized to arise from the child's interpretation of his or her experiences (e.g., family interaction, child abuse), social ecology (e.g., day care), and peer relations. To assess the models, Dodge, Bates, and Pettit (1990) initiated a longitudinal study beginning in preschool and continuing through the third grade. The large sample size and multiple indicator definition for the key concepts provide a powerful base for hypothesis testing. It was found that the SIP variables mediated the influence of abusive parenting practices on later measures of aggression. This longitudinal study represents an important step in establishing social cognition as a mediating construct.

Dodge (1991) suggests that different aspects of social information processing are related to reactive and proactive aggression. Reactive-aggressive children are hypothesized to experience particular deficits in encoding and interpretation, leading them to overreact to others. In contrast, proactive-aggressive children presumably have a limited and aggressively biased behavioral repertoire, and positively evaluate aggressive solutions.

The speed with which aggressive interchanges occur makes it important to ask whether there is sufficient time to accomplish these cognitive steps. The SIP model assumes that many of these steps are not consciously performed. The automatic processing feature of this model is intriguing and requires further exploration. We will discuss this further in the final section of this chapter.

Central to this model is the hypothesis that aggressive children exhibit a variety of information-processing deficits that collectively lead them to overestimate the amount of aggression directed toward them. Aggressive children, however, live in a world in which they are frequently attacked and consequently their "biases" may be an accurate reflection of their high base rates for such behavior. Patterson (1982) showed that aggressive children received attacks by their mothers 5% of the time when they were behaving prosocially. Similar rates for fathers and siblings were 4% and 3%, respectively. Aggressive children are more likely than others to be punished for deviant behavior as well as inappropriately attacked for behaving prosocially (Shinn, Ramsey, Walker, Stieber, & O'Neill, 1987; Trachenberg & Viken, 1994). Waas (1988) demonstrated that high base rates of received aggressive behavior increased the likelihood that the child will assume that ambiguous actions are hostile.

A variety of measurement problems emerge from assessment of SIP components. Although these are assessed in a structured and reliable laboratory assessment, it is possible to construe the individual's reactions to this as an elaborate self-report of the extent to which they are aggressive. R. B. Cairns and B. D. Cairns (1991) make a similar point.

> Examination of the scoring systems adopted in social skills inventories suggest that subjects who report aggressive behavior in concrete settings will be classified as deficient in social information processing. Hence, endorsement of aggressive behavior as a solution for interpersonal conflict is taken as evidence that the individual is (a) deficient in cognitive skills and/or interpersonal strategies and, (b) this deficiency accounts for his/her aggressive behavior. An al-

ternative possibility is that the children were merely reporting their likely behavior in that setting. (p. 62)

This illustrates the need to clarify the distinction between individual reports of antisocial attitudes and information-processing deficits. Furthermore, it is important to clarify the distinction between cognitive and behavioral acts. Are antisocial thoughts, statements, and attitudes really different from antisocial acts?

To the extent that we construe SIP variables as self-report, we must consider the possibility that method variance accounts for some of the findings. Consider the possibility that the environmental variable is defined by a method other than self-report, the mediational variable is defined by self-report, and the outcome variable is defined at least partially by self-report. In this case, support for the incremental power of the mediational construct over that of the environmental variable to predict the dependent variable is compromised by the monomethod bias (Bank et al., 1990; Cook & Campbell, 1979). To date, tests of the mediational model have not resolved this problem.

An extremely powerful test of the SIP model would be to show that experimental manipulation of one of the information-processing variables would lead to decreases in antisocial behavior. Numerous social cognitive intervention programs have been developed to address the problems of antisocial children (Lochman, White, & Wayland, 1990). The inconsistent reports of effectiveness, in conjunction with the failure to find specific linkages between social cognitive gains and behavioral improvement (e.g., Weissberg et al., 1981) illustrate the continued need to evaluate the SIP model through experimental trials.

To summarize, Dodge (1991) provides a comprehensive model attempting to account for multiple features of antisocial behavior including individual differences, continuity, consistency across settings, and severity. Individual differences in social information processing presumably arise out of experiences with families and peers. It is important to empirically test the explanatory power of SIP models against alternative models, particularly nonmediational models that stress direct effects of parenting practices. We hope the outcome will be clarification and expansion of models that will enlarge our understanding of development processes.

Future research might study the extent to which an individual's perception corresponds to behavior within specific interpersonal contexts. For example, are hostile biases of aggressive children consistent when they read the behaviors of their mothers, fathers, siblings, unfamiliar peers, or friends? Are social cognitive styles stable across development, underlying the stability observed in antisocial behavior? It is reasonable to assume that individuals shift their interpretations of social exchanges depending on their history and the type of relationship (unfamiliar, familiar, intimate).

Summary

A search for intrapersonal characteristics of the individual encompasses research on gender differences, behavior genetics, hyperactivity, temperament, and social cognition. It is generally agreed that there is evidence suggesting a heritable component to early-starting, life-course persistent antisocial behavior.

As an explanatory variable, however, the predictive effect is relatively weak in comparison with environmental circumstances. Dispositional characteristics of the child are thought to provide the mediating link between genotype, environment, and antisocial behavior. By far, hyperactivity shows the closest empirical linkage to childhood antisocial behavior, as well as to a long-term prognosis of antisocial behavior. This research suffers from problems in construct validity (conceptual overlap between hyperactivity ratings and antisocial behavior) and from a somewhat atheoretical stance. Recent applications of Gray's model are promising with respect to providing cohesion to a disparate body of research on temperament as an etiologic factor in antisocial behavior, and for stimulating research on the person-environment diathesis that may underlie more extreme and chronic forms of antisocial behavior. Another promising area of research focuses on social cognitive characteristics of the individual as a mediational link between environmental experiences and subsequent reactions. To date there has been no attempt to integrate social cognitive research into the biosocial literature on antisocial behavior.

Relationship Processes

Overview

Regardless of the researcher's theoretical perspective, it is generally agreed that in childhood and adolescence, relationships with parents, siblings, peers, and teachers are the basic social ecologies within which antisocial behavior is displayed, practiced, learned, accelerated, or suppressed. During adulthood, new relationships develop that are thought to add force to the stream of social development and affect the trajectories of antisocial behavior. Romantic relationships transform into long-term commitments and families. Peers become coworkers. Authority figures gradually change from teachers to supervisors. The developmental course of antisocial behavior mirrors the individual's adaptation to these evolving relationships at various stages of the life course.

From both a clinical and a developmental standpoint, parents are at center stage when considering the childhood emergence of antisocial behavior. For this reason, considerable research has been done in studying parent-child interactions as they relate to the development of antisocial behavior. Research and theory are emerging that clarify the unique role of peers in the development of antisocial behavior. Sibling relationships also contribute to these processes, and many of the findings that relate peer relationships to the development of antisocial behavior may apply to sibling relationships as well. Finally, relationships with teachers are probably the least studied relationship context.

Although there is little controversy regarding the importance of these relationships in the development of antisocial behavior, there is less agreement regarding the processes and mechanisms that explain observed correlations. As previously discussed, mediational approaches that employ constructs such as social cognition, bonding, or attachment provide one approach to explain the development of antisocial behavior.

A second class of models focuses on the action-reaction sequences that in aggregate define the relationship (see Figure 12.5b). This approach to studying relationships is reductionistic, in that interactions are broken down into their moment-by-moment sequences. In this approach, it is useful to think of antisocial behavior as being embedded in the social environment.

Social interactional models tend to focus on parenting practices (objective social exchange patterns) as having causal significance rather than subjective experiences that emerge from the relationship processes. As can be seen in Figure 12.5b, a social interactional model considers social cognitions to be outcomes of relationship processes, with a more limited role in the actual etiology of antisocial behavior. We now turn to the evidence relating more objective measures of parenting practices to the etiology of antisocial behavior in childhood.

Parenting Practices

The interest in the relation between parenting and the development of antisocial behavior cuts across disciplines. In longitudinal studies seeking to predict male adolescent antisocial behavior, parenting practices were among the most powerful predictors (Loeber & Dishion, 1983). Although the general relation is well established, there is variability from study to study in the magnitude of predictive validity, due primarily to differences in the measurement procedures used to define parenting. Use of parents' recall or reconstruction of their parenting behavior tends to produce lower predictability (Brook, Whiteman, Gordon, & Cohen, 1986; Patterson & Bank, 1986). Children's reports of parenting practices leads to somewhat higher predictive validity (e.g., Nye, 1958; Slocum & Stone, 1965). Outside sources for information on parenting, whether from official records of parent criminality, home visitor ratings, or direct observations, consistently produce the highest level of predictive validity for current and future antisocial behavior.

Criminologists attempting to predict subsequent delinquency from family factors have frequently used some version of the Glueck Social Prediction Table (Craig & Glick, 1968; Tait & Hodges, 1972; Trevett, 1972; Voss, 1963). This consists of home visitor impressions of parent discipline, supervision, cohesiveness, and chaotic family circumstances. Others, using similar comprehensive assessments of family functioning (e.g., Farrington, 1978; McCord, 1979; McCord, McCord, & Howard, 1961; Wadsworth, 1979; West & Farrington, 1973) have also successfully predicted adolescent antisocial behavior from family functioning in middle childhood. H. Wilson (1980) identified parent supervision practices as being a particularly important predictor of adolescent delinquency, especially in urban high-risk settings. Belson (1975) established a link between the child's retrospective recall of free-time in middle childhood and reports of theft in adolescence.

Patterson's (1982) coercion model focused specifically on the contributions of parent-child interactions to child antisocial behavior. This social interactional model, as indicated in Figure 12.5b, implies an emphasis on parent-child exchanges as the proximal cause of antisocial behavior throughout the life span. In Figure 12.5b, both the environment and the individuals' response tendencies are shown to provide the stimulus for individuals' social cognitive style. Thus, social cognition is seen as an outcome of social experience, not a mediating causal variable. On the other hand, social cognition may be a factor when individuals make selections about those with whom they enter relations. In contrast to a mediational model, the social interactional model posits that to change antisocial behavior, it is necessary to change the social exchanges within which behavior is embedded. Then, eventually, the individual's interpretation of the environment will change, as will the kinds of settings he or she selects (Patterson & Reid, 1984).

To date, the focus of the coercion model has been on the process by which the child learns antisocial behavior within parent-child exchanges. The concept of negative reinforcement is the key to understanding the interaction patterns we see occurring between parents and antisocial children, even in the toddler and preschool years. Figure 12.6 shows the early prototypes of parent-child coercive exchanges. Such interactions occur at some level in all families from time to time. A high rate of coercive exchanges, however, is hypothesized to train the child in an antisocial pattern. The long-term outcomes include failure to engage in socialization and skill-building tasks, such as homework and school.

The child learns to avoid parent demands through a process of negative reinforcement. Repeated over thousands of trials, the child learns to use coercive behaviors to gain control over a disrupted, chaotic, or unpleasant family environment. These patterns become overlearned and automatic, and operate without conscious, cognitive control. In the absence of countervailing forces, the child may progress from displaying these trivial aversive behaviors in the family to exhibiting similar patterns with other people in other settings, to engaging in other antisocial behaviors,

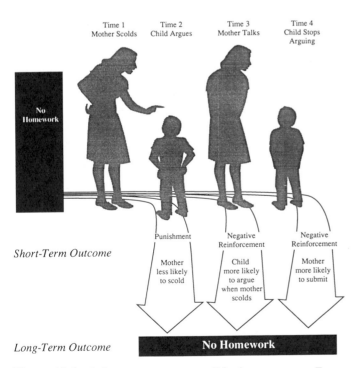

Figure 12.6 A four-step escape-conditioning sequence. From *Antisocial Boys* by G. R. Patterson, J. B. Reid, and T. J. Dishion, 1992, (p. 41). Copyright 1992 by Castalia Publishing Co. Used by permission.

including physical aggression, lying, or stealing. At the hub of the coercion process is the parents' inconsistent, harsh, or erratic efforts to set limits on their young child.

Often, the insidious coercion process is not recognized by the participants. Explanations evolve that suggest if the child is stubborn (like his or her father?), the marriage is bad, work is interfering, or the school is unfair. For this reason, parent reports yield low predictive validity. The development of observational methodology to record objectively the moment-by-moment interchanges between parents and their children has been critical in evaluating the coercion model. In the Oregon Youth Study (OYS), Patterson, Reid, and Dishion (1992) compared behavior observations and parent interview measures of discipline practices. They found that the correlations between these were abysmally low, barely satisfying the minimal requirements of convergent validity in construct validation.

Parents frequently believe they use good parenting practices, but the child fails to respond. In some respects, this may be accurate. Patterson, Reid, and Dishion (1992) provided data showing that aversive exchanges between the child and parent, even in the most disrupted families, constitute only about 10% of total interchanges. The remaining interchanges are positive and neutral. It has been our clinical observation that parents of problem children use a variety of positive parenting practices. These 10% of aversive practices appear to have the most saliency for establishing the developmental course of antisocial behaviors. Distressed and nondistressed marital relationships are similarly distinguished on the basis of aversive rather than positive exchanges (Gottman, 1979).

In some ways, the differences between the attachment and coercion models are quite subtle. For example, skilled family management subsumes positive relationship behaviors. Effective limit setting, when taught clinically, includes expressions of empathy and support. Parent training includes relationship-building skills such as communication and problem solving. Parents cannot effectively manage children without a positive relationship; it simply does not work. Within the social interactional framework, however, the conceptualization of the relationship processes is quite different. Consistent with its learning theory underpinnings, social exchanges are studied reductionistically; rather than being described globally, they are broken down into microsocial patterns, often occurring repeatedly within seconds. The question is, does this approach have any clinical merit?

The coercion model has been refined and tested using correlational methodologies, longitudinal study, and experimental manipulation in clinical trials. Patterson (1986) tested a structural equation model that demonstrated a strong correlation between harsh, abrasive, and inconsistent parent discipline and child antisocial behavior. This model was replicated across the two cohorts of the OYS with a single-parent sample and a clinical sample (Forgatch, 1991).

Consistent with a social interactional model (see Figure 12.5b), the causal arrows between the parent and child go both ways. The more coercive the child, the more difficult to manage. Parents' negative emotions (anger, depression, irritability) undermine their attempts to set limits, reinforce, and solve problems (Forgatch, 1984). In this sense, the more difficult children are, the more "control" they have over their immediate surroundings. In the short run, the child wins; in the long run, the child loses.

The link between parenting practices and the display of later antisocial behavior has been demonstrated in numerous longitudinal studies. Patterson and Bank (1989) and Vuchinich, Bank, and Patterson (1992) used structural equation modeling to test the relation between parent discipline during middle childhood and early adolescent antisocial behavior. In these analyses, they found that parent discipline practices were associated with child antisocial behavior in middle childhood and early adolescence. Moreover, the relation between parent discipline and antisocial behavior in early adolescence held, even when controlling for the stability of antisocial behavior from age 9 to 10 to age 11 to 12.

The coercion model holds as well for two-parent, middle-class families with preschool children (Eddy, 1991). In addition, Fagot (1990) has shown that coercive parenting in toddlerhood predicted problem behavior by age 6 to 7. Patterson and colleagues (Patterson & Dishion, 1985; Patterson & Stouthamer-Loeber, 1984) found an association between inept parent discipline practices, parent monitoring, and child antisocial behavior in midadolescence. The associations between parenting practices and antisocial behavior have been demonstrated in early childhood, middle childhood, and adolescence. At this stage of research, the evidence suggests that extreme deficits in family management skills, in combination with temperamentally difficult children, probably account for the life-course-persistent pattern described by Moffitt, Caspi, Belsky, and Silva (1992). Left on their own, these parents are least likely to improve their parenting practices to the normal range during their child's adolescence; thus, cumulative continuity (Caspi, Bem, & Elder, 1989) takes its toll by rendering a very antisocial and violence-prone adolescent (Capaldi & Patterson, 1991; Lykken, 1993).

As children move into adolescence, monitoring becomes an increasingly important aspect of parenting. Patterson and Dishion (1985) found a strong correlation between parent monitoring practices, adolescent delinquent behavior, and deviant peer associations. Inadequate parent monitoring seems to be important to the emergence and maintenance of antisocial behavior in children from middle childhood through adolescence. Similarly, French, Conrad, and Neill (1991) found that child report of lack of parent monitoring was associated with involvement with deviant peers as well as with smoking and alcohol use.

The strongest support for the involvement of parenting practices in the development of antisocial behavior comes from experimental trials in which changes in parenting led to reductions in antisocial behavior. Several investigators, using random assignment and control groups, have found that parent training leads to reductions in observed child aversiveness in the home (e.g., Forgatch, 1991; Forgatch & Toobert, 1979; Patterson, Chamberlain, & Reid, 1982; Webster-Stratton, 1990).

The key, however, to testing the coercion model experimentally is to demonstrate that improvement in family management skills results in reductions in coercive exchanges that, in turn, are associated with reductions in antisocial behavior. Dishion and Andrews (in press) randomly assigned parents of 150 problematic early adolescents (males and females) to the Adolescent Transitions Program (ATP) or to a nontreatment control group.

ATP consisted of three versions of intervention: parent-focused training; teen-focused training; and a joint focus on parent and teen. Involvement in ATP was associated with reductions in parent-child observed negative engagement, which in turn were reliability correlated with reductions in teacher ratings of antisocial behavior in school.

The evaluation of this intervention carefully selected independent and objective indexes of behavior (not parents' report) to minimize the Hawthorn effect on global ratings of functioning. To this extent, the study provided experimental support for the coercion model. Interventions with teens seemed to have an effect on their negative engagement with parents. Parent training was associated with parents' and teens' reduced reliance on negative interaction and parents' mastery of family management techniques. The specificity of the effects of the teen and parent interventions also supported the idea of mutual causation within family systems.

Although the coercion model has been extensively tested, gaps remain. For example, Gardner (1989) argued that the negative reinforcement aspect of the coercion model has not been adequately tested. This is a very subtle but accurate point. Coercion implies that positive outcomes result from aversive behavior. To date, we have only been able to approximate this process with microsocial indicators such as negative reciprocity (parent negative followed by child negative). The opposite side of the coin is that the lack of coercion implies that parent efforts to discipline are followed by compliance on the part of the child. Again, this interaction pattern has not been apparent in the microsocial analyses.

Progress on this issue has been made by Gardner (1989). She asserts that the problem has to be approached at a more macrosocial level. Gardner argues that it is necessary to look not only at the immediate reaction of compliance or noncompliance but also to consider the outcome of the conflict minutes afterward. Using this approach, she found that mothers of conduct-problem children were eight times more likely to relinquish demands than mothers of nonconduct-problem children. Also mothers of conduct-problem children handled 43% of the conflict episodes inconsistently compared with 5% of mothers of nonconduct-problem children.

Snyder (1991) also approached the problem of coercion at a more macrosocial level, although using a very different approach. He took microsocial interactions and aggregated them into conflict episodes, and then looked at the immediate reactions to conflicts in families with antisocial children versus families with control children. In antisocial families, he found the reaction to conflict was more likely to be escalation in the probability of aversive behavior, whereas the control families were more likely to deescalate. This study supported the central notion of escalation underlying a coercive family process (Patterson, 1982).

Another criticism of the coercion model is that it is too clinically oriented and does not fully consider the causal impact of positive features of the family environment. Within coercion theory, it is the use of aversive exchanges rather than positive exchanges that disrupts child development. In fact, the more entrenched the parents become in the coercion process, the further they shrink from relationship skills that they would enjoy under more favorable circumstances.

One answer to this criticism is to simply reverse-score the data and relabel the parenting constructs. An example is the research by R. D. Conger et al. (1992), in which the construct *Nurturing and Involved Parenting* was found to mediate the relation between economic stress and child adjustment. Another approach is to isolate the specific patterns of positive interactions that do not exist within families of antisocial children. Again, Gardner (1987) has made progress in this area. She successfully isolated deficits in positive interactions that characterize families with antisocial children. Limited engagement in *joint activity* and *joint conversation* differentiated the parent-child interactions of CD children from normal children. Although these positive practices may be disrupted due to the coercion process, the lack of joint activities may have a unique effect on multiple aspects of child social development not predicted by coercive interactions.

In summary, there is little doubt that parenting practices are highly correlated with child antisocial behavior, and improved behavior management practices by parents in intervention studies appear to be related to decreases in a child's antisocial behavior. What may be missing from the behavior management perspective is the quality of the parent-child relationship: In essence, what is the unique effect of love, or the lack thereof, on the development of antisocial behavior? A social interactional model of antisocial behavior assumes that a positive, responsive, and supportive parent-child relationship is embedded in high scores for parent behavior management (Patterson, Reid, & Dishion, 1992). In fact, poor behavior management is thought to undermine the feelings of love and acceptance that come naturally to most parents; the result is an atmosphere of conflict and rejection (Patterson & Dishion, 1988).

Others suggest that the quality of the parent-child relationship is fundamental to parenting practices and contributes uniquely to the child's sociocmotional adaptation. By far the richest theoretical model that emphasizes the role of the parent-child relationship is attachment theory.

Parent-Child Attachment

Attachment theory is an integration of psychodynamic models of ego development, ethology, and learning theory (Bowlby, 1969, 1973, 1980). From an ethological perspective, parent-child attachment serves as a key survival process, emanating from the child's and parent's readiness to form an emotional bond during infancy.

Central to attachment theory is the concept of the *internal working model,* or as described by some, *relationship prototype.* These are expectations regarding the availability and trustworthiness of others as well as the sense of self within a relationship that is applied throughout life in new interactional contexts. At the conclusion of infancy, these are well established, but malleable. Over the life span, they become increasingly solidified (Sroufe & Fleeson, 1988). In part, the increasing rigidity of the working models comes from the individual's active attempts to replicate these expectations in new relationships. For example, an individual who expects to be rejected in relationships frequently seeks out partners who will confirm that expectation.

Individual differences in the attachment relationship have been assessed by means of the Strange Situation developed by Ainsworth and colleagues (Ainsworth, Blehar, Waters, & Wall,

1978). Refinements of this procedure, which produce reliable and stable estimates of the attachment relationship, have made possible a plethora of studies on the nature of attachment across cultures, attachment relationships with fathers, and the effects of attachment on children's social-emotional adjustment (Bretherton, 1992).

In the Strange Situation, the young child is exposed to two major stressors for this developmental period: exposure to a stranger and separation from the mother. The child's reactions relative to his or her mother in a series of separations and reunions formulates the basis for three classifications (A, B, and C). Both A and C babies are described as insecurely attached: Avoidant (A) babies respond to the mother with avoidance or indifference, and Resistant (C) babies respond with anger or rejection. Securely attached babies (B) use the mother as a base of security. Recently, a new category, Disorganized (D), was added to describe children's disorganized and emotional reaction to the mother during reunion episodes (Main & Soloman, 1990). This type of attachment appears to be especially typical of maltreated children.

The internal working model can be construed as a mediational construct linking the environmental stimulus with connections between attachment theory and the social information-processing model proposed by Dodge (1993). Elicker, Englund, and Sroufe (1992) reviewed literature demonstrating that children with anxious-avoidant attachment histories were more likely to make unrealistic attributions or to display a hostile attributional bias than were individuals with more secure attachment histories. Attachment relations appear to serve as a marker of the parent-child relationship both currently and historically. Mothers of secure infants are more responsive, sensitive, accepting, and positive than are mothers of insecure infants (Ainsworth et al., 1978; Egeland & Farber, 1984). In contrast, neglectful, avoidant, or abusive child treatment leads to insecure attachment relationships (Cicchetti & Lynch, 1993). Maternal psychopathology also has an impact on the quality of the attachment relation (van Ijzendoorn, Goldberg, Kroonenberg, & Frenkel, 1992). The development of insecure attachment, however, is not dependent on severe parental dysfunctionality. As Waters, Posada, Crowell, and Lay (1993) note, "rather ordinary differences in early care can produce important differences in subsequent attachment behavior" (p. 217). Attachment relationships also change over time in response to alterations in the quality of parenting (Egeland & Farber, 1984). Consequently, the investigator must assess the status of both the current and past relationship to understand behavior (Waters et al., 1993).

Although Bowlby's (1969) original theoretical speculations regarding attachment processes were based on clinical observations of troublesome children, the application of attachment as a direct cause of child antisocial behavior is questionable. In fact, there have been relatively few longitudinal studies in which the predictability from infant attachment to preschool or childhood antisocial behavior was assessed.

Greenberg, Speltz, and DeKlyen (1993) reviewed the research relating assessments of attachment relationships to children's antisocial behavior (i.e., conduct problems, oppositional behavior) from preschool to middle childhood. These authors described two sets of opposing findings. Researchers who used relatively low-risk samples have generally failed to find children classified as insecurely attached at elevated risk for later antisocial behavior (Bates & Bayles, 1988; Bates, Maslin, & Frankel, 1985; Fagot & Kavanagh, 1990). On the other hand, researchers using high-risk samples found a modest level of predictive validity for the classification of resistant attachment to subsequent externalizing problems in the preschool years (Lewis, Feiring, McGuffog, & Jaskir, 1984; Renken, Egeland, Marvinney, Mangelsdorf, & Sroufe, 1989). The existence of predictive validity in high-risk versus low-risk samples seems to be a function of the higher incidence of behavior problems in high-risk samples.

It would seem that the disorganized, unattached (classification D) toddlers would show elevated risk for antisocial behavior in the middle school years. This troublesome affective reaction to maternal separation is associated, understandably, with severe conditions of maltreatment. There is no doubt that maltreated children have an elevated risk for psychopathology and, in particular, for antisocial behavior and diagnosis of CD. As of this writing, however, we await longitudinal data to test this hypothesis. Because the incidence of disorganized attachment is quite low, it would not account for the high proportion of antisocial behavior in middle childhood.

To date, there is little evidence that the attachment process has a major direct effect in the etiology of child antisocial behavior. Conclusive evidence could result from a longitudinal study that employed intensive measures of both parent behavior management practices, measures of children's early disposition, and their attachment to a primary caregiver. Does attachment provide a mediating effect between direct measures of poor parenting, the child's early disposition, and later antisocial behavior? If so, how much variance does it account for?

Recent speculation takes the judicious position that attachment processes do not need to constitute main effects in the etiology of antisocial behavior to be interesting and informative. Greenberg et al. (1993) considered attachment difficulties to be only one facet of a number of conditions that may be related to the etiology of early antisocial behavior. In their transactional model, insecure attachments combine or exacerbate factors such as the temperament of the child, parent behavior management practices, and the family's ecology in the etiology of antisocial behavior in young childhood. This transactional view emphasizes the importance of attachment as an indirect and/or direct effect on antisocial behavior (Greenberg et al., 1993; Waters et al., 1993). Although attachment theory may not account for substantial or unique variance in child antisocial behavior, understanding the nature of disruption in child social development, specific to poor parental attachment, considerably enriches our understanding of socialization. Furthermore, attachment can change over time as a consequence of changes in the relationship. Thus, accurate predictability depends, in part, on current as well as historical attachment relationships.

Attachment theorists have made additional long-term contributions to our models of development. In particular, their theoretical and empirical study of relationships (in contrast to the study of individual behavior) has broad range implications for the study of parent, child, and peer relationships. These relationships are of critical importance. Werner and Smith (1977), for example, showed that children from high-risk environments did well if they had a close relationship with a competent and prosocial adult.

Attachment theory may explain more about the development of relationships and prosocial behavior than it does about antisocial behavior. The connection between secure attachment and later preschool and childhood social competence and relationship development is well established (Elicker et al., 1992). The role of prosocial relationships in protecting individuals from antisocial behavior has been prominently highlighted in theories of bonding, which we will review in the next section.

Parent-Child Bonding

Research relating indexes of the parent-child relationship to antisocial behavior in adolescence was stimulated by the social control theory of Hirschi (1969). Within social control theory, the child's relationship with his or her parents in adolescence is conceptualized as a *bond*. *Bonding* as a construct refers to several dimensions of the parent-child relationship, including a sense of closeness, shared values, and identification. The basic idea is that a close bond to parents in adolescence serves a critical, social control function during the developmental period where the child is functioning more independently in the social world.

Hirschi (1969) argued that the best strategy for understanding adolescent antisocial behavior (i.e., delinquency) is to understand why some children *do not* engage in delinquency. According to the social control perspective, adolescents refrain from committing antisocial acts because they have a "stake in conformity." Close emotional relationships (i.e., bonds) with prosocial socialization agents translate to a commitment to prosocial lines of actions and institutions.

The social control model has stimulated a great deal of research activity; much of it was modeled after Hirschi's initial studies. Attachment to school, commitment to conventional norms, and involvement with delinquent companions are all reliably correlated (negatively and positively, respectively) with self-reported delinquency (Elliott et al., 1985; Hawkins & Lishner, 1987; Hirschi, 1969). More recently, Gottfried and Hirschi (1990) have updated the theoretical orientation of social control theory, much along the same lines suggested by Greenberg et al. (1993). In the reformulation, the parent-child relationship is considered as one facet of a parenting system and community context that is important in the etiology of adolescent antisocial behavior. In a reanalysis of the S. Glueck and E. Glueck (1959) data, Sampson and Laub (1990) provided support for the joint role of the parent-child relationship and family management practices in the etiology of adolescent delinquency.

Elliott and colleagues (1985, 1989) also integrated social control theory with social learning theory to account for the major contribution of deviant peer groups to adolescent antisocial behavior. Social control (i.e., bonding) is presumed to influence delinquency primarily through mediating adolescent bonding to deviant peer groups. Hawkins and Lishner (1987) provided a model that is conceptually similar to the Elliott et al. (1985) model, with the exception that family management constructs were included as more distal predictors of parent-child bonding. Virtually all studies that employ measures of the parent-child bonding during adolescence find a significant level of covariation with adolescent problem behavior. Before accepting this finding, however, some basic methodological issues require discussion.

A major difficulty with the research evaluations of social control theory in adolescence is that measures of bonding and adolescent problem behavior are both typically derived from self-reports, yielding the monomethod bias confound. In the investigations in which measures other than self-report have been used, the constructs have been measured with varying degrees of fidelity. Elliott et al. (1985) used a comprehensive assessment of delinquency, but used grade point average to measure bonding to school, and size of cohort to reflect the strain on resources. A more robust test of the model would be provided if constructs were measured using a multiagent assessment battery. Although the model reported by Elliott et al. (1985) has essentially been replicated by a number of investigators, each of the replications could be criticized because of the shared method variance of the key constructs.

Dishion and Brown (in press) used a multiagent and multimethod strategy in a sample of high-risk adolescents to measure parent monitoring, limit setting, and parent-child relationship quality and problem-solving skills. Observations, staff impressions, and child- and parent-report were used to define each construct, and multiple measures of adolescent problem behavior were employed. The first step in this research was to determine if a *construct model* of the data provided a superior fit-to-the-data than did a *method model*. In essence, did the conceptualization of parenting constructs provide a more reasonable account of the observed correlation among indicators than a model using constructs of parent-report, child-report, and staff impressions? A somewhat discouraging finding was that both models fit the data equally well. The method factors accounted for the data as well as the factors that represented specific parenting constructs. Furthermore, as expected, method constructs showed the highest predictive validity to antisocial behavior measured by the same method.

These data indicate that, as of this writing, there is considerable overlap in constructs describing parenting practices when measured comprehensively. In this sense, the literature on bonding has yet to establish this construct as uniquely contributing to the etiology of problem behavior in adolescents. At this stage of research, studies relying exclusively on one measurement method will not suffice to address this issue.

The model is also ambiguous in a more fundamental sense. *Lack of bonding* describes a socioemotional state that contributes to subsequent involvement with deviant peers and engagement in delinquent behavior during adolescence. The utility of lack of bonding as a mediational variable rests on the assumption that it contributes unique variance to predictions of involvement with deviant peers (as shown in Figure 12.5a), as well as subsequent delinquency when controlling for other environmental variables such as past behavior. For example, Dishion, Patterson, Stoolmiller, and Skinner (1991) showed that involvement with deviant peers in early adolescence (age 11 to 12) was predicted by prior (age 9 to 10) measures of peer relations and parenting behavior. Knowing that the child had been rejected, was antisocial, showed academic skill deficits, and was poorly supervised by parents accounted for 77% of the variance in deviant peer associations. Inclusion of a bonding construct would add little to this prediction. Similarly, they found that boys high in antisocial behavior at age 9 to 10 were highly likely to be involved in a deviant peer group by age 12 to 13, as represented by a longitudinal correlation of .79. These studies underscore the need for bonding theorists to control for prior behaviors when attempting to explain progressions in antisocial behavior from middle childhood to adolescence using bonding constructs.

Models that emphasize the importance of the parent-child relationship in the etiology of disorder do not help clarify developmental trends in antisocial behavior during adolescence and young adulthood. It is well known that delinquency peaks around age 16 and thereafter declines. Substance use, on the other hand, reaches its highest level in young adulthood. Adolescence and young adulthood are times when individuation and autonomy are normative, and this perhaps explains the peak in deviancy during this period. It does not explain, however, why antisocial behavior decreases later.

Most relationship-oriented models include the influence of the peer network in their models to explain such developmental trends. Parent-child relationships, however, continue to be important during this period and are used to better understand how the parent-child relationship changes during adolescence and adulthood and to find which practices promote further adaptation through young adulthood. We can imagine that many young people remain affectively close with their parents but are quite autonomous in their functioning. The young person's selection of peer environments and romantic relationships with peers that are consonant with the parents' values and attitudes is critical in maintaining affective closeness, yet full autonomy. There is very little data on the relation between parenting practices and the child's antisocial behavior in late adolescence or young adulthood. The influence of parents may be a subtle yet critical background factor that accounts for the maintenance or recovery (e.g., late starting, temporary delinquents) of a prosocial trajectory. Such parenting practices as financial, social, and emotional support promote prosocial behavior, modeling, and constructive problem solving. A critical skill for parents of older adolescents is to be a problem-solving resource for the more mature child. Skills such as emphasizing the positive, avoiding criticism, and constructive problem solving may greatly enhance the maturing child's use of parental support as well as facilitating positive adaptation for his or her initial foray into the adult world.

Parent Psychopathology

To this point, we have focused on parenting practices as a means by which the antisocial disposition could be transmitted across generations via socialization experiences, as well as biological or genetic mechanisms (Burgess & Youngblade, 1985; Elder, Caspi, & Van Nguyen, 1986; Widom, 1989; Zaidi, Knutson, & Mehm, 1989). This section will review evidence testing the hypothesis that parent psychopathology has an indirect effect on child antisocial behavior, primarily by disrupting parenting practices. This model of transmission illustrates how other contextual variables can impact the socialization process. Elder and colleagues (Elder, Caspi, & Van Nguyen, 1986; Elder, Van Nguyen, & Caspi, 1985) introduced the *amplifier hypothesis,* in which stress is assumed to amplify the maladaptive predispositions of parents and thereby disrupt family management and undermine parents' potentially supportive function. Parent antisocial behavior and depression are considered two of the most important forms of parent psychopathology related to the development of child antisocial behavior during childhood and adolescence.

Patterson and Dishion (1988) examined the role of parent antisocial behavior and social disadvantage on parenting practices and child antisocial behavior. Parent antisocial behavior was defined by the MMPI Psychopathic Deviant scale, records of moving traffic violations, license suspensions, and convictions for violations of the law. Structural equation modeling was used to test hypotheses regarding the link between stress, parent antisocial behavior, and child antisocial behavior. It was expected that parental antisocial behavior would be related to child antisocial behavior by virtue of parent discipline practices and that this would be exacerbated by stress. The models were analyzed separately for mothers and fathers.

There was a strong correlation between stress and antisocial behavior for both mothers and fathers. Mothers' and fathers' antisocial behavior significantly correlated with their discipline practices. After controlling for parent antisocial behavior, the relation between stress and discipline practices disappeared for both parents. For fathers, controlling for discipline practices resulted in a nonsignificant effect between fathers' and boys' antisocial behavior. For mothers, contrary to expectation, a correlation between child antisocial behavior and mother antisocial behavior remained after discipline practices and stress were entered. A variety of mechanisms could plausibly explain the direct link between mothers' and children's antisocial behavior. These mechanisms include mothers' modeling of antisocial behavior, a lack of sanctions for child engagement in antisocial behavior, or mothers' antisocial disposition as measured by the number of marital transitions in the family.

In its general outline, the link between stress, parent antisocial behavior, and child antisocial behavior is consistent with the amplifier hypothesis. A more stringent test could be applied by longitudinally examining the impact of a stressor on parenting practices of high-antisocial versus low-antisocial parents. One would expect the effect of stress to be more dramatic on the former. Very little research has explored the hypothesis that stress directly increases child antisocial behavior. Forgatch, Patterson, and Skinner (1985) tested a model that showed the impact of stress on child antisocial behavior was mediated through parent discipline.

Parent depression is also associated with child antisocial behavior. Again, causal loci are somewhat ambiguous, as an extremely antisocial child is likely to affect a caretaker's mood. The small sample of parent training outcome studies with antisocial children indicates that maternal depression was associated with the lack of clinical progress (e.g., Forehand, Furey, & McMahon, 1984; Lobitz & Johnson, 1975). Radke-Yarrow (1989) discovered that depressed mothers were more likely to back off in discipline confrontations and less likely to elicit child cooperation. Girls tended to be more negatively affected by this than boys. These data are consistent with the findings of Ensminger, Kellam, and Rubin (1983) in which mothers' psychological well-being was associated more with girls' subsequent delinquent behavior in adolescence than with boys' behavior.

Patterson, Reid, and Dishion (1992) found that maternal depression was correlated with boys' antisocial behavior in single-mother families, but this did not appear to be mediated by maternal parenting practices. For two-parent families, the findings were the opposite. Maternal depression was correlated with poor monitoring practices, but there was no relation between maternal depression and child antisocial behavior. There was no correlation between fathers' depression and either child antisocial behavior or family management practices. Wahler and Sansbury (1990) documented the poor tracking skills of troubled mothers by comparing their behavioral definitions with those of trained observers. Mothers with antisocial children tended to underreport child aversive behaviors.

In general, the links between child antisocial behavior and parental antisocial behavior appeared stronger than those for parental depression. The findings for parent depression at this stage are not clear with respect to the strength of the association, types of families, and the cause-effect relation.

Contributions of Siblings

It has been said that siblings are no more alike than two people chosen at random (Plomin & Daniels, 1987). It turns out that method variance again distorts our view of the contribution of siblings (Hoffman, 1991); that is, the lack of similarity among siblings ($r = .16$) found across samples may be an artifact of data based on personality inventories. Research employing alternative assessment methods, including direct obervation, paints a different picture of similarity between siblings on several indexes of adaptation in the home and school settings in the middle childhood years.

Studies that attempt to disentangle the influence of different family agents on the socialization of the child and the development of antisocial behavior are just beginning. Considerable evidence suggests that the influence of siblings is significant. One recalls the finding, first reported by West and Farrington (1973), that 10% of the families accounted for 50% of the crimes in an urban London sample. This finding implied that siblings share a common trait for antisocial behavior. We suspect that siblings are fellow travelers on the path to antisocial behavior (Patterson, 1986).

Clinical experience tells us that children referred for conduct problems often differ little from their nonreferred siblings. In their home, siblings' rates of aversive behavior frequently are comparable to that of the target child. Patterson (1986) reported a correlation of .61 among brothers referred for conduct problems who were observed in the home. Patterson et al. (1984) found a correlation of .43 among boys and their siblings as observed in the home. Patterson (1984) proposed that siblings, as well as other family members, shared a mutual trait toward aggressiveness. The thought is that the coercion process, as previously discussed, is elicited by inept parenting practices (Patterson, 1982; Patterson, Reid, & Dishion, 1992) and has an impact on all members of a family system. Strong support for the parenting hypothesis was provided by Arnold, Levine, and Patterson (1975), who found that all siblings decreased observed aversive behavior following parent training, even though only the problem child was targeted for treatment. To date, however, this finding has not been replicated with a randomly assigned experimental control group.

The high correlations between siblings on observed aggressive behavior are confounded because siblings are most often interacting with each other when observed in the home. We need to look at data on siblings in independent settings, such as the school, where they do not share the same classroom.

The work of Lewin et al. (1993) indicates considerable convergence among siblings on such measures as negative peer nominations ($r = .65$), teacher-ratings on aggression ($r = .26$), likability ($r = .55$), behavior adjustment ($r = .48$), and observed positive peer behavior in the classroom ($r = .47$). The correlation among siblings in teachers' reactions to each child in separate classrooms was surprising. Behavior observations in the classroom revealed a correlation of .72 ($p < .001$) in observed teacher disapproval. Note that these were independent observations of each of the siblings in separate classrooms with different teachers.

A simple generalization model cannot account for siblings' similarity in the school setting. Although siblings' behavior in the school setting is intercorrelated, as is siblings' behavior in the home setting, there is not a high correlation between children's aversive exchanges with their siblings and their peer acceptance or antisocial behavior in school (Dishion, 1987). Abramovitch, Corter, Pepler, and Stanhope (1986) also found no evidence for a direct transfer of interactions with siblings to those with peers. The analysis by Dishion (1987) seems to indicate that the most robust *interactional* index of generalizability was the family's behavior with the boy considered as a whole, rather than that of any one specific family member.

Presumably, relationships with siblings have a specific role in children's adaptation within a peer group, but the findings do not as yet clarify this unique role (Dunn, 1992). However, the extensive research on the contributions of peers to the development of antisocial behavior apply to siblings as well.

Contribution of Peers

A central assumption of developmental psychology is that children's peer relationships provide unique contributions to their development. Such relationships are contexts in which basic competencies emerge. They serve as resources that enhance children's competence as well as buffer them from stress. Finally, they may serve as precursors of other relationships (Hartup, 1992).

Peer relationships, however, are also implicated in the development of antisocial behavior. We see this as being accomplished in three major ways: (a) Antisocial behavior interferes with positive peer relations, depriving children of the positive benefits of peer learning and confining them within the social niches of marginal adjustment; (b) children may act as models and reinforcers for aggressive and antisocial behavior in other children; (c) children develop friendship networks that are predicated on activity themes. Within some friendship networks, support for antisocial behavior is established by providing both reinforcement and opportunity for such behavior. We will address each of these issues in turn.

Entry to school may be the first occasion during which the child is exposed to significant numbers of nonrelated agemates (French, 1987) and, as such, provides the conditions for establishing the peer culture. Patterson, Littman, and Bricker (1967) have shown that one of the consequences of exposure to other children is an increase in aggression. Their microanalysis of preschool children's interactions revealed that peers provide very rich schedules of positive reinforcement for coercive behavior, with 80% of coercive behavior producing successful outcomes. Instigators and victims are not random. Certain children provide reinforcement for aggression, with the consequence being an increase in the victimization of these children (Olweus, 1979). These reinforced patterns of aggression are common and continue into at least early adolescence.

The impact of peers on antisocial behavior is also seen in the work of Dodge, Price, Coie, and Christopoulos (1990). Using data from a series of playgroup sessions involving previously unacquainted peers, they found that 50% of the aggression observed in these play sessions was accounted for by a mere 20% of the dyads. As might be expected, these dyads consisted primarily of members identified by their aggressiveness. This research is complemented by a paper presented by Cillessen (1989), in which it was found that triads of low-status first-grade children were the most highly aggressive; mixed dyads (low- and high-status) produced considerably lower levels of aggressive behaviors. Thus, the antisocial traits of individuals merge to create a dyadic tendency to engage in antisocial behavior. When both members are antisocial, an amplification of maladaptive characteristics is likely. These data also raise the issue of deviant peer influences as early as middle childhood.

Much of the research on the role of peers in middle childhood antisocial behavior focuses on children's acceptance within the peer group, or sociometric status. Antisocial behavior has emerged as the most consistent correlate of social rejection in children (e.g., Coie & Dodge, 1988; French & Waas, 1987). Aggression is not, however, consistently associated with peer disapproval. Fighting back from a provoked attack may be positively associated with social status (Olweus, 1979), whereas unprovoked attacks seem to be a pathogenic sign of a general antisocial trait. Furthermore, antisocial behavior appears to account for only about 50% of peer rejection in boys (French, 1988) and somewhat less in girls (French, 1990).

The clearest evidence of the impact of aggression comes from observations of playgroups comprising previously unacquainted members. Coie and Kupersmidt (1983) formed playgroups consisting of four boys who differed in status. Rejected boys exhibited more physical and verbal aggression than other group members. Similar findings were obtained by Dodge (1983) in a study of unacquainted groups comprising eight boys unselected by status. Boys who eventually became rejected by their companions exhibited more physical aggression, inappropriate play, and more hostile verbalization than other group members.

There are also age-related and sex-related differences in the degree to which aggression is associated with peer rejection (Coie, Belding, & Underwood, 1987). Researchers have generally found stronger relations between aggression and peer status with boys than with girls and in elementary school more than in either preschool or adolescent populations. One explanation for these findings may be reliance on a construct of aggression, narrowly defined, rather than use of a broader construct of antisocial behavior. We argue that the construct of *antisocial behavior* may be more powerful than *aggression* in explaining rejection across the life span. Antisocial behavior accounts for developmental changes in topography and incorporates high frequency behaviors (e.g., whining or noncompliance with requests for stopping behaviors that are aversive and disruptive of social relations but do not fall under the definition of aggression).

The child's movement out of middle childhood into adolescence is marked by increased involvement with peers and affiliations with larger social groups. Much of the research on the contribution of peers to the development of antisocial behavior has focused on the impact of social groups. These are larger than friendship dyads and can be categorized as cliques or crowds (Brown, 1989). Cliques generally consist of fewer than 10 members who frequently interact with each other. In contrast, crowds are frequently defined on the basis of reputation, and members may or may not interact with each other.

There is evidence that children who are rejected by their peers (a significant percentage of whom exhibit antisocial behavior) begin to associate together during the elementary school years. These children are more likely to interact with younger peers, other rejected children, and individuals with whom they are not friends (Ladd, 1983).

These groups become increasingly solidified during early adolescence. Contributing to the formation of these groups is the adolescent quest for autonomy and vulnerability to peer pressure (Steinberg & Silverberg, 1986). An additional factor is the normative transition from the small elementary school environment to the larger, more impersonal middle and high school settings where there are large numbers of agemates with whom to associate and considerable freedom from adult scrutiny.

Dishion et al. (1991) found that low parent monitoring, poor academic skills, and peer rejection in middle childhood accounted for associations with deviant peers by early adolescence, even after controlling for prior levels of antisocial behavior. Although the deviant peer construct was stronger at a later age, there was indication that deviant peers were identifiable in the elementary school setting, as reported by children, teachers, and parents (Dishion, 1990). There was respectable stability in involvement with antisocial peers from ages 9 to 10 and 11 to 12, reflected in a standardized beta of .26 ($p < .01$) when controlling for family, school, and the child's behavior at age 9 to 10. R. B. Cairns, B. D. Cairns, et al. (1988) found that aggressive children in middle school tended to associate more as a function of mutual attraction than of peer rejection.

Of particular concern is the formation of the deviant peer group in adolescence. The large-scale, longitudinal study using a national probability sample reported by Elliott et al. (1985) focused on the role of deviant peers in the etiology of adolescent delinquent behavior. They found that self-reported involvement in a deviant peer group accounted for substantial variance in subsequent levels of self-reported delinquency in middle and late adolescence, even after accounting for previous levels of delinquency. This held for males and females and generalized from minor delinquency to more serious index offenses and serious substance use.

Not only do adolescents who engage in antisocial behavior tend to associate with other antisocial adolescents, but these groups often commit criminal acts. Aultman (1980) carefully reviewed juvenile records in Maryland and found that 63% of all recorded offenses were committed in the company of two to three peers.

Group involvement tended to vary with the type of offense, with 68% of property offenses and 43% of violent offenses committed by groups. Girls were also likely to commit offenses in the company of others, with 57% of their offenses committed in groups. In an analysis of self-reported delinquent acts, Gold (1970) estimated that 75% of all delinquent acts were committed in the company of friends.

The correlations between deviant peer involvement and antisocial behavior were quite high ($r = .40$ to .59) and held when both constructs were measured using multiple methods of measurement for both constructs (Patterson & Dishion, 1985). The relation held when the antisocial trait scores were correlated, based on independent reports, for two boys who were friends. For example, Dishion, Andrews, and Crosby (in press) found a correlation of .42 ($n = 181$) between the OYS boy's antisocial behavior and that of his best friend. Strong correlational support for the relation between these findings raises a question as to the possibility of an interactional mechanism in adolescent friendships that relates to the increase of antisocial behavior.

To study the friendship interactions associated with antisocial behavior, OYS boys 13 to 14 years old were asked to bring in their closest friend to complete a 25-minute videotaped problem-solving discussion. Dishion, Andrews, and Crosby (in press) found a tendency for the friendships of antisocial boys to be abrasive, less stable, and less satisfying to the boys themselves. As would be expected from coercion theory, the antisocial boys tended to be bossy with their friends, were involved in negative reciprocal cycles, and developed relationships that tended to end in disharmony within a year. No differences between antisocial and nonantisocial boys were found on the occurrence of positive behaviors. These findings indicate that the friendships of antisocial boys are compromised, apparently by means of their use of directives and coercion.

A mutual socialization process appears to operate in adolescent friendships and contribute to the ongoing development of antisocial attitudes and behavior. Cohen (1977) found that adolescent cliques that were the most stable over the course of 1 year were those who were most similar in attitudes and drug-use profiles. Acquiring a new group member tended to increase the homogeneity of the group, whereas a group member leaving (rejection) did not increase homogeneity. The author concluded that homophilic selection accounted for considerable variance in peer group homogeneity.

Kandel (1978) was able to disentangle the relations between homophily, friendship formation, and stability a bit more. She found that similarity in demographic characteristics was the most important determinant of friendship similarity. Second to demographic variables, however, was similarity in reported substance use, particularly marijuana use. Friendships between similar individuals were the most stable, whereas friendships that formed between dissimilar individuals tended to dissolve unless the members moved toward greater similarity over the course of a year.

Dishion, Andrews, Patterson, and Poe (1994) examined the videotapes of the boys with their friends to study the mutual influence process. The videotapes were coded for verbal content and affective reactions. Two topics were defined: *rule-breaking talk* and *normative talk.* The possible reactions were *positive, laugh,* and *pause* (most frequent negative reaction in friendship dyads). Two groups were compared: a group of early-starting antisocial boys and a normative group of boys. Rule-breaking talk occurred quite frequently in normal dyads but was more prevalent in antisocial dyads. Sequential analyses revealed that both groups of boys tended to laugh at a rule-breaking suggestion, indicating the function of such talk in male adolescent friendships. What distinguished the two groups, however, was the low likelihood that antisocial boys could elicit a laugh from their friend with normative talk. Thus, differential reinforcement for rule-breaking discussions was seen.

These findings suggest a developmental process fundamental to the role of intimate relationships in social development. In intimate relationships, there is a certain amount of merging of the characteristics of the members, referred to as *trait confluence.* This process may define the origins of assortative mating, which is a critical issue in understanding the etiology of antisocial behavior across disciplines. Individuals tend to merge in the context of shared activities and verbal behavior (see Figure 12.7). Antisocial boys tend to discuss and encourage rule-breaking talk and have little to say in prosocial or normative discussions. Within an intimate dyad, the relative rate of reinforcement for rule-breaking talk sets the occasion for rule-breaking behavior in other settings. If a friend laughs about stories of vandalism, chances are good that he or she may be amenable to such behavior when given the opportunity. With the marginal, unstable nature of these boys' friendships, it is likely that antisocial behavior and drug use activities form the hub of their friendships. Over time, the boys will become more similar with respect to antisocial behavior, and these behaviors may actually escalate in frequency and variety. Although the impact of these dyadic processes on developmental trajectories has yet to be established, this provides a possible explanatory mechanism for the findings of Cohen (1977) and Kandel (1978).

As with studies focusing on the role of parents in the etiology of antisocial behavior, we need intervention studies that provide clearer evidence of causal linkages. As of this writing, there are

Figure 12.7 Confluence of individual characteristics into dyadic traits. From "Peer Adaptation in the Development of Antisocial Behavior: A Confluence Model" by T. J. Dishion, G. R. Patterson, and P. C. Griesler, in L. R. Huesmann, (Ed.), *Aggressive Behavior,* (p. 68), New York: Plenum Press. Copyright 1994 by Plenum Publishing Corp. Used by permission.

few. Some experimental evidence is needed demonstrating that changes in the structure of adolescent peer networks can lead to changes in antisocial behavior. Feldman, Caplinger, and Wodarski (1983) showed that placing antisocial children in ongoing activities involving prosocial peers seemed to reduce their level of antisocial behavior. This finding is tentative, and it has not yet been studied with an experimental evaluation design.

The most ubiquitous finding in the study of antisocial behavior is that the rate of delinquent behavior begins to decrease in late adolescence and, across all cultures studied, continues to decrease throughout the adult years (Hirschi & Gottfredson, 1983). An unmet challenge of a socially oriented lifecourse model of antisocial behavior is to explain the pervasive age-crime relationship. However, Waas (1988) presents data suggesting that, in predicting self-report delinquency, age effects disappear when one also includes measures of peer influence, which show a developmental trend quite similar to that of antisocial behavior. In late adolescence and early adulthood, there is a shift away from same-gender friends to intimate and romantic relationships. Little is understood about the impact of this shift on antisocial behavior. Caspi and Herbener (1990) used a Q-sort methodology to assess assortative mating processes. Stability in marriage was accounted for largely by similarity in the profiles of spouses. Sociological studies of adult friendships revealed that similarity in demographics, religion, and substance use continued to be a major factor in the initial stages of relationship formation. Thus, because of the extent to which early-starting, life-persistent antisocial children continue to seek out companions with similar antisocial inclinations, they will continue to experience a large chasm between their social world and that of their prosocial compatriots.

Follow-up studies of boys moving from adolescence to young adulthood revealed that the maintenance of a delinquent lifestyle, partially indicated by friendships with deviant peers, is highly related to the maintenance of antisocial behavior into adulthood (West & Farrington, 1977). In contrast, marriage to spouses without an antisocial history, as well as moving from the neighborhood of origin, is related to desistance of antisocial conduct (Osborn, 1980; Osborn & West, 1979). Sampson and Laub (1990) reanalyzed the S. Glueck and E. Glueck (1950) data and presented convincing evidence that those antisocial individuals who attained stable jobs and positive marriages ceased to have contact with antisocial peers.

In some respects, desistance may be a misnomer. Although the illegal aspect of antisocial behavior may desist in the adult years, the coercive interpersonal style may persist. For individuals with a history of antisocial behavior who start families early, there are higher rates of divorce (Caspi et al., 1987; Kandel, Davies, & Kandel, 1984) and higher rates of spouse abuse (Huesmann et al., 1984). Both men and women with a history of antisocial behavior tend to use the abusive parenting practices that were used on them as children (Huesmann et al., 1984), forming the interactional basis for the transmission of antisocial behavior across generations. As if the behavioral transmission were not enough, there is evidence of assortative mating, whereby antisocial boys and girls select their marital partners on the basis of similarity to their own behavioral characteristics, such as antisocial behavior (Caspi et al., 1987). Assortative mating and behavioral continuity probably explain the startling crime statistics in Wolfgang, Figlio, and Sellin (1982) in which roughly 50% of the crimes reported seem to be committed by 10% of the families in any given community.

Thus, the topography of antisocial behavior changes as a function of maturity and social context. Continuity would seem to be the highest within highly similar contexts that occur in the life course. Military service is probably the clearest example of a constrained setting that demands rule compliance and cooperation with many peers, much as public school does. An early study by Roff (1961) illustrated the difficulties that antisocial young adults have in the military. Langan and Greenfeld (1983) reported that 57% of the habitual offenders in a population of prison inmates had records of dishonorable discharge from the military. Because of the rigid rule structure in the military service, as well as the intense demand on relationship skills, it would not be surprising to learn that those who have a high potential for antisocial behavior fail in the military as they do in the structured school setting.

Antisocial behavior also impairs the ability of young adults to succeed in the conventional workforce. Adults with a history of "ill temper" were more likely to be downwardly socially mobile than their family of origin and to display erratic work histories (Caspi et al., 1987; Kandel et al., 1984). A source of antisocial adults' troubles at work may be their difficulty in getting along with coworkers and supervisors, not just occupational skill deficits.

In summary, peer relationships are linked with antisocial behavior throughout the life span, ranging from early childhood to young adulthood. As yet, no data are conclusive on the question of causality. Longitudinal data analyses strongly suggest that deviant peer environments are potentially established early and demarcate a social habitat that contributes to the maintenance of antisocial behavior among some individuals over the life course (Dishion, Patterson, & Griesler, 1994).

Multiple Relationships

The challenge to developmental theorists and researchers is to think systemically about the joint influence of multiple relationship contexts on social behavior. Most of the work in this area has considered the joint influence of parents and peers. It is often said that parental influences diminish during adolescence whereas peer influences increase. Early in the study of antisocial behavior, Robins (1966) found that macrocharacteristics of children's peer groups, parent characteristics, and school performance in combination accounted for a substantial number of subsequent antisocial adolescents. For this reason, it is surprising that more data addressing the joint influence of parents and peers at different developmental stages are not available. Parent-peer models hold the most promise for guiding comprehensive intervention strategies that prevent or reduce antisocial behavior prior to adulthood.

Bronfenbrenner (1979, 1989) refers to such models as *mesosystem* models. A true mesosystem model not only incorporates the additive univariate effects into a multivariate model, thereby explaining variance in antisocial behavior, but it also assesses the interaction between the microsystems. The research reviewed in this section assesses the joint influence of parents and peers on antisocial behavior, as well as the impact of parent and peer systems on each other. Studies that incorporate these developmental questions are also included here.

Based on data collected on families and peer groups in the 1950s and 1960s, Elder (1980) found that adolescents coming from less nurturing, positive, and involved parent-child relationships were more likely to become invested in a deviant peer group and to respond to the deviant group norms with like behaviors. Conversely, children who had close and positive relationships with their parents tended to select values congruent with their parents, which were often prosocial and conventional. These findings suggest that a shift may occur in adolescence, when it becomes evermore critical for parents to maintain and enhance their relationship and involvement with adolescents. Close and rewarding family relationships may establish the affective tone for adoption of prosocial values, providing a cocoon of sorts against competing values inevitably confronted in the peer group. Psychodynamic models refer to this process as identification. Learning theorists could account for the same developmental mechanism using the rule-governed behavior framework (Hayes & Hayes, 1989). Similar to the findings reported by Dishion, Patterson, and Griesler (1994), positive affective exchanges between the parent and child provide the context for establishing prosocial norms. It may also be true that children are more at risk if they have a positive relationship with an antisocial parent, as these norms will become inculcated within the children's daily functioning.

In an earlier but related study, Siman (1977) reported that parent support of prosocial and antisocial behavior was related to teenage engagement in both types of behavior. In contrast, peer support seemed to be strongest for engagement in antisocial behavior. Boys were found to be more susceptible to peer pressure than girls. No effort was made in this study to examine the interaction between the child's experience within these two settings.

Elliott et al. (1985) developed an integrated model of delinquency causation, at the heart of which is the idea that children's relationships with their parents determine their selection of peer cliques. Focusing on delinquency and substance use, these authors showed that a weak bond with parents predicted an adolescent's involvement with a deviant peer group, which in turn accounted for unique variance in subsequent delinquent and substance-using behavior. The relation, however, was modest, even when both constructs were based on the same method. Hawkins and Weis (1985) proposed a nearly identical model that emphasized, in addition, the role of family management. In this model, poor family management leads to a weak parent-child relationship and both would influence the adolescent's social trajectory and commitment to conventional peers. The key element in the Elliott and Hawkins models is bonding to parents and peers. The social interactional model of antisocial behavior (Patterson, Reid, & Dishion, 1992) explicitly details the joint contribution of parent management and peer influence to antisocial behavior, along with research on how the two microsystems interrelate. The models varied with the age at which child antisocial behavior was being studied.

Patterson et al. (1984) tested a correlational model explaining physically aggressive behavior in boys of elementary school age. In this SEM model, inconsistent parenting was reciprocally related to negative microsocial exchanges with siblings, including sequential parameters such as startup of delinquency and synchronicity. A strong correlation was observed between the Parent Discipline and Child-Sibling Exchange constructs. Negative exchanges with siblings (as observed in the home) were strongly correlated with boys' physical aggression as rated by teachers, parents, and their own reports. A bidirectional effect between physical aggression and poor peer relations was also found. This research provided evidence of links between the child's experiences with parents, siblings, and peers.

As children move toward adolescence and spend more time outside direct adult scrutiny, parental monitoring becomes an increasingly important predictor of delinquent behavior. Stoolmiller (1990) referred to this as *child wandering*, and this can be added to the list of problematic behaviors exhibited by the persistently antisocial child. Snyder, Dishion, and Patterson (1986) found that the correlation between low parent monitoring and association with deviant peers increased from middle childhood to middle adolescence. Using the same sample, Patterson and Dishion (1985) found a very strong correlation between low parent monitoring and association with deviant peers in later adolescence. Parent monitoring practices were therefore directly and indirectly implicated. Direct effects were seen in parents' failure to closely track antisocial and delinquent behavior. Indirect effects were seen in the contribution of low parental monitoring to boys' increased opportunity to associate with deviant peers. Such association is predictive of increases in the frequency and variety of delinquent acts.

Longitudinal studies of antisocial behavior often confound two independent, temporal dimensions—the intercept and the slope. The intercept refers to the overall mean level of antisocial behavior over the temporal period examined, whereas the slope describes a decreasing, increasing, or other quadratic trend. Latent growth modeling applies SEM to the analysis of longitudinal data, providing the capability to model both intercept and slope. Patterson (1993) tested a model that accounted for both aspects of child antisocial behavior as measured from fourth grade to eighth grade (see Figure 12.8). In this model, the boy's relative ranking (i.e., intercept) over the 4-year interval was associated with parenting practices in the fourth grade, as defined by discipline (home observations) and monitoring. Linear growth in antisocial behavior, however, was independently accounted for by two factors: the child's increase in unsupervised wandering and his association with deviant peers. This model is particularly helpful because it points toward the synergistic influences of parents and peers on antisocial behavior. Parenting practices account for the boy's antisocial trait, and deviant peers account for the boy's learning new and creative forms of antisocial behavior. The model provides an intuitively appealing picture of the joint influences of parents and peers in the maintenance and course of antisocial behavior in adolescents.

These findings provide the basis for considering hypotheses regarding the social origins of the early- and late-starter developmental trajectories. It may be that children who start early are essentially adapting to coercive, chaotic parenting practices. In this sense, negative reinforcement may be the operating mechanism. For those who start late, positive reinforcement by peers may be the operating mechanism, whereby problem behavior becomes a

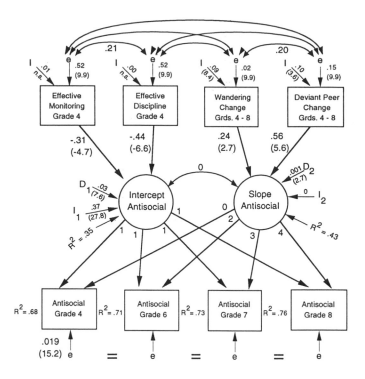

$\chi^2_{(22)} = 25.21, p = .29$

BBN = .960
BBNN = .993
CFI = .995
N = 201
Note: Only significant correlations shown

Figure 12.8 Developmental models for early and late starters. [χ^2 (22, N = 201) = 25.21, p = .29. Only the significant correlations are shown. Bentler Bonnett Normed (BBN) = .960; Bentler Bonnett Non-normed (BBNN) = .993; Comparative Fit Index (CFI) = .995; e = unstandardized error term; Grds = grades; n.s. = nonsignificant; I = mean for intercept (= .37); D = disturbance (unexplained variance)]. From "Orderly Change in a Stable World: The Antisocial Trait as a Chimera" by G. R. Patterson, 1993, *Journal of Consulting and Clinical Psychology, 61,* p. 915. Copyright 1993 by the American Psychological Association. Used by permission.

means to establish connectedness to a peer group. Thus, there is a temporary merging of the social worlds of early- and late-starters that seems to underlie the overall increase in antisocial behavior observed during this period (Dishion, Patterson, & Griesler, 1994). A constellation of family factors (relationships, interaction patterns, education) would seem to predict best those who ease out of the deviant peer group into positive adaptation in young adulthood.

Summary

Evidence was reviewed that provides overwhelming support for the hypothesis that socialization exchanges within relationships are both a cause and an outcome of antisocial behavior. Over the past 15 years, considerable progress has been made in understanding the impact of parenting practices. Reductionists' analyses of parent-child exchanges have been fruitful in identifying negative reinforcement as the key mechanism that accounts for child noncompliance and other behaviors prodromal to antisocial behavior in childhood and adolescence. Targeting these patterns in intervention trials produces reductions in antisocial behavior in other settings. Reductionistic models are not sufficient to account for long-term patterns of prosocial behavior, and evidence supports the idea that factors such as attachment and the parent-child relationship provide the emotional context for child and adolescent development. More recent developments provide impressive progress in isolating peers as causal agents for antisocial behavior in childhood, especially in adolescence. Selective dispensement of positive affect in these relationships may account for the power of the peer group to influence rule-breaking norms and behaviors. Studies of the joint influence of peers and parents support both agents as integral to both childhood onset and adolescent onset of antisocial behavior.

Behavior Settings

Overview

In much of the research on antisocial behavior, the impact of relationships is assessed as if it occurs in a vacuum. The ecological model alerts us to the importance of the context in which these relationships are embedded. Parenting occurs in homes that are placed within neighborhoods. Peer interactions take place in neighborhoods, schools, at the bus stop, on the street, in shopping malls, in organized activities, and in families. In the following sections, we discuss the family, neighborhood, and school behavior settings. A common approach for investigating setting effects has been to assess stress.

Family Stress

Various researchers have attempted to assess the effect of stress on the display of antisocial behavior in childhood. One index of stress is the number of transitions experienced by a family, in terms of changes or moves. Simmons, Burgeson, and Reef (1988) assessed transitions in the form of school changes, pubertal motivation, early dating, geographical mobility, and family disruption during the teenage years. As expected, the cumulative number of transitions was related to lower grades, higher problem behavior, and lower self-esteem. These effects were most pronounced in the European American subsample and also affected the self-esteem of African American girls. Apparently the impact of transitions is relative to other stressors occurring in the individual's life. They found no relation between the number of transitions and adjustment for the subsample of young adolescents in the lower socioeconomic status category. Such transition stresses were apparently minor relative to those already experienced. The lack of a relation between stress and adjustment among socially disadvantaged children was also found in the research by Sandler and Block (1979) among 5- to 8-year-old children. The findings relating stress directly to antisocial behavior in childhood and adolescence are weak.

Simcha-Fagan and Schwartz (1986) more successfully disentangled the temporal relation between perceived stress and antisocial behavior by assessing these interrelations over a 5-year time span. They found that stress was as likely to be a consequence of conduct disturbance as an antecedent. This research suggested that stressful family processes were the most likely antecedents to increased conduct disturbance.

Patterson (1983) showed how parenting practices covaried on a day-by-day basis with daily ratings of stress, as did the child's display of aversive behavior in the home. These findings linked stress to child antisocial behavior through parenting practices. Snyder (1991) replicated this set of findings with a sample of Headstart children, finding that the impact of levels of stress on children's antisocial behavior was mediated by parenting practices. The mediational model is consistent with ideas proposed by stress researchers, that children's immediate social context can serve as a key protective factor for children (Garmezy & Rutter, 1983; Rutter, 1979, 1983).

One of the more stressful family events is marital disruption (Bloom, Asher, & White, 1978). It is well known that divorce is often followed by temporary increases in boys' antisocial behavior. This effect is less pronounced in middle childhood for girls (Hetherington, 1988; Wallerstein & Kelly, 1980). What is less appreciated, however, is the influence of predivorce marital conflict on antisocial behavior. Studies that control for the level of conflict prior to divorce show that a minuscule amount of variance in antisocial behavior is accounted for by the actual breakup. In fact, J. H. Block, J. Block, and Gjerde (1986) found that child antisocial behavior tended to predict divorce. This is consistent with the view that family conflict may be the greatest risk factor for the development of child antisocial behavior (Emery & O'Leary, 1984), and the impact of divorce is very likely secondary to family disruption. Families who experienced little or no conflict prior to divorce have not been extensively studied to determine if the actual physical separation increased or decreased the antisocial behavior of the child. We could hypothesize that families who were able to maintain healthy levels of monitoring and limit setting would not show significant changes in the child's antisocial behavior. This does not preclude the possibility of other emotional sequelae. Evidence is strong, however, that these sequelae are minimal when children are not caught in the middle of conflict between divorced or separated spouses and when both parents maintain involvement with their children (Maccoby, Depner, & Mnookin, 1990).

There is evidence that divorce that occurs during early adolescence is marked by more severe child dysfunctionality than that which occurs either earlier or later. Hetherington and Clingempeel (1992) found heightened antisocial behavior of early adolescent males and females in both divorced and divorced-remarried families. Contributing to this antisocial behavior is disengagement from the family (particularly pronounced for stepfather families) as well as heightened conflict and negativity. Further, there is evidence of precocious sexuality of adolescents from divorced families. This behavior may stem from some of the same antecedents as antisocial behavior and may also impact antisocial behavior by increasing family conflict, accelerating adolescent disengagement from the family, and providing further involvement with a deviant peer group.

Capaldi and Patterson (1991) investigated the relation between antisocial behavior in boys and the number of marital transitions experienced by their families. Each breakup and remarriage was counted as a transition. The number of transitions experienced by the boys and their families was positively related to the mother's antisocial disposition and negatively related to the age at which she bore her first child. Boys' antisocial behavior was found to increase as a linear function of the number of transitions experienced by the family. This monotonic relation was also found for peer rejection, academic problems, low self-esteem, depression, and association with deviant peers.

As might be expected, parenting practices are most likely to mediate the impact of divorce on children's problem behavior. Hetherington, M. Cox, and R. Cox (1985) found an association between children's problem behavior and maternal uninvolvement following divorce. In addition, children who were more temperamentally difficult displayed more problem behavior subsequent to divorce.

Forgatch et al. (1985) found that parent discipline practices mediated the relation between maternal stress and child antisocial behavior. This study focused exclusively on recently divorced or separated mothers, and researchers carefully observed the families on repeated occasions in the home to assess the mother's parenting behavior with her children. Level of stress was correlated with the mother's noncontingent and negative parenting practices. The correlation between stress and child behavior was explained by maternal discipline. These findings were replicated in the single-parent families of the OYS (Patterson, Reid, & Dishion, 1992).

Neighborhood Settings

Child conduct problems are more prevalent in urban than in suburban areas (Rutter, 1978). Epidemiological data reveal that antisocial personality disorders as well as substance abuse problems and cognitive impairment are more than twice as prevalent in urban inner city settings than in suburban and rural settings (Robins et al., 1984). Ethnic differences in these forms of maladaption varied as a function of metropolitan area (New Haven, Baltimore, and St. Louis). Antisocial personality disorder was more prevalent among European Americans than African Americans in New Haven and Baltimore, but the reverse was true for St. Louis.

Rutter (1981) discussed how the physical design of a neighborhood, such as a housing project, can directly impact antisocial behavior. For example, the preponderance of semipublic space with unclear ownership has been associated with a high incidence of vandalism (Rutter, 1981). There are many ways in which the design and layout of living space in urban areas could reduce the incidence of antisocial behavior (Jacobs, 1963), but little systematic research has focused on this issue. It seems obvious, for example, that placing thousands of socially disadvantaged families in high-rise apartments sequestered away from the mainstream commerce is a bad idea (Jacobs, 1963). These neighborhoods are among the most dangerous areas in the United States and, perhaps, the world.

Evidence in support of the impact of neighborhoods on psychopathology comes from Crane (1991). Census data were used to look at the rate of high school dropout as a function of neighborhood risk status. As the percentage of high-status workers fell below 3.5%, the probability of adolescent dropout doubled from 11% to 22% in the largest metropolitan areas of the United States (see Figure 12.9). Crane asserted that the dramatic increase in the probability of dropout in the high-risk neighborhoods supports a contagion model of influence, where the effect of risk is nonlinear in the most pathogenic conditions. Again, we badly need data on the disrupting processes, as the contagionlike pattern could also be explained as an interaction effect: Children who are not monitored well and are exposed to a high density of deviant peers who live in settings with a low proportion of educationally accomplished adults are at high risk for school dropout.

In the highest risk settings (i.e., neighborhoods with the lowest percentage of middle-class residents), boys showed a dramatic nonlinear increase in the probability of dropout, whereas girls followed the predicted linear trend. This finding was replicated and extended in subsequent research by Connell, Clifford, and Crichlow (1992). They also found that African American boys were more sensitive to the quality of the neighborhood than girls in terms of risk for school dropout. Girls across ethnic status groups, on the other hand, were more sensitive to the hardships of family poverty and showed high rates of dropout in severely impoverished family contexts.

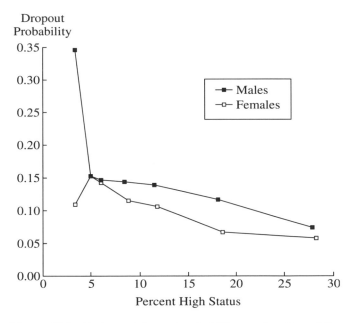

Figure 12.9 Estimated dropout probability as a function of the percentage of high-status workers in the neighborhood for black males and black females in the largest cities. From "The Epidemic Theory of Ghettos and Neighborhood Effects on Dropping Out and Teenage Childbearing" by J. Crane, 1991, *American Journal of Sociology, 100,* p. 1240. Copyright 1991 by the University of Chicago. Used by permission.

These dramatic effects of neighborhood may be described by a three-way interaction between ethnic status, gender, and neighborhood poverty level. To understand these effects, we must look at the developmental and interactional processes that occur in these settings, which has not yet been done. African American males may be less supervised than females in high-risk settings and, therefore, may be more at risk for intense involvement with a deviant peer group. In contrast, girls may be more in tune with the emotional atmosphere of the mother and so may be affected by the depression and distress associated with economic deprivation. Investigations assessing more microsocial aspects of peer and family relationships are necessary to disentangle these effects.

Simcha-Fagan and Schwartz (1986) compared parents' perceptions of neighborhood characteristics with objective information from census data. Parents' perceptions of the overall level of deviancy (Community Disorder-Criminal Subculture) were strongly associated with antisocial behavior and were associated with both self-reported antisocial behavior and police contacts. In addition, census records of the percentage of families with poverty-level income also accounted for unique variance in police contact. Direct effects of the neighborhood accounted for only small proportions of variance in police contact (7.1%) and severe antisocial behavior (1.7%). Simcha-Fagan and Schwartz concluded that neighborhood characteristics are most likely associated with child and adolescent antisocial behavior because of their impact on the primary socialization processes.

Some progress has been made toward understanding the process of disruption in urban environments. Brooks-Gunn, Duncan, Kato, and Sealand (1991) explored the impact of neighborhood on preschoolers and adolescents. They found that the density of neighborhood families classified as middle class was positively associated with intellectual functioning of preschool youth. The effects of neighborhood were mediated, however, by parents' scores on a general scale of their intellectual stimulation. No relations were found between neighborhood characteristics and Child Behavior Checklist ratings by parents of young children with behavior problems. The picture was somewhat different for the adolescent sample. At this age, there was a moderate level of covariation among the density of middle-class families, number of children who dropped out of school, and number out-of-wedlock parents.

Deviant peers are most prevalent in inner-city, urban environments. Consequently, it is likely that parent monitoring needs to be more diligent to prevent children's involvement with these peers. Elder and Ardelt (1992) compared impoverished with affluent neighborhoods in urban Philadelphia and found that parents in high-risk neighborhoods used more restrictive tactics to protect their children from life on the streets. These parents frequently kept their children inside, under the assumption that they simply could not control what would happen to their children on the streets.

Thus, we would expect that parenting practices would mediate the influence of the neighborhood context on antisocial behavior. Rutter (1981), in fact, found that the association between living context and antisocial behavior was in part mediated through the disruption of families as indexed by a Family Adversity scale. More specifically, in a study of urban living in London, Wilson

(1987) found that parental supervision practices were strongly correlated with antisocial behavior in an urban but not in a suburban setting. Studies are needed that link the effects of neighborhoods on the deviant peer network and family management practices. Because of the role of peers and the emerging autonomy of adolescents, it is likely that the impact of neighborhoods on child behavior will vary as a function of developmental status. High-risk neighborhoods for preschoolers may be those with very few peers, social isolation, few parents of young children to trade child care, and low socioeconomic resources. Such a neighborhood might increase the likelihood of child maltreatment (Gabarino & Sherman, 1980) and could possibly exacerbate coercive parent-child interactions. For older adolescents, neighborhoods with a high density of deviant peers may be the most problematic in contributing to gang involvement and more serious forms of antisocial behavior (Brooks-Gunn et al., 1991; Simcha-Fagan & Schwartz, 1986).

Schools

The child's entry into school presents new challenges and opportunities. The child is confronted with an environment in which there are consistent rules and expectations, where he or she is forced to share attention with unfamiliar adults, and where there are clear criteria and opportunities to succeed or fail.

Antisocial children tend to be poor academic achievers (Hawkins & Lishner, 1987). At least some of this may be explained by their low intellectual ability, as it has consistently been found that conduct-disordered children have lower intelligence than comparison children (Schonfeld, Shaffer, O'Connor, & Portnoy, 1988), and child aggression is negatively correlated with child IQ (e.g., Huesmann et al., 1984). Delinquency is also associated with lower intelligence even when race and social class are controlled (Hirschi & Hindelang, 1977).

Deficits in the academic skills of CD children, on the other hand, are only marginally explained by intellectual differences. As shown by Dishion (1990), poor parenting practices were associated with boys' antisocial behavior trait score as well as deficits in academic skills. After controlling for the influence of parenting practices, there was a significant correlation between the child's antisocial behavior and academic skills. We think that the correlation ($r = -.34$) between academic skills and antisocial behavior, once poor parenting practices are controlled for, is explained by the disruptive effect of antisocial behavior on skill acquisition (Patterson, Reid, & Dishion, 1992). This may also explain these children's lower performance on verbal IQ measures, which are heavily predicated on acquired academic skills. Their frequent lack of compliance with teacher's requests and school rules interferes with their development of academic skills. Patterson, Reid, and Dishion (1992) found a strong relation between child antisocial behavior and the on-task time the child devoted to academic activities. This variable was strongly correlated with subsequent performance on standardized academic achievement tests. These children are also deficient in other classroom survival skills, such as remaining at their desks, answering questions, and attending (Cobb, 1972; Cobb & Hops, 1972; Hops & Cobb, 1974). In examining the skill deficits of male adolescent delinquents by comparing interpersonal skill, standardized academic achievement scores, and homework completion, Dishion et al. (1984) found that the delinquent youth were most deficit in homework skills when compared with nondelinquent youth.

Antisocial children experience particular difficulty following school rules. In general, these are minor discipline infractions such as tardiness, insubordination to the teacher, and other mild disrupters. By themselves, these are trivial and are also committed by well-adjusted children, but the rate of these infractions for antisocial children far exceeds that of their conforming elementary (Walker, Shinn, O'Neill, & Ramsey, 1987) and middle school (French & Straight, 1991) classmates. The high frequency of these discipline infractions has multiple negative consequences. They may contribute to a negative interactional system between the child, teachers, and school officials that disrupts the child's commitment to school and, at the same time, reduces the willingness of school officials to work with the child. They may also lead to suspensions, expulsions, and out-of-class placement. Both aggression and school discipline problems are strongly associated with eventual school dropout (Cairns et al., 1989; Wehlage & Rutter, 1986), an outcome that further contributes to the negative life adjustment of the antisocial child.

In a series of studies conducted by H. M. Walker and his colleagues (Walker et al., 1987) that contrasted extremely antisocial boys with normal control boys, the former engaged in less on-task behavior in the classroom, more negative interactions with peers, were rated by teachers as less academically competent, and were more involved in disruptive school behavior. Patterson (1976) found that approximately 50% of boys who exhibited antisocial behavior at home also exhibited social and/or academic problems in school. Loeber and Dishion (1984) found that 30% of boys identified as physically aggressive at home were also identified as fighting at school. The causal link between parental discipline practices and antisocial behavior in school was assessed by Ramsey, Bank, Patterson, and H. M. Walker (1990). Using structural equation modeling with a subsample of the Oregon Youth Study, they found that inept parental discipline at fourth grade predicted fifth-grade antisocial behavior at school. Moreover, Dishion and Andrews (in press) found that improving parent-child interactions resulted in improvements in young adolescents' school behavior.

The previously described school experiences are basically products of antisocial behavior. But variations in school organization may also contribute to antisocial behavior. Gray, Smith, and Rutter (1980) found that enrollment in an impoverished school led to poor attendance, which then predicted early dropout, with the consequences being the increased likelihood of marginal employment and a poor work history. These effects were obtained even after controlling for both intelligence and SES.

Similarly, Rutter, Maughan, Mortimore, and Ouston (1979) found that negative secondary school experiences explained variability in subsequent delinquency after controlling for intake variables (study behavior, achievement, and SES). Positive school experiences, in contrast, served as protective factors. Rutter (1978) found that differences between schools that were successful and those that were unsuccessful in preventing subsequent delinquency were found in the structure of the interaction between children and teachers. More successful schools were characterized by clear homework completion requirements, high academic expectations, and clear and consistent discipline policies.

Many of the difficulties antisocial children have at school are due to their aversive behavior and poor compliance with rules. However, there appears to be an independent influence of school environment on youngsters' social trajectories. Some schools do not adequately address disruptive, antisocial behavior. One understudied aspect of school environments is the playground. These typically highly unstructured settings provide a potential training ground for antisocial and aggressive acts, as well as a context in which deviant peer networks are firmly established. Dishion, Duncan, Eddy, Fagot, and Fetrow (in press) tested a model that considered the multivariate influence of coercive parent-child and peer-child interactions and global ratings of elementary-school-age children's antisocial behavior. For both boys and girls, coercive peer-child interactions on the playground accounted for unique variance in antisocial behavior.

Nowhere is the evidence for a school effect more convincing than in the prevention literature. Programmatic work by Gottfredson and colleagues (Gottfredson, 1988; Gottfredson, Gottfredson, & Hybl, 1993) suggests that principles of family management associated with antisocial behavior apply to school management. These investigators found that systematic interventions on school rules, behavior management in the classroom, and incentives for appropriate behavior in school resulted in schoolwide reductions in problem behavior. These findings are exciting in two respects. First, considerable proportion of antisocial behavior is learned and practiced in the school setting; therefore, intervention procedures that reduce such behaviors could potentially reduce the overall rate of antisocial behavior. Second, this research demonstrates the utility of a learning theory for understanding and preventing pathology in settings other than the family. The school intervention programs of Gottfredson and colleagues resembles parent training family intervention programs. To what extent could the same principles be applied to prevent antisocial behavior in larger social units?

Community Contexts

Antisocial behavior varies widely across cultures, not necessarily in concordance with technological gains or material wealth. For example, B. B. Whiting and J. W. M. Whiting (1975) compared the rate of prosocial behavior across cultures and found that Third World cultures emphasizing interdependence were associated with higher rates of prosocial behavior. International crime statistics indicate that the United States is the most violent of all the industrialized nations, with a homicide rate of 8.4% per 100,000, which is more than double that of France, the United Kingdom, Germany, Japan, and Canada. Somewhat close is the homicide rate for Sweden (7.1%). The percentage for rapes is at least twice that of all other westernized countries. The United States also has the highest percentage of serious assaults (INTERPOL, 1988). It is tempting to consider high violence rates as an undesirable but inevitable accompaniment of high population density in urban centers. However, some very densely populated urban centers, such as Singapore, have very low violence rates (Rutter, 1980). It is therefore important to consider forces that operate within larger aggregate units to influence antisocial behavior rates at the community level (Biglan, Glasgow, & Singer, 1990). We consider media, economic and social resources, and ethnic minority status as three ecological dimensions that may indirectly impact the development of antisocial behavior.

Media.   The most pervasive media effect can be attributed to television. Television programming has a high density of antisocial and aggressive acts, especially in programs such as cartoons. The violent content seems to have a modest but lasting effect on aggressive and antisocial behavior for youngsters who watch a great deal of television (Eron, 1982). Although this holds for both boys and girls, it is more consistently seen for boys across various cultures (Eron & Huesmann, 1986). Children between the ages of 6 and 10 appear to be particularly vulnerable to the effects of violent programming on television, as are those who see aggressive events displayed on television as real. As might be expected, the more aggressive the child, the higher the preference for television violence (Eron & Huesmann, 1986). Standard attitudinal change techniques have been shown to reduce the correlation between television viewing and aggressive behavior (Eron & Huesmann, 1986), indicating that these relations can be somewhat modified.

The power of television programming to negatively impact children's aggressive behavior raises the question whether prosocial television programming would have a positive impact on children's social behavior. This appears to be the case, at least in the preschool years. Programs such as *Mr. Rogers' Neighborhood* have been shown to promote prosocial interaction among children (Eron & Huesmann, 1986). Television programming to teach child-rearing techniques that promote child adaptation and reduce antisocial behavior has not been tested, however. Parents with antisocial preschool children have benefited from viewing parenting videotapes emphasizing family management skills and have learned to significantly reduce their children's negative behaviors (Webster-Stratton, Kolpacoff, & Hollingsworth, 1988). Television programming could be a community asset in terms of communicating the means by which adults can affect prosocial and antisocial behavior in their children.

Resources.   Poverty is a pervasive disrupter of families. The effects of poverty and living in an inner-city environment are confounded in most research. Severe forms of antisocial behavior are more prevalent in families of lower socioeconomic status (Elliott & Ageton, 1979; Elliott et al., 1985), and low socioeconomic status in middle childhood modestly predicts antisocial behavior in adolescence (Loeber & Dishion, 1983).

The research by Elder and his colleagues is unique in its ability to disentangle the impact of poverty on antisocial behavior from other contextual factors (Elder, Caspi, & Van Nguyen, 1986; Elder, Van Nguyen, & Caspi, 1985). Elder used the data from the Oakland and Berkeley longitudinal studies to trace the impact of the Great Depression on parenting practices and assess the impact of this on child adjustment outcomes some years later. As might be expected, a general increase in child problem behavior resulted from dramatic income loss. In general, in the transitions between income loss, family process, and child problem behavior, stronger correlations were found between economic

difficulty and parenting irritability for fathers than for mothers. These increases in paternal irritability were associated with multiple negative outcomes in the children, including temper tantrums and problem behavior. Those children who exhibited behavior problems prior to the Depression were particularly likely to receive more negative and arbitrary parenting and to display an escalation in problem behaviors. Mothers appeared to play a buffering role. Mothers who were affectionate, demonstrative, and had a positive relationship with their children, mitigated the impact of fathers' irritability.

There were also gender differences in the consequences of the Depression on children. For boys, increases in fathers' irritability were associated with negative perceptions of their father. The impact of economic loss was somewhat different for girls, again, mediated primarily through the father. Girls' mood and self-perceptions were adversely affected by economic loss in the wake of increases in father rejection. The data also suggested that girls' physical attractiveness was negatively correlated with increases in father rejection during hard times.

The Elder study is also pioneering in that it capitalizes on "natural experiments" and traces the influence from the macroanalytic level to the specific processes associated with child outcomes. Some of the person-process-context findings, however, are based on relatively small subgroup sizes and, therefore, must be viewed with some caution.

More recently, Elder and Ardelt (1992) examined the impact of poverty, family adaptation, and parenting practices in a sample of 422 European American and African American families living in urban Philadelphia. In two-parent families, poverty was correlated with marital problems, which in turn were associated with the lack of parenting efficacy. In single-parent families, maternal depression seemed to have a mediating effect on parents' sense of efficacy in child rearing. This study, to date, has not yet tied these findings to child antisocial behavior.

R. D. Conger et al. (1992) recently assessed the effects of economic stress on male adolescent behavior in a farm community suffering an acute economic downturn. Economic stress resulted in increases in parental depression, marital conflict, and disrupted parenting. Consistent with the preceding findings, changes in child adjustment were mediated by disruptions in the quality of parenting.

A relative large sector of the population experiences permanent economic deprivations that often persist across generations. We refer to these people as the socially disadvantaged. Patterson and Dishion (1988) examined the relation between mother and father social disadvantage (education, occupation, low social skill), parenting practices, and child antisocial behavior. Social disadvantage was highly correlated with negative discipline practices as well as child antisocial behavior.

Larzelere and Patterson (1990) used a structural modeling approach to test the hypothesis that the correlation between socioeconomic status and adolescent antisocial behavior was mediated through family management. In this analysis, a hierarchical factor of family management was constructed with multiagent and multimethod indicators of both parent monitoring and discipline practices. Adolescent antisocial behavior was assessed with the boy's self-report and records of police contact for antisocial behavior. They found that the contribution of socioeconomic status as assessed by the Hollingshead Index disappeared after controlling for family management practices. The hypothesis that social disadvantage has an impact on antisocial behavior largely through alteration of family management practices appears to be supported for boys both in middle childhood (Patterson & Dishion, 1988) and adolescence (Larzelere & Patterson, 1990).

Ethnic Minority Status. Elevated rates of antisocial behavior have been observed for Hispanic American, African American, and Native American youth and adults in the United States (Elliott et al., 1985; Simcha-Fagan, Langer, Gersten, & Eisenberg, 1975). The processes explaining the relation between ethnic status and elevated rates of antisocial behavior has been woefully understudied, confined more to the arena of political debate than scientific inquiry. Ethnic status needs to be disentangled from disrupting influences such as economic hardship, limited employment opportunities, or residence in high-risk urban settings on basic socialization practices such as parenting and peer environments. As discussed earlier, these vestiges of minority status are strongly associated with antisocial behavior.

Studies that report differences in the incidence of antisocial behavior by ethnic status confound the impact of urban settings and poverty, both of which have a profound effect on socialization practices (McLloyd, 1990). Recent demographic trends underscore the increasing relation between pathogenic ecologies and ethnic status. These include the movement of the middle class from urban areas (McLloyd, 1990) and increases in the percentage of African American children living in poverty during the past decade: 36% in 1979 to 43% in 1989 (U.S. Bureau of the Census, 1991). The percentage of families living at the poverty level has also increased dramatically from the 1970s, as has the percentage of families headed by single parents (William T. Grant Foundation, 1988). The drop in family income is most precipitous for young African Americans and single-parent families. Among young single parents who have not completed a high school education, 92% experience extreme poverty. Poor families without opportunity, who live in communities with a high density of criminal and substance abuse activity, provide a breeding ground for child conduct disorders.

To say there is a confound between urban environments and ethnic status does not imply that either one accounts for elevated antisocial experiences, as both constructs are hopelessly vague. This is evident in the epidemiological data reported by Robin and Foster (1989), in which the diagnosis of antisocial personality disorder was the dependent variable. Here it was found that prevalence of chronic antisocial behavior was higher among European Americans in one urban setting and higher among African Americans in another urban setting.

The critical research question is the extent to which there are unique features of being a minority—aside from social disadvantage, single-parent status, neighborhood characteristics, urban settings, and economic deprivation—that are associated with ineffective family management practices. It is important to identify cultural and historical socialization of families of different ethnic status and assess how those behaviors interact with conditions of poverty and neighborhood to exacerbate or enhance antisocial behavior throughout the life course. The possibility of a direct effect between minority ethnic status and antisocial behavior requires

consideration. Being a recipient of racist actions or policies that are perceived as unfair may contribute to antisocial behavior, as illustrated by violent riots in inner-city settings. Perceived racism may also have an impact on the sense of community. Developmental models of antisocial behavior have yet to consider the impact of ethnic stigmatization on salient socialization and intrapersonal process as an important part of the etiology of antisocial behavior. For example, perceived ethnic stigmatization among children would likely contribute to social information processing, in particular, the likelihood of making hostile attributions in ambiguous situations.

McLloyd (1990) reviewed the impact of economic hardship on African American families and the socioemotional development of children. She used a process-oriented analysis of the linkages between minority status, economic and opportunity deprivation, and child socioemotional adjustment. Consistent with the literature discussed earlier, the impact on the context of the African American family is mediated through parenting practices and explained by two factors. The first is a person's appraisal of the reason for economic loss or poverty. Minority members might attribute their poverty to the verbal culture communicated in modern education or to racism. The availability of social support and controls may further moderate the link between poverty and parents' psychological distress. McLloyd argues that social support moderates the effect of poverty on the psychological stress of the parent, as well as directly helping parents' performance of family management skills.

Summary

The problem of how social contexts influence the development of antisocial behavior has been approached in several ways, largely depending on the investigator's discipline. Psychologists tend to operationalize context as stress, and are interested in the mediational effects of stress. Studies support the idea that experiences such as marital discord, divorce, the number of marital transitions, and unemployment influence the development of antisocial behavior through disrupted parenting practices. Sociologists are interested in how structural issues, such as poverty or single-parent status, directly affect the rates of crime in general, rather than looking at individual differences. Joining the two perspectives has provided a better understanding of the dynamics of structural features of contexts on basic socialization processes. More common conceptualization of context would enhance progress in this area. An ecological perspective that emphasizes the demarcation of behavior settings seems appropriate; for example, studies that focus on features of schools that covary with socialization experiences have been especially fruitful. Such research has led to the design of effective interventions that reduce problem behavior at the school level.

CONCLUSIONS AND IMPLICATIONS

Conclusions

Over the past 30 years, enormous progress has been made in understanding the development of antisocial behavior. Figure 12.10 is a summary of empirical linkages that have been well

CULTURAL AND COMMUNITY PATTERNS

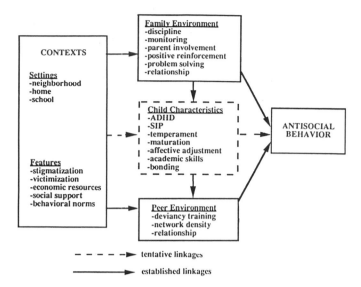

Figure 12.10   Factors influencing the development and maintenance of antisocial behavior.

established, as well as those that, at this writing, are tentative and require further testing. Three points are emphasized in this summary: (a) Parent-child interaction and management tactics play a dominant role in establishing the child's trajectory into antisocial behavior in early and middle childhood as well as adolescence; (b) although peer relationships are endogenous to family influences, they nevertheless seem to exert a veritable force in the development of antisocial behavior; and (c) child antisocial behavior is a global descriptive trait of the child that is an *outcome* of social interactional processes, but can in turn, contribute independently to maladaptive interactions with parents and peers.

The solid arrows represent hypotheses that are supported by previous longitudinal research, and the dotted lines are hypotheses that require further testing. Many of the established linkages are based on the study of European American boys in moderate-risk metropolitan areas. Further studies of the development of antisocial behavior in girls, in children in high-risk urban settings, and in children of diverse ethnicity are badly needed. We suspect that such research would reveal somewhat different processes for the development of antisocial behavior in males and females and would enrich our understanding of the impact of context on social development in general.

All children in high-risk settings do not become antisocial. In fact, many well-socialized adults making major contributions to today's community were socialized in such settings. Thus, protective and resiliency factors are of interest. The data suggest we do not have far to look. In the study of inner-city London children, W. J. Wilson (1987) found parental involvement and supervision was a key protective factor in reducing the risk of adolescent antisocial behavior. From a different angle, Werner and Smith (1982) found that a close relationship with one adult served as a key protective factor for children reared in high-risk

environments. Perhaps such close relationships offer an optimal combination of affection and management that provides successful adaptation. Unfortunately, the longitudinal studies in high-risk settings necessary to fill in the gaps regarding the nature of the developmental processes, as well as protective and resiliency factors, have yet to be completed. The ever-increasing rates of violent antisocial behavior in high-risk communities makes this task imperative.

This context moves to center stage in our research on the development of antisocial behavior. An ecological approach is suggested in Figure 12.10 that emphasizes the analysis of context as the influence of specific behavior settings on socialization processes. Following Barker and Wright (1955), behavior settings are differentiated along geographical dimensions (e.g., home, neighborhood, school, etc.) and qualified based on features particularly relevant to community living (stigmatization, victimization, economic and social resources, and social norms). This conceptualization of context is meant as a guide to developing specific operational constructs that could be used in the study of antisocial behavior. To systematically study contexts, we suggest assessing these dimensions within each setting and then comparing the impact of diverse behavior settings on antisocial behavior. Some data, for example, suggest that the same features of homes and schools lead to high levels of antisocial behavior. Ignoring one or more behavior settings runs the risk of misspecifying models of development. For example, researchers may overemphasize the influence of school settings on development of peer networks if they ignore the impact of neighborhood influences, which seems to be a major oversight of current developmental research.

There is a fundamental paradox in doing research on developmental psychopathology. On the one hand, there is enormous room for integration among diverse theoretical perspectives. For example, attachment theory and the information-processing model could be conceived as complementary. The information-processing paradigm could provide a mechanism that could explain the impact of parent-child attachment on the development of friendships. On the other hand, empirical progress emanates from testing competing hypotheses and pitting one construct against another. Because investigators are often attached to their theoretical model, this approach could be seen as adversarial, aggressive, or competitive. Paradoxically, tests of competing models require the collaboration of investigators with diverse theoretical orientations to appropriately represent and measure the competing constructs. Fortunately, the history of science tells us that testing competing hypotheses is not a zero-sum game.

Numerous influential models compete to explain antisocial behavior. These models include social information processing (Dodge, 1986; Dodge & Coie, 1987); bonding to parents, teachers, and conventional peers (Elliott et al., 1985); attachment (Greenberg et al., 1993); temperament (Chess & Thomas, 1984); maturation; affective adjustment; and academic skills. Research is needed to clarify the unique and complementary roles of these processes on the onset, frequency, or duration of antisocial behavior.

Enough is known, however, to fill in a rough sketch of the antisocial developmental process, especially for understanding boys who exhibit a persistent life-course pattern. The development of more serious and chronic antisocial behavior seems to follow a stagelike progression, consistent with notions of hierarchical integration. In the coercion model, the practice of aversive pain control in the family relates to the child's failure in other social arenas, among peers, in school, and in critical academic skills. Failure in these spheres influences later social development. Failing young adolescents create a social environment that is supportive of their maladaption within the deviant peer group. Deviant peer involvement is related to the support of new behaviors in the early-starting youngster, and the initiation of problem behavior in the late-starting adolescent. The choices, experiences, and modes of adaptation in the young adult years are affected by the individual's group of friends. Adolescents with a deviant peer group and delinquent lifestyle are more likely to run into difficulties in the adult years, whether it be with continued antisocial behavior and police contact, unstable work, or serious substance abuse problems (Robins & Przybeck, 1985). Selection of an antisocial spouse could permanently cement the developing adult into a life of maladaption through criminal behavior, incarceration, and ever more coercive family relationships.

Implications

Overview

Developmental psychopathology can be criticized as too narrowly focused on maladaption while virtually ignoring positive social development. Positive adaptation does not simply reflect the absence of pathology. On the other hand, a proven tenet of developmental psychopathology is that the study of pathology often reveals behavioral processes quite relevant to understanding normative development (Cicchetti & Toth, 1992).

Because of the sheer volume of research on antisocial behavior, especially during childhood and adolescence, patterns emerge that provide implications for future research. Much of what we have learned from the study of antisocial behavior is that we need to better understand the nature of our tools, more specifically our measurement methods. Findings regarding the etiology of antisocial behavior may elicit hypotheses regarding normal socialization processes. We will end this chapter, then, with a discussion of these implications for the study of development in general.

Measurement Theory Dialectic

Empirically based developmental models are predicated on measurement, regardless of whether development is perceived as qualitative holistic stages or a gradual growth process based on underlying dimensions. The study of antisocial behavior reveals the profound effect of measurement on our ability to define and test models. The most formidable problem is the volume of research in which the monomethod bias is present (Cook & Campbell, 1979). Measurement issues are often considered mundane and lacking theoretical substance. We propose that, within the context of a science of development, the distinction between measurement and theory is blurred. Some years ago, Fiske (1986) suggested that theoretical constructs might be defined in relation to the method of measurement. For example, constructs of antisocial behavior should be categorized by whether they were obtained from teacher ratings or observation in the home. Kellam

(1990) makes a similar case when he argues that certain assessors (i.e., natural raters) are particularly essential for defining problem components in the environment. Method bias may not be useless measurement error, but rather may contain judgmental biases that, if accurately measured and labeled, could be important components of a model of antisocial behavior. Although this approach is more cumbersome than multiagent and multimethod trait scores, there may be more to learn empirically. Through time and study, we can collectively learn and understand the behavior of our methods as well as our subjects.

This will be particularly important as we expand our testing of developmental models within randomized field experiments. Experimental manipulations tend to put models at a greater risk for falsification, and poor measurements are often used to explain the failure of a model to produce predicted effects (Meehl, 1978). Eventually those who develop the models will need to attend to the two inextricable submodels: measurement and causal models.

For reasons stated by Meehl (1978) and Popper (1972), the trend of grounding developmental psychopathology in intervention is ultimately to the advantage of behavioral science. The effort to test models within interventions leads to a better understanding of the mediational process between intervention and outcome (Cicchetti & Toth, 1992; Judd & Kenny, 1981). Kellam (1990) labels this approach *experimental epidemiology*. Studies of normal development might also benefit from the inclusion of experimental intervention to test the developmental hypotheses.

Failed measurements, in the D. T. Campbell and Fiske (1959) sense, may be theoretically informative. It is theoretically interesting that parents tend to be biased toward perceiving improvement following involvement in almost any intervention (Patterson, Dishion, & Chamberlain, 1993). This consistent finding raises questions about the origin and role of parental perceptions of child behavior. It seems likely that parents' immediate social context is critically important in determining the kinds of child behavior they desire, their feelings about the normalcy of their child's behavior, and their sense of distress (viz-à-viz social support) concerning their child's functioning.

Marginal Deviations

One function of natural raters' perceptions is to amplify relatively marginal deviations in children's competencies and temperament into major developmental trajectories, such as the life-course-persistent pattern of antisocial behavior described and studied by investigators (Moffitt, 1993a; Patterson, 1992). The idea is that characteristics of the child elicit reactions from adults and peers that may set the stage for maladaptive development. Caprara and Zimbardo (in press) have referred to this as the *marginal deviation hypothesis*. This idea may help in constructing "biosocial" models of both normative and pathological social development.

We have identified neuropsychological, behavioral, emotional, and temperamental contributors to antisocial behavior. There are also many associated features that frequently accompany antisocial behavior throughout the life span (e.g., relationship difficulties, skill deficits, and academic deficits). These features vary according to the stage of the life course that is examined. We need to know the extent to which these personal characteristics elicit environmental support for the child's, adolescent's, or adult's acquisition of the trait *antisocial*. Although it is important to continue documenting the associated skill deficits and multiple problems of antisocial people, only so much can be learned from this strategy (Meichenbaum, 1979). Instead, we need research that attempts to model how these experiences have an impact on the developmental course of antisocial behavior within the individual.

Consider the findings of the co-occurrence of hyperactivity and conduct disorder, as well as the poor prognosis for those children fitting both diagnostic categories. We can assume that the poor outcomes of ADHD-CD children may be due in part to social processes. We suspect that the marginal deviation hypothesis may help in understanding the processes underlying comorbidity.

In Figure 12.11, we offer a testable hypothesis. Note that a child with a difficult temperament, such as hyperactive, certainly taxes the skills and emotional resources of most parents. Perhaps such "marginal deviations" for some parents under some circumstances lead to rejection and erratic, ineffective parenting practices, yielding coercive parent-child exchanges. Over time, the child adds some antisocial behaviors to his or her list of marginal deviations, the parent becomes even more ineffective in managing the child's behavior, and the parent-child relationship slips further. Entering school, the child may experience more difficulties, including rejection and coercive teacher-child and peer-child interactions, academic failure, and reduced motivation to be in school and work. In an effort to adapt, the child creates social contexts that maximize positive interactions and minimize punishment. Unfortunately, such contexts can involve peers who model and reinforce antisocial behavior. Then more serious problem behaviors are added to the list by adolescence.

The marginal deviation hypothesis depends on feedback mechanisms that amplify existing characteristics of the individual. Such feedback mechanisms must also exist for the development of positive outcomes, like academic skills, but there are serious methodological difficulties in testing feedback. The main problem appears to be in accounting for changes in antisocial behavior that exceed the very high stability of the behavior pattern. A key to this research may be the study of developmental shifts or transitions.

For example, the child's transition from early childhood to middle childhood usually involves the beginning of public school-ing. Here, it may be possible to look at the child's behavior with family members to see how those behaviors predict school antisocial behavior and possibly add the feedback mechanism of parent rejection. The child's transition from middle childhood to adolescence allows us to examine how peer rejection, academic failure, and depression relate to the subsequent initiation of new forms of antisocial behavior such as illegal and delinquent use of substances, early dropouts in the developmental phases, and more serious behaviors that were not generally evident.

Micro Versus Macro

A debate nearly as old as psychology is whether to take a reductionistic (i.e., microsocial) or holistic (i.e., macrosocial) approach to studying development and personality. Learning theory approaches to studying social development are reductionistic in that there is an attempt to carefully disentangle antecedents, behavior, and consequences to determine whether a specific event is functional. In contrast, attachment and other organizational approaches to both normal and pathological development tend to consider behavior more holistically, much as Piaget (1954) considered cognitive development as a stagelike reorganization of specific cognitive abilities. Both approaches have their strength and weaknesses. We assume that both levels of analysis are complementary.

The coercion model of antisocial behavior supports the use of a microsocial approach, as does the social information-processing model. Patterson's (1982) research demonstrates how daily, seemingly trivial aversive interactions relate to dramatic patterns of maladaption, including chronic antisocial behavior.

The acceptance of a reductionistic approach to studying mechanisms underlying development hinges on the ability of researchers to provide a mapping between the two levels, micro and macro. The coercion model has been moderately successful in this effort. Although observations of parent-child interaction certainly show predictive validity, it is often the coders' global impressions that correlate most with macro level indexes of current and future antisocial behavior (Patterson, Reid, & Dishion, 1992; Dishion, Andrews, & Crosby, in press). In fact, close inspection of the early coercion studies reveals some basic misgivings regarding the functional utility of children's aversive behavior, which is the cornerstone of the coercion model. For example, Patterson (1982) reports that aversive behavior within normal families paid off as well or better than it did in families with an aggressive child.

Testing learning theory hypotheses in the natural environment has always been a tedious, complex task (see, e.g., Patterson & Cobb, 1971). We think that such studies have suffered from considering only half of the relevant information. Herrnstein's (1990) matching law notion makes clear the need to understand the *relative reinforcement* of a given behavior to understand the rate of performance. To date, the matching law paradigm has been used primarily as an equation to explain intraindividual changes in rates of behavior, primarily with nonhuman species (McDowell, 1988). It seems plausible that such an approach could be applied to understand interindividual differences in antisocial behavior.

Recall that analyses by Dishion, Patterson, and Griesler (1994) revealed that it was not that antisocial boys and their friends were more likely to react positively to rule-breaking talk;

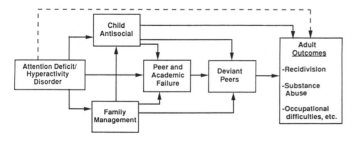

——— Direct effects significant after controlling for other model parameters

- - - Zero order correlations that are nonsignificant after controlling for other model parameters.

Figure 12.11 Marginal deviation hypothesis: Hyperactivity and temperament as disruptors of socialization.

rather, they were much more likely to react positively to rule-breaking talk than to normative talk. The relative rate of reinforcement was distinguishing. We think incorporating this basic principle in the study of microsocial processes will improve the prediction of macro-level outcomes (e.g., reports of antisocial behavior, attachment, relationship satisfaction, bonding) from moment-by-moment interactions between people. The matching law idea is also promising in furthering our understanding about how individuals select environments that reinforce the existing traits, referred to as "shopping."

Clinical experience with almost any population underscores the danger of using an holistic approach without a simultaneous understanding of underlying microsocial processes. Often real clinical change does not take place until the daily minutiae of social living is handled differently. For example, if the parent of a referred child would change two key patterns of responding, the child's behavior would eventually change as well. The two patterns are to acknowledge and support prosocial behavior and reduce escalations in the face of aversive behavior by ignoring or providing sane consequences.

The social information-processing model (Dodge & Coie, 1987) is useful because cognitive activity is separated into components. The greater specificity reveals the processes underlying aggressive responding. Thus, the fundamental processes and mechanisms that must change to prevent or reduce aggressive behavior are unveiled.

The advantages of macro level analyses are many. Ecological (Bronfenbrenner, 1979, 1989), ethnological (Hinde, 1989), transactional (Sameroff, 1981), and interactional (Magnusson, 1992) models all consider developmental, historical, and cultural forces in understanding individual development. A reductionistic study of interaction or perceptual processes would not reveal that early maturing girls tend to experience a burst in problem behavior, primarily due to their early involvement with older, more deviance-prone adolescents (Magnusson, 1992). Nor would it reveal that early-starting antisocial boys were those who acquired the most extensive court records and had the largest impact on the community's level of antisocial behavior.

Both micro and macro levels of analysis are needed to understand development across the life span. The two types of longitudinal studies in developmental psychopathology are those that study microsocial events, and those that employ analyses techniques such as event history and sequential or time series analysis. Studies are needed that assess subjects at wider time points, such as yearly or at developmental milestones. Both levels of analysis can be accomplished in the same study. Then the microsocial processes can be related to macro-level outcomes that provide the more holistic map of where the developmental process is going (Bank & Patterson, 1992).

This conclusion should hold for the study of normal development as well. Recent trends in cognitive development research show that the study of microsocial variables is highly relevant to understanding children's cognitive development. Stimulated by the contextual model of cognition and cognitive development proposed by Vygotsky (1978), investigators have been examining the interactional context of children's cognitive development. Studies by Rogoff and Wertsch (1984) and Tudge (1992), for example,

have used the concept of the *zone of proximal development* to better understand the role of the social environment in supporting growth in cognitive skills. This involves the study of the child's moment-by-moment interactions with parents and peers as related to macro-level measures of cognitive development.

Automatic Processing

The small correlations between global reports of parenting and direct observations testify to another issue in the study of development. Individuals may have only limited awareness of the patterns in which their behavior is embedded (Langer, 1978; Nisbett & Wilson, 1977). Thus, living in intimate relationships may be more like driving a car than preparing a talk for the next seminar.

These data on social development are painting a picture of social living as a programmed, emotional endeavor on which verbal histories are created that are considerably less than accurate. The study of abnormal development and clinical activity confronts the researcher with the simple fact that people develop seemingly "irrational" patterns, in the sense that long-term consequences of their behavior are often ignored.

Most models of social and emotional development integrate the notion of automatic processing. The social information-processing model certainly suggests that heuristic biases operate at the microsocial level, and that people are unaware of the many steps involved in reacting to a social event (perception, encoding, appraisal and attribution, response selection, etc.). Attachment theory relies on the internal working model notion, thought to operate within memory systems at the preconscious level. Currently, no models of antisocial behavior purpose that such behavior is a direct outcome of rational choices that weigh the costs and benefits or prosocial or antisocial behavior, and that people choose the latter.

The concept of automatic processing is consonant with psychodynamic notions of subconscious or preconscious processing, a key idea that arose out of Freud's (1922) intensive case studies of neurotic development. Now, automatic processing is integral to diverse perspectives of development, from those relying on learning theory to various social cognitive models. Hence the question, to what extent do the models describe different subconscious processes that determine behavior? The question is relevant to understanding both normal and atypical development, but it requires a new level of data and, to this extent, becomes a question to be addressed in the next generation of research.

Niche Finding

An emergent but central issue to all disciplines of development is the role of the individual in selecting his or her environment in determining developmental outcomes. Behavior genetics have pointed out that the selection of settings and relationships is influenced considerably by genetics. The most dramatic evidence of this is provided from the study of identical twins reared apart, who tended to become more similar to each other in their activities and relationships with age (Scarr & McCartney, 1983). This finding suggests that there are points at which individuals have an enormous influence on the course of their development.

The genetic influence, however, should not be overemphasized. Similarity between identical twins reared apart is no more than 50% of the explainable variance, and this may be an overestimate. In the case of schizophrenia, the outcome and trajectory of disorder for identical twins is likely to be dramatically different (Gottesman & Shields, 1982). The settings and relationships within which the individual exists may not account for much of this environmental influence. Seeking out environments that support established behavior patterns contributes to the individual's maintenance of personality (Elicker et al., 1992).

An important innovation to a learning-based model is the study of the child as an active agent in creating environmental contexts that shape or reinforce a trait, whether it be maladaptive or adaptive. To some extent, the child's behavior moves him or her into these environments. For example, wandering, school failure, and rejection by prosocial peers increase the likelihood of involvement with a deviant peer group. Parental problems in discipline and monitoring are increased by having a child who is difficult to discipline and who exhibits coercive behavior. This also increases the likelihood of involvement with deviant peers. Others, however, may also train the child in antisocial behavior. As suggested by Whiting (1980) as well as MacDonald and Parke (1984), the most powerful influence that parents may have is their role in selecting and managing their child's peer environment.

We are also making progress in understanding the processes that occur within relationships. Research on the development of normal friendships (e.g., Gottman, 1983) revealed that establishing a common-ground activity is the key, at least in the initial stages of children becoming friends. In studies of antisocial boys and their friendships, we found that positive exchanges within such relationships could actually exacerbate their deviance.

We suspect that the support of values and norms within close relationships may be an important mechanism that accounts for stability in many personality traits from adolescence through adulthood. The selection process is so sensitive that we probably know almost immediately when encountering a new person whether he or she is a likely candidate for a relationship. In Western industrialized cultures, the individual's dress, hair style, walk, car, etc., all provide relatively clear signals as to his or her system of values and norms. Five minutes of conversation provide even more data to make a selection for further or less involvement. Patterson et al. (1967), when studying the behavior of preschoolers, called this "shopping." Although considerably more sophisticated, the underlying process is probably quite the same in teenagers and adults.

Understanding the contextual forces and processes underlying antisocial boys' selection of friendships has implications for understanding normal personality development as well. In adulthood, individuals seem to select spouses with a personality similar to their own, and this strategy seems to promote both consistency and satisfaction within relationships (Caspi & Herbener, 1990). Through common activities, close relationships also have the power to create new trajectories and skills, and to provide a supportive context for change. Further study is needed of the processes leading to the formulation of close relationships at various stages of development and the extent to which these relationships influence subsequent adaptive and maladaptive development. Surely, through the joint consideration of relationship processes and ecological factors, new

strategies will emerge both for promoting prosocial adaptation and for reducing and preventing antisocial behavior.

Final Remarks

Evidence suggests that environmental factors are significant in the development of antisocial behavior, as well as in its cessation. At this stage of research, a diathesis-stress model seems quite appropriate, where dispositional characteristics of individuals define their range of reaction under specified environmental conditions. We are a long way, however, from being clear about which dispositional characteristics are most germane in different environmental and developmental contexts.

Bidirectional influences are evident in the socialization of antisocial behavior at the nature-nurture level as well as the person-to-person socialization processes within relationships. With regard to the former, environmental experiences influence constitutional factors such as neuropsychological status, temperament, and even genotype. Both genotype and constitutional factors of the individual can impact relationships. Certainly in peer relationships (friend, spouse), the influence process is mutual. In parent-child relationships, however, the dominant direction of influence is from the parent to the child. Even though a child's temperament may shape the parenting he or she experiences within a family, the data seem clear that a large proportion of the variance is in the interaction between family members.

From the existing literature, we could certainly suggest the kinds of environments where antisocial behavior would be extremely unlikely in children, adolescents, or adults; for example, a stable, loving family environment where parents teach their children cultural competence and effectively handle children's coercion and problem behaviors. Even under optimal family conditions, however, the absence of antisocial behavior could be guaranteed only if the family lived in a community with social and economic resources that explicitly supported the development of children and that espoused strong behavioral norms for prosocial as opposed to antisocial behavior. Unfortunately, current social structures do not often fit this warm picture. Economic and political systems seem to determine the contexts within which people socialize and are socialized. Inner-city settings, poverty, and racism create a disorganized social system that undermines adults' efforts to socialize children. As children learn to adapt within such systems, often adaptation consists of forming groups within which aggression and rule breaking are deemed a strength. It is no mystery, really, why one sees the escalating trends of substance abuse and violence among young people today in some pockets of the world.

The question is, how can a developmental psychopathology contribute to a solution to this problem? The concern for antisocial behavior reaches across disciplines. What the field of developmental psychopathology can contribute, we think, is understanding. Solutions based on a misunderstanding of the etiologic processes are doomed to long-term failure. Law-and-order policy decisions are often tempting, but poorly justified theoretically. Getting tough often means aggregating youthful offenders into pseudo institutions such as boot camps or juvenile detention centers. Rates of antisocial behavior often increase, even during a youth's containment. Long-term effects of institutionalizing children need further study, but it is safe to say there is no rehabilitative effect for the majority of children.

Within an ecological model, there is little justification for blaming "bad" parents, peers, children, or ethnic groups. A historical view would show that the faces change but the processes related to high rates of antisocial behavior remain the same. At one time in U.S. history, in one metropolitan area, for example, recent immigrant Irish-American families were the people with limited opportunities, resources, and disorganized communities (Sampson, 1994) and, not surprisingly, high rates of delinquency. Now other ethnic minorities have moved into a similar position of high-risk social contexts. High rates of serious antisocial behavior, however, can be observed in virtually all ethnic groups, although not in all cultures (Schlegel & Barry, 1991).

The promise of the developmental psychopathology perspective is to continue to focus on the intervention implications of etiologic research (Cicchetti & Toth, 1992). An explicit strategy for the programmatic integration of etiologic research and intervention trials has been proposed (Patterson, Reid, & Dishion, 1992). We can suggest alternative intervention strategies to reduce or prevent antisocial behavior (Reid, 1993). The key idea, however, is not only to get intervention effects (i.e., reductions in antisocial behavior) but to document how the intervention effects are achieved, that is, to understand the process of change (Dodge, 1993). Such an approach makes developmental psychopathology a dynamic science with the potential for constructive and democratic action.

REFERENCES

Abramovitch, R., Corter, C., Pepler, D. J., & Stanhope, L. (1986). Sibling and peer interaction: A final followup and a comparison. *Child Development, 57,* 217–229.

Achenbach, T. M. (1992). New developments in multiaxiel empirically-based assessment of child and adolescent psychopathology. In J. C. Rosen & P. McReynolds (Eds.), *Advances in psychological assessment* (Vol. 8, pp. 75–102.). New York: Plenum.

Achenbach, T. M., & Edelbrock, C. S. (1981). Behavioral problems and competencies reported by parents of normal and disturbed children aged four through sixteen. *Monographs of the Society for Research in Child Development, 46*(1, Serial No. 188).

Achenbach, T. M., McConaughy, S. H., & Howell, C. T. (1987). Child/adolescent behavioral and emotional problems: Implications of cross-informant correlations for situational specificity. *Psychological Bulletin, 101,* 213–232.

Ainsworth, M. D. S., Blehar, M. C., Waters, E., & Wall, S. (1978). *Patterns of attachment: A psychological study of the Strange Situation.* Hillsdale, NJ: Erlbaum.

Allport, G. W. (1937). *Personality: A psychological interpretation.* New York: Holt.

American Psychiatric Association (1980, 1987, 1994). *Diagnostic and statistical manual of mental disorders* (3rd ed., 3rd ed. rev., 4th ed.). Washington, DC: Author.

Anderson, J. C., Williams, S., McGee, R., & Silva, P. A. (1987). The prevalence of DSM-III disorders in pre-adolescent children: Prevalence in a large sample from the general population. *Archives of General Psychiatry, 44,* 69–76.

Arnold, J., Levine, A., & Patterson, G. R. (1975). Changes in sibling behavior following family intervention. *Journal of Consulting and Clinical Psychology, 43,* 683–688.

Asarnow, J. R. (1988). Peer status and social competence in child psychiatric inpatients: A comparison of children with depressive, externalizing, and concurrent depressive and externalizing disorders. *Journal of Abnormal Child Psychology, 16,* 151–162.

Aultman, M. (1980). Group involvement in delinquent acts: A study of offense type and male-female participation. *Criminal Justice and Behavior, 7,* 185–192.

Bandura, A. (1989). Social cognitive theory. In R. Vasta (Ed.), *Annals of child development* (Vol. 6, pp. 1–60). Greenwich, CT: JAI Press.

Bank, L., Dishion, T. J., Skinner, M. L., & Patterson, G. R. (1990). Method variance in structural equation modeling: Living with "glop." In G. R. Patterson (Ed.), *Depression and aggression in family interaction* (pp. 247–279). Hillsdale, NJ: Erlbaum.

Bank, L., & Patterson, G. R. (1992). The use of structural equation modeling in combining data from different types of assessment. In J. C. Rosen & P. McReynolds (Ed.), *Advances in psychological assessment* (Vol. 8, pp. 41–74). New York: Plenum.

Barker, R. G. (1960). Ecology and motivation. In M. R. Jones (Ed.), *Nebraska Symposium on Motivation* (pp. 1–50). Lincoln, NE: University of Nebraska.

Barker, R. G., & Wright, H. F. (1955). *Midwest and its children: The psychological ecology of an American town.* New York: Harper & Row.

Barkley, R. A. (1989). Attention deficit-hyperactivity disorder. In E. J. Mash & R. A. Barkley (Eds.), *Treatment of childhood disorders* (pp. 39–72). New York: Guilford.

Bates, J. E., & Bayles, K. (1988). Attachment and the development of behavior problems. In J. Belsky and T. Nezworski (Eds.), *Clinical implications of attachment* (pp. 253–294). Hillsdale, NJ: Erlbaum.

Bates, J. E., Bayles, K., Bennett, D. S., Ridge, B., & Brown, N. M. (1991). Origins of externalizing behavior problems at eight years of age. In D. J. Pepler & K. H. Rubin (Eds.), *The development and treatment of childhood aggression* (pp. 93–120). Hillsdale, NJ: Erlbaum.

Bates, J. E., Maslin, C. A., & Frankel, K. A. (1985). Attachment security, mother-child interaction, and temperament as predictors of behavior-problem ratings at age three years. In I. Bretherton & E. Waters (Eds.), *Growing points of attachment theory and research* (pp. 167–193). *Monographs of the Society for Research in Child Development, 50* (1–2, Serial No. 209).

Belson, W. A. (1975). *Juvenile theft: The causal factors.* London: Harper & Row.

Bentler, P. M. (1989). *EOS: Structural equations program manual.* Los Angeles: BMDP Statistical Software.

Bentler, P. M., & Bonett, D. G. (1980). Significance tests and goodness-of-fit in the analysis of covariance structures. *Psychological Bulletin, 88,* 588–606.

Bernal, M. E., Delfini, L. F., North, J. A., & Kreutzer, S. L. (1976). Comparison of boys' behavior in homes and classrooms. In E. Mash, L. Handy, & L. Hamerlynck (Eds.), *Behavior modification and families* (pp. 204–227). New York: Brunner/Mazel.

Biglan, A., Glasgow, R. E., & Singer, G. (1990). The need for a science of large social units: A contextual approach. *Behavior Therapy, 21,* 195–215.

Biglan, A., Metzler, C. W., Wirt, R., Ary, D., Noel, J., Ochs, L., French, C., & Hood, D. (1990). Social and behavioral factors associated with high-risk sexual behavior among adolescents. *Journal of Behavioral Medicine, 15,* 245–261.

Bird, H. R., Canino, G., Rubio-Stipec, M., & Ribera, J. C. (1988). Estimates of the prevalence of childhood maladjustment in a community survey of Puerto Rico: The use of combined measures. *Archives of General Psychiatry, 45,* 1120–1126.

Block, J. H., Block, J., & Gjerde, P. F. (1986). The personality of children prior to divorce: A prospective study. *Child Development, 57,* 827–840.

Bloom, B. L., Asher, S. J., & White, S. W. (1978). Marital disruption as a stressor: A review and analysis. *Psychological Bulletin, 85,* 867–894.

Bolger, N., Caspi, A., Downey, G., & Moorehouse, M. (1987). Development in context: Research perspectives. In N. Bolger, A. Caspi, G. Downey, & M. Moorehouse (Eds.), *Persons in context: Developmental processes.* New York: Cambridge Press.

Bowlby, J. (1969). *Attachment and loss: Vol. 1. Attachment.* New York: Basic Books.

Bowlby, J. (1973). *Attachment and loss: Vol. 2. Separation.* New York: Basic Books.

Bowlby, J. (1980). *Attachment and loss: Vol. 3. Loss.* New York: Basic Books.

Bretherton, I. (1992). The origins of attachment theory: John Bowlby and Mary Ainsworth. *Developmental Psychology, 28,* 759–775.

Bronfenbrenner, U. (1979). *The ecology of human development: Experiments by nature and by design.* Cambridge, MA: Harvard University Press.

Bronfenbrenner, U. (1986). Ecology of the family as a context for human development. *Developmental Psychology, 22,* 723–742.

Bronfenbrenner, U. (1989). Ecological systems theory. In R. Vasta (Ed.), *Annals of child development: Vol. 6. Six theories of child development: Revised formulations and current issues* (pp. 187–249). London: JAI Press.

Brook, J. S., Whiteman, M., Gordon, A. S., & Cohen, P. (1986). Some models and mechanisms for explaining the impact of maternal and adolescent characteristics on adolescent stage of drug use. *Developmental Psychology, 22,* 460–467.

Brooks-Gunn, J., Duncan, G. J., Kato, P., & Sealand, M. (1991, April). *Do neighborhoods influence child and adolescent behavior?* Paper presented at the biennial meeting of the Society for Research in Child Development, Seattle, WA.

Brown, B. B. (1989). The role of peer groups in adolescent's adjustment in secondary school. In T. J. Berndt & G. W. Ladd (Eds.), *Peer relationships in child development* (pp. 185–215). New York: Wiley.

Burgess, R. L., & Youngblade, L. (1985). *The intergenerational transmission of abusive parental practices: A social interactional analysis.* Unpublished manuscript, Department of Individual and Family Studies, Pennsylvania State University, Philadelphia.

Buss, D. M., & Craik, K. H. (1983). The act frequency approach to personality. *Psychological Review, 90,* 105–126.

Cairns, R. B., & Cairns, B. D. (1991). Social cognition and social networks: A developmental perspective. In D. J. Pepler & K. H. Rubin (Eds.), *The development and treatment of childhood aggression* (pp. 249–278). Hillsdale, NJ: Erlbaum.

Cairns, R. B., Cairns, B. D., & Neckerman, H. J. (1989). Early school dropout: Configurations and determinants. *Child Development, 60,* 1437–1452.

Cairns, R. B., Cairns, B. D., & Neckerman, H. J., Gest, S. D., & Gariepy, J. L. (1988). Social networks and aggressive behavior: Peer support or peer rejection. *Developmental Psychology, 24,* 815–823.

Cairns, R. B., & Gariepy, J. L. (1990). Dual genesis and the puzzle of aggressive mediation. In M. E. Hahn, J. K. Hewitt, N. D. Henderson, & R. H. Benno (Eds.), *Developmental behavior genetics: Neural, biometrical, and evolutionary approaches* (pp. 40–59). New York: Oxford University Press.

Cairns, R. B., Gariepy, J. L., & Hood, K. E. (1988). *Dual genesis and aggressive behavior.* Report from Social Development Laboratory, 1, 1–18, Department of Psychology, University of North Carolina, Chapel Hill.

Campbell, D. T., & Fiske, D. W. (1959). Conversant and discriminant validation of the multitrait and multimethod matrix. *Psychological Bulletin, 56,* 81–105.

Campbell, S. B., Breaux, A. M., Ewing, L. J., & Szumowski, E. K. (1986). Correlates and predictors of hyperactivity and aggression: A longitudinal study of parent-referred problem preschoolers. *Journal of Abnormal Child Psychology, 14,* 217–234.

Capaldi, D. M. (1991, April). *Fourth grade predictors of sexual intercourse by 9th grade for boys.* Paper presented at the biennial meeting of the Society for Research in Child Development, Seattle, WA.

Capaldi, D. M. (1992). The co-occurrence of conduct problems and depressive symptoms in early adolescent boys: II. A 2-year follow-up at Grade 8. *Development and Psychopathology, 4,* 125–144.

Capaldi, D. M., & Patterson, G. R. (1991). Relation of parental transitions to boys' adjustment problems: I. A linear hypothesis; II. Mothers at risk for transitions and unskilled parenting. *Developmental Psychology, 27,* 489–504.

Capaldi, D. M., & Patterson, G. R. (1994). Interrelated influences of contextual factors on antisocial behavior in childhood and adolescence for males. In D. Fowles, P. Sutker, & S. Goodman (Eds.), *Psychopathy and antisocial personality: A developmental perspective* (pp. 165–198). New York: Springer.

Caprara, G. V., Cinanni, V., D'Imperio, G., Passerini, S., Penzi, P., & Travaglia, G. (1985). Indicators of impulsive aggression: Present status of research on irritability and emotional susceptibility scales. *Personality and Individual Differences, 6,* 665–674.

Caprara, G. V., & Zimbardo, P. (in press). Aggregation and amplication of marginal deviations in the social construction of personality and maladjustment. *European Journal of Psychology.*

Carlson, G. A., & Cantwell, D. P. (1980). Unmasking masked depression in children and adolescents. *American Journal of Psychiatry, 137,* 445–449.

Caspi, A., Bem, D. J., & Elder, G. H. (1989). Continuities and consequences of interactional styles across the life course. *Journal of Personality, 56,* 375–406.

Caspi, A., Elder, G. H., & Bem, D. J. (1987). Moving against the world: Life-course patterns of explosive children. *Developmental Psychology, 23,* 308–313.

Caspi, A., & Herbener, E. S. (1990). Continuity and change: Assortive marriage and the consistency of personality in adulthood. *Journal of Personality and Social Psychology, 58,* 250–258.

Caspi, A., Lynam, D., Moffitt, T. E., & Silva, P. A. (1993). Unraveling girls' delinquency: Biological, disposition, and contextual contributions to adolescent misbehavior. *Developmental Psychology, 29,* 19–30.

Charlesbois, P., Tremblay, R. E., Gagnon, C., Larivee, S., & Laurent, D. (1989). Situational consistency in behavioral patterns of aggressive boys: Methodological considerations on observational measures. *Journal of Psychopathology and Behavioral Assessment, 11,* 15–27.

Chess, S., & Thomas, A. (1984). *Origins and evolution of behavior disorders: From infancy to early adult life.* New York: Brunner/Mazel.

Cicchetti, D. (1990). An historical perspective on the discipline of developmental psychopathology. In J. Rolf, A. Masten, D. Cicchetti, K. Nuechterlein, & S. Weintraub (Eds.), *Risk protective factors in development of psychopathology* (pp. 2–28). New York: Cambridge University Press.

Cicchetti, D. (1993). What developmental psychopathology is about: Reactions, reflections, projections. *Developmental Review, 13,* 471–502.

Cicchetti, D., & Lynch, M. (1993). Toward an ecological-transactional model of community violence and child maltreatment: Consequences for children's development. *Psychiatry, 56,* 96–119.

Cicchetti, D., & Toth, S. L. (1992). The role of development and theory in prevention and intervention. *Development and Psychology, 4,* 489–493.

Cillessen, T. (1989, April). *Aggression and liking in same-status versus different-status groups.* Paper presented at the biennial meeting for the Society for Research in Child Development, Kansas City, MO.

Cloninger, C. R., & Gottesman, I. J. (1987). Genetic and environmental factors in antisocial behavior disorders. In S. A. Mednick, T. E. Moffitt, & S. A. Stack (Eds.), *The causes of crime: New biological approaches* (pp. 92–109). New York: Cambridge University Press.

Cloward, R. A., & Ohlin, L. E. (1960). *Delinquency and opportunity.* Glencoe, IL: Free Press.

Cobb, J. A. (1972). *The relationship of discrete classroom behaviors to fourth-grade academic achievement.* Unpublished manuscript, Oregon Research Institute, Eugene.

Cobb, J. A., & Hops, H. (1972). Effects of survival skill training on low achieving first graders. *Journal of Educational Research, 2,* 54–63.

Cohen, J. M. (1977). Sources of peer group homogeneity, *Sociology of Education, 50,* 227–241.

Coie, J. D., Belding, M., & Underwood, M. (1987). Aggression and peer rejection in childhood. In B. B. Lahey & A. Kazdin (Eds.), *Advances in clinical child psychology* (Vol. 2, pp. 125–158). New York: Plenum.

Coie, J. D., & Dodge, K. (1988). Multiple sources of data on social behavior and social status in the school: A cross-age comparison. *Child Development, 59,* 815–829.

Coie, J. D., & Kupersmidt, J. B. (1983). A behavioral analysis of emerging social status in boys' groups. *Child Development, 54,* 1400–1416.

Conger, R. D., Conger, K. J., Elder, G. H., Jr., Lorenz, F. O., Simons, R. L., & Whitbeck, L. B. (1992). A family process model of economic hardship and adjustment of early adolescent boys. *Child Development, 63,* 526–541.

Connell, J. P., Clifford, E., & Crichlow, W. (1992, April). *Why do urban students leave school? Neighborhood, family and motivational influences.* Paper presented at research conference sponsored by the Committee for Research on the Urban Underclass and the Social Science Research Council, University of New York, Rochester.

Cook, T. D., & Campbell, D. T. (1979). *Quasi-experimentation: Design and analysis issues for field settings.* Boston: Houghton Mifflin.

Craig, M. M., & Glick, S. J. (1968). School behavior related to later delinquency and nondelinquency. *Criminologica, 5,* 17–27.

Crane, J. (1991). The epidemic theory of ghettos and neighborhood effects on dropping out and teenage childbearing. *American Journal of Sociology, 100,* 1226–1259.

Daugherty, T., & Quay, H. C. (1991). Response perseveration and delayed responding in childhood behavior disorders. *Journal of Child Psychology and Psychiatry, 32,* 453–461.

DiLalla, L. F., & Gottesman, I. J. (1989). Heterogeneity of causes for delinquency and criminality: Life span perspectives. *Development and Psychopathology, 1,* 339–349.

Dishion, T. J. (1987). *A developmental model for peer relations: Middle childhood correlates and one-year sequela.* Unpublished doctoral dissertation. Eugene: University of Oregon.

Dishion, T. J. (1990). Peer context of troublesome behavior in children and adolescents. In P. Leone (Ed.), *Understanding troubled and troublesome youth* (pp. 128–153). Beverly Hills, CA: Sage.

Dishion, T. J., & Andrews, D. W. (in press). A multicomponent intervention for families of young adolescents at risk: An analysis of short-term outcome. *Journal of Consulting and Clinical Psychology.*

Dishion, T. J., Andrews, D. W., & Crosby, L. (in press). Adolescent boys and their friends in adolescence: Relationship characteristics, quality, and interactional processes. *Child Development.*

Dishion, T. J., Andrews, D. W., Patterson, G. R., & Poe, J. (1994). *Adolescent antisocial boys and their friends: Accounting for behavioral confluence.* Unpublished manuscript, Oregon Social Learning Center, Eugene.

Dishion, T. J., & Brown, G. A. (in press). Measurement issues in studying parenting effects on adolescent problem behavior. In W. J. Bukoski & Z. Ansel (Eds.), *Drug abuse prevention: Source book on strategies and research.* Westport, CT: Greenwood Press.

Dishion, T. J., Capaldi, D., & Ray, J. (in press). The development and ecology of substance use in adolescent boys. *Child Development.*

Dishion, T. J., Duncan, T., Eddy, J. M., Fagot, B. I., & Fetrow, B. (in press). The world of parents and peers: Coercive exchanges and children's social adaptation. *Social Development.*

Dishion, T. J., Loeber, R. (1985). Male adolescent marijuana and alcohol use: The role of parents and peers revisited. *American Journal of Drug and Alcohol Abuse, 11,* 11–25.

Dishion, T. J., Loeber, R., Stouthamer-Loeber, M., & Patterson, G. R. (1984). Skill deficits and male adolescent delinquency. *Journal of Abnormal Child Psychology, 12,* 37–54.

Dishion, T. J., Patterson, G. R., & Griesler, P. C. (1994). Peer adaptation in the development of antisocial behavior: A confluence model. In L. R. Huesmann (Ed.), *Aggressive behavior: Current perspectives* (pp. 61–95). New York: Plenum.

Dishion, T. J., Patterson, G. R., Stoolmiller, M., & Skinner, M. (1991). Family, school, and behavioral antecedents to early adolescent involvement with antisocial peers. *Developmental Psychology, 27,* 172–180.

Dishion, T. J., Reid, J. B., & Patterson, G. R. (1988). Empirical guidelines for a family intervention for adolescent drug use. *Journal of Chemical Dependency Treatment, 1,* 189–224.

Dodge, K. A. (1983). Behavioral antecedents: A peer social status. *Child Development, 54,* 1386–1399.

Dodge, K. A. (1986). A social information processing model of social competence in children. In M. Perlmutter (Ed.), *Minnesota Symposium on Child Psychology* (Vol. 18, pp. 77–125). Hillsdale, NJ: Erlbaum.

Dodge, K. A. (1990). Nature versus nurture in childhood conduct disorder: It is time to ask a different question. *Developmental Psychology, 26,* 698–701.

Dodge, K. A. (1991). The structure and function of proactive and reactive aggression. In D. J. Pepler & K. H. Rubin (Eds.), *The development and treatment of childhood aggression* (pp. 201–218). Hillsdale, NJ: Erlbaum.

Dodge, K. A. (1993). Social-cognitive mechanisms in the development of conduct disorder and depression. *Annual Review of Psychology, 44,* 559–584.

Dodge, K. A., Bates, J. E., & Pettit, G. S. (1990). Mechanisms in the cycle of violence. *Science, 250,* 1678–1683.

Dodge, K. A., & Coie, J. D. (1987). Social-information processing factors in reactive and proactive aggression in children's peer groups. *Journal of Personality and Social Psychology, 53,* 1146–1157.

Dodge, K. A., Murphy, R. R., & Buchsbaum, K. (1984). The assessment of intention-cue detection skills in children: Implications for developmental psychopathology. *Child Development, 55,* 163–173.

Dodge, K. A., & Newman, J. P. (1981). Biased decision-making processes in aggressive boys. *Journal of Abnormal Psychology, 90,* 375–379.

Dodge, K. A., Price, J. M., Bachorowski, J. A., & Newman, J. P. (1990). Hostile attributional biases in severely aggressive adolescents. *Journal of Abnormal Psychology, 99,* 385–392.

Dodge, K. A., Price, J. M., Coie, J., & Christopoulos, D. (1990). On the development of aggressive dyadic relationships in boys' peer groups. *Human Development, 33,* 260–270.

Dodge, K. A., & Tomlin, A. M. (1987). Utilization of self-schemas as a mechanism of interpretational bias in aggressive children. *Social Cognition, 5,* 280–300.

Donovan, J. E., & Jessor, R. (1985). Structure of problem behavior in adolescence and young adulthood. *Journal of Consulting and Clinical Psychology, 53,* 890–904.

Dunn, J. (1992). Sisters and brothers: Current issues in developmental research. In F. Boer & J. Dunn (Eds.), *Children's sibling relationships. Developmental and clinical issues* (pp. 1–17). Hillsdale, NJ: Erlbaum.

Dwyer, J. H. (1983). *Statistical models for the social and behavior sciences.* New York: Oxford University Press.

Eddy, J. M. (1991). *Marital discord, parenting, and child antisocial behavior.* Unpublished doctoral dissertation, University of Oregon, Eugene.

Egeland, B., & Farber, E. A. (1984). Infant-mother attachment: Factors related to its development and changes over time. *Child Development, 55,* 753–771.

Elder, G. H. (1980). *Family structure and socialization.* New York: Arno.

Elder, G. H., & Ardelt, M. (1992, March). *Families adapting to economic pressure: Some consequences for parents and adolescents.* Paper presented at the Society for Research on Adolescence, Washington, DC.

Elder, G. H., Caspi, A., & Van Nguyen, T. (1986). Resourceful and vulnerable children: Family influences in hard times. In R. K. Silbereisen, K. Eyferth, & G. Rudinger (Eds.), *Development as action in context: Problem behavior and normal youth development* (pp. 167–186). New York: Springer-Verlag.

Elder, G. H., Van Nguyen, T., Caspi, A. (1985). Linking family hardship to children's lives. *Child Development, 56,* 361–375.

Elicker, J., Englund, M., & Sroufe, L. A. (1992). Predicting peer competence and peer relationships in childhood from early parent-child relationships. In R. D. Parke & G. W. Ladd (Eds.), *Family-peer relationships: Models of linkage* (pp. 77–106). Hillsdale, NJ: Erlbaum.

Elliott, D. S., & Ageton, S. (1979, May). *Reconciling race and class differences in self-reports and official estimates of delinquency.* Paper presented at Behavioral Research Institute Seminar, Boulder, CO.

Elliott, D. S., Huizinga, D., & Ageton, S. S. (1985). *Explaining delinquency and drug use.* Beverly Hills, CA: Sage.

Elliott, D. S., Huizinga, D., & Menard, S. (1989). *Multiple problem youth: Delinquency, substance use, and mental health problems.* New York: Springer-Verlag.

Elliott, D. S., & Morse, B. J. (1989). Delinquency and drug use as risk factors in teenage sexual activity. *Youth and Society, 21,* 32–62.

Ellis, S., Rogoff, B., & Cromer, C. (1981). Age segregation in children's interactions. *Developmental Psychology, 17,* 399–407.

Emde, R. N., Plomin, R., Robinson, J., Corley, R., Defries, J., Fulker, D. W., Resnick, J. S., Campos, J., Kagan, J., & Zahn-Waxler, C. (1992). Temperament, emotion, and cognition at fourteen months: The McArthur longitudinal twin study. *Child Development, 63,* 1437–1455.

Emery, E. R., & O'Leary, K. D. (1984). Marital discord and child behavior problems in a nonclinic sample. *Journal of Abnormal Child Psychology, 12,* 411–420.

Ensminger, M. E. (1990). Sexual activity and problem behaviors among black, urban, adolescents. *Child Development, 61,* 2032–2046.

Ensminger, M. E., Kellam, S. G., & Rubin, B. K. (1983). *School and family origins of delinquency: Comparisons by sex.* In K. Van Dusen & S. Mednick (Eds.), *Antecedents of antisocial behavior* (pp. 73–97). Hingman, MA: Nighoff Publishing.

Epstein, S. (1979). The stability of behavior: I. On predicting most of the people much of the time. *Journal of Personality and Social Psychology, 37,* 1097–1126.

Eron, L. D. (1982). Parent-child interaction, television violence, and aggression of children. *American Psychologist, 37,* 197–211.

Eron, L. D., & Huesmann, L. R. (1986). The role of television in the development of prosocial and antisocial behavior. In D. Olweus, J. Block, & M. Radke-Yarrow (Eds.), *Development of antisocial and prosocial behavior: Research, theories, & issues* (pp. 285–314). New York: Academic Press.

Fagin, J. (1989). The social organization of drug use and drug dealing among urban gangs. *Criminology, 27,* 633–669.

Fagot, B. I. (1990, January). *The relation of early parenting variables to aggressive and withdrawn behavior with peers.* Paper presented at the Society for Research in Child and Adolescent Psychopathology, Costa Mesa, CA.

Fagot, B. I., & Kavanagh, K. (1990). The prediction of antisocial behavior from avoidant attachment classifications. *Child Development, 61,* 864–873.

Farrington, D. P. (1978). The family backgrounds of aggressive youths. In L. A. Herson, M. Berger, & D. Shaffer (Eds.), *Aggression and antisocial behavior in childhood and adolescence* (pp. 73–93). Oxford, England: Pergamon.

Farrington, D. P. (1991). Childhood aggression and adult violence: Early precursors and later life outcomes. In D. J. Pepler & K. H. Rubin (Eds.), *The development and treatment of childhood aggression* (pp. 5–29). Hillsdale, NJ: Erlbaum.

Federal Bureau of Investigation. (1989). *Crime in the United States: Uniform crime reports. 1989.* Washington, DC: U.S. Government Printing Office.

Feldman, R. A., Caplinger, T. E., & Wodarski, J. S. (1983). *The St. Louis conundrum.* Englewood Cliffs, NJ: Prentice-Hall.

Fergusson, D. M., Horwood, L. J., & Lloyd, M. (1991). Confirmatory factor models of attention deficit and conduct disorder. *Journal of Child Psychology and Psychiatry, 32,* 257–274.

Fischler, G. L., & Kendall, P. C. (1988). Social cognitive problem-solving and childhood adjustment: Qualitative and topological analyses. *Cognitive Therapy and Research, 12,* 135–153.

Fiske, D. W. (1986). Specificity of method and knowledge in social science. In D. W. Fiske & R. A. Shweder (Eds.), *Metatheory in social science* (pp. 61–82). Chicago: University of Chicago Press.

Forehand, R., Furey, W. M., & McMahon, R. J. (1984). The role of maternal distress in parent training program to modify child noncompliance. *Behavioral Psychotherapy, 12,* 93–108.

Forgatch, M. S. (1984). *A two-stage analysis of family problem solving: Global and microsocial.* Unpublished doctoral dissertation, University of Oregon, Eugene.

Forgatch, M. S. (1991). The clinical science vortex: Developing a theory of antisocial behavior. In D. J. Pepler & K. Rubin (Eds.), *The development and creation of childhood aggression* (pp. 291–315.). Hillsdale, NJ: Erlbaum.

Forgatch, M. S., Patterson, G. R., & Skinner, M. L. (1985). A mediational model for the effect of divorce on antisocial behavior in boys. In E. M. Hetherington & J. D. Arasteh (Eds.), *Impact of divorce, single parenting and step-parenting on children* (pp. 135–154). Hillsdale, NJ: Erlbaum.

Forgatch, M. S., & Toobert, D. J. (1979). A cost effective parent training program for use with normal preschool children. *Journal of Pediatric Psychology, 4,* 129–145.

Fowles, D. C. (1984). Biological variables in psychopathology: A psychobiological perspective. In H. E. Adams & J. B. Sutker (Eds.), *Comprehensive handbook of psychopathology* (pp. 77–106). New York: Plenum.

Fowles, D. C. (1987). Application of a behavioral theory of motivation to the concepts of anxiety and impulsivity. *Journal of Research in Personality, 21,* 417–435.

French, D. C. (1987). Children's social interaction with older and younger peers. *Journal of Personal and Social Relations, 4,* 63–86.

French, D. C. (1988). Heterogeneity of peer-rejected boys: Aggressive and nonaggressive subtypes. *Child Development, 59,* 976–985.

French, D. C. (1990). Heterogeneity of peer rejected girls. *Child Development, 61,* 2028–2031.

French, D. C., Conrad, J., & Neill, S. (1991, April). *Social adjustment of antisocial and non-antisocial early adolescents.* Paper presented at the biennial meeting of the Society for Research in Child Development, Seattle, WA.

French, D. C., & Straight, A. L. (1991). Emergent leadership in children's small groups. *Small Group Behavior, 22,* 187–199.

French, D. C., & Waas, G. A. (1987). Social-cognitive and behavioral characteristics of peer-rejected boys. *Professional School Psychology, 2,* 103–112.

Freud, S. (1922). *Beyond the pleasure principle.* London: Psychoanalytic Press.

Garbarino, J., & Sherman, D. (1980). High-risk neighborhoods and high-risk families: The human ecology of child maltreatment. *Child Development, 51,* 188–198.

Gardner, F. M. (1987). Positive interaction between mothers and conduct-problem children: Is there training for harmony as well as fighting? *Journal of Abnormal Child Psychology, 15,* 283–293.

Gardner, F. M. (1989). Inconsistent parenting: Is there evidence for a link with children's conduct problems? *Journal of Abnormal Child Psychology, 17,* 223–233.

Garmezy, N., & Rutter, M. (1983). Acute reactions to stress. In M. Rutter & L. Herzov (Eds.), *Child psychiatry: A modern approach* (2nd ed.), (pp. 152–177). Oxford, England: Blackwell.

Gjerde, P. F., Block, J., & Block, J. H. (1988). Depressive symptoms and personality during late adolescence: Gender differences in the externalization-internalization of symptom expression. *Journal of Abnormal Psychology, 97,* 475–486.

Glueck, S., & Glueck, E. (1950). *Unraveling juvenile delinquency.* Cambridge, MA: Harvard University Press.

Glueck, S., & Glueck, E. (1959). *Predicting delinquency and crime.* Cambridge, MA: Harvard University Press.

Gold, M. (1970). *Delinquent behavior in an American city.* San Francisco: Brooks & Coleman.

Goldsmith, H. H. (1988). Human developmental behavioral genetics: Mapping the effects of genes and environments. *Annals of Child Development, 5,* 187–227.

Gollob, H. F., & Reichardt, C. S. (1987). Taking account of time lags in causal models. *Child Development, 58,* 80–92.

Gottesman, I. I., & Goldsmith, H. H. (in press). Developmental psychopathology of antisocial behavior: Inserting genes into ontogenesis and epigenesis. In C. Nelson (Ed.), *Minnesota Symposium on Child Psychology: Vol. 27. Infants and children at risk.* Hillsdale, NJ: Erlbaum.

Gottesman, I. I., & Shields, J. (1982). *Schizophrenia: The epigenetic puzzle.* New York: Cambridge University Press.

Gottfred, M. R., & Hirschi, T. (1990). *A general theory of crime.* Stanford, CA: Stanford University Press.

Gottfredson, D. (1988). An evaluation of an organization development approach to reducing school disorder. *Evaluation Review, 11,* 739–763.

Gottfredson, D. C., Gottfredson, G. D., & Hybl, L. G. (1993). Managing adolescent behavior: A multiyear, multischool study. *American Educational Research Journal, 30,* 179–215.

Gottman, J. M. (1979). *Marital interaction: Experimental investigations.* New York: Academic Press.

Gottman, J. M. (1983). How children become friends. *Monographs of the Society for Research in Child Development, 48*(3, Series No. 201).

Gottman, J. M., & Levenson, R. W. (1986). Assessing the role of emotion in marriage. *Behavioral Assessment, 8,* 31–48.

Gray, J. A. (1982). *The neuropsychology of anxiety: An inquiry into the functions of the septo-hypocampal system.* New York: Clarendon Press.

Gray, J. A. (1987). *The psychology of fear and stress* (2nd ed.). New York: Cambridge University Press.

Gray, G., Smith, A., & Rutter, M. (1980). School attendance and the first year of employment. In L. Hersov & I. Berg (Eds.), *In and out of school* (pp. 343–370). New York: Wiley.

Greenberg, M. T., Speltz, M. L., & DeKlyen, M. (1993). The role of attachment in early development of disruptive behavior problems. *Development and Psychopathology, 5,* 191–213.

Hare, R. D. (1968). Psychopathy, autonomic functioning, and the orienting response. *Journal of Abnormal Psychology Monograph Supplement, 73*(3), 1–24.

Hartup, W. W. (1992). Peer relations in early and middle childhood. In V. B. Hasselt & M. Hersen (Eds.), *Handbook of social development: A lifespan perspective* (pp. 257–282). New York: Plenum.

Hawkins, J. D., & Lishner, D. M. (1987). Schooling and delinquency. In E. H. Johnson (Ed.), *Handbook on crime and delinquency prevention* (pp. 179–221). New York: Greenwood Press.

Hawkins, J. D., & Weis, J. G. (1985). The social development model: An integrated approach to delinquency prevention. *Journal of Primary Prevention, 6,* 73–97.

Hayes, S. C., & Hayes, L. J. (1989). The verbal action of the listener as a basis for rule-governance. In S. C. Hayes (Ed.), *Rule-governed behavior: Cognition, contingencies and instructional control* (pp. 153–190). New York: Plenum.

Herrnstein, R. J. (1990). Rational-choice theory: Necessary but not sufficient. *American Psychologist, 45,* 356–367.

Hetherington, E. M. (Ed.). (1988). *Stress, coping, and resiliency in children and the family.* Hillsdale, NJ: Erlbaum.

Hetherington, E. M., & Clingempeel, W. G. (1992). Coping with marital transitions. *Monographs of the Society for Research in Child Development, 57*(2–3, Serial No. 27).

Hetherington, E. M., Cox, M., & Cox, R. (1985). Long-term effects of divorce and remarriage on the adjustment of children. *Journal of the American Academy of Child Psychiatry, 24,* 518–530.

Hinde, R. A. (1989). Theoretical and relationship approaches. In R. Vasta (Ed.), *Annals of Child Development: Vol. 6. Six theories of child development: Revised formulations and current issues* (pp. 251–285). London: JAI Press.

Hinshaw, S. P. (1987). On the distinction between attentional deficits/hyperactivity and conduct problems/aggression in child psychopathology. *Psychological Bulletin, 101,* 443–468.

Hirschi, T. (1969). *Causes of delinquency.* Berkeley: University of California Press.

Hirschi, T., & Gottfredson, M. (1983). Age and the explanation of crime. *American Journal of Sociology, 89,* 552–583.

Hirschi, T., & Hindelang, M. J. (1977). Intelligence and delinquency: A revisionist review. *American Sociological Review, 42,* 571–587.

Hoffman, L. W. (1991). The influence of the family environment on personality: Accounting for sibling differences. *Psychological Bulletin, 110,* 187–203.

Hops, H., & Cobb, J. A. (1974). Initial investigations into academic survival skill training, direct instruction, and first grade reading achievement. *Journal of Educational Psychology, 66,* 548–563.

Hops, H., Lewinsohn, P. M., Andrews, A., & Roberts, E. (1990). Psychosocial correlates of depressive symptomology among high school students. *Journal of Clinical Child Psychology, 19,* 211–220.

Huesmann, P. L., Eron, L. D., Lefkowitz, M. M., & Walder, L. O. (1984). The stability of aggression over time and generations. *Developmental Psychology, 20,* 1120–1134.

INTERPOL. (1988). *International crime statistics, 1987–1988.* International Criminal Police Organization.

Jackson, M. J. (1992). *Interactions of friends in early adolescence: Gender differences and relation to adjustment.* Unpublished doctoral dissertation, University of Oregon.

Jacobs, J. (1963). *Death and life in great American cities.* New York: Random House.

Jacobson, R. H., Lahey, B. B., & Strauss, C. C. (1983). Correlates of depressed mood in normal children. *Journal of Abnormal Child Psychology, 11,* 29–40.

Jessor, R., & Jessor, S. L. (1977). *Problem behavior and psychosocial development.* New York: Academic Press.

Joreskog, K. G., & Sorbom, D. (1989). *Lisrel 7: A guide to the program and applications* (2nd ed.). Chicago: SPSS.

Judd, C. M., & Kenny, D. A. (1981). Process analysis: Estimating mediation in treatment evaluations. *Evaluation Review, 5,* 602–619.

Kagan, J., Reznick, J. S., & Snidman, N. (1988). Biological bases of childhood shyness. *Science, 240,* 167–171.

Kandel, D. B. (1978). Homophily, selection, and socialization in adolescent friendships. *American Journal of Sociology, 84,* 427–436.

Kandel, D. B., Davies, D. H., & Kandel, P. L. (1984). *Continuity in discontinuities: Adjustment in young adulthood of former school absentees. Youth in Society, 15,* 325–354.

Kashani, J. H., Carlson, G. A., Beck, N. C., Hoeper, E. W., Corcoran, C. M., McAllister, J. A., Fallahi, C., Rosenberg, T. K., & Reid, J. C. (1987). Depression, depressive symptoms, and depressed mood among a community sample of adolescents. *American Journal of Psychiatry, 144,* 931–934.

Kazdin, A. (1987). Treatment of antisocial behavior in children: Current status and future directions. *Psychological Bulletin, 102,* 187–203.

Kellam, S. G. (1990). Developmental epidemiological framework for family research on depression and aggression. In G. R. Patterson (Ed.), *Depression and aggression in family interaction* (pp. 11–48). Hillsdale, NJ: Erlbaum.

Kellam, S. G., Brown, C. H., Rubin, B. R., & Ensminger, M. E. (1983). Paths leading to teenage psychiatric symptoms and substance use: Developmental epidemiological studies in Woodlawn. In S. B. Guze, F. J. Earls, & J. E. Barnett (Eds.), *Childhood psychopathology and development* (pp. 17–51). New York: Raven Press.

Kendall, P. C., & Fischler, G. L. (1984). Behavioral and adjustment correlates of problem-solving: Validational analyses of interpersonal cognitive problem-solving measures. *Child Development, 55,* 879–892.

Kolb, B. (1989). Brain development, plasticity and behavior. *American Psychologist, 44,* 1203–1212.

Kovacs, M., Paulauskas, S., Gatsonis, C., & Richards, C. (1988). Depressive disorders in childhood III: A longitudinal study of comorbidity with and risk for conduct disorders. *Journal of Affective Disorders, 15,* 205–217.

Ladd, G. W. (1983). Social networks of popular, average, and rejected children in school settings. *Merrill-Palmer Quarterly, 29,* 283–307.

Lahey, B. B., Hartdagen, S. E., Frick, P. J., McBurnett, K., Connor, R., & Hynd, G. W. (1988). Conduct disorder: Parsing the confounded relation to parental divorce and antisocial personality. *Journal of Abnormal Psychology, 97,* 334–337.

Lahey, B. B., Schaughency, B. S., Strauss, C. C., & Frame, C. L. (1984). Are attention deficit disorders with and without hyperactivity similar or dissimilar disorders? *Journal of the American Academy of Child Psychiatry, 23,* 302–309.

Langan, P. A., & Greenfeld, L. A. (1983, June). Career patterns in crime. *Bureau of Justice Statistics,* 1–8.

Langer, E. J. (1978). *Rethinking the role of thought in social interaction.* In J. H. Harvey, W. J. Ickes, & R. F. Kidd (Ed.), *New directions in attribution research* (Vol. 2, pp. 35–58). Hillsdale, NJ: Erlbaum.

Larzelere, R. E., & Patterson, G. R. (1990). Parental management: Mediators of the effect of socioeconomic status on early delinquency. *Criminology, 28,* 301–323.

Lewin, L. M., Hops, H., Davis, B., & Dishion, T. J. (1993). Multimethod comparison of similarity in school adjustment of siblings and unrelated children. *Developmental Psychology, 29,* 963–969.

Lewinsohn, P. M., Hobermand, H. M., Teri, L., & Hautziner, M. (1985). An integrative theory of unipolar depression. In S. Reiss & R. R. Bootzin (Eds.), *Theoretical issues in behavioral therapy* (pp. 313–359). New York: Academic Press.

Lewis, M., Feiring, C., McGuffog, C., & Jaskir, J. (1984). Predicting psychopathology in six-year-olds from early social relations. *Child Development, 55*, 123–136.

Lobitz, G. K., & Johnson, S. M. (1975). Normal versus deviant children: A multimethod comparison. *Journal of Abnormal Child Psychology, 3*, 353–374.

Lochman, J. E., White, K. J., & Wayland, K. K. (1990). In P. C. Kendall (Ed.), *Child and adolescent therapy* (pp. 25–65). New York: Guilford.

Loeber, R. (1982). The stability of antisocial and delinquent child behavior: A review. *Child Development, 53*, 1431–1446.

Loeber, R. (1988). Natural histories of conduct problems, delinquency, and associated substance use: Evidence for developmental progressions. In B. B. Lahey & A. E. Casdin (Eds.), *Advances in clinical child psychopathology* (Vol. II, pp. 73–124). New York: Plenum.

Loeber, R., & Dishion, T. J., (1983). Early predictors of male delinquency: A review. *Psychological Bulletin, 94*, 68–98.

Loeber, R., & Dishion, T. J. (1984). Boys who fight at home and school: Family conditions influencing cross-setting consistency. *Journal of Consulting and Clinical Psychology, 52*, 759–768.

Loeber, R., Green, S. M., Lahey, D. B., Christ, M. A. G., & Frick, P. J. (1992). Developmental sequences and the age of onset of disruptive child behaviors. *Journal of Family Studies, 1*, 21–41.

Loeber, R., & Schmaling, K. B. (1985). The utility of differentiating between mixed and pure forms of antisocial child behavior. *Journal of Abnormal Child Psychology, 13*, 315–336.

Loeber, R., Stouthamer-Loeber, M., & Green, S. M. (1991). Age at onset of problem behavior in boys and later disruptive and delinquent behavior. *Criminal Behavior and Mental Health, 1*, 229–246.

Long, J. S. (1983). *Confirmatory factor analysis.* Beverly Hills, CA: Sage.

Lykken, D. T. (1993). Predicting violence in a violent society. *Applied and Preventative Psychology, 2*, 13–20.

Maccoby, E. E., Depner, C. E., & Mnookin, R. H. (1990). Coparenting in the second year after divorce. *Journal of Marriage and the Family, 52*, 141–155.

Maccoby, E. E., & Jacklin, C. N. (1974). *The psychology of sex differences.* Stanford, CA: Stanford University Press.

MacDonald, K., & Parke, R. D. (1984). Bridging the gap: Parent-child play interaction and peer interactive competence. *Child Development, 55*, 1265–1277.

Magnusson, D. (1988). Aggressiveness, hyperactivity, and autonomic activity/reactivity in the development of social maladjustment. In D. Magnusson (Ed.), *Paths through life: Individual development from an interactionary perspective: A longitudinal study* (Vol. 1, pp. 153–175). Hillsdale, NJ: Erlbaum.

Magnusson, D. (1992). Individual development: A longitudinal perspective. *European Journal of Personality, 6*, 119–138.

Main, M., & Solomon, J. (1990). Procedures, findings, and implications for the classification of behavior. In M. Greenberg, D. Cicchetti, & E. M. Cummings (Eds.), *Attachment in the preschool years* (pp. 161–182). Chicago: University of Chicago Press.

Marriage, K., Fine, S., Moretti, M., & Haley, G. (1986). Relationship between depression and conduct disorder in children and adolescents. *Journal of the American Academy of Child Psychiatry, 25*, 687–691.

McBurnett, K., Lahey, B. B., Frick, P. J., Risch, C., Loeber, R., Hart, E. L., Christ, M. A. G., & Hanson, K. S. (1991). Anxiety, inhibition, and conduct disorders in children: II. Relation to salivary cortisol. *Journal of the American Academy of Child and Adolescent Psychiatry, 30*, 192–196.

McCord, J. (1979). Some child-rearing antecedents of criminal behavior in adult men. *Journal of Personality and Social Psychology, 37*, 1477–1486.

McCord, J. (1988). Identifying developmental paradigms leading to alcoholism. *Journal of Studies on Alcohol, 49*, 357–362.

McCord, W., McCord, J., & Howard, A. (1961). Familial correlates of aggression in nondelinquent male children. *Journal of Abnormal and Social Psychology, 62*, 79–93.

McDowell, J. J. (1988). Matching theory and natural human environments. *Behavior Analyst, 11*, 95–109.

McGee, R., Williams, S., & Silva, P. A. (1984). Background characteristics of aggressive, hyperactive, and aggressive-hyperactive boys. *Journal of the American Academy of Child Psychiatry, 23*, 280–284.

McLloyd, V. C. (1990). The impact of economic hardship on black families and children: Psychological distress, parenting, and socioemotional development. *Child Development, 61*, 311–346.

Meehl, P. E. (1978). Theoretical risks and tabular asterisks: Sir Karl, Sir Ronald and the slow progress of soft psychology. *Journal of Consulting and Clinical Psychology, 46*, 806–834.

Meichenbaum, D. (1979). *Cognitive-behavior modification: An integrative approach.* New York: Plenum.

Meyers, A. W., & Craighead, W. E. (Eds.). (1984). *Cognitive behavior therapy with children.* New York: Plenum.

Miller, W. R., & Brown, J. M. (1991). Self-regulation as a conceptual basis for the prevention and treatment of addictive behaviors. In N. Heather, W. R. Mill, & J. Greeley (Eds.), *Self-control and the addictive behaviours* (pp. 4–79). New York: Pergamon.

Miller, B. C., McCoy, J. K., Olson, T. D., & Wallace, C. M. (1986). Parental control attempts in relation to adolescent sexual attitudes and behavior. *Journal of Marriage and the Family, 48*, 503–512.

Moffitt, T. E. (1990). The neuropsychology of juvenile delinquency: A critical review. In M. Tonry & N. Morris (Eds.), *Crime and justice: A review of research* (Vol. 12, pp. 99–169). Chicago: University of Chicago Press.

Moffitt, T. E. (1993a). Adolescence-limited and life course persistent antisocial behavior: Developmental taxonomy. *Psychological Review, 100*, 674–701.

Moffitt, T. E. (1993b). The neuropsychology of conduct disorder. *Development and Psychopathology, 5*, 135–151.

Moffitt, T. E., Caspi, A., Belsky, J., & Silva, P. A. (1992). Childhood experience and the onset of menarche: A test of a sociobiological model. *Child Development, 63*, 47–58.

Moskowitz, D. S. (1982). Coherence and cross-situational generality in personality: A new analysis of old problems. *Journal of Personality and Social Psychology, 43*, 754–768.

Nagin, D. S., & Farrington, D. P. (1991). The stability of criminal potential from childhood to adulthood. *Criminology, 30*, 235–260.

Newman, J. P. (1987). Reaction to punishment in extroverts and psychopaths: Implications for the impulsive behavior of disinhibited individuals. *Journal of Research in Personality, 21*, 446–480.

Newman, J. P., Widom, C. S., & Nathan, S. (1985). Passive-avoidance in syndromes of disinhibition: Psychopathy and extraversion. *Journal of Personality and Social Psychology, 48*, 1316–1327.

Nisbett, R. E., & Wilson, T. D. (1977). The halo effect: Evidence for unconscious alteration of judgments. *Journal of Personality and Social Psychology, 35,* 250–256.

Nye, F. I. (1958). *Family relationships and delinquent behavior.* New York: Wiley.

Olweus, D. (1979). Stability of aggressive reaction patterns in males: A review. *Psychological Bulletin, 86,* 852–875.

Olweus, D. (1987). Testosterone adrenaline: Aggressive antisocial behavior in normal adolescent males. In S. A. Mednick, T. E. Moffitt, & S. A. Stack (Eds.), *The causes of crime: New biological approaches* (pp. 263–283). New York: Cambridge University Press.

Osborn, S. G. (1980). Moving home, leaving London and delinquent trends. *British Journal of Criminology, 20,* 54–61.

Osborn, S. G., & West, D. J. (1979). Marriage and delinquency: A postscript. *British Journal of Criminology, 18,* 254–256.

Parke, R. D., & Slaby, R. G. (1983). The development of aggression. In E. M. Hetherington (Ed.), P. H. Mussen (Series Ed.), *Handbook of child psychology: Vol. 4. Socialization, personality and social development* (pp. 547–641). New York: Wiley.

Patterson, G. R. (1976). The aggressive child: Victim and architect of a coercive system. In L. A. Hamerlynck, L. C. Handy, & E. J. Mash (Eds.), *Behavior modification and families: I. Theory and research; II. Applications and developments* (pp. 267–316). New York: Brunner/Mazel.

Patterson, G. R. (1982). *Coercive family process.* Eugene, OR: Castalia.

Patterson, G. R. (1983). Stress: A change agent for family process. In N. Garmezy & M. Rutter (Eds.), *Stress, coping, and development in children* (pp. 235–264). New York: McGraw-Hill.

Patterson, G. R. (1984). Siblings: Fellow travelers in coercive family processes. In R. J. Blanchard & D. C. Blanchard (Eds.), *Advances in the study of aggression* (Vol. 1, pp. 173–215). Orlando, FL: Academic Press.

Patterson, G. R. (1986). Maternal rejection: Determinant or product for deviant child behavior. In W. Hartup & Z. Rubin (Eds.), *Relationships and development* (pp. 73–94). Hillsdale, NJ: Erlbaum.

Patterson, G. R. (1992). Developmental changes in antisocial behavior. In R. D. Peters, R. J. McMahon, & V. L. Quinsey (Eds.), *Aggression and violence throughout the life span* (pp. 52–82). Newbury Park, CA: Sage.

Patterson, G. R. (1993). Orderly change in a stable world: The antisocial trait as a chimera. *Journal of Consulting and Clinical Psychology, 61*(6), 911–919.

Patterson, G. R., & Bank, L. (1986). Bootstrapping your way in the nomological thicket. *Behavioral Assessment, 8,* 49–73.

Patterson, G. R., & Bank, L. (1989). Some amplifying mechanisms for pathologic processes in families. In M. R. Gunnar & E. Thalen (Eds.) *Minnesota Symposium on Child Psychology: Vol. 22. Systems and development* (pp. 167–209). Hillsdale, NJ: Erlbaum.

Patterson, G. R., Capaldi, D., & Bank, L. (1991). An early starter model for predicting delinquency. In D. J. Pepler & K. H. Rubin (Eds.), *The development and treatment of childhood aggression* (pp. 139–168). Hillsdale, NJ: Erlbaum.

Patterson, G. R., Chamberlain, P., & Reid, J. R. (1982). A comparative evaluation of parent training procedures. *Behavior Therapy, 3,* 638–650.

Patterson, G. R., & Cobb, J. A. (1971). A dyadic analysis of "aggressive" behaviors. In J. P. Hill (Ed.), *Minnesota Symposia on Child Psychology* (Vol. 5, pp. 72–129). Minneapolis: University of Minnesota.

Patterson, G. R., & Dawes, R. M. (1975). A Guttman scale of children's coercive behavior. *Journal of Consulting and Clinical Psychology, 43,* 594.

Patterson, G. R., & Dishion, T. J. (1985). Contributions of families and peers to delinquency. *Criminology, 23,* 63–79.

Patterson, G. R., & Dishion, T. J. (1988). Multilevel modes of family process: Traits, interactions and relationships. In R. Hinde & J. Stevenson-Hinde (Eds.), *Relationships and families: Mutual influences* (pp. 283–310). Oxford, England: Clarendon Press.

Patterson, G. R., Dishion, T. J., & Bank, L. (1984). Family interaction: A process model of deviancy training [special issue]. In L. Eron (Ed.), *Aggressive Behavior, 10,* 253–267.

Patterson, G. R., Dishion, T. J., & Chamberlain, P. (1993). Outcomes and methodological issues relating to treatment of antisocial children. In T. R. Giles (Ed.), *Effective psychotherapy: A handbook of comparative research* (pp. 43–88). New York: Plenum.

Patterson, G. R., & Duncan, T. (1993). *Tests for continuity for preschool coercion progression.* Unpublished manuscript, Oregon Social Learning Center, Eugene.

Patterson, G. R., Littman, R. A., & Bricker, W. (1967). Assertive behavior in children: A step toward a theory of aggression. *Monographs of the Society for Research in Child Development, 32*(5, Serial No. 113).

Patterson, G. R., & Reid, J. B. (1984). Social interactional processes within the family: The study of the moment-by-moment family transactions in which human social development is imbedded. *Journal of Applied Developmental Psychology, 5,* 237–262.

Patterson, G. R., Reid, J. B., & Dishion, T. J. (1992). *Antisocial boys.* Eugene, OR: Castalia.

Patterson, G. R., & Stoolmiller, M. (1991). Replications of a dual failure model for boys' depressed mood. *Journal of Consulting and Clinical Psychology, 59,* 491–498.

Patterson, G. R., & Stouthamer-Loeber, M. (1984). The correlation of family management practices and delinquency. *Child Development, 55,* 1299–1307.

Patterson, G. R., & Yoerger, K. (1993). Developmental models for delinquent behavior. In S. Hodgins (Ed.), *Crime and mental disorder* (pp. 140–172). Newbury Park, CA: Sage.

Piaget, J. (1954). *The construction of reality in the child.* New York: Basic Books.

Pliszka, S. R., Rogeness, G. A., Hatch, J. P., Borcherding, S., & Maas, J. W. (1992). *A preliminary test of Quay's model of the psychobiology of ADHD.* Unpublished manuscript, University of Texas Health Science Center at San Antonio.

Plomin, R., & Daniels, D. (1987). Why are children in the same families so different from one another? *Behavioral and Brain Sciences, 10,* 1–60.

Plomin, R., Foch, T. T., & Rowe, D. C. (1981). Bobo-Yown aggression in childhood: Environment, not genes. *Journal of Research In Personality, 15,* 331–342.

Plomin, R., & Hershberger, S. (1991). Genotype-environment interaction. In T. D. Wachs & R. Plomin (Eds.), *Conceptualization and measurement of organism-environment interaction* (pp. 29–43). Washington, DC: American Psychological Association.

Ploman, R., Nitz, K., & Rowe, D. C. (1990). Behavior genetics and aggressive behavior in childhood. In M. Lewis & S. Miller (Eds.), *Handbook of developmental psychology* (pp. 119–133). New York: Plenum.

Popper, K. R. (1972). *Objective knowledge*. Oxford, England: Oxford University Press.

Puig-Antich, J. (1982). Major depression and conduct disorder in prepuberty. *Journal of the American Academy of Child Psychiatry, 21*, 118–128.

Pulkkinen, L. (1983). Youthful smoking and drinking in a longitudinal perspective. *Journal of Youth and Adolescence, 12*, 253–283.

Quay, H. C. (1964). Dimensions of personality in delinquent boys as inferred from the factor analysis of case history data. *Child Development, 35*, 479–484.

Quay, H. C. (1983). The behavioral reward and inhibition system in childhood behavior disorder. In L. M. Bloomingdale (Ed.), *Attention deficit disorder: Vol. 3. New Research in attention, treatment and psychopharmacology* (pp. 176–186). New York: Pergamon.

Quay, H. C. (1993). The psychobiology of undersocialized aggressive conduct disorder: A theoretical perspective. *Development and Psychopathology, 5*, 165–180.

Radke-Yarrow, M., & Brown, E. (1993). Resilience and vulnerability in children of multiple-risk families. *Development and Psychopathology, 5*, 581–592.

Ramsey, E., Bank, L., Patterson, G. R., & Walker, H. M. (1990). Generalization of the antisocial trait from home to school settings. *Journal of Applied Developmental Psychology, 11*, 209–223.

Reid, J. B. (Ed.). (1978). *A social learning approach to family intervention: II. Observation in home settings*. Eugene, OR: Castalia.

Reid, J. B. (1993). Prevention of conduct disorder before and after school entry: Relating interventions to developmental findings. *Development and Psychopathology, 5*, 243–262.

Rende, R., & Plomin, R. (1992). Diathesis-stress models of psychopathology: A quantitative perspective. *Applied and Preventative Psychology, 1*, 177–182.

Renken, B., Egeland, B., Marvinney, D., Mangelsdorf, S., & Sroufe, L. A. (1989). Early childhood antecedents of aggression and passive-withdrawal in early elementary school. *Journal of Personality, 57*, 257–281.

Roberts, M. A. (1990). A behavioral observation method for differentiating hyperactive and aggressive boys. *Journal of Abnormal Child Psychology, 18*(2), 131–142.

Robin, A. L., & Foster, S. L. (1989). *Negotiating parent-adolescent conflict*. New York: Guilford.

Robins, L. N. (1966). *Deviant children grow up: A sociological and psychiatric study of sociopathic personality*. Baltimore: Williams & Wilkens.

Robins, L. N., Helzer, J. E., Weissman, M. M., Orvaschel, H., Gruenberg, E., Burke, J. D., & Regier, D. A. (1984). Lifetime prevalence of specific psychiatric disorders in three sites. *Archives of General Psychiatry, 41*, 949–957.

Robins, L. N., & Przybeck, T. R. (1985). Age of onset of drug use as a factor in drug and other disorders. In C. L. Jones & R. J. Battjes (Eds.), *Etiology of drug abuse: Implications for prevention* (Research Monograph No. 56, pp. 178–193). Rockville, MD: National Institute on Drug Abuse.

Roff, M. (1961). Childhood social interactions and young adult bad conduct. *Journal of Abnormal Psychology, 63*, 33–337.

Rogoff, B., & Wertsch, J. V. (Eds.). (1984). Children's learning in the "zone of proximal development." In W. Damon (Series Ed.), *New directions for child development* (No. 23). San Francisco: Jossey-Bass.

Rosenzweig, M. R. (1984). Experience, memory, and the brain. *American Psychologist, 39*, 365–376.

Rothbart, M. K., & Derryberry, D. (1981). Development of individual differences in temperament. In M. E. Lamb & A. L. Brown (Eds.), *Advances in developmental psychology* (Vol. 1, pp. 37–86). Hillsdale, NJ: Erlbaum.

Rubin, K. H., Bream, L. A., & Rose-Krasnor, L. (1991). Social problem solving and aggression in childhood. In D. J. Pepler & K. H. Rubin (Eds.), *The development and treatment of childhood aggression* (pp. 219–245). Hillsdale, NJ: Erlbaum.

Rutter, M. (1978). Family, area, and school influences in the genesis of conduct disorders. In L. A. Hersov, M. Berger, & D. Schaffer (Eds.), *Aggression and antisocial behavior in childhood and adolescence* (pp. 95–114). New York: Pergamon.

Rutter, M. (1979). Protective factors in children's responses to stress and disadvantage. In K. W. Kent & E. J. Rolf (Eds.), *Primary prevention of psychopathology: Vol. III. Social competence in children* (pp. 117–131). Biddeford, ME: University of New England.

Rutter, M. (1980). *Changing youth in a changing society*. Cambridge, MA: Harvard University Press.

Rutter, M. (1981). The city and the child. *American Journal of Orthopsychiatry, 51*, 610–625.

Rutter, M. (1983). Stress, coping, and development: Some issues and some questions. In N. Garmezy & M. Rutter (Eds.), Stress, coping, and development in children (pp. 1–44). New York: McGraw-Hill.

Rutter, M. (1989). Pathways from childhood to adult life. *Journal of Child Psychology and Psychiatry, 30*, 23–51.

Rutter, M., MacDonald, H., LeCouteur, A., Harrington, R., Bolton, P., & Bailey, A. (1990). Genetic factors in child psychiatric disorders-II. *Empirical Findings, 31*, 39–48.

Rutter, M., Maughan, B., Mortimore, P., & Ouston, J. (1979). *Fifteen thousand hours: Secondary schools and their effects on children*. Cambridge, MA: Harvard University Press.

Sameroff, A. J. (1981). Development and the dialectic: The need for a systems approach. In W. A. Collins (Ed.), *Minnesota Symposium on Child Psychology* (Vol. 15, pp. 83–103). Hillsdale, NJ: Erlbaum.

Sampson, R. J. (1994). Urban poverty and the family context of delinquency: A new look at structure and process in a classic study. *Child Development, 65*, 523–540.

Sampson, R. J., & Laub, J. H. (1990). Crime and deviance over the life course: A salience of adult social bonds. *American Sociological Review, 55*, 609–627.

Sandler, I. N., & Block, M. (1979). Life stress and maladaption of children. *American Journal of Community Psychology, 7*, 425–440.

Scarr, S. (1985). Constructing psychology: Making facts and fables for our times. *American Psychologist, 40*, 499–512.

Scarr, S., & McCartney, K. (1983). How people make their own environments: A theory of genotype to environment effects. *Child Development, 54*, 424–435.

Schachar, R., Rutter, M., & Smith, A. (1981). The characteristics of situationally and pervasively hyperactive children: Implications for syndrome definition. *Journal of Child Psychology and Psychiatry, 22*, 375–392.

Schlegel, A., & Barry, H. (1991). *Adolescents: An anthropological inquiry*. New York: Free Press.

Schonfeld, I. S., Shaffer, D., O'Connor, P., & Portnoy, S. (1988). Conduct disorder and cognitive functioning: Testing three causal hypotheses. *Child Development, 59*, 993–1007.

Serbin, L. A., Moskowitz, D. S., Schwarzman, A. E., & Ledingham, J. E. (1991). In D. J. Pepler & K. H. Rubin (Eds.), *The development and treatment of childhood aggression,* (pp. 55–70). Hillsdale, NJ: Erlbaum.

Shapiro, S. K., Quay, H. C., Hogan, A. E., & Schwartz, K. P. (1988). Response preservation and delayed responding in undersocialized aggressive conduct disorder. *Journal of Abnormal Psychology, 97,* 371–373.

Shinn, M. R., Ramsey, E., Walker, H. M., Stieber, S., & O'Neill, R. E. (1987). Antisocial behavior in school settings: Initial differences in an at risk and normal population. *The Journal of Special Education, 21,* 69–84.

Siman, M. L. (1977). Application of a new model of peer group influence to naturally existing adolescent friendship groups. *Child Development, 48,* 270–274.

Simcha-Fagan, O., Langner, T. S., Gersten, J. C., & Eisenberg, J. G. (1975). *Violent and antisocial behavior: A longitudinal study of urban youth.* Unpublished interim report. NY: Columbia University, School of Public Health, Division of Epidemiology.

Simcha-Fagan, O., & Schwartz, J. E. (1986). Neighborhood and delinquency: An assessment of contextual effects. *Criminology, 24,* 667–700.

Simmons, R. G., Burgeson, R., & Reef, M. J. (1988). Cumulative change at entry to adolescence. In M. R. Gunnar & W. A. Collins (Eds.), *Minnesota Symposium on Child Psychology: Vol. 21. Development during the transition to adolescence* (pp. 123–150). Hillsdale, NJ: Erlbaum.

Slaby, R. G., & Guerra, N. G. (1988). Cognitive mediators of aggression in adolescent offenders: 1. Assessment. *Developmental Psychology, 24,* 580–588.

Slocum, W. I., & Stone, C. I. (1965). Family culture patterns and delinquent-type behavior. *Marriage and Family Living, 25,* 202–208.

Smith, G. M., & Fogg, C. P. (1979). Psychological antecedents of teenage drug use. *Research in Community Mental Health, 1,* 87–102.

Smith, R. E., Ptacek, J. T., & Smoll, F. L. (1992). Sensation seeking, stress, and adolescent injuries: A test of stress-buffering, risk-taking, and coping skills hypotheses. *Journal of Personality and Social Psychology, 62(6),* 1016–1024.

Snyder, J. (1991). Discipline as a mediator of the impact of maternal stress and mood on child conduct problems. *Development and Psychopathology, 3,* 263–276.

Snyder, J., Dishion, T. J., & Patterson, G. R. (1986). Determinants and consequences of associating with deviant peers. *Journal of Early Adolescence, 6,* 29–43.

Spence, S. H., & Marzillier, J. S. (1981). Social skills training with adolescent male offenders: II. Short-term, long-term, and generalized effects. *Behavior Research and Therapy, 19,* 349–368.

Sroufe, L. A., & Fleeson, J. (1988). The coherence of family relationships. In R. A. Hinde & J. Stevenson-Hinde (Eds.), *Relationships within families* (pp. 27–47). Oxford, England: Clarendon Press.

Steinberg, L., & Silverberg, S. B. (1986). The vicissitudes of autonomy in early adolescence. *Child Development, 57,* 841–851.

Stewart, M. A., DeBlos, C. S., & Cummings, C. (1979). Psychiatric disorder in the parents of hyperactive boys and those with conduct disorder. *Journal of Child Psychology and Psychiatry, 21,* 283–292.

Stoolmiller, M. S. (1990). *Parent supervision, child unsupervised wandering, and child antisocial behavior: A latent growth curve analysis.* Unpublished doctoral dissertation, University of Oregon, Eugene.

Tait, C. D., & Hodges, E. F. (1972). Follow-up study of Glueck table applied to a school population of problem boys and girls between the ages of five and fourteen. In S. Glueck & E. Glueck (Eds.), *Identification of predelinquents.* New York: Intercontinental Medical Books.

Tieger, T. (1980). On the biological basis of sex differences in aggression. *Child Development, 51,* 943–963.

Trachenberg, S., & Viken, R. J. (1994). Aggressive boys in the classroom: Biased attributions or shared perceptions? *Child Development, 65,* 829–835.

Tremblay, R. E. (1991). Aggression, prosocial behavior, and gender: Three magic words but no magic wand. In D. J. Pepler & K. H. Rubin (Eds.), *The development and treatment of childhood aggression* (pp. 71–78). Hillsdale, NJ: Erlbaum.

Trevett, N. B. (1972). Identifying delinquency-prone children. In S. Glueck & E. Glueck (Eds.), *Identification of predelinquents.* New York: Intercontinental Medical Books.

Tudge, J. R. H. (1992). Processes and consequences of peer collaboration: A Vygotskian analysis. *Child Development, 63,* 1364–1379.

U.S. Bureau of the Census. (1991). Washington, DC: U.S. Government Printing Office.

van Ijzendoorn, M. H., Goldberg, S., Kroonenberg, P. M., & Frenkel, O. J. (1992). The relative effects of maternal and child problems on the quality of attachment: A meta-analysis of attachment in clinical problems. *Child Development, 63,* 840–858.

Voss, H. T. (1963). The predictive efficiency of the Glueck Social Prediction Table. *Journal of Criminal Law and Criminology, 54,* 421–430.

Vuchinich, S., Bank, L., & Patterson, G. R. (1992). Parenting peers and the stability of antisocial behavior in preadolescent males. *Developmental Psychology, 28,* 510–521.

Vygotsky, L. S. (1978). *The mind in society: The development of higher psychological processes.* Cambridge, MA: Harvard University Press.

Waas, G. A. (1988). Social attributional biases of peer rejected and aggressive children. *Child Development, 59,* 969–975.

Waas, G. A., & French, D. C. (1989). Children's social problem solving: Comparison of the Open Middle Interview and the Children's Assertive Behavior Scale. *Behavioral Assessment, 11,* 219–230.

Wadsworth, M. E. J. (1979). *Roots of delinquency: Infancy, adolescence, and crime.* Oxford, England: Robertson.

Wahler, R. G., & Sansbury, L. E. (1990). The monitoring skills of troubled mothers: Their problems in defining child deviance. *Journal of Abnormal Child Psychology, 18,* 577–589.

Walker, J. L., Lahey, B. B., Hynd, G. W., & Frame, C. L. (1987). Comparison of specific patterns of antisocial behavior in children with conduct disorder with and without coexisting hyperactivity. *Journal of Consulting and Clinical Psychology, 55,* 910–913.

Walker, H. M., Shinn, M. R., O'Neill, R. E., & Ramsey, E. (1987). A longitudinal assessment of the development of antisocial behavior in boys: Rationale, methodology, and first year results. *Remedial and Special Education, 8,* 7–16.

Wallerstein, J. S., & Kelly, J. B. (1980). *Surviving the breakup: How children and parents cope with divorce.* New York: Basic Books.

Waters, E., Posada, G., Crowell, J., & Lay, K. (1993). Is attachment theory ready to contribute to our understanding of disruptive behavior problems? *Development and Psychopathology, 5,* 215–224.

Webster-Stratton, C. (1990). Long-term follow-up of families with young conduct problem children: From preschool to grade school. *Journal of Clinical Child Psychology, 19,* 144–149.

Webster-Stratton, C., Kolpacoff, M., & Hollingsworth, T. (1988). Self-administered videotape therapy for families with conduct problem children: Comparison with two cost-effective treatments and a control group. *Journal of Consulting and Clinical Psychology, 56,* 558–566.

Wehlage, G. C., & Rutter, R. A. (1986). Dropping out: How much do schools contribute to the problem? *Teachers College Record, 87,* 374–392.

Weissberg, R. P., Gesten, E. L., Rapkin, B. D., Cowen, E. L., Davidson, E., Flores de Apodaca, R., & McKim, B. J. (1981). Evaluation of a social problem-solving training program for suburban and inner city third grade children. *Journal of Consulting and Clinical Psychology, 49,* 251–261.

Werner, E. E., & Smith, R. S. (1977). *Kauai's children come of age.* Honolulu: University Press of Hawaii.

Werner, E. E., & Smith, R. S. (1982). *Vulnerable but invincible: A longitudinal study of resilient children and youth.* New York: McGraw-Hill.

Werry, J. S. (1988). The differential diagnosis of ADD and conduct disorder. In J. Swanson & L. Bloomingdale (Eds.), Attention deficit disorder. *Journal of Child Psychology and Psychiatry Monographs* (IV). New York: Pergamon.

Werry, J. S., Reeves, J. C., & Elkind, G. S. (1987). Attention deficit, conduct, oppositional, and anxiety disorders in children: I. A review of research on differentiating characteristics. *Journal of the American Academy of Child and Adolescent Psychiatry, 26,* 133–143.

West, D. J., & Farrington, D. P. (1973). *Who becomes delinquent?* New York: Crane, Russak.

West, D. J., & Farrington, D. P. (1977). *The delinquent way of life.* New York: Crane, Russak.

Whiting, B. B. (1980). Culture and social behavior: A model for the development of social behavior. *Ethos, 8,* 95–116.

Whiting, B. B., & Whiting, J. W. M. (1975). *Children of six cultures: A psychocultural analysis.* Cambridge, MA: Harvard University Press.

Widom, C. S. (1989, June). *Avoidance of criminality in abused/neglected children.* Paper presented at the meeting of the Life History Research Society, Montreal, Canada.

William T. Grant Foundation. (1988, November). *The forgotten half: Pathways to success for America's youth and young families* (Final Report). Washington, DC: Author.

Wilson, H. (1980). Parental supervision: A neglected aspect of delinquency. *British Journal of Criminology, 20,* 203–235.

Wilson, W. J. (1987). *The truly disadvantaged: The inner city, the underclass, and public policy.* Chicago: University of Chicago Press.

Wolfgang, M. E., Figlio, R., & Sellin, T. (1982). *Delinquency in a birth cohort.* Chicago: University of Chicago Press.

Zabin, L. S., & Hayward, S. C. (1993). *Adolescent sexual behavior and childbearing.* Newbury Park, CA: Sage.

Zaidi, L. Y., Knutson, J. F., & Mehm, J. G. (1989). Transgenerational patterns of abusive parenting: Analog and clinical tests. *Aggressive Behavior, 15,* 137–152.

Zoccolillo, M. (1993). Gender and the development of conduct disorder. *Development and Psychopathology, 5,* 65–78.

Zuckerman, M. (1979). *Sensation seeking.* Hillsdale, NJ: Erlbaum.

CHAPTER 13

The Continuity of Maladaptive Behavior: From Description to Understanding in the Study of Antisocial Behavior

AVSHALOM CASPI and TERRIE E. MOFFITT

There is a widespread assumption in modern social science that social continuity needs no explanation. Supposedly it is not problematical. Change is what requires explanation . . . The assumption of inertia, that . . . continuity [does] not require explanation, obliterates the fact that [continuity has] to be created anew in each generation, often with great pain and suffering.

—BARRINGTON MOORE, 1966

THE PROBLEM: CONTINUITIES IN ANTISOCIAL BEHAVIOR ACROSS THE LIFE COURSE

The continuity of maladaptive behavior especially poses a challenge to psychological theory. If behavior is largely sustained by its consequences, then adaptive behaviors should show continuity almost by definition. Indeed, the empirical observation that resilient, adaptable children grow into resilient, adaptable adults seems almost tautological. But maladaptive behaviors also show long-term continuities, and it is here that the need for a nontrivial explanation becomes more apparent. Why should maladaptive behaviors persist? What are the processes that sustain them across time and circumstance? We examine these questions by focusing on continuities in antisocial behavior.

Individual differences in antisocial behavior are very stable across the life course (Olweus, 1979). For example, children

with disorders in the preschool years continue to show disorders in late childhood (Richman, Stevenson, & Graham, 1982); disorders of conduct in late childhood are associated with a host of social, emotional, and relational difficulties in adolescence and young adulthood (Kazdin, 1987; Loeber & Dishion, 1983); a history of antisocial behavior in childhood and adolescence is also linked with criminal behavior later in life (Farrington & West, 1990; McCord, 1983b; Pulkkinen, 1982; Magnusson, 1988); and although most prospective studies have not yet traced their subjects beyond middle adulthood, we know that some individuals retain their antisocial tendencies into old age (Harpur & Hare, 1994). These robust continuities have been revealed over the past 50 years, in different nations, and with multiple methods of assessment; in Canada, England, Finland, New Zealand, Sweden, and the United States, data from teacher ratings, parent reports, and peer nominations of aggressive behavior have been found to predict important outcomes later in life.

In a summary of results from her studies of four male cohorts, Robins drew these five conclusions:

(1) adult antisocial behaviour virtually *requires* childhood antisocial behaviour; (2) most antisocial children do *not* become antisocial adults; (3) the variety of antisocial behaviour in childhood is a better predictor of adult antisocial behaviour than is any particular behaviour; (4) adult antisocial behaviour is better predicted by childhood *behaviour* than by family background or social class of rearing; (5) social class makes little contribution to the prediction of serious adult antisocial behaviour. (1978, p. 611)

Since then, we have learned the answers to several other questions.

Several components of this dual theory of antisocial behavior have been excluded from this chapter because they are beyond its scope. Other articles address the following topics in greater detail: peer relationships between the two hypothetical subtypes, why don't all adolescents commit delinquent acts, gender and race differences in antisocial behavior, historical changes in juvenile crime, and implications for the diagnosis of childhood behavioral disorders (e.g., Moffitt, 1993).

This work was supported by U.S. Public Health Service grants from the Personality and Social Processes Research Branch (MH-49414 to A. Caspi) and the Antisocial and Violent Behavior Research Branch (MH-45070 and MH-45548 to T. Moffitt) of the National Institute of Mental Health, and by the William T. Grant Foundation.

Are there individual differences in the stability of antisocial behavior? The rules of thumb asserted by Robins (1978) seem to simultaneously assert and deny the life-course stability of antisocial behavior: "Adult antisocial behaviour virtually *requires* childhood antisocial behaviour [yet] most antisocial children do *not* become antisocial adults." In fact, research has shown that antisocial behavior is remarkably stable across time and circumstance for some persons, but decidedly unstable for most other people.

Extremity of antisocial behavior is closely linked to its stability. In their study of 10,000 men, Wolfgang, Figlio, and Sellin (1972) found that 6% of offenders accounted for more than half the crimes committed by the sample; relative to other offenders, these high-rate offenders began their criminal careers earlier, and continued them for a longer time span. In his analysis of a sample of third-grade boys, Patterson (1982) found that the most aggressive 5% of the boys constituted the most persistent group as well; 38.5% of them ranked above the 95th percentile on aggression 10 years later, and 100% of them were still above the median. Similarly, Loeber (1982) has shown that stability of antisocial behavior across time is linked with stability across situations, and that both forms of stability are characteristic of a relatively small group of persons with extremely antisocial behavior.

Thus, in defiance of "regression to the mean," extremely antisocial persons remain extreme on measures taken at later ages and in different situations. Among less extreme persons, however, temporary and situational manifestations of antisocial behavior may be quite common. This point is vividly illustrated in the Dunedin (New Zealand) Multidisciplinary Health and Development Study, a longitudinal investigation of a representative cohort born in 1972 and 1973. In this sample, Moffitt (1991) identified a group of boys whose antisocial behavior was above average in each of seven biennial assessments (ages 3, 5, 7, 9, 11, 13, and 15) and pervasive across ratings by three different reporting agents (parents, teachers, and self). These boys constituted 5.9% of the representative sample of 536 New Zealand boys. Another 67% of the boys were rated as highly antisocial as well, but at only one age or by only one reporter (Henry, Moffitt, Robins, Earls, & Silva, 1993). Much of the measured stability in the New Zealand sample could be attributed to the 5.9% of boys whose behavior was extreme and consistent. For example, when these few boys were excluded from calculations, the 8-year stability coefficient for teacher reports was reduced by nearly half, from .28 to .16. In sum, there appear to be noteworthy individual differences in the stability of antisocial behavior.

How early can we tell? For at least some persons, antisocial behavior is manifest very early in life and remains stable thereafter (Campbell, 1991). Two recent longitudinal studies have shown that preschool variables can predict later antisocial outcomes, in boys and girls. J. Block, J. H. Block, and Keyes (1988) found that a constellation of preschool personality characteristics encompassed by the concept of ego control (e.g., inability to delay gratification, rapid tempo) predicted drug use later in adolescence. In the aforementioned New Zealand birth cohort, we have identified a host of personal characteristics at age 3 (e.g., mothers' reports that their 3-year-olds were "difficult to manage"; observers' ratings of restless, impulsive, and emotionally labile behaviors) that could prospectively differentiate adolescents with antisocial

disorders from those adolescents with other disorders or no disorders (Caspi, Henry, McGee, Moffitt, & Silva, in press; White, Moffitt, Earls, Robins, & Silva, 1990).

How can we best achieve prediction and understanding. As noted at the outset, individual differences in antisocial behavior are very stable. The longitudinal studies we have cited point to two kinds of stability (Kagan, 1969). *Homotypic continuity* refers to the continuity of similar behaviors or phenotypic attributes over time. The concept of coherence enlarges the definition of stability to include *heterotypic continuity*—continuity of an inferred genotypic attribute presumed to underlie diverse phenotypic behaviors. As Kagan and Moss (1962) suggest, a specific behavior in childhood might not be predictive or phenotypically similar behavior later in adulthood but may still be associated with behaviors that are conceptually consistent with the earlier behavior. Such phenotypically disparate but conceptually related responses may be viewed as derivatives of earlier behavior (Livson & Peskin, 1980; Moss & Susman, 1980).

Examples of heterotypic continuities were reported by Ryder (1967) who found that childhood aggression, sociability, physical adventurousness, and nonconformity were related to adult sexual behavior. Another example of coherence is provided in a 22-year follow-up study of men and women who had been rated as aggressive by their peers in late childhood (Huesmann, Eron, Lefkowitz, & Walder, 1984). As adults, the men were likely to commit serious criminal acts, abuse their spouses, and drive while intoxicated; whereas the women were likely to punish their offspring severely. Other examples of personality coherence include the finding that the developmental antecedents of erratic work histories may be found in phenotypically dissimilar temperamental attributes in childhood (Caspi, Elder, & Bem, 1987). And in their hallmark study, West and Farrington (1977) observed that stealing, drinking, sexual promiscuity, reckless driving, and violence were linked across the life course. The implied genotypic continuities thus exist in what they refer to as the individual's "antisocial tendency."

It is important to emphasize that coherence and heterotypic continuity refer to a *conceptual* rather than a literal continuity among behaviors. Accordingly, the investigator who claims to have discovered coherence must necessarily have a theory—no matter how rudimentary or implicit—that specifies the genotype or provides the basis on which the diverse behaviors and attributes can be said to belong to the same equivalence class. In what sense is adult sexual behavior a derivative of childhood physical adventurousness? In what ways is driving while intoxicated the same thing as pushing and shoving other children?

As these examples illustrate, the "theories" behind claims of coherence often amount to little more than appeals to the reader's intuitions. Developmental prediction and developmental understanding are not the same thing (Magnusson, 1988). Indeed, with the notable exception of the psychoanalytic theory of psychosexual stages and their adult sequelae, most personality theories do not specify the theoretical links between personality variables at different developmental periods. It's a bit ironic. Although the psychoanalytic enterprise is often belittled for its "postdictive" powers, Freudians may claim that at least they understand. Longitudinal researchers, although increasingly precise in their predictions, have yet to understand the behavioral connections so efficiently unraveled by prospective designs.

In this chapter, we build on the accumulated longitudinal-predictive data in an effort to understand *how* and *for whom* continuity in antisocial behavior is possible. We address each of these questions in successive sections: (a) How is continuity possible and (b) for whom is continuity the dominant pattern?

HOW IS CONTINUITY POSSIBLE? MECHANISMS OF CONTINUITY AND CHANGE

There is an extensive database of research documenting and describing the continuity of antisocial behavior across the life course. Efforts to go beyond description to the more difficult task of explanation are, however, far less developed. Nevertheless, recent attempts to integrate genetic, environmental, and interactional processes of personality functioning appear quite promising.

Genetic Contributions to the Continuity of Antisocial Behavior

Genotypic differences exert a powerful effect on behavioral variation (Plomin, 1990). And to the extent that genetic factors influence individual differences in social behavior, it is possible—*but not necessary*—that genetic factors may also influence the stability of those individual differences across time and circumstance. The quantitative methods that have traditionally been employed by behavioral geneticists to estimate the genetic and environmental components of phenotypic variance in cross-sectional studies have now been extended to estimate the components of stability and change across time in longitudinal studies (Plomin, 1986; Plomin & Nesselroade, 1990; Rowe, 1987), and we are beginning to learn more about genetic contributions to the continuity of behavior.

As yet, no clear-cut evidence suggests whether or not genetic factors contribute to the continuity of antisocial behavior across the life span. However, three lines of research may shed some light on this problem:

1. If cross-sectional studies show positive heritability effects on antisocial behavior among adults, adolescents, and children, we may conclude that genes help to control the expression of antisocial behavior at different points in the life course.

2. Although antisocial *behavior* per se is not inherited, a variety of biological traits may underlie the heritability coefficients for antisocial behavior by predisposing persons to develop an antisocial phenotype. These traits may be scrutinized empirically to determine if any are stable across development and if the process by which they initiate antisocial behavior might also serve to maintain such behavior.

3. In combination, these two lines of research are merely suggestive. The critical test of a genetic effect on the continuity of antisocial behavior will be revealed in longitudinal studies that estimate genetic contributions to cross-age correlations.

Behavior-Genetic Studies of Antisocial Behavior

Behavior-Genetic Studies of Antisocial Adults. The genetic contribution to criminality has been most soundly studied by Mednick and his colleagues using the Danish Adoption Cohort Register, which contains information on all 14,427 official extrafamilial adoptions carried out in Denmark between 1924 and 1947 (Mednick, Gabrielli, & Hutchings, 1984, 1985; Mednick, Moffitt, Gabrielli, & Hutchings, 1986; Mednick, Moffitt, Pollock, Talovic, & Gabrielli, 1983). In the adoption method, the deviant outcomes of adopted children (separated early in life from their biological parents) are compared with the outcomes of their adoptive parents and their biological parents. Similarity in outcome between adoptees and biological parents implicates a genetic effect. In addition, with the application of cross-fostering analysis, the relative contributions to deviance from biological parents and rearing parents may be compared.

Using court convictions as an index of criminal involvement, Mednick and colleagues tested the hypothesis that registered criminality in the biological parents is associated with an increased risk of registered criminal behavior in the adoptees. Their results are summarized in Table 13.1. The lower right-hand cell shows that if neither the biological nor adoptive parents were criminal, 13.5% of their sons were criminal. Moreover, if the biological parents were not criminal, but the adoptive parents evidenced criminality, this figure only rose to 14.7%. In the lower left-hand cell of Table 13.1, note that 20.0% of the sons were criminal if the adoptive parents were *not* criminal and one of the biological parents *was* criminal. If at least one biological parent and at least one adoptive parent were criminal, the figure rose to 24.5%. It appears that sons who have never seen their criminal, biological parents have an elevated probability of becoming criminal. This suggests that some biological characteristic is transmitted from the criminal biological parent to the son, which increases the son's risk of obtaining a court conviction for a criminal law offense.

Contrary to some expectations, the genetic effect found in the Danish adoption study was highly significant for property crime but not for violent crimes. Similar results have been reported in a large Swedish adoption study (Bohman, Cloninger,

Table 13.1   Adoption Analysis: Percentage of Adoptive Sons Who Have Been Convicted of Criminal Law Offenses[a]

	Are Biological Parents Criminal?	
	Yes	No
Are Adoptive Parents Criminal?		
Yes	24.5	14.7
	(143)	(207)
No	20.0	13.5
	(1226)	(2492)

From "Genetic Factors in Criminal Behavior" by S. A. Mednick, T. E. Moffitt, W. F. Gabrielli, and B. Hutchings, in *Development of Antisocial and Prosocial Behavior: Research, Theories, and Issues* by D. Olweus, J. Block, and M. Radke-Yarrow, (Eds.), 1986, Orlando, FL: Academic Press. Copyright 1986 by Academic Press. Reprinted by permission.

[a]The numbers in parentheses are the total N's for each cell.

von Knorring, & Sigvardsson, 1982). Although this suggests that violent behavior may not be genetically influenced, this conclusion could be hasty. A different model of genetic transmission than the direct pattern typically examined (biological parent *crime* predicting adoptee *crime*) could operate in the case of violent behavior. Such may be the case if some heritable factors, other than or in addition to those associated with parental criminal behavior, predispose individuals toward very poor behavioral control. A predisposition to mental illness may be such a factor. Certain types of mental disorders, especially the psychoses, personality disorders, and substance abuse disorders, are characterized by behavioral dyscontrol and have been demonstrated to have significant heritable components (Bohman, Cloninger, Sigvardsson, & von Knorring, 1982; Bohman et al., 1984).

Moffitt (1987) used the Danish Adoption Cohort Register to examine the contribution of mental disorder in the adoptees' biolgical backgrounds to their recidivistic and violent criminal offending. Recidivistic nonviolent criminal behavior was found at a significantly elevated rate in adopted-away sons when mental disorder and criminal involvement were characteristic of the adoptees' biological families. A similar, but nonsignificant, elevation was found for rates of violence. The types of parental mental illness contributing most strongly to sons' later criminal involvement were drug abuse, alcohol abuse, and personality disorders. Confidence in the validity of these findings is supported by adoption research demonstrating associations between alcohol abuse and crime (Bohman et al., 1984) and between substance abuse, personality disorder, and psychopathy (Schulsinger, 1974).

Investigators affiliated with the Danish adoption study have systematically evaluated alternatives to a genetic account of their data. Bias from missing data, effects of the child's age at transfer to the adoptive home, potential labeling of the infants of criminals by the adoption agencies, historical effects associated with the Great Depression, and effects of selective placement do not account for the observed genetic effects (Mednick et al., 1984, 1985).

Adoption studies are compelling "naturalistic experiments." However, they fail to control one important source of environmental variation: perinatal events surrounding the biological mothers' pregnancy. Mothers who plan to release their infants for adoption may be poorly motivated to invest effort in prenatal care, and prenatal care may be poorer still if the mother is involved in an antisocial lifestyle. This circumstance might contribute to effects on offspring that, although biological in nature, are environmental rather than genetic in etiology. Some portion of the association between deviance among biological parents and their children that is observed in adoption studies may be attributable to teratogenic effects on the infant. However, another behavior-genetic research design, the twin study, is free from perinatal confounds. Twin studies have provided corroborative evidence for a genetic effect on adult crime.

The twin study compares monozygotic (MZ) twins, who are genetically identical, to same-sex dizygotic (DZ) twins, who have no more genes in common than other siblings (50% on average). This research design assumes that the effect of hereditary factors

is demonstrated if MZ twins have more similar outcomes (concordance for deviance) than DZ twins. Christiansen (1977), and more recently DiLalla and Gottesman (1989), have reviewed studies of criminal arrest or conviction in adult twin pairs. Several small studies report positive heritability coefficients for adult criminal behavior, but perhaps the best study was one of 712 MZ and 1,390 same-sexed DZ pairs (Christiansen, 1977). The concordance rates were .74 for MZ twins and .47 for DZ twins.

Two large twin studies point to the heritability of individual differences in aggressiveness among adults. Data from an English twin register suggest that approximately 50% of twin variance in self-reports of altruism, empathy, nurturance, aggressiveness, and assertiveness can be assigned to additive genetic influence (Rushton, Fulker, Neale, Nias, & Eysenck, 1987).

Data from the Minnesota twin studies provide similar estimates (Tellegen et al., 1988). The Multidimensional Personality Questionnaire (MPQ) was administered to 331 pairs of twins reared together and 71 pairs of twins reared apart. In Table 13.2, we have reproduced the intraclass correlations for the three MPQ higher-order factors. Research using the MPQ has shown that greater delinquent participation (whether measured through self-reports, informant-reports, or official records) is associated with a personality configuration characterized by high Negative Emotionality and low Constraint (Krueger et al., 1994). Individuals high on *Negative Emotionality* have a low threshold for the experience of negative emotions, such as fear, anxiety, and anger, and tend to break down under stress; individuals low on *Constraint* tend to reject conventional social norms, seek dangerous situations, and act in an impulsive manner (Tellegen, 1982).

The correlations in Table 13.2, and subsequent model-fitting efforts, point to substantial genetic contributions to variability on those personality traits known to be associated with antisocial behavior. Of special interest is the finding that the correlations between monozygotic twins reared apart are very similar to the correlations between monozygotic twins reared together. It is sometimes claimed that MZ twins are more alike because they are treated as more similar by their parents (Lytton, 1980). But the Minnesota research findings about identical twins reared apart suggest this is far from the sole contributing factor to twin similarity.

Table 13.2 **Intraclass Correlations for Four Kinship Groups: Evidence for the Heritability of Personality Dimensions Assessed by the Multidimensional Personality Questionnaire (MPQ)**

| Personality Dimension | Kinship Groups | | | |
| | MZ Twins Reared | | DZ Twins Reared | |
	Apart	Together	Apart	Together
Constraint	.57	.58	.04	.25
Negative emotionality	.61	.54	.29	.41
Positive emotionality	.34	.63	−.07	.18

From "Personality Similarity in Twins Reared Apart and Together" by A. Tellegen, D. T. Lykken, T. J. Bouchard, Jr., K. J. Wilcox, N. L. Segal, and S. Rich, 1988, *Journal of Personality and Social Psychology, 6,* pp. 1031–1039. Copyright 1988 by the American Psychological Association. Reprinted by permission.

Behavior-Genetic Studies of Antisocial Adolescents.
Whereas the studies just reviewed point to a genetic predisposition to adult crime, studies of juvenile delinquency yield a more complicated picture. The contrast between the adult and adolescent findings is illustrated in Figure 13.1. According to DiLalla and Gottesman (1989; see also Cloninger & Gottesman, 1987), the weighted concordance rates for adult criminality across the several studies they reviewed are 51% for MZ twins and 22% for DZ twins. In contrast, the weighted concordance rates for juvenile delinquency are 87% for MZ twins and 72% for DZ twins. Whereas the MZ and DZ rates in adulthood are sufficiently different to suggest a genetic component for criminality, the difference between the MZ and DZ rates for juvenile delinquency is relatively small and does not implicate a genetic predisposition.

DiLalla and Gottesman (1989) note that the base rate of illegal behavior in the teenage twins studied was much higher than the base rate in the adult twins, a discrepancy that is found in the general population as well. They suggest that the very high base rate for juvenile delinquency in the population may simply obscure differences in concordance rates between MZ and DZ twins.

> It may be that only a minority of adolescents are significantly predisposed to delinquency for genetic reasons, and this minority continues to be criminal in adulthood. This does not necessarily mean that there is no genetic component to delinquency. Delinquency may be a developmental phase for most adolescents, but the subset of adults who are genetically predisposed to commit criminal acts may also be predisposed to behave delinquently when they are adolescents . . . [T]hose individuals, who, indeed, have a genetic predisposition toward antisociality and who manifest it in adolescence are masked by the high proportion of other adolescents who are passing through a "delinquent phase." (pp. 342–348)

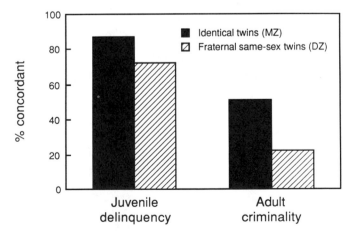

Figure 13.1   The heritability of crime: Weighted pairwise twin concordance rates for juvenile delinquency and adult criminality. From "Heterogeneity of Causes for Delinquency and Criminality: Lifespan Perspectives" by L. F. DiLalla and I. I. Gottesman, 1989, *Development and Psychopathology, 1,* pp. 339–349. Copyright 1989 by Cambridge University Press. Reprinted by permission of the authors.

It is also possible that many of the twin studies of juvenile delinquency are simply inadequate for detecting genetic effects, which are robust but small in adult studies. The pooled findings summarized by DiLalla and Gottesman (1989) are based on small numbers of twin pairs and the quality of the outcome measures from many of the early studies they review is apparently uncertain (Rutter et al., 1990).

In a recent study of 265 pairs of adolescent twins, Rowe (1983, 1986) did find that monozygotic twins were more alike than dizygotic twins in their self-reported delinquent behavior. The analyses established that the best fit to the twin data was a model including both genetic *and* shared environmental influences. Shared environmental effects refer to factors that are shared by members of a twin pair and that serve to make them similar to each other (e.g., social class, child-rearing practices). Rowe, however, has speculated that this shared-environment effect may not necessarily reflect criminogenic home environments as provided by parents of twins. Rather, the shared-environment effect may be the result of mutual influence within twin pairs. Twin pairs may commit crimes together and siblings may model delinquent behavior for one another (Rowe, 1983; Rowe, Rodgers, Meseck-Bushley, & St. John, 1989). Genetic factors and mutual influence may thus interact to produce delinquent behavior among members of the same family:

> Delinquent acts must be learned, and the key to this learning may be the availability of peer groups or, in this case, a twin sibling. However, for the social influence to be effective, the individual may have first to possess a disposition consisting of a combination of genetically influenced traits (e.g., intelligence, impulsivity, emotionality). If twins who cooperate in delinquency are also more genetically disposed to do so, then mutual sibling contact and the genetic factors are best regarded as interactive in the way they combine to produce delinquent behavior. (Rowe, 1983, p. 486)

Rowe's interpretation is consistent with the pooled twin results reported by DiLalla and Gottesman (1989). The high concordance rates for DZ twins (see Figure 13.1) suggest that the environment shared by siblings in their families of origin may exert an important influence on their antisocial behavior in adolescence.

Behavior-Genetic Studies of Antisocial Children.   Twin studies of aggressiveness earlier in life yield a much less consistent pattern of genetic influence (see Plomin, Nitz, & Rowe, 1990). But these studies have used small numbers of twin pairs and included diverse sets of measures. Some of the inconsistent results may be attributable to differences in measurement procedures. For example, Ghodsian-Carpey and Baker (1987) found that heritability coefficients for aggressive behavior in the same twin sample ranged from .24 to .94, depending on the measure of aggression that was analyzed. Direct comparisons between behavior-genetic findings from studies of children and older samples are also hampered by lack of comparability in the outcome measures used at different ages. Whereas adult and adolescent studies typically rely on official police records or self-report questionnaires, studies of children measure aggressive interactions or undercontrolled behaviors through the observations of mothers and teachers.

Some twin studies have pointed to the heritability of childhood temperamental attributes (e.g., anger, fear, activity) that may be associated with later aggression (Buss & Plomin, 1984). Other studies have implicated a genetic component in hyperactivity (see Rutter et al., 1990). The combination of aggressiveness and hyperactivity in childhood is known to be one of the best predictors of illegal behaviors that persist from adolescence into adulthood (Farrington, Loeber, & Van Kammen, 1990; Moffitt, 1990a). Thus, there appears to be some indication that genetic factors may influence some childhood characteristics that are linked with later crime, but clearly missing is a well-designed behavior-genetic study of childhood conduct disorder.

In summary, adoption and twin studies provide strong support for a detectable genetic contribution to crime and antisocial behavior during adulthood. The evidence from studies of adolescents and children is more equivocal, suggesting a genetic contribution to some forms of antisocial behavior. Collectively, these various studies suggest that genetic factors may influence the continuity of antisocial personality across the life course; however, they still do not address the mechanisms by which they do so. Research must focus on another level of analysis before it can be practically useful to us in developing theories and deriving hypotheses about the factors that predispose persons to antisocial behavior across the life course.

Mechanisms: What Is Inherited in Antisocial Behavior?

Genes exert their influence through heritable biological structures and processes. There have been numerous efforts to identify some of the biological factors involved in aggression in animals as well as in antisocial behavior in humans. The best researched candidates include sex-linked hormones such as testosterone, neurotransmitter substances such as serotonin, autonomic nervous system responsiveness to punishing stimuli, and electroencephalographic measures of subnormal brain arousal. Several reviews and edited volumes describe this large literature (Fishbein, 1990; Mednick, Moffitt, & Stack, 1987; Mednick & Volavka, 1980; Moffitt & Mednick, 1988; Raine, 1993). In addition, more mundane factors that are known to be partially heritable, such as physical size and strength, alcoholism, and low intelligence, have been advanced as explanations for the expression of antisocial behavior across generations.

Which of the aforementioned factors may best help to account for the *continuity* of antisocial behavior across the life course? Surprisingly, many of preceding variables are not competitive candidates. An inherited tendency to become disinhibited under the influence of alcohol may account for some adult violence, but its shortcomings as an explanation for preschool aggression are obvious. Neurotransmitter substances and hormones are known to fluctuate widely across age, and often their peaks and valleys do not coincide with changes in the prevalence of antisocial behavior. Relatively little is known about the heritability of psychophysiological and electroencephalographic measures or their stability from childhood to adulthood. Susman (1993) has noted that little is yet known about the longitudinal stability of most psychobiological measures.

Perhaps the best choice for our study of continuity is compromised cognitive ability. This variable offers several advantages as a candidate: The partial heritability of cognitive abilities is one of the most well-documented findings in the behavioral sciences (Plomin, 1988; 1990); the evidence for stability of intellective functions from childhood to adulthood is similarly convincing (Wohlwill, 1980); and the link between cognitive impairment and antisocial behavior has been repeatedly documented in studies of children's aggression, adolescents' delinquency, and adults' criminal conviction (e.g., Hirschi & Hindelang, 1977; Lynam, Moffitt, & Stouthamer-Loeber, 1993; Moffitt, Gabrielli, & Mednick, 1981). In addition, at least one longitudinal study has shown that neuropsychological deficits predict specifically the trajectory of delinquency that is both serious and stable from age 13 to 18 (Moffitt, Lynam, & Silva, 1994). We shall thus detail the possible contribution of intellectual ability to continuities in antisocial behavior.

In comprehensive reviews of research on the neuropsychology of juvenile delinquency, Moffitt (1990b; 1993; Moffitt & Henry, 1991) has suggested that two areas of mental function are especially pertinent to the question of antisocial behavior. Findings about (a) verbal functions and (b) executive functions provide especially intriguing theoretical implications for understanding sources of continuity in antisocial behavior.

Verbal Functions and Antisocial Behavior. On average, delinquents are less cognitively adept than their more law-abiding peers. One of the most robust findings in criminology is an IQ deficit of one-half standard deviation (about eight IQ points) for delinquents (e.g., Hirschi & Hindelang, 1977; Wilson & Herrnstein, 1985). This relation holds when IQ is assessed prospectively before the development of delinquency (Moffitt et al., 1981; West & Farrington, 1973). Moreover, IQ and delinquency share variance that is independent of social class (Moffitt et al., 1981; Reiss & Rhodes, 1961; Wolfgang et al., 1972; Lynam et al., 1993), of race (Short & Strodtbeck, 1965; Wolfgang et al., 1972), and of detection by police (Moffitt & Silva, 1988a). Delinquent siblings have been shown to have lower IQs than nondelinquent siblings within the same families (Healy & Bronner, 1936; Shulman, 1929). Just *why* low IQ predicts the development of antisocial behavior patterns remains unexplained, however.

Neuropsychologists know that specific distinct patterns of impaired cognitive functions can underlie an observed general IQ deficit. Individuals with identical omnibus IQ scores may have very different patterns of mental strengths and weaknesses because IQ can be broken down into a set of mental abilities that are hypothetically distinguishable (although not wholly orthogonal). A general low IQ score might result from specific and relatively isolated problems such as impaired social judgment, difficulty with language processing, poor auditory memory, or visual-motor integration failures (Lezak, 1988). Each deficit type could conceivably be more differentially predictive of antisocial behavior than the overall IQ, but each would contribute to the development of antisocial behavior through different theoretical causal chains. Elucidation of a possible delinquency-specific pattern of neuropsychological deficit has helped to clarify the relation between delinquency and cognitive test performance.

Since Wechsler's (1944) initial remarks about the diagnostic utility of a discrepancy between Performance and Verbal IQ scores, many studies have been published on the "PIQ > VIQ" sign in delinquency. The Verbal IQ is a composite score taken from tests of general factual knowledge, abstract reasoning, mental arithmetic, vocabulary, social comprehension and judgment, and immediate auditory memory. The Performance IQ is calculated from nonverbal tests of attention to detail, sequential reasoning, manual design construction, visual puzzle solving, symbolic encoding and decoding, and maze completion. The subtests used to calculate the VIQ score are administered orally, require an oral response, and are solved using language-based processing skills; the subtests used to calculate the PIQ are administered and solved in the visuo-spatial mode without the necessary use of language, and they require a manual, not an oral, response. PIQ and VIQ are probably the most well-researched and reliable measures used by psychologists. Prentice and Kelly (1963) reviewed 24 positive reports of the PIQ > VIQ sign in delinquents, West and Farrington (1973) reviewed still more, and the hypothesis continues to find empirical support (see Lynam et al., 1993).

The PIQ > VIQ effect suggests that delinquents may suffer from a specific deficit in language manipulation. This verbal deficit is pervasive, affecting receptive listening and reading, problem solving, expressive speech and writing, and memory for verbal material. Because language functions are subserved by the left cerebral hemisphere of the brain in almost all individuals (Benson & Zaidel, 1985), the PIQ > VIQ findings have also been interpreted as evidence for brain dysfunction in the etiology of antisocial behavior.

Although objections have been raised regarding the possible confounding of social disadvantage with low VIQ scores, several studies suggest that the PIQ > VIQ effect is too robust to be wholly discounted by this confounding factor. The verbal deficit effect has been found in studies where social class and family adversity effects, as well as race, are controlled (Denno, 1990; Moffitt & Silva, 1988b; Sobotowicz, Evans, & Laughlin, 1987). Furthermore, Moffitt (1990a) has reported an interaction effect between family adversity and verbal neuropsychological ability for self-reported aggressive delinquent acts (acts involving aggressive confrontation with a victim or adversary) in a prospective study of an unselected birth cohort of 1,037 children. The 75 children characterized by *both* low verbal scores and adverse family environments earned a mean aggression score more than four times greater than that of children with either low verbal ability, or an adverse home environment. This interaction suggests that neuropsychological deficit might make children more vulnerable to the effects of a criminogenic environment. Conversely, it appeared that strong verbal neuropsychological capacity might serve as a protector against development of aggressive behavior among children reared in even the most adverse family environments.

Several theorists have addressed the *processes* by which verbal neuropsychological deficits might contribute to children's antisocial behavior. A. R. Luria (1961; Luria & Homskaya, 1964) outlined a comprehensive theory of the importance of speech for the self-control of behavior. Luria ties the very young child's capacity for following verbal instructions to anatomic maturational development of the neuronal structures of the frontal lobes and left hemisphere of the brain. He also outlines

the developmental process through which external parental verbal instructions and reinforcements are converted to internal, verbally based self-control mechanisms. According to Luria, normal auditory verbal memory and verbal abstract reasoning are essential abilities in the development of self-control, and they influence socialization beginning with the earliest parent-child interactions. Speech-based mechanisms of self-control range from virtually automatic motor programming or inhibiting of simple childhood behaviors (e.g., "No!") to "thinking things through" before embarking on a course of complex adult behavior such as a robbery. Luria did not discuss antisocial behavior in his writings, but the notion that deficient verbal mediation characterizes children with aggressive behavior problems has received some empirical support (Camp, 1977; Kopp, 1982).

Other writers have also commented on the influence of childhood verbal deficits on the development of antisocial behavior. J. Q. Wilson and Herrnstein (1985) suggest that low verbal intelligence contributes to a present-oriented cognitive style, which in turn, fosters irresponsible and exploitative behavior. Humans use language as the medium for abstract reasoning; we keep things that are "out of sight" from also becoming "out of mind" by mentally representing them with words. Language is thus an essential ingredient in prosocial processes such as delaying gratification, anticipating consequences, and linking delayed punishments with earlier transgressions.

Eysenck (1977), in his autonomic conditioning theory of adult antisocial personality disorder, stated that stimulus generalization should be enhanced through parents' verbal labeling of misbehaviors as "naughty," "bad," or "wicked." But children with verbal-skill deficits might not profit from the labeling of a class of behaviors as punishment-attracting; they may have to learn by trial and error. Verbally impaired children should thus experience more frequent punishment events than verbally adept children, but with proportionately less result in curbing their problem behaviors. Consistent with Eysenck's prediction, Kaler and Kopp (1990) have demonstrated that much of toddler noncompliance can be explained by poor verbal comprehension.

Savitsky and Czyzewski (1978) speculate that a deficit in verbal skills may preclude delinquents' ability to label their perceptions of the emotions expressed by others (victims or adversaries). Such deficits might also limit delinquents' response options in threatening or ambiguous social situations and predispose them to physical reactions rather than verbal ones. Children who feel uncomfortable or inept with verbal communication may be more likely to strike out than to attempt to talk their way out of an altercation.

Tarter and his colleagues (Tarter, Hegedus, Winsten, & Alterman, 1984; Tarter, Hegedus, Alterman, & Katz-Garris, 1983) mention the intriguing notion that children with poor communication skills may elicit less positive interaction and more physical punishment from parents, especially if the family is stressed. Consistent with Tarter's prediction, McDermott and Rourke (cited in Rourke & Fiske, 1981) found fathers to be more negative, rejecting, and derogatory with their sons who had language deficits than with those boys' more verbal brothers. Following from Tarter's speculation, poor verbal abilities may hinder the development of healthy parent-child attachment bonds that might forestall and deter later delinquency.

The theories introduced in the previous paragraphs have emphasized neuropsychological effects on early parent-child interactions. Other theorists point to the limits placed on school achievement by verbal impairment (Lynam et al., 1993). Hirschi's (1969) version of social control theory predicts that differences in intellectual capacity will have implications for how children experience school, a crucial agency in the transfer of childrens' respect and obedience from parent's rules to society's laws. Cognitively able children are likely to receive rewards at school and to develop attachments to this social institution. Less able children may experience school as stressful and hence fail to form the social bonds that are thought to prevent illegal behavior. Regardless of attachment bonds, cognitive deficits interfere with youngsters' mastery of reading, writing, and arithmetic. Young adults who cannot read will find few alternatives to crime in the job market. Thus, in a follow-up study of men who had been retarded readers as children, Maughan, Gray, and Rutter (1985) reported that poor reading was linked with low pay, unskilled jobs, and unemployment, as well as with a record of arrest by police.

Although these diverse formulations make somewhat different predictions, they share the assumption that the child's complement of neuropsychological strengths and weaknesses is present very early in life, and its influence on personality and behavioral development begins to unfold with the child's earliest social interactions. Antisocial behavior patterns later in life may thus reflect early individual differences that are perpetuated or exacerbated by interactions with the social environment, with adults and peers, at home and in school. We will explore these specific interactional processes in a later section.

Executive Functions and Antisocial Behavior.   Antisocial behavior may also be associated with deficiencies in the brain's self-control functions. These mental functions are commonly referred to as "executive" functions, and they include sustaining attention and concentration, abstract reasoning and concept formation, goal formulation, anticipation and planning, programming and initiating purposive sequences of behavior, self-monitoring and self-awareness, and inhibition of unsuccessful, inappropriate, or impulsive behaviors with adaptive shifting to alternative behaviors. Experimental research with animals whose brains have been lesioned, as well as large numbers of clinical case studies of brain-damaged humans, have now fairly clearly established that these various executive functions are primarily subserved by the frontal lobes of the brain and by connective pathways between the frontal lobes and other brain systems (Stuss & Benson, 1986).

According to neuropsychological theory, executive dysfunctions should interfere with children's ability to control their own behavior, producing inattentive, impulsive children who are handicapped in considering the future implications of their acts. Such children have difficulty understanding the negative impact of their behavior on others, fail to hold in mind abstract ideas of ethical values and future rewards, and fail to inhibit inappropriate behavior or adapt their behavior to changing social circumstances. Executive deficits may thus give rise to early childhood behavior problems that in turn set the stage for emerging delinquent behavior as a child grows physically older, although not necessarily more cognitively mature.

Several studies that have applied batteries of formal tests of executive functions to delinquent subjects have now shown that the test scores can discriminate between delinquents and nondelinquents (Moffitt, 1990b). An important caveat in evaluating these studies is the limited measurement accuracy of tests of executive functions. Interpretation of these measures is complicated by the fact that they do not intercorrelate strongly (Cox & Evans, 1987; Hare, 1984), suggesting that executive function is not a unitary construct. The measures may also be less anatomically specific to the workings of the frontal lobes of the brain in the general population than has been implied by discriminative validity studies using brain-damaged patient samples (Robinson, Heaton, Lehman, & Stilson, 1980). Despite these cautions, there appear to be enough reports of positive results to warrant further research and theorizing in this area. An especially fertile area for investigation is the connection between deficits in self-control of attention and antisocial behavior.

There is good electrophysiological and neurochemical evidence pointing to frontal lobe mediation of attentional processes (Stamm & Kreder, 1979). In addition, research using positron-emission tomography (PET scan) to examine cerebral blood flow patterns, has found inadequate blood flow in the white matter tissues that connect the frontal lobes to the rest of the brain in a series of patients with attention deficit disorder (ADD), compared with controls (Lou, Henriksen, & Bruhn, 1984; also see Cohen et al., 1988). Moreover, the blood flow was improved by medication that suppressed attentional and hyperactive symptoms.

Evidence that attentional mechanisms may be primary among delinquents' executive deficits comes from their especially poor performance on the WISC-R Arithmetic subtest (e.g., Berman & Siegal, 1976; Brickman, McManus, Grapentine, & Alessi, 1984; Moffitt & Silva, 1988b; Voorhees, 1981). To the uninitiated, the Arithmetic subtest appears to be a test of calculating skills. To the neuropsychologist, the salient aspect of this test is that it is oral, not written; the subject is read a complex arithmetic problem, and must attend to concentrate while simultaneously recalling the problem and solving it mentally. Indeed, factor-analytic studies of WISC-R subtests reveal that Arithmetic loads most heavily on factors thought to represent "sustained concentration" or "freedom from distraction" (Cohen, 1959; also, Hubble & Groff, 1981, have obtained this factor structure with delinquents). Moreover, patients with frontal lobe injuries can often solve arithmetic problems with paper and pencil that they find impossible in an oral administration format because their attentional control is impaired, not their knowledge of arithmetic.

Are attention problems, and low scores on tests of executive function, associated with continuity of antisocial behavior? In a series of papers, Moffitt (Moffitt, 1990a; Moffitt & Henry, 1989; Moffitt & Silva, 1988c) has shown that New Zealand boys who exhibit comorbidity of conduct disorder and ADD score very poorly on neuropsychological tests of executive function and have histories of extreme antisocial behavior that remained stable from age 3 to age 15. Contrast groups of boys with single diagnoses of either conduct disorder or ADD did not have neuropsychological deficits and neither were their behavior problems stable. The New Zealand longitudinal data suggest that the cognitive problems manifested as poor scores on tests of self-control and as symptoms of ADD are linked with the continuity of antisocial behavior. In addition, there is some evidence that the persistent and impulsive behaviors characteristic of adults with antisocial personality disorder may be associated with executive deficits arising from problems in attention modulation.

Of special interest is the possibility that antisocial adults display executive deficits in the ability to inhibit behavior; they may perseverate with a previously rewarded response set even after contingencies change and the response is now punished (Gorenstein, 1982). Experiments by Newman (1987; Newman & Howland, 1989; Newman & Kosson, 1986) have shown that, once activated by the prospect of reward, individuals with antisocial personalities (a) form a rigid attentional set that is resistant to interruption, (b) pause and reflect less than others following punishment, and (c) have difficulty learning from feedback to inhibit punished behavior and to respond more appropriately on subsequent occasions. When an antisocial person's attention is fixated on the potential of obtaining a prize, he pursues it blindly, failing to be distracted by behavioral options that may, in fact, offer better paths toward obtaining the reward, or avoiding a punishment. Shapiro, Quay, Hogan, and Schwartz (1989) have implicated a similar process among conduct-disordered youngsters, using an adaptation of Newman's experimental procedures.

Raine's (1988) electrophysiological research has also pointed to an overfocus of attentional resources among adult prison inmates with a diagnosis of antisocial personality disorder. This attentional problem is quite similar to the difficulties experienced by ADD children; the latter exhibit impairments in sustaining attention, and in shifting attention strategically when warranted, but not in selective attention if motivation is adequate (Douglas & Peters, 1979). The theoretical structures linking individual differences in attentional processes among juvenile delinquents to behavioral disinhibition among adult antisocials suggests interesting hypotheses for neuropsychological factors in the continuity of antisocial behavior.

In summary, a wealth of consistent findings point to neuropsychological correlates of antisocial behavior, particularly in the verbal and executive (self-control) domains. We do not know, however, whether neuropsychological functions mediate genetic influences on the continuity of antisocial behavior. To address this issue, we shall need to investigate possible *sources* of neuropsychological dysfunctions. Although behavior-genetic studies have shown that some variation in different cognitive functions and abilities has heritable sources (e.g., Borecki & Ashton, 1984; Martin, Jardine, & Eaves, 1984; Plomin, 1988; Tambs, Sundet, & Magnus, 1984; Vandenberg, 1969), we still need to determine if genetic factors that produce individual differences in these functions during childhood and adolescence correlate with the genetic factors that produce these individual differences in adulthood. The chances are good that they do. Results from the Colorado Adoption Project, an ongoing study of nearly 500 adoptive and nonadoptive families (Plomin & De-Fries, 1985), suggest that much of the phenotypic stability for IQ is mediated genetically; that is, genetic factors that produce individual differences in children correlate significantly with

genetic factors that produce individual differences in adulthood (DeFries, Plomin, & LaBuda, 1987; Plomin, DeFries, & Fulker, 1988).

In addition, some work has begun to link two perinatal sources of cognitive deficit to the development of antisocial behavior. One possible source is disruption in the ontogenesis of the fetal brain caused by maternal drug abuse or poor prenatal nutrition (Kandel, Brennan, & Mednick, 1989). Another is brain insult suffered because of complications during birth (Szatmari, Reitsma-Street, & Offord, 1986). Kandel and Mednick (1991) found a weak, but significant, connection between delivery complications and later violent offending in adulthood. Some studies have also pointed to child abuse and neglect as possible sources of head injury in the histories of delinquents with neuropsychological impairment (e.g., Lewis, Shanok, Pincus, & Glaser, 1979; Tarter, Hegedus, Winsten, & Alterman, 1984). Prospective longitudinal designs are needed to unravel continuities in the relation between cognitive status, environmental experiences, and antisocial behavior over the life course.

The Missing Evidence: Longitudinal Studies of Antisocial Behavior and Genetic Factors

Different forms of antisocial behavior in childhood, adolescence, and adulthood may show some genetic influence; however, this does not necessarily mean that the genes that influence earlier forms of antisocial behavior also influence later forms of such behavior. Moreover, although biologically based cognitive impairments may be associated with antisocial behavior in children, adolescents, and adults, this does not necessarily mean that the genes that influence childhood aggression and adult crime do so through the same mechanisms.

Certain data support speculation that a heritable component may influence the stability of antisocial behavior. Perhaps the strongest predictor of a lengthy involvement in illegal behavior is the age at which such behavior begins. In a landmark study of 10,000 Philadelphia males, the rank-order correlation between age at first arrest and chronicity of subsequent arrests was −0.94 (Wolfgang et al., 1972). Summarizing a comprehensive review of empirical studies, Farrington et al. (1990, p. 283) concluded: "Those who begin offending at the earliest ages tend to commit large numbers of offenses over long time periods at high rates." Thus, if genes were to influence age at onset, we might infer that they also influence chronicity. Moffitt (1987) found a small link between adoptees' age at their first court conviction and the behavior of their biological parents in the Danish adoption cohort (unfortunately, data on age at first arrest were not available). In addition, these data revealed that criminals' recidivism was associated with stronger heritability. Most other adoption and twin studies have not specifically examined variability in the age at which illegal behavior was initiated or in recidivism, but the hypothesis is intriguing.

We need longitudinal studies that assess age-to-age genetic continuity and change. (Plomin, 1986). Such a definitive study would begin with twins or adoptees in childhood, and trace antisocial behavior and neuropsychological abilities (or other biological variables) across time in the same subjects.

Environmental Contributions to Behavioral Continuity

Behavioral patterns may show stability across the life course because the environment remains stable. In this section, we shall consider two sources of such environmental influence on behavioral continuity: the influence of *ecological constancy* and the influence of *continuities in the interpersonal environment.*

Ecological Constancy and the Stability of Antisocial Behavior

Denizens of every town and city are aware that antisocial behavior is disproportionately distributed throughout their communities. Parental admonitions about youth from "the wrong side of the tracks" reflect an ecological reality: Different community structures are related to different rates of crime. As Reiss (1986, pp. 1–2) observes, "Our sense of personal safety and potential victimization by crime is shaped less by knowledge of specific criminals than it is by knowledge of dangerous and safe places."

The ecological approach to the study of antisocial behavior is a distinctly sociological contribution; it seeks to examine the effects of the social context of the community on the behavioral development of its inhabitants. Community-level studies of antisocial behavior are thus able to identify characteristics of communities that are associated with antisocial behavior. They may also be used to ask whether criminogenic features of the community ecology can promote and sustain continuities in antisocial behavior. To explore this possibility, we first examine the community contexts and ecological correlates of adult crime, juvenile delinquency, and childhood disorder. We then examine whether these various forms of social and material disadvantage across the life course may account for the stability of antisocial behavior across the same time period.

The Community Context of Adult Crime.   Poverty and deprivation have long been cited as the most potent ecological correlates of crime rates (Sampson & Lauritsen, 1994). Recent studies have also used multivariate methods to isolate and identify several other endemic features of high-crime areas.

The assertion that poverty and deprivation are strongly linked to crime rates in urban areas may seem to contradict Robins' (1978) earlier-cited conclusion that social class is not related to criminal behavior in individuals. The controversy over whether or not economic disadvantage is linked to crime has a long history (see Gold, 1987, for a thoughtful review), and the controversy is fueled by two confusing issues. The first is the "data source fallacy": Whereas official crime statistics show that members of the lower social classes are more likely to be arrested and prosecuted, self-report surveys reveal that illegal behavior is equally common in all classes. Because early criminologists relied heavily on police data, it is possible that their theoretical and research emphasis on poverty was inadvertently guided by a now well-established measurement artifact. Poverty is important, but it may explain the behavior of the police better than the behavior of offenders. The second confusing issue is the "ecological fallacy": It is fallacious to deduce that poor individuals engage in crime simply because poor neighborhoods have higher crime rates.

The study of poverty and crime is also fraught with divisive disciplinary tensions. Whereas students of community effects highlight the effects of poverty, students of individual differences downplay its significance. Some may claim that these different slants are the outcome of scientific bickering: "One scientist's causal variable is another scientist's error term." We think it reflects something more fundamental about research designs. Students of individual offenders have generally collected data on their subjects' socioeconomic characteristics and, after controlling for the effects of SES, have concluded that the influences of other factors on criminal behavior are not significantly diminished. However, community researchers have not commonly controlled for the characteristics of individuals before concluding that disadvantage is linked to crime. This neglect results not from theoretical malice, but from lack of access to individual-level data in most community-level research designs.

Nevertheless, in our quest for sources of continuity in the behavior of individuals, we reviewed studies that have sought to identify the "active ingredients" in poverty (e.g., family instability). These ingredients or components may influence the continuity of antisocial behavior among middle-class children as well as poor children. Lack of money alone does not explain geographic differences in crime rates, and studies that attempt to "unpack" poverty into its component parts have revealed that family disruption and residential mobility are especially critical factors.

Neighborhoods characterized by high rates of family disruption tend to have higher rates of violence. Whether measured in terms of percentage of female-headed families or in divorce rates, community-level family disruption is associated with significant increases in rates of violent victimization, even after controlling for the effects of poverty and racial composition (Sampson, 1986).

Residential mobility also has a positive effect on crime rates above and beyond the effects of poverty. Using the National Crime Survey—a panel survey of nationally representative samples of households—Sampson (1985) reports that violent victimization rates are significantly higher in neighborhoods characterized by a large population turnover than in more stable areas. A longitudinal study spanning the 1970s in an American eastern seaboard city has also shown that rates of violent crimes (e.g., murder, aggravated assault) tended to increase as neighborhoods became more solidly "underclass" (Taylor & Covington, 1988). The combination of poverty and residential turnover is especially explosive.

Skogan (1990) has proposed that these various community factors influence crime because they lead to neighborhood *disorder,* a panoply of graffiti, broken windows, litter-strewn lots, and loitering youths—in sum, visible social and physical decay. Data from a study of 40 different areas in eight American cities showed that the effects of neighborhood poverty, instability, and racial composition were mediated by area disorder. Skogan suggests:

> Disorder may foster suspicion and distrust, undermine popular faith and commitment to the area, and discourage public and collective activities. Disorder may also undermine individual morale and the perceived efficacy of taking any positive action. Since there is little that individuals seem able to do about many forms of disorder, they may feel disheartened and frustrated, rather than motivated to do more, even to protect themselves. (1990, p. 72)

These characteristics may also lead to crime because they produce anonymity in the community. Psychological research on deindividuation has shown that circumstances in which individuals feel anonymous may produce weakened restraint against impulsive behavior as well as reduce inhibitions about committing crimes and engaging in antinormative behaviors (Diener, 1979; Diener, Fraser, Beaman, & Kelem, 1976; Zimbardo, 1970). In addition, persons who are in a deindividuated state are more likely to react to the cues in the immediate situation and are less likely to attend to the long-term consequences of their behavior (e.g., Prentice-Dunn & Rogers, 1980).

The Community Context of Juvenile Delinquency.   Survey studies and ethnographic materials similarly suggest that communities characterized by low socioeconomic status, residential mobility, and family disruption have high rates of juvenile delinquency. Sociologists have suggested these structural characteristics may give rise to conditions of community disorganization that, in turn, inhibit the creation of productive social relations and effective social norms.

According to Sampson and Groves (1989), three dimensions of community social organization are especially relevant for understanding delinquency and crime. The first dimension is the community's *ability to supervise and control teenage peer groups*. The second is the *extent and density of local friendship and acquaintanceship networks*. The third is the *rate of local participation in formal as well as voluntary community organizations*. To test this hypothesis, Sampson & Groves (1989) studied crime rates in 238 different localities throughout England. The results showed that these three dimensions of social organization mediated the effects of structural characteristics (e.g., poverty, residential mobility, family disruption) on crime and delinquency. For example, 80% of the effect of community SES on mugging and street robbery was mediated by unsupervised teenage groups. Similarly, nearly half the effect of residential mobility on mugging was mediated by the absence of local friendship networks. Communities that are characterized by unsupervised teenagers, limited friendship networks, and little participation in local organizations may have higher crime rates because their ability to construct effective norms and to exercise control over residents is greatly attenuated.

These survey findings assume emotive capacities on encountering Frank Furstenberg's (1990) ethnographic study of two Philadelphia neighborhoods; one is a public housing project; the other, a working-class enclave. Both neighborhoods are poor, but that is all they share in common. The former is anomic, characterized by little social trust, few family-neighborhood linkages, and an individualistic style of managing children and youth; the latter is cohesive, characterized by trustworthiness, extensive family-neighborhood linkages, and collective strategies of managing children and youth. Furstenberg wrote:

> Residents of the projects are inclined to adopt an individualistic style of family management in negotiating the world outside the household. Occasionally, they look for help in raising their children from formal institutions like schools or settlement houses or informal support from their kin or friends. But for the most part, they try to isolate themselves and their children from the surrounding community. They typically do not feel a part of their neighborhood institutions. They distrust the schools, regard local services suspiciously, and, to the extent that they use supportive services at all, take their business outside the community. The family system is largely disconnected from the community, and parents are left to manage on their own. (1990, pp. 13–14)

In contrast, parents in cohesive neighborhoods

> participate in a system that promotes shared parental responsibility through the delegation of control and sponsorship to both formal agencies and informal networks. The availability of resources, the relatively high degree of normative consensus, and strong social bonds forged by kinship and friendship all contribute to a close connection between local institutions and the family. Parents feel responsible to the schools and schools are responsible to parents. Youth cannot easily escape the scrutiny of neighborhood, schools, and families when these agencies are so interconnected. The high degree of observability keeps youth in check. The task of parents inside the home is reinforced by the support rendered by other parents outside the home . . . parenting [is] a collective activity, a style that distinctly contrasts to the individualistic mode of family management forced upon parents in more anomic neighborhoods. (1990, p. 20)

Thus, communities characterized by trust, wherein families are linked to each other and connected to other social networks, are communities that are able to construct effective social norms and facilitate opportunities for the next generation (Sampson & Groves, 1989).

The Community Context of Child Development.   Many of the community features associated with adult crime and adolescent delinquency are also implicated in psychosocial problems of early childhood development. Indeed, community influences appear in relation to infant mortality, child abuse, children's physical health as well as conduct problems (Bronfenbrenner, Moen, & Garbarino, 1984). Moreover, intervention programs suggest that the resources available in children's communities can affect their long-term antisocial outcomes. The suggestive data come from the Perry Preschool Project, a Head Start program in which disadvantaged black preschoolers (3-year-olds) were randomly assigned to treatment and control groups. The experimental group received 2 years of intensive intervention, at home and school. As has been the case with other interventions, gains in IQ were not sustained at long-term follow-up. However, in addition to IQ scores, this project's evaluators (Beruetta-Climent, Schweinhart, Barnett, Epstein, & Weikart, 1984) also measured outcomes of social competence. The experimental group scored better than the control group on teacher ratings of behavior problems at ages 6 to 9, on self-reported delinquent offending at age 15, and on official delinquency at age 19. For example, 51% of the untreated controls were arrested or charged by the police by age 19 in contrast to only 31% of the experimental group.

It is thus possible that the community contexts of early childhood may have long-lasting influences on later behavior. This point is nicely documented in Rutter's (1980, 1981; Rutter & Quinton, 1977) studies of ecological factors in human development in which he has observed that social and emotional problems are much more common in inner cities than in small towns. Of special interest to us is the finding that community differences are most pronounced in relation to chronic disorders with an early age of onset. Rutter (1981, p. 613) notes that "the problems most characteristic of city children are those beginning early, lasting a long time, and accompanied by many other problems in the family." He has further speculated that this difference may be attributable to the disruptive effect of city life on families. Although children may be shaped by their families, we must not forget that their families are shaped by conditions of the community (Wilson & Herrnstein, 1985).

In summary, a consistent body of research points to important ecological effects on a host of developmental difficulties across the life span. But as House (1981) notes, many of these demonstrations are wanting because they do not appraise the linkages between macro- and microsocial phenomena. Along these lines, Zigler and Child (1968) observed that psychologists are not likely to be content with evidence that shows the effect of social class on cognitive functioning; psychologists do not feel they understand the effect of social class on cognitive functioning until they have "reduced the sociological variable by conceptualizing it as a set of psychological events that cause the behavior being explained." This position is expressed also in Block's (1971, pp. 271–274) argument on "the necessity of psychologizing the notion of social class." If the term "psychologize" has troubling, reductionistic connotations, the intended message is clear enough. We must ask what it is about community conditions that has relevance for individuals' behavioral development.

We must also await longitudinal studies to answer the question we sought to address in this chapter: Do community features promote *continuity* in the development of antisocial behavior? Unfortunately, no evidence bears directly on this problem. This question can only be answered in the future by longitudinal studies that specify explicitly cross-level relations between features of the community ecology and attributes of the developing person across time. Such longitudinal studies should attend to the possibility that the relevant community features may also change developmentally. Just as the expression of antisocial behavior changes with age, so too do those features of the community that may promote or inhibit salutary developmental outcomes. In their review of research in criminology, Tonry, Ohlin, and Farrington (1991, p. 42) thus lament:

> Most individual-level research is inadequate because it neglects variation in community characteristics, while community-level research fails to take account of individual differences. Even when community context is considered, many important characteristics relevant to crime and delinquency have not been measured, especially factors central to early child development (e.g., variations in quality and access to prenatal health services, child-care facilities, community tolerance of a mother's substance abuse).

As illustrated in Figure 13.2, disorganized social communities are characterized by multiple sources of social and material disadvantage that are likely to inhibit healthy development at different points in the first two decades of life. Figure 13.2 summarizes some of what is known about community effects on

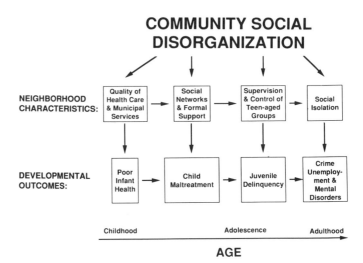

Figure 13.2 Community effects on the developing person across the life span.

the developing person across the life span: Access to health care systems is related to children's health (e.g., Bronfenbrenner et al., 1984); weak systems of neighborhood social support are related to child maltreatment (e.g., Garbarino & Sherman, 1980); the prevalence of unsupervised youth in a community is associated with crime (Sampson & Groves, 1989); and social isolation breeds crime and despair (Wilson, 1987). Figure 13.2 also summarizes some of what is known about the chain of continuity in antisocial behavior: Infants' health is related to maltreatment (e.g., Frodi et al., 1978); child maltreatment is linked with later violence (Widom, 1989); and juvenile delinquency is associated with a host of subsequent adult difficulties (e.g., Farrington, 1991). We do not know, however, whether the observed continuities between these various indexes of developmental risk can be accounted for by constancies in the community ecology. Answers to this question are most likely to emerge from studies of human development and criminal behavior that measure and monitor the structural and cultural features of community organization across the study members' lives (see Sampson and Lauritsen, 1994).

Studies of the community ecology are important because they can identify those features that may promote criminal activity and can suggest antidotes for dealing with disorder. However, studies of disorganized social communities often overlook the possibility that many features of the social ecology may reflect features of individuals who select themselves into particular ecological niches. After all, individuals make up the collective environment of the community, and families are not randomly assigned to neighborhoods. Consider poverty. This community-level effect on crime may be the result of a selection process whereby antisocial individuals who are unable to maintain stable employment select themselves into certain low-rent neighborhoods. As Mayer and Jencks (1989) explain, the social-selection hypothesis embraces two possibilities: "The people who move into different neighborhoods differ before they arrive, and the people who remain in a given neighborhood differ from those who leave"

(p. 1442). It is thus possible that social-selection processes create, to some unknown degree, the very criminogenic features of community social disorganization.

Whether or not the social composition of particular communities reflects entirely the selective aggregation of particular persons in those communities remains unclear. At the very least, the relations are most likely reciprocal. For example, neighborhood characteristics may weaken social controls that inhibit crime, attracting criminal activity that may then further accelerate neighborhood deterioration (Schuerman & Kobrin, 1986). This possibility can only be answered by longitudinal studies that track changing features of both communities and individuals.

Continuities in the Interpersonal Environment and the Stability of Antisocial Behavior

In addition to ecological constancies at the community level, environmental continuities may also exist at more proximal levels. Behavioral patterns may show stability across the life course because the interpersonal environments in which individuals reside remain stable. To the extent that parental demands, peer influences, and teacher expectancies remain stable over time, we could expect such environmental stability to promote behavioral continuities. Social behavior theorists have been telling us this for years, as have others (e.g., Bloom, 1964; Bradley, Caldwell, & Rock, 1988; Cairns & Hood, 1983; McCall, 1981), but few longitudinal studies have actually assessed the stability and change of the interpersonal environment alongside the stability and change of behavior patterns.

An approximation to this methodology was carried out by Hanson (1975), who reexamined the archives from the Fels Research Institute on which Kagan and Moss based their *Birth to Maturity* (1962). He found that 28 out of 30 environmental variables known to be related to IQ (e.g., parental involvement with the child, freedom to engage in verbal expression, direct teaching of language behavior) showed significant continuities from early to late childhood, with correlations corrected for attenuation ranging from .44 to .99.

Similar stabilities have also been found in parents' reports of child-rearing practices from childhood to adolescence (McNally, Eisenberg, & Harris, 1991; Roberts, Block, & Block, 1984); in global observations of maternal sensitivity from infancy to the preschool years in high-risk samples (Pianta, Sroufe, & Egeland, 1989); and in parenting practices that are correlated with children's aggressive acts (Patterson & Bank, 1990). In fact, Patterson, Bank, and Stoolmiller (1990) suggest that there are "parallel continuities" between children's aggressive behaviors and their parents' parenting skills. If the interpersonal environments of most children are as stable as all these data suggest, then the continuities observed in children's behavior over time may simply reflect the cumulative and continuing continuities of those environments.

The direct corollary of the assertion that behavioral continuities may reflect environmental constancies is that environmental change will produce behavioral change. For example, Rutter (1987) has noted that residential treatments have a marked influence on current behavior, but these influences do not persist when youngsters return home to an environment that maintains

its delinquency-promoting characteristics. Changes in the prosocial direction were shown by boys in England whose delinquent behavior diminished when their families moved out of London, a result that could not be attributed to selective migration (West, 1982). Also, Elliott and Voss (1974) reported that, for many delinquents, the rate of self-reported delinquency declined following dropout from schools, suggesting that a shift from environments associated with multiple failure experiences may serve to reduce delinquency. And finally, a longitudinal study of adolescent mothers shows that the sequelae of unplanned teen parenthood strongly depend on subsequent environmental events, such as further education, fertility control, marriage, and independence from the family of origin (Furstenberg, Brooks-Gunn, & Morgan, 1987).

It is important to note, however, that such environmental events are not random; they may themselves be a function of the individual's personality. Which women choose to return to school? Which choose to use contraception? Which are able to enter stable marriages? In short, the behavioral changes reported in many studies may derive from changes in environments that are themselves brought about by stable personality attributes. As we noted earlier, it is possible that features of the environment may reflect the stable and enduring features of individuals who make up the environment. It is even possible that features of the environment may reflect heritable characteristics of individuals.

Plomin and Bergeman (1991) have shown that the measures most commonly used by developmental psychologists to assess the influence of socialization environments on children and adolescents may be confounded with genetic variation. Using data from various twin and adoption studies, they decomposed the variance in measures of the environment into genetic and environmental components of variance. Environments per se

> have no DNA and can show no genetic influence. However *measures of the environment* . . . may be perfused with characteristics of individuals. To the extent that this is the case, measures of the environment can show genetic influence. Consider an environmental construct such as parental responsiveness. We might think of this construct as existing "out there" independent of individuals. However, when we measure the construct, we are in fact measuring parental behavior, and this measure can be analyzed as a phenotype in quantitative genetic analyses in order to investigate the extent to which inter-individual genetic differences and environmental differences contribute to phenotypic variance for this measure. If the measure is really "out there" independent of individuals, it will show no genetic influence. (p. 374)

Plomin and Bergeman (1991) reviewed multiple behavior-genetic studies to document that a variety of measures typically used to study children's environments (e.g., the HOME scales, the Moos Family Environment Scales) are subject to substantial genetic influence. Measures of the person and measures of the environment are *not* pure and distinct from each other. They are confounded. Although the mechanisms that produce genetic correlations between the two remain elusive, it is quite likely that genetic influences on measures of the environment reflect interactional processes wherein individuals evoke reactions and seek out situations that are compatible with their dispositions (Scarr & McCartney, 1983). We will discuss this topic in a later section.

Although we recognize the importance of social-selection effects, we must not forget that the ability to enact choices depends on opportunities and constraints in the physical and social environment. Social selections are exercised in a "field of eligibles," and this "field" must be surveyed before evaluating sources of continuity and change in social behavior.

In a recent study of the social context of pubertal development and juvenile delinquency. Caspi, Lynam, Moffitt, and Silva (1993) examined an unselected cohort of New Zealand girls whose psychological and biological development had been traced across childhood through adolescence when they entered either coed or all-girl secondary schools. They demonstrated that the impact of pubertal development on female delinquency was moderated by the sex composition of secondary schools; early-maturing girls in coed schools were at significantly greater risk for delinquency than girls in all-girl schools, even after controlling for intake differences between school types (*beta* = .28 vs. − .10). In addition, individual differences in antisocial behavior were significantly more stable and predictable throughout adolescence among girls who attended coed schools than among girls attending all-girl schools (*beta* = .63 vs. .32). This study provides one of the first demonstrations that an aspect of the social context can influence the continuity of antisocial behavior, while documenting that the obtained effect was not an artifact of social selection.

Caspi et al. (1993) argue that coed schools offered favorable conditions for the continuity of deviant behaviors because delinquent girls were more likely to find reinforcements and opportunities for their activities when in the company of boys. In contrast, the normative controls in all-girl schools appeared to suppress behavioral continuities in antisocial behavior, possibly because delinquent girls were more likely to be viewed as deviant in these settings; deviant individuals are often disliked and are thus more likely to be coerced into more modal patterns—what Cattell (1973) has called "coercion to the biosocial mean." In sum, it appears that environmental circumstances play an important role in regulating continuities in social development (Cairns & Hood, 1983). Deviant activities need the support of the social group not only for their initiation, but apparently for their maintenance as well. As J. P. Scott reminded his audience during the 1977 presidential address to the Behavior Genetics Association:

> Almost all behavior that is exhibited by members of highly social species . . . is expressed within social relationships. What little solitary behavior remains is expressed within social contexts derived from these relationships . . . the concept of the independent individual [and its corollary the independent environment] is a myth. (pp. 327–328, 345)

Clearly we are dealing with person-environment interactions, a topic to which we now turn.

Person-Environment Interactions

It is now widely acknowledged that personality and behavior are shaped in large measure by interactions between the person and the environment. There are many kinds of interactions, but we suggest that there are three that play particularly important roles both in promoting the continuity of personality across the life course and in controlling the trajectory of the life course itself (Buss, 1987; Plomin, DeFries, & Loehlin, 1977; Scarr & McCartney, 1983). *Reactive* interaction occurs when different individuals exposed to the same environment experience it, interpret it, and react to it differently. *Evocative* interaction occurs when an individual's personality evokes distinctive responses from others. *Proactive* interaction occurs when individuals select or create environments of their own (Caspi & Bem, 1990).

Reactive Person-Environment Interaction

Different individuals exposed to the same environment experience it, interpret it, and react to it differently. An anxious, sensitive child will experience and react to authoritarian parents in very different ways from a calm, resilient child. The person who interprets a hurtful act as the product of malice will react differently from one who interprets the same act as the product of incompetence. Each individual extracts a subjective psychological environment from the objective surroundings, and that subjective environment shapes both personality and subsequent interaction.

This is the basic tenet of the phenomenological approach historically favored by social psychology and embodied in the famous dictum that if people "define situations as real, they are real in their consequences" (Thomas & Thomas, 1928). It is also the assumption that connects Epstein's (1980; Epstein & Erskine, 1983) writings on the development of personal theories of reality; Tomkins' (1979) description of scripts about the self and interpersonal interactions; and Bowlby's (1973) analysis of working models—mental representations of the self and others—that develop in the context of interactional experiences.

All three theories suggest that early experiences can set up anticipatory attitudes that lead the individual to project particular interpretations onto new social relationships and ambiguous situations. This is accomplished through a variety of informational and behavioral processes in which the person interprets new events in a manner that is consistent with his or her experientially established understanding of the self and others.

All three theories also assert that people continually revise their "personal theories," "scripts," and "working models" as a function of experience. But if these function as filters for social information, the question is raised about how much revision actually occurs. In fact, social psychologists, who tend to focus on the cognitive rather than the motivational features of internal organizational structures, argue that self-schemata, psychological constructs of the self, screen and select from experience to maintain structural equilibrium (Greenwald, 1980). Once a schema becomes well organized, it filters experience and makes individuals selectively responsive to information that matches their expectations and views of themselves (Markus, 1977). A host of cognitive processes may promote consistency and also impair people's ability to change (e.g., Cantor & Kihlstrom, 1987; Nisbett & Ross, 1980; Snyder, 1984):

- *Primacy Effects.* The first information that people receive has a powerful influence on their overall impression of the world around them and affects their interpretation of new material.

- *Anchoring Bias.* While forming judgments about their world, people are quite reticent to adjust their initial solutions and are unlikely to depart from their initial "anchors."
- *Confirmatory Bias.* People preferentially seek evidence that confirms the propositions they are testing and they act in ways that generate disconfirmation for events and information that challenge their beliefs.

In these several ways, persistent ways of perceiving, thinking, and behaving may be preserved by features of the cognitive system. The course of personality development is likely to be quite conservative because features of the cognitive system may impair people's ability to change in response to new events that challenge their beliefs and self-conceptions.

According to contemporary theorists who view the self as "an arrangement of schemas that represent one's past experiences and personal characteristics," the self-concept is dynamic; it activates representations of particular situations and "carries" our responses to the interpersonal world (Markus & Cross, 1990, p. 594). If so, the self-concept of aggressive persons should differ from that of their nonaggressive peers. Indeed, antisocial persons appear to have different cognitive standards regarding the use of aggressive behavior. For example, they believe that aggression will yield tangible rewards and desirable results (Boldizar, Perry, & Perry, 1989; Perry, Perry, & Rasmussen, 1986). They are also more likely to believe that aggression is a legitimate response to solving problems (e.g., "It's OK to hit someone if you just go crazy with anger"); that behaving aggressively helps to avoid a negative image (e.g., "If you back down from a fight, everyone will think you are a coward"); that aggressive acts improve one's social reputation and increase self-esteem (e.g., "It's important to show everyone how tough you are"); and that victims don't suffer (Slaby & Guerra, 1988).

The self represents information not only about the past and present, but also about the future. For example, Markus maintains that the motivation for behavioral action depends on "possible selves," imaginal representations of the self in particular end-states:

> Possible selves are those conceptions of the self that one hopes, wants, or seeks to be, as well as those feared conceptions that one seeks to avoid or is afraid of becoming. (Markus & Cross, 1990, p. 595)

Possible selves are thus motivating, providing incentives for the future and blueprints for the life span. For a possible self to be motivationally effective, however, the person must strike a balance between *expected* possible selves and *feared* possible selves. A balance between expected and feared selves creates the possibility that persons will take action to avoid the realization of their fears. And it is here that aggressive youth encounter developmental difficulties (Oyserman & Markus, 1990): Juvenile delinquents are characterized by asymmetries between their fears and expectations. For example, they fear "not getting a job" but do not expect to "have a job"; they fear being "on drugs" but focus no expectations on avoiding drugs.

Although these delinquent youths have the type of feared selves that might be associated with the avoidance of delinquent activity, many of them seem to be missing the expected possible selves that could provide the organizing and energizing vision of how they might avoid criminal activity, and what they might expect if they do. (Oyserman & Markus, 1990, pp. 122–123)

Collectively, then, this arrangement of beliefs and self-conceptions may support the use of antisocial behavior in many social encounters. And, of course, the beliefs are not fictions. The social environment contains a rich reinforcement schedule for these antisocial acts and thus confirms the antisocial person's belief system (Patterson, 1982; Perry, Kusel, & Perry, 1988).

It is not clear, however, whether these beliefs guide behavioral action independent of information-processing biases, or whether—as is more likely—beliefs and self-conceptions influence the type of social information that is attended to and processed (Slaby & Guerra, 1988).

Numerous studies have focused on the social information-processing strategies of aggressive children. Most notable is the social-cognitive model proposed by Dodge (1986):

> A child comes to a particular social situation . . . with a biologically determined set of response capabilities . . . and a memory store of past experiences . . . and he or she receives as input from the environment a set of social cues. That child's behavioral response to those cues occurs as a function of the way that he or she processes the presented social information . . . [T]his processing occurs in sequential stages, or steps. Each step is a necessary part of competent responding . . . If the child processes the information skillfully, efficiently, and accurately, the probability is great that he or she will behaviorally respond in a manner that is judged by others to be competent. Failure to respond skillfully at a step or responding in a biased manner increases the probability that child will behave in a deviant, possibly aggressive, way. (p. 83)

Dodge (1986) posits five distinct social-information processing steps, and research has shown that aggressive behavior may be related to biases or deficits in processing information at any step and in different combinations of steps.

The first step is to *encode information* about the event; the child must search the situation for informative cues (e.g., the provocateur's facial expression) and focus attention to those cues. Research about this social information-processing step suggests that aggressive children search the situation for fewer cues before making an attributional decision (Dodge & Newman, 1981). Moreover, when defining and solving an interpersonal conflict, aggressive children seek out significantly less information about the event (Slaby & Guerra, 1988). These deficits may indicate a neuropsychological executive deficit in focusing attention on cues (Moffitt & Henry, 1989) and/or a perceptual readiness to interpret social encounters as hostile encounters (Dodge, 1986).

The second step is to *interpret the cues* and arrive at some decision about their meaning and significance. Individual differences in this social information-processing step have been studied extensively. Research has shown that aggressive children are prone to attribute hostile intention to ambiguous events (e.g., Dodge, 1980; Nasby, Hayden, & DePaulo, 1980; Steinberg & Dodge, 1983) and expect continued hostility from others in the social environment (e.g., Dodge & Frame, 1982).

The third step is to *search for possible responses* to the situation. Research about this information-processing step suggests that aggressive children differ in terms of both quality and quantity of responses. Aggressive children are more likely to generate aggressive responses (Dodge, 1986), and they also possess significantly less knowledge about interpersonal problem solving (e.g., Hains & Ryan, 1983; Platt, Spivak, Altman, & Altman, 1974; Slaby & Guerra, 1988). The variety of possible responses may also be important for continuity. In a longitudinal study of French-Canadian children, Tremblay (1991) found that aggressive children whose behavioral repertoire included incidents of prosocial behavior (as observed by classroom teachers) were less likely to remain in the aggressive group at follow-up than children whose behavioral repertoire at Time-1 was limited to aggressive acts.

The fourth step is to consider the consequences of each potential response and to *select a response* from the generated alternatives. Individual differences in emotional tempo or impulsivity may influence this fourth step; for example, rapidly escalating emotional reactions may truncate the process of weighing alternatives (Katz, 1989). Investigating this notion, Cairns & Cairns (1993) scrutinized the social interchanges of girls in conflict. Girls with an aggressive history tended to become entangled in a series of escalating angry interchanges, but nonaggressive girls allowed the argument to return to cooler levels at frequent points during the interaction.

The fifth step is to *carry out the selected response*. Research has pointed to several difficulties among aggressive persons in their ability to enact responses and to monitor the consequences of their actions. As we noted earlier, many antisocial individuals are characterized by verbal and self-control deficits that may place them at a disadvantage in interpersonal exchanges. If children feel uncomfortable or inept with verbal communication, they may be more likely to strike out physically than to try to talk their way out of an altercation. In addition, antisocial children may be more likely to have observed their parents and family members use physical violence to "solve" disagreements (see Snyder & Patterson, 1987). And finally, some evidence suggests that antisocial persons are also physically larger and stronger than average for their age (Wilson & Herrnstein, 1985). Although the causal structure among these sets of variables is far from clear, the combination of these characteristics would appear to favor agonistic responses; antisocial persons are likely to obtain greater and more immediate rewards from behaving menacingly than from arduous efforts aimed at verbal mediation.

In general, research has shown that individual differences in social-information processing patterns predict behavioral outcomes in naturalistic settings. In a series of studies, Dodge and his colleagues (Dodge, Pettit, McClaskey, & Brown, 1986) assessed children's social-information processing strategies through the use of video-recorded stimulus materials. At a later date, the children participated in a peer-group entry task and were exposed to a provocation by a peer. Social information-processing patterns predicted children's aggressiveness in these different situations. Moreover, these patterns were significantly associated with ratings of the children's aggressive behavior in the classroom and on the playground.

Some researchers doubt that purely cognitive models can account for individual differences in aggression (Dodge, 1991; Parke & Slaby, 1983) and have proposed that affective reactions mediate the relationship between information-processing variables and aggressive action patterns (e.g., Bell & Baron, 1990). Graham, Hudley, and Williams (1992) explored one version of this "cognition → affect → action" model. Children in their study were given different scenarios depicting different provocations by a peer and were asked to make judgments about the peer's intentions, as well as to indicate how they would feel and how they would act in response. The results pointed to the mediational role of emotion, in which attributions of hostile intent led to feelings of anger, and feelings of anger led to aggressive responses.

Whatever the mediating mechanisms, aggressive behavior is not greeted passively by the social world but is likely to evoke responses from the surrounding environment that confirm and sustain aggressive children's subjective interpretation of that environment as hostile. Thus begins a feedback process that militates more adaptive options and strengthens the chain of continuity.

Evocative Person-Environment Interactions

Each individual evokes distinctive responses from others. An infant who squirms and fusses when picked up will evoke less nurturance from a parent than one who likes to be cuddled. Docile children will evoke a less controlling style of child rearing from parents than will aggressive children. The person acts; the environment reacts; and the person reacts back in mutually interlocking evocative interaction. Such interactions continue throughout the life course and promote the continuity of aggressive behavior.

Even very early in life children evoke consistent responses from their social environment (Chess & Thomas, 1987). Numerous studies have shown that an infant's temperament may affect disciplinary strategies and subsequent interactions with adults and peers (Bell & Chapman, 1986). For example, children characterized by a "difficult" temperament in infancy are more likely to resist their mothers' efforts to control them in early childhood (Lee & Bates, 1985). Similarly, mothers of boys with a difficult temperament experience more problems in their efforts to socialize their children. Maccoby and Jacklin (1983) showed that over time these mothers reduce their active efforts to guide and direct their children's behavior and increasingly become less involved in the teaching process. Children with a difficult temperament appear to contribute to a socialization environment that exacerbates their difficulties.

As part of their ongoing longitudinal study of ego and cognitive development, J. Block and J. H. Block (1980) used an actometer to measure activity level in their subjects when the children were 3 and 4 years old. Observations of subsequent family interactions, when the children were 5 years old, revealed that children characterized by high levels of activity were more likely to evoke a variety of upper-limit control behaviors from their parents (Buss, 1981). Parents of highly active children were impatient and hostile with their children and frequently got into power struggles with them. Moreover, when the children were 7 years old, they were described by their teachers as aggressive, manipulative, noncompliant, and more likely to push limits and stretch the rules in many social encounters (Buss, Block, & Block, 1980). These findings, along with previous studies (e.g., Halverson & Waldrop, 1976), suggest that early developing temperamental differences are linked to a matrix of aversive interpersonal interactions with peers, parents, and teachers. Possibly, antisocial children evoke reactions from the social environment that then help to maintain and escalate a behavioral trajectory characterized by increasingly more serious problems.

Research on aggressive children at the Oregon Social Learning Center has shown in elegant detail how such evocative person-environment interactions can create and sustain destructive and aversive patterns of behavior (Patterson, 1982, 1986b; Patterson & Bank, 1990). By recording moment-to-moment interactions in families of antisocial boys, Patterson and his colleagues have been able to identify the peculiar reinforcement arrangements that typify the coercive family process. It appears that children's coercive behaviors often provoke and force adult family members to counter with highly punitive and angry responses, often escalating to an ever-widening gulf of irritation until the parents of such children eventually withdraw from aversive interactions with their children. One outcome of such *negative reinforcements* is that children who coerce others into providing short-term payoffs in the immediate situation may thereby learn an interactional style that continues to work in similar ways in later social encounters and with different interactional partners. The immediate reinforcement not only short-circuits the learning of more controlled interactional styles that might have greater adaptability in the long run, it also increases the likelihood that coercive behaviors will recur whenever similar interactional conditions arise again.

Children who coerce with one family member are likely to coerce with other family members (Patterson, 1986a). For example, analyses of sib interactions show that here too negative reinforcement contingencies serve to strengthen the target child's response (Snyder & Patterson, 1977). According to Patterson, the antisocial child is a "skilled architect," successfully constructing social interactions that maximize short-term payoffs; the child gets what he or she wants.

But the long-term costs associated with these short-term rewards are severe. Early coercive family interactions portend deteriorated family management practices when antisocial children reach adolescence. At this point, parents of antisocial children are less likely to supervise and monitor their pubescent boys; their inept disciplinary strategies, in turn, predict persistent and progressively more serious delinquency among their offspring (e.g., Laub & Sampson, 1988; Loeber & Stouthamer-Loeber, 1986).

The social learning interpretation of coercive family systems is that "family members and antisocial children alternate in the roles of aggressors and victims, each inadvertently reinforcing the coercive behavior of the other" (Patterson & Bank, 1990). Parents and children thus maintain and escalate coercive

cycles by evoking predictable reactions and counterreactions from each other. But there is an additional interpretation: Parents and children possess similar aggressive traits determined by their shared genes. Rowe (1987) observed that shared heredity may render the social learning interpretation incomplete and suggested that social-interactional analyses of biological and adoptive parent-child dyads are needed to estimate the contribution of social learning mechanisms to behavioral continuity independent of shared heredity.

However, experimental research has shown that children evoke predictable responses from adults independent of shared heredity. In a study of unrelated mothers and children, Anderson, Lytton, and Romney (1986) observed conduct-disordered and nonproblem boys interacting with their mothers in unrelated pairs. The conduct-disordered boys evoked more negative reactions from both types of mothers than did normal boys, but the two types of mothers did not differ from each other in their negative reactions. It appears that adults respond to the behaviors of children rather than create differences between the children. It may well be that early temperamental differences contribute to the development of conduct disorders by evoking responses from the interpersonal social environment that exacerbate the child's tendencies (Lytton, 1990).

Lytton's (1990) model does not simply substitute one "main effects" model (parental influence) with another such model (child influence). An interactional model recognizes that partners react back and forth in mutually interlocking evocative interaction; parents and children contribute to the maintenance of problem behavior by evoking congruent responses from each other. Just as children's aggression evokes maintaining responses from adults, adults' responses can evoke maintaining reactions from children. Moreover, these reciprocal behavioral influences are often mediated by belief systems (Sigel, 1986). Parents respond not only to children's actual behaviors, they also respond to children on the basis of expectations they have formed about their children's behavior. For example, many parents of preterm infants hold unrealistic expectations about their children's attainment of certain developmental milestones, and these may contribute to later dysfunctional parent-child relationships (Tinsley & Parke, 1983). Similarly, parental beliefs and expectations may exacerbate aversive interactions. For example, mothers of problem-behavior boys are more negative when interacting with their own children than when interacting with other children who are characterized by similar behavior problems (Anderson et al., 1986).

In an important demonstration, Bugenthal and Schennum (1984) showed that parental beliefs about the causes of caregiving outcomes determined adults' reactions to children's behavior and, inadvertently, served to maintain the children's behavioral styles. Using a synthetic family design, in which school-age boys were paired for social interactions with unrelated mothers, Bugenthal and Schennum (1984) demonstrated that women who ranked low on self-perceived power as caregivers were likely to find unresponsive children very difficult. Similarly, women who attributed power to children were likely to find assertive boys very difficult to handle. Moreover, these attributions were self-fulfilling; they elicited behavior from the children that confirmed the adults' belief systems.

It is also through evocative interaction that phenomenological interpretations of situations—the products of reactive interaction—are transformed into situations that are "real in their consequences." In particular, early experiences can set up expectations that lead an individual to project particular interpretations onto new situations and relationships and thence to behave in ways that corroborate those expectations.

For example, because aggressive children expect others to be hostile, they may behave in ways that elicit hostility from others, thereby confirming their initial suspicion and sustaining their aggression. Individuals also elicit and selectively attend to information that confirms rather than disconfirms their self-concepts (Darley & Fazio, 1980; Snyder, 1984; Swann, 1983, 1985, 1987). This promotes stability of the self-concept which, in turn, promotes the continuity of behavioral patterns that are congruent with that self-concept (Andrews, 1988; Backman, 1985, 1988; Secord & Backman, 1965. See also Carson, 1969; Snyder & Ickes, 1985).

Consider the case of a man named Otto, the son of a harsh authoritarian (Cottrell, 1969, p. 563). When Otto reached adolescence, he began vigorously to resist his father's martinettish behavior until the escalating tension led to Otto's removal to a foster home. As a young man, Otto was "placed in an unskilled job but walked out of it after a reprimand from his supervisor. This same sequence was repeated several times, and it became apparent than any exercise of authority evoked in Otto a very defiant reaction which usually lost him his job." This pattern continued in later years as Otto married and fathered a child: "In the situation where he was confronted with the negativistic behavior of his infant son he found he had learned quite well the harsh-father end of the self-other system."

Cottrell (1969) suggests that relational patterns learned in one situation will be repeated in later situations that are of similar structure, especially in new situations where the individual occupies one of the "action" positions defined by the earlier established self-other system (see also Sroufe & Fleeson, 1988). As a more general life-course process, such clinical evidence suggests the provocative hypothesis that the greater the perceived identity of situations across the life course, the greater the likelihood that characteristic behavior patterns will be reexpressed in these settings and will evoke confirming responses from new interaction partners (Cairns, 1979).

There is only scant empirical evidence to confirm this hypothesis. In an ingenious experimental analogue of life-course development, Gelfand and her colleagues (1974) showed that behavior patterns learned in one setting or relationship may generalize to novel settings and relationships. Specifically, they studied whether children trained with either punishment or reward techniques would subsequently apply these same techniques to train other children. Indeed, when asked to play the role of an adult, children tended to repeat whatever interactional pattern they had been exposed to previously, even though they now occupied—in Cottrell's language—the other action position in the relational system. It appears that the child, in later situations when assuming the role of the adult, fit the other child into the role he himself had formerly occupied. Early interactional experiences were thus recreated in later situations and relationships. In these several ways, reactive and evocative person-environment interactions enable an ensemble of behaviors, expectations, and self-concepts to evoke maintaining responses from others—thereby promoting continuity of antisocial styles across time and circumstance.

Proactive Person-Environment Interactions

Individuals often seek out situations that are compatible with their dispositions, and recent analyses have suggested that individuals' dispositions can lead them to select situations that, in turn, reinforce and sustain those same dispositions (Ickes, Snyder, & Garcia, in press; Snyder & Ickes, 1985). For example, when sensation-seekers preferentially seek out thrilling situations, they select themselves into environments that nourish and sustain their need for varied and novel sensations. What they cannot select, individuals can often create. For example, it is sensation seekers who suggest taking physical and social risks rather than staying put at home. As the name implies, proactive interaction is a process through which individuals become active agents in their own personality development.

It has been proposed that this dispositionally guided selection and creation of environments becomes increasingly influential as the individual gains increased autonomy from the imposed fetters of early childhood (Scarr, 1988; Scarr & McCartney, 1983). In fact, this phenomenon may account for the oft-noted age-related increase in the magnitude of stability coefficients across the life span (Caspi & Bem, 1990). Specifically, as self-regulatory competencies increase with age, individuals begin to make choices and display preferences that may reinforce and sustain their characteristics.

Examples of selections and their consequences are seen in leisure, educational, and occupational situations (Ickes et al., in press). But the most consequential environments for personality are probably our interpersonal environments; in friendship formation and mate selection, the personality-sustaining effects of proactive interaction are the most intriguing.

Friendship Formation. Friends tend to be similar with respect to values, attitudes, and behaviors (e.g., Billy & Udry, 1985; Cohen, 1977; Kandel, 1978a, 1978b; Newcomb, 1961). In addition, adolescents tend to affiliate selectively with others who resemble them somatically. For example, early-maturing girls tend to befriend other early-maturing girls as well as older peers (Magnusson, Stattin, & Allen, 1986). Even aggressive children, who are often unpopular with their classmates, succeed in forming close ties with particular subgroups of children. In particular, boys *and* girls tend to affiliate selectively with friends who match their antisocial behavior (Elliot, Huizinga, & Ageton, 1985; Rowe & Osgood, 1984). This observation is best documented in the Carolina Longitudinal Study, a prospective study of the development of antisocial behavior in two cohorts of boys and girls (Cairns & Cairns, 1993).

Table 13.3 summarizes results from social network analyses in which Cairns and his colleagues examined the correlations between their subjects' aggression (as reported by teachers) and their subjects' friends' aggression (as reported by teachers). The table indicates that, among males, the tendency to affiliate with others who were similar on a dimension

Table 13.3 Correlations between the Aggression Scores of Boys and Girls in the Carolina Longitudinal Study and the Aggression Scores of Their Friends

	Friends		
Sample Members	Reciprocal Friends	Nonreciprocal Friends	Sum across All Friends
Males			
Grade 4	.61*	.12	.41*
Grade 7	.63*	.40*	.49*
Females			
Grade 4	.07	.19	.08
Grade 7	.51*	.12	.34*

From "Social Networks and Aggressive Behavior: Peer Support or Peer Rejection" by R. B. Cairns, B. D. Cairns, H. J. Neckerman, S. D. Gest, and J. L. Gariepy, 1988, *Developmental Psychology, 24*, p. 821. Copyright 1988 by American Psychological Association. Reprinted by permission.
*p < .01

of aggressive expression had appeared already in fourth grade and became stronger with the advent of adolescence. Among females, there were only low levels of similarity in fourth grade. But by early adolescence, girls were as likely as their male counterparts to selectively affiliate with others who resembled them on aggressive expression (Cairns, Cairns, Neckerman, Gest, & Gariepy, 1988). Contrary to the assumptions of both psychological and sociological theories (e.g., Bowlby, 1988; Hirschi, 1969), deviant adolescents are neither disaffiliated nor are they incapable of forming meaningful personal bonds. In fact, most delinquents appear to have many friends (Giordano, Cernkovich, & Pugh, 1986), and importantly, their friends resemble them in terms of a deviant lifestyle.

In a series of studies, Billy and Udry (1985; Billy, Rodgers, & Udry, 1984) examined the contribution of three mechanisms to similarities between friends: *selection,* in which individuals acquire friends on the basis of behavioral similarity; *influence,* in which peers influence their friends to behave in certain ways; and *deselection,* in which individuals deselect friends whose behavior is different from their own. In general, it appears that social selection is the most important factor contributing to similarities in attitudes, behaviors, and, more generally, deviant lifestyles. Children and adolescents do not congregate randomly; they *choose* activities that are compatible with their own dispositions and *select* companions who are similar to themselves. Moreover, the similarity-attraction function appears to be continuous across the life span (Byrne & Griffitt, 1966).

Cairns and Cairns (1993) suggest:

similarity attracts because of the promise that the individuals who are alike on key dimensions will also have an adequate basis for interaction. [In addition] the rejection of dissimilarities may be functional in that some key characteristics in common are required for successful interactions to begin. But once the joint selection occurs, a new process is set into motion to ensure conjoint growth and further similarities, without which the embryonic relationship will dissolve. [Social] selection and socialization are mutually supportive.

The reciprocal dynamics of social selection and socialization are especially interesting with respect to problem behaviors.

Consistent with a social-learning formulation of differential association theory, Dishion and Patterson (Dishion, 1990; Dishion, Patterson, Stoolmiller, & Skinner, 1991; Patterson & Bank, 1990) have suggested that each individual "shops" for settings and people that maximize positive payoffs. The trial-and-error process of shopping and being rejected inevitably leads problem children to identify that group of peers that will reinforce their behaviors. In turn, membership in a delinquent peer group is a key determinant of drift into subsequent and more severe delinquency (Elliott & Menard, in press).

In their social-ecological analysis of the development of aggression, Cairns and his colleagues have found that the quality of aggressive children's social networks is quite stable over time (Cairns, Cairns, Neckerman, Ferguson, & Gariepy, 1989; Cairns, Perrin, & Cairns, 1985). Adolescents may switch alliances and cliques, but the new affiliations resemble the old ones in terms of deviance. Cairns and Cairns (1993) suggest that these affiliations may serve as guides for norm formation and the consolidation of behavior patterns of over time. Continuities in social networks may thus contribute to behavioral stability because the demands of the social environment remain relatively similar over time. Moreover, consistency in how members of the social network relate to the individual may contribute to behavioral stability because it affects how individuals view and define themselves. Consistent with these predictions, Cairns and colleagues have shown that stable pairs of friends are similar in their tendency to drop out of school (Cairns, Cairns, & Neckerman, 1989), and, tragically, in their propensity toward suicide (Cairns & Cairns, 1993).

The mutually supportive dynamics of social-selection and socialization are nicely revealed in research on the psychosocial implications of pubertal timing. Adolescent girls of the same age vary greatly in their level of pubertal development, and differences in the timing of puberty have important implications for behavioral development; in particular, early-maturing girls are more likely to engage in delinquent activities (e.g., Stattin & Magnusson, 1990). The association between early maturation and juvenile delinquency appears to be mediated by the composition of the girls' social networks. As we noted earlier, early-maturing girls are likely to gravitate toward chronologically older peers. Older peers, in turn, appear to function as norm transmitters, sanctioning and even encouraging a variety of norm-breaking behaviors among early-maturing girls.

Data from the Individual Development and Adjustment Study in Sweden reveal that the relation between early maturation and norm-breaking behaviors is conditioned by peers; the relation was strong and positive if the girls had older friends but practically absent if the girls affiliated exclusively with same-age peers. In further analyses, Stattin and Magnusson (1990) have shown that this effect may be attributable to the role that friends play as norm transmitters. Specifically, early-maturing girls with older friends expected weaker reactions after engaging in delinquent activities than did girls without older friends. Thus, the social network, whose composition is in part determined by direct social preferences, may serve as a convoy throughout development, producing support for acts of increasing deviance.

Recent findings from the adult follow-up of participants in the Cambridge study (Farrington, 1991) point to the importance of peer associations throughout the life course. When interviewed at age 32, those men had desisted from crime attributed their behavioral change to changes in their peer group; as they grew older, they simply stopped spending time with their delinquent friends. Indeed, the incidence of co-offending had declined by age 32 along with the incidence of crime in general. Still, adult burglary, robbery, and theft from vehicles were likely to involve co-offenders who were similar in age and background to the offending sample members. And, the sample members who were committing these serious offenses in adulthood were not newcomers to antisocial lifestyles; their behavior problems had been present 20 years earlier, at the beginning of the study.

Mate Selection.   People tend to marry partners who are similar to themselves. Positive marital assortment has been documented—in descending order of magnitude—for physical characteristics, cognitive abilities, values and attitudes, and personality traits (Epstein & Guttman, 1984; Jensen, 1978; Vandenberg, 1972). Moreover, it appears that similarities between spouses reflect active personal preferences, not simply the outcome of social homogamy (Mascie-Taylor & Vandenberg, 1988).

Few studies have directly examined assortative mating for aggressive reaction patterns, but there is a good deal of evidence of congruence for traits related to antisocial behavior (e.g., Zuckerman, 1979). We recently obtained data on married couples who are members of two longitudinal studies at the Institute of Human Development, University of California, Berkeley. Data were available on 82 couples who completed the California Psychological Inventory (CPI) on two occasions, in 1970 and in 1981 (Caspi & Herbener, 1993). Of special interest are spouse correlations for three scales: The *Socialization* scale "orders individuals along a continuum from asocial to social behavior and forecasts the likelihood that they will transgress the mores established by their particular cultures" (Megargee, 1972, p. 59); the *Self-control* scale "assesses the adequacy of self-regulation, self-control, and the degree of freedom from impulsivity" (p. 67); and the *Responsibility* scale "identifies people who are conscientious, responsible, dependable, articulate about rules and order, and who believe that life should be governed by reason" (p. 56).

Table 13.4 shows the spouse correlations for the three CPI scales that collectively index internalization and endorsement of normative conventions. Consistent with other studies of assortative mating for personality, the results point to relatively low but consistently positive correlations between spouses. The table also shows the spouse correlations for these three CPI

Table 13.4   Spouse Correlations: California Psychological Inventory (CPI) Scales

CPI Scale	IHD Samples		Buss (1984a) Sample
	Time 1	Time 2	
Responsibility	.35**	.37**	.36**
Socialization	.20*	.10	.17*
Self-control	.13	.18*	.07

*p < .05
**p < .01

scales reported by D. M. Buss (1984a) in an independent investigation. A comparison of these two sets of findings buttresses the evidence for nonrandom mating along traits related to antisocial behavior. Some evidence also points to significant but low correlations between spouses for criminal behavior (e.g., Baker, Mack, Moffitt, & Mednick, 1989).

Assortative mating has important genetic and social consequences (Buss, 1984b; Thiessen & Gregg, 1980), and it may also have important psychological implications. From the perspective of personality development, marriage to a similar partner serves to create an environment that reinforces initial tendencies; through assortative mating, people may set in motion processes of social interchange that help to sustain their dispositions across time and circumstance.

Using the archives of the Institute of Human Development, Caspi and Herbener (1990) sought to determine whether assortative mating of spouses on personality characteristics might promote personality continuity. When the original members of the Oakland Growth and Berkeley Guidance studies were interviewed in 1970 and 1980, so were their spouses, thereby providing personality profiles (in the form of individual Q-sorts) of subjects and spouses that could be directly correlated with each other. Caspi and Herbener divided the couples into three groups of equal size on the basis of the similarity between the spouses' 1970 Q-sorts and then examined the continuity of each person's personality from 1970 to 1980. They found that the least similar spouses showed individual continuities of .4 from 1970 to 1980; moderately similar spouses showed individual continuities of .5; and the most similar spouses showed continuities of .6. In two independent longitudinal studies, marriage to a similar partner appeared to promote consistency in the intraindividual organization of personality attributes across adulthood.

Perhaps more than any other social selection, then, marriage may contribute to personality continuities; for in selecting marriage partners, individuals also select the environments they will inhabit and the reinforcements to which they will be subject until death (or divorce) parts them (Buss, 1987). In addition, marital assortment may promote family transmission effects to the extent that marital assortment gives rise to shared experiences that create similarities between family members (Caspi, Herbener, & Ozer, 1992).

We have discussed the tendency to form friendships with similar others and the tendency to marry similar others as if these were different tendencies. But they are not. In a unique longitudinal design, Kandel, Davies, and Baydar (1990) examined continuities in the tendency to form dyadic relations with similar others. Using a sample of triads (i.e., longitudinal sample members matched with a best friend in adolescence and with a partner in adulthood), they examined the correlation between two latent variables; the first defining friendship similarity in adolescence, the second defining marital similarity in adulthood. The results revealed significant continuity from adolescence to adulthood—across different types of relationships—in the tendency of individuals to affiliate with others who are similar to themselves in terms of drug use and other (non)normative behaviors.

Just as assortative mating represents an important mechanism of continuity, cross-assortative mating may be a mechanism of change. Consider the case of deviant youth. What distinguishes the natural histories of men who are antisocial across the life course from those who defy the probabilities of a cumulative sequence of life disadvantage? Sampson and Laub (1990, 1993) addressed this question in their longitudinal study of 500 delinquents and 500 nondelinquent controls. The answer points to a set of informal social controls that may serve to reduce involvements in familiar and deviant social habits. In particular, marriage to a supportive spouse appears to modify trajectories of deviance across the life course. This effect was obtained in analyses that were performed separately among delinquents and nondelinquents and that controlled for original level of deviance.

Equally striking is an account of girls who grew up "in care." Quinton and Rutter (1988) found that, in general, institutional rearing was associated with a variety of psychosocial adversities in adulthood. Girls who were reared in institutions had worse outcomes than girls in the comparison group; for example, as adults, they were more likely to perform inadequately as mothers. However, as shown in Figure 13.3, this association was moderated by the quality of adult marital relationships. Thus, institutionally reared women who had a supportive spouse were just as likely to provide good parenting for their own children as were comparison-group women. Continuities in the life course and across generations were especially evident among institutionally reared women who lacked marital support.

Still, we have much more to learn about the mechanisms that allow problem youth to escape disadvantage through marriage. What distinguishes antisocial males who form bonds with supportive spouses from those who do not? The process is most likely not random. In their study, Quinton and Rutter (1988) note that women who escaped disadvantage through marriage differed from those who did not; the former were characterized already in adolescence by a constellation of attributes the authors dubbed "planfulness."

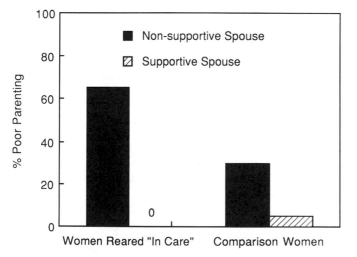

Figure 13.3 Spousal support as a moderator of the effect of childhood deprivation on adult parenting. From *Parenting Breakdown: The Making and Breaking of Inter-generational Links* by D. Quinton and M. Rutter, 1988. Copyright 1988 by Avebury. Reprinted by permission of the authors.

In combination, the studies we have reviewed suggest that continuities may emerge, not in spite of changing relationships and situations, but rather because individuals often select environments that are correlated with their backgrounds and dispositions. A more complete account of continuity and change thus requires that we examine the sustaining role of environmental conditions and, also, how individuals in various settings and relationships are successively drawn in as accomplices in the maintenance of behavior patterns across the life course (Wachtel, 1977). One does not have to embrace the most radical proposition contained in Sullivan's (1953, p. 111) conception of personality as the "relatively enduring pattern of recurrent interpersonal situations which characterize a human life" to appreciate its more subtle implication: Inquiries about sources of individual continuity and change may benefit from examining not only the individual but also those significant others in his or her life that contribute to the continuity and change of personality.

Life-Course Consequences of Person-Environment Interactions

We have noted that the processes of reactive, evocative, and proactive interaction enable an individual's personality both to shape itself and to promote its own continuity through the life course. These same processes also enable an individual's personality to influence the life course itself. In particular, person-environment interactions can produce two kinds of consequences in the life course: cumulative consequences and contemporary consequences.

Consider the case of a boy who, in late childhood, responds to frustration with explosive temper tantrums. His ill temper may provoke school authorities to expel him (*evocative interaction*) or cause him to experience school failure so negatively (*reactive interaction*) that he chooses to quit as soon as he is legally permitted to do so (*proactive interaction*). In either case, leaving school might limit his future career opportunities, channeling him into frustrating low-level jobs. This low occupational status might then lead to an erratic work life characterized by frequent job changes and bouts of unemployment, possibly disrupting his marriage and leading to divorce. In this hypothetical scenario, the occupational and marital outcomes are *cumulative* consequences of his childhood personality. Once set in motion by childhood temper tantrums, the chain of events takes over and culminates in the adult outcomes—even if he is no longer ill-tempered as an adult.

On the other hand, if he does carry his ill temper into adulthood, then contemporary *consequences* are also likely to arise. He is likely to explode when frustrations arise on the job or when conflicts arise in his marriage. This can lead to an erratic work life, low-level occupational status, and divorce. In this scenario, the same occupational and marital outcomes are contemporary consequences of his current personality rather than consequences of earlier events such as quitting school.

Caspi, Bem, and Elder (1989; Caspi, Elder, & Bem, 1987) explored these two hypothetical scenarios in their work using data from the longitudinal Berkeley Guidance Study. They identified men who had a history of temper tantrums during late childhood, and then traced the continuities and consequences of this personality style across the subsequent 30 years of the subjects' lives.

They began their research with the continuity question: Do ill-tempered boys become ill-tempered men? Apparently so. Correlations between the temper-tantrum scores in late childhood and Q-sort ratings 20 years later revealed that ill-tempered boys were later described as significantly more undercontrolled, irritable, and moody than their even-tempered peers.

They then examined the subjects' work histories. The major finding was that ill-tempered boys who came from middle-class homes suffered a progressive deterioration of socioeconomic status as they moved through the life course. They were somewhat more likely than their even-tempered peers to terminate their formal education earlier; the occupational status of their first jobs was significantly lower; and, by midlife (age 40), their occupational status was indistinguishable from that of men born into the working class. A majority of them held jobs of lower occupational status than those held by their fathers at a comparable age. They also had more erratic work lives, changing jobs more frequently and experiencing unemployment between ages 18 and 40.

Did these men become occupationally disadvantaged because their earlier ill-temperedness started them down a particular path (cumulative consequences) or because their current ill-temperedness handicapped them in the world of work (contemporary consequences)? The path analysis displayed in Figure 13.4 reveals evidence—albeit indirect—for both kinds of consequences.

Cumulative consequences are implied by the effect of childhood ill-temperedness on occupational status at midlife: Tantrums predict lower educational attainment (*beta* = −.34, *p* < .05), and educational attainment, in turn, predicts occupational status (*beta* = .59, *p* < .001). But there is no direct effect of ill-temperedness on occupational status (*beta* = −.10). In other words, middle-class boys with a history of childhood ill-temperedness arrive at lower occupational status at midlife because they truncated their formal education, not because they continue to be ill-tempered. (The subsequent path in Figure 13.4 between occupational status and occupational stability

cannot be interpreted unequivocally because they are contemporaneous variables.)

Contemporary consequences are implied by the strong direct link between ill-temperedness and occupational stability (*beta* = −.45, *p* < .01). Men with a childhood history of ill-temperedness continue to be ill-tempered in adulthood, where it gets them into trouble in the world of work. (A history of childhood ill-temperedness also affects the domestic sphere. Almost half (46%) of the men with histories of childhood ill-temperedness had divorced by age 40 compared with only 22% of other men.) As noted earlier, the processes of reactive, evocative, and proactive interaction not only shape personality and mediate its continuity over time; these processes also enable the personality to influence the trajectory of the life course itself.

FOR WHOM IS CONTINUITY THE DOMINANT PATTERN? A DEVELOPMENTAL-TAXONOMIC THEORY OF ANTISOCIAL BEHAVIOR

At the beginning of this chapter, we noted that there are large individual differences in the stability of antisocial behavior. Antisocial behavior is quite common in the population, but among most persons such behavior is temporary and situational. In contrast, antisocial behavior is highly stable and consistent in a relatively small number of males whose behavior problems are also quite extreme. In this section, we elaborate on the distinction between persistent and temporary antisocial behavior and review a new theory of delinquency based on this distinction. A central tenet of the theory is that persistent and temporary antisocial persons constitute two *qualitatively* distinct types of people, and each type must be accounted for and explained by different mechanisms (Moffitt, 1993).

The theory is best introduced with reference to the mysterious relation between age and antisocial behavior, the most robust yet bewildering empirical observation in criminology.

Age and Antisocial Behavior

When official rates of crime are plotted against age, the rates for both prevalence and incidence of offending appear highest during adolescence; they peak sharply at about age 17 and drop precipitously in young adulthood. The majority of criminal offenders are teenagers; by the early 20s, the number of active offenders decreases by over 50%; by age 28, almost 85% of former delinquents desist from offending (Blumstein & Cohen, 1987; Farrington, 1986). With slight variations, this general relation between age and crime obtains among males and females, for most types of crimes, during recent historical periods, and in numerous Western nations (Hirschi & Gottfredson, 1983).

Until recently, research on age and crime has relied on official data, primarily arrest and conviction records. As a result, the "left-hand" side of the age-crime curve has been censored. However, research on childhood conduct disorder has now documented that antisocial behavior begins long before the age when it is first encoded in police data banks. We now know that the

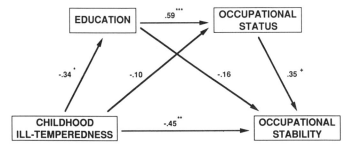

Figure 13.4 Midlife occupational stability of men with middle-class origins as a function of childhood ill-temperedness. From "Continuities and Consequences of Interactional Styles across the Life Course" by A. Caspi, G. H. Elder, Jr., and D. J. Bem, 1987, *Developmental Psychology, 23*. Copyright 1987 by the American Psychological Association. Reprinted by permission of the authors.

steep decline in antisocial behavior between ages 17 and 30 is mirrored by a steep incline in antisocial behavior between ages 7 and 17 (Loeber, Stouthamer-Loeber, Van Kammen & Farrington, 1989; Wolfgang et al., 1972).

And, with the advent of alternate measurement strategies—most notably self-reports of deviant behavior—we now know that arrest statistics merely reflect the tip of the deviance iceberg (Hood & Sparks, 1970; Klein, 1989). Actual rates of illegal behavior soar so high during adolescence that participation in delinquency appears to be a normal part of teen life (Elliott, Ageton, Huizinga, Knowles, & Canter, 1983). With the liberty of some artistic license, the solid curved line in Figure 13.5 may be taken to represent what is currently known about the prevalence of antisocial behavior over the life course.

Although there is widespread agreement about the shape of this curve, there are few convincing explanations for the relation between age and crime. Until recently, scholars still disagreed about whether the adolescent peak represented a change in prevalence or a change in incidence: Does adolescence bring an increment in the number of people who are willing to offend or does the small and constant number of offenders simply generate more criminal acts while they are adolescent? Empirical evaluations now suggest that the former explanation is correct. Farrington's (1983) study of offense rates over age, showed that the adolescent peak reflects a temporary increase in the number of people involved in antisocial behavior, not an acceleration in the offense rates of individuals.

But whence the increase? One possibility is that some phenomenon unique to adolescent development causes throngs of new adolescent offenders to temporarily join the few stable antisocial individuals in their delinquent ways. Figure 13.5 portrays these changes in prevalence graphically. A small group of persons engages in antisocial behavior of one sort or another at every stage of

life. We have labeled these persons "Life-Course-Persistent" to reflect the continuous course of their antisocial behavior. A larger group of persons fills out the age-crime curve with crime careers of short duration. We have labeled these persons "Adolescence-Limited," to reflect their more temporary involvement in antisocial behavior.

This simple distinction serves a powerful organizing function, with important implications for a theory about the cause of crime (Moffitt, 1993). We propose that for persons whose adolescent misbehavior is merely an inflection in a lifelong antisocial course, the origins of antisocial behavior must be found in early childhood, and we shall call on the aforementioned genetic, neuropsychological, environmental, and interactional effects to explain continuity in their troubled lives. In contrast, among delinquents whose misbehavior is confined to the adolescent years, the causal factors are proximal—specific to the period of adolescent development—and we shall have to account for the *discontinuity* in their lives. We suggest that *"juvenile delinquency" conceals two qualitatively distinct categories of individuals, each in need of its own distinct theoretical explanation* (Moffitt, 1993).

The next sections describe the two hypothetical types of antisocial youth: Life-Course-Persistent and Adolescence-Limited. The two groups differ in etiology, developmental course, demographic distribution, prognosis for intervention, and, importantly, in the classification of their behavior as either pathological or adaptive. Our goal is to proffer a description of the two hypothetical types in the form of a set of testable predictions.[1]

"Life-Course-Persistent" Antisocial Behavior

Continuity over the Life Course.   As implied by our label, continuity is the hallmark of this small group of persons. Across the life course, these individuals exhibit changing manifestations of antisocial behavior: biting at two, shoplifting at eight, selling drugs at 14, robbery at 20, and fraud at 28—the underlying disposition remains the same, but its expression changes form with the emergence of new social opportunities at different points in development. This pattern of heterotypic continuity is matched also by cross-situational consistency: Life-Course-Persistent antisocial persons lie at home, steal from shops, cheat at school, fight in bars, and embezzle at work (Loeber, 1982; Loeber & Baicker-McKee, 1989; Robins, 1966, 1978; White et al., 1990).

And what about the period beyond age 28? The pattern of official crime over age implies that antisocial behavior disappears in midlife, but there is no reason to suspect the miraculous assumption of prosocial tendencies in this phase of life. Although criminal psychopaths decrease their number of arrestible offenses at about age 40, the constellation of antisocial personality traits described by Cleckley (1976) persists in male samples until age 69 (Harpur & Hare, 1994). Developmental considerations suggest that, beyond young adulthood, antisocial behavior may be expressed in a form that is simply not yet well-measured by epidemiological surveys.

If, as we have asserted, age influences opportunities for the expression of antisocial behavior, it is likely that aging antisocial men increasingly lose opportunities to perform street crime; their physical strength declines, their networks of accomplices

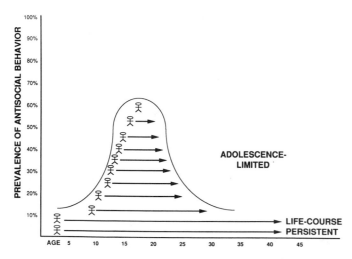

Figure 13.5   The changing prevalence of participation in antisocial behavior across the life span. From "Adolescence-Limited and Life-Course-Persistent Antisocial Behavior: A Developmental Taxonomy" by T. E. Moffitt, 1993, *Psychological Review, 100.* Copyright 1993 by the American Psychological Association. Reprinted by permission of the author.

dwindle, and prisons loom ever more threatening. Our theory predicts that offenders with a lifelong pattern of antisocial behavior would resort in midlife to antisocial acts that require less brawn and fewer accomplices, and that can be committed covertly. Excluded from street crime, Life-Course-Persistent persons may express their antisocial proclivities off the street, in settings where their behavior is less likely to come to the attention of authorities. Thus, family violence, wherein weaker victims are conveniently at hand in the privacy of home, may be but one more manifestation of heterotypic continuity in the lives of Life-Course-Persistent persons. Consistent with this hypothesis, crime statistics show that, whereas property crimes peak in the teen years and drop thereafter, family violence offenses show a steady increase with age (Gottfredson & Hirschi, 1986). Similarly, Farrington and West (1990) found that half the persistent offenders in the Cambridge longitudinal study self-reported having hit their spouses when they were interviewed at age 32. There is thus continuity in these men's lives, but the underlying disposition changes its manifestation across time and in diverse circumstances.

Low Prevalence in the Population. We have already alluded to the small number of Life-Course-Persistent persons in the general population. In fact, there is remarkable uniformity in the prevalence rates of different manifestations of antisocial behavior: Regardless of their age, under 10% of males warrant an antisocial designation. For example, about 5% of preschool boys are considered "very difficult to manage" (McGee, Partridge, Williams, & Silva, 1991); the prevalence of Conduct Disorder among school-age boys has been found to be between 4% and 9% in several countries (e.g., Costello, 1989; Rutter, Tizard, & Whitmore, 1970); about 6% of boys are first arrested as preteens (Moffitt & Silva, 1988d; Wolfgang et al., 1972); the rate of conviction for a violent offense in young adult males is between 3% and 6% (Moffitt, Mednick, & Gabrielli, 1989); and the prevalence of men with antisocial personality disorder (psychopathy) is estimated at about 5% (Davison & Neale, 1990).

Possibly, the persons who constitute these rates at different ages are different individuals. But the longitudinal data suggest otherwise: It is more likely that the remarkable constancy of prevalence rates reflects the co-occurrence of Life-Course-Persistent individuals in different antisocial categories at different ages. The professional nomenclature may change, but the faces remain the same as they drift through successive systems aimed at curbing their deviance—schools, juvenile-justice programs, psychiatric-treatment centers, and prisons.

There are still gaps in the epidemiological data base, but the consistency is more impressive: A substantial body of research consistently points to a very small group of males who display high rates of antisocial behavior across time and in diverse situations. The topography of their behavior may change with changing opportunities, but the underlying disposition persists throughout the life course.

Beginnings

If antisocial behavior is as stable as these data imply, we are compelled to look for its roots early in life, in factors that are present before or soon after birth. It is possible that the etiological chain begins with some factor capable of producing individual differences in the neuropsychological functions of the infant nervous system. Such differences may be heritable in origin (Plomin et al., 1990). In addition, such differences may result from pre- or postnatal exposure to toxic agents (Needleman & Beringer, 1981; Rodning, Beckwith, & Howard, 1989) or from delivery complications (Kandel et al., 1989; Szatmari et al., 1986). Finally, the brain may also be altered by neonatal deprivation of nutrition, stimulation, and even affection (Kraemer, 1988; Meany, Aitken, van Berkel, Bhatnager, & Sapolsky, 1988).

There are many routes by which compromised neuropsychological function might lead to antisocial behavior, and we have reviewed some of these processes in an earlier section of this chapter. According to one hypothetical scenario, toddlers with subtle neuropsychological deficits may be clumsy and awkward, overactive, inattentive, hard to keep on schedule, delayed in reaching developmental milestones, poor at verbal comprehension, deficient at expressing themselves, and may also show extreme emotional reactions. Such children pose a challenge to the most resourceful, loving, and patient parents. Unfortunately, the characteristics of parents and children tend to be correlated; parents of children who are difficult to manage are likely to lack the necessary resources, cognitive and temperamental, to cope constructively with a difficult child (Scarr & McCartney, 1983). The work of Patterson and his colleagues, reviewed earlier in this chapter, describes elegantly the ways in which difficult children may contribute to dysfunctional parenting. Patterson has also described the compounding effects of shared difficult temperament between parents and their children (e.g., Patterson, Bank, & Stoolmiller, 1990; Snyder & Patterson, 1987).

Cumulative Failure to Form Attachment Bonds. The child with subtle cognitive deficits is not merely difficult to manage, he or she is sometimes difficult to love. The cross-sectional association between juvenile delinquency and weak attachment bonds to parents is well known (Hirschi, 1969); less is known about the *developmental course* of antisocial children's attachment bonds. One possibility is that neuropsychological problems of Life-Course-Persistent persons disrupt the initial formation of healthy parent-infant bonds: "An excessively irritable, labile, or fearful infant is harder to nurture than a calm, stable, happy baby" (Kagan, Reznick, & Snidman, 1990; also see Goldsmith, Bradshow, & Rieser-Danner, 1986).

Waters, Vaughan, and Egeland (1980) found that aspects of neonatal adaptation that are typically included in infant neuropsychological examinations (such as orientation and motor maturity) predicted the quality of later infant-mother attachment. Irritable infant temperament has been shown to prospectively predict weak parent-child attachment (measured by the toddler's resistance to reunion with the mother after a separation from her), *especially* when the mother lacked her own supportive relationships (Crockenberg, 1981). Another study suggests that child-parent interactions influence attachment. Rodning, Beckwith, and Howard (1991) found that only 11% of a sample of prenatally drug-exposed toddlers were securely attached; the insecure children appeared dazed, aimless, confused, and unclear in communicating, while substance-abusing mothers treated the children with rejection, insensitivity, and little physical contact. Although the data are still sparse, an infant's neuropsychological health may combine with parent characteristics to cement attachment bonds (Kagan, 1984).

Theorists such as Bowlby (1973, 1988) and Ainsworth (1973) have proposed that failure to form secure relationships with parents during infancy has far-reaching implications for the capacity to form affectionate, trusting friendships and stable family relationships in later life. If first relationships constitute a "working model" for subsequent relationships, then childhood experiences of neglect, rejection, or conflict might be expected to color subsequent attitudes toward peers, spouses, employers, and even potential victims of crimes. Such harmful childhood experiences appear to be typical in the backgrounds of Life-Course-Persistent antisocial persons. Thus the "working model" of a Life-Course-Persistent antisocial person might be expected to yield a series of short-lived and exploitative relationships, void of any deep affection.

Absence of loyal friendships, unstable marital bonds, callous treatment of others, and irresponsible behavior toward offspring are the hallmarks of Life-Course-Persistent antisocial persons. Cleckley (1976) listed "incapacity for love" as a defining attribute of the psychopath. This construct has since been operationalized as the inability to maintain enduring attachments to a sexual partner, poor marital history, sexual promiscuity, lack of close friendships, failure to function as a responsible parent, and repeated violent confrontations with others, all of which are among the diagnostic criteria for antisocial personality disorder (American Psychiatric Association, 1987; Robins, 1966).

No empirical studies have yet linked prospective measures of parent-child attachment during the infant period with delinquent or criminal outcomes in later life. A few studies predicting childhood behavior problems from infant-mother attachment have been done, but findings are mixed (e.g., Fagot & Kavanaugh, 1990; Lewis, Feirling, McGuffog, & Jaskir, 1984; Lieberman, 1977). The implications of these studies are unclear because they have used small and/or middle-class samples, in which the base rates of insecure attachment, poor parenting, and conduct problems are each low. The studies have operationalized the quality of attachment through the Strange Situation procedure, yet the heuristic value of Bowlby's theory for this analysis of antisocial behavior need not be clouded by debate over the validity of the Strange Situation classification system. The study that is perhaps most pertinent to this review is the longitudinal Minnesota Mother-Child Study, which has examined outcomes of weak attachment in a sample at risk for poor parenting. In that sample, avoidant attachment measured in infancy was significantly correlated with boys' aggressive behavior in elementary school. A combination of avoidant child attachment, maternal hostility, and negative child affect explained almost one-third of the variance in the children's aggressive outcomes (Renken, Egeland, Marvinney, Mangelsdorf, & Sroufe, 1989).

There is some evidence that poor parent-child bonds can predict antisocial behavior beyond childhood. An exhaustive review of family studies concluded that, compared with all other aspects of family life and child-rearing that have been systematically studied, neglect by parents was the strongest predictor of later criminal careers (Loeber & Stouthamer-Loeber, 1986). Similarly, McCord (1983b) and Eron, Huesmann, & Zelli (1991) found that parental rejection was more strongly related to later criminal outcomes than other parenting practices (including discipline). Conversely, parental warmth and affection served to buffer boys who incurred risk for crime from other environmental disadvantages (McCord, 1983a).

Thus, the research evidence cited here suggests that abnormal parent-child relationships in early life may be related to a Life-Course-Persistent pattern of antisocial behavior in later years. In fact, disrupted affectional ties seem to be more influential than other family factors (e.g., social class, family structure, disciplinary strategies) in predicting long-term antisocial outcomes. It is conceivable that these early relational difficulties may have at least partial roots in children's neuropsychological endowments. This brief analysis of the theoretical long-term implications of disrupted attachments suggests the provocative hypothesis that delinquents who lack the capacity to form strong bonds with other people will more readily engage in antisocial behaviors of an interpersonal nature. If true, then Life-Course-Persistent delinquents, relative to other offenders, should be willing to engage in more violent or predatory confrontations with victims. And, they may be less discriminating about who they prey on, finding victims among their friends and families, as well as strangers. One study has shown that offenders who engage in the widest variety of different types of crimes, including violent crimes, described themselves on a personality assessment instrument as interpersonally alienated and lacking in need for social closeness (Krueger et al., 1994).

Cumulative Academic Failure. The perspectives introduced in the last section emphasized neuropsychological effects on early parent-child interactions. Other theorists point to the limits placed on school achievement by neuropsychological impairment. As previously mentioned, Hirschi's (1969) version of social control theory predicts that differences in intellectual capacity will have implications for how children experience school. For example, children with neuropsychological deficits have difficulty learning basic academic skills (Knights & Bakker, 1976; Rourke, 1975), and the formative educational experiences of many children with even subtle mild cognitive impairments includes frustration, failure, and humiliation (Maloney & Ward, 1976).

Cognitive deficits may also encourage antisocial behavior if they increase the likelihood that children will spend time in the company of already-delinquent pupils. Discussing the effects of individual differences on peer affiliation, Rowe and Osgood (1984) pointed out that scholarly students and failing students probably lack common vocabulary and common interests. Thus, underachieving students would feel more comfortable with peers of low verbal ability, and we have seen that such children are likely to be antisocial. More worrisome is systematic concentration of antisocial students in classrooms as an unintended side-effect of ability tracking. Kellam (1990) demonstrated that tracking produces segregation by antisocial behavior. Some first-grade classrooms had no aggressive pupils, but in other classrooms as many as 70% of the pupils were aggressive, as a result of tracking by pupils' reading-readiness scores. Regardless of social experiences at school, cognitive deficits interfere with youngsters' mastery of reading, writing, and arithmetic. Young adults who cannot read or understand basic mathematics will find few alternatives to crime in the job market (Maughan et al., 1985).

It must be said that there is controversy over the causal direction of the documented relation between measures of cognitive ability and antisocial behavior. Numerous studies conclude that antisocial behavior arises from cognitive deficit, others conclude that cognitive development is impeded by antisocial behavior. Hinshaw (1992) reviewed the evidence and pointed out that the entire database for the controversy is correlational, and thus can never be conclusive. Nonetheless, the mixed findings on causal direction are not problematic for the present theory because the theory posits that both causal relations occur sequentially in a series of person/environment interactions. The model is consistent with data from the New Zealand sample (Moffitt, 1990a). In 5% of the boys, difficult behavior and low scores on cognitive and motor tests coincided at age 3 years. Their antisocial behavior was exacerbated at the time of school entry, suggesting an effect of ability on behavior. From age 7 to age 13 their antisocial behavior remained stable while their reading attainment fell further and further behind their peers, suggesting an effect of behavior on ability. As adolescents, they were more aggressive than other delinquents, and their performance on neuropsychological tests was poorer. In light of their abject reading failure, it is likely that these boys will have poor employment prospects and continued delinquency, an effect of ability on behavior.

In summary, we propose a causal chain with origins in subtle neuropsychological dysfunctions during infancy. Such dysfunctions wreak their effects by setting limits on the growth of social behavior and interpersonal bonds at home and by limiting academic achievements at school. The subsequent links in this causal chain may culminate in Life-Course-Persistent antisocial behavior.

Maintenance over the Life Course

Neuropsychological deficits, disrupted attachment relationships, and learning disabilities may have long-term consequences for the continuity of antisocial behavior in part because these early individual differences set in motion cumulative continuities.

For example, children with poor self-control are often rejected by peers and adults (Coie, Belding, & Underwood, 1988; Dishion, 1990; Dodge, Coie, & Brakke, 1982). In turn, children who have learned to expect rejection, perhaps at home (Crittendon & DiLalla, 1988), are likely in later settings to interpret ambiguous encounters as threatening and thereby act preemptively, striking out against the world in an anticipatory fashion (Dodge, 1980; Dodge & Frame, 1982; Dodge & Newman, 1981). Or the following sequence of cumulative continuity may occur: Behavior problems at school and failure to attain basic math and reading skills place a low ceiling on job opportunities and thereby cut off alternatives to crime (Maughan et al., 1985; Moffitt, 1990b). Poor self-control, impulsivity, an inability to delay gratification, and foreshortened time horizons also increase the risk that antisocial persons will make irrevocable decisions that close the doors of opportunity: Teen parenthood, substance addiction, school dropout, disabling or disfiguring injuries, patchy work

histories, and time spent incarcerated extend the chain of cumulative continuity and diminish the probabilities of later success (Cairns & Cairns, 1993; Wilson & Herrnstein, 1985). Similarly, labels accrued early in life can influence later opportunities; an early arrest record or a "bad" reputation may rule out jobs, higher education, or an advantageous marriage (Farrington, 1977; Klein, 1986; West, 1982). In short, the behavior of Life-Course-Persistent antisocial persons in increasingly maintained and supported by narrowing options and opportunities.

In addition to cumulative continuity, the behavior of Life-Course-Persistent persons is maintained by contemporary continuity: Antisocial persons continue to carry into adulthood the same underlying constellation of traits that got them into trouble earlier in life.

For example, a mistrustful working model of relationships may limit the ability of Life-Course-Persistent men to form the kinds of close adult relationships with wives and children that deter crime (Belsky, Youngblade, & Pensky, 1990). Features of poor self-control may lead in adulthood to inauspicious decision making and contribute to impulsive crimes (Hare & McPherson, 1984). The same learning disabilities that precluded academic attainment in school may place a ceiling on the types of job skills these men can learn in later years. And even if Life-Course-Persistent persons are given the chance for remedial adult education, there is no reason to expect their cognitive deficits to remit spontaneously with age and allow them to learn more easily in adulthood the skills that eluded them in childhood.

Costs and Prognosis

It is now well documented that 5% to 7% of males, who have high-rate long-term antisocial careers, account for half of known crimes (e.g., Wolfgang et al., 1972). These high-rate offenders are also disproportionately likely to commit violent offenses (Moffitt et al., 1989). These epidemiological facts have been replicated around the world (see Farrington, Ohlin, & Wilson, 1986, for a review) and pose urgent policy considerations.

The prognosis for Life-Course-Persistent persons is bleak. Their path is likely to wend its way through a bewildering forest of unsavory outcomes (Farrington & West, 1990; Sampson & Laub, 1993). Drug and alcohol addiction, unsatisfactory employment, unpaid debts, homelessness, drunk driving, violent assault, multiple and unstable relationships with women, spouse battery, abandoned, neglected, or abused children, and psychiatric illness have all been reported at very high rates for offenders who persist past the age of 25 (Knight & West, 1975; Robins, 1966).

Because Life-Course-Persistent antisocial behavior extends across time and in diverse circumstances, its costs to society are incurred by an equally bewildering number of agencies and institutions. The best known costs are incurred by schools who must combat learning disabilities and control children with conduct disorders; by juvenile justice systems that seek to curb delinquency; and by penal systems that must incarcerate offenders. But the bill is more staggering still. There are health care costs for victims of violence, costs of health care systems for treating addictions and injuries, costs of unemployment and support for dependent children, costs to employers of worker absenteeism and retraining, and costs of preventing, controlling, and repairing property damage and theft.

Interventions with Life-Course-Persistent persons have met with dismal results (Martinson, 1974; Sechrest, White, & Brown, 1979). This does not surprise, considering that interventions are planned relatively late in the chain of cumulative continuity. As we have seen earlier in this chapter, the forces of continuity are formidable foes. And as we have also seen, opportunities for change are often actively transformed into opportunities for continuity: Rehabilitation programs provide a chance to selectively affiliate with antisocial peers, new jobs furnish the chance to steal, and new relationships provide a partner for abuse. We have contended that individual differences are likely to be accentuated when assuming new roles (Caspi & Moffitt, 1993) and our theory anticipates many such disappointing outcomes, especially when Life-Course-Persistent persons are thrust into new situations that purportedly offer the chance "to turn over a new leaf."

The implications from our study of continuity are that successful efforts to help Life-Course-Persistent individuals must come earlier in the chain of cumulative continuity, long before the antisocial style becomes ingrained and inflexible (Robins & Earls, 1986). Interventions might be directed toward specific aspects of development that are most often conscripted in the service of continuity (McGuire & Earls, 1991). We strongly urge that interventions be designed with a more realistic appreciation of the potency of the forces of continuity.

Life-Course-Persistent Antisocial Behavior Is Psychopathology

The syndrome of Life-Course-Persistent antisocial behavior meets many of the criteria for psychopathology:

- It is *statistically unusual,* characteristic of about 5% of males. Its rarity is thus consistent with a statistical definition of "abnormality."
- It is characterized by tenacious stability across time and in diverse circumstances. Life-Course-Persistent antisocial behavior is thus *maladaptive and inflexible.* The inflexibility of this antisocial style may be associated with a very limited repertoire of alternative prosocial behaviors (Tremblay, 1991).
- It may have a *biological basis* in subtle functions of the nervous system. (We hasten to add that assertions about biological origins are not deterministic. Rather, we have described how individual differences in nervous system variation provide raw material for subsequent person-environment interactions that may increase the risk of antisocial development.)
- It is *associated with other mental disorders.* Comorbidity of diagnoses is common among Life-Course-Persistent antisocial persons and research documents overlap with learning disabilities, hyperactivity, personality disorders, and addictions. Elliott, Huizinga, and Menard (1989) and Moffitt (1990a) have now shown that the presence of multiple psychological disorders predicts persistence of illegal behavior.

No one or two of these characteristics is enough to warrant a classification as psychopathology. Nonetheless, together they form a persuasive argument that persons whose antisocial behavior is stable and pervasive over the life course may be categorically distinct from persons demonstrating Adolescence-Limited antisocial behavior, which is short-term and situational.

"Adolescence-Limited" Antisocial Behavior

Discontinuity.   As implied by our label, discontinuity is the hallmark of teenage delinquents who have no notable history of antisocial behavior in childhood and no future for such behavior in adulthood. Compared with the Life-Course-Persistent type, Adolescence-Limited delinquents show relatively little continuity in their antisocial behavior. *Across age,* change in delinquent involvement is often abrupt, especially during the periods of onset and desistence. For example, in one longitudinal study of a representative sample of 536 boys, 12% of the youngsters were classified as new delinquents at age 13; they had no prior history of antisocial behavior from age 5 to age 11. From age 11 to age 13, they had changed from below the sample average to 1.5 SD above average on self-reported delinquency (Moffitt, 1990a). By age 15, another 20% of this sample of boys had joined the ranks of newcomers to delinquency, despite no prior history of antisocial behavior (Moffitt, 1991). Barely into mid-adolescence, 32% of the sample boys had joined a smaller group of antisocial boys—persistent through childhood (7% of the sample)—in their juvenile delinquency.

Adolescence-Limited delinquents also have sporadic, crime-free periods in the midst of their brief crime careers. And, in contrast to the Life-Course-Persistent type, they lack consistency in their antisocial behavior *across situations.* For example, they may shoplift in stores and use drugs with friends, but they continue to obey the rules at school. Because of the chimeric nature of their delinquency, different reporters (such as self, parent, and teacher) are less likely to agree about their behavior problems when asked to complete rating scales or clinical interviews (Loeber & Schmaling, 1985; Loeber, Green, Lahey, & Stouthamer-Loeber, 1990).

High Prevalence in the Population.   The brief tenure of Adolescence-Limiteds' delinquency should not obscure their frequency in the population. By contrast with the Life-Course-Persistent type, Adolescence-Limited delinquency is ubiquitous. Several studies have shown that about one-third of males are arrested during their lifetime for a serious criminal offense, and fully four-fifths of males have police contact for some minor infringement (Farrington et al., 1986). These contacts are generally made during the adolescent years. Participation in delinquent behavior is known to increase dramatically at puberty; for males, participation surges to a near-normative level at its peak, which is near age 17 in most Western nations (Farrington, 1986; Wolfgang, Thornberry, & Figlio, 1987). Our New Zealand sample has shown the surge; the mean number of offenses reported by the boys doubled from ages 13 to 15, then tripled between ages 15 and 18. At age 13, 40% of the boys denied offending in the past year, but by their 18th birthdays only 7% denied offending in the past year. Numerous other self-report studies have documented that it is statistically aberrant to refrain from crime during adolescence (Elliott et al., 1983; Hirschi, 1969; Moffitt & Silva, 1988d).

Our observation that the antisocial behavior of many youths lacks stability across time and consistency across situations is more than merely descriptive. It has implications for a theory of the etiology of Adolescence-Limited delinquency. The flexibility of most delinquents' behavior suggests that their engagement in deviant lifestyles may be under the control of reinforcement and punishment contingencies.

Unlike their Life-Course-Persistent peers—whose behavior is inflexible and refractory to changing aspects of different situations—Adolescence-Limited delinquents are likely to engage in antisocial behavior in circumstances where such responses are profitable, but they are also able to abandon antisocial behavior when prosocial styles are more rewarding. They maintain control over their antisocial responses, and use them only in situations where they may serve an instrumental function. Thus, principles of learning theory will be important to our theory of the cause of Adolescence-Limited delinquency.

Beginnings

A theory of Adolescence-Limited delinquency must account for several empirical observations: onset in early adolescence, recovery by young adulthood, widespread prevalence, and lack of continuity. Why do youngsters with no history of behavior problems in childhood suddenly become antisocial in adolescence? Why do they develop antisocial problems rather than other difficulties? Why is delinquency so common among teens? How are they able to spontaneously recover from an antisocial lifestyle within a few short years?

Just as the childhood onset of Life-Course-Persistent persons compelled us to look for causal factors early in their development, the coincidence of puberty with the rise in delinquent behavior compels us to look for clues in adolescent development. Critical features of this developmental period are variability in biological age, the increasing importance of peer relationships, and the budding of teenagers' self-conscious values, attitudes, and aspirations.

We suggest that the antisocial behavior of Adolescence-Limited delinquents is best regarded as *adaptable* social behavior. Such behavior is motivated by the gap between *biological maturity* and *social maturity;* it is learned from antisocial models who are easily mimicked and it is sustained according to the principles of learning theory.

Why do Adolescence-Limited delinquents begin delinquency? We believe their delinquency is *social mimicry* of the antisocial style of Life-Course-Persistent youth. The concept of social mimicry is borrowed from ethology. Social mimicry occurs when two animal species share a single niche and one of the species has cornered the market on a resource that is needed to promote fitness (Moynihan, 1968). In such circumstances, the "mimic" species adopts the social behavior of the more successful species to help obtain access to the valuable resource. For example, cowbird chicks—who are left by their mothers to be reared in the nests of unsuspecting parent birds—learn to behave like the parent birds' own true chicks and thus get the parents to drop food their way. Social mimicry may also allow some species to safely pass among a more successful group and thus share access to desired resources. For example, some monkey species have learned

to mimic bird calls and are thus able to share the delights of ripe fruit after the tree has been discovered and located by birds. Similarly, zebras are sensitive to the social signals of impalas and gazelles and thus benefit from the latter species' superior ability to detect predators (Wilson, 1975).

If social mimicry is to explain why Adolescence-Limited delinquents begin to mimic the antisocial behavior of their Life-Course-Persistent peers, then delinquency must be a social behavior that allows access to some desirable resource. We believe the "resource" is mature social status, with its consequent power and privilege.

In olden times, biological maturity came at a later age, social adult-status arrived at an earlier age, and rites of passage clearly delineated youths' assumption of new roles and responsibilities. In the past century, improved nutrition and health care have decreased the age of biological maturity at the rate of three-tenths of a year per decade (Tanner, 1978). Simultaneously, modernization of work has increased the age of social maturity to later points in development (Empey, 1978; Glaser & Kent, 1959). The ensuing gap leaves modern teenagers in a 5- to 10-year role vacuum (Csikszentmihalyi & Larson, 1984). They are biologically capable and compelled to be sexual beings, yet they are asked to delay most of the positive aspects of adult life (see Susman et al., 1987; and Udry & Talbert, 1988 for studies of the compelling influence of pubertal hormones on behavior and personality). In most American states, teens are not allowed to work before 16, get a driver's license before 17, marry or vote before 18, or buy alcohol before 21; and they are admonished to delay having children and establishing their own private dwellings until their education is completed at 22, sometimes more than 10 years after sexual maturity. They remain financially and socially dependent on their families of origin, and are allowed few decisions of any real import. Yet they want desperately to establish intimate bonds with the opposite sex, to accrue material belongings, to make their own decisions, and to be regarded as consequential by adults. Contemporary adolescents are thus trapped in a *maturity gap,* chronological hostages of a time warp between biological age and social age.

This emergent teen phenomenology begins to color the world for most boys between the ages of 13 and 15, a bit earlier for most girls. At the time of biological maturity, pubertal changes make the remoteness of ascribed social maturity painfully apparent to teens. This new awareness coincides with their entry into a high-school society dominated by older peers. Thus, just as teens begin to feel the discomfort of the maturity gap, they are initiated into a peer group that has endured this problem for three to four years and has already perfected some delinquent ways of coping with it. Several researchers have noted that this life-course transition may place teens at risk for antisocial behavior and have shown that exposure to older peers, when coupled with puberty, is an important determinant of Adolescence-Limited delinquency (Caspi et al., 1993; Magnusson, 1988; Simmons, & Blyth, 1987).

Life-Course-Persistent youth are the vanguard of this transition. Healthy adolescents are well aware that the few Life-Course-Persistent youth in their midst do not seem to suffer from the maturity gap. Already adept at deviance, Life-Course-Persistent youth are able to obtain possessions by theft or vice that are otherwise inaccessible to teens who have no independent incomes (cars, clothes, drugs, entry to "adults-only" leisure settings). Life-Course-Persistent boys seem more sexually experienced and confident with the opposite sex. They are often relatively free of their families of origin; they seem to go their own way, making their own rules. They take risks and do dangerous things that parents could not possibly endorse. Within the adolescent culture, the antisocial precocity of Life-Course-Persistent youths is an admired asset.

For teens who become Adolescence-Limited delinquents, antisocial behavior is an effective means of knifing-off childhood apron strings and of proving that they can act independently to conquer new challenges. The reinforcers for delinquency include damaging the quality of attachment relationships with parents, alienating adults such as teachers, finding new ways to look older (such as by smoking cigarettes, engaging in sexual intercourse), and tempting fate (risking pregnancy, trying LSD, shoplifting, playing "chicken"). None of this may seem desirable to the middle-aged academic, but each of the aforementioned events is a precious resource to the teenager and serves to reinforce delinquency. Every curfew broken, car stolen, joint smoked, and baby conceived is a statement of independence.

Life-Course-Persistent delinquents have been engaged in antisocial behavior for many years before other youngsters take notice of them in adolescence. In fact, evidence suggests that earlier in life Adolescence-Limited delinquents ignored and rejected Life-Course-Persistent kids because of their unpredictable, aggressive behavior in elementary school (Coie et al., 1988; Dodge et al., 1982). Only with adolescence does the antisocial behavior of Life-Course-Persistent youths become a valuable and alluring commodity for teens who are frustrated by the maturity gap. Life-Course-Persistent delinquents demonstrate the techniques, and Adolescence-Limited delinquents mimic their ways with care.

Critical to our theory is the supposition that the negative consequences of delinquency are paradoxically reinforcing to teens. Thus, the teenager who successfully frustrates his parents and alienates his teachers is reinforced for his delinquency. In contrast, most theories of delinquency emphasize weak social controls, such as lack of supervision by adults or weak attachments to parents, as the *cause* of burgeoning teen crime (e.g., Hirschi, 1969). But these theories do not explain why antisocial behavior per se is the outcome of these weakened social control systems. Why don't unsupervised teens mow lawns for the elderly? Why don't youth weakly attached to their parents get together and do more algebra homework? Social control theories rely on the philosophical assumption that all humans are inherently antisocial; crime must thus emerge spontaneously, by default, whenever social controls are weakened. Our taxonomic theory cannot afford the luxury of this philosophical premise about the mainsprings of human behavior. We have offered instead an answer that invokes individual motivation: Algebra does not make a statement about independence; it does not assert that a youth is entitled to be taken seriously. Crime does.

Desistence

Adolescence-Limited delinquents generally do not maintain their delinquent behavior into young adulthood. Our earlier analysis of Life-Course-Persistent persons demanded an analysis of maintenance factors. In contrast, our analysis of Adolescence-Limited delinquents demands that we analyze desistence: Why do Adolescence-Limited delinquents desist from delinquency? Our answer: They respond well to changing contingencies. If learning mechanisms initiate and maintain their delinquency, then, likewise, changing contingencies can extinguish such behavior.

According to our analysis of the maturity gap, Adolescence-Limited delinquents gradually experience a loss of motivation for delinquency as they exit this gap. With the inevitable progression of chronological age, more legitimate and tangible adult roles become available to teens. They graduate from high school (Elliott & Voss, 1974), join the army (Elder, 1986), marry a prosocial spouse (Rutter & Giller, 1984), move away from the old neighborhood (West, 1982), get a job (Sampson & Laub, 1993), have children, and settle down. As aging begins to entitle delinquents to the adult roles they so coveted as teens, the consequences of illegal behavior shift from rewarding to punishing. An adult arrest record will limit job opportunities, drug abuse keeps them from getting to work on time, drunk driving is costly, and bar fights lead partners to leave their mates. Adolescence-Limited delinquents have a lot to lose by persisting in their antisocial behavior beyond the teen years.

What enables Adolescence-Limited delinquents to make these (often abrupt) prosocial transitions? Unlike their Life-Course-Persistent counterparts, they are relatively exempt from the forces of cumulative and contemporary continuity. In general, these young adults have good social skills; they have a record of average or better academic achievement; their mental health is sturdy; they still possess the capacity to forge close attachment relationships; and they retain the good intelligence they had when they entered adolescence. With their self-control and flexible behavior, Adolescence-Limited delinquents are sensitive to the implications of moving from the juvenile justice system to its adult counterpart. When juvenile offense records are expunged and adult penalties for crimes ensue, Adolescence-Limited offenders alter their behavioral choices accordingly. Because the behavior of these delinquents is adaptable, it responds to the threat of punishment with extinction. These are the adults who say "I used to smoke marijuana every day, but now it just makes me sleepy"; "I used to drive drunk all the time, but now my child is in the back seat."

The availability of alternatives to crime may explain why some Adolescence-Limited delinquents desist later than others. Although the forces of cumulative continuity build up less momentum over the course of their short crime careers, some Adolescence-Limited youths will fall prey to many of the same snares that maintain continuity among Life-Course-Persistent persons. Those whose teen forays into delinquency inadvertently attracted damaging consequences may have more difficulty desisting. A drug habit, an incarceration, interrupted education, or a teen pregnancy are snares that require extra effort and time from which to escape. We thus predict that, among Adolescence-Limited offenders, variability in age at desistence should be accounted for by the number and type of ensnaring life events that detain persons in a deviant lifestyle.

Invoking learning theory to explain juvenile delinquency is not new. Other theories have suggested that delinquency follows the learning of cultural definitions conducive to crime (e.g., Sutherland & Cressey, 1978). We have asked ourselves what motivates that learning. What reinforces it? Why do so many people learn the definitions at the same life stage? Who are their "teachers"? Why are the definitions conducive to crime unlearned so readily a few years later? Our analysis invokes the maturity gap as an explanation for the motivation and timing of Adolescence-Limited antisocial behavior. We call on the process of social mimicry to explain why healthy adolescents adopt the style of boys who have been antisocial since early childhood. Thus, we attempt to answer some questions begged by earlier theories.

Adolescence-Limited Antisocial Behavior Is Not Pathological Behavior

Our theory of the etiology of Adolescence-Limited antisocial behavior posits three necessary conditions:

1. The maturity gap makes the consequences of antisocial behavior appear desirable to many adolescents and thus creates a motivational state for engaging in such behavior (Jessor & Jessor, 1977; Silbereisen & Noack, 1988).
2. Life-Course-Persistent peers must be available to demonstrate delinquent techniques so that social mimicry can occur.
3. Most delinquent careers are of relatively short duration because the consequences of crime—while reinforcing for youths caught inside the maturity gap—become punishing to youths as soon as they age out of the gap.

Earlier we contended that Life-Course-Persistent antisocial behavior represented an especially pernicious and tenacious form of psychopathology. Our view of Adolescence-Limited delinquency is strikingly different: It is normative rather than abnormal; it is flexible and adaptable rather than rigidly stable; instead of a biological basis in the nervous system, its origins lie in youngsters' efforts to cope with the gap between biological and social maturity that has been spurred by rapid secular changes; and neither our theory nor the empirical evidence suggest that it is closely linked with any other disorder.

Conclusions and Implications

Our developmental-taxonomic theory grew out of an effort to reconcile two robust empirical observations: Epidemiological data suggest that the prevalence of involvement in antisocial behavior changes dramatically over the life course, but longitudinal data point to the impressive continuity of antisocial behavior in individual lives. As a developmental rapprochement, we have offered a distinction between two hypothetical subtypes of antisocial individuals, each with its unique etiologic process and prognosis.

A notable feature of the theory is that developmental data are *required* for making the differential diagnosis between the two types of antisocial behavior. Yet the bulk of research on antisocial behavior continues to be performed on adolescent subjects and is still limited to cross-sectional comparisons of delinquents and nondelinquents. This is unfortunate because researchers and practitioners cannot yet effectively discriminate meaningful subtypes on the basis of their antisocial behavior in adolescence.

Elliott and Huizinga (1984, p. 98), in reviewing studies of delinquency, have noted:

> The problem is that so few of the serious career offenders are known to the police and that so many trivial and non-serious offenders are captured in the justice system process . . . [there is] no effective means for discriminating between the serious and non-serious offenders.

We are suggesting a new way of thinking about juvenile delinquency: a developmental taxonomic theory of antisocial behavior may enable us to unravel the causes of delinquenc*ies* by discriminating between genuine delinquents and mimic delinquents (Moffitt, 1993).

Another analogy from animal ethology may help to illustrate our point: Monarch butterflies, whose wings are a distinctive orange and black, contain noxious chemicals that discourage birds from eating them. Admiral butterflies have adopted mimicry as a strategy for evading predators: They too are orange and black, though they lack toxicity. Birds pay a price in nutrition for not being able to discriminate between the two insects in the butterfly stage. However, if birds could observe the butterflies at an earlier developmental stage, as cocoon or larvae, they could readily identify which insect is dangerous, and which is not. Social scientists, like birds, must look to an earlier developmental stage to discern which juvenile delinquents are dangerous, and which are not. Just as the distinction between subtypes of schizophrenias has had a liberating effect on investigations of psychoses (Meehl & Golden, 1982), we hope that our theory will exert a similar influence on investigations of antisocial behavior.

Our developmental taxonomic theory may serve to reconcile some of the following disagreements, feuds, and misunderstandings in research on antisocial behavior:

- The developmental taxonomy may resolve conceptual tensions between studies of peer rejection and studies of peer affiliation (e.g., Cairns et al., 1988). If antisocial children are rejected by their peers, how is it that juvenile delinquents have so many friends with whom to commit illicit acts? Sometimes competing effects are both true. Our developmental taxonomy suggests that peer-rejection and peer-affiliation explanations may be true for different subtypes at different developmental stages.

- The developmental taxonomy may account for effects that appear and disappear as a function of age. For example, behavior-genetic studies have shown that adult crime is heritable, whereas juvenile delinquency is less so (DiLalla & Gottesman, 1989). Similarly, childhood conduct disorder and adult criminal conviction are linked with reading disability, but the relation between reading problems and adolescent delinquency is weak or even reversed in sign. Similar age-related fluctuations in effect size have been noticed for the associations between antisocial behavior and social class (Elliott & Huizinga, 1983) and gender (Smith & Visher, 1980). These "disappearing effects" yield (unnecessary) controversy; they may be an inadvertent consequence of "mixing apples with oranges" when using adolescent research samples. According to our theory, the ratio of Life-Course-Persistents to their social mimics will change as a function of the age of the sample. Consequently, effect sizes may be attenuated in adolescent samples, and developmental interpretations of cross-sectional data will be confounded.

• The developmental taxonomy may prove instrumental in resolving debates about etiologic processes. Consider the robust cross-sectional correlation, observed among teen-agers, between weak and disrupted attachments to parents and involvement in antisocial behavior. The empirical finding is persuasive, but its interpretation may differ for different types of people. Among Life-Course-Persistent antisocial persons, disrupted attachments in adolescence are part of a cumulative causal chain of continuity that originates during infancy. Among Adolescence-Limited delinquents, disrupted attachment relationships are a reinforcing *consequence* of emerging delinquency. Thus, developmental interpretations of familiar findings can be elaborated by adopting a taxonomic approach.

• The developmental taxonomy also has implications for intervention research. For many years, evaluation studies have struggled to account for individual differences in delinquents' susceptibility to treatment programs (McGuire & Earls, 1991). Our theory suggests that all delinquents are not the same; it makes us more circumspect about many current interventions. Life-Course-Persistent youth are difficult to treat, especially if the treatment does not combat the active processes promoting behavioral continuity. Adolescence-Limited delinquents may be easy to "treat," but our theory suggests a more unsettling implication about their developmental course: If left untreated, Adolescence-Limited delinquents may improve their behavior naturally within a short time. The historically minded reader will be reminded of a similar fallacy in the annals of psychological treatment: Some years ago, before the natural course of depressive episodes was understood clearly, psychotherapists claimed, on the basis of within-subject designs, that they could relieve depression within one or two years. Lest the error be repeated, it is incumbent on harbingers of successful correctional programs to estimate "treatment effects" independent of developmental functions.

SPEAKING OF CHANGE ...

Longitudinal research has taught us to treat the stability and consistency of individual differences as a problematic phenomenon requiring both confirmation and explanation. No longer can we assume implicitly that continuities in antisocial behavior are simply manifestations of intrapersonal dispositions. We have learned instead to seek the explanation for continuity in the interaction between the person and the environment.

Our search has revealed some surprises. Continuity is not guided by inertia; rather, vigorous processes promote continuity across the life course. This observation, however, need not discourage would-be agents of therapeutic intervention in antisocial lives. On the contrary, this perspective encourages a more realistic appreciation of the special circumstances required for the successful genesis of change in conduct-disordered children, persistent juvenile delinquents, and adults with antisocial personality disorder. Oft-heard cries of "nothing works" (e.g., Bergin & Garfield, 1971; Gottschalk, Davidson, Gensheimer, & Mayer, 1987; Lipton, Mertinson, & Wilks, 1975; Zigler & Berman, 1983) might be countered with the observation that we have yet to try hard enough (Moffitt, Caspi, Harkness, & Silva, 1993).

Change is not impossible, but we are learning that the situational requisites that define turning points in behavioral development are more rigid and specialized than previously thought. The processes promoting continuity are aggressive foes. And those of us in the allied mental health and correctional professions must now recognize that, to promote salutary outcomes, we shall have to do more than provide our antisocial clients with opportunities for change. We also have to eliminate those opportunities that allow active processes of continuity to flourish and guide the trajectory of the life course.

REFERENCES

Ainsworth, M. D. S. (1973). The development of infant-mother attachment. In B. M. Caldwell & H. N. Ricciuti (Eds.), *Review of child development research* (Vol. 3, pp. 1–95). Chicago: University of Chicago Press.

American Psychiatric Association. (1987). *Diagnostic and Statistical Manual of Mental Disorders,* (3rd ed. rev.). Washington, DC: Author.

Anderson, K. E., Lytton, H., & Romney, D. M. (1986). Mothers' interactions with normal and conduct-disordered boys: Who affects whom? *Developmental Psychology, 22,* 604–609.

Andrews, J. D. W. (1988). *The active self in psychotherapy: An integration of therapeutic styles.* New York: Gardner Press.

Backman, C. W. (1985). Interpersonal congruency theory revisited: A revision and extension. *Journal of Social and Personal Relationships, 2,* 489–505.

Backman, C. W. (1988). The self: A dialectical approach. In L. Berkowitz (Ed.), *Advances in experimental social psychology* (pp. 229–260). New York: Academic Press.

Baker, L. A., Mack, W., Moffitt, T. E., & Mednick, S. A. (1989). Etiology of sex differences in property crime in a Danish adoption cohort. *Behavior Genetics, 19,* 355–370.

Bell, P. A., & Baron, R. A. (1990). Affect and aggression. In B. S. Moore & A. M. Isen (Eds.), *Affect and social behavior* (pp. 64–88). New York: Cambridge University Press.

Bell, R. Q., & Chapman, M. (1986). Child effects in studies using experimental or brief longitudinal approaches to socialization. *Developmental Psychology, 22,* 595–603.

Belsky, J., Youngblade, L., & Pensky, E. (1990). Childrearing history, marital quality, and maternal affect: Intergenerational transmission in a low-risk sample. *Development and Psychopathology, 1,* 291–304.

Benson, D. F., & Zaidel, E. (1985). *The dual brain.* New York: Guilford.

Bergin, A., & Garfield, S. (1971). *Handbook of psychotherapy and behavior change.* New York: Wiley.

Berman, A., & Siegal, A. W. (1976). Adaptive and learning skills in juvenile delinquents: A neuropsychological analysis. *Journal of Learning Disabilities, 9,* 51–58.

Billy, J. O. G., Rodgers, J. L., & Udry, R. (1984). Adolescent sexual behavior and friendship choice. *Social Forces, 62,* 653–678.

Billy, J. O. G., & Udry, R. (1985). Patterns of adolescent friendship and effects of sexual behavior. *Social Psychology Quarterly, 48,* 27–41.

Block, J. (1971). *Lives through time.* Berkeley, CA: Bancroft.

Block, J., & Block, J. H. (1980). The role of ego-control and ego-resilience in the organization of behavior. In W. A. Collins (Ed.), *Minnesota Symposia on Child Psychology* (Vol. 13, pp. 39–101). Hillsdale, NJ: Erlbaum.

Block, J., Block, J. H., & Keyes, S. (1988). Longitudinally foretelling drug usage in adolescence: Early childhood personality and environmental precursors. *Child Development, 59,* 336–355.

Bloom, B. S. (1964). *Stability and change in human characteristics.* New York: Wiley.

Blumstein, A., & Cohen, J. (1987). Characterizing criminal careers. *Science, 237,* 985–991.

Bohman, M., Cloninger, C. R., Sigvardsson, S., & von Knorring, A. (1982). Predisposition to petty criminality in Swedish adoptees. I. Genetic and environmental heterogeneity. *Archives of General Psychiatry, 39,* 1233–1241.

Bohman, M., Cloninger, R., von Knorring, A., & Sigvardson, S. (1984). An adoption study of somatoform disorders: III. Cross-fostering analysis and genetic relationship to alcoholism and criminality. *Archives of General Psychiatry, 41,* 872–878.

Boldizar, J. P., Perry, D. G., & Perry, L. C. (1989). Outcome values and aggression. *Child Development, 60,* 571–579.

Borecki, I. B., & Ashton, G. C. (1984). Evidence for a major gene influencing performance on a vocabulary test. *Behavior Genetics, 14,* 63–80.

Bowlby, J. (1973). *Attachment and loss: Vol. 2. Separation.* New York: Basic Books.

Bowlby, J. (1988). Developmental psychiatry comes of age. *American Journal of Psychiatry, 145,* 1–10.

Bradley, R. H., Caldwell, B. M., & Rock, S. L. (1988). Home environment and school performance: A ten-year follow-up examination of three models of environmental action. *Child Development, 59,* 852–867.

Brickman, A. S., McManus, M. M., Grapentine, W. L., & Alessi, N. (1984). Neuropsychology assessment of seriously delinquent adolescents. *Journal of the American Academy of Child Psychiatry, 23,* 453–457.

Bronfenbrenner, U., Moen, P., & Garbarino, J. (1984). Child, family, and community. In R. Parke (Ed.), *Review of child development research: Vol. 7. The family* (pp. 283–328). Chicago: University of Chicago Press.

Bugenthal, D. B., & Schennum, W. A. (1984). Difficult children as elicitors and targets of adult communication patterns: An attributional-behavioral transactional analysis. With commentary by P. Shaver; with reply by D. B. Bugenthal & W. A. Shennum. *Monographs of the Society for Research in Child Development, 49* (Serial No. 205). No. 1.

Buss, A. H., & Plomin, R. (1984). *Temperament: Early developing personality traits.* Hillsdale, NJ: Erlbaum.

Buss, D. M. (1981). Predicting parent-child interactions from children's activity level. *Developmental Psychology, 17,* 59–65.

Buss, D. M. (1984a). Marital assortment for personality dispositions: Assessment with three different data sources. *Behavior Genetics, 14,* 111–123.

Buss, D. M. (1984b). Toward a psychology of person-environment correspondence: The role of spouse selection. *Journal of Personality and Social Psychology, 47,* 361–377.

Buss, D. M. (1987). Selection, evocation, and manipulation. *Journal of Personality and Social Psychology, 53,* 1214–1221.

Buss, D. M., Block, J. H., & Block, J. (1980). Preschool activity level: Personality correlates and developmental implications. *Child Development, 51,* 401–408.

Byrne, D., & Griffitt, W. (1966). A developmental investigation of the law of attraction. *Journal of Personality and Social Psychology, 4,* 699–702.

Cairns, R. B. (1979). *Social development.* San Francisco: Freeman.

Cairns, R. B., & Cairns, B. D. (1993). *Adolescence in our time: Lifelines and risks.* Unpublished monograph, University of North Carolina, Chapel Hill.

Cairns, R. B., Cairns, B. D., & Neckerman, H. J. (1989). Early school dropout: Configurations and determinants. *Child Development, 60,* 1437–1452.

Cairns, R. B., Cairns, B. D., Neckerman, H. J., Ferguson, L. L., & Gariepy, J-L. (1989). Growth and aggression: I. Childhood to early adolescence. *Developmental Psychology, 25,* 320–330.

Cairns, R. B., Cairns, B. D., Neckerman, H. J., Gest, S. D., & Gariepy, J. L. (1988). Social networks and aggressive behavior: Peer support or peer rejection. *Developmental Psychology, 24,* 815–823.

Cairns, R. B., & Hood, K. E. (1983). Continuity in social development: A comparative perspective on individual difference prediction. In P. B. Baltes & O. G. Brim, Jr. (Eds.), *Life-span development and behavior* (Vol. 5, pp. 301–358). New York: Academic Press.

Cairns, R. B., Perrin, J. E., & Cairns, B. D. (1985). Social structure and social cognition in early adolescence: Affiliative patterns. *Journal of Early Adolescence, 5,* 339–355.

Camp, B. (1977). Verbal mediation in young aggressive boys. *Journal of Abnormal Psychology, 86,* 145–153.

Campbell, S. (1991). Longitudinal studies of hyperactive and aggressive preschoolers: Individual differences in early behavior and in outcome. In D. Cicchetti & S. L. Toth (Eds.), *Rochester Symposium on Developmental Psychopathology.* Hillsdale, NJ: Erlbaum.

Cantor, N., & Kihlstrom, J. (1987). *Personality and social intelligence.* Englewood Cliffs, NJ: Prentice-Hall.

Carson, R. C. (1969). *Interaction concepts of personality.* Chicago: Aldine.

Caspi, A., & Bem, D. J. (1990). Personality continuity and change across the life course. In L. Pervin (Ed.), *Handbook of personality: Theory and research* (pp. 549–575). New York, NY: Guilford.

Caspi, A., Bem, D. J., & Elder, G. H., Jr. (1989). Continuities and consequences of interactional styles across the life course. *Journal of Personality, 57,* 375–406.

Caspi, A., Elder, G. H., Jr., & Bem, D. J. (1987). Moving against the world: Life-course patterns of explosive children. *Developmental Psychology, 23,* 308–313.

Caspi, A., Henry, B., McGee, R. O., Moffitt, T. E., & Silva, P. A. (in press). Temperamental origins of child and adolescent behavior problems: From age 3 to age 15. *Child Development.*

Caspi, A., & Herbener, E. S. (1990). Continuity and change: Assortative marriage and the consistency of personality in adulthood. *Journal of Personality and Social Psychology, 58,* 250–258.

Caspi, A., & Herbener, E. S. (1993). Phenotypic convergence and marital assortment: Longitudinal evidence. *Social Biology, 40* 48–59.

Caspi, A., Herbener, E. S., & Ozer, D. J. (1992). Shared experiences and the similarity of personalities: A longitudinal study of married couples. *Journal of Personality and Social Psychology, 62,* 281–291.

Caspi, A., Lynam, D., Moffitt, T. E., & Silva, P. A. (1993). Unraveling girls' delinquency: Biological, dispositional, and contextual contributions to adolescent misbehavior. *Developmental Psychology, 29,* 19–30.

Caspi, A., & Moffitt, T. E. (1993). When do individual differences matter? A paradoxical theory of personality coherence. *Psychological Inquiry, 4,* 247–271.

Cattell, R. B. (1973). *Personality and mood by questionnaire.* San Francisco, CA: Jossey-Bass.

Chess, S., & Thomas, A. (1987). *Origins and evolution of behavior disorders: From infancy to early adult life.* Cambridge, MA: Harvard University Press.

Christiansen, K. O. (1977). A review of studies of criminality among twins. In S. Mednick & K. O. Christiansen (Eds.), *Biological bases of criminal behavior* (pp. 45–88). New York: Gardner Press.

Cleckley, H. (1976). *The mask of sanity* (5th ed.). St. Louis, MO: Mosby.

Cloninger, C. R., & Gottesman, I. I. (1987). Genetic and environmental factors in antisocial behavior disorders. In S. A. Mednick, T. E. Moffitt, & S. A. Stack (Eds.), *The causes of crime: New biological approaches* (pp. 92–109). New York: Cambridge University Press.

Cohen, J. (1959). The factorial structure of the WISC at ages 7.6, 10.6, and 13.6. *Journal of Consulting and Clinical Psychology, 23,* 285–299.

Cohen, J. (1977). Sources of peer group homogeneity. *Sociology of Education, 50,* 227–241.

Cohen, R. M., Semple, W. E., Gross, M., Holcomb, H. H., Dowling, M. S., & Nordahl, T. E. (1988). Functional localization of sustained attention: Comparison to sensory stimulation in the absence of instruction. *Neuropsychiatry, Neuropsychology, and Behavioral Neurology, 1,* 3–20.

Coie, J. D., Belding, M., & Underwood, M. (1988). Aggression and peer rejection in childhood. In B. Lahey & A. Kazdin (Eds.), *Advances in clinical child psychology* (Vol. 2, pp. 125–158). New York: Plenum.

Costello, E. J. (1989). Developments in child psychiatric epidemiology. *Journal of the American Academy of Child and Adolescent Psychiatry, 28,* 836–841.

Cottrell, L. S. (1969). Interpersonal interaction and the development of the self. In D. A. Goslin (Ed.), *Handbook of socialization theory and research.* Chicago: Rand McNally.

Cox, D. R., & Evans, W. (1987). Measures of frontal-lobe functioning in bright children. *Journal of Clinical and Experimental Psychology, 9,* 28.

Crittenden, P., & DiLalla, D. L. (1988). Compulsive compliance: The development of an inhibitory coping strategy in infancy. *Journal of Abnormal Psychology, 16,* 585–599.

Crockenberg, S. (1981). Infant irritability, mother responsiveness, and social influences on the security of infant-mother attachment. *Child Development, 52,* 857–865.

Csikszentmihalyi, M., & Larson, R. (1984). *Being adolescent: Conflict and growth in the teenage years.* New York: Basic Books.

Darley, J., & Fazio, R. H. (1980). Expectancy confirmation processes arising in the social interaction sequence. *American Psychologist, 35,* 867–881.

Davison, G. C., & Neale, J. M. (1990). *Abnormal psychology.* New York: Wiley.

DeFries, J. C., Plomin, R., & LaBuda, M. C. (1987). Genetic stability of cognitive development from childhood to adulthood. *Developmental Psychology, 23,* 4–12.

Denno, D. J. (1990). *Biology, crime, and violence: From birth to adulthood.* New York: Cambridge University Press.

Diener, E. (1979). Deindividuation, self-awareness, and disinhibition. *Journal of Personality and Social Psychology, 37,* 1160–1171.

Diener, E., Fraser, S. C., Beaman, A. L., & Kelem, T. R. (1976). Effects of deindividuation variables on stealing among Halloween trick-or-treaters. *Journal of Personality and Social Psychology, 33,* 178–183.

DiLalla, L. F., & Gottesman, I. I. (1989). Heterogeneity of causes for delinquency and criminality: Lifespan perspectives. *Development and Psychopathology, 1,* 339–349.

Dishion, T. J. (1990). The peer context of troublesome child and adolescent behavior. In P. Leone (Ed.), *Understanding troubled and troubling youth* (pp. 128–153). Newbury Park, CA: Sage.

Dishion, T. J., Patterson, G. R., Stoolmiller, M., & Skinner, M. L. (1991). Family, school, and behavioral antecedents to early adolescent involvement with antisocial peers. *Developmental Psychology, 27,* 172–180.

Dodge, K. A. (1980). Social cognition and children's aggressive behavior. *Child Development, 51,* 162–170.

Dodge, K. A. (1986). A social-information-processing model of social competence in children. In M. Perlmutter (Ed.), *Minnesota Symposia on Child Psychology* (Vol. 18, pp. 77–125). Hillsdale, NJ: Erlbaum.

Dodge, K. A. (1991). Emotion and social information processing. In J. Garber & K. A. Dodge (Eds.), *The development of emotion regulation and dysregulation* (pp. 159–181). New York: Cambridge University Press.

Dodge, K. A., Coie, J. D., & Brakke, N. P. (1982). Behavior patterns of socially rejected and neglected preadolescents: The roles of social approach and aggression. *Journal of Abnormal Child Psychology, 10,* 389–410.

Dodge, K. A., & Frame, C. L. (1982). Social cognitive biases and deficits in aggressive boys. *Child Development, 53,* 620–635.

Dodge, K. A., & Newman, J. P. (1981). Biased decision-making process in aggressive boys. *Journal of Abnormal Psychology, 90,* 375–379.

Dodge, K. A., Pettit, G. S., McClaskey, C. L., & Brown, M. M. (1986). Social competency in children. With commentary by J. M. Gottman. *Monographs of the Society for Research in Child Development, 51* (Serial No. 213). No. 2.

Douglas, V. I., & Peters, K. (1979). Towards a clearer definition of the attention deficit of hyperactive children. In G. Hale & M. Lewis (Eds.), *Attention and cognitive development,* (pp. 173–247). New York: Guilford.

Elder, G. H., Jr. (1986). Military times and turning points in men's lives. *Developmental Psychology, 22,* 233–245.

Elliott, D. S., Ageton, S. S., Huizinga, D., Knowles, B. A., & Canter, R. J. (1983). *The prevalence and incidence of delinquent behavior: 1976–1980.* Boulder, CO: Behavioral Research Institute.

Elliott, D. S., & Huizinga, D. (1983). Social class and delinquent behavior in a national youth panel: 1976–1980. *Criminology, 21,* 149–177.

Elliott, D. S., & Huizinga, D. (1984). The relationship between delinquent behavior and ADM problems. *Paper presented at the ADAMHA/OJJDP State of the Art Research Conference of Juvenile Offenders with Serious Drug, Alcohol and Mental Health Problems,* Rockville, MD.

Elliott, D. S., Huizinga, D., & Ageton, S. S. (1985). *Explaining delinquency and drug use.* Beverly Hills, CA: Sage.

Elliott, D. S., Huizinga, D., & Menard, S. (1989). *Multiple problem youth: Delinquency, substance use, and mental health problems.* New York: Springer-Verlag.

Elliott, D. S., & Menard, S. (in press). Delinquent friends and delinquent behavior: Temporal and developmental patterns. In D. Hawkins (Ed.), *Some current theories of deviance and crime.* New York: Springer-Verlag.

Elliott, D. S., & Voss, H. L. (1974). *Delinquency and dropout.* Lexington, MA: Heath.

Empey, L. T. (1978). *American delinquency.* Homewood, IL: Dorsey Press.

Epstein, E., & Guttman, R. (1984). Mate selection in man: Evidence, theory and outcome. *Social Biology, 31,* 243–278.

Epstein, S. (1980). The self-concept: A review and the proposal of an integrated theory of personality. In E. Staub (Ed.), *Personality: Basic issues and current research* (pp. 81–130). Englewood Cliffs, NJ: Prentice-Hall.

Epstein, S., & Erskine, N. (1983). The development of personal theories of reality from an interactional perspective. In D. Magnusson (Ed.), *Human development: An interactional perspective* (pp. 133–147). New York: Academic Press.

Eron, L. D., Huesmann, L. R., & Zelli, A. (1991). The role of parental variables in the learning of aggression. In D. Pepler & K. Rubin (Eds.), *The development and treatment of childhood aggression* (pp. 171–188). Hillsdale, NJ: Erlbaum.

Eysenck, H. J. (1977). *Crime and personality.* London: Routledge & Kegan Paul.

Fagot, B. I., & Kavanaugh, K. (1990). The prediction of antisocial behavior from attachment classifications. *Child Development, 61,* 864–873.

Farrington, D. P. (1977). The effects of public labelling. *British Journal of Criminology, 172,* 112–125.

Farrington, D. P. (1983). Offending from 10 to 25 years of age. In K. Van Dusen & S. A. Mednick (Eds.), *Prospective studies of crime and delinquency* (pp. 17–38). Boston: Kluwer-Nijhoff.

Farrington, D. P. (1986). Age and crime. In M. Tonry & N. Morris (Eds.), *Crime and Justice: An Annual Review of Research,* (Vol. 7, pp. 189–250). Chicago: University of Chicago Press.

Farrington, D. P. (1991). Antisocial personality from childhood to adulthood. *The Psychologist, 4,* 389–394.

Farrington, D. P., Loeber, R., Elliott, D. S., Hawkins, D. J., Kandel, D. B., Klein, M. W., McCord, J., Rowe, D., & Tremblay, R. (1990). Advancing knowledge about the onset of delinquency and crime. In B. Lahey & A. Kazdin (Eds.), *Advances in clinical child psychology* (Vol. 13, pp. 231–342). New York: Plenum.

Farrington, D. P., Loeber, R., & Van Kammen, W. B. (1990). Long-term criminal outcomes of hyperactivity-impulsivity-attention deficit and conduct problems in childhood. In L. N. Robins & M. R. Rutter (Eds.), *Straight and devious pathways to adulthood* (pp. 62–81). New York: Cambridge University Press.

Farrington, D. P., Ohlin, L., & Wilson, J. Q. (1986). *Understanding and controlling crime.* New York: Springer-Verlag.

Farrington, D. P., & West, D. J. (1990). The Cambridge study of delinquent development: A long-term follow-up of 411 London males. In H. J. Kerner & G. Kaiser (Eds.), *Kriminalitat* (pp. 117–138). New York: Springer-Verlag.

Fishbein, D. H. (1990). Biological perspectives in criminology. *Criminology, 28,* 27–72.

Frodi, A. M., Laub, M. E., Leavitt, L. E., Donovan, W. L., Neff, C., & Sherry, D. (1978). Fathers' and mothers' responses to the faces and cries of normal and premature infants. *Developmental Psychology, 14,* 490–498.

Furstenberg, F. F., Jr. (1990). *How families manage risk and opportunity in dangerous neighborhoods.* Unpublished manuscript, University of Pennsylvania.

Furstenberg, F. F., Jr., Brooks-Gunn, J., & Morgan, S. P. (1987). *Adolescent mothers in later life.* New York: Cambridge University Press.

Garbarino, J., & Sherman, D. (1980). High-risk neighborhoods and high risk families: The human ecology of child maltreatment. *Child Development, 51,* 188–198.

Gelfand, D. M., Hartmann, D. P., Lamb, A., Smith, C. L., Mahan, M. A., & Paul, S. C. (1974). The effects of adult models and described alternatives on children's choice of behavior management techniques. *Child Development, 45,* 585–593.

Ghodsian-Carpey, J., & Baker, L. A. (1987). Genetic and environmental influences on aggression in 4- to 7-year-old twins. *Aggressive Behavior, 13,* 173–186.

Giordano, P. C., Cernkovich, S. A., & Pugh, M. D. (1986). Friendship and delinquency. *American Journal of Sociology, 91,* 1170–1202.

Glaser, D., & Kent, R. (1959). Crime, age, and unemployment. *American Sociological Review, 24,* 679–686.

Gold, M. (1987). Social ecology. In H. Quay (Ed.), *Handbook of juvenile delinquency* (pp. 62–105). New York: Wiley.

Goldsmith, H. H., Bradshaw, D. L., & Rieser-Danner, L. A. (1986). Temperament as a potential developmental influence on attachment. In J. V. Lerner & R. M. Lerner (Eds.), *Temperament and social interaction during infancy and childhood* (pp. 5–34). San Francisco: Jossey-Bass.

Gorenstein, E. E. (1982). Frontal lobe functions in psychopaths. *Journal of Abnormal Psychology, 91,* 368–379.

Gottfredson, M., & Hirschi, T. (1986). The value of Lambda would appear to be zero: An essay of career criminals, criminal careers, selective incapacitation, cohort studies and related topics. *Criminology, 24,* 213–234.

Gottschalk, R., Davidson, W. S., Gensheimer, L. K., & Mayer, J. P. (1987). Community-based interventions. In H. C. Quay (Ed.), *Handbook of juvenile delinquency* (pp. 266–289). New York: Wiley.

Graham, S., Hudley, C. & Williams, E. (1992). Attributional and emotional determinants of aggression among African-American and Latino young adolescents. *Developmental Psychology, 28,* 731–740.

Greenwald, A. G. (1980). The totalitarian ego: Fabrication and revision of personal history. *American Psychologist, 35,* 603–618.

Hains, A. A., & Ryan, E. B. (1983). The development of social cognitive processes among juvenile delinquents and nondelinquent peers. *Child Development, 54,* 1536–1544.

Halverson, C. F., & Waldrop, M. F. (1976). Relations between preschool activity and aspects of intellectual and social behaviors at age 7½. *Developmental Psychology, 12,* 107–112.

Hanson, R. A. (1975). Consistency and stability of home environmental measures related to IQ. *Child Development, 46,* 470–480.

Hare, R. D. (1984). Performance of psychopaths on cognitive tasks related to frontal lobe function. *Journal of Abnormal Psychology, 93,* 133–140.

Hare, R. D., & McPherson, L. M. (1984). Violent and aggressive behavior by criminal psychopaths. *International Journal of Law and Psychiatry, 7,* 35–50.

Harpur, T. J., & Hare, R. D. (1994). The assessment of psychopathy as a function of age. *Journal of Abnormal Psychology, 103,* 604–609.

Healy, W., & Bronner, A. F. (1936). *New light on delinquency and its treatment.* New Haven, CT: Yale University Press.

Henry, B., Moffitt, T. E., Robins, L. N., Earls, F., & Silva, P. A. (1993). Early family predictors of child and adolescent antisocial behavior: Who are the mothers of delinquents? *Criminal Behaviour and Mental Health, 3,* 97–118.

Hinshaw, S. P. (1992). Externalizing behavior problems and academic underachievement in childhood and adolescence: Causal relationships and underlying mechanisms. *Psychological Bulletin, 111,* 127–155.

Hirschi, T. (1969). *Causes of delinquency.* Berkeley, CA: University of California.

Hirschi, T., & Gottfredson, M. (1983). Age and the explanation of crime. *American Journal of Sociology, 89,* 552–584.

Hirschi, T., & Hindelang, M. J. (1977). Intelligence and delinquency: A revisionist review. *American Sociological Review, 42,* 571–587.

Hood, R., & Sparks, R. (1970). *Key issues in criminology.* Wallop, Hampshire: BAS Printers.

House, J. (1981). Social structure and personality. In M. Rosenberg & R. H. Turner (Eds.), *Social psychology: Sociological perspectives* (pp. 525–561). New York: Basic Books.

Hubble, L. M., & Groff, M. (1981). Factor analysis of WISC-R scores of male delinquents referred for evaluation. *Journal of Consulting and Clinical Psychology, 49,* 738–739.

Huesmann, L. R., Eron, L. D., Lefkowitz, M. M., & Walder, L. O. (1984). Stability of aggression over time and generations. *Developmental Psychology, 20,* 1120–1134.

Ickes, W., Snyder, M., & Garcia, S. (in press). Personality influences on the choice of situations. In S. R. Briggs, R. Hogan, & W. H. Jones (Eds.), *Handbook of personality psychology.* Orlando, FL: Academic Press.

Jensen, A. R. (1978). Genetic and behavioral effects of non-random mating. In C. E. Noble, R. T. Osborne, & N. Weyle (Eds.), *Human variation: Biogenetics of age, race, and sex* (pp. 51–105). New York: Academic Press.

Jessor, R., & Jessor, S. L. (1977). *Problem behavior and psychosocial development: A longitudinal study of youth.* New York: Academic Press.

Kagan, J. (1969). The three faces of continuity in human development. In D. A. Goslin (Ed.), *Handbook of socialization theory and research* (pp. 983–1002). Chicago: Rand McNally.

Kagan, J. (1984). *The nature of the child.* New York: Basic Books.

Kagan, J. & Moss, H. A. (1962). *Birth to maturity.* New York: Wiley.

Kagan, J., Reznick, J. S., & Snidman, N. (1990). The temperamental qualities of inhibition and lack of inhibition. In M. Lewis & S. M. Miller (Eds.), *Handbook of developmental psychopathology* (pp. 219–226). New York: Plenum.

Kaler, S. R., & Kopp, C. B. (1990). Compliance and comprehension in very young toddlers. *Child Development, 61,* 1997–2003.

Kandel, D. B. (1978a). Similarity in real-life adolescent friendship pairs. *Journal of Personality and Social Psychology, 36,* 306–312.

Kandel, D. B. (1978b). Homophily, selection, and socialization in adolescent friendships. *American Journal of Sociology, 84,* 427–436.

Kandel, D. B., Davies, M., & Baydar, N. (1990). The creation of interpersonal contexts: Homophily in dyadic relationships in adolescence and young adulthood. In L. N. Robins & M. R. Rutter (Eds.), *Straight and devious pathways to adulthood* (pp. 221–241). New York: Cambridge University Press.

Kandel, E., Brennan, P., & Mednick, S. A. (1989). Minor physical anomalies and parental modeling of aggression predict to violent offending. *Journal of Consulting and Clinical Psychology, 78,* 1–5.

Kandel, E., & Mednick, S. A. (1991). Perinatal complications predict violent offending. *Criminology, 29,* 519–530.

Katz, J. (1989). *Seductions of crime.* New York: Basic Books.

Kazdin, A. E. (1987). *Conduct disorders in childhood and adolescence.* Beverly Hills, CA: Sage.

Kellam, S. (1990). Developmental epidemiological framework for family research on depression and aggression. In G. R. Patterson (Ed.), *Depression and aggression in family interaction* (pp. 11–48). Hillsdale, NJ: Erlbaum.

Klein, M. W. (1986). Labelling theory and delinquency policy. *Criminal Justice and Behavior, 13,* 47–79.

Klein, M. W. (1989). Watch out for that last variable. In S. Mednick, T. E. Moffitt, & S. A. Stack (Eds.), *The causes of crime: New biological approaches* (pp. 25–41). New York: Cambridge University Press.

Knight, B. J., & West, D. J. (1975). Temporary and continuing delinquency. *British Journal of Criminology, 15,* 43–50.

Knights, R. M., & Bakker, D. J. (1976). *The neuropsychiatry of learning disorders.* Baltimore: University Park Press.

Kopp, C. B. (1982). Antecedents of self-regulation: A developmental perspective. *Developmental Psychology, 18,* 199–214.

Kraemer, G. W. (1988). Speculations on the developmental neurobiology of protest and despair. In P. Simon, P. Soubrie, & D. Widlocher (Eds.), *Inquiry into schizophrenia and depression: Animal models of psychiatric disorders* (pp. 101–147). Basel: Karger.

Krueger, R. F., Schmutte, P., Caspi, A., Moffitt, T. E., Campbell, K., & Silva, P. A. (1994). Personality traits are linked to crime among males and females: Evidence from a birth cohort. *Journal of Abnormal Psychology, 103,* 328–338.

Laub, J. H., & Sampson, R. J. (1988). Unraveling families and delinquency: A reanalysis of the Gluecks' data. *Criminology, 26,* 355–380.

Lee, C. L., & Bates, J. E. (1985). Mother-child interaction at age two years and perceived difficult temperament. *Child Development, 56,* 1314–1323.

Lewis, D. O., Shanok, S. S., Pincus, J. H., & Glaser, G. H. (1979). Violent juvenile delinquents: Psychiatric, neurological, psychological and abuse factors. *Journal of the American Academy of Child Psychiatry, 2,* 307–319.

Lewis, M., Feirling, C., McGuffog, C., & Jaskir, J. (1984). Predicting psychopathology in six-year-olds from early social relations. *Child Development, 55,* 123–136.

Lezak, M. D. (1988). IQ: RIP. *Journal of Clinical and Experimental Neuropsychology, 10,* 351–361.

Lieberman, A. F. (1977). Preschoolers' competence with a peer: Influence of attachment and social experience. *Child Development, 48,* 1277–1287.

Lipton, D., Mertinson, R., & Wilks, J. (1975). *The effectiveness of correctional treatment: A survey of treatment evaluation studies.* New York: Praeger.

Livson, N., & Peskin, H. (1980). Perspectives on adolescence from longitudinal research. In J. Adelson (Ed.), *Handbook of adolescent psychology* (pp. 47–98). New York: Wiley.

Loeber, R. (1982). The stability of antisocial and delinquent child behavior: A review. *Child Development, 53,* 1431–1446.

Loeber, R., & Baicker-McKee, C. (1989). The changing manifestations of disruptive/antisocial behavior from childhood to early adulthood: Evolution or tautology? Unpublished manuscript, Western Psychiatric Institute, University of Pittsburgh.

Loeber, R., & Dishion, T. J. (1983). Early predictors of male adolescent delinquency: A review. *Psychological Bulletin, 94,* 68–99.

Loeber, R., Green, S., Lahey, B., & Stouthamer-Loeber, M. (1990). Optimal informants on childhood disruptive behaviors. *Development and Psychopathology, 1,* 317–337.

Loeber, R., & Schmaling, K. B. (1985). Empirical evidence for overt and covert patterns of antisocial conduct problems: A meta-analysis. *Journal of Abnormal Child Psychology, 13,* 337–352.

Loeber, R., & Stouthamer-Loeber, M. (1986). Family factors as correlates and predictors of juvenile conduct problems and delinquency. In M. Tonry & N. Morris (Eds.), *Crime and justice* (Vol. 7, pp. 29–149). Chicago: University of Chicago Press.

Loeber, R., Stouthamer-Loeber, M., Van Kammen, W., & Farrington, D. P. (1989). Development of a new measure of self-reported antisocial behavior for young children: Prevalence and reliability. In M. Klein (Ed.), *Cross-national research in self-reported crime and delinquency* (pp. 203–226). Boston: Kluwer-Nijhoff.

Lou, H. C., Henriksen, L., & Bruhn, P. (1984). Focal cerebral hypoperfusion in children with dysphasia and/or attention deficit disorder. *Archives of Neurology, 41,* 825–829.

Luria, A. R. (1961). *The role of speech in the regulation of normal and abnormal behavior.* New York: Basic Books.

Luria, A. R., & Homskaya, E. D. (1964). Disturbance in the regulative role of speech with frontal lobe lesions. In J. M. Warren & K. Akert (Eds.), *The frontal granular cortex and behavior* (pp. 353–371). New York: McGraw Hill.

Lynam, D., Moffitt, T. E., & Stouthamer-Loeber, M. (1993). Explaining the relationship between IQ and delinquency. *Journal of Abnormal Psychology, 102,* 187–196.

Lytton, H. (1980). *Parent-child interaction: The socialization process observed in twin and singleton families.* New York: Plenum.

Lytton, H. (1990). Child and parent effects in boys' conduct disorder: A reinterpretation. *Developmental Psychology, 26,* 683–697.

Maccoby, E. E., & Jacklin, C. N. (1983). The "person" characteristics of children and the family as environment. In D. Magnusson & V. L. Allen (Eds.). *Human development: An interactional perspective* (pp. 75–92). New York: Academic Press.

Magnusson, D. (1988). *Individual development from an interactional perspective.* Hillsdale, NJ: Erlbaum.

Magnusson, D., Stattin, H., & Allen, V. L. (1986). Differential maturation among girls and its relations of social adjustment: A longitudinal perspective. In P. B. Baltes, D. L. Featherman, & R. M. Lerner (Eds.). *Life-span development and behavior* (pp. 113–134). Hillsdale, NJ: Erlbaum.

Maloney, M. P., & Ward, M. P. (1976). *Psychological assessment: A conceptual approach.* New York: Oxford University Press.

Markus, H. (1977). Self-schemata and processing information about the self. *Journal of Personality and Social Psychology, 35,* 63–78.

Markus, H., & Cross, S. (1990). The interpersonal self. In L. Pervin (Ed.). *Handbook of personality: Theory and research* (pp. 576–608). New York: Guilford.

Martin, N. G., Jardine, R., & Eaves, L. J. (1984). Is there only one set of genes for different abilities? *Behavior Genetics, 14,* 355–370.

Martinson, R. (1974). What works? Questions & answers about prison reform. *Public Interest, 35,* 22–54.

Mascie-Taylor, C. G. N., & Vandenberg, S. G. (1988). Assortative mating for IQ and personality due to propinquity and personal preference. *Behavior Genetics, 18,* 339–345.

Maughan, B., Gray, G., & Rutter, M. (1985). Reading retardation and antisocial behavior: A follow-up into employment. *Journal of Child Psychology and Psychiatry, 26,* 741–758.

Mayer, S. E., & Jencks, C. (1989). Growing up in poor neighborhoods: How much does it matter? *Science, 243,* 1441–1445.

McCall, R. B. (1981). Nature-nurture and the two realms of development: A proposed integration with respect to mental development. *Child Development, 52,* 1–12.

McCord, J. (1983a). A forty-year perspective on the effects of child abuse and neglect. *Child Abuse and Neglect, 7,* 265–270.

McCord, J. (1983b). A longitudinal study of aggression and antisocial behavior. In K. T. Van Dusen & S. A. Mednick (Eds.), *Prospective studies of crime and delinquency* (pp. 269–279). Boston: Kluwer-Nijhoff.

McGee, R., Partridge, F., Williams, S. M., & Silva, P. A. (1991). A twelve year follow up of preschool hyperactive children. *Journal of the American Academy of Child and Adolescent Psychiatry, 30,* 224–232.

McGuire, J., & Earls, F. (1991). Prevention of psychiatric disorders in early childhood. *Journal of Child Psychology and Psychiatry, 32,* 129–153.

McNally, N., Eisenberg, N., & Harris, J. D. (1991). Consistency and change in maternal child-rearing practices and values: A longitudinal study. *Child Development, 62,* 190–198.

Meany, M. J., Aitken, D. H., van Berkel, C., Bhatnagar, S., & Sapolsky, R. M. (1988). Effect of neonatal handling on age-related impairments associated with the hippocampus. *Science, 239,* 766–768.

Mednick, S. A., Gabrielli, W. F., & Hutchings, B. (1984). Genetic factors in criminal behavior: Evidence from an adoption cohort. *Science, 224,* 891–893.

Mednick, S. A., Gabrielli, W. F., & Hutchings, B. (1985). Letter to the editor. *Science, 227,* 984.

Mednick, S. A., Moffitt, T. E., Gabrielli, W. F., & Hutchings, B. (1986). Genetic factors in criminal behavior. In J. Block, D. Olweus, & M. R. Yarrow (Eds.), *The development of antisocial and prosocial behavior* New York: Academic Press.

Mednick, S. A., Moffitt, T. E., Pollock, V., Talovic, S., & Gabrielli, W. F. (1983). The inheritance of human deviance. In D. Magnusson & V. L. Allen (Eds.), *Human development: An interactional perspective* New York: Academic Press.

Mednick, S. A., Moffitt, T. E., & Stack, S. A. (1987). *The causes of crime: New biological approaches.* New York: Cambridge University Press.

Mednick, S. A., & Volavka, J. (1980). Biology and crime. In N. Morris & M. Tonry (Eds.), *Crime and justice: An annual review of research* (Vol. 2, pp. 85–158). Chicago: University of Chicago Press.

Meehl, P. E., & Golden, R. R. (1982). Taxonomic methods. In P. C. Kendall & J. N. Butcher (Eds.), *Handbook of research methods in clinical psychology* (pp. 127–181). New York: Wiley.

Megargee, E. I. (1972). *The California Psychological Inventory handbook.* San Francisco, CA: Jossey-Bass.

Moffitt, T. E. (1987). Parental mental disorder and offspring criminal behavior: An adoption study. *Psychiatry, 50,* 346–360.

Moffitt, T. E. (1990a). Juvenile delinquency and attention-deficit disorder: Developmental trajectories from age three to fifteen. *Child Development, 61,* 893–910.

Moffitt, T. E. (1990b). The neuropsychology of juvenile delinquency: A critical review. In M. Tonry & N. Morris (Eds.), *Crime and justice:*

An annual review of research (Vol. 12, pp. 99–169). Chicago: University of Chicago Press.

Moffitt, T. E. (1991). *Juvenile delinquency: Seed of a career in violent crime, just sowing wild oats—or both?* Paper presented at the Science and Public Policy Seminars of the Federation of Behavioral, Psychological and Cognitive Sciences, Washington, DC.

Moffitt, T. E. (1993). Adolescence-limited and life-course-persistent antisocial behavior: A developmental taxonomy. *Psychological Review, 100,* 674–701.

Moffitt, T. E., Caspi, A., Harkness, A. R., & Silva, P. A. (1993). The natural history of change in intellectual performance: Who changes? How much? Is it meaningful? *Journal of Child Psychology and Psychiatry, 34,* 455–506.

Moffitt, T. E., Gabrielli, W. F., & Mednick, S. A. (1981). Socioeconomic status, IQ, and delinquency. *Journal of Abnormal Psychology, 90,* 152–156.

Moffitt, T. E., & Henry, B. (1989). Neuropsychological assessment of executive functions in self-reported delinquents. *Development and Psychopathology, 1,* 105–118.

Moffitt, T. E., & Henry, B. (1991). Neuropsychological studies of juvenile delinquency and juvenile violence. In J. S. Milner (Ed.), *The neuropsychology of aggression* (pp. 67–91). Boston: Kluwer.

Moffitt, T. E., Lynam, D., & Silva, P. A. (1994). Neuropsychological tests predict persistent male delinquency. *Criminology, 32,* 101–124.

Moffitt, T. E., & Mednick, S. A. (Eds.). (1988). *Biological contributions to crime causation.* Dordrecht, The Netherlands: Martinus-Nijhoff.

Moffitt, T. E., Mednick, S. A., & Gabrielli, W. F. (1989). Predicting criminal violence: Descriptive data and predispositional factors. In D. Brizer & M. Crowner (Eds.), *Current approaches to the prediction of violence* (pp. 13–34). New York: American Psychiatric Association Press.

Moffitt, T. E., & Silva, P. A. (1988a). IQ and delinquency: A direct test of the differential detection hypothesis. *Journal of Abnormal Psychology, 97,* 330–333.

Moffitt, T. E., & Silva, P. A. (1988b). Neuropsychological deficit and self-reported delinquency in an unselected birth cohort. *Journal of the American Academy of Child and Adolescent Psychiatry, 27,* 233–240.

Moffitt, T. E., & Silva, P. A. (1988c). Self-reported delinquency, neuropsychological deficit, and history of attention deficit disorder. *Journal of Abnormal Child Psychology, 16,* 553–569.

Moffitt, T. E., & Silva, P. A. (1988d). Self-reported delinquency: Results from an instrument for New Zealand. *Australian and New Zealand Journal of Criminology, 21,* 227–240.

Moore, B. (1966). *Social origins of dictatorship and democracy: Lord and peasant in the making of the modern world.* Boston: Beacon Press.

Moss, H. A., & Susman, E. J. (1980). Longitudinal study of personality development. In O. G. Brim, Jr., & J. Kagan (Eds.), *Constancy and change in human development* (pp. 530–595). Cambridge, MA: Harvard University Press.

Moynihan, M. (1968). Social mimicry: Character convergence versus character displacement. *Evolution, 22,* 315–331.

Nasby, W., Hayden, B., & DePaulo, B. M. (1980). Attributional bias among aggressive boys to interpret unambiguous social stimuli as displays of hostility. *Journal of Abnormal Psychology, 89,* 459–468.

Needleman, H. L., & Beringer, D. C. (1981). The epidemiology of low-level lead exposure in childhood. *Journal of Child Psychiatry, 20,* 496–512.

Newcomb, T. M. (1961). *The acquaintance process.* New York: Wiley.

Newman, J. P. (1987). Reaction to punishment in extroverts and psychopaths: Implications for the impulsive behavior of disinhibited individuals. *Journal of Research in Personality, 21,* 464–480.

Newman, J. P., & Howland, E. (1989). The effect of incentives on Wisconsin Card-sorting task performance in psychopaths. Unpublished manuscript. University of Wisconsin, Madison.

Newman, J. P., & Kosson, D. S. (1986). Passive avoidance learning in psychopathic and nonpsychopathic offenders. *Journal of Abnormal Psychology, 95,* 257–263.

Nisbett, R., & Ross, L. (1980). *Human inference: Strategies and shortcomings of social judgment.* Englewood Cliffs, NJ: Prentice-Hall.

Olweus, D. (1979). Stability of aggressive reaction patterns in males: A review. *Psychological Bulletin, 86,* 852–875.

Oyserman, D., & Markus, H. R. (1990). Possible selves and delinquency. *Journal of Personality and Social Psychology, 59,* 112–125.

Parke, R. D., & Slaby, R. (1983). The development of aggression. In P. H. Mussen & E. M. Hetherington (Eds.), *Handbook of child psychology: Vol. 4. Socialization, personality and social development* (4th ed., pp. 547–642). New York: Wiley.

Patterson, G. R. (1982). *Coercive family process.* Eugene, OR: Castalia.

Patterson, G. R. (1986a). Maternal rejection: Determinant or product for deviant child behavior? In W. Hartup & Z. Rubin (Eds.), *Relationships and development* (pp. 73–94). Hillsdale, NJ: Erlbaum.

Patterson, G. R. (1986b). Performance models for antisocial boys. *American Psychologist, 41,* 432–444.

Patterson, G. R., & Bank, L. (1990). Some amplifying mechanisms for pathologic processes in families. In M. R. Gunnar & E. Phelen (Eds.), *Minnesota Symposia on Child Psychology: Vol. 22. Systems and development* (pp. 167–209). Hillsdale, NJ: Erlbaum.

Patterson, G. R., Bank, L., & Stoolmiller, (1990). The preadolescent's contributions to disrupted family process. In R. Montemayor, G. R. Adams, & T. P. Gullotta (Eds.), *From childhood to adolescence* (pp. 107–133). Newbury Park, CA: Sage.

Perry, D. G., Kusel, S. J., & Perry, L. C. (1988). Victims of peer aggression. *Developmental Psychology, 24,* 807–814.

Perry, D. G., Perry, L. C., & Rasmussen, P. (1986). Cognitive social learning mediators of aggression. *Child Development, 57,* 700–711.

Pianta, R. C., Sroufe, L. A., & Egeland, B. (1989). Continuity and discontinuity in maternal sensitivity at 6, 24, and 42 months in a high risk sample. *Child Development, 60,* 481–487.

Platt, J. J., Spivak, G., Altman, N., & Altman, D. (1974). Adolescent problem-solving thinking. *Journal of Consulting and Clinical Psychology, 42,* 787–793.

Plomin, R. (1986). *Development, genetics, and psychology.* Hillsdale, NJ: Erlbaum.

Plomin, R. (1988). The nature and nurture of cognitive abilities. In R. Sternberg (Ed.), *Advances in the psychology of human intelligence* (Vol. 4, pp. 1–33). Hillsdale, NJ: Erlbaum.

Plomin, R. (1990). The role of inheritance in behavior. *Science, 248,* 183–188.

Plomin, R., & Bergeman, C. S. (1991). The nature of nurture: Genetic influence on "environmental" measures. *Behavioral and Brain Sciences, 14,* 373–386.

Plomin, R., & DeFries, J. C. (1985). *Origins of individual differences in infancy: The Colorado Adoption Project.* New York: Academic Press.

Plomin, R., DeFries, J. C., & Fulker, D. W. (1988). *Nature and nurture during infancy and early childhood.* New York: Cambridge University Press.

Plomin, R., DeFries, J. C., & Loehlin, J. C. (1977). Genotype-environment interaction and correlation in the analysis of human behavior. *Psychological Bulletin, 84,* 309–322.

Plomin, R., & Nesselroade, J. R. (1990). Behavioral genetics and personality change. *Journal of Personality, 58,* 191–220.

Plomin, R., Nitz, K., & Rowe, D. C. (1990). Behavioral genetics and aggressive behavior in childhood. In M. Lewis & S. M. Miller (Eds.), *Handbook of developmental psychopathology* (pp. 119–133). New York: Plenum.

Prentice, N. M., & Kelly, F. J. (1963). Intelligence and delinquency: A reconsideration. *Journal of Social Psychology, 60,* 327–337.

Prentice-Dunn, S., & Rodgers, R. (1980). Effects of deindividuating situational cues and aggressive models on subject deindividuation and aggression. *Journal of Personality and Social Psychology, 39,* 104–113.

Pulkkinen, L. (1982). Self-control and continuity from childhood to late adolescence. In P. B. Baltes & O. G. Brim, Jr. (Eds.), *Life-span development and behavior* (Vol. 4, pp. 63–105). New York: Academic Press.

Quinton, D., & Rutter, M. (1988). *Parenting breakdown: The making and breaking of intergenerational links.* Aldershot, England: Avebury.

Raine, A. (1988). Evoked potentials and antisocial behavior. In T. E. Moffitt, S. A. Mednick, & S. A. Stack (Eds.), *Biological contributions to crime and causation* (pp. 14–39). Dordrecht, The Netherlands: Nijhoff.

Raine, A. (1993). *The psychopathology of crime.* San Diego, CA: Academic Press.

Reiss, A. J., Jr. (1986). Why are communities important in understanding crime? In A. J. Reiss, Jr., & M. Tonry (Eds.), *Communities and crime* (pp. 1–34). Chicago: University of Chicago Press.

Reiss, A. J., & Rhodes, A. L. (1961). The distribution of juvenile delinquency in the social class structure. *American Sociological Review, 26,* 720–732.

Renken, B., Egeland, B., Marvinney, D., Mangelsdorf, S., & Sroufe, L. A. (1989). Early childhood antecedents of aggression and passive-withdrawal in early elementary school. *Journal of Personality, 57,* 257–281.

Richman, N., Stevenson, J., & Graham, P. J. (1982). *Preschool to school: A behavioural study.* London: Academic Press.

Roberts, G. C., Block, J. H., & Block, J. (1984). Continuity and change in parents' child rearing practices. *Child Development, 55,* 586–597.

Robins, L. N. (1966). *Deviant children grown up.* Baltimore: Williams & Wilkins.

Robins, L. N. (1978). Sturdy childhood predictors of adult antisocial behaviour: Replications from longitudinal studies. *Psychological Medicine, 8,* 611–622.

Robinson, A. L., Heaton, R. K., Lehman, R. A. W., & Stilson, D. W. (1980). The utility of the Wisconsin Card Sorting Test in detecting and locating frontal lobe lesions. *Journal of Consulting and Clinical Psychology, 30,* 911–920.

Rodning, C., Beckwith, L., & Howard, J. (1989). Characteristics of attachment organization and play organization in prenatally drug-exposed toddlers. *Development and Psychopathology, 1,* 277–289.

Rodning, C., Beckwith, L., & Howard, J. (1991). Quality of attachment and home environments in children prenatally exposed to PCP and cocaine. *Development and Psychopathology, 3,* 351–366.

Rourke, B. P. (1975). Brain-behavior relationships in children with learning disabilities: A research program. *American Psychologist, 30,* 911–920.

Rourke, B. P., & Fiske, J. L. (1981). Socio-emotional disturbances of learning disabled children: The role of central processing deficits. *Bulletin of the Orton Society, 31,* 77–88.

Rowe, D. C. (1983). Biometrical genetic models of self-reported delinquent behavior: A twin study. *Behavior Genetics, 13,* 473–489.

Rowe, D. C. (1986). Genetic and environmental components of antisocial behavior: A study of 265 twin pairs. *Criminology, 24,* 513–532.

Rowe, D. C. (1987). Resolving the person-situation debate: Invitation to an interdisciplinary dialogue. *American Psychologist, 42,* 218–227.

Rowe, D. C., & Osgood, D. W. (1984). Heredity and sociological theories of delinquency: A reconstruction. *American Sociological Review, 49,* 526–540.

Rowe, D. C., Rodgers, J. L., Meseck-Bushley, S., & St. John, C. (1989). Sexual behavior and nonsexual deviance: A sibling study of their relationship. *Developmental Psychology, 25,* 61–69.

Rushton, J. P., Fulker, D. W., Neale, M. C., Nias, D. K. B., & Eysenck, H. J. (1987). Altruism and aggression: The heritability of individual differences. *Journal of Personality and Social Psychology, 50,* 1192–1198.

Rutter, M. (1981). Epidemiological/longitudinal strategies and causal research in child psychiatry. *Journal of the American Academy of Child Psychiatry, 20,* 513–544.

Rutter, M. (1987). Psychosocial resilience and protective mechanisms. *American Journal of Orthopsychiatry, 57,* 316–331.

Rutter, M., & Giller, H. (1984). *Juvenile delinquency: Trends and perspectives.* Harmonsworth, England: Penguin.

Rutter, M., Macdonald, H., Le Couteur, A., Harrington, R., Bolton, P., & Bailey, A. (1990). Genetic factors in child psychiatric disorders: II. Empirical findings. *Journal of Child Psychology and Psychiatry, 31,* 39–83.

Rutter, M., & Quinton, D. (1977). Psychiatric disorder: Ecological factors and concepts of causation. In H. McGurk (Ed.), *Ecological factors in human development* (pp. 173–187). Amsterdam, The Netherlands: North-Holland.

Rutter, M., Tizard, J., & Whitmore, K. (1970). *Education, health, and behavior.* London: Longman.

Ryder, R. G. (1967). Birth to maturity revisited: A canonical analysis. *Journal of Personality and Social Psychology, 1,* 168–172.

Sampson, R. J. (1985). Neighborhood and crime: The structural determinants of personal victimization. *Journal of Research in Crime and Delinquency, 22,* 7–40.

Sampson, R. J. (1986). Neighborhood family structure and the risk of criminal victimization. In J. Byrne & R. Sampson (Eds.), *The social ecology of crime* (pp. 25–46). New York: Springer-Verlag.

Sampson, R. J., & Groves, W. B. (1989). Community structure and crime: Testing social disorganization theory. *American Journal of Sociology, 94,* 774–802.

Sampson, R. J., & Laub, J. H. (1990). Crime and deviance over the life course: The salience of adult social bonds. *American Sociological Review, 55,* 609–627.

Sampson, R. J., & Laub, J. H. (1993). *Crime in the making.* Cambridge, MA: Harvard University Press.

Sampson, R. J., & Lauritsen, K. (1994). Violent victimization and offending: Individual-, situational-, and community-level risk factors. In A. J. Reiss, Jr., & J. Roth (Eds.), *Understanding and preventing violence: Social influences* (Vol. 3, pp. 1–114). Washington, DC: National Academy Press.

Savitsky, J. C., & Czyzewski, D. (1978). The reaction of adolescent offenders and nonoffenders to nonverbal emotional displays. *Journal of Abnormal Child Psychology, 6,* 89–96.

Scarr, S. (1988). How genotypes and environments combine: Development and individual differences. In N. Bolger, A. Caspi, G. Downey, & M. Moorehouse (Eds.), *Persons in context: Developmental processes* (pp. 217–244). New York: Cambridge University Press.

Scarr, S., & McCartney, K. (1983). How people make their own environments: A theory of genotype → environment effects. *Child Development, 54,* 424–435.

Schuerman, L., & Kobrin, S. (1986). Community careers in crime. In A. J. Reiss, Jr., & M. Tonry (Eds.), *Communities and crime* (pp. 67–100). Chicago: University of Chicago Press.

Schulsinger, F. (1974). Psychopathy, heredity and environment. In S. A. Mednick, F. Schulsinger, J. Higgins, & B. Bell (Eds.). *Genetics, environment and psychopathology* New York: Elsevier/New Holland.

Schweinhart, L., Barnes, H., Weikart, D., Barnett, S., & Epstein, A. (1993). *Significant benefits.* Ypsilanti, MI: The High/Scope Press.

Scott, J. P. (1977). Social genetics. *Behavior Genetics, 7,* 327–346.

Sechrest, L., White, S. O., & Brown, E. D. (1979). *The rehabilitation of criminal offenders: Problems and prospects.* Washington, DC: National Academy of Sciences.

Secord, P. F., & Backman, C. W. (1965). Interpersonal approach to personality. In B. H. Maher (Ed.), *Progress in experimental personality research* (pp. 91–125). New York: Academic Press.

Shapiro, S. K., Quay, H. C., Hogan, A. E., & Schwartz, K. P. (1988). Response perseveration and delayed responding in undersocialized conduct disorder. *Journal of Abnormal Psychology, 97,* 371–373.

Short, J. F., & Strodbeck, F. L. (1965). *Group process and gang delinquency.* Chicago: University of Chicago Press.

Shulman, H. M. (1929). *A study of problem boys and their brothers.* Albany, NY: New York State Crime Commission.

Sigel, I. E. (1985). *Parental belief systems: The psychological consequences for children.* Hillsdale, NJ: Erlbaum.

Silbereisen, R. K., & Noack, P. (1988). On the constructive role of problem behavior in adolescence. In N. Bolger, A. Caspi, G. Downey, & M. Moorehouse (Eds.), *Persons in context: Developmental processes* (pp. 152–180). New York: Cambridge University Press.

Simmons, R. G., & Blyth, D. A. (1987). *Moving into adolescence: The impact of pubertal change and school context.* New York: Aldine de Gruyter.

Skogan, W. G. (1990). *Disorder and decline.* New York: Free Press.

Slaby, R. G., & Guerra, N. G. (1988). Cognitive mediators of aggression in adolescent offenders: 1. Assessment. *Developmental Psychology, 24,* 580–588.

Smith, D. A., & Visher, C. A. (1980). Sex and involvement in deviance/crime: A quantitative review of the empirical literature. *American Sociological Review, 45,* 691–701.

Snyder, J. (1977). Reinforcement analysis of interaction in problem and non-problem families. *Journal of Abnormal Psychology, 86,* 528–535.

Synder, J., & Patterson, G. (1987). Family interaction and delinquent behavior. In H. C. Quay (Ed.), *Handbook of juvenile delinquency* (pp. 216–243). New York: Wiley.

Snyder, M. (1984). When beliefs create reality. In L. Berkowitz (Ed.), *Advances in experimental social psychology* (pp. 248–305). Orlando, FL: Academic Press.

Snyder, M., & Ickes, W. (1985). Personality and social behavior. In E. Aronson & G. Lindzey (Eds.), *Handbook of social psychology* (3rd ed.) (Vol. 2, pp. 883–947). New York: Random House.

Sobotowicz, W., Evans, J. R., & Laughlin, J. (1987). Neuropsychological function and social support in delinquency and learning disability. *International Journal of Clinical Neuropsychology, 9,* 178–186.

Sroufe, L. A., & Fleeson, J. (1988). In R. A. Hinde & J. Stevenson-Hinde (Eds.), *Relationships within families: Mutual influences.* New York: Oxford University Press.

Stamm, J. S., & Kreder, S. V. (1979). Minimal brain dysfunction: Psychological and neuropsychological disorders in hyperkinetic children. In M. Gazzaniga (Ed.), *Handbook of behavioral neurology: Vol. 2. Neuropsychology* (pp. 119–152). New York: Plenum.

Stattin, H., & Magnusson, D. (1990). *Pubertal maturation in female development.* Hillsdale, NJ: Erlbaum.

Steinberg, M. S., & Dodge, K. A. (1983). Attributional bias in aggressive adolescent boys and girls. *Journal of Social and Clinical Psychology, 1,* 312–321.

Stuss, D. T., & Benson, D. F. (1986). *The frontal lobes.* New York: Raven Press.

Sullivan, H. S. (1953). *The interpersonal theory of psychiatry.* New York: Norton.

Susman, E. J. (1993). Psychological, contextual, and psychobiological interactions: A developmental perspective on conduct disorder. *Development and Psychopathology, 5,* 181–190.

Susman, E. J., Inoff-Germain, G., Nottleman, E. D., Loriaux, G. B., Cutler, G. B. Jr., & Chrousos, G. P. (1987). Hormones, emotional dispositions and aggressive attributes in young adolescents. *Child Development, 58,* 1114–1134.

Sutherland, E., & Cressey, D. R. (1978). *Criminology.* Philadelphia: Lippincott.

Swann, W. B., Jr. (1983). Self-verification: Bringing social reality into harmony with the self. In J. Suls & A. G. Greenwald (Eds.), *Psychological perspectives on the self* (Vol. 2, pp. 33–66). Hillsdale, NJ: Erlbaum.

Swann, W. B., Jr. (1985). The self as architect of social reality. In B. R. Schlemker (Ed.), *The self and social life* (pp. 100–125). New York: McGraw-Hill.

Swann, W. B., Jr. (1987). Identity negotiation: Where two roads meet. *Journal of Personality and Social Psychology, 53,* 1038–1051.

Szatmari, P., Reitsma-Street, M., & Offord, D. (1986). Pregnancy and birth complications in antisocial adolescents and their siblings. *Canadian Journal of Psychiatry, 31,* 513–516.

Tambs, K., Sundet, J. M., & Magnus, P. (1984). Heritability analysis of the WAIS subtests: A study of twins. *Intelligence, 8,* 283–293.

Tanner, J. M. (1978). *Fetus into man.* Cambridge, MA: Harvard University Press.

Tarter, R. E., Hegedus, A. M., Alterman, A. L., & Katz-Garris, L. (1983). Cognitive capacities of juvenile violent, nonviolent and sexual offenders. *Journal of Nervous and Mental Disorders, 171,* 564–567.

Tarter, R. E., Hegedus, A. M., Winsten, N. E., & Alterman, A. L. (1984). Neuropsychological, personality and familial characteristics of physically abused delinquents. *Journal of the American Academy of Child Psychiatry, 23,* 668–674.

Taylor, R. B., & Covington, J. (1988). Neighborhood changes in ecology and violence. *Criminology, 26,* 553–589.

Tellegen, A. (1982). *Brief manual for the Multidimensional Personality Questionnaire.* Minneapolis: University of Minnesota Press.

Tellegen, A., Lykken, D. T., Bouchard, T. J., Wilcox, K. J., Segal, N. L., & Rich, S. (1988). Personality similarity in twins reared apart and together. *Journal of Personality and Social Psychology, 6,* 1031–1039.

Thiessen, D., & Gregg, B. (1980). Human assortative mating and genetic equilibrium. *Ethology and Sociobiology, 1,* 111–140.

Thomas, W. I., & Thomas, D. (1928). *The child in America.* New York: Knopf.

Tinsley, B. R., & Parke, R. D. (1983). The person-environment relationship: Lessons from families with preterm infants. In D. Magnusson & V. L. Allen (Eds.), *Human development: An interactional perspective* (pp. 93–110). New York: Academic Press.

Tomkins, S. S. (1979). Script theory: Differential magnification of affects. In H. E. Howe, Jr., & R. A. Dienstbier (Eds.). *Nebraska Symposium on Motivation* (Vol. 26, pp. 201–236). Lincoln: University of Nebraska Press.

Tonry, M., Ohlin, L. E., & Farrington, D. P. (1991). *Human development and criminal behavior: New ways of advancing knowledge.* New York: Springer-Verlag.

Tremblay, R. E. (1991). Aggression, prosocial behavior and gender: Three magic words, but no magic wand. In D. Pepler & K. Rubin (Eds.), *The development and treatment of childhood aggression* (pp. 71–77). Hillsdale, NJ: Erlbaum.

Udry, J. R., & Talbert, L. M. (1988). Sex hormones effects on personality at puberty. *Journal of Personality and Social Psychology, 54,* 291–295.

Vandenberg, S. G. (1969). A twin study of spatial ability. *Multivariate Behavioral Research, 4,* 273–294.

Vandenberg, S. G. (1972). Assortative mating, or who marries whom? *Behavior Genetics, 2,* 127–157.

Voorhees, J. (1981). Neuropsychological differences between juvenile delinquents and functional adolescents: A preliminary study. *Adolescence, 16,* 57–66.

Wachtel, P. L. (1977). *Psychoanalysis and behavior therapy.* New York: Basic Books.

Waters, E., Vaughan, B., & Egeland, B. (1980). Individual differences in infant-mother attachment: Antecedents in neonatal behavior in an urban economically disadvantaged sample. *Child Development, 51,* 208–216.

Wechsler, D. (1944). *The measurement of adult intelligence.* Baltimore: Williams & Wilkins.

West, D. J. (1982). *Delinquency, its roots, careers and prospects.* Cambridge, MA: Harvard University Press.

West, D. J., & Farrington, D. P. (1973). *Who becomes delinquent?* London: Heinemann.

West, D. J., & Farrington, D. P. (1977). *The delinquent way of life.* New York: Crane Russak.

White, J., Moffitt, T. E., Earls, F., Robins, L. N., & Silva, P. A. (1990). How early can we tell? Predictors of childhood conduct disorder and adolescent delinquency. *Criminology, 28,* 507–533.

Widom, C. (1989). The cycle of violence. *Science, 244,* 160–166.

Wilson, E. O. (1975). *Sociobiology.* Cambridge, MA: Harvard University Press.

Wilson, J. Q., & Herrnstein, R. J. (1985). *Crime and human nature.* New York: Simon & Schuster.

Wilson, W. J. (1987). *The truly disadvantaged.* Chicago: University of Chicago Press.

Wohlwill, J. F. (1980). Cognitive development in childhood. In O. G. Brim, Jr., & J. Kagan (Eds.), *Constancy and change in human development,* (pp. 359–444). Cambridge, MA: Harvard University Press.

Wolfgang, M. E., Figlio, R. M., & Sellin, T. (1972). *Delinquency in a birth cohort.* Chicago: University of Chicago Press.

Wolfgang, M. E., Thornberry, T. P., & Figlio, R. M. (1987). *From boy to man, from delinquency to crime.* Chicago: University of Chicago Press.

Zigler, E., & Berman, W. (1983). Discerning the future of early childhood intervention. *American Psychologist, 38,* 894–906.

Zigler, E., & Child, I. (1969). Socialization. In G. Lindzey & E. Aronson (Eds.) *The handbook of social psychology* (Vol. 3, 2nd ed., pp. 450–589). Reading, MA: Addison-Wesley.

Zimbardo, P. (1970). The human choice: Individual, reason and order versus deindividuation, impulse and chaos. In W. J. Arnold & D. Levine (Eds.), *Nebraska Symposium on Motivation* (Vol. 16, pp. 237–307). Lincoln: University of Nebraska Press.

Zuckerman, M. (1979). *Sensation seeking: Beyond the optimal level of arousal.* Hillsdale, NJ: Erlbaum.

CHAPTER 14

Psychotic Processes

FRED R. VOLKMAR, DANIEL F. BECKER, ROBERT A. KING, and THOMAS H. McGLASHAN

The term *psychosis* is generally taken to imply some—usually serious degree of disturbance in "reality testing," reflected by specific pathological signs such as hallucinations, delusions, or disturbance in thinking; the term also sometimes refers to the group of disorders characterized by such disturbances. Although the term is often used imprecisely, psychotic processes are of considerable clinical and theoretical interest because of their tremendous morbidity, despite their relative infrequency in the general population. Although the term psychosis was once applied in a blanket fashion to individuals at all ages and levels of functioning, recent practice has been to use this, and related concepts, in more limited and restricted ways (Volkmar, 1991). This change in practice has reflected an awareness of the ambiguities inherent in the term and of earlier, and often incorrect, assumptions of continuities of conditions over the life span. In addition, advances in psychiatric taxonomy, as in the American Psychiatric Association's DSM-III (1980), DSM-III-R (1987), and DSM-IV (1994) have reflected an increasing commitment to reliable and valid definitions. Historically, several different lines of research have converged in the study of psychosis and its manifestations in both children and adults.

Although serious psychiatric and developmental disturbances have been recognized since antiquity, their scientific study, and the social policy implications of that study, are relatively much more recent historical phenomena (see Klerman, 1989). During the 1800s, advances were made in the humane care of the seriously mentally ill and in the classification of serious mental disturbance. Although interest in basic aspects of child development and in the care of severely developmentally impaired children also increased during this period, these lines of work generally remained separate. For example, Maudsley (1867) recognized that children could have serious psychiatric disorders beyond those attributable to severe mental subnormality. At the same time, major advances in psychiatric taxonomy, notably Kraepelin's description (1907) of dementia praecox (or what today would be termed schizophrenia), stimulated systematic research as it became possible for clinicians and researchers to agree on features central to

syndrome definition even while disagreeing on issues of syndrome pathogenesis and treatment (e.g., regarding issues of the "organic" bases of these conditions). In general, however, the presumption within this work was of continuity between expression of disorders in children and adults (see Rutter, 1985).

A related view arose from the interest of Freud and his colleagues in understanding psychiatric disturbance, particularly in adults, within the context of early life experiences and Freud's efforts to develop a truly general psychology. Early work focused on the pathogenesis of psychotic processes using models that postulated regression to earlier levels of functioning and attempted to understand mechanisms of the development of concepts of reality. As discussed subsequently, Freud's interest in phenomena such as dreams and associations provided material for understanding "primary" and "secondary" process thought, the nature of specific psychotic processes such as paranoia, and distinctions between psychotic and nonpsychotic processes (Freud, 1900/1957, 1911/1957, 1917/1957). Although Freud's enthusiasm for psychoanalytic treatment of psychoses waned after World War I, some of his followers maintained both clinical and theoretical interest in the area, and others—notably Anna Freud and Melanie Klein—extended his interest in early psychological development by the direct observation and analysis of children.

Despite the interest of psychoanalysis in the development of reality concepts and despite major advances in the classification of adult psychiatric disturbance, understanding of psychotic disorders in children showed comparatively less progress. This lag reflected several factors. There was a tendency to assume continuities of expression of psychotic disorders over the life span (e.g., all severe psychiatric disturbance in children must represent an early manifestation of schizophrenia). Theoretical speculations, such as the possibility of visual hallucinations as a form of "wish fulfillment" in normal infants, lent further credence to the ready generalization of concepts derived from work with adults to very impaired children. Because research and clinical work were not generally interdisciplinary, most clinical studies (primarily of adults), studies of children with severe developmental and behavioral problems, and studies of normal developmental processes proceeded independently. The advent of phenomenologically based descriptions of clinical disorders (e.g., of autism) led clinicians and researchers to question earlier assumptions about the continuity of psychotic processes over

From the Child Study Center (Drs. Volkmar and King) and Department of Psychiatry (Drs. Becker and McGlashan), Yale University School of Medicine, New Haven, CT 06510.

512

the life span. Similarly, a growing appreciation of Piaget's work (e.g., 1955) on the development of concepts of reality such as time and space caused many to question earlier assumptions of fundamental continuities in thought process between children and adults. The awareness of the importance of developmental issues in understanding psychotic processes has led to a substantive body of work over the past several decades. Refinements in diagnostic classification systems and an awareness of the importance of developmental factors have made it possible to select samples with greater precision. Similar advances have been made in the assessment of psychotic processes.

The traditional division of psychotic processes into the areas of hallucinations, delusions, and formal thought disorder is retained in this chapter. Apart from a certain continuity with tradition, this division also has its basis in the increasing separation of research in these areas. Nevertheless, the expression of psychotic processes, however these are defined, typically involves disturbances in multiple aspects of functioning. Within each area, the phenomenology and classification of the specific psychotic process is discussed and its relationship to clinical syndromes is reviewed. Knowledge regarding aspects of pathogenesis, both neurobiological and psychological, is critically reviewed. Finally, the importance of developmental factors in the expression and assessment of psychotic processes is discussed.

HALLUCINATIONS

Phenomenology

Two broad approaches dominate the literature on hallucinations. The first views hallucinations as a psychopathological symptom and focuses on the relationship of hallucinations to various forms of psychiatric disorder. The second approach postulates a continuum between normal mental imagery and hallucinations and notes that many individuals experience sensory experiences that are intermediate between normal images and hallucinations. From this perspective, hallucinations are similar both to normal perceptual phenomena, such as dreaming and mental imagery, and to common perceptual disturbances, such as illusions and hypnopompic and hypnogogic imagery. This perspective has fostered a large experimental literature aimed at identifying the circumstances that foster hallucinations and characterizing interindividual differences in proneness to induced or spontaneous hallucinations (e.g., see Bentall & Slade, 1985).

Although the goal of this chapter is to examine the phenomena of hallucinations in relation to psychosis, the study of hallucinations has important implications for our understanding of both normal and disturbed cognition and perception.

Like delusions, hallucinations raise philosophical questions about perception, the subject-object distinction, and the ultimate nature of reality that have persisted from the pre-Socratic philosophers to the present. One form of this perplexity is the philosophical skepticism associated with Descartes that questions how we can claim to know that anything about the sensory world is true or real. Much of the later work of Wittgenstein (1953) was concerned with showing a way out of this radical solipsism.

In a less radical fashion, hallucinations also raise the question of the extent to which perception (and our knowledge of the perceptual world) represents a passive registration of external sense objects *versus* an active constructive process.

Classification

Drawing on the work of Esquirol and others, Bleuler (1911/1951) gave the classic definition of *hallucinations* as "perceptions without corresponding stimuli from without." The more expansive definition of Slade and Bentall (1988, p. 23) provides a clearer picture of the spectrum of perceptual phenomena from which hallucinations must be distinguished. A hallucination may be defined as "any percept-like experience which (a) occurs in the absence of an appropriate stimulus, (b) has the full force or impact of the corresponding actual (real) perception, and (c) is not amenable to direct and voluntary control by the experiencer."

Hallucinations may be descriptively classified along several dimensions (Asaad, 1990):

- *Complexity.* Hallucinations range from simple, unformed percepts (indistinct shapes, shades, lights, sounds) to more complex organized percepts (identifiable figures, voices, sentences, melodies).

- *Modality.* Hallucinations may occur in one or more sensory modalities. *Auditory* hallucinations may take the form of voices or words heard as coming from inside the head or from without. The voice(s) may address the subject directly or order him or her to perform certain hurtful acts (command hallucinations). Alternatively, the voices may be heard in the third person discussing the subject. *Visual* hallucinations may take the form of people and animals or of inanimate lights, colors, or patterns. *Flashbacks* are recurrent intrusive visual hallucinatory experiences that occur intermittently following hallucinogen use or traumatic experiences. *Tactile (haptic)* hallucinations are false experiences of touch, which may be interpreted as insects crawling on the skin (formication). *Proprioceptive* hallucinations consist of false kinesthetic sensations or phantom phenomena experienced in an amputated limb. *Olfactory and gustatory* hallucinations are false perceptions of smell or taste, respectively.

- *Affective Tone.* Hallucinations may be neutral, kindly or benign, or threatening.

- *Level of Consciousness.* The term *hallucinosis* refers to florid hallucinations occurring in an otherwise alert and oriented subject without other psychotic symptoms. In contrast, the term *delirium* refers to an organic state in which there is a general disturbance of consciousness, including fluctuating alertness, memory, orientation, comprehension, and often hallucinations. *Hypnogogic and hypnopompic* hallucinations are false sensory perceptions that occur, respectively, while falling asleep or waking up.

- *Intactness of Reality Testing.* The term *pseudohallucination* has been used in two often confounded senses: first, to denote hallucinationlike experiences perceived as occurring within the body (e.g., locating voices within the head, rather than outside) or second, to denote hallucinations whose unreality is apparent to the subject (Bentall, 1990). In practice, however, subjects manifest a complex array of attitudes toward their hallucinations ranging from credulity to skepticism; hence, insight often cannot be described as simply present or absent.

- *Presence of External Sensory Stimulus.* Although historically the terms "illusion" and "hallucination" were used interchangeably, current usage follows the distinction drawn by Esquirol who defined illusions as false or distorted sensory perceptions of real external stimuli.

Epidemiology

The notion that hallucinations form part of a spectrum of perceptual disturbances that may occur in a wide range of individuals is supported by survey data suggesting that hallucinations and related sensory experiences are relatively common in nonclinical populations.

Despite sampling and assessment limitations, Sidgewick's (1894, cited in Tien, 1991) pioneering epidemiological study for the Society of Psychical Research provided data on the lifetime prevalence of hallucinations for 17,000 adults. Sidgewick found a lifetime prevalence of non-sleep-related hallucinations of 5.3% for males and 8.4% for females. Visual hallucinations were about three times more common than auditory ones, which in turn were more common than tactile ones.

Surveys of college students and other selected nonclinical samples found 25% to 71% of subjects reported having experienced at least briefly hallucinated voices when fully awake (McKellar, 1968; Posey & Losch, 1983). Having seen a face when no one was present was reported by 1.4% to 2.9% of college students (Young, Bentall, Slade, & Dewey, 1986; Bentall & Slade, 1985).

Data from the NIMH Epidemiologic Catchment Area (ECA) have been analyzed to estimate the age-group incidence of hallucinations occurring in the awake state including both those with and without distress or impairment (Tien, 1991). The incidence for adult males was 4.0% per year and 4.9% per year for females. Visual hallucinations were, in general, more common than auditory for all age groups, and the age-incidence of visual hallucinations was relatively constant until age 70 years; beyond that point, it showed a sharp rise. Nondistressing hallucinations exceeded distressing ones by severalfold.

Syndromic Issues

Because of their frequent occurrence in schizophrenia and other major neuropsychiatric disorders, hallucinations are sometimes incorrectly considered to be prima facie evidence of severe pathology. Hallucinations may occur naturally, however, or be induced in nonclinical subjects without other signs of psychopathology. On the one hand, the high prevalence of hallucinations in schizophrenia may point to important pathogenic processes shared by schizophrenia and hallucinations. On the other hand, the relative nonspecificity of hallucinations, even among psychiatric patients, and their occurrence in otherwise unimpaired individuals, caution against a purely syndrome-based approach to hallucinatory phenomena.

Hallucinations in Psychiatric Disorders

Zigler and Phillips (1961) reviewed the symptoms of 793 admissions to a psychiatric hospital over a 12-year period. Hallucinations were noted in 19% of the sample and were most common in patients diagnosed with schizophrenia (35%); the prevalence of hallucinations for patients in other diagnostic categories was 11% for manic-depressive disorder, 12% for character disorder, and 4% for neurosis.

Hallucinations are listed among the characteristics symptoms of schizophrenia by DSM-IV (American Psychiatric Association, 1994). Patients with schizophrenia may show any of the wide gamut of hallucinations described in the section on phenomenology. In a series of predominantly American and Swedish studies of schizophrenia, auditory hallucinations occurred in 34% to 94% of patients (mean 60.2% ± 19.9 SD) and visual hallucinations in 4% to 72% (mean 29.2% ± 20.8 SD) (Slade & Bentall, 1988).

Whether characteristic types of hallucination are specific to schizophrenia remains unclear. Schneider (1959) proposed that certain hallucinatory "first-rank" symptoms were specific to schizophrenia: hearing a running commentary on one's own actions; voices speaking about one in the third person; hearing one's thoughts spoken aloud. Similarly, in DSM-IV (American Psychiatric Association, 1994) hallucinations of a voice keeping up a running commentary on the person's behavior or thoughts, or two or more voices conversing with each other, are regarded as pathognomonic of schizophrenia, provided duration and impairment criteria are also met. The International Pilot Study of Psychotic Disorders found these two criteria, as well as voices speaking to the patient, to be highly predictive of schizophrenic and paranoid psychosis, but not affective or other psychoses (World Health Organization, 1975). On the other hand, questionnaire-based studies of college students found that 14% to 18% endorsed the Schneiderian symptom "I often hear a voice speaking my thoughts aloud" (Bentall & Slade, 1985; Young et al., 1986).

DSM-IV includes hallucinations among the symptoms diagnostic of affective disorders such as Major Depressive Disorder or Bipolar Disorder with Psychotic Features. Hallucinations are less common, however, in patients with bipolar and depressive disorder than in those with schizophrenia. When hallucinations do occur, auditory hallucinations are the commonest modality (Goodwin, Alderson, & Rosenthal, 1971). For both the hallucinations and delusions accompanying affective disorders, a common distinction is between *mood-congruent* and *mood-incongruent* psychotic features. In depression, the content of mood-congruent hallucinations or delusions is concerned with "typical depressive themes of personal inadequacy, guilt, disease, death, nihilism, or deserved punishment" (p. 223). Thus, hallucinations in depression with mood-congruent psychotic features may include derogatory voices, somatic and olfactory hallucinations of self-putrefaction, and so on. In contrast, the mood-congruent hallucinations or delusions of mania are concerned with "the typical manic themes of inflated worth, power, knowledge, identity, or special relationship to a deity or famous person" (p. 218). Sexually charged somatic hallucinations may also accompany the hypersexuality of the manic phase.

Although language impairments hinder assessment, hallucinations appear to be rare among patients with "early-onset" pervasive disorders, such as *infantile autism.* In contrast, hallucinations are more common in children diagnosed with later-onset psychosis or strictly defined DSM-IV schizophrenia. As discussed later, this distinction formed one of the bases for abandoning the once-popular global concept of "childhood psychosis" or "childhood schizophrenia" in favor of the more narrowly defined DSM-IV categories of Autistic Disorder and Schizophrenia occurring in childhood (King & Noshpitz, 1991).

Transient hallucinations (which may resemble illusions or pseudohallucinations) are sometimes seen in *Schizotypal Personality Disorder* and *Borderline Personality Disorder;* these hallucinations, however, usually lack the vividness, intrusiveness, and distress associated with hallucinations in schizophrenia or affective disorder, two conditions to which these personality disorders may be genetically related.

In *Dissociative* and *Posttraumatic Stress Disorder* hallucinatory phenomena can constitute part of the recurrent, intrusive flashbacks experienced by victims of posttraumatic stress disorder (PTSD) following acute or chronic violence, accidents, or natural disaster; in addition, hallucinations can also be an immediate concomitant of severe acute stress. These hallucinations or pseudohallucinations may recapitulate aspects of the traumatic event and be accompanied by anxiety or depersonalization. Although such hallucinations may be limited to reliving the trauma, they may also include command hallucinations (e.g., telling the subject to commit suicide) or be accompanied by delusions (Mueser & Butler, 1987; Waldfogel & Mueser, 1988).

From at least the time of Freud, Breuer, Charcot, and Janet, hallucinations were noted to be a common component of a dissociative syndrome that was then widely prevalent and frequently included rapidly fluctuating and abnormal forms of consciousness, fugue states, affective lability, and sensorimotor conversion phenomena (Breuer & Freud, 1895/1955). Diagnosed under the broad rubric of hysteria, these disorders were early on recognized as "ideogenic" (although a constitutional vulnerability was sometimes postulated). Although Freud was later to invoke internal instinctual conflicts as the principal pathogenic agent, he initially hypothesized that these disorders were the result of psychic trauma, most often sexual in nature. Over the decades, such symptoms have been conceptualized under a variety of labels, including *hysteria* and *hysterical psychosis.*

Interest in the relationship of such hallucinations to trauma has been revived by the recent increased recognition of the posttraumatic nature of many dissociative conditions, including flashbacks, multiple personality disorder, and conversion disorder. Nurcombe and colleagues (in press) have coined the term *dissociative hallucinosis* to describe an adolescent syndrome of acute, transient hallucinations accompanied by emotional turmoil, altered consciousness, disorganized thinking, and impulsive aggression and have noted its frequent link to severe, most often chronic, trauma. To what extent borderline personality disorder (which may also be characterized by lability and "micropsychotic" episodes) is a concomitant or a risk factor for the development of such a condition remains to be determined.

Hallucinations in Medical Conditions

In addition to these major psychiatric disorders, hallucinations may occur in many toxic, metabolic, and neurological conditions (Asaad, 1990). Hallucinations associated with chronic alcohol abuse usually fall under the classification of *alcoholic hallucinosis* or *delirium tremens.* The vivid hallucinations of *delirium tremens* (the "DTs") form part of a time-limited organic withdrawal syndrome of disorientation, tremulousness, agitation, autonomic hyperactivity, and fluctuating consciousness occurring with a few days of partial or complete abstinence following a period of heavy drinking (Asaad, 1990). Such hallucinations are frequently threatening in nature and most commonly visual and tactile, such as complex and fantastical visual images (e.g., the "pink elephants" of popular fiction) and a sensation of crawling insects on the skin (formication).

Unlike delirium tremens, *alcoholic hallucinosis* occurs without confusion or fluctuating alertness. These predominantly auditory hallucinations, occurring a few days after the cessation of heavy chronic drinking of several years' duration, range from indistinct noises through vivid voices that may be threatening or accusatory. Although usually transient, the condition may become chronic or become complicated by referential thinking, delusions, and disordered thought that is difficult to distinguish from schizophrenia.

A variety of other metabolic or toxic conditions can produce hallucinations and delirium. These include fever, starvation, thirst, hypoglycemia, electrolyte imbalances, hepatic encephalopathy, renal failure, porphyria, mineral deficiencies, mercury or bromide poisoning, and respiratory disturbances such as hyperventilation, hypoxia, or hypercarbia. In the general hospital setting, hallucinations are most commonly seen in intensive care units or recovery rooms. The patients most susceptible to such "ICU psychosis" are those exposed to the physiological (and psychological) stresses of major surgery, periods of hypoxia or brain ischemia, multiple medications, or sensory deprivation (including paralyzed and ventilator-dependent patients). The "sundowning" phenomena of disorientation and/or hallucinations at dusk or night is seen in hospitals and nursing homes in elderly and other compromised patients, presumably due to loss of daytime structure and sensory stimulation (see discussion of sensory deprivation later in this chapter).

Hallucinations may occur as a consequence of seizure disorders, either as part of the aura, the seizure proper, or the postictal phase (Asaad, 1990). These hallucinations may vary from simple, unformed percepts to complex and highly organized images. Consistent with Penfield and Perot's (1963) evocation of hallucinatory sensory experiences by means of direct cortical stimulation, the sensory mode and content of seizure-linked hallucinations often reflect the seizure focus. For example, olfactory hallucinations (most often of unpleasant odors) are associated with the uncal portion of the temporal lobe. Gustatory hallucinations are associated with a parietal or temporal focus (Hausser & Bancaud, 1987). Visual hallucinations, which may range from unformed lights, spots, colors, or darkness through elaborate scenes or images, are often associated with a posterior temporal or occipital focus (Strub & Black, 1988). Auditory hallucinations such as music or voices may be associated with superior temporal foci.

Especially with the partial complex seizures of temporal lobe epilepsy, hallucinations may come to be associated with other psychotic phenomena, including thought disorder, delusions, dissociative phenomena (such as fugue states and déjà or jamais vu experiences), and excessive religious preoccupations.

Hallucinations may also be found in a wide variety of neurological disorders, including migraine, narcolepsy, head injury, infarcts, vasculitides, and tumors. Hallucinations also occur in the degenerative dementias of later life, such as Alzheimer's disease or multi-infarct dementia (Crystal, Wolfson, & Ewing, 1988). A variety of basal ganglia disorders may also be accompanied by hallucinations (Asaad, 1990), including Huntington's and Sydenham's choreas, Parkinson's disease, and idiopathic basal ganglia calcification (Francis, 1979). Among the central nervous system infections producing delirium and hallucinations, the syndrome of general paresis of the insane associated with tertiary syphilis was common in the preantibiotic era; in our era, HIV-related organic psychoses and dementias are increasingly common.

Hallucinations have been noted as occasional side effects of almost every class of drugs. Some drugs, such as psilocybin or LSD, produce hallucinations in almost all who take them. In contrast, other drugs produce hallucinations in only a small number of individuals. Whether individuals who develop medication-related hallucinations share distinctive features is unknown. It is often assumed that patients with a genetic (or other constitutional) vulnerability to schizophrenia or bipolar disorder may be especially prone to developing psychotic symptoms on drugs such as the antidepressants or stimulants.

Hallucinations in the Absence of Specific Medical or Psychiatric Conditions

Reports of hallucinations in substantial numbers of nonclinical subjects raise the question, What conditions contribute to hallucinations and are some individuals predisposed to such experiences? A related question is, To what extent are such hallucinations similar to those seen in the previously discussed psychiatric and medical disorders?

Dreams. Experimental subjects wakened during REM sleep report vivid imagery (most often visual), that is often bizarre, implausible, and affectively charged. Dreamlike *hypnogogic* or *hypnopompic* hallucinations, often accompanied by sleep paralysis, are experienced while falling asleep or sudden awakening, and appear to represent the intrusion of REM state mental phenomena into the waking states.

The similarity between hallucinations and dreams has long been noted. Schopenhauer wrote, "A dream is a short-lasting psychosis, and a psychosis is a long-lasting dream" (cited in Fischman, 1983, p. 73). Freud saw shared regressive, primary processes underlying the genesis of both dreams and hallucinations. Many authors have speculated on the relationship between dreams, acute psychosis, and hallucinogenic drug states that share a disruption of a coherent sense of the self and the emergence of primary process characterized loss of reality testing and abstract thinking (Asaad, 1990; Fischman, 1983; Horowitz,

1983). Drawing on the effects of various pharmacological agents, such speculation has also focused on the role played by various neurotransmitter systems (e.g., dopaminergic and serotonergic) and their neuroanatomic pathways in modulating both sleep architecture and hallucinatory phenomena (Fischman, 1983).

Sleep Deprivation. Prolonged sleep deprivation or circadian rhythm disruption (such as that experienced by long-distance fliers) can lead to perceptual illusions and visual or auditory hallucinations that may be accompanied by depersonalization, disorientation, and sometimes sleep paralysis; wide interindividual differences exist in the vulnerability to such experiences (Horowitz, 1983; Mullaney, Kripke, Fleck, & Johnson, 1983; Snyder, 1983). The work of Dement et al. (1969) suggests that, like hypnogogic and hypnopompic hallucinations, such experiences may represent intrusions of some aspects of REM sleep into waking experience.

Sensory Deprivation. Beginning with the studies of Hebb and colleagues in the 1950s, sensory deprivation became a widely used paradigm for studying the induction of hallucinatorylike experiences. The experimental conditions employed (e.g., darkness or eye patches, soundproofing or white noise) provide an experimental analogue to the natural conditions known to foster hallucinations (e.g., solitary confinement; postcataract surgery; prolonged exposure to the perceptual monotony of the desert, open sea, or arctic landscape).

Many nonclinical subjects exposed to such conditions experience an increased vividness of their usual mental imagery or entoptic images; with additional exposure, volitional control of such images diminishes to the point that some subjects experience apparent hallucinations (Horowitz, 1983; Zuckerman & Cohen, 1964). (This body of research has been criticized as lacking a consistent operational definition of hallucination and failing to take into account the element of suggestion in the experimental procedures.) As many as half of subjects experience simple percepts, such as spots of light, geometric forms or patterns, and humming noises; more complex and meaningful complex auditory or visual percepts are experienced by 15% to 20% of subjects (Slade, 1984; Zuckerman, 1969). Examining the personality correlates of such experiences, Goldberger and Holt (1961) found that subjects who were more compliant and intellectually flexible and less emotionally constricted reported more images.

Hallucinations Related to Stress or Grief. Auditory or visual hallucinations may be associated with bereavement. For example, as many as 13% of recently widowed men and women reported hallucinating their deceased spouse's voice (Reese, 1971). These hallucinations may not be limited to seeing or hearing the deceased (Wells, 1980). Although such hallucinations are usually transient, they may be more persistent in cases of pathological mourning or where culturally supported by a belief in ghosts or spirits.

Exposure to severe stress can produce hallucinations in vulnerable individuals. For example, Spivak, Trottern, Mark, Bleich, and Weizman (1992) reported several young Israeli draftees who experienced hallucinations during their first days in basic training.

Such hallucinations may be hostile and threatening, or wish fulfilling and reparative as in the case of trapped miners who hallucinated doorways, stairs, and the Pope (Comer, Madow, & Dixon, 1976). Hallucinations may be more common in patients exposed to isolation and life-threatening situations (Mueser & Butler, 1987; Siegel, 1984).

Charles Bonnet Syndrome—Isolated, Vivid Visual Hallucinations. In 1769, the naturalist Charles Bonnet described pleasant, complex, visual hallucinations in his cataract-ridden, but cognitively intact grandfather. Subsequently, the term *Charles Bonnet syndrome* has come to be applied to isolated complex visual hallucinations, with awareness of their unreality, occurring in alert, usually elderly, individuals in the absence of psychopathology or obvious cognitive impairment (Damas-Mora, Skelton-Robinson, & Jenner, 1982; Gold & Rabins, 1989). Rosenbaum and colleagues (1987) used the phrase "visual hallucinations in sane people" to describe the syndrome. There is no consensus whether eye disease or diagnosable neurological disorder should be necessary or exclusionary criteria, and this broadly inclusive eponymic disorder includes cases of diverse etiology.

Many but not all the patients with this syndrome have some form of visual impairment. Hallucinations can occur with pathology at any level of the visual system. "Black patch delirium" and "cataract psychoses" are well-known syndromes in eye patients. In a case control study of 100 elderly patients with macular degeneration, Holroyd, Rabins, Finkelstein, and Nicholson (1992) found 13% reported visual hallucinations, usually following an acute change in vision. Living alone, lower cognitive scores, history of stroke, and bilaterally worse visual acuity emerged as predisposing factors, but not personal or family history of psychiatric disorder or maladaptive personality traits. Possible toxic reactions to drugs, such as anticholinergic eye drops, should be excluded (Gold & Rabins, 1989).

The Charles Bonnet syndrome can occur in patients without detectable visual, neurological, or psychiatric pathology. For example, Bhatia, Khastgir, and Malik (1992) reported a case of Charles Bonnet syndrome in an extensively evaluated 38-year-old man, whose symptoms improved on carbamazepine, but not haloperidol. In some patients, however, the underlying pathology becomes diagnosable only on follow-up; in Gold and Rabins' (1989) series, two patients subsequently proved to have dementia.

Pathogenesis

Neurobiological Perspectives

The occurrence of hallucinations as a potential side effect of a diverse array of pharmacological agents suggests that disturbances in neurotransmitter regulation may play a role in the genesis of hallucinations. Among the systems that have been suggested to play a role are the cholinergic, dopaminergic, serotonergic, noradrenergic, and the glutamatergic and other excitatory amino acid systems (Asaad, 1990; Heresco-Levy, Javitt, & Zukin, 1993). Hallucinogenic and psychotomimetic drugs, such as LSD and phencyclidine (PCP) have provided useful models for the experimental study of the neurochemistry and neurobiology of hallucinations.

The similarity of PCP-induced psychosis to schizophrenia has led to increased interest in the N-methyl-D-aspartate (NMDA) receptor complex to which PCP selectively binds. The NMDA receptor is a subtype of glutamate receptor, the major excitatory neurotransmitter of the brain.

Modern imaging techniques have begun to elucidate the functional neuroanatomic basis of hallucinations. Regional cerebral blood flow studies of patients with chronic auditory hallucinations have found increased blood flow in the anterior basal ganglia, hippocampal, and medial temporal areas compared with normal controls; such studies also point to distinctive patterns of regional blood flow in patients with auditory as contrasted with tactile hallucinations (Musalek et al., 1989). Partially consistent with these findings, a positron-emission tomography (PET) study comparing schizophrenic patients with and without auditory hallucinations found hallucinations correlated with decreased metabolism in cortical language areas (Wernicke's and auditory cortical areas) and increased relative metabolism in the striatal and anterior cingulate areas (Cleghorn et al., 1992). A recent single photon emission computed tomography (SPECT) study compared the scans of 12 subjects as they experienced auditory hallucinations with scans of the same subjects in a nonhallucinating state; blood flow to Broca's area was increased in the hallucinating state (McGuire, Shah, & Murray, 1993). This pattern of cortical activity is similar to that observed in subjects speaking and listening to their own voices or subvocalizing (Waddington, 1993; Cleghorn et al., 1992). During active auditory hallucinations, response delays are noted in auditory evoked potentials and magnetic fields, an effect similar to that produced by external speech or sound-masking stimuli (Tiihonen et al., 1992).

Psychological Perspectives

Most psychological theories of hallucination are variants of what Slade and Bentall (1988) term "seepage theories." Such theories see hallucinations as "a 'seepage' into consciousness of mental activity that would normally remain preconscious" (p. 114). Slade and Bentall's own five-factor theory and West's "perceptual release" theory (1975) represent exemplars of this type.

Seepage theories draw on the influential work of Hughlings Jackson (1932) who speculated that hallucinations represented a release phenomenon secondary to impairment of higher cortical structures that normally inhibited the activity of midbrain structures; as a result of this disinhibition, internal stimuli emerged into consciousness in the form of hallucinations.

West (1975) proposed that the contents of conscious awareness represent a balance between external sensory input and internal stimuli (the neural activity underlying memory, thought, imagination). Under ordinary circumstances, West suggested, external stimuli exert an organizing effect, increasing arousal and sharpening the screening and scanning processes that focus attention and exclude from awareness low-priority, static, or unwanted information from internal and external sources. According to this model, if the level of external sensory input is insufficient to maintain the organizing activity of these screening and scanning functions (or if the press of internal stimuli is too great), perceptual memory traces will emerge into awareness and be perceived as "real" or external, provided there is sufficient arousal for awareness to be maintained. West provides the analogy of a man standing in front of a fireplace looking at an outside scene through a glass window. In broad daylight, all he sees through the window is the outside. As twilight falls, he may be able to see in the window not only the outside scene but also the reflected interior lit by the fire and seen in the glass as though outside. With night, all he sees is the reflected interior. Finally, as the fire dies down, it is dark both outside and within, save for occasional reappearances of the vision in the glass as the fire momentarily flares up. Using this model, West attempted to show how the levels of arousal and effective sensory input in various situations might account for the hallucinatory phenomena associated with sensory deprivation, hypnopompic and hypnogic states, and normal dreaming.

Empirical support for West's theory is provided by the studies of Slade (1974) and colleagues (Margo, Hemsley, & Slade, 1981), who examined the influence of various environmental stimulus conditions on hallucinating subjects. The studies concluded that low or unpatterned stimulation increased the probability of hallucinations, whereas meaningful stimulation (especially verbal tasks such as reading) seemed to inhibit hallucinations (Bentall, 1990; Slade & Bentall, 1988).

Individuals differ markedly in their vulnerability to spontaneous or experimentally induced hallucinations. A better understanding of these interindividual differences may shed light on the pathogenesis of hallucinations.

Suggestibility is an important dimension of individual differences. As might be expected from the significant influence of cultural and social factors on both the occurrence and content of hallucinations, suggestion can serve as a potent inducer of reported hallucinations. For example, reported hallucinations can be induced in many subjects under hypnosis; it is difficult, however, to ascertain whether it is hallucinations or compliant reporting that is being induced. Experimental studies suggest that hallucinators are more suggestible than nonhallucinators; whether this suggestibility is limited to the realm of perceptual judgments is unclear (Bentall, 1990).

Barber and Calverly (1964) developed a paradigm for studying the effect of suggestions to hallucinate in nonhypnotic subjects, who were asked to "close your eyes and hear a phonograph" playing "White Christmas." Of these subjects, 49% reported having clearly heard the record; 5% additionally reported that they had believed the record was actually played. Variations on this paradigm demonstrate the impact of context and social desirability factors on subjects' responses (Slade & Bentall, 1988; Spanos, 1986). However, even when subjects in one visual version of the experiment were given the option that they "imagined" rather than "saw" the suggested stimulus, 1% persisted in reporting that they had seen it (McPeake & Spanos, 1973).

An interesting converse experimental paradigm was developed by Perky (1910) to assess subjects' propensity to mistakenly identify real percepts as the products of their imagination. Subjects were asked to imagine an object on a white screen. An actual image of the object was than back-projected onto the screen with gradually increasing intensity until visible. All subjects reported experiencing the image as imaginary.

Differences in susceptibility to social influences do not account for all the interindividual differences on reality discrimination. Perceptual discrimination experiments suggest that in a variety of ways, hallucinators are prone to make impulsive and overconfident judgments about the nature and source of their perceptions (e.g., localizing sounds in space, discriminating voices or the meaning of words against white noise) (Bentall, 1990).

Integrating these findings, Bentall and Slade suggest that paralleling the continuum between hallucinatory and nonhallucinatory experiences are wide individual differences in the capacity to discriminate inner and outer reality. Rather than regarding "reality testing" as an all-or-nothing phenomenon, Bentall and Slade (1988) suggest that reality discrimination is a metacognitive skill that may be exercised with greater or lesser accuracy and that involves weighing a variety of perceptual, social, and contextual cues. Hallucinations, from this perspective, may stem from a variety of deficits in distinguishing internal and external phenomena.

Sociocultural Perspectives

In contrast to the view of hallucinations as necessarily, or even usually, psychopathological, some societies view various hallucinations as culturally sanctioned or positively valued experiences. Certain types of hallucinations may be actively sought after either as a rite of passage (e.g., vision quest) or as a means of communicating with spirits or departed ancestors (Al-Issa, 1977; Bourguignon, 1970).

Geographic and historical variations in the form and content of hallucinations suggest the influence of social and cultural factors (Bentall & Slade, 1988; Mitchell & Vierkant, 1989; Wilkins, 1987). For example, international studies of schizophrenia suggest that visual hallucinations may be more common in developing countries than in the industrialized world (Bentall, 1990).

Hallucinations over the Life Span

Hallucinations are difficult to ascertain in children prior to a certain level of language development and must be differentiated from such phenomena as imaginary companions and sleep-related phenomena. Nonetheless, hallucinations have been noted to occur in children as young as three or four years of age, with and without major psychiatric disorders (King & Noshpitz, 1991).

Although there are several case series of hallucinations in childhood, many suffer from overly broad or vague inclusion criteria, and a lack of controls, systematic assessment, or follow-up (Despert, 1948; Egdell & Kolvin, 1972; Kemph, 1987; Kotsopoulos, Kanigsberg, Coke, & Fiedorowicz, 1987; Pilowsky & Chambers, 1986; Rothstein, 1981; see Werry, 1992, for a discussion). Virtually all reports are drawn from clinical populations and are limited by the selection biases that clinical samples pose. The current NIMH multisite Methodologic Epidemiologic study of Children and Adolescents may provide community-based prevalence data for hallucinations in older children and adolescents similar to the Epidemiologic Catchment Area study data previously reported for adults; it has proven difficult, however, to develop a structured epidemiological interview to elicit reliable and valid data on psychotic phenomena in children, in view of the importance of the child as the primary informant for such phenomena.

Although hallucinations can occur in childhood as part of the major psychiatric disorders, more prognostically benign transient hallucinations also occur in preschool children, especially in reaction to acute anxiety or situational stresses (Aug & Ables, 1971; Esman, 1962; Ravenscroft, 1980; Rothstein, 1981; Schreier & Libow, 1986; Wilking & Paoli, 1966). These transient, primarily visual and tactile hallucinations in otherwise healthy preschoolers are usually of acute onset and often begin at night, suggesting in some cases a dream-state-related origin, but persist, sometimes for several days, even when the child is fully alert. Such children commonly have tactile hallucinations of bugs crawling on their skin or in their bed or clothes, and frantically try to brush them off. Visual hallucinations may include insects and other threatening animals. Even as the hallucinations subside, the children continue for a while to be clingy, frightened, and avoidant of bed or sleep. Dynamically, these hallucinations may occur in the context of heightened anxiety over oedipal or aggressive concerns. The similarity of these symptoms to the animal phobias of childhood led Ravenscroft (1980) to coin the term "acute phobic hallucinosis" and to view them as "a more intense regressive variant of an acute anxiety attack of childhood."

In contrast to the acute, transient hallucinations reported in otherwise healthy school-age children, hallucinations in older children and adolescents are often more persistent (Del Beccaro, Burke, & McCauley, 1988) and associated with more serious pathology, including schizophrenia (Russell, Bott, & Sammons, 1989; Volkmar, Cohen, Hoshino, Rende, & Paul, 1988); mania (Ballenger, Reus, & Post, 1982); major depression (Carlson & Kashani, 1988; Chambers, 1986); conduct disorder and personality disorder (Aug & Ables, 1971); and retardation. Like the delusions of childhood schizophrenia, these hallucinations are more fluid and less complex than those of adult schizophrenics and, reflecting the developmental concerns of childhood, are more often concerned with animals, toys, or monsters, rather than sexual themes (Russell et al., 1989).

Hallucinations occur in up to 80% of children with childhood-onset schizophrenia (Green, Padron-Gayol, Hardesty, & Bassiri, 1992; Russell et al., 1989; Volkmar et al., 1988). This condition is, however, only very rarely reported in preschool children likely reflecting intrinsic maturational aspects of the schizophrenic process, rather than problems in ascertaining the presence of hallucinations or delusions in preschool children (King, 1994).

As with adults, childhood hallucinations can occur in the context of a wide variety of organic syndromes. Progressive deteriorative neurological disorders, such as subacute sclerosing panencephalitis (SSPE) can present initially as an organic psychosis (Caplan, Tanguay, & Szekely, 1987). The term "periodic psychosis of puberty" has been used to describe a transient, but recurrent premenstrual psychosis seen in adolescent girls (Berlin, Bergey, & Money, 1982). An "Alice in Wonderland" syndrome of visual distortions of size, form, movement, or color may accompany an otherwise undiagnosed bout of infectious mononucleosis (Lahat, Eshel, & Arlazoroff, 1990).

From a developmental perspective, the pattern of drug-induced hallucinations may vary across the life span. In the pediatric age group, hallucinations have been noted as uncommon side effects of stimulants, antihistamines, decongestants, antibiotics, barbiturates, dilantin, and aspirin. Elderly patients may be more prone to medication side effects, in part because of great difficulty metabolizing and excreting various drugs.

DELUSIONS

Phenomenology

A *delusion* is a false personal belief that is firmly held in the face of contradictory evidence, and that is not held by other members of the individual's culture or subculture (American Psychiatric Association, 1994; Kaplan & Sadock, 1991; Leon, Bowden, & Faber, 1989; Yager, 1989). Delusions are further classified in many ways. A *simple* delusion contains few elements, while a *complex* delusion has multiple aspects. A *systematized* delusion is a group of elaborate false beliefs all related to a single event, person, or theme; *nonsystematized* (or *fragmentary*) delusions, by contrast, are poorly elaborated and lacking in thematic unity. *Primary* delusions occur without apparent preexisting psychopathology, such as hallucinations or a disordered mood; *secondary* delusions appear to emerge in response to specific experiences or pathology. A primary delusion that forms instantaneously is referred to as an *autochthonous* delusion. A *bizarre* delusion concerns a phenomenon that would be considered completely implausible within the individual's culture; a *nonbizarre* delusion, on the other hand, involves a phenomenon that—however improbable—is indeed plausible within the cultural belief system. Finally, an *encapsulated* delusion is one that has no significant effect on the person's behavior.

Kendler, Glazer, and Morgenstern (1983) suggest that delusions can be characterized along five dimensions: (a) *conviction*—the degree to which the individual is convinced of the reality of the delusion; (b) *extension*—the degree to which the delusion involves multiple areas of the person's life (this dimension captures the distinction between "complex" and "simple" delusions); (c) *bizarreness*—the degree to which the belief departs from culturally sanctioned reality; (d) *disorganization*—the degree to which delusional beliefs are internally consistent (this dimension relates to the distinction between "systematized" and "nonsystematized" delusions); and (e) *pressure*—the degree to which the individual is preoccupied with the delusion.

In addition to these general classification schemes, delusions can be typed according to their content (American Psychiatric Association, 1994; Kaplan & Sadock, 1991; Leon et al., 1989). A *persecutory* delusion involves being conspired against, attacked, or harassed; this type is sometimes incorrectly referred to as a "paranoid delusion." In a *delusion of reference,* events, objects, or others' behavior have a particular significance—usually negative—for the individual. A *delusion of influence* (or "delusion of control") centers on the belief that the individual's thoughts, feelings, or actions are imposed by an outside force. A *grandiose* delusion (or "delusion of grandeur") involves exaggerated status or ability. A *religious* delusion pertains to a diety or a related manifestation; these delusions are often also grandiose in nature.

The theme of nonexistence is of central importance in a *nihilistic* delusion ("delusion of negation" or "Cotard's syndrome"). A *somatic* delusion (or "hypochondriacal delusion") pertains to the functioning of the individual's body; on occasion, a somatic delusion may be nihilistic as well. A delusion of *poverty* is the false belief that one is or will be without material possessions; a delusion of *guilt*, that one has sinned or committed some other serious transgression. A delusion of *jealousy* ("delusion of infidelity" or "Othello syndrome") represents the belief that one's sexual partner is unfaithful. A delusion of *erotic attachment* ("erotomania" or "de Clérambault's syndrome") is the belief that a stranger, usually someone of higher social status, is in love with the individual. In a delusion of *replacement* ("Capgras' syndrome"), the individual believes that a significant other has been replaced by an imposter with some kind of persecutory intent; "Fregoli's syndrome" is a variant in which a persecutor is believed to be presenting himself or herself as a variety of people near to the individual (Hart & McClure, 1989). ("Reduplicative paramnesia" is a related syndrome in which the individual believes his or her physical surroundings have been replaced; this syndrome has traditionally—perhaps somewhat arbitrarily—been considered to be a neurological disorder instead of a psychiatric one, Crichton & Lewis, 1990).

Thought broadcasting, thought insertion, and *thought withdrawal* are, respectively, the individual's beliefs that his or her thoughts are projected into the environment, are being placed in the mind by others, and are being removed from the mind by others. A *delusional mood* is an unfounded fear of impending disaster, which may in turn result in the secondary elaboration of an explanatory delusional idea. A *delusional perception* occurs when a normal perception is followed by a delusional conclusion from that perception.

Finally, *shared* delusions (e.g., "folie à deux," "folie à trois," or "folie à famille") occur when one or more related individuals hold the same false beliefs, which are not held by other members of the subculture. Folie à deux has been subclassified as follows: (a) In "folie imposée," which is most common, the delusion of a dominant individual is adopted by a passive, suggestible individual; (b) in "folie simultanée," two individuals who are close to each other develop similar delusional symptoms at about the same time; (c) in "folie communiquée," two individuals who are close develop delusional illnesses, but at slightly different times, and the two illnesses have distinctive characteristics; and (d) in "folie induite," which is least common, two individuals with preexisting illnesses adopt parts of each other's delusions (Hart & McClure, 1989).

Syndromic Issues

Human behavior is distinguished from all other biological activity in its reliance on signs, symbols, concepts, and meanings. Rational and voluntary action is seen as rational and voluntary by its being in response to a meaning-scheme (Fingarette, 1963). An impairment in one's ability to discern culture-syntonic meanings in the world is a significant adaptive disadvantage. Therefore, the presence of a delusion in a patient is of considerable diagnostic importance. The symptom is pathognomonic of psychosis—though not all psychotic individuals have delusions (Nicholi, 1978). Although delusions occur most commonly in schizophrenia, they are found in other mental disorders as well.

Kraepelin's (1907, 1921) detailed descriptive work allowed the first clear differentiation of psychotic syndromes. He distinguished between the chronic delusions resulting from the mental deterioration of "dementia praecox" and the delusions of "manic-depressive insanity," resulting from profound emotional disturbance and resolving with the resolution of this disturbance. He further described "paranoia" as a delusional belief system occurring in the absence of the generalized deterioration typical of dementia praecox. Kraepelin subtyped paranoia into "delusions of persecution," "delusions of jealousy," and "delusions of grandeur." The latter subtype was in turn subdivided into the "delusion of being a great inventor," the "delusion of being descended from royalty," the "delusion of being a prophet or saint," and the "delusion of eroticism" ("erotomania"). Despite various attempts at reclassification over the middle portion of this century, the scheme embodied in DSM-IV (American Psychiatric Association, 1994) bears remarkable resemblance to Kraepelin's observations (Segal, 1989).

Within DSM-IV, delusions are among the defining characteristics of several diagnostic entities. The diagnostic criteria for Schizophrenia may include—but do not require—delusions. A special emphasis on bizarre delusions is built into the criteria, though it is still a matter of dispute whether this emphasis is warranted (Goldman, Hien, Haas, Sweeney, & Frances, 1992). Certain types of delusions are found much more commonly in Schizophrenia than in other disorders; these include thought broadcasting, thought insertion, thought withdrawal, and delusions of being controlled. These delusions are among Schneider's (1959) "first-rank" symptoms, which—though highly discriminating for Schizophrenia—are not pathognomonic, in that they can be found in one-fourth of manic-depressive patients (Carpenter, Strauss, & Muleh, 1973). Among the subtypes of Schizophrenia, delusions are a prominent feature of the *Paranoid Type,* which can be characterized by preoccupation with one or more systematized delusions. Delusions can also be found in the *Catatonic, Disorganized,* and *Undifferentiated Types,* though they are not seen in the *Residual Type* of Schizophrenia.

Delusions can also be observed in the major Mood Disorders. In DSM-IV, delusions are associated features of *Manic Episodes* and *Major Depressive Episodes*—and, as such, can be seen in *Bipolar Disorders* and *Major Depressive Disorders*. In general, delusions found within the context of a Mood Disorder are nonbizarre and "mood-congruent," though "mood-incongruent" delusions are seen as well. Though there has been some controversy about whether mood-incongruent psychotic affective illness should be viewed as indistinguishable from other forms of psychotic affective illness—or, alternatively, as a type of Schizoaffective Disorder or Schizophrenia—most of the evidence seems to support the DSM-IV approach of considering it to be a subtype of psychotic affective illness (Kendler, 1991). In a similar vein, the current classification system emphasizes the similarities between Mood Disorders with and without psychotic features. Nonetheless, there has been some support for the notion that Major Depressive Disorder with Psychotic Features ("delusional depression") should be viewed as a separate diagnostic entity (Schatzberg & Rothschild, 1992).

The diagnostic criteria for *Schizoaffective Disorder* include the same prominent psychotic symptomatology (the "A criterion") required for Schizophrenia; these must occur during a major mood episode. In addition, either delusions or hallucinations must occur for at least 2 weeks in the absence of any mood syndrome. Delusions can also be seen in *Schizophreniform Disorder;* here again, the "A criterion" for schizophrenia is required to make the diagnosis. *Brief Psychotic Disorder* is a psychotic disorder of limited duration and of sudden onset; transient delusions are common. DSM-IV describes a *Shared Psychotic Disorder,* in which a delusional system develops in a second person as a result of a close relationship with another person (the "primary case") who already has a delusional illness; this is the "folie imposée," described earlier. Delusions are typically nonbizarre, though bizarre delusions are occasionally induced; persecutory delusions seem to be particularly common. The most common diagnosis in the primary case is Paranoid Schizophrenia, followed by Delusional Disorder and Mood Disorder with Psychotic Features (Kendler, Spitzer, & Williams, 1989).

Delusional disorder is a DSM-IV category in which the central feature is the presence of delusions not due to a Schizophrenic, Mood, or organic mental disorder. This category bears considerable resemblance to Kraepelin's "paranoia." Delusions must persist for at least one month and must be nonbizarre; auditory and visual hallucinations, if present, must not be prominent. The disorder is subdivided into *Erotomanic Grandiose, Jealous, Persecutory, Somatic, Mixed,* and *Unspecified Types.* This uncommon disorder is probably slightly more common in females. Though marital and social functioning may be impaired in afflicted individuals, occupational functioning is usually intact. The course is variable. In contrast with most of the disorders described earlier, which have typical onset during the first few decades of life, delusional disorder usually occurs initially during the fifth or sixth decade.

Finally, delusions are commonly found in several organic mental syndromes. They may be the sole symptom of central nervous system disturbance, or they may occur along with dementia, delirium, or hallucinations (Cummings, 1985). An organic delusional syndrome can be the result of many different neurological and systemic etiologies; it can also be found within certain specific *DSM-IV* disorders, such as *Primary Degenerative Dementia of the Alzheimer's Type with Delusions* and *Vascular Dementia with Delusions*—as well as in various *Substance-Induced Psychotic Disorders with Delusions.* Nonsystematized delusions, often of a paranoid nature and secondary to hallucinosis, are occasionally noted in *Delirium.*

In general, organic delusions cannot be distinguished readily from those found in Schizophrenia: the differential diagnosis must be made on the basis of the higher frequency of other signs and symptoms of organicity, the relative absence of negative symptoms of Schizophrenia, and the reduced prominence of thought disorder in patients with organic delusional syndrome (Cornelius et al., 1991). Cummings's prospective study of 20 patients with organic delusions revealed that the most common types were simple persecutory delusions, complex persecutory delusions, grandiose delusions, and those associated with specific perceptual deficits (e.g., visual agnosia). In general, he found that the complexity of delusions diminishes with increasing cognitive impairment. In comparison with the syndromes discussed earlier, organic delusional syndrome occurs most

commonly later in life, with average onset during the seventh decade (Cornelius et al., 1991; Cummings, 1985).

Pathogenesis

The inference of meanings and the construction of belief is a complex process that requires the contributions of many aspects of mental functioning and social interaction. What follows is a brief review of some of the most obvious biopsychosocial factors in the etiology of delusions.

Neurobiological Perspectives

An initial approach to the problem of the neural mechanisms of delusional thinking can be made by considering the neuropathology of delusional syndromes. Cummings' extensive review of the literature (1985) suggests that delusions can be found in patients with virtually every form of disorder that affects the functioning of the central nervous system—including systemic illnesses, metabolic disorders, toxic conditions, and neurological disease. Most commonly, organic delusions occur in toxic-metabolic disorders and in diseases affecting the limbic system and basal ganglia. Cummings suggests that organic delusions are caused by the disruption of limbic-cortical associations.

Studies of interictal and postictal psychosis also point to the importance of limbic system disturbance in the pathogenesis of delusions (Logsdail & Toone, 1988). Most instances of psychosis occurring in patients with seizure disorders involve temporal lobe epilepsy. Signer and Benson (1990) also implicate disturbance of the limbic regions in the pathogenesis of delusions in their description of three patients with temporal lobe epilepsy who presented with symptoms of eating disorder accompanied by somatic delusions.

Another body of literature has focused on the contributions of misperceptions to the process of delusion formation. In a study of over 200 patients with Alzheimer's disease, Deutsch, Bylsma, Rovner, Steele, and Folstein (1991) found that almost half had delusions; many of these, in turn, also had experienced hallucinations, illusions, or misidentifications.

There have been many reports of delusions occurring in patients with right-hemisphere deficits. Crichton and Lewis (1990) report the case of a patient with AIDS who developed a delusional misidentification syndrome—or Capgras' syndrome—along with reduplicative paramnesia in the context of nondominant hemispheric dysfunction. Neuroimaging showed a right-sided parietal lesion; the psychotic symptoms improved when the lesion resolved. These investigators conclude that this case of Capgras' syndrome was caused by a transient right parietal lesion resulting in a visuospatial amnestic deficit. Levine and Grek (1984) did a controlled study of 25 patients without preexisting dementia who suffered right cerebral infarction—9 of whom subsequently experienced some form of delusion, and 16 of whom did not. The authors found no relationship between the size or location of the lesion and the development of delusions. They did find that even a small stroke in the context of significant brain atrophy is associated with delusional impairment—whereas patients with mild to moderate cerebral atrophy showed no such symptoms. They conclude that delusion formation after right-hemisphere stroke depends on the interaction between a focal lesion and diffuse brain atrophy.

Finally, some hypotheses and evidence relevant to the pathogenesis of delusions are not limited to the problem of delusion formation, but apply more generally to the origin of the positive symptoms of schizophrenia. Weinberger (1987) proposes a compelling developmental model that involves a lesion in the mesocortical dopaminergic system, occurring early in development. This deficit leads to reduced prefrontal activation, loss of inhibitory feedback to the limbic areas and to the mesolimbic dopaminergic system, and consequent positive symptomatology. His thesis is based in part on the observation that early adulthood—the typical period of schizophrenic onset—is the time of peak brain dopamine activity. He further notes that positive symptoms tend to diminish over the years, in parallel with the decline in subcortical dopaminergic activity that accompanies aging.

Cannon, Mednick, and Parnas (1990) take another approach to the genesis of positive schizophrenic symptoms. They found that individuals at genetic risk for schizophrenia, who had experienced early family disruption and who manifested high autonomic responsiveness in adolescence, had a higher than expected rate of predominantly positive-symptom schizophrenia. The interaction of these two factors was a better predictor of positive-symptom schizophrenic outcome than either factor independently. One explanation offered is that defective thalamic "gating" of sensory input results in autonomic hyperarousal and other symptoms of turmoil. The evidence points to a longitudinal pathogenic process beginning in preadolescence and adolescence. The investigators note that positive-symptom schizophrenia is often preceded by overexcitability, irritability, distractibility, and aggressiveness in school.

Psychological Perspectives

Cognition.   The study of the effects of cognition on the formation and maintenance of delusions has focused on the debate about whether delusions are "rational" responses to perceptual aberrations—or whether, alternatively, they represent errors in logical reasoning. Garety, Hemsley, and Wessely (1991) review this controversy and report on an experiment involving subjects with delusions due to either schizophrenia or delusional disorder, as well as a nondeluded control group. They found that the deluded subjects requested less information on a probabilistic inference task before reaching a decision; there was no difference between the two deluded groups. The authors further found that subjects with reasoning abnormalities were also more likely to be experiencing aberrant perceptions. They conclude that perceptual abnormalities and reasoning biases may both result from a failure to recall past regularities in processing new information.

Affect.   Another psychological factor influencing the formation, maintenance, and nature of delusions is mood or affect. That "mood-congruent" delusions are prominent in major affective disorders is itself suggestive of the importance of the current emotional state in the genesis of false beliefs. Delusional depression is classically characterized by nihilistic delusions, delusions of guilt, and somatic delusions involving poison, sickness, and decay. By contrast, grandiosity is commonly associated with manic psychosis. Signer and Swinson (1987) emphasize the relationship of erotic delusions to affective disorder and to mood fluctuations in their report of two cases of erotomania in patients with bipolar disorder. Others have emphasized the role of fear and anger in persecutory delusion formation (Kennedy, Kemp, & Dyer, 1992). Even in patients with misidentifications and delusions secondary to Alzheimer's disease, prevailing mood has been shown to affect the specific nature of the delusion and the way in which it is experienced by the individual (Molchan, Martinez, Lawlor, Grafman, & Sunderland, 1990). Finally, it is worth considering the role of affectively charged memory in the pathogenesis of delusions. Freud's (1911/1957) understanding of the formation of delusions was based on the defense mechanism of projection operating in relation to childhood experiences. More recently, others have shown that delusions of possession are more common in psychotic patients with childhood histories of physical or sexual abuse (Goff, Brotman, Kindlon, Waites, & Amico, 1991).

Sociocultural Perspectives

The effect of culture and culturally sanctioned belief on delusion formation is well illustrated by the phenomenon of the delusion of possession. Though possession states were culturally believable within Western societies during recent centuries, they are now acceptable forms of belief and expression only within isolated subcultures of the industrialized world. In those nonindustrialized cultures where possession is still common, the form that it takes is highly dependent on the prevailing religious belief system; cultures may manifest possession by gods, demons, animal spirits, and so on (Goff et al., 1991). In these cultural settings, such beliefs cannot be said to be delusional. Similarly, lycanthropy—the delusion of being an animal—was apparently common in the medical literature several centuries ago, when it was attributed by some to demonic possession. More recently, it is an extremely rare condition (Kulick, Pope, & Keck, 1990). Thus, cultural forces not only determine whether a given belief is delusional, but they also appear to affect the content of delusions. For instance, delusions of being followed by the CIA, of being abducted by aliens from outer space, or of having a radio transmitter in one's head would have been unlikely a century ago. A good example of a delusion that is rather specific to a non-Western culture is found in koro—the belief that one's genitals are shrinking and that this will result in death. This syndrome is found almost exclusively in Asian cultures and occurs in isolation as well as in epidemic form (Bernstein & Gaw, 1990).

Subcultural variations are also important in determining the content of delusions. In 1962, Lucas, Sainsbury, and Collins reported on a study of over 400 hospitalized schizophrenics, in which the content of delusions was examined in relation to various social factors. These investigators found that religious and grandiose delusions were most common in people of higher social status, that persecutory delusions were more common in immigrants to the region than in natives, and that sexual delusions were more common in women and in married people.

Delusions over the Life Span

In Kolvin's (1971) seminal work on childhood schizophrenia ("late-onset psychosis"), he defines the syndrome, then notes that allowances need to be made in this definition for the "language limitations," the "limited ability for complex abstractions," and the "vivid imagination and extensive fantasying which may be seen in the early school era" (p. 384). Piaget (1951) demonstrated that children do not use logic in the same ways as adults. Children's tendency to blur the distinction between fantasy and reality, in combination with their inability to fully utilize logical reason, renders it difficult to define delusions in individuals much younger than 5 years old. These same factors also affect the ways in which delusions manifest at different stages in childhood.

Several important studies have described the phenomenology of delusions in childhood schizophrenia. In general, delusions are found less commonly than they are in adults with the same disorder. Delusions are found least frequently in children under the age of 10; they tend to be simple, nonsystematized, and centered on disturbances in identity. Hypochondriacal, persecutory, and grandiose delusions appear slightly more often in prepubertal children—and considerably more often in adolescents (Beitchman, 1985; Cantor, Evans, Pearce, & Pezzot-Pearce, 1982; Eggers, 1978; Garralda, 1985; Jordan & Prugh, 1971; Kolvin, Ounsted, Humphrey, & McNay, 1971; Kydd & Werry, 1982; Russell et al., 1989; Volkmar et al., 1988).

Despite the phenomenological similarities between childhood schizophrenia and its adult equivalent, this syndrome is much less common in children (Beitchman, 1985); therefore, delusions remain an infrequent finding in the younger age groups. Delusions begin to be seen much more frequently in early adulthood, when the incidence of schizophrenia rises dramatically. During adulthood, delusions accompany occurrences of the schizophrenia spectrum disorders, bipolar disorder, psychotic depression, and delusional disorder.

DSM-III-R removed the upper age limit for schizophrenia, so that individuals over 45 years old can receive this diagnosis. Accordingly, attention has been focused on the phenomenological differences between "late-onset" and "early-onset" schizophrenia. Pearlson et al. (1989) compared a group of late-onset patients with a group of younger patients; they also included a group of elderly patients with early-onset illness. Both elderly groups were more likely to manifest delusions. Persecutory delusions were most common in the late-onset group, followed by the elderly early-onset group; grandiose delusions were most common in the elderly early-onset group, followed by the late-onset group; there were no differences in the frequency of somatic delusions. The Lucas et al. (1962) study of the social influences on delusions also found that, as age of schizophrenia onset increased, delusions became more prominent.

As individuals enter senescence, delusions become more prominent for other reasons as well. We have reviewed the literature suggesting that delusions can be prompted by generalized atrophy, focal neurological deficits, systemic disease, and perceptual difficulties. A recent study by Morriss, Rovner, Folstein, and German (1990) found that over 20% of patients admitted to nursing homes had delusions. The majority of these individuals were afflicted with a dementia—most commonly Alzheimer's disease. As previously noted, most of these patients' delusions would be expected to be relatively simple, nonsystematized, and related to their cognitive and perceptual deficits—for example, delusions secondary to misidentification, or delusions of having been robbed (Devanand et al., 1992; Drevets & Rubin, 1989). It would seem, then, that as individuals move into the later decades of life, their delusions become increasing simple and—though perhaps for different reasons—similar to those seen occasionally in children.

THOUGHT DISORDER

Phenomenology

The term *thought disorder,* sometimes referred to as *formal thought disorder* or as *thought process disorder,* includes a rather heterogeneous group of difficulties in the form, rather than the content, of thought. The nature of the difficulties subsumed within this construct has varied widely (Andreasen & Grove, 1986; Butler & Braff, 1991). At times, the term has been seen to be synonymous with schizophrenia or to refer to the totality of unusual symptoms of thought (form and content) exhibited in that condition. In more recent works (and in this chapter), the term refers in general terms to a group of specific clinical signs related to the organization and presentation of thoughts in the clinical context (Holzman, 1986). In this view, hallucinations and delusions are manifestations of psychotic thinking related to content, rather than form, of thought. A recent trend has been to emphasize the overtly observable signs (e.g., disorganized speech) rather than thought process difficulties that are presumed to be somewhat more difficult to assess and to emphasize that a complex set of clinical, linguistic, and cognitive factors are important in assessment (Andreasen & Grove, 1986; Docherty, Schnur, & Harvey, 1988; George & Neufeld, 1985). Research in this area has been complicated by inconsistency in use of terms and a lack of generally agreed on definitions and, at least until relatively recently, of assessment instruments.

Although disagreement continues about certain aspects of the boundaries of the term, there is consensus on at least some concepts that should be included within it. These difficulties all reflect problems in the organization and expression of thought processes. Differences in terminology, however, continue to complicate research in this area, and terms often may have similar, if not precisely overlapping meanings. For example, the concept of "loose associations" is closely related to that of "tangential thinking" and so forth.

Loosening of associations is observed in speech in which shifts in topic are apparently unconnected, or only very loosely connected, to each other and when the speaker is oblivious to the failure to connect the topics. When loosening of associations is severe, speech may be incomprehensible *(incoherence).* In speech that is *circumstantial,* statements may be overly wordy and long but relevant points of ideational "connectedness" are maintained. Usually, the term "loosening of association" is not used when the lack of connection appears primarily to reflect extremely rapid speech and thought *(flight of ideas)*. In flight of ideas, the rapidly changing topics usually have understandable points of connection. As with loosening of associations, incoherence may result if flight of ideas is severe.

Related concepts include "derailment," and "illogicality." The term *derailment* refers to marked disruption in thought process in which the topic is readily changed during discourse. *Illogicality* refers to statements that violate basic logical rules (i.e., basic violations in logical thought occur).

Thought *blocking* is observed if the continuous expression of organized speech is interrupted before being completed; usually individuals describe a failure to recall the content or goal of the speech and may indicate that they have "lost the train" of thought. *Neologisms* are new, generally meaningless, words given a highly personal and idiosyncratic meaning; neologisms can include totally new words or use of words in idiosyncratic ways. *Clang associations,* sometimes referred to as clanging, are those in which the relationship of words in speech reflect their sounds rather than their meanings; this may include use of rhyme. *Echolalia* refers to the repetitive echoing of others' speech. In contrast, *perseveration* refers to repetition of words or topics (i.e., the speaker appears "stuck" on his or her own word or idea).

Poverty of content of thought or speech refers to speech that is adequate in quantity but fails to convey any, or very little, information. For example, an individual may speak for some time in response to a question but fail to answer it. The term is not usually used to describe situations where speech is so chaotic as not to be understandable (i.e., *incoherence*) nor where the amount of speech is highly limited *(poverty of speech)*.

Distinctions have sometimes been drawn between positive and negative symptoms of thought disorder—whether a symptom is suggested by its presence (e.g., flight of ideas) or absence (e.g., poverty of content of speech). Evaluation of each feature of thought process disorder requires careful consideration of the totality of the communicative transaction (i.e., of the individual's medical/psychiatric status, developmental level, and sociocultural background). For example, the term incoherence would not generally be applied if a person's verbal difficulties reflected the aftereffects of a stroke, nor if discourse deficits were seen in a young child or a person functioning at a low developmental level. In DSM-IV (American Psychiatric Association, 1994), four aspects of formal thought disorder are particularly emphasized: incoherence, illogical thinking, loosening of associations, and poverty of speech content.

Although the concept of thought disorder has, historically, been central in the definition of schizophrenia (e.g., see Bleuler, 1911/1951) disturbances in the organization of speech may be observed in a broad range of disorders in addition to schizophrenia (e.g., in mood disorders during manic episodes, and in certain "organic" conditions such as drug intoxication or dementia). Issues of culture, educational background, and developmental status may also give rise to misattributions of thought process disorder. For example, echolalia is observed in other pathological conditions such as autism as well as during normal language learning. For the most part, research employing a developmental perspective on these conditions has been rather limited.

Other difficulties with the overarching concept of thought disorder stem from the rather diverse clinical uses of the concept and the lack of generally agreed on definitions of specific constructs. Some investigators have proposed definitions based primarily on severity, whereas other focus more on the form of thought. Frequently, it is assumed that the patient's speech straightforwardly reflects impairment in thought process. Studies of patients with other conditions (e.g., those with aphasia; Critchley, 1970; Faber et al., 1983), suggested some apparent similarities to the speech of individuals with schizophrenia as well as some differences, but the similarities argue for incorporation of an explicit linguistic perspective into assessment. This has, in part, also led to the trend to focus more on disorganization of speech rather than on thought process per se (George & Neufeld, 1985). The advent of more precise diagnostic criteria and of reliable and valid assessment instruments has facilitated work in this area in both child and adult populations (e.g., Andreasen, 1979; Andreasen & Grove, 1986; Andreasen & Olsen, 1982; Caplan, Foy, Asarnow, & Sherman, 1990; Caplan, Guthrie, & Foy, 1992; Caplan, Perdue, Tanguay, & Fish, 1990; Holzman, 1986).

The Thought, Language, and Communication scale (TLC) (Andreasen, 1979) includes various signs of formal thought disorder such as poverty of speech, tangentiality, and illogicality and has provided reliable and valid measures of thought disorder. Andreasen (1979) noted that signs of formal thought disorder were not specific to schizophrenia. Other studies (e.g., Andreasen and Olsen, 1982) have suggested that certain aspects of thought disorder, such as loose association and tangential speech, are more closely related to positive signs of schizophrenia (Crow, 1980), whereas aspects such as illogicality and poverty of speech, are more closely related to negative signs of the disorder. Although subsequent research (e.g., Fenton & McGlashan, 1991) has suggested that these relationships are somewhat more complex, this approach has stimulated a series of studies on adults with thought process problems in which relationships of specific signs of thought disorder are related to aspects of clinical presentation, associated biological and psychological features, response to pharmacological intervention, and so forth (Andreasen, Flaum, Swayze, Tyrell, & Arndt, 1990; Braff et al., 1991; Liddle, Friston, & Hirsch, 1990; Marks & Luchins, 1990).

Syndromic Issues

In Bleuler's (1911/1951) view, loosening of associations was one of the four cardinal signs of schizophrenia—the thought processes of individuals with schizophrenia were guided not by usual conventions but by principles unique to the individual. In this view, hallucinations and delusions in schizophrenia were secondary phenomena to the underlying disturbances in thought and affect. Although the concept of thought disorder was seen, for many years, as specific to schizophrenia, other studies (e.g., Andreasen, 1979), noted apparent disturbances of thought such as loosening of associations in patients with mania. With the advent of the Research Diagnostic Criteria (RDC) approach (Spitzer, Endicott, & Robins, 1978), issues of definition assumed a greater importance in the definition of thought process disorder. The emphasis on careful definition of specific clinical features and the appreciation that problems in thought process were not unique to schizophrenia produced important changes in the conceptualization of thought disorder in clinical groups.

In DSM-IV (American Psychiatric Association, 1994) formal thought disorder, as such, is not listed as a necessary diagnostic feature for any condition. Rather many of the concepts traditionally included in this term (e.g., loosening of associations) are included as essential or associated features in various diagnostic categories. The attention to the importance of reliable operational definitions has also been associated with a trend toward emphasis of the observable rather than the inferred (e.g., disorganized speech rather than disorganized thinking).

The DSM-IV definition of *schizophrenia* includes incoherence or frequent incoherence in a list of characteristics symptoms during the active phase of the disorder. In DSM-IV, it is possible to achieve a diagnosis of schizophrenia if other signs (e.g., delusions and prominent hallucinations) are present even without loosening of associations (as noted earlier, this emphasis has been questioned; Goldman et al., 1992). During a *manic episode,* loosening of associations, clang associations, and/or flight of ideas may be observed (delusions and hallucinations are not present for more than 2 weeks in the absence of mood disturbance). Incoherence can be observed during the course of either schizophrenia or a manic episode.

Poverty of speech is sometimes observed during a *major depressive episode* but usually features of thought process disturbance are not otherwise marked. In *organic mental disorders,* symptoms such as hallucinations and delusions are often most prominent, but disturbances of thought process may be observed including flight of ideas, echolalia, and incoherence. In *autism* and the *pervasive developmental disorders,* echolalia is frequently observed in verbal individuals; however, this echolalia appears to be different from that observed in schizophrenia and may have important adaptive functions. Although there was a period in which individuals with autism were thought to exhibit a form of schizophrenia, it appears that the two conditions are unrelated (Rutter, 1972), and although individuals with autism may exhibit some features usually associated with thought disorder, (e.g., poverty of speech and illogicality; Dykens, Volkmar, & Glick, 1991) they are not, apparently, at markedly increased risk for schizophrenia (Volkmar & Cohen, 1991). Certain features of thought disorder, such as neologisms, loosening of associations, and incoherence, are potentially observable in any psychotic condition and thus have little specific diagnostic significance other than in guiding the differential diagnosis to focus on psychotic conditions.

As noted previously, the advent of valid and reliable metrics has stimulated research, particularly in the adult population. Comparatively, most of the empirical work with adults in the area of comparison of diagnostic groups has focused on schizophrenia and manic-depressive illness. Andreasen and Olsen (1982) noted that patients with schizophrenia were more likely to have symptoms of negative thought disorder, whereas manic patients were more likely to have positive symptoms. Similarly, Holzman, Shenton, and Solovay (1986) reported similar differences using the Thought Disorder Index (TDI). Studies with child populations have been much less common and are discussed subsequently.

Pathogenesis

Neurobiological Perspectives

Although the neurobiological basis, or bases, of thought disorder remain unclear, several lines of research suggest the importance of neurobiological factors in the pathogenesis of disordered thinking. The available research is, however, limited in important respects: Most studies relate to one diagnostic group (i.e., schizophrenia), and studies tend to be correlational in nature. Finally, explication remains very limited for mechanisms of pathogenesis of thought disorder in clinical populations.

Several studies have been concerned with the response of some index of thought disorder to specific pharmacological interventions such as use of major tranquilizers (Hurt, Holzman, & Davis, 1983; Marder, Asarnow, & Van Putten, 1984). Similarly, measures of severity of thought disorder have been related to specific neurobiological factors (e.g., Liddle et al., 1990).

Psychological Perspectives

Various approaches have been employed in the study of the psychology of thought disorder, particularly in adult populations. One group of studies has focused on the relationship between verbal and perceptual responses using projective techniques. Other approaches have been based on attempts to quantify unusual responses during projective testing; for example, the Thought Disorder Index (TDI; Johnston & Holzman, 1979). Johnston and Holzman (1979) noted different patterns of response in groups of patients with schizophrenia, other psychiatric and nonpsychotic clinical populations, and normal adults. Other studies have focused on response bias, word association, or interpretation of proverbs among adult patients with schizophrenia in an effort to demonstrate whether or not associational patterns differed from those usually observed (e.g., Schwartz, 1982).

Studies of attentional processes have similarly revealed deficits in clinically disordered population using diverse measures such as indexes of attention (Cornblatt & Erlenmeyer-Kimling, 1985), reaction time (Holzman, 1986), span of apprehension, and so forth. Clinical assessments of thought disorder have been related to deficits in information processing (e.g., Harvey, Earle-Boyer, & Levinson, 1988). There is a similar, although smaller, literature on this topic in children. Asarnow and Ben-Meir (1988) reported that children with schizophrenia and similar disorders had lower distractibility factor scores on the WISC-R; deficits in visual information processing have also been noted (Asarnow & Sherman, 1984). A measure of loosening of association has been related to distractibility indexes in children with schizophrenia (Caplan et al., 1990). Although studies of cognition and information processing generally suggest similarities between children and adults with schizophrenia, some potential differences between children and adults with schizophrenia have also been noted (Schneider & Asarnow, 1987). In both groups, however, measures of illogicality and loosening of associations are related to the severity of thought disorder.

Another line of research has focused on the language/communication of individuals with thought disorder. Measures of thought disorder are related to measures of communicative dysfunction. For example, the speech of adults with schizophrenia has been noted to be less predictable than that of individuals without overt psychopathology (Salzinger, Portnoy, & Feldman, 1964). The linguistic productions of patients with schizophrenia have also been observed to have specific deficits in processing verbal information (Koh, 1978) and differences in pragmatic skills (Harvey, 1983; Hoffman, Stopek, & Andreasen, 1986; Rochester & Martin, 1979; Rutter, 1985). Pragmatic deficits included differences in providing cohesive information to the listener (Harvey, 1983) and ambiguous references (Harvey & Brault, 1986).

The diagnostic specificity of language/communication deficits remains controversial (Harvey et al., 1988; Hoffman et al., 1986). Studies of these deficits in thought-disordered children (mostly in those with schizophrenia) have been relatively even less frequent. Caplan et al. (1992) reported similarities of children to adults with schizophrenia in terms of pragmatic deficits, such as the relative failure to use cohesive devices.

Sociocultural Perspectives

Relative to either delusions or hallucinations, sociocultural aspects of thought disorder have been less frequently studied. The expression of certain disorders associated with thought disorder may have noteworthy sociocultural aspects, and the expression of problems in thought content (e.g., hallucinations and delusions), may vary depending on cultural context. With the possible exception of a few disorders that appear to be primarily culture bound, the expression of thought disorder appears to be less variable. At the same time modifications in usual standards for the evaluation of thought disorder are needed for assessing individuals with origins outside the predominant cultural context.

Thought Disorder over the Life Span

The vast majority of work in the area of thought process disturbance has centered on adults, particularly those with schizophrenia. Several factors impeded a greater appreciation of developmental issues in understanding thought disorders in children. As noted previously, there was an early presumption that thought disturbance (or certain aspects of thought disturbance), was specific to schizophrenia. Work on the developmental aspects of thinking, notably that of Piaget (1962), was not appreciated by or integrated into the clinical literature. In addition, broad views of schizophrenia in the United States were associated with a simple downward extrapolation of concepts to children (the presumption was that children with very severe disorders must have schizophrenia). The debate about the continuity of childhood autism and schizophrenia was particularly notable in this regard.

Despite some early attempts (e.g., Potter, 1933) to employ more stringent definitions of childhood schizophrenia, most clinicians and investigators assumed continuity of the condition with autism after the latter was described by Kanner (1943). Assumptions about underlying psychopathology, and thought process and

content disturbance, were made even about children who had never talked. This practice contributed to further blurring of the boundaries of more traditional conceptualizations of thought process disturbance in children. On the other hand, as verbal autistic children became older, their speech, which was characterized by extreme literalness, echolalia, and pronoun reversal, did bear some general similarity to that of adults with schizophrenic disorders. In the first two editions of the American Psychiatric Association's *Diagnostic and Statistical Manual* (1952, 1968), only the term "childhood schizophrenia" was available for children with very severe psychiatric disturbance.

By 1980, when DSM-III appeared, a substantial body of evidence suggested that autism and schizophrenia were not, in fact, related (e.g., Kolvin, 1971; Makita, 1966; Volkmar et al., 1988) and differed in terms of clinical features, family history, and course. Although a few investigators (e.g., Cantor et al., 1982) continued to argue that thought disorder was characteristic of autism, most were persuaded by the substantial body of data that this was not the case (Volkmar et al., 1988). Consistent with Kolvin's original report (1971), individuals with autism do not appear to be at higher than population-expected risk for schizophrenia (Volkmar & Cohen, 1981).

The radical reconceptualization of childhood schizophrenia embodied in DSM-III also marked a period in which studies of the condition became very uncommon. Subsequent research (see Werry, 1992) has, however, suggested that childhood schizophrenia is observed—although at very low rates—and that the same criteria used for diagnosis in adults work reasonably well, with some consideration of developmental factors, in children. For example, disturbances of thought content and process may be difficult to diagnose in preschool children (Green et al., 1984; Russell et al., 1989; Volkmar et al., 1988) but become more like those observed in adults as children enter middle childhood (Bettes & Walker, 1987; Garralda, 1984).

An interesting, and relatively consistent, finding has been that age at onset of the condition is a major prognostic feature and is associated with severity of disorder; children with very early-onset schizophrenia tend to have the worst prognosis (Werry, 1992) and to have higher levels of apparent thought disorder (Caplan et al., 1990). As noted by Caplan (1994), it is also possible that early onset is associated with impaired acquisition of pragmatic and cognitive skills.

The interpretation of early studies on thought disorder in childhood is limited in various respects, but certain results are relevant to consideration of developmental factors in psychotic thinking. Despert (1948) employed a developmental approach in considering thought disturbance in schizophrenia and noted that young, normally developing children could distinguish fantasy and reality and that certain psychotic symptoms (e.g., delusions) were uncommon in very young children. Confusion about diagnostic concepts in the 1950s and 1960s resulted in the inability to interpret many publications dating from this period.

Following the publication of DSM-III, greater consistency was employed in diagnosing childhood schizophrenia, and studies of thought disorder in this age group began to appear. Various research strategies have been employed focusing, for example, on aspects of clinical expression (Arboleda & Holzman, 1985), on cognitive processes (Watkins & Asarnow, 1992), and on communication (Caplan, Foy, Sigman, & Perdue, 1990). Children at risk for schizophrenia have higher levels of thought disturbance as assessed by the TDI than normal children (Johnson & Holzman, 1979) or depressed children. Johnston and Holzman (1979) also noted the importance of controlling for developmental level in assessment of thought disturbance in preadolescent children.

Caplan and colleagues (Caplan, Guthrie, Fish, Tanguay, & David-Lando, 1989; Caplan, Foy, Asarnow, & Sherman, 1990) developed the Kiddie Formal Thought Disorder Rating Scale (K-FTDS) based on Andreasen's Thought, Language, and Communication Scale (1979) as well as an indirect interview (Caplan et al., 1989). The K-FTDS employs operational definitions of illogical thinking, incoherence, loosening of association, and poverty of speech content. Illogical thinking and loose associations were noted to differentiate children with schizophrenia from normal children and normal children from those with schizotypal personality disorder (Caplan et al., 1989; Caplan, Foy, Sigman, & Perdue, 1990); differentiation of schizophrenia and schizotypal personality disorder was not, however, as robust.

Studies using these and similar techniques have suggested that children with schizophrenia share many features with adults who have the disorder and that, as with adults, features of thought disorder are not necessarily specific to schizophrenia, but are observed, often at lower rates, in children with other conditions. Some apparent differences were also noted; both incoherence and poverty of content of speech occurred at very low rates in children with schizophrenia. Caplan and colleagues (Caplan, Foy, Asarnow, & Sherman, 1990) also observed that, in normally developing children, loose associations are not observed after age 7 and that illogical thinking decreases markedly in the normal population after that time. Children with complex partial seizure disorder may exhibit illogical thinking without, however, the loosening of association observed in schizophrenia (Caplan, 1994).

In general, it appears that of the various features of thought disorder in children, loosening of association appears to be most specific to schizophrenia. The absence of research using similar methods with other conditions complicates the interpretation of the available data, and many of the procedures developed for research purposes are not necessarily readily extended into clinical settings.

IMPLICATIONS FOR THE STUDY OF NORMAL DEVELOPMENT

The existing empirical literature that relates aspects of psychotic processes to developmental context is limited in important respects. The rather larger theoretical literature, particularly the psychoanalytic literature, does tend to place such phenomena squarely within a developmental context but empirical studies based on this, and other, theoretical frameworks are uncommon. Studies that are available often have limited value because of methodological problems (e.g., inconsistencies in methods and diagnostic terminology, differences in ages studied). Changing views of basic concepts, such as the nature and definition of thought disorder, and differences in diagnostic practice severely limit the interpretability of much early work. From a developmental perspective, it is also frustrating, while understandable, that most empirical studies that have addressed the pathogenesis of psychotic phenomena have utilized adult—often geriatric—populations. It is, however, worth considering what can be learned about development through the study of psychotic phenomena because this endeavor provides an opportunity to examine the highly complex and uniquely human adaptation of constructing meanings and of forming beliefs and sharing such experiences with others.

As reviewed earlier, many theories of hallucinations view these phenomena as originating in irritative phenomena, disinhibition, or other sensory processing difficulties. If Slade and Bentall (1988) are correct in regarding reality discrimination (i.e., the ability to discern the source of a sensation) as a critical metacognitive skill, it is important to inquire about the developmental history of this capacity (or set of capacities).

Many psychoanalytic theorists, such as Mahler and Klein, propose that the infant, with its inchoate sense of self, is unable to discriminate between internal and external stimuli. Freud's own approach to hallucinations was a fundamentally developmental one, in that he saw them as reflecting in part a regression to an earlier primary process mode of experience, akin to that underlying dreams (Freud, 1900/1957). Referring to the primary process transformations found in dreams, he suggested that thoughts were transformed into visual images, that representations of words were made back into things. Aspects of the primary process mode were also then viewed as basic to thought process disturbance. Like Arieti's (1955) notion of "perceptualization of the concept," Freud's description of primitive perceptually rooted modes of thought has parallels in Piaget's (1962) notion of sensorimotor thought. Freud also emphasized the relationship of hallucinations to affect, wish fulfillment, and restitutive fantasies. He hypothesized that the hungry infant, while waiting to be fed, is able, at least temporarily, to soothe itself by hallucinating the breast.

The view of the young infant as intrinsically solipsistic or unable to distinguish between internal and external experience has been criticized in detail by Stern (1985) and others. Among the infant's early capacities emphasized by Stern is that of *amodal perception,* the ability to coordinate information coming through diverse perceptual modalities—seen, heard, touched—as though emanating from the same external thing. Whether this ability to construct external objects is innate or learned by coordination of sensory schema (Piaget, 1955) remains a matter of both theoretical and experimental controversy. Philosophical and psychological critiques of "imagist" theories have argued that the occurrence of hallucinatory phenomena should not lead us to the misguided metaphorical notion that our knowledge of the world consists of images that are then judged (correctly or incorrectly) to be either "internal" or "external" (Wittgenstein, 1953; Gardner, 1985).

In actual practice, the presence of psychotic phenomena is difficult, if not impossible, to ascertain in children prior to the development of language. Even with the development of language, the child's imaginative play and conceptual immaturity may occasionally mislead the examiner. By 3 or 4 years, however, most children have learned to use culturally appropriate verbal and paraverbal conventions to demarcate "pretend" play and utterances (Cohen et al., 1987). Thus, although imaginary companions are common developmental phenomena, it is usually easy to determine in most cases that they represent imaginative suspensions of disbelief rather than psychotic phenomena.

These issues are illustrated in the experience of dreams. Very young children may not realize that their dreams are not publicly accessible and may ascribe to them an external location, rather than a conventional internal one (Piaget, 1951); certain cultures, however, retain aspects of this developmentally early view of dreams. By age 3 years, children give evidence of understanding that people can think of or imagine things and that these images are private and in that sense internal or "not real" (Wellman, 1993). Despite Piaget's (1951) pioneering work, this area of normal development has not been well described.

Although early investigators assumed continuity between deficits in social relatedness and language in severely impaired children with what they assumed would become more typical thought process disturbances in later life, considerable evidence (e.g., Kolvin, 1971) now questions this view. More recent research (e.g., Caplan, Foy, Asarnow, & Sherman, 1990; Caplan, Guthrie, Fish, Tanguay, & David-Lando, 1990; Caplan, Perdue, Tanguay, & Fish, 1989; Caplan, et al., 1993) suggests important continuities in expression of thought process disturbance if subjects are carefully selected diagnostically and if the concept of thought process disturbance is specifically, rather than globally, defined. Deficits observed in children with schizophrenia include problems with illogical thinking and loosening of associations similar in many ways to the difficulties observed in adolescents and adults with the disorder. Important developmental differences associated with this condition (e.g., in relation to deficits in cognitive processing and discourse), are beginning to be explored.

The suggestion that auditory hallucinations represent misattributed subvocalized or inner speech (Slade & Bentall, 1988) recalls Vygotsky's developmental hypothesis that the "egocentric" speech of the young child is self-directed and represents a transitional stage in the development of inner speech. Further studies are needed of the developmental course of this phenomenon, including its physiological concomitants, its regulatory function, and how it is conceptualized by the child.

Although vivid hallucinations in anxious, but otherwise nonsymptomatic children are rare beyond the preschool period, hallucinations do not otherwise seem to be more common in younger children, contrary to what might be expected if they represented a developmental lag in reality discrimination.

Studies of older populations (Deutsch et al., 1991; Drevets & Rubin, 1989; Morriss et al., 1990) demonstrate the importance of relatively intact perception and cognition to the maintenance of a culturally syntonic reality orientation. There is now considerable evidence that one of the pathogenic pathways to delusion formation is some combination of perceptual deficit, focal cognitive deficit, and/or diffuse cognitive deficit (Crichton & Lewis, 1990; Garety et al., 1991; Levine & Grek, 1984). What, then, are the roles of normally developing perception and cognition to the formation of a culturally syntonic reality orientation? Moreover, what role do relatively subtle

delays in these areas play in the genesis of subtle distortions of social meanings and personal belief? An increasing body of literature is addressing the relationships between cognitive and perceptual deficit, social information processing, and socially maladaptive behavior (Burke, Crenshaw, Green, Schlosser, & Strocchia-Rivera, 1988; Dodge, Bates, & Pettit, 1990; Milich & Dodge, 1984; Moffitt & Silva, 1988; Tarter, Hegedus, Winsten, & Alterman, 1984). It is possible that the antisocial behavior of a cognitively impaired child, say, is pathophysiologically related to—though developmentally distinct from—the delusion-driven, aggressive behavior of the elderly patients described by Deutsch and colleagues (1991).

The phenomenon of delusions may also shed some light on another aspect of cognitive development—namely the capacity to tolerate ambiguity and ambiguous meaning. At least some individuals who manifest delusions appear either to have failed to develop, or else to have failed to maintain, a tolerance for ambiguity—or for "not knowing." The delusion provides a way "to know," and a "certain" solution—albeit often a maladaptive one—to an ambiguous situation.

CONCLUSIONS

Despite the continuing limitations of the literature on developmental aspects of psychotic phenomena, important progress has been made. In general, the trend in this area has been to move toward more objective definitions and measurements with a corresponding increase in the replicability of results obtained. The move away from broad theoretical notions toward examination of more discrete but well-defined processes has been a major accomplishment. However, partly reflecting the early history of work in this area, there has been a certain reluctance to place findings within a broader context, theoretically or developmentally (Fish & Ritvo, 1978). Certain issues for future research have been previously noted. In our conclusion of this review we would like to highlight a few issues that appear to us to be of particular importance for a developmental perspective on psychotic processes.

An important line of research suggested by the problem of psychotic phenomena is that of better understanding the normal development of children's theory of mind—how children come to describe and distinguish between publicly accessible stimuli and private phenomena such as dreams, inner speech, thoughts, and mental imagery (Piaget, 1951; Wellman, 1993). The developmental study of the child's sense of ownership toward his or her mental contents is germane not only to the study of hallucinations, but of obsessions and compulsions as well. In the adult realm, more reliable and empirically robust methods of studying mental imagery are needed (Gardner, 1985; Slade & Bentall, 1988). Further studies of these phenomena in blind and deaf children, as well as those with language impairments, would contribute to our understanding of normal development.

Both in children and adults, better data are needed concerning the epidemiology and personality correlates of susceptibility to psychotic processes. This work is intimately related to the development of increasingly better diagnostic criteria and other methodological advances.

Advances in understanding the neurobiology of schizophrenia and of normal mental functioning are likely to deepen our understanding of psychotic phenomena as well. For example, recent neuroimaging studies find that auditory hallucinations, like subvocalization, are accompanied by increased activity in expressive, rather than receptive speech areas; this parallel is of interest in light of various theories and therapeutic approaches based on the notion that auditory hallucinations represent misattributed subvocalizations or inner speech (Slade & Bentall, 1988). Similarly, the observation that levels of formal thought disorder decrease in children with intractable complex partial seizures after temporal lobectomy (Caplan et al., 1993) suggests an important area for neurobiological studies.

A developmental perspective for future research on psychotic phenomena is critically needed. Longitudinal studies that examine the frequency, severity, and nature of delusional manifestations in individuals over time will be important. Optimally, such studies would consider the phenomenology of delusions within the contexts of psychiatric diagnosis, personality traits, developmental stage, stressful life events, and neuropsychological deficit or damage. Such studies, by including disordered and at-risk children, would make the effects imparted by early developmental change more easily discernible.

Cross-sectional research will also be of value. More studies such as the one by Goff and coworkers (1991) will help to determine the extent and the specificity of the relationship between early traumatic experiences and certain types of psychotic experience. Although several careful studies concerning the relationship between cognitive deficit and psychotic phenomena (e.g., delusions) have been conducted in elderly populations, there is a need for future studies to include younger adults and children—and for such studies to consider subtle processing differences in addition to gross deficits. The study by Garety and colleagues (1991) that utilized a probabilistic inference task is a good example in this respect.

Finally, the work by Weinberger (1987) linking delusions to the vicissitudes of dopaminergic development bears further elaboration. A useful approach may be through observing symptomatology during dopaminergic-specific pharmacological intervention—such as a case report involving the combined use of a neuroleptic and a psychostimulant in a schizophrenic child (Rogeness & Macedo, 1983), and a more recent study involving an analogous combination of medications in 21 adults with the same disorder (Goldberg, Bigelow, Weinberger, Daniel, & Kleinman, 1991). The advantage of this approach is in its potential for selectively manipulating various dopaminergic systems. Another correlational approach (Bracha, Livingston, Clothier, Linington, & Karson, 1993) involves the comparison of a dopaminergic sign (i.e., left-turning behavior) with a dopaminergic symptom (i.e., delusions) in a sample of psychotic patients. Eventually, studies such as these—which probe the contributions of dopaminergic dysregulation to delusion formation—should be conducted across various age groups, so that the developmental aspects of these perturbations may be better understood.

REFERENCES

Al-Issa, I. (1977). Social and cultural aspects of hallucinations. *Psychological Bulletin, 84,* 570–587.

American Psychiatric Association. (1952, 1968, 1980, 1987, 1994). *Diagnostic and statistical manual of mental disorders.* Washington, DC: Author.

Andreasen, N. C. (1979). Thought, language, and communication disorders: I. Clinical assessment, definition of terms, and evaluation of their reliability. *Archives of General Psychiatry, 36,* 1315–1323.

Andreasen, N. C., Flaum, M., Swayze, V. W., Tyrell, G., & Arndt, S. (1990). Positive and negative symptoms in schizophrenia. *Archives of General Psychiatry, 47,* 615–621.

Andreasen, N. C., & Grove, W. M. (1986). Thought, language, and communication in schizophrenia: Diagnosis and prognosis. *Schizophrenia Bulletin, 12,* 346–359.

Andreasen, N. C., & Olsen, S. (1982). Negative vs. positive schizophrenia: Definition and validation. *Archives of General Psychiatry, 39,* 789–794.

Arboleda, C., & Holzman, P. S. (1985). Thought disorder in children at risk for psychosis. *Archives of General Psychiatry, 42,* 1004–1013.

Arieti, S. (1955). Interpretation of schizophrenia. *Schizophrenia Bulletin,* New York: Brunner.

Asaad, G. (1990). *Hallucinations in clinical psychiatry: A guide for mental health professionals.* New York: Brunner/Mazel.

Asarnow, J. R., & Ben-Meir, S. (1988). Children with schizophrenia spectrum and depressive disorders: A comparative study of premorbid adjustment, onset pattern, and severity of impairment. *Journal of Child Psychology and Psychiatry, 29,* 477–489.

Asarnow, R. F., & Sherman, T. (1984). Studies of visual information processing in schizophrenic children. *Child Development, 55,* 249–261.

Aug, R., & Ables, B. (1971). Hallucinations in nonpsychotic children. *Child Psychiatry and Human Development, 1,* 153–167.

Ballenger, J. C., Reus, V. I., & Post, R. M. (1982). The "atypical" clinical picture of adolescent mania. *American Journal of Psychiatry, 139,* 602–606.

Barber, T. X., & Calverly, D. S. (1964). An experimental study of hypnotic (auditory and visual) hallucinations. *Journal of Abnormal and Social Psychology, 63,* 13–20.

Beitchman, J. H. (1985). Childhood schizophrenia: A review and comparison with adult-onset schizophrenia. *Psychiatric Clinics of North America, 8,* 793–814.

Bentall, R. P. (1990). The illusion of reality: A review and integration of psychological research on hallucinations. *Psychological Bulletin, 107,* 82–95.

Bentall, R. P., & Slade, P. D. (1985). Reliability of a measure of disposition towards hallucination. *Personality and Individual Differences, 6,* 527–529.

Berlin, F., Bergey, G., & Money, J. (1982). Periodic psychosis of puberty: A case report. *American Journal of Psychiatry, 139,* 119–120.

Bernstein, R. L., & Gaw, A. C. (1990). Koro: Proposed classification for *DSM-IV. American Journal of Psychiatry, 147,* 1670–1674.

Bettes, B. A., & Walker, E. (1987). Positive and negative symptoms in psychotic and other psychiatrically disturbed children. *Journal of Child Psychology and Psychiatry, 28,* 555–568.

Bhatia, M. S., Khastgir, V., & Malik, S. C. (1992). Charles Bonnet syndrome. *British Journal of Psychiatry, 161,* 409–410.

Bleuler, E. (1951). Dementia praecox, or the group of schizophrenia (J. Zinkin, Trans.). New York: International Universities Press. (Original work published 1911)

Bourguignon, E. (1970). Hallucinations and trance: An anthropologist's perspective. In W. Keup (Ed.), *Origin and mechanisms of hallucinations*, (pp. 183–190). New York: Plenum.

Bracha, H. S., Livingston, R. L., Clothier, J., Linington, B. B., & Karson, C. N. (1993). Correlation of severity of psychiatric patients' delusions with right hemispatial inattention (left-turning behavior). *American Journal of Psychiatry, 150,* 330–332.

Braff, D. L., Heaton, R., Kuck, J., Cullum, M., Moranville, J., Grant, I., & Zisook, S. (1991). The generalized pattern of neuropsychological deficits in outpatients with chronic schizophrenia with heterogeneous Wisconsin Card Sorting Test results. *Archives of General Psychiatry, 48,* 891–898.

Breuer, J., & Freud, S. (1955). Studies on hysteria. In J. Strachey (Ed. and Trans.), *The standard edition of the complete psychological works of Sigmund Freud* (Vol. 2). London: Hogarth Press. (Original work published 1895)

Burke, A. E., Crenshaw, D. A., Green, J., Schlosser, M. A., & Strocchia-Rivera, L. (1988). Influence of verbal ability on the expression of aggression in physically abused children. *Journal of the American Academy of Child and Adolescent Psychiatry, 28,* 215–218.

Butler, R. W., & Braff, D. L. (1991). Delusions: A review and integration. *Schizophrenia Bulletin, 17,* 633–647.

Cannon, T. D., Mednick, S. A., & Parnas, J. (1990). Antecedents of predominantly negative- and predominantly positive-symptom schizophrenia in a high-risk population. *Archives of General Psychiatry, 47,* 622–632.

Cantor, S., Evans, J., Pearce, J., & Pezzot-Pearce, T. (1982). Childhood schizophrenia: Present but not accounted for. *American Journal of Psychiatry, 139,* 758–763.

Caplan, R. (1994). Childhood schizophrenia assessment and treatment—A developmental approach. *Child Adolescent Psychiatry Clinic North America, 3,* 15–30.

Caplan, R., Foy, J. G., Asarnow, R. F., & Sherman, T. (1990). Information processing deficits of schizophrenic children with formal thought disorder. *Psychiatry Research, 31,* 169–177.

Caplan, R., Foy, J. G., Sigman, M., & Perdue, S. (1990). Conservation and formal thought disorder in schizophrenia and schizotypal children. *Developmental Psychopathology, 2,* 183–190.

Caplan, R., Guthrie, D., Fish, B., Tanguay, P. E., & David-Lando, G. (1989). The Kiddie Formal Thought Disorder Rating Scale (K-FTDS). Clinical assessment, reliability, and validity. *Journal of the American Academy of Child and Adolescent Psychiatry, 28,* 208–216.

Caplan, R., Guthrie, D., & Foy, J. G. (1992). Communication deficits and formal thought disorder in schizophrenic children. *Journal of the American Academy of Child and Adolescent Psychiatry, 31,* 151–159.

Caplan, R., Guthrie, D., Sheilds, D., Peacock, W. J., Vinters, H. V., & Yudovin, S. (1993). Communication deficits in children undergoing temporal lobectomy. *Journal of the American Academy of Child and Adolescent Psychiatry, 32,* 604–611.

Caplan, R., Perdue, S., Tanguay, P. E., & Fish, B. (1990). Formal thought disorder in childhood onset schizophrenia and schizotypal personality disorder. *Journal of Child Psychology and Psychiatry, 31,* 1103–1114.

Caplan, R., Tanguay, P. E., & Szekely, A. G. (1987). Subacute sclerosing panencephalitis presenting as childhood psychosis: A case study. *Journal of the American Academy of Child Psychiatry, 26,* 440–443.

Carlson, G. A., & Kashani, J. H. (1988). Phenomenology of major depression from childhood through adulthood: Analysis of three studies. *American Journal of Psychiatry, 145,* 1222–1225.

Carpenter, W. T., Strauss, J. S., & Muleh, S. (1973). Are there pathognomonic symptoms in schizophrenia? An empiric investigation of Schneider's first-rank symptoms. *Archives of General Psychiatry, 28,* 847–852.

Chambers, W. (1986). Hallucinations in psychotic and depressed children. In D. Pilowsky & W. Chambers (Eds.), *Hallucinations in children.* Washington, DC: American Psychiatric Press.

Cleghorn, J. M., Franco, S., Szechtman, B., Kaplan, R. D., Szechtman, H., Brown, G. M., Nahmias, C., & Garnett, E. S. (1992). Toward a brain map of auditory hallucinations. *American Journal of Psychiatry, 149,* 1062–1069.

Cohen, D. J., Marans, S., Dahl, K., Marans, W., Cohen, P., & Lewis, M. (1987). Discussions with oedipal children. *Psychoanalytic Study of the Child, 42,* 59–83.

Comer, N. L., Madow, L., & Dixon, J. J. (1967). Observations of sensory deprivation in a life-threatening situation. *American Journal of Psychiatry, 124,* 164–169.

Cornblatt, B. A., & Erlenmeyer-Kimling, L. (1985). Global attentional deviance as a marker of risk for schizophrenia: Specificity and predictive validity. *Journal of Abnormal Psychology, 94,* 470–486.

Cornelius, J. R., Day, N. L., Fabrega, H., Mezzich, J., Cornelius, M. D., & Ulrich, R. F. (1991). Characterizing organic delusional syndrome. *Archives of General Psychiatry, 48,* 749–753.

Crichton, P., & Lewis, S. (1990). Delusional misidentification, AIDS, and the right hemisphere. *British Journal of Psychiatry, 157,* 608–610.

Critchley, M. (1970). The neurology of psychotic speech. In M. Critchley (Ed.), *Aphasiology and other aspects of language* (pp. 348–362). London: Arnold.

Crow, T. J. (1980). Molecular pathology of schizophrenia: More than one disease process? *British Medical Journal, 20,* 66–68.

Crystal, H. A., Wolfson, L. I., & Ewing, S. (1988). Visual hallucinations as first symptoms of Alzheimer's disease. *American Journal of Psychiatry, 145,* 1318.

Cummings, J. L. (1985). Organic delusions: Phenomenology, anatomical correlations, and review. *British Journal of Psychiatry, 146,* 184–197.

Damas-Mora, J., Skelton-Robinson, M., & Jenner, F. A. (1982). The Charles Bonnet syndrome in perspective. *Psychological Medicine, 12,* 251–261.

Del Beccaro, M. A., Burke, P., & McCauley, E. (1988). Hallucinations in children: A follow-up study. *Journal of the American Academy of Child and Adolescent Psychiatry, 27,* 462–465.

Dement, W., Zarcone, V., Ferguson, J., Cohen, H., Pivik, T., & Barchas, J. (1969). Some parallel findings in schizophrenic patients and serotonin-depleted cats. In D. V. S. Sankar (Ed.), *Schizophrenia: Current concepts and research* (pp. 775–811). Hicksville, NY: P.J.D. Publications.

Despert, L. (1948). Delusional and hallucinatory experiences in children. *American Journal of Psychiatry, 1*(4), 528–537.

Deutsch, L. H., Bylsma, F. W., Rovner, B. W., Steele, C., & Folstein, M. F. (1991). Psychosis and physical aggression in probable Alzheimer's disease. *American Journal of Psychiatry, 148,* 1159–1163.

Devanand, D. P., Miller, L., Richards, M., Marder, K., Bell, K., Mayeux, R., & Stern, Y. (1992). The Columbia University Scale for Psychopathology in Alzheimer's disease. *Archives of Neurology, 49,* 371–376.

Docherty, D., Schnur, M., & Harvey, P. D. (1988). Reference performance and negative thought disorder: A follow-up study of manics and schizophrenics. *Journal of Abnormal Psychology, 4,* 437–442.

Dodge, K. A., Bates, J. E., & Pettit, G. S. (1990). Mechanisms in the cycle of violence. *Science, 250,* 1678–1683.

Drevets, W. C., & Rubin, E. H. (1989). Psychotic symptoms and the longitudinal course of senile dementia of the Alzheimer type. *Biological Psychiatry, 25,* 39–48.

Dykens, E., Volkmar, F., & Glick, M. (1991). Thought disorder in high functioning autistic adults. *Journal of Autism and Developmental Disorders, 21,* 291–301.

Egdell, H. G., & Kolvin, I. (1972). Childhood hallucinations. *Journal of Child Psychology and Psychiatry, 13,* 279–287.

Eggers, C. (1978). Course and prognosis of childhood schizophrenia. *Journal of Autism and Childhood Schizophrenia, 8,* 21–36.

Esman, A. (1962). Visual hallucinosis in young children. *Psychoanalytic Study of the Child, 17,* 334–343.

Faber, R., Abrams, R., Tayor, M. A., Kasprison, A., Morris, C., & Weisc, R. (1983). Comparison of schizophrenic patients with formal thought disorder and neurogically impaired patients with aphasia. *American Journal of Psychiatry, 140,* 1348–1351.

Fenton, W. S., & McGlashan, T. H. (1991). Natural history of schizophrenia subtypes: II. Positive and negative symptoms and long-term course. *Archives of General Psychiatry, 48,* 978–986.

Fingarette, H. (1963). *The self in transformation: Psychoanalysis, philosophy, and the life of the spirit.* New York: Basic Books.

Fischman, L. G. (1983). Dreams, hallucinations, drug states, and schizophrenia: A psychological and biological comparison. *Schizophrenia Bulletin, 9,* 73–94.

Fish, B., & Ritvo, E. R. (1978). Psychoses of childhood. In J. Noshpitz (Ed.), *Basic handbook of child psychiatry* (Vol. 2, pp. 249–304). New York: Basic Books.

Francis, A. F. (1979). Familial basal ganglia calcification and schizophreniform psychosis. *British Journal of Psychiatry, 135,* 360–362.

Freud, S. (1957). The interpretation of dreams. In J. Strachey & A. Freud (Eds.), *The standard edition of the complete works of Sigmund Freud* (Vol. 5). London: Hogarth Press. (Original work published 1900)

Freud, S. (1957). Psychoanalytic notes on an autobiographical account of a case of paranoia. In J. Strachey & A. Freud (Eds.), *The standard edition of the complete works of Sigmund Freud,* (Vol. 12). London: Hogarth Press. (Original work published 1911)

Freud, S. (1957). A metapsychological supplement to the theory of dreams. In J. Strachey & A. Freud (Eds.), *The standard edition of the complete works of Sigmund Freud,* (Vol. 14, pp. 222–235). London: Hogarth Press. (Original work published 1917)

Gardner, H. (1985). The mind's new science: A history of the cognitive revolution. New York: Basic Books.

Garety, P. A., Hemsley, D. R., & Wessely, S. (1991). Reasoning in deluded schizophrenic and paranoid patients: Biases in performance on a probabilistic inference task. *Journal of Nervous and Mental Disorders, 179,* 194–201.

Garralda, M. E. (1984). Hallucinations in children with conduct and emotional disorders: I. The clinical phenomena. *Psychological Medicine, 14,* 589–596.

Garralda, M. E. (1985). Characteristics of the psychoses of late onset in children and adolescents: A comparative study of hallucinating children. *Journal of Adolescence, 8,* 195–207.

Geller, B., Fox, L. W., & Fletcher, M. (1993). Effect of tricyclic antidepressants on switching to mania and on the onset of bipolarity in depressed 6- to 12-year-olds. *Journal of the American Academy of Child and Adolescent Psychiatry, 32*(1), 43.

George, L., & Neufeld, R. W. J. (1985). Cognition and symptomatology in schizophrenia. *Schizophrenia Bulletin, 11,* 264–285.

Goff, D. C., Brotman, A. W., Kindlon, D., Waites, M., & Amico, E. (1991). The delusion of possession in chronically psychotic patients. *Journal of Nervous and Mental Disorders, 179,* 567–571.

Gold, K., & Rabins, P. V. (1989). Isolated visual hallucinations and the Charles Bonnet syndrome: A review of the literature and presentation of six cases. *Comprehensive Psychiatry, 30,* 90–98.

Goldberg, T. E., Bigelow, L. B., Weinberger, D. R., Daniel, D. G., & Kleinman, J. E. (1991). Cognitive and behavioral effects of the coadministration of dextroamphetamine and haloperidol in schizophrenia. *American Journal of Psychiatry, 148,* 78–84.

Goldberger, L., & Holt, R. (1961). A comparison of isolation effects and their personality correlates in two divergent samples. *New York University ASD Tech Report, 61,* 417.

Goldman, D., Hien, D. A., Haas, G. L., Sweeney, J. A., & Frances, A. J. (1992). Bizarre delusions and *DSM-III-R* schizophrenia. *American Journal of Psychiatry, 149,* 494–499.

Goodwin, D. W., Alderson, P., & Rosenthal, R. (1971). Clinical significance of hallucinations in psychiatric disorders. *Archives of General Psychiatry, 24,* 76–80.

Green, W. H., Campbell, M., Hardesty, A. S., Grega, D. M., Padron-Gaylor, M., Shell, J., & Erlenmeyer-Kimling, L. (1984). A comparison of schizophrenic and autistic children. *Journal of the American Academy of Child Psychiatry, 4,* 399–409.

Green, W. H., Padron-Gayol, M., Hardesty, A., & Bassiri, M. (1992). Schizophrenia with childhood onset: A phenomenological study of 38 cases. *Journal of the American Academy of Child and Adolescent Psychiatry, 31,* 968–976.

Hart, J., & McClure, G. M. G. (1989). Capgras' syndrome and folie à deux involving mother and child. *British Journal of Psychiatry, 154,* 552–554.

Harvey, P. D. (1983). Speech competence in manic and schizophrenic psychoses: The association between clinically rated thought disorder and performance. *Journal of Abnormal Psychology, 92,* 368–377.

Harvey, P. D., & Brault, J. (1986). Speech performance in mania and schizophrenia: The association of positive and negative thought disorders and reference failure. *Journal of Communicative Disorders, 19,* 161–174.

Harvey, P. D., Earle-Boyer, E. A., & Levinson, J. C. (1988). Cognitive deficits and thought disorder: A retest study. *Schizophrenia Bulletin, 14,* 57–66.

Hassibi, M., & Breuer, H., Jr. (1980). *Disordered thinking and communication in children.* New York: Plenum.

Hausser, H. C., & Bancaud, J. (1987). Gustatory hallucinations in epileptic seizures: Electrophysiological, clinical, and anatomical correlates. *Brain, 110,* 339–359.

Heresco-Levy, U., Javitt, D. C., & Zukin, S. R. (1993). The phencyclidine/N-methyl-D-asparate (PCP/NMDA) model of schizophrenia: Theoretical and clinical implications. *Psychiatric Annals, 23,* 135.

Hoffman, R. E., Stopek, S., & Andreasen, N. C. (1986). A comparative study of manic vs. schizophrenic speech disorganization. *Archives of General Psychiatry, 43,* 831–838.

Holroyd, S., Rabins, P. V., Finkelstein, D., Nicholson, M. C., Chase, G. A., & Wisniewski, S. C. (1992). Visual hallucinations in patients with macular degeneration. *American Journal of Psychiatry, 149,* 1701–1706.

Holzman, P. S. (1986). Thought disorder in schizophrenia: Editor's introduction. *Schizophrenia Bulletin, 12,* 342–345.

Holzman, P. S., Shenton, M. E., & Solovay, M. R. (1986). Quality of thought disorder in differential diagnosis. *Schizophrenic Bulletin, 12,* 360–371.

Horowitz, M. (1983). *Image formation and psychotherapy.* New York: Jason Aronson.

Hurt, S. S., Holzman, P. S., & Davis, J. M. (1983). Thought disorder: The measurement of its change. *Archives of General Psychiatry, 40,* 1281–1285.

Jackson, J. H. (1932). *Selected writings.* London: Hoddor & Stoughton.

Johnston, M. H., & Holzman, P. S. (1979). *Assessing schizophrenic thinking* (pp. 56–101). San Francisco: Jossey-Bass.

Jordan, K., & Prugh, D. G. (1971). Schizophreniform psychosis of childhood. *American Journal of Psychiatry, 128,* 323–329.

Kanner, L. (1943). Autistic disturbances of affective contact. *Nervous Child, 2,* 217–250.

Kaplan, H. I., & Sadock, B. J. (1991). *Comprehensive glossary of psychiatry and psychology.* Baltimore: Williams & Wilkins.

Kemph, J. P. (1987). Hallucinations in psychotic children. *Journal of the American Academy of Child and Adolescent Psychiatry, 26,* 556–559.

Kendler, K. S. (1991). Mood-incongruent psychotic affective illness: A historical and empirical review. *Archives of General Psychiatry, 48,* 362–369.

Kendler, K. S., Glazer, W. M., & Morgenstern, H. (1983). Dimensions of delusional experience. *American Journal of Psychiatry, 140,* 466–469.

Kendler, K. S., Spitzer, R. L., & Williams, J. B. W. (1989). Psychotic disorders in *DSM-III-R, American Journal of Psychiatry, 146,* 943–962.

Kennedy, H. G., Kemp, L. I., & Dyer, D. E. (1992). Fear and anger in delusional (paranoid) disorder: The association with violence. *British Journal of Psychiatry, 160,* 488–492.

King, R. (1994). Childhood schizophrenia development and pathogenesis. *Child Adolescent Psychiatric Clinic North America, 3,* 1–14.

King, R. A., & Noshpitz, J. (1991). *Pathways of growth: Essentials of child psychiatry: Vol. 2. Psychopathology.* New York: Wiley.

Klerman, G. S. (1989). Historical background. In R. Michaels (Series Ed.), *Psychiatry* (Vol. 1, ch. 52). Philadelphia: Lippincott.

Koh, S. D. (1978). Remembering verbal materials by schizophrenic young adults. In S. Schwartz (Ed.), *Language and cognition in schizophrenia* (pp. 251–273). Hillsdale: Erlbaum.

Kolvin, I. (1971). Studies in the childhood psychoses: I. Diagnostic criteria and classification. *British Journal of Psychiatry, 118,* 381–384.

Kolvin, I., Ounsted, C., Humphrey, M., & McNay, A. (1971). Studies in the childhood psychoses: I. The phenomenology of childhood psychoses. *British Journal of Psychiatry, 118,* 385–395.

Kotsopoulos, S., Kanigsberg, J., Cote, A., & Fiedorowicz, C. (1987). Hallucinatory experiences in nonpsychotic children. *Journal of the American Academy of Child and Adolescent Psychiatry, 26,* 375–380.

Kraepelin, E. (1907). *Clinical psychiatry: A textbook for students and physicians* (A. R. Diefendorf, Trans.). New York: Macmillan.

Kraepelin, E. (1921). *Manic-depressive insanity and paranoia* (R. M. Barclay, Trans.). Edinburgh: Livingstone.

Kulick, A. R., Pope, H. G., & Keck, P. E. (1990). Lycanthropy and self-identification. *Journal of Nervous and Mental Disorders, 178,* 134–137.

Kydd, R. R., & Werry, J. S. (1982). Schizophrenia in children under 16 years. *Journal of Autism and Developmental Disorders, 12,* 343–357.

Lahat, E., Eshel, G., & Arlazoroff, A. (1990). "Alice in Wonderland" syndrome and infectious mononucleosis in children (letter). *Journal of Neurology, Neurosurgery, and Psychiatry, 53,* 1104–1111.

Leon, R. L., Bowden, C. L., & Faber, R. A. (1989). The psychiatric interview, history, and mental status examination. In H. I. Kaplan & B. J. Sadock (Eds.), *Comprehensive textbook of psychiatry* (5th ed.) (pp. 449–462). Baltimore: Williams & Wilkins.

Levine, D. N., & Grek, A. (1984). The anatomic basis of delusions after right cerebral infarction. *Neurology, 34,* 577–582.

Liddle, P. F., Friston, S. R., & Hirsch, S. R. (1990). Regional cerebral metabolic activity in chronic schizophrenia (abstract). *Schizophrenia Research, 3,* 23–24.

Logsdail, S. J., & Toone, B. K. (1988). Post-ictal psychoses: A clinical and phenomenological description. *British Journal of Psychiatry, 152,* 246–252.

Lucas, C. J., Sainsbury, P., & Collins, J. G. (1962). A social and clinical study of delusions in schizophrenia. *Journal Men. Sci., 108,* 747–758.

Makita, K. (1966). The age of onset of childhood schizophrenia. *Folia Psychiatrica Neurologica Japonica, 20,* 111–121.

Marder, S., Asarnow, R. F., & Van Putten, C. (1984). Informal processing and neuroleptic response in acute and stabilized schizophrenic patients. *Psychiatry Research, 13,* 41–49.

Margo, A., Hemsley, D. R., & Slade, P. D. (1981). The effects of varying auditory input on schizophrenic hallucinations. *British Journal of Psychiatry, 139,* 122–127.

Marks, R. C., & Luchins, D. J. (1990). Relationship between brain image findings in schizophrenia and psychopathology: A review of the literature relating positive and negative symptoms. In N. C. Andreasen (Ed.), *Modern problems of pharmacopsychiatry: Positive and negative symptoms and syndromes* (pp. 89–123). Basel: Karger.

Maudsley, H. (1867). *The physiology and pathology of the mind.* London: Macmillan.

McGuire, P. K., Shah, G. M. S., & Murray, R. M. (1993). Increased blood flow in Broca's area during auditory hallucinations in schizophrenia. *Lancet, 342,* 703–706.

McKellar, P. (1968). *Experience and behaviour.* Harmondsworth, England: Penguin.

McPeake, J. D., & Spanos, N. P. (1973). The effects of the wording of rating scales on hypnotic subjects' descriptions of visual hallucinations. *American Journal of Clinical Hypnosis, 15,* 239–244.

Milich, R., & Dodge, K. A. (1984). Social information processing in child psychiatric populations. *Journal of Abnormal Child Psychology, 12,* 471–490.

Mitchell, J., & Vierkant, A. D. (1989). Delusions and hallucinations as a reflection of the subcultural milieu among psychotic patients of the 1930s and 1980s. *Journal of Psychology, 123*(3), 269–274.

Moffitt, T. E., & Silva, P. A. (1988). Neuropsychological deficit and self-reported delinquency in an unselected birth cohort. *Journal of the American Academy of Child and Adolescent Psychiatry, 27,* 233–240.

Molchan, S. E., Martinez, R. A., Lawlor, B. A., Grafman, J. H., & Sunderland, T. (1990). Reflections of the self: Atypical misidentification and delusional syndromes in two patients with Alzheimer's disease. *British Journal of Psychiatry, 157,* 605–608.

Morriss, R. K., Rovner, B. W., Folstein, M. F., & German, P. S. (1990). Delusions in newly admitted residents of nursing homes. *American Journal of Psychiatry, 147,* 299–302.

Mueser, K. T., & Butler, R. W. (1987). Auditory hallucinations in combat-related chronic post-traumatic stress disorder. *American Journal of Psychiatry, 144,* 299–302.

Mullaney, D. J., Kripke, D. F., Fleck, P. A., & Johnson, L. C. (1983). Sleep loss and nap effects on sustained continuous performance. *Psychophysiology, 20,* 643–651.

Musalek, M., Podreka, I., Walter, H., Suess, E., Passweg, V., Nutzinger, D., Strobl, R., & Lesch, O. M. (1989). Regional brain function in hallucinations: A study of regional cerebral blood flow with 99m-Tc-HMPAO-SPECT in patients with auditory hallucinations, tactile hallucinations, and normal controls. *Comprehensive Psychiatry, 30,* 99–108.

Nicholi, A. M. (1978). History and mental status. In A. M. Nicholi (Ed.), *The Harvard guide to modern psychiatry* (pp. 25–40). Cambridge, MA: Belknap Press.

Nurcombe, B., Mitchell, W., Begtrup, R., Tramontana, M., LaBarbera, J., & Pruitt, J. (in press). Dissociative hallucinosis and allied conditions. In F. Volkmar (Ed.), *Psychoses and pervasive developmental disorders in childhood and adolescence.* Washington, DC: American Psychiatric Association.

Pearlson, G. D., Kreger, L., Rabins, P. V., Chase, G. A., Cohen, B., Wirth, J. B., Schlaepfer, T. B., & Tune, L. E. (1989). A chart review study of late-onset and early-onset schizophrenia. *American Journal of Psychiatry, 146,* 1568–1574.

Penfield, W., & Perot, P. (1963). The brain's record of auditory and visual experience: A final summary and conclusion. *Brain, 86,* 595–696.

Perky, C. W. (1910). An experimental study of imagination. *American Journal of Psychology, 21,* 422–452.

Piaget, J. (1951). Play, dream and imitation in childhood. New York: Norton.

Piaget, J. (1955). The child's construction of reality. London: Routledge & Kegan Paul.

Piaget, J. (1962). The stages of the intellectual development of the child. *Bulletin of the Menninger Clinic, 26,* 120–132.

Pilowsky, D., & Chambers, W. (1986). *Hallucinations in children.* Washington, DC: American Psychiatric Press.

Posey, T. B., & Losch, M. E. (1983). Auditory hallucinations of hearing voices in 375 normal subjects. *Imagination, Cognition and Personality, 2,* 99–113.

Potter, H. W. (1933). Schizophrenia in children. *American Journal of Psychiatry, 12,* 1253–1270.

Ravenscroft, J. (1980, October). *Acute phobic hallucinoisis of childhood.* Paper presented at the American Academy of Child Psychiatry Convention, Chicago.

Reese, W. D. (1971). The hallucinations of widowhood. *British Medical Journal, 210,* 37–41.

Rochester, S. R., & Martin, J. R. (1979). *Crazy talk: A study of the discourse of schizophrenic speakers.* New York: Plenum.

Rogeness, G. A., & Macedo, C. A. (1983). Therapeutic response of a schizophrenic boy to a methylphenidate-chlorpromazine combination. *American Journal of Psychiatry, 140,* 932–933.

Rosenbaum, F., Harati, Y., Rolak, L., & Freedman, M. (1987). Visual hallucinations in sane people: Charles Bonnet syndrome. *Journal of the American Geriatrics Society, 35,* 66–68.

Rothstein, A. (1981). Hallucinatory phenomena in childhood: A critique of the literature. *Journal of the American Academy of Child Psychiatry, 20,* 623–635.

Russell, A. T., Bott, L., & Sammons, C. (1989). The phenomenology of schizophrenia occurring in childhood. *Journal of the American Academy of Child and Adolescent Psychiatry, 28,* 399–407.

Rutter, D. R. (1985). Language in schizophrenia. The structure of monologues and conversations. *British Journal of Psychiatry, 146,* 399–404.

Rutter, M. (1972). Childhood schizophrenia reconsidered. *Journal of Autism and Childhood Schizophrenia, 2,* 315–337.

Rutter, M. (1985). Infantile autism and other pervasive developmental disorders. In M. Rutter & L. Hersov (Eds.), *Child and adolescent psychiatry: Modern approaches* (pp. 545–566). Oxford, England: Blackwell.

Salzinger, K., Portnoy, S., & Feldman, R. S. (1964). Verbal behavior of schizophrenic and normal subjects. *Annals of the New York Academy of Science, 105,* 845–860.

Schatzberg, A. F., & Rothschild, A. J. (1992). Psychotic (delusional) major depression: Should it be included as a distinct syndrome in *DSM-IV? American Journal of Psychiatry, 149,* 733–745.

Schneider, K. (1959). *Clinical psychopathology.* New York: Grune & Stratton.

Schneider, S. G., & Asarnow, R. F. (1987). A comparison of cognitive/neuropsychological impairments of nonautistic and schizophrenic children. *Journal of Abnormal Child Psychology, 15,* 29–36.

Schreier, H. A., & Libow, J. A. (1986). Acute phobic hallucinations in very young children. *Journal of the American Academy of Child Psychiatry, 25,* 574–578.

Schwartz, S. (1982). Is there a schizophrenic language? *Behavioral and Brain Sciences, 5,* 579–626.

Segal, J. H. (1989). Erotomania revisited: From Kraepelin to *DSM-III-R. American Journal of Psychiatry, 146,* 1261–1266.

Sherman, T., & Asarnow, R. F. (1985). The cognitive disabilities of the schizophrenic child. In M. Sigman (Ed.), *Children with emotional disorders and developmental disabilities: Assessment and treatment* (pp. 153–170). New York: Grune & Stratton.

Sidgewick, H. A. (1894). Report of the census of hallucinations. *Proceedings of the Society for Psychical Research, 26,* 259–394.

Siegel, R. K. (1984). Hostage hallucinations: Visual imagery induced by isolation and life-threatening stress. *Journal of Nervous and Mental Disease, 172,* 264–272.

Signer, S. F., & Benson, D. F. (1990). Three cases of anorexia nervosa associated with temporal lobe epilepsy. *American Journal of Psychiatry, 147,* 235–238.

Signer, S. F., & Swinson, R. P. (1987). Two cases of erotomania (de Clérambault's syndrome) in bipolar affective disorder. *British Journal of Psychiatry, 151,* 853–855.

Slade, P. D. (1974). The external control of auditory hallucinations: An information theory analysis. *British Journal of Social and Clinical Psychology, 13,* 73–79.

Slade, P. D. (1984). Sensory deprivation and clinical psychiatry. *British Journal of Hospital Medicine, 35,* 256–260.

Slade, P. D., & Bentall, R. P. (1988). *Sensory deception: A scientific analysis of hallucination.* Baltimore: Johns Hopkins University Press.

Snyder, S. (1983). Isolated sleep paralysis after rapid time zone change ("jet lag") syndrome. *Chronobiologia, 10,* 377–379.

Spanos, N. P. (1986). Hallucinations and contextually generated interpretations. *Behavioral and Brain Sciences, 9,* 533–534.

Spitzer, R. L., Endicott, J. R., & Robins, E. (1978). Research diagnostic criteria. *Archives of General Psychiatry, 25:* 733–782.

Spivak, B., Trottern, S. F., Mark, M., Bleich, A., & Weizman, A. (1992). Acute transient stress-induced hallucinations in soldiers. *British Journal of Psychiatry, 160,* 412–414.

Spohn, H. E., Lolafaye, C., Larson, J., Mittleman, J. S., & Hayes, K. (1986). Episodic and residual thought pathology in chronic schizophrenics: Effect of neuroleptics. *Schizophrenia Bulletin, 12,* 394–407.

Stern, D. (1985). The interpersonal world of the infant. New York: Basic Books.

Strub, R. L., & Black, F. W. (1988). *Neurobehavioral disorders: A clinical approach.* Philadelphia: Davis.

Tarter, R. E., Hegedus, A. M., Winsten, N. E., & Alterman, A. I. (1984). Neuropsychological, personality, and familial characteristics of physically abused delinquents. *Journal of the American Academy Child and Adolescent Psychiatry, 23,* 668–674.

Tien, A. Y. (1991). Distributions of hallucinations in the population. *Social Psychiatry and Psychiatric Epidemiology, 26,* 287–292.

Tiihonen, J., Hari, R., Naukkarinen, H., Rimon, R., Jousmaki, V., & Kajola, M. (1992). Modified activity of the human auditory cortex during auditory hallucinations. *American Journal of Psychiatry, 149,* 255–257.

Volkmar, F. R. (1991). Childhood schizophrenia. In M. Lewis (Ed.), *Child and adolescent psychiatry* (pp. 621–628). Baltimore: Williams & Wilkins.

Volkmar, F. R., & Cohen, D. J. (1991). Comorbid association of autism and schizophrenia. *American Journal of Psychiatry, 148,* 1705–1707.

Volkmar, F. R., Cohen, D. J., Hoshino, Y., Rende, R. D., & Paul, R. (1988). Phenomenology and classification of the childhood psychoses. *Psychological Medicine, 18,* 191–201.

Waddington, J. L. (1993). Sight and insight: "Visualisation" of auditory hallucinations in schizophrenia? *Lancet, 342,* 692–693.

Waldfogel, S., & Mueser, K. T. (1988). Another case of chronic PTSD with auditory hallucinations (letter). *American Journal of Psychiatry, 145,* 1314.

Weinberger, D. R. (1987). Implications of normal brain development for the pathogenesis of schizophrenia. *Archives of General Psychiatry, 44,* 660–669.

Wellman, H. M. (1993). Early understanding of mind: The normal case. In S. Baron-Cohen, H. Tager-Flusberg, and D. J. Cohen (Eds.), *Understanding other minds* (pp. 10–39). Oxford, England: Oxford University Press.

Wells, L. A. (1980). Hallucinations associated with pathologic grief reaction. *Journal of Psychiatric Treatment and Evaluation, 5,* 259–261.

Werry, J. S. (1992). Child and adolescent (early onset) schizophrenia: A review in light of DSM-III-R. *Journal of Autism and Developmental Disorders, 22(4),* 601–624.

West, L. J. (1975). A clinical and theoretical overview of hallucinatory phenomena. In R. K. Siegel & L. J. West (Eds.), *Hallucinations: Behaviour, experience, and theory* (pp. 275–291). New York: Wiley.

Wilking, V., & Paoli, C. (1966). The hallucinatory experience. *Journal of the American Academy of Child and Adolescent Psychiatry, 5,* 431–440.

Wilkins, R. (1987). Hallucinations in children and teenagers admitted to Bethlehem Royal Hospital in the nineteenth century and their possible relevance to the incidence of schizophrenia. *Journal of Child Psychology and Psychiatry, 28,* 569–580.

Wittgenstein, L. (1953). *Philosophical investigations.* London, England: Blackwell.

World Health Organization. (1975). *Schizophrenia: A multinational study.* Geneva: Author.

Yager, J. (1989). Clinical manifestations of psychiatric disorders. In H. I. Kaplan & B. J. Sadock (Eds.), *Comprehensive textbook of psychiatry* (5th ed.) (pp. 553–582). Baltimore: Williams & Wilkins.

Young, H. F., Bentall, R. P., Slade, P. D., & Dewey, M. E. (1986). Disposition towards hallucination, gender, and IQ scores. *Personality and Individual Differences, 7,* 247–249.

Zigler, E., & Phillips, L. (1961). Psychiatric diagnosis and symptomatology. *Journal of Abnormal and Social Psychology, 63,* 69–75.

Zuckerman, M. (1969). Variables affecting deprivation results. In J. P. Zubek (Ed.), *Sensory deprivation.* New York: Appleton-Crofts.

Zuckerman, M., & Cohen, N. (1964). Sources of reports on visual and auditory sensations in perceptual isolation experiments. *Psychological Bulletin, 62,* 1–20.

CHAPTER 15

Schizophrenia through the Lens of a Developmental Psychopathology Perspective

DIANE C. GOODING and WILLIAM G. IACONO

Schizophrenia is a clinical syndrome whose symptoms are manifest in multiple domains of behavior: attention, perception, and information processing; language and thought; affect; motor behavior; and interpersonal relationships. To date, an understanding of the underlying pathophysiological mechanisms and etiologic factors implicated in the development of schizophrenia remains elusive. Since its introduction in the 1980s by developmentalists such as Garmezy, Sroufe, Rutter, Zigler, and Cicchetti, the interdisciplinary framework of developmental psychopathology has emerged as a provocative new area of study. The purpose of this chapter is to demonstrate the ways in which consideration of the general principles of developmental psychopathology may enhance our attempts to conceptualize and study schizophrenia.

First, we outline and define the framework of developmental psychopathology and discuss different ways of conceptualizing schizophrenia. We selectively review the research literature, and evaluate whether our current state of knowledge regarding schizophrenia is consistent with developmental hypotheses of the disorder considering phenomenological and etiologic heterogeneity. We discuss how well extant data fit the models posited to account for the transmission and/or development of schizophrenia, and how a developmental life-span view of psychopathology is consistent with the models. Drawing on advances from the fields of biology, developmental neuroscience, and genetics, we offer speculations about possible etiologic factors. We describe and discuss research strategies aimed at identifying indicators of heightened risk for schizophrenia prior to the manifestation of the disorder. We examine ways in which a developmental psychopathology perspective may enhance the inquiry into risk factors and developmental precursors of schizophrenia. Finally, we suggest that the application of a developmental life span perspective can enhance our investigation of currently unanswered issues in the study of schizophrenia.

A DEVELOPMENTAL ANALYSIS OF PSYCHOPATHOLOGY

Developmental psychopathology incorporates a developmental life-span perspective into the study of abnormal behavior. There are several major principles inherent to the developmental psychopathology perspective. The tenets of developmental psychopathology are briefly summarized here; readers are referred to other sources (Cicchetti, 1990, 1993; Sroufe & Rutter, 1984; Zigler & Glick, 1986) for a more detailed explication.

According to this perspective, the path between risk and outcome is not invariant. Developmental psychopathologists view the ultimate outcome of risk to be the result of transactions between the organism, its environment, and the mechanisms and/or processes underlying the diathesis (Cicchetti, 1990; Cicchetti & Schneider-Rosen, 1986). Thus, the same risk may have multiple possible outcomes; this principle is known as multifinality. The principle of multifinality accounts for the observation that a given anomaly does not necessarily lead to the same outcome in each individual possessing that trait. An example of this is multiple sclerosis, a demyelinating disorder in which different organs and systems are affected to varying degrees, resulting in various symptom pictures. A disease process that is characterized by multifinality would have a variable clinical picture, depending on when the organism was exposed to the etiologic factor(s), what stage of development the organism was in, and what resiliency-promoting factors were also present. The notion that there is an interaction between the individual's premorbid state and developmental processes is central to the principle of multifinality. Because not all individuals at increased risk for a disorder will exhibit the disorder, a developmental analysis of psychopathology involves the identification of resiliency-producing factors as well as risk factors (Cicchetti, 1990, 1993).

Another important principle to developmental psychopathology is equifinality. Equifinality involves the notion that multiple pathways lead to the same developmental outcome (Cicchetti, 1990, 1993). Mental retardation provides an example of how different diseases may share a common final pathway. Different etiologic factors, such as chromosomal anomalies, the pairing of deleterious recessive genes, lead poisoning, maternal alcoholism, and anoxia, may all affect the central nervous system, resulting in

This chapter was written while the first author (D. G.) was under the support of NIMH Neurobehavioral Training Grant (MH17069).

The authors wish to thank D. Cicchetti, S. Nicol, I. Gottesman, and L. Erlenmeyer-Kimling for their helpful comments during the preparation of this chapter.

diminished cognitive development. In this way, the manifest disorder represents a gross neurological response to a variety of adverse factors that may have exerted their effects pre-, peri- and/or postnatally. Due to this principle of multiple determination, a developmental analysis of psychopathology involves elucidating the different pathways by which the same outcome may be achieved (Cicchetti, 1993).

Rather than viewing abnormal behavior as fixed and stereotyped, a developmental analysis of psychopathology focuses on heterogeneity in behavioral outcomes as well as heterogeneity in the developmental process, thereby emphasizing the continuities and discontinuities of psychopathology over time (Rutter, 1986). In such a conceptual framework, the influence of age and timing on psychopathology cannot be overestimated. A developmental perspective considers the possibility that the same experiences may affect developing organisms differently, depending on the age and developmental maturity of the organism at the time of the operating factors (Rutter, 1988). One related issue that is explicitly considered in the developmental approach is that the meaning of a particular variable may change across the life span (Rutter, 1989). The issues of heterotypic continuity, namely, the possibility that the meaning of behaviors will vary with age, and that different behaviors at different times may represent the same underlying phenomenon, is a methodological consideration that is addressed in the developmental approach.

A developmental psychopathology perspective posits a continuum between normal and abnormal behaviors, as well as the existence of an interface between the study of normal and atypical development (Cicchetti, 1993). As such, knowledge of normal development permits the understanding of psychopathology and the study of pathology enhances the understanding of normal development. In its assumption of a continuum between normal and abnormal behavior, a developmental psychopathology perspective deviates from a disease model of psychopathology (Zubin, Feldman, & Salzinger, 1991). According to this view, because the expression of a disorder may be modified by developmental changes, the possibility of reclaiming the normal developmental trajectory remains so that ". . . no one is ever completely inoculated against or totally doomed to psychopathological and/or maladaptive outcome" (Cicchetti, 1993, p. 482).

Andreasen and Carpenter (1993) summarized three main explanatory constructs currently posited to account for the variation in clinical manifestations of schizophrenia. These explanatory constructs are consistent with a developmental psychopathology perspective. The first maintains that schizophrenia is a neurological insult that can be manifest in several distinct ways. The hypothesis that a single underlying pathophysiological process may lead to multiple diverse outcomes is consistent with the developmental principle of multifinality.

Rather than regarding schizophrenia as a singular disorder, the second explanatory construct considers schizophrenia as comprising several syndromes, each with its own distinct etiology. In this conceptualization of schizophrenia, schizophrenia is a final common path that reflects different underlying dysfunctional processes (Andreasen & Carpenter, 1993). The hypothesis that multiple disease entities lead to a single outcome

through different etiopathological processes is consistent with the developmental principle of equifinality.

In contrast to the notion of schizophrenia as a final common pattern of reaction, the third explanation discussed by Andreasen and Carpenter (1993) suggests that several processes may be associated with specific aspects of schizophrenia, and these processes may coexist in varying combinations in different patients. This notion—that specific symptom constellations reflecting diverse pathological processes may combine in different patterns in different individuals—is also consistent with the developmental principle of equifinality. Implicit in this view is the developmental notion of a complex transactional process whereby the pathological factors may interact with the developing organism and recombine at later developmental stages, resulting in potentially different manifestations (Asarnow & Goldstein, 1986; Cicchetti, 1990, 1993).

We assert that schizophrenia may be appropriately characterized by either equifinality or multifinality and, to the extent that it represents a collection of disorders, possibly by both developmental notions. In this view, different combinations of genetic and environmental factors lead to central nervous system dysfunction (the final common path). The resultant brain disease, schizophrenia, will be manifest in multiple behavioral domains to varying degrees, depending on the developmental competencies of the individual and the presence of interacting risk and protective factors. Moreover, if there is a group of distinct schizophrenias, then the notion of equifinality may only be applicable within each subtype.

CONCEPTUALIZING SCHIZOPHRENIA: HISTORICAL OVERVIEW FROM A DEVELOPMENTAL PERSPECTIVE

In this section, we review past and present conceptualizations of schizophrenia with the aim of demonstrating the ways in which schizophrenia has been and currently is implicitly defined as a developmental disorder. In this discussion, we also address the "appropriateness of fit" between a developmental approach and our current state of knowledge regarding schizophrenia.

Since Kraepelin's introduction of the term dementia praecox, the definition of schizophrenia has caused considerable debate. According to Kraepelin (1919/1971), schizophrenia is a developmental disorder characterized by an early onset, an organic basis, and a deteriorating course. Although E. Bleuler (1911/1950) also asserted that there was an organic basis to schizophrenia, he placed a greater emphasis on the phenomenology of the disorder. According to Bleuler's view of schizophrenia, all forms of the disorder could be characterized by a constellation of symptoms that he believed to be fundamental (the four A's: affective disturbance, autism, ambivalence, and associative distortion). Bleuler distinguished between these primary symptoms and accessory, or secondary, ones. Bleuler's list of accessory symptoms included delusions, hallucinations, and psychomotor disturbances. Readers are referred to Neale and Oltmanns (1980) for a well-explicated definition and description of the primary and accessory symptoms.

Others, namely, Meyer (1910), Kasanin (1933), and Langfeldt (1937), further broadened the way in which schizophrenia was defined. According to Meyer, a disorder such as schizophrenia could be precipitated by negative life experiences as well as by heritable defects. Kasanin introduced the term schizoaffective disorder to describe another proposed variant of schizophrenia in which affective symptoms were prominent. Langfeldt, as did Kraepelin, emphasized course and outcome as important criteria in his definition of schizophrenia. However, by introducing the concept of schizophreniform psychosis, Langfeldt asserted the existence of a form of schizophrenia that differed from Kraepelin's dementia praecox. Schizophreniform psychosis represented a compromise between Meyer's belief that some forms of schizophrenia could result from an experiential trauma and have a better prognosis, and Kraepelin's dementia praecox, which was most often characterized by a poor prognosis.

Schneider's first-rank symptoms also made an impact on the operational definition of schizophrenia. Schneider (1959) proposed that 11 symptoms, including specific types of hallucinations, delusions, and thought disorder, might be pathognomonic of the disorder. However, these first-rank symptoms have been criticized for being nonspecific indicators of psychosis (Carpenter, Strauss, & Bartko, 1974; Kety, 1985; Pfohl & Winokur, 1982). Despite Schneider's concept of first-rank symptoms and the ensuing controversy, few would dispute that schizophrenia is typically characterized by problems in thought, perception, affect, interpersonal relationships, and motor activity. In contrast, the reliance on poor prognosis as a defining feature of schizophrenia is a topic of considerable debate (Harding, 1986; Neale & Oltmanns, 1980).

Various diagnostic formulations have relied on the classic Kraepelinian or Bleulerian definitions of schizophrenia to differing degrees. In the United States for most of this century, a Bleulerian approach, heavily emphasizing the presence of thought disorder, was used to diagnose schizophrenia. This approach was cross-sectional with the diagnosis largely dependent on the presence of acute psychotic symptoms. Because of the belief that schizophrenia was a disorder of both thought form and content, most nonorganic psychotic people with odd speech, hallucinations, and/or delusions were considered to be schizophrenic. This broad, poorly formed concept of schizophrenia was provided for in the first two editions of the American Psychiatric Association's first two *Diagnostic and Statistical Manual of Mental Disorders* (DSM, DSM-II; 1952, 1968) which were in effect until the introduction of DSM-III in 1980.

Several factors led to a reconceptualization of schizophrenia in DSM-III (American Psychiatric Association, 1980). Chief among them was the success of earlier efforts to narrow the concept of schizophrenia using explicit diagnostic criteria. One of the earliest attempts to operationally define schizophrenia was that of Feighner et al., (1972). These Washington University psychiatrists were strongly influenced by Kraepelin's views of schizophrenia and proposed a definition in which the developmental course of the disorder played a prominent role. The subsequently introduced Research Diagnostic Criteria (RDC) of Spitzer, Endicott, and Robins (1978) deemphasized the importance of course, relying instead on the

types of hallucinations and delusions that Schneider noted were evident among those with this disorder to make the diagnosis. Eccentric individuals with odd speech and behavior but no overt psychotic symptoms tended to receive a schizophrenia diagnosis under DSM-II. In the RDC, these individuals were identified as having "schizotypal features." The diagnostic criteria for schizotypal features anticipated those for DSM-III schizotypal personality disorder, a type of disorder believed to fall into the schizophrenia "spectrum." Schizoaffective disorder, which was a subtype of schizophrenia in DSM-II, was placed in a special category in the RDC. DSM-III combined features of both the Feighner et al. (1972) and Spitzer et al. (1978) diagnostic systems in its reformulation and narrowing of the concept of schizophrenia.

Unlike DSM-II and the RDC, the DSM-III did not allow schizophrenia to be diagnosed solely on the presence of acute symptoms without taking into account developmental considerations. DSM-III defines schizophrenia essentially as a chronic disorder, lasting at least 6 months, characterized by deteriorated vocational and interpersonal functioning. Superimposed on this enduring state are one or more "active phases" or episodes characterized by the presence of acute psychotic symptoms. Mild symptoms and/or impaired functioning preceding or following the acute episode are used to differentiate schizophrenia from schizophreniform disorder. Individuals with long-standing schizotypal or paranoid characteristics in the absence of an acute episode are considered to have personality disorders. One difficulty inherent to the DSM-III concept of schizophrenia is that if it emerges relatively early in the life span, deterioration of functioning may be less apparent because of the individual's failure to develop normally. The DSM-III-R (American Psychiatric Association, 1987) essentially simplified the DSM-III rules for diagnosing schizophrenia. Like its predecessor, DSM-III-R continues to emphasize the developmental, Kraepelinian view of the natural history of schizophrenia being one of deterioration. The DSM-III-R broadened developmental considerations in its definition of schizophrenia by requiring that the individual in question show evidence of either a decline in functioning or a failure to achieve expected levels of achievement. The DSM-IV (APA, 1994) is very similar to DSM-III-R in that it maintains a similar developmental emphasis.

THE IMPORTANCE OF SUBTYPES

Any effort to achieve a comprehensive understanding of schizophrenia has to deal at some level with its manifest heterogeneity. It is likely that schizophrenia is etiologically heterogeneous, which could account in part for the many inconsistencies that plague the schizophrenia literature. However, despite the prevalence of this belief among those researching this disorder, there is little hard evidence in support of such a conclusion, and few good leads regarding how best to subclassify schizophrenia in a way that is etiologically relevant. Instead, the common approach to subtyping those with this disorder involves producing phenomenologically homogeneous subgroups and then identifying the nonsymptomatic correlates of subgroup membership to determine whether subgroups differing in clinical picture also differ in other important ways.

Phenomenological Subtyping

One method of subtyping schizophrenia involves an obvious developmental perspective but now is largely of historical significance. A distinction was made between process and reactive schizophrenia on the basis of premorbid adjustment, rate of development of the disorder, and prognosis (Garmezy, 1970; Neale & Oltmanns, 1980). The process-reactive dimension took into account the competencies and milestones mastered at the time of the manifestation of the disorder. Process schizophrenics were thought to have an early onset, a lengthy prodromal period, and a poor prognosis. This conceptualization of process schizophrenia approximates the strict Kraepelinian definition of schizophrenia. The current DSM definition of schizophrenia is, by and large, process schizophrenia. Under this system, patients who would have previously been considered to have reactive schizophrenia are now likely to be diagnosed with schizophreniform disorder.

Several other strategies are commonly employed for subtyping schizophrenia. The DSM-IV maintains the Kraepelin-Bleuler scheme of classifying patients according to the presence or absence of other clinical features such as paranoia or disorganization (hebephrenia). This classical subtyping approach has been criticized, largely because of failures (e.g., Tsuang, Woolson, Winokur, & Crowe, 1981) to demonstrate temporal stability. A notable exception is a report by Parnas, Jorgensen, Teasdale, Schulsinger, and Mednick (1988) based on their 6-year follow-up of schizophrenic women who were mothers in the Copenhagen High-Risk Project. Out of 64 DSM-III-R diagnosed schizophrenics, there were only 10 cases in which the investigators found evidence of a significant change in the patients' subtype picture. Although the issue of temporal stability in paranoid and non-paranoid subtypes is unresolved, family studies of schizophrenics (e.g., Kendler, Gruenberg, & Tsuang, 1988) indicate that these subtypes do not necessarily breed true in the first-degree relatives of patients.

In the early 1980s, several investigators (Andreasen, 1982; Andreasen & Olsen, 1982; Crow, Cross, Johnstone, & Owen, 1982) advocated subtyping schizophrenic patients according to the relative prominence of positive and negative symptoms. The positive (or expressive) symptoms consist of behavioral and/or perceptual excesses such as delusions, hallucinations, and bizarre or disorganized speech or actions. The negative symptoms consist of behavioral and/or perceptual deficits, such as poverty of speech, anhedonia, blunted or restricted affect, and avolition. Andreasen (Andreasen, 1982; Andreasen & Olsen, 1982) proposed three types of schizophrenia: positive, negative, and mixed: Patients who displayed both positive and negative symptoms of schizophrenia concurrently were considered to have the mixed subtype of the disorder.

Crow (1985) proposed two distinct schizophrenic syndromes associated with different neuropathologies. According to this hypothesis, Type I schizophrenia is characterized by dopaminergic overactivity due to increased D2 dopamine receptors, a predominance of positive symptoms, good response to neuroleptics, and a relatively favorable outcome. In contrast, the Type II schizophrenia syndrome, characterized primarily by negative symptoms, appears to be related to process schizophrenia and Kraepelin's original conceptualization of dementia praecox (Crow, 1985). According to Crow, Type II schizophrenia is related to neuronal loss in temporal lobe structures and is characterized by a predominance of negative symptoms, poor response to neuroleptics, and less favorable outcome.

Numerous reports have lent support for subtyping schizophrenic patients according to the relative prominence of positive or negative symptoms. Schizophrenics with a predominance of negative symptoms tend to display chronicity, neurological soft signs, and brain abnormalities on CT and MRI scans (Andreasen, 1985; Crow, 1985; Jackson et al., 1989). Negative symptom schizophrenics tend to be less educated (Pogue-Geile & Harrow, 1984) and appear more likely to display premorbid cognitive impairment (Kay, Opler, & Fiszbein, 1986) and/or neurological indications of prefrontal dysfunction (Bilder, 1985; Merriam, Kay, Opler, Kushner, & van Praag, 1990).

However, the view that positive schizophrenia and negative schizophrenia are different "types" has been increasingly called into question. Considerable research (Kay et al., 1986; Kulhara & Chandiramani, 1990; Rosen et al., 1984) suggests that rather than representing opposite ends of a bipolar dimension, as Andreasen and Olsen (1982) suggested, positive and negative symptomatology are independent of each other, and both may be prominent in the same patients. Both positive and negative symptoms may occur concurrently, or at different phases during the illness (Liddle, 1990). Positive symptoms reportedly decrease over time, whereas negative symptoms appear to be stable (Bleuler, 1988; Jackson et al., 1989; Kulhara & Chandiramani, 1990), or even become more apparent over time (Weinberger, 1986). To the extent that negative symptoms are stable over time, Husted, Beiser, and Iacono (1992) have shown they are identified with poor outcome in first-episode schizophrenics. As Schulsinger and Parnas (1990) argue, many schizophrenic patients who show poor response to neuroleptics and poor outcome would be classified as negative schizophrenics, even though they frequently display many Schneiderian first-rank (i.e., positive) symptoms.

Pogue-Geile and Harrow (1985) suggested several ways to account for the association between schizophrenia and negative symptoms: Negative symptoms may serve as a moderating variable that affects the phenotypic expression of schizophrenia; they may increase the individual's risk for developing the disorder; or they may reflect a greater accumulation of multifactorial influences that produce the disorder. Furthermore, Pogue-Geile and Harrow (1985) asserted, as have others, that the presence of negative symptomatology does not imply the absence of positive symptomatology.

Negative symptoms have been negatively correlated with social skills (Jackson et al., 1989; Pogue-Geile & Harrow, 1984). However, some negative symptoms may be secondary to medication, rather than reflective of the patients' core level of interpersonal functioning. Even when negative symptoms appear independent of medication effects, it is unclear whether these symptoms are natural accompaniments, or the sequelae of, patients' social development. Pogue-Geile and Harrow

(1985) suggest that prominent negative symptoms may occur concurrently with poor functioning. This hypothesis warrants further investigation, especially in view of Pogue-Geile and Harrow's (1984) prior suggestion to divide negative symptoms into two classes: those associated with deficits in interpersonal behavior and those associated with deficits in cognitive and psychomotor functioning. Although this area of inquiry appears promising, future work is necessary before the prominence of negative symptomatology, either in terms of interpersonal functioning or neuropsychological functioning, can be utilized to define a subtype of schizophrenia.

These criticisms have led Crow (1987) and others to modify their conceptualization of the role of positive and negative symptoms in schizophrenia. Rather than representing distinct diseases, Crow (1987) asserted that the positive and negative syndromes reflect separate parts of a singular disease process. According to this view, the positive syndrome is characteristic of acute phases of the disease, whereas the negative syndrome is more likely to be present in chronic stages of the disorder.

Crow's (1987) revised two-syndrome concept not only takes into account differential response to neuroleptics and relative presence of intellectual impairment, but also tries to link possible neuroendocrine correlates. For example, according to Crow (1987), Type I syndrome is associated with an increase in D2 dopamine receptors, and a reduction in gonadotropin responsivity. Type II syndrome, on the other hand, is associated with cell loss in the temporal region, and blunted growth hormone response to apomorphine, a dopamine agonist. Preliminary findings from a prospective study of psychobiological variables in first-episode schizophrenics (Lieberman et al., 1992) indicated the existence of two latent classes of patients distinguished on the basis of brain morphology, negative symptomatology, first-episode remission, and gender. For assignment to the more severe subtype of the disorder, male patients had to show either prominent negative symptomatology or nonremission status, whereas female patients had to display both abnormal MRI findings and prominent negative symptomatology. Although the investigators did not emphasize this finding, it appeared that their two latent classes also differed in terms of their mean growth hormone response to apomorphine.

Another view is that rather than being related to different dimensions of pathology, the neurochemical anomaly and structural anomalies are related; the sign(s) of pathology that are most prominent may depend not only on the site of the lesion but also on the developmental stage at which it occurred. This provocative view is likely to continue to spark research interest, especially in terms of what the presence, timing, and predominance of these syndromes can tell us about the development and/or course of the disorder.

Psychophysiological and Biological Subtyping

Attempts to classify schizophrenia into phenomenologically homogeneous subtypes have been only marginally successful. We assert that the time is ripe for a different approach to the identification of distinct subgroups of schizophrenics—one based on psychophysiological and/or neuroanatomic variables, either alone, or in combination with other biological and clinical attributes.

Biological variables, such as psychophysiological measures and brain structural features, present an alternative or complementary strategy for subtyping schizophrenic patients. One advantage of using such variables is that they can be assessed using noninvasive techniques. A specific advantage of using psychophysiological variables to subclassify schizophrenics is that many of them are candidate markers for genetic vulnerability for schizophrenia (see Holzman, 1987; Iacono, 1985; Iacono & Clementz, 1993; Iacono & Ficken, 1989 for reviews). Such variables have obvious potential to provide clues to the etiology of schizophrenia among those patients who manifest the deviant psychophysiology. Psychophysiological variables that are likely to assist researchers in identifying different subgroups of schizophrenics include smooth pursuit eye-tracking performance, electrodermal responsivity, and cortical event-related potentials (Iacono, 1991).

Smooth Pursuit Eye Movements

One of the most robust findings in the psychopathology literature is schizophrenics' impaired ability to visually follow a continuously moving, low-velocity target. The smooth pursuit eye-tracking deficit observed in a disproportionate number of schizophrenic patients was first reported by Holzman, Proctor, and Hughes in 1973. Since then, there have been many independent replications of this finding (see Holzman, 1987; Iacono, 1985; Iacono & Clementz, 1993; Levy, Holzman, Matthysse, & Mendell, 1993 for reviews). Although most studies of pursuit eye tracking have examined patients with long-standing schizophrenia, smooth pursuit eye-tracking impairment has been observed in first-episode and recent-onset schizophrenic patients as well.

One of the advantages of studying first-episode and/or recent-onset schizophrenic patients is that abnormal performance on a given measure cannot be attributed to the potentially confounding effects known to plague schizophrenia research such as chronic illness, institutionalization, or any sequelae of neuroleptic or other treatment. Investigations of smooth pursuit eye tracking in first-episode schizophrenia (Iacono, Moreau, Beiser, & Lin, 1992; Lieberman et al., 1993; Sweeney, Haas, & Li, 1992) have consistently indicated performance deficits. Moreover, pursuit tracking has been shown to be stable even in first-episode schizophrenics, over an average period of 9.5 months, despite significant changes in psychiatric symptomatology and medication (Gooding, Iacono, & Beiser, 1994). These findings provide a nice complement to prior reports (see, e.g., Iacono, Tuason, & Johnson, 1981) showing that impaired smooth pursuit performance is displayed by remitted, nonsymptomatic schizophrenics. Taken together, these reports show that the impaired eye movements displayed by schizophrenics cannot be accounted for by state-dependent variables such as presence of psychotic symptoms or medication effects.

Studies of twins (see, e.g., Holzman, Kringlen, Levy, & Haberman, 1980; Iacono, 1982) indicate that smooth pursuit eye-tracking performance is heritable. Iacono, Bassett, and Jones (1988) described an interesting family in which abnormal pursuit segregated with schizophrenia and partial trisomy of chromosome 5 in relatives. Several groups (see Iacono & Clementz, 1993, for a review) have reported that first-degree relatives of schizophrenics show impaired tracking performance. Iacono et al. (1992) demonstrated that schizophrenic patients with eye-tracking dysfunction tend to have relatives with abnormal pursuit. Furthermore, in a multitrait family study of eye tracking, Grove and colleagues (1991) observed a correlation between eye-tracking dysfunction and personality and information-processing characteristics purportedly associated with schizophrenia proneness, such as physical anhedonia and impairment on a continuous performance test.

However, not all schizophrenic patients exhibit oculomotor dysfunction. There have been several reports (Blackwood, St. Clair, Muir, & Duffy, 1991; Clementz, Grove, Iacono, & Sweeney, 1992; Iacono et al., 1992; Ross et al., 1988; Sweeney et al., 1993) indicating that the eye-tracking performance of schizophrenics divides them into two overlapping but separate groups, one with close to normal and the other with abnormal tracking performance. There are findings suggesting that eye-tracking dysfunction is related to schizophrenia even in patients who produce normal eye tracking. Holzman's group (Holzman, Kringlen, Levy, & Haberman, 1980) reported cases of twins discordant for schizophrenia in which the proband produced normal pursuit, whereas the clinically normal cotwin displayed pursuit impairments. Iacono et al. (1992) and Grove, Clementz, Iacono, and Katsanis (1992) also demonstrated that among large families of schizophrenic probands who did not display eye-tracking dysfunction, there were psychiatrically normal relatives who produced deviant pursuit. These findings have been interpreted as evidence for pleiotropy—multiple effects of a single gene, with the underlying pathophysiology of the proband's disorder leading to eye-tracking dysfunction, schizophrenia, or both.

On the basis of extant eye-tracking data, there appears to be a group of schizophrenics for whom eye tracking dysfunction is familially related, and a group of schizophrenic patients for whom it is not familially related. Although researchers engaged in genetic modeling based on eye tracking data concur that abnormal pursuit tracking may be a manifestation of a single major gene with pleiotropic effects, there is some controversy regarding the mechanism by which the eye-tracking dysfunction is transmitted as well as the proportion of families displaying aberrant tracking. Holzman and his colleagues have posited the existence of a latent trait, an underlying neurobiological characteristic transmitted through a dominant, major gene. Furthermore, Holzman et al. (Holzman et al., 1988; Holzman & Matthysse, 1990; Matthysse, Holzman, & Lange, 1986) asserted that the latent trait is present in nearly 90% of all families with a schizophrenic member.

In contrast, Iacono and colleagues (Iacono & Grove, 1993; Iacono et al., 1992) maintain that eye-tracking dysfunction is present in only about 50% to 60% of all schizophrenic pedigrees. In a complex segregation analysis, in which Grove, Clementz, Iacono, and Katsanis (1992) tested various genetic models of eye-tracking dysfunction using oculomotor data pooled from three separate studies, they observed a major gene effect, though their data were not consistent with a dominant gene theory for eye tracking. Unlike Holzman and his associates, Iacono and his group proposed that if a single major gene is at work, it tends toward recessivity and is transmitted along with a group of polygenes. The differences between the Holzman-Matthysse and Iacono-Grove models also have implications in terms of the question of genetic

heterogeneity, with a potential strategy for elucidating discrete subgroups of schizophrenic patients implicit to the latter model.

Although both groups' models have been supported by the empirical data from their respective laboratories, the discrepant prevalence rates of eye-tracking dysfunction may be attributable in part to differences in scoring methodology. The eye-tracking data on which the Holzman-Matthysse model has been based used a dichotomous, qualitative rating of pursuit performance, whereas Iacono et al. (1992) yielded considerably lower rates of poor tracking using a quantitative measure known as root-mean-square error. The findings of Iacono et al. (1992) were replicated and extended by Clementz et al. (1992) who found that both root-mean-square error and another index of impaired smooth pursuit, reduced gain, identified similar rates of poor tracking. Similar results for root-mean-square error were also obtained by Sweeney and associates (1993; Sweeney, Haas, Clementz, Escobar, Drake, & Frances, 1994).

Schizophrenics with poor eye tracking differ from those with normal pursuit performance. Investigations of neuropsychological test performance in chronic schizophrenic patients have shown that frontal lobe dysfunction is associated with poor tracking (Bartfai, Levander, Nyback, Berggren, & Schalling, 1985; Katsanis & Iacono, 1991; Litman, et al., 1991). Schizophrenic probands with eye-tracking dysfunction are also more likely to display negative symptoms (Katsanis & Iacono, 1991; Blackwood, Young, et al., 1991; Sweeney et al., 1994). Although some investigators (Bartfai et al., 1985; Blackwood, St. Clair, Muir, & Duffy, 1991; Blackwood, Young et al., 1991) have found an association between lateral ventricular enlargement and deviant pursuit tracking, others (e.g., Katsanis & Iacono, 1991) did not observe such an association. Similarly, Katsanis, Iacono, and Beiser (1991) found no association between tracking performance and third ventricle width in their sample of first-episode patients. However, morphological abnormalities in the mesiotemporal and third ventricular brain regions were associated with normal eye tracking in some first-episode schizophrenics (Lieberman et al., 1993).

The Clementz et al. (1992) investigation of eye-tracking performance in schizophrenic probands and their first-degree relatives indicated that it is only families in which oculomotor dysfunction is present that eye-tracking performance may relate to other variables such as schizotypy. Clementz et al. (1992) found significant phenotypic correlations between tracking proficiency (as measured either by root-mean-square error or oculomotor gain) and schizophrenia-related personality factors in families in which poor tracking is familially related. Moreover, in these families, oculomotor dysfunction accounted for up to 56% of the schizophrenia spectrum diagnosis variance.

Event-Related Potentials

Another psychophysiological technique that has been applied to the study of schizophrenia involves the recording of event-related potentials, the averaged electroencephalographic signals generated in response to repetitions of a stimulus presentation. The late, positive component of the event-related potential (labeled P3 or P300) has application as an index of cognitive processing. The P300 amplitude is believed to be a function of three factors: (a) the amount of information transmitted, (b) the subjective probability of the stimulus occurrence, and (c) the stimulus meaning (task complexity, stimulus complexity, and stimulus value; Johnson, 1986). Several psychophysiological investigations of schizophrenia have indicated that adult schizophrenics display attenuated P300 amplitudes (Blackwood, St. Clair, Muir, & Duffy, 1991; Ebmeier et al., 1990; Holzman, 1987; Pritchard, 1986; Strik, Dierks, & Maurer, 1993). There have also been reports of an association between delayed P300 latency and schizophrenia (Blackwood, St. Clair, & Muir, 1991; Blackwood, St. Clair, Muir, & Duffy, 1991; Roxborough, Muir, Blackwood, Walker, & Blackburn, 1993). Prolonged P300 latency is thought to reflect impairments in selective attention and/or stimulus discrimination. Studies have indicated that schizophrenic probands displaying P300 deviations are more likely to display prominent negative symptoms (Strik, Dierks, & Maurer, 1993), or frontal and temporal lobe deficits on neuropsychological testing (Roxborough et al., 1993).

There have also been reports of biological relatives of schizophrenics displaying abnormal P300 responses (see Black, Mowry, Barton, & de Roach, 1992; Blackwood, St. Clair, Muir, & Duffy, 1991). To date, there has been one published investigation (Blackwood, St. Clair, Muir, & Duffy, 1991) of the prevalence of P300 and smooth pursuit eye-tracking abnormalities in the relatives of schizophrenic. In this pedigree study, Blackwood and colleagues observed that in most families of schizophrenic patients, relatives displayed either one or both of the psychophysiological abnormalities; their analyses revealed that the eye-tracking dysfunction was independent of the P300 abnormality in these relatives. Blackwood, St. Clair, Muir, and Duffy (1991) also observed a small subgroup (15%) of families in which no member produced abnormal eye tracking or deviant P300 responses. The investigators concluded that there may be heterogeneity among schizophrenic pedigrees, with some families displaying psychophysiological abnormalities and other families appearing psychophysiologically normal.

In addition to the reports of P300 abnormalities, other event-related potential studies have focused on an early, positive-going component labeled P50. The P50 wave is typically elicited through a conditioning-testing paradigm, in which two loud clicks are presented in close succession. The first stimulus, called the conditioning stimulus, purportedly activates or conditions an inhibitory mechanism, whereas the second (testing) stimulus tests the strength of the inhibitory mechanism. The P50 component of the event-related potential is typically smaller in response to the test than to the conditioning stimulus. Freedman's group (Adler, et al., 1982; Siegel, Waldo, Mizner, Adler, & Freedman, 1984) demonstrated that in schizophrenics, the response to the test stimulus is approximately 90% of that to the conditioning stimulus, compared with 10% in normal subjects. Siegel et al. (1984) observed that impaired smooth pursuit eye tracking and the nonsuppression of the P50 component in the event-related potential existed independently in some schizophrenics, though they identified a subset of probands who displayed both deficits. Perhaps future investigations, in which both psychophysiological traits are assessed, will enable schizophrenic probands to be subtyped based on the concordance or discordance of these two abnormalities.

P50 nonsuppression has been observed in other laboratories as well (Boutros, Zouridakis, & Overall, 1991; Judd, McAdams,

Budnick, & Braff, 1992). Boutros and colleagues (Boutros, Zouridakis, Rustin, Peabody, & Warner, 1993) observed that their samples of paranoid and nonparanoid schizophrenics differed in terms of their P50 amplitudes. They also observed that neuroleptic treatment normalized P50 amplitudes in nonparanoid schizophrenics, but had no effect on paranoid schizophrenics. They suggested that P50 measurements could be a useful way of identifying subtypes of schizophrenic patients.

Freedman's group has provided evidence indicating that P50 nonsuppression displayed by schizophrenic patients is also seen in some of their first-degree relatives (Adler, Hoffer, Griffith, Waldo, & Freedman, 1992; Siegel et al., 1984). Waldo et al. (1991)'s pedigree analysis of the families of schizophrenic patients who displayed P50 nonsuppression provided further evidence that this sensory gating deficit is familial. Biological relatives (of schizophrenic probands) who display the sensory gating deficit (the P50 effect) are also more likely to have higher scores on the Schizophrenia Scale (scale 8) of the Minnesota Multiphasic Personality Inventory (MMPI; Hathaway & McKinley, 1943). This finding suggests that the failure to suppress P50 is familially associated with schizophrenia-proneness.

Electrodermal Activity

Electrodermal responsivity is another psychophysiological variable that differentiates groups of schizophrenics. Many adult schizophrenic patients display some form of aberrant electrodermal activity. Some fail to display a skin conductance orienting response to innocuous stimuli (Dawson & Nuechterlein, 1984; Holzman, 1987; Iacono, 1985), whereas others show electrodermal habituation abnormalities (Bernstein et al., 1983; Dawson & Nuechterlein, 1984; Iacono, 1985). Overall, the electrodermal nonresponders tend to appear more withdrawn and conceptually disorganized than responsive schizophrenic patients (Dawson & Nuechterlein, 1984). Katsanis and Iacono (1992) found an association between electrodermal nonresponsiveness and poor performance on neuropsychological tests sensitive to temporal lobe dysfunction.

Brain Morphology

Neuroanatomic imaging may also identify different groups of schizophrenic patients. Some schizophrenic individuals display nonlocalizing brain structural abnormalities. Investigations using neuroanatomic imaging techniques such as computerized tomography (CT) and magnetic resonance imaging (MRI) often find lateral ventricular enlargement in schizophrenic patients (Kelsoe, Cadet, Pickar, & Weinberger, 1988; Shelton & Weinberger, 1986; Suddath et al., 1989).

In addition to reports of nonlocalizing structural abnormalities, there has also been suggestive evidence of neuropathological abnormalities in the frontal cortex of some schizophrenics. A number of computerized tomography (CT) studies (see Shelton & Weinberger, 1986) have indicated that schizophrenics show signs of cortical atrophy in the prefrontal region. Compared with CT scans, magnetic resonance imaging (MRI) provides greater resolution, thereby permitting more detailed investigation of smaller brain structures. Previous findings based on MRI have indicated that compared with normals, schizophrenic patients have less frontal white matter (Smith et al., 1984) and/or smaller frontal lobes (Andreasen et al., 1986). However, subsequent investigation by Andreasen's group (Andreasen et al., 1990) indicated that when demographic factors such as socioeconomic status (SES) and educational attainment were controlled for, significant differences in frontal area did not emerge.

One study (Kelsoe, et al., 1988) that compared schizophrenics and controls in terms of prefrontal volume also failed to detect significant group differences. The studies conducted by Andreasen et al. (1990) and Kelsoe et al. (1988) are not directly comparable due to differences in operational definition of the frontal region under study as well as the latter group's not matching patients and controls for educational level. A more recent study, performed by Raine et al. (1992) has indicated that schizophrenics have smaller frontal areas compared with normal controls. This study is particularly compelling because the investigators, unlike some of their predecessors, improved on earlier studies by controlling for age, gender, parental SES, and education.

The majority of CT (Bogerts, 1989; Shelton & Weinberger, 1986) and MRI studies (Shenton et al., 1992; Suddath et al., 1989) also reveal supportive evidence of structural abnormalities in the temporal lobe, particularly the hippocampal formation. Suddath et al. (1989) found that chronic schizophrenic patients had significantly smaller temporal lobe gray matter volume than age- and sex-matched normal subjects. Shenton et al. (1992) demonstrated that chronic schizophrenic subjects displayed decreased volume in the left posterior temporal cortex, relative to nonaffected controls. Degreef et al. (1992) reported that first-episode schizophrenics had smaller mesiotemporal volumes compared with age- and sex-matched healthy controls.

Ventriculomegaly has been observed in patients experiencing their first episode of schizophrenia (Degreef et al., 1992; Iacono, Smith et al., 1988) or schizophreniform disorder (Holsenbeck et al., 1992; Weinberger, DeLisi, Perman, Targum, & Wyatt, 1982). Holsenbeck and associates (1992) found evidence of ventricular enlargement in the CT scans of first-episode schizophreniform patients assessed an average of 3.8 days following the onset of symptomatology. This finding suggests that such structural brain abnormality is present at the onset of psychotic symptomatology. The results of work by Sponheim, Iacono, and Beiser (1991) provide additional evidence suggesting that ventriculomegaly is not progressive. Sponheim et al. (1991) rescanned a group of first-episode schizophrenic patients who had undergone CT scanning approximately 2 years earlier and found that subjects displayed temporally stable ventricular size. These results suggest that ventricular enlargement is not simply a reflection of progressive changes that accompany aging, nor is it dependent on the progression of psychosis.

At present, it is not clear what causes some schizophrenics to have structural abnormalities. Although DeLisi et al. (1986) observed increased ventricular size in families with more than one affected member of the same generation, which suggests that ventricular enlargement is present in schizophrenic patients with an inherited vulnerability toward the disorder, the findings of Suddath, Christison, Torrey, Casanova, and Weinberger (1990) and Sacchetti et al. (1992) suggest that extragenetic factors are implicated in the ventricular enlargement displayed by some schizophrenics. Suddath et al. (1990) studied monozygotic

twins discordant for schizophrenia and observed that the affected cotwins could be distinguished from their siblings by their larger ventricles. Sacchetti et al. (1992) found that schizophrenics born during winter months, especially those who did not have a familial history of schizophrenia, had an increased likelihood of displaying ventricular enlargement. These research findings suggest that one criterion for subtyping schizophrenics might be based on evidence of neuroanatomic abnormalities such as ventriculomegaly, smaller temporal lobe structures, and/or frontal atrophy.

FURTHER EVIDENCE OF ETIOLOGIC HETEROGENEITY

The preceding sections attest to the behavioral, psychophysiological, and brain morphological heterogeneity present in schizophrenia. In our view, etiologic studies of schizophrenia stand to be more productive if this complex phenotype is reduced to subtypes defined by psychophysiological and brain structural features. Consistent with the notion of equifinality, we believe that the evidence points to the existence of etiologically distinct subgroups of schizophrenics, defined by the relative presence or absence of eye tracking, electrophysiological, and brain morphological deviations, that may reflect different genetic and neurological etiologies. Other studies of biological variables, although they do not provide a ready means of subtyping the disorder, also point to schizophrenia's possible etiologic heterogeneity.

Neurochemistry

Studies of neurochemical pathology can assist in elucidating the genetic etiology of schizophrenia in part because alterations in neurotransmission are likely to have a genetic basis (Heston & White, 1991). Alterations in dopaminergic neurotransmission have been implicated in the pathogenesis of schizophrenia since the mid-1960s. According to the simplest form of the dopamine hypothesis, increased central dopaminergic activity plays a pathogenic role in schizophrenia (Cooper, Bloom, & Roth, 1991; Neale & Oltmanns, 1980). There are several possible mechanisms for the excess dopaminergic activity: excess production, excess release, or deficient reuptake of dopamine by presynaptic neurons (Neale & Oltmanns, 1980), as well as heightened sensitivity at the level of the postsynaptic neuron and/or an increased number of dopaminergic receptors (Owen, et al., 1978). One of the most convincing, though indirect arguments in support of the dopamine hypothesis is the observation that the classic neuroleptics, which block dopamine D2 receptors (Cooper et al., 1991; Kebabian & Calne, 1979; Owen et al., 1978), are effective in reducing the positive symptoms associated with schizophrenia (Henn, 1982; Neale & Oltmanns, 1980; Swerdlow & Koob, 1987). However, it is well known that some patients are refractory to treatment with dopamine antagonists.

Evidence of increased sensitivity of dopamine receptors (Owen et al., 1978), as well as increased numbers of D2 receptors have been found in the brains of schizophrenics. Because previous neuroleptic treatment increases the number of postsynaptic DA receptors (Bannet, Belmaker, & Ebstein, 1981; Burt, Creese, & Snyder, 1977; Karson, Goldberg, & Leleszi, 1986; Mackay, Bird, Spokes, Rosser, & Iversen, 1980), evidence of elevated D2 receptor density in the brains of neuroleptic-naive schizophrenics (Swerdlow & Koob, 1987) provides particularly cogent support of the dopamine hypothesis.

Advances in the genetic field of cloning and characterization of genes for dopamine receptor regions have rendered it possible to investigate evidence of gene mutation for dopaminergic transmission in schizophrenic families (Coon, Byerley et al., 1993). To date, research attempts to demonstrate linkage between the genes for five dopamine receptors and schizophrenia have been unsuccessful (Coon, Byerley et al., 1993; Moises et al., 1991; Sabate et al., 1994; Su et al., 1993). These linkage studies, however, have examined relatively small pedigrees. As several investigators (such as Crowe, Black, Andreasen, & Heuther, 1990) have asserted, it is imperative to study large multiplex families to obtain adequate estimation of the lod score, the standard statistical test used in linkage analyses. One way to reconcile these negative findings with the compelling evidence implicating dopamine in the pathophysiology of schizophrenia is genetic heterogeneity. Linkage between some familial forms of schizophrenia and at least one of the dopamine receptor gene regions may ultimately be discovered in some families or subgroups.

Swerdlow and Koob (1987) proposed a multiple neurotransmitter, multiple circuit hypothesis to account for schizophrenia. Since the Swerdlow and Koob (1987) model, there has been increasing evidence of the complexity of the neurotransmitter interactions. Investigators (Beart, 1987; Carlsson & Carlsson, 1990a, 1990b) have pointed to glutamate as another neurotransmitter likely to be implicated in the neurochemistry of schizophrenia. Clozapine, an atypical neuroleptic, has been found to be clinically efficacious in those schizophrenic patients whose illness has proven refractory to typical neuroleptics. Moreover, clozapine has been associated with serotonergic and muscarinic receptors as well as dopaminergic receptors (Ereshefsky, Watanabe, & Tran-Johnson, 1989). It appears that the neurochemistry of schizophrenia is too complex to be easily explained by activity in a single neurotransmitter system. The recent reports of different subgroups of schizophrenic patients (as determined by relative prominence of positive and negative symptoms), and their differential response to typical neuroleptics and clozapine supports the notion that clinically diagnosed schizophrenia is neurochemically heterogeneous. Thus, there may be linkage between schizophrenia and mutations at other neurotransmitter receptor loci. On balance, however, although they appear to hold promise, investigations of neurochemical processes in schizophrenia have not provided clear evidence of etiological heterogeneity, despite reports of differential efficacy of traditional neuroleptics targeting dopamine and newer drugs such as clozapine, which affects both dopamine and serotonin. Recent failures to support genetic linkage between dopamine receptor regions and schizophrenia provide further incentive to search for evidence of multiple pathophysiological mechanisms associated with schizophrenia.

Molecular Genetics

We assume that readers accept the compelling evidence, based on results of family, twin, and adoption studies, of the substantial influence of genetic factors in the etiology of schizophrenia (Faraone & Tsuang, 1985; Gottesman, 1991; Gottesman, Shields, & Hanson, 1982; Neale & Oltmanns, 1980). Increasingly, there is evidence that other psychiatric disorders such as dementia (Heston & White, 1991) are etiologically heterogeneous (i.e., have multiple distinct genetic mechanisms). Few would argue that the best way to demonstrate that a disorder is etiologically heterogeneous would be to provide evidence at the molecular level. Linkage analysis tests the likelihood of nonindependent transmission of an illness and a genetic marker within a family. Linkage studies involve the localization of disease-associated DNA segments on a specific chromosome; such studies have the potential for identifying those deoxyribonucleic acid (DNA) marker alleles that increase the risk of the disorder (Heston & White, 1991).

On the basis of a reported association between partial trisomy of chromosome 5 and schizophrenia in a Canadian family (Bassett, Jones, McGillivray, & Pantzar, 1988), Sherrington and colleagues (1988) investigated linkage between chromosome 5 and increased risk for schizophrenia in several British and Icelandic families. Although Sherrington et al. (1988) observed linkage between the chromosome 5q region and schizophrenia susceptibility, attempts to replicate this finding have not been successful (see, e.g., Crowe, Black, Andreasen, & Heuther, 1990; Crowe et al., 1991; Detera-Wadleigh et al., 1989; St. Clair et al., 1989). In the Sherrington study, a broad definition of the phenotype was used that went beyond the disorders typically considered to be part of the schizophrenia spectrum. As a result, some investigators speculated that failure of confirmation of this linkage in other pedigrees could be attributed to differences in diagnostic practices and the lack of an objective index of what constitutes the presence of the genotype. On the other hand, a linkage analysis performed by Blackwood, St. Clair, & Muir (1991), which used both clinical diagnosis and the presence of a P300 abnormality to define the schizophrenic phenotype, confirmed previous reports (such as St. Clair et al., 1989) of no linkage between schizophrenia and chromosome 5. Although we would agree that failures to replicate a linkage study could be due to genetic heterogeneity, the weight of evidence to date offers little support for linkage between schizophrenia and chromosome 5.

Based on the observations of cytogenetic abnormalities of the sex chromosomes in many schizophrenic patients, as well as reports that schizophrenic siblings are more often concordant for sex, Crow, DeLisi, and Johnstone (1989) hypothesized that schizophrenia susceptibility may be associated with the pseudo-autosomal region of the sex chromosomes. This possibility led to several attempts to find evidence of a schizophrenia susceptibility gene on the sex chromosomes. Collinge et al. (1991) reported evidence for a genetic linkage between DXYS14, a pseudoautosomal region of the sex chromosomes, and susceptibility to schizophrenia. This finding has been independently replicated by some investigators (D'Amato et al., 1992) but not others (Asherson et al., 1992).

Unless researchers accept replication failures as evidence of molecular genetic heterogeneity, linkage studies have shed little light on the etiologic heterogeneity question. To date, linkage studies of schizophrenia have been plagued with difficulties, such as phenotype definition (including the diagnostic criteria for the selection of probands, selection criteria for considering relatives as affected, and the dilemma of handling spectrum diagnoses), uncertain modes of transmission of susceptibility, and uncertainty regarding degree of penetrance (Bassett, 1991; Gill, Taylor, & Murray, 1989; Levinson & Mowry, 1991). Despite these obstacles, linkage studies hold promise for elucidating the nature of schizophrenia.

Bassett and Honer (1994) suggested a strategy for enhancing the productivity of molecular genetic investigations of schizophrenia, based on an unusual pattern of inheritance called genetic anticipation. Genetic anticipation, a pattern of inheritance in which there is increasing severity of disorder and decreasing age of onset over successive generations, is caused by the presence of novel genes with trinucleotide (triplet) repeats. Bassett and Honer (1994) found evidence of anticipation in their sample of multigenerational families of schizophrenics. In their clinical study, all eight multigenerational families exhibited increasing rates of hospitalized psychotic illness, progressively earlier ages of onset, and increasing severity of illness across successive generations. Although these findings may not be generalizable to most cases of schizophrenia, they suggest another strategy for conducting genetic linkage analysis of schizophrenia. Bassett and Honer (1994) proposed screening for the trinucleotide repeat mutations as a complementary strategy in linkage studies. They also asserted that the genetic modeling parameters which are used in linkage studies (such as penetrance) may need to be modified to reflect the effects of anticipation.

We suggest that the inclusion of psychophysiological variables, such as smooth pursuit eye-tracking performance and the P50 auditory evoked response, may enhance the productivity of molecular genetic investigations of schizophrenia. A recent investigation by Coon, Plaetke et al. (1993) illustrates this strategy. Coon, Plaetke et al. (1993) used the P50 auditory evoked response in their linkage analysis of nine multigenerational families. Although they did not observe strong evidence for linkage to P50 in the pedigrees studied, the investigators identified genomic areas for further study on four different chromosomes (4, 7, 11, and 15).

GENETIC MODELS OF SCHIZOPHRENIA

As we noted earlier, the results of family, twin, and adoption studies provide compelling evidence that genetic factors are strongly implicated in the etiology, transmission, and development of schizophrenia. Compared with the risk of approximately 1% in the general population, having a schizophrenic first-degree relative places one at heightened (5–15 times higher) statistical risk for developing schizophrenia. Indeed, yet another comparison (Onstad, Skre, Torgersen, & Kringlen, 1991) of the concordance rates for DSM-III-R schizophrenia in monozygotic (MZ) and dizygotic (DZ) twins confirmed once again that the

probandwise rates were considerably higher in MZ twins than in DZ twins (48% vs. 4% concordance).

Psychopathologists are cognizant that individuals do not inherit schizophrenia; rather, they inherit a vulnerability for developing the disorder. Several theories have been posited to account for the genetic mechanism underlying the diathesis for schizophrenia. In the next section, we discuss and summarize selected genetic models of schizophrenia. We evaluate these models in terms of the following criteria: parsimony versus comprehensiveness, adherence to developmental principles, heuristic value, and congruence with extant data about schizophrenia.

Single Major Gene Models

Single major gene models of schizophrenia involve the hypothesis that there is an abnormal gene at one chromosomal locus that accounts for the transmission of schizophrenia. Such a model posits that schizophrenia is transmitted through a simple, Mendelian pattern associated with either dominant or recessive modes of inheritance. The single major locus model has already been demonstrated to hold true for some disorders such as Huntington's disease. However, when compared with extant epidemiological data, most monogenic models of transmission appear inadequate to account for the transmission of schizophrenia risk (Faraone & Tsuang, 1985; Gottesman, 1991; Gottesman, Shields, & Hanson, 1982; McGue & Gottesman, 1989a). More specifically, the gene segregation ratios that would be predicted from a generalized single locus model cannot account for the high rate of concordance in monozygotic twins or the high rates of risk for offspring of dual matings (Gottesman, 1991; Gottesman, Shields & Hanson, 1982; McGue & Gottesman, 1989b).

One variant of the monogenic model of schizophrenia, discussed earlier in this chapter, is the latent trait hypothesis posited by Holzman and Matthysse (Holzman et al., 1988; Holzman & Matthysse, 1990). The latent trait model attributes most cases of schizophrenia to a single major gene that operates according to pleiotropy, with the gene expressing itself as schizophrenia, eye-tracking dysfunction, or both. Such a mode of transmission has been observed previously in disorders such as von Recklinghausen's disease or neurofibromatosis (Holzman et al., 1988). As with other single major locus models, predictions made using the latent trait model are inconsistent with some of the epidemiological findings regarding the risk for schizophrenia among some relatives of probands. The latent trait model underestimates the risk for schizophrenia in the monozygotic co-twins of schizophrenics, as well as in offspring of two schizophrenics (McGue & Gottesman, 1989a).

The Distinct-Heterogeneity Model

According to the distinct-heterogeneity model, schizophrenia is a cluster of qualitatively distinct diseases, each of which have separate etiologies (Gottesman, 1991; Gottesman, Shields & Hanson, 1982). Such a model assumes that each distinct type of schizophrenia is caused by a different genetic mechanism perhaps involving different types of Mendelian genes and/or polygenes. The distinct-heterogeneity model has the advantage that different phenotypic variants of the disorder can be viewed as influenced by different alleles at different loci. Such an explanation has been observed to account for severe mental retardation; phenylketonuria and Tay-Sach's disease are just two of the different diseases subsumed under the umbrella term "mental retardation." Similarly, dementia is another psychiatric disorder that can be accounted for by a variant of the distinct-heterogeneity model. Alzheimer's disease appears to have several distinct genetic variants (Tsuang, 1994) and, as Heston and White (1991) illustrated, dementia of the Alzheimer type, Pick's dementia, and Huntington's disease all involve very different etiologies, despite having important common features.

The distinct-heterogeneity model is an embodiment of the developmental principle of equifinality. The distinct-heterogeneity model also appears consistent with extant epidemiological and psychophysiological data. However, unlike the situation with mental retardation and dementia, it remains uncertain how best to split schizophrenia into subtypes with potentially distinct genetic etiologies. As long as this situation prevails, the heuristic value of this model will be limited. Testing the model would require the epidemiological study of such large numbers of families that it would not be feasible without a multiyear, multicenter, collaborative effort. Alternatively, it may be possible to simplify the task if a psychophysiological marker that putatively identifies carriers of the schizophrenia genotype, such as eye-tracking dysfunction, were studied in conjunction with manifest schizophrenia (see Iacono & Grove, 1993).

Multifactorial, Interactional Models

Multifactorial models involve the notion of an interaction between a combination of genes and experiential or environmental factors. There are several variants of interactional models, which differ in terms of the contributory roles of genetic factors, and the ways in which the genetic liability or diathesis may become manifest. These models traditionally emphasize the diathesis-stress notion as an explanatory construct for schizophrenia. In the medical literature, multifactorial, interactional explanations have been posited to account for cerebrovascular accidents or strokes. Obesity, hypertension, "life style," and hypercholesterolemia are all factors implicated in the development of cerebrovascular accidents.

One of the earliest multifactorial, interactional models was proposed by Meehl (1962). According to Meehl, only individuals possessing the specific genetic diathesis to schizophrenia, namely the dominant gene and some potentiating factors, would be at risk for the development of schizophrenia. In his model, the diathesis produces a neurointegrative defect; Meehl termed this neurointegrative defect "schizotaxia." Meehl conceptualized schizophrenia as the resultant interaction between the diathesis or innate predisposition and a variety of stressors.

An alternative to Meehl's model is the multifactorial polygenic threshold model of schizophrenia that was originally proposed by Gottesman and Shields in the late 1960s. In this model, multiple genetic factors and multiple environmental factors are distributed on a normal liability continuum. The genes are proposed to be of small, equal, and additive effect that in combination with environmental insults and stressors, forms the diathesis. In this completely additive polygenic model, there are both genetic assets and liabilities, as well as environmental assets and liabilities. Gottesman's model also includes the notion of an explicit, quantifiable threshold. In this model, if the cumulative amount of liability exceeds the hypothesized threshold, the individual will manifest psychiatric disorder (Gottesman, 1974, 1991). According to Gottesman, the hypothesized threshold for schizophrenia spectrum disorders is lower than the hypothesized threshold for the development of schizophrenia. Gottesman's multifactorial polygenic (MFP) model has continued to evolve in that he now allows for some genes to have relatively larger effects than others. This modification of Gottesman's model makes it conceptually similar to a mixed model, differing only in the number and influence of "major" genes postulated (Prescott & Gottesman, 1993).

Similarly, Meehl (1972, 1989, 1990) has continued to develop and refine his diathesis-stress model. Meehl (1972) coined the term "hypokrisia" for the "synaptic slippage" or disturbed neuronal signal selectivity (see Meehl, 1962) posited to underlie schizophrenia. In Meehl's theory, the causal chain involves a dominant gene that causes hypokrisia, which in turn leads to schizoptypic features such as cognitive slippage and soft neurological signs. Polygenes serve as potentiators accounting for other features such as hypohedonia and social introversion. Hence Meehl's multifactorial model is also a type of mixed model with a single gene working against a polygenic background.

Like Gottesman's model, Meehl's (1989, 1990) model includes a threshold component. If the person has the constitutional diathesis for developing schizotaxia, given a certain level of stress, that person will develop schizophrenia and/or a schizophrenia spectrum disorder. According to Meehl, even among schizotypes there is a continuum of risk; those schizotypes with the highest probability of developing schizophrenia are those who possess other potentiating risk factors, such as social introversion and anhedonia. The developmental principle of multifinality is consistent with Meehl's suggestion that exposure to various etiologic factors may render some individuals more affected than others. The differential outcome in individuals, all of whom possess the necessary genetic makeup for schizotaxia, may be related to differences in timing, number, and type of potentiating factors. Implicit in Meehl's conceptualization of the interaction between diathesis and stressor(s) is the notion that the stressor(s) may precede the phenotypic expression of illness by several years.

Iacono and Grove (1993) presented another multifactorial, interactional model to account for the subgroup of schizophrenics for whom deviant eye tracking is a putative marker. In this alternative diathesis-stress model, they posit a single major pathogene working along with polygenes that interact with random environmental effects. The Iacono-Grove model is similar to Meehl's diathesis-stress model, though the former model posits recessivity. Not only is their model consistent with extant eye-tracking data (as described previously in this chapter), it also accounts for the reports of schizotypal features and attentional deficits observed in schizophrenics' families.

Although the proponents of these multifactorial, diathesis-stress models devote much attention to describing the diathesis, they have been criticized by some for displaying "benign neglect" toward the stress component in their models. In the general diathesis stress model, the diathesis is posited as an initial, unchanging genetic factor, and the stress is characterized as something environmental or experiential. Typically, in diathesis-stress models, environmental and psychological factors may ameliorate or exacerbate the biological vulnerability, though they are typically not thought of as potential predisposing factors (Zubin, Feldman, & Salzinger, 1991). Indeed, in diathesis-stress models, the individual's genetic endowment determines the threshold, above which psychopathology is manifested (Cicchetti & Schneider-Rosen, 1984). However, Gottesman has allowed for the diathesis to vary over time as well as across individuals. In this way, liability varies according to the interaction between the initial diathesis, environmental and biological stressors, and the turning on and off of genetic mechanisms (Prescott & Gottesman, 1993).

From the perspective of developmental psychopathologists, the stressor is most likely some experience that interacts developmentally with the diathesis, and, in turn, may compose part of the resultant liability; this position is typically held by psychopathologists who posit vulnerability, rather than diathesis-stress, models.

The diathesis-stress model was further expanded by Zubin and Spring (1977), who referred to their revision as a vulnerability model. According to this view, low-risk individuals would not be expected to succumb to illness unless they were exposed to a high level of stress. The Zubin and Spring (1977) model also predicts that individuals possessing a stronger predisposition to illness would be more likely to decompensate with little stress. Vulnerability models account for the development of disorder by positing that, in addition to the influence of a person's initial diathesis and stress, the person's status at that time will be a factor in the determination of his or her state at a later point (Cicchetti & Schneider-Rosen, 1984). In the vulnerability model, stress may either trigger an episode of disorder, or render the individual more vulnerable to developing pathology. In this view, an increase in the number or degree of stressors would interact with the diathesis, and result in an increased level of psychopathology. The diathesis in Zubin's model is typically, though not necessarily, a genetic one. The Zubin vulnerability model contrasts with that of Meehl's (1962) diathesis-stress model in that it accounts for nongenetic forms of schizophrenia. According to Zubin, given a sufficiently high level of stress, some individuals might succumb to schizophrenia, despite their not possessing a genetic vulnerability to the disease.

Vulnerability models have been criticized because that they are typically disorder-specific. According to Cicchetti and Schneider-Rosen (1984, 1986), by being disorder-specific, such constructs of vulnerability are not likely to shed light on normal development. Thus, vulnerability models, though viewed by some as an improvement over traditional diathesis-stress models, would not be considered wholly consistent with a developmental psychopathology perspective because one of the tenets of a developmental psychopathology approach is that the study of pathology can enhance the understanding of normal development.

Both types of interactional models—diathesis-stress and vulnerability—are consistent with extant epidemiological data on schizophrenia and the developmental principle of multifinality. These models provide accounts for the development of schizophrenia spectrum disorders as well as schizophrenia. However, these interactional models have been criticized for being mechanistically, rather than organismically, oriented (Sameroff & Zax, 1973; Cicchetti & Schneider-Rosen, 1984, 1986). In a mechanistic view, the individual is portrayed as a passive, reactive organism (Cicchetti, 1990). An organismic orientation is more congruent with a developmental psychopathology perspective because in this view, the individual affects and is affected by, his or her dynamic interactions with the environment.

Transactional Models

Proponents of a developmental psychopathology perspective (such as Cicchetti & Schneider-Rosen, 1984, 1986) suggest that a developmental, transactional model is necessary to account for complex disorders such as schizophrenia. In developmental, transactional models, outcomes are viewed as the product of dynamic interchanges between the organism and the environment. Transactional models consider two types of potentiating factors that increase the likelihood of a pathological outcome: enduring factors (the vulnerability factors) and transient factors (challengers) (Cicchetti & Schneider-Rosen, 1984). In a developmental, transactional view, there are also two types of resiliency factors: long-term factors (the compensatory factors) and relatively short-term factors (buffers) (Cicchetti & Schneider-Rosen, 1984).

Like the interactional models, a transactional model includes a hypothesized threshold, above which psychopathology becomes manifest. However, developmental, transactional models are nonlinear models that lend greater prominence to factors such as contextual environment, age, and developmental level. In a transactional perspective, factors such as age, timing, and developmental level are posited as dynamic influences that, along with potentiating and compensatory factors, account for each individual's psychiatric outcome.

The concepts of both equifinality and multifinality can be incorporated into a developmental, transactional view. In such a view, there is consideration of a greater range of outcomes at each point along the life span, because the relative influence of potentiating and resiliency-promoting factors will vary with age and developmental level (Cicchetti & Schneider-Rosen, 1984). Nuechterlein (1987) proposed a transactional model of schizophrenia, in which he talked about complex interactions involving personal vulnerability factors, environmental potentiators and stressors, personal resiliency-promoting factors, and environmental resiliency-promoting factors. Through this transactional perspective, Nuechterlein's model allows for greater plasticity in terms of individuals' functioning. Such a model appears consistent with extant data, though its complexity renders it difficult both to specify and to test each of its components.

We assert that the diathesis-stress concept is not wholly inconsistent with a developmental, transactional view. Indeed, modifications of the diathesis-stress notion can result in a model that is both parsimonious and comprehensive, while explicitly addressing the complexities of a developing organism. A necessary modification of the diathesis-stress conceptualization of schizophrenia concerns the influence of age, timing, and development on both the potentiating and compensatory factors involved in the development of the disorder. In the next section, we discuss neurodevelopmental models of schizophrenia, and illustrate how a diathesis-stress model can accommodate a more organismic (rather than wholly mechanistic) conceptualization of the processes, which may dynamically interact to give rise to a schizophrenic outcome.

IDENTIFYING CANDIDATE STRESSORS IN DIATHESIS-STRESS MODELS

Since Meehl's early writings on schizotaxia (Meehl, 1962), several investigators (Crow, 1987; Mednick, Machon, & Huttunen, 1989; Murray & Lewis, 1987; Sacchetti et al., 1992; Swerdlow & Koob, 1987; Weinberger, 1987) have suggested that schizophrenia reflects some neurodevelopmental deviance that occurs early in life. In this section, we consider hypothesized mechanisms by which an early neurodevelopmental injury might occur.

Obstetrical Complications

There have been several intriguing reports of an excess of pregnancy and birth complications among schizophrenics (Goodman, 1988; McNeil & Kaij, 1978; Murray & Lewis, 1987). As a result, obstetric complications, broadly defined as any factors in the pre- or perinatal environment that raise the risk of fetal mortality (Lewis, Owen, & Murray, 1989), have been implicated as factors that increase risk for the development of manifest schizophrenia. Specifically implicated as possible potentiators of the schizophrenic diathesis are the following: prenatal factors, such as maternal age, viral infection, and gestation under 36 weeks; perinatal factors, such as multiple births, low (<6) Apgar score, and physical trauma; and neonatal factors, such as respiratory distress, convulsions, and hypoxia (Nasrallah, 1986).

Regardless of the specific manner in which obstetric complications are implicated in schizophrenia, empirical support exists for their importance. Mednick, Mura, Schulsinger, & Meednick, (1971) found that compared with the low-risk group, a disproportionate number of children at high risk for schizophrenia had a history of pregnancy and birth complications. Drawing on data from the Copenhagen High-Risk Study, Parnas et al. (1982b) observed that the offspring of schizophrenic mothers who had a higher than normal level of perinatal birth complications were the ones who later developed schizophrenia. There have been a few reports of an association between enlarged ventricles and low birth weight (see, e.g., DeLisi et al., 1986; Owen, Lewis, & Murray, 1988; Reveley, Reveley, & Murray, 1984). A retrospective examination of records of schizophrenics treated at the Maudsley Hospital between 1980 and 1984 indicated that schizophrenic patients with a history of obstetric complications were more likely than those with apparently normal births to show structural brain deficits (Owen, Lewis, & Murray, 1988). Cannon,

Mednick, and Parnas (1989) observed an interaction between the degree of genetic risk for schizophrenia and perinatal insult in terms of predicting later ventricular enlargement. As Lewis, Owen, and Murray (1989) pointed out, obstetric complications can result in cerebrovascular accidents that produce structural deficits similar to those observed in schizophrenics, namely, ventricular enlargement, widening of cortical sulci, cerebellar atrophy, and hypofrontality. Obstetric complications could also account for findings of lower interneuronal densities in the anterior cingulate and prefrontal cortex of schizophrenic brains (Benes, McSparren, Bird, San Giovanni, & Vincent, 1991).

There has been some controversy regarding whether obstetric complications have a specific etiologic role in the development of schizophrenia, or whether they are simply contributing factors that, when coupled with a genetic diathesis, heighten the individual's risk for schizophrenia. According to Gottesman, Shields, and Hanson (1982), obstetric complications are moderator variables in the development of schizophrenia, whereas they are specific etiologic factors in other disorders such as mental retardation. The authors use genetic data, such as an equal prevalence of schizophrenia in male and female monozygotic twins, as well as the observation of equal prevalences of schizophrenia in males and females, to argue that obstetric complications are more likely to increase liability.

Nonetheless, several researchers (Parnas et al., 1982b; Parnas & Mednick, 1990) concur that obstetric complications may only be pathogenic in the presence of a genetic diathesis to schizophrenia. Obstetric complications may potentiate the genetic diathesis for schizophrenia by leaving the central nervous system (CNS) of the developing organism in an immature state, rendering it more sensitive to other insults that may occur during development (Lewis, Owen, & Murray, 1989), or by leading directly to aberrant neural development (Mednick, Machon, & Huttunen, 1989). Support for the latter possibility is derived from a more recent report on the Copenhagen high-risk sample (Cannon et al., 1993) which indicated that the presence of developmental brain abnormalities, such as ventricular enlargement, could be predicted by the interaction of genetic risk and obstetric complications.

Season of Birth and Viral Agents

In addition to obstetric complications, season of birth and viral infections have been implicated as underlying pathophysiological factors in the development of schizophrenia. Since Menninger, investigators have hypothesized that an environmental factor associated with winter birth, whether dietary or infectious in nature, causes neural damage in the developing fetus or infant (Goodman, 1988; Mednick, Machon, & Huttenen, 1989; Murray & Lewis, 1987; Sacchetti et al., 1992). Individuals born during winter months may be exposed to seasonally varying factors that adversely affect the CNS, possibly increasing the risk for schizophrenia. Investigators have observed an excess of schizophrenic births in the winter months, especially in years with particularly cold winters (Hare & Moran, 1981; Kendell & Kemp, 1989; Watson, Kucala, Tilleskjor, & Jacobs, 1984).

In some populations, there appears to be an association between prenatal exposure to maternal influenza and schizophrenia.

After examining a Helsinki birth cohort consisting of those who were fetuses during the 1957 Type A influenza epidemic, Mednick et al. (1988, 1989) reported an increased rate of schizophrenia among individuals who were in their second trimester of fetal development during a severe flu epidemic. Adults who were in their second trimester of gestation during the 1957 Type A influenza epidemic in England and Wales also showed increased rates of schizophrenia (Callaghan, Sham, Takei, Glover, & Murray, 1991). Takei et al. (1994) analyzed population data from England and Wales between 1938 and 1965. Their findings supported the hypothesized association between exposure to influenza five months before birth and an increased rate of adult schizophrenia, though the association appeared to be significant only for females. The investigators suggested that the prevalence of neurodevelopmental insults other than influenza may be greater in schizophrenic males, thus rendering it more difficult to demonstrate the association between their in utero exposure to influenza epidemics and adult schizophrenia.

An attempt to replicate these findings in Dutch and Croatian birth cohorts was not successful (Erlenmeyer-Kimling et al., 1994; Susser et al., 1994). These negative results are intriguing because of the inclusion of population denominators in order to estimate risk of schizophrenia, as well as relatively complete case ascertainment. Moreover, Susser et al. (1994) did not observe an association between risk of schizophrenia and prenatal exposure to influenza even after separate analyses for males and females were conducted. Based on their negative findings, along with those of Crow, Done, and Johnstone (1991), Susser et al. (1994) hypothesized that additional mediating factors, such as prenatal nutritional deficiency, may affect the hypothesized association between prenatal exposure to influenza and risk of schizophrenia. This explanation appears plausible, especially given the observation that the second trimester is the most active period for the formation of cortical neurons, and, as Huttunlocher (1994) points out, rapidly developing structures are more sensitive to the damaging effects of stressors such as anoxia, metabolic disturbances, or malnutrition. This account for conflicting findings would be supported by data indicating that there was a greater prevalence of nutritional deficiencies in the United Kingdom than in Holland.

Early exposure to other infectious agents, such as diptheria, pneumonia, measles, and polio have also been associated with the later development of schizophrenia (Torrey, Rawlings, & Waldman, 1988; Watson et al., 1984). Other evidence indirectly supports the hypothesis that exposure to viral agents early in development may render individuals at greater risk for schizophrenia. Guy, Majorski, Wallace, and Guy (1983) observed that adult schizophrenics appear to have significantly more physical anomalies; physical anomalies and alterations in dermatoglyphics have been proposed as markers of deleterious intrauterine experiences, such as in utero viral infections (Torrey & Kaufmann, 1986).

Sacchetti et al. (1992) observed that schizophrenics born between December and April had an increased likelihood of displaying ventricular enlargement; they noted that this pattern was particularly true for patients lacking a family history of schizophrenia. These results, along with reports (i.e., Katsanis, Ficken, Iacono, & Beiser, 1992; Ohlund, Ohman, Alm, Ost, & Lindstrom, 1990) of an association between winter birth and diminished

electrodermal activity in schizophrenic patients, are consistent with the hypothesis that the seasonality of schizophrenic births may be mediated by some form of CNS damage.

Several investigators (Sacchetti et al., 1992; Suddath et al., 1990) have posited that ventricular enlargement is the result of a stressor that may either potentiate a genetic diathesis for the development of schizophrenia, or constitute a by-product of the diathesis for the disorder. Suddath's observation of ventricular enlargement in the brains of the affected cotwins of monozygotic twins discordant for schizophrenia suggests that the cause of the ventricular enlargement is extragenetic. On the basis of their observations of the association between winter births and ventricular enlargement, especially among schizophrenic patients without a family history of the illness, Sacchetti et al. (1992) proposed that winter birth was a stressor that leads to brain damage (ventricular enlargement), which, in turn, constitutes a predisposition to schizophrenia.

At present, investigators might argue that the aforementioned hypothesized mechanisms for the diathesis are overly accommodating; it is precisely because they fail to explain any of the variables in a specific way that they also cannot be refuted. Moreover, until recently, most diathesis-stress models did not consider the influence that the developmental state of the organism might have in terms of the cumulative effect of the diathesis. Because the development of schizophrenia may reflect an interaction between the timing of the etiologic factor(s) and the status of the developing organism, it is useful to identify periods in which individuals appear most vulnerable to such factors. An understanding of the notion of sensitive periods is crucial to application of such a developmental perspective to the study of schizophrenia.

THE IMPORTANCE OF TIMING: THE CONCEPT OF SENSITIVE PERIODS

Biologists, developmentalists, and psychologists agree that experiences occurring at a certain period in the life span may have a dramatic effect on the future developmental course of the organism (Bornstein, 1989). However, the notion of certain periods being critical to development has been largely replaced by the concept of sensitive periods. Sensitive periods are defined as periods in the life course of the organism that are either maximally optimal for development or maximally vulnerable to insult. Such a notion reflects the observation that all periods in the life course are important, thereby minimizing the connotations associated with the term "critical period" (Bornstein, 1989).

Sensitive periods tend to coincide with periods of rapid neural organization or reorganization; during these periods, experiences are thought to have their maximal influence. The notion of sensitive periods can be applied to the development of schizophrenia in the following manner: there are two main types of sensitive periods, one relating to the onset of the neurodevelopmental injury and another relating to the onset of manifestations of the sequelae of the neurodevelopmental injury (i.e., in most cases, the onset of the disorder).

Greenough, Black, and Wallace (1987) distinguish between experience-expectant and experience-dependent processes.

Experience-expectant neural processes are posited as mechanisms by which all members of a species incorporate common environmental information. Experience-dependent neural processes are posited as mechanisms by which each organism incorporates environmental information that is specific to its experience. According to this perspective, experience-expectant processes are more active during early stages in the life course, whereas experience-dependent processes are more active in later stages of development. Thus, experience-expectant processes are likely to have a major role during the sensitive periods relating to the onset of the neurodevelopmental injury because experience-expectant neural processes must precede experience-dependent processes. A prime example of experience-expectant processes would be the development of ocular dominance columns in mammals (Greenough et al., 1987; Purves & Lichtman, 1985). Similarly, experience-dependent processes are likely to be more involved during the sensitive periods relating to the onset of the manifestations of the disorder. In addition, the type and quality of the experience may influence how long the developing organism remains sensitive to experiential effects (Greenough et al., 1987). In the next section, sensitive periods for the occurrence of neurodevelopmental injury are discussed, along with the ways in which experience-expectant processes may influence the duration of these periods.

Sensitive Periods for the Occurrence of a Neurodevelopmental Injury

Developmental periods that have been posited as potential sensitive periods for the occurrence of a neurodevelopmental injury include the fetal, neonatal, and early childhood periods as well as adolescence. The span from fetal development to approximately 3 years of age is an important period in terms of neuroanatomic cortical changes. There is considerable evidence that in the early development of the CNS, cellular proliferation, neuronal migration, and cellular death are important processes that affect later cerebral functioning (Huttenlocher, 1994; Purves & Lichtman, 1985).

Massive neural migration occurs in the second prenatal trimester (Huttenlocher, 1994). A specific marker for environmental insult during the second prenatal trimester is fingerprint ridge count; not only do fingertip dermal cells migrate to form fingerprint ridges during this period, but finger ridge count directly correlates with second-trimester fetal size (Schaumann & Alter, 1976). Because of its status as a neurodevelopmental marker, Gottesman, Torrey, and others (Bracha, Torrey, Gottesman, Bigelow, & Cunniff, 1992) compared the finger ridge counts of 23 pairs of monozygotic twins discordant for schizophrenia with those of 7 twin pairs in which both members were normal. They observed that the discordant twin group had a significantly greater difference in total finger ridge count as well as a greater percentage of intrapair differences than the comparison group of twins. As the investigators pointed out, intrapair differences in either direction could be accounted for by some form of prenatal complication such as anoxia, maternal toxin exposure, or prenatal infection. These findings suggest that in the presence of an environmental stressor, a genetic diathesis for schizophrenia is more

likely to develop into manifest disorder. The results of Bracha et al. (1992) also buttress the assertion the second prenatal trimester is a sensitive period for the occurrence of neurodevelopmental injury.

The findings of Huttenlocher (1979) suggest that the third prenatal trimester is another likely sensitive period. Huttenlocher (1979) observed that during infancy, synaptic density was approximately 50% above the adult mean. The subsequent decline of synaptic density between the ages of 2 and 16 years is a direct result of neuronal axon retraction. Because neuronal axon retraction is greatest during the last 2 months of gestation, this time before birth is another likely sensitive period. Greenough et al. (1987) discuss the ways in which experience-expectant processes "produce a surplus of synapses which are then pruned back by experience to a functional subset" (p. 550). Almli and Finger (1987) described the process in the following manner: "Axons and dendrites differentiate and branch, interneuronal (synaptic) connections between elements are made, and the process of myelination begins. The retrogressive processes of cell death, axon retraction, and synaptic elimination appear to contribute to the functional development and fine-tuning of the developing nervous system" (p. 127). Saugstad (1989) asserted that schizophrenia may result from an early central nervous system (CNS) insult that occurs during the second trimester and the period between 1–2 years of age, when excessive synapses are eliminated.

Another sensitive period probably occurs between the ages of 7 and 12, during which most myelination is completed. Myelination has been proposed as a neurodevelopmental landmark in which the CNS is especially responsive to modification. Although it is extremely difficult to pinpoint exactly when cerebral lateralization is complete, readings (see, e.g., Witelson & Kigar, 1988) suggest that structural lateralization, as evidenced by the development of the corpus callosum, is becoming fixed between the ages of 8 and 14. There have been reports of cerebral asymmetries in schizophrenia (see, e.g., Crow, 1986; Crow, Ball et al., 1989); a neurodevelopmental injury that occurred during middle childhood to early adolescence may be implicated in the etiology of these asymmetries.

It appears that in addition to infancy and/or middle childhood, late puberty may be a sensitive period. During the final regressive event, which is thought to occur after puberty is reached, approximately 40% of neuronal synapses are eliminated (Saugstad, 1989). The experience-expectant processes posited by Greenough et al. (1987) would be expected to determine which synapses survived the regressive events. According to Saugstad's model, schizophrenia is the result of excessive elimination of synapses. Supportive evidence for this model would derive from findings that preschizophrenic children, compared with normal children, lacked certain key experiences, suggesting, as a result, that they would have fewer synapses to begin with.[1] Zubin (1989)

---

[1] Social attachment has been posited as an example of experience-expectant learning (Bowlby, 1969; Collins & Depue, 1992). De Haan, Luciana, Malone, Matheny, and Richards (1994) suggested that the consolidation of this attachment parallels the development of the prefrontal cortex. Moreover, they propose that aberrations in the psychosocial experience of attachment may affect the synaptic structure of prefrontal

also suggested that the early age of onset for schizophrenia could be accounted for by the sloughing off of supernumerary neural cells at mid-adolescence. Perhaps such a synaptic deficiency could account for Meehl's (1990) notion of hypokrisia, which he described as "an insufficiency of separation, differentiation, or discrimination" (p. 15).

The role of synaptic connections in neuronal death or survival are also taken into account in Weinberger's (1986, 1987) neurodevelopmental model of schizophrenia. His model posits the development of a lesion early in life, which involves the dorsolateral prefrontal cortex. According to this model, the early structural defect interacts with later maturational events, such as synaptic pruning and myelination. The effects of the early fixed lesion are thought to remain latent until the affected brain regions have reached maturation, typically 15–20 years later, in late adolescence or early adulthood.

Like Weinberger (1986, 1987), Benes (1989) also posits a neurodevelopmental model of schizophrenia. Benes pointed at late adolescence as a potential sensitive period, at least for the development of temporal brain regions such as the parahippocampal cortex. During the late adolescent period, there is evidence of increased myelination of neuronal inputs to the hippocampus. Aberration during the time of such changes has been implicated as causing disruptions in corticolimbic integration.

The models discussed thus far suggest that many, if not all, cases of schizophrenia are developmental in origin. Most of these models point toward fetal and/or early infancy periods as sensitive periods for the onset of the neurodevelopmental insult, because those periods are marked by numerous neuronal changes, such as cellular proliferation, migration, and retrogressive events such as synaptic elimination.

Sensitive Periods for the Manifestation of the Disorder

In the previous section, we discussed how experience-expectant processes may influence the duration of periods during which the CNS is maximally vulnerable to a neurodevelopmental injury. Similarly, experience-dependent processes can affect the development of the CNS on the basis of the type and quality of experiential input. In this section, we discuss periods during which neurodevelopmental injury is most likely to interact with potentiating factors to give rise to manifest disorder. As part of this discussion, possible experience-dependent processes are discussed in terms of the process by which risk factors interact with the developing organism to determine whether and when the disorder will be expressed.

In Weinberger's (1986, 1987) neurodevelopmental model of schizophrenia, he posits a period during which the neurodevelopmental injury remains latent. Support for Weinberger's hypothesized latent period can be derived from primate studies in which experimentally induced prenatal dorsolateral frontal lesions did not cause obvious behavioral disturbances for several years (Goldman & Galkin, 1978). Weinberger's model would also be

cortex in a similar manner because aberrant visual input can result in asymmetric synapse elimination in the visual cortex.

consistent with Greenough et al.'s (1987) hypothesis that cortical regions differ in terms of their developmental course and experiential sensitivities.

Hudspeth and Pribram (1992) observed psychophysiological findings that are consistent with neuroscientists' reports that the rate of brain maturation, as assessed by density of cortical volume and cortical neuron packing densities, is different for different areas. Hudspeth and Pribram (1992) investigated indexes of cerebral maturation in a large sample of individuals aged 1 through 21 by examining their quantitative electroencephalographic frequency spectra for cortical regions. They observed synchronous maturation across cortical regions (defined functionally as visuoauditory, visuospatial, somatic, and frontal executive) during the first 10.5 years of life, following which the maturation trajectories were independent. Although the visuoauditory, visuospatial, and somatic regions had reached their maturational peak by 14, 15, and 16 years, respectively, cortical activity in the frontal executive region did not appear to change until later. Hudspeth and Pribram (1992) observed that cortical maturation was confined to the frontal executive regions during the period spanning 17 to 21 years of age.

To date, findings consistently indicate that in humans, the prefrontal cortex is the last brain region to develop. As many investigators have noted, the maturation of the prefrontal region during adolescence coincides with the beginning of the high-risk period for the onset of schizophrenia. "Since the symptoms of schizophrenia may be linked to dysfunction of neural systems that normally reach physiological maturity in late adolescence and early adulthood, the clinical onset of the illness may be a function of this normal maturational process" (Weinberger, 1987, p. 663). Weinberger's model not only predicts that schizophrenics will show deficits in frontal functioning, but predicts that other cortical regions may be involved as well, depending on the extent of the lesion. In this way, Weinberger accounts for the clinical and biological heterogeneity often observed among schizophrenic patients.

Two periods that have been posited as potentially sensitive for the manifestation of schizophrenia are late adolescence and early adulthood. The support for this assertion is twofold: First, the onset of schizophrenia is typically associated with these periods (see, e.g., Iacono & Beiser, 1989). Second, neurochemical imbalances have been implicated in the etiology of schizophrenia; both late adolescence and early adulthood are periods in which there are massive changes in biochemistry, both at the level of brain neurotransmitters and body hormones.

Differential activity in dopamine receptors as a function of age may partly explain why schizophrenia and some of its symptoms are more likely at certain ages. Morgan, May, and Finch (1987) proposed that the generally young age of onset of schizophrenia is attributable to normative age-related declines in the nigrostriatal dopaminergic system. Evidence based on animal and clinical studies of dopamine levels indicates an age-related reduction in postsynaptic D2 dopamine receptor binding in the caudate nucleus. According to Morgan et al. (1987), the decline in dopaminergic transmission that accompanies the normative aging process can account for the declining risk of developing schizophrenia during middle age, because aberrant increases in dopaminergic activity would be less likely to exceed some hypothetical threshold for the appearance of schizophrenic symptoms.

Walker (1993) hypothesized the existence of multiple, functionally discrete neural circuits that are differentially activated as a function of maturational processes. According to this model, the reduction of florid psychotic symptoms and the increase in movement abnormalities that reportedly accompany advanced age can be accounted for by the relative activation of D1 and D2 dopaminergic receptors. According to Walker's model, the D1 receptors, which mediate a direct, excitatory pathway, decline in activation relative to the D2 receptors, which mediate the inhibitory, indirect pathway that is implicated in motor disturbances.

In addition to providing an account for sex differences in age of onset, and interindividual differences in terms of clinical manifestations, these hypothesized neurochemical imbalances are consistent with the notion of the intraindividual differences over time. The flow of information between the multiple neurotransmitter systems affects the functioning of the organism (Teychenne, Feuerstein, Lake, & Ziegler, 1985); a neurochemical imbalance may disturb interactions between neurotransmitter systems. The altered interplay between neurotransmitter systems may, in turn, impair the functioning of various target structures, resulting in primary lesions in various brain regions (Braff & Geyer, 1989). Because various brain regions develop at different rates, it is likely that the sequelae of neurochemical disturbance will be differentially manifest over time.

There are several findings of gender differences in terms of age of onset. For males, the peak incidence of schizophrenia is 5 to 10 years earlier than that observed in females (Loranger, 1984; Murray & Lewis, 1987; Riecher et al.,1990; Zubin, 1989). Studies that examine chronic patients risk confounding the estimates of sex distribution with gender differences in the course of psychotic illness, which is known to be more severe in schizophrenic men (Goldstein, 1988). First-episode schizophrenic patients are particularly well suited for the study of gender differences. In the MAP project, Iacono and Beiser (1989, 1992) observed a higher incidence of schizophrenia in males. This finding buttresses support for neurodevelopmental hypotheses of the etiology of schizophrenia. Additionally, the finding of gender differences in terms of prevalence and age of onset support our present assumption of phenotypic heterogeneity.

Gottesman, Shields, and Hanson (1982) reviewed data suggesting that the age of risk for the development of schizophrenia could extend beyond early adulthood, affecting men and women differently. A review of the literature (see Harris & Jeste, 1988; Yassa, 1991) supports the notion that some individuals may have their first experience of psychotic symptoms during middle and late adulthood. Reports also suggest that patients displaying late-onset schizophrenia, defined as incidence of schizophrenia after 40, are more likely to be female and to have sensory impairments, particularly auditory loss.

Several biological explanations have been posited to account for the sex difference in age at onset. One account for this gender difference is based on the sexes' differential age of puberty. Extremely late maturation is thought to reflect a neurodevelopmental deviation in which there is an excessive reduction of synaptic density. In general, females experience puberty at a younger age, have a lower proportion of extremely late maturers, and therefore, may have a lower risk of schizophrenia (Saugstad, 1989).

Although the age at onset of schizophrenia is not identical to the hormonal changes associated with puberty and menopause, there are some interesting parallels. An increase in hormonal levels may serve as a risk factor for males; Seeman (1985) suggests that the pubescent increase of androgens in males may lead males to engage in more aggressive and risk-taking behaviors, with greater risk of infections and physical trauma. Some investigators (such as Hafner, 1990) have suggested that male gonadal hormones have a sensitizing, possibly dopaminergic effect.

In contrast, hormonal levels are hypothesized to exert a protective effect in females (Hafner, 1990; Seeman, 1982, 1985; Torrey, 1989). Estrogens exert an antidopaminergic effect (Raymond et al., 1978; Seeman, 1982, 1985). This antidopaminergic effect has been posited to account for the typically better prognosis of female schizophrenics. Although females typically have a later age of onset than males (i.e. 5–10 years later), there is no evidence suggesting an increase in incidence of schizophrenia among females during the adulthood period immediately following menopause. One might speculate, therefore, that during the adulthood period immediately following menopause, the dopaminergic (DA) and estrogen curves are declining in parallel.

CHILDHOOD PSYCHOSES AND ADULT SCHIZOPHRENIA

Is Autism Related to Adult Schizophrenia?

If schizophrenia is an end product of an earlier developmental insult in the broadest sense, then it is feasible to explore the ways in which other forms of childhood psychopathology may be related to later adult schizophrenia. The possibility that experiences and processes at one developmental phase may modify responses at later developmental stages (Asarnow, 1988) renders it necessary and important to look at the relationship between childhood psychopathology and later risk for adult schizophrenia. There have been several case reports (e.g., Petty, Ornitz, Michelman, & Zimmerman, 1984; Watkins, Asarnow, & Tanguay, 1988) of children with infantile autism who subsequently developed schizophrenia in childhood or adolescence. Watkins et al. (1988) examined the development of psychiatric symptoms in children (n = 18) who met DSM-III criteria for childhood schizophrenia. Records of behavior, scholastic performance, and physical health were retrospectively examined and independently rated at four age ranges: 0 to 30 months; 31 months to 5 years, 11 months; 6 to 8 years, 11 months; and 9 to 11 years, 11 months. Over one-third of the children had a history of autistic symptoms, and 17% met criteria for pervasive developmental disorder prior to the onset of schizophrenia. Compared with their affected peers who had no prior history of autism, the childhood schizophrenics with a history of infantile autism had an earlier age of onset.

The possible continuity between autism and childhood schizophrenia may indicate that such early-onset childhood disorders place children at risk for the later development of schizophrenia.

However, investigators cannot conclude from studies of autistic youngsters who grew up to have some schizophrenic symptoms that childhood autism is a variant of schizophrenia. This result could be an artifact of the imprecision and overinclusiveness of the adult diagnostic criteria for schizophrenia, which were not developed with this issue in mind (although the authors of DSM-IV forbade the diagnosis of schizophrenia in autistic adults unless hallucinations or delusions are present). Gottesman, Shields, and Hanson (1982), who concluded that autism was not determined by genetic etiologic factors, also appeared skeptical about any link between autism and adult schizophrenia (see also Smalley, Asarnow, & Spence, 1988). Additional research is needed to determine whether the adult form of schizophrenia that is preceded by childhood autism is the same as that which is not preceded by such early psychopathology.

Is Childhood Schizophrenia Related to Adult Schizophrenia?

Both E. Bleuler (1911/1950) and Kraepelin (1919/1971) noted that a small percentage of their schizophrenic patients had been disordered since childhood. Since the early writings of Kraepelin and Bleuler, there have been several reports (see Asarnow, Asarnow, Hornstein, & Russell, 1991; Werry, 1992 for reviews) suggesting that cases of childhood-onset schizophrenia exist. However, there has been relatively little research conducted on childhood-onset schizophrenia.

Childhood schizophrenia has been compared with adult schizophrenia in terms of family history, phenomenology, and premorbid adjustment. On the basis of their adoption study data, Kety, Rosenthal, Wender, and Schulsinger (1968) asserted that childhood onset schizophrenia was related to adult schizophrenia. Hanson and Gottesman (1976) investigated the prevalence of schizophrenia among parents of childhood schizophrenics and found an increased prevalence of schizophrenia. These results suggest that childhood schizophrenia is genetically related to adult schizophrenia. The prevalence of schizophrenia among parents of childhood schizophrenics exceeded that of parents of adult-onset schizophrenics, a finding that is consistent with the hypothesis that childhood schizophrenia is a more severe form of adult schizophrenia. However compelling these findings are, bear in mind that they are based on samples diagnosed prior to the introduction of the narrow DSM-III (American Psychiatric Association, 1980) concept of schizophrenia.

Childhood schizophrenia as diagnosed with earlier diagnostic systems is distinctly different from the current clinical diagnosis. Former definitions of childhood schizophrenia did not differentiate among autism, childhood-onset schizophrenia, and other childhood psychotic disorders. For example, there was only one childhood psychotic category in the DSM-II (American Psychiatric Association, 1968). Data from Kolvin (1971), Rutter (1972), and others suggested that autism and childhood schizophrenia could be meaningfully distinguished. Subsequent research comparing children meeting DSM-III criteria for schizophrenia, infantile autism, or conduct disorder (Green et al., 1984) also indicated that such distinctions could be made. Since the Hanson and Gottesman (1976) analysis, there have been a few reports

(e.g., Werry, McClellan, & Chard, 1991) of an increased family history of schizophrenia in the pedigrees of children diagnosed with DSM-III schizophrenia. However, most of these studies have been criticized (Werry, 1992) for not being as methodologically rigorous as earlier studies such as the Hanson and Gottesman (1976) investigation.

Because many of the earlier studies can be criticized for their diagnostic ambiguity, we are limiting the rest of our review of the literature to studies that have been conducted since the introduction of the DSM-III system. Although investigators differ in terms of their nomenclature, we have opted, like Asarnow's group (cf. Asarnow et al., 1991), to define childhood-onset schizophrenia as cases of DSM-III or DSM-III-R schizophrenia that are diagnosed prior to age 14. Unfortunately, some studies were difficult to interpret due to their inclusion of samples with a large age variation, rendering it nearly impossible to distinguish between youths exhibiting childhood-onset schizophrenia and youths exhibiting early onset of adult-type schizophrenia. We advocate distinguishing between cases occurring prior to age 14, and those cases occurring between the ages of 14 and 18, which we will refer to as early-onset (adult) schizophrenia.

Currently, childhood-onset schizophrenia is a very infrequent disorder; population-based estimates put the frequency as low as 20 or fewer cases per 10,000 (Asarnow et al., 1991; Beitchman, 1985; Burd & Kerbeshian, 1987; Cantor, 1988). In the DSM-III, its revision, and DSM-IV, the criteria for childhood onset schizophrenia are the same as those for adult schizophrenia. Hence, modern DSM criteria require the presence of positive symptoms—hallucinations, delusions, and/or thought disorder. One implication of such a requirement is that it is extremely difficult to diagnose schizophrenia in preverbal children. Although there have been reports of cases of childhood onset schizophrenia as early as age 5 (see, e.g., Cantor, Evans, Pearce, & Pezzot-Pearce, 1982), most investigators agree that it is difficult to reliably diagnose schizophrenia in children under the age of 7 or 8 (Tanguay & Cantor, 1986).

Phenomenological Comparisons

Although there are some similarities between the clinical symptoms observed in schizophrenic children and those typically associated with adult schizophrenia (Beitchman, 1985; Caplan, Foy, Asarnow, & Sherman, 1990a; Caplan, Perdue, Tanguay, & Fish, 1990; Green et al., 1984), the content of the psychotic symptoms differs according to the developmental level and age of the patients. Caplan et al. (1990b) observed a developmental component involved in the formal thought disorder displayed by childhood schizophrenic patients. Caplan and colleagues (1990b) compared the thinking patterns and loose associations ratings in a sample of schizophrenic and schizophrenia spectrum (schizotypal personality disorder) subjects (ages 7.2–12.5 years) with that of normal children matched on sex, age, and IQ. They noted that the schizophrenic and schizotypal children displayed significantly higher ratings on the measure of illogical thinking and loose associations.

In contrast to reports that the majority of schizophrenic children display signs of thought disorder, Russell, Bott, and Sammons (1989) found that only 40% of their sample (ages 4.7 to 13.1

years) displayed signs of thought disorder. The investigators attributed this finding partly to the inherent difficulty in reliably rating a symptom whose severity requirement was not operationally defined. It is also likely that the inclusion of preschool children in the Russell et al. sample (1989) may have compounded the problem of diagnosing thought disorder.

Caplan et al. (1990b) also noted developmental differences between the younger and older children, with younger children in all three groups displaying more illogical thinking and loose associations than the older children. Similarly, Watkins, Asarnow, and Tanguay (1988) discovered that the manifestations of psychopathology displayed by schizophrenic children were age-dependent. On the basis of retrospective data, Watkins, Asarnow, and Tanguay (1988) described the symptom development of child schizophrenics, from birth through age 12 years. Watkins and colleagues reported that motor abnormalities as well as social impairment are present as early as infancy, whereas delusions and hallucinations do not emerge until approximately age 9 years.

There are several indications that the elaboration, complexity, and systematization of the child schizophrenic's delusions depends on age as well as verbal and cognitive ability. Compared with adult schizophrenics, children displaying childhood onset schizophrenia have considerably less frequent systematic delusions (McClellan & Werry, 1992). Russell et al. (1989) confirmed earlier findings indicating that the content of delusional thinking displayed by schizophrenic children varied according to age, and these researchers extended the literature by providing evidence that hallucinations also become more complex and elaborate with increasing developmental level of the children.

Other data suggest that childhood schizophrenia is a variant of adult schizophrenia. Asarnow and Ben-Meir (1988) compared depressed, dysthymic, schizophrenic, and schizotypal-personality-disordered children (ages 7–12) in terms of their premorbid adjustment, onset patterns, and severity of impairment. They concluded that the children diagnosed with either schizophrenia or schizotypal personality disorder had poorer premorbid adjustment than the mood-disordered children. Additionally, the ratings of premorbid adjustment for the schizophrenic children were poorer than those reported for adult schizophrenics. On the basis of this finding, along with the observation that early age of onset is associated with poorer premorbid adjustment in schizophrenic adults, Asarnow and Ben-Meir (1988) asserted that childhood schizophrenia may represent an early-onset form of adult-onset schizophrenia. To date, there have been no prospective longitudinal studies of childhood schizophrenia. Such studies are necessary to evaluate whether there is continuity between childhood schizophrenia and adult-onset schizophrenia.

According to the tenets of developmental psychopathology, prior adaptation, or lack thereof, places constraints on subsequent adaptation (Cicchetti, 1994). Given the possibility that early dysfunction renders the individual less equipped to achieve later developmental competencies, it is possible that individuals with early-onset schizophrenia have a more severe form of disorder than those who develop schizophrenia during the typical ages of risk, namely, ages 18 through 35. On the basis of retrospective data, Watkins et al. (1988) described the symptom development of child schizophrenics, from birth through age 12. They observed that children diagnosed with schizophrenia displayed more severe symptoms and social impairment prior to disease onset than the symptoms reported in childhood histories of schizophrenic adults. Because the Watkins et al. (1988) sample all had an onset at or prior to age 10, it is not certain that these findings would generalize to children with a later age of onset. Given the relative rarity of childhood onset schizophrenia prior to that age, these researchers may have had a different (possibly even more severely disturbed) subgroup of childhood schizophrenics. Moreover, a sizable percentage of the Watkins et al. (1988) sample had a history of infantile autism.

Some outcome studies of childhood schizophrenics suggest that the younger the age of onset, the less favorable the outcome (Beitchman, 1985). Howells and Guirguis (1984) conducted a 20-year follow-up study of patients who met diagnostic criteria for schizophrenia at or before the age of 12 years. Half of their sample had an extremely early onset (before age 30 months). On the basis of a semistructured interview, Howells and Guirguis assessed the group using two sets of criteria: Schneider's first-rank symptoms and the criteria of Feighner and colleagues. These investigators found evidence of temporal stability for measures of social impairment, language abnormalities, and level of intellectual functioning. Based on their results, it appeared that the symptoms of childhood schizophrenia remained stable throughout adulthood. Interestingly enough, the use of the different sets of diagnostic criteria for adult schizophrenia produced conflicting findings. When the investigators required the presence of Schneider's first-rank symptoms, none of the subjects with childhood schizophrenia met criteria for adult schizophrenia. In contrast, all the subjects met the Feighner et al. criteria for adult schizophrenia, though the criterion of family history was notably absent. As the authors concluded, ". . . whether or not childhood schizophrenics grow up to be adult schizophrenics does not depend on the nature of the illness as much as on the criteria used for diagnosing adult schizophrenia" (Howells & Guirguis, 1984, p. 127). The Howells and Guirguis analysis has been criticized, however, for its broad application of the Feighner et al. criteria to a group of adult autistic subjects (Tanguay & Cantor, 1986).

Although there appears to be some striking phenomenological similarities between the childhood and adult forms of schizophrenia, this may simply reflect that similar diagnostic criteria are typically used to define them (Beitchman, 1985). For example, in DSMs III, III-R, and IV, the adult criteria for schizophrenia are applied to preadolescent children because no lower age limit has been set (Perlmutter, Greenhill, Chambers, & Kestenbaum, 1989). Because the expression of symptoms seems to be mediated by the child's level of cognitive development (Watkins et al., 1988), applying adult criteria for schizophrenia to preadolescent children may be misleading and possibly obscures phenomenological differences between children and adults. Nonetheless, at present, it appears that children diagnosed with schizophrenia share similarities with adult schizophrenics that cannot be attributed simply to an artifact of how the diagnosis was made. The assertion that childhood schizophrenia may be related or similar to adult schizophrenia is consistent with some of the biobehavioral research findings on childhood onset schizophrenia.

Biobehavioral Investigations of Childhood Schizophrenia

Findings from investigations of attention and information processing in children have consistently indicated that schizophrenic children, like adults with schizophrenia, display deficits. The assessments of attention and information processing have used either a span of apprehension task or a continuous performance test. Span of apprehension involves a complex visual discrimination in which subjects are exposed to stimuli for very brief intervals, typically, 50 to 70 milliseconds. The stimuli are presented either alone or embedded in an array of irrelevant stimuli (Holzman, 1987; Rund & Landro, 1990). A continuous performance test is a rapidly paced visual vigilance task during which subjects monitor a series of randomly ordered individual stimuli and indicate each time they detect a predesignated target stimulus (Nuechterlein, 1991; Nuechterlein & Dawson, 1984; Nuechterlein, Phipps-Yonas, Driscoll, & Garmezy, 1990).

A series of studies conducted by Asarnow's group (Asarnow et al., 1991; Asarnow & Sherman, 1984; Asarnow, Sherman, & Strandburg, 1986; Caplan et al., 1990a; Strandburg et al., 1990, 1991) demonstrated that schizophrenic and schizotypal children display reduced efficiency in their information-acquisition strategies. A sample of children (mean age 12 years) who met DSM-III criteria for schizophrenia displayed significantly greater impairment on the partial-report version of a span of apprehension task when compared with a nonpatient group (Asarnow & Sherman, 1984). Caplan et al. (1990) examined the relations between aspects of formal thought disorder, span of apprehension scores, and the distractibility factor on the Weschler Intelligence Scale for Children-Revised (WISC-R; Wechsler, 1974) in a group of schizophrenic children (mean age = 10.4 ± 1.4 years). On the basis of the observed correlations, Caplan et al. (1990a) concluded that illogical thinking was related to poor performance on the span of apprehension task, whereas loose associations reflected distractibility.

An investigation conducted by Erwin, Edwards, Tanguay, Buchwald, and Letai (1986) also indicated that schizophrenic children display information-processing deficits. Erwin et al. (1986) used a more complex "oddball paradigm" that included both an unattended rare stimulus and an attended rare (target) stimulus to compare the P300 responses in a group of schizophrenic or schizotypal children (mean age = 11.5 years), age-matched normal children, and younger normal children (mean age = 7.25 years). Although both groups of normal children displayed P300 responses that were larger for rare and target stimuli than for frequent stimuli, the group of schizophrenic and schizotypal children had smaller responses to rare and target stimuli that did not differ from each other. The investigators interpreted these findings as indicating that the schizophrenic children used an inefficient information-processing strategy.

Reports (Strandburg et al., 1990) on a sample of schizophrenic children (mean age 11.2 ± 1.5 years) indicated that they not only showed worse performance on a continuous performance task, but they also showed reduced P3 amplitude to the target stimuli, relative to gender- and age-matched controls. Strandburg et al. (1991) also investigated event-related potential activity during performance on the span of apprehension task.

They observed that the schizophrenic children produced attention-related negative potentials that were significantly smaller than those produced by an age-matched control group.

Early-Onset Schizophrenia

There has been interest in assessing the performance of individuals diagnosed with early-onset schizophrenia on biobehavioral variables that differentiate adult schizophrenics from control subjects. Research findings on adolescent (aged 14 through 18) samples suggest that early-onset schizophrenia is similar to adult onset schizophrenia. A CT scanning investigation of teenage patients (mean age of 16.5 ± 1.5) with schizophrenia or a schizophrenia spectrum disorder indicated that these patients displayed significantly enlarged ventricles relative to controls and other nonschizophrenic psychiatric patients (Schulz et al., 1983). The ventricle-to-brain ratios of these young schizophrenic patients were also noted to be comparable to that of adult schizophrenics.

Jenkins (1989) assessed the smooth pursuit eye movements produced by a sample of psychotic adolescents (mean age 14, range, 11–18 years). When compared with a group of age-matched normal controls, the smooth pursuit eye tracking of the psychotic patients did not appear significantly different. We assert that the lack of significant differences between the pursuit tracking of psychotic children and that of nonpatient controls may be attributable to the sample's inclusion of prepubescent youths as well as those in their early adolescence, and that the physiological systems subserving pursuit eye movements may not have reached maturity in the control group. This assertion is strengthened by the results of a comparison of pursuit performance in normal preadolescent (11-year-old) and adolescent (17-year-old) males (Ficken & Iacono, 1991). Ficken and Iacono (1991) observed that deviant smooth pursuit eye movements were relatively common in the 11-year-olds, though not in the 17-year-olds. Ficken and Iacono attributed these differential findings to the likelihood that, at age 11, the pursuit system is underdeveloped, whereas by age 17, it appears to have matured. Such an explanatory account is also consistent with the Levin (1984) hypothesis that pursuit eye movements are mediated in part by the frontal cortex; the frontal lobes reach maturity during late adolescence (Weinberger, 1986, 1987). There is a need for further investigation of biobehavioral variables in both nonpatient samples of children (to determine normative development) as well as in children diagnosed as schizophrenic.

Etiology of Childhood-Onset and Early-Onset Schizophrenia

Earlier in this chapter, we discussed ways in which the developmental psychopathology perspective can account for variable age of onset, as well as a gender difference in age of onset, among adult schizophrenic patients. More specifically, we discussed neurodevelopmental hypotheses posited to account for the diagnosis of schizophrenia after the typical ages of risk—18 to 35 years. We then turned our attention to cases that are diagnosed before the typical ages of risk, reviewed phenomenological and biobehavioral investigations of childhood schizophrenia, and summarized the biobehavioral research on early-onset schizophrenia. Due to the scarcity of relevant data, we advise caution regarding claims of continuity between childhood and adult types of schizophrenia. In contrast, we tentatively conclude that early-onset schizophrenia is likely to be a variant of adult schizophrenia.

If childhood-onset and/or early-onset schizophrenia are variant forms of adult schizophrenia, then etiologic models of schizophrenia must account for onset of the disorder both before and after the typical risk period. Unfortunately, the research literature on schizophrenia expressed early in life is such that it is difficult to determine how well the existing etiologic models for adult schizophrenia mesh with childhood-onset data. The most widely held adult models posit a genetic vulnerability for schizophrenia. Determining the applicability of these models to children requires examination of pedigrees of probands diagnosed with childhood schizophrenia to see if there is a genetic relationship to adult schizophrenia. More of this type of research is needed.

One hypothesis posited to account for the genetic relationship between early-onset schizophrenia and adult schizophrenia involves the notion of an unusual pattern of inheritance called genetic anticipation. Observations of genetically determined neurological disorders such as Huntington's disease have indicated that the earlier the onset of the disorder, the more severe the course (Currier, Jackson, & Meydrech, 1982). In a recent paper, Ross, McInnis, Margolis, and Li (1993) reviewed data suggesting that the genetic basis for several disorders, including Huntington's disease and fragile X syndrome, is the expansion of a trinucleotide (triplet) repeat in a gene. The presence of novel genes with triplet repeats leads to the pattern of inheritance called genetic anticipation, whereby the severity of the disorder increases and the age of onset decreases in successive generations of a pedigree (Ross et al., 1993). Ross and colleagues report that in the case of Huntington's disease, there appears to be a high correlation between the length of a repeating DNA triplet region and age of onset. Moreover, a gender difference was observed in which affected offspring of affected fathers are more likely to exhibit this pattern of genetic anticipation (i.e., have an age of onset several years earlier than their fathers) than affected offspring of affected mothers.

Ross and colleagues (1993) suggest that genes with triplet repeats may also be the cause of psychiatric disorders such as schizophrenia; it is plausible to speculate that such a pattern of transmission could also account for the disproportionate number of affected males among those patients diagnosed with early-onset schizophrenia. Pedigree analysis of patients diagnosed with early-onset schizophrenia are necessary to test the hypothesis that genetic anticipation can account for such forms of schizophrenia. For such a hypothesis to be supported, it would be necessary to demonstrate that not only does the age of onset decrease but the severity of the disease increases; that is, the affected member with early-onset schizophrenia would be expected to be the most severely affected individual among all the affected family members. To date, there has been one report (Bassett & Honer, 1994) of genetic anticipation in schizophrenia. Unfortunately, however, the researchers excluded any subjects under the age of 15 years in their index group, rendering it difficult to explore hypotheses regarding early-onset schizophrenia.

Childhood- and Early-Onset Schizophrenia as Potential Leads for the Study of Adult Schizophrenia

A developmental approach to the etiology of childhood-onset schizophrenia and early-onset schizophrenia may enable us to identify processes that are specific to the form(s) of schizophrenia that occur prior to the typical risk period. To date, empirical investigations of childhood schizophrenia have yielded limited information because of reliance on diagnostic nomenclature that is too broad, a paucity of phenomenological descriptions of childhood schizophrenia, and the use of adult diagnostic criteria of uncertain validity for diagnosing children across a wide age span. These methodological shortcomings, along with the relatively low incidence of the disorder, have made it difficult to empirically study either childhood- or early-onset schizophrenia. Further research should employ diagnostic criteria that allow adequate definition and age-appropriate specificity for studying meaningful groups of child schizophrenics.

Published reports suggest that children diagnosed as having schizophrenia or a schizophrenia spectrum disorder show the following anomalies: enlarged ventricle-to-brain ratio (VBR), poor performance on tests of attention and information processing, and aberrant cortical responses. In contrast to other investigations of psychophysiological performance in children diagnosed as schizophrenic, eye-tracking studies do not indicate that psychotic youths can be distinguished from their normal peers. Significant differences between the pursuit eye tracking of psychotic children and that of nonpatient controls may be lacking because the physiological systems subserving ocular motor functioning do not fully mature until mid-to-late adolescence. Because extant data suggest that normal children produce aberrant pursuit performance, smooth pursuit tracking performance is not likely to be an informative variable when applied to children.

As Gottesman and Goldsmith (1994) assert, "The genetics of explicitly developmental aspects of behavior, such as age of onset and course of disorders is seldom investigated" (p. 98). There is a need to examine the developmental course of youths diagnosed with childhood schizophrenia, early-onset schizophrenia, and/or other forms of childhood psychopathology to determine whether they are at increased risk for the later development of adult schizophrenia. The unusual pattern of transmission referred to as genetic anticipation is compatible with several of the extant etiologic models of schizophrenia and could also account for early-onset schizophrenia. Testing such a hypothesis requires pedigree studies of individuals diagnosed with early-onset schizophrenia. It is also imperative that researchers investigate whether individuals diagnosed with early-onset schizophrenia appear to have a poorer course and prognosis than those individuals diagnosed with adult schizophrenia.

The prospective, longitudinal study of patients diagnosed with schizophrenia during childhood is interesting and valuable in terms of its potential to inform us about the continuities and discontinuities of psychopathology over the life span. However, such studies may be of limited usefulness in identifying developmental precursors of adult schizophrenia because expression of the variables in question may have been altered by the childhood disorder. Moreover, most adult schizophrenics have no history of childhood clinical disorder (Walker, 1991).

HIGH-RISK STUDIES AS A MEANS OF IDENTIFYING DEVELOPMENTAL PRECURSORS

A developmental framework permits us to identify deficits that may precede overt clinical symptoms of adult schizophrenia. Applying a developmental life-span approach to the study of schizophrenia entails determining whether there are any early behavioral precursors of schizophrenia. The possibility that the constitutional predisposition gives rise to signs of dysfunction several years prior to any overt manifestation of the disease process has provided the impetus for longitudinal high-risk studies of schizophrenia.

Implicit in our discussion of potential sensitive periods both for the onset of a neuropathological process and for the manifestation of illness is the assumption that these two periods do not necessarily overlap in time. Research on neurodevelopment suggests that the behavioral sequelae of a neuropathological process may not become manifest until the organism has reached a sufficient level of maturity; in some cases, this may be decades later. Applying a developmental perspective to the study of schizophrenia permits us to determine when, in the life course, signs of psychopathology are first manifest. "Because the emergence of clinical symptoms probably does not mark the onset of the neuropathological process, documenting the developmental trajectories leading to schizophrenia takes on greater importance" (Walker, 1991, p. 2).

One strategy used to examine the developmental precursors of adult schizophrenia is the longitudinal prospective assessment of individuals believed to be at increased risk for developing the disorder. The aim of such a study is to determine the precursors of the disorder without the confounds of either the consequences of the illness itself or the interventions employed in the treatment of the illness. There are several strategies for identifying groups thought to be at heightened risk for schizophrenia, including the genetic and biobehavioral high-risk methods. These strategies differ in their selection criteria for the identification of at-risk subjects.

Defining Risk

In the genetic high-risk approach, first proposed by Pearson and Kley (1957), risk is determined by the individual's genetic relatedness to an affected proband. Individuals with a higher than normal genetic loading for schizophrenia, by virtue of having at least one affected first-degree relative (usually a parent), are identified and studied longitudinally. Individuals with one schizophrenic parent have a slightly greater than 10% chance of developing the disorder, whereas individuals with two affected parents have a risk greater than 40% (Gottesman, 1991; Nicol & Gottesman, 1983). Hence, selecting offspring of schizophrenic parents is one way to obtain a sample of at-risk persons. This design involves

determining whether a given measure, assessed at one time point, predicts later manifestation of schizophrenia and related disorders. The identification of developmental precursors of schizophrenia entails the hope that characteristics assessed early in life can be used to differentiate offspring who develop psychopathology from those who do not.

The biobehavioral high-risk strategy involves studying nonschizophrenic individuals believed to be at high risk for schizophrenia because they show the same deviations on biobehavioral measures that schizophrenic individuals do. These measures may be derived from psychophysiological variables, indexes of brain morphology, cognitive performance, neuropsychological function, and scores on psychometric instruments assessing characteristics evident in schizophrenics.

Iacono (1985) defined a vulnerability marker as any symptom, trait, or performance characteristic that identifies an individual's risk for the eventual manifestation of the disorder. Of special interest here is his notion of vulnerability markers that identify the genetic predisposition for the disorder. Indicators of the genetic diathesis for schizophrenia would be expected to have a relatively low base rate in the general population, have a heritable component, and show temporal stability. This traitlike characteristic must precede the onset of the disorder in affected persons, be present in affected individuals during symptom remission as well as symptom exacerbation, and segregate with the illness in affected relatives. Such a vulnerability indicator would be expected to be present in a higher rate among first-degree relatives of affected persons compared with the general population. Several biobehavioral variables have been posited as potential markers of liability for schizophrenia, including deviant performance on measures of attention and information processing, smooth pursuit tracking, electrodermal responsivity, and ventricular-to-brain ratio (Holzman, 1987; Iacono, 1985; Iacono & Ficken, 1989). These candidate markers have been employed in several investigations of the developmental precursors of schizophrenia. Studying individuals who possess markers associated with heightened risk of schizophrenia, but yet do not develop the disorder, can yield much information regarding the contingencies that influence the manifestation of a schizophrenic diathesis.

Many of the genetic high-risk projects included measures of smooth pursuit eye tracking, electrodermal responsivity, and attention and information processing in their assessment batteries. The underlying rationale for the inclusion of these specific biobehavioral variables in high-risk offspring was twofold: (a) these variables have been found repeatedly to differentiate schizophrenic samples from control samples, and (b) these variables have been posited as potential biological markers of liability for schizophrenia.

The Genetic High-Risk Strategy

Because schizophrenia has a relatively low population base rate (about 1%), the task of identifying vulnerability markers or deficits that may precede overt symptoms of schizophrenia is made all the more difficult. Systematic examination of the young offspring of schizophrenics increases the probability of obtaining a preschizophrenic subsample, thereby offering a parsimonious method in which to study vulnerability indicators as well as possible deficits that precede the onset of schizophrenia. In addition, these high-risk studies permit the opportunity to observe the developmental course of schizophrenia (Winters, Cornblatt, & Erlenmeyer-Kimling, 1991). The genetic high-risk research strategy has been employed by several research groups (see Asarnow, 1988; Garmezy, 1974; Garmezy & Streitman, 1974; and Walker & Aylward, 1984, for excellent summaries of high-risk research).

One of the first studies to embody the genetic high-risk approach was initiated by Mednick, Schulsinger, and their colleagues. The Copenhagen High-Risk Study began in 1962, with 207 offspring of schizophrenic mothers and 104 comparison offspring with psychiatrically normal mothers. At the time of intake, the study subjects ranged in age from 10 to 19 years (mean age, 15.1 years) and none were psychiatrically ill. A 10-year follow-up assessment included 173 high-risk and 91 low-risk subjects (Schulsinger, 1976). The sample was assessed again 18 years after the initial investigation, with diagnoses made according to DSM-III criteria. One strength of this study is that although maternal diagnoses were initially made prior to DSM-II, they have been subsequently confirmed using DSM-III criteria.

Another intriguing aspect of the Copenhagen High-Risk Project involves the subsequent determination of paternity and diagnostic study of the high-risk subjects' biological fathers (see Parnas et al., 1993). This further inquiry permitted the investigators to classify their sample into three subgroups: those at very high risk ("super high-risk"), by virtue of being the offspring of two parents with schizophrenia-spectrum diagnoses; high-risk subjects who had one parent with a schizophrenia-spectrum diagnosis; and low-risk subjects, both of whose parents were free of psychiatric illness. Hence, this study has been strengthened by the knowledge of which individuals are the product of dual-matings.

A second study of particular note is the New York High-Risk Project of Erlenmeyer-Kimling and associates (Erlenmeyer-Kimling & Cornblatt, 1987a, 1987b). In the New York High-Risk Project, investigators followed two independent samples of three groups of children: those with at least one schizophrenic parent; those with one or two parents with major affective disorder; and those with two psychiatrically normal parents. The inclusion of an at-risk comparison group, consisting of offspring of other psychiatric patients is a particular strength of this study. Comparisons with offspring of other psychiatrically disturbed individuals are especially useful, in that such research can assist us in identifying behavioral precursors specifically associated with the development of schizophrenia, rather than psychiatric outcome in general.

At the time of entry into the New York High-Risk Project, the children ranged in age from 7 to 12. Sample A was first tested between 1971 and 1972, whereas Sample B was first tested between 1977 and 1979. By including two independent samples that represent different birth cohorts, this study makes it possible to disentangle two different aspects of developmental change, namely, age and time. The two samples also endow the project with a built-in mechanism for checking the replicability of findings.

This is important in high-risk research because it is still not certain which variables are most likely to be predictive and because the large number of variables typically employed increases the likelihood of making a Type II error.

Thus far, the New York-High Risk Study is one of a select number of projects (Erlenmeyer-Kimling & Cornblatt, 1987a; Fish, 1987; Marcus et al., 1987; Mirsky, 1988; Parnas et al., 1993) that have followed high-risk samples into early adulthood. Nonetheless, the findings from studies in which high-risk samples have not yet reached the age of major risk have been valuable by suggesting ways in which offspring of schizophrenics differ from normal controls and offspring of affectively disordered individuals. Following our developmental life-span approach, our review and analysis of studies using the genetic high-risk strategy are organized by developmental periods: infancy (ages birth to 2 years) and early childhood (2 to 5), middle childhood (6 to 11), puberty and adolescence (12 to 18), young adulthood (19 to 30), and middle adulthood (31 to 55). Our review concludes with an integrative overview spanning these developmental periods and a critique of this approach to investigating schizophrenia's development.

Infancy

Fish (1977) studied 12 infants of schizophrenic mothers along with a comparison group matched for socioeconomic background. Fish reported that infants with elevated genetic risk for schizophrenia showed signs of underactivity, hypotonia, and an overall abnormally quiet state; she termed this pattern of behavior "pandevelopmental retardation." This early finding has been the impetus for other investigations of the activity level and motor development of offspring of schizophrenic probands. A report from the Jerusalem Infant Development Study (Marcus, Auerbach, Wilkinson, & Burack, 1981) revealed that almost one-fourth of infants born to schizophrenics (13 of 58) displayed poor motor and sensorimotor performance during their first days and throughout their first year of life.

Early Childhood

Retrospective data from the Copenhagen High-Risk Study has indicated that individuals who later became schizophrenic were characterized by passivity, low energy, and shortened attention span during early childhood (Parnas et al., 1982a; Parnas & Mednick, 1990). As part of a larger prospective study of child development, Hanson, Gottesman, and Heston (1976) examined the obstetric and follow-up records of schizophrenic mothers, spouses of schizophrenic fathers, and their offspring. They observed that at age 4 years, children of schizophrenic patients showed abnormalities in both gross and fine motor performance.

Middle Childhood

Results from the Israeli High-Risk Study (Mirsky, 1988; Mirsky et al., 1986) indicate that the at-risk children differed from the control sample during middle childhood. The at-risk sample displayed deficient discrimination between meaningful and neutral stimuli on a continuous performance task. High-risk cases displayed significant impairment on a number of other attention-related skills as well, such as digit span, letter cancellation, and the Wisconsin Card Sorting Test (Mirsky,

1988). In fact, the attentional deficits displayed at that time (mean age 11) were good predictors of which genetically vulnerable subjects would be diagnosed with schizophrenia or a schizophrenia spectrum disorder by the time of adult follow-up, when they were between 26 and 32 years old (Mirsky, 1988; Mirsky et al., 1986).

Findings from the New York High-Risk Project (Erlenmeyer-Kimling & Cornblatt, 1984) indicate that during middle childhood, the offspring of schizophrenics showed delayed neuromotor development as well as impairments in fine motor coordination. However, subsequent analyses (Erlenmeyer-Kimling & Cornblatt, 1987a, 1987b) indicated that neuromotor deviance in high-risk children at school age proved neither specific to nor predictive of psychiatric adjustment in young adulthood.

In Sample A of the New York High-Risk Project (Cornblatt, Winters, & Erlenmeyer-Kimling, 1989), the offspring of schizophrenics were the only subjects who displayed attentional deficits across all three waves of testing (a period spanning 7 years). In fact, nearly 25% of the schizophrenia high-risk group showed attentional deficits, as measured by a battery that included the Continuous Performance Task,[2] Digit Span subtest of the Wechsler Intelligence Scale for Children (WISC; Wechsler, 1974), and an attention span task. These results were replicated in the second sample (Winters, Cornblatt, & Erlenmeyer-Kimling, 1991), in which a subgroup of high-risk children displayed attentional deficits, as measured by the Continuous Performance Test at the first round of testing (mean age = 9 years) and at subsequent data collection waves. This finding suggests that among some offspring of schizophrenic parents, attentional dysfunction is a temporally stable trait.

Other studies using the genetic high-risk method have also indicated an association between the display of attentional deficits and the presence of a schizophrenic diathesis. Investigators from the Stony Brook High-Risk Project (Winters, Stone, Weintraub, & Neale, 1981) assessed the ability of children to sustain attention in a visual search task. Compared with the offspring of normal controls, the at-risk children were less efficient at detecting a designated target letter among an array of high-similarity irrelevant letters.

As part of Garmezy's Minnesota High-Risk Research Project, Nuechterlein, Garmezy, and Devine (1989) assessed the following subgroups on the Continuous Performance Test: children of schizophrenic mothers, hyperactive children, children of nonpsychotic, psychiatrically disordered mothers, and children of normal controls. In contrast to the other children, the offspring of schizophrenics displayed significantly poorer levels of perceptual sensitivity and lower attentional functioning on the more cognitively demanding task conditions. This finding is particularly interesting in light of a review of the literature by Nuechterlein and Dawson (1984) that suggests complex versions of the Continuous Performance Test (i.e., those involving relatively heavy processing loads) are needed to affect performance in adult schizophrenic patients.

There have been several investigations of electrodermal activity in high-risk children during middle childhood. Janes, Hesselbrock, and Stern (1978) examined the electrodermal responsivity in children (mean age = 9.5 years) of schizophrenic, manic-depressive, physically ill, and normal parents. The groups, matched according to age, sex, and race, were not observed to differ on any of the indexes of electrodermal activity. Similarly, Kugelmass, Marcus, and Schmueli (1985) and Prentky, Salzman, and Klein (1981) reported no difference in skin conductance response between their at-risk and comparison samples. A comparison of the offspring of schizophrenic, depressed, and normal parents in terms of their half-amplitude recovery of electrodermal responses yielded no significant group differences (Erlenmeyer-Kimling, Friedman, Cornblatt, & Jacobsen, 1985).

Investigators in the University of Rochester Child and Family Study (Wynne, Cole, & Perkins, 1987) did not detect any significant differences in eye-tracking performance between the offspring of schizophrenics and the offspring of normal controls, all of whom were tested at ages 7, 10, and 13. The failure to detect any significant differences in the tracking performance of these children may reflect that the smooth pursuit eye-tracking variable is not age appropriate.

Puberty and Adolescence

Mednick and Schulsinger (1968) measured the electrodermal activity in offspring of schizophrenic mothers (mean age = 15) and compared their pattern of response to that displayed by age-matched children of controls. The at-risk group showed greater response amplitudes and faster response recovery. A subgroup of the at-risk sample who appeared deviant in terms of their electrodermal response patterns during adolescence were the individuals who showed signs of psychopathology at the time of the 5-year follow-up.

Subsequent analysis of the Copenhagen data (Hollister, Mednick, Brennan, & Cannon, 1994) revealed an association between spontaneous fluctuations in electrodermal activity and increasing level of genetic risk for schizophrenia. Subjects in their "super high-risk" group (i.e., schizophrenia in the mother and schizophrenia spectrum disorder in the father) showed no habituation in their spontaneous fluctuation rate, whereas subjects in the high-risk group (one affected parent) showed some habituation and those in the low-risk group (neither parent affected) displayed a prominent decline in spontaneous activity over time. In addition, these investigators found that at-risk subjects who became schizophrenic in adulthood displayed the habituation anomaly as children. Hence, the Copenhagen High-Risk Study has shown that deviations in electrodermal activity could be detected during adolescence, before any overt behavioral symptoms of psychopathology, and that they tended to predict adult schizophrenia.

Other investigators have attempted to determine whether individuals at heightened risk for schizophrenia differed from normal controls in terms of their cognitive processing. In the New York High-Risk Study (Friedman, Cornblatt, Vaughan, & Erlenmeyer-Kimling, 1986), the individuals at risk did not differ from the psychiatric comparison or control subjects in terms of their P300 response latency to visual stimuli, nor did they

---

[2] The Continuous Performance Test (CPT) is not a unitary measure, but rather, it is a family of stimulus-discrimination measures (see Cornblatt & Keilp, 1994, and Nuechterlein, 1991).

display evidence of P300 amplitude reduction. There are several possible explanations for these negative findings. The failure to detect significant group differences may be attributable to efforts to measure event related potentials in the visual modality. The results of Duncan, Morihisa, Fawcett, and Kirch (1987) suggested that the trait or state status of reduced P300 amplitude may be modality specific, with the evoked responses to visual stimuli being dependent upon clinical state. It would be imprudent to expect at-risk individuals who do not yet manifest behavioral disturbance to exhibit attenuated P300 amplitude if this phenomenon were elicited in the visual modality.

Due to this reasoning, along with indications that reduced P300 amplitude to auditory stimuli reflects a trait indicator, Friedman, Cornblatt, Vaughan, and Erlenmeyer-Kimling (1988) measured cortical activity in response to auditory stimuli. They found no group differences in the amplitude of evoked responses. Moreover, they failed to observe any association between attentional deviance, as measured in an earlier test wave, and P300 amplitude.

An alternative explanation for the failure of the high-risk subjects to display attenuated P300 amplitude similar to that observed in adult schizophrenics is that, due to developmental differences, the measure is not suitable for studies of individuals who have not yet completed adolescence. This explanation seems less tenable given the positive findings (Asarnow & Sherman, 1984; Strandburg et al., 1990) of information processing deficits in children with early-onset schizophrenia.

To date, there have been two reports indicating that high-risk adolescents display attention and information processing deficits as measured by event-related potentials. Schreiber, Stolz, Rothmann, Kohnhuber, and Born (1989) reported that twelve at-risk offspring, ages 9 to 16, displayed slowed target classification (as defined by P300 latency) in comparison to control children who were matched for age, sex, and socioeconomic status. Schreiber and colleagues (1991) replicated their finding using an independent group of high-risk offspring, ages 7 to 17. Based on their positive findings, they suggested that prolonged P300 latency may serve as an indicator of vulnerability to schizophrenia. It is interesting to note that although the high-risk subjects showed reduced mean peak amplitude of the P300 component, due to considerable variability between subjects, no significant group differences were found.

It is difficult to reconcile the seemingly discrepant findings of Schreiber's group and the New York investigators. The New York high-risk sample is considerably larger than the samples used in the Schreiber investigations, though the latter sample included a higher percentage of offspring of dual matings. Moreover, although both tasks presented the stimuli in the auditory modality, it is unclear how comparable the tasks are in terms of their level of difficulty.

The failure to detect significant group differences in the New York High-Risk Study (Friedman et al., 1986, 1988) may be attributable to the use of a task that had a relatively low processing demand load. Further investigation, using a cognitive task with a high processing load, is warranted to determine whether high-risk subjects display deviant event-related potentials during adolescence.

The lack of a psychiatric comparison group in the Schreiber studies also leaves unclear whether prolonged P300 latency is an indicator of vulnerability to psychiatric disorder in general or a specific indicator of risk for schizophrenia. The issue of specificity is particularly salient, given the recent findings of Squires-Wheeler, Friedman, Skodol, and Erlenmeyer-Kimling (1993). Squires-Wheeler et al. (1993) examined the relationship between evoked responses at age 15 and clinical outcome approximately 10 years later. Reductions in P300 were associated with poor global personality functioning in each of the three groups studied (the high-risk, psychiatric comparison, and normal control). This finding suggests that event-related potential abnormalities in adolescence may serve as a nonspecific predictor of later psychiatric dysfunction.

Mather (1985) reported that the offspring of schizophrenic parents (mean age, 17, range, 12–19) revealed significantly poorer oculomotor performance than the offspring of normal controls. These results, when considered with other findings of aberrant oculomotion in first-degree relatives of schizophrenics (Clementz & Sweeney, 1990; Holzman, 1987; Iacono, Moreau, Beiser, & Lin, 1992), suggest that abnormal eye tracking in some at-risk offspring may be a possible precursor of subsequent psychiatric disturbance. For eye-tracking dysfunction to serve as a vulnerability indicator of a schizophrenic diathesis in adolescence, the proportion of adolescents with abnormal tracking performance would have to be higher among offspring of schizophrenics (the high-risk subjects) than among the offspring of normal controls and offspring of parents with nonschizophrenic psychiatric disturbance.

A subgroup (15 of 80) of high-risk offspring in the New York High Risk Project (Erlenmeyer-Kimling et al., 1987a) were identified on the basis of their performance on a battery of attentional measures. Cornblatt and Erlenmeyer-Kimling (1989) reported that this subgroup, who had shown signs of global attentional deviance during childhood, were displaying signs of clinical deviance and/or were diagnosed with schizophrenia or schizophrenia-spectrum disorders by the mean age of 17.5 years.

Young Adulthood

Thus far, Fish's (1977) New York sample is the only high-risk sample that has been followed from infancy into adulthood. Fish (1984) observed that 75% of the high-risk offspring who had demonstrated abnormal passivity during infancy were later diagnosed as displaying schizophrenia spectrum disorders.

Hanson, Gottesman, and Heston (1990) followed their high-risk sample into young adulthood. When the children were 7 years old, they identified a subset of high-risk offspring as being at especially heightened risk for schizophrenia by virtue of displaying poor motor performance, behavioral problems, and large intraindividual differences on a psychological test battery. However, among the subset of children (80%) who were followed up into young adulthood, none of them have been diagnosed with either schizophrenia or schizophrenia-spectrum disorder.

The offspring in the New York High-Risk Project have also been followed into young adulthood. By young adulthood (ages 22–29), 22% (12 of 55) of the high-risk and 11% (4 of 38) of the psychiatric comparison group had been hospitalized for psychiatric treatment (Erlenmeyer-Kimling, Rock, Squires-Wheeler, Roberts, & Yang, 1991). Another 38% (21 of 55) of high-risk subjects had received some form of psychiatric treatment short of hospitalization compared with 29% (11 of 38) of the psychiatric comparison group. Erlenmeyer-Kimling's group (Erlenmeyer-Kimling et al., 1991) applied path analysis to their data from Sample A and observed that having a schizophrenic parent was a robust and direct predictor of psychiatric illness and/or hospitalization in adulthood. However, as noted before, only a subset of the at-risk offspring of schizophrenic parents displayed psychiatric dysfunction.

Erlenmeyer-Kimling, Golden, and Cornblatt (1989) applied a taxometric model to the childhood data from the New York High Risk Project. The indicator variables they used included response indexes from the Continuous Performance Test, as well as scores of motor impairment, visuomotor development, and intellectual functioning. Most (73%) of the subsample identified as taxon members were from the high-risk group; 47% of the offspring of schizophrenic parents (compared with 13% of the other children) were classified as being at exceptionally high risk for developing schizophrenia or a schizophrenia spectrum disorder. Erlenmeyer-Kimling and her associates (1989) found that taxon membership was a good predictor of psychiatric hospitalization in young adulthood. In terms of predictive value, the taxometric method had higher sensitivity but less specificity than the attention-deviance method that had previously been applied to the data.

Findings from the Copenhagen High-Risk study sample (Parnas, Cannon, Jacobsen, Schulsinger, Schulsinger, & Mednick, 1993) demonstrated directly that the offspring of a schizophrenic parent were at heightened risk for schizophrenia and/or schizophrenia spectrum disorders in adulthood. The results of this follow-up study of the offspring of schizophrenic mothers and their matched controls indicated that at-risk individuals had a significantly higher lifetime prevalence of DSM-III-R schizophrenia and schizophrenia spectrum disorders. The high-risk group did not show evidence of an increased prevalence of mood disorders, an observation that strengthens the hypothesized specificity of the genetic diathesis.

Although most of the studies using the genetic high-risk strategy have focused on the offspring of affected probands, there have been a few investigations (Maier, Franke, Hain, Koop, & Rist, 1992; Saitoh et al., 1984; Weinberger, De Lisi, Neophytides, & Wyatt, 1981) of the siblings of schizophrenic patients. Weinberger and his associates (1981) assessed the VBR of nonschizophrenic adults (mean age 26.1, range 19–41). The siblings of the schizophrenic patients were observed to display significantly larger ventricles than the controls. Within the sibship pairs that included a schizophrenic proband, the patients had larger ventricle-to-brain ratios than their unaffected siblings.

In another sibling study, Saitoh, Niwa, Hkiramatsu, Kameyama, Rymar, and Itoh (1984) observed that at-risk subjects (mean age 28.5) showed significantly smaller P3 amplitudes to target stimuli, compared with age-matched controls. Additionally, the at-risk subjects displayed patterns of response similar to those of their affected siblings, namely, a failure to produce augmentation of P3 amplitude in response to the detection of target stimuli.

Maier's group (1992) selected siblings of schizophrenic patients who had not yet passed "the period of risk," which they operationally defined as ending at age 30. The at-risk sample, who had a mean age of 26 years, were administered a battery of attention and information-processing tasks. The high-risk group members reportedly performed similarly to their affected siblings on the more difficult versions of the CPT and span of apprehension tasks. These findings provide further support for the oft-cited assertion that attention and information-processing deficits are markers of vulnerability to schizophrenia.

Middle Adulthood

F. Schulsinger et al. (1984) reassessed at-risk offspring from the Copenhagen High-Risk Project at the mean age of 33. They compared lateral ventricular size among the high-risk offspring, who were diagnosed as schizophrenic, schizophrenic spectrum, or mentally healthy. The investigators found that the at-risk subjects who had developed schizophrenia had greater ventricular enlargement than the other two groups. They also noted that the at-risk subjects who had not received any psychiatric diagnosis displayed ventricular size that was intermediate relative to the two pathological groups.

Suddath et al. (1990) compared the MRI scans of monozygotic (MZ) twins who were discordant for schizophrenia. In 80% of the MZ pairs discordant for schizophrenia, the affected twin could be identified by visual inspection of the MRI scan alone. Compared with their unaffected cotwins, the schizophrenic twins showed subtle enlargement of the lateral and third ventricles. Significant differences between the MZ twins discordant for schizophrenia were also observed in the volume of the anterior hippocampal region and in the grey matter volume of the left temporal lobe. Among the psychiatrically healthy MZ twin pairs who were studied as controls, no differences in cerebral anatomy were observed. The Copenhagen sample was reassessed when their average age was 42 (Cannon et al., 1993). In addition to psychiatric interviews, computerized tomography (CT) scans were obtained. The risk status of the offspring was classified according to whether neither ("low-risk"), one ("high-risk"), or both ("super high-risk") of the parents had received a schizophrenia-spectrum diagnosis. The at-risk subjects displayed a pattern of ventricular enlargement that increased with increasing level of genetic risk for schizophrenia. Considered together, the results of the within-pair comparison of siblings (Weinberger et al., 1981), the within-group comparison of high-risk subjects (Schulsinger et al., 1984) the within-pair comparison of MZ twins discordant for schizophrenia (Suddath et al., 1990), and the between-group comparison of subjects at varying genetic risks for schizophrenia (Cannon et al., 1993), provide further support for the hypothesis that neurological insult, manifested as ventricular enlargement, may be a stressor that contributes to decompensation and ultimately manifest schizophrenia in at-risk individuals.

A Life-Span Overview

In the preceding section, we examined the extent to which it is possible to detect the presence of a schizophrenia diathesis before the appearance of manifest schizophrenia in adulthood. The genetic high-risk strategy has proven to be an important source of information regarding developmental precursors of adult schizophrenia. The results of these studies, though far from conclusive, suggest that the predisposition for schizophrenia may be detectable at an early age.

One consistently replicated finding relates to the presence of attention and information-processing deficits. Across all ages, at-risk individuals displayed impaired stimulus discrimination, signal detection, and/or decreased attention span (Cornblatt & Erlenmeyer-Kimling, 1989; Cornblatt & Keilp, 1994; Cornblatt, Winters, & Erlenmeyer-Kimling, 1989; Erlenmeyer-Kimling & Cornblatt, 1987a; Maier et al., 1992; Mirsky et al., 1986; Nuechterlein et al., 1989; Parnas & Mednick, 1990; Parnas et al., 1982a; Winters et al., 1991; Winters et al., 1981).

The findings from psychophysiological investigations are more equivocal. Adult siblings of probands have shown event-related potential (P300) deviations similar to those seen in schizophrenia (Saitoh et al., 1984). Investigations of the P300 in the offspring of schizophrenics had yielded intriguing, albeit inconclusive results. There have been two reports of positive findings (Schreiber et al., 1989, 1991) and an equal number of negative findings (Friedman et al., 1986, 1988). Two limitations make it difficult to conclude much from the current data regarding event-related potentials in high-risk children: (a) even if P300 anomalies are present in high-risk children, because similar effects are evident in children with or at-risk for other types of psychopathology, the specificity of P300 findings to schizophrenia remains unresolved; and (b) it remains possible that at-risk children would consistently show attenuated P300 amplitude if tasks with greater processing demands were used.

With regard to electrodermal activity (EDA), although several investigators (Erlenmeyer-Kimling et al., 1985; Janes et al., 1978; Kugelmass et al., 1985; Prentky et al., 1981) failed to detect any differences in at-risk offspring under age 12, the results from the Copenhagen High Risk Study (Mednick & Schulsinger, 1968) indicated that among at-risk adolescents, significant differences were present. The repeated failures to replicate the early findings of Mednick and Schulsinger might be the result of sample differences. This is a reasonable hypothesis because the Copenhagen sample consisted of adolescents, whereas the mean age of the children in the other high-risk samples was 9.5 years. Until the Erlenmeyer-Kimling (1985) investigation, none of the investigations of EDA in high-risk children had used the same measures and/or paradigm as Mednick and Schulsinger. Thus, although several studies had been performed in the same domain, they were not replications; as such, it is difficult to determine whether the differential findings could be attributed to age differences in the samples, or varying designs and measures. In view of the expense of implementing these studies, it is imperative that investigators make available the programs and designs that may be necessary to fully replicate a study.

In the case of pursuit eye-tracking performance, the Rochester group (Wynne et al., 1987) observed no differences between at-risk and normal children, though Mather (1985) detected poorer tracking in her sample of high-risk adolescents. These findings are not inconsistent if age mediates whether oculomotor deficits are manifest. In a cross-sectional comparison of normal children aged 7 to 15, Ross, Radant, and Hommer (1993) observed a correlation between age and smooth pursuit tracking performance. A longitudinal investigation of pursuit tracking performance in children and adolescents is necessary before drawing conclusions regarding the potential of eye-tracking dysfunction as a marker of vulnerability in high-risk youths.

Overall, findings from the genetic high-risk studies suggest that offspring as well as other first-degree relatives of schizophrenics are more likely to appear deviant on measures which discriminate schizophrenic probands from normals. In fact, evidence from some genetic high-risk projects, such as the New York High-Risk Project, indicates that at least a subset of high-risk children become increasingly deviant with age. Not enough high-risk research has been carried out using infants and very young children. This is unfortunate given the current hypothesis that an insult early in life (e.g., viral exposure or obstetrical complications) may play an important role in the etiology of schizophrenia.

Looking to the Future

After more than three decades of investigation, it is reasonable to evaluate the progress of this line of research, in terms of how well it has fulfilled its mission. In this section, we critically appraise this methodology. First, we assess the advantages of this approach. We then describe the limitations of the genetic high-risk strategy and discuss why the findings of such studies warrant both caution and optimism.

A particular advantage of the genetic high-risk approach is that currently, it is the only strategy that involves studying the entire life span. Especially in those studies that employ a longitudinal design, there is the opportunity to explore the extent to which deficits progress over time. As Zubin, Feldman, and Salzinger (1991) point out, deficits may remain stable over time, though the individual appears increasingly more deviant from peers because the deficit becomes manifest in a broader array of systems. Deficits may also increase over time, such that the individual is becoming more dysfunctional and hence, appears more deviant. Data from Fish's New York sample, the Copenhagen High-Risk Project, and the New York High-Risk Project indicate that in at least some offspring of schizophrenics, both processes are likely to be occurring.

Among at-risk individuals, there is considerable heterogeneity: Only a subset of the at-risk group—those possessing greater liability for schizophrenia—will manifest a schizophrenic outcome (Hanson, Gottesman, & Meehl, 1977). Indeed, even among the high-risk subjects who display early signs of deviance, there will be heterogeneity in outcome. Several investigators have suggested ways of resolving within-group heterogeneity. Many (Cornblatt & Marcus, 1986; Erlenmeyer-Kimling & Cornblatt, 1987a, 1987b; Hans & Mirsky, 1987; Hanson, Gottesman, & Heston, 1976, 1990; Marcus et al., 1987; Tienari, 1987) advocate the use of composite measures rather than individual measures to identify those high-risk subjects who are most likely to develop schizophrenia. The use of profiles based on independent, multiple measures is advantageous, because at present, a sensitive and specific indicator of heightened risk for schizophrenia does not exist (Hanson, Gottesman, & Heston, 1990). Another way of resolving within-group heterogeneity would be to apply taxometric analysis using objective psychometric measures to identify the subset of at-risk subjects who are most liable for a schizophrenic outcome (Moldin, Rice, Gottesman, & Erlenmeyer-Kimling, 1990a, 1990b, Moldin, Gottesman, Rice, & Erlenmeyer-Kimling, 1991).

In studies using the genetic high-risk strategy, even the "false positives" (i.e., those individuals predicted to be at heightened risk who do not eventually develop schizophrenia) are interesting and potentially informative. These individuals who "beat the odds" can teach us much about resiliency factors (Garmezy, 1987). Such information is likely to have implications in terms of preventive interventions (Walker & Emory, 1983).

Despite the promise of genetic high-risk studies, there are several reasons why caution is warranted. Many of these investigations were started prior to the inception of the DSM-III diagnostic system. Thus, some of the subjects who were classified as schizophrenic probands may not have met the stricter diagnostic criteria of the DSM-III system. Most of the investigations used different measures (even when purportedly assessing the same variables), thereby rendering it difficult to make between-study comparisons.

One criticism of the studies that have relied on the genetic high-risk strategy concerns their failure to compare the offspring of schizophrenic parents with offspring of psychiatric control parents (i.e., nonschizophrenic parents who are affected with some other form of psychopathology) (Erlenmeyer-Kimling & Cornblatt, 1987b; Zubin et al., 1991). Such a comparison group is necessary to determine whether the variables of interest are actually specific to a liability for schizophrenia, as opposed to indicating liability for psychiatric outcome in general. Moreover, even in the best of designs in which appropriate comparison groups are included, the expected yield from genetic high-risk studies is likely to be low. Due to problems of subject attrition, small samples, and even smaller yield of affected individuals, these high-risk studies are often plagued by low statistical power (Erlenmeyer-Kimling & Cornblatt, 1987b). Investigators such as Erlenmeyer-Kimling and Cornblatt (1987b) have advocated multicenter collaboration to increase statistical power. As Richters and Weintraub (1990) assert, "The few measures on which high risk-for-schizophrenia offspring have been distinguishable from offspring of psychiatric control parents await replication on new samples" (p. 71).

A related problem involves the choice of dependent variables and the methodologies used to examine them. Progress in schizophrenia research has been notoriously slow, in part because of methodological inadequacies and because of the failure to replicate studies with what appear to be interesting findings. An assessment employed in a longitudinal high-risk investigation reflects the prevailing wisdom, at the time of the assessment, regarding what to measure and how to measure it. Unfortunately, many of the chosen variables may turn out, with hindsight, not to have been interesting choices for study. Even if they seem relevant, the possibility remains that they were not assessed using optimal methods. The only solution to this problem is for the investigator to include in the assessment a broad array of variables with the hope that some will both stand the test of time and prove predictive of schizophrenia.

When utilizing the genetic high-risk strategy, the issue of external validity must be considered. A variable may have high positive predictive value within a group at known risk

for schizophrenia, such as first-degree relatives of affected probands but may not replicate when applied to the general population (Erlenmeyer-Kimling, Golden, & Cornblatt, 1989; Shields, Heston, & Gottesman, 1975). The generalizability of the results to other subgroups of schizophrenia (i.e. those without an affected first-degree relative) is thus unknown (Walker & Aylward, 1984).

Because schizophrenia may be characterized by equifinality, individuals are expected to differ in terms of the antecedent factors and developmental precursors implicated in the clinical manifestation of the disorder. As Asarnow (1988) has noted, "When genetic heterogeneity and/or developmental complexity exist, associations between schizophrenia and putative antecedents are likely to vary because different persons will have different antecedents . . . our task is to identify multiple pathways, in which risk indicators may vary for different forms of schizophrenia . . ." (p. 614). Even in the largest high-risk samples, the number of individuals likely to succumb to schizophrenia is apt to be too small to deal effectively with the challenge raised by Asarnow.

Many extant high-risk studies are subject to criticism because of their assumption of continuity between the functioning of adult schizophrenics and that of preschizophrenic children and adolescents (Richters & Weintraub, 1990), without concomitant consideration of developmental issues. To date, most high-risk studies have failed to address ways in which developmental competencies may affect the expression of a deficit. The developmental perspective in risk research, exemplified in the Asarnow (Asarnow & Goldstein, 1986; Asarnow, 1988) reviews, is imperative because, as Kandel (1986) asserts, "no single variable is a strongly positive predictor at all stages" (p. 166). Although attentional deficits appear to be a positive predictor at many of the stages of development of schizophrenia, issues of homotypic versus heterotypic continuity render it difficult to ensure that we are measuring the same construct at different times, even when the same measure is used. Heterotypic continuity, the possibility that the meaning of behaviors will vary with age, and that different behaviors at different times may represent the same underlying phenomenon (Rutter, 1989), must be considered.

For example, it is possible that the physiological nature and the psychological meaning of a construct such as attention changes as the child progresses through Piagetian stages of cognitive development. Several subprocesses are coordinated in the attentional system; they include regulation and maintenance of a state of arousal, orientation and signal detection, perception (stimulus encoding and analysis), resource allocation, response planning, response execution, and storage and retrieval of previous operations (Groner & Groner, 1989; Levin, 1984). With increasing cognitive development, the complexity of attention is likely to increase from simple arousal and sensory awareness, to relative freedom from distractibility, and perhaps, as cortical maturity continues, to allocation of resources and response planning.

Not only may the meaning of a behavior vary with age and level of developmental competency, but as Richters and Weintraub (1990) remind us, phenotypically similar behaviors may serve different functions in different children. Hence, there is a need for investigators using the genetic high-risk strategy to move beyond simply describing the differences between the high-risk subjects and comparison samples, to investigating why the deviance is manifest in the ways that it is. The task, then, is to go beyond the description of differences to elucidating their meaning, and identifying the processes by which behavioral deficits may be altered phenotypically by concomitant developmental changes.

In the transactional, developmental approach, there is a posited integration of competencies between behavioral and biological systems. Hence, developmental lags or other forms of atypical development in one system may affect the development of other behavioral systems (Cicchetti, 1990; Cicchetti & Schneider-Rosen, 1986). Few researchers have explicitly examined whether there is an association between delayed achievement of early developmental milestones and risk for schizophrenia. Erlenmeyer-Kimling, Rock, Squires-Wheeler, Roberts, and Yang (1991) hypothesized that early developmental milestones—first sitting up, standing and walking, and first word—might be negatively related to later psychiatric outcome. They applied path analysis to life-history variables from the first sample (Sample A) of the New York High Risk Project. Although there was no indication that early developmental milestones are significantly related to psychiatric outcome in young adulthood, this negative finding may reflect that in the Sample A high-risk offspring, the developmental milestones appeared early. In cases where developmental milestones are delayed, there may be a negative correlation between the timing of developmental milestones and later psychiatric outcome.

Most of the longitudinal high-risk studies have focused on early to middle childhood. Because adolescence is a time of developmental transitions, it is likely to be a particularly good period in which to examine the processes of normal behavior as well as abnormal development (Masten, 1987). During adolescence, individuals are faced with the challenges of adapting to physiological changes, increasingly complex social roles and expectations, and cognitive changes. Masten (1987) speculated that those individuals who display signs of maladjustment in middle childhood will be more vulnerable during the adolescent transitions.

Harvey (1991) also suggests that adolescence is a potentially sensitive period in the premorbid course of schizophrenia. He asserts that adolescence is "the time when those individuals who will eventually develop schizophrenia can best be differentiated from those who will not" (p. 139). Currently, however, we do not have enough data either to support or refute such a claim. Future risk research should explore adolescence as a sensitive period. Use of a cross-sequential longitudinal design (see Livson & Peskin, 1980 for a detailed description), in which at least two cohorts (namely, middle-childhood and adolescent samples) are studied simultaneously and longitudinally, is likely to be of great assistance in exploring the ways in which adolescence presents special challenges for an at-risk individual.

How can investigators ascertain whether they are identifying vulnerability indicators and precursors to schizophrenia, as opposed to prodromal symptoms of the disorder? The variables that differentiate a subset of high-risk offspring from other high-risk children and comparison groups (i.e., both at-risk offspring of nonschizophrenic psychiatric patients and normal controls) may

actually represent early prodromal signs of schizophrenia rather than being indicators of a schizophrenia diathesis. If this were the case, these variables would not be useful for elucidating the path(s) from diathesis to disorder, nor would these variables be useful for identifying factors that contribute to liability (Gottesman, 1991). However, if these variables represented early prodromal signs of the disorder rather than being risk indicators, these early signs of psychopathology could be used as signals for the initiation of intervention (Gottesman, 1991; Walker & Emory, 1983). Until recently, there has been little research on schizophrenia-spectrum disorders (paranoid, schizotypal, and schizoid personality disorders), either in the general population, or among the offspring of schizophrenic parents. Further investigation of such schizophrenia-spectrum disorders, especially longitudinal studies exploring their developmental relationship to schizophrenia, will undoubtedly assist us in our understanding of vulnerability indicators, and the ways in which they may differ from prodromal symptoms.

The Biobehavioral High-Risk Strategy

Investigators such as Siever and Coursey (1985) have advocated the identification of at-risk individuals on the basis of variables that have been observed to differentiate schizophrenics from normal controls. This alternative research strategy is particularly important because the majority of schizophrenic patients do not have schizophrenic parents, siblings, or offspring. As such, defining an individual's risk status on the basis of his or her own biobehavioral deviation is likely to yield a subgroup of schizophrenia-prone individuals who would be overlooked using the classical genetic high-risk strategy.

A limitation of investigations employing this approach for the selection of at-risk samples is that its utility is dependent on the extent to which such a deviation is a valid and relatively specific indicator of vulnerability to schizophrenia. Fortunately, there are some measures, such as smooth pursuit performance, which, as we have noted previously, appear to be robust and valid indicators of increased liability for schizophrenia. Siever, Coursey, Alterman, Buchsbaum, and Murphy (1982) assessed the clinical characteristics of adults identified as being at risk because of their poor performance during pursuit tracking tasks. They noted that college students with low-accuracy pursuit tracking were more likely to display schizotypal characteristics such as social introversion, anhedonia, and difficulty in interpersonal relations.

The biobehavioral high-risk strategy has proven more difficult to implement in studies of children. Although it is advisable to look first for deviant performance on variables that have differentiated affected adults from controls (Cornblatt & Marcuse, 1986), a difficulty with such a strategy is the instability of psychophysiological function in a rapidly developing organism. As Garmezy (1974) indicated, it may not be prudent to rely on deviant psychophysiological functioning in children as a criterion of risk because such functioning may not be longitudinally stable. Until we have more normative data for children's performance on psychophysiological measures, the strategy of longitudinally following individuals from the general population who show anomalous performance on some candidate markers such as smooth pursuit eye movements or electrodermal activity may only be suitable for use with postpubescent or older individuals. Not only do we need more normative data on children's psychophysiological functioning, but we also need data that address the issue of temporal stability of such measures during childhood.

Studying young children with an anomaly seen in adult schizophrenia may nonetheless be fruitful; this is evident in preliminary findings from the Mauritius study (Venables et al., 1978). Venables et al. (1978) screened the entire population of 3-year-olds on the island of Mauritius and used their patterns of electrodermal activity as the criterion for determining risk for schizophrenia. These investigators identified two distinct groups of at-risk children, namely, those with electrodermal hyperactivity and those with electrodermal hyporesponsiveness. When the subjects had reached nearly 11 years old, they were reassessed, using a battery of psychophysiological (electrodermal, cardiovascular, and oculomotor) measures. A comparison of the smooth pursuit eye-tracking performance of the risk and control subjects did not reveal any significant group differences. However, when the groups were divided by IQ scores, Venables (1989) observed that in one subset of the at-risk population, namely, the electrodermal hyperresponders, children with low intelligence displayed significantly poorer pursuit tracking performance than their high-IQ peers. This strategy of classifying subjects by IQ seems plausible, given prior research findings (see Aylward, Walker, & Bettes, 1984) indicating that preschizophrenic individuals tend to have lower IQ than their peers, as well as the report from the New York High-Risk Project (Erlenmeyer-Kimling, Kestenbaum, Bird, & Hilldoff, 1984) that the at-risk offspring who had succumbed to illness displayed lower IQ than the at-risk offspring who were psychiatrically healthy.

According to Venables (1989), a measure of psychophysiological functioning during early childhood may have predictive value in terms of later behavior, which may, in fact, serve as a precursor of schizophrenia. Venables (1990) concluded that although the early markers of electrodermal activity were not useful for predicting schizophrenic outcome in adulthood, hyperresponsivity appeared useful for predicting deviant eye tracking, which in other studies has been an indication of vulnerability to schizophrenia. This is a particularly intriguing assertion, in view of a report by Bartfai, Levander, and Sedvall (1983) indicating that schizophrenic patients with poor pursuit tracking performance also showed slower habituation of skin conductance responses. The selection of at-risk individuals on the basis of deviant electrodermal activity during childhood may yield a cost-effective high-risk sample, especially if low intelligence is included in the selection criterion.

An additional group of children predicted to be at heightened risk for a schizophrenic outcome would be preterm infants who have intra- or periventricular bleeding at birth. A disproportionate number of these infants show ventricular enlargement in early childhood. Ventricular enlargement has been associated with increased risk for later manifestation of soft neurological signs, and perceptual and cognitive impairments (Williams, Lewandowski, Coplan, & D'Eugenio, 1987). The observations of ventricular enlargement and cognitive deficits among a subgroup of adult schizophrenics suggest that the longitudinal investigation of children displaying these symptoms may prove fruitful (Murray & Lewis, 1987).

Another valid criticism of investigations that use the biobehavioral high-risk strategy is that for some of these variables the functional significance of the deficits remains unknown. Therefore, it is unknown whether the deficits, when found, are simply correlates of the schizophrenia and schizophrenia spectrum disorders, or whether they are part of the underlying pathophysiology of the disorder.

A variant of the biobehavioral high-risk strategy uses scores on psychometric scales to define the high-risk group. In this psychometric high-risk approach, questionnaires that are believed to identify subjects at heightened risk for psychosis are administered to nonclinical populations, and individuals with extreme scores are examined to identify how they are like schizophrenic subjects. To date, investigators have identified subjects as schizotypal on the basis of their performance on questionnaire measures such as the Physical Anhedonia Scale (Chapman, Chapman, & Raulin, 1976), the Perceptual Aberration Scale (Chapman, Chapman, & Raulin, 1978), and the MMPI (Hathaway & McKinley, 1943). Lengthy discussions regarding the construct validity of these psychometric measures can be found elsewhere; readers are referred to published reviews (i.e., Grove, 1982) and reports such as that of L. J. Chapman, Edell, and J. P. Chapman (1980) and Lenzenweger and Loranger (1989) for further information regarding the psychometric detection of schizotypy.

Simons (1981) studied an undergraduate volunteer sample selected on the basis of aberrant scores on the Chapman Physical Anhedonia Scale (Chapman, Chapman, & Raulin, 1976), a questionnaire that measures an inability to experience pleasure. As predicted, Simons observed an association between anhedonia and electrodermal hyporesponsivity. In a study involving the measurement of ERPs, Simons, MacMillan, and Ireland (1982) reported that at-risk (as determined by high scores on the physical anhedonia scale) subjects' cortical responses to hedonic and neutral stimuli did not differ, a finding consistent with that observed in schizophrenic patients.

Josiassen, Shagass, Roemer, and Straumanis (1985) assessed college students with extreme scores on either Chapman's Physical Anhedonia Scale (Chapman, Chapman, & Raulin, 1976) or Perceptual Aberration Scale (Chapman, Chapman, & Raulin, 1978). They observed that subjects with extreme scores on the anhedonia scale produced late positive ERP components whose amplitudes were significantly reduced relative to those produced by control subjects. These findings suggest that the anhedonia scale identifies subjects who are likely to display psychophysiological aberrations similar to those shown by schizophrenic patients. The ability of the Physical Anhedonia Scale to identify nonclinical samples who display "schizophreniclike" patterns of responding has been replicated several times (Bernstein & Riedel, 1987; Drewer & Shean, 1993).

Simons and Katkin (1985) examined the eye-tracking performance of undergraduate students who scored high on the Physical Anhedonia Scale and observed that their tracking performance was more variable than that of the control group. They interpreted this finding as supportive of the association between schizotypal symptoms and deviant smooth pursuit eye tracking. Similarly, a group of individuals classified as schizotypes based on their scores on the Perceptual Aberration Scale, which measures perceived distortions of one's body and other objects, displayed deviant eye-tracking ability.

There have been mixed findings regarding the use of the Perceptual Aberration Scale to identify at-risk individuals. Simons (1981) observed that a group of students who frequently endorsed items on the Perceptual Aberration Scale did not differ from controls in electrodermal responsivity. Josiassen et al. (1985) reported that the ERP amplitudes of subjects considered at heightened risk for psychopathology by virtue of having extreme scores on the Perceptual Aberration Scale did not differ from those of control subjects.

Although the Perceptual Aberration Scale has not been found to identify at-risk subjects in nonclinical populations based on their electrodermal activity or event-related potentials, the scale has been used to identify schizotypic subjects who show other information-processing deficits. Lenzenweger, Cornblatt, and Putnick (1991) observed that subjects identified as schizotypic on the basis of the Perceptual Aberration Scale displayed significantly poorer performance on the Continuous Performance Test, a measure of sustained attention. When Clementz, Grove, Katsanis, and Iacono (1991) compared the two Chapman scales in terms of their ability to indicate liability for schizophrenia among the relatives of affected probands, they observed that the Physical Anhedonia Scale, but not the Perceptual Aberration Scale, appeared to be familial in schizophrenics and their relatives.

Hanson, Gottesman, and Heston (1990) reported findings from a follow-up study conducted on the Hathaway-Monachesi sample of 15,000 adolescents who were administered the Minnesota Multiphasic Personality Inventory (MMPI) during ninth grade. Hanson and associates compared the mean MMPI profiles of the ninth graders who later developed schizophrenia with that of their sex- and age-matched classmate controls. The adolescents who later became schizophrenic displayed a pattern of statistically significant differences, most notably on MMPI Scales 8 (schizophrenic) and 4 (psychopathic deviate). However, based on their observation that some individuals who produced normal MMPI profiles at age 15 later developed schizophrenia, the authors concluded that the MMPI alone is not sufficient to detect the presence of a schizophrenic genotype in a nonclinical population.

Moldin, Rice, Gottesman, and Erlenmeyer-Kimling (1990a, 1990b) used the psychometric high-risk strategy to identify who, among individuals already classified as at risk on the basis of their genetic relatedness to an affected person, was most likely to manifest schizophrenia and/or a schizophrenia-spectrum disorder. They performed admixture analysis on the adolescent data from the New York High Risk-Project using an index of liability derived from the MMPI. Of the high-risk group, 17% fell into the deviant range of the bimodal distribution; these subjects were predicted to be at greatest risk for manifesting a schizophrenic outcome. The positive predictive value of this psychometric index was subsequently cross-validated (Moldin, Gottesman et al., 1991). Thus, the MMPI profiles may be useful in identifying a subset of at-risk individuals who are most likely to possess a schizophrenic diathesis.

Lencz et al. (1993) evaluated the smooth pursuit eye-tracking performance of college undergraduates with extreme scores on a scale purported to assess schizotypal personality disorder. They observed that subjects with extreme scores on the schizotypy scale also produced qualitatively poor eye tracking. This finding suggests that several personality measures may identify individuals in the general population who are at increased risk for schizophrenia.

A strategy to explore whether psychological variables can serve as predisposing factors for the development of schizophrenia is to identify potentially vulnerable individuals from nonclinical populations (using the psychometric high-risk strategy) and longitudinally follow them. L. J. Chapman and colleagues (Chapman, Chapman, Kwapil, Eckblad, & Zinser, 1994) employed this strategy and recently reported the results of their 10-year follow-up evaluation of subjects who were identified as high risk on the basis of scores on the Chapman questionnaires. They observed that high-scoring subjects on either or both of the Perceptual Aberration Scale and the Magical Ideation Scale (Eckblad & Chapman, 1983) were more likely to display DSM-III-R psychosis than control subjects. High-scoring subjects were also more likely to report psychotic experiences, schizotypal personality characteristics, and having psychotic relatives. Their findings suggest that the Perceptual Aberration and Magical Ideation Scales are valid indicators of psychosis-proneness, in general rather than schizophrenia per se.

Overall, the biobehavioral high-risk strategy, whether employing psychophysiological or psychometric indicators of risk, has not been exploited as a methodology for understanding how schizophrenia develops. Almost all the studies in this area do little more than provide evidence for the construct validity of the biobehavioral measure as one related to schizophrenia risk. The failure to use this approach to full advantage is no doubt in part due to the lack of developmental, normative data regarding biobehavioral measures. Until we know at what age variables like eye-tracking ability have stabilized or how electrodermal activity in children of different ages relates to that of adults, it would be unwise to launch too many projects mirroring the ambitious Mauritius undertaking. Nevertheless, because most biobehavioral variables probably are stabilized by around age 16, they could probably be used to effect in prospective studies of appropriately aged adolescents who possess the biobehavioral deviation but do not yet show signs of clinical schizophrenia or related disorders.

Walker and her research group (Walker, Grimes, Davis, & Smith, 1993; Walker & Lewine, 1990) advocate the use of an archival-observational approach as another strategy for investigating the developmental precursors of schizophrenia. In their strategy, they examine home movies of individuals whose adult psychiatric outcome is known to identify the ways in which individuals who develop adult schizophrenia may be distinguished from control subjects during childhood. Preliminary findings (Walker & Lewine, 1990) as well as more recent reports (see, e.g., Walker et al., 1993) suggest that behavioral measures such as facial expressiveness may distinguish preschizophrenic and normal subjects early in life. Overall, the preschizophrenic children showed greater negative affect than their healthy siblings. Indeed, the raters were able to identify the preschizophrenic child among the sibship groups at above-chance levels as early as the period from birth to 4 years. This strategy appears especially promising, in view of developmental, normative data regarding facial expressiveness.

CONTRIBUTIONS THE STUDY OF SCHIZOPHRENIA CAN MAKE TO NORMAL DEVELOPMENT

Earlier, we discussed the basic tenets of developmental psycho-pathology. In our discussion of strategies to identify developmental precursors of schizophrenia, we provided examples of ways in which a developmental life-span perspective may improve already existing research protocols. According to a developmental psychopathology perspective, the study of atypical or abnormal populations can be informative about normal development as well as psychopathology (Cicchetti, 1993). In this section, we discuss the ways in which the study of schizophrenia contributes to our knowledge of normal development. The study of schizophrenia may contribute to our understanding of normal development by providing further information about developmental events throughout the life span, helping to delineate the boundaries of pathology, and refining theories of normal development.

Recovery of Function

Because prior adaptation places constraints on subsequent adaptation and/or functioning, the more prolonged the pathological state, the harder it will be for the organism to reclaim a normal developmental trajectory (Cicchetti, 1990). It is particularly important to longitudinally study individuals experiencing their first lifetime episode of schizophrenia to examine the developmental course of the disorder. Moreover, studying first-episode schizophrenia permits us to examine developmental events, course, and outcome across the life span. Longitudinal investigations such as the one currently being carried out by Nuechterlein and his associates (Nuechterlein et al., 1992) and Iacono and Beiser (1989; Erickson, Beiser, Iacono, Fleming, & Lin, 1989) are likely to provide much information about how different events, (e.g., emancipation, loss of a significant other, physical maturation) serve different functions and have differential impact, depending on the nature of the developing organism.

A related issue is the relative plasticity and/or flexibility of different behavioral and psychological systems; the study of schizophrenic patients, especially those experiencing early episodes of the disorder, is likely to provide information about the development and/or deterioration of functioning across the life span. In traditional neurology and neuropsychology, ontogeny of functions can be identified by studying lesion patients as they undergo recovery. That is possible, in part, because the functioning of the lesion patient is likely to be on the same continuum as normal functioning; that is, there are likely to be quantitative though not necessarily qualitative differences in behavior. However, schizophrenia represents a special case, in that there is rarely full recovery of functioning; overall, the extant studies indicate that schizophrenic patients may experience recovery from an acute episode, but, due to residual symptomatology, they rarely exhibit full recovery of functioning (see Harding, 1986, however, for a differing view). In a transactional, developmental perspective, the developmental trajectory of the individual and the stage of the disorder will affect the individual's interactions with the environment; such dynamic transactions are expected to affect the course of the disorder (Strauss & Harding, 1990). Studying schizophrenic patients may assist behavioral scientists in identifying factors that are ameliorative in assisting individuals to regain the normal developmental trajectory, or at least, in arresting any patterns of decompensation.

The Boundaries of Pathology

In a developmental psychopathology perspective, there is the assumption of an interface between normalcy and pathology. The assertion that schizophrenia is continuous with normal development can be supported if one considers schizophrenia-spectrum disorders to be intermediate forms of schizophrenia-related disorder. As Cicchetti and Schneider-Rosen (1986) have indicated, an atypical individual may take several alternate pathways. The study of individuals with schizophrenia-spectrum disorders, and the longitudinal study of high-risk individuals who exhibit characteristics that distinguish them from their normal peers, can enhance our knowledge regarding the boundaries of pathology. The study of schizophrenia has led to the development of questionnaire measures, such as the Chapman scales (Chapman, Chapman, & Raulin, 1976, 1978), that can be used in nonclinical populations.

In a transactional, developmental perspective, there is a posited integration of competencies between behavioral and biological systems (Cicchetti, 1990). Developmental psychopathologists assert that lags or atypical development in one behavioral system affect the development of other behavioral systems (Cicchetti & Schneider-Rosen, 1986). The study of schizophrenia, especially in terms of high-risk investigations, has provided us with further information about the interactions between various behavioral and biological systems, such as the association between social behavior and attentional functioning. Several investigators (such as Cornblatt et al., 1989; Cornblatt & Erlenmeyer-Kimling, 1989; Nuechterlein et al., 1990) have noted that a specific subset of high-risk children show attention and information-processing deficits. Many of these at-risk children also displayed signs of social withdrawal or other potential indicators of schizotypy. This led to investigation of associations between information processing and social behavior, to determine whether attentional deficits were secondary to abnormal social functioning, or whether a certain level of attentional competency is necessary for the age-appropriate development of social abilities. Nuechterlein, Phipps-Yonas, Driscoll, and Garmezy (1990) observed that among normal children, there was a significant relationship between abnormal social functioning and attentional deficits, whereas the relationship was not present among the children of schizophrenic parents.

Refining Theories of Normal Development

The study of schizophrenia from a developmental perspective can enhance our knowledge of normal development by contributing greater precision to existing theories (Cicchetti & Schneider-Rosen, 1984). Since Kraepelin, psychopathologists have noted that one of the core deficits in schizophrenia appears to involve attention and information processing. The study of the attentional impairments displayed by many schizophrenics has enriched the understanding of the development and functioning of the human attentional system.

Shakow's (1962, 1977) writings on the disintegration and deterioration observed in schizophrenic disorders focused on the inability of schizophrenic patients to maintain a normal attentional set. According to Shakow, schizophrenic patients were only able to achieve a "segmental set"; in this way, he accounted for their inability to respond to incoming stimuli in an appropriate manner, without either habituating or perseverating. Shakow also described attention as a hierarchically organized system, in which higher cortical centers are involved in goal-directed situations, and lower systems deal with peripheral or irrelevant stimuli. Shakow's concept of a "major" or "generalized set" as opposed to a "segmental set," along with his notion of hierarchical control over attentional subsystems has influenced both students of psychopathology and cognitive psychology.

Investigators attempting to explain the attention and information-processing deficits observed in schizophrenics have refined existing theories of information processing. Callaway and Naghdi (1982)'s discussion of schizophrenics' performance on information-processing tasks helped to expand Posner's (1978) concepts of automatic parallel and controlled serial processes. Similarly, Nuechterlein and Dawson (Nuechterlein, 1985; Nuechterlein & Dawson, 1984) revised and refined currently available models of human information processing, encouraging cognitive psychologists to move beyond stage models of selective attention to more complex processing capacity models of attention. The Nuechterlein and Dawson (1984) discussion of schizophrenics' impaired performance on high-demand processing tasks incorporated both Kahneman's (1973) flexible allocation model and Posner's (1978) notion of limited capacity in the attentional system. In this way, Nuechterlein and Dawson (1984) helped to clarify that subsystems underlying attention do not operate solely in terms of either strict seriality or unlimited parallel processing.

Moreover, the frontal lobe dysfunction exhibited by many schizophrenics (Levin, 1984; Weinberger, 1986, 1987) has provided an example of the importance of studying pathological processes to elucidate the hierarchically integrated nature of the central nervous system (CNS). For example, the perseverative responses displayed by schizophrenics during neuropsychological tasks such as the Wisconsin Card Sorting Test (Berg, 1948; Grant & Berg, 1948) have affirmed hypotheses regarding the executive function of the prefrontal cortex over the phylogenetically older structures of the CNS, such as the thalamic regions and pontine reticular activating system.

CONCLUSIONS

In earlier sections, we discussed past and present conceptualizations of schizophrenia. We illustrated the ways in which many of the principles inherent to developmental psychopathology are consistent with current conceptualizations of schizophrenia. Throughout the chapter, we noted how adopting a developmental psychopathology perspective can enhance the study of schizophrenia. Because of the relative youth of the field of developmental psychopathology, it is not surprising that few investigators studying schizophrenia have included consideration of developmental principles in their research designs and/or explanatory constructs.

In this chapter, we reviewed and evaluated several etiologic models of the transmission of risk for schizophrenia, including main effects (distinct heterogeneity and single major gene), multifactorial, interactional (diathesis-stress and vulnerability), and transactional models. Because of the necessity of accounting for such issues as heterogeneity, variable age of onset, and variable course and outcome, a more complex, nonlinear developmental explanatory model is required. We offered suggestions for enhancing existing diathesis-stress models with more transactional considerations; this has been attempted by such investigators as Nuechterlein. We now expand further on these suggestions.

At present, individuals diagnosed with schizophrenia appear to be a clinically heterogeneous group. Such heterogeneity is demonstrated by symptom pictures that differ in terms of the relative prominence of positive and negative symptoms, response to different types of neuroleptics, and the presence of psychophysiological deficits (smooth pursuit eye movements, event-related potentials, electrodermal anomalies) and neuroanatomic anomalies (ventriculomegaly, frontal lobe atrophy, temporal lobe anomalies). Schizophrenia, then, appears to be characterized by multifinality.

We also discussed the evidence supporting the hypothesis that schizophrenia is characterized by equifinality. Currently, schizophrenia is viewed as a complex phenotype resulting from interactions of genetic and extragenetic factors. Identification of specific underlying etiologic factors for the development of schizophrenia remains elusive. Moreover, present data regarding the hypothesized etiologic heterogeneity of schizophrenia is inconclusive. In this section, we present ways in which researchers can incorporate developmental themes in their attempts to empirically investigate the etiology, transmission, and manifestation of schizophrenia.

Genetic linkage analysis is a promising tool for identifying the genes implicated in the disorder provided that single genes exerting major effects exist. However, efforts to date have been unsuccessful, hindered perhaps by the etiologic heterogeneity believed to characterize individuals diagnosed schizophrenic. Impaired smooth pursuit eye tracking, failure to habituate to paired auditory stimuli presented in rapid succession (the P50 effect), reduced cortical response to novel or significant stimuli (the P300 effect), and ventricular enlargement are all candidate biobehavioral markers of a schizophrenic diathesis. Assessment of such biobehavioral markers may assist investigators by enabling the identification of homogeneous subgroups of schizophrenics for use in linkage analyses.

Another strategy for investigating etiologic factors implicated in schizophrenia involves the study of first-episode patients. Studying patients experiencing their first lifetime episode of schizophrenia is preferable to studying chronic patients because the use of a first-episode sample permits the separation of causal factors from effects of the illness, such as sequelae of treatment and/or institutionalization. Schizophrenics have been observed to differ in their clinical responsiveness to pharmacological interventions (i.e., traditional neuroleptics vs. newer pharmacological agents such as clozapine); the identification of two or more subgroups of first-episode schizophrenics who differ in their clinical responsiveness to different antipsychotic drugs would provide support for etiologic heterogeneity because these antipsychotics have been demonstrated to involve different receptor types.

The results of high-risk studies suggest that some individuals show early indicators of an increased liability for the manifestation of schizophrenia. To date, most investigations of developmental precursors have employed the genetic high-risk method. These studies have illustrated that at least some offspring of schizophrenics display signs of deviant functioning as early as childhood. Awareness of heterogeneity of outcome, as evidenced by differences among offspring of schizophrenics, and monozygotic cotwins discordant for psychopathology, as well as consideration of the developmental principle of equifinality, leads us to conclude that a linear model of development is not sufficient to account for the developmental trajectories leading to schizophrenia. Application of a transactional model is needed to yield further information regarding why some at-risk individuals succumb to the disorder, whereas others do not. One way to identify those offspring of schizophrenic probands who are most likely to possess a schizophrenic genotype would be to identify individuals who are biologically related to a proband, and select those who also show signs of attentional difficulties, deviant event-related potentials, or eye-tracking impairment. Combining the genetic high-risk and biobehavioral high-risk strategies is likely to yield a larger sample of individuals who possess the schizophrenic genotype than using either strategy in isolation.

Based on what we have already learned from these high-risk studies, there are several directions for further empirical inquiry:

- What is the meaning of the biobehavioral anomalies that appear early in the life span of at-risk individuals?

- Among those at-risk individuals who display a deficit, why is the schizophrenic diathesis manifest through this particular deficit?

- In what ways are these deviations the same over time, and in what ways do they differ? More specifically, is there biobehavioral isomorphism in some domains, and/or how do emergent developmental competencies and more complex experiential processes modify the expression of such deviations?

- For the at-risk individuals who display abnormalities early in the life course, how do they differ from at-risk individuals who display abnormalities later in the life course, closer to the time of the first episode of disorder? In what ways does development, an ongoing transaction between biological competence and psychological experience, lead to further dysfunction in the same domain, dysfunction in additional domains, and/or possibly, compensatory behaviors?

One of the next tasks in the high-risk line of inquiry is to move from simply describing the differences (i.e., between at-risk offspring who display deficits, at-risk offspring who do not, and normal controls) to elucidating the processes that give rise to such differences. The study of persons at genetic risk for developing schizophrenia who do not succumb to the disorder could

also identify psychosocial factors, such as social support networks or higher intelligence, which serve as potential protective or resiliency factors.

Other areas meriting inquiry from a developmental psychopathology perspective include the investigation of psychological variables that can serve as predisposing factors, rather than as factors that simply potentiate the schizophrenic diathesis. One way to explore this possibility would be to identify individuals from nonclinical populations (using the psychometric high-risk strategy) and assess them for the presence of psychophysiological or neuroanatomic anomalies. Individuals deviant on both the psychometric and biological screens could then be recruited for participation in a prospective, longitudinal study, in which a battery of measures, including assessment of psychological and psychosocial variables, would be administered at regular intervals. Such an investigation would not only provide information about the role of psychological factors in the development of schizophrenia, it also has the potential to inform us about the precursors of schizophrenia.

As we have discussed in this chapter, not everyone at risk for schizophrenia by virtue of genetic relatedness to a proband, the presence of a biobehavioral anomaly, and/or signs of schizotypy will develop schizophrenia. Some individuals may develop schizophrenia-spectrum disorders, whereas others will remain clinically healthy. Despite advances made in identifying and studying schizophrenia-spectrum personality disorders, the precise relationship between these disorders and schizophrenia remains elusive. Viewing schizophrenia through the lens of a developmental psychopathology perspective leads us to the following issues:

- In what ways do individuals diagnosed with schizophrenia-spectrum disorders differ from individuals in the prodromal phase of schizophrenia?

- How do persons with a schizophrenia-spectrum disorder differ from individuals who display schizophreniclike deviant performance on psychophysiological tasks but do not develop either schizophrenia or a schizophrenia-spectrum disorder?

- How do individuals with a schizophrenia-spectrum disorder differ from schizophrenic probands who appear clinically normal until near the time of their first episode?

- What determines whether individuals with schizophrenia-spectrum personality disorders or schizophreniform disorder go on to become schizophrenic?

- How might the onset of prodromal symptoms affect subsequent development?

We reviewed several reports indicating that the biological relatives of schizophrenics display psychophysiological deficits, such as impaired smooth pursuit eye tracking and diminished P300 waves. Although there are indications that relatives who show such deficits are also more likely to display schizotypal features, there is little to indicate whether these individuals are more likely to develop schizophrenia than biological relatives of schizophrenics who do not display the psychophysiological deficits. A longitudinal study of probands' first-degree relatives, especially those near the beginning of the age-of-risk window, (e.g., like the Copenhagen High-Risk Project) would be helpful for exploring whether relatives with smooth pursuit or cerebral evoked potential anomalies are at greater risk for the manifestation of psychopathology.

It is reasonable to speculate that the term "schizophrenia," like the term "mood disorder," can be conceptualized as a group of disorders, each with different etiologies, and/or combinations of different disease processes. On the basis of our review of the phenomenological and biobehavioral investigations of children diagnosed with schizophrenia, we cannot rule out the possibility that childhood-onset schizophrenia may be a variant of adult-onset schizophrenia. Confirmation of this possibility would provide evidence for etiologic homogeneity. To the extent that etiologic heterogeneity exists, some forms of schizophrenia will be better accounted for by the neurodevelopmental models reviewed in this chapter than others. With such a conceptualization, it would be possible for the clinical presentation of schizophrenia to be dependent on the length of exposure to the etiologic factors, the developments (whether in terms of neurogenesis, psychosocial, or intrapsychic factors) that had already occurred at the time of the etiologic insult, and the phase of development that the individual is currently in.

A related issue would be the extent to which the disorder varies as a function of age of onset, gender, and premorbid functioning. Individuals with a later age of onset, for example, young adulthood, may be more competent and have more social resources than an individual who develops the disorder during early adolescence. On the other hand, the early adolescent may have the transient buffers of a more structured environment (i.e., the parental home environment, or school) and be faced with less transient stressors, such as the societal expectations to progress toward financial and emotional emancipation. Further research is also necessary to assess what accounts for the gender differences that have been reported in the symptomatology, course, and outcome of schizophrenia.

Developmental research on schizophrenia represents an exciting and daunting challenge. In this chapter, we illustrated the ways in which a developmental psychopathology perspective may assist investigators in examining many currently unanswered questions about schizophrenia. We also touched on ways in which the study of schizophrenia has enhanced knowledge concerning normal development. It is our belief that assessment of biobehavioral markers is likely to assist the increasingly complex study of schizophrenia, in terms of classifying patients into more homogeneous subgroups, defining the schizophrenia phenotype for linkage analyses, providing an alternative high-risk strategy for identifying the developmental precursors of schizophrenia, and delineating the boundaries of the schizophrenia spectrum. The application of psychophysiological and neuroanatomical assessment has great potential to enhance the study of both atypical and normal development.

REFERENCES

Adler, L. E., Hoffer, L. J., Griffith, J., Waldo, M. C., & Freedman, R. (1992). Normalization by nicotine of deficient auditory sensory gating in the relatives of schizophrenics. *Biological Psychiatry, 32,* 607–616.

Adler, L. E., Pachtman, E., Franks, R. D., Percevich, M., Waldo, M. C., & Freedman, R. (1982). Neurophysiological evidence for a defect in neuronal mechanisms involved in sensory gating in schizophrenia. *Biological Psychiatry, 17,* 639–654.

Almli, C. R., & Finger, S. (1987). Neural insult and critical period concepts. In M. H. Bornstein (Ed.), *Sensitive periods in development: Interdisciplinary perspectives* (pp. 123–143). Hillsdale, NJ: Erlbaum.

American Psychiatric Association. (1952, 1968, 1980, 1987, 1994). *Diagnostic and statistical manual of mental disorders* (1st ed., 2nd ed., 3rd ed., 3rd ed. rev., 4th ed.). Washington, DC: Author.

Andreasen, N. C. (1982). Negative symptoms in schizophrenia. Definition and reliability. *Archives of General Psychiatry, 39,* 784–788.

Andreasen, N. C. (1985). Positive vs. negative schizophrenia: A critical evaluation. *Schizophrenia Bulletin, 11,* 380–389.

Andreasen, N. C., & Carpenter, W. T. (1993). Diagnosis and classification of schizophrenia. *Schizophrenia Bulletin, 19,* 199–214.

Andreasen, N. C., Ehrhardt, J. C., Swayze, V. W., Alliger, R. J., Yuh, W. T. C., Cohen, G., & Ziebell, S. (1990). Magnetic resonance imaging of the brain in schizophrenia. *Archives of General Psychiatry, 47,* 35–44.

Andreasen, N. C., Nasrallah, H. A., Dunn, V., Olsen, S. C., Grove, W. M., Ehrhardt, J. C., Coffman, J. A., Crossett, J. H. (1986). Structural abnormalities in the frontal system in schizophrenia. *Archives of General Psychiatry, 43,* 136–144.

Andreasen, N. C., & Olsen, S. (1982). Negative vs. positive schizophrenia. Definition and validation. *Archives of General Psychiatry, 39,* 789–794.

Asarnow, J. R. (1988). Children at risk for schizophrenia: Converging lines of evidence. *Schizophrenia Bulletin, 14,* 613–631.

Asarnow, J. R., Asarnow, R. F., Hornstein, N., & Russell, A. (1991). Childhood-onset schizophrenia: Developmental perspectives on schizophrenic disorders. In E. F. Walker (Ed.), *Schizophrenia: A life-course developmental perspective* (pp. 95–122). San Diego: Academic Press.

Asarnow, J. R., & Ben-Meir, S. (1988). Children with schizophrenia spectrum and depressive disorders: A comparative study of premorbid adjustment, onset pattern, and severity of impairment. *Journal of Child Psychology and Psychiatry, 29,* 477–488.

Asarnow, J. R., & Goldstein, M. J. (1986). Schizophrenia during adolescence and early adulthood: A developmental perspective on risk research. *Clinical Psychology Review, 6,* 211–235.

Asarnow, R. F., & Sherman, T. (1984). Studies of visual information processing in schizophrenic children. *Child Development, 55,* 249–261.

Asarnow, R. F., Sherman, T., & Strandburg, R. (1986). The search for the psychobiological substrate of childhood onset schizophrenia. *Journal of the American Academy of Child Psychiatry, 26,* 601–614.

Asherson, P., Parfitt, E., Sargeant, M., Tidmarsh, S., Buckland, P., Taylor, C., Clements, A., Gill, M., McGuffin, P., & Owen, M. (1992). No evidence for a pseudoautosomal locus for schizophrenia: Linkage analysis of multiply affected families. *British Journal of Psychiatry, 161,* 63–68.

Aylward, E., Walker, E., & Bettes, B. (1984). Intelligence in schizophrenia: Meta-analysis of the research. *Schizophrenia Bulletin, 10,* 430–459.

Bannet, J., Belmaker, R. H., & Ebstein, R. P. (1981). Individual differences in the response of dopamine receptor number to chronic haloperidol treatment. *Biological Psychiatry, 16,* 1059–1065.

Bartfai, A., Levander, S. E., Nyback, H., Berggren, B. M., & Schalling, D. (1985). Smooth pursuit eye tracking, neuropsychological test performance, and computed tomography in schizophrenia. *Psychiatry Research, 15,* 49–62.

Bartfai, A., Levander, S. E., & Sedvall, G. (1983). Smooth pursuit eye movements, clinical symptoms, CSF metabolites, and skin conductance habituation in schizophrenic patients. *Biological Psychiatry, 18,* 971–986.

Bassett, A. S. (1991). Linkage analysis of schizophrenia: Challenges and promise. *Social Biology, 38,* 189–196.

Bassett, A. S., & Honer, W. G. (1994). Evidence for anticipation in schizophrenia. *American Journal of Human Genetics, 54,* 864–870.

Bassett, A. S., Jones, B. D., McGillivray, B. C., & Pantzar, J. T. (1988). Partial trisomy chromosome 5 segregating with schizophrenia. *Lancet,* 799–801.

Beart, P. M. (1987). Roles for glutamate and norepinephrine in limbic circuitry and psychopathology. *Behavioral and Brain Sciences, 10,* 208–209.

Beitchman, J. H. (1985). Childhood schizophrenia. *Psychiatric Clinics of North America, 8,* 793–814.

Benes, F. M. (1989). Myelination of cortical-hippocampal relays during late adolescence. *Schizophrenia Bulletin, 15,* 585–593.

Benes, F. M., McSparren, J., Bird, E. D., San Giovanni, J. P., & Vincent, S. L. (1991). Deficits in small interneurons in prefrontal and cingulate cortices of schizophrenic and schizoaffective patients. *Archives of General Psychiatry, 48,* 996–1001.

Berg, E. A. (1948). A simple objective test for measuring flexibility in thinking. *Journal of General Psychology, 39,* 15–22.

Bernstein, A. S., & Riedel, J. A. (1987). Psychophysiological response patterns in college students with high physical anhedonia: Scores appear to reflect schizotypy rather than depression. *Biological Psychiatry, 22,* 829–847.

Bernstein, A. V., Taylor, K. W., Starkey, P., Lubowsky, J., Juni, S., & Paley, H. (1983). The effect of prolonged stimulus repetition on autonomic response and EEG activity in normal subjects, schizophrenic, and nonschizophrenic patients. *Psychophysiology, 20,* 332–342.

Bilder, R. M. (1985). *Subtyping in chronic schizophrenia: Clinical, neuropsychological, and structural indices of deterioration.* University Microfilms, Ann Arbor, MI.

Black, J. L., Mowery, B. J., Barton, D. A., & de Roach, J. N. (1992). Auditory P300 studies in schizophrenic subjects and their first-degree relatives. *Australasian Physical and Engineering Sciences in Medicine, 15,* 65–73.

Blackwood, D. H., St. Clair, D., & Muir, W. (1991). DNA markers and vulnerability markers in families multiply affected with schizophrenia. *European Archives of Psychiatry and Clinical Neuroscience, 240,* 191–196.

Blackwood, D. H., St. Clair, D. M., Muir, W. J., & Duffy, J. C. (1991). Auditory P300 and eye tracking dysfunction in schizophrenic pedigrees. *Archives of General Psychiatry, 48,* 899–909.

Blackwood, D. H., Young, A. H., McQueen, J. K., Martin, M. J., Roxborough, H. M., Muir, W. J., St. Clair, D. M., & Kean, D. M. (1991). Magnetic resonance imaging in schizophrenia: Altered brain morphology associated with P300 abnormalities and eye tracking dysfunction. *Biological Psychiatry, 30,* 753–769.

Bleuler, E. (1950). *Dementia praecox or the group of schizophrenias* (H. Zinkin, Trans.). New York: International Universities Press. (Original work published 1911)

Bleuler, M. (1988). The course, outcome, and prognosis of schizophrenic psychoses. In F. Flach (Ed.), *The schizophrenias* (pp. 11–21). New York: Norton.

Bogerts, B. (1989). Limbic and paralimbic pathology in schizophrenia: Interaction with age- and stress-related factors. In S. C. Schulz & C. A. Tamminga (Eds.), *Schizophrenia: Scientific Progress* (pp. 216–226). New York: Oxford University Press.

Bornstein, M. H. (1989). Sensitive periods in development: Structural characteristics and causal interpretations. *Psychological Bulletin, 105,* 179–197.

Boutros, N. N., Zouridakis, G., & Overall, J. (1991). Replication and extension of P50 findings in schizophrenia. *Clinical Electroencephalography, 22,* 40–45.

Boutros, N. N., Zouridakis, G., Rustin, T., Peabody, C., & Warner, D. (1993). The P50 component of the auditory evoked potential and subtypes of schizophrenia. *Psychiatry Research, 47,* 243–254.

Bowlby, J. (1969). *Attachment and loss: Vol. 1. Attachment.* New York: Basic Books.

Bracha, H. S., Torrey, E. F., Gottesman, I. I., Bigelow, L. B., & Cunniff, C. (1992). Second-trimester markers of fetal size in schizophrenia: A study of monozygotic twins. *American Journal of Psychiatry, 149,* 1355–1361.

Braff, D. L., & Geyer, M. A. (1989). Sensorimotor gating and the neurobiology of schizophrenia: Human and animal studies. In S. C. Schulz & C. A. Tamminga (Eds.), *Schizophrenia: Scientific progress* (pp. 124–136). New York: Oxford University Press.

Burd, L., & Kerbeshian, J. (1987). A North Dakota prevalence study of schizophrenia presenting in childhood. *Journal of American Academy of Child & Adolescent Psychiatry, 26,* 347–350.

Burt, D. R., Creese, I., & Snyder, S. H. (1977). Antischizophrenic drugs: Chronic treatment elevates dopamine receptor binding in brain. *Science, 196,* 326–328.

Callaghan, E., Sham, P., Takei, N., Glover, G., & Murray, R. M. (1991). Schizophrenia after prenatal exposure to 1957 A2 influenza epidemic. *Lancet, 337,* 1248–1250.

Callaway, E., & Naghdi, S. (1982). An information processing model for schizophrenia. *Archives of General Psychiatry, 39,* 339–347.

Cannon, T. D., Mednick, S. A., & Parnas, J. (1989). Genetic and perinatal determinants of structural brain deficits in schizophrenia. *Archives of General Psychiatry, 46,* 883–889.

Cannon, T. D., Mednick, S. A., Parnas, J., Schulsinger, F., Praestholm, J., & Vestergaard, A. (1993). Developmental brain abnormalities in the offspring of schizophrenic mothers. I. Contributions of genetic and perinatal factors. *Archives of General Psychiatry, 50,* 551–564.

Cantor, S. (1988). *Childhood schizophrenia.* New York: Guilford.

Cantor, S., Evans, J., Pearce, J., & Pezzot-Pearce, T. (1982). Childhood schizophrenia: Present but not accounted for. *American Journal of Psychiatry, 139,* 758–762.

Caplan, R., Foy, J. G., Asarnow, R. F., & Sherman, T. (1990a). Information processing deficits of schizophrenic children with formal thought disorder. *Psychiatry Research, 31,* 169–177.

Caplan, R., Perdue, S., Tanguay, P. E., & Fish, B. (1990b). Formal thought disorder in childhood. *Journal of Child Psychology and Psychiatry, 31,* 1103–1114.

Carlsson, M., & Carlsson, A. (1990a). Interactions between glutamatergic and monoaminergic systems within the basal ganglia—implications for schizophrenia and Parkinson's disease. *Trends in Neurosciences, 13,* 272–276.

Carlsson, M., & Carlsson, A. (1990b). Schizophrenia: A subcortical neurotransmitter imbalance syndrome? *Schizophrenia Bulletin, 16,* 425–432.

Carpenter, W. T., Strauss, J. S., & Bartko, J. J. (1974). Use of signs and symptoms for the identification of schizophrenic patients. *Schizophrenia Bulletin, 2,* 37–49.

Chapman, L. J., Chapman, J. P., Kwapil, T. R., Eckblad, M., & Zinser, M. C. (1994). Putatively psychosis-prone subjects ten years later. *Journal of Abnormal Psychology, 103,* 171–183.

Chapman, L. J., Chapman, J. P., & Raulin, M. L. (1976). Scales for physical and social anhedonia. *Journal of Abnormal Psychology, 85,* 374–382.

Chapman, L. J., Chapman, J. P., & Raulin, M. (1978). Body-image aberration in schizophrenia. *Journal of Abnormal Psychology, 87,* 399–407.

Chapman, L. J., Edell, W. S., & Chapman, J. P. (1980). Physical anhedonia, perceptual aberration, and psychosis proneness. *Schizophrenia Bulletin, 6,* 639–653.

Cicchetti, D. (1990). An historical perspective on the discipline of developmental psychopathology. In J. Rolf, A. Masten, D. Cicchetti, K. Nuechterlein, & S. Weintraub (Eds.), *Risk and protective factors in the development of psychopathology* (pp. 2–28). New York: Cambridge University Press.

Cicchetti, D. (1993). Developmental psychopathology: Reactions, reflections, projections. *Developmental Review, 13,* 471–502.

Cicchetti, D. (1994). Integrating developmental risk factors: Perspectives from developmental psychopathology. In C. A. Nelson (Ed.), *The Minnesota symposia on child psychology: Vol. 27. Threats to optimal development* (pp. 285–325). Minneapolis: University of Minnesota Press.

Cicchetti, D., & Schneider-Rosen, K. (1984). Toward a transactional model of childhood depression. *New Directions for Child Development, 26,* 5–27.

Cicchetti, D., & Schneider-Rosen, K. (1986). An organizational approach to childhood depression. In M. Rutter, C. Izard, & P. Read (Eds.), *Depression in young people: Clinical and developmental perspectives* (pp. 71–134). New York: Guilford.

Clementz, B. A., Grove, W. M., Iacono, W. G., & Sweeney, J. A. (1992). Smooth pursuit eye movement dysfunction and liability for schizophrenia: Implications for genetic modeling. *Journal of Abnormal Psychology, 101,* 117–129.

Clementz, B. A., Grove, W. M., Katsanis, J., & Iacono, W. G. (1991). Psychometric detection of schizotypy: Perceptual aberration and physical anhedonia in relatives of schizophrenics. *Journal of Abnormal Psychology, 100,* 607–612.

Clementz, B. A., & Sweeney, J. A. (1990). Is eye movement dysfunction a biological marker for schizophrenia? A methodologic review. *Psychological Bulletin, 108,* 77–92.

Collinge, J., DeLisi, L. E., Boccio, A., Johnstone, E. C., Lane, A., Larkin, C., Leach, M., Lofthouse, R., Owen, F., Poulter, M., Shah, T., Walsh, C., & Crow, T. J. (1991). Evidence for a pseudo-autosomal locus for schizophrenia using the method of affected sibling pairs. *British Journal of Psychiatry, 158,* 624–629.

Collins, P. F., & Depue, R. A. (1992). A neurobehavioral systems approach to developmental psychopathology: Implications for disorders of affect. In D. Cicchetti & S. L. Toth (Eds.), *Rochester symposium on developmental psychopathology: Vol. 4. Developmental perspectives on depression* (pp. 29–101). Rochester, NY: University of Rochester Press.

Coon, H., Byerley, W., Holik, J., Hoff, M., Myles-Worsley, M., Lannfelt, L., Sokoloff, P., Schwartz, J. -C., Waldo, M., Freedman, R., &
Plaetke, R. (1993). Linkage analysis of schizophrenia with five dopamine receptor genes in nine pedigrees. *American Journal of Human Genetics, 52,* 327–334.

Coon, H., Plaetke, R., Holik, J., Hoff, M., Myles-Worsley, M., Waldo, M., Freedman, R., & Byerley, W. (1993). Use of a neurophysiological trait in linkage analysis of schizophrenia. *Biological Psychiatry, 34,* 277–289.

Cooper, J. R., Bloom, F. E., & Roth, R. H. (1991). *The biochemical basis of neuropharmacology* (6th ed.). New York: Oxford University Press.

Cornblatt, B., & Erlenmeyer-Kimling, L. (1989). Attention and schizophrenia. *Schizophrenia Research, 2,* 58.

Cornblatt, B., & Keilp, J. (1994). Impaired attention, genetics, and the pathophysiology of schizophrenia. *Schizophrenia Bulletin, 20,* 31–46.

Cornblatt, B., & Marcus, Y. (1986). Children at high risk for schizophrenia: Predictions from childhood to adolescence. In L. Erlenmeyer-Kimling & N. E. Miller (Eds.), *Life-span research on the prediction of psychopathology* (pp. 101–117). Hillsdale, NJ: Erlbaum.

Cornblatt, B., Winters, L., & Erlenmeyer-Kimling, L. (1989). Attentional markers of schizophrenia: Evidence from the New York High-Risk Study. In S. C. Schulz & C. A. Tamminga (Eds.), *Schizophrenia: Scientific progress* (pp. 83–92). New York: Oxford University Press.

Crow, T. J. (1985). The two-syndrome concept: Origins and current status. *Schizophrenia Bulletin, 11,* 471–486.

Crow, T. J. (1986). Left brain, retrotransposons, and schizophrenia. *British Medical Journal, 293,* 3–4.

Crow, T. J. (1987). Two syndromes of schizophrenia as one pole of the continuum of psychosis. A concept of the nature of the pathogen and its genomic locus. In F. A. Henn & L. E. DeLisi (Eds.), *Handbook of schizophrenia: Vol. 2. Neurochemistry and neuropharmacology of schizophrenia* (pp. 17–48). London: Elsevier.

Crow, T. J., Ball, J., Bloom, S. R., Brown, R., Bruton, C. J., Colter, N., Frith, C. D., Johnstone, E. C., Owens, D. G. C., & Roberts, G. W. (1989). Schizophrenia as an anomaly of development of cerebral asymmetry. *Archives of General Psychiatry, 46,* 1145–1150.

Crow, T. J., Cross, A. J., Johnstone, E. C., & Owen, F. (1982). Two syndromes in schizophrenia and their pathogenesis. In F. A. Henn & H. A. Nasrallah (Eds.), *Schizophrenia as a brain disease* (pp. 196–234). New York: Oxford University Press.

Crow, T. J., DeLisi, L. E. & Johnstone, E. C. (1989). Concordance by sex in sibling pairs with schizophrenia is paternally inherited: Evidence for a pseudoautosomal locus. *British Journal of Psychiatry, 155,* 92–97.

Crow, T. J., Done, D. J., & Johnstone, E. C. (1991). Schizophrenia and influenza. *Lancet, 338,* 116–117.

Crowe, R. R., Black, D. W., Andreasen, N. C., & Heuther, M. (1990). The Iowa Multiplex Family study of schizophrenia: Linkage analyses on chromosome 5. *European Archives of Psychiatry and Neurological Sciences, 239,* 290–292.

Crowe, R. R., Black, D. W., Wesner, R., Andreasen, N. C., Cookman, A., & Roby, J. (1991). Lack of linkage to chromosome 5q11–q13 markers in six schizophrenia pedigrees. *Archives of General Psychiatry, 48,* 357–361.

Currier, R. D., Jackson, J. F., & Meydrech, E. F. (1982). Progression rate and age of onset are related in autosomal dominant neurologic diseases. *Neurology, 32,* 907–909.

D'Amato, T., Campion, D., Gorwood, P., Jay, M., Sabate, O., Petit, C., Abbar, M., Malafosse, A., Leboyer, M., Hillaire, D., Clerget-Darpousx, F., Feingold, J., Waksman, G., & Mallet, J. (1992). Evidence for a pseudoautosomal locus for schizophrenia: II. Replication of a non-random segregation of alleles at the DXYS14 locus. *British Journal of Psychiatry, 161,* 59–62.

Dawson, M. E., & Nuechterlein, K. H. (1984). Psychophysiological dysfunctions in the developmental course of schizophrenic disorders. *Schizophrenia Bulletin, 10,* 204–232.

Degreef, G., Ashtari, M., Bogerts, B., Bilder, R. M., Jody, D. N., Alvir, J. M. J., Lieberman, J. A. (1992). Volumes of ventricular system subdivisions measured from magnetic resonance images in first-episode schizophrenic patients. *Archives of General Psychiatry, 49,* 531–537.

deHaan, M., Luciana, M., Malone, S. M., Matheny, L. S., & Richards, M. L. M. (1994). Development, plasticity, and risk: Commentary on Huttenlocher, Pollitt and Gorman, and Gottesman and Goldsmith. In C. A. Nelson (Ed.), *The Minnesota symposia on child psychology: Vol. 27. Threats to optimal development* (pp. 285–325). Minneapolis: University of Minnesota Press.

DeLisi, L. E., Goldin, L. R., Hamovit, J. R., Maxwell, E., Kurtz, D., & Gershon, E. S. (1986). A family study of the association of increased ventricular size with schizophrenia. *Archives of General Psychiatry, 43,* 148–153.

Detera-Wadleigh, S. D., Goldin, L. R., Sherrington, R., Encio, I., de Miguel, C., Berrettini, W., Gurling, H., & Gershon, E. S. (1989). Exclusion of linkage to 5q11–13 in families with schizophrenia and other psychiatric disorders. *Nature, 340,* 391–393.

Drewer, H. B., & Shean, G. D. (1993). Reaction time crossover in schizotypal subjects. *Journal of Nervous and Mental Disease, 181,* 27–30.

Duncan, C. C., Morihisa, J. M., Fawcett, R. W., & Kirch, D. G. (1987). P300 in schizophrenia: State or trait marker? *Psychopharmacology Bulletin, 23,* 497–501.

Ebmeier, K. P., Potter, D. D., Cochrane, R. H. B., Mackenzie, A. R., McAllister, H., Besson, J. A. O., & Salzen, E. A. (1990). P300 and smooth eye pursuit: Concordance of abnormalities and relation to clinical features in DSM-III schizophrenia. *Acta Psychiatrica Scandinavica, 82,* 283–288.

Eckblad, M., & Chapman, L. J. (1983). Magical ideation as an indicator of schizotypy. *Journal of Consulting and Clinical Psychology, 51,* 215–225.

Ereshefsky, L., Watanabe, M. D., & Tran-Johnson, T. K. (1989). Clozapine: An atypical antipsychotic agent. *Clinical Pharmacy, 8,* 691–709.

Erickson, D. H., Beiser, M., Iacono, W. G., Fleming, J. A. E., & Lin, T. (1989). The role of social relationships in the course of first-episode schizophrenia and affective psychosis. *American Journal of Psychiatry, 146,* 1456–1461.

Erlenmeyer-Kimling, L., & Cornblatt, B. (1984). Biobehavioral risk factors in children of schizophrenic parents. *Journal of Autism and Developmental Disabilities, 14,* 357–374.

Erlenmeyer-Kimling, L., & Cornblatt, B. (1987a). The New York High-Risk Project: A follow-up report. *Schizophrenia Bulletin, 13,* 451–461.

Erlenmeyer-Kimling, L., & Cornblatt, B. (1987b). High-risk research in schizophrenia: A summary of what has been learned. *Journal of Psychiatry Research, 21,* 401–411.

Erlenmeyer-Kimling, L., Folnegovic, Z., Hrabak-Zerjavic, V., Borcic, B., Folnegovic-Smalc, V., & Susser, E. (1994). Schizophrenia and prenatal exposure to the 1957 A2 influenza epidemic in Croatia. *American Journal of Psychiatry, 151,* 1496–1498.

Erlenmeyer-Kimling, L., Friedman, D., Cornblatt, B., & Jacobsen, R. (1985). Electrodermal recovery data on children of schizophrenic parents. *Psychiatry Research, 14,* 149–161.

Erlenmeyer-Kimling, L., Golden, R., & Cornblatt, B. (1989). A taxometric analysis of cognitive and neuromotor variables in children at risk for schizophrenia. *Journal of Abnormal Psychology, 98,* 203–208.

Erlenmeyer-Kimling, L., Kestenbaum, C. J., Bird, H., & Hilldoff, U. (1984). Assessment of the New York High Risk Project subjects in Sample A who are now clinically deviant. In N. Watt, E. J. Anthony, L. C. Wynne, & J. Rolf (Eds.), *Children at risk for schizophrenia: A longitudinal perspective* (pp. 227–239). New York: Cambridge University Press.

Erlenmeyer-Kimling, L., Rock, D., Squires-Wheeler, E., Roberts, S., & Yang, J. (1991). Early life precursors of psychiatric outcomes in adulthood in subjects at risk for schizophrenia or affective disorders. *Psychiatry Research, 39,* 239–256.

Erwin, R. J., Edwards, R., Tanguay, P. E., Buchwald, J., & Letai, D. (1986). Abnormal P300 responses in schizophrenic children. *Journal of the American Academy of Child Psychiatry, 25,* 615–622.

Faraone, S. V., & Tsuang, M. T. (1985). Quantitative models of the genetic transmission of schizophrenia. *Psychological Bulletin, 98,* 41–66.

Feighner, J. P., Robins, E., Guze, S. B., Woodruff, R. A., Jr., Winokur, G., & Munoz, R. (1972). Diagnostic criteria for use in psychiatric research. *Archives of General Psychiatry, 26,* 57–63.

Ficken, J., & Iacono, W. G. (1991, October). Eye tracking proficiency in preadolescent and adolescent males. Poster presented at the meeting of the Society for Psychophysiological Research. Chicago.

Fish, B. (1977). Neurobiologic antecedents of schizophrenia in children. Evidence for an inherited, congenital neurointegrative defect. *Archives of General Psychiatry, 34,* 1297–1313.

Fish, B. (1984). Characteristics and sequelae of the neurointegrative disorder in infants at risk for schizophrenia (1952–1982). In N. F. Watt, E. J. Anthony, L. C. Wynne, & J. E. Rolf (Eds.), *Children at risk for schizophrenia* (pp. 423–439). New York: Cambridge University Press.

Fish, B. (1987). Infant predictors of the longitudinal course of schizophrenic development. *Schizophrenia Bulletin, 13,* 395–409.

Friedman, D., Cornblatt, B., Vaughan, H., & Erlenmeyer-Kimling, L. (1986). Event-related potentials in children at risk for schizophrenia during two versions of the Continuous Performance Test. *Psychiatry Research, 18,* 161–177.

Friedman, D., Cornblatt, B., Vaughan, H., & Erlenmeyer-Kimling, L. (1988). Auditory event-related potentials in children at risk for schizophrenia: The complete initial sample. *Psychiatry Research, 26,* 203–221.

Garmezy, N. (1970). Process and reactive schizophrenia: Some conceptions and issues. *Schizophrenia Bulletin, 2,* 30–74.

Garmezy, N. (1974). Children at risk: The search for antecedents of schizophrenia. Part 2. Ongoing research programs, issues, and intervention. *Schizophrenia Bulletin, 1,* 55–125.

Garmezy, N. (1987). Stress, competence, and development: Continuities in the study of schizophrenic adults, children vulnerable to psychopathology, and the search for stress-resistant children. *American Journal of Orthopsychiatry, 57,* 159–174.

Garmezy, N., & Streitman, S. (1974). Children at risk: The search for the antecedents of schizophrenia: Part 1. Conceptual models and research methods. *Schizophrenia Bulletin, 1,* 14–90.

Gill, M., Taylor, C., & Murray, R. M. (1989). Schizophrenia research: Attempting to integrate genetics, neurodevelopment and nosology. *International Review of Psychiatry, 1,* 277–286.

Goldman, P. S., & Galkin, T. W. (1978). Prenatal removal of frontal association cortex in the fetal rhesus monkey: Anatomical and functional consequences in postnatal life. *Brain Research, 152,* 451–485.

Goldstein, J. M. (1988). Gender differences in the course of schizophrenia. *American Journal of Psychiatry, 145,* 684–689.

Gooding, D. C., Iacono, W. G., & Beiser, M. (1994). Temporal stability of smooth pursuit eye tracking in first episode psychosis. *Psychophysiology, 31,* 62–67.

Goodman, R. (1988). Are complications of pregnancy and birth causes of schizophrenia? *Developmental Medicine and Child Neurology, 30,* 391–406.

Gottesman, I. I. (1974). Developmental genetics and ontogenetic psychology: Overdue detente and propositions from a matchmaker. In A. Pick (Ed.), *The Minnesota symposia on child psychology: Vol. 8.* (pp. 55–80). Minneapolis: University of Minnesota Press.

Gottesman, I. I. (1991). *Schizophrenia Genesis: The origins of madness.* New York: Freeman.

Gottesman, I. I., & Goldsmith, H. H. (1994). Developmental psychopathology of antisocial behavior: Inserting genes into its ontogenesis and epigenesis. In C. A. Nelson (Ed.), *The Minnesota symposia on child psychology: Vol. 27. Threats to optimal development.* (pp. 55–80). Minneapolis: University of Minnesota Press.

Gottesman, I., Shields, J., & Hanson, D. R. (1982). *Schizophrenia: The epigenetic puzzle.* Cambridge, England: Cambridge University Press.

Grant, D. A., & Berg, E. A. (1948). A behavioral analysis of degree of reinforcement and ease of shifting to new responses in a Weigl-type card sorting problem. *Journal of Experimental Psychology, 38,* 404–411.

Green, W. H., Campbell, M., Hardesty, A. S., Grega, D. M., Padron-Gayol, M., Shell, J., & Erlenmeyer-Kimling, L. (1984). A comparison of schizophrenic and autistic children. *Journal of the American Academy of Child Psychiatry, 23,* 399–409.

Greenough, W. T., Black, J. E., & Wallace, C. S. (1987). Experience and brain development. *Child Development, 58,* 539–559.

Groner, R., & Groner, M. T. (1989). Attention and eye movement control: An overview. *European Archives of Psychiatry and Neurological Sciences, 239,* 8–16.

Grove, W. M. (1982). Psychometric detection of schizotypy. *Psychological Bulletin, 92,* 27–38.

Grove, W. M., Clementz, B. A., Iacono, W. G., & Katsanis, J. (1992). Smooth pursuit ocular motor dysfunction in schizophrenia: Evidence for a major gene. *American Journal of Psychiatry, 149,* 1362–1368.

Grove, W. M., Lebow, B. S., Clementz, B. A., Cerri, A., Medus, C., & Iacono, W. G. (1991). Familial prevalence and coaggregation of schizotypy indicators: A multitrait family study. *Journal of Abnormal Psychology, 100,* 115–121.

Guy, J. D., Majorski, L. V., Wallace, C. J., & Guy, M. P. (1983). The incidence of minor physical abnormalities in adult male schizophrenics. *Schizophrenia Bulletin, 9,* 571–582.

Hafner, H. (1990). New perspectives in the epidemiology of schizophrenia. In H. Hafner & W. F. Gattaz (Eds.), *Search for the Causes of Schizophrenia* (Vol. II, pp. 408–431). Berlin: Springer-Verlag.

Hanson, D. R., & Gottesman, I. I. (1976). The genetics, if any, of infantile autism and childhood schizophrenia. *Journal of Autism and Childhood Schizophrenia, 6,* 209–234.

Hanson, D. R., Gottesman, I. I., & Heston, L. L. (1976). Some possible childhood indicators of adult schizophrenia inferred from children of schizophrenics. *British Journal of Psychiatry, 129,* 142–154.

Hanson, D. R., Gottesman, I. I., & Heston, L. L. (1990). Long-range schizophrenia forecasting: Many a slip twixt cup and lip. In J. Rolf, A. Masten, D. Cicchetti, K. Nuechterlein, & S. Weintraub (Eds.), *Risk and protective factors in the development of psychopathology* (pp. 424–444). New York: Cambridge University Press.

Hanson, D. R., Gottesman, I. I., & Meehl, P. E. (1977). Genetic theories and the validation of psychiatric diagnoses: Implications for the study of children of schizophrenics. *Journal of Abnormal Psychology, 86,* 575–588.

Harding, C. M. (1986). Speculations on the measurement of recovery from severe psychiatric disorder and the human condition. *Psychiatric Journal of the University of Ottawa, 11,* 199–204.

Hare, E., & Moran, P. (1981). A relation between seasonal temperature and the birth rate of schizophrenic patients. *Acta Psychiatrica Scandinavica, 63,* 396–405.

Harris, M. J., & Jeste, D. V. (1988). Late onset schizophrenia: An overview. *Schizophrenia Bulletin, 14,* 39–55.

Harvey, P. D. (1991). Cognitive and linguistic functions of adolescent children at risk for schizophrenia. In E. F. Walker (Ed.), *Schizophrenia: A life-course developmental perspective* (pp. 140–157). San Diego: Academic Press.

Hathaway, S. R., & McKinley, J. C. (1943). *The Minnesota Multiphasic Personality Inventory.* Minneapolis: University of Minnesota Press.

Henn, F. A. (1982). Dopamine: A role in psychosis or schizophrenia. In F. A. Henn & H. A. Nasrallah (Eds.), *Schizophrenia as a brain disease* (pp. 176–195). New York: Oxford University Press.

Heston, L. L., & White, J. A. (1991). *The vanishing mind: A practical guide to Alzheimer's disease and other dementias.* New York: Freeman.

Hollister, J. M., Mednick, S. A., Brennan, P., & Cannon, T. D. (1994). Impaired autonomic nervous system habituation in those at genetic risk for schizophrenia. *Archives of General Psychiatry, 51,* 552–558.

Holsenbeck, L. S., Davidson, L. M., Hostetter, R. E., Casanova, M. F., Taylor, D. O., Kelley, C. T., Perrotta, C., Borison, R. L., & Diamond, B. (1992). Ventricle-to-brain ratio and symptoms at the onset of first-break schizophrenia. *Schizophrenia Bulletin, 18,* 427–435.

Holzman, P. S. (1987). Recent studies of psychophysiology in schizophrenia. *Schizophrenia Bulletin, 13,* 49–75.

Holzman, P. S., Kringlen, E., Levy, D. L., & Haberman, S. (1980). Deviant eye tracking in twins discordant for psychosis: A replication. *Archives of General Psychiatry, 37,* 627–631.

Holzman, P. S., Kringlen, E., Matthysse, S., Flanagan, S. D., Lipton, R. B., Cramer, G., Levin, S., Lange, K., & Levy, D. L. (1988). A single dominant gene can account for eye tracking dysfunctions and schizophrenia in offspring of discordant twins. *Archives of General Psychiatry, 45,* 641–647.

Holzman, P. S., & Matthysse, S. (1990). The genetics of schizophrenia: A review. *Psychological Science, 1,* 279–286.

Holzman, P. S., Proctor, L. R., & Hughes, D. W. (1973). Eye tracking patterns in schizophrenia. *Science, 181,* 179–181.

Howells, J. G., & Guirguis, W. R. (1984). Childhood schizophrenia 20 years later. *Archives of General Psychiatry, 41,* 123–128.

Hudspeth, W. J., & Pribram, K. H. (1992). Psychophysiological indexes of cerebral maturation. *International Journal of Psychophysiology, 1,* 19–29.

Husted, J. A., Beiser, M., & Iacono, W. G. (1992). Negative symptoms and the early course of schizophrenia. *Psychiatry Research, 43,* 215–222.

Huttenlocher, P. R. (1979). Synaptic density in human frontal cortex: Developmental changes and effects of aging. *Brain Research, 163,* 195–205.

Huttenlocher, P. R. (1994). Synaptogenesis, synapse elimination, and neural plasticity in human cerebral cortex. In C. A. Nelson (Ed.), *The Minnesota symposia on child psychology: Vol. 27. Threats to optimal development.* (pp. 35–54). Minneapolis: University of Minnesota Press.

Iacono, W. G. (1982). Eye tracking in normal twins. *Behavior Genetics, 12,* 517–526.

Iacono, W. G. (1985). Psychophysiologic markers of psychopathology: A review. *Canadian Psychology, 26,* 96–112.

Iacono, W. G. (1991). Psychophysiological assessment of psychopathology. *Psychological Assessment, 3,* 309–320.

Iacono, W. G., Bassett, A. S., & Jones, B. D. (1988). Eye tracking dysfunction is associated with partial trisomy of chromosome 5 and schizophrenia. *Archives of General Psychiatry, 45,* 1140–1141.

Iacono, W. G., & Beiser, M. (1989). Age of onset, temporal stability, and eighteen-month course of first-episode psychosis. In D. Cicchetti (Ed.), *Rochester Symposium on Developmental Psychopathology: Vol. 1. The emergence of a new discipline* (pp. 221–260). Hillsdale, NJ: Erlbaum.

Iacono, W. G., & Beiser, M. (1992). Where are the women in first-episode studies of schizophrenia? *Schizophrenia Bulletin, 18,* 471–480.

Iacono, W. G., & Clementz, B. A. (1993). A strategy for elucidating genetic influences on complex psychopathological syndromes (with special reference to ocular motor functioning and schizophrenia). In L. J. Chapman, J. P. Chapman, & D. C. Fowles (Eds.), *Progress in experimental personality and psychopathology research* (Vol. 16, pp. 11–65). New York: Springer.

Iacono, W. G., & Ficken, J. W. (1989). Research strategies employing psychophysiological measures: Identifying and using psychophysiological markers. In G. Turpin (Ed.), *Handbook of clinical psychophysiology* (pp. 45–70). London: Wiley.

Iacono, W. G., & Grove, W. M. (1993). Schizophrenia reviewed: Toward an integrative genetic model. *Psychological Science, 4,* 273–276.

Iacono, W. G., Moreau, M., Beiser, M., & Lin, T. (1992). Smooth pursuit eye tracking in first-episode psychotic patients and their relatives. *Journal of Abnormal Psychology, 101,* 104–116.

Iacono, W. G., Smith, G. N., Moreau, M., Beiser, M., Fleming, J. A. E., Lin, T., & Flak, B. (1988). Ventricular and sulcal size at the onset of psychosis. *American Journal of Psychiatry, 145,* 820–824.

Iacono, W. G., Tuason, V. B., & Johnson, R. A. (1981). Dissociation of smooth pursuit and saccadic eye tracking in remitted schizophrenics: An ocular reaction time task that schizophrenics perform well. *Archives of General Psychiatry, 38,* 991–996.

Jackson, H. J., Minas, I. H., Burgess, P. M., Joshua, S. D., Charisiou, J., & Campbell, I. M. (1989). Is social skills performance a correlate of schizophrenia subtypes? *Schizophrenia Research, 2,* 301–309.

Janes, C. L., Hesselbrock, V., & Stern, J. A. (1978). Parental psychopathology, age, and race as related to electrodermal activity of children. *Psychophysiology, 15,* 24–34.

Jenkins, D. M. F. (1989). *A developmental study of smooth pursuit eye movements in psychotic children and adolescents.* Unpublished doctoral dissertation, Harvard University.

Johnson, R. (1986). A triarchic model of P300 amplitude. *Psychophysiology, 23,* 367–384.

Josiassen, R. C., Shagass, C., Roemer, R. A., & Straumanis, J. J. (1985). Attention-related effects on somatosensory evoked potentials in college students at high risk for psychopathology. *Journal of Abnormal Psychology, 94,* 507–518.

Judd, L. L., McAdams, L., Budnick, B., & Braff, D. L. (1992). Sensory gating deficits in schizophrenia: New results. *American Journal of Psychiatry, 149,* 488–493.

Kahneman, D. (1973). *Attention and effort.* Englewood Cliffs, NJ: Prentice-Hall.

Kandel, D. B. (1986). Improving prediction in longitudinal research: Equivalence, developmental stages, and other issues. In L. Erlenmeyer-Kimling & N. E. Miller (Eds.), *Life-span research on the prediction of psychopathology* (pp. 157–167). Hillsdale, NJ: Erlbaum.

Karson, C. N., Goldberg, T. E., & Leleszi, J. P. (1986). Increased blink rate in adolescent patients with psychosis. *Psychiatry Research, 17,* 195–198.

Kasanin, J. (1933). The acute schizoaffective psychoses. *American Journal of Psychiatry, 13,* 97–123.

Katsanis, J., Ficken, J., Iacono, W. G., & Beiser, M. (1992). Season of birth and electrodermal activity in functional psychoses. *Biological Psychiatry, 31,* 841–855.

Katsanis, J., & Iacono, W. G. (1991). Clinical, neuropsychological, and brain structural of smooth-pursuit eye tracking performance in chronic schizophrenia. *Journal of Abnormal Psychology, 100,* 526–534.

Katsanis, J., & Iacono, W. G. (1992). Temporal lobe dysfunction and electrodermal nonresponding in schizophrenia. *Biological Psychiatry, 31,* 159–170.

Katsanis, J., Iacono, W. G., & Beiser, M. (1991). Clinical and psychophysiological correlates of lateral ventricle size in first-episode psychotic patients. *Psychiatry Research, 37,* 115–127.

Kay, S. R., Opler, L. A., & Fiszbein, A. (1986). Significance of positive and negative syndromes in chronic schizophrenia. *British Journal of Psychiatry, 149,* 439–448.

Kebabian, J. W., & Calne, D. B. (1979). Multiple receptors for dopamine. *Nature, 277,* 93–96.

Kelsoe, J. R., Cadet, J. L., Pickar, D., & Weinberger, D. R. (1988). Quantitative neuroanatomy in schizophrenia. *Archives of General Psychiatry, 45,* 533–541.

Kendell, R. E., & Kemp, I. W. (1989). Comparison of winter- and summer-born schizophrenics and winter- and summer-born affectives. In S. C. Schulz & C. A. Tamminga (Eds.), *Schizophrenia: Scientific progress* (pp. 28–35). New York: Oxford University Press.

Kendler, K. S., Gruenberg, A. M., & Tsuang, M. T. (1988). A family study of the subtypes of schizophrenia. *American Journal of Psychiatry, 145,* 57–62.

Kety, S. S. (1985). The concept of schizophrenia. In M. Alpert (Ed.), *Controversies in schizophrenia: Changes and constancies* (pp. 3–11). New York: Guilford.

Kety, S. S., Rosenthal, D., Wender, P. A., & Schulsinger, F. (1968). The types and prevalence of mental illness in the biological and adoptive families of adopted schizophrenics. In D. Rosenthal & S. S. Kety (Eds.), *The transmission of schizophrenia* (pp. 345–362). New York: Pergamon.

Kolvin, I. (1971). Studies in the childhood psychoses: I. Diagnostic criteria and classification. *British Journal of Psychiatry, 118,* 381–384.

Kraepelin, E. (1971). *Dementia praecox and paraphrenia* (R. M. Barclay, Trans.). Huntington, NY: Krieger. (Original work published 1919)

Kugelmass, S., Marcus, J., & Schmueli, J. (1985). Psychophysiological reactivity in high-risk children. *Schizophrenia Bulletin, 11,* 66–73.

Kulhara, P., & Chandiramani, K. (1990). Positive and negative subtypes of schizophrenia: A follow-up study from India. *Schizophrenia Research, 3,* 107–116.

Langfeldt, G. (1937). The prognosis in schizophrenia and the factors influencing the course of the disease. *Acta Psychiatrica et Neurologica Scandinavica* (Suppl. 13).

Lencz, T., Raine, A., Scerbo, A., Redmon, M., Brodish, S., Holt, L., & Bird, L. (1993). Impaired eye tracking in undergraduates with schizotypal personality disorder. *American Journal of Psychiatry, 150,* 152–154.

Lenzenweger, M. F., Cornblatt, B. A., & Putnick, M. (1991). Schizotypy and sustained attention. *Journal of Abnormal Psychology, 100,* 84–89.

Lenzenweger, M. F., & Loranger, A. W. (1989). Detection of familial schizophrenia using a psychometric measure of schizotypy. *Archives of General Psychiatry, 46,* 902–907.

Levin, S. (1984). Frontal lobe dysfunctions in schizophrenia: I. Eye movement impairments. *Journal of Psychiatric Research, 18,* 27–55.

Levinson, D. F., & Mowry, B. J. (1991). Defining the schizophrenia spectrum: Issues for genetic linkage studies. *Schizophrenia Research, 17,* 491–514.

Levy, D. L., Holzman, P. S., Matthysse, S., & Mendell, N. R. (1993). Eye tracking dysfunction and schizophrenia: A critical perspective. *Schizophrenia Bulletin, 19,* 461–536.

Lewis, S. W., Owen, M. J., & Murray, R. M. (1989). Obstetric complications and schizophrenia: Methodology and mechanisms. In S. C. Schulz & C. A. Tamminga (Eds.), *Schizophrenia: Scientific progress* (pp. 56–68). New York: Oxford University Press.

Liddle, P. F. (1990). Prefrontal and subcortical dysfunction in schizophrenia. In M. Weller (Ed.), *International perspectives in schizophrenia: Biological, social, and epidemiological findings* (pp. 85–95). London: Libbey Press.

Lieberman, J. A., Alvir, J., Woerner, M., Degreef, G., Bilder, R. M., Ashtari, M., Bogerts, B., Mayerhoff, D. I., Geisler, S. H., Loebel, A., Levy, D. L., Hinrichsen, G., Szymanski, S., Chakos, M., Koreen, A., Borenstein, M., & Kane, J. M. (1992). Prospective study of psychobiology in first-episode schizophrenia at Hillside Hospital. *Schizophrenia Bulletin, 18,* 351–371.

Lieberman, J. A., Jody, D., Alvir, J. M., Ashtari, M., Levy, D. L., Bogerts, B., Degreef, G., Mayerhoff, D. I., & Cooper, T. (1993). Brain morphology, dopamine, and eye-tracking abnormalities in first-episode schizophrenia. Prevalence and clinical correlates. *Archives of General Psychiatry, 50,* 357–368.

Litman, R. E., Hommer, D. W., Clem, T., Ornsteen, M. L., Ollo, C., & Pickar, D. (1991). Correlation of Wisconsin Card Sorting Test performance with eye tracking in schizophrenia. *American Journal of Psychiatry, 148,* 1580–1582.

Livson, N., & Peskin, H. (1980). Perspectives on adolescence from longitudinal research. In J. Adelson (Ed.), *Handbook of adolescent psychology* (pp. 47–98). New York: Wiley.

Loranger, A. W. (1984). Sex difference in age at onset of schizophrenia. *Archives of General Psychiatry, 41,* 157–161.

Mackay, A. V., Bird, E. D., Spokes, E. G., Rossor, M., & Iversen, L. L. (1980). Dopamine receptors and schizophrenia: Drug effect or illness? *Lancet,* 915–916.

Maier, W., Franke, P., Hain, C., Kopp, B., & Rist, F. (1992). Neuropsychological indicators of the vulnerability to schizophrenia. *Progress in Neuro-Psychopharmacology and Biological Psychiatry, 16,* 703–715.

Marcus, J., Auerbach, J., Wilkinson, L., & Burack, C. M. (1981). Infants at risk for schizophrenia. *Archives of General Psychiatry, 38,* 703–713.

Marcus, J., Hans, S. L., Nagler, S., Auerbach, J. G., Mirsky, A. F., & Aubrey, A. (1987). Review of the NIMH Israeli kibbutz-city study and the Jerusalem infant development study. *Schizophrenia Bulletin, 13,* 425–438.

Masten, A. (1987). Toward a developmental psychopathology of early adolescence. In M. D. Levin & E. R. McArnarney (Eds.), *Early adolescent transitions* (pp. 261–278). Lexington, MA: Heath.

Mather, J. A. (1985). Eye movements of teenage children of schizophrenics: A possible inherited marker of susceptibility to the disease. *Journal of Psychiatric Research, 19,* 523–532.

Matthysse, S., Holzman, P. S., & Lange, K. (1986). The genetic transmission of schizophrenia: Application of Mendelian latent structure analysis of eye tracking dysfunctions in schizophrenia and affective disorder. *Journal of Psychiatric Research, 20,* 57–76.

McClellan, J. M., & Werry, J. S. (1992). Schizophrenia. *Pediatric Psychopharmacology, 15,* 131–148.

McGue, M., & Gottesman, I. I. (1989a). A single dominant gene still cannot account for the transmission of schizophrenia. *Archives of General Psychiatry, 46,* 478–479.

McGue, M., & Gottesman, I. I. (1989b). Genetic linkage in schizophrenia. *Schizophrenia Bulletin, 15,* 453–464.

McNeil, T., & Kaij, L. (1978). Obstetric factors in the development of schizophrenia. Complications in the births of preschizophrenics and in reproduction by schizophrenic parents. In L. C. Wynne, R. L. Cromwell, & S. Matthysse (Eds.), *The nature of schizophrenia* (pp. 401–429). New York: Wiley.

Mednick, S. A., Machon, R. A., & Huttunen, M. (1989). Disturbances of fetal neural development and adult schizophrenia. In S. C. Schulz & C. A. Tamminga (Eds.), *Schizophrenia: Scientific progress* (pp. 69–77). New York: Oxford University Press.

Mednick, S. A., Machon, R. A., Huttunen, M. O., & Bonett, D. (1988). Adult schizophrenia following prenatal exposure to an influenza epidemic. *Archives of General Psychiatry, 45,* 189–192.

Mednick, S. A., Mura, E., Schulsinger, F., & Meednick, B. (1971). Perinatal conditions and infant development in children with schizophrenic parents. *Social Biology, 18,* 103–113.

Mednick, S. A., & Schulsinger, F. (1968). Some premorbid characteristics related to breakdown in children with schizophrenic mothers. In D. Rosenthal & S. S. Kety (Eds.), *The transmission of schizophrenia* (pp. 267–291). Oxford, England: Pergamon.

Meehl, P. E. (1962). Schizotaxia, schizotypy, schizophrenia. *American Psychologist, 17,* 827–838.

Meehl, P. E. (1972). Specific genetic etiology, psychodynamics, and therapeutic nihilism. *International Journal of Mental Health, 1,* 10–27.

Meehl, P. E. (1989). Schizotaxia revisited. *Archives of General Psychiatry, 46,* 935–944.

Meehl, P. E. (1990). Toward an integrated theory of schizotaxia, schizotypy, and schizophrenia. *Journal of Personality Disorders, 4,* 1–99.

Merriam, A. E., Kay, S. R., Opler, L. A., Kushner, S. F., van Praag, H. M. (1990). Neurological signs and the positive-negative dimension in schizophrenia. *Biological Psychiatry, 28,* 181–192.

Meyer, A. (1910). The dynamic interpretation of dementia praecox. *American Journal of Psychology, 21,* 385–403.

Mirsky, A. F. (1988). Research on schizophrenia in the NIMH laboratory of psychology and psychopathology, 1954–1987. *Schizophrenia Bulletin, 14,* 151–156.

Mirsky, A. F., Duncan, C., Silberman, E., Nagler, S., Kugelmass, S., Sohlberg, S., & Shotten, J. (1986). Early neuropsychological and other behavioral predictors of later psychotic disorders. In C. Shagass, G. Simpson, W. Bridges, R. Josiassen, D. Staff, K. Weiss (Eds.), *Biological psychiatry* (pp. 1118–1120). New York: Elsevier.

Moises, H. W., Gelernter, J., Giuffra, L. A., Zarcone, V., Wetterberg, L., Civelli, O., Kidd, K. K., & Cavalli-Sforza, L. L. (1991). No linkage between D-2 dopamine receptor gene region and schizophrenia. *Archives of General Psychiatry, 48,* 643–647.

Moldin, S. O., Gottesman, I. I., Rice, J., & Erlenmeyer-Kimling, L. (1991). Replicated psychometric correlates of schizophrenia. *American Journal of Psychiatry, 148,* 762–767.

Moldin, S. O., Rice, J. P., Gottesman, I. I., & Erlenmeyer-Kimling, L. (1990a). Psychometric deviance in offspring at risk for schizophrenia: I. Initial delineation of a distinct subgroup. *Psychiatry Research, 32,* 297–310.

Moldin, S. O., Rice, J. P., Gottesman, I. I., & Erlenmeyer-Kimling, L. (1990b). Psychometric deviance in offspring at risk for schizophrenia: II. Resolving heterogeneity through admixture analysis. *Psychiatry Research, 32,* 311–322.

Morgan, D. G., May, P. C., & Finch, C. E. (1987). Dopamine and serotonin systems in human and rodent brain: Effects of age and neurodegenerative disease. *Journal of the American Geriatrics Society, 35,* 334–345.

Murray, R. M., & Lewis, S. W. (1987). Is schizophrenia a neurodevelopmental disorder? *British Medical Journal, 295,* 681–682.

Murray, R. M., & Lewis, S. W. (1988). Is schizophrenia a neurodevelopmental disorder? Response. *British Medical Journal, 296,* 63.

Nasrallah, H. A. (1986). The differential diagnosis of schizophrenia: Genetic, perinatal, neurological, pharamacological, and psychiatric factors. In H. A. Nasrallah & D. R. Weinberger (Eds.), *Handbook of schizophrenia: Vol. 1. The neurology of schizophrenia* (pp. 49–64). London: Elsevier Science.

Neale, J. M., & Oltmanns, T. F. (1980). *Schizophrenia.* New York: Wiley.

Nicol, S. E., & Gottesman, I. I. (1983). Clues to the genetics and neurobiology of schizophrenia. *American Scientist, 71,* 398–404.

Nuechterlein, K. H. (1985). Converging evidence for vigilance deficit as a vulnerability indicator for schizophrenic disorders. In M. Alpert (Ed.), *Controversies in schizophrenia* (pp. 175–198). New York: Guilford.

Nuechterlein, K. H. (1987). Vulnerability models for schizophrenia: State of the art. In H. Hafner, W. F. Gattaz, & W. Janzarik (Eds.), *Search for the causes of schizophrenia* (pp. 297–316). Berlin: Springer-Verlag.

Nuechterlein, K. H. (1991). Vigilance in schizophrenia and related disorders. In S. R. Steinhauer, J. H. Gruzelier, & J. Zubin (Eds.), *Handbook of schizophrenia: Vol. 5. Neuropsychology, psychophysiology, and information processing* (pp. 397–430). New York: Elsevier.

Nuechterlein, K. H., & Dawson, M. (1984). Information processing and attentional functioning in the developmental course of schizophrenic disorders. *Schizophrenia Bulletin, 10,* 160–203.

Nuechterlein, K. H., Dawson, M. E., Gitlin, M., Ventura, J., Goldstein, M. J., Snyder, K. S., Yee, C. M., & Mintz, J. (1992). Developmental processes in schizophrenic disorders: Longitudinal studies of vulnerability and stress. *Schizophrenia Bulletin, 18,* 387–425.

Nuechterlein, K. H., Garmezy, N., & Devine, V. T. (1989). Sustained, focused attention under high processing loads: Relevance to vulnerability to schizophrenia. In S. C. Schulz & C. A. Tamminga, (Eds.), *Schizophrenia: Scientific progress,* (pp. 95–109). New York: Oxford University Press.

Nuechterlein, K. H., Phipps-Yonas, S., Driscoll, R., & Garmezy, N. (1990). Vulnerability factors in children at risk: Anomalies in attentional functioning and social behavior. In J. Rolf, A. S. Masten, D. Cicchetti, K. H. Nuechterlein, & S. Weintraub (Eds.), *Risk and protective factors in the development of psychopathology* (pp. 445–479). New York: Cambridge University Press.

Ohlund, L. S., Ohman, A., Alm, T., Ost, L. -G., Lindstrom, L. H. (1990). Season of birth and electrodermal unresponsiveness in male schizophrenics. *Biological Psychiatry, 27,* 328–340.

Onstad, S., Skre, I., Torgersen, S., & Kringlen, E. (1991). Twin concordance for DSM-III-R schizophrenia. *Acta Psychiatrica Scandivavica, 83,* 395–401.

Owen, F., Crow, T. J., Poulter, M., Cross, A. J., Longden, A., & Riley, G. J. (1978). Increased dopamine-receptor sensitivity in schizophrenia. *The Lancet,* 223–225.

Owen, M. J., Lewis, S. W., & Murray, R. M. (1988). Obstetric complications and schizophrenia: A computed tomographic study. *Psychological Medicine, 18,* 331–339.

Parnas, J., Cannon, T. D., Jacobsen, B., Schulsinger, H., Schulsinger, F., & Mednick, S. A. (1993). Lifetime DSM-III-R diagnostic outcomes in the offspring of schizophrenic mothers. Results from the Copenhagen High-Risk Study. *Archives of General Psychiatry, 50,* 707–714.

Parnas, J., Jorgensen, A., Teasdale, T. W., Schulsinger, F., & Mednick, S. A. (1988). Temporal course of symptoms and social functioning in relapsing schizophrenics: A 6-year follow-up. *Comprehensive Psychiatry, 29,* 361–371.

Parnas, J., & Mednick, S. A. (1990). Early predictors of onset and course of schizophrenia and schizophrenia spectrum. In H. Hafner & W. F. Gattaz (Eds.), *Search for the causes of schizophrenia* (Vol. II, pp. 34–47). Berlin: Springer-Verlag.

Parnas, J., Schulsinger, F., Schulsinger, H., Mednick, S. & Teasdale, T. (1982a). Behavioral precursors of schizophrenia spectrum. *Archives of General Psychiatry, 39,* 658–664.

Parnas, J., Schulsinger, F., Teasdale, T., Schulsinger, H., Feldman, P., & Mednick, S. (1982b). Perinatal complications and clinical outcome within the schizophrenia spectrum. *British Journal of Psychiatry, 140,* 421–424.

Pearson, J. S., & Kley, I. B. (1957). On the application of genetic expectancies as age specific base rates in the study of human behavior disorders. *Psychological Bulletin, 54,* 406–420.

Perlmutter, I. R., Greenhill, L. L., Chambers, W., & Kestenbaum, C. J. (1989). Childhood schizophrenia: Theoretical and treatment issues. *Journal of American Academy of Child and Adolescent Psychiatry, 28,* 956–962.

Petty, L. K., Ornitz, E. M., Michelman, J. D., & Zimmerman, E. G. (1984). Autistic children who become schizophrenic. *Archives of General Psychiatry, 41,* 129–135.

Pfohl, B., & Winokur, G. (1982). Schizophrenia: Course and outcome. In F. A. Henn & H. A. Nasrallah (Eds.), *Schizophrenia as a brain disease* (pp. 26–39). New York: Oxford University Press.

Pogue-Geile, M. F., & Harrow, M. (1984). Negative and positive symptoms in schizophrenia and depression: A follow-up. *Schizophrenia Bulletin, 10,* 371–387.

Pogue-Geile, M. F., & Harrow, M. (1985). Negative symptoms in schizophrenia: Their longitudinal course and prognostic importance. *Schizophrenia Bulletin, 11,* 427–439.

Posner, M. I. (1978). *Chronometric explorations of mind.* Hillsdale, NJ: Erlbaum.

Prentky, R. A., Salzman, L. F., & Klein, R. H. (1981). Habituation and conditioning of skin conductance responses in children at risk. *Schizophrenia Bulletin, 7,* 281–291.

Prescott, C. A., & Gottesman, I. I. (1993). Genetically mediated vulnerability to schizophrenia. *Psychiatric Clinics of North America, 16,* 245–267.

Pritchard, W. S. (1986). Cognitive event-related potential correlates of schizophrenia. *Psychological Bulletin, 100,* 43–66.

Purves, D., & Lichtman, J. W. (1985). *Principles of neural development.* Sunderland, MA: Sinauer.

Raine, A., Lencz, T., Reynolds, G. P., Harrison, G., Sheard, C., Medley, Reynolds, L. M., & Cooper, J. E. (1992). An evaluation of structural and functional prefrontal deficits in schizophrenia: MRI and neuropsychological measures. *Psychiatry Research, 45,* 123–137.

Raymond, V., Beaulieu, M., Labrie, F., & Boissier, J. (1978). Potent antidopaminergic activity of estradiol at the pituitary level on prolactin release. *Science, 200,* 1173–1175.

Reveley, A. M., Reveley, M. A., & Murray, R. M. (1984). Cerebral ventricular enlargement in nongenetic schizophrenia: A controlled twin study. *British Journal of Psychiatry, 144,* 89–93.

Richters, J., & Weintraub, S. (1990). Beyond diathesis: Toward an understanding of high-risk environments. In J. Rolf, A. Masten, D. Cicchetti, K. Nuechterlein, & S. Weintraub (Eds.), *Risk and protective factors in the development of psychopathology* (pp. 67–96). New York: Cambridge University Press.

Riecher, A., Maurer, K., Loffler, W., Fatkenheurer, B., an Der Heiden, W., Munk-Jorgensen, P., Stromgren, E., & Hafner, H. (1990). Gender differences in age at onset and course of schizophrenic disorders. In H. Hafner & W. F. Gattaz (Eds.), *Search for the causes of schizophrenia* (Vol. II, pp. 14–34). Berlin: Springer-Verlag.

Rosen, W. G., Mohs, R. C., Johns, C. A., Small, N. S., Kendler, K. S., Horvath, T. B., & Davis, K. L. (1984). Positive and negative symptoms in schizophrenia. *Psychiatry Research, 13,* 277–284.

Ross, C. A., McInnis, M. G., Margolis, R. L., & Li, S. -H. (1993). Genes with triplet repeats: Candidate mediators of neuropsychiatric disorders. *Trends in Neuroscience, 16,* 254–260.

Ross, D. E., Ochs, A. L., Hill, M. R., Goldberg, S. C., Pandurangi, A. K., & Winfrey, C. J. (1988). Erratic eye tracking in schizophrenic patients as revealed by high resolution techniques. *Biological Psychiatry, 24,* 675–688.

Ross, R. G., Radant, A. D., & Hommer, D. W. (1993). A developmental study of smooth pursuit eye movements in normal children from 7 to 15 years of age. *Journal of the American Academy of Child and Adolescent Psychiatry, 32,* 783–791.

Roxborough, H., Muir, W. J., Blackwood, D. H., Walker, M. T., & Blackburn, I. M. (1993). Neuropsychological and P300 abnormalities in schizophrenics and their relatives. *Psychological Medicine, 23,* 305–314.

Rund, B. R., & Landro, N. I. (1990). Information processing: A new model for understanding cognitive disturbances in psychiatric patients. *Acta Psychiatrica Scandinavica, 81,* 305–316.

Russell, A. T., Bott, L., & Sammons, C. (1989). The phenomenology of schizophrenia occurring in childhood. *Journal of American Academy of Child Adolescent & Psychiatry, 28,* 399–407.

Rutter, M. (1972). Childhood schizophrenia reconsidered. *Journal of Autism and Childhood Schizophrenia, 2,* 315–337.

Rutter, M. L. (1986). Child psychiatry: The interface between clinical and developmental research. *Psychological Medicine, 16,* 151–169.

Rutter, M. (1988). Epidemiological approaches to developmental psychopathology. *Archives of General Psychiatry, 45,* 486–495.

Rutter, M. (1989). Age as an ambiguous variable in developmental research: Some epidemiological considerations from developmental psychopathology. *International Journal of Behavioral Development, 12,* 1–34.

Sabate, O., Campion, D., d'Amato, T., Martres, M. P., Sokoloff, P., Giros, B., Leboyer, M., Jay, M., Guedj, F., Thibaut, F., Dollfus, S., Preterre, P., Petit, M., Babron, M. -C., Waksman, G., Mallet, J., & Schwartz, J. C. (1994). Failure to find evidence for linkage or association between the dopamine D3 receptor gene and schizophrenia. *American Journal of Psychiatry, 151,* 107–111.

Sacchetti, E., Calzeroni, A., Vita, A., Terzi, A., Pollastro, F., & Cazzullo C. L. (1992). The brain damage hypothesis of the seasonality of births in schizophrenia and major affective disorders: Evidence from computerised tomography. *British Journal of Psychiatry, 160,* 390–397.

Saitoh, O., Niwa, S., Hiramatsu, K., Kameyama, T., Rymar, K., & Itoh, K. (1984). Abnormalities in late positive components of event-related potentials may reflect a genetic predisposition to schizophrenia. *Biological Psychiatry, 19,* 293–303.

Sameroff, A., & Zax, M. (1973). Schizotaxia revisited: Model issues in the etiology of schizophrenia. *American Journal of Orthopsychiatry, 43,* 744–754.

Saugstad, L. F. (1989). Age at puberty and mental illness. Towards a neurodevelopmental aetiology of Kraepelin's endogenous psychoses. *British Journal of Psychiatry, 155,* 536–544.

Schaumann, B., & Alter, M. (1976). *Dermatoglyphics in medical disorders.* New York: Springer-Verlag.

Schneider, K. (1959). *Clinical psychopathology.* New York: Grune & Stratton.

Schulsinger, F., & Parnas, J. (1990). Risk factors in schizophrenia: Interaction between genetic liability and environmental factors. In A. Kales, C. N. Stefanis, & J. A. Talbott (Eds.), *Recent advances in schizophrenia* (pp. 119–129). New York: Springer-Verlag.

Schulsinger, F., Parnas, J., Petersen, E. T., Schulsinger, H., Teasdale, T. W., Mednick, S. A., Moller, L., & Silverton, L. (1984). Cerebral ventricular size in the offspring of schizophrenic mothers. *Archives of General Psychiatry, 41,* 602–606.

Schulsinger, H. (1976). A ten year follow-up of children of schizophrenic mothers: Clinical assessment. *Acta Psychiatrica Scandinavica, 53,* 371–386.

Schulz, S. C., Koller, M. M., Kishore, P. R., Hamer, R. M., Gehl, J. J., & Friedel, R. O. (1983). Ventricular enlargement in teenage patients with schizophrenia spectrum disorder. *American Journal of Psychiatry, 140,* 1592–1595.

Schreiber, H., Stolz, G., Rothmeier, J., Kornhuber, H. H., & Born, J. (1989). Prolonged latencies of the N2 and P3 of the auditory event-related potential in children at risk for schizophrenia: A preliminary report. *European Archives of Psychiatry and Neurological Sciences, 238,* 185–188.

Schreiber, H., Stolz-Born, G., Rothmeier, J., Kornhuber, A., Kornhuber, H. H., & Born, J. (1991). Endogenous event-related brain potentials and psychometric performance in children at risk for schizophrenia. *Biological Psychiatry, 30,* 177–189.

Seeman, M. V. (1982). Gender differences in schizophrenia. *Canadian Journal of Psychiatry, 27,* 107–112.

Seeman, M. V. (1985). Sex and schizophrenia. *Canadian Journal of Psychiatry, 30,* 313–315.

Shakow, D. (1962). Segmental set: A theory of the formal psychological deficit in schizophrenia. *Archives of General Psychiatry, 6,* 1–17.

Shakow, D. (1977). *Schizophrenia: Selected papers.* New York: International Universities Press.

Shelton, R. C., & Weinberger, D. R. (1986). X-ray computerized tomography studies in schizophrenia: A review and synthesis. In H. A. Nasrallah & D. R. Weinberger (Eds.), *Handbook of Schizophrenia: Vol. 1. The neurology of schizophrenia* (pp. 207–250). London: Elsevier.

Shenton, M. E., Kikinis, R., Jolesz, F. A., Pollak, S. D., LeMay, M., Wible, C., Hokama, J., Martin, J., Metcalf, D., Coleman, M., & McCarley, R. W. (1992). Abnormalities of the left temporal lobe and thought disorder in schizophrenia. A quantitative magnetic imaging study. *New England Journal of Medicine, 327,* 604–612.

Sherrington, R., Brynjolfsson, J., Tetursson, H., Potter, M., Dudleston, K., Barraclough, B., Wasmuth, J., Dobbs, M., & Gurling, H. (1988). Localization of a susceptibility locus for schizophrenia on chromosome 5. *Nature, 336,* 164–166.

Shields, J., Heston, L., & Gottesman, I. (1975). Schizophrenia and the schizoid. The problem for genetic analysis. In D. Rosenthal & H. Brill (Eds.), *Genetic research in psychiatry* (pp. 167–197). Baltimore: Johns Hopkins Press.

Siegel, C., Waldo, M., Mizner, G., Adler, L. E., & Freedman, R. (1984). Deficits in sensory gating in schizophrenic patients and their relatives. *Archives of General Psychiatry, 41,* 607–612.

Siever, L. J., & Coursey, R. D. (1985). Biological markers for schizophrenia and the biological high-risk approach. *Journal of Nervous and Mental Disease, 173,* 4–16.

Siever, L. J., Coursey, R. D., Alterman, I. S., Buchsbaum, M. S., & Murphy, D. L. (1982). Psychological and physiological correlates of variations in smooth pursuit eye movements. In E. Usdin & I. Hanin (Eds.), *Biological markers in psychiatry and neurology* (pp. 359–370). Elmsford, NY: Pergamon.

Simons, R. F. (1981). Electrodermal and cardiac orienting in psychometrically defined high-risk subjects. *Psychiatry Research, 4,* 347–356.

Simons, R. F., & Katkin, W. (1985). Smooth pursuit eye movements in subjects reporting physical anhedonia and perceptual aberrations. *Psychiatry Research, 14,* 275–289.

Simons, R. F., MacMillan, F. W., & Ireland, F. B. (1982). Anticipatory pleasure deficit in subjects reporting physical anhedonia: Slow cortical evidence. *Biological Psychology, 14,* 297–310.

Smalley, S. L., Asarnow, R. F., & Spence, M. A. (1988). Autism and genetics: A decade of research. *Archives of General Psychiatry, 45,* 953–961.

Smith, R. C., Calderon, M., Ravichandran, G. K., Largen, J., Vroulis, G., Shvartsburd, A., Gordon, J., & Schoolar, J. C. (1984). Nuclear magnetic resonance in schizophrenia: A preliminary study. *Psychiatry Research, 12,* 137–147.

Spitzer, R. L., Endicott, J., & Robins, E. (1978). Research diagnostic criteria. *Archives of General Psychiatry, 35,* 773–782.

Sponheim, S. R., Iacono, W. G., & Beiser, M. (1991). Stability of ventricular size after the onset of psychosis in schizophrenia. *Psychiatry Research, 40,* 21–29.

Squires-Wheeler, E., Friedman, D., Skodol, A. E., & Erlenmeyer-Kimling, L. (1993). A longitudinal study relating P3 amplitude to schizophrenia spectrum disorders and to global personality functioning. *Biological Psychiatry, 33,* 774–785.

Sroufe, L. A., & Rutter, M. (1984). The domain of developmental psychopathology. *Child Development, 83,* 173–189.

Strandburg, R. J., Marsh, J. T., Brown, W. S., Asarnow, R. F., Guthrie, D., & Higa, J. (1990). Event-related potential correlates of impaired attention in schizophrenic children. *Biological Psychiatry, 27,* 1103–1115.

Strandburg, R. J., Marsh, J. T., Brown, W. S., Asarnow, R. F., Guthrie, D., & Higa, J. (1991). Reduced attention-related negative potentials in schizophrenic children. *Electroencephalography and Clinical Neurophysiology, 79,* 291–307.

Strauss, J. S., & Harding, C. M. (1990). Relationships between adult development and the course of mental disorder. In J. Rolf, A. S. Masten, D. Cicchetti, K. H. Nuechterlein, & S. Weintraub (Eds.), *Risk and protective factors in the development of psychopathology* (pp. 514–525). New York: Cambridge University Press.

Strik, W. K., Dierks, T., & Maurer, K. (1993). Amplitudes of auditory P300 in remitted and residual schizophrenics: Correlations with clinical features. *Neuropsychobiology, 27,* 54–60.

St. Clair, D., Blackwood, D., Muir, W., Baillie, D., Hubbard, A., Wright, A., & Evans, H. J. (1989). No linkage of chromosome 5q11–q13 markers to schizophrenia in Scottish families. *Nature, 399,* 305–309.

Su, Y., Burke, J., O'Neill, F. A., Murphy, B., Nie, L., Kipps, B., Bray, J., Shinkwin, R., Nuallin, M. N., MacLean, C. J., Walsh, D., Diehl, S. R., & Kendler, K. S. (1993). Exclusion of linkage between schizophrenia and the D2 dopamine receptor gene region of chromosome 11q in 112 Irish multiplex families. *Archives of General Psychiatry, 50,* 205–211.

Suddath, R. L., Casanova, M. F., Goldberg, T. E., Daniel, D. G., Kelsoe, J. R., & Weinberger, D. R. (1989). Temporal lobe pathology in schizophrenia: A quantitative magnetic resonance imaging study. *American Journal of Psychiatry, 146,* 464–472.

Suddath, R. L., Christison, G. W., Torrey, E. F., Casanova, M. F., & Weinberger, D. R. (1990). Anatomical abnormalities in the brains of monozygotic twins discordant for schizophrenia. *New England Journal of Medicine, 322,* 789–794.

Susser, E., Lin, S. P., Brown, A. S., Lumey, L. H., & Erlenmeyer-Kimling, L. (1994). No relation between risk of schizophrenia and prenatal exposure to influenza in Holland. *American Journal of Psychiatry, 151,* 922–924.

Sweeney, J. A., Clementz, B. A., Escobar, M. D., Li, S., Pauler, D. K., & Haas, G. L. (1993). Mixture analysis of pursuit eye-tracking dysfunction in schizophrenia. *Biological Psychiatry, 34,* 331–340.

Sweeney, J. A., Haas, G. L., Clementz, B. A., Escobar, M. D., Drake, K., & Frances, A. J. (1994). Eye tracking dysfunction in schizophrenia: Characterization of component eye movement abnormalities, diagnostic specificity, and the role of attention. *Journal of Abnormal Psychology, 103,* 222–230.

Sweeney, J. A., Haas, G. L., & Li, S. (1992). Neuropsychological and eye movement abnormalities in first-episode and chronic schizophrenia. *Schizophrenia Bulletin, 18,* 283–293.

Swerdlow, N. R., & Koob, G. F. (1987). Dopamine, schizophrenia, mania, and depression: Toward a unified hypothesis of cortico-striato-pallido-thalamic function. *Behavioral and Brain Sciences, 10,* 197–245.

Tanguay, P. E., & Cantor, S. L. (1986). Schizophrenia in children. *Journal of the American Academy of Child Psychiatry, 25,* 591–594.

Takei, N., Sham, P., O'Callaghan, E., Murray, G. K., Glover, G., & Murray, R. M. (1994). Prenatal exposure to influenza and the development of schizophrenia: Is the effect confined to females? *American Journal of Psychiatry, 151,* 117–119.

Teychenne, P. F., Feuerstein, G., Lake, C. R., & Ziegler, M. G. (1985). Central catecholamine systems: Interaction with neurotransmitters in normal subjects and in patients with selected neurologic diseases. In C. R. Lake & M. G. Ziegler (Eds.), *The catecholamines in psychiatric and neurologic diseases* (pp. 91–123). Boston: Butterworth.

Tienari, P., Sorri, A., Lahti, I., Naarala, M., Wahlberg, K. E., Moring, J., Pohjola, J., & Wynne, L. C. (1987). Interaction of genetic and psychosocial factors in schizophrenia: The Finnish adoption study. *Schizophrenia Bulletin, 13,* 477–484.

Torrey, E. F. (1989). The epidemiology of schizophrenia: Questions needing answers. In S. C. Schulz & C. A. Tamminga (Eds.), *Schizophrenia: Scientific progress* (pp. 45–51). New York: Oxford University Press.

Torrey, E. F., & Kaufmann, C. A. (1986). Schizophrenia and neuroviruses. In H. A. Nasrallah & D. R. Weinberger (Eds.), *Handbook of schizophrenia: Vol. I. The neurology of schizophrenia* (pp. 361–376). New York: Elsevier.

Torrey, E. F., Rawlings, R., & Waldman, I. N. (1988). Schizophrenic births and viral diseases in two states. *Schizophrenia Research, 1,* 73–77.

Tsuang, M. T. (1994). Genetics, epidemiology, and the search for causes of schizophrenia. *American Journal of Psychiatry, 151,* 3–6.

Tsuang, M. T., Woolson, R. F., Winokur, G., & Crowe, R. R. (1981). Stability of psychiatric diagnosis: Schizophrenia and affective disorders followed up over a 30- to 40-year period. *Archives of General Psychiatry, 38,* 535–539.

Venables, P. H. (1989). The Emanuel Miller memorial lecture. Childhood markers for adult disorders. *Journal of Child Psychology and Psychiatry, 30,* 347–364.

Venables, P. H. (1990). Developmental precursors of adult disorders. In M. Weller (Ed.), *International perspectives in schizophrenia: Biological, social, and epidemiological findings* (pp. 77–84). London: Libbey Press.

Venables, P. H., Mednick, S. A., Schulsinger, S. F., Raman, A. C., Bell, B., Dalais, J. C., & Fletcher, R. P. (1978). Screening for risk in mental illness. In G. M. Serban (Ed.), *Cognitive defects in the development of mental illness* (pp. 273–303). New York: Brunner/Mazel.

Waldo, M. C., Carey, G., Myles-Worsley, M., Cawthra, E., Adler, L. E., Nagamoto, H. T., Wender, P., Byerley, W., Plaetke, R., & Freedman, R. (1991). Codistribution of a sensory gating deficit and schizophrenia in multi-affected families. *Psychiatry Research, 39,* 257–268.

Walker, E. F. (1991). Research on life-span development in schizophrenia. In E. F. Walker (Ed.), *Schizophrenia: A life-course developmental perspective* (pp. 1–6). San Diego: Academic Press.

Walker, E. F. (1993, April). *Neurodevelopmental models on schizophrenia.* Paper presented at the International Congress on Schizophrenia Research, Colorado Springs, Colorado.

Walker, E. F., & Aylward, E. (1984). Longitudinal research in schizophrenia: The high-risk method. In S. A. Mednick, M. Harway, &

K. M. Finello (Eds.), *Handbook of longitudinal research: Vol. II: Teenage and adult cohorts* (pp. 451–486). New York: Praeger.

Walker, E. F., & Emory, E. (1983). Infants at risk for psychopathology: Offspring of schizophrenic parents. *Child Development, 54,* 1269–1285.

Walker, E. F., Grimes, K. E., Davis, D. M., & Smith, A. J. (1993). Childhood precursors of schizophrenia: Facial expressions of emotion. *American Journal of Psychiatry, 150,* 1654–1660.

Walker, E. F., & Lewine, R. J. (1990). Prediction of adult-onset schizophrenia from childhood home movies of the patients. *American Journal of Psychiatry, 147,* 1052–1056.

Watkins, J. M., Asarnow, R. F., & Tanguay, P. E. (1988). Symptom development in childhood onset schizophrenia. *Journal of Child Psychology and Psychiatry, 29,* 865–878.

Watson, C. G., Kucala, T., Tilleskjor, C., & Jacobs, L. (1984). Schizophrenic birth seasonality in relation to the incidence of infectious diseases and temperature extremes. *Archives of General Psychiatry, 41,* 85–90.

Wechsler, D. (1974). *Wechsler intelligence scale for children—revised.* New York: Psychological Corporation.

Weinberger, D. R. (1986). The pathogenesis of schizophrenia: A neurodevelopmental theory. In H. A. Nasrallah & D. R. Weinberger (Eds.), *Handbook of schizophrenia: Vol. I. The neurology of schizophrenia* (pp. 397–406). New York: Elsevier.

Weinberger, D. R. (1987). Implications of normal brain development for the pathogenesis of schizophrenia. *Archives of General Psychiatry, 44,* 660–669.

Weinberger, D. R., DeLisi, L. E., Neophytides, A. N., & Wyatt, R. J. (1981). Familial aspects of CT scan abnormalities in chronic schizophrenic patients. *Psychiatry Research, 4,* 65–71.

Weinberger, D. R., DeLisi, L. E., Perman, G. P., Targum, S., & Wyatt, R. J. (1982). Computed tomography in schizophreniform disorder and other acute psychiatric disorders. *Archives of General Psychiatry, 39,* 778–783.

Werry, J. S. (1992). Child and adolescent (early onset) schizophrenia: A review in light of DSM-III-R. *Journal of Autism and Developmental Disorders, 22,* 601–624.

Werry, J. S., McClellan, J. M., & Chard, L. (1991). Childhood and adolescent schizophrenia, bipolar, and schizoaffective disorders: A clinical and outcome study. *Journal of the American Academy of Child and Adolescent Psychiatry, 30,* 457–465.

Williams, M. L., Lewandowski, L. J., Coplan, J., & D'Eugenio, D. B. (1987). Neurodevelopmental outcome of preschool children born preterm with and without intracranial hemorrhage. *Developmental Medicine and Child Neurology, 29,* 243–249.

Winters, K. C., Stone, A. A., Weintraub, S., & Neale, J. M. (1981). Cognitive and attentional deficits in children vulnerable to psychopathology. *Journal of Abnormal Psychology, 9,* 435–453.

Winters, L., Cornblatt, B. A., & Erlenmeyer-Kimling, L. (1991). The prediction of psychiatric disorders in late adolescence. In E. F. Walker (Ed.), *Schizophrenia: A life-course developmental perspective* (pp. 123–137). San Diego: Academic Press.

Witelson, S. F., & Kigar, D. L. (1988). Anatomical development of the corpus callosum in humans: A review with reference to sex and cognition. In D. L. Molfese & S. J. Segalowitz (Eds.), *Brain lateralization in children: Developmental implications* (pp. 35–57). New York: Guilford.

Wynne, L. C., Cole, R. E., & Perkins, P. (1987). University of Rochester Child and Family Study: Risk research in progress. *Schizophrenia Bulletin, 13,* 463–476.

Yassa, R. (1991). Late-onset schizophrenia. In E. F. Walker (Ed.), *Schizophrenia: A life-course developmental perspective* (pp. 243–255). San Diego: Academic Press.

Zigler, E., & Glick, M. (1986). *A developmental approach to adult psychopathology.* New York: Wiley.

Zubin, J. (1989). Suiting therapeutic intervention to the scientific models of aetiology. *British Journal of Psychiatry, 155* (Suppl. 5), 9–14.

Zubin, J., Feldman, R. S., & Salzinger, S. (1991). A developmental model for the etiology of schizophrenia. In W. M. Grove & D. Cicchetti (Eds.), *Thinking clearly about psychology. Vol. 2. Personality and psychopathology* (pp. 410–429). Minnesota: University of Minnesota Press.

Zubin, J., & Spring, B. (1977). Vulnerability: A new view of schizophrenia. *Journal of Abnormal Psychology, 96,* 103–126.

CHAPTER 16

Development of Dissociative Disorders

FRANK W. PUTNAM

WHY IS DISSOCIATION INTERESTING FROM A DEVELOPMENTAL PERSPECTIVE?

The dissociative disorders (psychogenic amnesia, psychogenic fugue states, depersonalization disorder, and multiple personality disorder (MPD)) were among the very first psychiatric conditions studied. First described in the 1600s, these unusual conditions caught the attention of psychologists and psychiatrists during the late 1800s. Multiple personality in particular served as a model for many of the polypsychic theories of mind that collectively spurred the evolution of dynamic psychiatry around the beginning of this century (Ellenberger, 1970). The recent resurgence of interest in the dissociative disorders, now linked to traumatic precipitants, has stimulated a powerful new developmental perspective to our understanding of these painful conditions. Multiple personality disorder in particular may serve as a unique testing ground for exploring theories of developmental psychopathology because it involves a dramatic deviation in the development of self, a core domain of developmental psychopathology. This unusual condition, characterized by the individual's psychological organization into a series of semiautonomous dissociative states of consciousness, serves as a common meeting ground for many theoretical perspectives.

Dissociation represents a powerful isomorphic construct that cuts across divergent psychological domains of knowledge. Dissociation can be operationally defined and quantified, and increasingly sophisticated approaches are being applied to its measurement. Psychophysiological correlates of dissociative states have been identified, providing an important neurobiological window into somatization and related mind/body processes. Neuropsychological studies have begun to elucidate the nature of the amnesias and other memory disturbances that characterize the disorder and torment afflicted individuals. The close linkage of MPD to early childhood traumatic experiences provides an opportunity to examine the alteration of an initially defensive process into an increasingly maladaptive condition over the life course of the individual. A number of normative capacities (e.g., fantasy, hypnotizability, regulation of behavioral state) have been identified as potential substrates for the development of dissociative defenses.

From the first psychiatric descriptions, clinicians and psychologists have sought to use dissociation as a centerpiece for models of the mind. Models and theoretical perspectives currently brought to bear on dissociation include classical psychoanalytic perspectives (Berman, 1981; Marmer, 1991), object relations (Crisp, 1983), classical and operant conditioning (Braun, 1984), neurobiology (Demitrack, Putnam, Brewerton, Brandt, & Gold, 1990; Devinsky, Putnam, Grafman, Bromfield, & Theodore, 1989; Good, 1989), computer models (Andorfer, 1985; Li & Spiegel, 1992) and social role theory (Spanos, 1986). For more than a century, multiple personality disorder and related dissociative phenomena have served as a psychopathological focus around which models of the mind and behavior have been organized.

The primary purpose of this chapter is to provide an in-depth review of the dissociative disorders, particularly multiple personality disorder, for readers not familiar with these conditions. Whenever possible, aspects and issues relevant to developmental psychopathology will be highlighted. At present, however, few data actually link dissociative disorders to developmental psychopathological constructs. It is hoped that this overview will encourage developmental psychopathologists and others in related disciplines to undertake the study of dissociative disorders and to include measures of dissociation in research on developmental processes likely to be impacted by pathological dissociation.

The review begins with a brief history of the waxing and waning of psychiatric interest in the dissociative disorders, followed by an examination of current diagnostic formulations. Although the dissociative disorders are viewed categorically in the *Diagnostic and Statistical Manual of Mental Disorders* (DSM-IV; American Psychiatric Association, 1994), much of this chapter will treat dissociation as a widely distributed, continuum process that becomes pathological only in its extreme forms. As this is an important conceptualization of dissociation, evidence for the continuum nature of dissociation and its underlying dimensions will be detailed. Most clinical formulations regard dissociation as serving psychological defensive functions. These functions will be discussed in detail along with a brief review of the data linking significant levels of dissociation to traumatic antecedents. The question of a developmental window for the creation of multiple personality will be raised at this point.

Much progress has been made in the assessment of dissociation, both as a continuum process and as categorical diagnoses. A review of the instruments and issues of measurement and diagnosis is included to acquaint potential investigators with the state of the art. Unlike many other psychiatric disorders, something is also known about the cognitive and physiological mechanisms underlying dissociative symptoms. Research in this area is described, with an emphasis on how these mechanisms produce or contribute to symptoms and behaviors. Principles derived from the laboratory study of dissociation will be invoked in the final section on the developmental basis of the dissociative disorders.

Having laid this foundation, the chapter next addresses the clinical features of the adult dissociative disorders, which are the best studied examples. This review includes sections on epidemiology, clinical presentations, the alter personalities of MPD patients, life course, treatment, and outcome. The reader is then introduced to current theories of dissociation and MPD, which are largely offered to account for the adult clinical data. Whenever possible, research supporting or refuting these theories is cited.

Some of these theories and models emphasize the role of childhood trauma; therefore the limited information available on dissociation in childhood is summarized in the concluding sections of the chapter. Beginning with clinical data, the reader is introduced to the signs and symptoms of dissociation in children and adolescents. This is followed by a discussion of normative dissociation in children. Many readers may be dismayed by the limited and tenuous nature of the information contained here—but this dearth of hard data accurately represents the state of the field and to suggest otherwise would be misleading. The final section on the developmental basis of the dissociative disorders is largely speculative and concerns the connections between dissociation and important research constructs operationalized in developmental psychology and psychopathology. The intention here is to provide researchers in these disciplines with broad hypotheses for investigation. Again, the tentative and hypothetical nature of these connections may frustrate some readers. This area is in its infancy, however, and to overextend current knowledge would be a mistake.

In general, this chapter seeks to move from what is known to what is speculative. The wish is to thoroughly ground the reader in dissociation theory and the clinical phenomenology of the dissociative disorders, as is appropriate in a manual on psychopathology. The dissociative disorders represent potentially very rich models for understanding the ontogeny of environmentally produced psychiatric conditions. It is hoped that this chapter will stimulate the interest of readers who have the ability to add to our knowledge in the area.

BRIEF HISTORY OF DISSOCIATION AND MULTIPLE PERSONALITY DISORDER

Dramatic and powerful examples of dissociation exist in every culture. Possession states, shamanistic transformation, conversion symptoms, and religious healing are dissociative phenomena that are as old as humankind. In one form or another, culturally determined variants of these processes are widely distributed throughout all societies (Bliss, 1986; Bourguignon, 1968; Mulhern, 1991). Temple and religious healing through the induction of trance states, the "royal touch," and other dissociative interventions are part of Western medical tradition, dating back at least to the Greeks (Bliss, 1986; Ellenberger, 1970). These "suggestive" interventions continue to constitute core therapeutic elements of many modern non-Western psychotherapies.

Paracelsus is credited by Bliss (1986) as being the first physician to describe a case of multiple personality disorder: a woman whose alter personality filched her money while she remembered nothing about it. Important early cases were reported by Benjamin Rush, personal physician to George Washington and father of American psychiatry, in 1812, and by S. L. Mitchell in 1817 (Bliss, 1986; Carlson, 1981). Mitchell's case of Mary Reynolds, redescribed by others over the years, became the stereotype for multiple personality until Morton Prince's patient, "Miss Beauchamp," now known to have been Clara Norton Fowler, caught the imagination of both the general public and professionals at the turn of the century (Putnam, 1989a). Despine's 1836 treatment of Estelle, an 11-year-old Swiss girl, is a recently rediscovered classic that first puts forward the basic axioms of psychotherapy for dissociative disorders (Ellenberger, 1970; Fine, 1988).

Pierre Janet's work at the beginning of the 20th century crowned a period of intense interest in the dissociative disorders (van der Hart & Friedman, 1989). Janet and his contemporaries, William James, Morton Prince, and others on both sides of the Atlantic, elucidated the core principles of the dissociative disorders, including the role of discrete states of consciousness and the linkage of dissociation to overwhelming psychological or physical experiences (Putnam, 1989b). The seminal discoveries of Janet and others were lost, however. They were drowned, as Morton Prince had gloomily predicted, by the rising tide of a militant psychoanalytic movement (Hale, 1975). Prince and his followers were subsequently held up to ridicule for allegedly creating a *folié à deux* with their patients. Among additional factors contributing to the disappearance of the diagnosis, most notable was its inclusion under the diagnosis of schizophrenia, introduced by Bleuler in 1908 (Rosenbaum, 1980).

Dissociation and multiple personality disorder never really disappeared from the medical scene or the clinical literature. Psychogenic amnesia, psychogenic fugue cases, and conversion symptoms accounted for a substantial percentage of the psychiatric casualties in both World Wars. Following the successful abreactive treatment of the massive dissociative casualities from Dunkirk, allied military physicians were routinely trained in hypnotic and barbiturate-facilitated abreactive therapies (Putnam, 1992b). Occasional cases of MPD continued to appear in reputable journals, the authors often expressing astonishment at the distinctiveness of the alter personalities (Putnam, 1989a).

During the latter 1950s, the book and movie *The Three Faces of Eve,* which described a case of multiple personality disorder, attracted a great deal of notoriety (Thigpen & Cleckley, 1957). The authors, however, knew little about the disorder and contributed to the popularization of an erroneous stereotype that even today continues to mislead professionals and the public. *Sybil,* an account that is far more accurate and useful, is often credited with reigniting an awareness of the disorder among mental health professionals (Schreiber, 1974). Sybil's psychiatrist, Cornelia Wilbur, together with Arnold Ludwig and others at the University of Kentucky aggressively investigated MPD during the 1970s, contributing several classic studies that paved the way for the inclusion of a separate dissociative disorder category in the DSM-III (American Psychiatric Association, 1980; Brandsma & Ludwig, 1974; Ludwig, Brandsma, Wilbur, Bendfeldt, & Jameson, 1972).

Following a decade of growing clinical recognition and increasingly sophisticated research, a great deal has been learned about dissociation and its disorders, much of which confirms the forgotten knowledge of Janet and his colleagues (Putnam, 1989b). Current research, though grossly underfunded, is broad based and supports the construct of dissociation through a series of converging validities. Reliable and valid measures are available to screen for, verify, and quantify dissociation (Bernstein & Putnam, 1986; Carlson, Putnam, Ross et al., 1993; Ross, Heber, Norton, Anderson, Anderson, & Barchet, 1989; Steinberg, 1990). For the first time, acceptable epidemiological data are becoming available for high-risk populations and the general public (Ross, 1991). In addition to their clinical utility, these measures have greatly enhanced the scientific investigation of dissociation, permitting the identification of biological and clinical correlates (Putnam, 1991c). Recent studies confirm that elevated levels of dissociation are significantly related to an interesting array of psychopathological processes. Most importantly, the confirmation of the role of traumatic childhood antecedents in adult cases has led to the active identification of these disorders in abused and traumatized children.

DEFINITIONS OF DISSOCIATION

The DSM-III and DSM-IV Perspectives

The conceptualizations of dissociation and dissociative disorders in DSM-III and DSM-IV (American Psychiatric Association, 1987, 1994) reflect a long-standing trend toward understanding dissociation as a disruption in the integrative functions of identity and memory. The earliest diagnostic definitions, dating to the 1890s, were descriptive, usually referencing a famous case for comparison (Putnam, 1989a). The definitions of multiple personality focused primarily on the separateness and distinctness of the alter personalities but often acknowledged varying degrees of amnesia or disinterest among alter personalities. Around 1900, a classification system for different types of multiple personality cases was based on the directional nature of the amnesia among alters and included "one-way amnesia" (A knows about B, but not vice versa) and "two-way amnesia" (mutual amnesia). Subsequent work has shown that most MPD cases have complex combinations of directional amnesia, which vary depending on the nature of the memory task involved. Literature reviews by Sutcliffe and Jones (1962) and Taylor and Martin (1944) gradually refined the syndromal definitions for multiple personality. The work of Ludwig and colleagues in the 1970s greatly influenced the DSM-III criteria, which were based exclusively on establishing that the personalities were discrete and separate complex entities that recurrently assumed full control over the individual's behavior (Brandsma & Ludwig, 1974; Larmore, Ludwig, & Cain, 1977; Ludwig et al., 1972).

The DSM-III (American Psychiatric Association, 1980) approval of MPD brought many cases to light that had been quietly treated by therapists concerned about credibility issues. Taken together with the increasing number of newly diagnosed cases, they led to general, statistically based, syndromic profiles, less influenced by idiosyncratic features of dramatized cases such as Eve. For example, in most instances it was discovered that although there were usually some alter personalities with verifiably unique behaviors and individualized social patterns, many of these entities are extremely limited in the range and depth of the dimensions that collectively constitute the construct of "personality." For example, many alter personalities can express only a single or at best, a very limited range of affect. Recognition that the Hollywood Stereotype of each personality as a fully developed person was in error, contributed to the dropping in the DSM-III-R (American Psychiatric Association, 1987) of the DSM-III requirement that each of the alter personalities have "its own unique behavior patterns and social relationships."

Subsequently, the DSM-III-R criteria have been criticized for being too general and vague. The DSM-IV criteria seek to redress this critique by adding a requirement for amnesia. The amnesia criterion is based on analyses of several cases series showing that some form of amnesia is detectable 98% to 100% of the time. However, at least one prominent authority has argued strongly against this position (Kluft, 1991b). As more information accrues, many new subtypes of MPD are being proposed. For example, a recent review of the features of MPD listed over 20 contrasting clinical presentations suggesting that MPD may be more heterogeneous than previously recognized (Kluft, 1991b). The comorbidity of MPD with Axis II personality disorders also requires further clarification. Although MPD can be distinguished from these disorders, it nonetheless shares symptom clusters with a number of Axis II disorders including borderline personality disorder, antisocial personality disorder, and avoidant personality disorder (Fink, 1991).

The DSM-III introduced a catchall category called Atypical Dissociative Disorder for individuals who did not satisfy criteria for a specific dissociative disorder but who experienced prolonged trancelike states or dissociative symptoms. Although there is virtually no published data on this diagnosis, the prevailing clinical impression is that there are a substantial number of these cases. The DSM-III-R and DSM-IV have continued this category, with a number of additions, as the diagnosis of Dissociative Disorder Not Otherwise Specified (DDNOS). DDNOS cases appear to share much of the diffuse clinical phenomenology of MPD with the exception that they do not exhibit clear-cut alter personality states (Coons, 1992).

The Dissociative Continuum

Although the DSM treats the dissociative disorders as a set of discrete diagnoses, the conceptualization of dissociation as a continuum process that becomes pathological only in its extreme forms dates back at least to the writings of Morton Prince and has been echoed by many others over the years (Hale, 1975; Putnam, 1989a). Examples of normative dissociation experienced by most adults include daydreaming and highway hypnosis. Daydreaming often occurs during times when the individual is bored or in situations where he or she does not want to be. Typically, the individual "tunes out" of the immediate environment and becomes involved in a directed reverie that often involves an alteration in the individual's sense of self, (e.g., appearance, physical, mental abilities, or sexual prowess). On termination or interruption of the fantasy, the individual may have little recall of the immediate events around him (e.g., missing information in a lecture he or she is attending).

Highway hypnosis, the induction of a trancelike state by monotonous activity such as driving a car on an interstate highway, is not uncommon. Similar trancelike states, sometimes called "breakaway" by the military and accident investigators, have been reported in helmsmen aboard ships and high-altitude pilots (Barnes, 1980). They are also thought to play a role in some sport parachuting deaths (Cancio, 1991). In most instances, however, highway hypnosis occurs without mishap and the individual merely finds him- or herself miles farther on down the road with little or no recollection of having driven the distance. This common experience illustrates that complex activities such as driving a car in high-speed traffic can occur largely out of conscious awareness. Automatization of complex behaviors is thought to be one of the adaptive functions of normal dissociation, permitting an individual to divide attention between two dissimilar tasks (e.g., driving a car and planning the day's work activities).

Evidence for a continuum of dissociative phenomena ranging from minor everyday mini- and microdissociation to chronic pathological conditions comes from two principal sources. The first is the study of hypnosis, a controlled and structured dissociative process characterized by total absorption, compartmentalization of experience and heightened suggestibility (Spiegel, 1991). For adults, pathological dissociation is strongly correlated with high hypnotizability (Frischholz, 1985; Spiegel, 1991; Stutman & Bliss, 1985). However, high hypnotizability is not necessarily related to pathological dissociation (Carlson & Putnam, 1989). Studies of hypnotizability indicate that this capacity is distributed in a non-Gaussian fashion throughout the general population with roughly 10% of individuals scoring high, 45% being moderately hypnotizable, and 45% showing low hypnotizability (Hilgard, 1965, 1986) (see Figure 16.1).

The second major source of data bearing on the continuum nature of dissociation comes from studies using the Dissociative Experiences Scale (DES) and other instruments. The DES quantifies three major factors thought to underlie pathological dissociation: (a) psychogenic amnesia; (b) depersonalization and identity disturbances; and (c) absorption and enthrallment phenomena (Armstrong & Loewenstein, 1990; Bernstein & Putnam, 1986; Carlson & Putnam, 1989; Ross, Norton, & Anderson, 1988). About 5% to 9% of the general population score in the high range on this instrument, though some of these individuals appear to be asymptomatic when evaluated in depth by structured clinical interviews (Ross, 1991). DES scores are strongly influenced by childhood histories of stress and trauma and appear to share other developmental factors in common with hypnotizability and fantasy proneness discussed later in this chapter.

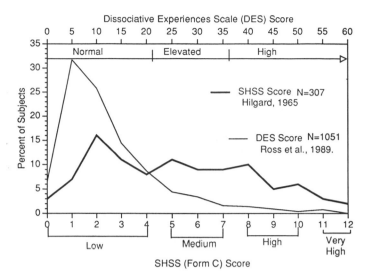

Figure 16.1 Distribution of hypnotizability and dissociativity in general population samples.

DIMENSIONS OF DISSOCIATION

Dissociation is a complex process composed of a number of related domains. Different measures tap varying combinations of these domains resulting in significant correlations between measures but sufficient differences remain so that they are not interchangeable. Furthermore, none of the measures can rule out the possibility that there may be a qualitative shift in the nature of dissociation at some point along the continuum (Frankel, 1990). In addition to the disruptions of memory and identity that are a core feature of the dissociative disorders, dissociation involves experiences of intense absorption. Measures of absorption such as the Tellegen Absorption Scale (Tellegen & Atkinson, 1974), correlate significantly with measures of hypnotizability and with measures of pathological dissociation (Nash, Hulsey, Sexton, Harralson, & Lambert, 1993).

Dissociation is often discussed from another perspective, however, that of the discrete state of consciousness (Putnam, 1991c). Dissociation is conceived as the entry into a specific state of consciousness, the dissociative state. The concept of a dissociative state of consciousness, was present in the earliest writings about hypnosis and dissociative disorders. Dissociative states were a core feature of Janet's thinking about dissociative disorders and continue to be routinely invoked in discussions of hypnosis and the dissociative disorders today (Putnam, 1989b). From this perspective, an individual experiencing dissociation, enters into a unique state of consciousness—the dissociative state—that has certain specific features including: (a) isolation of memory and affects from normal states of consciousness; (b) disturbance in sense of identity or sense of self; (c) intense absorption of focused concentration and, in the case of the hypnotic state, increased suggestibility.

How can investigators reconcile these two different conceptualizations of dissociation as both a discrete state of consciousness and a continuum process? To some extent, the requirement for more than one model to account for all the facts is analogous to the physicist's need to characterize light as both a particle and a wave. In the case of dissociation, however, the two models can be layered such that dissociation is conceptualized as a specific state of consciousness with certain properties that individuals enter into with different frequencies and/or for different lengths of time, thereby creating a continuum distribution of the degree of dissociation. Those individuals who enter into a dissociative state(s) more often and/or for longer periods, experience significantly more dissociative phenomena and thus score higher on current instruments that are to some extent predicated on the continuum conceptualization. An individual's dissociativity can be defined as a function of the frequency and duration with which the individual spontaneously enters into a dissociative state of consciousness in naturally occurring situations (Carlson, 1981; Putnam, 1991b).

THE DEFENSIVE FUNCTIONS OF DISSOCIATION

Irrespective of whether dissociation is conceptualized as a discrete state of consciousness, a continuum process, or an isomorphic combination thereof, dissociation is widely regarded as a defensive operation invoked by individuals caught in situations that they wish to escape or avoid (Bliss, 1986; Fink, 1988; Ludwig, 1983; Putnam, 1985; Spiegel, 1991). From Janet (1901) onward, it has been recognized that dissociation serves to defend an individual against unacceptable psychological or physical experiences. Ludwig (1983) proposed a set of adaptive and defensive functions performed by dissociation including automatization of certain behaviors, efficiency and economy of effort, resolution of irreconcilable conflicts, escape from the constraints of reality, isolation of catastrophic experiences cathartic discharge of feelings, and the enhancement of herd sense. Additional defensive operations such as analgesia and detachment from self have been identified by others (Putnam, 1991b; Spiegel, 1991).

For heuristic purposes, I have grouped these proposed defensive functions into four overriding defensive operations: (a) automatization; (b) compartmentalization; (c) alteration of identity; and (d) protection from unbearable pain. These dissociative subprocesses work independently and in combination to produce the psychological and clinical phenomena identified as dissociative behavior. During the following discussion, it should be kept in mind that although dissociation is commonly present in a variety of minor forms in everyday life, it is in many respects a last-ditch psychological defensive response, and as such it exacts a severe price with chronic use.

Automatization

Many of the examples of "everyday" normal dissociative behaviors involve automatization of complex actions such as driving a car in high-speed traffic. Automatization involves a redirection of conscious awareness away from an activity. Usually attention is withdrawn from a repetitive or procedural activity that can be done by routine or rote. Conscious awareness is frequently redirected from external activities to internal preoccupations. The ability to divide attention, particularly in situations where the individual is facing a boring but potentially demanding task, increases the ability to accomplish necessary mental chores such as planning and solving problems. Ludwig (1983) likened this capacity to the simultaneous foreground- and background-processing capabilities of some computers.

Automatization may occur in varying degrees, with a dynamic waxing and waning of conscious awareness of the activity depending on changing circumstances. Automatized activities may range from complex tasks such as driving an automobile to minor mental overflow activities such as doodling while talking on the telephone. Hilgard (1986) has suggested that dissociative automatization extends to activities occurring in conscious awareness over which the individual feels that he or she has no control such as passive influence experiences like automatic writing.

Automatization may also increase the efficiency of certain repetitive activities that become "paralyzed" by self-conscious scrutiny and analysis. Creative abilities such as playing music likewise may be enhanced by the suspension of consciously directed performance. Return of conscious awareness to the automatized task may be rapid and abrupt, however, such as the electric adrenaline jolt a person experiences when things start to go seriously wrong on the highway.

Compartmentalization

A second, critical component of defensive dissociation is compartmentalization, the partitioning off of areas of conscious experiences from each other. This complicated process, which appears to be mechanistically based on the principles of state-dependent learning and memory retrieval, produces many complex psychological effects (Putnam, 1991c). Defensively, compartmentalization permits the isolation of catastrophic experiences. Overwhelming perceptions, sensations, affects and ideation can be walled off from everyday waking consciousness, allowing the individual to function in other areas of life. The dissociation of traumatic experiences from normal consciousness, however, impedes their psychological resolution so that walled-off trauma remains "raw" and psychologically fresh despite the passage of time. Dissociated traumatic material often seems to have a life of its own, periodically intruding into awareness through dreams and nightmares, flashbacks, intrusive images, affects and memories (van der Kolk & Kadish, 1987). The induction of altered states of consciousness by alcohol, drugs, hypnosis, or other procedures frequently increases the leakage of dissociated material into conscious awareness.

The segregation of emotionally charged material allows the individual to tolerate the side-by-side existence of irreconcilable conflicts and impulses. As such, opposing drives and desires are sequentially expressed, often as doing and undoing behaviors, in an unintegrated fashion (Ludwig, 1983). On the other hand, compartmentalization may work synergistically with automatization to further isolate and enhance the performance of demanding tasks or functions. In addition to sequestering traumatic material, compartmentalization can act to preserve sensitive psychological functions and capacities by rigidly isolating them from disruptive and intrusive material. Such single-mindedness of purpose may significantly contribute to the practice of artistic talents. Dissociative states also permit the cathartic expression of intense emotions—aggressive and libidinal urges—within a contained arena (Ludwig, 1983). Many cultures use music, dance, drugs, pain, and other trance-inducing, mental state-altering tools to both unleash and reframe these impulses during ritual and religious rites (Ludwig, 1983; Mulhern, 1991).

Alterations and Estrangements of Self

Dissociative defensive alterations of identity take a variety of forms. In many instances, the psychological dynamics behind the alteration are transparently obvious to an observer. For example, in psychogenic amnesia, the individual may "forget" who and what he is in a global or selective way as necessary to protect himself from the effects of a traumatic event (Loewenstein, 1991b; Putnam, 1985). While in a psychogenic fugue, an individual may elaborate another identity, remaining largely amnesic for his original identity and its problems. In multiple personality disorder, the individual usually switches among a series of alter identities that personify specific functions, capacities, or experiences. In depersonalization, the individual experiences a loss of or a distortion in his or her sense of reality of self, often accompanied by feelings of detachment and "numbness" (Putnam, 1985; Steinberg, 1991).

Profound alterations of identity, in concert with compartmentalization, can effectively, if only transiently, isolate catastrophic psychological experiences. The withdrawal of investment in self that accompanies traumatically induced depersonalization acts to protect the individual from the loss or annihilation of self in the face of death. Out-of-body experiences, characterized by the individual's experience of viewing himself as if from a distance or as in a "movie" and often accompanied by a sense of sharpened but detachment mental acuity, are common in near-death situations (Putnam, 1985, 1991b; Spiegel, 1991; Steinberg, 1991). Ludwig (1983) has speculated that dissociation in near-death situations may be analogous to the freezing and sham-death reflexes evoked by predators in the young of many prey species.

The alter personalities of MPD represent complex disturbances of identity and self that contain conflicts, preserve functions, and express forbidden impulses. The partial or complete obliteration of identity in psychogenic amnesia often serves to "stop time" until the individual can safely process the overwhelming event. Depersonalization, detachment from self, and even obliteration of self-awareness serve to psychologically distance overwhelming personal experiences. Dissociative alterations in self and identity transform the denial process from "it is not happening" to "it is not happening to me."

Dissociative alterations of identity also include a variety of disturbances in body image. Many authorities believe that the dissociative process is central to somatization and conversion symptoms (Loewenstein, 1991b; Nemiah, 1991). Dissociative distortions of identity are a common feature of the alter personalities of MPD, which may see "themselves" as physically being of a different gender, age, or body size, or as having other body-image attributes that differ from the actual body (Putnam, 1989a). It is speculated that the increased dissociativity of many anoretic patients may contribute to the profound distortions of body image in the eating disorders (Demitrack et al., 1990). Group process mediated dissociative alterations in identity may contribute to submergence of the individual identity in religious or patriotic causes, mob psychology or mass hysteria (Ludwig, 1983). Impairment of reality testing, submission to charismatic leaders, heightened suggestibility, self-sacrifice, and other lapses in logic and judgment, and pursuit of self-interest are common in such situations.

Protection from Unbearable Pain

In the last analysis, most of the defensive operations of dissociation act to spare the individual from overwhelming psychological and physical pain. These defensive processes operate synergistically at psychological and psychophysiological levels providing an extraordinary opportunity for insight into mind-body mechanisms. Analgesia or even complete anesthesia for pain are commonly reported during traumatically induced dissociative reactions and can be routinely demonstrated in the hypnosis laboratory (Hilgard, 1986). Gioloas and Sanders have demonstrated that in normal subjects, high dissociators tolerate pain significantly longer than low dissociators (Gioloas & Sanders, 1992). Protection from physical pain, together with depersonalization of self, permit some individuals to dispassionately endure horrible experiences such as rape or torture in a detached and often analytic manner. The cessation of struggling and the calm, detached, peaceful acceptance of death reported by many near-death survivors may be the ultimate manifestation of the protective functions of dissociation. An analogous "peaceful acceptance of death" has been observed in mortally wounded prey succumbing to predators suggesting the existence of a primitive, biologically based escape from unbearable pain.

DISSOCIATION AND TRAUMA

The connection between dissociation and trauma has been known for a long time. Janet was among the first to systematically elaborate this linkage (Putnam, 1989b; van der Hart & Friedman, 1989). Clinical reports and studies from World War I and World War II also routinely connected dissociation to stress and trauma, even correlating the degree of combat exposure with the incidence of dissociative disorders, a finding that recent studies confirm (Branscomb, 1991; Bremner et al., 1992; Loewenstein, 1991b; Putnam, 1985). Classic studies of civilian populations also established connections between dissociative disorders and overwhelming psychological trauma (Abeles & Schilder, 1935; Kanzer, 1939; Loewenstein, 1991b; Putnam, 1985; Stengel, 1941). The data linking dissociation and trauma have been demonstrated and reviewed extensively elsewhere and will not be discussed in full detail here (Albini & Pease, 1989; Bliss, 1986; Boor, 1982; Bowman, Blix, & Coons, 1985; Braun & Sachs,

1985; Briere & Runtz, 1988; Chu & Dill, 1990; Fink, 1988; Frischholz, 1985; Greaves, 1980; Kluft, 1985a; Nemiah, 1980; Putnam, 1985; Ross, Miller, Bjornson, Reagor, Fraser, & Anderson, 1991; Schultz, Braun, & Kluft, 1989; Spiegel, 1991; West, 1967). Given the existence of this knowledge, the question is, Why was this information not better assimilated by psychiatry?

Some have suggested that there is a long-standing, tacit conspiracy on the part of our society to avoid looking at what we do to children (Donovan 1991; Rothenberg, 1980). Bowman (1990) wryly notes that late 19th and early 20th century clinicians resorted to Latin to discuss "hallucinosis incestus patris," indicating a reluctance to openly acknowledge patients' allegations of incest and abuse in common language. Within the MPD therapist community, many presenters analogize society's dissociation of the connection between dissociation and trauma and the patient's dissociation of the same information at the personal level.

Whatever the reasons, the general recognition of the existence of a range of posttraumatic psychiatric sequelae and the more specific linkage between dissociation and trauma has just recently been accepted by the larger mental health establishment. This recognition, coupled with the recent availability of reliable and valid measures of dissociation, has prompted widespread exploration for dissociative disorders and symptoms in at-risk populations. The many published and presented surveys and studies of psychiatric and normal samples have begun to clarify the incidence and prevalence of these conditions, although a great deal of work remains to be done. The apparent explosion in the numbers of dissociative disorder cases, however, has led some to worry about a possible iatrogenic or fad effect as a result of increased attention (Fahy, 1988; Frankel, 1990). Time and work will resolve many of these controversies.

Among the best demonstrated connections between trauma and dissociation is the finding of massive early childhood trauma in the vast majority of cases of multiple personality disorder. The rediscovery of this connection in the late 1960s by Cornelia Wibur and her colleagues was first confirmed retrospectively in adult case series (e.g., see Coons, Bowman, & Milstein, 1998; Loewenstein & Putnam, 1990; Putnam, Guroff, Silberman, Barban, & Post, 1986; Ross et al., 1991; Schultz et al., 1989). Subsequently, this connection has also been established in much smaller series of child and adolescent cases (Bowman et al., 1985; Dell & Eisenhower, 1990; Fagan & McMahon, 1984; Hornstein & Putnam, 1992; Hornstein & Tyson, 1991; Kluft, 1984; Malenbaum & Russel, 1987; Peterson, 1990; Riley & Mead, 1988; Vincent & Pickering, 1988; Weiss, Sutton, & Utecht, 1985). Although the bulk of these data are retrospective self-report in nature, and thus subject to all the criticisms thereof, sufficient founded cases exist to convincingly demonstrate that there are extraordinarily high levels of physical, sexual, and other abuses and a variety of other types of trauma in the childhoods of MPD patients.

DEVELOPMENTAL WINDOW OF VULNERABILITY

The establishment of a presumably causal relationship between childhood traumatic antecedents and adult MPD outcomes has spurred a developmental approach to MPD. Many theoretical papers have been written and models proposed (Albini & Pease, 1989; Bliss, 1986; Boor, 1982; Braun & Sachs, 1985; Fink, 1988; Kluft, 1985a; Putnam, 1989a). An interesting feature of this posited causal relationship is the consistent finding that patients with MPD report that their abusive experiences occurred in early childhood and that the alter personalities first appeared in this context, although at the time they were generally not recognized as such.

In reviews of MPD, Greaves (1980) and Boor (1982) both found that in the majority of reported cases there was a history of early childhood trauma. Greaves noted that alter selves appeared in early childhood, and typically were present by age 8. The first modern case series was collected by Bliss (1980), who found that in every instance, the first alter personality was created between ages 4 and 6 years in the context of "unpleasant or intolerable" events. A large survey by Putnam et al. (1986) found a mean age of 5.98 years and a median age of 4 years for the creation of the first alter personalities. A subsequent large case series by Coons et al. (1988) reported a mean age of 6.7 years for the first appearance of an alter personality. An extensive survey of cases in treatment by Schultz et al. found a mean age for the onset of child abuse of 3.3 years in MPD patients but did not report data on first appearance of alter personalities. In addition, two studies, one with adult psychiatric inpatients and the other with a non-clinical sample of sexually abused girls demonstrate that histories of earlier onset of maltreatment are significantly associated with increased levels of dissociation (Kirby, Chu, & Dill, 1993; Putnam, Helmer, Horowitz, & Trickett, in press).

In aggregate, these data have been taken to infer the existence of a developmental window of vulnerability for the creation of MPD. The upper limits of this window are generally thought to be about 9 to 10 years of age. Estimates of the lower limits range from "in utereo" to about 3 to 3½ years but are confounded by seemingly impossible claims for vivid memories of abuse in very early infancy. Cases alleging the first occurrence of MPD in adulthood have been published, however (Young, 1987).

Implications of a developmental window of vulnerability include the possibility of differential effects depending on whether the trauma occurred near the beginning or the end of this sensitive period. As early as 1980, Allison and Schwartz suggested that there were two main types of MPD cases, depending on whether the first alter personalities appear before age 6 or after age 8 years. Early trauma produced cases with large numbers of personalities and chaotic disorganization. Late occurring trauma (after age 8 years) produced patients with few personalities and good "ego strength." Subsequently Putnam et al. (1986) found a significant negative correlation between the age of first appearance of an alter personality and the number of alter personalities. There was a significant positive correlation between the number of alter personalities and the number of types of abuse or trauma the individual was exposed to (e.g., physical abuse, sexual abuse, witnessing violence).

The existence of such a window of vulnerability may serve to highlight the developmental substrates and processes on which the trauma acts to produce the fragmentation of self and memory that characterize the dissociative disorders. The study of the self is a central concern of developmental psychology and developmental psychopathology providing a rich source of data and theory (Cicchetti & Beeghly, 1990). Traumatically induced dissociative disturbances of self may provide a unique opportunity to observe the deviation or disruption of self-development and to test developmentally restorative interventions.

THE NATURE OF DISSOCIATION

Measurement and Correlates of Dissociation

The measurement of dissociation has been operationalized around the manifestation of a set of signs and behaviors and the subjective reporting of a set of symptoms and experiences. The set of subjective experiences include amnesias, alterations in perceptions of self and the world and absorption and enthrallment phenomena. Many of these internal experiences are outwardly expressed as signs and behaviors that are quantified by dissociation scales and measures. In addition to assessing spontaneously emitted behaviors, dissociation and hypnosis scales can also measure performance with structured tasks and probes. The scales and measures in current use should be regarded as first-generation measures that can be further expanded and refined.

Hypnotizability is commonly measured by three established instruments: the Stanford Hypnotic Susceptibility Scale (SHSS), usually Form C; the Harvard Group Scale of Hypnotic Susceptibility (HGSHS); and the Hypnotic Induction Profile (HIP) (Hilgard, 1965; Shor & Orne, 1962; Spiegel & Spiegel, 1978). Although the SHSS and the HGSHS are generally well correlated with each other (typically in the .65–.75 range), the HIP is only moderately correlated with either (typically .25–.35) and appears to tap other dimensions that may be more directly related to psychopathology (Spiegel & Spiegel, 1978). The SHSS and the HIP are individually administered, and the HGSHS is designed to be given to a group.

The SHSS measures a number of motor, sensory, and behavioral phenomena in the hypnotic state. For example, Form C includes 12 items, such as degree of difficulty in moving locked hands apart after the experimenter suggests that your fingers are "so tightly interlocked that you wonder very much if you could take fingers and hands apart" (Hilgard, 1965, p. 213). Other items included a suggested taste hallucination, age regression to the fifth grade in school, suggestion that the person cannot smell a stimulus of undiluted household ammonia, and a negative hallucination in which the individual is unable to see a standard stimulus present in front of him or her. (Hilgard, 1965).

The HIP generates two summary scores based on six items (Spiegel & Spiegel, 1978). Perhaps the most interesting aspect of the HIP is its inclusion of an eye roll task, thought to have a biological basis. The degree of eye roll is measured by observing the amount of cornea visible when a subject rolls his or her eyes as far upward as possible. Highly hypnotizable individuals typically roll their eyes upward so that only the white of the eye (sclera) can be seen. A similar eye roll is often observed when MPD patients switch alter personality states (Putnam, 1988).

Research on hypnosis has largely been conducted with normal populations, most frequently undergraduate and graduate students.

Using tabular data from Hilgard's seminal work, *Hypnotic Susceptibility*, Figure 16.1 illustrates the distribution of hypnotizability scores in a sample of Stanford students. Most laboratory research has focused on individuals scoring in the medium to high ranges of the various scales.

A variety of interesting disturbances of memory and self can be demonstrated in highly hypnotizable individuals. One of the most dramatic hypnotic alterations of self involves the "hidden observer." The hidden observer is a metaphor coined by Hilgard (1986) to describe the existence of a condition of simultaneous divided cognition as manifest by two separate reporting systems—overt and covert—operating in parallel. Hidden observers can be found in approximately half of highly hypnotizable individuals (Hilgard, 1979; Zamansky & Bartis, 1986).

The typical experimental paradigm involves the hypnotic manipulation of a sensation that is differentially reported by the conscious individual and the hidden observer function. For example, pain is induced by ice water (cold presser test) or with a tight tourniquet (ischemic pain) in a hypnotized subject who has received a suggestion of analgesia or anesthesia. The individual periodically reports on his or her sense of pain using a standard scale. Hilgard found that some highly hypnotizable individuals could differentially report two separate levels of pain awareness that were consciously separated from each other by amnesic barriers. Differential reporting occurs simultaneously through different mechanisms (e.g., by verbal report and automatic writing or automatic key pressing). This phenomenon has subsequently been widely replicated in many hypnosis laboratories, though some controversies about its nature and origin are unresolved.

Another important and dramatic hypnotic alteration of self is age regression. An age regression task is included as an item on some hypnosis scales and this capacity is most often present in highly hypnotizable subjects. In the laboratory, subjects are usually age regressed to a standard point and the degree of regression tested (e.g., by change in handwriting, speech, language usage). Individuals who exhibit some degree of age regression may differ in their subjective perspective—whether they witnessed it as if observing from outside or experienced the sense of regression directly (Hilgard, 1986). There has been much debate on the age consistency of behaviors in age-regressed subjects compared with simulator controls (Hilgard, 1986). Claims of reincarnation are sometimes put forward based on age-regression experiences. In many instances, resourceful investigators have been able to demonstrate that the individual had prior exposure to information relevant to his or her reports of a past life. However, recovery of childhood abilities and talents with hypnotic age regression has been demonstrated in some experiments (Hilgard, 1986; Walker, Garrett, & Wallace, 1976).

Dissociativity has been thought of as the clinical analogue of hypnotizability. A number of recently developed measures including the Dissociative Experiences Scale (DES) (Bernstein & Putnam, 1986), Perceptual Alteration Scale (PAS) (Sanders, 1986), and the Dissociative Experiences Questionnaire (Riley, 1988) seek to quantify dissociativity. The DES, developed by Bernstein and Putnam, is the most widely used measure to date. Factor-analytic studies indicate that the DES measures amnesia, depersonalization/derealization, and experiences of intense absorption (Carlson & Putnam, 1993). The DES uses a visual analogue format to capture the frequency of a set of subjective experiences clinically noted in dissociative patients. Subjects are asked to indicate where they fall along a continuum of frequency for each example. The reliability and validity of the DES have been tested in various ways, and the scale performs quite credibly in most instances (Carlson & Putnam, 1993).

Although many DES studies have been conducted in college populations, the real utility of the instrument has been in the exploration of clinical samples. A number of studies strongly link elevated DES scores to childhood stress and trauma in both normal and clinical populations (Chu & Dill, 1990; Demitrack et al., 1990; Frischholz, et al., 1990; Kirby et al., 1993; Ross et al., 1988). For example, studies of adolescent and college populations by Sanders found strong associations between stress, psychological abuse, physical abuse, and a combination with higher DES scores in college students and disturbed adolescents (Sanders & Gioloas, 1991; Sanders, McRoberts, & Tollefson, 1989). Studies by Chu and colleagues at McLean hospital have demonstrated strong relationships between DES scores and a history of early childhood trauma, particularly sexual abuse, in psychiatric patients (Chu & Dill, 1990; Kirby et al., 1993). DES scores are also elevated in combat veterans with posttraumatic stress disorder (PTSD) (Branscomb, 1991; Bremner et al., 1992; Loewenstein & Putnam, 1988).

In addition to the research done with dissociation scales, testing profiles of dissociative patients are emerging on established measures (Armstrong, 1991). Work by Bliss (1984) and Coons and Fine (1990) have established good discriminant validity for MMPI profiles of dissociative patients. Coons and Fines demonstrated an overall hit rate of 71% for blind classification of 63 cases as either MPD or non-MPD based on a set of MMPI characteristics. Although not pathognomonic for MPD, the relative specificity of the MMPI profile for MPD compares favorably with other attempts at diagnostic discrimination with this instrument. There is a long history of Rorschach studies in MPD (for a summary see Armstrong, 1991; Armstrong & Loewenstein, 1990). Briere (1990) has altered the Hopkins Symptom Checklist to capture dissociation and other investigators are known to be working on this and other frequently employed adult measures. Assessment of dissociation in children has lagged beyond in terms of the development and validation of measures.

The Child Dissociative Checklist (CDC) developed to capture and quantify dissociative behaviors in children (Putnam, Helmers, & Trickett, 1993). Originally paired with a structured interview that was later discontinued because of poor reliability, the CDC has evolved over a decade, passing through several versions. Pressed into service as a screening instrument in clinical settings, it is also increasingly used as a research tool. Two essentially equivalent versions (Version 2.2 dated 2/88 and Version 3.0, dated 2/90) are in circulation. Version 3.0 includes the same items and item ordering as Version 2.0 with four items added at the end of the scale. The CDC has good test-retest reliability. Individual items show similar test-retest coefficients ranging from .57 ($p = .005$) to .92 ($p = .0001$) over a 1-year interval. Cronbach's alpha, split-half reliability, and other measures of internal consistency are all robust.

The CDC readily discriminates between normal and traumatized children as a group (Malinosky-Rummell & Hoeir, 1991; Putnam et al., 1993; Wherry, Jolly, Feldman, Adam, & Manjanatha, in press). The vast majority of children with formally diagnosed dissociative disorders (95%) score 12 or more, whereas only 1% of controls achieve this level. The scale does have limitations and further work on its psychometric properties is needed; however, the preliminary data indicate that it is measuring something that approximates clinical dissociation.

The CDC is an observer-completed rating scale with a response format patterned after the Child Behavioral Checklist (Achenbach & Edelbrock, 1981). Clinical experience with dissociative behavior indicates that it is often context-dependent. Thus, the CDC is intended to be completed by an observer who is familiar with the child's behavior across different settings and situations (e.g., parents, guardians, and teachers). The scale inquires about a number of dimensions of dissociative behavior including amnesias, trance states, shifts in ease of retrieval of implicit and explicit information, rapid shifts in demeanor and personality characteristics including age regression, hallucinations, and alterations in identity. The scale also includes items that tap behaviors clinically associated with dissociative disorders (lying, self-injury, explosive temper, promiscuous sexuality). The scale is scored by simply summing the item scores.

Diagnosis of Dissociative Disorders

The diagnosis of a dissociative disorder is made the same way as all other DSM-IV psychiatric diagnoses, by the application of clinical criteria to interview, historical, and observational data. The mainstay of early work in this area was the clinical interview developed by Kluft, Braun, Wilbur, Caul, and others and taught at an annual workshop held in conjunction with the American Psychiatric Association from 1978 to present. Examples of this interview technique are covered in books by Ross (1989) and Putnam (1989a). This approach was refined and updated by Loewenstein (1991a) into a more efficient, office-based clinical interview. Two structured interviews have been developed, the SCID-D developed by Marlene Steinberg and colleagues at Yale (Steinberg, Rounsaville, & Cicchetti, 1990), and the Dissociative Disorders Interview Schedule (DDIS) by Colin Ross and colleagues (Ross, Heber, Norton, Anderson, Anderson, & Barchet, 1989). Both interviews have demonstrated high reliability and good validity and are proving useful in a range of research efforts. DES scores are generally predictive of structured interview results, although investigators disagree on the appropriate cutoff score to use for the best combination of sensitivity and specificity (Carlson et al., 1993; Frischholz et al., 1990; Steinberg, Rounsaville, & Cicchetti, 1991).

Dissociative Disturbances of Memory

Dissociative disorders are characterized by a set of memory disturbances that are manifest clinically and documentable in the laboratory. Dissociative disturbances of memory include (a) amnesias for autobiographical information, (b) an ability to compartmentalize information more tightly than is usual in normal individuals, (c) differential transfer rates for different types of information across alter personality states, and (d) difficulties in determining whether a recalled event is a real memory or a pseudomemory. These disturbances of memory synergistically contribute to disturbances of sense of self and other clinical manifestations of dissociative psychopathology.

Autobiographical Amnesias

Among the most dramatic dissociative disturbances of memory is psychogenic amnesia for identity and self-referential information. Loewenstein (1991b) defines psychogenic amnesia "as a reversible memory impairment in which groups of memories for personal experience that would ordinarily be available for recall to the conscious mind cannot be retrieved or retained in consciousness" (p. 191). He notes that the diagnosis of psychogenic amnesia connotes four factors. The first is that the amnesia is for a large group of memories rather than a single memory or event. Second, the information that is unavailable would ordinarily be considered a routine part of conscious awareness (e.g., what my name is, where I went and what I did, thought, and felt at the time). Third, the ability to learn, retrieve, and utilize new information is intact, together with normal cognitive function and language capacity. And finally, dissociated memories and information reveal their presence in disguised and symbolic forms (e.g., intrusive imagery, somatoform symptoms, conversion symptoms, nightmares, and "unconscious" behavioral reenactments). A variety of clinical subtypes of psychogenic amnesia have been identified in the DSM-IV though often more than one subtype is present.

The study of autobiographical memory and its dynamics is a relatively young area of inquiry that draws on the methods and theories of cognitive psychology (Rubin, 1988; Rubin & Nebes, 1988). Impairments in autobiographical memory, especially extensive childhood amnesia, have long been noted in MPD patients (Putnam, 1989a). Schacter et al. (Schacter, Kihlstrom, Kihlstrom, & Berren, 1989) have empirically demonstrated significant deficits in autobiographical memory in an in-depth case study of an MPD subject. The contributions of dissociative impairments in autobiographical memory to disturbances in the continuity of self are discussed later in this chapter.

Compartmentalization of Memory

Clinically, compartmentalization of memories, knowledge, experiences, skills, and affects is a central feature of the dissociative disorders. Multiple personality disorder patients in particular continually maintain mutually discrepant autobiographical versions of events, diametrically opposed responses to the same stimulus, and other glaring inconsistencies side by side without dissonance. Many of the striking moral and behavioral differences between alter personalities that make MPD such a dramatic disorder are a manifestation of this dissociative capacity for compartmentalization of memory.

Silberman et al. experimentally demonstrated that compartmentalization of neutral information is significantly enhanced in MPD subjects compared with simulating controls (Silberman, Putnam, Weingartner, Braun, & Post, 1985). Within a single alter personality state, the ability of MPD subjects to keep two highly similar lists of words separate was equivalent to control subjects.

However, across alter personalities states that were reported to be mutually amnesic for each other, MPD subjects showed an enhanced capacity to keep highly similar information separate. Controls who were simulating alter personalities actually showed a decreased capacity to keep information compartmentalized compared to their within-personality state levels. The increased compartmentalization of information within the MPD subjects was far from perfect, however, indicating that extensive leakage of neutral information occurs even between subjectively amnesic alter personalities.

Based on several intensive single case studies, Ludwig et al. concluded that the more affectively loaded a memory task was, the greater the degree of compartmentalization (Brandsma & Ludwig, 1974; Ludwig et al., 1972). Nissen et al., summarizing their experience with an intensive single case, observed that the degree of compartmentalization was to some extent dependent on the way that the knowledge was uniquely interpreted by a specific personality state (Nissen, Ross, Willingham, Mackenzie, & Schacter, 1988). Further work is required to delineate the role of affective valence and other attributes that contribute to the degree of compartmentalization of specific information.

Implicit and Explicit Memory Disturbances

Memory tasks are commonly classified in two broad categories, declarative or explicit memory and nondeclarative or implicit memory. Explicit memory consists of memory for facts and events and includes autobiographical memory. Explicit memory is available to conscious recall and is typically tested with verbal tasks. Implicit memory includes several kinds of abilities, all of which are expressed through performance and are not consciously available to recall (Squires & Zola-Morgan, 1991). Examples of implicit memory functions include skills and habits, simple classical conditioning, and habituation.

MPD patients show a peculiar set of implicit and explicit memory disturbances that vary in complicated ways among the alter personalities. When pairs of alter personalities are trained and tested against each other, it is apparent that information transfer between any given pair of alter personalities (A&B) is differentially polarized. The degree of transfer is a function of the type of memory task and the direction of the transfer, e.g., A → B but B ⇸ A. Figure 16.2 presents a schematic example of demonstrated rates of information transfer between a pair of alter personalities "A" and "B" as a function of the type of information. This figure should be interpreted as a simplified and generalized example based on limited information (Ludwig et al., 1972; Nissen et al., 1988; Putnam, 1991c; Schacter et al., 1989; Silberman et al., 1985). It conveys the range of disruptions in transfer of information between alter personalities for different types of memory. No study to date has tested for all types of information in a given pair of alter personalities.

As schematized in Figure 16.2, the disruption of memory occurs in the transfer of information across a "dissociative barrier." Most authorities have interpreted this barrier to be the separation between two behavioral states of consciousness. In this framework, the dissociative disruptions of memory seen in MPD subjects are representative of classical state-dependent learning and retrieval (SDL/R) phenomena. State-dependent learning and retrieval refer to an empirically demonstrated phenomenon that

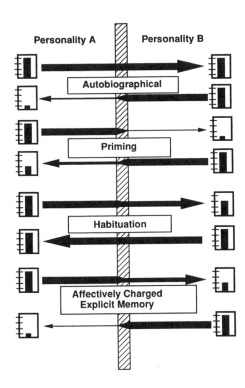

Figure 16.2 Schematic representation of the memory disturbances found in patients with multiple personality disorder.

information learned in a given state of consciousness, defined by mood, arousal level, or pharmacology, is best retrieved in the same state of consciousness compared with other states of consciousness (Weingartner, 1978). The classic SDL/R experiment involves a 2 × 2 design in which information is learned in one state (e.g., while under the influence of alcohol) and is later retrieved while sober and while under the influence of alcohol. The same experiment is then repeated with the information being learned in the sober state and retrieved in intoxicated and sober states. Information learned in an intoxicated state is recalled significantly better in an intoxicated state compared with a sober state. In 1891 Ribot proposed a SDL/R explanation for the memory disturbances of alter personalities in MPD (Ribot, 1891). Others have echoed this hypothesis in varying forms across the years (Braun, 1984; Putnam, 1986; Silberman et al., 1985). The research findings to date are most congruent with this explanation (Putnam, 1991c).

Psychophysiology of Dissociation

A number of psychophysiological studies suggest that the alter personality states of MPD subjects exhibit unique psychophysiological differences (for reviews, see Coons, 1988; Putnam, 1991c). Studies of averaged evoked responses (AERs), such as visual, auditory, and somatosensory evoked potentials, indicate that alter personalities may vary in sensory functioning (Putnam, 1984). Although many artifacts and confounds remain to be sorted through, differential EEG activity at certain frequencies also appears to be a function of personality

state (Coons, Milstein, & Marley, 1982; Flor-Henry, Tomer, Kumpula, Koles, & Yeudall, 1990; Hughes, Kuhlman, Fichtner, & Gruenfeld, 1990; Putnam, 1991c). Spiegel and others have demonstrated that visual and somatosensory AERs are susceptible to hypnotic alterations (Spiegel, Bierre, & Rootenberg, 1989; Spiegel, Cutcomb, Ren, & Pribram, 1985). Differential cerebral blood flow (CBF) has been reported across alter personalities in the same MPD patient (Mathew, Jack, & West, 1985). Taken together, these studies suggest that both resting and stimulus-evoked measures of central nervous system (CNS) activity can be altered by varying dissociative state.

Likewise, a number of studies demonstrate the existence of differential autonomic nervous system (ANS) activity across MPD alter personalities (Bahnson & Smith, 1975; Coons, 1988; Putnam, Zahn, & Post, 1990). The study by Putnam and colleagues (1990) found that unique alter personality-specific psychophysiological patterns were stable across a period of 1 to 2 weeks. In the same study, a number of simulating controls using hypnosis as one of their three states of consciousness were also able to produce unique and replicable psychophysiological patterns over the same time period. The hypnotic state patterns shared only 9% of the same variables with the dissociative states in the MPD subjects, suggesting that hypnosis and clinical dissociation tap different physiological mechanisms. In two studies, Miller and his colleagues demonstrated that compared with simulating controls, MPD subjects exhibit an interesting array of significant differences in subjective and objective measures of vision (Miller, 1989; Miller, Blackburn, Scholes, White, & Mamalis, 1991).

The CNS and ANS differences among alter personality states as demonstrated in the laboratory do not surprise clinicians working with these patients. From the first reported cases, clinicians have described an astonishing array of psychological and physiological differences between alter personalities (Alvarado, 1989; Putnam, 1986). In fact, it is these striking psychophysiological differences that give credibility to the subjective sense of separateness voiced by the alter personalities. As with the memory disturbances discussed earlier, the most parsimonious explanation for these data is the existence of dissociative state-dependent physiology. In the animal experimental community, the state-dependent nature of psychophysiology is a well-established fact (Lydic, 1987). Surprisingly, this conceptualization of "state" as a major source of biological variability has received little attention in psychiatric research.

An intriguing area of psychophysiology that is as yet little studied is the switch process (Putnam, 1988, 1991c). Switching is the transition from one state of consciousness to another. Some form of switching is observed in a variety of psychiatric conditions such as panic attacks, transitions among mania, depression and euthymia in bipolar disorders, onset and offset of catatonic states in schizophrenia, acute drug and alcohol intoxication, and dissociative abreactions in PTSD patients. A heightened susceptibility to environmental stimuli that trigger switching to inappropriate, dysfunctional, or dysphoric state is a significant pathological feature of MPD. In MPD, alter personality switches are typically rapid events that can be captured and analyzed behaviorally and physiologically (Putnam, 1988). In many respects, MPD switches resemble behavioral state transitions reported in infants and young children (Putnam, 1988; Wolff, 1987). The clinical behaviors associated with switching are discussed in greater detail later in this chapter.

THE DISSOCIATIVE DISORDERS

Epidemiology

Adult dissociative disorders were considered extremely rare until recently. Their true incidence and prevalence remain to be established, but preliminary epidemiological data are pointing to much higher rates than previously believed. Using the DES, Ross and his colleagues conducted a large-scale survey study of a stratified ransom sample of the population age 18 years and older in Winnipeg, Canada (Ross, Joshi, & Currie, 1989). Ross then followed up with a structured diagnostic interview for dissociative disorders in a subsample of this population. They reported an overall rate of 11.2% for some form of dissociative disorder with 3.1% of cases making DSM-III-R criteria for MPD (Ross, 1991).

They note, however, that many of the diagnosed cases in their general population cases were not symptomatic. They estimate that only about 1% of the entire sample had clinically significant MPD. This figure agrees well with an estimate calculated using data derived from a large multicenter discriminant analysis study of the DES (Carlson et al., 1993). This estimate is based on the relative frequencies of dissociative disorder patients scoring above and below 30, an empirically determined cutoff score. Applying these figures to the Ross et al. data would suggest that about 1% of their general population sample had clinically relevant dissociative disorders. Studies of the frequency of dissociative disorders in psychiatric settings suggest that about 1% to 10% of general psychiatric patients have a diagnosable dissociative disorder (Bliss & Jeppsen, 1985; Graves, 1989; Ross, 1991; Ross, Anderson, Fleisher, & Norton, 1991; Ross, Norton, & Wozney, 1989). At this point, it seems reasonable to estimate that about 1% of the North American general population and about 3% to 5% of North American psychiatric patients qualify for a dissociative disorder diagnosis.

Few data are available on the worldwide distribution of dissociative disorders. Modestin (1992) conducted a questionnaire study of all of the psychiatrists practicing in Switzerland and calculated a prevalence rate of 0.1% for MPD in that country. Several studies coming out of Holland (Boon & Draijer, 1991; Ensink, 1992; Ensink & van Otterloo, 1989) indicate that MPD can be readily found in cultures where it was not officially recognized until very recently. Dissociative disorder diagnoses have been incorporated in the 1992 drafted ICD-10, though some of the ICD categories are at odds with the DSM-III-R/IV nosology (e.g., see Garcia, 1990, and related commentaries).

Clinical Presentations

Early views of the clinical presentation of multiple personality disorder were strongly influenced by a handful of cases largely known from their portrayals in the media. The advent of systematic studies of clinical phenomenology using questionnaire surveys (Putnam et al., 1986; Ross et al., 1989; Schultz et al., 1989), large case series (Coons et al., 1988; Kluft, 1991b; Loewenstein & Putnam, 1990) and structured interviews (Ross et al., 1989; Steinberg et al., 1990) has significantly changed our view of this complex disorder. In his seminal review of the clinical presentations of MPD, Kluft describes more than 20 variations (Kluft, 1991a). He notes that only about 20% of cases come to attention because of overt florid dissociative symptoms that are sustained for any length of time. Most MPD patients are only transiently symptomatic with "classic" symptoms; many remain extremely covert and are only discovered late in the course of treatment for other disorders that they mimic. A longitudinal look at the clinical course of these patients indicate that most manifest an array of different psychiatric presentations over time. The best clinical predictor of MPD continues to be a patient with a history of treatment failure for multiple psychiatric diagnoses.

Classic MPD is characterized by a plethora of dissociative and posttraumatic symptoms including amnesias, depersonalization, and derealization; passive influence experiences; and switching behaviors (Kluft, 1991a; Putnam, 1989a). Patients usually can give clear examples of "time loss," fugue episodes, disremembered behavior, perplexing forgetfulness, and other indications of extensive amnesia. The diagnostic evaluation process is often replete with examples of miniamnesias, spacing out, and other spontaneous dissociative symptoms, providing the alert clinician with ample reason to suspect the disorder. Examples of executive control by alter personalities can often be elicited in the history taking, and frequently an experienced clinician can meet alter personalities within the first or second interview. Some patients, motivated to deny the condition, may disavow these behaviors or cleverly conceal them—misleading even experts at times.

Not infrequently, the first overt manifestations of MPD in adulthood appear closely following an acute stressor such as a rape, an accident, or loss of a significant other. In many such instances, the individual gives a history suggestive of early childhood MPD that has sealed over or become dormant and which appears to have been reactivated by the stressor (Kluft, 1991a; Putnam, 1989a). These clinical data, together with cross-sectional looks at the life course of MPD (Kluft, 1985b), suggest that there are windows of diagnosability for MPD that vary over the life cycle and that interact with situational stress. Kluft's work on the natural history of MPD further indicates that the clinical presentation changes in predictable ways with age.

Despite the varying clinical presentations of MPD and DDNOS, a core set of dissociative and posttraumatic symptoms is found in the majority of cases. Most pertinent to this chapter are the amnesia, process, and trance symptoms. Amnesia symptoms are usually manifest as a set of perplexing life experiences that adult patients recognize as abnormal, and therefore struggle to conceal and deny. Foremost among these amnesia experiences is "time loss," which is the vernacular for periods when the individual cannot account for his or her behavior and activities. The MPD or DDNOS patient loses variable lengths of time; often just a few hours cannot be accounted for. This occurs frequently, however, and in ways that embarrass or frighten the person.

Fugue episodes, in which the person finds him- or herself in some location or situation and has no idea of how he or she came to be there, are a common form of time loss. Although dramatic fugues occur, such as finding oneself in another state or country, the more typical example would be finding oneself in a store buying an item and having no memory of coming to the store or of the reason for purchasing the item.

Finding unexplained possessions or evidence complex, goal-directed activities for which the individual has no recollection are common manifestations of dissociative amnesias. As discussed in the previous section on the experimental study of memory disturbances in MPD patients, fluctuations in skills, habits, and implicit knowledge are very common in these cases, at times, depriving dissociative patients of the ability to perform their jobs or other crucial life activities. This erratic availability of fundamental skills and information plays havoc in the lives of these people, profoundly undermining their self-confidence.

Most MPD patients exhibit extensive amnesias for childhood. Although careful search may reveal this symptom in other psychiatric disorders (Loewenstein, 1991b), the childhood amnesias found in dissociative patients are characterized by extensive gaps in autobiographical memory. These deficits do not show the retention gradient typically noted in studies of autobiographical memory (Rubin & Nebes, 1988). For example, an MPD patient may report no recollections from ages 10 to 13 years, but have appropriate recall of the period prior to and after these missing memories. There is often a sharply demarcated, "punched out" quality to the childhood amnesia.

Experiences of depersonalization, derealization, and diffusion of identity are common in MPD and DDNOS patients. These are extremely distressing and may precipitate suicide attempts or episodes of self-mutilation intended to restore a sense of reality through experiencing pain. Sensory distortions—voices sounding muffled, people and objects appearing small and far away, and sensations of being physically partitioned off from the world in a "glass bubble"—are commonly reported by patients. Many DDNOS in particular, identify experiences of depersonalization as the most disturbing symptom they endure.

Equally distressing are the frequent auditory hallucinations that plague MPD and DDNOS patients. Although many clinicians mistakenly equate hallucinations with psychosis, auditory hallucinations in nonpsychotic individuals are actually not uncommon (e.g., Ross found that 27% of his general population sample reported hearing voices). This is particularly true in children (Asaad & Sharpiro, 1986; Kotsopoulos, Kanigsberg, Cote, & Fiedorowicz, 1987; Schreier & Libow, 1986). The misdiagnosis of schizophrenia, made in about half of MPD patients, is often attributable to the presence of auditory hallucinations.

The auditory hallucinations reported in MPD and DDNOS patients are usually heard as voices within the head as opposed to coming from outside the individual. The voices are generally reported to have specific attributes such as age, gender, race, and affect. The content may be pejorative or supportive. Dissociative auditory hallucinations typically include experiences of hostile berating voices that command the patient to hurt him- or herself, voices of children, often frightened or crying, and voices that provide solace and comfort. MPD and DDNOS patients generally recognize that these voices are hallucinations and attempt to ignore or suppress them. Fearing that he or she will be labeled as "crazy," it is not usual for MPD patients to conceal the existence of these voices from their therapists until years into treatment.

Richard Kluft was instrumental in calling attention to the frequency of passive influence experiences in MPD patients. His classic study demonstrated that these experiences of being made to do or feel something against one's will were far more common in dissociative patients than in schizophrenia or bipolar illness, two disorders previously thought to account for the vast majority of such symptoms (Kluft, 1987a). Subsequent studies by Ross and colleagues (1990) and Fink (1991) have confirmed Kluft's findings. Passive influence experiences may produce a "possessiform" clinical presentation of MPD reminiscent of demonic possession. It is likely that many cases of demonic possession are cultural variants of MPD.

Switching symptoms are under process symptoms. Switches are abrupt and discernible shifts in alter personality state. Like state-dependent memory and state-dependent psychophysiology, switching between discrete states of consciousness has been described in a number of psychiatric disorders, most notably bipolar illness, panic attacks, and catatonic reactions. Clinically, switching is manifest by abrupt changes in facial expression, intonation, accent, and word choice; focus and content of thought processes; and posture, motor activity, and body language.

Experimentally, switching is characterized by abrupt, nonlinear shifts in psychophysiological variables such as heart rate, respiration, skin conductance, electromyographic (EMG), and electroencephalographic (EEG) activity (Putnam, 1988, 1991c). Switches are often elicited by experiences of external or internal dissonance triggered by environmental or situational stimuli. Little is known about the natural course of switching behavior outside the clinical or laboratory setting, although a case study conducted by Loewenstein, Hamilton, Alagna, Reid, & Devries (1987) demonstrated differences between the patterns of alter personality state emergence in clinical and social settings.

The Alter Personalities

The most dramatic manifestations of multiple personality disorder are the alter personality states. Although experienced clinicians seek to minimize fascination with these entities, dramatized alter personalities continue to capture the attention of the general public. It is clinically well established that the alter personalities are not individual "people" by any stretch of the imagination (Kluft, 1991b; Putnam, 1989a, 1992a). Yet they continue to be portrayed this way by the popular media. Typical MPD cases average about 10 to 20 alter personalities, with women having more than men (Loewenstein & Putnam, 1990; Putnam et al., 1986). There are some patients who report having hundreds of alter personalities. Such reports should not be interpreted literally, but are better understood as reflecting a psychological organization characterized by extreme diffusion and diversity of identity (Kluft, 1991b). The number of alter personality states is positively correlated with the number of different categorical types of trauma reported by patients and negatively correlated with the age at which the trauma was reported to have begun (Putnam et al., 1986). Patients with larger systems of alter personalities tend to take longer to treat, although there are many exceptions to this rule (Putnam, 1989a).

Most authorities agree that the sum total of all the patient's alter personalities constitutes the individual's "personality" (Kluft, 1991b; Putnam, 1989a). The alter personalities seem to be best conceptualized as unique patterns of psychological and physiological variables that constitute discrete behavioral states organized around a prevailing affect, sense of self (including body image), a limited repertoire of behaviors and a set of state-dependent memories (Putnam, 1989a). This model is most parsimonious with the current psychophysiological data (Putnam 1991c). Treatment should focus on the person as a whole and not on specific alter personalities, although at times the clinician must therapeutically interact with them individually to effect change in the patient's behavior.

MPD patients have an array of alter personalities that perform specific functions for the individual. Common types of alters have been described across different studies (Coons et al., 1988; Putnam, et al., 1986; Ross, Norton, & Wozney, 1989). Beyond cataloguing the types of alter personalities found in MPD patients, little attention has been paid to how different constellations of alters influence the clinical course. The physiological and behavioral differences between alter personalities are most apparent to an observer, but it is their inner psychological landscape of contrasting beliefs, values, cognition, and relationships that constitute the core of their differences.

When an MPD subject switches executive control from one alter personality state to another, he or she shifts cognitive sets. These different knowledge bases and cognitive styles influence how the individual regards him- or herself at that moment and how he or she relates to the world. As discussed earlier, laboratory studies indicate that specific types of information, particularly *implicit* information, is very strongly alter personality state-dependent. State-dependent learning and memory retrieval are probably largely responsible for the alter personality differences in cognition (Putnam, 1991c).

Life Course

With the exception of a few single cases followed over long periods of time, most of what is known about the life course of MPD comes from the work of Richard Kluft, who has treated over 200 MPD patients. Drawing on both a cross-sectional perspective and long-term treatment and follow-up, Kluft (1985b) has sketched out a natural history of MPD. His work remains to be replicated but is congruent with the experience of most experts in the field. His follow-up of untreated cases strongly suggests that MPD does not spontaneously remit, although the symptomatic presentation does change with time.

Patients diagnosed in their 20s are more likely to display florid dissociative symptoms, while those in their 30s tend to present as depressed, anxious, and obsessional. Patients first diagnosed in their 40s have often managed to conceal the disorder from themselves and others until a major life event destroyed their internal equilibrium and reactivated latent alter personality states formed in response to much earlier stressors. In patients diagnosed in

their 50s and beyond, there is often evidence that their alter personality systems have simplified over time, with many previously contentious and conflicting alter personality states becoming dormant. This process was also observed in Rosenbaum's patient, Maud, followed over the course of more than 30 years (Rosenbaum & Weaver, 1980).

Treatment and Outcome

Although a range of therapeutic modalities have been advocated for treatment of MPD, DDNOS, and related dissociative disorders, there are few data on the efficacy of any form of treatment. Most authorities advocate that the primary treatment is an individual, dynamically oriented psychotherapy augmented by hypnosis and medication (Kluft, 1991b; Putnam, 1989a). A recent survey of therapists found that the vast majority rated this combination as more effective than any other combination of standard psychiatric or psychological therapies in their selected case (Putnam & Loewenstein, 1993).

With respect to treatment goals, Kluft (1991b) has classified four therapeutic positions that he believes are emerging in the field: (a) integrationalism, which advocates the unification of the alter personalities; (b) personality-oriented interventions designed to promote internal harmony without integration; (c) adaptationalism, which focuses on solving here-and-now life problems; and (d) minimalism, which discourages treatment and often glorifies MPD as a "highly creative" personal solution to overwhelming trauma. The last position is primarily advanced for social, personal, or political rather than clinical reasons. Debate over appropriate treatment goals is likely to intensify in the future as the MPD treatment community struggles with cost-effective therapeutic approaches.

The case report literature is replete with optimistic short-term outcomes, but the few systematic data available would suggest a more guarded prognosis. The recent survey study by Putnam and Loewenstein found that the median MPD patient had been in a twice weekly psychotherapy for almost 4 years at the time of sampling, and most of these patients will require many additional years of treatment (Putnam & Loewenstein, 1993). A follow-up study by Coons (1986) also suggests that although many MPD patients were substantially improved compared with their initial presentations, most were far from being cured. Poor outcomes were associated with histories of continued trauma and stress. The most optimistic outcome data have come from Kluft's large case series. He reports that 94% of his "unified" patients were asymptomatic when reevaluated 2 years after termination of treatment (Kluft, 1988). Future outcome studies should include multicenter designs to collect large, representative samples.

Clinically, the treatment of MPD seems to proceed in a stepwise fashion as was first suggested by Ralph Allison (1978; Coons, 1986). Acceptance of the diagnosis is often followed by more active engagement in treatment and cooperation among the alter personality states. This improved internal communication leads to the erosion of the dissociative barriers and development of coconscious awareness among the alter personality states. Increased internal awareness facilitates the recovery and working through of the traumatic material thought to have initially generated and subsequently perpetuated the dissociative divisions of consciousness. Therapeutic transformation of traumata often leads to a series of spontaneous integrations of various combinations of alter personality states sharing common traumatic origins. Final integrations involve resolving the differences that separate the larger groups or "families" of alter personality states. Generally several "final" integrations occur before the patient is stable. Integration does not mark the end of treatment, however. Most patients require substantial psychotherapy following their final integration to assist them in developing nondissociative defenses against the stresses of life (Putnam, 1989a).

THEORIES OF DISSOCIATION

The long history of dissociative disorders in psychiatry, dating well into the last century, has spawn many theories. Like many other ideas in psychology, theories of dissociation and MPD are periodically updated and recirculated as "new" hypotheses. The four major categories of theories are: (a) multiple personality disorder as an enacted social role, perhaps even a role suggested by the therapist to a susceptible patient; (b) neurological theories of dissociation either as a form of epilepsy or as the result of a disconnection between the two cerebral hemispheres; (c) dissociation as a form of autohypnotic disorder; and (d) dissociation as a form of discrete behavioral state. For the first time, however, there are data that permit these hypotheses to be empirically tested.

Social Role Model

The social role model theory dates back to Pierre Janet although there is ample evidence that he did not believe role playing accounted for the core dissociative process. Rather, he conceived suggestion and role playing as a shaping influence that crystallized the clinical presentation (Janet, 1889). The principal modern advocate of a social role theory of MPD is Nicholas Spanos, who has published a series of studies purporting to induce multiple personality disorder through social manipulations such as by asking psychology undergraduate students to simulate an accused murderer being interrogated in the fashion of the Hillside Strangler case (Spanos, 1986). Critics of Spanos' studies point to the wide range of differences between his transparently simulating undergraduates and actual clinical cases (Kluft, 1989b; Putnam, 1991b). Although MPD has been and will continue to be malingered by a few criminals in pursuit of an insanity defense, there is no evidence that the vast majority of patients derive any secondary gain by simulating this condition. The issues of iatrogenesis and suggestibility in MPD have been thoroughly discussed in a recent journal special issue (Kluft, 1989a).

Neurological Theories

Neurological theories of MPD have been tested by a number of recent studies and found wanting. Charcot (Charcot & Marie, 1892) originally proposed that MPD was a form of epilepsy, a hypothesis that has been repeatedly reinvoked over the following century (Putnam, 1986). However, a series of recent studies investigating epileptic phenomena in MPD patients (Devinsky et al., 1989) and dissociation in epileptic patients (Loewenstein & Putnam, 1988; Ross, Heber, & Norton, 1989) have uniformly failed to find any convincing evidence that these two disorders are causally related.

The theory that MPD is caused by a functional disconnection between the two cerebral hemispheres dates back to Benjamin Rush (Carlson, 1981). Dusted off and updated with the neuropsychological lingo of the split-brain research, this theory retains an intrinsic appeal. A few single case studies purport to demonstrate differences in the lateralization of physiological measures across alter personalities in MPD patients (see review in Putnam et al., 1990). In addition, changes in dominant handedness between alter personalities are commonly reported in MPD patients (Loewenstein & Putnam, 1990; Putnam et al., 1986). The only controlled, multiple patient psychophysiological study did not, however, detect evidence of lateralization in autonomic nervous system measures (Putnam et al., 1990). The lateralization theory remains to be definitively tested, but the absence of MPD-like phenomena in surgically disconnected "split-brain" patients (Sidis, 1986), together with the failure to find clear evidence of lateralization in controlled physiological studies, would dictate caution in acceptance of this hypothesis.

Autohypnotic Model

The autohypnotic theory of MPD has many adherents. The auto- or self-hypnosis theory of MPD posits that the individual makes use of self-hypnosis to escape from overwhelming trauma and then later generalizes this defensive response to other stressors. First proposed by Janet (1889) and elaborated by Morton Prince (1890), it was revived by Bliss (1986) in his important studies during the early 1980s. Three lines of evidence link pathological dissociation with hypnotizability. The first is that MPD patients are highly hypnotizable (Bliss, 1986; Frischholz, 1985). Second, many MPD-like phenomena can be produced by hypnosis in highly hypnotizable subjects, for example, amnesias, conversion symptoms, hallucinations, and hidden observers (Putnam, 1986). Third, hypnosis is highly useful in the treatment of MPD and dissociative disorders (Putnam, 1989a; Ross, 1989).

Recent studies, however, demonstrate that hypnotizability, as measured by standardized scales, is only moderately correlated with measures of clinical dissociation such as the DES (Carlson & Putnam, 1989). Although one preliminary report initially linked histories of child abuse to increased hypnotizability in adults (Nash, Lynn, & Givens, 1984), more carefully controlled studies have failed to replicate this finding (Nash et al., 1993). These and other studies do find significant correlations between DES scores and histories of childhood trauma (Chu & Dill, 1990; Coons et al., 1988; Ensink, 1992; Frischholz et al., 1990; Ross et al., 1988; Sanders et al., 1989; van der Kolk, Perry, & Herman, 1991). Prospective studies of hypnotizability in children also show no differences in standardized scores between abused and matched control children, even when followed longitudinally over a 2-year period (Putnam et al., in press).

At this time, the best reading of the data suggests that hypnotic capacity and dissociative capacity intersect in certain ways (e.g., they are both moderately correlated with measures of absorption and enthrallment), but they are not synonymous processes. Carlson and Putnam note that the data indicate that highly dissociative individuals are generally highly hypnotizable, but highly hypnotizable subjects are often not clinically dissociative (Carlson & Putnam, 1989). The simple, unqualified clinical equation of hypnosis and clinical dissociation must be abandoned for a more complex and ambiguous relationship that overlaps in some domains and diverges in others.

Developmental Models

The discovery of the linkage between child abuse and MPD in the early 1980s led to a number of retrospectively derived, developmentally slanted theories or models. Kluft's (1984) four-factor theory and Braun and Sachs's "3 P" theory (1985) are representative of a class of models that posit that a given child's biological predisposition to dissociate is initially utilized defensively in the context of overwhelming trauma. The traumatized child's dissociative capacity and dissociative defenses may then be perpetuated or even enhanced by repeated trauma and by the failure of significant others to provide adequate soothing and nurturance.

These models only abstractly acknowledge the nature of the alter personalities and their possible origins. None of these models systematically traces any developmental constructs or themes, nor do they account for the "window of vulnerability" or principal dissociative symptoms. Fink (1988) has extended this class of models considerably by focusing on the impact of dissociation on development of self, a developmental theme also stressed by a number of others (Putnam, 1994).

This first set of developmental models was generated by clinicians primarily for heuristic purposes to account for the etiology of MPD as taught in workshops and symposia. More sophisticated models can be anticipated as the developmental research community undertakes the study of the effects of trauma and maltreatment.

PATHOLOGICAL DISSOCIATION IN CHILDREN AND ADOLESCENTS

Children and adolescents with dissociative disorders were described in 19th- and early 20th-century medical journals (Bowman, 1990; Fine, 1988). Clinical awareness of this condition in children, like adults, disappeared during the nadir of dissociation theory, the period between the late 1920s to early 1970s. The dramatic rise in diagnosed adult cases from 1980 to present has refocused attention on this condition in minors. Systematically collected cases series (Dell & Eisenhower, 1990; Hornstein & Putnam, 1992; Hornstein & Tyson, 1991) are supplanting the first case reports of early pioneers. Although these preliminary data suggest that child and adolescent cases closely resemble adult cases, many clinicians report actually seeing many more ambiguous dissociative presentations than clear-cut, adultlike disorders. This discrepancy between clinical experience and the clinical literature likely reflects that conventional-appearing cases are more publishable. In response to these ambiguities, Peterson (1990) has proposed the creation of a new DSM-IV diagnosis, Dissociative disorder of Childhood. Unfortunately, it appears as if these crucial concerns are ignored in the DSM-IV (American Psychiatric Association, 1994).

In children, like adults, dissociation occurs on a continuum. In children and adolescents, however, dissociativity is strongly influenced by chronological age and developmental stage. Clinicians must take into careful account these variables, together with a confusing array of individual differences and the child's life situation and context, when attempting to determine whether a given child's dissociation is "pathological." Following the approach set forth in the overview of this chapter, we begin the discussion of dissociation in children with an examination of the clinical manifestations of pathological dissociation. The chapter concludes with a discussion of developmental processes that are believed to contribute to both normative and pathological dissociation.

Clinical Profiles of Pathological Dissociation in Children and Adolescents

Hornstein and Putnam (1992) compared the clinical phenomenology of two independently collected samples of children and adolescents with diagnoses of MPD and DDNOS. They found that, in general, children with either diagnosis suffered from a plethora of affective, anxiety, conduct, posttraumatic, and dissociative symptoms. The symptomatology of MPD and DDNOS cases were similar in many areas but differed in that MPD cases were older as a group and had more amnesias, hallucinations, and identity disturbances. In addition, the MPD group showed strong trends for higher levels of depression, dissociative process symptoms, and aggression. Child Dissociative Checklist scores were significantly different between the two groups (Hornstein & Putnam, 1992). The similarity of the two series collected in differing clinical settings was interpreted as supporting the basic construct validity of MPD and DDNOS diagnoses in children and adolescents (Hornstein & Putnam, 1992).

The prominent affective symptoms seen in these children resemble clinical presentations common during early to middle adulthood. High rates of depression and suicidal ideation were found in both diagnostic groups, though MPD children made significantly more suicide attempts than DDNOS cases. Rapid mood swings, irritability, and explosive anger were almost universally present across both diagnoses. High rates of conduct problems were common, though the classic "sociopathic" triad of enuresis, cruelty to animals, and fire setting was only rarely present. Chronic lying was frequently reported by caretakers and, like adult patients, appears in many instances to reflect disavowal of disremembered behavior rather than deliberate falsehood. Inappropriate, promiscuous, and precocious sexuality were seen in over half of cases and are a likely sequelae of sexual abuse and other eroticizing experiences (Yates, 1987). A substantial percentage of these children (15%) were already identified as perpetrators of sexual abuse and assaults on other children.

Like adult cases, dissociative children manifest an extensive array of amnesias, disremembered behavior, and perplexing forgetfulness. Passive influence symptoms, auditory and visual hallucinations, and other process symptoms are common and similar to adult counterparts. Disturbances in thought processes, particularly thought insertion, were common. Rapid age regression, often in the context of stimuli evocative of traumatic memories, was common for both diagnoses. Trancelike, or spacey, unresponsive states were seen in virtually all cases.

As would be expected, school performance was profoundly affected by this array of affective, posttraumatic, dissociative, and conduct symptoms. Many of the children were labeled as hyperactive, attention disordered, and/or learning disordered by their schools. Difficulty concentrating and easy distractibility were frequently reported by teachers. Many showed spotty and inconsistent performance on standardized tests. Mean IQ was 95.5 ± 16.7. Truancy and antisocial acting-out behaviors were increasingly frequent with age in this sample.

In summary, the presenting symptoms, high rates of depression, suicidality, hallucinations, and behavioral problems described in child and adolescent dissociative disorder patients closely resemble the clinical profiles described for adults. Similarly, the high rates of trauma and abuse in youth samples replicates the trauma histories reported in adult series. These and other correspondences strongly argue for the continuity of child and adolescent dissociative disorders with adult dissociative outcomes. However, no longitudinal studies have, as yet, actually established such continuity.

THE DEVELOPMENTAL BASIS OF THE DISSOCIATIVE DISORDERS

Normative Dissociation in Children

Very little is known about the developmental basis of dissociation and the dissociative disorders. However, dissociation is believed to be related to or associated with a number of developmental processes that have been subjected to more systematic study. Much may be learned from attempts to integrate this wealth of existing information around a dissociative focus. Potentially relevant domains of knowledge include: (a) research on the developmental basis of hypnotizability; (b) studies of behavioral states in infants; (c) the array of diverse theoretical perspectives and empirical data on the nature and development of imagination and fantasy in children; (d) research on attachment and attunement, particularly as it relates to dissociative behavior between the mother and child; and (e) studies of the development and integration of self. Each of these domains of knowledge is extensive and complicated. The intention in this chapter is to highlight specific potential connections to stimulate interest and research by developmentally informed investigators.

Most authorities believe that children are normatively more dissociative than adults (Kluft, 1984; Putnam, 1991a). In actual fact, this belief is based more on clinical experience than on empirical data. Experimental knowledge about one form of normal dissociation in children comes from studies of hypnotizability, a moderate correlate of clinical dissociation in adults and only a presumed correlate of clinical dissociation in children. A second and still preliminary source of data comes from research with the Child Dissociative Checklist. In sum, these data lend support to the clinical conceptualization that children are more dissociative than adults. They also indicate that dissociative capacity declines over the course of childhood and adolescence.

Beyond these general impressions, however, virtually nothing is known for certain about the developmental trajectory of normative dissociation.

Data on hypnotizability in children show an interesting curvilinear relationship with age, initially rising to a peak at about age 9 to 10 years and then declining during adolescence (Putnam, 1991a). Cross-sectional studies of adults reveal that hypnotizability continues to decline over the life cycle, though the slope becomes more gradual by the third decade (Putnam, 1991b). The relationship of hypnotizability, as measured by standardized scales, to clinical dissociation in children has not been established. As discussed previously, in adults, these two constructs are only at best moderately correlated. Preliminary data from the longitudinal study by Trickett and Putnam, indicate that there is little correlation between clinical dissociation, as measured by the CDC, and hypnotizability measured by the child version of the Stanford Hypnotic Susceptibility Scale (SHSS) (Putnam et al., in press). In addition, there are no significant differences in SHSS scores between groups of sexually abused and control children, aged 6 to 16 years. Furthermore, hypnotizability does not seem to be significantly associated with any of the measures of psychopathology analyzed to date. In comparison, CDC scores are highly correlated with Child Behavior Checklist scores and many other measures of psychopathology.

These are surprising findings, in view of the theories now in vogue that are predicated on hypnotizability and clinical dissociation being one and the same or at least highly overlapping constructs (Spiegel, 1991). Furthermore, the same theories predict that hypnotizability should be increased by traumatic experiences (Spiegel, Hunt, & Dondershine, 1988). In the Trickett and Putnam study, sexually abused and control children were retested with the SHSS after 1 year. Again there were no differences between the two groups. Both abused and control children did, however, show the expected curvilinear relationship between hypnotizability and age reported by other investigators (Putnam, 1991b). Over the same interval, the CDC scores of the abused children increased by 10%, whereas the control children had a 52% reduction in their group means.

Cross-sectional analyses indicate that CDC scores decline with age at different rates in different populations (Putnam et al., 1993). Negative correlations between CDC scores and age are greatest for sexual abuse and DDNOS samples and are not significant for control subjects and MPD patients, who show floor and ceiling effects respectively. Not surprisingly, correlations with measures of psychopathology, e.g., CBCL scores, are higher in younger age groups, though they remain significant for all ages from 6 to 16 years. These correlations are of equal magnitude in both sexual abuse and control groups, supporting the concept of dissociation as a dimension rather than a diagnosis.

The CDC also discriminates between the two dissociative disorder diagnoses in children. DDNOS cases were clustered around a median and mean score of about 16, whereas MPD subjects similarly scored close to 25. The sexually abused girls exhibit the greatest variance of currently studied samples with a subset of girls (20%) scoring in the range of children with clinically diagnosed dissociative disorders. Predictive validity studies remain to be completed on this subgroup. The relationship of

CDC scores to other issues such as measures of family environment, and presence of other psychopathology also remains to be explored. The CDC should prove a useful first-generation instrument that can lead to further advances in studying the developmental course of dissociation.

Behavioral States of Consciousness

Much of the research on the psychophysiology of multiple personality disorder indicates that this condition is characterized by a series of discrete behavioral states demarcated by the alter personalities (Putnam, 1988, 1991c). Behavioral states appear to be such a ubiquitous component of human behavior that they rarely come under scrutiny except in the form of altered states of consciousness (Zinberg, 1977). Tart (1972) who studied drug-induced and other altered states of consciousness, has suggested that there should be a state-specific sciences of human behavior. Many of the "dissociative properties" of the alter personalities are simply dramatic exaggeration of normal state-dependent memory retrieval and state-dependent psychophysiology previously demonstrated in drug-induced and affective states of consciousness. The behavioral states model of dissociation and MPD serves as an important conceptualization that can be tested from a developmental perspective.

Discrete behavioral states are easily identified in infants and young children, though their scientific study has been primarily limited to the first year of life (Wolff, 1987). Wolff, one of the leading advocates of this model, defines behavioral states as self-organizing discrete patterns of critical variables such as motor activity, eye movement patterns, facial display, skin color, vocalization, and respiration. Taken individually, these variables are continuous functions, but when considered in aggregate, they serve to classify discrete, discontinuous domains of behavior. Infant behavioral states can be operationally defined and reliably discriminated using these observable patterns of variables.

Specific infant states can be induced, prolonged, or terminated by experimental manipulations. Transitions between behavioral states in infants are hypothesized to be analogous to the switching seen in MPD patients and involve the destabilization of the current state and its replacement by another stable behavioral state. Transitions are discontinuous or saltatory jumps and are brief compared with the time spent in the stable behavioral states. The similarity of state transition phenomena among a number of psychiatric disorders (e.g., bipolar illness, panic attacks, catatonia) and with the infant behavioral state transitions suggest that a common underlying neurobiological mechanism may be involved (Putnam, 1988).

It has been suggested that dissociative states induced by overwhelming traumatic events may serve as the nidus around which the alter personalities of MPD patients are created (Putnam, 1991b, 1991c). The defensive properties of the dissociative states compartmentalize the traumatic affects and memories, to distance the child from the experience and to protect him or her from physical and psychological pain. In the context of recurrent trauma, e.g., incest, this state (or set of states) is repeatedly evoked and acquires increasing behavioral complexity, including state-dependently bound memories and affects, and a differentiated sense of self. With recurrent activation, such a state may ultimately crystallize into an alter personality. In the framework of this model, the postulated developmental window of vulnerability for the development of MPD would reflect a need for this process to begin early in development, prior to the appearance of other psychological defenses against trauma and/or a developmental alteration in behavioral state dynamics with maturation.

Imagination and Fantasy

One of the most important windows on the development of dissociative disorders may come through the study of imagination and fantasy. Long a subject of interest to developmental psychologists, much has been learned about the range and course of imagination and fantasy capacities over development. A separate but complementary body of data exists in the hypnosis literature concerning "fantasy proneness," a term coined by Wilson and Barber in 1981 (Lynn, Rhue, & Green, 1988). These two sources of knowledge can guide investigations of the posited role of imaginary companionship and other fantasy capacities in the creation of multiple personality disorder and related dissociative conditions.

Pretense, role playing, fantasy, and other aspects of make-believe have received periodic attention by developmental psychologists (Bretherton, 1989; Fein, 1981). These activities have been studied primarily in play or storytelling contexts with samples of normal children, typically preschoolers. Investigation of pretend play reveals a great deal of complexity and richness, even in young children. Of particular relevance to the dissociative disorders is the identity shifts that children manifest during pretend play. In addition to being "actors" in their make-believe worlds, children are also "playwrights" and "stage directors" (Bretherton, 1989). With regard to this last role, Giffin (1984) has identified a series of surprisingly sophisticated directing strategies employed by young children to comanage a shared pretend world. Children switch back and forth among these roles so seamlessly that this function was overlooked by researchers until recently (Bretherton, 1989). Only rarely do children become confused about which role they or their partner are in at a given moment. A better understanding of role-playing and role-exchanging capacities in normal and traumatized children may shed light on dissociative disturbances in the modulation of identity transformation.

A second area of developmental research has focused on the ability of children to distinguish between reality and fantasy (DiLalla & Watson, 1988; Harris, Brown, Marriott, Whittal, & Harmer, 1991). With age, children develop an increasing ability to distinguish between these domains. Even 3-year-olds can reliably differentiate between real and mental representations of those same objects (Harris et al., 1991). Scarlett and Wolf (1979) postulate that children develop the concept of a boundary between fantasy and reality realms that becomes more sophisticated with time. Children appear to have more difficulty making this differentiation in the area of fantasies about monsters, ghosts, and other scary beings. The studies of children's wary reactions to a box that contains an imagined monster convincingly demonstrate that even 6-year-olds can become frightened by their own fantasy creations (Harris et al., 1991). They explain their finding by speculating that children may be unsure of the rules that govern transformation of mental objects into physical objects.

An extension of the Harris et al. hypothesis is that perhaps monsters, ghosts, and scary creatures represent a special class of mental objects that differ from mental representations of common physical objects (cups, toothbrushes, etc.) used in other studies of reality testing. It may be that imagined "living" entities, be they good or evil, are more real for children (and adults) than are imagined physical objects. The ability of children to imbue transitional objects, stuffed animals, dolls, toy soldiers, and the like with life and personality is a little-understood capacity. Yet, it is one of the core imaginative capacities invoked in make-believe, particularly solitary pretend play. This ability has particular relevance for understanding the nature and reality of alter personalities created in MPD patients abused in childhood.

A third related area of research concerns the nature of imaginary companionship. Most developmental studies use Svendsen's definition of an imaginary companion as " . . . an invisible character, named and referred to in conversation with other persons or played with directly for a period of time . . . having an air of reality for the child but no apparent objective basis" (Svendsen, 1934, p. 988). Imaginary companionship is a relatively common normative phenomenon, beginning about age 4 and usually disappearing around school age (Manosevitz, Prentice, & Wilson, 1973). Estimates of prevalence range from 12% to 65% of children depending on the definitions and survey methodology (Bretherton, 1989; Harris et al., 1991; Manosevitz et al., 1973). Parents are often unaware of the existence or number of imaginary companions their child has. A variety of purposes have been proposed for imaginary companionship. Psychoanalytic writings concentrate on association with stress, loneliness, or discharge of forbidden impulses, the developmental literature emphasizes socialization. Firstborn and only children are more likely to have imaginary companions, and children with imaginary companions are more adept at talking and interacting with adults and score higher on measures of socialization (Manosevitz et al., 1973).

Imaginary companionship has been identified as a possible developmental substrate for the creation of alter personalities in MPD patients (Bliss, 1986; Lovinger, 1983; Lynn et al., 1988; Putnam, 1989a). Many adult MPD patients report that their alter personalities first existed as externalized imaginary companions created for companionship during times of loneliness or physical confinement. A recent study of children and adolescents with dissociative disorders found that 84% had imaginary companions currently or by history (Hornstein & Putnam, 1992). Congruent with the adult reports, the alter personality systems of children with MPD are sometimes externalized by the children as vivid imaginary companionship rather than internalized alter personalities (Putnam, 1991a). Although this impression remains to be systematically documented, clinical evidence suggests that these externalized alter personalities are later internalized around puberty. A comparison study of the imaginary companions of maltreated children with those of nontraumatized samples may be very revealing.

The developmental literature views imagination and fantasy capacities as normative and more likely to be associated with socialization and creativity, whereas the psychoanalytic literature regards these processes as serving defensive purposes. Among the defensive functions ascribed to fantasy are escape, wish fulfillment, restitution of self-esteem, and revenge. A dramatic example of the escape function of fantasy emerges from the accounts of the hostages held in Lebanon. Kept in isolation for long periods, most hostages report constructing elaborate fantasy worlds that they visited on a daily basis. For example, Reed constructed buildings in Islesboro, Maine; Cicippio designed his dream home (a common escape fantasy reported by Vietnam POWs); Polhill taught himself to play 37 instruments and conducted band concerts in his head; and Terry Anderson, held captive the longest, took elaborate, step-by-step walking tours of Tokyo in his mind (Boustany & Priest, 1992). It seems reasonable that if adults retreat into imaginary worlds during times of isolation and maltreatment, that traumatized children, with their developmentally heightened imaginary capacities, must also make use of this escape route. Investigation of the defensive use of fantasy may prove a profitable area for the field of developmental psychopathology.

One branch of research on hypnosis has concentrated on the identification and study of "fantasy-prone individuals." Fantasy-prone persons denote a group of individuals, who ". . . live much of their time in a world of their own making—a world of imagery, imagination and fantasy" (Wilson & Barber quoted in Lynn et al., 1988, p. 138). It is estimated that about 4% of the population are fantasy prone. Extensive studies by Lynn and Rhue (Lynn et al., 1988) document the tendency of these individuals to hallucinate vividly, experience fantasy as reality, and to have difficulty in differentiating fantasy events from real experiences. Fantasy-prone individuals report a variety of identity alteration processes including believing that they become someone else while in fantasy and having out-of-body experiences. Fantasy-prone individuals are also highly hypnotizable (Lynn et al., 1988; Plotnick, Payne, & O'Grady, 1991). Of particular interest is the observation that fantasy-prone individuals generally share a childhood background of abuse, neglect, and hardship (Lynn et al., 1988).

The relationship of fantasy proneness, as defined in the hypnosis literature, and the evolution of fantasy capacities described in the developmental literature remains to be determined. In addition to being highly hypnotizable, some investigators believe that fantasy-prone individuals are also highly dissociative (Lynn et al., 1988). This important hypothesis remains to be tested. However, there is reason to believe that dissociative disorder patients are likely to be fantasy prone. There is a set of items on the DES that inquire about difficulties distinguishing between actual events and remembered or imagined events. Dissociative disorder patients have significantly higher scores on this set of items compared with 20 other DSM-III-R Axis I psychiatric disorders (Putnam, 1994). In fact, these are the DES items that most robustly distinguish dissociative disorder patients from other psychiatric patients. Other clinical evidence indicates that dissociative disorder patients have a great deal of difficulty differentiating memories generated by fantasy from those produced by actual events (Ganaway, 1989).

In summary, several lines of evidence connect dissociation with imagination and fantasy capacities. Daydreaming and fantasy excursions are considered part of the normal range of the dissociative continuum (Hilgard, 1986; Putnam, 1991b).

Developmental investigations of fantasy role playing, role transitioning, and identity alterations may yield insights into the disturbances of identity modulation and stability inherent in the dissociative disorders. In people with MPD, the experience of the compelling reality of their alter personalities may result from traumatic disruptions in the evolution of the fantasy-reality boundary posited by Scarlet and Wolff and other investigators (DiLalla & Watson, 1988; Scarlett & Wolf, 1979). Work by Harris and colleagues (1991) suggests that whereas this boundary firms up with respect to common mental representations of physical objects by age 3 years, it remains in flux until age 6 years for "animate" imaginary objects. And fantasy proneness, particularly the tendency to confuse imaginary and real events, may significantly overlap with the dissociative disorders. Researchers in developmental psychopathology should alert to these and other potential connections between dissociation and fantasy capacities.

Dissociation and Attachment Theory

Bowlby's (1969) concept of attachment has proven to be a powerful construct, driving much current research in the fields of developmental psychology and developmental psychopathology (Cicchetti & Greenberg, 1991). The impact of maltreatment on attachment behavior in children has been investigated by several studies (Cicchetti & Barnett, 1991; Crittenden & Ainsworth, 1989; Gaensbauer & Harmon, 1982). Histories of insecure attachment are significantly related to self-destructive behaviors in adults abused or neglected as children (van der Kolk et al., 1991). High levels of dissociation were predictive of self-mutilation and suicide attempts in this same sample (van der Kolk et al., 1991). Significant levels of dissociation, on the part of the child and/or caretaker(s), are likely to influence the display of attachment behaviors in certain contexts and to influence the quality of the attachment relationship.

Although no formal studies of attachment behavior exist for MPD or dissociative patients, clinicians have invoked attachment theory in explanations of MPD. Barach (1991) equates the detachment phase of the separation response described by Bowlby with dissociation in that the abandoned child is sequestering information and behavior related to attachment stimuli. Bowlby (1988) viewed the detachment response as a deactivation of the attachment behavioral system that excluded from awareness " . . . signals, arising from both inside and outside the person, that would activate their attachment behavior and that would enable them both to love and to experience being loved" (pp. 34–35). Certainly the dissociative memory disturbances described earlier could serve as a mechanism for screening out attachment cues or for decoupling attachment behavior from attachment stimuli. Clinically, detachment from self and surroundings, usually manifest as depersonalization and derealization, is a common feature of dissociative disorders and is often evoked by overwhelming trauma.

At present, the strongest line of evidence supporting the argument that MPD involves significant disturbances in attachment comes from interpretations of the typical transferential responses of MPD patients in psychotherapy. The clinical literature on transference and countertransference issues in MPD is replete with examples of approach-avoidance behaviors acted out by these patients toward their therapists (Loewenstein, 1993; Putnam, 1989a). Early in treatment, MPD patients characteristically "test" their therapists with frequent emergencies, demands for extra sessions, and requests for special treatment. At the same time, they usually make threats and attempts to leave treatment, citing the therapist's failure to meet their needs as justification. Barach (1991) interprets these behaviors as evidence for the activation/deactivation of attachment behaviors. He also astutely observes that the child alter personalities of adult MPD patients often elicit powerful caretaking countertransferential responses in neophyte therapists, suggesting that this is one of their functions. One of the core principles of treatment for MPD is that the therapist provide a constancy of demeanor and behavior in couterresponse to the perturbations in the therapeutic relationship resulting from the alter personalities' differential transference responses (Putnam, 1989a). Perhaps this therapeutic stance succeeds, in part, by addressing disturbances in attachment.

Although these clinical explanations are intriguing, they lack the rigor necessary to test theories of the impact of chronic dissociation on attachment. One potential area of investigation is the effects of dissociation on the integration of the internal representational models that are postulated to underlie the meaning and organization of attachment responses (Crittenden, 1990). A pathologically dissociating child could be expected to have several different working models of an attachment relationship with his or her abuser—each associated with a specific set of dissociatively compartmentalized memories. Such cases have been described in the clinical literature. For example, Riley and Mead (1988) describe a 3-year-old girl with MPD, who manifested different attachment relationships to her biological mother who abused her and her nonabusing guardian depending on which alter personality was in control. The dissociative barriers discussed earlier in this chapter would act to impede the integration of different attachment representations. Consequently, the child would show very different attachment behaviors depending on which set of memories and representational model is currently being activated. The discrete behavioral states framework previously discussed would posit that the internal representational models would be dissociative state-dependently accessible.

Drawing on Tulving's division of memory into episodic, semantic, and procedural systems, Crittenden (1990) discusses a roughly analogous situation regarding the integration of attachment models confined to different memory systems. In the case of a dissociating individual, the problem of integrating representational models would be compounded because the effects of dissociation on memory are not neatly confined to a specific system such as episodic or semantic memory, but cut differential across memory systems. Furthermore, retrieval of memories associated with attachment figures would be influenced by the directional issues discussed earlier in this chapter and diagrammed in Figure 16.2. In MPD, clinicians often find within the same individual alter personalities that hate the abusing parent, alter personalities that idealize the same parent, and alter personalities that disclaim any relationship, positive or negative, with the parent (Putnam, 1989a). The ability of abused children to maintain strong attachments to their abusers may reflect, in part, some form of dissociation of their internal representational models.

Pathological dissociation, particularly MPD, produces rapid and dramatic behavioral shifts, particularly in interpersonal relatedness. It is common for MPD parents to have alter personalities that vehemently deny any relationship with their biological children. In reaction to these different maternal responses, children of MPD parents regularly describe having "many mothers" (Putnam, 1989a). Researchers might anticipate that pathological dissociation in a primary caretaker, particularly the mother, would produce disturbances in parenting and in attachment behaviors in both the parent and child.

Only two studies have attempted to examine the effects of MPD on parenting. Relying on the mother's description of her own behavior, Kluft (1987b) examined the parenting practices of 75 MPD patients. He did not evaluate the children. He found that about 16% of the parents reported abuse of their children and that 45% were classified as compromised or impaired in their parenting abilities. Commonly reported problems included failures to provide continuous care because of amnesias or personality switching, abdication of parenting by alter personalities who did not view the children as theirs, and "affective absence."

Coons (1985) examined the children of parents with MPD and compared them with the children of psychiatric patients with equivalent chronicity of illness. He found that the children of parents with MPD were significantly more disturbed than those of the other psychiatric patients. However, based on clinical interview, they did not exhibit higher levels of dissociation.

These clinical studies did not attempt to assess attachment behaviors in any fashion. Based on current attachment classification schemes, investigators might hypothesize that children of dissociative mothers would exhibit type "D," "disorganized/disoriented" behaviors. Type "D" attachment behavior has been identified in maltreated children (Carlson, Cicchetti, Barnett, & Braunwald, 1989). It is thought to result more from inconsistent maternal behavior than from bizarre or consistently rejecting behaviors. Particularly interesting is the interpretation that type "D" behavior represents a conflict between two or more attachment models such that the child first invokes one then another model, producing the apparent disorganization.

Type "D" responses may reflect the attempts of the child to invoke and attachment model that is congruent with the parent's behavioral state. A pathologically dissociating parent, especially a parent with MPD, can be expected to have very dissimilar behavioral states. Therefore, a child attempting to relate to a dissociating parent may be forced to choose among unlike and even contradictory attachment models. The consequences of choosing the "wrong" model may also be more severe in such cases.

Often a type "D" child manifests a momentary "stilling" of all behavior in an attachment situation. This behavioral "stilling," sometimes described as "trancelike," may reflect switching behaviors analogous to those described in the discussions of switching in MPD patients and behavioral state transitions in infants and young children. In MPD patients, a trancelike or "void" state is sometimes an intermediate transition state between two dissimilar alter personality states. Perhaps a similar principle applies to

shifting between two dissimilar attachment representational models for young children.

Although a disturbance in attachment formation is a compelling explanation invoked by clinicians to account for certain behaviors in MPD patients, systematic investigation of this hypothesis must come from developmental psychologists versed in all the subtle nuances of the measurement of attachment. Using tools and clinical indicators derived from clinical sources, developmental psychopathologists can study the contribution of dissociation in both parent and child to attachment behaviors. At least two studies, using the DES to assess dissociation in the mothers of maltreated children, are currently underway (Mary Main, personal communication, 1991; Dante Cicchetti, personal communication, 1993).

Impact of Pathological Dissociation on the Development of Self

A core clinical feature of the dissociative disorders is disturbance in sense of self. This disturbance can take several forms. In psychogenic amnesia, the individual is unable to recall important personal information that is too familiar or too extensive to be accounted for by normal forgetfulness (often his or her name, age, and marital status) (Loewenstein, 1991b). In depersonalization, the individual experiences a persistent feeling of unreality of self and estrangement from body and surroundings (Steinberg, 1991). In cases of psychogenic fugue, individuals often assume a transient secondary identity and are amnesic for their primary identity (Loewenstein, 1991b). And in multiple personality disorder, the individual experiences him- or herself as organized into a series of alternate identities (Putnam, 1989a).

Understanding "self" is the province of many disciplines and philosophies. Developmental psychology has primarily concerned itself with investigating the development of the self, the relationship of self to others and disruptions of the self (Cicchetti & Beeghly, 1990). Emerging from these studies, as well as from philosophical inquiry, is the concept of the self as a system of functions or subselves (Stern, 1985; Wolff, 1987). Within the developmental literature alone, there are many ways to conceptualize the organization of self. It is beyond the scope of this chapter to summarize and integrate these different models. The intention here is to illustrate, using for heuristic purposes one developmental model, how chronic dissociation could interfere with the ontogeny of self.

Daniel Stern (1985) has divided self into four basic component processes: self-agency, self-coherence, self-affectivity, and self-continuity. Self-agency involves a sense of authorship of one's behavior and the nonauthorship of the behavior of others, the sense of volition over one's actions, and the expectation of specific consequences resulting from one's actions. Wolf (1987) has studied the authorial function in young children and finds that by age 3 years, they adopt different voices to signal different perspectives that they take on personal experiences. The development of an authorial self-function, in fact, permits children to create new experiences of self. The authorial function also implies the simultaneous existence of different versions of self depending on the stance that the child takes toward the situation. Examination of the language of young children illustrates that the child is continually juggling several versions of self (Wolff, 1987). This process is well illustrated by the fluid but controlled exchange of roles—from actor to narrator to director—discussed in the prior section on imagination and fantasy.

Pathological dissociation can be expected to interfere with self-agency functions on several levels. With respect to authorship functions, the rigidity of the boundaries between dissociative versions of self interfere with the coordination and integration of role shifts and perspective taking. The sense of authorship and ownership of behavior must be undermined by the individual's discovery of having done things that he or she cannot remember and that may be against his or her best interests, judgment, or moral code. Dissociative memory disturbances, particularly the failure to integrate autobiographical memory, undercuts the individual's ability to access different versions of self.

Dissociative phenomena such as the passive influence experiences discussed earlier interrupt the volitional quality of self-generated behavior. Although well oriented to person, place, and situation, dissociative patients experiencing passive influence symptoms feel compelled to perform acts against their will. For its victims, these powerful, "possessionlike" experiences are one of the most frightening aspects of MPD. Not uncommonly, the patient is seized by an irresistible impulse to harm him- or herself. Intense depersonalization or out-of-body experiences frequently accompany these self-harm experiences, further eroding the sense of authorship and volition. The high rates of self-mutilation and suicidal behavior reported in dissociative patient samples reflect, in part, these nonvolitional self-destructive processes in operation.

The expectability of consequences and the logical continuity of cause-and-effect relationships, important to self-agency and other aspects of self, are interrupted by dissociative amnesias and switching behaviors. Adults (Putnam, 1989a) and children (Hornstein & Putnam, 1992; Putnam, 1991b) with dissociative disorders have a great deal of difficulty learning from experience. It is believed that, in part, this failure results from dissociative interference with the subjective continuity of behavior. Consequences of unremembered acts are experienced without insight into how they stem from earlier behavior. And conversely, dissociating individuals, may have no awareness of the later consequences of their acts.

Self-coherence, the second of Stern's four elements of self, is predicated on the experience of a coherent, nonfragmented, physical whole with boundaries and a locus of action across different contexts. Coherence of self depends to a large extent on the coherence of temporal experience and the stability of perception, cognition and identity. Obviously, many aspects of chronic dissociation interfere with self-coherence. One of the core subjective experiences of pathological dissociation is the "loss of time." Disruptions and even subjective reversals (e.g., when a dissociating individual experiences "age-regression") in the flow of time destroy temporal coherence. Dissociative distortions in body image (e.g., different alter personalities viewing the body as having a different appearance and gender) undercut a sense of physical coherence and stability. Dissociative state-specific differences in perception, cognition, and physiology, such as those documented in the previous section on psychophysiology, further contribute to fragmentation of self. And finally, depersonalization and passive influence experiences undercut the unity of locus of control.

Self-affectivity, the third component in Stern's model, requires the stability of internal self-events associated with specific emotional states such as joy, fear, surprise, and anger. Stern argues that for each emotional state there is a set of invariant internal self-events including (a) proprioceptive feedback patterns to/from facial display, respiratory rate, and rhythm and vocalization; (b) internal patterns of activation and arousal; and (c) emotion-specific qualities of feeling (Stern, 1985). Stern further argues that the constancy of these internal experiences over the entire life span makes them an excellent warrant for the stability of self over time.

In MPD, different affective responses to the same stimuli are commonly observed between alter personality states of the same individual. In fact, these differences in affective response to equivalent stimuli often seem, in part, to define, for the individual and others the "separateness" of the alter personalities. As discussed in the earlier section on alter personalities, most of these entities are organized around a single prevailing affect and cannot express a wide range of affect. Thus, the multiplicity of affective responses to a given situation, the differential dissociative state-dependent psychophysiological patterns associated with specific alter personality states, and the inaccessibility of the larger affective repertoire of the individual as a whole, undercut the contribution of self-affectivity to the continuity of self.

Stern's final component, self-continuity, is the cement that binds the other functions of self into an integrated whole (Fink, 1988; Stern, 1985). Failures in self-continuity are inherent in dissociative disturbances of the self-agency, self-coherence, and self-affectivity. Continuity of memory is central to continuity of self. Dissociative disturbances of memory—particularly compartmentalization, impairments of information retrieval, and difficulties in determining whether a memory reflects an experienced or imagined event—seriously undermine the continuity of memory. The extensive gaps in autobiographical memory noted in MPD patients break their historical warrants of self-continuity. The fragmentation of continuity in the present and the disruption of historical links with the past must contribute in profound ways to the failures in integration of self-organization manifest in dissociative disorder patients.

In summary, it is likely that chronic dissociation produces profound disturbances in the development of self. The nature of these disruptions will be conceptualized differently depending upon the organizational model of self used. Irrespective of the particular framework, pathological dissociation can be expected to produce fragmentation of self, particularly along the dimensions of agency and continuity. The dissociative disorders provide an excellent model for developmental psychopathologists to explore the ontogenesis of self-systems. Cole and Putnam (1992) have argued elsewhere that disruptions in the development of self are common to all psychiatric disorders associated with childhood sexual abuse.

CONCLUSIONS

This chapter provides an in-depth introduction to dissociation and the dissociative disorders for developmental psychologists and psychopathologists. Among the first psychopathological processes studied, dissociation is generally conceptualized as occurring along a continuum ranging from the normal dissociations of everyday life to extreme conditions characterized by profound disturbances in memory and identity. Multiple personality disorder in particular, with its bizarre disturbances of self, has often been cited as a key example of the polypsychic nature of the human mind and historically is credited with stimulating the development of modern psychiatry.

Clinical evidence strongly supports the interpretation that dissociation serves as a psychological defense for individuals confronted with an overwhelming traumatic situation. Defensive functions of dissociation include (a) automatization of complex behaviors—allowing the individual to focus conscious attention on other matters, (b) compartmentalization and sequestration of emotionally charged material out of conscious awareness, (c) alterations and estrangements from self that protect individuals facing imminent death, and (d) protection from unbearable physical and psychological pain. At least in some instances, dissociative disorders are thought to arise when the individual generalized acutely induced dissociative defenses to lessor stressors. A possible developmental window, closing around age 9 to 10 years, may exist for the creation of multiple personality disorder.

Recent progress in the measurement of dissociation is producing the first meaningful data on the distribution of dissociativity in normal and clinical samples and of the prevalence of dissociative disorders. Laboratory research is shedding light on the cognitive and physiological basis of dissociation. Dissociative disturbances of memory include autobiographical amnesias, compartmentalizations of memory, and disturbances in the retrieval of explicit and implicit information, the latter showing the most robust effects. Studies of the psychophysiology of dissociation suggest that dissociation is a special state(s) of consciousness that involves alterations in basic regulatory physiology, stimulus processing, and cognition. Individuals with MPD often rapidly switch among several dissociative states of consciousness (the alter personalities) producing precipitous changes in their behavior.

Both adult and child dissociative disorders present with a plethora of psychiatric symptoms. The typical symptom array includes affective symptoms, self-destructive behaviors, hallucinations, passive influence symptoms, amnesias, identity disturbances, and depersonalization. The alter personalities of MPD patients appear to represent discrete states of consciousness that are organized around a predominant affect, a state-dependent cognitive and behavioral repertoire, and a sense of self. Most MPD patients have an array of alter personalities that perform specific psychological or social functions. The symptomatic floridness of MPD waxes and wanes across the life cycle and in response to stress. Although clinicians working with these patients are enthusiastic about their response to treatment, little systematic data on outcome is available. A variety of theories, ranging from iatrogenic suggestion to epilepsy have been advanced to account for MPD in particular.

Little is known about the developmental roots of normative dissociation of the dissociative disorders. Many theories have implicated hypnotizability as a potential substrate for pathological dissociation. However, recent research indicates that it is at best a moderate correlate of dissociativity in adults. Preliminary research finds no relationship between hypnotizability and dissociativity in normal or traumatized children. Other developmental processes theoretically linked to dissociation include behavioral states, imagination and fantasy, attachment theory, and the development and integration of self-systems. Much work remains on the developmental substrates of dissociation and on the effects of pathological dissociation on other developmental processes. Further advances in this area will require the active involvement of researchers trained in developmental psychology.

REFERENCES

Abeles, M., & Schilder, P. (1935). Psychogenic loss of personal identity. *Archives of Neurology and Psychiatry, 34*, 587–604.

Achenbach, T., & Edelbrock, C. (1981). Behavioral problems and competencies reported by parents of normal and disturbed children aged 4 through 16. *Monographs of the Society for Research in Child Development, 46.*

Albini, T. K., & Pease, T. E. (1989). Normal and pathological dissociations of early childhood. *Dissociation, 2*, 144–150.

Allison, R. B. (1978). A rational psychotherapy plan for multiplicity. *Sven Tidskrift Hypnos, 3*, 9–16.

Allison, R. B., & Schwartz, T. (1980). *Minds in many pieces.* New York: Rawson, Wade.

Alvarado, C. (1989). Dissociation and state-specific psychophysiology during the nineteenth century. *Dissociation, 2*, 160–168.

American Psychiatric Association. (1980, 1987, 1994). *Diagnostic and statistical manual of mental disorders.* (3rd ed., 3rd ed. rev., 4th ed.). Washington, DC: Author.

American Psychiatric Association. (1993). *DSM-IV Draft Criteria.* Washington, DC: Author.

Andorfer, J. C. (1985). Multiple personality in the human information-processor: A case history and theoretical formulation. *Journal of Clinical Psychology, 41*, 309–324.

Armstrong, J. (1991). The psychological organization of multiple personality disordered patients as revealed in psychological testing. *Psychiatric Clinics of North America, 14*, 533–546.

Armstrong, J. G., & Loewenstein, R. J. (1990). Characteristics of patients with multiple personality and dissociative disorders on psychological testing. *Journal of Nervous Mental Disease, 178*, 448–453.

Asaad, G., & Sharpiro, B. (1986). Hallucinations: Theorectical and clinical overview. *American Journal of Psychiatry, 143*, 1088–1097.

Bahnson, C. B., & Smith, K. (1975). Autonomic changes in a multiple personality. *Psychosomatic Medicine, 37*, 85–86.

Barach, P. M. M. (1991). Multiple personality as an attachment disorder. *Dissociation, 4*, 117–123.

Barnes, F. F. (1980). Travel and fatigue as causes of partial dissociative reactions. *Comprehensive Psychiatry, 21*, 55–61.

Berman, E. (1981). Multiple personality: Psychoanalytic perspectives. *International Journal of Psychoanalysis, 62*, 283–300.

Bernstein, E., & Putnam, F. W. (1986). Development, reliability and validity of a dissociation scale. *Journal of Nervous and Mental Disease, 174,* 727–735.

Bliss, E. (1984). A symptom profile of patients with multiple personalities, including MMPI results. *Journal of Nervous and Mental Disease, 174,* 197–202.

Bliss, E. L. (1980). Multiple personalities. *Archives of General Psychiatry, 37,* 1388–1397.

Bliss, E. L. (1986). *Multiple personality, allied disorders and hypnosis.* New York: Oxford University Press.

Bliss, E. L., & Jeppsen, E. A. (1985). Prevalence of multiple personality among inpatients and outpatients. *American Journal of Psychiatry, 142,* 250–251.

Boon, S., & Draijer, N. (1991). Diagnosing dissociative disorders in the Netherlands: A pilot study with the structured clinical interview for DSM-III-R dissociative disorders. *American Journal of Psychiatry, 148,* 458–462.

Boor, M. (1982). The multiple personality epidemic. *Journal of Nervous and Mental Disease, 170*(5), 302–304.

Bourguignon, E. (1968). World distribution and patterns of possession states. In R. Prince (Ed.), *Trance and possession states* (pp. 3–35). Montreal: R. M. Bucke Memorial Society.

Boustany, N., & Priest, D. (1992, February 23). For ex-hostages, "Pain has not gone away." *Washington Post,* pp. 1A & 18A.

Bowlby, J. (1969). *Attachment.* New York: Basic Books.

Bowlby, J. (1988). *A secure base: Parent-child attachment and healthy human development.* New York: Basic Books.

Bowman, E. S. (1990). Adolescent multiple personality disorder in the nineteenth and early twentieth century. *Dissociation, 3,*(4), 179–187.

Bowman, E. S., Blix, S., & Coons, P. M. (1985). Multiple personality in adolescence: Relationship to incestual experiences. *Journal of the American Academy of Child Psychiatry, 24*(1), 109–114.

Brandsma, J. M., & Ludwig, A. M. (1974). A case of multiple personality: Diagnosis and therapy. *International Journal of Experimental and Clinical Hypnosis, 22,* 216–233.

Branscomb, L. (1991). Dissociation in combat-related posttraumatic stress disorder. *Dissociation, 4,* 13–20.

Braun, B. G. (1984). Towards a theory of multiple personality and other dissociative phenomena. *Psychiatric Clinics of North America, 7,* 171–193.

Braun, B. G., & Sachs, R. G. (1985). The development of multiple personality disorder: Predisposing, precipitating and perpetuating factors. In R. P. Kluft (Ed.), *Childhood antecedants of multiple personality disorder* (pp. 37–64). Washington, DC: American Psychiatric Press.

Bremner, J. D., Southwick, S., Brett, E., Fontana, A., Rosenheck, R., & Charney, D. S. (1992). Dissociation and posttraumatic stress disorder in Vietnam combat veterans. *American Journal of Psychiatry, 149,* 328–332.

Bretherton, I. (1989). Pretense: The form and function of make-believe play. *Developmental Review, 9,* 383–401.

Briere, J. (1990). Augmenting Hopkins SCL scales to measure dissociative symptoms. *Journal of Personality Assessment, 55,* 376–379.

Briere, J., & Runtz, M. (1988). Symptomatology associated with childhood sexual victimization in a nonclinical adult sample. *Child Abuse and Neglect, 12,* 51–59.

Cancio, L. C. (1991). Stress and trance in freefall parachuting: A pilot study. *American Journal of Clinical Hypnosis, 33,* 225–234.

Carlson, E. B., & Putnam, F. W. (1989). Integrating research on dissociation and hypnotizability: Are there two pathways to hypnotizability? *Dissociation, 2*(1), 32–38.

Carlson, E. B., & Putnam, F. W. (1993). An update on the Dissociative Experience Scale. *Dissociation, 6,* 15–26.

Carlson, E. B., Putnam, F. W., Ross, C. A., Torem, M., Coons, P. M., Dill, D. L., Loewenstein, R. J., & Braun, B. G. (1993). Validity of the Dissociative Experiences Scale in screening for multiple personality disorder: A multicenter study. *American Journal of Psychiatry, 150,* 1030–1036.

Carlson, E. T. (1981). The history of multiple personality in the United States: I. The beginnings. *American Journal of Psychiatry, 138*(5), 666–668.

Carlson, V., Cicchetti, D., Barnett, D., & Braunwald, K. G. (1989). Disorganized/disoriented attachment relationships in maltreated infants. *Developmental Psychology, 25,* 525.

Charcot, J. M., & Marie, P. (1892). On hysteroepilepsy. In H. Tuke (Ed.), *A dictionary of psychological medicine.* London: Churchill.

Chu, J. A., & Dill, D. L. (1990). Dissociative symptoms in relation to childhood physical and sexual abuse. *American Journal of Psychiatry, 147,* 887–892.

Cicchetti, D., & Barnett, D. (1991). Attachment organization in preschool aged maltreated children. *Development and Psychopathology, 3,* 397–411.

Cicchetti, D., & Beeghly, M. (1990). Perspectives on the study of the self in transition. In D. Cicchetti & M. Beeghly (Eds.), *The self in transition* (pp. 1–16). Chicago: University of Chicago Press.

Cicchetti, D., & Greenberg, M. (1991). Attachment and psychopathology (special issue). *Development and psychopathology, 3.*

Cole, P. M., & Putnam, F. W. (1992). Effect of incest on self and social functioning: A developmental psychopathology perspective. *Journal of Clinical and Consulting Psychology, 60.*

Coons, P. M. (1985). Children of parents with multiple personality disorder. In R. P. Kluft (Ed.), *Childhood antecedents of multiple personality* (pp. 151–165). Washington, DC: American Psychiatric Press.

Coons, P. M. (1986). Treatment progress in 20 patients with multiple personality disorder. *Journal of Nervous and Mental Disease, 174,* 715–721.

Coons, P. M. (1988). Psychophysiologic aspects of multiple personality disorder: A review. *Dissociation, 1,* 47–53.

Coons, P. M. (1992). Dissociative disorder not otherwise specified: A clinical investigation of 50 cases with suggestions for typology and treatment. *Dissociation, 5,* 187–195.

Coons, P. M., Bowman, E. S., & Milstein, V. (1988). Multiple personality disorder: A clinical investigation of 50 cases. *Journal of Nervous and Mental Disease, 176,* 519–527.

Coons, P. M., & Fine, C. G. (1990). Accuracy of the MMPI in identifying multiple personality disorder. *Psychological Reports, 66,* 831–834.

Coons, P. M., Milstein, V., & Marley, C. (1982). EEG studies of two multiple personalities and a control. *Archives of General Psychiatry, 39,* 823–825.

Crisp, P. (1983). Object relations and multiple personality: An exploration of the literature. *Psychoanalytic Review, 70,* 221–234.

Crittenden, P. M. (1990). Internal representational models of attachment relationships. *Infant Mental Health Journal, 11,* 259–277.

Crittenden, P. M., & Ainsworth, M. D. S. (1989). Child maltreatment and attachment theory. In D. Cicchetti & V. Carlson (Eds.), *Child maltreatment* (pp. 432–463). Cambridge, England: Cambridge University Press.

Dell, P. F., & Eisenhower, J. W. (1990). Adolescent multiple personality disorder. *Journal of the American Academy of Child and Adolescent Psychiatry, 29,* 359–366.

Demitrack, M. A., Putnam, F. W., Brewerton, T. D., Brandt, H. A., & Gold, P. W. (1990). Relation of clinical variables to dissociative phenomena in eating disorders. *American Journal of Psychiatry, 147,* 1184–1188.

Devinsky, O., Putnam, F. W., Grafman, J., Bromfield, E., & Theodore, W. H. (1989). Dissociative states and epilepsy. *Neurology, 39,* 835–840.

DiLalla, L. F., & Watson, M. W. (1988). Differentiation of fantasy and reality: Preschoolers' reactions to interruptions in their play. *Developmental Psychology, 24,* 286–291.

Donovan, D. M. (1991). Darkness invisible. *Journal of Psychohistory, 19,* 165–184.

Ellenberger, H. F. (1970). *The discovery of the unconscious: The history and evolution of dynamic psychiatry.* New York: Basic Books.

Ensink, B. J. (1992). *Confusing realities: A study of child sexual abuse and psychiatric symptoms.* Amsterdam: VU University Press.

Ensink, B. J., & van Otterloo, D. (1989). A validation of the Dissociative Experiences Scale in the Netherlands. *Dissociation, 2,* 221–224.

Fagan, J., & McMahon, P. P. (1984). Incipient multiple personality in children: Four cases. *Journal of Nervous and Mental Disease, 172*(1), 26–36.

Fahy, T. A. (1988). The diagnosis of multiple personality disorder: A critical review. *British Journal of Psychiatry, 153,* 597–606.

Fein, G. G. (1981). Pretend play in childhood: An integrative review. *Child Development, 52,* 1095–1118.

Fine, C. G. (1988). The work of Antoine Despine: The first scientific report on the diagnosis and treatment of a child with multiple personality disorder. *American Journal of Clinical Hypnosis, 31*(1), 33–39.

Fink, D. L. (1988). The core self: A developmental perspective on the dissociative disorders. *Dissociation, 1*(2), 43–47.

Fink, D. L. (1991). The comorbidity of multiple personality disorder and DSM-III-R Axis II disorders. *Psychiatric Clinics of North America, 14*(3), 547–566.

Flor-Henry, R., Tomer, R., Kumpula, I., Koles, Z. J., & Yeudall, L. T. (1990). Neurophysiological and neuropsychological study of two cases of multiple personality syndrome and comparison with chronic hysteria. *International Journal of Psychophysiology, 10,* 151–161.

Frankel, F. H. (1990). Hypnotizability and dissociation. *American Journal of Psychiatry, 147,* 823–829.

Frischholz, E. J., Braun, B. G., Sachs, R. G., Hopkins, L., Shaeffer, D. M., Lewis, J., Leavitt, F., Pasquotto, J. N., & Schwartz, D. R. (1990). The Dissociative Experiences Scale: Further replication and validation. *Dissociation, 3,* 151–153.

Frischholz, M. A. (1985). The relationship among dissociation, hypnosis, and child abuse in the development of multiple personality disorder. In R. P. Kluft (Ed.), *Childhood antecedents of multiple personality* (pp. 100–126). Washington, DC: American Psychiatric Press.

Gaensbauer, T. J., & Harmon, R. J. (1982). Attachment behavior in abused/neglected and premature infants: Implications for the concept of attachment. In R. N. Emde & R. J. Harmon (Eds.), *The development of attachment and affiliative systems.* New York: Plenum.

Ganaway, G. K. (1989). Historical truth versus narrative truth: Clarifying the role of exogenous trauma in the etiology of multiple personality disorder and its variants. *Dissociation, 2,* 205–220.

Garcia, F. O. (1990). The concept of dissociation and conversion in the new edition of the *International Classification of Diseases* (ICD-10). *Dissociation, 3,* 204–208.

Giffin, H. (1984). The coordination of meaning in the creation of shared make-believe reality. In I. Bretherton (Ed.), *Symbolic play: The development of social understanding* (pp. 73–100). New York: Academic Press.

Gioloas, M. H., & Sanders, B. (1992). Pain and suffering as a function of dissociation level and instructional set. *Dissociation, 5,* 205–209.

Good, M. I. (1989). Substance-induced dissociative disorders and psychiatric nosology. *Journal of Clinical Psychopharmacology, 9*(2), 88–93.

Graves, S. M. (1989). Dissociative disorders and dissociative symptoms at a community health center. *Dissociation, 2,* 119–127.

Greaves, G. B. (1980). Multiple personality: 165 years after Mary Reynolds. *Journal of Nervous and Mental Disease, 168*(10), 577–596.

Hale, N. G. (Ed.). (1975). *Morton Prince. Psychotherapy and multiple personality disorder: Selected essays.* Cambridge: Harvard University Press.

Harris, P. L., Brown, E., Marriott, C., Whittal, S., & Harmer, S. (1991). Monsters, ghosts and witches: Testing the limits of fantasy-reality distinction in young children. *British Journal of Developmental Psychology, 9,* 105–123.

Hilgard, E. R. (1965). *Hypnotic susceptibility.* New York: Harcourt Brace Jovanovich.

Hilgard, E. R. (1979). Divided consciousness in hypnosis: The implications of the hidden observer. In E. Fromm & R. E. Shor (Eds.), *Hypnosis: Developments in research and new perspectives (2nd ed.)* (pp. 45–79). New York: Aldine.

Hilgard, E. R. (1986). *Divided consciousness: Multiple controls in human thought and action (rev. ed.).* New York: Wiley.

Hornstein, N. L., & Putnam, F. W. (1992). Clinical phenomenology of child and adolescent dissociative disorders. *Journal of the American Academy of Child and Adolescent Psychiatry, 31,* 1077–1085.

Hornstein, N. L., & Tyson, S. (1991). Inpatient treatment of children with multiple personality/dissociative disorders and their families. *Psychiatric Clinics of North America, 14*(3), 631–648.

Hughes, J. R., Kuhlman, D. T., Fichtner, C. G., & Gruenfeld, M. J. (1990). Brain mapping in a case of multiple personality. *Clinical Electroencephalography, 21,* 200–209.

Janet, P. (1889). *L'automatisme psychologue.* Paris: Pans Balliere.

Janet, P. (1901). *The mental state of hystericals. A study of mental stigmata and mental accidents* (C. R. Corson, Trans.) (2 vols. in 1). New York: Putnam.

Kanzer, M. (1939). Amnesia: A statisical study. *American Journal of Psychiatry, 96,* 711–716.

Kirby, J. S., Chu, J. A., & Dill, D. L. (1993). Correlates of dissociative symptomatology in patients with physical and sexual abuse histories. *Comprehensive Psychiatry, 34,* 258–263.

Kluft, R. P. (1984). Multiple personality in childhood. *Psychiatric Clinics of North America, 7*(1), 121–134.

Kluft, R. P. (1985a). Childhood multiple personality disorder: Predictors, clinical findings and treatment results. In R. P. Kluft (Ed.), *Childhood antecedents of multiple personality* (pp. 167–196). Washington, DC: American Psychiatric Press.

Kluft, R. P. (1985b). The natural history of multiple personality disorder. In R. P. Kluft (Ed.), *Childhood antecedents of multiple personality* (pp. 197–238). Washington, DC: American Psychiatric Press.

Kluft, R. P. (1987a). First-rank symptoms as a diagnostic clue to multiple personality disorder. *American Journal of Psychiatry, 144,* 293–298.

Kluft, R. P. (1987b). The parental fitness of mothers with multiple personality disorder: A preliminary study. *Child Abuse and Neglect, 11,* 273–280.

Kluft, R. P. (1988). The postunification treatment of multiple personality disorder: First findings. *American Journal of Psychotherapy, 62,* 212–228.

Kluft, R. P. (1989a). The David Caul Memorial Symposium Papers: Iatrogenesis and MPD. *Dissociation, 2,* 66–104.

Kluft, R. P. (1989b). Iatrogenic creation of new alter personalities. *Dissociation, 2,* 83–91.

Kluft, R. P. (1991a). Clinical presentations of multiple personality disorder. *Psychiatric Clinics of North America, 14*(3), 605–630.

Kluft, R. P. (1991b). Multiple personality disorder. In A. Tasman & S. M. Goldfinger (Eds.), *American Psychiatric Press annual review of psychiatry* (Vol. 10, pp. 161–181). Washington, DC: American Psychiatric Press.

Kotsopoulos, S., Kanigsberg, J., Cote, A., & Fiedorowicz, C. (1987). Hallucinatory experiences in nonpsychotic children. *Journal of the American Academy of Child and Adolescent Psychiatry, 26,* 375–380.

Larmore, K., Ludwig, A., & Cain, R. (1977). Multiple personality: An objective case study. *British Journal of Psychiatry, 131,* 35–40.

Li, D., & Spiegel, D. (1992). A neural network model of dissociative disorders. *Psychiatric Annals, 22,* 144–147.

Loewenstein, R. J. (1991a). An office mental status examination for complex chronic dissociative symptoms and multiple personality disorder. *Psychiatric Clinics of North America, 14*(3), 567–604.

Loewenstein, R. J. (1991b). Psychogenic amnesia and psychogenic fugue: A comprehensive review. In A. Tasman & S. M. Goldfinger (Eds.), *American Psychiatric Press annual review of psychiatry* (pp. 189–221). Washington, DC: American Psychiatric Press.

Loewenstein, R. J. (1993). Post-traumatic and dissociative aspects of transference and countertransference in the treatment of multiple personality disorder. In R. P. Kluft & C. G. Fine (Eds.), *Clinical perspectives on multiple personality disorder* (pp. 287–301). Washington, DC: American Psychiatric Press.

Loewenstein, R. J., Hamilton, J., Alagna, S., Reid, N., & Devries, M. (1987). Experiential sampling in the study of multiple personality disorder. *American Journal of Psychiatry, 144,* 19–21.

Loewenstein, R. J., & Putnam, F. W. (1988). A comparison study of dissociative symptoms in patients with partial complex seizures, MPD, and posttraumatic stress disorder. *Dissociation, 1*(4), 17–32.

Loewenstein, R. J., & Putnam, F. W. (1990). The clinical phenomenology of males with multiple personality disorder: A report of 21 cases. *Dissociation, 3,* 135–143.

Lovinger, S. L. (1983). Multiple personality: A theorectical view. *Psychotherapy: theory, research and practice, 20,* 425–434.

Ludwig, A. M. (1983). The psychobiological functions of dissociation. *American Journal of Clinical Hypnosis, 26,* 93–99.

Ludwig, A. M., Brandsman, J. M., Wilbur, C. B., Bendfeldt, F., & Jameson, D. H. (1972). The objective study of a multiple personality. *Archives of General Psychiatry, 26,* 298–310.

Lydic, R. (1987). State-dependent aspects of regulatory physiology. *Journal of the Federation of the American Society of Experimental Biology, 1,* 6–15.

Lynn, S. J., Rhue, J. W., & Green, J. P. (1988). Multiple personality and fantasy proness: Is there an association or dissociation? *British Journal of Experimental and Clinical Hypnosis, 5,* 138–142.

Malenbaum, R., & Russel, A. J. (1987). Multiple personality disorder in an 11 year-old boy and his mother. *Journal of the American Academy of Child and Adolescent Psychiatry, 26,* 436–439.

Malinosky-Rummell, R. R., & Hoeir, T. S. (1991). Validating measures of dissociation in sexually abused and nonabused children. *Behavioral Assessment, 13,* 341–357.

Manosevitz, M., Prentice, N. M., & Wilson, F. (1973). Individual and family correlates of imaginary companions in preschool children. *Developmental Psychology, 8,* 72–79.

Marmer, S. S. (1991). Multiple personality disorder: A psychoanalytic perspective. *Psychiatric Clinics of North America,* 677–694.

Mathew, R. J., Jack, R. A., & West, W. S. (1985). Regional cerebral blood flow in a patient with multiple personality. *American Journal of Psychiatry, 142,* 504–505.

Miller, S. D. (1989). Optical differences in cases of multiple personality disorder. *Journal of Nervous and Mental Disease, 177*(8), 480–486.

Miller, S. D., Blackburn, T., Scholes, G., White, G. L., & Mamalis, N. (1991). Optical differences in multiple personality disorder: A second look. *Journal of Nervous and Mental Disease, 179,* 132–135.

Modestin, J. (1992). Multiple personality disorder in Switzerland. *American Journal of Psychiatry, 149,* 88–92.

Mulhern, S. (1991). Embodied alternative identities: Bearing witness to a world that might have been. *Psychiatric Clinics of North America, 14*(3), 769–786.

Nash, M. R., Hulsey, T. L., Sexton, M. C., Harralson, T. L., & Lambert, W. (1993). Long-term sequelae of childhood sexual abuse: Perceived family environment, psychopathology, and dissociation. *Journal of Clinical and Consult Psychology, 61,* 276–283.

Nash, M. R., Lynn, S. J., & Givens, D. L. (1984). Adult hypnotic susceptibility, childhood punishment, and child abuse: A brief communication. *International Journal of Clinical and Experimental Hypnosis, 32,* 6–11.

Nemiah, J. C. (1980). Dissociative disorders. In A. M. Freedman & H. I. Kaplan (Eds.), *Comprehensive textbook of psychiatry* (pp. 1544–1561). Baltimore: Williams & Wilkins.

Nemiah, J. C. (1991). Dissociation, conversion and somatization. In A. Tasman & S. M. Goldfinger (Eds.), *American Psychiatric Press annual review of psychiatry* (pp. 248–260). Washington, DC: American Psychiatric Press.

Nissen, M. J., Ross, J. L., Willingham, D. B., Mackenzie, T. B., & Schacter, D. L. (1988). Memory and awareness in a patient with multiple personality disorder. *Brain & Cognition, 8,* 117–134.

Peterson, G. (1990). Diagnosis of childhood multiple personality. *Dissociation, 3,* 3–9.

Plotnick, A. B., Payne, P. A., & O'Grady, D. J. (1991). Correlates of hypnotizability in children: Absorption, vividness of imagery, fantasy play and social desirability. *American Journal of Clinical Hypnosis, 34,* 51–58.

Prince, M. (1890). Some of the revelations of hypnotism. *Boston Medical and Surgical Journal, 122,* 463–467.

Putnam, F. W. (1984). The psychophysiologic investigation of multiple personality disorder. *Psychiatric Clinics of North America, 7,* 31–40.

Putnam, F. W. (1985). Dissociation as a response to extreme trauma. In R. P. Kluft (Ed.), *Childhood antecedents of multiple personality* (pp. 66–97). Washington, DC: American Psychiatric Press.

Putnam, F. W. (1986). The scientific investigation of multiple personality. In J. M. Quen (Ed.), *Split minds split brains* (pp. 109–126). New York: New York University Press.

Putnam, F. W. (1988). The switch process in multiple personality disorder and other state-change disorders. *Dissociation, 1*(1), 24–32.

Putnam, F. W. (1989a). *Diagnosis and treatment of multiple personality disorder*. New York: Guilford.

Putnam, F. W. (1989b). Pierre Janet and modern views of dissociation. *Journal of Traumatic Stress, 2*(4), 413–429.

Putnam, F. W. (1991a). Dissociative disorders in children and adolescents: A developmental perspective. *Psychiatric Clinics of North America, 14*(3), 519–532.

Putnam, F. W. (1991b). Dissociative phenomena. In A. Tasman & S. M. Goldfinger (Eds.), *American Psychiatric Press annual review of psychiatry* (pp. 145–160). Washington, DC: American Psychiatric Press.

Putnam, F. W. (1991c). Recent research on multiple personality disorder. *Psychiatric Clinics of North America, 14*, 489–502.

Putnam, F. W. (1992a). Are alter personalities fragments or figments? *Psychoanalytic Inquiry, 12*, 95–111.

Putnam, F. W. (1992b). Using hypnosis for therapeutic abreactions. *Psychiatric Medicine, 10*, 51–56.

Putnam, F. W. (1994). Dissociation and disturbances of self. In D. Cicchetti & S. L. Toth (Eds.), *The self and its disorders* (Vol. 5). Rochester, NY: University of Rochester Press.

Putnam, F. W., Guroff, J. J., Silberman, E. K., Barban, L., & Post, R. M. (1986). The clinical phenomenology of multiple personality disorder: Review of 100 recent cases. *Journal of Clinical Psychiatry, 47*, 285–293.

Putnam, F. W., Helmer, K., Horowitz, L. A., & Trickett, P. A. (in press). Hypnotizability and dissociativity in sexually abused girls. *Child Abuse and Neglect.*

Putnam, F. W., Helmers, K., & Trickett, P. K. (1993). Development, reliability and validity of a child dissociation scale. *Child Abuse and Neglect, 17*, 731–741.

Putnam, F. W., & Loewenstein, R. J. (1993). Treatment of multiple personality disorder: A survey of current practices. *American Journal of Psychiatry, 150*, 1048–1052.

Putnam, F. W., Zahn, T. P., & Post, R. M. (1990). Differential autonomic nervous system activity in multiple personality disorder. *Psychiatric Research, 31*, 251–260.

Ribot, T. (1891). *The diseases of personality.* Chicago: Open Court Publishing.

Riley, K. C. (1988). Measurement of dissociation. *Journal of Nervous and Mental Disease, 176*, 449–450.

Riley, R. L., & Mead, J. (1988). The development of symptoms of multiple personality disorder in a child of three. *Dissociation, 1*, 41–46.

Rosenbaum, M. (1980). The role of the term schizophrenia in the decline of multiple personality. *Archives of General Psychiatry, 37*, 1383–1385.

Rosenbaum, M., & Weaver, G. M. (1980). Dissociated state: Status of a case after 38 years. *Journal of Nervous and Mental Disease, 168*, 597–603.

Ross, C. A. (1989). *Multiple personality disorder: Diagnosis, clinical features and treatment.* New York: Wiley.

Ross, C. A. (1991). Epidemiology of multiple personality disorder. *Psychiatric Clinics of North America, 14*(3), 503–518.

Ross, C. A., Anderson, G., Fleisher, W., & Norton, G. (1991). The frequency of multiple personality disorder among psychiatric inpatients. *American Journal of Psychiatry, 148*, 1717–1720.

Ross, C. A., Heber, S., & Norton, G. R. (1989). Differentiating multiple personality disorder and complex seizures. *General Hospital Psychiatry, 11*, 54–58.

Ross, C. A., Heber, S., Norton, G., Anderson, D., Anderson, G., & Barchet, P. (1989). The Dissociative Disorders Interview Schedule: A structured interview. *Dissociation, 2*, 169–189.

Ross, C. A., Joshi, S., & Currie, R. (1989). Dissociative experiences in the general population. *American Journal of Psychiatry, 147*, 1547–1552.

Ross, C. A., Miller, S. D., Bjornson, L., Reagor, P., Fraser, G., & Anderson, G. (1990). Structured interview data on 102 cases of multiple personality disorder from four centers. *American Journal of Psychiatry, 147*, 596–601.

Ross, C. A., Miller, S. D., Bjornson, L., Reagor, P., Fraser, G. A., & Anderson, G. (1991). Abuse histories in 102 cases of multiple personality disorder. *Canadian Journal of Psychiatry, 36*, 97–101.

Ross, C. A., Norton, G. R., & Anderson, G. (1988). The Dissociative Experiences Scale: A replication study. *Dissociation, 1*(2), 21–22.

Ross, C. A., Norton, G. R., & Wozney, K. (1989). Multiple personality disorder: An analysis of 239 cases. *Canadian Journal of Psychiatry, 34*, 413–418.

Rothenberg, M. B. (1980). Is there an unconscious national conspiracy against children in the United States? *Clinical Pediatrics, 19*, 10–24.

Rubin, D. C. (1988). Introduction. In D. C. Rubin (Ed.), *Autobiographical memory* (pp. 3–18). Cambridge, England: Cambridge University Press.

Rubin, D. C., & Nebes, R. D. (1988). Autobiographical memory across the lifespan. In D. C. Rubin (Ed.), *Autobiographical memory* (pp. 202–221). Cambridge, England: Cambridge University Press.

Sanders, B., & Gioloas, M. H. (1991). Dissociation and childhood trauma in psychologically disturbed adolescents. *American Journal of Psychiatry, 148*, 50–54.

Sanders, B., McRoberts, G., & Tollefson, C. (1989). Childhood stress and dissociation in a college population. *Dissociation, 2*, 17–23.

Sanders, S. (1986). The Perceptual Alteration Scale: A scale measuring dissociation. *American Journal of Clinical Hypnosis, 29*, 95–102.

Scarlett, W. G., & Wolf, D. (1979). When it's only make-believe: The construction of a boundary between fantasy and reality in storytelling. In E. Winner & H. Gardner (Eds.), *New directions for child development: Fact, fiction and fantasy in childhood* (pp. 15–28). San Francisco: Jossey-Bass.

Schacter, D. L., Kihlstrom, J. F., Kihlstrom, L. C., & Berren, M. B. (1989). Autobiographical memory in a case of multiple personality disorder. *Journal of Abnormal Psychology, 98*, 1–7.

Schreiber, F. R. (1974). *Sybil.* New York: Warner.

Schreier, H. A., & Libow, J. A. (1986). Acute phobic hallucinations in very young children. *Journal of the American Academy of Child and Adolescent Psychiatry, 25*, 574–578.

Schultz, R., Braun, B. G., & Kluft, R. P. (1989). Multiple personality disorder: Phenomenology of selected variables in comparison to major depression. *Dissociation, 2*, 45–51.

Shor, R. E., & Orne, E. (1962). *Harvard group scale of hypnotic susceptibility.* Palo Alto: Consulting Psychologists Press.

Sidis, J. J. (1986). Can neurological disconnection account for psychiatric dissociation? In J. M. Quen (Ed.), *Split minds split brains* (pp. 127–148). New York: New York University Press.

Silberman, E. K., Putnam, F. W., Weingartner, H., Braun, B. G., & Post, R. M. (1985). Dissociative states in multiple personality disorder: A quantitative study. *Psychiatric Research, 15,* 253–260.

Spanos, N. P. (1986). Hypnosis, nonvolutional responding, and multiple personality: A social psychological perspective. *Progress in Experimental Personality Research, 14,* 1–62.

Spiegel, D. (1991). Dissociation and trauma. In A. Tasman (Ed.), *American Psychiatric Press annual review of psychiatry* (pp. 261–275). Washington, DC: American Psychiatric Press.

Spiegel, D., Bierre, P., & Rootenberg, J. (1989). Hypnotic alteration of somatosensory perception. *American Journal of Psychiatry, 146,* 749–754.

Spiegel, D., Cutcomb, S., Ren, C., & Pribram, K. (1985). Hypnotic hallucination alters evoked potentials. *Journal of Abnormal Psychology, 94,* 249–255.

Spiegel, D., Hunt, T., & Dondershine, H. E. (1988). Dissociation and hypnotizability in posttraumatic stress disorder. *American Journal of Psychiatry, 145,* 301–305.

Spiegel, H., & Spiegel, D. (1978). *Trance and treatment.* New York: Basic Books.

Squires, L. R., & Zola-Morgan, S. (1991). The medial temporal lobe memory system. *Science, 295,* 1380–1386.

Steinberg, M. (1990). Transcultural issues in psychiatry: The Atague and multiple personality disorder. *Dissociation, 3,* 31–33.

Steinberg, M. (1991). The spectrum of depersonalization: Assessment and treatment. In A. Tasman & S. M. Goldfinger (Eds.), *American Psychiatric Press annual review of psychiatry* (pp. 223–247). Washington, DC: American Psychiatric Press.

Steinberg, M., Rounsaville, B., & Cicchetti, D. (1990). The structured clinical interview for DSM-III-R dissociative disorders: Preliminary report on a new diagnostic instrument. *American Journal of Psychiatry, 147,* 76–82.

Steinberg, M., Rounsaville, B., & Cicchetti, D. (1991). Detection of dissociative disorders in psychiatric patients by a screening instrument and a structured interview. *American Journal of Psychiatry, 148,* 1050–1054.

Stengel, E. (1941). On the aetiology of fugue states. *Journal of Mental Science, 87,* 572–599.

Stern, D. N. (1985). *The interpersonal world of the infant.* New York: Basic Books.

Stutman, R. K., & Bliss, E. L. (1985). Posttraumatic stress disorder, hypnotizability, and imagery. *American Journal of Psychiatry, 142,* 741–743.

Sutcliffe, J. P., & Jones, J. (1962). Personal identity, multiple personality, and hypnosis. *International Journal of Clinical and Experimental Hypnosis, 10,* 231–269.

Svendsen, M. (1934). Children's imaginary companions. *Archives of Neurology and Psychiatry, 2,* 985–999.

Tart, C. (1972). States of consciousness and state-specific sciences. *Science, 176,* 1203–1210.

Taylor, W. S., & Martin, M. F. (1944). Multiple personality. *Journal of Abnormal Social Psychology, 39,* 281–300.

Tellegen, A., & Atkinson, G. (1974). Openness to absorbing and self-altering experience ("absorption"), a trait related to hypnotic susceptibility. *Journal of Abnormal Psychology, 83,* 268–277.

Thigpen, C. H., & Cleckley, H. (1957). *The three faces of Eve.* New York: McGraw-Hill.

van der Hart, O., & Friedman, B. (1989). A reader's guide to Pierre Janet on dissociation: A neglected intellectual heritage. *Dissociation, 2*(1), 3–16.

van der Kolk, B., Perry, J., & Herman, J. (1991). Childhood origins of self-destructive behavior. *American Journal of Psychiatry, 148,* 1665–1671.

van der Kolk, B. A., & Kadish, W. (1987). Amnesia, dissociation, and the return of the repressed. In B. A. van der Kolk (Ed.), *Psychological trauma* (pp. 173–192). Washington, DC: American Psychiatric Press.

Vincent, M., & Pickering, M. R. (1988). Multiple personality disorder in childhood. *Canadian Journal of Psychiatry, 33,* 524–529.

Walker, N. S., Garrett, J. B., & Wallace, B. (1976). Restoration of eidetic imagery via hypnotic age regression. *Journal of Abnormal Psychology, 85,* 335–337.

Weingartner, H. (1978). Human state dependent learning. In B. T. Ho, D. W. Richards, & D. C. Chute (Eds.), *Drug discrimination and state dependent learning* (pp. 361–382). New York: Academic Press.

Weiss, M., Sutton, P. J., & Utecht, A. J. (1985). Multiple personality in a 10-year-old girl. *Journal of the American Academy of Child Psychiatry, 24,* 495–501.

West, L. (1967). Dissociative reaction. In A. M. Freedman & H. I. Kaplan (Eds.), *Comprehensive textbook of psychiatry* (pp. 885–899). Baltimore: Williams & Wilkins.

Wherry, J. N., Jolly, J. B., Feldman, J., Adam, B., & Manjanatha, S. (in press). Concurrent and discriminant validity of the Child Dissociative Checklist. *Journal of Child Sexual Abuse.*

Wolff, P. H. (1987). *The development of behavioral states and the expression of emotions in early infancy.* Chicago: University of Chicago Press.

Yates, A. (1987). Psychological damage associated with extreme eroticism in young children. *Psychiatric Annals, 17,* 257–261.

Young, W. C. (1987). Emergence of a multiple personality in a posttraumatic stress disorder of adulthood. *American Journal of Clinical Hypnosis, 29,* 249–254.

Zamansky, H. S., & Bartis, S. P. (1986). The dissociation of an experience: The hidden observer observed. *Journal of Abnormal Psychology, 94,* 243–248.

Zinberg, N. E. (1977). The study of consciousness states: Problems and progress. In N. E. Zinberg (Ed.), *Alternate states of consciousness* (pp. 1–36). New York: Free Press.

CHAPTER 17

The Development of Obsessionality: Continuities and Discontinuities

ALICE S. CARTER, DAVID L. PAULS, and JAMES F. LECKMAN

The purpose of this chapter is (a) to present empirical and theoretical knowledge about the development and maintenance of obsessions and compulsions throughout the life span; (b) to explore issues of continuity and discontinuity between normal and pathological obsessions and compulsions through development; and (c) to suggest directions for future research. First, we will present definitions and clinical descriptions of obsessions, compulsions, and related phenomena as manifested across developmental epochs. Next, we will present available epidemiological, genetic, and neurobiological evidence, reviewed in the context of historical and current theories relevant to the etiology of both adaptive and maladaptive obsessions and compulsions. Throughout the chapter, the limited empirical evidence dealing directly with developmental issues will be presented and discussed within a framework intended to promote new research in this area of developmental psychopathology.

Although the goal of this chapter is to describe the broad spectrum of obsessionality in development by including both adaptive and maladaptive manifestations, considerably more empirical information is available regarding pathological forms of obsessionality. Hence, greater attention is paid to pathological forms.

DEFINITIONS AND CLINICAL DESCRIPTIONS

Definitions

Obsessional Thoughts

Obsessions are cognitive activities that are experienced by individuals in the general population and by individuals suffering from several forms of psychopathology (Turner, Beidel, & Stanley, 1992). Obsessions are repetitive and intrusive thoughts, images, and ideational impulses that are considered inappropriate, lead to subjective distress, and typically are accompanied by some form of resistance, or effort to dismiss the obsession (Hoogduin, 1986; Insel, 1984; Rachman, 1985). The individual generally experiences these cognitive events as uncontrollable, and frequently the contents of the obsessions are seemingly unrelated to activities of daily living. Further, adult obsessions are usually considered pointless, nonsensical, bizarre, repulsive, and/or obscene (Rachman, 1985). Often, obsessions

and their associated symptoms may relate to the development or maintenance of interpersonal connections that are crucial to the individual. These interpersonally oriented obsessions are often very disturbing aggressive and/or sexual images and thoughts involving family members.

In both pathological and nonpathological forms, obsessions can be distinguished from cognitive processes observed in other psychiatric disorders. Thus, obsessions differ from the kinds of excessive worries about real-life events that are seen in generalized anxiety disorders (GAD). Further, in contrast to cognitive processes associated with psychotic processes (e.g., thought insertion), obsessions are recognized as the product of the individual's own mind and are not experienced as externally imposed.

Because of the unwanted nature of these mental events and the individual's recognition that they are emerging in his or her own mind, the attempts to resist or suppress their occurrence are not surprising. Individuals with disturbing obsessions usually try to resist, ignore, or suppress such thoughts or impulses, or to neutralize them with another thought or action (i.e., compulsion).

Compulsions

Compulsions are repetitive behaviors (e.g., checking, hand washing, cleaning) and mental activities (e.g., counting, repeating specific words over and over) that are employed to prevent or diminish anxiety, tension, or distress (American Psychiatric Association, [APA] 1994). The content of the compulsive behavior is not in and of itself rewarding or oriented toward an intrinsic goal. Compulsive behaviors may be functionally related to obsessive thoughts (e.g., checking to ensure that the stove is off in response to an obsessional thought about leaving the stove on), but typically they are not connected in a realistic way to the source of the distress (e.g., counting to 100 four times in 4 minutes).

In adaptive forms, the compulsions are related to the obsession in a realistic manner or are brief in duration, and the individual experiences relief following the behavior. In nonpathological forms, many obsessive and compulsive behaviors can serve adaptive purposes for the individual, his or her family, and the broader community as they involve attending to safety and health concerns and/or establishing the experience of security with the familiarity of an ordered environment. Nonclinical checking behaviors may represent the individual's attempt to reestablish control over the environment (Frost, Sher, & Geen, 1986). In contrast, nonclinical cleaning behaviors may involve restorative efforts and less a concern with controlling future harm (Rachman & Hodgson, 1980).

In pathological forms, the compulsions are excessive and often must be performed in a rigid stereotyped manner and/or sequence for which the individual cannot provide a rationale (e.g., getting dressed or cleaning the house in a particular order). Some individuals will initiate a long sequence of compulsive behaviors repeatedly, until they complete each step of the entire sequence perfectly or until it feels "just right." In pathological forms, compulsions can occupy hours of the individual's day and can disrupt personal health, interpersonal relationships, and occupational functioning.

Obsessive Compulsive Disorder (OCD)

Obsessive Compulsive Disorder (OCD) is the psychiatric diagnostic label that is assigned to individuals who evidence pathological obsessions and/or compulsions. To distinguish between pathological and nonpathological obsessional phenomena, the DSM-IV (APA, 1994) criteria for OCD require that the obsessions and/or compulsions be experienced at some point during the disturbance as inappropriate and that they are of sufficient intensity, frequency, and/or duration to be a significant source of distress to the individual. The thoughts, impulses or images that characterize OCD are distinguished from excessive worries about real-life behavior and interfere with the individual's typical routine, occupational functioning, and/or relationships with others. In addition, the DSM-IV (APA, 1994) criteria require that the individual regards the content of the thoughts as the product of his or her mind and that significant efforts to resist, ignore, or suppress the thoughts are present and ineffective. If another psychiatric diagnosis is present, the content of the obsessions must be unrelated to it. For example, when there is an Axis I eating disorder present, the cognitive content of the obsession is not about food or dieting.

For compulsions, the repetitive behavior is performed in response to an obsession or according to rigid rules that must be adhered to strictly. The compulsion is not gratifying, but is performed to reduce anxiety or distress associated with a dreaded event or situation. Further, the activity is either excessive or unconnected with the feared event or situation.

The DSM-IV (APA, 1994) has deemphasized the importance of resistance in the definition of obsessions and in the diagnostic criteria for OCD. This is in part due to the recognition that over time, some individuals adapt to the disorder by engaging in efforts to neutralize the obsessions so quickly and in such a practiced, rote manner, that they no longer are aware of, and therefore do not report the experience of resistance.

Because the definitive symptoms of OCD involve cognitive ideation, the diagnosis relies on the individual's subjective accounts of his or her symptoms. With younger informants, the measurement and quantification of mental processes such as resistance, interference, and ego-dystonicity pose major difficulties because young children are limited in their abilities to reflect on their own cognitions and behaviors (King, 1991). In response to concerns about children's ability to serve as informants about their cognitive processes, the DSM-IV has added a caveat that children do not need to recognize that the obsessions and compulsions are excessive or unreasonable. Thus, the issue of ego-dystonicity must be viewed within the context of the child's emerging cognitive capacities. The most significant aspect in this process is the development of metacognition, or the ability to reflect on one's own cognitive processes. As the developing child's cognitive structures undergo qualitative transformations, the manner in which the child construes and organizes the external world as well as his or her emotions, cognitions, and behaviors will change, becoming more complex. These cognitive shifts must also be examined within the transaction of currently changing biological systems (e.g., brain structures and neurochemical processes) and environment (e.g., interpersonal relationships and roles) (Cicchetti, 1993).

Obsessive Compulsive Personality Disorder (OCPD)

While Obsessive Compulsive Personality Disorder (OCPD) shares the words "Obsessive" and "Compulsive" with OCD, the presence of obsessions is not a defining characteristic of this extreme personality type. Rather, OCPD is characterized by "a preoccupation with orderliness, perfectionism and mental and interpersonal control, at the expense of flexibility, openness and efficiency" (APA, 1994, p. 669). The pattern must be present by early adulthood and seen in a variety of contexts. To receive a diagnosis of OCPD the DSM-IV criteria require that at least four of the following are present: (a) a preoccupation with details, rules, lists, order, organization, or schedules such that activity is disrupted; (b) perfectionism that interferes with task completion; (c) overconscientiousness, scrupulousness, and/or inflexibility about matters of morality, ethics, or values (that are not a function of religious or cultural proscriptions); (d) excessive devotion to work and productivity to the exclusion of leisure activities and relationships; (e) the inability to discard worn-out or worthless objects even when they have no sentimental value; (f) a reluctance to delegate responsibility due to a fear that others will not perform a task correctly (i.e., according to his or her exacting standards); (g) a lack of generosity or miserly spending style toward both self and others; and (h) the exhibition of rigidity and stubbornness.

One of the DSM-III-R (APA, 1987) criteria for OCPD—indecisiveness that is sufficient to interfere with decision making—was not included in the DSM-IV (APA, 1994). This symptom is similar to obsessional doubting. The only DSM-IV criteria for OCPD that are similar to features of OCD are the inability to discard worthless objects and possibly a miserly spending style. Both of these can be seen as variants of hoarding behavior, as the miserly style can be interpreted as hoarding money to protect against a future catastrophe. Thus, there is minimal overlap in the current diagnostic features of OCPD and OCD. Further, in OCPD, the individual does not consciously experience ego-dystonicity, a lack of controllability or resistance—the features of OCD that are most helpful in discriminating between pathological and nonpathological obsessional phenomena. There are no modifications of the criteria for evaluating children and adolescents.

NONPATHOLOGICAL FORMS OF OBSESSIONS AND COMPULSIONS

Child and Adolescent Obsessionality

Obsessions

Children do not develop metacognitive capacities that are sufficient for reporting on obsessive ideation reliably until elementary school age. It is not surprising, therefore, that more is known about young children's development of observable rituals and compulsions than about normative or pathological forms of obsessive ideation. A study that employed a survey form of the Leyton Obsessional Inventory-Child Version with nonreferred adolescents, provides some preliminary information on obsessionality among a nonclinical sample (Berg, Whitaker, Davies, Flament, & Rapoport, 1988). Items that are considered obsessive symptoms were endorsed by more than 46% of the sample. These items included thinking repetitive thoughts and words, hating dirt and dirty things, worrying about being clean enough, being fussy about keeping one's hands clean, and having trouble making decisions. Females in this sample endorsed a greater number of obsessional items and had significantly higher interference scores (an index of the degree to which obsessions interrupted their functioning) than males. This finding is consistent with other findings suggesting that females are more likely than their male counterparts to engage in ruminative responses when depressed and that these responses tend to maintain dysphoria and interfere with functioning (Nolen-Hoeksema, 1990). The gender difference in obsessionality does not appear to influence clinical rates of the disorder; females and males were equally represented in the highest quartile in this sample (Berg et al., 1988). This is consistent with clinical studies that find an equal ratio of postpubertal male-to-female patients (Swedo, Rapoport, Leonard, Lenane, & Cheslow, 1989).

Despite the inclusion of adolescents in 9th through 12th grades, responses did not differ significantly with age. Consistent with the adult evidence, nonpathological obsessions that are similar in content to those that become part of maladaptive patterns when accompanied by a lack of controllability, appear to be quite typical among adolescents. It is critical to conduct similar epidemiologically based surveys with younger children as there is currently no adequate empirical description of the emergence, prevalence, or course of obsessions or compulsions in normative samples. The only available information about obsessionality and compulsions in younger children is based on samples of convenience and clinical observations.

Compulsive Behaviors

Developing rituals, adhering to rules, and repeating a particular activity or game as well as varying degrees of compulsiveness are important aspects of normal human development. From a cognitive-developmental perspective, Piaget (1962) described the critical role of repetition in the first year of life, prior to the emergence of formal play. Indeed, Piaget (1962) accords a central role to repetition in the young infant's efforts to (a) create schemata, aggregated action patterns that are both motor and perceptive; and (b) maintain these schemata through assimilation. According to Piaget (1962), the earliest schemata are acquired through the repetition of reflexive behaviors. In this repetition, the behavior becomes incorporated into a set of action plans that the child can then apply in a nonreflexive manner. In describing the normal emergence of imitation, Piaget (1962) suggested that the typically developing infant engages in repetition of a pattern of action only in relation to a purpose or goal. When the infant develops the capacity for imitation, the repetition of familiar behaviors becomes the basis for many new games between infants and their caregivers (e.g., the infant's waving bye-bye, lifting up his or her arms, or performing another motor behavior in response to a specific question).

Repetitive Play

More recent developmental studies of repetition have focused on perseveration, defined as the inability to shift easily from one mental set or activity to another (e.g., Sophian & Wellman, 1983; Welsh, Pennington, & Groisser, 1991). Neuropsychologists have become interested in normative developmental trends in perseverative behaviors that are associated with frontal lobe dysfunction in adults (e.g., Diamond, 1988; Welsh & Pennington, 1988).

The association between these kinds of perseveration and typically occurring behaviors in infancy and the preschool years that may be associated with obsessions and compulsions (e.g., insisting on specific rituals, hoarding) is not clear. For example, many crawling 7- to 10-month-olds become preoccupied with examining and at times collecting small particles that are barely observable to the adult eye. Similarly, preschoolers often insist on sameness or precision in food habits (e.g., desiring the same menu of plain spaghetti in the same bowl) and/or in dressing (e.g., insisting on wearing the same t-shirt day after day). Anna Freud (1965) reflected on the normality of such childhood repetitive behaviors but did not conduct any systematic studies of the phenomenon.

Gesell, Ames, and Ilg (1974) reported that at approximately $2\frac{1}{2}$ years of age toddlers begin to insist that routines be done in a consistent manner. These authors noted that such behavior was most likely to occur during stressful periods of transition in the day (e.g., bedtime, bathing, mealtimes) and attributed importance to the roles of separation anxiety, mastery, and cognitive control. The bedtime ritual is typically developed in collaboration with the parent(s), but toddlers and preschoolers often perseverate on a particular aspect of the ritual or require that a specific component of the ritual be performed "just so" (e.g., the same book must be reread in exactly the same manner, a special stuffed toy must be in the same position). Many children have elaborate bedtime rituals that last 30 minutes or more. Unfortunately, empirical studies of such rituals and their functions for the child and within the family are lacking. The early emergence of ritualistic behavior and the more extreme symptoms observed in the adult condition of OCD appear to share an association with situational stressors.

Adams (1973) described the important functions that early emerging rituals may serve and suggested that toddlers and preschoolers employ rituals to magically ward off uncertainty and lack of predictability, especially with regard to separations. This is certainly consistent with the adoption by many toddlers of a special transitional object (e.g., a beloved stuffed animal or blanket) that must accompany them, especially when venturing into unfamiliar and/or familiar stressful situations.

Repetitious play most likely serves different functions at different ages and for different individuals. However, across a wide range of ages, repetitious play can provide opportunities to experience mastery, control, and self-efficacy. The child's experience of repetitious play may contain both soothing and exciting aspects (King, 1991) and may be performed in interaction with another (e.g., infant and toddler games such as pat-a-cake and peekaboo, elementary school jump-rope rhymes) or independently (e.g., rehearsing the same real or imagined scenario with dolls and props). In typical pretend play at home and in play therapy sessions, young children often repeat the same theme or even an exact sequence of behaviors while working through the emotions aroused by enacting those events.

Marans, Mayes, and Colonna (1993), discussing the psychoanalytic view of children's play, identified two forms of repetition in children's play. One form allows the child to establish an experience as familiar and can be construed as mastery play. This repetitive play is posited to result in both the pleasure and relief associated with the predictability of familiar experiences. A second form of repetition is seen as children attempt to master previously traumatic experiences. In working through the conflicts associated with traumatic experiences, the child may be limited in his or her ability to use play flexibly to adopt a variety of internal mental viewpoints and may not experience pleasure in the repetition.

A third form of behavior that may emerge in the context of play, and that may share some of the behavioral features associated with play in the service of conflict, can be speculatively related to obsessions rather than compulsions. Specifically, some children appear to become "stuck" in behavioral sequences or to experience intrusive behavioral sequences. In contrast to play associated with a previous trauma or conflict, in which the thematic content of the repetition is connected to real-life events, this repetitious play is not obviously associated with day-to-day experiences. Further, in contrast to mastery play, the perseverative play is not associated with pleasure in the familiarity of the behavioral chain. The notion of ego-dystonicity can be interpreted as the lack of connection between the intrusive thought and the goals of the individual (i.e., not associated with the goals of the ego). Thus, infant and/or toddler repetition that is dissociated from a goal may be functionally associated with later obsessionality.

This hypothesized form of repetitive play is distinct from repetition that is observed in the study of normally emerging and dysfunctional executive functioning. The perseveration or repetition observed on executive functioning tasks is associated with difficulty in flexibly shifting plans once a goal-oriented strategy is practiced. Thus, in this hypothesized third form of repetition, the initial behavioral sequence is not goal directed. It is likely that these non-goal-directed repetitive behaviors can be seen in both normal and atypical development and across multiple forms of psychopathology. For example, perseveration (or repetitive behaviors that do not appear to be in the service of a goal) is also seen in children with autism. However, some perseveration in autism appears to be related to a more general difficulty shifting

cognitive sets or strategies (Ozonoff, Pennington, & Rogers, 1991; Rumsey & Hamberger, 1988). This form of repetitive behavior may also be associated with stereotypies, purposeless repetition with rhythmicity such as head rocking and tics (cf. Hodes & Cohen, 1991).

A fourth form of repetitive play may more be closely linked to compulsions and shares some features of play in the service of conflict. The stuck behaviors that are observed in some young children may be interpreted as secondary to the distress engendered by experiencing a frightening and confusing thought or image. Thus, consistent with the use of compulsions in older children and adults, the child retreats into the sameness and/or familiarity of a repetitive behavioral sequence to avoid focusing on the upsetting thoughts or images.

Although repetitious play often is enacted in the service of healthy cognitive and social-emotional development, it may at times represent maladaptive functioning. Some very young children may have difficulty disengaging from or inhibiting repetitive patterns that are not enacted in the service of experiences of mastery, control, or self-efficacy. Such children appear to become stuck in perseverative behavioral sequences and may experience a lack of control that is consistent with the reports of adult pathological obsessions.

The preschool years appear to be an important period for developmental shifts in multiple aspects of perseveration on cognitive tasks (Cuneo & Welsh, 1992; Diamond, 1988). Further, preliminary evidence supports the notion that there are significant stable individual differences in these perseverative aspects of cognition and behavior (Cuneo & Welsh, 1992). Future research must address the ways in which these aspects of cognitive perseveration may influence and/or be associated with the emergence of both pathological and nonpathological obsessions and compulsions as well as more general individual differences in social-emotional development.

Rule-Governed Play and Superstitious Behaviors

By the time children reach elementary school, their play begins to involve increasingly complex sets of rules (e.g., dodgeball, board games). Although no empirical studies of obsessions or compulsions have been reported to date, the elementary school years are also marked by the appearance of rule-based superstitious behavior (e.g., "step on a crack—break your mother's back" or the need to hold one's breath while passing a cemetery to avoid waking the dead). Similarly, the commonly played game of "cooties," in which a particular child is avoided because he or she has an amorphous something that is bad and contagious, shares some aspects of contamination fears (King, 1991). These normally emerging superstitious beliefs and behaviors appear to be similar to successful OCD compulsions that serve to decrease anxiety associated with aggressive or disturbing thoughts or impulses.

Jahoda (1969) suggested that adult superstitions arise when individuals do not feel in control of circumstances in their lives. Consistent with this, Peterson (1978) found superstitiousness in adults to be correlated with an external locus of control—a belief that factors outside the self are the most important determinants of life events). Frost and colleagues (1993) reported an association between superstitious beliefs and behaviors with measures of compulsivity and obsessionality among female college students. Compulsive checking but not cleaning was associated with superstitious behaviors and beliefs. Both superstitiousness and checking are efforts to prevent harm from occurring. Cleaning, however, may serve a more reparative function and be associated with restoring a sense of well-being and less with a concern for avoiding future harm (Rachman & Hodgson, 1980). In contrast, a study that compared children with OCD and unaffected children found no association between superstitious behaviors and compulsivity (Leonard, Goldberger, Rapoport, Cheslow, & Swedo, 1990). Many alternative explanations can be offered for this null result: (a) The association between compulsiveness and superstitiousness emerges later in the life-span; (b) the association between superstitiousness and compulsiveness is only present for compulsions that function to prevent future harm, suggesting the need for subtyping in clinical studies; and/or (c) the relation is seen across normal and pathological groups and does not readily discriminate between these groups.

Ritualistic play, repetitive behaviors, and rule-governed games, as well as superstitious beliefs, behaviors, and prohibitions, have all been viewed on a continuum with the more extreme variants of these behaviors that present in OCD (Leonard et al., 1990; Nemiah, 1985; Peller, 1954). Yet, as observed by Leonard and colleagues (1990), we do not have systematic longitudinal data addressing the issue of the continuity between early developmental behaviors that are morphologically similar to the more extreme behaviors associated with childhood or adult-onset OCD. If we are to further our understanding of continuities and discontinuities in the development of obsessions and compulsions, it is critical to acquire empirical data regarding the full range of obsessions and compulsions and to examine carefully the developmental contexts in which these behaviors arise.

Adult Obsessions and Compulsions

Approximately 80% to 90% of adult nonclinical samples report experiencing obsessional or intrusive thoughts at some time (Niler & Beck, 1989; Rachman & de Silva, 1978; Salkovskis & Harrison, 1984). Further, the obsessions reported among nonclinical populations appear to be similar to the obsessions reported among clinical populations, both in the content reported and in the increased distress associated with the inability to dismiss the thoughts (Rachman & de Silva, 1978; Salkovskis & Harrison, 1984). However, compared with clinical populations, the obsessions of nonclinical subjects tend to be less frequent, briefer in duration, and more easily dismissed.

Uncontrollability and Unacceptability

In discriminating between nonpathological and pathological intrusive thoughts, Turner and colleagues (1992) argue that the two critical features are the uncontrollability and unacceptability of thoughts. Controllability refers to the degree to which individuals assume responsibility for and believe they regulate the occurrence and maintenance of their obsessions. Unacceptability refers to the degree to which the thoughts are ego-dystonic or upsetting. Barlow (1988) also noted the role of unacceptability and suggested that negative intrusive thoughts, which are a common response to

stressful situations, are more likely to be perceived as unacceptable by patients with OCD. Barlow (1988) suggested that the degree of unacceptability may be mediated by a combination of biological and psychological vulnerability that heightens the ego-dystonicity of the obsessions. In contrast, England and Dickerson (1988) suggested that uncontrollability rather than unacceptability is the most critical factor in distinguishing nonpathological and pathological obsessional thoughts. They have demonstrated in nonclinical samples that even intrusive thoughts with pleasant content are perceived as distressing if they are experienced as difficult to control. This emphasis on controllability in the adult literature is consistent with the hypothesized central role of mastery and cognitive control for very young children in coping with difficult transitions such as bedtime (Gesell et al., 1974).

PATHOLOGICAL FORMS OF OBSESSIONS AND COMPULSIONS

Adult Obsessive Compulsive Disorder

The phenomenological clinical presentation of OCD appears to be fairly consistent across the life span. Several attempts have been made to classify characteristic phenomenological presentations of the obsessional phenomena associated with OCD in adulthood. An early effort was made by Akhtar, Wig, Varma, Pershad, and Verma (1975) who described six types of obsessions: (a) obsessive doubt, (b) obsessive thinking, (c) obsessive impulse, (d) obsessive fear, (e) obsessive image, and (f) a miscellaneous type. The most commonly occurring type of obsession was obsessive doubting, experienced by 75% of the sample. Akhtar and colleagues (1975) also characterized six categories of contents: (a) dirt and contamination, (b) aggression, (c) inanimate-interpersonal (e.g., safety mechanisms, arranging things in an orderly manner), (d) sex, (e) religion, and (f) miscellaneous. The most commonly occurring content was dirt and contamination, experienced by 46% of the sample.

Early research on adult community samples suggested that obsessions were accompanied by compulsions or rituals in approximately 70% to 75% of cases (Akhtar et al., 1975; Welner, Reich, Robins, Fishman, & Van Doren, 1976). More recent research among an adult patient sample suggests that as many as 93% of individuals who meet DSM-III-R criteria for OCD have obsessions that are accompanied by compulsions (Rasmussen & Tsuang, 1986). Recent research on the perceptual and sensory phenomena that frequently precede and/or accompany compulsions in a large clinic-referred sample suggests that as many as 92% of subjects with OCD reported being aware of experiencing a need to perform compulsions until they were "just right" at some point during their illness (Leckman et al., 1994). This experience was most often associated with visual or tactile aspects of compulsions (reported by 80% and 66% of the sample, respectively) as compared with the auditory aspects of the compulsions (reported by 20% of the sample). Moreover, the percentage of the patients' time that was consumed with psychasthenic feelings (i.e., feelings of being "incomplete," "insufficient," or "imperfect") that are typically associated with the "just right" perceptions was significantly associated with OCD severity.

A different strategy for addressing phenomenological issues involves developing categorical schemes based on the function of the phenomena being classified. Mavissakalian (1979) defined obsessions as anxiety-producing behaviors and compulsions as anxiety-reducing behaviors. Overt compulsions and obsessions were considered to be functionally equivalent based on their impact on the anxiety levels. Four categories were proposed: (a) obsessions; (b) obsessions plus successful compulsions; (c) obsessions plus obsessionalized compulsions; and (d) rituals involving predominantly stereotyped behaviors that did not impact on anxiety states. Mavissakalian, Turner, and Michelson (1985) noted that compulsions can lose their anxiety-reducing effect and become obsessionalized compulsions that increase anxiety. He suggested that the frustration associated with the failure of previously successful strategies may increase depressive moods and that this is the point at which individuals often seek treatment for their obsessive-compulsive behaviors.

Rasmussen and Eisen (1991) described some of the common phenomenological presentations of adult OCD. The most common is an obsessive fear of contamination coupled with hand-washing compulsions. The primary emotion that is reported is anxiety, but disgust and shame are also commonly seen (Straus, 1948). Somatic obsessions, major depression, and panic disorder are often found in OCD along with checking compulsions. Recurrent and abhorrent sexual and aggressive obsessions plague another group of individuals who suffer from OCD. In addition, there is often the experience of uncertainty regarding whether or not the unacceptable act was committed. The primary emotions accompanying such thoughts are guilt and anxiety. The compulsion to confess is often present as is checking to ensure that the aggressive or sexual act was not committed. Another subgroup of individuals with OCD present with obsessions that involve the wish to have objects or events in a certain order or place, to perform certain motor actions in a precise fashion, to feel things in a specific manner, or to have things exactly symmetrical or "evened up." These symptoms are accompanied by minimal anxiety and may not be ego-dystonic. The subjective feeling reported when things are not properly placed is predominantly discontent or tension rather than anxiety.

Rasmussen and Eisen (1991) reported that those individuals whose primary obsession involves symmetry or other just right phenomena can be further divided into those individuals with primary obsessive slowness and those with primary magical thinking. Consistent with the excessive amount of time and the repetition involved in executing a particular behavior just right, individuals with primary obsessive slowness appear to have lost their goal directedness. Rather, they become preoccupied with the execution of the behavior per se. In contrast, individuals who are preoccupied with the need for symmetry and precision and evidence magical thinking experience their obsessions and rituals as a mechanism of warding off an imagined disaster that they believe is out of their control. The predominant emotion associated with preventing the imagined disaster is anxiety. Superstitious rituals including the repetition of lucky and unlucky numbers and counting rituals often accompany such a presentation. Hoarding, pathological responsibility or doubt, and religious obsessions are also common presenting complaints.

Childhood Obsessive Compulsive Disorder

Until quite recently, childhood OCD received little empirical attention, perhaps due to its perceived rarity. The question of normal variation in obsessionality or the developmental emergence of obsessionality has received even less attention. Children diagnosed with OCD present with very similar symptom patterns as adult patients (Johnson, 1993; Rapoport, Swedo, & Leonard, 1992; Swedo et al., 1989). Rituals are a more common presenting complaint than obsessions in young children (Rapoport et al., 1992), which most likely reflects that young children do not self-refer and rarely report obsessions. Parents who refer their children for help become concerned when they observe their children engaging in excessive rituals or when their children exhibit severe negative reactions to the disruption of their rituals.

Consistent with adults (Rasmussen & Eisen, 1991), the most common pattern observed in children is an obsessive fear of contamination that is coupled with washing and cleaning compulsions and avoidance of contaminated objects (Swedo et al., 1989). Another common presentation involves obsessive doubt that leads to checking compulsions typically involving determining the safety of a potentially dangerous object or situation (e.g., a sharp knife that could fall, an oven left on). A less commonly occurring clinical presentation involves pure obsessions without any compulsions. The contents observed in children are consistent with those observed in adults and involve sexual and/or aggressive imagery that often is accompanied by guilt and shame in addition to anxiety, counting rituals, and/or repetition of specific phrases. Although these pure obsessions are not accompanied by overt compulsions, children may employ cognitive rituals or counterthoughts to ward off the initial recurrent and intrusive thought (Insel, 1990). Often, there is tremendous fear concerning the power of the thoughts to do actual damage or that a disturbing image could become reality.

Epidemiology and Natural History

Until quite recently, OCD was thought to be a rare disorder. Public perception regarding adult OCD shifted with the publication of the Epidemiology Catchment Area (ECA) study, which reported a lifetime prevalence of 2.5% in the general population (Robins et al., 1984). Subsequent work utilizing lay interviewers and structured interviews in community samples have reported similar results (Bland, Newman, & Orn, 1988; Karno, Golding, Sorenson, & Burnam, 1988). However, a follow-up study of a subsample in the ECA study that employed semistructured interviews conducted by psychiatrists, reported significantly lower prevalence rates than those obtained with lay interviewers in the initial ECA study (Anthony et al., 1985; Helzer et al., 1985). These findings suggest that the prevalence of clinically relevant obsessions and compulsions may be lower than 2.5%. On the other hand, the ECA results suggest that the rate of obsessions and compulsions may be much higher than previously thought. It would be quite helpful to know the difference between individuals who report OC behaviors and those who are deemed to have a clinically relevant disorder. These data would allow a more thorough examination of the continuity in the general population and would possibly help our understanding of the developmental continuity of these behaviors. An important research question is the determination of when these behaviors become impairing and distressing to the individuals experiencing them.

The ECA and follow-up studies focused on adults' current functioning. Retrospective studies of adults with OCD suggest that approximately one-third had the onset of their first symptom before age 15 (Beech, 1974; Black, 1974). Several authors have reported that approximately one-third of OCD cases onset during childhood (Black, 1974; Ingram, 1961; Rapoport, 1986). Furthermore, studies of child and adolescent cases report that a majority of children first showed symptoms during the period from 10 to 14 years of age with another third reporting first symptoms before age 9 (Riddle et al., 1990; Swedo et al., 1989; Toro, Cervera, Osejo, & Salamero, 1992). In addition, retrospective data suggests that many adults with OCD experienced "micro episodes" several years before developing the full disorder. Thus, although OCD appears to be more rare in childhood than in adulthood, it is possible that it is more prevalent than was once believed.

Unfortunately, the true prevalence in the childhood population is not known because appropriate epidemiological studies with school-age children have not yet been completed. In the classic Isle of Wight survey, Rutter, Tizard, and Whitmore (1970) found that only 7 (0.3%) of the 2,199 children who were screened had prominent obsessive features and none met criteria for OCD. However, this study was completed before currently used assessment instruments were developed, making it impossible to compare with more recent research.

A methodologically rigorous study of the prevalence of OCD in 5,596 adolescents employed both continuous ratings of obsessive symptomatology (i.e., the Leyton Obsessional Inventory–Child Version) and psychiatric interviews to determine diagnostic status (Flament et al., 1988). Of the subsample of adolescents who were interviewed, 20 subjects received a lifetime diagnosis of OCD yielding a weighted prevalence estimate of 1.9%—a prevalence remarkably similar to the rate reported in the adult ECA (Robins et al., 1984). As many as 2% of adolescents in the Flament study reported obsessive preoccupations or behaviors that were either quite frequent and/or interfered with normal functioning. The latter group with "subclinical OCD" revels an important population, especially for prospective studies. These individuals do not meet the full criteria for OCD but do show one or two obsessive symptoms that (a) have a definite onset date; (b) do not appear developmentally continuous; (c) are not easily attributed to situational or personality factors; and (d) are seen by the adolescent as undesirable or abnormal (Flament et al., 1988).

Flament and colleagues (1988) inferred that OCD is more common in adolescents than usually assumed. Furthermore, it appears that OCD is frequently underdiagnosed and untreated in adolescents. This does not appear to be due to a symptomatological difference in the community sample. The symptom presentation and rates of associated disorders in the community sample were similar to those found in clinic-based populations (Rapoport et al., 1992). A 2-year follow-up study of the community sample of adolescents diagnosed as having OCD revealed that there was continuity in symptom presentation and levels of impairment (Berg

et al., 1989). Thus, at least over a short period of time, there did not appear to be an effect of age on the type of symptoms experienced in this adolescent sample.

Consistent with this lack of age effect, Rettew, Swedo, Leonard, Lenane, and Rapoport (1992) found no association with the number or type of obsessions or compulsions and age in a follow-up study of the community population Flament and colleagues (1988) assessed initially despite a larger age range (i.e., pre-, early-, mid-, and late-adolescents) than was employed in the initial community survey. Of note is that while all patients had a somewhat different constellation of symptoms at the follow-up, there was no discernible pattern with regard to specific symptoms and age. On the other hand, however, there is some evidence that compulsions appear before obsessions, particularly for those individuals who experience them at a very young age (Honjo et al., 1989; Rettew et al., 1992). The emergence of compulsions prior to obsessions is consistent with the normative sequencing of ritualistic and obsessional behaviors and the inability of young children to reflect on or develop rational explanations about their behavior.

Chart review studies of child psychiatric clinic records suggest that children and adolescents diagnosed with OCD account for 0.2% to 1.2% of child and adolescent clinic populations (Hollingsworth, Tanguay, Grossman, & Pabst, 1980; Judd, 1965; Toro et al., 1992). This may be changing. With the advent of improved behavioral and pharmacological interventions for OCD, increasing numbers of children and adolescents are presenting to clinics for treatment (Berg et al., 1989; Flament et al., 1985; Leonard et al., 1993). Thus, these figures may not be representative for current clinic populations. Indeed, Honjo and colleagues (1989), reviewed the charts of children presenting to an outpatient clinic in Japan between 1982 to 1986 and reported that 5% had obsessive-compulsive symptoms. A concern with dirt was the most common obsession, and cleaning was the most common compulsion. Unfortunately, it is difficult to make direct comparisons between this Japanese sample and studies in other cultures, because Honjo and colleagues' (1989) report provides rates of obsessive-compulsive symptoms rather than rates of OCD diagnoses. Nevertheless, the rate is similar to one reported by Johnson (1993), who reviewed cases presenting to Maudsley and Bethlehem Royal Hospitals between 1968 to 1983. This investigator reported a rate of 3.1% of children with obsessions who did not have autism, psychosis, personality disorder, sexual deviance, or substance dependence. However, only 0.7% of children in this report actually received an Axis I diagnosis of OCD from their attending physician.

Considerable research is needed to understand the developmental emergence of obsessions and compulsions. This research should utilize a prospective design because of the potential bias inherent in retrospective reporting of symptomatology. Retrospective reporting may be biased, in part due to the possibility that children may not initially experience symptoms of obsessions and compulsions as ego-dystonic. Given the similarity of the rate of OCD among Flament and colleagues (1988) adolescent sample and the adult prevalence rates (Bland et al., 1988; Karno et al., 1988), the possibility that adults are unreliable reporters of age of onset cannot be ignored. Prospective longitudinal population-based studies of young children are needed to obtain data about the typical emergence of specific obsessions and compulsions and the prevalence, age of onset and developmental course (e.g., severity, duration) of subsequent obsessions and compulsions that persist into clinically significant symptoms of disorder. Only when the normal developmental course of these behaviors is well documented and it is known when certain behaviors emerge and subsequently disappear and/or change will it be possible to understand more fully the differences between normal OC behaviors and "disordered" OC symptoms.

The Apparent Discontinuity between Obsessive Compulsive Disorder (OCD) and Obsessive Compulsive Personality (OCPD)

The relationship between OCPD and OCD is a topic of ongoing debate and controversy (Black, Yates, Noyes, Pfohl, & Kelley, 1989; Marks, 1987). If the personality type and disorder were on a continuum, one would expect to find high comorbidity for OCD and OCPD and a higher rate of OCPD among the first-degree relatives of individuals with OCD. Neither of these patterns have been observed in adult, adolescent, or child samples. In both adolescent community (Flament et al., 1988) and child-onset patient samples (Swedo et al., 1989) fewer than 20% of children diagnosed with OCD also had a compulsive personality disorder (17% and 16% respectively). Although this rate of OCPD is higher that would be expected in a nonclinical sample, the majority of adolescents with OCD do not also exhibit OCPD symptoms.

Rapoport and colleagues (1981) argued that OCD is a distinct condition that is not on a continuum with obsessive traits or OCPD. The issue of whether OCD and OCPD lie on a continuum may be best resolved by examining family genetic studies. Black, Noyes, Pfohl, Goldstein, and Blum (1993) evaluated 32 individuals with OCD and 33 age- and sex-matched control subjects and their first-degree relatives with a semistructured diagnostic interview designed to assess personality disorders as well as several self-report instruments. Individuals with OCD were more likely than controls to exhibit a personality disorder, with OCPD was not the most prevalent personality disorder. This is similar to findings in an earlier study where individuals with OCD scored higher on the harm avoidance dimension of a continuous measure of personality (Black, Yates, Noyes, Pfohl, & Kelley, 1989). However, no significant differences in rates of OCPD or obsessional, hysterical, or oral character traits were found in the first-degree relatives of individuals with OCD as compared with first-degree relatives of the control subjects. Therefore, although personality disorders appear to be more prevalent among patients with OCD who present for treatment, this family study did not support an underlying genetic relationship between OCD and OCPD.

A further line of evidence that does not support an etiologic association between OCD and OCPD is the follow-up of child-onset OCD patients in adulthood. Thomsen and Mikkelsen (1993) reported an increased rate of avoidant personality disorder but no increased incidence of OCPD when comparing adults who presented to a child clinic for OCD and adults who presented to a child clinic for another psychiatric disorder. This finding is consistent with Mavissakalian and colleagues (Mavissakalian, Hamann, Haidar, & de Groot, 1993; Mavissakalian, Hamann, & Jones, 1990) who also reported an increased rate of personality dysfunction that was not limited to compulsive personality disorder among individuals affected with OCD relative to individuals affected with panic and generalized anxiety disorders.

Associated (Co-Morbid) Conditions

Anxiety Disorders

As the preceding phenomenological descriptions suggest, the clinical presentation of obsessive ideation is often accompanied by dysregulated emotions. Currently, OCD is classified within the anxiety disorders. The high frequency of the co-occurrence of anxiety disorders among individuals diagnosed with OCD suggests that they may be vulnerable to multiple kinds of anxiety (Rasmussen & Eisen, 1991). Barlow, DiNardo, Vermilyea, Vermilyea, & Blanchard (1986) reported that 83% of a sample of OCD patients reported panic attacks and Kringlen (1965) reported that over half of 91 adult OCD patients reported the presence of phobias. Further, adult OCD patients exhibit increased levels of somatic arousal that are typical of those observed in other anxiety states (e.g., Kelly, 1980). Rachman and Hodgson (1980) summarized the physiology of obsessional symptoms as including increases in heart rate, heart rate variability, and skin conductance in response to the presentation of real or imagined obsessional stimuli. These measures of arousal diminish gradually over time but may be diminished more readily with the performance of successful rituals.

Of particular interest in understanding developmental aspects of the emergence of anxiety disorders is the high lifetime prevalence of separation anxiety in individuals suffering from either OCD (Rasmussen & Eisen, 1991) or other anxiety disorders such as panic disorder (Gittelman & Klein, 1985). The overt behavioral manifestations of separation anxiety are readily identified in early childhood and may contribute to it being the most common anxiety disorder diagnosed in young children. As no longitudinal studies of children at-risk for OCD have been completed, it is not known what precurser behaviors may be present in children who later develop OCD. Thus, separation anxiety may be a marker for later vulnerability to OCD and/or other anxiety disorders. It is possible that separation anxiety may reflect a developmentally appropriate manifestation or an early onset of a variety of anxiety disorders (e.g., OCD, panic, GAD) that will take on a more distinctive profile later in development. This would be consistent with typical development, in which the complexity of organization increases over time (Gottlieb, 1991; Werner, 1957). As the child with separation anxiety develops, differentiation in multiple linguistic, cognitive, emotional, behavioral, psychophysiological, and anatomic structures may allow for the emergence of more distinct disorders. Therefore, a consequence of simpler systems in early development may be greater restriction on the range of possible behavioral manifestations. Although a similar early course for multiple anxiety disorders can be used as evidence for a common underlying etiology, it is equally plausible that multiple genetic and environmental etiologic agents share a common early phenotypic expression.

Major Depression and Dysthymia

Along with anxiety-related difficulties, individuals who suffer from OCD show high rates of depression. The incidence of depression among adult individuals with OCD exceeds 65% in at least two studies (Barlow et al., 1986; Pauls, Leckman, & Cohen, 1994). As will be discussed in greater detail, because of the lack of control associated with the obsessional symptomatology and the ego-dystonic symptoms, OCD could be conceptualized as depressogenic from the reformulated learned helplessness perspective (Abramson, Seligman, & Teasdale, 1978). Turner and colleagues (1992) suggest that anxiety may constitute an initial emotional response to very stressful or conflictual stimuli and situations. If the stress is not decreased or the conflict is not resolved, however, depression is likely to develop.

The association between obsessional thoughts and negative mood is evident in both adult nonclinical and patient samples. For example, Welner and Horowitz (1975) found that there was an increase in intrusive thoughts in a nonclinical sample following a depressive mood induction procedure. In patients, an association between severity of depressive symptomatology and the uncontrollability of intrusive thoughts has been noted (Edwards & Dickerson, 1987; Sutherland, Newman, & Rachman, 1982). Other affective and motivational states may also be associated with obsessive ideation. For example, in a nonclinical sample, self-reported characterological guilt was a better predictor of frequency, duration, difficulty dismissing, and distress associated with intrusive thoughts than was anxiety or depression (Niler & Beck, 1989). One explanation for this pattern of associations would be that attributional styles, which were not assessed in this study, contribute to increased obsessional symptoms and increased feelings of guilt. In other words, both guilt and increased difficulty with obsessions may be the consequences of applying internal, stable, uncontrollable attributions of causality (i.e., a view of self as inefficacious and responsible) to explain the obsessions.

Consistent with the adult data, approximately 40% of children with severe OCD have a current or past history of another anxiety disorder (Swedo et al., 1989; Toro et al., 1992). Among patient populations, over 60% receive comorbid diagnoses (Riddle et al., 1990; Swedo et al., 1989). Approximately one-third of children with OCD also suffer from depression (Swedo et al., 1989). In approximately half of the child cases, the depressive symptoms followed the onset of the OCD symptoms.

Gille de la Tourette's Syndrome (GTS) and Tic Disorders

The hypothesis that there is an association between OCD and Gilles de la Tourette's syndrome (GTS) is as old as the description of GTS itself. In his original report of the syndrome, Gilles de la Tourette (1885) documented that obsessions and compulsions were experienced by some of his patients with tics. Interest in this association were rejuvenated early in the century when Meige and Feindel (1907) wrote about the similarities between obsessions, compulsions, and tics. Subsequent studies have documented that obsessions and compulsions are experienced by a substantial number of patients with GTS (cf. Pauls, Raymond, & Robertson, 1991). In addition, family studies of GTS suggest

that OCD without tics may sometimes represent a variant expression of GTS. The relation between OCD and GTS is further supported by the results of a family study of OCD (Pauls, Alsobrook, Goodman, Rasmussen, & Leckman, in press), which suggests that the rate of GTS and tics in relatives of OCD patients is elevated in some, but not all, families. Thus, it appears that not all forms of OCD are related to GTS.

Individuals who are suffering from OCD accompanied by Tourette's syndrome are more likely to present with the need for symmetry and precision than OCD patients without Tourette's syndrome (Leckman et al., in press). Individuals with tic-related OCD often present with a rich assortment of obsessions and compulsions including those with sexual and religious themes. No differences in just right perceptions or psychasthenia have been reported between individuals suffering from OCD with and without Tourette's syndrome. The data further suggest that these symptoms may be associated with the overall level of severity rather than with one subtype of OCD versus another (Leckman et al., in press).

In summary, individuals suffering from OCD appear to be at increased risk for several anxiety disorders and depression and a subset are also at increased risk for GTS and related tic disorders. Although the few family genetic studies offer some suggestive evidence in support of these associations, many of the studies addressing issues of associated symptomatology, or comorbidity, must be interpreted with care because of a reliance on clinic-based populations. As described by Berkson (1946) for a range of medical conditions, individuals who seek treatment are more likely to present with multiple disorders. Population-based studies are needed to obtain unbiased rates of comorbidity within and across different forms of OCD.

ETIOLOGIC PERSPECTIVES

Most current theorists believe that individuals who develop clinical manifestations or pathological forms of obsessions and compulsions carry an underlying biological vulnerability for these behaviors. The specific mechanisms involved in this biological vulnerability have not yet been identified, but genetic and neurobiological evidence is accumulating. This is in contrast to earlier etiologic attributions. The earliest detailed descriptions of individuals who suffered from what may now be recognized as Obsessive Compulsive Disorder appeared centuries ago (Hunter & MacAlpine, 1963). At that time, the obsessional symptoms were attributed to spiritual causes such as demonic possession. Newer etiologic models can also be contrasted with older psychological models that attributed obsessions and compulsions to unconscious conflicts. Recent psychological models that emphasize cognitive-behavioral and neurocognitive functions can be integrated with biological explanations to provide a more comprehensive framework for attempts to understand the development and maintenance of adaptive and pathological obsessions and compulsions. An adequate integrated framework must involve the multiple systems, or levels of analysis, that contribute to the understanding of human behavior. Genetic, neurobiological, and psychological levels of analysis have received the most attention in the study of obsessions and compulsions.

Genetic Factors

Little is known about the genetic contribution to the development of normal obsessions and compulsions. Only a handful of studies have examined normally occurring obsessions and compulsions and there is a modest literature addressing the possible contribution of genetic factors to the manifestation of maladaptive obsessions and compulsions. The evidence that genetic factors are important in the manifestation of obsessive-compulsive symptomatology has come from two types of studies: twin studies and family studies.

Clifford (1983) and Clifford, Murray, and Fulker (1984) performed genetic analyses on data collected from 419 pairs of unselected twins who had been given the Eysenck Personality Questionnaire (EPQ) to assess obsessional and compulsive traits and the 42-item version of the Leyton Obsessional Inventory (LOI) to assess obsessive and compulsive symptoms. Multivariate analyses provided separate heritability estimates of 44% for obsessional traits and 47% for obsessional symptoms. There appeared to be little overlap between the two types of behaviors.

These findings suggested that the genetic factors important for obsessive-compulsive personality traits are in part independent from those genetic factors important for the expression of symptoms necessary for a diagnosis of OCD. Thus, separate genetic factors appear to play a role in the development and expression of obsessive-compulsive personality traits and the manifestation of those symptoms necessary for a diagnosis of OCD. What is not clear, however, is the extent to which the genetic factors for traits and/or symptoms contribute to the expression of normally occurring obsessions and compulsions.

Additional twin studies focusing on OCD have been reported. Rasmussen and Tsuang (1986) reviewed the OCD literature on twins and found that approximately 65% of monozygotic (MZ) twins were concordant for OCD. However, these results need to be interpreted with caution because no data from dizogotic (DZ) twins were available for comparisons. It is not possible with these twin data to determine the extent to which they support the hypothesis that genetic factors contribute to the expression of OCD.

A subsequent twin study included data from DZ twins. Carey and Gottesman (1981) reported on a sample of 30 twins (15 MZ and 15 DZ) ascertained through an affected twin with OCD. This sample was quite small, limiting rigorous statistical analyses, but these investigators reported several interesting trends. The most intriguing finding with regard to the involvement of genetic factors in the development of obsessive and compulsive symptoms came from an analysis that included obsessional features as the criteria for concordance. When the presence of a full spectrum of obsessive features was used instead of the more restrictive diagnostic criteria, 87% of the MZ twins were concordant compared with 47% of the DZ pairs. Obsessional features were defined as obsessive phenomena that met criteria for being symptoms (not traits) but that did not necessarily involve social incapacitation. Thus, obsessional features could include

those behaviors that occur quite frequently in the normal population. In this study, individuals with obsessive-compulsive features failed to meet diagnostic criteria either because the symptoms were not a significant source of distress or did not interfere with social role functioning. It should be noted, however, that these individuals did have sufficient obsessive-compulsive symptoms to otherwise satisfy diagnostic criteria for OCD.

Not all twin studies support the hypothesis that OCD by itself is heritable. Two recent twin studies (Andrews, Stewart, Allen, & Henderson, 1990; Andrews, Stewart, Morris-Yates, Holt, & Henderson, 1990; Torgerson, 1983) demonstrated that genetic factors were important for the manifestation of anxiety disorders in general, but not specifically OCD. The authors suggested that, to the extent obsessions and compulsions are symptoms of anxiety, genetic factors play a role in their expression.

Family studies of OCD patients provide further evidence that genetic factors play a role in the manifestation of the obsessions and compulsions. The familial nature of OCD has been observed since the 1930s (cf., Pauls et al., 1991). Nevertheless, the area remains controversial with some studies reporting rates as high as 35% among first-degree relatives (Lenane et al., 1990) and others reporting no increase (Insel, Hoover, & Murphy, 1983; McKeon & Murray, 1987; Rosenburg, 1967). Many of these studies are difficult to interpret because of differences in diagnostic criteria and assessment methodologies. Most studies did not directly interview relatives, and others failed to include a control sample. It is important to interview relatives directly because it has been shown that family history data alone can significantly underestimate the rates of illness (Orvaschel, Thompson, Belanger, Prusoff, & Kidd, 1982). This may be especially true for OCD where patients can be secretive about their symptoms. Whereas it is possible that individuals with OCD could both hide symptoms from relatives and deny those symptoms in a direct interview, it is less likely that they will be able to do both over their lifetime. Therefore, an approach that uses both direct interviews and family history information from multiple informants seems best suited for the study of OCD.

Five studies of OCD addressed some of the short-comings of earlier research (Bellodi, Sciuto, Diaferia, Ronchi, & Smeraldi, 1992; Black, 1992; Lenane et al., 1990; Leonard et al., 1992; Riddle et al., 1990); these studies directly interviewed relatives and used standard diagnostic criteria. Their findings provide further support for the hypothesis that a familial component is important for the expression of obsessions and compulsions. Three of the studies focused on families of children with OCD (Lenane et al., 1990; Leonard et al., 1992; Riddle et al., 1990); the remaining two investigated families of adults (Bellodi et al., 1992; Black et al., 1992).

Lenane and coworkers (1990) studied 145 first-degree relatives of 46 children and adolescents with severe primary OCD. Relatives were personally interviewed with clinical and structured psychiatric interviews. Among the parents, 25% of fathers and 9% of mothers had OCD. When subthreshold OCD was included, the age-corrected morbid risk for all first-degree relatives was 35%. In a second study of childhood OCD families, Riddle et al. (1990) interviewed the parents of 21 clinically referred children and adolescents with OCD. Of 42 parents, 15 (35.7%)

received a diagnosis of clinical ($N = 4$) or subthreshold ($N = 11$) OCD. In both studies, subthreshold OCD was defined in a way similar to the OCD features described by Carey and Gottesman (1981). Thus, these studies provide additional support for the hypothesis that at least some of the nonclinical symptoms observed in these families could be due to the same underlying etiologic factors responsible for OCD. In a third investigation of the families of childhood-onset OCD, Leonard et al. (1992) examined 170 first-degree relatives of 54 childhood probands. Thirteen percent of all first-degree relatives met criteria for OCD.

Bellodi and colleagues (1992) studies the families of 92 adult patients with OCD. The rate of OCD among parents and siblings was only 3.4%. However, when probands were separated on the basis of age at onset, the rates were significantly higher among the relatives of probands who onset before age 14. The morbid risk for OCD among relatives of the 21 early-onset probands was 8.8% compared with 3.4% among the relatives of later-onset probands.

A significant methodological weakness of the previous four studies is the lack of a control sample. Thus, it is not possible to determine whether the rates observed among the family members for OCD or subthreshold OCD are significantly higher than would be observed by these investigators employing the same diagnostic methods in a sample of families that were ascertained through unaffected individuals. Although the rates for OCD in these studies can be compared with rates obtained in epidemiological investigations, no studies have been conducted using similar methods to allow for an appropriate comparison for subthreshold OCD.

Black and colleagues (1992) reported the results of a study on the genetics of OCD that included a control group. They studied families of 32 adult OCD probands and 33 normal controls and found no evidence that OCD was familial. However, the risk of a more broadly defined OCD (i.e., subthreshold OCD) was increased among the parents of OCD probands when compared with parents of controls. In addition, the rates of anxiety disorders were significantly increased among relatives of obsessional probands compared with relatives of controls. Once again, these data suggest that there may be a relationship between the normally occurring obsessions and compulsions as well as other symptoms of anxiety.

These studies provide additional evidence that genetic factors play a role in the manifestation of some obsessions and compulsions and that there may also be a relationship to other anxiety traits that are transmitted within families. Although these findings support the hypothesis that genes play a role in the expression of obsessions and compulsions, it is not clear to what extent these same factors play a role in the development of normal obsessions and compulsions.

To address these questions and to obtain additional evidence that genetic and familial factors are important for the expression of normal obsessions and compulsions and OCD, additional well-controlled studies are needed. These studies should include both twins and families. Twins and families should be ascertained through patients with OCD as well as through individuals manifesting nonclinical obsessions and compulsions. All subjects and their relatives should be directly evaluated to assess the presence of all obsessions and compulsions. Finally, family history data should be systematically collected from relatives

and controls. To begin to understand genetic and environmental contributions to the course of these behaviors, family history data should attempt to document the occurrence of all obsessions and compulsions throughout a given individual's lifetime.

Two elegant designs that would allow a direct examination of the importance of genetic factors in the development of obsessions and compulsions would be studies of children at risk for OCD and studies of twins discordant for the clinical manifestation of OCD. By observing children at risk at critical stages of development and carefully documenting all behaviors possibly related to the manifestation of obsessions and compulsions, researchers would be able to determine whether there is a relationship between clinical and nonclinical symptoms. In addition, they would be able to examine factors in the family environment that might be associated with the movement from nonclinical to clinical. Studies of discordant twins would allow an examination of the manifestation of nonclinical obsessions and compulsions in the cotwin. Should the frequency of these symptoms be much higher than the mean of the normal population, it could be argued that some of the genetic factors for OCD also play a role in the manifestation of OC symptoms. Data from such studies would help make it possible to understand more completely the familial transmission of obsessive-compulsive behaviors and the possible role of genetic factors in their development.

Neurobiology

Multiple converging lines of evidence suggest that neurobiology plays a significant role in the etiology and maintenance of obsessional phenomena. During the past decade, there has been considerable progress in attempting to identify the neuroanatomic substrates involved in the expression of obsessive compulsive disorder. It is not certain that these substrates are also involved in the development of normal obsessions and compulsions, but it is hoped that an understanding of the functioning of the brain in individuals identified as having clinically significant obsessions and compulsions may lead to a better understanding of how these processes function in normal development.

The brain areas most frequently identified by in vivo neuroimaging studies as potentially involved in the manifestation of OCD are the orbitofrontal cortex (OFC), the anterior cingulate area (ACA), and the head of the caudate nucleus (Insel, 1992). The OFC, which maintains extensive connections with the amygdala and hypothalamus as well as projections to the basal forebrain and autonomic centers in the brain stem, has consistently been shown to have increased rates of glucose utilization in unmedicated OCD patients (Baxter et al., 1987; Nordahl et al., 1989; Swale, Hymas, Lees, & Frackowiak, 1991; Swedo, Leonard, et al., 1992; Swedo, Pietrini et al., 1992). Furthermore, the ACA has been strongly implicated in the pathobiology of OCD by the encouraging results of neurosurgical procedures directed at this structure and related fiber tracts (Bingley, Leskell, Meyerson, & Rylander, 1977; Fodstad, Strandman, Karlsson, & West, 1982; Jenike et al., 1991). Unfortunately, these interventions do not localize a lesion since interrupting a circuit only decreases neural transmission and does not indicate where in the circuit neural activity may have been abnormal.

Another region of the brain to have been implicated in OCD is the caudate nucleus and the closely associated nucleus acumbens. This region receives input from both the OFC and the ACA. Two in vivo neuroimaging studies have demonstrated changes in glucose utilization in the head of the caudate nucleus that appear to be correlated with both behavioral and pharmacological treatment response (Baxter et al., 1992; Benkelfat et al., 1990; Swedo, Leonard et al., 1992; Swedo, Pietrini et al., 1992). These studies suggest that treatments that effectively decrease symptoms of OCD are associated with decreases in metabolic activity in these regions. Of note is that these findings are associated with OCD symptoms, since scans of healthy controls done 10 weeks apart showed no differences.

All of these brain areas (the OFC, ACA, and the head of the caudate) are functionally interrelated limbic structures that are part of the cortico-striato-thalamo-cortical (CSTC) circuits. It is believed that these circuits channel and subchannel emotionally laden information (Alexander, DeLong, & Strick, 1986). Furthermore, they may be important in the neuronal encoding of active avoidance behaviors (see Sparenborg & Gabriel, 1990). A number of investigators (Baxter et al., 1992; Model, Mountz, Curtis, & Greden, 1989; Pitman, 1989; Rapoport & Wise, 1988) have speculated that these circuits are hyperactive in individuals with OCD. This hyperactivity could result in a self-reinforcing cycle that is difficult to break. On the other hand, Insel (1992) suggests that the hypermetabolic state observed in the OFC may be caused by the individual's resistance to the obsessive-compulsive symptoms. Although in vivo imaging studies identify increases in brain activity, the lack of methods that can distinguish inhibitory from excitatory increases in brain activity make it impossible to resolve these differing hypotheses.

In addition to the imaging studies just described, pharmacological and neurobiological studies have implicated several central neurotransmitter systems in the pathophysiology of OCD and related conditions. The strongest pharmacological evidence concerns the serotonergic system and the well-established efficacy of potent serotonin reuptake inhibitors in the treatment of OCD (cf. Goodman et al., 1989; Zohar & Insel, 1987). However, other systems have also been implicated. Specifically, central dopaminergic and opioid systems seem to be important in the expression of some forms of OCD (Goodman et al., 1990; Hanna, McCracken, & Cantwell, 1991; Insel & Pickar, 1983; McDougle et al., 1993; McDougle et al., 1994; Senjo, 1989). More recently, several studies have implicated two closely related neuropeptides, arginine vasopressin (AVP), and oxytocin (OT) in the pathobiology of some forms of OCD (Altemus et al., 1992; Annsseau et al., 1987; de Boer & Westenberg, 1992; Leckman et al., 1994; Swedo, Leonard et al., 1992). Both AVP and OT have been implicated in the manifestation of memory, grooming, sexual, and aggressive behaviors (see Leckman et al., 1994).

OT has been called the "amnesic" neuropeptide because of its action to attenuate memory consolidation and retrieval. This property has led some clinical investigators to administer OT to OCD patients in the hope that it would help to extinguish compulsions. The results of these trials are mixed, with some patients showing slight worsening of OC symptoms (Leckman et al., 1994). Animal data suggest that the OT effects on memory are

bimodal and site dependent. Whereas low doses attenuate memory, moderate doses can actually improve memory.

Grooming behavior can be elicited pharmacologically with the administration of either AVP or OT. The effect of centrally administered OT is a clear dose-response relationship. Increased doses lead to increased grooming behavior. The pattern of OT-related grooming involves autogrooming of the head and anogenital regions in many species. Given the close association of animal models of grooming behaviors and human compulsions (e.g., hand washing), AVP and OT continue to be of interest as potential mediators of obsessive and compulsive behaviors.

Some of the most compelling data in animals concern the bimodal behavioral effects of OT in sexual behavior (Carter, 1992) and aggression (Winslow & Insel, 1991). With regard to sexual behavior, findings from animal and human studies suggest that OT participates at several levels of the sexual response. Small amounts might facilitate precopulatory events and, through positive feedback, result in more OT being released. Subsequent pulsatile release of OT may lead to orgasmic responses involving activation of limbic and autonomic centers, followed by a refractory period of satiety. The relation of these OT-mediated sexual responses to human obsessionality is less clear than the association with grooming behaviors. Most sexually related symptoms involve obsessions and not compulsions and the content of the intrusive sexual imagery is often distressing. Relatively less is known about the role of OT in aggressive behaviors, although the central administration of OT can lead to a dose-response increase in aggressive behavior in dominant male monkeys (Winslow & Insel, 1991).

The existence of structural and functional differences, specific pharmacological responses in humans exhibiting clinically significant manifestations of obsessions and compulsions, and neurobiological findings consistent with animal models of obsessive and compulsive behaviors, suggest that these biological mechanisms might play a role in the development of normal obsessions and compulsions. To date, however, little is known about the specific neurobiological mechanisms involved in the normal emergence of ritualistic behavior and obsessional thought. Neurobiological findings with individuals suffering from maladaptive forms of obsessions and compulsions may inform the development of these behaviors in the general population (Insel, 1992).

While there is considerable disagreement about the specific brain regions that may be involved in OCD and/or nonpathological forms of obsessions and compulsions, frontal lobe and basal ganglia systems have received considerable attention (cf. Otto, 1990). The model of an overactive cortical-striatal-thalamic cortical circuit appears promising (Insel, 1992). Baxter and colleagues (Baxter, Schwartz, Guze, Bergman, & Szuba, 1990) hypothesized that the caudate nucleus might be central, whereas Insel (1992) highlights the orbitofrontal region of the cortex. Lesion studies in primates suggest that the orbitofrontal region of the cortex is involved in the ability to disregard irrelevant stimuli and to inhibit previously learned responses that are no longer appropriate (Drewe, 1975; Iverson & Mishkin, 1970). Insel (1992) refers to these processes as "interference control." Recent studies demonstrate that differences in metabolic functions between OCD and normal controls disappear when OCD patients respond to either pharmacological and behavioral treatment with diminished symptoms (Baxter et al., 1992). Thus, the observed difference in metabolic function may not reflect an etiologic cause of the disorder, but rather a compensatory increase in activity for decreases in regions that have not yet been identified. Further, increases may not be a function of the obsessive symptoms but of the resistance to the symptoms or an effort to exert interference control (Insel, 1992). Thus, whereas the evidence for structural and functional differences in OCD is accumulating, the interpretation of these findings remains ambiguous.

Psychological Models

Conflict Models

Freud. The earliest psychological models to explain the occurrence of obsessions and compulsions involved conflict models. OCD played a significant role in the development of Freud's thinking about the role of unconscious conflicts. Freud (1913) understood the predisposition toward the development of obsessionality as arising from anxiety-provoking conflicts, associated with aggressive and sexual urges and impulses organized within a fixation or regression to the anal psychosexual phase of development. He posited that when such conflict arises, the sadistic-anal-erotic sexual organization produces impulses to hurt, control, and soil that generate tremendous anxiety. He noted that the obsessional individual attempts to contain this anxiety through characteristic defenses that he believed were commonly associated with obsessive neurosis: denial, reaction formation, isolation, magical thinking, doubting, intellectualization, and undoing. Obsessive-compulsive symptoms were thus produced by the ego-dystonic negative impulses and defenses against these impulses. Freud (1913) was influenced by biological theory, and hypothesized that the specific symptoms chosen were strongly influenced by constitutional or hereditary factors. More recent psychoanalytic authors have emphasized the obsessional child's difficulties as involving maladaptive defenses against guilt, anxiety, and uncertainty while recognizing the role of biological factors (King, 1991).

Janet. Whereas Freud's theory of obsessive-compulsive symptoms was based on psychosexual conflict, Janet (1903/1976) viewed obsessions and compulsions within a broader symptom profile that included tics, phobias, and depersonalization (Pitman, 1987b). He termed these symptoms *forced agitations* and the condition that marked the disorder involving these symptoms *psychasthenia*. Janet conceived a hierarchy of psychological functions that culminated with the "reality functions." These functions included "presentification," a capacity to be fully in the present moment, to perform real actions involving considerable effort such as adapting to novel situations, and to experience emotions appropriate to the current reality. Below the reality functions, Janet included habitual actions and nonchallenging mental activities, imagination and abstract reasoning, visceral emotional reactions, and useless muscle movements. The level of psychological functioning was positively determined by the level of psychological tension. For Janet, psychasthenia reflected a deficit in psychological tension. He also proposed the existence of psychic

energy that flows through nerves as blood flows through the circulatory system. He suggested that the diversion of this psychic energy caused the appearance of obsessions, compulsions, ruminations, tics, phobias, and anxieties. According to Janet, the inability to complete a high-level operation, as a result of low levels of psychological tension, leads to lower level diversions, such that "other phenomena are produced that are both unanticipated and unnecessary" (Janet, 1913/1976, p. 555). Further, because high-level phenomena require more psychic energy than low-level phenomena, multiple forced agitations may appear following the diversion of an uncompleted high-level phenomenon (Pitman, 1987b). In light of the greater emphasis on tics and other motor movements, it is possible that, compared with Freud, Janet observed more patients who suffered from OCD with tic disorders than from OCD alone.

Ethological and Animal Models. Mechanistic energy models have received no scientific validation, but the idea of displacement has received some support from ethological theory. Observed in a wide array of species, displacement activities involve out-of-context actions that occur when motivated behaviors cannot be executed. The most commonly observed classes of displacement activities involve fixed-action patterns associated with grooming, feeding, cleaning, and nest building. These displacement activities often arise when an animal is faced with a conflict between aggression and escape motivations. Pitman (1991) noted the similarity between ethologists' observations of displacement activities and Janet's characterization of forced agitations in humans as well as the central role Freud assigned to conflict in the emergence of obsessive-compulsive symptoms.

These displacement activities have been proposed as an animal model for studying OCD (Holland, 1974). There is considerable comparability between the content of human rituals and compulsions and the fixed action patterns observed across species (e.g., washing, hoarding, ensuring safety). In addition, the universality of symptoms observed in OCD across cultures and time (Akhtar, et al., 1975; Okasha, Kamel, & Hassen, 1968; Rasmussen & Tsuang, 1986) suggests that compulsive behaviors may represent response tendencies selected for through evolution, which become activated out of context in OCD.

Neurocognitive and Affective Perspectives

Learning Theory and Conditioning Models. The learning theory that has received the most attention in OCD is Mowrer's (1960) two-factor theory, which states that obsessive thoughts produce anxiety because they have been associated previously with an unconditioned, anxiety-arousing stimulus. Obsessions, then elicit conditioned anxiety independently, the reduction of which is reinforcing. Compulsions are thereby established and maintained as they are reinforced by the subsequent reduction in anxiety. These compulsions can become elaborated through response chaining. Thus, the first factor constitutes the classical conditioning of the anxiety response, and the second factor involves the instrumental conditioning of compulsive behaviors that are maintained through the negative reinforcement inherent in the reduction of anxiety. This theory has a difficult time explaining the minority of individuals who engage in compulsions but do not report obsessions and do not know why they are engaging in compulsions.

Neurocognitive Theories. Gray (1982) developed a neuropsychological theory of anxiety that is relevant to OCD. Gray proposed a behavioral inhibition system that constitutes the anxiety response and that is available to respond to the following three kinds of stimuli: (a) novel stimuli; (b) stimuli associated with punishment; and (c) stimuli associated with nonreward. The behavioral inhibition system is involved in the following: (a) increasing arousal; (b) increasing attention; and (c) inhibiting ongoing behavior. Gray (1982) also proposed a comparator function, that compares actual sensory stimuli with expected stimuli generated by the cortex. When the comparator function identifies a mismatch between incoming and expected signals, the stimuli is "tagged" as in need of checking or problematic. Such labeling may include an association of the stimulus as important, with regard to safety concerns in situations of novelty; or aversive, with regard to potentially threatening situations (Gray, 1982). Further, he postulated that stimuli labeled in this manner would be responded to more slowly, as the comparator function engages in increased monitoring or checking for match-mismatch phenomena.

Cybernetic Models. Cybernetic comparator systems have also been hypothesized to explain the underlying dysfunction in OCD (Pitman, 1989, 1991). For example, Pitman (1987a) has proposed a cybernetic model of OCD that recognizes that obsessions and compulsions are purposeful behaviors. In this model, obsessive-compulsive symptoms result from an exaggerated attempt to match a perceptual signal to an internal reference signal, or goal for the perception. Pitman (1987a) hypothesized that the core problem of OCD is the persistence of mismatches between perceptual signals and internal reference signals that cannot be reduced to a zero (or matching) state by behavioral output. The phenomenological experience of the mismatch is feelings of incompleteness, sensations that are not quite right, and doubt. Thus, according to this theory, the repetitive and stereotyped symptoms of OCD represent behavioral programs that are executed repeatedly in an effort to reduce the mismatch of perceptual signals. At the neuroanatomic level, the frontocaudate loop is implicated in the assimilation of tertiary sensory information and its integration with prior knowledge as a means to planning strategies or actions and selecting motor plans. As previously noted, imaging studies have demonstrated that the orbitomedial frontal areas as well as the caudate and nucleus accumbens appear abnormal in individuals suffering from OCD. These regions are believed to be involved in the integration of limbic or emotional content with other sensory and stored information during planning and strategy generation.

In Gray's (1982) neuropsychological model, Pitman's (1991) cybernetic model, and Freud's (1913) conflict model, the source of the dysfunction is not specified. Thus, it is not clear whether the incoming stimuli or conflict (obsessional thought) is greater or has higher signal value than in nonpathological states or whether there is a problem in the threshold or monitoring system that is being employed to evaluate the incoming signal.

Consistent with learning theory and neurocognitive models, individuals who are prone to obsessionality tend to be highly

conditionable for negatively reinforced events. In general, they are willing to forgo positive reinforcers to minimize the risk of punishment. Animal models demonstrate that serotonergic neurons are involved in the behavioral punishment system and that abnormalities in serotonin may result in an animal that is particularly susceptible to negative contingencies in operant conditioning (Gray, 1982). The serotonergic system also appears to be implicated in human investigations. For example, when individuals suffering from OCD benefit from a therapeutic response to serotonin uptake inhibitors, they become more able to tolerate rather than become anxious and avoid unlikely negative contingencies and ambiguity.

Other neurocognitive mechanisms have also been implicated in OCD. Neuropsychological studies of individuals suffering from OCD have assessed the following abilities: shifting attention and cognitive set flexibly; inhibiting attention toward irrelevant stimuli; and/or disinhibiting attention to objects, images, or thoughts when necessary to maintain an orientation toward a goal. Unfortunately, only a small number of studies address neuropsychological functioning in individuals affected with OCD. Furthermore, methodological limitations and differences in these studies contribute to a pattern of disparate findings that are not readily interpreted as supporting any specific profile of neurocognitive strengths and/or weaknesses (cf. Christensen, Kim, Dysken, & Hoover, 1992; Otto, 1990). These limitations include the following: small sample sizes, the use of measures with differential sensitivity, reliance on published norms rather than control groups, and a lack of attention to the effects of age, sex, severity of disorder, and comorbid conditions. Further, few studies have employed comprehensive assessment strategies that permit differentiation of specific impairments in functioning. Results of these studies must therefore be viewed with extreme caution.

Patterns that do emerge suggest that individuals with OCD may have relative impairments in recent nonverbal memory (but not verbal or immediate nonverbal memory) (Boone, Ananth, Philpott, Kaur, & Djenderedjian, 1991; Christensen et al., 1992). They also show relative deficits on tasks across domains that measure speed of performance (Christensen et al., 1992). These differences may be a consequence of the symptoms of OCD rather than evidence of underlying etiologic factors. Specifically, the internal distraction of ongoing obsessions (which may be verbal and/or nonverbal in content) may interfere with both recent nonverbal memory and performance on timed tasks. There also appears to be some converging evidence for a relative deficit in visual-spatial abilities (Boone et al., 1991; Cox, Fedio, & Rapoport, 1989; Head, Bolton, & Hymas, 1989; Zielinski, Taylor, & Juzwin, 1991). Evidence for difficulties in executive functioning, the ability to flexibly shift cognitive strategies when the demands of the task change, are inconsistent across studies and warrant further investigation before conclusions can be drawn. Indeed, studies of executive functioning in patients with OCD utilizing more sophisticated methods have yielded nonsignificant results (e.g., Christensen et al., 1992; Martin et al., 1993). An alternative explanation for the lack of results on executive tasks is that they are measuring goal-directed behaviors that are no longer appropriate to the environmental demands. If obsessions can be reconceptualized as non-goal-directed behaviors, we would not necessarily anticipate difficulties in this domain.

In light of the previously described anatomical and functional findings, it is surprising that the current neuropsychological literature is so sparse. To advance our understanding of the role of neurobiology in pathological and nonpathological forms of OCD, it is necessary to examine the behavioral concomitants of observable structural and/or functional differences in a more systematic and comprehensive manner. It is quite likely that this approach with disordered populations will inform our understanding of the role of these structures and functions in typical development.

Attention Bias, Attributions, and Emotion Regulation

Attention Bias. Examining the impact of attention and affect regulation on the experience of obsessions may inform our understanding of continuities and discontinuities in adaptive and pathological forms of obsessionality. Consistent with neuropsychological theories that highlight the role of attention and arousal, studies have shown that attentional and affective factors within the individual may influence the perceived uncontrollability and degree of displeasure that is associated with the intrusive content of obsessional thoughts. Dickerson and colleagues (Edwards & Dickerson, 1987; England & Dickerson, 1988) argued that uncontrollability is predicted by the attentional salience of a particular thought. Studies of patients with anxiety disorders (e.g., GAD, panic disorder, social phobia, OCD) show attentional biases toward fear-relevant stimuli across a variety of cognitive processing tasks (e.g., Foa & McNally, 1986; McNally, Foa, & Donell, 1989). However, it is not clear whether this association precedes or is concomitant with the onset of these disorders. If Dickerson and colleagues (Edwards & Dickerson, 1987; England & Dickerson, 1988) are correct, and (a) uncontrollability is the most critical phenomenological variable distinguishing pathological and nonpathological forms of obsessionality; and (b) obsessionality is predicted by the attentional salience of particular thoughts, then attentional bias is a critical construct to evaluate when documenting the onset and course of pathological obsessions. Methods are available that could be utilized to study self-report (e.g., mood ratings), psychophysiological (e.g., evoked potential, heart-rate reactivity), and cognitive processing (e.g., Stroupe, depth of processing memory paradigms) responses to a wide range of obsessional contents and other potentially anxiety-eliciting stimuli to delineate the scope of the attention bias phenomenon.

Attributional Theories and Emotion Regulation. Rachman (1992) argued that an inflated sense of responsibility is part of the process that drives obsessional and compulsive behavior. He suggested that individuals with maladaptive obsessions make distorted attributions regarding their role in a variety of situations and that an exaggerated sense of responsibility can involve viewing their influence on others and the environment as being too extensive, too intense, too personal, and/or too exclusive. The person whose general attributional style involves an inflated sense of responsibility will feel more blameworthy for obsessional thoughts (e.g., impulses to harm others, sexual images), and the likely emotional response to this attribution is guilt. If an attribution about the source of the intrusive cognition is external, the resulting emotion is more likely to be anger (Rachman, 1992).

It is of interest that the presence of another person may diminish the discomfort or distress associated with an obsession, especially for individuals whose compulsions involve checking behaviors. Rachman and Hodgson (1980) suggest that this may be because the individual may experience a diffusion of responsibility such that the burden of maintaining a safe environment is shared with others. This diminution in symptoms has been observed when individuals with checking compulsions present for laboratory studies and when they are first admitted for inpatient hospitalization. Although a diminished sense of responsibility does not eradicate obsessions involving safety and the subsequent compulsions employed to neutralize these obsessions completely, it does reduce negative arousal and checking rituals are carried out more effectively and quickly. Unfortunately, as the checkers habituate to the new environment, their distortions in attributions of responsibility increase, with a concomitant increase in negative arousal.

A second possible explanation for familiar environments being more often associated with high levels of obsessional symptoms than are novel environments concerns violations of expectancy sets. Thus, the individual's perception that a knife is out of place in his or her own kitchen appears to create more distress than perceiving that a similar knife is out of place in a restaurant. The mismatch between the person's experience of threat and uncertainty and the expectation of feeling secure in his or her own home may in part contribute to the resulting negative emotional response.

A third alternative explanation from an attentional bias perspective would also account for the observed diminution in compulsions involving checking contents in experimental and inpatient settings. It is possible that when individuals who are particularly concerned with issues of safety encounter a novel environment, they must allocate a significant portion of their attentional resources to the novel features of the environment to ensure a successful (and safe) adaptation. Although individuals with checking compulsions may continue to experience the same frequency of obsessions, their attention is distracted by other, more salient features of the new external environment. Therefore, the experience of uncontrollability is diminished, and there is less urgency with regard to neutralizing the obsession with a compulsion. When such individuals habituate to the new environment (i.e., the novelty in the external world is less distracting), their attentional resources are more available to focus on the obsessions.

The attributional style described by Rachman (1992) is similar to the pessimistic attributional style that is described in the reformulated learned helplessness model (Abramson et al., 1978). The pessimistic attributional style has been shown to place individuals at risk for depressive episodes (Peterson & Seligman, 1984; Peterson, Seligman, & Vaillant, 1988; Sweeney, Anderson, & Bailey, 1986). Thus, in addition to providing a possible mechanism whereby an obsessional thought becomes dysfunctional, evaluating the attributions of responsibility along with other attributional dimensions may discriminate within the group of individuals with pathological forms of obsessionality who have or are at-risk for depression from those who are less vulnerable to depression.

The reformulated learned helplessness model posits that causal explanations can be analyzed along three attributional dimensions: (a) internality-externality; (b) stability; and (c) globality (Abramson, Seligman, & Teasdale, 1978). A multidimensional approach may help to distinguish pathological and nonpathological obsessions. Further, greater differentiation of specific attributions may be especially useful for understanding the wide range of affective responses (e.g., guilt, shame, anger) associated with obsessions. An internal attributional style suggests that the individual is more likely to explain a variety of events by attributing causal factors within the self (e.g., intelligence, skill, aptitude, effort, and personality). In contrast, an external attributional style suggests that the individual has a tendency to attribute causality to factors outside the self (e.g., task difficulty, skill of an opponent, help received, and luck).

Each dimension is associated with different emotional and cognitive consequences. According to the reformulated learned helplessness model, an internal style places individuals at risk for loss of self esteem. Stability differentiates causes on the basis of their relative endurance. A stable style is associated with the chronicity of helplessness and depression following a negative event. Globality refers to how inclusive the individual is in attributing causality, or the extent to which the individual generalizes from the specific incident to broader events and/or life domains. The globality dimension is related to the pervasiveness of the perceived deficits. A specific attribution will circumscribe feelings of helplessness to the domain of obsessions and compulsions. A global attribution may lead to impairment across multiple life domains. An individual's attributional set will depend on his or her developmental level and previous experiences as well as on contextual factors in the environment.

Although very young children engage in behaviors that provide them with a sense of mastery and control and/or that lead them to develop generalized expectations of helplessness, their experience of these states is not comparable to that of older children, adolescents, and adults. Thus, another important developmental issue to consider in the study of obsessions is that young children do not employ similar rules when making attributions about cognitions, emotions, and behavior (Weiner & Graham, 1984). Therefore, it is quite likely that young children will make different attributions of internality-externality, stability, globality, and controllability about their own cognitive processes and behaviors (including the occurrence and duration of obsessions and compulsions) than older children and adults.

Researchers in the area of attribution-emotion relations generally find that children as young as 5 years of age can distinguish the underlying property of controllability (cf. Rehm & Carter, 1990). However, developmental investigations that focus on children's attributions regarding success and failure have concluded that prior to age 9, children cannot fully distinguish between outcomes that are a function of ability as opposed to effort (Weiner & Handel, 1985). Because young children tend to attribute negative outcomes such as having a bad thought to insufficient effort, as opposed to lack of ability (Dweck & Repucci, 1973), they may be at greater risk for experiencing obsessions as uncontrollable. Thus, young children may have more difficulty comprehending that they are not to blame for the inability to get the thought or image out of their minds.

Repeated experience with the failure of not being able to terminate thoughts and images may lead them to attribute the failure to limited ability. Further, children's greater propensity toward global attributions places them at greater risk for overgeneralizing these failure experiences. Seligman (1975) suggested that children's generalized sense of mastery is formulated at a very early age and that the failure to acquire this characteristic would lead to a predisposition toward helplessness and depression. Thus, children who experience maladaptive obsessions prior to age 9 may be at increased risk for attributing the obsessions to internal, uncontrollable, stable, and/or global causes. If this set of attributions becomes characteristic of their general attributional style, it will place them at greater risk for later depression. Thus, consistent with the promise of utilizing a multidimensional attributional approach to study adult obsessionality, identifying the existence and consequences of attributional styles developmentally through the life span may help us to understand whether or not developmental changes in attributional processes contribute to or are a consequence of adaptive and maladaptive forms of obsessions and compulsions. In addition, a careful developmental analysis of these attributional processes will likely contribute to our understanding of emotional concomitants such as the observed high rate of depressive symptoms among children whose thoughts or images get stuck in their minds.

External Situational Factors

Although obsessions are events that may be influenced by internal attentional, affective, cognitive-attributional, and motivational factors, it is also important to recognize the influence of external situational stressors (Parkinson & Rachman, 1981). These external influences include exposure to stimuli that are associated with obsessions (e.g., dangerous objects, an ill individual) or to general life stressors (Rasmussen & Tsuang, 1984). Individuals who exhibit pathological forms of obsessionality, or OCD may be particularly vulnerable to external situational factors that are consistent with their obsessional thoughts. In addition, specific developmental transitions may heighten the salience of particular social and nonsocial threats. For example, the transition to parenthood may be associated with a heightened sense of interpersonal threat of loss for both parents, due to the real dangers surrounding childbirth for the mother and infant, and a recognition of the infant's dependency on the parents for survival. New parents often report that they frequently awaken in the night to check on their baby, concerned that the child may have stopped breathing (Jones, 1990). For a majority of new parents, this heightened awareness of threat diminishes after a few weeks or months. The decreasing salience of the threat is most likely the result of the parents obtaining feedback from the following: (a) the checking behaviors that confirm the baby's health (i.e., the baby is breathing each time they check); (b) the experience of a broader sense of competence in parenting; and (c) their infant's increasing predictability and developmental progress. Although there is limited empirical evidence on the relationship of pregnancy and birth to OCD, there may be some association between reproductive events such as pregnancy and miscarriage and either the emergence of clinical OCD or the worsening of symptoms (Neziroglu, Anemone, & Yaryura-Tobias, 1992; Sichel, Cohen, Dimmock, & Rosenbaum, 1993).

Consistent with Rachman's (1992) assertions that distorted feelings of responsibility increase negative arousal (particularly guilt) associated with intrusive thoughts, developmental transitions that involve increased responsibility may promote intense anxiety that in turn increases the salience of preexisting obsessions. Similarly, developmental transitions that heighten the experience of uncontrollability may be particularly difficult. Adolescence may be one such developmental transition. The adolescent experiences marked physical changes along with new challenges in interpersonal, academic/vocational and societal arenas. Further, cognitive changes in adolescence may also contribute to risk for obsessive psychopathology. Elkind (1967, 1978) described adolescents' heightened self-consciousness and egocentrism. In response to new cognitive capacities, some adolescents become fascinated and absorbed with the products of their own minds and are egocentric in believing that no one else could possibly share their experiences. An adolescent who experiences new, uncontrollable negative obsessions (e.g., perhaps associated with a romantic affiliation) may become preoccupied with these thoughts and may also feel solely responsible for the thought. Consistent with this hypothesis that adolescence may represent a sensitive developmental stage or period, there appears to be a marked increase in the prevalence of OCD during adolescence (Flament et al., 1988; Goodwin, Guze, & Robins, 1969; Rasmussen & Tsuang, 1986).

CONCLUSIONS

This chapter has reviewed the existing knowledge regarding the development of obsessions and compulsions with an emphasis on continuities and discontinuities in normative and maladaptive forms. Unfortunately, due to the limited number of studies conducted in these areas, we have encountered more questions than answers. Specifically, no definitive statements can be made regarding whether there is etiologic and developmental continuity between the following: (a) childhood rituals and preadolescent through adult obsessions; (b) pathological and normative forms of obsessionality; (c) obsessive-compulsive symptoms and other affective symptomatology; or (d) OCD and OCPD. Thus, in the concluding section of this chapter, we offer suggestions for future research to address these issues.

The future study of developmental continuities and discontinuities in obsessionality must be informed from a developmental psychopathology perspective (Cicchetti, 1993; Sroufe & Rutter, 1984). It is critical that researchers and clinicians working in this area become cognizant of the interface between psychological and biological processes in normal and abnormal development. In addition, the research on obsessions and compulsions must move from the descriptive level to address developmental mechanisms and processes across the life span. Further, a comprehensive understanding of each of these questions will likely require a multidisciplinary, multimethod effort that includes research designs and techniques from the following fields: epidemiology, genetics, neurobiology, neuropsychology, developmental psychology, social psychology, and social learning theory.

First, one of the major tenets of developmental psychopathology is that we must understand normal development to fully comprehend the nuances of psychopathological conditions. Thus, to understand fully developmental aspects of maladaptive patterns of obsessions and compulsions, more normative information must be gathered. To date, information about the emergence of typical ritualistic and compulsive behaviors is based on very small samples of convenience or clinical observations. These rich descriptions are useful for hypothesis generation, but developmental studies of maladaptive compulsive and obsessional behaviors are severely constrained by the lack of a normative context. Further, whereas many theoreticians (e.g., Adams, 1973) discuss the adaptive value of ritualistic behaviors and obsessionality, empirical efforts have not addressed the possible functional significance of these behaviors.

A second tenet of developmental psychopathology is that information from the study of disordered conditions can be utilized to enhance our understanding of normal functions. This issue has been addressed most directly within the areas of neurobiology and genetics. In the realm of neurobiology, the identification of structural abnormalities coupled with an understanding of the behavioral concomitants informs our understanding of the role of these regions in normal functioning (Insel, 1992). Similarly, genetic strategies that identify a disordered proband may inform our understanding of the etiology of the normal range of phenotypic functioning. For example, genetic strategies including both twin and family studies, can be useful in the examination of the relationship between clinically significant symptoms and normally occurring obsessions and compulsions. DeFries and Fulker (1985, 1988) have developed a twin study method that allows an examination of whether extreme scores on a continuous measure have the same underlying genetic basis as scores in the normal range. For this analysis, twin pairs identified through one twin with an extreme score are needed. It is also necessary to have population data for the continuous measure. If there are common genetic factors for the normally occurring obsessions and compulsions and clinically significant symptoms, the mean scores of the cotwins will deviate from the population mean toward the scores of the extreme twin. The difference between the means of the less extreme cotwin and the population mean provide an estimate of the magnitude of the genetic influence. If the means of the cotwins are not different from the population means, it would suggest that there are not common genetic factors for the normally occurring and extreme behaviors.

Family study data can also allow the examination of the association between clinically significant and normative obsessions and compulsions. By examining the rate of normally occurring obsessions and compulsions among the relatives of individuals with OCD, it is possible to determine if the patterns within families are consistent with the hypothesis that the two are genetically related. Once again, it is necessary to have estimates of the rates of the normally occurring behaviors so that it is possible to determine if the frequencies of these behaviors are increased among the relatives. These estimates can be obtained through population studies using the same instruments or by including control families in the design.

Third, given the multiple systems that are likely to be implicated in a full understanding of the origins and course of pathological and nonpathological obsessions and compulsions, a multidisciplinary approach will likely lead to the most illuminating findings. Consistent with this, the approach to assessment must be developmentally sensitive throughout the life span. Furthermore, the assessment approach must be comprehensive, addressing multiple domains of functioning as well as the multiple contexts in which behaviors may manifest (Cicchetti & Wagner, 1990; Sparrow, Carter, Racusin, & Morris, in press). Excellent candidate domains for the study of obsessionality include (a) cognitive processes (e.g., attentional biases, multidimensional attributions); (b) neurocognitive functioning (e.g., memory, visual-spatial perception and production, cognitive flexibility, tactile perception); (c) emotional responses to obsessions and compulsions (e.g., guilt, shame, anger); (d) physiological responses (e.g., reactivity and regulation following the presentation of a range of obsessional contents and fear-evoking stimuli); and (e) neuroanatomic structures and functions.

Within the multimethod, multidomain assessment approach, an analysis of the risk and protective factors and mechanisms operating in the individual and his or her environment across the life span is critical (Cicchetti & Aber, 1986). The investigation of how emergent functions, competencies, and developmental tasks modify the expression of obsessions and compulsions or lead to new symptoms and difficulties (e.g., depressions and other anxiety disorders) is crucial for a comprehensive understanding of the full range of obsessions and compulsions. As noted by Zigler and Glick (1986), a central tenet of developmental psychopathology is that individuals move from pathological to nonpathological states of functioning. Further, even while exhibiting significant symptoms of psychopathology, individuals may display highly adaptive coping mechanisms (Cicchetti, 1993) that will be integral to understanding pathological forms and their sequelae. There must also be greater emphasis on the developmental contexts in which behaviors appear, especially in light of the recognition that a particular stress or vulnerability factor may express itself differently at various points in development and/or in different environmental contexts (Cicchetti & Aber, 1986; Rutter, 1989). Further, environmental stressors and protective factors as well as the intraindividual experience of specific emotions, behaviors, and cognitions will have very different meanings and subsequent representations depending on the timing, nature, and context of the experience (Rutter, 1989).

High-risk longitudinal prospective designs provide a powerful research tool for examining questions of continuity between normally emerging ritualistic behavior and later obsessionality as well as continuity in the phenomenology of child, adolescent, and adult forms of pathological obsessive and compulsive behaviors. Ideally, high-risk longitudinal prospective designs can be embedded within larger family genetic studies, and multiple levels and domains of assessment can be addressed. There is a growing consensus that the process of identifying those individuals who experience obsessional thoughts to a pathological degree is in part regulated by biological vulnerability. However, the parameters that govern the individual variation observed have yet to be demarcated (Turner et al., 1992).

The high-risk prospective method involves identifying a sample of children who may be at risk for the development of maladaptive obsessionality. This identification can be based on family membership (i.e., selecting children who have a high family loading for obsessional and compulsive behaviors) or on characteristics of the child. Focusing on children with a high

family loading assumes that there is genetic and/or environmental familial transmission of OCD and obsessional symptoms. A very reasonable strategy for identifying children and/or adolescents based on their own characteristics would be to follow children and/or adolescents who are exhibiting subclinical manifestations of OCD. Because the estimates for lifetime prevalence of adult OCD based on community samples is 1.2% to 2.5% (Bland et al., 1988; Karno et al., 1988), it is unlikely that the entire 2% of the population in the adolescent community sample who were exhibiting subclinical symptoms of obsessionality (Flament et al., 1988) will develop clinically significant OCD.

Including assessments of affective, cognitive-attributional and motivational factors as well as neurotransmitters that are hypothesized to influence the severity and perceived distress associated with obsessionality in such a prospective design would greatly inform our understanding of the interplay of such factors. Information regarding the critical issue of directionality of effects can be broached in this manner. Our current body of knowledge does not preclude the possibility that the observed neurobiological findings are the sequelae of the complex behaviors observed in maladaptive forms of OCD and obsessionality. Thus, the identification and longitudinal study of adolescents who are evidencing subclinical OCD can provide an unusual opportunity to learn more about the factors that contribute to the onset of diagnosable OCD. One weakness in this design is that the early course of obsessionality and the importance of early emerging ritualistic behavior cannot be addressed.

Another potentially powerful design would be a modification of the previously discussed high-risk prospective study, in which children would be selected based on both a high family loading for OCD and individual characteristics of the children. Given the association of OCD and other anxiety disorders, findings of higher rates of behavioral inhibition among offspring of adults with anxiety disorders (Rosenbaum et al, 1990), and higher rates of anxiety disorders in behaviorally inhibited adolescents (Biederman et al., 1993), behavioral inhibition may be a marker of heightened risk for obsessions and compulsions (Rosenbaum, Biederman, Hirshfeld, Boduc, & Chaloff, 1991). Behavioral inhibition is a fairly stable temperament style associated with extreme shyness, caution, and emotional reserve, a lower threshold for external stimulation, and reduced heart rate variability (i.e., high stable heart rates) (Kagan, 1989; Kagan, Reznick, & Snidman, 1988; Kagan & Snidman, 1991). Children who are behaviorally inhibited may be predisposed toward attentional biases that are consistent with those observed in adults with obsessionality. In addition, similar neurobiological explanations have been advocated to account for maladaptive obsessional states and behavioral inhibition (Kagan & Snidman, 1991).

Finally, little attention has been paid to the role of context or the circumstances that are likely to lead to the manifestation and/or intensification of obsessional behaviors. A vehicle for addressing contextual effects would be to examine developmental transitions hypothesized to influence affective, cognitive-behavioral, and motivational states related to obsessionality. For example, the transition to parenthood presents unique challenges in terms of increased responsibility and unpredictability as well as a wide range of other stressors that may lower an individual's threshold for obsessionality. For women, the transition to parenthood may also involve neurobiological challenges. Adolescence is another developmental transition that deserves further attention.

In conclusion, developmentally sensitive integrative models are required to fully understand the range of obsessionality through the life span. Although it is rarely possible to address all the relevant levels of the system simultaneously, methodological approaches that acknowledge the complexity of transactions across genetic, epidemiological, neurobiological, phenomenological, cognitive-behavioral, and environmental stressors are needed.

REFERENCES

Abramson, L. Y., Seligman, M. E. P., & Teasdale, J. (1978). Learned helplessness in humans: Critique and reformulation. *Journal of Abnormal Psychology, 87,* 32–48.

Adams, P. (1973). *Obsessive children.* New York: Penguin Books.

Akhtar, S., Wig, N. N., Varma, V. K., Pershad, D., & Verma, S. K. (1975). A phenomenological analysis of symptoms in obsessive-compulsive neurosis. *British Journal of Psychiatry, 127,* 342–348.

Alexander, G. E., DeLong, M. R., & Strick, P. L. (1986). Parallel organization of functionally segregated circuits linking basal ganglia and cortex. *Annual Review of Neuroscience, 9,* 357–381.

Altemus, M., Pigott, T., Kalogeras, K. T., Demitrack, M., Dubbert, B., Murphy, D. L., & Gold, P. W. (1992). Abnormalities in the regulation of vasopressin and corticotropin releasing factor secretion in obsessive-compulsive disorder. *Archives of General Psychiatry, 49,* 9–20.

American Psychiatric Association. (1980, 1987, 1994). *Diagnostic and statistical manual of mental disorders* (3rd ed., 3rd ed. rev., 4th ed.). Washington, DC: Author.

Andrews, G., Stewart, G., Allen, R., & Henderson, A. S. (1990). The genetics of six neurotic disorders: A twin study. *Journal of Affective Disorders, 19,* 23–29.

Andrews, G., Stewart, G., Morris-Yates, A., Holt, P., & Henderson, A. S. (1990). Evidence for a general neurotic syndrome. *British Journal of Psychiatry, 157,* 6–12.

Ansseau, M., Legros, J. J., Mormont, C., Cerfontaine, J., Papart, P., Geenen, V., Adam, F., & Franck, G. (1987). Intranasal oxytocin in obsessive-compulsive disorder. *Psychoneuroendocrinology, 12,* 231–236.

Anthony, J. C., Folstein, M., Romanoski, A. J., Von Korff, M. R., Nestadt, G. R., Chahal, R., Merchant, A., Brown, C. H., Shapiro, S., Kramer, M., & Gruenberg, E. (1985). Comparison of the lay Diagnostic Interview Schedule and a standardized psychiatric diagnosis: Experience in eastern Baltimore. *Archives of General Psychiatry, 42,* 667–675.

Barlow, D. H. (1988). *Anxiety and its disorders.* New York: Guilford.

Barlow, D. H., DiNardo, P. A., Vermilyea, B. B., Vermilyea, J., & Blanchard, E. B. (1986). Co-morbidity and depression among the anxiety disorders: Issues in diagnosis and classification. *Journal of Nervous and Mental Disease, 174,* 63–72.

Baxter, L. R., Phelps, M. E., Mazziotta, J. C., Guze, B. H., Schwartz, J. M., & Selin, C. E. (1987). Local cerebral glucose metabolic rates in obsessive compulsive disorder. *Archives of General Psychiatry, 44,* 211–218.

Baxter, L. R., Schwartz, J. M., Bergman, K. S., Szuba, M. P., Guze, B. H., Mazziotta, J. C., Alazraki, A., Selin, C. E., Ferng, H. K., Munford, P., & Phelps, M. E. (1992). Caudate glucose metabolic rate changes with both drug and behavior therapy for obsessive-compulsive disorder. *Archives of General Psychiatry, 49,* 681–689.

Baxter, L. R., Schwartz, J., Guze, B., Bergman, K., & Szuba, M. (1990). Neuroimaging in obsessive compulsive disorder: seeking the mediating neuroanatomy. In M. Jenike, L. Baer, & W. E. Minichiello (Eds.), *Obsessive compulsive disorders: Theory and management* (2nd ed.) (pp. 167–188). Chicago: Year Book Medical.

Beech, H. R. (1974). Approaches to understanding obsessional illness. In H. R. Beech (Ed.), *Obsessional states* (pp. 3–17). London: Methuen.

Bellodi, L., Sciuto, G., Diaferia, G., Ronchi, P., & Smeraldi, E. (1992). Psychiatric disorders in the families of patients with obsessive-compulsive disorder. *Psychiatry Research, 42,* 111–120.

Benkelfat, C., Nordahl, T. E., Semple, W. E., King, A. C., Murphy, D. L., & Cohen, R. M. (1990). Local cerebral glucose metabolic rates in obsessive-compulsive disorder: Patients treated with clomipramine. *Archives of General Psychiatry, 47,* 840–848.

Berg, C. Z., Rapoport, J. L., Whitaker, A., Davies, M., Leonard, H., Swedo, S., Braiman, S., & Lenane, M. (1989). Childhood obsessive compulsive disorder: A two-year prospective follow-up of a community sample. *Journal of the American Academy of Child and Adolescent Psychiatry, 28,* 528–533.

Berg, C. Z., Whitaker, A., Davies, M., Flament, M. F., & Rapoport, J. L. (1988). The survey form of the Leyton Obsessional Inventory–Child Version: Norms from an epidemiological study. *Journal of the American Academy of Child and Adolescent Psychiatry, 27,* 759–763.

Berkson, J. (1946). Limitations of the application of fourfold table analysis to hospital data. *Biometrics, 2,* 47–51.

Biederman, J., Rosenbaum, J. F., Bolduc-Murphy, E. A., Faraone, S. V., Chaloff, J., Hirschfeld, D. R., & Kagan, J. (1993). A 3-year follow-up of children with and without behavioral inhibition. *Journal of the American Academy of Child and Adolescent Psychiatry, 32,* 814–821.

Bingley, T., Leskell, L., Meyerson, B. A., & Rylander, G. (1977). Long-term results of sterotactic anterior capsulotomy in chronic obsessive-compulsive neurosis. In W. H. Sweet, S. Obrador, & J. G. Martin-Rodriguez (Eds.), *Neurosurgical treatment in psychiatry* (pp. 287–289). Baltimore: University Park Press.

Black, A. (1974). The natural history of obsessional neurosis. In H. R. Beech (Ed.), *Obsessional states* (pp. 19–54). London: Methuen.

Black, D. W., Noyes, R., Jr., Goldstein, R. B., & Blum, N. (1992). A family study of obsessive-compulsive disorder. *Archives of General Psychiatry, 49,* 362–368.

Black, D. W., Noyes, R., Pfohl, B., Goldstein, R. B., & Blum, N. (1993). Personality disorder in obsessive compulsive volunteers, well comparison subjects, and their first degree relatives. *American Journal of Psychiatry, 150,* 1226–1232.

Black, D. W., Yates, W. R., Noyes, R., Pfohl, B., & Kelley, M. (1989). DSM-III personality disorder in obsessive-compulsive study volunteers: A controlled study. *Journal of Personality Disorders, 3,* 58–62.

Bland, R. C., Newman, S. C., & Orn, H. (1988). Lifetime prevalence of psychiatric disorders in Edmonton. *Acta Psychiatrica Scandinavica, 77,* 24–32.

Boone, K. B., Ananth, J., Philpott, L., Kaur, A., & Djenderedjian, A. (1991). Neuropsychological characteristics of nondepressed adults with obsessive-compulsive disorder. *Neuropsychiatry, Neuropsychology, and Behavioral Neurology, 4,* 96–109.

Carey, G., & Gottesman, I. I. (1981). Twin and family studies of anxiety, phobic, and obsessive disorders. In D. F. Klein & J. Rabkin

(Eds.), *Anxiety: New research and changing concepts* (pp. 117–136). New York: Raven Press.

Carter, C. S. (1992). Oxytocin and sexual behavior. *Neuroscience and Biobehavioral Review, 16,* 131–144.

Christensen, K. J., Kim, S. W., Dysken, M. W., & Hoover, K. M. (1992). Neuropsychological performance in obsessive-compulsive disorder. *Biological Psychiatry, 31,* 4–18.

Cicchetti, D. (1993). Developmental psychopathology: Reactions, reflections, and projections. *Developmental Review, 13,* 471–502.

Cicchetti, D., & Aber, J. L. (1986). Early precursors to later depression: An organizational perspective. In L. Lipsitt, & C. Rovee-Collier (Eds.), *Advances in infancy* (Vol. 4, pp. 87–137). Norwood, NJ: Ablex.

Cicchetti, D., & Wagner, S. (1990). Alternative assessment strategies for the evaluation of infants and toddlers: An organizational perspective. In S. Meisels & J. Shonkoff (Eds.), *Handbook of early intervention* (pp. 246–277). New York: Cambridge University Press.

Clifford, C. A. (1983). Twin studies of drinking behavior and obsessionality. Unpublished doctoral dissertation, Institute of Psychiatry, London.

Clifford, C. A., Murrary, R. M., & Fulker, D. W. (1984). Genetic and environmental influences on obsessional traits and symptoms. *Psychological Medicine, 14,* 791–800.

Cox, C. S., Fedio, P., & Rapoport, J. L. (1989). Neuropsychological testing of obsessive-compulsive adolescents. In J. L. Rapoport (Ed.), *Obsessive-compulsive disorder in children and adolescents* (pp. 73–85). Washington, DC: American Psychiatric Press.

Cuneo, K. M., & Welsh, M. C. (1992). Perception in young children: Developmental and neuropsychological perspectives. *Child Study Journal, 22,* 73–92.

de Boer, J. A., & Westenberg, H. G. M. (1992). Oxytocin in obsessive compulsive disorder. *Peptides, 13,* 1083–1085.

DeFries, J. C., & Fulker, D. W. (1985). Multiple regression analysis of twin data. *Behavior Genetics, 15,* 467–473.

DeFries, J. C., & Fulker, D. W. (1988). Multiple regression analysis of twin data: Etiology of deviant scores versus individual differences. *Acta Geneticae, 37,* 205–216.

Diamond, A. (1988). Abilities and neural mechanisms underlying AB performance. *Child Development, 59,* 523–527.

Drewe, E. (1975). Go-no go learning after frontal lobe lesions in humans. *Cortex, 11,* 8–16.

Dweck, C. S., & Repucci, N. D. (1973). Learned helplessness and reinforcement responsibility in children. *Journal of Personality and Social Psychology, 25,* 109–116.

Edwards, S., & Dickerson, M. (1987). Intrusive unwanted thoughts: A two-stage model of control. *British Journal of Medical Psychology, 60,* 317–328.

Elkind, D. (1967). Egocentrism in adolescence. *Child Development, 38,* 1025–1034.

Elkind, D. (1978). Understanding the young adolescent. *Adolescence, 13,* 127–134.

England, S. L., & Dickerson, M. (1988). Intrusive thoughts: Unpleasantness not the major cause of uncontrollability. *Behavioral Research and Therapy, 26,* 279–282.

Flament, M. F., Whitaker, A., Rapoport, J. L., Davies, M., ZarembaBerg, C., Kalikow, K., Sceery, W., & Shaffer, D. (1988). Obsessive compulsive disorder in adolescence: An epidemiologic study.

Journal of the American Academy of Child and Adolescent Psychiatry, 27, 764–771.

Foa, E. B., & McNally, R. J. (1986). Sensitivity to feared stimuli in obsessive-compulsives: A dichotic listening analysis. *Cognitive Therapy and Research, 10,* 477–485.

Fodstad, H., Strandman, E., Karlsson, B., & West, K. A. (1982). Treatment of chronic obsessive compulsive states with stereotactic anterior capsulotomy or cingulotomy. *Acta Neurochirurgica, 62,* 1–23.

Freud, A. (1965). *Normality and pathology in childhood.* New York: International Universities Press.

Freud, S. (1958). The disposition to obsessional neurosis. A contribution to the problem of choice of neurosis. In J. Strachey (Ed. and Trans.) *The standard edition of the complete psychological works of Sigmund Freud* (Vol. 12, pp. 317–326). London: Hogarth Press. (Original work published in 1913)

Frost, R. O., Krause, M. S., McMahon, M. J., Peppe, J., Evans, M., McPhee, A. E., & Holden, M. (1993). Compulsivity and superstitiousness. *Behavior Research and Therapy, 31,* 423–425.

Frost, R. O., Sher, K., & Geen, T. (1986). Psychopathology and personality characteristics of nonclinical compulsive checkers. *Behavior Research and Therapy, 24,* 133–143.

Gesell, A., Ames, L. B., & Ilg, F. L. (1974). *Infant and child in the culture of today.* New York: Harper & Row.

Gille de la Tourette, G. (1885). Etude sur une affection nerveuse caracterisee par de l'indoordination motrics accompagnee d'echolalie et de copralalie. *Archives of Neurology, 9,* 19–42.

Gittelman, R., & Klein, D. F. (1985). Childhood separation anxiety and adult agoraphobia. In A. Y. Tuma & J. D. Maser (Eds.), *Anxiety and the anxiety disorders* (pp. 389–402). Hillsdale, NJ: Erlbaum.

Goodman, W. K., McDougle, C. J., Price, L. H., Riddle, M. A., Pauls, D. L., & Leckman, J. F. (1990). Beyond the serotonin hypothesis: A role for dopamine in some forms of obsessive compulsive disorder? *Journal of Clinical Psychiatry, 51,* 36–43.

Goodman, W. K., Price, L. H., Rasmussen, S. A., Delgado, P. L., Heninger, G. R., & Charney, D. S. (1989). Efficacy of fluvoxamine in obsessive-compulsive disorder: A double-blind comparison with placebo. *Archives of General Psychiatry, 46,* 36–44.

Goodwin, D. W., Guze, S. B., & Robins, E. (1969). Follow-up studies in obsessional neurosis. *Archives of General Psychiatry, 20,* 182–187.

Gottlieb, G. (1991). Experiential canalization of behavioral development: Theory. *Developmental Psychology, 27,* 4–13.

Gray, J. A. (1982). *The neuropsychology of anxiety: An enquiry into the functions of the septo-hippocampal system.* Oxford, England: Oxford University Press.

Hanna, G. L., McCracken, J. T., & Cantwell, D. P. (1991). Prolactin in childhood obsessive-compulsive disorder: Clinical correlates and response to clomipramine. *Journal of the American Academy of Child and Adolescent Psychiatry, 30,* 173–178.

Head, D., Bolton, D., & Hymas, N. (1989). Deficit in cognitive shifting ability in patients with obsessive-compulsive disorders. *Biological Psychiatry, 25,* 929–937.

Helzer, J. E., Robins, L. N., McEvoy, L. T., Spitznagel, E. L., Stoltzman, R. K., Farmer, A., & Brockington, I. F. (1985). A comparison of clinical and diagnostic interview schedule diagnoses. Physician reexamination of lay-interviewed cases in the general population. *Archives of General Psychiatry, 42,* 657–666.

Hodes, E. L., & Cohen, D. J. (1991). Repetitive behaviors of childhood. In M. Levine & W. Carey (Eds.), *Developmental-behavioral pediatrics* (2nd Ed., pp. 607–622). Philadelphia, PA: Saunders.

Holland, H. C. (1974). Displacement activity as a form of abnormal behavior in animals. In H. R. Beech (Ed.), *Obsessional states* (pp. 161–173). London: Methuen.

Hollingsworth, C. E., Tanguay, P. E., Grossman, L., & Pabst, P. (1980). Long-term outcome of obsessive-compulsive disorder in children. *Journal of the American Academy of Child Psychiatry, 19,* 134–144.

Honjo, S., Hirano, C., Murase, S., Kaneko, T., Sugiyama, T., Ohtaka, K., Aoyama, T., Takei, Y., Inoko, K., & Wakabayashi, S. (1989). Obsessive-compulsive symptoms in childhood and adolescence. *Acta Psychiatrica Scandinavica, 80,* 83–91.

Hoogduin, K. (1986). On the diagnosis of obsessive-compulsive disorder. *American Journal of Psychotherapy, 40,* 36–51.

Hunter, R., & MacAlpine, I. (1963). *Three hundred years of psychiatry.* London: Oxford University Press.

Ingram, I. M. (1961). Obsessional illness in mental hospital patients. *Journal of Mental Science, 107,* 382–402.

Insel, T. R. (1984). Obsessive compulsive disorder: The clinical picture. In T. R. Insel (Ed.), *New findings in obsessive compulsive disorder* (pp. 2–22). Washington, DC: American Psychiatric Press.

Insel, T. R. (1990). Phenomenology of obsessive-compulsive disorder. *Journal of Clinical Psychiatry, 51*(Suppl.), 4–9.

Insel, T. R. (1992). A neuropeptide for affiliation: Evidence from behavioral, receptor, autoradiographic, and comparative studies. *Psychoneuroendocrinology, 17,* 3–35.

Insel, T. R., Hoover, C., & Murphy, D. L. (1983). Parents of patients with obsessive compulsive disorder. *Psychological Medicine, 13,* 807–811.

Insel, T. R., & Pickar, D. (1983). Naloxone administration in obsessive-compulsive disorder: Report of two cases. *American Journal of Psychiatry, 140,* 1219–1220.

Iverson, S., & Mishkin, M. (1970). Perseverative-interference in monkeys following selective lesions of the inferior prefrontal cortex. *Experimental Brain Research, 11,* 376–386.

Jahoda, G. (1969). *The psychology of superstition.* London: Allen Lane; Penguin Press.

Janet, P. (1976). *Les obsessions et la Psychiasthenie* (Vol. I). New York: Arno. (Original work published 1903)

Jenike, M., Baer, L., Ballantine, T., Martuza, R., Tynes, S., Giriunas, I., Buttolph, L., & Cassem, N. (1991). Singulatomy for refractory obsessive-compulsive disorder: A long-term follow-up of 33 patients. *Archives of General Psychiatry, 48,* 548–555.

Johnson, B. A. (1993). The Maudsley's obsessional children: Phenomenology, classification, and associated neurobiological and comorbid features. *European Child and Adolescent Psychiatry, 2,* 192–204.

Jones, D. (1990). Inner tidiness. *Nature, 344,* 24.

Judd, L. L. (1965). Obsessive compulsive neurosis in children. *Archives of General Psychiatry, 12,* 136–143.

Kagan, J. (1989). Temperamental contributions to social behavior. *American Psychologist, 44,* 668–674.

Kagan, J., Reznick, J. S., & Snidman, N. (1988). Biological bases of childhood shyness. *Science, 240,* 167–171.

Kagan, J., & Snidman, N. (1991). Infant predictors of inhibited and uninhibited profiles. *Psychological Science, 2,* 40–44.

Karno, M., Golding, J. M., Sorenson, S. B., & Burnam, M. A. (1988). The epidemiology of obsessive-compulsive disorder in five U.S. communities. *Archives of General Psychiatry, 45,* 1094–1099.

Kelly, D. (1980). *Anxiety and emotions: Physiological basis and treatment.* Springfield, IL: Thomas.

King, R. A. (1991). Obsessive-compulsive disorder. In R. A. King & J. D. Noshpitz (Eds.), *Pathways of growth: Essentials of child psychiatry* (Vol. 2, pp. 265–298). New York: Wiley.

Kringlen, E. (1965). Obsessional neurotics: A long term follow-up. *British Journal of Psychiatry, 111,* 709–722.

Leckman, J. F., Goodman, W. K., North, W. G., Chappell, P. B., Price, L. H., Pauls, D. L., Anderson, G. M., Riddle, M. A., McSwiggan-Hardin, M., McDougle, C. J., Barr, L. C., & Cohen, D. J. (1994). The role of central oxytocin in obsessive compulsive disorder and related normal behavior. *Psychoneuroendocrinology, 19,* 723–749.

Leckman, J. F., Grice, D. E., Barr, L. C., de Vries, A. L. C., Martin, C., Cohen, D. J., Goodman, W. K., & Rasmussen, S. A. (in press). Tic-related vs. non-tic-related obsessive compulsive disorder. *Anxiety.*

Lenane, M. C., Swedo, S. E., Leonard, H., Pauls, D. L., Sceery, W., & Rapoport, J. (1990). Psychiatric disorders in first degree relatives of children and adolescents with obsessive-compulsive disorder. *Journal of the American Academy of Child and Adolescent Psychiatry, 29,* 407–412.

Leonard, H. L., Goldberger, E. L., Rapoport, J. L., Cheslow, D. L., & Swedo, S. E. (1990). Childhood rituals: Normal development or obsessive-compulsive symptoms. *Journal of the American Academy of Child and Adolescent Psychiatry, 29,* 17–23.

Leonard, H. L., Lenane, M. C., Swedo, S. E., Rettew, D. C., Gershon, E. S., & Rapoport, J. L. (1992). Tics and Tourette's disorder: A 2- to 7-year follow-up of 54 obsessive-compulsive children. *American Journal of Psychiatry, 149,* 1244–1251.

Leonard, H. L., Swedo, S. E., Lenane, M. C., Rettew, D. C., Hamburger, S. D., Bartko, J. J., & Rapoport, J. L. (1993). A 2- to 7-year follow-up study of 54 obsessive-compulsive children and adolescents. *Archives of General Psychiatry, 50,* 429–439.

Marans, S., Mayes, L. C., & Colonna, A. B. (1993). Psychoanalytic views of children's play. In A. J. Solnit, D. J. Cohen, & P. B. Neubauer (Eds.), *The many meanings of play: A psychoanalytic perspective* (pp. 9–28). New Haven, CT: Yale University Press.

Marks, I. M. (1987). *Fears, phobias, and rituals.* New York: Oxford University Press.

Martin, A., Pigott, T. A., Lalonde, F. M., Dalton, I., Dubbert, B., & Murphy, D. L. (1993). Lack of evidence for Huntington's disease-like cognitive dysfunction in obsessive-compulsive disorder. *Biological Psychiatry, 33,* 345–353.

Mavissakalian, M. R. (1979). Functional classification of obsessive compulsive phenomena. *Journal of Behavioral Assessment, 1,* 271–279.

Mavissakalian, M. R., Hamann, M. S., Haidar, S. A., & de Groot, C. M. (1993). DSM-III personality disorders in generalized anxiety, panic/agoraphobia, and obsessive-compulsive disorders. *Comprehensive Psychiatry, 34,* 243–248.

Mavissakalian, M. R., Hamann, M. S., & Jones, B. (1990). Correlates of DSM-III personality disorder in obsessive-compulsive children. *Comprehensive Psychiatry, 31,* 481–489.

Mavissakalian, M. R., Turner, F. M., & Michelson, L. (1985). Future directions in the assessment and treatment of obsessive compulsive disorder. In M. Mavissakalian, S. M. Turner, & L. Michelson (Eds.), *Obsessive compulsive disorder: Psychological and pharmacological treatments* (pp. 213–248). New York: Plenum.

McDougle, C. J., Goodman, W. K., Leckman, J. F., Barr, L. C., Heninger, G. R., & Price, L. H. (1993). The efficacy of fluvoxamine in obsessive compulsive disorder: Effects of comorbid chronic tic disorder. *Journal of Clinical Psychopharmacology, 13,* 354–358.

McDougle, C. J., Goodman, W. K., Leckman, J. F., Lee, N. C., Heninger, G. R., & Price, L. H. (1994). Haloperidol addition in fluvoxamine-refractory obsessive compulsive disorder: A double blind, placebo-controlled study in patients with and without tics. *Archives of General Psychiatry, 51,* 302–308.

McKeon, P., & Murray, R. (1987). Familial aspects of obsessive-compulsive neurosis. *British Journal of Psychiatry, 151,* 528–534.

McNally, R. J., Foa, E. B., & Donell, C. D. (1989). Memory bias for anxiety information in patients with panic disorder. *Cognition and Emotions, 3,* 27–44.

Meige, H., & Feindel, E. (1907). *Tics and their treatment* (S. A. K. Wilson, Trans.). New York: William Wood.

Model, J., Mountz, J., Curtis, G., & Greden, J. (1989). Neurophysiologic dysfunction in basal ganglia/limbic striatal and thalamocortical circuits as a pathogenetic mechanism of obsessive-compulsive disorder. *Journal of Neuropsychiatrica, 1,* 27–36.

Mowrer, O. H. (1960). *Learning theory and behavior.* New York: Wiley.

Nemiah, J. (1985). Obsessive compulsive neurosis. In A. Freedman, H. Kaplan, & B. Sadock (Eds.), *A comprehensive textbook of psychiatry* (pp. 1241–1255). Baltimore: Williams & Wilkins.

Neziroglu, F., Anemone, R., & Yaryura-Tobias, J. A. (1992). Onset of obsessive compulsive disorder in pregnancy. *American Journal of Psychiatry, 149,* 947–950.

Niler, E. R., & Beck, S. J. (1989). The relationship among guilt, dysphoria, anxiety, and obsessions in a normal population. *Behavior Research and Therapy, 27,* 213–220.

Nolen-Hoeksema, S. (1990). *Sex differences in depression.* Stanford, CA: Stanford University Press.

Nordahl, T. E., Benkelfat, C., Semple, W., Gross, M., King, A. C., & Cohen, R. M. (1989). Cerebral glucose metabolic rates in obsessive-compulsive disorder. *Neuropsychopharmacology, 2,* 23–28.

Okasha, A., Kamel, M., & Hassan, A. H. (1968). Preliminary psychiatric observations in Egypt. *American Journal of Psychiatry, 114,* 949–955.

Orvaschel, H., Thompson, W. D., Belanger, A., Prusoff, B. A., & Kidd, K. K. (1982). Comparison of the family history method to direct interview: Factors affecting the diagnosis of depression. *Journal of Affective Disorders, 4,* 49–59.

Otto, M. W. (1990). Neuropsychological approaches to obsessive-compulsive disorder. In M. A. Jenike, L. Baer, & W. E. Minichiello (Eds.), *Obsessive compulsive disorders: Theory and management* (pp. 132–148). Chicago: Yearbook Medical.

Ozonoff, S., Pennington, B. F., & Rogers, S. J. (1991). Executive function deficits in high-functioning autistic individuals: Relationship to theory of mind. *Journal of Child Psychology and Psychiatry, 32,* 1081–1105.

Parkinson, L., & Rachman, S. J. (1981). The nature of intrusive thoughts. *Advances in Behavior Research and Therapy, 3,* 101–110.

Pauls, D. L., Alsobrook, J. P., II, Goodman, W. K., Rasmussen, S., & Leckman, J. F. (in press). A family study of obsessive compulsive disorder. *American Journal of Psychiatry.*

Pauls, D. L., Leckman, J. F., & Cohen, D. J. (1994). Evidence against a genetic relationship between the Gilles de la Tourette syndrome and anxiety, depression, panic and phobic disorders. *British Journal of Psychiatry, 164,* 215–221.

Pauls, D. L., Raymond, C. L., & Robertson, M. M. (1991). The genetics of obsessive compulsive disorder. In Y. Zohar, T. Insel, & S. Rasmussen (Eds.), *Psychobiological aspects of OCD* (pp. 89–100). New York: Springer.

Peller, L. (1954). Libidinal phases, ego development and play. *Psychoanalytic Study of the Child, 10,* 178–199.

Peterson, C. (1978). Locus of control and belief in self-oriented superstitions. *Journal of Social Psychology, 105,* 305–306.

Peterson, C., & Seligman, M. E. P. (1984). Causal explanations as a risk factor for depression: Theory and evidence. *Psychological Review, 91,* 347–374.

Peterson, C., Seligman, M. E. P., & Vaillant, G. (1988). Pessimistic explanatory style is a risk factor for physical illness: A thirty-five-year longitudinal study. *Journal of Personality and Social Psychology, 55,* 23–27.

Piaget, J. (1962). *Play, dreams and imitation in childhood.* New York: Norton.

Pitman, R. K. (1987a). A cybernetic model of obsessive-compulsive psychopathology. *Comprehensive Psychiatry, 28,* 334–343.

Pitman, R. K. (1987b). Pierre Janet on obsessive-compulsive disorder (1903): Review and commentary. *Archives of General Psychiatry, 44,* 226–232.

Pitman, R. K. (1989). Animal models of compulsive behavior. *Biological Psychiatry, 26,* 189–198.

Pitman, R. K. (1991). Historical considerations. In J. Zohar, T. Insel, & S. Rasmussen (Eds.), *The psychobiology of obsessive-compulsive disorder* (pp. 1–12). New York: Springer.

Rachman, S. J. (1985). An overview of clinical and research issues in obsessive-compulsive disorders. In M. Mavissakalian, S. M. Turner, & L. Michelson (Eds.), *Obsessive-compulsive disorders: Psychological and pharmacological treatment* (pp. 1–47). New York: Plenum.

Rachman, S. J. (1992). Obsessions, responsibility and guilt. *Behavior Research and Therapy, 31,* 149–154.

Rachman, S. J., & de Silva, P. (1978). Abnormal and normal obsessions. *Behavior Research and Therapy, 16,* 233–248.

Rachman, S. J., & Hodgson, R. J. (1980). *Obsessions and compulsions.* Englewood Cliffs, NJ: Prentice-Hall.

Rapoport, J. L. (1986). Childhood obsessive compulsive disorder. *Journal of Child Psychology and Psychiatry, 27,* 289–295.

Rapoport, J. L., Elkins, R., Langer, D., Sceery, W., Buchsbaum, M., Gillin, J. C., Murphy, D., Zahn, T., Lake, R., Ludlow, C., & Mendelson, W. (1981). Childhood obsessive compulsive disorder. *American Journal of Psychiatry, 138,* 1545–1553.

Rapoport, J. L., Swedo, S. E., & Leonard, H. L. (1992). Childhood obsessive compulsive disorder. *Journal of Clinical Psychiatry, 53,* 11–16.

Rapoport, J. L., & Wise, S. P. (1988). Obsessive-compulsive disorder: Is it a basal ganglia dysfunction? *Psychopharmacological Bulletin, 24,* 380–384.

Rasmussen, S. A., & Eisen, J. L. (1991). Phenomenology of OCD: Clinical subtypes, heterogeneity and coexistence. In J. Zohar, T. Insel, & S. Rasmussen (Eds.), *The psychobiology of obsessive-compulsive disorder* (pp. 13–43). New York: Springer.

Rasmussen, S. A., & Tsuang, M. T. (1984). The epidemiology of obsessive-compulsive disorder. *Journal of Clinical Psychiatry, 45,* 450–457.

Rasmussen, S. A., & Tsuang, M. T. (1986). Clinical characteristics and family history in DSM-III obsessive-compulsive disorder. *American Journal of Psychiatry, 143,* 317–322.

Rehm, L. P., & Carter, A. S. (1990). Cognitive components of depression. In M. Lewis & S. M. Miller (Eds.), *Handbook of developmental psychopathology* (pp. 341–351). New York: Plenum.

Rettew, D. C., Swedo, S. E., Leonard, H. L., Lenane, M. C., & Rapoport, J. L. (1992). Obsessions and compulsions across time in 79 children and adolescents with obsessive compulsive disorder. *Journal of the American Academy of Child and Adolescent Psychiatry, 31,* 1050–1056.

Riddle, M. A., Scahill, L., King, R., Hardin, M. T., Towbin, K. E., Ort, S. I., Leckman, J. F., & Cohen, D. J. (1990). Obsessive compulsive disorder in children and adolescents: Phenomenology and family history. *Journal of the American Academy of Child and Adolescent Psychiatry, 29,* 766–772.

Robins, L. N., Helzer, J. E., Weissman, M. M., Orvaschel, H., Gruenberg, E., Burke, J. D., & Regier, D. A. (1984). Lifetime prevalence of specific psychiatric disorders in three sites. *Archives of General Psychiatry, 41,* 949–959.

Rosenbaum, J. F., Biederman, J., Gersten, M., Meminger, S. R., Herman, J. B., Kagan, J., Reznick, J. S., Snidman, N. (1990). Behavioral inhibition in children of parents with panic disorder and agoraphobia: A controlled study. *Archives of General Psychiatry, 45,* 463–470.

Rosenbaum, J. F., Biederman, J., Hirshfeld, D. R., Boduc, E. A., & Chaloff, J. (1991). Behavioral inhibition in children: A possible precursor to panic disorder or social phobia. *Journal of Clinical Psychiatry, 52* (Nov. Suppl.), 5–9.

Rosenberg, C. M. (1967). Familial aspects of obsessional neurosis. *British Journal of Psychiatry, 113,* 405–413.

Rumsey, J. M., & Hamburger, S. D. (1988). Neuropsychological findings in high-functioning autistic men with infantile autism, residual state. *Journal of Clinical and Experimental Neuropsychology, 10,* 201–221.

Rutter, M. (1989). Pathways from childhood to adult life. *Journal of Child Psychology and Psychiatry, 30,* 23–51.

Rutter, M., Tizard, J., & Whitmore, K. (1970). *Education, health and behavior.* London: Longmans.

Salkovskis, P. M., & Harrison, J. (1984). Abnormal and normal obsessions—a replication. *Behavior Research and Therapy, 22,* 549–552.

Seligman, M. E. P. (1975). *Helplessness: On depression, development, and death.* San Francisco: Freeman.

Senjo, M. (1989). Obsessive-compulsive disorder in people that abuse codeine. *Acta Psychiatrica Scandinavica, 79,* 619–620.

Sichel, D. A., Cohen, L. S., Dimmock, J. A., & Rosenbaum, J. F. (1993). Postpartum obsessive compulsive disorder: A case series. *Journal of Clinical Psychiatry, 54,* 156–159.

Sophian, C., & Wellman, H. M. (1983). Selective information use and perseveration in the search behavior of infants and young children. *Journal of Experimental Child Psychology, 35,* 369–390.

Sparenborg, S., & Gabriel, M. (1990). Neuronal encoding of conditional stimulus duration in the cigulate cortex and the limbic thalamus of rabbits. *Behavioral Neuroscience, 104,* 919–933.

Sparrow, S. S., Carter, A. S., Racusin, G. R., & Morris, R. (in press). Comprehensive psychological assessment: A lifespan developmental approach. In D. V. Cicchetti & D. J. Cohen (Eds.), *Manual of developmental psychopathology,* New York: Wiley.

Sroufe, L. A., & Rutter, M. (1984). The domain of developmental psychopathology. *Child Development, 55,* 17–29.

Straus, E. W. M. (1948). On obsession: A clinical and methodological study. *Nervous and Mental Disease Monographs, 73,* 1–124.

Sutherland, G., Newman, B., & Rachman, S. (1982). Experimental investigations of the relations between mood and intrusive unwanted cognitions. *British Journal of Medical Psychology, 55,* 127–138.

Swale, G., Hymas, N., Lees, A., & Frackowiak, R. (1991). Obsessional slowness: Functional studies with positron emission tomography. *Brain, 114,* 2191–2202.

Swedo, S. E., Leonard, H. L., Kruesi, M. J. P., Rettew, D. C., Listwak, S. J., Berrettini, W., Stipec, M., Hamburger, S., Gold, P. W., Potter, W. Z., & Rapoport, J. L. (1992). Cerebrospinal fluid neurochemistry in children and adolescents with obsessive-compulsive disorder. *Archives of General Psychiatry, 49,* 29–36.

Swedo, S. E., Pietrini, P., Leonard, H. L., Schapiro, M. B., Rettew, D. C., Goldberger, E. L., Rapoport, S. I., Rapoport, J. L., & Grady, C. L. (1992). Cerebral glucose metabolism in childhood-onset obsessive-compulsive disorder: Revisualization during pharmacotherapy. *Archives of General Psychiatry, 49,* 690–694.

Swedo, S. E., Rapoport, J. L., Leonard, H., Lenane, M., & Cheslow, D. (1989). Obsessive-compulsive disorder in children and adolescents. Clinical phenomenology of 70 consecutive cases. *Archives of General Psychiatry, 46,* 335–341.

Sweeney, P. D., Anderson, K., & Bailey, S. (1986). Attributional style in depression: A meta-analytic review. *Journal of Personality and Social Psychology, 50,* 974–991.

Thomsen, P. H., & Mikkelsen, H. U. (1993). Development of personality disorders in children and adolescents with obsessive-compulsive disorder: A 6- to 22-year follow-up study. *Acta Psychiatrica Scandinavica, 87,* 456–462.

Torgerson, S. (1983). Genetic factors in anxiety disorder. *Archives of General Psychiatry, 40,* 1085–1089.

Toro, J., Cervera, M., Osejo, E., & Salamero, M. (1992). Obsessive-compulsive disorder in childhood and adolescence: A clinical study. *Journal of Child Psychology and Psychiatry, 33,* 1025–1037.

Turner, S. M., Beidel, D. C., & Stanley, M. A. (1992). Are obsessional thoughts and worry different cognitive phenomena? *Clinical Psychology Review, 12,* 257–270.

Weiner, B., & Graham, S. (1984). An attributional approach to emotional development. In C. E. Izard, J. Kagan, & R. B. Zajonc (Eds.), *Emotions, cognitions, and behavior* (pp. 167–191). Cambridge, England: Cambridge University Press.

Weiner, B., & Handel, S. (1985). Anticipated emotional consequences of causal communications and reported communication strategy. *Developmental Psychology, 21,* 102–107.

Welner, A., Reich, T., Robins, E., Fishman, R., & Van Doren, T. (1976). Obsessive-compulsive neurosis: Record, follow-up and family studies: I. Inpatient record study. *Comprehensive Psychiatry, 17,* 527–539.

Welner, N., & Horowitz, M. (1975). Intrusive and repetitive thoughts after a depressing film: A pilot study. *Psychological Reports, 37,* 135–138.

Welsh, M. C., & Pennington, B. F. (1988). Assessing frontal lobe functioning in children: Views from developmental psychology. *Developmental Neuropsychology, 4,* 199–230.

Welsh, M. C., Pennington, B. F., & Groisser, D. B. (1991). A normative-developmental study of executive functioning: A window on prefrontal function in children. *Developmental Neuropsychology, 7,* 131–149.

Werner, H. (1957). The concept of development from a comparative and organismic point of view. In D. B. Harris (Ed.), *The concept of development* (pp. 125–148). Minneapolis: University of Minnesota Press.

Winslow, J. T., & Insel, T. R. (1991). Social status in pairs of squirrel monkeys determines the behavioural response to central oxytocin administration. *Journal of Neuroscience, 11,* 2032–2038.

Zielinski, C. V., Taylor, M. A., & Juzwin, K. R. (1991). Neuropsychological deficits in obsessive-compulsive disorder. *Neuropsychiatry, Neuropsychology, and Behavioral Neurology, 4,* 110–126.

Zigler, E., & Glick, M. (1986). *A developmental approach to adult psychopathology.* New York: Wiley.

Zohar, J., & Insel, T. R. (1987). Obsessive-compulsive disorder: Psychobiological approaches to diagnosis, treatment, and pathophysiology. *Biological Psychiatry, 2,* 667–687.

CHAPTER 18

The Development of Personality Disorders

THEODORE MILLON and ROGER D. DAVIS

Personality disorders are not disorders in the medical sense. Rather, they are reified constructs employed to represent varied styles or patterns in which the personality system functions *maladaptively* in relation to its environment.

This relational aspect is an important one, because it is an interactional conception of personality disorder: Normal persons exhibit flexibility in their interactions with their environment. Their responses or behaviors are appropriate to the given situation and over time. If person and environment are conceptualized as a dynamic system, then the evolution of the system through successive states must be subject to constraints that lie both in the person and in the environment. When environmental constraints dominate, the behavior of individuals tends to converge, regardless of their prepotent dispositions: Almost everyone stops when stop lights are red. When environmental constraints are few or not well-defined, there is opportunity for flexibility, novelty, and the expression of individual differences in behavior.

However, if the person-environment interaction is pervasively constrained by personological factors, the variability of an individual's behavior is no longer appropriate and proportional to what the environment requires. The interaction is driven by the person. When the alternative strategies employed to achieve goals, relate to others, and cope with stress are few in number and rigidly practiced (*adaptive inflexibility*), when habitual perceptions, needs, and behaviors perpetuate and intensify preexisting difficulties (*vicious circles*), and when the person tends to lack resilience under conditions of stress (*tenuous stability*), we speak of a clinically interesting personality pattern. Borrowing terminology from the medical model, we may even say that a personality "disorder" exists, if we keep in mind that the disorder is an interactional aberration with degrees, shading gently from normality to clinicality, and has at a latent level no single underlying cause or disease pathogen, but instead must be as multidetermined as the personality system itself is multifaceted.

For pedagogical purposes, the multifaceted personality system can be heuristically decomposed into various domains, as given in Table 18.1. While these facilitate clinical investigation and experimental research, no such division exists in reality. Personality development represents the complex interplay of elements within and across each of these domains. Not only is there an interaction between person and environment; there are interactions and complex feedback loops operating within the person as well at levels of organization both biological and psychological. It is the

essentially *stochastic* character of these interactions, together with the person's own unique history, that binds the individual together as an organic whole with its own unique coloration we call personality. Our guiding metaphor, then, is organismic and dynamic, rather than mechanistic and reductionistic. (See Cicchetti, 1990, for an interesting historical perspective on these paradigms.)

Unfortunately, this very organismic-dynamic metaphor leads to a curious paradox between what is desired of an exposition of personality development and what is possible. Because all scientific theories are to some extent simplifications of reality, the map rather than the territory, all theories involve trade-offs between scope and precision. Most modern developmental theories are organismic and contextual in character. By embracing a multidomain organismic-contextual model we aspire to *completely* explain personality disorder development as a totality. However, we must simultaneously accept the impossibility of any such explanation given the stochastic character of the interactions espoused by the model we have assumed. Despite our aspirations, a certain amount of ontological imprecision is built into the guiding metaphor. The term ontological is aptly used, since its posits the existence or reality of experimental error, that is, that the interaction of personality variables is very often synergistic or nonlinear rather than additive.

Certain conceptual gimmicks could be used to recover this imprecision or to present an illusion of precision. We might give an exposition of personality disorder development from a "one-

TABLE 18.1 Functional and Structural Domains of Personality

Functional Domains	Structural Domains
Behavioral Level	
Expressive acts	
Interpersonal conduct	
Phenomenological Level	
Cognitive style	Object representations
	Self-image
Intrapsychic Level	
Regulatory mechanisms	Morphologic organization
Biophysical Level	
	Mood/temperament

domain" perspective, whether cognitive, psychodynamic, or behavioral. Such explanations might increase the precision of their derived theses, but this feat would be accomplished only by denying essential aspects of the whole person. Such reductionism with respect to content is incommensurate with the guiding metaphor, that of the total organism. Thus, while any one of these personologic domains could be abstracted from the whole in order to give an exposition of personality disorder development from a particular and narrow perspective, this would not do justice to a "pathology" that "pervades" the entire matrix of the person.

Accordingly, interaction and continuity are the major themes of this chapter. The discussion stresses the fact that numerous biogenic and psychogenic determinants covary to shape personality disorders, the relative weights of each varying as a function of time and circumstance. Further, this interaction of influences persists over time. The course of later characteristics is related intrinsically to earlier events; individual history itself is a constraint on future development. Personality disorder development must be viewed, therefore, as a process in which organismic and environmental forces display not only a mutuality and circularity of influence, but also an orderly and sequential continuity throughout the life of the individual.

For pedagogical purposes, it is necessary to separate biogenic from psychogenic factors as influences in personality disorder development; as noted, this bifurcation does not exist in reality. Biological and experiential determinants combine in an inextricable interplay throughout life. Thus, constitutional dispositions not only shape the character of experience but also are themselves modified through constant transactions with the environment. This sequence of biogenic-psychogenic interaction creates a never-ending spiral; each step in the interplay builds upon prior interactions and creates, in turn, new potentials and constraints for future reactivity and experience. There are no unidirectional effects in development; it is a multideterminant transaction in which unique biogenic potentials and distinctive psychogenic influences mold each other in reciprocal and successively more intricate ways. The circular feedback and the serially unfolding character of the developmental process defy simplification, and must constantly be kept in mind when analyzing the background of personality disorders.

BIOLOGICAL INFLUENCES

That characteristics of anatomic morphology, endocrine physiology, and brain chemistry would not be instrumental in shaping the development of personality is inconceivable. Biological scientists know that the central nervous system cannot be viewed as a simple and faithful follower of what is fed into it from the environment; not only does it maintain a rhythmic activity of its own, it also plays an active role in regulating sensitivity and controlling the amplitude of what is picked up by peripheral organs. Unlike a machine, which passively responds to external stimulation, the brain has a directing function that determines substantially what, when, and how events will be experienced. Each individual's nervous system selects, transforms, and registers objective events in accord with its distinctive biological characteristics.

Unusual sensitivities in this delicate orienting system can lead to marked distortions in perception and behavior. Any disturbance which produces a breakdown in the smooth integration of functions, or a failure to retrieve previously stored information, is likely to create chaos and pathology. Normal psychological functioning depends on the integrity of certain key areas of biological structure, and any impairment of this substrate will result in disturbed thought, emotion, and behavior. It must be carefully noted, however, that although biogenic dysfunctions or defects may produce the basic break from normality, psychological and social determinants almost invariably shape the *form* of its expression. Acceptance of the role of biogenic influences, therefore, does *not* negate the role of social experience and learning (Eysenck, 1967; Meehl, 1962, 1990; Millon, 1981, 1990).

Although the exact mechanisms by which biological functions undergird personality disorders remain obscure, the belief that biogenic factors are intimately involved is not new. Scientists have been gathering data for decades, applying a wide variety of research methods across a broad spectrum of biophysical functions. The number of techniques used and the variety of variables studied are legion. These variables often are different avenues for exploring the same basic hypotheses. For example, researchers focusing on biochemical dysfunctions often assume that these dysfunctions result from genetic error. However, the methods they employ and the data they produce are quite different from those of researchers who approach the role of heredity through research comparing monozygotic with dizygotic twins. With this in mind, this chapter proceeds to subdivide the subject of development into several arbitrary (but traditional) compartments, beginning with heredity.

Heredity

The role of heredity is usually inferred from evidence based on correlations among traits in members of the same family. Most psychopathologists admit that heredity must play a role in personality disorder development, but they insist that genetic dispositions are modified substantially by the operation of environmental factors. This view states that heredity operates not as a fixed constant but as a disposition that takes different forms depending on the circumstances of an individual's upbringing. Hereditary theorists may take a more inflexible position, referring to a body of data that implicate genetic factors in a wide range of psychopathologies. Although they are likely to agree that variations in these disorders may be produced by environmental conditions, they are equally likely to assert that these are merely superficial influences that cannot prevent the individual from succumbing to his or her hereditary inclination. The overall evidence seems to suggest that genetic factors serve as predispositions to certain traits, but, with few exceptions, similarly affected individuals display important differences in their symptoms and developmental histories. Moreover, genetically disposed disorders can be aided by psychological therapies, and similar symptomatologies often arise without such genetic dispositions.

A number of theorists have suggested that the milder pathologies, such as personality disorders, represent undeveloped or minimally expressed defective genes; for example, the schizoid personality may possess a schizophrenic genotype, but in this case the defective gene is weakened by the operation of beneficial modifying genes or favorable environmental experiences (Meehl, 1990). An alternate explanation might be formulated in terms of polygenic action; polygenes have minute, quantitatively similar, and cumulative effects. Thus, a continuum of increasing pathological severity can be accounted for by the cumulative effects of a large number of minor genes acting upon the same trait.

The idea that psychopathological syndromes comprise well-circumscribed disease entities is an attractive assumption for those who seek a Mendelian or single-gene model of inheritance. Recent thinking forces us to question the validity of this approach to nosology and to the relevance of Mendelian genetic action. Defects in the infinitely complex central nervous system can arise from innumerable genetic anomalies (Plomin, 1990). Moreover, even convinced geneticists make reference to the notion of phenocopies, a concept signifying that characteristics usually traceable to genetic action can be simulated by environmental factors; thus, overtly identical forms of pathology may arise from either genetic or environmental sources. As a consequence, the clinical picture of a disorder may give no clue to its origins since similar appearances do not necessarily signify similar etiologies. To complicate matters further, different genes vary in their responsiveness to environmental influences; some produce uniform effects under all environmental conditions, whereas others can be entirely suppressed in certain environments (Plomin, DeFries, & McClearn, 1990). Moreover, it appears that genes have their effects at particular times of maturation and that their interaction with environmental conditions is minimal both before and after these periods.

Despite these ambiguities and complications, there can be little question that genetic factors do play some dispositional role in shaping the morphological and biochemical substrate of certain traits. However, these factors are by no means necessary to the development of personality pathology, nor are they likely to be sufficient in themselves to elicit pathological behaviors. They may serve, however, as a physiological base that makes the person susceptible to dysfunction under stress or inclined to learn behaviors which prove socially troublesome.

Temperament

Each child enters the world with a distinctive pattern of dispositions and sensitivities. Nurses know that infants differ from the moment they are born, and perceptive parents notice distinct differences in their successive offspring. Some infants suck vigorously; others seem indifferent and hold the nipple feebly. Some infants have a regular cycle of hunger, elimination, and sleep, whereas others vary unpredictably (Michelsson, Rinne, & Paajanen, 1990). Some twist fitfully in their sleep, while others lie peacefully awake in hectic surroundings. Some are robust and energetic; others seem tense and cranky.

The question that must be posed, however, is not whether children differ temperamentally but whether a particular sequence of subsequent life experiences will result as a consequence of these differences; childhood temperament would be of little significance if it did not constrain subsequent patterns

of functioning. In this regard the clinician must ask whether the child's characteristics evoke distinctive reactions from his or her parents and whether these reactions have a beneficial or a detrimental effect upon the child's development (Kagan, Reznick, & Snidman, 1989; Maccoby & Martin, 1983). Rather than limit attention to the traditional question of what effect the environment has upon the child, the focus might be changed to ask what effect the child has on the environment and what are the consequences on the child's development.

Patterns of behavior observed in the first few months of life are apparently more biogenic rather than psychogenic origin. Some researchers speak of these patterns as "primary" because they are displayed before postnatal experience can fully account for them. Investigators have found that infants show a consistent pattern of autonomic system reactivity; others have reported stable differences on such biological measures as sensory threshold, quality and intensity of emotional tone, and electroencephalographic waves. Because the pertinence of psychophysiological differences to later personality is unknown, investigators have turned attention to the relationship between observable behavior and later development.

The studies of a number of research groups (Escalona, 1968; Escalona & Heider, 1959; Escalona & Leitch, 1953; Murphy & Moriarty, 1976; Thomas & Chess, 1977; Thomas, Chess, & Birch, 1963, 1968) have been especially fruitful in this regard. Their work has contributed not only to an understanding of personality development in general but also to the development of personality pathology in particular. Several behavioral dimensions were found to differentiate the temperament patterns of infants. Children differ in the regularity of their biological functions, including autonomic reactivity, gauged by initial responses to new situations; sensory alertness to stimuli and in adaptability to change; characteristic moods; and in intensities of response, distractibility, and persistence. Although early patterns were modified only slightly from infancy to childhood, this continuity could not be attributed entirely to the persistence of innate endowments. Subsequent experiences served to reinforce the characteristics that were displayed in early life (Kagan, 1989). This occurred in great measure because the infant's initial behaviors transformed the environment in ways that intensified and accentuated initial behaviors.

Theorists have often viewed disorders to be the result of experiences that individuals have no part in producing themselves (Jones & Raag, 1989; Zanolli, Saudargas, & Twardosz, 1990). This is a simplification of a complex interaction (Sroufe & Waters, 1976). Each infant possesses a biologically based pattern of sensitivities and dispositions that shape the nature of his or her experiences. The interaction of biological dispositions and environmental experience is not a readily disentangled web but an intricate feedback system of crisscrossing influences. Two components of this process are elaborated because of their pertinence to development.

The biological dispositions of the maturing child are important because they strengthen the probability that certain traits will become prepotent (Bates, 1980, 1987; Thomas, Chess, & Korn, 1982). For example, highly active and responsive children relate to and rapidly acquire knowledge about events and persons in their environment. Their zest and energy may lead them to experience personal gratification quickly or, conversely, their lively and exploratory behavior may result in painful frustrations if they run repetitively into insuperable barriers. Unable to fulfill their activity needs, they may strike out in erratic and maladaptive ways. Moreover, temperament also influences the expression of psychological variables such as attachment (Belsky & Rovine, 1987).

Organismic action in passive children is shaped also by their biological constitution. Ill-disposed to deal with their environment assertively and disinclined to discharge their tensions physically, they may learn to avoid conflicts and step aside when difficulties arise. They may be less likely to develop guilt feelings about misbehavior than active youngsters, who more frequently get into trouble and receive punishment, and who are therefore inclined to develop aggressive feelings toward others. Passive youngsters may also deprive themselves of rewarding experiences, feel "left out of things," and depend on others to protect them from events they feel ill-equipped to handle on their own.

Interpersonal Reciprocity

Previously we spoke of personality as a system. However, a systems notion need not be confined to operations that take place within the organism. Interpersonal theorists often speak of dyads and triads as systems of reciprocal influence. Childhood temperament evokes counterreactions from others that confirm and accentuate initial temperamental dispositions (Papousek & Papousek, 1975). Biological moods and activity levels shape not only the child's own behaviors but also those of the child's parents. If the infant's disposition is cheerful and adaptable and care is easy, the mother will quickly display a positive reciprocal attitude (Osofsky & Danzger, 1974). Conversely, if the child is tense, or if his or her care is difficult and time-consuming, the mother may react with dismay, fatigue, or hostility. Thourgh this distinctive behavioral disposition, the child elicits parental reactions that reinforce the initial pattern. Innate dispositions can be reversed by strong environmental pressures. A cheerful outlook can be crushed by parental contempt and ridicule. Conversely, shy and reticent children may become more self-confident in a thoroughly encouraging family atmosphere (Smith & Pederson, 1988).

Although the idea that biophysical aspects constrain future development is easily understood, it must also be remembered that not all features of an individual's constitution are activated at the moment of birth. Individuals mature at different rates. Potentials may unfold only gradually as maturation progresses. Thus, some biologically-rooted influences may not emerge until the youngster is well into adolescence, and it is not inconceivable that these late-blooming patterns may supplant those displayed earlier.

A crucial determinant of whether a particular temperament will lead to personality pathology appears to be parental acceptance of the child's individuality. Parents who accept their child's temperament, and then modify their practices accordingly, can deter what might otherwise become pathological. On the other hand, if parents experience daily feelings of failure, frustration, anger, and guilt, regardless of the child's disposition, they are likely to contribute to a progressive worsening of the child's adjustment. These comments point once more to the fact that biogenic and psychogenic factors interact in complex ways.

Biophysical Individuality

The general role that neurological lesions and physiochemical imbalances play in producing pathology can be grasped with only a minimal understanding of the structural organization and functional character of the brain. However, it is important that naive misconceptions be avoided. Among these is the belief that psychological functions can be localized in neurohormonal depots or precise regions of the brain. Psychological processes such as thought, behavior, and emotion derive from complex and circular feedback properties of brain activity. Unless the awesomely intricate connections within the brain that subserve these psychological functions are recognized, the result will be simplistic propositions that clinical or personality traits can arise as a consequence of specific chemical imbalances or focal lesions (Purves & Lichtman, 1985). Psychological concepts such as emotion, behavior, and thought represent diverse and complex processes that are grouped together by theorists and researchers as a means of simplifying their observations. These conceptual labels must not be confused with tangible events and properties within the brain. Certain regions are more involved in particular psychological functions than others, but it is clear that higher processes are a product of brain area interactions. For example, the frontal lobes of the cortex orchestrate a dynamic pattern of impulses by selectively enhancing the sensitivity of receptors, comparing impulses arising in other brain spheres and guiding them along myriad arrangements and sequences. In this regnant function it facilitates or inhibits a wide range of psychological functions.

The point to be emphasized is that clinical signs and symptoms cannot be conceived as localized or fixed to one or another sphere of the brain. Rather, they arise from a network of complex interactions and feedbacks (Purves & Lichtman, 1985). We might say that all stimuli, whether generated externally or internally, follow long chains of reverberating circuits that modulate a wide range of activities. Psychological traits and processes must be conceived, therefore, as the product of a widespread and self-regulating pattern of interneuronal stimulation. If we keep in mind the intricate neural interdependencies underlying these functions, we should avoid falling prey to the error of interpretive simplification.

Nevertheless, if the above caveats are kept in mind, certain broad hypotheses seem tenable. Possessing more or less of the interactive neurological substrates for a particular function, for example, such as pleasure or pain, can markedly influence the character of experience and the course of learning and development. Quite evidently, the role of neuroanatomical structures in psychopathology is not limited to problems of tissue defect or damage. Natural interindividual differences in structural anatomy and organization can result in a wide continuum of relevant psychological effects (Davidson, 1986). If we recognize the network of neural structures that are upset by a specific lesion, and add the tremendous individual differences in brain morphology, the difficulties involved in tracing the role of a neurological disturbance become apparent. If the technical skills required to assess the psychological consequences of a specific brain lesion are difficult, one can only begin to imagine the staggering task of determining the psychological correlates of natural anatomic differences.

EARLY DEVELOPMENT

The previous section stressed the view that biological functions play an active role in regulating what, when, and how events will be experienced; the nervous and endocrine systems do not passively accept what is fed into them. Moreover, although behavior pathology may be activated by biogenic abnormalities, the mere specification of a biogenic constraint is not sufficient for etiologic analysis. Even where clear-cut biogenic factors can be identified, it is necessary to trace the sequence of experiences that transform them into manifest forms of pathology (Davidson, 1986). Some persons with biological defects function effectively, whereas other, similarly afflicted individuals succumb to maladaptation. The biological defect is necessary, but not sufficient to account for such divergences. Pathological behaviors that are precipitated initially by biological abnormalities are not simple products of these defects; rather, they emerge through a complex sequence of interactions that include environmental experiences and reciprocal interpersonal relationships. Such interactions begin at conception and continue throughout life. Personality patterns unfold as new maturations interweave with new environmental encounters. In time, a distinctive hierarchy of traits stabilizes that remains relatively consistent throughout life.

Maturational Plasticity

The interaction between biological and psychological factors is not unidirectional such that biological determinants always precede and influence the development of behavior. The direction of effects may be reversed. Deeply embedded behavior patterns may arise as a consequence of psychological experiences that affect developing biological structures so profoundly as to transform them into something substantially different from what they might otherwise have been. Circumstances that exert so profound an effect are usually those experienced during infancy and early childhood, a view that can be traced to the seminal writings of Freud at the turn of the century. The observations of ethologists on the consequences of early stimulation on adult animal behaviors add substantial evidence for this position (Rakic, 1985, 1988). Experimental work on early developmental periods also has shown that environmental stimulation is crucial to the maturation of psychological functions. In essence, psychological capacities fail to develop fully if their biological substrates are subjected to impoverished stimulation; conversely, these capacities may develop to an excessive degree as a consequence of enriched stimulation (Lipton & Kater, 1989).

Maturation refers to the intricate sequence of ontogenetic development in which initially inchoate bodily structures progressively unfold into specific functional units. Early stages of differentiation precede and overlap with more advanced states such that simpler and more diffuse structures interweave and connect into a complex and integrated network of functions displayed ultimately in the adult organism. It was once believed that the course of maturation from—diffusion to differentiation to integration—arose exclusively from inexorable forces within the genes. Maturation was thought to evolve according to a preset timetable that unfolded independently of environmental conditions. This view is no longer tenable. Maturation follows an orderly progression, but the developmental sequence and level of ultimate biological function are substantially dependent on environmental stimuli and nutritional supplies. Thus, maturation does not progress in a fixed course leading to a predetermined level but is subject to numerous variations that reflect the character of environmental experience.

The answer to why early experiences are more central to development than later experiences derives in part from the fact that peak periods of structural maturation occur from prenatal stages through the first years of postnatal life. For example, in the nervous system, prenatal deficiencies in nutrition will retard the differentiation of gross tissue into separable neural cells; early postnatal deficiencies will deter the proliferation of neural collaterals and their integration. However, deficiencies arising later in life will have but little effect on the development of these neural structures.

Organismic Nutrition

Nutrition should be viewed more broadly than is commonly done in order to understand biological maturation. Nutrition includes not only obvious components, such as food, but additionally what Rapaport has termed "stimulus nutriment" (1958). This concept suggests that the impingement of environmental and psychological stimuli upon the maturing organism has a direct bearing on the chemical composition, ultimate size, and patterns of neural branching within the brain (Lipton & Kater, 1989; Purves & Lichtman, 1985).

The belief that the maturing organism requires periodic psychological nutriments for proper development has led some to suggest that the organism actively seeks an optimum level of stimulation. Thus, just as the infant cries out in search of food when deprived or wails in response to pain, so too may it engage in behaviors that provide it with psychosensory stimulation requisite to maturation (Butler & Rice, 1963; Murphy, 1947). Although infants are restricted largely to stimulation supplied by others, they often engage in what appear to be random exercises that, in effect, furnish them with feedback experiences. In the first months of life, infants can track auditory and visual stimuli; as they mature further, they grasp incidental objects and then mouth and fondle them. Furthermore, the young of all species display more exploratory and frolicsome behavior than adults. These seemingly "functionless" play activities are not functionless at all; they may be essential to growth, a means of self-stimulation indispensable to the maturation and maintenance of biological capacities (Ainsworth, Blehar, Waters, & Wall, 1978; Bowlby, 1969/1982; Bretherton, 1985; Volkmar & Provence, 1990). In sum, unless certain chemicals and structures are activated by environmental stimulation, the biological substrate for a variety of psychological functions may be impaired irrevocably. In turn, deficiencies or abnormalities in functions that normally mature in early life set the stage for progressive constraints on later functioning.

What evidence is there that serious consequences may result from an inadequate supply of early psychological and psychosensory stimulation?

Numerous investigators (e.g., Beach & Jaynes, 1954; Killackey, 1990; Melzack, 1965; Rakic, 1985, 1988; Scott, 1968; Thompson & Schaefer, 1961) have shown that an impoverished early environment results in permanent adaptational difficulties. For example, primates reared in isolation tend to be deficient in traits such as emotionality, activity level, social behavior, curiosity, and learning ability. As adult organisms they possess a reduced capacity to cope with their environments, to discriminate essentials, to devise strategies and manage stress. Comparable results are found among humans. Children reared under unusually severe restrictions, such as in orphanages, evidence deficits in social awareness and reactivity, are impulsive and susceptible to sensorimotor dysfunctions, and display a generally low resistance to stress and disease. These early difficulties have double-barreled effects. Not only is the child hampered by specific deficiencies, but each of them yields to progressive and long-range consequences in that they retard the development of more complex capacities (Ainsworth et al., 1978; Bowlby, 1960; Bretherton, 1985; Volkmar & Provence, 1990).

Conversely, intense levels of early stimulation also appear to have effects, at least in animals. Several investigators have demonstrated that enriched environments in early life resulted in measurable changes in brain chemistry and brain weight. Others have found that early stimulation accelerated the maturation of the pituitaryadrenal system, whereas equivalent later stimulation was ineffective. On the behavioral level, enriched environments in animals enhance problem-solving abilities and the capacity to withstand stress.

More interesting, however, is the possibility that some kinds of overstimulation may produce detrimental effects. Accordingly, excess stimulation would result in overdevelopments in biological substrates that are disruptive to effective psychological functioning. Just as excess food leads to obesity and physical ill health, so too may the psychostimulation of certain neural substrates, such as those subserving emotional reactivity, dispose the organism to overreact to social situations. Thus, when schemas which subserve problematic personality traits become prepotent, they may disrupt what would otherwise be a more balanced pattern of functioning.

EVOLUTIONARY-NEUROPSYCHOLOGICAL STAGES

Does the timing of the specific environmental events have any bearing on their effect? The concept of sensitive periods of development states that there are limited time periods during which particular stimuli are necessary for the full maturation of an organism, after which they will have minimal or no effects. Without the requisite stimulation, the organism will suffer various maldevelopments which are irremediable and cannot be compensated for at a later date.

Embryological research suggests that the effects of environmental stimuli upon morphological structure are most pronounced when tissue growth is rapid (Killackey, 1990; Rakic, 1985, 1988). The mechanisms that account for the special interaction between stimulation and periods of rapid neural growth are as yet unclear. Psychological stimulation itself promotes a proliferation of neural collaterals, an effect most pronounced when growth potential is greatest. Moreover, early psychological stimulation creates selective growth so that certain collaterals establish

particular interneuronal connections to the exclusion of others. In behavioral terms: Once these connections are biologically embedded, the first sets of stimuli that traverse them, especially if pervasive, appear to preempt the circuit, thereby decreasing the chance that subsequent stimuli will co-opt the circuit for other effects. In cognitive terms: Once schemas are in place for perceiving objective events in a particular way, these schemas co-opt future interpretations of similar events.

Numerous theorists have proposed, either by intention or inadvertently, developmental schemas based on a concept of sensitive periods. Among these are Heinz Werner (1940), Jean Piaget (1952), and both Sigmund Freud (1908) and Erik Erikson (1950). None, however, have presented their notions in terms of evolutionary-neuropsychological growth stages, although G. Stanley Hall (1916) sought to formulate a developmental theory of "recapitulation" anchored to Darwin's model. Although such compound terminology may seem formidable, it is intended to communicate first the fact that personological developmental constraints derive from the history of human adaptation, and second that the ultimate instantiation of these constraints lies in universal evolutionary principles, whether they be expressed in personality traits, cognitive schemas, or sociocultural customs (Wilson, 1978).

Evolutionary Phases

Broadly speaking, there are four "stages" that an individual human organism must pass through and a parallel set of four "tasks" that must be fulfilled to perform adequately in life. The first three pairs of these stages and tasks, and in part the fourth as well, are shared by lower species and may be thought of as recapitulating four phases of *evolution* (Millon, 1990). Each stage and task corresponds to one of the four evolutionary phases: Existence, Adaptation, Replication, and Abstraction. Polarities, that is, contrasting functional directions, representing the first three of these phases (pleasure-pain, passive-active, other-self) have been used to construct a theoretically anchored classification of personality styles and disorders, such as described in this text. Such biopolar or dimensional schemes are almost universally present throughout the literature's of mankind, as well as in psychology-at-large (Millon, 1990). The earliest may be traced to ancient Eastern religions, most notably the Chinese *I Ching* texts and the Hebrew *Kabala*.

In the life of the individual organism, each evolutionary phase is recapitulated and expressed ontogenetically; that is, each individual organism moves through developmental stages which have functional goals related to their respective phases of evolution. Within each stage, every individual acquires personologic dispositions representing a balance or predilection toward one of the two polarity inclinations; which inclination emerges as dominant over time results from the inextricable and reciprocal interplay of intraorganismic and extraorganismic factors. Thus, during early infancy, the primary organismic function is to "continue to exist." Here, evolution has supplied mechanisms which orient the infant toward life-enhancing environments (pleasure) and away from life-threatening ones (pain).

The expression of traits or dispositions acquired in early stages of development may have their expression transformed as later faculties or dispositions develop (Millon, 1969). Temperament is perhaps a classic example. An individual with an active temperament may develop, contingent on contextual factors, into an avoidant or an antisocial personality. The transformation of earlier temperamental characteristics takes the form of what we will call "personological bifurcations." Thus, if the individual is inclined toward a passive orientation and later learns to be self-directed, a narcissistic style ensues. But if the individual possesses an active orientation and later learns to be self-directed, an antisocial style ensues. Thus, early developing dispositions may undergo "vicissitudes," whereby their meaning in the context of the whole organism is subsequently re-formed into more complex personality trait configurations.

As previously noted, the authors believe that the development of personality disorders should be organized in terms of fundamental personological axes embedded in evolutionary theory. These are discussed next.

Phase 1: Existence

The first phase, existence, concerns the survival of integrative phenomena, whether a nuclear particle, virus, or human being, against the forces of entropic decompensation. Evolutionary mechanisms associated with this stage relate to the processes of *life-enhancement* and *life-preservation*. The former are concerned with orienting individuals toward improving the quality of life; the latter with orienting individuals away from actions or environments that decrease the quality of life, or even jeopardize existence itself. These two superordinate processes may be called *existential aims*. At the highest level of abstraction such mechanisms form, phenomenologically or metaphorically, a pleasure-pain polarity. Most humans exhibit both processes, those oriented toward enhancing pleasure and avoiding pain. Some individuals, however, appear to be conflicted in regard to existential aims (e.g., the sadistic), while others possess deficits in such aims (e.g., the schizoid). In terms of evolutionary-neuropsychological stages (Millon, 1969, 1981, 1990), orientations on the pleasure-pain polarity are set during a "sensory-attachment" developmental stage, the purpose of which is to further mature and selectively refine and focus the largely innate ability to discriminate between pain and pleasure signals.

Phase 2: Adaptation

Everything which exists, exists in an environment. To come into existence as a surviving particle or living creature is but an initial phase. Once an integrated structure exists, it must maintain its existence through exchanges of energy and information with its environment. This second evolutionary phase relates to what is termed the modes of adaptation; it also is framed as a two-part polarity: a passive orientation, that is, to be *ecologically accommodating* in one's environmental niche, versus an active orientation, that is, to be *ecologically modifying* and to intervene in or to alter one's surrounds. These *modes of adaptation* differ from the first phase of evolution, in that they relate to how that which has come to exist, endures. In terms of neuropsychological development, this polarity is ontogenetically expressed as the "sensorimotor-autonomy stage," during which the child typically progresses from an earlier, relatively passive style of accommodation to a relatively active style of modifying his or her physical and social environment.

The accommodating-modifying polarity necessarily derives from an expansion of the systems concept. Whereas in the Existence phase the system is seen as being mainly intraorganismic in character, the Adaptation phase expands the systems concept to its logical progression, from person to person-in-context. Some individuals, those of an active-orientation, operate as genuine agencies, tending to modify their environments according to their desires. For these individuals, an active-organism model is appropriate. Other persons, however, seek to accommodate to whatever is offered, or, rather than work to change what exists, seek out new, more hospitable venues when current ones become problematic. For these individuals, a passive-organism model is appropriate.

Phase 3: Replication

Although organisms may be well-adapted to their environments, the existence of any life-form is time-limited. To circumvent this limitation, organisms exhibit patterns of the third polarity, *replicatory strategies,* by which they leave progeny. These strategies relate to what biologists have referred to as an *r-* or *self-*propagating strategy, at one polar extreme, and a *K-* or *other*-nurturing strategy at the second extreme. Psychologically, the former is disposed toward individually-oriented actions which are perceived by others as egotistic, insensitive, inconsiderate, and uncaring; while the latter is disposed toward nurturant-oriented actions which are seen as affiliative, intimate, protective, and solicitous (Gilligan, 1981; Rushton, 1985; Wilson, 1978). Like pleasure-pain, the self-other polarity is not unidimensional. Whereas most humans exhibit a reasonable balance between the two polar extremes, some personality disorders are quite conflicted on this polarity, as are the compulsive and negativistic personalities. In terms of a neuropsychological growth stages, an individual's orientation toward self and others evolves largely during the "pubertal-gender identity" stage.

As with the passive-active polarity, the self-other bipolarity necessarily derives from an expansion of the systems concept. Whereas with the adaptation phase the system was seen as existing within an environment, here the system is seen as evolving over time. As before, the goal of the organism is its survival or continuance. When expressed across time, however, survival means reproducing, and strategies for doing so.

Phase 4: Abstraction

The reflective capacity to transcend the immediate and concrete, to interrelate and synthesize diversity, to represent events and processes symbolically, to weigh, reason and anticipate, each signifies a quantum leap in evolution's potential for change and adaptation (Millon, 1990). Emancipated from the real and present, unanticipated possibilities and novel constructions may routinely be created by various styles of abstract processing. It is these capacities that are represented in the neuropsychological stage of "intracortical-integration."

The capacity to sort and to recompose, to coordinate and to arrange the symbolic representations of experience into new configurations is, in certain ways, analogous to the random processes of recombinant replication, though they are more focused and intentional: to extend this rhetorical liberty, genetic replication represents the recombinant mechanism underlying the adaptive progression of phylogeny, whereas abstraction represents the recombinant mechanism underlying the cognitive progression of ontogeny. The uses of replication are limited, constrained by the finite potentials inherent in parental genes. In contrast, experiences, internalized and recombined, through cognitive processes are infinite. Over one lifetime, innumerable events of a random, logical or irrational character transpire, construed and reformulated time and again, some of which proving more, and others less adaptive than their originating circumstances may have called forth. Whereas the actions of most subhuman species derive from successfully evolved genetic programs, activating behaviors of a relatively fixed nature suitable for a modest range of environmental settings, the capabilities of both implicit and intentional abstraction give rise to adaptive competencies that are suited to radically divergent ecologic circumstances, circumstances which themselves may be the result of far-reaching acts of symbolic and technologic creativity.

The abstract mind may mirror outer realities, but reconstructs them in the process, reflectively transforming them into subjective modes of phenomenologic reality, rendering external events subject to individualistic designs. Every act of apprehension is transformed by processes of abstract symbolism. Not only are internal and external images emancipated from direct sensory and imaginal realities, allowing them to become entities, but contemporaneous time also loses its immediacy and impact, becoming as much a construction as a substance. Cognitive abstractions bring the past effectively into the present, and their power of anticipation brings the future into the present, as well. With past and future embedded in the here and now, humans can encompass, at once, not only the totality of our cosmos, but its origins and nature, its evolution, and how they have come to pass. Most impressive of all are the many visions humans have of life's indeterminate future, where no reality as yet exists.

Comment

Because any classification system is a simplification of nature, the most important aspect of a taxonomy is where the boundaries are drawn. The authors believe their evolutionary systems conception, linked to fundamental stages of development, provides the most secure foundation for dissecting the personologic sphere. Accordingly, and in contrast to earlier formulations (e.g., Erikson, Freud, Piaget), it seems more reasonable to us to construct a developmental model on the basis of evolutionary phases and their related neuropsychological stages and tasks, rather than on ones oriented to psychosexual or cognitive processes and periods. As noted, part-function models such as the latter two fail to encompass the entire person, are unconnected to the deeper laws of evolutionary progression and, hence, cannot form either a comprehensive or a firm grounding for a modern developmental theory.

A qualification should be noted before describing the developmental stages derived from the model. First, individuals differ with regard to the degree to which they are constrained at each level of organization. Biologically speaking, children of the same chronological age, for example, often are not comparable in the level and character of their biological capacities. Not only does each infant start life with distinctive neurological, physiochemical, and sensory equipment, each also progresses at his or her own maturational rate toward some ultimate but unknown level of potential. The same is true for constraints of a sociocultural nature.

Second, although we differentiate four seemingly distinct stages of development in the following section, it is important to state at the outset that all four stages and their related primary processes begin in utero and continue throughout life, that is, they proceed simultaneously and overlap throughout the developmental process. For example, the elements that give shape to "gender identity" are underway during the sensory-attachment phase, although at a modest level, as do the elements that give rise to attachment behaviors continue and extend well into puberty. Stages are differentiated only to bring attention to periods of development when certain processes and tasks are prominent and central. The concept of sensitive periods implies that developmental stages are not exclusionary; rather, they merely demarcate a period in life when certain developmental potentialities are salient in their maturation and in their receptivity to relevant life experiences.

The characteristics and consequences of the four "overlapping" stages of neuropsychological development are discussed next, as are their roots in the evolutionary phase theory.

NEUROPSYCHOLOGICAL STAGES

The four stages of development parallel the four evolutionary phases discussed previously. Moreover, each evolutionary phase is related to a different stage of ontogenetic development (Millon, 1969). For example, life enhancement-life preservation corresponds to the sensory-attachment stage of development in that the latter represents a period when the young child learns to discriminate between those experiences that are enhancing and those that are threatening.

Stage 1. Sensory-Attachment: The Life-Enhancement (Pleasure)-Life-Preservation (Pain) Polarity

The first year of life is dominated by sensory processes, functions basic to subsequent development in that they enable the infant to construct some order out of the initial diffusion experienced in the stimulus world, especially that based on distinguishing pleasurable from painful "objects." This period has also been termed that of attachment because infants cannot survive on their own (Fox, Kimmerly, & Schafer, 1991) but must "fasten" themselves to others who will protect, nurture, and stimulate them, that is, provide them with experiences of pleasure rather than those of pain.

Such themes are readily understood through an evolutionary theory of personality development. While evolution has endowed adult humans with the cognitive ability to project future threats and difficulties as well as potential rewards, human infants are comparably impoverished, being as yet without the benefit of these abstract capacities. Evolution has therefore "provided" mechanisms or substrates which orient the child toward those activities or venues which are life-enhancing (pleasure), and away from those which are potentially life-threatening (pain). Existence during this highly vulnerable stage is quite literally a to-be or not-to-be matter.

As noted previously, life-enhancing actions or sensations can be subsumed under the rubric of "pleasure," while life-threatening actions or sensations can be subsumed under the metaphorical term "pain." Such a "pleasure-pain polarity" simply recognizes that while the behavioral repertoire of the young child, the operational means, so to speak, may be manifestly diverse, e.g. smiles, coos, stranger anxiety, and primitive reflexes, the end, or *existential aim,* is universal and has as its bare minimum the maintenance of life itself. In the normal organism, both pleasure and pain are coordinated toward ontogenetic continuity. However, whether as a result of genetic factors, early experiences, or their interaction, some pathological patterns display aberrations in their orientation toward pleasure or pain. Deficits in the strength of both painful and pleasurable drives, for example, either constitutionally given or experientially derived are involved in the schizoid pattern, while a reversed or conflicted pleasure-pain orientation inclines toward the masochistic or sadistic disorders.

Development of Sensory Capacities

The early neonatal period is characterized by undifferentiation. The organism behaves in a diffuse and unintegrated way, and perceptions are unfocused and gross. Accordingly, the orientation of the infant is toward sensations which are proportionately broad and undifferentiated, although increasingly the distinction between pleasure and pain becomes central to subsequent refinements. Freud recognized that the mouth region is a richly endowed receptor system through which neonates establish their first significant relationship to the world, but it is clear that this oral unit is merely the focal point of a more diverse system of sensory capacities for making significant distinctions. Through oral and other tactile contacts the infant establishes a sense, or "feel," of the environment which evokes pleasurable or painful responses.

According to neuropsychological and evolutionary theories, it would be expected that the amount and quality of tactile stimulation to which the neonate is exposed will contribute significantly to the infant's development as precocities or retardations, depending on the level of stimulation. Moreover, it is likely that the quality and patterning of this stimulation may lead the infant to experience inchoate feelings tentatively drawn against the background of pleasure-pain. These form the phenomenological prototypes of such later-evolving emotions such as fear, joy, sadness, anger.

Development of Attachment Behaviors

The neonate cannot differentiate between objects and persons; both are experienced simply as stimuli. How does this initial indiscriminateness become progressively refined into specific attachments? For all essential purposes, the infant is helpless and dependent on others to avoid pain and supply its pleasurable needs. Separated from the womb, the neonate has lost its physical attachment to the mother's body and the protection and nurturance it provided; it must turn toward other regions or sources of attachment if it is to survive and obtain nourishment and stimulation for further development (Bowlby, 1969/1982; Gewirtz, 1963; Hinde, 1982; Lamb, Thompson, & Gardner, 1985; Ribble, 1943; Spitz, 1965). Attachment behaviors may be viewed, albeit figuratively, as an attempt to reestablish the unity lost at birth that enhanced and protected life. In fact, recent investigations show that while initial attachments are transformed across stages of development, they remain important across the lifespan (e.g., Sroufe & Fleeson, 1986). Whether the infant's world is conceptualized as a buzz or a blank slate, it must begin to differentiate venues or objects which further its existential aims, supplying nourishment, preservation, and stimulation, from those that diminish, frustrate, or threaten them. These initial relationships, or, "internal representational models" (e.g., Crittenden, 1990), apparently "prepared" by evolution, become the context through which other relationships develop.

Consequences of Impoverishment

A wealth of clinical evidence is available showing that humans deprived of adequate maternal care in infancy display a variety of pathological behaviors. We cannot design studies to disentangle precisely which of the complex of variables that compromise maternal care account for these irreparable consequences; the lives of babies cannot be manipulated to meet our scientific needs.

However, extensive reviews of the consequences in animals of early stimulus impoverishment show that sensory neural fibers atrophy and cannot be regenerated by subsequent stimulation (Beach & Jaynes, 1954; Riesen, 1961). Inadequate stimulation in any major receptor function usually results in decrements in the capacity to utilize these sensory processes in later life. The profound effects of social isolation have been studied thoroughly and show that deprived monkeys are incapable at maturity of relating to peers, of participating effectively in sexual activity, and of assuming adequate roles as mothers. Abstracting to those substrates and pathways which undergird pleasure-pain, we might expect that such under-elaboration, if pervasive, might at the least render emotional discriminations of a more refined or narrow character impossible, or worse, result in the wholesale impoverishment of all affective reactions, as seen in the schizoid pattern.

The potential effects of moderate levels of early sensory impoverishment have been little researched. The reader should note, however, that the degree of sensory impoverishment varies along a gradient or continuum, it is not an all-or-none effect. Children who receive less than an optimum degree of sensory stimulation will be likely to grow up less "sensory-oriented" and less "socially-attached" than those who have experienced more (Bowlby, 1952, 1969/1982, 1973; Goldfarb, 1955; Yarrow, 1961). Such variations are especially relevant to the study of personality disorders, which lie on a continuum with normal functioning.

Consequences of Enrichment

Data on the consequences of too much, or enriched, early sensory stimulation are few and far between; researchers have been concerned with the effects of deficit, rather than excess, stimulation.

A not unreasonable hypothesis, however, is that excess stimulation during the sensory-attachment stage would result in overdevelopments among associated neural structures (Rosenzweig & Diamond, 1962); these may lead to oversensitivities which might, in turn, result in potentially maladaptive dominance of sensory functions or pleasurable substrates. Along this same line, Freud hypothesized that excess indulgence at the oral stage was conducive to fixations at that period. Eschewing both oral and fixation notions, the authors propose that excess sensory development in childhood will require a high level of maintenance in adulthood, as seen in persistent sensory-seeking or pleasure-seeking behaviors. These individuals might be characterized by their repetitive search for excitement and stimulation, their boredom with routine, and their involvement in incidental and momentarily gratifying adventures. Exactly what neural or chemical mechanisms undergird such a stimulus-seeking pattern is a matter for speculation. Whatever the mechanisms may be, it appears plausible both neurologically and clinically that overenriched early stimulation can result in pathological stimulus-seeking behavior, a pattern dominated by relatively capricious and cognitively unelaborated, pleasurable pursuits.

Excess stimulation, especially if anchored exclusively to a parental figure, might result in an overattachment to him or her. This is demonstrated most clearly in the symbiotic child, where an abnormal clinging to the mother and a persistent resistance to stimulation from other sources often result in overwhelming feelings of isolation and panic, as when they are sent to nursery school or "replaced" by a newborn sibling.

Stage 2. Sensorimotor-Autonomy: The Ecologically Accommodating (Passive)-Ecologically Modifying (Active) Polarity

Not until the end of the first year has the infant matured sufficiently to engage in actions independent of parental support. Holding the drinking cup, the first few steps, or a word or two, all signify a growing capacity to act autonomously. As the child develops the functions that characterize this stage, he or she begins to comprehend the attitudes and feelings communicated by stimulative sources. No longer is rough parental handling merely excess stimulation, undistinguished from the playful tossing of an affectionate father; the child now discerns the difference between harshness and good-natured roughhousing.

In the sensorimotor-autonomy stage, the focus shifts from existence in itself to existence within an environment. From an evolutionary perspective, the child in this stage is learning a *mode of adaptation,* an *active* tendency to modify its ecologic niche, versus a *passive* tendency to accommodate to whatever the environment has provided. The former reflects a disposition toward taking the initiative in shaping the course of life events; the latter a disposition to be quiescent, placid, unassertive, to react rather than act, to wait for things to happen, and to accept what is given. In the prior sensory-attachment stage, the infant was in its native mode, so to speak, largely passive, mostly dependent upon parental figures to meet its existential needs. While the child may have engaged in behaviors, for example, crying, which seemed active by virtue of the arousal they evoked in others, these signals were intended to recruit others in the service of fundamental needs. Here it was parental figures, rather than the child itself, who either modified the ecologic milieu or sought out a more hospitable one. With the development of autonomous capacities, the young child finds itself embedded in an environment, an environment either to be explored and later modified, or feared and accommodated to. The child must "decide" whether to "break out" of dependence on parental figures or to perpetuate this dependent pattern into later years. Whatever alternative is pursued, it is a matter of degree rather than a yes-no decision.

Undoubtedly important in the child's orientation toward the environment are its attachments. Those children which possess a "secure base" will explore their environments without becoming fearful that their attachment figure cannot be recovered (Ainsworth, 1967). On the other hand, those without such a base tend to remain close to their caretakers, assuming the more passive mode, one likely to ultimately restrict their range of coping resources through decreased or retarded sociocognitive competence (Millon, 1969).

Development of Sensorimotor Capacities

The unorganized movements of the neonate progressively give way to focused muscular activity. As the neural substrate for muscular control unfolds, the aimless motor behavior of the infant is supplanted by focused movements. These newly emergent functions coordinate with sensory capacities to enable the child to explore, manipulate, play, sit, crawl, babble, throw, walk, catch, talk, and otherwise intervene in its ecologic milieu as desired. The maturing fusion between the substrates of sensory and motor functions is strengthened by the child's exploratory behavior. Manipulative play and the formation of babbling sounds are methods of self-stimulation that facilitate the growth of action-oriented interneuronal connections; the child is building a neural foundation for more complicated and refined skills such as running, handling utensils, controlling sphincter muscles, and articulating precise speech. Children's intrinsic tendency to "entertain" themselves represents a necessary step in establishing capacities that are more substantial than maturation alone would have furnished. Stimulative experiences, either self-provided or provided by relations with others, are requisites for the development of normal, activity-oriented sensorimotor skills. Unless retarded by environmental restrictions, biological handicaps, or insecure attachments, toddlers' growing sensorimotor capacities prepare them to take an active rather than passive role in coping with their environment.

Development of Autonomous Behaviors

Perhaps the most significant aspect of sensorimotor development is that it enables children to begin to take an active stance in doing things for themselves, to influence their environment, to free themselves from domination, and to outgrow the dependencies of their first years. Children become aware of their increasing competence and seek new ventures. Needless to say, conflicts and restrictions arise as they assert themselves (Erikson, 1959; White, 1960). These are seen clearly during toilet training, when youngsters often resist submitting to the demands of their parents. A delicate exchange of power and cunning often ensues. Opportunities arise for the child to actively extract promises or deny wishes; in response, parents may mete out punishments, submit meekly, or shift inconsistently. Important precedents for attitudes toward authority, power and autonomy are generated during this period of parent-child interaction.

Consequences of Impoverishment

A lack of stimulation of sensorimotor capacities can lead to retardations in functions necessary to the development of autonomy and initiative, leading children to remain within a passive adaptational mode. This is seen most clearly in children of overprotective parents. Spoon-fed, excused from "chores," restrained from exploration, curtailed in friendships, and protected from "danger"—all illustrate controls that restrict growing children's opportunities to exercise their sensorimotor skills and develop the means for autonomous behavior. A self-perpetuating cycle often unfolds. These children may fear abandoning their overlearned dependency upon their parents since they are ill-equipped to meet other children on the latter's terms. They may become timid and submissive when forced to venture out into the world, likely to avoid the give and take of competition with their peers, and they may seek out older children who will protect them and upon whom they can lean. Here the passive mode which began as dependence on parental figures is continued in the larger social context (Millon, 1969).

Consequences of Enrichment

The consequences of excessive enrichment during the sensorimotor-autonomy stage are found most often in children of excessively lax, permissive, or overindulgent parents. Given free rein with minimal restraint, stimulated to explore and manipulate things to their suiting without guidance or control, these children will often become irresponsibly undisciplined in their behaviors. Their active style compels these children to view the entire ecologic milieu as a playground or medium to be modified according to their whims. Carried into the wider social context, these behaviors run up against the desires of other children and the restrictions of less permissive adults. Unless the youngsters are extremely adept, they will find that their actively self-centered and free-wheeling tactics fail miserably. For the few who succeed, however, a pattern of egocentrism, unbridled self-expression, and social arrogance may become dominant. The majority of these youngsters fail to gain acceptance by peers and never quite acquire the flexibility to shift between active and passive styles according to contextual demands. Such children are conspicuous in their lack of the normal give and-take skills which form the basis of genuine social relationships.

Equally important as a form of enrichment is the intensity of attachments. Children acquire representations about the world, themselves, and others through their interactions with attachment figures (Bowlby, 1969/1982; 1973). Constant concern about a child's welfare may cause it to view itself as an object of frailty, resulting later in a passive style wherein the older child

or adult constantly makes bids for others to take the initiative in transforming the environment.

Stage 3. Pubertal-Gender Identity: The Progeny Nurturance (Other)-Individual Propagation (Self) Polarity

Somewhere between the eleventh and fifteenth years a rather sweeping series of hormonal changes unsettle the psychic state that had been so carefully constructed in preceding years. These changes reflect the onset of puberty and the instantiation of sexual and gender-related characteristics which are preparatory for the emergence of the r- and K-strategies—strong sexual impulses and adultlike features of anatomy, voice, and bearing. Erratic moods, changing self-images, reinterpretations of one's view of others, new urges, hopeful expectancies, and a growing physical and social awkwardness, all upset the relative equanimity of an earlier age. Disruptive as it may be, this turbulent stage of growth bifurcates and focuses many of the remaining elements of the youngster's biological potential. It is not only a preparatory phase for the forthcoming independence from parental direction, but is when the psychological equivalent of the r- and K- strategies, self (male) and other (female) orientations, begin to diverge and then coalesce into distinct gender roles.

With the unsettling influences of adolescence, both physiological and social, and the emergence of the individual as a being of genuine reproductive potential, the r- and K- strategies begin to take on an implicitly criterial role in the selection of the behaviors of the moment, as well as future goals, from a universe of implicit alternatives. These strategies are psychologically expressed, at the highest level of abstraction, in an orientation toward self and an orientation toward others. Here the male can be prototypally described as more dominant, imperial, and acquisitive, and the female more communal, nurturant, and deferent.

These representations—self and other and their coordination—are essential to the genesis of the personality system. Both attachment theory and the evolutionary model presented here recognize the importance of self and other constructs. From an attachment perspective, these constructs represent inchoate interpersonal relationships, the intricacies of which are made possible by cognitive developments. No longer is the world an unorganized swirl of events; increasingly, it is organized around relationships and expectations. While relationships are organic wholes (Sroufe and Fleeson, 1986), within these wholes the individual's orientation, that is, expectations about future states of the relationship and outcomes desired from the relationship, are oriented toward self and other, and the individual may possess positive or negative models of each (Bartholomew & Horowitz, 1991).

Development of Pubertal Maturation

Pubescence is characterized by the rapidity of body growth, genital maturity, and sexual awareness. A series of transformations take place that are qualitatively different from those developed earlier in childhood. They create an element of discontinuity from prior experiences, confronting the youngster, not only with an internal "revolution" of a physiological nature, but also with a series of psychological tasks that are prompted by emergent sexual feelings. Perhaps more applicable to this stage of life than those which Freud considered paramount in infancy, the emergence of pubertal sexuality is central to the psychic development of the adolescent. Much effort is invested both consciously and unconsciously to incorporate these new bodily impulses into one's sense of self and one's relationship to others. Youngsters must establish a gender identity that incorporates physiological changes and the powerful libidinal feelings with which they are associated. The increase in pubertal libidinal drives requires a reorganization of one's sense of adolescent identity. Developed in a satisfactory manner, the adolescent is enabled to search out relevant extrafamilial love objects.

Development of Gender Identity

Developing a gender identity is not so much acquiring a means for satisfying libidinal impulses as it is a process of refining the youngster's previously diffused and undifferentiated sense of self. This is achieved most effectively by reflecting the admiration of a beloved other. The feedback received in real and fantasized love relationships assists the teenager to revise and define their gender-identity. It serves also to clarify and further develop a new self-concept that encompasses relationships with peer companions of both genders, rather than parents or siblings.

Not uncommonly, the definition of one's own gender identity brings forth a rejection of the opposite sex. "They" are treated with derision and contempt. A turning toward the same-sex peer group is of value in defining one's identity, a process that is deeply embedded by a self-conscious selection and alliance of same-sex peers. Pubertal boys avoid girls, belittle them and strongly reject female sentimentality. Girls turn for affection and support toward their same-sex peers, sharing secrets, intimacies, and erotically tinged fantasies and romances. All these efforts add a psychosocial dimension and gender definition to increasingly powerful pubertal processes.

Consequences of Impoverishment

The goal of the adolescent is in part to achieve a libidinous extrafamilial object, an aim ultimately resulting in a richer and more mature emotional life. As noted, with the onset of puberty, parental identification declines and is replaced by identifications with valued peers, both real friendships and romanticized heroes. The lack of such identifications and role models during adolescence may culminate in imaginary infatuations, unreal and ineffectual substitutes for the desirable qualities that usually emerge from everyday personal relationships.

Without direct tuition from his elders, the teenager will be left to his own devices to master the complexities of a varied world, to control intense aggressive and sexual urges which well up within him, to channel his fantasies and to pursue the goals to which he aspires. He may become a victim of his own growth, unable to discipline his impulses or fashion acceptable means for expressing his desires. Scattered and unguided, he cannot get hold of a sense of personal identity, a consistent direction and purpose to his existence. He becomes an "other-directed" person, one who vacillates at every turn, overly responsive to fleeting stimuli and who shifts from one erratic course to another. Ultimately, without an

inner core or anchor to guide his future, he may flounder or stagnate. Deficient gender identifications and inadequate sexual initiations may interfere in significant ways with the development of his emotional maturity.

Borderline personality disorders often characterize this pattern of gender diffusion. Their aimlessness and disaffiliation from the mainstream of traditional American life may be traced, in part, to the failure of experience to provide a coherent set of gender role-models and values around which they can focus their lives and orient themselves toward a meaningful future.

Consequences of Enrichment

In contrast to the problems that arise from a deficiency of gender-role models, we frequently observe excessive dependency on peer group sexual habits and values. Some adolescents who have been ill-disposed to the values of problematic peer groups may find themselves isolated and avoided, if not ridiculed and ostracized. To protect themselves against this discomforting possibility the teenager may submerge his identity to fit the roles given him by others. He may adopt gender models that have been explicitly or implicitly established by group customs. They act, dress, use language, and enact their gender roles in terms of peer-group standards.

Not untypically, peer groups provide a formal structure to guide the youngster, with uniforms, rituals, and even specified heroes as imitative models. Such identities, gender and otherwise, are provided by belonging to neighborhood gangs or "hippie" subcultures. Many high-school students conform unquestioningly to the sexual standards of their peers in order to be accepted, to be enmeshed in the good feeling of group solidarity, and to boost their sense of identity through identification. In effect, these youngsters have jettisoned parental norms for peer group norms, and it is these latter norms that foreclose independent thought and feeling. What is seen in these identifications is an increase in narcissism, a posture of arrogance and rebellion, as well as defiance against conventional societal norms.

As the diffusion of earlier bisexual trends give way to a distinct heterosexual orientation, sexuality becomes the most prominent feature of these "enriched" youngsters. Many become sensitive, almost exclusively, to erotic stimuli, in contrast to the more global and varied aspects of normal heterosexual relationships. Such adolescents often "back-off," stating that they are worried that they might be getting "too involved." Hence, pubertal maturation in these youngsters may not only intensify their libidinal drives, but may also increase in equal measure their aggressive/hostile drives. As a consequence of these developments and transformations, these youngsters may now have developed behaviors that accentuate the stereotypical roles of masculinity and femininity.

Stage 4. Intracortical-Integration: The Intellective Reasoning (Thinking)-Affective Resonance (Feeling) Polarity

The intracortical-integration stage coordinates with the fourth phase of the evolutionary progression, the thinking-feeling polarity. The peak period of neurological maturation for certain psychological functions generally occurs between the ages of 4 and 18. The amount and kind of intrapsychic and contextual stimulation at these times of rapid growth will have a strong bearing on the degree to which these functions mature. Thinking and feeling are broad and multifaceted constructs with diverse manifestations. While the focus in the first three stages of development was on the child's existential aims, modes of adaptation, and gender identification, here the focus shifts to the individual as a being-in-time.

Initially, the child must acquire abstract capacities that enable it to transcend the purely concrete reality of the present moment and project the self-as-object into myriad futures contingent upon its own style of action or accommodation. Such capacities are both cognitive and emotional, and may have wide-ranging consequences for the personality system if they fail to cohere as integrated structures, as in the more severe personality disorders, e.g., borderline and schizotypal.

What are the capacities which unfold during this stage, and what consequences can be attributed to differences in the quality and intensity of relevant experience?

Development of Intracortical Capacities

Progressively more complex arrangements of neural cells become possible as children advance in maturation. Although these higher-order connections begin in early infancy, they do not form into structures capable of rational foresight and adult-level planning until the youngsters have fully developed their more basic sensorimotor skills and pubertal maturations. With these capacities as a base, they are able to differentiate and arrange the objects of the physical world. As verbal skills unfold, they learn to symbolize concrete objects; soon they are able to manipulate and coordinate these symbols as well as, if not better than, the tangible events themselves. Free of the need to make direct reference to the concrete world, they are able to recall past events and anticipate future ones. As increasingly complex cortical connections are established, higher conceptual abstractions are formulated, enabling the children to transfer, associate, and coordinate these symbols into ideas of finer differentiation, greater intricacy, and broader integration. These internal representations of reality, the product of symbolic thought, the construction of events past, present, and future, take over as the primary elements of the representational world. Especially significant at this period is a fusion between the capacities to think and to feel.

Development of Integrative Processes

When the inner world of symbols is mastered, giving objective reality an order and integration, youngsters are able to create some consistency and continuity in their lives. No longer are they buffeted from one mood or action to another by the swirl of changing events; they now have an internal anchor, a nucleus of cognitions that serves as a base and imposes a sense of sameness and continuity upon an otherwise fluid environment. As they grow in their capacity to organize and integrate their world, one configuration becomes increasingly differentiated and begins to predominate. Accrued from experiences with others and their reactions to the child, an image or representation of self-as-object has taken shape. This highest order of abstraction, the sense of

individual identity as distinct from others becomes the dominant source of stimuli that guides the youngster's thoughts and feelings. External events no longer have the power they once exerted; the youngster now has an ever-present and stable sphere of internal representations, transformed by rational and emotional reflections, which govern one's course of action and from which behaviors are initiated.

Consequences of Impoverishment

The task of integrating a consistent self-other differentiation, as well as consolidating the divergencies of thought and feeling are not easy in a world of changing events and pluralistic values. From what sources can a genuine balance between reason and emotion be developed?

The institutions which interweave to form the complex fabric of society are implicitly designed to shape the assumptive world of its younger members. Family, school, and church transmit implicit values and explicit rules by which the child is guided in behaving and thinking in a manner consonant with those of others. The youngster not only is subject to cultural pressures but requires them to give direction to his/her proliferating capacities and impulses. Without them, potentials may become overly diffuse and scattered; conversely, too much guidance may narrow the child's potentials and restrict their adaptiveness. In either case, the sense of self and other, as well as the relationship of thought and emotion, are no longer expressed in personally elaborated and multifaceted forms. Instead, they are manifested narrowly or rigidly, with the result that the individual lacks the flexibility required to successfully navigate life's social contexts on his own. Once basic patterns of thought and feeling are shaped during this period, it is difficult to orient them along new pathways.

What are the effects of inadequate or erratic stimulation during the peak years of intracortical integration?

Without direct tuition from elders, youngsters are left to their own devices to master the complexities of a varied world, to control intense urges, to channel fantasies, and to pursue the goals to which they aspire. They may become victims of their own growth, unable to orient their impulses or fashion acceptable means for expressing their desires. Scattered and unguided, they may be unable to construct a sense of internal cohesion, nor a consistent direction and purpose to their existence. They may vacillate at every turn, overly responsive to fleeting stimuli, shifting from one erratic course to another. Without an inner core or anchor to guide their future, they may flounder or stagnate.

Evidently, the impoverishment of integrative stimuli will have a profound effect. Fortunately, with proper guidance, the "immaturity and irresponsibility" of many adolescents may be salvaged in later years. But for others, the inability to settle down into a consolidated path may become a problem of increasingly severe proportions.

Consequences of Enrichment

The negative consequences of overenrichment at the fourth stage usually occur when parents are controlling and perfectionistic. The overly trained, overly disciplined and overly integrated youngster is given little opportunity to shape his own destiny.

Whether by coercion or enticement, the child who, too early, is led to control his emergent feelings, to focus his thoughts along narrowly defined paths and to follow the prescriptions of parental demands, has been subverted into adopting the identities of others. Whatever individuality he may have acquired is drowned in a model of adult orderliness, propriety and virtue. Such over-socialized and rigid youngsters lack the spontaneity, flexibility and creativeness we expect of the young; they have been trained to be old men before their time, too narrow in perspective to respond to excitement, variety and the challenge of new events. Overenrichment at this stage has fixed them on a restrictive course, and has deprived them of the rewards of being themselves.

Comment

It would be an error to leave this discussion of evolutionary-neuropsychological development with the impression that personality growth is merely a function of stimulation at sensitive maturational periods. Impoverishment and enrichment have their profound effects, but the quality or kind of stimulation the youngster experiences is often of greater importance. The impact of parental harshness or inconsistency, of sibling rivalry or social failure, is more than a matter of stimulus volume and timing. Different dimensions of experience take precedence as the meaning conveyed by the source of stimulation becomes clear to the growing child. This facet of psychogenesis will be considered shortly, as will our discussion of the central tasks that must be undertaken at each of the four sequential stages of development.

Normal psychological processes depend on a substrate of orderly neuronal connections. The development of this intricate neural substrate unfolds within the organism in accord with genetically determined mechanisms, but there remain substantial numbers of fibers whose direction of growth is modifiable. To summarize the previous section, it might be said that the basic architecture of the nervous system is laid down in a relatively fixed manner, but refinements in this linkage system do not develop without the aid of additional experiences. Environmental experience not only activates neural collaterals but alters these structures so as to preempt them for similar subsequent experiences. Thus, early experiences not only construct new neural pathways but, in addition, selectively prepare them to be receptive to later stimuli that are qualitatively similar.

This second consequence of experience, representing the selective lowering of thresholds for the transmission of similar subsequent stimuli, is described in the conceptual language of psychology as learning. It reflects the observation that behaviors that have been subject to prior experience are reactivated with increasing ease. With this second consequence of stimulation, we begin to conceive the nervous system as more than a network of abstract pathways; it is now viewed as possessing the residues of specific classes of environmental stimuli. These environmentally anchored neural connections interweave to form patterns of perception and behavior that relate to discriminable events in the external world. By including qualitatively discriminable features of the stimulus world within our purview, we shift our attention to observational units that transcend neural mechanisms located strictly within the anatomical limits of the body. It is necessary to

represent these complex external-internal relationships in a conceptual language that is broader in scope than that of neurology.

Both neurological and learning concepts can be utilized to describe changes in response probabilities arising from prior stimulus exposure. But, since learning concepts are formulated in terms of behavior-environment interactions, it would appear reasonable, when discussing the specific properties of qualitatively discriminable stimulus events, to utilize the conceptual language of learning. Moreover, the principles derived from learning theory and research describe subtle features of psychological behavior that cannot begin to be handled intelligently in neurological terms. With the principles and conceptual language of learning, we can formulate precisely our ideas about the effects of qualitatively discriminable stimulus events, that is, differences not only in the magnitude but in the variety and content of the stimulus world as we experience it.

Keep in mind that learning concepts and neurological concepts do not represent intrinsically different processes; we are using the former because they have been more finely differentiated and, therefore, are more fruitful tools for formulating notions about qualitatively different stimulus-behavior interactions.

DEVELOPMENTAL TASKS

As has been noted in prior sections, experience is likely to have a more profound effect at certain stages in the developmental sequence than at others. This statement reiterates a conviction stated earlier that pronounced environmental influences occur at periods of rapid neurological growth. A further reason for the stage-specific significance of experience is the observation that children are exposed to a succession of social tasks that they are expected to fulfill at different points in the developmental sequence. These stage-specific tasks are timed to coincide with periods of rapid neurological growth (e.g., the training of bladder control is begun when the child possesses the requisite neural equipment for such control; similarly, children are taught to read when intracortical development has advanced sufficiently to enable a measure of consistent success). In short, a reciprocity appears between periods of rapid neurological growth and exposure to related experiences and tasks. To use Erikson's (1950) terms, the child's newly emerging neurological potentials are challenged by a series of "crises" with the environment. Children are especially vulnerable at these critical stages since experience both shapes their neurological patterns and results in learning a series of fundamental attitudes about themselves and others.

What experiences typically arise at the four neuropsychological stages described earlier, and what are the central attitudes learned during these periods?

In seeking answers to these questions, this discussion turns briefly to the fertile ideas of Freud and Erikson. During the sensory-attachment stage, when pleasure and pain discriminations are central, the critical attitude learned deals with one's "trust of others." The sensorimotor-autonomy stage, when the progression from passive to active modes of adaptation occurs, is noted by learning attitudes concerning "adaptive confidence." During the pubertal-gender identity stage, when the separation between self and other roles is sharpened, we see the development of reasonably distinct "sexual roles." The intracortical-integrative stage, when the coordination between intellectual and affective processes develop, may best be characterized by the acquisition of a balance between "reason and emotion." A brief elaboration of these is in order.

Task 1: Developing Trust of Others (Pain-Pleasure Polarity)

Trust may be described as a feeling that one can rely on the affections and support of others. There are few periods of life when an individual is so wholly dependent on the goodwill and care of others than during the relatively helpless state of infancy. Nothing is more crucial to the infant's well-being than the nurturance and protection afforded by his/her caretakers. Through the quality and consistency of this support, deeply ingrained feelings of trust are etched within the child. From the evolutionary model presented earlier, trust and mistrust represent facets of the pleasure and pain constructs, generalized to adaptational venues within the physical environment, such as the nursery, as well as to the environment of prototypal social objects. Within the infant's world, of course, trust and mistrust lack their phenomenological and moral dimensions, resembling more global and undifferentiated feelings of soothing calm (pleasure) or tense apprehension (pain) than consciously abstracted states.

Such perceptual indiscriminateness of associations is highly significant. Thus, feelings and expectancies arising from specific experiences become highly generalized and come to characterize the child's image of the entire environment. Because children are unable to make fine discriminations their early attachments become pervasive and widespread. Nurtured well and given comfort and affection, they will acquire a far-reaching trust of others; they learn that discomfort will be moderated and that others will assist them and provide for their needs. Deprived of warmth and security or handled severely and painfully, they will learn to mistrust their environment, to anticipate further stress, and view others as harsh and undependable. Rather than developing an optimistic and confident attitude toward the future, they will be disposed to withdraw and avoid people for fear that these persons will recreate the discomfort and anguish that were experienced in the past.

Task 2: Acquiring Adaptive Confidence (Active-Passive Polarity)

Children become progressively less dependent on their caretakers during the sensorimotor-autonomy stage. By the second and third years, they are ambulatory and possess the power of speech and control over many elements in their environment. They have acquired the manipulative skills to venture forth and test their competence to handle events on their own (White, 1960). In terms of the evolutionary model, this stage concerns the active-passive polarity. Here children struggle to break out of the inherently dependent and passive mode of infancy. Rather than remain a passive receptacle for environmental forces, clay to be molded, they acquire competencies which enlarge their vistas and allow them to become legitimate actors in their environments.

However, subtle, as well as obvious, parental attitudes shape children's confidence in their ability to exercise their competencies. These attitudes markedly influence behavior since it is not only what the children can do that determines their actions but how they feel about what they can do. The rewards and punishments to which they are exposed and the degree of encouragement and affection surrounding their first performances will contribute to their confidence in themselves. Severe discipline for transgressions, humiliating comments in response to efforts at self-achievement, embarrassment over social awkwardness, deprecations associated with poor school performance, and shame among one's peers as a result of physical inadequacies, all weigh heavily to diminish self-esteem. Faced with rebuffs and ridicule, children learn to doubt their competence and adequacy. Whether they actually possess the skills to handle events is no longer the issue; they simply lack the confidence to try, to venture out or to compete. Believing their efforts will be ineffectual and futile, these children often adopt a passive, wait-and-see attitude toward their environment and their future.

Task 3: Assimilating Sexual Roles (Self-Other Polarity)

The many crushes and infatuations experienced during the pubertal period serves as a genuine source of development. Gender roles emerge in significant ways by interacting with others, especially as enacted in peer group relationships. Adhering to the models of peer behaviors helps the youngster find and evaluate how certain gender roles fit. The high-school clique, the neighborhood gang, the athletic team, all aid the teenager in discovering his/her gender identity, providing both useful role models and instant social feedback. The "bull" session among boys and the endless phone conversations between girls serve significant goals by providing evaluative feedback as the youngster searches to define his or herself. It is particularly during the time of rapid body changes when genital impulses stimulate sexual fantasies that the adolescent learns to rely on peers as important guides and sounding boards.

Security is found in peer relationships in that youngsters share a code as to what constitutes appropriate gender behaviors. No less important is the mutuality they experience in struggling through the same pubertal issues. The importance of the influence of the peer group is perhaps nowhere more significant than in the realm of sexual behaviors. For the most part, the adolescent finds security in accepting the peer-gender norms as preliminary guides regarding how one can regulate one's impulses, feelings, and sexual inclinations.

Task 4: Balancing Reason and Emotion (Intracortical-Integration Polarity)

The emergence of this final developmental stage—with its capacities for thinking, feeling, evaluating, and planning—leads children to formulate a clear image of themselves as a certain "kind of adult," an identity discernible from others, one capable of having independent judgments and of fashioning their own course of action. Healthy children must acquire a coherent system of internalized values that will guide them through a changing and varied environment. They must find their own anchor and compass by which to coordinate both their feelings and ideas about life. Equipped by successful efforts toward autonomy, they will have confidence that they possess a direction in life that is valued by others and one that can safely withstand the buffeting of changing events. In terms of the evolutionary model, such children are capable of integrating their feelings and thoughts, setting their own agendas, and becoming masters of their own fate.

Conversely, if deprived of rewarded achievements and unable to construct a picture of a valued identity, they will lack the means to meet life's tasks rationally and be unable to handle discouraging emotional forces that may arise. In such cases, their identity may come to be defined through the goals and needs of others rather than through self. Without an integrated and consistent integration of thought and feeling, the growing adolescent or adult will flounder from one tentative course to another and be beset with amorphous and vague feelings of discontent and uselessness.

PATHOGENIC SOURCES

Behavior and attitudes may be learned from explicit indoctrination, but most of what is learned stems from haphazard and casual events to which the child is incidentally exposed. Not only are rewards and punishments meted out most often in a spontaneous and erratic fashion, the everyday and ordinary activities of parents also provide the child with unintended models to imitate.

Without awareness or intention, parents suggest through incidental behaviors how "people" think, talk, fear, love, solve problems, and relate to others. Aversions, irritabilities, anxieties, and styles of relating and communicating are adopted by children as they observe the everyday actions of parents and older siblings. Children mirror complex behaviors without understanding their significance and without parental intentions to transmit them. Since many pathological patterns have their beginnings in offhand behaviors and attitudes to which children are incidentally exposed, it is important to recognize that such learnings accrue less from intentional training than from adventitious experience.

Pathogenic learnings arise essentially from three sources. First, there are events that create intense anxieties because they undermine feelings of security. When these events persist they elicit adaptive and self-protective reactions that (though successful in diminishing discomfort in the short run) may establish long-term coping styles and anticipations that ultimately intrude upon and undermine healthy functioning. Second are emotionally neutral conditions or models of behavior that do not activate protective or defensive behaviors, as do emotionally disruptive events. However, they do suggest styles of behavior that prove deleterious when exhibited or generalized to settings other than those for which they are suitable. The roots of these difficulties do not lie in anxious events or unconscious defense mechanisms but in the simple conditioning or imitation of maladaptive behaviors. The third source of pathogenicity reflects an insufficiency of experiences requisite to learning adaptive behaviors. Thus, stimulus impoverishment or minimal social experience

may produce deficits in learned coping behaviors. The lack of skills and competencies for mastering the environment is a form of pathological underlearning that may prove as severe as those generated by stress or defective models of behavior.

Feelings and Attitudes

Since the ebb and flow of life consists of many interwoven elements, keep in mind that the features we may separate for analysis represent only single facets of an ongoing and inextricable constellation of events.

An atmosphere, a way of handling the routine of life, a tone to ways of relating and communicating day in and day out, all come to characterize the family setting within which the child develops (Emde, 1989; Maccoby & Martin, 1983). In contrast to the occasional and scattered events of the outside environment, the circumstances of daily family life have cumulative effects upon the entire fabric of children's learning. Within this setting children establish feelings of security, imitate the way people relate interpersonally, acquire impressions of how others feel about them, develop a sense of self-worth, and learn to cope with the stresses of life (Billings & Moos, 1982; Lewinsohn, 1974).

The most pervasive and perhaps most important aspect of learned experience is the extent to which children develop a feeling of acceptance or rejection by parents. To be exposed throughout one's early life to parents who view one as unwanted or troublesome can establish only a deep and overriding feeling of isolation and worthlessness (Cicchetti & Beeghly, 1987). Deprived of security at home, the child may be disinclined to venture forth to face struggles in the outer world. Rejected by parents, the child is likely to anticipate equal devaluation by others (Dodge, Murphy, & Buchsbaum, 1984; Dornbusch, Ritter, Leiderman et al., 1987; Steinberg, Elmen, & Mounts, 1989). As a defense against further pain, the child may learn to avoid others and utilize indifference as a protective cloak to minimize what is now expected from others. Different strategies may evolve, of course. Thus, some rejected children may imitate parental scorn and ridicule, and learn to handle their disturbed feelings by acting in a hostile and vindictive fashion (Cicchetti & Carlson, 1989; Mueller & Silverman, 1989).

Rejection is not the only parental attitude that can produce insidious damage. Attitudes such as seduction, exploitation, and deception contribute their share of damage as well. However, it is usually the sense of being unwanted and unloved that proves to have the most pervasive and destructive of effects. Children can usually tolerate considerable buffeting from their environment if they sense a basic feeling of love and support from their parents (Rutter, 1989).

Behavior Control

Parents disposed to intimidate their offspring, using punitive or repressive measures of control, may set the stage for a variety of maladaptive patterns (El Sheikh, Cummings, & Goetsch, 1989; Loeber & Stouthamer-Loeber, 1986). If children submit and fulfill parental expectations, they are apt to become overly obedient and circumspect. These children not only learn to keep their impulses and contrary thoughts in check but alas, by observations and imitation, often adopt the parental model and become punitive themselves in response to the deviant behaviors of others. Should these youngsters fail to satisfy parental demands and be subject to continued harassment, they may develop a pervasive anxiety about personal relationships, leading to feeling discouraged and resulting in social avoidance and withdrawal. Others, faced with similar punitive experiences, may incorporate the pattern of parental harshness and develop hostile and aggressively rebellious behaviors. Which learned strategy evolves depends on the larger configuration of factors involved (Ferster, 1973; Lazarus, 1968; Lewinsohn, 1974; Patterson, 1977).

Some parents rarely are punitive but expect that certain behaviors will be performed prior to giving recognition. Approval or praise is contingent, therefore, upon approved performance. Youngsters reared under these conditions tend to be socially pleasant and affable but, quite often, seem to have an insatiable and indiscriminate need for social acceptance. Contingent reward methods appear to condition children to develop an excessive need for approval.

Other parental methods of control may be characteristically inconsistent, contradictory, and capricious (Maccoby & Martin, 1983). Some degree of variability is inevitable in every child's life, but there are parents who display an extreme inconsistency in their standards and expectations, and an extreme unpredictability in their application of rewards and punishments. Youngsters exposed to such chaotic or capricious treatment cannot learn consistently and cannot devise a nonconflictive style of adaptive behavior. To avoid the anxiety of unpredictable reactions, the child may become protectively noncommittal. Others, imitating what they have been exposed to, may come to be characterized by their own ambivalent tendency to vacillate from one action or feeling to another.

Some parents protectively narrow the experiences to which their children are exposed such that the youngsters fail to learn the rudiments of autonomous behaviors (Baumrind, 1967; Lewis, 1981). Overprotective parents not only succeed in forestalling the growth of normal competencies but, indirectly, give children a feeling that they are inferior and frail. And, observing their actual inadequacies, the children have verification that they are, in fact, weak, inept, and dependent (Millon, 1981; Parker, 1983).

Overly indulgent, lax or undisciplined parents may allow children full rein to explore and assert their every whim. Moreover, by their own lack of discipline these parents provide a model to be imitated, which only further strengthens the child's tendency to be irresponsible. Unconstrained by parental control, these youngsters display inconsiderate and tyrannical characteristics, and are often exploitive, uncooperative, and antisocially aggressive. Unless rebuffed by external discipline, they frequently become difficult members of society (Millon, 1969).

Styles of Communication

The styles of interpersonal communication to which children are exposed serve as models for attending, organizing, and reacting to the expressions, thoughts, and feelings of others. Unless this framework of communication is rational and reciprocal, they will be ill-equipped to relate in an effective way with others. Thus, the very capacity which enables humans to symbolize their environment so successfully may lend itself to serious misdirections and confusions. Illogical ideas, irrational reactions, and irrelevant and bizarre verbalizations most often arise as a consequence of emotional stress, but the roots can also be traced to an early exposure to peculiar or disjointed styles of interpersonal communication (Campbell, 1973; Mash & Johnston, 1982; Morrison, 1980; Tizard & Hodges, 1978).

The effects of amorphous, fragmented, or confusing communications have been explored by numerous investigators (Singer & Wynne, 1965). Not only are messages attended to in certain families in a vague or erratic fashion, with a consequent disjunctiveness and loss of focus, but when they are attended to, they frequently convey equivocal or contradictory meanings. Exposed to such communications, the child's conception of reality may become deviant, if not precarious (Reid, Patterson, & Loeber, 1982; Reiss, 1981). To avoid these confusions, some children may learn to distort or deny conflicting signals, but in this defensive maneuver they may succumb even further to irrational thinking. Unable to interpret intentions and feelings correctly, they may fall prey to an increasing estrangement from others.

Content of Experiences

Parents transmit values and attitudes through either direct tuition or unintentional commentary (Dorr, 1985; Emde, 1979). Through these explicit and implicit teachings the child learns to think about and react to events and people in particular ways. What teachings lend themselves to potentially pathological attitudes and behaviors?

The most insidious of these teachings is training in anxiety. Parents who fret over health, investigate every potential ailment, or are preoccupied with failures and the dismal turn of events, teach and furnish models for anxiety proneness in their children (Coolidge & Brodie, 1974; Parker, 1983; Waldron, Shrier, Stone, & Tobin, 1975). Few attitudes transcend the pernicious effects of a chronically anxious and apprehensive household.

Guilt and shame are generated in the teachings of many homes. Failure to live up to parental expectations, a feeling that one has caused undue sacrifices, or that one has transgressed rules and embarrassed the family, illustrate events that undermine the individual's self-worth and produce marked feelings of shame and guilt. The sacrificing and guilt-laden atmosphere of such parental homes often provides a model for behavioral imitation. Admonished and reproached repeatedly for minor digressions, such children develop a deep and pervasive self-image of failure. To protect against feelings of self-condemnation, these youngsters may restrict their activities, deny themselves the normal joys and indulgences of life, and learn to control their impulses far beyond that required to eschew shame and guilt.

Other destructive attitudes can be taught directly through narrow parental outlooks. Particularly damaging are those associated with anger, affection, and sexual urges. Unrealistic standards which condemn these common behaviors and feelings create unnecessary fears and strong guilt feelings.

Family Structure

The formal composition of the childhood family unit often sets the stage for learning pathogenic attitudes and relationships. The lack of significant adult figures within the family often deprives children of the opportunity to acquire, through observation, many of the complex patterns of behavior required in adult life (Emery, 1982; Ferri, 1976; Millon, 1987). The most serious deficit usually is the unavailability of the same-sex parental model (Hetherington, Cox, & Cox, 1982). For example, the frequent absence of fathers in underprivileged homes, or the vocational preoccupations of fathers in well-to-do homes, may give rise to a lack among sons of a mature sense of masculine identity.

Children subject to persistent parental bickering are not only exposed to destructive models but also are faced with a repeated upsetting influence (Crockenberg, 1985; Cummings, Pellegrini, Notarius, & Cummings, 1989; Rutter & Giller, 1983). The stability of life necessary for acquiring a consistent pattern of behaving and thinking is shattered when strife and controversy prevail. Children frequently become scapegoats, subject to displaced parental hostilities, constantly dragged into the arena of parental strife or involved in competitions and coalitions that determine who receives affection and who receives antagonism (Hetherington, 1972).

Sibling relationships often are overlooked as a major element in shaping the pattern of peer and other intimate "competitions" (Circirelli, 1982; Dunn & Kendrick, 1981; Wagner, Schubert, & Schubert, 1979). When disproportionate affections are allocated to one child, seeds of discontent and rivalry flourish. Since hostility fails to eliminate the competitor and gains, not the sought-for attention, but parental disapproval, the aggrieved child often reverts to maneuvers such as pouting, illness, or depression. If these methods succeed in gaining parental love, the youngster will have been reinforced to continue these ultimately troublesome techniques. More often than not, however, efforts to alter parental preferences succeed only partially, and the child continues both to display these partially successful maneuvers and still experience deep resentment and insecurity. Such persons often acquire a distrust of affections, fearing that those who express them will prove to be as fickle as their parents.

Traumatic Experiences

Popular psychology has it that most forms of psychopathology can be traced to a single, very severe experience, the residues of which account for the manifest disorder. Freud's early writings gave impetus to this notion, but he reversed himself when he was made aware that patient reports of trauma often were imaginative fabrications. Current thinking indicates that most pathological behaviors accrue gradually through repetitive experiences. Thus, childhood abuse, considered so central to several personality disorders, does not usually reflect a single traumatic event, but rather a series of continuing debasements on the part of others.

There are occasions, however, when a particularly painful event can shatter equanimity and leave deeply embedded attitudes that cannot be readily extinguished. The impact of these events may be especially severe with young children since they are usually ill-prepared for them and lack a perspective that might serve as a context for moderating their effects (Field, 1985; Garmezy, 1986; Weissman & Paykel, 1974). If a traumatic event is the first exposure to a particular class of experiences, the feelings it evokes may intrude and color all subsequent events of that kind.

The consequences of single, intense traumatic events are likely to persevere for essentially two reasons. First, a high level of neural activation occurs in response to situations of marked distress. This suggests that many and diverse neural associations become connected to the event; the greater the level of neural involvement, the more ingrained and pervasive will be the learned reaction. Second, during heightened stress there is often a decrement in the ability to make clear distinctions among the elements of the environment. As a consequence, the traumatized individual is likely to generalize the emotional reaction to a variety of objects and persons only incidentally associated with the traumatic source. More is said in the next section about the difficulty in extinguishing such attitudes and feelings.

PERSISTENCE AND CONTINUITY OF EARLY EXPERIENCES

This section concentrates on the notion of continuity in behavior since the authors believe that the significance of early experience lies not only in the intensity of its impact but also in its durability and persistence. Early experiences are not only ingrained more pervasively and forcefully, but their effects tend to persist and are more difficult to modify than the effects of later experiences. Although part of this continuity may be ascribed to the stability of constitutional and temperamental factors, there are numerous psychological processes that contribute to it as well (Chess & Thomas, 1984; Kagan, Reznick, & Snidman, 1989; Plomin & Dunn, 1986; Robins & Rutter, 1990).

Presymbolic Experiences

The nervous system of young infants is primitive and incomplete; they perceive the world from momentary and changing vantage points and are unable to discriminate many of the elements of their experience. What they learn about the environment through their infantile perceptual and cognitive systems will never again be experienced in the same manner in later life.

This presymbolic world of fleeting impressions recedes gradually as children acquire the ability to identify and symbolize experience. By the time they are 4 or 5 years old, they group and symbolize objects and events in a stable way, a way quite different from that of infancy. Once the children's perceptions have taken on symbolic forms, they can no longer duplicate the perceptually amorphous and diffusely inchoate experiences of their earlier years. These early learnings will persist beneath the level of symbolic awareness in the form of feelings, attitudes, and expectancies that crop up in a vague and diffuse way.

Interpersonal Reciprocity

A systems conception is one of the fundamental themes of this chapter. As noted earlier, personality patterns develop as a consequence of enduring experiences generated in everyday, incidental relationships with members of one's immediate family. What aspects of family relationships strengthen and perpetuate personality traits which are inchoate in existence?

Contextual Constriction

The typical life of daily activities in which young children participate is restricted and repetitive. Day after day they play with the same toys, remain in the same physical environment, and relate to the same people. Repeated exposure to a narrow range of family attitudes and training methods not only builds deeply etched traits and expectational schemas but also prevents children from having new experiences that are essential to changing old patterns. The dependency of children keeps them restricted to a tight little world with few alternatives for the disconfirmation of old cognitive schemas and their replacement by the formation of new ones. Early traits may fail to change, therefore, not because they have jelled permanently but because the same slender hand of experiences that formed them initially continue and persist for many years.

Caretaker Feedback

The notion that children's early behaviors may be accentuated by their parents' response to them was raised earlier. For example, unusually sensitive or cranky infants frequently elicit feelings on the part of their mothers that perpetuate the infants' original tendencies.

This model of circular, or reciprocal, influences applies not only to the perpetuation of biological dispositions but also to traits that are acquired interpersonally. Many distinctive and potentially troublesome behaviors provoke or "pull" from others certain reactions that result in their repetition (Leary, 1957). For example, a chip-on-the-shoulder, defiant child eventually will force others to counter with exasperation and anger. An ever-widening gulf of irritation and defiance may develop as parents of such children withdraw, become punitive, or "throw up their hands in disgust." Each participant, in feedback fashion, contributes fuel to the fire, and the original level of hostile behavior is further aggravated. Once the process has gotten out of hand, it may continue its inexorable course until some benign influence interferes or until it deteriorates further (Gottman & Katz, 1989).

Social Stereotypes

The child's early behaviors form a distinct impression upon others. Once established, people expect the child to behave in this manner, and, in time, they develop a fixed image of "what kind of person the child is." The term stereotype represents this tendency to simplify and categorize the attributes of others in order to achieve cognitive economy.

People no longer view a child with deliberation once they have formed a representational model of the child (Farrington, 1977). Because they are sensitized to those distinctive features rendered prepotent by expectations derived from the model, a stereotype begins to operate as a screen through which the child's behaviors are selectively perceived so as to fit the attributed characteristics. Cast in such a mold, children begin to experience a consistency in the way in which others interact with them, ways which more often than not fail to take cognizance of the complexities of the child. Once formed, these representational models are difficult to alter or falsify. Thus children may find that their behaviors are interpreted in the same fixed and rigid manner. Unable to break the stereotypes in to which they have been cast, children may give up and continue to behave as they did originally, thus confirming the expectations of others or elaborating other's representational models in expected directions.

Self-Perpetuation

The residues of past experiences and relationships are never fully lost, persisting as influences into the present. Moreover, they shape and distort the present, as described by Millon (1969):

> Significant experiences of early life may never recur again, but their effects remain and leave their mark. Physiologically, we may say they have etched a neurochemical change; psychologically, they are registered as memories, a permanent trace and an embedded internal stimulus. In contrast to the fleeting stimuli of the external world, these memory traces become part and parcel of every stimulus complex which activates behavior. Once registered, the effects of the past are indelible, incessant and inescapable. They now are intrinsic elements of the individual's make-up; they latch on and intrude into the current events of life, coloring, transforming and distorting the passing scene. Although the residuals of subsequent experiences may override them, becoming more dominant internal stimuli, the presence of earlier memory traces remains in one form or another. In every thought and action, the individual cannot help but carry these remnants into the present. Every current behavior is a perpetuation, then, of the past, a continuation and intrusion of these inner stimulus traces.
>
> The residuals of the past do more than passively contribute their share to the present. By temporal precedence, if nothing else, they guide, shape, or distort the character of current events. Not only are they ever present, then, but they operate insidiously to transform new stimulus experiences in line with past. (p. 200)

A number of these self-perpetuating processes are elaborated here.

Protective Constriction

Personality disorders clients tend to perpetuate painful patterns of interaction with others (vicious circles). To do so, they must actively avoid that which would force them into new and perhaps ultimately more adaptive directions. Painful memories may kept out of consciousness, a process referred to as repression. Similarly, experiences which reactivate repressed memories are judiciously avoided. The individual develops a network of protective maneuvers to decrease the likelihood that distressing memories or distressing experiences will recur.

While this strategy results in short term gains, the person's world is constricted as a consequence. Repression, for example, thwarts the individual from processing disturbed feelings or learning new, potentially more constructive ways of coping with them. Likewise, by reducing activities to situations that will not activate painful memories, the individual precludes the possibility of expanding his or her boundaries in order to become less anxious than in the past. These persons preserve unaltered the experiences, memories, and representational models of the past, thus perpetuating them into the future. A positive feedback loop ensues: The more vigilant the protective steps and the more constrictive the individual's boundaries, the more limited will be the challenges which build competencies for effective functioning, and the more unlikely it is that the individual will be able to cope in an effective manner.

Perceptual and Cognitive Distortion

Certain actions not only preserve the past but also transform the present in line with the past. Once individuals acquire a system of expectancies, they respond with increasing alertness to similar elements in their life situation. For example, persons who develop bodily anxieties often become hyperalert to physiological signs that most people experience but ignore.

People acquire anticipatory attitudes as a consequence of all forms of past experience. These cognitions guide, screen, code, and evaluate new experiences in line with expectancies (Folkman & Lazarus, 1988; Sroufe, 1979). The role of habits of language as factors in shaping perceptions is of particular interest. The words we use transform our experiences in line with the meaning of these words. For example, children whose parents respond to every minor mishap as "a shattering experience" will tend to use these terms themselves and conceive every setback they experience as "shattering" because they consistently labeled it as such. These children have developed a representational model which interprets every frustration as defeat.

The importance of expectancies, sensitivities, and language habits lies in their distortion of objective realities. These distortions channel attention, magnify awareness of insignificant or irrelevant features of the environment, and intrude constantly to obscure and warp an accurate perception of reality. The following quote from Beck (1963) illustrates this process well:

> A depressed patient reported the following sequence of events which occurred within a period of half an hour before he left the house: His wife was upset because the children were slow in getting dressed. He thought, "I'm a poor father because the children are not better disciplined." He then noticed a faucet was leaky and thought this showed he was also a poor husband. While driving to work, he thought, "I must be a poor driver or other cars would not be passing me." As he arrived at work he noticed some other personnel had already arrived. He thought, "I can't be very dedicated or I would have come earlier." When he noticed folders and papers piled up on his desk, he concluded, "I'm a poor organizer because I have so much work to do." (p. 329)

Such distortions may have an insidiously cumulative and spiraling effect. By misconstruing reality to make it corroborate expectancies, individuals intensify their misery. These persons subjectively experience neutral events as if they were threatening; in this process, they create painful experiences for themselves where none, in fact, exist. Once a pathological process of distortion has begun, these patients may become caught in a downward spiral in which everything, no matter how objectively "good" it might be, is perceived as distressing. Distortion has created its own momentum, resulting not only in its perpetuation but in its intensification.

Generalization of Representational Expectancies

From the viewpoint of cognitive efficiency, representational models simplify reality, allowing us to react in similar ways to persons and situations that are subjectively comparable. However, a problem arises when representational modes are applied incorrectly to situations that are objectively dissimilar, for example, when reacting to novel circumstances in the present as if they were duplicates of the past. The tendency to universalize maladaptive representational models has far-reaching consequences. Reactions are inevitably elicited from others that not only perpetuate these behaviors but also aggravate the conditions that gave rise to them.

An example may help illustrate this point. Youngsters who anticipate punishment from their parents may become hypersensitive to signs of rejection from others. They may distort innocuous comments, seeing them as indications of hostility. In preparing themselves to counter the hostility they expect, they freeze their posture, stare coldly and rigidly, or comment aggressively. These actions communicate a message quickly sensed by others as antagonistic. Before long, others begin to withdraw and display real, rather than imagined, hostility. Thus, the youngsters' suspiciousness has evoked the very punitive responses expected. They now have experienced an objective form of rejection similar to that received at the hands of their parents, which leads them to be even more suspicious and arrogant, beginning the vicious circle over again. In personality disordered clients, reciprocal interactions intensify maladaptive behavior; docile or fearful actions, for example, draw domineering and manipulative responses, and confidence and self-assurance elicit admiration and submissiveness.

DEVELOPMENT OF SPECIFIC PERSONALITY DISORDERS

Here we will attempt to specify probable biogenic and psychogenic contributors to personality disorder development, a set of necessary, though perhaps not sufficient, factors. Again, we must note that personality is a multidetermined construct with referents across a variety of domains. Our analysis, therefore, especially when presented interactionally, rather than as a simplistic "main-effects" model, must be considered speculative. Our detailed discussion will be limited to several of the more popular and interesting personality disorders. Additional clinical patterns are elaborated in Millon (1981) and Millon and Davis (1995).

Before listing a number of influences that ostensibly shape each personality disorder, three points should be reiterated.

First, most hypotheses (especially interactional or across-domain hypotheses) in psychopathology are conjectural. Second, a role ascribed to constitutional or biological determinants in no way precludes comparable effects at a uniquely psychological level of organization. Third, biogenic and psychogenic factors interact; they are separated only for pedagogic purposes.

Dependent Personality Disorder

Hypothesized Biogenic Factors

Dependency per se is never inherited, but certain types of genetic endowments are likely to have reasonably high probabilities of evolving, under normal life experiences, into a dependent style of functioning. If one's constitutional makeup is moderately consistent throughout life, it would seem reasonable to hypothesize that many adult dependents would have displayed a tendency to a soft, gentle, peaceful, and perhaps, somewhat sad quality in early childhood. Similarly, they may have shown hesitance about asserting themselves, a restraint in new situations, and a fear of venturing into the world to assert their growing capacities.

The dependent's early temperamental dispositions elicit distinctive reactions from parents. A gentle but fearful infant is likely to evoke warmth and overprotectiveness from a concerned mother. Such children invite excessive care from others, which may eventuate in their being overly dependent and comfortable with caretakers. Rather than overcoming their initial dispositions, they evoke dominant reactions from others and force them to take the initiative, leading the dependent to be even less assertive and venturesome than they would otherwise have been.

A somewhat intricate pattern of neural organization may be hypothesized to account for the development of dependent personality traits. Reticular arousal mechanisms may be sluggish in these individuals, giving rise to deficit coping under conditions of stress. At the same time, they may be overly endowed in limbic regions associated with fear, pain, and sadness. Given these neural characteristics, such persons may learn to turn to others for assistance. Their "limbic" attributes dispose them to feel difficulties intensely, and their "reticular" attributes prevent them from mustering the reactive powers needed to cope with these difficulties. Fortunate in having thoughtful and protective caretakers, such persons quickly learn to depend on others to execute the defensive actions they cannot manage on their own. Turning more and more to their caretakers to aid them in coping only "binds" them further to others and the protection they provide. As a consequence, they may progress into increasingly greater dependencies.

Experiential History

A score of experiential influences might be enumerated which contribute to the development of the dependent personality. The conditions described in this section have been chosen because they appear often in the history of these individuals and seem to carry weight in initiating, as well in shaping, their personality style. They are relevant because they contribute both to the development of attachment styles and to the avoidance of independent behaviors.

Every infant is helplessly dependent on caretakers for both protection and nurturance. During the first months of life, the child acquires a notion of which objects are associated with increments in comfort and gratification; as a consequence, the child becomes "attached" to these objects. Difficulties arise if these attachments are too narrowly restricted or so rooted as to deter the growth of the child's competencies for self-direction and autonomy. It may be of interest to follow the course of these pathological attachments through the first three stages of evolutionary-neuropsychological development outlined earlier in this chapter.

The first stage of development, the sensory attachment stage (concerned with the pleasure-pain polarity), serves as a foundation for future growth. Supplied with pleasurable stimulation, the child is likely to develop interpersonal sensitivity and trust. However, infants who receive excessive stimulation and nurturance, and experience these almost exclusively from one source, usually the mother, will be disposed to develop passively dependent traits. As a consequence of a narrow sphere of object relations, the infant may form a singular attachment, a fixation, if you will, to one object source to the exclusion of others. A variety of events may give rise to this exclusive attachment. Unusual illnesses or prolonged physical complications in the child's health may prompt a parent to tend excessively to the infant. On the other hand, an overly worrisome and anxious parent may be hypersensitive to real and fantasized needs seen in a normal child, resulting in undue attention and cuddling. Occasionally, special circumstances, such as a father leaving for an overseas war assignment, may throw the infant and mother together into a "symbiotic" dependency.

Infants who retain their exclusive parental attachments during the second evolutionary-neuropsychological stage, that of sensorimotor-autonomy (concerned with the active-passive polarity), will have their earlier training in passivity and dependency strengthened and perpetuated. However, many youngsters who are not especially attached to a parent in the first stage also develop the dependent pattern. The second evolutionary stage is distinguished by the opportunity to learn skills associated with competence, independent behaviors and, in general, the active modification of the environment. Circumstances that undermine the acquisition of these competencies may foster pathological dependency.

What conditions in this stage may result in pathological dependency patterns? A not uncommon factor is the child's own deficits and temperament dispositions, such as physical inadequacies, fear of new challenges, anguish when left alone, and so on. Whether by virtue of constitutional temperament or early experiences, some children evoke protective reactions from others. Parents may be induced to overprotect an exceptionally timid or insecure child. The child's reluctance or even refusal to exercise independence "forces" them to do so. Similarly, children who have suffered prolonged illnesses may have been prevented from exercising their maturing capacities because of a realistic physical limitation or the judgments of justifiably concerned parents.

Barring constitutional or physical deficits, normal youngsters assert their growing capacities and strive to do more things by themselves. This progression toward self-competence and active environmental mastery may be interfered with by excessive parental anxieties. Thus, some parents discourage independence for fear of "losing their baby." These parents actively or insidiously place barriers and diversionary pitfalls which prevent their children from gaining autonomy. They may restrict ventures outside the home, worry lest children strain themselves, make no demands for self-responsibility, or provide children with every comfort and reward so long as they keep close to the protective parent. Rather than let children stumble and fumble with their new skills, the parents do things for them and make challenging developmental tasks unnecessarily easy. Time and again children may be discouraged from "going it alone." Because of the ease with which they can obtain gratification by leaning on their parents, these children may give up their feeble efforts at independence. Hence, they may never acquire the wherewithal to act on their own in order to secure the rewards of life. There is no need to acquire self-initiated instrumental behaviors. From needing to modify their ecologic niche, all the dependent must do is sit back passively and let others take control.

Parental overprotection that is continued into the third evolutionary-neuropsychological stage, that which concerns the self-other polarity, may devastate and impoverish a child's self-image. These children may fail to develop a representational model of themselves apart from their caretakers: Their dependence on others denies them the opportunity to do things for themselves, to form an impression of what they are good at and who they are: Dependency deprives them of experiences necessary for the development of a self-image that distinguishes them as individuals. Moreover, parental over-protection implies that these children cannot take care of themselves. Thus, pampered children are likely to view themselves just as their parents do, as persons who need special care and supervision because they are incompetent, prone to illness, oversensitive, constitutionally weak, and so on. Their representational model of themselves mirrors that of parental figures. They see themselves as weak and inferior. Upon venturing into the outside world, such individuals are likely to find their subjective inferiority confirmed: By this point, they are objectively less competent and mature than their cohorts. Viewing themselves to be inadequate, they have little recourse but to again turn to others to arrange their life and to provide for them.

Some nonparental factors may also predispose children toward a dependent pattern. The major factor here concerns events of relationships that lead children either to believe that they cannot compete with others or to learn that a passive and submissive rather than and active and assertive role will assure less discomfort and more reward. For example, a family situation in which the growing youngster is exposed to a more aggressive, competent, or troublesome sibling may set the stage for a dependent personality style. A more assertive and effective sibling may lead to unfavorable self-comparisons. Similarly, a difficult-to-manage sibling may invite the child to adopt the "good boy" image, one who acquiesces to mother's every mood and wish so as to gain comparative favor. In a third family, a child who is repeatedly subjected to the lashing of an angry or jealous sib may run so often for parental cover that the child learns to cling to more powerful others whenever a difficult world must be confronted.

Similar difficulties may be generated in experiences with one's peer group. Feelings of unattractiveness and inadequacy,

especially during adolescence, often result in social humiliation and self-doubt. These youngsters are fortunate in the sense that they can usually retreat to their parents, where they find both love and acceptance. Although the immediate refuge of home is not to be demeaned, it may, in the long run, prove a disservice to these children since they must ultimately learn to stand on their own.

Histrionic Personality Disorder

As with the dependent pattern, the influences posited here as significant in forming the histrionic personality must be recognized as conjectural. Further, the distinction made in grouping these influences into biogenic and experiential sections is merely pedagogic; the pattern of constraints is not only interactive but is reciprocally and sequentially interconnected. With these caveats, discussion of the topic proceeds.

Hypothesized Biogenic Factors

The biological underpinnings of the histrionic personality are difficult to infer. Conceived in temperamental terms, histrionic behavior suggests both a high level of energy and activation, and a low threshold for autonomic reactivity. Histrionics tend, in general, to be quick and responsive, especially with regard to the expression of emotions. Feelings of both a positive and negative variety come forth with extreme ease, suggesting either an unusually high degree of sensory irritability, excessive sympathetic activity, or a lack of cortical inhibition. No single temperament label readily captures the intense, erratic, and wide range of emotions to which histrionics are disposed.

Histrionic adults likely display a high degree of emotional responsiveness in infancy and early childhood. This inference derives from the facts that constitutional traits are essentially stable throughout life and that active and responsive children are likely to foster and intensify their initial responsiveness by evoking stimulating reactions from others.

Among the possible brain sites that may be posited for the emotional responsivity of the histrionic are the limbic and reticular systems. A neurally dense or abundantly branched limbic region may account for both the intensity and ease with which emotions are expressed. Low thresholds for reticular activation, stemming from idiosyncratic features of that region, may underlie their excitability and diffuse reactivity. Similarly, ease of sympathetic arousal, adrenal hyperreactivity, and neurochemical imbalances may facilitate a rapid transmission of impulses across synaptic junctions, resulting in the tendency of histrionics to be labile, distractible, and excitable. Such hypotheses are, however, highly conjectural.

Experiential History

Constitutionally alert and responsive infants are likely to experience greater and more diverse stimulation in their first months of life than dull and phlegmatic infants. As a consequence, their active dispositions are reinforced to look "outward" to the external world for rewards rather than "inward" to themselves. Similarly, normally alert infants may develop this exteroceptive attitude if their caretakers, by virtue of indulgence and playfulness, expose them to excessive stimulation during the first, or what we have termed the sensory-attachment stage (concerned with the pleasure-pain polarity). Future histrionic personalities may have been exposed to a number of different sources that provided brief, highly charged, and irregular stimulus reinforcements. For example, they may have had many different caretakers in infancy (parents, siblings, grandparents, and foster parents) who supplied them with intense, short-lived gratifications at irregular or haphazard intervals. Such experiences may not only have built in a high level of sensory capacity, requiring constant "feeding" to be sustained, but may also have lead to the development of representational models through which the child expects positive stimulation in short, concentrated bursts from a melange of different sources. Viewed in this way, the persistent yet erratic dependency behaviors of the histrionic personality may reflect a pathological form of intense object seeking that is traceable to highly charged, varied, and irregular conditions characterizing early attachments. Shifting from one source of gratification to another, the histrionic's search for new, stimulating adventures, penchant for creating excitement, and inability to tolerate boredom and routine, all may represent the consequences of these unusual early experiences.

In addition to differences in the variety, regularity, and intensity of object enrichments in the pain-pleasure (sensory-attachment) stage, the childhood experiences of the histrionic may be distinguished from those of the dependent personality. For dependents, the attention and affection of caretakers is not contingent on the dependent's own behavior—they do not need to "perform" to elicit parental nurturance and protection. As a consequence of passively waiting for their parents to tend to their needs, dependents failed to develop adequate competencies and autonomy. Future histrionics, in contrast, must engage in particular sanctioned behaviors and satisfy particular parental desires and expectations in order to receive attention and affection. In other words, future histrionics learn that parental approval is contingent on performance, such as "looking pretty" or showing their latest "artistic masterpiece," or the "fancy ballet steps" just learned in dancing school. Thus, while both the dependent and histrionic patterns are other-oriented, the dependent is passively, and the histrionic actively, so.

Speaking behaviorally, we might say that the conditions for learning histrionic behaviors seem to be characterized by three features: minimal negative reinforcement and punishment (e.g., parents tend not to harshly criticize or punish the child), positive reinforcement contingent upon performance of parentally approved behaviors (e.g., favorable comments are conveyed only if one "is pretty" or "did well"), and irregularity in positive reinforcement (e.g., parents periodically fail to take cognizance of the child's efforts even when the child attempts to attract their attention). Speaking in terms of object relations, we might say that future histrionics possess representational models of the parents as irregular in their approval and praise, perhaps even as inconsistent or fickle with regard to activities previously approved. Stated colloquially, the parents of the future histrionic infrequently punish their children, distribute reward only for what they approve and admire, but often fail to bestow these rewards even when the child behaves acceptably.

Such experiences have several consequences for personality development. They reinforce behaviors designed primarily to evoke rewards, create a feeling of competence and acceptance only if others acknowledge and commend one's performances, and build a habit of seeking approval for its own sake. All three characterize the histrionic personality. The following paragraphs consider their development in some detail.

Children who receive few punishments and many rewards develop strong and unambivalent inclinations to relate to others. When such a child learns that the achievement of rewards is dependent on fulfilling the expectations and desires of others, he or she develops a set of instrumental behaviors designed to please others and thereby elicit these rewards. However, if these behaviors succeed irregularly, the child may persist in using them well beyond all reason—until they do succeed, which they eventually will. Such reward- and attention-seeking behaviors do not easily extinguish, even if they fail much of the time. As a consequence, these children become actively, rather than passively, oriented toward others. Furthermore, they will learn to look to others rather than to themselves for rewards, since their actions are a preliminary, but not a sufficient condition for achieving reinforcement. Despite invariably behaving to please and perform for others, the fact remains that it is others who determine whether the child will be rewarded. Future histrionics look to others for their judgment of whether the histrionic's efforts justify approval: Others define the adequacy of the child's behavior. In its most superficial incarnation, appeal and achievement are gauged solely by the attentions of others, not by the intrinsic merit or lack of merit of the histrionic's objective actions. Moreover, since favorable recognition of acceptance occurs only irregularly—that is, not every time the child performs—future histrionics are never sure of their appeal and attractiveness, and therefore continue to look to others, even after repeated failures, to express a favorable response. Because of the irregularity with which attention is bestowed, the search takes on a "life of its own," a habit of soliciting signs of approval that becomes so firmly established that it eventually is pursued for its own sake.

Two additional features of family life often contribute to the development of the histrionic pattern—parental models who themselves are histrionic and certain patterns of sibling rivalry.

As previously discussed, children learn, quite unconsciously and unintentionally, to mimic that to which they are regularly exposed. Representationally speaking, they incorporate the representational models of others as their own: Prevailing attitudes, feelings, and incidental behaviors displayed every day by family members serve as models which children imitate and take as their own long before they can recognize what they are doing or why. Such incorporation is made especially easy if parental behaviors and feelings are unusually pronounced or dramatic. When parents bring attention to themselves and create strong emotional reactions in their child, the child cannot help but see and learn clearly how people behave and feel. Thus, the daily input of a histrionic parent who exhibits feelings and attitudes rather dramatically provides a sharply defined model that can be identified with and appropriated by the child.

Another family condition conducive to development of the histrionic pattern arises among children who must compete for parental attention and affection under conditions of sibling rivalry. These children may sometimes continue their attention-getting devices into adulthood. Thus, if the child learned to employ cuteness, charm, attractiveness, and seduction as a strategy to secure parental attention, these interpersonal behaviors may persist and take the form of a lifelong histrionic pattern.

Finally, there are parents who fail to provide their children with a consistent or stabilizing set of values. Some are intellectually committed to a laissez-faire policy; others are vacillating themselves; a third group is so preoccupied that they have little time to guide their child's development. Whatever the reason, many children are left to fend for themselves, to discover their own direction in the complex and changing world which surrounds them. Given the character of an evolving society, these children find little clarity or consistency; one set of values is espoused here, and another, entirely contradictory set is presented there. No firm footing is to be found anywhere. As a consequence, such children may learn that the best course of action is to size up each situation as they face it and to guide themselves in accord with the particulars of that situation, and no other. Rather than establishing an internal set of consistent standards, they acquire a hyperflexibility, a facile and quick adaptiveness to changing circumstances. To believe in anything wholeheartedly is foolish since events change and one must be ready to adjust to them. Such youngsters are devoid of any internal and stable belief system to which they are committed. Their identities are multiple and diffuse. Life progresses, not with an internal gyroscope, but with a radar system that is sensitive to changing values and expectations. Unsure of who they are, these youngsters must remain hyperalert and hyperadaptive to their environment. Restlessly shifting from one belief and fleeting course of action to another is a trait that often comes to characterize the future histrionic, especially those who exhibit borderline personality features.

Histrionics orient their attention to the external world and their perceptions and cognitions tend to be fleeting, impressionistic, and undeveloped. This preoccupation with incidental and passing details prevents experiences from being digested and embedded within the individual's inner world. In effect, histrionics show little integration and few well-examined reflective processes that intervene between perception and action; histrionics act before their actions can be connected and organized by the operation of memory and thought. The disadvantages of this hyperalertness to external stimuli may outweigh its advantages. Unless life events are digested and integrated, the individual gains little from them. Interpersonal transactions and experience pass through the person as if he or she were a sieve. There is little opportunity to develop inner skills and few memories against which future experience can be evaluated. Indiscriminate and scattered responsiveness leaves the person devoid of an inner reservoir of articulated memories and a storehouse of examined ideas and thoughts. In short, an excessive preoccupation with external events perpetuates the histrionic's "empty shell" and further fosters dependence on others as the only source of guidance.

The histrionic personality requires a retinue of changing events and people to replenish the need for stimulation and approval. Thus, as life progresses, histrionics move capriciously from one source to another. One consequence of these fleeting and erratic relationships is that histrionics can never be sure of securing the affection and support they crave. By moving constantly and by devouring the affections of one person and then another, they place themselves in jeopardy of having nothing to tide them over the times between. They may be left high and dry, alone and abandoned with nothing to do and no excitement with which to be preoccupied. Cut off from external supplies, histrionics are likely either to engage in a frantic search for stimulation and approval or to become dejected and forlorn. They may proceed through cyclical swings, alternating moments of simulated euphoria and excitement intermingled with longer periods of hopelessness, futility, and self-condemnation. Should deprivation be frequent or prolonged, the probability is high that these personalities will display the signs of a clear and serious affective disorder.

Narcissistic Personality Disorder

Whatever the reason may be, some parents come to view their child as "God's gift to mankind." These parents pamper and indulge their youngsters as if their every wish were the parent's command, teaching them that they can receive without giving in return, and that they deserve prominence without even minimal effort. An excerpt from Freud's seminal paper "On Narcissism" is reproduced to highlight this contributor's view to the development of narcissism. It signifies Freud's awareness that narcissism need not stem from rejection or disillusion, as the analysts Kernberg and Kohut contend, but may be a direct consequence of parental overvaluation. In describing these parents, Freud wrote:

> They are impelled to ascribe to the child all manner of perfections which sober observation would not confirm, to gloss over and forget all his shortcomings . . . Moreover, they are inclined to suspend in the child's favor the operation of all those cultural requirements which their own narcissism has been forced to respect, and to renew in his person the claims for privileges which were long ago given up by themselves. The child shall have things better than his parents; he shall not be subject to the necessities which they have recognized as dominating life . . . restrictions on his own will are not to touch him; the laws of nature, like those of society, are to be abrogated in his favor; he is really to be the center and heart of creation. (1914, p. 48)

Horney presented a similar developmental history in the following quote:

> Parents who transfer their own ambitions to the child and regard the boy as an embryonic genius or the girl as a princess thereby develop in the child the feeling that he is loved for imaginary qualities rather than for his true self. (1939, p. 91)

In short order, children with such experiences begin to view themselves as special beings. They expect subservience from others, and begin to recognize that their mere existence is sufficient to provide pleasure to others and that their every action evokes commendation and praise. Unfortunately, they fail to learn how to cooperate and share or to think of the desires and interests of others. They acquire little sense of interpersonal responsibility and few skills for the give-and-take of social life. The family world revolves about them. They are egotistic in their attentions and narcissistic in the expression of their love and affect.

Children that have been exposed repeatedly to acquiescent and indulgent parents will expect comparable treatment from others, and they learn to employ the presumptuous and demanding strategies that quickly elicited favored reactions when these were not immediately forthcoming from their parents. Thus, when their desires are frustrated, they need act only in that way, feeling entitled and assuming that their wishes will automatically be met.

Such youngsters learn not only to take others for granted and to exploit them for personal benefit, but they also learn to see others as weak and subservient. By their fawning and self-demeaning behaviors, the parents of future narcissists have provided them with a representational model of others as manipulable, docile, and yielding. This view not only enhances narcissists' image of their own specialness but also serves to strengthen their inclination to exploit others. Seeing others as weak and submissive allows them to ride roughshod over their interests with impunity.

It may be useful to trace the effects of parental overvaluation through the evolutionary-neuropsychology stages of development.

Feelings of omnipotence begin shortly after birth but do not take hold in a meaningful fashion until the sensorimotor-autonomy stage (concerned with the active-passive polarity). Every minor achievement of future narcissists is responded to with such favor as to give them a deluded sense of their own extraordinary self-worth. While extreme confidence in one's child need not be a disservice if it is well earned, in the case of the future narcissist, a marked disparity exists between the child's actual competence and the impression he/she has of it.

Failure in parental guidance and control will play an important role during the intracortical-initiative stage (concerned with the self-other polarity). The child is encouraged to imagine, explore, and act without discipline and regulation. Unrestrained by the imposition of parental limits, the child's thoughts and behaviors may stray far beyond accepted boundaries of social reality. Untutored by parental discipline regarding the constraints of fear, guilt, and shame, the child may fail to develop those internal regulating mechanisms that result in self-control and social responsibility. Thus, the child acquires an excessive orientation toward the self. He or she becomes the absolute center of the object world.

Mention should be made of the high frequency with which the conditions noted here arise among only children. Such youngsters often are cherished by their parents as possessions of extraordinary value. Not only are these children fawned over, they also frequently experience few of the restrictions and few of the responsibilities of sharing acquired by youngsters with siblings.

As with all personalities, narcissists exhibit their style with persistence and inflexibility. They cannot alter their strategy since these patterns are deeply ingrained. Rather than modifying their behavior when faced with failure, they may revert more intractably to their characteristic style; this is likely to intensify and foster new difficulties. In their attempts to cope with shame and defeat, they set up vicious circles that only perpetuate their problems. These are elaborated next.

Narcissists assume that the presumption of superiority will suffice as its proof. Conditioned to think of themselves as able and admirable, they see little reason to waste the effort needed to acquire these virtues. Why bother engaging in such demeaning labors as systematic and disciplined study if one already possesses talent and aptitude? Moreover, it is beneath one's dignity to struggle as others do. Since they believe that they are well endowed from the start, there is no need to exert their energies to achieve what they already have. They simply assume that what they wish will come to them with little or no effort on their part.

Many narcissists begin to recognize in time that they cannot "live up" to their self-made publicity and fear trying themselves out in the real world. Rather than face genuine challenges, they may temporize and boast, but they never venture to test their adequacy. By acting in this way, they can retain their illusion of superiority without fear of disproof. As a consequence, however, narcissists paralyze themselves. Their unfounded sense of confidence and their omnipotent belief in their perfection inhibit them from developing whatever aptitudes they may in fact possess. Unwilling or fearful of expending the effort, they may slip increasingly behind others in actual attainments. Their deficits may become pronounced over time, making them, as well as others, increasingly aware of their shortcomings. Since the belief in their superiority is the bedrock of their existence, the disparity between their genuine and their illusory competence becomes extraordinarily painful. The strain of maintaining their false self-image may cause them to feel fraudulent, empty, and disconsolate. They may succumb to periodic depressions or may slip slowly into paranoid irritabilities and delusions.

The narcissist's illusion of superiority and entitlement is but one facet of a more generalized disdain for reality. Narcissists are neither disposed to stick to objective facts nor to restrict their actions within the boundaries of social custom or cooperative living. Unrestrained by childhood discipline and confident of their worth and prowess, they may take liberties with rules and reality, and prevaricate and fantasize at will. Free to wander in their private world of fiction, narcissists may lose touch with reality, lose their sense of proportion, and begin to think along peculiar and deviant lines. Their facile imagination may ultimately evoke comments from others concerning their arrogance and conceit. Ill-disposed to accept critical comments about their "creativity" and needing to retain their admirable self-image, narcissists are likely to turn further to their habit of self-glorification. Lacking social or self-controls, however, their fantasies may take flight and recede increasingly from objective reality.

Were narcissists able to respect others, allow themselves to value others' opinions, or see the world through others' eyes, their tendencies toward illusion and unreality might be checked or curtailed. Unfortunately, narcissists have learned to devalue others, not to trust their judgments, and to think of them as naive and simpleminded. Thus, rather than question the correctness of their own beliefs, they assume that it is the views of others that are at fault. Hence, the more disagreement they have with others, the more convinced they are of their own superiority and the more isolated and alienated they are likely to become. These ideational difficulties are magnified further by their inability to participate skillfully in the give-and-take of shared social life. Their characteristic selfishness and ungenerosity often evoke condemnation and disparagement from others. These reactions drive narcissists further into their world of fantasy and only strengthen their alienation. And this isolation further prevents them from understanding the intentions and actions of others. They are increasingly unable to assess situations objectively, thereby failing further to grasp why they have been rebuffed and misunderstood. Distressed by these repeated and perplexing social failures, they are likely, at first, to become depressed and morose. However, true to their fashion, they will begin to elaborate new and fantastic rationales to account for their fate. But the more they conjecture and ruminate, the more they will lose touch, distort, and perceive things that are not there. They may begin to be suspicious of others, to question the latter's intentions, and to criticize them for ostensive deceptions. In time, narcissists' actions will drive away potential well-wishers, a reaction that will only serve to "prove" their suspicions.

Deficient in social controls and self-discipline, the narcissist's tendency to fantasize and distort may speed up. The air of grandiosity may become more flagrant. They may find hidden and deprecatory meanings in the incidental behavior of others, becoming convinced of others' malicious motives, claims upon them, and attempts to undo them. As their behaviors and thoughts transgress the line of reality, their alienation will mount, and they may seek to protect their phantom image of superiority more vigorously and vigilantly than ever. Trapped by the consequences of their own actions, they may become bewildered and frightened as the downward spiral progresses through its inexorable course. No longer in touch with reality, they begin to accuse others and hold them responsible for their own shame and failures. They may build a "logic" based on irrelevant and entirely circumstantial "evidence" and ultimately construct a delusional system to protect themselves from unbearable reality.

Antisocial Personality Disorder

For pedagogic purposes, biogenic factors are again differentiated from experiential influences. The usual caveat concerning the conjectural nature of the hypotheses that follow is also applicable. There is a marked paucity of established empirical findings, even in this group of disorders where more research has been undertaken than in any other personality syndrome. Although some of the conjectures proposed in the following paragraphs derive from findings that are reasonably consistent, it would still be wise to view them with a skeptical eye.

Hypothesized Biogenic Factors

A number of constitutional features have been reported to occur with disproportionately high frequency among these personalities. In the realm of activation, for example, they have been judged to be energetic, to react with high intensity to stimuli, and to have a low threshold for responding physically but a high threshold for responding emotionally. Unbounded in energy, they appear assertive and intrude upon others like the proverbial "bull in a china shop." Others display an irritability upon stimulation, respond before thinking, act impulsively, and are unable to delay or inhibit their first reaction, and therefore behave in an unreflective and uncontrolled manner. With regard to affect and temperament, there are indications that many of these personalities are constitutionally fearless, unaffected by events that most people experience as dangerous and frightening. Some evidence a foolhardy courageousness, a venturesomeness seemingly blind

to the potential of serious consequences. Others appear easily provoked to anger; they appear so constituted as to respond with hostility "at the drop of a hat." Thus, in contrast to their high threshold for experiencing fear or anxiety, their threshold for anger is so low that the mildest of provocations can elicit intensely hostile reactions.

Parents who bring their acting-out children to clinics often report that their youngsters "always were that way." A common complaint is that the child displayed temper tantrums from infancy and would get furious when frustrated, either when awaiting the bottle or feeling uncomfortable in a wet diaper. As these children mature, they are often described as having had a "hot temper" and a bullying attitude toward sibs and other children. Quite commonly, parents remark that these children were undaunted by punishment and generally quite unmanageable. Moreover, many evidenced a daring boldness, an audacious and foolhardy willingness to chance physical harm. Many seemed thick-skinned and unaffected by pain.

Temperamental dispositions such as these in early life are significant not only in themselves but also for the experiences they produce and the reactions they evoke from others. More venturesome, such children explore, challenge, and compete in their environment assertively. Moreover, they intrude and upset the peaceful existence that others seek. Not only are they likely to precipitate more trouble than most, their seeming recalcitrance results in their receiving more punishment than that required to control most children. Thus, given a "nasty" and "incorrigible" disposition from the start, these children provoke an excess of exasperation and counterhostility from others. Their temperament initiates a vicious circle in which they not only prompt frequent aggression but also learn to expect it.

As suggested earlier, a disposition to hostile and irritable behaviors may be based in part on low thresholds for activation. Similarly, the insensitivity to pain and anxiety often attributed to these personalities may derive from high thresholds for autonomic reactivity. Moreover, should reticular pathways for arousal be unusually dense or laid out to short circuit the inhibitory effects of cortical intervention, the individual may exhibit the characteristic intense and impulsive behaviors. An unusual anatomical distribution in the limbic system also may contribute to the distinctive pattern of affectivity and to the bold and seemingly fearless outlook. We may speculate, finally, that the biophysical substrate for "rage and anger" may be copious or extensively branched, resulting in the rapid and frequently activated hostile behaviors.

Experiential History

Although the characteristics of this personality may be traced, albeit quite speculatively, to biogenic dispositions, psychogenic factors also undoubtedly shape the content and direction of these inclinations. Moreover, experience itself may be sufficient to prompt these behaviors. Keep in mind, however, that as far as personality patterns are concerned, biogenic and psychogenic factors inevitably weave a complex sequence of influences difficult to disentangle.

The primary experiential agent for this pattern is likely to be parental rejection, discontent, or hostility. This reaction may be prompted in part when the newborn infant, for constitutional reasons, proves to be "cold," sullen, testy, or otherwise difficult to manage. It does not take too long for a child with a disposition such as this to be stereotyped as a "miserable, ill-tempered, and disagreeable little beast." Once categorized in this manner, reciprocal negative feelings build up into a lifelong cycle of parent-child feuding.

Parental hostility may stem from any number of sources other than the child's initial disposition. Many children are convenient scapegoats for displaced anger that has been generated elsewhere, such as in a parent's occupational, marital, or social frustrations. Whatever its initial source, a major cause for the development of this personality pattern is exposure to parental cruelty or indifference. The reason that these experiences have so pronounced an impact is fairly straightforward. Hostility breeds hostility, and indifference breeds indifference, not only in generating intense feelings of anger and resentment on the part of the recipient but, even more importantly, also by establishing a model for vicarious learning. It makes little difference as to whether the child desires consciously to imitate parental indifference or hostility; mere exposure to these behaviors—especially in childhood, when there are few alternatives to be observed—serves as a template or model as to how people feel and relate to one another. Thus, neglectful, irresponsible, and abusive parents arouse and release strong counter feelings of personal indifference and hostility in their children. Moreover, they demonstrate in their roughshod and inconsiderate behaviors both a model for imitation and an implicit sanction for similar abusive behaviors whenever the children themselves feel a rush of anger or frustration.

Tracing the effects of parental neglectfulness and abuse in line with the three evolutionary-neuropsychological stages of development will provide additional insights into the complex pattern of habits and attitudes displayed by both major variants of this personality.

The distinguishing feature of the sensory-attachment stage (pleasure-pain polarity) is not likely to have been the amount of stimulation to which the infant was exposed, but rather its quality. Rough or harsh treatment conveys a tone, a "feeling" in the neonate that the world is an unkind, painful, and dangerous place, that discomfort and frustration are to be expected and to be prepared for. Early parental abuse and neglect cue the infant to mistrust the environment and to view it with suspicion.

Having learned to expect a world that will treat them indifferently or harshly, these children enter the sensorimotor-autonomy stage (active-passive polarity) with a feeling that they cannot depend on others, that they must turn to themselves to provide pleasure and to avoid pain. Having no alternatives, the youngsters rapidly acquire the skills of autonomy and self-reliance. By the "end" of the second neuropsychological stage, they are both deeply mistrustful and substantially independent of their parents.

Being both suspicious of others and increasingly confident in their powers of self-sufficiency, these youngsters begin the intracortical-initiative (self-other polarity) stage with a determination to reject the guidance and domination of others. Why should they accept the restrictions and demands that others seek to impose upon them when they have nothing to gain and, in addition, are convinced that they can manage better on their own? Subjected to parental abuse and disinterest throughout these growing

years, the children learn not only to reject their parents but to oppose the values and standards of the adult world they represent. Thus, they set out to shape their own identity, one that is contrary to those espoused by their elders; in so doing, they embark on a course of self-sufficiency and mistrust.

One consequence of rejecting "authorities" is to lose the guidance society provides for handling and directing impulses. By rejecting traditional values and customs, these youngsters are left on their own. They must devise, either on their own or by imitating peer models, ways and means to handle their emotions. During this period, when adolescent children are driven strongly by both erotic and hostile impulses, we find that few acquire self-developed controls adequate to their emotions. Most have difficult in deferring gratifications, in resisting temptations, and in inhibiting angry reactions to even the slightest of frustrations. Such youngsters pursue their desires with little concern for the dangers or complications they invite.

In summary, children who are exposed to parental neglect or abuse acquire enduring resentments toward others, and they incorporate the parental model of indifference or hostility as a guide for venting these feelings. This background is one of the most common found among the antisocial personality, but by no means is it the only, pathogenic source for this pattern.

Another important contributor in shaping antisocial types is the lack of parental models. If parents provide little or no guidance for their children, they are left to fend for themselves, to observe and to emulate whatever models they can for guidance. Broken families, especially those in which the father has abandoned both wife and children, often characterize this state of affairs. With the model and authority of the breadwinner out of sight, and the mother frequently harassed by overwork and financial insecurity, the youngster is often left to roam the streets, unguided and unrestrained by the affection and controls of an attending parent. Moreover, the disappearance of the father and the preoccupations of a distracted mother are felt as rejections. To find a model or belief by which their identity can be mobilized and given meaning, these children must often turn to their peers, to those other barren and lost souls who are also bereft of parental attention, and who likewise wander aimlessly in an indifferent, if not hostile, world.

Together with their fellow outcasts, these nascent antisocial personalities quickly learn that they are viewed by others as society's misfits, and that their misfortunes will only be further compounded by the deprecatory and closed-minded attitudes of the larger community. They soon learn that it is only by toughness and cunning that they will find a means of survival. Unfortunately, this adaptive strategy sets into play a vicious circle. As they venture into the deviant remains left behind for them and their fellow scavengers by the larger society, that very same society points a finger of disapproval and castigates and condemns them. As their resentments mount over the injustice and entrapment they feel, the circle of hostility and counter hostility feeds back and gains momentum. With little hope of changing their fate and little promise of advancement—and struggling mightily, if cunningly and brutally, to keep a foothold in the dog-eat-dog world into which they have been cast—they are driven further and further into an antisocial and vindictive life-style.

Most of what is communicated and experienced in life is fragmentary in nature—a few words, an intonation, a gesture. On the basis of these suggestive, but incomplete, messages we come to some conclusion or inference as to what others seek to convey. We constantly "read between the lines" on the basis of past experiences, enabling us thereby to give these incidental cues their coherence and meaning. Among the determinants of what we "fill in" are our moods and anticipations. If we expect someone to be cruel and abusive we are likely to piece together the hazy elements of the communication in line with this expectancy. If we feel downhearted some days, it appears that the whole world is downcast and gloomy with us. Since the outlook and moods of most of us are episodic and temporary, these intrusions tend to be counterbalanced. That is, we may be suspicious of certain persons but overly naive with others; we may feel "blue" some days but cheerful and optimistic on others. This pattern of variability and balancing of mood and attitude is less typical of pathological than "normal" personalities. In the aggressively antisocial individual, for example, there is an ever-present undertone of anger and resentment, a persistent expectation that others will be devious and hostile. Because these moods and expectancies endure, these personalities are likely to repeatedly distort incidental remarks and actions so that they appear deprecatory and vilifying. They persist in misinterpreting what they see and hear, and magnify minor slights into major insults and slanders.

Despite the fact that this personality's antisocial reaction to external threat is understandable, given past experience, it promotes repetitive self-defeating consequences. For example, by perceiving rejection where none exists, these individuals prevent themselves from recognizing and appreciating whatever goodwill of others actually exists. Their reality is what they perceive, not what objectively exists. Thus, their vulnerability to rejection blocks them from recognizing the presence of experiences that might prove gratifying and thereby change the course of their outlook and attitudes. Moreover, their distortion aggravates their misfortunes by creating, through anticipation, fictitious dangers that duplicate those of the past. Rather than avoiding further pain and abuse, the antisocial's hypersensitivity uncovers them where they do not exist. In essence, their moods and defenses have fabricated dangers from which antisocials cannot escape since they derive from within themselves.

Both the basic aggressive and overtly antisocial variants of this personality evoke hostility, not only as an incidental consequence of their behaviors and attitudes but also because they intentionally provoke others in to conflict. They carry a "chip on their shoulder," often seem to be spoiling for a fight, and appear to enjoy tangling with others to prove their strength and test their competencies and powers. Having been periodically successful in past antisocial ventures, they feel confident of their prowess. They may seek out dangers and challenges. Not only are they unconcerned and reckless, they also appear poised and bristling, ready to vent resentments, demonstrate their invulnerability, and restore their pride.

Unfortunately, as with their perceptions and attitudes, these aggressive, conflict-seeking behaviors only perpetuate their fears and misery. More than merely fostering distance and rejection, they have now provoked others into justified counterhostility. By spoiling for a fight and by precipitous and irrational arrogance, they create not only a distant reserve on the part of others but intense and well-justified animosity. Now they must face real aggression, and now they have a real basis for anticipating retaliation. Objective threats and resentments do exist in the environment now, and the vicious circle is perpetuated anew. Their vigilant state cannot be relaxed, they must ready themselves, no longer for suspected threat and imagined hostility, but for the real thing.

Obsessive-Compulsive Personality Disorders

Hypothesized Biogenic Factors

Few obsessive-compulsives evidence a lively or ebullient manner; most are rigidly controlled and emotionally tight, and their failure to release pent-up energies is likely to dispose them to psychophysiologic disorders. Any speculation that the ambivalence of compulsives might reflect some intrinsic antagonism between opposing temperamental dispositions would seem presumptuous. Yet we do observe an opposition between intense fear and intense anger among these individuals. Both tendencies may be great and may account in part for their frequent indecisiveness and immobilization. Given their grim and joyless quality, we might also conjecture that many possess a constitutionally based anhedonic temperament. Translating these notions into tangible substrates, it might be hypothesized that regions of the limbic system associated with both "fear" and "anger" may be usually dense or well branched; conflicting signals from these areas might underlie the hesitancy, doubting, and indecisive behaviors seen in these patients. Similarly, the substrate for experiencing pleasure may be poorly developed, leading to the compulsive's typical stern countenance. Speculations such as these are highly conjectural.

Experiential History

The determinants of the compulsive style are rooted primarily in interpersonal experience and reflect the behaviors the child learns as a means of coping with these experiences. This discussion formulates a developmental history with reference to a social learning model that parallels many of the views of psychoanalytic theorists.

"Overcontrol" is a major concept in understanding how compulsives were trained to become what they are. It explains how compulsives acquired their style of behavior, as well as being descriptive of that style. The notion of overcontrol as a concept of child rearing may best be understood by contrasting it with other child-rearing practices. First, it differs from "overprotection" in that it reflects an attitude of parental firmness, if not repressiveness. Overprotection, most common in the history of the dependent personality, usually reflects a gentle and loving parental concern, a desire to cuddle and care for the child without harshness or hostility. Overcontrolling parents may also be "caring," but display this concern by "keeping the child in line"; they prevent children from causing trouble not only for themselves but also for the parents. Overcontrolling parents are frequently punitive in response to transgression, whereas overprotective parents are likely to restrain the child more gently and lovingly, not with anger or threats.

Parental overcontrol is similar to parental hostility, a training process more typical of the history of the antisocial personality pattern. But there are important distinctions here as well. Hostile parents are punitive regardless of the child's behavior, whereas overcontrolling parents are punitive only if the child misbehaves. Thus, the parents of future compulsives are likely to expect their children to live up to their expectations and condemn them only if they fail to achieve the standards imposed. Overcontrol may be conceived, therefore, as a method of contingent punishment; that is, punishment is selective, occurring only under clearly defined conditions.

The contingency aspect of parental overcontrol makes it similar to the child-rearing experiences that characterize the history of the histrionic personality. Here, again, there are important differences. Future histrionics experience irregular attention and praise that is contingent on "good" performances; they tend not to receive overt punishment or disapproval for "bad behavior." In contrast, future compulsives receive their praise, not irregularly but consistently, and they experience mostly negative or punitive reactions rather than positive comments and rewards. They become experts in learning what they must not do, so as to avoid punishment and condemnation, whereas histrionics learn what they can do, so as to achieve attention and praise. Future compulsives learn to heed parental restrictions and rules; for them, the lines of disapproved behaviors are set rigidly. However, as a consequence of experiencing mostly negative injunctions, they have little idea of what is approved. They know well what they must not do but do not know so well what they can do. The positive achievements of young compulsives often are "taken for granted" and only occasionally acknowledged by their parents; comments and judgments are almost exclusively limited to pointing out infractions of rules and boundaries the child must never transgress.

In sum, parental overcontrol is a restrictive method of child rearing in which punitive procedures are used to set strict limits upon the child's behavior. As long as these children operate within the approved boundaries they are likely to be secure from parental criticism and condemnation. Although overcontrol is a highly efficient training procedure, it is one fraught with pathological possibilities. These consequences during the second and third stages of neuropsychological development are examined next (the first stage is likely to have been "highly scheduled," but this is neither pathogenic nor distinctive to the development of the compulsive personality).

The second stage of development, concerning the active-passive polarity, is notable for the fact that children begin their struggle to acquire autonomous skills and to achieve a sense of self-competence. At this time, children become more assertive and resistant to parental directions and admonitions. Overcontrolling parents are likely to respond to these efforts with firm and harsh discipline. Some will physically curtail their children, berate them, withdraw love, and so on. Others will be relentless in their desire to squelch any bothersome transgression. Children who cannot find refuge from the parental onslaught either will submit entirely, withdraw into a shell, or be adamant and rebel. However, if these children can identify a sphere of behavior that is free of parental condemnation, they are likely to overvalue and indulge it. Not only will they restrict their activities to areas that meet parental approval, they also may become "experts" at them, perfectionists, if you will. Needless to say,

they will stick within parentally circumscribed boundaries and not venture beyond.

Several consequences flow from this solution. Autonomy will be sharply curtailed, and the future compulsives will fail to develop the full range of competence feelings that other, less restricted children typically acquire. They are likely to develop marked doubts about their ability to deal with events beyond the confines to which they have been bound. They will hesitate to deviate from the "straight and narrow path," withdraw from new situations, and, hence, lack spontaneity, curiosity, and venturesomeness. Having little confidence in themselves and fearing parental wrath for even trivial misdeeds, they will learn to submerge their impulse toward independence and autonomy, and avoid exploring the unknown lest it lead them beyond approved boundaries. The future compulsive is like the dependent child in this regard; in contrast, however, the compulsive has accepted dependency, not for its comforts, love, and affection, but from guilt, shame, punishment, and the fear of rejection.

The third neuropsychological stage is characterized by the acquisition of self-initiative and a growing sense of one's personal identity and orientation on the self-other polarity. A prerequisite to their development is a well-established feeling of personal competence and autonomy, two features already impaired in the future compulsive. And to add insult to prior injury, overcontrolling parents continue to restrict and overdirect their children. They proffer advice and admonishments by which the children are expected to guide their behavior. Not only do they continue to be shaped excessively by parental directives, the latter's counsel usually follows a narrow and well-defined course also. As a consequence, young compulsives not only fail to learn to think for themselves but in addition are guided in their thinking along highly conventional and adult lines. Rather than feeling free to engage in the imaginative play and creativity of childhood thinking, they are shaped to think in an overly mature fashion. They are led at an accelerated pace toward adulthood and are expected to "toe the line" in acquiring proper and upright attitudes. Parental overcontrol at this stage undermines children's opportunities to take the initiative and to acquire their own identity. They quickly become caricatures of adult propriety, "gentlemen" and "ladies," but automatons as well. Unable to face the novel and the unanticipated, they can act only if they are certain that their narrow band of approved behaviors is applicable and correct. They dare not venture on their own for fear that they are ill-equipped to meet challenges, or that they may overstep accepted boundaries. Their only recourse, then, is to simplify and organize their world, to be absolutely sure of what they can do, and to eliminate complexities that require decisions and initiative. Their environment must be a familiar one guided by explicit rules and standards; one in which they know beforehand what course of action is expected and approved.

To restate the foregoing in behavioral terms: The children learn instrumentally to avoid punishment by obediently acquiescing to parental demands and strictures. They are "shaped" by fear and intimidation to conform to the expectations and standards set down by their elders. Further, the children learn vicariously and by imitation. They acquire representational models of themselves according to their parents' image by incorporating "whole hog" the rules and inhibitions that characterize their parents' standards and values. Moreover, they make a virtue of necessity. Thus, they feel proud and self-satisfied being good and proper, thus not only to master their dread of parental rejection but also gaining their parents' commendation. Adoption of parental models has its problematic side, however. Along with adult propriety, future compulsives incorporate parents' strictness and punitive attitudes. In their representational models, they place themselves in a role that parallels their parents'; as a result, they become stern, intolerant, and self-righteous tyrants who condemn the "immaturity and irresponsibility" of others. Another characteristic of the compulsive's learning history is its insufficiency, its narrow range of competencies and its inadequacies for dealing with novel and unforeseen events. Thus, compulsives not only are fearful of violating rules but also lack the wherewithal to change the unknown. Their behavioral narrowness is partly a matter of adaptive object choices and partly a matter of having no alternatives.

There is another feature common to the developmental history of the compulsive: exposure to conditions that teach responsibility to others and a feeling of guilt when these responsibilities have not been met. As noted earlier, these youngsters are often "moralized" to inhibit their inclinations toward frivolous play and impulse gratification. Many are impressed by the shameful nature of such activities and are warned against the terrible consequences of mischief and "sin." Others may be told how pained and troubled their parents will be if they cause them embarrassment or deviate from the "path of righteousness." Long before children can understand the significance of these injunctions, they learn that they must adopt them as their own. In time, they will internalize these strictures and develop self-discipline and self-criticism, a "conscience" that will prevent them from transgressing the rights of others. They will be made to feel disloyal and disrespectful of their "well-meaning" parents if they balk at the latter's impositions and restraints. How inconsiderate a child must be "after all the things they have done." By promoting guilt, the child's anger is diverted from its original object and turned inward toward the self. It can be used to further curtail the child's inclinations toward disobedience or independence. Not only are these children now fearful of the consequences of their defiant impulses, they also have learned to feel guilty for merely thinking them. Now, by condemning themselves, they demonstrate their "good" intentions and thereby ward off reproach and criticism. And, as their own conscience and persecutor, they can always anticipate and avoid social condemnation.

Given the conflicts and anxieties engendered by their strategy, why do compulsives resist exploring alternative coping methods? One answer is that they experience less pain by continuing, rather than changing. Thus, discomforting as the strategy may be, it is less anguishing and more rewarding than any other they can envisage. Another answer is that much of what they do is merely the persistence of habit, the sheer continuation of the past. Thus, compulsives persevere, in part at least, not because their behavior is so rewarding but because it is deeply ingrained, so much so that it persists automatically. None of this is unique to the compulsive personality. It is true of all personality disorders. Each style fosters a vicious circle such that the individual's adaptive strategy promotes conditions similar to those that gave

rise initially to that strategy. Pathological personality traits are traps, self-made prisons that are perniciously self-defeating in that they promote their own continuation.

Compulsives dread making mistakes and fear taking risks lest they provoke disapproval. Defensively, they learn to restrict themselves to situations with which they are familiar and to actions they feel confident will be approved. They keep themselves within narrow boundaries and confine themselves to the repetition of the familiar. Rarely do they wander or view things from a different perspective than they have in the past. Moreover, compulsives are characteristically single-minded, have sharply defined interests, and can stick to "the facts" without deviation. To avoid the unknown—that is, the potentially dangerous, they maintain a tight and well-organized approach to life. They hold onto the "tried and true" and keep their nose to old and familiar grindstones. The price paid for this rigid and narrow outlook is high. Subtle emotions and creative imagination are simply incompatible with the deliberate and mechanical quality of the compulsive's style. Further, the repetitious going over the same dull routine prevents these persons from experiencing new perceptions and new ways of approaching their environment. By following the same narrow path, compulsives block their chances of breaking the bonds of the past. Their horizons are confined as they duplicate the same old grind.

By the time compulsives attain adolescence, they are likely to have fully incorporated the strictures and regulations of their elders. Even if they could "get away with it" and be certain that no external power would judge them severely, they now carry within themselves a merciless internal "conscience," an inescapable inner gauge that ruthlessly evaluates and controls them, one that intrudes relentlessly to make them doubt and hesitate before they act. The proscriptions of "proper" behavior have been well learned and they dare not deviate irresponsibly.

Avoidant Personality Disorder

As stated previously, personality represents the individual's pervasive style of functioning and arises as a consequence of the intricate and sequential interplay of both biological and psychological influences. As with other disorders discussed in this chapter, the present section outlines several of the more plausible biogenic and psychogenic factors that underlie the development personality pathology. Note again that the influences hypothesized here are neither necessary, sufficient, mutually exclusive, nor even contributory causes in all cases. They are posited as reasonable conjectures, and the authors believe that any number of combinations of these determinants may shape the course of pathological personality development.

Hypothesized Biogenic Factors

The hypervigilance that characterizes the avoidant signifies a habitual high level of somatic arousal. The exterior appearance of sluggishness and inactivity is deceptive, overlaying an extremely low threshold for alertness and reactive readiness, which the avoidant goes to great pains to cover up. Chronic tension may be discerned in spasmodic and uncoordinated motor behaviors, and in a high degree of sensory distractibility. While many avoidants appear to the undiscerning eye to be quiet and shy, unperturbed by external events, the converse is actually true. Avoidants are preoccupied with and hyperalert to their surroundings, so much so that they often cannot concentrate on their work or responsibilities.

The hyperarousal of avoidants may reflect a biophysical sensory irritability or a more centrally involved somatic imbalance or dysfunction. Using a different conceptual language to refer to this biophysical speculation, it might be hypothesized that these individuals possess a constitutionally based fearful or anxious temperament, that is, a hypersensitivity to potential threat. The conjectures suggested here may be no more than different conceptual approaches to the same thesis; for example, a fearful temperamental disposition may simply be a "behavioral" term to represent a "biophysical" limbic system imbalance.

Genetic or hereditary predispositions to avoidant behavior cannot be overlooked. Diverse anatomic structures and processes provide the substrate for such complex psychological functions as those called "affective disharmony," "interpersonal aversiveness," and so on. These biophysical substrates may vary substantially from person to person (Williams, 1973) and are clearly influenced in their structure by heredity. Studies that demonstrate a higher than chance correspondence among family members in such behaviors as social apprehensiveness and aversiveness are attributable in large measure to learning but there is reason to believe, at least in some cases, that this correspondence can be ascribed in part to the common genotypic pool within families.

Infants who display temperamentally based hyperirritability, crankiness, tension, and withdrawal may not only possess a constitutional disposition toward an avoidant pattern but may prompt rejecting and hostile attitudes from their parents. Easily frightened and hypertense babies who are easily awakened, cry, and are colicky rarely afford their parents much comfort and joy. Such infants typically induce parental weariness, feelings of inadequacy, exasperation, and anger, attitudes and feelings that may give rise to a stereotype of a troublesome, whining, and difficult-to-manage child. In these cases, an initial temperamental tendency toward anxiety and tension may be aggravated further by parental rejection and deprecation.

Delayed or uneven maturation in any of the major spheres of sensory, sensorimotor, or cognitive functioning may signify an impaired biophysical substrate that can limit these children's capacity to cope adequately with the normal tasks they face at each developmental stage. Intrinsic deficiencies such as these may also be compounded by the children's self-conscious awareness of their inadequacies. Of no less potential as a factor intensifying these deficits are parental reactions to the child's atypical development. Parents who expect their children to progress successfully and rapidly through the usual developmental sequence may experience considerable dismay over the deviations and failures they observe. Perceived in this manner, delayed achievements often result in parental condemnation and ridicule, experiences that evoke feelings of social alienation and low self-regard on the part of the child.

A few speculations of an anatomical and biochemical nature may be in order. For example, avoidant personalities may experience aversive events more intensely and more frequently than others because they possess an especially dense or overabundantly branched neural substrate in the "aversive" center of the limbic system. Another plausible speculation for their avoidant tendencies is a possible functional dominance of the sympathetic nervous system. Thus, excess adrenalin owing to any one of a number of autonomic or pituitary adrenal axis dysfunctions may give rise to the hypervigilant and irritable characteristics of this personality. Imbalances of this kind may lead also to the affective disharmony and cognitive interference found among these patients. Deficiencies or excesses in certain brain neurohormones may facilitate rapid synaptic transmission and result in a flooding and scattering of neural impulses. Such individuals will not only appear overalert and overactive but also may experience the avoidant's characteristic cognitive interference and generalized emotional dysphoria. Although individual differences in anatomy and physiology have been well demonstrated, we must recognize that speculations attributing complex forms of clinical behavior to biophysical variations such as proposed here are not only conjectural but also rather simplistic. Even if differences in aversiveness ultimately were found to be connected to biological substrates, the psychological form and content of these tendencies would take on their specific character only as a function of the individual's particular life experiences and learnings, factors to which the discussion turns next.

Experiential History

Any attempt to list the diverse life experiences that may give rise to an avoidant personality would be not only futile but misleading. It is not so much the particulars of the timing, setting, or source of these events that make them important, but rather the message these experiences convey to the individual. Diverse though they may be, these experiences possess one crucial theme in common: They depreciate the individual's self-esteem through either explicit or implicit rejection, humiliation, or denigration. Moreover, repeated exposure to such events not only fosters a deflated sense of self-worth but also tends, ultimately, to produce the affective dysphoria, cognitive interference, alienated self-image, interpersonal distrust, and active social detachment so characteristic of this personality. Two of the primary sources of these derogating experiences are elaborated in the following paragraphs.

The first and major source is parental rejection and deprecation. Attractive and healthy infants may be subjected to parental devaluation, malignment, and rejection no less so than troublesome youngsters. Reared in a family setting in which they are belittled, abandoned, and censured, these children will have their natural robustness and optimism crushed, and will acquire instead attitudes of self-depreciation and feelings of social alienation (Cicchetti & Beeghly, 1987). Before elaborating some of the features associated with parental derogation and hostility that lead to the avoidant personality, it may be instructive to note some points in common between the experiences of the antisocial personality and those of the avoidant. They are quite similar in certain respects; both are exposed to parental devaluation or condemnation, and both learn to be suspicious and to view the world as hostile and dangerous. There appear to be two main reasons why avoidants learn to actively detach from others, whereas the aggressive antisocials learn to rise up with counterhostility and assertive independence.

First, close inspection of the childhood of the avoidant personality indicates that parental rejection takes the form primarily of belittlement, depreciation, and humiliation. Although these youngsters may have borne the brunt of occasional physical cruelty, the essential nature of the message conveyed by the persecutor is that the child was weak, worthless, and beneath contempt. As a consequence of being demeaned and belittled, these children also learn to devalue themselves and, hence, develop little or no sense of self-esteem. Considered worthless, derided, and forlorn, they feel powerless to counterattack and overcome the humiliation and ridicule to which they were exposed. Antisocial children were objects of similar derogation from their parents, but they received or experienced a different message than did the future avoidants. Rather than being devalued in the attack, future antisocials learned to feel that they were a "power" that had to be contended with, that they could upset others, that they had the wherewithal to disrupt the moods, attitudes, and behaviors of others. Instead of feeling humiliated and belittled, each hostile onslaught to which they were exposed served to strengthen an image of their own influence and potency. Judging themselves as possessing the power to "cause trouble," they were spurred on to vigorous counter-hostility.

A second distinction between the avoidant and the antisocial may be traced to possible differences in temperament. It is not implausible that constitutionally apprehensive and timorous children and constitutionally fearless and hardy youngsters would respond differentially to parental derogation and hostility. Parental attitudes such as these would be likely to produce an avoidant pattern in an anxious and fearful youngster, hence an avoidant personality, and an antisocial pattern in a dauntless and bold youngster.

The consequences of parental rejection and humiliation are undoubtedly many and diverse. Returning to the avoidant personality's development, some of these consequences are outlined as they might arise during each of the first stages of neuropsychological development.

Parents who manage their infants in a cold and indelicate manner during the sensory-attachment stage will promote feelings of tension and insecurity on the part of their offspring. Such infants are likely to acquire a diffuse sense that the world is harsh, unwelcoming, and discomforting. In their primitive and highly generalized way, they will be disinclined to attach themselves to others. Moreover, they may acquire a vague, yet deeply felt, mistrust of their human surroundings and, as a result, feel an ever-present sense of being isolated, helpless, and abandoned. Self-protectively, these youngsters may learn to "turn off" their growing sensory capacities and thereby diminish the discomfort they experience. By doing so, however, they may set the stage for an enduring and generalized habit of interpersonal withdrawal.

Parents who ridicule and belittle their offspring's first stumbling efforts during the sensorimotor-autonomy stage will markedly diminish these children's feelings of competence and confidence. Although these youngsters may develop fully normal language skills and motor aptitudes, they may begin to utilize these competencies in a hesitant and self-doubting manner. In effect, they have internalized as "valid" their parents' criticisms and derogations, and, in time, they may come to disparage and

revile themselves just as their parents had done. Harsh and self-critical attitudes such as these have far-reaching and devastating consequences. By belittling their own worth, these children have undone themselves as a source for soothing their wounds or gaining the esteem they cannot obtain elsewhere. As a consequence of this self-derogation, they have not only lost the approval and respect of others but also can no longer obtain these from themselves. They are caught now in a web of both social and self-reproval. Moreover, they, themselves, have become prime agents of their own derogation and belittling, which sets the roots of another cardinal feature of the avoidant, self-alienation.

The roots of self-depreciation begun in the sensorimotor-autonomy phase take firmer hold in the pubertal-identity and intracortical-integration stages. The image of being a weak, unlovable, and unworthy person becomes implanted in a strong cognitive base as a representational model of the self as unattractive, pitiful persons who deserve to be scoffed at and ridiculed. Few efforts may be expended on their part to alter this image since nothing they attempt "can ever" succeed, given the deficits and inadequacies they see within themselves.

Avoidant youngsters often compound their plight by identifying with an ineffectual parent or parental surrogate. Seeking and finding a modicum of love and affection in this model, they learn to identify themselves with this "unwholesome" parental figure and thereby seal their fate. By abdicating their own identity for the dubious rewards provided by this ineffectual mode, they undermine whatever possibilities they may have had for finding a more satisfying style of life. They now copy the insecurities and inadequacies of their sorrowful exemplar, learning to display the same social deficits and ineffectualities they observe.

Signs of the avoidant pattern are usually evident well before the child begins to participate in the give-and-take or peer relationships, school and athletic competitions, heterosexual dating (with its attendant anxieties), and so on. These early signs may stem from constitutional dispositions or the circumstances of family life. Whatever their origins, most school-age children already possess the hesitations and aversive tendencies that will characterize them more clearly in later life. But for other youngsters, the rudiments of social withdrawal and self-alienation have developed only minimally when they first encounter the challenges of peer group activities in the pubertal-gender identity stage. Opportunities for enhancing competencies and for developing effective social skills remain good, unless they experience rejection, isolation, or the devastating ridicule that can so often be meted out by age-mates. As hesitant children venture to meet their peers at school, on the athletic field, at school dances, and so on, they are exposed to challenges that may tear down their sense of competence and self-esteem. Some will be shattered by daily reminders of their scholastic ineptitude; a few will be ridiculed for deficits in athletic prowess; others will experience cruel derogation because of a lack of attractiveness, vitality, and so on. Unable to prove themselves in any of the myriad intellectual, physical, or social spheres of peer competition, they are not only derided and isolated by other but become sharply critical toward themselves for their own lack of worthiness and esteem. Their feelings of loneliness and shame are now compounded by severe self-judgments of personal inferiority and unattractiveness. They can turn neither to others for solace and gratification nor to themselves as they progress into the intracortical-integration stage.

The coping maneuvers of avoidants prove self-defeating. There is a driven and frightened quality to their behaviors. Moreover, avoidants are adaptively inflexible because they cannot explore alternative actions without feeling trepidation and anxiety. In contrast to other personalities, the avoidant coping style is essentially negative. Rather than venturing outward or drawing upon what aptitudes they possess, they retreat defensively and become increasingly remote from others and removed from sources of potential growth. As a consequence of their protective withdrawal, avoidants are left to be alone with their inner turmoil, conflicts, and self-alienation. They have succeeded in minimizing their external dangers, but they have trapped themselves in a situation equally devastating.

Avoidant personalities assume that the experiences to which they were exposed in early life will continue forever. Defensively they narrow the range of activities in which they allow themselves to participate. By sharply circumscribing their life, they preclude the possibility of corrective experiences that might lead them to see that "all is not lost" and that there are kindly persons who will neither disparage nor humiliate them.

A further consequence of detaching themselves from others is that they are left to be preoccupied with their own thoughts and impulses. Limited to the inner world of stimuli, they will reflect and ruminate about the past, with all the discomforts it brings forth. Since their experiences have become restricted largely to thinking about past events, life becomes a series of duplications. As a consequence, avoidants are left to relive the painful experiences of earlier times rather than be exposed to new and different events that might alter their outlook and feelings. Moreover, these self-preoccupations serve only to further widen the breach between themselves and others. A vicious circle may take hold. The more they turn inward, the more they lose contact with the typical interests and thoughts of those around them. They become progressively more estranged from their environment, increasingly out of touch with reality and the checks against irrational thought provided by social contact and communication. Away from the controls and stabilizing influences of ordinary human interactions, they begin to lose their sense of balance and perspective, often feeling puzzled, peculiar, unreal, and "crazy."

Detached and mistrustful behaviors not only establish distance from others but also evoke reciprocal reactions of disaffiliation and rejection. An attitude that communicates weakness, self-effacement, and fear invariably attracts those who enjoy deprecating and ridiculing others. Thus, the hesitant posture, suspicious demeanor, and self-deprecating attitudes of the avoidant will tend to evoke interpersonal responses that lead to further experiences of humiliation, contempt, and derogation—in short, a repetition of the past. Any apparent sensitivity to rebuff or obviously fearful and unassertive style will tend to evoke ridicule from peers, an experience that will only reinforce and intensify this personality's aversive inclinations.

Avoidant personalities are painfully alert to signs of deception, humiliation, and deprecation. As noted in an earlier case presentation, these patients detect the most minute traces of indifference or annoyance on the part of others and make the

molehills of minor and passing slights into mountains of personal ridicule and condemnation. They are incredibly sensitive instruments for picking up and magnifying incidental actions and for interpreting them as indications of derision and rejection. This hypersensitivity functions well in the service of self-protection but fosters a deepening of the person's plight. As a result of their extensive scanning of the environment, avoidants actually increase the likelihood that they will encounter precisely those stimuli they wish most to avoid. Their exquisite antennae pick up and transform what most people overlook. In effect, their hypersensitivity backfires by becoming an instrument that brings to their awareness, time and again, the very pain they wish to escape. Their defensive vigilance thus intensifies rather than diminishes their anguish.

Avoidants must counter the flood of threatening stimuli that they register as a consequence of their emotional and perceptual hypersensitivities. To assure a modicum of personal tranquillity, they engage constantly in a series of cognitive reinterpretations and digressions. They may actively block, destroy, and fragment their own thoughts, seeking to disconnect relationships between what they see, what meanings they attribute to their perceptions, and what feelings they experience in response. Defensively, then, they intentionally destroy the clarity of their thought by intruding irrelevant distractions, tangential ideas, and discordant emotions. This coping maneuver exacts its price. By upsetting the smooth and logical pattern of their cognitive processes, avoidants further diminish their ability to deal with events efficiently and rationally. No longer can they attend to the most salient features of their environment, nor can they focus their thoughts or respond rationally to events. Moreover, they cannot learn new ways to handle and resolve their difficulties since their thinking is cluttered and scattered. Social communications take on a tangential and irrelevant quality, and they may begin to talk and act in an erratic and halting manner. In sum, in their attempt to diminish intrusively disturbing thoughts, they fall prey to a coping mechanism that further aggravates their original difficulties and ultimately intensifies their alienation from both themselves and others.

Schizoid Personality Disorder

Diagnostic differentiations between schizoid and avoidant personalities may be difficult to make upon initial observations. Both tend to be socially hesitant and unresponsive. A nonempirical source of difficulty in this regard may arise among clinicians who consider all "bland exteriors" to signify an adaptive or defensive emotional blunting and withdrawal consequent to repressed childhood disappointments, conflicts, and anxieties. This theoretical assumption does not apply to the formulations of the schizoid as conceived in the DSM. Though presented atheoretically insofar as etiology is concerned, the DSM schizoid is seen as not conflicted, nor suffering either ambivalence or deep disillusion; this patient's affectless and detached qualities stem from inherent deficits. For those who hold to the conflict, disillusion, and defense models, the avoidant personality designation represents the syndrome that derives from experiences of early rebuff or affectional deprivation. Avoidant types desire affect and social acceptance, whereas the similarly appearing schizoid is intrinsically unresponsive and indifferent to them. Avoidants may appear coolly detached, but they actually are restrained and fearful lest their intense desires be met with further rejection and humiliation.

Hypothesized Biogenic Factors

Schizoids may display an autonomic-endocrine imbalance favoring the cholinergic or parasympathetic system. Similarly, measures of arousal and activation should suggest high thresholds and sluggish responsivity. An ectomorphic body build, signifying inadequate nutritional reserves and lowered physical and energy capacities, has also been reported with some regularity. Behavioral observations lead us to infer, further, that schizoids have not only an anhedonic temperament but also a temperament that is characterized by a broadly generalized emotional unresponsiveness. We might suggest, therefore, that biological substrates for a number of drive states, such as sex and hunger, are also especially weak. Speculations concerning the particular brain regions involved in these deficits are noted later. Again, one must recall that the role of biophysical processes in psychopathology is almost entirely conjectural. With this caveat in mind, a few of the more plausible hypotheses are detailed.

Since children inherit overt physical features from their parents, it is safe to assume that features of internal morphology and physiochemistry are similarly inherited. Specifically, it would seem that parents who are biologically limited in their capacity to experience intense emotions, or to be vigorous and active, possess associated structural and physiological deficiencies that they transmit genetically to their children. Translated in terms relevant to our topic, the schizoid pattern may arise because an individual is at the low end of a genetically based continuum of individual differences in neurological structures and physiochemical processes that subserve affectivity, interpersonal sensitivity, activation, and so on.

Another frankly speculative hypothesis is that a substantial number of adult schizoid personalities displayed low sensory responsivity, motor passivity, and a generally placid mood in infancy and early childhood. They may have been easy to handle and care for, but it is likely that they provided their parents with few of the blissful and exuberant responses experienced with more vibrant and expressive youngsters. As a consequence of their undemanding and unresponsive nature, they are likely to have evoked few reciprocal responses of overt affection and stimulation from their caretakers. This reciprocal deficit in sheer physical handling and warmth may have compounded the child's initial tendencies toward inactivity, emotional flatness, and general insipidity.

Given that the schizoid is not obviously organic, it is probable that biophysical defects, if any, would take the form, not of gross tissue damage, but of a numerical sparseness of neural cells or of thinly dispersed branching systems emanating from relevant functional regions. For example, a congenital aplasia in any of the centers of the limbic system may give rise to affectivity deficits. Since the subregions of this complex anatomical system may be differentially impaired, no two persons will possess identical deficits. Thus, some schizoid personalities may exhibit the consequences of deficiencies in the "pleasure" center, whereas others may display behaviors associated with an underdeveloped "aversive" center, and so on.

The apathetic character of the schizoid pattern may be traced to deficits in the reticular system. Our understanding of the diverse functions carried out by this widely ramified system is far from complete, but we do have reason to think that it subserves arousal and activation. Thus a feebly branched reticular formation may underlie the lethargy and lack of alertness that characterize this personality. The view that the reticular system is a major relay situation for intrabrain circuitry is also unverified, but it is plausible. Dysfunctions in the reticular system may give rise, therefore, to chaotic interneuronal transmissions, and these may lead, in turn, to deficient emotional learnings. In a disorganized system, the emotional dimension of an experience may be circuited peculiarly or fail to be anchored to the cognitive awareness of that experience. As a result of such "discoordinations," the person may possess an intellectual grasp of human relationships but obscure them with irrelevant or deficient emotional correlates. This breakdown in reticular coordination may account for the schizoid's deficiency in connecting cognitions with their normally associated emotions.

Hypotheses implicating neurohormonal disturbances have become increasingly popular, and specific attention has been drawn to the role of these chemicals in maintaining synaptic control. Excesses or deficiencies in various neurohormones may result in the proliferation and scattering of neural impulses or in the inhibition of efficient neural sequences. Any chemically induced source of synaptic dyscontrol could give rise to the cognitive or affective deficits that characterize the schizoid.

Experiential History

The variety of influences that may shape personality are legion. Unfortunately, there is a paucity of well-designed research in the field. Despite the lack of consistent confirmatory data, there is sufficient reason to believe that the psychogenic hypotheses that follow have merit as plausible conjectures.

A lack of functional stimuli normally provided by the infant's caretakers will inevitably set the foundation for maturational and learning deficits. Insufficient stimulus nourishment during the first year of life is likely to result in the underdevelopment of neural substrates for affectivity and a deficient learning of interpersonal attachments. Constitutionally unresponsive infants who have a built-in stimulus barrier, or who elicit few reactions from their environment, may be subject to a compounding of their initial activation and sensory deficits. Such children receive little cuddling and affection from their parents and, as a consequence, are deprived of the social and emotional cues requisite to learning human attachment behaviors. Some may provide stimulation for themselves, but this is likely to take the form of inanimate objects (dolls, blankets, or blocks), which may result in attachments to things rather than to people. Given an inborn sensory or energy deficit, these "schizoid-prone" infants are likely to be deprived of stimuli necessary for the maturation of their "emotional" brain centers and for the learning of human attachment behaviors.

Similar consequences may occur among infants with entirely normal constitutional capacities and dispositions. An "average" child who is reared with minimal human warmth, either in an impersonal atmosphere or with cold and unaffectionate parents, will also be deprived of the early sensory and affective stimulation necessary for normal development. As a consequence, these youngsters are likely to acquire the interpersonally detached and affectless symptomatology of the schizoid pattern.

Families that are characterized by interpersonal reserve and formality, or that possess a bleak and cold atmosphere in which members relate to each other in a remote or disaffiliated way, are likely breeding grounds for schizoid-prone children who will acquire deeply ingrained habits of social ineptness or insensitivity.

Fragmented or amorphous styles of family communication also set the stage for the schizoid style. Thus, to relate successfully with others requires the capacity to focus on what others are experiencing and communicating, and to convey appropriate and relevant reactions in response. Some children fail to learn how to attend and interpret the signals that others communicate, or to fail to learn how to respond in meaningful and rational ways. Learning effective styles of interpersonal communication is a requisite to shared social behaviors. Without these skills, the individual cannot function comfortably with others and will appear detached, unresponsive, cold, and insensitive—traits we associate with the schizoid pattern. Family styles of communicating in which ideas are aborted or are transmitted in circumstantial or amorphous ways are likely to be mirrored in the growing child's own manner of communication. Moreover, being exposed to unfocused and murky patterns of thought, these children will, both by imitation and by the need to follow the "logic" that surrounds them, attend to peripheral or tangential aspects of human communication, that is, to signs and cues that most people view as irrelevant and distracting. This way of attending to, thinking about, and reacting to events, when generalized beyond the family setting, will give rise to perplexity and confusion on the part of others. As a consequence, disjointed and meaningless transactions may come to characterize many of these children's interpersonal relations, leading them into isolation and social distance. These events can only foster cognitive obscurities and emotional deficiencies, traits that characterize this passive-detached, or schizoid pattern.

The impassivity and lack of color of schizoids enable them to maintain a comfortable distance from others. But their preferred state of detachment is itself pathogenic, not only because it fails to elicit experiences that could promote a more vibrant and rewarding style of life but also because it fosters conditions that are conducive to more serious forms of psychopathology.

The inarticulateness and affective unresponsiveness that characterize schizoids do little to make them attractive to others. Most persons are not inclined to relate to schizoids for any period, tending to overlook their presence in most settings and, when interacting socially, doing so in a perfunctory and unemotional way. The fact that others consider them as boring and colorless suits the asocial predilections of schizoids quite well. However, this preference for remaining apart and alone only perpetuates and intensifies their tendencies toward detachment. The schizoid pattern not only is social imperceptive but also tends to "flatten" emotional events, that is, to blur and homogenize experiences that are intrinsically distinct and varied. In effect, these personalities project their murky and undifferentiated cognitions upon discriminable and complex social events.

Borderline Personality Disorder

Those who function at the borderline personality level may begin with less adequate constitutional equipment or be subjected to a series of more adverse early experiences than most other personality disorders. As a consequence of their more troublesome histories, they either fail to develop an adequate coping style in the first place or decompensate slowly under the weight of repeated and unrelieved difficulties. The authors' view, however, is that most borderline cases progress sequentially through a more adaptive or higher level of functioning before deteriorating to the advanced dysfunctional state. Some patients, however, notably childhood variants, never appear to "get off the ground" and give evidence of a borderline pattern from their earliest years.

The developmental history of the borderline personality reviewed here by should help clarify the varied pictures that are seen among patients diagnosed as borderline.

Hypothesized Biogenic Factors

The biogenic background of borderlines who exhibit dependent personality features is likely to include a disproportionately high number of bland and unenergetic relatives. A melancholic and fearful infantile pattern is not infrequent and often gives rise to parental overprotection. Speculations may be proposed regarding various limbic, reticular, or adrenal imbalances to account for their typical low activation levels and their vulnerability to fear, both of which may elicit protective and nurturing responses in beneficent environments.

Biogenically, the borderline with histrionic or antisocial features may have close relatives who exhibit high autonomic reactivity. Other evidence suggesting a constitutional predisposition is hyperresponsivity in early childhood. A temperamental inclination such as this not only exposed them to a high degree of sensory stimulation but also may have elicited frequent and intense reactions from others. Another speculation might suggest neurally dense or low-threshold limbic, reticular, or adrenal systems as underlying their sensory reactivity.

Characteristic Experiential Histories

The negativistic, discontented, and erratic quality of these patients is largely attributable to early parental inconsistency. Most failed to be treated in even a moderately predictable fashion, being doted upon one moment and castigated the next—ignored, abused, nurtured, exploited, promised, denied, and so on, with little rhyme or reason as seen from a child's perspective. These borderlines learned to anticipate irrationality, to expect contradictions, and to know, however painfully, that their actions would bring them rewards one time but condemnation the next. Parental behaviors may have served as models for vacillation, capriciousness, and unpredictability. In others, schisms may have existed between parents, tearing the child's loyalties first one way and then the other. These borderline types learned that nothing is free of conflict and that they are trapped in a bind. Despite feeling mishandled and cheated, they received enough attention and affection to keep them hoping for some harmony and a secure dependency. Unfortunately for these borderlines, these hopes rarely were fulfilled. Not only did external circumstances continue to be inconsistent, the patients themselves also perpetuated further inconsistencies by their own vacillations, unpredictability, unreasonableness, sullenness, and revengeful nature. Having learned to anticipate disappointment, they often "jumped the gun," thereby alienating others before the latter rejected them. In addition, inner tensions kept churning close to the surface, leading them to act impulsively and precipitously. This lack of controls resulted in endless wrangles with others and precluded achieving the affections these patients so desperately sought. Angry and pessimistic, they may have become violent at times, exploding with bitter complaints and recriminations against the world, or, conversely, they may have turned against themselves, becoming self-sacrificing, pleading forgiveness, and derogating themselves through impulsively self-damaging acts. Unable to "get hold" of themselves, control their churning resentments and conflicts, or elicit even the slightest degree of approval and support from others, and guilt-ridden and self-condemnatory, this borderline will often slide from impulsive actions into more serious psychotic disorders.

Sociocultural forces also play a significant role in the development of borderlines. Thus, where a society's values and practices are fluid and inconsistent, so, too, will its residents evolve deficits in psychic solidity and stability. This more amorphous cultural state, so characteristic of our modern times, is clearly mirrored in the interpersonal vacillations and affective instabilities that typify the borderline personality. Central to our recent culture have been the increased pace of social change and the growing pervasiveness of ambiguous and discordant customs to which children are expected to subscribe. Under the cumulative impact of rapid industrialization, immigration, mobility, technology, and mass communication, there has been a steady erosion of traditional values and standards. Instead of a simple and coherent body of practices and beliefs, children find themselves confronted with constantly shifting styles and increasingly questioned norms whose durability is uncertain and precarious (Millon, 1987).

No longer do youngsters find the certainties and absolutes which guided earlier generations. The complexity and diversity of everyday experience play havoc with simple "archaic" beliefs, and render them useless as instruments to deal with contemporary realities. Lacking a coherent view of life, maturing youngsters find themselves groping and bewildered, swinging from one set of principles and models to another, unable to find stability either in their relationships or in the flux of events; each of these elements are core characteristics of the borderline disorder. Few times in history have so many children faced the tasks of life without the aid of accepted and durable traditions. Not only does the strain of making choices among discordant standards and goals beset them at every turn, but these competing beliefs and divergent demands also prevent them from developing either internal stability or external consistency. And no less problematic in generating such disjoined psychic structures is the escalation of emotionally capricious and interpersonally discordant role models.

The fabric of traditional and organized societies not only comprises standards designed to indoctrinate and inculcate the young, but it also provides "insurance," if you will, backups to compensate and repair system defects and failures. Extended families, church leaders, schoolteachers, and neighbors provide nurturance and role models by which children experiencing troubling parental relationships can find a means of support and affection, enabling them thereby to be receptive to society's established body of norms and values. Youngsters subject to any of the diffusing and divisive forces so typical in the developmental background of borderlines (Millon, 1987), must find one or another of these culturally sanctioned sources of surrogate modeling and sustenance to give structure and direction to their emerging capacities and impulses. Without such bolstering, maturing potentials are likely to become diffuse and scattered. Without admired and stable roles to emulate, such youngsters are left to their own devices to master the complexities of their varied and changing worlds, to control the intense aggressive and sexual urges which well up within them, to channel their fantasies, and to pursue the goals to which they may aspire. Many borderlines become victims of their own growth, unable to discipline their impulses or find acceptable means for expressing their desires. Scattered and unguided, they are unable to fashion a clear sense of personal identity, a consistent direction for feelings and attitudes, a coherent purpose to existence.

Tendencies toward borderline decompensation are usually aggravated by the accumulation of repetitive pathogenic experiences. Not only are early behaviors and attitudes difficult to distinguish, but, in addition, the individual may be exposed to a continuous stream of destructive events that accelerate the pathological decline. Not the least of these accelerating factors are the borderline's own coping behaviors, which foster new problems and perpetuate vicious circles. As with other more advanced personality dysfunctions, borderlines experience serious incursions upon their psychic equilibrium, giving rise to short-lived, but usually reversible psychotic episodes. These bizarre periods normally subside following the reduction of stress. In some cases, however, psychotic episodes persist until they become an ingrained and enduring pattern. Perhaps the circumstances of stress failed to diminish or the patient became trapped, so to speak, in the web of his/her own coping maneuvers. Not infrequently, the rewards and comforts acquired during the episode were greater than those the patient obtained preceding it. Whatever the cause or combination of causes, some borderline patients fail to "pull themselves together" and override what is usually a transient psychotic period. It is in these cases that we often see the progressive deterioration into a decompensated borderline pattern. At these times, patients begin to feel that their "normal" relations with others are bogged down and hopeless. They also experience an intolerable decline in their self-worth. As they defensively isolate themselves from social pain and humiliation, their feelings of helplessness and self-derogation increase. They may soon experience a measure of relief as they accept the inevitability of invalidism. There are gains to be eked out through collapse and withdrawal. Not only will others care for them, they also need meet no responsibilities nor struggle to achieve goals in a world with which they cannot cope. They give up their struggle for a meaningful social existence and allow themselves to sink increasingly into a pervasive listlessness, a disorganization of control and thought, an invalidism in which they care little and do little to care for themselves.

Schizotypal Personality Disorder

The specific term "schizotypal" was coined by S. Rado in a paper delivered in 1950. Conceiving the label as an abbreviation of "schizophrenia phenotype" (indicating its ostensive representation in overt form of an underlying hereditary predisposition or genotype), Rado specified the existence of two inherited defects, that of an "integrative pleasure deficiency" and a "proprioceptive diathesis." The former defect typified by a lack of affect and by feelings devoid of "pleasure, desire, love, and pride," features of a passive character akin to the schizoid personality. By contrast (although somehow overlapping), the latter defect produced a more active or avoidant type of schizotypal functioning, one characterized by a lack of self-confidence, a psychic "brittleness," and the feeling that one "is hopelessly different from other people."

Attracted by Rado's schizotypal formulation, P. Meehl (1962, 1990) has constructed a brilliant, speculative theoretical model. Essentially, Meehl sought to articulate how an inherited "neural integrative defect," which he labeled "schizotaxia," evolved through "all known forms of social history" into the phenotypic personality organization that Rado termed the "schizotype." The reader is referred to Meehl's papers for his masterly neurologic-social-learning thesis. A brief quote from his first paper on this thesis will suffice here:

> I hypothesize that the statistical relation between schizotaxia, schizotypy, and schizophrenia is class inclusion: All schizotaxics become, *on all actually existing social learning regimens,* schizotypic in personality organization; but most of these remain compensated. A minority, disadvantaged by other (largely polygenically determined) constitutional weaknesses, and put on a bad regimen by schizophrenogenic mothers (most of whom are themselves schizotypes) are thereby potentiated into clinical schizophrenia. What makes schizotaxia etiologically specific is its role as a necessary condition. I postulate that a nonschizotaxic individual, whatever his other genetic makeup and whatever his learning history, would at most develop a character disorder or a psychoneurosis; but he would not become a schizotype and therefore could never manifest its decompensated form, schizophrenia. (1962, p. 832)

Hypothesized Biogenic Factors

The more passively oriented schizotypals may be unfortunate carriers of a defective family inheritance. There are some data supporting the contention that genetic factors conducive to affective and cognitive deficits underlie the eccentricities of many of these personalities. Although families do "breed" the characteristics of these schizotypals, it is difficult to conceptualize the nature of the genetic mechanisms involved or even to state unequivocally that such mechanisms do in fact operate. Meehl's (1990) developmental speculations on this matter deserve careful reading. Among other biogenic factors that may be conducive to the development of this schizotypal is a passive infantile pattern, which may initiate a sequence of impoverished stimulation and parental indifference. Also possible, though speculative, are anatomic deficits or neurochemical dysfunctions in either reticular, limbic, sympathetic, or synaptic control systems, resulting in diminished activation, minimal pleasure-pain sensibilities, and cognitive dysfunctions.

By contrast, there is evidence that the more "active" variant of the schizotypal have a family history of apprehensive or cognitively "muddled" relatives, suggesting the possibility that genetic dispositions may be operative. A fearful infantile pattern was not uncommon in this personality, often precipitating parental exasperation and rejection. Some have evidenced an irregular sequence of maturation, resulting in the development of an imbalance among competencies, an inability to handle excess emotionality, and the emergence of social peculiarities. The possibility of an underlying excess in limbic and sympathetic system reactivity, or a neurochemical acceleration of synaptic transmission, likewise may be posited. Dysfunctions such as these could give rise to the hypersensitivity and cognitive "flooding" that characterize these schizotypal patients.

Characteristic Experiential History

Passively oriented schizotypals hindered in early life with constitutional insensitivities often experience marked stimulus impoverishment during their "oral," or sensory-attachment stage. This may set in motion an underdeveloped biophysical substrate for affectivity and deficient learning of social attachment behaviors. Other experiential factors of note are family atmospheres of indifference, impassivity, or formality, which may provide models for imitative learning and thereby establish the roots for lifelong patterns of social reticence, interpersonal insensitivity, and discomfort with personal affection and closeness. Family styles of fragmented and amorphous communication may also contribute. Thus, exposure to disjointed, vague, and pointless interactions may give rise to the development, not only of inner cognitive confusions, but also to unfocused, irrelevant, and tangential interpersonal relations. Experiences paralleling those of early childhood are often repeated and cumulative. In addition, stereotypes of the child's early "character" often take firm root, shape subsequent social attitudes, and preclude any changes in interpersonal style. Problematic relationships of this nature often get caught in a web of reciprocally destructive reactions, which then only aggravate earlier maladaptive tendencies.

Often overlooked among processes that perpetuate the individual's initial experiences are his or her own behaviors and coping styles. In the developmental background of the more passive schizotypals, the following appear to be especially self-defeating: affective deficits that "flatten" emotional experiences and perceptual insensitivities and cognitive obscurities that blur distinctions among events that might otherwise enhance and enrich their lives. As a consequence, opportunities for realizing stimulating and varied experiences, so necessary to alter the characteristically apathetic state, are precluded or diluted. To add further insult to these injuries, the early passive and cognitively insensitive behaviors of these schizoid-like schizotypals make them unattractive and unrewarding social companions. Unable to communicate with either affect or clarity, they likely were shunned, overlooked, and invited to share few of the more interesting experiences to which others were drawn. Failing to interchange ideas and feelings with others, they remained fixed and undeveloped, continuing therefore in their disjointed, amorphous, and affectless state. Restricted in their social experiences, they acquired few social skills, found it increasingly difficult to relate socially, and perpetuated a vicious circle that not only fostered their isolated life but also accentuated their social inadequacies and cognitive deficiencies.

Alienated from others and marginal members of society, these passive schizotypals turn increasingly to solitary thoughts. Over time, shared social behaviors became fully subordinate to private fantasy. In solitude their thoughts were left to wander unchecked by the logic and control of reciprocal social communication and activity. What they found within themselves was hardly rewarding, a barren, colorless void that offered no basis for joyful fantasy. Their inner personal world proved to be as "dead" and ungratifying as objective reality. They had no choice, so it seemed, but to turn to "unreal" fantasies. These, at least, might fill in the void and give their existence some substance. Interest moved toward the mystical and magical, to "needed" illusions and ideation that enabled the person to become a central, rather than a peripheral and insignificant figure.

Many of the active or avoidant type of schizotypal were exposed to an early history of deprecation, rejection, and humiliation, resulting in feelings of low self-esteem and a marked distrust of interpersonal relations. Others may have been subjected to belittlement, censure, and ridicule, not only from parents but also from sibs and peers. During the sensory-attachment phase of development they may have been treated in a harsh and unwelcoming fashion, thereby learning protectively to keep distance from their environment and to insulate their feelings. Ridicule from others in response to their efforts during the sensorimotor-autonomy stage may have led to feelings of personal incompetence and low self-worth. A further consequence of these experiences is that the children learn not only to avoid the appraisals of others but also to demean themselves as persons. Continuation into the pubertal-gender identity and intracortical-integration stages only intensified feelings of low self-esteem and increases self-critical attitudes. Future active and anxious schizotypals now devalue, censure, and belittle themselves as others had in the past. Some are subjected to deprecation and humiliation at the hands of their adolescent peers. Social alienation heterosexual failure, and minimal vocational and competitive success during this period add further insults to the earlier injuries.

Unfortunately, the coping strategies acquired by these anxious schizotypals to fend off the pain of life fostered rather than resolved their difficulties. In an effort to minimize their awareness of external discomfort, they turned inward to fantasy and rumination, but this also proved to be self-defeating. Not only were their inner conflicts intense, they also spent much of their reflective time reliving and duplicating the painful events of the past. Their protective efforts only reinforced their distress. Moreover, given their low self-esteem, their inner reflections often took the form of self-reproval. Not only did they fail to gain solace from themselves, they also found that they could not readily escape from their own thoughts of self-derogation, from feelings of personal worthlessness and the futility of being themselves. In an effort to counter these oppressive inner thoughts, they may have sought to block and destroy their cognitive clarity, that is, to interfere with the anguish of their discordant inner emotions and ideas. This maneuver not only proved self-defeating, in that it diminished their ability to deal with events rationally, it also further estranged them from communicating effectively with others. Even more destructive self-reproval and cognitive interference alienated them from their own existence. Having no place to go, they began to create a new, inner world, one populated by "magical" fantasies, illusions, telepathic relationships, and other odd thoughts that would provide them not only with an existence but also one that was more significant and potentially rewarding than that found in reality.

Why does the schizotypal deteriorate further? Certainly these patients have had little reason to face reality, a life full of anguish and humiliation. Having failed repeatedly to cope with their adversity, they had no option but to withdraw, "tune out" reality and reduce contact with events that evoked nothing but shame and agony. At first, they sought this respite from painful reality. Unchecked by social judgment, their fantasies had free rein to salve their wounds. These reveries often blurred into a dreamlike state, lost any organization, and became fragmented, discontinuous, and ephemeral, especially as they progressed into the intracortical-integration stage. Despite its usefulness in blocking reality, these patients found that their dream world was not a haven but a nightmare. Whatever meaning they drew from these reveries reminded them of their misery, of past misfortunes, and of having become nothing but failures, humiliated nonentities bereft of status and hope. Their inner personal world proved no less painful than that of reality. Faced with the pain of being themselves, they turned away, not only from others but also from their own being. But this was no simple task. This effort, like so many that preceded it, proved a further undoing. Trapped in the web of self-made confusions, they could not gain a clear focus and could not organize themselves to find some meaningful purposes to their existence. Ultimately, they began to sink into an abyss of nothingness, an estrangement from both the outer world and subjective self.

It is evident from the preceding that the emergence of the schizotypal pattern is a progressive and insidious process. The kernel was set in place in childhood and developed into manifest clinical form through imperceptible steps. It is not necessary to elaborate each step in the developmental sequence preceding the final pattern.

At this deteriorated schizotypal stage, external events are seen as a distant screen upon which phantoms move in a strange and purposeless automaticity. Voices appear to emanate from alien sources, creating a muted cacophony of obscure and bewildering sounds. A visual fog descends, enshrouding the patient's eyes and ears, dampening the senses and giving events a shadowy, pantomimic quality. Inner thoughts are no more articulate or meaningful. Within the self is a boundless region of fantasy, delusion, inchoate images, and sensations. An unanchored and rudderless ship in a whirling sea, the patient drifts without a compass, hither any yon, buffeted by waves of past memories and future illusions. Dreams, reality, past, and present, a potpourri of random pieces merge and are then dismembered. To these patients, their own physical presence is foreign, a detached corpse. They sense themselves floating, a disembodied mind filled with fleeting, disconnected, jumbled, and affectless impressions. There is a frightening collapse of meaning and existence as the very sense of life is lost.

Summary

What is remarkable about the above portraits is their coordination to the set of fundamental principles or polarities presented earlier. Rather than simply assume the current set of personality disorders, we have sought to cast the development of these personologic types within a coherent, holistic conception, one derived from foundational principles of evolution and neurological growth. Thus, while at an idiographic level, the level of detail of the individual life, each appears to possess its own unique antecedents, at a more abstract level certain commonalities can be discerned across the development of the various types. Both the dependent and histrionic, for example, become oriented toward others in their development. However, the functional significance of this orientation differs in the overall organizational character of their personalities: The dependent deliberately keeps the range of coping resources to a minimum in a bid to solicit attention and caring of others. The histrionic, however, is impressive in the intensity of its need for social stimulation and its highly flexible or flighty attempts to gain attention and praise. One is a passive drawing in, the other an active seeking out. Likewise, while both the narcissistic and dependent styles are passively oriented toward their environment and social interactions, it is toward different ends, the former toward the aggrandizement or perpetuation of self, the latter toward that of soliciting the nurturance of others. Unlike trait psychologists, who are content to study a particular facet of personality in isolation, developmentalists in the organismic-dynamic tradition readily recognize the essential holism of personality and consequently the veracity of the organizational thesis (e.g., Sroufe & Fleeson, 1986). One advantage of a deductive taxonomy is its offer of a nonarbitrary source of constraint at the molar organizational level, one that should appeal to developmental theorists.

RELATION BETWEEN NORMAL AND ABNORMAL PERSONALITY DEVELOPMENT

This is a time of rapid scientific and clinical advances, a time that seems propitious for ventures designed to bridge new ideas and syntheses. The intersection between the study of "abnormality" and the study of "normality" is one of these spheres of significant academic activity and clinical responsibility (Cicchetti, 1990; Millon, 1990). Theoretical formulations that bridge this intersection would represent a major and valued intellectual step, but to limit our focus to traditional concepts addressing this junction will lead to overlook the solid footing provided by our more mature sciences (such as physics and evolutionary biology). By failing to coordinate propositions and constructs to principles and laws established in these advanced disciplines, the different facets of our subject will continue to float, so to speak, at their current level, requiring that we return to this task another day (Millon, 1990).

To take this integrative view is not to argue that different spheres of scientific inquiry should be equated, nor it is to insist that there is only one possible conceptual system that may encompass normality and abnormality. Arguing in favor of building explicit links between these domains does not call for a reductionistic philosophy, a belief in substantive identicality, or efforts to so fashion them by formal logic. Rather we should seek to illustrate their substantive concordance and conceptual interfacing. By tracing their characteristics to the same underlying principles, we may demonstrate that they are merely different expressions of nature's basic processes.

There is no better sphere within the psychological sciences to undertake such a synthesis than the study of persons, normal or abnormal. Persons are the only organically integrated systems in the psychological and psychiatric domain, evolved through the millennia and inherently created from birth as natural entities, rather than culture-bound and experience-derived gestalts. The intrinsic cohesion is not merely a rhetorical construction but an authentic substantive unity. Personologic features may be differentiated into normal or abnormal and may be partitioned conceptually for pragmatic or scientific purposes, but they are segments of an inseparable biopsychosocial entity.

Numerous attempts have been made to develop definitive criteria for distinguishing psychological normality from abnormality. Some of these criteria focus on features that characterize the so-called normal, or ideal, state of mental health; others have sought to specify criteria for concepts such as abnormality or psychopathology. The most common criterion employed is a statistical one in which normality is determined by those behaviors that are found most frequently in a social group; and pathology or abnormality, by features that are uncommon in that population. Among diverse criteria used to signify normality are a capacity to function autonomously and competently, a tendency to adjust to one's social environment effectively and efficiently, a subjective sense of contentment and satisfaction, and the ability to self-actualize or to fulfill one's potentials. Psychopathology would be noted by deficits among the preceding.

Central to our understanding of these terms is the recognition that normality and abnormality are relative concepts; they represent arbitrary points on a continuum or gradient, since no sharp line divides normal from pathological behavior. Not only is personality so complex that certain areas of psychological functioning operate normality while others do not, but environmental circumstances also change such that behaviors and strategies that prove adaptive at one time fail to do so at another. Moreover, features differentiating normal from abnormal functioning must be extracted from a complex of signs that not only wax and wane but often develop in an insidious and unpredictable manner.

Pathology results from the same forces as involved in the development of normal functioning. Important differences in the character, timing, and intensity of these influences will lead some individuals to acquire more abnormal traits and others to develop more normal traits. When an individual develops an ability to cope with the environment in a flexible manner, and when his or her learned perceptions and behaviors foster increments in personal satisfaction, then the person may be said to have developed a normal or healthy personality. Conversely, when average or everyday responsibilities have been responded to inflexibly or defectively, or when the perceptions and behaviors the individual has acquired result in increments in personal discomfort or curtail opportunities to learn and to grow, then we may speak of an abnormal or maladaptive pattern.

Despite the tenuous and fluctuating nature of the normality-abnormality distinction, three features of development, mentioned earlier, may be abstracted from the flow of behavioral characteristics to serve as differentiating criteria; these relate to the acquisition of an adaptive inflexibility, learning to foster vicious or self-defeating circles, and a developing tenuous emotional stability under conditions of stress (Millon, 1969). Each is elaborated briefly here.

Adaptive inflexibility signifies that the alternative strategies the individual has learned for relating to others, for achieving goals, and for coping with stress are not only few in number but also appear to be practiced rigidly; that is, they are imposed upon conditions for which they are ill-suited. The individual not only is unable to adapt effectively to the circumstances of his or her life but has in addition learned to arrange the environment to avoid objectively neutral events that are perceived as stressful. As a consequence, the individual's opportunities for acquiring new, more adaptive behaviors are reduced and his/her life experiences become ever more narrowly circumscribed.

All of us learn to manipulate our environments to suit our needs. What distinguishes abnormal from normal patterns is not only their rigidity and inflexibility but also their tendency to foster vicious circles. What this means is that the person's acquired perceptions, needs, and behaviors perpetuate and intensify preexisting difficulties. These acquired maneuvers are processes by which individuals restrict their opportunities for new learning, misconstrue essentially benign events, and provoke reactions from others that reactivate earlier problems. In effect, then, abnormal personality patterns become themselves pathogenic; that is, they generate and perpetuate existent dilemmas, provoke new predicaments, and set into motion self-defeating sequences with others, which cause their already established difficulties not only to persist but also to be aggravated further.

The third feature that distinguishes abnormal from normal personalities is an acquired fragility or lack of resilience under conditions of subjective stress. Given the ease with which the already troubled are vulnerable to events that reactivate the past, and given their inflexibility and paucity of effective coping mechanisms, they are now extremely susceptible to new difficulties and disruptions. Faced with recurrent failures, anxious lest old and unresolved conflicts reemerge, and unable to recruit new adaptive strategies. These persons are likely to revert to previously developed and abnormal ways of coping, to less adequate control over their emotions, and, ultimately, to increasingly subjective and distorted perceptions of reality.

FINAL COMMENTS AND FUTURE DIRECTIONS

In this chapter many notions that theorists have used to identify the principal psychogenic sources of personality pathology have been brought together. Only rarely has the discussion commented on the soundness of these notions or the data in deriving them. The presentation would be amiss if it failed to comment, albeit briefly, on the soundness of the evidence.

That early experience plays a decisive part in constraining personality development is assumed by psychiatrists and psychologists of all theoretical persuasions. The "hard data," the unequivocal evidence derived from well-designed and well-executed research, are sorely lacking, however. There are findings that show no substantial difference in deleterious childhood experiences between normal persons and psychiatric patients. Furthermore, some adults reared in devastating childhood environments not only survive but also thrive, whereas others, raised under ideal conditions, deteriorate into severe pathological patterns. The events and sequences involved in producing pathology are awesomely complex and difficult to unravel. Limited reference to specific research has been made in this chapter, lest the reader be led to believe that there are supportive data from many well-designed studies. The authors believe that the notions presented here are fundamentally sound and justified. However, the reader should approach them as propositions to be sustained in ongoing and future research.

An important advance toward the end of strengthening research was introduced in the third edition of the American Psychiatric Association's Diagnostic and Statistical Manual of Mental Disorders (DSM-III). Particularly significant was the specification of relatively explicit "diagnostic criteria" for each disorder. Rather than a discursive description, each category was composed of a set of clearly articulated behavior and biographic characteristics. Henceforth, a specified number of these criteria were required for a patient to be assigned a diagnostic label. Despite minor controversies concerning the theoretical and empirical adequacy of the DSM's criteria, there was considerable agreement regarding their ultimate utility (Millon, 1986, 1987). Nevertheless, the DSM-III's introduction of diagnostic criteria provided a promise and not an achievement. In the ensuing years, especially from 1980 to the present, there was an increasing emphasis in psychiatry on the importance of empirically validating their diagnostic processes. Similarly, within psychology this emphasis was reinforced by its strong tradition of psychometric research. With the growth of research studies employing standardized instruments and interviews the body of data on the personality disorders has grown sufficiently to justify increasing confidence in the reliability and validity of its diagnostic criteria sets.

The major emphasis for DSM-IV, Axis II was to optimize the impact of accumulated research on its Work Group deliberations and to document where possible the empirical basis for any planned revisions. In addition to well-organized literature reviews, analyses of various systematic studies carried out by the Work Group members and associates, a number of field trials were carried out to help clarify conceptual issues regarding disorder definitions (e.g., Antisocial Personality). Data analyses were extensive and included a wide range of diagnostic efficiency statistics, including: (a) conditional probability of each personality disorder given each other personality disorder, (b) the sensitivity, specificity, positive and negative predictive power, and phi coefficient or point biserial correlations of each criterion to its parent diagnosis, (c) the interrater reliability of each criterion, and (d) the sensitivity, specificity, positive and negative predictive power, phi coefficient, and point biserial correlation of each criterion to all of the other personality disorders. All in all, these analyses give both a good foundation as well as a basis for future developments grounded in a sound empirical base.

Ideally, the goals of such research would be to specify (1) the necessary and sufficient conditions for the development of personality pathology, as well as (2) conditions which "immunize" persons against the development of personality pathology. Both will be necessary if developmental knowledge is to be instrumental as part of an applied clinical science of personology. Criteria derived from the former would enable clinicians to identify children at risk, while the latter would suggest some definite course of intervention.

Conceptual considerations, however, suggest that achieving these goals may be substantially more difficult than enumerating them. The shift in DSM-III from monothetic to polythetic criteria sets recognized that while singly necessary and jointly sufficient criteria (monothetic) are appropriate for abstract entities (Frances & Widiger, 1986), they are not appropriate for the classification of natural objects. As Horowitz, Post, French, Wallis, and Siegelman (1981, p. 575) note, "All of the prototype's properties are assumed to characterize at least some members of the category, but no one property is necessary or sufficient for membership in the category." The prototype concept recognizes that nature never expresses itself in pure (monotypic) forms, and that class membership is probabilistic rather than certain. Just as there exist no necessary or sufficient conditions whereby category membership can be established cross-sectionally, it is likely that there are no necessary or sufficient conditions by which to specify the developmental pathways of personality pathology, except perhaps at very gross levels of description (e.g., a troubled home). If so, then nature expresses itself neither in pure forms, nor in pure pathways.

Such considerations are especially important when planning prospective studies of personality disorder development. As we have noted throughout this chapter, although a generative theoretical basis and much clinical lore exists from which the developmental antecedents of these disorders can be extrapolated, longitudinal studies are sorely lacking. An essential thesis of developmental theory is that past events and developments constrain those which may develop in the future. If the serially unfolding character of personality disorders is to be fully understood and documented, rather than inferred from clinical lore or case studies, longitudinal studies must be done. These studies may be especially useful in delineating risk factors for personality disorder development. Such risk factors are essentially the longitudinal equivalent of the DSM's diagnostic attributes. Just as the possession of more diagnostic attributes increases the likelihood of disorder, possessing more risk factors increases the likelihood that one is "on the road" or latent pathway to personality pathology.

One item potential researchers should keep in mind is the kind of theory which has been presented. While the evolutionary theory is essentially a recapitulational theory, and while the theory has been presented as a stage theory, it is both an organismic and a contextual theory. By definition, evolution, whether of the individual life or the universe at large, proceeds within an ecological milieu. The stages presented are inherently contextualized. In fact, as we have seen, it is the role which context plays in the theory which prevents any simplistic exposition

of personality pathology development. Nor does the theory posit a teleological progression toward some final end-state, a prototypal characteristic of organismic theories, such as those of Piaget and Kohlberg, and a characteristic which minimizes the importance of individual differences through the postulation of a predetermined outcome. Instead, and unlike Piaget or Kohlberg, the subject domain of the theory is the entire person, and the theory seeks a level of abstraction at once necessary to address personological or molar-level concerns, and yet sufficient to allow the derivation of a taxonomy of personological prototypes diverse enough to be clinically useful.

In addition to providing a nonarbitrary basis from which to derive a taxonomy, a good theory also makes predictions and serves a generative function. An evolutionary theory of personality disorders makes specific predictions concerning the developmental time-frames during which "personological bifurcations" are likely to occur, as well as the directions these bifurcations may take, described in terms of the four broad evolutionary polarities of pleasure-pain, active-passive, self-other, and thinking-feeling. In other words, to borrow a psychodynamic term, the manifestations of these evolutionary polarities are subject to certain vicissitudes depending on maturational factors, as well as temperamental disposition, family interactions, object relationships, and so on. During early infancy, for example, pleasurable substrates are gross and undifferentiated, associated largely with certain sensory experiences. At later stages, these substrates are recruited in the transformation of objective realities, giving the construct definite phenomenological expression, allowing it to play its own legitimate role at this level in the personality system. Such intraorganismic multilevel complexity is predicted by the theory. Personologic domains which develop sooner constrain those which develop later, and the expression of certain latent principles in domains which develop later vary as a function of those which develop earlier. A highly active temperament, for example, does not exclude a phlegmatic phenomenology, but it does considerably diminish the likelihood of this kind of occurrence. Again one sees the probabilistic character of personologic science, expressed here longitudinally rather than cross-sectionally, as with the prototype construct. Future research in the development of personality pathology will have to contend with such probabilism. Fortunately, the generative theoretical basis necessary for such investigations is already in place.

REFERENCES

Ainsworth, M. D. S. (1967). *Infancy in Uganda.* Baltimore: John Hopkins University Press.

Ainsworth, M. D. S., Blehar, M., Waters, E., & Wall, S. (1978). *Patterns of attachment: A psychological study of the strange situation.* Hillsdale, NJ: Erlbaum.

Bartholomew, K., & Horowitz, L. M. (1991). Attachment styles among young adults: A test of a four-category model. *Journal of Personality and Social Psychology, 61,* 226–244.

Bates, J. E. (1980). The concept of difficult temperament. *Merrill-Palmer Quarterly, 26,* 299–319.

Bates, J. E. (1987). Temperament in infancy. In J. D. Osofsky (Ed.), *Handbook of infancy* (2nd ed., pp. 1101–1149). New York: Wiley.

Baumrind, D. (1967). Child care practices anteceding three patterns of preschool behavior. *Genetic Psychology Monographs, 75,* 43–83.

Beach, F., & Jaynes, J. (1954). Effects of early experience upon the behavior of animals. *Psychological Bulletin, 51,* 239–262.

Beck, A. T. (1963). Thinking and depression. *Archives of General Psychiatry, 9,* 324–333.

Belsky, J., & Rovine, M. (1987). Temperament and attachment security in the strange situation: An empirical rapprochement. *Child Development, 58,* 787–795.

Billings, A. G., & Moos, R. H. (1982). Psychosocial theory and research on depression: An integrative framework and review. *Clinical Psychology Review, 2,* 213–237.

Bowlby, J. (1952). *Maternal care and mental health.* Geneva: World Health Organization.

Bowlby, J. (1960). Grief and mourning in infancy and early childhood. *Psychoanalytic Study of the Child, 15,* 9–52.

Bowlby, J. (1982). *Attachment and loss: Vol 1: Attachment.* New York: Basic Books. (Original work published 1969)

Bowlby, J. (1973). Attachment and loss: Vol 2: Separation. New York: Basic Books.

Bretherton, I. (1985). Attachment theory: Retrospect and Prospect. *Monograph of Social Research in Child Development, 50* (No. 209), 3–35.

Butler, J. M., & Rice, L. N. (1963). Adience, self-actualization, and drive theory. In J. Wepman, & R. Heine (Eds.), *Concepts of personality.* Chicago: Aldine.

Campbell, S. B. (1973). Mother-infant interaction in reflective, impulsive, and hyperactive children. *Developmental Psychology, 8,* 341–349.

Chess, S., & Thomas, A. (1984). *Origins and evolution of behavior disorders.* New York: Brunner/Mazel.

Cicchetti, D. (1990). A historical perspective on the discipline of developmental psychopathology. In J. Rolf, A. S. Masten, D. Cicchetti, K. H. Nuechterlein, & S. Weintraub (Eds.), *Risk and protective factors in the development of psychopathology* (pp. 2–28). New York: Cambridge University Press.

Cicchetti, D., & Beeghly, M. (1987). Symbolic development in maltreated youngsters: An organizational perspective. In D. Cicchetti & M. Beeghly (Eds.), *Atypical symbolic development.* San Francisco: Jossey-Bass.

Cicchetti, D., & Carlson, V. (Eds.). (1989). *Child maltreatment: Theory and research on the causes and consequences of child abuse and neglect.* New York: Cambridge University Press.

Circirelli, V. G. (1982). Sibling influence throughout the lifespan. In M. E. Lamb & B. Sutton-Smith (Eds.), *Sibling relationships* (pp. 267–284). Hillsdale, NJ: Erlbaum.

Coolidge, J. C., & Brodie, R. D. (1974). Observations of mothers of 49 school phobic children. *Journal of the American Academy of Child Psychiatry, 13,* 275–285.

Crittenden, P. M. (1990). Internal representational models of attachment. *Infant Mental Health Journal, 11,* 259–277.

Crockenberg, S. (1985). Toddler's reaction to maternal anger. *Merrill-Palmer Quarterly, 31,* 361–373.

Cummings, J. S., Pellegrini, D. S., Notarius, C. I., & Cummings. (1989). Children's responses to angry adults as a function of marital distress and history of interparent hostility. *Child Development, 60,* 1035–1043.

Davidson, E. H. (1986). *Gene activity in early development.* Orlando, FL: Academic Press.

Dodge, K., Murphy, R., & Buchsbaum, K. C. (1984). The assessment of intention-cue detection skills in children: Implications for developmental psychopathology. *Child Development, 55,* 163–173.

Dornbusch, S. M., Ritter, P. L., & Leiderman, P. H. (1987). The relation of parenting style to adolescent school performance. *Child Development, 58,* 1244–1257.

Dorr, A. (1985). Contexts for experience with emotion, with special attention to television. In M. Lewis & C. Saarni (Eds.), *The socialization of emotions* (pp. 55–85). New York: Plenum.

Dunn, J., & Kendrick, C. (1981). Interaction between young siblings: Associations with the interactions between mothers and first-born. *Developmental Psychology, 17,* 336–343.

El Sheikh, M., Cummings, E. M., & Goetsch, V. (1989). Coping with adult's angry behavior: Behavioral, physiological, and verbal responses in preschoolers. *Developmental Psychology, 25,* 490–498.

Emde, R. N. (1989). The infant's relationship experience: Developmental and affective aspects. In A. Sameroff & R. N. Emde (Eds.), *Relationship disturbances in early childhood: A developmental approach* (pp. 33–51). New York: Basic Books.

Emery, R. E. (1982). Interparental conflict and the children of discord and divorce. *Psychological Bulletin, 92,* 310–330.

Erikson, E. (1950). *Childhood and society.* New York: Norton.

Erikson, E. (1959). Growth and crises of the healthy personality. In G. S. Klein (Ed.), *Psychological issues.* New York: International University Press.

Escalona, S. (1968). *Roots of individuality.* Chicago: Aldine.

Escalona, S., & Heider, G. (1959). *Prediction and outcome.* New York: Basic Books.

Escalona, S., & Leitch, M. (1953). *Early phases of personality development.* Evanston: Child Development Publications.

Eysenck, H. J. (1967). *The biological basis of personality.* Springfield, IL: Charles C. Thomas.

Farrington, D. P. (1977). The effects of public labeling. *British Journal of Criminology, 17,* 112–125.

Ferri, E. (1976). *Growing up in a one-parent family.* Slough England: NFER.

Ferster, C. B. (1973). A functional analysis of depression. *American Psychologist, 28,* 857–871.

Field, T. M. (1985). Affective responses to separation. In T. B. Brazelton & M. W. Yogman (Eds.), *Affective development in infancy.* Norwood, NJ: Ablex.

Folkman, S., & Lazarus, R. S. (1988). Coping as a mediator of emotion. *Journal of Personality and Social Psychology, 54,* 466–475.

Fox, N. A., Kimmerly, N. L., & Schafer, W. D. (1991). Attachment to mother/attachment to father: A meta-analysis. *Child Development, 62,* 210–225.

Freud, S. (1908). Character and anal eroticism. In *Collected papers* (English trans., Vol. 2, 1925). London: Hogarth.

Freud, S. (1914). On narcissism: An introduction. In *Collected papers* (English trans., Vol. 4, 1925). London: Hogarth.

Frances, A., & Widiger, T. A. (1986). Methodological issues in personality disorder diagnoses. In T. Millon & G. Klerman (Eds.), *Contemporary directions in psychopathology: Towards the DSM-IV* (pp. 381–400). New York: Guilford.

Garmezy, N. (1986). Developmental aspects of children's responses to the stress of separation and loss. In M. Rutter, C. E. Izard, & P. B.

Read (Eds.), *Depression in young people: Developmental and clinical perspectives* (pp. 297–323). New York: Guilford.

Gewirtz, J. L. (1963). A learning analysis of the effects of normal stimulation upon social and exploratory behavior in the human infant. In B. M. Foss (Ed.), *Determinants of infant behavior II*. New York: Wiley.

Gilligan, C. (1981). *In a different voice*. Cambridge, MA: Harvard University Press.

Goldfarb, W. (1955). Emotional and intellectual consequences of psychologic deprivation in infancy: A reevaluation. In P. Hoch & J. Zubin (Eds.), *Psychopathology of Childhood*. New York: Grune & Stratton.

Goldsmith, H. H., & Gottesman, I. I. (1981). Origins of variation in behavioral style: A longitudinal study of temperament in young twins. *Child Development, 52,* 91–103.

Gottman, J. M., & Katz, L. F. (1989). Effects of marital discord on young children's peer interaction and health. *Developmental Psychology, 25,* 373–381.

Hall, G. S. (1916) *Adolescence,* New York: Appleton.

Hetherington, E. M. (1972). Effects of paternal absence on personality development in adolescent daughters. *Developmental Psychology, 7,* 313–326.

Hetherington, E. M., Cox, M., & Cox, C. R. (1982). Effects of divorce on parents and children. In M. Lamb (Ed.), *Nontraditional families* (pp. 223–288). Hillsdale, NJ: Erlbaum.

Hinde, R. A. (1982). Attachment: Some conceptual and biological issues. In J. Stevenson-Hinde & C. P. Parkes (Eds.), *The place of attachment in human behavior* (pp. 60–76). New York: Basic Books.

Horney, K. (1939). *New Ways in Psychoanalysis*. New York: Norton.

Horowitz, L. M., Post, D. L., French, R. de S., Wallis, K. D., & Siegelman, E. Y. (1981). The prototype as a construct in abnormal psychology: 2. Clarifying disagreement in psychiatric judgments. *Journal of Abnormal Psychology, 90,* 575–585.

Jones, S. S., & Raag, T. (1989). Smile production in older infants: The importance of a social recipient for the facial signal. *Child Development, 13,* 147–165.

Kagan, J. (1989). Temperamental contribution to social behavior. *American Psychologist, 44,* 668–674.

Kagan, J., Reznick, J. S., & Snidman, N. (1989). Issues in the study of temperament. In G. A. Kohnstamm, J. E. Bates, & M. K. Rothbart (Eds.), *Temperament in childhood*. New York: Wiley.

Killackey, H. P. (1990). Neocortical expansion: An attempt toward relating phylogeny and ontogeny. *Journal of Cognitive Neuroscience, 2,* 1–17.

Lamb, M. E., Thompson, R. A., Gardner, W., & Estes, D. (1985). Infant-mother attachment. Hillsdale, NJ: Erlbaum.

Lazarus, A. A. (1968). Learning theory and the treatment of depression. *Behavior Research and Therapy, 6,* 83–89.

Leary, T. (1957). *Interpersonal diagnosis of personality*. New York: Ronald.

Lewinsohn, P. M. (1974). A behavioral approach to depression. In R. J. Friedman & M. M. Katz (Eds.), *The psychology of depression: Contemporary theory and research*. Washington, DC: Winston.

Lewis, C. C. (1981). The effects of parental firm control: A reinterpretation of findings. *Psychological Bulletin, 90,* 547–563.

Lipton, S. A., & Kater, S. B. (1989). Neurotransmitter regulation of neuronal outgrowth, plasticity, and survival. *Trends in Neuroscience, 12,* 265–269.

Loeber, R., & Stouthamer-Loeber, M. (1986). Family factors as correlates and predictors of juvenile conduct problems and delinquency.

In M. Toury & N. Morris (Eds.), *Crime and Justice* (Vol. 7). Chicago: University of Chicago Press.

Maccoby, E., & Martin, J. (1983). Socialization in the context of the family: Parent-child interaction. In E. M. Hetherington (Ed.), *Handbook of child psychology, Vol 4: Socialization, personality, and social development*. New York: Wiley.

Mash, E. J., & Johnston, C. (1982). A comparison of the mother-child interactions of younger and older hyperactive and normal children. *Child Development, 53,* 1371–1381.

Meehl, P. E. (1962). Schizotaxia, schizotypy, schizophrenia. *American Psychologist, 17,* 827–838.

Meehl, P. E. (1990). Toward an integrated theory of schizotaxia, schizotypy, and schizophrenia. *Journal of Personality Disorders, 4,* 1–99.

Melzack, R. (1965). Effects of early experience upon behavior: Experimental and conceptual considerations. In P. Hoch & J. Zubin (Eds.), *Psychopathology of perception*. New York: Grune & Stratton.

Michelsson, K., Rinne, A., & Paajanen, S. (1990). Crying, feeding and sleeping patterns in 1- to 12-month-old infants. *Child Care, Health, and Development, 16,* 99–111.

Millon, T. (1969). *Modern psychopathology: A biosocial approach to maladaptive learning and functioning*. Philadelphia: Saunders.

Millon, T. (1981). *Disorders of personality: DSM-III, Axis II*. New York: Wiley.

Millon, T. (1986). On the past and future of the DSM-III: Personal recollections and projections. In T. Millon & G. L. Klerman (Eds.), *Contemporary directions in psychopathology: Towards the DSM-IV* (pp. 29–70). New York: Guilford.

Millon, T. (1987). On the genesis and prevalence of the borderline personality disorder: A social learning thesis. *Journal of Personality Disorders, 1,* 354–372.

Millon, T. (1990). *Toward a new personology*. New York: Wiley.

Millon, T., & Davis, R. D. (1995). Disorders of personality: DSM-IV, Axis II. New York: Wiley.

Morrison, J. R. (1980). Adult psychiatric disorders in parents of hyperactive children. *American Journal of Psychiatry, 137,* 825–827.

Mueller, E., & Silverman, N. (1989). Peer relations in maltreated children. In D. Cicchetti & V. Carlson (Eds.), *Child maltreatment: Theory and research on the causes and consequences of child abuse and neglect* (pp. 529–578). New York: Cambridge University Press.

Murphy, G. (1947). *Personality: A biosocial approach to origins and structures*. New York: Harper.

Murphy, L. B., & Moriarty, A. E. (1976). *Vulnerability, coping, and growth*. New Haven: Yale University Press.

Osofsky, J. D., & Danzger, B. (1974). Relationships between neonatal characteristics and mother-infant interaction. *Developmental Psychology, 10,* 124–130.

Papousek, H., & Papousek, M. (1975). Cognitive aspects of preverbal social interaction between human infants and adults. In R. Porter & M. O'Conner (Eds.), *Parent-infant interaction* (pp. 241–260). Amsterdam: Elsevier.

Parker, G. (1983). *Parental overprotection: A risk factor in psychosocial development*. New York: Grune & Stratton.

Patterson, G. R. (1977). Accelerating stimuli for two classes of coercive behaviors. *Journal of Abnormal Child Psychology, 5,* 335–350.

Piaget, J. (1952). *The origins of intelligence in children*. New York: International Universities Press.

Plomin, R. (1990). The role of inheritance in behavior. *Science, 248,* 183–188.

Plomin, R., Defries, J. C., & McClearn, G. E. (1990). *Behavioral genetics: A primer* (2nd ed.). New York: Freeman.

Plomin, R., & Dunn, J. (Eds.). (1986). *The study of temperament: Changes, continuities, and challenge.* Hillsdale, NJ: Erlbaum.

Purves, D., & Lichtman, J. W. (1985). *Principles of neural development.* Sunderland, MA: Sinauer.

Rado, S. (1956). Schizotypal organization: Preliminary report on a clinical study of schizophrenia. In S. Rado & G. E. Daniels (Eds.), *Changing concepts of psychoanalytic medicine,* pp. 225–236. New York: Grune & Stratton.

Rakic, P. (1985). Limits of neurogenesis in primates. *Science, 227,* 154–156.

Rakic, P. (1988). Specification of cerebral cortical areas. *Science, 241,* 170–176.

Rapaport, D. (1958). The theory of ego autonomy: A generalization. *Bulletin of the Menninger Clinic, 22,* 13–35.

Reid, J. B., Patterson, G. R., & Loeber, R. (1982). The abused child: Victim, instigator, or innocent bystander. In D. Bernstein (Ed.), *Response, structure and organization.* Lincoln: University of Nebraska Press.

Reiss, D. (1981). *The families' construction of reality.* Cambridge, MA: Harvard University Press.

Ribble, M. A. (1943). *The rights of infants.* New York: Columbia University Press.

Riesen, A. H. (1961). Stimulation as a requirement for growth and function in behavioral development. In D. Fiske & S. Maddi (Eds.), *Functions of varied experience* (pp. 57–80). Homewood, IL: Dorsey.

Robins, L., & Rutter, M. (Eds.). (1990). *Straight and devious pathways from childhood to adulthood.* New York: Cambridge University Press.

Rosenzweig, M. R., & Diamond, M. (1962). Effect of environmental complexity and training on brain chemistry and anatomy: A replication and extension. *Journal of Comparative Physiological Psychology, 55,* 429–437.

Rushton, J. P. (1985). Differential K theory: The sociobiology of individual and group differences. *Personality and Individual Differences, 6,* 441–452.

Rutter, M. (1989). Intergenerational continuities and discontinuities in serious parenting difficulties. In D. Cicchetti & V. Carlson (Eds.), *Child maltreatment: Theory and research on the causes and consequences of child abuse and neglect* (pp. 317–348). Cambridge: Cambridge University Press.

Rutter, M., & Giller, H. (1983). *Juvenile delinquency: Trends and perspectives.* Harmondsworth, England: Penguin.

Scott, J. P. (1968). *Early experience and the organization of behavior.* Belmont, CA: Brooks-Cole.

Singer, M. T., & Wynne, L. C. (1965). Thought disorder and family relations of schizophrenics, III: Methodology using projective techniques. *A.M.A. Archives of General Psychiatry, 12,* 187–212.

Smith, P. B. & Pederson, D. R. (1988). Maternal sensitivity and patterns of infant-mother attachment. *Child Development, 59,* 1097–1101.

Spitz, R. A. (1965). *The first year of life.* New York: International University Press.

Sroufe, L. A. (1979). Socioemotional development. In J. Osofsky (Ed.), *Handbook of infant development, 1st edition* (pp. 462–515). New York: Wiley.

Sroufe, L. A., & Fleeson, J. (1986). Attachment and the construction of relationships. In W. Hartup & Z. Rubin (Eds.), *Relationships and development* (pp. 51–71). Hillsdale, NJ: Erlbaum.

Sroufe, L. A., & Waters, E. (1976). The ontogenesis of smiling and laughter: A perspective on the organization of development in infancy. *Psychological Review, 83,* 173–189.

Steinberg, L., Elmen, J. D., & Mounts, N. S. (1989). Authoritative parenting, psychosocial maturity, and academic success among adolescents. *Child Development, 60,* 1424–1436.

Thomas, A., & Chess, S. (1977). *Temperament and development.* New York: Brunner/Mazel.

Thomas, A., Chess, S., & Birch, H. G. (1963). *Behavioral individuality in early childhood.* New York: New York University Press.

Thomas, A., Chess, S., & Birch, H. G. (1968). *Temperament and behavior disorders in children.* New York: New York University Press.

Thomas, A., Chess, S., & Korn, S. J. (1982). The reality of difficult temperament. *Merrill-Palmer Quarterly, 28,* 1–20.

Thompson, W. R., & Schaefer, T. (1961). Early environmental stimulation. In D. Fiske & S. Maddi (Eds.), *Functions of varied experience* (pp. 81–105). Homewood, IL: Dorsey.

Tizard, B., & Hodges, J. (1978). The effect of early institutional rearing on the development of 8-year-old children. *Journal of Child Psychology and Psychiatry, 19,* 99–118.

Volkmar, F., & Provence, S. (1990). *Disorders of affect* (Yale Child Study Center Working Paper). New Haven, CT: Yale Child Study Center.

Wagner, M. E., Schubert, H. J. P., & Schubert, D. S. P. (1979). Sibship-constellation effects on psychosocial development, creativity, and health. In H. W. Reese & L. P. Lipsitt (Eds.), *Advances in child development and behavior* (Vol. 14, pp. 58–148). New York: Academic Press.

Waldron, S., Shrier, D. K., Stone, B., & Tobin, F. (1975). School phobia and other childhood neuroses: A systematic study of the children and their families. *American Journal of Psychiatry, 132,* 802–808.

Weissman, M. M., & Paykel, E. S. (1974). *The depressed woman: A study of social relationships.* Chicago: University of Chicago Press.

Werner, H. (1940). *Comparative psychology of mental development.* New York: Follett.

White, R. W. (1960). Competence and the psychosexual stages of development. In M. R. Jones (Ed.), *Nebraska symposium on motivation.* Lincoln: University of Nebraska Press.

Williams, R. J. (1973). The biological approach to the study of personality. In T. Millon (Ed.), *Theories of psychopathology and personality* (2nd ed., 1973). Philadelphia: Saunders.

Wilson, E. O. (1978). *On human nature.* Cambridge, MA: Harvard University Press.

Yarrow, L. J. (1961). Maternal deprivation: Toward and empirical and conceptual reevaluation. *Psychological Bulletin, 58,* 459–490.

Zanolli, K., Saudargas, R., & Twardosz, S. (1990). Two-year-olds' responses to affectionate and caregiving teacher behavior. *Child Study Journal, 20,* 35–54.

CHAPTER 19

Emergence of Alcohol Problems and the Several Alcoholisms: A Developmental Perspective on Etiologic Theory and Life Course Trajectory

ROBERT A. ZUCKER, HIRAM E. FITZGERALD, and HELENE D. MOSES

This volume is guided by a powerful theoretical framework that is second nature to developmentalists, but one that has yet to be fully appreciated by psychopathologists. That heuristic is developmental theory, and its core tenets involve the observations that the structure of events is anchored in time, and that the careful study of adjacency, both of co-occurrence in context, and of sequence (i.e., precedence), allows one to disentangle the flow of causal process more readily than by any other means. The theory also posits a different paradigm for the observation of structure, that is, crystallization of relationships over time, as in the structure of a diagnostic syndrome. Structure is not to be taken as a given, but rather must be accounted for. Thus the achievement of what appears to be steady state crystallization must instead be initially regarded as a dynamic organization that is potentially fluid, and held together by a series of ongoing processes. Within this perspective, change, or instability, is as likely as is stability, and the occurrence of either must be accounted for. Finally, given the importance of both adjacent and time-based relationships, the notion that one needs to understand casual interplay by way of systemic interrelationships (Ford & Lerner, 1992; von Bertalanffy, 1968) is also a central tenet of the theory.

The editors of these volumes hope that this framework will become the core theory by which the ebb, flow, and maintenance of psychopathological process is understood. The authors of this chapter hope that this theory, taken along with the body of evidence reviewed here, will persuade readers to re-organize their thinking about the nature of causal processes regulating the acquisition, use, abuse, and more severe symptomatic manifestations of alcohol involvement over the life course. The particular focus of this chapter involves these phenomena in the early and middle portions of the life span and developmental outcomes in the later stages of life are only briefly commented on.

THE MAGNITUDE OF ALCOHOL USE, ALCOHOL PROBLEMS, AND ALCOHOLISM IN AMERICAN SOCIETY[1]

On the basis of national summary statistics, it is clear that alcohol use is a ubiquitous part of American life for large age segments of the population (Table 19.1). Even among 14-year-olds, national data (Johnston, O'Malley, & Bachman, 1993) indicate that more than half of both boys and girls have used beverage alcohol in the past year, with more than a quarter reporting some use during the last month. When one turns to data on adults (also Table 19.1), a recent report based upon the 1992 National Household Survey on Drug Abuse (Substance Abuse and Mental Health Services Administration, 1993) indicates that 80% of men in the 18 to 25-year-old age range and 84% in the 26 to 34-year-old age range reported some consumption in the past year. These figures drop to 69% among those aged 35 and older, and other data, not presented here, show that the decline continues even further, with only 49% of men aged 65 and older reporting any use (Williams & De-Bakey, 1992). Among women, 76% and 75%, respectively of 18 to 25 and 26 to 34-year-olds are drinkers. The figure drops to 57% among those 35 and older; and among those over 65, only 25% of the population are involved in this activity. Similarly dramatic variations (and disparities) are found on the basis of racial and ethnic group differences.

While the adult and youth data over the last half generation also provide clear evidence that historical changes are operating

---

This work was supported in part by grants from the National Institute on Alcohol Abuse and Alcoholism (2 RO1 AA 07065).

---

[1] We use the term alcoholism here to refer to that envelope of clinically severe and long-standing alcohol problems which has been described under a variety of guises in the last generation. The current and most commonly used classification scheme is the DSM-IV (American Psychiatric Association, 1994) cluster of alcohol abuse/dependence. While there is extensive discussion of the differences in population accessed via different definitional schemes (see Secretary of Health and Human Services, 1993, Chapter 14), the generic term alcoholism is used here to refer to this larger umbrella. When we wish to make distinctions among differently defined clusters, we will move to a more specific terminology.

TABLE 19.1 Some Background Statistics on Alcohol Use and Life Course Variation: U.S. Population Estimates for 1992 (Percent Users—Last Year)

	Males	Females
Total population (12+)	70	60
By age group:		
12–17	34	31
18–25	80	76
26–54	84	75
35+	69	57
Adolescent population		
8th grade (ca. age 14)	54	54
10th grade (ca. age 16)	70	71
12th grade (ca. age 18)	77	76

Note: Sources for these data are Substance Abuse and Mental Health Services Administration, 1993 (National Household Survey on Drug Abuse, 1992, p. 85), and Johnston, O'Malley, & Bachman, 1993 (National Survey Results on Drug Use, 1975–1992, p. 56).

to reduce the general pattern of consumption, the magnitude of the differences in level of use among the different age groups is not explainable by simple cohort effects, nor by the small amounts of historical change being brought about by an increasingly health conscious and temperance valuing American society. Rather, these marked, age-graded shifts in alcohol-seeking (and using) behavior that show equally dramatic variations as a function of gender and ethnic group membership and that in some form are detectable even before the age 14, require the use of a multicausal explanatory structure that reaches far beyond concepts relating to alcohol use alone to account for the variety of observed developmental trajectories. It is for this reason that the study of alcohol-related phenomena has been of interest not only to alcohol researchers, but also to developmentalists and scholars from a wide variety of other disciplines for at least half a century (Jessor, Graves, Hanson, & Jessor, 1968; Kandel, 1978; Pittman & Snyder, 1968; Quarterly Journal of Studies on Alcohol, 1945). The provision of an adequate explanatory framework is thus a challenging theoretical backdrop for the core focus of this chapter, namely, the charting and understanding of variations in a subpart of this domain, pertaining to *problem* alcohol use over the life course.

Given the ubiquity of normal drinking behavior and the strong gender difference in adulthood, it is perhaps not surprising that alcohol abuse/dependence, as an index of drinking practices at the psychopathological end of the use continuum shows a high level of prevalence, involving one in four men over the course of a lifetime, and one in nine women. What is not as well appreciated is that this disorder is the *most common* of all DSM-III disorders *for men* (Robins & Regier, 1991). Lifetime prevalence for alcohol abuse/dependence is 23.8% (one-year prevalence = 11.7%) contrasted against a lifetime rate for *any* mental disorder of 36%. The comparable figures for women are much lower, with a 4.6% lifetime prevalence for alcohol abuse/dependence (one-year prevalence = 2.1%) and an overall rate for any mental disorder of

30% (Helzer & Pryzbeck, 1988; Secretary of Health and Human Services, 1993).[2]

GOALS OF THE CHAPTER

Perhaps because alcohol involvement and its problems, even at the extreme, are so common, perhaps also because the pathological version of alcohol use shades into patterns of regular drinking in a still heavily alcohol using society, the magnitude of alcohol abuse/dependence, and its importance as a social problem has still to a substantial degree been unappreciated by mental health professionals. In addition, the degree to which the normal phenomena of alcohol use, their ebb and flow over the life span, and the degree to which they may be explained within the framework of developmental theory, has to a large degree been ignored by psychopathologists as the benchmark against which the various clinical/pathological adaptations need to be contrasted. This is a major goal of this chapter. A second goal is to illustrate the utility of the developmental heuristic as a framework around which to organize the disparate and, in some instances, apparently contradictory array of clinical and etiologic data that currently exist.

To attempt this task for the entirety of the literature on the evolution of alcohol problems is an impossible task for a work of this length. Instead, we selectively focus on seven issues: (a) the nature of the explanatory net one needs to spread in order to adequately capture developmental variation and etiologic processes pertaining to problem alcohol use; (b) the development of clinical "caseness," as a concept that more easily allows the linkage of child and adult psychopathological phenomena; (c) the definitional and conceptual problem of defining the onset of alcohol-related difficulty; (d) the influence of contexts upon epigenetic progression; (e) the evidence for multiple developmental trajectories (multiple alcoholisms); (f) implications of the etiologic literature for issues of prevention/intervention, and finally (g) a section on conclusions and needed work for the future. We do not deal with the literature relating to fetal alcohol syndrome and its longer term developmental course. Although this is an issue that has frequently been researched by developmental psychologists, outcomes here have less to do with the development of patterns of alcohol abuse in adolescence and adulthood, and more to do with issues about developmental delays relating to the effects of this teratogenic insult (cf. Day, 1992).

AN EXPLANATORY NET FOR DEVELOPMENTAL VARIATION

The long biopsychosocial process that results in the appearance of alcohol problems at the individual level begins with the manufacture and distribution of this beverage/drug, and is in place

---

[2] Figures based upon Epidemiologic Catchment Area study data weighted to estimate prevalence for the U.S. population aged 18 and over (cf. Regier et al., 1990).

long before the chain of individual causal events pertaining to consumption and consequences has started. From a contextual standpoint, it is important to note that one cannot have alcohol problems without the presence of alcohol. This is only superficially a trivial issue, given that the presence of the drug is regulated by societal norms about appropriate contexts of use, and actual availability of the drug within the society. Thus, alcohol use and the problems that come from such use are phenomena that are deeply embedded in a social matrix. It is likely therefore, that a systems perspective, one that accounts for larger economic forces, employment and unemployment, the production of alcohol in the society, and even population density (as it relates to living in an urban vs. rural environment) is vital in accounting for some of the variation that ultimately relates to consumption and problems at the individual level (e.g., Brenner, 1973; Fitzgerald & Zucker, in press).

Such phenomena are all macrolevel events, determined by collectives. They change, but they change slowly, and individual and small group level variation is contained within such macrolevel structures. At a level supraordinate to the family, group influences—by way of laws and other control structures pertaining to availability and penalties for use by young people—play a role (O'Malley & Wagenaar, 1991). As the explanatory lens is moved closer to the individual, within-culture variation in socialization practices play themselves out, by way of differential inculcation of values pertaining to drugs, and expectancies about drug effects. Evidence is already substantial that such learning plays a causal role in eventual alcohol involvement. But the panoramic view requires examination of socialization practices pertaining to alcohol nonspecific variation (for example, related to the development of aggressiveness), given the strong relationship between comorbid symptomatology and later severe alcohol problems (Pihl & Peterson, 1991; Zucker & Fitzgerald, 1991).

A society is a macrostructure, moving through historical time. As this structure moves along, within its mass, individuals mate, conceive, and new lives begin their developmental course. Even here the larger culture mediates developmental processes. Social factors affect prenatal care, and alcohol availability impacts use, which in turn impacts fetal development, which in turn will influence longer term developmental process (Streissguth et al., 1991; Streissguth, Clarren & Jones, 1985). The problem at the individual level only begins at this juncture. Time, maturational process, biological function, all start to play out, and are influenced by a multitude of factors as developmental course proceeds. Causal factors do not operate in a constant manner over the life course. For example, genes turn on and off at different times in development and create a different neurochemical and hormonal environment as they do. Nonetheless, from a systems or nonlinear dynamics view, the organism is subject to epigenetic process. Evolution has given the species gene pool a set of highly developmentally stable characteristics, such that a minimally reasonable environment fosters the unfolding of organism-environment opponent process in an orderly fashion even though aspects of multifinality come into play. One child's gait will be different than another's but they both end up with upright locomotion despite differences in time to organize.

On the other hand, when a minimally normal environment is not encountered, maturation does not do anything to rebut the consequences of deprivation (cf. Spitz, 1945, on what happens when infants are neglected in orphanages).

In parallel fashion, the larger culture's age stages create different expectations within the social structure, and peer groups, as both teachers and enhancers of behavior, change their quality and the behavioral repertoire that they elicit and also reinforce (Patterson, 1993). And finally, the complexity of this influencing structure is even greater, given the likelihood that the relationship between macrolevel social influences (such as the "wetness or dryness" of the society (Skog, 1985)) and those operating at the microculture or family level, are not related in a linear fashion. Macrolevel cultural influences change the threshold within which microlevel phenomena (e.g., alcoholism subtypes), appear (Helzer & Canino, 1992; Reich, Cloninger, Van Eerdewegh, Rice, & Mullaney, 1988), so that differences in level of genetic susceptibility will be capable of being expressed in higher versus lower consumption cultures. Nonetheless, once such threshold values are passed, at the microlevel, different rules of operation may operate (Salthe, 1985). It is this panorama of causal structures which must be addressed to adequately map alcohol-related difficulty. In this section, we discuss the developmental method as a paradigm for the understanding of risk evolution, present a probabilistic, multidomain model as a framework within which to map the interplay of across domain and across time processes, and proceed to lay out the critical domains and the accumulating evidence for a time-based, multiple process model of the etiology of alcoholism and alcohol-related problems.

Developmental Systems Theory and Problem Alcohol Involvement

The developmental systems perspective is concerned with change as it occurs through the life span. Living systems are hierarchically organized, dynamic, self-regulating, holistic, purposeful, and open (Laszlo, 1972; Miller, 1978; Miller & Miller, 1992; von Bertalanffy, 1968). As systems organize and develop, their dynamic structure emerges via a network of *feedback loops* that regulate the growth, collapse, oscillation, and inhibition of the system (Levine & Fitzgerald, 1992). The dynamic structure of a system includes not only the individual variables in the system, but also the pattern of feedback loops that form the mechanisms underlying the functioning of the system. It is the relationships among system components and not the individual components per se that generate patterns or levels of organization. Moreover, the transactions among components always occur in context such that context becomes part of the transaction. This is precisely what is meant by the dictum that the observer is always an integral part of the observed event. The state or stability of a system, therefore, is tied as much to context as it is to patterns of relationship generated by system components. Feedback loops play a critical role in state regulation.

Feedback loops can be positive or negative. Positive feedback loops amplify change; they are associated with growth or collapse of a system. Negative feedback loops counteract change; they are associated with inhibition or self-correction of the system. For example, a family system that is organized and regulated by paternal alcoholism can be destabilized if the father shifts from alcohol dependence to abstinence (Steinglass, Bennett, Wolin, & Reiss, 1987). The bifurcation precipitated by the marked change in the father's behavior will inevitably lead to a reorganization of the family system. Members of the family may act to re-establish the family system encouraging the father to resume drinking (negative feedback). They may redefine the family system, with or without the inclusion of father, in order to facilitate change and growth (positive feedback). Ford and Lerner (1992) also refer to feedforward processes, which are goal-directed strategies or actions that attempt to project or anticipate bifurcations in the system at some point in the future. For example, developing outside interests or hobbies in anticipation of retirement, or in anticipation of the youngest child's leaving home. Note, that whereas there may be a finite range of possible outcomes (reaction range) when a system reorganizes, there is no predetermined or a priori program that determines the outcome or form of systemic reorganization. The reorganized system emerges from the newly formed relationships or patterns generated by the system.

This emergent process is *epigenetic* (Gottlieb, 1991b), which means that the structures and functions that organize over time are probabilistically determined. It is not the case, however, that dynamic systems are random. The boundaries that delineate a system (subsystems, primary system, adjunctive system, etc.) and the transitional points between systems, define the parameters within which nonlinear processes operate. Each individual's developmental and experiential history is unique (Gottlieb, 1991a), regardless of whether the behavior in question is developmentally stable (e.g., motor and language skills) or developmentally labile (cognitive skills). The development of motor behavior (Thelen, 1992; Thelen, Kelso, & Fogel, 1987) and language (van Geert, 1991) seem to be regulated by the same nonlinear dynamics that we assert are regulating the individual's risk for substance abuse. Consider, for example, two siblings with the same alcoholic father. Each of the children experiences the same contextual event (their father's alcoholism), yet their subjective reactions to the event may differ markedly. If the siblings are not monozygotic twins, they will differ in various ways (e.g., sex, birth order, temperament, genetic vulnerability, sensitivity to particular drug actions, age at onset of paternal alcoholism, parent-child interaction, family SES, family structure, peer group, interests, and values). As Hoffman (1991) points out in her poignant review of research on the influence of family environment on personality development:

> The same family event can thus be interpreted differently, producing a different emotional response and self-attribution, and can have a different impact on personality development. This approach views children as endlessly coding and interpreting their surroundings and contrasting themselves to others. (Hoffman, 1991, p. 191)

This approach views social and personality development to be regulated by nonlinear dynamics. Thus, each child in the alcoholic family not only has access to possible developmental pathways, but also the possible pathways for one child are not necessarily those of another child. This is what is meant by reaction range; the possible phenotypes available will depend on the dynamic relationships between genotype and the organism's environment. Similarly, different families have different presenting state characteristics. The family with an alcoholic father whose only dependence is alcohol differs sharply from the family with an alcoholic father who abuses other substances as well (Gonzalez, Zucker, & Fitzgerald, 1993). Similarly, the family in which both parents are alcoholic is different from that in which only one is alcoholic. The task for alcoholism researchers is to begin to take such contextual variation into account in their etiological models and in their search for alcohol types.

Cultural and Ethnic Variation in Alcohol-Related Difficulty

There is, at this point, overwhelming evidence that alcohol problems vary with culture and social class, just as they do as a function of gender. Alcohol problems, even at their most severe end stages, are manifestations of a biopsychosocial process (Zucker & Gomberg, 1986). From a behavioral standpoint, they require self-administration of a substance and involve the more or less conscious, more or less volitional pursuit of an external object (drug) in order for the syndrome's activity to be maintained. So they require the presence of a much larger set of contexts that not only allow such use, but also make the drug available, and even encourage its use. For these reasons, understandings of cultural and ethnic variation are crucial, and the manner in which diatheses interact with these contexts becomes a critical issue in understanding how alcoholic disorder will play out. We follow with a broad range of examples that illustrate this point.

Drunkenness is more prevalent in hunter-gatherer societies than it is in herding-agricultural societies (Field, 1991); public drinking is acceptable among the Navaho but not among the Hopi (Levy & Kunitz, 1974); adult Korean males have one of the highest alcohol consumption rates in the world (Lee, 1992), whereas Korean-Americans living in Los Angeles had the highest number of abstainers of four Asian-American groups studied by Kitano and Chi (1986/87). And in the general U.S. population, substantial differences occur in different geographic regions in both problem drinking and abstention (Hilton, 1991). Heath's (1991) description of the changes in drinking patterns of the Camba of Bolivia provides one example of the regulatory role that culture, context, and historical change play in shaping changes in drinking patterns. A cultural pattern of intense group drinking organized around secular and religious holiday celebrations was disrupted by marked changes in the ecosystem that provided the infrastructure for Camba culture and their binge drinking practices. Industrialization and cultivation of land for sugar cane and coca production led to changes in the social ecology of the Camba, with the result that contemporary youth show little interest in participating in the rituals of the Camba drinking party (Heath, 1991). Another example is provided by changes in the economic climate in China and the related emergence of a new mercantile class. Although alcohol has been a part of Chinese culture for nearly 4000 years, its use traditionally is mandated by ceremonial and social customs (Wang et al., 1992). As a result, China is a culture in which alcohol abuse and dependence occur at extraordinarily low rates, 0.4 to 3.5 percent (Wang et al., 1992). However, as members of the emergent mercantile class acquire greater wealth and social privilege, the rates of drinking have increased, including the rates of alcohol abuse and dependence (Wang et al., 1992).

Closer to home, the rate of antisocial alcoholism is higher among urban men of lower socioeconomic status (SES) than among lower SES urban women (Fitzgerald & Zucker, in press); acculturation processes are positively related to increased rates of drunkenness among Mexican-American, Cuban-American, and Puerto Rican men (Caetano, 1986/87). Historically, the field has provided substantial evidence about variations among drinking patterns in Caucasian immigrant groups who arrived earlier to American shores (e.g., the Irish, Italians, Jews, and Slavs; Gomberg, White, & Carpenter, 1982; Pittman & Snyder, 1968; Pittman & White, 1992) so that we know more about variation among these groups than we do about variation among America's contemporary ethnic minorities.

The search for clearcut information about the relationship between ethnicity and alcohol use and abuse is complicated by the fact that the boundaries delimiting ethnic group membership are becoming more like sieves than semi-permeable membranes (Aboud, 1987; Root, 1992). For example, what does it mean to classify individuals on the basis of Spanish surnames? As Rotheram and Phinney (1987) point out, Blacks, Whites, Native-Americans, and Asians can have Spanish surnames. Moreover, ". . . it is estimated that 30% to 70% of African-Americans by multigenerational history are multiracial . . . virtually all Latinos . . . and Filipinos . . . are multiracial, as are the majority of American Indians . . . and Native Hawaiians" (Root, 1992, p. 9). Consideration of alcohol use and abuse among ethnic minorities, therefore, must be considered with such multiracial multigenerational diversity in mind.

African-Americans

Since the mid-1940s, the incidence of cirrhosis of the liver, heart disease, and cancer have increased dramatically among African-Americans (Ronan, 1986/87), with an incidence of cirrhosis of the liver twice that of the nonwhite population of the United States, but less than that of Native-Americans (Lex, 1987). In an even more recent update on U.S. population data, Herd notes that "except for the youth population, blacks are over-represented on most indirect measures of alcohol problems" (1991, p. 309). However, she also notes a substantial set of possible contextual confounds in almost all of the literature on indicators of alcohol related disorder, including such factors as high hepatitis rates, inferior nutritional status, and lower socioeconomic status.

Lex (1987) found that among 18 to 59-year-old African-Americans living in San Francisco, five factors (marital problems, job problems, family problems, victims of crime, police problems) were associated with alcohol consumption on 17 or more days during the previous month.

Analysis of data in the 1984 National Survey pointed to many similarities between African-American and white men with rates of abstinence, infrequent drinkers, and heavy drinkers roughly the same (Herd, 1991). On the other hand, African-American women have higher abstention rates than white women. There were differences between African-American men and white men. For example, African-American men who become heavy drinkers show a pattern of late onset drinking (30 to 39 years) compared with whites (18 to 29 years) (Ronan, 1986/87). Higher income levels were associated with increased rates of drinking among white men, but decreased rates among African-American men; the heaviest drinking whites tended to live in more urban areas of the North and Midwest, whereas, the heaviest drinking African-Americans tended to live in more suburban and rural areas of the South (Herd, 1991). Consistent with other research, African-American men had higher rates of acute and chronic health problems. African-American women, on the other hand, reported fewer problems than white women, especially for drinking and driving and some social problems.

Native-Americans

Although Native-Americans comprise less than 1% of the general population, they are one of the fastest growing ethnic groups in the United States as well as one of the youngest. The median age for Native-Americans is just short of 23 years compared with a median age of 30 years for the general population (Young, 1988). Slightly more than half of the Native-American population resides in an urban area (Manson, Shore, Baron, Ackerson, & Neligh, 1992). Reservations are characterized by high unemployment and high levels of drug use, with poverty, prejudice, and poor education presenting nearly insurmountable barriers for positive change. Consistent with popular stereotype, the Native-American population is characterized by high rates of heavy drinking. Inconsistent with the stereotype, the Native-American population also is characterized by high rates of abstinence (Lex, 1987). What is most clear is that there is great variation within the Native-American population with respect both to use and abuse of alcohol. To give perspective to rates of heavy drinking in selective tribes, consider that studies of the general population indicate that from 9% to 18% of the population uses alcohol heavily. Rates of heavy drinking for the Standing Rock Sioux range from 9% to 24%, those for the Navajo 14%, the Ute 26%, and the Ojibwa 42% (Manson et al., 1992). The Creek and Cherokee of Oklahoma have very low rates of alcohol-related deaths or problems with the police, whereas the Cheyenne-Arapaho account for a significant percentage of alcohol-related deaths and arrests for public drunkenness despite the fact that they comprise less than 2% of Oklahoma's Native-American population (Weibel-Orlando 1986/87).

In many ways, Native-American do not differ from other populations with respect to alcohol abuse and dependence: Men have higher rates than women (except for Sioux women who are reported to drink more than men); married and widowed individuals have lower rates than never married or divorced individuals; and poor education, low occupational status, and early age of first intoxication all predict higher risk for heavy drinking (Lex, 1987; Manson et al., 1992; Oetting, Edwards, & Beauvais, 1989; Weibel-Orlando, 1986/87; Young, 1988). On the other hand, in many ways Native-American differ from other populations, most saliently with respect to the consequences of heavy drinking. For example, Manson et al. (1992) found alcohol abuse to be related to five of the 10 leading causes of death in Native-American. Mortality was 5.5 times higher for automobile accidents, 2.4 times higher for cirrhosis of the liver, 2.4 times higher for suicide, and 2.8 times higher for homicides. As is the case with other minority populations, little is known about the etiology of alcohol use and abuse among Native-American. It is clear, however, that contextual factors play a key role in regulating drinking behavior, and that these factors play out differently from one tribe to another.

Hispanic-Americans

As noted, the term Hispanic-American encompasses a rich diversity of racial and ethnic people who share at least one of the following: Spanish language, a specific cultural heritage, or a Spanish surname. Among people who can appropriately be referred to as Hispanic, Cuban-Americans, Puerto Ricans, and Mexican-Americans have been the most frequent participants in studies of alcohol use and abuse. As is the case for some other minority groups, Hispanic men have a high rate of heavy drinking, whereas Hispanic women have higher abstention rates than the general population. More Hispanic men and women in higher income brackets have lower rates of abstinence than occur in the general population. Men in the highest income group have high a rate of frequent heavy drinking. Caetano (1991) contends that acculturation is related to lower rates of abstention and increased rates of frequent heavy drinking.

Caetano (1988) designed a provocative study to examine variation in alcohol use between cultures and within cultures simultaneously. He compared Mexicans (Michaocan), Hispanics in the United States (Mexican-American, Puerto Ricans, and Cuban-Americans), and Spanish in Madrid on a variety of measures of alcohol use and abuse. Men in Madrid drank more frequently, but in smaller amounts. Drinking in the Michaocan was less frequent, but in larger amounts, with higher rates of drunkenness. In the U.S. sample, the order of drinking ranging from high maximum to low maximum was Mexican-American, Cuban-American, and Puerto Rican. Frequent heavy drinking occurred when the men were in their 30s rather than during the early 20s as is the case for the general U.S. population. Drinking norms reflected strong moderation in Madrid, and all three cultures reject drinking during work or when driving.

A study by Golding, Burnam, Benjamin, and Wells (1992) provides some insight into why people drink, and at the same time challenges researchers to think about the ways in which they report and interpret their findings. Golding and colleagues examined reasons for drinking in 725 Mexican Americans (some born in the United States and some born in Mexico), and 915 non-Hispanic whites, all of whom were 18 years-of-age or older. Golding et al. found that reasons for drinking did not account for cultural differences in alcohol involvement. More normative than deviant reasons were associated with heavy drinking. Two

reasons (i.e., loosen up around people, cheers you up) were more common among Mexican American and immigrant men, and were associated with heavy drinking and abuse and dependence. Drinking to induce sleep was more common among non-Hispanic white men and was associated with alcohol use diagnoses in men born in the United States, but not in men born in Mexico. Reasons seem to be related to culture: Men in the Mexican-American culture drink to celebrate occasions, whereas non-Hispanic whites drink small amounts more frequently. Golding et al. found that particular reasons were cited more or less often by individuals from the different groups, implying marked between group differences in the types of reasons cited for drinking. However, when the 10 reasons are rank-ordered within groups, a different picture emerges. It is one thing, for example, to report that 54.3% of Mexican-Americans born in Mexico drink "to relax," whereas 75.3% non-Hispanic whites drink "to relax," and another thing to report that both groups rank "to relax" as the most important reason why they drink. In other words, does culture exacerbate underlying similarities, or does it produce fundamental differences between groups? Put differently, how would the data reported by Golding et al. differ, if the white contrast group had been Irish born in the United States and immigrant Irish? As Rotheram and Phinney (1987) so forcefully point out in their discussion of children's ethnic socialization, ethnicity means a great deal more than minority. From a developmental contextualist perspective, it is essential for alcohol use/abuse researchers to pay more careful attention to issues related to ethnicity and culture, avoiding the insidious equation of ethnicity with race.

Asian-Americans

Kitano and Chi (1986/87) studied four Asian groups residing in Los Angeles. Japanese and Filipinos were twice as likely as Chinese and Koreans to report heavy drinking. Compared to Filipinos, Chinese, and Japanese, Koreans had the most abstainers. Within this population of Asian-Americans, predictors linked to drinking included such contextual factors as social status (high), white collar occupation, urban residence, permissive attitudes toward drinking, and peer tolerance of drinking. Compared to white Americans, overall drinking rates among Asians and Asian-Americans are low. Chinese, for example, have the lowest reported death rates for chronic liver disease (Yu & Liu, 1986/87), although as we noted previously, the rates are increasing among the newly emerging Chinese merchant class as they gain in economic and social prestige (Wang et al., 1992). The well-documented flushing response, evident as early as the newborn period, suggests that acetaldehyde dehydrogenase Type 1 (ALDH-1) deficiency may represent a protective factor against alcohol abuse, especially among Japanese and/or Japanese-Americans (Nakawatase, Yamamoto, & Sasao, 1993). On the other hand, the flushing response does not seem to have the same inhibitory influence on drinking in Korea, which is among the highest consumption countries in the world (Lee, 1992). Drinking in Korea is tied heavily to ritual and tradition, is male dominant, and is social (solitary drinking is rare). In contrast to the inverted U-shaped developmental function evident in most countries, the rate of alcoholism in Korea increases linearly with age (Lee, 1992).

Most generally, although it is clear that culture, social class, and gender are powerful determinants of the rule structures that govern roles and regulate the use of alcohol, in recent years, attention to the cultural context of alcohol use and abuse has not been a major focal issue among alcoholism researchers. This has been particularly true for research with minority groups. But partly out of federal efforts, partly out of a more general awareness that the ethnic mix of the U.S. population is in the midst of major change, and partly out of a recognition that there is a larger biracial and multiracial segment to our society than is typically acknowledged (Root, 1992), this knowledge base is slowly beginning to change (Boyd, Howard & Zucker, 1994; Clark & Hilton, 1991).

Summary

This overview of the role of culture and ethnicity in the etiology of alcohol use and abuse has been selective and brief. Nonetheless, the background of literature that lies behind is sufficient to prompt several generalizations that we offer as working hypotheses about this area of alcohol research.

1. With rare exception, alcohol use and abuse is more prevalent among men than among women in the world's cultures and ethnic groups.

2. Within all cultures and ethnic groups, there is considerable heterogeneity with respect to alcohol use and abstention such that there is little basis to substantiate broad cultural and ethnic stereotypes.

3. Within many cultures, the prevalence of problem drinking increases as socioeconomic class decreases, or as rapid transitions in upward social mobility occur. In the former case, problem drinking seems to be related to the aggregation of social problems, related to class rather than to inherent intraindividual characteristics. In the latter case, problem drinking seems to be related to increases in economic power and social prestige.

4. Cultures where drinking is highly related to ceremony and ritual tend to follow a pattern of low frequency drinking but with the consumption of large quantities of alcohol per drinking session. When social, economic, and political forces evoke rapid transitions in such cultures, the frequency of drinking seems to increase as does the pervasiveness of problem drinking.

5. There is only beginning attention to the relationship between ethnic group diversity and alcohol consumption in the United States. This is due in part to a cultural failure to recognize the role of biracial/biethnic and multiracial/multiethnic influences on family functioning and individual development. This is perhaps most clearly illustrated by the continued use of the term Hispanic to characterize an extremely large population of heterogeneous individuals.

6. The study of cultural and ethnic influences on alcohol consumption tends to focus more on prevalence of drinking patterns as a function of group membership than it does on the role of attitudes, values, and beliefs related to the individual's perceived ethnicity including cultural attributions about the individual's ethnic group. Yet full models of cultural and ethnic influence need to include both sets of characteristics in order to adequately understand the interplay between such macrosystem variables and individual level drinking behavior, abuse, and dependence.

THE ONSET OF THE CLINICAL CASE: A DEVELOPMENTAL PHENOMENON

In the last section we described the breadth of the spectrum of influencing structures that has been brought to bear in characterizing variation in problem alcohol use. In this section we move to consider the time-based nature of these processes. Clinicians, in contrast to epidemiologists, are typically confronted with an already largely crystallized entity, or "case." In contrast, as soon as one moves away from practice frameworks wherein chronic forms of disorder show themselves, the question of what is or is not a case becomes an issue. This problem is more than an arbitrary one of cut-off points and definitional criteria for inclusion. It lies at the very base of the notion that there is such a beast as a psychopathological entity, or structure, and is as well, at odds with a dimensional notion of symptomatic or trait variation. Here, beginning with the disease concept of alcoholism, we briefly review this issue, as it has been variously conceptualized within the alcohol literature. At the end of the section we also briefly discuss several methodological implications of this problem.

A Brief History of the Concept of Alcoholism/Alcohol Dependence as Disease

Notions of mental disorder as disease, with an inevitable course and a clearly demarcated and unchanging structure are nowhere better found than in the clinical literature on alcoholism (Jellinek, 1960). Perhaps because the disease concept has been an effective framework within which to destigmatize the experience of severe, alcohol-related behavior for the general public and also for alcoholics, perhaps also because the notion that alcoholism is an "addictive disease" has been a core part of the moral explanatory structure pertaining to public outrage about excesses of use, vestiges of the disease concept continue even in a substantial part of the scientific literature of the present day (Secretary of Health and Human Services, 1993). As we describe next, from a developmental perspective, this explanatory structure ignores issues pertaining to the ebb and flow of disorder, and is also blind to ways in which both normal and preclinical manifestations of difficulty are conceptually as well as substantively linked to the etiology of the end-state "disease." Thus, its continuation as a core heuristic paradigm for the disorder is likely to severely restrict attempts at etiologic understanding.

Levine (1978), in his definitive historical review of the concept of addiction notes that "the idea that alcoholism is a progressive disease"—the chief symptom of which is loss of control over drinking behavior, and whose only remedy is abstinence from all alcoholic beverages—is now about 175 or 200 years old, but no older. He continues:

> This new paradigm constituted a radical break with traditional ideas about the problems involved in drinking alcohol. During the 17th century, and for most of the 18th, the assumption was that people drank and got drunk because they wanted to, and not because they "had" to. In colonial thought, alcohol did not permanently disable the will; it was not addicting, and habitual drunkenness was not regarded as a disease. With very few exceptions, colonial Americans did not use a vocabulary of compulsion with regard to alcoholic beverages.
>
> At the end of the 18th century and in the early years of the 19th some Americans began to report for the first time that they were addicted to alcohol: They said they experienced overwhelming and irresistible desires for liquor. Laymen and physicians associated with the newly created temperance organizations developed theories about addiction and brought the experience of it to public attention. Throughout the 19th century, people associated with the Temperance Movement argued that inebriety, intemperance or habitual drunkenness was a disease, and a natural consequence of the moderate use of alcoholic beverages. Indeed, the idea that drugs are inherently addicting was first systematically worked out for alcohol and then extended to other substances. Long before opium was popularly accepted as addicting, alcohol was so regarded. (Levine, 1978, pp. 143–144)

In his analysis Levine demonstrated that there was a basic continuity of position between the ideology of the Temperance Movement and the post-Prohibition paradigm of alcoholism as a progressive disorder/disease, marked by loss of control. Although the temperance position was the dominant one, there was another anti-temperance thread to be identified during this nineteenth-century period. This was the moral position that drunkenness was a vice, not a disease (Todd, 1882) that involved both lack of will-power and the continuance and repetition of vicious conditions. "The cause of vice is always moral . . . and it is from first, to last, the choice of a depraved and wicked will." This "minority position" is of special interest because it is a clear precursor to the notion of psychopathy as "moral insanity" (Cleckley, 1950), which itself is the intellectual forbearer of the position that some forms of alcoholism are associated with antisocial character (Cadoret, O'Gorman, Troughton, & Haywood, 1985; Cloninger, Bohman, & Sigvardsson, 1981; Zucker, 1987).

Although Jellinek is usually considered to be the father of the disease concept, one can find origins for this notion as far back as the work of Benjamin Rush, including characterization of the four elements necessary to satisfy an addictive disease paradigm: (1) loss of control; (2) a causal agent—what is sometimes referred to as the *sine qua non* (Meehl, 1990); (3) the identification of the involvement as a disease (of the will, i.e., inability to abstain); and (4) the cure: abstinence (Levine, 1978). Nonetheless, Jellinek's work most clearly articulated the modern notion of alcoholism as a disease. Although he was willing to embrace a broad definition of alcoholism, involving "any use of alcoholic beverages that causes any damage to the individual or society or both" (1960, p. 35), he ended up reserving the notion of a disease entity for only two clusters of alcoholic symptomatology, *gamma* and *delta alcoholism*. From a developmental standpoint, it is important to note that these two are the only syndromes posited to involve a progression, as well as presume an underlying physiological *process* (cf. pp. 37–38). Both of these subspecies are seen as having acquired tissue tolerance, adaptive cell metabolism, withdrawal symptoms and "craving" (i.e., physical dependence), and for gamma alcoholism, loss of control. (For delta alcoholism, the fourth critical characteristic is inability to abstain.) Excluded from the disease classification are those forms of "alcoholism" that are seen as purely psychologically motivated (e.g., *alpha alcoholism*), that do not involve progression (e.g., periodic but not progressive dipsomania), or that may be the residue of an underlying psychopathological rather than a physiological etiology.

Although major changes in the level of understanding of the vagaries of display, unfolding, and natural history of alcohol problems have occurred since Jellinek's time, his basic definitional paradigm had strong connections to the one used in the DSM-III-R (American Psychiatric Association, 1987), where there was a heavy emphasis on characteristics of the alcohol dependence syndrome (Edwards & Gross, 1976) as critical in establishing the presence of *alcohol dependence*, as well as relative downplay of criteria concerned with impaired social and occupational functioning (Institute of Medicine, 1987). With the advent of the DSM-IV (American Psychiatric Association, 1994), there is some moving back from this perspective, given that the alternative of "dependence without physiological dependence" is provided as a diagnostic possibility, but a theme of compulsive use remains. Alcohol dependence symptoms include tolerance, withdrawal, drinking to relieve withdrawal, greater use than the person intends, inability to cut down or control use, much time spent in activities related to obtaining alcohol or recovering from use, continuing use despite problems connected to use, and reduction of role involvements because of use. A minimum of three of these symptoms must be present, in the same 12-month period, in order to make the diagnosis.

Problems with the Existing Schemas

From a developmental standpoint, there are three main problems with the addictive, disease, and dependence typologies described here:

1. There is a failure to adequately represent the contextual embeddedness within which alcohol problems evolve. The simplest way to summarize this deficit is to note that the contribution of psychosocial factors to the onset, maintenance, and exacerbation of alcohol related difficulties is downplayed in clinical accounts and in formal, medically based definitions these facts are frequently ignored. Thus, in Jellinek's description of disease process, contextual influences are excluded as irrelevant to the disease process simply because they are necessary for onset but do not in an obvious way drive the addictive time sequence. And in both DSM-III-R and DSM-IV, these influences are minimized, are brought in by way of the back door of time [". . . a great deal of time is spent in activities necessary to obtain the substance . . ." (American Psychiatric Association, 1994, p. 181)], and there is no awareness that time takes place within social process, and that social factors may in fact drive the pathognomic process rather than simply be a passive surround which allows the disease to unfold.

2. With the exception of attention paid to etiological factors at the biological level, there is a failure to deal with how best to represent the underlying, or core processes involved in the production of the disorder(s). A disease is a system whose structure and operation is more than the sum of its subsidiary parts (von Bertalanffy, 1968). One reason why the alcohol dependence syndrome is attractive is because it articulates a concept that embodies a set of interdependent characteristics that are best understood at the holon rather than the characteristics level, albeit with a data language that is primarily alcohol specific, and heavily neurophysiological. But the evidence at this point in time is clearly indicative of a multifactorial, biopsychosocial set of processes that eventually coalesce into structures that are larger than their immediate addictive determinants. The lack of a developmental perspective impedes the field's ability to generate an adequate representational structure for these phenomena. In order to produce one, researchers would need to more clearly embrace developmental notions of process, that include the possibility of evolutionary change at a level beyond the specific differentiated subprocesses (Kandel, 1988). Heinz Werner in 1948 postulated the *orthogenetic principle* which specifies that when development occurs, it proceeds from relative lack of structure and global functioning, to increasing levels of differentiation, articulation and hierarchic integration (Werner, 1957). It is this latter characteristic that needs to be emphasized: alcoholism (or alcohol dependence) is the manifestation of a hierarchically integrated structure that is superordinate to the classes of influence that contributed to its ontogenesis. Before the structure is sufficiently evolved, we have an agglomeration of different phenomena that may or may not move further. The core issue, from a developmental perspective, is to be able to construct a more accurate, time and context based representation of the hierarchic structures that evolve when the accretion processes maintain themselves.

3. Related to this last point, the conceptual structure for alcoholic disorder has been heavily based upon observations of clinical phenomena made by clinicians, or by researchers who are using clinical contexts as the base from which to recruit their subjects. If one's goal is to accurately chart process and document differences in process flow, the major problem with such observations is that they are likely to be biased in the direction of showing continuity of time flow and process agglomeration. All instances that do not show agglomeration are simply lost to the clinical observer, and diminution of symptoms is viewed primarily as remission, wherein the disorder's structure is considered still to be present but not visible. What is most unfortunate is that these boundary limiting conditions have not influenced the etiologic models that are constructed. This is a central issue, and it underscores the need to more fully understand not only the processes of accretion, but also those of dissolution and/or epiphenomenality of symptom display. If one reads Jellinek or the DSM III-R closely, one becomes aware that the authors of these documents were in an intuitive way aware of this anomaly;

one notes observations which indicate that progress does not always take place at the same rate, and also does not always completely unfold. In other places, one finds notations concerning reversibility and remission. The DSM-IV has made some strides in this direction by articulating a series of remission subdiagnoses, and also by acknowledging a very limited set of context factors (being on agonist medication; being in a controlled environment) that influence symptomatic status. Such processes need to be much more carefully articulated and understood.

A Contrasting View of Diagnostic Categories: More about Ephiphenomenality, Chronicity, and Course

The evidence for a substantial degree of instability/epiphenomenality of alcohol problems over the life course is now significant. Heavily based upon population samples, it ranges from studies of youth (Andersson & Magnusson, 1988; Donovan, Jessor, & Jessor, 1983; Temple & Fillmore, 1985/86) to studies of adults (Cahalan, 1970; Clark & Cahalan, 1976; Hasin, Grant, & Endicott, 1990; Knupfer, 1972; Roizen, Cahalan, & Shanks, 1978; Skog & Duckert, 1993) to studies of the elderly (Atkinson, Tolson, & Turner, 1990; Gomberg, 1982; 1989). All of this work reports significant shifts into and out of problem drinking classifications over intervals even as short as one year, and over all segments of the age span, thus indicating that consumption level and related problems are unstable over longer intervals of time for large segments of the problem drinking population.

By the same token, evidence for stability of drinking patterns and for the operation of a cumulative process is likewise present in a subset of longitudinal databases (Grant, Harford, & Grigson, 1988; Penick, Powell, Liskow, Jackson, & Nickel, 1988). Given that some of these studies are the same ones that provide evidence for instability and shift (Andersson & Magnusson, 1988; Skog & Duckert, 1993; Windle, 1994), we are left with the conclusion that the issue of change vs. stability has more to do with how one analyzes the data, and what specific attributes of the problem one looks at, than it has to do with an intrinsic characteristic of the time flow of alcohol-related processes. Thus, Fillmore in two papers has suggested that this paradox is age-connected (Fillmore, 1985; Fillmore & Midanik, 1984), with instability being the rule in the younger years and old age, and chronicity being more common in the middle years. The Skog & Duckert (1993) data indicate that stability is most likely to take place among those with greater (more chronic) levels of problematic drinking.

What the mechanisms might be that lead to these segregated effects have yet to be understood, but a variety of lines of evidence are convergent in establishing that when chronicity takes place, it is because it is driven by cumulation of a variety of processes (Andersson & Magnusson, 1988; Brook, Whiteman, Gordon, & Cohen, 1986; McCord, 1988; Zucker, 1989). This leads to the observation that current, "magic bullet" versions of course (Zucker, 1994), which characterize the trajectory from risk to clinical outcome as straightforward and undeviating—no matter what the intervening contextual pressure—are not adequate for the job. We move now to an alternative framework.

A Probabilistic-Developmental Framework for Course[3]

The notion of process implies the notion of *course,* of a specified sequence of events. Such a perspective also implies coherency across transitions and some ability to specify what the nature of the latent coherency of mechanism might be. Given the evidence for the operation of multiple processes in the development of alcohol problems, the notion of a single progressive and irreversible pathway of outcome is no longer workable. A more appropriate way to encompass multiple processes is to move to a probabilistic conceptual framework of both risk and clinical disorder (Zucker, 1987; 1989). Within such a framework, with an appropriate set of predisposing etiologic factors operating within the model, one can conceive of risk as a fluid characteristic that increases or decreases depending upon the interplay of ongoing trajectory (what one might call the momentum of earlier risk, or, alternately the operation of a high risk structure which is in equilibrium) and the influence of new external and internal (stage-triggered) causative agents. Risk needs to be construed as the end result of a set of dynamic processes; level of risk is thus anchored within both developmental and sociohistorical time, and operates in varying degrees throughout the lifespan of the individual. As summations, subtractions, interactions occur, risk ebbs and flows.

Within this framework, the onset of "caseness" (i.e., the discovery that a clinical case has developed) is best understood as a threshold phenomenon. Previously epiphenomenal symptomatic manifestations become clearly observable, and show a pattern of continuity/regularity of display that is sufficiently large to become labelled as an entity. This may occur because previous manifestations now display with greater intensity, frequency, or regularity than was previously the case. Or they may move to a different display system (e.g., from covert to overt). Under those circumstances, "going critical" now involves a set of behavioral/physiological manifestations that become regarded as symptomatic. At that point, clinically one no longer speaks about "risk" but instead talks about "disease" or "disorder." But the additive, subtractive, and potentiating processes have been operating before as well as after the "disease threshold" event.

This reformulation is offered as a more accurate rendition of the probabilistic nature of the event-cumulation interplay; it allows for an increasingly precise specification of interactional (transactional) processes, which occur in microtime, and which result in some instances in the development of "disease" and in other instances in the development of a "resilient outcome" (Richters & Cicchetti, 1993; Rutter, 1987). This causal framework differs from the commonly held view of the etiology of clinical disorder in several ways. The probabilistic model is prospective in focus, and is closer to a hierarchic developmental paradigm (Loevinger, 1966; Zucker, 1979). It makes no presumptions about the necessity for automatic progression, nor about the irrevocable nature of a particular pathway. A move to a higher or lower probability of flow toward caseness is possible via one particular pattern of risk additivity, but branching and enhancement of risk by way of other influencing structures also is possible.

Edwards (1984) has likened such a progression to the course of a career rather than to a "natural history"; the former implies the possibility of branching and changing, which the latter implies predictable and largely invariant unfolding of course. Thus, the commonly held disease models, although ostensibly prospective in focus, are retrospectively derived cascade models. They begin with the end case, where there has in a particular subset of individuals been evidence for cascade (irrevocability, of course). Arguing back from the positive (cumulation) instances of outcome, such models tend to ignore instances of negative outcome and noncumulation. In addition, as in Freud's psychosexual stage theory, they tend to be based on an embryonic model of development wherein course through a disorder is seen as fixed and invariant, once the cascade has begun. Contextual influences are seen as playing only a moderating role (i.e., to attenuate or accentuate an already existing pattern). In contrast, a probabilistic model allows for the occurrence of mediator variation, wherein process may be heavily influenced by earlier stage developmental experience, yet also influenced by the impact of more recent state dependent learning or triggering experiences (Baron & Kenny, 1986; Sher, 1991).

Three examples illustrate this point:

1. Age of onset for alcohol involvement and for harder drug use has in recent years been regarded as a proxy indicator of a gateway phenomenon. Thus, if onset of drug use can be prevented until the early 20s, then risk for later drug problems becomes negligible (Kandel & Yamaguchi, 1985; Robins, 1984). This process is best understood within the context of age-stage influences and the transition from adolescent stage pressures to those of early adulthood. One of the dominant themes of adolescence in our society is increasing development of independence, along with increasing rebelliousness, heightened peer socialization for deviant behavior, and heightened alcohol and other drug involvement (Jessor & Jessor, 1977). In contrast, the role demands of early adulthood are for achievement, conventionality, and marriage, all of which are conducive to lessened alcohol and other drug use (Donovan et al., 1983). Thus, if one makes it through adolescence without drug involvement, one misses the window of exposure, availability, and peer pressure which drives onset of the phenomenon. Thereafter, without earlier use, even if the biopsychological structure is appropriate for a pattern of abuse, the environmental triggers and the significant substance availability are absent— hence the notion of a critical period for risk based upon the mediating effects of stage-specific contextual factors.

2. Our second example is not only stage-connected but also incorporates processes involving the momentum from earlier trajectory. Studies examining problem drinking among the elderly suggest the operation of at least two different sets of processes, one of continuity (i.e., continuation of a pattern of earlier onset problem drinking), and the other of late-onset abuse (Rosin & Glatt, 1971; Sobell, Cunningham, Sobell, & Toneatto, 1993). Insofar as aging frequently brings with it a number of role changes leading to the exacerbation of stress level (e.g., retirement, widowhood), it has also been noted to be a time wherein risk for alcohol abuse increases. But the available data suggest a variety of both main effects and interactions operating at this age stage. For

---

[3] The material presented in this section is adapted from another recent but more extended discussion of these issues (Zucker, 1994).

some who already have a history of problems, the stress of this new life period appears to sustain a process of continued alcohol involvement, even though the main effect for this period would be an anticipated drop off in use/abuse (Drew, 1968). For others, albeit a minority of the population, stresses of the new period (both role-related and also personal, e.g., depression) appear to be contributory to the emergence of new patterns of abuse (Finney & Moos, 1984; Sobell et al., 1993). For still others, a main effect pattern is indicated, wherein late onset alcoholism is marked by a more circumscribed and milder set of problems, and where both family alcoholism and psychosocial indicators suggest a milder set of risk factors than is the case for the early onset (continuity of process) cases (Atkinson et al., 1990).

3. The last example is not primarily alcohol-related, but it illustrates the complexity of interactions across systems of influence. Testosterone has been related to the presence of dominance, sensation seeking, and aggressiveness in humans (Daitzman & Zuckerman, 1980; Olweus, 1983) and to the display of aggression and dominance in primates (Bernstein, Rose, & Gordon, 1974). However, data from several recent studies suggest that biology-behavior relationships are neither entirely unidirectional, nor best conceived as simple main effects. In some instances they appear to be modifiable by contextually driven factors that relate to the context in which the hormonal output is displayed. In other instances, the biological variable appears to operate in obverse fashion, by moderating the impact of the social context. Thus Dabbs and Morris (1990) not only found main effects relating high serum testosterone level to a number of indices of adolescent and adult antisocial and impulsive activity (including alcohol, marijuana, and other hard drug involvement), but also discovered that the relationship was substantially moderated by socioeconomic status (SES). Higher SES attenuated most of the testosterone-behavior relationships; lower SES strengthened it. The Dabbs and Morris study does not allow any sorting out of direction of effect, but other studies of adolescence, involving both alcohol abuse (experience of drunkenness) (Udry, 1991) and menstrual cycle synchronicity among women living together (McClintock, 1981), suggest that the influencing structure may be a two-way street. The Udry study indicates that social behavior (e.g., good vs. poor school performance) interacts with biological substrate (testosterone level) in a straightforwardly moderating capacity, such that drunkenness occurs differentially as a function of both of these contributory influences. When testosterone level is low and school achievement is high, the probability of drunkenness is uniformly low; when testosterone level is low and school achievement is low, the probability of drunkenness is quite high. In contrast, adolescents with high testosterone levels systematically are more likely to have reported drunkenness, irrespective of school achievement level. On the other hand, the McClintock study implicates the psychosocial environment as operating directly, as a simple main effect in the regulation of biological function. The definitive longitudinal studies of these phenomena have yet to be done, but the existing data are suggestive of a broader range of effects than has generally been posited in the earlier literature.

Within the framework of probabilistic theory, we now move to consideration of how one defines onset of alcoholism, and a series of related issues concerning the interpretation of data on the progression of alcohol-related difficulty.

HOW EARLY DOES ALCOHOLISM BEGIN? DEFINING ONSET AND INTERPRETING DATA ON THE PROGRESSION OF ALCOHOL-RELATED DIFFICULTY

In this section we review the existing literature pertaining to what is known about the earliest manifestations of alcohol problems, and then move to consider what is known about the structure of events which leads to their early appearance. We also attend to a related "downstream" question, namely, what evidence is there that the appearance of early, alcohol-related difficulty, has anything to do with the adult disorder?

The question, "When (or how early) does alcoholism begin?" can be addressed at a variety of different levels. From the perspective of ultimate causes, insofar as some forms of alcoholism have a substantial genetic basis (Secretary of Health and Human Services, 1993; National Institute on Alcohol Abuse and Alcoholism, 1985), onset of the diathesis occurs at conception even though the full-fledged disorder does not show itself until much later. From a clinical standpoint, alcoholism begins only at the time there is a sufficient aggregation of symptoms to make the diagnosis and move into formal case status. Here onset is defined in terms of the presence of a large complement of overt symptoms. Somewhere in between these two poles lies a middle ground; before the clinical case appears, subclinical, but clearly problematic indicators of alcohol related difficulty have to show themselves. This is the first point of indexing of what may, if nurtured, become the clinical syndrome. Without these first indicators, the more problematic versions cannot flower. With them, it may or may not, depending upon what else drives the system into fuller form. It is this middle area that we attend to first, examining data on alcohol use and some indices of problem alcohol involvement among youth, at a time when most authorities would suggest that "alcoholism" has not yet emerged.

Evidence for the Very Early Onset of Alcohol-Related Difficulty in One Subpopulation

Table 19.2 presents recent, albeit retrospective data on grade of first alcohol use, and first drunkenness in the United States (Johnston et al., 1993). The 10th graders' data are utilized here rather than those from another age group because, as the authors note, younger informants are likely to more literally interpret questions about first use, and over report on "first drink" experience. Conversely, to use 12th grade informants is to lengthen the time interval for retrospection, and also to increasingly lose heavier using respondents because of their greater likelihood for school drop-out. These reports indicate that alcohol use has already begun for one out of thirteen 10-year-olds, and that by age 14 more than half the population have had some alcohol consumption experience. The drunkenness data, as an indicator of escape and therefore incipient problem alcohol involvement, show that 1.3% of 10-year-olds have already crossed

TABLE 19.2   Grade of First Alcohol Use and Drunkenness as Retrospectively Reported by Tenth Graders (Percentage of U.S. Population)

	Grade	Approximate Age	Use	Cumulative User Population	First Time Drunk	Cumulative Drunk Population
Grade school	4	10	7.6	7.6	1.3	1.3
	5	11	4.4	12.0	1.1	2.4
	6	12	8.5	20.5	3.2	5.6
Middle school	7	13	15.2	35.7	7.0	12.6
	8	14	19.7	55.4	11.1	23.7
High school	9	15	19.6	75.0	16.0	39.7
	10	16	7.2	82.2	8.0	47.7

Note: Source is 1992 national survey data from *Monitoring the Future* (Johnston, O'Malley, & Bachman, 1993, Table 18b, p. 135).

this threshold. The Monitoring the Future 30-day prevalence data (Johnston et al., 1993, p. 99), as an index of subjects' immediately past experiences, converges with the retrospective onset figures given that 8% of 8th graders, 18% of 10th graders, and 30% of 12th graders report they have had at least one drunkenness experience in the last month.

There are other ways of approaching this issue from the same database. Thus, 13% of eighth graders report they have had five or more drinks in a row at least once in the last two weeks, and a 4% subset of this group reports this consumption level for 3 to 5 times or more (Johnston et al., 1993, p. 47). To recast these figures, given that drinking for adolescents is heavily confined to weekends, this high end group of approximately 1 out of 8 is reporting drinking at adult heavy drinking levels, and a third of that group, or 4% of the population, is suggesting that they are drinking at adult heavy drinking rates at every available opportunity. On the grounds of DSM-IV criteria, with the presence of any recurring additional trouble related to the drinking (a not unreasonable assumption at this age), behavior sufficient to achieve a diagnosis of Alcohol Abuse has already been attained.[4]

Given these problem prevalence figures and the fact that alcohol-related difficulty does not develop overnight, one can only assume that this subset of the population have entered into a problem alcohol trajectory well before adolescence, and that etiologic factors have already been in place, relating to the emergence of these behaviors for some time. Despite the ready availability of these incidence data, which drive home the point, to our knowledge this conclusion has not been made before on the basis of population statistics although here and there one can find accounts

in the clinical literature of the last generation, (e.g., Mitchell, Hong, & Corman, 1979) and even as far back as a century ago (e.g., Madden, 1884), which call attention to this apparently not so rare occurrence of very early and very severe child alcohol involvement. In making this point, we are also suggesting that detection of risk for severe alcohol-related difficulty may be feasible at the least during the middle childhood years, and conceivably even quite a bit earlier, given the nature of the contextual structure in which the risks are embedded. In the latter part of this section, we build this case and also suggest that this is the group most likely to maintain continuity of alcohol problems on into adulthood. But before getting into this evidence, we describe another, very different set of alcohol involvement data, that have received the bulk of attention in the alcohol problem literature, and that have largely obscured the point we have just made.

Later Onset of Another Trajectory of Alcohol Involvement: Normative Drinking in Adolescence

From the standpoint of population prevalence, the importance of the 10-year-olds' data on first experience of drunkenness, as a marker of having crossed a use threshold into problem alcohol involvement, may also be evaluated as minuscule since the figures show this experience has touched only one in 75. Even the patterns of sustained problem use described by a subset of the 14-year-olds (the 8th graders) may be viewed as quite small since they still involve only one in 25. If these phenomena are approached developmentally from the other side, by starting with data on the magnitude of the adult disorder, this conclusion is underscored. Using U.S. population estimates for abuse/dependence in the past year that are based upon the 1988 National Health Interview Survey (Grant et al., 1991), 18% of persons in the 18 to 29-year age range qualify for a DSM-III-R diagnosis (by gender these figures are 26% of men and 11% of women). In other words, a shift approximating a four- to five-fold increase in symptom level occurs over approximately the four-year age span between ages 14 and 18. Given that this level of symptomatology does not build up overnight, and given the low level of alcohol-related difficulty at age 14, a different set of developmental questions now emerges: (a) What is it that turns the population so heavily into this symptomatic channel over such a short timeframe? And

---

[4] In order to achieve an *abuse* diagnosis, one must be involved in a maladaptive pattern of substance use leading to clinically significant impairment or distress that manifests itself in failure to fulfill major role obligations, recurrent use in situations of physical hazard, recurrent substance-related legal problems, or continued use despite persistent or recurrent social or interpersonal problems caused or exacerbated by the effects of the substance (American Psychiatric Association, 1994, pp. 182–183). The period over which the recurrence/persistence is estimated is as long as 12 months, although if it is judged to be repeated, conceivably a substantially shorter period of time could elapse within which the diagnosis would be established.

(b), given this dramatic shift, involving increase in alcohol-related difficulty, is there any obverse evidence indicating substantial shifts away from problem use as development proceeds?

This set of questions is different than those we have posed earlier about the early onset subgroup. The stimulus for the latter questions are the data on rapid developmental change, while the stimulus for the former pertain to the early appearance of alcohol problems and the possibility of potentially strong stability/continuity from childhood on through adolescence into adulthood. Although infrequently recognized, the majority of the literature on adolescent problem alcohol use has focused on this second subset—that part of the population that has undergone rapid onset of alcohol use in adolescence, along with a subset who develop concomitant alcohol-related problems and this juncture, and the bulk of work in the adolescent area has addressed these phenomena. Early onset users were specifically excluded from the Columbia group's major longitudinal study of transitioning into different stages of alcohol and other drug involvement, *because they had already begun alcohol involvement* (Margulies, Kessler, & Kandel, 1977). In addition, two of the other major studies in this area either accessed primarily middle class samples, who would not fall in this early onset group (Jessor & Jessor, 1975), or had very heavy initial nonparticipation rates by minority, male, and more disopportunitied segments of the population where such phenomena would be more likely to show up (Huba & Bentler, 1980; Newcomb, Huba, & Bentler, 1983).

The main focus of this section—adolescent onset—has been extensively reviewed by Kandel (1978), Jessor and Jessor (1977), Newcomb and Bentler (1988) and Zucker (1979; Zucker & Noll, 1987) and these papers detail a limited number of factors that contribute to the emergence of these normative behaviors. We briefly summarize this explanatory net here, and turn to two still classic theoretical models, one sociological, the other social psychological, as heuristic structures around which to organize the voluminous empirical literature.

As Maddox and McCall (1964) noted a generation and a half ago, teenage drinking occurs in a social world. It is part of the age-graded structure of a society wherein the majority of adults consume alcohol and regard it also as a privilege of adult status (along with driving, being able to vote, etc.). By way of the formal legal structure on minimum age drinking laws, as well as by way of informal rites of passage like going out and buying one's first legal beer, the normative structure clearly ties alcoholic beverage use into age grades. Thus child-expected abstinence can also be expected to give way to adult use, and adolescence, as the precursive age stage, is the developmental place where this transition begins to take place. Thus also, teenagers see adults as drinkers, aspire to adult status, and in a variety of other ways begin to experiment with crossing the boundary into adultlike behavior. Such excursions, as explorations, are viewed within the peer structure as generally worthy of regard.[5] In support of this theory, the epidemiologic data show major increases in both use of alcohol as well as concomitant increases in problem rates during the teen years, slowing down and leveling off in the 21 to 23-year-old age range, and then showing significant decline during the rest of the 20s (Grant, Harford, & Grigson, 1988; Temple & Fillmore, 1985/86). In other words, with the onset of adult roles, like marriage, childbearing, and entry into the permanent workforce, rates of both problem and nonproblem alcohol involvement decline, *for most of the population.* So the answer to the question posed above, about whether there is a drop off, is positive, although the decline is not of the same magnitude as the onset.

The Jessors and their colleague, John Donovan, have provided a parallel explanatory structure to account for this variation at the individual level. They have constructed one of the few theories of adolescent psychological development that explicitly incorporates the emergence of drug-taking behavior, as well as the development of problem alcohol use, into a general model of adolescent social behavior, growth, and change. Problem behavior theory (Donovan & Jessor, 1985; Jessor & Jessor, 1977) views the acquisition and maintenance of patterns of alcohol-seeking behavior as part of a broader process that encompasses the social context of neighborhood, religious membership, social class, and family, the personality system (including values and expectancies not only about alcohol and other drugs, but also about the social environment itself—including the valuing of independence vs. achievement, one's personal sense of alienation and of being controlled by internal vs. external forces, one's acceptance or rejection of deviance as acceptable or unacceptable behavior) and the behavior system. By way of a series of analyses across several age groups and populations, these investigators and others have been able to show that the transition to a number of putatively problem behaviors of adolescence is predictable by the same theoretical model, and also that each of these "problem behavior" variables, including the earlier use of alcohol, the use of marijuana as well as other illicit drugs, involvement in problem alcohol use, earlier sexual experience, have substantial variance in common, and may all be subsumed under a "general deviance" rubric (Donovan, Jessor, & Costa, 1988; McGee & Newcomb, 1992; Sadava, 1985). The advantages of the theory are that it connects a number of behaviors previously regarded as unconnected, it predicts who will transition into "use," as well as progress to more problematic alcohol or other drug involvement, and it ties these behavioral adaptations into a much broader matrix of both personality structure and the social environment. In the context of the subsidence question being examined here, what is of special interest is that the theory also predicts decline in these activities as development proceeds from adolescence into early adulthood (Jessor, Donovan, & Costa, 1991).

Although not heavily emphasized by the Colorado group, from the perspective of socialization theory, Problem Behavior Theory is of special interest because it focuses on, and develops operational measures of a core transition, from socialization involving the valuing of parents and acceptance of their guidance, to the valuing and reliance on peers as a source of both norms and social reinforcement. Insofar as the adolescent, Euro-American peer culture emphasizes independence from parents and experimentation with deviant behavior, this becomes the normative choice of that age stage. With a shift to adult status, the same, now older cohort emphasizes a different set of valued

---

[5] Given the recent changes to a more temperate value structure in the larger society, the degree to which this entire process may have more recently been disrupted has yet to be explored.

behaviors, involving greater conformity; and cohort behavior changes in an obverse direction. This is a highly useful and powerful theory.

We now return to further consideration of the early onset population, and address the two issues posed earlier:

1. If significant problem alcohol involvement can be detected even in middle childhood, what is the nature of the risk structure that relates to this outcome, and how much earlier can it be detected?

2. Does the extant literature provide any evidence pertaining to long-term course, as related to the issue of progression into both adolescence and adulthood for this population?

SPECIFYING THE ETIOLOGIC MATRIX FOR EARLY-ONSET ALCOHOL PROBLEMS

If risk is to be detected early, we need to know where to look. The work reviewed in the preceding section, on causal factors relating to the emergence of more normative patterns of alcohol use and alcohol problems, highlights one of the most significant, but frequently unarticulated issues in literature on the etiology of alcohol-related problems, that is, that two parallel processes need to be charted in order to specify outcome:

1. Those concerned with *alcohol specific behavior,* and

2. Those concerned with *alcohol nonspecific co-occurring processes,* that are necessary but not sufficient parts of the causal matrix (e.g., problem proneness or deviance, self-derogation processes, alcohol nonspecific biological variations that make this particular drug more attractive, or that might even throw one into earlier exposure to the drug).

Given the operation of these dual processes, etiologic specification has to deal not only with timing, onset, and course of alcohol-specific unfolding, but also with the parallel processes, and eventually must articulate the junctures where intermingling starts to take place. Thus, full causal models need to identify alcohol-specific variation (which is necessary, and in some instances may even be a sufficient explanatory structure for alcohol problem variability), and also model another large set of causal factors that are alcohol-nonspecific, but that are a major part of the risk structure for later alcohol problems. Because these latter causal structures do not involve alcohol, they are by no means etiologically sufficient; in some instances, they appear to operate in a mediational capacity, and in others as moderators. More about this as we proceed.

Tracking Early Alcohol-Specific Risk

Any comprehensive review of this area would have to deal with two distinct literatures, one on the biology of alcohol use, the other on the development of cognitions and expectancies about alcohol. Both sets of factors have been clearly linked to individual differences in one's experience of alcohol as a drug, and the

degree to which one is likely to continue to pursue a second dose, once the first consumption experience has occurred. The biological literature by itself is very large, and includes substantial animal as well as human work on genetic differences in appetitive interest, biological variability in the ability to develop tolerance (Schuckit, Risch, & Gold, 1988) and in the experience of intoxication (those experiencing less of an effect would be anticipated to be at higher risk to drink more). Other biologically mediated mechanisms likely to drive variability in consumption include differences in the effects of alcohol, as a reinforcer, on the brain's reward mechanism system, and variability in processes pertaining to ethanol metabolism, insofar as timing, as well as individual differences in the production and retention of metabolic byproducts lead to a different subjective experience of the alcohol high. For coverage of this work, consult reviews by Newlin (1994), Sayette (1993), and the NIAAA's most recent summary report to Congress (Secretary of Health and Human Services, 1993). But given that alcohol consumption by children is prohibited in most Atlantic Basin countries, empirical work on individual differences in alcohol consumption and biological variation is limited to studies of adults of legal drinking age, or of animals. Also, because regular consumption of this drug, even in the very early onset group, commences some time in middle childhood, subjective experience from the pharmacological feedback system would not be available until that developmental juncture. Thus, it is reasonable to assume that early alcohol experiences in this area almost exclusively pertain to the acquisition and development of cognitions, expectancies, and affective schemas about alcohol and other drugs, and that the sources of information that contribute to these experiences come from feedback systems other than those linked to personal consumption. That is, they come from exposure to the media, and from a variety of personal family (including sibling) experiences, including those involving the sense of smell as well as of sight and sound (cf. Brook, Whiteman, Brook, & Gordon, 1991; Noll, Zucker, & Greenberg, 1990). Conceivably they may also, in a small way, come from whatever is gleaned from peers at this early an age, but given that same age peers are in the same (nonuse) boat, it is likely that such influences are of smaller import than those from the other two sources.[6]

A generation or so ago, much of the empirical work and theory in this area was based on the presumption that early expectancies about drugs emerged from two environments: (a) peer exposure during adolescence; and (b) one's parents' attitudes, values and use patterns (Kandel, 1978; Wechsler & Thum, 1973). In the intervening period, a substantial body of research has shown that children's ability to recognize alcoholic beverages and name them (i.e., their ability to categorize them as objects), their awareness of these beverages as a special class of substances that have effects different than other substances, their awareness of some of the cultural rule structures about use (e.g., that adults drink more than children, and males more than females), and their emerging capacity to formulate expectancies about what alcohol will produce in the way of cognitive and behavioral effects,

---

[6] As far as we are aware, the area of potential peer influence at this early age has not yet been examined.

is detectable well before adolescence (Gaines, Brooks, Maisto, & Dietrich, 1988; Miller, Smith, & Goldman, 1990), and in some instances as early as the preschool years (Noll, Zucker, & Greenberg, 1990; Zucker & Noll, 1987). In addition, both the Miller and the Noll studies, as well as some of our own ongoing work on the development of cognitive schemas about alcohol (Zucker, Fitzgerald, & Kincaid, 1994), show that family patterns of heavier or problematic alcohol use are already predictive of the children's emergent cognitive structures, even before the age of six. Children with exposure to heavier drinking environments, as well as preschooler children of alcoholics (COAs), are more precocious in the emergence of these category systems. Thus, at the least, the nature of this early manifestation is a risk pertaining to the precocious acquisition of a knowledge base, and an interest in this class of objects. It is likely also that such socialization involves significant affective-emotional components as well as cognitive ones, given the intensity of affective experience surrounding alcohol consumption in heavy use/abuse home environments. It remains for longitudinal work to chart how the appearance of these cognitive and affective structures interfaces with the later acquisition of drinking behavior. Of special interest here is the question of how expectancies layer onto affect, and how these two sources of variation drive each other to eventuate in a system adaptation that either moves toward problematic alcohol involvement . . . or moves in the other direction. Other data collected on older children and adolescents are suggestive. Thus, parallel processes have been observed whereby heavier parental drinking behavior has been linked to the emergence of cognitive expectancies about alcohol, and these expectancies, in turn, have been linked to use patterns in adolescence (Brown, Creamer, & Stetson, 1987; Christiansen, Smith, Roehling, & Goldman, 1989). McCord's (1988) work on the Cambridge-Somerville study has provided one of the few studies that articulates the contribution of affective components to this process. In following up COAs from middle childhood into middle adulthood, McCord found that when mothers held the alcoholic father in high esteem, the boy was significantly more likely to later become alcoholic. In families where the mother did not, the boy was less likely to enter this problem path.

Taken together, these studies have significant implications for our understanding of when socialization to alcohol involvement begins, particularly for the early onset group of children. Results are consistent with the following six propositions:

1. The process of socialization to alcohol/drug involvement begins much earlier than adolescence, and involves learning about drugs as a class of objects (i.e., being able to identify them by name and smell and class);

2. The early socialization process involves being able to articulate differences between these substances and other "adult-use" substances in the child's environment;

3. The socialization process involves not only learning the drug schema, but also includes affective socialization that pertains to the likelihood that the drug-using models in the child's environment will be perceived as positive (and therefore to be emulated), or negative (and therefore to be avoided);

4. Knowledge of the primary rule structure about alcohol use that exists in the adult culture already can be detected during the preschool years;

5. Some children in this age range can already begin to articulate a belief structure about drug effects, and describe expectancies about planned use and like/dislike of these substances;

6. Individual differences in precocity of such learning can be tied to both cognitive capacity differences (i.e., I.Q.), and to differences in exposure to alcoholic beverages within the child's home environment. Those environments that have been identified, during the child's adolescence, as fostering the emergence of heavier and more problematic alcohol use, are also the environments identified as those most likely to foster the even earlier emergence of schemas about alcohol and other drugs. We turn now to the other literature, pertaining to the early identification of alcohol nonspecific factors of risk that may relate to the emergence of early-onset alcohol problems and alcoholism.

Tracking Early-Alcohol Nonspecific Risk Factors for Later Alcoholic Outcome

The presence of a family history positive (FH +) for alcoholism is one obvious marker that is connected to a large number of childhood problem outcomes (West & Prinz, 1987). Also, a greater density of FH+ is associated with development of early-onset alcoholism among children of alcoholics (COAs). But this index is still an imprecise marker of risk, given that substantially less than half of those with an alcoholic parent themselves become alcoholic, and of those who are alcoholic, only about one-third are themselves COAs (Russell, 1990). In addition, as Russell so carefully documents, we are still left with the issue of what it is that is producing the risk, given that offspring show different morbidity rates as a function of both age and ethnicity. Jacob and Leonard (1986) document that even putative risk variation among child and adolescent COAs is related to level of alcoholic symptomatology as well as the presence of greater other psychopathology among the parents. Thus the marker of family history leaves unclear whether the pathogenesis is communicated genetically, via modeling or other types of learning, and the degree to which the transmission process is *alcoholism* specific is also not well specified.

Ultimately, the method of choice to establish etiologic progression is by way of a prospective study with sufficient at risk individuals, and a sufficiently rich variable matrix to allow adequate tracking of both intervening process, as well as causal factors predicting adult outcome (Garmezy & Streitman, 1974; Zucker & Fitzgerald, 1991). Our own group is specifically addressing this missing link by way of the Michigan State University–University of Michigan (MSU-UofM) Longitudinal Study (Zucker, Noll, & Fitzgerald, 1986; Zucker & Fitzgerald, 1991), an ongoing prospective investigation of families who vary in degree of parental alcoholism visibility and severity, and where all families have sons (and most have daughters) initially in the 3 to 5-year age range. An extensive array of measures that focus upon both alcohol specific as well as more general regulatory and psychopathological behaviors among the children, and a parallel set of data among the parents, are being collected at three-year intervals. The study, currently in the midst of Wave Two and Wave Three data collection (children at mean ages 7.5 and 10.5 years of age), is planned to run at least until the children reach adulthood. This study, along with New Zealand's Dunedin Multidisciplinary Health and Development Study (Casswell, Gilmore, Silva, & Brasch, 1988; Silva, 1990), are, to our knowledge, currently the developmentally earliest beginning longitudinal projects worldwide, that explicitly focus upon the evolution of alcohol-related risk from early childhood. Neither is yet at a place to report long term findings, although early childhood findings are summarized at relevant places throughout this chapter.

Rather than waiting another 10 to 15 years, another strategy for approximating etiologic risk can be used to fill in some of the gaps. If longitudinal studies relevant to the outcome variable can be found that cover shorter portions of the developmental span, but their results can be dovetailed, then it becomes possible to assemble a jigsaw puzzle that should approximate the longer term pattern of development. This is tantamount to using the literature as a base for a cohort sequential longitudinal design. We follow that strategy here.

A systematic review by Zucker and Gomberg (1986) of the extant longitudinal studies which tracked characteristics in childhood to whether or not subjects become alcoholic in adulthood identified six studies; the preponderance of them began in adolescence. Eight across-study etiologic consistencies were noted:[7]

1. The presence of childhood antisocial behavior was consistently related to later alcoholic outcome (5 studies).

2. More childhood difficulty in achievement related activity (i.e., school work) was noted among those who later become alcoholic (4 studies).

3. Boys who later become alcoholic were more loosely interpersonally connected to others (e.g., they were rated as less dependent, less considerate of others, and were more likely to leave home earlier) than were those who did not (4 studies).

4. Heightened marital conflict was reported with consistently greater frequency in the pre-alcoholic homes (4 studies).

5. Greater activity level in childhood was identified as a precursor to alcoholic outcome (2 studies).

6. Parent-child interaction in homes of children more likely to later become alcoholic was to a greater degree characterized by inadequate parenting and by the child's lack of contact with the parent(s) (all 6 studies).

7. Parents of pre-alcoholics were also more often inadequate role models for later normality; they were more likely to be alcoholic, antisocial, or sexually deviant (4 studies).

8. Ethnic differences were systematically linked to alcoholic outcomes; within the range of ethnic heritages sampled, alcoholics were more likely to come from Irish than Italian backgrounds (3 studies).

The strength of these connections is heightened by the fact that, even in instances where a nonreplication took place, it was always the absence of an effect rather than the presence of an obverse finding. Sher's (1991) more recent review of the older COA, primarily cross-sectional literature is also heavily confirmatory of the differentiating power of the content domains noted as precursive here, and longitudinal study analyses reported since the earlier summary (i.e., Beardslee, Son, & Vaillant, 1986; McCord, 1988) offer other replication for points 6 and 7. Nonetheless, given that these studies largely began their observations when middle childhood was over, etiologic process only is established from adolescence on. Insofar as we wish to evaluate causal processes related to early-onset alcohol related difficulty, the developmental period that is of primary interest has been missed.

The analytic strategy that allows this problem to be segued is to posit continuity of process from childhood to adulthood; then the areas of known etiologic significance for the period from adolescence to adulthood become a template for what to examine earlier on. In that case, earlier high risk, longitudinal studies that have been able to establish characteristics of risk which predict early-onset adolescent alcohol use and alcohol problems become a test arena for the continuity proposition. If the same characteristics that predict alcoholic outcome from adolescence to adulthood also predict childhood functioning to adolescent problems, we can have some confidence that the causal structure from early childhood to adulthood has been mapped; if different characteristics appear in the two developmental periods, then a much more complex set of possibilities exists.

Table 19.3 lists the relevant earlier childhood-to-adolescence studies, and summarizes their background characteristics. Table 19.4 lists the six etiologic predictors for the adolescent to adult studies,[8] and summarizes the degree to which correspondence of etiologic process was observed in the earlier stage developmental studies. A replication was judged to exist if, in the child study, the risk characteristic already identified as predicting alcoholism in adulthood was likewise identified as precursive to later, greater alcohol involvement, more alcohol-related problems, or a later stage of alcohol/drug use at adolescent follow-up in the developmental study.

As shown in Table 19.4, in the six etiologic areas where data were available, findings—in most instances involving three to four studies—consistently replicate the adolescent to adult work, and again, *no instances of obverse effects were observed*. Altogether, these data, encompassing two very diverse groups of studies, provide impressive evidence for a pattern of relationships that are initially detectable in early childhood, that predict problematic alcohol outcomes in adolescence, and that continue to predict alcoholic outcomes into early to middle adulthood.

How are these findings to be understood, and what is still missing from this picture? First to the limitations: The pattern of relationships described here assumes that the etiologic conditions in place in early childhood will also be present in adolescence, given that the set of independent variables we utilized were the

---

[7] The Zucker and Gomberg paper contains the specific study references.

[8] Although the original review also found marital conflict and ethnic differences as predictive of adult alcoholism, none of the child studies covered these aspects of functioning.

TABLE 19.3   Prospective Studies of Influences during Earlier Childhood Related to Alcohol and Drug Involvement in Adolescence: Study Characteristics

Study	Subject Characteristics and Source	Age at First Contact	Age at Follow-Up
1. Rydelius (1981); Nylander (1960)	229 Stockholm Ss with severly alcoholic clinic treated fathers (50% male) and 163 matched "social twins" without paternal alcoholism	4–12	24–32
2. Kellam, Brown, Rubin, and Ensminger (1983); Kellam, Ensminger, and Simon (1980); Ensminger, Brown, and Kellam (1982); Ensminger, Kellam, and Rubin (1983); Woodlawn Project	1242 inner-city black 1st graders from South Side Chicago (50% male)	6	6–7; 9; 16–17
3. Brook, Gordon, Whiteman, and Cohen (1986); Brook, Whiteman, Gordon, and Brook (1990); Brook, Whiteman Gordon, and Cohen (1986, 1989)	356 Ss randomly selected from 2 NY counties (49% male; 94% Caucasian)	5–10	13–18
4. Block, Block, and Keyes (1988)	105 middle-class Ss selected from nursery schools (49% male; 67% Caucasian)	3	4; 5; 7; 11; 14
5. Werner (1986, 1989); Kauai Study	698 Kauai (Hawaii) Ss (45% male) born in 1955	prenatal	mid-childhood; 18; 30+
6. Matejcek, Drytrych, and Schuller (1988); Prague Cohort	220 Prague Ss (50% male) identified prenatally after mothers denied access to abortions	9	16–18; 21–23
7. Pulkkinen (1983)	369 Finnish Ss (53% male) drawn from half urban and half suburban schools; 144 followed at T2; Full N at T3	8	14; 20

same for the two developmental intervals. While this is probably not an unreasonable assumption, it does require that either context, or individual factors enhancing continuity (e.g., temperament) insure that such stability is present.

It is also likely that some of these etiologic influences are correlated (for example, inadequate parenting and the presence of parental psychopathology). The fact that associations are noted for eight different areas of influence does not insure that each

will contribute an equal amount to outcome, once causal models are constructed that effectively analyze for covariation. This has not yet been done in any of the existing studies. Related to this last point, because virtually all of the existing studies have relied almost exclusively upon univariate analysis (in only one instance were multiple regression techniques utilized) and only examined direct effects, it is likely that carefully thought out analytic strategies utilizing latent variable approaches and path modeling

TABLE 19.4   Etiologic Continuity: Correspondences between Earlier State Developmental Studies and Longitudinal Studies of Child/Adolescent Risk Leading to Adult Alcoholism

Etiologic Characteristics Identified in Longitudinal Studies with Older Ss	Replications	Obverse Findings
1. Childhood antisocial behavior/aggression	6[1,3–7] + 1 male only[2]	0
2. Childhood achievement problems	4[1, 2, 5, 6]	0
3. Poorer childhood interpersonal connections	5[2, 5, 6, 7]	0
4. Heightened activity in childhood	3[1, 6, 7] + 1 male only[4]	1
5. Less parent-child contact and more inadequate parenting in childhood	5[1, 2, 5, 6, 7] + 1 female only[4]	0
6. Parents more often inadequate role models with more psychopathology and no alcoholism and other psychopathology	2[1, 7]	0

Note: Superscripts in table refer to studies described in Table 19.3 that share the predictive characteristic. A replication is judged to exist when the developmental study predicted precocious or problem alcohol use in adolescence on the basis of the same child/adolescent risk characteristics that predicted alcoholism in adulthood.

will uncover mediational causal processes in addition to direct paths of effect (Windle, 1994). And last, the databases assembled in these studies did not evaluate biological variation, so that the separate and interactive effects of this major source of influence are left unestimated.[9]

Despite these limitations, these effects should be regarded as quite robust, given the diversity of samples in which they appeared, the variety of initial levels of risk load in the early childhood studies, (which would work to attenuate effects among the more advantaged samples), and the major variation in cultural and socioeconomic background found among the studies. It is also clear that the base of findings identified here—as a network of heightened risk for the development of both alcohol problems and eventual alcoholism, comes into play much earlier than had previously been noted, with some studies indicating causal processes may already be detectable in the preschool years. In fact, cross-sectional findings from Wave One of the MSU-UofM study, involving children in the 3 to 5-year-old age range, are directly interpretable as confirming the antisocial and achievement connections (areas 1 and 2 above), given that children from high risk families were already developmentally delayed in terms of intellectual functioning (Noll, Zucker, Fitzgerald, & Curtis, 1992), and were rated as having more aggressive and externalizing symptomatology than controls (Fitzgerald et al., 1993; Zucker & Fitzgerald, 1991). In addition, children from families where parents were more deviant and antisocial (i.e., area 7 above) were themselves higher in aggressiveness and difficult temperament, both of which factors are reasonably considered proxies at this young age for earlier and more heavily alcohol abusing outcome (Ellis, 1993).

These studies provide no information about how best to link the eight different influencing structures identified, but it is possible, on the basis of general developmental theory, to mark some influences as more distal and some as more proximal to adult later outcomes. For example, although it is not reasonable to assume ethnic differences are invariant across historical time, they nonetheless embody a level of expectancy structure that is certainly more stable (at least under noncrisis or nonwar conditions) than are individual and familial level variables, that would be anticipated to vary widely with developmental stage changes. Using this strategy, a reasonable flow model for this early onset alcoholic trajectory (which would include problem alcohol involvement along the way) would include the following:

1. Heightened activity level in early childhood. This is a high-risk indicator that needs to be placed quite distally in any etiologic flow diagram, given its linkages to constitutional differences, and ultimately to a variety of different, biologically driven diatheses (Lerner & Lerner, 1983; Tarter, Alterman, & Edwards, 1985; Tarter, Moss, & Vanukov, in press). Activity level variations are present even in utero, yet also are modifiable as epigenesis unfolds, and in combination with attributes of the rearing

environment (e.g., parent disciplinary practices), may be expected to be shaped into more immediately risky personality and behavioral attributes (Tarter, Blackson, Martin, Loeber, & Moss, 1993; Windle, 1990).

At the same time, it is important to note that this influencing structure is a broad one, that has commonly been poorly defined. Within the longitudinal databases reviewed here the label has had sufficient breadth to be linked also to constructs of arousability and excitability, and the broad definitional base that has been included under this rubric encompasses not only high gross motor activity, but also (a) hyperactivity—with its component substructure of inattentiveness/distractibility (Windle, 1990); (b) impulsivity and its later developmental manifestations of behavioral undercontrol (Sher, 1991; Tarter, 1988); and (c) approach behavior, including sociability and boldness (Windle, in press), as well as novelty and sensation seeking (Cloninger, 1987; Zuckerman, 1979). A fourth characteristic, (d) early aggressiveness (Zucker, 1987; Zucker & Noll, 1982) also has ties to impulsivity and high activity, but it can also develop independently, and there is a significant animal literature which indicates the sources of this variation are not derivative simply from undercontrol. So the precise nature of this influencing structure, as well as the underlying diathesis base, remains to be clarified.

2. Moving a life-stage-step closer to adulthood, both longitudinal data sets mark the etiologic impact of three individual level child variables: two of these, problems of misbehavior and conduct that move into later delinquency and antisociality, and problems of interpersonal attachment to intimate others are directly linked both to the behavioral undercontrol/activity level findings and the early aggression findings just described, but they begin to take a more negative cast, and they also involve a more clearly relational component as they display in older samples. The third characteristic, achievement-related deficits, has obvious social implications but its antecedents are most directly linked to attentional deficits that would impede the development of cognitive processing skills, as well as to the "difficult temperament" cluster, which includes activity level, (negative) emotionality, and social withdrawal.

All of these variables have been identified as predictive of later alcoholism, as well as problematic alcohol use in earlier life stages. Here again, the extent to which these variables are separable at all developmental stages is not yet well enough charted. Conduct deficits lead to school difficulty as well as longer term relational deficits, and trouble with school, as well as difficulties in one's involvement with intimate others throws one more quickly into a peer network of like behaving children—who are similarly either missing parental involvement, or are estranged from it (cf., Dishion, Capaldi, & Ray, 1993; Patterson, De-Baryshe, & Ramsey, 1989).

3. Parallel to the child sequence, both sets of studies implicate the parenting system, involving the parent as child-rearing provider, teacher, and shaper, of social behavior. Parent impact is identified in two ways, one by direct shaping/rearing, the other by way of provision of models for imitation (as an alcoholic or problem user, as well as in alcohol nonspecific ways, e.g., in modeling marital conflict as a style of interpersonal relatedness). And as just noted in the context of the child's

---

[9] Vaillant's (1983) study is the only one, among the adolescent to adult longitudinal studies, that explicitly attempted to estimate biological variation by way of a family history of alcoholism index; none of the child to adolescent studies provided any estimation of this variance.

contribution to developmental outcome, the parent as an inadequate provider of contact, will similarly be creating an interpersonal space into which peer influences may move earlier in the developmental sequence. On these grounds also, early alcohol use would be anticipated.

4. The parent findings indirectly implicate another form of parental transmission, by way of genetically mediated processes. Such influences, more likely than not involving the heritability of alcohol nonspecific characteristics relating to impulsivity, undercontrol, and antisociality (see 2 above), have been especially linked to the early-onset form of alcohol related difficulty (Cloninger, Bohman, & Sigvardsson, 1981; McGue, Pickens, & Svikis, 1992). Genetically based variation also plays out over time and not always in a constant way (McGue, 1994). Since experiential events interact with the genotype differently in different contexts and at different times during development (Fillmore, 1987; Searles, 1990), there may well be critical periods when individuals who are genotypically at-risk for early-onset alcohol-related difficulty are more vulnerable to environmental organizers than at other times, just as there may be different contexts that affect susceptibility to a greater or lesser degree.

The precise character of these interactions has yet to be charted, but we also note that the search for the specific diathesis(es) producing the phenotypic variability continues aggressively at this time, and the Collaborative Genetics Project (Begleiter et al., 1993) has this as its primary goal. Recent reviewers of this literature are increasingly of the opinion that there are likely several diatheses, rather than just one. Thus, Stone and Gottesman's (1993) definitive and dispassionate review concludes that "a multifactorial-polygenic mode of transmission accounts for the familiality and differences in severity better than does a simple Mendelian mode of transmission" (p. 127). They also suggest that "biologically significant effects of genes related to alcoholism are more likely to appear in severe rather than mild forms of the disorder" (p. 127) (i.e., be related more to the early-onset form that we are focused upon here).

What might the nature of these diatheses be? Some significant confluences exist in the literature. A recent meta-analysis of the event related potential (ERP) literature on high-risk-for-alcoholism (FH+) subjects by Polich, Pollock, and Bloom (1994) concluded that the smaller P300 amplitude consistently observed with FH+ males was a robust finding, and was an indicator of cognitive deficits pertaining to the speed with which attentional resources are allocated when memory updating is taking place. Working from these same studies, as well as other evidence, both Begleiter (1992) and Tarter et al., (in press) have suggested that what is heritable in COAs is a genetic predisposition to a nonspecific biobehavioral dysregulatory function, which under the proper contextual circumstances, increasingly moves into a pathway of risk to early alcohol problems, and early onset alcoholism thereafter. The Tarter group, in particular, have suggested that it is the "difficult temperament" cluster identified out of the New York Longitudinal Study (Lerner & Vicary, 1984; Thomas & Chess, 1977), involving early behavioral manifestations of slow adaptability, dysrhythmia, negative mood, social withdrawal, and high intensity

of emotional reactions, that is the core early liability complex in this early-onset, very high risk subpopulation. These hypotheses are in close concert with the behavioral studies of difference noted in section 2 above; they also continue to be supported in the recent literature (Wills & DuHamel, 1993; Windle, 1990).

One final point: the interplay of this disparate array of influencing structures needs to continue over long periods of time in order for damaged outcomes to occur, and there is currently substantial debate about the degree to which these processes are best viewed as operating in a stochastic fashion, as a function of life's vagaries, or in some more constrained progression. This is a critical issue, because it raises the question about whether or not the presumed orderliness of progression observed in the clinical case is simply a happenstance based upon retrospectively noted random coalescence, or contrastingly, an orderly progression that is driven by some combination of internal and external factors which ultimately give structure to the syndrome. We turn to that issue now.

TRAJECTORY ISSUES: THE IMPACT OF NESTEDNESS ON EPIGENETIC PROGRESSIONS

In an attempt to bring order to the trajectory issue, Johnson and Rolf (1990) have suggested that the expression of early biobehavioral maladaptation may follow one of four possible trajectories. Maladaptive functioning may first become evident during childhood and continue to manifest itself into adulthood. This is a strong continuity model that requires evidence of early etiological factors that are then maintained over time. (This is the model we have been utilizing for the early-onset, high problem subset of children.) A second trajectory involves the appearance of maladaptive behavior in childhood, becoming masked during adolescence, and then reappearing in adulthood. This is a weak continuity model in that it predicts that maladaptive behavior merely is dampened during a particular time period, only to resurface later in development. The other two models posit onset of maladaptive behavior during adolescence and continuing into adulthood, or onsetting for the first time in adulthood.[10]

The more general point is that some ordering has become necessary in order to describe the less than completely random variation and progression that characterized the relationship of risk factors for substance abuse to the end point of problem alcohol involvement/alcoholism. At the same time, trajectory models are descriptive rather than causal; they offer no explanatory net for why one outcome rather than another, except that the interaction of environment (broadly conceived), and genotype creates a unique path. While positing that course is more than an agglomeration of factors that, at the organismic level, appear to hold together over time, trajectory propositions do not deal with issues of constraints upon the system, including the fact that the

---

[10] A fifth and a sixth model, involving onset of maladaptive behavior in childhood which ceases in adolescence, and onset in adolescence which ceases in adulthood, are not considered within the framework of the Johnson/Rolf exposition.

envelope of risk and protective factors is never a completely unbounded one. None of us lives within a world of unlimited choice, and the envelope of opportunity is restricted by way of one's genotype, by way of the opportunity structure offered in the family and larger social environment within which we make our lives, and by way of the timing of the changes that take place, which simultaneously impose a bounding structure on external variation, on internal variation, and on the opportunity structure within which change can take place.

Ever since the appearance of Scarr and McCartney's (1983) important paper, it has become increasingly popular to note that organisms seek, create, and shape environments. While acknowledging the substantial evidence for that position, we believe that simultaneously, an obverse proposition needs to be entertained, that environments not only constrain the range of variation of organisms—a relatively old developmental concept—but by so doing, they play a role in shaping and channelling the trajectories that are possible within their boundaries. Restriction of range is also provision of a particular, and *specialized* opportunity structure, which in some instances drives the organism into particular directions of opportunity, and in others may even drive the organism back onto itself. This is the concept of nestedness.

The first part of this nestedness proposition is not new to developmentalists and is contained within the range of variation concept. The second half, pertaining to the impact on trajectories, is less well-articulated although there is significant evidence for it in a diverse array of literatures. Thus, there is by now a substantial literature on the capacity of cultures to shape and render more or less deviant that which temperamentally appears early on as externalizing behavior (Weisz, 1989). Similarly, there is beginning evidence that even the manifestations of risk that occur will be shaped as a function of the cultural or social structure within which they are embedded. Adolescents in Denmark are at risk for bicycling while intoxicated, not driving, and the fatalities that occur are of substantially lesser magnitude because the vehicles are inherently less danger producing (Arnett & Balle-Jensen, 1993). So different longer term outcomes (for self and for close others) occur as a result of earlier and greater involvement in antisociality fatality than do as a result of injury. It is in this manner that nests alter trajectories.

Recent studies from two other, quite different arenas, one involving alcohol problems, the other not, lead in a similar direction, out of very different data. Thus, prevalence rates for alcoholism among two-parent families are higher in neighborhoods that have heavier indicators of social disorganization (number of single parent households, percent of families at poverty level) (Pallas, 1992). In other words, from the perspective of child conception as well as rearing, it appears that the matrix of heightened risk may show itself at greater frequency in some environments. Similarly, rates of juvenile offending have been found to vary by neighborhood, with lower SES characterizing the higher rate areas. Pathways of progression also differed by neighborhood. Boys living in low SES neighborhoods advanced further into a pathway of offending than did boys living in the high SES neighborhoods (Loeber & Wikstrom, 1993). The definitive studies that will track order of progression here have not yet been done. But these new studies are suggestive, at the least, and indicate the need to chart more completely how the microenvironment may offer different opportunity structures within which risk is nurtured and develops (also cf. Patterson & Yoerger, 1993).

Variation in onset time provides another clear example of nesting phenomena. As noted in an earlier section of this chapter, delaying onset of alcohol and other drug involvement alters trajectory, such that onset occurring at the end of adolescence effectively disengages such use from deviance and thus prevents escalation/progression (Kandel, 1988). Recent evidence in other areas of psychopathology—and from other phases of the life cycle—provides an example of how this process may work. Thus, schizophrenics with earlier life onset (before age 45) show distinct differences in symptomatic pattern from those with late onset, and different patterns of etiology appear to be implicated. Early onset and dense family history have been implicated in a neurodevelopmental form, and late onset has been observed more commonly in women than in men, and has been closely tied to family histories of affective disorder rather than schizophrenia (Castle & Murray, 1993). Similarly, schizophrenics with very early onset (between the ages of 14 and 18) show a higher likelihood of chronicity in course (Krausz & Muller-Thomsen, 1993), which in turn has been linked to the impact of the disorder upon normal, but not yet sufficiently stabilized developmental processes. Thus, the experience of a psychotic episode when "the patient has not yet developed a sufficient degree of social and emotional independence and maturity" (p. 831) is likely to have greater impact upon later functioning than would be the case after an adult adaptation is achieved. The degree of disorganization as well as the experience of self-failure are likely to be greater when there is less in the way of personality coherency to fall back on.

It is a major tenet of developmental psychopathology that even within the framework of that which is abnormal in childhood, normal processes are present and operating (Cicchetti, 1984; Sroufe & Rutter, 1984). Another tenet is that developmental pressure—especially in younger organisms—is toward adaptation and resolution of trauma (Sameroff & Chandler, 1975). Thus, only under repeated insult does normal developmental process fail to assert itself. From a systems perspective, these positions advocate an organismic primacy view of human development, and there is very substantial evidence to be marshalled in support of it. Here, however, we are encouraging simultaneous consideration of issues of sustained harshness of environment, which make such evolutionarily adaptive behavior less easy to sustain. Insofar as these bounding structures operate in concert, coalescences begin to appear, and covariation occurs that makes the process substantially less than random, and in some instances appears to make it increasingly unlikely that resilience can operate. Data from the MSU-UofM study underscores this point. In an extensive series of analyses of the interplay between risk and protective factors in this generally high-risk but very young sample, Moses, Zucker and Fitzgerald (1993) found that indices of social and intellectual competence among parents (which all loaded on a Protectiveness factor) were negatively ($r = -.4$) associated with level of parental psychopathology. Both factors operated independently (and in opposite directions) in predicting the outcome variable of level of child behavior problems, but there was no interaction. That is, level of protectiveness did not operate as a moderator of the risk-damaged outcome relationships. Given the direct negative relationship between risk and familial difficulty, the idea that protectiveness (and resilience) are possible under all circumstances may be a romanticized notion, especially for those coming out of densely risk laden environments.

MULTIPLE TRAJECTORIES AND MULTIPLE ETIOLOGIES: THEREFORE MULTIPLE ALCOHOLISMS

One of the core points of nestedness theory, then, is that a random probabilistic model of the development of alcohol related difficulty is not an appropriate one to explain the diversity of influencing structures. At the same time, a heavily contextual model is also inappropriate. How then may any order be made of the diversity of trajectories that are possible? We suggest that those circumstances which regularly pair high-risk environments with a dense set of individual risk factors are the ones most likely to produce developmental continuity. In early stages, such pairing would be anticipated to create a situation of fluid risk, but as the coalescence is maintained over a substantial interval, regularity of both elicitation and action would occur, which in turn would be expected to evolve into a behavioral structure of some coherence and stability. This proposition, outlined within the arena of developmental psychopathology, is actually a specific corollary to a more general proposition about canalization through epigenetic progression (cf. Gottlieb, 1991a). What it articulates, and what is essential to note, is that the action structure that evolves begins to have a life of its own, and would be anticipated thereafter to have motivational (guiding and stabilizing) properties that did not exist when both risk and context were present but the behavioral repertoire driving the symptomatic display had not yet been sufficiently overlearned. What is also essential to note is that the stable symptomatic display becomes the clue that a structure is present. And when the stability is not present, the outcome is dilution of risk and epiphenomenality of symptomatic presence.

This general set of propositions has immediate relevance as an organizing framework for the variety of factors described as both risky and facilitative of risk in the last two sections. On the basis of our review, one may still pose the question: How do we get from the diatheses to early onset of problem drinking and a longer term trajectory, given these multiple diatheses, multiple individual risk factors and multiple environments? The key is the behavioral organization that begins to emerge, involving the early and steadfast presence of antisocial behavior, which appears to be the crystallized action matrix that sustains the trajectory, *provided it occurs in a nesting environment that can maintain it* (cf. Cairns, 1991). Under circumstances of greater density of macrostructure risk as well as of individual risk, there is early introduction to alcohol use, a rapid onset of alcohol-related problems, sustaining and facilitating models which encourage overlearning, the emergence of other life difficulty, including both school difficulty and other psychopathology, and the emergence of a pattern of increasing momentum, which continues on even into adulthood (Patterson, 1993; Pihl & Peterson,

1991; Zucker & Fitzgerald, 1991). Where it has been examined, one of the critical factors differentiating it from the other trajectory is the *early and sustained presence* of antisociality (Robins, 1993; Stabenau, 1990; Zucker, Ellis, & Fitzgerald, 1993). The existing data also imply that if the antisociality is not sustained, for whatever reason, then the structure will fail to crystallize.

We end this point with a quotation from the Swedish National Conscript Study analysis of the social, behavioral and psychological factors involved in high alcohol consumption among the entire population of Swedish males aged 18 to 21 ($N = 49,464$):

> The concept of a high risk group might be helpful in reconciling what appears as conflicting results from earlier research. The high risk group had a high proportion of fathers who often drank alcohol, several indicators of early social maladjustment, psychological symptoms, and multidrug misuse. . . . antisocial behavior is a strong predictor of high alcohol consumption, (but) its predictive power appears largely limited to the high risk group described. (Andreasson, Allebeck, Brandt & Romelsjo, 1992, p. 713)

Thus, even moving into early adulthood, evidence continues to exist for more than one trajectory of alcohol related difficulty. When timing, lack of concentration of nests, and individual risk load vary with developmental change, then the confluence of these factors operates to produce a fluid, heavily life-stage dependent set of drinking problems. As developmental time proceeds, we get discontinuity of alcohol problems for this subset. These two different trajectories have already been described elsewhere in some detail (Zucker, 1987, 1994); the early onset, continuous trajectory has been termed *Antisocial Alcoholism,* the other, stage-dependent pattern of problem alcohol involvement has been termed *Developmentally Limited Alcoholism.*

The evidence we have reviewed to this point has been mainly drawn from the childhood and adolescent risk and epidemiologic literature. Given that most alcohol researchers, to say nothing of psychopathology researchers more generally, are largely unacquainted with these literatures, the databases we have described have tended to either be ignored or else used as evidence for markers of risk which only manifest themselves in adult disorder, without there being consideration of the possibility that the markers are in fact part of the intervening process, and need to be present in order for the adult pathology to manifest itself.

This state of affairs is beginning to change, and there is some evidence that process differences are being attended to in recent work. The Andreassen et al. (1992) study just cited is one example. Others of special relevance to this review include (a) a paper by Weber, Graham, Hansen, Flay, & Anderson (1989), identifying differences in trajectory for problem prone vs. more normally socialized adolescents that closely parallels the argument we have been advancing; (b) the Tarter group's work characterizing the epigenesis of early onset alcoholism (Tarter et al., in press); (c) the Monitoring the Future Project's recent work charting differences in trajectory for patterns of binge drinking during the transition from adolescence to young adulthood, and identifying differences in causal structure for these different trajectories (Schulenberg, Wadsworth, O'Malley, Bachman, & Johnston, 1994) and (d) our own group's work characterizing differences in path models of risk structure among preschoolers, that already are

TABLE 19.5   Replication of the Antisocial-Nonantisocial Alcoholism Typology in Recent Literature

| Investigative Group | Antisocial Type | Other Types | | Comments |
		Number	Name	
Cloninger (1987); Cloninger et al. (1981)	Type II (male limited)	1	Type I (Milieu limited)	Type II has denser fam hx alcoholism and antisocialtiy; earlier onset of antisociality and alcoholism; more severe alcohol-related consequences.
von Knorring, von Knorring, Smigan, Lindberg, and Edholm (1987)	Type II (male limited)	1	Type I (Milieu limited)	Divided Ss on age of onset and presence of 23 alcohol-related psychosocial consequences. Type I and Type II alcoholics differ on similar characteristics as Cloninger's classification based primarily on fam hx.
Hesselbrock, Hesselbrock, and Stabenau (1985)	Alcoholism with Antisocial Personality Disorder (ASP)	1	Alcoholism without ASP	History of antisociality better predictor of alcoholism course than density of fam hx. Alc w/ASP > Alc w/o ASP on age of first drunkenness, first regular intoxicat., and recog. of alcoholism. Alc w/ASP > in bilateral FH+ grp than unilateral FH+ and FH− grps; bilateral FH+ > other grps on many psychosocial consequences.
Hesselbrock, Hesselbrock, and Workman-Daniels (1986)	Alcoholism with Antisocial Personality Disorder (ASP)	2	Alcoholism only; alcoholism with depression	Alc w/ASP grp had earliest onset of alcohol difficulty.
Powell et al. (1982)	Alcoholism with antisocial personality	3	Alcoholism only; alcohol/drug; alcohol with depression	Alc/ASP and Alc/Drug had earlier onset of abusive drinking and age of residential rx. Alc/ASP group had most probs. with the law.
Babor et al. (1992)	Type B	1	Type A	Type B > Type A on earlier onset, more childhood risk factors, higher degree of familial alc., more current psychopath., greater sever. of dependence, more life stress, more polydrug use, more chronic Rx Hx. At 12 and 36 months, Type B > Type A in alcohol recidivism, other psychopath., life stress.
Zucker (1987, 1994)	Antisocial alcoholics	3	Developmentally limited; negative affect; the primary alcoholisms: (a) Isolated alc. abuse; (b) Episode alc.; (c) Developmentally cumulative alc.	Develop Limited ends and Antisocial continues in adulthood. Negative Affect has late onset + Dep., and Anx. comorbidity. Primary Alc.: initially no comorbidity and Alc. specific causal structure; more react. to envt'l stress.
Zucker et al. (1993); Zucker, Ellis, and Fitzgerald (1994a)	Antisocial alcoholics (AALs)	1	Non-antisocial alcoholics alcoholics (NAALs)	AALs stronger relationship between bio. risk and life-time alc. problems; greater assoc. between childhood conduct problems and current dysfunction. AALs tend to show downward socioeconomic mobility re: fy of origin. Children of AALs > behav. prob. than children of NAALs.

suggestive of potential differences in long-term trajectory, even into adulthood (Zucker, Ellis, & Fitzgerald, 1994a).

Interestingly, as soon as one moves into the adult literature, there is a proliferation of discussion about subtypes that has been going on as far back as the last century. Babor and his colleagues (Babor & Dolinsky, 1988; Babor et al., 1992; Babor & Lauerman, 1986) in a series of definitive reviews of this area conclude that there is substantial and long-standing evidence for at least two types, one of which is the early onset type we have already described. Babor et al. (1992) describe it as "characterized by early onset, a more rapid course, more severe symptoms, greater psychological vulnerability, and poorer prognosis" (p. 600). The other "is characterized by later onset, a slower course, fewer complications, less psychological impairment, and better prognosis" (p. 600). To give some sense of the large background of studies upon which this conclusion is founded, in Table 19.5 we present a summary of the recent major studies that address the question of typological variation. Note, as an aside, that this work has primarily been done among male alcoholics, and our remarks are addressed to that subset. We briefly comment upon these issues among women, in the concluding section of the chapter.

From a developmental perspective what is striking about this proliferation of studies is that (a) they consistently replicate the early-onset, antisocial type, and (b) they also uncover at least one other type, marked in some instances simply by lesser psychopathology, and in others by depression. Note also that the residual type (or types) are not the same as the developmentally limited trajectory we have described earlier. In short, counting the two trajectories already identified, there is at least one more, and perhaps more than that. A logical next question is, how many more?

One of us has addressed this issue in more complete form in other publications (Zucker, 1987, 1994); space limitations allow for only a brief recapitulation of that work here. Making use of the proposition that stability of behavioral organization is one of the keys to identifying trajectory differences, and utilizing the Epidemiologic Catchment Area population estimates of comorbidity (Regier et al., 1990) as a route into identifying the major types of behavioral covariation found with alcoholism in adulthood, six trajectory variants have been proposed. Along the way, special attention has been given to contextual influences that may enhance or dilute trajectory by way of age-stage demands, and to a second level of problem that begins to become much more salient for adult psychopathology, namely, the secondary symptomatic effects produced by the chronicity of the disorder itself.

Figures 19.1 and 19.2 graphically represent the trajectories of the different types. Three have other comorbidities associated with them, one of long standing (i.e., the antisociality that is at the core of Antisocial Alcoholism), another that is also conduct disordered and antisocial but stage limited (i.e., the delinquent and impulsive activity of the problem behavior syndrome), and a third involves the emergence in childhood and adolescence of internalizing symptomatology in high-risk populations (e.g., Colder & Chassin, in press; Earls, Reich, Jung, & Cloninger, 1988; Rolf, Johnson, Israel, Baldwin, & Chandra, 1988; Sher, Walitzer, Wood, & Brent, 1991; Schuckit, Irwin, & Brown, 1990), but appears to be linked to a trajectory of severe, and sustained alcohol related difficulty only in adulthood. This third pattern, *negative*

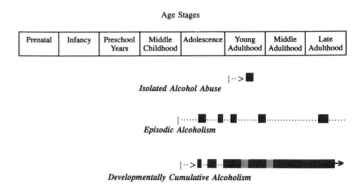

Figure 19.1 The comorbid alcoholisms.

affect alcoholism, is more common among women (Schuckit, Pitts, & Reich, 1969; Turnbull & Gomberg, 1990) and has also been tied to the special role demands that women face (Wilsnack, Klassen, Schur, & Wilsnack, 1991), as well as to the influence of genetic factors common to both major depression and alcoholism (Kendler, Heath, Neale, Kessler, & Eaves, 1993; Merikangas, Leckman, Prusoff, Pauls, & Weissman, 1985).

The trajectories shown in Figure 19.2 describe a subset of alcoholisms that have no apparent parallel in childhood. They involve sustained alcohol intake, which leads to severe, alcohol-related symptomatology; no other behavioral covariation is known to have linkages to their onset. The hypothesis, still relatively untested, is that these trajectories are driven by the presence of elevated environmental stress, occurring in a social context that provides a support and value structure for alcohol as the "drug of choice" for tension reduction. When these two conditions are met and are coupled with a third set of risk factors involving alcohol-specific vulnerabilities that make the consumption of this drug even more reinforcing (or less aversive), then the best-fit scenario exists for alcohol abuse. Under circumstances of nonsustained stress (e.g., immediately preceding or following the break-up of a marriage, cf. Cahalan, 1970), isolated abuse may occur. Under circumstances where the interval is more episodic (e.g., times of heightened stress

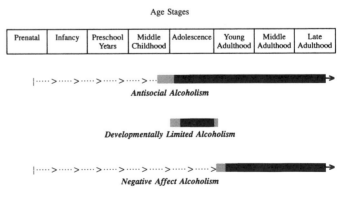

Figure 19.2 The primary alcoholisms (alcoholisms without initial continuity or → comorbidity).

related to unemployment, or for those in intermittently high stress occupations) the pattern may move to become episodic. For those whose contextual and individual vulnerability match is greatest, the pattern would eventually move into a chronic adaptation. This later trajectory has been termed *developmentally cumulative alcoholism*. The reader will also note that there are parallels between these latter three trajectories and the developmentally limited pattern. Although the form of all four of these types is similar, for the developmentally limited pattern, individual level etiologic risk factors have already been identified, but the onset and termination of the disorder is bounded by nonindividual level contextual factors. This may ultimately also be the case for the episodic and developmentally cumulative variants, and in fact the San Diego group has been specially focused on this issue (e.g., Schuckit, 1988, 1994). But at the moment, their causal structure has been less well charted.

IMPLICATIONS FOR PREVENTION AND INTERVENTION

The overall thrust of this review has been that the emergence and course of alcohol-related difficulties is best understood as involving multiple trajectories and multiple etiologies. And to make the matter even more interesting, developmental variation means that even those on the same trajectory may be differently influenced and shifted, depending on where in the trajectory the attempts at change are being carried out. On these grounds it is not surprising that the recent prevention and intervention literatures are increasingly advocating multiple strategies, based upon life stage, problem severity, and the special characteristics of the subpopulation being encountered (Baer, Marlatt, & McMahon, 1993; Beutler et al., 1993; Project Match Research Group, 1993). Thus, it is no longer appropriate to presume that a single method will be successful with all populations, at all levels of risk. There are a variety of other, derivative conclusions that emerge, some directly from the literature we have reviewed on etiology and trajectory, and some from recent prevention/early intervention and clinical studies:

1. One is that intervention activity is also best framed as a multi-stage, developmental endeavor. Thus, while early stage work may simply involve consciousness raising, later stage work may need to involve graded and much more focused programs, that are specially tailored to the known needs of the clientele. This type of stepped strategy probably needs to be considered as an essential part of the prevention/treatment armamentarium, even before the "treatment" begins (Pentz, 1993; Sobell & Sobell, 1993).

2. Apropos our extensive discussion of the origins of antisocial alcoholism, it should also be recognized that severe early use is almost invariably a nested problem, involving poverty, major psychiatric comorbidity, depression, unemployment, poor job performance, damaged social relationships (marital instability, damaged family relationships and family violence, damaged caretaker roles). Thus, prevention efforts for this subset of the population are more likely to have long-term success if the nested, multiproblem nature of the problematic

alcohol use is addressed from the beginning (Hawkins, Catalano, & Miller, 1992; Maguin, Zucker, & Fitzgerald, 1994). Given that the causal structure is to a very significant degree intertwined, to intervene on a single factor without addressing the larger causal matrix is likely to provide short-term effects that will not sustain themselves.

Early on in the process, the social network of intimate relationships (parents, siblings, other relatives) is at close range and is to some degree the pump primer for moving into a more deviant social environment. Thus, programmatic efforts need to move more closely into the intimate social relationship structure than simply school and peers, if we are to have more effective impact for this early-onset group (Dielman, Butchart, & Shope, 1993; Patterson et al., 1989; Yoshikawa, 1994).

3. More generally, the multiproblem nature of the matrix means that a chronic disease model is a more appropriate one for very high risk populations, wherein one needs to think in terms of long-term, multiple inoculation strategies, that will slowly bring the level of risk in the matrix down to less risky levels (Barnett, 1993; Henderson, Ross, & Pike, 1991; Tinsley, 1992). Intervention strategies that attempt to settle the difficulty in one inoculation are almost certainly likely to have poor long-term outcomes.

4. At the same time, the concept of nestedness does not end at the microenvironment structure of family and intimate others. Manipulations at the community and legal levels have very significant influences upon both consumption and problems (Wagenaar & Perry, 1994), although the degree to which these levels of influence interface with each other is not well understood. Even more critical as an issue to settle is the extent to which such macrolevel influences have equal or different levels of impact upon very high vs. lower risk (e.g., later onset) populations. This question is a high priority one for new research.

5. Moving to intervention programming after adolescence, a developmental perspective would support the view that clinical change is a process that occurs step by step, in an orderly way, provided the relevant maintaining factors are addressed. Parallel to this view is the theoretical perspective offered by Marlatt, Miller, and their colleagues in the recent treatment literature, relating to utilization of harm reduction strategies for the reduction of alcohol problems (Marlatt & Tapert, 1993; Miller & Page, 1991). Rather than adopting an abstinence standard as the only one for problem use, these writers have amassed a substantial amount of data indicating that intermediary level strategies, which reduce consumption and require the abuser to anticipate and problem solve their manner of dealing with situations of high risk for the creation of new problems, will effectively change long-term trajectories of abuse. Evidence also indicates that, for a subset of the risk population, such strategies will be all that are needed to solve the problem. And where this is not the case, other data indicate that this early work may effectively serve as an entree into later more sustained risk reduction activity.

6. Also in the arena of adulthood, a systems perspective would encourage a view even of severe alcohol related difficulty, as occurring in a matrix that sometimes may support and

sometimes may drive the ongoing individual difficulty (Seilhammer & Jacob, 1990). On these grounds, ignoring that matrix is likely to ignore significant portions of causal variance. Thus to address this problem at an individual level, without intervening in helping the family that is partner to and facilitator of the disability, is likely to lead toward degradation of the effect.

7. Nonetheless, not all levels of system are equally important contributors to process at different points during the trajectory of problem alcohol involvement. A chronic problem may be best addressed initially by pharmacological means, and only later may be amenable to intervention at a social relational level. Similarly, less severe problems are likely more easily defined as occurring within the bounds and under the control of the organism (i.e., the client), and hence may best be addressed by way of cognitive interventions. Intervention theory has not yet reached this level of articulation; it needs to.

ABNORMAL AND NORMAL DEVELOPMENT: A BIDIRECTIONAL PERSPECTIVE

How does the study of "abnormal" development inform us about normal development? There are a number of approaches to this question, but they all revolve around two propositions: First, that abnormal development more adequately specifies what are the limits of the envelope of behavioral plasticity. Second, and simultaneously, the study of the abnormal tests our theories of the applicability of the normal (Cicchetti, 1984). After all, what is psychopathological is also lawful and "normal." So the deviant requires us to attend more carefully to the explanatory network that we need to have in place. Under less "deviant" circumstances, less complete explanatory models may do the job, and obscure other typically "quieter" structures, that do not surface under usual circumstances.

Thus, the study of the abnormal provides information about the relative plasticity of the boundaries that frame the system, and also provides covert evidence about trajectory. Deviant adaptations that run counter to a normative trajectory require the hypothesis that different processes must be operating. This was precisely the reasoning that led to the proposition that there is more than one kind of alcohol problem trajectory in adolescence. For one subset, the problems alleviate (i.e., those with the developmentally limited trajectory), for another subset (the antisocial one), they do not. At that point, the developmentalist will need to posit either contextual variation in the current system (i.e., a process that produces branching) (cf. Schulenberg et al., 1994), or alternatively hypothesize the operation of a different history that appears superficially indistinguishable, but that must have a different structure and momentum insofar as it has begun earlier and carries on into adulthood without the subsidence. The puzzle then becomes how to distinguish these phenotypes at the time when they appear relatively indistinguishable. The detective work that is carried out in studying the deviant case is more likely to provide clues to underlying process and structure simply because the deviance exacerbates that which is "normal," and thus is more likely to show in highlighted form.

The reverse is also true. There are instances where the robustness of normal developmental phenomena may be observed even within the framework of that which is grossly deviant. Thus, as noted earlier in this chapter, early onset of schizophrenia has far different developmental ramifications than it does when onsetting later. The disturbance of normal trajectories, and the offsetting of the life task time clock has different, and far more serious implications when disturbance appears earlier than when it shows later. A parallel set of ramifications exists for antisocial alcoholism. When contrasted against later onset forms (e.g., the primary alcoholisms), the likelihood of remission-dissolution of the late-onset type is far greater. Insofar as the appearance of psychopathology is an overlay on an already largely effective life course, the level of life invasiveness should be less, and the likelihood of persistence of the overlay phenomena (in this instance, the alcohol problems) is lessened. Conversely, an alcohol involvement pattern that is interwoven with other life experience over a long part of the life course is likely much more resistant to remission.

The empirical evidence in adulthood is consistent with this hypothesis (Babor et al., 1992), and prevention theory in the substance abuse area has already embraced this perspective. In fact, as we have already noted, delay of onset (i.e., altering normal developmental trajectory) has been proposed as one of the strongest routes into the prevention of substance abuse.

Insofar as normal developmental processes may be identified within the midst of that which is deviant, such data provide added grounds for the destigmatization of psychopathological phenomena. By the same token, such findings encourage a redefinition of psychopathology within the bounds of a theory that embraces both normal and abnormal. This revised explanatory structure would challenge extant clinical theory to incorporate that which is adaptive even within the bounds of that which appears to be maladaptive. Reframing of this nature, at the level of the clinical encounter, can sometimes dramatically provide hope and sow the seeds for a trajectory of later functioning that departs radically from the earlier more obviously maladaptive one (cf. Erikson, 1956). Perhaps developmental psychopathological theory may likewise dramatically modify our current paradigms for understanding clinical phenomena.

One last hypothesis about how the abnormal may inform our understanding of the normal: Given the greater presence of extremes of behavioral adaptation, the study of the abnormal is more likely to provide evidence of the importance of feedback in system maintenance (negative) and disorder (positive). In other words, it helps in the search for patterns underlying chaos. Put differently, traditional developmental psychology focuses on mapping a modal developmental pathway rather than describing individual developmental pathway variations; thus issues of multifinality and equifinality are not addressed. The stokers of developmental systems theory, on the other hand, are fueled by variation, contexts, alternative pathways, attractors, bifurcations, perturbations, transitions, reorganizations, and individual differences (Cicchetti, 1993; Ford & Lerner, 1992; Gollin, Stahl, & Morgan, 1989; Levine & Fitzgerald, 1992; Silvern, 1984). From a systems perspective, "pathological" or "high-risk" systems are like natural experiments in system organization, disorganization, and reorganization, which can only be viewed properly with a prospective longitudinal methodology. While organized experience is more likely to produce steady state adaptations, and serves a maintenance function, chaos drives system reorganization. Change facilitates or induces reorganization . . . or to put this in systems language: dynamic systems bifurcate into new attractor states via destabilization of a currently stable system.

We close with a description of Chauvin's (1977) Rule of the Unusual:

> The more unusual the situation, or the less likely it is to be met in nature, the more variable will be the animal's behavior and the more likely that its adaptation will rise above the stereotyped behavior of the species. As Lecomte said, the titmouse "knows" how to build its nest, but it "seeks" the solution to à repair problem. (pp. 47–48)

CONCLUSIONS AND FUTURE WORK

This review only begins to scratch the surface of a field that has burgeoned in the last decade, but that still is at the beginnings of embracing a developmental perspective on behavior. The majority of our review has focused upon content and has attempted to organize the diverse array of findings involving the emergence and maintenance of problem alcohol involvement, in its various forms in the interval between birth and midadulthood. Given the joint truths that "God is in the details," and that the way a field advances is through advances in method, it is fitting for us to focus explicitly on what we regard as some of the core methodological issues that still remain insufficiently attended to in current work.

Measurement Issues: The Problem of Defining the Dependent Variable Developmentally

Undergirding this review has been a family of questions pertaining to the issues of tracking continuity and discontinuity of risk, and the degree to which a broad spectrum of potentially explanatory factors do or do not have impact upon this process. In virtually all of this work, the dependent variable indices of risk either have been proxy measures (such as aggressiveness or deviance), or what the epidemiologists call point prevalence measures of outcome. Given developmentalists avowed interest in epigenetic structure, it is puzzling to us why, at the dependent variable end of the equation, an avowedly developmental analytic strategy has not more frequently been utilized in constructing measures of outcome that might reflect structure and the potential for momentum (i.e., mass).

Current diagnostic and assessment frameworks for scaling both alcohol, as well as other drug related difficulty have not yet systematically addressed this issue. The DSM-III-R classification, with its effort to scale severity of symptomatic display in fact confused the issue of current life invasiveness and long-term damage. As is true of all point-prevalence measures, sheer number of current troubles is not an index of long-term life difficulty (or, in the preclinical arena, of sustained risk). Perhaps for this reason, DSM-IV has moved away from a seventy classification

scheme, and has made some beginning forays into categorizing course.

In the substance abuse area, to date there have been only limited forays into addressing this issue. The construction of life history-based measures has been driven more out of interest by treatment researchers in the practical problem of gauging prognosis (e.g., McLellan et al., 1985; Skinner & Allen, 1982), than out of interest in dealing with the developmental question of what took place ahead of time, and how this may have some predictive relevance to later trajectory. Nonetheless, both the McLellan group's Addiction Severity Index (ASI), as well as Skinner and Allen's Lifetime Drinking History are beginning attempts at evaluating the degree to which alcohol problems (and for the ASI, also drug problems) invade other aspects of the life space currently, as well as historically. In the same vein, our own group has had substantial early success in creating a developmentally focused index called the Lifetime Alcohol Problems Score (LAPS) (Zucker, 1991), which gauges onset, breadth of symptom structure, and also extent of life course invasiveness of alcohol-related difficulty. The index has proven highly effective as a measure of extent of child exposure to adult risk (Fitzgerald et al., 1993), and also as an indicator of level of alcohol-related damage among adults (Zucker, Ellis, & Fitzgerald, 1993). More work of this kind, which attempts to summate the components of developmental momentum, needs to take place.

Sampling Issues

The failure to adequately specify, and then sample the range of alcohol problem variation, has been a major difficulty not only in the clinical literature but also in the existing longitudinal high risk literature. Given what is already known from cross-sectional but large scale population studies, of the wide variation in both comorbidity and socioeconomic differences among different types of alcoholics and alcohol abusers, it is essential that such specification be carried out better. This issue is of intrinsic importance, but there is a measurement issue, as well, that is directly connected to the problem of inadequate sampling specification and inadequate sample representation. The predictive value of an indicator is related both to its validity and also to the prevalence of the condition or attribute in the population being studied. Thus the lack of replication of findings in many of the existing studies may just as easily be attributable to sampling differences as to unreliability of findings, or imprecise specification of the construct being evaluated. Until this issue is better sorted out, the literature is likely to remain confused.

As we have already indicated, this problem is nowhere more prominent than in the arena pertaining to fluidity versus stability of risk in childhood. But it extends beyond this arena as well. Even high-risk designs contrasting COA (and ostensibly high risk) vs. nonCOA (and ostensibly lower risk) subjects are likely to be confounded if the COA population being accessed happens to come from families where there is low comorbidity.

Another sampling issue that has special relevance to those of developmental bent is the need to better specify elements of course when one characterizes clinical samples. Given the major differences between acute and chronic conditions, involving not just symptoms but differences in nesting experience over long periods of time, the issue of how long the symptomatology has been in place becomes a critical factor in characterizing the sample and in specifying etiologic process. Attempts to approximate this, by way of specification of age do the job only imprecisely, given the likelihood of differences in age of onset for the different subtypes.

Conceptual Issues

Distinguishing between Alcohol-Related and Alcohol-Nonspecific Variance, and Assessing Both Domains

This point has already been made earlier, but we reiterate it here. In understanding the etiology of alcohol-related problems, these two, sometimes parallel and sometimes separate processes need to be adequately charted. They still are commonly not both evaluated. Given their dual operation, and the importance of nonspecific variance for the more severe forms of alcohol-related difficulty, full etiologic specification needs to include not only timing, onset, and course of alcohol-specific unfolding, but also of the parallel processes. It also must eventually articulate the junctures where intermingling starts to take place. Unfortunately, in the chronic state, melding has long since taken place; and in the acute state, the two appear only loosely related.

Failures to Adequately Map the Envelope of What Is Alcoholism Specific and What Is Drug General

A parallel issue to the one just raised is the need for better understanding of the differences between influencing structures that are drug specific as compared to drug general. Denise Kandel's (1975) now classic mapping of drug sequencing at the onset end documented the interplay between alcohol use and other drug use. Beer and wine most often are first drugs of use, followed by cigarettes for some, and hard liquor for others. A subset of the population moves thereafter from cigarettes to marijuana use, a second subset from liquor to marijuana, but the two most common paths (for those who travel that far into the sequence) were from cigarettes to liquor, and afterward to marijuana use, and from liquor to cigarettes, and after to marijuana. Donovan and Jessor (1983) contributed the important revision/observation that problem-drinking onset typically occurred prior to harder drug use but after first marijuana use, thus further documented the interplay between alcohol and other drug involvement. Thereafter, all paths lead to illicit drug use of other kinds. While this schema has needed some revision in the generation since it was published, its general pattern continues to have validity. The sequencing provides a straightforward illustration of the manner in which alcohol use is tied to involvement with other drugs, in some instances being preceded by other drug involvement (e.g., when involving hard liquor use), in other instances serving as a gateway to other drugs. On these grounds, it is likely that what has frequently been depicted in the alcohol literature as a specific, alcohol-related effect (e.g., for expectancies, or for differences in consumption) is also, in part a general drug using effect. Evidence even into adulthood continues to accumulate that the dimension of other drug involvement is to some degree correlated with

problem-alcohol involvement (Regier et al., 1990), but also to a degree cross-cuts this dimension, and is linked more heavily to some forms of alcoholism, most particularly the antisocial type, than it is to others (Babor et al., 1992; Gonzalez et al., 1993). Thus, when a finding implicates problem alcohol use, it likely also implicates marijuana use, and when problem alcohol use is being assessed, cigarette smoking is likely already a baseline phenomenon for the population. The implications of this interplay are not yet well enough understood.

Problems of Conceptual and Empirical Poverty

Issues of the interplay of macrolevel and microlevel influences are still virtually completely unresearched, and most investigators in the alcohol field do not even indicate an awareness of the problem. For example, we know that laws change consumption levels as well as the display of rates of alcohol-related problems (Wagenaar & Perry, 1994). What is not known is whether such macrolevel influences have differential effects upon the less deviant as compared to the more deviant (e.g., already alcoholic) segments of the population. From both a public health perspective as well as an intervention perspective, it is essential that these phenomena be better understood.

Another example: as far back as fifty years ago, a significant association was observed between heavy as well as problem (antisocial) alcohol use and lower socioeconomic status (Dollard, 1945), and the association continues to be noted even today (Helzer, Burnam, & McEvoy, 1991). What is not often articulated is that these data indirectly indicate there is a link between higher rates of alcohol problems and the occurrence of poverty. Despite this long-standing connection, the precise nature of this linkage has yet to be understood. Does alcoholism (or problem drinking more generally) maintain chronic poverty? Does poverty drive the alcoholism? Or is there a third causal structure which accounts for both? Common social explanations have been based on a theory that posits the causal chain running from macrolevel process (poor social conditions) to microlevel (individual) alcohol problems and alcoholism. But the extent to which chronic economic disadvantage is either maintained, or even enhanced by high rates of alcohol use has not been examined. Only by way of longitudinal designs will it be possible to disentangle these processes.

Still another example: The field still has virtually no understanding of the relationship between biological and psychosocial variation. There is almost no across-domain work yet in the literature, although several groups (e.g., the Tarter-Moss group at Pittsburgh, the McGue et al., study in Minnesota, and the Schuckit et al. San Diego group) will eventually be able to address these questions. From both an etiological as well as an intervention perspective, it is essential that these phenomena be better understood.

Forgotten Populations

We began this chapter with the observation that alcohol use and alcohol-related difficulty were most prevalent among males, and also among males of younger ages. For eminently practical reasons, researchers have for a long time focused heavily on this subset of the universe of drinkers. But as the world changes, and as the population shifts, there is increasing evidence that women's problem alcohol use is increasing (Secretary of Health & Human Services, 1993), and that significant problem alcohol involvement among the aged appears also to be rising. These populations present special challenges but they also offer special opportunities, to test general theories of developmental process in arenas which will challenge existing models. To give but two examples: the old notion, that one could not develop alcohol problems in later life if one did not have some problematic experience earlier on in the life course appears now to be an inappropriate one (Atkinson et al., 1990; Sobell et al., 1993). As such, it raises questions about old notions of fixity versus plasticity of behavior over long spans of the life cycle. Similarly, the notion that women's patterns of drinking were different in a process sense, from men's (Bohman, Sigvardsson, & Cloninger, 1981) appears now to be in jeopardy, as new studies more carefully sample the range of variation that is present, but that, for women, may be harder to come by (Hill & Smith, 1991).

Nonetheless, with the application of developmental constructs as a guiding heuristic, we anticipate that the processes governing these newly uncovered variations in patterning of the world's most domesticated drug will become better understood. Along the way, this work should also inform us about the processes and mechanisms that more generally govern life course stability and change.

REFERENCES

Aboud, F. E. (1987). The development of ethnic self-identification and attitudes. In J. S. Phinney & M. J. Rotheram (Eds.), *Children's ethnic socialization* (pp. 32–55). Newbury Park, CA: Sage.

American Psychiatric Association (1987). *Diagnostic and statistical manual of mental disorders* (3rd ed. rev.). Washington, DC: American Psychiatric Association.

American Psychiatric Association (1994). *Diagnostic and statistical manual of mental disorders*, 4th ed. Washington, DC: American Psychiatric Association.

Andersson, T., & Magnusson, D. (1988). Drinking habits and alcohol abuse among young men: A prospective longitudinal study. *Journal of Studies on Alcohol, 49*, 245–252.

Andreasson, S., Allenbeck, P., Brandt, L., & Romelsjo, A. (1992). Antecedents and covariates of high school consumption in young men. *Alcoholism: Clinical and Experimental Research, 16*, 708–713.

Arnett, J. & Balle-Jensen, L. (1993). Cultural bases of risk behavior: Danish adolescents. *Child Development, 64*, 1842–1855.

Atkinson, R. M., Tolson, R. L., & Turner, J. A. (1990). Late versus early onset problem drinking in older men. *Alcoholism: Clinical and Experimental Research, 14*, 574–579.

Babor , T. F., & Dolinsky, Z. S. (1988). Alcoholic typologies: Historical evolution and empirical evaluation of some common classification schemes. In R. M. Rose, & J. Barret (Eds.), *Alcoholism: Origins and Outcome* (pp. 245–266). New York: Raven Press.

Babor, T. F., Hoffmann, M., DelBoca, F. K., Hesselbrock, V., Meyer, R. E., Dolinsky, Z. S., & Rounsaville, B. (1992). Types of alcoholics, I: Evidence for an empirically derived typology based on indicators of vulnerability and severity. *Archives of General Psychiatry, 49.* 599–608.

Babor, T. F., & Lauerman, R. J. (1986). Classification and forms of inebriety: Historical antecedents of alcoholic typologies. In M. Galanter (Ed.), *Recent Developments in Alcoholism, 5*, 113–144. New York: Plenum.

Baer, J. S., Marlatt, G. A., & McMahon, R. J. (Eds.). (1993). *Addictive behaviors across the life span: Prevention, treatment and policy.* Newbury Park, CA: Sage.

Barnett, W. S. (1993). Benefit-cost analysis of preschool education: Findings from a 25 year follow-up. *American Journal of Orthopsychiatry, 63*, 500–508.

Baron, R. M., & Kenny, D. A. (1986). The moderator-mediator variable distinction in social psychological research: Conceptual, strategic, and statistical considerations. *Journal of Personality and Social Psychology, 51*, 1173–1182.

Beardslee, W. R., Son, L., & Vaillant, G. E. (1986). Exposure to parental alcoholism during childhood and outcome during adulthood: A prospective longitudinal study. *British Journal of Psychiatry, 149*, 584–591.

Begleiter, H. (1992, June). A potential phenotypic marker for the development of alcoholism. Distinguished Research Awardee Address, Annual meeting of the Research Society on Alcoholism, San Diego, CA.

Begleiter, H., Gordis, E., Reich, T., Hesselbrock, V., Bucholz, K., Li, T-K., Porjesz, B., Edenberg, H., Goate, A., Schuckit, M., & Rice, J. (1993, June). Symposium on the Collaborative Genetics Study. Research Society on Alcoholism, San Antonio, TX.

Bernstein, I. S., Rose, R. M., & Gordon, T. P. (1974). Behavioral and environmental events influencing primate testosterone levels. *Journal of Human Evolution, 3*, 517–525.

Beutler, L. E., Patterson, K. M., Jacob, T., Shoham, V., Yost, E., & Rohrbaugh, M. (1993). Matching treatment to alcoholism subtypes. *Psychotherapy, 30*, 463–472.

Block, J., Block, J. H., & Keyes, S. (1988). Longitudinally foretelling drug usage in adolescence: Early childhood personality and environmental precursors. *Child Development, 59*, 336–355.

Bohman, M., Sigvardsson, S., & Cloninger, C. R. (1981). Maternal inheritance of alcohol abuse: cross-fostering analysis of adopted women. *The Archives of General Psychiatry, 38*, 965–969.

Boyd, G. M., Howard, J., & Zucker, R. A. (1994). Youth and risk: An integrated perspective. In R. A. Zucker, G. M. Boyd, & J. Howard (Eds.), *The development of alcohol problems: Exploring the biopsychosocial matrix of risk* (NIAAA Research Monograph 26, pp. v–xx). Rockville, MD: Department of Health and Human Services.

Brenner, M. H. (1973). *Mental illness and the economy.* Cambridge: Harvard University Press.

Brook, J. S., Gordon, A. S., Whiteman, M., & Cohen, P. (1986). Dynamics of childhood and adolescent personality traits and adolescent drug use. *Development Psychology, 22*, 403–413.

Brook, J. S., Whiteman, M., Brook, D. W., & Gordon, A. S. (1991). Sibling influences on adolescent drug use: Older brothers on younger brothers. *Journal of the American Academy of Child and Adolescent Psychiatry, 30*, 958–966.

Brook, J. S., Whiteman, M., Gordon, A. S., & Brook, D. W. (1990). The role of older brothers in younger brothers' drug use viewed in the context of parent and peer influences. *Journal of Genetic Psychology, 151*, 59–75.

Brook, J. S., Whiteman, M., Gordon, A. S., & Cohen, P. (1986). Some models and mechanisms for explaining the impact of maternal and adolescent characteristics on adolescent stage of drug use. *Developmental Psychology, 22*, 460–467.

Brook, J. S., Whiteman, M., Gordon, A. S., & Cohen, P. (1989). Changes in drug involvement: A longitudinal study of childhood and adolescent determinants. *Psychological Reports, 65,* 707–726.

Brown, S. A., Creamer, V. A., & Stetson, B. A. (1987). Adolescent alcohol expectancies in relation to personal and parental drinking patterns. *Journal of Abnormal Psychology, 96,* 117–121.

Cadoret, R. J., O'Gorman, T., Troughton, E., & Haywood, E. (1985). Alcoholism and antisocial personality: Interrelationships, genetic and environmental factors. *Archives of General Psychiatry, 42,* 161–167.

Caetano, R. (1986/87). Drinking and Hispanic-American family life. *Alcohol Health and Research World, 11,* 26–34.

Caetano, R. (1988) A comparative analysis of drinking among Hispanics in the United States, Spaniards in Madrid, and Mexicans in the Michoacan. In T. Harford, & L. Towle (Eds.), *Cultural influences and drinking patterns: A focus on Hispanic and Japanese populations* (pp. 273–311). Washington, DC: NIAAA Monographs.

Caetano, R. (1991). Findings from the 1984 National Survey of alcohol use among United States Hispanics. In W. B. Clark & M. E. Hilton (Eds.), *Alcohol in America* (pp. 293–307). New York: State University of New York Press.

Cahalan, D. (1970). *Problem drinkers.* San Francisco: Jossey-Bass.

Cairns, R. B. (1991). Multiple metaphors for a singular idea. *Developmental Psychology, 27,* 23–26.

Casswell, S., Gilmore, L. L., Silva, P., & Brasch, P. (1988). What children know about alcohol and how they know it. *British Journal of Addictions, 83,* 223–227.

Castle, D. J., & Murray, R. M. (1993). The epidemiology of late-onset schizophrenia. *Schizophrenia Bulletin, 19,* 691–700.

Chauvin, R. (1977). *Ethology: The biological study of animal behavior.* (Trans.) (pp. 47–48). New York: International University Press.

Christiansen, B. A., Smith, G. T., Roehling, P. V., & Goldman, M. S. (1989). Using alcohol expectancies to predict adolescent drinking behavior after one year. *Journal of Consulting and Clinical Psychology, 57,* 93–99.

Cicchetti, D. (1984). The emergence of developmental psychopathology. *Child Development, 55,* 1–7.

Cicchetti, D. (1993). Developmental psychopathology: Reactions, reflections, projections. *Developmental Review, 13,* 471–502.

Clark, W., & Cahalan, D. (1976). Changes in problem drinking over a four-year span. *Addictive Behaviors, 1,* 251–259.

Clark, W. B., & Hilton, M. E. (1991). *Alcohol in America.* New York: State University of New York Press.

Cleckley, H. (1950). *The mask of sanity.* St. Louis: Mosby.

Cloninger, R. (1987). Neurogenetic adaptive mechanisms in alcoholism. *Science, 236.* 410–416.

Cloninger, R., Bohman, M., & Sigvardsson, S. (1981). Inheritance of substance abuse: Cross-fostering analysis of adopted men. *Archives of General Psychiatry, 38,* 861–867.

Colder, C. R., & Chassin, L. (in press). The stress and negative affect model of adolescent alcohol use and the moderating effects of behavioral undercontrol. *Journal of Studies on Alcohol.*

Dabbs, J. M., Jr., & Morris, R. (1990). Testosterone, social class, and antisocial behavior in a sample of 4,462 men. *Psychological Science, 1,* 209–211.

Daitzman, R. J., & Zuckerman, M. (1980). Disinhibitory sensation seeking, personality and gonadal hormones. *Personality and Individual Differences, 1,* 103–108.

Day, N. L. (1992). The effects of prenatal exposure to alcohol. *Alcohol Health and Research World, 16,* 238–244.

Dielman, T. E., Butchart, B. A., & Shope, J. A. (1993). Structural equation model tests of patterns of family interaction, peer alcohol use, and intrapersonal predictors of adolescent alcohol use and misuse. *Journal of Drug Education, 23,* 273–316.

Dishion, T. J., Capaldi, D. M., & Ray, J. (1993). *A multivariate model for early-onset substance use in boys: Direct and indirect effects of prior antisocial behavior.* Unpublished paper, Oregon Social Learning Center, Eugene, OR.

Dollard, J. (1945). Drinking mores of the social classes. In *Alcohol, science and society: Twenty-nine lectures with discussions as given at the Yale Summer School of Alcohol Studies* (pp. 95–104). New Haven: Quarterly Journal of Studies on Alcohol.

Donovan, J. E., & Jessor, R. (1983). Problem drinking and the dimension of involvement with drugs: A Guttman scalogram analysis of adolescent drug use. *American Journal of Public Health, 73,* 543–552.

Donovan, J. E., & Jessor, R. (1985). Structure of problem behavior in adolescence and young adulthood. *Journal of Consulting and Clinical Psychology, 53,* 890–904.

Donovan, J. E., Jessor, R., & Costa, F. (1988). The syndrome of problem behavior in adolescence: A replication. *Journal of Consulting and Clinical Psychology, 56,* 762–765.

Donovan, J. E., Jessor, R., & Jessor, S. L. (1983). Problem drinking in adolescence and early adulthood: A follow-up study. *Journal of Studies on Alcohol, 44,* 109–137.

Drew, L. R. H. (1968). Alcoholism as a self-limiting disease. *Quarterly Journal of Studies on Alcohol, 29,* 956–967.

Earls, F., Reich, W., Jung, K. G., & Cloninger, C. R. (1988). Psychopathology in children of alcoholic and antisocial parents. *Alcohol: Clinical and Experimental Research, 12,* 481–487.

Edwards, G. (1984). Drinking in longitudinal perspective: Career and natural history. *British Journal of Addiction, 79,* 175–183.

Edwards, G., & Gross, M. M. (1976). Alcohol dependence: Provisional description of a clinical syndrome. *British Medical Journal, 1,* 1058–1061.

Ellis, D. A. (1993). *Typological differences in patterns of risk among young children of alcoholics.* Unpublished doctoral dissertation, Department of Psychology, Michigan State University, East Lansing, MI.

Ensminger, M. E., Brown, C. H., & Kellam, S. G. (1982). Sex differences in antecedents of substance use among adolescents. *Journal of Social Issues, 38,* 25–42.

Ensminger, M. E., Kellam, S. G., & Rubin, B. R. (1983). School and family origins of delinquency: Comparison by sex. In S. A. Mednick (Ed.), *Prospective studies of crime and delinquency.* Boston: Kluwer-Nijhoff.

Erikson, E. H. (1956). The problem of ego identity. *Journal of the American Psychoanalytic Association, 4,* 56–121.

Field, P. B. (1991). A new cross-cultural study of drunkenness. In D. J. Pittman & H. R. White (Eds.), *Society, culture, and drinking patterns reexamined* (pp. 32–61). New Brunswick, NJ: Rutgers Center of Alcohol Studies.

Fillmore, K. M. (1985). The social victims of drinking. *British Journal of Addiction, 80,* 307–314.

Fillmore, K. M. (1987). Prevalence, incidence, and chronicity of drinking patterns and problems among men as a function of age: A longitudinal and cohort analysis. *British Journal of the Addictions, 82,* 77–83.

Fillmore, K. M., & Midanik, L. (1984). Chronicity of drinking problems among men: A longitudinal study. *Journal of Studies of Alcohol, 45,* 228–236.

Finney, J. W., & Moos, R. H. (1984). Life stressors and problem drinking among older persons. In M. Galanter (Ed.), *Recent developments in alcoholism, Vol. 2.* New York: Plenum.

Fitzgerald, H. E., Sullivan, L. A., Ham, H. P., Zucker, R. A., Bruckel, S., & Schneider, A. (1993). Predictors of behavior problems in three-year-old sons of alcoholics: Early evidence for the onset of risk. *Child Development, 64,* 110–123.

Fitzgerald, H. E., & Zucker, R. A. (in press). Socioeconomic status, antisociality, and alcoholism: Stucturing developmental pathways of addiction. In H. E. Fitzgerald, B. M. Lester, & B. Zuckerman (Eds.), *Children of poverty.* New York: Garland.

Ford, D. H., & Lerner, R. M. (1992). *Developmental systems theory.* Newbury Park, CA: Sage.

Gaines, L. S., Brooks, P. H., Maisto, S., & Dietrich, M. (1988). The development of children's knowledge of alcohol and the role of drinking. *Journal of Applied Developmental Psychology, 9,* 441–457.

Garmezy, N., & Streitman, S. (1974). Children at risk: The search for the antecedents of schizophrenia. Part I. Conceptual models and research methods. *Schizophrenia Bulletin, No. 8,* 14–90.

Golding, J. M., Burnam, M. A., Benjamin, B., & Wells, K. B. (1992). Reasons for drinking, alcohol use, and alcoholism among Mexican-Americans and non-Hispanic whites. *Psychology of Addictive Behaviors, 6,* 155–167.

Gollin, E. S., Stahl, G., & Morgan, E. (1989). On the uses of the concept of normality in developmental biology and psychology. In H. W. Reese (Ed.), *Advances in child development and behavior* (pp. 49–71). New York: Academic Press.

Gomberg, E. S. L. (1982). Alcohol use and alcohol problems among the elderly. *NIAAA Alcohol and Health Monograph 4. Special Population Issues.*

Gomberg, E. S. L. (1989). Drugs, alcohol, and aging. *Research advances in alcohol and drug problems* (Vol. 10). New York: Plenum.

Gomberg, E. L., White, H. R., & Carpenter, J. A. (Eds.). (1982). *Alcohol, science and society revisted.* Ann Arbor: University of Michigan Press.

Gonzalez, F., Zucker, R. A., & Fitzgerald, H. E. (1993). *Adaptation and psychopathology among drug-involved and non-drug-involved alcoholic men: Testing a devlopmental hypothesis.* Unpublished manuscript, Michigan State University, East Lansing, MI.

Gottlieb, G. (1991a). Experiential canalization of behavior development: Theory. *Developmental Psychology, 27,* 4–13.

Gottlieb, G. (1991b). Epigenetic systems view of human development. *Developmental Psychology, 27,* 33–34.

Grant, B. F., Harford, T. C., Chou, P., Pickering, R., Dawson, D. A., Stinson, F. S., & Noble, J. (1991). Epidemiologic Bulletin No. 27: Prevalence of DSM-III-R alcohol abuse and dependence: United States, 1988. *Alcohol Health and Research World, 15,* 91–96.

Grant, B. F., Harford, T. C., & Grigson, M. B. (1988). Stability of alcohol consumption among youth: A national longitudinal survey. *Journal of Studies on Alcohol, 49,* 253–260.

Grant, B. F., Harford, T. C., Hasin, D. S., Chou, P., & Pickering, R. (1992). DSM-III-R and the proposed DSM-IV alcohol use disorders, United States 1988: A nosological comparison. *Alcoholism: Clinical and Experimental Research, 16,* 215–221.

Hasin, D. S., Grant, B., & Endicott, J. (1990). The natural history of alcohol abuse: Implications for definitions of alcohol use disorders. *American Journal of Psychiatry, 147,* 1537–1541.

Hawkins, J. D., Catalano, R. F., & Miller, J. Y. (1992). Risk and protective factors for alcohol and other drug problems in adolescence and early adulthood: Implications for substance abuse prevention. *Psychological Bulletin, 112,* 64–105.

Heath, D. B. (1991). Continuity and change in drinking patterns of the Bolivian Camba. In D. J. Pittman & H. R. White (Eds.), *Society, culture, and drinking patterns* (pp. 78–108). New Brunswick, NJ: Rutgers Center of Alcohol Studies.

Helzer, J. E., Burnam, A., & McEvoy, L. T. (1991). Alcohol abuse and dependence. In L. N. Robins & D. A. Regier (Eds.), *Psychiatric disorders in America: The epidemiologic catchment area studies* (pp. 81–115). New York: Free Press.

Helzer, J. E., & Canino, G. J. (Eds.). (1992). *Alcoholism in North America, Europe, and Asia.* New York: Oxford.

Helzer, J. E., & Pryzbeck, T. R. (1988). The co-occurrence of alcoholism with other psychiatric disorders in the current population and its impact on treatment. *Journal of Studies on Alcohol, 49,* 219–224.

Henderson, B. E., Ross, R. K., & Pike, M. C. (1991). Toward the primary prevention of cancer. *Science, 254,* 1131–1138.

Herd, D. (1991). Drinking patterns in the Black population. In W. B. Clark & M. E. Hilton (Eds.), *Alcohol in America* (pp. 308–328). New York: State University of New York Press.

Hesselbrock, V. M., Hesselbrock, M. N., & Stabenau, J. B. (1985). Alcoholism in men patients subtyped by family history and antisocial personality. *Journal of Studies on Alcohol, 46,* 59–64.

Hesselbrock, V. M., Hesselbrock, M. N., & Workman-Daniels, K. L. (1986). Effect of major depression and antisocial personality on alcoholism: Course and motivational patterns. *Journal of Studies on Alcohol, 47,* 207–212.

Hill, S. Y., & Smith, T. R. (1991). Evidence for genetic mediation of alcoholism in women. *Journal of Substance Abuse, 3,* 159–174.

Hilton, M. E. (1991). Regional diversity in United States drinking practices. In W. B. Clark & M. E. Hilton (Eds.), *Alcohol in America* (pp. 256–280). New York: State University of New York Press.

Hoffman, L. W. (1991). The influence of the family environment on personality: Accounting for sibling differences. *Psychological Bulletin, 110,* 187–203.

Huba, G. J., & Bentler, P. M. (1980). The role of peer and adult models for drug taking at different stages in adolescence. *Journal of Youth and Adolescence, 9,* 449–465.

Institute of Medicine (1987). *Causes and consequences of alcohol problems: An agenda for research.* Washington, DC: National Academy Press.

Jacob, T., & Leonard, K. (1986). Psychosocial functioning in children of alcoholic fathers. *Journal of Studies on Alcohol, 47,* 373–380.

Jellinek, E. M. (1960). *The disease concept of alcoholism.* New Haven, CT: Hillhouse Press.

Jessor, R., Donovan, J. E., & Costa, F. M. (1991). *Beyond adolescence: Problem behavior and young adult development.* New York: Cambridge University Press.

Jessor, R., Graves, T. D., Hanson, R. C., & Jessor, S. L. (1968). *Society, personality, and deviant behavior: A study of a tri-ethnic community.* New York: Holt, Rinehart & Winston.

Jessor, R., & Jessor, S. L. (1975). Adolescent development and the onset of drinking: A longitudinal study. *Journal of Studies on Alcohol, 36,* 27–51.

Jessor, R., & Jessor, S. L. (1977). *Problem behavior and psychosocial development: A longitudinal study of youth.* New York: Academic Press.

Johnson, J. L., & Rolf, J. E. (1990). When children change: Research perspectives on children of alcholics. In R. L. Collins, K. E. Leonard, & J. S. Searles (Eds.), *Alcohol and the family: Research and clinical perspectives* (pp. 162–193). New York: Guilford.

Johnston, L. D., O'Malley, P. M., & Bachman, J. G. (1993). *National survey results on drug use from the Monitoring the Future study, 1975–1992: Vol. 1: Secondary School Students.* Rockville, MD: National Institute on Drug Abuse.

Kandel, D. B. (1975). Stages in adolescent involvement in drug use. *Science, 190,* 912–914.

Kandel, D. B. (1978). Convergences in prospective longitudinal surveys of drug use in normal populations. In D. B. Kandel (Ed.), *Longitudinal research on drug use* (pp. 3–38). Washington, DC: Hemisphere.

Kandel, D. B. (1988). Issues of sequencing of adolescent drug use and other problem behaviors. *Drugs and Society, 3,* 55–76.

Kandel, D. B., & Yamaguchi, K. (1985). Developmental patterns of the use of legal, illegal, and medically prescribed psychotropic drugs from adolescence to young adulthood. In C. L. Jones & R. J. Battjes (Eds.), *Etiology of drug abuse: Implications for prevention.* N.I.D.A. Monograph 56 (pp. 193–235). Rockville, MD: National Institute on Drug Abuse.

Kellam, S. G., Brown, C. H., Rubin, B. R., & Ensminger, M. E. (1983). Paths leading to teenage psychiatric symptoms and substance use: Developmental epidemiological studies in Woodlawn. In S. B. Guze, F. J. Earls, & J. E. Barrett (Eds.), *Childhood psychopathology and development* (pp. 17–47). New York: Plenum.

Kellam, S. G., Ensminger, M. E., & Simon, M. B. (1980). Mental health in first grade and teenage drug, alcohol, and cigarette use. *Drug and Alcohol Dependency, 5,* 273–304.

Kendler, K. S., Heath, A. C., Neale, M. C., Kessler, R. C., & Eaves, L. J. (1993). Alcoholism and major depression in women: A twin study of the causes of comorbidity. *Archives of General Psychiatry, 50,* 690–698.

Kitano, H. H. L., & Chi, L. (1986/87). Asian-Americans and alcohol use. *Alcohol Health and Research World, 11,* 42–47.

Knupfer, G. (1972). Ex-problem drinkers. In M. Roff, L. Robins, & M. Pollock (Eds.), *Life history research in psychopathology* (Vol. 2, pp. 256–280). Minneapolis: University of Minnesota Press.

Krausz, M., & Muller-Thomsen, T. (1993). Schizophrenia with onset in adolescence: An 11-year follow-up. *Schizophrenia Bulletin, 19,* 831–841.

Laszlo, G. (1972). *The systems view of the world.* New York: Braziller.

Lee, C. K. (1992). Alcoholism in Korea. In J. E. Helzer & G. J. Canino (Eds.), *Alcoholism in North America, Europe, and Asia* (pp. 247–263). New York: State University of New York Press.

Lerner, J. V., & Lerner, R. M. (1983). Temperament and adaptation across life: Theoretical and empirical issues. In P. B. Baltes & O. G. Brim, Jr. (Eds.), *Lifespan development and behavior* (Vol. 5, pp. 197–231). New York: Academic Press.

Lerner, J. V., & Vicary, J. (1984). Difficult temperament and drug use: Analysis from the New York Longitudinal Study. *Journal of Drug Education, 14,* 1–8.

Levine, H. G. (1978). The discovery of addiction; changing conceptions of habitual drunkenness in America. *Journal of Studies on Alcohol, 39* (1), 143–174.

Levine, R. L., & Fitzgerald, H. E. (1992). Living systems, dynamical systems, and cybernetics: Historical overview and introduction to system dynamics. In R. L. Levine & H. E. Fitzgerald, (Eds.), *Analysis of dynamic psychological systems: Basic approaches to general systems, dynamic systems, and cybernetics* (Vol. 1, pp. 1–6). New York: Plenum.

Levy, J. E., & Kunitz, S. J. (1974). *Indian drinking.* New York: Wiley.

Lex, B. W. (1987). Review of alcohol problems in ethnic minority groups. *Journal of Consulting and Clinical Psychology, 55,* 293–300.

Loeber, R., & Wikstrom, P. H. (1993). Individual pathways to crime in different types of neighborhoods. In D. P. Farrington, R. J. Sampson, & P. H. Wikstrom (Eds.), *Integrating individual and ecological aspects of crime* (pp. 169–204). (BRA-report 1993:1).

Loevinger, J. (1966). The meaning and measurement of ego development. *American Psychologist, 21,* 195–206.

Madden, T. M. (1884). Alcoholism in childhood and youth. *British Medical Journal* (Proceedings of the 52nd Annual Meeting), 358–359.

Maddox, G. L., & McCall, B. C. (1964). *Drinking among teenagers.* New Brunswick, NJ: Rutgers Center of Alcohol Studies.

Maguin, E., Zucker, R. A., & Fitzgerald, H. E. (1994). The path to alcohol problems through conduct problems: A family based approach to very early intervention with risk. *Journal of Research on Adolescence, 4,* 249–269.

Manson, S. M., Shore, J. H., Baron, A. E., Ackerson, L., & Neligh, G. (1992). Alcohol abuse and dependence among American Indians. In J. E. Helzer & G. J. Canino (Eds.), *Alcoholism in North America, Europe, and Asia* (pp. 113–130). New York: Oxford University Press.

Margulies, R. Z., Kessler, R. C., & Kandel, D. B. (1977). A longitudinal study of onset of drinking among high school students. *Journal of Studies on Alcohol, 38,* 897–912.

Marlatt, G. A., & Tapert, S. (1993). Harm reduction: Reducing the risks of addictive behaviors. In J. S. Baer, G. A. Marlatt, & R. J. McMahon (Eds.), *Addictive behaviors across the life span: Prevention, treatment, and policy issues* (pp. 243–273). Newbury Park, CA: Sage.

Matejcek, Z., Dytrych, Z., & Schuller, V. (1988). The Prague cohort through age nine. In H. P. David, Z. Dytrych, Z. Matejcek, & V. Schuller, (Eds.), *Born unwanted: Developmental effects of denied abortion* (pp. 53–86). Prague: Avicenum, Czechoslovak Medical Press.

McClintock, J. M. (1981). Social control of the ovarian cycle and the function of estrous synchrony. *American Zoologist, 21,* 243–256.

McCord, J. (1988). Identifying developmental paradigms leading to alcoholism. *Journal of Studies on Alcohol, 49,* 357–362.

McGee, L., & Newcomb, M. D. (1992). General deviance syndrome: Expanded hierarchical evaluations at four ages from early adolescence to adulthood. *Journal of Consulting and Clinical Psychology, 60,* 766–776.

McGue, M. (1994). Evidence for causal mechanisms from human genetics data bases. In R. A. Zucker, G. M. Boyd, & J. Howard, (Eds.), *The development of alcohol problems: Exploring the biopsychosocial matrix of risk* (Research Monograph No. 26, pp. 1–40). Rockville, MD: National Institute on Alcohol Abuse and Alcoholism.

McGue, M., Pickens, R. W., & Svikis, D. S. (1992). Sex and age effects on the inheritance of alcohol problems: A twin study. *Journal of Abnormal Psychology, 101,* 3–17.

McLellan, A. T., Luborsky, L., Cacciola, J., Griffith, J. E., Evans, F., & Barr, H. (1985). New data from the Addiction Severity Index: Reliability and validity in three centers. *Journal of Nervous and Mental Disorders, 173,* 412–423.

Meehl, P. E. (1990). Schizotaxia as an open concept. In A. I. Rabin, R. A. Zucker, R. A. Emmons, & S. Frank (Eds.), *Studying persons and lives* (pp. 248–303). New York: Springer.

Merikangas, K. R., Leckman, J. F., Prusoff, B., Pauls, D. L., & Weissman, M. M. (1985). Familial transmission of depression and alcoholism. *Archives of General Psychiatry, 42,* 367–371.

Miller, J. G. (1978). *Living systems.* New York: McGraw-Hill.

Miller, J. G., & Miller, J. L. (1992). Cybernetics, general systems theory, and living systems theory. In R. L. Levine & H. E. Fitzgerald, (Eds.), *Analysis of dynamic psychological systems.* (pp. 9–34). New York: Plenum.

Miller, P. M., Smith, G. T., & Goldman, M. S. (1990). Emergence of alcohol expectancies in childhood: A possible critical period. *Journal of Studies on Alcohol, 51,* 343–349.

Miller, W. R., & Page, A. C. (1991). Warm turkey: Other routes to abstinence. *Journal of Substance Abuse Treatment, 8,* 227–232.

Mitchell, J. E., Hong, K. M., & Corman, C. (1979). Childhood onset of alcohol abuse. *American Journal of Orthopsychiatry, 49,* 511–513.

Moses, H. D., Zucker, R. A., & Fitzgerald, H. E. (1993, March). Moderators of the effects of father alcohol problems on child behavior problems (abstract). *Abstracts of the Society for Research in Child Development:* Biennial meetings of the Society for Research in Child Development, New Orleans, LA.

Nakawatase, T. V., Yamamoto, J., & Sasao, T. (1993). The association between fast-flushing response and alcohol use among Japanese Americans. *Journal of Studies on Alcohol, 54,* 48–53.

National Institute on Alcohol Abuse and Alcoholism (1985). *Alcoholism: An inherited disease.* (DHHS Publication No. ADM 85–1426). Washington, DC: U.S. Government Printing Office.

Newcomb, M. D., & Bentler, P. M. (1988). *Consequences of adolescent drug use: Impact on the lives of young adults.* Newbury Park, CA: Sage.

Newcomb, M. D., Huba, G. J., & Bentler, P. M. (1983). Mothers' influence on the drug use of their children: Confirmatory tests of direct modeling and mediational theories. *Developmental Psychology, 19,* 714–726.

Newlin, D. B. (1994). Alcohol challenge in high-risk individuals. In R. A. Zucker, G. M. Boyd, & J. Howard (Eds.), *The development of alcohol problems: Exploring the biopsychosocial matrix of risk* (Research Monograph No. 26, pp. 47–68). Rockville, MD: National Institute on Alcohol Abuse and Alcoholism.

Noll, R. B., Zucker, R. A., Fitzgerald, H. E., & Curtis, W. J. (1992). Cognitive and motor achievement of sons of alcoholic fathers and controls: The early childhood years. *Developmental Psychology, 28,* 665–675.

Noll, R. B., Zucker, R. A., & Greenberg, G. S. (1990). Identification of alcohol by smell among preschoolers: Evidence for early socialization about drugs occurring in the home. *Child Development, 61,* 1520–1527.

Nylander, I. (1960). Children of alcoholic fathers. *Acta Paediatrica Scandinavica (Suppl.), 49:*121.

Oetting, E. R., Edwards, R. W., & Beauvais, F. (1989). Drugs and Native-American youth. *Drugs and Society, 3,* 5–38.

Olweus, D. (1983). Testosterone in the development of antisocial behavior in adolescents. In K. T. VanDusen & S. A. Mednick (Eds.), *Prospective studies of crime and delinquency.* Boston: Kluwer-Nijhoff.

O'Malley, P. M., & Wagenaar, A. C. (1991). Effects of minimum drinking age laws on alcohol use, related behaviors, and traffic crash involvement among American youth: 1976–1987. *Journal of Studies on Alcohol, 52,* 478–491.

Pallas, D. M. (1992). *The ecological distribution of alcoholic families: A community study in Mid-Michigan.* Unpublished master's thesis, University of Wisconsin, Oshkosh.

Patterson, G. R. (1993). Orderly change in a stable world: The antisocial trait as a chimera. *Journal of Consulting and Clinical Psychology, 61,* 911–919.

Patterson, G. R., DeBaryshe, B. D., & Ramsey, E. (1989). A developmental perspective on antisocial behavior. *American Psychologist, 44,* 329–335.

Patterson, G. R., & Yoerger, K. (1993, October). *Differentiating outcomes and histories for early and late onset arrests.* Paper presented at the annual conference for the American Society of Criminology, Phoenix, AZ.

Penick, E. C., Powell, B. J., Liskow, B. I., Jackson, J. O., & Nickel, E. J. (1988). The stability of coexisting psychiatric syndromes in alcoholic men after one year. *Journal of Studies on Alcohol, 49,* 395–405.

Pentz, M. A. (1993). Comparative effects of community-based drug abuse prevention. In J. S. Baer, G. A. Marlatt, & R. J. McMahon (Eds.), *Addictive behaviors across the life span: Prevention, treatment, and policy issues* (pp. 69–87). Newbury Park, CA: Sage.

Pihl, R. O., & Peterson, J. B. (1991). Attention-deficit hyperactivity disorder, childhood conduct disorder, and alcoholism: Is there an association? *Alcohol Health and Research World, 15,* 25–31.

Pittman, D., & Snyder, C. R. (Eds.). (1968). *Society, culture and drinking patterns.* New York: Wiley.

Pittman, D., & White, H. R. (Eds.). (1992). *Society, culture and drinking patterns re-examined.* New Brunswick, NJ: Rutgers Center of Alcohol Studies.

Polich, J., Pollock, V. E., & Bloom, F. E. (1994). Meta-analysis of P300 amplitude from males at risk for alcoholism. *Psychological Bulletin, 115,* 55–73.

Powell, B. J., Penick, E. C., Othmer, E., Bingham, S. F., & Rice, A. S. (1982). Prevalence of additional psychiatric syndromes among male alcoholics. *Journal of Clinical Psychiatry, 43,* 404–407.

Project Match Research Group (1993). Project MATCH: Rationale and methods for a multisite clinical trial matching patients to alcoholism treatment. *Alcoholism: Clinical and Experimental Research, 17,* 1130–1145.

Pulkkinen, L. (1983). Youthful smoking and drinking in a longitudinal perspective. *Journal of Youth and Adolescence, 12,* 253–283.

Quarterly Journal of Studies on Alcohol (1945). *Alcohol, science and society.* New Haven, CT: Author.

Regier, D. A., Farmer, M. E., Rae, D. S., Locke, B. Z., Keith, S. J., Judd, L. L., & Goodwin, F. K. (1990). Comorbidity of mental disorders with alcohol and other drug use. *Journal of the American Medical Association, 264,* 19, 2511–2518.

Reich, T. R., Cloninger, C. R., Van Eerdewegh, P., Rice, J. P., & Mullaney, J. (1988). Secular trends in the familial transmission of alcoholism. *Alcoholism: Clinical and Experimental Research, 12,* 458–464.

Richters, J. E., & Cicchetti, D. (1993). Mark Twain meets DSM-III-R: Conduct disorder, development, and the concept of harmful dysfunction. Special issue: Toward a developmental perspective on conduct disorder. *Development and Psychopathology, 5,* 5–29.

Robins, L. N. (1984). The natural history of adolescent drug use. *American Journal of Public Health, 74.* 656–657.

Robins, L. N. (1993). Childhood conduct problems, adult psychopathology, and crime. In S. Hodgins (Ed.), *Mental disorder and crime* (pp. 173–193). Newbury Park, CA: Sage.

Robins, L. N., & Regier, D. A. (1991). *Psychiatric disorders in America: The epidemiologic catchment area study.* New York: Free Press.

Roizen, R., Cahalan, D., & Shanks, P. (1978). "Spontaneous remission" among untreated problem drinkers. In D. B. Kandel (Ed.), *Longitudinal research on drug use* (pp. 197–221). Washington, DC: Wiley.

Rolf, J. E., Johnson, J. L., Israel, E., Baldwin, J., & Chandra, A. (1988). Depressive affect in school-aged children of alcoholics. *British Journal of Addiction, 83,* 841–848.

Ronan, L. (1986/87). Alcohol-related health risks among black Americans. *Alcohol Health and Research World, 11,* 36–39, 65.

Root, M. P. P. (1992). Within, between, and beyond race. In M. P. P. Root (Ed.), *Racially mixed people in America* (pp. 3–11). Newbury Park, CA: Sage.

Rosin, A. J., & Glatt, M. M. (1971). Alcohol excess in the elderly. *Quarterly Journal of Studies on Alcohol, 32,* 53–59.

Rotheram, M. J., & Phinney, J. S. (1987). Introduction: Definitions and perspectives in the study of children's ethnic sociliation. In J. S. Phinney & M. J. Rotheram (Eds.), *Children's ethnic socialization.* (pp. 10–28). Newbury Park, CA: Sage.

Russell, M. (1990). Prevalence of alcoholism among children of alcoholics. In M. Windle & J. S. Searles (Eds.), *Children of alcoholics: Critical perspectives* (pp. 9–48). New York: Guilford.

Rutter, M. (1987). Psychological resilience and protective mechanisms. *American Journal of Orthopsychiatry, 57,* 316–331.

Rutter, M. (1990). Psychosocial resilience and protective mechanisms. In J. Rolf, A. S. Masten, D. Cicchetti, K. H. Nuechterlein, & S. Weintraub (Eds.), *Risk and protective factors in the development of psychopathology* (pp. 182–214). Cambridge: Cambridge University Press.

Rydelius, P. (1981). Children of alcoholic fathers: Their social adjustment and their health status over 20 years. *Acta Paediatrica Scandinavica, 286,* 1–83.

Sadava, S. W. (1985). Problem-behavior theory and consumption and consequences of alcohol use. *Journal of Studies on Alcohol, 46,* 392–397.

Salthe, S. N. (1985). *Evolving hierarchical systems: Their structure and representation.* New York: Columbia University Press.

Sameroff, A. J., & Chandler, M. J. (1975). Perinatal risk and the continuum of caretaker casualty. In F. D. Horowitz, M. Heatherington, S. Scarr-Salaptek, & G. Siegel (Eds.), *Review of child development research* (Vol. 4). Chicago: University of Chicago Press.

Sayette, M. A. (1993). An appraisal-disruption model of alcohol's effects on stress responses in social drinkers. *Psychological Bulletin, 114,* 459–476.

Scarr, S., & McCartney, K. (1983). How people make their own environments: A theory of genotype—environment effects. *Child Development, 54,* 424–435.

Schubert, D. S., Wolf, A. W., Patterson, M. B., Grande, T. P., & Pendleton, L. (1988). A statistical evaluation of the literature regarding the associations among alcoholism, drug abuse, and antisocial personality disorder. *International Journal of the Addictions, 23,* 797–808.

Schuckit, M. A. (1988). Reactions to alcohol in sons of alcoholics and controls. *Alcoholism: Clinical and Experimental Research, 12,* 465–470.

Schuckit, M. A. (1994). Low levels of response to alcohol as a predictor of future alcoholism. *American Journal of Psychiatry, 151,* 184–189.

Schuckit, M. A., Irwin, M., & Brown, S. A. (1990). The history of anxiety symptoms among 171 primary alcoholics. *Journal of Studies on Alcohol, 51,* 34–41.

Schuckit, M. A., Pitts, F. N., & Reich, T. (1969) Alcoholism, I: Two types of alcoholism in women. *Archives of General Psychiatry, 20,* 301–306.

Schuckit, M. A., Risch, S. C., & Gold, E. O. (1988). Alcohol consumption, ACTH level, and family history of alcoholism. *American Journal of Psychiatry, 145,* 1391–1395.

Schulenberg, J., Wadsworth, K. N., O'Malley, P. M., Bachman, J. G., & Johnston, L. D. (1994). *Adolescent risk factors for binge drinking during the transition to young adulthood: Variable- and pattern-centered approaches to understanding change.* Unpublished manuscript, Institute for Social Research, University of Michigan.

Searles, J. S. (1990). The contribution of genetic factors to the development of alcoholism: A critical review. In R. L. Collins, E. K. Leonard, & J. S. Searles, (Eds.), *Alcohol and alcoholism* (Vol. 1). New York: Oxford University Press.

Secretary of Health and Human Services. (1993). *Eighth Special Report to the U.S. Congress on alcohol and health.* Washington, DC: U.S. Department of Health and Human Services.

Seilhamer, R. A., & Jacob, T. (1990). Family factors and adjustment of children of alcoholics. In M. Windle & J. S. Searles (Eds.), *Children of alcoholics: Critical perspectives* (pp. 168–186). New York: Guilford.

Sher, K. J. (1991). *Children of alcoholics: A critical appraisal of theory and research.* Chicago: University of Chicago Press.

Sher, K. J., Walitzer, K. S., Wood, P. K., & Brent, E. E. (1991). Characteristics of children of alcoholics: Putative risk factors, substance use and abuse, and psychopathology. *Journal of Abnormal Psychology, 100,* 427–448.

Silva, P. A. (1990). The Dunedin multidisciplinary health and development study: A fifteen year longitudinal study. *Paediatric and Perinatal Epidemiology, 4,* 96–127.

Silvern, L. E. (1984). Emotional-behavioral disorders: A failure of system functions. In E. S. Gollin (Ed.), *Malformations of development* (pp. 95–152). New York: Academic Press.

Skinner, H. A., & Allen, B. A. (1982). Alccohol dependence syndrome: measurement and validation. *Journal of Abnormal Psychology, 91,* 199–209.

Skog, O.-J. (1985). The collectivity of drinking cultures: A theory of the distribution of alcohol consumption. *British Journal of Addiction, 80,* 83–99.

Skog, O.-J., & Duckert, F. (1993). The stability of alcoholics' and heavy drinkers' consumption: A longitudinal study. *Journal of Studies on Alcohol, 53,* 178–188.

Sobell, L. C., Cunningham, J. A., Sobell, M. B., & Toneatto, T. (1993). A life-span perspective on natural recovery (self-change) from alcohol problems. In J. S. Baer, G. A. Marlatt, & R. J. McMahon (Eds.), *Addictive behaviors across the life span: Prevention, treatment, and policy* (pp. 34–66). Newbury Park, CA: Sage.

Sobell, M. B., & Sobell, L. C. (1993). Treatment for problem drinkers: A public health priority. In J. S. Baer, G. A. Marlatt, & R. J. McMahon (Eds.), *Addictive behaviors across the life span: Prevention, treatment, and policy issues* (pp. 138–157). Newbury Park, CA: Sage.

Spitz, R. A. (1945). Hospitalism: An inquiry into the genesis of psychiatric conditions in early childhood. *Psychoanalytic Study of the Child, 1,* 153–172.

Sroufe, L. A., & Rutter, M. (1984). The domain of developmental psychopathology. *Child Development, 55,* 17–29.

Stabenau, J. R. (1990). Additive independent factors that predict risk for alcoholism. *Journal of Studies on Alcohol, 51,* 164–174.

Steinglass, P., Bennett, L. A., Wolin, S. J., & Reiss, D. (1987). *The alcoholic family.* New York: Basic Books.

Stone, W. S., & Gottesman, I. I. (1993). A perspective on the search for the causes of alcoholism: Slow down the rush to genetical judgements. *Neurology, Psychiatry, and Brain Research, 1,* 123–132.

Streissguth, A. P., Aase, J. M., Clarren, S. K., Randels, S. P., LaDue, R., & Smith, D. F. (1991). Fetal alcohol syndrome in adolescents and adults. *Journal of the American Medical Association, 265,* 1961–1967.

Streissguth, A. P., Clarren, S. K., & Jones, K. L. (1985). Natural history of the fetal alcohol syndrome: A 10-year follow-up of eleven patients. *Lancet, 2,* 85–91.

Substance Abuse and Mental Health Services Administration. (1993). *National household survey on drug abuse: 1992.* Washington, DC: U.S. Dept. of Health and Human Services, Author (DHHS Publication No. (SMA) 93–2053).

Tarter, R. E. (1988). Are there inherited traits that predispose to substance abuse? *Journal of Consulting and Clinical Psychology, 56,* 189–196.

Tarter, R. E., Alterman, A. I., & Edwards, K. L. (1985). Vulnerability to alcoholism in men: A behavior-genetic perspective. *Journal of Studies on Alcohol, 46,* 329–356.

Tarter, R. E., Blackson, T., Martin, C., Loeber, R., & Moss, H. B. (1993). Characteristics and correlates of child discipline practices in substance abuse and normal families. *American Journal on Addictions, 2,* 18–25.

Tarter, R. E., Moss, H. B., & Vanukov, M. W. (in press). Behavior genetic perspective of alcoholism etiology. In H. Begleiter & B. Kissin (Eds.), *Alcohol and alcoholism* (Vol. 1). New York: Oxford University Press.

Temple, M., & Fillmore, K. M. (1985/86). The variability of drinking patterns and problems among young men, age 16–31: A longitudinal study. *International Journal of the Addictions, 20,* 1595–1620.

Thelen, E. (1992). Development as a dynamic system. *Current Directions in Psychological Science, 1,* 189–193.

Thelen, E., Kelso, J. A. S., & Fogel, A. (1987). Self-organizing systems and infant motor development. *Developmental Review, 7,* 39–65.

Thomas, A., & Chess, S. (1977). *Temperament and development.* New York: Brunner/Mazel.

Tinsley, B. J. (1992). Multiple influences on the acquisition and socialization of children's health attitudes and behavior: An integrative review. *Child Development, 63,* 1043–1069.

Todd, J. E. (1882). *Drunkenness: A vice, not a disease.* Hartford, CT: Case, Lockwood, & Brainard, Cited in E. M. Jellinek. (1960). *The disease concept of alcoholism.* New Haven: Hillhouse Press.

Turnbull, J. E., & Gomberg, E. S. L. (1990). The structure of depression in alcoholic women. *Journal of Studies on Alcohol, 51,* 148–154.

Udry, J. R. (1991). Predicting alcohol use by adolescent males. *Journal of Biosocial Science, 23,* 381–386.

Vaillant, G. (1983). *The natural history of alcoholism.* Cambridge: Harvard University Press.

van Geert, P. (1991). A dynamic systems model of cognitive and language growth. *Psychological Review, 98,* 3–53.

von Bertalanffy, L., (Ed.). (1968). *General system theory.* New York: Braziller.

von Knorring, L., von Knorring, A., Smigan, L., Lindberg, U., & Edholm, M. (1987). Personality traits in subtypes of alcoholics. *Journal of Studies on Alcohol, 48,* 523–527.

Wagenaar, A. C., & Perry, C. L. (1994). Community strategies for the reduction of youthful drinking: Theory and application. *Journal of Research on Adolescence,* 319–345.

Wang, C-H., Liu, W. T., Zhang, M-Y., Yu, E. S. H., Xia, Z-Y., Fernandez, M., Lung, C-T., Xu, C-L., & Qu, G-Y. (1992). In J. E. Hlezer & G. J. Canino Eds.), *Alcoholism in North America, Europe, and Asia.* (pp. 264–286). New York: Oxford University Press.

Weber, M. D., Graham, J. W., Hansen, W. B., Flay, B. R., & Anderson, C. A. (1989). Evidence for two paths of alcohol use onset in adolescents. *Addictive Behaviors, 14,* 399–408.

Wechsler, H., & Thum, D. (1973). Teen-age drinking, drug use, and social correlates. *Quarterly Journal of Studies on Alcohol, 34,* 1220–1227.

Weibel-Orlando, J. C. (1986/87). Drinking patterns of urban and rural American Indians. *Alcohol Health and Research World, 11,* 8–13.

Weisz, J. R. (1989). Culture and the development of child psychopathology: Lessons from Thailand. In D. Cicchetti (Ed.), *The emergence of a discipline: Rochester Symposium on developmental psychopathology* (Vol. 1). Hillsdale, NJ: Erlbaum.

Werner, E. E. (1986). Resilient offspring of alcoholics: A longitudinal study from birth to age 18. *Journal of Studies on Alcohol, 47,* 34–40.

Werner, E. E. (1989). High-risk children in young adulthood: A longitudinal study from birth to 32 years. *American Journal of Orthopsychiatry, 59,* 72–81.

Werner, H. (1957). The concept of development from a comparative and organismic point of view. In D. B. Harris (Ed.), *The concept of development* (pp. 125–148). Minneapolis: University of Minnesota Press.

West, M. O., & Prinz, R. J. (1987). Parental alcoholism and childhood psychopathology. *Psychological Bulletin, 102,* 204–218.

Williams, G. D., & DeBakey, S. F. (1992). Changes in levels of alcohol consumption: United States, 1983–1988. *British Journal of the Addictions, 87,* 643–648.

Wills, T. A., & DuHamel, K. (1993). *Relation of children's temperament to early-onset substance abuse.* Paper presented at the annual meetings of the American Psychological Association, Toronto, Ontario, Canada.

Wilsnack, S. C., Klassen, A. D., Schur, B. E., & Wilsnack, R. W. (1991). Predicting onset and chronicity of women's problem drinking: A five-year longitudinal analysis. *American Journal of Public Health, 81,* 305–318.

Windle, M. (1990). Temperament and personality attributes of children of alcoholics. In M. Windle & J. S. Searles (Eds.), *Children of alcoholics: Critical perspectives.* (pp. 129–167). New York: Guilford.

Windle, M. (1994a). Commentary: Covariance structure models and other statistical procedures for analyzing longitudinal data. In R. A. Zucker, G. M. Boyd, & J. Howard, (Eds.), *The development of alcohol problems: Exploring the biopsychosocial matrix of risk.* (Research Monograph No. 26, pp. 387–398). Rockville, MD: National Institute of Alcohol Abuse and Alcoholism.

Windle, M. (1994b). Temperamental inhibition and activation: Hormonal and psychosocial correlates and associated psychiatric disorders. *Personality and Individual Differences, 17,* 61–70.

Windle, M., & Searles, J. S. (1990). *Children of alcoholics: Critical perspectives.* New York: Guilford.

Yoshikawa, H. (1994). Prevention as cumulative protection: Effects of early family support and education on chronic delinquency and its risks. *Psychological Bulletin, 115*, 28–54.

Young, T. J. (1988). Substance use and abuse among Native-American. *Clinical Psychology Review, 8*, 125–138.

Yu, E. S. H., & Liu, W. T. (1986/87). Alcohol use and abuse among Chinese-Americans. *Alcohol Health and Research World, 11*, 14–17, 60–61.

Zucker, R. A. (1979). Developmental aspects of drinking through the young adult years. In H. T. Blane & M. E. Chafetz (Eds.), *Youth, alcohol, and social policy*. (Chap. 4, pp. 91–146). New York: Plenum.

Zucker, R. A. (1987). The four alcoholisms: A developmental account of the etiologic process. In P. C. Rivers (Ed.), *Alcohol and addictive behaviors: Nebraska Symposium on motivation* (pp. 27–83). Lincoln, NE: University of Nebraska Press.

Zucker, R. A. (1989). Is risk for alcoholism predictable? A probabilistic approach to a developmental problem. *Drugs and Society, 4*, 69–93.

Zucker, R. A. (1991). Scaling the developmental momentum of alcoholic process via the Lifetime Alcohol Problems Scores. *Alcohol and Alcoholism,* (Suppl. No. 1). 505–510.

Zucker, R. A. (1994). Pathways to alcohol problems and alcoholism: A developmental account of the evidence for multiple alcoholisms and for contextual contributions to risk. In R. A. Zucker, G. M. Boyd, & J. Howard, (Eds.), *The development of alcohol problems: Exploring the biopsychosocial matrix of risk* (NIAAA Research Monograph 26, pp. 255–289). Rockville, MD: Department of Health and Human Services.

Zucker, R. A., Boyd, G. M., & Howard, J. (1994). Alcohol involvement and the biopsychosocial panorama of risk: An introduction. In R. A. Zucker, G. M. Boyd, & J. Howard, (Eds.), *The development of alcohol problems: Exploring the biopsychosocial matrix of risk* (Research Monograph No. 26). Rockville, MD: Department of Health and Human Services.

Zucker, R. A., Ellis, D. A., & Fitzgerald, H. E. (1993). *Other evidence for at least two alcoholisms, II: The case for lifetime antisociality as a basis of differentiation*. Unpublished manuscript, Michigan State University, East Lansing, MI.

Zucker, R. A., Ellis, D. A., & Fitzgerald, H. E. (1994a). Developmental evidence for at least two alcoholisms: I. Biopsychosocial variation among pathways into symptomatic difficulty. *Annals of the New York Academy of Sciences, 708*, 134–146.

Zucker, R. A., Ellis, D. A., & Fitzgerald, H. E. (1994b). *Characterizing risk load definition among COAs in early childhood: Varieties of familial alcoholism, child behavior problems, and cognitive functioning*. Unpublished paper, University of Michigan, Ann Arbor, MI.

Zucker, R. A., & Fitzgerald, H. E. (1991). Early developmental factors and risk for alcohol problems. *Alcohol Health and Research World, 15*, 18–24.

Zucker, R. A., Fitgerald, H. E., & Kincaid, S. B. (1994, August). Alcohol concepts, attitudes, and schemas: Their development in early childhood. Paper presented at the symposium, "Attitudes about alcohol," at the annual meetings of the American Psychological Association.

Zucker, R. A., & Gomberg, E. S. L. (1986). Etiology of alcoholism reconsidered: The case for a biopsychosocial process. *American Psychologists, 41*, 783–793.

Zucker, R. A., & Noll, R. B. (1982). Precursors and developmental influences on drinking and alcoholism: Etiology from a longitudinal perspective. In NIAAA (Ed.), *Alcohol and Health Monographs, No. 1: Alcohol consumption and related problems*. Rockville, MD: National Institute on Alcohol Abuse and Alcoholism, 289–327.

Zucker, R. A., & Noll, R. B. (1987). The interaction of child and environment in the early development of drug involvement: A far ranging review and a planned very early intervention. *Drugs and Society, 2*, 57–97.

Zucker, R. A., Noll, R. B., & Fitzgerald, H. E. (1986). *Risk and coping in children of alcoholics*. Unpublished grant application, NIAAA Grant ROI AA07065. Unpublished paper, Michigan State University, East Lansing, MI.

Zuckerman, M. (1979). *Sensation-seeking: Beyond the optimal level of arousal*. Hillsdale, NJ: Erlbaum.

PART THREE

Adaptation and Protective Processes

CHAPTER 20

Competence, Resilience, and Psychopathology

ANN S. MASTEN and J. DOUGLAS COATSWORTH

The concept of adaptation is central to developmental psychopathology as a comprehensive effort to understand psychological problems in the context of development. This effort has been described as "the study of the origins and course of individual patterns of behavioral maladaptation" (Sroufe and Rutter, 1984, p. 18) and "the study of adaptation, its variations and vicissitudes" (Masten, 1989, p. 289). Moreover, developmental psychopathologists have asserted that the adaptational processes leading to good developmental outcomes are important for understanding, ameliorating, and preventing psychopathology (Cicchetti, 1984, 1990a, 1990b; Garmezy, 1974; Masten, 1989; Masten & Braswell, 1991; Sroufe, 1990; Sroufe & Rutter, 1984). It follows that competence, resilience, and protective processes need to be studied in conjunction with maladaptive behavior, vulnerability, and risk factors for disorder.

It is a fundamental premise of developmental psychopathology that psychopathology is defined with respect to variations in human development and expectations for behavior that are developmentally, culturally, and historically based (Masten & Braswell, 1991; Sroufe, 1990). Knowledge about normative development and developmental tasks provides key benchmarks by which behavior is evaluated as deviant and maladaptive or effective and successful. Understanding the origins and course of psychopathology in developmental context requires the study of pathways toward and away from deviance, and the "roads not taken." Those roads include the many other paths of development taken by individuals who at one time shared similar backgrounds or genes or

behavior but who now have much more successful developmental trajectories.

Adaptation, the broadest term for sustaining and perpetuating life, includes homeostatic self-regulatory processes, effective transactions with the environment, and development. Human individuals, as living organisms, must maintain coherence and organization as a unit, while they interact with the environment, including other individuals, and also function as part of larger systems (Cicchetti & Schneider-Rosen, 1986; Ford, 1987; Ford & Lerner, 1992; Gunnar & Thelen, 1989). Development requires both the maintenance of internal organization and regulation and effective organism-environment transactions. In addition to growth, maturation, and learning, "development" refers to the processes by which living systems reorganize themselves to function in ways that are more complex, diverse, differentiated, and/or superordinate to previous organizations of structures and functions (Cicchetti & Schneider-Rosen, 1986; Ford, 1987; Ford & Lerner, 1992; Gunnar & Thelen, 1989; Sameroff, 1982, 1989; Werner, 1957).

The organizational perspective in developmental theory emphasizes the qualitative transformations in ontogeny that flow from adaptational processes (Cicchetti, 1990b; Cicchetti & Schneider-Rosen, 1986; Cicchetti & Sroufe, 1978; Sroufe, 1979; Sroufe & Waters, 1976). These developmental processes include differentiation combined with hierarchical integration (Werner, 1948, 1957), as well as assimilation and accommodation (Piaget, 1952). Adaptational processes in developmental theory are invoked to account for the continuities and coherence of development in spite of dramatic maturational changes and shifts in the environment (Cicchetti, 1990b; Sroufe, 1979).

Disruptions in internal equilibrium or in the smooth executions of interactions with the environment, precipitated by internal or external phenomena, may stimulate transformations in the functional systems of development. A resulting reorganization may represent a developmental advance, what Ford and Lerner (1992) have termed, "elaborative change" (p. 50). However, disruptions may also lead to the derailment of development, what Ford and Lerner termed a "decremental change" (p. 51). Thus, challenges to a developmental system could produce either adaptive or maladaptive outcomes.

"Successful" adaptation has been defined from many perspectives, ranging from propagation of a species by successful, successive reproduction in evolutionary biology to "self-actualization"

Our thinking about competence, resilience, and developmental psychopathology has been profoundly influenced over the years by Norman Garmezy, Auke Tellegen, and our other colleagues on Project Competence, and by Michael Rutter, Alan Sroufe, Dante Cicchetti, and faculty and students in the Institute of Child Development at the University of Minnesota. Our interactions with William Charlesworth, Scott Gest, Jennifer Neemann, Jon Hubbard, and Marie Reed were particularly important for this chapter. Support for the first author in the preparation of this chapter was provided by the William T. Grant Foundation, the National Institute of Mental Health (MH33222), the National Institute of Child Health and Human Development through the Minnesota Center for Research on Developmental Disabilities (RD30-HD24051), and the University of Minnesota. Support for the second author was provided by an NIMH grant for postdoctoral training in prevention research to the Arizona State University Preventive Intervention Research Center (5T 32 MH18387-03).

in humanistic psychology. Some psychological theories have focused on individual internal adaptation, including such concepts as "ego-strength," "psychological well-being," "defense mechanisms," or "self-regulation." Psychological problems and symptoms associated with failures of internal adaptation include internalizing symptoms such as depressed mood, anxiety, distress, negative self-perceptions, and disorganization of psychological functioning (i.e., "decompensation"). Other theories have focused on external adaptation, examining social adjustment and achievements. Problems in this aspect of adaptation include externalizing symptoms such as trouble with the law, school or job failure, and social rejection.

"Competence" and "resilience" also have varied meanings in psychological usage, but generally refer to the capability for, or manifestation of, favorable adaptation. Ford (1985) identified five interrelated but distinct meanings of competence: (a) motivational phenomena, (b) beliefs about one's own effectiveness, (c) specific abilities or skills, (d) personality traits, and (e) manifest accomplishments. All refer to effective functioning, but they differ in their focus on internal processes, mental structures, abilities or behavioral outcomes. Similarly, the term resilience has been used to describe successful adaptation following perturbations in internal functioning as well as the maintenance or recovery to effective functioning despite exogenous threats (Masten, 1994; Masten, Best, & Garmezy, 1990). It has been used to refer to the general capacity for such recovery or maintenance, and the outcome of good adaptation despite adversity or risk. Murphy and Moriarty labelled these two aspects of psychological adaptation, the externally directed and the internally directed, as "Coping I" and "Coping II." Coping I referred to the "capacity to cope with opportunities, challenges, frustrations, threats in the environment" while Coping II referred to the "maintenance of internal integration" (Murphy & Moriarty, 1976).

Psychopathology usually refers to patterns of maladaptive behavior or psychological distress that interfere with some aspect of adaptation. The role clinical judgments of adaptation play in diagnosing psychopathology is evident in the current diagnostic manual of the American Psychiatric Association (1994), "DSM-IV," both in the diagnostic criteria for the syndromes included in the manual and in the description of "impairment" associated with most syndromes. Some disorders are *defined* in part by declines in or failures to achieve developmentally based benchmarks of adaptation. Others are defined by behaviors or internal symptoms that are assumed to carry a high risk for compromising external adaptation or development. In most cases, significant impairments in social functioning are described as typical of people meeting the diagnostic criteria for a disorder. These criteria and observations about impairment are based on a combination of pooled clinical wisdom and empirical data. Extensive studies of disordered behavior implicate the role of adaptation, developmental benchmarks, and competence in defining and treating psychopathology.

Developmental theory, traditional definitions of disorders, and empirical evidence all suggest that competence and psychopathology are integrally related. In this chapter, we examine the conceptual and empirical linkages between competence and psychopathology and the implications of these linkages for developmental psychopathology. In the first of four sections, we examine competence as a family of constructs and set forth a working definition of competence. In the second section, we focus on models of how competence and psychopathology might be related and then examine data pertinent to these models. This section is not intended to be exhaustive because many other authors in this manual address this linkage from the perspective of specific disorders and problems. In the third section, we examine concepts and studies of risk and resilience as potential bridges between competence and psychopathology. In the concluding section, we discuss the implications of the concepts and data examined in this chapter for theory and research in normal and deviant psychological development.

COMPETENCE AS A FAMILY OF CONSTRUCTS IN PSYCHOLOGY

Psychological competence constructs share roots with the broader construct of adaptation. The roots of all these constructs run deep. In *The Republic,* for example, Plato discussed who should be chosen as a Ruler according to differential aptitudes for the position. However, systematic study of variations in human adaptation or success in life originated primarily in the 19th century. That century gave rise to mental testing, the child guidance movement, and psychoanalysis, each of which focused on human individual differences in adaptation (Borstelmann, 1983; Cairns, 1983).

Biology as a systematic science also emerged in the 19th century (Mayr, 1982), with the publication of *The Origin of Species* (Darwin, 1859/1964) serving as a milestone for both the history of biology and the idea of adaptation. It marked a shift in the concept of adaptation, which took on its dynamic character during the same century (Mayr, 1982). Previously, adaptation was conceptualized in European thought as a static reflection of a creator's genius or the perfect harmony of nature (Mayr, 1982).

Individual differences were crucial to Darwin's theory. Natural selection, characterized by differential reproductive success of individuals that varied in heritable ways, provided the mechanism of evolution. In Darwin's theory, individual adaptation was both the result of and a contributor to evolution. Adaptation in the individual was "influenced" through inheritance by the natural selection of ancestors who had traits that provided a reproductive advantage. Individual adaptation to the environment in turn served as the proximal mediator for ongoing processes of natural selection, since a highly maladaptive organism probably would have reduced reproductive fitness (e.g., if the organism did not survive long enough to reproduce or the offspring were not viable due to that maladaptation). Darwin's observations of variations within and across species, his theory of evolution, and the debates surrounding it undoubtedly increased attention to individual differences and to the concept of adaptation (Brandon, 1990; Dobzhansky, 1962; Mayr, 1982).

In this section, we review the family of constructs closely associated with competence in psychological theories of adaptation. These theories emerged from the ethos of 19th century thought, but they were nourished by 20th-century science and the experiences of practitioners concerned with human welfare and child development.

Developmental Ego Psychology

The concept of "ego" in psychology, either as a structure or function of the human mind, has played an important role in theories of personality development (Breger, 1974; Loevinger, 1976). The concept of adaptation entered psychological theory through these theories of how the mind operates. (See also the chapters by Fonagy and Moran, and Hauser and Safier in this manual.)

The beginnings of modern ego psychology were initiated by Freud in his later works and by the increased emphasis on the ego in his structural theory (Blanck & Blanck, 1979). In *The Ego and the Id* (or the "I" and the "it"), Freud (1923/1960) elaborated on his evolving concept of a structure in the mind that served the purpose of both self-preservation and adaptation to the world. The ego, "a coherent organization of mental processes," mediated conflicts among "three masters": the instinct-driven id, the exacting superego, and the environment. Guided by a "self-preservation instinct," the ego functioned to balance the requirements of these three masters. If the ego was threatened by imbalance or conflict, anxiety resulted. A primary goal of psychoanalysis in Freud's structural theory was to strengthen the functioning of the ego.

Further evolution of Freud's thinking about the ego can be gleaned from a very late paper on humor (Freud, 1928). In an earlier book, Freud (1905/1960) analyzed the pleasures derived from jokes and comedy in terms of his mechanistic, economic theory of energy savings. Jokes, for example, allowed for the safe release of sexual and aggressive impulses. In contrast, the later essay focused on the *elevating* qualities of humor. Freud described gallows humor as an effort of the ego to assert its mastery in the face of an untenable situation, "the ego's victorious assertion of its own invulnerability" (p. 2). Freud clearly admired how a human being, in the face of insurmountable adversity, could psychologically triumph over despair and maintain integrity of ego-functioning, through humor.

Freud's ideas about the ego evolved over time. Nonetheless, it was left to others to elaborate the role of the ego. One psychoanalyst who took up the challenge was Freud's daughter Anna, whose 1936 volume *The Ego and the Mechanisms of Defense* (Freud, 1966) has been recognized as an important turning point in developmental ego psychology (Felsman & Vaillant, 1987). In this manual and in other works, she emphasized adaptive functions of the ego in its defense mechanisms. This conceptualization of defenses as psychologically healthy shifted the course of psychoanalytic thought and set the stage for future theories of healthy psychodynamic development.

Another important milestone in the evolution of the ego construct in psychoanalytic theory was Heinz Hartmann's 1939 monograph, *Ego Psychology and the Problem of Adaptation,* published the year Freud died. The focus of Hartmann's book was autonomous ego functioning, independent of the id and conflict, and the inborn human potential for mastering the environment. His monograph focused on adaptation and development, emphasizing the integrative functions of the ego in adaptation, while deemphasizing its role as solver of conflicts. Hartmann distinguished between a state of adaptedness and the processes of adaptation, "we call a man well-adapted if his productivity, his ability to enjoy life, and his mental equilibrium are undisturbed" (p. 23). The

ego and its development provided the processes of adaptation in Hartmann's view.

Hartmann's perspectives on ego development were influenced by Werner's (1929) theory of development as a process of differentiation and integration. Hartmann described inborn capacities for ego development that are shaped through differentiation and integration. Hartmann's ego psychology brought forth the functions of adaptation and achievement in the external world as the centerpiece of mental health. He saw his monograph as part of the efforts to broaden psychoanalysis beyond the focus on conflicts and psychopathology to a general theory of mental life. The goal of psychoanalysis, in his words, was "to help men achieve a better functioning synthesis and relation to the environment" (p. 81).

Hartmann was undoubtedly influenced by many ideas of his time, particularly developmental and evolutionary theory, but his brilliant synthesis of ideas from psychoanalysis, biology, and child development was a landmark that foreshadowed many of the themes that characterize developmental psychopathology decades later. His view was fundamentally *transactional,* although he did not use this term. He viewed adaptation as influenced by constitution, environment, and "ontogenetic phase" in interaction. Hartmann argued that "the search for a favorable environment among those available should probably be given a far more central position among adaptation processes—in the broader sense—than is customary" (p. 20) and that "human action adapts the environment to human functions, and then the human being adapts (secondarily) to the environment which he has helped to create" (p. 26f.). He recognized the role of context and the importance of an individual's "fit" with the environment in attained adaptedness. The role of society was recognized in deciding "which forms of behavior shall have the greatest adaptive chance" (p. 31).

In Hartmann's theory, there were several inborn instincts and "apparatuses" that would come to serve the ego in the course of development. These included perception and intelligence and "self-preservation." Hartmann did not elaborate on these processes, expressing his hope in his closing chapter for more precise delineation of the "self-preservation drives" in psychoanalytic theory.

Ives Hendrick, a contemporary of Hartmann's, took up the motivational theme of self-preservation in ego psychology and proposed an "instinct to master" the environment. Based on research and observations of children, Hendrick (1942) argued for an "inborn drive to do and to learn how to do" (p. 40):

> I shall propose the thesis that psychoanalysis has neglected the overwhelming evidence that the need to learn how to do things, manifested in the infant's practice of its sensory, motor, and intellectual means for mastering its environment, is at least as important as pleasure seeking mechanisms in determining its behavior and development during the first two years of life (p. 34).

The idea of an instinct to master the environment, while not well-received by many of his psychoanalytic colleagues (see Hendrick, 1943), anticipated the great synthesis of Robert White on the motivational system underlying competence. Hendrick's focus on the integrative functions of the ego in accomplishing this task also anticipated modern developmental ego psychology.

These themes were further elaborated by Erik Erikson and Jane Loevinger, among others. In his theory of psychosocial development, Erikson (1963, 1968) emphasized the adaptive nature of the ego and the processes of adaptation during eight stages of development (discussed further later). Loevinger (1976) subsequently focused on the ego as a process rather than a structure, with the function of "striving to master, to integrate, to make sense of experience" (p. 59). In Loevinger's integration of ego psychology, ego development was the process by which individuals organize and find coherence in their cognitions, affects and behaviors. Like Erikson, Loevinger proposed sequential stages of ego development. She also proposed a typology of personality based on individual differences in level of ego development within an age cohort.

Jack and Jeanne Block have also described personality types that reflect individual differences in ego functioning (Block & Block, 1980). Their theory attempted to integrate concepts from Lewinian and psychoanalytic thought. The adaptive functions of the ego were elaborated in their concepts of *ego-control* and *ego-resiliency*. Ego-control refers to "degree of impulse control and modulation," while ego-resiliency refers to "ability to modify one's behavior in accordance with contextual demands." In their longitudinal study of these constructs, children and youth high on ego-resiliency, for example, were found to have many positive qualities and successes in the environment. Those also high on ego-control, "resilient overcontrollers," were described as calm, empathic, and compliant while "resilient undercontrollers" were described as energetic, curious, and interesting.

Motivation and Mastery

> When parallel trends can be observed in realms as far apart as animal behavior and psychoanalytic ego psychology, there is reason to suppose that we are witnessing a significant evolution of ideas. (White, 1959, p. 297)

With this statement, Robert White began his seminal essay, "Motivation reconsidered: The Concept of Competence." In this article, White linked ideas from ego psychology with observations of animal behavior and human development, to argue that the force behind the development of the capacity for effective interactions with the environment was a motivational system independent of other drives or instincts. When not occupied by "homeostatic" crises, or other pressing needs, people and animals seek environmental interaction. These behaviors are directed and persistent and appear to be engaged in for their own sake, with no apparent "drive-reduction" or "consummatory response" involved. Hence, White posited that such behavior was motivated. Exploratory behavior in monkeys, activity wheel behavior in rats, and the play of human infants were connected in his argument that humans and animals are biologically predisposed to interact with the environment in ways that promote effective adaptation. White termed the motivation behind such behavior, "effectance" and the feelings resulting from its satisfaction, "efficacy."

White's theory provided a link between adaptation in the evolutionary context and adaptation in ontogenesis. In an advanced species like humans, with a great deal to learn, competence motivation was highly adaptive. The individual, however, worked for the feelings of efficacy that result from the process of achieving competence, not the evolutionary goal of adaptedness. Although White speculated that competence motivation becomes differentiated over ontogeny, he did not elaborate on its developmental course.

Harter (1978) later argued that a more detailed examination of effectance was needed, particularly in regard to its development, the role of failure (White focused on success), and the role of perceptions of one's competence and control. Harter proposed a model of effectance motivation that differentiated three domains of competence (cognitive, social, physical), and that included processes by which success or failure influenced effectance. Given success, intrinsic pleasure follows and effectance is increased, particularly when the individual attributes to his or her own efforts the major credit for meeting the challenge of the situation. In her model, greater pleasure is derived from optimally challenging tasks. In contrast, failure can produce varying degrees of anxiety or decreased effectance, depending on an individual's interpretation of the experience.

Harter's model attempted to fill in the broad strokes left by White, by linking effectance motivation to theory and research on concepts such as intrinsic versus extrinsic motivation, locus of control, perceived competence, and mastery. She described processes by which effectance for a given domain of competence would increase or decrease and vary across individuals, depending on perceptions, experiences, and development.

Connell and Wellborn (Connell, 1990; Connell & Wellborn, 1991) have also extended the motivational aspect of adaptation. They have proposed that people have psychological needs for competence, autonomy and relatedness, which motivate interactions in the environment, and influence the development of the self-system, discussed next.

Individual cognitive appraisal, beliefs, and values played a substantial role in these processes. In the next section, the role of self-perception is considered, in the work of Harter and others on perceived competence and Bandura on self-efficacy.

Perceived Competence and Self-Efficacy

The past 25 years have produced an extensive literature on the role of the "self" in behavior and development (Gunnar & Sroufe, 1991; Harter, 1982). Theoretical and empirical papers have elaborated on the function of self-systems in adaptation. This work has emphasized the important of a persons' beliefs and perceptions about their own competence for adaptation.

Much of Harter's work has focused on the multidimensional nature of perceived competence (Harter, 1982, 1985, 1990). For example, she has found that 8- to 12-year-old children differentiate among their scholastic competence, athletic competence, and social competence. Adolescents evaluate their competence along several additional dimensions, including romantic appeal, close friendships, and job competence. At the same time, individuals have a global sense of self-worth that is not simply a sum or average of these components, but also reflects the relative value they place on success in these different realms of behavior.

Albert Bandura (1977, 1982, 1989) has described a "self-efficacy mechanism" that explains the reciprocal influence of effective functioning on a person's beliefs about their effectiveness (self-efficacy) and how those beliefs influence motivation and subsequent behavior. Success engenders confidence; confidence in turn engenders effort. Self-efficacy can be altered in several ways, including verbal persuasion and physiological state, but actual attainments appear to be a powerful source of influence. Cognitive, affective, and motivational processes are linked in this model, which has been supported by elegant experiments.

Self-efficacy also provides a mechanism for resilience. Bandura argued that people with a positive and sturdy sense of their own efficacy are more likely to persevere in the face of failure, rejection, and challenge. Because they expect to do well, they avoid the distress of anticipating failure. Robust self-efficacy develops from experiences of overcoming manageable setbacks and challenges in life.

A maladaptive cousin to the adaptive concept of self-efficacy is the concept of "learned helplessness" (Abramson, Seligman, & Teasdale, 1978; Garber & Seligman, 1980; Seligman, 1975). In the "reformulated" theory of learned helplessness (Abramson et al., 1978), attributing one's failure to stable, global, and internal causes is expected to produce depressive affect. Learned helplessness also reflects diminution of motivation: faced with failure, the "helpless" individual gives up.

Perceptions of control clearly influence self-efficacy and the consequences of failure in these models. The relation of perceived control to the effectiveness of behavior has been theoretically and empirically elaborated by a number of investigators (Connell & Wellborn, 1991; Harter, 1985; Skinner, 1991; Skinner, Chapman, & Baltes, 1988). For example, beliefs about control have been differentiated into three components: control beliefs, means-ends beliefs, and agency beliefs (Skinner et al., 1988). Control beliefs refer to a child's expectations about whether he or she can produce success or avoid failure, without regard to the means. High expectations about control increase the likelihood of action and persistence, which enhance the likelihood of success. If credit is taken for successes, then control beliefs are enhanced or confirmed, a kind of self-fulfilling prophecy. Similarly, low perceived control can contribute to less action, less success, and decreasing beliefs in control, a downward spiral to learned helplessness and less effective behavior. Beliefs about the causes of outcomes, means-end beliefs (e.g., luck versus ability), have been differentiated from beliefs about one's self in regard to the causes of outcomes (e.g., "I am lucky" versus "I am smart") (Skinner, 1991). These beliefs influence the consequences of outcomes—successes and failures—on self-perception. Research has suggested general development shifts in beliefs about causes (e.g., belief in luck as a cause decreases in middle childhood) and a tendency for control beliefs to become more self-regulatory and less influenced by outcomes (Skinner, 1991).

Perceived competence or self-efficacy, along with perceived control and values placed on effectiveness in different domains of competence, are all facets of modern "self" theory. Each of

these ideas brings the role of human cognition and appraisal into the complex interactions of organism and environment in the process of adaptation. Each of these lines of thought also explicitly or implicitly emphasizes the importance of effective performance in valued domains to psychological well-being.

Developmental Tasks

The evaluation of effective adaptation, whether by self or others, requires criteria. The concept of "developmental tasks" focuses attention on the developmental nature of the standards by which success in adaptation is judged.

The general concept of developmental tasks, though anticipated by psychoanalytic theories of psychosexual, psychosocial, and ego development, was fully articulated by Robert Havighurst. He originally introduced this notion in a 1948 pamphlet designed for use in a course he was teaching at the University of Chicago (Havighurst, 1972). Havighurst's concept incorporated both the perspectives of an individual's needs and of societal regulations. He suggested that living in a modern society imposed a long series of tasks for its members to learn. Learning these tasks well brought satisfaction and reward, while poor learning brought forth unhappiness and disapproval. It is with regard to learning these tasks that an individual judges himself or herself, or is judged by others, to be a reasonably successful person (Havighurst, 1972).

Havighurst's primary interest was in the educational implications of developmental tasks and how the educational system could help children accomplish the tasks. However, he adopted a life-span perspective and outlined a series of tasks that ranged from infancy through "later maturity." The resultant taxonomy of developmental issues suggested milestones that "constitute[d] healthy and satisfactory growth in our society" (Havighurst, 1972, p. 2). It included the following examples: learning to walk, talk, and distinguish right from wrong in infancy and early childhood; learning to read, write, and calculate in middle childhood; achieving emotional independence in adolescence; entering marriage and starting a family in early adulthood; achieving adult social and civic responsibility in middle adulthood; and adjusting to retirement and reduced income in later maturity. As evident in this abbreviated list, the importance and timing of some of these tasks will be determined primarily by biological maturation (e.g., learning to walk) while others will be defined at least partially by the sociocultural values of the group under study (e.g., emotional independence, marriage). Havighurst's list of tasks uses the American middle-class as a referent, but the general concept of developmental tasks does not exclude the possibility of varying taxonomies for different racial, cultural, or economic groups. Despite these possible differences, the basic idea is that these tasks can be used as markers of successful adaptation, or global competence.

Havighurst credits Erik Erikson's theory of psychosocial development (Erikson, 1963, 1968) with popularizing the use of the developmental task concept. Erikson's well-known epigenetic theory outlined eight stages of development from infancy through adulthood, each with its own psychosocial crisis for the individual to confront. Erikson's tasks include such social developmental milestones as forming a trusting relationship with the parent, establishing an integrated identity in adolescence, assisting and guiding the younger generation during one's middle adulthood, and maintaining a sense of satisfaction and integrity in late adulthood. Each of the eight tasks remains a lifelong issue, but rises to ascendancy at particular times in the life-cycle. It is during that period that the task becomes foremost for the individual's development, and when adaptive responses to the crisis at hand leaves one better equipped to meet the challenges of successive stages.

Erikson's developmental model was the basis for assessments of children and adults in the study of Adult Development at Harvard by Vaillant and colleagues (Felsman & Vaillant, 1987). This classic study followed up to adulthood an urban sample of nondelinquent boys originally assessed in early adolescence. "Boyhood Competence" was a composite of six scales based on Erikson's "industry versus inferiority" stage of development. It included items such as "school grades relative to IQ" and a coping index, "planfulness, making the best of the environment" (see Felsman & Vaillant, 1987, p. 293). This composite was the best predictor of adult adjustment on a variety of outcome measures that also reflected Eriksonian theory.

The idea of developmental tasks also was central to the conceptualization of "premorbid competence" in studies of risk for psychopathology (Feffer & Phillips, 1953; Garmezy, 1970; Phillips, 1953, 1968; Phillips & Cowitz, 1953; Zigler & Glick, 1986). Early pioneers in this area utilized principles from organismic developmental theory (Werner, 1948, 1957) to develop measures of premorbid competence that documented an individual's success in adaptive tasks as a broad gauge of developmental level. The Phillips Premorbid Scale (Phillips, 1953) and its successor, the Zigler-Phillips Social Competence Scale (Zigler & Glick, 1986; Zigler & Phillips, 1961) assessed performance in multiple aspects of adult life in U.S. society, and scores were found to have considerable predictive validity for prognosis (Zigler & Glick, 1986).

Waters and Sroufe (1983) explicitly linked the construct of competence to the organizational theory of development as well as to developmental tasks. In their view, competence is best viewed as a molar, developmental construct which is characterized by the individual's ability to use intrapersonal and environmental resources to achieve a good developmental outcome. They emphasized that competence is indicated by the coordination of behavior, cognition and affect in producing positive development, and suggested that the key to age-appropriate assessment of competence lies in the identification of select issues (developmental tasks) for each developmental period. Mastering a developmental task requires an individual to integrate behavioral, affective, and cognitive responses into a coherent pattern of person-environment interaction, and thus provides an excellent marker of competence. They also predicted that competence will show coherence through time, even though the criteria for competence change from one period of development to another. Proper assessments of competence, in their view, are broad-based in scope, tap success in salient developmental tasks, and emphasize the integrative coordination of cognition, emotion, and behavior to achieve adaptive outcomes. Measures that challenge the individual to adapt in naturally occurring situations were recommended.

Although Hartmann and Erikson each took a life-span approach to developmental tasks, most investigators and theorists have concentrated on specific period of development, such as infancy or adolescence. Considerable research has provided convergent validity regarding the important developmental tasks of various age periods. The salient developmental issues of infancy and early childhood have been discussed by Greenspan (1981), Sander (1975), Sroufe (Sroufe, 1979; Waters & Sroufe, 1983), and others, with striking similarities. The period of adolescence is currently receiving a great deal of research attention with corresponding delineation of and consideration for the salient tasks that characterize this developmental stage (e.g., Feldman & Elliott, 1990; Hill, 1980, 1983; Klaczynski, 1990). Still others have begun to look more closely at the development of adaptive competence in adulthood (Perlmutter, Kaplan, & Nyquist, 1990), and at how individuals confront the developmental tasks in retirement (Antonovsky & Sagy, 1990). These various literatures provide researchers with critical developmentally appropriate criteria by which to judge competence across the life span.

It is important to reiterate that developmental tasks are defined within a historical and social milieu. Some developmental tasks, such as attachment, may be universal in general form, but vary substantially across cultures in specific content. Developmental tasks such as school success may be limited to cultures that have adopted "school" as a mechanism for formal learning. Similarities in developmental tasks across cultures and history may reflect commonalities in the constraints inherent in the human species, commonalities in the environmental resources and challenges faced by humans living on the same planet, and shared knowledge across cultures and time. Differences may reflect variations in phenotypes, natural environmental differences, or societies. Any measure of competence is likely to reflect those values held strongly within the society (Zigler & Trickett, 1978). This also can be said for developmental tasks as they may have been "selected" by historical and social processes which found them to be the most effective in promoting positive development within a given culture (Oerter, 1986; Ogbu, 1985).

IQ and Competence

The concepts of intelligence and adaptation have been intricately linked. Many of the early intelligence theorists adopted broad definitions of intelligence that included some aspects of environmental adaptation. These definitions frequently included mention of intelligence as adaptive behavior in real world environments. However, most current day theorizing about, and measurement of, intelligence neglects the individual's external adaptation and focuses almost exclusively on the individual's internal world of cognitive processes, skills, and structures (Charlesworth, 1979; Sternberg, 1985).

The diversity of views on the nature and definition of intelligence has been demonstrated effectively in a comparison of two symposia, one held in 1921 and the second in 1986 (Sternberg & Detterman, 1986). Each symposium brought together some of the foremost psychologists of the time to discuss what intelligence was and what were the crucial steps for researching this difficult construct (Sternberg & Detterman, 1986). Each meeting produced a variety of definitions from which several common themes emerged. Attributes such as adaptation to the environment, basic mental processes, and higher order thinking (e.g., reasoning, problem solving) were prominent in both lists. However, several differences were also apparent, including the greater focus on metacognition and the role of context in the 1986 definitions (Sternberg & Berg, 1986).

These symposia illustrate the inherent difficulty in trying to define intelligence simply. It is a broad, complex construct and to define it adequately requires a broad, complex theory which takes into account the nature of intelligence in terms of its relation to the internal world of the individual, the external world, and the interrelation between them (Sternberg, 1985). Most definitions of intelligence emphasize one or two of these elements at the expense of the others.

Early theorists did attempt to propose broad theories that incorporated multiple aspects of this construct. For example, Alfred Binet believed that intelligence was a collection of abilities that included such things as judgment, practical sense, initiative, and the faculty of adapting oneself to circumstances (Binet & Simon, 1905/1916; Sattler, 1988).

Jean Piaget proposed several complementary definitions of intelligence, including intelligence as "a particular instance of biological adaptation," "the form of equilibrium toward which successive adaptations and exchanges between the organization and the environment are directed," and "a system of living and acting operations" (quoted by Ginsberg & Opper, 1988, p. 13). Each of these definitions incorporates the notion that intelligence is defined primarily by adaptation to environmental demands.

In Piaget's (1952) theory, intellectual development shared two basic properties of living organisms: organization and adaptation (Flavell, 1963). Two facets of adaptation that Piaget applied to his theory of intellectual development were assimilation and accommodation (Flavell, 1963). Assimilation referred to the process whereby an organism changes so as to incorporate food (physiological adaptation) or information (intellectual adaptation), for example, into the organization of the organism (physical or cognitive). Accommodation referred to the process by which the organism itself changes in order to adapt, as by cutting up the food or opening one's mouth to ingest it, or changing one's concepts in accordance with new information. Organization and adaptation were inseparable parts of the process of intellectual development in this theory (Flavell, 1963). Piaget described them as "two complementary processes of a single mechanism, the first being the internal aspect of the cycle of which adaptation constitutes the external aspect" (Piaget, 1952, pp. 7–8).

Like his predecessors, David Wechsler also defined intelligence broadly, as "the aggregate or global capacity of the individual to act purposefully, to think rationally and to deal effectively with his environment" (Wechsler, 1958). Wechsler believed that intelligence was most constructively interpreted as a portion of the total personality, and as a resultant of interactions of abilities rather than as a cause. In its broadest sense, Wechsler's theory of general intelligence also included nonintellective factors such as temperament and personality traits that are not directly related to logical or analytic skills, but help produce intelligent behavior.

Evident in each of these three prominent theories of intelligence is the notion of effective interaction with the environment. However, *measuring* that aspect of the construct has proven difficult and tools used to assess intelligence have generally concentrated on the internal mechanisms, with little attention given to the environmental adaptation (Sternberg, 1985). Although the original Stanford-Binet test and its subsequent revisions may have done an excellent job in tapping analytic skills and in predicting success in school, it may not have done justice to Binet's original broad theory of intelligence (Sternberg, 1988). Wechsler was well aware of the limits in trying to measure intelligence as he defined it. Wechsler wrote that factor analysis alone was not the answer, and psychology required a new psychometric that would measure "what is purported in our definitions of intelligence" (Wechsler, 1950).

Other individuals, not wedded to the psychometric approach to assessment, have noted its limitations (e.g., Charlesworth, 1978, 1979). Charlesworth acknowledged that the psychometric tradition has identified a number of cognitive operations which appear intuitively to relate to everyday life situations, but cautions that it has taught us little about how, or how frequently, these operations function in everyday life. Adopting an ethological perspective, Charlesworth clearly differentiated intelligence, as an inferred disposition, and intelligent behavior, which is an observed portion of the individual's overall behavior. Intelligent behavior was defined as those behaviors that are under cognitive control (as opposed to reflexes or fixed action patterns) and are "employed toward the solution of problems which challenge the well-being, needs, plans, and survival of the individual" (Charlesworth, 1979). Within the ethological view, intelligence is a mode of adaptation to everyday challenges in the environment and it is most effectively studied through comprehensive naturalistic observations of behavior.

One theory that has received considerable attention in recent years is Robert Sternberg's triarchic theory of intelligence (Sternberg, 1985). After reviewing earlier theories of intelligence, Sternberg concluded that the older theories of intelligence were more incomplete than incorrect. His theorizing on intelligence, which adheres to the information processing models of cognition, reflects an attempt to bridge the gap between the psychometric approach with its focus on internal cognitive structures or process and approaches such as the ethological which focus on intelligence as adaptation to real world environments. Sternberg describes intelligence as, "mental activity directed toward purposive adaptation to, and selection and shaping of, real-world environments relevant to one's life" (p. 45). His definition of intelligence focuses on the *mental activity* involved in adaptive processes, rather than their results, but the emphasis on adaptation is also salient.

Sternberg posited that a comprehensive theory of intelligence should include descriptions of how it relates to the internal world of the individual, the external world of the individual, and the experiences which mediate the relationship between internal and external worlds. Thus, Sternberg's triarchic theory is composed of three separate subtheories: the componential, the experiential and the contextual. In the real world, these three separate components are thought to work in an integrated fashion to produce more or less intelligent behavior.

The componential subtheory is the portion that addresses intelligence and its relationship to the internal world of the individual. It focuses on the mental processes involved in thinking. The experiential subtheory considers the relationships between intelligence and a person's level of experience with particular tasks. It proposes that intelligence requires dealing with novel tasks and that once these tasks are understood and confronted more frequently, the mental operations become more automatized. According to this theory, more intelligent individuals can better automatize information processing (Sternberg, 1988).

The final component of the triarchic theory is the contextual subtheory, which seeks to understand how individuals adapt to, select, and seek relevant environments. It is in this portion of the theory that Sternberg defines intelligence in everyday life. But, like the other two components, this is a theory of mental events that contribute to the individual's selection of, and adaptation to the environment. Although this portion of the triarchic theory comes closest to the idea of competence as behavioral effectiveness in the environment, it has a distinct emphasis on mental events that mediate contextual adaptation (Sternberg, 1985), rather than behavioral adaptation itself.

Other areas of research have also indicated the close relationship between the constructs of competence and intelligence. In several studies investigating both experts' and laypersons' implicit theories of intelligence, a clear factor of social competence has emerged, along with expected factors of problem solving and verbal abilities (Sternberg, 1985). In his subsequent work, Sternberg divides this factor into two related, but distinct, kinds of intelligence: social intelligence and practical intelligence. His research on social intelligence has concentrated on people's abilities to decode nonverbal messages in interpersonal situations. Results from studies in this area were not promising in implicating a stable social decoding ability across social situations. However, his work on practical intelligence, and more specifically an aspect of this he labels "tacit knowledge" have been more promising.

Tacit knowledge refers to a practical knowledge and understanding that relates directly to success in real world tasks. For example, success in various occupations is assumed to be due in part to a tacit knowledge of the "ins and outs" of the occupation, above and beyond any academic or other preparation for the job. Sternberg and his colleagues have investigated these ideas and developed a methodology in a series of studies (see Wagner & Sternberg, 1986). The studies demonstrate that tacit knowledge is predictive of real world occupational success. Sternberg also has suggested that this tacit knowledge might generalize to aspects of real world performance beyond the occupations investigated in the studies.

Adaptive Behavior

The inability of a single measure of IQ to fully explain an individual's functioning in the everyday world is also evident in the definition of mental retardation (MR). A diagnosis of MR requires impaired adaptive functioning as well as a significantly below-average IQ score on a standard test (American Association

of Mental Retardation, 1992). Although many individuals in the early decades of the 20th century wrote of social competency, social skills, or adaptability to the environment as an important aspect for defining mental retardation, it was not until 1959 that the definition of mental retardation included the additional requirement of impairment in adaptive behavior (Heber, 1959).

The contemporary beginnings of this construct can be found in Edgar Doll's creation of the Vineland Social Maturity Scale (Doll, 1935, 1953). Doll believed that the main criteria for defining mental deficiency should not be performance on a standardized intelligence scale, but the individual's inability to function independently in the world. The secondary and tertiary criteria of the definition were low intelligence and arrested development (Doll, 1935). Doll argued that adaptive behavior, or in his terms "social competence," was evident only in manifest, typical performance in the environment.

Since Doll's pioneering work, the construct of adaptive behavior has continued to change with various researchers emphasizing different aspects to advance new definitions. Throughout these changes several common themes have persisted. McGrew (1989) identified these as follows: (a) a developmental criterion in which adaptive behavior is expected to vary with age; (b) a cultural/environmental criterion suggesting that adaptive behavior must be evaluated in relation to specific cultural, social or environmental contexts; and (c) a consensus that the general domains of *independent functioning* and *social responsibility* should be included in the definition. Despite this apparent agreement about some of the common themes in the definition of adaptive behavior, disagreement and dissatisfaction with the existing measures of adaptive behavior remain (McGrew & Bruininks, 1989). Most important, however, has been the recognition that mental retardation must include some degree of failure to adapt to specific environmental contexts as evidenced in manifest behavior. In this respect the adaptive behavior construct most closely approximates Charlesworth's (1976, 1978, 1979) ethological approach to intelligent behavior.

Toward a Working Definition of Competence

This review of competence-related constructs in psychological theory suggests that there are common themes, basic differences in focus, and fundamental issues to be considered in formulating a definition of competence. These themes and issues will be summarized and then competence will be defined for the purposes of this chapter.

Common Themes among Competence Constructs

The rubric of "competence" has encompassed a number of different constructs that, in part, may reflect different phenomena (Ford, 1985). Nonetheless, common themes are evident across these constructs, suggesting a family resemblance. Many of these constructs share the following features.

1. Competence-related constructs refer to skills, processes or outcomes related to the effectiveness of adaptation in the environment.

2. It is assumed that the there are individual differences in the quality of adaptation that can be evaluated.

3. Competence behaviors, or the markers of it, have developmental properties: these behaviors and processes show transformation over time, including differentiation and reorganization at more complex levels. Thus, this family of constructs requires that one link adaptation to development.

4. The behavioral manifestations and the underlying processes involved are organized, integrative, coordinated, and actively directed toward effective transactions with the environment.

5. Many underlying processes are implicated in the capacity for, or achievement of, competence; what these processes have in common is their role in facilitating effective functioning in the environment. These processes include a wide array of complex cognitive, affective, and motivational mental functions and their integration in adaptive behavior.

6. Competence is multidimensional.

Major Differences in Competence Constructs

Competence constructs also differ in several major respects, including the following.

1. Although all the competence constructs concern effective adaptation in the environment, they differ in their focus on internal versus external behavior (mental versus observable behavior). This dichotomy of focus reflects, at least in part, the dual tasks of living systems, which must maintain integrity as an organized system while at the same time functioning as part of larger systems (Ford, 1987). This duality has been described repeatedly by theorists concerned with competence, coping, resilience, and adaptation (Ford, 1985; Koestler, 1978; Murphy & Moriarty, 1976). Attempts have been made to transcend this dichotomy by defining competence as the coordinated directing of internal processes in order to achieve good adaptational outcomes (e.g., Waters & Sroufe, 1983). The focus in such efforts is the *transactional* processes between organism and environment.

2. There are corresponding differences in the systems level of focus among the competence constructs. Some focus on the individual system and its equilibrium while others focus on the individual system's functioning in larger ecological systems.

3. Competence constructs differ in their respective emphasis upon processes versus manifestations.

4. Constructs differ in their focus on cognitive, temperamental, or motivational processes.

5. Finally, the scope of the constructs differ. Some of the constructs refer to narrow domains or aspects of functioning, others to a general capacity for adaptation or broad behavioral accomplishments.

Major Issues in Defining Competence

A number of issues have been raised about the nature and measurement of competence (Ford, 1985; Waters & Sroufe, 1983). Two major issues stand out.

1. Perhaps the most central issue concerns the evaluative aspect of competence. Judgments about competence require criteria, values, or normative expectations. They also require a frame of reference and evaluations may vary from different perspectives. Evaluations of effectiveness in the environment also reflect the context for behavior and transactions between organism and environment. Early on, Hartmann (1939/1958) emphasized the "reciprocal relationship between the organism and its environment" in his discussion of the ego and adaptation. An individual's effectiveness may vary in different contexts. Some theories include as one of the internal dispositions toward competence, the ability to find or create the environment that maximizes one's own effectiveness. This process is often referred to as "niche-building" (Scarr & McCartney, 1983). As a species, humans excel in the ability to manipulate the environment to suit their own adaptational needs.

2. A second fundamental issue concerns proximal versus ultimate success in adaptation. It is conceivable that behavior patterns that function to maintain integrated functioning or adaptation to the environment at one point in time, ultimately undermine adaptation and development in the long run because these behaviors foreclose opportunities or linger past the time and place of their usefulness.

In their developmental definition of competence, Waters and Sroufe (1983) argued that the criteria for evaluating competence from a developmental perspective must include both proximate and ultimate criteria of adaptation. Assessments of success in meeting the challenges of developmental tasks at one period of development would be proximal indicators. Solutions to these challenges also would have to pass a longer term test. If adaptations worked in the short-term but compromised future development or adaptation, a child would not be viewed as competent by the standard of Waters and Sroufe (1983). Presumably, developmental tasks in a given culture, and particularly those tasks shared across many cultures, have evolved over time partly in accordance with their significance for long-term adaptation. Solutions to developmental tasks that compromise development and adult adaptation in large segments of a population should eventually change in more favorable directions or undermine the ultimate viability of the population.

A Performance-Based Working Definition of Competence

The following propositions are the basis for our working definition of competence:

1. Competence is a generalization about adaptation or performance based on a "track record." When one refers to an individual as "competent," it is based on a history of manifested effectiveness. A single poor performance does not mean that competence is poor, either for a musician or for an 8-year-old school student. Thus, in the narrow domain case, one is not a competent pianist if one has never played the piano, regardless of one's talent for piano playing, but it is possible for a competent musician to have a bad performance. Similarly, in the broad case, one is not a competent 8-year-old unless there

is a track record of accomplishing the developmental tasks for children of this age, gender, society, and so on. It is possible for a competent 8-year-old to have a bad day.

Competence is judged from previous behavior, but it also conveys an expectation for future competence and an assumption that the person has the capacity for competence, at least under some conditions. Thus, when "competence" is used to mean "a state of being competent" or the "capacity for effective functioning," an inference generally has been made based on prior behavior that leads others to predict that a person can perform effectively in the future.

Competence carries a dual connotation of both capacity and accomplishment. The term "fitness" in evolutionary biology has an analogous ambiguity of meaning in Darwinian theory. Brandon (1990) has indicated that fitness can refer to either actual reproductive success ("realized fitness") or the potential for reproductive success ("expected fitness").

2. Competence carries the connotation of at least "good," but not necessarily "superb" effectiveness. It is used to refer to a broader range of quality than the term "expertise," which conveys a history of very high level performances. The goal of a concert pianist is higher than "competence."

3. Competence refers to patterns of human behavior that require the organization and coordination of a myriad of mental and physical processes to perform complex tasks in the environment. These may be directed toward effective piano performances or, more generally, toward effective performances in the tasks of living.

4. Given that many processes are involved in effective functioning in the environment, there are likely to be many different ways in which the same outcome could be achieved. Given the complexity of these processes, it could be advantageous, as a practical matter, to begin to study such phenomena at the point of observable outcomes, rather than in the middle of complex processes. The study of competence could be anchored by measuring the most readily observed aspects of the phenomena of interest. At the same time, one would need to remember that "outcomes" are part of the ongoing processes and inherently dynamic rather than static in nature.

5. Competence is inherently contextual. It is defined and evaluated in terms of developmental, cultural, ecological, and historical frames of reference. Because we are a social species, adaptation to the social environment is of great importance to society and to the viability of the individuals within them. In most cases, external behavior will be of greater concern to a society than inner states or processes, until such time as inner processes are understood well enough to make direct causal ties between the internal processes and external social behavior.

Based on these propositions, the broad psychological construct of individual competence is defined as

a pattern of effective performance in the environment, evaluated from the perspective of development in ecological and cultural context.

Effectiveness is judged on the basis of normative, developmentally-based standards for individual behavior in a particular ecological and historical context. These standards evolve and vary from one culture to another, yet also share commonalities across history and culture. Such similarities may be due to evolutionary capacities and constraints shared by members of the species as well as to similarities in the ecologies in which humans live. These standards have been described as "salient developmental tasks."

This working definition closely resembles other efforts to define competence by Ford (1985) and Waters and Sroufe (1983). It also reflects the influence of Garmezy (1971, 1974; Garmezy & Nuechterlein, 1972), Hartmann (1939/1958), Phillips (1968), White (1959), and Zigler (Zigler & Glick, 1986).

Competence, by this definition, could be influenced by many mental processes within the organism and transactions between organism and environment (experiences). Therefore, it could be undermined or handicapped in many different ways. Damage, problems, or deficiencies in the central nervous system that affect mental operations and behavior, shortcomings in the social environment for development, limited opportunities, and environmental adversities all could interfere with competence. By definition, anything that substantially diminishes or derails basic development will affect competence. The implications of this definition for the relation of competence and psychopathology will be examined in the following section.

COMPETENCE AND PSYCHOPATHOLOGY

As in the case of competence, "psychopathology" is a term connected to a family of constructs. Reviewing these constructs is beyond the scope of this chapter. Generally, however, psychopathology refers to patterns of psychological functioning, internal or external, that are both deviant and maladaptive (i.e., abnormal behavior). There are many terms and constructs associated with psychopathology. For example, internal and external indicators of maladaptive patterns of behavior have been called "symptoms." In the glossary of DSM-IV (American Psychiatric Association, 1994), "symptom" is defined, in the medical tradition, as "a subjective manifestation of a pathological condition" (p. 771). Patterns of symptoms that consistently occur together and persist over time (at least for some minimal time) have been labelled "syndromes" or "disorders." In DSM-IV, a syndrome is defined as "a grouping of signs and symptoms, based on their frequent co-occurrence" (p. 771). A "behavior problem" usually refers to a repeated maladaptive behavior, that may or may not be one of the symptoms defining a syndrome. These and many other terms and constructs concerned with psychopathology may be found throughout this handbook.

Our goal in this section is to examine the conceptual and empirical linkages between competence and psychopathology. First, we examine the relation of competence to mental disorders through an analysis of the role of competence in the DSM-IV classification system for mental disorders. Then we delineate models of possible linkages between competence and psychopathology. Finally, we review the empirical evidence of linkage.

Mental Disorder and Competence: An Examination of DSM-IV from the Perspective of Competence

The close relation between competence and psychopathology is evident in the Diagnostic and Statistical Manual of the American Psychiatric Association (APA, 1994). The effectiveness of adaptation is implicitly or explicitly incorporated in the definition of mental disorder, the criteria for some disorders, the associated complications of many disorders, the associated impairments of disorders, the course of many disorders, and in Axis V of this multiaxial system, the Global Assessment of Functioning Scale.

The Definition of Mental Disorder

The definition of mental disorder, adopted by the framers of DSM-IV for specifying whether a condition should be included in the manual, highlights three important elements:

1. The mental condition causes significant distress (painful symptom) or disability (impairment in one or more important areas of functioning).
2. It is not merely an expectable and culturally sanctioned response to a particular event.
3. It is a manifestation of a mental dysfunction (see Wakefield, 1992b).

Spitzer and Williams (1982) argued that the *consequences* of a condition, rather than its etiology should determine whether it is a disorder. Because of DSM-IV's non-etiological stance, the diagnostic criteria for any of the disorders included in the manual emphasize point number one, that there exists significant distress or disability. For the most part, true to Spitzer and Williams, these criteria are consequences, evident in observable, manifest behaviors, or reported subjective distress. It is in the disability clause, or impairment in important areas of functioning, that considerable overlap with the definition of competence is evident.

Criteria for Disorder

One way competence is reflected in the diagnostic categories of DSM-IV is simply that clinical judgments, or standardized assessments, of competence (or lack thereof) are listed as diagnostic criteria. Some disorders are defined in part by criteria reflecting how well an individual is functioning in the environment, or, in other words, by competence criteria. The prototypical examples of this are the developmental disorders of Mental Retardation, Pervasive Developmental Disorders, and Learning Disorders. Each of these diagnostic categories meets the definition of mental disorder not because it causes distress, although it may, but because it entails maladaptation with respect to broadly or narrowly defined developmental expectations for functioning in the environment. This set of disorders reflects an assumption of dysfunctions that lead to general delays, or qualitative distortions in the normal processes underlying the development of cognitive, language, motor, or social skills. Along with below-average intellectual functioning, one of the essential features of Mental Retardation is "concurrent deficits or impairments in adaptive functioning" (p. 46). DSM-IV notes that impairments in adaptive functioning, rather than low IQ scores, are usually the presenting

problem in Mental Retardation (p. 40). Here, adaptive functioning refers to "how effectively individuals cope with common life demands and how well they meet the standards of personal independence expected of someone in their particular age group, sociocultural background and community setting" (p. 40). These criteria reflect considerable overlap with the definition of competence. Without this competence deficit, a diagnosis of Mental Retardation cannot be given.

Inclusion of the Learning Disorders in a manual of Mental Disorders remains controversial, as was noted in DSM-III-R (APA, 1987), but these disorders conform to the definition of mental illness by reflecting impairment in important areas of functioning for children. Most frequently, Learning Disorders interfere with a child's functioning in the school setting, but they may also cause more general problems with the activities of daily living.

In contrast to the developmental *delays* of Mental Retardation and Learning Disorders, Pervasive Developmental Disorders reflect *qualitative* impairment in normal adaptive functioning. This impairment is most evident in an individual's social behavior, in what might be termed social competence. Although DSM-IV remains atheoretical as to the etiology of these disorders, it is noted that they are sometimes observed in association with a neurological or other medical condition. There appears to be an underlying assumption that central nervous system dysfunctions cause the distortions in development of competence in this class of disorders.

Another childhood disorder that reflects the inclusion of competence in DSM-IV diagnostic criteria is Conduct Disorder (CD). Children with this diagnosis demonstrate impairments in an important domain of competence, involving adherence to social regulation and rule-governed behavior. Examination of the specific diagnostic criteria for CD indicates that in keeping with the DSM-IV definition of mental disorder, this is *exclusively* a disorder of "disability." In contrast to many of the DSM-IV disorders, in which symptoms of distress may impair a person's ability to function, CD reflects symptoms of maladaptation which may, or may not, lead to distress. Although symptoms of anxiety or depression are common in children with CD, they are considered independent for diagnostic purposes. If severe enough, these symptoms would warrant a second diagnosis of a mood or anxiety disorder in addition to CD. Since distress does not enter into the diagnosis of CD, and no assumption appears to be made about basic mental dysfunctions underlying the disorder, conduct disorder might be considered a competence disorder. (See Richters & Cicchetti, 1993, for a provocative discussion of competence and dysfunction.)

A second way in which competence is reflected in the diagnostic criteria for certain disorders is through a criterion of social or occupational dysfunction. This criterion may require that functioning in important areas of work, interpersonal relations, or self care are markedly below prior levels of functioning. Dysfunction may also be evident in failure to achieve expected levels of interpersonal, academic or occupational achievement. For example, the diagnostic criteria for Schizophrenia include a stipulation of decreased functioning in areas such as work, social relations, and self-care. The disorder is frequently conceptualized as incorporating two phases: an active phase and a prodromal phase. The active phase of the disorder is characterized by psychotic symptoms such as loose associations, hallucinations, and delusions. The development of the active phase is generally preceded by a prodromal phase characterized by symptoms that reflect competence criteria. It is during this phase that decline and failures in social and/or occupational functioning become apparent. Prodromal criteria typically are characterized by negative symptoms such as affective flattening, or alogia, but may also include such social competence indicators as marked social isolation or withdrawal, impairment as either a wage-earner, a student, or a homemaker, and impairment in personal hygiene and grooming.

Deterioration or impairment in functioning may also be evident in the mood disorders. One of the diagnostic criteria for a Manic episode includes significant impairment in social functioning, occupational functioning, or usual social activities or relationships with others. Some impairment in the same areas may be evident in a Hypomanic episode. Similarly, competence criteria are also included in the diagnostic criteria for a Major Depressive episode (MDE). The essential features of the latter involve the symptoms of depressed mood and loss of interest or pleasure in activities which reflect a change from a previous level. However, in order to meet diagnostic criteria for MDE, the symptom pattern must also cause significant distress, *or* impairment in social, occupational, or other important areas of functioning. In severe cases, the person may "lose the ability to function socially or occupationally" (p. 322).

Associated Features of Disorder

Competence also enters into the DSM-IV classification system in the form of "associated features" of some disorders. For these disorders, there is no assumption that competence problems are necessary for the diagnosis, rather the symptoms of the disorder may lead to subsequent competence problems. For example, the essential symptoms of Attention-Deficit Hyperactivity Disorder (ADHD) are developmentally inappropriate levels of inattention, impulsivity, and hyperactivity. The manifest behaviors by which these symptoms are judged, (e.g., "often interrupts or intrudes on others," p. 84) may be single indicators of incompetent behavior, but they do not meet broader definitions of competence. Instead, it is the associated features of this symptom picture that are most related to competence as broadly defined. The associated features of ADHD include such broad-based competence indicators as impaired academic performance and problems with peer and family relationships. DSM-IV also notes that individuals with ADHD may obtain less schooling than their peers and have poorer vocational achievement, and that in its severe form, "the disorder is very impairing, affecting social, familial, and scholastic adjustment" (p. 81). The empirical evidence for these impairments is discussed in more detail later in this chapter.

Course and Prognosis—Axis V

In addition to incorporating competence into the diagnostic criteria for some disorders, DSM-IV also includes the Global Assessment of Functioning Scale (GAF) on Axis V. Clinicians use this scale to make ratings of the individual's psychological, occupational, and social functioning. These ratings provide nondiagnostic information about a patient's course of disorder and prognosis.

The ratings originally were intended to provide prognostic information because it was believed that individuals usually return to their previous level of functioning following an episode of illness. It is suggested in DSM-IV that it may be helpful in some cases to rate the GAF at several time points in order to document changes in level of functioning over time.

With regard to making these ratings, clinicians are given little instruction as to what criteria to consider and the descriptors of each anchor point on the scale are left quite global. This scale allows for ratings of patient functioning (competence) regardless of diagnosis, however, it also includes symptoms as criteria. Thus, it confounds the very purpose for which it was intended: to provide valuable nondiagnostic information. Skodol, Link, Shrout, and Horwath (1988) demonstrated that in a mixed sample of 362 psychiatric inpatients and outpatients, ranging in age from 18 to "over 50," and including a variety of diagnoses, symptoms explained more of the variance in DSM-III Axis V ratings than did adaptive functioning variables. It appears that by including symptoms in its Axis V ratings, DSM-III-R did not improve on this matter (cf. Richters, Cicchetti, Sparrow, & Volkmar, 1993). If the objective of providing independent nondiagnostic information is retained, then it would be preferable to exclude symptoms and to provide clearer guidelines in how to rate important aspects of social and occupational functioning.

The authors of DSM-IV have already begun to attend to this issue by proposing the Social and Occupational Functioning Assessment Scale (SOFAS) as an axis provided for further study. The SOFAS represents an attempt to assess occupational and social functioning independent of overall severity of an individual's psychological symptoms. Any impairment must be due to mental or physical health problems and not simply to lack of opportunity or environmental limitations. Such efforts signify a recognition of the importance of elucidating the meaning and relations between competence and psychopathology.

Conclusions about the Definition of Mental Disorder in DSM-IV as It Relates to Competence

The definition of mental disorder in DSM-IV, both as explicitly defined and as inferred from diagnostic criteria and associated features, is integrally related to adaptive functioning. However, the precise relation of the two concepts is not articulated in this document. Some disorders are defined solely by external adaptive functioning, others by internal symptoms, others by both. In the case of disorders defined without relying on competence-related symptoms, it seems clear that impairment in external adaptation is assumed or predicted. The role of externally adaptive functioning, and thereby competence, is so pervasive that it seems reasonable to pose this question: If there is no impairment in adaptive functioning in the environment, is there mental disorder? Certainly, external adaptation could be impaired for other reasons besides mental disorder, such as extremely adverse environments, discrimination, physical handicaps, or nonmental diseases. Thus, mental disorder cannot be defined solely in terms of external adaptation or "failures of competence." Then what are the essential features of a mental disorder?

Wakefield (1992a, 1992b) has argued that a mental disorder is a "harmful dysfunction." Dysfunction is defined by Wakefield as "the failure of an internal mechanism to perform a natural [evolved through natural selection] function" (1992a, p. 374). "Harmful" refers to negative consequences as defined by sociocultural standards (Wakefield, 1992a). Thus, Wakefield's definition emphasizes how internal mental operations are related to external adaptation. A dysfunction that significantly impairs competence (as defined in this chapter) would be harmful.

Models of How Competence Could Be Related to Psychopathology

Theoretically, there are a number of reasons competence might be related to psychopathology. Several of them will be discussed next.

The Criteria for Judging Competence and Psychopathology Overlap

One reason competence may be related to psychopathology is because there is an overlap in the indicators used to measure the two constructs. For example, externalizing symptoms could lie on the negative end of a dimension of social competence while compliance with rules and authority and other prosocial behaviors could fall on the opposite pole. Academic achievement and social acceptance are common indicators of competence where failures could be treated as symptoms. In other words, disorders could be comprised of symptom patterns that reflect, in part or entirely, poor performance on developmental tasks, using the same implicit criteria by which competence is judged.

Psychopathology Interferes with Competence or Its Development

Competence requires the successful coordination of many psychological processes in interactions with the environment. If psychopathology reflects dysfunction in these processes or deficits in basic central nervous system functioning required for competence, then competence could be compromised or undermined by psychopathology. This could occur in several ways: (a) permanent deficits in brain functioning could continuously impair learning and effective transactions with the environment; (b) a disease process in the brain could alter or disrupt the basic mental activities (e.g., perception, attention, motivation, problem solving) required for competence, either temporarily or progressively; or (c) symptoms of disorder could lead to the development of behaviors that eventually have adverse effects on competence. In the first two cases, the basic tools for competence that could be disrupted include complex cognitive, affective, or motivational processes that have a range of individual differences and many different possibilities for dysfunction. In the last case, if the symptoms of a disorder are aversive to other people, for example, the environmental supports for competence could be altered unfavorably.

Since competence refers in this discussion to a pattern of effective *external* functioning, it is conceivable that a person with internal symptoms could still behave effectively. In theory, a person could feel distressed but still do well in school, although at severe levels of internal distress, competence presumably would suffer. Given this theoretical possibility, the relation of internalizing symptoms and competence may be particularly interesting to examine.

Failure to Achieve Competence Contributes to Psychopathology

It is conceivable that failures of competence could contribute to psychopathology, primarily through the effects on psychological well-being. Loss of face, peer rejection, school failure, or perceived lack of success in any area valued by the person could produce symptoms of distress, frustration, or other reactions. A chain reaction is also possible, wherein symptoms of a disorder lead to competence failures which then in turn exacerbate symptoms or cause new symptoms. Organizational theories suggest that there may be lawful causal sequencing of behavior patterns, including psychopathology as well as competence, resulting from developmental processes and organism-environment transactions (Cicchetti, 1990b; Cicchetti & Schneider-Rosen, 1986; Sroufe, 1979; Sroufe & Rutter, 1984).

A Common Etiological Factor Produces both Problems in Competence and Characteristic Symptoms of a Disorder

Shared biological or environmental causal influences could independently contribute to two distinct classes of problems, both symptoms and diminished competence. This could be due to a general risk factor such as parental neglect or a brain disorder, that by differing mechanisms, leads to a classic set of symptoms comprising a disorder as well as competence problems.

Studies Linking Competence and Psychopathology

Because the empirical literature pertinent to the linkages of competence and psychopathology is extensive and diverse, the following review is necessarily selective rather than inclusive. Additional data relevant to this topic may be found in many other chapters of this manual. Highlighted here are studies of children and adolescents that explicitly include both measures of competence and measures of symptoms or disorder. The emphasis is on school-aged children and adolescents. Very relevant research on infants and toddlers, such as longitudinal studies linking attachment to later competence and symptoms are excluded (see Carlson & Sroufe, this manual). Studies linking broad indicators of psychopathology or multiple disorders and competence are reviewed first. Next, studies of internalizing and externalizing symptoms are examined in relation to competence, followed by studies on peer relations. Finally, data on selected disorders are examined in relation to competence.

Comprehensive or Multifaceted Studies Encompassing Competence and Psychopathology

Most broad studies linking competence and psychopathology focus on dimensions of psychopathology, such as internalizing and externalizing symptoms, psychiatric disorders, or what is often termed "adjustment" outcomes, variously defined, and link these to school achievement, peer relations, and behavioral conduct. The choice of indicators of adequate versus inadequate functioning may reflect developmental tasks and expectations, although this is rarely articulated.

In their classic reviews of the data on childhood predictors of adult adjustment, Kohlberg and colleagues (Kohlberg, LaCrosse,

& Ricks, 1972; Kohlberg, Ricks, & Snarey, 1984) reached several conclusions:

1. Academic achievement is a good global predictor of adult outcomes, including social adaptation and mental disorders, but primarily through its covariance with developmental-adaptational traits such as IQ and antisocial behavior.
2. Antisocial behavior is a powerful predictor of later adjustment.
3. The quality of peer relations, particularly peer acceptance or rejection, is a good general predictor of later outcomes.

They also concluded that emotional symptoms, withdrawal, and dependency had much less or little predictive power over time.

These authors argued that "developmental-adaptational" achievements, such as academic achievement, are cumulative by nature and heavily based on cognitive development. For these reasons, these adaptational achievements tended not to be "lost." Poor adaptation would tend, if anything, to improve. Meanwhile, emotional disturbances were expected to wax and wane with little cumulative effect and thus were expected to be less stable and less predictive of later problems.

There have been many empirical studies of the structure and classification of psychopathology, yet little attention has been given to exploring the dimensional structure of competence and how these dimensions may relate to pathological dimensions. An exception is the work of Kohn and Rosman (1972, 1973). These investigators explicitly examined the structure of symptom and social competence measures in preschoolers. Their analysis revealed that each type of measure yielded two broad dimensions of socio-emotional functioning. Both the competence set of measures and the symptom set included a dimension of social withdrawal or isolation, the main difference being that in the competence set of measures, this dimension was bipolar, with a positive pole describing general involvement and interest with people and activities. The second factor of each measure included antisocial behavior, but again, the competence set had a positive pole of cooperative, compliant behavior. These two parallel dimensions correlated 0.75 and 0.79, respectively, across the two types of measures. Allowing for measurement error, these strong correlations suggest the possibility that the same two basic dimensions of behavior are being tapped by the competence and by the symptom sets of measures.

In a longitudinal study of these two dimensions, Kohn (1977) followed a large sample of preschoolers in New York City for five years. Combining the symptom and competence measures, composite measures of two global dimensions of social-emotional functioning were formed. Termed "apathy-withdrawal" and "anger-defiance" (named for the negative poles), these dimensions were modestly correlated ($r = 0.35$). Each was found to have significant stability over time. Both dimensions predicted later academic problems. The withdrawal dimension was more strongly related to reading problems than the defiance dimension. However, each dimension predicted the other over time, hence the effects of the defiance dimension on academic achievement may have been partially mediated by its effects on apathy-withdrawal.

The explicit relation of competence to current and future problems has been examined in a number of studies. One study

identified four groups of elementary school children according to median splits on two relatively independent dimensions of social and academic competence (Blechman, Tinsley, Carella, & McEnroe, 1985). Competent children (high on both) had the lowest scores on a problem checklist while incompetent children (low on both) had the highest scores.

The classic Woodlawn studies also have provided data linking earlier competence to later problems (Kellam, Brown, Rubin, & Ensminger, 1983). Two facets of adaptation ("mental health") were assessed in this study: psychological well-being and social adaptational status. The latter refers to "the adequacy of the individual's role function in the major social fields appropriate to his or her place in the life cycle" (Kellam et al., 1983, p. 18) and, according to the definition adopted in this chapter, to competence.

The Woodlawn participants were drawn from a poor, African-American community on the south side of Chicago. In the longitudinal analyses described by Kellam et al. (1983), data from a large cohort of first graders assessed in 1966/1967 and followed up in 1975/1976 were examined to identify possible developmental pathways to psychiatric problems and substance abuse in adolescence. Well-being and social adaptation were assessed in first grade and related to these psychopathology outcomes at ages 16 to 17. Social adaptational status in several areas of functioning was primarily assessed by teacher observations and ratings. Results were quite different for males and females. Well-being had little predictive significance for males but was related to later symptoms, particularly depression, in females. Early learning problems related to adolescent psychiatric symptoms, particularly in males. In addition, aggressive behavior predicted later substance abuse in males, while shyness alone had little relation to this outcome. However, the combination of shyness and aggressive behavior was strongly related to substance abuse in males.

A small number of empirical studies have examined the concurrent or antecedent competence of children with various disorders. Several studies have drawn on longitudinal data sets with broad assessments of adaptation over time.

The Dunedin, New Zealand, cohort, for example, has provided data relevant to the topic of competence and disorder (see Caspi & Moffitt, this manual). This cohort includes about 1000 children born in 1972/1973. One study of this cohort examined the current and antecedent competence of children with a single or multiple DSM-III disorders diagnosed at age 11 (Anderson, Williams, McGee, & Silva, 1989). Children with attention deficit disorder and those with multiple disorders at age 11 had significantly lower reading and spelling achievement at ages 7, 9, and 11. When disorders occurred together, diagnoses usually included attention deficit disorder and either conduct or oppositional disorder. At age 11, these children (mostly boys) were disliked and isolated from their peers and this effect had increased over time since they were age 5. Anxious-depressed children also were less liked or more solitary than nondisordered peers and antecedent data suggested that these effects had increased since age 7.

Another analysis of the Dunedin data shed additional light on the antecedent competence of boys with attention deficit disorder alone versus those with multiple problems. Moffitt (1990) analyzed the developmental trajectories of 4 groups of boys from this cohort: (a) those with no disorder; (b) those with attention deficit disorder (ADD) only; (c) those with ADD plus delinquency; and (d) those with only delinquency, as diagnosed at age 11 (ADD) or 13 (delinquency). Boys with both problems had worse developmental histories than other groups. Both reading and verbal IQ scores were lowest among this group for assessments beginning at age 5 (verbal IQ only), and subsequently at ages 7, 9, and 11 (verbal IQ and reading). Boys with only ADD had mild reading problems and no IQ deficits. The delinquent-only group showed no evidence of reading or IQ problems.

The linkage between social competence and disorder in the Dunedin sample was examined directly in a subsequent analysis of data from the 11-and 15-year-old assessments of this cohort (McGee & Williams, 1991). A composite rating of social competence included the quality of relationships with parents and peers, school involvement, and involvement in activities. At age 11, social competence was related to disorder and to the level of internalizing and externalizing symptom scores, particularly for boys. Competence at age 11 did not add to the prediction of disorder at age 15 over and above the role of stability in internalizing and externalizing symptoms over time. However, among children with an externalizing disorder at age 11, poor social competence predicted persistence of externalizing disorder, suggesting a moderating influence of competence on prognosis. For boys, ongoing externalizing symptoms appeared to have a small effect on social competence at age 15. By age 15, the rate of disorder, particularly for externalizing disorders, was much higher in adolescents with poor social competence. Internalizing disorders had some current relation to social competence in girls and no relation in boys.

Another cohort followed for many years, the New York Child Longitudinal Study, comprised of white, middle, and upper class, primarily Jewish children, also has provided relevant data. One study linked school failure to disorder (Velez, Johnson, & Cohen, 1989). Repeating a grade was a significant risk factor for all five of the disorders assessed at ages 11 and 20, including conduct disorder, attention deficit disorder, oppositional disorder, overanxiety disorder, and major depression. The association was strongest for attention deficit disorder. However, the role of comorbidity in these associations was not examined.

Another analysis of this data set focused on two dimensions of negative functioning: labeled "Aggression" (aggressive, noncompliant) and "Affect" (emotional disturbance) assessed at ages 1 to 12. Their significance for later adolescent functioning was examined for three major domains of positive adjustment: school, social, and family (Lerner, Hertzog, Hooker, Hassibi, & Thomas, 1988). Structural modeling results indicated that the aggression construct was highly stable and was strongly and negatively related to all three adjustment outcomes. The affect construct was stable but not predictive of adjustment outcomes.

An epidemiological study of mental health in a large sample of children 4 to 16 years old in Ontario, Canada, has provided data on academic competence in relation to four composite disorders: conduct disorder, hyperactivity, emotional disorder, and somatization (Offord, Boyle, & Racine, 1989). Results were inconsistent by informant. Children identified by parents as having attention deficit hyperactivity disorder had elevated rates of school failure whereas children with other disorders did not. In contrast, when children were identified by teacher (age 4 to 11) or self (age 12 to 16) as disordered, only those children with conduct disorder had more school failure.

A subsequent follow-up study of this sample indicated that initial "problems getting along" predicted the persistence of disorder four years later (Offord et al., 1992). Problems getting along included relations with peers, teachers, and parents. Children originally diagnosed with conduct disorders had the highest rates of conduct and other disorders and worse problems getting along 4 years later compared to other groups, significantly greater than a nondisordered control group (significance of differences with other disordered groups are not reported). In contrast, the highest rates of school problems were observed for children who originally had hyperactivity or emotional disorders. Children with conduct disorder did not differ significantly from nondisordered controls in the rate of poor school performance four years later.

These longitudinal findings from the Ontario study need to be viewed with some caution for two reasons. First, as noted by the authors, there was substantial attrition and missing data in the follow-up. Analyses indicated that attrition was higher for children with greater pathology and family adversity, suggesting the possibility of greater attrition among severe cases of conduct disorder and children with multiple diagnoses. Second, the role of comorbidity was not sorted out in the analyses. A high percentage of children had more than one disorder in this study and it would have been much more informative if analyses had systematically examined the role of comorbidity for prognosis.

Many of the studies reviewed here as well as the more extensive literature reviewed by Kohlberg have suggested that emotional symptoms, such as anxiety and depression, have different relations to competence than conduct-related symptoms, such as aggression, noncompliance, and hyperactivity. In part, this could be due to the overlap in the conduct aspect of behavior that is often a criterion for both competence or adjustment (compliant, obeys rules and laws) and symptoms (externalizing, antisocial, conduct-disordered). While this confound may be evident in some of the relations between competence and symptoms, externalizing problems also appear to have strong correlations with other domains of adaptation that do not overlap in concept or content, such as academic achievement and peer relations.

Studies reviewed in this section also suggest a connection between symptoms of attention deficit/hyperactivity disorder and antisocial behavior that is associated with worse competence or prognosis. This finding will be explored further in the following sections.

Affective symptoms appear to be associated with withdrawal and sometimes with reduced social competence. The differential correlates of emotional and conduct symptoms with competence are examined further in the next section.

Internalizing and Externalizing Symptoms Related to Competence

Measures of child behavior problems and symptoms frequently index two major dimensions, often termed "internalizing" and "externalizing," or "overcontrolled" and "undercontrolled" (see Achenbach, this manual; Achenbach, 1966, 1991a, 1991b; Achenbach & Edelbrock, 1978). Popular measures, such as the

Child Behavior Checklist (Achenbach & Edelbrock, 1983) have been widely used in research and hence there are many studies relating these problem dimensions to other variables, including competence indicators.

The Child Behavior Checklist (CBCL) and the ACQ Behavior Checklist (a composite of leading child behavior checklists developed by Achenbach, Conners, and Quay) include an assessment of social competence as well as the two symptom dimensions. The rationally based competence scores include a Total Competence Score and three subscales: Activities, Social and School. Competence scores significantly differentiate clinic from non-clinic samples (Achenbach, 1991b; Achenbach & Edelbrock, 1983; Achenbach, Howell, Quay, & Conners, 1991).

There is also a Teacher Report Form (TRF) version of Achenbach's behavior checklist measures (Achenbach, 1991c). The TRF includes scales to measure academic performance, four aspects of "adaptive functioning" (Working Hard, Behaving Appropriately, Learning, and Happy), and a Total Adaptive Functioning composite of the four. These scales also discriminate between normative and clinic samples (Achenbach, 1991c) for boys and girls between the ages of 5 and 18. The Manual for the TRF (Achenbach, 1991c) also reports strong correlations of TRF adaptive functioning scores with another widely used scale, the Conners Revised Teacher Rating Scale. For example, the "Hyperactivity Index" scores on the Conners correlated −0.40 to −0.62 with the 4 subscales and −0.66 with the Total Adaptive scores for a small sample of children referred for evaluation.

Children can be identified as "Internalizers" or "Externalizers" according to their overall profile patterns on the CBCL. Children with Internalizing profiles have been found to have better scores on the academic and sometimes the social competence scales of the CBCL than children with Externalizing profiles (Edelbrock & Achenbach, 1980). In a study of clinic-referred children, 6- to 11-year-old Internalizing boys had higher scores on the Activities and Social subscales of the CBCL and better scores on teacher ratings of Adaptive Classroom Functioning (McConaughy, Achenbach, & Gent, 1988). Internalizers also had better "on-task" performance judged by classroom observers blind to CBCL scores. Although individually assessed achievement scores were higher in some, but not all, areas for Internalizers, neither teachers nor parents rated Internalizers differently than Externalizers on school performance. However, the Externalizing subgroup of children with a Hyperactive profile had the lowest school performance ratings as well as the lowest overall competence ratings by both parents and teachers. Verbal and Full Scale IQ scores were also higher for Internalizers than Externalizers.

Another study relating parent CBCL scores to competence in a 6- to 12-year-old referred sample also found externalizing scores more strongly related to negative scores on competence indicators (Cohen, Kershner, & Wehrspann, 1988). Parent-reported externalizing scores were associated with more teacher-rated conduct problems and hyperactivity. Lower externalizing scores were associated with better teacher ratings of academic performance, rule compliance, and peer sociability. Internalizing symptoms were significantly related only to teacher ratings of lower peer sociability. In other words, teachers' ratings of competence were

related more strongly to parent ratings of externalizing symptoms than to internalizing symptoms. Neither symptom profile as rated by parents was correlated with reading or IQ scores in this clinic sample. Parent ratings of school competence were related to teacher ratings of academic competence, rule compliance, inattention, but not to other conduct problems or peer sociability. Parent ratings of social competence were not related to any teacher rating or test result.

Longitudinal data on the CBCL has been provided by a study of divorce that followed children from ages 4 to 10 (Hetherington, Cox, & Cox, 1985). High externalizing symptoms in preschool predicted lower competence at age 10 as well as higher internalizing and externalizing scores. Internalizing scores had less predictive significance; externalizing scores generally were as good or better predictors of internalizing scores at age 10 than earlier internalizing symptoms. Early competence scores predicted later competence, but had little predictive significance for either symptom dimension.

Other longitudinal studies of internalizing and externalizing symptoms on the CBCL or ACQ have demonstrated stability for both dimensions (Koot & Verhulst, 1992; McConaughy, Stanger, & Achenbach, 1992; Stanger, McConaughy, & Achenbach, 1992; Verhulst & van der Ende, 1992). In a four-year follow-up of a Dutch cohort of 4- to 12-year-olds, Koot and Verhulst (1992) found that problem scores predicted later problems better than competence scores, although the School subscale did predict later academic problems. Global Externalizing scores and the Aggressive subscale were particularly predictive of mental health referral and trouble with the law, but did not predict special education services. In contrast, Internalizing scores and the Attention problems score predicted referral for special education services as well as mental health services, but not police contacts, the measure of trouble with the law. Notably, the Anxious/Depressed subscale of Internalizing did not have unique predictive significance for any of these outcomes.

These studies of internalizing and externalizing symptoms are generally congruent with findings from the broad studies reviewed in the previous section. Strong concurrent and predictive relations are found between externalizing symptoms and competence in various domains. These studies support other findings suggesting that a subgroup of hyperactive externalizing children appear to have worse academic competence than either internalizing or externalizing children. Studies of internalizing problems have less consistent findings, but data suggest stability in internalizing symptoms and some association with less peer sociability. On the whole, data also suggest that internalizing symptoms have less significance for academic achievement problems than externalizing symptoms.

These studies have not been as informative as one might hope for on the question of how the two dimensions are uniquely, and in combination, related to competence. This problem is difficult to clarify in part because internalizing and externalizing symptoms tend to be highly correlated. For example, the 1991 CBCL Manual reports an average correlation of 0.54 for clinic and 0.59 for nonreferred samples (Achenbach, 1991b). In studies of profile types, both dimensions are used to classify children as "Internalizers" or "Externalizers," making it difficult to know whether the predictive power derives more from one dimension than the other. Moreover, the interaction of these two dimensions rarely have been examined, perhaps because of multicollinearity problems. Thus, it is not clear whether children with both kinds of symptoms simply have more problems for additive reasons and thereby correspondingly lower competence, or if there is a synergistic effect of the two kinds of symptoms. These questions may be important for understanding the widespread phenomenon of "comorbidity" in clinic or hospital samples of children.

Peer Relations, Competence, and Psychopathology

Quality of peer relations is widely held to be key index of competence in childhood and adolescence. As salient developmental tasks, getting along with peers and peer friendships should predict subsequent adaptation (Waters & Sroufe, 1983). A considerable body of evidence supports both the concurrent and predictive validity of peer relations as a marker of competence and correlate of adaptation (Asher & Hymel, 1981; Hartup, 1983; Morison & Masten, 1991; Parker & Rubin, this manual; Rubin & Coplan, 1992). Concurrent problems with peers, including peer rejection (i.e., being generally disliked), have been widely reported among children with symptoms of psychopathology or diagnosed disorders (Hartup, 1983; Rolf, 1972; Strauss, Lahey, Frick, Frame, & Hynd, 1988). Peer rejection has also been linked with a variety of symptoms, including hyperactivity, anxiety, and most particularly, aggressive and disruptive behavior (French, & Waas, 1985; Hartup, 1983; Parker & Asher, 1987; Rubin & Coplan, 1992).

The linkage of peer relations and later psychopathology has interested investigators for some time. Parker and Asher (1987) reviewed the evidence implicating poor peer relations as a risk factor for later psychopathology. Three major indices of peer problems were examined: low peer acceptance or rejection (not liked or disliked), aggression, and shyness/withdrawal. Earlier rejection and aggression were clearly related to later dropping out and delinquency. Much less evidence supported the relation of shyness or withdrawal to poor later adjustment. However, the reviewers concluded that there were too few adequate studies of these indicators to conclude that shyness or withdrawal had no predictive significance. They suggested that greater differentiation of peer problems was needed in studies using more sophisticated models of causal linkages among peer relations and adaptation. Parker and Asher also noted that while retrospective and follow-back studies of adults with serious psychopathology, particularly schizophrenia, have often found evidence of peer problems, prospective evidence for this link was sparse.

Subsequent research has emphasized more fine-grained classification of peer-rejected children in various ways. Social isolation as a risk factor has been examined more closely by Rubin, Hymel, and colleagues (Hymel, Rubin, Rowden, & LeMare, 1990; Rubin, Hymel, Mills, & Rose-Krasnor, 1991). They have argued that social isolation is a complex construct with multiple meanings. Some children may actively isolate themselves (withdraw) from peers due to anxiety, for example, while others are ostracized by peers because of their aggressive behavior. They predict that children who self-isolate due to anxiety would be at some risk for internalizing problems. In a longitudinal study of withdrawn children, these investigators have found some evidence to support

this view. Especially as such children grew older, withdrawal was related to internalizing symptoms and lower self-perceptions of social competence. The degree to which these results reflected the stability of internalizing behavior rather than the added risk of social isolation was not clear.

"Withdrawal," of course, has long been considered an internalizing symptom. For example, on the CBCL, the "withdrawn" items, which factor together as a narrow-band symptom dimension, load with two other narrow-band dimensions, anxious/depressed and somatic complaints, on the higher order internalizing dimension (Achenbach, 1991b).

Additional cross-sectional data are consistent with the findings of Rubin's group. A study of peer-rejected 7th and 8th grade students found two groups: one more disruptive/aggressive, and the other more submissive (Parkhurst & Asher, 1992). Children in the submissive-rejected group were lonelier than average students and also had more concerns about being humiliated and rejected, but were not more aggressive or disruptive than average students. Another study (Strauss, Forehand, Smith, & Frame, 1986) has found that children in 2nd to 5th grade who interact very little with peers have more symptoms of depression and anxiety (discussed further later in this chapter).

The possible long-term effects of a "shy" interpersonal style (children rated as socially anxious or inhibited) have been examined in the archival data of the Berkeley Guidance Study (Caspi, Elder, & Bem, 1988). Shy boys were more likely to delay entrance into adult social roles, including marriage, having children, and establishing careers. In contrast, shy girls were not delayed and were more likely than other girls to follow a traditional pattern of marriage, homemaking, and childrearing. Neither shy boys or girls showed a greater likelihood of serious pathological outcomes in this small normative study.

Very few longitudinal studies have examined the association of peer relations to subsequent adaptation in terms of both competence and symptoms. One study examined the predictive significance of three dimensions of peer reputation in middle childhood for adolescent adaptation seven years later (Morison & Masten, 1991). Positive peer reputation, based on ratings of sociability and leadership qualities, was broadly predictive of adolescent adaptation, correlating both with internalizing and externalizing symptoms as well as with social, academic, and job competence. Adolescent social competence scores included ratings of social acceptance, quality of friendships, and activeness of social life. Peer reputation as disruptive and aggressive was related to adolescent academic and job competence, as well as externalizing symptoms. Sensitive-isolated reputation was related to lower social competence in adolescence. However, interesting sex differences emerged for peer reputation as sensitive-isolated. Boys with this reputation in middle childhood were less involved in sports and activities later (perhaps because they had been less athletically involved earlier on). Girls with this reputation were more involved in sports and activities and had fewer externalizing symptoms in adolescence, despite somewhat lower social competence. Sensitive-isolated reputation was not related to later internalizing symptoms for either boys or girls.

Peer rejection predicted a broad array of problems five years later in another study of children assessed sociometrically in the

4th grade (Ollendick, Weist, Borden, & Greene, 1992). On follow-up, rejected children had failed more grades, had more adjudicated offenses, were more likely to drop out, and were rated as more aggressive.

Peer rejection was explicitly compared to aggressive behavior as a predictor of later adaptation in another longitudinal study where sociometric status in 5th grade was analyzed as a general, or specific, predictor of externalizing problems in adolescence (Kupersmidt & Coie, 1990). Aggression was a better predictor of negative outcomes than peer rejection. Only for the white subsample were both rejection and aggression significant predictors. Aggression and school absences were the only significant unique predictors of subsequent school dropout. Results of this study highlighted the need for studies testing alternative causal models linking peer relations to psychopathology, for example, to sort out the causal influences of aggression and peer rejection on competence and psychopathology.

A subsequent longitudinal study also directly compared the unique predictive significance of childhood aggression and peer rejection for later adjustment (Coie, Lochman, Terry, & Hyman, 1992). Peer assessments in 3rd grade included social status and peer ratings of aggressive behavior. In 6th grade, after a transition to middle school, the sample was rated by teachers on academic achievement and school conduct, which yielded a single "Adjustment" score. Parents completed the CBCL and adolescents were interviewed. Although results were not consistent across all outcomes, peer rejection and aggression scores each made unique contributions to the prediction of several key outcomes, including parent ratings of externalizing symptoms, adolescent ratings of internalizing symptoms, and teacher ratings of adjustment.

The role of aggression in peer rejection is undoubtedly complex. Many aggressive children are not rejected and many rejected children are not aggressive (Dunn & McGuire, 1992; French, 1988). Moreover, "aggression" is a very broad construct. Qualitative differences in the nature of aggressive behavior and its context may be crucial to the processes that underlie rejection. One study found differential patterns of relations linking bullying, reactive, and instrumental types of aggression to peer rejection in first and third grade boys (Coie, Dodge, Terry, & Wright, 1991). Social norms for these behaviors appeared to be important as well. Rejected, aggressive boys were more hostile and violated peer norms for aggressive interactions. Instrumental aggression was a prominent correlate of rejection even in first grade. In keeping with other studies, findings also suggested that aggression often "works": in the short-term, it is reinforced, even though the long-term cost may be high.

A number of studies have suggested that the combination of aggression and isolation in peer relations has greater significance than aggression alone. Woodlawn data described above suggested that "shy/withdrawn" children who were also aggressive had a particularly high risk of later substance abuse (Kellam et al., 1983). Other studies have found that aggressive/withdrawn or aggressive/rejected children have more problems than children who are only aggressive (Ledingham, 1981; Ledingham & Schwartzman, 1984; Milich & Landau, 1984). Some boys with both reputations may have the symptoms of two disorders, attention deficit hyperactivity disorder and conduct disorder, a combination in the

psychiatric literature that has been associated with early onset of problems and poor prognosis.

The processes by which problems in peer relations become linked to psychopathology have not been well-established. One of the most developed models to date has been proposed and tested by investigators from the Oregon Social Learning Center (Dishion, 1990; Dishion, Patterson, Stoolmiller, & Skinner, 1991; Patterson, 1986; Patterson & Capaldi, 1990; Patterson & Stoolmiller, 1991; Vuchinich, Bank, & Patterson, 1992). This group has proposed that inept parenting leads to antisocial behavior in boys that in turn leads to peer difficulties. Antisocial behavior in boys also contributes to negative parenting in a reciprocal fashion. Both parenting and antisocial behavior contribute to academic problems, which also purportedly have a negative influence on peer relations. Poor academic performance and normative peer rejection are hypothesized to lead eventually to association with deviant peer groups that promote delinquent behavior. This view is congruent with delinquency theorists who support the "birds of a feather" hypothesis of co-offending (Reiss & Farrington, 1991). These patterns have been supported by structural modeling of cross-sectional and longitudinal data in studies by the Oregon group and by close observations of coercive sequences of behavior in the homes of antisocial children.

"Dual failure" (in school and with peers) has been posited to lead to depressed mood as well (Capaldi, 1991; Patterson & Stoolmiller, 1991). Thus far, however, data support the possible influence of failure with peers on depressed mood more consistently than the influence of academic failure (Patterson, Reid, & Dishion, 1992). (This model is discussed further later.)

Deviant peer groups have been the subject of intense theoretical interest in the criminology literature (Gillmore, Hawkins, Day, & Catalano, 1992). "Cultural deviance" theories propose that peer relations in delinquent groups are similar to other adolescent peer groups except that the group holds deviant norms which reinforce delinquent behavior. "Social control" theories, in contrast, emphasize lack of bonding to other people and to society. From this perspective, association with deviant peer groups is thought to result more from a lack of alternatives (due to rejection by prosocial peers) than from preference. Thus, peer relations among deviant delinquents would be expected to differ from that of conventional adolescents, particularly in social skills and friendship quality. Evidence has been mixed on the nature and quality of peer relations among delinquent adolescents and does not clearly refute either perspective (Gillmore et al., 1992). It is possible that each view is true, at least for some adolescents.

Another process by which aggressive children come to be rejected by peers has been proposed and tested by Dodge and colleagues in a series of studies (Dodge, 1986; Dodge & Frame, 1982; Dodge, Murphy, & Buchsbaum, 1984; Dodge, Pettit, McClaskey, & Brown, 1986). They have argued that the social cognitions of aggressive children lead them to ascribe hostile intentions to other people under specific conditions (threat to self, ambiguity) and to respond accordingly. Peers in turn observe hostile behavior that seems unprovoked, leading to further dislike and rejection. These transactions exacerbate the aggressive behavior of the aggressive child and his rejections by peers, in a negative cycle. The source of the aggression and attributions of aggressive children is another question. One possibility is that aggression and hostile attributional styles develop in the context of child maltreatment (Dodge, Bates, & Pettit, 1990; Rieder & Cicchetti, 1989).

These two research groups have begun to identify and test processes by which aggressive, noncompliant children may inadvertently undermine the development of their own competence. Their behavior not only may elicit responses from others that have a negative effect on them, it may also alter their opportunities for participation and learning in positive social groups and for high quality educational experiences. Caspi, Elder, and Bem (1987) have suggested that maladaptive behaviors in such cases persist as a result of two processes, termed "cumulative continuity" and "interactional continuity." The former refers to the process by which and individual's behaviors "channel him into environments that perpetuate those behaviors" (Caspi et al., 1987). They also propose that individuals have maladaptive interactional styles with other people that evoke responses that maintain maladaptive behavior, a process they term "interactional continuity." The coercion cycles Patterson and colleagues have described in the interactions of parents and antisocial children are one example of interactional continuity. Caspi and coworkers suggested these processes to explain the maladaptive outcomes of children with temper tantrums. These children as adults tended to have declining SES (indexed by occupation for men and marriage for women), more divorces, and erratic work (males) or parenting (females) histories.

In summary, data support the importance of peer relations as correlates of current and future competence and psychopathology. Peer rejection is associated with worse adaptation in other domains of competence, currently and in the future. Strong evidence points to aggression as a contributor to peer rejection and later problems. The reciprocal role of peer rejection for exacerbating antisocial behavior has not been adequately examined, although evidence suggests that it may contribute to the entry (by default or selection) into antisocial peer groups. In comparison, evidence is weaker on the possible role of shy/withdrawn peer relations for future development. However, it is not clear whether weaker predictions are found from withdrawn behavior to later adaptation because of methodological shortcomings or because withdrawal from peers has less adaptational significance than rejection by peers. Current evidence is consistent with the hypothesis that withdrawal predicts a narrower range of problems in later competence than does peer rejection.

Despite the importance ascribed to friendship as an important developmental task in middle childhood and adolescence (Hartup, 1983, 1992; Hartup & Sancilio, 1986; Sullivan, 1953), little research has specifically considered friendship as distinct from peer acceptance or rejection in relation to psychopathology. Aggressive children and adolescents rejected by peers may have social networks with similarly aggressive peers and antisocial friends, both of which support and encourage further escalations of aggressive behavior (Cairns, Cairns, Neckerman, Gest, & Gariepy, 1988). "Socialized delinquency" has been associated with such deviant peer clusters. Nonetheless, the quality of friend relationships in adolescence has been related to

better adjustment, which is consistent with developmental theory that includes intimacy and close friendships as important developmental tasks of adolescence (Buhrmester, 1990). There is also evidence that friendships ease school adjustment among younger children (Ladd, 1990). In their review, Parker and Asher (1987) also called for further research on lack of friendship as a risk factor for development.

Competence in Children with Specific Disorders

There is a diverse and very extensive literature linking competence to specific categories of disorder. Two externalizing and two internalizing classes of disorders were chosen as examples for the purposes of this chapter: attention deficit/hyperactivity disorders (here referred to as ADHD, but including studies that may use definitional criteria that differ from DSM-III-R or DSM-IV for diagnosis) and conduct disorder as examples of externalizing disorders; depression and anxiety disorders as illustrations of internalizing disorders. There has been considerable research on these four groups of disorders, and there is considerable comorbidity among them. Moreover, they relate to competence in diverse ways. An exhaustive review of competence across all disorders was beyond the scope of this chapter. The reader is referred to many other chapters of this manual for further discussions of adaptation in relation to specific disorders.

Attention-Deficit Hyperactivity Disorder and Competence

The diagnosis of ADHD (and similar diagnostic labels) has been linked to many different indicators of competence. Some of the associated features of this disorder include impairment in social, academic, and vocational adaptation. Conduct Disorder or Oppositional Disorder is frequently seen as a co-occurring problem in children with ADHD.

ADHD has been tied strongly to academic achievement problems (Barkley, 1990; Hinshaw, 1992; Schachar, 1991). There is a high risk of specific reading disorder and school failure reported in children with ADHD. The academic problems of children with ADHD has been attributed most often to the symptoms of the disorder (e.g., impulsivity, inattention, and disorganized overactivity) interfering with academic work and to co-occurring learning disabilities (Barkley, 1990; Schachar, 1991). Even using relatively strict criteria for diagnosing learning disorder, about one quarter of children with ADHD have some type of specific learning disorder (Barkley, 1990).

Studies documenting improvements in cognitive performance as a function of stimulant medication are consistent with the "symptom interference" notion of how ADHD becomes related to academic achievement (Barkley, 1990; Schachar, 1991). Behaviors important for academic *performance* apparently improve, although long-term effects on cumulative academic *achievement* have not yet been established (Carlson, Pelham, Milich, & Dixon, 1992).

Despite data supporting the symptom interference hypothesis, the reasons for the association of ADHD and learning disabilities have not been clearly established (Schachar, 1991). Several hypotheses are reasonable. ADHD symptoms could result from or lead to learning problems. Some studies support transactional relations between the two types of problems (Rowe & Rowe, 1992). Both problems could coincide by chance, by common genetic mediation, or some other common causal factor. Twin data from the Colorado Reading Project (Gilger, Pennington, & De-Fries, 1992) support the possibility of a genetic basis for the co-occurrence of ADHD and reading disability, at least in some cases. Data from the Dunedin, New Zealand, cohort suggests that reading readiness problems, aggression and hyperactivity already are associated when school begins, although reading failure may exacerbate behavior problems (McGee & Share, 1988; McGee, Williams, Share, Anderson, & Silva, 1986). Finally, all these reasons for the co-occurrence of ADHD and learning disabilities could be true, for different children.

Complicating the relation is the issue of comorbidity between ADHD and Conduct Disorder. Few studies have attempted to differentiate the unique relation of academic problems to ADHD when there is comorbidity with conduct disorder. One study found that lower academic achievement was related to both disorders considered individually, but only to ADHD when considered jointly (Frick et al., 1991). In other words, when the relation of ADHD and achievement was controlled, conduct disorder had little relation to academic problems.

Children with ADHD frequently experience social problems, particularly in troubled parent and peer relationships (Barkley, 1990; Buhrmester, Whalen, Henker, MacDonald, & Hinshaw, 1992; Campbell, 1990). Medication has been shown to improve parent-child interactions, suggesting that the social problems are, at least in part, "child-driven," presumably by symptoms or behaviors related to symptoms of the disorder (Barkley, 1990). Data on the effects of methylphenidate on peer relations appear to be complex or inconsistent (see Buhrmester et al., 1992). Moreover, the degree to which these problems are related to social ineptness versus aggression (and the comorbidity of conduct disorder) is not yet clear. Few studies of peer problems in these children have controlled for aggression and conduct disorder. One study that has examined the relation of hyperactivity and aggression to peer acceptance and rejection in elementary children found that, although there was high co-occurrence, each symptom dimension was independently related to peer rejection (Pope, Bierman, & Mumma, 1989). Only hyperactivity was inversely related to peer acceptance. Hyperactivity symptoms had broader relations to peer sociometric status when aggression was controlled than vice versa. Among the "hyperactivity" symptoms, inattentiveness and impulsivity accounted for more peer problems than high levels of activity.

Although ADHD has been consistently linked to antisocial outcomes, the high rate of comorbidity of ADHD and conduct disorder (CD) raises the possibility that the linkage of ADHD and later antisocial behavior is attributable to continuities in antisocial behavior rather than any added risk of ADHD (Farrington, Loeber, & Van Kammern, 1990; Hinshaw, 1987; Lilienfeld & Waldman, 1990; Schachar, 1991). On the other hand, as indicated above, a number of broad studies of symptoms and adaptation have suggested that the *combination* of these two types of disorders or their component symptoms (hyperactivity and aggression in particular), has worse outcomes. More specific studies of the two disorders also suggest additive and/or interaction effects (Schachar, 1991).

The Cambridge Study in Delinquent Development (Farrington et al., 1990) has provided important data pertinent to teasing apart the unique, additive, and interactive effects of these two disorders. Four groups were identified by high and low ADHD symptoms (hyperactivity, impulsivity, attention problems) and CD symptoms (e.g., stealing, lying, destructiveness, defiance), based on data collected at ages 8 to 10. Both types of symptoms were found to be independent, additive predictors of juvenile convictions and chronic offending. Interestingly, the level of ADHD symptoms was not an independent predictor of juvenile convictions when both CD symptoms and the risk factor of criminal parents were both controlled, suggesting the possibility that parental variables account for the linkage of ADHD to later conduct disorder.

Conduct Disorder and Competence

The definition of CD implies competence problems in age-appropriate rule-governed behavior and compliance, which are important life-long developmental tasks. Thus, the conceptualization of this disorder overlaps with the working definition of competence and it would not be very surprising or illuminating to find that CD is related to low scores on socialization or conduct indicators of competence. However, CD and component problems also have been linked to additional domains of competence.

Conduct disorder has been associated with past, current, and future academic achievement problems (Hinshaw, 1992; Martin & Hoffman, 1990). Yet, it is not clear if these associations would hold up if IQ and SES were consistently controlled (Martin & Hoffman, 1990). Moreover, as noted above, co-occurring ADHD or specific learning disabilities, most notably reading disabilities, appear to play a role in some cases. There are very few longitudinal studies that allow one to sort out the likely multiplicity of causal pathways by which conduct disorder and academic achievement become related.

The social behavior of children with CD has led to the subtyping of this disorder. Based on empirical studies, DSM-III-R distinguished "solitary aggressive type" and "group type." In the latter case, misconduct occurs primarily in deviant peer groups with evidence of group loyalty and even friendships, and there is some evidence of rule-based behavior (even if these are gang rules). In the former case, previously termed "undersocialized aggressive," aggression is prominent and there is little evidence of peer acceptance or friendship. This solitary type has been more associated with ADHD as well (Loeber, 1990). This distinction has been supported by data on differential onset patterns and outcomes in these two groups (Henn, Bardwell, & Jenkins, 1980; Loeber, 1990). The aggressive, isolated subtype has early onset. Group types, especially if nonaggressive, have later onset and more favorable outcomes. DSM-IV has altered the sub-typing of this disorder to reflect the age of onset, rather than solitary or group affiliation. The new subtypes are "childhood onset" and "adolescent onset."

Social competence thus appears to be related to the developmental form (patterning of symptoms in time and ontogeny) of conduct disorder. Children with earlier onset conduct problems experience less peer acceptance and more peer rejection. The conjunction of aggression, hyperactivity, and impulsivity has been implicated as a culprit in this early onset path and each has been identified as a risk factor for more serious antisocial outcome. Harsh, inconsistent parenting, and parental rejection have been implicated as causal factors for this path. Potential correcting influences of normative school and peer environments may be averted by the behavior of these children, leading to a "snowball" accumulation of antisocial behavior and negative environments.

Better social competence usually precedes the later onset, group type of conduct disorder, and better outcomes follow the period of adolescent delinquency. Deviant peer influences, coupled with lack of supervision, appear to play a role in this antisocial path, but there appears to be a greater likelihood of recovery to competence. On the whole, this group may have less vulnerability coupled with more favorable early childhood experiences. The development of social and academic competence could proceed more normally up to a point, digress for a time, and then return to a more normative path. Members of this subgroup may have developed more of the fundamental tools for effective adult adaptation in majority society. They may be more responsive to developmental processes in late adolescence that shift behavior in more normative directions (Mulvey & LaRosa, 1986; Pulkkinen, 1988).

Conduct disorder has also been identified as a general risk factor for a wide variety of adult problems (Robins, 1991). These include marital problems, job problems, and higher mortality. The independence of these predictions for other risk factors (such as IQ) and comorbidity (such as ADHD) is not clear at this time.

Depressed mood and depression also have been linked to conduct disorder (Capaldi, 1991, 1992; Patterson & Capaldi, 1990). As discussed earlier, one causal model for these linkages is that conduct problems and aggressive behavior lead to failure in developmental tasks, including academic problems and peer rejection, with these failures and/or perceived failure leading to depression (cf. Cicchetti & Schneider-Rosen, 1986). Results of several longitudinal studies are consistent with this model (e.g., Capaldi, 1991, 1992; Panak & Garber, 1992). The relation of competence to depression is examined further in the next section.

Childhood Depression and Competence

Empirical evidence regarding the relation between depressive disorders and competence in school-age children is limited to a handful of studies. However, this growing body of literature does indicate that childhood depression is related to problems in academic achievement (e.g., Cole, 1990; Slotkin, Forehand, Fauber, McCombs, & Long, 1988), social competence and peer popularity (e.g., Blechman, McEnroe, Carella, & Audette, 1986; Cole, 1990; Lefkowitz & Tesiny, 1985), and conduct problems (e.g., Capaldi, 1991, 1992; Cole & Carpentieri, 1990). As yet, however, causal processes underlying these linkages are unclear.

The relation between academic achievement and depression has been demonstrated in studies using multiple reporters (self, parent, and teacher reports) and different measures to assess depressive symptoms. Leon, Kendall, and Garber (1980) found that children's depression and parent-rated learning problems were moderately correlated ($r = 0.43$). Slotkin et al. (1988) found moderate negative correlations between grades and self-reported CDI depression scores ($r = -0.38$), grades and mother-reported CDI scores ($r = -0.50$), teacher-rated academic competence and mother rated depression ($r = -0.36$), and

teacher-rated academic competence and self-reports of depression ($r = -0.45$). Cole (1990) used confirmatory factor analysis to account for measurement error and method variance and found a much stronger correlation between a factor of depression and a factor of academic competence ($r = -0.80$). Some additional evidence suggests that these problems in achievement may be transitory, with children who have sustained affective recovery returning to a level of performance indistinguishable from normal controls (Puig-Antich et al., 1985b), or only slightly lower than nonproblem children (Capaldi, 1992).

Childhood depression has also been linked strongly with peer relationships and peer social status. Jacobsen, Lahey, and Strauss (1983) found that depression scores on the CDI and the Peer Nomination Inventory for Depression (the PNID) were significantly correlated with teacher ratings of peer popularity. These patterns of correlation varied by gender but for the full sample, the correlations were as strong as 0.61 between teacher ratings of popularity and PNID scores. Other studies have indicated that the relation is not that strong, with researchers generally reporting correlations of the magnitude of 0.30 (Fauber, Forehand, Long, Burke, & Faust, 1987; Slotkin et al., 1988). However, again Cole (1990) used confirmatory factor analyses to control for error and method variance and obtained a much stronger relationship between a factor of social competence and a factor of depression ($r = -0.82$). Similarly, Patterson and Stoolmiller (1991) used Structural Equation Modeling (SEM) techniques to find a strong negative relationship between a "good peer relations" construct and a "depressed mood" construct for three separate samples of 9- to 12-year-old boys.

The data indicate a significant relationship between indicators of social competence and depressed mood. Some data suggest that the relationship between peer problems, such as peer rejection, and depression might be due to a subgroup of depressed children who also manifest symptoms of conduct disorder (Cole & Carpentieri, 1990). Given the high rates of comorbidity of these two problems (cf. Cole & Carpentieri, 1990; Puig-Antich, 1982), this seems to be a plausible hypothesis for study. Capaldi (1991, 1992) compared four groups of boys diagnosed with depressed mood only, conduct problems only, co-occurring depressed mood and conduct problems, or neither problem in 6th and 8th grades. She found that depressed only boys reported some difficulties with peers, and were significantly different than boys with neither problem. However, the boys with co-occurring problems manifested more persistent and more severe adjustment problems than either of the single problem groups. These boys manifested both the problems typically associated with conduct disorder (e.g., peer rejection) and the competence problems associated with depressed children. (e.g., low self-esteem and negative self-reports of relationships with peers and parents).

Results from these studies and others (e.g., Patterson & Capaldi, 1990; Patterson & Stoolmiller, 1991) support a failure model of depressed mood. In the dual failure model, achievement problems in the domains of peer relations and academics are expected to contribute to depressed mood. Patterson and Capaldi (1990) originally tested a model in which low academic competence, low self-esteem, and peer rejection were expected to contribute uniquely to depressed mood. Instead, a mediational model fit the data better: the relation between low academic skills and depressed mood was mediated through peer rejection and peer rejection had independent direct effects on self-esteem and depressed mood. Patterson and Stoolmiller (1991) altered the model to exclude self-esteem, and tested it in three separate samples. For all three, the path coefficients from peer relations to dysphoric mood were highly significant (−0.50 to −0.77). In contrast, the path from academic achievement to depressed mood was of low magnitude and less stable across samples.

Results of these studies also are consistent with a broader developmental approach to childhood depression which proposes that lack of competence at an earlier period of development contributes to later childhood depression (Cicchetti & Schneider-Rosen, 1986). In this theory, failure to master the social, cognitive, and emotional tasks in one stage of development leaves children ill-equipped to cope with later challenges in their lives, and thus, vulnerable to depressed mood.

Childhood Anxiety Disorders and Competence

Even less attention has been directed toward the study of competence correlates of anxiety disorders in children. What little data do exist focus on the competence dimensions of academic performance and peer relations. There is still some debate regarding whether anxious behavior is significant in terms of children's development and overall psychosocial adaptation or whether it is a relatively benign aspect of normal development (Orvaschel & Weissman, 1986; Strauss, Frame & Forehand, 1987). Additionally, there is little evidence that anxious behavior in childhood has long-term implications for maladjustment in adulthood (Orvaschel & Weissman, 1986).

One of the early studies in this area examined the relation between anxiety and academic achievement in a group of adolescents with school phobia (Berg, Collins, McGuire, & O'Melia, 1975). Results from this study indicated that these children did not manifest problems in school achievement, were working at a level appropriate for their IQ, and were indistinguishable from other psychiatric controls. More recently, Hodges and Plow (1990) compared intellectual ability and academic achievement scores for psychiatrically hospitalized children with DSM-III-R diagnoses of conduct disorder, oppositional disorder, depression, and anxiety disorder. Results indicated that children with anxiety disorders had significantly lower Full Scale IQ scores on the WISC-R, but surprisingly did not show lower academic achievement as measured by the Woodcock Johnson Psychoeducational Battery. However, the study allowed for multiple diagnoses and failed to examine the effects of comorbidity.

Other researchers have identified lower academic performance as a correlate of childhood anxiety (Strauss et al., 1987). In this study, 24 children who received extremely high teacher ratings on the Anxiety-Withdrawal factor of the Revised Behavior Problem Checklist (RBPC) were drawn from a sample of 325 second-through-fifth grade children. Teachers also perceived these 24 children as demonstrating deficits in academic performance relative to non-anxious children. However, lack of rater independence between judgments of anxiety and school performance limit the interpretability of this study.

The peer relations and social status of anxious children has received slightly more attention, and there is a small, but growing body of literature suggesting that anxiety and maladaptive social functioning may be interrelated (Strauss et al., 1986; Strauss et al., 1988; Strauss, Lease, Kazdin, Dulcan, & Last, 1989). As noted in the section on peer relations, cross-sectional data suggest that some anxious children may self-isolate from peers (Hymel et al., 1990; Rubin et al., 1991; Rubin & Mills, 1988). However, the longitudinal implications of the converse, peer isolation leading to later anxiety is less clear. Cross-sectionally, the data are fairly consistent, with the relationship between anxiety and problematic peer relationships found in both non-clinic samples (e.g., Panella & Henggeler, 1986; Strauss et al., 1987), and clinic referred samples (Puig-Antich et al., 1985a; Strauss et al., 1988; Strauss et al., 1989). Both sets of samples have yielded fairly consistent findings using various reporters (i.e., self-, parent, and teacher reports) and methods (i.e., behavioral observations, sociometric measurements, and peer evaluations) (Strauss et al., 1989).

In one example, a nonclinic sample of 24 teacher-identified highly anxious children was found to be significantly less popular on peer ratings using the "like most/like least" nomination method (Strauss et al., 1987). These children were also rated by peers as more shy and socially withdrawn than non-anxious peers. Two additional studies conducted by Strauss and colleagues (Strauss et al., 1988; Strauss et al., 1989), compared the peer relations of clinic referred anxious children with separate groups of clinic controls and nonreferred children. In these samples too, anxious children were liked significantly less by peers and rated by teachers as less socially competent than nonreferred children. When compared to conduct disordered and non-referred children, anxious children also were more likely to have low social impact scores (liked most + liked least) (Perry, 1979), and to be classified as "neglected" (low social impact, negative social preference).

Several cautions should be made when examining these findings. First, the samples in these studies are relatively small, ranging from 16 to 55. In addition, exploratory analyses in the Strauss et al. (1988) study suggested that the lack of popularity of children with anxiety disorders may have been limited to those children with concurrent depression. More research with this population is needed to examine the relations between anxiety disorders and competence, and to tease apart issues of comorbidity.

Conclusions from the Data on Competence and Psychopathology

A broad spectrum of research indicates that competence, defined in terms of effective performance in age-salient developmental tasks, is related to externalizing symptoms and disorders both concurrently and predictively from an early age. This linkage is not limited to the overlap between the constructs of competence and symptoms in the domain of rule-governed behavior or adherence to social conduct norms and expectations. Preschool externalizing behavior predicts later academic and peer problems. Childhood externalizing behavior predicts lower adolescent and adult competence in multiple areas, including academic and job achievement and social problems, such as peer relations and marital difficulties.

Two major disorders or clusters of externalizing symptoms have been linked to competence: ADHD symptoms and aggression or conduct disorder symptoms. ADHD symptoms are associated with early and persistent academic problems, due in part, it appears, to symptoms that interfere with learning and also to co-occurring specific reading disability. Conduct disorder, on the other hand, does not appear to have a strong, independent relation to academic attainment until adolescence. Moreover, the role of low SES and IQ in this relation is not clear. Disengagement from school, truancy, and substance abuse, all of which may increase in antisocial children in adolescence, may play a role in the strengthened relations between conduct disorder and academic achievement in adolescence.

Persistent disruptive, aggressive behavior appears to interfere with the development of social and academic competence. The combination of ADHD symptoms plus aggression (and later CD) is associated with both persistence of externalizing problems and high risk for competence problems. Isolated and aggressive conduct-disordered children also appear to be a high risk group. It is not clear to what degree these two groups overlap. These high-risk patterns are more common in boys and are associated with high-risk family backgrounds.

Competence also predicts externalizing symptoms and disorders, although the evidence is more limited. Early academic achievement and school failure predict a broad spectrum of later problems, including externalizing symptoms in adolescence. However, it seems likely that in many cases externalizing symptoms were already present (but unmeasured) at the time of the school failure. The evidence is sketchy by which to determine whether academic failure exacerbates externalizing symptoms.

Social competence problems with peers in childhood also predict later externalizing problems in adolescence and adulthood. Again, however, it seems likely that ongoing aggression or ADHD or both may have already been associated with peer status. As yet, only limited data support the causal role of peer treatment or status on subsequent externalizing problems. Rejection by normative peer groups may contribute to association with deviant peers, but this process, which is an example of "cumulative continuity" (Caspi et al., 1987) has proven difficult to track empirically.

The data also suggest moderate relations among internalizing disorders, such as depression and anxiety, and different dimensions of competence including academic achievement, peer relationships, and conduct. The existing data speak primarily to cross-sectional relationships and do not illuminate the potential longitudinal and transactional relations between competence and internalizing disorders. Some data do indicate that recovery from internalizing symptoms may also help alleviate the problems in academic competence, and to a lesser extent social competence (Capaldi, 1992; Puig-Antich et al., 1985b). However, these results are not conclusive and further longitudinal evidence is necessary before definitive conclusions are warranted.

Additionally, it is important for future studies to investigate the temporal and transactional relationships between competence and depression in longitudinal studies. Whether depression leads to later incompetence, or vice versa, the transactional nature of development suggests that this is a fruitful area for study. Developmental models suggest that depressive symptoms will inhibit the acquisition of competencies required for effective adaptation (e.g., Cicchetti & Schneider-Rosen, 1986), as well as suggesting that lack of competence, and feedback regarding incompetence, may be of etiological significance for depression (Cicchetti & Schneider-Rosen, 1986; Cole, 1991).

Issues of comorbidity must also be confronted. Longitudinal relations between depression and competence could be due in part to the co-occurrance of depression and conduct problems. Conduct problems have demonstrated long-term negative effects on competence and researchers must account for this relationship when investigating the effects of childhood depression on later competence. Longitudinal studies that can clearly identify the primacy of conduct problems or depressive mood, and can document change in diagnosis and adjustment over time will help clarify these relations proximally and distally.

RISK AND RESILIENCE

The concepts of "risk" and "resilience" in psychology both focus attention on the criteria for judging developmental outcomes (Horowitz, 1989; Masten, 1994; Masten & Garmezy, 1985; Masten et al., 1990). Predictors of problems in adaptation, judged either in terms of symptoms or competence, have been called risk factors. When risk is judged to be high, yet children develop well, resilience is sometimes inferred. Resilience refers to achieving desirable outcomes in spite of significant challenges to adaptation or development. The study of competence and psychopathology can be unified in studies of risk and resilience.

Risk generally refers to elevated probabilities of undesired outcomes among members of a group who share one or more characteristics. Risk indicators are based on group data; usually, it is not known which individuals will be exposed to, much less succumb, to the causal influences underlying the risk status of the group. In psychological studies of children, the criteria for evaluating risk outcomes often include failures to reach desired levels of competence as well as symptoms of psychopathology.

In the literature on resilience, the term "protective factors" has been used to refer to individual or environmental characteristics that predict or correlate with good outcomes in children at risk. Protective factors are correlates of resilience that suggest processes have operated to buffer a child or ameliorate the effects of adversities. Inferring resilience requires evidence that a person has overcome challenges or averted harmful outcomes. Simply having a better outcome because one was exposed to fewer hazards or challenges is not usually interpretable as resilience. This requirement presents a dilemma in many studies of children at risk. Usually, it is not clear whether good outcomes are due to less exposure to hazard or to lower vulnerability rather than to the resilience of an individual or the operation of protective processes that buffer the individual in some way (Masten, 1994; Masten et al., 1990). In other words, two individuals, both categorized as "high risk," may actually have quite different net risk if additional factors that vary within the group or actual exposure to the risk mechanism are examined more closely. Better outcomes may be the result of lower overall risk rather than resilience mechanisms.

In this section, we review the literature bearing on the relations of competence and psychopathology through the study of risk factors, stressors, and resilience. First, we describe models linking risk and adversity to competence and psychopathology. Then we examine three areas of research on risk and adversity in relation to competence and psychopathology: (a) broad studies of cumulative risk, (b) studies of stressful life events, and (c) studies of acute trauma and chronic adversity. Our discussion is highly selective, focusing on research that considers competence and resilience as well as psychopathology. Many other chapters of this manual review risk and resilience research in the context of specific risk categories or undesirable outcomes, such as disorder (see especially the chapter by Cohler, Stott, & Musick).

Models Linking Risks and Adversity to Competence and Psychopathology

There are several ways in which risks and experiential hazards could contribute to an association between competence and psychopathology.

1. Assets and advantages for development may contribute independently to the promotion of competence and the mitigation of symptoms. For example, parenting behavior, intellectual skills and socioeconomic advantages are widely reported correlates of both symptoms and, inversely, competence (Masten et al., 1988). This could occur through many overlapping and independent processes.

2. Adversity could erode competence at the same time that it increases symptoms of psychopathology. Again, this could involve many processes, some of which differ for specific aspects of competence and symptoms.

3. Genetically based psychopathology in a parent could produce both worse environmental rearing conditions for a child as a result of parent symptoms, as well as vulnerability in the child due to genetic transmission of the diathesis. This could produce a child in double jeopardy for a particular disorder. Simultaneously, the adverse environment could interfere with the development of competence independently of its effects on the development of the genetically-based disorder.

4. It is also conceivable that the causal factors that facilitate the development of competence could also play a protective role in ameliorating the effects of hazardous experiences. Parental monitoring, for example, may bolster academic achievement and also reduce the effects of dangerous neighborhoods on development. A child could be genetically vulnerable to some disorder but effectively buffered from developing it by good caregiving, which also promotes competence.

5. Competence attainments or their lack could function as a risk or protective factor for subsequent psychopathology. Competence processes could bolster the stress-resistance of a child. On the other hand, failures to attain competence in domains valued by self, parents, or society could result in increased

vulnerability to psychological distress or other symptoms of psychopathology in the context of risk or adversity.

Broad Studies of Risk and Resilience: Cumulative Risk and Protective Factors

Risk factors often co-occur and multiple risk factors often prove to be more predictive than single risk factors. Therefore, it often makes more sense to study cumulative risk rather than individual risk factors. Investigators of infants at risk due to perinatal complications or medical problems have long recognized the power of combined risk indicators (Meisels & Wasik, 1990; O'Dougherty & Wright, 1990; Sameroff & Chandler, 1975).

Several important research programs have shown the significance of cumulative risk for psychopathology and competence outcomes. Two important studies of cumulative risk have focused on disorder and criminality. Rutter and his colleagues have shown the strong relation of 6 predictors to psychiatric disorder in children: severe marital discord, low social status, overcrowding or large family size, paternal criminality, maternal psychiatric disorder, and out-of-home placement of the child (Rutter, 1979). With only one of these risk factors, the risk of psychiatric disorder was low, but with two it quadrupled. With four, it jumped dramatically again. These results suggested synergistic effects of combined risk factors.

In the second project, the Newcastle Thousand Family Study, criminality was the outcome of interest to Kolvin, Miller, Fleeting, and Kolvin (1988). The cumulative risk indicators were very similar to the Rutter studies: marital instability, parental illness, poor care of children and home, welfare dependency, overcrowded housing, and poor mothering ability. Cumulative risk was a strong predictor of later criminality. Causal influences were suggested by this study's finding that when deprivation, as defined by risk, increased for a child, subsequent criminality rates increased, and when cumulative risk decreased, those rates also decreased.

Early childhood protective factors implicated in this study included good mothering, good maternal health, and an employed breadwinner, good health and physical development in the child and being elder-born. In the school years, intellectual functioning, school achievement, good parental supervision, and belonging to positive youth clubs predicted better outcomes (lower criminality rates).

Two other important research programs include competence indicators in their outcome evaluations of risk and protective factors. One is the classic study of risk and resilience conducted by Werner and Smith on the Hawaiian Island of Kauai (Werner, Bierman, & French, 1971; Werner & Smith 1977, 1982, 1992). These investigators have followed for over 30 years a cohort of more than 500 children born on the island in 1955. Many of these children were reared under conditions of poverty and disadvantage.

Initial findings of the Kauai study demonstrated the role of prenatal care in lowering the risk for birth complications. Results also showed the protective effect of higher SES as a risk-moderator when perinatal complications occurred. Within the group who experienced birth complications, developmental outcomes were much better in children reared in more socioeconomically advantaged homes as compared to lower SES homes. This finding has been replicated in a number of other studies (Kopp, 1983; Masten & Garmezy, 1985; Sameroff & Chandler, 1975).

Later analyses indicated a number of risk factors for mental health problems and lower competence in this cohort. Risk factors included perinatal stress, poverty, family dysfunction, and low maternal education. Based on such risk factors, a high-risk subsample of these children was identified, constituting about a third of the whole. Two-thirds of this high-risk sample had competence and/or mental health problems at age 10 or 18 in follow-ups, including learning and behavior problems, mental health problems, and trouble with the law. However, one-third of this group had good outcomes, defined in terms of positive academic and social competence and absence of psychopathology. These two groups of high-risk children differed in many respects from early childhood, suggesting either greater vulnerability in the troubled group or protective processes in the resilient group or variation in composite risk even among a high-risk sample. As infants, the resilient group were healthier and had fewer separations from caregivers. The next sibling was at least two years younger. As infants and toddlers, these children were engaging to adults and had good care from a primary caregiver. In the childhood years, the resilient group had better intellectual and reading skills than the nonresilient high risk group, and also demonstrated good peer relations. As adolescents, they were more positive about themselves and had more internal locus of control, but also more structured and rule-governed households.

In the adult follow-up, when the cohort was 31 to 32 years old, the resilient group continued to succeed in most respects, including academic and vocational achievements. None had trouble with the law. Very few sought psychiatric services. However, there were some signs that this group may have been affected by their stressful experiences, particularly when there was a dysfunctional family. They had more stress-related health problems than similarly competent but low-risk-history peers and they seemed to keep some emotional distance in their interpersonal relationships.

Among the other high-risk children, many of whom did not fare well in adolescence, there was considerable improvement for many. New opportunities opened for some as they moved into the adult world. Jobs, military service, higher education, and religious involvements seemed to play a role in the redirecting of the lives of these youth. Nonetheless, a substantial minority continued to have problems. This was particularly true for males. Adolescents with four or more juvenile convictions were at considerable risk of adult criminality and a host of other problems. Most of this group had been described as aggressive in childhood. Males with mental health problems in adolescence also had a high risk of future problems in terms of both psychopathology and lower competence.

Another research program concerned with competence as well as psychopathology outcomes is the Rochester Longitudinal Study (Sameroff & Seifer, 1983, 1990; Sameroff, Seifer, & Zax, 1982; Sameroff, Seifer, Zax, & Barocas, 1987). Ten family risk factors served as a cumulative risk index in children born to mothers with schizophrenia, a group at elevated risk

for this disorder. These included family size, low maternal education, maternal anxiety, low occupational status of the head of household, disadvantaged minority status, and stressful life events, among others. This index was related to child IQ and social-emotional functioning at age 4. The relations were linear: as risk increased, IQ and adaptive functioning decreased.

In a subsequent follow-up study, a subsample of 50 of these high-risk children (with four or more risk factors at age 4) were compared with 102 lower risk children (Seifer, Sameroff, Baldwin, & Baldwin, 1992). Both at age 4 and age 13, IQ and adjustment scores of these two groups were examined. Good adjustment ratings encompassed both competence and the absence of symptoms, while poor adjustment was a composite of low academic achievement, poor conduct, distress, aggression, and impulsiveness. Several variables were related to improved status on adjustment measured over time, both for low and high risk groups. These included fewer stressful life events, less depression in mothers, and less dissatisfaction and criticism experienced by mothers about the child. One variable that consistently predicted improvement in adjustment was the mother's level of expressed concern about the child, assessed at age 13, which was lower in children who had more positive developmental trajectories. Given that this variable was assessed at the time of outcome, the direction of this effect was not clear: positive change in a child could reduce parental concerns.

These studies of cumulative risk suggest that there are general predictors of adaptation in development that cut across competence and psychopathology outcomes. In the child these would include physical health and intellectual functioning. In the family, these would include the quality of parenting and socioeconomic advantage or disadvantage. Stressful life experiences also appear to play a role for both outcomes. Many of the same predictors have been implicated in studies of risk for delinquency (Loeber, 1990) and in studies of perinatal risk as broadly predictive of developmental outcomes (O'Dougherty & Wright, 1990; Sameroff & Chandler, 1975).

Studies of Stressful Life Events and Resilience

A diverse literature on life events has suggested that cumulative negative life events have some relation to both competence and psychopathology indicators in children and adolescents (Compas, 1987; Johnson, 1986). However, this area of research has been fraught with methodological and conceptual difficulties that, for the most part, preclude clear inferences about these linkages. Outcomes and predictors have been confounded in some cases, because some of the "life events" used to predict child outcomes are themselves indicators of symptoms or could be precipitated by the child's own behavior (Compas, 1987; Garmezy, 1985; Garmezy & Rutter, 1985; Johnson, 1986; Masten, Neemann, & Andenas, 1994).

One solution to the confounding issue has been to tally negative life events that are independent of a person's behavior and then correlate this life event score with adjustment indicators. Results of such studies have been inconsistent (Cohen, 1988). Some studies have found relations between recent major life events and adjustment (e.g., Cowen, Weissberg, & Guare, 1984;

Dubois, Felner, Brand, Adan, & Evans, 1992; Newcomb, Huba, & Bentler, 1986; Sandler & Block, 1979; Sterling, Cowen, Weissberg, Lotyczewski, & Boike, 1985). Other studies, particularly prospective studies, have not (Cohen, Burt, Bjorck, 1987; Gersten, Langner, Eisenberg, & Simcha-Fagan, 1977).

Few studies have examined the linkages between cumulative life events and specific mental disorders in children and adolescents. Goodyer and colleagues (Goodyer, Kolvin, & Gatzanis, 1985) found a greater number of major threatening life events among child and adolescent outpatient psychiatric cases (ages 4 to 15) than among case controls. Psychiatric cases included conduct disorder, mild mood disorder, severe emotional disorder, and somatic disorder. Recent life events were higher in all the psychiatric groups compared to community controls. Recent life events were also found to be higher in a clinic sample of 7- to 16-year-old children with emotional disorders than in a group of community controls (Goodyer, Wright, & Altham, 1990). In both studies, only events classified as independent of illness were included.

A longitudinal study of children during 3rd and 4th grade has linked major life events to depressive symptoms concurrently and over time (Nolen-Hoeksema, Girgus, & Seligman, 1992). More negative life events predicted increases in negative mood.

Several research projects have focused on potential moderators of the relations between stressful life events and outcomes. Most of this work has been cross-sectional rather than longitudinal. Data from the Project Competence group suggested that IQ and SES may moderate the relation of recent life events to current disruptive/aggressive behavior in 3rd to 6th grade children (Masten et al., 1988). These data are consistent with the possibility that IQ and SES function as protective factors. For girls, high quality parenting appeared to mitigate disruptiveness under conditions of high stress exposure. Unexpectedly, however, good parenting quality also appeared to function as a vulnerability factor for social disengagement at high adversity levels. Subsequent longitudinal analyses from this project support a different protective process in which parenting alters the level of exposure rather than its consequences (Gest, Neemann, Hubbard, Masten, & Tellegen, 1993). Competent parents appeared to produce less parent-related adversity for their children. Once stressful life experiences occurred, however, there was a small but significant increase in rule-breaking behavior associated with experiencing adversity.

Using similar analytic strategies, Luthar (1991) found internal locus of control and social skills moderated the relation of life events to competence in a sample of inner city 9th graders, while intelligence appeared to be a vulnerability factor. Among high intelligence adolescents, school grades and "assertive-responsible" behavior were high when stress was low but lower (more like their lower intelligence peers) at high stress levels. In other words, the intelligent children seemed to lose their advantage in these competence domains when adversity was high.

Results of this study also suggested that competent children with high stress exposure had more depressed mood and anxiety than competent children with lower stress. This finding again raises the possibility that one may attain competence under adverse conditions but still suffer psychologically, perhaps from the adversity itself, or perhaps from the strain of achieving competence under such difficult circumstances. It would also indicate an adaptive strategy that has lower risk for damaging one's reputation at the same time that it raises the risk for internalizing symptoms. Such findings also reinforce the importance of considering both internalizing and externalizing aspects of adaptation.

The Rochester Child Resilience Project also has focused on resilience in urban children who have experienced high levels of stressful life events (Cowen, Wyman, Work, & Parker, 1990; Wyman, Cowen, Work, & Parker, 1991; Wyman et al., 1992). Two groups of 4th to 6th grade children have been compared: "stress-resilient" and "stress-affected." Stressors included ongoing chronic adversities as well as discrete events. Adjustment measures included peer acceptance, school achievement, conduct, and behavior problems. The resilient group had more positive perceptions of self and family and better social skills. Parent interviews corroborated a number of the differences observed between resilient and troubled high-risk children in the Kauai study, including a close relationships with a caregiver, fewer separations from caregiver in infancy, and an "easy" engaging disposition in infancy. Parents of resilient children also appeared to be more competent and satisfied.

One prospective study, mentioned above, has tested for the interaction of major negative life events and negative explanatory styles in predicting depressive symptoms (Nolen-Hoeksema et al., 1992). As predicted by the reformulated helplessness theory of depression (Abramson et al., 1978), in a diathesis-stressor framework, as children grew older (in early adolescence), a pessimistic explanatory style increased the effect of negative life events on depression. Results of this study also suggested that earlier negative events contribute to the formation of a pessimistic explanatory style. Thus, negative life events lead to a diathesis which increases the impact of subsequent negative events on depressed mood.

Cumulative life event studies suggest that negative life experiences may pose some hazards for development of competence, but the processes involved in that risk may be quite complex or intertwined with other risk and protective factors. The role of stressful life events as risk factors for childhood disorders or decreased competence remains obscure at this time.

Studies of Acute Trauma and Chronic Adversities

Both severe experiences of brief duration and prolonged adversities have been implicated as causal influences in the development of psychopathology and reduced competence (Garmezy & Masten, 1994; Garmezy & Rutter, 1985; Masten & Wright, in press; Wright & Masten, in press; Yule, 1994). Some severe, isolated traumas such as experiencing a tornado or witnessing a murder appear to have little lasting effect when the duration is brief and there is no lasting bodily damage or disruption of care and support to the child as a consequence. However, if there is physical damage to the child or the perpetrator or victim of a traumatic experience is a parent, or the community is destroyed, lasting effects may occur as a result of enduring adverse experiential sequelae.

An examination of the extensive literature on acute and chronic adversities is beyond the scope of this chapter (see

Ammerman & Hersen, 1990; Bentovim & Smith, 1994; Cicchetti & Carlson, 1989; Garmezy & Masten, 1994; Garmezy & Rutter, 1985; Skuse & Bentovim, 1994; Wright & Masten, in press; Yule, 1994). Specific adversities are examined in other chapters of this manual (see chapters by Cicchetti & Lynch, Emery, and Pynoos, this manual). We will highlight the recent findings from the research on children of depressed parents and children who experience parental discord and divorce. These topics illustrate the nature of the cumulative risks associated with chronic adversities and their relation to competence and symptoms.

Children of Depressed Parents

Children of mentally ill parents have been the focus of extensive research (e.g., Cicchetti & Toth, 1992a; Downey & Coyne, 1990; Watt, Anthony, Wynne, & Rolf, 1984). Parental mental illness, including schizophrenia, antisocial personality disorder, and mood disorders, may pose considerable multiple risk conditions for their offspring, including genetic risk for a specific disorder, poor parenting, high stress exposure, and instability of both family life and housing.

In the children of depressed parents, investigators have found a broad spectrum of behavior problems, poor academic achievement, impaired social functioning and elevated prevalence of psychiatric disorders (Downey & Coyne, 1990). Many of these problems appear to be the result of the multiple risk factors that are not specific to depression in the parent or the child. Hammen and her colleagues (Conrad & Hammen, 1989; Gordon et al., 1989; Hammen, 1992; Hammen et al., 1987; Hammen, Burge, & Adrian, 1990; Hammen, Burge, & Stansbury, 1991) have observed that these children experience high cumulative stress exposure, similar to other children at multiple risk for different reasons. It is also not clear whether the genetic risk for depression is distinct for risk for anxiety disorders in children (Compas & Hammen, 1994). However, children and mothers have been found to have episodes of depression in close proximity to one another, a phenomenon that may be specific to depression (Hammen et al., 1991).

Resilience in children of affectively disordered parents has not received much research attention. The studies of Hammen and her colleagues indicated that children with better outcomes in terms of mental disorders had lower overall risk, more parental resources, and higher self-concept, as well as greater social and academic competence. One case study of four children of parents with mood disorders suggested that competence was associated with better intellectual skills, social appealingness, and possession of an attribute valued by the family, such as being a boy or having athletic talent (Radke-Yarrow & Sherman, 1990).

Interparental Conflict and Divorce

Another area of extensive study has been interparental discord and divorce (Emery, 1982, 1988, 1989; Hetherington, 1989; Hetherington, Stanley-Hagan, & Anderson, 1989; Kitson & Morgan, 1990). Neither discord nor divorce are isolated experiences. Divorce is a complex process, often complicated before and after, by multiple stressors, including conflict, moving, economic strain, and remarriage. A wide variety of problems in behavior,

encompassing both competence and symptoms have been reported among children subsequent to divorce. Such problems could result from the added stressors or declines in parental functioning that may accompany or follow divorce. However, some of these problems probably preceded the divorce (see Block, Block, & Gjerde, 1986; Cherlin et al., 1991). Other problems may result from dysfunctional parenting and relate more to the risky conditions preceding separation, such as long-standing conflict (Capaldi & Patterson, 1991; Emery, 1988; Forgatch, Patterson, & Skinner, 1988; Hetherington, 1989). Parents who divorce may also have ongoing mental disorders, such as antisocial personality disorder (see Capaldi & Patterson, 1991; Lahey et al., 1988). These studies indicate a very complex admixture of chronic adversity, stressful life events, and cumulative risk in many of the families with interparental conflict and divorce. The degree of cumulative risk often appears to be the key to prediction of adjustment in the children. In addition, there may be important protective processes that need to be explored further in research. Many children whose parents divorce appear to adjust and carry on with their lives (Emery & Forehand, 1994). Once again, a good relationship with one of the parents is consistently indicated as a protective factor in studies of discord and divorce, as in studies of other adversities (Garmezy & Masten, 1994; Masten et al., 1990).

Conclusions from the Studies of Risk and Resilience

Diverse studies of risk and resilience are consistent with one, several, or all of the five proposed models by which competence and psychopathology may be linked by shared risk and protective factors. It is difficult to evaluate the differential evidence supporting each model because this area of research has not advanced to the point of testing alternative models. Such studies are rare.

However, the data are consistent with the possibility that there are key risk or protective factors that have generalized influences. Stressors, parenting qualities, intellectual functioning, and socioeconomic variables are broadly implicated as predictors, correlates, and moderators of both competence and psychopathology. These qualities may signify that general conditions for development have been and will continue to be favorable and that neurological development is proceeding favorably. Under such conditions, human development is robust, competence is likely and psychopathology is less likely.

There are also data supporting the possible role of competence attainments as vulnerability or protective factors with respect to the effects of stressors on the development of psychopathology. However, virtually no longitudinal studies are available on this question.

Despite evidence that competence and psychopathology share predictive correlates, very little is known at this time about the processes that underlie either risk or protective factors (Masten, 1994; Masten et al., 1990; Rolf, Masten, Cicchetti, Nuechterlein, & Weintraub, 1990; Rutter, 1990). It will not be easy to sort out the specific causal processes by which risk factors, including adverse life experiences, influence the development of competence and psychopathology, or how resilience works. Nonetheless, it is clear that more comprehensive, longitudinal studies and better specified models will be needed.

CONCLUSIONS AND FUTURE DIRECTIONS

The emerging tenets of developmental psychopathology suggest that it is important to integrate the concepts and study of competence and psychopathology (Masten & Braswell, 1991). This chapter has examined the network of meanings attached to competence in psychology, data on the structure of competence, and selected evidence linking competence with psychopathology. Results of this review support the utility of a more unified approach to the study of adaptation in development for understanding both deviant and normative psychological development.

Conclusions from the Literature Review

In order to examine competence in relation to psychopathology, we began with a detailed review of the family of constructs focused on the successfulness of psychological adaptation, ranging from the ego to IQ. A working definition of competence was set forth, emphasizing the multidimensional nature of developmentally and culturally-based expectations for behavior in children and adolescence. This set the stage for an examination of how and why competence and psychopathology may be related.

Four possibilities were considered for explaining relations between competence and psychopathology:

1. The criteria overlap for judging these two facets of adaptation outcomes;
2. Psychopathology interferes with competence;
3. Competence failures contribute to psychopathology; and
4. Common etiological factors produce effects on both types of outcomes.

The benefits of better differentiation of competence and psychopathology in theory and research were discussed and the evidence for causal linkages was examined.

Conceptual overlaps were noted in the definition and measures of competence and psychopathology. Antisocial behavior, academic performance, and peer relations, for example, all have been viewed as indicators of both psychopathology and competence. Competence was found to play a pervasive role in the current diagnostic manual for mental disorder of the American Psychiatric Association, yet the relation of competence and psychopathology in this document is not well articulated. DSM-IV provides an elaborate organizational scheme for disorder but a weak and diffuse treatment of adaptive functioning. Further examination of the concept of psychopathology in relation to adaptation and, more specifically competence, may clarify the meaning of both and provide guidance for a better classification system. If competence were given as much attention in classification systems as psychopathology, the result might be a different conceptualization and organization of mental disorders. Encompassing competence might prove particularly useful for the diagnosis and treatment of children and adolescents.

Many facets of competence at different ages have been described, in terms of developmental tasks, social competence, academic achievement, and so on. Yet there has been very little analysis of the structure of competence in terms of adaptive functioning, much less to identify meaningful patterns of good or poor adaptation. In other words, the indicators of positive psychosocial development have not received nearly the emphasis as have the indicators of deviant functioning and development. Indirectly, the structure of competence has been analyzed through the analysis of symptoms, when symptoms include the "low scores" on competence indicators. This neglect may have impeded advances in the understanding of both psychopathology and competence.

Our review also indicated how few longitudinal studies are available by which to consider causal relations between various facets and patterns of competence and psychopathology. This neglect is analogous to ignoring the role of comorbidity in studies purporting to examine single disorders and presents a similar dilemma for drawing inferences for the existing data on competence and psychopathology. Nonetheless, some conclusions were consistently supported.

Some forms of psychopathology appear to undermine competence. Evidence strongly suggests that the configuration of symptoms described in DSM-IV terminology as Attention-Deficit Hyperactivity Disorder (ADHD), including hyperactivity, attentional problems, and impulsivity symptoms, has a negative effect on academic performance and peer relations. Moreover, this impact is evident early in the school years and this link does not seem to be accounted for by specific learning disabilities or aggression. The configuration of symptoms usually grouped under the category of conduct disorder, particularly including aggressive, antisocial actions and rule-breaking behavior, appears to undermine academic and job competence by adolescence. Prior to adolescence, antisocial behavior characterized by aggression appears to contribute to rejection by normative peers and probably undermines relations with parents and teachers, as well.

The mechanisms by which these influences may occur have not been well-established, although research is promising. Symptoms of these disorders (e.g., ADHD and Conduct Disorder) may interfere with performance and learning of academic or social skills. It is also conceivable that failures to perform age-salient developmental tasks precipitate changes in the learning or socialization environment, such as placement in alternative classrooms or limited choices of peer groups, extracurricular activities, and so on. Selection into "deviant" environments may have crucial long-term effects on the course of development.

The causal roles of competence successes and failures in the development of, recovery from, or avoidance of psychopathology have received less attention. The role of competence failures in contributing to psychopathology has only recently been the subject of research and little evidence is available. At this point, the best case could be made for peer rejection as a contributor to depression. The role of competence in compensating for psychopathology or moderating the development or course of disorder has also received little direct examination. Previous competence appears to be a good predictor of course, likelihood or timing of relapse, and eventual outcome in children and adults with mental disorders (APA, 1994; Zigler & Glick, 1986). Yet, particularly little research on this topic has been done with children.

The possibility that one set of causal influences linking competence and psychopathology relates to shared vulnerability or environmental risk factors is consistent with an extensive body of research on risk for different disorders and facets of competence. However, very little is known about the possible mechanisms that underlie risk or vulnerability. Moreover, the risk factors are often very global. Ironically, studies that employ cumulative risk indicators of adaptation (either in terms of disorder or competence) often show powerful effects but the level of aggregation obscures the processes by which risk may operate (Masten, 1994).

The correlates of competence in children from risk groups or exposed to adversity point to a familiar list of possible protective factors. Many of these factors, such as intellectual functioning in the child or parenting quality, are widely implicated as general correlates of competence as well as resilience. These assets appear to work as predictors of better developmental outcome under many conditions, particularly under adverse rearing conditions. Such assets are likely to have multifaceted roles in adaptation, although the actual processes of resilience have not been established as yet.

Investigators of resilience have hypothesized that a number of basic adaptational mechanisms may be involved in resilience (Masten, 1994; Rutter, 1990). These include attachment processes, proactive buffering of children by adults, problem solving, modeling, self-efficacy processes, opening up of opportunities, niche-seeking, and others. The human species has a rich and varied repertoire of adaptive strategies. However, there appear to be many individual differences in the type and extent of functional protection or resiliency available to a child. Moreover, there are undoubtedly contextual influences, where the fit of protection to challenges plays a role in resilience.

Psychopathology may undermine these protective systems. A child's behavior could "turn off" or wear out the protective involvement of caregivers or other adults. Symptoms of disorder could also interfere with learning and motivational processes associated with protection. Parental problems also may interfere with protective systems at the same time that these problems generate more stressors for children. Moreover, those parent problems may have a partly genetic basis. Hence, if that genetic vulnerability has been passed on to a child, that child who needs greater protection may have fewer protective resources available.

Contributions from the Study of Risk and Psychopathology to Theories about the Normal Development of Competence

One of the primary goals of developmental psychopathology is to understand developmental trajectories over time. These developmental pathways cannot be fully delineated without consideration of both pathology and competence. Considering normal and abnormal behavior together lies at the heart of developmental psychopathology (Sroufe, 1990). In this chapter, we have described general models of how competence and psychopathology may become related and reviewed relevant literature. We have attempted to illustrate how attention to competence in the full context of adaptation in which psychopathology unfolds has the potential to sharpen our understanding of disorder. Moreover, the study of risk and psychopathology may illuminate the processes of normal development, including the processes by which competence is achieved.

Historically, competence theory is rooted in both the study of normative populations as well as the study of risk and psychopathology. However, it is interesting to note the extent to which efforts to understand and operationalize competence have come from studies of risk and adversity. As investigators began to track the development of risk groups, it became necessary to define and measure good psychological development along with signs of incipient problems. These investigators recognized that the absence of symptoms does not adequately describe a developmental pathway.

The study of resilience also emerged from studies of children at risk for mental disorders (Masten & Braswell, 1991). Longitudinal studies of risk and resilience afford opportunities to unify the study of competence and psychopathology. Studies of resilience in children at risk underscore the importance of several basic adaptational systems in human development, including parenting, self-efficacy, and intelligence. Yet this work also points to the need for more refined analyses of how these systems work to promote different aspects of competence. Longitudinal studies that attend to both competence and psychopathology will provide the data needed to compare resilient and troubled developmental trajectories and to test models of how adaptational systems work in human development.

Even the early stages of integrative studies encompassing competence and psychopathology have yielded a host of questions about the nature and development of competence. It is not clear, for example, exactly how parental monitoring or parental expectations, friends, or school environments foster the development of success in society or how differentiated these roles are with respect to different domains of competence. Moreover, it is essential that we consider how we define success and the implications of this definition for bicultural children or children whose proximal rearing environment is life-threatening. Developmental tasks in a society are shaped by biological and cultural history; these expectations and benchmarks for development in turn shape socialization systems, such as schools and families, and thereby individual children. In modern pluralistic societies, there may be conflicting "tasks" and an enormous range of ecological niches to consider.

A more integrative view also emphasizes the significance of knowledge about normal development for prevention and treatment. Acceptance by nondeviant peers may have a protective role with respect to conduct problems and depression in children. Knowing when and how to foster peer acceptance requires a solid knowledge of social development. Similarly, a knowledge base on the development of rule-governed behavior may be essential information for preventing delinquency or violence.

Much of the impetus for understanding competence derives from two related goals: (a) preventing problems and (b) fostering more effective adaptation in society. The latter would include facilitating better recovery from disorder or trauma. Society has a considerable stake in these goals, given the advantages of a competent citizenry and the costs of dysfunction or underachievement. Studies of risk and resilience underscore the importance of understanding the complex biological, social, cognitive, and ecocultural processes involved in effective adaptation, as an area of basic developmental research. Knowledge from such studies is critical for prevention and intervention effects. At the same time, intervention research can serve to corroborate theories and hypotheses about adaptation in development.

Future Directions for Research

This review has three major implications for research: (a) the potential benefit of examining the structure and development of competence as closely as symptoms and disorders have been analyzed; (b) the need for more comprehensive longitudinal studies; and, (c) the need for studies of risk and resilience mechanisms.

The structure and classification of adaptive functioning has not been given the same quality of serious empirical attention as symptoms and disorder. Developmental tasks and different facets of competence have been described and assumed in many studies, rather than studied empirically to learn how they cluster and covary in people over time.

More comprehensive analyses of competence and symptoms will yield more powerful predictions of future development and may result in a more developmentally appropriate classification system for disorders. Classification systems such as DSM-IV classify only a relatively small portion of adaptive behavior. The consideration of competence is typically fragmented, indirect, and inconsistent. Important competence-related predictors of course and outcome are omitted or only partially considered in this system. It may be time for a serious reevaluation of the scope of behavior classified in this and other systems of mental disorder.

There are few longitudinal studies that have considered both competence and symptoms over time so that unidirectional and bidirectional causal models can be evaluated. Larger scale archival data sets, such as the Dunedin, New Zealand study (e.g, McGee & Williams, 1991; McGee et al., 1986, Moffitt, 1990) may provide initial opportunities for such studies. However, it is likely that existing data sets have limitations based on the interests of the original investigators. Either competence or psychopathology may be neglected. Thus, new studies may be required to address some of the unanswered questions on how competence and psychopathology may be related. Furthermore, it would be particularly informative if some future longitudinal studies also incorporate a genetic design, such as long-term twin studies, so that genetic and experiential models can be compared and contrasted simultaneously in relation to competence and psychopathology.

Studies of risk and resilience have shown that these constructs tap important sources of variance in individuals that may underlie the covariation of competence and psychopathology and explain some of the differences in developmental outcome of individuals in specific contexts. However, this research has been largely descriptive and global. Several research directions may prove fruitful.

It has been noted by a number of investigators that the *number* of risk factors appear to be more important for prediction than the precise nature of any one risk variable. Determining the degree to which this is true and why are important research tasks.

The patterning of risk within and across risk categories may prove illuminating. Studies of "resilience" in children among a risk group often amounts to better assessment of differential net risk among members of the group (Masten, 1994). Recent interest in risk and adaptation among siblings and nonshared environmental effects in behavioral genetics research represent important strategies for future risk studies (Beardsall & Dunn, 1992; Plomin & Daniels, 1987).

Intervention can be conceptualized as a deliberate effort to redirect development in more favorable directions or to improve adaptive functioning, as well as to reduce symptoms or "cure" disorder (Masten, 1994). Intervention research offers the opportunity to test hypothesized protective processes in controlled experiments. Thus, intervention research can be informative about adaptational theory as well as about "what works." Strategic, theory-driven interventions are an important avenue for understanding adaptation and its relation to psychopathology (Cicchetti & Toth, 1992b; Masten, 1994).

FINAL COMMENTS

Comprehensive theories and studies of competence and psychopathology are fundamental to developmental psychopathology. These two aspects of adaptation are inseparably related, such that it is not possible to study one without the other, whether one is attentive to the other aspect of adaptation or not. This review suggests that there is much to be gained by analyzing these two facets of adaptation in the same developmental context. Above all, integrative theories and studies of psychopathology and competence will provide a better scientific foundation for designing policies and programs to foster competence and prevent or ameliorate psychopathology.

REFERENCES

Abramson, L. Y., Seligman, M. E. P., & Teasdale, J. D. (1978). Learned helplessness in humans: Critique and reformulation. *Journal of Abnormal Psychology, 87,* 49–74.

Achenbach, T. M. (1966). The classification of children's psychiatric symptoms. *Psychological Monographs, 80* (No. 7, Whole No. 615), 1–37.

Achenbach, T. M. (1991a). *Integrative Guide for the 1991 CBCL/4-18, YSR, and TRF Profiles.* Burlington, VT: University of Vermont Department of Psychiatry.

Achenbach, T. M. (1991b). *Manual for the Child Behavior Checklist/4-18 and 1991 Profile.* Burlington, VT: University of Vermont Department of Psychiatry.

Achenbach, T. M. (1991c). *Manual for the Teacher's Report Form and 1991 Profile.* Burlington, VT: University of Vermont Department of Psychiatry.

Achenbach, T. M., & Edelbrock, C. S. (1978). The classification of child psychopathology: A review and analysis of empirical efforts. *Psychological Bulletin, 85,* 1275–1301.

Achenbach, T. M., & Edelbrock, C. (1983). *Manual for the Child Behavior Checklist and Revised Child Behavior Profile.* Burlington: University of Vermont, Department of Psychiatry.

Achenbach, T. M., Howell, C. T., Quay, H. C., & Conners, C. K. (1991). National survey of problems and competencies among four- to sixteen-year-olds. *Monographs of the Society for Research in Child Development, 56* (Serial No. 225).

American Association on Mental Retardation (1992). *Mental retardation: Definition, classification, and systems of supports* (9th ed.). Washington, DC: Author.

American Psychiatric Association (1987). *Diagnostic and statistical manual of mental disorders* (3rd ed.). Washington, DC: Author.

American Psychiatric Association (1994). *Diagnostic and statistical manual of mental disorders* (4th ed.). Washington, DC: Author.

Ammerman, R. T., & Hersen, M. (1990). *Children at risk: An evaluation of factors contributing to child abuse and neglect.* Plenum, New York.

Anderson, J., Williams, S., McGee, R., & Silva, P. (1989). Cognitive and social correlates of DSM-III disorders in preadolescent children. *Journal of the American Academy of Child and Adolescent Psychiatry, 28,* 842–846.

Antonovsky, A., & Sagy, S. (1990). Confronting developmental tasks in the retirement transition. *The Gerontologist, 30,* 362–368.

Asher, S. R., & Hymel, S. (1981). Children's social competence in peer relations: Sociometric and behavioral assessment. In J. D. Wine & M. D. Smye (Eds.), *Social competence* (pp. 125–157). New York: Guilford.

Bandura, A. (1977). Self-efficacy: Toward a unifying theory of behavioral change. *Psychological Review, 84,* 191–215.

Bandura, A. (1982). Self-efficacy mechanism in human agency. *American Psychologist, 37,* 122–147.

Bandura, A. (1989). Human agency in social cognitive theory. *American Psychologist, 44,* 1175–1184.

Barkley, R. A. (1990). *Attention Deficit Hyperactivity Disorder: A handbook for diagnosis and treatment.* New York: Guilford.

Beardsall, L., & Dunn, J. (1992). Adversities in childhood: siblings' experience, and their relations to self-esteem. *Journal of Child Psychology and Psychiatry, 33,* 349–359.

Bentovim, A., & Smith, M. (1994). Sexual abuse. In M. Rutter, L. Hersov, & E. Taylor (Eds.), *Child and adolescent psychiatry: Modern approaches* (3rd ed.) (pp. 230–251). Oxford: Blackwell.

Berg, I., Collins, T., McGuire, R., & O'Melia, J. (1975). Educational attainment in adolescent school phobia. *British Journal of Psychiatry, 126,* 435–438.

Binet, A., & Simon, T. (1916). *The development of intelligence in children* [translation by E. S. Kite]. Baltimore: Williams & Wilkins. (Original work published 1905)

Blanck, G., & Blanck, R. (Eds.). (1979). *Ego psychology: Psychoanalytic theory and practice.* New York: Columbia University Press.

Blechman, E. A., McEnroe, M. J., Carella, E. T., & Audette, D. P. (1986). Childhood competence and depression. *Journal of Abnormal Psychology, 95,* 223–227.

Blechman, E. A., Tinsley, B., Carella, E. T., & McEnroe, M. J. (1985). Childhood competence and behavior problems. *Journal of Abnormal Psychology, 94,* 70–77.

Block, J. H., & Block, J. (1980). The role of ego-control and ego-resiliency in the organization of behavior. In W. A. Collins (Ed.), *Development of cognition, affect, and social relations* (pp. 39–101). Hillsdale, NJ: Erlbaum.

Block, J. H., Block, J., & Gjerde, P. F. (1986). The personality of children prior to divorce: A prospective study. *Child Development, 57,* 827–840.

Borstelmann, L. J. (1983). Children before psychology: Ideas about children from antiquity to the late 1800s. In W. Kessen (Ed.), P. H. Mussen's (Series Ed.), *Handbook of child psychology: Vol. 1. History, theory, and methods* (1–40). New York: Wiley.

Brandon, R. N. (1990). *Adaptation and environment.* Princeton, NJ: Princeton University Press.

Breger, L. (1974). *From instinct to identity: The development of personality.* Englewood Cliffs, NJ: Prentice-Hall.

Buhrmester, D. (1990). Intimacy of friendship, interpersonal competence, and adjustment during preadolescence and adolescence. *Child Development, 61,* 1101–1111.

Buhrmester, D., Whalen, C. K., Henker, B., MacDonald, V., & Hinshaw, S. P. (1992). Prosocial behavior in hyperactive boys: Effects of stimulant medication and comparison with normal boys. *Journal of Abnormal Child Psychology, 20,* 103–121.

Cairns, R. B. (1983). The emergence of developmental psychology. In W. Kessen (Ed.), P. H. Mussen's (Series Ed.), *Handbook of child psychology: Vol. 1. History, theory, and methods* (41–102). New York: Wiley.

Cairns, R. B., Cairns, B. D., Neckerman, H. J., Gest, S. D., & Gariepy, J.-L. (1988). Social networks and aggressive behavior: Peer support or peer rejection? *Developmental Psychology, 24,* 815–823.

Campbell, S. B. (1990). The socialization and social development of hyperactive children. In M. Lewis & S. M. Miller (Eds.), *Handbook of developmental psychopathology* (pp. 77–91). New York: Plenum.

Capaldi, D. M. (1991). Co-occurrence of conduct problems and depressive symptoms in early adolescent boys: I. Familial factors and general adjustment at Grade 6. *Development and Psychopathology, 3,* 277–300.

Capaldi, D. M. (1992). Co-occurrence of conduct problems and depressive symptoms in early adolescent boys: II. A 2-year follow-up at grade 8. *Development and Psychopathology, 4,* 125–144.

Capaldi, D. M., & Patterson, G. R. (1991). Relation of parental transitions to boys' adjustment problems: I. A linear hypothesis. II. Mothers at risk for transitions and unskilled parenting. *Developmental Psychology, 27,* 489–504.

Carlson, C. L., Pelham, W. E., Milich, R., & Dixon, J. (1992). Single and combined effects of methylphenidate and behavior therapy on the classroom performance of children with attention-deficit hyperactivity disorder. *Journal of Abnormal Child Psychology, 20,* 213–232.

Caspi, A., Elder, G. H., & Bem, D. J. (1987). Moving against the world: life-course patterns of explosive children. *Developmental Psychology, 23,* 308–313.

Caspi, A., Elder, G. H., & Bem, D. J. (1988). Moving away from the world: Life-Course patterns of shy children. *Developmental Psychology, 24,* 824–831.

Charlesworth, W. R. (1976). Human intelligence as adaptation: An ethological approach. In L. B. Resnick (Ed.), *The nature of intelligence* (pp. 147–168). Hillsdale, NJ: Erlbaum.

Charlesworth, W. R. (1978). Ethology: Its relevance for observational studies of human adaptation. In G. Sackett (Ed.), *Observing behavior: Theory and applications in mental retardation* (Vol. 1, pp. 7–32). Baltimore: University Park Press.

Charlesworth, W. R. (1979). Ethology: understanding the other half of intelligence. In M. von Cranach, K. Foppa, W. Lepenies, & D. Ploog (Eds.), *Human ethology: Claims and limits of a new discipline* (pp. 491–519). Cambridge: Cambridge University Press.

Cherlin, A. J., Furstenberg, F. F., Jr., Chase-Lansdale, P. L., Kiernan, K. E., Robins, P. K., Morrison, D. R., & Teitler, J. O. (1991). Longitudinal studies of divorce on children in Great Britain and the United States. *Science, 252,* 1386–1389.

Cicchetti, D. (1984). The emergence of developmental psychopathology. *Child Development, 55,* 1–7.

Cicchetti, D. (1990a). An historical perspective on the discipline of developmental psychopathology. In J. Rolf, A. S. Masten, D. Cicchetti, K. H. Nuechterlein, & S. Weintraub (Eds.), *Risk and protective factors in the development of psychopathology* (pp. 2–28). New York: Cambridge University Press.

Cicchetti, D. (1990b). The organization and coherence of socioemotional, cognitive, and representational development: Illustrations through a developmental psychopathology perspective on Down Syndrome and child maltreatment. In R. Thompson (Ed.), *Socioemotional development: Nebraska symposium on motivation* (Vol. 36) (pp. 259–366). Lincoln, NE: Cambridge University Press.

Cicchetti, D., & Carlson, V. (Eds.) (1989). *Child maltreatment.* New York: Cambridge University Press.

Cicchetti, D., & Schneider-Rosen, K. (1986). An organizational approach to childhood depression. In M. Rutter, C. Izard, & P. Read (Eds.), *Depression in young people: Clinical and developmental perspectives* (pp. 71–134). New York: Guilford.

Cicchetti, D., & Sroufe, L. A. (1978). An organizational view of affect: Illustration from the study of Down's syndrome infants. In M. Lewis & L. Rosenblum (Eds), *The development of affect* (pp. 309–350). New York: Plenum.

Cicchetti, D., & Toth, S. L. (1992a) (Eds.). *Rochester Symposium on Developmental Psychopathology (Vol. 4): Developmental perspectives on depression.* Rochester: University of Rochester Press.

Cicchetti, D., & Toth, S. L. (1992b). The role of developmental theory in prevention and intervention. *Development and Psychopathology, 4,* 489–493.

Cohen, L. H. (1988). *Life events and psychological functioning: Theoretical and methodological issues.* Newbury Park, CA: Sage.

Cohen, L. H., Burt, C. E., & Bjorck, J. P. (1987). Life stress and adjustment: Effects of life events experienced by young adolescents and their parents. *Developmental Psychology, 23,* 583–592.

Cohen, N. J., Kershner, J., & Wehrspann, W. (1988). Correlates of competence in a child psychiatric population. *Journal of Consulting and Clinical Psychology, 56,* 97–103.

Coie, J. D., Dodge, K. A., Terry, R., & Wright, V. (1991). The role of aggression in peer relations: An analysis of aggression episodes in boys' play groups. *Child Development, 62,* 812–826.

Coie, J. D., Lochman, J. E., Terry, R., & Hyman, C. (1992). Predicting early adolescent disorder from childhood aggression and peer rejection. *Journal of Consulting and Clinical Psychology, 60,* 783–792.

Cole, D. A. (1990). Relation of social and academic competence to depressive symptoms in childhood. *Journal of Abnormal Psychology, 99,* 422–429.

Cole, D. A. (1991). Preliminary support for a competency-based model of depression in children. *Journal of Abnormal Psychology, 100,* 181–190.

Cole, D. A., & Carpentieri, S. (1990). Social status and the comorbidity of child depression and conduct disorder. *Journal of Consulting and Clinical Psychology, 58,* 748–757.

Compas, B. E. (1987). Stress and life events during childhood and adolescence. *Clinical Psychology Review, 7,* 275–302.

Compas, B. E., & Hammen, C. L. (1994). Child and adolescent depression: Covariation and comorbidity in development. In R. J. Haggerty, L. R. Sherrod, N. Garmezy, & M. Rutter (Eds.), *Stress, risk and resilience in children and adolescents: Processes, mechanisms, and interventions* (pp. 225–267). New York: Cambridge University Press.

Connell, J. P. (1990). Context, self, and action: A motivational analysis of self-system processes across the life span. In D. Cicchetti &

M. Beeghly (Eds.), *The self in transition: Infancy to childhood* (61–97). Chicago: University of Chicago Press.

Connell, J. P., & Wellborn, J. G. (1991). Competence, autonomy, and relatedness: A motivational analysis of self-system processes. In M. R. Gunnar & L. A. Sroufe (Eds.), *Self processes and development: The Minnesota symposia on child development* (Vol. 23, pp. 43–77). Hillsdale, NJ: Erlbaum.

Conrad, M., & Hammen, C. (1989). Role of maternal depression in perceptions of child maladjustment. *Journal of Consulting and Clinical Psychology, 57,* 663–667.

Cowen, E. L., Weissberg, R. P., & Guare, J. (1984). Differentiating attributes of children referred to a school mental health program. *Journal of Abnormal Child Psychology, 12,* 397–410.

Cowen, E. L., Wyman, P. A., Work, W. C., & Parker, G. R. (1990). The Rochester child resilience project: Overview and summary of first year. *Development and Psychopathology, 2,* 193–212.

Darwin, C. (1964). *On the origin of species.* A facsimile of the first edition (edited by E. Mayr). Cambridge: Harvard University Press. (Original work published 1859)

Dishion, T. J. (1990). The family ecology of boys' peer relations in middle childhood. *Child Development, 61,* 874–892.

Dishion, T. J., Patterson, G. R., Stoolmiller, M., & Skinner, M. L. (1991). Family, school, and behavioral antecedents to early adolescent involvement with antisocial peers. *Developmental Psychology, 27,* 172–180.

Dobzhansky, T. (1962). *Mankind evolving: The evolution of the human species.* New Haven: Yale University Press.

Dodge, K. A. (1986). A social information processing model of social competence in children. In M. Perlmutter (Ed.), *Cognitive perspectives on children's social and behavioral development: The Minnesota Symposia on Child Psychology* (Vol. 18) (pp.77–125). Hillsdale, NJ: Erlbaum.

Dodge, K. A., Bates, J. E., & Pettit, G. S. (1990). Mechanisms in the cycle of violence. *Science, 250,* 1678–1683.

Dodge, K. A., & Frame, C. L. (1982). Social cognitive biases and deficits in aggressive boys. *Child Development, 53,* 620–635.

Dodge, K. A., Murphy, R. R., & Buchsbaum, K. (1984). The assessment of intention-cue detection skills in children: Implications for developmental psychopathology. *Child Development, 55,* 163–173.

Dodge, K. A., Pettit, G. S., McClaskey, C. L., & Brown, M. M. (1986). Social competence in children. *Monographs of the Society for Research in Child Development, 51* (2, Serial No. 213).

Doll, E. A. (1935). A genetic scale of social maturity. *American Journal of Orthopsychiatry, 5,* 180–188.

Doll, E. A. (1953). *The measurement of social competence: A manual for the Vineland Social Maturity Scale.* Minneapolis: Educational Publishers.

Downey, G., & Coyne, J. C. (1990). Children of depressed parents: An integrative review. *Psychological Bulletin, 108,* 50–76.

Dubois, D. L., Felner, R. D., Brand, S., Adan, A. M., & Evans, E. G. (1992). A prospective study of life stress, social support, and adaptation in early adolescence. *Child Development, 63,* 542–557.

Dunn, J., & McGuire, S. (1992). Sibling and peer relationships in childhood. *Journal of Child Psychology and Psychiatry, 33,* 67–105.

Edelbrock, C., & Achenbach, T. M. (1980). A typology of Child Behavior Profile Patterns: Distribution and correlates in disturbed children aged 6 to 16. *Journal of Abnormal Child Psychology, 8,* 441–470.

Emery, R. E. (1982). Interparental conflict and the children of discord and divorce. *Psychological Bulletin, 92*, 310–330.

Emery, R. E. (1988). *Marriage, divorce, and children's adjustment.* Newbury Park, CA: Sage.

Emery, R. E. (1989). Family violence. *American Psychologist, 44*, 321–328.

Emery, R. E., & Forehand, R. (1994). Parental divorce in children's well-being: A focus on resilience. In R. J. Haggerty, L. R. Sherrod, N. Garmezy, & M. Rutter, (Eds.), *Stress, risk and resilience in children and adolescents: Processes, mechanisms, and interventions* (pp. 64–99). New York: Cambridge University Press.

Erikson, E. H. (1963). *Childhood and society* (2nd ed.). New York: Norton.

Erikson, E. H. (1968). *Identity, youth and crisis.* New York: Norton.

Farrington, D. P., Loeber, R., & van Kammen, W. B. (1990). Long-term criminal outcomes of hyperactivity-impulsivity-attention deficit and conduct problems in childhood. In L. N. Robins & M. Rutter (Eds.), *Straight and devious pathways from childhood to adulthood* (pp. 62–81). New York: Cambridge University Press.

Fauber, R., Forehand, R., Long, N., Burke, M., & Faust, J. (1987). The relationship of young adolescent Children's Depression Inventory (CDI) scores to their social and cognitive functioning. *Journal of Psychopathology and Behavioral Assessment, 9*, 161–172.

Feffer, M., & Phillips, L. (1953). Social attainment and performance under stress. *Journal of Personality, 22*, 284–297.

Feldman, S. S., & Elliott, G. R. (1990). *At the threshold: The developing adolescent.* Cambridge, MA: Harvard University Press.

Felsman, J. K., & Vaillant, G. E. (1987). Resilient children as adults: A 40-year study. In E. J. Anthony & B. J. Cohler (Eds.), *The invulnerable child* (pp. 289–314). New York: Guilford.

Flavell, J. H. (1963). *The developmental psychology of Jean Piaget.* New York: Van Nostrand.

Ford, D. H. (1987). *Humans as self-constructing living systems: A developmental perspective on behavior and personality.* Hillsdale, NJ: Erlbaum.

Ford, D. H., & Lerner, R. M. (1992). *Developmental systems theory: An integrative approach.* Newbury Park, CA: Sage.

Ford, M. E. (1985). The concept of competence: Themes and variations. In H. A. Marlowe, Jr. & R. B. Weinberg (Eds.), *Competence Development: Theory and practice in special populations* (pp. 3–49). Springfield, IL: Thomas.

Forgatch, M. S., Patterson, G. R., & Skinner, M. L. (1988). A mediational model for the effect of divorce on antisocial behavior in boys. In E. M. Hetherington & J. D. Arasteh (Eds.), *Impact of divorce, single parenting, and stepparenting on children* (pp. 135–154). Hillsdale, NJ: Erlbaum.

French, D. C. (1988). Heterogeneity of peer-rejected boys: Aggressive and nonaggressive subtypes. *Child Development, 59*, 976–985.

French, D. C., & Waas, G. A. (1985). Behavior problems of peer-neglected and peer rejected elementary-age children: Parent and teacher perspectives. *Child Development, 56*, 246–252.

Freud, A. (1966). *Ego and the mechanisms of defense.* New York: International Universities Press. (Original work published 1936)

Freud, S. (1928). Humour. *The International Journal of Psycho-analysis, 9*(1), 1–6.

Freud, S. (1960). *Jokes and their relation to the unconscious.* New York: Norton. (Original work published 1905)

Freud, S. (1960). *The ego and the id.* New York: Norton. (Original work published 1923)

Frick, P. J., Kamphaus, R. W., Lahey, B. B., Loeber, R., Christ, M. A. G., Hart, E. L., & Tannenbaum, L. E. (1991). Academic underachievement and the disruptive behavior disorders. *Journal of Consulting and Clinical Psychology, 59*, 289–294.

Garber, J., & Seligman, M. E. P. (Eds.). (1980). *Human helplessness: Theory and applications.* New York: Academic Press.

Garmezy, N. (1970). Process and reactive schizophrenia: Some conceptions and issues. *Schizophrenia Bulletin, 2*, 30–74.

Garmezy, N. (1971). Vulnerability research and the issue of primary prevention. *American Journal of Orthopsychiatry, 41*, 101–116.

Garmezy, N. (1974). The study of competence in children at risk for severe psychopathology. In A. Koupernik (Ed.), *The child in his family—Children at psychiatric risk* (Vol. 3) (pp. 77–97). New York: Wiley.

Garmezy, N. (1985). Stress-resistant children: The search for protective factors. In J. E. Stevenson (Ed.), *Recent research in developmental psychopathology. Journal of Child Psychology and Psychiatry Book Supplement No. 4* (pp. 213–233). Oxford: Pergamon.

Garmezy, N., & Masten, A. S. (1994). Chronic adversities. In M. Rutter, L. Herzov, & E. Taylor (Eds.), *Child and adolescent psychiatry: Modern approaches* (3rd ed) (pp. 191–208). Oxford: Blackwell.

Garmezy, N., & Nuechterlein, K. (1972). Invulnerable children: The fact and fiction of competence and disadvantage. *American Journal of Orthopsychiatry, 42*, 328–329.

Garmezy, N., & Rutter, M. (1985). Acute reactions to stress. In M. Rutter & L. Hersov (Eds.), *Child psychiatry: Modern approaches* (2nd ed.) (pp. 152–176). Oxford: Blackwell.

Gest, S. D., Neemann, J., Hubbard, J. J., Masten, A. S., & Tellegen, A. (1993). Parenting quality, adversity, and conduct problems in adolescence: Testing process-oriented models of resilience. *Development and Psychopathology, 5*, 663–682.

Gersten, J. C., Langner, T. S., Eisenberg, J. G., & Simcha-Fagan, O. (1977). An evaluation of the etiologic role of stressful life-change events in psychological disorders. *Journal of Health and Social Behavior, 18*, 228–244.

Gilger, J. W., Pennington, B. F., & DeFries, J. C. (1992). A twin study of the etiology of comorbidity: Attention-deficit hyperactivity disorder and dyslexia. *Journal of the Academy of Child and Adolescent Psychiatry, 31*, 343–348.

Gillmore, R. R., Hawkins, J. D., Day, L. E., & Catalano, R. F. (1992). Friendship and deviance: New evidence on an old controversy. *Journal of Early Adolescence, 12*, 80–95.

Ginsburg, H. P., & Opper, S. (1988). *Piaget's theory of intellectual development* (3rd ed.). Englewood Cliffs NJ: Prentice-Hall.

Goodyer, I., Kolvin, I., & Gatzanis, S. (1985). Recent undesirable life events and psychiatric disorder in childhood and adolescence. *British Journal of Psychiatry, 147*, 517–523.

Goodyer, I., Wright, C., & Altham, P. (1990). The friendships and recent life events of anxious and depressed school-age children. *British Journal of Psychiatry, 156*, 689–698.

Gordon, D., Burge, D., Hammen, C., Adrian, C., Jaenicke, C., & Hiroto, D. (1989). Observations of interactions of depressed women with their children. *American Journal of Psychiatry, 146*, 50–55.

Greenspan, S. I. (1981). *Psychopathology and adaptation in infant and early childhood: Principles of clinical diagnosis and preventive intervention.* New York: International Universities Press.

Gunnar, M. R., & Sroufe, L. A. (Eds.) (1991). *Competence, autonomy, and relatedness: A motivational analysis of self-system processes.* Hillsdale, NJ: Erlbaum.

Gunnar, M. R., & Thelen, E. (1989). Systems and development: The Minnesota Symposia on Child Psychology (Vol. 22). Hillsdale, NJ: Erlbaum.

Hammen, C. (1992). The family-environmental context of depression: A perspective on children's risk. In D. Cicchetti & S. Toth (Eds.), *Rochester Symposium on Developmental Psychopathology (Vol. 4): Developmental perspectives on depression* (pp. 251–281). Hillsdale, NJ: Erlbaum.

Hammen, C., Adrian, C., Gordon, D., Burge, D., Jaenicke, C., & Hiroto, D. (1987). Children of depressed mothers: Maternal strain and symptom predictors of dysfunction. *Journal of Consulting and Clinical Psychology, 59,* 341–345.

Hammen, C., Burge, D., & Adrian, C. (1991). Timing of mother and child depression in a longitudinal study of children at risk. *Journal of Consulting and Clinical Psychology, 59,* 341–345.

Hammen, C., Burge, D., & Stansbury, K. (1990). Relationship of mother and child variables to child outcomes in a high-risk sample: A causal modeling analysis. *Developmental Psychology, 26,* 24–30.

Harter, S. (1978). Effectance motivation reconsidered: Toward a developmental model. *Human Development, 21,* 34–64.

Harter, S. (1982). The perceived competence scale for children. *Child Development, 53,* 87–97.

Harter, S. (1985). Competence as a dimension of self-evaluation: Toward a comprehensive model of self-worth. In R. L. Leahy (Ed.), *The development of the self* (pp. 55–121). New York: Academic Press.

Harter, S. (1990). Self and identity development. In S. S. Feldman & G. R. Elliott (Eds.), *At the threshold: The developing adolescent* (pp. 352–387). Cambridge: Harvard University Press.

Hartmann, H. (1958). *Ego psychology and the problem of adaptation.* New York: International Universities Press. (Original work published 1939)

Hartup, W. W. (1983). Peer relations. In E. M. Hetherington (Ed.), P. H. Mussen (Series Ed.), *Handbook of child psychology: Vol. 4. Socialization, personality , and social development* (pp. 103–198). New York: Wiley.

Hartup, W. W. (1992). Friendships and their developmental significance. In H. McGurk (Ed.), *Childhood Social Development: Contemporary perspectives* (pp. 175–205). Hove, UK: Erlbaum.

Hartup, W. W., & Sancilio, M. F. (1986). Children's friendships. In E. Schopler & G. B. Mesibov (Eds.), *Social behavior in autism* (pp. 61–79). New York: Plenum.

Havighurst, R. J. (1972). *Developmental tasks and education* (3rd ed.). New York: David McKay.

Heber, R. (1959). A manual on terminology and classification in mental retardation. *American Journal of Mental Deficiency, 64* (Monograph Supplement).

Hendrick, I. (1942). Instinct and the ego during infancy. *Psychoanalytic Quarterly, 11,* 33–58.

Hendrick, I. (1943). Work and the pleasure principle. *Psychoanalytic Quarterly, 12,* 311–329.

Henn, F. A., Bardwell, R., & Jenkins, R. L. (1980). Juvenile delinquents revisited: Adult criminal activity. *Archives of General Psychiatry, 37,* 1160–1163.

Hetherington, E. M. (1989). Coping with family transitions: Winners, losers, and survivors. *Child Development, 60,* 1–14.

Hetherington, E. M., Cox, M., & Cox, R. (1985). Long-term effects of divorce and remarriage on the adjustment of children. *Journal of the American Academy of Child Psychiatry, 24,* 518–530.

Hetherington, E. M., Stanley-Hagan, M., & Anderson, E. R. (1989). Marital transitions: A child's perspective. *American Psychologist, 44,* 303–312.

Hill, J. (1980). Understanding early adolescence: A framework. Chapel Hill, NC: Center for Early Adolescence.

Hill, J. (1983). Early adolescence: A research agenda. *Journal of Early Adolescence, 3,* 1–21.

Hinshaw, S. P. (1987). On the distinction between attentional deficits/hyperactivity and conduct problems/aggression in child psychopathology. *Psychological Bulletin, 101,* 443–463.

Hinshaw, S. P. (1992). Externalizing behavior problems and academic underachievement in childhood and adolescence: Causal relationships and underlying mechanisms. *Psychological Bulletin, 111,* 127–155.

Hodges, K., & Plow, J. (1990). Intellectual ability and achievement in psychiatrically hospitalized children with conduct, anxiety, and affective disorders. *Journal of Consulting and Clinical Psychology, 58,* 589–595.

Horowitz, F. (1989, April). The concept of risk: A re-evaluation. Invited address, biennial meeting of the Society for Research in Child Development, Kansas City, MO.

Hymel, S., Rubin, K. H., Rowden, L., & LeMare, L. (1990). Children's peer relationships: Longitudinal prediction of internalizing and externalizing problems from middle to late childhood. *Child Development, 61,* 2004–2021.

Jacobson, R. H., Lahey, B. B., & Strauss, C. C. (1983). Correlates of depressed mood in normal children. *Journal of Abnormal Child Psychology, 11,* 29–40.

Johnson, J. H. (1986). *Life events as stressors in children and adolescents.* Beverly Hills, CA: Sage.

Kellam, S. G., Brown, C. H., Rubin, B. R., & Ensminger, M. E. (1983). Paths leading to teenage psychiatric symptoms and substance use: Developmental epidemiological studies in woodlawn. In S. B. Guze, F. J. Earls, & J. E. Barrett (Eds.), *Childhood psychopathology and development* (pp. 17–47). New York: Raven Press.

Kitson, G. C., & Morgan, L. A. (1990). The multiple consequences of divorce: A decade review. *Journal of Marriage and the Family, 52,* 913–924.

Klaczynski, P. A. (1990). Cultural-developmental tasks and adolescent development: Theoretical and methodological considerations. *Adolescence, 25,* 811–823.

Koestler, A. (1978). *Janus: A summing up.* New York: Random House.

Kohlberg, L., LaCrosse, J., & Ricks, D. (1972). The predictability of adult mental health from childhood behavior. In B. B. Wolman (Ed.), *Manual of child psychopathology* (pp. 1217–1284). New York: McGraw-Hill.

Kohlberg, L., Ricks, D., & Snarey, J. (1984). Childhood development as a predictor of adaptation in adulthood. *Genetic Psychology Monographs, 110,* 91–172.

Kohn, M. (1977). *Social competence, symptoms and underachievement in childhood: A longitudinal perspective.* New York: Wiley.

Kohn, M., & Rosman, B. L. (1972). A social competence scale and symptom checklist for the preschool child. *Developmental Psychology, 6,* 430–444.

Kohn, M., & Rosman, B. L. (1973). Cognitive functioning in five-year-old boys as related to social-emotional and background-demographic variables. *Developmental Psychology, 8,* 177–194.

Kolvin, I., Miller, F. J. W., Fleeting, M., & Kolvin, P. A. (1988). Risk/protective factors for offending with particular reference to deprivation. In M. Rutter (Ed.), *Studies of psychosocial risk: The power of longitudinal data* (pp. 77–95). New York: Cambridge University Press.

Koot, H. M., & Verhulst, F. C. (1992). Prediction of children's referral to mental health and special education services from earlier adjustment. *Journal of Child Psychology and Psychiatry, 33,* 717–729.

Kopp, C. B. (1983). Risk factors in development. In P. H. Mussen (Ed.), *Handbook of child psychology* (4th ed.). Vol. 2: M. M. Haith & J. J. Campos (Eds.), *Infancy and developmental psychobiology* (pp. 1081–1188). New York: Wiley.

Kupersmidt, J. B., & Coie, J. D. (1990). Preadolescent peer status, aggression, and school adjustment as predictors of externalizing problems in adolescence. *Child Development, 61,* 1350–1362.

Ladd, G. W. (1990). Having friends, keeping friends, making friends, and being liked by peers in the classroom: Predictors of children's early school adjustment? *Child Development, 61,* 1081–1100.

Lahey, B. B., Hartdagen, S. E., Frick, P. J., McBurnett, K., Connor, R., & Hynd, G. W. (1988). Conduct disorder: Parsing the confounded relation to parental divorce and antisocial personality. *Journal of Abnormal Psychology, 97,* 334–337.

Ledingham, J. E. (1981). Developmental patterns of aggressive and withdrawn behavior in childhood: A possible method for identifying preschizophrenics. *Journal of Abnormal Child Psychology, 9,* 1–22.

Ledingham, J. E., & Schwartzman, A. E. (1984). A 3-year follow-up of aggressive and withdrawn behavior in childhood: Preliminary findings. *Journal of Abnormal Child Psychology, 12,* 157–168.

Lefkowitz, M. M., & Tesiny, E. P. (1985). Depression in childhood: Prevalence and correlates. *Journal of Consulting and Clinical Psychology, 53,* 647–656.

Leon, G. R., Kendall, P. C., & Garber, J. (1980). Depression in children: Parent, teacher, and child perspectives. *Journal of Abnormal Child Psychology, 8,* 221–235.

Lerner, J. V., Hertzog, C., Hooker, K. A., Hassibi, M., & Thomas, A. (1988). A longitudinal study of negative emotional states and adjustment from early childhood through adolescence. *Child Development, 59,* 356–366.

Lilienfeld, S. O., & Waldman, I. D. (1990). The relation between childhood attention-deficit hyperactivity disorder and adult antisocial behavior reexamined: The problem of heterogeneity. *Clinical Psychology Review, 10,* 699–725.

Loeber, R. (1990). Development and risk factors of juvenile antisocial behavior and delinquency. *Clinical Psychology Review, 10,* 1–41.

Loevinger, J. (1976). *Ego development.* San Francisco: Jossey-Bass.

Luthar, S. S. (1991). Vulnerability and resilience: A study of high-risk adolescents. *Child Development, 62,* 600–616.

Martin, B., & Hoffman, J. A. (1990). Conduct disorders. In M. Lewis & S. M. Miller (Eds.), *Handbook of developmental psychopathology* (pp. 109–118). New York: Plenum.

Masten, A. S. (1989). Resilience in development: Implications of the study of successful adaptation for developmental psychopathology. In D. Cicchetti (Ed.), *The emergence of a discipline: Rochester Symposium on Developmental Psychopathology* (Vol. 1; pp. 261–294). Rochester: University of Rochester Press.

Masten, A. S. (1994). Resilience in individual development: Successful adaptation despite risk and adversity. In M. C. Wang & E. Gordon (Eds.), *Educational resilience in inner city America: Challenges and prospects* (pp. 3–25). Hillsdale, NJ: Erlbaum.

Masten, A. S., Best, K. M., & Garmezy, N. (1990). Resilience and development: Contributions from the study of children who overcome adversity. *Development and psychopathology, 2,* 425–444.

Masten, A. S., & Braswell, L. (1991). Developmental psychopathology: An integrative framework. In P. R. Martin (Ed.), *Handbook of behavior therapy and psychological science: An integrative approach* (pp. 35–56). New York: Pergamon.

Masten, A. S., & Garmezy, N. (1985). Risk, vulnerability, and protective factors in developmental psychopathology. In B. B. Lahey & A. E. Kazdin (Eds.), *Advances in clinical child psychology* (Vol. 8) (pp. 1–52). New York: Plenum.

Masten, A. S., Garmezy, N., Tellegen, A., Pellegrini, D. S., Larkin, K., & Larsen, A. (1988). Competence and stress in school children: The moderating effects of individual and family qualities. *Journal of Child Psychology and Psychiatry, 29,* 745–764.

Masten, A. S., Neemann, J., & Andenas, S. (1994). Life events and adjustment in adolescents: The significance of event independence, chronicity, and desirability. *Journal of Research on Adolescence, 4,* 71–97.

Masten, A. S., & Wright, M. O'D. (in press). Cumulative risk and protective models of maltreatment. In B. B. R. Rossman & M. S. Rosenberg (Eds.). *Multiple victimization of children.* Haworth.

Mayr, E. (1982). The growth of biological thought: Diversity, evolution, and inheritance. Cambridge, MA: Harvard University Press.

McConaughy, S. H., Achenbach, T. M., & Gent, C. L. (1988). Multiaxial empirically based assessment: Parent, teacher, observational, cognitive, and personality correlates of child behavior profile types for 6- to 11-year-old boys. *Journal of Abnormal Child Psychology, 16,* 485–509.

McConaughy, S. H., Stanger, C., & Achenbach, T. M. (1992). Three-year course of behavioral/emotional problems in a national sample of 4- to 16-year-olds: I. Agreement among informants. *Journal of the American Academy of Child and Adolescent Psychiatry, 31,* 932–940.

McGee, R., & Share, D. L. (1988). Attention deficit disorder-hyperactivity and academic failure: Which comes first and what should be treated? *Journal of the American Academy of child and Adolescent Psychiatry, 27,* 318–325.

McGee, R., & Williams, S. (1991). Social competence in adolescence: Preliminary findings from a longitudinal study of New Zealand 15-year-olds. *Psychiatry, 54,* 281–291.

McGee, R., Williams, S., Share, D. L., Anderson, J., & Silva, P. A. (1986). The relationship between specific reading retardation, general reading backwardness and behavioural problems in a large sample of Dunedin boys: a longitudinal study from five to eleven years. *Journal of Child Psychology and Psychiatry, 27,* 597–610.

McGrew, K. S. (1989). *Defining the constructs of adaptive, and maladaptive behavior within a model of personal competence.* Unpublished doctoral dissertation.

McGrew, K., & Bruininks, R. (1989). Factor structure of adaptive behavior. *School Psychology Review, 18,* 64–81.

Meisels, S. J., & Wasik, B. A. (1990). Who should be served? Identifying children in need of early intervention. In S. J. Meisels & J. P. Shonkoff (Ed.), *Handbook of early childhood intervention* (pp. 605–632). New York: Cambridge University Press.

Milich, R., & Landau, S. (1984). A comparison of the social status and social behavior of aggressive and aggressive/withdrawn boys. *Journal of Abnormal Child Psychology, 12,* 277–288.

Moffitt, T. E. (1990). Juvenile delinquency and attention deficit disorder: Boys' developmental trajectories from age 3 to age 15. *Child Development, 61,* 893–910.

Morison, P., & Masten, A. S. (1991). Peer reputation in middle childhood as a predictor of adaptation in adolescence: A seven-year follow-up. *Child Development, 62,* 991–1007.

Mulvey, E. P., & LaRosa, J. F. (1986). Delinquency cessation and adolescent development: Preliminary data. *American Journal of Orthopsychiatry, 56,* 212–224.

Murphy, L. B., & Moriarty, A. E. (1976). *Vulnerability, coping, and growth: From infancy to adolescence.* New Haven: Yale University Press.

Newcomb, M. D., Huba, G. J., & Bentler, P. M. (1986). Life change events among adolescents: An empirical consideration of some methodological issues. *The Journal of Nervous and Mental Disease, 174,* 280–289.

Nolen-Hoeksema, S., Girgus, J. S., & Seligman, M. E. P. (1992). Predictors and consequences of childhood depressive symptoms: A 5-year longitudinal study. *Journal of Abnormal Psychology, 101,* 405–422.

O'Dougherty, M., & Wright, F. S. (1990). Children born at medical risk: factors affecting vulnerability and resilience. In J. Rolf, A. S. Masten, D. Cicchetti, K. H. Nuechterlein, & S. Weintraub (1990). *Risk and protective factors in the development of psychopathology* (pp. 120–140). New York: Cambridge University Press.

Oerter, R. (1986). Developmental tasks throughout the life span: A new approach to an old concept. In P. A. Baltes, D. L. Featherman, & R. M. Lerner (Eds.), *Life span development and behavior* (Vol. 7) (pp. 233–269). Hillsdale, NJ: Erlbaum.

Offord, D. R., Boyle, M. H., & Racine, Y. (1989). Ontario Child Health Study: Correlates of disorder. *Journal of the American Academy of Child and Adolescent Psychiatry, 28,* 856–860.

Offord, D. R., Boyle, M. H., Racine, Y. A., Fleming, J. E., Cadman, D. T., Blum, H. M., Byrne, C., Links, P. S., Lipman, E. L., MacMillan, H. L., RaeGrant, N. I., Sanford, M. N., Szatmari, P., Thomas, H., & Woodward, C. A. (1992). Outcome, prognosis, and risk in a longitudinal follow-up study. *Journal of the American Academy of Child and Adolescent Psychiatry, 31,* 916–923.

Ogbu, J. U. (1985). A cultural ecology of competence among inner-city blacks. In M. B. Spencer, G. K. Brookins, & W. R. Allen (Eds.), *Beginnings: The social and affective development of black children* (pp. 45–66). Hillsdale, NJ: Erlbaum.

Ollendick, T. H., Weist, M. D., Borden, M. C., & Greene, R. W. (1992). Sociometric status and academic, behavioral, and psychological adjustment: A five-year longitudinal study. *Journal of Consulting and Clinical Psychology, 60,* 80–87.

Orvaschel, H., & Weissman, M. M. (1986). Epidemiology of anxiety disorders in children: A review. In R. Gittelman (Ed.), *Anxiety disorders of childhood* (pp. 58–72). New York: Guilford.

Panak, W. F., & Garber, J. (1992). Role of aggression, rejection, and attributions in the prediction of depression in children. *Development and Psychopathology, 4,* 145–165.

Panella, D., & Henggler, S. W., (1986). Peer interactions of conduct-disordered, anxious,-withdrawn, and well-adjusted Black adolescents. *Journal of Abnormal Child Psychology, 14,* 1–11.

Parker, J. G., & Asher, S. R. (1987). Peer relations and later personal adjustment: Are low-accepted children at risk? *Psychological Bulletin, 102,* 357–389.

Parkhurst, J. T., & Asher, S. R. (1992). Peer rejection in middle school: Subgroup differences in behavior, loneliness, and interpersonal concerns. *Developmental Psychology, 28,* 231–241.

Patterson, G. R. (1986). Performance models for antisocial boys. *American Psychologist, 41,* 432–444.

Patterson, G. R., & Capaldi, D. M. (1990). A mediational model for boys' depressed mood. In J. Rolf, A. S. Masten, D. Cicchetti, K. H. Nuechterlein, & S. Weintraub (Eds.), *Risk and protective factors in the development of psychopathology* (pp. 141–163). New York: Cambridge University Press.

Patterson, G. R., Reid, J. B., & Dishion, T. J. (1992). *A social interactional approach (Vol. 4): Antisocial boys.* Eugene OR: Castaglia.

Patterson, G. R., & Stoolmiller, M. (1991). Replications of a dual failure model for boys' depressed mood. *Journal of Consulting and Clinical Psychology, 59,* 491–498.

Perlmutter, M., Kaplan, M., & Nyquist, L. (1990). Development of adaptive competence in adulthood. *Human Development, 33,* 185–197.

Perry, C. (1979). Popular, amiable, isolated, rejected: A reconceptualization of sociometric status in pre-school children. *Child Development, 50,* 1231–1234.

Phillips, L. (1953). Case history data and prognosis in schizophrenia. *Journal of Nervous and Mental Disease, 117,* 515–525.

Phillips, L. (1968). *Human adaptation and its failures.* New York: Academic Press.

Phillips, L., & Cowitz, B. (1953). Social attainment and reaction to stress. *Journal of Personality, 22,* 270–283.

Piaget, J. (1952). *The origins of intelligence in children.* New York: International University Press.

Plomin, R., & Daniels, D. (1987). Why are children in the same family so different from one another? *The Behavioral and Brain Sciences, 10,* 1–15.

Pope, A., Bierman, K. L., & Mumma, G. H. (1989). Relations between hyperactive and aggressive behaviors and peer relations at three elementary grade levels. *Journal of Abnormal Psychology, 17,* 253–268.

Puig-Antich, J. (1982). Major depression and conduct disorder in prepuberty. *Journal of the American Academy of Child Psychiatry, 21,* 118–121.

Puig-Antich, J., Lukens, E., Davies, M., Goetz, D., Brennan-Quattrock, J., & Todak, G. (1985a). Psychosocial functioning in prepubertal major depressive disorders: I. Interpersonal relationships during the depressive episode. *Archives of General Psychiatry, 42,* 500–507.

Puig-Antich, J., Lukens, E., Davies, M., Goetz, D., Brennan-Quattrock, J., & Todak, G. (1985b). Psychosocial functioning in prepubertal major depressive disorders: II. Interpersonal relationships after sustained recovery from affective episode. *Archives of General Psychiatry, 42,* 511–517.

Pulkkinen, L. (1988). Delinquent development: theoretical and empirical considerations. In M. Rutter (Ed.), *Studies of psychosocial risk: the power of longitudinal data* (pp. 184–199). New York: Cambridge University Press.

Radke-Yarrow, M., & Sherman, T. (1990). Hard growing: Children who survive. In J. Rolf, A. S. Masten, D. Cicchetti, K. H. Nuechterlein, & S. Weintraub (Eds.), *Risk and protective factors in the development of psychopathology* (pp. 97–119). New York: Cambridge University Press.

Reiss, A. J., & Farrington, D. P. (1991). Advancing knowledge about co-offending: Results from a prospective longitudinal survey of London males. *Journal of Criminal Law and Criminology, 82,* 360–395.

Richters, J. E., & Cicchetti, D. (1993). Mark Twin meets DSM-III-R: Conduct disorder, development, and the concept of harmful dysfunction. *Development and Psychopathology, 5,* 5–29.

Richters, M. M., Cicchetti, D., Sparrow, S., & Volkmar, F. R. (1993). Axis V: A closer look at its reliability and viability. Poster presented at the 40th annual meeting of the American Academy of Child and Adolescent Psychiatry, San Antonio, TX.

Rieder, C., & Cicchetti, D. (1989). Organizational perspective on cognitive control functioning and cognitive-affective balance in maltreated children. *Developmental Psychology, 25,* 382–393.

Robins, L. N. (1991). Conduct disorder. *Journal of Child Psychology and Psychiatry, 32,* 193–212.

Rolf, J. E. (1972). The social and academic competence of children vulnerable to schizophrenia and other behavior pathologies. *Journal of Abnormal Psychology, 80,* 225–243.

Rolf, J., Masten, A. S., Cicchetti, D., Nuechterlein, K. H., & Weintraub, S. (1990). *Risk and protective factors in the development of psychopathology.* New York: Cambridge University Press.

Rowe, K. J., & Rowe, K. S. (1992). The relationship between inattentiveness in the classroom and reading achievement (part B): An exploratory study. *Journal of the American Academy of Child and Adolescent Psychiatry, 31,* 357–368.

Rubin, K. H., & Coplan, R. J. (1992). Peer relationships in childhood. In M. H. Bornstein & M. E. Lamb (Eds.), *Developmental psychology: An advanced textbook* (3rd ed.) (pp. 519–578). Hillsdale, NJ: Erlbaum.

Rubin, K. H., Hymel, S., Mills, R. S. L., & Rose-Krasnor, L. (1991). Conceptualizing different developmental pathways to and from social isolation in childhood. In D. Cicchetti & S. L. Toth (Eds.), *Internalizing and externalizing expressions of dysfunction: Rochester Symposium on developmental psychopathology* (Vol. 2) (pp. 91–122). Hillsdale, NJ: Erlbaum.

Rubin, K. H., & Mills, R. S. L. (1988). The many faces of social isolation in childhood. *Journal of Consulting and Clinical Psychology, 56,* 916–924.

Rutter, M. (1979). Protective factors in children's responses to stress and disadvantage. *Annals of the Academy of Medicine, Singapore, 8,* 324–338.

Rutter, M. (1990). Psychosocial resilience and protective mechanisms. In J. Rolf, A. S. Masten, D. Cicchetti, K. H. Nuechterlein, & S. Weintraub (Eds.), *Risk and protective factors in the development of psychopathology* (pp. 181–214). New York: Cambridge University Press.

Sameroff, A. J. (1982). Development and the dialectic: The need for a systems approach. In W. A. Collins (Ed.), *The concept of development: The Minnesota Symposia on Child Psychology* (Vol. 15) (pp. 83–103). Hillsdale, NJ: Erlbaum.

Sameroff, A. J. (1989). Commentary: General systems and the regulation of development. In M. R. Gunnar & E. Thelen (Ed.), *Systems and development: The Minnesota symposia on child psychology* (pp. 219–235). Hillsdale, NJ: Erlbaum.

Sameroff, A. J., & Chandler, M. J. (1975). Reproductive risk and the continuum of caretaking casualty. *Review of Child Development Research, 4,* 187–244.

Sameroff, A. J., & Seifer, R. (1983). Familial risk and child competence. *Child Development, 36,* 413–424.

Sameroff, A. J., & Seifer, R. (1990). Early contributors to developmental risk. In J. Rolf, A. S. Masten, D. Cicchetti, K. H. Nuechterlein, & S. Weintraub (Eds.), *Risk and protective factors in the development of psychopathology* (pp. 52–66). New York: Cambridge University Press.

Sameroff, A. J., Seifer, R., & Zax, M. (1982). Early development of children at risk for emotional disorder. *Monographs of the Society for Research in Child Development, 47* (7, Serial No. 199).

Sameroff, A. J., Seifer, R., Zax, M., & Barocas, R. (1987). Early indicators of developmental risk: Rochester longitudinal study. *Schizophrenia Bulletin, 13,* 383–394.

Sander, L. W. (1975). Infant and caretaking environment: Investigation and conceptualization of adaptive behavior in a system of increasing complexity. In E. J. Anthony (Ed.), *Explorations in child psychiatry* (pp. 129–166). New York: Plenum.

Sandler, I. N., & Block, M. (1979). Life stress and maladaptation of children. *American Journal of Community Psychology, 7,* 425–439.

Sattler, J. M. (1988). *Assessment of children* (3rd ed.). San Diego: Sattler.

Scarr, S., & McCartney, K. (1983). How people make their own environments: A theory of genotype—environment effects. *Child Development, 54,* 424–435.

Schachar, R. (1991). Childhood hyperactivity. *Journal of Child Psychology and Psychiatry, 32,* 155–191.

Seifer, R., Sameroff, A. J., Baldwin, C. P., & Baldwin, A. (1992). Child and family factors that ameliorate risk between 4 and 13 years of age. *Journal of the American Academy of Child and Adolescent Psychiatry, 31,* 893–903.

Seligman, M. E. P. (1975). *Helplessness: On depression, development, and death.* San Francisco: Freeman.

Skinner, E. A. (1991). Development and perceived control: A dynamic model of action in context. In M. R. Gunnar & L. Alan Sroufe (Eds.), *Self processes and development: The Minnesota Symposia on Child Development* (Vol. 23) (pp. 167–216). Hillsdale, NJ: Erlbaum.

Skinner, E. A., Chapman, M., & Baltes, P. B. (1988). Control, means-ends, and agency beliefs: A new conceptualization and its measurement during childhood. *Journal of Personality and Social Psychology, 54,* 117–133.

Skodol, A. W., Link, B. G., Shrout, P. E., & Horwath, E. (1988). The revision of Axis V in DSM-III-R: Should symptoms have been included? *American Journal of Psychiatry, 145,* 825–829.

Skuse, D., & Bentovim, A. (1994). Physical and emotional maltreatment. In M. Rutter, L. Herzov, & E. Taylor (Eds.), *Child and adolescent psychiatry: Modern approaches* (3rd ed.) (pp. 209–229). Oxford: Blackwell.

Slotkin, J., Forehand, R., Fauber, R., McCombs, A., & Long, N. (1988). Parent-completed and adolescent-completed CDIs: Relationships to adolescent social and cognitive functioning. *Journal of Abnormal Child Psychology, 16,* 207–217.

Spitzer, R. L., & Williams, J. B. W. (1982). The definition and diagnosis of mental disorder. In W. R. Gove (Ed.), *Deviance and mental illness* (pp. 15–31). Beverly Hills, CA: Sage.

Sroufe, L. A. (1979). The coherence of individual development: Early care, attachment, and subsequent developmental issues. *American Psychologist, 34,* 834–841.

Sroufe, L. A. (1990). Considering normal and abnormal together: The essence of developmental psychopathology. *Development and Psychopathology, 2,* 335–347.

Sroufe, L. A., & Rutter, M. (Eds.) (1984). The domain of developmental psychopathology. *Child Development, 55,* 17–29.

Sroufe, L. A., & Waters, E. (1976). The ontogenesis of smiling and laughter: A perspective on the organization of development in infancy. *Psychological Review, 83,* 173–189.

Stanger, C., McConaughy, S. H., & Achenbach, T. M. (1992). Three-year course of behavioral/emotional problems in a national sample of 4-to 16-year-olds: II. Predictors of syndromes. *Journal of the American Academy of Child and Adolescent Psychiatry, 31,* 941–950.

Sterling, S., Cowen, E. L., Weissberg, R. P., Lotyczewski, B. S., & Boike, M. (1985). Recent stressful life events and young children's school adjustment. *American Journal of Community Psychology, 13,* 87–98.

Sternberg, R. J. (1985). *Beyond IQ: A triarchic theory of human intelligence.* Cambridge: Cambridge University Press.

Sternberg, R. J. (1988). *The triarchic mind: A new theory of human intelligence.* New York: Viking.

Sternberg, R. J., & Berg, C. A. (1986). Quantitative integration: Definitions of intelligence. A comparison of the 1921 and 1986 symposia. In R. J. Sternberg & D. K. Detterman (Eds.), *What is intelligence: Contemporary viewpoints on its nature and definition* (pp. 155–162). Norwood, NJ: Ablex.

Sternberg, R. J., & Detterman, D. K. (Eds.) (1986). *What is intelligence? Contemporary viewpoints on its nature and definition.* Norwood NJ: Ablex.

Strauss, C. C., Forehand, R., Smith, K., & Frame, C. L. (1986). The association between social withdrawal and internalizing problems of children. *Journal of Abnormal Child Psychology, 14,* 525–535.

Strauss, C. C., Frame, C. L., & Forehand, R. L. (1987). Psychosocial impairment associated with anxiety in children. *Journal of Clinical Child Psychology, 16,* 235–239.

Strauss, C. C., Lahey, B. B., Frick, P., Frame, C. L., & Hynd, G. W. (1988). Peer social status of children with anxiety disorders. *Journal of Consulting and Clinical Psychology, 56,* 137–141.

Strauss, C. C., Lease, C. A., Kazdin, A. E., Dulcan, M. K., & Last, C. G. (1989). Multimethod assessment of the social competence of children with anxiety disorders. *Journal of Clinical Child Psychology, 18,* 184–189.

Sullivan, H. S. (1953). *The interpersonal theory of psychiatry.* New York: Norton.

Velez, C. M., Johnson, J., & Cohen, P. (1989). A longitudinal analysis of selected risk factors for childhood psychopathology. *Journal of the American Academy of Child and Adolescent Psychiatry, 28,* 861–864.

Verhulst, F. C., & van der Ende, J. (1992). Six-year developmental course of internalizing and externalizing problem behaviors. *Journal of the American Academy of Child and Adolescent Psychiatry, 31,* 924–931.

Vuchinich, S., Bank, L., & Patterson, G. R. (1992). Parenting, peers, and the stability of antisocial behavior in preadolescent boys. *Developmental Psychology, 28,* 510–521.

Wagner, R. K., & Sternberg, R. J. (1986). Tacet knowledge and intelligence in the everyday world. In R. J. Sternberg & R. K. Wagner (Eds.), *Practical intelligence: Nature and origins of competence in the everyday world* (pp. 51–83). New York: Cambridge University Press.

Wakefield, J. C. (1992a). The concept of mental disorder: On the boundary between biological facts and social values. *American Psychologist, 47,* 373–388.

Wakefield, J. C. (1992b). Disorder as harmful dysfunction: A conceptual critique of DSM-III-R's definition of mental disorder. *Psychological Review, 99,* 233–247.

Waters, E., & Sroufe, L. A. (1983). Social competence as a developmental construct. *Developmental Review, 3,* 79–97.

Watt, N. F., Anthony, E. J., Wynne, L. C., & Rolf, J. E. (1984). Children at risk for schizophrenia: A longitudinal perspective. New York: Cambridge University Press.

Wechsler, D. (1950). Cognitive, conative, and non-intellective intelligence. *American Psychologist, 5,* 78–83.

Wechsler, D. (1958). *The measurement and appraisal of adult intelligence.* Baltimore: Williams & Wilkins.

Werner, E. E., Bierman, J. M., & French, F. E. (1971). *The children of Kauai.* Honolulu: University of Hawaii Press.

Werner, E. E., & Smith, R. S. (1977). *Kauai's children come of age.* Honolulu: University of Hawaii Press.

Werner, E. E., & Smith, R. S. (1982). *Vulnerable but invincible: A study of resilient children.* New York: McGraw-Hill.

Werner, E. E., & Smith, R. S. (1992). *Overcoming the odds: High risk children from birth to adulthood.* Ithaca: Cornell University Press.

Werner, H. (1929). *Comparative psychology of mental development* (3rd ed.). New York: International Universities Press.

Werner, H. (1948). *Comparative psychology of mental development* (rev. ed.). Chicago: Follett.

Werner, H. (1957). The concept of development from a comparative and organismic point of view. In D. B. Harris (Ed.), *The concept of development* (pp. 125–148). Minneapolis: University of Minnesota Press.

White, R. W. (1959). Motivation reconsidered: The concept of competence. *Psychological Review, 66,* 297–333.

Wright, M. O'D., & Masten, A. S. (in press). Vulnerability and resilience in young children. In S. I. Greenspan, J.D. Osofsky, & K. Pruett (Eds.), *Handbook of child and adolescent psychiatry: Infancy and early childhood: Theory and issues.* New York: Basic Books.

Wyman, P. A., Cowen, E. L., Work, W. C., & Parker, G. R. (1991). Developmental and family milieu correlates of resilience in urban children who have experienced major life stress. *American Journal of Community Psychology, 19,* 405–426.

Wyman, P. A., Cowen, E. L., Work, W. C., Raoof, A., Gribble, P. A., Parker, G. R., & Wannon, J. (1992). Interviews with children who experienced major life stress: Family and child attributes that predict resilient outcomes. *Journal of the American Academy of Child and Adolescent Psychiatry, 31,* 904–910.

Yule, W. (1994). Posttraumatic stress disorders. In M. Rutter, L. Herzov, & E. Taylor (Eds.), *Child and adolescent psychiatry: Modern approaches* (3rd ed) (pp. 392–406). Oxford: Blackwell.

Zigler, E., & Glick, M. (1986). *A developmental approach to adult psychopathology.* New York: Wiley.

Zigler, E., & Phillips, L. (1961). Social competence and outcome in psychiatric disorder. *Journal of Abnormal and Social Psychology, 61,* 231–238.

Zigler, E., & Trickett, P. (1978). IQ, social competence and evaluation of early childhood intervention programs. *American Psychologist, 33,* 789–798.

CHAPTER 21

Adversity, Vulnerability, and Resilience:
Cultural and Developmental Perspectives

BERTRAM J. COHLER, FRANCES M. STOTT, and JUDITH S. MUSICK

The field of developmental psychopathology has systematically explored the balance between continuity and discontinuity in adjustment and personality over time (Achenbach, 1990; Caspi, Elder, & Herbener, 1990; Kazdin, 1989; Lewis, 1990a, 1990b; Overton & Horowitz, 1991; Rutter, 1990; Rutter & Garmezy, 1983; Sroufe, 1989, 1990; Sroufe & Rutter, 1984). Relying on concepts from epidemiology, such as risk and incidence, much of this study has been concerned with factors associated with the emergence of psychological distress, for example among offspring who have earlier been subject to prenatal and perinatal complications (Werner, Bierman, & French, 1971; Werner & Smith, 1977, 1982), or to significant, lengthy, parental physical separation or emotional withdrawal across the first years of life (Felner, 1984; Garmezy, 1986; LeVine & Miller, 1990; Robertson, 1958/1970; Rutter, 1972/1981, 1979a; Winnicott, 1960). There has been less study of otherwise vulnerable persons who retain psychological resilience even as confronted by such adversity as poverty or large-scale social disorganization or cultural change (Luthar & Ziegler, 1991a), particularly interacting with temperamentally based vulnerability due to factors, such as increased genetic loading for major psychiatric disorder (Tseng & Hsu, 1980).

Much of the study of vulnerability and resilience has failed to consider the place of culture or ethnicity as a factor associated with origin and course of personal distress across the life span. Culturally constructed meanings of psychological illness and healing provide the context in which distress and intervention must be understood for both patient and family caregivers. Factors, such as poverty and social disorganization, together with constitutional proclivity to psychopathology, contribute to episodes of psychiatric illness and lead to enhanced likelihood for the emergence of personal distress. Growing up in disorganized environments, such as Belfast, Lebanon, or the South Bronx, may tax personal coping resources and lead to enhanced personal distress, which is then compounded by the lack of intervention services (Garmezy & Masten, 1986). However, it is difficult to understand individual differences in sensitivity to such environmentally determined adversity (Cottrell, 1976; French, Rodgers, & Cobb, 1974).

Conflict between family values and those of the community may further interfere in the possibility of obtaining assistance. However, some otherwise vulnerable persons may remain relatively resilient, even as confronted by personal and collective misfortune. Bettelheim (1943/1986, 1960) observed that those inmates of the concentration camps who were most resilient when confronted with atrocity and imminent death had strong ethical and moral commitments and a clear cultural tradition that they could rely on at time of crisis. More resilient inmates (often from marginal groups within the community) had strong religious beliefs or political ideology that permitted them to maintain morale, whereas persons lacking in such strong convictions often gave up hope. These observations pose interesting questions regarding the significance of culture in enhancing resilience for individuals who are confronted with misfortune and in helping them maintain adjustment even when they are confronted with major life changes.

Recognition of psychological development in context is essential for the study of psychological resilience to major psychopathology across the life course. Both expected and eruptive life changes, as well as shared knowledge of self and others, can provide constraints and opportunities for understanding particular life experiences. Research, such as that of Elder and his colleagues, continues to focus on sociohistorical change and cross-sequential developmental study (Elder & Caspi, 1990; Elder & Rockwell, 1979), but there has been very little investigation of psychological development and mental health across the life span that takes into account both sociohistorical events and culture. Adjustment takes place within a culture that comprises shared understandings of meanings, including those about the passage of time and expectable changes with time, continuity of self, and relations with others within both family and society (Ewing, 1991; Geertz, 1966/1973b; Obeyesekere, 1990; Ogbu, 1981).

Just as life-course perspectives have enlarged our understanding of both normative developmental processes and also origins and course of psychopathology, cultural perspectives further qualify and enlarge our understanding of variation in personal adjustment over time. Variation includes both enhanced vulnerability that might interfere with continued capacity to cope with adversity, leading to episodes of disturbance, and also experienced modes of resilience that mitigate otherwise noxious impact of adverse life changes on continued adjustment (French, Rodgers, & Cobb, 1974). This chapter considers the interplay of psychological development, culture, and adversity in understanding enhanced resilience to psychopathology among persons varying in risk and vulnerability.

RISK, VULNERABILITY, AND RESILIENCE

Psychological resilience represents all those means used to maintain adjustment by reducing the otherwise noxious effects imposed by unfortunate life experiences. Resilience reflects the present outcome of the available repertoire of protective factors, including techniques for coping with misfortune, which are founded on the interplay of temperamental and environmental characteristics, and which become significant for adjustment as culturally constructed modes of dealing with misfortune.[1] Studies of children within our own culture who are psychologically vulnerable but remain resilient to the impact of adversity suggest a number of personal attributes associated with this enhanced resilience: enhanced capacity to interest others, high personal energy level, and enhanced cognitive and social intelligence. Additional contributions to resilience may be attributed to family attributes such as constancy of care during early childhood, absence of undue parental strife, and freedom from unexpected misfortune (e.g., parental physical or psychiatric illness and hospitalization, or early off-time parental death) together with positive community attributes (e.g., stability of school) and the absence of poverty-related factors (e.g., gangs or enhanced possibility of substance abuse) (Garmezy, 1985a, 1985b; Kagan, 1983; Luthar, 1993; Luthar & Ziegler, 1991b; Maughan, 1988).

Risk and Vulnerability

Study of the association of particular risk factors and later adjustment has provided important information about determinants of adjustment. At the same time, particular emphasis on adverse outcome following exposure to risk factors may disregard the significance of coping mechanisms that enhance resilience to adversity. In understanding determinants of continuity and change within lives over time, the study of resilience may be as significant as the study of the emergence of psychological symptoms. Luthar (1993)

---

[1] Rutter defines resilience in terms of the enhanced presence of "protective factors, . . . influences that modify, ameliorate, or alter a person's response to some environmental hazard that predisposes to a maladaptive outcome (1985, p. 600)." First, Rutter has observed that reliance on these protective factors should not be equated with a pleasant experience. Coping with the effects of stress may indeed be painful. Second, the protective factor may be more important in the future than in the present; a positive caregiving experience in childhood may be most important in adolescence or adulthood at time of adversity (Greenson, 1971). Third, culturally significant attributes such as gender may provide inherent protective factors beyond any personal effort; boys appear much more often than girls in child guidance clinics and have a greater number of learning disorders, whereas girls, particularly after adolescence, become physically ill more often and are more often likely to experience depressive sentiments. Finally, factors that are protective at one point across the course of life may not be protective at another point. For example, being a girl is protective factor during childhood, but much less a factor across the adult years.

notes the confusion surrounding the terms *risk, resilience, protective factors, ameliorative effects,* or *compensatory factors.* It is not clear whether focus should be on factors providing enhanced resistance to adversity, such as living in poverty or conflict, or on those factors that reduce the impact of adversity or provide enhanced coping at times of increased vulnerability. Further, issues of continuity and change must be more carefully considered than they have up to the present time. It is hardly surprising that such risk factors as early life spent in abject poverty might be associated with subsequent poverty and enhanced personal distress; it is much more interesting to study those persons who are able to remain resilient, even when confronted with adversity, and to study those attributes that are associated with enhanced ability to cope with misfortune (Brown, 1983; Farber & Egeland, 1987; Fisher, Kokes, Cole, Perkins, & Wynne, 1987; Jacobs, Fischhoff, & Davis, 1993; Jessor, 1993; Phillips & Zimmerman, 1990; Robins, 1978; Wrubel, Benner, & Lazarus, 1981).

The concept of risk is derived from epidemiological study, concerned with factors enhancing the probability of contracting particular illness. Applied to the study of mental health, the concept of risk highlights those innate and situational factors that might be expected to enhance the probability of developing particular forms of impairment in psychological functioning. Escalona (1974) has observed that the concept of risk assumes identification of particular attributes, including both temperament and context, that increase the probability of subsequent distress. For example, genetic studies suggest that the presence of major psychopathology within one parent increases the risk tenfold that an offspring will develop major psychopathology (Gottesman & Shields, 1982).

Both developmental trajectory and cultural context play a role in determining episodes of psychiatric illness. Following Scarr and McCartney's (1983) paradigm for understanding the relationship of innate and environmental characteristics, Werner and Smith (1992) suggest that both development and experience alter the impact of genetic predisposition. During infancy and early childhood, genetic effects may make the most direct contribution to mental health status, determining the infant's initial capacity to both elicit and respond to care, which may shape the subsequent mother-child tie (Bell, 1977; Harper, 1975; Hoffman & Manis, 1978; Lerner & Busch-Rossnagel, 1981; Lerner & Spanier, 1978). Subsequently, these genetic influences may be observed most directly in the child's robustness and capacity to interest others and evoke a positive environmental response across the childhood years. Cultural and situational factors such as immigration, followed by a life spent living in poverty, increase vulnerability to episodes of psychiatric illness (Tseng & Hsu, 1980). Again, the point at which these changes take place across the life span is significant for adjustment over time. Loss of a parent through death or other disruptions in the continuity of family life across the first decade of life may lead to greater long-term adverse impact on adjustment than parent loss experienced across adolescence and young adulthood (Altschul & Pollock, 1988; Tennant, Bebbington, & Hurry, 1982).

The adult's capacity to find a congenial milieu directly contributes to mental health outcome. For example, adults reared within families marked by discord and conflict but who are able to leave home for military service or the Peace Corps, may realize a more benign environment than that available to brothers and sisters who remain at home, enmeshed within continuing conflict. The pileup of adverse life changes in the context of enhanced vulnerability may contribute to an episode of psychiatric illness. Although no single event is capable of evoking an episode, the accumulation of these events may have that effect. As Rutter (1981/1983) and Werner and Smith (1992) have noted, study that fails to consider the impact of multiple intertwined risk factors will not provide accurate information about the risk factors that might be associated with actual episodes of psychopathology.

Baldwin, Baldwin, and Cole (1990) have suggested a distinction between proximal risk factors in the social environment, such as maternal psychopathology and disruption in child care, and more distal risk factors, including poverty, reduced access to medical care, and poor nutrition, that directly impinge on children and are mediated by the proximal factors. Masten, Best, and Garmezy (1990) have suggested that whereas enhanced distal risk places an additional burden on the family to compensate for it, this risk may also encourage the family to take a more active role in protecting the child against its impact. In the development of major psychopathology among the offspring of troubled parents, tragic life-changes, such as early off-time parental death or adverse life circumstances, such as community disorganization and conflict or poverty, all contribute to episodes of illness. It is the interaction of multiple risk factors, considered together with personal and collective misfortune that is particularly critical in the emergence of psychopathology. Increased genetic loading as a risk factor may not be significant except in the context of adverse life circumstances.

The impact of loss and disruption becomes intertwined with adverse impact resulting from day-to-day strains and tensions within the family and may further contribute to vulnerability (Tseng & Hsu, 1980; Wertlieb, Weigel, Springer, & Feldstein, 1987). Wertlieb and his colleagues report that the major impact of temperament on personal distress is among behaviorally disruptive (externalizing) children, rather than among those whose problems are expressed as troublesome thoughts and feelings (internalizing). Where temperament makes a difference, it may be confined largely to those children who are more difficult to manage in the classroom, in the community, and at home. Significantly, both follow-through studies (Watt, 1974; Watt, Stolorow, Lubensky, & McClelland, 1970) and follow-back studies of children first seen in child guidance clinics (Ricks & Berry, 1970) suggest that behaviorally disruptive children are most likely to show later major psychopathology like schizophrenia.

When personal resources are sufficient to sustain resilience, persons can maintain adequate adjustment, even though vulnerable to psychopathology, and can recover from adversity, often at higher levels of adjustment than prior to experiencing this adversity. However, we still do not understand the manner in which persons deploy personal resources to cope with misfortune. Individuals not only vary in resilience, but this variation also fluctuates across the course of life. Some persons remain resilient to the impact of cumulative adversity across the first half of life, only to succumb to episodes of psychiatric illness in later years (Gutmann, Griffin, & Grunes, 1982). There is little

understanding of the manner in which both culture and context contribute to resilience (Cottrell, 1976). A convoy of consociates already dealing with on-time losses like widowhood may provide examples based on their own experiences for the new widow struggling to manage this adversity and may provide support during periods of crisis (Antonucci, 1985; Antonucci & Akiymama, 1987; Bankoff, 1983; Kahn, 1979; Kahn & Antonucci, 1980; Plath, 1980). Some persons, however, find that use of others for support and assistance during crises may lead to additional demands on coping ability; seeking help from others may increase rather than reduce the negative impact of adversity (Cohler, 1983; Pruchno, Blow, & Smyer, 1984).

Personal misfortune may affect not only the person experiencing this difficulty but also a wide circle of family and friends. The impact of misfortune among relatives and friends is similar to the impact of throwing a stone into a pond. As news of the adversity spreads, there is an ever-widening circle of family and friends expected to offer assistance. The circles of impact radiate outward from the event, touching the lives of many friends and family members (Cohler, 1983; Cohler & Grunebaum, 1981; Pruchno et al., 1984). Occurrence of a particular adverse life change for one family member may impose additional burden on others, which may heighten their own vulnerability to stress and provide increased possibility for the emergence of psychiatric symptoms. Whereas there has been much emphasis on the impact of social support as a major factor buffering the impact of adversity (Barrera, 1988; Dean & Lin, 1977), there has been less attention to the impact of this support on those providing support during misfortune.

Family members are expected to assist each other in dealing with crises such as serious illness or death among kindred. However, this assistance may interrupt work and interfere with family responsibilities that are intertwined with relatives' own efforts to cope with this misfortune (Cohler, 1983; Pruchno, Blow, & Smyer, 1984). The impact on the family of loss and change is further magnified within those ethnic groups in our own society in which significant relationships with collateral kindred are particularly emphasized (Cohler & Grunebaum, 1981; Leichter & Mitchell, 1967; Spiegel, 1971). As one older Italian-American woman observed when asked about the nearly simultaneous deaths of several friends and family members, "Who has time to grieve; I've been too busy having to arrange wakes." Among already more vulnerable persons, cumulative experience of misfortune within the family may contribute to the event that precipitates an episode of psychiatric illness.

Hanson, Gottesman, and Heston (1976, 1990) have observed that there is no reason to believe that the entire continuum of risk for psychopathology will have been realized within the first years of life. Further, although some temperamentally based attributes may remain constant (Kagan & Moss, 1963), studying discontinuity in personality and adjustment may be both more interesting and significant than accounting for continuity in personality and mental health across the life course. Risk for serious psychopathology may continue throughout the life span; vulnerability may be particularly significant at particular points, reflecting the consequence of both life experiences and temperament interacting with type of disorder (Clausen, 1985; Cohler & Ferrono,

1987; Gutmann, Griffin, & Grunes, 1982; Hanson, Gottesman, & Meehl, 1977; Heston & Denny, 1968). Although adjustment may be successful across the first half of life, eruptive life changes across middle or later life may have particularly adverse impact among psychologically vulnerable persons.

Whereas Lewis (1990a) has emphasized the contribution of developmental psychopathology as a field for the study of abnormal or maladaptive behaviors, Cicchetti (1984) has emphasized the contribution of developmental studies to personality and adjustment, noting the importance of normative developmental study, together with study of the emergence of psychopathology, as interrelated approaches. The study of the deviant instance informs normative approaches, and normative developmental study fosters an understanding of expectable changes over time as the context for studying vulnerabilities that lead to episodes of psychiatric illness. Kazdin (1989) and other investigators within developmental psychopathology emphasize the first decade of life as critical for the study of psychopathology, whereas Caspi et al. (1990) and Elder and Hareven (1993) show the importance of a life-course context for the study of mental health.

Increased psychological impairment over time may be viewed as the consequence of a complex interplay of temperamental factors together with past and present life circumstances. These circumstances include all those adverse, accidental factors, (e.g., parental illness or death early in the child's life) that challenge present adjustment, as well as personal misfortunes beyond the years of early childhood that pose particular problems for present mental health. Pioneering study of the interplay between personal style and response of others, such as among children who were initially shy or explosive (Caspi, Elder, & Bem, 1987, 1988; Caspi et al., 1990; Kagan & Moss, 1963), shows the significance of childhood attributes as the foundation for particular responses from others in fostering particular modes of adult adjustment.[2]

Longitudinal study, which focuses additionally on life course and mental health in the cross-sequential study of multiple cohorts, allows a more precise estimate of the impact of sociohistorical change on expectable developmental processes. For example, the transition from adolescence to youth or young adulthood is often viewed as a critical point in the emergence of major psychopathology, such as schizophrenia (Ebata, Petersen, & Conger, 1990; Walker, Davis, & Gottlieb, 1991; Weiner, 1970). Across successive cohorts, particular sociohistorical life changes may pose quite different consequences than for their predecessors. For example, the intertwined issues of rapid social change and the danger posed by conscription into the Vietnam conflict posed

quite different challenges for the generation reaching young adulthood in the late 1960s than the problems of redundancy and underemployment presently facing young adults. Further, such demographic factors as cohort size may shape patterns of transition from adolescence to young adulthood. As Easterlin (1987) and Guttentag and Secord (1983) have observed, large birth cohorts induce greater lifelong competition than smaller birth cohorts for realization of expectable transitions, such as college entrance, entry into the workforce, mate selection and marriage, and even retirement (Galatzer-Levy & Cohler, 1993). To date, there has been little integration of this perspective with the study of developmental psychopathology (Elder & Rockwell, 1979; Overton & Horowitz, 1991).

Risk and Resilience

Just as some heritable characteristics and life circumstances may increase risk for an episode of psychiatric illness, other factors may provide enhanced protection against the impact of these risk factors. Masten, Best, and Garmezy (1990) define resilience as:

> the process of, capacity for, or outcome of successful adaptation despite challenging or threatening circumstances. Psychological resilience is concerned with behavioral adaptation, usually defined in terms of internal states of well-being or effective functioning in the environment or both.
>
> "Protective factors" *moderate* the effects of individual vulnerabilities or environmental hazards so that the adaptational trajectory is more positive than would be the case if the protective factor were not operational. Protective factors do not necessarily yield resilience: It is conceivable that protective processes, such as efforts by a parent to foster adaptation, may not be adequate if the vulnerability of the individual or the severity of the adversity is too great to overcome. (p. 426)

Werner and Smith (1992) note that resilience and protective factors serve as positive counterparts to risk and vulnerability. Protective factors such as concern for a child's welfare by teachers and other relatives may counteract the impact of both genetic loading and adverse life circumstances that might otherwise increase risk. From this perspective, resilience and protective factors are the counterpart of increased risk and vulnerability for psychiatric disorder. Risk is transformed into psychopathology through the pileup of day-to-day tensions and adverse life-changes and in the absence of protective factors. Significant misfortune, besides having a direct adverse effect on the adjustment of close family members and friends, has indirect effects over time: The experience of misfortune has both a direct effect due to loss and change, and also an indirect effect through increasing existing role strain or day-to-day hassles within the family (Folkman & Lazarus, 1980; Lazarus & Folkman, 1984; Zautra, Guarnaccia, & Dohrenwend, 1986; Zautra, Guarnaccia, Reich, & Dohrenwend, 1988).

Reviewing his own pioneering study of childhood resilience, Rutter (1990) has stressed the extent to which resilience reflects individual differences in response to variation in risk. He observed that resilience reflects a process leading to enhanced protective (or coping) mechanisms transforming potential sources of threat to personal adjustment into opportunities for maintaining personal adjustment:

---

[2] Although long-standing problems in the relationship between parents and children may lead to childhood adjustment problems that enhance subsequent vulnerability, there is little evidence regarding the direct impact of child rearing on emergence of psychiatric illness. There has also been little evidence regarding the value of early intervention programs among the offspring of parents with major psychiatric illness as a means of forestalling the later onset of psychiatric illness. Efforts to provide cognitive enrichment and social facilitation that may be missing in the home environment undoubtedly enhance the quality of children's lives, but these programs provide little assurance regarding the subsequent course of adjustment or psychological resilience later in life; nor do they ameliorate the impact of otherwise devastating psychiatric illness.

The crucial difference between vulnerability/protection processes and risk mechanisms is that the latter lead directly to disorder (either strongly or weakly), whereas the former operate indirectly, with their effects apparent only by virtue of their interactions with the risk variable. The implication is that psychological processes involved in risk and in protection are likely to differ in important respects. The key feature lies in the process . . . the term "protection" is to be preferred over "lack of vulnerability" when the process involves a change in life-trajectory from risk to adaptation. (p. 189)

For example, the ability of persons whose families experienced economic privation during the Great Depression to use this actuality as an incentive for enhanced personal success, rather than as an excuse for personal failure (Elder & Rockwell, 1979) reflects this capacity for turning disadvantage into advantage, and for turning adversity into enhanced personal adjustment.

Anthony (1987b) concurs with Murphy (1962) in his observation that the resilient child is responsive to others, shows good self-esteem, has a good sense of humor, takes moderate risks, is realistic but hopeful about self and others, is both self-reliant and sociable, responds flexibly to new challenges, and maintains a sense of personal coherence even when confronted by challenges. To a large extent, this view is characteristic of expectations for both children and adults in our culture. However, resilience is also relative: Useful coping strategies at one point in life might enhance vulnerability at another; early off-time death of a parent evokes far greater personal turmoil than parental death across the middle-adult years. Temperament, life experiences, and larger sociohistorical factors all help determine the extent of vulnerability.

There is always a close relationship between the kind of risk for personal distress that the child encounters, the context in which this risk arises, and the capacity to remain resilient when confronting it. Rutter stresses the significance for adjustment of concurrent risk factors, such as the presence of other family members able to assist children whose parents have suffered psychiatric or other illness, or who have lost a parent through death or desertion. The concept of risk must be studied in the context of the culturally constructed protective circumstances mitigating that risk, the significance of particular adversity for the child or adult as determined by particular life circumstances, and the complex interplay of risk and experienced personal resources available in managing adversity. The child who can turn to another adult for comfort on experiencing parental illness or death is better able to manage other associated adversity such as poverty or family relocation; the extent of risk found in adversity is mitigated by the child's capacity to find solace.

The concept of risk is closely intertwined with the concept of vulnerability. Rutter (1990) views vulnerability as long-standing biosocial processes predisposing differential response to circumstances presenting challenge to adjustment.[3] Failure to recognize

and deal with this challenge poses increased risk for personal distress. Life changes represent transition points with opportunities either for enhanced protection as the outcome of coping with misfortune, or for the emergence of heightened personal distress, reflected in particular, recognizable, psychological symptoms. Enhanced resilience is reflected in the increased capacity for using personal attributes (e.g., humor) and both emotion- and problem-centered coping (Lazarus & Folkman, 1984) in responding to the threat to adjustment posed by adverse life changes.

Vulnerability reflects the failure of resilience, increasing the probability of psychological distress. Consistent with the formulations of Murphy and Moriarty (1976), Rutter (1985, 1987, 1990), Schuldberg (1993), and Zubin and Spring (1977), resilience and vulnerability may be understood as relative rather than absolute processes. Each of us is subject to particular forms of adversity that reflect extreme situations beyond our capacity to remain resilient (Bettelheim, 1943/1986, 1960). The significant factor for adjustment is not vulnerability, which at least to some extent is inevitable. Rather, it is the capacity to protect the self from the impact of this vulnerability Murphy (1982). Murphy and Moriarty (1976), Moriarty (1987), Pasamanick and Knobloch (1960), and Sameroff and Chandler (1975) all support a view of vulnerability as a continuum in which heritable characteristics, such as those associated with prenatal and postnatal development, together with subsequent life experiences, are intertwined in determining the degree of resilience that persons can muster at any one point in time, in response to challenges to adjustment (Sameroff, 1989).

Factors such as gender may provide protection at one point in life but not at another: Rutter (1970, 1990) has summarized the literature on the role of gender, noting that young boys are more likely than young girls both to experience increased distress in response to family misfortune and to witness parental quarrels, intensifying misfortune in their lives. However, Dornbusch (1989), Ebata et al. (1990), Kessler and McLeod (1984), Petersen (1988), and Weissman and Klerman (1977) are among the many observers of gender, psychopathology, and the life course who have noted the reversal of gender and vulnerability beginning in adolescence: Boys are particularly at risk earlier in life as a result of delayed neurodevelopment, but over time, this initial developmental imbalance favoring girls recedes before the reality of increased strain and burden confronting women in contemporary society. Gender vulnerability thus contributes to the marked reduction in morale and increased physical illness reported by adult women from young adulthood through midlife.

Werner (1990) has suggested that, among boys, innate individual differences may be the most important determinant of resilience whereas among girls, the impact of early life within the family may be the primary factor determining resilience. The sources of resilience across the first decade of life may be somewhat different for boys and for girls, and subsequent study must consider issues of risk, vulnerability, and resilience separately for boys and girls of different ages and over time (Luthar,

---

[3] Consistent with Bibring's (1959) earlier formulation of risk, Rutter views vulnerability simply in terms of challenge to present adjustment demanded by particular events. Although the literature on life changes has struggled with questions concerning the extent of anticipation or preparedness for an event and the extent of adversity reflected by an event (Dohrenwend & Dohrenwend, 1974; Holmes & Rahe, 1967), much of the evidence regarding the impact of life changes suggests that

it is not change as such that poses a challenge but, more specifically, those life changes that are early off-time in terms of sociocultural definition, and that spell serious adversity and particular misfortune (Pearlin, 1975, 1983).

Doernbeger, & Ziglcr, 1993). However, F. Grossman ct al. (1992) report that adolescent girls reporting a large number of psychosocial risk factors such as parental divorce appeared more resilient in responding to this adversity than adolescent boys; in this study, girls seemed to be better able than boys to reach out and seek help from both family and other adults.

CULTURE AND THE MANAGEMENT OF MISFORTUNE

A generation of research has shown the adverse impact of factors such as poverty and underclass life on adjustment and advent of psychiatric illness (Kessler & Cleary, 1980; Kessler, Price, & Wortman, 1985; Mishler & Scotch, 1963; Myers & Bean, 1968). However, there has been little study of vulnerability to personal distress or resilience to episodes of major mental illness from the perspective of culture or particular shared symbolic constructions of reality (Geertz, 1966/1973b, 1973). Proximal and distal risk factors (Baldwin, Baldwin, & Cole, 1990), such as family conflict, social disorganization, and social change, have particular impact because of the way these events are understood by those living within a culture (Dressler, 1991; Garmezy, 1983; Mishler & Scotch, 1963; Ogbu, 1981; Rutter, 1979b). Within our own culture, the very fact of parental psychiatric illness is believed to increase the risk for an episode of psychopathology among offspring. How we portray the origins, course, and treatment of syndromes like schizophrenia has a direct bearing on how persons with varying degrees of vulnerability or risk for psychopathology manage resilience when confronted by risk.

As Elder (1974, 1979) has shown in his study of response among offspring within families suffering catastrophic decline in income during the Great Depression, family members fashioned meanings of this experience that directly influenced the subsequent experience of self and others. These meanings included enhanced concern with economic security and determination to overcome the impact of this earlier loss. Systematic study has shown both the value of cross-cultural comparative study for understanding the expectable course of development over the life course and has also provided important information regarding the place of cultural variation in the symbolic construction of self and others. From the pioneering studies of Whiting (1941) and J. W. M. Whiting and Child (1953) to the reports of LeVine and his colleagues (LeVine, Dixon, LeVine, Richman, Leiderman, Keefer, & Brazelton, 1994) and Lutz (1988), cross-cultural study has shown both the variation in child care across cultures and also the complex interplay of natural ecology, the shared historical and cultural symbol system, and the social structure in establishing child-rearing practices. Climate, mode of subsistence, and historical tradition are among the factors that determine expectable modes of relationship between parent and child (Whiting & Whiting, 1978). The next step in this study is to explore the relationship between cultural study and response to threats to adjustment experienced across the course of life.

Cultural study provides a natural laboratory in which to observe the impact of child care on personality development (Monroe & Monroe, 1980; Price-Williams, 1985). Pioneering

work in psychological anthropology rcportcd by Margaret Mead on the basis of her studies in Micronesia showed that adolescence in other cultures does not present the problems so often associated with this indeterminate phase of life within our own culture. Systematic cross-cultural study of child care and personality, from that reported by the Whitings (B. Whiting, 1963) to the most recent work of R. LeVine and his colleagues (1994) in East Africa or Weisz (1989) in Thailand, S. LeVine (1979), and Lutz (1988), have explored how culturally constructed understandings of self, others, and the natural world, or "local knowledge," (Geertz, 1983b, 1974/1984) shape parents' child-rearing practices as well as the accepted view of the very process of development from birth to adulthood.

Patterns of child care reflect the particular understanding of self, others, and the relationship of person and environment that characterizes particular cultures. These child-rearing patterns, together with other aspects of those symbol systems collectively portrayed as culture, provide important information regarding the manner in which meaning systems determine particular developmental outcomes, the meanings attached to expression of thought and feeling, and the very manner in which past and present are understood across cultures. Particular forms of local knowledge govern the course of life from infancy to oldest age and provide important information regarding the impact of these cultural conceptions of self, others, and experience over the course of time and age.

Culture: Meaning and Adjustment

The concept of culture, understood as a part of a larger concern with the interplay of culture and psychological process, remains an enduring issue for study within the social sciences (Geertz, 1966b; Kluckhohn & Kroeber, 1963; Parsons, 1951). Study of person and culture was earlier portrayed as the outcome of inevitable conflict between personal intentions and shared expectations regarding a common orientation toward life as a consequence of participating in shared institutions (Kluckhohn, Murray, & Schneider, 1961). This earlier view of person and culture was based on a Western concept of the relationship of person and social life.[4] Across the past two decades, however, there has been a dramatic reconsideration of the role of person within culture. As a result of this reconsideration of person and culture, attention has shifted from concern with the fit between person and culture, or with the study of presumed universals in culture, to a much more detailed, descriptive study of the manner in which cultures construct categories of meaning regarding experience

---

[4] Finding it difficult to convey the concepts of otherness reflected in non-Western contexts, LeVine (1973) had recommended that persons be brought from their home cultures to study Western social science in American universities, so that these dual participants in non-Western and Western cultures could return to their home culture and "explain" the dynamics of that culture in terms understandable to American social scientists. An alternative approach is for Western social scientists to steep themselves in the culture they wish to study and then attempt to portray that culture in terms understandable to members of our own culture.

and the factors that account for change in these meanings over time (Levi-Strauss, 1962/1966).

As D'Andrade (1984) has observed, within the study of culture, there has been a shift away from the study of habit and behavior to concern with the ways in which persons think, represented by knowledge within symbolic systems.[5] Much of contemporary study of culture emphasizes abstraction from interaction, ordered in ways viewed as meaningful among those others sharing particular conceptions of self, others, and natural surround, including conceptions of time and space (Kluckhohn & Kroeber, 1963). Perhaps the most succinct definition has been provided by Geertz (1966/1973c) who observes:

> [culture consists of] a historically transmitted pattern of meanings embodied in symbols, a system of inherited conceptions expressed in symbolic forms by means of which persons communicate, perpetuate, and develop their knowledge about and attitudes toward life. (p. 89)

Shared symbol systems define the very context of thought itself, and are the particular focus of cultural study. As Geertz (1966/1973a) has observed, the goal of this cultural study is increased understanding of how characteristic members of a culture make sense of experience at any one point in time.

Although culture has most often been viewed in terms of actual artifacts or particular customs, Geertz's definition is more encompassing and includes meanings attributed to all aspects of the external social world. The meanings we attribute to all aspects of our surround, including their representation in particular rituals and myths, are learned through communication with others from earliest infancy through oldest age. Study of symbol systems is actually the study of meaning systems contained within those symbol systems; cultural study focuses on

the dialogue between personal experience and meanings continually reinterpreted and refashioned by each of us in an effort to maintain a coherent, ordered, and integrated understanding of self and experience (Vygotsky, 1930-1935/1978; Wertsch, 1985, 1991). These meanings are formed through language, become increasingly complex and intertwined over time, and contain an evocative quality sometimes termed affect. Meanings make order out of experiences that are at one and the same time both personal and collective, and that guide and direct adjustment to the external world (D'Andrade, 1984).

For example, contemporary study of the life course focuses less on parents' actions in caring for their children than with the study of shared understandings regarding what constitutes childhood and parenthood, the language used to portray these categories of personhood, and the manner in which these meanings determine child-care practices among members of the culture. Persons within particular cultures share fundamental concepts such as the definition of the self: Our own culture emphasizes a concept of self founded on individuality and self-reliance, whereas Japanese culture emphasizes group solidarity and interdependence as the foundation of the experience of self (Doi, 1986; Heller, Sosna, & Wellbery, 1986; MacFarlane, 1987).

Parallel with the shift from action to meaning, there has been a shift of concern from study of such particular institutional constellations as law, family, or education to study of the means by which persons construct understandings of these and other aspects of social life, and to the history of changes in the portrayal of these symbolic systems, represented by oral history and available documents. The focus of interest in these historical records is less with representation of institutional change than with the symbolic representation of these practices over time through either written or spoken discourse. The turn to history (Bloch, 1977; Sahlins, 1981; Vansina, 1970), just as with the general trend toward the methods of traditional humanistic study, reflects Geertz's (1980/1983a) observation regarding the blurring of genres in contemporary cultural study. Renewed concern with the construction of the past as an active, imaginative process, is particularly relevant in understanding how cultures continually reinterpret the past (Mink, 1987; Stanford, 1986; White, 1978). Concern with cultural change has increased as anthropology has become increasingly aware of the impact of the industrialized West on traditional societies, and as historical study itself has become increasingly concerned with oral history and shared narratives of the past (Stone, 1979; Vansina, 1985). History also reflects particular constructions of self and experience located not only in space, but also in time: The presently recounted story of a culture reflects salient symbol systems and serves as a guide to action.

This marked shift of emphasis within the study of culture and person has been inspired by important changes in the philosophy of science (Toulmin, 1990), shift within developmental psychology toward a social cognitive perspective on development (Wertsch, 1991), and by increasing concern with issues of narrative and language as first formulated within the humanities (Bakhtin, 1975/1981; Bohman, Hiley, & Shusterman, 1991; Fernandez, 1986; Levi-Strauss, 1962/1966; Lutz, 1985, 1988; Marcus & Fischer, 1986; Schieffelin & Ochs, 1986; Taylor, 1971/1979,

---

[5] D'Andrade (1984, 1990) attributes this shift in the study of culture from action to thought to the computer revolution as reflected in the work of Bruner (1990) but Bruner maintains that he never advocated a computational model in the study of cognitive processes, and that from the outset, the focus of his interest was on the construction of meanings rather than processing information. Citing the work of the Soviet psychologists (e.g., Vygotsky, 1930–1935/1978; 1934/1986), Bruner maintains that meaning systems are entrenched in culture, and that these systems provide the basis for meanings constructed by particular members of the community through the use of language. Bruner observes that psychology is so immersed in culture that it must always be thought of as "folk psychology," organized around the shared meaning systems of particular cultures. The mentation of particular persons within a culture reflects shared knowledge; implicitly relying on Levi-Strauss's (1962/1966) formulation, members of a culture construct narratives of particular experience based on the available symbol systems within a particular culture. Life experience provides the foundation for these particular narratives of experience. D'Andrade's emphasis on the information-processing aspect of culture emphasizes but one of the important functions of culture. Bruner's critique of meanings fashioned solely on a computational model highlights the problems implicit in approaches to the study of culture that do not fully integrate affect, thought, and the continual refashioning of experience within a transactional perspective in which experience and culture meet and mutually influence each other.

1991). This study has been informed by ethnopsychology, or concern with culturally constructed categories for understanding the concept of person and psychological process, as well as by appreciation for the manner in which persons symbolically fashion history, nature, and experience into an organized worldview or explanation of self, other, and experience (Comaroff & Comaroff, 1992; Hill, 1988; Reeve, 1988; Levi-Strauss, 1963; Ohnuki-Tierney, 1990). This new symbolic anthropology focuses less on the fit of personal adjustment and culture than with the very meaning which a culture ascribes to deviance and distress, and the manner in which culture constructs explanations of the origins, course, and intervention in psychological distress.

Cultural Construction of the Concept of Person

Reflecting the strong influence of Soviet psychology and criticism, particularly the work of Bakhtin (1975/1981), Vygotsky (1930–1935/1978, 1934/1986), and the extension of constructive developmentalism (Laboratory of Comparative Human Cognition, 1983; Wertsch, 1985, 1991), together with a shift away from the structuralism of Piaget's epigenetic formulation, the focus within both developmental psychology and anthropology has shifted toward the means by which attributes of a culturally defined personhood are elaborated across the course of life. For example, Lutz's (1988) study of the portrayal of emotions among the Ifaluk shows that, just as members of a culture share a common language, they share a common set of understandings regarding words used to talk about persons. As Lutz's (1988) study shows, even the use of the personal pronoun is culturally defined; for example, within the corporate culture of the Ifaluk, the use of "I" represents a deviant and often unacceptable reference.

Speech provides the many implicit, shared referents for portraying self and others. Everyday conversation within culture reflects these shared referents; considered together, aspects of everyday speech contain a culturally defined conception of self, others, relationships, and feeling states. Within particular cultures persons maintain distinctive understandings about fundamental attributes—personhood, the relationship among persons, and basic aspects of human development, such as the conception of the life-cycle itself, time, age, and explanations of the origins, course, treatment, and outcome of illness. Sometimes referred to as ethnopsychology (Briggs, 1970; Geertz, 1973; Lutz, 1988; White & Kirkpatrick, 1985), even this term fails to portray the variation across cultures that is possible in understanding the human condition.

Particular lives reflect variation in life experience within shared meaning systems. The life history, or narrative of lived experience (Schutz & Luckmann, 1973–1989), although founded in shared symbolic systems, reflects the unique ordering of experiences that the individual constructs on the basis of these shared meanings. The infinite variety of experiences leads the richness of personal expression within this larger nexus of meaning. Persons sharing the same culture are better able to understand each other than persons from different cultures, including shared understanding of adversity and resilience across the course of life (Modell & Siegler, 1993). From the perspective of contemporary cultural theory, the task of interpretation involves explicating the meanings that persons implicitly assign to their lives, or understanding the foundations of everyday lived experience.

Uniquely within the West, offspring characteristics are assumed as primarily the consequence of heritability of temperament and particular cognitive styles, together with forward socialization in which aspects of parental personality and adjustment are believed to be responsible for their children's personal development and later life adjustment. Even older adults presenting with psychopathology attribute aspects of their present dilemma to aspects of child rearing some six to seven decades earlier. It should come as little surprise that, contrasting parents across six cultures, Minturn and Lambert (1964) report that American parents ranked second in terms of both hostility and guilt regarding care of young children. The bourgeois West is relatively unique among the world's cultures in attributing parental factors and family interaction to later offspring characteristics such as achievement, psychological well-being, vulnerability to physical and psychiatric illness, or variation in resilience to misfortune (Fischer & Fischer, 1963; Kirkpatrick & White, 1985; Kleinman, 1988; Lutz, 1988; Marsella, 1980; Riesman, 1992; Sanua, 1980; Shweder, 1990). Mental health outcomes must be understood in terms of both individual variation in vulnerability to psychiatric disorder and culturally constructed understandings of physical and psychiatric illness, including episode, course, and treatment. This chapter reviews what is known about personal resilience to the impact of psychopathology as influenced by personal variation in vulnerability as well as by cultural values and social change.

From Culture to Ethnicity

Arriving at a university-affiliated state psychiatric hospital, a second-generation Italian American mother with a diagnosis of schizophrenia, and her 1½-year-old baby girl, presented for admission, together with her mother and with the baby's older sister. The response of the admitting psychiatrist was to assume a mother-daughter symbiosis contributing to the illness, which would be resolved across the course of hospitalization. This formulation, however, neglected to recognize the mother's position within Italian American and other southern Mediterranean families (Parsons, 1969). Parsons argues that the role of the mother in Southern Italian culture is to act as the mediator between a harsh and unsympathetic father and supplicant offspring. In Italy, this maternal role is well reflected in the Roman Catholic Church, where the priest and parishioners pray to the mother of Jesus (the Madonna) to mediate on their behalf. From the perspective of Southern Italian culture, the appearance of the patient's mother at the hospital was entirely consistent her role as mediator between her troubled daughter and the hospital bureaucracy.

The perspective from social psychiatry, reflected in the studies of Opler (1959a, 1959b, 1967), Opler and Singer (1956), and Singer and Opler (1959a, 1959b) on the Italian American family, and in Cohler and Grunebaum's (1981) study of the multigeneration Italian American family, challenges the assumption that the appearance of mother and daughter at the hospital together necessarily reflects symbiotic family psychopathology. Further, the emphasis on individuality and self-reliance within our own culture is in marked contrast with the emphasis placed on extended family ties across most of the world's cultures (Cohler, 1983; Cohler & Grunebaum, 1981; Cohler & Stott, 1987; Ewing, 1991; Pruchno et al., 1984; Rudolph & Rudolph, 1978). For example, over the past decade, there has been detailed study of the role of family process in determining posthospital adjustment among offspring with schizophrenia. The place of family process in the inception of the first episode, rehospitalization, and subsequent life course has been a subject of much controversy within psychiatry.

Earlier psychiatric study had suggested that communication processes within the family were responsible for socializing offspring into deviant modes for processing reality, which led to the development of psychiatric illness among offspring (Lidz, 1963; Lidz, Fleck, & Cornelison, 1965; Wynne, 1981; Wynne, Singer, Bartko, & Toohey, 1977). With the accumulated weight of biological study showing that origins of schizophrenic disturbance might be better traced to brain processes, psychological study shifted from study of the origin of schizophrenic disorders to concern with course of illness in the aftermath of the first hospitalization. In particular, although family conflict could not be directly implicated in the origins of the illness, the impact of family response to the burden of caring for an episodically troubled offspring, which is so often disruptive for both family and community, could impair offspring adjustment, leading to an early return to the hospital.

Initial study by Brown and his colleagues (Brown, 1959; Brown, Monck, Carstairs, & Wing, 1962) showed that former patients showed lower rates of rehospitalization when living in board-and-care facilities than when living at home. Within board-and-care facilities, there was a much lower level of criticism directed at residents than when these former patients lived at home. This difference in hostility and criticism directed at the former patient was presumed to differentiate the two living arrangements and explained the lower rate of rehospitalization within a setting whose impersonality would ordinarily be expected to contribute to increased rates of rehospitalization. Continuing study of psychiatric patients and their relatives has portrayed this family conflict as "expressed emotion," or hostility and criticism that parents direct particularly toward a formerly schizophrenic offspring due to the former patient's continuing antisocial conduct (Birely & Brown, 1970; Brown, Birley, & Wing, 1972; Brown & Birley, 1968; Brown, Bone, Dalison, & Wing, 1966; Falloon, 1985; Leff & Vaughn, 1985; Vaughn & Leff, 1976; Vaughn, Snyder, Jones, Freeman, & Falloon, 1984).[6]

At least within Anglo-American families, continuing offspring psychopathology poses significant problems for the care of either impaired offspring or infirm parents (Cohler, Groves, Borden, & Lazarus, 1989; Cohler, Pickett, & Cook, 1991; Cook & Cohler, 1986; Cook, Hoffschmidt, Cohler, & Pickett, 1992; Cook, Lefley, Pickett, & Cohler, in press). Recognizing the particular hostility expressed more generally by parents within Anglo-American culture regarding child rearing (Fischer & Fischer, 1963; Minturn & Lambert, 1964), evidence for this continuing hostility across the course of life, and in situations of adversity, should hardly be surprising. Because of the emphasis within our culture on individuality and self-reliance (McFarlane, 1987; Parker, 1972), families are not comfortable providing care for troubled members over long periods, and caregiving is particularly difficult when family members with illnesses such as schizophrenia or late phase Alzheimer's disease act in socially inappropriate ways. On the other hand, comparative study suggests that the phenomenon of "expressed emotion" is limited largely to our own culture (Cook, Lefley, Pickett, & Cohler, in press; Jenkins, 1984, 1991; Jenkins, Karno, de la Selva, Santana, Telles, Lopez, & Mintz, 1986; Karno, Jenkins, de la Selva, & Santana, 1987; Leff, Wig, Ghosh, & Bedi, 1987; Lefley, 1985; Wig, Menon, Bedi, & Ghosh, 1987; Wig, Menon, Bedi, & Leff, 1987). Much less expressed emotion has been found among families such as the Mexican Americans of California, who maintain traditional extended family ties and who explicitly recognize interdependence within the family, and where intergenerational living is expected, than among Anglo counterpart families.[7]

Culture and Symbolic Representation of Experience

The Italian concept of relations within the family, assumed by members of that culture to be universal, is but one of a number of alternatives used across cultures for ordering relationships among persons. Within a home culture, particular solutions or value orientations for common human dilemmas are assumed to be universal. These value orientations have been defined by C. Kluckhohn (1951) as:

> generalized and organized conception, influencing behavior, of nature, man's place in it, of man's relation to man, and of the desirable and nondesirable, as they relate to man-environment and interhuman relations. (p. 400)

---

[6] From the perspective of families providing care for formerly hospitalized offspring, emphasis on parental hostility and criticism does not differ in focus from earlier concern with the "schizogenic" parent or family communication processes responsible for the initial episode of illness. A powerful volume edited by members of the Boston Family Collective (Dearth, Labenski, Mott, Pellegrini, et al., 1986) notes that the Expressed-Emotion (EE) approach is no different in philosophical assumptions than earlier studies of family and communication process. This view is consistent more generally with the position of the National Alliance for the Mentally Ill (NAMI), which has raised similar concerns. In each instance, family process is assumed to be responsible for offspring illness. This perspective is consistent with the prevalent assumption in our own culture that parents are responsible for offspring adjustment over the course of life (Fischer & Fischer, 1963; Minturn &

Lambert, 1964). The same factors that lead mothers in our culture to feel guilty and resentful about the parental role are reflected in the continuing assumption of parental responsibility for offspring illness. Even if the focus has shifted from origin to course of the illness, the presumption remains that family processes largely determine posthospital adjustment. The fact that families in other cultures respond in quite different ways to offspring misfortune (Jenkins, 1991) shows that cultural factors largely determine variation in caregiving across the course of life.

[7] It is significant that efforts to intervene within the family to reduce both feelings of burden on the part of caregivers, and consequent expression of hostility and criticism (Leff & Vaughn, 1985) rely on techniques consistent with the acceptance expressed normatively by family members in other cultures regarding their psychiatrically ill relatives.

Kluckhohn and Strodtbeck (1961) note further:

> Value orientations are complex but definitely patterned (rank-ordered) principles, resulting from the transactional interplay of three non-analytically distinguishable elements of the evaluative process—the cognitive, the affective, and the directive elements—which give order and direction to the ever-flowing stream of human acts and thoughts as these relate to the solution of "common human" problems. These principles are variable from culture to culture but are . . . variable only in the *ranking patterns* of component parts which are themselves cultural universals. (p. 4)

The significance of this approach to the study of values has been demonstrated in F. Kluckhohn and Strodtbeck's (1961) study of culture and intergroup relations among Anglo, Native American and Hispanic ethnic groups in the American Southwest, as well as in Clark's (1972) and Clark and Anderson's (1967) study of Japanese and Mexican American ethnic groups in San Francisco, and Spiegel's studies of family and psychopathology (Papajohn & Spiegel, 1975; Spiegel, 1971). These studies of Greek and Italian American culture document the impact of culture change and threat of "mazeway disintegration" (Wallace, 1956) on the family, including such intergenerational conflict as offspring struggles to make accommodation between the culture of home and school, or conflict between family and the mental health system.[8] Spiegel (1971) has noted that the classification of values in terms of value orientations presumes that (a) there are a limited number of solutions for common human problems, (b) solutions to these problems are not limitless or random, and (c) all possible solutions can be found as variants within any one culture, with a particular solution being preferred by most people.

Five value orientations have been viewed as worth particular consideration: (a) the relation of humans to nature (person-nature orientation), (b) the temporal focus of human life (time orientation), (c) the modality of human activity (activity orientation), (d) view of human nature, and (c) the relationship among persons (relational orientation). Within each of these five value orientations, while all possible solutions may be expressed within a culture, there is a rank ordering. For example, considering the time orientation, some cultures may be characterized as preferring to live in the past, others in the present, or in the future. American culture is preeminent in the preference for living in the future as the highest ranked preference, whereas most peasant societies prefer living in the present as the first ranked preference, and the great Eastern civilizations prefer living in the past as a first-ranked time orientation alternative.

Again, in terms of relations with others, our own culture prefers an individualistic/nuclear solution, whereas the Southern Italian family prefers a corporate/extended solution, and the preferred East Asian family solution focuses on a lineal alternative

---

[8] Wallace's (1956) use of the term "mazeway" was borrowed from learning theory (particularly that of the influential cognitively oriented theorist Edward Chace Tolman), which tested essential postulates by sending or "running" rats through a maze or mazeway to determine the potency of certain learned responses. Tolman (1951) in particular suggested that intrinsic satisfaction may be of greater significance than the desire to increase pleasure or avoid pain.

emphasizing deference to elders. The problem with an Italian American family presenting at a psychiatric hospital, within a culture characterized by individualistic relationships, is that conflict develops between the preferred solutions to the relational value orientations of family, hospital, and community; the family assumes that the corporate/extended preference is first-ranked within the culture, whereas the larger Anglo culture assumes that the individualistic/nuclear solution is the first-ranked or preferred solution. Within each value orientation, there are more and less preferable solutions: These solutions can be rank ordered within any one culture.

Culture and Ethnicity

Culture becomes ethnicity as this rank ordering, previously assumed to be universal, is discovered to be but one of several alternatives, and one that has shifted from the first-ranked position in the home culture to a less preferable rank in the new culture. As these assumed universal solutions become alternatives, they often are not the preferred solutions. This "discovery" of alternatives reflects what Wallace (1956) has portrayed as the threat of mazeway disintegration, or lack of certainty regarding the most appropriate solutions for common human dilemmas that previously were assumed to have been resolved. A sense of personal and collective crisis then leads to confusion about the value of the traditional modes of resolution.

More than a half century of social science study has suggested that adjustment is promoted by living with others who share common values. Community studies have shown that persons distinguish between face-to-face, or "primary group," relations and "secondary group," or more impersonal relationships of school and workplace (Cohler & Grunebaum, 1981; Park, Burgess, & McKenzie, 1925/1967; Suttles, 1968; Wirth, 1928, 1945). Participants living in a homogeneous culture of origin generally share values. For example, the concept of mazeway disintegration formulated by Wallace (1956), when applied to the problem of contact between the Seneca Indian tribe of northern New England and white settlers from the time of the late 18th century (Wallace, 1972), suggests the impact of immigration on these presumed core values. The discovery that previously assumed universals are but one possible variant leads to a collective and personal sense of disorganization and reformulation in a more rigid and less adaptive manner than existed prior to this threat. This initial disruption of traditions is refashioned in the new culture. Living in a neighborhood with others from the same cultural traditions fosters emergence of primary group relations reflecting shared values. Recognize that these values may no longer reflect those of the culture of origin, as immigration turns culture into ethnicity, neighborhood residents who return home each day from experiences in the larger society, meet others reading and speaking the same language, and sharing a common outlook on experience. These similar views enhance social support and personal integration. Support from others of the same ethnic group, realized through continuing supportive primary groups ties is essential for preserving present adjustment.

The absence of such continuing contact with others sharing similar dilemmas and similar solutions from within the same ethnic group interferes with adjustment and appears associated with impaired mental health. Community survey findings reported by Mintz and Schwartz (1964) have shown that persons living in neighborhoods with a greater density of others from within the same ethnic group are less likely to be hospitalized for psychiatric illness than residents of less ethnically dense neighborhoods. The impact of mazeway disintegration is also dramatically illustrated by studies showing that immigrant groups are more likely than their nonemigrant counterparts to show evidence of psychiatric illness (Sanua, 1969, 1980; Struening, Rabkin, & Peck, 1969; Tseng & Hsu, 1980). It is not clear what factors might be associated with increased impairment in mental health within the first or immigrant generation as contrasted with later generations. It is possible that immigrants represent more troubled and dissatisfied persons in their native land who are consequently more marginal and more likely to migrate.

Although enhanced marginality and vulnerability to psychiatric illness may be common both to the decision to migrate and to higher rates of psychiatric impairment within the immigrant generation, increased psychiatric impairment also may be a consequence of the strain attending immigration and settling in a new country, including the mazeway disintegration inevitable on moving to a new culture, together with stigma felt following this settlement. The experience of stigma and prejudice, combined with the discovery that once assumed universal values are only one solution for common human dilemmas—and one that is also criticized and held in low regard—has an adverse impact on mental health. Exposure to stigma and marginality within particular minority or ethnic groups fosters social disorganization and increases personal distress (Tseng & Hsu, 1980).

Consistent with Wallace's initial formulation of culture change and personal adjustment, the consequence of immigration is that aspects of the original culture now become distorted and lack their initial flexibility. This is well exemplified by language use; the French spoken in Quebec is more like that of the 17th-century colonists than that spoken in France today. Again, Italian and Polish immigrants, returning to their homeland several decades later, are generally distressed to discover that the culture of the remembered past is so discrepant from the contemporary culture. In a study of aging and ethnicity in a large city (Cohler & Lieberman, 1978, 1979, 1980), many older Polish respondents still had maps of Warsaw published before World War I. It was difficult for these older adults to accept the possibility of dramatic change within their home culture, and the impact of modernity on a less urbanized past.

It is this remembered past, rather than the present culture, that is of particular significance in the lives of these immigrants. Initially preferred rankings within the culture of origin now become distorted and reified as culture becomes ethnicity, reflecting a relatively homogeneous set of values, customs, and other symbols abstracted from behavior. This distinctive ethnicity is preserved through particular socialization practices in a society that is historically and culturally separate from the one in which the meaning systems and customs originally were formulated. To maintain their commitment to the beliefs and customs of the home culture, persons seek to live in face-to-face relations with others from the same ethnic group thus confirming these earlier presumed universal solutions now discovered to be alternatives

among many solutions, and not even necessarily the preferred ones (Wirth, 1928).

Over time, and across generations, with continuing separation from the home culture, the customs of the ethnic group become ever more discrepant and separate, leading to a way of life that resembles neither the home culture nor the new land, but something altogether separate. Max Weber (1968) observed that ethnicity refers to:

> those human groups that entertain a subjective belief in the common descent because of similarities of physical type or of customs or of both, or because of memories of colonization and migration; this belief must be important for the propagation of group formation; conversely, it does not matter whether or not an objective blood relationship exists. Ethnic membership (*Gemeinsamkeit*) differs from the kinship group precisely by being a presumed identity, not a group with concrete social action, like the latter. (p. 389)

Weber's view also emphasizes shared meaning systems leading to enhanced communality as members of a community experience fellow feeling, or gemeinschaft (Tonnies, 1887/1957). Indeed, one of the few generalization that can be made within the social sciences is that persons generally prefer being with others like themselves, who share common values or worldview (Wirth, 1928). Emphasis on meaning as the foundation of ethnicity, and on ethnicity as a subjective experience, contrasts with those definitions of ethnicity based simply on intergroup conflict. It assumes (a) some shared value expressed through the development of particular institutions; (b) a defined historical period during which these institutions developed in a culturally different and polyethnic society sponsoring cultural diversity within a common political entity or "state"; (c) determination to preserve such customs through endogenous marriage; and (d) awareness by most members of the ethnic group (and generally the larger society as well) that these institutions are being realized or expressed in ways that differ from other such ethnic groups—usually as a consequence of migration to a new society (Barth, 1969).

Ethnicity as the embodiment of cultural traditions perpetuated across generations provides identity for its members and leads to assurance that familiar customs and beliefs will be preserved and that socioemotional support will be provided for group members who go out during the day to participate in the larger society (Francis, 1947). More recent formulations of the concept of ethnicity are generally consistent with this view of ethnicity as presented in Weber's classic definition (Barth, 1969; 1981; Greeley & McCready, 1974; Kolm, 1971; Schermerhorn, 1970).

Culture, Ethnicity, and the Expression of Personal Distress

Viewing ethnic groups as culture-bearing units, Barth (1969) and Blom (1969) show the importance of a shared culture that is accepted both by members of the particular ethnic group and by the larger society. This category for understanding self and others is made possible through the acceptance of particular boundaries between an ethnic group and the larger society. Whereas in other cultures, the boundaries may be geographic as well as social, boundaries are largely social in pluralistic Western society:

Children go to school and adults go to work during the day, returning home to family and community of residence of a particular ethnic group. These face-to-face, or primary-group, relations sustain personal adjustment and provide enhanced sense of identity as a member of an ethnic group (Wirth, 1928).

Many of the problems in the study of mental health and ethnicity understood as a "culture-bearing unit" (Barth, 1969), or system of meanings, have been reviewed by Ogbu (1990a), who has provided a comprehensive study of culture including the significance of symbolic and social action perspectives. A pioneer in the study of literacy and schooling among minority (primarily African American) children, Ogbu (1981, 1982, 1983, 1990) has long argued for a reconsideration of the problems of learning in school among children whose home environment differs markedly from the assumptions and expectations of mainstream American society. Ogbu (1990) has proposed a "cultural model" that is:

> . . . an understanding that a people have of their universe—social, physical, or both—as well as their understanding of the behavior in that universe. The cultural model of a population serves its members as a guide in their interpretation of events and elements within their universe; it also serves as a guide to their expectations and actions in that universe or environment. Furthermore, the cultural model underlies their folk theories or folk explanations of recurrent circumstances, events, and situations in various domains of life. It is used by members of the population to organize their knowledge about such recurrent events and situations. Members of a society or its segment develop their cultural model from collective historical experiences. The cultural model is sustained or modified by subsequent events or experiences in their universe. (p. 523)

From this perspective, the problem of literacy and academic attainment for some minority groups is that the model of school and society that is maintained within their ethnic groups is not congruent with the dominant view. Ogbu (1990a, 1990b) further argues that African Americans represent an involuntary minority forced to adopt the cultural beliefs and practices of the larger culture rather than, as among recent immigration of East Asian groups, a voluntary migration with values and beliefs already anticipating those of contemporary American culture. Just as in the discussions of culture and conflict provided by Clyde Kluckhohn (1951) and by F. Kluckhohn & Strodtbeck (1961) and by Wallace (1956), conflict between a pervasive understanding of self and others and competing orientations in values leads to problems of adaptation within culture. Dressler (1991), elaborating this perspective, has studied morale and patterns of social relationships among African American families in the South as they encounter social change.

Ogbu (1981, 1983) and Wallace (1956) agree on the threat of mazeway disintegration, which so often accompanies immigration, but also note a difference between the *voluntary* migrations of persons from Old World cultures in search of increased opportunities, and the *forced* migration of persons transported to the United States through slavery, conquest, and colonization. For example, voluntary migrants regarded obstacles to achievement as temporary, to be overcome over time through hard work, whereas involuntary migrants had little hope for the future. Again, consistent with the observations of F. Kluckhohn and Strodtbeck (1961)

and Spiegel (1971) regarding the hierarchy of solutions within each of several value orientations, and Wallace's (1956) formulation of threat of mazeway disintegration to an older culture that contacts a new culture, Ogbu (1990b) recognizes that primary cultural differences may pose problems in migrant adjustment to the new culture. Involuntary migrants suffer the additional problem of not being able to identify as a group with a homeland or primary group who provide support in the process of making increasingly more effective adaptation to American society.

Renewed emphasis on African roots of the black experience in American society accounts, at least in part, for the recent change in self-definition from black Americans to African Americans. This is the case even though the migration from Africa took place more than 300 years ago and may be far less important in American black society than subsequent experiences within the United States such as slavery, reconstruction in the latter part of the 19th century, or the move North to the "Rust Belt" cities following World War II (Fogel & Engerman, 1974; Grossman, 1989; Gutman, 1976; Henri, 1975). Just as in the study of families (Schneider, 1968; Spiegel, 1971), kin more distant in time or geography may become more significant for personal adjustment than those more immediate as a reference group. As in Ogbu's discussion of migration and culture, the significance of both involuntary migration and conflict in cultural orientations poses problems for the African American child in school and, more generally, in realizing a sense of effectance (White, 1959, 1960, 1963) within a culture very different from that of the homeland.

The significance for mental health of this sense of a shared commitment to a worldview for mental health is reflected in the finding that rates of major psychiatric illness are associated with density of ethnic group membership within a neighborhood: Those census tract areas having higher rates of ethnic group membership also show reduced rates of psychiatric illness among members of the dominant ethnic group (Mintz & Schwartz, 1964). Wirth's emphasis on the importance of a shared world view for adjustment is consistent with the recent emphasis on the significance of social relationships for mental health within disciplines as diverse as sociology and psychoanalysis (Kahn & Antonnucci, 1980; Kohut, 1977). Living with others who share a common view of culture supports the individual's own preferred modes of dealing with problems, and confirms accepted modes of understanding self and others within a multiethnic or pluralistic society in which competing alternatives may appear equally cogent.

It is particularly important to consider the role of culture as the foundation for determining change within lives over time. Shared understandings of self and others, of the course of life, and of the determinants of psychological health and illness (Kleinman, 1988), all reflect symbolic systems that serve as a template for action. These culturally constructed beliefs, which are the foundation for thought and action (Laboratory of Comparative Human Cognition, 1983), are first learned within the family and among peers, and are transmitted across successive generations. Harkness and Super (1990) have discussed these shared belief systems as "culture-bound syndromes" (patterns that in our own culture might be termed psychological illness). This cultural perspective questions fundamental assumptions of

Western psychiatry regarding the origins, course, and treatment of psychiatric distress (Kleinman & Good, 1985; Tseng & Hsu, 1980).[9]

Even within the major psychiatric disorders such as schizophrenia or depression, "local knowledge" (Geertz, 1983b) regarding origins, course, and outcome shows such variation across cultures that it is difficult to discuss these presumably universal, biologically determined disorders in any universal manner. Harkness and Super (1990) maintain that all illness is culture bound and must be understood in culturally specific terms. Culture determines explanations of cause, intervention, and outcome of disease processes, including psychiatric illness. It has been difficult for Western psychiatry, committed to a means-end rationality, to understand that the assumptions of biological causation and psychopharmacological treatment of psychiatric illness reflect the culturally bound interpretation that is most relevant within our own culture. As Harkness and Super (1990) cogently observe:

> Culture labels psychological distress or dysfunction, organizing it into categories and thus further influencing its manifestations. This principle, derived from anthropological and epidemiological research on psychopathology, across cultures, does not deny the reality of the biological dimension of psychological illness. In contrast to disease-based epidemiological research, however, recognition of the cultural organization of psychopathology leads to the conclusion that there is no universal "ultimate reality" of mental disorders that can be captured beyond purely medical models. (p. 48)

The implications for mental health based on cultural study are much more complex. From the time of Sigmund Freud (1913), there has been controversy regarding the contributions of cultural studies in understanding mental health and adjustment (Harkness & Super, 1990). Psychoanalytically informed anthropologists (Henry, 1963; Mead, 1928, 1930) maintained that contemporary Western culture provided obstacles to personal fulfillment that contrasted with the support for spontaneous personal development fostered by such cultures as the New Guinea highlands and the Amazon Basin. This view of anthropology as cultural critique was replaced with a view emphasizing culture as the repository of diversity. According to this view, those persons not able to adjust to the demands of our own industrial society should be able to find cultures supporting their particular character structure. It was assumed that even persons with psychiatric illness, deviant in terms of Western norms, could find a culture in which their symptoms might be congruent and syntonic. According to this view, concepts of normal and abnormal are relevant only in terms of particular cultures; hysterical conversion and spirit possession, which might be regarded as aberrant in our own culture, are expectable aspects of the expression of the woman's voice in the North Sudan

(Boddy, 1989). Psychological symptoms may be more a reflection of the role assigned to men and women within society than a consequence of personal psychopathology.

Addressing this issue of cultural relativism, Spiro (1965/1987) has differentiated between social relativism, which maintains that psychiatric illness is deviant only in terms of the dominant norms or beliefs within a particular society, and cultural relativism, which suggests that phenomena such as delusions, which might be a sign of serious psychiatric illness in the West, would be acceptable within other cultures. However, Spiro argues that modes of personal expression must always be judged within a particular culture and that persons expressing personal distress within a particular culture are not likely to be able to fit into other cultures with any greater ease. As Spiro (1965/1987) observes:

> A psychiatrically diagnosed psychotic is not only incapable of participating in his own society, he is incapable of participating in any society. An American psychotic would function no better in a Buddhist monastery than in an American city. (p. 157)

From this perspective, major psychopathology interferes with adjustment within any cultural context; there is little reason to assume that problems in maintaining adjustment within one culture might be acceptable within another.

Study of culturally sanctioned practices like shamanism has sometimes been used in the argument for cultural relativism (Levi-Strauss, 1963). As both Boddy (1989) and Kakar (1982) have shown, shamanism is a complex, cultural practice that is not comparable to hysteria, schizophrenia, or other forms of personal distress recognized within our own culture. Although the mode of expression of symptoms may be constructed according to historically determined meanings characteristic of a particular culture, significant disruptions in maintaining adjustment would lead to problems in other cultures as well although expressed in modes consonant with that culture. From this perspective, it is difficult to accept the view that a major psychiatric illness such as schizophrenia, which leads to profound disruption of adjustment within one culture would provide an acceptable mode of adjustment within another culture.

The very significance of psychological symptoms for personal adjustment and family continuity may be culturally specific. Our own culture finds it more difficult to tolerate the thought disorder and accompanying disruption of personal functioning among schizophrenic family members than is characteristic of other cultures (Jenkins, 1991; Kleinman, 1988). A cultural perspective, focusing on determinants of shared understanding of self and others, considered together with a developmental perspective founded on shared understanding of expectable changes over time, provides an important means for understanding the experience of living with personally troubled family members over periods of many years. As Harkness and Super (1990) have observed, an important next step in study of the interplay of culture and psychopathology is to understand variation in cultural response not only in the origins of psychopathology but also in the subsequent course and outcome of personal distress.

Understanding of the complex interplay of meaning system, social relations, and psychiatric illness reflects changing

---

[9] There is some difference within the literature regarding the interplay of culture and psychopathology in the construction of symptoms. Whereas Kleinman and his colleagues focus on the significance of cultural elements, Draguns (1980) suggests that the psychoses (particularly schizophrenia and psychotic bipolar depression) may present with symptoms more transculturally universal than nonpsychotic disorders. Draguns suggests that the cultural plasticity of psychiatric symptoms may have been overstated.

perspectives on the origins and course of major psychiatric illness. In the first place, cultures understand the impact of psychiatric disorder in quite different ways: Symptoms characteristic of major psychiatric disorders in one culture may not be those relevant for another culture (Harkness & Super, 1990). For example, Kleinman (1988) notes the emotional expression of unipolar disorders differs not just across cultures but also across ethnic groups within particular cultures. In the United States at the present time, conversion symptoms are rarely found among urban residents presenting with psychoneuroses (hysteria); the extraordinary dissociation characterizing the syndrome of multiple personality is even less frequently observed. However, it is not uncommon to find conversion hysteria in rural areas where the psychosomatic hypothesis (that emotions or feelings are related to bodily states) is less a shared belief, or even to encounter cases of multiple personality or personal dissociation. Sophisticated urban culture promotes the notion that the body may symbolize psychological conflict and that wishes may be represented by physical symptoms. This understanding of the body as symbol for wishes and feelings is largely absent within rural culture.

In the second place, culture not only defines the very terms in which symptoms are expressed, it also sets the parameters for the expression of personal distress. Findings from the study of an impoverished, largely rural, Eastern Canadian province (Leighton, Harding, Macklin, Macmillan, & Leighton, 1963), and two urban areas with marked variation in social status (Hollingshead & Redlich, 1958; Rogler & Hollingshead, 1965), together with study of a more affluent urban community in the now classic study of midtown Manhattan (Srole & Fischer, 1962), all show an association between extent of community social disorganization, enhanced anomie, and increased personal distress. These earlier studies were very important in showing the association between social status and mental health, but they assumed that psychiatric illness could be understood in similar terms across cultures. The meaning of psychiatric illness varies between individuals living in rural Canadian provinces and sophisticated urban residents of midtown New York.[10]

This consideration of the place of shared culture for personal adjustment presents problems in terms of an "ecological fallacy," equating personal disposition and larger social process, and

---

[10] Much of the study involving community characteristics and mental health has focused on the function of social status in the origin of psychological disorder. The implication of this work is that the reduced life chances and lack of sense of empowerment contribute to lowered morale, which, in turn, is associated with increased vulnerability. Lack of economic resources also directly contributes to this increased vulnerability. Poverty may construct a culture characterized by shared meanings and characteristic means for understanding self and others that is intertwined with economic privation. Further, since poverty may be most characteristic among particular ethnic groups, privation and culture become intertwined as "ethclass" leading to a culture of poverty. Much of this perspective is represented in Glazer and Moynihan's (1963) classic study of social status and ethnicity in New York. In studying social status and mental health, it is important to view the impact of poverty in more than sheerly economic terms.

assuming a causal role for aspects of social surround (Hughes, Tremblay, Rapoport, & Leighton, 1960; Kleinman, 1988; Leighton et al., 1963; Mishler & Scotch, 1963; Sanua, 1980; Warner, 1985). Faris and Dunham (1939) had earlier suggested a "social drift" hypothesis, suggesting that the association between increased rates of psychiatric illness and lower social status was due to the tendency of less well functioning members of society to congregate in the most marginal and disorganized parts of the city. Other studies suggested that aspects of poverty and family disorganization contributed to the association between lower social status and increased psychiatric disorder. As Banfield (1958), Kleinman (1988), and Stack (1974) all have observed, poverty is directly responsible for much of human misery. The impact of poverty, with associated family and social disorganization, may lead to sense of "demoralization" in which persons feel helpless, hopeless, and unable to manage the tasks of daily living.

In its more pervasive form, an initial crisis state, such as accompanies unemployment, leads to a "social breakdown" syndrome, and to reliance on such deviant solutions as substance abuse and crime in an effort to regain the sense of personhood lost through continuing struggle with social disorganization or disintegration (Kohut, 1971, 1977). As Hughes et al. (1960) have observed, communities characterized by marked social disintegration, including both parts of the Canadian community, and large sections of contemporary American cities, foster enhanced feelings of demoralization and higher rates of both physical and psychiatric illness. S. Parker and Sasaki (1965) report on the comparative study of two socially disintegrated rural areas, a Navajo community in the American Southwest, and a French-Canadian village in an Eastern Canadian province. The impact of poverty on the rigidly controlled Navajo personality leads to higher rates of psychophysiological disorder, but there is less explicit evidence of anomie within a functioning extended family system. On the other hand, among the French-Canadians, who are more explicitly a part of the larger society, feelings of lowered self-regard are particularly evident.

This perspective becomes important when considering the issue of risk for major psychiatric disorder among offspring of parents with psychiatric disorder. Poverty and other aspects of social disorganization compound personal vulnerability, leading to increased possibility of personal breakdown or an episode of psychiatric illness. It may well be that the very high rates of psychiatric illness observed among offspring of schizophrenic parents in the New York Longitudinal Study (Erlenmeyer-Kimling & Cornblatt, 1987; Erlenmeyer-Kimling et al., 1990) reflect a complex pattern of poverty magnifying the potential impact of genetic factors in the origin of the major psychiatric illness. Social disintegration within the community in which many of these families live, together with accompanying demoralization, intensifies possible genetic loading for psychiatric illness, leading to episodes of major psychopathology among otherwise vulnerable offspring to a greater extent than would be found in more organized neighborhoods (Sanua, 1980).

The issue of diagnosis has been pervasive in psychiatry; the shift to a descriptive nosology (Spitzer, Endicott, & Robins, 1978) did not resolve the problems of diagnosis but merely standardized the decision-making process. Particularly in the diagnosis of the major psychiatric disorders (especially schizophrenia and the unipolar and bipolar affective disorders), although there is fairly high reliability on diagnosis within American psychiatry, the criteria in the *Diagnostic and Statistical Manual of Mental Disorders* (DSM-IV; American Psychiatric Association, 1994) are still discrepant from those used in the World Health Organization classification (1990). Even disregarding problems in the diagnosis of the disorder, distributed around the world with a 1% prevalence rate, Kleinman (1988) has shown that there is marked variation both in rates of schizophrenic illness among culture, and also in expression of symptoms, course of illness, and mode of treatment.

Meaning systems embedded within culture, together with aspects of social surround, may elicit particular psychiatric illness with greater frequency; social disorganization and other prevailing conflicts may lead to a host of problems from malnutrition to social and personal chaos resulting in increased rates of both physical and mental illness. Industrialization and larger economic dislocation may affect both the manner of onset and course of schizophrenia among otherwise more vulnerable prospective patients (Warner, 1985) and may determine the particular form of their positive symptoms (Andreasen, 1987, 1991; Savage, Leighton, & Leighton, 1965). For example, Caudill (1958) recounts a visit to a Japanese psychiatric hospital where a catatonic patient sat huddled in a corner of his room. On being greeted by his psychiatrist and Caudill, the patient rose, bowed deeply in the characteristic Japanese manner of respect, and then returned to the corner.

Whereas the structure of delusions may be readily identified across cultures, the content of these delusions is strongly influenced by culture. On the other hand, content that we would consider delusional in our own culture may be normative elsewhere. Savage, A. Leighton, and D. Leighton (1965), and Kakar (1989) both provide examples of ideational content that would seem delusional if expressed by a member of bourgeois Western culture even though it would be characteristic of thought processes for participants of Indian culture.[11] Hallucinations are also strongly influenced by cultural context and may not be readily differentiated from visual and auditory experiences of other cultures except as characterized by their duration.[12] Regardless of the factors

determining an episode of psychiatric illness, once it has become manifest, the particular form assumed by psychiatric symptoms is culturally constructed and must be understood within the terms of a particular culture.

Culture, Psychological Development, and Vulnerability

Meanings attached to the child's intentions play an important part in determining parental response which, in turn, fosters the child's own particular understandings of wish and intent. Culture also provides an opportunity for studying the impact of modernity and industrialization on child rearing. For example, comparative study by the Whitings and their collaborators (Whiting, 1963) has also shown that children from cultures more characteristically thought of as "simple" in contrast to more highly developed and industrialized Western cultures show greater nurturance and less dominance in their social relations. Findings reported by Kagan, Klein, Finley, Rogoff, and Nolan (1979) on school-age children in a Guatemalan village show that the relative sensory deprivation imposed by spending long periods inside the parental dwelling are quickly overcome when these children are permitted out into village life. The children are able to overcome earlier deficits and do not differ from same age counterparts in our own society. These findings suggest the possibility of remediation for children suffering privation and neglect within our own society and show the advantage of comparative cross-cultural study in understanding not only onset of psychopathology but also resilience across the course of life, even among more vulnerable persons.

Culture and the Study of Risk and Psychological Resilience

The interplay of culture and personal development across the life span is relevant in the study of vulnerability and determinants of psychiatric disorder, as well as the emergence of those attributes that protect against the impact of psychopathology. Concern with means used to manage adversity and to remain resilient to psychological disorder has been a particular focus of study over the past several decades. Beginning with Lois Murphy's (1962) classic study of the means used by children to master novelty, loss, and change in their lives, together with R. W. White's (1959, 1960) discussion of competence, interest shifted from sole concern with the origins and course of psychopathology to the determinants and course of means used to manage personal distress that otherwise might lead to psychopathology (Albee, 1980). Just as with the origins of personal distress, life experiences within

---

[11] Although the content of psychiatric symptoms reflects meanings embedded within culture, as Spiro (1965/1987) has suggested, adjustment does not simply reflect the fit between person and culture, nor is it the case that the person dissatisfied in one culture would necessarily be better adjusted living within another culture. Relativist perspectives cannot be used to understand origins, course, and treatment of major psychiatric illness; symptoms of thought disorder have the same significance in Delhi as in New York. However, just as with other meanings fashioned out of the symbolic surround, the content of delusions and hallucinations must be understood within the context of the patient's particular culture.

[12] Savage et al. (1965), in reviewing the criteria important in making a diagnosis of schizophrenia at that time, questioned whether flattened affect should be used for the diagnosis of schizophrenia across cultures since there are many cultures in which the expression of affect toward strangers outside the household is considered inappropriate. This problem is also evident in studying affective disorders across cultures; although extreme cases of bipolar disorder may be readily recognized within any particular culture, manic states may be hard to recognize,

---

such as within some African cultures in which expression of excitement is assumed to be normative (Carothers, 1953; Wittoker & Fried, 1959), or in India, where emotions are to be understated and not readily expressed to strangers. Culture may mask the appearance of psychiatric disorder. Incongruity between culturally defined meanings and expectations and the expression of delusions, hallucinations, and inappropriate affects, together with a personal history of interpersonal conflict, may be the most important means for making a psychiatric diagnosis across cultures.

particular cultures, at particular points across the course of life, determine relative success in managing adversity.[13] Personal resources called into play to foster resilience at one point in life may not provide equal protection at subsequent points across the life span.

Beginning with findings reported by Anthony (1974a, 1987a), Garmezy (1974, 1975, 1981, 1985a, 1985b, 1987b), Garmezy and Devine, (1984), Rutter (1979a, 1987), and their research groups, interest has focused on the means by which persons remain resilient during times of misfortune. As Elder's (1974) work initially showed, persons in our own culture are able to successively rewrite their life story using past struggle with misfortune as the foundation of present resilience (Cohler, 1991b). To date, there has been little systematic study of this issue, and even less study of the manner in which cultural conceptions of person, time, and place might determine how the past is used as a psychological resource in the present (Cohler, 1991b; Daniel, 1984; Geertz, 1966/1973a, 1966/1973b; Kakar, 1982; Lutz, 1988; White & Kirkpatrick, 1985).

For example, within our own culture children recognize parental psychiatric disorder as malignant and as a threat to continuity in child care and provision of a consistent environment for the child's development. Children of parents recurrently hospitalized for psychiatric illness within the bourgeois West soon learn the significance of particular changes in parental symptoms, and respond with alarm to the first indications of the onset of an additional episode (Cohler, Gallant, Grunebaum, & Kauffman, 1983). Other cultures may code the significance of parental psychiatric illness and its implications for the well-being of the family in ways quite different from our own (Lutz, 1988). Certainly, the assumption that parental attributes determine the child's present and future adjustment is uniquely a belief within our own culture helping to explain the guilt and anxiety that mothers report associated with child care (Minturn & Lambert, 1964). Availability of kindred to assist in child care also mitigates the impact of psychiatric illness within the family for the child's present life (Jenkins, 1991; Kleinman, 1988).

Although intensive study has not yet located the genetic markers for major psychopathology, there is agreement that a complex interplay of life circumstances and biologically determined predisposition is responsible for both first and subsequent episodes of disturbance.[14] Integrated life-course and genetic perspectives

within our culture suggest a model of vulnerability in which biological predisposition, meaning systems, and life circumstances are significant in the origins of psychiatric disorder and also are essential in providing effective intervention. Epidemiological perspectives, such as those of Leighton and his colleagues in the Sterling County studies of mental health and illness have demonstrated the capacity of social surround to affect adjustment.

The same threat of mazeway disintegration (Wallace, 1956) that impacts personality and adjustment as culture is transformed into ethnicity also affects reciprocal socialization processes within the family. Parents brought up in a different culture from that of their offspring often find it difficult to follow the prescriptions of the new culture that conflict with dominant value orientations, including meanings assigned to interpersonal relationships and other aspects of experience. Ethnic group variation in socialization practices continues across successive generations or cohorts. Italian American mothers foster expressivity and indulgence in their young children to a far greater extent than Irish American mothers, who expect a high degree of personal control over feelings and conduct. Again, the impact of culture on child rearing is most dramatically illustrated in the comparative six-culture study (Minturn & Lambert, 1964; Whiting, 1963).

The approach followed by the Whitings and their associates represents the most systematic effort to date to study the impact of environment and culture on personality and adjustment. Much of this study, however, was carried out across six cultures on children between ages 3 and 11 with little follow-up possible regarding these children and their families.[15] In the light of more recent emphasis within anthropology on the study of local knowledge (Geertz, 1983b) or culturally determined meanings of person and intent (Lutz, 1988; White, 1980; White & Kirkpatrick, 1985), the efforts to standardized meanings or to assume invariant understandings of human behavior across cultures raise questions about the significance of comparative studies such as the six-culture study. Regarding culture largely as independent variations in a controlled experimental study does not allow for recognition of the complexity that more recent

---

[13] Except for some detailed study of culture and psychopathology (Kleinman, 1988) and some very limited attention to culture and developmental perspectives on psychopathology (Harkness & Super, 1990), there has been very little focus on culture and psychological resilience and coping. There has been even less consideration of the manner in which culture shapes coping responses to what is defined within that culture as distress and psychological illness.

[14] There is an additional problem in attributing the origins of the major mental disorders to biology interacting with the life surround. From a cultural perspective, attribution of psychiatric disorder to a biological substratum within the bourgeois West is but one of the modes of explanation for this disorder found around the world. There is an assumption that Western rational-experimental science has "demonstrated" the

existence of this biological determination of schizophrenia and affective disorders. However, as Levi-Strauss (1962/1966) has argued in *The Savage Mind,* ultimately the science of the concrete permits alternative modes of explanation that are as convincing as the ones we favor in the West. Indeed, much of the argument made regarding causation within psychiatry is founded on the process of working "backward" from the presumed actions of a particular psychotropic medication to a probable cause. It is important to maintain a perspective that focuses less on presumed natural science origins of major mental illness than on "local" or culturally shaped explanations of psychiatric illness as being operative in modes of treatment. There is little evidence that treatment with phenothiazine is preferable to the approach of traditional Japanese treatment, which relies heavily on an interpersonal perspective.

[15] LeVine and his associates (R. LeVine et al., 1994; S. LeVine, 1979) have returned to the same East African culture area as that in which LeVine's earlier work had been carried out and have reported on issues of socialization and transition to modernity characteristic of this community.

study in ethnopsychology has shown to be important in persons' understanding of self and others.

Culture, Ecology, and Child Care: Determinants of Personal Adjustment

Perhaps the most comprehensive formulation to date regarding the function of culture in development and emergence of psychopathology has been provided by John and Beatrice Whiting and their colleagues at the Laboratory of Human Development (Palfrey House), Harvard University. Over nearly four decades, the Whitings, and their associates and students, systematically explored a paradigm for understanding culture and personal development, and for sampling culture as related to the emergence of sentiment and intent in childhood. As R. LeVine (1970) observed, much of the focus in this work has been to demonstrate variation rather than uniformity across the world's cultures in the study of child rearing and both childhood and adulthood personality and adjustment in the manner first portrayed by J. W. M. Whiting and Child (1953) in their exploration of social learning and psychological development.[16]

J. W. M. Whiting and B. Whiting (1959) defined a "custom complex" referring to the way that cultural beliefs and practices might influence behavior. Culture comprises a value system or ethics, a belief system regarding human behavior, and the pragmatics or set of technical skills and knowledge of culture that, together with socially recognized attributes of child, parent, and family (e.g., status, honor, kinship, and lineage structure and density) and age and gender of offspring, all play a part in determining the child's actions. Within American culture, families are structurally independent; generations may live together for brief periods, as among young adults returning home while finding a job following college, but it is considered desirable for offspring to live apart from their parents.[17] Even though a majority of the

mothers of young children presently work at least part time, the wife and mother is still viewed as the kin-keeper and "emotional manager" within the family, whereas the father is viewed as primarily responsible for the family's economic support. It is still the case that the wife's income and status as a worker is typically viewed as discretionary, particularly prior to the time when all children are in high school (Cohler & Grunebaum, 1981).

This structural isolation and stereotypy of the woman's role within the family when children are young is among the many factors accounting for the particular hostility expressed by women in our culture regarding the parental role and the task of child care. Other cultures show culturally constructed hostility toward the parental role based on traditional patterns of social structure and traditional meanings associated with particular family roles. For example, Turnbull (1974a) notes the wide kinship variation among African cultures, together with the fluidity of kinship attributions: Among the Mbuti pygmies, organized into hunting bands, family members leaving to join another band also lose their kinship affiliations. Other groups reckon kinship in terms of age-grade or generation, with many persons of the mother's generation called "mother." The names that persons are called parallel obligations and responsibilities, and these responsibilities are, in turn, affected by mode of subsistence.

The Whitings and their associates view social structure, particularly household composition and sleeping arrangements, as critical in determining childhood socialization practices that, in turn, determine child and adult personality. However, from the outset, they also emphasized the significance of mode of subsistence and other geographic factors in determining social structure: Geography and climate have a direct effect on the daily routine of both children and adults, and remain an important influence on both social structure and child care (Whiting, 1981; Whiting et al., 1966; Whiting & Whiting, 1978). J. Whiting (1981) reports that history and climate influence important aspects of socialization, such as physical closeness of mother and infant. For example, contrasting the two most common types of infant carriers, the sling and the cradle, the sling or shawl is most often found in warm climates where the infant wears little clothing and is cuddled closely against the mother's body.

The cradle with accompanying swaddling clothes is characteristic of cold climates, where the infant is bound and carried on the mother's back. In sum, infants in warm climates show more sustained and intimate contact with their mother than infants in cold climates. Extent of body contact between mother and infant is associated with a broad range of socialization practices that also show systematic variation with climate. The open physical arrangement of the residence, which is common in tropical climates, also fosters a high degree of social interaction, leading to quite different assignment of meanings to concepts of being with others or alone, and to privacy, than within our own culture. The Whitings (1966) also observe that the most economical manner of providing shelter within cold climates is a house for an extended family, which provides maximum heat and lowest cost for building materials. Child care within these northern climate, extended-family households is characterized by emphasis on quiet, respect for others' privacy and little tolerance for aggressive or loud behaviors.

---

[16] Particularly in the Whitings' innovative "Six Cultures" study (Whiting, 1963; Whiting & Whiting, 1975), they and their students attempted to systematize methods of collecting data (detailed mother interviews regarding child care and 5-minute participant observer behavior samples transformed into ratings of children's actions and parental responses), and also variables to be used in the analysis. As R. LeVine (1970) has observed, whereas other groups claim to have employed these same methods in their own work, variation in the methods of these other studies comprise the comparability of data obtained from the six-culture study and later extensions of this work.

[17] While T. Parsons (1949, 1955a, 1955b) had portrayed the structural isolation of the nuclear family unit, later discussion of Parsons' views led to the misunderstanding that marital families were interpersonally isolated as well. In fact, even when they do not live together, kindred have frequent contact. Residential proximity and good transportation mean that the urban multigenerational family is able to enjoy frequent visits. Cohler and Grunebaum (1981) review much of the literature in family sociology showing that residential mobility over large distances is much less common than once assumed. Further, there is a matrifocal "tilt" in the choice of living arrangements (Fischer & Fischer, 1963; Sweetser, 1963, 1964); where possible, it is assumed desirable for the young couple to live near to the wife's parents. It is also assumed that the daughter will have a special commitment to caring for her own kindred.

The cold northern climate forces families indoors for much of the year; living together indoors stresses overcontrol in childhood socialization. Crowded living conditions exaggerate these problems of the enclosed house and make particularly severe demands on interpersonal harmony and expression of aggression. Climate determines the mode of adult supervision which, in turn, is an important determinant of child behavior. For example, Mexican children are required to remain within the family compound, under direct adult supervision, playing with brothers and sisters within eyesight of the mother (Romney in B. Whiting, 1963). Okinawan children are expected to play in large groups near their compound, whereas Gusii children are encouraged to take responsibility for the solitary task of tending cattle far from the compound (LeVine & Lloyd in B. Whiting, 1963). R. LeVine (1974) also notes that these Gusii children continue to be carried over longer durations of childhood than children in many other cultures; the particular dangers for toddlers wandering near ever-present cooking fires is overcome through keeping these children out of harm's way (Collomb & Valantin, 1970).

The approach of the Palfrey House-Laboratory of Human Development group at Harvard is consistent with much of the study of the impact of ecology and climate on modes of subsistence, which, in turn, determine psychological attributes transmitted through socialization practices across generations. This close interrelationship of ecology and child care has been dramatically illustrated in Turnbull's (1974b), report on his study of the Ilk, a desert-dwelling African hunting people. Food is very scarce in this harsh desert ecology; even two persons dare not cooperate if subsistence for either is to be possible. Self-interest is essential for self-preservation and sociality is dysfunctional; Turnbull describes a case in which a mother who cared for her child in the loving manner of Western culture, and who tried to protect her child from privation and starvation was viewed by others as acting in a dysfunctional manner.

Perhaps of even greater significance in the interplay of ecology, culture, child rearing, and vulnerability, the daughter of this caring and concerned mother, at least as viewed by Western standards, was taught that others could be depended on to be helpful and thus was insufficiently personally resourceful. This daughter died of starvation in middle childhood when her mother was finally forced to throw her out of the house because there was nothing to eat, and when no one else in the village would provide resources. Similar circumstances of what would be seen as increased risk for psychopathology in contemporary culture, as a consequence of parental neglect, have been reported by Aries (1962) as expectable within Western culture during the Middle Ages when privation and starvation were characteristic across much of European society. Resilience within such a culture is a function of enhanced personal autonomy and resourcefulness, and those persons more predisposed to sociality, or those more dependent on others, may not be able to survive.

Spiro (1965/1987) has argued that adjustment represents a fit between personal attributes and modal characteristics of the culture. Consistent with Goldschmidt's (1971, 1976) emphasis on ecology in understanding social structure and culture, Edgerton's (1971) comparative study of four East African groups shows the significance of subsistence for personality, adjustment, and family structure.[18] Factors such as ease in expressing feelings and comfort in being with others vary with mode of subsistence: a pastoral life of herding flocks versus a settled and stable agricultural life.[19] As Goldschmidt (1971) notes in his introduction to the study, food and shelter are essential for social life to continue across generations: This activity is carried on in connection with others, and is subject to the same activity of making meaning or symbolic activity as other aspects of culture. Mode of subsistence then becomes an inherently symbolic activity, mediating between ecology, including climate and geography, and social organization. Pastoralists (herders), living in areas difficult to cultivate, tend to be brave, to act directly and forcefully, and to be concerned with pride and shame. Farmers, living where cultivation of crops is possible, tend to emphasize industriousness, sociability, and constancy of action, including chastity and fidelity.

Edgerton's findings largely confirm Goldschmidt's assumptions. Culture emerged as more important than demographic factors of age or gender in determining responses on a number of psychological measures. Mode of subsistence was nearly as important as culture in determining psychological attributes: Pastoralists across the four groups were concerned with issues of independence and shame, emphasizing bravery and both open and direct expression of feelings. Pastoralists were fiercely loyal to their fellows and were directly concerned with preservation of direct and intense ties, helping to ensure survival. Farmers were concerned with issues of respect and resentment of authority, together with firm control over the expression of feelings. However, farmers also showed greater difficulty than pastoralists in forming tightly knit communities, and they were more likely to express feelings of jealousy and lack of respect for the wishes of others. The comparatively greater luxury of the farmer's circumstances permitted expression of feelings of jealousy and resentment of others that might be potentially disruptive to the community. This risk was not acceptable among herders, whose circumstances are

---

[18] Collomb and Valantin (1970) have noted the continent of Africa is a particularly adverse environment for family life and child care. The diverse landscape poses difficult conditions for child care, from the poverty that is intrinsic to the desert areas to the sparse human communities of the bush. Climate and hygiene foster spread of disease; this climatic adversity is reflected in the fear and suspiciousness that so often make the environment appear especially malignant. Rapid economic development has further contributed to processes of social disorganization that are adverse for the care of young children (Lambo, 1974). Rutter (1979b) identifies the social disorganization and poverty, associated with enhanced family discord, of the London slum as an ecological factor contributing in significant ways to the increased rate of psychiatric disturbance in a London borough as contrasted with the more rural and socially functional Isle of Wight.

[19] Goldschmidt (1971) notes that this distinction among "ideal types" is itself too global. In some groups, herding and farming are totally separate, whereas in other groups, they may be integrated. The herd itself may be the means of subsistence, as in the herding of sheep or cattle, or a form of capitalism, as in the herding of horses. Farming is also diverse; cultivation techniques show great variation and may also vary in productivity and labor demand (Goldschmidt notes that societies using draft animals are almost always patrilineal, while hoe farming may be associated with matrilineality as well).

necessarily more precarious, and whose interdependence and ability to call on each other for help and assistance might be critical at times of emergency.

This personality pattern continues even after mode of subsistence shifts from herding to settled agriculture. Particular ecologies make particular demands on persons and require modes of adaptation that shape social structure, including child rearing and methods of coping with life changes (Berry, 1976). Although mode of subsistence is linked to a particular lifestyle and accompanying dispositions, it is not simply the case that one form of subsistence and accompanying character style is better than another, or more likely to foster adaptation. Edgerton (1992) does show, however, that not all cultures are equally successful in fostering adaptation. Particular cultural practices and beliefs may threaten not only the adjustment of particular members of a culture but the actual survival of entire populations.

Environments vary in the extent to which they are forgiving of maladaptive beliefs and practices just as cultures can succeed effectively until internal or external forces demand change to realize continued adaptation (Cottrell, 1976; Edgerton, 1971, 1992; French, Rodgers, & Cobb, 1974). Spiro (1965/1987) has suggested that the important question regarding the fit between personal and collective adaptation concerns the manner in which persons living within particular circumstances are able to adapt to those circumstances and to make a positive adjustment. Psychopathology is similarly idiosyncratic and disruptive (Tseng & Hsu, 1980). Culturally constructed modes of thought and action transmitted across generations provide the foundation for individual adjustment; as Edgerton (1992) has emphasized, particular cultural beliefs and practices may interfere in realization of personal well-being. The expression of independence and loyalty is adaptive among the pastoralists, whereas hard work and routine within one's own self-interest are particularly relevant among farmers.

Within the bourgeois West, ecology and child care have seldom been the focus of study. However, Bronfenbrenner (1979) has portrayed a concept of ecological developmental study, fitting context and developmental process together; and Minuchin (1970) has proposed the concept of "ecological psychiatry," assuming concern with the child as embedded within the context of family, neighborhood, school, and community. Mental health and efforts at intervention must take account of the child's life within these "behavior settings" (Barker & Wright, 1951, 1955). However, beyond the pioneering ethnographic studies of J. Fischer and A. Fischer (1963), reporting on Orchard Town (New England) in the six-culture study; Barker and Wright's (1955) study of ecology and behavior in a small midwestern community; the Topeka coping study of Lois Barclay Murphy and her collaborators (Murphy, 1962; Murphy & Moriarty, 1976); and Shirley Brice Heath's (1989, 1991) work on language, develop, and culture, researchers have seldom employed this perspective in the study of child care and development within our culture (Jahoda, 1980; Monroe & Monroe, 1980).

Murphy's extensive observational, longitudinal study was carried out in the midwestern United States, and is notable for its focus on the ways that climate and geography affect child-rearing practices (child rearing takes on quite different significance in regions where harsh winters force children and parents indoors living in close proximity than in mild climates like that of southern California, where children can play outdoors for large parts of the year, and where there is not a perpetual struggle to get into the snowsuit). Murphy and her associates note other aspects of community ecology and composition as particularly influential, including the problems presented by the great seasonal variations in weather, with the concomitant threat of tornado activity as a danger and source of anxiety for parents and children alike (so well portrayed by Dorothy in *The Wizard of Oz*), and homogeneity of social status (although virtually all families considered themselves "Americans" and made few social class comparisons). For example, Murphy and Moriarty (1976) note that working-class children had more play equipment than middle-class children, whose fathers were less handy with tools and less able to produce play structures than working-class counterparts.

Finally, and consistent with renewed concern for actual historical processes in the study of culture, factors such as migration, ethnicity, and traditional beliefs, which have all been shaped by particular events and transmitted across generations through narrative or story, must be understood as relevant to socialization. Within American culture, both the behaviorism of the 1930s and the psychoanalytic humanism of the 1950s led to particular recommendations regarding child rearing that have been widely read and discussed (Clarke-Stewart, 1978). Even if parents are not able to remember specific recommendations and advice, popular guides to child rearing have had wide impact on particular cohorts. Views on child rearing are further emphasized within the media, in classes for prospective parents, and even by the family physician. Particularly with the advent of television, the impact of this advice has been enhanced by the appearances of "experts" on network talk shows.

Cross-cultural studies (e.g., those of the Whitings and their associates at Palfrey house; Cole, Wertsch, and their associates at the Laboratory of Comparative Cognition at the University of California at San Diego), and the literacy studies of Ogbu (1982, 1983, 1990a, 1990b) and Heath (1989, 1991) have provided means for portraying the significance of environment for adaptation. From the perspective of the vulnerability model initially proposed by Zubin and Spring (1977), and extended by Goldstein (1990), Neufield & Mothersill, (1980), Nicholson and Neufeld (1989, 1992), and others, conflict in value orientation predisposes to enhanced risk for psychopathology. Although by no means underestimating the impact of poverty on psychological development and personal adjustment, Banfield (1958) has shown, in his studies of southern Italy, that particular symbolic constructions of self and others are associated with efforts at coping (Pearlin & Schooler, 1978) and may conflict with dominant cultural orientations.[20]

---

[20] This view should not be understood as an endorsement of cultural relativism. Consistent with Spiro's (1965/1987) critique, it is not simply that there is a cultural niche in which particular cultural orientations might foster adaptation. As Wallace (1956, 1972) has suggested, particular cultural orientations may reflect rather brittle efforts to maintain older ways in a wooden manner when confronted by the orientations of a new culture. The concept of "cargo-cult" or emphasis on older ways such as in the Seneca cult of Handsome Lake is a response to cultural change. As Geertz (1959) has noted in his portrayal of the impact of

Ecology and Psychological Vulnerability

Few studies of children at risk for psychopathology founded in parental psychiatric illness have shown the magnitude of impairment reported by Erlenmeyer-Kimling (1984, 1990). These children, largely from African American families living in high-rise slums, are the descendants of an involuntary migration; they also are the survivors of nearly three centuries of poverty, neglect, and abuse by the larger society, including the deliberate effort to destroy family and culture. Sheer economic distress makes a distinctive contribution to the high rates of psychopathology among these children of psychiatrically ill parents. Whereas the association between poverty and psychiatric illness has been well documented (Mishler & Scotch, 1963), there has been less detailed study of the manner in which this negative impact is realized.

Poverty within African American families may have a meaning quite different from that within families from other cultures. Three decades of prejudice and deliberate, externally created disruption of the family have taken a toll on children's coping ability and resilience, thus enhancing their vulnerability from other causes such as increased genetic loading and hazardous living circumstances. The culture of African American poverty, combined with a sense of stigma and stereotyping, has led to the construction of a particular set of meanings that make it difficult to reach out to others and encourage feelings of hopelessness and helplessness. It is significant that, among studies of the adjustment of inner-city African American children at risk for major psychopathology as a consequence of parental psychopathology, the adjustment of children reported in continuing studies of Erlenmeyer-Kimling and her associates (1984, 1990) is markedly more impaired than in any other single study. A large proportion of the families followed by the New York group are from within this urban African American poverty. Our own research group, attempting intervention with similar children at risk at Thresholds in Chicago, finds similar marked psychopathology among children living in the most abject poverty of the high-rise public housing projects.

Although Zubin and Spring's formulation is based on the study of schizophrenia, their model is relevant more generally in the study of developmental psychopathology. Building on models derived from field theory or forces emanating from without that threaten equilibrium, as well as behavioral and learning models, and those emphasizing biological (principally genetic) factors in the origins and course of psychopathology, Zubin and Spring (1977) have proposed that each person "is endowed with a degree

of vulnerability that under suitable circumstances will express itself in an episode of schizophrenic illness" (p. 109). Zubin and Spring carefully differentiate vulnerability from episode. Although some genetic loading for major mental disorders is continually present, realization of an episode of illness depends on a variety of factors, including those in the social and cultural surround.

Over the past decade, there has been much discussion of the nature of life changes and psychological vulnerability (Brown & Harris, 1978; Pearlin, Lieberman, Menaghan, & Mullan, 1981; Pearlin & Schooler, 1978). As Pearlin (1975) has observed, much of this discussion has confused so-called stress factors as being associated with increased vulnerability to personal distress. Within the large literature on stress, some reports (Lazarus & Folkman, 1984; Zautra et al., 1986; Zautra et al., 1988) refer to stress as everyday hassles or role strain and overload, caused by the often overwhelming role portfolio of contemporary life, in which exhausted persons scramble between housekeeping, child care, career, and community (Pearlin, 1983; Pearlin & Lieberman, 1979; Pearlin, Lieberman, Menaghan, & Mullan, 1981). Luthar and Ziegler (1991b) emphasize particularly the contribution of everyday strains and tensions to vulnerability and the emergence of episodes of psychopathology. Daily strains and hassles appear to predict better to the onset of both physical and psychological illness than those more major, eruptive forms of adversity. It may be, however, that major adversity exacerbates exiting role strains and tensions, magnifying the negative impact of these tensions on mental health (Luthar & Zigler, 1991a, 1991b; Zautra et al., 1988). Other reports (Billings & Moos, 1981; Cohen, 1988; Dohrenwend, & Dohrenwend, 1981a, 1981b; Holmes & Rahe, 1967; Paykel, Prusoff, & Uhlenhuth, 1972; Paykel & Uhlenhuth, 1972) refer to stress in terms of life changes, often confusing expectable changes, such as school graduation or retirement, with off-time (generally early in terms of expectable life changes) adverse events, such as death of a parent, adolescent pregnancy, loss of a job, or experience of a life-threatening illness.

Life strain and life changes must be differentiated because they have quite different implications for mental health. A life-course perspective, emphasizing expectable transitions over time, focuses principally on how children, adolescents, and adults adjust to such expectable changes as beginning or completing school, becoming married, or beginning a job. Ironically, more is known about adjustment to these expectable transitions across the second half of life than across the first half of life. Whereas both retirement and on-time widowhood have been studied extensively, (Galatzer-Levy & Cohler, 1993), there has been little study of expectable response to issues like starting school, a parental move, or the birth of a sibling (Dunn, 1988; Hay, 1988). Only a small number of children adjust poorly to these expectable transitions, but this poor adjustment appears to persist over time, and is associated with a more complex pattern of conflicted relationships within the child's family.[21]

---

new ways on burial practices in Javanese society, reintegration of the traditional mode in a brittle manner would not be effective in any circumstance of cultural change. Distorted modes of adaptation, whether in Java, Nova Scotia (Leighton et al., 1963), or the inner city of our own time are equally problematic. Alternatively, modes of adaptation that take value orientation into account reflect culturally constituted modes of adaptation. Particular modes of adaptation may be culturally saturated, such as those shown by recent East Asian voluntary migrations in which an exaggerated achievement ethos is particularly consistent with the cultural orientation of dominant American culture from Plymouth Plantation to the present time (Potter, 1954).

---

[21] Generally, among children and adolescents, the experience of being the recipient of an early-off time adverse event is the principal problem.

The approach first developed by Holmes and Rahe has many inherent problems of method, including cultural bias and failure to distinguish between role strain and both expectable and eruptive life changes, and between adverse and positive changes (Pearlin, 1975, 1980, 1983; Pearlin et al., 1981). Many of these problems are highlighted in studies of children and adolescents, but the changes viewed by children as most adverse generally focus on separation and loss—death of a parent or sibling, death of a pet, or parental marital conflict and separation. These losses represent unexpected and adverse life changes with immediate and obvious implications for mental health.

Garmezy (1983, 1986) reports few studies of children's response to bereavement, and even fewer studies using a systematic design such as that of Arthur and Kemme (1964), who showed a marked relationship between early parental death and subsequent offspring adjustment among children referred to a child guidance clinic. Follow-up studies show a positive association between early off-time parental death and subsequent adult psychiatric disorder, particularly depression and enhanced mood variation (Roy, 1985; Tennant et al., 1982). Examining this relationship separately for men and for women, McLeod (1991) has shown that this relationship is much more significant among women than among men.

Studies of early parental loss and adult mood confirm clinical case reports (Altschul & Pollock, 1988), of adults who lost parents through death in childhood or adolescence. Garmezy questions the significance of findings based nonclinical study; his review of findings from systematic epidemiological comparative study of children of bereaved surviving spouses and a community comparison group (Van Eerdewegh, Bieri, Parilla, & Clayton, 1982) showed that dramatic symptoms of depression following parental death had largely disappeared by the end of the first year of bereavement. However, this epidemiological study was based entirely on parental reports of offspring adjustment, with several children within a family interviewed, so that the children in these families were not statistically independent.[22]

Extent of vulnerability determines the ease with which life changes, particularly those that are early off-time and adverse (e.g., teenage pregnancy, death of spouse in early to mid-adulthood, death of offspring), will culminate in an episode of major psychiatric illness (Pearlin, 1980). Extending the concept of adversity and life changes, Coddington (1972a, 1972b), Garmezy and Rutter (1985), Garmezy and Tellegen (1984), and Yeaworth, York, Hussey, Ingle, and Goodwin (1980), have modified Holmes and Rahe's (1967) life-changes scale for use with children. This modification of the scale includes items more relevant for the lives of children than adults.

[22] Continuing study of a very large number of children referred to the Barr-Harris Clinic of the Institute for Psychoanalysis in Chicago for a consultation also supports the Arthur and Kemme findings. Most of the children in this group were not referred by the school but were seen at the request of the surviving parent, generally in the absence of particular psychiatric symptoms among the children, with the goal of preventing possible distress. Although this group of children could not be considered to be a clinic sample, rates of personal distress among children and adolescents, including both depression and such depressive equivalents as substance abuse and conflict with siblings were marked.

Garmezy (1974) has developed a model of adversity and response that was first applied to the study of children at risk for psychopathology, focusing largely on the impact of parental (maternal) psychiatric illness as an eruptive life change demanding particular adaptation. Subsequently, this model was extended in the Minnesota Competence Project to include such continuing adversity as economic disadvantage. Zubin and Spring (1977) have suggested that an episode of psychiatric disorder occurs when the threat from an adverse, generally eruptive, off-time life change exceeds the person's capacity to adjust to this change in the context of enhanced genetic loading for the particular disorder. Zubin and Spring (1977) do not consider the meaning of particular episodes of psychiatric illness for particular lives; over time, the experience of psychiatric disorder, no matter how time limited, markedly changes experience of self, leading to lowered self-regard and personal confidence. The experience of being labeled as a psychiatric patient, makes it further difficult to overcome the impact of an episode (Scheff, 1966).

Further, at least in the case of schizophrenia, there may be several subtypes of the illness, differentiated not only in terms of symptoms, but also in terms of the course of the illness and response to intervention (Marcus, Auerbach, Wilkinson, & Burack, 1981). A first episode may enhance the probability of subsequent episodes in response to adversity: once a pathway to the expression of personal distress has been found, its use may become increasingly frequent over time. Bleuler's (1911/1950) concept of dementia praecox reflects several of the life-course pathways into personal distress that may reflect the reality for at least some persons presenting with a schizophrenic illness. This first episode is but the initial stage in a process that sooner or later ends with dementia if the patient should live on into old age. Schizophrenia is perhaps best thought of in its original terms as the "group of schizophrenias," with multiple forms of course and outcomes possible, although not yet predictable at this stage in the study of schizophrenia and life course.

Significant in Zubin and Spring's formulation is the realization that particular study of the life history of each patient is critical in understanding illness origin and course. Beck and Worthen (1972) have shown that observed life changes, idiosyncratic or unique to a particular life history, may contribute to illness episodes. Particular patient accounts of life changes significant in leading to a schizophrenic episode were not those rated as adverse on the basis of scales such as those of Holmes and Rahe (1967). Rather, these changes included subjectively significant disappointments and experiences that would not appear on lists of commonly rated adverse changes. The individual's experience of the extent to which life changes are adverse is the critical factor determining the impact of life changes on adjustment. Nicholson and Neufeld (1989, 1992) note further that the whole issue of the nature and timing of events assumed to be related to episodes of

---

Consultation with area elementary and high schools further confirms systematic clinic surveys and interviews with the children: The impact of early off-time parental death is devastating over periods of many years and predisposes children and adolescents to enhanced vulnerability for subsequent psychopathology.

psychiatric illness must be more carefully studied. Not only are there questions regarding the causal nature of adverse life changes for episodes of illness (Brown, Harris, & Peto, 1973), but also questions have been raised regarding the relative significance of major adversity as contrasted with day-to-day problems in determining present adjustment (Zautra et al., 1988).

In spite of the wide recognition that illness and contributing factors are closely interrelated, there has been little detailed study of the necessary reciprocal relationship between adversity and episode (Nicholson & Neufeld, 1992). Finally, as Beck and Worthen (1972) and Nicholson and Neufeld (1989, 1992) have shown, the particular manner in which persons interpret everyday problems may be as critical as the problems themselves. Interpretive modes of study (Bohman et al., 1991; Rabinow & Sullivan, 1979) must necessarily supplement more checklist measures (Holmes & Rahe, 1967; Paykel et al., 1972) in understanding the relationship between life stress and emergence of psychiatric symptoms. Narrative perspectives are necessary to understand the complex interplay between temperament; particular life circumstances associated with birth, family life, and personality development; and response to major developmental tasks (e.g., leaving school and entering the adult world), together with unexpected misfortune and management of strains or hassles associated with characteristic adult roles including work, marriage, and parenthood. All these factors are assumed to be formative in determining adult adjustment.

It is also necessary to study the life history of vulnerability and response more carefully over many years (Clausen, 1985; Cohler & Ferrono, 1987). Nicholson and Neufeld (1992) note that discrete time periods dichotomize what is essentially a continuous process. Considered together with more detailed study of what constitutes major misfortune occurring within lives over time, and everyday strain within particular cultures, this more extended study will add to our understanding of the factors meaningfully associated with breakdown and recovery from episodes of psychiatric distress. Further, greater attention must be paid to how these episodes are related to later life outcome. At least within our own culture, the side effects of antipsychotic medication lead to those telltale signs that may stigmatize recovering psychiatric patients and make it difficult to find work or to establish intimate ties. Considered together with the residual impact of negative symptoms such as lethargy (Andreasen, 1990), it is not surprising to learn that recovery from schizophrenia is so difficult to realize.

Zubin and his colleagues (Zubin, 1978; Zubin, Magaziner, & Steinhauer, 1983; Zubin & Spring, 1977; Zubin & Steinhauer, 1981), as well as Goldstein (1987), and Mirsky and Duncan (1986) have enhanced understanding of the interplay of developmentally determined vulnerability and eruptive, generally adverse life changes that increase the chances for an episode of major psychiatric illness.[23] Nicholson and Neufeld (1989, 1991)

have extended this perspective in their dynamic vulnerability formulation, which places additional emphasis on vulnerability, episode, course of illness, and available coping techniques in portraying the impact of these factors on first and subsequent episodes. Consistent with detailed discussion of coping processes reported by Folkman and Lazarus (1980), Lazarus and Folkman (1984), Pearlin and Schooler (1978), and Stone, Helder, and Schneider (1988), Nicholson and Neufeld (1992) emphasize on magnitude of impairment in the capacity for cognitive appraisal as a factor associated with onset of both initial and later episode. Maintaining that enough is presently known to construct a causal model of both initial and subsequent episodes, Nicholson and Neufeld present a model suitable for study using statistical procedures such as Jureskog's structural equation approach (LISREL).

Increased genetic diathesis for psychopathology, exacerbated by intrauterine and birth events, may lead to cognitive deficits in information processing as well as impairment in sensorimotor performance and associated "pandysmaturation" or marked developmental deviation (Fish, 1977, 1984, 1987). The significance of these cognitive deficits in determining vulnerability to an episode of major psychiatric illness is enhanced by pervasive family conflict and disruption in the continuity of child care, together with eruptive, generally adverse, life changes, and conflict in cultural or value orientation. This enhanced vulnerability compounds problems in adjusting to expectable role transitions and the increased role strain characteristic even for children and adolescents in urban industrial society (Pearlin, 1975, 1980, 1983; Pearlin & Schooler, 1978).[24]

---

[23] Goldstein (1987) includes family interactional process among risk factors associated with increased vulnerability. Initially, so-called transactional thought disorder or communication deviance (Goldstein, 1987; Lidz et al., 1965; Miklowitz, Goldstein, & Falloon, 1983; Wynne, 1981; Wynne et al., 1977) was assumed as predisposing to offspring illness through induction into deviant modes of thought and communication. Models of socialization assuming that transactions between parents and offspring involve both forward and backward socialization (Cook & Cohler, 1986) call such forward socialization models into question. More recent work on communication process within the family, particularly those on the role of parental hostility and criticism ("expressed-emotion" or EE), still assume forward socialization process as instrumental in rehospitalization, although now focused not on the origin of the illness but on additional episodes.

Living with a schizophrenic offspring is a difficult and burdensome process; American culture, with its stress on self-reliance and autonomy, fosters particular conflict regarding caregiving within the family generally, and particular conflict within the family of adulthood, whether the issue is children caring for troubled or infirm older parents or parents caring for troubled adult children (Cohler et al., 1989; Cohler, Pickett & Cook, 1991). It is important to understand family process in a cultural context (Kleinmann, 1988) and, as already noted, to view family interactional processes from a cultural perspective. Family communication processes may not be similar to other aspects of vulnerability in the stress-diathesis or risk-vulnerability model proposed by Zubin and his associates.

[24] Cognitive deficits and other developmentally determined limitations in coping ability are intertwined with personal misfortune to a varying extent in contributing to illness episodes. It is important to recognize that even within particular modes of psychopathology such as schizophrenia, there may be a number of subtypes (Marcus et al., 1981). An overall term such as schizophrenia does not do justice either to the pathways associated with the origins of the illness or its subsequent course.

The relevance of mode of subsistence and associated socialization processes for study of psychopathology might at first appear moot; the appearance of major psychopathology does not appear to vary by culture. Further, since children within particular cohorts and cultures experience similar socialization, the vulnerability-risk-resilience approach would seem to hold socialization as a constant. However, variation within culture is also significant, as is the intertwined impact of both culture and long-standing family psychopathology on socialization practices. For example, B. Whiting (1980) has shown the significance of setting as a determinant of socialization in a manner that extends Barker and Wright's (1951, 1955) earlier studies of community ecology and behavior settings: Children are expected to act differently in the classroom and at home.

Children growing up in suburban homes, with a room of their own, learn quite different modes of getting along with both children and adults than children who sleep in a common area with several other siblings and adults. The child of a single parent with a psychiatric disorder, living in the midst of the social disorganization characteristic of urban high-rise slums, suffers greater adversity than an equally at-risk child who lives in a single-family house in a small southern community. The at-risk child living in a climate that permits outside play most of the year—able to come and go without the terrifying dangers posed by gangs of the urban high-rise slums—has greater ease in leaving the house and escaping the continuing impact of parental psychiatric distress. There are also greater opportunities for continuing contact with family and neighbors who will take an interest in the child's development. Further, parents and other family members who live in single-family homes have an easier time supervising their children than caregivers of children living in a high-risk slum.

Culture, Psychological Vulnerability, and Resilience

Culture is significant for individual adjustment precisely because shared symbolic representations of self and others provide a template for wish, sentiment, and action. The significance of culture is intensified within polyethnic states that comprise a number of different groups with particular traditions, further shaped by migration and adaptation to a society in which primary-group or face-to-face relations at home are separated from secondary-group relations at school or at work (Barth, 1969; Wirth, 1928). Ethnicity is critical as a determinant of personal adjustment. The particular symbolic system or cultural model characteristic of a particular ethnic group determines modes of thought and action that may prove disruptive of personal adjustment.

This perspective regarding ethnicity as cultural model is explicitly portrayed by Ogbu (1981, 1990a, 1990b) in his discussion of the problems posed for African American children struggling with issues of literacy in a culture whose demands are different from those of the primary group culture of early childhood. Mismatch between the cultural model of early childhood and that of the larger society leads to conflict between these cultural models. Modes of adjustment that are effective on the streets of the inner city may not be effective when employed at school or in the larger community; as Ogbu suggests, the concept of competence must be understood within the context of a particular ethnic group. Discussing the study of competence among disadvantaged children,

Garmezy and Masten (1986) have also noted the importance of including "street-smarts" as a factor in understanding competence, but lament that this factor is difficult to study using the traditional approaches of developmental psychology.

Recognition that the concept of competence is culturally defined, with attributes contributing to success within one ethnic group or culture less appreciated within another, suggests an important source of collaboration between anthropology, relying on ethnographic approaches, and developmental psychopathology, relying on observation and psychometric methods. The same perspective underlies much of the study of ethnicity, from F. Kluckhohn and Strodtbeck's (1961) study in the American Southwest to studies of African and New Guinea cultures reported by Barth (1969, 1981, 1987), Bohannan (1957), Collomb and Valantin (1970), Evans-Pritchard (1937, 1940), and Turner (1967). Spiegel (1971) has documented the significance of this perspective for mental health in his reports regarding culture and psychopathology within Italian-American families. Although some capacity for realizing expectable, socially sanctioned skills is essential for secondary group relations (e.g., in school or workplace), considerable cultural variation in modes of understanding self and others contribute to this strength in adapting to the demands of the larger society. Covello (1944/1972) and Barnes (1980) have reported similar issues in the assimilation of immigrant children into a common school system, documenting the contradictory pressures posed for children who speak different languages at home and at school, and who have quite different experiences of the goals and expectations of parents and teachers.

Because American culture views the process of development as both linear and cumulative (Kluckhohn & Strodtbeck, 1961; Spiegel, 1971), it may be assumed that children who are subject to disadvantage and discontinuity in child care also experience deficits in managing self-esteem, conflict, and lack of satisfaction from relations with family and friends, and in realizing socially recognized achievement. As a group, however, children having the adversity of a parent with a history of major psychiatric illness—who might be expected to show greater psychopathology than counterparts from psychologically well families—show little later impact on their own adjustment. These children make maximum use of support and help offered by relatives, teachers, and other caring adults, and are able to use their adversity as inspiration to overcome problems evoked by family conflict and distress. Our own studies show that these children of parents with major psychopathology, who are at increased risk and psychologically more vulnerable as a consequence of genetic endowment and life experience, are reported by teachers to show unusual persistence in school and are especially adept in enlisting the teacher's help with their work.

Developmental Psychopathology, Culture, and Study of Resilience

Developmental psychopathology provides an important perspective on risk factors associated with psychological distress; factors that are most significant in contributing to psychological symptoms at one point in the life cycle may not be equally responsible for the emergence of psychological symptoms at some later point (Sroufe & Rutter, 1984). The translation of vulnerability into psychological distress depends on the combination of innate factors and life circumstances that are beyond the capacity to cope with the distress.

Following more than a decade of study of children experiencing adversities such as parental illness and poverty, Garmezy and his colleagues (Garmezy, 1985a, 1985b; Garmezy & Masten, 1986; Garmezy, Masten, Nordstrom, & Ferrarese, 1979; Masten, 1985, 1989; Masten & Garmezy, 1985; Masten, Morison, Pellegrini, & Tellegen, 1990), Rutter (1987, 1990), and Werner and her colleagues (Werner, 1990; Werner & Smith, 1992) summarize findings from their longitudinal studies regarding protective factors that may reduce the noxious impact of personal, family, and collective misfortune. Garmezy's (1986) review, based on his study of poverty, urban conflict, and parental psychiatric illness, supports Rutter's conclusions. He concludes that the child's personality, social intelligence, and temperament; a supportive family socioemotional climate; and community support for nascent coping efforts, all are critical in fostering resilience. Based on studies of psychiatrically ill mothers living in poverty and in working-class neighborhoods, Cohler and his colleagues (Kauffman, Grunebaum, Cohler, & Gamer, 1979; Musick, Stott, Spencer, Goldman, & Cohler, 1987; Strom, 1992) have concluded that the presence of a single concerned and caring adult may do much to offset the impact of misfortune in the lives of young children. Similar conclusions have been suggested in the psychoanalytic literature by Kohut (1979), discussing the resilience of a young man raised in a family characterized by marital conflict and parental emotional withdrawal.

Reviewing the concept of resilience from the perspective of the developing child, Werner (1990) notes that the infant and young child who is attractive to others—responsive and engaging—can elicit increased concern and help from others that, in turn, fosters enhanced resilience. This perspective suggests the complex interplay between children as producers of their own development (Lamb, 1978; Lerner & Busch-Rossnagel, 1981; Lerner & Spanier, 1978), and the influences of family and community. In one of the few follow-through studies to adulthood of children at risk for major psychopathology, resulting from temperamental characteristics and/or socially disorganized family circumstances, Emily Werner and her colleagues have reported findings from a large group of children in Hawaii (Werner, 1985, 1989, 1990; Werner, Bierman, & French, 1971; Werner & Smith, 1977, 1982, 1992). This study involved a group of nearly 4,000 pregnancies constituting two separate birth cohorts over the years 1955 and 1956–1957 on the island of Kauai in Hawaii, from pregnancy and birth to adulthood. The majority of children were from very poor Oriental or Polynesian families working as migrant laborer families. Beginning with nearly 1,700 infants evaluated at birth, the 1955 birth cohort was followed up at 2 years and 10 years of age, and, for more than a third of the initial group, successively through high school and into adulthood.

Earlier reports from the study had documented the extent of problems characteristic of this unique cohort. Intertwined biological and psychosocial vulnerability had taken its toll on these children. Prenatal damage and low birth weight were among the factors contributing to developmental delay, intellectual deficit,

and poor social skills among nearly a fifth of this group during the first decade of life. The impact of these biological factors was greatest among those children living in the most abject poverty. During adolescence, more than 15% of the group was involved in delinquency or crime, while more than 10% had required psychiatric services. Across the first two decades of life, more than a third of the group had shown learning or behavior problems, and while 20% had been involved with the state's legal or mental health systems. Early life misfortune continued to have a negative impact on the lives of this group of young people followed into adulthood (representing more than four-fifths of the original cohorts) (Werner, 1989). Close birth spacing of brothers and sisters, family conflict, father absence, and disruptions of parenting were associated with higher rates of criminal activity and marital and parental irresponsibility among men, and early off-time parenthood and parenting problems among women.

Whereas Werner and her colleagues had noted limitations in coping among the most impoverished young people in their earlier work, their more recent work (Werner, 1989, 1990; Werner & Smith, 1982) has particularly focused on the issues of resilience and coping in a group of children showing personal and social competence into adulthood even though exposed to multiple risk factors of poverty and family dysfunction during infancy and childhood (Werner, 1990; Werner & Smith, 1982). These more resilient adults began life as particularly responsive infants who elicited great warmth from their caretakers. Particularly resilient men, followed back to infancy, were more often the firstborn and were able to obtain parental affection. These men were also characterized during childhood as showing vigor and energy in developmental testing sessions, and they were especially responsive to others. Cheerful, self-confident, and independent toddlers were less likely to show later learning and behavioral problems than less responsive and engaging infants.

Across middle childhood, these children rated as more resilient in infancy showed continued positive adjustment, particularly in school, even when confronted by poverty and family disruption. They were better able to talk about themselves than peers earlier rated as less robust and vigorous, and to be more effective in solving problems in the psychological testing situation. These children were less conventional in their social views and less stereotyped in their conceptions of themselves as boys and girls than their less resilient counterparts. They showed a sense of effectance, expressed confidence in their ability to overcome problems, and expressed positive self-regard. More resilient girls remained sociable in the classroom and with friends, and were also more independent than their equally vulnerable but less resilient counterparts.

Continued resilience was less common among adolescents than among younger children. Further, the finding regarding gender and mental health, common in so many mental health studies (Weissman & Klerman, 1977) was repeated in this longitudinal work as well: across the first decade of life, boys were more at risk than girls for personal distress and school problems; at adolescence, however, this trend was reversed, with girls becoming more at risk than boys for personal distress. Adolescents in the Hawaii study who were less likely to be involved with the criminal justice or mental health systems were more likely to live in multigeneration households that provided greater continuity in caretaking. Caretaking responsibilities by girls fostered a sense of enhanced competence, whereas the most competent boys were most often firstborn and had less competition for parental attention during the early years of life. More competent adolescents had increased emphasis on personal control and responsibility and a more positive self-concept; they were more conscientious and achievement oriented than their less resilient counterparts.

Werner (1990) has emphasized the importance of persistence, a more reflective cognitive style, open and nonstereotyped responses to others, a variety of interests and hobbies, and both sociability and increased capacity for self-solace as factors contributing to resilience in middle childhood. Concern with achievement, social maturity, and sociability, together with firm determination to overcome adversity, and belief in the ability to succeed were also characteristic of resilient adolescents in the Hawaii study (Werner, 1990; Werner & Smith, 1992). Overall, increased interest in other people and the capacity to elicit the interest of others helped maintain resilience across the first two decades of life in this study.

Following up their resilient and vulnerable high-risk children into their early 30s, Werner and Smith (1992) have reported that time may heal many of the psychological wounds associated with early childhood risk due to such earlier adversity as difficulties in the child's birth, and growing up in families marked by poverty and discord. For example, even among those showing mental health problems across the teenage years, the majority had shown a good recovery by their early 30s. The impact of early biological insult as a factor shaping present adjustment had largely diminished by young adulthood, although a very small number of the most troubled adults had childhood histories characterized by rather marked perinatal insults with evidence of neurological damage. Perinatal trauma emerged as a significant factor in accounting for later distress only among those who had suffered neurological damage as a consequence of difficulties with labor and delivery. Protective factors leading to successful outcomes in adulthood included at least average intelligence, personal attractiveness and vitality noted during infancy, good physical health, positive relations with parents and extended family members, and community supports through school and church. Women initially at risk in childhood appeared better able than their male counterparts to make use of these resources and to remain resilient through their early 30s. Although the first decade of life had favored the high-risk girls, the second decade of life had favored the boys.

By the third decade of life, women were once again favored as better able to adjust to life circumstances than masculine counterparts. Considering the relationship between infant status and adult outcomes, the children most likely to have poor mental health outcomes in adulthood were boys with the following characteristics: unmarried mothers, prolonged disruptions in receipt of care, birth of a sibling while still a toddler, physically less robust health, and a continuing history of family discord and inability to achieve in school. It was somewhat easier for Werner and Smith (1992) to identify early childhood factors associated with this satisfactory adult outcome at age 32 among women than among men. Events during childhood rather than

the original high-risk infant status seemed most significant among women, particularly family discord and disruption due to parental death or family conflict. Problems in the adolescent years, such as financial difficulties or early off-time marriage and pregnancy, as well as increased conflict with peers, all predicted to more adverse mental health outcomes during early adulthood. Boys experiencing marked perinatal insult, conditions of marked poverty, and less robust physical condition during early childhood appeared particularly at risk for subsequent adult psychiatric distress.

Rutter (1979b, 1981/1983) has contrasted the adjustment of children living on the Isle of Wight with children living in an impoverished London housing project. These findings show that marital conflict, poverty, poor living conditions, parental personal disorganization, and failure of the continuity of child care, particularly characteristic of the London setting, were primary factors associated with poor child mental health outcomes. On the other hand, a supportive home and school environment fostered personal resilience, even when the family lived in impoverished circumstances. Further consistent with this perspective, Milgram and Palti (1993) report that more psychologically resilient, high-achieving boys, from culturally disadvantaged families living in Israel were more self-confident and, in particular, were better able than their less resilient counterparts to elicit the interest of others in them. These more successful boys received greater attention, made more friends, and were more helpful and sociable than their lesser achieving counterparts from similarly impoverished and disorganized circumstances.

From initial concern with such details of child care as breast versus bottle feeding (Sears, Maccoby, & Levin, 1957) to more recent emphasis on living with parents over longer periods of time (Winnicott, 1960) as the "anlage" of predisposing factor to regularized patterns of interaction leading to the child's expectations for self and others (Stern, 1985), studies of caregiving have shown the importance of parent-child relations to vulnerability (Garmezy, 1985a, 1985b; Rutter, 1972/1981, 1979a, 1987; Stern, 1984, 1985, 1989; Werner, 1990). However, as Minturn and Lambert (1964) have shown, emphasis on parental psychological attributes as a determinant of subsequent adjustment or mental health is unique to our own culture. This emphasis places a particular burden and marked strain on parents who feel that each miscalculation will adversely and permanently affect the child's development of coping ability. As parents attempt to live up to this ideal of child care, they may actually disturb the benign environment needed for optimal psychological development.

Resilience and the Life Course

Anthony (1987b) has cautioned that over the course of life there may be a shift in the direction of either enhanced resilience or enhanced vulnerability. Consistent with Anthony's observations, Gottesman and Shields (1982) have argued that temperamental factors (variation in genetic loading for psychopathology) leads to lifelong risk; there is little evidence that this risk is greater in childhood than later in life, or that protective factors in childhood can mitigate against the impact of adversity that is experienced as particularly overwhelming at some subsequent point in life. Further, as Murphy and Moriarty's (1976) longitudinal reports on mastery have suggested, there is some fluctuation in resilience over the short term. For example, children use the experience of illness in quite different ways: Over the short term, serious illness may lead to increased vulnerability to personal distress, whereas over the longer term, conquered illness becomes part of a life story or personal narrative of overcoming misfortune that fosters enhanced resilience (Cohler, 1991b).

Although Rutter (1985) and Anthony (1987) favor the concept of a continuum of vulnerability-invulnerability, problems arise in understanding what Anthony refers to as the "invulnerables" (Garmezy, 1974; Garmezy & Nuechterlein, 1972).[25] It is unlikely that anyone is so well steeled against misfortune as to be protected from all adversity. Rather, consistent with Murphy and

---

[25] Following Garmezy (1971, 1974), Anthony (1974, 1987a) has portrayed the "syndrome" of the psychologically invulnerable child. Anthony reviews Segal and Yahraes's (1978) work on resilience as further support for this concept of invulnerability. Garmezy (1974) had originally distinguished between "vulnerables" and "invulnerables" in terms of children thought to have a heightened predisposition to psychopathology by virtue of personality, temperament, or life circumstances, but who also showed protective factors mitigating against emergence of the disease process. Subsequently, both his work and that of Michael Rutter (1981/1983, 1985, 1987) has focused more generally on the question of the emergence of competence in children, following the model initially portrayed by R. W. White (1959, 1960, 1963, 1974, 1979). Enhanced resilience is associated with the following characteristics: capacity to deploy attention and to sustain attention through concentration; effectiveness in work, play, and intimate relationships; optimism and positive self-esteem; self-motivated goals and ability to follow through in efforts to attain these goals; and control of wishes and flexible and creative thought.

Sroufe and Rutter (1984) note further that resilience must also be portrayed in developmental terms, focusing on issues particularly salient for the child or adult at any one point across the course of life. Anthony (1974, 1987a) has also adopted the concept of competence in efforts to evaluate degree of vulnerability and resilience, carefully differentiating between two types of invulnerables: the true heroes—self-effacing and robust, competent and generous—and those who have overcome earlier adversity, adopting an optimistic attitude as the consequence of some charismatic or inspirational experience. "Pseudoinvulnerable" persons are self-absorbed and isolated from others, and are unable to form close relationships. Such persons were truly the "apple of their mother's eye," but they are also self-centered. Risk-taking pseudoheros, who are largely foolish, should not be included within the group of true invulnerables.

It may be questioned whether the true hero portrayed by Anthony ever existed. Garmezy questions the value of concepts such as invulnerability, or "super-kids," as used by Kauffman et al. (1979). Consistent with the point of view systematized by Zubin and Spring (1977), Garmezy observed that few persons are absolutely invulnerable in the sense of the enduring psychological protection suggested by Anthony. Garmezy prefers instead the concept of stress-resistant as a descriptive term. The problem with this term is that the concept of stress has such surplus meaning that it is important to define the intended meaning precisely, apart from role strain or adverse life changes. The somewhat more awkward term "relatively resilient when confronted by adversity" more completely captures the phenomenon, recognizing that even resilience is relative and that, for each of us, some adverse life-changes so tax the capacity to cope with adversity that we succumb to an episode of illness (Neufield & Mothersill, 1980).

Moriarty's (1976) observation, and Zubin and Spring's (1977) formulation, we all have a "checkerboard of strengths and weaknesses" leading to relative degrees of resilience across particular situations. Rutter (1979b) has suggested that focus on psychopathology has detracted from concern with characteristic adjustment or positive mental health in terms of expectable adjustment among persons confronted by adversity (Jahoda, 1958; Offer & Sabshin, 1974). As already noted, Beck and Worthen (1972) report that the particular forms of adversity leading prospective schizophrenic patients to express positive signs of illness were highly idiosyncratic and meaningful only within the context of a particular patient's life story. Certain forms of adversity, such as the death of a parent, spouse, or child, represent universal threats to present adjustment. Even the most seriously troubled persons seem to respond more effectively to these major forms of adversity than to less significant losses and disappointments.

Personally troublesome events in life are those experienced as uniquely adverse, even though these events may not be represented on checklists of positive and adverse life changes. Indeed, G. Brown and Birley (1968) found little evidence that misfortune itself induced episodes of psychiatric illness. The role of life changes in producing episodes is complex and intertwined—meanings are attributed to these changes in their cultural or symbolic context as well as in the context of the life history. However, findings from a number of studies (Clarke & Clarke, 1976; Kagan, 1980, 1984; Kagan et al., 1979) suggest that persons may be inherently more resilient to the impact of adversity than has been suggested by socialization theories, including social learning theory and earlier psychoanalytic formulations of development. Reviewing the biographies of several hundred of the most distinguished men and women of the past century, V. Goertzel and M. G. Goertzel (1962) found marked early childhood deprivation and family conflict to be the rule rather than the exception.

Culture, Defense, and Coping

In ways still not well understood, early privation may serve as a stimulus for determination to overcome adversity. Within our own culture, however, enhanced resilience may come at the price of enhanced self-preoccupation (Anthony, 1987a; Kohut, 1977). Particularly among persons who have overcome early life economic disadvantage, there may be an attitude of disdain for those who have been less fortunate, and the attribution that continued misfortune reflects individual moral failing. These persons correspond in some way to Anthony's (1987a) "sociopathic" pseudoinvulnerable adult. Enhanced focus on personal attainments at the expense of concern with the welfare of others is an often observed outcome of overcoming early adversity. Further, it is still not clear whether the early ability to conquer adversity is maintained across the life span, or what personal costs accompany enhanced resilience in response to adversity. In a follow-up of some children, now adults, studied in the pioneering Joint Admission intervention project of parents with major psychiatric illness (Grunebaum, Weiss, Cohler, Hartman, & Gallant, 1975/1982), the subjects show career success but greater difficulty maintaining intimate relationships.

Two major contributions, Robert White's (1959, 1963, 1979) formulation of the concept of effectance or competence, and the

pioneering studies of coping by Lois Barclay Murphy and her associates (Murphy, 1962, 1974; Murphy & Moriarty, 1976), were followed by more systematic study of variation in coping in early childhood (Dibble & Cohen, 1974; Earls, Beardslee, & Garrison, 1987; White, 1978; White, Kaban, & Attanucci, 1979; White & J. Watts, 1973). Murphy and her associates have explored the manner in which children confront novel and challenging situations (e.g., a birthday party or mastering fear of a thunderstorm) and struggle to overcome adversity (e.g., chronic and debilitating illness, or a scary accident). Murphy and her associates were principally concerned with the child's efforts to deal with environmental pressures requiring intentional effort to overcome obstacles. Significantly, the same adaptive processes that may be effective at one point may not be successful at another.

In her original formulation of means of personal protection against the vicissitudes of psychological conflict, Anna Freud (1936/1966) was emphatic that the defense mechanisms that she portrayed—denial, hysterical, and obsessional defenses—could not be neatly portrayed in any straightforward genetic-developmental order. From this first, formative, monograph, through her later (1965) study of normality and psychopathology in childhood as well as Sandler's (1985) report of conversations with Anna Freud regarding the process of ego and defense (Sandler & A. Freud, 1985), she repeatedly emphasized the danger of the "genetic fallacy" (Hartmann, 1939/1958) of assuming a linear relationship between original conflict situations and later defensive postures.

The question to be resolved through both psychoanalytic and observational-developmental study concerns the relationship between original conflict in personality development and later mode of adaptation. Swanson (1961) has also emphasized the problems posed by assuming a relationship between the epigenetic phase of personality development (Abraham, 1924/1953; Erikson, 1950/1963), and particular, preferred modes of defense in adulthood. Miss Freud has observed that the healthy person uses a variety of defenses from all presumed levels of personality development; there is little evidence for assuming a hierarchy of defenses ordered in any regular, developmental sequence. At the same time, following S. Freud (1926), A. Freud, Miller and Swanson (1960), Vaillant (1971, 1976, 1977), and Vaillant and Milofsky (1980) all have shown, defenses may be ordered in terms of the extent to which they are complex, reality adaptive, and sophisticated.

Haan and her associates (Haan, 1977; Kroeber, 1963) have argued that defense against psychological conflict should be considered as a separate process rather than as a mode of defense, in the terms originally portrayed by A. Freud. Kroeber has provided detailed descriptions of the defensive and coping responses attached to each of the so-called ego functions. For example, intellectualization, used as a defense against the awareness of instinctual conflict, should not be considered as functioning in the same manner as intellectual activity, or the satisfaction derived from productive intellectual activity such as studying or writing. Repression as a means of impulse control should be differentiated from suppression, viewed as a means of appropriately managing wish, action, and sentiment.

Using Rorschach and MMPI indexes akin to those originally developed by Schafer (1954) for the defenses, Kroeber argued that for each of the standard defenses, there was a coping alternative.

For example, alert concern with the world about one was seen as the coping alternative to projection as a psychological defense. Haan (1977, 1982) has developed paper-and-pencil test scales (MMPI) for these constructs that are akin to those developed by Kroeber as an alternative to the original focus on defense against conflict.

Psychological Resilience, Mastery, and American Culture

Much of the concern in Haan and Kroeber's reformulation of the concept of defense was to emphasize issues of adaptation and mastery as initially formulated in psychoanalysis by Nunberg (1931, 1932/1965) and Hartmann (1939/1958). Consistent with R. W. White's (1959) concept of effectance as an intrinsic, growth-promoting activity, studies of the development of mastery in childhood by Murphy and her colleagues (Murphy, 1962, 1987; Murphy & Moriarty, 1976), support Kroeber's (1963) theoretical formulation of coping as apart from defense or psychological protection against psychological distress. Unless interfered with, children and adults seek growth-promoting activity. Consistent with the optimistic and pragmatic emphasis characteristic of American psychology, intervention is presumed to be devoted to removing obstacles to continued forward psychological growth. Coping reflects a struggle toward mastery of skills in which the process of mastery is more important than any particular outcome (Murphy, 1960a, 1960b, 1970, 1974).

This view of mastery is consistent with American emphasis on achievement and in proving one's worth: Life is a challenge, and particular activities are devoted to mastering challenges for their own sake. Murphy (1962) observes that coping involves emphasis on the "pioneer spirit." Kagan (1980) and Murphy and Moriarty (1976) emphasize the robust nature of psychological development, recognition of the capacity for self-repair, and the vitality of mastery processes that may be observed across the first decades of life. Emphasis is on normalcy, adjustment, and drive to integration within a life characterized by personal commitment and self-rewarding activity. The social-psychological portrait of American character provided by D. Riesman, Glazer, and Denny (1950) the community interview studies of Fischer and Fischer (1963), Sears et al. (1957), and Winterbottom (1958), and the detailed observational studies of American children in Little League games (Fine, 1987) have made clear that the primary emphasis on competence within American culture involves rugged self-reliance and enjoyment of mastery as an intrinsic activity (Felsman & Vaillant, 1987). The 19th-century series of novels focusing on Heratio Alger's hero "Ragged Dick" is precisely about the pleasure that comes from self-rewarding, effectance activity. Dick attains success sheerly because of the pleasure that this activity provides.

Contemporary American culture has inherited an emphasis on rugged individualism that was shaped by the 17th-century northeastern American colonial experience. American culture might be quite different today if the founding of the American commonwealth had proceeded from the more traditional and hierarchical emphasis of Jamestown instead of from the innovative and individualistic emphasis of the Plymouth plantation, which was committed to hard work as evidence of election and the enhanced glory of God. The social theorist Max Weber (1904–1905), portrayed the impact of Protestant thought on character. He noted the impact of the changed relationship of God and man with the removal of the priest as mediator. With good works no longer available to assure a sense of salvation, the problem of conviction of salvation loomed large in the Reformation. Calvinist doctrines regarding predestination placed a demand for certainty of election through demonstrated success in this world, leading to a this-worldly asceticism that replaced the other-worldly asceticism of the Catholic monastery. The experience of this worldly success, although in no way altering predetermined election, contributed to the increased conviction of election.

The New England Puritan experience was very much the heir of these Calvinist doctrines and fostered an ethos that both encouraged innovation and exploitation of the vast wilderness of the American continent. Success in controlling the environment, in turning forest into farm, and in realizing success due to individual initiative, contrasts markedly with concepts of interdependency characteristic of the world's cultures. Emphasis on "making it" on one's own, apart from family and community, provided particular certainty regarding the possibility of election. Individual competence and personal skills were featured as dramatic evidence of success consistent with the reality of election (Greven, 1977). Sayings such as "the Lord helps those who help themselves" became 19th-century success mottos that were demonstrated through novels regarding success and manuals guiding individual competence (Cawelti, 1965).

Over time, the religious foundation underlying individual attainment was replaced by an ethos fostering individual attainment and effort that was intrinsically self-rewarding. Much of this ethos is portrayed in Benjamin Franklin's biography (incorrectly viewed by Weber, 1904–05, as the ideal type of the Protestant ethos). Franklin advocates systematic accumulation of wealth through prudent, innovative, calculated efforts. Little possibility is provided for collective support fostering such attainment. The ideal successful American regards adversity as a challenge to be overcome through individual initiative, bravery, and an undaunted spirit (Cawelti, 1965). The capacity to rely on others, or recourse to help provided by family and friends, is not a part of the American success ethos. Accounts of successful coping provided by Murphy (1962) and by Felsman and Vaillant (1987) stress this capacity for individual attainment. Although good-enough parenting (Winnicott, 1960) is believed to provide a critical foundation for later coping efforts, beyond the early years of life, coping is largely a product of individual effort; those persons who succumb through heightened vulnerability and insufficient resilience are viewed as personally inadequate, tantamount to evidence that election was not preordained.

Other cultures than our own recognize that continued resilience when confronted with adversity is a collective rather than personal attainment (Cohler, 1983; Cohler & Stott, 1987). Kakar (1982) has dramatically portrayed the role of physician, family, and community in the support of persons with marked vulnerability for depression. Caudill (1958) portrays the role of the society in the treatment of Japanese schizophrenics. Whereas psychotropic medication is featured as the critical element in intervention with profoundly troubled persons in American and Western European society, often coupled with psychosocial therapy to foster work-readiness and capacity for independent living, treatment in Japanese psychiatry has focused on restoration of function of the person within the community. Individual initiative is much less important than restoration of the capacity to work within the context of family and community. Family plays a critical role in the development of the capacity to overcome adversity: the Family maintains its traditional function within Japanese society in the period following misfortune. The capacity to call on family members for help without increased sense of shame at having to become the "client" of other family members, owing them more than is owed, and of losing face for admitting the need for help (Doi, 1986) is critical in maintaining adjustment within Japanese culture.

There has been very little cross-cultural study of coping with adversity. Culture is treated either from the perspective of epidemiology, providing further evidence regarding the distribution of psychiatric symptoms across the world, or as a means of replicating findings based on study of a particular culture. The role of symbolic systems in determining culture and as the foundation of action has largely been absent in developmental psychopathology. The present chapter has argued that symbolic systems, transmitted across generations through socialization, across the course of life, and over historical time periods, are responsible for determining the conception of self and other; this perspective, however, has seldom been applied to the study of vulnerability and resilience. There has been considerable cross-national study of children at risk for psychopathology, but much of this work has been strictly epidemiological and has focused on rates and proportions of offspring at risk.

Even within our own country, in spite of concern expressed by Ogbu (1990a, 1990b) and others, there has been little focus on ethnic variation in coping with adversity. Particular problems are posed for ethnic groups, such as Italian Americans or African Americans, who place much emphasis on family as a resource in solving problems, in a culture emphasizing principally individual rather than collective means of coping with conflict (Dressler, 1991; Ogbu, 1981; Papajohn & Spiegel, 1975; Spiegel, 1971). Much of the study of vulnerable children has focused on replication of British and American findings in other cultures, with little attention to issues of culture and competence, or the manner in which symbolic processes might be associated with particular, culturally recognized, modes of coping.

Clues regarding the value of this cultural perspective in subsequent study might be obtained from cross-cultural studies of risk and resilience, particularly those reported by Anthony and his colleagues within the International Association for Child and Adolescent Psychiatry (Anthony & Chiland, 1978, 1980; Anthony & Koupernik, 1974). Within our own society, the first steps in understanding culture and resilience are reflected in the following studies of ethnicity, poverty, and psychopathology: the reports on inner-city socially disorganized families by C. Goodman and the Pace Project at New York's Bronx State Hospital, the New York High-Risk Project (Erlenmeyer-Kimling et al., 1984; Watt, Grub, & Erlenmeyer-Kimling, 1984); S. Goodman's studies of psychopathology among underclass mothers in a Southern city (Goodman, 1987; Goodman & Brumley, 1990; Goodman &

Johnson, 1986); and studies by Lyons-Ruth and her colleagues of parents and children living in disadvantaged neighborhoods in the Boston area (Lyons-Ruth, Botein, & Grunebaum, 1984; Lyons-Ruth, Zoll, Connell, & Grunebaum, 1986; Lyons-Ruth, Connell, Grunebaum, & Botein, 1990).

There has been much study of the development of social and cognitive competence (White & et al., 1978; White et al., 1979; White & Watts, 1973). However, consistent with Ogbu's (1981) critique, little discussion has focused on cultural or ethnic variations in what constitutes competence. As Garmezy and Masten (1986) have observed, most measures of mental health and adjustment in childhood assume psychopathology rather than "normalcy" as the standard, and fail to focus on areas of competence and effectance. Modes of dealing with such problems as family conflict are intertwined with understanding of meanings attributed to relationships by family members within a culture.

We must understand how persons within a culture or ethnic group symbolically construct concepts such as self and others before we can understand factors attributed to vulnerability and resilience as well as the role of particular cultures in resolving problems caused by increased vulnerability. American culture is predisposed to attribute vulnerability to temperamental factors that decrease the significance of personal responsibility in maintaining adjustment over time. As reflected in the new consumer movement in major mental disorders, attribution of "cause" strictly to biological factors "explains" the origins of the major mental disorders without involving personal or social factors in the origins, course, and treatment of terribly debilitating disorders such as schizophrenia and bipolar mood disorders.

The problem of cultural variation, intrinsically involved in methods of study, causes additional difficulties. The challenge of devising a culture-free intelligence test has plagued psychometric study since Binet's initial study of French schoolchildren in the late 19th century. Problems have also been highlighted in the use of paper-and-pencil and projective psychological measures with unstructured or semistructured stimuli such as the Rorschach or picture-thematic materials. It has long been recognized that culture shapes mode of perception, and even capacity to deal with novel stimuli. If the Rorschach plates elicit such responses as "color shock" on Plate VIII within our own culture, then it must be assumed that persons in other cultures also respond affectively to stimuli in ways that have not been systematically studied, and even the attempt to carry out such study poses problems of interpretation. Problems of rapport and meaning are also evident in both interview schedules and participant observation.

TOWARD THE FUTURE: MAKING MEANING AND THE MANAGEMENT OF MISFORTUNE

Reviewing research on the intertwined concepts of vulnerability and resilience, Luthar and Zigler (1991b) consider the interplay of psychological development and social context in the construction of psychological symptoms. More vulnerable persons are already predisposed or at risk for psychopathology as a result of inborn characteristics, psychologically toxic social environment, and such personal misfortune as parental psychiatric illness or divorce

across the early years of the child's life. Luthar and Zigler regard social status as a "social address," or shorthand for these interrelated characteristics assumed to shape development. Substandard housing, poor nutrition, inconsistent and disrupted parenting, exposure to physical violence that threatens personal safety, and socialization into the experience of social defeat are among the characteristics coded as low social status among both those experiencing privation and the larger community (Polansky, Chalmers, Buttenweiser, & Williams, 1981). Consistent with discussion of adjustment to life among the disadvantaged and disenfranchised (Dressler, 1982, 1991; Ogbu, 1981, 1983, 1990a, 1990b), Luthar and Zigler accept the concept of low social status as a mode of locating persons within society.

Growing up in the underclass (Wilson, 1987, 1989) may be viewed as a social address that implicitly refers to a set of interrelated characteristics believed to adversely affect cognitive and social development, which necessarily threatens adjustment. However, it is possible to view the concept of social status not only as a social address, locating a group of persons within the social system, but also as a distinctive culture, reflecting a unique means for portraying self and others, and for explaining the social and natural world. This focus on symbolic systems rather than institutional context has two particularly significant implications. In the first place, emphasis shifts from action to experience as a unity including both thought and action, and to the manner in which persons symbolize and enact meanings associated with particular conceptions of self and others. Social address is a shorthand reference to a world of meanings regarding self, others, and the course of life that requires more detailed study (Geertz, 1973, 1983b; Stack, 1974).

Understanding symbolic systems requires that the ethnographer assume an experience-near rather than an experience-distant stance toward the phenomenon being studied. With this empathic stance, the anthropologist attempts to enter into the subjectivity of the informants of the inquiry. As Geertz (1972/1973) has shown in his review of the manner in which a Balinese cockfight characterizes enduring tensions within the culture, this understanding of the symbolic world presumes "local knowledge" or knowledge from the informant's point of view. The cockfight becomes a miniature for all of Balinese society, with its formality and multidimensional view of personhood. However, recognizing that the ethnographer's own experience of the phenomena provides important information regarding the subject of the study, this empathic mode of inquiry also means relinquishing the traditional objectivity of the anthropologist.

Within the human sciences, including anthropology, this interpretive turn (Bohman et al., 1991; Schafer, 1992; Taylor, 1971/1979), focusing on the study of the symbolic realm, characterizes much of contemporary inquiry. This perspective has been most completely formulated by Crapanzano (1992), Geertz (1972/1973, 1973, 1974/1984, 1983b), Rabinow and Sullivan (1979), and Turner (1967), who have stressed the importance of understanding the world from the perspective of those who live in it. The focus of this symbolic perspective is on portrayal of those who inhabit this world. Just as among persons in other cultures whose fundamental understandings of self and the social and nonsocial world are fundamentally different from our own views, underclass life must be understood in its own terms. Turner notes the distinction between the indigenous or exegetical meaning that persons living within a culture attribute to all aspects of culture, and both the operational or observational significance of the culture "at work," as well as the positional meaning derived from the complex interplay of symbolic systems as interpreted by the ethnographer (Turner, 1967).

Bohman et al. (1991) observe four particularly distinctive elements that characterize that the new interpretive perspective disputes the distinction between explanation and understanding, maintaining that realist and essentialist claims regarding wish and sentiment are not tenable in the study of meanings embedded within complex symbolic systems or cultures. This perspective also assumes that coherence or sense of conviction provides the only possible test of the adequacy of interpretations within the human sciences. It is less relevant to judge accounts in terms of some external and enduring test of accuracy or validity than to judge these accounts in terms of the extent to which they presently provide a convincing and coherent account of phenomena being studied. Changes in theory over time inevitably lead to subsequent interpretations that "work better" than accepted modes of understanding person and culture.

This approach to the interpretation of culture appears to lead to the problem of the "hermeneutic circle," a solipsistic perspective in which the interpretation is validated by the interpretation. However, culture is constituted through language; language, expressed through discourse, provides the foundation for intersubjectivity. Ultimately, there is nothing more or less than the story that is told (Ricoeur, 1991). The central task of culture is to "make sense" of experience. We devote much of our time trying to understand each other, and this understanding takes place primarily using the medium of language. As Lutz (1985, 1988) has shown, cultures use language in quite different ways, including to express ideas. The ethnographer attends to this self-critical activity of understanding the other and uses language for reporting observations. Further, this activity of understanding the other through language is recognized as one of a number of stories that might be told (Lutz, 1985, 1988). Language remains a central medium both in listening to the story of another, and in reporting that is learned through participant observation as a form of listening.

Contemporary cultural study recognizes that an ethnography is less a record of another culture than a report authored with a particular intent and read by others in a particular manner (Comaroff & Comaroff, 1992) just as more generally, in the study of both history and culture, the important issue in telling about the event is the sense or meanings presently attributed to the phenomenon rather than its occurrence. As historians long have noted in discussing historiography, the important issue is not whether an event such as the Battle of Waterloo took place (an often cited event in debates within historiography), but what the meaning of this battle was for the subsequent course of events (H. White, 1978).[26] Discussion about the use of the past in

history has informed current debate regarding the significance of the study of otherness within anthropology. Ohnuki-Tierney (1990) and John and Jean Comaroff (1992) cite Braudel's (1980) observation regarding the use of history to gain perspective on the present, and they note that the two disciplines share concern with studying distance to gain enhanced understanding of ourselves, either in time (history) or space (anthropology).

History has helped anthropology in understanding that this record of the past is but one story about the past that could be told. The primary criterion for judging this account concerns the meaning or "followability" of stories of the past (Ricoeur, 1991). Ethnographic study has shown that the important issues in the study of culture is meaning or sense-making activity based on the study of particular lives. This perspective on ethnographic study, in turn, has led many historians to shift concern from study of battles and other global events to increasing concern with the lives of ordinary persons at a particular time. From Power's (1924/1992) classic study of the lives of ordinary persons in the Middle Ages, to Le Roy Ladurie's (1979) account of a French village of the late Middle Ages, based on historical materials gathered in connection with the Inquisition, and Ginzburg's (1980) detailed account of the life of a 16th-century miller, the focus of this historical study has been on the life story or biography of particular persons living during particular historical periods, and on the meanings that they assigned to the time in which they lived (Ginzburg, 1989; Gurevich, 1992). Mode of inquiry, particularly in the work of Le Roy Ladurie and Ginzburg, owes a significant intellectual debt to ethnographic inquiry.

The interpretive turn in anthropology has a number of important implications for the method of study of psychological resilience. First, focus in this work is on the variety of subjectivities, or constraints and opportunities, that are provided by culture for portraying self and experience. Geertz is cautious regarding the extent to which one not living within a culture is ever able to fathom the set of experiences and meanings attendant on life within a particular culture. As inexact as this task may be, the only method available for understanding local knowledge, and providing "thick description" is to view culture as a text to be interpreted in the manner of literary criticism (Clifford & Marcus, 1986; Marcus & Fischer, 1986). "Reading" culture is similar to reading any other text: Focus is on the story presently constructed that accounts most coherently for presently observed culture. The ability to understand the experiences of otherness depend, in turn, on the capacity for reflexive self-awareness. At least to some extent, as Kracke (1981) has suggested in his paper on Kagwev mourning, experiences such as death of a parent, spouse, or offspring, evoke similar responses across cultures. However, the capacity for appreciating the culturally determined response to crises of affliction such

---

[26] Aspects of experience are a function of both place and history. Experiences of people over time are critical in understanding the particular mode in which they encode and enact these symbolic elements of culture.

An inland living group of persons may have a seashore dwelling bird as a totem reflecting their previous environment. A group of persons living in a temperate climate may still swaddle children in the manner necessary for survival in an earlier, harsh winter climate (Levi-Strauss, 1962/1966).

as loss through death of a loved one (Lutz, 1985, 1988), involves the observer's recognition of his or her own responses reciprocally to those of the other.

Issues like loss and change are present across all cultures as a part of the human experience. Perhaps a part of the enduring significance of Van Gennep's (1908/1960) study of crises of affliction across the life course reflects the reality of changes to which persons in all cultures must respond. A birth in the family, the transformation from childhood to adolescence, or the death of a family member provides the impetus for refashioning meanings. The particular manner in which these crises of loss and change are resolved will obviously vary across cultures but must be recognized by all cultures. Those day-to-day hassles and annoyances that so directly impact present adjustment will vary across cultures but may be more directly related to issues of vulnerability and resilience than major losses and changes.

Culturally constructed responses to these life crises, together with issues particular to any culture, require particular self-awareness, including the observer's capacity to bear his or her own anxiety and remain responsive to the study of the phenomenon (Devereux, 1968). Experience-near observation (Geertz, 1974; Kohut, 1959, 1971), provides a method for understanding the immanent characteristics used by persons within a culture to order and portray experience, and lays the foundation for both the mundane actions of everyday life and complex religious rituals and civic ceremonies.

Second, it is not necessary to search for distant and presumably "primitive" cultures that may be different from our own modern culture to impart a moral message regarding the hazards of modernity. The other is all of us, and contemporary Western European and American culture is as much subject to symbolic analysis as the most primitive and presumably unspoiled culture in a distant land (Fernandez, 1990). Modes of cultural analysis are inherently reflexive and require a new orientation to fieldwork. Empathic modes of data collection, concerned with the ethnographer's experience of culture, have replaced the experience-distant natural science orientation of much previous ethnographic study. Since the posthumous publication of Malinowski's (1967/1989) diary, there has been important reconsideration of the role of the ethnographer within the culture being studied (Marcus & Fischer, 1986; Ruby, 1982). Although Malinowski's fieldwork was exemplary for its wealth of detail regarding Trobriand beliefs and ritual practices, his posthumous diary reveals the complexity of his feelings regarding his fieldwork and the people he studied.

Acknowledgement of the reality of the ethnographer's own subjectivity in response to the people being studied has had an important impact on ethnography. Ethnographic reports by Briggs (1970), Crapanzano (1980), Rabinow (1977), and P. Riesman (1977) relied on the author's experience of the relationship with informants as an important guide to meanings and intents characteristic of the culture. For example, the social marginality of one of the most important informants in Crapanzano's (1981) study, experienced by Crapanzano as an elusive quality within their own relationship, reflected a particular concept of self and other characteristics more generally in Morocco culture. This perspective makes it difficult to conceive ethnography as a mirror of a culture. Just as more generally in

history and the human sciences (Comaroff & Comaroff, 1992; Polkinghorne, 1983, 1988), the ethnographer brings particular concerns and preconceptions to the study of a culture that frame the nature of inquiry. Since Geertz's pioneering study, the comprehensive statement of Marcus and Fischer (1986), the publication of Malinowksi's (1967/1989) posthumous diary, critical reflexive perspectives on the nature of fieldwork (Ruby, 1982), and ethnographic study such as that of Rabinow (1977) and Crapanzano (1980), it has been difficult to conceive ethnography apart from the perspective of the ethnographer and the relationship of ethnographer and informant.

Other more recent study of subjectivity within culture has focused on ethnopsychological perspectives, including characteristic conceptions of personhood within particular cultures (Lutz, 1985, 1988; White & Kirkpatrick, 1985). Characteristic meanings representing a particular culture are less studied in the formal context of institutions such as the family, government, or religion than in the subjectivity of persons' representations of self and others. These representations are embodied in language and in the way that particular linguistic patterns structure reality (Fernandez, 1986; Lutz, 1988). This study also reflects focus on particular interpretations of this subjectivity observed in the relationship of ethnographer with informant, and in the informant's characterizations of person and experience.

Just as more generally in research studies, conversations become texts to be interpreted (Ricoeur, 1991). Once fieldwork notes have been transcribed, the interpretive process focuses on the relationship to the text rather than on the interaction between informant and ethnographer. Culture becomes text and the problem of interpreting culture becomes similar to the problem of interpreting other texts (Clifford & Marcus, 1986; Cottom, 1989; Marcus & Fisher, 1986). Although this emphasis on "anthropological poetic" (Marcus & Fischer, 1986) has been criticized as too removed from the phenomena being studied to provide a meaningful and significant understanding of another culture (Kracke & Herdt, 1987), it has directed attention away from the experience-distant ethnography of traditional study and has emphasized the significance of the ethnographer as intrinsic to the phenomena being studied.

Contemporary study of culture as text raises important questions regarding methods such as those used by Kluckhohn and Strodtbeck and their colleagues (1961) in their study of acculturation. This study, which relied so heavily on rating scales and forced-choice interview responses, has the appearance of a replicable scientific study but may actually elude the most important aspects of the phenomena being studied. Covello's (1944/1972) report of the relations between Italian-American families and a lower East Side high school in New York provides a more experience-near perspective on the struggles of immigrant groups coming to terms with a meaning system alien to their own worldview. An even more powerful example of this perspective is Crapanzano's (1985) study of the white South African response to the black population of South Africa, which raises the question of why apartheid would have been so tenaciously maintained in the face of intensified black-white conflict and negative world opinion. Crapanzano explores the worldview of a group whose views he finds difficult to accept with tact and sensitivity, portraying the experience of culture becoming ethnicity in a manner unique in the literature on ethnicity.

As with much of the study of culture and mental health, few discussions of culture as text factors such as the ethnographer's response to the phenomena, the language and composition of cultural narratives, and the subjectivity of the phenomenon. Ironically, Jules Henry (1965) may have pioneered this study in his idiosyncratic report of living with families of very troubled youngsters. Although his work was heavily influenced by the assumptions popular at the time (e.g., parents were responsible for inducting their offspring into faulty modes of managing reality, and for encouraging distortions in reality processing that led to subsequent episodes of psychiatric illness among more vulnerable offspring), Henry focused on the experience-near world of the family and portrayed shared meaning systems within family and culture.

There has been little other study of culture and mental health reflecting the approach pioneered by Henry and Crapanzano. Murphy (1962) implicitly focuses on the world of middle- and working-class Kansas families coping with such everyday hassles and tensions as birthday parties, school outings, and holidays. Murphy provides a wonderful opportunity for observing how children respond to everyday novelty. This study shows the value of focus on the everyday events that may intensify role strain and lead to impaired morale (Dohrenwend & Shrout, 1985; Lazarus & Folkman, 1984; Monroe, 1983; and Zautra et al., 1988). Many small events may be more important as a threat to adjustment among otherwise vulnerable persons than major adverse life changes (e.g., early loss of parent through death or divorce) that have been the focus of so much study in the area of risk for psychopathology. Clinical observation suggests that persons are mostly able to respond to terrible misfortune with a maturity not always possible to fathom in advance of the event. Rather, it is the accumulation of day-to-day hassles and annoyances that may make the difference in the ability to remain resilient. Just as more generally in the study of adversity, these often random annoyances contribute in a cumulative manner to mood and sense of effectance. Further, although many annoyances may be beyond personal control, others reflect more enduring problems in transactions with others and may negatively rebound on sense of self as effective.

Although Murphy (1962) has highlighted the significance of such everyday experiences as a child's response to a birthday party for a particular community, there has been very little study of these daily events as they affect adjustment across communities or cultures. It would appear that the difference between daily annoyance and major misfortune reflects a distinction greater than that within our own culture; future study will have to determine how such distinctions are made elsewhere. What does seem clear is that an experience-near or empathic mode of study, focusing on the life story of participants within a culture or ethnic group, may provide unique information that may be more comprehensive and rich in detail for understanding the interplay between culture and mental health than much of previous study. This perspective was pioneered as early as 1918 by Thomas and Znaniecki (1918/1974) in their massive study of the

adjustment of Polish peasant immigrants to the New World. This rich and informative two-volume report provides important detail based on life-history narratives that has yet to be carefully explored. These narratives reveal quite different responses to immigration and adjustment following relocation from Europe to the United States.

The next stage in the study of culture and resilience must take advantage of the emerging narrative perspective regarding culture. Detailed inquiry about the worldview of persons who are vulnerable, as defined by the interplay of constitutional and environmental factors (e.g., first-generation immigrants with a history of familial psychiatric illness), similar to Guiteras-Holmes's (1961) study of the world of an Tzotzil Indian in Mexico, Daniel's (1984) study of Tamil culture, or Crapanzano's (1985) study of the white South Africans will provide important understanding of the ways that persons make sense of adversity. This detailed narrative inquiry makes possible study of the interplay between major misfortune and day-to-day difficulties in determining threat to present adjustment. A first important step in such study may be the journalistic account of the travails of a chronically ill woman with major psychiatric illness (Sheehan, 1982). Sheehan simply recounts the experiences of this patient and her family as she moves between hospital and home. Although the account is largely descriptive and does not include sufficient detail about this patient's responses to loss and change within her life, or the author's method of study, it provides some understanding of how even small hassles or setbacks, such as the failure to respond to innovative medication, further erode the patient's confidence in the possibility of receiving help and increase her vulnerability to additional episodes of psychiatric illness.

Living with such families in the manner of Jules Henry (1965), focusing on the daily round in the manner of Lois Murphy (1962), being concerned with narratives of everyday experience (Nelson, 1989), and including the observer's own near response to the phenomena, in the manner pioneered by Crapanzano (1980), all might lead to important new information that could inform our understanding of the interplay of culture and experience in determining past adjustment. For example, what is it about everyday life in Mexican-American or South Asian families that allows them to provide support for relatives with a tenuous adjustment, whereas everyday experiences of vulnerable relatives within bourgeois Western European and American urban families are associated with enhanced probability of an episode of psychiatric illness (Jenkins, 1991)? We still do not understand the factors that lead some underclass families to be successful in fostering the development of children who achieve adjustment against all odds and who are able to be creative, empathic, and effective as adults despite growing up in the midst of abject poverty or episodic parental psychiatric illness (Meissner, 1970). Systematic study of narratives of resilience would enhance understanding of how culture and life experience interact in determining different responses to the complex interplay of wrenching misfortune and everyday annoyance. These responses, in turn, contributed to different outcomes in mental health ranging from enhanced competence and realization of expectable life attainments to social breakdown and repeated rehospitalizations.

CONCLUSION

Developmental perspectives suggest that mental health and adjustment must be considered within the context of the life course as a whole, and that issues both of resilience and vulnerability are relative rather than absolute. Conceiving lives as structured according to shared symbolic understandings about expectable transitions over time, culture determines both the differentiation of the life course and the experience of the finitude of life (Geertz, 1966/1973). Within Western European and American culture, the passage of time is assumed to be linear. Both lives and stories are presumed to reflect this linear time orientation with a beginning, a middle, and an end. This linear life course is divided into epochs marked by transitions based on this shared understanding of time and age from early to middle childhood, childhood to adolescence, stable adult years to middle age, and middle age to later life (Cohler & Boxer, 1984; Neugarten, 1979; Neugarten & Hagestad, 1976; Neugarten & Moore, 1968; Neugarten, Moore, & Lowe, 1965; Sorokin & Merton, 1937). Each of these recognized age-status changes is accompanied by particular transitions and role changes, such as entrance into school marking the transition from early to middle childhood, or retirement marking the transition from middle to later life.

These expectable transitions must be differentiated from unexpected, generally adverse life changes, such as the early off-time illness or death of a parent, or parental discord, psychopathology and hospitalization, illness, or job loss, all of which pose a threat to the stability of the family and the adjustment within the larger family group. Early off-time adversity is particularly difficult to manage because of lack of contact with others having the same experience who might share problems, and because of lack of prior experience gained by watching others struggle with a similar problem. Transitions across the course of life, together with the manner in which adversity associated with these transitions is managed, reflect those shared symbolic systems constituting culture (Cohler, 1991a). The complex interplay of time and particular adversity is experienced in quite different ways, and with different consequences, among cultures varying in their construction of time, relations among persons, and between person and natural surround. Within cultures stressing the significance of extended family ties, such as India, family adversity (e.g., illness or death of a parent, when children are still young) has quite different consequences for the continuity of child care than among cultures emphasizing the nuclear family unit.

Cultural factors are critical in determining resilience within particular lives, providing psychological protection against the impact of misfortune, even in the presence of increased vulnerability which, itself, is codetermined by those symbolic properties constituting culture. As Ogbu (1981), and Musick, Stott, Spencer, Goldman, and Cohler (1987) have shown, social disorganization accompanying poverty contributes to increased vulnerability of both parents and children to psychopathology. Increased vulnerability among adolescents living in the inner city may be a result of diverse factors: early off-time pregnancy among teenage girls, or expectation of gang membership and violent actions among teenage boys. Personal charm and cleverness, street-smarts, and a quick wit may provide enhanced resilience against the impact of poverty and social disorganization. The teenage boy who can get along with gang counterparts without becoming involved in gang membership and delinquent activity demonstrates a mode of resilience that is particularly adaptive within a particular culture and that may be much less relevant for a suburban teenage boy from more advantaged social circumstances (Ogbu, 1981, 1990a, 1990b). Luthar (1993) suggests that although suburban adolescents may rely on intellectual abilities to get them through periods of difficulty, inner-city teenagers may rely on talents other than intellectual ability.

Culturally constructed modes of adaptation, first learned in the family, and at school, become the foundation for resilience across the years of childhood and adulthood. Resilience is fostered by the presence of a parent or other family member who can teach the young child means for coping with the social disorganization in the community. Although by no means guaranteeing lifelong resilience, these family coping skills make it possible for otherwise vulnerable children to maintain a positive adjustment over the short term. Further, to the extent that the child living in the inner city experiences family, school, and community as consistent in supporting literacy, and a strong sense of self-worth, the environment fosters efforts to remain resilient.

Personal attractiveness, intelligence, sense of humor, and presence of others willing to provide support and encouragement, all foster the self-esteem so essential for resilience even as children are confronted by enhanced vulnerability. Developmental perspectives suggest that these so-called protective factors are only relative and that persons showing resilience at one point in life may be much less resilient when confronted by later adversity. Further, the pileup of significant adversity over time may exceed the capacity to cope with misfortune. Vulnerability and resilience both vary over time: Protective factors available for coping with misfortune at any one point in time may not be available at other points in time. Further, the advent of large-scale social dysfunction (e.g., national socialism in Germany, the subsequent totalitarian regime, and World War II) poses serious problems that accentuate personal misfortune.

At the same time, for reasons not yet understood, this same misfortune may strength personal resolve to overcome adversity. Some persons seem to function best at times of great personal or collective crisis. Day-to-day hassles (Lazarus & Folkman, 1984), or idiosyncratically defined adversity (Beck & Worthen, 1972), rather than significant misfortune, may pose a greater threat to continued adjustment and may tax personal resilience to the extent that resilience succumbs to psychopathology. Finally, as Cohler (1987), Luthar (1991), and Luthar and Zielger all have emphasized, persons may appear to be resilient to the impact of adversity at particular points in time even though more detailed study may show that there were high personal costs in remaining resilient. Overall resilience may be a less interesting index than study of particular areas of adjustment such as capacity for close social ties that could be important in maintaining resilience. Further, present adjustment to adversity may not predict well to later adjustment.

There has been very little study of resilience relying on the perspective elaborated in this chapter. Even in those studies, such as in the Hawaiian longitudinal research, which include diverse ethnic groups and contrasting cultures, there has been little attention to the significance of culture and social context as factors enhancing resilience. The Hawaii study includes evaluation of social disorganization and dislocation as factors related to vulnerability but does not consider ethnically determined resilience within the several groups represented in the study. Findings reported by Garmezy and his associates, and by Rutter (1985), do not include the range of cultural diversity potentially accessible in the Hawaii study. However, the comparative study of London and the Isle of Wight includes sufficiently diverse ethnic groups that stronger focus on culture would have made possible increased study of the role of culture in fostering psychological resilience.

Significantly, the reports on vulnerable children across cultures in the volume edited by Anthony and Koupernik (1974) reflect African societies varying along the dimension of modernization. These reports, however, are essentially concerned with a view of vulnerability to psychopathology as a universal, which largely disregards culture. These papers show little explicit concern with culture in the construction of particular modes of resilience to adversity. For example, these papers fail to consider such culturally relevant issues in their study of coping as concern with subsistence and changes in child rearing that accompany the shift in mode of production from subsistence farming to factory labor (Edgerton, 1971). The rapid advance of modernity poses a marked challenge for psychological resilience. Traditional societies make fewer demands on individual adjustment than societies undergoing the rapid social change that accompanies the transition to modernity. Future study must address issues of vulnerability and resilience from within the framework of cultural study. The very concept of resilience must be understood within a cultural perspective that takes into account symbolic construction of self and others, values, and the personal significance of particular life experiences as reflected in the personal narrative or life story.

Future study must also address the implications of this cultural framework for studying resilience for prevention and intervention in personal distress. Appreciation of the role of ecology and culture for optimal mode of adjustment, and for expression of psychological distress, leads to enhanced understanding of persons who may be at risk for psychopathology. Modern families living in rural communities and children of stem families without extensive kinship ties both reflect increased risk for psychopathology and also offer opportunity for preventive intervention that might forestall psychological distress (Hughes et al., 1960). However, Luthar (1993) has questioned whether prevailing statistical technique are able to manage interactions of the complexity required to systematically study the interplay of cultural and developmental forces relevant to resilience over the course of life. More systematic and methodologically innovative study is needed to understand the complex interweaving of culture, temperament,

individual experience, and change over time, and for planning particular intervention modalities among persons otherwise at risk for enhanced psychopathology within particular cultures.

REFERENCES

Abraham, K. (1953). A short study of the libido viewed in the light of mental disorders (1924). In K. Abraham, *Selected papers on psychoanalysis.* (pp. 418–501). New York: Basic Books. (Original work published 1924)

Achenbach, T. (1990). Conceptualization of developmental psychopathology. In M. Lewis & S. Miller (Eds.), *Handbook of developmental psychopathology.* (pp. 3–14). New York: Plenum.

Albee, G. (1980). A competency model must replace the defect model. In L. A. Bond & J. C. Rosen (Eds.), *Competence and coping during adulthood* (pp. 75–104). Hanover, NH: University of Vermont Press and University Press of New England.

Altschul, S., & Pollock, G. (1988). (Eds.), *Childhood bereavement and its aftermath.* New York: International Universities Press.

American Psychiatric Association. (1994). *The diagnostic and statistical manual of mental disorders.* Washington, DC: Author.

Andreasen, N. (1987). The diagnosis of schizophrenia. *Schizophrenia Bulletin, 13,* 9–22.

Andreasen, N. (1990). *Schizophrenia: Positive and negative symptoms and syndromes.* New York: Karger.

Anthony, E. J. (1976). How children cope in families with a psychotic parent. In E. Rexford, L. Sander, & T. Shapiro (Eds.), *Infant psychiatry: A new synthesis.* (pp. 239–250). New Haven: Yale University Press. (Original work published 1971)

Anthony, E. J. (1974). The syndrome of the psychologically invulnerable child. In E. J. Anthony & C. Koupernik (Eds.), *The child in his family: Children at psychiatric risk.* (pp. 529–544). New York: Wiley.

Anthony, E. J. (1987a). Risk, vulnerability, and resilience: An overview. In E. J. Anthony & B. J. Cohler (Eds.), *The invulnerable child.* (pp. 3–48). New York: Guilford.

Anthony, E. J. (1987b). Children at high risk for psychosis growing up successfully. In E. J. Anthony & B. J. Cohler (Eds.), *The invulnerable child.* (pp. 147–184). New York: Guilford.

Anthony, E. J., & Chiland, C. (Eds.). (1978). *The child in his family: Children and their parents in a changing world* (Vol. 5, Yearbook of the international association for child and adolescent psychiatry and allied professions). New York: Wiley.

Anthony, E. J., & Chiland, C. (Eds.). (1982). *The child in his family: Children in turmoil: Tomorrow's parents.* (Vol. 7, Yearbook of the international association for child and adolescent psychiatry and allied professions). New York: Wiley.

Anthony, E. J., & Koupernik, C. (Eds.). (1974). *The child in his family: Children at psychiatric risk* (Vol. 3, Yearbook of the international association for child and adolescent psychiatry and allied professions). New York: Wiley.

Antonucci, T. (1985). Personal characteristics, social support, and social behavior. In R. Binstock & E. Shanas (Eds.), *Handbook of aging and the social sciences* (2nd ed.). (pp. 94–128). New York: Van Nostrand-Reinhold.

Antonucci, T., & Akiyama, H. (1987). Social networks in adult life and a preliminary examination of the convoy model. *Journal of Gerontology, 42,* 519–527.

Aries, P. (1962). *Centuries of childhood: A social history of family life* (R. Baldrick, Trans.). New York: Random House/Vintage.

Arthur, B., & Kemme, M. (1964). Bereavement in childhood. *Journal of Child Psychology and Psychiatry, 5,* 37–49.

Bakhtin, M. M. (1981). *The dialogic imagination* (C. Emerson & M. Holquist, Trans.). Austin, TX: University of Texas Press. (Original work published 1975)

Baldwin, A., Baldwin, C., & Cole, R. (1990). Stress-resistant families and stress-resistant children. In J. Rolf, A. Masten, D. Cicchetti, K. Nuechterlein, & S. Weintraub (Eds.), *Risk and protective factors in the development of psychopathology* (pp. 257–280). New York: Cambridge University Press.

Banfield, E. (1958). *The moral basis of a backward society.* New York: Free Press.

Bankoff, L. (1983). Social support and adaptation to widowhood. *Journal of Marriage and the Family, 45,* 827–839.

Barker, R., & Wright, H. (1951). *One boy's day.* New York: Harper & Row.

Barker, R., & Wright, H. (1955). *Midwest and its children.* New York: Harper & Row.

Barnes, P. (1980). Comparative study of Punjabi and English child-rearing practices in England. In E. J. Anthony & C. Chiland (Eds.), *The child in his family: Preventive child psychiatry in an age of transition.* (pp. 197–209). New York: Wiley.

Barrera, M. (1988). Models of social support and life stress. In L. Cohen (Ed.), *Life events and psychological functioning: Theoretical and methodological issues.* (pp. 211–236). Newbury Park, CA: Sage.

Barth, F. (1969). Introduction. In F. Barth (Ed.), *Ethnic groups and boundaries: The social organization of culture difference.* (pp. 9–38). Boston: Little Brown.

Barth, F. (1981). *Process and form in social life: Selected essays of Fredrick Barth* (Vol. I). Boston: Routledge & Kegan Paul.

Barth, F. (1987). *Cosmologies in the making: A generative approach to cultural variation in inner New Guinea.* New York: Cambridge University Press.

Beck, J., & Worthen, K. (1972). Precipitating stress, crisis theory, and hospitalization in schizophrenia and depression. *Archives of General Psychiatry, 26,* 123–129.

Berry, J. (1976). Human ecology and cognitive style: Comparative studies in cultural and psychological adaptation. New York: Sage-Halsted-Wiley.

Bell, R. Q. (1964). The effect on the family of a limitation in coping ability in the child: A research approach and a finding. *Merrill-Palmer Quarterly, 10.*

Bell, R. Q. (1977). Socialization findings reexamined. In R. Q. Bell & L. Harper (Eds.), *Child effects on adults.* (pp. 53–84). Hillsdale, NJ: Erlbaum.

Bettelheim, B. (1986). Mass behavior in extreme situations. In B. Bettelheim, *Surviving the holocaust.* (pp. 60–96). London: Fontana/Collins. (Original work published 1943)

Bettelheim, B. (1960). *The informed heart.* New York: Free Press/Macmillan.

Bibring, G. (1959). Some considerations of the psychological process in pregnancy. *Psychoanalytic Study of the Child, 14,* 113–121.

Billings, A., & Moos, R. (1981). The role of coping responses and social resources in attenuating the stress of life events. *Journal of Behavioral Medicine, 4,* 139–157.

Birely, L., & Brown, G. (1970). Crises and life changes preceding the onset or relapse of acute schizophrenia: Clinical aspects. *British Journal of Psychiatry, 116,* 327–333.

Bleuler, E. (1950). *Dementia Praecox or The Group of Schizophrenias* (J. Zinkin, Trans.). New York: International Universities Press. (Original work published 1911)

Bloch, M. (1977). The past in the present. *Man, 12,* 278–292.

Blom, J. P. (1969). Ethnic and cultural differentiation. In F. Barth (Ed.), *Ethnic groups and boundaries: The social organization of culture difference.* (pp. 74–85). Boston: Little, Brown.

Boddy, J. (1989). *Wombs and alien spirits: Women, men and the Zar cult in Northern Sudan.* Madison, WI: University of Wisconsin Press.

Bohannan, P. (1957). *Justice and judgment among the Tiv.* New York: Oxford University Press.

Bohannan, P. (1963). *Africa and Africans.* Garden City, NY: American Museum of Natural History Press.

Bohman, J., Hiley, R., & Shusterman, R. (1991). Introduction: The interpretive turn. In D. Hiley, J. Bohman, & R. Shusterman (Eds.), *The interpretive turn: Philosophy, science, culture* (pp. 304–314). Ithaca, NY: Cornell University Press.

Braudel, F. (1980). *On history.* (S. Matthews, Trans.). Chicago: University of Chicago Press.

Briggs, J. L. (1970). *Never in anger: Portrait of an Eskimo family.* Cambridge, MA: Harvard University Press.

Bronfenbrenner, U. (1979). *The ecology of human development.* Cambridge, MA: Harvard University Press.

Brown, G. (1959). Experiences of discharged chronic schizophrenic mental hospital patients in various types of living groups. *Millbank Memorial Fund Quarterly, 37,* 105–131.

Brown, G., & Birley, J. (1968). Crises and life changes and the onset of schizophrenia. *Journal of Health and Social Behavior, 9,* 203–214.

Brown, G., Birley, J., & Wing, J. (1972). Influence of family life on the course of schizophrenic disorders: A replication. *British Journal of Psychiatry, 121,* 241–258.

Brown, G., & Birley, L. (1968). Crises and life changes and the onset of schizophrenia. *Journal of Health and Human Behavior, 9,* 203–214.

Brown, G., Bone, M., Dalison, B., & Wing, J. (1966). Schizophrenia and social care. London: Oxford University Press.

Brown, G., & Harris, T. (1978). *Social origins of depression: A study of psychiatric disorder in women.* New York: Free Press.

Brown, G., Harris, T., & Peto, J. (1973). Life events and psychiatric disorders: Part 2. Nature of the causal link. *Psychological Medicine, 3,* 159–170.

Brown, G., Monck, E., Carstairs, G., & Wing, J. (1962). Influence of family life on the course of schizophrenic illness. *British Journal of Preventive and Social Medicine, 16,* 55–68.

Brown, W. (1983). *The other side of delinquency.* New Brunswick, NJ: Rutgers University Press.

Bruner, J. (1990). *Acts of meaning.* Cambridge, MA: Harvard University Press.

Carothers, J. C. (1953). *The African mind in health and disease.* Geneva: World Health Organization.

Caspi, A., Elder, G., & Bem, D. (1987). Moving against the world: Life-course patterns of explosive children. *Developmental Psychology, 23,* 308–313.

Caspi, A., Elder, G., & Bem, D. (1988). Moving away from the world: Life-course patterns of shy children. *Child Development, 24,* 824–831.

Caspi, A., Elder, G., & Herbener, E. (1990). Childhood personality and the prediction of life-course patterns. In L. Robins & M. Rutter (Eds.), *Straight and devious pathways from childhood to adulthood* (pp. 13–35). New York: Cambridge University Press.

Caudill, W. (1958). *The psychiatric hospital as a small society.* Cambridge, MA: Harvard University Press.

Cawelti, J. (1965). *Apostles of the self-made man.* Chicago: University of Chicago Press.

Cicchetti, D. (1984). The emergence of developmental psychopathology. *Child Development, 55,* 1–7.

Clark, M. (1972). Cultural values and dependency in later life. In D. O. Cowgill & L. D. Holmes (Eds.), *Aging and modernization* (pp. 263–274). New York: Appleton-Century-Crofts.

Clark, M., & Anderson, B. G. (1967). *Culture and aging.* Springfield, IL: Thomas.

Clarke, S. D., & Clarke, A. M. (Eds.). (1976). *Early experience: Myth and evidence.* New York: Free Press.

Clarke-Stewart, A. (1978). Popular primers for parents. *American Psychologist, 33,* 359–369.

Clausen, J. (1985). Mental illness and the life course. In P. Baltes & O. G. Brim, Jr. (Eds.), *Life-span development and behavior* (Vol. 6). New York: Academic Press, 1984, 204–243.

Clifford, J., & Marcus, G. (1986). *Writing culture.* Berkeley: University of California Press.

Coddington, R. D. (1972a). The significance of life events as etiologic factors in the diseases of children: I. A survey of professional workers. *Journal of Psychosomatic Research, 16,* 7–18.

Coddington, R. D. (1972b). The significance of life events as etiologic factors in the diseases of children: II. A study of a normal population. *Journal of Psychosomatic Research, 16,* 205–213.

Cohen, L. (1988). Measurement of life events. In L. Cohen (Ed.), *Life-events and psychological functioning: Theoretical and methodological issues* (pp. 11–30). Newbury Park, CA: Sage.

Cohler, B. (1983). Autonomy and interdependence in the family of adulthood: A psychological perspective. *Gerontologist, 23,* 33–39.

Cohler, B. (1985). Aging in the old and new world: Variations in the peasant tradition. In J. A. Meacham (Ed.), *Family and individual development.* (Contributions to *Human Development,* No. 14, pp. 65–79). New York: Karger.

Cohler, B. (1987). Adversity, resilience, and the study of lives. In E. J. Anthony & B. J. Cohler (Eds.), *The invulnerable child* (pp. 363–424). New York: Guilford.

Cohler, B. (1991a). Stress, coping, and the course of life. In E. M. Cummings, A. L. Greene, & K. H. Karraker (Eds.), *Life-span developmental psychology: Stress and coping across the life-span* (Vol. 11, pp. 297–326). Hillsdale, NJ: Erlbaum.

Cohler, B. (1991b). The life story and the study of resilience and response to adversity. *Journal of Narrative and Life History, 1,* 169–200.

Cohler, B., & Boxer, A. (1984). Middle adulthood: Settling into the world-person, time and context. In D. Offer & M. Sabshin (Eds.), *Normality and the life course: A critical integration* (pp. 145–203). New York: Basic Books.

Cohler, B., & Ferrono, C. (1987). Schizophrenia and the life course. In N. Miller & G. Cohen (Eds.), *Schizophrenia and aging* (pp. 189–199). New York: Guilford.

Cohler, B., Gallant, D., Grunebaum, H., & Kauffman, C. (1983). Social adjustment among schizophrenic, depressed and well mothers and the school aged children. In H. Morrison (Ed.), *Children of depressed parents: Risk, identification and intervention* (pp. 65–98). New York: Grune & Stratton.

Cohler, B., Groves, L., Borden, W., & Lazarus, L. (1989). Caring for family members with Alzheimer's disease. In E. Light & B. Lebowitz (Eds.), *Alzheimer's disease, treatment and family stress: Directions for research* (pp. 50–105). Washington, DC: U.S. Government Printing Office.

Cohler, B., & Grunebaum, H. (1981). *Mothers, grandmothers, and daughters: Personality and child-care in three-generation families.* New York: Wiley.

Cohler, B., & Lieberman, M. (1978). Ethnicity and personal adjustment. *International Journal of Group Tensions, 7,* 20–41.

Cohler, B., & Lieberman, M. (1979). Personality change across the second half of life: Findings from a study of Irish, Italian and Polish-American men and women. In D. Gelfand & A. Kutznik (Eds.), *Ethnicity and aging* (pp. 227–245). New York: Springer.

Cohler, B., & Lieberman, M. (1980). Social relations and mental health: Middle-aged and older men and women from three European ethnic groups. *Research on Aging, 2,* 4454–4469.

Cohler, B., Pickett, S., & Cook, J. (1991). The psychiatric patient grows older: Issues in family care. In E. Light & B. Lebowitz (Eds.), *The elderly with chronic mental illness* (pp. 82–110). New York: Springer.

Cohler, B., & Stott, F. (1987). Separation, interdependence, and social relations across the second half of life. In J. Bloom-Feshbach & S. Bloom-Feshbach (Eds.), *The psychology of separation and loss* (pp. 165–204). San Francisco: Jossey-Bass. (Selection of the Behavioral Sciences Book Service)

Collomb, H., & Valantin, S. (1970). The Black African family. In E. J. Anthony & C. Koupernik (Eds.), *The child in his family* (Vol. 1, pp. 359–388). New York: Wiley.

Comaroff, J., & Comaroff, J. (1992). *Ethnography and the historical imagination.* Boulder, CO: Westview Press.

Comer, J. (1974). The Black American child in school. In E. J. Anthony & C. Koupernik (Eds.), *The child in his family: Children at psychiatric risk* (pp. 341–355). New York: Wiley.

Cook, J., & Cohler, B. (1986). Reciprocal socialization and the care of offspring with cancer and with schizophrenia. In N. Datan, A. Greene, & H. Reese (Eds.), *Intergenerational networks: Families in context* (pp. 223–243). Hillsdale, NJ: Erlbaum.

Cook, J., Hoffschmidt, S., Cohler, B., & Pickett, S. (1992). Marital satisfaction among parents of offspring with severe mental illness living in the community. *American Journal of Orthopsychiatry,* 552–563.

Cook, J., Lefley, H., Pickett, S., & Cohler, B. (in press). Parental aging and family burden in major mental illness. *American Journal of Orthopsychiatry.*

Cottrell, L. (1976). The competent community. In B. Kaplan, R. Wilson, & A. Leighton (Eds.), *Further explorations in social psychiatry* (pp. 195–209). New York: Basic Books.

Cottom, D. (1989). *Theory and history of literature: Vol. 62. Text and culture: The politics of interpretation.* Minneapolis, MN: University of Minnesota Press.

Covello, L. (1972). *The social background of the Italo-American school child.* Totowa, NJ: Rowman and Littlefield. (Original work published 1944)

Crapanzano, V. (1980). *Tuhami: Portrait of a Moroccan.* Chicago: University of Chicago Press.

Crapanzano, V. (1985). *Waiting: The Whites of South Africa.* New York: Random House.

Crapanzano, V. (1992). *Hermes' dilemma and Hamlet's desire: On the epistemology of interpretation.* Cambridge, MA: Harvard University Press.

D'Andrade, R. (1984). Cultural meaning systems. In R. Shweder & R. LeVine (Eds.), *Culture theory: Essays on mind, self, and emotion* (pp. 88–119). New York: Cambridge University Press.

D'Andrade, R. (1990). Some propositions about the relations between culture and human cognition. In J. Stigler, R. Shweder, & G. Herdt (Eds.), *Cultural psychology* (pp. 65–129). New York: Cambridge University Press.

Daniel, E. V. (1984). *Fluid signs: Being a person the Tamil Way.* Berkeley: University of California Press.

Dean, A., & Lin, N. (1977). The stress-buffering role of social support: Problems and prospects for systematic investigation. *Journal of Nervous and Mental Disease, 165,* 403–417.

Dearth, N., Labenski, B., Mott, E., & Pellegrini, L., and Families of the Mentally Ill Collective. (1986). *Families helping families: Living with schizophrenia.* New York: Norton.

Devereux, G. (1968). *From anxiety to method in the behavioral sciences.* The Hague: Mouton.

Dibble, E., & Cohen, D. (1974). Companion instruments for measuring children's competence and parental style. *Archives of General Psychiatry, 30,* 805–815.

Dohrenwend, B. S., & Dohrenwend, B. P. (1974). *Stressful life-events: Their nature and effects.* New York: Wiley.

Dohrenwend, B. S., & Dohrenwend, B. P. (1981a). Life stress and illness: Formulation of the issues. In B. S. Dohrenwend & B. P. Dohrenwend (Eds.), *Stressful life events and their contexts* (pp. 1–27). New York: Prodist-Neale Watson.

Dohrenwend, B., & Dohrenwend, B. (1981b). Life-stress and psychopathology. In D. Regier & G. Allen (Eds.), *Risk factor research in the major mental disorders* (pp. 131–141). (DHHS Publication No. ADM 81-1068). Washington, DC: U.S. Government Printing Office.

Dohrenwend, B., & Shrout, P. (1985). "Hassles" in the conceptualization measurement of life stress variables. *American Psychologist, 40,* 780–785.

Doi, T. (1986). *The anatomy of self. The individual versus society.* (M. Harbison, Trans.). New York: Kodansha International.

Dornbusch, S. (1989). The sociology of adolescence. *Annual Review of Sociology, 15,* 233–259.

Draguns, J. (1980). Psychological disorders of clinical severity. In H. Triandis & J. Draguns (Eds.), *Handbook of cultural psychology. VI: Psychopathology* (pp. 99–174). Boston: Allyn & Bacon.

Dressler, W. (1982). *Hypertension and culture change: Acculturation and disease in the West Indies.* South Salem, NY: Redgrave.

Dressler, W. (1991). *Stress and adaptation in the context of culture: Depression in a southern black community.* Albany, NY: SUNY Press.

Dunn, J. (1988). Normative life-events as risk factors in childhood. In M. Rutter (Ed.), *Studies of Psychosocial risk: The power of longitudinal data* (pp. 227–244). New York: Cambridge University Press.

Earls, F., Beardslee, W., & Garrison, W. (1987). Correlates and predictors of competence in young children. In E. J. Anthony & B. J. Cohler (Eds.), *The invulnerable child* (pp. 70–83). New York: Guilford.

Easterlin, R. (1987). *Birth and fortune: The impact of numbers on personal welfare* (2nd ed.). Chicago: University of Chicago Press.

Ebata, A., Petersen, A., & Conger, J. (1990). The development of psychopathology in adolescence. In J. Rolf, A. Masten, D. Cicchetti, K. Nuechterlein, & S. Weintraub (Eds.), *Risk and protective factors in the development of psychopathology* (pp. 308–333). New York: Cambridge University Press.

Edgerton, R. (1971). *The individual in cultural adaptation: A study of four East African peoples.* Berkeley: University of California Press.

Edgerton, R. (1992). *Sick societies: Challenging the myth of primitive harmony.* New York: Free Press.

Elder, G. H., Jr. (1974). *Children of the Great Depression.* Chicago: University of Chicago Press.

Elder, G. H., Jr. (1979). Historical change in life patterns and personality. In P. B. Baltes & O. G. Brim, Jr. (Eds.), *Life span development and behavior* (Vol. 2, pp. 118–161). New York: Academic Press.

Elder, G. H., Jr., & Caspi, A. (1990). Studying lives in a changing society: Sociological and personological explanations. In A. I. Rabin, R. Zucker, R. Emmons, & S. Frank (Eds.), *Studying persons and lives* (pp. 201–247). New York: Springer.

Elder, G., Jr., & Hareven, T. (1993). Rising above life's disadvantage: From the Great Depression to the war. In G. H. Elder, Jr., J. Modell, & R. D. Parke (Eds.), *Children in time and place: Developmental and historical insights* (pp. 47–72). New York: Cambridge University Press.

Elder, G., Jr., & Rockwell, R. (1979). The life-course and human development: An ecological perspective. *International Journal of Behavioral Development, 2,* 1–21.

Erikson, E. H. (1963). *Childhood and society (rev. ed.).* New York: Norton. (Original work published 1950)

Erlenmeyer-Kimling, L., & Cornblatt, B. (1987). The New York High-Risk Project: A follow-up report. *Schizophrenia Bulletin, 13,* 451–463.

Erlenmeyer-Kimling, L., Cornblatt, B., Bassett, A., Moldin, S., Hilldoff-Adamo, U., & Roberts, S. (1990). High-risk children in adolescence and young adulthood: Course of global adjustment. In L. Robins & M. Rutter (Eds.), *Straight and devious pathways from childhood to adulthood* (pp. 351–364). New York: Cambridge University Press.

Erlenmeyer-Kimling, L., Marcuse, Y., Cornblatt, B., Friedman, D., Rainer, J., & Rutschmann, J. (1984). The New York High-Risk Project. In N. Watt, E. J. Anthony, L. C. Wynne, & J. Rolf (Eds.), *Children at risk for schizophrenia: A longitudinal perspective* (pp. 169–190). New York: Free Press.

Escalona, S. (1974). Intervention programs for children at psychiatric risk: The contribution of child psychology and developmental theory. In E. J. Anthony & C. Koupernik (Eds.), *The child in his family: Children at psychiatric risk* (pp. 35–46). New York: Wiley.

Evans-Pritchard, E. E. (1937). *Witchcraft, oracles, and magic among the Azande.* Oxford: Clarendon Press.

Evans-Pritchard, E. E. (1940). *The Nuer: A description of the modes of livelihood and political institutions of a Nilotic People.* Oxford, England: Clarendon Press.

Ewing, K. (1991). Can psychoanalytic theories explain the Pakistani woman? Intrapsychic autonomy and interpersonal engagement in the extended family. *Ethos, 19,* 131–160.

Falloon, I. (1985). *Family management of schizophrenia: A study of clinical, social, family, and economic benefits.* Baltimore: Johns Hopkins University Press.

Farber, E., & Egeland, B. (1987). Invulnerability among abused and neglected children. In E. J. Anthony & B. J. Cohler (Eds.), *The invulnerable child* (pp. 253–288). New York: Guilford.

Faris, R., & Dunham, H. (1939). *Mental disorders in urban areas.* Chicago: University of Chicago Press.

Felner, R. (1984). Vulnerability in childhood: A preventive framework for understanding children's efforts to cope with life stress and transition. In M. Roberts & L. Peterson (Eds.), *Prevention of problems in childhood: Psychological research and applications* (pp. 133–169). New York: Wiley.

Felsman, J. K., & Vaillant, G. (1987). Resilient children as adults: A forty year study. In E. J. Anthony & B. J. Cohler (Eds.), *The invulnerable child* (pp. 289–314). New York: Guilford.

Fernandez, J. (1986). *Persuasions and performances: The play of Tropes in culture.* Bloomington: Indiana University Press.

Fernandez, J. (1990). Enclosures: Boundary maintenance and its representations over time in Austrian mountain villages (Spain). In E. Ohnuki-Tierney (Ed.), *Culture through time: Anthropological approaches* (pp. 94–127). Stanford, CA: Stanford University Press.

Fine, G. (1987). *With the boys: Little league baseball and preadolescent culture.* Chicago: University of Chicago Press.

Fischer, J., & Fischer, A. (1963). The New Englanders of Orchard Town. In B. Whiting (Ed.), *Six cultures* (Vol. 5). New York: Wiley.

Fish, B. (1977). Neurologic antecedents of schizophrenia in children: Evidence for an inherited, congenital neurointegrative deficit. *Archives of General Psychiatry, 34,* 1297–1313.

Fish, B. (1984). Characteristics and sequelae of the neurointegrative disorder in infants at risk for schizophrenia. In N. Watt, E. J. Anthony, L. C. Wynne, & J. Rolf (Eds.), *Children at risk for schizophrenia: A longitudinal perspective* (pp. 423–439). New York: Free Press.

Fish, B. (1987). Infant predictors of the longitudinal course of schizophrenic development. *Schizophrenia Bulletin, 13,* 395–410.

Fisher, L., Kokes, R., Cole, R., Perkins, P., & Wynne, L. (1987). Competent children at risk: A study of well functioning offspring of disturbed parents. In E. J. Anthony & B. J. Cohler (Eds.), *The invulnerable child* (pp. 211–258). New York: Guilford.

Fogel, R., & Engerman, S. (1974). *Time on the cross: The economics of American Negro slavery.* Boston: Little Brown.

Folkman, S., & Lazarus, R. (1980). An analysis of coping in a middle-aged community sample. *Journal of Health and Social Behavior, 21,* 219–239.

Francis, E. K. (1947). The nature of the ethnic group. *American Journal of Sociology, 52,* 393–400.

French, J. R. P., Jr., Rodgers, W., & Cobb, S. (1974). Adjustment as a person-environment fit. In G. C. Coelho, D. Hamburg, & J. Adams (Eds.), *Coping and adaptation* (pp. 316–333). New York: Basic Books.

Freud, A. (1966). *The writings of Anna Freud: Vol. II. The ego and the mechanisms of defense.* New York: International Universities Press. (Original work published 1936)

Freud, A. (1965). *The writings of Anna Freud: Vol. VI. Normality and psychopathology in childhood: Assessments of development.* New York: International Universities Press.

Freud, S. (1955). Totem and taboo: Some points of agreement between the mental lives of savages and neurotics. In J. Strachey (Ed. and Trans.), *The standard edition of the complete psychological works of Sigmund Freud* (Vol. 13, pp. 1–161). London: Hogarth Press. (Original work publised 1912–1913)

Freud, S. (1959). Inhibitions, symptoms and anxiety. In J. Strachey (Ed. & Trans.), *The standard edition of the complete works of Sigmund Freud* (Vol. 20, pp. 75–172). London: Hogarth Press. (Original work published 1926)

Galatzer-Levy, R., & Cohler, B. (1993). *The essential other.* New York: International Universities Press.

Garmezy, N. (1971). Vulnerability research and the issue of primary prevention. *American Journal of Orthopsychiatry, 41,* 101–116.

Garmezy, N. (1974). The study of competence in children at risk for severe psychopathology. In E. J. Anthony & C. Koupernik (Eds.), *The child in his family: Children at psychiatric risk* (pp. 77–98). New York: Wiley.

Garmezy, N. (1975). The experimental study of children vulnerable to psychopathology. In A. Davids (Ed.), *Child personality and psychopathology: Current topics* (pp. 171–216). New York: Wiley.

Garmezy, N. (1981). Children under stress: Perspectives on antecedents and correlates of vulnerability and resistance to psychopathology. In A. I. Rabin, J. Aronoff, A. M. Barclay, & R. Zucker (Eds.), *Further explorations in personality* (pp. 196–269). New York: Wiley.

Garmezy, N. (1983). Stressors of childhood. In N. Garmezy & M. Rutter (Eds.), *Stress, coping and development in children* (pp. 43–84). New York: McGraw-Hill.

Garmezy, N. (1985a). Broadening research on developmental risk: Implications from studies of vulnerable and stress-resistant children. In W. Frankenburg, R. Emde, & J. Sullivan (Eds.), *Early identification of children at risk: An international perspective* (pp. 45–58). New York and London: Plenum.

Garmezy, N. (1985b). Stress-resistant children: The search for protective factors. In J. E. Stevenson (Ed.), *Recent research in developmental psychopathology* (pp. 213–233). Oxford: Pergamon. (Suppl. N. 4, *Journal of Child Psychology and Psychiatry*)

Garmezy, N. (1986). Developmental aspects of children's responses to the stress of separation and loss. In M. Rutter, C. Izard, & P. Read (Eds.), *Depression in young people: Clinical and developmental perspectives* (pp. 297–324). New York: Guilford.

Garmezy, N. (1987a). Children vulnerable to major mental disorders: Risk and protective factors. In (Ed.), *Psychiatry update, III* (pp. 91–103). Washington, DC: American Psychiatric Press.

Garmezy, N. (1987b). Stress, competence, and development: Continuities in the study of schizophrenic adults, children vulnerable to psychopathology, and the search for stress-resistant children. *American Journal of Orthopsychiatry, 57,* 159–174.

Garmezy, N., & Devine, V. (1984). Project competence: The Minnesota studies of children vulnerable to psychopathology. In N. F. Watt, E. J. Anthony, L. C. Wynne, & J. E. Rolf (Eds.), *Children at risk for schizophrenia: A longitudinal perspective* (pp. 289–303). New York: Cambridge University Press.

Garmezy, N., & Masten, A. (1986). Stress, competence, and resilience: Common frontiers for therapist and psychopathologist. *Behavior Therapy, 17,* 500–521.

Garmezy, N., Masten, A., Nordstrom, L., & Ferrarese, M. (1979). The nature of competence in normal and deviant children. In M. W. Kent & J. E. Rolf (Eds.), *Primary prevention of psychopathology: Vol. III. Social competence in children* (pp. 23–43). Hanover, NH: The University of Vermont Press and The University Press of New England.

Garmezy, N., & Nuechterlein, K. H. (1972). Invulnerable children: The fact and fiction of competence and disadvantage (Abstract). *American Journal of Orthopsychiatry, 42,* 328–329.

Garmezy, N., & Rutter, M. (1985). Acute reactions to stress. In M. Rutter & L. Hersov (Eds.), *Child psychiatry: Modern approaches* (2nd ed.) (pp. 152–176). Oxford, England: Blackwell.

Garmezy, N., & Tellegen, A. (1984). Studies of stress-resistant children: Methods, variables, and preliminary findings. In F. L. Morrison, C. Lord, & D. P. Keating (Eds.), *Applied developmental psychology.* (Vol. 1, pp. 231–287). New York: Academic Press.

Geertz, C. (1973). Deep play: Notes on the Balinese cockfight. In C. Geertz, *The interpretation of cultures: Selected essays* (pp. 412–454). New York: Basic Books. (Original work published 1972)

Geertz, C. (1973a). The impact of the concept of culture on the concept of man. In C. Geertz, *The interpretation of cultures: Selected essays* (pp. 33–55). New York: Basic Books. (Original work published 1966)

Geertz, C. (1973b). Person, time and conduct in Bali. In C. Geertz, *The interpretation of cultures: Selected essays* (pp. 360–411). New York: Basic Books. (Original work published 1966)

Geertz, C. (1973c). Religion as a cultural system. In C. Geertz, *The interpretation of cultures: Selected essays* (pp. 87–125). New York: Basic Books. (Original work published 1966)

Geertz, C. (1973). Ritual and social change: A Javanese example. In C. Geertz, *The interpretation of cultures: Selected essays* (pp. 142–169). New York: Basic Books. (Original work published 1959)

Geertz, C. (1973). Thick description: Toward an interpretive theory of culture. In C. Geertz, *The interpretation of cultures: Selected essays* (pp. 3–32). New York: Basic Books.

Geertz, C. (1983a). Blurred genres: The reconfiguration of social thought. In C. Geertz, *Local knowledge: Further essays in interpretive anthropology* (pp. 19–35). New York: Basic Books. (Original work published 1980)

Geertz, C. (1983b). Local knowledge: Fact and law in comparative perspective. In C. Geertz, *Local knowledge: Further essays in interpretive anthropology* (pp. 167–234). New York: Basic Books.

Geertz, C. (1984). From the native's point of view: On the nature of anthropological understanding. In C. Geertz, *Local knowledge: Further essays in interpretive anthropology* (pp. 167–234). New York: Basic Books. (Original work published 1974)

Ginzburg, C. (1980). *The cheese and the worm: The cosmos of a sixteenth century miller* (J. Tedeschi & A. Tedeschi, Trans.). Baltimore: Johns Hopkins University Press.

Ginzburg, C. (1989). *Clues, myths, and the historical method.* (J. Tedeschi & A. Tedeschi, Trans.). Baltimore: Johns Hopkins University Press.

Glazer, N., & Moynihan, D. (1963/1967). *Beyond the melting pot: The Negroes, Puerto Ricans, Jews, Italian and Irish of New York City.* Cambridge, MA: The M.I.T. Press.

Goertzel, V., & Goertzel, M. G. (1962). *Cradles of eminence.* Boston: Little Brown.

Goldschmidt, W. (1971). The theory of cultural adaptation: Introduction to R. Edgerton, *The individual in cultural adaptation* (pp. 1–21). Berkeley: University of California Press.

Goldschmidt, W. (1976). *Culture and behavior of the Sebei.* Berkeley: University of California Press.

Goldstein, M. (1987). Psychosocial issues. *Schizophrenia Bulletin, 13,* 157–171.

Goldstein, M. (1990). Family relations as risk factors for the onset and course of schizophrenia. In J. Rolf, A. Masten, D. Cicchetti, K. Nuechterlein, & S. Weintraub (Eds.), *Risk and protective factors in the development of psychopathology* (pp. 408–423). New York: Cambridge University Press.

Goodman, S. (1987). Emory University project on children of disturbed parents. *Schizophrenia Bulletin, 13,* 411–423.

Goodman, S., & Brumley, H. (1990). Schizophrenic and depressed mothers: Relational deficits in parenting. *Developmental Psychology, 26,* 31–39.

Goodman, S., & Johnson, M. (1986). Life problems, social supports, and psychological functioning of emotionally disturbed and well low-income women. *Journal of Community Psychology, 14,* 150–158.

Gordon, H. (1934). Psychiatry in Kenya Colony. *Journal of Mental Science, 80,* 167.

Gottesman, I., & Shields, J. (1982). *Schizophrenia: The epigenetic puzzle.* New York: Cambridge University Press.

Greeley, A., & McCready, W. (1974). Does ethnicity matter? *Ethnicity, 1,* 89–108.

Greenson, R. (1971). A dream while drowning. In J. McDevitt & C. Settlage (Eds.), *Separation-individuation: Essays in honor of Margaret S. Mahler* (pp. 377–384). New York: International Universities Press.

Greven, P. (1977). The Protestant temperament: Patterns of child-rearing, religious experience, and the self in early America. Chicago: University of Chicago Press.

Grossman, F., Beinashowitz, J., Anderson, L., Sakurai, M., Finnin, L., & Flaherty, M. (1992). Risk and resilience in young adolescents. *Journal of Youth and Adolescence, 21,* 529–550.

Grossman, J. (1989). *Land of hope: Chicago, black southerners and the Great Depression.* Chicago: University of Chicago Press.

Grunebaum, H., Weiss, J., Cohler, B., Hartman, C., & Gallant, D. (1982). *Mentally ill mothers and their children (rev. ed.).* Chicago: University of Chicago Press. (Original work published 1975)

Gurevich, A. (1992). *Historical anthropology of the middle ages.* Chicago: University of Chicago Press.

Guiteras-Holmes, C. (1961). *Parts of the soul: The world view of a Tzotzil Indian.* New York: Free Press/Macmillan.

Gutman, H. (1976). *The black family in slavery and freedom, 1750–1925.* New York: Pantheon Books.

Gutmann, D., Griffin, B., & Grunes, J. (1982). Developmental contributions to late-onset affective disorders. In P. B. Baltes & O. G. Brim, Jr. (Eds.), *Life-span development and behavior.* (Vol. 4, pp. 244–263). New York: Academic Press.

Guttentag, M., & Secord, P. (1983). *Too many women: The sex ratio question.* Beverly Hills, CA: Sage.

Haan, N. (1977). *Coping and defending: Processes of self-environment organization.* New York: Academic Press.

Haan, N. (1982). The assessment of coping, defense, and stress. In L. Goldberg & S. Breznitz (Eds.), *Handbook of stress* (pp. 254–269). New York: Free Press/Macmillan.

Hanson, D., Gottesman, I. I., & Heston, L. (1976). Some possible childhood indicators of adult schizophrenia inferred from children of schizophrenics. *British Journal of Psychiatry, 129,* 142–154.

Hanson, D., Gottesman, I., & Heston, L. (1990). Long-range schizophrenia forecasting: Many a slip twixt cup and lip. In J. Rolf, A. Masten, D. Cicchetti, K. Nuechterlein, & S. Weintraub (Eds.), *Risk and protective factors in the development of psychopathology* (pp. 424–444). New York: Cambridge University Press.

Hanson, D., Gottesman, I. I., & Meehl, P. E. (1977). Genetic theories and the validation of psychiatric diagnosis: Implications for the study of children of schizophrenics. *Journal of Abnormal Psychology, 6,* 575–588.

Harkness, S., & Super, C. (1990). Culture and psychopathology. In M. Lewis & S. Miller (Eds.), *Handbook of developmental psychopathology* (pp. 41–52). New York: Plenum.

Harper, L. (1975). The scope of offspring effects: From caregiver to culture. *Psychological Bulletin, 82,* 784–801.

Hartmann, H. (1958). *Ego psychology and the problem of adaptation* (D. Rapaport, Trans.). New York: International Universities Press. (Original work published 1939)

Hay, D. (1988). Studying the impact of ordinary life: A developmental model research plan and words of caution. In M. Rutter (Ed.), *Studies of psychosocial risk: The power of longitudinal data* (pp. 245–254). New York: Cambridge University Press.

Heath, S. B. (1989). The learner as cultural member. In M. Rice & R. Schiefelbusch (Eds.), *The teachability of language* (pp. 333–350). Baltimore: Brooks.

Heath, S. B. (1991). The children of Trackton's children: Spoken and written language in social change. In J. Stigler, R. Shweder, & G. Herdt (Eds.), *Cultural psychology: Essays on comparative human development* (pp. 496–519). New York: Cambridge University Press.

Heller, T., Sosna, M., & Wellbery, D. (Eds.) (1986). *Reconstructing individualism: Autonomy, individuality and the self in western thought.* Stanford, CA: Stanford University Press.

Henry, J. (1963). *Culture against man.* New York: Random House.

Henry, J. (1965). *Pathways to madness.* New York: Random House.

Heston, L., & Denny, D. (1968). Interactions between early life experience and biological factors in schizophrenia. In D. Rosenthal & S. Kety (Eds.), *The transmission of schizophrenia* (pp. 363–376). New York: Pergamon.

Henri, F. (1975). *Black migration: Movement north: 1900–1920.* New York: Anchor Press.

Hill, J. (Ed.). (1988). *Rethinking history and myth: Indigenous South American perspectives on the past.* Urbana: University of Illinois Press.

Hoffman, L., & Manis, J. (1978). Influence of children on marital interaction and parental satisfactions and dissatisfactions. In R. M. Lerner & G. Spanier (Eds.), *Child influence on marital and family interaction: A life-span perspective* (pp. 165–213). New York: Academic Press.

Hollingshead, A., & Redlich, F. (1958). *Social class and mental illness.* New York: Wiley.

Holmes, T., & Rahe, R. R. (1967). The social readjustment rating scale. *Journal of Psychosomatic Research, 11,* 213–218.

Hughes, C., Tremblay, M., Rapoport, R., & Leighton, A. (1960). *The Stirling County study of psychiatric disorder and sociocultural environment: Vol. II. People of Cove and Woodlot: Communities from the viewpoint of social psychiatry.* New York: Basic Books.

Jacobs, M., Fischhoff, B., & Davis, W. (1993). Adolescent (in)vulnerability. *American Psychologist, 48,* 102–116.

Jahoda, G. (1980). The land systematic approaches in cross-cultural psychology. In H. Triandis & J. Draguns (Eds.), *Handbook of cultural psychology: I. Perspectives* (pp. 69–141). Boston: Allyn & Bacon.

Jahoda, M. (1958). *Current concepts of positive mental health.* New York: Basic Books.

Jenkins, J. (1984). Schizophrenia and the family: Expressed emotion among Mexican-Americans and Anglo-Americans. *Dissertation Abstracts International, 45*(6-A), 1806.

Jenkins, J. (1991). Anthropology, expressed emotion and schizophrenia. *Ethos, 10,* 387–432.

Jenkins, J., Karno, M., de la Selva, A., Santana, F., Telles, C., Lopez, S., & Mintz, J. (1986). Expressed emotion, maintenance pharmacotherapy and schizophrenic relapse among Mexican-Americans. *Psychopharmacology Bulletin, 22,* 621–627.

Jessor, R. (1993). Successful adolescent development among youth in high-risk settings. *American Psychologist, 48,* 117–126.

Kagan, J. (1980). Perspectives on continuity. In O. G. Brim, Jr., & J. Kagan (Eds.), *Continuity and change in human development* (pp. 26–74). Cambridge, MA: Harvard University Press.

Kagan, J. (1983). Stress and coping in early development. In N. Garmezy & M. Rutter (Eds.), *Stress, coping, and development in children* (pp. 191–216). New York: McGraw-Hill.

Kagan, J. (1984). Continuity and change in the opening years of life. In R. Emde & R. Harmon (Eds.), *Continuities and discontinuities in development* (pp. 15–40). New York: Plenum.

Kagan, J., Klein, R., Finley, G., Rogoff, B., & Nolan, E. (1979). A cross-cultural study of cognitive development. *Monographs of the Society for Research in Child Development, 44,* (Serial No. 180).

Kagan, J., & Moss, H. (1963). *From birth to maturity.* New York: Wiley.

Kahn, R. (1979). Aging and social support. In M. Riley (Ed.), *Aging from birth to death* (pp. 77–91). Boulder, CO: Westview Press.

Kahn, R., & Antonucci, T. (1980). Convoys over the life course: Attachment, roles, and social support. In P. B. Baltes & O. G. Brim, Jr. (Eds.), *Life-span development and behavior* (Vol. 3, pp. 254–286). New York: Academic Press.

Kakar, S. (1982). *Shamans, mystics and doctors: A psychological inquiry into India and its healing traditions.* New York: Knopf.

Kakar, S. (1989). The maternal-feminine in Indian psychoanalysis. *International Journal of Psychoanalysis, 16,* 355–362.

Karno, M., Jenkins, J., de la Selva, A., & Santana, F. (1987). Expressed emotion and schizophrenic outcome among Mexican-American families. *Journal of Nervous and Mental Disease, 175,* 143–151.

Karno, M., & Associates (1987). Mental disorder among Mexican Americans and non-Hispanic whites in Los Angeles. In M. Gaviria & J. D. Arana (Eds.), *Health and behavior: Research agenda for Hispanics.* Chicago: University of Illinois and Simon Bolivar Hispanic Research Program.

Kauffman, C., Grunebaum, H., Cohler, B., & Gamer, E. (1979). Superkids: Competent children of schizophrenic mothers. *American Journal of Psychiatry, 136,* 1398–1402.

Kazdin, A. (1989). Developmental psychopathology: Current research, issues and directions. *American Psychologist, 44,* 180–187.

Kazdin, A. (1993). Adolescent mental health: Prevention and treatment programs. *American Psychologist, 48,* 127–141.

Kent, M. W., & Rolf, J. (Eds.). (1979). *Primary prevention of psychopathology: III. Social competence in children.* Hanover, NH: The University of Vermont Press and The University Press of New England.

Kessler, R. C., & Cleary, P. (1980). Social class and psychological distress. *American Sociological Review, 45,* 463–478.

Kessler, R. C., & McLeod, J. (1984). Sex differences in vulnerability to undesirable life events. *American Sociological Review, 49,* 620–631.

Kessler, R. C., Price, R., & Wortman, C. (1985). Social factors in psychopathology: Stress, social support, and coping processes. *Annual Review of Psychology, 36,* 531–572.

Kirkpatrick, J., & White, G. (1985). Exploring ethnopsychologies. In G. White & J. Kirkpatrick (Eds.), *Person, self, and experience: Exploring pacific ethnopsychologies* (pp. 3–34). Berkeley: University of California Press.

Kleinman, A. (1988). *Rethinking psychiatry: From cultural category to personal experience.* New York: Free Press.

Kleinman, A., & Good, B. (1985). *Culture and depression: Studies in the anthropology and cross-cultural psychiatry of affect and disorder.* Berkeley: University of California Press.

Kluckhohn, C. (1951). Values and value orientations. In T. Parsons & E. Shils (Eds.), *Toward a general theory of action* (pp. 388–433). Cambridge, MA: Harvard University Press.

Kluckhohn, C., & Kroeber, A. L. (1963). *Culture: A critical review of concepts and definitions.* New York: Random House/Vintage.

Kluckhohn, C., Murray, H., & Schneider, D. (Eds.). (1961). *Personality in nature, culture, and society.* New York: Knopf.

Kluckhohn, F., & Strodtbeck, F. (1961). *Variations in value orientations.* Evanston, IL: Harper & Row.

Kohut, H. (1959/1978). Introspection, empathy and psychoanalysis: An examination of the relationship between mode of observation and theory. In P. Ornstein (Ed.), *The Search for the Self: Selected Writings of Heinz Kohut, 1950–1978.* (Vol. I, pp. 205–232). New York: International Universities Press.

Kohut, H. (1971). *The analysis of the self* (*Monographs of the Psychoanalytic Study of the Child,* No. 1). New York: International Universities Press.

Kohut, H. (1977). *The restoration of the self.* New York: International Universities Press.

Kohut, H. (1979). The two analyses of Mr. Z. *International Journal of Psychoanalysis, 60,* 3–27.

Kolm, R. (1971). Ethnicity in society and community. In O. Feinstein (Ed.), *Ethnic groups in the city: Culture, institutions and power* (pp. 57–77). Lexington, MA: Lexington Books/Heath.

Kracke, W. (1981). Kagwahiv Mourning: Dreams of a Bereaved Father. *Ethos 9:* 258–275.

Kracke, W. (1987). Encounter with other cultures: Psychological and epistemological aspects. *Ethos, 15,* 58–82.

Kracke, W., & Herdt, G. (1987). Introduction: Interpretation in psychoanalytic anthropology. *Ethos, 15,* 3–8.

Kroeber, T. (1963). The coping functions of the ego mechanisms. In R. W. White (Ed.), *The study of lives* (pp. 178–199). New York: Aldine/Atherton.

Laboratory of Comparative Human Cognition. (1983). Culture and cognitive development. In P. H. Mussen (Ed.), W. Kessen (Vol. Ed.), *Handbook of child psychology (formerly Carmichael's manual of child psychology) (4th ed.)* (pp. 295–356). New York: Wiley.

Lamb, M. (1978). Influence of the child on marital quality and family interaction during the prenatal, perinatal and infancy periods. In R. Lerner & G. Spanier (Eds.), *Child influences on marital and family interaction: A life-span perspective* (pp. 137–164). New York: Academic Press.

Lambo, T. A. (1974). The vulnerable African child. In E. J. Anthony & C. Koupernik (Eds.), *The child in his family: Children at psychiatric risk* (pp. 259–278). New York: Wiley.

Lazarus, R., & Folkman, S. (1984). *Stress, appraisal and coping.* New York: Springer.

Leff, J., & Vaughn, C. (1985). *Expressed emotion in families.* New York: Guilford.

Leff, J., Wig, N., Ghosh, A., & Bedi, H. (1987). Influence of relatives' expressed emotion on the course of schizophrenia in Chandigarh: III. *British Journal of Psychiatry, 151,* 166–173.

Lefley, H. (1985). Families of the mentally ill in cross-cultural perspective. *Psychosocial Rehabilitation Journal, 8,* 57–75.

Leichter, H., & Mitchell, W. (1967). *Kinship and casework.* New York: Russell-Sage Foundation.

Leighton, A. (1959). *The Stirling County study of psychiatric disorder and sociocultural environment: Vol. I. My name is legion: Foundations for a theory of man in relation to culture.* New York: Basic Books.

Leighton, A. (1976). Conceptual perspectives. In B. Kaplan, R. Wilson, & A. Leighton (Eds.), *Further explorations in social psychiatry* (pp. 14–24). New York: Basic Books.

Leighton, D., Harding, J., Macklin, D., Macmillan, A., & Leighton, A. (1963). *The Stirling County study of psychiatric disorder and sociocultural environment: Vol. III. The character of danger: Psychiatric symptoms in selected communities.* New York: Basic Books.

Lerner, R., & Busch-Rossnagel, N. (1981). Individuals as producers of their own development: Conceptual and empirical issues. In R. Lerner & N. Busch-Rossnagel (Eds.), *Individuals as producers of their own development* (pp. 1–36). New York: Academic Press.

Lerner, R., & Spanier, G. (1978). A dynamic interactional view of child and family development. In R. Lerner & G. Spanier (Eds.), *Child influences on marital and family interaction: A life-span perspective* (pp. 1–22). New York: Academic Press.

Le Roy Ladurie, E. (1979). *Montaillou: The promised land of error* (B. Bray, Trans.). New York: Vintage Books.

LeVine, R. (1970). Cross-cultural study in child psychology. In P. H. Mussen (Ed.), *Carmichael's manual of child psychology (3rd ed.)* (pp. 559–614). New York: Wiley.

LeVine, R. (1973). *Culture, behavior, and personality.* New York: Aldine/Atherton.

LeVine, R. (1974). Parental goals: A cross-cultural view. In H. Leichter (Ed.), *The family as educator.* New York: Teachers College Press.

LeVine, R., Dixon, S., LeVine, S., Richman, A., Leiderman, P., Keefer, C., & Brazelton, T. B. (1994). *Childcare and culture: Lessons from Africa.* New York: Cambridge University Press.

LeVine, R., & LeVine, B. [Lloyd] (1963). Nyangsongo: A Gusii community in Kenya. In B. Whiting (Ed.), *Six cultures* (Vol. 2) New York: Wiley.

LeVine, R., & Miller, P. (1990). Commentary (Cross-cultural validity of attachment theory). *Human Development, 33,* 73–79.

LeVine, S. (1979). *Mothers and wives: Gusii women of East Africa.* Chicago: University of Chicago Press.

Levi-Strauss, C. (1963). *Structural anthropology.* (C. Jacobson & B. Grundfest Schoepf, Trans.). New York: Basic Books.

Levi-Strauss, C. (1966). *The savage mind.* Chicago: University of Chicago Press. (Original work published 1962)

Lewis, M. (1990a). Challenges to the study of psychopathology. In M. Lewis & S. Miller (Eds.), *Handbook of developmental psychopathology* (pp. 29–40). New York: Plenum.

Lewis, M. (1990b). Models of developmental psychopathology. In M. Lewis & S. Miller (Eds.), *Handbook of developmental psychopathology* (pp. 15–27). New York: Plenum.

Lidz, T. (1963). *The family and human adaptation: Three lectures.* New York: International Universities Press.

Lidz, T., Fleck, S., & Cornelison, A. (1965). *Schizophrenia and the family.* New York: International Universities Press.

Luthar, S. (1991). Vulnerability and resilience: A study of high-risk adolescents. *Child Development, 62,* 600–616.

Luthar, S. (1993). Annotation: Methodological and conceptual issues in research on childhood resilience. *Journal of Child Psychology and Psychiatry and Allied Disciplines, 34,* 441–453.

Luthar, S., Doernberger, C., & Zigler, E. (1993). Resilience is not a unidimensional construct: Insights from a prospective study of inner-city adolescents. Special Issue: Milestones in the development resilience, *Development and Psychopathology, 5,* 703–717.

Luthar, S., & Ziegler, E. (1991a). Vulnerability and competence: A review of research on resilience in childhood. *American Journal of Orthopsychiatry, 61,* 6–22.

Luthar, S., & Ziegler, E. (1991b). Vulnerability and resilience: A study of high risk adolescents. *Child Development, 62,* 600–616.

Luthar, S., & Ziegler, E. (1992). Intelligence and social competence among high-risk adolescents. *Development and Psychopathology, 4,* 287–299.

Lutz, C. (1985). Ethnopsychology compared to what? Explaining behavior and consciousness among the Ifaluk. In G. White & J. Kirkpatrick (Eds.), *Person, self, and experience: Exploring pacific ethnopsychologies* (pp. 35–79). Berkeley: University of California Press.

Lutz, C. (1988). *Unnatural emotions: Everyday sentiments on a micronesian atoll.* Chicago: University of Chicago Press.

Lyons-Ruth, K., Botein, S., & Grunebaum, H. (1984). Reaching the hard-to-reach: Serving isolated and depressed mothers with infants in the community. *New Directions for Mental Health Services, 24,* 94–122.

Lyons-Ruth, K., Connell, D., Grunebaum, H., & Botein, S. (1990). Infants at social risk: Maternal depression and family support services as mediators of infant development and security of attachment. *Child Development, 61,* 85–98.

Lyons-Ruth, K., Zoll, D., Connell, D., & Grunebaum, H. (1986). The depressed mother and her one year infant: Environment, interaction, attachment and infant development. *New Directions for Child Development, 34,* 61–82.

Malinowski, B. (1989). *A diary in the strictest sense of the word* (N. Guterman, Trans.). Stanford, CA: Stanford University Press. (Original work published 1967)

MacFarlane, A. (1987). *The culture of capitalism.* Oxford, England: Basil Blackwell.

Marcus, G., & Fischer, M. (1986). *Anthropology as cultural critique: An experiential moment in the human sciences.* Chicago: University of Chicago Press.

Marcus, J., Auerbach, J., Wilkinson, L., & Burack, C. (1981). Infants at risk for schizophrenia: The Jerusalem development study. *Archives of General Psychiatry, 38,* 703–713.

Marsella, A. (1980). Depressive experience and disorder across cultures. In H. Triandis & J. Draguns (Eds.), *Handbook of cross-cultural psychology: Vol. VI. Psychopathology* (pp. 237–290). Boston: Allyn & Bacon.

Masten, A. (1985). Risk, vulnerability and protective factors in developmental psychopathology. In B. Lahey & A. Kazdin (Eds.), *Advances in clinical child psychology* (Vol. 8, pp. 1–52). New York: Plenum.

Masten, A. (1989). Resilience in development: Implications of the study of successful adaptation for developmental psychopathology. In D. Cicchetti (Ed.), *The emergence of a discipline: The Rochester Symposium on Developmental Psychopathology: I* (pp. 261–294). Hillsdale, NJ: Erlbaum.

Masten, A., Best, K., & Garmezy, N. (1990). Resilience and development: Contributions from the study of children who overcome adversity. *Development and Psychopathology, 2,* 425–444.

Masten, A., & Garmezy, N. (1985). Risk, vulnerability, and protective factors in developmental psychopathology. In B. Lahey & A. Kazdin (Eds.), *Advances in clinical child psychology,* (Vol. 8, pp. 1–52). New York: Plenum.

Masten, A., Morison, P., Pellegrini, D., & Tellegen, A. (1990). Competence under stress: Risk and protective factors. In J. Rolf, A. Masten, D. Cicchetti, K. Nuechterlein, & S. Weintraub (Eds.), *Risk and protective factors in the development of psychopathology* (pp. 236–256). New York: Cambridge University Press.

Maughan, B. (1988). School experiences as risk/protective factors. In M. Rutter (Ed.), *Studies of psychosocial risk: The power of longitudinal data* (pp. 200–226). New York: Cambridge University Press.

Mauss, M. (1967). *The gift.* (I. Cunnison, Trans.). New York: Norton. (Original work published 1925)

McLeod, J. (1991). Childhood parental loss and adult depression. *Journal of Health and Social Behavior, 32,* 205–220.

Mead, M. (1928). *Coming of age in Samoa: A psychological study of primitive youth for Western civilization.* New York: Morrow.

Mead, M. (1930). *Growing up in New Guinea: A comparative study of primitive education.* New York: Morrow.

Meissner, W. (1970). Sibling relations in the schizophrenic family. *Family Process, 9,* 1–26.

Menaghan, E. (1983). Individual coping efforts: Moderators of the relationship between life stress and mental health outcomes. In H. Kaplan (Ed.), *Psychosocial stress: Trends in theory and research* (pp. 157–191). New York: Academic Press.

Miklowitz, D., Goldstein, M., & Falloon, I. (1983). Premorbid and symptomatic characteristics of schizophrenics from families with high and low levels of expressed emotion. *Journal of Abnormal Psychology, 92,* 359–367.

Miklowitz, D., Goldstein, M., Falloon, I, & Doane, J. (1984). Interactional correlates of expressed emotion in the families of schizophrenics. *British Journal of Psychiatry, 144,* 482–487.

Milgram, N., & Palti, G. (1993). Psychosocial characteristics of resilient children. *Journal of Research in Personality, 27,* 207–221.

Miller, D., & Swanson, G. (1960). *Inner conflict and defense.* New York: Henry Holt-Dryden.

Mink, L. (1987). *Historical understanding.* (B. Fay, E. Golob, & R. Vann, Eds.). Ithaca, NY: Cornell University Press.

Minturn, L., & Lambert, W. (1964). *Mothers of six cultures: Studies of child-rearing.* New York: Wiley.

Mintz, N., & Schwartz, D. (1964). Urban ecology and psychosis: Community factors in the incidence of schizophrenic and manic-depression among Italians in greater Boston. *International Journal of Social Psychiatry, 10,* 101–118.

Minuchin, S. (1970). The use of an ecological framework in the treatment of a child. In E. J. Anthony & C. Koupernik (Eds.), *The child in his family* (pp. 41–58). New York: Wiley.

Mirsky, A., & Duncan, C. (1986). Etiology and expression of schizophrenia: Neurobiological and psychosocial factors. *Annual Review of Psychology, 37,* 291–319.

Mishler, E., & Scotch, N. (1963). Sociocultural factors in the epidemiology of schizophrenia. *Psychiatry, 26,* 315–353.

Modell, J., & Siegler, R. (1993). Child development and human diversity. In G. H. Elder, Jr., J. Modell, & R. D. Parke (Eds.), *Children in time and place: Developmental and historical insights* (pp. 73–105). New York: Cambridge University Press.

Monroe, S. (1983). Major and minor life-events as predictors of psychological distress: Further issues and findings. *Journal of Behavioral Medicine, 6,* 189–205.

Moriarty, A. (1987). John: A boy who acquired resilience. In E. J. Anthony & B. J. Cohler (Eds.), *The invulnerable child* (pp. 106–144). New York: Guilford.

Monroe, R., & Monroe, R. (1980). Perspectives suggested by psychological data. In H. Triandis & J. Draguns (Eds.), *Handbook of cultural psychology. I: Perspectives* (pp. 253–317). Boston: Allyn & Bacon.

Murphy, L. B. (1960a). The child's way of coping: A longitudinal study of normal children. *Bulletin of the Menninger Clinic, 24,* 136–143.

Murphy, L. B. (1960b). Coping devices and defense mechanisms in relation to autonomous ego functions. *Bulletin of the Menninger Clinic, 24,* 114–153.

Murphy, L. B. (1962). *The widening world of childhood.* New York: Basic Books.

Murphy, L. B. (1970). The problem of defense and the concept of coping. In E. J. Anthony & C. Koupernik (Eds.), *The child in his family:* (Vol. II, pp. 65–86). New York: Wiley.

Murphy, L. B. (1974). Coping, vulnerability, and resilience in childhood. In G. V. Coelho, D. Hamburg, & J. Adams (Eds.), *Coping and adaptation* (pp. 69–100). New York: Basic Books.

Murphy, L. B. (1982). *Robin: Comprehensive treatment of a vulnerable adolescent.* New York: Basic Books.

Murphy, L. B. (1987). Further reflections on resilience. In E. J. Anthony & B. J. Cohler (Eds.), *The invulnerable child* (pp. 84–105). New York: Guilford.

Murphy, L. B., & Moriarty, A. (1976). *Vulnerability, coping, and growth: From infancy to adolescence.* New Haven, CT: Yale University Press.

Musick, J., Stott, F., Spencer, K. K., Goldman, J., & Cohler, B. (1987). Maternal factors related to vulnerability and resiliency in young children at risk. In E. J. Anthony & B. J. Cohler (Eds.), *The invulnerable child* (pp. 229–252). New York: Guilford.

Myers, J. K., & Bean, L. L. (1968). *A decade later: A follow-up of social class and mental illness.* New York: Wiley.

Nelson, K. (1989). *Narrative From the Crib.* Cambridge, MA: Harvard University Press.

Neufield, R. W. J., & Mothersill, K. (1980). Stress as an irritant of psychopathology. In I. Sarason & C. Spielberger (Eds.), *Stress and anxiety, III* (pp. 31–56). New York: Hemisphere.

Neugarten, B. (1979). Time, age and the life-cycle. *American Journal of Psychiatry, 136,* 887–894.

Neugarten, B., & Hagestad, G. (1976). Aging and the life-course. In R. Binstock & E. Shanas (Eds.), *Handbook of aging and the social sciences* (pp. 35–57). New York: Van Nostrand-Reinhold.

Neugarten, B., & Moore, J. (1968). The changing age-status system. In B. Neugarten (Ed.), *Middle-age and aging: A reader in social psychology* (pp. 5–20). Chicago: University of Chicago Press.

Neugarten, B., Moore, J., & Lowe, J. (1965). Age norms, age constraints, and adult socialization. *American Journal of Sociology, 70,* 710–717.

Neugebauer, B., Dohrenwend, B. P., & Dohrenwend, B. S. (1980). Formulation of hypotheses about the true prevalence of functional psychiatric disorders among adults in the United States. In B. P. Dohrenwend, B. S. Dohrenwend, M. S. Gould, B. Link, R. Neugebauer, & R. Wunsch-Hitzig (Eds.), *Mental disorders in the United States: Epidemiological estimates* (pp. 45–94). New York: Praeger.

Nicholson, I., & Neufeld, R. (1989). Forms and mechanisms of susceptibility to stress in schizophrenia. In R. Neufeld (Ed.), *Advances in the investigation of psychological stress* (pp. 392–420). New York: Wiley.

Nicholson, I., & Neufeld, R. (1992). A dynamic vulnerability perspective on stress and schizophrenia. *American Journal of Orthopsychiatry, 62,* 117–130.

Nunberg, H. (1931). The synthetic function of the ego. *International Journal of Psychoanalysis, 12,* 123–140.

Nunberg, H. (1965). *Principles of psychoanalysis: Their application to the neuroses* (M. Kahr, & S. Kahr, Trans.). New York: International Universities Press. (Original work published 1932)

Obeyesekere, G. (1990). *The work of culture: Symbolic transformation in psychoanalysis and anthropology.* Chicago: University of Chicago Press.

Offer, D., & Sabshin, M. (1974). *Normality: Clinical and theoretical concepts of mental health.* New York: Basic Books.

Ogbu, J. (1981). Origins of human competence: A cultural-ecological perspective. *Child Development, 52,* 413–429.

Ogbu, J. (1982). Cultural discontinuities and schooling. *Anthropology and Education, 13,* 290–307.

Ogbu, J. (1983). Minority status and schooling in plural societies. *Comparative Education Review, 27,* 168–190.

Ogbu, J. (1990a). Cultural model, identity, and literacy. In J. Stigler, R. Shweder, & G. Herdt (Eds.), *Cultural psychology: Essays on comparative human development* (pp. 520–541). New York: Cambridge University Press.

Ogbu, J. (1990b). Minority status and literacy in a comparative perspective. *Daedalus, 119,* 141–168.

Ohnuki-Tierney, E. (Ed.). (1990). *Culture through time: Anthropological approaches.* Stanford, CA: Stanford University Press.

Opler, M. (1959a). Cultural differences in mental disorders: An Italian and Irish contrast in the schizophrenias-U.S.A. In M. Opler (Ed.), *Culture and mental health: Cross-cultural studies* (pp. 425–444). New York: Macmillan.

Opler, M. K. (Ed.). (1959b). *Culture and mental health: Cross-cultural studies.* New York: Macmillan.

Opler, M. (1967). *Culture and social psychiatry.* New York: Atherton Press.

Opler, M., & Singer, J. (1956). Ethnic differences in behavior and psychopathology: Italian and Irish. *International Journal of Social Psychiatry, 2,* 11–22.

Overton, W., & Horowitz, H. (1991). Developmental psychopathology: Integrations and differentiations. In D. Cicchetti & S. L. Toth (Eds.), *Models and integrations: Rochester Symposium on Developmental Psychopathology* (Vol. 3, pp. 1–42). Rochester, NY: University of Rochester Press.

Papajohn, J., & Spiegel, J. (1975). *Transactions in families.* San Francisco: Jossey-Bass.

Park, R., Burgess, E., & McKenzie, R. (1925/1967). *The City.* Chicago: The University of Chicago Press.

Parker, B. (1972). *A mingled yarn: Chronicle of a troubled family.* New Haven: Yale University Press.

Parker, S., & Sasaki, T. (1965). Society and sentiments in two contrasting socially disturbed areas. In J. Murphy & A. H. Leighton (Eds.), *Approaches to cross-cultural psychiatry* (pp. 329–360). Ithaca, NY: Cornell University Press.

Parsons, A. (1969). *Belief, magic and anomie: Essays in psychosocial anthropology.* New York: Free Press/Macmillan.

Parsons, T. (1949). The social structure of the family. In R. Anshen (Ed.), *The family: Its function and destiny* (p. 190). New York: Harper & Row.

Parsons, T. (1951). *The social system.* New York: Free Press.

Parsons, T. (1955a). The American family: Its relations to personality and to the social structure. In T. Parsons & R. F. Bales (Eds.), *Family, socialization, and interaction* (pp. 3–34). New York: Free Press/Macmillan.

Parsons, T. (1955b). Family structure and the socialization of the child. In T. Parsons & R. F. Bales (Eds.), *Family, socialization, and interaction* (pp. 35–132). New York: Free Press/Macmillan.

Pasamanick, B., & Knobloch, H. (1960). Brain damage and reproductive casualty. *American Journal of Orthopsychiatry, 30,* 298–305.

Paykel, E., Prusoff, B., & Uhlenhuth, E. (1972). Scaling of life events. *Archives of General Psychiatry, 25,* 340–347.

Paykel, E., & Uhlenhuth, E. (1972). Rating the magnitude of life stress. *Canadian Psychiatric Association Journal, 17,* SS93-SS100.

Pearlin, L. (1975). Sex roles and depression. In N. Datan & L. Ginsberg (Eds.), *Life-span developmental psychology: Normative life crises* (pp. 191–207). New York: Academic Press.

Pearlin, L. (1980). The life-cycle and life strains. In H. Blalock, Jr. (Ed.), *Sociological theory and research* (pp. 349–360). New York: Free Press/Macmillan.

Pearlin, L. (1983). Role strains and personal stress. In H. B. Kaplan (Ed.), *Psychosocial stress: Trends in theory and research* (pp. 3–32). New York: Academic Press.

Pearlin, L., & Lieberman, M. (1979). Social sources of emotional distress. In R. Simmons (Ed.), *Research in community and mental health, Vol. 1* (pp. 217–248). Greenwich, CT: JAI Press.

Pearlin, L., Lieberman, M., Menaghan, E., & Mullan, J. (1981). The stress process. *Journal of Health and Social Behavior, 22,* 337–356.

Pearlin, L., & Schooler, C. (1978). The structure of coping. *Journal of Health and Social Behavior, 19,* 2–21.

Petersen, A. (1988). Adolescent development. *Annual Review of Psychology, 39,* 583–607.

Phillips, D., & Zimmerman, M. (1990). The developmental course of perceived competence and incompetence among competent children. In R. Sternberg & J. Kolligan, Jr. (Eds.), *Competence considered* (pp. 41–66). New Haven, CT: Yale University Press.

Plath, D. (1980). Contours of consociation: Lessons from a Japanese narrative. In P. Baltes & O. G. Brim, Jr. (Eds.), *Life span development and behavior* (pp. 287–307). New York: Academic Press.

Polansky, N., Chalmers, M. A., Buttenweiser, E., & Williams, D. (1981). *Damaged parents: An anatomy of child neglect.* Chicago: University of Chicago Press.

Polkinghorne, D. (1983). Methodology for the Human Sciences: Systems of Inquiry. Albany, NY: State University of New York Press.

Polkinghorne, D. (1988). Narrative Knowing and the Human Sciences. Albany, NY: State University of New York Press.

Power, E. (1992). Medieval people. New York: HarperCollins. (Original work published 1924)

Potter, D. (1954). *People of plenty.* Chicago: University of Chicago Press.

Price-Williams, D. R. (1985). Cultural psychology. In G. Lindzey & E. Aronson (Eds.), *Handbook of social psychology. Vol. II: Applications* (pp. 993–1042). New York: Random House.

Pruchno, R., Blow, F., & Smyer, M. (1984). Life events and interdependent lives: Implications for research and intervention. *Human Development, 27,* 31–41.

Rabinow, P. (1977). *Reflections on fieldwork in Morocco.* Berkeley: University of California Press.

Rabinow, P., & Sullivan, W. M. (1979). The interpretive turn: Emergence of an approach. In P. Rabinow & W. Sullivan (Eds.), *Interpretive Social Science: A Reader.* Berkeley, CA: The University of California Press, 1–24.

Radke-Yarrow, M., & Sherman, T. (1990). Hard growing: Children who survive. In J. Rolf, A. Masten, D. Cicchetti, K. Nechterlein, & S. Weintraub (Eds.), *Risk and protective factors in the development of psychopathology* (pp. 97–119). New York: Cambridge University Press.

Reeve, M-E. (1988). Cauchu Uras: Lowland Quichua Histories of the Amazon Rubber Basin. In J. Hill (Ed.), *Rethinking history and myth: Indigenous South American perspectives on the past* (pp. 19–34). Urbana: University of Illinois Press.

Ricks, D., & Berry, J. (1970). Family and symptom patterns that precede schizophrenia. In M. Roff & D. Ricks (Eds.), *Life-history research in psychopathology,* (Vol. 1, pp. 31–50). Minneapolis: University of Minnesota Press.

Ricoeur, P. (1991). From the hermeneutics of texts to the hermeneutics of action, Part II. *From text to action: Essays in hermeneutics* (K. Blamey & J. B. Thompson, Trans.) (Vol. II, pp. 105–226). Evanston, IL: Northwestern University Press.

Riesman, D., Glazer, N., & Denney, R. (1950). *The lonely crowd.* New Haven, CT: Yale University Press.

Riesman, P. (1977). *Freedom in Fulani social life: An introspective ethnography.* Chicago: University of Chicago Press.

Riesman, P. (1992). *First find your child a good mother: The construction of self in two African communities.* New Brunswick, NJ: Rutgers University Press.

Robertson, J. (1970). *Young children in the hospital* (2nd ed. with postscript). London: Tavistock. (Original work published 1958)

Robins, L. (1978). Study of childhood predictors of adult outcome: Replication from longitudinal studies. *Psychological Medicine, 8,* 611–622.

Rogler, L., & Hollingshead, A. (1965). *Trapped: Families and schizophrenia.* New York: Wiley.

Romney, A. K., & Romney, R. (1963). The Mixtecans of Juxtlahuaca. In B. Whiting (Ed.), *Six cultures* (Vol. 4). New York: Wiley.

Rosaldo, R. (1980). *Ilongot headhunting, 1883–1974: A study in society and history.* Stanford, CA: Stanford University Press.

Rothenberg, A. (1983). Psychopathology and creative cognition: A comparison of hospitalized patients, nobel laureates, and controls. *Archives of General Psychiatry, 40,* 937–942.

Roy, A. (1985). Early parental separation and adult depression. *Archives of General Psychiatry, 42,* 987–991.

Ruby, J. (Ed.). (1982). *A crack in the mirror: Reflexive perspectives in anthropology.* Philadelphia: University of Pennsylvania Press.

Rudolph, S., & Rudolph, L. (1978). Rajput adulthood: Reflections on the Amar Singh diary. In E. Erikson (Ed.), *Adulthood* (pp. 149–172). New York: Norton.

Rutter, M. (1970). Sex differences in children's responses to family stress. In E. J. Anthony & C. Koupernik (Eds.), *The child in his family* (pp. 165–169). New York: Wiley.

Rutter, M. (1979a). Maternal deprivation, 1972–1978: New findings, new concepts, new approachs. *Child Development, 50,* 283–305.

Rutter, M. (1979b). Protective factors in children's responses to stress and disadvantage. In M. W. Kent & J. E. Rolf (Eds.), *Primary prevention of psychopathology: Vol. III. Social competence in children* (pp. 49–74). Hanover, NH: University of Vermont Press and University Press of New England.

Rutter, M. (1981). *Maternal deprivation reassessed (2nd ed.).* London: Penguin. (Original work published 1972)

Rutter, M. (1983). Stress, coping and development: Some issues and some questions. In N. Garmezy & M. Rutter (Eds.), *Stress, coping and development* (pp. 1–41). New York: McGraw-Hill. (Original work published 1981)

Rutter, M. (1985). Resilience in the face of adversity. *British Journal of Psychiatry, 17,* 598–611.

Rutter, M. (1987). Psychosocial resilience and protective mechanisms. *American Journal of Orthopsychiatry, 57,* 316–331.

Rutter, M. (1989). Pathways from childhood to adult life. *Journal of Child Psychology and Psychiatry, 30,* 23–51.

Rutter, M. (1990). Psychosocial resilience and protective mechanisms. In J. Rolf, A. Masten, D. Cicchetti, K. Nuechterlein, & S. Weintraub (Eds.), *Risk and protective factors in the development of psychopathology* (pp. 181–214). New York: Cambridge University Press.

Rutter, M., & Garmezy, N. (1983). Developmental Psychopathology. In E. M. Hetherington (Ed.), *Handbook of child psychology (4th ed.)* (pp. 775–911). New York: Wiley.

Rutter, M., Quinton, D., & Hill, J. (1990). Adult outcome of institution-reared children: Males and females compared. In L. Robins & M. Rutter (Eds.), *Straight and devious pathways from childhood to adulthood* (pp. 135–157). New York: Cambridge University Press.

Sahlins, M. (1981). *Historical metaphors and mythical realities.* Ann Arbor, MI: University of Michigan Press.

Sameroff, A. (1989). Models of developmental regulation: The environtype. In D. Cicchetti (Ed.), *The emergence of a discipline: The Rochester Symposium on Developmental Psychopathology* (Vol. I, pp. 41–68). Hillsdale, NJ: Erlbaum.

Sameroff, A., & Chandler, M. (1975). Reproductive risk and the continuum of caretaking casualty. In F. D. Horowitz, M. Hetherington, S. Scarr-Salapatek, & G. Siegel (Eds.), *Review of Child Development Research, 4,* 187–244.

Sandler, J., & Freud, A. (1985). *The analysis of defense: The ego and the mechanisms of defense revisited.* New York: International Universities Press.

Sanua, V. (1969). Immigration, migration and mental illness: A review of the literature with special emphasis on schizophrenia. In E. Brody (Ed.), *Behavior in new environments: Adaptation of migrant populations* (pp. 291–352). Beverly Hills, CA: Sage.

Sanua, V. (1980). Familial and sociocultural antecedents of psychopathology. In H. Triandis & J. Draguns (Eds.), *Handbook of cross-cultural psychology: VI. Psychopathology* (pp. 175–236). Boston: Allyn & Bacon.

Savage, C., Leighton, A., & Leighton, D. (1965). The problem of cross-cultural identification of psychiatric disorders. In J. Murphy & A. H. Leighton (Eds.), *Approaches to cross-cultural psychiatry* (pp. 21–63). Ithaca, NY: Cornell University Press.

Scarr, S., & McCartney, K. (1983). How people make their own environments: A theory of genotype → environment effects. *Child Development, 54,* 424–435.

Schafer, R. (1954). *Psychoanalytic interpetative Rorschach testing.* New York: Grune and Stratton.

Schafer, R. (1992). *Retelling the life-story.* New York: Basic Books.

Scheff, T. (1966). *Being mentally ill: A sociological theory.* Chicago: Aldine.

Schieffelin, B., & Ochs, E. (1986). *Language socialization across cultures.* New York: Cambridge University Press

Schermerhorn, A. (1970). *Comparative ethnic relations: A framework for theory and research.* New York: Random House.

Schneider, D. (1968). *American kinship: A cultural account.* New York: Random House.

Schuldberg, D. (1993). Personal resourcefulness: Positive aspects of functioning in high-risk research. *Psychiatry, 56,* 137–152.

Schutz, A., & Luckmann, T. (1973–1989). *The structures of the life world* (Vols. 1–2) (R. M. Zander, H. T. Engelhardt, Jr., & D. J. Parent, Trans.). Evanston, IL: Northwestern University Press.

Sears, R., Maccoby, E., & Levin, H. (1957). *Patterns of child rearing.* Evanston, IL: Row-Peterson.

Segal, J., & Yahraes, H. (1978). *A child's journey: Forces that shape the lives of our young.* New York: McGraw-Hill.

Seifer, R., & Sameroff, A. (1986). Multiple determinants of risk and invulnerability. In E. J. Anthony & B. J. Cohler (Eds.), *The invulnerable child* (pp. 51–69). New York: Guilford.

Sheehan, S. (1982). *Is there no place on earth for me?* Boston: Houghton-Mifflin.

Shweder, R. (1990). Cultural psychology—What is it? In J. Stigler, R. Shweder, & G. Herdt (Eds.), *Cultural psychology: Essays on comparative human development* (pp. 1–46). New York: Cambridge University Press.

Singer, J., & Opler, M. (1956a). Contrasting patterns of fantasy and motility in Irish and Italian schizophrenics. *Journal of Abnormal and Social Psychology, 53,* 42–47.

Singer, J., & Opler, M. (1956b). Ethnic differences in behavior and psychopathology. *International Journal of Social Psychiatry, 2,* 11–23.

Sorokin, P., & Merton, R. (1937). Social time: A methodological and functional analysis. *American Sociological Review, 42,* 615–629.

Spiegel, J. (1971). *Transactions: The interplay between individual, family and society.* New York: Science House-Aronson.

Spiro, M. (1987). Religious systems as culturally constituted defense mechanisms. In B. Kilborne & L. L. Langness (Eds.), *Culture and human nature: Theoretical papers of Melford E. Spiro* (pp. 145–160). Chicago: University of Chicago Press. (Original work published 1965)

Spitzer, R., Endicott, J., & Robins, E. (1978). Research diagnostic criteria. *Archives of General Psychiatry, 35,* 773–783.

Srole, L., & Fischer, A. K. (Eds.). (1962). *Mental health in the metropolis: The Midtown Study.* (rev. ed., Vols. 1–2). New York: Harper & Row.

Sroufe, A. (1989). Pathways to adaptation and maladaptation: Psychopathology as developmental deviation. In D. Cicchetti (Ed.), *The emergence of a discipline: The Rochester Symposium on Developmental Psychopathology* (Vol. I, pp. 13–40). Hillsdale, NJ: Erlbaum.

Sroufe, A. (1990). Considering normal and abnormal together: The essence of developmental psychopathology. *Development and Psychopathology, 2,* 329–344.

Sroufe, A., & Rutter, M. (1984). The domain of developmental psychopathology. *Child Development, 55,* 17–29.

Stack, C. (1974). *All our kin: Strategies for survival in a black community.* New York: Harper Torchbooks.

Stanford, M. (1986). *The nature of historical understanding.* New York: Basil Blackwell.

Stern, D. (1984). Affect attunement. In J. Call, E. Galenson, & R. Tyson (Eds.), *Frontiers of infant psychiatry* (Vol. II, pp. 3–14). New York: Basic Books.

Stern, D. (1985). *The interpersonal world of the infant: A view from psychoanalysis and developmental psychology.* New York: Basic Books.

Stern, D. (1989). The representation of relational patterns: Developmental considerations. In A. Sameroff & R. Emde (Eds.), *Relationship disturbances in early childhood: A developmental approach* (pp. 53–69). New York: Basic Books.

Stone, A., Helder, L., & Schneider, M. (1988). Coping with stressful events: Coping dimensions and issues. In L. Cohen (Ed.), *Life events and psychological functioning: Theoretical and methodological issues* (pp. 182–210). Newbury Park, CA: Sage.

Stone, L. (1979). The revival of narrative. *Past and Present, 85,* 3–24.

Strohm, A. H. (1992). *Coping and vulnerability in children of psychiatrically ill mothers: A longitudinal follow-up.* Unpublished doctoral dissertation, Northwestern University.

Straus, J. (1989). Subjective experiences of schizophrenia and related disorders. *Schizophrenic Bulletin, 15,* 177–324.

Struening, E., Rabkin, G., & Peck, H. (1969). Migration and ethnic membership in relation to social problems. In E. Brody (Ed.), *Behavior in new environments: Adaptation of migrant populations* (pp. 217–247). Beverly Hills, CA: Sage.

Suttles, G. (1968). *The social order of the slums: Ethnicity and territory in the inner city.* Chicago: The University of Chicago Press.

Swanson, G. (1961). Determinants of the individual's defenses against her inner conflict: Review and reformulation. In J. G. Glidewell (Ed.), *Parental attitudes and child behavior* (pp. 5–41). Springfield, IL: Thomas.

Sweetser, D. (1963). Mother-daughter ties between generations in industrial societies. *Family Process, 3,* 332–343.

Sweetser, D. (1964). The effect of industrialization on intergenerational solidarity. *Rural Sociology, 31,* 156–170.

Taylor, C. (1979). Interpretation and the sciences of man. In P. Rabinow & W. Sullivan (Eds.), *Interpretive social science: A reader* (pp. 25–72). Berkeley: University of California Press. (Original work published 1971)

Taylor, C. (1991). The dialogical self. In D. Hiley, J. Bohman, & R. Shusterman (Eds.), *The interpretive turn: philosophy, science, culture* (pp. 304–314). Ithaca, NY: Cornell University Press.

Tennant, C., Bebbington, P., & Hurry, J. (1982). Social experiences in childhood and adult psychiatric morbidity: A multiple regression analysis. *Psychological Medicine, 12,* 321–327.

Thomas, W. I., & Znaniecki, F. (1974). *The Polish peasant in Europe and America* (Vols. 1–2). New York: Octagon Books-Farrar, Straus, and Giroux. (Original work published 1918)

Tolman, E. C. (1951). *Collected papers in psychology.* Berkeley: University of California Press.

Tonnies, F. (1957). *Community and society.* New York: Harper Torchbooks. (Original work published 1887)

Toulmin, S. (1990). *Cosmopolis: The hidden agenda of modernity.* New York: Free Press/Macmillan.

Turnbull, C. (1974a). Introduction: The African condition. In E. J. Anthony & C. Koupernik (Eds.), *The child in his family: Children at psychiatric risk* (pp. 227–244). New York: Wiley.

Turnbull, C. (1974b). Normality and tribal society. In E. J. Anthony & C. Koupernik (Eds.), *The child in his family: Children at psychiatric risk* (pp. 287–304). New York: Wiley.

Turner, V. (1967). *The forest of symbols: Aspects of ndembu ritual.* Ithaca, NY: Cornell University Press.

Tseng, W-S., & Hsu, J. (1980). Minor psychological disturbances of everyday life. In H. Triandis & J. G. Draguns (Eds.), *Handbook of cross-cultural psychology: Vol. VI. Psychopathology* (pp. 61–97). Boston: Allyn & Bacon.

Vaillant, G. (1971). Theoretical hierarchy of adaptive ego mechanisms: A thirty year follow-up of 30 men selected for psychological health. *Archives of General Psychiatry, 24,* 107–118.

Vaillant, G. (1976). Natural history of male mental health: V. The relation of choice of ego mechanisms of defense to adult adjustment. *Archives of General Psychiatry, 33,* 535–545.

Vaillant, G. (1977). *Adaptation to life.* Boston: Little Brown.

Vaillant, G. (1986). (Ed.). *Empirical studies of ego mechanisms of defense.* Washington, DC: American Psychiatric Press.

Vaillant, G., & Milofsky, E. (1980). Natural history of male psychological health: IX. Empirical evidence for Erikson's model of the life cycle. *American Journal of Psychiatry, 137,* 1348–1359.

Van Eerdewegh, M., Bieri, M., Parilla, R., & Clayton, P. (1982). The bereaved child. *British Journal of Psychiatry, 140,* 23–29.

Van Gennep, A. (1960). *Rites of passage.* (M. B. Vizedom & G. L. Caffee, Trans.). Chicago: University of Chicago Press. (Original work published 1908)

Vansina, J. (1970). Cultures through time. In R. Naroll & R. Cohen (Eds.), *A handbook of methods in cultural anthropology* (pp. 165–179). Garden City, NY: Natural History Press.

Vansina, J. (1985). *Oral tradition as history.* Madison: University of Wisconsin Press.

Vaughn, C., & Leff, J. P. (1976). The influence of family and social factors on the course of psychiatric illness: A comparison of schizophrenic and depressed neurotic patients. *British Journal of Psychiatry, 129,* 125–137.

Vaughn, C., Snyder, K., Jones, S., Freeman, W., & Falloon, I. (1984). Family factors in schizophrenic relapse: Replication in California of the British research on expressed emotion. *Archives of General Psychiatry, 41,* 1169–1177.

Vygotsky, L. (1978). *Mind in society.* (M. Cole, V. John-Steiner, S. Scribner, & E. Souberman, Trans.). Cambridge, MA: Harvard University Press. (Original work published 1930–1935)

Vygotsky, L. (1986). *Thought and language.* (A. Kozulin, Ed.). Cambridge, MA: MIT Press. (Original work published 1934)

Walker, E., Davis, D., & Gottlieb, L. (1991). Charting the developmental trajectories to schizophrenia. In D. Cicchetti & S. L. Toth (Eds.), *Models and integrations: Rochester Symposium on Developmental Psychopathology* (Vol. 3, pp. 186–206). Rochester, NY: University of Rochester Press.

Wallace, A. F. C. (1956). Revitalization movements: Some theoretical considerations for their comparative study. *American Anthropologist, LVIII,* 264–281.

Wallace, A. F. C. (1972). *The death and the rebirth of the seneca.* New York: Random House/Vintage.

Warner, R. (1985). *Recovery from schizophrenia: Psychiatry and political economy.* New York: Routledge & Kegan Paul.

Watt, N. (1974). Childhood and adolescent routes to schizophrenia. In D. Ricks, A. Thomas, & M. Roff (Eds.), *Life-history research in psychopathology* (Vol. 3, pp. 194–211). Minneapolis: University of Minnesota Press.

Watt, N., Grubb, T., & Erlenmeyer-Kimling, L. (1984). Social, emotional, and intellectual behavior at school among children at risk for schizophrenia. In N. Watt, E. J. Anthony, L. C. Wynne, & J. Rolf

(Eds.), *Children at risk for schizophrenia: A longitudinal perspective* (pp. 212–226). New York: Free Press.

Watt, N., Stolorow, R., Lubensky, A., & McClelland, D. C. (1970). School adjustment and behavior of children hospitalized for schizophrenia as adults. *American Journal of Orthopsychiatry, 40*, 637–657.

Weber, M. (1904–05/1955). *The Protestant ethic and the spirit of capitalism.* New York: Scribners. (Original work published 1906)

Weber, M. (1968). Ethnic Groups. In G. Roth & C. Wittick (Eds.), *Economy and society* (pp. 385–398). New York: Bedminster Press.

Weiner, I. (1970). *Psychological disturbance in adolescence.* New York: Wiley.

Weissman, M., & Klerman, G. (1977). Sex differences in the epidemiology of depression. *Archives of General Psychiatry, 34*, 98–111.

Weisz, J. (1989). Culture and the development of child psychopathology: Lessons from Thailand. In D. Cicchetti (Ed.), *The emergence of a discipline: The Rochester Symposium on developmental psychopathology* (Vol. I, pp. 89–118). Hillsdale, NJ: Erlbaum.

Werner, E. (1985). Stress and protective factors in children's lives. In A. R. Nicol (Ed.), *Longitudinal studies in child psychology and psychiatry* (pp. 335–355). New York: Wiley.

Werner, E. (1989). High-risk children in young adulthood: A longitudinal study from birth to 32 years. *American Journal of Orthopsychiatry, 59*, 72–81.

Werner, E. (1990). Protective factors and individual resilience. In S. Meisels & J. Shonkoff (Eds.), *Handbook of early childhood intervention* (pp. 97–116). New York: Cambridge University Press.

Werner, E., Bierman, J., & French, F. (1971). *The children of Kauai: A longitudinal study from the prenatal period to age ten.* Honolulu: University Press of Hawaii.

Werner, E., & Smith, R. (1977). *Kauai's children come of age.* Honolulu: University Press of Hawaii.

Werner, E., & Smith, R. (1982). *Vulnerable but invincible: A study of resilient children.* New York: McGraw-Hill.

Werner, E., & Smith, R. (1992). *Overcoming the odds: High risk children from birth to adulthood.* Ithaca, NY: Cornell University Press.

Wertlieb, D., Weigel, C., Springer, T., & Feldstein, M. (1987). Temperament as a moderator of children's stressful experiences. *American Journal of Orthopsychiatry, 57*, 234–245.

Wertsch, J. (1985). *Vygotsky and the social formation of mind.* Cambridge, MA: Harvard University Press.

Wertsch, J. (1991). *Voices of the mind: A sociocultural approach to mediated action.* Cambridge, MA: Harvard University Press.

White, B. L., et al. (1978). *Experience and environment* (Vol. 2). Englewood Cliffs, NJ: Prentice-Hall.

White, B. L., Kaban, B., & Attanucci, J. (1979). *The origins of human competence: The final report of the Harvard Preschool Project.* Lexington, MA: Lexington Books/Heath.

White, B. L., & Watts, J. C. (1973). *Experience and environment* (Vol. 1). Englewood Cliffs, NJ: Prentice-Hall.

White, G. (1980). Conceptual universals in interpersonal language. *American Anthropologist, 82*, 759–781.

White, G., & Kirkpatrick, J. (1985). *Person, self and experience: Exploring pacific ethnopsychologies.* Berkeley: University of California Press.

White, H. (1978). *The tropics of discourse: Essays in cultural criticism.* Baltimore, MD: Johns Hopkins University Press.

White, R. W. (1959). Motivation reconsidered: The concept of competence. *Psychological Review, 66*, 297–333.

White, R. W. (1960). Competence and the psychosexual stages. In M. Jones (Ed.), *Nebraska symposium on motivation* (pp. 97–140). Lincoln: University of Nebraska Press.

White, R. W. (1963). *Ego and reality in psychoanalytic theory: A proposal regarding independent ego energies* (Psychological Issues Monograph 11). New York: International Universities Press.

White, R. W. (1974). Strategies of adaptation: An attempt at systematic description. In G. V. Coelho, D. A. Hamburg, & J. E. Adams (Eds.), *Copying and adaptation* (pp. 47–68). New York: Basic Books.

White, R. W. (1979). Competence as an aspect for personal growth. In M. Wahlen & J. Rolf (Eds.), *Primary prevention of psychopathology. III: Social competence in children* (pp. 5–22). Hanover, NH: University Press of New England.

Whiting, B. (Ed.). (1963). *Six cultures: Studies of child rearing.* New York: Wiley.

Whiting, B. (1980). Culture and social behavior: A model for the development of social behavior. *Ethos, 8*, 95–116.

Whiting, B., & Whiting, J. (1975). *Children of six cultures: A psychocultural analysis.* Cambridge, MA: Harvard University Press.

Whiting, J. W. M. (1941). *Becoming a Kwoma: Teaching and learning in a New Guinea tribe.* New Haven: Yale University Press.

Whiting, J. W. M. (1981). Environmental constraints on infant care practices. In R. Munroe, R. Munroe, & B. Whiting (Eds.), *Handbook of cross-cultural development* (pp. 155–180). New York: Garland-STPM Press.

Whiting, J. W. M., & Child, I. (1953). *Child-training and personality.* New Haven, CT: Yale University Press.

Whiting, J. W. M., Child, I., Lambert, W., Fischer, A., Fischer, J., Nydegger, C., Nydegger, W., Maretzki, H., Maretzki, T., Minturn, L., Romney, A. K., & Romney, R. (1966). *Field guide for a study of socialization.* (Vol. I.) New York: Wiley.

Whiting, J. W. M., & Whiting, B. (1959). Contributions of anthropology to methods of studying child rearing. In P. H. Mussen (Ed.), *Handbook of research methods in child development* (pp. 918–944). New York: Wiley.

Whiting, J., & Whiting, B. (1978). A strategy for psychocultural research. In G. Spindler (Ed.), *The making of psychological anthropology* (pp. 39–61). Berkeley: University of California Press.

Wig, N., Menon, D., Bedi, H., & Ghosh, A. (1987). Expressed emotion and schizophrenia in North India: I. Cross-cultural transfer of ratings of relatives' expressed emotion. *British Journal of Psychiatry, 151*, 156–160.

Wig, N., Menon, D., Bedi, H., & Leff, J. (1987). Distribution of expressed emotion components among relatives of schizophrenic patients in Aarhus and Chandigarh: II. *British Journal of Psychiatry, 151*, 160–165.

Wilson, W. J. (1987). *The truly disadvantaged: The inner city, the underclass, and public policy.* Chicago: University of Chicago Press.

Wilson, W. J. (1989). *The ghetto underclass: Social science perspectives.* Newbury Park, CA: Sage.

Winnicott, D. W. (1960). The theory of the parent-infant relationship. *International Journal of Psychoanalysis, 41*, 585–595.

Winterbottom, M. (1958). The relation of need for achievement to learning experiences in independence and mastery. In J. W. Atkinson (Ed.), *Motives in fantasy, action, and society* (pp. 453–478). New York: Van Nostrand-Reinhold.

Wirth, L. (1928). *The ghetto*. Chicago: University of Chicago Press.

Wirth, L. (1945). The problem of minority groups. In R. Linton (Ed.), *The science of man in the world crisis* (pp. 347–372). New York: Columbia University Press.

Wittoker, E., & Fried, J. (1959). Some problems of transcultural psychiatry. In M. K. Opler (Ed.), *Culture and mental health* (pp. 489–500). New York: Macmillan.

World Health Organization (WHO). (1990). Evalaution of the use of the international classification of impairments, disabilities and handicaps (ICIDH) in surveys and health related statistics: Technical report drawn up by an ad hoc working group for the Committee of Experts on the Application of the WHO Classification of Impairments, Disabilities and Handicaps/Council of Europe. Strasbourg: The Council.

Wrubel, J., Benner, P., & Lazarus, R. (1981). Social competence from the perspective of stress and coping. In J. D. Wine & M. D. Syme (Eds.), *Social competence* (pp. 61–99). New York: Guilford.

Wynne, L. (1981). Current concepts about schizophrenia and family relationships. *Journal of Nervous and Mental Disease, 169,* 82–89.

Wynne, L., Singer, M., Bartko, J., & Toohey, M. (1977). Schizophrenics and their families: Recent research on parental communication. In J. M. Tanner (Ed.), *Developments in psychiatric research* (pp. 254–286). London: Hodder and Stoughton.

Yeaworth, R. C., York, J., Hussey, M., Ingle, M., & Goodwin, T. (1980). The development of an adolescent life change event scale. *Adolescence, 15,* 91–97.

Zautra, A., Guarnaccia, C., & Dohrenwend, B. (1986). Measuring small events. *American Journal of Community Psychology, 14,* 629–655.

Zautra, A., Guarnaccia, C., Reich, J., & Dohrenwend, B. (1988). The contribution of small events to stress and distress. In L. Cohen (Ed.), *Life-events and psychological functioning: Theoretical and methodological issues* (pp. 123–148). Newbury Park, CA: Sage.

Zubin, J. (1978). Concluding remarks. In L. Wynne, R. Cromwell, & S. Matthysee (Eds.), *The nature of schizophrenia: New approaches to research and treatment* (pp. 641–643). New York: Wiley.

Zubin, J., Magaziner, J., & Steinhauer, S. (1983). The metamorphosis of schizophrenia. *Psychological Medicine, 13,* 551–571.

Zubin, J., & Spring, B. (1977). Vulnerability—A new view of schizophrenia. *Journal of Abnormal Psychology, 86,* 103–126.

Zubin, J., & Steinhauer, S. (1981). How to break the logjam in schizophrenia: A look beyond genetics. *Journal of Nervous and Mental Disease, 169,* 447–492.

CHAPTER 22

Resilience and Reserve Capacity in Later Adulthood: Potentials and Limits of Development across the Life Span

URSULA M. STAUDINGER, MICHAEL MARSISKE, and PAUL B. BALTES

In this chapter we explore the potential and limits of development across the life span. Our exploration is conducted with explicit concern for identifying similarities and differences between life-span theory and developmental psychopathology (see also Staudinger, Marsiske, & Baltes, 1993). To facilitate the comparison, we focus on two concepts that are embedded in the life-span and the developmental psychopathology research traditions, respectively—reserve capacity and resilience.

Resilience is a major concept in research on developmental psychopathology; it conveys the idea that individuals can avoid negative outcomes despite the presence of significant risk factors in their environments. It also includes the idea that individuals can regain normal levels of functioning after developmental setbacks, both with and without the help of external interventions (e.g., Garmezy, 1991; Rutter, 1987). In contrast, stereotypic conceptions of late life and the process of aging have historically tended to see late life as a time of uniformly negative changes and losses; in other words, a period of the life span not characterized by much resilience.

Reserve capacity is a construct from the realm of life-span theory (e.g., Baltes, 1987; Kliegl & Baltes, 1987); it refers to an individual's potential for change and especially his or her potential for growth. In this chapter, we shall elaborate on one of the fundamental propositions of the life-span developmental perspective, which is that, across the entire age range, development is simultaneously comprised of "gains and losses;" that is, of increases, decreases, and stability of functioning. Individuals have "reserve capacity" and are capable of functional "plasticity" throughout the entire life course. Implicit in this life-span perspective is the idea that resilient functioning—the ability to

maintain and regain adequate levels of functioning in the face of risks and losses—is a potential that, in varying degrees and expressions, continues to be possible throughout adulthood and old age (Baltes & Baltes, 1990a).

The central goal of this paper is to show, drawing on life-span psychological research, that resilience is a major feature of psychological aging. Moreover, we will suggest that resilience is not only a "naturally occurring" phenomenon (i.e., older adults spontaneously show resilient functioning despite the presence of risks), but that resilience can be supported and enhanced by interventions and "age-friendly" environments. In the process, we highlight similarities and differences between two domains of developmental research—developmental psychopathology and life-span development. There has been a paucity of formal connections between these subdisciplines, despite the fact that the two areas may be able to nurture one another (e.g., Cicchetti, 1993; Datan & Ginsberg, 1975).

We begin by introducing some of the major concepts from the psychology of life-span development. Focusing on old age, we identify resilience within this theoretical framework and highlight two facets of research on reserve capacity and resilience. We then provide a selective review of the literature in three areas of psychological aging (cognition, self and personality, social relations) in order to illustrate resilience and reserve capacity in later life. The third major component of this paper presents an evolving model in which resilience is integrated into the framework of life-span development.

A LIFE-SPAN PERSPECTIVE ON THE RANGE AND LIMITS OF DEVELOPMENT IN LATER ADULTHOOD

What is life-span developmental theory? Since our joint discussion of resilience and reserve capacity in later life is nested within a life-span perspective on development, we begin by presenting an overview of the central concepts and assumptions of this orientation. Many concepts in life-span theory, such as plasticity and multidirectionality, can be found in other developmental schools as well. What is unique about life-span theory

The authors wish to thank John R. Nesselroade, Laura L. Carstensen, Margret M. Baltes, David F. Lopez, and Frieder Lang for helpful comments on earlier versions of the paper. In addition, we would like to acknowledge the many valuable discussions with our colleagues from the Max Planck Institute for Human Development and Education, the Berlin Aging Study, and the Network on Successful Midlife Development of the MacArthur Foundation. This chapter expands on work originally presented in Staudinger, Marsiske, & Baltes (1993).

Table 22.1   Summary of Family of Theoretical Propositions Characteristic of Life-Span Developmental Psychology

Concepts	Propositions
Life-span development	Ontogenetic development is a lifelong process. No age period holds supremacy in regulating the nature of development.
Multidirectionality	Considerable diversity or pluralism is found in the directionality of changes that constitute ontogenesis, even within the same domain.
Development as gain/loss	The process of development is not a simple movement toward higher efficacy, such as incremental growth. Rather, through life, development always consists of the joint occurrence of gain (growth) and loss (decline).
Plasticity	Much intraindividual plasticity (within-person modifiability) is found in psychological development. The key developmental agenda is the search for the range of plasticity and its constraints.
Historical embeddedness	How ontogenetic (age-related) development proceeds is markedly influenced by the kind of sociocultural conditions existing in a given historical period, and by how these evolve over time.
Contextualism as paradigm	Any particular course of individual development can be understood as the outcome of the interactions (dialectics) among three systems of developmental influences: age-graded, history-graded, and non-normative.

Note: After Baltes (1987).

is its attempt at synthesis, viewing such concepts as a family of perspectives characterizing psychosocial and behavioral development (see also Table 22.1; Baltes, 1987; Baltes, Reese, & Lipsitt, 1980; Lerner, 1984). The life-span approach may be more metatheoretical than theoretical, to the extent that it identifies an orientation to the study of stability and change across the life span that encompasses multiple domains of functioning.

Extending the research focus of "mainstream" developmental psychology beyond infancy, childhood, and adolescence, life-span developmental psychology defines its territory as encompassing the entire life course, from infancy into old age. Many life-span researchers, however, work in the field of adult development and aging. More recently, as childhood longitudinal research has come of age, a new cohort of researchers is joining the effort to construct a life-span view of human development (Eichorn, Clausen, Haan, Honzik, & Mussen, 1981; Hetherington, Lerner, & Perlmutter, 1988; Reese, 1993; Sørensen, Weinert, & Sherrod, 1986).

For many, the second half of life is connected with negative stereotypic expectations, such as the belief that old age is largely a period of decline and despair. The life-span view presented here argues against such simplistic and unidirectional views of development. Conceptualizing development across the life span as being multidirectional and modifiable, and applying these notions to aging research, this theoretical orientation signals a view that challenges models of aging that are oriented *exclusively* toward decrements (Baltes, 1993; Riley & Riley, 1989; Rowe & Kahn, 1987).

As will be discussed in more detail, at all ages, development implies concurrent and successive gains and losses, which can be either dependent upon or independent of each other (see also Uttal & Perlmutter, 1989). Contrary to widely held beliefs

about childhood as a period of universal progression, losses occur even early in life. Piaget (1965), for example, described some visual illusions that increase with age and others that decrease with age. He ascribed this loss in visual accuracy to advancement in cognitive stage, in this case the development of conceptual schemata. Similarly, in contrast to equally widely held beliefs about the pervasiveness of decline with aging, there continue to be gains in later life. In language development, for example, individuals may continue to modify and expand their verbal knowledge even into very old age (e.g., Horn & Hofer, 1992). Similarly, there is evidence that at least some older adults demonstrate advances in areas such as wisdom and work-related expertise (e.g., Baltes, Smith, & Staudinger, 1992). Even in the field of memory research, which is "notorious" for its findings of age-related declines, there is a facet called implicit memory (i.e., unintentional memory), which evinces stability and some increase across the life span (e.g., Graf, 1990; Howard, 1991). The notion of what constitutes a loss and what constitutes a gain is highly complex and dependent, for example, on age-graded, history-graded, and idiosyncratic influences.

Development as Life-Long Transactional Adaptation

The core assumption of life-span developmental psychology is that development occurs from birth until death. The central feature of the developmental process is "transactional adaptation" (e.g., Lerner, 1984, 1986) or "person-environment interaction" (e.g., Magnusson, 1990). That is, development is not simply the passive unfolding of "pre-wired" maturational programs, or the mechanistic reaction of organisms to environmental stimuli.

Development is the outcome of a constant and active process of the individual's transactions with changing contextual influences, including age-graded changes of the genome and historical transformations of society. Transactional adaptation comprises the view that the individual is actively selecting developmental contexts; the individual can simultaneously change contexts and be changed by contexts at the same time.

Development occurs at multiple levels. Not only psychological functioning changes with age, but also the contexts (and their associated risks and resources) and the functional consequences (evaluative criteria) of development change with age. Returning to the examples of language and cognitive development, it is not only proficiency that changes or develops with age, but also the contexts of their acquisition and application in everyday life. Furthermore, the criteria according to which language and cognitive proficiency are evaluated undergo age-related changes. Whenever development is considered from a life-span perspective, it is these three interlocking constants of development (i.e., level of functioning, sources or contexts, functional consequences) which are at the focus of analysis.

If one assumes that development occurs through transactional adaptation, then the stability or change of these internal and external developmental contexts becomes analytically important. Development can be brought about by continuous (cumulative/atrophic) or discontinuous (innovative/disruptive) processes. In the intellectual domain, for example, both continuous and discontinuous developmental processes are constantly at work. With regard to continuity, for instance, at both the mean level, and in terms of *interindividual* retest stability (i.e., of rank order of performance), adults show substantial stability of intelligence test performance over multiple retest occasions (e.g., Hertzog & Schaie, 1988; Schaie, 1994). The same seems to be true for personality development as measured by standard personality tests (e.g., Costa & McCrae, 1988; Siegler, George, & Okun, 1979). At the same time, however, as persuasively argued by Nesselroade (1991) and discussed in more detail below, both on theoretical and empirical grounds there is also sizable *intraindividual* (within-person) variability. Thus, there are two sides to consider when it comes to the continuity of development: interindividual continuity or stability on a group-level of analysis can be concurrent with intraindividual change (see also Brim & Kagan, 1980).

Development is also characterized by discontinuity; that is, innovation or disruption. New influences on development can emerge over the life span. As we develop or age, we are continuously confronted with new internal and external developmental contexts that may give rise to discontinuity. This phenomenon is captured by the theoretical concept of "developmental tasks" (both in the practical and intrapsychic sense) which change over the life course (e.g., Erikson, Erikson, & Kivnick, 1986; Havighurst, 1973; Labouvie-Vief, 1982; Levinson, 1978; Oerter, 1986). The cognitive and social effects of participation in the work force, for example, represent new contexts for development that were not present when the same individuals were still in school (e.g., Smith & Marsiske, in press). Retirement (e.g., Atchley, 1982) and widowhood (e.g., Wortman & Silver, 1990) are other life-span contexts where issues of discontinuity take center stage. Furthermore, health and functional changes that arise as a consequence of biological aging, such as decreases in sensory functioning, can serve as sources for developmental innovation and/or disruption late in life (Lindenberger & Baltes, 1994).

Multidirectionality and Multidimensionality of Life-Span Development

We have argued that according to the life-span perspective, development throughout life is characterized by the *simultaneous* and *successive* occurrence of increases (gains), decreases (losses), and maintenance (stability) in transactional-adaptive capacity. This conception of development involving gains *and* losses is highlighted by the notion of *multidirectionality*. Multidirectionality of life-span development encompasses the increase, maintenance, and decrease of functioning within one behavioral domain across time. Furthermore, multidirectionality becomes paramount if development is considered not to be uni- but *multidimensional* (e.g., intellectual functioning involves distinct categories such as fluid versus crystallized intelligence). Thus, when development is approached from a life-span perspective, it is important to distinguish between the overall balance of developmental gains and losses across domains and the domain-specific trajectories for particular functions. Such a point of view is consistent with a *multilevel* or systemic approach to development (Ford, 1987).

Development is a process that unfolds in many different domains of functioning. There is no unitary developmental process that affects all dimensions of an individual in the same way. Although changes in some domains of functioning in an individual will tend to be correlated, it is quite possible for individuals to experience changes in some areas that are quite independent of changes in others. For example, in the psychological sphere, personality functioning in adulthood can develop rather independently of physical functioning (e.g., Baltes, 1993; Smith & Baltes, 1993). When studying development, then, it may often be more meaningful to speak of domain-specific trajectories for particular functions (e.g., Karmiloff-Smith, 1992; Weinert & Helmke, in press). The "overall development" of a person would represent some complex admixture of development along specific dimensions.

Within the same individual, at the same moment in time, some functions may be increasing while others are decreasing or remaining stable. Normal development in adolescence, for example, may include increases in physical competence that are concurrent with decreases in the ability to acquire additional languages. Normal aging includes normative biological losses (e.g., Finch, 1990), and losses in some areas of intellectual functioning, while other domains of intellectual functioning and personality functioning may show stability or even increase (e.g., Baltes, 1993; Baltes & Graf, in press). Taken together, the multidimensionality and multidirectionality perspectives argue against overly simplistic conceptions of development across the life span; even in individuals of advanced old age with a pattern of predominant decline, increments in some domains may be present. Consider, for instance, possible advances in the psychological intimacy of a father-son relationship emanating from contacts initiated by the father's impending death. From a life-span perspective, therefore, aging is

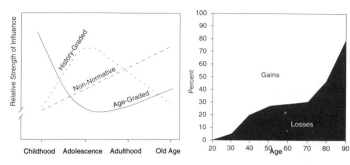

Figure 22.1 Shifting weight and valence of developmental influences. On average aging is characterized by an increasing proportion of losses relative to gains (right; after Heckhausen, Dixon, & Baltes, 1989). From a life-span developmental perspective, increases in non-normative influences (e.g., illness, unexpected death of social network members) and age-graded influences (e.g., biological decline, social role loss after retirement) with primarily negative valence may constitute the most important sources for this shifting ratio (left; Baltes, Reese, & Lipsitt, 1980).

not synonymous with decline. With increasing age, however, the balance of gains to losses in level of functioning and available reserves across different domains of development does become less positive (Baltes, 1987; see right panel of Figure 22.1).

Heterogeneity of Life-Span Development

Not only may particular individuals be demonstrating different developmental trajectories for different abilities at the same time, but individuals differ from one another with regard to their developmental profile. Even when a particular developmental change is considered "normative" in the statistical sense, this does not imply universality. Rather, there may be substantial *interindividual differences* in the magnitude, timing, sequencing, and even directionality of the change. Not all children begin to walk by their first birthday. Some will have begun to walk before, while others may begin to walk later than their age peers. Some may start to walk before they talk and vice versa. In some cases (i.e., individuals with pathological conditions), the ability to walk may be delayed for years, or even permanently. In late life, negative changes in some cognitive domains (e.g., memory, speed of information processing) seem to become normative in the seventh or eighth decade (e.g., Salthouse, 1991a). Despite this, many individuals may not have experienced declines, or may have experienced declines of smaller magnitude, while other individuals may have experienced intellectual losses earlier in adulthood (e.g., Nelson & Dannefer, 1992; Schaie, 1989). With age, some individuals may first experience health-related declines and only much later declines in cognitive functioning and others may first show cognitive deficits and stay healthy much longer.

Heterogeneity of development does not concern only the comparison between individuals but also the comparison within one individual at different points in time, or in different domains of functioning. Thus, there is *intraindividual variability*

within and between domains (Buss, 1973; Nesselroade, 1989). The notions of domain- and time-related intraindividual variability of development are conceptually important, because they guard against global conceptions or what may be called a halo effect of developmental achievement or decline. It is not necessarily true that an individual low in performance in one domain is also low in all other domains of development. An older person, for example, who has become physically feeble may still be quite alert intellectually (e.g., Smith & Baltes, 1993). Similarly, at the early end of the life span, a child with reading disabilities may be quite proficient when it comes to mathematics (Karmiloff-Smith, 1992; Stanovich, 1991).

One specific aspect of intraindividual variability is *plasticity* (Baltes, 1987; Gollin, 1981; Lerner, 1984). Plasticity denotes the range of latent reserves of functioning. It encompasses both the reserves currently available and the reserves that may become available in the future. This is a concept we shall consider in much greater detail later in this chapter. It is important to note that not only will an individual differ in his or her developmental status across different domains, but the same individual may also differ within one domain at different points in time (Nesselroade, 1991). A one-time assessment of intellectual functioning, for example, ignores the fact that individuals may score differently on intelligence tests depending on factors like anxiety, fatigue, perceived relevance of the test, and level of baseline performance (Cornelius, 1986; Labouvie-Vief, Hoyer, Baltes, & Baltes, 1974). Individuals can also improve their performance substantially as a simple function of practice (i.e., "warming up" to the task); in other words, as a function of the degree to which currently available reserve capacity is activated.

Taken together, concepts like multidimensionality, multidirectionality, inter- and intraindividual differences highlight the need to carefully consider *individuals* and their contexts when studying development, and to consider the *domain-specificity* and *latent reserves* of development. Not all children will acquire language, walking, and toileting skills at the same ages, or in the same sequences. Particular children may also vary from day to day in their expressions of these competencies; the child who has been toilet trained may still have an occasional "accident." A child early in acquiring toileting may be a late walker. Across the life span, this highly differentiated view of development becomes even more significant because of a decrease in biological functions and an increase in individuation (Baltes, 1993; Nelson & Dannefer, 1992).

Development as a Gain/Loss Dynamic

Throughout this consideration of life-span developmental perspectives, we have argued that it is useful to define development—despite its longstanding association with progression (Harris, 1957; Nisbett, 1980)—as a concept without a priori direction. Stated differently, development includes the full range of directional possibilities—from gain, to stability, to loss. The process of development should not solely be described as a continued progression to higher levels of functioning, or positive growth.

The life-span perspective conceives of development as a system of changes that encompasses positive and negative directions and consequences (Baltes, 1987; Weinert, 1994). When considering the overall balance between gains and losses across domains, a generally positive or negative picture may emerge. As we shall suggest below, however, aging may be a portion of the life-span where the balance of gains and losses shifts, and becomes increasingly negative. Viewing overall development as a system of positive and negative changes implies the possibility of dysfunctional ("unsuccessful") developmental outcomes. We will see in more detail later that this conception of development is one of the natural links between the life-span developmental perspective and developmental psychopathology. Research on risk and protective factors in the field of developmental psychopathology is aimed, for example, at identifying the developmental constellations (considering internal and external developmental contexts) that lead to adaptive or maladaptive developmental outcomes, respectively (e.g., Cicchetti, 1993; Cicchetti & Garmezy, 1993; Jessor, 1993; Rutter, 1987).

The gain/loss argument goes beyond the simple observation of multidirectionality in one or more developmental domains. It also includes the idea of considering the developing human organism as a complex system (see Ford, 1987). Thus, developmental domains are not independent of each other and a dynamic interplay between gains and losses ensues. In one model of developmental adaptation, the model of *selective optimization with compensation* (to be discussed below), Baltes and Baltes (1990) highlight the idea that organisms have limited amounts of adaptive resources and that these resources change in their range and fixedness across the life span (see also Marsiske, Lang, Baltes, & Baltes, in press).

A first limitation on resources results from investment into a specific path of development. No individual can do all things; there must be a selection of courses of action from the broader universe of possible action plans. This idea has a long history in developmental science and has similarity to Waddington's idea of canalization (Edelman, 1987; Waddington, 1975). Under the assumption of limited adaptive resources, every selection of a developmental path necessarily implies that other action possibilities have not been selected; the selection of one developmental alternative (even if such selection has been "preselected," e.g., by the genome) necessarily implies the loss of potential to engage in many other developmental courses. In this sense, all development, including developments we would traditionally classify as exemplifying progressive growth, are complemented by an element of loss. One example is the often confirmed negative side effects of professional specialization. As one becomes increasingly proficient in a particular career, one loses some potential to invest in proficiency in other careers. Similarly, as one learns to walk, one loses some efficacy in other earlier motor behaviors (e.g., creeping, crawling). This idea of development as increasing canalization of resources sets the stage for life scenarios that are likely to exhaust an individual's transactional-adaptive resources. Midlife is one example. It is a life stage which presents the individual with many competing developmental task domains including career, children, parents, and so on. Although an individual in midlife usually also has a large amount of internal and external resources available, the sheer amount of demands can still present a risk situation by exceeding resources at hand (e.g., Brim, 1992).

A second limitation on resources and their development ensues from age-related changes in the overall range (level) and scope (variability) of resources. Across the life span, the totality of resources available for development changes. This is particularly true for early and late life. In the case of old age, as we will see in more detail below, it is not so much the demands of the external contexts which exhaust resources, but rather the decay of physical resources in combination with the loss of external resources that characterize potential risk situations. This suggests that the gain-loss dynamic shows configurations specific to age and life period that should be considered when life-span scenarios for developmental optimization, protection against losses (maintenance of functioning), and recovery from dysfunction are evaluated.

Life-Span Development and Contextualism

When development is described as the outcome of ongoing processes of transactional adaptation, analytic attention must shift to the question: What are the intra- and extra-personal conditions that are transacting in producing a developmental outcome? Developmental contextualism (Lerner & Kauffman, 1985; Reese & Overton, 1970; Riegel, 1976), and its allied idea of probabilistic epigenesis (Lerner, 1984), reflect the classic interactionist position (e.g., Anastasi, 1970) that development is always the simultaneous and complex outcome of forces of nature and nurture, of genes and environment, of intra- and extra-personal influences.

In life-span work on this topic, Baltes and his colleagues (Baltes, Cornelius, & Nesselroade, 1979; Baltes et al., 1980) have proposed a tri-factor model of internal and external contextual influences (age-graded, history-graded, and non-normative), which delineates the macrosystem of developmental sources (explicated further below). The point to be made here, however, is that these systems of biological and contextual influence may serve important analytic and explanatory functions in understanding both interpersonal and intercultural regularities of developmental trajectories, as well as in understanding the sources of inter-individual differences (e.g., Baltes & Nesselroade, 1984; Dannefer, 1984). In other words, due to biological and sociogenic differentiation, individuals will find themselves with similarities and differences in developmental challenges and opportunities.

We take an example from the development of eating behavior. All organisms must eat, for example, but the conditions of food availability and nutritional needs will vary. Ontogeny (or age-graded influences) shapes some of these issues: infants need particular nutrients in the service of their rapid cellular growth and differentiation; older adults have typically been reported as having fewer caloric requirements relative to their younger age peers (Masoro & McCarter, 1990). Not all of this is biological; when older adults are in societies that retire them from active work, for example, lowered physical activity may also reduce caloric requirements. History-graded influences are also relevant to eating behavior: food availability (both in amount and in kind) varies dramatically over time (Elder & O'Rand, in press), as do social norms about eating and desired weight (Garner, Garfinkel, Schwartz, & Thompson, 1980). The recent historical growth of reported eating disorders like anorexia nervosa and bulimia in some Western countries highlights the potential power of changing norms about food to influence individual behavior (e.g., Klingenspor, 1994). There are also non-normative, more idiosyncratic influences (Cooper & Fairburn, 1992). Individuals may be born with differential sensitivity to feelings of satiety, and individual family and cultural constellations can also shape attitudes toward desirable foods and caloric intake (Johnson, McPhee, & Birch, 1991; Petersen, 1988).

Contextualism, then, is a world view (Pepper, 1942) or metatheoretical paradigm which is central to the life-span perspective. It highlights the commitment of life-span scholars to understanding the transactional and probabilistic role of biological, social, cultural, and historical changes in development. It signals an analytic posture that looks to internal and external influences on various levels of analysis *and* how they mutually influence each other in understanding human development. Context is not merely viewed as monolithic and determined, but rather as a complex and probabilistic system of interdependent areas or territories of influence ranging from inner biological to outer physical and sociocultural ones (e.g., Bronfenbrenner, 1979; Lawton & Nehemow, 1973). Contextualism also highlights an orientation toward understanding both the reasons for commonalities across individuals and cultures, the sources of their differences, as well as the degree to which there are as yet untapped reserves for further growth or alternative pathways.

Development Is Embedded within History

Cultural and historical influences represent, in effect, one area or one level of the broader set of contextual influences that affect development (e.g., Lerner & von Eye, 1992). In the development of life-span theory and research, they have always obtained special attention. Historical periods and cultural changes condition and shape the opportunity structures to which individuals have access. Social structures are constantly evolving, and vary across cultures and socioeconomic groups. Major historical events (e.g., war, economic depression, migrations) and historical changes in technology (e.g., introduction of antibiotics, increasing availability of food, the growing role of the computer in society) have had an effect on the level and direction of psychological development (e.g., Baltes, 1968; Caspi, 1987; Elder & O'Rand, in press; Riegel, 1972; Riley, 1986; Schaie, 1965). Elder (1979), for example, showed that the Great Depression had long-term effects on the psychosocial adjustment of American men. The nature of that effect, however, was moderated by age during the Depression, and prior family socialization practices.

One major demonstration of the important role of history has been suggested by life-span developmental research on *cohort differences* (e.g., Baltes et al., 1979; Labouvie & Nesselroade, 1985; Schaie, 1965, 1994). In longitudinal and cross-sectional sequential research methodology, multiple birth cohorts of individuals (i.e., individuals born at about the same period in historical time) can be followed over time. Such designs permit the examination of whether individuals born in different sociocultural conditions evince differences in developmental trajectories. That is, when comparing the developmental trajectories from different birth

cohorts (here, taken as an *index* of the broad body of contextual differences in such variables as education, medicine, economic conditions), are there differences in level, direction, and dispersion of functioning?

In adolescent personality development, for instance, Nesselroade and Baltes (1974) have shown that even over short periods of historical time (1970–1972) age trajectories of personality dimensions such as achievement motivation, social anxiety, and independence can vary substantially between cohorts of adolescents (see also Petersen, 1988). In the intellectual domain and for adulthood and old age, Schaie (1983, 1994) demonstrated that cohort differences in intellectual functioning can be sizeable: over historical time, comparing adults in the range from early adulthood to old age born from 1889 until 1966, some intellectual abilities studied have shown increase (e.g., verbal, spatial, and reasoning ability), while others have shown stability (numerical ability) or even decrease (word fluency) over generational birth cohorts. Moreover, as was true for adolescent personality development, the identification of historical effects may not require such a broad sampling of birth cohorts. Even when birth cohorts separated by an average of 15 years are studied over only a three-year longitudinal interval, a substantial influence of birth cohort on cognitive functioning has been detected (Hultsch, Hertzog, Small, McDonald-Miszczak, & Dixon, 1992). In a similar way, a recent study of psychosocial development in adulthood, also employing a cohort-sequential design, identified cohort effects (Whitbourne, Zuschlag, Elliot, & Waterman, 1992). Using an inventory based on Erik Erikson's model of psychosocial development, Whitbourne and her colleagues found that the late-life developmental task of reaching integrity versus falling into despair was less favorably resolved by the later-born cohorts. The authors suggested that this may have been due to a historical erosion in philosophical values in the society (Whitbourne et al., 1992).

The implications of historical and cultural embeddedness are related to notions of interindividual and intraindividual differences. That is, in considering development, it is also important to consider intercohort or interhistorical period differences. It would not be correct to assume that the developmental trajectories obtained for today's cohort of older adults in some domain will necessarily continue to hold for future cohorts. For example, Fries' (1983) work suggests that future cohorts of older adults may show less medical comorbidity and disability prior to death, due to changes in nutrition and general life style as well as medical treatment. Life-span psychologists proffer that one must be continuously aware of the historical and cultural relativity of any putatively "normative" developmental trends.

The Study of Development Asks for Multidisciplinarity

Life-span developmental psychologists naturally tend to focus on antecedents and outcomes of a psychological nature. Following from the contextualistic paradigm, however, is the notion that development is constituted by both psychological and nonpsychological domains, and their constant interplay. Aging, for example, is associated with a large number of normal biological changes (e.g., Birren & Schaie, 1990; Finch, 1990; Maddox,

1987). Psychological development occurs concurrently with these biological changes, and it is reasonable to think of the dynamic interplay between them. Age-related changes in musculoskeletal, neuronal, or sensory systems, for example, may influence such psychological domains as social participation or information processing. Moreover, the motivational system may influence biological health: individuals who select physical fitness as a goal may engage in different health-maintaining behaviors than individuals who select other goals. The study of development, with all its facets, is a fundamentally multidisciplinary enterprise, and no single-discipline account of it is likely to be adequate (Mayer & Baltes, in press).

As psychologists interested in development across the life span, we must acknowledge the fundamental incompleteness of psychological inquiry into development. Even accounts of psychological phenomena may need to include non-psychological variables be it from the realms of sociology, history, anthropology, economics, social work, or biology and medicine. It may be particularly fruitful to consider interdisciplinary collaboration when working on certain developmental topics. Some recent examples of this approach include work by M. Baltes, Mayr, Borchelt, Maas, and Wilms (1993), who investigated the influence of biomedical, sociological, and psychological variables on everyday activity patterns of 70- to 100-year-old persons. They found, for instance, that biological-medical variables were particularly important in determining "basic" levels of everyday activity such as self-care behaviors. In predicting "expanded" domains of competence, such as leisure and social activities, psychological factors like intellectual functioning gained in prominence. Similarly, Featherman, Smith, and Peterson (1990) investigated the joint and distinct role of both social and psychological variables in understanding the career development and specialization (e.g., planners versus practitioners) of engineers.

Before we move on to the final major theoretical orientation from life-span psychology, the plasticity of functioning, the main focus of this chapter, we will briefly summarize our key points thus far. We have described a number of crucial characteristics of the development of psychological functioning as life-span theory views them (see also Table 22.1). Such characteristics included an emphasis on the active role of the individual in development, which is reflected in the conceptualization of development as the outcome of a process of transactional adaptation to changing internal and external developmental contexts. Furthermore, development has been characterized as encompassing concurrent (and successive) gains and losses. The notion of gains and losses presupposes the multidimensionality and multidirectionality of development. Development is not "governed" by one uniform process, but rather by multiple and variable processes. Variability of development is observed between individuals within the same domain and between different domains of functioning. Variability across time and across domains is also observed within one individual. This latter aspect of variability leads to the central concept of this paper, the plasticity of psychological functioning.

Plasticity can be viewed as a special case of intraindividual variability in level of functioning. The phenotype of behavior observed at a given point in time is not fixed. There are reserves in performance capacity which can become apparent under certain conditions. We will also see that reserves in performance capacity are not fixed in time but follow a developmental course of their own.

Levels of Reserve Capacity and Variations in Plasticity of Development

The concept of *plasticity,* which includes both the consideration of the range and limits of behavioral change, is the final central concept in life-span theory and research which we want to consider (Baltes, 1987; Lerner, 1984). If human development is the product of dynamic and probabilistic transactions among diverse sources of developmental influences and selection processes, then development must also be characterized by plasticity.

As we have already suggested, the course of psychological development is not completely predetermined, neither within nor across domains. It includes both fixed, variable, and latent components. These variable components, we have argued, are reflected in interindividual differences, intraindividual differences and modifiability, and cross-cultural differences as well as historical relativity. Latent components denote level and domains of functioning which, while possible in principle, have not been activated or become manifest. In this sense, plasticity is conceptualized, not unlike the "norm of reaction" in behavior genetics which asserts that genetic inheritance sets the upper and lower boundaries of behavioral development (Dunn, 1965; Lerner, 1984), as the potential for change in transactional-adaptive capacity. Although plasticity is often used to denote an increase in level of adaptation, definitionally it is a concept that does not imply the direction of change but, rather, aims at characterizing the range and limits of development.

Plasticity of development can also be considered at different levels of analysis and across time: Is there one overall degree of plasticity or is the plasticity of development—like development itself—also a multidimensional and multidirectional concept? Does the degree of plasticity change with age? The first type of question is still difficult to answer. There is an indication from training transfer studies that training gains in one domain of functioning, such as a specific cognitive task which has demonstrated plasticity, do not always transfer to other cognitive tasks (Detterman & Sternberg, 1993; Guberman & Greenfield, 1991; Karmiloff-Smith, 1992; Royer, Cisero, & Carlo, 1993). This suggests that plasticity of development, like development itself, may require a distinction between general-purpose and task- or domain-specific resources.

The concept of plasticity provides an index of an individual's manifest and latent change potential and how flexible and robust he or she might be in dealing with developmental challenges and demands. In life-span work, the degree of plasticity has been denoted as an individual's *reserve capacity* (or reserves), which is constituted by internal (e.g., cognitive capacity, physical health) and external (e.g., social network, financial status) resources available to the individual at any given time. Furthermore, taking a systemic approach, plasticity in one domain of functioning may serve as a resource for another domain. To illustrate this point, consider an older person who demonstrates plasticity in the domain of social relations by establishing new social ties.

These new social relationships could later serve as important sources of support if bodily deterioration increases the need for assistance. It is important to note that an individual's resources need not be fixed, but may themselves change over time. The gains and losses discussed above not only concern the development of phenotypically manifested behavior, but also the latent plasticity of development. This implies that sometimes losses may not become immediately obvious on the behavioral level. Phenotypic behavior may show stability even as the related reserves or the behavioral potential undergoes a gradual age-related decrease. It is also possible that losses in plasticity will only become visible under especially demanding performance settings which require these reserves (e.g., Baltes, 1987; Kliegl & Baltes, 1987).

The concept of reserve capacity has been further differentiated. To denote both concurrent and future change potential, life-span researchers have offered a two-tier classification of reserve capacity: (a) baseline reserve capacity, and (b) developmental reserve capacity. *Baseline reserve capacity* denotes an individual's current maximum performance potential, that is, the most an individual can do with current internal and external resources. Resources, however, can be activated or increased, for instance, through optimizing interventions or new age-related changes of the positive or negative kind. This temporal (ontogenetic) trajectory of plasticity is subsumed under the label of *developmental reserve capacity.* As reserve capacity increases or decreases, so does the potential for (positive) plasticity. The investigation of the *range and limits of plasticity,* in both senses, is a major focus of life-span developmental research (Baltes, 1987; Kliegl & Baltes, 1987).

Building on the distinction between performance and competence (Flavell & Wohlwill, 1969), the differentiation between tiers of reserve capacity (baseline vs. developmental) helps in the interpretation of possible sources of loss and decline in functioning. This is particularly important for understanding aging. A decline or loss in performance level can be, but does not have to be, related to a decline in reserve capacity. Declines in performance can be due to contextual ("phenotypic") rather than "genotypic" conditions involving levels of reserve capacity. As we argue later, it is necessary to conduct research oriented toward testing the range *and* limits of reserve capacity, such as training research in the areas of physical and cognitive functioning, in order to ascertain whether or not the source of age-related performance differences is due to age differences in developmental reserve capacity (Coper, Jänicke, & Schulze, 1986; Kliegl, Smith, & Baltes, 1990; Salthouse, 1991a).

RESILIENCE AS A TYPE OF RESERVE CAPACITY

How can the resilience concept be understood in the context of life-span developmental psychology? To date there has been little integration of these two research streams. We suspect there are at least two reasons for this: First, resilience is a construct that, in psychology, originated in research on the development of psychopathology rather than on normal development (e.g., Cicchetti, 1989; Garmezy, 1991; Masten, Best, & Garmezy, 1991; Rutter,

1987). Most adult developmental research, aside from relatively recent efforts concerned with old age in the area of mental health (e.g., Birren & Sloane, 1980) and senile dementia (e.g., Cohen, 1989; Smyer, Zarit, & Qualls, 1990), has focused on "normal" aging (e.g., Birren & Schaie, 1990). Second, resilience is a term which has been used and applied primarily in research on childhood and adolescence, rather than adulthood and old age. One exception has been the work of the MacArthur Foundation Network on Successful Aging (Rowe & Kahn, 1987).

In our view, there is substantial overlap between definitions of resilience and life-span views of developmental reserve capacity. Garmezy (1991, p. 459), for example, has defined resilience as "the capacity for recovery and maintained adaptive behavior that may follow initial retreat or incapacity upon initiating a stressful event." For Rutter, resilience describes "the positive pole of individual differences in people's response to stress and adversity" (Rutter, 1987, p. 316).

Thus, definitions of resilience in the literature seem to contain reference to two kinds of adaptive response: (a) the maintenance of normal development despite the presence of threats or risks (internal and external), and (b) recovery from trauma. Unlike the notion of invulnerability, resilience is not considered to be trait-like. Rather, it is assumed that an individual's resilience changes in transaction with specific circumstances and challenges (Magnusson & Öhman, 1987; Rutter, 1987). Consequently, resilience demonstrated in one situation is not automatically sustained over time or transferred to other circumstances and challenges. An individual's degree of resilience is considered a function of protective factors (internal and external) that modify the person's response to some environmental hazards that "normally" result in maladaptive outcomes (Garmezy, 1991; Rutter, 1987).

Mapping definitions of resilience onto the concepts of reserve capacity and plasticity suggests that resilience can be conceptualized as one *type* of plasticity. While plasticity, in principle, can be seen as encompassing the potential for any change in adaptive capacity (including increase, maintenance, decrease), resilience refers to the potential for the maintenance and regaining of levels of normal adaptation; that is, resilience is a subtype of the broader range of changes in adaptive capacity encompassed by plasticity. Like reserve capacity, resilience implies the presence of latent resources which can be activated. However, unlike resilience, reserve capacity is not only relevant to maintaining or regaining *normal* levels of adaptation. Reserve capacity also refers to factors and resources that promote *growth beyond* the current and normal level of functioning (Staudinger, Marsiske, & Baltes, 1993; see also Figure 22.3).

Although notions of plasticity and resilience serve a heuristic purpose, conceptual problems remain with both lines of research. For example, the distinction between the protective factors and mechanisms underlying resilience, and resilience as an outcome can be quite arbitrary. In a similar way, this is true for the distinction between resources on the one hand and plasticity on the other; that is, plasticity itself can serve as a kind of resource. Moreover, in both lines of research the criteria for what constitutes a protective factor or a resource are not easy to define. What may be a protective factor in one context can be a risk factor in another, and vice versa.

These and similar issues have been subsumed in the life-span literature under the concept of *multifunctionality* of development and associated variations in developmental outcomes (e.g., Baltes & Silverberg, 1994; Chapman, 1988). Is there only one adequate criterion for a loss with respect to intellectual functioning in old age, for example? Is school or college performance in young adulthood an adequate reference point for assessing intellectual efficacy in older adults, or should we also consider changes in intellectual task demands and in later adulthood and criteria of "normal" intellectual functioning in late life? Another example comes from the study of autonomy versus dependency in old age. Is the advent of dependent behavior in old age only to be considered a loss, or can dependency under certain conditions also imply gains (e.g., provision of social contact of freeing up resources for other desirable activities; Baltes, in press)? In other words, what is *labeled* as decline or loss may actually be quite adaptive within the everyday ecology of older adults.

If one takes the person-in-context definition of resilience seriously, then one should specify both the developmental domain or unit "at stake," as well as the selected marker(s) for assessing and evaluating resilience. More concretely, one should be aware that speaking about *the* resilience of a person in general, and about life-span development in general, rather than about resilience within a specific domain of functioning, may be overly ambitious. Optimization of adaptation at any given point in the life course needs to take into consideration *positive and negative transfer effects across domains of functioning and across time.* For instance, high-level physical functioning at one point in time, as in the case of top college athletes, can have long-term negative effects on health. Or as another example, career-oriented achievement motivation in early adulthood, for instance, is generally considered a protective and optimizing factor. In later adulthood, and especially during retirement, such a personality characteristic can become quite dysfunctional.

Resilience and Reserve Capacity in Later Adulthood as a Function of Risk and Protective Factors

Having introduced the central life-span propositions that are relevant to the investigation of the whole life course and how resilience fits into this framework, we will now shift to the central focus of this chapter, which is later adulthood. What are the potential risks, challenges, and gains of old age? We have argued before that according to life-span theory, limiters and facilitators of development can be categorized into three broad systems of developmental influences: (a) age-graded, (b) history-graded, and (c) non-normative (Baltes, 1987; Baltes et al., 1980). Individuals act and react within the setting of these influences.

Age-graded influences are defined as biological and environmental determinants that have a fairly strong relationship to chronological age and are therefore quite predictable in their temporal course. Their direction of influence is assumed to be rather similar across individuals. *History-graded* influences also involve environmental and biological determinants, but they are associated with historical time. Individuals develop within the framework of evolution and culture; the influences of pharmacology

on health, or the nature of educational opportunities, for example, vary across cultures and historical time. Finally, another set of biological and environmental determinants is *non-normative,* in the statistical sense. Non-normative influences do not follow a general and predictable course; rather, they differ in onset, duration, and prevalence from individual to individual and are not clearly tied to ontogenetic or historical time. Non-normative influences represent the idiosyncratic facet of development, and are contained in factors such as unique life experiences (e.g., migration, winning in a lottery) or biomedical conditions of health or endowment (e.g., physical injury due to an accident, special musical talent) and varying constellations of these influences.

These three systems of developmental influences manifest themselves as both facilitators (supportive of gains) and limiters (supportive of losses) of life-span changes in functioning and the mastery of life tasks. Translating life-span ideas into the language of resilience, we could define facilitators and their related gains as protective factors, and the limiters and their related losses as risk factors. There have been speculations about the relative influence of these three systems of developmental influences across the life span (Baltes et al., 1980), which are schematically illustrated on the left side of Figure 22.1. In addition to the relative weight, the functional valence (e.g., value expectation) of the three streams of influences also changes with age. In old age, idiosyncratic and normative influences become increasingly negative, threatening current levels of adaptation. This shifting balance in the functional valence of developmental influences is also captured in subjective beliefs about the life-span trajectories of gains and losses as shown in the right panel of Figure 22.1.

Indeed, old age has been described as the period of life which is generally characterized by a depletion of reserves (and thus resources) through multiple losses, often occurring simultaneously or within a short period of time (e.g., Baltes, 1991; Finch, 1990; Fries, 1990; Schaie, 1989). Negative non-normative and age-graded events (see left panel Figure 22.1), such as death of spouse, death of friends, running out of one's own life time, decline of physical health and physical functioning, loss of social status, prestige, and sometimes financial insecurity, on average, all become increasingly prevalent in late life. In fact, one could argue that some events (e.g., illness), judged to be rare or non-normative in earlier periods of life, may become relatively normative in old age. Together these perspectives on the risks, challenges, and gains of old age suggest a high likelihood for an increasing call upon reserves and resilience in old age, if adaptive functioning is to be maintained (see also Figure 22.3 below).

Dealing with this relative age-related increase in losses will test the limits, and may exhaust the internal and external resources that individuals have available. Furthermore, if aging individuals are engaged in managing many losses, they will have fewer developmental reserves available to invest in their development and growth. This is not to conclude that protective factors do not operate in old age, or that resources are entirely depleted. The critical issue in old age, however, is the overall ratio of gains to losses (e.g., Baltes & Baltes, 1990b; Brandtstädter, Wentura, & Greve, 1993; Hobfoll, 1989). Any one of the losses mentioned above, such as loss of spouse or loss of employment, also may occur at earlier times in the life span. At younger ages, however, it is unlikely that an individual would also have to deal simultaneously with many concurrent losses. Thus, it may well be that older persons have access to some protective factors, but nevertheless the overall need for resources more and more often surpasses those available.

In summary, old age is characterized by a general restriction in the range of plasticity or reserve capacity and an increase in challenges with negative valence. Nevertheless, within specific domains of functioning, declines might still be modulated, and there may still be potential to repair and enhance functioning to or beyond earlier levels. Indeed, there is evidence that in some domains of psychological functioning even continued growth can be promoted by means of enhancement programs. In the following sections, we review some research selected from three domains of psychological functioning in which we and our colleagues at the Max Planck Institute for Human Development and Education in Berlin have conducted research (cognitive functioning, self and personality, and social transactions), in order to provide some illustrative evidence for protective mechanisms and resilience in old age. Along the line, we also point to the consistency of this evidence with concepts of life-span developmental psychology. In addition, we discuss a model of "successful aging" that describes how aging individuals might focus and optimize their reserves in effective ways including the generation and enlisting of compensatory efforts.

Two Facets of Research on Reserve Capacity and Resilience in Later Adulthood

Following the dual conception of resilience as (a) the maintenance of normal development despite the presence of risks, and (b) recovery from trauma, two research themes of plasticity and resilience can be distinguished with regard to aging. The first approach is research on the "real-life" or *natural* (in vivo) occurrence of resilience or plasticity. This refers to studies that demonstrate reserve capacity in old age by investigating how old adults "naturally" adapt to and master circumstances that could potentially threaten the normal developmental trajectory in everyday life. Here, it is important to underscore that we mean "natural" in the sense of a high degree of everyday prevalence, and not in the sense of a biologically determined phenomenon. Research on coping, and also on cognitive enrichment through work-related specialization, and selective and compensatory processes of the self fits this aspect of plasticity.

The second stream of plasticity research in old age has moved beyond the natural context of everyday functioning, and has focused on different forms of *intervention*. In this approach, the focus is on what is possible in principle and if "natural" conditions were different. Two kinds of intervention research can be identified. One set of studies focuses on remediation and treatment of existing declines and pathologies (e.g., Baltes & Danish, 1979; Riley & Riley, 1989), challenging the view based on negative stereotypes of old age that age-associated losses cannot be minimized or reversed. There is accumulating evidence that remediation is often possible (e.g., Baltes, 1988; Baltes & Lindenberger, 1988; Carstensen, 1988; Danish, Smyer, & Nowak, 1980; Fries, 1989). A second kind of intervention research focuses

explicitly on prevention and optimization; that is, on interventions that, through both domain-general and domain-specific strategies, enhance developmental reserve capacity, promote growth, and move individuals beyond the normal developmental trajectory toward optimal levels of functioning. As do younger people, older people have considerable developmental reserve capacity that might be activated under specific cultural conditions related to the social and physical environment, and that might facilitate their attainment of such positive late-life goals as maintenance of social productivity, independent functioning, or advanced states of well-being (Baltes & Baltes, 1990b; Riley & Riley, 1989; Ryff, 1984, 1991). In the following sections, we will illustrate psychological research on those two facets of plasticity and resilience by reviewing studies from the areas of cognitive functioning, self and personality, and social transactions. We begin by considering cognitive and intellectual resilience.

COGNITIVE RESILIENCE IN ADULTHOOD AND OLD AGE

In the following sections on the aging mind, we examine three broad streams of research as more in-depth illustrations of the themes we have mentioned above. We first consider descriptive evidence regarding the nature of developmental changes in adult intellectual performance. Second, we focus on those aspects of the aging mind, such as professional expertise, which may be less likely to demonstrate normative losses in old age; that is, where cognitive resilience in real-life (natural) contexts is a frequent outcome. Finally, given that some features of adult intelligence are expected to evince losses in advanced old age, we consider the potentials for and limits to modifiability (improvement) in these domains.

A Dual-Process Conception of the Aging Mind: Is There Need for Cognitive Resilience?

Historically, the level of intellectual functioning in late life, if studied from a resilience perspective, would more likely have been categorized as a "risk factor" than as a "protective factor with regared to the overall balance of development." There is widespread empirical support from both cross-sectional and longitudinal studies using omnibus and ability-specific measures of intelligence that older adults do not perform as well as younger adults on a variety of measures of intellectual functioning (Salthouse, 1991a).

There is evidence, however, to moderate a *general* view of cognitive aging as decline. With the onset of longitudinal and cohort-sequential investigations (see Maddox, 1987) and increasing reliance on multifactorial conceptions of intelligence (e.g., Horn & Hofer, 1992), a more complex picture of adult intellectual functioning has emerged (Lindenberger & Baltes, in press). Current empirical perspectives suggest that there is substantial inter-individual variability in the onset and rate of negative changes, that the magnitude of negative change differs by domain of intellectual functioning, and that for a sizable number of persons the outcome is one of stability of intellectual functioning through much of adulthood (Schaie, 1989). Normative decline (i.e., ability-general losses for most individuals) is not visible until later adulthood, often in the seventh decade and beyond (Hertzog & Schaie, 1988; Lindenberger, Mayr, & Kliegl, 1993). After age 70 to 75 (Schaie, 1989), in part because of an increase in age-associated illnesses, ability-general decline becomes increasingly likely.

In this context of multifactorial models of intelligence, the distinction between fluid and crystallized intelligence (Cattell, 1971; Horn & Hofer, 1992) has been one of the most fruitful taxonomies of intellectual abilities in the life-span developmental literature. In our own work, we have combined the Horn-Cattell framework with perspectives from cognitive and evolutionary psychology. As a result, we have proposed the distinction between two higher order "idealized" constructs of intellectual functioning: the fluid-like *mechanics,* and the crystallized *pragmatics* of the mind (Baltes, 1987, 1993; Baltes, Dittmann-Kohli, & Dixon, 1984). In this scheme, the cognitive mechanics reflect the neurophysiological architecture of the brain as it developed during ontogeny and has been largely prepared by processes of evolution. The cognitive pragmatics can be understood as the kind of knowledge and information that cultures offer about the world and human affairs, and that developing individuals acquire as they participate in culture-based socialization.

Based on this theoretical position regarding the different primary sources for the development of the cognitive mechanics and pragmatics, it is assumed that the two facets to the aging mind evince different life-span trajectories. The evidence concurs. The cognitive mechanics or fluid intelligence, as captured, for instance, in the speed and accuracy of basic information processing, demonstrate age-related declines beginning as early as middle adulthood (e.g., Salthouse, 1991a). Conversely, there is growing evidence that, given positive cultural and personal circumstances, stability and even positive age change during adulthood are possible in the knowledge-based pragmatic facets of the mind, such as in tests of vocabulary or professional expertise (Baltes, 1993; Staudinger, Cornelius, & Baltes, 1989).

The Cognitive Pragmatics: "Natural" Resilience through Knowledge

The cognitive pragmatics refer to the *enrichment* of the cognitive system by bodies of knowledge, and the associated potential *compensatory* power of culture-based knowledge in the face of biologically determined losses in the mechanics of the mind. This possibility for the cognitive pragmatics to serve as a reservoir for enrichment and as a compensatory resource we have termed "natural" resilience. This is not meant to imply that only losses in the cognitive mechanics cause gains in the mental pragmatics (Uttal & Perlmutter, 1989); pragmatics do not only serve a compensatory function. Rather, we argue that the development of knowledge systems in old age is a potential gain in its own right that may also serve as a source of protection. In other words, people may have reserve capacity in the crystallized pragmatics, even when there is age-related loss in the mechanics of intelligence, and they may use pragmatic reserves to offset these losses in the mechanics.

The developmental research tradition contains several interrelated efforts to highlight the important role of knowledge for cognitive advances (e.g., Brown, 1982; Chi, Glaser, & Rees, 1982; Glaser, 1984; Weinert & Waldmann, 1988). One important model of cognitive development in knowledge domains is the "expertise" model. Here, we are guided by the general view of expert knowledge systems recently summarized in Ericsson and Smith (1991). We draw from this literature general perspectives on how living longer may result in a movement *toward* high levels of functioning in select areas of cognition and intelligence. In principle, research on expertise suggests that a coalition of factors must be present, and that their presence must extend over time, so that performance moves in the direction of higher and higher levels until expertise is reached. In the following sections, we illustrate two resilience-related phenomena. First, it is shown that living longer (i.e., being older), under particular conditions, may result in the acquisition of certain bodies of knowledge, which are conducive to higher levels of psychological functioning. Second, we demonstrate that pragmatic knowledge can be used to compensate for age-associated losses in the cognitive mechanics.

The Performance of Older Experts

The question of whether expertise, or the availability of a rich procedural and factual knowledge base, is a protective factor against age-related losses in intellectual functioning has only recently begun to be addressed. In one study of expert typists, described in Salthouse (1991a), younger typists showed superiority on several measures of perceptual-motor speed (reaction time, tapping speed, rate of digit symbol substitution). Such evidence is suggestive of a performance advantage on the part of the younger typists in sheer response speed while typing. However, the older *expert* typists selected for the study could achieve *equally good* performance levels on a typing task when they were provided with larger typing preview spans. In other words, acquired procedural knowledge involving reading ahead in the to-be-typed text (reserves in pragmatics) was used to offset developmental losses in the cognitive mechanics; that is, age-related slowing of reaction time and of tapping speed. Similar findings were reported by Krampe (1994; see also Ericsson, Krampe, & Tesch-Römer, 1993) who compared young and old expert pianists. Specifically, despite the presence of age-related "mechanical" decline in reaction and tapping times, older expert pianists were able to play well and fast, most likely by preparing and coordinating multiple finger movements in advance through "deliberate practice." Charness (1985) also reported that older chess players seemed to differ from younger players in their evaluative chess strategies. In each case, "pragmatic" procedural strategies appeared to compensate for the loss in the cognitive mechanics (see also Erikson & Charness, 1994).

In summary, research is supportive of the contention that knowledge-based expertise yields a pattern of age-maintenance or age-increase in expertise-related functioning. Moreover, process-oriented research designed to understand the components of age-invariant expertise suggests that high levels of pragmatic knowledge may be used to produce more effective and efficient response strategies, despite age-associated losses in relevant cognitive mechanics (Clancy & Hoyer, 1994). Similar interpretations can be derived from research on the late-life accomplishments of some artists and scientists (e.g., Perlmutter, 1990; Simonton, 1991).

Wisdom: Expertise in the Fundamental Pragmatics of Life

Besides investigating expertise in professional and in leisure domains, "knowledge about life and the human condition" has been identified as another example of the cognitive pragmatics. Research on wisdom is a sample case. In our own work, we have defined wisdom as an "expert knowledge system in the fundamental pragmatics of life permitting excellent judgment and advice involving important and uncertain matters of life" (e.g., Baltes, Smith, & Staudinger, 1992; Baltes & Staudinger, 1993). This body of knowledge entails insights into the quintessential aspects of the human condition, including its biological finitude, cultural conditioning, and individual variations. At the center of this body of knowledge are questions concerning the conduct, interpretation, and management of life.

The central idea of this line of research is to explore whether individuals, during adulthood and old age and under favorable personal and experiential conditions, can acquire and refine knowledge and skills dealing with life review, life planning, and life management and thereby attain higher levels of wisdom-related knowledge. In several studies with adults of differing ages and professional background, individuals were presented with life dilemmas and asked to think aloud as they went about solving them. The tasks varied in difficulty and age-relevance. Thinking-aloud responses were transcribed and scored according to five wisdom-related criteria that were defined as essential to wisdom (Baltes & Smith, 1990; Baltes & Staudinger, 1993). Two of these criteria (rich factual and rich procedural knowledge about life) represent basic criteria and are taken from general theories of expert systems (e.g., Ericsson & Smith, 1991). The three remaining meta-criteria (life-span contextualism, relativism of values and life goals, recognition and management of uncertainty) are informed by life-span research on adult cognitive and personality development (e.g., Alexander & Langer, 1990; Erikson et al., 1986; Maciel, Heckhausen, & Baltes, 1994; Sinnott & Cavanaugh, 1991; Sternberg & Berg, 1992).

The definition of wisdom as an expert knowledge system (expertise) implies the presence of high standards which relatively few individuals will reach. Therefore, as expected, relatively few truly "wise" responses were identified. Despite this relative lack of high-level responses, performances in the middle-level range demonstrated a pattern dramatically different from those derived from research on the cognitive mechanics in aging. On average, older persons performed as well as younger adults on the wisdom-related tasks (Smith & Baltes, 1990; Staudinger, 1989). Also, older adults, that is, 60- to 80-year-olds, produced as many of the top 20% of performances as younger adults. Besides, the performance of older adults was best when they responded to a life dilemma that was typical for their own period in life. Moreover, there was evidence that being older, when *combined* with certain experiential contexts conducive to the accumulation and refinement of wisdom-related knowledge, was associated with the relatively highest levels of performance. In addition, it was found that certain personality traits (such as Openness to Experience) were correlated with higher levels of wisdom-related performance.

One experiential context studied was that of certain professional specializations, such as clinical psychology or family law. The results indicated the presence of an age by experience interaction: Older clinical psychologists not only performed better than age-matched professional controls, but in some tasks they actually outperformed their younger professional colleagues (Smith, Staudinger, & Baltes, in press; Staudinger, Smith, & Baltes, 1992). Subsequent research included a sample of distinguished citizens nominated as wise and characterized by wisdom-facilitative biographical constellations. Two examples may highlight the special character of this group: 57% have published their autobiographies, and 41% were members of the German anti-Nazi resistance movement during the Third Reich. This sample had an average age of 67 years (ranging from 41 to 88 years). Findings from this study further verified the enhancing effect of certain experiential settings, and again documented the absence of negative age effects in wisdom-related performance. Older wisdom nominees performed at least as well as the next group, the old clinical psychologists, and both groups performed better than the two professional control groups. When considering the top range of performances, the wisdom nominees produced more than their share and more than any other group of the best performances (Baltes, Staudinger, Macreker, & Smith, in press).

In research on wisdom-related performance, we witness an example of the "natural" resilience of the mind as well as its potential for enrichment (Staudinger & Baltes, in press). This research also reminds us that chronological age in itself is not the most important resource which contributes to these mental reserves. Rather, it is the combination of features such as facilitative experiential contexts, personality characteristics, motivational constellations, and age-related accumulation of experiences which seem to be generative of higher levels of wisdom-related performance.

Everyday Competence: "Natural" Resilience in Tasks of Daily Living

Another domain of complex, high-level functioning is that of everyday problem solving or everyday competence. Everyday competence is a complex concept, and has been studied from a variety of multidisciplinary perspectives, including medical/biological (Katz, Ford, & Moskowitz, 1963; Mahoney & Barthel, 1965), sociological/epidemiological (Manton, Stallard, & Liu, 1993; Wolinsky, Callahan, Fitzgerald, & Johnson, 1992), and psychological (Baltes, Mayr, Borchelt, Maas, & Wilms, 1993; Lawton, 1991; Lawton & Brody, 1969; Willis, 1991).

In the context of the present chapter, we want to focus on cognitive components of everyday competence, which we shall discuss here as *everyday problem solving*. The emphasis has been on objective, performance-based measurement (i.e., studying what individuals can do, or performance potential, rather than what individuals say they can do). Everyday problem solving and its allied concept of practical intelligence (e.g., Sternberg & Wagner, 1986) encompass the total spectrum of situations in which mental abilities are used in the conduct of daily life (e.g., Lave, 1988). As a result, individual research attempts have tended to be selective, and relatively unrelated to one another (Hartley, 1989; Marsiske & Willis, in press a).

Most life-span theory about everyday cognition has tended to emphasize the ideas of contextualism and adaptive fit discussed at the beginning of this chapter. With regard to the study of older adults, for example, a number of theorists have proposed that the everyday tasks confronted by older adults should have features of self-selection, personal relevance, and high familiarity (e.g., Baltes & Baltes, 1990b; Berg & Sternberg, 1985). They represent often-encountered tasks for which individuals may have well-developed action plans, knowledge structures, and scripts. Theories which emphasize this pragmatic, knowledge-based aspect of everyday competence would predict that, in those task domains which are personally salient and familiar, late life may be a time of differential preservation of competence and selectively maintained high levels of performance (e.g., Salthouse, 1991b). Some research on everyday cognition has tended to support these assertions, with older adults typically performing as well as, or better than, younger adults on tasks of everyday information use and social strategy use (e.g., Cornelius & Caspi, 1987; Demming & Pressey, 1957; Denney, 1984; Gardner & Monge, 1977; Heidrich & Denney, 1994).

A second stream of life-span theory and research on everyday cognition has more specifically emphasized normatively defined tasks of "basic competence" (e.g., food preparation, medication use, housekeeping; see Morrell, Park, & Poon, 1990; Willis, 1991). In addition, consistent with lay (implicit) conceptions of everyday competence (e.g., Berg & Sternberg, 1992; Cornelius & Caspi, 1987; Sternberg, Conway, Ketron, & Bernstein, 1981) these studies emphasize adults' abilities to adapt to unexpected but potentially relevant life situations (e.g., dealing with widowhood, poor weather; see Denney & Pearce, 1989) and thereby tap more into the cognitive mechanics than the pragmatics of the mind (Marsiske & Willis, in press b). Consequently in this research, there has been less evidence for preservation of functioning in late life.

Willis, Jay, Diehl, and Marsiske (1992) showed that older adults, followed longitudinally over a seven-year interval, as they moved from 70 to 77 years of age, on average experienced significant mean decline in performance on a measure of reasoning and document literacy involving everyday texts (e.g., prescription labels, bus schedules, recipes), which was predicted by associated losses in psychometric intelligence functioning. Despite this decline at the group level, when intraindividual change trajectories were examined, the majority of the sample (62%) was judged to have performed at levels close to what they had shown seven years earlier. The findings of mean decline from 70 to 77 years of age are consistent with cross-sectional research reported by Denney and her colleagues on adult problem solving. Over several cross-sectional studies, Denney (see Denney, 1989, for a review) has demonstrated that peak performances in adults' ability to generate solutions to everyday problems, even when those problems are drawn from the experiences of older adults, is typically highest in middle-aged subjects (subjects aged 40 to 50).

The research on everyday problem solving in later life is still too sparse to permit broad generalizations about age-related resilience. Despite this, given findings regarding the different trajectories for the mechanics and pragmatics of intelligence across adulthood, it is possible to conclude that "natural" resilience will be observed primarily in those everyday tasks which emphasize the crystallized pragmatics and which draw on individuals' reservoirs of procedural and declarative knowledge in the domains in which they have specialized. The major exception from this pattern, as we shall argue for the cognitive mechanics (Baltes, Kühl, & Sowarka, 1992), are persons who are afflicted by severe brain-related diseases such as Senile Dementia of the Alzheimer's Type.

In sum: A major aspect of successful aging concerns knowledge about the nature of life-span development itself, and the human condition, and how such knowledge about the course and conditions of life might be useful for managing the peaks and valleys of everyday behavior (Baltes & Baltes, 1990a; Baltes, Smith, & Staudinger, 1992; Brim, 1992; Fries, 1989). As for the dynamics between the crystallized pragmatics and the fluid mechanics, research suggests that level of performance can be maintained in select domains despite losses in the cognitive mechanics. Drawing on rich levels of procedural and factual knowledge, older adults seem able to compensate for age-related reductions in the cognitive mechanics by the use of knowledge-based pragmatic resources. Capacity reserves in the cognitive pragmatics, then, seem to provide a rich and "natural" source for cognitive resilience. In many ways, such findings and perspectives are consistent with a view held in sociology and also the educational sciences (e.g., Featherman, 1983; Mayer, 1994; Maddox, 1987). It is the view that—at the macrolevel—education and stimulating work careers serve as major facilitators of aging well.

Potential for Resilience and Growth in the Cognitive Mechanics: Training Results

It would be incorrect to assume that, even if normal age-related losses in performance on measures of the fluid mechanics exist, they *necessarily* imply underlying losses in cognitive competence (baseline reserves), and the absence of potential for resilience in the mechanical components of intellectual functioning. Indeed, as suggested by cohort studies, some of the negative age differences observed in cross-sectional studies not only reflect "genotypic" decline associated with the biology of aging, but also cohort- or generational disadvantages associated with education and societal status (Schaie, in press), and occupational complexity (e.g., Schooler, 1990). Such findings do suggest that there is "room" for cultural factors to influence the level and rate of normative aging of the cognitive mechanics. Indeed, from a civilization point of view, the period of "old age" is still "young" (Baltes & Baltes, 1990b), and we are only beginning to understand what it takes to optimize individual aging, and what role cultural factors might play.

Exploring the range of modifiability and optimization has been at the center of cognitive training research (Baltes, 1993; Baltes & Willis, 1982; Denney, 1984; Labouvie-Vief, 1977; Willis, 1987). A growing body of cognitive intervention research has suggested that, as is true for younger age groups, older persons also possess substantial baseline reserves concurrently with the "normative" losses in baseline performance. These reserves can be activated and enriched under appropriate conditions. The most direct evidence comes from cognitive training research.

Activation of Current Maximum Performance (Baseline Reserves) in the Cognitive Mechanics: Cognitive Resilience After Intervention

For almost two decades, research findings have documented robust individual plasticity (modifiability) in the performance of older adults on tests of fluid intelligence and the cognitive mechanics (e.g., working memory). The general paradigm has involved tutored or self-guided instruction of older adults, ranging from about 60 to 90 years of age, in the strategies needed to successfully solve fluid intelligence problems. With slight variations across studies, the broad pattern of findings suggests: (a) older subjects demonstrate significant performance gains on the tests selected for training and practice, and (b) training group superiority, relative to untrained controls, is often maintained for periods up to one year or more. Training gains on selected tests are in the range of one-half to one standard deviation. Generally, however, training effects do not generalize beyond the abilities selected for training (e.g., Bäckman, Mäntylä, & Herlitz, 1990; Baltes & Lindenberger, 1988; Baltes, Sowarka, & Kliegl, 1989; Denney, 1984; Verhaeghen, Marcoen, & Goosens, 1992; Willis, 1987).

Taken together, the literature on training the cognitive mechanics of the mind (e.g., fluid intelligence and working memory) seems to support the presence of substantial levels of baseline reserve capacity in the cognitive mechanics, that exist concurrently with normal age-related losses. The only major exception seems to be research with older persons with, or at risk for, Senile Dementia of the Alzheimer's Type (Baltes, Kühl, & Sowarka, 1992). Such persons do not seem to profit from cognitive training. Despite this caveat, for most older persons, changes in practice and in contextual support allow for significant improvement in performance levels. One implication is that the presence of enriching cognitive environments, either by providing for formal practice, or by providing in vivo practice associated with social tasks and roles for older adults, may constitute one protective factor for the management of decline in the cognitive mechanics.

It will be interesting to explore to what degree such practice- and training-related activities reduce the onset and rate of decline, and thus, could function as protective factors in the sense of prevention. Training and practice results from longitudinal research in the age range from 64 to 95 years have suggested that, in the majority of older subjects who had experienced reliable intellectual decline, intervention could remediate performance on the trained tests to levels approximating that displayed by the same subjects fourteen years earlier (Willis & Schaie, 1986). For subjects who had not declined, training and practice could enhance performance above younger baseline levels. Further, there is growing evidence that subjects evince significantly less decline in the seven years following training and practice, relative to untrained controls (Willis & Nesselroade, 1990; Willis & Schaie, 1994). In general, longitudinal research with subjects who have experienced *memory* training has been less positive. Two studies reported no maintenance of training gains over a three-year period (Anschutz, Camp, Markley, & Kramer, 1987; Scogin & Bienias, 1988). More recently, however, Nealy and Bäckman (1993) have reported that very intensive memory training did

show maintenance over a three-year span, suggesting that lack of durability may be a partial function of intervention intensity. One problematic feature of longitudinal analysis with older adults is selective survivorship; that is, longitudinal results are based on a positively selected subset of subjects. Moreover, we need to be careful not to generalize from improvement in select trained tasks and functions to a wider spectrum of cognitive functioning. So far, if anything, the lack of such transfer to a wide spectrum has been demonstrated.

Another unaddressed question in the cognitive training research reviewed here is that of age differences in the magnitude of training gain; that is, whether young adults would have profited more, the same, or less than older adults (Salthouse, 1991a). There are good reasons for the dearth of substantial age-comparative training studies. In the usual age comparisons, a myriad of factors make it almost impossible to differentiate between differences in competence (genotype) or reserve capacity and differences in performance (phenotype) (e.g., Salthouse, 1991a; Willis & Baltes, 1981). To make this distinction possible, it is necessary to move beyond the given and explore the range and limits of developmental reserve. This is done within a testing-the-limits paradigm which, by means of intensive and extensive intervention, aims at (a) enhancing existing reserves and (b) estimating asymptotic levels of "best" performance potential (Baltes, 1987; Kliegl & Baltes, 1987).

Enhancing Developmental Reserves in the Cognitive Mechanics: Potentials and Limits

Testing the limits, as a paradigm in life-span research, was designed for two main purposes. The first was to identify limits to performance by means of variation in difficulty and difficulty-related performance conditions. The basic metaphor is the "stress test" used in biology and medicine, designed to assess the upper range of adaptive fitness and early indications of emerging dysfunctions (Baltes & Kindermann, 1985; Coper et al., 1986). The second goal of testing-the-limits research was to explore an "optimal" range of functioning, not unlike practice and training research in athletics. The building theme for this kind of research was the search for "developmental" reserve capacity.

In this vein, testing-the-limits work was aimed at engineering and testing of high levels of performance (Baltes & Lindenberger, 1988; Kliegl & Baltes, 1987). One way in which this was illustrated was through the use of a mnemonic technique, the so-called Method of Loci. The key feature of this method is to first acquire a mental map of fixed locations, and then to create mental images for each word that link it to one of the locations. The goal of this research was not to train memory experts, but to use the Method of Loci as a research model and as a means of manipulating and studying more general processes associated with the cognitive mechanics (Baltes, 1993; Kliegl et al., 1990).

In an illustrative example of this line of research, a sample of young and old (65 to 83 years) highly intelligent subjects was recruited. Training and practice in the Method of Loci continued for more than thirty sessions, until subjects approximated a level of asymptotic performance. As was true for earlier cognitive training research, substantial performance plasticity was demonstrated in all subjects: mean performance increased from recall of 5 to 7 words to recall of a mean of about 15 words in correct order (Baltes & Kliegl, 1992; Kliegl et al., 1990). However, under conditions of high levels of difficulty and "stress," as the speed of the task was increased, as well as under conditions of extensive practice, negative age differences in plasticity (developmental reserve capacity) became more and more apparent and were magnified over those age differences present at baseline. Indeed, under conditions of high difficulty and near individual limits or best performance levels, there was virtually no overlap in the performance distributions of young and old subjects, with significant performance superiority in the younger subjects. The negative age differences obtained in this research were sizable and robust (Baltes & Kliegl, 1992): After few sessions of training and practice, the mean performance of young adults exceeded the mean performance that older adults would achieve after about 35 sessions of training and practice.

In summary: There are two facets to the aging of the cognitive mechanics: (a) Substantial training improvements in performance can be observed in older persons unless they are afflicted by a brain-related illness such as senile dementia; and (b) at least with regard to fluid intelligence, gains appear to be task-specific and long-lasting. On the other hand, however, when the highest possible levels of functioning of older adults are studied in comparison with younger adults (i.e., following intensive training), seemingly irremediable losses in developmental reserve capacity become manifest. Older adults have slower cognitive mechanics and they are more likely to make errors than younger adults.

Such results can be interpreted as suggesting that cognitive reserves of the mechanics kind are reduced with increasing age. For several reasons, these reductions may not become manifest in actual cognitive functioning. First, despite losses, for many tasks there may still be a surplus of reserves beyond current levels of functioning. Second, knowledge-based compensation seems to be possible in tasks related to domains of expertise. Third, reductions in reserves are less likely to become noticeable under average everyday conditions of cognitive functioning. One can expect, however, that aging losses in reserves of the mechanics may become evident if an older person has to operate under high challenge or complex conditions, especially under conditions where cognitive speed, parallel processing, and new learning are required. A simple everyday example of such a high-challenge situation might be that of having to decide quickly whether to cross an intersection in the face of oncoming traffic.

Intervention-Supported Resilience in the Face of Cognitive Pathology: The Sample Case of Dementia

Aside from case studies, there is relatively little systematic research on the regaining of resilience after older adults have suffered from pathology in cognitive functioning. One of the most widely known cognitive pathologies of advanced old age is senile dementia. Although this is frequently discussed as a mental health problem (see Smyer et al., 1990), it comprises a complex set of disorders that seem to have primarily biological origins (Cohen, 1989). Senile Dementia of the Alzheimer's Type (SDAT) and multi-infarct dementia are among the most

prevalent types (Fratiglioni et al., 1991). At present, exact diagnosis of dementia type is possible only at autopsy. To provide adequate treatment, it is important to distinguish senile dementia from other potentially treatable dementing conditions, like depression (Blazer, 1989) and adverse drug reactions (Callahan, 1992; Morrison & Katz, 1989).

One of the major defining features of dementing conditions is their influence on cognitive functioning. Memory impairment, in particular, is one of the first noticeable symptoms of the disease. Although, as we suggested in our review of cognitive mechanics, there are normal age-related deficits in memory functioning (e.g., Craik & Jennings, 1992; Hultsch & Dixon, 1990), one major difference between normal and pathological (i.e., demented) cognitive aging seems to center on the relative magnitude of cognitive reserve capacity. While there is strong evidence that, with a variety of supportive conditions including training and modification of task instructions or material to-be-remembered, healthy older adults can demonstrate substantial improvement in memory performance (Craik, Byrd, & Swanson, 1987; Herlitz, Lipinska, & Bäckman, 1992; Kliegl et al., 1990), the literature on the effect of supportive memory conditions (e.g., Craik, 1977) in demented elders is less positive. Supportive memory conditions that do not seem to work particularly well for individuals with cognitive impairment—as compared to non-impaired elders—include the use of pictorial and highly concrete verbal stimuli at encoding (e.g., Butters et al., 1983; Wilson, Bacon, Kramer, Fox, & Kaszniak, 1983), increasing the semantic organization of the to-be-remembered words (e.g., Cushman, Como, Booth, & Caine, 1988), using interventions which increase the strength of memory traces (e.g., Corkin, 1982), or using subject-generated word lists as the to-be-remembered words (Dick, Kean, & Sands, 1989).

In a similar way, research attempting to use fluid intelligence training paradigms with demented elders or even persons at risk for dementia has documented a lack of improvement in performance. One generalization about dementia seems to be that it is characterized by the relative absence of cognitive reserve capacity, as instantiated, for instance, by the relative inability to profit from cognitive training (Baltes, Kühl, & Sowarka, 1992).

As the life-span perspective on inter-individual variability suggests, global generalizations about the effects of cognitive interventions on persons with dementia must be tempered by the acknowledgment of heterogeneity. In one detailed review of cognitive intervention research in dementia, Herlitz and her colleagues (1992) noted that the effectiveness of supportive memory conditions shows some inconsistencies over studies. One reason for this is weak validity of the diagnosis. The severity of dementia is often not systematically examined. Using intervention techniques primarily informed by a cognitive processing approach, some memory improvement is possible in mildly demented subjects, but virtually no improvement has been documented in the memory performance of moderately or severely demented individuals.

Within the cognitive processing approach, in line with our earlier discussion of normal cognitive aging, the most effective interventions seem to fall into two categories: those which minimize the demands of the task drawing on the cognitive mechanics, and those which increase the "pragmatic," knowledge-related component of the task.

Reduction of Demands on Speed of Information Processing

A number of studies have reported that decreasing presentation rates (i.e., increasing the study time individuals have with to-be-remembered items) can be beneficial. When demented elders were given up to eight times more study time per item to be remembered relative to normal older adults (i.e., 16 seconds instead of only 2 seconds), memory performance in demented and non-demented elders was about the same (e.g., Corkin et al., 1984; Huppert & Piercy, 1979; Kopelman, 1985). Thus, there is some support for the notion that when mechanical demands (e.g., on speed of information processing) are relaxed, demented elders may be able to show improved memory performance.

Focus on Prior Knowledge

Bäckman and his colleagues have shown that memory interventions that rely on the preserved knowledge of demented elders can be effective. In general, persons with dementia display some similarity to normal older adults in their better memory for information from the remote past than from the recent past. In one study, Bäckman and Herlitz (1990) presented both mildly demented and normal older adults with pictures of famous faces. Half the faces were of persons whose fame was at its highest in the 1940s, while the other half of the faces were of the recently famous. Not surprisingly, normal elders generally outperformed demented subjects. An interesting differential pattern of results was found, however, by using two different test conditions. In the first test condition, both groups were asked whether they knew the famous faces from their past. In this condition, both groups showed superior face and name recognition of the more dated famous individuals. In a subsequent second test condition, subjects were asked whether they recognized the famous faces from having just seen them in the research situation. In this condition, normal elders also showed superiority for dated faces, but demented subjects showed no difference between dated and recent famous faces.

In a second study, Lipinska, Bäckman, and Herlitz (1992) attempted to increase the activation of knowledge from past life by having subjects generate statements about each picture, and by keeping names and faces associated at all times, both at study and at test. Under these circumstances, when past knowledge was more active, demented subjects also showed a superior memory for dated faces in the condition which asked whether they had seen the person in a previous research situation. These results are suggestive of the view that increased reliance on intact knowledge could compensate, in part, for some dementia-related deficits in the cognitive mechanics.

The evidence for the effectiveness of cognitive training and support interventions with demented persons is weak. Despite this pessimistic pattern of results arising from intervention research within the cognitive processing tradition, however, it would be incorrect to conclude that there is *no* cognitive reserve capacity in demented elders at all. Even within the cognitive processing tradition of intervention research, it seems that external resources can contribute to the reserves of demented persons

when external investment of time and effort in intervention is high, and the intervention is task-specific. Furthermore, there are other forms of intervention which have not yet been sufficiently explored. As an example, intervention research within the tradition of behavior modification has suggested the potential for regaining at least some resilience even in cases of severe dementia. As we will discuss next, this latter strategy emphasizes the systematic use of reinforcement principles and engineering of age-friendly environmental conditions (e.g., Baltes & Barton, 1977; Lawton, 1988; Skinner, 1983).

Strategies of Behavior Modification and Operant Psychology

Principles of behavior modification and operant psychology have been successfully applied in maintaining functioning and reversing dysfunctioning in various cognitive and behavioral domains, and in a variety of groups with pathological conditions, including older adults (e.g., Baltes, 1988; Baltes & Barton, 1977; Carstensen, 1988; Horgas, Wahl, & Baltes, in press; Skinner, 1983). Operant procedures, in general, require fewer cognitive resources on the part of the target person. They are characterized by rather creative treatment combinations involving, for example, stimulus control, reinforcement schedules, and shaping. Thus, they appear to be promising as potentially effective interventions to use with demented elders.

Unfortunately, relatively few developmental and cognitive studies, so far, explicitly engaged in experimental or functional analyses of behaviors, their specific micro-ecological antecedents and consequences (i.e., their eliciting, prompting, reinforcing, and punishing conditions; Baltes & Barton, 1979). Developmental operant research carefully considers the acquisition, maintenance, and extinction schedule of behaviors. It also offers the opportunity to "engineer" quite complex behaviors out of simpler behavioral units (e.g., Baltes, in press; Carstensen, 1988; Mosher-Ashley, 1986-87; Wisocki, 1991). In the field of mental retardation, for instance, the use of operant procedures has offered a rich world of possibilities to enhance development and everyday functioning. Therefore, it seems plausible to expect similar outcomes for the field of dementia.

Early behavior-modification research with demented old persons has demonstrated its effectiveness in treating such specific dysfunctions as inability to eat independently and disturbing vocal behavior (Baltes & Barton, 1979). Recently, Camp and his colleagues (Camp et al., 1993; Camp & Schaeller, 1989; Foss, Camp, & O'Hanlon, 1993; McKitrick, Camp, & Black, 1992) have documented the success of the joint application of memory and behavior modification principles in the case of spaced-retrieval memory training in persons with dementia. Spaced retrieval involves repeatedly retesting the recall of specific information, and doing so at increasingly longer intervals. In its simplest form, a subject is presented with a stimulus and asked to recall it after some interval. If the stimulus is not recalled, there is corrective feedback. After each correct recall, the interstimulus interval is systematically lengthened; after incorrect recall, the interstimulus interval is reduced to a prior level. Using this procedure in several small studies with demented individuals, one subject could remember the name of a nurse for periods of up to six months (but could recall no other staff members). Other subjects learned to extract a colored coupon from an array of distractors for a period of up to a week (subjects were reinforced with money for correct selections). On one level of interpretation, and when restricting one's attention to a carefully defined behavior, this research quite impressively documents the effectiveness of operant conditioning. In addition, Camp and his colleagues have argued that the success of this intervention program may in part be due to the fact that it circumvents deficits in explicit, effortful memory by relying on less effortful, and more preserved, implicit (unintentional) memory capabilities (e.g., Graf & Schachter, 1987).

Taken together, the results of memory training and operant interventions with demented older adults can be summarized in two points. First, regarding the results of intervention studies in the cognitive processing tradition, it seems that after the onset of pathological cognitive loss, an increased weakening of reserve capacity is observed (Baltes, Kühl, & Sowarka, 1992). The potential modifiability of memory functioning seems to be very closely related to the severity of dementia. As long as there are at least some intact cognitive processes (e.g., encoding, activation of prior knowledge), however, some reserves can be activated and some resilience can be regained. Second, in terms of intervention studies applying classical behavior modification principles and linking these approaches to cognitive psychology, it seems that the implementation of operant principles may represent a relatively untapped resource for achieving limited improvements in persons with dementia (Camp et al., 1993), and may also have positive secondary gains with regard to social relations and self esteem (e.g., if subjects recognize and can name their families, colleagues and caregivers, they may be able to increase their amount of social participation). Thus, intervention-supported cognitive resilience, albeit within limits, may be possible through creative and combinatorial use of a variety of behavioral engineering techniques even in older adults with substantial brain-based cognitive dysfunctions.

The complexity and degree of investment increase as the severity of the dysfunction increases. However, even in cases when resilience seems irretrievably lost at the individual level because of severe losses of biological and cognitive resources, a whole structure of external and interpersonal resources (e.g., behavior modification principles, formal and informal caregiving) can be called upon to recover to a certain degree the resilient functioning of older adults. Of particular importance in this intervention effort is the physical environment. With regard to physical environmental resources such as housing, Lawton (e.g., 1982, 1988) has provided an extensive review and suggestions for architectural design that are all based on behavioral modification principles, behavioral ecology, and person-environment transactions. As to the role of interpersonal and social factors, we shall consider these in greater detail in our section on social transactions.

RESILIENCE AND RESERVE CAPACITY IN ADULTHOOD AND OLD AGE: SELF AND PERSONALITY

What about personality and self-related functioning in old age? Not unlike the pragmatics of the mind and contrary to the mechanics, self-regulated functioning shows much stability and even age-related growth. There is little correlation between age and various indicators of self-related functioning (e.g., Baltes, 1993; Brandtstädter et al., 1993), including self-esteem (e.g., Bengtson, Reedy, & Gordon, 1985), sense of personal control (e.g., Lachman, 1986), or happiness and subjective well-being (e.g., Costa et al., 1987; Ryff, 1989). This also includes 80- to 100-year-olds (Smith & Baltes, 1993). Thus, on the group level, age does not seem to be a "risk" factor for the self and its sense of control and well-being.

The absence of strong relationships between age and self-related functioning, despite what we have characterized as an increase in risks and potential losses with advancing age, is theoretically important. Indeed, the discrepancy between an increasing number of risks on one hand, and maintenance of adaptive functioning in the self on the other, has been labeled a "paradox" (Baltes & Baltes, 1990b; Brandtstädter & Greve, 1994). Implicit in the paradox formulation is the assumption that the self exhibits resilience, or reserve capacity, in the face of age-related risks and primarily health-related losses.

In contrast to the domain of cognitive functioning, research in areas of the aging self has only started to link the mechanisms hypothesized to underlie resilience to self-related criteria of resilience. Rather, in many cases, chronological age is simply used as a proxy variable for all risks allegedly linked to old age, without precise specification of what particular risk factors might be. Relatively few studies have made a point of (a) identifying a group of old adults actually at risk for self-related dysfunction and comparing it with same-aged controls, and (b) examining some of the mechanisms hypothesized to underlie maintained well-being in the high-risk group (e.g., Staudinger, Freund, Linden, & Maas, in press).

Furthermore, evidence is emerging that maintenance or optimization of self-related functioning not only illustrates domain-specific resilience in areas of the self, but that certain processes and mechanisms of the self may also serve as resources for resilience and growth in *other* domains of psychological functioning. One hypothesis is, not unlike findings on the role of self-efficacy and agency (Bandura, 1986), that effective functioning in some self-related domains increases the likelihood that individuals will maintain and optimize their functioning in other domains, such as intelligence, memory, or health. In this sense, adaptive processes of the self can take on the character of "general purpose" mechanisms (cf. Karmiloff-Smith, 1992).

Self-Regulatory Processes and "Natural" Resilience in the Aging Self

In our selection of theoretical and empirical work (see also Baltes 1991, 1993; Brandtstädter et al., 1993; Carstensen & Freund, 1994; Hobfoll, 1989; Magai & Hunziker, 1993; Markus & Herzog, 1991; Rosenberg, 1979; Ryff, 1991; Whitbourne, 1987), we first consider research which provides evidence for the "natural" resilience of the aging self. It comprises studies from three areas: (a) recent social-cognitive research on the transactional-adaptive capacities of the self, (b) research on life-span development of personality, and (c) research on emotional management, and coping. Finally, we return to the questions of whether, and to what degree, self-related functioning can be seen as a general resource for resilience and developmental reserve capacity, and whether there is resilience in the face of pathology.

Multiple and Possible Selves

Most current conceptions describe the self as a multifaceted dynamic structure comprised of a relatively stable array of self-conceptions (e.g., Greenwald & Pratkanis, 1984; Markus & Wurf, 1987). Different situations or contexts, however, activate different subsets of this composite structure. Markus and Wurf (1987) have called this the working self-concept. This view of the self as both stable and dynamic fits life-span conceptions that emphasize the potential for continuity as well as change as a characteristic feature of transactional adaptation during development. Furthermore, evidence is accruing that a multifocal and diversified structure of priorities and self-conceptions, or identity projects, makes transactive adaptation to developmental changes easier (e.g., Linville, 1987; Thoits, 1983). Older adults who define their "selves" through multiple identities which are richly construed, positively evaluated and anchored in the present, are more successful (as measured by subjective well-being) in their mastery of negative developmental changes associated with their health condition (Freund, 1993). Similarly, a variety of sociologically oriented studies suggest that a greater number of identities (e.g., family and work) is related to better mental health (Coleman & Antonucci, 1982; Kessler & McRae, 1982).

Along these lines, research by Markus and others (e.g., Cross & Markus, 1991; Markus & Nurius, 1986) for example, has demonstrated that in negotiating the changes and transitions of adulthood, "possible selves" (i.e., those identities which are either feared or hoped for presently, in the past, or in the future) are used as resources to motivate and defend the individual. For instance, an individual currently dissatisfied in the workplace might use the hoped-for possibility of a future promotion as a facilitator for subjective well-being or self-esteem and as a motivator for continued engagement. Such findings point to the possibility that having access to a larger set of well-developed possible selves may be a protective factor as we confront and manage growing old. In one study on possible selves and perceived health, the majority of older adults had possible selves in the domain of health and also the most important possible self was in the realm of health. In addition, self-regulatory processes (e.g., perceived efficacy, outcome expectancy) explained over half of the variance in self-perceived health when it was also listed as most important hoped-for self component (Hooker, 1992). In other words, older adults felt subjectively healthier if at the same time they reported hopes for their health and believed that they had some control over their health. When it came to dreaded possible selves in the health domain, such as increasing morbidity and physical suffering, self-regulatory processes had almost no predictive power with regard to perceived health. That is, "health pessimism" seems to be unimportant when it comes to subjective health in the present.

Selection of Goals and Life Priorities

Possible selves act as motivational sources, and are linked to goals that are either strived for or avoided. Indeed, the content and priorities of life goals and self-defining components seem to change with age. In one study of 70- to 100-year-olds, for instance, health, well-being of family members, cognitive fitness, and thinking about life had highest priority with regard to goal investment for older adults (Staudinger et al., 1994b). Similar to earlier findings on cognitive pragmatics of the mind (e.g., expertise research), these results also point to selection into individual life contexts and the importance of internal and external contexts in defining salient features of the self in old age (see also Brandtstädter & Rothermund, 1994; Carstensen, 1993). In a study on the effects of community relocation on mental health in old age, Ryff and Essex (1992) found that the psychological centrality of certain life domains (e.g., family, economics) moderated the resilience-increasing effect of certain interpretative mechanisms of the self.

Age-related changes in goal structures were also found on a meta-level of aggregation. Using a sentence completion technique, Dittmann-Kohli (1991) demonstrated that older adults find meaning in life predominantly by searching for "contentment," whereas younger adults more often reported that they searched for happiness. Furthermore, Ryff (1989) found that younger people are more likely to assess their subjective well-being in terms of accomplishments and careers, whereas older people are more likely to associate well-being with good health and the ability to accept change. It seems to be highly protective to renounce or relegate to the periphery of importance those roles and commitments that are no longer serviceable, and to invest in others more "in tune" with current conditions of living (e.g., Brim, 1992; Dittmann-Kohli, 1991; Lazarus & DeLongis, 1983). Again, the general line of argument is that selection and resetting of priorities are facilitated if there is a rich variety of self-defining concepts to select from and to rearrange.

Adjustment of Aspirational Levels through Social Comparisons

In addition to the change in content and ranking of self-concepts and goals, there is evidence for other self-regulatory processes protecting the aging self. Research on the self also suggests that aging individuals modify their aspirational levels within given domains of functioning in order to adapt to decreases in, for instance, their behavioral competence or negative changes in their health condition.

Adjustment of aspirational levels can occur through a variety of mechanisms. Quite often, it is related to processes of social comparison. New reference groups are selected in order to permit a reorganization of personal standards of evaluation. This might be done, for example, by comparing oneself to specific subgroups, such as age, gender, and ethnic-cultural groups, rather than the population at large. Downward comparisons, in which individuals compare themselves to people who are worse off in a relevant domain of functioning, may become more and more important with age (Heckhausen & Krueger, 1993; Taylor & Lobel, 1989; Wood, 1989). Costa and McCrae (1980), for example, found that health expectations decline with age regardless of the individual's own health status. In a study of the effect of community relocation on subjective well-being, it was demonstrated that endorsement of social comparisons predicted various aspects of well-being (e.g., personal growth, self-acceptance; Ryff & Essex,

1992). Downward social comparisons also play an important role in the evaluation of goal investment: It seems that we select reference groups which make the age-related difference in goal investment disappear or at least appear to be much smaller. Indeed, in one study, chronological age was substituted by cognitive and physical status of participants. When old subjects (70 to 105 years) were divided into two groups according to "high" and "low" level of functioning in terms of cognitive-physical status, no group difference in current goal investment ratings was obtained. A significant group difference emerged only when both groups were asked to use their past status as a comparison referent; lower functioning subjects then indicated greater perceived declines in goal investment (Staudinger et al., 1994b).

In general, then, the contention is that selection of appropriate comparison groups is an important protective mechanism that empowers the aging individual to manage the gains and losses of old age. Better functioning groups are selected for comparison if the goal is to maintain and to improve, while more poorly functioning group referents tend to be selected if the goal is to deal with losses. Note that despite the discussion of these comparison strategies as though they were operating at a conscious level, little is known about the level of consciousness at which such mechanisms operate. Later we shall suggest that the most critical question regarding the adaptiveness of such mechanisms concerns the use of the "right" (functional) comparison at the "right" time.

Lifetime (Temporal) Comparisons

Besides social comparisons, comparisons across one's own lifetime constitute an important resource of the self. Suls and Mullen (1982) have suggested that temporal comparisons, especially retrospective temporal comparisons, provide an additional strategy for effective self-management and self-evaluation in old age. Indeed, they have argued that with increasing age, social comparisons become less frequent and lifetime (temporal) comparisons increase in frequency. The evidence to support this hypothesis, however, is still scarce. Again, one must realize that it is not the temporal comparison per se that is protective; rather, depending on the characteristic or the domain selected, lifetime comparisons can result in either the realization of, or loss in, self enhancement.

In earlier age-comparative research on beliefs about development across the life span, it was demonstrated that such beliefs differ when people are asked to generate expectations about themselves versus about a generalized other versus about the personal ideal, and retrospectively versus prospectively (Ahammer & Baltes, 1972; Harris, 1975; Ryff & Baltes, 1976). More recently, this approach of systematic instructional variation (e.g., age referent, social referent) has been explored with regard to the question of age-related change versus stability of subjective well-being. In this vein, it seems that for many older adults shifting the temporal point of reference may be an effective strategy in maintaining high subjective well-being across the life span Ryff (1991) has found when different age groups are asked to report on their current functioning in different facets of personality (such as autonomy, social relations, personal growth, etc.), they do not differ. Age differences become apparent, however, when instructional variations in temporal referent are introduced. Younger adults have a more positive evaluation of their future and a less positive

evaluation of their past than older adults. Conversely, it seems that older adults, perhaps due to fewer opportunities to achieve in the present and a richer set of positive experiences in the past, increasingly refer to successes of the past. Indeed, reference to earlier achievements may fortify current levels of optimism and energy for dealing with present challenges. Selectively attending to positive aspects of the self at different points in the lifetime can serve to support a positive sense of self at the present. The endorsement of selective lifetime comparisons makes it plausible that in concurrent (present-day) self evaluations only few age differences emerge (see also Fleeson & Baltes, 1994).

Life Review

With respect to self-enhancing and self-maintaining lifetime comparisons, another self-related process often discussed as taking on special meaning in old age is that of life review (e.g., Butler, 1963). Research on the aging self has identified life review as a potentially relevant activity involved in the construction, maintenance, and transformation of the self (Breytspraak, 1984). In this respect, life review is seen as a highly complex process of self regulation encompassing the reconstruction, explanation, and evaluation of the past. It is not to be confused (as often done in the literature) with reminiscence as remembering past episodes or the wandering of the mind back in time (Staudinger, 1989). In our view, effective use of life review can be considered as another protective mechanism or resource of the self.

Various developmental theorists (e.g., Bühler & Massarik, 1968; Erikson et al., 1986) have conceptualized an individual's life review as a rich resource for the restoration of psychological balance in the face of life transitions and in old age, especially in the face of death. Molinari and Reichlin (1984/85) present a model of life review as "psychological action," proposing that life review is a deliberately initiated action to consolidate and redefine the self-concept in the face of experiences of aging which are incompatible with a person's self-concept. When experiences of aging have a negative impact on a person's current sense of self, reviewing past experiences can redefine one's current sense of self in light of past achievements. Other researchers have also suggested that thinking and/or talking about past events and trying to make sense out of them operate as protective mechanisms to help an older person cope with the losses of aging (e.g., Lewis, 1971; Staudinger, 1989).

Regarding the protective function of life review, Coleman (1974) found that among older adults dissatisfied with their past, "noticeable" life reviewers exhibited higher life satisfaction and less depression than "slight" life reviewers. In a similar vein, a study by Wong and Watt (1991) demonstrated that successful aging was related to integrative reminiscence (life review). Studies on autobiographical memory in depressed and nondepressed elderly (e.g., Yang & Rehm, 1993) are also consistent with the so-called self-enhancement view of life review. Nondepressed subjects recalled more positive events and they also evaluated them as happier now as compared to when the event had happened in the past.

Furthermore, life review has been suggested and employed as a therapeutic means of optimizing and enhancing adaptation in late life (e.g., Birren & Deutchman, 1991; Sherman, 1991). The underlying rationale is, not unlike psychoanalysis, that life review therapy can be used to facilitate the individual's reconciliation with his or her past life, and thereby support the identification of meaning in life. Although life review groups are an increasingly common phenomenon, empirical evidence in terms of evaluation research on life review groups or guided autobiography groups unfortunately is still scarce or methodologically problematic (Sherman, 1991; Staudinger, 1989).

Personality, Emotional Management and Coping as "Naturally" Protective Factors of the Aging Self

The Aging Personality

Another avenue for exploring self-related resilience and reserves is the study of personality structure and individual differences. What is the adaptive potential of various personality traits in old age?

The current body of research suggests that, in addition to self-management and coping processes, personality traits might also serve a mediating function between age and indicators of self-related resilience such as subjective well-being (Costa et al., 1987; Staudinger, Freund, Linden, & Maas, in press). Individuals with certain patterns of personality characteristics are likely to master challenging events better than others. Neuroticism and extraversion have been shown, for example, to evince significant predictive relations to subjective well-being as measured by the Bradburn Affect Balance Scale. Over a period of 10 years, neuroticism was found to predict the degree of negative affect and extraversion the level of positive affect (Costa, McCrae, & Norris, 1981). Using other measures of personality, it has often been reported that a high standing on dimensions such as ego strength, cognitive investment, and competence (e.g., Block, 1981; Haan, 1981; Helson & Wink, 1987) are positively related to various measures of well-being and adaptation, both cross-sectionally and longitudinally.

Furthermore, there is an indication that individuals with a greater degree of openness to experience (Costa & McCrae, 1985) are better able to adapt to changes. An aging individual who is experientially open, as captured by characteristics such as being emotionally responsive, seeking variety, being intellectually curious, and broad-minded, may be more aware of bodily changes, and may also be able to devise innovative strategies to adapt to them. Empirical evidence with regard to the adaptivity of openness to experience is still scarce (Whitbourne, 1987). From early research on the personality correlates of wisdom, however, there is a suggestion that individuals who are more open to new experiences and who hold a middle position on the introversion-extraversion dimension also evince higher levels of wisdom-related performance (Baltes & Staudinger, 1993). In the same vein, research from the Seattle Longitudinal Study (Schaie, Dutta, & Willis, 1991) has suggested that maintained "behavioral flexibility" may be an important covariate of late-life adaptation: The progression of intellectual ability from middle to old age was substantially related to a flexible personality style over time. Taken together, these findings imply that in addition to a lack of neuroticism, an intermediate degree of extraversion and a high degree of openness to experience seems to be a protective factor when it comes to managing the self-related challenges of old age.

Similarly, and not unlike the work on the role of self-efficacy (e.g. Bandura, 1986) and optimism (e.g., Seligman, 1990) in earlier phases of life, optimism or future time perspective has been demonstrated to possess protective power in old age (e.g., Reker & Wong, 1988). Taylor and Brown (1988; see also Taylor, 1989) suggested that unrealistic optimism ("positive illusions") about the future may be generally adaptive, in that it promotes feelings of self worth, the ability to care for others, persistence and creativity in the pursuit of goals and the ability to deal with stress. In a more recent study, Taylor and others (Taylor et al., 1992) could provide some evidence for the conclusion that optimism is psychologically functional without necessarily compromising health behavior. Most recently the position that inaccurately positive self-knowledge is related to well-being has received increasing theoretical and empirical criticism (Colvin & Block, 1994; Taylor & Brown, 1994). Longitudinal studies, for instance, have suggested that optimism often has a positive impact initially, but that when persistently negative objective circumstances prevail, the cumulative impact of unrealistic optimism turns into being negative. Evidence is also increasing that under certain circumstances realistic pessimism can have highly adaptive outcomes (e.g., Frese, 1993).

Besides the trait model of personality, which describes individual differences in temporally rather stable personality characteristics, one must also consider what have been called the developmental stage models of personality. One of the central historical figures of this school is probably Erikson (1959, 1963; see also Levinson, 1980), with his theory of eight ego-developmental stages. Erikson's theory, for instance, predicts that in the second half of life, individuals in the post-reproductive phase of life either develop generativity or fall into stagnation (Erikson et al., 1986). In dealing with the final developmental task, old adults may achieve ego maturity by integrating their past lives and finding new meaning in them or they may fall into despair.

By and large, the empirical evidence to support these theoretical contentions is still scarce, not only generally but also regarding the analysis of temporally ordered causal sequences. With respect to generativity, there is research suggesting that older adults redirect their ambition toward offspring rather than toward their own achievements (Ochse & Plug, 1986). Considering ego integrity, Ryff (1991) has reported that older adults displayed higher levels of current self-acceptance than they reported in ratings of their own past. Current self-acceptance of older adults was also higher than that reported by younger adults.

Related to this notion that knowledge about one's self becomes better integrated with increasing age is a finding that older adults are more likely than younger adults to behave in accordance with their own feelings and attitudes rather than in response to social expectations (Reifman, Klein, & Murphy, 1989). In addition, relative to younger adults, elders seem more able to integrate self-knowledge, building more realistic self-conceptions. With increasing age, ideal selves are adjusted, so that they approach present selves (Cross & Markus, 1991; Ryff, 1991). Given reduced time left for accomplishments, and the reduced "degrees of freedom" available to make life choices with advancing age, this increased realism seems to be a valuable protective mechanism of the aging self. As mentioned above,

Dittmann-Kohli (1991) characterized this age trend as one from a search for "happiness" to one for "contentment." However, it may be crucial to find the optimal discrepancy between the real and the ideal in order to stay motivated without becoming frustrated by failure (e.g., Thomae, 1970). The "optimal" discrepancy seems to be related to a higher level of life satisfaction (Cross & Markus, 1991).

The idea of ego maturity and its putative benefits for functioning and subsequent development have also been discussed in other approaches to the study of personality development such as Loevinger's model of ego development (Loevinger, 1976), Vaillant's model of adult adjustment (e.g., Vaillant, 1977, 1990), Haan's development of ego structures (Haan, 1977), or concepts of maturity as derived from scales of the California Personality Inventory (CPI; e.g., Helson & Wink, 1987). Ego level as measured according to Loevinger's Sentence Completion Test is reported to display a positive relation with reality-oriented and flexible coping (e.g., Picano, 1989) as well as with tolerance, sensitivity, and responsibility (e.g., White, 1985). With regard to its relation to higher levels of adjustment, the empirical evidence is equivocal (e.g., McCrae & Costa, 1983). In a longitudinal study, comparing two conceptions of maturity, Helson and Wink (1987) found that different measures of maturity predicted different aspects of adjustment (e.g., self-related, other-related).

In his model of adult adjustment, Vaillant (e.g., 1977, 1990) extended psychoanalytical conceptions of defense mechanisms into a developmental framework of more or less mature or adaptive defense mechanisms. Vaillant (e.g., 1983) argued that mature defenses may provide an explanation for some of the so-called invulnerabilities among the disadvantaged, or in the terminology of this chapter, they may carry protective and development-enhancing power. More recently, he provided evidence from long-term longitudinal data for this protective and development-enhancing power of mature defenses in middle and later adulthood (Vaillant, 1990).

Emotional Management: A Protective Facet of the Resilient Self in Old Age

In addition to thinking about ego maturity as a personality characteristic, one can also think about it as adults' ability to manage their emotions. Thus, what Erikson has called ego integrity, and what other developmental theorists have referred to as maturity (e.g., Loevinger, 1976; Vaillant, 1977), can also be conceptualized as a process of gaining perspective and competence in mastering one's own emotional life. In this vein, several studies suggest that older adults seem to be better able to manage their emotions and deal with emotional issues (e.g., Blanchard-Fields, 1986; Cornelius & Caspi, 1987; Staudinger, 1989). Labouvie-Vief and her colleagues (Labouvie-Vief, Hakim-Larson, DeVoe, & Schoeberlein, 1989), for example, have developed a four-level assessment scheme for the understanding and control of emotional states, such as anger, sadness, fear, and happiness during adulthood. They reported that older subjects demonstrated developmentally higher levels of emotional understanding and control than young adults. Being able to manage one's emotions seems to be an especially important protective factor in the context of all the losses (e.g., friends, spouse, social status, physical strength)

an aging individual might have to confront. Weiner and Graham (1989), for example, reported that feelings of pity and helping increased and anger decreased in frequency across the life span. This finding is also congruent with notions of greater generativity at advanced ages. In a similar vein, Levenson, Carstensen, and Gottmann (1993) demonstrated that when comparing old and young married couples who describe themselves as *unhappily* married on measures of life satisfaction, older couples report relatively higher levels of life satisfaction.

The processes underlying such changes in emotional management are not yet identified, neither is it clear how far the effectiveness of emotional management extends into the very late phases of life, that is very old age. Recent evidence from the Berlin Aging Study suggests that even into very old age (70 to 105 yrs.), no significant age differences in the frequency of negative emotions are found. However, negative age differences in the frequency of positive emotions are obtained (Staudinger et al., in press). From research on emotional intensity and expressivity, we do know that the greater ability of older adults to manage their emotions is not just due to an age-related decrease in expressivity and intensity of emotions (Levenson, Carstensen, Friesen, & Ekman, 1991; Malatesta, 1990). The appraisal-model of emotion (e.g., Lazarus, 1993) would suggest that increased capability in emotional management reflects an increase in knowledge about life and oneself (e.g., Baltes & Staudinger, 1993; Edelstein & Noam, 1982; Staudinger, 1989), and/or age-related changes in values, and commitments (Dittmann-Kohli, 1991; Lazarus & DeLongis, 1983). Such development- and resilience-enhancing knowledge and skills involving emotions and emotional regulation can be seen as another instantiation of the knowledge-based mental pragmatics which were identified earlier as having protective and enhancing power with regard to intellectual functioning in old age. In this instance, as well, these seem to serve a protective function for older adults.

Self-Related Resilience through Coping

Another concept which has attracted attention as an integrated and "general purpose" mechanism of adjustment and mastery across the life span is coping. The capacity to cope successfully is another potential protective factor in old age.

In the seventies, Pfeiffer (1977) speculated that with increasing age, *regressive* coping tendencies increase. In the same year, however, Vaillant (1977) reported an age-related increase in *mature* coping mechanisms. In a similar vein, Folkman, Lazarus, Pimley, and Novacek (1987), for example, found that older respondents were less likely to seek social support or use confrontive coping and more likely to use distancing and positive reappraisal. In fact, more and more of the recent evidence supports this "growth" view of coping in adulthood and old age (e.g., Aldwin, 1991; Irion & Blanchard-Fields, 1987; Labouvie-Vief, Hakim-Larson, & Hobart, 1987; McCrae, 1989) or at least speaks for stability in coping behavior.

With respect to the developmental stability of coping behavior during adult life it has been observed, for instance, that individual differences in the endorsement of coping mechanisms are more a function of the type of stressful event than of age

(McCrae, 1989). This finding is extended by evidence from the Berlin Aging Study. In that study, based on data from a representative sample of 70- to 103-year-olds, it is suggested that those old individuals who reported employing a large number of different coping strategies also demonstrated the highest level of well-being (Staudinger et al., 1994a). Similar findings are reported in research on depression in old age. Rather than any particular form of coping, it seems that self-related resilience as indicated by measures of mental health is related to the availability of a large number of different forms of coping (Forster & Gallagher, 1986). We have argued above that the multiplicity of self definitions has protective value and we will see further below that, similarly, social relations with multiple functions are a richer resource than other types of relationships. This evidence suggests that access to a wide repertoire in functioning (e.g., coping, self definitions, multiplexity of a relationship) may be a key resource as it facilitates the person-situation fit.

Furthermore, older adults seem to be more flexible in adapting their coping response to the characteristics of the situation (e.g., controllability) than younger adults (e.g., Aldwin, 1991). Such evidence is congruent with findings that, in comparison to younger adults, older individuals have been found to demonstrate an accommodative coping style in the face of adversity or failure; that is, older adults were more flexible and better able to adjust their strivings to changed circumstances than young adults (Brandtstädter & Renner, 1990). Conversely, younger adults were more likely to adhere to their once established goals (i.e., assimilative coping), even if they were no longer realizable. With age, Brandtstädter and Renner (1990) have demonstrated that adults favor accommodative (goal flexible) over assimilative (goal persistent) coping. In a similar vein, Heckhausen and Schulz (1993; in press) have more recently proposed an age-related shift from primary to secondary control strategies in order to master the tasks of aging.

In our view, such evidence on age-related stability and positive transformations in coping efficiency is significant for two reasons. First, if late adulthood and old age are characterized by an increasing number of varied stressful events, then the findings on coping efficiency seem to suggest the presence of another component of self-related reserve capacity. Second, in contrast to stereotypical conceptions of the elderly as rigid, the evidence suggests that, based on processes of self-representation, self-regulation, and self-enhancement, older adults possess a substantial capacity for adjustment and flexible mastery of demands.

Regaining Self-Related Resilience after Breakdown: Intervention in Depression

In the following section, we attempt to summarize the evidence available on the regaining of adjustment after "breakdown" in one area of self-related functioning, that is depressivity and depression. While clinical depression is not more but rather less frequent in old age when compared to younger ages, depressive affect and symptoms show an age-related increase after middle adulthood (Anthony & Aboraya, 1992; Gatz & Hurwicz, 1990; Häfner, 1994; Kessler, Foster, Webster, & House, 1992). In addition, our

everyday expectations may suggest that older adults may have increasing difficulty in recovery.

To discuss depression under the heading of the self, however, is to a certain degree arbitrary in the same way as to discuss Senile Dementia of the Alzheimer Type (SDAT) under the heading of cognition. These categorizations are related to a relative priority of self-related and cognitive symptoms, respectively, but both disorders encompass a very complex and variegated system of manifestations involving biomedical, cognitive, and personality-related aspects. The differential diagnosis of depression versus SDAT, for example, is a major technical problem, especially at lower levels of severity or at earlier stages in the progression of the illness. Indeed, it seems to be one of the important characteristics of geriatric pathology that the multidimensional specificity of psychological functioning decreases and eventually is lost altogether (e.g., Helmchen & Linden, 1993).

It is exactly this complexity of symptoms grouped under the heading of depression which results in little consensus in the psychiatric literature regarding issues of prevalence and incidence of depression (e.g., Carstensen & Edelstein, 1987; Cohen, 1989; Häfner, 1994; Helmchen & Linden, 1993). Many symptoms associated with depressive illness in later life (e.g., change in sleep patterns, change in sexual interest, dread of death) are overlooked, and may be dismissed as inevitable manifestations of the aging process. As mentioned before, diagnosis is further complicated by the multimorbidity of many older patients (see Gaylord & Zung, 1987; Kinzie, Lewinsohn, Maricle, & Teri, 1986). In addition, the situation is exacerbated by the fact that epidemiological studies differ dramatically with respect to diagnostic and classification criteria.

Owing to differences in methodology and definition, however, estimates of the prevalence of depression in old age (over 64 years) vary widely, from less than 5%, to almost 44% (Blazer & Williams, 1980). Given the cross-sectional nature of most of this epidemiological research, Lewinsohn, Rohde, Seeley, and Fischer (1991, 1993) have argued that one complication may be a difference in the lifetime occurrence of depression across different birth cohorts. More recent birth cohorts seem to report a higher prevalence of depression, perhaps due to variables including the changing social desirability of acknowledging depressive symptoms. Nonetheless, there seems to be a growing consensus that the prevalence of *major depressive disorder* does not show an age-related increase (Cohen, 1989; Gatz & Hurwicz, 1990; Häfner, 1994). Rather, any age-related increase in depressive symptomatology, if it occurs, may be attributable more to *reactive depressions* (depressivity) arising in association with increasing somatic illnesses, medication effects, or critical life events, rather than specific psychiatric disorders such as depression (e.g., Teri, Baer, & Reifler, 1991).

This lack of an increase in depression in old age highlights the relative age-related robustness and reserve capacity of the self-system from a different perspective. Perhaps most importantly, this fact counteracts the frequently held view that therapeutic interventions are less promising in old age than at earlier age periods. To illustrate, we briefly consider some research concerning the effectiveness of treatment of depression in old age.

Aside from drug therapies, three psychotherapeutic approaches are particularly common for the treatment of depression in later life: psychoanalytic, behavioral, and cognitive-behavioral therapy (Smyer et al., 1990). These therapies seem especially useful in the case of depressivity, or depressive reactions, rather than depression as a nosological category. In each case, treatment results seem to be generally supportive of the notion that there is much self-related resilience in aging individuals, even after the onset of depressive symptomatology. Studies including psychodynamic therapies, usually with adults in their sixties and seventies, have generally reported effectiveness rates which are comparable to those of behavioral and cognitive approaches (e.g., Marmar, Gaston, Gallagher, & Thompson, 1989; Thompson, Gallagher, & Breckenridge, 1987; Thompson, Gallagher, & Czirr, 1988). The gerontological research literature on adult mental health, however, focuses most heavily on behavioral and cognitive approaches to the treatment of depression. We will consider these in greater detail.

Behavioral Approaches

In examining the etiology of depressive symptomatology, behavioral approaches pay particular attention to the negative aspects of the life environments of clients (Carstensen & Edelstein, 1987; Zeiss & Lewinsohn, 1986). In the case of older adults, many normative environmental events have been shown to be potential risk factors for depressive symptomatology, including social role loss and the resultant potential loss of pleasant life events (e.g., Zeiss & Lewinsohn, 1986), coping with chronic illnesses of aging and its resultant pain (e.g., Parmalee, Katz, & Lawton, 1991; Williamson & Schulz, 1992), coping with the illness and caregiving responsibility for a loved one (Pruchno, Kleban, Michaels, & Dempsey, 1990), widowhood and bereavement (e.g., Gilewski, Farberow, Gallagher, & Thompson, 1991) as well as iatrogenic consequences of formal care institutions (e.g., Johnson, 1987; Parmalee, Katz, & Lawton, 1992; Smyer, Cohn, & Brannon, 1988). It is important to note that the age range covered in such studies ranges from the late fifties to the nineties.

Late-life depressivity is also predicted by or correlated with learned helplessness (e.g., Seligman & Elder, 1986). Individuals, aged 65 to 96 years, with higher levels of depression were more likely to attribute failure to a lack of ability, and success to luck; the reverse pattern was found in nondepressed older adults (Maiden, 1987). Not surprisingly, the literature on the provision of more positive life environments (e.g., increasing the number of personally salient pleasant events) to older adults has documented substantial success, even with highly depressed subjects (Goddard & Carstensen, 1986; Teri & Gallagher-Thompson, 1991). Part of the success of this therapeutic strategy may result from the provision of increased control opportunities to older adults (e.g., Baltes & Baltes, 1986; Bandura, 1986; Lachman, 1993; Langer & Rodin, 1976; Rodin, 1986), as they are encouraged to choose events and situations that are pleasing to them (Goddard & Carstensen, 1986). It seems that the transaction between certain external (i.e., environmental features) and internal (i.e., self efficacy) resources contribute to a regaining of resilience.

Cognitive-Behavioral Approaches

Cognitive-behavioral therapy has evolved in varied forms and as the result of joining principles of behavior modification with principles of cognitive psychology and social-learning conceptions of personality. In its traditional form, one major feature of cognitive therapy is to challenge individuals' negative cognitions. The goal is to reduce distortions in thinking about the self and one's relationship to others, and to model more adaptive ways of viewing situations and the world (Beck, 1979). The effectiveness of such therapy presumes, at the least, that individuals have a minimum level of cognitive competency (Krantz & Gallagher-Thompson, 1990). Consequently, pure cognitive therapies are not appropriate for individuals with moderate or severe dementia; in this case, the use of behavioral therapies may be much more effective (Teri & Gallagher-Thompson, 1991). For those older individuals whose level of cognitive functioning is normal, however, numerous studies suggest that cognitive approaches can be highly effective in remediating depression and maintaining treatment gains (e.g., Florsheim, Leavesley, Hanley-Peterson, Gallagher-Thompson, 1991; Gallagher-Thompson, Hanley-Peterson, & Thompson, 1990; Rodman, Gantz, Schneider, Gallagher & Thompson, 1991). However, cognitive status is frequently confounded with age in many intervention studies, since subjects are typically in the young-old (60 to 75 years) range.

Cognitive-behavioral therapy represents a mix of behavioral and cognitive approaches (Meichenbaum, 1974). As outlined for the field of aging by Thompson, Gallagher-Thompson, and their colleagues, it involves producing both changes in clients' environment, and challenging particular cognitions. In the case of chronically ill elderly, for example, the behavioral component involves reinforcing both participation in therapy and in regular self-maintenance activities. Individuals are encouraged to remain as active as possible. Simultaneously, the cognitive component challenges such beliefs as the irreversibility of depression, or the perception of being a "burden." Case reviews suggest that such treatments can be highly effective (e.g., Rybarczyk, Gallagher-Thompson, Rodman, Zeiss, & Thompson, 1992).

In summary, outcome studies regarding the treatment of depressivity have found that structured short-term psychotherapy of almost any kind can evince impressive results with older people (Marmar et al., 1989; Thompson et al., 1987). In those few cases where depression seems to be resistant to treatment, the origins of depressive symptoms are likely located primarily in biological conditions (Goff & Jenicke, 1986). These positive findings stand in contrast both to the historically negative statements in the mental health professions regarding the prognosis of late-life depression, and to the negative aging stereotype which has assumed relatively little mental health-related plasticity in aging individuals (Butler, 1989). In fact, one of the major challenges to the effectiveness of therapeutic interventions with older adults seems to be the latent or manifest unwillingness of mental health professionals to engage in such treatment. Indeed, surveys of mental health professionals frequently reveal high levels of ageism (Gatz & Pearson, 1988), and a general disinterest or resistance in treating older adults (Teri & Logsdon, 1992). Thus, one of the pressing problems of therapeutic environments for older adults (e.g., nursing homes) is the relative absence of trained mental health practitioners in their settings (e.g., Smyer et al., 1988). More supportive and available therapeutic environments could constitute a critical variable in enhancing the resilient functioning of older adults with depressive symptomatology (e.g., Blazer, 1986; Lewinsohn & Tilson, 1987).

Social Relations (Transactions) and Resilience or Reserve Capacity in Later Adulthood

The final domain of psychological functioning in which we have selected to investigate resilience and reserve capacity in later adulthood is the area of social relationships, or, as we would prefer to call it, "social transactions." We prefer to use the term social transactions to emphasize the exchange or interactive aspect of this domain of psychological functioning (see also Sameroff, 1975). Since James, Mead or Vygotsky we know that any domain of psychological functioning involving cognition and the self is social-interactive in nature (e.g., Baltes & Staudinger, in press; Cole, in press). The domain of social relations is one where this social-interactive nature becomes most obvious. Nevertheless, psychological research in this area has only begun to transcend the classical person-centered research approach. Furthermore, the domain of social transactions provides an instance of how external and interpersonal resources may contribute to the resilience and reserve capacity of an individual. Returning to Figure 22.1, this capacity to profit from and turn to others as resources becomes increasingly important given the age-related increase in physical morbidity and frailty.

In the following section, we attempt to integrate several streams of research relevant to the topic of social transactions: (a) social network approach (e.g., Fischer, 1982); (b) social support and coping (e.g., House, Umberson, & Landis, 1988; Schwarzer & Leppin, 1992); and (c) personal relationships (e.g., Blumstein & Kollock, 1988). As the topic of social transaction lies "between" the individual and the social, various disciplines contribute to this field, including sociology, epidemiology, and psychology. Different disciplines use different emphases and different methodologies in their pursuits. It may be due to this diversity that the field of social relationships is, on the one hand, characterized by a high productivity in terms of empirical studies, and, on the other hand, still awaiting the formulation of unifying theoretical frameworks.

We have selected the family of life-span propositions introduced in the beginning of this chapter as an integrative framework to highlight the nature of developmental changes in social transactions during adulthood and old age (see Table 22.1). Throughout this section, we will illustrate how the propositions of multidimensionality, multidirectionality, the dynamics of gains and losses, potential and limits, and contextualism apply to the field of social transactions. Given the richness of the available empirical material, this review is necessarily selective. Our selection of research was guided by the goal of exploring social transactions as a potentially protective factor or as an instance of resilience in old age but also as a risk factor for normal functioning in later adulthood.

House and Kahn (1985) have introduced the notion of the multidimensionality of social support. We extend this argument, and assert that multiple dimensions of social transactions can be identified which also follow different life-span trajectories. The dimensions considered are: (a) the *function or content* (borrowing from the world of economics one could also talk about the "currency" of exchange) of the social transactions (e.g., social affiliation, emotional support, instrumental support, social control); (b) the *quantity* of social transactions taking place and of the associated "currency" of exchange; and (c) the *quality and structure* of the system of social transactions (e.g., types, density, durability, homogeneity, or reciprocity).

Usually, handbook chapters and review articles on social relations—especially on social relationships and aging—subsume all these aspects explicitly or implicitly under the umbrella of "social support." Social affiliation, for example, is either discussed as the quantitative aspect of social transactions; that is, the mere frequency of social contact, number of relationships or amount of time spent in social transactions, or it is categorized as one type of support. Recently, an increasing number of authors have come to acknowledge that with this exclusive focus on support, both the potential negative effects of relationships, as well as the other functions of relationships besides support, such as social affiliation and sense of personal control, are neglected in their contribution to the social world and the well-being of individuals, especially old people (e.g., Baltes & Silverberg, 1994; Morgan, 1990; Rook, 1990). Two broad themes have been identified as especially suited to illustrate the resilience-related qualities of social transactions in adulthood and old age: Social affiliation or companionship, and social support. By resilience-related we mean that (a) social relationships themselves contribute to a person's reserves, and (b) support provided by social relationships can be a resource in the face of stress.

Social Affiliation: An Interpersonal Resource in Adulthood and Old Age

According to the still prevailing negative aging stereotypes, social transactions and their quantity might be categorized as another risk factor for the achievement of resilience in old age (e.g., Palmore, 1988). As will be demonstrated, the lonely and socially isolated old person is one of the most well-known negative myths of aging.

Social Contact across the Life Span: More Stability Than Change

Two kinds of empirical evidence have actually demonstrated that the expectation that most older persons are lonely and socially isolated is a myth. First, multiple longitudinal studies have found that neither the number of network members, nor the frequency of contacts, show dramatic changes over the life span (for summary see e.g., Carstensen, 1992; Palmore, 1981; Schulz & Rau, 1985). Covering an age range from 20 to 95 years, adults on average report network sizes of 8 to 15 people (see Schulz & Rau, 1985; Smith & Baltes, 1993). A significant drop in frequency of social contacts already occurs between early and middle age

(Carstensen, 1992). This finding of stability is especially true with regard to kin relationships, and with regard to persons categorized as very close (Carstensen, 1992). Due to losses, for example, in peers and siblings, however, a reduction in the number of less close people is found, particularly after age 85 and 90 (Lang & Carstensen, 1994).

A third indicator of social contact, besides number of close network members, and frequency of social contact, is time spent with others. With regard to this third indicator, time spent with other people, Larson and colleagues (Larson, Cskiszentmihalyi, & Graef, 1982), for instance, reported, using a time-sampling and beeper methodology, that older people over age 65 spend 48% of their waking time alone as compared to 25% in adolescence and 30% below age 65. Time spent with friends stays about the same, that is 7%, across the age range studied. Only adolescents spend much more time with friends (i.e., 29%). In a more recent study of a heterogeneous city sample of German elders (mean age M = 72 years), using a diary methodology to assess daily activity patterns, it was found that people in that age group spent 59% of their time alone and 6% with friends (Baltes, Wahl, & Schmid-Fürstoss, 1990). This finding is supported by another study using a slightly modified diary methodology. In this study, participants of the Berlin Aging Study (age range: 70 to 103 years) reported a complete list of activities in which they had engaged on a typical day. A major finding of this study was that older people differed to a large degree as to how much time they spent with others. It ranged from as little as 10 minutes for a group characterized primarily by rest activities to 1.5 hours for the most active group (Baltes, Wilms, & Horgas, 1993). Physical status was one predictor of the amount of time spent with others. This study nicely illustrates the range of interindividual variability of social functioning in old age, and it shows that decreases in functioning and reserves in one domain (i.e., health) cut across to other domains and result in decreases in other domains as well (i.e., social transactions). In sum, it seems that number of close social network members and frequency of contact with close friends and family members stay about the same across the adult life span, whereas the time spent with others declines with age. Although some of the quantitative indicators of social contact evince age-related decline, it still would be incorrect to conclude that old people must feel lonely as a result.

The correlational pattern characterizing the relationship between quantity of social contact and subjective well-being is not consistent across studies. In general, it seems that there is a modest positive relationship between life satisfaction and frequency of social contact across the life span. This relationship seems to be especially strong for non-kin interactions (e.g., Larson, 1978). The modest size of the correlation and the inconsistency across studies suggests that there is no isomorphy between amount of social contact (e.g., frequency, time spent with others) and subjective well-being.

Social Contact, Isolation, and Loneliness

In this vein, a second type of evidence has helped to challenge the myth of pervasive loneliness in old age. A clarification in terminology resolves a large portion of the inconsistencies of findings regarding age, social contact, and subjective well-being.

Living alone is not the same as being socially isolated, and neither term is equivalent to loneliness. An important distinction introduced, therefore, is one between so-called social and emotional (or psychological) isolation (e.g., Townsend, 1957; Weiss, 1982) on the one hand and loneliness on the other. Social isolation speaks to the amount of time individuals are alone, while emotional isolation refers to the perceived lack of confidants or close personal relationships. The latter type of isolation seems to primarily contribute to the feeling of loneliness. Frequency, number and type of social contacts or social and emotional isolation are constructs that correspond to "objective" conditions, whereas loneliness refers to the subjective evaluation of these "objective" conditions (Baltes, Tesch-Römer, & Lang, 1994).

Across the life span, individuals may differ on how much contact they need in order to feel well and not lonely. In other words, independent of whether the age trajectories of contact frequency remain stable, increase or decrease, old people may or may not *feel* lonely. The empirical evidence, which is primarily from cross-sectional studies, shows that older adults do not feel more lonely than their younger counterparts (e.g., Mellor & Edelmann, 1988; Peplau, Bikson, Rook, & Goodchilds, 1982). If anything there seems to be a tendency with increasing age for adults to report more, rather than less, satisfaction with their social transactions (Antonucci, 1985). The empirical evidence changes, however, when we consider the age range above age 80. Fifty-three percent of adults above the age of 80 feel lonely (e.g., Kaufman & Adams, 1987; Smith & Baltes, 1993). Again, there is evidence suggesting that it may be useful to distinguish between loneliness with regard to kin and non-kin relationships. Schmitt and Kurdek (1985) reported, for instance, that older women felt especially lonely with regard to friendship and love relationships whereas younger women felt more lonely with regard to family relationships.

Companionship and Social Affiliation: Evaluative Dimensions of Social Contact

Although the correlations are not very high, there are many studies that report a positive relationship, or main effect, of frequency of social contact on psychological well-being. Thus, amount of social contact in itself seems to constitute an important resource for adaptive psychological functioning. These studies, however, seldom consider the possible mediating processes involved in this correlation. This is probably a consequence of the exclusive analytic focus on the "support function" of social transactions.

Companionship has been introduced as one theoretical construct which may help to understand such processes. Rook (1990), for example, defined the need for companionship as the intrinsic motivation to voluntarily share pleasure with others. Companionship defines an important part of the fabric of daily life. She argues that companionship is one way to temporarily escape daily hassles, or preoccupation with one's own faults and failures. Furthermore, companionship may be interpreted as the behavioral affirmation of the focal person's self esteem, since it comes about by a mutual agreement between people who want to share time with each other. The mutuality of companionship may reduce one of the major risks of social support relationships, which is the asymmetry between helper and helpee. Having to accept support without being able to give something in return may undermine rather than affirm the helpee's self esteem.

We had reported above that the positive relation between frequency of social contact and subjective well-being is especially strong for social relations outside the family (Larson, 1978). The concept of companionship offers an explanation for this differential effect. When a particular activity is carried out with friends, it is likely to be characterized by greater spontaneity, less habitualization, less obligation, and perhaps also by more novelty as compared to sharing this activity with a family member. In selecting companions, we do have a choice which is not available in the case of kin relationship and in turn, this feature is mutual. We are selected by our companions, but usually not by our family.

Is Satisfaction with the Frequency of Social Contacts Always a Resource for Resilience and Enhancement?

Given this positive effect of social contact on well-being, it is interesting to note that although older people over age 65 spend about 50% of their waking time alone (as compared to 25% in adolescence and 30% below age 65; Larson, Cskiszentmihalyi, & Graef, 1982), they do not fill that time with companionship or social contact, neither do they seem to feel bad about it (e.g., Baltes et al., 1994). Multiple explanations are possible: Is it lack of opportunity to be with friends, or do individuals self-select to not spend more time with friends? Resolving this question poses empirical challenges, which illustrates the importance of a type of measurement in assessing social transactions and their role as risk, protective, and enhancing factors in old age.

One approach might be to ask people how satisfied they are with their social relationships. People who select not to spend more time with friends should be more satisfied than those people who would like to, but do not have the opportunity. Unfortunately, researchers typically find that such differences in the evaluative basis do not become visible in satisfaction ratings. Both potential groups of people (self selection, lack of opportunity) tend to give similar satisfaction ratings. We have seen in our discussion of the resilient self that the transformational processes at work within the self can be quite effective in adjusting to almost any living circumstances (e.g., well-being paradox). People come to accept and sometimes even appreciate what they cannot have.

In an attempt to disentangle the paradox, researchers (Campbell, Converse, & Rodgers, 1976; Rook & Thuras, 1988) have distinguished, for example, between satisfaction of contentment (self selected), satisfaction of resignation (lack of opportunity), and defensive denial (lack of opportunity). Any of those three states can underlie the same satisfaction rating. Refinement in measurement is necessary to empirically distinguish these varied forms of satisfaction. The separation of these different types clearly has also implications with respect to resilience in later adulthood. Satisfaction based on defensive denial or satisfaction based on resignation may be less of a resource than satisfaction based on self selection and contentment. Depending on which operationalization of resilience (e.g., presence of well-being or lack of depression) and which evaluative dimension of social relationships (importance, frequency, satisfaction, etc.) are used, these differences can remain obscure or become visible (Rook & Thuras, 1988).

Social Affiliation: Life-Span Changes in Motivation

Another important piece in the explanatory puzzle of the social time pattern of older people and its contribution to their well-being (e.g., Baltes et al., 1990; Larson et al., 1982) is provided by socioemotional selectivity theory (e.g., Carstensen, 1993). In socioemotional selectivity theory, Carstensen argues that older people, as an example of persons approaching social endings, become very selective about which contacts to engage in and which ones to avoid or to give up. Carstensen claims that in later adulthood emotional and affective benefits, and not information seeking, are the driving forces for contacts. Fredrickson and Carstensen (1990) found, for instance, that older people, in contrast to younger adults, reported preferring familiar over novel social partners. Older people—in contrast to younger adults—also reported that they preferred social relationships which are related to anticipated affect rather than information seeking or future contact. When asked why, older people quite explicitly said that they had no time to waste and had to be careful about their choices.

Applied to the notion of companionship, Carstensen's approach and findings imply that, in old age, only highly selected companions will fulfill affiliation needs. If old friends have died, the likelihood that they will be replaced by new ones should be rather low. New friends do not share a long history of common experiences and therefore do not provide the degree of emotional closeness that is desired. Therefore, turning to companionship as a resource in old age is characterized by conditions that are based on the age-specific nature of social goals.

The Dynamic between Affiliation and Solitude as a Potential Resource

Self-selection of reduced social participation in late life may be motivated not only by the goal of optimizing emotional closeness, but also by the need to balance contrasting goals. Considering the developmental tasks of old age (Havighurst, 1948), it would be defensible to argue that the need for affiliation or companionship is paralleled by an age-related increase in the need for solitude or privacy (e.g., Rook, 1990). In discussing social transactions as potential resource for resilience, and possibly growth, one should not forget the potential resources related to the *dialectic* between social contact and solitude (Lowenthal & Robinson, 1976). In this respect, one should distinguish between two dimensions; that is, affiliation and solitude, rather than considering only the amount of social contact. There is, for example, an indication that in very old age (above age 85), the investment (in terms of mental time and effort) in relations with friends and with family decreases and investment in dealing with one's death and dying and one's past life increases (Staudinger, Freund, & Smith, 1993b). Congruent with theories of personality development and developmental tasks (e.g., Erikson et al., 1986; Jung, 1971), solitude and interiority seem to gain importance in very old age. Thus, it becomes plausible from still another vantage point that being alone in old age is not synonymous with feeling lonely (see also Baltes et al., 1994).

Whether solitude can be considered a protective or a risk factor emphasizes, again, the importance of considering a person's developmental context. Across the life span, we find telling examples. Take, for instance, the breastfeeding mother of a newborn who wishes to have at least half an hour to herself. In contrast, a single young person may invest a lot of effort into escaping her solitude. Another example might be the overburdened adult at midlife, whose time is completely taken up by professional, family, and sometimes societal obligations so that no time is left for privacy. When it comes to old age, it seems that for older married adults, solitude can be energizing, while for unmarried elders living alone, it can be depleting (Larson, Zuzanek, & Mannell, 1985). This is not meant to imply that it is marriage which "does the trick" but rather that marriage, in this case, stands for the potential availability of social contact. On the one hand, solitude has the potential to be a resource if it is self-selected, and if the individual perceives an opportunity to counterbalance it with intimacy and companionship. On the other hand, it seems that affiliation also needs to be counterbalanced with solitude in order for the protective function of social affiliation to develop to its fullest.

Social Support in Later Adulthood: The Interplay between Risk and Protective Factors

So far, our discussion of the function of social relations in old age has considered social transactions as a resource for strengthening current well-being, without considering the presence of immediate stressors. We now turn to the social support function of social relations, which considers social transactions as a resource in the face of age-related threats or challenges.

Across the life span, and especially in old age (see left panel of Figure 22.1), social support is considered to be a resource when psychological functioning needs to be maintained or restored after the occurrence of a stressor (e.g., Antonucci, 1985). In other words, research on social support primarily focuses on the maintenance or recovery of normal functioning. This matches closely with our definition of resilience. In contrast, research on social contact and social affiliation also emphasizes the potential for enhancement of well-being, which is more consistent with our definition of reserve capacity and its function of supporting growth. This analogy demonstrates once more how important it is, from a perspective encompassing both resilience and reserve capacity, to separate and include both fields of study in the investigation of social transactions as conditions of risk, protection, and enhancement in adulthood and old age.

Social Support: Conceptual and Methodological Issues

During recent decades, this area of research has grown not only in terms of number of studies, but also in terms of differentiation of theoretical concepts. Reviewing the recent literature with regard to the life-span implications of social support for questions of resilience and reserve capacity suggests that it is useful to consider the following differentiations when characterizing interpersonal systems and determining whether or not a given support relationship has the potential to contribute to the focal person's resilience and reserve capacity: (a) perceived availability of support (prospective) versus perceived received (retrospective) support versus observed support; (b) quantity (frequency, amount) versus quality (satisfaction) of support; (c) presence versus absence of needed support; (d) type of support provided (emotional, instrumental); (e) single relationships versus the support network as a whole; (f) characteristics of the support network (e.g., density, homogeneity, reciprocity); (g) long-term versus short-term support relationships (convoy versus network); (h) support provided by family members versus non-family members; (i) informal versus formal helpers; (j) type of event necessitating support (normative, non-normative, etc.) versus generalized stress aggregated across different events; (k) acute versus chronic stress.

This list of variables speaks, on the one hand, to the complexity of the topic of social support. On the other hand, it also illustrates the relative lack of coherent theory, which is perhaps typical of work at the interface of social psychology and sociology. Keeping in mind the recency of aging research and the complexity of this list, it is obvious that the state of knowledge in this field and its relevance for aging is far from well explicated. Despite these limitations, we subsequently attempt to illustrate issues and questions relevant for aging and aging well.

Social Support as a Resource in the Face of Generalized Stress and Specific Stressful Life Events in Adulthood and Old Age

When the relationship between received social support and psychological well-being has been studied without considering the moderating effect of stress, results have been very inconsistent across different studies. Some studies have documented a positive relationship between social support and well-being in old age, and others have not (cf., Schulz & Rau, 1985). Investigations of the effectiveness of support in response to specific critical life events during adulthood and old age, however, have consistently shown a positive relationship with mental health or subjective well-being (e.g., Cohen & Wills, 1985; Schulz & Rau, 1985). Using data from a prospective longitudinal study (Social Security Administration's Longitudinal Retirement History Study), Wan (1982) concluded that social support has a positive effect on gerontological health during certain stressful events, but that this relationship is considerably more complicated than has previously been suggested. This evidence seems to support the notion of domain-specific reserves. It seems that the protective function of social support is more domain-specific, or in this case, event-specific in nature, than of a "general-purpose" type.

The buffering effect of social support in the case of chronic stress, such as chronic illnesses, seems to be even stronger. This result should still be interpreted with caution, as it is yet based on relatively few studies. For instance, the analysis of coping with chronic strain—a topic of high relevance for old age—has been sorely neglected in the epidemiological literature (Kessler & McLeod, 1985). Singer and Lord (1984), for example, pointed out that in the case of chronic stress the sudden loss of support might become a stressor itself which counteracts the protective effects of provided support.

Consistent with the contextualism proposition of life-span theory, it has been demonstrated that life events can present different types and amount of stress, depending on the point in the life span at which they occur (e.g., Baltes, 1987; Brim & Ryff, 1980). Schulz and Rau (1985), for example, reported that with increasing age, the stress-inducing effect of widowhood decreases while that of divorce increases. Morgan (1976) suggested that the higher morale of widows over age 70 is related to their experience of fewer negative outcomes. An older widow, for example, may be more likely to have available a reference peer group of supportive, empathic individuals (i.e., other widows). Divorce presents the complementary picture. With increasing age and time spent in a relationship, divorce becomes less and less normative and expected (see also Cooney & Uhlenberg, 1990). As a consequence, no empathic support group is available at older ages, whereas at younger ages one is much more likely to have other divorcees in one's network.

With respect to the buffering effects of support in the case of specific critical life events, some structural features of the network have also been identified as relevant. Depending on the type of life event, the positive effect of network density is linked to a critical threshold. If density is too high, that is if too many network members know each other, this can be—primarily in the case of non-normative life crises—dysfunctional. Certain support functions can no longer be performed by such a network (Hirsch, 1980). The family, as the typical example of a high-density network (which in the case of normative life crises may be highly supportive) may become dysfunctional, for example, in the case of non-normative life events such as divorce, remarriage after widowhood, or marriage in late life (Schulz & Rau, 1985). The dysfunctionality of the family network seems to be related to the presence of homogeneous expectations within the network concerning which behavior is appropriate for the focal person to display. Diversified, less closely knit networks, like friendship networks, increase the probability of finding appropriate models or adequate support needed for coping with non-normative events (e.g., Granovetter, 1973; Wilcox, 1981).

In summary, the findings that the protective function of social support depends on the type of event and the age of the focal person at the time of occurrence provides further evidence for the specificity of reserves. In an earlier section, we offered this notion of domain-specific resources with regard to cognitive training research. The evidence on social support networks seems to suggest that the protective and possibly enhancing function is dependent on the match between a specific constellation of the support network and a particular critical event. In the following section, we try to demonstrate that the protective effect of social support is complicated even further through intervening self-related characteristics.

Personality Characteristics Seem to Mediate the Protective Effect of Social Support

The perceived availability of social support must be distinguished from the retrospectively reported received support in the face of stress (e.g., Schwarzer & Leppin, 1992). In research covering the adult age range, it has been repeatedly demonstrated that the concepts are almost orthogonal. Differentiating between perceived (anticipated) and received support is especially relevant with regard to instrumental support and less so with regard to emotional support (e.g., Dunkel-Schetter & Bennett, 1990; Newcomb, 1990).

As we will see in a later section, the proportion of instrumental support received increases with age (e.g., Depner & Ingersoll-Dayton, 1988). Thus, the differentiation between anticipated and received support may be of special relevance in old age. Usually, perceived social support (i.e., self-reported anticipation or prediction) is more strongly related to adaptive outcomes than reported received support (i.e., self-report on actually received support; Wethington & Kessler, 1986). This seems to suggest that the social-cognitive processes concerning social relations and support can be fairly powerful mediating variables with regard to the stress buffering effect of social support.

It is these and similar findings that have caused some researchers to argue that perceived anticipated social support is, to a certain degree, measuring stable personality characteristics (e.g., Sarason, Pierce, & Sarason, 1990). Social competence, self esteem, and self efficacy have been identified as some of the relevant constructs in predicting, but also in activating and maintaining systems of social support (e.g., Gottlieb, 1983; Krause, 1987; Schwarzer & Leppin, 1992). At the same time, the stronger positive relationship between anticipated support and well-being as compared to received support may also be an illustration of the potential negative effects of provided support. The measure of reported received support is an evaluation of the experience of having received support which includes, for example, having experienced receiving support without being able to reciprocate; that is, having experienced relational asymmetry (e.g., Rook, 1984). The potential negative effects of support (particularly in terms of unequal exchanges) may especially accrue in old age.

Based on the considerations just mentioned and other, similar ones, most current attempts at modeling the causal links between stress, social support and mental health in old age include personality dimensions at various points in the model (e.g., Krause, Liang, & Yatomi, 1989). Personality characteristics such as self efficacy, for example, have been shown experimentally to influence the degree to which others are willing to provide support. Those who show the initiative to help themselves are also more likely to be supported by others (e.g., Schwarzer & Weiner, 1990). Turning this around, it has also been argued, based on life-span research, that the supporter's beliefs concerning the recipient's abilities may become reflected in an increase or decrease of the recipient's own self efficacy beliefs (Antonucci & Jackson, 1987). Considering this from a life-span perspective, it opens a vista on how powerful long-term social relations may be in terms of modifying an individual's resilience and reserves (Antonucci & Akijama, 1987). Returning to the ideas of Mead and others mentioned at the beginning of this section, we can also speculate about the role that social transactions may play in regard to developing and/or maintaining positive or negative illusions about the self and thus contributing to or diminishing self-related reserves (cf. Colvin & Block, 1994; Taylor & Brown, 1988).

A further example concerning the mediating function of personality characteristics makes the close linkage between personal and social-environmental factors in the regulation of resilience through social support equally clear. People with a trait-like tendency for negative affect such as neuroticism, or depressivity, are less likely to be satisfied with anything, and therefore will also tend to be less satisfied with their perceived and received social support. This in turn, may influence the likelihood of others offering support in the future (Schwarzer & Leppin, 1992). Considering stereotypic expectations and also empirical findings concerning old age which suggest more depressive symptoms in elders (Kessler et al., 1992), this may become a vicious cycle.

Social Support as a Function of Relationship Type (Kin versus Nonkin)

On average, different types of relationships are likely to provide specific types of support. In the language of this paper, we may also say that they represent different kinds of reserves. Some of these patterns have been identified in the literature. The life-span concepts of multidimensionality and multidirectionality are very nicely exemplified in such patterns. In old age, children and the spouse, if living, are the primary source of instrumental support. We will talk about the special role of the daughter with regard to caretaking activities further below. Emotional support is provided by a variety of sources, including spouse, children, friends and sometimes formal organizations such as religious communities or self help groups (e.g., Seeman & Berkman, 1988). In middle age, the spouse is the primary provider of emotional support, and the focus in relationships with friends and colleagues is on informational support (Schulz & Rau, 1985).

A "wildcard" reserve in any support network seems to be socalled multifunctional or multiplex relationships. Such relations carry the potential to fulfill the need for different kinds of support depending on the situation (Hirsch, 1980). The prototype of a multifunctional relationship is the spouse. For instance, it is a well established finding in the aging literature that marriage protects against morbidity (e.g., Depner & Ingersoll-Dayton, 1985; House, Robbins, & Metzner, 1982). This seems to be especially true for men, whereas for women marriage serves a protective function only if they are happily married (e.g., Hess & Soldo, 1985). All their lives, women tend to have a greater number of close relationships than men and therefore seem to adapt more easily to widowhood in old age than men. It has also been reported that being married and having children is among the most important factors keeping older people out of institutions (Hanson & Sauer, 1985). This finding is mediated through the fact that married people do have access to better support networks than unmarried people. At the same time, childless married people tend to have smaller support networks than unmarried people (e.g., Hanson & Sauer, 1985; Lang, 1994).

Usually, specific types of support are best provided by certain types of relationships. For example, support that requires residential proximity is often provided by neighbors, support requiring long-term commitment (as for example in the case of a chronic illness) is provided by family members, while support presupposing a similarity in life style is best earned by friends. A spouse (especially a female one), however, is more likely qualified to provide all these different types of support (Dykstra, 1993).

To date, in aging research, different studies have identified different patterns of support functions as characteristic of certain types or relationships (e.g., kin versus nonkin). Some studies identified clear complementary functional profiles for family versus non-family relationships in later adulthood, while other studies failed to do so (e.g., Dykstra, 1993). Dykstra drew the

conclusion that it may not be very helpful to use broad categories such as kin versus nonkin. She proposed differentiation according to (a) characteristics of these relationship types such as degree of consanguinity or degree of friendship, and (b) the kind of network of which these relationships are a part (non-married network, childless network, no acquaintances network, etc.). Concerning these latter context effects, it was demonstrated that relationships with children and friends were nominated as more supportive by those not cohabiting than by those cohabiting. It has been suggested that compensation between types of relationships along a "hierarchy of compensation," may be possible (Cantor, 1979). At the same time, compensatory processes between relationship types clearly seem to have their limits as well. There is evidence, for example, that married and non-married elders differed less than expected in terms of the degree of emotional and instrumental support they received from friends (Dykstra, 1993). There seem to be limits to what a friend (who is defined by voluntary provision of help) can be asked for without threatening the relationship.

Research on personal or close relationships also suggests, however, that such multifunctionality may have high costs (e.g., Morgan, 1990; Rook & Pietromonaco, 1987). A study investigating the process of coping with an acute illness such as a heart attack demonstrated, for example, that spouses not only provided support, but were also active participants in the exchange process. They brought their own vulnerabilities, goals, and demands to the situation which increased rather than decreased the stressfulness of the situation. Despite this, there is evidence suggesting that support from other sources cannot fully compensate for deficiencies in intimate or close relationships (Coyne, Ellard, & Smith, 1990); close relationships generally offer more gains than losses. What distinguishes intimate or close relationships from most other relationships is that they tend to be communal rather than exchange-based. Close relationships tend to be characterized by ongoing mutual commitment and responsiveness and are not constituted by specific exchanges.

The "take home" message with regard to social support, type of social relationship, resilience and reserves in old age may run as follows: It seems to be a great resource in old age to be (happily) married, both in terms of support provided by the spouse, and also in terms of related size of the support network. At the same time, this resource may be diminished by some costs resulting from the closeness of the spouse relationship. Furthermore, non-married or widowed elders are not without resources either. They may be able to compensate for the lack of a multiplex spousal relationship, but only to a certain degree, by activating other types of relationships available in their support network (e.g., Blieszner & Adams, 1992; Lang & Carstensen, 1994).

Reciprocity and Types of Support

Across the life span, the balance sheet of received and provided support changes. Midlife (up to age 65) is characterized by a surplus of provided as compared to received help. Later in life, this gap between support provided and received is increasingly closed. Older people provide about as much support as they receive (Antonucci & Akiyama, 1987; Depner & Ingersoll-Dayton, 1988). To some, this in itself may be a surprising finding.

The life-span trajectory of different types of support can be characterized as follows. Within their families, old people provide a considerable amount of financial support (e.g., Hauser & Wagner, 1994; Johnson, 1988) and assistance with child care (e.g., Bengtson, Rosenthal, & Burton, 1990), while they themselves primarily receive health-related support. Emotional support does not fluctuate in a similar fashion but is a rather stable component of the support system (provision and receipt) throughout the life span.

Reciprocity of support exchange has been demonstrated to be positively related to well-being *over and above* support received (Ingersoll-Dayton & Antonucci, 1988; Israel & Antonucci, 1987; Lang, 1994). This is a finding with specific relevance to the planning of interventions in old age. Not only is it important to think that providing support is a resource for the old person, but so as providing opportunities for the older person to provide support to others. Creating opportunities to provide support can be seen as a protective factor or a resource for the old person. Unmarried or widowed elders, for example, do seem to be able to compensate for a lack of social affiliation due to smaller networks. Data from Berlin Aging Study participants, age 70 to 103 years, demonstrated that unmarried or widowed elders seemed to compensate for this lack of reserve (as indicated by lower levels of well-being) by *providing* (rather than receiving) support to others (e.g., Lang, 1994).

From a life-span perspective, reciprocity is not only a characteristic of a single exchange of support, but can also be traced over a life time or at least over a longer amount of time, and across different domains or "currencies" of support (e.g., Burgess & Hustin, 1979). Different kinds of relationships differ in the degree to which they are based on longer time perspectives or more immediate pay-back loops. Again, the spouse relationship is the prototype of a support relationship with a long-term exchange budget. The parent-child relationship also carries this characteristic. In the latter case, the relationship even has the added advantage that the times of highest need of children and parents respectively are distributed over the life span in sequential order and, therefore, permit anticipated as well as realized effects. Antonucci (1985) coined the term "support bank" to describe that flow of intergenerational exchange. Early in adulthood, parents primarily provide largely unreciprocated support to their children. This way, they make a deposit into their support bank which, later in life, when they themselves may be less able to reciprocate for received support they are able to "cash in" without feelings of overbenefitting. Feelings of overbenefitting have been shown to have resilience-diminishing effects (e.g., Rook, 1984).

From a life-span perspective, a concept like that of the support bank raises the question of possible cohort changes in values which may "devalue" earlier deposits. Although the empirical investigation of the effectiveness of norms of reciprocity has only begun (Rossi & Rossi, 1990), it seems fair to say that those norms are firmly rooted across cohorts. In comparing three cohorts (born in 1920, 1950, 1980), Bengtson and Schütze (1994) came to the conclusion that the effectiveness of the norm of reciprocity has not weakened.

Taking into consideration the *accumulation and anticipation of reserves over time*—as it is done with the concept of a lifelong and intergenerational support bank—opens new perspectives on prevention as well. The idea of long-term investment, or "lagged reserves," is similar to recently reported findings from research on the prevention of juvenile delinquency (e.g., Yoshikawa, 1994). In his review article, Yoshikawa suggests a cumulative protection model to explain the successful prevention of chronic juvenile delinquency, a good demonstration of the principle of life-span continuity of resources.

Social Support in the Case of Disability and Illness: A Contribution to Resilience in Old Age

So far, we have discussed the social support provided to "normal" relatively healthy middle-aged and older adults. In old age support is increasingly needed in the health domain, however, because the focal person has an increasing likelihood of becoming disabled or ill. In the literature, support of the increasing numbers of frail elders is discussed under the heading of caregiving. Formal and informal sources of help are distinguished. A number of studies report that female spouses and children are the sole informal caregivers to elderly persons, with little extension to siblings and other kin (e.g., Lopata, 1978; Streib & Beck, 1980). In order to interpret these results, one has to take into consideration, however, that studies often have a family bias, so that nonkin age peers are excluded. Nevertheless, it seems safe to conclude that the family is the primary *informal* caregiving source for non-institutionalized elders. Counter to widely spread beliefs about the historical weakening of the family, present-day society is characterized by a continuation of the extended family, substantial intergenerational ties, and continuity of responsible filial behavior (e.g., Bengtson & Schütze, 1994; Brody & Brody, 1989; Field & Minkler, 1988; Rossi & Rossi, 1990).

Most care (80%) provided to older adults comes from informal sources including family members, friends, acquaintances, and neighbors (e.g., Brody & Brody, 1989). The person most likely to take prime responsibility for the care of an elder in the community is the spouse. If there is no spouse, there is a predictable sequence of the next most probable relatives to become primary caregivers, beginning with the adult daughter of the frail individual (Gatz, Bengtson, & Blum, 1990). This suggests that caregiving follows a combination of kinship and gender lines. Costs and benefits on both sides of the caregiving relationship need to be considered. On the side of the caregiver, it is certainly an immense burden with regard to time and investment. At the same time, studies reported that by providing this instrumental support the emotional relationship between frail parent and caregiving adult child can become richer (e.g., Walker, 1990). On the side of the care recipient, family caregiving, for instance, has the advantage that the old person can stay in their familiar environment. However, some studies have also indicated that negative social interactions had a stronger effect on the old person's morale than positive interactions (e.g., Stephens, Kinney, Ritchie, & Norris, 1987).

Formal caregiving structures are—compared to informal structures—underdeveloped, both in terms of long-term care institutions and with regard to community-based ambulatory help systems (e.g., Chappell, 1990). The latter has become a particular focus of social policy. It has been shown that the availability of informal or ambulatory formal support represent external resources which delay or reduce the need for institutionalization (e.g., Antonucci, 1990). Currently, there is much engagement in articulating the goal that old persons should maintain their "independent" living in their own home as long as possible. The behavioral and social costs of such an approach are not yet fully understood, however. If no ambulatory caregiving system is available, it is still sometimes the case that old people who have no or only limited access to an informal care network (i.e., lack of interpersonal resources) are sent to long-term care institutions, not for medical reasons, but because of the lack of social support (e.g., Cantor, 1983).

As already indicated, it is especially in this context of providing assistance in the basic activities of daily living that the "dilemmas of helping" (Coyne et al., 1990), that is, the potential negative resilience-diminishing effects of support, can become most obvious. In a research program on dependence in old age, M. Baltes and her colleagues have shown that caregivers in institutions, and also, though to a lesser degree, in family settings, tend to display a behavioral pattern which reinforces dependent rather than independent behavior in nursing or family home residents who are in need of physical care (e.g., Baltes, in press; Baltes & Wahl, 1987; Horgas, Wahl, & Baltes, in press). Based on social learning principles, one can conclude that—due to such dependence-support and independence-ignore scripts on the part of the caregivers—care recipients become more dependent than their reserve capacity would permit. Indeed, intervention studies in nursing homes conducted within the same research program, drawing on the operant principles mentioned earlier, have demonstrated that once the caregiver's behavioral pattern was more focused on providing support for independence, it was possible to successfully increase the older person's independent behavior.

Similarly, research on married couples' coping with the acute life-threatening illnesses of one partner found that, under certain conditions, support can become dysfunctional (Coyne et al., 1990). In this study, support became maladaptive whenever the helper primarily had her or his own goals in mind (e.g., getting things done more quickly), rather than also considering the goals of the recipient. In such situations, less support would often constitute more of a resource for the care receiver. Based on these results, Coyne and others (1990) have made a strong pledge for viewing social support from the perspective of interdependence between recipient and provider and not as a "one-way street" concept (see also Baltes & Silverberg, 1994). Social support must be interpreted as the dynamic outcome of negotiations between the parties involved. More support is not always functional. It is possible, therefore, to "overcare."

The concept of functionality or multifunctionality of support has been explored in great detail within the just mentioned research program of M. Baltes and her colleagues on dependency (Baltes, in press). Being dependent and "exercising" dependency is not only indicative of a loss of reserves, but at the same time it can involve gains in reserve capacity; an issue which has been discussed in the clinical literature under the heading of secondary gain of the illness or disorder (e.g., Freud, 1989). First, a certain degree of dependency reduces the aging person's concern with everyday self-care and thereby frees resources for other activities. Second, dependent behavior on the part of the elderly does not only result in one outcome, that is, care. At the

same time, it can, for instance, provide a sense of control over social partners on the part of the old person. As observational research both in family and in institutional settings has demonstrated (Baltes, in press), it is dependent rather than independent behaviors on the part of the elderly which resulted in immediate and positive social responses from the social environment. In particular, dependent behaviors initiated and provided social contact. In other words, losing or "giving up" reserves in one domain (i.e., independent self care) may be a worthwhile "investment" with regard to gaining resources in another domain (i.e., social affiliation). This evidence again suggests that it is useful to consider any reserve-diminishing and augmenting behaviors in a given domain of functioning within the larger system of multiple domains of functioning and reserves.

In the caregiving literature this perspective on multifunctionality and contextual embeddedness is receiving increasing attention. This is, for example, reflected in the recent concern with the caregiving family member or the caregiving family as a family system (e.g., Gatz et al., 1990). Traditionally, in the caregiving literature, the support for the care provider has primarily been reflected in the study of the caregiver burnout syndromes, which threaten the breakdown of the established support system for a given care recipient (e.g., Anthony-Bergstone, Zarit, & Gatz, 1988; MaloneBeach & Zarit, 1991; Pearlin, Turner, & Semple, 1989). Recently, there is growing interest in the system effects and the gains and losses of the various members involved in care giving. These considerations illustrate that the optimization of social support as a resource, which contributes to increased resilience for times of stress and to enhancement of reserves, takes more than finding a provider of support and the optimization of a unidirectional stream of transaction. Social transactions involve reciprocal as well as conflictual goals.

To summarize, research in the domain of social transactions has provided evidence for the maintenance (e.g., social support) but also for the decrease (e.g., social contact) in level of functioning with increasing age. Primarily due to age-graded context effects (e.g., developmental tasks of old age, change in motivation structure), social resilience and reserves, on average, continue to be present at sizeable levels into advanced age. Moreover, domain-specific reserves (e.g., support bank, kin vs. non-kin relations) are often available to compensate for losses and to provide for enhancement (e.g., companionship). With regard to everyday functioning, social support was identified as one of the major resources in the face of physical decline. To optimize this resource, recent research endeavors have started to identify the importance of reciprocity (concurrent or lifetime) and of system effects involving all members of the network. Recent research has also shown how giving up a certain level of independence on the part of the elderly (a loss at first sight) can have also positive consequences (secondary gains).

TOWARD MODELS OF AGING WELL

Our review has shown that all three areas of psychological functioning reviewed here, cognition, self, and social transactions, provide evidence for both "natural" resilience and reserve capacity, as well as the successful regaining and increase of resilience and reserves through intervention. At the same time, all three areas of functioning are not only resources for development in later adulthood, but also present developmental risks which require resilience. How can this illustrative evidence on cognition, the self, and social transactions help us to understand resilience and reserves in old age in general? We take these findings to represent the influence of two major categories of determinants, biology and culture, and their interactions, which seem to underlie a Janus-like face of aging (e.g., Baltes, 1993; Baltes et al., 1980). It seems that whenever biology and physical health are primary with respect to functioning in a given domain, one predicts age-related decline in performance, especially baseline performance and developmental reserve capacity. In our review, the decline in cognitive mechanics provided an example of this side of the Janus face. Stability and growth of cognitive functioning characterize the other side. Culture-based bodies of knowledge, the unique human capacity for self-reflection and self-agency, and social embeddedness are key resources for the reconstitution, maintenance, and sometimes even enhancement of psychological functioning. Based on such resources, the self seems to serve an executive function with respect to orchestrating gains and losses in various domains of functioning.

Thus far, we have described resilience and reserves in old age more or less separately by domain of functioning (cognition, self, social transactions), and by the processes involved (e.g., practice, learning, coping, social comparison, affiliation, social support). As a next step, we will argue on a different level of aggregation and discuss several *general* strategies of aging well. In the gerontological literature, we find a number of models that attempt to describe how gains and losses, the risk and protective factors of old age, are coordinated in order to achieve successful adaptation (e.g., Atchley, 1993; Baltes, 1991, 1993; Brandtstädter et al., 1993; Carstensen, 1993; Hobfoll, 1989). Baltes and Baltes (1990b; see also Baltes & Carstensen, in press; Marsiske, Lang, Baltes, & Baltes, in press), for example, have suggested that throughout life "successful" development can be characterized by a strategy of *selective optimization with compensation.* The processes of selection, optimization, and compensation are coordinated such that the two main overarching goals of human development can be achieved: (a) movement toward higher levels of functioning (growth), and (b) avoidance of negative outcomes (maintenance). It is important to underscore that selection, optimization and compensation may operate on both a conscious and an unconscious level, and, in addition, may be driven by internal and external conditions.

In old age, this general strategy of successful life-span development continues to operate, however with different weights and in different constellations. The shifting balance between gains and losses in old age presents a particularly strong new challenge. For example, due to an overall loss in reserve capacity or resources and increasing constraints on resource replacement (Hobfoll, 1989), it becomes more difficult to maintain high-level or desired levels of functioning in all previously active domains. It then becomes necessary to select domains where one would like or need to preserve high levels of functioning, often at the expense of functioning in other domains. Furthermore, it may become necessary to change the ways by which certain levels of

performance are achieved. Compensation becomes increasingly important (e.g., Bäckman & Dixon, 1992). In those domains where high performance has continued adaptive value, under conditions of declining performance levels, new strategies must be derived, and reserves must be tapped and pooled across different domains of functioning to maintain high-level performance. Figure 22.2 illustrates the operation of selective optimization with compensation summarizing the precursor conditions under which it is evoked in old age and listing its potential consequences.

The research reviewed herein provides illustrations for all three mechanisms, optimization, selection, and compensation. We have seen that, via training and the acquisition of new bodies of knowledge, cognitive functioning can be *optimized.* On a much smaller scale, similar evidence is available from training research in the area of the self. Another important self-related protective factor that supports optimization as a general-purpose mechanism, which we have not reviewed in detail, is self-efficacy and agency beliefs (e.g., Bandura, 1986). Efficacy and agency beliefs can serve as motivators and skill resources in striving for higher levels of performance. Furthermore, self-efficacy has been demonstrated to have positive effects on the availability of social support. In the social domain, we have seen that the reciprocity of social support exchanges contributes to well-being over and above the support received.

With regard to *compensation,* the cognitive area provided evidence for the compensatory power of culture-based bodies of knowledge in the face of declines in the cognitive mechanics. In the area of self and personality functioning, we find, as described above, a rich variety of compensatory processes such as varied use of social comparison at work. Research on personality has

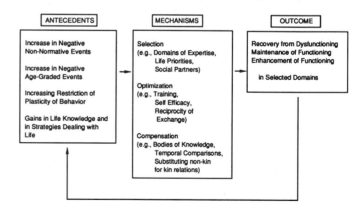

Figure 22.2 A model of successful aging (modified after Baltes & Baltes, 1990b). A coalition of antecedent influences will tend to change the balance of losses and gains in late life. In order to maintain functioning in critical task domains, or even to experience growth in selected areas, three processes are proposed: Selection of domains to maintain or enhance functioning, optimization of functioning in selected domains, and compensation (including substitution) for lowered functioning in those domains which cannot be maintained. Although these processes are assumed to operate throughout life, they take on special salience in late life under conditions of accumulating losses.

been focused more on the identification of mechanisms, rather than documenting their use under conditions of risk and challenge. Utilization of social and temporal comparison processes, availability of many different coping behaviors, coping styles such as flexible goal adjustment, certain personality dimensions (generativity, integrity), and well-balanced emotional management are examples of self-based compensatory factors. Finally, in the area of social transactions it was demonstrated, for example, that some compensation between different types of relationships (kin for nonkin) is possible with regard to the provision of social support.

Another area of compensation refers to compensatory processes that cut across different domains of functioning. For example, in cases when the self has exhausted its resources (e.g., depressivity), it has been demonstrated that compensation by means of external and interpersonal resources, that is relying on members of the social network is possible. The same is true for cognitive functioning, also including in this case the use of "mechanical" assistive devices such as hearing aids, glasses, notebooks, and age-friendly environments (Bäckman & Dixon, 1992).

We find *selection* at work when the self extracts from its broader set of goals and commitments and from the opportunities provided by society those in which maintained functioning is important. In the cognitive area, this strategy of selection is seen in the development of individualized, domain-specific expertises (Ericsson & Smith, 1991). In the social domain, it may involve the selection of emotionally meaningful social relationships (Carstensen, 1993).

This strategy of "aging well" is meant to describe universal adaptive processes. Based on individual life constellations, the specific outcomes of this strategy are bound to exhibit large individual and cultural variations (Baltes & Baltes, 1990b). Using the strategy of selective optimization with compensation, with changed emphases and new weightings, it seems possible that older persons enlist and transform their resources in effective ways. Employment of this strategy not only allows one to recover and maintain adaptation, but also provides the basis for continued growth in select domains.

BEYOND NORMS: INDIVIDUAL CRITERIA OF SUCCESSFUL ADAPTATION

Models of successful development and aging present us with the problem of delineating criteria for what we consider to be optimal aging. They present us with the problem of determining a "best" direction of development. What is the desirable end state of life? Is there one, or are there many potentially incompatible ends depending on the outcome criteria we examine? For example, if we take good physical health in old age as an aspired goal this would necessitate a certain life style, which would in turn demand sacrifices in other domains, such as enjoying certain foods or spending more time in physically inactive ways.

As long as we consider, for example, laboratory training research for cognitive functioning, this criterion problem is perhaps less obvious. In the laboratory training studies, higher levels of performance are often selected as the criterion for reasons of experimental paradigm. The more words one can remember, the better; the faster we can complete the task, the higher the level of performance. However, as soon as we think about everyday life, the criterion needs to be adapted to ecological demands and characteristics. It then often becomes a question of the right measure: Which kind of behavior is to be endorsed at which time, for how long, and to which degree? What may be a gain in one domain of functioning leads to a loss in another domain, and what may be successful in the short run, may be detrimental when it comes to long-term effects.

Thus, while the focus of cognitive training research has been on demonstrating, in principle, plasticity and limits of plasticity in intellectual functioning, the question of what level of performance is necessary for everyday functioning remains largely unaddressed. In this respect, we also need to ask about the long-term and ecologically valid transfer effects of intellectual training. With regard to the self and the social domain, similar problems have been identified: In coping research, for example, a high domain-specificity of coping behaviors has been identified. Furthermore, coping behaviors which are adaptive as immediate responses need not be adaptive in the long run. Thus, even with regard to coping, implications for everyday functioning are not fully known (Filipp & Klauer, 1991). Similarly, as we have seen in the social domain, it is very important to strike a balance between affiliation and solitude.

The dilemma of defining criteria for adequate as well as optimal functioning in everyday life becomes especially evident when we think about old age. For some, old age is the phase in life characterized by liberation, while for others it becomes the final testing ground of physical health (Baltes & Baltes, 1990b; Fries, 1989). What is the optimal level of self-efficacy beliefs to have? What is the optimal way to grieve? What is the optimal network configuration? What is optimal memory? These examples illustrate that, in old age, general norms may apply even less than in earlier phases of life. Given the wide range of individual differences in levels of functioning and personality make-up (Nelson & Dannefer, 1992), it may be crucial to define reserves on the level of person-in-context units. Given the increasing variability between individuals and the absence of a well-developed culture of old age (Baltes, 1993), this is of particular relevance.

Defining criteria for enhancement seems to be a less difficult task with regard to single individuals and to narrowly defined domains of functioning. For a given person with a particular problem, an intervention could be directed toward increasing the level of functioning within the specific person-in-context condition. Thus, for a newly widowed older man who cannot cook and would like to continue to eat at home, for example, an intervention might be aimed at teaching new skills in the kitchen. However, when conceiving of intervention programs for widowers in general, criteria are less obvious. Some would rather go out to eat, or convince a friend to do the cooking. If the selective optimization with compensation model is an appropriate characterization of how successful adaptation might occur in late life, perhaps individuals could be instructed in the need to select critical life domains, and could be given suggestions about when and how optimization, selection, and compensation strategies could be applied. The domain-specific optimization process would be left to the particular person-in-context constellation, which is very much congruent with the notion of multidirectional and individualized development (cf., Chapman, 1988).

Earlier, we described the key function of knowledge-based and self-related functioning in orchestrating the optimization of development by processes such as selection and compensation. An important consideration in this respect is the appraisal of resources (Hobfoll, 1989), in this case when to accept a loss and reorient one's life, and when to still strive harder because current behavior is not yet employed to its fullest capability (Staudinger, Cornelius, & Baltes, 1989). With respect to optimizing development, Brim has argued, for example, that one criterion for making this decision could be to consider something like a "performance/capacity ratio" (Brim, 1992). According to this ratio, acceptance of a certain loss becomes necessary when the display of the behavior requires a "dysfunctionally" high amount of reserve capacity. For example, when climbing stairs becomes so exhausting that it threatens an older adult's ability to perform other central everyday tasks, acceptance of this functional loss is desirable. If the inability to continue climbing stairs threatens continued viability, then compensatory strategies (e.g., installation of stair-climbing machinery, change of residence, employment of caregivers, engagement in physical therapy) become necessary. A certain degree of acceptance of the loss is required, however, before one can initiate compensation. These examples illustrate how important it is to realize that what constitutes resilience in old age requires a dynamic, person-in-context view. Multiple levels of meaning and consequences, as well as individual and cultural variations, need consideration.

The Study of Resilience in Later Adulthood and Its Relationship to Normal Development

In conclusion, we would like to reconsider the topic of similarity and differences between concepts from life-span developmental work such as plasticity and reserve capacity on the one hand, and resilience on the other. Life-span research on reserve capacity has an emphasis on the conditions under which development is "optimized." It extends beyond the recovery from maladaptation or the maintenance of normal functioning. In other words, rather than emphasizing the identification of conditions leading to problems and their avoidance (risk and protective factors of mainstream resilience research), the enhancement and optimization model espoused by life-span developmentalists also focuses on the identification of conditions that can lead to growth, even before any threat or challenge has come on stage (cf., Brandtstädter & Schneewind, 1977). We suspect that these differences in emphasis are related to several issues, including the historical distinction between health and disease, as well as between normality and growth. Resilience research in psychology emerged out of epidemiological risk research and the prevention of pathology (cf., Rutter, 1987). Conversely, enhancement research is focused on the optimization in the sense of progress and movement toward some individualized ideal end state (Nisbett, 1980).

We have developed a schematic model that suggests one possible way of integrating the notions of resilience and levels of reserve capacity. With this working model (see Figure 22.3) we do

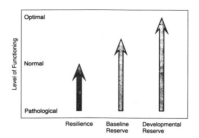 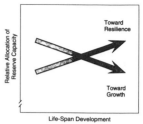

Figure 22.3   Resilience and levels of reserve capacity. Resilience focuses primarily on the maintenance and recovery of "normal" developmental functioning. Reserve capacity serves in addition the attainment of further growth and "optimal" levels of functioning (left). In old age, less overall reserve capacity is available. Therefore, an increasing share needs to be allocated to the avoidance of negative or "pathological" outcomes (right).

not aim so much at reflecting the use of such concepts in the literature, but rather to suggest a theoretical framework which may foster an increased exchange between the two lines of scholarship.

The model distinguishes between three levels of developmental functioning, pathological, normal, and optimal. We prefer to use the term "optimal" rather than "successful" to make the distinction from normal aging more pronounced. Rowe and Kahn (1987) have pointed out, especially with respect to aging, that the term normal has at least two connotations. One is normal in the sense of usual (i.e., the statistical average, which may include losses), and the other is normal in the sense of successful (i.e., free of pathology). We have argued, however, that normal aging in the sense of statistical average increasingly resembles pathological functioning in that it includes a growing feature of loss. That is, the distinction between statistically normal and pathological becomes increasingly blurred with age. We would like to disentangle the notion of "optimal" development conceptually from this blending. While successful aging, in the sense of normal, may be defined by the relative absence of pathology, we want to underscore that a growth-oriented concept of successful aging, in the sense of "optimal," is also possible in principle.

The overlap between the three arrows connotes that resilience can be supported not only by reserves currently available (baseline reserve capacity, "natural" resilience) but also by reserves activated through intervention or development (developmental reserve capacity, resilience through intervention). Furthermore, we would also like to briefly mention that this model is complicated when we consider the issue of domain-specific development and development in general, a topic which deserves more discussion in its own right. For instance, the activation of developmental reserve capacity in one domain of functioning can support resilience in another domain but can also be a risk factor. Becoming too dedicated at work can also maximize financial resources, but may come at the cost of losses in the health or family domain.

What happens when we put this general model in an ontogenetic framework with a focus on old age? Given the changing gains-losses ratio which, on average, is characteristic of old age, an increasing amount of reserve capacity has to be invested in coping with losses, and in the prevention of dysfunction. Thus, reserves are increasingly unavailable to support growth. We have depicted this age-related change in the relative allocation of reserve capacity on the right-hand side of Figure 22.3. This implies that research on resilience in old age, with its focus on how to prevent dysfunction, and research on reserve capacity, with its focus on how to optimize development, become more closely linked than they are when earlier phases of life are the period under study.

This "life-span convergence" between research on resilience and research on reserve capacity should not lead us to blur the theoretical distinction between the two concepts (see left panel Figure 22.3). While the "resilient move" between "pathological" and "normal" levels of functioning may, in certain cases, involve the activation of reserve capacity, plasticity is a concept that underlies *more* than the avoidance of pathology. Reserve capacity supports the full *range* of adaptive change, or plasticity. In our view, resilience is that type of plasticity concerned with the avoidance of pathology and the maintenance of "normal" functioning. We suggest keeping the resilience concept separate from the movement toward optimal development per se. To restate the definition of resilience from the beginning of the paper, resilience has been defined as that kind of plasticity that ensures "normal" (and not "optimal") development despite the presence of threats, risks, and insults.

OUTLOOK

By reviewing the evidence on potential and reserve capacity in old age, we have perhaps generated the impression that the state of optimization and prevention research in human aging is a healthy one. This is not so. Systematic research and theory-building with respect to prevention, intervention, rehabilitation in old age, not to mention growth-oriented enhancement, did not get the attention it deserved for a long time (e.g., Baltes & Danish, 1979). Even now, such attempts are still fighting ageism (Riley & Riley, 1989). Any attempt at intervention may profit from taking into account the characteristics of development as they are described in the propositions of life-span theory. To highlight just a few: Development as transactional adaptation suggests that not only the individual but also the developmental context should be the target of intervention. The gain/loss dynamic alerts to potential negative effects of intervention either with regard to other domains of functioning or with regard to the future. Finally, the model of successful aging through selective optimization with compensation suggests that rather than targeting specific symptoms with certain intervention programs, it may be worthwhile spending time exploring what the most fruitful domains of intervention might be. To advance research on resilient and optimal aging in a more coordinated manner, life-span researchers interested in the range and limits of reserve capacity, and clinical researchers interested in resilience, need to become partners. It is time to move beyond courtship and into active collaboration.

REFERENCES

Ahammer, I. M., & Baltes, P. B. (1972). Objective vs. perceived age differences in personality: How do adolescents, adults, and older people view themselves and each other? *Journal of Gerontology, 27*, 46–51.

Aldwin, C. M. (1991). Does age affect the stress and coping process? Implications of age differences in perceived control. *Journals of Gerontology, 46*, 174–180.

Alexander, C., & Langer, E. J. (Eds.). (1990). *Beyond formal operations: Alternative endpoints to human development.* New York: Oxford University Press.

Anastasi, A. (1970). On the formation of psychological traits. *American Psychologist, 25*, 899–910.

Anschutz, L., Camp, C. J., Markley, R. P., & Kramer, J. J. (1987). A three-year follow-up on the effects of mnemonics training in elderly adults. *Experimental Aging Research, 13*, 141–143.

Anthony, J. C., & Aboraya, A. (1992). The epidemiology of selected mental disorders in later life. In J. E. Birren, R. B. Sloane, & G. D. Cohen (Eds.), *Handbook of mental health and aging* (pp. 28–74). San Diego, CA: Academic Press.

Anthony-Bergstone, C. R., Zarit, S. H., & Gatz, M. (1988). Symptoms of psychological distress among caregivers of dementia patients. *Psychology and Aging, 3*, 245–248.

Antonucci, T. C. (1985). Personal characteristics, social support, and social behavior. In R. H. Binstock & E. Shanas (Eds.), *Handbook of aging and the social sciences* (2nd ed., pp. 94–128). New York: Van Nostrand-Reinhold.

Antonucci, T. C. (1990). Social support and social relationships. In R. H. Binstock & E. Shanas (Eds.), *Handbook of aging and the social sciences* (pp. 205–227). New York: Academic Press.

Antonucci, T. C., & Akiyama, H. (1987). Social networks in adult life and a preliminary examination of the convoy model. *Journals of Gerontology, 42*, 519–527.

Antonucci, T. C., & Jackson, J. S. (1987). Social support, interpersonal efficacy, and health: A life course perspective. In L. L. Carstensen & B. A. Edelstein (Eds.), *Handbook of clinical gerontology* (pp. 291–311). New York: Pergamon.

Atchley, R. C. (1982). Retirement as a social institution. *Annual Review of Sociology, 8*, 263–287.

Atchley, R. C. (1993). Continuity theory and the evolution of activity in later adulthood. In J. R. Kelly (Ed.), *Activity and aging: Staying involved in later life* (pp. 5–16). Newbury Park, CA: Sage.

Bäckman, L., & Dixon, R. A. (1992). Psychological compensation: A theoretical framework. *Psychological Bulletin, 112*, 259–283.

Bäckman, L., & Herlitz, A. (1990). The relationship between prior knowledge and face recognition memory in normal aging and Alzheimer's disease. *Journals of Gerontology, 45*, 94–100.

Bäckman, L., Mäntylä, T., & Herlitz, A. (1990). The optimization of episodic remembering in old age. In P. B. Baltes & M. M. Baltes (Eds.), *Successful aging: Perspectives from the behavioral sciences* (pp. 118–163). New York: Cambridge University Press.

Baltes, M. M. (1988). The etiology and maintenance of dependency in the elderly: Three phases of operant research. *Behavior Therapy, 19*, 301–319.

Baltes, M. M. (in press). Dependency in old age: Gains and losses. *Current Directions in Psychological Science.*

Baltes, M. M., & Baltes, P. B. (Eds.). (1986). *The psychology of control and aging.* Hillsdale, NJ: Erlbaum.

Baltes, M. M., & Barton, E. M. (1977). New approaches toward aging: A case for the operant model. *Educational Gerontology: An International Quarterly, 2,* 383–405.

Baltes, M. M., & Barton, E. M. (1979). Behavioral analysis of aging: A review of the operant model and research. *International Journal of Behavior Development, 2,* 297–320.

Baltes, M. M., & Carstensen, L. L. (in press). The process of successful aging: A critical commentary and proposal. *Ageing and Society.*

Baltes, M. M., & Kindermann, T. (1985). Die Bedeutung der Plastizität für die klinische Beurteilung des Leistungsverhaltens im Alter [The significance of plasticity for the clinical assessment of competence in later life]. In D. Bente, H. Coper, & S. Kanowski (Eds.), *Hirnorganische Psychosyndrome im Alter: Methoden zur Objektivierung pharmakotherapeutischer Wirkung* (Vol. 2, pp. 171–184). Berlin: Springer.

Baltes, M. M., Kühl, K. -P., & Sowarka, D. (1992). Testing for limits of cognitive reserve capacity: A promising strategy for early diagnosis of dementia? *Journals of Gerontology, 47,* 165–167.

Baltes, M. M., Mayr, U., Borchelt, M., Maas, I., & Wilms, H. -U. (1993). Everyday competence in old and very old age: An interdisciplinary perspective. *Ageing and Society, 13,* 657–680.

Baltes, M. M., & Silverberg, S. B. (1994). The dynamics between dependency and autonomy: Illustrations across the life-span. In D. L. Featherman, R. M. Lerner, & M. Perlmutter (Eds.), *Life-span development and behavior* (Vol. 12, pp. 42–90). New York: Academic Press.

Baltes, M. M., Tesch-Römer, C., & Lang, F. (1994). *Einsamkeit und Alter* [Loneliness in old age]. Unpublished manuscript, Free University, Berlin.

Baltes, M. M., & Wahl, H. -W. (1987). Dependence in aging. In L. L. Carstensen & B. A. Edelstein (Eds.), *Handbook of clinical gerontology* (pp. 204–221). New York: Pergamon.

Baltes, M. M., Wahl, H. -W., & Schmid-Fürstoss (1990). The daily life of elderly Germans: Activity patterns, personal control, and functional health. *Journals of Gerontology, 45,* 173–179.

Baltes, M. M., Wilms, H. -U., & Horgas, A. L. (1993). *Alltagskompetenz, Ökologie und entwicklungspsychologische Überlegungen [Everyday competence, ecology, and developmental psychological considerations].* Paper presented at the 11. Tagung Entwicklungspsychologie, September 1993, Osnabrück, Germany.

Baltes, P. B. (1968). Longitudinal and cross-sectional sequences in the study of age and generation effects. *Human Development, 11,* 145–171.

Baltes, P. B. (1987). Theoretical propositions of life-span developmental psychology: On the dynamics between growth and decline. *Developmental Psychology, 23,* 611–626.

Baltes, P. B. (1991). The many faces of human aging: Toward a psychological culture of old age. *Psychological Medicine, 21,* 837–854.

Baltes, P. B. (1993). The aging mind: Potentials and limits. *Gerontologist, 33,* 580–594.

Baltes, P. B., & Baltes, M. M. (Eds.). (1990a). *Successful aging: Perspectives from the behavioral sciences.* New York: Cambridge University Press.

Baltes, P. B., & Baltes, M. M. (1990b). Psychological perspectives on successful aging: The model of selective optimization with compensation. In P. B. Baltes & M. M. Baltes (Eds.), *Successful aging: Perspectives from the behavioral sciences* (pp. 1–34). New York: Cambridge University Press.

Baltes, P. B., Cornelius, S. W., & Nesselroade, J. R. (1979). Cohort effects in developmental psychology. In J. R. Nesselroade & P. B. Baltes (Eds.), *Longitudinal research in the study of behavior and development* (pp. 61–87). New York: Academic Press.

Baltes, P. B., & Danish, S. J. (1979). Intervention in life-span development and aging: Concepts and issues. In R. Turner & H. W. Reese (Eds.), *Life-span developmental psychology: Intervention* (pp. 49–78). New York: Academic Press.

Baltes, P. B., Dittmann-Kohli, F., & Dixon, R. A. (1984). New perspectives on the development of intelligence in adulthood: Toward a dual process conception and a model of selective optimization with compensation. In P. B. Baltes & O. G. Brim (Eds.), *Life-span development and behavior* (Vol. 6, pp. 33–76). New York: Academic Press.

Baltes, P. B., & Graf, P. (in press). Psychological and social aspects of aging: Facts and frontiers. In D. Magnusson et al. (Eds.), *Individual development over the lifespan: Biological and psychosocial perspectives.* Cambridge, MA: Cambridge University Press.

Baltes, P. B., & Kliegl, R. (1992). Further testing of limits of cognitive plasticity: Negative age differences in a mnemonic skill are robust. *Developmental Psychology, 28,* 121–125.

Baltes, P. B., & Lindenberger, U. (1988). On the range of cognitive plasticity in old age as a function of experience: Fifteen years of intervention research. *Behavior Therapy, 19,* 283–300.

Baltes, P. B., & Nesselroade, J. R. (1984). Paradigm lost and paradigm regained: Critique of Dannefer's portrayal of life-span developmental psychology. *American Sociological Review, 49,* 841–846.

Baltes, P. B., Reese, H. W., & Lipsitt, L. P. (1980). Life-span developmental psychology. *Annual Review of Psychology, 31,* 65–110.

Baltes, P. B., & Smith, J. (1990). The psychology of wisdom and its ontogenesis. In R. J. Sternberg (Ed.), *Wisdom: Its nature, origins, and development* (pp. 87–120). New York: Cambridge University Press.

Baltes, P. B., Smith, J., & Staudinger, U. M. (1992). Wisdom and successful aging. In T. Sonderegger (Ed.), *Nebraska Symposium on Motivation* (Vol. 39, pp. 123–167). Lincoln, NB: University of Nebraska Press.

Baltes, P. B., Sowarka, D., & Kliegl, R. (1989). Cognitive training research on fluid intelligence in old age: What can older adults achieve by themselves? *Psychology and Aging, 4,* 217–221.

Baltes, P. B., & Staudinger, U. M. (1993). The search for a psychology of wisdom. *Current Directions in Psychological Science, 2,* 75–80.

Baltes, P. B., & Staudinger, U. M. (Eds.). (in press). *Interactive minds: Life-span perspectives on the social foundation of cognition.* New York: Cambridge University Press.

Baltes, P. B., Staudinger, U. M., Macreker, A., & Smith, J. (in press). Peolpe nominated as wise: A comparative study of wisdom-related knowledge. *Psychology and Aging.*

Baltes, P. B., & Willis, S. L. (1982). Plasticity and enhancement of intellectual functioning in old age: Penn State's Adult Development and Enrichment Project (ADEPT). In F. I. M. Craik & S. E. Trehub (Eds.), *Aging and cognitive processes* (pp. 353–389). New York: Plenum.

Bandura, A. (1986). *Social foundations of thought and action: A social-cognitive theory.* Englewood Cliffs, NJ: Prentice-Hall.

Beck, A. T. (1979). *Cognitive therapy and the emotional disorders.* New York: NAL-Dutton.

Bengtson, V. L., Reedy, M. N., & Gordon, C. (1985). Aging and self-conceptions: Personality processes and social contexts. In J. E. Birren & K. W. Schaie (Eds.), *Handbook of the psychology of aging* (2nd ed., pp. 544–593). New York: Van Nostrand-Reinhold.

Bengtson, V., Rosenthal, C., & Burton, L. (1990). Families and aging: Diversity and heterogeneity. In R. H. Binstock & L. K. George (Eds.), *Handbook of aging and the social sciences* (pp. 263–287). San Diego, CA: Academic Press.

Bengston, V. L., & Schütze, Y. (1994). Altern und Generationen-beziehungen. Aussichten für das kommende Jahrhundert [Aging and intergenerational relations: Perspectives for the next century]. In P. B. Baltes, J. Mittelstrass, & U. M. Staudinger (Eds.), *Alter und Altern: Ein interdisziplinärer Studientext zur Gerontologie* [Old age and aging: An interdisciplinary reader in Gerontology] (pp. 492–517). Berlin: De Gruyter.

Berg, C. A., & Sternberg, R. J. (1985). A triarchic theory of intellectual development during adulthood. *Developmental Review, 5,* 334–370.

Berg, C. A., & Sternberg, R. J. (1992). Adults' conceptions of intelligence across the adult life-span. *Psychology and Aging, 7,* 221–231.

Birren, J. E., & Deutchman, D. E. (1991). *Guiding autobiography groups for older adults.* Baltimore, MD: John Hopkins University Press.

Birren, J. E., & Schaie, K. W. (Eds.). (1990). *Handbook of the psychology of aging* (3rd ed.). San Diego, CA: Academic Press.

Birren, J. E., & Sloane, R. B. (Eds.). (1980). *Handbook of mental health & aging.* Englewood Cliffs, NJ: Prentice-Hall.

Blanchard-Fields, F. (1986). Reasoning in adolescents and adults on social dilemmas varying in emotional saliency: An adult developmental perspective. *Psychology and Aging, 1,* 325–333.

Blazer, D. G. (1986). Depression: Paradoxically, a cause for hope. *Generations, 10,* 21–23.

Blazer, D. G. (1989). Depression in late life: An update. In M. P. Lawton (Ed.), *Annual review of gerontology and geriatrics* (Vol. 9, pp. 197–215). New York: Springer.

Blazer, D. G., & Williams, C. D. (1980). Epidemiology of dysphoria and depression in an elderly population. *American Journal of Psychiatry, 137,* 439–444.

Blieszner, R., & Adams, R. G. (Eds.). (1992). *Adult friendship.* Newbury Park, CA: Sage.

Block, J. (1981). Some enduring and consequential structures of personality. In A. I. Rabin (Ed.), *Further explorations in personality* (pp. 27–43). New York: Wiley.

Blumstein, P., & Kollock, P. (1988). Personal relationships. *Annual Review of Sociology, 14,* 467–490.

Brandtstädter, J., & Greve, W. (1994). The aging self: Stabilizing and protective processes. *Developmental Review, 14,* 52–80.

Brandtstädter, J., & Renner, G. (1990). Tenacious goal pursuit and flexible goal adjustment: Explication and age-related analysis of assimilative and accomodative strategies of coping. *Psychology and Aging, 5,* 58–67.

Brandtstädter, J., & Rothermund, K. (1994). Self-perceptions of control in middle and later adulthood: Buffering losses by rescaling goals. *Psychology and Aging, 9,* 265–273.

Brandtstädter, J., & Schneewind, K. A. (1977). Optimal human development: Some implications for psychology. *Human Development, 20,* 48–64.

Brandtstädter, J., Wentura, D., & Greve, W. (1993). Adaptive resources of the aging self: Outlines of an emergent perspective. *International Journal of Behavioral Development, 16,* 323–349.

Breytspraak, L. M. (1984). *The development of self in later life.* Boston, MA: Little Brown.

Brim, O. G. (1992). *Ambition. How we manage success and failure throughout our lives.* New York: Basic Books.

Brim, O. G., & Kagan, J. (1980). Constancy and change: A view of the issues. In O. G. Brim, & J. Kagan (Eds.), *Constancy and change in human development* (pp. 1–25). Cambridge, MA: Harvard University Press.

Brim, O. G., & Ryff, C. D. (1980). On the properties of life events. In P. B. Baltes & O. G. Brim (Eds.), *Life-span development and behavior* (Vol. 3, pp. 368–387). New York: Academic Press.

Brody, E. M., & Brody, S. J. (1989). Long term care: The long and the short of it. In C. Eisdorfer, D. A. Kessler, & A. N. Spector (Eds.), *Caring for the elderly: Reshaping health policy* (pp. 259–273). Baltimore, MA: John Hopkins University Press.

Bronfenbrenner, U. (1979). *The ecology of human development.* Cambridge, MA: Harvard University Press.

Brown, A. L. (1982). Learning and development: The problem of compatibility, access and induction. *Human Development, 25,* 89–115.

Bühler, C., & Massarik, F. (Eds.). (1968). *The course of human life.* New York: Springer.

Burgess, R. L., & Huston, T. L. (Eds.). (1979). *Social exchange in developing relationships.* New York: Academic Press.

Buss, A. R. (1973). An extension of developmental models that separate ontogenetic change and cohort differences. *Psychological Bulletin, 80,* 466–479.

Butler, R. N. (1963). The life-review: An interpretation of reminiscence in the aged. *Psychiatry, 26,* 65–76.

Butler, R. N. (1989). Dispelling ageism: The cross-cutting intervention. *The Annals of the American Academy of Political and Social Science, 503,* 138–147.

Butters, N., Albert, M. S., Sax, D. S., Miliotis, P., Nagode, J., & Sterste, A. (1983). The effect of verbal mediators on the pictorial memory of brain-damaged patients. *Neuropsychologia, 21,* 307–323.

Callahan, C. M. (1992). Psychiatric symptoms in elderly patients due to medication. In J. W. Rowe & J. C. Ahronheim (Eds.), *Annual review of gerontology and geriatrics* (Vol. 12, pp. 41–75). New York: Springer.

Camp, C. J., Foss, J. W., Stevens, A. B., Reichard, C. C., McKitrick, L. A., & O'Hanlon, A. M. (1993). Memory training in normal and demented elderly populations: The E-I-E-I-O model. *Experimental Aging Research, 19,* 277–290.

Camp, C. J., & Schaeller, J. R. (1989). Epilogue: Spaced-retrieval memory training in an adult day-care center. *Educational Gerontology, 15,* 641–648.

Campbell, A., Converse, P. E., & Rodgers, W. L. (1976). *The quality of American life.* New York: Sage.

Cantor, M. H. (1979). The informal support system of New York's inner city elderly: Is ethnicity a factor? In D. Gelfand & A. Kutzik (Eds.), *Ethnicity and aging* (pp. 153–174). New York: Springer.

Cantor, M. H. (1983). Strain among caregivers: A study of experience in the United States. *Gerontologist, 23,* 597–604.

Carstensen, L. L. (1988). The emerging field of behavioral gerontology. *Behavior Therapy, 19,* 259–281.

Carstensen, L. L. (1992). Social and emotional patterns in adulthood: Support for socioemotional selectivity theory. *Psychology and Aging, 7,* 331–338.

Carstensen, L. L. (1993). Motivation for social contact across the life span: A theory of socioemotional selectivity. In J. Jacobs (Ed.), *Nebraska Symposium on Motivation* (Vol. 40, pp. 205–254). Lincoln, NB: University of Nebraska Press.

Carstensen, L. L., & Edelstein, B. A. (Eds.). (1987). *Handbook of clinical gerontology.* Elmsford, NY: Pergamon.

Carstensen, L. L., & Freund, A. (1994). The resilience of the aging self. *Developmental Review, 14*, 81–92.

Caspi, A. (1987). Personality in the life course. *Journal of Personality and Social Psychology, 53*, 1203–1213.

Cattell, R. B. (1971). *Abilities: Their structure, growth, and action.* Boston, MA: Houghton Mifflin.

Chapman, M. (1988). Contextuality and directionality of cognitive development. *Human Development, 31*, 92–106.

Chappell, N. L. (1990). Aging and social care. In R. H. Binstock & E. Shanas (Eds.), *Handbook of aging and the social sciences* (3rd ed., pp. 438–454). New York: Academic Press.

Charness, N. (Ed.). (1985). *Aging and human performance.* Chichester, England: Wiley.

Chi, M. T. H., Glaser, R., & Rees, E. (1982). Expertise in problem solving. In R. J. Sternberg (Ed.), *Advances in the psychology of human intelligence* (Vol. 1, pp. 7–75). Hillsdale, NJ: Erlbaum.

Cicchetti, D. (1989). Developmental psychopathology: Past, present, and future. In D. Cicchetti (Ed.), *The emergence of a discipline: Rochester Symposium on Developmental Psychology* (Vol. 1, pp. 1–12). Hillsdale, NJ: Erlbaum.

Cicchetti, D. (1993). Developmental psychopathology: Reactions, reflections, projections. *Developmental Review, 13*, 471–502.

Cicchetti, D., & Garmezy, N. (Eds.). (1993). Special Issue: Milestones in the development of resilience. *Development and Psychopathology, 5*(4).

Clancy, S. M., & Hoyer, W. J. (1994). Age and skill in visual search. *Developmental Psychology, 30*, 545–552.

Cohen, G. D. (1989). Biopsychiatry in Alzheimer's disease. In M. P. Lawton (Ed.), *Annual review of gerontology and geriatrics* (Vol. 9, pp. 216–231). New York: Springer.

Cohen, S., & Wills, T. A. (1985). Stress, social support, and the buffering hypothesis. *Psychological Bulletin, 98*, 310–357.

Cole, M. (in press). Interacting minds in a life-span perspective: A cultural/historical approach to culture and cognitive development. In P. B. Baltes & U. M. Staudinger (Eds.), *Interactive minds: Life-span perspectives on the social foundation of cognition.* New York: Cambridge University Press.

Coleman, P. G. (1974). Measuring reminiscence characteristics from conversation as adaptive features of old age. *International Journal of Aging and Human Development, 5*, 281–294.

Coleman, L. M., & Antonucci, T. C. (1982). Impact of work on women at midlife. *Developmental Psychology, 19*, 290–294.

Colvin, C. R., & Block, J. (1994). Do positive illusions foster mental health? An examination of the Taylor and Brown formulation. *Psychological Bulletin, 116*, 3–20.

Cooney, T. M., & Uhlenberg, P. (1990). Family size and mother-child relations in later life. *Gerontologist, 30*, 618–625.

Cooper, M. J., & Fairburn, C. G. (1992). Thoughts about eating, weight and shape in anorexia nervosa and bulimia nervosa. *Behavioral Research and Theory, 30*, 501–511.

Coper, H., Jänicke, B., & Schulze, G. (1986). Biopsychological research on adaptivity across the life span of animals. In P. B. Baltes, D. L. Featherman, & R. M. Lerner (Eds.), *Life-span development and behavior* (Vol. 7, pp. 207–232). Hillsdale, NJ: Erlbaum.

Corkin, S. (1982). Some relationships between global amnesias and the memory impairments in Alzheimer's disease. In S. Corkin, K. L. Davies, J. H. Growdon, E. Usdin, & R. J. Wurtman (Eds.), *Alzheimer's disease: Advances in basic research and therapies* (pp. 149–177). Cambridge MA: Center for Brain Sciences and Metabolism Trust.

Corkin, S., Growdon, J. H., Nissen, M. J., Huff, F. J., Freed, D. M., & Sagar, H. J. (1984). Recent advances in the neuropsychological study of Alzheimer's disease. In R. J. Wurtman, S. Corkin, & J. H. Growdon (Eds.), *Alzheimer's disease: Advances in basic research and therapies* (pp. 74–95). Cambridge, MA: Center for Brain Sciences and Metabolism Trust.

Cornelius, S. W. (1986). Classic pattern of intellectual aging: Test familiarity, difficulty and performance. *Journals of Gerontology, 39*, 201–206.

Cornelius, S. W., & Caspi, A. (1987). Everyday problem solving in adulthood and old age. *Psychology and Aging, 2*, 144–153.

Costa, P. T., & McCrae, R. R. (1980). Still stable after all these years: Personality as a key to some issues in adulthood and old age. In P. B. Baltes & O. G. Brim (Eds.), *Life-span development and behavior* (Vol. 39, pp. 66–102). New York: Academic Press.

Costa, P. T., & McCrae, R. R. (1985). *The NEO personality inventory manual.* Odessa, FL: Psychological Assessment Resources.

Costa, P. T., & McCrae, R. R. (1988). Personality in adulthood: A six-year longitudinal study of self-reports and spouse ratings on the NEO Personality Inventory. *Journal of Personality and Social Psychology, 54*, 853–863.

Costa, P. T., McCrae, R. R., & Norris, A. H. (1981). Personal adjustment to aging: Longitudinal prediction from neuroticism and extraversion. *Journals of Gerontology, 36*, 78–85.

Costa, P. T., Zoderman, A. B., McCrae, R. R., Cornoni-Huntley, J., Locke, B. Z., & Barbano, H. E. (1987). Longitudinal analyses of psychological well-being in a national sample: Stability of mean levels. *Journals of Gerontology, 42*, 50–55.

Coyne, J. C., Ellard, J. H., & Smith, D. A. F. (1990). Social support, interdependence, and the dilemmas of helping. In B. R. Sarason, I. G. Sarason, & G. R. Pierce (Eds.), *Social support: An interactional view* (pp. 129–199). New York: Wiley.

Craik, F. I. M. (1977). Age differences in human memory. In J. E. Birren & K. W. Schaie (Eds.), *Handbook of the psychology of aging* (pp. 384–420). New York: Van Nostrand-Reinhold.

Craik, F. I. M., Byrd, M., & Swanson, J. M. (1987). Patterns of memory loss in three elderly samples. *Psychology and Aging, 2*, 79–86.

Craik, F. I. M., & Jennings, J. M. (1992). Human memory. In F. I. M. Craik & T. A. Salthouse (Eds.), *Handbook of aging and cognition* (pp. 51–110). Hillsdale, NJ: Erlbaum.

Cross, S., & Markus, H. (1991). Possible selves across the life span. *Human Development, 34*, 230–255.

Cushman, L. A., Como, P. G., Booth, H., & Caine, E. D. (1988). Cued recall and release from proactive interference in Alzheimer's disease. *Journal of Clinical and Experimental Neuropsychology, 10*, 685–692.

Danish, S. J., Smyer, M. A., & Nowak, C. A. (1980). Developmental intervention: Enhancing life-event processes. In P. B. Baltes & O. G. Brim (Eds.), *Life-span development and behavior* (Vol. 3, pp. 339–366). New York: Academic Press.

Dannefer, D. (1984). Adult development and social theory: A paradigmatic reappraisal. *American Sociological Review, 49*, 100–116.

Datan, N., & Ginsberg, L. H. (Eds.). (1975). *Life-span developmental psychology: Normative life crises.* New York: Academic Press.

Demming, J. A., & Pressey, S. L. (1957). Tests 'indigenous' to the adult and older years. *Journal of Counseling Psychology, 4*, 144–148.

Denney, N. W. (1984). A model of cognitive development across the life span. *Developmental Review, 4*, 171–191.

Denney, N. W. (1989). Everyday problem solving: Methodological issues, research findings, and a model. In L. W. Poon, D. C. Rubin, & B. A. Wilson (Eds.), *Everyday cognition in adulthood and late life* (pp. 330–351). New York: Cambridge University Press.

Denney, N. W., & Pearce, K. A. (1989). A developmental study of practical problem solving in adults. *Psychology and Aging, 4,* 438–442.

Depner, C. E., & Ingersoll-Dayton, B. (1985). Conjugal social support: Patterns in later life. *Journals of Gerontology, 40,* 761–766.

Depner, C. E., & Ingersoll-Dayton, B. (1988). Supportive relationships in later life. *Psychology and Aging, 3,* 348–357.

Detterman, D. K., & Sternberg, R. J. (Eds.). (1993). *Transfer on trial: Intelligence, cognition, and instruction.* Norwood, NJ: Ablex.

Dick, M. B., Kean, M. -L., & Sands, S. (1989). Memory for internally generated words in Alzheimer-type dementia: Breakdown in encoding and semantic memory. *Brain and Cognition, 9,* 88–108.

Dittmann-Kohli, F. (1991). Meaning and personality change from early to late adulthood. *European Journal of Gerontology, 1,* 98–103.

Dunkel-Schetter, C., & Bennett, T. L. (1990). The availability of social support and its activation in times of stress. In B. R. Sarason, I. G. Sarason, & G. R. Pierce (Eds.), *Social support: An interactional view* (pp. 267–296). New York: Wiley.

Dunn, L. L. (1965). *A short history of genetics.* New York: McGraw-Hill.

Dykstra, P. A. (1993). The differential availability of relationships and the provision and effectiveness of support to older adults. *Journal of Social and Personal Relationships, 10,* 355–370.

Edelman, G. M. (1987). *Neural Darwinism: The theory of neuronal group selection.* New York: Basic Books.

Edelstein, W., & Noam, G. (1982). Regulatory structures of the self and postformal stages in adulthood. *Human Development, 25,* 407–422.

Eichorn, D. H., Clausen, J. A., Haan, N., Honzik, M. P., & Mussen, P. H. (Eds.). (1981). *Present and past in middle life.* New York: Academic Press.

Elder, G. H., Jr. (1979). Historical change in life patterns and personality. In P. B. Baltes & O. G. Brim (Eds.), *Life-span development and behavior,* (Vol. 2, pp. 117–159). New York: Academic.

Elder, G. H., Jr., & O'Rand, A. M. (in press). Adult lives in a changing society. In K. Cook, G. Fine, & J. S. House (Eds.), *Sociological perspectives on social psychology.*

Ericsson, K. A., & Charness, N. (1994). Expert performance: Its structure and acquisition. *American Psychologist, 49,* 725–747.

Ericsson, K. A., Krampe, R. Th., & Tesch-Römer, C. (1993). The role of deliberate practice in the acquisition of expert performance. *Psychological Review, 100,* 363–406.

Ericsson, K. A., & Smith, J. (Eds.). (1991). *Towards a general theory of expertise: Prospects and limits.* New York: Cambridge University Press.

Erikson, E. (1959). Identity and the life cycle. *Psychological Issues* (Monograph 1). New York: International University Press.

Erikson, E. (1963). *Childhood and society* (2nd Ed.). New York: Norton.

Erikson, E., Erikson, J. M., & Kivnick, H. (1986). *Vital involvement in old age: The experience of old age in our time.* London, England: Norton.

Featherman, D. L. (1983). The life-span perspective in social science research. In P. B. Baltes & O. G. Brim (Eds.), *Life-span development and behavior* (Vol. 5, pp. 1–59). New York: Academic Press.

Featherman, D. L., Smith, J., & Peterson, J. G. (1990). Successful aging in a 'post-retired' society. In P. B. Baltes & M. M. Baltes (Eds.), *Successful aging: Perspectives from the behavioral sciences* (pp. 50–93). New York: Cambridge University Press.

Field, D., & Minkler, M. (1988). Continuity and change in social support between young-old and old-old or very-old age. *Journals of Gerontology, 43,* 100–106.

Filipp, S. H., & Klauer, T. (1991). Subjective well-being in the face of critical life events: The case of successful coping. In F. Strack, M. Argyle, & N. Schwarz (Eds.), *The social psychology of subjective well-being* (pp. 213–235). Oxford, England: Pergamon.

Finch, C. E. (1990). *Longevity, senescence, and the genome.* Chicago: University of Chicago Press.

Fischer, C. S. (1982). *To dwell among friends.* Chicago: University of Chicago Press.

Flavell, J. H., & Wohlwill, J. F. (1969). Formal and functional aspects of cognitive development. In D. Elkind & J. H. Flavell (Eds.), *Studies in cognitive development* (pp. 67–120). New York: Oxford University Press.

Fleeson, W., & Baltes, P. B. (1994). *The predictive power of perceived change and life time comparisons in personality assessments.* Unpublished manuscript, Max Planck Institute for Human Development and Education, Berlin.

Florsheim, M. J., Leavesley, G., Hanley-Peterson, P., & Gallagher-Thompson, D. (1991). An expansion of the A-B-C approach to cognitive/behavioral therapy. *Clinical Gerontologist, 10,* 65–69.

Folkman, S., Lazarus, R. S., Pimley, S., & Novacek, J. (1987). Age differences in stress and coping processes. *Psychology and Aging, 2,* 171–184.

Ford, D. H. (1987). *Humans as self-constructing living systems: A developmental perspective on behavior and personality.* Hillsdale, NJ: Erlbaum.

Forster, J. M., & Gallagher, D. (1986). An exploratory study comparing depressed and nondepressed elder's coping strategies. *Journals of Gerontology, 41,* 91–93.

Foss, J. W., Camp, C. J., & O'Hanlon, A. M. (1993, November). *Spaced retrieval method in strategy training with AD populations.* Paper presented at the 46th Annual Scientific Meeting of the Gerontological Society of America, New Orleans, LA.

Fratiglioni, L., Grut, M., Forsell, Y., Viitanen, M., Grafstrom, M., Holmen, K., Ericsson, K., Bäckman, L., Ahlbom, A., & Winblad, B. (1991). Prevalence of Alzheimer's disease and other dementias in an elderly urban population: Relationship with age, sex, and education. *Neurology, 41,* 1886–1892.

Fredrickson, B. L., & Carstensen, L. L. (1990). Choosing social partners: How old age and anticipated endings make people more selective. *Psychology and Aging, 5,* 163–171.

Frese, M. (1992). A plea for realistic pessimism: On objective reality, coping with stress, and psychological dysfunction. In L. Montada, S. Filipp, & M. J. Lerner (Eds.), *Life crises and experiences of loss in adulthood* (pp. 81–94). Hillsdale, NJ: Erlbaum.

Freud, S. (1989). *Gesammelte Werke* [Collected Works]. Frankfurt: Fischer.

Freund, A. (1993). *Wer bin ich? Die Selbstdarstellung alter Menschen* [Who am I? The self-descriptions of older persons]. Unpublished doctoral dissertation. Berlin: Free University Berlin.

Fries, J. F. (1983). The compression of morbidity. *Milbank Memorial Fund Quarterly, 61,* 397–419.

Fries, J. F. (1989). *Aging well.* Reading, MA: Addison-Wesley.

Fries, J. F. (1990). Medical perspectives upon successful aging. In P. B. Baltes & M. M. Baltes (Eds.), *Successful aging: Perspectives from the behavioral sciences* (pp. 34–49). New York: Cambridge University Press.

Gallagher-Thompson, D., Hanley-Peterson, P., & Thompson, L. W. (1990). Maintenance of gains versus relapse following brief psychotherapy for depression. *Journal of Consulting and Clinical Psychology, 58,* 371–374.

Gardner, E. F., & Monge, R. H. (1977). Adult age differences in cognitive abilities and educational background. *Experimental Aging Research, 3,* 337–383.

Garmezy, N. (1991). Resilience in children's adaptation to negative life events and stressed environments. *Pediatric Annals, 20,* 459–466.

Garner, D. M., Garfinkel, P. E., Schwartz, D., & Thompson, M. (1980). Cultural expectations of thinness in women. *Psychological Reports, 47,* 483–491.

Gatz, M., Bengtson, V. L., & Blum, M. J. (1990). Caregiving families. In J. E. Birren & K. W. Schaie (Eds.), *Handbook of the psychology of aging* (pp. 404–426). San Diego, CA: Academic Press.

Gatz, M., & Hurwicz, M. L. (1990). Are old people more depressed? Cross-sectional data on Center for Epidemiological Studies Depression Scale factors. *Psychology and Aging, 5,* 284–290.

Gatz, M., & Pearson, C. G. (1988). Ageism revised and the provision of psychological services. *American Psychologist, 43,* 184–188.

Gaylord, S. A., & Zung, W. W. K. (1987). Affective disorders among the aging. In L. L. Carstensen & B. A. Edelstein (Eds.), *Handbook of clinical gerontology* (pp. 76–95). Elmsford, NY: Pergamon.

Gilewski, M. J., Farberow, N. L., Gallagher, D. E., & Thompson, L. W. (1991). Interaction of depression and bereavement on mental health in the elderly. *Psychology and Aging, 6,* 67–75.

Glaser, R. (1984). Education and thinking. *American Psychologist, 39,* 93–104.

Goddard, P., & Carstensen, L. L. (1986). Behavioral treatment of chronic depression in an elderly nursing home resident. *Clinical Gerontologist, 4,* 13–20.

Goff, D. C., & Jenicke, M. A. (1986). Treatment-resistant depression in the elderly. *Journal of the American Geriatrics Society, 34,* 63–70.

Gollin, E. S. (1981). Development and plasticity. In E. S. Gollin (Ed.), *Developmental plasticity: Behavioral and biological aspects of variations in development* (pp. 231–251). New York: Academic Press.

Gottlieb, B. H. (1983). Social support as a focus for integrative research in psychology. *American Psychologist, 38,* 278–287.

Granovetter, M. S. (1973). The strength of weak ties. *American Journal of Sociology, 78,* 1360–1380.

Graf, P. (1990). Life-span change in implicit and explicit memory. *Bulletin of the Psychonomic Society, 28,* 353–358.

Graf, P., & Schacter, D. L. (1987). Selective effects of interference on implicit and explicit memory for new associations. *Journal of Experimental Psychology: Learning, Memory and Cognition, 13,* 45–53.

Greenwald, A. G., & Pratkanis, A. R. (1984). The self. In R. S. Wyer & T. K. Srull (Eds.), *Handbook of social cognition* (Vol. 3, pp. 129–178). Hillsdale, NJ: Erlbaum.

Guberman, S. R., & Greenfield, P. M. (1991). Learning and transfer in everyday cognition. *Cognitive Development, 6,* 233–260.

Häfner, H. (1994). Psychiatrie des höheren Lebensalters [Psychiatry of old age]. In P. B. Baltes, J. Mittelstrass, & U. M. Staudinger (Eds.), *Alter und Altern: Ein interdisziplinärer Studientext zur Gerontologie* [Old age and aging: An interdisciplinary reader in Gerontology] (pp. 151–179). Berlin: De Gruyter.

Haan, N. (1977). *Coping and defending: Processes of self-environment organization.* New York: Academic Press.

Haan, N. (1981). Common dimensions of personality development: Early adolescence to middle life. In D. H. Eichorn, J. A. Clausen,

N. Haan, M. P. Honzik, & P. H. Mussen (Eds.), *Present and past in middle life* (pp. 117–151). New York: Academic Press.

Hanson, S. H., & Sauer, W. G. (1985). Children and their elderly parents. In W. J. Sauer & R. T. Coward (Eds.), *Social support networks and the care of the elderly: Theory, research, and practice* (pp. 41–66). New York: Springer.

Harris, D. B. (Ed.). (1957). *The concept of development.* Minneapolis, MN: University of Minnesota Press.

Harris, L. (1975). *The myth and reality of aging in America.* Washington, DC: National Council on the Aging.

Hartley, A. A. (1989). The cognitive ecology of problem solving. In L. W. Poon, D. C. Rubin, & B. A. Wilson (Eds.), *Everyday cognition in adulthood and late life* (pp. 300–329). Cambridge, MA: Cambridge University Press.

Hauser, R., & Wagner, G. (1994). Altern und soziale Sicherung [Aging and social security]. In P. B. Baltes, J. Mittelstrass, & U. M. Staudinger (Eds.), *Alter und Altern: Ein interdisziplinärer Studientext zur Gerontologie* [Old age and aging: An interdisciplinary reader in Gerontology] (pp. 581–613). Berlin: De Gruyter.

Havighurst, R. J. (1948). *Developmental tasks and education.* New York: McKay.

Havighurst, R. J. (1973). History of developmental psychology: Socialization and personality development through the life-span. In P. B. Baltes & K. W. Schaie (Eds.), *Life-span developmental psychology: Personality and socialization* (pp. 3–24). New York: Academic Press.

Heckhausen, J., Dixon, R. A., & Baltes, P. B. (1989). Gains and losses in development throughout adulthood as perceived by different adult age groups. *Developmental Psychology, 25,* 109–121.

Heckhausen, J., & Krueger, J. (1993). Developmental expectations for the self and most other people: Age grading in three functions of social comparison. *Developmental Psychology, 29,* 539–548.

Heckhausen, J., & Schulz, R. (1993). Optimisation by selection and compensation: Balancing primary and secondary control in life-span development. *International Journal of Behavioral Development, 16,* 287–303.

Heckhausen, J., & Schulz, R. (in press). A life-span theory of control. *Psychological Review.*

Heidrich, S. M., & Denney, N. W. (1994). Does social problem solving differ from other types of problem solving during the adult years? *Experimental Aging Research, 20,* 105–126.

Helmchen, H., & Linden, M. (1993). The differentiation between depression and dementia in the very old. *Ageing and Society, 13,* 589–617.

Helson, R., & Wink, P. (1987). Two conceptions of maturity examined in the findings of a longitudinal study. *Journal of Personality and Social Psychology, 53,* 531–541.

Herlitz, A., Lipinska, B., & Bäckman, L. (1992). Utilization of cognitive support for episodic remembering in Alzheimer's disease. In L. Bäckman (Ed.), *Memory functioning in dementia* (pp. 73–96). Amsterdam: Elsevier.

Hertzog, C., & Schaie, K. W. (1988). Stability and change in adult intelligence: 2. Simultaneous analysis of longitudinal means and covariance structures. *Psychology and Aging, 3,* 122–130.

Hess, B. B., & Soldo, B. J. (1985). Husband and wife networks. In W. J. Sauer & R. T. Coward (Eds.), *Social support networks and the care of the elderly: Theory, research and practice* (pp. 67–92). New York: Springer.

Hetherington, E. M., Lerner, R. M., & Perlmutter, M. (Eds.). (1988). *Child development in life-span perspective.* Hillsdale, NJ: Erlbaum.

Hirsch, B. J. (1980). Natural support systems and coping with major life changes. *American Journal of Community Psychology, 8,* 159–172.

Hobfoll, S. E. (1989). Conservation of resources. *American Psychologist, 44,* 513–524.

Hooker, K. (1992). Possible selves and perceived health in older adults and college students. *Journals of Gerontology, 47,* 85–95.

Horgas, A. L., Wahl, H. -W., & Baltes, M. M. (in press). Dependency in late life. In L. L. Carstensen, B. A. Edelstein, & L. Dornbrand (Eds.), *The practical handbook of clinical gerontology.* Newbury Park, CA: Sage.

Horn, J. L., & Hofer, S. M. (1992). Major abilities and development in the adult period. In R. J. Sternberg & C. A. Berg (Eds.), *Intellectual development* (pp. 44–49). New York: Cambridge University Press.

House, J. S., & Kahn, R. L. (1985). Measures and concepts of social support. In S. Cohen & S. L. Syme (Eds.), *Social support and health* (pp. 83–108). Orlando, FL: Academic Press.

House, J. S., Robbins, C., & Metzner, H. L. (1982). The association of social relationships and activities with mortality: Prospective evidence from the Tecumseh Community Health Study. *American Journal of Epidemiology, 116,* 123–140.

House, J. S., Umberson, D., & Landis, K. R. (1988). Structures and processes of social support. *Annual Review of Sociology, 14,* 293–318.

Howard, D. V. (1991). Implicit memory: An expanding picture of cognitive aging. *Annual Review of Gerontology and Geriatrics, 11,* 1–22.

Hultsch, D. F., & Dixon, R. A. (1990). Learning and memory in aging. In J. E. Birren & K. W. Schaie (Eds.), *Handbook of the psychology of aging* (Vol. 3, pp. 258–273). New York: Academic Press.

Hultsch, D. F., Hertzog, C., Small, B. J., McDonald-Miszczak, L., & Dixon, R. A. (1992). Short-term longitudinal change in cognitive performance in later life. *Psychology and Aging, 7,* 571–584.

Huppert, F. A., & Piercy, M. (1979). Normal and abnormal forgetting in organic amnesia: Effects of locus of lesion. *Cortex, 15,* 385–390.

Ingersoll-Dayton, B., & Antonucci, T. C. (1988). Reciprocal and non-reciprocal social support: Contrasting sides of intimate relationships. *Journals of Gerontology, 43,* 65–73.

Irion, J. C., & Blanchard-Fields, F. (1987). A cross-sectional comparison of adaptive coping in adulthood. *Journals of Gerontology, 42,* 502–504.

Israel, B. A., & Antonucci, T. C. (1987). Social network characteristics and psychological well-being: A replication and extension. *Health Education Quarterly, 14,* 461–481.

Jessor, R. (1993). Successful adolescent development among youth in high-risk settings. *American Psychologist, 48,* 117–126.

Johnson, C. L. (1987). The institutional segregation of the aged. In P. Silverman (Ed.), *The elderly as modern pioneers* (pp. 375–388). Bloomington, IL: Indiana University Press.

Johnson, C. L. (1988). *Ex familia.* New Brunswick, NJ: Rutgers University Press.

Johnson, S. L., McPhee, L., & Birch, L. L. (1991). Conditioned preferences: Young children prefer flavors associated with high dietary fat. *Physiology and Behavior, 50,* 1245–1251.

Jung, C. G. (1971). The stages of life. In J. Cambell (Ed.), *The portable Jung* (pp. 3–46). New York: Viking.

Karmiloff-Smith, A. (1992). *Beyond modularity: A developmental perspective on cognitive science.* Cambridge, MA: MIT Press.

Katz, S. C., Ford, A. B., & Moskowitz, R. M. (1963). Studies of illness in the aged. The index of ADL: A standardized measure of biological and psychosocial function. *Journal of the American Medical Association, 185,* 914–919.

Kaufman, A. V., & Adams, J. P. (1987). Interaction and loneliness: A dimensional analysis of the social isolation of a sample of older Southern adults. *Journal of Applied Family Relations, 35,* 389–395.

Kessler, R. C., Foster, C., Webster, P. S., & House, J. S. (1992). The relationship between age and depressive symptoms in two national surveys. *Psychology and Aging, 7,* 119–126.

Kessler, R. C., & McLeod, J. D. (1985). Social support and mental health in community samples. In S. Cohen & S. L. Syme (Eds.), *Social support and health* (pp. 219–240). Orlando, FL: Academic Press.

Kessler, R. C., & McRae, J. A. (1982). The effect of wives' employment on the mental health of married men and women. *American Sociological Review, 47,* 216–227.

Kinzie, J. D., Lewinsohn, P., Maricle, R., & Teri, L. (1986). The relationship of depression to medical illness in an older community population. *Comprehensive Psychiatry, 27,* 241–246.

Kliegl, R., & Baltes, P. B. (1987). Theory-guided analysis of mechanisms of development and aging mechanisms through testing-the-limits and research on expertise. In C. Schooler & K. W. Schaie (Eds.), *Cognitive functioning and social structure over the life course* (pp. 95–119). Norwood, NJ: Ablex.

Kliegl, R., Smith, J., & Baltes, P. B. (1990). On the locus and process of magnification of age differences during mnemonic training. *Developmental Psychology, 26,* 894–904.

Klingenspor, B. (1994). Gender identity and bulimic eating behavior. *Sex Roles, 31,* 407–431.

Kopelman, M. D. (1985). Rates of forgetting in Alzheimer-type dementia and Korsakoff's syndrome. *Neuropsychologia, 23,* 623–638.

Krampe, R. Th. (1994). *Maintaining excellence: Cognitive-motor performance in pianists differing in age and skill level.* Berlin: Edition Sigma.

Krantz, S. E., & Gallagher-Thompson, D. (1990). Depression and information valence influence depressive cognition. *Cognitive Therapy and Research, 14,* 95–108.

Krause, N. (1987). Life stress, social support, and self esteem in an elderly population. *Psychology and Aging, 2,* 349–356.

Krause, N., Liang, J., & Yatomi, N. (1989). Satisfaction with social support and depressive symptoms: A panel analysis. *Psychology and Aging, 4,* 88–97.

Labouvie, E. W., & Nesselroade, J. R. (1985). Age, period, and cohort analysis and the study of individual development and social change. In J. R. Nesselroade & A. von Eye (Eds.), *Development and social change: Explanatory analysis* (pp. 189–212). New York: Academic Press.

Labouvie-Vief, G. (1977). Adult cognitive development: In search of alternative interpretations. *Merrill Palmer Quarterly, 23,* 263–277.

Labouvie-Vief, G. (1982). Dynamic development and mature autonomy: A theoretical prologue. *Human Development, 25,* 161–191.

Labouvie-Vief, G., Hakim-Larson, J., DeVoe, M., & Schoeberlein, S. (1989). Emotions and self-regulation: A life-span view. *Human Development, 32,* 279–299.

Labouvie-Vief, G., Hakim-Larson, J., & Hobart, C. J. (1987). Age, ego level, and the life-span development of coping and defense processes. *Psychology and Aging, 2,* 286–293.

Labouvie-Vief, G., Hoyer, W. J., Baltes, M. M., & Baltes, P. B. (1974). Operant analysis of intellectual behavior in old age. *Human Development, 17,* 259–272.

Lachman, M. E. (1986). Personal control in later life: Stability, change, and cognitive correlates. In M. M. Baltes & P. B. Baltes (Eds.), *The psychology of control and aging* (pp. 207–236). Hillsdale, NJ: Erlbaum.

Lachman, M. E. (Ed.). (1993). Special Issue: Planning and control processes across the life span. *International Journal of Behavioral Development, 16*(2).

Lang, F. R. (1994). *Soziale Einbindung im hohen Alter-Eltern und Kinderlose gestalten Hilfebeziehungen* [Social relations in very old age: Support relationships of parents and non-parents]. Berlin: Edition Sigma.

Lang, F. R., & Carstensen, L. L. (1994). Close emotional relationships in late life: Further support for proactive aging in the social domain. *Psychology and Aging, 14,* 315–324.

Langer, E. J., & Rodin, J. (1976). The effects of choice and enhanced personal responsibility for the aged: A field experiment in an institutional setting. *Journal of Personality and Social Psychology, 34,* 191–198.

Larson, R. (1978). Thirty years of research on the subjective well-being of older Americans. *Journals of Gerontology, 33,* 109–125.

Larson, R., Cskiszentmihalyi, M., & Graef, R. (1982). Time alone in daily experience: Loneliness or renewal? In L. A. Peplau & D. Perlman (Eds.), *Loneliness: A sourcebook of current theory, research and therapy* (pp. 41–53). New York: Wiley.

Larson, R., Zuzanek, J., & Mannell, R. (1985). Being alone versus being with people: Disengagement in the daily experience of older adults. *Journals of Gerontology, 33,* 109–125.

Lave, J. (1988). *Cognition in practice: Mind, mathematics, and culture in everyday life.* Cambridge, MA: Cambridge University Press.

Lawton, M. P. (1982). Environments and living arrangements. In R. H. Binstock, W. -S. Chow, & J. H. Schulz (Eds.), *International perspectives on aging* (pp. 159–192). New York: United Nations Fund for Population Activities.

Lawton, M. P. (1988). Behavior-relevant ecological factors. In K. W. Schaie & C. Schooler (Eds.), *Social structures and aging: Psychological processes* (pp. 57–78). Hillsdale, NJ: Erlbaum.

Lawton, M. P. (1991). Functional status and aging well. *Generations, 15,* 31–34.

Lawton, M. P., & Brody, E. M. (1969). Assessment of older people: Self-maintaining and instrumental activities of daily living. *Gerontologist, 9,* 179–185.

Lawton, M. P., & Nehemow, L. (1973). Ecology and the aging process. In C. Eisdorfer & M. P. Lawton (Eds.), *The psychology of adult development and aging* (pp. 619–674). Washington, DC: American Psychological Association.

Lazarus, R. S. (1993). From psychological stress to the emotions: A history of changing outlooks. *Annual Review of Psychology, 44,* 1–21.

Lazarus, R. S., & DeLongis, A. (1983). Psychological stress and coping in aging. *American Psychologist, 38,* 245–254.

Lerner, R. M. (1984). *On the nature of human plasticity.* New York: Cambridge University Press.

Lerner, R. M. (1986). *Concepts and theories of human development.* New York: Random House.

Lerner, R. M., & Kauffman, M. B. (1985). The concept of development in contextualism. *Developmental Review, 5,* 309–333.

Lerner, R. M., & von Eye, A. (1992). Sociobiology and human development: Arguments and evidence. *Human Development, 35,* 12–33.

Levenson, R. W., Carstensen, L. L., Friesen, W. V., & Ekman, P. (1991). Emotion, physiology, and expression in old age. *Psychology and Aging, 6,* 28–35.

Levenson, R. W., Carstensen, L. L., & Gottman, J. M. (1993). Longterm marriage: Age, gender and satisfaction. *Psychology and Aging, 8,* 301–313.

Levinson, D. J. (1978). *The seasons of a man's life.* New York: Knopf.

Levinson D. J. (1980). Toward a conception of the adult life course. In N. J. Smelser & E. H. Erikson (Eds.), *Themes of work and love in adulthood* (pp. 265–290). Cambridge, MA: Harvard University Press.

Lewinsohn, P. M., Rohde, P., Seeley, J. R., & Fischer, S. A. (1991). Age and depression: Unique and shared effects. *Psychology and Aging, 6,* 247–260.

Lewinsohn, P. M., Rohde, P., Seeley, J. R., & Fischer, S. A. (1993). Age-cohort changes in the lifetime occurrence of depression and other mental disorders. *Journal of Abnormal Psychology, 102,* 110–120.

Lewinsohn, P. M., & Tilson, M. D. (1987). Psychotherapy services for older adults: Innovative roles for the clinical geropsychologist. *Gerontology and Geriatrics Education, 7,* 111–123.

Lewis, C. N. (1971). Reminiscing and self-concept in old age. *Journals of Gerontology, 26,* 240–243.

Lindenberger, U., & Baltes, P. B. (in press). Intellectual aging. In R. J. Sternberg et al. (Eds.), *Encyclopedia of intelligence.* New York: Macmillan.

Lindenberger, U., & Baltes, P. B. (1994). Sensory functioning and intelligence in old age: A strong connection. *Psychology and Aging, 9,* 339–355.

Lindenberger, U., Mayr, U., & Kliegl, R. (1993). Speed and intelligence in old age. *Psychology and Aging, 8,* 207–220.

Linville, P. W. (1987). Self-complexity as a cognitive buffer against stress-related illness and depression. *Journal of Personality and Social Psychology, 52,* 663–676.

Lipinska, B., Bäckman, L., & Herlitz, A. (1992). When Greta Garbo is easier to remember than Stefan Edberg: Influences of prior knowledge on recognition memory in Alzheimer's disease. *Psychology and Aging, 7,* 214–220.

Loevinger, J. (1976). *Ego development: Conception and theory.* San Francisco: Jossey-Bass.

Lopata, H. (1978). Contributions of extended families to the support system of metropolitan area widows: Limitations of the modified kin network. *Journal of Marriage and the Family, 40,* 355–364.

Lowenthal, M., & Robinson, B. (1976). Social networks and isolation. In R. H. Binstock & E. Shanas (Eds.), *Handbook of aging and the social sciences* (pp. 432–456). New York: Van Nostrand-Reinhold.

Maciel, A., Heckhausen, J., & Baltes, P. B. (1994). Life-span views on the interface between personality and intelligence. In R. J. Sternberg & P. Ruzgis (Eds.), *Intelligence and personality.* (pp. 61–103). New York: Cambridge University Press.

Maddox, G. L. (Ed.). (1987). *The encyclopedia of aging.* New York: Springer.

Magai, C., & Hunziker, J. (1993). Tolstoy and the riddle of developmental transformation: A lifespan analysis of the role of emotions in personality development. In M. Lewis & J. M. Haviland (Eds.), *Handbook of Emotions* (pp. 247–259). New York: Guilford.

Magnusson, D. (1990). Personality development from an interactional perspective. In L. A. Pervin (Ed.), *Handbook of personality: Theory and research* (pp. 193–222). New York: Guilford.

Magnusson, D., & Öhman, A. (Eds.). (1987). *Psychopathology. An interactional perspective.* Orlando, FL: Academic Press.

Mahoney, F. I., & Barthel, D. W. (1965). Functional evaluation: The Barthel Index. *Maryland State Medical Journal, 14,* 61–65.

Maiden, R. J. (1987). Learned helplessness and depression: A test of the reformulated model. *Journals of Gerontology, 42,* 60–64.

Malatesta, C. Z. (1990). The role of emotions in the development and organization of personality. In R. A. Thompson (Ed.), *Nebraska Symposium on Motivation* (Vol. 36, pp. 1–56). Lincoln, NB: University of Nebraska Press.

MaloneBeach, E. E., & Zarit, S. H. (1991). Current research issue in caregiving to the elderly. *International Journal of Aging and Human Development, 32,* 103–114.

Manton, K. G., Stallard, E., & Liu, K. (1993). Forecasts of active life expectancy: Policy and fiscal implications. *Journals of Gerontology, 48* (Special Issue), 11–26.

Markus, H. R., & Herzog, A. R. (1991). The role of the self-concept in aging. *Annual Review of Gerontology and Geriatrics, 11,* 111–143.

Markus, H., & Nurius, P. (1986). Possible selves. *American Psychologist, 41,* 954–969.

Markus, H., & Wurf, E. (1987). The dynamic self-concept: A social psychological perspective. *Annual Review of Psychology, 38,* 299–337.

Marmar, C. R., Gaston, L., Gallagher, D., & Thompson, L. W. (1989). Alliance and outcome in late life depression. *Journal of Nervous and Mental Disease, 177,* 464–472.

Marsiske, M., Lang, F. R., Baltes, P. B., & Baltes, M. M. (in press). Selective optimization with compensation: Life-span perspectives. In R. A. Dixon & L. Bäckman (Eds.), *Psychological compensation: Managing losses and promoting gains.* New York: Springer.

Marsiske, M., & Willis, S. L. (in press a). Dimensionality of everyday problem solving in older adults. *Psychology and Aging.*

Marsiske, M., & Willis, S. L. (in press b). Practical creativity in older adults' everyday problem solving: Life-span perspectives. In C. E. Adams-Price (Ed.), *Creativity and aging: Theoretical and empirical approaches.* New York: Springer.

Masoro, E. J., & McCarter, R. J. M. (1990). Dietary restriction as a probe of mechanisms of senescence. *Annual Review of Gerontology and Geriatrics, 10,* 183–197.

Masten, A. S., Best, K. M., & Garmezy, N. (1990). Resilience and development: Contributions from the study of children who overcome adversity. *Development and Psychopathology, 2,* 425–444.

Mayer, K. U. (1994). Bildung und Arbeit in einer alternden Bevölkerung [Education and work in an aging population]. In P. B. Baltes, J. Mittelstrass, & U. M. Staudinger (Eds.), *Alter und Altern: Ein interdisziplinärer Studientext zur Gerontologie* [Old age and aging: An interdisciplinary reader in Gerontology] (pp. 518–543). Berlin: De Gruyter.

Mayer, K. U., & Baltes, P. B. (Eds.). (in press). *Die Berliner Altersstudie: Die vielen Gesichter des Alterns* [The Berlin Aging Study: The many faces of aging]. Berlin: Akademie Verlag.

McCrae, R. R. (1989). Age differences and changes in the use of coping mechanisms. *Journals of Gerontology, 44,* 919–928.

McCrae, R. R., & Costa, P. T. (1983). Psychological maturity and subjective well-being: Toward a new synthesis. *Developmental Psychology, 19,* 243–248.

McKitrick, L. A., Camp, C. J., & Black, F. W. (1992). Prospective memory intervention in Alzheimer's disease. *Journals of Gerontology, 47,* 337–343.

Meichenbaum, D. (1974). *Cognitive behavior modification.* Morristown, NJ: General Learning Press.

Mellor, K. S., & Edelmann, R. J. (1988). Mobility, social support, loneliness, and well-being among two groups of older adults. *Personality and Individual Differences, 9,* 1–5.

Molinari, V., & Reichlin, R. E. (1984/85). Life review and reminiscence in the elderly: A review of the literature. *International Journal of Aging and Human Development, 20,* 81–92.

Morgan, D. L. (1990). Combining the strengths of social networks, social support, and personal relationships. In S. Duck & R. C. Silver (Eds.), *Personal relationships and social support* (pp. 191–215). London: Sage.

Morgan, L. A. (1976). A re-examination of widowhood and morale. *Journals of Gerontology, 31,* 687–695.

Morrell, R. W., Park, D. C., & Poon, L. W. (1990). Effects of labelling techniques on memory and comprehension of prescription information in young and older adults. *Journals of Gerontology, 45,* 166–172.

Morrison, R. L., & Katz, I. R. (1989). Drug-related cognitive impairment: Current progress and recurrent problems. *Annual Review of Gerontology and Geriatrics, 9,* 232–279.

Mosher-Ashley, P. M. (1986/87). Procedural and methodological parameters in behavioral-gerontological research: A review. *International Journal of Aging and Human Development, 24,* 189–229.

Nealy, A. S., & Bäckman, L. (1993). Long-term maintenance of gains from memory training in older adults: Two 3.5 year follow-up studies. *Journals of Gerontology, 48,* 233–237.

Nelson, E. A., & Dannefer, D. (1992). Aged heterogeneity: Fact or fiction? The fate of diversity in gerontological research. *Gerontologist, 32,* 17–23.

Nesselroade, J. R. (1989). Adult personality development: Issues in addressing constancy and change. In A. I. Rabin, R. A. Zucker, R. A. Emmons, & S. Frank (Eds.), *Studying persons and lives* (pp. 41–85). New York: Springer.

Nesselroade, J. R. (1991). Interindividual differences in intraindividual change. In L. M. Collins & J. L. Horn (Eds.), *Best methods for the analysis of change* (pp. 92–105). Washington, DC: American Psychological Association.

Nesselroade, J. R., & Baltes, P. B. (1974). Adolescent personality development and historical change: 1970–1972. *Monographs of the Society for Research in Child Development, 39,* (1, Serial No. 154).

Newcomb, M. D. (1990). What structural equation modeling can tell us about social support. In B. R. Sarason, I. G. Sarason, & G. R. Pierce (Eds.), *Social support: An interactional view* (pp. 26–63). New York: Wiley.

Nisbett, R. E. (1980). *History of the idea of progress.* New York: Basic Books.

Ochse, R., & Plug, C. (1986). Cross-cultural investigation of the validity of Erikson's theory of personality development. *Journal of Personality and Social Psychology, 50,* 1240–1252.

Oerter, R. (1986). Developmental tasks through the life span: A new approach to an old concept. In P. B. Baltes, D. L. Featherman, & R. M. Lerner (Eds.), *Life-span development and behavior* (Vol. 7, pp. 233–269). Hillsdale, NJ: Erlbaum.

Palmore, E. B. (1981). *Social patterns in normal aging: Findings from the Duke Longitudinal Study.* Durham, NC: Duke University Press.

Palmore, E. B. (1988). *The facts on aging quiz.* New York: Springer.

Parmalee, P. A., Katz, I. R., & Lawton, M. P. (1991). The relation of pain to depression among institutionalized aged. *Journals of Gerontology, 46,* 15–21.

Parmalee, P. A., Katz, I. R., & Lawton, M. P. (1992). Incidence of depression in long-term care settings. *Journals of Gerontology, 47,* 189–196.

Pearlin, L. I., Turner, H., & Semple, S. (1989). Coping and the mediation of caregiver stress. In E. Light & B. D. Lebowitz (Eds.), *Alzheimer's disease treatment and family stress: Directions for research.* Washington, DC: National Institute of Mental Health (DHHS Publication No. ADM 89-1569).

Pepper, S. C. (1942). *World hypotheses: A study in evidence.* Berkeley: University of California Press.

Peplau, L. A., Bikson, T. K., Rook, K. S., & Goodchilds, J. D. (1982). Being old and living alone. In L. A. Peplau & D. Perlman (Eds.), *Loneliness: A sourcebook of current theory, research and therapy* (pp. 135–151). New York: Wiley.

Perlmutter, M. (Ed.). (1990). *Late-life potential.* Washington, DC: Gerontological Society of America.

Petersen, A. C. (1988). Adolescent development. *Annual Review of Psychology, 39,* 583–608.

Pfeiffer, E. (1977). Psychopathology and social pathology. In J. E. Birren & K. W. Schaie (Eds.), *Handbook of the psychology of aging* (pp. 650–671). New York: Van Nostrand-Reinhold.

Piaget, J. (1965). *The moral judgment of the child.* New York: Free Press.

Picano, J. J. (1989). Development and validation of a life history index of adult adjustment for women. *Journal of Personality Assessment, 53,* 308–318.

Pruchno, R. A., Kleban, M. H., Michaels, J. E., & Dempsey, N. P. (1990). Mental and physical health of caregiving spouses. Development of a causal model. *Journals of Gerontology, 45,* 192–199.

Reese, H. W. (1993). Developments in child psychology from the 1960s to the 1990s. *Developmental Review, 13,* 503–524.

Reese, H. W., & Overton, W. F. (1970). Models of development and theories of development. In L. R. Goulet & P. B. Baltes (Eds.), *Lifespan developmental psychology: Research and theory* (pp. 115–145). New York: Academic Press.

Reifman, A., Klein, J. G., & Murphy, S. T. (1989). Self-monitoring and age. *Psychology and Aging, 4,* 245–246.

Reker, G. T., & Wong, P. T. P. (1988). Aging as an individual process. Toward a theory of personal meaning. In J. E. Birren & V. L. Bengtson (Eds.), *Emergent theories of aging* (pp. 214–246). New York: Springer.

Riegel, K. F. (1972). The influence of economic and political ideologies on the development of developmental psychology. *Psychological Bulletin, 78,* 129–141.

Riegel, K. F. (1976). The dialectics of human development. *American Psychologist, 31,* 689–700.

Riley, M. W. (1986). The dynamisms of life stages: Roles, people, and age. *Human Development, 29,* 150–156.

Riley, M. W., & Riley, J. W., Jr. (Eds.). (1989). The quality of aging: Strategies for interventions. *The Annals of the American Academy of Political and Social Science, 503.*

Rodin, J. (1986). Health, control, and aging. In M. M. Baltes & P. B. Baltes (Eds.), *The psychology of control and aging* (pp. 139–166). Hillsdale, NJ: Erlbaum.

Rodman, J. L., Gantz, F. E., Schneider, J., & Gallagher-Thompson, D. (1991). Short term treatment of endogenous depression using cognitive-behavioral therapy and pharmacotherapy. *Clinical Gerontologist, 10,* 81–84.

Rook, K. S. (1984). Promoting social bonding: Strategies for helping the lonely and socially isolated. *American Psychologist, 39,* 1389–1407.

Rook, K. S. (1990). Social relationships as a source of companionship: Implications for older adults' psychological well-being. In B. R. Sarason, I. G. Sarason, & A. G. R. Pierce (Eds.), *Social support: An interactional view* (pp. 219–250). New York: Wiley.

Rook, K. S., & Pietromonaco, P. (1987). Close relationships: Ties that heal or ties that bind? In W. H. Jones & D. Perlman (Eds.), *Advances in personal relationships* (Vol. 1, pp. 1–35). Greenwich, CT: JAI Press.

Rook, K. S., & Thuras, P. (1988, November). *Denial of social needs: Implications for social network satisfaction and psychological health.* Paper presented at the Annual Meeting of the Gerontological Society of America, San Francisco.

Rosenberg, M. (1979). *Conceiving the self.* New York: Basic Books.

Rossi, A. S., & Rossi, P. H. (Eds.). (1990). *Of human bonding: Parent-child relations across the life course.* New York: De Gruyter.

Rowe, J. W., & Kahn, R. L. (1987). Human aging: Usual and successful. *Science, 237,* 143–149.

Royer, J. M., Cisero, C. A., & Carlo, M. S. (1993). Techniques and procedures for assessing cognitive skills. *Review of Educational Research, 63,* 201–243.

Rutter, M. (1987). Resilience in the face of adversity. Protective factors and resistance to psychiatric disorder. *British Journal of Psychiatry, 147,* 598–611.

Ryff, C. D. (1984). Personality development from the inside: The subjective experience of change in adulthood and aging. In P. B. Baltes & O. G. Brim (Eds.), *Life-span development and behavior* (Vol. 6, pp. 243–279). New York: Academic Press.

Ryff, C. D. (1989). In the eye of the beholder: Views of psychological well-being among middle-aged and older adults. *Psychology and Aging, 4,* 195–210.

Ryff, C. D. (1991). Possible selves in adulthood and old age: A tale of shifting horizons. *Psychology and Aging, 6,* 286–295.

Ryff, C. D., & Baltes, P. B. (1976). Values and transitions in adult development of women: The instrumentality-terminality sequence hypothesis. *Developmental Psychology, 12,* 567–568.

Ryff, C. D., & Essex, M. J. (1992). The interpretation of life experience and well-being: The sample case of relocation. *Psychology and Aging, 7,* 507–517.

Rybarczyk, B., Gallagher-Thompson, D., Rodman, J., Zeiss, A., & Thompson, L. (1992). Applying cognitive behavioral psychotherapy to the chronically ill elderly: Treatment issues and case illustration. *International Psychogeriatrics, 4,* 127–140.

Salthouse, T. A. (1991a). *Theoretical perspectives on cognitive aging.* Hillsdale, NJ: Erlbaum.

Salthouse, T. A. (1991b). Expertise as the circumvention of human processing limitations. In K. A. Ericsson & J. Smith (Eds.), *Toward a general theory of expertise* (pp. 286–300). New York: Cambridge University Press.

Sameroff, A. J. (1975). Transactional models in early social relations. *Human Development, 18,* 65–79.

Sarason, I. G., Pierce, G. R., & Sarason, B. R. (1990). Social support and interactional processes: A triadic hypothesis. *Journal of Social and Personal Relationships, 7,* 495–506.

Schaie, K. W. (1965). A general model of the study of developmental problems. *Psychological Bulletin, 64,* 92–107.

Schaie, K. W. (1983). The Seattle Longitudinal Study: A twenty-one year exploration of psychometric intelligence in adulthood. In K. W. Schaie (Ed.), *Longitudinal studies of adult psychological development* (pp. 64–135). New York: Guilford.

Schaie, K. W. (1989). The hazards of cognitive aging. *Gerontologist, 29,* 484–493.

Schaie, K. W. (1994). The course of adult intellectual development. *American Psychologist, 49* 304–313.

Schaie, K. W., Dutta, R., & Willis, S. L. (1991). Relationship between rigidity-flexibility and cognitive abilities in adulthood. *Psychology & Aging, 6,* 371–383.

Schmitt, J. P., & Kurdeck, L. A. (1985). Age and gender differences in and personality correlates of loneliness in different relationships. *Journal of Personality Assessment, 49,* 485–496.

Schooler, C. (1990). Psychosocial factors and effective cognitive functioning in adulthood. In J. E. Birren & K. W. Schaie (Eds.), *Handbook of the psychology of aging* (pp. 347–358). San Diego, CA: Academic Press.

Schulz, R., & Rau, M. T. (1985). Social support through the life course. In S. Cohen & S. L. Syme (Eds.), *Social support and health* (pp. 129–149). Orlando, FL: Academic Press.

Schwarzer, R., & Leppin, A. (1992). Social support and mental health: A conceptual and empirical overview. In L. Montada, S.-H. Filipp, & M.-J. Lerner (Eds.), *Life crises and experiences of loss in adulthood* (pp. 435–458). Hillsdale, NJ: Erlbaum.

Schwarzer, R., & Weiner, B. (1990). Die Wirkung von Kontrollierbarkeit und Bewältigungsverhalten auf Emotionen und soziale Unterstützung [The effect of controllability and coping on emotions and social support]. *Zeitschrift für Sozialpsychologie* [Journal of Social Psychology], *21,* 118–125.

Scogin, F., & Bienias, J. L. (1988). A three-year followup of older adult participants in a memory-skills training program. *Psychology and Aging, 3,* 334–337.

Seeman, T. E., & Berkman, L. F. (1988). Structural characteristics of social networks and their relationship with social support in the elderly: Who provides support? *Social Science and Medicine, 26,* 737–749.

Seligman, M. E. P. (1990). *Learned optimism.* New York: Knopf.

Seligman, M. E. P., & Elder, G. H. (1986). Learned helplessness and lifespan development. In A. B. Sørensen, F. E. Weinert, & L. R. Sherrod (Eds.), *Human development and the life course: Multidisciplinary perspectives* (pp. 377–428). Hillsdale, NJ: Erlbaum.

Sherman, E. (1991). *Reminiscence and the self in old age.* New York: Springer.

Siegler, I. C., George, L. K., & Okun, M. A. (1979). Cross-sequential analysis of adult personality. *Developmental Psychology, 15,* 350–351.

Simonton, D. K. (1991). Creativity in the later years: Optimistic prospects for achievement. *Gerontologist, 30,* 626–631.

Singer, J. E., & Lord, D. (1984). The role of social support in coping with chronic or life-threatening illness. In A. Baum, S. E. Tayor, & J. E. Singer (Eds.), *Handbook of psychology and health* (pp. 269–277). Hillsdale, NJ: Erlbaum.

Sinnott, J. D., & Cavanaugh, J. C. (Eds.). (1991). *Bridging paradigms. Positive development in adulthood and old age.* New York: Praeger.

Skinner, B. F. (1983). Intellectual self-management in old age. *American Psychologist, 38,* 239–244.

Smith, J., & Baltes, P. B. (1990). A study of wisdom-related knowledge: Age/cohort differences in responses to life planning problems. *Developmental Psychology, 26,* 494–505.

Smith, J., & Baltes, P. B. (1993). Differential psychological aging: Profiles of the oldest old. *Ageing and Society, 13,* 551–587.

Smith, J., & Marsiske, M. (in press). Definitions and taxonomies of foundation skills and adult competencies: Life-span perspectives. In A. Tuijnman, I. Kirsch, & D. A. Wagner (Eds.), *Adult basic skills: Innovations in measurement and policy analysis.* Cresskill, NJ: Hampton Press.

Smith, J., Staudinger, U. M., & Baltes, P. B. (in press). Settings facilitating wisdom-related knowledge: The sample case of clinical psychologists. *Journal of Consulting and Clinical Psychology.*

Smyer, M., Cohn, M. D., & Brannon, D. (1988). *Mental health consultation in nursing homes.* New York: New York University Press.

Smyer, M. A., Zarit, S. H., & Qualls, S. H. (1990). Psychological intervention with the aging individual. In J. E. Birren & K. W. Schaie (Eds.), *Handbook of the psychology of aging* (3rd. ed., pp. 375–403). New York: Academic Press.

Sørensen, A. B., Weinert, F. E., & Sherrod, L. (Eds.). (1986). *Human development and the life course: Multidisciplinary perspectives.* Hillsdale, NJ: Erlbaum.

Stanovich, K. E. (1991). Discrepancy definitions of reading disability: Has intelligence led us astray? *Reading Research Quarterly, 26,* 7–29.

Staudinger, U. M. (1989). *The study of life review. An approach to the investigation of intellectual development across the life span.* Berlin: Edition Sigma.

Staudinger, U. M., & Baltes, P. B. (in press). The psychology of wisdom. In R. J. Sternberg et al. (Eds.), *Encyclopedia of intelligence.* New York: Macmillan.

Staudinger, U. M., Cornelius, S. W., & Baltes, P. B. (1989). The aging of intelligence: Potential and limits. *The Annals of the American Academy of Political and Social Science, 503,* 43–49.

Staudinger, U. M., Freund, A., & Smith, J. (1994a). *Differential coping patterns in old age.* Unpublished manuscript. Berlin: Max Planck Institute for Human Development and Education.

Staudinger, U. M., Freund, A., & Smith, J. (1994b). *The goal system: A facet of the resilient self in old age?* Unpublished manuscript. Berlin: Max Planck Institute for Human Development and Education.

Staudinger, U. M., Freund, A., Linden, M., & Maas, I. (in press). Selbst, Persönlichkeit und Lebensbewältigung: Psychologische Widerstandsfähigkeit und Vulnerabilität [Self, personality, and life management: Psychological resilience and vulnerability]. In K. U. Mayer & P. B. Baltes (Eds.), *Die Berliner Altersstudie: Die vielen Gesichter des Alterns [The Berlin Aging Study: The many faces of aging].* Berlin: Akademie Verlag.

Staudinger, U. M., Marsiske, M., & Baltes, P. B. (1993). Resilience and levels of reserve capacity in later adulthood: Perspectives from lifespan theory. *Development and Psychopathology, 5,* 541–566.

Staudinger, U. M., Smith, J., & Baltes, P. B. (1992). Wisdom-related knowledge in a life review task: Age differences and the role of professional specialization. *Psychology and Aging, 7,* 271–281.

Stephens, M. A. P., Kinney, J. M., Ritchie, S. W., & Norris, V. K. (1987). Social networks as assets and liabilities in recovery from stroke by geriatric patients. *Psychology and Aging, 2,* 125–129.

Sternberg, R. J., & Berg, C. A. (Eds.). (1992). *Intellectual development.* Cambridge, MA: Cambridge University Press.

Sternberg, R. J., Conway, B. E., Ketron, J. L., & Bernstein, M. (1981). People's conceptions of intelligence. *Journal of Personality and Social Psychology, 41,* 37–55.

Sternberg, R. J., & Wagner, R. K. (Eds.). (1986). *Practical intelligence: Nature and origins of competence in the everyday world.* New York: Cambridge University Press.

Streib, G. F., & Beck, R. W. (1980). Older families: A decade review. *Journal of Marriage and the Family, 42,* 937–956.

Suls, J. N., & Mullen, B. (1982). From the cradle to the grave: Comparison and self-evaluation across the life-span. In J. Suls (Ed.), *Psychological perspectives on the self* (Vol. 1, pp. 97–128). Hillsdale, NJ: Erlbaum.

Taylor, S. E. (1989). *Positive illusions.* New York: Basic Books.

Taylor, S. E., & Brown, J. D. (1988). Illusion and well-being: A social psychological perspective on mental health. *Psychological Bulletin, 103,* 193–210.

Taylor, S. E., & Brown, J. D. (1994). Positive illusions and well-being revisited: Seperating fact from fiction. *Psychological Bulletin, 116*(1), 21–27.

Taylor, S. E., Kemeny, M. E., Aspinwall, L. G., Schneider, S. G., Rodriguez, R., & Herbert, M. (1992). Optimism, coping, psychological distress, and high-risk sexual behavior among men at risk for acquired immunodeficiency syndrome (AIDS). *Journal of Personality and Social Psychology, 63,* 460–473.

Taylor, S. E., & Lobel, M. (1989). Social comparison activity under threat: Downward evaluation and upward contacts. *Psychological Bulletin, 96,* 569–575.

Teri, L., Baer, L. C., & Reifler, B. V. (1991). Depression in Alzheimer's patients: Investigation of symptom patterns and frequency. *Clinical Gerontologist, 11,* 47–57.

Teri, L., & Gallagher-Thompson, D. (1991). Cognitive-behavioral interventions for treatment of depression in Alzheimer's patients. *Gerontologist, 31,* 413–416.

Teri, L., & Logsdon, R. G. (1992). The future of psychotherapy with older adults. *Psychotherapy, 29,* 81–87.

Thoits, P. A. (1983). Multiple identities and psychological well-being: A reformulation and test of the social isolation hypothesis. *American Sociological Review, 8,* 174–187.

Thomae, H. (1970). Theory of aging and cognitive theory of personality. *Human Development, 12,* 1–16.

Thompson, L. W., Gallagher, D., & Breckenridge, J. S. (1987). Comparative effectiveness of psychotherapies for depressed elders. *Journal of Consulting and Clinical Psychology, 55,* 385–390.

Thompson, L. W., Gallagher, D., & Czirr, R. (1988). Personality disorder and outcome in the treatment of late-life depression. *Journal of Geriatric Psychiatry, 21,* 133–146.

Townsend, P. (1957). *The family life of old people.* Glencoe, IL: Free Press.

Uttal, D. H., & Perlmutter, M. (1989). Toward a broader conceptualization of development: The role of gains and losses across the lifespan. *Developmental Review, 9,* 101–132.

Vaillant, G. E. (1977). *Adaptation to life.* Boston: Little Brown.

Vaillant, G. E. (1983). *The natural history of alcoholism: Causes, patterns and paths to recovery.* Cambridge, MA: Harvard University Press.

Vaillant, G. E. (1990). Avoiding negative life outcomes. Evidence from a forty-five year study. In P. B. Baltes & M. M. Baltes (Eds.), *Successful aging: Perspectives from the behavioral sciences* (pp. 332–355). New York: Cambridge University Press.

Verhaeghen, P., Marcoen, A., & Goosens, L. (1992). Improving memory performance in the aged through mnemonic training: A meta-analytic study. *Psychology and Aging, 7,* 242–251.

Waddington, C. H. (1975). *The evolution of an evolutionist.* Edinburgh, England: Edinburgh University Press.

Walker, A. (1990, July). *The economic burden of aging and the prospect of intergenerational conflict.* Paper presented at the 12th World Congress of Sociology, Research Committee on Aging, Madrid, Spain.

Wan, T. T. H. (1982). *Stressful life events, social-support networks and gerontological health.* Lexington, MA: Heath.

Weiner, B., & Graham, S. (1989). Understanding the motivational role of affect: Life-span research from an attributional perspective. *Cognition and Emotion, 3,* 410–419.

Weinert, F. E. (1994). Altern in psychologischer Perspektive [Aging in psychological perspective]. In P. B. Baltes, J. Mittelstrass, & U. M. Staudinger (Eds.), *Alter und Altern: Ein interdisziplinärer Studientext zur Gerontologie* [Old age and aging: An interdisciplinary reader in Gerontology] (pp. 180–203). Berlin: De Gruyter.

Weinert, F. E., & Helmke, A. (in press). The neglected role of individual differences in theoretical models of cognitive development. *Learning and Instruction, 4.*

Weinert, F. E., & Waldmann, M. R. (1988). Wissensentwicklung und Wissenserwerb [Knowledge development and knowledge acquisition]. In H. Mandl & H. Spada (Eds.), *Wissenspsychologie* [Psychology of Knowledge] (pp. 161–199). Munich: Psychologie Verlags Union.

Weiss, R. S. (1982). Issues in the study of loneliness. In L. Peplau & D. Perlman (Eds.), *Loneliness: A sourcebook of current theory, research and therapy* (pp. 71–80). New York: Wiley.

Wethington, E., & Kessler, R. C. (1986). Perceived support, received support, and adjustment to stressful life events. *Journal of Health and Social Behavior, 27,* 78–89.

Whitbourne, S. K. (1987). Personality development in adulthood and old age: Relationships among identity style, health, and well-being. *Annual Review of Gerontology and Geriatrics, 7,* 189–216.

Whitbourne, S. K., Zuschlag, M. K., Elliot, L. B., & Waterman, A. S. (1992). Psychosocial development in adulthood: A 22-year sequential study. *Journal of Personality and Social Psychology, 63,* 260–271.

White, M. S. (1985). Ego development in adulthood. *Journal of Personality, 53,* 561–574.

Wilcox, B. L. (1981). Social support in adjusting to marital disruption: A network analysis. In B. H. Gottlieb (Ed.), *Social networks and social support* (pp. 97–115). Beverly Hills, CA: Sage.

Williamson, G. M., & Schulz, R. (1992). Pain, activity restriction, and symptoms of depression among community-residing elderly adults. *Journals of Gerontology, 47,* 367–372.

Willis, S. L. (1987). Cognitive training and everyday competence. *Annual Review of Gerontology and Geriatrics, 7,* 159–188.

Willis, S. L. (1991). Cognition and everyday competence. *Annual Review of Gerontology and Geriatrics, 11,* 80–109.

Willis, S. L., & Baltes, P. B. (1981). Letters to the editor. On cognitive training research in aging: Reply to Donaldson. *Journals of Gerontology, 36,* 636–638.

Willis, S. L., Jay, G. M., Diehl, M., & Marsiske, M. (1992). Longitudinal change and the prediction of everyday task competence in the elderly. *Research on Aging, 14,* 68–91.

Willis, S. L., & Nesselroade, C. S. (1990). Long-term effects of fluid ability training in old-old age. *Developmental Psychology, 26,* 905–910.

Willis, S. L., & Schaie, K. W. (1986). Training the elderly on the ability factors of spatial orientation and inductive reasoning. *Psychology and Aging, 1,* 7–12.

Willis, S. L., & Schaie, K. W. (1994). Cognitive training in the normal elderly. In F. Forette, Y. Christen, & F. Boller (Eds.), *Plasticité cérébrale et stimulation cognitive.* Paris: Foundation Nationale de Gérontologie.

Wilson, R. S., Bacon, L. D., Kramer, R. L., Fox, J. H., & Kaszniak, A. W. (1983). Word frequency effect and recognition memory in dementia of the Alzheimer type. *Journal of Clinical Neuropsychology, 5,* 97–104.

Wisocki, P. (Ed.). (1991). *Handbook of clinical behavior therapy with the elderly client.* New York: Plenum.

Wolinsky, F. D., Callahan, C. M., Fitzgerald, J. F., & Johnson, R. J. (1992). The risk of nursing home placement and subsequent death among older adults. *Journals of Gerontology, 47,* 173–182.

Wong, P. T. P., & Watt, L. M. (1991). What types of reminiscence are associated with successful aging? *Psychology and Aging, 6,* 272–279.

Wood, J. V. (1989). Theory and research concerning social comparisons of personal attributes. *Psychological Bulletin, 106,* 231–248.

Wortman, C. B., & Silver, R. C. (1990). Successful mastery of bereavement and widowhood: A life-course perspective. In P. B. Baltes & M. M. Baltes (Eds.), *Successful aging. Perspectives from the behavioral sciences* (pp. 225–264). New York: Cambridge University Press.

Yang, J. A., & Rehm, L. P. (1993). A study of autobiographical memories in depressed and nondepressed elderly individuals. *International Journal of Aging and Human Development, 36,* 39–55.

Yoshikawa, H. (1994). Prevention as cumulative protection: Effects of early family support and education on chronic delinquency and its risks. *Psychological Bulletin, 115,* 28–54.

Zeiss, A. M., & Lewinsohn, P. M. (1986). Adapting behavioral treatment for depression to meet the needs of the elderly. *Clinical Psychologist, 39,* 98–100.

Author Index

Subject Index

Relationship prototype, 441
Relationships, *see specific types of relationships*
cognitive screening, 50
cross-sex, 167
kinship, 23, 769
opposite-sex, 167, 169, 172
parental divorce and, 9
representational models of, 49
Relativism, culture and, 767
Religious affiliation, significance of, 39
Religious delusion, 519, 522
REM sleep, dreams, 516
Remarriage:
custody arrangements, 13–14
demographics, 4
education and, 20
impact of, 12, 450–451
Remission, 404, 407
Reparative fantasy, 87
Repetition compulsion, 85
Repetition Test of Information Processing, 276–278
Replacement, delusion of, 520
Replication stage, personality disorder, 639
Representation skills, 383
Representational expectancies, 652
Representational models, in maltreated children, 46, 49–50, 57
Repression, 84, 86, 651–652, 779
Reputation, peer acceptance and, 136
Research Diagnostic Criteria (RDC), 525, 537
Reserve capacity, plasticity of development, 807–808
Resilience:
childhood, 756
cognitive:
intervention-supported, 815–817
need for, 810–811
potential for, 813–815
defined, 756, 808
developmental psychopathology research, 775–777
friendships and, 113
life course and, 777–778
in maltreated children, 55–56
mastery and, 779–780
narratives of, 784
natural, 811–813, 817–820
in old age, *see* Old age, resilience issues
peer relationships and, 144
psychological, 767–769, 779–781
as reserve capacity, 808–810, 817
risk and, *see* Risk, resilence and
self-esteem and, 785
social relations, 824
traumatic stress and, 84–86
Resistance, 51, 78–79, 610
Response-accessing, 436, 487
Response-decision, 436, 487
Restriction fragment length polymorphisms (RFLPs), 219

Restrictive parenting, 78
Retirement, 772
Rett's Disorder, 119–120
Revenge fantasy, 85, 87
Revictimization, in maltreated child, 43
Revised Behavior Problem Checklist (RBPC), 736
Reward dependence, 353
Rheumatic fever, 223
Right-handedness, 226, 228
Rigidity, 316, 348
Risk, *see specific disorders*
enduring, 36
resilience and:
acute trauma and, 740–741
adversity and competency, 738
chronic adversities, 740–741
defined, 716
future directions, 744
overview, 737–738, 756–758
protective factors, 738–739
stressful life events and, 739–470
vulnerability and, 754–758
Rites of passage, 518
Rituals:
checking, 623
in children, 611, 614
compulsive behaviors, 611, 613–614
obsessive-compulsive disorder and, 614
Tourette's syndrome and, 217
Rochester Child Resilience Project, 740
Role models, alcoholism and, 692
Role play, 89, 598, 600
Role strain, 773, 784
Role transitioning, 600
Rorschach, 779, 781
Rule-breaking talk, 446–447, 458–459

Sadomasochistic behavior, 87
Scanning, 253–256
Schedule for Affective Disorders and Schizophrenia for School-Age Children—Epidemiologic Version, 54
Schizoaffective Disorder, 520–521
Schizoid personality disorder, development of, 666–667
Schizophrenia:
in adults:
autism and, 551–552
childhood schizophrenia related to, 552–554
age at onset, 550–551, 554–556
attention impairment, 247
attention tests, changes in, 263–264
autism and, 551–552
Catatonic, 520
in children, 523, 525–527
adult schizophrenia relation:
biobehavioral investigations, 554
onset of, 553, 555–556
phenomenological comparisons, 552
onset, 554–555

definitions, 536–537
delusions in, 520, 522, 524
developmental perspective:
attention impairment, types of, 264
longitudinal course, 264–265
diathesis-stress model:
candidate stressors:
obstetrical complications, 547
season of birth and viral agents, 547–548
multifactorial, interactional models, 545–546
Disorganized, 520
early-onset, 523
etiologic heterogeneity:
molecular genetics, 543–544
neurochemistry, 542–543
family support and, 187–188
first episode, 761, 773
first rank symptoms, 520
genetic models of:
distinct-heterogeneity models, 544–545
multifactorial, interactional models, 545–546
single major gene models, 544
transactional models, 546–547
genetic vulnerability, 213
hallucinations, 514, 519, 524
high-risk studies:
biobehavioral high-risk strategy, 563–565
conclusions, 568–569
genetic high-risk strategy, 556–563
risk, defined, 556
historical overview, 536–537
hyperprosexia, 244
late-onset, 523
manifestations, 550–551
as multiple syndromes, 536
neurobiological perspective, 529
as neurological insult, 536
normal development implications:
pathology boundaries, 566
recovery of function, 566
refining theories, 566–567
obstetrical complications and, 222
Paranoid Type, 520–521
parental, 264, 556, 560
peer adjustment and, 123
phases of, 725–726
recovery from, 774
Residual Type, 520
social competence of, 124, 187
social support:
developmental changes, 188
enacted support, 187–188
need for, 186
perceived support, 186–187
quality of, 195
social networks, 186–188
social theories, 185–186